E.G. SCHUMACHER MEM. LIBRARY--NORTH
3 4829 00008 913 8

P9-CAY-038

MACMILLAN
COMPENDIUM

SOCIAL ISSUES

MACMILLAN

COMPENDIUM

SOCIAL ISSUES

SELECTIONS FROM MACMILLAN'S FOUR-VOLUME

Encyclopedia of Sociology

Robert D. Benford

Editor-in-Chief

MACMILLAN LIBRARY REFERENCE USA

New York

Macmillan Library Reference USA
1633 Broadway, 5th Floor
New York, NY 10019

Manufactured in the United States of America.

printing number
1 2 3 4 5 6 7 8 9 10

Library of Congress Cataloging-in-Publication Data

Social issues / [edited by] Robert Benford.
p. cm. — (Macmillan compendium)
"Selections from Macmillan's four-volume Encyclopedia of sociology and from Twayne's Social movement past and present series."
Includes bibliographical references and index.
ISBN 0-02-865055-7 (hardcover : alk. paper)
1. Sociology—Encyclopedias. 2. Social problems—Encyclopedias. 3. Social movements—Encyclopedias. I. Benford, Robert D. II. Series.
HM17.S576 1998
301′.03—dc21 98-46461
CIP

This paper meets the requirements of ANSI/NISO Z39.48-1992 (Permanence of Paper).

Contents

Preface

The twenty-first century no longer looms as some distant, ominous future. It is now upon us. The inhabitants of this new millennium find themselves living in a world that is shrinking in size and yet increasingly complex. The planet's myriad of complexities can be conceived of as *social issues.* Social issues are essentially any recurrent pattern of human interaction that is meaningful. Social issues include social problems such as poverty, racism, sexism, drug abuse, crime, and genocide; social institutions such as family, religion, economy, polity, education, sport, medicine, and science; and other social dynamics such as socialization, courtship, marriage, divorce, migration, and revolutions. Macmillan's *Social Issues* seeks to shed new light on these and numerous other social issues that affect our daily lives, our communities, and our world.

Students, library patrons, practitioners, and social scientists have indicated a need for a single-volume that elaborates on such social issues. Fortunately, the basis for crafting such a volume already existed in the form of Macmillan's *Encyclopedia of Sociology.* This impressive four-volume set was written under the erudite editorship of Edgar F. and Marie L. Borgatta. An extraordinary collection of many of the most eminent social scientists wrote the original articles comprising the *Encyclopedia of Sociology.* The authors and editors of the *Encyclopedia of Sociology* deserve all of the credit for the high quality and extensive coverage found in the present volume.

Of the 350 articles published in the original volumes, I selected approximately half for inclusion in *Social Issues.* The articles were selected in order to ensure maximum coverage of the full range of social issues we face in this new millennium. In addition to selecting articles on the basis of their relevance to the twenty-first century, I also selected only those articles that could be readily comprehended by readers who are not familiar with the latest social scientific jargon. Methodological, purely theoretical, and other articles that are of interest only to academic sociologists were omitted from *Social Issues.* Kathy Acklin, a sociology doctoral student, carefully updated the statistical data contained in several of the articles to ensure that this volume reflects current conditions.

Many of the social problems included among the social issues covered in *Social Issues* have led to the formation of social movements, extra-institutional groups organized for the purpose of changing some aspect of a society or the world. These include civil rights, disability rights, human rights, animal rights, children's rights, women's equality, and environmental rights movements to name but a few. Given the vital role social movements play in affecting our understanding of various social issues as well as their impact on the contours of social life, we decided to include several social movement selections from Scribner's 1996 *Supplement* to the *Dictionary of American History.* Members of Macmillan's reference staff made the selections from the *Dictionary of American History* for the inclusion in *Social Issues.*

Whether you are a student, teacher, researcher, or scholar specializing in one of the social issues covered in this compendium, or perhaps an inquisitive, concerned citizen who would like to learn more about the social issues we confront in the twenty-first century, I hope you will find *Social Issues* useful and stimulating.

—Robert D. Benford
University of Nebraska-Lincoln
Editor-in-Chief

ADULTHOOD

Becoming an adult is a life-cycle transition signified not by a single event but by a series of markers or activities designating adult status. The diversity of the more formal markers (completion of education, independent residence, economic self-sufficiency, marriage, parenthood, voting, military service, and entry into full-time work) and the variability in the ages at which they typically occur make the timing of this transition rather ambiguous (Buchmann 1989). There has been a trend in the United States and Western Europe toward earlier assumption of full adult civil rights (e.g., permission to vote or to marry without parental consent), from age twenty-one to age eighteen (Coleman and Husen 1985). However, with the extension of formal education, youth are remaining economically dependent on their parents for longer periods of time. Adolescents are sometimes restrained from "growing up" when assuming adult-like statuses threatens adult interests and values. For example, the extension of required schooling has been seen as motivated, at least in part, by a desire to curb youth unemployment and to allay older workers' fears of job competition (Osterman 1980).

The extension of required schooling has been motivated by a desire to curb youth unemployment and to allay older workers' fears of job competition.

In addition to the more visible, formal markers, there are informal but nonetheless clearly recognized prerogatives of adult status (e.g., smoking, alcohol use, and sexuality) that are widely frowned upon or legally prohibited when engaged in by minors. Youth's engagement in these "problem behaviors" can represent attempts to affirm maturity or to negotiate adult status. Jessor and Jessor (1977, p. 206) view them as "transition behaviors . . . a syndrome of activities oriented toward accession to a developmentally later status." Finally, there are even more subtle indicators—differences in psychological orientation considered appropriate for preadult and adult persons. Young adults are expected to give up the dependent, playful, experimental, carefree, even reckless stances of adolescence and youth and become financially and emotionally independent, productive, hard-working, and responsible (Klein 1990). Whereas it is sometimes alleged that the timing of transition to adulthood is especially unclear in contemporary Western societies, Foner and Kertzer (1978) describe similar ambiguity in premodern contexts, where elders and the rising adult generation struggle over the timing of age-set transitions and corresponding transfers of power, wealth, and privilege.

Historical Change in the Transition to Adulthood

Historical studies demonstrate that both the timing and the process of becoming adult are in no way universalistic or biologically determined. Through the centuries in Western societies, there has been increasing differentiation of early life stages, postponement of entry to adulthood, and changes in the status positions from which adulthood is launched (Klein 1990). In medieval times persons moved directly from infancy, when small size and limited strength precluded productive work, to adulthood, at which time younger persons worked alongside their elders (Aries 1962). A new stage of childhood, intermediate between infancy and adulthood, arose with the emergence of formal schooling. As economic production shifted from agriculture to trade and industry, persons increasingly entered adulthood after a stage of apprenticeship or "child labor." By the beginning of the twentieth century, with schooling extended and child labor curtailed, a new stage of adolescence was recognized (Hall 1904). The adolescent came to be seen as free of adult responsibilities; oriented to fun, sports, popular music, and peers; receptive to change; and ready to experiment with alternative identities and, sometimes, mood-altering substances.

With the majority of young people now obtaining some form of higher education (or entering military service) in the United States, a new stage of "youth" or "postadolescence" has emerged, extending into the twenties and characterized by limited autonomy but continued economic dependence and concern with the establishment of adult identity (Keniston 1970; Coleman and Husen 1985; Buchmann 1989). Youth's residence in dormitories or military barracks provides independence from familial monitoring, while a formal institution assumes a greater or lesser degree of control (Klein 1990). It has been suggested that societal wealth encourages postponement of adulthood and the exten-

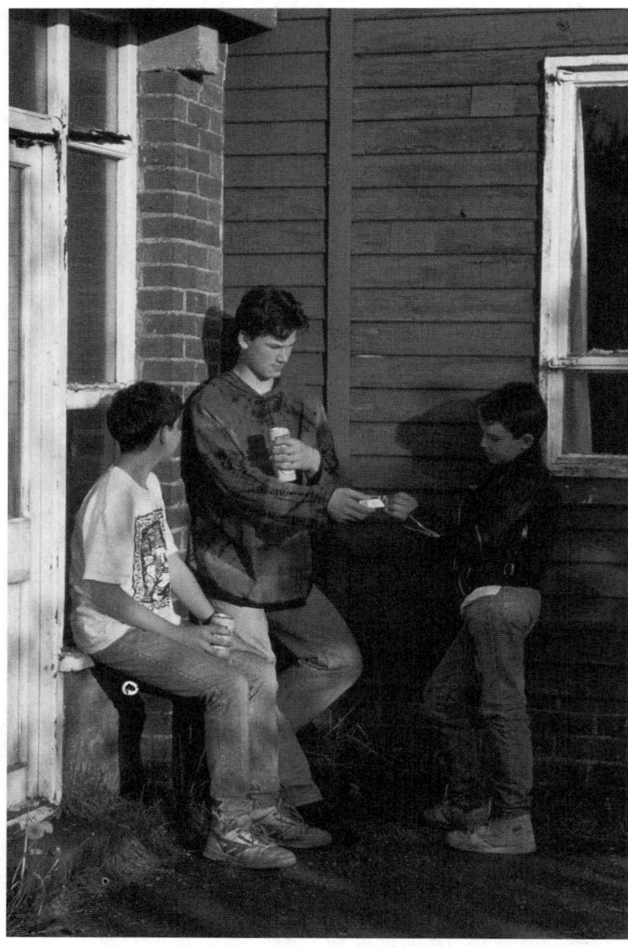

Becoming an adult is a process marked by formal as well as less formal but clearly recognized rituals. Adolescents smoking and drinking know that these activities are forbidden to minors, and they view it as adult behavior. (Jennie Woodcock; Reflections Photolibrary/Corbis)

sion of "youthful" values and life-styles to older ages. Japanese young people, traditionally oriented to the extended family, obedience, educational achievement, and hard work, are apparently becoming more rebellious and are seeking immediate enjoyment as delayed gratification becomes more difficult to sustain in an increasingly affluent society (Connor and De Vos 1989).

For those who enter the labor force after high school, there is also a continued "moratorium" period (Osterman 1989) lasting several years, in which youth hold jobs in the secondary sector of the economy and experience high unemployment and job instability. Such youth lack career orientation and instead emphasize peer relationships, travel, adventure, and short-term jobs to satisfy immediate consumption needs. At the same time, employers express preference for low-wage workers who do not require fringe benefits and are not likely to unionize. When filling adult-like "primary" jobs, such employers seek evidence of stability or "settling down." Comparative research in the United States and West Germany indicates that youth "irresponsibility" and employer reluctance to fill primary jobs with youthful recruits are not universal in modern societies. Instead, they are functions of particular institutional arrangements, specifically, the absence of clear channels of mobility from education to the industrial sector in the United States. According to Hamilton (1990), the highly developed institution of apprenticeship in West Germany effectively provides such linkage.

Whereas the onset of adulthood has been increasingly delayed through historical time, during the past century in the United States the various changes marking the transition have come to take place first in quicker, then in more lengthy, succession. Movement into adulthood (as indicated by school exit, work entry, departure from the family, marriage, and the establishment of an independent household) took place over a longer period of time in 1880 than in 1970 (Modell, Furstenberg, and Hershberg 1976). Historical census records show that while the age of departure from school and entry to the work force rose, leaving home, marriage, and the establishment of a separate household occurred at younger ages in the mid-twentieth century (a similar pattern of cohort change occurred in Norway; see Featherman and Sorensen 1983).

However, this trend toward accelerated timing of family events and more uniform passages to adulthood has reversed in recent decades, as evidenced by later marriage, delayed childbearing (Rindfuss, Morgan, and Swicegood 1988), increasing variability in the ages of first marriage and initial childbearing, increasing divorce rates, and other demographic changes (Buchmann 1989, p. 52). There is also some indication that youth are returning to their parental homes, after leaving for college or other destinations, more frequently today than in the past. Largely as a result of technological change and increasing educational requirements, the entry to adulthood has been extended, diversified, and individualized; and it has become less well defined (Buchmann 1989). Increasing diversity of the sequencing and combination of transitional life events and activities (schooling and work, parenting and women's employment) have promoted more autonomous courses of action. The greater individualization of the adult transition and early life course in recent times may have increased the potential for freedom as well as stress.

Modell's (1989) social history of the transition to adulthood in twentieth-century America finds youth increasingly taking charge of their heterosexual relationships and the formation of new families, becoming ever freer of adult surveillance and control. At the turn of the century, parents closely supervised the practices of "calling," "keeping company," "courtship," and "engagement" and retained veto power over developing relationships. With the emergence of the comprehensive high school came a new autonomous meeting ground for socializing away from parents' watchful eyes. By the 1920s, new patterns of dating, thrill-seeking, music, and dancing were fueled by technological advances (the car, telephone, motion picture) as well as by economic affluence.

Thus, each new generation's experience of transition to adulthood may be somewhat unique and depend on the particular economic, political, and social currents of the time (Mannheim 1952). Historical events and broad macroprocesses clearly influence the process of family formation, an important marker of the adult transition (Modell 1989). When the Great Depression limited material support for new families, engagement was extended. Subsequent mobilization for war, economic growth, and support for returning servicemen promoted earlier marriage. Familistic values during the baby boom were reflected in a gender-asymmetric youth dating system and in the practice of "going steady." Those who moved through adolescence in the 1950s married and became parents earlier than both earlier and later cohorts (Marini 1984a; 1987). By the mid-1960s, the feminist movement, criticism of contemporary life-styles, and weakening restrictions on sexual expression contributed to the erosion of the dating system, declining marriage rates, and growing interest on the part of young women in careers (Modell 1989). Inflation and slower economic growth at the same time lessened the availability of resources for early marriage and parenthood. By the 1970s, young people were no longer as interested in dating, and youth were negotiating their sexual relationships in an even more individualistic fashion. Cohabitation, slow movement into parenthood, and divorce became more prevalent.

It is pertinent to note the changing symbolic meanings of the institutions and experiences that structure the early life course (Modell 1989). In the 1950s, independence and the rejection of adult authority were expressed in dating, going steady, and early marriage. Disenchanted youth, alienated from school, moved directly into marriage and parenthood. But by the 1970s, youthful independence was expressed by immersion in the youth subculture. Many young people saw dating, still linked to marriage, as a conservative, even anachronistic, institution.

The Timing and Sequencing of Events in the Adult Transition

It is widely believed that age norms, specifying the timing of key life events, structure passage through the life course (Neugarten, Moore, and Lowe 1965; Neugarten and Datan 1973). Those who are "off-time" (too early or too late) are thought to be the target of negative social sanctions and to experience strain (Rossi 1980). Divergence from normative timing or sequencing sometimes generates public alarm and comes to be seen as a social problem. Thus, teenage pregnancy and childbearing mark a too early transition to adulthood, and youth unemployment signifies unacceptable delay in entering adult roles. However, the extent to which the timing of transition to adulthood is normatively driven has been questioned. Marini (1984b) notes that there is little direct evidence regarding the existence or content of social norms governing the timing of life events signifying adult status. National polls asking about the ideal age to marry and to become a parent yield age distributions that cluster around the modal ages at which these changes actually occur. Evidence that age preferences ("ideal" ages) lag behind behavioral change (Modell 1980) contradicts the notion that norms actually control timing behavior (for evidence that expectations about life-course activities follow aggregate behavioral change, see McLaughlin et al. 1988, Chapter 9).

Marini (1984b) draws a clear distinction between norms—involving a sense of "ought" or "should" and linked to sanctions for transgression—and behavioral preferences arising through socialization and observation of typical patterns. Teenage childbearing is clearly linked to school dropout, difficulties in the job market, restricted income, and marital instability (Furstenberg, Brooks-Gunn, and Morgan 1987), but these consequences may have little to do with the operation of social sanctions. Moreover, Furstenberg, Brooks-Gunn, and Morgan's (1987) study of a panel of black adolescent mothers sixteen to seventeen years after their children were born showed considerable diversity in maternal socio-economic outcomes. Marini (1984b) notes that if norms (and associated sanctions) do exist, they probably vary by population subgroup (e.g., by socioeconomic status, gender, and ethnicity) and may designate such a wide range of acceptable ages for given transitions that they lack causal significance.

Demographers have charted changes in the linkages among transition events (Hogan and Astone 1986). There is considerable variability in the United States in their sequencing; many people, for example, experience the atypical pattern of entering full-time employment before completing schooling (Marini 1984a). The sequencing and the amount of time spent in various combinations of role activities during the adult transition vary by gender, as do the socioeconomic consequences of these transitional patterns (Marini, Shin, and Raymond 1989). In a cohort of young people born in the early 1940s, males ages sixteen to twenty-nine were found to spend more time in school and in simultaneous schooling and employment (Marini 1987). Higher educational attainment predicted labor-force entry prior to finishing full-time schooling, especially for males (Marini 1984a). Males were also more likely to experience familial role changes before finishing school (Marini 1987). Primarily because of earlier marriage and parenthood, women moved through the transition to adulthood at a faster rate than males (Marini 1987, p. 24). But females who attained high levels of education were more likely to delay family roles (marriage, parenthood) until they completed school. Marini (1987, p. 28) explains these patterns as follows: "Males are more likely to continue their educations after entry into adult family roles because education contributes to fulfillment of the traditional male roles of husband and father by improving a man's ability to provide for the family financially. Education bears a less important relationship to fulfillment of the traditional roles of wife and mother."

Cross-national comparison of Britain and the United States reveals considerable differences in transitional patterns (Kerckhoff 1990). British youth (of the cohort born in 1958) leave school and enter the full-time work force earlier than their American peers but leave the parental home and marry later. They are also more likely to reenter the educational system on a part-time basis to gain credentials after leaving full-time schooling. The period of transition to adulthood is shorter in the United States, and it is also characterized by greater diversity in event sequences.

Factors Influencing Adult Status Placement and Adjustment

The U.S. school assigns children to grades based on age and, with some exceptions, allows movement to the next level each year. Since it is customary for the completion of education to precede other transitional events (Marini 1984b), individual educational attainment largely determines the timing and portal of entry to adult occupational positions and other roles marking entry to adulthood. Critics of contemporary high schools argue that their internal structure—the division into college preparatory, vocational, and commercial "tracks"—perpetuates inequality intergenerationally (Bowles and Gintis 1976; Rosenbaum 1976). The cognitive learning, occupational preferences, and career expectations fostered by formal schooling are most useful as preparation for white-collar and, especially, professional or managerial employment (Coleman and Husen 1985). While vocational education programs in secondary schools are designed for noncollege youth, their effectiveness may be limited given their detachment from actual employment settings (Grubb 1989).

As Hogan and Astone (1986, p. 115) remark, "the organizational structures of schools, military service, and labor markets differ across societies, producing unique institutional bases of age-grading, and societal variability in age-stratification systems." But there is considerable variation within societies in such age-grading and status allocation processes. While in the United States the timing of passage through the various institutional pathways to adulthood is to some extent legally regulated (e.g., by age criteria for compulsory schooling, marriage, employment, military entry, etc.), such rules set only minimum standards. Moreover, there may be asynchronies in the age-grading systems of different societal institutions, and these asynchronies generate status inconsistencies (Buchmann 1989). Adult identities confirmed in some contexts may not be confirmed in others, and this situation can generate strain. It is widely believed that adolescence and youth are stressful life stages and that problems diminish with successful acquisition of adult roles (Modell, Furstenberg, and Hershberg 1976). Consistent with this supposition, men's self-perceptions of personal well-being and competence were found to decline during college and to rise during the following decade (Mortimer, Finch, and Kumka 1982).

Several factors facilitate adult socialization and adjustment (Mortimer and Simmons 1978). For example, the degree of institutionalization of the transition has implications for adaptation, as it influences recognition of the newcomer (by the self and others) as having a new status and identity, carrying with it new rights and obligations. Rituals such as marriage and graduation allow public recognition of successful passage to adulthood.

Employed adolescents have more cynical attitudes toward work than those who are not employed.

The availability of opportunities for anticipatory socialization or practice of adult roles may also affect adjustment. It is sometimes said that youth are isolated in schools, cut off from meaningful contact with adult workers (excepting their teachers), and prevented from engaging in processes of anticipatory socialization to adulthood (Panel on Youth of the President's Science Advisory Committee 1974). Many parents encourage adolescent children to work, believing that this experience will help them to become responsible and independent, to learn to handle money, and to manage their time effectively (Phillips and Sandstrom 1990). However, "youth jobs" are quite different from adult work, as they generally involve rather simple, repetitive tasks requiring little training or skills. Greenberger and Steinberg (1986), doubting the benefits of such work experience, report that employed adolescents have more cynical attitudes toward work than those who are not employed. While the full impact of employment in adolescence on the transition to adulthood is not known, there is evidence that investment in adolescent work is related to restricted educational aspirations and attainment, which would limit adult career options (Mortimer and Finch 1986). However, several studies have shown that employment during high school predicts more stable work histories and higher earnings in the years immediately following (Freeman and Wise 1979; Meyer and Wise 1982; Mortimer and Finch 1986). Stern and Nakata (1989), using data from noncollege youth in the National Longitudinal Survey of Youth, report that more complex work activity in adolescence is associated with lower incidence of unemployment and higher earnings three years after high school.

There is further evidence that the quality of adolescent work experience matters for psychological outcomes that influence adult attainment (Mortimer, et al. forthcoming). An ongoing longitudinal study of working in adolescence shows that adolescent boys who feel that they are obtaining useful skills and who perceive opportunities for advancement in their jobs increased in their sense of mastery (internal control) over a one-year period. Girls who thought that they were being paid well for their work similarly manifested increasing levels of self-efficacy over time (Finch et al. 1990).

The character and outcomes of the transition to adulthood clearly depend on diverse resources that are differentially distributed among young people. Socioeconomic differences can affect the age at which individuals acquire adult roles, the character of marking events, and even the availability of opportunities to assume adult status positions. The socioeconomic level of the family of origin sets the level of available resources that can facilitate or lessen the likelihood of a successful adult transition, fostering intergenerational continuities in attainment (Blau and Duncan 1967; Sewell and Hauser 1976). Postsecondary education and the purchase of a home may depend, at least in part, on the financial status of the family of origin. Moreover, there is growing recognition that the socioeconomic context of the family of origin may change over time and that this change could affect young people's developing aspirations and plans (Featherman and Spenner 1988). Relative advantage or disadvantage can also derive from placement in familial and other networks that provide information (Granovetter 1974; Osterman 1989), for example, about higher educational opportunities, jobs, or even prospective marital partners.

Personal resources facilitating the educational and occupational attainment process have been linked to social class background. Adolescents' educational and occupational aspirations are important mediators of the effects of occupational origins on destinations (Featherman 1980). The transmission of self-directed values may also constitute a mechanism through which socioeconomic status is perpetuated across generations. The more self-directed values of men in higher occupational positions can be attributed largely to the complexity and autonomy of their work tasks (Kohn and Schooler 1983). Importantly, self-directed values influence the qualities that parents seek to instill in their children, and parental self-directed values influence adolescent and young-adult children's own values as well (Kohn, Slomczynski, and Schoenbach 1986).

Parents of higher socioeconomic level typically engage in more supportive child-rearing behavior (Gecas 1979), which fosters the development of personality traits that are conducive to adult attainment. In a panel of highly educated youth, closer, more supportive relationships with fathers fostered a sense of competence, work involvement, and positive work values, which facilitated early adult socioeconomic attainments (Mortimer, Lorence, and Kumka 1986). Social support from parents became a less important source of these psychological traits as sons moved from late adolescence to early adulthood. (A similar pattern of diminishing effects of parents' views on daughters' political orientations has been observed; see Alwin, Cohen, and Newcomb forthcoming). Close father-son relationships in late adolescence also engender similarity in paternal occupations and sons' early adult occupational destinations (Mortimer and Kumka 1982).

Of course, parents may not provide role models of successful adult functioning, and, as a result of social learning or inadequate resources, a problematic transition to adulthood may result. If the family is an important institutional context for the acquisition of economic and other resources for the adult transition, family poverty or disintegration may be expected to have negative consequences. Experiences in youth may thus set in motion a train of events that have profound impact on the early life course. Quinton (1988) finds that institutionally reared girls from disrupted homes were more likely to become pregnant before age nineteen, to marry deviant men, and to experience disturbed family relationships in early adulthood, irrespective of their level of functioning in early adolescence. Moreover, when these women were beset with marital and economic problems similar to those experienced earlier in life, difficulties arose in early parenting.

Disruption and single parenthood in the family of origin, and the economic loss and emotional turmoil that frequently ensue, may clearly jeopardize investment in children and youth. However, Coleman and Husen (1985) argue that declining investments in the next generation may occur even in more favorable and affluent circumstances. As the functions of the family are transferred to other agencies in welfare states (e.g., as the government takes over education, welfare, support of the aged, and other functions), there is a declining economic dependence of family members on one another. As the multigenerational organization and functions of the family weaken, parental motivation to invest attention, time, and effort in the younger generation may also decrease throughout the population.

While psychological resources (e.g., a sense of mastery or internal control, self-esteem) are influenced by formative experiences in the contexts of family, school, peer group, and workplace, once formed they constitute important assets in the transition to adulthood. Increasingly it is recognized that early orientations toward and expectancies about competent action are critical for later adult success (Mainquist and Eichorn 1989). Jordaan and Super (1974) report that adolescents' planfulness, responsibility, and future orientation predicted their level of occupational attainment at the age of twenty-five. The more explorative adolescents, who actively engaged the environment, had more positive early adult outcomes. "Planful competence," denoting self-confidence, intellectual investment, and dependability in adolescence, has also been linked to men's adult occupational status (Clausen 1991). These attributes imply planfulness, delayed gratification, and a sense of control over goal attainment. The propensity to plan early in life is also related to positive adult outcomes among institution-reared girls (Quinton and Rutter 1988).

The "What's the use of trying?" stance of young blacks contrasts sharply with the "effort optimism" characteristic of middle-class whites and some immigrant groups.

Ogbu (1989) implicates beliefs about success as critical to understanding the paradox of high black adolescent aspirations coupled with low subsequent achievement. The "folk culture of success," fostered by a history of discrimination and reinforced by everyday experience (e.g., the observation of black career ceilings, inflated job qualifications, housing discrimination, and poor occupational achievement despite success in school), convinces many young blacks that desired occupational outcomes will not be assured by educational attainment. Given the belief that external forces controlled by whites determine success, alternative strategies for achievement are endorsed—hustling, collective action, or dependence on a more powerful white person. These, in turn, diminish the effort in school that is necessary to obtain good grades and educational credentials. The "What's the use of trying?" stance of young blacks contrasts sharply with the "effort optimism" characteristic of middle-class whites and some immigrant groups.

For the most disadvantaged segments of society there is concern that poor educational opportunities and a rapidly deteriorating economic base in the inner cities preclude access to viable adult roles (Wilson 1987), irrespective of personal efficacy, ambition, or other traits. Black males' lack of stable employment limits their ability to assume the adult family role (as male provider) and fosters the increasing prevalence and legitimacy of female-headed families. This concern about the availability of adult work roles and high youth unemployment extends beyond U.S. inner cities. With increasing technological complexity of occupations in advanced industrial economies, and the exportation of low-skill work to less developed countries, there are declining work opportunities for youth who lack formal educational qualifications and technical skills (Coleman and Husen 1985). Further exacerbating the problems of unskilled youth, increasing postsecondary education inflates educational requirements for job entry well beyond task requirements.

The Transition to Adulthood as a Critical Period of Human Development

The transition to adulthood is recognized as a critical period for the crystallization of certain psychological orientations that tend to remain stable throughout the adult life course. Evidence for such "aging stability," or increasing attitudinal stability following the adult transition, is fairly substantial in the realm of political attitudes and preferences (Glenn 1980). Alwin, Cohen, and Newcomb's (forthcoming) study of a panel of Bennington college women from the 1930s to the 1980s reports extraordinary persistence of political attitudes formed while in college over an approximately fifty-year period (a stability coefficient of 0.781). There is also evidence that work orientations become more stable following early adulthood (Lorence and Mortimer 1985; Mortimer, Finch, and Maruyama 1988). Three explanations have been put forward to account for this pattern. The first implicates the environment; the second, features of the person; and the third combines both elements.

According to the first line of reasoning, the relatively dense spacing of major life events during the transition to adulthood (completion of education, marriage, parenthood, entry into the work force or the military) generates external pressures to form new attitudes or to change previous views (Glenn 1980). While the same kinds of events sometimes occur later in life, they are usually spaced more widely and involve a revision of previous experiences rather than wholly new circumstances requiring adaptation (e.g., a job or career change, remarriage, or entry into an adult education program). Similarly, experiences at work generally assume greater constancy after an initial period of job instability (Osterman 1980). Primary relationships, which provide support for attitudes, are often in flux during the transition to adulthood; thereafter, stable primary groups may provide continuing support for previously crystallized attitudinal positions (Sears 1981; Backman 1981). According to this perspective, there may be continuing capacity to change throughout life (Baltes, Reese, and Lipsitt 1980), but if environments become more stable after the adult transition, there will be less impetus for such change over time (Moss and Susman 1980).

Another set of explanations links the "aging stability" pattern to individual attributes that foster growing resistance to change. Mannheim's (1952) classic concept of generation implies that the young are especially receptive to influences generated by the important historical changes of their time (economic upheaval, war, or political revolution). Alwin, Cohen, and Newcomb (forthcoming) find evidence for a "generational/persistence model," which similarly combines notions of vulnerability in youth and persistence thereafter. Before role and character identities are formed, a person may be quite malleable. However, preserving a consistent, stable sense of self is a major motivational goal (Rosenberg 1979); and once self-identities are linked to key attitudes and values, a person's self may become inextricably tied to those views (Sears 1981). Moreover, feelings of dissonance (Festinger 1957) arise when attitudes and beliefs that provide a sense of understanding are threatened (Glenn 1980). Consistent with the notion that young adults may be more ready to change, occupational experiences (i.e., experiences related to autonomy) have been found to have stronger influences on the work orientations of younger workers, ages sixteen to twenty-nine, than on those who are older (Lorence and Mortimer 1985; Mortimer, Finch, and Maruyama 1988).

According to a third point of view, an interaction between a young person and the environment fosters a process of "accentuation" of preexisting traits. While early experiences provide initial impetus for personal development, attitudes and values formed in childhood or adolescence are later strengthened through the individual's active selection, production, or maintenance of environmental circumstances that support earlier dispositions. According to this view, youth making the transition to adulthood are not passive recipients of environmental forces; instead they select or mold their environments (Lerner and Busch-Rossnagel 1981) so as to maintain or reinforce initial psychological states. As a result, there may be an "increase in emphasis of already prominent characteristics during social transitions in the life course" (Elder and Caspi 1990, p. 218).

Illustrations of such processes abound in the literature. For example, students choosing particular college majors become increasingly similar in interests and values over time (Feldman and Weiler 1976). Mortimer, Lorence, and Kumka's (1986) study of a panel of young men showed that competence measured in the senior year of college predicted work autonomy ten years later, which in turn fostered an increasing sense of competence over time. Similarly, intrinsic, extrinsic, and people-oriented values prior to adult entry to the work force led to the selection of occupational experiences that served to maintain and strengthen these value preferences. Psychological well-being in late adolescence increased the likelihood of marriage, which further heightened subsequent well-being. Alwin, Cohen, and Newcomb's (forthcoming) follow-up study of women who attended Bennington College in the 1930s indicated that the choice of associates and the formation of supportive reference groups—spouses, friends, and children—played a substantial part in maintaining the women's political values.

Elder's longitudinal study of young people growing up during the Great Depression has amassed evidence that successful encounters with problems in adolescence can build confidence and resources that promote effective coping with events later in life, fostering personality continuity (Elder 1974; Elder, Liker, and Cross 1984). For members of the Oakland cohort, early economic deprivation provided opportunity to help the family in a time of crisis, and the consequent self-efficacy, motivation, and capacity to mobilize effort fostered adult work and family security. Elder and Caspi (1990) similarly found that adolescents with more resilient personalities reacted more positively as young adults to combat in World War II. Negative early events may, however, set in motion processes that accentuate problems. For example, traumatic war experiences in early adulthood can threaten marriage and thereby reinforce a cycle of irritability (Elder and Caspi 1990, p. 235).

Whereas sociologists emphasize the social determination of early adult outcomes, and social psychologists have noted enduring personality and character traits that influence the process of transition to adulthood, it must be recognized that changes in both socioeconomic and personal trajectories do occur, frequently at times of life-course transition. Change can occur as a result of "fortuitous events" that intervene in the developmental process rather than reinforcing patterns of preadult behavior (Elder and Caspi 1988, p. 102). For example, the quality of a first marriage may lead to a change in direction of a previously disorderly or otherwise problematic early life course (Rutter and Quinton 1984).

[See also Socialization.]

BIBLIOGRAPHY

Alwin, Duane F., Ronald L. Cohen, and Theodore M. Newcomb (Forthcoming) *Aging, Personality, and Social Change: Attitude Persistence and Change over the Life-Span.* Madison: University of Wisconsin Press.

Aries, Philippe 1962 *Centuries of Childhood: A Social History of Family Life.* New York: Vintage.

Backman, Carl W. 1981 "Attraction in Interpersonal Relationships." In M. Rosenberg and R. H. Turner, eds., *Social Psychology: Sociological Perspective.* New York: Basic Books.

Baltes, Paul B., Hayne W. Reese, and Lewis P. Lipsitt 1980 "Life-Span Developmental Psychology." *Annual Review of Psychology* 31:65–110.

Blau, Peter M., and Otis Dudley Duncan 1967 *The American Occupational Structure.* New York: Wiley.

Bowles, Samuel, and Herbert Gintis 1976 *Schooling in Capitalist America.* New York: Basic Books.

Buchmann, Marlis 1989 *The Script of Life in Modern Society: Entry into Adulthood in a Changing World.* Chicago: University of Chicago Press.

Clausen, John 1991 "Adolescent Competence and the Shaping of the Life Course." *American Journal of Sociology* 96:805–842.

Coleman, James S., and Torsten Husen 1985 *Becoming Adult in a Changing Society.* Paris: Organization for Economic Co-operation and Development.

Connor, John W., and George A. De Vos 1989 "Cultural Influences on Achievement Motivation and Orientation toward Work in Japanese and American Youth." In D. Stern and D. Eichorn, eds., *Adolescence and Work: Influences of Social Structure, Labor Markets, and Culture.* Hillsdale, NJ.: Lawrence Erlbaum.

Elder, Glen H., Jr. 1974 *Children of the Great Depression.* Chicago: University of Chicago Press.

———, and Avshalom Caspi 1988 "Human Development and Social Change: An Emerging Perspective on the Life Course." In N. Bolger, A. Caspi, G. Downey, and M. Moorehouse, eds., *Persons in Context: Developmental Processes.* New York: Cambridge University Press.

——— 1990 "Studying Lives in a Changing Society: Sociological and Personological Explorations." In A. I. Rabin, R. A. Zucker, and S. Frank, eds., *Studying Persons and Lives.* New York: Springer-Verlag.

Elder, Glen H., Jr., J. K. Liker, and C. E. Cross 1984 "Parent-Child Behavior in the Great Depression: Life Course and Intergenerational Influences." In P. B. Baltes, ed., *Life-Span Development and Behavior.* New York: Academic Press.

Featherman, David L. 1980 "Schooling and Occupational Careers: Constancy and Change in Worldly Success." In O. G. Brim, Jr., and J. Kagan, eds., *Constancy and Change in Human Development.* Cambridge, Mass.: Harvard University Press.

———, and Annemette Sorensen 1983 "Societal Transformation in Norway and Change in the Life Course Transition into Adulthood." *Acta Sociologica* 26:105–126.

———, and Kenneth I. Spenner 1988 "Class and the Socialization of Children: Constancy, Change, or Irrelevance?" In E. Mavis Hetherington, R. M. Lerner, and M. Perlmutter, eds., *Child Development in Perspective.* Hillsdale, N.J.: Lawrence Erlbaum.

Feldman, Kenneth A., and John Weiler 1976 "Changes in Initial Differences among Major-Field Groups: An Exploration of the 'Accentuation Effect.' " In W. H. Sewell, R. M. Hauser, and D. L Featherman, eds., *Schooling and Achievement in American Society.* New York: Academic Press.

Festinger, Leon 1957 *A Theory of Cognitive Dissonance.* Stanford, Calif.: Stanford University Press.

Finch, Michael D., Michael J. Shanahan, Jeylan T. Mortimer, and Seongryeol Ryu 1990 "Work Experience and Control Orientation in Adolescence." Paper presented at the 1990 American Sociological Association Meeting, Washington, D.C., August.

Foner, Anne, and David Kertzer 1978 "Transitions over the Life Course: Lessons from Age-Set Societies." *American Journal of Sociology* 83:1,081–1,104.

Freeman, Richard B., and David A. Wise 1979 *Youth Unemployment.* Cambridge, Mass.: National Bureau of Economic Research.

Furstenberg, Frank F., Jr., J. Brooks-Gunn, and S. Philip Morgan 1987 *Adolescent Mothers in Later Life.* Cambridge: Cambridge University Press.

Gecas, Viktor 1979 "The Influence of Social Class on Socialization." In W. R. Burr, R. Hill, F. I. Nye, and I. L. Reiss, *Contemporary Theories about the Family.* Vol. 1, *Research-Based Theories.* New York: Free Press.

Glenn, Norval D. 1980 "Values, Attitudes, and Beliefs." In O. G. Brim, Jr., and J. Kagan, eds., *Constancy and Change in Human Development.* Cambridge, Mass.: Harvard University Press.

Granovetter, Mark S. 1974 *Getting a Job.* Cambridge, Mass.: Harvard University Press.

Greenberger, Ellen, and Laurence Steinberg 1986 *When Teenagers Work.* New York: Basic Books.

Grubb, W. Norton 1989 "Preparing Youth for Work: The Dilemmas of Education and Training Programs." In D. Stern and D. Eichorn, eds., *Adolescence and Work: Influences of Social Structure, Labor Markets, and Culture.* Hillsdale, N.J.: Lawrence Erlbaum.

Hall, G. S. 1904 *Adolescence: Its Psychology and Its Relations to Physiology, Anthropology, Sociology, Sex, Crime, Religion, and Education.* New York: Appleton.

Hamilton, Stephen F. 1990 *Apprenticeship for Adulthood Preparing Youth for the Future.* New York: Free Press.

Hogan, Dennis P., and Nan Marie Astone 1986 "The Transition to Adulthood." *Annual Review of Sociology* 12:109–130.

Jessor, Richard, and Shirley L. Jessor 1977 *Problem Behavior and Psychosocial Development: A Longitudinal Study of Youth.* New York: Academic Press.

Jordaan, Jean Pierre, and Donald E. Super 1974 "The Prediction of Early Adult Vocational Behavior." In D. F. Ricks, A. Thomas, and M. Roff, eds. *Life History Research in Psychopathology.* Minneapolis: University of Minnesota Press.

Keniston, Kenneth 1970 "Youth as a Stage of Life." *American Scholar* 39:631–654.

Kerckhoff, Alan C. 1990 *Getting Started: Transition to Adulthood in Great Britain.* Boulder, Colo.: Westview Press.

Klein, Hugh 1990 "Adolescence, Youth, and Young Adulthood: Rethinking Current Conceptualizations of Life Stage." *Youth and Society* 21:446–471.

Kohn, Melvin L., and Carmi Schooler 1983 *Work and Personality: An Inquiry into the Impact of Social Stratification.* Norwood, NJ.: Ablex Publishing.

———, Kazimierz M. Slomczynski, and Carrie Schoenbach 1986 "Social Stratification and the Transmission of Values in the Family: A Cross-National Assessment." *Sociological Forum* 1:73–102.

Lerner, Richard M., and N. A. Busch-Rossnagel (eds.) 1981 *Individuals as Producers of Their Development: A Life-Span Perspective.* New York: Academic Press.

Lorence, Jon, and Jeylan T. Mortimer 1985 "Job Involvement through the Life Course: A Panel Study of Three Age Groups." *American Sociological Review* 50:618–638.

McLaughlin, Steven D., Barbara D. Melber, John O. G. Billy, Denise M. Zimmerle, Linda D. Winges, and Terry R. Johnson 1988 *The Changing Lives of American Women.* Chapel Hill: University of North Carolina Press.

Mainquist, Sheri, and Dorothy Eichorn 1989 "Competence in Work Settings." In D. Stern and D. Eichorn, eds., *Adolescence and Work: Influences of Social Structure, Labor Markets, and Culture.* Hillsdale, N.J.: Lawrence Erlbaum.

Mannheim, Karl 1952 "The Problem of Generations." In P. Kecskemeti, ed., *Essays in the Sociology of Knowledge.* London: Routledge and Kegan Paul.

Marini, Margaret Mooney 1984a "The Order of Events in the Transition to Adulthood." *Sociology of Education* 57:63–84.

——— 1984b "Age and Sequencing Norms in the Transition to Adulthood." *Social Forces* 63:229–244.

——— 1987 "Measuring the Process of Role Change during the Transition to Adulthood." *Social Science Research* 6:1–38.

———, Hee-Choon Shin, and Jennie Raymond 1989 "Socioeconomic Consequences of the Process of Transition to Adulthood." *Social Science Research* 13:89–135.

Meyer, Robert M., and David A. Wise 1982 "High School Preparation and Early Labor Force Experience." In R. B. Freeman and D. A. Wise, eds., *The Youth Labor Market Problem: Its Nature, Causes, and Consequences.* Chicago: University of Chicago Press.

Modell, John 1980 "Normative Aspects of American Marriage Timing since World War II." *Journal of Family History* 5:210–234.

——— 1989 *Into One's Own: From Youth to Adulthood in the United States, 1920–1975.* Berkeley: University of California Press.

———, Frank Furstenberg, and Theodore Hershberg 1976 "Social Change and Transitions to Adulthood in Historical Perspective." *Journal of Family History* 1:7–32.

Mortimer, Jeylan T., and Michael D. Finch 1986 "The Effects of Part-Time Work on Self-Concept and Achievement." In K. Borman and J. Reisman, eds., *Becoming a Worker.* Norwood, N.J.: Ablex Publishing.

———, Michael D. Finch, and Donald S. Kumka 1982 "Persistence and Change in Development: The Multidimensional Self-Concept." In P. D. Baltes and O. G. Brim, Jr., eds., *Life-Span Development and Behavior.* New York: Academic Press.

———, Michael D. Finch, and Geoffrey Maruyama 1988 "Work Experience and Job Satisfaction: Variation by Age and Gender." In J. T. Mortimer and K. M. Borman, eds., *Work Experience and Psychological Development through the Life Span.* Boulder, Colo.: Westview Press.

———, Michael D. Finch, Michael Shanahan, and Seongryeol Ryu (Forthcoming) "Work Experience, Mental Health, and Behavioral Adjustment in Adolescence." *Journal of Research on Adolescence.*

———, and Donald S. Kumka 1982 "A Further Examination of the 'Occupational Linkage Hypothesis.' " *Sociological Quarterly* 23:3–16.

———, Jon Lorence, and Donald S. Kumka 1986 *Work, Family, and Personality: Transition to Adulthood.* Norwood, N.J.: Ablex Publishing.

———, and Roberta G. Simmons 1978 "Adult Socialization." *Annual Review of Sociology* 4:421–454.

Moss, Howard A., and Elizabeth J. Susman 1980 "Longitudinal Study of Personality Development." In O. G. Brim, Jr., and J. Kagan, eds., *Constancy and Change in Human Development.* Cambridge, Mass.: Harvard University Press.

Neugarten, Bernice L., and Nancy Datan 1973 "Sociological Perspectives on the Life Cycle." In P. B. Baltes and K. Warner Schaie, eds., *Life Span Developmental Psychology: Personality and Socialization.* New York: Academic Press.

Neugarten, Bernice L., Joan W. Moore, and John C. Lowe 1965 "Age Norms, Age Constraints, and Adult Socialization." *American Journal of Sociology* 70:710–717.

Ogbu, John U. 1989 "Cultural Boundaries and Minority Youth Orientation toward Work Preparation." In D. Stern and D. Eichorn, eds., *Adolescence and Work: Influences of Social Structure, Labor Markets, and Culture.* Hillsdale, N.J.: Lawrence Erlbaum.

Osterman, Paul 1980 *Getting Started: The Youth Labor Market.* Cambridge, Mass.: MIT Press.

——— 1989 "The Job Market for Adolescents." In D. Stern and D. Eichorn, eds., *Adolescence and Work: Influences of Social Structure, Labor Markets, and Culture,* Hillsdale, N.J.: Lawrence Erlbaum.

Panel on Youth of the President's Science Advisory Committee 1974 *Youth: Transition to Adulthood.* Chicago: University of Chicago Press.

Phillips, Sarah, and Kent Sandstrom 1990 "Parental Attitudes toward 'Youthwork.' " *Youth and Society* 22:160–183.

Quinton, David 1988 "Longitudinal Approaches to Intergenerational Studies: Definition, Design, and Use." In M. Rutter, ed., *Studies of Psychosocial Risk: The Power of Longitudinal Data.* Cambridge: Cambridge University Press.

———, and Michael Rutter 1988 *Parenting Breakdown: The Making and Breaking of Intergenerational Links.* Aldershot, U.K.: Gower.

Rindfuss, Ronald R., S. Philip Morgan, and Gray Swicegood 1988 *First Births in America: Changes in the Timing of Parenthood.* Berkeley: University of California Press.

Rosenbaum, James 1976 *Making Inequality: The Hidden Curriculum of High School Tracking.* New York: Wiley.

Rosenberg, Morris 1979 *Conceiving the Self.* New York: Basic Books.

Rossi, Alice S. 1980 "Life-Span Theories and Women's Lives." *Signs: Journal of Women in Culture and Society* 6:4–32.

Rutter, Michael, and David Quinton 1984 "Long-Term Follow-Up of Women Institutionalized in Childhood: Factors Promoting Good Functioning in Adult Life." *British Journal of Developmental Psychology* 2:191–204.

Sears, David O. 1981 "Life-Stage Effects on Attitude Change, Especially among the Elderly." In B. Kiesler, J. N. Morgan, and V.

Kincade Oppenheimer, eds., *Aging: Social Change.* New York: Academic Press.

Sewell, William H., and Robert M. Hauser 1976 "Causes and Consequences of Higher Education: Models of the Status Attainment Process." In W. H. Sewell, R. M. Hauser, and D. L. Featherman, eds., *Schooling and Achievement in American Society.* New York: Academic Press.

Stern, David, and Yoshi-Fumi Nakata 1989 "Characteristics of High School Students' Paid Jobs, and Employment Experience after Graduation." In D. Stern and D. Eichorn, eds., *Adolescence and Work: Influences of Social Structure, Labor Markets, and Culture.* Hillsdale, N.J.: Lawrence Erlbaum.

Wilson, William Julius 1987 *The Truly Disadvantaged: The Inner City, the Underclass, and Public Policy.* Chicago: University of Chicago Press.

– JEYLAN T. MORTIMER

AFFIRMATIVE ACTION

The term *affirmative action* has been used in the United States since the late 1960s to refer to policies that go beyond the simple prohibition of discrimination on grounds of race, national origin, and sex in employment practices and educational programs. These policies require some further action, "affirmative action," to make jobs and promotions and admissions to educational programs available to individuals from groups that have historically suffered from discrimination in gaining these opportunities or are, whether discriminated against or not by formal policies and informal practices, infrequently found in certain occupations or educational institutions and programs.

Affirmative action policies may be policies of governments or governmental units, affecting their own procedures in employment or in granting contracts; or they may be policies of governments, affecting the employment procedures of companies or nonprofit agencies and organizations over whom the governments have power or with whom they deal; or they may be the policies of profit and nonprofit employers, adopted voluntarily or under varying degrees of public or private pressure. Affirmative action policies may include the policies of philanthropic foundations, when they affect the employment policies of their grantees, or educational accrediting agencies, when they affect the employment or admissions policies of the institutions they accredit.

The range of policies that can be called affirmative action is wide, but the term also has a specific legal meaning. It was first used in a legal context in the United States in an executive order of President John F. Kennedy. Subsequent presidential executive orders and other administrative requirements have expanded its scope and meaning, and since 1971 affirmative action so defined has set employment practice standards for contractors of the United States, that is, every company, college, university, hospital, or other institution that has business with the U.S. government. These standards are enforced by an office of the Department of Labor, the Office of Federal Contract Compliance Programs. Because of the wide sweep of the executive order and its reach into the employment practices of almost every large employer, affirmative action policies have become extremely controversial.

Affirmative action, under other names, is also to be found in other countries to help groups, whether majority or minority, that have not fared as well as others in gaining employment in higher status occupations or admissions to advanced educational programs.

Affirmative action has been controversial because it appears to contradict a central objective of traditional liberalism and the U.S. civil rights movement, that is, the treatment of individuals on the basis of their individual talents and not on the basis of their color, race, national origin, or sex. Affirmative action, as it has developed, requires surveys by employers of the race, national origin, and sex of their employees to uncover patterns of "underutilization" and to develop programs to overcome this underutilization and thus to take account of the race, national origin, and sex of applicants for employment and of candidates for promotion. To many advocates of expanded civil rights, this is seen as only the next and a most necessary step in achieving equality for groups that have in the past faced discrimination. To others who deem themselves advocates of civil rights and of the interests of minority groups, affirmative action, in the form in which it has developed, is seen as a violation of the first requirement for a society that promises equal opportunity, that is, to treat individuals as individuals independent of race, national origin, or sex.

This apparent contradiction between civil rights and affirmative action may be glimpsed in the very language of the Civil Rights Act of 1964, the central piece of legislation that banned discrimination in government programs, public facilities, and employment. In the debate over that act, fears were expressed that the prohibition of discrimination in employment, as codified in Title VII, would be implemented by requiring certain numbers of employees to be of a given race. This fear was dealt with by placing language in the act that was understood at the time specifically to forbid the practices that are required under affirmative action since the late 1960s and early 1970s. Tide 703 (j) reads:

> Nothing contained in this title shall be interpreted to require any employer . . . to grant preferential treatment to any individual or to any group because of the

> race, color, religion, sex, or national origin of such individual or group on account of an imbalance which may exist with respect to the total number or percentage of persons of any race, color, religion, sex, or national origin employed by any employer.

However, federal executive orders governing how the federal government does its business may set their own standards, independent of statutory law. The first executive order using the term *affirmative action* was issued by President John F. Kennedy in 1961. It created a President's Committee on Equal Employment Opportunity to monitor the obligations contractors undertook to extend affirmative action. At this time, the general understanding of affirmative action was that it required such things as giving public notice that the employer did not discriminate, making the availability of positions and promotions widely known, advertising in minority media, and the like. With the Civil Rights Act of 1964—which not only prohibited discrimination on grounds of race, color, and national origin but also on grounds of sex—a new executive order, no. 11,246, was formulated by President Lyndon B. Johnson and came into effect. It replaced the President's Committee on Equal Employment Opportunity with an Office of Federal Contract Compliance Programs (which still operates). Subsequent federal regulations of the late 1960s and early 1970s specified what was meant by affirmative action in the executive order, and the meaning of affirmative action was considerably expanded into the full-fledged program that has existed since 1971. Revised order no. 4 of that year, which is part of the *Code of Federal Regulations* and is still in effect, reads in part:

> An affirmative action program is a set of specific and result-oriented procedures to which a contractor commits itself to apply every good effort. The objective of those procedures plus such efforts is equal employment opportunity. Procedures without efforts to make them work are meaningless; and effort, undirected by specific and meaningful procedures, is inadequate. An effective affirmative action program must include an analysis of areas within which the contractor is deficient in the utilization of minority groups and women, and further, goals and timetables to which the contractor's good faith efforts must be directed to correct the deficiencies and, [sic] thus to achieve prompt and full utilization of minorities and women, at all levels and in all segments of its work force where deficiencies exist. (Code of Federal Regulations 1990, pp. 121–122)

Much of the controversy over affirmative action is over the term *goals and timetables:* Are these "quotas"? Supporters of affirmative action say not—only good faith efforts are required, and if they fail the contractor is not penalized. Further controversy exists over the term *utilization:* What is the basis on which a group is found "underutilized," and to what extent is this evidence of discrimination?

President Ronald Reagan was an avowed opponent of affirmative action, but despite his eight-year administration no modification of the program took place.

Controversy also arises over the categories of employees that contractors must report on and over whose utilization they must be concerned. The executive order lists four categories: blacks, Spanish-surnamed Americans, American Indians, and Orientals. (These are the terms in the order as of 1971 and are still used in the *Code of Federal Regulations.*) The preferred names of these groups have changed since then to Afro- or African-Americans, Hispanics or Latinos, Native Americans, and Asians. While the original executive order and the Civil Rights Act was a response to the political action of black civil rights groups, and it was the plight of blacks that motivated both the executive order and the Civil Rights Act, it was apparently deemed unwise in the mid-1960s to limit affirmative action requirements to blacks alone. The Civil Rights Act bans discrimination against any person on grounds of race, national origin, and sex and specifies no group in particular for protection; but the Equal Employment Opportunity Commission, set up by the Civil Rights Act to monitor discrimination in employment, from the beginning required reports on the four groups listed above, despite the fact that even in the 1960s it could be argued that discrimination against Asians was far less acute and much less of a problem than discrimination against blacks, that discrimination against American Indians also differed in severity and character from discrimination against blacks, and that discrimination against Spanish-surnamed Americans ranged from the nonexistent or hardly existent (Spaniards from Spain? Cubans? Sephardic Jews?) to the possibly significant. Nevertheless, these four categories set up in the mid-1960s are still the groups that governmental programs of affirmative action target for special attention (Glazer 1987).

Since affirmative action is a governmental program operated by government agencies that grant contracts and is overseen by the Office of Federal Contract Compliance Programs, one major issue of controversy has been over the degree to which these programs are really enforced. It is generally believed that enforcement is more severe under Democratic administrations than under Republican administrations, even though the program was first fully developed under the Republican administration of President Richard Nixon. President Ronald Reagan was an avowed opponent of affirmative action, but despite his eight-year administration no modification of the program took place. Changes were proposed by some parts of the Republican administration but opposed by others. Business, in particular big business, had learned to live with affirmative action and was not eager to upset the apple cart (Belz 1990).

Perhaps the most controversial area in which affirmative action is applied is in the employment and promotion of police, firefighting and sanitation personnel, and teachers and other local government employees. Here strict racial quotas often do apply. They are strongly resented by many employees when new employees are hired by race and even more when promotions are given out by race and layoffs are determined by race. The basis of these quotas is not the presidential executive order but rather consent decrees entered into by local government on the basis of charges of discrimination brought by the federal government. These charges are brought on the basis of the Civil Rights Act; under this act, if is found, quotas can be required by courts as a remedy. Since local government employment is generally on the basis of tests, one very controversial aspect of such cases is the role of civil service examinations. Blacks and Hispanics characteristically do worse than white applicants. Are these poorer results to be taken as evidence of discrimination? A complex body of law has been built up on the basis of various cases determining when a test should be considered discriminatory. In the Civil Rights Act of 1964, one provision read "it shall not be an unlawful employment practice . . . for an employer to give and act upon the results of any professionally developed ability test provided that such test . . . is not designed, intended, or used to dis-

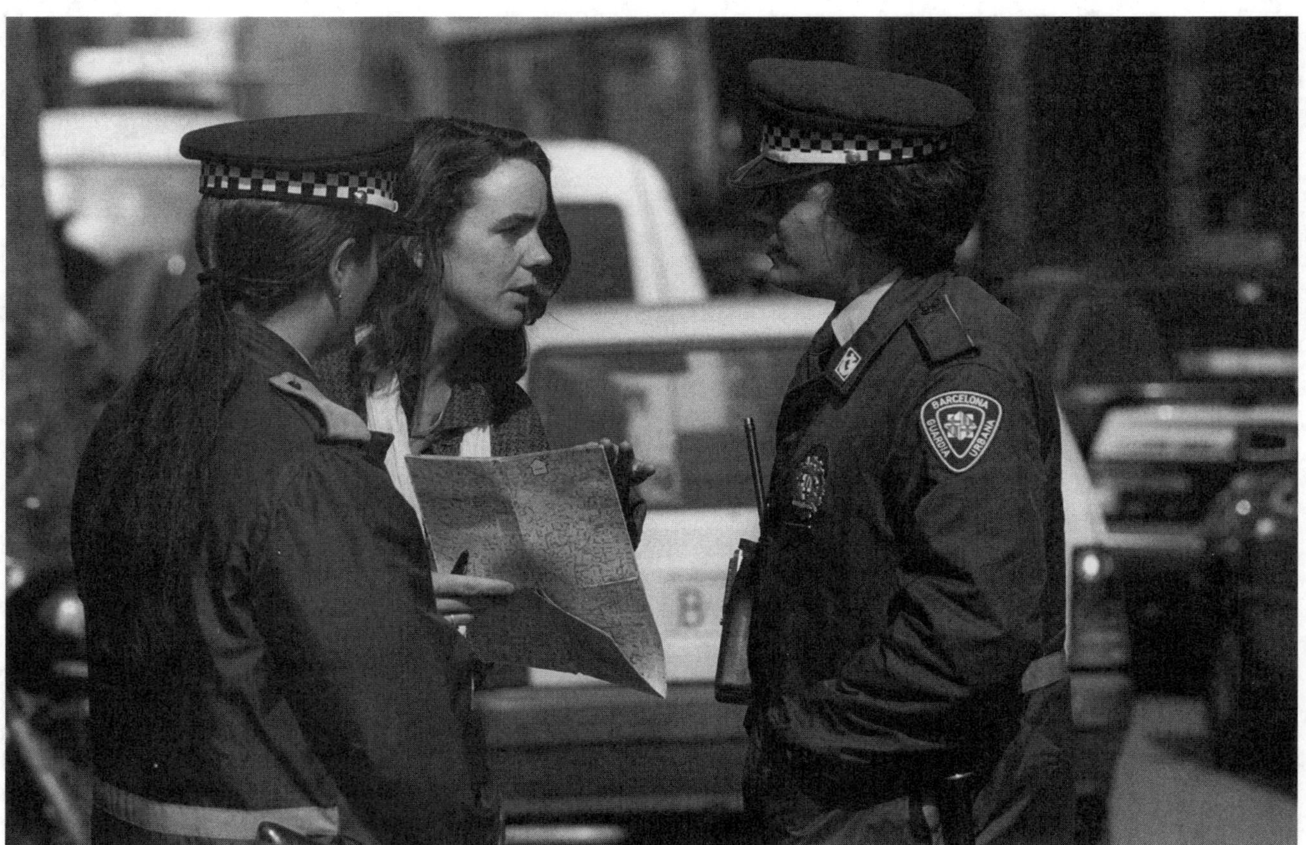

Allowing women and minorities a fair chance at good jobs is the intended consequence of affirmative action policies. However, some workers complain that these policies often allow less qualified people into positions that are denied to qualified white males. (Owen Franken/Corbis)

criminate." But the courts decide whether the test is "designed, intended, or used to discriminate." Because of the frequency with which courts have found tests for the police, fire, or sanitation force discriminatory, and because state and local governments believe they will lose such cases, many have entered into "consent decrees" in which they agree to hire and promote on the basis of racial and sex criteria.

Affirmative action is also used in the granting of government contracts on the basis of either statutes (federal, state, or local) or administrative procedures. Such procedures in granting contracts have also been attacked in the courts. Some have been upheld, while some have been struck down by the Supreme Court. The state of the law will of course change with the composition of the Court, but as of this writing the Court requires some previous showing of discrimination as a basis for establishing preference for minority contractors in getting contracts.

One issue in preferring minority contractors has been that of possible fraud, as various contractors find it to their advantage to take on black partners so as to present themselves as minority contractors and thus to get whatever advantages in bidding that status provides. In this area, as in other areas where advantage might follow from minority status, there have been debates over what groups may be included as minorities. It was unclear, for example, whether Asian Indians—immigrants and American citizens of Indian origin—were to be considered Asian. Asian Indian Americans were divided among themselves on this question, but during the Reagan administration they were reclassified as Asian, presumably in part for the modest political advantage this gave the Republican administration.

Affirmative action also governs the employment practices of colleges and universities, whether public or private, because they all make use of federal grants and loans for their students, and many have government research contracts. Colleges and universities therefore must also survey their faculties and other staffs for underutilization, and they develop elaborate affirmative action programs. Affirmative action applies to women as well as to racial and ethnic minority groups. There has been, perhaps in part because of affirmative action programs, a substantial increase in female faculty. But there has been little increase in black faculty during the 1980s. The numbers of blacks taking doctorates in arts and sciences has been small and has not increased. Possibly the higher rewards of law, business, and medicine have attracted into those fields black students who could prepare themselves for an academic career. Many campuses have been shaken by controversies over the small number of black faculty, with administrators arguing that few were available and protestors, often black students, arguing that greater effort would change the situation.

The term *affirmative action* is also used to describe admissions to undergraduate colleges and graduate and professional programs in which preference is given to black, Hispanic, and Native American students. This kind of affirmative action is not required by government regulations, as in the case of employment, except in the special case of southern public higher education institutions. There parallel and separate black and white institutions existed, and while all of these institutions have been open to both white and black students since at least the early 1970s, an extended lawsuit has charged that they still preserve their identity as traditionally black and traditionally white institutions. As a result of this litigation, many of these institutions accept goals that require them to recruit a certain number of black students. But the major pressure on many other institutions to increase the number of black students has come from goals voluntarily accepted by administrators or as a result of black student demands. (In one case, that of the University of California, the state legislature has called on the institution to mirror in its racial-ethnic composition the graduating classes of California high schools.) Voluntary affirmative action programs for admission of students, targeted on black, Hispanic, and Native American students, became quite popular in the late 1960s and early 1970s, particularly after the death of Martin Luther King. They have led to legal controversies as well as, according to observers, some tension between white and black students (Bunzel 1988).

The first affirmative action cases to reach the Supreme Court challenged such programs of preference for black and other minority students. A rejected Jewish applicant for admission to the University of Washington Law School, which had set a quota to increase the number of its minority students, sued for admission, and his case reached the Supreme Court. It did not rule on it. The Court did rule on a subsequent case, that of Allan Bakke, a rejected applicant to the University of California, Davis, Medical School, which also had set a quota. The Court, splitting into a number of factions, rejected fixed numerical quotas but asserted race was a factor that could be taken into account in admissions decisions for purposes of promoting academic diversity. Most American colleges and universities of any reputation do give such preference to black, Hispanic, and Native American applicants; in the 1970s they may have given such preference to Asian applicants, but this practice ceased in the 1980s as the number of qualified Asian applicants rapidly increased. Indeed, Asian applicants have charged that they now face discrimination (Bunzel and Au 1987).

Since these 1970s cases there have been many Supreme Court cases on many aspects of affirmative action in employment, in the granting of contracts, and in college and university admissions. On the whole, the policies have survived. The Supreme Court has made and continues to make many fine distinctions between legitimate and illegitimate practices. Affirmative action has been a divisive issue in American political life and has sometimes been raised effectively in political campaigns. It has divided former allies on civil rights issues, in particular American Jews, normally liberal, from blacks. Jews oppose quotas in admissions to medical and law schools because they were in the past victims of very low quotas imposed by American universities.

Affirmative action has divided former allies on civil rights issues, in particular American Jews, normally liberal, from blacks.

Affirmative action under various names and legal arrangements is found in many countries: in India, to provide opportunities to scheduled castes, scheduled tribes, and other backward classes, where different requirements operate at the national level and within the states and where some degree of preference has existed in some areas and for some purposes as far back as the 1920s (Galanter 1984); in Malaysia, to protect the native Malay population; in Sri Lanka, to benefit the majority Sri Lankan population (Sowell 1990); and in Australia and Canada, where milder forms of affirmative action than those found in the United States operate. The policies called affirmative action in the United States are called "reservations" in India, and "positive discrimination" in other countries.

There is considerable debate as to the effects of affirmative action policies and how weighty these can be as against other factors affecting employment, promotion, and educational achievement (Leonard 1984a; 1984b). A summary judgment is difficult to make. Black leaders generally consider affirmative action an essential foundation for black progress, but some black intellectuals and publicists have been skeptical. Black leaders often denounce opponents of affirmative action as racists, hidden or otherwise, yet it is clear that many opponents simply find the use, required or otherwise, of racial and sexual characteristics to determine job and promotion opportunities and admission to selective college programs in contradiction with the basic liberal principles of treating individuals without regard to race, national origin, color, and sex. Affirmative action has undoubtedly increased the number of blacks who hold good jobs and gain admission to selective programs. But it has also had other costs in the form of increased racial tensions. It has coincided with a period in which a pattern of black advancement occupationally and educationally since World War II has been surprisingly checked. The defenders of affirmative action argue that this is because it has not yet been applied vigorously enough. The opponents argue that the concentration on affirmative action encourages the neglect of the key factors that promote educational and occupational progress, which are basically the acquisition of qualifications for better jobs and superior educational programs.

[See also Discrimination; Equality of Opportunity.]

BIBLIOGRAPHY

Belz, Herman 1990 *Equality Transformed: A Quarter-Century of Affirmative Action.* New Brunswick, N.J.: Transaction Books.

Bunzel, John H. 1988 "Affirmative-Action Admissions: How It 'Works' at UC Berkeley." *The Public Interest* 93:111–129.

———, and Jeffrey K. D. Au 1987 "Diversity or Discrimination? Asian Americans in College." *The Public Interest* 87:49–62.

Code of Federal Regulations 1990 Title 41, section 60-2.10, pp. 121–122.

Galanter, Marc 1984 *Competing Equalities: Law and the Backward Classes in India.* Berkeley: University of California Press.

Glazer, Nathan 1987 *Affirmative Discrimination: Ethnic Inequality and Public Policy.* Cambridge, Mass.: Harvard University Press. (Originally published 1975 and 1978, New York: Basic Books.)

Leonard, Jonathan 1984a "The Impact of Affirmative Action on Employment." Working Paper No. 1,310. Cambridge, Mass.: National Bureau of Economic Research.

——— 1984b "What Promises Are Worth: The Impact of Affirmative Action Goals." Working Paper no. 1,346. Cambridge, Mass.: National Bureau of Economic Research. (Also published in *Journal of Human Resources* (1985) 20:3–20.)

Sowell, Thomas 1990 *Preferential Policies: An International Perspective.* New York: William Morrow.

– NATHAN GLAZER

AFRICAN-AMERICAN STUDIES

African-American research has expanded greatly in recent years. This article covers only selected aspects of this research: certain theoretical debates, the sociological interpretation of slavery, the debate on the underclass, and analyses of current discrimination.

Theories of Black-White Relations

Explanatory theories of U.S. racial relations can be classified roughly into "order-deficit" theories and "power-conflict" theories. Order-deficit theories accent the gradual inclusion of an out-group such as African-

Americans into the dominant white society and culture of the United States, and emphasize the internal subcultural barriers to further progress—that is, those that lie within the African-American outgroup—or both. Power-conflict theories, in contrast, emphasize external structural barriers preventing racial integration, such as the huge power and resource imbalance between black and white Americans.

Hirschman has suggested that one major order-deficit viewpoint, the assimilationist perspective, remains the major theoretical framework guiding most sociological research in the field of racial and ethnic relations (Hirschman 1983). One major scholar, Milton Gordon (1964, 1978), distinguishes several types of initial encounters between racial and ethnic groups and an array of subsequent assimilation outcomes ranging from acculturation to intermarriage. In his view immigrants in the United States have adapted by conforming substantially and by giving up much of their heritage for the dominant white Anglo-Saxon Protestant core culture. Gordon applies this scheme to African-Americans, whom he sees as substantially assimilated at the cultural level (for example, in regard to language) yet with some cultural differences remaining because of the "lower class subculture" among blacks. Beyond this acculturation Gordon sees modest integration at the primary-group level and little intermarriage. In more recent work Gordon (1981) has criticized affirmative action programs and adopted some arguments of the underclass perspective (see below). He is optimistic about the full assimilation and integration of the black middle class (see also Glazer 1975).

Power-conflict analysts reject the assimilationist view of eventual African-American inclusion and assimilation and assimilationists' inclination to focus on deficits within African-American subculture as major barriers to further integration. From the power-conflict perspective, the current condition of African-Americans is more oppressive than that of other U.S. immigrant groups because of its roots in the enslavement of Africans and in the subsequent semislavery of low-wage jobs and poor living conditions. Once a system of extreme subordination is established historically, those in the superior position continue to inherit and monopolize disproportionate socioeconomic resources over many generations. One important power-conflict analyst was Oliver C. Cox, who adopted a neo-Marxist approach: From the 1500s onward black-white stratification in North America arose out of the European imperialistic system of profit-oriented capitalism. The African slave trade was in Cox's view "a way of recruiting labor for the purpose of exploiting the great natural resources of America." The color of Africans was not important; they were chosen "simply because they were the best workers to be found for the heavy labor in the mines and plantations across the Atlantic" (Cox 1948, p. 342; see also Willhelm 1983).

Reflecting a power-conflict perspective, Bob Blauner (1972) argues that there are major differences between black Americans and the white immigrant groups at the center of much assimilationist analysis. The Africans brought across the Atlantic Ocean became part of an internal subordinated colony; they were incorporated against their will, providing much hard labor to build the new society—first as slaves, then as sharecroppers and tenant farmers, and later as low-wage urban laborers. As a result of the northward migration accelerating after 1900, African-Americans also became a subordinate part of the urban socioeconomic system.

Slavery

Recent research on slavery has underscored the importance of the power-conflict perspective for understanding the history and conditions of African-Americans. Manning Marable (1985, p. 5) demonstrates that before the African slave trade began, Western Europeans were predisposed to accept slavery. Slavery was accepted by such Western intellectuals as Plato, Aristotle, and Sir Thomas More, and the European words for "black" had long been associated with the devil, barbarians, and slavery. North American enslavement of Africans was facilitated by this European background.

African-Americans constitute the only U.S. racial-ethnic group that is substantially the result of the forced miscegenation of its ancestors with members of the dominant racial group.

Research by sociologists, social historians, and legal scholars underscores the point that slavery is the foundation of African-American subordination. Legal scholar Patricia Williams has accented the dramatic difference between the oppression faced by the enslaved immigrants and that faced by all white immigrant groups: "The black slave experience was that of lost languages, cultures, tribal ties, kinship bonds, and even of the power to procreate in the image of oneself and not that of an alien master" (Williams, 1987, p. 415). Williams illustrates this last point by relating the story of Austin Miller, her great-great-grandfather, a thirty-five-year-old white lawyer who bought Williams's eleven-year-old black great-great-grandmother, Sophie, and her parents. Miller forced the young Sophie to become the mother of Williams's great-grandmother Mary. Williams's white great-great-grandfather was thus a child molester. African-Americans today constitute the only U.S. racial-ethnic group that is substantially the result of the forced miscegenation of its ancestors with members of the dominant racial group.

A central dilemma for the underclass is the departure of middle-class families from traditional black areas into better neighborhoods farther away.

This negative impact of slavery did not mean that African-American slaves did not resist. Social historian Eugene Genovese (1974) has demonstrated that the extreme conditions of African-American slaves could produce both servile accommodation and violent rebellion. The slaves also created their own distinctive African-American culture out of African cultural fragments remaining to them and out of their creativity in coping with the immediate oppressiveness of New World culture. Herbert Gutman (1976) has demonstrated the extensive cultural and family resiliency and creativity the slaves possessed.

Recent social science research has made it clear why not only white southerners but also many white northerners were willing to perpetuate African-American slavery. Whites in the North built their society in part on slave labor and in part on white immigrant labor from Europe. By the mid-1600s there were strict slave codes in the North. For example, in 1641, three years after whites brought slaves into Massachusetts, the whites enshrined this slavery in law; and Massachusetts merchants and shippers played crucial roles in the North American slave trade. Not until the 1780s did public opinion and court cases come together to abolish New England slavery (Higginbotham 1978, pp. 63–65). By 1786 slaves made up 7 percent of the New York population. Only in 1799 was a partial emancipation statue passed; not until the 1850s were all slaves freed. Moreover, an intense political and economic subordination of free African-Americans accompanied the emancipation of slaves in the North (Higginbotham 1978, pp. 144–149). As Benjamin Ringer put it, "despite the early emancipation of slaves in the North it [racial subordination] remained there, not merely as fossilized remains but as a deeply engrained coding for the future" (1983, p. 533). This important sociological point helps to explain the extensive system of antiblack discrimination and "Jim Crow" segregation that existed in the northern states before and after the Civil War. The freed slaves and their descendants who migrated from the South to northern cities after 1870 migrated into a socioeconomic system already coded to subordinate African-Americans.

The Underclass

Since the 1980s many social scientists, journalists, and government policy analysts have focused on the black "underclass," usually defined as low-income African-Americans, as the root of contemporary black problems. Many analysts have adopted some version of an order-deficit perspective, one that sees in the values and family structures of the black underclass the barriers to assimilation into middle class society. Recent underclass analysts have rehabilitated a viewpoint developed in a 1965 U.S. government publication, *The Negro Family.* There Daniel P. Moynihan argued that a tangle of pathology characterized much of black America and that "there is considerable evidence that the Negro community is, in fact, dividing between a stable middle class group that is steadily growing stronger and more successful and an increasingly disorganized and disadvantaged lower class group" (Moynihan 1965, pp. 5–6).

Since the late 1970s many white journalists and scholarly analysts have adopted and developed this perspective. For example, Ken Auletta produced an influential series of articles published in the *New Yorker* and later developed into a book entitled *The Underclass* (1982). Auletta discusses the black, white, and Hispanic underclasses but emphasizes black Americans. For Auletta, discrimination plays no significant part in the problems of the underclass, described as those with a lifestyle characterized by poverty and antisocial life patterns including immorality, broken families, and a poorly developed work ethic. About the same time black sociologist William J. Wilson became a major exponent of the underclass perspective. Wilson's 1978 work, *The Declining Significance of Race,* contended that affirmative action programs had widened the gap between the increasingly successful black middle class and the deteriorating underclass (for a thorough analysis of middle class conditions, see Farley 1984; Landry 1987). Most readers interpreted Wilson's book as suggesting that discrimination had little significance for African-Americans moving into the middle class and that class differences were more important than antiblack discrimination in explaining the condition of African-Americans.

In *The Truly Disadvantaged* (1987) Wilson further developed his view of the underclass. There he discusses numerous fallacies in the analysis of order-deficit authors such as Moynihan and Auletta. In *The Truly Disadvantaged* Wilson prefers a structural rather than a value-oriented or subcultural explanation for the plight of the underclass. As he sees it, a central dilemma for the underclass is the departure of middle-class families from traditional black areas into better neighborhoods farther away. As a result, not only are there fewer role models for low-income families but there are also fewer supportive institutions, including small stores and churches. Coupled with the resulting social isolation are the concentration effects of having single-parent families, criminals, and the unemployed crowded into one area. Wilson emphasizes joblessness as the important causal factor in the troubles of the underclass: If young black men and women cannot afford to get married, rent an apartment, and live together in a stable economic situation, young black women set up their own households, raise their children, and often depend on welfare benefits.

Other scholars have amplified Wilson's structural critique of order-deficit interpretations of the underclass. Douglas Glasgow (1987) takes issue with the deficit theory's major assumptions: that a value deficiency in the black community created the underclass; that the underclass problem is mainly a female or family problem rather than a racial discrimination problem; and that 1960s poverty programs helped create the underclass. Sidney Willhelm (1983) shows that the restructuring of U.S. capitalism since World War II substantially created the underclass of unemployed and underemployed African-Americans. Those African-Americans who were able to move into better-paying blue-collar jobs during the 1960s and 1970s often faced their industries' decline because of automation and capital flight in the 1980s and 1990s. The movement of jobs from northern cities to Sunbelt cities and overseas is not just part of a routine fluctuation in U.S. history but signals rather that capitalists are moving capital once reinvested in the United States to areas with cheap labor and weak governmental regulation. While the agricultural South and the industrializing cities of the North once needed African-American labor on a significant scale, "today," Willhelm argues, "the economics of corporate capitalism, by turning to automation, makes black labor unessential" (p. 240). The changing investment strategies of corporate executives, not deficits in black values and family organization, are the major villains in creating an African-American underclass.

Discrimination

One additional weakness in most order-deficit arguments is the rejection of racial discrimination as a significant reason for current African-American difficulties. Some, such as Wilson, who criticize the order-deficit interpretation of the underclass problem do not accent continuing racial discrimination. In interviews with rank-and-file whites in the late 1970s and early 1980s, Blauner (1989, p. 197) found that all but one viewed recent decades as an era of great racial progress for black Americans; most viewed racial discrimination as no longer a serious problem in the United States.

Racial discrimination can be defined in social-contextual terms as "practices carried out by members of dominant racial groups which have a differential and negative impact on members of subordinate racial groups" (Eckberg and Feagin 1980; see also Pettigrew 1975). Major dimensions of this discrimination include (a) the motivation for discrimination; (b) the discriminatory action; (c) the effects; (d) the relationship between motivation and action; (e) the relationship between action and effects; (f) the immediate organizational context; and (g) the societal context. Much discrimination research concentrates on (c), the effects of discrimination. A major report by the National Research Council (Jaynes and Williams 1989) summarizes social science evidence on the effects of antiblack discrimination: One in three African-Americans lives in poverty; median African-American family income is 60 percent of median white family income; most African-Americans remain segregated in predominantly minority neighborhoods and schools; and significant inequality remains in political participation.

Within employment settings black Americans face much subtle and blatant discrimination. One example of subtle discrimination is tokenism.

During recent decades the number of black professional, technical, managerial, and administrative workers has increased significantly. Yet African-Americans in these categories have been disproportionately concentrated in jobs with status lower than those that whites fill. Within the professional and technical categories, African-Americans today are most commonly found in such fields as social and recreational work, elementary school teaching, vocational counseling, personnel, dietetics, and health-care work; they are least often found among lawyers and judges, dentists, writers and artists, engineers, and university teachers. Within the managerial and administrative categories, African-Americans are most commonly found among restaurant and bar managers, health administrators, and government officials; they are least commonly found among top corporate executives, bank and financial managers, and wholesale sales managers (Brimmer 1976; Feagin 1989, p. 226).

Within employment settings black Americans face much subtle and blatant discrimination. One example of subtle discrimination is tokenism. Reluctantly tearing down blatant discriminatory barriers over the last two decades, many white officials and executives have retreated to a second line of defense including tokenism. The tokenist strategy is to hire African-Americans for conspicuous but powerless positions. Kenneth Clark (1980) has noted that well-educated African-Americans moving into nontraditional jobs in corporate America have frequently found themselves tracked into positions in "ghettos" within organizations, positions such as a manager of a department of "community affairs" or "special markets." Clark notes that blacks "are rarely found in line positions concerned with developing or controlling production, supervising the work of large numbers of whites or competing with their white 'peers' for significant positions" (p. 30).

Edward Jones (1985; 1986) has reported on a nationwide survey of black corporate executives, all of whom had graduate-level business degrees. Nearly all (98 percent) felt that black managers had not achieved equal opportunity with white managers in their companies. More than 90 percent felt there was much antiblack hostility in corporations and that black managers had less opportunity than whites to succeed in their firms solely on the basis of ability. Two-thirds felt that many whites in corporations still believe African-Americans are intellectually inferior. Most reported that this adverse racial climate had a negative impact on the evaluations, assignments, and promotions of black executives.

In addition, research on cities reveals high levels of residential segregation and housing discrimination. Using 1980 data, Denton and Massey (1988) found that in twenty metropolitan areas with the largest black populations, blacks at all socioeconomic levels continued to be highly segregated into their own residential areas. There has been some increase in the number of African-Americans living in suburban areas, but researchers have found this is mostly because black residents of central cities have spilled into adjacent, often predominantly black, suburbs. In addition, housing search studies in Dallas, Boston, and Denver have found differential treatment favoring white owners and renters looking for housing; whites were more likely to be shown or told about more housing units than were African-Americans with comparable socioeconomic status (Yinger 1984).

The aforementioned National Research Council report noted that by the mid-1970s "many Americans believed that . . . the Civil Rights Act of 1964 had led to broad-scale elimination of discrimination against Afro-Americans in public accommodations" (Jaynes and Williams 1989, p. 84). Yet recent research (Feagin 1990) based on interviews with middle class African-Americans in fourteen cities found significant discrimination in public accommodations such as restaurants, department stores, and hotels, as well as on the street. African-Americans frequently received poor service in public accommodations and suffered racially motivated hostility from white strangers and white police officers on the street.

Contemporary discrimination for most black Americans entails a lifetime of blatant and subtle acts of differential treatment by whites

Low-income and middle-income African-Americans experience discrimination in a number of different areas. This discrimination has a cumulative impact. Contemporary discrimination for most black Americans entails more than an occasional discriminatory act; it entails, rather, a lifetime of blatant and subtle acts of differential treatment by whites that often cumulate to a severely oppressive psychological and group impact. African-Americans cope with this recurrent discrimination in a variety of ways ranging from repressed rage to angry aggression and retaliation (Cobbs 1988; on response patterns of minorities to discrimination, see Allport 1954). This cumulative and persisting discrimination is a major reason for the periodic resurgence of civil rights organizations and protest movements among African-Americans (see Bloom 1987; Morris 1984). Future research on African-Americans will need to focus more centrally on the significance and impact of cumulative racial discrimination.

[See also Discrimination; Race; Segregation and Desegregation; Slavery and Involuntary Servitude; Urban Underclass.]

BIBLIOGRAPHY

Allport, Gordon 1954 *The Nature of Prejudice.* Reading, Mass.: Addison-Wesley.

Auletta, Ken 1982 *The Underclass.* New York: Random House.

Blauner, Bob 1972 *Racial Oppression in America.* New York: Harper and Row.

——— 1989 *Black Lives, White Lives.* Berkeley. University of California Press.

Bloom, Jack M. 1987 *Class, Race and the Civil Rights Movement.* Bloomington: Indiana University Press.

Brimmer, Andrew F. 1976 *The Economic Position of Black Americans.* Washington, D.C.: National Commission for Manpower Policy.

Clark, Kenneth B. 1980 "The Role of Race." *New York Times Magazine,* October 5, p. 30.

Cobbs, Price M. 1988 "Critical Perspectives on the Psychology of Race." In *The State of Black America: 1988.* New York: National Urban League.

Cox, Oliver C. 1948 *Caste, Class, and Race.* Garden City, N.Y.: Doubleday.

Denton, Nancy A., and Douglas S. Massey 1988 "Residential Segregation of Blacks, Hispanics, and Asians by Socioeconomic Status and Generation." *Social Science Quarterly* 69:797–817.

Eckberg, Douglas, and Joe R. Feagin 1980 "Discrimination: Motivation, Action, Effects, and Context." *Annual Review of Sociology.* 6:1–23.

Farley, Reynolds 1984 *Blacks and Whites. Narrowing the Gap.* Cambridge: Harvard University Press.

Feagin, Joe R. 1989 *Racial and Ethnic Relations,* 3rd ed. Englewood Cliffs, N.J.: Prentice-Hall.

——— 1991 "The Continuing Significance of Race: The Black Middle Class in Public Places." *American Sociological Review* 56:101–116.

Genovese, Eugene D. 1974 *Roll, Jordan, Roll: The World the Slaves Made.* New York: Pantheon.

Glazer, Nathan 1975 *Affirmative Discrimination.* New York: Basic Books.

Glasgow, Douglas G. 1987 "The Black Underclass in Perspective." In *The State of Black America: 1987.* New York: National Urban League.

Gordon, Milton 1964 *Assimilation in American Life.* New York: Oxford University Press.

——— 1978 *Human Nature, Class and Ethnicity.* New York: Oxford University Press.

——— 1981 "Models of Pluralism." *Annals of the American Academy of Political and Social Science* 454:178–188.

Gutman, Herbert 1976 *The Black Family in Slavery and Freedom, 1790–1925.* New York. Pantheon.

Higginbotham, A. Leon 1978 *In the Matter of Color.* New York: Oxford University Press.

Hirschman, Charles 1983 "America's Melting Pot Reconsidered." *Annual Review of Sociology* 9:397–423.

Jaynes, Gerald D., and Robin Williams, Jr. (eds.) 1989 *A Common Destiny: Blacks and American Society.* Washington, D.C.: National Academy Press.

Jones, Edward 1985 "Beneficiaries or Victims? Progress or Process." Unpublished research report. South Orange, N.J.

——— 1986 "What It's Like to Be a Black Manager." *Harvard Business Review* (May–June):84–93.

Landry, Bart 1987 *The New Black Middle Class.* Berkeley: University of California Press.

Marable, Manning 1985 *Black American Politics.* London: New Left Books.

Moynihan, Daniel P. 1965 *The New Family: The Case for National Action.* Washington, D.C.: U.S. Government Printing Office.

Morris, Aldon D. 1984 *The Origins of the Civil Rights Movement.* New York: Free Press.

Ringer, Benjamin B. 1983 *"We the People" and Others.* New York: Tavistock.

Pettigrew, Thomas 1975 *Racial Discrimination in the United States.* New York: Harper and Row.

Willhelm, Sidney 1983 *Black in a White America.* Cambridge, Mass.: Schenkman.

Williams, Patricia 1987 "Alchemical Notes: Reconstructing Ideals from Deconstructed Rights." *Harvard Civil Rights and Civil Liberties Review* 22: 401–434.

Wilson, William J. 1978 *The Declining Significance of Race.* Chicago: University of Chicago Press.

——— 1987 *The Truly Disadvantaged: The Inner City, the Underclass, and Public Policy.* Chicago: University of Chicago Press.

Yinger, John 1984 "Measuring Racial and Ethnic Discrimination with Fair Housing Audits: A Review of Existing Evidence and Research Methodology." Washington, D.C.: HUD Conference on Fair Housing Testing.

– JOE R. FEAGIN

AGGRESSION

Perhaps no other construct in social psychology subsumes a broader range of behaviors than does aggression. At a purely descriptive level, swatting a fly, teasing, criticizing, or rendering someone unconscious (either to take a life or to save it) could all be considered aggressive acts. Treating diverse behaviors as indicators of a unitary construct is undoubtedly a reason for many of the empirical inconsistencies observed in research on aggression over the past fifty years. Nonetheless, recent analyses of the various laboratory response measures that have been used to represent aggressive behavior support the notion of a common underlying construct of aggression (Carlson, Marcus-Newhall, and Miller 1989).

Theories put forth to explain aggressive behavior have generally focused on differing aspects of the aggressive act. The ethological/instinctivist approach emphasizes the biological basis of aggressive behavior; frustration-aggression theory emphasizes the antecedent conditions; learning theory looks primarily at the outcomes of the behavior; and the social cognitive perspective focuses on the attributions that people make in social situations. Although there is substantial overlap among them, these approaches differ not only in their primary focus but in their ability to explain the acquisition, persistence, and control of aggressive behavior.

Ethological/Instinctive Theories

The work of Lorenz (1966) illustrates the ethological approach to the study of aggression. Lorenz views aggression in animals and humans as a "species-preserving instinct" that performs an adaptive function. The energy for aggression is seen as occurring naturally within the organism and is regulated by appropriate stimuli within the environment. Aggression is considered adaptive for several reasons: (1) Territorial aggression serves an ecological function by regulating the dispersion of a species; (2) aggression promotes selection of the fittest for reproduction; and (3) it serves to protect the young. Major drawbacks to the ethological approach concern the minor role allocated to learning principles and the validity of generalizing from infrahumans to humans.

In contrast to the ethological approach, Freud (1927) posited a substantially different type of instinctive, aggressive drive, which he termed *Thanatos* or *the death instinct.* The aim of the death instinct is Nirvana, or the ultimate cessation of all stimulation. Thanatos was invoked to explain sadistic and masochistic behaviors in humans, and aggression was seen as Thanatos turned outward. Although psychoanalytic theory is historically very important in the study of aggression, Freud's notion of a death instinct was highly speculative and never popularly accepted, even among psychoanalysts.

Frustration-Aggression Theory

Frustration-aggression theory can be viewed as a conceptual bridge between the psychoanalytic, instinctive view of aggression and the subsequently emerging behavioristic view. The link between frustration and aggression was formalized by the proposition of Dollard et al. (1939, p. 1) that "the occurrence of aggressive behavior always presupposes the existence of frustration and, contrariwise, that the existence of frustration always leads to some form of aggression." Frustration was defined by Dollard et al. as "an interference with the occurrence of an instigated goal response at its proper time in the behavior sequence" (1939, p. 7); and aggression was defined as a "sequence of behavior, the goal response of which is the injury of the person toward whom it is directed" (1939, p. 9). According to the theory, the strongest instigation is to aggress against the agent perceived to be responsible for the frustration. If such "direct" aggression is inhibited, "indirect" or "displaced" aggression is expected to occur. Inhibition is presumed to vary directly with the strength of the punishment anticipated for the aggressive act.

Although research has shown that frustration can cause aggression in both animals and humans, it soon became clear that the initial statement of frustration-aggression theory was too restrictive. Miller (1941), in collaboration with the original theorists, acknowledged that frustration could have consequences other than aggression. Subsequent research has also shown that aggression may occur even when there is no apparent frustration, that it can be learned much as any other response, and that it may be instrumental rather than hostile in its intent. Additional research has shown that the presence of aggressive cues (i.e., stimuli associated with aggressive acts in general or with specific characteristics of the frustrating agent) can heighten the probability of aggressive behavior.

Berkowitz (1989) has advanced a reformulation of the frustration-aggression hypothesis in what he has termed a *cognitive-neoassociationistic* model of aggression. This view holds that aversive conditions or events initiate a sequence of responses in which aversive stimulation first gives rise to negative affect (i.e., any feeling that individuals generally seek to avoid). It is this negative affect that, in turn, gives rise to aggression. Thus, frustrations, along with other stimuli such as noxious odors, disgusting scenes, and high temperatures, create an instigation to aggression because they are aversive and lead to negative affect. This negative affect is presumed to activate a variety of expressive-motor reactions, memories, and feeling states that are associated with both fighting and fleeing. A variety of other learned, situational, and dispositional factors then determine the relative strengths of the inclinations toward fleeing and fighting. After these initial, relatively automatic responses have taken place, thinking (cognition) may enter the process to influence subsequent emotional and behavioral reactions. Thus, according to the cognitive-neoassociationistic model, it is only during the later stages of the process that persons make causal attributions about the negative experience and attempt to control their feelings and aggressive actions.

Learning Theory Approaches

All of the major theoretical explanations of aggression allow for the acquisition of aggressive behavior; they differ, however, in the importance of learning as a determinant of aggression. From the learning theory perspective, aggression can be viewed as a learned operant that is reinforced whenever aggression leads to goal attainment. Using this framework, Sears (1958) has argued that the motivation to aggress could also be acquired through a process of secondary reinforcement in which successful goal attainment is consistently paired with the suffering of the victims. For example, when a bully takes candy from another child, the latter's distress is paired with the drive reduction and satisfaction on the part of the bully associated with having the candy for himself. In this manner, distress in others becomes rewarding in itself.

From the learning theory perspective, aggression can be viewed as a learned operant that is reinforced whenever aggression leads to goal attainment.

Bandura (1973) has noted that more complicated forms of aggressive behavior (or any behavior for that matter) are unlikely to be emitted as free operants. Similarly, trial and error processes and behavioral shaping techniques are too inefficient to explain the initial occurrence of an aggressive act. Instead, Bandura suggested that aggressive behaviors can be acquired through a four-step process of observational or imitative learning involving (1) attentional processes; (2) memory and retention processes; (3) behavioral acquisition and enactment processes; and (4) reinforcement and motivational processes including self-reinforcement. Self-generated consequences for behavior have important implications for the regulation of aggression. For example, individuals for whom aggressive conduct is a source of pride will experience a sense of satisfaction (i.e., positive self-reinforcement), whereas others may experience a sense of shame.

Social Cognition Theories

More recently, a social cognitive approach, developed by Kenneth Dodge and others (e.g., see Dodge and Crick 1990) has built on the work of Bandura, especially with regard to self-regulatory processes. It incorporates developments in a number of social psychological fields including attribution, decision making, and information processing. According to this approach, individuals in social situations proceed through a series of information-processing steps which begin with encoding and interpreting information, and are followed by the consideration, selection, and performance of a behavior. Effective processing at each step will lead to a socially acceptable performance within the situation, whereas deficient processing may result in aggressive behavior.

In the first step of processing, relevant information is encoded. Ineffective processing at this stage, for example the failure to recognize an important facial cue such as a smile by another, may increase the likelihood of an aggressive response. Step 2 is an interpretive step in which the cues encoded in the prior step are given meaning and represented in long-term memory. Thus, a smile may be interpreted to mean that another is "only kidding." Step 3 involves the search of long-term memory for an appropriate response. Some responses will have strong associations with specific mental representations of the relevant cues, and these are most likely to emerge as potential responses within the social situation. The next step in processing involves selecting the most appropriate response. The exact decision strategy that individuals use to select a response is unknown, although idiosyncratic factors are likely to influence the process. The final step is to perform the selected response. An important aspect of behavioral enactment is response monitoring, in which the behavioral response and its effects are observed by the actor. Since this process involves attention to social cues, the five-step process is hypothesized to begin anew.

Current Status of Theories of Aggression

Each of the theories examined makes a compelling case for focusing on specific aspects of the aggressive response such as the role of biological factors in initiating the response and the role of learning and cognitive processes in maintaining it. Although there has been a greater emphasis on cognitive factors in recent time, it appears that any satisfactory explanation must incorporate the influences of biological, psychological, situational, and cultural factors. As yet, no overarching theory has emerged to integrate these diverse factors.

BIBLIOGRAPHY

Bandura, Albert 1973 *Aggression: A Social Learning Analysis.* New York. Holt.

Berkowitz, Leonard 1989 "Frustration-Aggression Hypothesis: Examination and Reformulation." *Psychological Bulletin* 106:59–73.

Carlson, Michael, Amy Marcus-Newhall, and Norman Miller 1989 "Evidence for a General Construct of Aggression." *Personality and Social Psychology Bulletin* 15:377–389.

Dodge, Kenneth, and Nicki Crick 1990 "Social Information-Processing Bases of Aggressive Behavior in Children." *Personality and Social Psychology Bulletin* 16:8–22.

Dollard, John, Leonard Doob, Neal Miller, O. H. Miller, and Robert Sears 1939 *Frustration and Aggression.* New Haven: Yale University Press.

Freud, Sigmund 1927 *Beyond the Pleasure Principle.* New York: Boni and Liveright.

Lorenz, Konrad 1966 *On Aggression.* New York: Harcourt, Brace and World.

Miller, Neal 1941 "The Frustration-Aggression Hypothesis." *Psychological Review* 48:337–342.

Sears, Robert 1958 "Personality Development in the Family." In J. M. Seidman, ed., *The Child.* New York: Rinehart.

– KARL KOSLOSKI

ALCOHOL

The sociological study of alcohol in society is concerned with two broad areas. The first area is the study of alcohol behavior, which includes (1) social and other factors in alcohol behavior; (2) the prevalence of drinking in society; and (3) group and individual variations in drinking and alcoholism. The second major area of study has to do with social control of alcohol, which includes (1) the social and legal acceptance or disapproval of alcohol (social norms); (2) the sociolegal regulations and control of alcohol in society; and (3) efforts to change or limit deviant drinking behavior (informal sanctions, law enforcement, treatment, and prevention).

Only issues related to the first area of study, sociology of alcohol behavior, will be reviewed here.

Physical Effects of Alcohol

Three major forms of beverages containing alcohol (ethanol) are regularly consumed. Wine is made from fermentation of fruits and usually contains up to 14 percent ethanol by volume. Beer is brewed from grains and hops and contains 3 to 6 percent ethanol. Liquor (whisky, gin, vodka, and other distilled spirits) is 40 to 50 percent ethanol (80 to 100 proof). A bottle of beer (12 ounces), a glass of wine (4 ounces), and a cocktail or mixed drink with a shot of liquor in it, therefore, each have about the same absolute alcohol content, one-half to three-fourths of an ounce of ethanol.

Alcohol is a central nervous system depressant, and its physiological effects are a direct function of the percentage of alcohol concentrated in the body's total blood volume (which is determined mainly by the person's body weight). This concentration is usually referred to as the BAC (blood alcohol content) or BAL (blood alcohol level). A 150-pound man can consume one alcoholic drink (about three-fourths of an ounce of ethanol) every hour essentially without physiological effect. The BAC increases with each additional drink during that same time, and the intoxicating effects of alcohol will become noticeable. If a 150-pound man has four drinks in an hour, he will have an alcohol blood content of 0.10 percent, enough for recognizable motor-skills impairment. In almost all states, if he operates a motor vehicle with this BAC (determined by breathalyzer or blood test), he is violating a law and is subject to arrest on a charge of DWI (driving while intoxicated). At 0.25 percent BAC (about ten drinks in an hour) the person is extremely drunk, and at 0.40 percent BAC the person loses consciousness. Excessive drinking of alcohol over time is associated with numerous health problems. Cirrhosis of the liver, hepatitis, heart disease, high blood pressure, brain dysfunction, neurological disorders, sexual and reproductive dysfunction, low blood sugar, and cancer are among the illnesses brought on by alcohol abuse (National Institute of Alcohol Abuse and Alcoholism 1981, 1987; Royce 1989).

Social Factors in Alcohol Behavior

Alcohol has direct effects on the brain, affecting motor skills, perception, and eventually consciousness. The way people actually behave while drinking, however, is only partly a function of the direct physical effects of ethanol. Overt behavior while under the influence of alcohol depends also on how individuals have learned to behave in the setting in which they are drinking and with whom they are drinking at the time. Variations in individual experience, group drinking customs, and the social setting produce variations in observable behavior while drinking. Actions reflecting impairment of coordination and perception are direct physical effects of alcohol on the body. These physical factors, however, do not account for "drunken comportment"—the behavior of those who are "drunk" with alcohol before reaching the stage of impaired muscular coordination (MacAndrew and Edgerton 1969). Social, cultural, and psychological factors are more important in overt drinking behavior. Cross-cultural studies (MacAndrew and Edgerton 1969), surveys in the United States (Kantor and Straus 1987), and social pyschological experiments (Marlatt and Rohsenow 1981) have shown that both conforming and deviant behavior while "under the influence" are more a function of sociocultural and individual expectations and attitudes than of the physiological effects of alcohol.

Overt behavior while under the influence of alcohol depends on how individuals have learned to behave and with whom they are drinking at the time.

Sociological explanations of alcohol behavior emphasize these social, cultural, and social psychological variables not only in understanding the way people act when they are under, or think they are under, the influence of alcohol but also in understanding differences in drinking patterns at both the group and the individual level. Sociologists see all drinking behavior as socially patterned, from abstinence, to moderate drinking, to alcoholism. Within a society persons are subject to different group and cultural influences, depending on the communities in which they reside, their group memberships, and their location in the social structure as defined by their age, sex, class, religion, ethnic, and other statuses in society. Whatever other biological or personality factors and mechanisms may be involved, both conforming and deviant alcohol behavior are explained sociologically as products of the general culture and the more immediate groups and social situations with which individuals are confronted. Differences in rates of drinking and alcoholism across groups in the same society and cross-nationally reflect the varied cultural traditions regarding the functions alcohol serves and the extent to which it is integrated into eating, ceremonial, leisure, and other social contexts.

The more immediate groups within these socio-cultural milieux provide social learning environments and social control systems in which the positive and negative sanctions applied to behavior sustain or discourage certain drinking according to group norms. The most significant groups through which the general cultural, religious, and community orientations toward drinking have an impact on the individual are family, peer, and friendship groups, but secondary groups and the media also have an impact. (For a social learning theory of drinking and alcoholism that specifically incorporates these factors in the social and cultural context see Akers 1985; Akers and La Greca, forthcoming. For a review of sociological, psychological, and biological theories of alcohol and drug behavior see Goode 1989.)

Social Characteristics and Trends in Drinking Behavior

AGE. Table 1 shows that the percentages of high school seniors who have used alcohol (under the legal age in most states) rival those of young adults and exceed those of older adults. The peak years for drinking are this last year of high school (seventeen to eighteen years of age) and the young adult years of ages eighteen to twenty-five when about eight out of ten are drinkers, two-thirds are current drinkers, and one in twenty are daily drinkers. The many young men and women of this age who are in college are even more likely to drink (Berkowitz and Perkins 1986). For both men and women, the probability that one will drink at all stays relatively high up to about age thirty-five. Heavy or frequent drinking peaks out in later years, somewhat sooner for men than for women. After that the probability for both drinking and heavy drinking declines noticeably, particularly among the elderly. After age sixty, the proportion of both drinkers and of heavy or frequent drinkers decreases. Studies in the general population have found consistently that the elderly are less likely than younger persons to be drinkers, heavy drinkers, and problem drinkers (Cahalan, Cisin, and Crossley 1967; Fitzgerald and Mulford 1981; Meyers et al. 1981–1982; Borgatta, Montgomery, and Borgatta 1982; Holzer et al. 1984).

SEX. The difference is not as great as it once was, but more men than women drink, and men have higher rates of problem drinking in all age, religious, racial, social class, and ethnic groups and in all regions and communities. Teenage boys are more likely to drink and to drink more frequently than teenage girls, but the difference between male and female percentages of current drinkers at this age is less than it is in any older age group. Among adults, men are three to four times more likely than women (among the elderly as much as ten times more likely) to be heavy drinkers and two to three times more likely to report negative personal and social consequences of drinking (National Institute on Alcohol Abuse and Alcoholism 1987).

TABLE 1

PERCENTAGES OF ALCOHOL USE BY AGE GROUP, 1974–1988

	Year			
Age Group	**1974**	**1979**	**1985**	**1988**
12–17				
Ever used	54	70	55	50
Past year	51	54	52	45
Past month	34	37	31	25
High school seniors				
Ever used	90*	93	92	92
Past year	85	88	86	85
Past month	68	72	66	64
18–25				
Ever used	81	95	93	90
Past year	77	87	87	82
Past month	69	76	71	65
26+				
Ever used	73	91	89	87
Past year	63	72	74	69
Past month	54	61	61	55

Sources: National Institute on Drug Abuse 1988; 1989; Johnston, O'Malley, and Bachman 1989.

* Figures in this column for high school seniors are for the year 1975.

SOCIAL CLASS. The proportion of men and women who drink is higher in the middle class and upper class than in the lower class. The more highly educated and the fully employed are more likely to be current drinkers than the less educated and unemployed. Drinking by elderly adults increases as education increases, but there are either mixed or inconsistent findings regarding the variations in drinking by occupational status, employment status, and income (Holzer 1984; Borgatta, Montgomery, and Borgatta 1982; Akers and La Greca, forthcoming).

COMMUNITY AND LOCATION. Rates of drinking are higher in urban and suburban areas than in small towns and rural areas. As the whole country has become more urbanized the regional differences have leveled out so that, while the South continues to have the lowest proportion of drinkers, the most recent studies show no difference in the proportions of teenage and adult drinkers among the other regions. Although there are fewer drinkers in the South, those who do drink tend to drink more per person than drinkers in other regions (National Institute on Alcohol Abuse and Alcoholism 1987).

RACE, ETHNICITY, AND RELIGION. The percent of drinking is higher among both white males and females than among African-American men and women. Drinking among non-Hispanic whites is also higher than among Hispanic whites. The proportion of problem or heavy drinkers is about the same for African-Americans and white Americans (National Institute on Alcohol Abuse and Alcoholism 1981; Fishburne, Abelson, and Cisin 1980; National Institute on Drug Abuse 1988). There may be a tendency for blacks to fall into the two extreme categories, heavy drinkers or abstainers (Brown and Tooley 1989), and black males suffer the highest rate of mortality from cirrhosis of the liver (National Institute on Alcohol Abuse and Alcoholism 1987). American Indians and Alaskan Natives have rates of alcohol abuse and problems several times the rates in the general population (National Institute on Alcohol Abuse and Alcoholism 1987).

Catholics, Lutherans, and Episcopalians have relatively high rates of drinking. Relatively few fundamentalist Protestants, Baptists, and Mormons drink. Jews have low rates of problem drinking, and Catholics have relatively high rates of alcoholism. Irish-Americans have high rates of both drinking and alcoholism. Italian-Americans drink frequently and heavily but apparently do not have high rates of alcoholism (see Cahalan, Cisin, and Crossley 1967; Mulford 1964). Strong religious beliefs and commitment, regardless of denominational affiliation, inhibit both drinking and heavy drinking among teenagers and college students (Cochran and Akers 1989; Berkowitz and Perkins 1986).

TRENDS IN PREVALENCE OF DRINKING. There has been a century-long decline in the amount of absolute alcohol consumed by the average drinker in the United States. There was a period in the 1970s when the per capita consumption increased (see Table 1), and the proportion of drinkers in the population was generally higher by the end of the 1970s than at the beginning of the decade, although there were yearly fluctuations up and down. The level of drinking among men was already high, and the increases came mainly among youth and women. But in the 1980s the general downward trend resumed (Keller 1958; National Institute on Alcohol Abuse and Alcoholism 1981, 1987). Until the 1980s, this trend was caused mainly by the increased use of lower-content beer and wine and the declining popularity of distilled spirits rather than by a decreasing proportion of the population who are drinkers. In the 1980s the prevalence of drinking alcohol declined for both men and women and all age groups.

In 1979 more than two-thirds of American adolescents (twelve to seventeen years of age) had some experience with alcohol, and nearly four out of ten were current drinkers (drank within the past month). In 1988 these proportions had dropped to one-half and one-fourth, respectively. Lifetime prevalence of alcohol use (ever used) has remained essentially the same for the older age groups in the last decade. Lifetime prevalence is not a sensitive measure of change in the adult population, however, because it can be changed only by the lifetime drinking experience of those newly entering the adult years (since the lifetime prevalence is already fixed for the cohort of adults already sampled in previous surveys). There have been declines in both annual (past year) prevalence of drinking (decreases of 3 to 5 percent) and current (past month) prevalence of drinking (decreases of 7 to 10 percent) among high school seniors, young adults, and older adults. Current use in the general American population twelve years of age and older declined from 59 percent in 1985 to 53 percent in 1988. Among the adult population eighteen years of age and older, current use declined from 71 percent in 1985 to 57 percent in 1988.

The relative size of the reductions in drinking prevalence in recent years has not been great, however, and proportions of drinkers remain high. By the time of high school graduation, two-thirds of adolescents are current drinkers, and the proportion of drinkers in the population remains at this level through the young adult years. Eight out of ten high school seniors and young adults and 70 percent of adults over the age of twenty-five have consumed alcohol in the past year. It should be remembered, however, that most of this is light to moderate consumption; the modal pattern of drinking for all age groups in the United States has long been and continues to be nondeviant, light to moderate social drinking. The moderation in drinking behavior may have become more pronounced in recent years; not only has current drinking declined, there are some indications that frequent (daily) drinking also has moderated. A further indication is that both high school seniors and young adults reported less likelihood of heavy drinking (consumed five or more drinks in a row sometime during the last two weeks) in 1988 than a decade earlier (National Institute on Drug Abuse 1989; Johnston, O'Malley, and Bachman 1989).

ESTIMATES OF PREVALENCE OF ALCOHOLISM. In spite of these trends in lower levels of drinking, alcoholism remains one of the most serious problems in American society. Alcohol abuse and all of the problems related to it cause enormous personal, social, health, and financial costs in American society. In a 1965 national survey Cahalan, Cisin, and Crossley (1967) characterized 6 percent of the general adult population and 9 percent of the drinkers as "heavy-escape" drinkers, the same figures reported for a 1967 survey (Cahalan 1970). These figures do not seem to have changed very much in the years since. They are similar to findings in national surveys from 1979 to 1988 (National Institute on Alcohol Abuse and Alcoholism 1981; Clark and Midanik 1982; National Institute on Alcohol Abuse and Alcoholism 1987; National Institute on Drug Abuse 1988, 1989), which support an estimate that 6 percent of the general population are problem drinkers and that about 9 percent of those who are drinkers will abuse or fail to control their intake of alcohol. Royce (1989) and Vaillant (1983) both estimate that 4 percent of the general population in the United States are "true" alcoholics. This estimate would mean that there about eight million alcoholics in American society. How many alcoholics or how much alcohol abuse there is in our society is not easily determined because the very concept of alcoholism (and therefore what gets counted in the surveys and estimates) has long been and remains controversial.

The Concept of Alcoholism

The idea of alcoholism as a sickness traces back at least 200 years (Conrad and Schneider 1980). There is no single unified disease concept, but the prevailing concepts of alcoholism today revolve around the one developed by Jellinek (1960) from 1940 to 1960. Jellinek defined alcoholism as a disease entity that is diagnosed by the "loss of control" over one's drinking and that progresses through a series of clear-cut "phases." The final phase of alcoholism means that the disease renders a person powerless to drink in a controlled, moderate, nonproblematic way.

The disease of alcoholism is viewed as a disorder or illness for which the individual is not personally responsible for having contracted. It is viewed as incurable in the sense that alcoholics can never truly control their drinking. That is, sobriety can be achieved only by total abstention: Even if one drink is taken, the alcoholic cannot control how much more he or she will consume. Alcoholism is a "primary" self-contained disease that produces the problems, abuse, and loss of control over drinking associated with the disease. It can be controlled through proper treatment to the point where the alcoholic can be helped to stop drinking so that he or she is in "remission" or is "recovering." "Once an alcoholic, always an alcoholic" is a central tenet of the disease concept. Thus, one can be a sober alcoholic, which means that one can still suffer from the disease even though one is consuming no alcohol at all. Although the person is not responsible for becoming sick, he or she is viewed as responsible for aiding in the cure by cooperating with the treatment regimen or participation in groups such as Alcoholics Anonymous.

The disease concept is the predominant one in public opinion and discourse on alcohol (according to a 1987 Gallup Poll, 87 percent of the public believes that alcoholism is a disease). It is the principal concept used by the vast majority of the treatment professionals and personnel offering programs for alcohol problems. It receives widespread support among alcohol experts and continues to be vigorously defended by many alcohol researchers (Keller 1976; Vaillant 1983; Royce 1989). Alcoholics Anonymous, the largest single program for alcoholics in the world, defines alcoholism as a disease (Rudy 1986). The concept of alcoholism as a disease is the officially stated position of the American Medical Association and of the federal agency most responsible for alcohol research and treatment, the National Institute on Alcohol Abuse and Alcoholism (1987).

Nonetheless, many sociologists and behavioral scientists remain highly skeptical and critical of the disease concept of alcoholism (Trice 1966; Cahalan and Room 1974; Conrad and Schneider 1980; Rudy 1986; Fingarette 1988; Peele 1989). The concept may do more harm than good by discouraging many heavy drinkers who are having problems with alcohol, but who do not identify themselves as alcoholics or do not want others to view them as sick, from seeking help. The disease concept is a tautological (and therefore untestable) explanation for the behavior of people diagnosed as alcoholic. That is, the diagnosis of the disease is made on the basis of excessive, problematic alcohol behavior that seems to be out of control, and then this diagnosed disease entity is, in turn, used to explain the excessive, problematic, out-of-control behavior.

In so far as claim about alcoholism as a disease can be tested, "almost everything that the American public believes to be the scientific truth about alcoholism is false" (Fingarette 1988, p. 1; see also Peele 1989; Conrad and Schneider 1980). The concept preferred by these authors and by other sociologists is one that refers only to observable behavior and drinking problems. The term *alcoholism* then is nothing more than a label attached to a drinking pattern characterized by personal and social dysfunctions (Mulford and Miller 1960; Conrad and Schneider 1980; Rudy 1986). That is, the drinking is so frequent, heavy, and abusive that it produces or exacerbates financial, familial, occupational, physical, and interpersonal problems for the drinker and those around him. The heavy drinking behavior and its attendant problems are themselves the focus of explanation and treatment. They are not seen as merely symptoms of some underlying disease pathology. When drinking stops or moderate drinking is resumed and drinking does not cause social and personal problems, one is no longer alcoholic. Behavior we label as alcoholic is problem drinking that lies at one extreme of a continuum of drinking behavior, with abstinence at the other end and various other drinking patterns in between (Cahalan, Cisin, and Crossley 1967). From this point of view, alcoholism is a disease only because it has been socially defined as a disease (Conrad and Schneider 1980).

Many sociologists and behavioral scientists remain highly skeptical and critical of the disease concept of alcoholism.

GENETIC FACTORS IN ALCOHOLISM. Contrary to what is regularly asserted, evidence that there may be genetic, biological factors in alcohol abuse is evidence neither in favor of nor against the disease concept, any more than evidence that there may be genetic variables in criminal behavior demonstrates that crime is a disease. Few serious researchers claim to have found evidence that a specific disease entity is inherited or that there is a genetically programmed and unalterable craving or desire for alcohol. It is genetic susceptibility to alcoholism that interacts with the social environment and the person's drinking experiences, rather than genetic determinism, that is the predominant perspective.

The major evidence for the existence of hereditary factors in alcoholism comes from studies that have found greater "concordance" between the alcoholism of identical twins than between siblings and from studies of adoptees in which offspring of alcoholic fathers were found to have an increased risk of alcoholism even though raised by nonalcoholic adoptive parents (Goodwin 1976; National Institute on Alcohol Abuse and Alcoholism 1982; U.S. Department of Health and Human Services 1987). Some have pointed to serious methodological problem in these studies that limit their support for inherited alcoholism (Lester 1987). Even the studies finding evidence for inherited alcoholism report that only a small minority of those judged to have the inherited traits become alcoholic and an even smaller portion of all alcoholics have indications of hereditary tendencies. Whatever genetic variables there are in alcoholism apparently come into play in a small portion of cases. Depending on the definition of alcoholism used, the research shows that biological inheritance either makes no difference at all or makes a difference for only about one out of ten alcoholics. Social and social psychological factors are the principal variables in alcohol behavior, including that which is socially labeled and diagnosed as alcoholism (Fingarette 1988; Peele 1989).

[See also Drug Abuse.]

BIBLIOGRAPHY

Akers, Ronald L. 1985 *Deviant Behavior A Social Learning Approach.* Belmont, Calif.: Wadsworth.

———, and Anthony J. La Greca (forthcoming) "Alcohol Use among the Elderly: Social Learning, Community Context, and Life Events." In David J. Pittman and Helene White, eds., *Society, Culture, and Drinking Patterns Re-Examined.* New Brunswick, NJ.: Rutgers University Press.

Berkowitz, Alan D., and H. Wesley Perkins 1986 "Problem Drinking among College Students: A Review of Recent Research." *Journal of American College Health* 35:21–28.

Borgatta, Edgar F., Rhonda J. V. Montgomery, and Marie L. Borgatta 1982 "Alcohol Use and Abuse, Life Crisis Events, and the Elderly." *Research on Aging* 4:378–408.

Brown, Frieda, and Joan Tooley 1989 "Alcoholism in the Black Community." In Gary W. Lawson and Ann W. Lawson, eds., *Alcohol and Substance Abuse in Special Populations.* Rockville, Md.: Aspen Publishers.

Cahalan, Don 1970 *Problem Drinkers: A National Survey.* San Francisco: Jossey-Bass.

———, Ira H. Cisin, and Helen M. Crossley 1967 *American Drinking Practices.* Washington, D.C.: George Washington University Press.

———, and Robin Room 1974 *Problem Drinking Among American Men.* New Haven, Conn.: College and University Press.

Clark, Walter B., and Lorraine Midanik 1982 "Alcohol Use and Alcohol Problems Among U.S. Adults: Results of the 1979 Survey." *Alcohol Consumption and Related Problems.* Department of

Health and Human Services, No. 82-1190. Washington, D.C.: U. S. Government Printing Office.

Cochran, John K., and Ronald L. Akers 1989 "Beyond Hellfire: An Exploration of the Variable Effects of Religiosity on Adolescent Marijuana and Alcohol Use." *Journal of Research on Crime and Delinquency* 26:198–225.

Conrad, Peter, and Joseph W. Schneider 1980 *Deviance and Medicalization.* St. Louis: C. V. Mosby.

Fingarette, Herbert 1988 *Heavy Drinking: The Myth of Alcoholism as a Disease.* Berkeley: University of California Press.

Fishburne, Patricia, Herbert I. Abelson, and Ira Cisin 1980 *National Survey on Drug Abuse: Main Findings.* Washington, D.C.: U.S. Government Printing Office.

Fitzgerald, J. L., and Harold A. Mulford 1981 "The Prevalence and Extent of Drinking in Iowa, 1979." *Journal of Studies on Alcohol* 42:38–47.

Goode, Erich 1989 *Drugs in American Society,* 3rd ed. New York: Alfred A. Knopf.

Goodwin, Donald 1976 *Is Alcoholism Hereditary?* New York: Oxford University Press.

Holzer, C., Lee Robins, Jerome Meyers, M. Weissman, G. Tischler, P. Leaf, J. Anthony, and P. Bednarski 1984 "Antecedents and Correlates of Alcohol Abuse and Dependence in the Elderly." In George Maddox, Lee Robins, and Nathan Rosenberg, eds., *Nature and Extent of Alcohol Abuse Among the Elderly.* Department of Health and Human Services No. 84-1321. Washington, D.C.: U.S. Government Printing Office.

Jellinek, E. M. 1960 *The Disease Concept of Alcoholism.* New Haven, Conn.: Hillhouse Press.

Johnston, Lloyd D., Patrick M. O'Malley, and Jerald G. Bachman 1989 *Drug Use, Drinking, and Smoking: National Survey Results from High School, College, and Young Adult Populations, 1975–1988.* Washington, D.C.: U.S. Government Printing Office.

Kantor, Glenda K., and Murray A. Straus 1987 "The 'Drunken Bum' Theory of Wife Beating." *Social Problems* 34:213–230.

Keller, Mark 1958 "Alcoholism: Nature and Extent of the Problem." *Annals of the American Academy of Political and Social Sciences* 315:1–11.

——— 1976 "The Disease Concept of Alcoholism Revisited." *Journal of Studies on Alcohol* 37:1694–1717.

Lester, David 1987 *Genetic Theory: An Assessment of the Heritability of Alcoholism.* New Brunswick, N.J.: Center of Alcohol Studies, Rutgers University.

MacAndrew, Craig, and Robert B. Edgerton 1969 *Drunken Component: A Social Explanation.* Chicago: Aldine.

Marlatt, G. Alan, and Damaris J. Rohsenow 1981 "The Think-Drink Effect." *Psychology Today* (Dec.):60–69, 93.

Meyers, A. R., E. Goldman, R. Hingson, N. Scotch, and T. Mangione 1981–1982 "Evidence of Cohort and Generational Differences in Drinking Behavior of Older Adults." *International Journal of Aging and Human Development* 14:31–44.

Mulford, Harold A. 1964 "Drinking and Deviant Drinking, USA, 1963." *Quarterly Journal of Studies on Alcohol* 25:634–650.

———, and Donald Miller 1960 "Drinking in Iowa IV: Preoccupation with Alcohol and Definitions of Alcoholism, Heavy Drinking, and Trouble Due to Drinking." *Quarterly Journal of Studies on Alcohol* 21:279–296.

National Institute on Alcohol Abuse and Alcoholism 1981 *Fourth Special Report to the U.S. Congress on Alcohol and Health.* Washington, D.C.: U.S. Government Printing Office.

——— 1982 *"Researchers Investigating Inherited Alcohol Problems." NIAAA Information and Feature Service* No. 99, August 30. Rockville, Md.: National Institute on Alcohol Abuse and Alcoholism.

——— 1987 *Alcohol and Health: Sixth Special Report to the U. S. Congress from the Secretary of Health and Human Services.* Rockville, Md.: National Institute on Alcohol Abuse and Alcoholism.

National Institute on Drug Abuse 1988 *National Household Survey on Drug Abuse: Main Findings 1985.* Rockville, Md.: National Institute on Drug Abuse.

——— 1989 "Highlights of the 1988 Household Survey on Drug Abuse." *NIDA Capsules,* August. Rockville, Md.: National Institute on Drug Abuse.

Peele, Stanton 1989 *Diseasing of America: Addiction Treatment Out of Control.* Lexington, Mass.: Lexington Books.

Royce, James E. 1989 *Alcohol Problems and Alcoholism,* rev. ed. New York. Free Press.

Rudy, David 1986 *Becoming Alcoholic: Alcoholics Anonymous and the Reality of Alcoholism.* Carbondale: Southern Illinois University Press.

Trice, Harrison 1966 *Alcoholism in America.* New York. McGraw-Hill.

U. S. Department of Health and Human Services 1987 *Sixth Special Report to the U S. Congress on Alcohol and Health from the Secretary of Health and Human Services.* Rockville, Md.: National Institute on Alcohol Abuse and Alcoholism.

Vaillant, George 1983 *The Natural History of Alcoholism.* Cambridge, Mass.: Harvard University Press.

– RONALD L. AAKERS

ALIENATION

Between 1964 and 1974, many commentators were speaking of a crisis of confidence in the United States, a malaise marked by a widespread public belief that major institutions—businesses, labor unions, and especially the government, political parties, and political leaders—were unresponsive, remote, ineffective, and not to be trusted (Lipset and Schneider 1983). The word *alienation* became the catchword for these sentiments and a host of other problems including discontented workers, wayward youth, and militant minority groups. Leaders concerned about the apparent increase in alienation found new relevance in an ongoing discussion among sociologists and other social scientists, who over the years have defined the term *alienation,* used public opinion polls to measure the level of alienation in society, and debated the causes, significance, and consequences of alienation and particularly political alienation.

Dimensions of Alienation and Political Alienation

Sociological researchers and theorists have developed different definitions for the word *alienation* (Seeman 1975). Alienation sometimes refers to the isolation of individuals from a community—a detachment from the activities, identifications, and the ties to relatives and friends that a community can provide. In contrast, scholars influenced by the philosophical writings of Karl

Marx have used the word to mean self-estrangement and the lack of self-realization (Blauner 1964). Marx argued that although humans by their very nature are capable of creative and intrinsically rewarding work, the Industrial Revolution reduced workers to the unskilled tenders of machines (Braverman 1974). The machinery and other commodities that are produced become part of a system of hierarchies at work and global markets that the worker cannot control. Rather, the system dominates workers as an alienated, "reified" force, apart from the will and interests of workers (Meszaros 1970).

The concept of alienation has included the notion of cultural radicalism, or estrangement from the established values of a society. Ingelhart (1981) has argued that the highly educated generation that came of age in the counterculture of the 1960s has rejected the elders' traditional values of materialism, order, and discipline and instead espouses "postmaterialist" values emphasizing the quality of life, self-realization, and participatory democracy.

Much of the recent discussion of alienation has been on the topic of political alienation and, ironically, has described the politics not of authoritarian regimes but rather of the highly developed democracies of Western Europe and the United States. Sociologists have been particularly interested in measuring the extent to which individuals in political contexts feel powerless (i.e., unable to influence government decisions or secure desired outcomes) and perceive political affairs as meaningless (i.e., too complicated, unclear, or incomprehensible) (Seeman 1975). Sociologists have tried not only to measure political alienation but also to determine its causes and consequences. Powerlessness and meaninglessness may be connected to normlessness, or anomie, which occurs when individuals are no longer guided by the political rules of the game (Lipset and Raab 1978). Thus, social scientists have been concerned that alienation might lead to nonconventional actions like protest movements and collective violence, while reducing participation through conventional political channels such as voting and interest group activity.

Measurement and Consequences of Political Alienation

Political alienation consists of several specific attitudes whereby citizens evaluate government and politics. Specifically, political alienation is composed of the attitudes of distrust and inefficacy. *Distrust* (also called cynicism) is a generalized negative attitude about governmental outputs: the policies, operations, and conditions produced by government. Compared to the simple dislike of a particular governmental policy or official, distrust is a negative reaction that is broader in scope. Whereas distrust is an evaluation of governmental outputs, *inefficacy* is an expectation about inputs to government, the processes by which groups influence government. People have a sense of inefficacy when they feel they cannot influence government policies or deliberations (Gamson 1971).

Mason, House, and Martin (1985) argue that two specific questions used in opinion polls are the most "internally valid" measures of distrust (i.e., the questions yield answers correlated to only one particular underlying attitude): "How much of the time do you think you can trust the government in Washington to do what is right—just about all of the time, most of the time, or only some of the time?" and "Would you say that the government is pretty much run by a few big interests looking out for themselves or that it is run for the benefit of all people?" Similarly, a person's sense of inefficacy can be measured by asking the person to agree or disagree with statements containing the words "like me": "People like me don't have any say about what the government does" and "I don't think public officials care much what people like me think."

During election years since the 1950s, the Center for Political Studies at the University of Michigan at Ann Arbor has addressed these (and numerous other) questions to national samples of citizens. Those replying that you can trust the government only some of the time or none of the time composed 22 percent in 1964 but 73 percent in 1980. Those disagreeing with the statement that public officials care rose from 25 percent in 1960 to 52 percent in 1980.

Furthermore, polls indicated that in the 1960s and 1970s, increasing numbers of citizens felt that government was less responsive and paid less attention to what the people thought (Lipset and Schneider 1983, pp. 13–29). This feeling, which can be termed *system unresponsiveness,* was measured by asking questions that did not use the words "like me." Responses to the questions thus contained no evaluations of the respondent's own personal power, but rather expressed the respondent's views of the external political system. (Craig 1979 conceptualizes system unresponsiveness as "output inefficacy.")

What are the consequences of the increase in alienated political attitudes among Americans? Social scientists have investigated whether individuals with highly alienated attitudes are more likely to engage in certain types of political actions and behaviors.

Research findings have been complicated by the fact that the same specific attitude of political alienation has been compatible with many different behavioral orientations including withdrawal or the favoring of reform movements or political violence (Schwartz 1973, pp. 162–177).

Social scientists have generally agreed that politically alienated individuals are less likely to participate in conventional political processes. During four presidential elections from 1956 to 1968, citizens with a low sense of efficacy and a low level of trust were less likely to vote, attend political meetings, contribute money, work for candidates, or even pay attention to the mass media coverage of politics. The alienated showed little tendency to support extremist candidates for office. (The only exception was that high-status alienated citizens supported Goldwater's presidential campaign in 1964. See Wright 1976, pp. 227, 251; Herring 1989, p. 98.) Although some studies fail to confirm that those with low *trust* are likely to be apathetic (Citrin 1974, p. 982), those with low political *efficacy* are indeed likely to be nonvoters, mainly because they are also less educated (Lipset and Schneider 1983, p. 341). In the United States, the percentage of eligible voters who actually cast ballots has declined since 1960, dropping to 53 percent in 1980, while the percentage expressing political inefficacy has risen in the same period; Abramson and Aldrich (1982) estimate that about 27 percent of the former trend is caused by the latter. (See Shaffer 1981 for confirmation but Cassel and Hill 1981 and Miller 1980 for contrary evidence.)

Some researchers have found that the politically alienated are more likely to participate in politics using nonconventional tactics such as demonstrations or violence.

Piven and Cloward (1988) vigorously dispute the notion that the alienated attitudes of individuals are the main cause for the large numbers of nonvoters in the United States. Piven and Cloward construct a historical explanation—that in the early twentieth century, political reformers weakened local party organizations in cities, increased the qualifications for suffrage, and made voting registration procedures more difficult. Legal and institutional changes caused a sharp decrease in voting, which only then led to widespread political alienation. Legal requirements to register in advance of election day and after a change in residence, along with limited locations to register, continue to reduce voting participation, especially among the minority poor in large cities.

Some researchers have found that the politically alienated are more likely to participate in politics using nonconventional tactics such as demonstrations or violence. College students who participated in a march on Washington against the Vietnam War, compared to a matched sample of students from the same classes at the same schools, expressed more alienated attitudes, which in turn stemmed from a sense of inefficacy and system unresponsiveness (Schwartz 1973, pp. 138–142). Paige's (1971) widely influential study drew on Gamson's distinction between trust and efficacy and showed that blacks who participated in the 1967 riot in Newark, New Jersey, had low levels of political trust but high levels of political efficacy (i.e., high capabilities and skills to affect politics, measured indirectly in this instance by the respondent's level of political knowledge). Sigelman and Feldman (1983) attempted to confirm these findings in a study of seven nations. They discovered that those who supported and participated in unconventional forms of politics were only slightly more likely to be both efficacious *and* distrusting. In some nations, however, respondents were more likely to be dissatisfied about specific policies (rather than generally distrusting; see also Citrin 1974, p. 982, and Craig and Maggiotto 1981 for the importance of specific dissatisfactions over policies).

Even though politically alienated individuals may be more likely to participate in social movements, the alienation of individuals is not necessarily cause of social movements. McCarthy and Zald (1977) have argued that alienation, policy dissatisfactions, and other grievances are quite common in societies. Whether or not a social movement arises depends on the availability of resources and the opportunities for success. The civil rights movement, according to McAdam (1982), succeeded not when blacks believed that the political system was unresponsive but rather when blacks felt that federal authorities were beginning to change the system.

Distribution and Significance of Political Alienation

Social scientists have argued that political alienation is concentrated in different types of groups—first, among those who dislike the administration in Washington; second, in certain socioeconomic classes; and finally, among those dissatisfied with government policy. Each of these findings supports a different assessment of the causes and the importance of political alienation.

PARTISAN BICKERING? First of all, high levels of political distrust can be found among those who have a negative view of the performance of the presidential administration then in office. Citrin (1974) concludes that widespread expressions of political distrust (cynicism) merely indicate partisan politics as usual. Cynicism, rather than being an expression of deep discontent, is just rhetoric and ritual. Citrin argues that political distrust is not a threat to the system; even those who intensely distrust incumbent politicians are proud of the form of the government in the United States and want to keep it as it is.

BLUE-COLLAR BACKLASH? Second, other researchers interested in determining the distribution of political alienation have searched for concentrations not among people with certain attitudes and opinions but rather in demographic groups defined by such variables as age, gender, education, and socioeconomic class. Some studies have found alienation only weakly concentrated among such groups. In the 1960s, inefficacy increased uniformly throughout the entire U.S. population rather than increasing in certain demographic groups such as blacks or youth (House and Mason 1975). Using a 1970 survey, Wright (1976) noted that inefficacy and distrust were somewhat concentrated among the elderly, the poorly educated, and the working class. Still, Wright's conclusion was that the alienated were a diverse group that consisted of both rich and poor, black and white, and old and young, making it very unlikely that the alienated as a group could ever become a unified political force.

The alienated have become habituated from an early age to their own lack of power.

Most studies have shown that the politically alienated are indeed concentrated among persons with less education and lower income and occupational status (Wright 1976, p. 136; Lipset and Schneider 1983, pp. 311–315; Finifter 1970; Form and Huber Rytina 1971). Wright argues that even though sizable numbers of such persons express alienated attitudes, these people pose little threat to the stability of regimes because they rarely take political actions and even lack the requisite resources and skills. The alienated have become habituated from an early age to their own lack of power. The alienated are preoccupied with their personal problems and concerns and thus passively give their assent to the regime.

Lipset (1963) has argued that such mass apathy is a virtue because it allows elites in democratic societies to better exert leadership. (For a critique see Wolfe 1977, p. 301.) In fact, for many social scientists in the 1950s, mass apathy was a welcome alternative to the alleged mass activism that had produced the fascist regimes in Germany and Italy. However, Wright (1976, pp. 257–301) counters that since the alienated masses actually pose no threat to the contemporary political system, an increase in mass democratic participation, perhaps the mobilization of workers on the issues of class division, could very well be beneficial, producing more enlightened and humane public policies for the majority in society.

But the class mobilization that Wright envisions might turn out to be a middle-class affair rather than a working-class revolt. Whereas Lipset and Wright have been concerned about the concentration of political alienation in the lower socioeconomic strata, Warren (1976) emphasizes the alienation among "middle American radicals," who believe that they are disfavored by a government that gives its benefits to the poor and the very wealthy. Inefficacy and distrust increased the most, not among the poor or the capitalist class, but rather among the middle strata—private sector managers, middle-income workers, and a "new layer" of public sector professionals (Herring 1989).

Unlike the poor, the middle strata have the resources and capacity to protest and to organize social movements and electoral campaigns, exemplified by the protests against the property tax that culminated with the passage of Proposition 13 in California and Proposition 2½ in Massachusetts. Property tax protesters were middle class homeowners concerned about "taxation without representation." Citizens who felt cut off from political decision making were the most likely to support the tax revolt (Lowery and Sigelman 1981). Protests centered on unresponsive government officials who continued to increase assessments and tax rates without heeding the periodic angry responses of homeowners. Movement activists interpreted their own powerlessness in community and metropolitan politics, thereby shaping the emerging tactics and goals of a grass roots citizen's movement (Lo 1990).

A CRISIS FOR DEMOCRACY? Finally, other social scientists, who have found concentrations of political alienation among those with intense dissatisfactions about government policy, reach the more pessimistic conclusion that political alienation makes effective democratic government almost impossible. Miller (1974) argued that between 1964 and 1970, political distrust (cynicism) increased simultaneously among those favoring withdrawal and those favoring military escalation in the Vietnam War. Distrust increased both among blacks who thought that the civil rights movement was making too little progress and among white segregationists who held the opposite view. The 1960s produced two groups—cynics of the left and cynics of the right, each favoring a set of polarized policy alternatives (see also Lipset and Schneider 1983, p. 332).

Cynics of the right, for example, rejected both the Democratic and Republican parties as too liberal. (Herring 1989 has developed a similar "welfare split" thesis: that more social spending has different effects on the distrust of different groups and, overall, raises political distrust.) Miller concludes that increases in cynicism, along with the concomitant extreme positions on issues, make it difficult for political leaders to find compromises and build support for centrist policy options. While agreeing with Wright that the alienated are divided among themselves, Miller argues that this fragmentation does indeed constitute a crisis of legitimacy for American politics.

For some theorists, widespread political alienation not only makes it difficult to choose among polarized policy options, but also is a sign of even deeper political and economic contradictions in American society. Throughout American history, as citizens have fought to extend their democratic freedoms and personal rights, businesses have used the notion of property rights to protect their own interests and stifle reform (Bowles and Gintis 1987). Wolfe (1977) sees political alienation as a symptom of how the democratic aspirations of the citizenry have been frustrated by the state, which has attempted to foster the growth of capitalism while at the same time attempting to maintain popular support. Alienation, once a Marxist concept depicting the economic deprivations of industrial workers, is now a political concept portraying the plight of citizens increasingly subjected to the authority and the bureaucracy of the state in advanced capitalist societies.

BIBLIOGRAPHY

Abramson, Paul, and John Aldrich 1982 "Decline of Electoral Participation in America." *American Political Science Review* 76:502–521.

Blauner, Robert 1964 *Alienation and Freedom: The Factory Worker and His Industry.* Chicago: University of Chicago Press.

Bowles, Samuel, and Herbert Gintis 1987 *Democracy and Capitalism: Property, Community, and the Contradictions of Modern Social Thought.* New York: Basic Books.

Braverman, Harry 1974 *Labor and Monopoly Capital.* New York. Monthly Review Press.

Cassel, Carol A., and David B. Hill 1981 "Explanations of Turnout Decline: A Multivariate Test." *American Politics Quarterly* 9:181–195.

These Polish citizens ultimately changed the political system of their nation through their mass protests. (Peter Turnley/© Corbis)

Citrin, Jack 1974 "Comment: The Political Relevance of Trust in Government." *American Political Science Review* 68:973–988.

Craig, Stephen C. 1979 "Efficacy, Trust, and Political Behavior: An Attempt to Resolve a Lingering Conceptual Dilemma." *American Politics Quarterly* 7:225–239.

———, and Michael Maggiotto 1981 "Political Discontent and Political Action." *Journal of Politics* 43:514–522.

Finifter, Ada W. 1970 "Dimensions of Political Alienation." *American Political Science Review* 64:389–410.

Form, William H., and Joan Huber Rytina 1971 "Income, Race, and the Ideology of Political Efficacy." *Journal of Politics* 33:659–688.

Gamson, William 1971 "Political Trust and Its Ramifications." In Gilbert Abcarian and John W. Soule, eds., *Social Psychology and Political Behavior Problems and Prospects.* Columbus, Ohio: Merrill.

Herring, Cedric 1989 *Splitting the Middle: Political Alienation Acquiescence, and Activism among America's Middle Layers.* New York: Praeger.

House, James, and William Mason 1975 "Political Alienation in America, 1952–1968." *American Sociological Review* 40:123–147.

Ingelhart, Ronald 1981 "Post-Materialism in an Environment of Insecurity." *American Political Science Review* 75:880–900.

Lipset, Seymour Martin 1963 *Political Man.* Garden City, N.Y.: Anchor.

———, and Earl Raab 1978 *The Politics of Unreason: Right-Wing Extremism in America, 1790–1977.* Chicago: University of Chicago Press.

——— and William Schneider 1983 *The Confidence Gap: Business, Labor, and Government in the Public Mind.* New York: Free Press.

Lo, Clarence Y. H. 1990 *Small Property versus Big Government: Social Origins of the Property Tax Revolt.* Berkeley and Los Angeles: University of California Press.

Lowrey, David, and Lee Sigelman 1981 "Understanding the Tax Revolt: Eight Explanations." *American Political Science Review* 75:963–974.

McAdam, Doug 1982 *Political Process and the Development of Black Insurgency.* Chicago: University of Chicago Press.

McCarthy, John D., and Mayer N. Zald 1977 "Resource Mobilization and Social Movements: A Partial Theory." *American Journal of Sociology* 82:1112–1141.

Mason, William W., James S. House, and Steven S. Martin 1985 "On the Dimensions of Political Alienation in America." In Nancy Brandon Tuma, ed., *Sociological Methodology.* San Francisco: Jossey-Bass.

Meszaros, I. 1970 *Marx's Theory of Alienation.* London: Merlin.

Miller, Arthur 1974 "Political Issues and Trust in Government: 1964–1970." *American Political Science Review* 68:951–972.

Miller, Warren E. 1980 "Disinterest, Disaffection, and Participation in Presidential Politics." *Political Behavior* 2:7–32.

Paige, Jeffery 1971 "Political Orientation and Riot Participation." *American Sociological Review* 36:801–820.

Piven, Frances Fox, and Richard A. Cloward 1988 *Why Americans Don't Vote.* New York: Pantheon.

Schwartz, David C. 1973 *Political Alienation and Political Behavior.* Chicago: Aldine.

Seeman, Melvin 1975 "Alienation Studies." In Alex Inkeles, James Coleman, and Neil Smelser, eds., *Annual Review of Sociology,* vol. 8. Palo Alto, Calif.: Annual Reviews.

Shaffer, Stephen D. 1981 "A Multivariate Explanation of Decreasing Turnout in Presidential Elections, 1960–1976." *American Journal of Political Science* 25:68–95.

Sigelman, Lee, and Stanley Feldman 1983 "Efficacy, Mistrust, and Political Mobilization: A Cross-National Analysis." *Comparative Political Studies* 16:118–143.

Warren, Donald I. 1976 *The Radical Center: Middle Americans and the Politics of Alienation.* Notre Dame, Ind.: University of Notre Dame Press.

Wolfe, Alan 1977 *The Limits of Legitimacy: Political Contradictions of Contemporary Capitalism.* New York: Free Press.

Wright, James D. 1976 *The Dissent of the Governed Alienation and Democracy in America.* New York: Academic Press.

– CLARENCE Y. H. LO

ALTERNATIVE LIFE-STYLES

Considerable concern is voiced from certain segments of the population over the "demise" of the family. The high divorce rate, increased rates of premarital sexuality, cohabitation, and extramarital sex are pointed to as both the culprits and the consequences of the deterioration of family values. This distress, however, is not particularly new; for at least a century American observers and social critics have warned against the negative consequences of changes in the family.

Thanks to books, television, movies, and a variety of other sources, we all know what the family "should" look like. What invariably comes to mind is the white, middle-class, two-parent family in which the father works outside the home and the mother stays at home to take care of the children, at least while they are young. This monolithic model, however, excludes the majority of the population; indeed, a growing number of persons do not desire such a model even if it was attainable. It is based on the false notion of a single and uniform intimate experience that many argue has racist, sexist, and classist connotations.

There are, nonetheless, new reasons for the latest wave of concern of family demise that began to emerge during the 1960s and 1970s. During this period the utility and the structure of many social institutions were seriously questioned, and the family was not exempt. What is the purpose of the family? Is it a useful social institution? Why or why not? How can it be improved? The given cultural milieu of the period exacerbated these questions: the resurgence of the women's movement and the subsequent analysis of gender roles, concern about human rights more generally, and improvements in our reproductive and contraceptive technology. In increasing numbers, individuals began to experiment with alternative ways in which to develop meaningful relationships, including nonmarital sexual relationships, cohabitation, open marriage, and communal living arrangements. A flurry of literature soon abounded among both the academic community and the popular press describing and deliberating on these new life-styles. In 1972 a special issue of *The Family Coordinator* was devoted to the subject of alternative life-styles, with a follow-up issue published in 1975. The subject was firmly entrenched within the field of family sociology by 1980 when the *Journal of Marriage and Family* devoted a chapter to alternative family life-styles in their decade review of research and theory.

Notwithstanding the interest, curiosity, and concern with alternative life-styles, it should be noted that most of the experiments during the 1960s and 1970s attracted only a very small portion of the population, particularly those lifestyles considered to be the most "radical" or alien to the traditional family, such as communal living or open marriage. The vast majority of the population, both then and now, prefer to marry, have children, and live in a committed, monogamous relationship. The most profound changes to date have not occurred in alternatives *to* marriage but rather in alternatives *prior* to marriage, and alternative ways in *structuring* marriage itself yet keeping the basic structure and purposes intact. For example, nonmarital sex, delayed marriage, and cohabitation are practiced with increasing frequency, and are tolerated by a larger percentage of the population than ever before. Within marriage itself, certain changes are becoming increasingly popular, such as greater equality between men and women (although gender equality is more an ideal than a reality in most marriages, at least within the United States). The perceived "threats" to the institution of marriage, such as extramarital sex, gay and lesbian relationships, and communal living groups, are not increasing in popularity to the same degree. Generally the public holds these life-styles in greater suspicion because they question the basic values and norms of the traditional family systems: monogamous intimacy and the bearing and socialization of young children. Voluntary childlessness is somewhat unique; while still strongly disapproved of generally, an increasing number of persons are adopting this life-style nonetheless.

Never-Married Singles

A small but growing percentage of adult men and women remain single throughout their lives. In the United States, approximately 5 percent never marry. These individuals experience life without the support and obligations of a spouse and, most often, children. While often stereotyped as either "swingers" or "lonely losers," Stein reports that both categorizations are largely incorrect (1981). Instead, singles cannot be easily categorized and do not constitute a single social type. Some have chosen singlehood as a preferred option, perhaps due to career decisions, sexual preference, or other family responsibilities. Others have lived in locations in which demographic imbalances have affected the pool of eligibles for mate selection. And others have been lifelong isolates, have poor social skills, or have significant health impairments that have limited social contacts.

By the mid-1970s singlehood was not only tolerated but even viewed by many as an avenue for enhancing one's happiness.

Attitudes toward singlehood have been quite negative historically, especially in the United States, although change has been noted in recent years. Studies report that during the 1950s, remaining single was viewed as a pathology, but by the mid-1970s singlehood was not only tolerated but even viewed by many as an avenue for enhancing one's happiness. Single males are still viewed more favorably than are single females; the former are stereotyped as carefree "bachelors," while single women are characterized as unattractive and unfortunate "spinsters." Oudijk (1983) found that the Dutch population generally affords greater life-style options to women, and only one-quarter of his sample of married and unmarried persons reported that married persons are necessarily happier than are singles.

Shostak (1987) has developed a typology in which to illustrate the divergence among the never-married single population. It is based on two major criteria: the voluntary verses involuntary nature of one's singlehood, and whether their singlehood is viewed as temporary or stable. *Ambivalents* are those who may not at this point be seeking mates but who are open to the idea of marriage at some time in the future. They may be deferring marriage for reasons related to schooling or career, or they may simply enjoy experimenting with a variety of relationships. *Wishfuls* are actively seeking a mate but have been unsuccessful in finding one. They are, generally, dissatisfied with their single state and would prefer to be married. The *resolved* consciously prefer singlehood. They are committed to this life-style for a variety of reasons; career, sexual orientation, or other personal considerations. A study of 482 single Canadians reported that nearly half considered themselves to fall within this category (Austrom and Hanel 1985). They have made a conscious decision to forgo marriage for the sake of a single life-style. A small but important component of this group are priests; nuns; and others who, for religious reasons, choose not to marry. Finally, *regretfuls* are those who would rather marry but who have given up their search for a mate and are resigned to singlehood. They are involuntarily stable singles. Many bright, well-educated, and successful career women are within this category. Because our marital norms decree that men will marry women who are younger or less educated than they, successful older women often find a shortage of men they deem "suitable" mates.

While the diversity and heterogeneity among the never-married population is becoming increasingly apparent, one variable is suspected to be of extreme importance in explaining at least some of the variation: gender. Based on data gathered in numerous treatises, the emerging profiles of male and females singles is in stark contrast. As Bernard (1973) bluntly puts it, the never-married men represent the "bottom of the barrel," while the never-married women are the "cream of the crop." Single women are generally thought to be more intelligent, are better educated, and are more successful in their occupations than are single men, or women who marry. Additionally, research finds that single women report to be happier, less lonely, and have a greater sense of psychological well-being than do their single male counterparts.

Despite the fact that only 2 percent of the population identified singlehood as their preferred choice a decade ago (Roper Organization 1980), social demographers predict that the proportion of singles in our population is likely to increase in the future. As singlehood continues to become a viable and respectable alternative to marriage, more adults may choose to remain single throughout their lives. Others may remain single not out of choice but due to demographic and social trends. The postponement of marriage and the increasing educational level and occupational aspirations of women, coupled with our continued norms of marital homogamy, help to ensure that the number of never-married single persons—women in particular—are likely to increase into the next century. Basing his projections on current patterns, Glick (1984) predicts that 10 percent of males who were between the ages of 25 and 29 in 1980 and 12 percent of females in that age group will never marry.

Child-Free Adults

There is reason to believe that fundamental changes are occurring in the values associated with having children. As economic opportunities for women increase; as birth control, including abortion, becomes more available and reliable; and as tolerance increases for an array of lifestyles, having children is likely to become increasing viewed as an option rather than a mandate. Evidence is accumulating to suggest that men and women are reevaluating the costs and benefits of parenthood. This trend is occurring not only in the United States but in many industrialized countries in Europe as well. The decline in childbearing there has been referred to as the "second demographic transition" (Van de Kaa 1987). Davis (1987) posits that features of industrial societies weaken the individual's desire for children. He lists several interrelated traits of industrialization, including the postponement of marriage, cohabitation, out-of-wedlock births, female labor force participation, and high rates of divorce, claiming that these trends decrease the need for both marriage and childbearing.

Remaining child-free is not a new phenomenon, however. In 1940, for example, 17 percent of married white women between ages thirty-five and thirty-nine were child-free. Some of these women were simply delaying parenthood until their forties; however, in all likelihood most remained child-free. This percentage began to drop considerably after World War II, and by the late 1970s approximately 7 percent of women in the thirty-five to thirty-nine age group remained child-free. Today the figure is rising dramatically. Eighteen percent of women in this age group were without children in 1988. It is predicted that 20 percent to 25 percent of the cohort referred to as "baby-boomers" will remain child-free. This increase is due to a multitude of factors: delayed childbearing, infertility, and voluntary childlessness.

Among married persons under age forty who have no children, wives are more likely than their husbands to report a preference for remaining child-free.

An important distinction to make in the discussion of childlessness is whether the decision was voluntary or involuntary. *Involuntary* childlessness involves those who are infecund or subfecund. They do not have a choice and, unless they adopt or create some other social arrangement, are inevitably committed to this life-style. *Voluntary* childlessness, the focus of this discussion, involves those who choose to remain child-free. Large differences exist within members of this group; *early articulators* have made their decision early in their lives and are committed to their choice. *Postponers,* on the other hand, begin first by delaying their childbearing, but wind up being child-free due to their continual postponement. Early articulators generally exhibit less stereotypical gender roles, are more likely to cohabit, and enjoy the company of children less than do postponers. Seccombe (1990) found that among married persons under age forty who have no children, wives are more likely than their husbands to report a preference for remaining childfree (19 percent and 13 percent, respectively).

Despite increasing rates of voluntary childlessness, most research conducted within the United States documents the pervasiveness of pronatalist sentiment. Those who voluntarily opt to remain child-free are viewed as selfish, immature, lonely, unfulfilled, insensitive, and more likely to have mental problems than are those who choose parenthood. Females, those persons with less education, with large families of their own, Catholics, and those residing in rural areas are most apt to judge the child-free harshly.

Most studies report that those persons who opt to remain child-free are well aware of the sanctions surrounding their decision yet are rarely upset by them (see Houseknecht 1987 for review). In her review of twelve studies, Houseknecht found only three that reported that child-free individuals had trouble dealing with the reaction from others. Sanctions apparently are not strong enough to detract certain persons from what they perceive as the attractiveness of a child-free lifestyle. Houseknecht (1987), in a content analysis of twenty-nine studies reporting the rationales for remaining child-free, identified nine primary motivations. These are, in order of the frequency in which they were found: (1) freedom from child-care responsibilities: greater opportunity for self-fulfillment and spontaneous mobility, (2) more satisfactory marital relationship, (3) female career considerations, (4) monetary advantages, (5) concern about population growth, (6) general dislike of children, (7) negative early socialization experience and doubts about the ability to parent, (8) concern about physical aspects of childbirth and recovery, and (9) concern for children given world conditions. Gender differences were evidenced in a number of areas. Overall, females were more likely to offer altruistic rationales (e.g., concern about population growth, doubts about the ability to parent, concern for children given world conditions). The male samples, conversely, were more apt to offer personal motives (e.g., general dislike of children, monetary advantages).

The consequences of large numbers of persons in industrialized societies forgoing parenthood are far-reaching. For example, the demographic structure in many countries is in the process of radical change; populations are becoming increasingly aged. More persons are reaching old age than ever before, those persons are living longer, and birth rates are low. The cohort age eighty-five or older, in fact, is the fastest-growing cohort in the United States. The question remains: Who will care for the elderly? Some Western European countries provide a variety of services to assist elderly persons in maintaining their independence within the community as long as possible. But social policies in other countries, including the United States, rely heavily on adult children to provide needed care to elderly parents. Formal support services, when available, tend to be uncoordinated and expensive. The question of who will provide that needed care to the large numbers of adults who are predicted to have no children has yet to be answered.

Communal Living Groups

Recent history has witnessed a wide variety of types of communal living groups, including collectives, shared households, experimental communities, and group marriage. Communal living arrangements of these types were more prevalent during the 1960s and 1970s than during any other point in history. It is estimated that within the United States during this period there were approximately 50,000 communal groups with 755,000 participants. These groups coalesce for divergent reasons: simple convenience; political, philosophical, or religious ideologies; sexual variety; economic considerations; or personal growth. Kanter (1972) distinguishes communal living groups during this era as distinctive from previous ones: Communes prior to 1845 generally contained religious themes; after that period economic and political themes were central; and beginning in the 1960s we see that the severe erosion of faith in American institutions was the cornerstone of the formation of communal living groups.

Commune members are a highly divergent group, but certain generalizations can be made. According to the findings of research conducted during the 1970s, most members were young, college-educated, single, and had no children. Approximately three-quarters had never been married, and most were under age thirty. Although most members considered themselves to be politically liberal, commune members resembled the mainstream more so than most people imagine. Most were from middle-class origins, and a higher percentage came from intact families than found among the national average. Many communes had a religious orientation, but even among those that did not, a high number of members reported to have experimented with religious philosophies.

Of the variety of alternative life-styles discussed here, communal living may be the least understood and the most disapproved of. A study conducted in the early 1970s, in the heyday of such living groups, found that only 20 percent of the U.S. population approved of them, and the percentage reporting that they were interested in such living arrangements was much lower still (Yankelovich 1974).

Given the lack of societal support, it is not surprising that communal living groups are unstable. Most arrangements dissolve within a year. The Constantines' study of over a hundred communal living groups in the early 1970s reported that 44 percent of groups lasted for a year or more, 17 percent for three years, and only 7 percent survived for more than five years (Constantine and Constantine 1973).

Today very few persons live in such arrangements. It is estimated that communal living groups contain no more that 250,000 persons in the United States. Other Western countries report similar trends. Studies conducted in the Netherlands and Denmark indicate that not only do very few communal groups exist in these countries, but also they are relatively small, containing only six members per group on average.

Cohabitation

Cohabitation is generally defined as nonmarried heterosexual persons who share intimacy, sexual relations, and who coreside. Cohabitation is not a recent phenomenon nor a uniquely Western one; many societies today and in the past note within their populations couples who were legally married, and those who reside in the generally less honored state of cohabitation. In Sweden, unlike the United States, cohabitation has become so common that it is considered a social institution in and of itself. It is a variant of marriage rather than of courtship; approximately 20 percent of all couples in Sweden who live together are unmarried.

In Sweden, unlike the United States, cohabitation has become so common that it is considered a social institution. It is a variant of marriage rather than of courtship.

Cohabitation is becoming increasingly common in the United States, although it has not achieved the same status as in Scandinavia. In 1988 there were 2.6 million couples in the United States, or more than 5 million adults, living together outside of marriage at any given time. National data indicate that the increase since 1970 is almost fivefold. From 1970 to 1980 the percentage of couples who had cohabited prior to marriage, as reported in one specific county in Oregon, rose from 13 percent to 53 percent (Gwartney-Gibbs 1986). Another study, of eighty-seven Canadian couples located through newspaper wedding announcements, reported that 64 percent of the couples had cohabited for some period, 43 percent of these for over three months. Thus cohabitation is now seen as an institutionalized component to the larger progression involving dating, courtship, engagement, and marriage.

Cohabitors tend to differ from noncohabitors in a variety of sociodemographic characteristics. For example, cohabitors tend to see themselves as being more androgynous and more politically liberal, are less apt to be religious, are more experienced sexually, and are younger than married persons. The data on the quality of their home life within their families of orientation is mixed. See Macklin (1987) and Buunk and Van Driel (1989) for two divergent views. Although cohabitors may argue that living together prior to marriage will enhance the latter relationship by increasing their knowledge of their compatibility with day-to-day living prior to legalizing the union, such optimism is generally not supported. While some studies indicate no differences in the quality of marriages among those who first cohabited and those that did not, others indicate that the noncohabitors seem to have the advantage. This may, however, have nothing to do with cohabitation per se but rather may be due to other differences in the personalities and expectations of marriage between the two groups.

A wide variety of personal relationships exist among cohabiting couples. Several typologies have been created to try to capture the diversity found within these relationships. One particularly useful one, articulated by Macklin (1983), is designed to exemplify the diversity in the stability of such relationships. She discusses four types of cohabiting relationships: (1) *temporary or casual* relationships, in which the couple cohabits for convenience or for pragmatic reasons; (2) *going together,* in which the couple is affectionately involved but has no plans for marriage in the future; (3) *transitional,* which serves as a preparation for marriage; and (4) *alternative to marriage,* wherein the couple opposes marriage on ideological or other grounds.

Attitudes toward cohabitation have become increasingly positive, especially among younger persons. However, the majority of persons in the United States still disapprove of living together without the legal ties of marriage. Buunk and Van Driel (1989) remind us that cohabitation in several U.S. states is still a felony, based on a legal code outlawing "crimes against chastity." These laws, however, are rarely if ever enforced. In the Netherlands, or in other countries where cohabitation is institutionalized, the majority of the population sees few distinctions between cohabitation and marriage.

Both are viewed as appropriate avenues for intimacy, and the two life-styles resemble one another much more so than in the United States in terms of commitment and stability.

The future of cohabitation, and the subsequent changes in the attitudes toward it, are of considerable interest to sociologists. Many predict that cohabitation will become institutionalized in the United States to a greater degree within the near future, shifting from a pattern of courtship to an alternative to marriage. Whether it will ever achieve the status found within other countries, particularly in Scandinavia, remains to be seen.

Gay and Lesbian Relationships

Not long ago homosexuality was viewed by many professionals as an illness or a perversion. It was only as recently as 1973, for example, that the American Psychiatric Association removed homosexuality from its list of psychiatric disorders. Today, due in large part to the efforts of researchers such as Kinsey and associates (1948, 1953), Masters and Johnson (1979), and to organizations such as the Gay Liberation Front during the late 1960s, homosexuality has generally become to be viewed as a life-style rather than an illness, at least within academic circles. The work of Kinsey and associates illustrated that a sizable minority of the population, particularly males, had experimented with same-sex sexual relationships, although few considered themselves exclusively homosexual. Thirty-seven percent of males, he reported, had experienced at least one homosexual contact to the point of orgasm, although only 4 percent were exclusively homosexual. Among females, 13 percent had a same-sex sexual contact to the point of orgasm, while only 2 percent were exclusively homosexual in their orientation. A national probability sample of adult males interviewed by telephone found that 3.7 percent reported to be either homosexual or bisexual (Harry 1990).

Cross-cultural evidence suggests that the majority of cultures recognize the existence of homosexual behavior, particularly in certain age categories such as adolescence, and most are tolerant of homosexual behavior. Culturally speaking, it is rare to find an actual *preference* for same-sex relations; they tend to occur only in societies that define homosexuality and heterosexuality as mutually exclusive, as in many industrial countries.

Among nonacademic circles, attitudes toward homosexuality are less accepting or tolerant. Many states within the United States, particularly those in the South and in the West, still have laws barring homosexual activity among consenting adults. Attitudes among the United States populace parallel such statutes. The results of a Gallup poll indicate that 60 percent of adults believe that homosexuals should not be hired as elementary-school teachers (Gallup 1987). According to a statewide study in Alaska, gays and lesbians report that their sexual orientation has caused a variety of problems in securing housing and in the job market. Additionally, almost two-thirds of the respondents reported at least one instance of violence or verbal abuse due to their sexual orientation (Green and Brause 1989). This contrasts sharply with the view toward homosexuality in the Scandinavian countries. Not only are homosexual relations between consenting adults legal, but also the majority of the population considers it to be normal behavior. The AIDS crisis, however, has made the public less tolerant of homosexual behavior in both the United States and Europe.

Gender differences emerge in homosexual relations within a variety of contexts.

There is a growing amount of research illuminating various aspects of homosexual relationships, such as gender roles; degree of commitment; quality of relationship; and the couples' interface with other relationships, such as children, ex-spouses, or parents. However, because of unique historical reactions to gays and lesbians, and to the differential socialization of men and women in our society, it is important to explore the nature of lesbian and gay relationships separately. Gender differences emerge in homosexual relations within a variety of contexts; for example, lesbians are more apt to have monogamous, stable relationships than are gay men, although the popular stereotype of gays as sexually "promiscuous" has been exaggerated. The majority of gay men, just like lesbians, are interested in monogamous, long-term relationships. The lack of institutional support for gay and lesbian relationships and the wide variety of obstacles not encountered among heterosexuals, such as prejudice and discriminatory behavior, take their toll on these relationships, however.

The AIDS epidemic has had an enormous impact on the gay subculture. While the impact on lesbians is significantly less, they have not been untouched by the social impact of this devastating medical issue (see Kaplan et al. 1987 for a thorough review of the sociological impact of AIDS). The high mortality rates among AIDS victims has particularly struck San Francisco, New York, Los Angeles, and Miami, and the devastation attributed to this epidemic cannot be ignored, despite the slow response of the world's governments.

Concluding Comments

There is considerable accumulating evidence to suggest that family life-styles are becoming more varied and that the public is becoming increasingly tolerant of this diversity. The data indicate that marriage itself per se may be less important in sanctioning intimacy. The review by Buunk and Hupka (1986) of seven countries reveals that individualism, as expressed by following one's own personal interests in intimate relationships, was more prevalent in affluent democratic countries such as the United States and in most of Western Europe than in poorer and nondemocratic nations such as the Soviet Union.

This does not mean, however, that people are discarding the institution of marriage. In the United States, as elsewhere, the vast majority of the population continues to endorse marriage and parenthood in general, and for themselves personally. Most still plan to marry and have children, and optimism remains high that theirs will be a lasting union despite high national frequencies of divorce.

Alternative life-styles are not replacing marriage. Instead, they are gaining acceptance because they involve, for some, modifications of the family structure as an adaptation to changing conditions in society. The life-styles discussed here, as well as others such as single-parent families, commuter marriages, sexually open marriages, dual-career families, and stepfamilies, reflect the broader social changes in values, relationships, and even technology that are found within society as a whole. As Macklin notes, the family is not disappearing, but "continuing its age-old process of gradual evolution, maintaining many of its traditional functions and structures while adapting to changing economic circumstances and cultural ideologies" (1987, p. 317). This process has merely accelerated during the past several decades, and these changes have caught the attention of the general public. College classes and their corresponding textbooks within this discipline of sociology are still often titled *Marriage and the Family,* as if there were only one model of intimacy. Yet perhaps a more appropriate title would be Marriages and Families. This

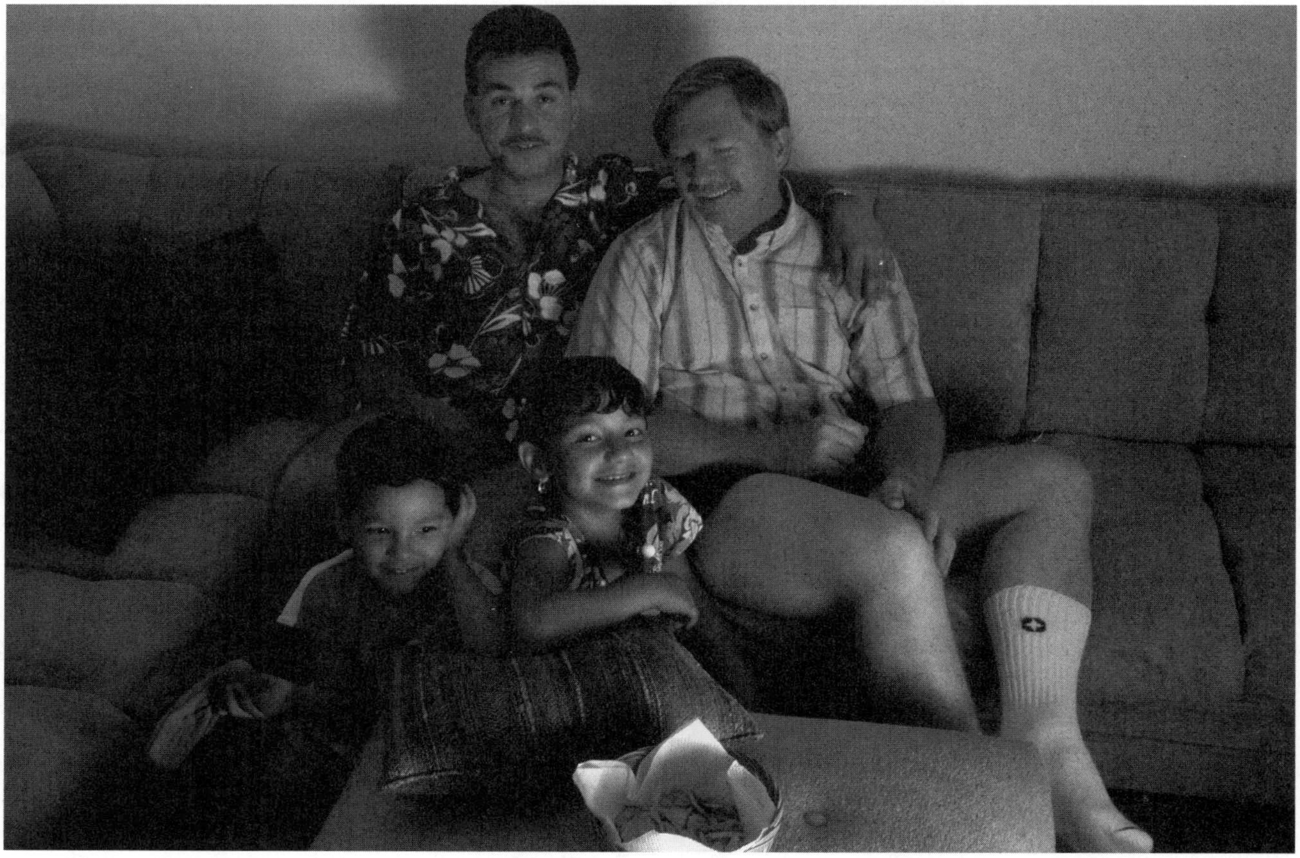

Most gay men are interested in long-term monogamous relationships, which sometimes includes raising children together. (Shelley Gazin/Corbis)

would reflect not only the diversity illustrated here but would also acknowledge the tremendous ethnic and class variations that make for rich and meaningful intimate relations.

[See also American Families; Courtship; Marriage; Mate Selection Theories; Sexual Orientation.]

BIBLIOGRAPHY

Austrom, Douglas, and Kim Hanel 1985 "Psychological Issues of Single Life in Canada: An Exploratory Study." *International Journal of Women's Studies* 8:12–23.

Bernard, Jessie 1973 *The Future of Marriage.* New York: Bantam Books.

Buunk, Bram P., and R. B. Hupka 1986 "Autonomy in Close Relationships: A Cross-cultural Study." *Family Perspective* 20:209–221.

———, and Barry Van Driel 1989 Variant Lifestyles and Relationships. Newbury Park, Calif.: Sage Publications.

Constantine L., and J. M. Constantine 1973 *Group Marriage.* New York. Collier Books.

Davis, Kingsley 1987 "Low Fertility in Evolutionary Perspective." In K. Davis, M. S. Bernstam, and R. Ricardo-Campbell, eds., *Below Replacement Fertility in Industrial Societies.* Cambridge: Cambridge University Press.

Gallup Report 1987 Report Nos. 244–245:2–9.

Glick, Paul C. 1984 "Marriage, Divorce, and Living Arrangements: Perspective Changes." *Journal of Family Issues* 5:7–26.

Green, Melissa S., and Jay K. Brause 1989 *Identity Reports: Sexual Orientation Bias in Alaska.* Anchorage, Alaska: Identity Inc.

Gwartney-Gibbs, Patricia A. 1986 "The Institutionalization of Premarital Cohabitation: Estimates from Marriage License Applications." *Journal of Marriage and the Family* 48:423–434.

Harry, Joseph 1990 "A Probability Sample of Gay Men." *Journal of Homosexuality* 19:89–104.

Houseknecht, Sharon K. 1987 "Voluntary Childlessness." In M. B. Sussman and S. K. Steinmetz, eds., *Handbook of Marriage and the Family.* New York: Plenum Press.

Kanter, Rosabeth Moss 1972 *Commitment and Community: Communes and Utopias in Sociological Perspective.* Cambridge, Mass.: Harvard University Press.

Kaplan, Howard B., Robert J. Johnson, Carol A. Bailey, and William Simon 1987 "The Sociological Study of AIDS: A Critical Review of the Literature and Suggested Research Agenda." *Journal of Health and Social Behavior* 28:140–157.

Kinsey, Alfred, W. Pomeroy, P. H. Gebhard, and C. E. Martin 1953 *Sexual Behavior in the Human Female.* Philadelphia: W. B. Saunders.

Kinsey, Alfred, W. Pomeroy, and C. E. Martin 1948 *Sexual Behavior in the Human Male.* Philadelphia: W. B. Saunders.

Macklin, Eleanor D. 1983 "Nonmarital Heterosexual Cohabitation: An Overview." In E. D. Macklin and R. H. Rubin, eds., *Contemporary Families and Alternative Lifestyles: Handbook on Research and Theory.* Beverly Hills, Calif.: Sage Publications.

——— 1987 "Nontraditional Family Forms." In M. B. Sussman and S. K. Steinmetz, eds., *Handbook of Marriage and the Family.* New York: Plenum Press.

Masters, William H., and Virginia E. Johnson 1979 *Homosexuality in Perspective.* Boston: Little, Brown.

Oudijk, C. 1983 *Social Atlas of Women* (in Dutch). The Hague: Staatsuitgeverij.

Roper Organization 1980 *The Virginia Slims American Women's Poll.* Storrs, Conn.: Author.

Seccombe, Karen 1990 "Assessing the Costs and Benefits of Children: Gender Comparisons among Child-free Husbands and Wives." *Journal of Marriage and the Family* 53:191–202.

Shostak, Arthur B. 1987 "Singlehood." In M. B. Sussman and S. K. Steinmetz, eds., *Handbook of Marriage and the Family.* New York: Plenum Press.

Stein, Peter J. 1981 *Single Life: Unmarried Adults in Social Context.* New York: St. Martin's Press.

Van de Kaa, Dick J. 1987 "Europe's Second Demographic Transition." *Population Bulletin* 42:1–57.

Yankelovich, Daniel 1974 *The New Morality: Profile of American Youth in the Seventies.* New York: McGraw-Hill.

– KAREN SECCOMBE

AMERICAN FAMILIES

Many longstanding assumptions about American families have been challenged in recent years. Among these assumptions is the belief that in colonial times the American family was extended in its structure, with three generations living together under one roof. It has been commonly believed that the nuclear family came about as a result of industrialization, with smaller families better able to meet the demands of an industrialized economy. However, historical data show that the extended family was not typical in the colonial era and that the earliest families arriving from Great Britain and other western European countries were already nuclear in structure (Demos 1970; Laslett and Wall 1972).

More generally, family scholars have successfully challenged the notion of "the American family." As Howe (1972, p. 11) puts it, "the first thing to remember about the American family is that it doesn't exist. Families exist. All kinds of families in all kinds of economic and marital situations." This review will show the great diversity of family patterns that characterize the United States of the past, the present, and the foreseeable future.

Historical Overview

It is unfortunate that textbooks intended for courses on the family rarely include a discussion of Native Americans, for a historical examination of these groups shows a striking range of variation in family patterns. In fact, virtually all the variations in marriage customs, residence patterns, and family structures found the world over could be found in North America alone (Driver 1969). Though some of these traditional family patterns have survived to the present day, others have been disrupted over the course of U.S. history. It is important to note, however, that research has not confirmed the commonly held assumption that Native American societies were placid and unchanging prior to European contact and subsequent subjugation. Important changes were taking place in Native American societies long before the arrival of Europeans (Lurie 1985).

As has been noted, European immigrants to the American colonies came in nuclear rather than extended families (and also came as single persons—for example, as indentured servants). It was long believed that colonial families were very large, with some early writers claiming an average of ten to twelve children per family. More recently, family scholars have cited evidence showing somewhat lower numbers of children, with an average of eight children born to colonial women (Zinn and Eitzen 1987). Scholars also have distinguished between number of children born per woman and family size at a given point in time. Average family size was somewhat smaller than the average number of children born, due to high infant mortality and because the oldest children often left home prior to the birth of the last child. Evidence suggests an average family size of five to six members during colonial times (Nock 1987). Thus, although the average size of colonial families was somewhat larger than today's families, they are not as large as have been commonly assumed.

"The first thing to remember about the American family is that it doesn't exist."

To understand the size of colonial households, consideration must also be given to nonrelated persons living in the home. Servants often lived with prosperous colonial families, and other families took in boarders and lodgers when economic conditions required such an arrangement (Zinn and Eitzen 1987). Households might also include apprentices and other employees. The presence of nonfamily members has important implications for family life. Laslett (1973) has argued that the presence of nonkin meant that households offered less privacy to families and hence provided the opportunity for greater scrutiny by "outsiders." Colonial homes also had fewer rooms than most American homes today, which also contributed to the relatively public nature of these households.

Colonial communities placed great importance on marriage, particularly in New England, where sanctions were imposed on those who did not marry (for example, taxes were imposed on single men in some New England colonies). However, historical records indicate that colonists did not marry at especially young ages. The average age at marriage was twenty-four to twenty-five for men and twenty-two to twenty-three for women (Leslie and Korman 1989). Older ages at marriage during this era reflect parental control of sons' labor on the farm (with many sons delaying marriage until their fathers ceded land to them) and also reflect the lower relative numbers of women (Nock 1987). Parents also typically exerted strong influence over the process of mate selection but did not control the decision. Divorce was rare during this period. The low divorce rate cannot be equated with intact marriages, however. Spousal desertion and early widowhood were far more common experiences than they are today.

The population for the American colonies came primarily from Great Britain, other western European countries, and from western Africa. Initially brought to the colonies in 1619 as indentured servants, hundreds of thousands of Africans were enslaved and transported to America during the colonial period (by 1790, the date of the first U.S. census, African-Americans composed almost 20 percent of the population; Zinn and Eitzen 1987). It has been commonly assumed that slavery destroyed the cultural traditions and family life of African-Americans. The reasoning behind this assumption was that slave families often were separated for sale to other masters, males were unable to provide for or protect their families, and slave marriages were not legal. The stereotype of "matriarchal" black families, in which women are the family heads and authorities, usually assumes that slavery produced this family form. Recent research challenges these assumptions. Though slave families lived in constant fear of separation (Genovese 1986), many slave marriages were strong and long-lasting (Gutman 1976). Marriages were legitimized within the slave community (symbolized, for example, by the ritual of "jumping over a broomstick"; Boris and Bardaglio 1987), and two-parent families were common among slaves as well as among free blacks in the North and the South (Gutman 1976). A variety of family structures, including female-headed households, were found in the slave community and attested to the importance placed on kin ties. Rather than the "absent family" assumed to characterize slave life, slaves were connected to one another through extensive kinship networks (Genovese 1986). Extended kin ties continue to be an important aspect of African-American families today.

For decades, the heritage of slavery and its presumed effects on family life has been invoked to explain social problem in poor black communities (e.g., Moynihan 1965). The historical evidence described above does not lend support to this explanation. Most recent writers argue that social problems experienced in poor black communities can more accurately be attributed to the effects of discrimination and the disorganizing effects of mass migration to the urbanized North rather than to the heritage of slavery (e.g., Staples 1986).

Societal changes associated with the Industrial Revolution profoundly affected all types of American families, though the specific nature and extent of these effects varied by social class, race, ethnic origins, and geographic region. Prior to the Industrial Revolution, family members worked together as an economic unit. Their workplace was the home or family farm, with families producing much of what they consumed. Family life and economic life were one and the same, and the boundaries between "private life" in the family and "public life" in the community were blurred. With the development of a commercial economy, the workplace was located away from the family unit. Separation of work and family life created a sharp distinction between the "public" realm of work and the "private" realm of family. Particularly for women's roles, changes initiated by the Industrial Revolution have been long-lasting and far-reaching. Increasingly, women's roles were defined by activities assumed to be noneconomic, in the form of nurturing and caring for family members. This was especially true for middle class women, and married women were excluded from many jobs. Poor and working-class women often participated in wage labor, but this work was generally seen as secondary to their family roles. Men were viewed as having primary responsibility for the economic welfare of their families. No longer an economically interdependent unit, families were transformed such that women and children became economically dependent on the primary wage earner.

Thus, children's roles and family relationships also changed with industrialization. In contrast to earlier times, in which children were viewed as miniature adults and engaged in many of the same tasks they would also perform as adults, childhood came to be seen as a special stage of life characterized by dependence in the home. And although children in working-class homes were more likely to work for pay, the evidence suggests that these families also viewed childhood as a stage of life distinct from adulthood (Zinn and Eitzen 1987). Overall, the family became increasingly defined as a private place specializing in the nurturance of children and the satisfaction of emotional needs, a "haven in a heartless world" (Lasch 1977).

Family structures also changed during the 1800s. Family size declined to an average of four to five members. (Of course, average numbers obscure variation in family sizes across social classes and other important dimensions such as race and ethnicity.) Though the average size of nineteenth-century American families was close to that of today's families, women bore more children during their lifetimes than do American women today. Infant and child mortality was higher and births were spaced further apart, thus decreasing the average size of families at a given point in time. Household size also declined, with fewer households including nonrelated persons such as boarders or apprentices. The average ages at which women and men married were similar to those of colonial times, with an average of twenty-two years for women and twenty-six for men. However, greater life expectancy meant that marriages typically lasted longer than they did during the colonial period (Nock 1987).

From 1830 to 1930 the United States experienced two large waves of immigration. The first wave, from 1830 to 1882, witnessed the arrival of more than ten million immigrants from England, Ireland, Germany, and the Scandinavian countries. During the second wave, from 1882 to 1930, over twenty-two million immigrated to the United States. Peoples from northern and western Europe continued to come to the United States during this second wave, but a large proportion of immigrants came from southern and eastern Europe as well (Zinn and Eitzen 1987). Immigrants' family lives were shaped by their ethnic origins as well as by the diverse social and economic structures of the cities and communities in which they settled.

Ethnic traditions also helped Mexican-American families adapt to changing circumstances. Annexation of territory from Mexico in 1848 and subsequent immigration from Mexico produced sizable Mexican-American communities in the Southwest. Immigrants from Mexico often reconstructed their original family units within the United States, typically including extended as well as nuclear family members. Extended family households are more common today among Mexican-Americans than among non-Hispanic whites, reflecting Mexican-Americans' strong family orientation (or "familism") as well as their less advantaged economic circumstances (Zinn and Eitzen 1987).

Imbalanced sex ratios among Chinese and Japanese immigrants greatly influenced the family experiences of these groups. First coming to the United States in the early 1900s, Chinese immigrants were predominantly male. The Chinese Exclusion Act of 1882 barred further immigration, and only wealthy Chinese men were able to bring brides to the United States (Boris and Bardaglio 1987). As of 1910, there were 1,413 Chinese men in the United States to every 100 Chinese women. This sex ratio was still skewed in 1940, when there were 258 men to every 100 women. In contrast to the extended family networks typical of traditional Chinese culture, until recent decades many Chinese-American households consisted of single men living alone (Marden and Meyer 1973).

Substantial immigration from Japan took place between 1885 and 1924. Like traditional Chinese families, Japanese families were based on strong extended kin networks. As was true for Chinese immigration, most Japanese immigrants were male. In addition to immigration restrictions, Japanese-American families (especially those on the West Coast) were disrupted by property confiscation and the mass relocations that took place during World War II (Marden and Meyer 1973).

In addition to the "old" immigration of the mid-nineteenth century and the "new" immigration of the late nineteenth and early twentieth centuries, a third wave of large-scale immigration to the United States began in the mid-1960s. In contrast to the earlier waves, when most immigrants came from European countries, most immigration in this third wave has been from Latin America and Asia. However, as has been true of earlier periods of immigration, public controversies surround the economic and social absorption of these new groups (Marger 1991). In addition to occupational and economic challenges facing immigrant families, social challenges include the continuing debate over whether schools should provide bilingual education to non-English-speaking children.

Trends Since 1900

The separation of paid work and family life, associated with the transition to an industrialized society, gave rise to profound changes in family life. Over the course of the twentieth century, women's roles have been defined primarily by family responsibilities within the "private sphere" of the home, but women's labor-force participation has risen steadily (except for a brief period following World War II; Andersen 1988). Increases in labor-force participation have been especially great among married women. In 1900, only 6 percent of all married women were in the labor force. By 1984, that figure had risen to 53 percent (Scanzoni and Scanzoni 1988). However, as has been true historically, African-American and other minority women are more likely to work for pay than non-Hispanic white women. As discussed below, women's labor-force participation has important implications for many dimensions of family life.

Though American families have changed in important ways over the past 100 years, examination of historical trends also reveals continuation of some family patterns begun long ago. Notably, the period of the 1950s is commonly thought to mark the end of a golden age of family life. However, historical data show that for a number of family patterns, the 1950s, rather than the 1970s and 1980s, was an unusual period. Lower rates of divorce, lower ages at marriage, and higher rates of childbearing observed during the 1950s have been attributed mainly to greater economic prosperity following the Great Depression and World War II (Cherlin 1981).

AGE AT FIRST MARRIAGE. As of 1986, the average (median) age at first marriage in the United States was twenty-three years for women and almost twenty-six years for men (Scanzoni and Scanzoni 1988). Available evidence suggests somewhat higher ages at first marriage in the future (Sweet and Bumpass 1987). Although some consider the trend toward later marriage a deviation from traditional patterns of family formation, historical data do not support this belief. The timing of marriage today is similar to that observed from the colonial period through the late 1800s (Cherlin 1981; Scanzoni and Scanzoni 1988). Between the early 1900s and the late 1960s, average age at marriage declined to approximately 20.5 years for women and twenty-three years for men. Subsequent to the late 1960s, average age at marriage began to climb once more. Examination of non-Hispanic whites, blacks, and Hispanic whites shows that age at first marriage has climbed more rapidly for blacks than for non-Hispanic whites, with blacks now marrying later than non-Hispanic whites. In contrast, Hispanics marry at younger ages than do other groups. It is difficult to assess whether Hispanics' lower age at marriage reflects long-term trends within the United States due to the large numbers of Mexican-Americans who have immigrated in recent years (Sweet and Bumpass 1987).

Although some consider the trend toward later marriage a deviation from traditional patterns of family formation, historical data do not support this belief.

Factors promoting later age at marriage in recent decades include greater societal acceptance of singlehood and cohabitation as well as greater emphasis on educational attainment (Zinn and Eitzen 1987). The relationship between age at marriage and level of education is nearly linear for non-Hispanic white men and women, with more education associated with later age at marriage. This relationship is more complex for minority groups, and especially for black and Hispanic men. For these men, later age at marriage is associated *both* with lower and higher educational levels, producing a U-shaped relationship between education and age at marriage. Minority men with low education are likely to have especially poor job prospects, which in turn affect prospects for marriage. Overall, less racial and ethnic diversity in age at marriage is shown for those with higher educational attainment (Sweet and Bumpass 1987).

SINGLES. The size of the unmarried population is increasing, due primarily to later ages at marriage and increases in divorce (to be discussed below). In addition to those who are divorced, separated, or widowed, the single adult population includes persons who have never married. Throughout U.S. history a small but significant proportion of individuals have remained unmarried throughout their lives. In 1980, 5.4 percent of men and 5 percent of women ages fifty-five to sixty-four had never married. Among blacks, 7.9 percent of men and 6.4 percent of women in this age group had never married (Bumpass and Sweet 1987). Due to the continuing stigmatization of homosexuality, it is difficult to ascertain the numbers of single persons who are gay or lesbian. Researchers have estimated that 4 percent of men and 2 percent of women are exclusively homosexual (Collins 1988). Though homosexual marriages are not legally recognized, many gay and lesbian couples form lasting unions.

Diverse factors help to explain the rise in singleness. The pattern of women marrying men several years older than themselves, observed since colonial times, is important to consider. Since 1940, the number of women aged twenty-two (women's "peak marrying year") has been greater than the number of men aged twenty-five (men's peak marrying year). The imbalance of available male partners for women increases with age. Among

American family life of the 1950s has often been idealized in retrospect, but it was unusual in the history of family patterns. (Corbis-Bettmann)

those ages forty-five to sixty-four, the number of single women is three times greater than the number of single men. The imbalance of available male partners also is greater for black women. The shortage of black men as marital partners for black women has been attributed to various factors, including interracial marriage and black men's greater likelihood of unemployment and incarceration (see Zinn and Eitzen 1987). Women's changing roles have also been linked with the rise in singleness. Women with higher education and higher personal income are less likely to marry or have children (Andersen 1988). Also, in contrast to earlier eras, there is greater societal tolerance of singlehood, providing greater freedom for both women and men to choose a single life-style.

Though women with greater personal resources are less likely to marry, the proportion of single women who are poor has risen steadily in recent decades. Of those adults whose income fell below the official poverty line in 1983, two out of three were women (Gerstel and Gross 1987). Minority women, older women, and those with children are especially at risk. Both women and men face the potential for economic hardship when they become widowed, divorced, or separated. The economic consequences are greater for women than for men, however (Keith 1986). Among those who divorce, women's subsequent income averages 24 percent of previous family income, while men's is 87 percent (Andersen 1988).

CHILDBEARING. Childbearing patterns have varied somewhat over the past 100 years. Women born in 1891 had an average of three children. Women born in 1908, who bore children during the Great Depression, had an average of two children. This figure increased to three children per mother during the 1950s and has since declined to a little less than two per mother today. In addition to fewer numbers of children born, current trends in childbearing include higher age at first childbirth and longer intervals of time between births. These trends are interrelated. Waiting longer to have a first child and spacing births further apart decrease the average number of children born per mother. The timing of childbearing also has important effects on other life experiences, including educational and occupational attainment. Lower rates of childbearing are associated with higher educational levels and higher incomes (Cherlin 1981; Sweet and Bumpass 1987).

Fewer married couples are having their first child in the period immediately following marriage, but there are some important differences by race. In 1960, 54 percent of non-Hispanic white couples had children within twelve to seventeen months of marriage. In 1980 this figure dropped to 36 percent. Little change was shown over this period for black couples, who had children within twelve to seventeen months of marriage. Compared to the total population, black couples are likely to have more children on average and to have a child present at the time of marriage. For whites (Hispanics and non-Hispanics) as well as blacks, nine-tenths of all couples have children within seven to eight years of marriage (Sweet and Bumpass 1987).

Childbearing among single women has increased substantially. For single women ages twenty and over, rates of childbearing rose between 1940 and the 1960s, declined for about ten years, then continued the upward trend. Childbearing among teens ages fifteen to nineteen has increased continuously since the 1940s. In 1960, 5 percent of all births were to single women. In 1985, this figure climbed to 18 percent, or one of every six children born in the United States. Nonmarital childbearing is much higher for blacks than for whites. Among blacks, 55 percent of all children are born to single women, compared to 12 percent among whites. However, childbearing rates among single black women have declined since 1965, while whites' rates have continued to increase. For all races, nonmarital childbearing is highest among those who are poor (Collins 1988; Sweet and Bumpass 1987). Socioeconomic factors can help to explain why blacks, who are disproportionately likely to be poor, have had higher rates of childbearing.

DIVORCE. Divorce rates have been rising in the United States since the Civil War. Over the past century, the proportion of adults currently divorced rose from one in 300 to one in thirteen women and one in eighteen men (Sweet and Bumpass 1987). This long-term trend does not show a smooth and progressive rise, however. Divorce rates have risen more sharply after every major war during this century. Divorce also increased following the Great Depression, apparently reflecting stresses associated with unemployment and economic deprivation. Economic prosperity, as well as greater emphasis on family life, have been linked to the lower divorce rate observed from 1950 to 1962. Following 1962, dramatic increases in the divorce rate have occurred, with a 100 percent increase between 1963 and 1975 (Cherlin 1981). By the early 1970s, the chance of eventual divorce reached almost 50 percent. The divorce rate has more or less stabilized since that time, such that approximately 50 percent of all marriages begun today are estimated to end in divorce (Collins 1988).

Population trends have been linked with the increased rate of divorce. Among these trends is greater longevity, with an average life expectancy at birth of seventy-eight years for women and seventy-one years for men born in 1985. When they reach the age of sixty-five, women born in 1985 can expect to live an additional nineteen years, while men can expect to live fifteen more years. (These figures are for the total population. Life expectancies are lower for members of racial and ethnic minorities.) In contrast, the life expectancy at birth for those born in 1900 was forty-eight years for women and forty-six years for men (Grambs 1989). Unsatisfactory marriages that formerly may have been terminated by the death of one partner are now more likely to be dissolved by divorce (Uhlenberg 1986). Writers have also noted the apparent connection between women's increasing levels of labor-force participation and the increased rate of divorce in the United States. Studies do show that divorce is more likely to occur in couples where the wife is able to support herself financially (Cherlin 1981).

Studies show that divorce is more likely to occur in couples where the wife is able to support herself financially.

The risk of divorce also varies with age at marriage, duration of the marriage, education, race, and ethnicity. Age at marriage is one of the most important factors, with the likelihood of divorce twice as great among couples where the wife was seventeen or younger than among couples where the wife was in her early twenties. Further, most divorces take place within the first few years of marriage. The longer a couple has been together, the less likely they will be to get divorced. This pattern also holds among couples in which one or both partners have remarried. Education also seems to be an important factor, with a higher divorce rate observed among high school dropouts than among college graduates. However, the effect of education is due in large part to the fact that college graduates tend to marry at later ages. Looking across racial and ethnic groups, the risk of divorce is greater among African-Americans than among whites, and especially high divorce rates are observed for Hispanics (Puerto Ricans in particular), Native Americans, and Hawaiians. Divorce is less common among Asian-Americans (Sweet and Bumpass 1987).

WIDOWHOOD. The average age of widowhood has increased with rises in life expectancy. Among women, the median age at widowhood was fifty-one in 1900, compared to fifty-nine in 1964 and sixty-eight in 1979. Median age at widowhood for men was forty-five in 1900, sixty-five in 1964, and seventy-one in 1979. Women today are widowed at younger ages than men and can also expect to live longer in a widowed status due to higher female life expectancy. Of all women over age seventy-five who have been married, two-thirds will be widowed. This figure rises to almost 78 percent for African-American women (Grambs 1989).

REMARRIAGE. Most persons who divorce eventually remarry, as do a large proportion of those who are widowed during their prime adult years. Especially for women, remarriage rates are tied closely with age. Among women who divorce prior to age thirty, 75 percent will eventually remarry. In comparison, 50 percent of women who divorce between the ages of thirty and forty will remarry, and 28 percent of women who divorce at forty and older will remarry (Scanzoni and Scanzoni 1988). As is true for rates of marriage and divorce, large race and ethnic differences are observed for remarriage. The proportion of women who remarry in ten years or less following separation is almost three-quarters for non-Hispanic whites, about one-half for Mexican-Americans, and about one-third for blacks. Men are more likely to remarry than women, but similar race and ethnic differences in remarriage rates are observed for both genders (Sweet and Bumpass 1987).

Increased rates of divorce and remarriage are transforming American families. "Blended" families are becoming increasingly common. These can consist of couples who have previously been married to different partners, the children born in those previous marriages, and the children born to the current marital partners. In 1980 41 percent of all marriages involved one previously married partner. In 1970 this figure was 30 percent (Furstenberg 1980).

HOUSEHOLD STRUCTURE. As defined by the U.S. Census Bureau, "family households" are those containing persons who are related to the household head (the person in whose name the home is owned or rented). "Nonfamily households" consist of one or more unrelated persons. Historically, most American households have been family households, and most of these have included married couples. In 1910 80 percent of all households included married couples. By 1980 this percentage had declined to 61 percent. A breakdown of all U.S. households in 1980 shows that 31 percent were married couples with children under age eighteen; 30 percent were married couples with no children under age eighteen; 7 percent were single parents with children under age eighteen; 6 percent were family households that did not include a married couple or any children of the householder; and 26 percent were "nonfamily." Of the nonfamily households, 86 percent consisted of individuals who were living alone. The proportion of single-person households has risen dramatically over the century. In 1890, only 4 percent of all households were of this type.

Breakdowns of family structure by race and ethnicity show that Americans of Korean, Filipino, Vietnamese, and Mexican heritage are most likely to live in family households (for each group, about 84 percent live in family households). African-Americans and non-Hispanic whites are somewhat less likely to live in family households. Also, compared to other racial and ethnic groups, Puerto Ricans are most likely to live in a household consisting of a mother and one or more children (with 23 percent living in this type of household), followed by African-Americans, Native Americans, and Hawaiians (Sweet and Bumpass 1987).

Type of household is tied closely with economic status. Children are more likely to be poor today as a result of greater poverty among women. Among households headed by women (with no adult male present), almost one-half of all non-Hispanic white children lived in poverty in 1985, compared with 69 percent of all black children and 71 percent of all Hispanic children (Folbre 1987; Sweet and Bumpass 1987).

Likely due to economic as well as cultural factors, racial and ethnic minority groups are more likely than majority whites to live in extended family settings. Groups most likely to do so are of Vietnamese, Filipino, and African heritage. While 35 percent of all Vietnamese-American children live in an extended family setting, only 8 percent of non-Hispanic white children live with relatives in addition to (or other than) one or both parents (Sweet and Bumpass 1987).

American Families and the Future

Traditional distinctions between "family" and "nonfamily" are increasingly challenged. Though still a relatively small proportion of all households (about 4 percent; Scanzoni and Scanzoni 1988), the number of cohabiting heterosexual couples has increased greatly in the past several decades. Marriage between homosexuals is not legally recognized, but some have elected to adopt each other legally, and a growing number are raising children. In addition to the "traditional" nuclear family form of two parents with children, other family types can be expected to continue in the future. These include single parents, blended families resulting from remarriage, and households in which other relatives such as grandparents reside.

Increased longevity has brought about some of the most important changes in American family life over the past century. Children are more likely than ever before to interact with their grandparents. Further, many persons are becoming grandparents while their own parents are still alive (Uhlenberg 1986). Research has documented the prevalence and importance of social interaction, emotional support, financial help, and other assistance between the generations (Horowitz 1985). For all types of American families, indications are that high levels of interaction and assistance between the generations will continue in the future.

[See also Alternative Life-Styles, Courtship; Marital Adjustment; Marriage; Marriage and Divorce Rates; Mate Selection Theories; Parental Roles; Remarriage.]

BIBLIOGRAPHY

Andersen, Margaret L. 1988 *Thinking about Women: Sociological Perspectives on Sex and Gender.* 2d ed. New York: Macmillan.

Boris, Eileen, and Peter Bardaglio 1987 "Gender, Race, and Class: The Impact of the State on the Family and the Economy, 1790–1945." In Naomi Gerstel and Harriet Engel Gross, eds., *Families and Work.* Philadelphia: Temple University Press.

Cherlin, Andrew J. 1981 *Marriage, Divorce, Remarriage.* Cambridge, Mass.: Harvard University Press.

Collins, Randall 1988 *Sociology of Marriage and the Family: Gender, Love, and Property.* 2d ed. Chicago: Nelson-Hall.

Demos, John 1970 *A Little Commonwealth.* New York: Oxford University Press.

Driver, Harold E. 1969 *Indians of North America.* 2d ed. Chicago: University of Chicago Press.

Folbre, Nancy 1987 "The Pauperization of Motherhood: Patriarchy and Public Policy in the United States." In N. Gerstel and H. E. Gross, eds., *Families and Work.* Philadelphia: Temple University Press.

Furstenberg, Frank F. Jr. 1980 "Reflections on Remarriage." *Journal of Family Issues* 1:443–453.

Genovese, Eugene D. 1986 "The Myth of the Absent Family." In Robert Staples, ed., The *Black Family: Essays and Studies.* 3d ed. Belmont, Calif.: Wadsworth.

Gerstel, Naomi, and Harriet Engel Gross, eds. 1987 *Families and Work.* Philadelphia: Temple University Press.

Grambs, Jean Dresden 1989 *Women over Forty: Visions and Realities.* New York: Springer.

Gutman, Herbert 1976 *The Black Family in Slavery and Freedom, 1750–1923.* New York: Pantheon.

Horowitz, Amy 1985 "Family Caregiving to the Frail Elderly." In M. P. Lawton and G. L. Maddox, *Annual Review of Gerontology and Geriatrics.* New York: Springer.

Howe, Louise Knapp 1972 *The Future of the Family.* New York: Simon and Schuster.

Keith, Pat M. 1986 "The Social Context and Resources of the Unmarried in Old Age." *International Journal of Aging and Human Development* 23(2):81–96.

Lasch, Christopher 1977 *Haven in a Heartless World: The Family Besieged.* New York: Basic Books.

Laslett, Barbara 1973 "The Family as a Public and Private Institution: An Historical Perspective." *Journal of Marriage and the Family* 35:480–494.

Laslett, Peter, and Richard A. Wall, eds. 1972 *Household and Family in Past Time.* New York: Cambridge University Press.

Leslie, Gerald R., and Sheila K. Korman 1989 *The Family in Social Context.* 7th ed. New York: Oxford University Press.

Lurie, Nancy Oestreich 1985 "The American Indian: Historical Background." In N. R. Yetman, ed., *Majority and Minority.* 4th ed. Boston: Allyn and Bacon.

Marden, Charles F., and Gladys Meyer 1973 *Minorities in American Society.* 4th ed. New York: D. Van Nostrand.

Marger, Martin N. 1991 *Race and Ethnic Relations: American and Global Perspectives.* Belmont, Calif.: Wadsworth.

Moynihan, Daniel P. 1965 *The Negro Family: The Case for National Action.* Washington, D.C.: Office of Policy Planning and Research, U.S. Department of Labor.

Nock, Steven L. 1987 *Sociology of the Family.* Englewood Cliffs, N.J.: Prentice-Hall.

Scanzoni, Letha Dawson, and John Scanzoni 1988 *Men, Women, and Change: A Sociology of Marriage and Family.* New York: McGraw-Hill.

Staples, Robert, ed. 1986 *The Black Family: Essays and Studies.* 3d ed. Belmont, Calif.: Wadsworth.

Sweet, James A., and Larry L. Bumpass 1987 *American Families and Households.* New York: Russell Sage.

Uhlenberg, Andrew 1986 "Death and the Family." In A. S. Skolnick and J. H. Skolnick, eds., *Family in Transition.* Boston: Little, Brown.

Zinn, Maxine Baca, and D. Stanley Eitzen 1987 *Diversity in American Families.* New York: Harper and Row.

– LAURIE RUSSELL HATCH

AMERICAN INDIAN STUDIES

American Indian Studies blends many fields in the social sciences and humanities; history and anthropology have been especially prominent, along with education, sociology, psychology, economics, and political science. For convenience, this literature can be grouped into several subject areas: demographic behavior, socioeconomic conditions, political and legal institutions, and culture and religion. Of course, there is a great deal of overlap. To date, this literature deals almost exclusively with aboriginal North Americans and their descendants. As the field has evolved, relatively little attention has been devoted to the natives of South America or the Pacific Islanders.

Demography

HISTORICAL DEMOGRAPHY. Historical demography is important for understanding the complexity of indigenous North American societies and for assessing the results of their contacts with Europeans. For example, complex societies require large populations to generate economic surpluses for trade, and large populations often entail highly developed systems of religion, culture, and governance. Because American Indians almost disappeared in the late nineteenth century, large numbers of pre-Columbian Indians would indicate that devastating mortality rates and profound changes in native social organization followed the arrival of Europeans.

No one knows with certainty when populations of *homo sapiens* first appeared in the Western hemisphere. The first immigrants to North America probably followed game from what is now Siberia across the Beringia land bridge, now submerged in the Bering Sea. This land bridge has surfaced during several ice ages, leading to speculation that the first populations arrived as early as 40,000 years ago or as recently as 15,000 years ago—25,000 years ago is a credible estimate (Thornton 1987, p. 9).

In 1918 a Smithsonian anthropologist, James Mooney, published the first systematic estimates of the American Indian population. He reckoned that 1.15 million American Indians were living around 1600. Alfred Kroeber (1934) subsequently reviewed Mooney's early estimates and deemed them correct, though he adjusted the estimate downward to 900,000 (Deneven 1976). The Mooney-Kroeber estimates of approximately one million American Indians in 1600 have been the benchmark for scholars throughout most of this century. These estimates were flawed, however, because they failed to take epidemic disease into account; European pathogens devastated native populations.

Noting the shortcomings of the Mooney-Kroeber figures, Henry Dobyns (1966) revised the estimate for the 1492 precontact population, suggesting that it was as large as twelve million. His article ignited an intense debate that is still not fully resolved. Conservative estimates now number the indigenous 1492 population at approximately three to five million (Snipp 1989). Dobyns's (1983) most recent estimates raise the figure to eighteen million.

The fluidity of the American Indian population underscores a particularly problematic concern for demographers: namely, defining population boundaries.

Population estimates substantially larger than the Mooney-Kroeber figures are consistent with the archaeological record, which indicates that relatively complex societies occupied the Southwest, the Pacific Northwest, and the Mississippi River valley before the Europeans arrived (Thornton 1987). The effects of European contact were certainly greater than once believed. European diseases, slavery, genocidal practices, and the intensification of conflicts nearly exterminated the native people. Huge population losses undoubtedly caused large-scale amalgamation and reorganization of groups struggling to survive and wrought profound changes in their cultures and social structures.

CONTEMPORARY DEMOGRAPHY. During the twentieth century, the American Indian population grew very quickly, from about 228,000 in 1890 to about 1.4 million in 1980. American Indian fertility is exceedingly high, even higher than that of blacks (Snipp 1989). Indians often have better access to health care (from the Indian Health Service) than other equally impoverished groups, and they are experiencing diminishing infant mortality and increasing longevity (Snipp 1989).

A peculiar characteristic of American Indian population growth, at least since 1970, is that a large share of the increase has resulted from persons switching the racial identification they report to the census from another category (such as black or white) to American Indian (Passell and Berman 1986). The U.S. census, virtually the only comprehensive source of data for American Indians, depends on voluntary racial self-identification. Declining racial discrimination, growing ethnic pride, and a resurgence in tribal organization have been cited as reasons that persons of mixed heritage may choose to report themselves as American Indian (Passell and Berman 1986).

The fluidity of the American Indian population underscores a particularly problematic concern for demographers: namely, defining population boundaries. Definitions abound, and there is no single agreed-upon standard. Some federal agencies and a number of tribes use an arbitrary measure of descent, such as one-fourth blood quantum; standards for tribal membership vary greatly from one-half to one-sixty-fourth Indian blood.

For many other applications, genealogical verification of blood quantum standards is too complex. Agencies such as the Census Bureau thus simply rely on self-identification. By default, most studies of American Indians also rely on self-identification, especially if they use secondary data from federal government sources. To complicate the matter, the Canadian government uses a somewhat different set of standards to define the boundaries of its native Indian population.

Beyond the complexities of counting, studies show that American Indians, more than other minorities, are concentrated in rural areas; slightly less than one-half reside in cities. Most live west of the Mississippi River, primarily because nineteenth-century removal programs were directed at eastern American Indians. A large number of studies document that American Indians are one of the least educated, most often unemployed, poorest, and least healthy groups in American society (see Snipp 1989). Nonetheless, American Indians are more likely than other groups, especially blacks, to live in a large husband-wife household, and about one-third of them speak an Indian language—provisional evidence of the continuing influence of traditional culture in family organization and language use (Sandefur and Sakamoto 1988).

Studies of Social and Economic Status

Most recent studies of the early social and economic status of American Indians focus on the historical development of so-called dependency relations between them and Euro-Americans (White 1983). Dependency theory, a variant of neo-Marxist World Systems Theory, has been widely criticized for its shortcomings, but it has gained some acceptance among scholars of white—Indian relations (Wolf 1982; White 1983; Hall 1989). In this view, economic dependency arose from trade relations in which Euro-Americans enjoyed disproportionate economic advantage stemming from a near monopoly over items such as manufactured goods and rum (Wolf 1982; White 1983). European business practices, such as the use of credit, also fostered dependency.

Dependency relations promoted highly exploitative conditions that were a frequent source of conflict and periodically erupted into serious violence. Unscrupulous traders and a growing commerce in Indian captives, for example, spawned the Yamassee War, which ended Indian slavery in the Southeast (Merrell 1989). Early colonial officials frequently complained about the conflicts created by the unethical practices of frontier traders and sought to curb their abuses, though with little success (Bateman 1989).

Nevertheless, European traders introduced innovations that altered cultures and lifestyles forever. In the Southwest, for example, guns and horses revolutionized relations between nomadic and sedentary groups and allowed the Spanish to exploit their traditional antagonisms (Hall 1989).

The emergence of industrial capitalism, large-scale manufacturing, growing urbanization, and an influx of immigrants from Europe and slaves from Africa changed dramatically the relations between Euro-Americans and indigenous peoples. Trading with Indians subsided in favor of policies and measures designed to remove them from lands desired for development (Jacobsen 1984). Throughout the nineteenth century, American Indians were more or less forcibly induced to cede their lands for the development of agriculture, timber, and water. In the late nineteenth century, U.S. corporations began to develop petroleum, coal, and other minerals on tribal lands (Miner 1976).

Exploitation of Indian lands has continued, prompting some scholars to argue that American Indian tribes have a quasi-colonial status within the U.S. economy (Snipp 1986). Natural resources such as timber, water, and minerals are extracted from reservations and exported to distant urban centers where they are processed. In exchange, manufactured goods are imported for consumption. The value of the imported goods typically exceeds the value of the exported resources. The deficit between imports and exports contributes to the persistent poverty and low levels of economic development on many reservations.

The Meriam Report, published in 1928, furnished the first systematic empirical assessment of the economic status of American Indians. Since its publication, numerous studies have documented the disadvantaged status of American Indians (Levitan and Hetrick 1971). Although many reports have described economic conditions in detail, fewer have attempted to isolate the causes of poverty and unemployment. Clearly, a number of factors can be blamed. American Indians have very little formal education, limiting their access to jobs. Whether racial discrimination limits opportunities is unclear. Some research suggests that discrimination is not a significant disadvantage for American Indians (Sandefur and Scott 1983), but other studies disagree (Gwartney and Long 1978).

Conditions on reservations, where about one-third of all American Indians live, are particularly harsh. Unemployment rates above 50 percent are not unusual. Studies of reservation economies usually blame the isolated locales for many of their woes. Economic development in Indian country is frequently complicated by the collision of traditional native values and the ethics of capitalism (Virje 1982). In recent years, however, some reservations have enjoyed limited (and in a few instances, spectacular) success in spurring economic development, especially in tourism, gambling, and light manufacturing (Snipp and Summers 1991).

Urban American Indians enjoy a higher standard of living than their counterparts in reservation areas (Sorkin 1978). Even so, there is disagreement about the benefits of rural-urban migration for American Indians; some studies have identified tangible benefits for urban immigrants (Clinton, Chadwick, and Bahr 1975; Sorkin 1978), but other research finds contrary evidence (Gundlach and Roberts 1978; Snipp and Sandefur 1988). Federal programs that encouraged urban immigration for American Indians in the 1950s and 1960s were abandoned amid controversies over their effectiveness and overall results (Fixico 1986).

The economic hardship facing rural and urban American Indians alike have been a major source of

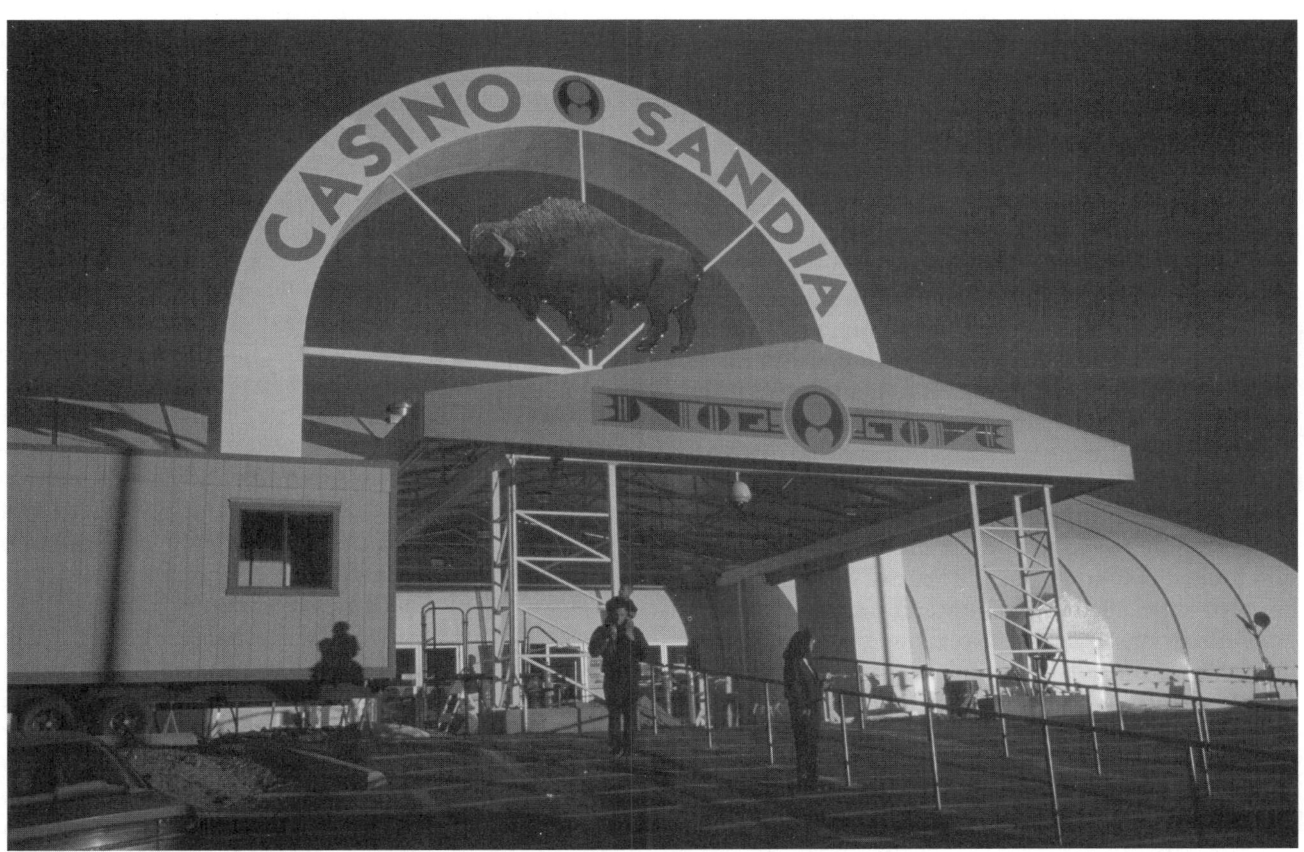

Federal legislation in the early 1990s allowed commercial gambling on American Indian reservations. The casinos that many of the Indians built pulled some tribes out of the poverty that is typical of Indian reservations. (Miguel Gandert/© Corbis)

other serious distress. Alcoholism, suicide, and homicide are leading causes of death for American Indians (OTA 1986).

Political Organization and Legal Institutions

The political and legal status of American Indians is an extremely complicated subject, tangled in conflicting treaties, formal laws, bureaucratic regulations, and court decisions. Unlike any other racial or ethnic group in U.S. society, American Indians have a distinctive niche in the legal system. As a result of this legal history, a separate agency within the federal government (the Bureau of Indian Affairs [BIA]), a volume of the Code of Federal Regulations, and a multiplicity of other rules exist for dealing with American Indians.

Exploitation of Indian lands has continued, prompting some scholars to argue that American Indian tribes have a quasi-colonial status within the U.S. economy.

The political status of American Indian tribes is difficult to characterize. In 1831, Chief Justice John Marshall described tribes as "domestic, dependent nations," setting forth the principle that tribes are autonomous political entities that enjoy a quasi-sovereignty yet are subject to the authority of the federal government (Barsh and Henderson 1980). The limits on tribal political autonomy have fluctuated as a result of court decisions and federal legislation curtailing or extending tribal powers. Since the early 1900s, tribal governments have greatly increased their autonomy (Gross 1989).

One of the most significant political developments in this century for American Indians, was the passage of the Wheeler-Howard Indian Reorganization Act (IRA) of 1934. This legislation made it possible for tribes legally to reconstitute themselves for the purpose of limited self-government (Prucha 1984, chap. 37). Subject to the democratic precepts imposed by the federal government, tribes were allowed to have representative governments with judicial, executive, and legislative branches. Other forms of tribal governance—based on the inheritance of authority, for example—were not permitted by the IRA legislation. Today, virtually every reservation has a form of representative government.

Tribal sovereignty is a complex legal doctrine affecting the political autonomy of tribal governments. It is distinct from a closely aligned political principle known as self-determination. The principle of self-determination, unlike tribal sovereignty, is relatively recent in origin and was first posed as a claim for administrative control of reservation affairs. As a political ideology, self-determination developed in response to the unilateral actions of the federal government in implementing policies such as the Termination legislation of the 1950s. In the 1960s, it was a rallying theme for promoting greater tribal involvement in federal policies affecting American Indians. The principle was formally enacted into public law with the passage of the Indian Self-Determination and Educational Assistance Act of 1975. Since its passage, federal agencies have gradually divested control over programs and services such as those once administered by the BIA. For example, many tribal governments have contracts to provide social services similar to the arrangements made with state and local governments.

In recent years, arguments promoting self-determination have developed to the point where self-determination is nearly indistinguishable from tribal sovereignty (Gross 1989). The most influential statement merging the two is a report presented to the Senate by the American Indian Policy Review Commission in 1976. The AIPRC report was a comprehensive though highly controversial evaluation of federal Indian policy. The Reagan and Bush administrations have accepted self-determination only as narrowly defined, and currently there is no indication that the Bush administration is willing to adopt self-determination as promoted by the AIPRC.

The political revitalization of American Indians accelerated with the civil rights movement. Some observers have suggested that Indian political activism in the 1960s was a response to postwar termination policies (Cornell 1988), which tried to dissolve the federal reservation system and liquidate the special status of the tribes. Relocation programs in the 1950s accelerated the urbanization of American Indians and, at the very least, may have contributed to the political mobilization of urban Indians, as well as their reservation counterparts (Fixico 1986). Though often complementary, the political agendas of urban and reservation Indians are not always in strict accord.

The diverse tribal composition of urban Indian populations has meant that it is virtually impossible to organize them around issues affecting only one or a few tribes. In the face of this constraint, the ideology of "pan-Indianism" is particularly appealing to urban Indian groups (Hertzberg 1971). Pan-Indianism is a supratribal ideology committed to broad issues such as economic opportunity and social justice and to cultural events such as intertribal pow-wows.

The roots of modern pan-Indian organizations can be traced first to the Ottawa leader Pontiac and later to the Shawnee leader Tecumseh and Joseph Brant, a Mohawk. These men led pan-Indian movements opposing Euro-American frontier settlement in the late eighteenth and early nineteenth centuries (e.g., Pontiac's Revolt, 1763). In the late nineteenth century, pan-Indian messianic movements known as Ghost Dances swept across the West (Thornton 1986).

Pan-Indian organizations have been active throughout the twentieth century, but urbanization hastened their development in the 1950s and 1960s (Cornell 1988). Some, such as the National Congress of American Indians (founded in 1944), have moderate political agendas focused on lobbying; others, such as the American Indian Movement, are highly militant. The latter was involved in the sacking of the Washington, D.C., BIA office in 1972 and in the armed occupation of Wounded Knee, South Dakota, in 1973. Today, most cities with large Indian populations have pan-Indian organizations involved in political organization, cultural events, and social service delivery.

Culture and Religion

The cultures of American Indians are extremely diverse, and the same can be said, in particular, about their religious beliefs. Not much is known about the spiritual life of American Indians before the fifteenth century. Only from archaeological evidence is such knowledge available, and this seldom captures the rich complexity of religious symbol systems. Most of what is known about American Indian religions is based on the later reports of explorers, missionaries, traders, and anthropologists (Brown 1982).

Contemporary spiritual practices reflect several different types of religious observances: Christian, neotraditional, and traditional. Participation in one type does not necessarily preclude participation in another. Furthermore, there is a great deal of tribal variation.

American Indians who are practicing Christians represent the legacy of European missionaries. The Christian affiliation of many, perhaps most, American Indians reflects their tribal membership and the denomination of the missionaries responsible for their tribe's conversion. Numerical estimates are not available, but there are many Catholic Indians in the Southwest, and American Indians in the Midwest are often Lutheran, to mention only two examples.

American Indians who participate in neotraditional religions often belong to a branch of the Native American Church (NAC). NAC is a pan-Indian religion practiced throughout the United States and Canada. It combines elements of Christianity with traditional religious beliefs and practices.

Traditional religions are often practiced in informally organized groups such as sweatlodge or feasting societies. Some of these groups are remnants of older religious movements such as the Ghost Dance. Not much is written about them because they are ordinarily not open to outsiders; the Sun Dance is an exception. It is perhaps best known for the ritual scarification and trances of its participants (Jorgenson 1972).

The diverse tribal composition of urban Indian populations has meant that it is virtually impossible to organize them around issues affecting only a few tribes.

The secrecy in which many traditional religions are practiced may be due to the intense repression once directed at their observances by the federal government. In 1883, the BIA established Courts of Indian Offenses that prosecuted people for practicing native religions. Among other things, the courts forbade traditional medicines, shaman healers, and all traditional ceremonial observances. Despite their dubious legal foundation, the Courts of Indian Offenses were active until their mandate was rewritten in 1935 (Prucha 1984).

In 1935, the federal government ended its official repression of tribal culture and religion. But the conflicts between government authorities and American Indians trying to practice non-Christian religions did not end. Many Indians regard freedom of religion as an elusive promise. Most controversies involve NAC ceremonies, the preservation of sacred areas, and the repatriation of religious artifacts and skeletal remains in museum collections (Loftin 1989).

NAC ceremonies are controversial because they sometimes involve the use of peyote (a hallucinogen) as a sacrament. Although peyote was once outlawed, the NAC won the right to use it within narrowly defined limits prescribed by the courts. The Supreme Court recently upheld a case in which Oregon banned the use of peyote, however, raising concerns about how the conservative court will interpret freedom of religion cases in the future.

Preservation of sacred areas places Indian groups at odds with land developers, property owners, local governments, and others who would use sites deemed sacred by spiritual leaders. In one case, the Navajo and Hopi in 1983 went to court to petition against the development of a ski resort that intruded on sacred grounds. In this case and several similar ones, the courts ruled against the Indians (Loftin 1989). Similar conflicts have arisen over the repatriation of religious artifacts and skeletal remains in museums. These issues pit academics such as scientists and museum curators against Indian groups. In some instances, remains and artifacts have been returned to tribes; Stanford University returned burial remains to the Ohlone tribe in California, for example. Other institutions have opposed repatriation or are studying the matter. The Smithsonian has developed a complex policy for repatriation, and the University of California appointed a committee to develop a policy. For the foreseeable future, the controversy is likely to linger in the courts, Congress, and academic institutions.

The secrecy in which many traditional religions are practiced may be due to the intense repression once directed at their observances by the federal government.

Compared to repatriation, cultural studies are a less controversial though no less important domain of American Indian Studies. Indian religion represents one of the central forms of native culture, but cultural studies also emphasize other elements of Indian lifestyles, values, and symbol systems. Some of these studies focus on the content of tribal culture; other research deals with the consequences of tribal culture.

For decades, studies of American Indians were dominated by ethnologists recording for posterity details about Indian culture, especially material culture, or documenting the ways that European contact influenced the content of tribal culture. The popularity of this type of research has declined significantly, partly because there are few "pristine" cultures left anywhere in the world, much less in North America. Another reason, perhaps more damaging, is the growing realization that studies purporting to document precontact Indian culture were based on secondhand accounts of groups that were not truly pristine. The influence of European diseases and trade goods often arrived far in advance of Europeans (Dobyns 1983).

Many studies of American Indian culture now resemble literary or artistic criticism. Others focus on how European innovations have been incorporated into tribal culture in unique ways; silversmithing and rug weaving are two well-known examples (Highwater 1981). A related set of studies deals with the resurgence of traditional culture, such as the recent increase in the use of American Indian languages (Leap 1988).

The behavioral consequences of culture are perhaps most prominent in a large literature on American Indian mental health, education, and rehabilitation (Bennett and Ames 1985; Foster 1988). Many studies show that education and rehabilitation efforts can be made more effective if they are sensitive to cultural nuances. In fact, many specialists take this idea as a point of departure and focus their research instead on the ways in which Euro-American educational and therapeutic practices can be adapted to the cultural predisposition of American Indian clients.

Like the American Indian population, American Indian Studies is a highly diverse and growing field of inquiry. It is interdisciplinary and eclectic in the perspectives it uses. Once primarily the domain of historians and anthropologists, American Indian Studies has rapidly expanded beyond the bounds of these disciplines with contributions from scholars in a wide variety of fields.

[See also Discrimination; Race.]

BIBLIOGRAPHY

Barsh, Russel Lawrence, and James Youngblood Henderson 1980 *The Road: Indian Tribes and Political Liberty.* Berkeley: University of California Press.

Bateman, Rebecca 1989 "The Deerskin Trade in the Southeast." Unpublished manuscript. Baltimore, Md.: Department of Anthropology, Johns Hopkins University.

Bennett, Linda A., and Genevieve M. Ames, eds. 1985 *The American Experience with Alcohol Contrasting Cultural Perspectives.* New York: Plenum.

Brown, Joseph Epes 1982 *The Spiritual Legacy of the American Indians.* New York: Crossroad.

Clinton, Lawrence, Bruce A. Chadwick, and Howard M. Bahr 1975 "Urban Relocation Reconsidered: Antecedents of Employment among Indian Males." *Rural Sociology* 40:117–133.

Cornell, Stephen 1988 *The Return of the Native: American Indian Political Resurgence.* New York: Oxford University Press.

Deneven, William M., ed. 1976 *The Native Population of the Americas in 1492.* Madison: University of Wisconsin Press.

Dobyns, Henry F. 1966 "Estimating Aboriginal American Population: An Appraisal of Techniques with a New Hemispheric Estimate." *Current Anthropology* 7:395–416.

——— 1983 *Their Number Become Thinned: Native American Population Dynamics in Eastern North America.* Knoxville: University of Tennessee Press.

Fixico, Donald L. 1986 *Termination and Relocation, 1945–1960.* Albuquerque: University of New Mexico Press.

Foster, Daniel V. 1988 "Consideration of Treatment Issues with American Indians in the Federal Bureau of Prisons." *Psychiatric Annals* 18:698–701.

French, Laurence 1987 *Psychocultural Change and the American Indian.* New York: Garland.
Gross, Emma R. 1989 *Contemporary Federal Policy Toward American Indians.* Westport, Conn.: Greenwood Press.
Gundlach, James H., and Alden E. Roberts 1978 "Native American Indian Migration and Relocation: Success or Failure." *Pacific Sociological Review* 21:117–128.
Gwartney, James D., and James E. Long 1978 "The Relative Earnings of Blacks and Other Minorities." *Industrial and Labor Relations Review* 31:336–346.
Hall, Thomas D. 1989 *Social Change in the Southwest, 1350–1880.* Lawrence: University Press of Kansas.
Hertzberg, Hazel W. 1971 *The Search for an American Indian Identity.* Syracuse, N.Y.: Syracuse University Press.
Highwater, Jamake 1981 *The Primal Mind: Vision and Reality in Indian America.* New York: Harper and Row.
Jacobsen, Cardell K. 1984 "Internal Colonialism and Native Americans: Indian Labor in the United States from 1871 to World War II." *Social Science Quarterly* 65:158–171.
Jorgenson, Joseph G. 1972 *The Sun Dance Religion: Power for the Powerless.* Chicago: University of Chicago Press.
Kroeber, Alfred L 1934 "Native American Population." *American Anthropologist* 36:1–25.
Leap, William L. 1988 "Indian Language Renewal." *Human Organization* 47:283–291.
Levitan, Sar A., and Barbara Hetrick 1971 *Big Brother's Indian Programs: With Reservations.* New York: McGraw-Hill.
Loftin, John D. 1989 "Anglo-American Jurisprudence and the Native American Tribal Quest for Religious Freedom." *American Indian Culture and Research Journal* 13:1–52.
Merrell, James H. 1989 *The Indian's New World: Catawbas and Their Neighbors from European Contact Through the Era of Removal.* Chapel Hill: University of North Carolina Press.
Miner, H. Craig 1976 *The Corporation and the Indian: Tribal Sovereignty and Industrial Civilization in Indian Territory, 1865–1907.* Columbia: University of Missouri Press.
Office of Technology Assessment (OTA) 1986 *Indian Health Care* OTA-H-290. Washington, D.C.: U.S. Government Printing Office.
Passel, Jeffrey S., and Patricia A. Berman 1986 "Quality of 1980 Census Data for American Indians." *Social Biology* 33:163–182.
Prucha, Francis Paul 1984 *The Great Father: The United States Government and the American Indians.* Lincoln: University of Nebraska Press.
Sandefur, Gary D., and Arthur Sakamoto 1988 "American Indian Household Structure and Income." *Demography* 25:71–80.
Sandefur, Gary D., and Wilbur J. Scott 1983 "Minority Group Status and the Wages of Indian and Black Males." *Social Science Research* 12:44–68.
Snipp, C. Matthew 1986 "The Changing Political and Economic Status of American Indians: From Captive Nations to Internal Colonies." *American Journal of Economics and Sociology* 45:145–157.
——— 1989 *American Indians: The First of This Land.* New York: Russell Sage Foundation.
Snipp, C. Matthew, and Gary D. Sandefur 1988 "Earnings of American Indians and Alaska Natives: The Effects of Residence and Migration." *Social Forces* 66:994–1008.
Snipp, C. Matthew, and Gene F. Summers 1991 "American Indians and Economic Poverty." In Cynthia M. Duncan, ed., *Rural Poverty in America.* Westport, Conn.: Greenwood Press.
Sorkin, Alan L. 1978 *The Urban American Indian.* Lexington, Mass.: D. C. Heath.
——— 1988 "Health and Economic Development on American Indian Reservations." In C. Matthew Snipp, ed., *Public Policy Impacts on American Indian Economic Development.* Albuquerque: Institute for Native American Development, University of New Mexico.
Thornton, Russell 1986 *We Shall Live Again: The 1870 and 1890 Ghost Dance Movements as Demographic Revitalization.* New York: Cambridge University Press.
——— 1987 *American Indian Holocaust and Survival: A Population History Since 1492.* Norman: University of Oklahoma Press.
Vinje, David L. 1982 "Cultural Values and Economic Development: U.S. Indian Reservations." *Social Science Journal* 19:87–99.
White, Richard 1983 *The Roots of Dependency: Subsistence, Environment, and Social Change among the Choctaws, Pawnees, and Navajos.* Lincoln: University of Nebraska Press.
Wolf, Eric R. 1982 *Europe and the People Without History.* Berkeley. University of California Press.

– C. MATTHEW SNIPP

ANIMAL RIGHTS MOVEMENT

The animal rights movement in America traces its roots to the first settlers. In 1641 Massachusetts Bay Colony Puritans enacted two provisions prohibiting cruelty to animals as part of the colony's Body of Liberties. New York State passed a law protecting animals in 1829, with Massachusetts passing a similar law seven years later. Despite these measures, it was not until after the Civil War that animal rights became a major public issue. In 1866 Henry Bergh organized the American Society for the Prevention of Cruelty to Animals. Heir to a shipbuilding fortune, Bergh became a defender of abused carriage horses in New York City and prosecuted butchers, carters, carriage drivers, and organizers of dog fights and cock fights. Bergh's efforts gained support from influential business and government leaders and inspired the formation of the Massachusetts Society for the Prevention of Cruelty to Animals by George Angell and the American Anti-Vivisection Society, started by Caroline Earle White. The early animal rights movement encountered opposition over the use of dogs, cats, and other animals for medical experiments, forcing its leaders to drop the issue.

By 1907 every state had an anticruelty law in place. For the next seventy years several laws prohibiting specific practices were enacted, but there was an increased use of animals in medical laboratories, on factory farms, and for other business purposes. In the 1970s civil rights, feminist, environmental, and antiwar activists turned their attention to animal rights. Publication of *Animal Liberation* by Peter Singer in 1975 revealed many of the practices used in factory farms and research laboratories, and three highly publicized incidents changed animal rights into a national grass-roots movement: protests organized by Henry Spira against the American Museum of Natural History in New York

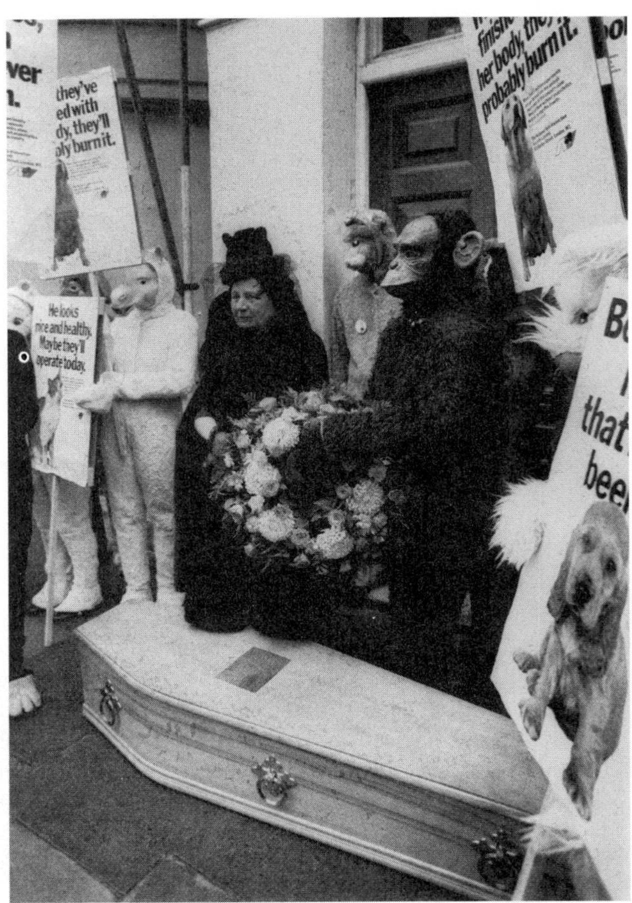

Animal rights activists protest such activities as the use of primates in research experiments and the wearing of animal fur. (Hulton-Deutsch Collection/Corbis)

City for its experiments on cats; the arrest and conviction of Dr. Edward Taub in 1981 for abusive practices on monkeys at the federally funded Institute for Behavioral Research; and the 1984 release of the documentary *Unnecessary Fuss* by the Animal Liberation Front, which showed baboons at the University of Pennsylvania being bashed in the head for experiments on trauma. An estimated 30,000–40,000 people took part in the 1990 March for the Animals in Washington, D.C. By the mid-1990s there were hundreds of local, regional, and national organizations, such as the People for Ethical Treatment of Animals and the National Anti-Vivisection Society, that devoted themselves to a variety of animal rights issues, including the ethical treatment of animals in laboratories, protection of endangered species, the humane treatment of farm animals, antifur campaigns, and the overpopulation of pets.

– ERIC BRUUN

ASIAN-AMERICAN STUDIES

The term Asian-American is used in the United States by federal, state, and local governments to designate people of Asian descent, including Pacific Islanders (residents from the Pacific islands that are under U.S. jurisdiction, such as Guam and American Somoa). Although historically relevant and geographically appropriate, inclusion of the Pacific islands in the generic term *Asian-American* stemmed from administrative convenience for the federal government rather than from race or ethnic identifications.

Historically, in 1917 the Congress of the United States created the Asiatic Barred Zone, which stretched from Japan in the east to India in the west. People from within the zone were banned from immigration. The geographic concept was incorporated into the Immigration Act of 1924 (Oriental Exclusion Act), a law that had a profound impact on the demographic structure of Asian-American communities as well as on U.S. foreign policy. Although it is generally assumed that the term *Asian-American* has a racial basis, particularly from the perspective of U.S. immigration history, the racial overtone is muted by the inclusion in the 1980 census of people from India in the "Asian and Pacific Islander" category; they had been classified as "white" prior to 1980.

Immigration and Restrictions of Asian-Americans

Asian immigration can be divided into two periods: the old and the new. The old immigration period was marked by nonoverlapping waves of distinct Asian populations who came largely in response to the sociopolitical conditions in their homelands and to the shortage of unskilled labor experienced by special-interest groups in the United States. The new immigration was characterized by the simultaneous arrival of people from the Asia-Pacific Triangle, spurred principally by the 1965 legislative reforms in U.S. immigration policy, shortages of certain skilled and professional labor, the involvement of the United States in Asia, and the sociopolitical situations in Asia.

The year 1848 marked the beginning of Asian immigration to the United States when the coastal Chinese—mostly from Guangdong—responded to failures in the rural economy of China and the gold rush in California, seeking new opportunities on the West Coast. Within less than thirty-five years, the Chinese became the first group in U.S. history to be legally barred from becoming citizens because of race. The 1882 Anti-Chinese Exclusion Act was followed by an influx of immigrants from the southern prefectures of Japan during the last decade of the nineteenth century—until that flow ended abruptly with the Gentlemen's Agreement of 1907–1908. Unlike the termination of Chinese immigration, cessation of entry by Japanese was accomplished through a diplomatic compromise between the two governments rather than through an act of Congress. Without a continuous flow of Japanese farm workers to ease the labor shortage on the Hawaiian plantations, contractors turned to the Philippine Islands—which had been a U.S. possession since 1898—for cheap labor. From 1906 to the independence of the Republic of the Philippines in 1946, over 125,000 (predominantly single) Filipino males, the majority of them from the Ilocos region, labored on Hawaiian sugar plantations.

The Chinese became the first group in U.S. history to be legally barred from becoming citizens because of race.

The exclusions of Asians enacted into the National Origins Act of 1924 essentially remained in effect until 1965. By Act of Congress in 1943, however, 105 Chinese were permitted to immigrate annually, and in 1952, under the 1952 McCarran-Walter Act, a token one hundred persons from each Asian country were allowed entry. The symbolic opening of immigration doors to Asians was attributed to Walter Judd, a congressman from Minnesota who had spent many years in China as a medical missionary. The provision of a quota of one hundred persons seemed to be an important moral victory for those who wanted the elimination of the exclusion act, but it was in fact a restatement of the 1924 national origin quota basis for immigration.

The new stream of Asian immigrants to the United States is the artifact of the 1965 legislative reform that allowed an equal number of persons (20,000) from each country outside the Western Hemisphere to immigrate. Furthermore, family unification and needed skills became the major admission criteria, replacing national origin. Besides China and the Philippines, Korea and the Indian subcontinent became, and continue to be, the major countries of origin of many newly arrived Asian immigrants. Refugees from Vietnam, Cambodia, and Laos began to enter the United States in 1975. By 1990, peoples from Indochina had become the third largest Asian group, following Chinese and Filipinos. In contrast, Japan's immigration to the United States practically ceased from 1945 to 1965, when it resumed at a much lower rate than those reported for other Asian countries.

Social Consequences of Immigration Restrictions

Several distinct demographic characteristics illustrate most graphically past restrictions and recent reforms in the immigration laws. Earlier immigrants from China and the Philippines were predominantly single males. As a result of racial prejudice that culminated in the passage of anti-miscegenation laws directed primarily against people of color in many western and southwestern states, the majority of these earlier Asian immigrants remained unmarried. The lack of family life caused unattached immigrants to depend on one another, creating an apparent great solidarity among people of the same ethnic group. Many of the earlier studies of Chinese and Filipino communities depicted themes of social isolation and loneliness, which did not apply to the Japanese community. A well-known portrayal of the extreme social isolation of Chinese laundrymen in Chicago was published by Paul Siu (1952) only as a paper entitled "The Sojourner." Although Siu's work was written under the direction of Robert E. Park and Ernest W. Burgess, it was not included in the Chicago School sociological series published by the University of Chicago Press. Thus, a major piece of Asian-American research, *The Chinese Laundryman: A Study in Social Isolation* (Siu 1987), remained unpublished until after the author's death.

The existence of single-gender communities of Filipinos and Chinese is clearly demonstrated in the U.S. censuses between 1860 and 1970. In 1860, the sex ratio for Chinese was 1,858 men for every 100 women. By 1890, following the peak of Chinese immigration during the previous decade, the ratio was 2,678 males for every 100 females—the highest recorded. Sex ratios for the Chinese population later declined steadily as the result of legislative revisions in 1930 (46 U.S. Stat. 581) and 1931 (46 U.S. Stat. 1511) that enabled women from China to enter the United States.

A second factor that helped to balance the sex ratio in the Chinese community, particularly among the younger age cohorts, was the presence of an American-born generation. In 1900, U.S.-born persons constituted only 10 percent of the Chinese-American population. By 1970, the figure was 53 percent. Nevertheless, in the 1980 census, the sex ratio remained high for some age groups within certain Asian-American subpopulations; among Filipinos, for example, the highest sex ratio was found in those sixty-five and older.

The demographic characteristics of Japanese-Americans present yet another unusual feature. Under the "Gentlemen's Agreement" between Japan and the

United States, Japanese women were allowed to land on the West Coast to join their men even though the immigration of male laborers was curtailed. The majority of the women came as picture brides (Glenn 1986, pp. 31–35) within a narrow span of time. Thus, the years following 1910 were the decade of family building for the first (*issei*) generation of Japanese-Americans. Since almost all issei were young and their brides were chosen from a cohort of marriageable applicants of about the same age, it was not surprising that issei began their families at about the same time after marriage. The historical accident of controlled migration of brides resulted in a uniform age cohort of the second-generation Japanese Americans (*nisei*). The relatively homogeneous age group of the nisei generation meant that their children, the third generation (known as *sansei*), were also of about the same age. The fourth generation followed the same pattern. The amazingly nonoverlapping age and generational cohorts among Japanese-Americans is not known to have had parallels in other population groups.

Third, while Asian-Americans in general continue to grow in number as a result of new immigration, the size of the Japanese-American population increases primarily by the addition of new generations of U.S.-born babies. It is generally believed that offspring of Japanese women who marry Caucasians have lost their Japanese identity, even though there are no estimates of the impact of intermarriages upon the shrinkage of the Japanese-American community. Given the fact that Japanese immigrants had lower fertility rates than women in Japan during the period prior to and shortly after World War II, and that the number of new immigrants since the war has remained small, Japanese-American communities have larger percentages of older people than do other ethnic minority populations, including other Asian-Americans. In short, Japanese-Americans will be a much smaller ethnic minority in the future.

One more demographic fact is worthy of note. Hawaii and the West Coast states continue to draw large numbers of new immigrants from Asia. Through a process known as chain migration, relatives are likely to follow the immigrants soon after their arrival. This leads to sudden increases in population within the ethnic enclaves. The post-1965 pattern of population growth in many Chinatowns, for instance, is an example of the renewal and revitalization of ethnic communities—which prior to 1965, were experiencing a decline—as are the formation and expansion of Koreantowns and Filipinotowns. Moreover, the settlement of post-1965 immigrants from Asia is more dispersed than that of the earlier groups, owing to the fact that the need for professional and skilled manpower is widely distributed throughout the country. The emergence of Thai, Malaysian, and Vietnamese communities in major metropolitan areas has added a new dimension to the ethnic composition of Asian-Americans.

Two separate chains of immigration resulted from the new immigration legislation of 1965. One chain, largely found in Chinese and Filipino communities, is kin-selective in that the process of settlement follows the family ties of earlier immigrants. The other process is occupation-selective, based on skills and professional qualifications. These two processes created significantly different immigrant populations, with clearly discerned bimodal distributions of status characteristics. It is therefore common to find recent immigrants from Asia among the high-income groups as well as among the families living below the poverty level; some find their homes in the ethnic enclaves of central cities while others live in posh suburban communities. Any attempt to describe Asian-Americans by using average measures of social status characteristics, such as income, education, and occupation, can produce a distorted profile that fits no particular group except in the combined abstractions of a myth that is of little use to either researchers or planners. A more useful description would be the use of standard errors—to show the polarities or deviations of the immigrant group from the norm of the majority.

In short, the sociodemographic and socioeconomic characteristics of all Asian-American communities since 1850 have been greatly influenced by federal immigration legislation. It is impossible to have a clear grasp of the structure and change of Asian-American communities without an understanding of the history of immigration legislation.

Asian-American Research

Asian-American research may be divided into five periods: (1) the early period before World War II, which was influenced by the Chicago School of thought; (2) the World War II period, which saw a preponderance of Japanese-American studies; (3) the postwar era, with a strong emphasis on culture and personality studies; (4) a shift toward "ethnic studies" as a result of the civil-rights movement; (5) the emergence of a new generation of Asian-American studies in the 1980s.

THE EARLY PERIOD. The pioneer sociological studies on the assimilation of immigrants in American urban communities may be attributed to the work of Robert E. Park. Although Park had done little empirical investigation, he had supervised a large number of graduate students and had formulated what was known as the theory of race cycle, which stressed the unidirectional process of competition, accommodation, and assimilation as the basis of race relations in urban America. Park later led a group of researchers to study Chinese and Japanese communities on the Pacific Coast. The results failed to prove the race-cycle theory. In defending his theory, according to Lyman (1977, p. 4), Park employed the Aristotelian doctrine of "obstacles," which suggests that among Chinese and Japanese the assimilation progress in the hypothesized direction was delayed.

Early published sociological research on Asian-Americans included the works of Bogardus (1928, 1930), who attempted to delineate degrees of prejudice against minorities in terms of social distance. There were special topics such as "Oriental crime" in California (Beach 1932); school achievement of Japanese-American children (Bell 1935); and anti-Asian sentiments (Sandmeyer 1939; Ichihashi 1932). A noted pioneer community study of Japanese-Americans conducted by Frank Miyamoto (1939) in Seattle in the late 1930s paved the way for the long and significant bibliography on Japanese-American studies that followed.

Perhaps the most significant and ambitious piece of work during the prewar era was the study of the social isolation of Chinese immigrants, which took more than a decade to complete. The author, Paul Siu, lived and observed, in extreme poverty, the life of Chinese laundrymen. The product of his research endeavors offers a classic text in the study of "unmeltable" immigrants, from which new sociological concepts were developed (Siu 1952, 1987).

WORLD WAR II AND JAPANESE-AMERICAN STUDIES. Large-scale systematic studies on Asian-Americans began shortly after the Japanese attack on Pearl Harbor, when the United States declared war on Japan. The U.S. government stripped Japanese-Americans of their property, relocated them, and housed them in internment camps for several years. Alexander Leighton, a psychiatrist, recruited nisei social-science graduates to assist in his work in the camps, monitoring the morale and loyalty of internees; this perhaps was the pioneer work in assessing their group cohesion and structure. A few of Leighton's nisei assistants completed their doctoral studies after the war, maintaining a close and affectionate relationship with him. All had made their

Chinatown in San Francisco is a prominent example of the post-1965 pattern of growth of such Asian-American neighborhoods. (Kevin Fleming/ © Corbis)

own contributions as social scientists and as Asian-American specialists. Leighton's work on the internment of these civilians (both citizens and noncitizens) resulted in the publication of a classic text on loyalty (Leighton 1945).

Careful documentation of the situation was made by Thomas and Nishimoto (1946), Thomas (1952), and Broom and Kitsuse (1955). U.S. home front conditions had sparked an area of development in social-science research, and it had increased the general knowledge base on Japanese-Americans, including their families, their communities, and their sacrifices and contributions during a time of trial.

CULTURE AND PERSONALITY STUDIES IN THE POST-WAR ERA. During World War II, the U.S. government had the reason and the opportunity to question the suitability of Asians as American citizens in regard to loyalty and civic responsibilities. It was also a time to test the myth that Asian immigrants could not assimilate into American society. Social scientists were intrigued by the way culture shapes the personality. Ruth Benedict's classic work on the Japanese personality and society (Benedict 1946) opened a new vista for research. A cohort of young scholars at the University of Chicago, which included Japanese-American graduate students, became known for their pioneer work in studying Japanese behavioral patterns. It had a profound effect on a generation of interested social scientists and resulted in the publication of many classic works in culture and personality (Caudill 1952; Jacobson and Rainwater 1953; Caudill and DeVos 1956; DeVos 1955; Kitano 1961, 1962, 1964; Caudill and Scarr, 1961; Babcock and Caudill 1958; Meredith 1966; and Vogel 1961). Similar studies on other Asian-American groups are conspicuously absent.

ETHNIC STUDIES AND THE CIVIL-RIGHTS MOVEMENT. In the 1960s, the civil-rights movement, sparked by the death of Martin Luther King, Jr., led, perhaps indirectly, to the passage of an unprecedented immigration-legislation reform. At the time there existed among Asian-Americans a collective search for identity that shared many of the goals and rhetoric of the black movement on the Pacific Coast, principally in California. Research into ethnic (Asian) U.S. communities had added two dimensions. The first was the need to raise consciousness as a part of the social movement. Personal testimonials of experiences as members of an oppressed minority provided insight into the psychology of ethnic minorities. The cathartic as well as the cathectic quality in much of the writings of the postwar era reflected the mood of the period and was perhaps necessary in the absence of an appropriate theoretical model, with empirical data, to argue against the assimilation model in standard texts on racial and ethnic studies. Second, consistent with the radical theme, was the apparent influence of Marxian views on race and ethnic relations, which posited that African-American and other minorities are victims of oppression in a capitalist society.

Expectedly, the civil-rights movement began a renewed interest in research on the experiences of the earliest Asian-Americans. With time the titles ranged from well-documented academic publication to insightful popular readings for the lay public (Chen 1980; Daniels 1988; Choy 1979; Ichioka 1988; Miller 1969; Nee and de Bary 1973; Saxton 1971; Sung 1971; Takaki 1989; Wilson and Hosokawa 1980).

Asian-American studies was established as an academic discipline at a time when there were only a few major publications as sources of information for undergraduates (see Kitano 1961–1976; Lyman 1974; Petersen 1971). The birth of the specialty was marked by the conspicuous absence of available materials, particularly on Filipinos, Koreans, Vietnamese, and the peoples of India. In response to this void, the Asian-American Studies Center at the University of California at Los Angeles published two collection of papers (*Roots* and *Counterpoint*) and a quarterly journal, *The Amerasian.* On the Atlantic Coast, a group of U.S.-born professionals published an intellectual nonacademic monthly, *The Bridge,* for nearly a decade. For more than a decade, these publications were popular reading materials for college students interested in Asian-American studies.

New Generation of Asian-American Studies and Research

Stanley Lyman is generally acknowledged as a pioneer in Asian-American research at the University of California, Berkeley. Through his numerous papers and books, he has demonstrated a combination of theoretical relevance and historical insight into the origin and growth of Asian-American communities, especially those of the Chinese and Japanese. As a social historian, he based his research, by and large, on archival documents (see Lyman 1970b).

In the 1980s, some well-trained sociologists began to emerge, many of them foreign-born and foreign-educated—the "first-generation new immigrants"—scholars who pursued advanced degrees in the United States. Arriving at a time when the United States as a whole had become sensitive to diverse cultures, the new Asian-American researchers are increasingly vocal, questioning traditional sociological theories and concepts based on studies of European-based cultures. Their studies of Asian-American communities have added much to a field that had been underserved by the social sciences. Similarly, they have even questioned neutral and descriptive federal statistics on Asian and Pacific Islander populations, both in terms of inadequate sample design and in terms of their culturally biased instrument design.

Members of the new generation of researchers generally work on specific topical areas that previously had not been systematically scrutinized. The works of Bonacich (1972, 1978, 1980) and her associates (Bonacich, Light, and Wong 1976; Bonacich and Modell 1980) have concentrated on the theory of the split labor market and Asian-American—particularly Korean immigrant—small business in America. Light has begun to build an impressive series of research works on Asian-American small businesses (Light 1972; Light and Wong 1975). Korean communities have become the favorite subject for many publications that have contributed significantly to the literature on new immigrant communities and urban America (S.D. Kim 1975; Hurh and Kim 1984; Kim, Kim, and Hurh 1981; Ilsoo Kim 1981; Yu 1977).

A lack of statistics has been a major problem in Asian-American studies.

However, a lack of statistics has been a major problem in Asian-American studies. Whereas estimates of the social and economic characteristics of white, African-American, and other groups may be obtained from Current Population Surveys and other special surveys, as well as from the U.S. Bureau of the Census, the only useful and comprehensive source materials for Asian-Americans are census data. However, such information is available for only three major Asian groups from 1940 through 1970 (Chinese, Japanese, Filipino). In 1980, for the first time, the census provided separate counts for three other major Asian groups: Koreans, Asian Indians, and Vietnamese. Through special publications, the Census Bureau has provided excellent data on the socioeconomic status and social mobility of Asian-Americans (Gardner, Robey, and Smith 1985; Hirschman and Wong 1984; Wong 1982), but by and large the information is rather limited; and it is not always possible to disaggregate the different Asian subgroups from the generic category "Asian-Americans."

The use of averages to represent the social and economic characteristics of diverse groups of Asians in the United States, or the reliance on data from a few older immigrant groups of Asians (such as Japanese, Chinese, and Filipinos) to represent all Asian-Americans, masks the significantly different levels of social attainment experienced by subgroups of Asian-Americans, thereby furthering the myth, popularized in the 1970s, that Asians are a "model minority."

During the 1980s, a number of studies began to counter the myth of Asians as a model minority; they cover a wide spectrum of specific topics that had not been previously published. These include the achievement of Asian-Americans in school (Hsia 1988; Stevenson, Lee, and Stigler 1986; Stevenson et al. 1985; Vernon 1982); health statistics and mental-health issues (Sue and Morishima 1982; Yu et al. 1987, 1989; Liu and Yu 1985, 1986a, 1986b; Liu et al. 1990); families and kinship (Glenn 1986; Liu et al. 1988; Liu 1987; Li 1977; Fernandez and Liu 1988); political participation (Jo 1979); religion; (Kim, Kim, and Hurh 1978; Cho 1979); and business and income (Zhou and Logan 1989; Chiswick 1978, 1980).

Though rigorous and systematic studies on Asian America are still in their infancy, a solid beginning was launched in the late 1980s. Asian America as field of academic study and as a research topic became a new section of the American Sociological Association, with more than 300 members in 1990. Nearly all major universities on the Pacific Coast have established Asian-American Studies programs, and new Pacific or Asian Centers have been set up on the East Coast. In addition, many academic programs on Asian-Americans are available as part of broader and undifferentiated ethnic-studies programs throughout the country.

[See also Discrimination; Race.]

BIBLIOGRAPHY

Babcock, Charlotte E., and William Caudill 1958 "Personal and Cultural Factors in Treating a Nisei Man." In Georgene Seward, ed., *Social Studies in Culture Conflict.* New York: Ronald Press.

Barth, Gunther 1964 *Bitter Strength: A History of the Chinese in the United States, 1850–1870.* Cambridge, Mass.: Harvard University Press.

Beach, W. C. 1932 *Oriental Crime in California.* Stanford, Calif.: Stanford University Press.

Bell, Richard 1935 *Public School Education of Second Generation Japanese in California.* Stanford, Calif.: Stanford University Press.

Benedict, Ruth 1946 *The Chrysanthemum and the Sword.* Boston: Houghton Mifflin.

Bogardus, Emory S. 1928 *Immigration and Race Attitudes.* Boston: D. C. Heath.

——— 1930 "A Race Relations Cycle." *American Journal of Sociology* 35.

——— 1949 "Cultural Pluralism and Acculturation." *Sociolinguistics and Sociology* 34.

Bonacich, Edna 1972 "A Theory of Ethnic Antagonism: The Split Labor Market." *American Sociological Review* 37:549–559.

——— 1978 "U.S. Capitalism and Korean Immigrant Small Business." Paper read at the Ninth World Congress of Sociology, Uppsala, Sweden, August 14–19.

——— 1980 "Small Business and Japanese American Ethnic Solidarity." In R. Endo, S. Sue, and N. Wagner, eds., *Asian Americans: Social and Psychological Perspectives,* vol. 2. Palo Alto, Calif.: Science & Behavior Books.

———, Ivan Light, and Charles C. Wong 1976 "Korean Immigrant Small Business in Los Angeles." In R. S. Bryce-Laporte, ed., *Sourcebook on New Immigration.* New Brunswick, N.J.: Transaction Books.

———, and John Modell 1980 *The Economic Base of Ethnic Solidarity: Small Business in the Japanese American Community.* Berkeley: University of California Press.

Broom, Leonard, and John Kitsuse 1956 *The Managed Casualty.* Berkeley: University of California Press.

Brunhouse, Robert L. 1940 "Lascars in Pennsylvania." *Pennsylvania History* 7.

Caudill, William 1952 "Japanese-American Personality & Acculturation." *Genetic Psychology Monographs.*

———, and G. DeVos 1956 "Achievement, Culture, and Personality: The Case of Japanese Americans." *American Anthropologist* 58:1107.

———, and Harry A. Scarr 1961 "Japanese Value Orientations and Cultural Change." *Ethnology* 1:53–91.

Chen, Jack 1980 *The Chinese of America.* New York: Harper and Row.

Chiswick, B. R. 1978 "The Effect of Americanization on the Earnings of Foreign Born Men." *Journal of Population Economy* 96:891–921.

——— 1980 "Immigrant Earnings Patterns by Sex, Race and Ethnic Groupings." *Monthly Labor Review* pp. 22–25.

Cho, Pill Jay 1979 "The Korean Church in America: A Dahrendorf Model." Paper read at the Asian American Sociological Meeting, Boston, August 28.

Choy, Bong Youn 1979 *Koreans in America.* Chicago: Nelson-Hall.

Daniels, Roger 1962 *The Politics of Prejudice: The Anti-Japanese Movement in California and the Struggle for Japanese Exclusion.* Berkeley: University of California Press.

——— 1988 *Asian America: Chinese and Japanese in the United States Since 1850.* Seattle: University of Washington Press.

DeVos, George 1955 "A Quantitative Rorschach Assessment of Maladjustment and Rigidity in Acculturating Japanese Americans." *Genetic Psychology Monographs.*

Gardner, R. W., B. Robey, and P. C. Smith 1985 *Asian Americans: Growth, Change and Diversity.* Washington, D.C.: The Population Reference Bureau.

Glenn, Evelyn Nakano 1986 *Issei, Nisei, War Bride.* Philadelphia: Temple University Press.

Hirschman, C., and M. G. Wong 1984 "Socioeconomic Gains of Asian Americans, Blacks and Hispanics: 1960–1976." *American Journal of Sociology* 90:584–607.

Hsia, Jayjia 1988 *Asian Americans in Higher Education and at Work.* Hillsdale, N.J.: Lawrence Erlbaum Associates.

Hurh, Won Moo, and Kwang Chung Kim 1984 *Korean Immigrants in America.* Teaneck, N.J.: Fairleigh Dickinson University Press.

Ichihashi, Y. 1932 *Japanese in the United States.* Stanford, Calif.: Stanford University Press.

Ichioka, Yuji 1988 *The Issei.* New York: The Free Press.

Jacobson, Alan, and Lee Rainwater 1953 "A Study of Management Representative Evaluations of Nisei Workers." *Social Forces* 32:35–41.

Kim, David S., and Charles C. Wong 1977 "Business Development in Koreatown, Los Angeles." In Hyung-chan Kim, ed., *The Korean Diaspora.* Santa Barbara, Calif.: ABC-Clio.

Kim, Ilsoo 1981 *New Urban Immigrants: The Korean Community in New York.* Princeton, N.J.: Princeton University Press.

Kim, K. C., H. C. Kim, and W. M. Hurh 1981 "Job Information Deprivation in the United States: A Case Study of Korean Immigrants." *Ethnicity* 8:219–232.

Kim, S. D. 1975 "Findings of National Inquiries on Asian Women of U.S. Servicemen." Paper read at the Methodist Conference, Tacoma, Washington, March 20–21.

Kitano, Harry H. L. 1961 "Differential Child-Rearing Attitudes Between First and Second Generation Japanese in the U.S." *Journal of Social Psychology* 53:13–19.

——— 1962 "Changing Achievement Patterns of the Japanese in the United States." *Journal of Social Psychology* 58:257–264.

——— 1964 "Inter-generational Differences in Maternal Attitudes Towards Child-Rearing." *Journal of Social Psychology* 63:215–220.

——— 1976 *Japanese Americans: The Evolution of a Subculture.* Englewood Cliffs, N.J.: Prentice-Hall.

Lee, Rose Hum 1949 "The Decline of Chinatowns in the United States." *American Journal of Sociology.*

——— 1960 *The Chinese in the United States of America.* Hong Kong: Hong Kong University Press.

Leighton, Alexander 1945 *The Governing of Men.* Princeton, N.J.: Princeton University Press.

Li, Peter 1977 "Fictive Kinship, Conjugal Ties, and Kinship Chain Among Chinese Immigrants in the United States." *Journal of Comparative Family Studies* 8:47–63.

Light, Ivan H. 1972 *Ethnic Enterprise in America.* Berkeley: University of California Press.

———, and C. C. Wong 1975 "Protest or Work." *American Journal of Sociology* 80:1342–1368.

Liu, William T., and Elena Yu 1985 "Ethnicity and Mental Health: An Overview," In L. Maldonaldo and J. Moore, eds., *Urban Ethnicity in U.S.: New Immigrants and Old Minorities.* Beverly Hills, Calif.: Sage.

——— 1986a "Asian/Pacific American Elderly: Mortality Differentials, Health Status, and Use of Health Services." *Journal of Applied Gerontology* 4:35–64.

——— 1986b "Health Services for Asian Elderly." *Research on Aging* 8:156–183.

———, Elena Yu, C. F. Chang, and M. Fernandez 1990 "The Mental Health of Asian American Teenagers." In A. R. Stiffman and L. E. Davis, eds., *Ethnic Issues in Adolescent Mental Health.* Newbury Park, Calif.: Sage.

Lyman, Stanford 1961 "The Structure of Chinese Society in Nineteenth Century America." Ph.D. diss., University of California, Berkeley.

——— 1964 "The Chinese Secret Societies in the Occident: Notes and Suggestions for Research in the Sociology of Secrecy." *Canadian Review of Sociology and Anthropology* 1:2.

——— 1968 "Contrasts in the Community Organization of Chinese and Japanese in North America." *Canadian Review of Sociology and Anthropology* 5:2.

——— 1970a *Asians in the West.* Reno: University of Nevada Press.

——— 1970b *The Asian in North America.* Santa Barbara, Calif.: ABC-Clio.

——— 1974a "Conflict and the Web of Group Affiliation in San Francisco's Chinatown, 1850–1910." *Pacific Historical Review* 43:4.

——— 1974b *Chinese Americans.* New York: Random House.

——— 1977 *The Asian in North America.* Santa Barbara, Calif.: ABC-Clio.

Meredith, Gerald M. 1966 "Amae and Acculturation Among Japanese College Students in Hawaii." *Journal of Social Psychology* 68:171–180.

Miller, Stuart Creighton 1969 *The Unwelcome Immigrant: The American Image of the Chinese, 1775–1882.* Berkeley: University of California Press.

Miyamoto, Frank 1939 "Social Solidarity Among the Japanese in Seattle." *University of Washington Publications in the Social Sciences* 11(2):57–130.

Nee, Victor G., and Brett de Bary 1973 *Longtime Californ: A Documentary Study of an American Chinatown.* New York: Pantheon.

Petersen, William 1971 *Japanese Americans.* New York: Random House.

Reimers, David M. 1985 *Still the Golden Door.* New York: Columbia University Press.

Sandmeyer, Elmer C. 1939 *The Anti-Chinese Movement in California.* Urbana: University of Illinois Press.

Saxton, Alexander 1971 *The Indispensable Enemy: Labor and Anti-Chinese Movement in California.* Berkeley: University of California Press.

Siu, Paul C. P. 1952 "The Sojourner." *American Journal of Sociology.*

——— 1987 *The Chinese Laundryman: A Study in Social Isolation.* New York: New York University Press.

Stevenson, H. W., S. Y. Lee, and J. W. Stigler 1986 "Mathematics Achievement of Chinese, Japanese and American Children." *Science* 231:693–699.

Stevenson, H. W., et al. 1985 "Cognitive Performance and Academic Achievement of Japanese, Chinese, and American Children." *Child Development* 56:718–734.

Sue, Stanley, and James Morishima 1982 *The Mental Health of Asian Americans.* San Francisco: Jossey-Bass.

Sung, Betty Lee 1971 *The Story of the Chinese in America.* New York: Collier Books.

Takaki, Ronald 1989 *Strangers from a Different Shore: A History of Asian Americans.* Boston: Little, Brown.

Thomas, Dorothy S. 1952 *The Salvage.* Berkeley: University of California Press.

———, and R. Nishimoto 1946 *The Spoilage.* Berkeley: University of California Press.

Vernon, P. E. 1982 *The Abilities and Achievements of Orientals in North America.* New York: Academic Press.

Vogel, Ezra 1961 "The Go-between in a Developing Society: The Case of the Japanese Marriage Arranger." *Human Organization* 20:112–120.

Wilson, Robert A., and Bill Hosokawa 1980 *East to America: A History of the Japanese in the U.S.* New York: William Morrow.

Wong, Morrison 1982 "The Cost of Being Chinese, Japanese and Filipino in the United States, 1960, 1970, 1976." *Pacific Sociological Review* 25:59–78.

Yu, Elena, and William T. Liu 1987 "The Underutilization of Mental Health Services by Asian Americans: Implication for Manpower Training." In W. T. Liu, ed., *A Decade Review of Mental Health Research, Training, and Services.* Chicago: University of Illinois Press.

Yu, Elena, et al. 1987 "Measurement of Depression in a Chinatown Clinic." In W. T. Liu, ed., *A Decade Review of Mental Health Research, Training, and Services.* Chicago: University of Illinois Press.

——— 1989 "Suicide Prevention and Intervention Among Asian Youths." In ADAMHA, *Report of the Secretary's Task Force on Youth Suicide,* vol. 3. DHHS Publication no. (ADM)89-1623. Washington, D.C.: U.S. Government Printing Office.

Yu, Eui-Yong 1977 "Koreans in America." *Amerasia Journal* 4:117–131.

Zhou, Min, and John R. Logan 1989 "Returns on Human Capital in Ethnic Enclaves: New York City's Chinatown." *American Sociological Review* 54:809–820.

– WILLIAM T. LIU
ELENA S. H. YU

ATTITUDES

Attitude "is probably the most distinctive and indispensable concept in contemporary American social psychology" (Allport 1985, p. 35). Hundreds of books and thousands of articles have been published on the topic. A brief review of this literature may be found in McGuire (1985). Despite this popularity, there is considerable disagreement about such basics as terminology. Several terms are frequently used as synonyms for attitude, including *opinion* and *belief.* Contemporary writers often distinguish attitudes from *cognitions,* which is broader and includes attitudes as well as perceptions of one's environment. Most analysts distinguish attitude from *value,* the latter referring to a person's ultimate concerns or preferred modes of conduct.

The viewing of programs intentionally designed to teach positive attitudes toward racial or ethnic minorities does increase children's acceptance of such persons.

An attitude is a learned predisposition to respond to a particular object in a generally favorable or unfavorable way. Every attitude is about an object, and the object may be a person, product, idea, or event. Each attitude has three components: (1) a belief, (2) a favorable or unfavorable evaluation, and (3) a behavioral disposition. This definition is used by most contemporary writers. However, a minority define attitude as consisting only of the positive or negative evaluation of an object.

A *stereotype* is one type of attitude. Originally, the term referred to a rigid and simplistic "picture in the head." In current usage, a stereotype is a belief about the characteristics of members of some specified social group. A stereotype may be positive (Asian-Americans are good at math) or negative (women are bad at math). Most stereotypes are resistant to change.

Attitudes link the person to other individuals, groups, and social organizations and institutions. Each person has literally hundreds of attitudes, one for each significant object in the person's physical and social environment. By implication, the individual's attitudes should reflect his or her location in society. Thus, attitudes are influenced by gender, race, religion, education, and social class. Considerable research on the relationship between social position and attitudes has been carried out; this literature is reviewed by Kiecolt (1988).

Attitude Formation

Many attitudes are learned through direct experience with the object. Attitudes toward one's school, job, church, and the groups to which one belongs are examples. Attitudes toward the significant persons in one's life are also learned in this way. More often, attitudes are learned through interactions with others. Socialization by parents, explicit teaching in educational and religious settings, and interactions with friends are important sources of attitudes. Research shows that children's attitudes toward a variety of objects, including gender roles and political issues, are similar to those held by then parents.

Another source of attitudes is the person's observations of the world. A topic of substantial interest since the early 1970s has been the impact of mass media on the attitudes (and behavior) of users. A thorough review of the literature on this topic (Roberts and Maccoby 1985) concludes that television viewing affects both children's and adolescents' attitudes about gender roles. Further, the viewing of programs intentionally designed to teach positive attitudes toward racial or ethnic minorities does increase children's acceptance of such persons. With regard to adults, evidence supports the "agenda setting" hypothesis; the amount and quality of coverage by the media (press, radio, and television) of an issue influences the public's perception of the importance of that issue.

Stereotypes are also learned. A stereotype may arise out of direct experience with a member of the stereotyped group. A person who knows a musically talented black may create a stereotype by overgeneralizing, inferring that all African-Americans are gifted musically. More often, however, stereotypes are learned from those with whom we interact. Other stereotypes may be acquired from books, television, or film. Research indicates that television programming portrays women, the elderly, and members of some ethnic minorities in negative ways and that these portrayals create (or reinforce) misperceptions and negative stereotypes in viewers (McGuire 1985).

Social institutions influence the attitudes one learns in several ways. Adults' ties to particular ethnic, religious, and other institutions influence the attitudes they teach their children. The instruction given in schools reflects the perspectives of the dominant political and economic institutions in society. The amount and quality of media coverage of people and events reflects the interests of particular groups in society. Through these mechanisms, the individual's attitudes reflect the society, institutions, and groups of which she or he is a member.

Each attitude fulfills one or more of four functions for the individual. First, some attitudes serve an instrumental function: An individual develops favorable attitudes toward objects that aid or reward the individual and unfavorable attitudes toward objects that thwart or punish the individual. For example, a person who earns a large salary will have a positive attitude toward the job. Second, attitudes often serve a knowledge function. They provide the person with a meaningful and structured environment. Third, some attitudes express the individual's basic values and reinforce self-image. Whites' attitudes toward black Americans reflect the importance that whites place on the values of freedom and equality. Fourth, some attitudes protect the person from recognizing certain thoughts or feelings that threaten his or her self-image or adjustment.

Attitude Measurement

Because attitudes are mental states, they cannot be directly observed. Social scientists have developed a variety of methods for measuring attitudes, some direct and some indirect.

DIRECT METHODS. These methods involve asking the person questions and recording the answers. Direct methods include various rating scales and several sophisticated scaling techniques.

The three most frequently used rating scales involve a single item, Likert scales, and the semantic differential. The *single-item scale* usually consists of a direct positive or negative statement about the object, and the respondent indicates whether he or she agrees, disagrees, or is unsure. Such a measure is easy to score, but it is not precise. A *Likert scale* typically involves several statements, and the respondent is asked to indicate the degree to which she or he agrees or disagrees with each. By analyzing differences in the pattern of responses across respondents, the investigator can order individuals from greatest agreement to greatest disagreement. Whereas Likert scales assess the denotative (literal) meaning of an object to a respondent, the *semantic differential* technique assesses the connotative (personal) meaning of the object. Here, an investigator presents the respondent with a series of bipolar adjective scales. Each of these is a scale whose poles are two adjectives having opposite meanings, for example, good-bad, exciting-boring. The respondent rates the attitude object, such as "my job," on each scale. After the data are col-

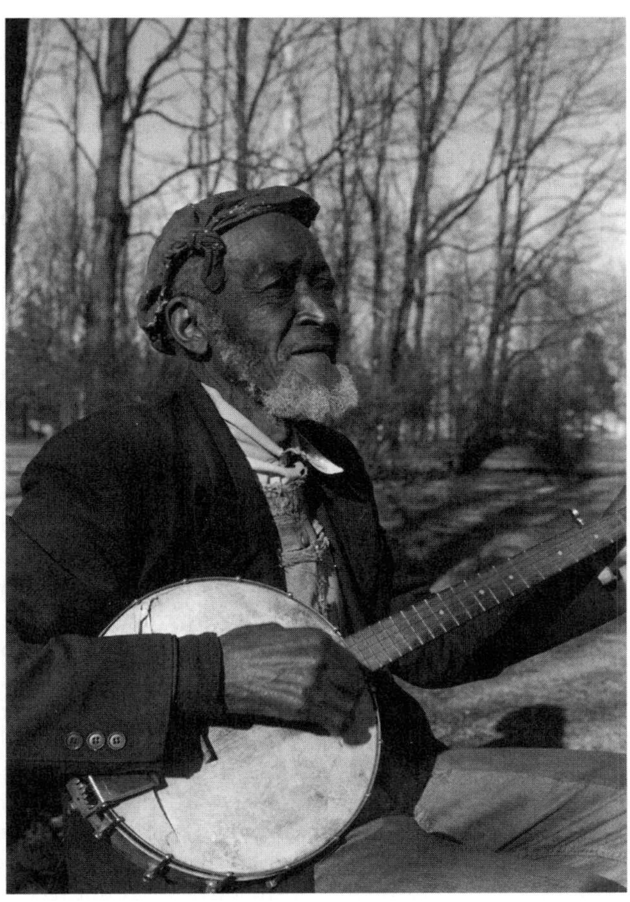

Stereotypes are often learned from family and friends, but they can also be learned through direct experience. A person who knows a black musician, for instance, may overgeneralize and think that all African-Americans are musically talented. (Corbis-Bettmann)

lected, the researcher can analyze them by various statistical techniques.

A variety of more sophisticated scaling techniques have been developed. These typically involve asking a series of questions about a class of objects, for example, occupations, crimes, or political figures, and then applying various statistical techniques to arrive at a summary measure. These include magnitude techniques (e.g., the Thurstone scale), interlocking techniques (e.g., the Guttman scale), proximity techniques (e.g., smallest space analysis), and the unfolding technique developed by Coombs. None of these has been widely used.

INDIRECT METHODS. Direct methods assume that people will report honestly their attitudes toward the object of interest. But when questions deal with sensitive issues, such as attitudes toward members of minority groups or abortion, respondents may not report accurately. In an attempt to avoid such reactivity, investigators have developed various indirect methods.

Some methods involve keeping respondents unaware of what is being measured. The "lost letter" technique involves dropping letters in public areas and observing the behavior of the person who finds it. The researcher can measure attitudes toward abortion by addressing one-half of the letters to a prochoice group and the other half to an antiabortion group. If a greater percentage of letters to the latter group are returned, it suggests people have antiabortion attitudes. Another indirect measure of attitude is pupil dilation, which increases when the person observes an object she or he likes and decreases when the object is disliked.

Some indirect measures involve deceiving respondents. A person may be asked to sort a large number of statements into groups, and the individual's attitude may be inferred from the number or type of categories used. Similarly, a respondent may be asked to write statements characterizing other people's beliefs on an issue, and the content and extremity of the respondent's statements are used to measure his or her own attitude. A third technique is the "bogus pipeline." This involves attaching the person with electrodes to a device and telling the person that the device measures his or her true feelings. The respondent is told that some signal, such as a blinking light, pointer, or buzzer, will indicate the person's real attitude, then the person is asked direct questions.

While these techniques may reduce inaccurate reporting, some of them yield measures whose meaning is not obvious or is of questionable validity. Does mailing a letter reflect one's attitude toward the addressee or the desire to help? There is also evidence that measures based on these techniques are not reliable. Finally, some researchers believe it is unethical to use the techniques that involve deception. Because of the importance of obtaining reliable and valid measures, research has been carried out on how to ask questions about sensitive issues. This research is reviewed by DeLamater (1982). Sudman and Bradburn (1983) provide guidelines for constructing and asking such questions.

For a comprehensive discussion of attitude measurement techniques and issues, see Dawes and Smith (1985).

Attitude Organization and Change

An individual's attitude toward some object usually is not an isolated psychological unit. It is embedded in a cognitive structure and linked with a variety of other attitudes. Several theories of attitude organization are based on the assumption that individuals prefer consistency among the elements of cognitive structure, that is, among attitudes and perceptions. Two of these are balance theory and dissonance theory.

BALANCE THEORY. Balance theory, developed by Heider, is concerned with cognitive systems composed of two or three elements. The elements can be either persons or objects. Consider the statement "I will vote for Mary Sweeney; she supports parental leave legislation." This system contains three elements—the speaker, P; another person (candidate Mary Sweeney), O; and an impersonal object (parental leave legislation), X. According to balance theory, two types of relationships may exist between elements. *Sentiment relations* refer to sentiments or evaluations directed toward objects and people; a sentiment may be either positive (liking, endorsing) or negative (disliking, opposing). *Unit relations* refer to the extent of perceived association between elements. For example, a positive unit relation may result from ownership, a relationship (such as friendship or marriage), or causality. A negative relation indicates dissociation, like that between ex-spouses or members of groups with opposing interests. A null relation exists when there is no association between elements.

An indirect measure of attitude is pupil dilation, which increases when the person observes an object she or he likes.

Balance theory is concerned with the elements and their interrelations from P's viewpoint. In the example, the speaker favors parental leave legislation, perceives Mary Sweeney as favoring it, and intends to vote for her. This system is balanced. By definition, a *balanced state* is one in which all three relations are positive or in which one is positive and the other two are negative. An *imbalanced state* is one in which two of the relationships between elements are positive and one is negative or in which all three are negative. For example, "I love (+) Jane; Jane loves (+) opera; I hate (−) opera" is imbalanced.

The theory assumes that an imbalanced state is unpleasant and that when one occurs, the person will try to restore balance. There is considerable empirical evidence that people do prefer balanced states and that attitude change often occurs in response to imbalance. Furthermore, people maintain consistency by responding selectively to new information. There is evidence that people accept information consistent with their existing attitudes and reject information inconsistent with their cognitions. This is the major mechanism by which stereotypes are maintained.

DISSONANCE THEORY. Dissonance theory assumes that there are three possible relationships between any two cognitions. Cognitions are consistent, or *consonant,* if one naturally or logically follows from the other; they are *dissonant* when one implies the opposite of the other. The logic involved is psycho logic—logic as it appears to the individual, not logic in a formal sense. Two cognitive elements may also be irrelevant; one may have nothing to do with the other.

Cognitive dissonance is a state of psychological tension induced by dissonant relationships between cognitive elements. There are three situations in which dissonance commonly occurs. First, dissonance occurs following a decision whenever the decision is dissonant with some cognitive elements. Thus, choice between two (or more) attractive alternatives creates dissonance because knowledge that one chose A is dissonant with the positive features of B. The magnitude of the dissonance experienced is a function of the proportion of elements consonant and dissonant with the choice. Second, if a person engages in a behavior that is dissonant with his or her attitudes, dissonance will be created. Third, when events disconfirm an important belief, dissonance will be created if the person had taken action based on that belief. For example, a person who buys an expensive car in anticipation of a large salary increase will experience dissonance if she or he does not receive the expected raise.

Since dissonance is an unpleasant state, the theory predicts that the person will attempt to reduce it. Usually, dissonance reduction involves changes in the person's attitudes. Thus, following a decision, the person may evaluate the chosen alternative more favorably and the unchosen one more negatively. Following behavior that is dissonant with his or her prior attitude, the person's attitude toward the behavior may become more positive. An alternative mode of dissonance reduction is to change the importance one places on one or more of the attitudes. Following a decision, the person may reduce the importance of the cognitions that are dissonant with the choice; this is the well-known "sour grapes" phenomenon. Following disconfirmation of a belief, one may increase the importance attached to disconfirmed belief. A third way to reduce dissonance is to change behavior. If the dissonance following a choice is great, the person may decide to choose B instead of A. Following disconfirmation, the person may change behaviors that were based on the belief.

Several books and hundreds of articles about dissonance theory have been published since it was introduced by Festinger in 1957. There is a substantial body of research evidence that supports various predictions from and elaborations of the theory. Taken together, this literature has produced a detailed taxonomy of situations that produce dissonance and of preferred modes of dissonance reduction in various types of situations.

Both balance and dissonance theories identify the desire for consistency as a major source of stability and change in attitudes. The desire to maintain consistency leads the individual either to interpret new information as congruent with his or her existing cognitions (assimilation) or to reject it as not relevant (contrast) if it would challenge existing attitudes. At the same time, the desire for consistency will lead to attitude change when imbalance or dissonance occurs. Dissonance theory explicitly considers the link between behavior and attitudes. It predicts that engaging in counterattitudinal behavior may lead to attitude change. This is one mechanism by which social influences on behavior can indirectly affect attitudes. This mechanism may come into play when the person experiences changes in roles and the requirements of the new role are inconsistent with his or her prior attitudes.

Attitude-Behavior Relation

The attitude-behavior relation has been the focus of considerable research since the early 1970s. This research has identified a number of variables that influence the extent to which one can predict a person's behavior from his or her attitudes.

Some of these variables involve the measurement of the attitude and of the behavior. The correspondence of the two measures is one such variable; one can predict behavior more accurately if the two measures are at the same level of specificity. An opinion poll can predict the outcome of an election because there is high correspondence between the attitude ("Which candidate do you prefer for mayor in next month's election?") and the behavior (voting for a candidate in that election). The length of time between the measure of attitude and the occurrence and measure of the behavior is also an important variable. The shorter the time, the stronger the relationship. The longer the elapsed time, the more likely the person's attitude will change, although some attitudes are stable over long periods, for example, twenty years.

The characteristics of the attitude also influence the degree to which one can predict behavior from it. In order for an attitude to influence behavior, it must be activated, that is, brought from memory into conscious awareness. An attitude is usually activated by a person's exposure to the attitude object. Attitudes vary in *accessibility,* the ease with which they are activated. There is evidence that the more accessible an attitude is, the more likely it is to guide future behavior. Another variable is the source of the attitude. Attitudes based on direct experience with the object are more predictive of behavior.

The attitude-behavior relation is also influenced by situational constraints—the social norms governing behavior in a situation. An attitude is more likely to be expressed in behavior when the behavior is consistent with these norms.

An important attempt to specify the relationship between attitude and behavior is the theory of reasoned action, developed by Fishbein and Ajzen. According to this theory, behavior is determined by behavioral intention. Behavioral intention is determined by two factors, attitude and subjective norm. Attitude is one's beliefs about the likely consequences of the behavior and one's evaluation—positive or negative—of each of those outcomes. Subjective norm is the person's belief about other important persons' or groups' reactions to the behavior and the person's motivation to comply with the expectations of each. One of the strengths of the theory is this precise specification of the influences on behavioral intention. It is possible to measure quantitatively each of the four components (likely consequences, evaluations, likely reactions, motivation to comply) and use these to make precise predictions of behavior. A number of empirical studies from the 1980s report results consistent with such predictions. The theory applies primarily to behavior that is under conscious, volitional control; in some situations, behavior may be determined primarily by habit rather than intention.

Attitude as Indicator

Increasingly, attitudes are employed as indicators. Some researchers use attitude measures as indicators of concepts, while others study changes in attitudes over time as indicators of social change.

INDICATORS OF CONCEPTS. Measures of specific attitudes are frequently used as indicators of more general concepts. For example, agreement with the following statement is interpreted as an indicator of powerlessness: "This world is run by the few people in power, and there is not much the little guy can do about it." Powerlessness is considered to be a general orientation toward the social world and is a sense that one has little or no control over events. Feelings of powerlessness may be related to such varied behaviors as vandalism, not voting in elections, and chronic unemployment.

Attitude measures have been used to assess many other concepts used in the analysis of political attitudes and behavior. These include the liberalism-conservatism dimension, political tolerance (of radical or unpopular groups), trust in or disaffection with national institutions, and relative deprivation. (For a review of this literature, see Kinder and Sears 1985.) Attitude measures are used to assess many other characteristics of persons. In the realm of work these include occupational values, job satisfaction, and leadership style.

An attitude is more likely to be expressed in behavior when the behavior is consistent with these social norms.

A major concern when attitudes are employed as indicators is *construct validity,* that is, whether the specific items used are valid measures of the underlying concept. In the powerlessness example, the connection between the content of the item and the concept may seem obvious, but even in cases like this it is important to demonstrate validity. A variety of analytic techniques may be used, including interitem correlations, factor analysis, and LISREL.

INDICATORS OF SOCIAL CHANGE. Two methodological developments have made it possible to use attitudes to study social change. The first was the development of probability sampling techniques, which allow the investigator to make inferences about the characteristics of a population from the results obtained by surveying a sample of that population. The second is the use of the same attitude measures in surveys of representative samples at two or more points in time.

A major source of such data is the General Social Survey, an annual survey of a probability sample of adults. The GSS repeats a core set of items on a roughly annual basis, making possible the study of changes over a period of twenty years. Many of these items were drawn directly from earlier surveys, making comparisons over a thirty- or forty-year timespan possible. A recently published book describes these items and presents the responses obtained each time the item was used (Niemi, Mueller, and Smith 1989). Other sources of such data include the National Election Studies and the Gallup Polls.

This use of attitude items reflects a general concern with social change at the societal level (Hill 1981). The investigator uses aggregate measures of attitudes in the population as an index of changes in cultural values and social institutions. Two areas of particular interest are attitudes toward race and gender roles. In both areas, efforts have been made to improve access to educational programs, jobs, and professions, increase wages and salaries, and provide greater opportunity for advancement. The availability of responses to the same attitude items over time allows us to assess the consistency between these social changes and attitudes in the population. Consider the question "Do you think civil rights leaders are trying to push too fast, are going too slowly, or are moving at about the right speed?" This question was asked in surveys of national samples every two years from 1964 to 1976 and in 1980. The percentage of whites replying "Too fast" declined from 74 percent in 1964 to 40 percent in 1980 (Bobo 1988), suggesting increased white support for the black movement. In general, research indicates that both racial and gender-role attitudes became more liberal between 1960 and 1985, and this finding is consistent with the social changes in these areas. Other topics that have been studied include attitudes toward abortion, social class identification, and subjective quality of life.

There are several issues involved in this use of attitude items. The first is the problem of "non-attitudes" (Converse 1970). Respondents may answer survey questions or endorse statements even though they have no attitude toward the object. In fact, when respondents are questioned about fictional objects or organizations, some of them will express an opinion. Schuman and Kalton (1985) discuss this issue in detail and suggest ways to reduce the extent to which nonattitudes are given by respondents.

The second issue involves the interpretation of responses to items. In the example above, the analyst assumes that white respondents who reply "Too fast" feel threatened by the movement. However, there is evidence that small changes in the wording of survey items can produce substantial changes in aggregate response patterns. This evidence and guidelines for writing survey items are discussed in Schuman and Presser (1981) and Sudman and Bradburn (1983).

Finally, there is the problem of equivalence in meaning over time. In order to make meaningful comparisons across time, the items need to be the same or equivalent. Yet over time the meaning of an item may change. Consider the item "Are you in favor of *desegregation,* strict *segregation,* or something in between?" This question was asked of national samples in 1964 and every two years from 1968 to 1978. From 1964 to 1970, the percentage of white, college-educated adults endorsing desegregation increased; from 1970 to 1978, the percentage decreased steadily. Until 1970, desegregation efforts were focused on the South; after 1970, desegregation efforts focused on school integration in northern cities. Evidence suggests that endorsement of desegregation changed because the meaning of the question for white adults changed (Schuman, Steeh, and Bobo 1985).

[See also Prejudice.]

BIBLIOGRAPHY

Allport, Gordon W. 1985 "The Historical Background of Social Psychology." In G. Lindzey and E. Aronson, eds., *Handbook of Social Psychology,* 3rd ed. New York: Random House.

Bobo, Lawrence 1988 "Attitudes toward the Black Political Movement: Trends, Meaning, and Effects on Racial Policy Preference." *Social Psychology Quarterly* 51:287–302.

Converse, Philip 1970 "Attitudes and Nonattitudes: Continuation of a Dialogue." In E.R. Tufte, ed., *The Quantitative Analysis of Social Problems.* Reading, Mass.: Addison-Wesley.

Dawes, Robyn M., and Tom L. Smith 1985 "Attitude and Opinion Measurement." In G. Lindzey and E. Aronson, eds., *Handbook of Social Psychology,* 3rd ed. New York: Random House.

DeLamater, John 1982 "Response-Effects of Question Content." In W. Dijkstra and J. van der Zouwen, eds., *Response Behavior in the Survey-Interview.* London: Academic Press.

Festinger, Leon 1957 *A Theory of Cognitive Dissonance.* Stanford, Calif.: Stanford University Press.

Fishbein, Martin, and Icek Ajzen 1975 *Belief, Attitude, Intention, and Behavior.* Reading, Mass.: Addison-Wesley.

Hill, Richard 1981 "Attitudes and Behavior." In M. Rosenberg and R. H. Turner, eds., *Social Psychology: Sociological Perspectives.* New York: Basic Books.

Kiecolt, K. Jill 1988 "Recent Developments in Attitudes and Social Structure." In W. R. Scott and J. Blake, eds., *Annual Review of Sociology,* Vol. 14. Palo Alto, Calif.: Annual Reviews.

Kinder, Donald R., and David O. Sears 1985 "Public Opinion and Political Action." In G. Lindzey and E. Aronson, eds., *Handbook of Social Psychology,* 3rd ed. New York: Random House.

McGuire, William J. 1985 "Attitudes and Attitude Change." In G. Lindzey and E. Aronson, eds., *Handbook of Social Psychology,* 3rd ed. New York: Random House.

Niemi, Richard G., John Mueller, and Tom W. Smith 1989 *Trends in Public Opinion: A Compendium of Survey Data.* New York: Greenwood Press.

Roberts, Donald F., and Nathan Maccoby 1985 "Effects of Mass Communication." In G. Lindzey and E. Aronson, eds., *Handbook of Social Psychology,* 3rd ed. New York: Random House.

Schuman, Howard, and Graham Kalton 1985 "Survey Methods." In G. Lindzey and E. Aronson, eds., *Handbook of Social Psychology,* 3rd ed. New York: Random House.

Schuman, Howard, and Stanley Presser 1981 *Questions and Answers in Attitude Surveys. Experiments on Question Form, Wording, and Context.* New York: Academic Press.

Schuman, Howard, Charlotte Steeh, and Lawrence Bobo 1985 *Racial Attitudes in America.* Cambridge, Mass.: Harvard University Press.

Sudman, Seymour, and Norman R. Bradburn 1983 *Asking Questions: A Practical Guide to Questionnaire Design.* San Francisco: Jossey-Bass.

– JOHN D. DELAMATER

B

BIRTH AND DEATH RATES

Much of the birth and death information published by individual governments and compiled by the United Nations is in absolute numbers. These raw data are difficult to interpret. For example, a comparison of the 10,678 births in Alaska with the 21,375 births in West Virginia in 1994 reveals nothing about the relative levels of fertility because West Virginia has a larger population (National Center for Health Statistics).

To control for the effect of population size, analyses of fertility and mortality usually use rates. A rate measures the number of times an event such as birth occurs in a given period of time divided by the population at risk to that event. The period is usually a year, and the rate is usually expressed per 1,000 people in the population to eliminate the decimal point. Dividing West Virginia's births by the state's population and multiplying by 1,000 yields a birth rate of 12 per 1,000. A similar calculation for Alaska yields 22 per 1,000, evidence that fertility makes a greater contribution to population growth in the younger state.

Birth Rates

The crude birth rate calculated in the preceding example,

$$\text{Crude birth rate} = \frac{\text{Live births in year } x}{\text{Midyear population in year } x} \times 1{,}000 \qquad (1)$$

is the most common measure of fertility because it requires the least amount of data and measures the impact of fertility on population growth.

Crude birth rates range from over 40 per 1,000 in most African countries and some western and southern Asian countries to less than 18 in the slower growing or declining countries of Europe, North America, Australia, New Zealand, Japan, Taiwan, South Korea, and Hong Kong (Population Reference Bureau 1990).

The crude birth rate is aptly named when used to compare childbearing levels between populations. Its estimate of the population at risk to giving birth includes men, children, and postmenopausal women. If women of childbearing age compose different proportions in the populations under consideration or within the same population in a longitudinal analysis, the crude birth rate is an unreliable indicator of the relative level of childbearing. A small portion of Alaska's 83 percent higher crude birth rate is due to the state's higher proportion of childbearing age women, 25 percent, versus 23 percent in West Virginia (United States Bureau of the Census).

Other rates that more precisely specify the population at risk are better comparative measures of childbearing, although only the crude birth rate measures the impact of fertility on population growth. If the number of women in childbearing ages is known, general fertility rates can be used:

$$\text{General fertility rate} = \frac{\text{Live births in year } x}{\text{Women 15–44 in year } x} \times 1{,}000 \qquad (2)$$

This measure reveals that Alaskan women of childbearing age produce more births, given their number, than their West Virginian counterparts, 89 versus 51 births per 1,000 women between ages 15–44 (National Center for Health Statistics 1989a, p. 21). The 74 percent difference in the two states' general fertility rates is not as great as that indicated by their crude birth rates, which also measure the full impact of age-composition differences.

The general fertility rate is sensitive only to the distribution of childbearing-age women. When women are heavily concentrated in the younger, more fecund ages, such as in the United States in 1980, or in the less fecund older ages, such as in the United States in 2000, the general fertility rate is not the best choice for fertility analysis. It inflates the relative level of fertility in the former population and deflates the estimate in the latter.

Age-specific fertility rates eliminate potential distortions from age compositions. These rates are calculated for five-year age groups beginning with ages 15–19 and ending with ages 45–49:

$$\text{Age-specific fertility rate} = \frac{\text{Live births in year } x \text{ to women age } a}{\text{Women age } a \text{ in year } x} \times 1{,}000 \qquad (3)$$

Age-specific fertility rates also provide a rudimentary measure of the tempo of childbearing. The four countries in Figure 1 have distinct patterns. Honduras, a less developed country with extremely high fertility, has

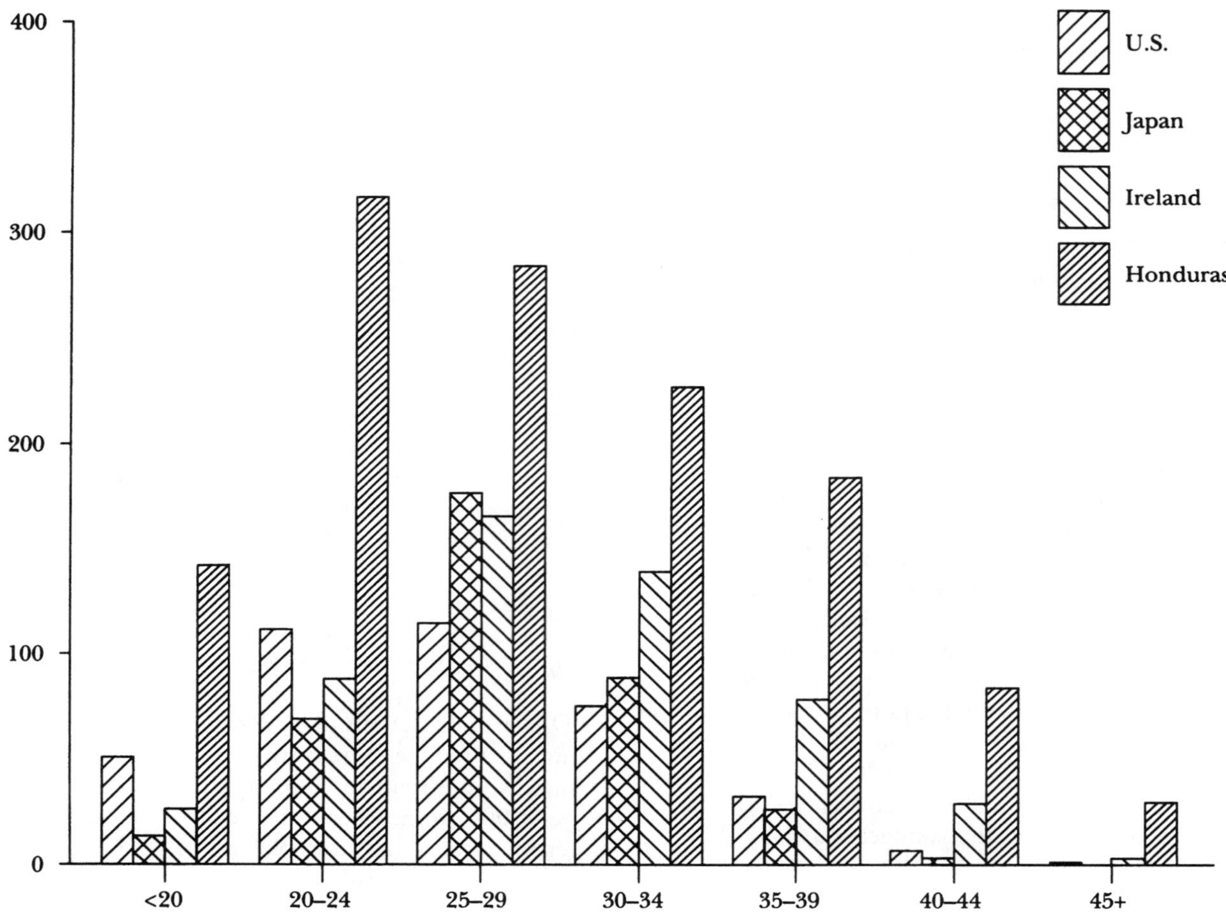

Figure 1. Age-Specific Fertility Rates: Selected Countries, Mid-1980s. (United Nations, Demographic Yearbook, 1987*)*

higher rates at all ages. At the other extreme, Japan's low fertility is highly concentrated between the ages of twenty-five and thirty-four, even though these Japanese rates are well below those in Honduras. In contrast, young women in the United States have higher fertility than young women in Japan and most other developed countries, whereas older women in Ireland have unusually high rates.

More detailed analyses of the tempo of childbearing require extensive information about live birth order to make fertility rates for each age group specific for first births, second births, third births, and so forth (Shryock and Siegel 1976, p. 280). A comparison of these age-order-specific rates in 1976 and 1987 (National Center for Health Statistics 1978, p. 10; 1989a, p. 16) reveals a shift toward later childbearing in the United States. Rates for first and second births increased for women over thirty and first birth rates declined for women ages twenty to twenty-four.

When the tempo of fertility is not of interest, the advantages of age-specific fertility rates are outweighed by the cumbersome task of comparing many rates between more than a few populations. In this case each population's age-specific rates can be condensed in an age-sex adjusted birth rate (Shryock and Siegel 1976, pp. 284–288). The most frequently used age-sex adjusted rate is calculated:

$$\text{Total fertility rate} = \frac{\text{sum (age-specific fertility rates}}{} \times 5), \qquad (4)$$

if the age-specific fertility rates are for five-year age groups. Single-year age-specific rates are summed without the five-year adjustment. When expressed per single woman, the total fertility rate can be interpreted as the average number of births that a hypothetical group would have at the end of their reproduction if they

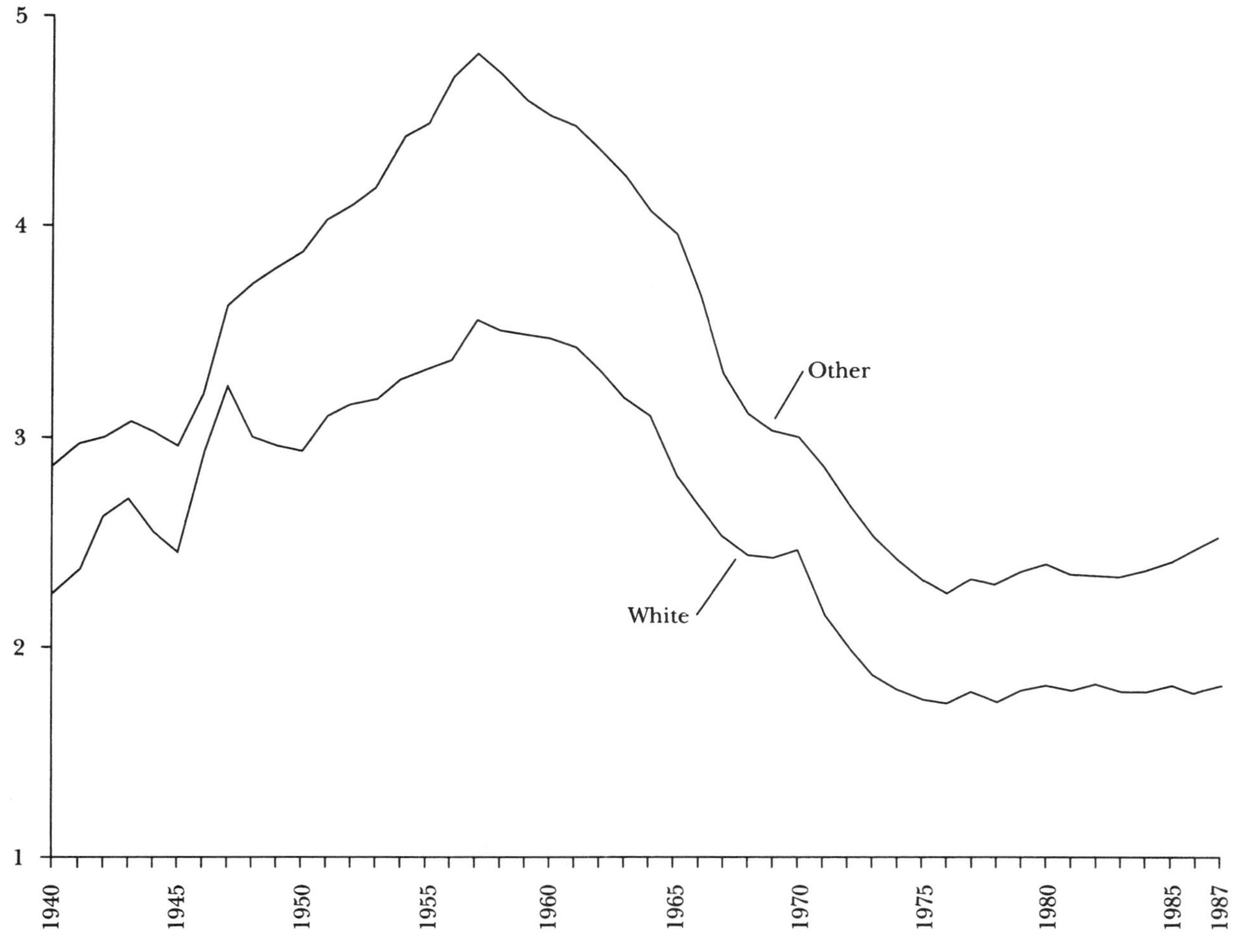

Figure 2. Total Fertility Rates by Race: United States, 1940 to 1987. (National Center for Health Statistics, "Advance Report of Final Natality Statistics, 1987," Monthly Vital Statistics Report *and U.S. Bureau of the Census,* Historical Statistics of the United States, Colonial Times to 1970. *Part 1)*

experienced the age-specific fertility observed in a particular year over the course of their childbearing years.

In reality, age-specific rates in populations that consciously control fertility can be volatile. For example, the fertility rate of American women ages 30–34 fell to 71 per 1,000 in the middle of the Great Depression and climbed back to 119 during the postwar baby boom, only to fall again to 53 in 1975 and rebound to 71 in 1987 (U.S. Bureau of the Census 1975, p. 50; National Center for Health Statistics 1989a, p. 18). Consequently, a total fertility rate calculated from one year's observed age-specific rates is not a good estimate of the eventual completed fertility of childbearing-age women. It is, however, an excellent index of the level of fertility observed in a year that is unaffected by age composition.

The total fertility rate's insensitivity to age composition makes it useful for examining trends in a population with a changing age composition, such as the United States, or between populations with different age compositions, such as whites and nonwhites in this country (Figure 2). After declining since before the turn of the century, American fertility rose sharply after World War II, peaked in the late 1950s, and sank to a historic low in the mid-1970s. Since then, the national rate has crept back to nearly two births per woman. Non-whites average about one-half a child more than whites. The racial difference narrowed only during the immediate postwar years of the mid-1940s and widened during the peak years of the baby boom, when the economy was expanding rapidly.

The total fertility rate also can be interpreted as an estimate of the reproductivity of a population. Reproductivity is the extent to which a generation exactly replaces its eventual deaths. Theoretically, women would need to average only two births, one of each sex, to maintain a constant population size, if all female newborns survived to the end of their childbearing years. In real populations some females die before menopause. As a result, the total fertility rate must exceed two for a generation to replace all of its deaths. In populations with a low risk of dying before age fifty, such as in the more developed countries of the world, the total fertility rate needs to be only about 2.1 for replacement. Developing countries with higher mortality need a higher total fertility rate for replacement. Nigeria, for example, with an infant mortality rate of 121 per 1,000 live births and a life expectancy of only forty-eight needs a rate of about three births per woman for replacement.

Most developed countries have total fertility rates below replacement (Population Reference Bureau 1990). Many western and southern European countries as well as Japan, Hong Kong, and South Korea have total fertility rates below 1.7 births per woman. Those without net in-migration will decline if their rates do not rebound as they are doing in Finland, Iceland, Sweden, West Germany, and the United States.

In contrast, the total fertility rates of most developing countries far exceed replacement (Population Reference Bureau 1990). The highest rates are found in Africa and western Asia, where most countries have rates greater than six births per woman. These populations are growing by more than 2.5 percent per year. A few such as Kenya, Zambia, and Iraq are growing 3.8 percent per year or more. If unchanged, these populations will double in eighteen years, but change is evident. Thailand's rate declined from 4.5 births per woman in 1980 to 2.6 in 1990 (Population Reference Bureau 1980; 1990). A few developing countries, including China, Taiwan, South Korea, Sri Lanka, Cyprus, Barbados, Cuba, Puerto Rico, Jamaica, Chile, and Uruguay, are averaging less than 2.5 births per woman. Others with very high fertility, such as Kenya, India, Bangladesh, and Egypt, have begun to show a decline.

The fertility measures discussed up to this point are period rates. They are based on data for a particular year and represent the behavior of a cross-section of age groups in the population in that year. Fertility also can be measured over the lifetime of birth cohorts. Cu-

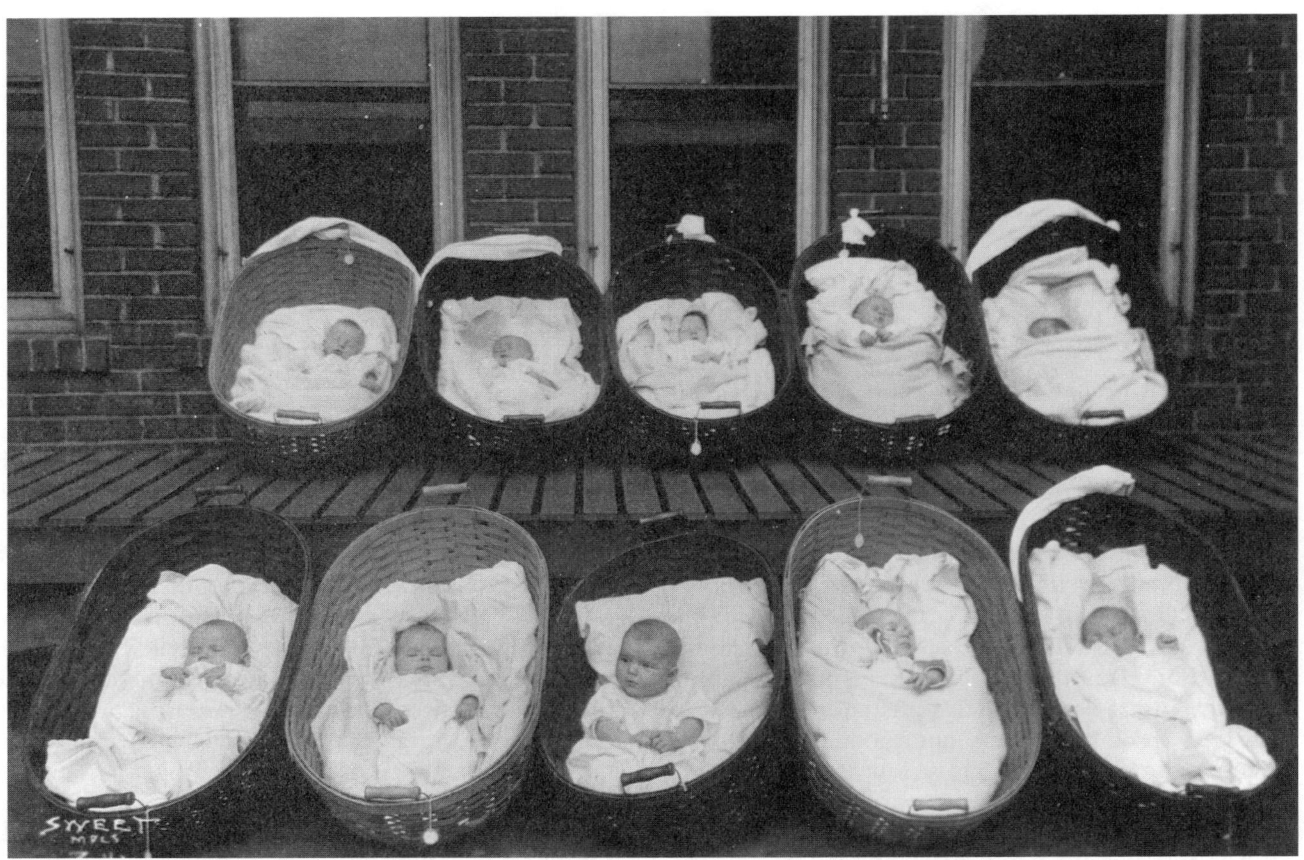

Total fertility rate can be interpreted as an estimate of the reproductivity of a population. Reproductivity is the extent to which a generation exactly replaces its eventual deaths. (Minnesota Historical Society/Corbis)

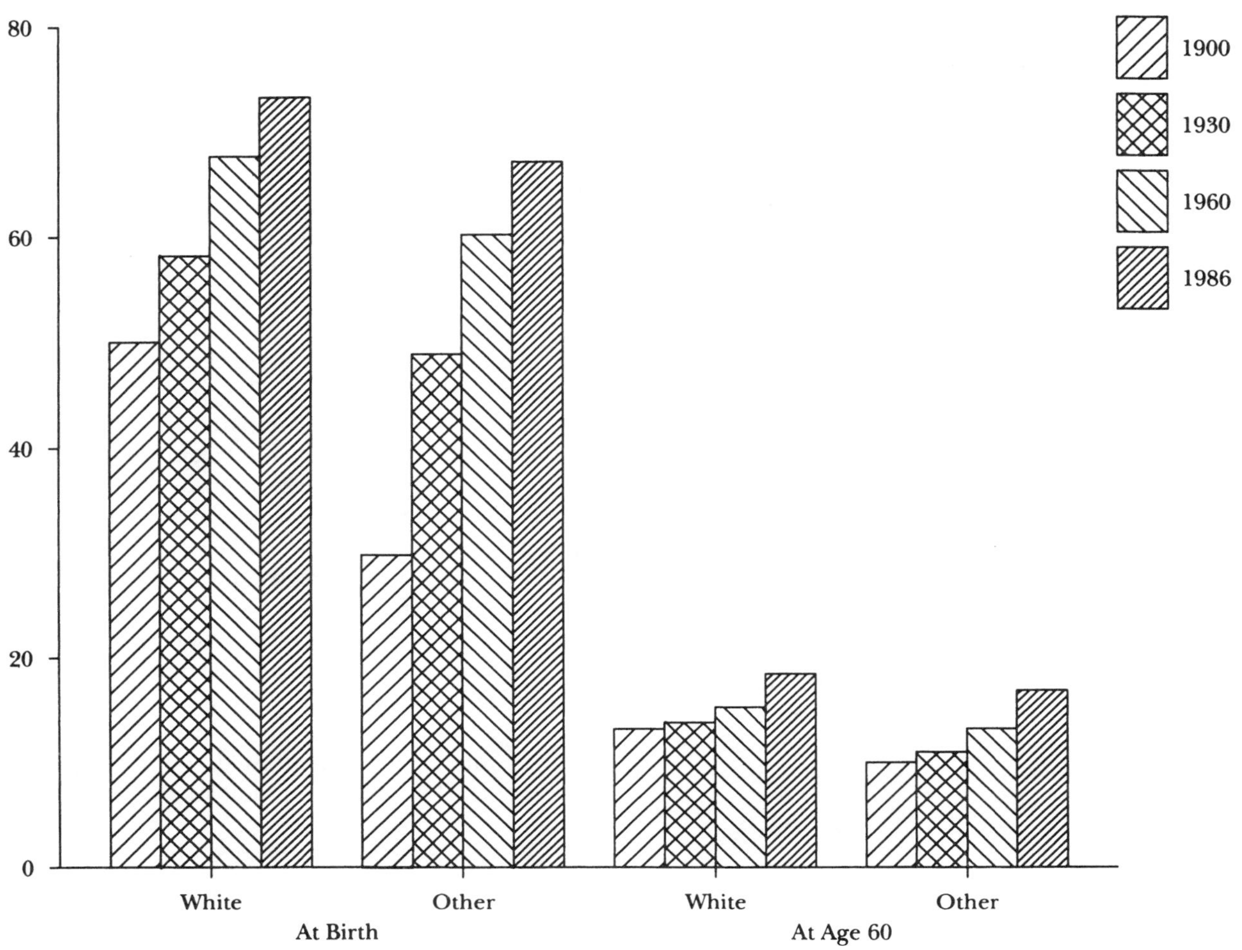

Figure 3. Male Life Expectancy (in Number of Years) at Birth and Age 60 by Race: United States. (National Center for Health Statistics, 1986 Mortality, *Part A and U.S. Bureau of the Census,* Historical Statistics of the United States, Colonial Times to 1970, *Part 1. Note: Life expectancy data for 1900 and 1930 for "Other" indicate blacks only)*

mulative fertility rates can be calculated for each birth cohort of women by summing the age-specific fertility rates that prevailed as they passed through each age (Shryock and Siegel 1976, p. 289). This calculation yields a completed fertility rate for birth cohorts that have reached the end of their reproductive years. It is the cohort equivalent of the period total fertility rate.

Death Rates

The measurement of mortality raises many of the same issues discussed with fertility. Rates are more informative than absolute numbers, and those rates that more precisely define the population at risk to dying are more accurate. Unlike fertility, however, the entire population is at risk to dying, and this universal experience happens only once to an individual.

The impact of mortality on population growth can be calculated with a crude death rate:

$$\text{Crude death rate} = \frac{\text{Deaths in year } x}{\text{Midyear population in year } x} \times 1{,}000 \quad (5)$$

Crude death rates vary from over 20 per 1,000 in some African countries and Afghanistan to as low as 2 or 3 per 1,000. The lowest rates are not in the developed countries of Europe, North America, Oceania, and the Soviet Union, which have rates between 7 and 12 per 1,000 (Population Reference Bureau 1990). Instead, the lowest crude death rates are found in developing countries with high fertility and declining mortality. This anomaly results from the older age composition of developed countries compared to developing countries. The proportion of people age sixty-five and over ranges between 12 and 18 percent in developed countries compared to less than 5 percent in most African, Asian, and Latin American populations. Although the entire population is at risk of dying, the risk rises with age after childhood. Consequently, populations with a higher

The total fertility rate must exceed two for a generation to replace all of its deaths.

proportion of elderly have higher crude death rates even when there is no difference in the risk of dying at each age.

To control for the strong influence of age on mortality, age-specific rates can be calculated for five-year age groups:

$$\text{Age-specific mortality rate} = \frac{\text{Deaths in year } x \text{ to the population age } a}{\text{Population age } a \text{ in year } x} \times 1{,}000 \qquad (6)$$

Before age five, the age-specific mortality rate usually is subdivided to capture the higher risk of dying immediately after birth. The rate for one- to four-year olds, like other age-specific rates, is based on the midyear estimate of this population. The conventional infant mortality rate, however, is based on the number of live births:

$$\text{Infant mortality rate} = \frac{\text{Deaths under age 1 in year } x}{\text{Live births in year } x} \times 1{,}000 \qquad (7)$$

The infant mortality rate is often disaggregated into the neonatal mortality rate for the first month of life and the postneonatal rate for the rest of the year:

$$\text{Neonatal mortality rate} = \frac{\text{Deaths under 28 days in year } x}{\text{Live births in year } x} \times 1{,}000 \qquad (8)$$

$$\text{Postneonatal} = \frac{\text{Deaths from 29 days to age 1 in year } x}{\text{Live births in year } x} \times 1{,}000 \qquad (9)$$

Infant mortality varies widely throughout the world. Many African and some Asian countries have 1993 rates that still exceed 100 per 1,000 births, although they have declined (Population Reference Bureau 1993). Latin American infant mortality rates have declined as well. They now range from 15.2 in Cuba to 89 in Haiti. In contrast, developed countries with market economies have rates at or below 10, led by Japan with under 5 infant deaths per 1,000 live births.

The U.S. infant mortality rate for 1996 was double that of Japan's, and the downward trend in this rate has slowed (National Center for Health Statistics) as the proportion of premature births has increased (National Center for Health Statistics). The country's largest minority, blacks, have more than double the rates of premature births and infant mortality of whites, but not all minorities have higher infant mortality. Data from eighteen states and the District of Columbia reveal that Hispanic infant mortality is slightly lower than the Anglo rate of 8.4 (National Center for Health Statistics).

Infant mortality also varies by sex in the United States and other countries. The rate for U.S. male newborns is 11 per 1,000 compared to 9 per 1,000 for females (National Center for Health Statistics 1989b, p. 13). This sex difference in mortality is evident at all ages. The greatest gap is among young adults; U.S. males are three times more likely to die than females between twenty and twenty-four, due largely to motor vehicle fatalities.

Age-specific mortality rates usually are specific for sex as well because of the large differences. This results in thirty-eight rates with the usual age categories, and this can be awkward. When the age pattern of mortality is not of interest, an age-adjusted composite measure is preferable. The most common of these is life expectancy.

Life expectancy is the average number of years that members of an age group would live if they were to experience the age-specific death rates prevailing in a given year. It is calculated for each age group in a life table (Shryock and Siegel 1976, pp. 249–68). All developed countries and some developing countries in Asia, Latin America, and Oceania have life expectancies at birth of over seventy (Population Reference Bureau 1990). Japan has the longest, seventy-nine years, due to extremely low infant mortality. African countries, in contrast, with their relatively high infant and child mortality, generally have life expectancies in the forties or fifties.

U.S. males are three times more likely to die than females between twenty and twenty-four, due largely to motor vehicle fatalities.

Declines in infant and child mortality from infectious diseases have been largely responsible for the historical increase in life expectancy in all developed and most developing countries. As a result, life expectancy in the United States has increased far more at birth than at age sixty (Figure 3), and cardiovascular disease and cancer have become the major causes of death (National Center for Health Statistics 1989, p. 6). If cardiovascular mortality continues to decline and the slight reduction in cancer mortality observed in 1986 and 1987 grows, gains in life expectancy at age sixty will accelerate.

[See also Infant and Child Mortality; Life Expectancy.]

BIBLIOGRAPHY

National Center for Health Statistics 1978 "Advance Report of Final Natality Statistics, 1976." *Monthly Vital Statistics Report,* Vol. 26, no. 12, suppl. Hyattsville, Md.: Public Health Service.

——— 1988 *1986 Mortality,* Vol. 2, part A. Washington, D.C.: U.S. Government Printing Office.

——— 1989a "Advance Report of Final Natality Statistics, 1987." *Monthly Vital Statistics Report,* Vol. 38, no. 3, suppl. Hyattsville, Md.: Public Health Service.

——— 1989b "Advance Report of Final Mortality Statistics, 1987." *Monthly Vital Statistics Report,* vol. 38, no. 5, suppl. Hyattsville, Md.: Public Health Service.

Population Reference Bureau 1980 *1980 World Population Data Sheet.* Washington, D.C.: Population Reference Bureau.

——— 1990 *1990 World Population Data Sheet.* Washington, D.C.: Population Reference Bureau.

Shryock, Henry S., and Jacob S. Siegel 1976 *The Methods and Materials of Demography.* San Francisco: Academic Press.

United Nations 1989 *Demographic Yearbook, 1987.* New York: United Nations.

U.S. Bureau of the Census 1975 *Historical Statistics of the United States, Colonial Times to 1970.* Washington D.C.: Government Printing Office.

——— 1988 "Projections of the Population of States by Age, Sex, and Race: 1988–2010." *Current Population Reports,* series P-25, no. 1017. Washington, D.C.: Government Printing Office.

– DEBORAH A. SULLIVAN

BUREAUCRACY

The origin of the term *bureaucracy* can be traced to eighteenth-century French literature (Albrow 1970). In this early usage, the term referred to the workplace of officials whose activities were routinely determined by fairly explicit rules and regulations. In contradistinction to other forms of administration, modern bureaucracies represent highly formalized and intensely rational systems of administration. As systems of management and supervision, bureaucracies are designed to provide for the rational coordination of duties and responsibilities of officials and employees of organizations. It is important to recognize that this notion of the rational organization of individual behavior pertains to an organizational and not to an individual level of concern. Consequently, bureaucracies represent devices by which the private, idiosyncratic, and uniquely personal interests and actions of individuals are formally orchestrated and constrained in order to achieve specified organizational goals in an efficient way. This orchestration of individual action is accomplished by the use of rules and formal programs of activity (March and Simon 1958) intended to provide a clear outline of mandated duties and responsibilities. With such a delineation of duties and responsibilities, this system of administration tends to ensure that the actions and activities of individuals contribute to the interests of the organizations within which they are employed.

The Contribution of Max Weber

Interest in bureaucracy, both as a process and as an outcome, has been long standing in sociology. Early concern is evident in the work of Karl Marx ([1852] 1963) and of Alexis de Tocqueville (1877), who were among the first to recognize the relatively recent historical trend toward increasing bureaucratization at the level of distinct organizations, especially military organizations, as well as in Western European society in general. Further understanding of the bureaucratic process was provided by Michels's (1949) analysis of the dynamics of power distribution within bureaucratic organizations and the development of oligarchical tendencies detrimental to democratic principles. However, the emergence of the study of bureaucracy as a major and independent line of sociological inquiry is fundamentally based upon the work of Max Weber (1864–1920). Although Weber conducted his study immediately prior and subsequent to the turn of the century, his work was not widely recognized by English-speaking theorists until its translation during the late 1940s (Weber 1946, 1947).

Weber's ambitious and richly informative work most notably includes consideration of Chinese, Egyptian, Roman, Prussian, and French administrative systems. In his comparative analysis of this vast array of diverse cultural systems of administration, Weber recognized an inexorable relationship between power and authority, on the one hand, and differing systems of administration on the other. Thus, in Weber's analysis, the bureaucratic form of administration reflects one of three particular ways in which power is legitimated. Consequently, in order to gain a clear appreciation of the unique features of bureaucratic structure and processes, it is necessary briefly to address Weber's notion of the relationship among power, authority, and systems of administration.

Power, for Weber, represents the ability or capacity to have other people behave in accordance with certain orders or dictates, irrespective of whether those affected regard its application as rightful or legitimate. *Authority* represents the legitimation of this power by those individuals whose activities are so ordered such that the application of power is perceived to be rightful. In Weber's analysis, three different types of authority are recognized: traditional, charismatic, and rational-legal (Weber 1947, p. 328). Traditional authority represents a system in which the use of power is regarded as legitimate when it is predicated upon belief in the sanctity of time-honored traditions. Charismatic authority has a much more limited focus, in that it is based on intensely personal acts of devotion. Under these circumstances, authority is conferred upon a specific individual who is regarded by devoted followers to exhibit exceptional, sacred, and/or heroic characteristics. Thus, the authority of the charismatic leader is predicated upon the granting of power by these devoted followers. Rational-legal authority derives from the belief in the legitimacy of law, specifically in the legality of rules and the authority of officials and employees to perform certain legally sanctioned and mandated duties that are assigned to them.

Associated with each type of authority are distinctive *systems of administration.* Over the course of premodern social history, traditional authority was the principal means by which social organization was achieved. This type of authority structure resulted in the development of a wide variety of highly stable but nonetheless particularistic systems of administration, in which personal relations of dependence or loyalty provided the underpinning. In general, these systems of administration are most clearly exemplified by patrimonial and feudal systems of administration.

Systems of administration under the dominion of charismatic authority tend to be inherently transitory and are most likely to arise during periods of crisis or unprecedented change.

Charismatic authority results in the emergence of highly unstable systems of administration, because the foundation of these systems, the profoundly personal relationships between charismatic leaders and followers, is decisively limited in both time and circumstance. Given the notably conditional foundations of charismatic authority structures, it is not surprising that the systems of administration that arise in such situations encounter difficulties in generating stable administrative practices. In this regard, problems pertaining to the routinization of authority and leadership succession are particularly salient and acute (Weber 1947, pp. 358–373). Thus, systems of administration under the dominion of charismatic authority tend to be inherently transitory and are most likely to arise during periods of crisis or unprecedented change.

Rational-legal authority culminates in the emergence of highly precise and universalistic systems of administration that are most clearly exemplified by the modern rational bureaucracy. Weber clearly regards such bureaucratic practices to be relatively recent in their development: "Bureaucracy . . . is fully developed in political and ecclesiastical communities only in the modern state, and in the private economy only in the most advanced institutions of capitalism" (Weber 1978, p. 956).

Characteristics of Bureaucracies

Perhaps the most distinguishing feature of modern rational bureaucracies is the fact that individual activity is formally controlled, prescribed, and regulated through the enforcement of rules. Moreover, the intent of enforcing these rules is the efficient achievement of specific organizational goals. In orchestrating individual action, a succinct and unambiguous specification of the official duties and responsibilities is provided, to minimize, if not to eliminate, the influence of personal interests, ambitions, and interests upon the performance of official duties. The official or employee is thus able to concentrate exclusively upon the technical aspects of the work, in particular the efficient and rational completion of assigned tasks. In addition to this attempt to separate individuals' private concerns from their official duties and responsibilities, distinguishing characteristics of bureaucracies include the following:

1. A pervasive hierarchical ordering of authority relations that limits the areas of command and responsibility for subordinate as well as superordinate personnel
2. The recruitment and selective promotion of individuals solely on the basis of technical expertise and competence
3. A structuring of the work environment in ways that ensure continuous and full-time employment, the development and fulfillment of career expectations, and the elimination of other sources of employment competing for the time and attention of officials and employees
4. A clearly defined division of labor in which a high degree of specialization and training is required for the performance of assigned tasks
5. The impersonality and impartiality of relationships involving both organization members and those outside the organization, such as customers or clients
6. An emphasis upon formal and written documentation in the form of "official records."

Bureaucratic organization thus represents an attempt to coordinate individual action on the basis of rational rules, rules that are intended to insulate and contain individual action in ways that promote the technical efficiency of an organization. The distinctive feature of bureaucratic organization is not the use of rules per se but, rather, the type of rules employed within an organization as well as the justification for the use of rules.

The distinctive feature of bureaucratic organization is not the use of rules per se but, rather, the type of rules employed within an organization.

Rules have been, and continue to be, used in other forms of administration to control individual action; however, the rules used in the other administrative forms (such as rules based on tradition in feudal administration or on dependency in patrimonial bureaucracy) are not necessarily based on technical knowledge and the rational and efficient achievement of specific goals. By contrast, within a modern bureaucracy explicit rules are designed to assure uniformity of performance in accordance with technical requirements. Thus, bureaucracies represent systems of control which attempt to ensure that the technical abilities of individuals are effectively utilized. Factors that would reduce the prospect of an official's or employee's performance being anything other than organizationally focused, affectively neutral, and achievement oriented (Parsons and Shils 1951, pp. 76–91) are thereby systematically excluded.

The Ideal Type Construct

By underscoring the unique features of modern bureaucratic systems of administration out-lined above, Weber implicitly provides an ideal-type characterization of bureaucracies. Despite subsequent confusion as to the value of such a portrayal of bureaucracies, Weber did not intend to provide an accurate description of the reality of bureaucratic processes. As noted in the introduction to one of his edited works, "Situations of such pure type have never existed in history. . . . The ideal types of Weber's sociology are simply mental constructs to serve as categories of thought, the use of which will help us to catch the infinite manifoldness of reality . . ." (Rhinestein 1954, pp. xxix–xxx). Thus, the ideal-type characterization is not suggestive of either extreme cases or distinct logical categories of phenomena (Mouzelis 1967). Rather, it provides a simplification and exaggeration of empirical events so that one can appreciate more clearly the features of the phenomena in question. Actual bureaucratic organizations may exhibit only a limited number of these properties or may possess them in varying degrees, a point understood and documented by Weber. In contradistinction to this ideal bureaucratic characterization of organizations are collectivist organizations of the type identified by Rothschild-Whitt (1979). This type of organization, with its explicit rejection of a rational-legal basis for authority, provides an obvious alternative to the bureaucratic model of organization.

Empirical Assessment

Stanley Udy (1959) was among the first to propose that, rather than regarding the specification of bureaucracies to be strictly a matter of definition, we need to ascertain empirically the extent to which bureaucratic characteristics are associated with one another in actual organizations. In the subsequent efforts at empirical assessment of the extent to which organizations exhibit bureaucratic properties, the works of Richard Hall (1963) and the Aston University research group (Pugh et al. 1968) are especially noteworthy. Hall's (1963) findings suggest that among samples of U.S. organizations, bureaucratic features of organizations may vary independently of one another. As is illustrated by the negative relationship between an emphasis on technical qualifications and other bureaucratic features—in particular hierarchy of authority and rule enforcement—Hall's study suggests that bureaucratic systems of organization may be indicative of multidimensional rather than unitary processes.

Similar findings for organizations in Britain were reported by the Aston University research group (Pugh et al. 1968). On the basis of their measurements of the bureaucratic characteristics of organizations specified by Weber, these researchers found four mutually independent dimensions of organizational structure rather than a single overarching bureaucratic dimension. With this finding, the authors concluded that bureaucracy is a multidimensional phenomenon and that it ". . . is not unitary, but that organizations may be bureaucratic in any number of ways" (Pugh et al. 1968, p. 101). However, these findings have not been unchallenged. The contentious nature of inquiry into the precise structure of bureaucratic organization is succinctly reflected in the work of Blau (1970) and of Child (1972), the adoption of a modified position by one of the investigators in the original Aston group (Hickson and McMillan 1981), and the subsequent reply by Pugh (1981).

The Paradox of Bureaucratic Efficiency: A Revelation of Underlying Complexity

Although bureaucracy existed in imperial Rome and ancient China, as well as in various national monarchies, the complexity of legislative issues in the modern state has caused an enormous growth of administrative function within both government and the private sector. Consequently, with respect to affairs of the state, the power and authority of permanent nonelected officials to control policy within the modern state has, over time, increased appreciably. As Weber noted,

> The bureaucratic structure is everywhere a late product of historical development. The further back we trace our steps, the more typical is the absence of bureaucracy and of officialdom in general. Since bureaucracy has a rational character, with rules, means-ends calculus, and matter-of-factness predominating, its rise and expansion has everywhere had revolutionary results. (1978, p. 1002)

Further, Weber contended that traditional authority structures have been, and will continue to be, replaced by the rational-legal authority structures of modern bureaucracies, given their "purely technical superiority over any other form of organization" (Weber 1946, p. 214). Nevertheless, the increased prominence of bureaucracies in both the public and the private sectors is not without its problems. The principal concern is that these bureaucracies are often unresponsive to the very public sectors they were designed to serve. To exacerbate the situation still further, few, if any, techniques of control are available to the public to ensure that bureaucracies and their officials become more responsive. As Weber acknowledged, certain negative consequences may be attendant upon the development of bureaucratic systems of administration, including the following:

1. The monopolization of information and the creation of "official secrets"
2. The relative inability to effect change from either inside or outside the bureaucratic structure because of vested incentive and reward systems, as well as the continuing social need for the level of specialization and expertise provided by the bureaucracy.
3. The tendency for bureaucracies to act in an autocratic, self-appointed manner, indifferent to variations not previously articulated within the bureaucracy. (Weber 1947, pp. 224–233)

Hence, on the one hand, bureaucracies are to be regarded as highly efficient and technically superior forms

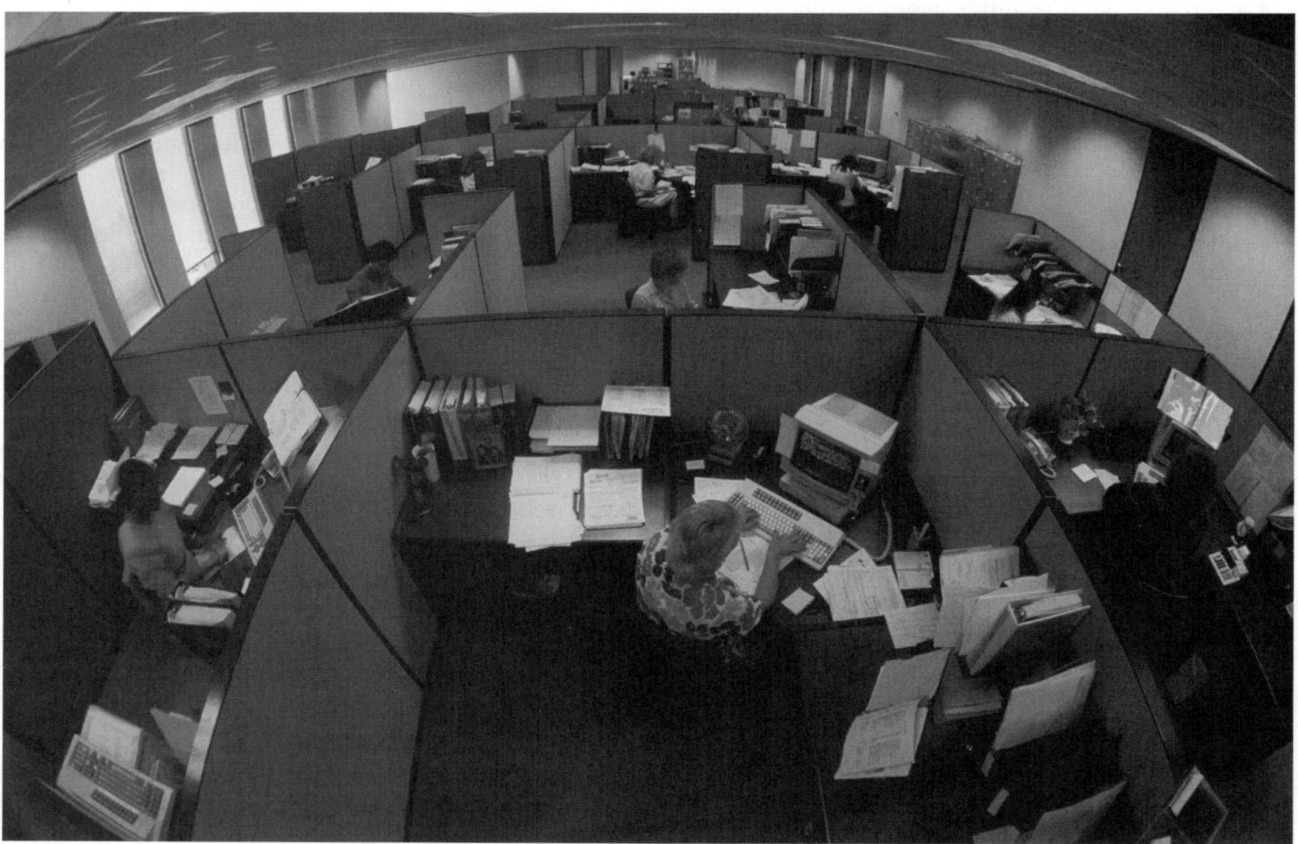

Modern bureaucracies achieve uniformity of performance among employees through rules that focus their attention on the goals of the organization. (Kit Kittle/Corbis)

of administration that have proven to be indispensable to large, complex organizations and modern society; however, on the other hand, various practical problems arise within these administrative structures that can result in outcomes at variance with notions of efficiency and technical superiority. These outcomes include implied incompetence, an overly constrained and myopic outlook, the unwarranted application of rules and regulations, the duplication of effort, and a certain unconcerned and even cavalier attitude among officials and employees. As a result, bureaucratic forms of administration may lead to certain paradoxical and dysfunctional developments. As Perrow has noted (1972), criticism of bureaucracies frequently relates to the fact that the actions of officials and employees are not bureaucratic enough.

The classic works of Merton (1940) and of Gouldner (1954) illustrate certain ways in which dysfunctional and unanticipated developments can adversely impact the intended effectiveness of bureaucratic procedures. Merton notes that, commencing with the need for bureaucratic control, individual compliance with rules is enforced, subsequently allowing for the development of routinely prescribed, reliable patterns of activity. However, when this agenda of rule compliance is implemented in a dynamic and fluctuating set of circumstances requiring more spontaneous responses, these prescribed patterns of bureaucratic activity can lead to adverse unintended consequences. Even though the circumstances require a different type of response, prescribed and fixed patterns of response may still be adopted because such responses are legitimated and defensible within the bureaucracy, given the extent to which they enhance individual reliability. Consequently, officials and employees do not accommodate the unique features of the situation, efficiency is undermined, and difficulties with clients and customers ensue.

"Adherence to the rules, originally conceived of as a means, becomes transformed into an end in itself."

Eventually, troublesome experiences with customers and clients may contribute to an even greater emphasis on bureaucratically reliable behavior rather than attenuating this encapsulated and counterproductive type of behavior. Thus, as Merton (1940) notes, "Adherence to the rules, originally conceived of as a means, becomes transformed into an end in itself; there occurs the familiar process of displacement of goals whereby an instrumental value becomes a terminal value. . . ." Recognizing that not all behavior within bureaucracies is prescribed by rules and that highly adaptive and flexible behavior also occurs, Merton's model serves as a reminder that, regardless of the type of behavior, various sets of structural constraints operate to promote such behavior (Blau and Meyer 1987; Allinson 1984).

Like Merton, Gouldner (1954) is concerned with possible unintended effects of formal rule enforcement. In Gouldner's model, the implications of the use of general and impersonal rules as a means of enforcing organizational control are investigated. The intended result of the use of such rules is to mask or partially conceal differential power relations between subordinates and their superiors. In societies with egalitarian norms, such as the United States, this serves to enhance the legitimacy of supervisory positions, thereby reducing the prospect of tensions among groups of differing power. However, the use of general and impersonal rules also has the unintended consequence of providing only minimal guidelines as to acceptable organizational behavior. Further, if only minimum standards of performance are specified and if individuals conform only to these standards, then a disparity arises between the stated goals of the organization, which require a level of performance beyond minimally acceptable and specified standards, and the actual level of individual performance. Since a greater level of individual output and performance is required, more personal forms of control are employed, in the form of closer supervision. However, increased closeness of supervision increases the visibility of power relations, an effect contrary to that previously achieved by the use of general and impersonal rules. Thus, Gouldner's study underscores the fact that in actual organizational settings the enforcement of bureaucratic rules does not necessarily represent a "machinelike" procedure in which the actions of individuals and the organizational implications of these actions represent axioms of efficiency.

As further indications that bureaucratic processes may reflect processes other than those dictated by the principle of efficiency, the satirical works of Peter and Hull (1969) and of Parkinson (1957) are suggestive. Peter and Hull contend that even though individual talent and expertise are the formal requisites for recruitment and promotion within a bureaucracy, individuals often are promoted to positions that exceed their level of competence. Instead of being relocated to more suitable positions, the individuals remain in these elevated positions. Consequently, Peter and Hull argue, individuals are promoted to their level of incompetence, a representation at variance with the image of operational efficiency.

As an illustration of the law that bears his name ("Work expands to fill the time available for its completion"), Parkinson (1957) highlights certain correlates of increasing organizational size. In particular, he notes that within the field of public administration, an increase in the number of officials is not necessarily related to the amount of work to be performed. Thus, an increase in the number of officials may be associated with factors other than increasing work demands, which would be the assumption of an efficiency-based assessment of organizational development. Consequently, increases in the number of public officials can be attributed to the opportunity officials have to minimize competition among themselves by creating subordinate positions. In the process of this increase of personnel, previously nonexistent work is created by having to supervise personnel assigned to these new positions.

Besides a valuefree view of bureaucracy that focuses upon the operational efficiency of bureaucratic procedures, an alternative, more "humanistic" approach to the study of bureaucracy is also needed (Kamenka 1989, ch. 5). This alternative approach highlights the situational constraints to which individuals and groups both within and outside bureaucracies are exposed. As Martin Albrow has noted, bureaucracy is "a term of strong emotive overtones and elusive connotations" (1970, p. 13), and as such it represents more than a straightforward technical process. Consequently, comprehensive inquiry into the complexities of bureaucratic processes necessitates a genuinely eclectic perspective.

[See also Complex Organizations.]

BIBLIOGRAPHY

Albrow, Martin 1970 *Bureaucracy.* London: Pall Mall Press.

Allinson, Christopher W. 1984 *Bureaucratic Personality and Organization Structure.* Aldershot, England: Gower.

Blau, Peter M. 1970 "Decentralization in Bureaucracies." In Mayer N. Zald, ed., *Power in Organizations.* Nashville, Tenn.: Vanderbilt University Press.

———, and Marshall W. Meyer 1987 *Bureaucracy in Modern Society,* 3rd ed. New York: Random House.

Child, John 1972 "Organization, Structure, and Strategies of Control." *Administrative Science Quarterly* 17:163–177.

Gouldner, Alvin W. 1954 *Patterns of Industrial Bureaucracy.* Glencoe, Ill.: Free Press.

Hall, Richard 1963 "The Concept of Bureaucracy: An Empirical Assessment." *American Journal of Sociology* 69:32–40.

Hickson, David, and C. J. McMillan 1981 *Organization and Nation: The Aston Programme IV.* Westmead, England: Gower.

Kamenka, Eugene 1989 *Bureaucracy.* Oxford: Basil Blackwell.

March, James G., and Herbert A. Simon 1958 *Organizations.* New York: Wiley.

Marx, Karl (1852) 1963 *The Eighteenth Brumaire of Louis Bonaparte.* New York: International Publishing Co.

Merton, Robert K. 1940. "Bureaucratic Structure and Personality." *Social Forces* 18:560–568.

Michels, Robert 1949 *Political Parties: A Sociological Study of the Oligarchial Tendencies of Modern Democracy.* New York: Free Press.

Mouzelis, Nicos P. 1967 *Organization and Bureaucracy.* London: Routledge and Kegan Paul.

Parkinson, C. Northcote 1957 *Parkinson's Law.* Boston: Houghton Mifflin.

Parsons, Talcott, and E. A. Shils 1951 *Toward a General Theory of Action.* Cambridge, Mass: Harvard University Press.

Perrow, Charles 1972 *Complex Organizations: A Critical Essay.* Glenview, Ill.: Scott Foresman.

Peter, Laurence F., and Raymond Hull 1969 *The Peter Principle.* New York: Morrow.

Pugh, D. S. 1981 "The Aston Programme of Research: Retrospect and Prospect." In Andrew H. Van de Ven and W. F. Joyce, eds., *Perspectives on Organization Design and Behavior.* New York: Wiley.

———, et al. 1968 "Dimensions of Organization Structure." *Administrative Science Quarterly* 13:65–105.

Rhinestein, Max 1954 *Max Weber on Law in Economy and Society.* New York: Simon and Schuster.

Rothschild-Whitt, Joyce 1979 "The Collectivist Organization: An Alternative to Rational Bureaucratic Models." *American Sociological Review* 44:50–527.

Tocqueville, Alexis de (1877) 1955 *L'ancien régime and the French Revolution,* J. P. Mayer and A. P. Kerr, eds. Garden City, N.Y.: Doubleday.

Udy, Stanley H. Jr. 1959 " 'Bureaucracy' and 'Rationality' in Weber's Organization Theory." *American Sociological Review* 24:591–595.

Weber, Max 1946 *From Max Weber: Essays in Sociology,* H. H. Gerth and C. W. Mills, eds. London: Oxford University Press.

——— 1947 *The Theory of Social and Economic Organization,* A. M. Henderson and T. Parsons, eds. Glencoe, Ill.: Free Press.

——— 1978 *Economy and Society: An Outline of Interpretive Sociology,* Guenther Roth and Claus Wittich, eds. Berkeley: University of California Press.

– DAVID G. NICKINOVICH

C

CAPITALISM

Sociology has no complete, formal consensus on a specific definition of capitalism. The discipline of sociology itself arose as an attempt to understand and explain the emergence and nature of modern capitalist societies. Sociology's founding theorists were very much concerned with the development of capitalism. Émile Durkheim sought to find the bases of new forms of morality and social solidarity in the division of labor, which capitalism both expanded and accelerated (Durkheim 1984). Karl Marx, of course, spent his adult life analyzing and criticizing capitalist society. Marx's project was guided by his hope and expectation that capitalism would be displaced as history moved toward a socialist, and then communist, future. Max Weber, too, devoted considerable attention to the origins of modern capitalism and the historically specific character of Western society under capitalist expansion. Contemporary sociology's treatment of capitalism is grounded in the works of these theorists. The works of Marx and Weber, insofar as they more explicitly focused attention on the dynamics of capitalism, provide a point of departure for discussing modern sociology's approaches to capitalism.

The term *capitalism* is sometimes used to refer to the entire social structure of a capitalist society. Unless otherwise indicated, it is used here with specific reference to a form of economy to which multiple social institutions are effectively bound in relatively compatible ways. Weber used the term *capitalism* in a very general way: 'wealth used to gain profit in commerce' (Weber 1976, p. 48). This understanding of capitalism permits the discovery of capitalism in a wide variety of social and historical settings. Weber describes this general form of capitalism in traditional India and China, ancient Babylon, Egypt, and Rome and in medieval and modern Europe. However, Weber also constructs a more specific typology that pertains to the form that capitalism has taken in more contemporary Western society. This form of capitalism is referred to as modern, or Western, capitalism. In *The Protestant Ethic and the Spirit of Capitalism,* Weber (1958 pp. 21–22) contends that this is "a very different form of capitalism which has appeared nowhere else" and that it is unique in its rational "organization of formally free labor." Other important characteristics of modern capitalism, such as the separation of business from the household and rational bookkeeping, derive their significance from this peculiar organization of labor. In this emphasis on the importance of free labor, or the creation of a labor market, Weber's definition of capitalism moves much closer to Marx's use of the term.

Laborers are compelled to sell their labor by the "whip of hunger."

For Marx, it is the creation of a market for human labor that is the essence of capitalism. Marx wrote that capitalism can "spring into life only when the owner of the means of production and subsistence meets in the market with the free laborer selling his labor power" (Marx, quoted in Sweezy 1970 pp. 56–57). The emergence of the free laborer represents the destruction of other noncapitalist economic forms. Feudal or slave economies, for example, are not characterized by the recognized right of laborers to sell their own labor power as a commodity. Simple commodity production, or economies in which laborers own their own means of production (tools, equipment, etc.), are not characterized by the need for laborers to sell their labor power as a commodity. In the latter case, Weber concurs with Marx that this freedom is only formal since such laborers are compelled to sell their labor by the "whip of hunger."

The sociological conception of capitalism also varies with particular theoretical understandings of the nature of history. Marxists, guided by an evolutionlike vision of history, tend to see capitalism as a stage in humanity's progressive movement to a communist future. In this manner, Marxist sociology also often refers to various phases of capitalism. Wright (1978 pp. 168–169), for example, describes six stages of capitalist development: primitive accumulation, manufacture, machinofacture, monopoly capital, advanced monopoly capital, and state-directed monopoly capitalism. The implicit assumptions of law-like forces at work in the historical process are evident in the Marxist confidence that capitalism, like all previous socioeconomic orders, will eventually be destroyed by the internal contradictions it generates. References to the current stage of capitalism as "late capitalism" (e.g., Mandel 1978), for instance, reveal a belief in the inevitability of capitalism's demise.

The Weberian tradition, on the other hand, rejects the assumption of history's governance by "iron laws." This leads to a recognition of various types of capitalism but without the presumption that capitalism must eventually be eliminated. The Weberian tradition discovers in the history of Western capitalism a process of rationalization toward depersonalization, improved monetary calculability, increased specialization, and greater technical control over nature as well as over persons (Brubaker 1984). However, while the Weberian tradition can expect the *probability* of continued capitalist rationalization, it does not predict the *inevitability* of such a course for history. It is important to note that, for Weber, a transition from capitalism to socialism would probably only further this rationalization. Such developments were seen as associated with industrial society and bureaucratic forms of domination rather than with capitalism per se.

This background permits a more detailed examination of contemporary sociology's treatment of capitalism. Already, it can be seen that sociology's understanding of capitalism is more specific than popular conceptions of capitalism as simply "free-market" or "free-enterprise" systems. This is especially so insofar as sociology focuses its attention on modern society. It is the emergence of a "free market" in human labor that sociology tends to recognize as the distinguishing characteristic of modern capitalism. For Durkheimian sociology, this market guides the normal division of labor that is the basis of social solidarity. In this view, the absolute freedom of such a market is necessary to generate the conditions of equal opportunity that are required to guarantee norms by which people come to accept capitalism's highly developed division of labor. Under conditions of a truly free labor market, the stratification system is seen as legitimate since individuals attain their position through their own achievement and not by means of some ascribed status (e.g., caste, gender, race, ethnicity, nepotism) or political patronage. For Marxian sociology, it is in this labor market that the two fundamental and opposing classes of capitalism meet: the owners of the means of production or capitalists (bourgeoisie) and the workers (proletariat). In this view, the struggle between these two classes is the dynamic force behind capitalist development. For Weberian sociology, this market for human labor is necessary for the development of the advanced and superior calculability of capitalist economic action. This calculability is, in turn, a fundamental component of the rationalization process in modern Western society.

This transformation of human labor into a commodity is the force behind both capitalism's internal dynamism as well as its outward expansion. On the one hand, capitalism is constantly driven to enhance its productivity. This compulsion of modern capitalism continuously to develop its technical capacity to produce is not driven simply by competition among capitalists but is related to the unique role that human labor plays in capitalist production. Prior to the emergence of a market for human labor, premodern forms of capitalism exhibited no such pressure constantly to revolutionize the technical means of production. Modern capitalism's dependence on human labor as a commodity, however, demands that this cost of production be kept as low as possible. First, technological development can lower the cost of labor as a commodity by vastly increasing the production of mass consumer goods. The subsequent reduction in the cost of items like food and clothing translates into reductions in the cost of wages to sustain laborers and their families. Another means to this end is automation, the creation of technology that can replace or enhance human labor. Such technological development also permits capitalists to circumvent the natural limits of the human body to labor and the tendency of laborers to organize and demand higher wages, especially important spurs to technological development in capitalist's societies characterized by a shortage of labor. However, under such conditions the capitalist's demand for profitability may limit the internal expansion of technology as a means of increasing production (i.e., capital-intensive production) in favor of an outward expansion that draws upon new sources of labor. This expansion of capitalism can take two basic forms. On the one hand, there is a drive toward proletarianization, or the inclusion of more and more of society's population segments that have previously escaped the labor market. On the other hand, there is a tendency to reach outside of the society itself toward other societies, thus incorporating ever larger regions of the world into the sphere of capitalism.

In the early development of capitalist societies, peasants are freed from feudal relations and slaves are freed from slave relations to add to the available pool of labor. This transformation is rarely a smooth one. The great revolutions in Western Europe and the U.S. Civil War forced these precapitalist classes to surrender their workers to the capitalist labor market. Another major source of labor for capitalist expansion has been independent laborers or persons who "work for themselves." Farmers who own their own land and equipment and work without hired labor are a good example of the type of self-employed producer that sociologists commonly refer to as simple commodity producers. There are other occupations in this general classification, of course. Highly skilled laborers have at times been able to retain independence from capitalist labor markets. However, capitalism has displayed a powerful capacity to bring these laborers into the sphere of capitalist, wage labor relations. For example, carpenters, mechanics, butchers, even doctors and lawyers increasingly find themselves working for wages or a salary in a capitalist firm rather than working for themselves. From time to time, the number of self-employed appears actually to rise in certain capitalist societies (Bechhofer and Elliott 1985). This is usually the result of the introduction of some new technology or new service. Sometimes persons who strongly wish to be their "own bosses" are able to take advantage of specific market conditions or are willing to sacrifice potential income to achieve this status. But clearly, if capitalist societies are examined over the course of the last 200 to 300 years, the tendency is strongly toward increased absorption of persons into the capitalist labor market.

In recent times, labor markets in nations like the United States have found another major source of labor power in women. The traditional role of homemaker impeded the inclusion of women in the labor market. That role of women within the home has changed somewhat, but the role played by women in expanding the pool of labor available to capital has increased tremendously. Ethnic minorities have often performed a similar function in expanding the size of the labor market. Succeeding waves of immigrants have frequently played an initially marginal role in the labor market, only to be gradually absorbed into more routine participation as time passes.

Capitalism's inherent expansionary tendencies also push the capitalist society to reach beyond the borders of the nation. This expansion occurs as capitalism seeks markets for its products but also in the search for raw materials and cheaper labor to produce goods for the home market. Eventually, capitalism may simply seek profitable investment outlets outside the nation of origin. Sociology has analyzed capitalism's transnational expansion with two general but conflicting theoretical approaches. Modernization theory views this expansion in a positive way, seeing it as a means by which undeveloped societies are enabled to begin the process of development that the developed societies have already achieved. This theoretical orientation has been especially important in shaping development policies directed at the "third world" by many Western governments, the World Bank, and even the United Nations (Giddens 1987).

Sociology's other basic approach to the emergence of a world-scale capitalist economy involves a more critical interpretation. This view tends to see capitalist expansion as having actually caused underdevelopment. The underdevelopment approach sees the lack of development in less-developed societies (periphery) as a consequence of systematic exploitation of their people and resources by the advanced societies (core). This process of underdevelopment is generally viewed as having occurred in three stages. The first stage, that of merchant capitalism, persisted from the sixteenth century to the late nineteenth century. Merchant capitalism, supported by military force, transferred vast amounts of wealth from the periphery to the European nations to help finance initial industrial development in what are now the advanced capitalist societies. The second stage, colonialism, persisted until about ten to fifteen years after World War II, when many colonial nations were granted formal independence. In the colonial stage, the developed societies organized economic and political institutions in the less-developed nations to serve the needs of industrial capitalism in the advanced nations. In the postcolonial period, formal political independence has been granted, but the persistent economic inequalities between developed and underdeveloped nations strongly favor the more-developed capitalist societies. Even when raw materials and finished products remain in the lesser-developed nation, the profits derived from such production are taken from the periphery and returned to the advanced core societies. Thus, the pattern of underdevelopment continues in the face of formal independence.

The shift of much industrial production to underdeveloped regions is generating a process of deindustrialization in the advanced capitalist societies.

Traditionally, much of sociology's attention to international capitalist expansion has focused on relations between nations. Increasingly, sociology is examining these matters with greater attention to relations between classes. This shift of emphasis reflects the increasing importance of the transnational corporation in recent times. The transnational corporation's greater capacity to use several international sites for component production and the shift of much industrial production to underdeveloped regions are generating a process of deindustrialization in the advanced capitalist societies. While capitalism has long been a world system, many sociologists contend that the transnational, or "stateless," corporation has significantly less commitment or loyalty to any specific nation. Capital flows ever more rapidly throughout the world, seeking the cheapest

source of labor. Modern computer technology has facilitated this trend. Asian, European, and North American capital markets are increasingly interdependent. Sociology's shift of emphasis reflects this tendency for the U.S. capitalist to have more in common, sociologically, with the Japanese or German capitalist than the U.S. investor has in common with the American worker. Sociology's new attention to the internationalization of capital may present a need for rethinking the usefulness of the nation as the typical boundary of a society. The emergence of the "new Europe" and the demise of state socialism in Eastern Europe and the USSR may also lead to a more flexible notion of what constitutes a society.

The preceding discussion has focused on capitalism as a specific form of economy that is defined by the expansion of a labor market in which propertyless workers sell their labor power for money. Capitalist societies are, of course, far more complex than this. There are a number of distinct economic forms that coexist with capitalism in both complementary and conflictual relations. The capitalist economy itself may be broken down into two basic sectors, one representing big business and one representing small business. Sociologists usually refer to these as the monopoly sector and the competitive sector. This dual economy is reflected in a segmented, or dual, labor market. Monopoly sector workers are more likely to be male, unionized, receive better wages and benefits, have greater job security, and work in a more clearly defined hierarchy of authority based on credentials. Competitive sector workers are less likely to possess strong credentials, more likely to be female, receive lower pay, work under more dangerous conditions, and work without union protection, benefits, or job security.

Noncapitalist economic forms also exist alongside this dual capitalist economy. The self-employed reflect a form distinct from modern capitalism that sociologists commonly refer to as simple commodity producers or petite bourgeoisie. These people produce goods and services (commodities) for sale on the market, but they work for themselves and use only their own labor in production. Most capitalist societies also contain cooperative economic organizations that are distinct from

Minorities often serve marginal roles in the labor market, eventually making their way into mainstream participation. (Dave G. Houser/Corbis)

capitalist enterprises. Cooperatives are commercial, nonprofit enterprises, owned and democratically controlled by the members. The nonprofit status and democratic distribution of control (one member, one vote) set cooperatives apart. The cooperative is an especially important form of economic organization for those simple commodity producers, like farmers, described above. All capitalist societies today also contain elements of socialist economy. Key social services, such as health care, and even some commodity production are provided by the state in many societies commonly recognized as capitalist. The United States is perhaps among the most resistant to this movement toward mixed economy. Yet even the United States has, to some extent, socialized education, mail delivery, libraries, police and fire protection, scientific research and technological development, transportation networks (e.g., highways, airports, urban transit), military production, industrial infrastructure provision, and so on. The mixed character of this economy is further indicated by the common practice of the government contracting capitalist firms to produce many goods and services. In a related way, the development of welfare has influenced the nature of capitalist society. The increased intervention of government into the economy has generated the notion of the welfare state. While popular conceptions of the welfare state tend to focus on the role that government plays in alleviating the impacts of poverty on individuals, sociology also recognizes that welfare reduces the cost of reproducing the commodity—labor. In this sense, welfare functions, in the long run, as a subsidy to capital. Further, many of the socialized sectors of capitalist economies function to ensure a profitable environment for capitalist firms (O'Connor 1973; Offe 1984). In many instances, such subsidization of capital is biased toward the largest corporations.

Some sociologists have contended that the rise of the large capitalist corporation, with its dispersed stock ownership and bureaucratic form of organization, has eroded the power of individual capitalists to control the corporation in which they have invested their capital. Instead, it is argued, bureaucratic managers have gained control over corporate capital. Such managers are thought to be relatively free of the drive to maximize profits and are willing to accept average rates of profit. In this way, the ruthless character of earlier forms of capitalism are seen as giving way to a capitalism that is managed with broader interests in mind. Further, the dispersal of ownership and control is said to eliminate the misuse of capital in the interests of an elite and wealthy minority. This "managerialist" position complements pluralist political theory by providing greater authority for institutions of representative democracy to control the allocation of society's resources.

This view is challenged in a variety of ways. Other sociologists contend that while management may have gained some formal independence, its job requires devotion to profit maximization, and its performance is assessed on this criteria. In this view, the larger companies' executives and owners are able to use interlocking directorates and their common class background (e.g., elite schools, private clubs, policy-planning organizations) to minimize price competition and thus sustain high profit levels. Others argue that those informal ties are of less consequence than their common dependency on banks. In this view, banks, or finance capital, play a disproportionately powerful role in centralizing control over the allocation of capital resources. This position strongly opposes the managerialist arguments and those who envision an independent corporate elite whose power lies in the control of corporate bureaucracies rather than in personal wealth (Glasberg and Schwartz 1983). Further, to the extent that it is valid, this argument is particularly important given the increasing internationalization of capital discussed above, since a great deal of that development has occurred in the sphere of finance capital.

The tremendous inequality of wealth generated by modern capitalism impedes the possibility of political equality.

These sorts of arguments reflect an important shift in sociology's understanding of the relationship between capitalism and democracy. Sociology's Enlightenment roots provided a traditional legacy of viewing capitalism and democracy as intertwined in the process of modernization. While this parallel development is certainly recognizable in early forms of modern capitalism, more recent forms of capitalism call into question the extent to which capitalism and democracy are inevitably bound together. Indeed, recent works suggest that capitalism and democracy are now opposed to one another (e.g., Piven and Cloward 1982). This view holds that the tremendous inequality of wealth generated by modern capitalism impedes the possibility of political equality. Even conservative writers (e.g., Huntington 1975) have noted the problematic relationship between contemporary capitalism and democracy, suggesting a retrenchment of democratic forms in defense of capitalism. The future of capitalism will be shaped by this tension with democracy, but that tension itself is located in an increasingly global economy. At the moment, the politics of capitalist society seem to lag behind the economic changes. The individual is increasingly pressured to sell his or her labor as a commodity on a world market, yet at the same time that individual remains a citizen, not of the world, but of the nation. The transnational capitalist enterprise and the flow of capital, on the other hand, are ever more free of such national borders.

BIBLIOGRAPHY

Bechhofer, F., and B. Elliott 1985 "The Petite Bourgeoisie in Late Capitalism." *Annual Review of Sociology* 11:181–207.

Brubaker, Rogers 1984 *The Limits of Rationality.* London: Allen and Unwin.

Christensen, Kathleen 1987 "Women and Contingent Work." *Social Policy* 17:15–18.

Durkheim, Emile 1984 *The Division of Labor in Society.* New York: Free Press.

Giddens, Anthony 1987 *Sociology: A Brief but Critical Introduction,* 2d ed. New York: Harcourt Brace Jovanovich.

Glasberg, Davita Silfen, and Michael Schwartz 1983 "Ownership and Control of Corporations." *Annual Review of Sociology* 9:311–332.

Huntington, Samuel P. 1975 "The United States." In Michael Crozier, Samuel P. Huntington, and Joji Watanuki, eds., *The Crisis of Democracy: Report on the Governability of Democracies to the Trilateral Commission.* New York: New York University Press.

Mandel, Ernest 1978 *Late Capitalism.* London: Verso.

O'Connor, James 1973 *The Fiscal Crisis of the State.* New York: St. Martin's Press.

Offe, Claus 1984 *Contradictions of the Welfare State.* Cambridge, Mass.: M.I.T. Press.

Piven, Frances Fox, and Richard A. Cloward 1982 *The New Class War.* New York: Pantheon Books.

Sweezy, Paul M. 1970 *The Theory of Capitalist Development.* New York: Monthly Review Press.

Weber, Max 1958 *The Protestant Ethic and the Spirit of Capitalism.* Talcott Parsons, trans. New York: Scribners.

——— 1976 *The Agrarian Sociology of Ancient Civilizations.* R. I. Frank, trans. London: New Left Books.

Wright, Erik Olin 1978 *Class, Crisis, and the State.* London: New Left Books.

– PATRICK H. MOONEY

CASTE AND CLASS

The term "caste" is often used to denote large-scale kinship groups that are hierarchically organized within a rigid system of stratification. In such a system a person's social position is determined by birth, and marital connection outside one's caste is prohibited. Sociologists who study stratification frequently contrast caste systems with class systems. In class systems one's opportunities in life, at least in theory, are determined by one's actions, allowing a degree of individual mobility that is not possible in caste systems.

Caste systems are to be found among the Hindus in India and among societies where groups are ranked and closed. Early Hindu literary classics describe a society divided into four *varnas:* Brahman (poet-priest), Kshatriya (warrior-chief), Vaishya (traders), and Shudras (menials, servants). The *varnas* formed ranked categories characterized by differential access to spiritual and material privileges. It excluded the Untouchables, who were despised because they engaged in occupations that were considered unclean and polluting.

The *varna* model of social ranking persisted throughout the Hindu subcontinent for over a millennia. The basis of caste ranking was the sacred concept of purity and pollution with Brahmans, because they were engaged in priestly duties considered ritually pure, while those who engaged in manual labor and with ritually polluting objects were regarded as impure. Usually those who had high ritual status also had economic and political power. Beliefs about pollution generally regulated all relations between castes. Members were not allowed to marry outside their caste; there were strict rules about the kind of food and drink one could accept and from what castes; and there were restrictions on approaching and visiting members of another caste. Violations of these rules entailed purifactory rites and sometimes expulsion from the caste (Ghurye 1969).

The *varna* scheme refers only to broad categories of society, for in reality the small endogamous group or subcaste (*jati*) forms the unit of social organization. In each linguistic area there are about two thousand such subcastes. The status of the subcaste, its cultural traditions, and its numerical strength vary from one region to another, often from village to village.

Field studies of local caste structures revealed that the caste system was more dynamic than the earlier works by social scientists had indicated. For example, at the local level, the position of the middle castes, between the Brahmans and the Untouchables, is often not very clear. This is because castes were often able to change their ritual position after they had acquired economic and political power. A low caste would adopt the Brahminic way of life, such as vegetarianism and teetotalism, and in several generations attain a higher position in the hierarchy. Upward mobility occurred for an entire caste, not for an individual or the family. This process of upward mobility, known as Sanskritization (Srinivas 1962), did not, however, affect the movement of castes at the extremes. Brahmans in most parts of the country were found at the top, and Untouchables everywhere occupied a degrading status because of their economic dependency and low ritual status.

The operation of this hierarchical society was justified with reference to traditional Hindu religious beliefs about *samsara* (reincarnation) and *karma* (quality of actions). A person's position in this life was determined by his or her actions in previous lives. Persons who were born in a Brahman family must have performed good deeds in their earlier lives. Being born a Shudra or an Untouchable was punishment for the sinful acts committed in previous lives.

Some scholars (Leach 1960; Dumont 1970) saw the caste system as a cooperative, inclusive arrangement where each caste formed an integral part of the local socioeconomic system and had its special privileges. In a *jajmani* system, as this arrangement between castes was known, a village was controlled by a dominant caste, which used its wealth, numerical majority, and high status to dominate the other castes in the village. Most other castes provided services to this caste. Some worked on the land as laborers and tenants. Other castes provided goods and services to the landowning households and to other castes. A village would thus have a potter, blacksmith, carpenter, tailor, shoemaker, barber,

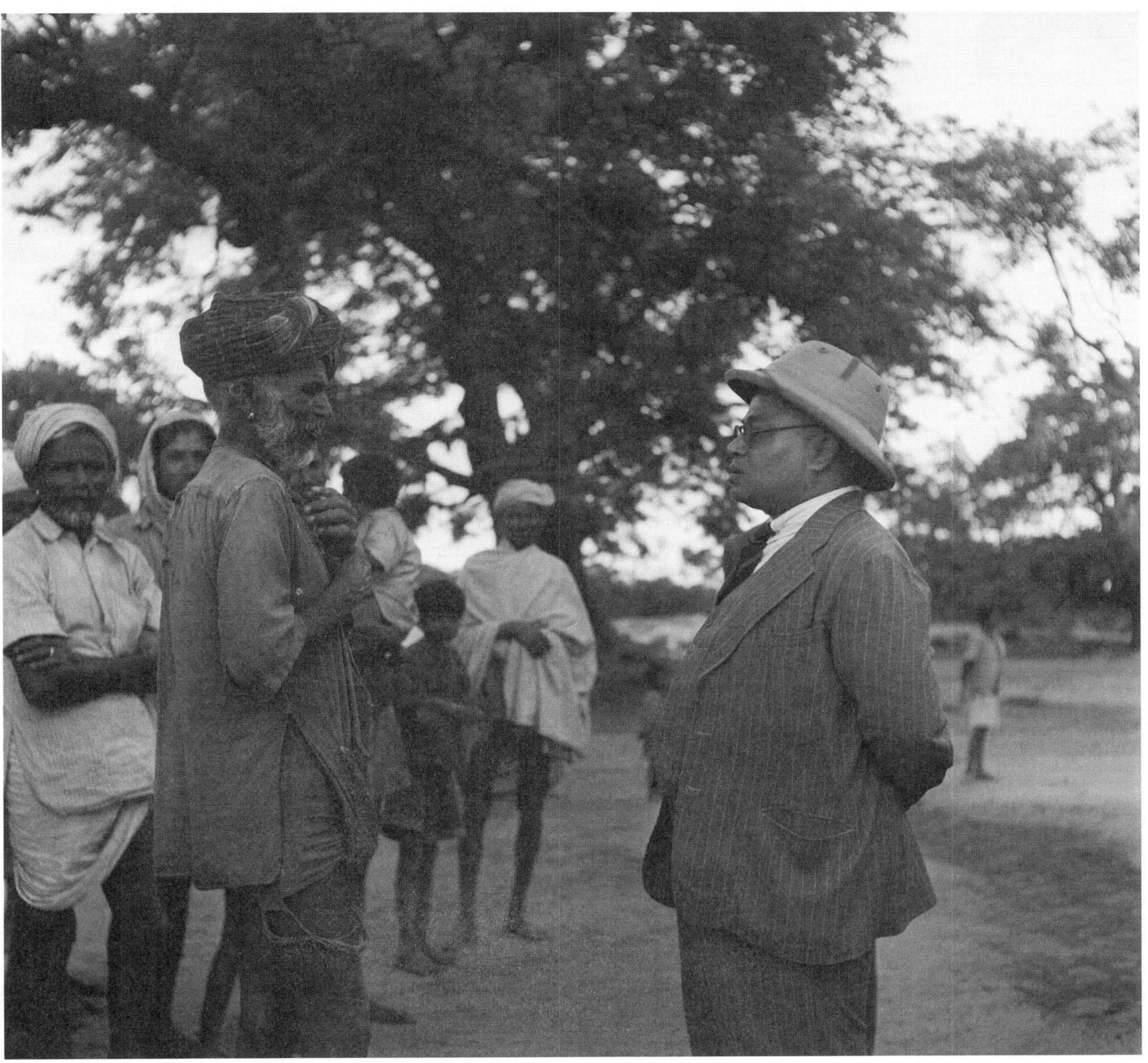

In a caste system, such as that of the Hindus of India, a person's social position is determined by birth. Hindus of the lowest class, such as this man in the turban, are known as Untouchables. (Bradley Smith/Corbis)

sweeper, and a washer-man, with each caste specializing in different occupations. These were hereditary occupations. In return for their services castes would be paid in kind, usually farm produce. These patron-client relationships continued for generations, and it was the religious duty of the *jajman* (patron) to take care of others.

Relations between castes are now governed by rules of competitive politics.

Although the system did provide security for all, it was essentially exploitative and oppressive (Berreman 1981; Beidelman 1959; Freeman 1986), particularly for the Untouchables, who were confined to menial, despised jobs, working as sweepers, gutter and latrine cleaners, scavengers, watchmen, farm laborers, and curers of hides. They were denied access to Hindu temples; were not allowed to read religious Sanskrit books and remained illiterate; could not use village wells and tanks; were forced to live in settlements outside the village; and were forbidden to enter the residential areas of the upper castes.

Changes in the Caste System

British rule profoundly affected the Indian social order. The ideas of Western culture; the opening of English educational institutions; the legal system, which introduced the principle of equality before the law; and the new economic activities and the kind of employment they generated all brought new opportunities for greater advancement. Although these new developments resulted in greater mobility and opened doors for even the low castes, those castes that benefited most were the ones already in advantageous positions. Thus, Brahmans with a tradition of literacy were the first to avail themselves of English education and occupy administrative positions in the colonial bureaucracy.

The spread of communications enabled local subcastes to link together and form caste associations. These organizations, although initially concerned with raising the caste status in terms of Brahmanical values, later sought educational, economic, and social benefits from the British (Rudolph and Rudolph 1960). When the colonial authorities widened political participation by allowing elections in some provinces, castes organized to make claims for political representation. In some regions, such as the South, the non-Brahman castes were successful in restricting entry of Brahmans in educational institutions and administrative services.

To assuage the fears of communities about upper-caste Hindu rule in independent India and also to weaken the nationalist movement, the British granted special political representation to some groups such as the Untouchables. They had become politically mobilized under the leadership of Dr. B. R. Ambedkar and had learned, like other castes and communities, the use of political means to secure status and power (Zelliot 1970).

After the country became independent from British rule in 1947, the Indian leaders hoped that legislative and legal measures would reorder an entrenched social structure. A new Constitution was adopted, which abolished untouchability and prohibited discrimination in public places. In addition, special places were reserved for Untouchables in higher educational institutions, government services, and in the lower houses of the central and state legislatures.

What progress has the country made toward improving the lives of the Untouchables, who form nearly 16 percent of the population? Has the traditional caste system disintegrated?

The movement from a traditional to a modern economy—increase in educational facilities; expansion of white-collar jobs, especially in the state sector; expansion of the transportation and communication networks; increase in agricultural production (known as the Green Revolution)—has had a significant impact on the institution of caste. However, political factors have been equally if not more important in producing changes in the caste system. One is the democratic electoral system. The other is the state's impact on intercaste relations through its policy of preferences for selected disadvantaged castes.

The close association between caste and traditional occupation is breaking down because of the expansion of modern education and the urban-industrial sector. In India, an urban middle class has formed whose members are drawn from various caste groups. This has reduced the structural and cultural differences between castes, as divisions based on income, education, and occupation become more important than caste cleavages for social and economic purposes. The reduction, however, is most prominent among the upper socioeconomic strata—the urban, Western-educated, professional, and higher-income groups—whose members share a common life-style (Beteille 1969).

For most Indians, especially those who live in rural areas (73 percent of the Indian population is still rural), caste factors are an integral part of their daily lives. In many parts of the country Scheduled Castes (the common term for Untouchables now) are not allowed inside temples and cannot use village water wells. Marriages are generally arranged between persons of the same caste.

With the support of government scholarships and reservation benefits, a small proportion of Scheduled Castes has managed to gain entry into the middle class—as schoolteachers, clerks, bank tellers, typists, and government officials. Reservation of seats in the legislature has made the political arena somewhat more accessible, although most politicians belonging to the Scheduled Caste community have little say in party matters and government policymaking. The majority of Scheduled Caste members remain landless agricultural laborers, powerless, desperately poor, and illiterate.

Modern economic forces are changing the rural landscape. The increase in cash-crop production, which has made grain payments in exchange for services unprofitable; the introduction of mechanized farming, which has displaced manual labor; the preference for manufactured goods over handmade ones; and the migration to cities and to prosperous agricultural areas for work and better wages have all weakened the traditional patron-client ties and the security it provided. The Scheduled Castes and other low castes have been particularly affected as the other sectors of the economy have not grown fast enough to absorb them.

The rural social structure has been transformed in yet another way. The dominant castes are no longer from the higher castes but belong to the middle and lower peasant castes—the profit-maximizing "bullock capitalists" (Rudolph and Rudolph 1987) who were the chief beneficiaries of land reform and state subsidies to the agricultural sector (Blair 1980; Brass 1985). They have displaced the high-caste absentee landlords, who have moved to cities and taken up modern occupations.

Modern political institutions have also brought about changes in the traditional leadership and power structure of local communities. Relations between castes are now governed by rules of competitive politics, and leaders are selected for their political skills and not because they are members of a particular caste. The role of caste varies at different levels of political action. At the village and district levels caste loyalties are effectively used for political mobilization. But at the state and national levels, caste factors become less important for political parties because one caste rarely commands a majority at these levels.

In recent years there have been numerous instances of confrontations between the middle peasant castes and Scheduled Castes in rural areas. Violence and repression against Scheduled Castes has increased as they have begun to assert themselves. With the support of Communist and Dalit movements (the latter a movement formed of militant Scheduled Castes), they are demanding better wages, the right to till government-granted land, and the use of village wells.

In urban areas, caste conflict has mainly centered around the issue of "reservation." The other backward castes (who belong mainly to the Shudra caste and form approximately 50 percent of the country's population) have demanded from the government benefits similar to those available to Scheduled Castes in government service and educational institutions. Under electoral pressures the state governments have extended these reservation benefits to the other backward castes, leading to discontent among the upper castes.

Extension of preferential treatment from Scheduled Castes to the more numerous and in some states somewhat better-off backward castes has not only created great resentment among the upper castes but also has reduced public support for the policy of special benefits for the Scheduled Castes. In cities they have often been victims during anti-reservation agitations. That this is happening at the very time when the preferential programs have gradually succeeded in improving the educational and economic conditions for Scheduled Castes is not accidental (Sheth 1987).

As education and the meaning of the vote and the ideas of equality and justice spread, the rural and urban areas will witness severe intercaste conflicts. What is significant, however, is that these conflicts are not over caste beliefs and values, but like conflicts elsewhere between ethnic groups, have to do with control over political and economic resources.

Caste in Other Societies

Do castes exist outside India? Is it a unique social phenomenon distinct from other systems of social stratification? Opinion among scholars is divided over this issue. Castelike systems have been observed in the South Asian subcontinent and beyond (in Japan, Africa, Iran, and Polynesia). Caste has also been used to describe the systems of racial stratification in South Africa and the southern United States.

Those who focus on its religious foundations argue that caste is a particular species of structural organization found only in the Indian world.

Whether the term *caste* is applicable to societies outside the South Asian region depends on how the term is defined. Those who focus on its religious foundations argue that caste is a particular species of structural organization found only in the Indian world. Louis Dumont (1970), for example, contends that caste systems are noncomparable to systems of racial stratification because of the differences in ideology—one based on the ideology of hierarchy, the other on an equalitarian ideology.

Others, such as Gerald Berreman (1981) argue, that cultural differences notwithstanding, both systems are alike in their structure and in their effect on the life experiences of those most oppressed. Recently, scholars (Weiner 1983) have shown that similarities also exist in the political consequences of preferential policies that culturally distinct societies such as the United States and India have adopted to reduce group disparities.

[See also Social Stratification.]

BIBLIOGRAPHY

Beidelman, T. O. 1959 *A Comparative Analysis of the Jajmani System.* Monograph VII of the Association of Asian Studies. Locust Valley, NY: J. J. Augustin.

Berreman, Gerald 1981 *Caste and Other Inequities.* Delhi: Manohar.

Beteille, André 1969 *Caste: Old and New.* Bombay: Asia Publishing House.

Blair, Harry W. 1980 "Rising Kulaks and Backward Castes in Bihar: Social Change in the Late 1970's." *Economic and Political Weekly,* 12 (Jan.): 64–73.

Brass, Paul R. 1983 *Caste, Faction and Party in Indian Politics: Faction and Party,* vol. 1. Delhi: Chanakya Publications.

——— 1985 *Caste, Faction and Party in Indian Politics: Election Studies,* vol. 2. Delhi: Chanakya Publications.

Breman, Jan 1974 *Patronage and Exploitation.* Berkeley: University of California Press.

Dumont, Louis 1970 *Homo Hierarchicus.* Chicago: University of Chicago Press.

Freeman, James M. 1986 "The Consciousness of Freedom among India's Untouchables." In D. K. Basu and R. Sisson, eds., *Social and Economic Development in India.* Beverly Hills, Calif.: Sage.

Galanter, Marc 1984 *Competing Equalities: Law and the Backward Classes in India.* Berkeley: University of California Press.

Ghurye, G. S. 1969 *Caste and Race in India,* 5th ed. Bombay: Popular Prakashan.

Gould, Harold A. 1987 *The Hindu Caste System: The Sacralization of a Social Order.* Delhi: Chanakya.

Hutton, J. H. 1961 *Caste in India,* 4th ed. Oxford: Oxford University Press.

Kolenda, Pauline 1978 *Caste in Contemporary India: Beyond Organic Solidarity.* Menlo Park, Calif.: Benjamin/Cummings.

Kothari, Rajni 1970 *Caste in Indian Politics.* New Delhi: Orient Longman.

Leach, E. R. (ed.) 1960 *Aspects of Caste in South India, Ceylon, and North-West Pakistan.* Cambridge: Cambridge University Press.

Mahar, J. M. (ed.) 1972 *The Untouchables in Contemporary India.* Tucson: University of Arizona Press.

Rudolph, L. I., and S. H. Rudolph 1960 "The Political Role of India's Caste Associations." *Pacific Affairs* 33(1):5–22.

——— 1987 *In Pursuit of Laxmi.* Chicago: University of Chicago Press.

Sheth, D. L. 1987 "Reservation Policy Revisited." *Economic and Political Weekly,* vol. 22, Nov. 14.

Srinivas, M. N. 1962 *Caste in Modern India.* London: Asia Publishing House.

——— 1969 *Social Change in Modern India.* Berkeley: University of California Press.

Weiner, Myron 1983 "The Political Consequences of Preferential Policies: A Comparative Perspective." *Comparative Politics* 16(1):35–52.

Zelliot, Eleanor 1970 "Learning the Uses of Political Means: The Mahars of Maharashtra." In Rajni Kothari, ed., *Caste in Indian Politics.* Delhi: Orient Longman.

– RITA JALALI

CENSUS

A census is a procedure for establishing the size and characteristics of a total population by attempting to count each of the individuals in the population. A census of a school, church, or other local organization may be quite easy, requiring only a review of membership records and a count of the total number of names. A national census, by contrast, requires attention to an array of definitional issues and the development of elaborate procedures. Planning, execution, and tabulation of the 1990 U.S. Census of Population extended over more than ten years. Hundreds of thousands of people were employed at a cost of nearly three-billion dollars.

A modern national census is "the total process of collecting, compiling, evaluating, analysing and publishing or otherwise disseminating demographic, economic, and social data pertaining, at a specified time, to all persons in a country" (United Nations 1980, p. 2). The United Nations encourages its members to take regular censuses and provides technical assistance. It also publishes an annual demographic yearbook that reports census data and other population information for many countries.

The actual enumeration for a national population census is usually spread over a period of weeks or months, but an attempt is made to record circumstances as of the census day (April 1 for the 1990 U.S. census). In some censuses, persons are recorded in their legal or usual place of residence (a *de jure enumeration*). The Bible reports that a census decree issued by the government in Rome ordered that persons be counted and taxed in their home towns; therefore, for example, Joseph and his pregnant wife, Mary, traveled from Nazareth to Bethlehem. Other censuses record people where they are on the census day (a *de facto enumeration*). Whatever residency rule is followed, a variety of special circumstances must be anticipated and fieldworkers trained to record people appropriately.

A few examples from the 1990 U.S. census illustrate problems that arise in fieldwork and later tallying. On a designated night in March, persons in hotels and rooming houses filled in special census forms indicating their usual place of residence; these forms were later compared to the regular schedules to confirm that these persons were properly reported at their homes. College students, even if they happened to be at home or on spring break when enumerated, were recorded as living in their college residences. Citizens working in another country for the U.S. government, and their families, were included in state population counts for reapportionment purposes but were otherwise reported separately as nonresident population.

The United States conducts many regular censuses, including those on population, housing, business firms, agriculture, and local governments. Each census provides information on the particular population at a specified time. Other parts of the statistical system provide information on the flows of units into and out of the population. For the U.S. population, people are added by birth and immigration and subtracted by death and emigration. Information based on birth and death registrations is of high quality, whereas information on immigration and emigration, both legal and illegal, is grossly deficient.

Some countries keep population registries, continuous records of where their people live and of some of their characteristics. Citizens in the United States are wary of governmental dossiers. The U.S. Census Bureau therefore conducts a series of regular and special sample surveys to provide population information between ten-year-censuses.

The Southern states wanted to increase their representation in Congress by including slaves in the population count.

When a country takes a population census, there is great public interest in the official total. Two very large countries reported new census totals in 1990: for the United States, 249,632,692; for China, 1,133,682,501. The total count is one tiny part of the results of a modern census. Censuses provide information on the population sizes of states, counties, cities, villages, and other administrative units. Censuses also record important characteristics about individuals, such as age, sex, relationship to others living in the same household, educational level, occupation, and so on. The 1990 U.S. census form asked seven questions about each person and twenty-six additional questions of a sample of one of every six persons. Recording and this information for the entire country and for the thousands of cities and other subareas results in the production of hundreds of printed reports and the equivalent of millions of additional pages in computer-readable files.

In the United States, the idea for a regular census emerged during debates about the problem of creating a representative form of government. The U.S. Constitution (Article I, Section 2) directs that membership in the House of Representatives be based on population: "The actual enumeration shall be made within three years after the first meeting of the Congress of the United States, and within every subsequent term of ten years, in such manner as they shall by law direct."

The questions asked in a census reflect political and social issues of the day and often provoke spirited debate. For example, a divisive issue for the Constitutional Convention was how to deal with slavery. The Southern states wanted to increase their representation in Congress by including slaves in the population count. A compromise (Article I, Section 2) provided that: "Representatives . . . shall be apportioned among the several states . . . according to their respective numbers, which shall be determined by adding to the whole number of free persons, excluding Indians not taxed, three-fifths of all other persons."

The 1790 census was modest in scope. Assistants to federal marshals made lists of households, recording for each the number of persons in five categories: free white males over sixteen and under sixteen, free white females, other free persons, and slaves (Anderson 1988, p. 13).

The 1790 census and the next five decennial censuses were conducted with little central organization or statistical expertise. A temporary federal census office was established to conduct the 1850 census. The individual rather than the household became the focus of the enumeration, and the content of the census was expanded to include occupation, country or state of birth, and other items. Experienced statisticians were consulted, and the United States participated in the first International. Statistical Congress in 1853.

The conduct of U.S. censuses became increasingly difficult. Population size was growing rapidly and census content was expanding. For the 1890 census, the temporary census office became one of the largest federal agencies, employing 47,000 enumerators and 3,000 clerical workers. To help with the enormous task of tallying the data from the census forms, census officials encouraged the work of a young inventor, Herman Hollerith, who developed an electrical tabulating machine. His punched-card system proved effective in census operations and later contributed to the growth of the IBM company.

A permanent census office was established in 1902, and an increasingly professional staff assumed responsibility for the population censuses and a broad range of other statistical activities. During the early decades of the twentieth century, massive immigrations from Europe were of continuing political interest, and census figures were important evidence in debates over the need for immigration controls.

Deficiencies in the federal statistical systems became apparent during the 1930s as the nation tried to assess the effects of the Great Depression and to analyze an array of new programs and policies. Social scientists in several federal agencies supported expansion of the social and economic content of the 1940 and later population censuses. New questions in 1940 asked about participation in the labor force, earnings, education, migration (place of residence in 1935), and fertility. A housing census was paired with the population census to provide information about housing values and rents, mortgages, condition of dwellings, water supply, and other property issues. Greatly expanded population and housing information was provided for subareas of large cities.

Governmental statistical agencies are often rather set in their ways, concerned with continuity rather than innovation and removed from the higher levels of policymaking. For several decades beginning in the late 1930s, the U.S. Bureau of the Census was extraordinarily creative. Social scientists and statisticians employed by the Bureau were active in research and scholarly publication and played leadership roles in professional organizations. Bureau personnel pioneered in development of the theory and practice of population sampling. To accommodate large increases in content and geographic scope of the 1940 census, the census questionnaire was divided into two parts. A set of basic questions was asked of everyone, while a set of supplementary questions was asked of a one-in-twenty sample. Subsequent U.S. censuses have continued to use sampling, as with the one-in-six long-form version of the 1990 questionnaire. Sampling theory was also applied to the development of periodic sample surveys to provide timely information between censuses.

As they had in 1890, the processing needs of the Bureau led it in 1950 to participate actively in the development and utilization of a new technology, the computer. In later censuses, the schedules were microfilmed and optically scanned for direct input of information (without names and addresses) into a computer for error checking, coding, and tabulating. In the 1960s, the Bureau began issuing special computer-readable files of census data, and these files enabled scholars, policy analysts, and others to conduct their own analyses of population information without relying solely on the Bureau's printed volumes.

Through 1950, census taking in the United States was accomplished almost entirely by personal interview. By 1990, most census questionnaires were distributed and returned to the Bureau by mail, with telephone follow-up replacing many personal visits.

The questions asked in each census have changed more slowly than the procedures. There are three reasons for this. First, keeping the same topics and the same wordings of questions helps the government measure change from one census to the next. This reason appeals more strongly to university researchers and government policy analysts than it does to those policymakers whose attention is focused mainly on current programs and next year's budget. Second, the census is an expensive and visible tool. A lengthy review process confronts any agency that seeks to add, delete, or alter a question. Both the executive branch and the Congress must approve the final census schedule and other aspects of the census process. For example, a question on pet ownership has been regularly proposed but rejected

Through the 1950 United States census, census takers interviewed residents in person. By the 1990 census, residents answered questionnaires that they received and returned by mail. (UPI/Corbis-Bettmann)

on two grounds: There is no compelling governmental interest in such a question, and, even if there were, separate sample surveys would be more appropriate than the census. A third reason the content of the questionnaire changes little is that citizen cooperation is needed. The Census Bureau thinks that a longer questionnaire would be burdensome and discourage people from completing and returning the forms. The Bureau resists additions to the schedule unless there are compensating cuts. Proponents of new topics and questions must overcome the proponents of topics and questions that were on the previous census. This competition requires extensive lobbying and mobilization of support from federal agencies, congressional committees, lobbyists, and other interest groups.

One domain of growing national policy interest that has an increasing presence on the U.S. census schedules is race and ethnicity. Special tallies were made from the 1950 and 1960 censuses of persons with Spanish surnames, but only for five southwestern states. Beginning in 1970, and with increased elaboration in later censuses, persons were asked if they were of Spanish/Hispanic origin. A contrasting approach was taken by the United Kingdom. Controversy about a proposed ethnic minority question led to its omission from the 1981 census schedule, thus hindering factual analyses of their increasingly diverse population.

Reform of U.S. immigration laws in the mid-1960s led to more immigration and a change in dominant national origins from Europe to several Asian and Latin American countries. The national surge of interest in ethinicity led to a new question asking everyone to report an ancestry or ethnic origin (such as German, Italian, Afro-American, etc.). Other questions asked year of immigration, language spoken at home, and, for those not using English at home, how well the person spoke English.

The most contentious issue about recent U.S. censuses is not their content but their accuracy. Concern with census undercount arises from the growth in federal, state, and local programs that distribute funds based in part on census information. The recipients of those funds, including states, cities, and many classes of persons represented by interest groups, have become more aware of how they may be affected by inaccuracies in the census. The word *undercount* has acquired symbolic status as an indicator of being shortchanged or deprived of rights.

A second reason for interest in the accuracy of the census is the success of the Bureau in publicizing the census. To encourage citizen cooperation, the Bureau works hard to make each decennial census a mass media event. It has succeeded to the degree that the media report not only the official press releases but also their own investigations of procedural difficulties and interviews with those opposed to or upset by the census.

A third reason for increased concern with undercount is increased knowledge of census accuracy. President George Washington commented about the first census that "our real numbers will exceed, greatly, the official returns of them; because the religious scruples of some would not allow them to give in their lists; the fears of others that it was intended as the foundation of a tax induced them to conceal or diminish theirs; and through the indolence of the people and the negligence of many of the Officers, numbers are omitted" (quoted in Scott 1968, p. 20). Lacking methods for determining "our real numbers," census results, whatever their apparent shortcomings, have remained the agreed-upon basis for legislative reapportionment.

The word undercount *has acquired symbolic status as an indicator of being shortchanged or deprived of rights.*

Studies comparing birth certificates and other lists of names to the persons reported in the 1940 census documented a sizable net undercount. To provide more information on census coverage and accuracy, a postenumeration survey was conducted following the 1950 census using specially selected and closely supervised enumerators. One finding from the resurvey was that the undercount of infants in the census did not arise, as had been thought, from a tendency for new parents to forget to mention a new baby to the census enumerator. The problem, rather, was that many young couples and single parents had irregular and difficult-to-find living arrangements, and entire households were missed by census enumerators. Based on this and related findings, much effort has been given in subsequent censuses to precensus and postcensus review of lists of dwelling units.

Improved techniques of demographic analysis have led to new estimates of net undercount, first by demographers outside the Census Bureau and finally by Bureau staff (e.g., Fay, Passel, and Robinson 1988). The infant who was missed in the 1940 census may have been listed in the registry of births during 1939, appeared as a ten-year-old in the 1950 census, been missed as a twenty-year-old in 1960, and been recorded at ages thirty, forty, and fifty in later censuses. Estimates are made by analyzing the numbers of persons of each age, sex, and race in succesive censuses and using plausibly adjusted information on births and deaths by age, sex, and race. Based on demographic analysis, the estimated undercount was about 5.6 percent in 1940, 1.4 percent in 1980 (Fay, Passel, and Robinson 1988, Table 3.2) and 1.8 percent in 1990.

The percentage net undercount understates the total coverage error in the census because omissions of some transients, homeless persons, families doubled up with relatives, and others are accompanied by double counting of persons such as college students counted correctly at a dormitory but also reported improperly as living with parents.

If the net undercount were uniform for all population groups and geographic regions, it would not affect equity in the distribution of congressional seats or public funds. But census errors are not uniform. The estimates for 1980 show net undercounts exceeding 10 percent for adult black males and small net overcounts for some age and race groups.

In 1980, the mayor of Detroit, the City of Detroit, New York City, and others sued the federal government, alleging violation of their constitutional rights to equal representation and fair distribution of federal funds (Mitroff, Mason, and Barabba 1983). The issue remained alive through the 1980s, and the federal government agreed to analyze early 1990 census results and conduct methodological investigations and then decide whether to produce a set of officially adjusted 1990 results (Robey 1989).

One of the difficulties in the U.S. undercount debates arises from confusion between the ideal of the census as a true count and the reality of the census as a procedure for obtaining a population estimate. There is, no feasible method for determining with perfect accuracy the size and characteristics of any large population. A national census is a set of procedures adopted in a political, economic, and social context to produce population figures.

Every nation confronts political and social problems with census taking. Many regularly scheduled censuses have been postponed or abandoned because of international conflict. The United States and the United Kingdom have canceled plans for mid-decade censuses because of national budget constraints. West Germany was unable to take a census for several years because of citizen fears about invasions of privacy (Starr 1987, p. 32). Ethnic conflict has interfered with census taking in India, Lebanon, and many other nations.

The processes by which census procedures are determined, the ways in which census figures are used, and the conflicts that occur about these procedures and numbers are a social process worthy of specific study. The "sociology of official statistics" (Starr 1987) is an area in need of development.

[See also Population.]

BIBLIOGRAPHY

Anderson, Margo J. 1988 *The American Census: A Social History.* New Haven: Yale University Press.

Fay, Robert E., Jeffrey S. Passel, and J. Gregory Robinson 1988 *The Coverage of Population in the 1980 Census.* PHC80-E4. Washington, D.C.: U.S. Government Printing Office.

Mitroff, Ian I., Richard O. Mason, and Vincent P. Barabba 1983 *The 1980 Census Policymaking amid Turbulence.* Lexington, Mass.: Lexington Books.

Robey, Bryant 1989 "Two Hundred Years and Counting: The 1990 Census." *Population Bulletin* 44, no. 1.

Scott, Ann H. 1968 *Census, USA: Fact Finding for the American People, 1790–1970.* New York: Seabury Press.

Starr, Paul 1987 "The Sociology of Official Statistics." In W. Alonso and P. Starr, eds., *The Politics of Numbers.* New York: Russell Sage Foundation.

United Nations 1980 *Principles and Recommendations of Population and Housing Censuses.* ST/ESA/STAT/SER.M/67. New York: United Nations.

– KARL TAEUBER

CHILDREN'S RIGHTS MOVEMENT

Children are those persons who have not reached the age of majority (usually eighteen or twenty-one) as defined by state and federal law. Children's rights are the moral and legal obligations shared by a child, its parents, and the state. Tension exists between the rights of parents to raise their children as they wish, the state's interest in how children are raised, and children's own rights. The concept of children's rights arose from two outlooks, one being that of the "child savers," who believe children should have a legal right to intervention to protect their welfare, and the "kiddie libbers," who think that children should have more power to make decisions that affect their lives and that children should have many of the constitutional rights granted to adults.

The child savers first appeared in the nineteenth century with the movement to enact child labor laws, compulsory school attendance laws, and child welfare laws and to establish juvenile courts to handle children in a more humane way than the criminal justice system. Prior to that time children were the chattel of their parents, and parents were responsible for providing for their children. When parents failed to meet this responsibility, the church and, to a limited extent, the state intervened by placing the children in orphanages. The kiddie libbers emerged in the 1960s and were instrumental in the granting of constitutional rights to children. *In re Gault,* which was heard before the Supreme Court in 1967, granted children due process rights, including the right to counsel, to notice of charges, to freedom from self-incrimination, and to examine and cross-examine witnesses. By the mid-1990s, however, children still did not have the federal right to bail, to a speedy trial, or to a jury trial and could be arrested for acts that would not be considered crimes if the child

Prior to child labor laws enacted in the late 1800s, the state regarded children as chattel of their parents and did not place age limits on employment of minors. (Library of Congress/Corbis)

were an adult. *Gault* led the way to extending due process rights to neglect cases, to divorce proceedings where children sometimes have their own independent counsel, and to due process rights in schools.

Children gained the constitutional right to peaceful protest in 1969, but in 1988 the Supreme Court upheld the right of school authorities to censor student publications. With the ratification of the Twenty-sixth Amendment in 1971, eighteen-year-olds were granted the right to vote. While children gained privacy rights regarding abortion (*Planned Parenthood* v. *Danforth,* 1976) and contraception (*Carey* v. *Population Services,* 1977), many states required parental notification when children exercised these rights. Other health care decisions remained the choice of a child's parents. While adults could not be committed involuntarily to a mental health facility unless it was proven that they were dangerous to themselves or others, parents could commit their children to such facilities without any sort of judicial review. Similarly, although adults increasingly chose not to secure medical treatment when such treatment would do no more than prolong life, children could rarely make such choices, even when they had reached an age when they can be determined to know the consequences of their decisions. Illegitimate children gained rights similar to those of legitimate children (*Weber* v. *Aetna Casualty and Surety Company,* 1972). Prior to this time illegitimate children did not necessarily have the right to be supported by their parents or the right to inherit property from their parents.

In 1988 the Supreme Court upheld the right of school authorities to censor student publications.

Congress also became active on behalf of children in the 1970s. While much congressional attention focused on education, federal legislation also addressed child welfare—laws for adoption assistance, child abuse and neglect prevention and treatment, child support enforcement, education for handicapped children, protection of children against sexual exploitation, Native American child welfare, juvenile justice and delinquency prevention, missing children, parental kidnapping prevention, family support, better child care, victims of child abuse, and the family and parental leave. Through expansion of the Medicaid program during the 1980s, children became eligible for more health care. Congress addressed the nutritional needs of poor children through the National School Lunch Program (1962), and the Women's Infant and Children Program (1972) provided food for pregnant women and their preschool children.

– DORIS-JEAN BURTON

CITIES

A city is a relatively large, dense, permanent, heterogeneous, and politically autonomous settlement whose population engages in a range of nonagricultural occupations. Various definitions have been developed for cities and their associated phenomena (Shryock, Siegel, and associates 1976, pp. 83–104). The city is often defined in terms of administrative area, which may be larger than, smaller than, or equal to the area of relatively dense settlement that comprises what is otherwise known as the city proper (Davis 1959). The suburb is a less dense but permanent settlement that is located outside the city proper and contains populations that are socially and economically tied to the city. Urban definitions vary by nation; in the United States the term *urban* refers to populations of 2,500 or more living in towns or cities and to populations living in urbanized areas, including suburbs. *Urbanization* refers to the economic and social changes that accompany population concentration in urban areas and the growth of cities and their surrounding areas.

Cities have always been centers of markets, governments, religion, and culture (Harris and Ullman 1945; Weber 1958, pp. 65–89). The community is a population sharing a physical environment and leading a common and interdependent life. The size, density, and heterogeneity of the urban community have been described as leading to "urbanism as a way of life," which includes organizational, attitudinal, and ecological components different from those of rural areas (Wirth 1938).

The City in History

The development of towns and cities was tied to a technological revolution in agriculture that increased food production, thereby freeing agriculturalists to engage in nonagricultural occupations. This resulted in urban living and led eventually to industrial production (Childe 1950). A contrasting Marxian-related view is that urban development is better explained by the needs of capitalist production for a malleable labor force (Jaret 1983, p. 449). Towns, and then cities, first developed in the fourth to third millennium B.C. in the rich valleys of the Indus River, the delta area of the Tigris and Euphrates rivers, the lower Nile valley, and the east coast of China. Increasing complexity of social organization, environmental adaptation, and technology led to the emergence of cities (Childe 1950; Duncan 1964).

Small agricultural surpluses and limits on transportation meant that the first towns were small and few in number, and contained only a small proportion of the populations of their regions. After the rise of towns in the Middle East, trading centers appeared on the shores and islands of the Mediterranean; some, such as Athens, became city-states. After developing more effective communication and social organization, some city-states expanded and acquired empires, such as those of Alexander the Great and of Rome. Following the decline of Rome, complex city life continued in the West in the Byzantine and Muslim empires while the population of Europe declined and reverted, for the most part, to subsistence agriculture and organized into small territories held together by the Catholic Church (Hawley 1981, pp. 1–35).

Sjoberg (1960) has argued that preindustrial cities were feudal in nature and shared social, ecological, economic, family, class, political, religious, and educational characteristics different from those in modern industrial cities. In the former, the city center, with its government and religious and economic activities, dominated the remainder of the city and was the locale of the upper social classes. Homogeneous residential areas could be differentiated throughout the city, but nonresidential activities were not confined to distinct neighborhoods (Sjoberg 1960).

Beginning in the tenth century, further town development in the West was facilitated by increases in agricultural technology, population, trade, and communication; the rise of an entrepreneurial class; and an expanding web of social norms regarding economic activity. Communication and manufacturing were revived, which led to the growth of towns with local autonomy and public administration, and eventually to networks of cities. Surplus rural population's migrated to cities, which grew because of their specialization and larger markets, becoming focal points of European societies (Hawley 1981, pp. 37–83).

Western Cities Since the Industrial Revolution

In most countries of the developed world, urbanization and urban growth have occurred at an increasing rate since the beginning of the Industrial Revolution. After 1820, the numbers and sizes of urban areas and cities in the United States increased as a result of employment concentration in construction and manufacturing, so urban areas began to grow more rapidly than rural ones. The population classified as urban by the United States census (based on aggregations of 2,500 or more and including the surrounding densely populated territories) increased from 5 percent in 1790 to 74 percent in 1980. In 1790 the largest urban place in the United States had less than 50,000 inhabitants. As late as 1840, not a single urban place in the United States had more than half a million inhabitants. There were four such places in 1890, fourteen in 1940, and twenty-two in 1980 (U.S. Bureau of the Census 1983, pp. 36–38).

City growth in the United States during the nineteenth century was driven by migration, since there were sometimes excesses of urban deaths over births in the early part of that century and lower birthrates in the last part of that century. Population concentration facilitated greater divisions of labor within and among families and individuals, as well as increasing numbers of voluntary associations centered on new urban interests and problems. At first, cities were compact, growth was vertical, and workers resided near their workplaces. The outward expansion of the residential population was facilitated in the last part of the century by steam and electric railways, the outward expansion of industry, and the increasing role of the central business district in integrating economic activities (Hawley 1981, pp. 61–145).

The increasing scale of production in the United States led to the development of a system of cities differentiated from each other by their degree of dominance over or subordination to other cities, some of which were engaged in centralized manufacturing, others of which depended on transportation, commercial, administrative, or other functions. According to Hawley (1986), cities may have certain key functions that dominate other cities: that is, integrating, controlling, or coordinating activities with these cities. Examples of key functions are administration, commerce, finance, transportation, and communication (Duncan et al. 1960; Wilson 1984). Since each city exists within its own organizational environment, the expansion of linkages of urban organizations has accompanied the development of urban systems (Turk 1977).

In the United States, the nature of key functions in city systems changed with the expansion of settlements westward, as colonial seaports, river ports, midwestern railway towns, central places on the Great Plains, extractive centers, and government centers were integrated into an urban system. A nationwide manufacturing base was established by 1900, as were commercial and financial centers (Duncan and Lieberson 1970). By 1960 a fully developed system of differentiated urban centers existed within the United States (Duncan and Lieberson 1970).

Metropolitan Areas

In the United States, metropolitan areas (as of 1990) are defined as being of two kinds. Metropolitan statistical areas (MSAs) are areas including one or more central cities with a population of 50,000 or more, or areas with a less densely populated central city but with a combined urban population of at least 100,000 (75,000 in New England), including surrounding counties or towns. Consolidated metropolitan statistical areas (CMSAs) contain at least one million population and may have subareas called primary metropolitan statistical areas (PMSAs) (Frey 1990, p. 6).

New urban-population-density patterns have appeared with the development of metropolitan areas. Growth has been characterized by increases in population density in central cities, followed by increases in density in the metropolitan ring. Transport and communication technologies have facilitated linkages of diverse neighborhoods into metropolitan communities dominated by more densely populated central cities. These linkages in turn have organized relationships between central cities and less densely populated hinterlands and subcenters. Older metropolitan areas have become the centers of CMSAs, while newer areas have been the frontiers of expansion, growing by natural increase and especially by net migration. Metropolitan sprawl extends beyond many former nonurban functions, as well as more centrally located older features of the cityscape. In the 1970s the redistribution of population within metropolitan areas favored lower-density areas (White 1987, p. 250).

The pattern of population concentration into larger cities and metropolitan areas changed during the 1970s, leading to a population turnaround, as populations in smaller metropolitan areas grew more rapidly than those in larger metropolitan areas and as nonmetropolitan counties grew more rapidly than did metropolitan counties (Frey 1990; Frey and Speare 1988). This change has been described as temporary and unique, representing a shift of growth to new regions, or as one more deconcentration of population (Frey 1987; 1990, pp. 10–11).

Intracity and intrametropolitan residential mobility—the individual counterpart of population redistribution processes—is affected by population characteristics and factors influencing mobility decisions. These decisions are tied to socioeconomic and psychological factors pertaining to the family and the family life cycle, housing and the local environment, and occupational and social mobility (Sabagh et al. 1969). For each of these factors, conditions may restrain persons from moving, or push or pull them to new locations. Information concerning new housing opportunities, the state of the housing market, and availability of resources may impede or facilitate moves; subsequent mobility may stem from recent migration or residential turnover in the metropolitan areas (Long 1988, pp. 219–224; Roseman 1971).

Explaining Cities

During the nineteenth century the character of the city was seen as different from that of noncity areas. Beginning with the public-health movement and concerns with urban housing, social scientists documented "pathologies" of urban life through the use of social surveys, the purpose of which was to provide policy-relevant findings (Young 1956). But since "urbanism as a way of life" has permeated the United States, many of the social and economic problems of cities have spread into smaller towns and rural areas, thus rendering the notion of unique urban pathologies less valid than when it was formulated.

In the twentieth century, efforts have been made to form theoretical explanations of city development, and disagreements have arisen (Sjoberg 1968, p. 455). Theories based on social Darwinism (Park [1916–1939] 1952) and economics (Burgess 1924) were first used to explain the internal structures of cities. "Subsocial" aspects of social and economic organization—which did not involve direct interpersonal interaction—were: viewed as generating population aggregation and expansion. Competitive-cooperative processes—including aggregation-thinning out, expansion-contraction, centralization, displacement, segregation, migration, and mobility—were believed to determine the structures and patterns of urban neighborhoods (Quinn 1950; Hawley 1950). The competition of differing urban populations and activities for optimal locations was described as creating relatively homogeneous communities, labeled "natural areas," which display gradient patterns of decreasing densities of social and economic activities and problems with increasing distance from the city center.

On the basis of competitive-cooperative processes, city growth was assumed to result in characteristic urban shapes. The Burgess hypothesis specifies that in the absence of countervailing factors, the American city takes the form of a series of concentric zones, ranging from the organizing central business district to a commuters' zone (Burgess 1925, pp. 47–52). Other scholars emphasized star-shaped, multiple-nuclei, or cluster patterns of development. These views were descriptive rather than theoretical; assumed a capitalist commercial-industrial city; were distorted by topography, and street and transportation networks; and generally failed to take into account use of land for industrial purposes, which is found in most city zones.

Theodorson (1964, 1982) and Michaelson (1970, pp. 3–32) have described research on American cities as reflecting neo-orthodox, social-area analysis, and sociocultural approaches, each with its own frame of reference and methods.

Neo-orthodox approaches have emphasized the interdependence of components of an ecological system, including population, organization, technology, and environment (Duncan 1964). This view has been applied to larger ecological systems that can extend beyond the urban community. Sustenance organization is an important focus of study (Hawley 1986; Gibbs and Martin 1958). While the neo-orthodox ecologists have not integrated the notion of social Darwinism into their work, the economic aspects of their approach have helped to guide studies of population phenomena, including urban differentiation (White 1987), residential mobility (Long 1988, pp. 189–251), and segregation (Farley and Allen 1987, pp. 103–159; Lieberson and Waters 1988, pp. 51–93).

Social-area analysis, however, regards modern industrial society as based on increasing scale, which represents "increased rates and intensities of social relation," "increased functional differentiation," and "increased complexity of social organization" (Shevky and William 1949; Shevky and Bell 1955). These concepts are related to neighborhood dimensions of social rank, urbanization, and segregation, which are delimited by the factor analysis of neighborhood or census tract measures (Janson 1980; Van Arsdol et al. 1958). The system has been used for classifying census tracts. Janson (1980, p. 454) has argued that factor analysis studies of internal urban social structure, which are associated with social-area analysis and similar approaches, have led to empirical generalizations that are theoretically relevant, but that factorial studies making use of larger urban units lead to less specific generalizations.

Sociocultural ecology has used social values to explain land use in central Boston (Firey 1947) and the movement of Norwegians within greater New York City (Jonassen 1949). While values are relevant to explanations of city phenomena, this perspective had not led to a fully developed line of investigation.

William Michaelson (1970, pp. 17–32) has argued that none of these aforementioned ecological approaches to the city explicitly study the relationship between the physical and the social environment, for the following reasons: (1) their incomplete view of the environment; (2) their focus on population aggregates; (3)

Nearly half of the world's population resided in urban areas by the year 2000. Los Angeles, California, ranked eleventh in size among world cities. (William Boyce/Corbis)

their failure to consider contributions of other fields of study; and (4) the newness of the field. Since Michaelson wrote his critique, sociologists are giving more attention to the urban environment.

Retrospect and Prospect

The interior of large Western metropolitan areas represents a merging of urban areas into complex overlapping spatial patterns. The blurring of neighborhood distinctions, facilitated by freeway networks, facilitates interaction among "social circles" of people who are not neighborhood-based. Meanwhile, urban neighborhoods organized around such factors as status, ethnicity, or life-style, may also persist. As the city ages, so does suburban as well as centrally located housing—a delayed consequence of the spread of urban settlement.

"Urbanism as a way of life" has permeated the United States.

Constraints on future city growth include economic decline, shortages of resources and infra-structures, environmental and social problems making cities less attractive, and adoption of growth limitation policies. Sooner or later all cities reach such limits, at which point growth becomes more vertical or new growth centers are established.

Urbanization in developing countries does not necessarily follow the Western pattern. City growth may absorb national population increments and reflect a lack of rural employment, a migration of the rural unemployed to the city, and a lack of urban industrial development. Increasing concentration of population in larger cities may be followed by the emergence of more "Westernstyle" hierarchies of cities, functions, and interorganizational relationships. Many cities in developing countries experience the environmental hazards of Western cities, a compartmentalization of life, persistent poverty and unemployment, a rapidly worsening housing situation, and other symptoms of Western social disorganization. The juxtaposition of local urbanism and some degree of Western urbanization may vitiate a number of traditional Western solutions to urban problems.

Developing countries are sometimes characterized by primate cities, that is, the largest cities in the country are larger than would be expected on the basis of a "rank-size" rule, which indicates that the rank of a population aggregation times its size equals a constant, thus resulting in an underdeveloped supporting hierarchy of smaller cities (Jefferson 1939; Zipf 1941; Shryock, Siegel, and associates 1976). Primate cities often appear in small countries, and in countries with a dual economy, but are not as apparent in large countries or those with long urban histories (Berry 1964).

By the year 2000, approximately half of the earth's population will be urban, with the vast majority in developing areas (Population Crisis Committee 1990). While cities in developing nations lack resources when compared with those in developed nations, cities in both types of nations are becoming more responsive to changes in local and worldwide conditions (Friedman and Wolff 1982; Frey 1990, p. 39).

These trends are apparent, for example, in Los Angeles and Mexico City, which ranked eleventh and second in size, respectively, in a recent compilation of data on the world's metropolitan areas (Population Crisis Committee 1990). After World War II and until the 1970s, Los Angeles's industrial and population growth and suburban sprawl made it a prototype for urban development that brought with it many inner-city, energy, suburban, environmental, state-management, ethnic, and capital-accumulation problems.

Since the early 1970s, Los Angeles has become a radically changed giant global city based on reindustrialization, communications, accumulation of global capital, and access to new international markets (Soja, Morales, and Wolff 1983). The reorganization of Los Angeles has greatly affected labor-force demands and the character of both native and immigrant populations. Ivan Light (1987) has emphasized that Los Angeles has a great concentration of industrial technology and great international cultural importance, is dependent on the private automobile, and has air hazards, limited water supplies, housing shortages, serious crime, and uncontrolled intergroup conflicts. Mexico City, while not commanding the same stature as Los Angeles, appears to share many of Los Angeles's problems, including lack of housing and services, expansion of low-income settlements, dependence on the private automobile, lack of sufficient transportation, and air pollution (Schteingart 1987). These consequences suggest that cities at somewhat similar levels of influence within their respective countries share similar characteristics, whether in the developed or in the developing world.

[See also Suburbanization; Urbanization; Urban Underclass.]

BIBLIOGRAPHY

Berry, Brian J. L. 1964 "Cities as Systems Within Systems of Cities." In J. Friedman and W. Alonso, eds., *Regional Development and Planning*. Cambridge, Mass.: MIT Press.

Burgess, Ernest W. 1925 "The Growth of the City, an Introduction to a Research Project." In Robert E. Park, Ernest W. Burgess, and R. D. McKenzie, eds. Chicago: University of Chicago Press.

Childe, V. Gordon 1950 "The Urban Revolution." *Town Planning Review* 21:3–17.

Davis, Kingsley 1959 *The World's Metropolitan Areas.* Berkeley and Los Angeles: University of California Press.

Duncan, Beverly, and Stanley Lieberson 1970 *Metropolis and Region in Transition.* Beverly Hills, Calif.: Sage.

Duncan, Otis D. 1961 "From Social System to Ecosystem." *Sociological Inquiry* 31:140–149.

——— 1964 "Social Organization and the Ecosystem." In Robert E. L. Faris, ed., *Handbook of Modern Sociology.* Chicago: Rand McNally.

———, William R. Scott, Stanley Lieberson, Beverly Duncan, and Haliman H. Winsborough 1960 *Metropolis and Region.* Baltimore: Johns Hopkins University Press.

Farley, Reynolds, and Walter R. Allen 1987 *The Color Line and the Quality of Life m America.* New York: Russell Sage Foundation.

Firey, Walter 1947 *Land Use in Central Boston.* Cambridge, Mass.: Harvard University Press.

Frey, William, II 1987 "Migration and Depopulation of the Metropolis: Regional Restructuring or Rural Renaissance?" *American Sociological Review* 52:240–257.

——— 1990 "Metropolitan America: Beyond the Transition." *Population Bulletin* 45, no. 2:1–53.

———, and Alden Speare, Jr. 1988 *Regional and Metropolitan Growth and Decline in the United States.* New York: Russell Sage Foundation.

Friechmann, John F., and Goetz Wolff 1982 "World City Formation: An Agenda for Research and Action." *International Journal of Urban and Regional Research* 6:309–344.

Gibbs, Jack P., and Walter T. Martin 1958 "Urbanization and Natural Resources: A Study in Organizational Ecology." *American Sociological Review* 23:266–277.

Harris, Chauncy D., and Edward L. Ullman 1945 "The Nature of Cities." *Annals of the American Academy of Political and Social Science* 242:7–17.

Hawley, Amos H. 1950 *Human Ecology.* New York: Ronald Press.

——— 1981 *Urban Society: An Ecological Approach,* 2nd ed. New York: Wiley.

——— 1986 *Human Ecology: A Theoretical Essay.* Chicago: University of Chicago Press.

Janson, Carl-Gunnar 1980 "Factorial Social Ecology: An Attempt at Summary and Evaluation." In *Annual Review of Sociology,* vol. 6, ed. by A. Inkeles, N. J. Smelser, and R. H. Turner. Palo Alto, Calif.: Annual Reviews.

Jaret, Charles 1983 "Recent Neo Marxist Urban Analysis." In *Annual Review of Sociology,* vol. 9, ed. by Ralph H. Turner and James F. Short, Jr., Palo Alto, Calif.: Annual Reviews.

Jefferson, M. 1939 "The Law of the Primate City." *Geographical Review* 29, no. 7:226–232.

Jonassen, C. T. 1949 "Cultural Variables in the Ecology of an Ethnic Group." *American Sociological Review* 14:32–41.

Lieberson, Stanley, and Mary C. Waters 1988 *From Many Strands: Ethnic and Racial Groups in Contemporary America.* New York: Russell Sage Foundation.

Light, Ivan 1987 "Los Angeles." In M. Dogan and J. D. Kasarda, eds., *The Metropolis Era,* vol. 2, *Mega Cities.* New York: Russell Sage Foundation.

Long, Larry 1988 *Migration and Residential Mobility in the United States.* New York: Russell Sage Foundation.

Michaelson, William 1970 *Man and His Urban Environment: A Sociological Approach.* Reading, Mass.: Addison-Wesley.

Park, R. E. (1916–1939) 1952 "Human Communities: The City and Human Ecology." *Collected Papers,* vol. 2. Glencoe, Ill.: Free Press.

Population Crisis Committee 1990 *Cities: Life in the World's 100 Largest Metropolitan Areas.* Washington, D.C.: Population Crisis Committee.

Quinn, James 1950 *Human Ecology.* New York: Prentice-Hall.

Roseman, Curtis C. 1971 "Migration as a Spatial and Temporal Process." *Annals of the Association of American Geographers* 61:589–598.

Sabagh, Georges, Maurice D. Van Arsdol, Jr., and Edgar W. Butler 1969 "Determinants of Intrametropolitan Residential Mobility: Conceptual Consideration." *Social Forces* 48, no. 1:88–97.

Schteingart, Martha 1987 "Mexico City." In M. Dogan and J. D. Kasarda, eds., *The Metropolis Era,* vol. 2, *Mega Cities.* New York: Russell Sage Foundation.

Shevky, Eshref, and Wendell Bell 1955 *Social Area Analysis: Theory, Illustrative Applications and Computational Procedures.* Stanford Sociological Series, no. 1. Stanford, Calif.: Stanford University Press.

Shevky, Eshref, and Marilyn Williams 1949 *The Social Areas of Los Angeles: Analysis and Typology.* Berkeley and Los Angeles: University of California Press.

Shryock, Henry S., Jacob S. Siegel, and associates 1976 *The Materials and Methods of Demography,* condensed edition ed. by Edward G. Stockwell. San Diego: Academic Press/Harcourt Brace Jovanovich.

Sjoberg, Gideon 1960 *The Pre-Industrial City: Past and Present.* New York: Free Press.

——— 1965 "Theory and Research in Urban Sociology." In P. M. Hauser and L. F. Schnore, eds., *The Study of Urbanization.* New York: Wiley.

——— 1968 "The Modern City." In David L. Sills, ed. *International Encyclopedia of the Social Sciences,* vol. 1. New York: Macmillan and Free Press.

Soja, Edward, Rebecca Morales, and Goetz Wolff 1983 "Urban Restructuring: An Analysis of Social and Spatial Change in Los Angeles." *Economic Geography* 59:195–230.

Theodorson, George A. 1964 *Studies in Human Ecology.* Evanston, Ill.: Row, Peterson.

——— 1982 *Urban Patterns: Studies in Human Ecology.* University Park: Pennsylvania State University Press.

Turk, Herman 1977 *Organizations in Modern Life: Cities and Other Large Networks.* San Francisco: Jossey-Bass.

U.S. Bureau of the Census 1983 *1980 Characteristics of the Population,* vol. 1. Washington, D.C.: U.S. Government Printing Office.

Van Arsdol, Maurice D., Jr., Santo F. Camilleri, and Calvin F. Schmid 1958 "The Generality of Urban Social Areas Indexes." *American Sociological Review* 23:277–284.

Weber, M. 1958 "The Nature of the City." In Don Martindale and Gertrud Neuwirth, eds., *The City.* New York: Free Press.

White, Michael J. 1987 *American Neighborhoods and Residential Differentiation.* New York: Russell Sage Foundation.

Wilson, Franklin D. 1984 "Urban Ecology: Urbanization and Systems of Cities." In *Annual Review of Sociology,* vol. 10, ed. by Ralph H. Turner and James F. Short, Jr., Palo Alto, Calif.: Annual Reviews.

Wirth, Louis 1938 "Urbanism as a Way of Life." *American Journal of Sociology* 44:1–24.

Young, Pauline V. 1956 *Scientific Social Surveys and Social Research.* New York: Prentice-Hall.

Zipf, G. K. 1941 *National Unity and Disunity.* Bloomington, Ind.: Principia Press.

– MAURICE D. VAN ARSDOL, JR.

CIVIL RIGHTS MOVEMENT

In the years since passage of the 1965 Voting Rights Act, generally considered the culmination of the civil rights movement, the struggle among African Americans to achieve full political, social, and economic justice has been marked by significant progress in some areas and frustration in others. In the South, the immediate results of the Voting Rights Act and the 1964 Civil Rights Act were breathtaking given the context of a century of institutionalized segregation. Public accommodations immediately and with little protest from whites opened their doors to black customers on an equal basis. Voting rolls bulged with new black voters. Prior to 1965 less than 20 percent of the eligible black electorate was registered to vote. Within three years more than two-thirds of eligible African Americans had registered to vote. Perhaps most important, the movement and its successes had imparted a sense of personhood, identity, and destiny to the South's blacks, a people told by both words and actions that they had counted for little in the region's development. No longer did black citizens endure the daily sense of humiliation and inferiority imparted by the words "white" and "colored," and the denial of the basic tenet of U.S. citizenship embodied in the right to vote. The South stood poised for an economic takeoff, with the historic partnership between two ancient and unequal cohabitants.

Once blacks had demonstrated both the folly and tragedy of racial separation, many whites felt relieved to have the burden of justifying the unjustifiable lifted from themselves and their region.

The movement liberated southern whites as well. Most whites had acquiesced in maintaining a segregated society. Once blacks had demonstrated both the folly and tragedy of racial separation, many whites felt relieved to have the burden of justifying the unjustifiable lifted from themselves and their region. Blacks and whites had lived in the South together for centuries and had shared the same soil, the same work, the same history, and the same blood, but they had been strangers to one another. Through the civil rights movement blacks had demonstrated to their white neighbors that it was possible to be both southern and integrated. Using the language of evangelical Protestantism, of suffering and redemption, blacks spoke to whites in a familiar language. Through their dignity and their appeals to a higher moral ground, black southerners spoke to the better instincts of southern whites. The civil rights movement as a piece of southern vernacular accounts, in part, for the difficulties Martin Luther King, Jr., and his colleagues experienced in trying to translate the movement to the ghettos of the urban North. There, amid family and institutional breakdown, the message of hope, redemption, and interracial harmony had much less resonance.

The forces that propelled the civil rights movement to its greatest legislative victories in 1964 and 1965 disintegrated shortly after the passage of the 1965 Voting Rights Act. The coalition of civil rights organizations, never cohesive to begin with, split over differences in strategies, white involvement, and personalities. The riot in the Watts section of Los Angeles less than a week after President Lyndon B. Johnson signed the Voting Rights Act in August 1965 inaugurated a series of long hot summers in the black ghettos of the North. The violence and accompanying calls for "black power" evaporated the reservoir of white northern goodwill toward black demands for civil and social equality. The Vietnam War diverted energy, attention, and funds from civil rights. The assassinations of King and Robert F. Kennedy in 1968 removed from the national scene two of the most articulate advocates for equality. When the Kerner Commission, appointed by President Lyndon B. Johnson to investigate the disturbances in the nation's cities, argued in 1968 that "the nation is rapidly moving toward two increasingly separate Americas . . . a white society principally located in suburbs . . . and a Negro society largely concentrated within large central cities," few challenged the conclusion.

Still, the civil rights movement generated important changes for the better, particularly in the South. Title VI of the 1964 Civil Rights Act prohibited job discrimination and southern blacks benefited immediately. More than 100,000 black workers entered the textile industry. While the provisions of the act outlawing segregation in public accommodations did not result in a totally integrated society, many public facilities, such as parks, playgrounds, theaters, hotels, and restaurants, now opened to the black community. Southern blacks benefited more from the 1965 Voting Rights Act. The sudden injection of blacks into southern politics moderated race-baiting, initiated an era of two-party politics, and resulted in the election of many black officeholders. By the 1980s the South led the nation with

4,000 African-American elected officials, including the mayors of such cities as Atlanta, Charlotte, Richmond, New Orleans, Birmingham, and Little Rock.

As a result of the *Swann* v. *Charlotte-Mecklenburg Board of Education* case in 1971, the federal government forced cities across the South to achieve racial desegregation in public schools, sometimes by using the controversial method of busing. By the 1980s the South had the most integrated public school system in the nation. With policies such as affirmative action (initially part of the 1964 Civil Rights Act, but strengthened during Richard Nixon's administration and by the federal courts) and the booming Sun Belt economy, the numbers of middle-income blacks in the South rapidly increased. One estimate held that between 1975 and 1990 the black urban middle class in the South grew from 12 percent of the black population to nearly half.

Nationally, results after 1968 were less promising. The transformation from a manufacturing to a service-oriented economy heavily affected the mainly semi-skilled and unskilled black labor force. While the northern black middle class grew in size and affluence, a bifurcation emerged in black society with expansion of the black underclass. Affirmative action, especially in education and employment, boosted the black middle class, but for those mired in poverty, it proved irrelevant or elusive. The decline in federal funding for poverty programs during the Ronald Reagan and George Bush administrations exacerbated the socioeconomic split in the black community. Immigration from Latin America and Asia during the 1980s and 1990s added ethnic conflicts and competition to an already inauspicious future for the black poor. In the South the political transformation wrought by the entrance of blacks into the electoral process gave rise to a predominantly white, conservative Republican party. Also, given changes in the U.S. economy and the decline of federal funding, black officeholders were unable to offer much surcease for their poorest constituents. In addition, urban school districts became increasingly black or, as in the cases of Norfolk and Little Rock, voluntarily resegregated to maintain racial balance in the rest of the system.

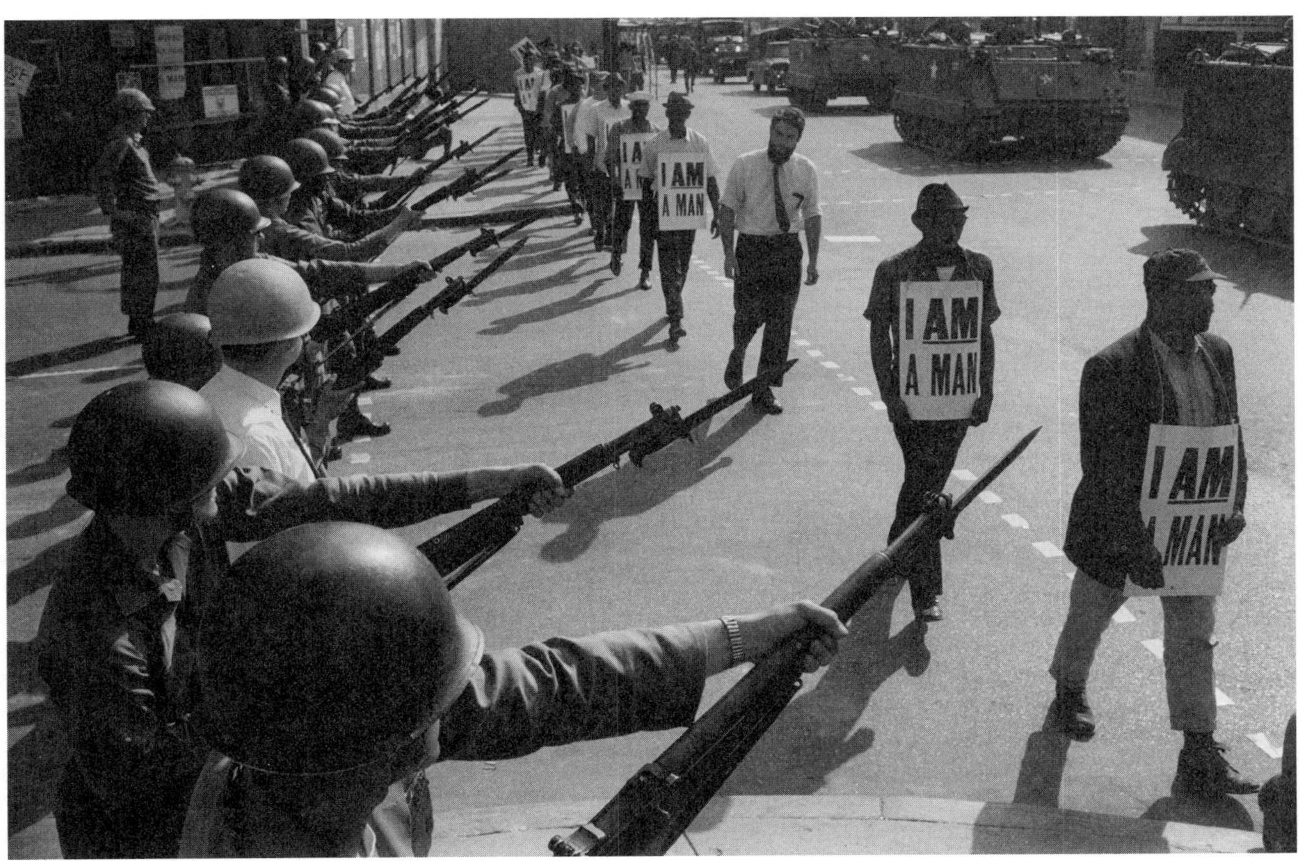

In the civil rights movement of the 1960s, Southern African Americans demanded their rights to political, social, and economic justice. (UPI/Corbis-Bettmann)

If the 1960s were years of civil rights confrontation, when southern blacks confronted whites with their consciences and their past, and the 1970s and 1980s were decades of consolidation, when blacks, especially in the urban South, built on the gains of the 1960s, then the 1990s were the decade of confusion and contradiction—an era of incomparable black middle class affluence and unprecedented numbers of impoverished blacks. The old interracial coalition of the 1960s disintegrated into numerous competing groups and interracial and religious antagonisms. Even the major purpose of the old movement—integration—appeared anachronistic in an era that promoted diversity and multiculturalism. Some black leaders reminisced about the era of segregation and the strength and identity blacks derived from building and maintaining their own communities and institutions.

Polls in the 1990s indicated that black and white Americans had sharply different understandings of the role of government in solving social problems, and affirmative action guidelines and set-aside programs came under national attack after the election of a conservative Republican Congress in 1994. The targets for civil rights activism were more elusive and ambiguous than ever before. Experts offered up economic explanations, genetics, and cultural theories to explain the persistent dilemma of race. Racism alone no longer seemed the clear-cut explication of race relations that it was in the 1960s, nor did the solutions seem obvious in terms of legislation and court rulings. Although venerable civil rights organizations, such as the National Association for the Advancement of Colored People, the Congress of Racial Equality, the Urban League, and Southern Christian Leadership Conference, persisted into the 1990s, their influence among rank-and-file blacks had diminished. The Reverend Jesse Jackson's Rainbow Coalition, an antipoverty organization, achieved some success, beginning in the mid-1980s, and Nation of Islam leader Louis Farrakhan's message of self-help and race pride won him a growing following, as evidenced by the Million Man March on Washington, D.C., in October 1995. Farrakhan's rhetorical attacks on other races and religious groups, however, often divided rather than united blacks. The true spirit of the civil rights movement lies with hundreds of local organizations that sponsor day-care facilities, lunch programs, after-school activities, and other grass-roots efforts.

The civil rights movement of the 1960s, one may conclude, reflected the best in U.S. society, the struggle to live up to the ideals of the Declaration of Independence and the Constitution. If that struggle fell short in certain areas, it succeeded in others. Perhaps the greatest legacy of the movement is that it serves as a reminder that Americans can overcome racial problems given the willingness of whites to change behavior and of the federal government to encourage change.

– DAVID GOLDFIELD

CLASS AND RACE

There is considerable debate in the sociology of race relations over how social inequality based on class and that based on race intertwine or intersect. Are these separate dimensions of inequality that simply coexist? Or are they part of the same reality? A similar question has been raised about gender inequality.

In studies conducted in southern towns of the United States, a parallel was drawn between the racial order and the Indian caste system.

Efforts to develop an understanding of the relationship between class and race have a long history in sociology. In the 1930s and 1940s it was common to conceptualize the issue as "caste and class" (Davis, Gardner, and Gardner 1941; Dollard 1937). Studies were conducted in southern towns of the United States, and a parallel was drawn between the racial order and the Indian caste system. Class differentiation was observed within each of the two racial "castes," but a caste line divided them, severely limiting the social status of upper class African-Americans. This view, while descriptively illuminating, was challenged by Cox (1948), who saw U.S. race relations as only superficially similar to caste and based on a very different dynamic.

Today the relationship between class and race is mainly of concern to Marxist scholars of race and racism. Some authors, particularly those influenced by the New Left of the 1960s (Omi and Winant 1986), assert the independence of race from class and resist the reduction of race to class forces. They see race and racism as having an independent dynamic. They claim that the United States is organized along racial lines from top to bottom and that race is a more primary category than class. (A similar argument is made by some feminist sociologists regarding gender.)

However, for most Marxist sociologists of race relations, class and race cannot be treated as separate dimensions of inequality that somehow intersect. Rather, these Marxist sociologists argue that race and class are both part of the same system and need to be understood through an analysis of that system. Modern race relations are seen as distinctive products of world capitalism. The central question then becomes: How has capitalism, as a system based on class exploitation, shaped the phenomenon of race and racism?

Although ethnic and racial differences have provided a basis for intergroup conflicts for the entire history of humanity, the expansion of Europe, starting in the sixteenth century, set the stage for a new form of intergroup relations. Never before was conquest so widespread and thorough. Nor was it ever associated with such a total ideology of biological and cultural inferiority. Modern racism, with its "scientific" claims of inferiority, is a unique phenomenon.

An understanding of European expansion, and its impact on peoples of color, begins with an analysis of capitalism as it developed in Europe. Capitalism is a system that depends on the private ownership of productive property. In order to earn profits on property, the owners of it depend on the existence of a nonowning class that has no alternative but to sell its labor-power to the owners. The owners accumulate wealth through profit, that is, the surplus they extract from labor. Hence, a class struggle develops between capitalists and workers over the rights of capitalists to the surplus.

In Europe, labor came to be "free," that is, people were no longer bound by serfdom or other forms of servitude but were free to sell their labor-power on an open market to the highest bidder. Being free in this sense gave European workers a certain political capacity, even though they were often driven to conditions of misery and poverty.

Capitalism is an expansionary system. Not only does it unleash great economic growth, but it also tends to move beyond national boundaries. The expansive tendencies lie in a need for new markets and raw materials, a search for investment opportunities, and a pursuit of cheaper labor in the face of political advances by national labor forces. European capitalism thus developed into an imperialistic system (Lenin 1939).

European imperialism led to a virtually total conquest of the globe. Europe carved up the entire world into spheres of influence and colonial domination. Since Europeans are "white," the colonial period, which reached its height in the early twentieth century, is a period of "white domination." Europeans, or whites, imposed their political, economic, cultural, and religious rule on the rest of the world, which consisted of peoples of color: "black" Africans, "yellow" Asians, "red" American Indians, and so forth. "White" became associated with a certain form of domination and oppression.

European domination took multiple forms, from unequal treaties, unfair trade relations, conquest, and the establishment of alien rule to annihilation and white settlement in places where once other peoples had thrived. Imperialism received ideological justification in beliefs that non-European cultures were "primitive," "uncivilized," "barbaric," and "savage," and their religions were pagan and superstitious. Europeans were convinced that they had the true religion in Christianity and that all other peoples needed to be "saved." The denigration of other cultures was accompanied by beliefs in "natural," biological inferiority. Dark skin color was a mark of such inferiority, while white skin was viewed as more highly evolved. Africans, in particular, were seen as closer to the apes. These kinds of ideas received "scientific" support in the form of studies of cranial capacity and culturally biased intelligence tests. The totalizing oppression and dehumanization of colonial domination is well captured in Albert Memmi's *The Colonizer and the Colonized* (1967).

European economic domination had many aspects, but a major aspect was the exploitation of colonized workers. Unlike white labor, which was "free," colonial labor was typically subjected to various forms of coercion. As conquered peoples, colonized nations could be denied any political rights and were treated openly as beings whose sole purpose was to enhance white wealth. Throughout the colonial world, various forms of slavery, serfdom, forced migrant labor, indentured servitude, and contract labor were common.

The coercion of colonized workers makes for a vast divide within the working class along color lines. Generally, white labor has been free, with certain political rights, while labor of color has been unfree and denied political rights. The result has been a greater oppression of workers of color as well as secondary conflicts between white workers and workers of color over their different circumstances and needs.

Not only did European imperialists exploit colonized workers in their homelands, but they also moved many people around to other areas of the colonial world where they were needed. The most notorious instance was the African slave trade, under which Africans were brought in bondage to the Caribbean area and sections of North and South America. However, other examples include the movement of contract workers from China and India all over the colonial world. Britain, as the chief imperialist power, moved Indians to southern Africa, Fiji, Trinidad, Mauritius, and other places to serve as laborers in remote parts of the British Empire. These movements created "internal colonies" (Blauner 1972), where workers of color were again subject to special coercion.

Even seemingly free immigrants of color have been subjected to special constraints. For example, Chinese immigrants to the United States in the late nineteenth century were denied naturalization rights, in contrast to European immigrants, and as a result were subjected to special legal disabilities. In the United States, Australia, Canada, and elsewhere, Chinese were singled out for "exclusion" legislation, limiting their access as free immigrants.

The sections of the world with the worst racial conflicts are the "white settler colonies." In the British Empire, these include the United States, South Africa, Zimbabwe (Rhodesia), Canada, Australia, and New Zealand. These societies established large white working classes that came into conflict with colonial capitalists over the use of coerced labor (Harris 1964).

So far we have talked only of the relations between white capital, white labor, and colonized labor. The colonial world was, of course, more complex than this. Not only did colonized people have their own middle or upper classes, but sometimes outside peoples immigrated or were brought in and served as indirect rulers of the colonized.

Middle strata from among the colonized peoples can play a dualistic role in the system. On the one hand, they can help the imperialists exploit more effectively. Examples include labor contractors, police, or small business owners who make use of ethnic ties to exploit members of their own group. In these types of situations, the dominant white group can benefit by having members of the colonized population help to control the workers primarily for the dominant whites while also taking a cut of the surplus for themselves. On the other hand, middle strata can also be the leaders of nationalist movements to rid their people of the colonial yoke.

Outsider middle strata, sometimes known as middleman minorities, can be invaluable to the colonial ruling class. As strangers to the colonized, they have no ambivalence about the aspirations of the colonized for self-determination. They take their cut of profits while not seriously threatening to take over from the Europeans. Because middleman groups tend to serve as the chief interactors with the colonized, they often become a major butt of hostility, deflecting the hostility that would otherwise be directed at the colonial elite.

Thus, the class and race relations resulting from the development of European capitalism and imperialism have been complex and world-shaping. Even though formal colonialism as outright political domination has been successfully challenged by national liberation movements, and even though the most oppressive forms of coerced labor have been legally banned in most of the world, neocolonialism and racial oppression continue in various guises.

For example, African-Americans in the United States remain a relatively disenfranchised and impoverished population. Although illegal, racial discrimination persists in everyday practice, and racist ideology and attitudes pervade the society. Many whites continue to believe that blacks are innately inferior and object to social integration in the schools or through intermarriage. African-Americans are almost totally absent from positions of power in any of the major political, economic, and social institutions of the society. Meanwhile, they suffer from every imaginable social deprivation in such areas as housing, health care, and education.

The capitalist system maintains racism in part because racially oppressed populations are profitable. Racial oppression (along with gender oppression) is a mechanism for obtaining cheap labor. It allows private owners of capital to reduce labor costs and increase their share of the surplus derived from social production. In general, the people of color do the menial work in most white-dominated societies, while a sector of the white population reaps the benefit.

With an increasingly globalized world capitalism, these processes have taken on an international dimension. Not only do capitalists take advantage of oppressed groups in their own nation-states, but they seek them out wherever in the world they can be found. Such people are, once again, of color. Of course, the rise of Japan as a major capitalist power has changed the complexion of the ruling capitalist elite, but the oppressed remain primarily African, Latin American, and Asian.

Claiming that the antiwhite sentiments of blacks are as racist as white racism is a form of denial of the historically specific basis of white racism.

It is common today for people to assume that prejudice goes both ways and that everyone is equally prejudiced, that African-Americans have just as much animosity toward whites as whites have toward blacks. According to this thinking, whites should not be singled out for special blame because prejudice against those who are different is a universal human trait: We are all equally guilty of prejudice. This view totally disregards the history described above. Europe was never conquered and humiliated by other societies, and its culture and biology were never denigrated. To the extent that peoples of color are antiwhite, it is a reaction to a long history of abuse. Claiming that the antiwhite sentiments of blacks are equally racist and on the same level as white racism is a form of denial of the historically specific basis of white racism.

At the foundation of the problem of race and class oppression lies the value system of capitalism, which asserts that pursuit of self-interest in a competitive marketplace will lead to social enhancement for all and that therefore the social welfare need not be attended to directly. This assumption is patently untrue. The United States, perhaps the worst offender, has let this social philosophy run amok, resulting in the creation of a vast chasm between excessive wealth and grinding poverty, both heavily correlated with color. Without intervention in "free market" processes, the United States is heading toward increased racial polarization and even possible violence.

Societies need to attend to racial issues directly. Their solution lies not only in "affirmative-action" types of programs, where a minority of people of color experience some upward mobility in an otherwise unchanged class system, but rather, the whole system of inequality based on appropriation of surplus wealth by a few, mainly white, private property owners needs to be challenged. Neither class-based nor racial inequality and domination can be attacked alone. They are linked with each other and must be overthrown together.

[See also African-American Studies.]

BIBILIOGRAPHY

Blauner, Robert 1972 *Racial Oppression in America.* New York: Harper and Row.

Cox, Oliver Cromwell 1948 *Caste, Class, and Race.* New York: Modern Reader.

Davis, Allison, Burleigh B. Gardner, and Mary R. Gardner 1941 *Deep South.* Chicago: University of Chicago Press.

Dollard, John 1937 *Caste and Class in a Southern Town.* Garden City, N.Y.: Doubleday.

Harris, Marvin 1964 *Patterns of Race in the Americas.* New York: Walker.

Lenin V. I. 1939 *Imperialism: Highest Stage of Capitalism.* New York: International.

Memmi, Albert 1967 *The Colonizer and the Colonized.* Boston: Beacon Press.

Omi, Michael, and Howard Winant 1986 *Racial Formation in the United States.* New York: Routledge and Kegan Paul.

– EDNA BONACICH

COALITIONS

Originally a word for union or fusion, the term *coalition* came in the eighteenth century to mean a temporary alliance of political parties. In modern social science, the meaning has broadened to include any combination of two or more social actors formed for mutual advantage in contention with other actors in the same social system. In most contemporary theories of coalition formation, it is taken for granted that the principles governing coalition formation are not much affected by the size of the actors, who may be small children or large nations, but are significantly affected by the number of actors in the system. In the sociological and social-psychological literature, interest has focused on coalition formation in social systems containing three actors, commonly known as *triads,* and on the factors that influence the formation of coalitions in that configuration. Coalitions in triads have certain properties that are very useful in the analysis of power relationships in and among organizations. Moreover, tetrads, pentads, and higher-order social systems can be viewed for analytical purposes as clusters of linked triads.

The social science perspective on coalitions derives from two major sources: the formal sociology of Georg Simmel (1858–1918) and the *n*-person game theory of John von Neumann (1903–1957). Simmel had the fundamental insight that conflict and cooperation are opposite sides of the same coin so that no functioning social system can be free of internal conflicts or of internal coalitions. Simmel also proposed that the geometry of social relationships is independent of the size of the actors in a social system but heavily influenced by their number; that social systems are held together by internal differentiation; that relationships between superiors and subordinates are intrinsically ambivalent; that groups of three tend to develop coalitions of two against one; and that, in stable social systems, coalitions shift continually from one situation to another.

While the basic ideas are attributable to Simmel, the analytical framework for most of the empirical research on coalitions that has been undertaken so far is that of Von Neumann (and his collaborator Oskar Morgenstern). Any social interaction involving costs and rewards can be described as an *n*-person game. In two-person games, the problem for each player is to find a winning strategy, but in games with three or more players, the formation of a winning coalition is likely to be the major strategic objective. The theory distinguishes between zero-sum games, in which one side loses whatever the other side gains, and non-zero-sum games with more complex pay-off schedules. And it provides a mathematical argument for the equal division of gains among coalition partners, the gist of which is that any essential member of a winning coalition who is offered less than an equal share of the joint winnings can be induced to desert the coalition and join an adversary who offers more favorable terms. In the various experimental and real-life settings in which coalitions are studied, this solution has only limited application, but game theory continues to furnish the vocabulary of observation.

Modern empirical work on coalitions falls into two major categories: experimental studies of small groups playing games that have been devised by the experimenter to test hypotheses about the choice of coalition partners and the division of coalition winnings under specified conditions, and observational studies of coalitions in the real world. Stimulated by the publication of divergent theories of coalition formation (Mills 1953; Caplow 1956; Gamson 1961) in the *American Sociological Review,* coalition experiments became part of the standard repertory of social psychology in the 1960s and continue to be so to this day. A great deal has been learned about how the choice of coalition partners and the division of coalition winnings are affected by variations in game rules and player attributes (Miller and Crandall 1980). Much, although by no means all, of this work has focused on three-player games in which the players have unequal resources and any coalition is a winning coalition, the distribution of resources falling into one of three types: (1) $A>B>C$, $A<B+C$; (2) $A=B$, $B>C$, $A<B+C$; (3) $A>B$, $B=C$, $A<B+C$. With respect to the choice of coalition partners, the leading question has been whether subjects will consistently choose the partner with whom they can form the minimum winning coalition, or the stronger partner, or the partner who offers the more favorable terms, or the partner who resembles themselves in attributes or ideology. The general finding is that each of these results can be produced with fair consistency by varying the rules of the experimental game. The division of winnings between coalition partners has attracted even more attention than the choice of partners. The question has been whether winnings will be divided on the principle of *equality,* as suggested by game theory; or of *parity,* proportionate to the contribution of each partner, as suggested by exchange theory; or at an intermediate ratio established by *bargaining.* Although many experimenters have claimed that one or the other of these principles is primary, their collective results seem to show that all three modes of division occur spontaneously and that subjects may be tilted one way or another by appropriate instructions. Additional nuances of coalition formation have been explored in games having more than three players, variable payoffs, or incomplete information. Non-zero-sum games and sequential games with continually changing weights have been particularly instructive. The findings readily lend themselves to mathematical expression (Kahan and Rapoport 1984).

The explicit application of coalition analysis to real-life situations began with Riker's (1962) study of political coalitions in legislative bodies; he discerned a consistent preference for minimal winning coalitions and emphasized the pivotal role of weak factions. Caplow (1968) showed how the developing theory of coalitions in triads could be used to analyze conflict and competition in nuclear and extended families, organizational hierarchies, revolutionary politics, international relations, and other contexts. The subsequent development of observational studies has been slow and uneven compared with the proliferation of laboratory studies, but there have been some notable achievements, particularly in family dynamics and international relations, where coalition models fit gracefully into earlier lines of investigation. Coalition theory has also been applied, albeit in a more tentative way, to work groups, intra- and interorganizational relationships, litigation and criminal justice, class and ethnic conflict, and military strategy.

The initial distribution of power between husband and wife is always transformed by the arrival of children.

Whatever the field of application, the examination of coalition, especially the simple coalition of two against one, provides a key to the social geometry of situations involving conflict, competition, and cooperation. In nearly every conflict, each of the contending parties seeks the support of relevant third parties, and the side that gains that support is likely to prevail. In very many competitive situations, the outcome is eventually decided by the formation of a winning coalition. And any system of cooperation that involves a status order must rely on the routine formation of coalitions of superiors against subordinates and be able to counter coalitions of subordinates against superiors.

All of these situations are susceptible to coalitions of two against one, which tend to transform strength into weakness and weakness into strength. Under many conditions, in the first of the triads mentioned above ($A>B>C$, $A<B+C$), both A and B will prefer C as a coalition partner; his initial weakness ensures his inclusion in the winning coalition. When $A>B$, $B=C$, $A<B+C$, B and C will often prefer each other as coalition partners; A's initial strength ensures his exclusion from the winning coalition. When $A=B$, $A>C$, C's initial weakness again makes him a likely winner. The first purpose of any hierarchy must be to restrain in one way or another the inherent tendency of subordinates to combine against superiors. Although force and ritual are often deployed for this purpose, the stability of complex status orders depends on certain interactive effects that appear in triads with overlapping membership, called linked triads. In such clusters, the choice of coalition partners in one triad influences the choices made in other triads. The natural rules that seem to govern the formation of coalitions in linked hierarchical triads are that a coalition adversary in one triad may not be chosen as a coalition partner in another triad, and that actors offered a choice between incompatible winning coalitions will choose the one in the higher-ranking triad. The net effect favors conservative coalitions of superiors against subordinates without entirely suppressing revolutionary coalitions of subordinates against superiors.

Cross-cutting the coalition preferences that arise from unequal distributions of power and resources are preferences based on affinity, compatibility, and prior experience with potential partners. These other bases of coalition formation are conspicuous in intimate groups such as the family, where same-sex coalitions alternate with same-generation coalitions.

The study of coalitions in nuclear families is particularly rewarding because the distribution of power in the triad of mother-father-child changes so dramatically as the child grows up, and because same-sex coalitions are differently valued than cross-sex coalitions. The initial distribution of power between husband and wife is always transformed by the arrival of children. Most cultures encourage certain patterns, such as the Oedipus and Electra complexes described by Sigmund Freud: coalitions of mother and son against father and of father and daughter against mother. Research on the contemporary American family suggests that parental coalitions are quite durable, both mother-daughter and mother-son coalitions against the father are very common, father-daughter coalitions against the mother much less so, and father-son coalitions against the mother comparatively rare. Sibling coalitions are most likely among same-sex siblings adjacent in age. Sibling aggression is endemic in families of this type, especially in the presence of parents. An interesting study by Felson and Russo (1988) suggests that parents usually take side with the weaker child in these incidents, and this leads to more frequent aggression by the excluded child. There are very few family conflicts that cannot be instructively described by a coalition model.

The application of coalition theory to international relations has concentrated on the "strategic triangle" of the United States, China, and the Soviet Union during the Cold War era of 1950–1985. In one of the many studies that have examined the internal dynamics of this triad, Hsiung (1987) concluded that China as the weak player in this triad benefited much more than either of the superpowers from the various coalitional shifts that occurred over time, as would be theoretically expected in a triad of this type ($A = B$, $B > C$, $A < B + C$). A recent study by Caplow (1989) explains the failure of peace planning in 1815, 1919, and 1945, by showing how efforts to put an end to the war system were undermined by the formation of coalitions to prevent the domination of the peacekeeping organization by the strongest of the victorious powers. Many older studies of international balances of power visualize international relations as a game in which the first priority of every major player is to block the domination of the entire system by any other player. Zagare's (1984) analysis of the Geneva Conference on Vietnam in 1954 as a three-person game broadened this approach by comparing the preference schedules of the three players and showing how they combined to produce the unexpected outcome of the negotiations.

Both family dynamics and international relations in peacetime exemplify situations of continuous conflict, wherein relationships have long histories and are expected to persist indefinitely, and the opposition of interests is qualified by the necessity for cooperation. The choice of coalition partners and the division of winnings is strongly influenced by the past transactions of the parties and by the fact that payoffs are not completely predictable. Continuous conflict triads with $A > B > C$, $A < B + C$ often alternate the three possible coalitions according to circumstances: the *conservative coalition* AB reinforces the existing status order; the *revolutionary coalition* BC challenges it; and the *improper coalition* AC subverts it.

In the triad of judge and courtroom adversaries, there is a clear tendency for judges to favor the litigant to whom they are socially closer.

Episodic conflicts, by contrast, involve discrete zero-sum games played under strict rules. The passage of any measure in a legislative body necessarily involves the formation of a coalition. Even when one party has a solid majority, its members will seldom be in complete agreement on an issue. The formation of a coalition for the passage of a specific measure usually involves hard bargaining and payoffs negotiated in advance. Under these conditions, the tendency to minimize costs by forming the minimal winning coalitions is very strong. When $A > B > C$, $A < B + C$, a BC coalition is highly probable. Empirical studies of legislative voting bear this out, although more than minimal coalitions also occur, for various reasons.

The resolution of disputes by civil and criminal litigation is another variety of episodic conflict that has begun to be studied as a coalition process. Black (1989) explores the triad of judge and courtroom adversaries and discovers a clear tendency for judges to favor the litigant to whom they are socially closer, ordinarily the litigant of higher status—a tacit conservative coalition. But in forms of dispute resolution where the third party is less authoritative, the weaker adversary may be favored. Marital counselors, for example, often side with wives against husbands, and ombudsmen and other relatively powerless mediators normally incline toward the weaker party.

In terminal conflicts, the object is the permanent destruction of adversaries, and the formation of coalitions is a delicate matter. In the triad where A>B>C, A<B+C, a successful BC coalition that destroys A leaves C at the mercy of B. Indeed, any winning coalition is hazardous for the weaker partner. A fragile peace can be maintained if A>B>C and A=B+C; the BC coalition forms as a matter of course, creating what is known as a balance of power. This has been the key configuration in European affairs for the past several centuries. The balance breaks down with any significant shift in the relative power of the parties; for example, if A grows stronger than the BC coalition, it will be tempted to conquer them. If B becomes equal to A, an AB coalition may be tempted to attack and partition C. If C grows stronger and the triad assumes the form A>B, B=C, B+C>A, the formation of a BC coalition to overthrow A is likely. In the eighteenth century, the breakdown of a balance of power led to war without delay. Under current conditions, the breakdown of a balance of power among major industrialized states does not involve an automatic resort to arms, but in several regional arenas, such as Southeast Asia and the Middle East, the old mechanism is still intact.

Terminal conflicts occur also within nations as coups, resistance movements, and revolutions. One common pattern is the urban uprising against a dictatorial regime, in which the players are the government, the army, and the populace. If the army continues to support the government and is willing to fire on the populace, the uprising fails. If the army sides with the populace, the government is overthrown. Often the issue is undecided until the moment when the troops confront the demonstrators. At a more fundamental level, successful revolutions require a coalition of formerly separate factions against the ruling group.

Every organization generates both internal and boundary coalitions. Internal coalitions are activated whenever persons or groups of unequal status interact before witnesses. In general, the presence of a high-status witness reinforces the authority of a superior, while the presence of a low-status witness reduces it; examined in detail, these catalytic effects are delicate and precise. Boundary coalitions occur whenever one organization has permanent relations with another. Their respective agents must form a coalition with each other to perform their functions, and that coalition pits them both against their own colleagues, always with interesting consequences.

In a long-term perspective, the two bodies of coalition studies, experimental and observational, exemplify two extremes of scholarly development. The experimental studies have explored nearly every possibility suggested by the available theories, run down every lead, manipulated every variable. Further progress probably waits on a new theoretical framework. The observational studies have scarcely tapped the rich possibilities suggested by the available theories and confirmed by the few empirical studies that have been done thus far. The social psychology of coalitions is well developed; most of the macrosociological work remains to be done.

BIBLIOGRAPHY

Adams, Wesley J. 1985 "The Missing Triad: The Case of Two-Child Families." *Family Process* 24:409–413.

Black, Donald 1989 *Sociological Justice.* New York: Oxford University Press.

Bonacich, Phillip, Oscar Grusky, and Mark Peyrot 1985 "Family Coalitions: A New Approach and Method." *Social Psychology Quarterly* 44:42–50.

Caplow, Theodore 1956 "A Theory of Coalitions in the Triad." *American Sociological Review* 21:480–493.

——— 1968 *Two Against One: Coalitions in Triads.* Englewood Cliffs, N.J.: Prentice-Hall.

——— 1989 *Peace Games.* Middletown, Conn.: Wesleyan University Press.

Felson, Richard B., and Natalie Russo 1988 "Parental Punishment and Sibling Aggression." *Social Psychology Quarterly* 51:11–18.

Gamson, William A. 1961 "A Theory of Coalition Formation." *American Sociological Review* 26:565–573.

Hsiung, James C. 1987 "Internal Dynamics in the Sino-Soviet-U.S. Triad," In I. J. Kim, ed., *The Strategic Triangle.* New York: Paragon.

Kahan, James P., and Amnon Rapoport 1984 *Theories of Coalition Formation.* Hillsdale, N.J.: Lawrence Erlbaum Associates.

Komorita, S. S., and Charles E. Miller 1986 "Bargaining Strength as a Function of Coalition Alternatives." *Journal of Personality and Social Psychology* 51:325–332.

Miller, Charles E., and R. Crandall 1980 "Experimental Research on the Social Psychology of Bargaining and Coalition Formation." In R. Paulus, ed., *Psychology of Group Influence,* Hillsdale, N.J.: Lawrence Erlbaum Associates.

Mills, Theodore M. 1953 "Power Relations in Three-Person Groups." *American Sociological Review* 18:351–357.

Murnighan, Keith 1978 "Models of Coalition Behavior: Game Theoretic, Social Psychological, and Political Perspectives." *Psychological Bulletin* 85:1130–1153.

Nail, Paul, and Steven G. Cole 1985 "Three Theories of Coalition Behavior: A Probabilistic Extension." *British Journal of Social Psychology* 24:181–190.

Riker, William H. 1962 *The Theory of Political Coalitions.* New Haven, Conn.: Yale University Press.

Rodgers, Joseph Lee, and Vaida D. Thompson 1986 "Towards a General Framework of Family Structure: A Review of Theory-Based Empirical Research." *Population and Environment* 8:143–171.

Rose, Irene Kathryn 1986 "Testing Coalition Theory in the Great Gatsby, and the Rabbit Trilogy." Ph.D. diss., University of Oklahoma.

Simmel, Georg 1902 "The Number of Members as Determining the Sociological Form of the Group." *American Journal of Sociology* 8:1–46, 158–196.

——— 1966 *The Social Theory of George Simmel,* ed. Nicholas J. Spykman. New York: Atherton.

Von Neumann, John, and Oskar Morgenstern 1944 *Theory of Games and Economic Behavior.* Princeton, N.J.: Princeton University Press.

Zagare, Frank C. 1984 *Game Theory: Concepts and Applications.* Beverly Hills, Calif.: Sage Publications.

– THEODORE CAPLOW

COLLECTIVE BEHAVIOR

Collective behavior consists of those forms of social behavior in which the usual conventions cease to guide social action and people collectively transcend, bypass, or subvert established institutional patterns and structures. As the name indicates, the behavior is collective rather than individual. Unlike small group behavior, it is not principally coordinated by each-to-each personal relationships, though such relationships do play an important part. Unlike organizational behavior, it is not coordinated by formally established goals, authority, roles, and membership designations, though emergent leadership and an informal role structure are important components. The best-known forms of collective behavior are rumor episodes; spontaneous collective response to crises such as natural disasters; crowds; collective panics; crazes, fads, and fashions; publics; cults; followings; and reform and revolutionary movements. Social movements are sometimes treated as forms of collective behavior but are often viewed as a different order of phenomena because of the degree of organization necessary to sustain social action. This essay will include only those social movement theories that also have relevance for the more elementary forms of collective behavior.

Theories of collective behavior can be classified broadly as focusing on the activity itself (micro level or interactional) or on the larger social and cultural settings within which the activity occurs (macro level or structural). An adequate theory at the micro level must answer three questions, namely: How is it that people come to transcend, bypass, or subvert institutional patterns and structures in their activity; how do people come to translate their attitudes into significant overt action; and how do people come to act collectively rather than singly? Structural theories identify the processes and conditions in culture and social structure that are conducive to the development of collective behavior.

Micro-Level Convergence Theories

Micro-level theories can be further divided into *action* theories and *interaction* theories. Action or *convergence* theories assume that when a critical mass of individuals with the same disposition to act in a situation comes together, collective action occurs almost automatically.

Collective behavior has been conceived as a collective pursuit of meaning and personal identity when strains and imbalances in social institutions have made meaning and identity problematic.

The psychological hypothesis that frustration leads to aggression has been widely applied in this way to explain racial lynchings and riots, rebellion and revolution, and other forms of collective violence. Collective behavior has been conceived as a collective pursuit of meaning and personal identity when strains and imbalances in social institutions have made meaning and identity problematic (Klapp 1972). In order to explain the convergence of a critical mass of people experiencing similar frustrations, investigators posit deprivation shared by members of a social class, ethnic group, gender group, age group, or other social category. Because empirical evidence has shown consistently that the most deprived are not the most likely to engage in collective protest, more sophisticated investigators assume a condition of *relative deprivation* (Gurr 1970), or a discrepancy between expectations and actual conditions. Relative deprivation frequently follows a period of rising expectations brought on by improving conditions, then interrupted by a setback, as in the J-curve hypothesis of revolution (Davies 1962). Early explanations for collective behavior, generally contradicted by empirical evidence and repudiated by serious scholars, characterized much crowd behavior and many social movements as the work of criminals, the mentally disturbed, persons suffering from personal identity problems, and other deviants. In all convergence theories it is assumed that "the individual in the crowd behaves just as he would behave alone, *only more so,*" (Allport 1924, p. 295), meaning that individuals in collective behavior are doing what they wanted to do anyway but could not do or feared to do without the "facilitating" effect of similar behavior by others.

RATIONAL DECISION THEORIES. Several recent convergence theories assume that people make rational decisions to participate or not to participate in collective behavior, and that they make these decisions on the basis of self-interest. Two important theories of this sort are those of Richard Berk and Mark Granovetter.

Berk (1974) defines collective behavior as the behavior of people in crowds, which means activity that is transitory, not well planned, and that involves face-to-face contact among participants and considerable cooperation, though he also includes panic as competitive collective behavior. Fundamental to his theory is the assumption that crowd activity involves rational, goal-directed action, in which possible rewards and costs are considered along with the chances of support from others in the crowd. Hence, he looks to decision theory. Rational decision making means reviewing viable options, reviewing events that may occur, arranging information and choices in chronological order, evaluating the consequences of alternative courses of action, judging the chances that uncertain events will occur, and choosing actions with minimal outcomes. Since the best outcome for an individual in collective behavior depends fundamentally on what other people will do, the decision process is analyzed in terms of *game theory.* Participants attempt to advance their own interests by recruiting others and through negotiation. Berk's theory does not explain the origin and nature of the proposals for action that are heard in the crowd but describes the process by which these proposals are sifted as the crowd moves toward collaborative action, usually involving a division of labor. To explain decision making, he offers a simple equation in which the probability of a person beginning to act (e.g., to loot) is a function of the product of the net anticipated personal payoff for acting and the probability of group support in that action.

Granovetter's (1978) application of rational decision theory focuses on the concept of *threshold.* He assumes that each person, in a given situation, has a threshold number or percentage of other people who must already be engaging in a particular action before he or she will join in. Since it can be less risky for the individual to engage in collective behavior (riotous behavior, for example) when many others are doing so than when few are involved, the benefit-to-cost ratio improves as participation increases. Based on the personal importance of the action in question, individual estimation of risk, and a host of other conditions, individual thresholds will vary widely in any situation. Thresholds determine the order in which individuals will join in collective behavior. More interestingly, collective behavior cannot develop without low-threshold individuals to get it started, and development will stop when there is no one with the threshold necessary for the next step in escalation. Collective behavior reaches an equilibrium (which can be ascertained in advance from knowing the distribution of thresholds) when this point is reached. While the mathematical version of the model assigns each additional participant a uniform value of one, Granovetter makes allowance for the possibility that participating friends may count for more than one and that physical dispersion of the participants may modify the threshold effect. Like Berk, Granovetter makes no effort to explain what actions people will value. Furthermore, intuitively appealing as the theory may be, operationalizing and measuring individual thresholds may be, for all practical purposes, impossible.

Micro-Level Interaction Theories

CONTAGION THEORIES. Early interaction theories, which lay more emphasis on what happens to people in the context of a crowd or other collectivity than on the dispositions people bring to the collectivity, stressed either the emergence of a group mind or processes of imitation, suggestion, or social contagion. While the concept of a group mind is no longer taken seriously, the contagion approach as formulated by Herbert Blumer (1939) has many followers.

Blumer explains that the fitting together of individual actions in most group behavior is based on shared understandings, which are influenced by custom, tradition, conventions, rules, or institutional regulations. In contrast, collective behavior is group behavior that arises spontaneously and not under the guidance of preestablished understandings, traditions, or rules of any kind. If sociology in general studies the social order, collective behavior consists of the processes by which that order comes into existence. While coordination in publics and social movements involves more complex cognitive processes, coordination in the crowd and in other elementary forms of collective behavior is accomplished through a process of *circular reaction.* Circular reaction is a type of interstimulation in which the response by others to one individual's expression of feeling simply reproduces that feeling, thereby reinforcing the first individual's feeling, which in turn reinforces the feelings of the others, setting in motion an escalating spiral of emotion. Circular reaction is contrasted to *interpretative interaction,* which characterizes most human response, including the coordination in publics and social movements. Circular reaction begins with individual restlessness, when people have a blocked impulse to act. When many people share such restlessness and are already sensitized to one another, circular reaction can set in and create a process of *social unrest,* in which the restless state is mutually intensified into a state of milling. In milling, people move or shift their attention aimlessly among each other, thereby becoming preoccupied with each other and decreasingly responsive to ordinary objects and events. In the state of rapport, collective excitement readily takes over, leading to a final stage of *social contagion,* the "relatively rapid, unwitting, and non-rational dissemination of a mood, impulse, or form of conduct" (Blumer 1939, p. 176). Social unrest is also a prelude to the formation of publics and social movements. In the case of the public, the identification of an issue rather than a mood or point of view converts the interaction into discussion rather than circular reaction. Social movements begin with circular reaction, but with persisting concerns they acquire organization and programs, and interpretative interaction prevails.

EMERGENT NORM THEORY. Turner and Killian ([1957] 1987) criticized convergence theories for underemphasizing the contribution of interaction processes in the development of collective behavior and found both convergence and contagion theories at fault for assuming that participants in collective behavior become homogeneous in their moods and attitudes. Instead of emotional contagion, it is the emergence of a norm or norms in collective behavior that facilitates coordinated action and creates the illusion of unanimity. The emergent norm is characteristically based on established norms but transforms or applies those norms in ways that would not ordinarily be acceptable. What the emergent norm permits or requires people to believe, feel, and do corresponds to a disposition that is prevalent but not universal among the participants. In contrast to convergence theories, however, it is assumed that participants are usually somewhat ambivalent; people could have felt and acted in quite different ways if the emergent norm had been different. Striking events, symbols, and keynoting—a gesture or symbolic utterance that crystallizes sentiment in an undecided and ambivalent audience—shape the norm and supply the normative power, introducing an element of unpredictability into the development and direction of all collective behavior.

Emergent norm theory differs from contagion theories in at least six important and empirically testable ways. First, the appearance of unanimity in crowds, social movements, and other forms of collective behavior is an illusion, produced by the effect of the emergent norm in silencing dissent. Second, while the collectivity's mood and definition of the situation are spontaneously induced in some of the participants, many participants experience group pressure first and only later, if at all, come to share the collectivity's mood and definition of the situation. Third, unlike collective excitement and contagion, normative pressure is as applicable to quiet states such as dread and sorrow as it is to excited states. Fourth, according to emergent norm theory, a conspicuous component in the symbolic exchange connected with the development of collective behavior should consist of seeking and supplying justifications for the collectivity's definition of the situation and action, whereas there should be no need for justifications if the feelings were spontaneously induced through contagion. Fifth, a norm not only requires or permits certain definitions and behaviors; it also sets acceptable limits, while limits are difficult to explain in terms of a circular reaction spiral. Finally, while contagion theories stress anonymity within the collectivity as facilitating the diffusion of definitions and behavior that deviate from conventional norms, emergent norm theory asserts that familiarity among participants in collective behavior enhances the controlling effect of the emergent norm.

Common action occurs when observers perceive a situation as critical, think there is limited time for action, and view the crisis as having a simple cause and being susceptible to influence by simple acts.

Recently, emergent norm theory has been broadened to make explicit the answers to all three of the key questions micro-level theories must answer. The emergent normative process is the principal answer to the question of why people adopt definitions and behavior that transcend, bypass, or contravene established social norms. Participants translate their attitudes into overt action rather than remaining passive, principally because they see action as feasible and timely. Action is collective rather than individual primarily because of preexisting groupings and networks and because an event or events that challenge conventional understandings impel people to turn to others for help in fashioning a convincing definition of the problematic situation. In addition, the three sets of processes interact and are mutually reinforcing in the development and maintenance of collective behavior. This elaboration of emergent norm theory is presented as equally applicable to elementary forms of collective behavior such as crowds and to highly developed and organized forms such as social movements.

OTHER INTERACTION THEORIES. Although all interactional theories presume that collective behavior develops through a cumulative process, Heirich (1971) makes this central to his theory of collective conflict, formulated to explain the 1964–65 year of spiraling conflict between students and the administration at the University of California, Berkeley. Common action occurs when observers perceive a situation as critical, think there is limited time for action, and view the crisis as having a simple cause and being susceptible to influence by simple acts. Heirich specifies determinants of the process by which such common perceptions are created and the process by which successive redefinitions of the situation take place. Under organizational conditions that create unbridged cleavages between groups that must interact regularly, conflict escalates through successive encounters in which cleavages become wider, issues shift, and new participants join the fray, until the conflict becomes focused on the major points of structural strain in the organization.

Also studying collective conflict as a cumulative process, Useem and Kimball (1989) developed a sequence of stages for prison riots, proceeding from preriot conditions to initiation, expansion, siege, and finally termination. While they identify disorganization of the governing body as the key causative factor, they stress that what happens at any one stage is important in determining what happens at the next stage.

Less fully developed as a theory, the *social behaviorist/interactionist* approach of McPhail and Miller (1973) and of Miller (1985) conceives collective behavior as individuals' actions that converge on the basis of explicit instructions or other cues to conduct. Rather than positing an overarching principle such as contagion or norm emergence, this approach uses detailed observation of individual actions and interactions within collectivities and seeks explanations at this level.

Structural Theories

Micro-level theories attempt first to understand the internal dynamics of collective behavior, then use that understanding to infer the nature of conditions in the society most likely to give rise to collective behavior. In contrast, structural theories depend primarily on an understanding of the dynamics of society as the basis for developing propositions concerning when and where collective behavior will occur. Historically, most theories of elementary collective behavior have been micro-level theories, while most theories of social movements have been structural. Neil Smelser's (1963) *value-added* theory is primarily structural but encompasses the full range from panic and crazes to social movements.

Smelser attempted to integrate major elements from the Blumer and Turner-Killian tradition of micro-level theory into an action and structural theory derived from the work of Talcott Parsons. Smelser describes the normal flow of social action as proceeding from values to norms to mobilization into social roles and finally to situational facilities. Values are the more general guides to behavior; norms specify more precisely how values are to be applied. Mobilization into roles is organization for action in terms of the relevant values and norms. Situational facilities are the means and obstacles that facilitate and hinder attainment of concrete goals. The four "components of social action" are placed in a hierarchy: Any redefinition of a component requires adjustment in the components below it but not necessarily in those above. Each of the four components in turn has seven levels of specificity with the same hierarchical ordering as the components. Types of collective behavior differ in the level of the action components they aim to restructure. Social movements address either values, in the case of most revolutionary movements, or norms, in the case of most reform movements. Elementary collective behavior is focused at either the mobilization or the situational facilities level. Collective behavior is characterized formally as "an uninstitutionalized mobilization for action in order to modify one or more kinds of strain on the basis of a generalized reconstitution of a component of action" (Smelser 1963, p. 71). The distinguishing feature of this action is that it short-circuits the normal flow of action from the general to the specific, jumping from extremely high levels of generality to specific, concrete situations, without attention to the intervening components and their levels of specificity. Thus, in Smelser's view, collective behavior is intrinsically irrational.

In order for collective behavior to occur, six conditions must be met, each of which is necessary but insufficient without the others. Smelser likens the relationship among the six determinants to the value-added process in economics, with each determinant adding an essential component to the finished product. The first determinant is *structural conduciveness,* meaning that the social structure is organized in a way that makes the particular pattern of action feasible. The second determinant is *structural strain,* consisting of ambiguities, deprivations, conflicts, and discrepancies experienced by particular population segments. Third, and central in Smelser's theorizing, is the growth and spread of a *generalized belief.* The generalized belief identifies and characterizes the supposed source of strain and specifies appropriate responses. The generalized belief incorporates the short-circuiting of the components of action that is a distinctive feature of collective behavior. Fourth are *precipitating factors,* usually a dramatic event or series of events that give the generalized belief concrete and immediate substance and provide a concrete setting toward which collective action can be directed. The fifth determinant is *mobilization of participants for action,* in which leadership behavior is critical. The final determinant is the *operation of social control.* Controls may serve to minimize conduciveness and strain, thus preventing the occurrence of an episode of collective behavior, or they may come into action only after collective behavior has begun to materialize, either dampening or intensifying the action by the way controls are applied. Although these determinants are often read as sequential stages in development of collective behavior, Smelser insists that they need not occur in any particular order.

Addressing a more limited range of phenomena, Waddington, Jones, and Critcher (1989) have formulated a *flashpoint* model to explain public disorders, and this model bears some resemblance to the value-added component of Smelser's theory. Public disorders typically begin when some ostensibly trivial incident becomes a flashpoint. The flashpoint model is a theory of the conditions that give a minor incident such grave significance. Explanatory conditions exist at six levels. At the *structural* level are conflicts inherent in material and ideological differences between social groups, which conflicts are not easily resolvable within the existing social structure, especially the state. At the *political/ideological* level, dissenting groups are unable to express their dissent through established channels, and their declared ends and means are considered illegitimate. At the *cultural* level, the existence of groups with incompatible definitions of the situation, appropriate behavior, or legitimate rights can lead to conflict. At the *contextual* level, a history of past conflicts between a dissenting group and police or other authorities enhances the likelihood that a minor incident will become a flashpoint. At the *situational* level, immediate spatial and social conditions can make public control and effective negotiation difficult. Finally, at the *interactional* level, the dynamics of interaction between police and protesters, as influenced by meanings derived from the other five levels, ultimately determine whether there will or will not be public disorder and how severe it will be. Unlike Smelser, Waddington, Jones, and Critcher make no assumption that all levels of determinants must be operative. Also, they make no explicit assumption that disorderly behavior is irrational, though their goal is to formulate public policy that will minimize the incidence of public disorders.

Resource mobilization theories have been advanced as alternatives to Smelser's value-added theory and to most micro-level theories. Although they have generally been formulated to explain social movements and usually disavow continuity between social movements and elementary collective behavior, they have some obvious implications for most forms of collective behavior. Although there are now several versions of resource mobilization theory, certain core assumptions can be identified. Resource mobilization theorists are critical of previous collective behavior and social movement theories for placing too much emphasis on "structural strain," social unrest, or grievances; on "generalized beliefs," values, ideologies, or ideas of any kind; and on grass roots spontaneity in accounting for the development and characteristics of collective behavior. They assume that there is always sufficient grievance and unrest in society to serve as the basis for collective protest (McCarthy and Zald 1977) and that the ideas and beliefs exploited in protest are readily available in the culture (Oberschall 1973). They see collective protest as centrally organized, with the bulk of the participants "mobilized" much as soldiers in an army are mobilized and directed by their commanders. In explaining the rise of collective protest, they emphasize the availability of essential resources, such as money, skills, disposable time, media access, and access to centers of power, and prior organization as the basis for effectively mobilizing the resources. Resource mobilization theorists favor the use of rational decision models to explain the formulation of strategy and tactics and emphasize the role of social movement professionals in directing protest.

Collective action is the product of purposeful negotiations whereby a plurality of perspectives, meanings, and relationships crystallize into a pattern of action.

In recent years there has been some convergence between resource mobilization theorists and the theorists they criticize. The broadened formulation of emergent norm theory to incorporate resources (under "feasibility") and prior organization as determinants of collective behavior takes account of the resource mobilization contribution without, however, giving primacy to these elements. Similarly, many resource mobilization theorists have incorporated social psychological variables in their models.

Recently introduced to English-speaking audiences, Alberto Melucci (1989) offers a *constructivist* view of collective action, combining macro and micro orientations. Collective action is the product of purposeful negotiations whereby a plurality of perspectives, meanings, and relationships crystallize into a pattern of action. Action is constructed to take account of the goals of action, the means to be utilized, and the environment within which action takes place, all of which remain in a continual state of tension. The critical process is the negotiation of collective identities for the participants. In the current postindustrial era, conflicts leading to collective action develop in those areas of communities and complex organizations in which there is greatest pressure on individuals to conform to the institutions that produce and circulate information and symbolic codes.

[See also Crowds and Riots; Disaster Research; Social Movements.]

BIBLIOGRAPHY

Allport, Floyd H. 1924 *Social Psychology.* Boston: Houghton Mifflin.

Berk, Richard A. 1974 "A Gaming Approach to Crowd Behavior." *American Sociological Review* 39:355–373.

Blumer, Herbert 1939 "Collective Behavior." In Robert E. Park, ed., *An Outline of the Principles of Sociology.* New York: Barnes and Noble.

Davies, James C. 1962 "Toward a Theory of Revolution." *American Journal of Sociology* 27:5–19.

Granovetter, Mark 1978 "Threshold Models of Collective Behavior." *American Journal of Sociology* 83:1420–1443.

Gurr, Ted R. 1970 *Why Men Rebel.* Princeton: Princeton University Press.

Heirich, Max 1971 *The Spiral of Conflict: Berkeley, 1964.* Berkeley: University of California Press.

Klapp, Orrin E. 1972 *Currents of Unrest: An Introduction to Collective Behavior.* New York: Holt, Rinehart, and Winston.

McCarthy, John D., and Mayer N. Zald 1977 "Resource Mobilization and Social Movements: A Partial Theory." *American Journal of Sociology* 82:1212–1241.

McPhail, Clark, and David Miller 1973 "The Assembling Process: A Theoretical and Empirical Examination." *American Sociological Review* 38:721–735.

Melucci, Alberto 1989 *Nomads of the Present: Social Movements and Individual Needs in Contemporary Society.* Philadelphia: Temple University Press.

Miller, David L. 1985 *Introduction to Collective Behavior.* Belmont, Calif.: Wadsworth.

Oberschall, Anthony 1973 *Social Conflicts and Social Movements.* Englewood Cliffs, N.J.: Prentice-Hall.

Smelser, Neil J. 1963 *Theory of Collective Behavior.* New York: Free Press.

Turner, Ralph H., and Lewis M. Killian (1957) 1987 *Collective Behavior.* Englewood Cliffs, N.J.: Prentice-Hall.

Useem, Bert, and Peter Kimball 1989 *States of Siege: U.S. Prison Riots, 1971–1986.* New York: Oxford University Press.

Waddington, David, Karen Jones, and Chas Critcher 1989 *Flashpoints: Studies in Public Disorder.* London: Routledge.

– RALPH H. TURNER

COMMUNITY

The sociology of community has been a dominant source of sociological inquiry since the earliest days of the discipline. Each of the three most influential nineteenth century sociologists (Marx, Durkheim, and Weber) regarded the social transformation of community in its various forms as a fundamental problem of sociology and sociological theory. The problem of community has also long been a concern of the social sciences in general. Some fifty years ago sociologist Carle C. Zimmerman observed that the notion of community "has been discussed either directly or incidentally by nearly everyone who has written in the social sciences since Aristotle" (Zimmerman 1938, p. 11). Concerning specifically the emergence of sociology, Bender (1978) suggested that as early social thinkers observed the disruption of the traditional social order and traditional patterns of social life associated with industrialization, urbanization, and the rise of capitalism, significant attention was focused on the social transformation of community and communal life. It should be emphasized that contemporary sociology remains, at its core, a discipline largely concerned with the definition and persistence of community as a form of social organization, social existence, and social experience.

Contemporary sociology remains a discipline largely concerned with the definition and persistence of community as a form of social organization, social existence, and social experience.

The definition of community in sociology has been problematic for several reasons, not the least of which has been nostalgic attachment to the idealized notion that the existence of community is embodied in the village or small town where human associations are characterized as *Gemeinschaft*—that is, associations that are intimate, familiar, sympathetic, mutually interdependent, and reflective of a shared social consciousness (in contrast to relationships that are *Gesellschaft*—casual, transitory, without emotional investment, and based on self-interest). According to this notion, the requirements of community or communal existence are met only in the context of a certain quality of human association occurring within the confines of limited, shared physical territory.

The classic perspective on community offered by Zimmerman (1938) is consistent with this theme in that the basic four characteristics argued by Zimmerman to define community (social fact, specification, association, and limited area) require a territorial context. Hillary (1955), in a content analysis of ninety-four definitions of community advanced in sociological literature, discovered basic consensus on only three definitional elements: social interaction between people, one or more shared ties, and an area context. An alternative, less restrictive, conception of community that accommodates the recognition of communal experience and the persistence of community in a highly mobile, urbanized society argues that community can be achieved independently of territorial arrangements and attachments where social networks exist sufficient to sustain a *Gemeinschaft* quality of interaction and association (e.g. Lindeman 1930; Bender 1978). Although Zimmerman opposed the notion that the requirements of community could be achieved by social interaction without shared territorial attachments, the findings of Hillary (1955) indicated that of the three unifying elements of community found in the literature (social interaction, common bonds, and area) "area" or "territory" was the least required to achieve a high level of consistency among definitions of community. Although many other definitions of community have been advanced in the decades since Hillary's analysis, the dominant discriminating element and point of debate among definitions remain the role of territorial arrangements.

Major Questions

The major questions that concern the sociology of community include the distinguishing characteristics and definition of community; the bases of communal experience and integration; the unique functions and tasks of community; the units of social structure within the community and the relationships and interactions between structural units; the economic and social bases of the community social structure; the relationship and distinction between internal community social structure and macrosocial structures external to the community; the relationship between individual experience and behavior and communal experience and behavior; the causes and processes of transformation from *Gemeinschaft* to *Gesellschaft* states of social existence; and processes of community persistence and adaptation in the face of social change.

Community studies undertaken by sociologists over the past sixty years have to a large extent sought to address some if not all of these issues. The most famous and controversial include Robert Lynd and Helen Lynd's Middletown studies (1929, 1937) and the Yankee City series by W. Lloyd Warner and his associates. The more well-known studies that have focused on the problem of community within large cities have included William Whyte's *Street Corner Society* and Gerald Suttles' *The Social Order of the Slum*, which themselves are aligned with earlier conceptions (associated with Robert Park and Ernest Burgess of the University of Chicago Department of Sociology) of the "natural community" arising within the confines of a seemingly faceless, anonymous, large city (Suttles 1972, pp. 7–9). Descriptive studies that emphasize field work and examine social structure as a spatial phenomenon are the hallmark of the highly influential Chicago School that arose and flourished under Park and Burgess during the 1920s and 1930s.

Robert Lynd and Helen Lynd carried out two studies involving extensive personal field work on the town of Muncie, Indiana, respectively *Middletown* (1929) and *Middletown in Transition* (1937). In the first Middletown study, the Lynds spent the years 1924 and 1925 participating in and observing the community life of Muncie (population 36,500) and performing extensive survey work. Their objective was to address all aspects of social life and social structure of the community. A fundamental focus of this analysis was the consequences of technological change (industrialization) for the social structure of Muncie, in particular the emergence of social class conflicts subsequent to turn-of-the-century industrialization.

Although the Lynds found distinctions between the living conditions and opportunity structures of business- and working-class families that were consistent with their Marxist expectations (i.e., children of the working class were more likely to drop out of school to help support the family, working-class families worked longer hours for less pay and less financial security, and living conditions in general were more harsh for working-class families), they failed to discover a disparate value structure or alienation among the working class. At all levels of social class the Middletown of 1925 shared a common conservative value structure that entailed a belief in hard work, self-reliance, and faith in the future. The subsequent study, undertaken in 1935 by Robert Lynd and a staff of five assistants, addressed the effects on Muncie of certain events during the period between 1925 and 1935, some of which were economic boom times, a 37-percent population increase, and the emergence of the Great Depression. The Lynds' fundamental questions in the later study addressed the persistence of the social fabric and culture of the community in the face of the "hard times" and other aspects of social change, the stability of community values concerning self-reliance and faith in the future when confronted by structurally induced poverty and dependence, whether the depression promoted a sense of community or undermined community solidarity by introducing new social cleavages, and the outcomes of latent conflicts observed in the mid-1920s (Lynd and Lynd 1937, p. 4). The conclusion reached by the Lynds was that the years of depression did little to diminish or otherwise change the essentially bourgeois value structure and way of life in Middletown, and that in almost all fundamental respects the community culture of Middletown remained much as it did a tumultuous decade earlier: "In the main, a Rip Van Winkle, fallen asleep in 1925 while addressing Rotary or the Central Labor Union, could have awakened in 1935 and gone right on with his interrupted address to the same people with much the same ideas" (Lynd and Lynd 1937, p. 490).

Although this remark seems to reflect some amount of disappointment on the Lynds' part that Middletown's bourgeois value system and class structure remained so unchanged in the face of widespread and unprecedented destitution, the Lynds still remained convinced that the Middletown family was in jeopardy, as evidenced by (among other things) an ever-widening generation gap. The Lynds' apprehensions concerning the survival of the American family were (and are) in keeping with the popular belief concerning the decline of the American family as its socialization functions are assumed by other formal social institutions external to the family. The conclusions of the Middletown III study, undertaken from 1976 to 1978 by Theodore Caplow, Howard M. Bahr, and Bruce A. Chadwick, who attempted to replicate the methodology of the Lynds, firmly reject this point of view. In contrast to the Lynds' foreboding in 1935 and popular sociology since that time, Caplow and his associates contend that Middletown's families of the 1970s have "increased family solidarity, a smaller generation gap, closer marital communication, more religion, and less mobility" (Caplow et al. 1982, p. 323). The conclusions derived from the third Middletown study also reject similar assumptions concerning consistent linear trends in equalization, secularization, bureaucratization, and depersonalization consistent with the relentless *Gemeinschaft*-to-*Gesellschaft* theme (Bahr, Caplow, and Chadwick 1983).

Although many of the Lynds' predictions concerning the social transformation of Middletown failed to come true as history unfolded, their work and remarkable powers of observation remain unparalleled in many respects. Of equal importance, the early Middletown studies helped to inspire such other works as *Street Corner Society* and the Yankee City studies, and remain the standard by which all other community studies are judged.

The largest-scale community study undertaken remains W. Lloyd Warner's Yankee City, published in a five-volume series from 1941 through 1959 (Warner and Lund 1941, 1942; Warner and Srole 1945; Warner and Low 1947; Warner 1959). The Yankee City project was undertaken by Warner and his associates in Newburyport, Massachusetts, during the late 1930s. Warner, an anthropologist whose most recent work prior to the Yankee City project was with Australian aborigines (Vidich, Bensman, and Stein 1964), attempted to obtain a complete ethnographic account of a "representative" American small community with a population range from 10,000 to 20,000. To accomplish this task, Warner's staff (numbering in the thirties) conducted aerial surveys of Newburyport and its surrounding communities, gathered some 17,000 "social personality" cards on every member of the community, gathered data on the professed and de facto reading preferences of its citizens, and even subjected plots of local plays to content analysis (Thernstrom 1964, pp. 227–228). In his criticism of the Yankee City study, Thernstrom (1964) provides the following comment pertaining to the size and scope of Warner's endeavor: "One breathes a sigh of sympathy at the image of a haunted [upper-class citizen] of Warner's Newburyport seeking furtively to pick up his monthly *Esquire* under the cool stare of a Radcliffe graduate student in sociology" (Thernstrom 1964, p. 228).

Warner's conception of Yankee City was that of a stable, rather closed community with a social structure being transformed in very negative ways by the latter stages of industrialization. According to Warner's vision of *Yankee City*, the loss of local economic control over its industries through a factory system controlled by "outsiders" disrupted traditional management—labor relations and communal identification with local leadership. Moreover, the factory system was seen by Warner as promoting an increasingly rigid class structure and decreased opportunities for social mobility. In particular, Warner's discussion of the loss of local economic control through horizontal and vertical affiliation, orientation, and delegation of authority seems to have offered a prophetic glimpse into the future for many American communities.

Although the Yankee City study produced a voluminous ethnographic record of an American city that has remained untouched in scale, Warner found little support for his contention that the ethnographic portrait of Newburyport produced by the Yankee City series could be generalized to other small American communities. Moreover, Warner's contention that social mobility was made more difficult by industrialization was not supported by the quality of his data and is in conflict with social history both before and subsequent to *Yankee City*. The most devastating criticisms of *Yankee City*, however, concerned Warner's ahistorical approach and system of social stratification.

Warner's ahistorical strategy relied almost wholly on original ethnographic information produced by the research team as the principal basis for the formation of their ideas about the community and rejected substantial use of historical record. The rationale for this approach pertained to a wish to escape the ethnocentric biases of previous historical information. However, Thernstrom (1964) suggested that the exclusive reliance on the community's time-bound perspective and beliefs about itself promoted the very biased ethnocentric perceptions Warner wished to avoid. Warner's system of stratification, which rejected economic criteria in favor of six discrete social classes determined through subjective ranking by community informants, provoked the most devastating attacks upon the Yankee City study. The criticisms included the observations that (1) Warner's measure of social class was limited to a measure of social prestige; (2) affixing someone in a particular social class by the representative polling of others was unwieldy and inherently arbitrary; (3) there is difficulty in observing social mobility under a stratification system based on "communal ranking"; and (4) there were references by Warner himself in Yankee City that indicated members of the working class ranked people by the simple economic criteria Warner eschewed.

The findings of the various community studies have aided enormously in the struggle to refine conceptualization of the social transformation process among American communities.

Both Gerald Suttle's *The Social Order of the Slum* (1968) and William Whyte's *Street Corner Society* (1943) provide sociology with unparalleled ethnographic accounts of neighborhood social structure and communal life in urban environs. Suttle's work focused on the territorial relationships, neighborhood social structure, and communal life among Italian, Hispanic, and black slum inhabitants of the Near West Side of Chicago in the 1960s. Whyte's *Street Corner Society,* based on Whyte's residence in a Chicago Italian slum district a generation earlier, provided an understanding of the complex and stable social organization that existed within slum neighborhoods conventionally believed to have epitomized social disorganization. Whyte's observations and keen insights concerning small-group behavior were pioneering contributions to that area of sociology. Both studies, in method, theory, and substance, are classic examples of Chicago School sociology.

Social Theory and the Transformation of the American Community

The findings of the various community studies have aided enormously in the struggle to refine conceptualization of the social transformation process among American communities. Warren (1978) describes the modern social transformation of community as a change of orientation by the local community units toward the extracommunity systems of which they are a part, with a corresponding decrease in community cohesion and autonomy (Warren 1978, pp. 52–53). In Warren's conception of social transformation, the owner-operated corner cafe is transformed to a franchise with rotating upwardly mobile management personnel and an emphasis on consistency of product over what is unique and local. Warren identifies seven areas through which social transformation can be analyzed: division of labor, differentiation of interests and association, increasing systemic relationships to the larger society, bureaucratization and impersonalization, transfer of functions to profit enterprise and government, urbanization and suburbanization, and changing values. The framework suggested by Warren offers a rich conceptualization of community transformation that goes well beyond an elaboration of the traditional *Gemeinschaft–Gesellschaft* dichotomy.

Like Warren, Bender (1978) speaks the language of social transformation of community rather than disappearance or collapse. Bender proposes that the observations by various community scholars at different points in historical time, each suggesting that theirs is *the* historical tipping point from community to mass society, contradict linear decline or an interpretation of history that stresses the collapse of community. Although Bender acknowledges the ascendance of *Gesellschaft* in American social experience during the period following the Civil War, he suggests that a "bifurcation of social experience" or sharpening of the distinction between *Gemeinschaft* and *Gesellschaft* realms of social interaction is a more accurate interpretation of the historical transformation of community than that provided by the linear *Gemeinschaft*-to-*Gesellschaft* framework.

The Decline of Community Debate

Ever since nineteenth-century social thinker Ferdinand Tonnies offered sociology *Gemeinschaft* and *Gesellschaft* as contrasting qualities of human association, the fundamental focus of debate within the sociology of community has concerned the hypotheses emphasizing the decline of community. According to this hypothesis and its variations, the intimate, sustained, and mutually interdependent human associations based on shared fate and shared consciousness observed in traditional communal society are relentless giving way to the casual, impersonal, transitory, and instrumental relationships based on self-interest that are characteristic of social existence in modern mass society.

Of the many works that derive their perspective from the decline-of-community hypothesis, the most famous is Louis Wirth's "Urbanism as a Way of Life" (1938). Wirth's eloquent essay presents a perspective of urban existence and urban social relationships that managed to capture much sociological thinking about the emergence of a heterogenous urban mass society characterized by a breakdown of informal communal ways of meeting human need and by "human relations which are largely anonymous, superficial, and transitory" (Wirth 1938, p. 1). All other works pertaining to the decline-of-community hypothesis are either a reply to Wirth or an elaboration of Wirth's succinct presentation of the thesis.

Although many of Wirth's observations about the nature of human association, the disruption of a communal social structure, and the rise of formal, impersonal social institutions are difficult to refute, replies to the decline-of-community theme generally offer either (1) an alternative, albeit more limited, communal social structure or (2) evidence that suggests the march from a *Gemeinschaft* to a *Gesellschaft* state of human association has neither been linear nor relentless.

Of the former approach, the most notable is the conception of the "community of limited liability." According to the community-of-limited-liability thesis, networks of human association and interdependence are argued to exist at various levels of social organization, and social status characteristics are identified that are associated with differentiated levels of participation in community life (e.g., family life-cycle phase). The idea of "limited liability" poses the argument that, in a highly mobile society, the attachments to community tend to be based on rationalism rather than on sentiment and that even those "invested" in the community are limited in their sense of personal commitment (Janowitz 1952; Greer 1962).

The approaches that challenge the decline-of-community thesis on the basis of its vision of a linear transformation from a communal *Gemeinschaft* society to an urban mass *Gesellschaft* society do so by offering evidence suggesting that Wirth's vision of the relentless social forces of urbanism is both overly deterministic and blind to the reality that patterns of *Gemeinschaft* and *Gesellschaft* human associations can be found to exist side by side in very complex ways. For example, Bahr, Caplow, and Chadwick (1983) argue that their analysis of Muncie, Indiana (forty years after the Lynds' *Middletown in Transition*), failed to find the singular trends in bureaucratization, secularization, mobility, and depersonalization that would be predicted from a linear decline-of-community hypothesis. Janowitz (1952) suggests that while the *Gemeinschaft*-to-*Gesellschaft* social transformation might be a long-term trend, long-term trends are not useful to the interpretation of contemporary social reality. Redfield (1955), in his reformulation of the folk-urban society contrast, offers an alternative perspective to the Wirth linear transformation of folk (*Gemeinschaft*) society to urban (*Gesellschaft*) society, proposing that both urban ways and folkways can be observed in contemporary communities and cities: "In every isolated little community there is civilization; in every city there is the folk society" (Redfield 1955, p. 146).

While much of the evidence from community studies appears to support Redfield's vision of *Gemeinschaft–Gesellschaft* coexistence in contemporary society, it is left to future sociological investigation to determine where and under what conditions particular patterns of *Gemeinschaft* and *Gesellschaft* social existence emerge.

BIBLIOGRAPHY

Bahr, Howard M., Theodore Caplow, and Bruce Chadwick 1983 "Middletown III: Problems of Replication, Longitudinal Measurement, and Triangulation." *Annual Review of Sociology* 9:249–258.

Bender, Thomas 1978 *Community and Social Change in America.* New Brunswick, N.J.: Rutgers University Press.

Caplow, Theodore, Howard M. Bahr, Bruce A. Chadwick, Reuben Hill, and Margaret Holmes Williamson 1982 *Middletown Families: Fifty Years of Change and Continuity.* Minneapolis: University of Minnesota Press.

Greer, Scott 1962 *The Emerging City: Myth and Reality.* New York: Free Press of Glencoe.

Hillary, George A., Jr. 1955 "Definitions of Community: Areas of Agreement." *Rural Sociology* 20:111–123.

Janowitz, Morris 1952 *The Community Press in an Urban Setting: The Social Elements of Urbanism.* Chicago: University of Chicago Press.

Lindeman, E. C. 1930 "Community." In Edwin R. A. Seligman, ed. *The Encyclopedia of Social Sciences.* New York: Macmillan.

Lynd, Robert, and Helen Lynd 1929 *Middletown: A Study in American Culture.* New York: Harcourt, Brace and Company.

——— 1937 *Middletown in Transition: A Study in Cultural Conflicts.* New York: Harcourt, Brace and Company.

Redfield, Robert 1955 *The Little Community.* Chicago: University of Chicago Press.

——— 1968 *The Social Order of the Slum: Ethnicity and Territory in the Inner City.* Chicago: University of Chicago Press.

Suttles, Gerald 1972 *The Social Construction of Communities.* Chicago: University of Chicago Press.

Thernstrom, Stephen 1964 *Poverty and Progress.* Cambridge, Mass.: Harvard University Press.

Vidich, Arthur, Joseph Bensman, and Maurice Stein 1964 *Reflections on Community Studies.* New York: Wiley.

Warner, W. Lloyd 1959 *The Living and the Dead: A Study of the Symbolic Life of Americans.* New Haven: Yale University Press.

———, and J. O. Low 1947 *The Social System of the Modern Factory: The Strike, A Social Analysis.* New Haven: Yale University Press.

———, J. O. Low, Paul S. Lund, and Leo Srole 1963 *Yankee City.* New Haven: Yale University Press.

———, and Paul S. Lund 1941 *The Social Life of a Modern Community.* New Haven: Yale University Press.

——— 1942 *The Status System of a Modern Community.* New Haven: Yale University Press.

———, and Leo Srole 1945 *The Social Systems of American Ethnic Groups.* New Haven, Conn.: Yale University Press.

Warren, Roland 1978 *The Community in America.* Chicago: Rand McNally.

Whyte, William Foote 1943 *Street Corner Society: The Social Structure of an Italian Slum.* Chicago: University of Chicago Press.

Wirth, Louis 1938 "Urbanism as a Way of Life." *American Journal of Sociology* 44:1–24.

Zimmerman, Carle C. 1938 *The Changing Community.* New York: Harper and Brothers.

– GUNNAR ALMGREN

COMMUNITY HEALTH

Community health represents an organized community effort to ensure a healthy population. It is both an approach and a discipline. The basic distinction is whether service or science is stressed. As an approach, community health refers to the provision of health services. As a discipline, community health is the science of disease, illness, and health maintenance.

The community health approach includes the institutions and persons that constitute the health care system of a community. Thus, the official public health agencies, the physicians who may practice as community medicine specialists, and all other health practitioners and professionals involved with organized health care delivery in a community are incorporated, as well as a variety of service agencies.

The community health discipline is the population-based study of the causes, control, and prevention of health problems. It uses the science of epidemiology to investigate health and health services.

Community Health Services

Community health services are wide in scope. The services involve (1) official activities of local, state, and federal public health departments, and (2) services delivered by persons or institutions in the private and semipublic sectors. The former are conducted with public funds by agencies designated as official public health departments. The latter are not publicly funded and can include the services of hospitals, long-term care institutions, health education facilities, human service agencies, health administrators, health planners, and staff of community agencies. This last group is rapidly increasing its community health efforts as society moves away from formal institutional care for long-term and mental health problems to community-based and home care.

The American Public Health Association is also integrally involved in community health efforts. It has a national membership of persons working to improve the health of communities and has called for legislation to provide breast and cervical cancer screening, long-term care for the elderly, drug and alcohol treatment centers, a new focus on TB as a health problem, and new policies for the care and education of AIDS patients.

Public Health Services

Public health departments are organized at federal, state, and local levels. They represent a community's official line of defense against disease and injury. Until the middle of the twentieth century public health departments were concerned primarily with the spread of infectious disease. At the present time they concentrate on chronic diseases, with the exception of AIDS and sexually transmitted diseases.

Public health agencies engage in many activities that are prevention-oriented. They attempt to reduce the threat of disease by emphasizing prevention. These activities encompass several areas: providing a safe physical environment; preventing the spread of infectious disease; ensuring maternal and infant health; protecting the public from unintentional injuries; ensuring adequate nutrition; and enhancing the public's knowledge of health maintenance and disease prevention behaviors. Thus, safe disposal of sewage and hazardous waste, monitoring the spread of AIDS and related disorders, providing pregnant women with health care and infant health information, and determining occupational hazards fall within the domain of the public health sector.

Local public health services have existed in the United States since the colonial period (Shonick 1988). Port cities established in the seventeenth century quickly discovered that they had to face the problem of epidemics spread by sailors and new settlers. Local officials began to enforce quarantines on persons or ships to prevent the spread of dread diseases. In the twentieth century major cities typically have a public health department, and counties may also have public health agencies.

Each state has a public health division. The functions of most state public health departments include: maintaining data bases for vital statistics and rates of specific diseases; providing laboratory services to diagnose disease; assessing environmental hazards; and providing aid to expectant mothers and young children. Many states are also involved in health education and nursing service programs and may regulate licensure of health facilities.

Federal legislation governing the health of the public dates from 1796 (Shonick 1988). Early efforts concerned the need to prevent the spread of infectious disease, but the lack of knowledge of the cause and spread of disease hampered these efforts. The U.S. Public Health Service was given its present name in 1912. By 1925, accurate information was available about the methods of transmission of most communicable diseases. Because food, water, insects, and animals were often implicated, federal and local agencies focused their efforts on sanitation, water control, and elimination of pests as disease agents.

At the present time the U.S. Public Health Service conducts a wide range of health activities that include establishing health policies and regulations, enforcement, health education, disease monitoring, and health research. With regard to the latter, the National Institutes of Health sponsor most of the health-related research in this country. These institutes operate under the jurisdiction of the U.S. Public Health Services.

The Center for Disease Control is also an important arm of the U.S. Public Health Service because of its surveillance efforts. This agency collects and circulates a complete set of statistics that detail disease prevalence (rates indicating the presence of specific diseases) and incidence (rates indicating the number of new cases during a particular period, such as a week). It also is involved in major disease-prevention efforts.

Community-Based Health Facilities

Many community agencies are involved in the community health effort. These agencies may include typical health-focused service agencies (e.g., local heart or muscular dystrophy associations, among others). They may also include human and social service agencies (e.g., an aging service agency that institutes a day care center for frail elderly). These agencies may be publicly or privately funded. Their activities can be very diverse.

Community-based agencies may implement health fairs, community-based screening programs, and infant care services or provide health education material. Outreach service programs are often included. They may also mobilize a community to intervene directly. There is renewed interest in the term *empowerment,* which refers to efforts of a community to exert local control over conditions that are troublesome. In some communities persons march to influence officials to remove unsafe housing or clean up dumpsites. Other communities contribute money to clean up lots that can provide safe play areas for children. Still others resort to dubious tactics (such as trying to deny schooling to young AIDS patients) to control the spread of AIDS.

Community Medicine

Medical specialties that physicians can pursue on a postgraduate basis now include community medicine. This is a medical practice area directed toward community health. Community medicine had its birth in the 1960s. Health professionals acknowledged that there must be a program responsible for professional development, direction, and coordination of a wide range of ambulatory health care services. Thus, departments of community medicine were established in leading medical schools.

The major premise of community medicine programs is that "the main factors that determine a community's health are to be found within the community itself—in its social, cultural, or biological features, or in its environment, natural and man-made" (Clark 1981, p. 14). At the heart of the statement is the assumption that community health cannot be promoted nor assured without recognizing that resources, circumstances, attitudes, and population characteristics of the community can cause or prevent disease; furthermore, these things determine the medical treatment that ill people can receive.

Community medicine programs acquire and provide information on health and health problems of the community, the health services available, and the planning and management of health care. They also provide the expertise to advise community health and human service agencies on health status concerns. Therefore, persons trained in community medicine programs recognize that the physical and social environments, the behaviors of the citizens, and the way the health care system of the community is organized all govern the health of that community.

Epidemiology

Community health and health problems are best understood by utilizing a scientific approach. This relies on epidemiological studies. Epidemiology is defined as the study of the determinants and distribution of disease in a population. It is a population-based effort to understand disease and is widely used in community and public health research.

Determining the population at risk for a particular disease or injury is critical if it is to be controlled.

Epidemiological studies investigate (1) the segment of the population at risk for a disease or injury; (2) the biomedical, environmental, and psychosocial factors that influence the onset of the problem; and (3) the factors associated with the course and progression of an illness.

Determining the population at risk for a particular disease or injury is critical if it is to be controlled. Until epidemiological research established that AIDS was primarily confined to hemophiliacs, intravenous drug users, homosexuals, sexual partners of the groups named, and children of infected mothers, it was impossible to plan intervention strategies. In earlier times, people with dread diseases were isolated because the principle of an at-risk individual was unknown, and it was believed that every person was susceptible. Hence, the diseased citizen was kept from everyone.

The biomedical, environmental, and psychosocial factors that can influence the onset of a disease must be identified before preventive efforts can be successful. Clearly, medical experts could not accurately begin to address lung cancer prevention until sufficient causal linkages of cigarette smoking and lung pathology were established.

Research that identifies factors that exacerbate or ameliorate progression of a disease can provide a major breakthrough. Such research yields important information about slowing the course of a disease or preventing further bodily deterioration. The Framingham Heart Study showed that stress and personality characteristics such as Type A Behavior increase the likelihood of death from a heart attack (Haynes et al. 1978; Haynes, Feinleib, and Kannel 1980). After this epidemiological study, both prevention and treatment efforts began to concentrate on behavioral change and psychosocial phenomena that affect the course of an illness.

Conclusions About Community Health

Community health is the approach that addresses health service provision; community health is also the population-based discipline that determines the distribution and causes of health problems in a community. The terms *community health* and *public health* are often used interchangeably, but they are quite different. Public health technically refers to a society's efforts to deal with disease and injury on an official basis, using public funds. Community health, on the other hand is a much broader health effort. It involves many prevention- and treatment-oriented services and includes numerous people and institutions associated with both the public and nonpublic sectors. Preserving health, preventing disease and injury wherever possible, and organizing and providing adequate health care services are ongoing major community health activities.

[See also Comparative Health-Care Systems; Health Promotion.]

BIBLIOGRAPHY

Clark, Duncan W. 1981 "A Vocabulary for Preventive and Community Medicine." In Duncan W. Clark and Brian MacMahon, eds., *Preventive and Community Medicine.* Boston: Little, Brown.

Haynes, Suzanne G., Manning Feinleib, and William B. Kannel 1980 "The Relationship of Psychosocial Factors to Coronary Heart Disease in the Framingham Study: III. Eight-Year Incidence of Coronary Heart Disease." *American Journal of Epidemiology* 111:37–58.

Haynes, Suzanne G., Manning Feinleib, Sol Levine, Nathan Scotch, and William B. Kannel 1978 "The Relationship of Psychosocial Factors to Coronary Heart Disease in the Framingham Study: II. Prevalence of Coronary Heart Disease." *American Journal of Epidemiology* 107:384–402.

Nation's Health 1990 "Bills Would Fund Breast, Cervical Cancer Screening." *The Nation's Health* 20(4):1, 13.

Shonick, William 1988 "Public Health Services: Background and Present Status." In Stephen J. Williams and Paul R. Torrens, eds., *Introduction to Health Services,* 3rd ed. New York: Wiley.

– ROSALIE F. YOUNG

COMPARABLE WORTH

Comparable worth refers to equal pay for work of equal value. Like affirmative action policies, it has been proposed as a way to remedy the effects of past discrimination and, like affirmative action policies, it is controversial. Comparable worth advocates would extend the right of equal pay for equal work provided by Title VII of the Civil Rights Act of 1964 to a broader concept of equal pay for work requiring comparable levels of effort, skills, and responsibility. A number of legal actions, including one heard in the Supreme Court (*County of Washington* v. *Gunther,* 452 U.S. 161 [1981]), have been based on the premise of comparable worth. The Supreme Court ruling in this case removed a major legal obstacle to comparable worth as the basis for equalizing wages. Although it did not endorse the comparable worth approach, it did rule that a man and woman need not do "equal work" in order to establish pay discrimination under Title VII (Heen 1984). Subsequent lower court rulings have not resulted in clear-cut decisions regarding comparable worth, and at present it seems unlikely that court decisions will mandate the comparable worth approach. Nevertheless, the concept remains important in public policy debates.

The issue of comparable worth arose primarily in response to concern over continued wage inequality between men and women. (Although comparable worth policies also have significant implications for minorities, the debate has centered primarily on gender inequalities, and the discussion here focuses on gender.) The concern over the inequality of wages for men and women is not a new one. In the 1922 presidential address to the British Association of Economists, F. Y. Edgeworth (1922) spoke on "Equal Pay to Men and Women for Equal Work." The major issues he outlined are much as they remain: First, that men and women work in different jobs, albeit jobs that often require similar levels of effort and skill; second, that jobs held by women are paid far less than those held by men; and third, whether removing overt discrimination will equalize wages for men and women.

There is considerable evidence demonstrating that men and women work in different occupations. During the 1980s more than half of the workers of one sex would have had to change occupations in order to equalize the distribution of men and women across occupations (Jacobs 1989). Researchers using more specific job titles within firms have found that almost no men and women occupy positions with the same title in the same firm (Bielby and Baron 1986). Comparisons of occupational segregation by sex since 1900 show that levels have remained about the same (Gross 1968; Jacobs 1989).

The difference in wages paid to women relative to men has also changed little during the twentieth century (Marini 1989). In 1993 in the United States, women sixteen years and older working full time brought home about 66 percent of what men earned (U.S. Bureau of the Census 1997). A number of factors account for this wage gap. Some of the difference can be attributed to individual differences in labor-market capital, such as education, training, and experience; however, these differences account for less than half of the difference in wages (U.S. Bureau of the Census 1997). On average, across a number of studies, the concentration of women in low-paying female-dominated occupations accounts for about 25 percent of the gap between men's and women's wages (Sorensen 1986).

A number of skill or work-environment explanations for the lower wages in female-dominated occupations have been proposed. Comparisons of the skill requirements of male- and female-dominated occupations do not support these explanations. Instead, these comparisons have shown that the premium paid for skills in male-dominated occupations is higher. That is, a specific skill requirement in male-dominated occupations increases the wage more than the same skill requirement increases the wage in female-dominated occupations (McLaughlin 1978; Kemp and Beck 1986). Empirical evidence has not supported other possible explanations, such as that female-dominated occupations have greater nonmonetary compensations (Jencks, Perman, and Rainwater 1988) or that they are more accommodating to intermittent careers (England 1982).

The conclusion of J. S. Mill in 1865, as quoted by Edgeworth in 1922—"The remuneration of the peculiar employments of women is always, I believe, greatly below that of employments of equal skill and equal disagreeableness carried on by men"—is similar to the conclusion reached by the Norton-commissioned National Research Council/National Academy of Sciences committee report in 1981:

> [Such] differential earnings patterns have existed for many decades. They may arise in part because women and minority men are paid less than white men for doing the same (or very similar) jobs within the same firm, or in part because the job structure is substantially segregated by sex, race, and ethnicity and the jobs held mainly by women and minority men pay less than the jobs held mainly by non-minority men. (Treiman and Hartmann 1981, p. 92).

Proponents of comparable worth argue that the lack of improvement in women's wages over past decades demonstrates the need for direct intervention to equalize wage rates. The justification for using comparable worth to adjust wages lies in two basic positions: (1) that the lower wages in historically female jobs represent a form of discrimination, and (2) that job-evaluation systems provide an acceptable remedy to this form of discrimination.

First, certain jobs have been systematically undervalued because the work has been and continues to be done primarily by women and minorities. This process has resulted in wages paid for historically female or minority work being *artificially depressed* relative to wages for jobs historically performed by white males. Thus, past discrimination is embedded in the current wage structure (Remick 1984; Marini 1989). Continued labor-market segregation combined with the systematic undervaluation of jobs held by women and minorities is thereby a principal cause of continued inequality and a form of labor-market discrimination.

Second, job-evaluation techniques provide a viable procedure for identifying and remedying this type of discrimination. The use of job-evaluation plans is neither new nor unusual. Currently, job evaluation is often used to determine pay scales, not only by governments, but also by many businesses.

Job evaluations are used for a variety of reasons; however, they are primarily used when employers cannot rely on the market to establish wages. (See Spilerman 1986, for a discussion of the types of organizations that use nonmarket wage-allocation mechanisms.) Employers must determine wages, for example, when positions are filled entirely from within an organizational unit (e.g., through promotion of an existing work force) or when they fill jobs that are unique to a particular firm. In these cases, "going rates" for all jobs are not always available in local labor markets.

Methods of job evaluation involve the establishment of equivalences for a variety of educational fields and degrees, types of skills, responsibilities, and work environments in order to compare the value to the firm of workers employed in different jobs. In addition to considering the training and work requirements for jobs within the firm, systems of job evaluation often also take into account whatever information is available on prevailing wages for different types of labor.

While in theory various jobs can be assigned values objectively, existing job-evaluation schemes have been criticized for undervaluing the skills and abilities that are emphasized in female jobs.

Actual methods of job evaluation differ, but the usual approach is to start by describing all jobs within a given organization. Next, a list of various requirements that are believed to determine pay differentials is developed and jobs are rated on each requirement. For instance, one requirement could be the use of mathematics. In this case each job would be rated from "low" (e.g., addition and subtraction of whole numbers) to "high" (use of differential equations and the calculus). Most job-evaluation methods have only included technical requirements of the job, such as level of education, skills, level of responsibility, and the environment in which the work is performed. Some job-evaluation methods also include such characteristics of job incumbents as average education, training, and experience. More ambitious job-evaluation models consider how jobs rank with regard to fringe benefits (e.g., sick leave), hours (e.g., shift work), training and promotion opportunities, hazards, autonomy (e.g., employees who may leave work without permission), authority (e.g., supervises others), and organizational setting (e.g., organizational size) as well as the technical and educational requirements of jobs (see Jencks, Perman, and Rainwater 1988). After each job is rated and given a score for each requirement, scores are combined to create an overall score for each job. These composite scores are then used to rank jobs in order to help determine appropriate wages (Blau and Ferber 1986). (Job-evaluation methods are also used in research on stratification and occupational mobility.) The implementation of comparable worth requires an evaluation of the contribution of many different jobs within an organization or firm.

Whereas a number of studies have successfully used this technique (Remick 1984; Steinberg and Cook 1982), there are a number of limitations to these methods in establishing comparable worth. First, while in theory various jobs can be assigned values objectively (i.e., not influenced by the sex and race of the incumbent), existing job-evaluation schemes have been criticized for undervaluing the skills and abilities that are emphasized in female jobs (Beatty and Beatty 1984). Second, job-evaluation methods are designed to be used *within* a particular firm or organization rather than across organizations. This is especially limiting because most organizations are staffed by individuals in a relatively narrow span of occupations. For example, a female occupation, such as nurse, and a male occupation, such as fire fighter, might have similar overall scores—but nurses and fire fighters seldom are incumbents in the same organization. Hence, it is unlikely that job-evaluation methods could be used to equalize wages of nurses and fire fighters. While these limitations prevent the use of job evaluation from being a complete solution to wage inequality arising from the segregation of women into undercompensated occupations, job-evaluation methods are certainly feasible, and a comparable worth strategy could have a substantial impact on reducing this source of inequality.

Although it is unlikely, as noted earlier, that comparable worth will be mandated under Title VII, it may be an important component of changes in the labor-market wage structures. For instance, it may serve as a bargaining chip in union negotiations. Unions in the public sector, especially those in organizations such as universities where public image is important, are particularly likely to pursue the comparable worth agenda (Remick 1984). Therefore, even without a strong legal mandate, comparable worth will likely influence labor-market outcomes.

[See also Gender; Work and Occupations.]

BIBLIOGRAPHY

Beatty, R. W., and J. R. Beatty 1984 "Some Problems with Contemporary Job Evaluation Systems." In H. Remick, ed., *Comparable Worth and Wage Discrimination: Technical Possibilities and Political Realities.* Philadelphia: Temple University Press.

Bielby, W. T., and J. N. Baron 1986 "Men and Women at Work: Sex Segregation and Statistical Discrimination." *American Journal of Sociology* 91:759–799.

Blau, F. D., and M. A. Ferber 1986 *The Economics of Women, Men and Work.* New York: Prentice-Hall.

Edgeworth, F. Y. 1922 "Equal Pay to Men and Women for Equal Work." *The Economic Journal* 32:431–456.

England, P. 1982 "The Failure of Human Capital Theory to Explain Occupational Sex Segregation." *Journal of Human Resources* 17:358–370.

Gross, E. 1968 "Plus ça change . . . ? The Sexual Structure of Occupations over Time." *Social Problems* 16:198–208.

Heen, M. 1984 "A Review of Federal Court Decisions Under Title VII of the Civil Rights Act of 1964." In H. Remick, ed., *Comparable Worth and Wage Discrimination: Technical Possibilities and Political Realities.* Philadelphia: Temple University Press.

Jacobs, J. A. 1989 "Long Term Trends in Occupational Segregation by Sex." *American Journal of Sociology* 95:160–173.

Jencks, C., L. Perman, and L. Rainwater 1988 "What Is a Good Job? A New Measure of Labor-Market Success." *American Journal of Sociology* 93:1322–1357.

Kemp, A. A., and E. M. Beck 1986 "Equal Work, Unequal Pay: Gender Discrimination within Work-similar Occupations." *Work and Occupations* 13:324–347.

Marini, M. M. 1989 "Sex Differences in Earnings in the U.S." In W. R. Scott, ed., *Annual Review of Sociology*, vol. 15. Palo Alto, Calif.: Annual Reviews.

McLaughlin, S. 1978 "Occupational Sex Identification and the Assessment of Male and Female Earnings Inequality." *American Sociological Review* 43:909–921.

Remick, H. (ed.) 1984 *Comparable Worth and Wage Discrimination: Technical Possibilities and Political Realities.* Philadelphia: Temple University Press.

Sorensen, E. 1986 "Implementing Comparable Worth: A Survey of Recent Job Evaluation Studies." *American Economic Review* (Papers and Proceedings) 76:364–367.

Spilerman, S. 1986 "Organizational Rules and the Features of Work Careers." *Research in Social Stratification and Mobility* 5:41–102.

Steinberg, Ronnie, and Alice Cook 1982 "Women, Unions and Equal Employment Opportunity." *Working Paper no. 3.* Albany, N.Y.: Center for Women in Government.

Treiman, D. J., and H. I. Hartman 1981 *Woman, Work and Wages: Equal Pay for Jobs of Equal Value.* Washington, D.C.: National Academy Press.

U.S. Bureau of the Census 1986 *Statistical Abstract of the United States.* 1987, 107th ed. Washington, D.C.: U.S. Government Printing Office.

——— 1987 *Male-Female Differences in Work Experience, Occupation and Earnings: 1984.* Current Population Report P-70, No. 10. Washington, D.C.: U.S. Government Printing Office.

– NANCY E. DURBIN

COMPARATIVE HEALTH-CARE SYSTEMS

With increasing pressure during the 1990s for restructuring the U.S. health-care system, social scientists as well as political activists have renewed interest in finding successful models abroad. A health-care system can be defined as the set of institutions designed to deliver health services, with mechanisms for financing these services, provisions for assuring access to the services, structures of the division of labor for delivering the services, and the arrangements for training those who provide the services. How these parts are organized and integrated into a system is a key issue in making cross-cultural comparisons. The situation can range from fragmentation, in which potentially there is no system at all, to a tightly interlinked set of structures and procedures.

Light (1986) has noted that the values espoused by a society underlie and partially explain the society's method of delivering health care. He posits four models of a health-care system—the mutual aid, professional, state, and corporatist models. The first of these, the mutual aid model, is not currently typical of any industrialized country and in the past applied chiefly among groups of workers who developed sickness funds. It involves people getting together to provide for their care in sickness and to promote health. It could be argued that this model no longer applies in the modern world, although vestiges remain in such movements as the Boston Women's Health Collective. For comparative purposes applicable to countries as a whole, the other three models are more relevant.

In the professional model, according to Light, the health system is run by medical professionals and is characterized by physician control and autonomy, fee-for-service reimbursement, emphasis on high quality care, and use of advanced technology. The only country that has approached this model is the United States. It does not apply elsewhere, with the possible exception of South Africa, and indeed can be characterized as a nonsystem, a "cottage industry," because of its basis in a market economy and the absence of national planning (Anderson 1989). In understanding the health-care systems in other countries, this model is of limited utility.

In the state model the goal is to keep people healthy at minimum cost in order to maintain the strength of the state. Consequently, the emphasis is on primary care and health promotion, with all planning and coordination centralized. Several countries may fit this model, including Great Britain and the People's Republic of China.

In Light's corporatist model, the interests of consumers, government, and providers are counterbalanced through negotiations that result in jointly agreeable health-care financing and organizational structure. The state may intervene to see that the terms of the agreement are carried out but does not itself run the system. According to Light, examples include Canada, the former West Germany, and Italy.

In reviewing information on health-care systems, it may not always be possible to force them into the state or corporatist mold, but these conceptualizations will be useful in understanding the diversity of organizational forms for providing health services in countries throughout the world, both industrialized (developed) and those still in the process of industrialization (developing). As "ideal types" in the Weberian sense, they are not expected to fit precisely to reality. Roemer (1977) had specified in more detail the aspects of national systems that should be considered in any analysis, namely economic support, manpower, facilities, delivery patterns, preventive services, regulation, and administration and planning. Again, these may constitute an ideal list since these issues may not all be addressed in reviews of comparative health-care systems. Moreover, Elling (1980, p. 84) complains that this perspective is ahistorical and fails to take into account "the continuing class struggle in a variety of political-economic forms."

Another complexity in comparative research in the health field is the fact that systems are often in flux, in some cases as a result of conscious planning for change, as in Cuba and Ghana, in others as the consequences (perhaps unintended) of changes in the structure of an entire society, as in the case of the People's Republic of China or in the joining of East and West Germany. As a consequence of the fluidity and multiplicity of health-care systems, it is not possible in this brief space to describe them all or indeed with any confidence to use descriptions that date back a decade or more. Thus, the Appendix in Kohn and White (1976), which describes the characteristics of health-services provisions and organization in the six foreign countries used in their WHO comparative study, is chiefly of historical interest, as are Elling's (1980) comparisons of systems in Africa, Asia, Latin America, the Middle East, Europe, Japan, and the USSR. The countries whose systems will be briefly summarized here are Japan, the People's Republic of China, Italy, Great Britain, Ghana, and Cuba. In each of these countries relatively recent information is available.

In Japan, based on its cultural beliefs, the physician, who has the title of *sensei* (teacher), is accepted as the leader of the health-care team, in which everyone knows his or her place, and patients accept the hierarchical order as well (Powell and Anesaki 1990). The Health Insurance Law provides for universal compulsory health insurance, but there are diverse insurance carriers and fee coverage rules, producing complex paper work requirements for reimbursement. Most physicians have private practices with open, no-appointment clinics, and also sell medicines.

Recently, the government, in an attempt to cut costs, has mandated that by 1995 each individual will pay 20 percent of medical care costs up to a prescribed ceiling. This has lead to the growth of private insurance, which individuals purchase to cover their 20-percent share, as well as to the merger of some of the health insurance carriers to reduce administrative costs. There is no government evaluation system for quality of services, not even in hospitals, where the average length of stay is the longest in the world, 49.1 days in 1983 (a figure that may be skewed by the inclusion of long-term care for leprosy cases and some elderly). The absence of an evaluation procedure arises, according to Powell and Anesaki (1990, pp. 234–235) from the paternalistic hierarchical system, in which employees and staff monitor themselves in order to gain respect. Among all the models in Light's terminology, Japan's health-care system comes closest to fitting the corporatist. But further change is coming to the system in Japan. Despite the fact that the health status of the Japanese people is very high, the extent to which the state should be more directly involved with the organization, financing, and delivery of health services is open for debate in the last decade of the twentieth century (Steslicke 1989). That Japan will shift to a state model remains a possibility.

In contrast to the island nation of industrialized Japan, the People's Republic of China inhabits a vast land mass and consists mainly of an agricultural population. Its health system from the time of "liberation" in 1949 focused on prevention and the delivery of primary care (Sidel and Sidel 1982). The well-known "barefoot doctor," briefly trained in public health, disease prevention, sanitation, and the care of minor, everyday illness, serves as the first level of health services in the countryside. If necessary, patients are referred to regional health clinics, which in turn may refer patients to hospitals, institutions largely concentrated in the cities (Mechanic and Kleinman 1980). Payments for health services have in the past been made at the commune or production brigade level; this system amounts to a form of mutual aid insurance. Annual membership fees were about 3 percent of family income, but members also had to pay a service fee for clinic visits. If referred to a hospital, the commune fund covered up to 50 percent of the costs, with the balance up to the patient. In urban areas, neighborhood medical workers provided the same services as the barefoot doctors. In all these efforts, integration of traditional Chinese and Western medicine has been a goal.

This description is put in the past tense because in recent years economic reform in China has fostered a market economy that has diminished the role of the commune, particularly in rural areas. As of 1984 only 40 to 45 percent of the rural population was covered by health insurance (Hsiao 1984). The collapse of the rural cooperative system has brought about a drop in the number of barefoot doctors, with some going back into agriculture to increase their income, while others have set up private practices. Some voluntary insurance program remain in production brigades and farms, but many seriously ill must pay the costs of hospital care. One lesson to be learned, according to Hsaio (1984, p. 935), is that economic structure affects health labor power, service demands, and the organization and financing of health care.

The British health-care system, also a state-run enterprise, has been described in detail by Gill (1980). Like Japan, Britain is an island, is highly industrialized, has a culture steeped in respect for royalty, and has a class-based hierarchy. The National Health Service has a tripartite structure: Primary care is delivered by general practitioners in small dispensaries throughout the country, a medical elite of specialists work in the hospitals (where general practitioners have no role after their patients are admitted), and a public health sector is responsible for preventive and health promotion programs. The conditions for delivery of services were successfully negotiated between organizations of the medical professions and the state at the initiation of the National Health Service. A national insurance program, based on deductions from wages and salaries, was originally supposed to cover all costs of care, but rising demand for care and increases in its costs later required partial payment for services for some conditions. British general practitioners, as in the USSR, play a gatekeeper role by validating illness pay claims or expediting admission to "council housing" for the elderly (Haug 1976, p. 93). They also play a role in rationing high technology hospital care such as kidney dialysis and organ transplants (Aaron and Schwartz 1984). British rationing is based on hard cost-benefit decisions, which affect the delivery of care to the elderly and the terminally ill.

Reorganizations in the system have attempted to equalize regional differences in services and bring about integration between public health, primary care, and hospital services. During the 1980s a conservative government policy focused on cutting costs. A private sector exists side by side with the National Health Service, particularly in more well-to-do areas and for specialist care. This private sector has grown in recent years because of long waits under the NHS for nonemergency hospital care, and it has spawned a growth in private insurance schemes (Aaron and Schwartz 1984). Thus, although a state system is the basic form of British health care, it coexists with a private enterprise structure as well.

The Italian Health Service serves as an example of a corporatist Western European system. In a country fragmented by regional differences, sometimes in language and frequently by political party ideology (between the Communist party and the Christian Democrats), there has really not been a national health-care system. As described by Krause (1988), Italy has historically had physicians on the public payroll. They are now grouped into *ordini,* the regional organizations to which all persons practicing medicine must belong by law and that have both licensing and disciplinary power. Prior to 1978, there was a proliferation of private health insurance plans covering different population segments—professionals, blue-collar workers, farmers, and civil servants. Although almost everyone was covered for some services, poor primary care facilities meant that treatment for all but minor illnesses required hospitalization. When these insurance schemes went bankrupt, the Italian National Health Service was created in 1978 as a cost-cutting measure. It was given an all-encompassing public fund, which was to be centrally managed but with budgets allocated to regional governments. Doctors were put on full salary. However, the Italian National Health Service is not a health service but a cost-control funding mechanism according to Krause (1988, p. 157), and it is not national but regional. The Italian medical organizations must contract for fees and payment methods with each regional and local government Health Service Administration. Three-year contracts are negotiated for patient panel reimbursements and hospital salaries. The *ordini* became the bargaining agents with the regional governments, who are trying to hold the line in costs. Strike threats could be used as bargaining strategies, and strikes could actually occur. It is the existence of this fragmented system of financing by contracts with medical groups that fits Italy into the category of Light's corporatist model.

An example of the tribulations of a health-care system in a small underdeveloped country in Africa forms a balance to the description of major systems in Asia and Europe. In Ghana, consistent with the WHO goal of health for all by the year 2000, a system of primary health care was adopted before 1980. It was viewed as a first step in developing a comprehensive health-care program. Ghana, like many poor countries, has a high infant and maternal mortality rate, problems of malnutrition, and extensive infective and parasitic diseases, which accounted for a third of all deaths in 1983 (Anyinam 1989). Among reasons for this poor health record has been the poverty of the country, the lack of good drinking water, and, as a hangover from former colonial policies, a tendency to put more funds into hospitals rather than in the system of free regional polyclinics.

In an attempt at cost containment undertaken by a new regime in 1983, "user fees" were introduced in all public health facilities, both primary care and specialist clinics, as well as for hospital inpatient care. These user fees were increased in 1985, with only leprosy and tuberculosis patients completely exempt and hospital care for a specified list of twenty-four diseases partially exempt. A health insurance program has also been instituted, but considering that 60 percent of rural and 45 percent of urban dwellers live below the poverty line, it is likely to be limited in coverage (Anyinam 1989, p. 541). With the help of an International Monetary Fund loan, Ghana has attempted to improve the availability of drugs and equipment. At the same time a decentralization policy has been adopted to make all physicians and hospitals autonomous, whether they are private or public. In the communities, primary health care involves village health workers, not unlike the barefoot doctors in China, supervised by nurses and public health officers. At a district level, a public health and medical team attempts to integrate these activities. But all are plagued by lack of trained staff and the poverty of the people. Ghana's experiences demonstrate the difficulties of implementing a state system when it is not centralized and when the economic context is inadequate to support the needed services.

In sharp contrast to the situation in Ghana is that of another small third world country. Cuba, on the opposite side of the globe, also suffered high infant mortality and was plagued with infectious diseases in the past. In Cuba, the government provides all medical care free; in 1983 this cost 15 percent of the gross national product. Ubell (1983) has described a system run by the Ministry of Public Health, which pays the salaries of all physicians and other health care workers, and runs all the local polyclinics, hospitals, and nursing homes. The polyclinics are the chief sources of ambulatory services, not only primary care but also some specialty care. Teams of physicians and nurses may make house calls, check up on persons at risk, and assess community health and sanitation conditions. Patients are seen by their own doctors, who provide entry into specialist and hospital care. Hospitals, formerly concentrated in Havana, are spread throughout the country, with 60 percent of beds in rural areas and towns. There are national medical institutes for high technology procedures including kidney transplants and heart operations. Sophisticated equipment, including computers and a CAT scan, is available at a major hospital attached to the Havana Medical School; much of this equipment is imported from Japan. Graduates of the medical school, which selects students on the basis of a high grade point average in the equivalent of high school, must perform three years of service in rural areas in community medicine.

Cuba's success has been comparable to that of the most advanced countries in cutting infant mortality, increasing life expectancy, and controlling of infectious diseases.

Local health policy making is shared to some extent with community organizations, particularly women's groups, but physicians have considerable local authority. In the end, the Ministry of Public Health, which controls the whole system, is responsible for the health advances that have been achieved. According to reports (Ubell 1983), Cuba's success has been comparable to that of the most advanced countries in cutting infant mortality, increasing life expectancy, and eradicating or controlling of infectious diseases. As far back as 1984, Cuba claimed a physician ratio of one for every 750 people, compared to one for every 540 in the United States and one for every 1,750 in Brazil (Ubell 1983, p. 1,472). Part of this success was due to financial aid from the Soviet Union but also to a national commitment to health promotion and health care that is unusual among hardpressed developing countries. Cuba is an example of a successful state system, and it has survived despite a U.S. embargo and many economic problems in the small island nation.

These few examples by no means exhaust the list of varying health-care systems. Partial information, rather than a comprehensive explanation of a total system, often appears in edited books or in journals. A sampling of recent reports of this type include articles about Peru (Andes 1989), Chile (Scarpaci 1985), Nepal (Subedi 1989), Singapore (Quah 1989), the Philippines (de Brun and Elling 1987), South Korea (Cho 1989), Egypt (Abu-Zeid and Daum 1985), New Zealand (Raffel 1989), Australia (Rees and Gibbons 1986), Switzerland (Lehman, Gutzmiller, and Martin 1989), Spain (de Miguel and Guillen 1989), Poland (Sokolowka and Rychard 1989), and the former Yugoslavia (Parmelee 1989). Besides the occasional book, among the best sources for understanding cross-cultural developments in the health field are the journals *Social Science and Medicine,* published in Great Britain, and the *International Journal of Health Services,* whose editor is located in the United States.

The lessons to be learned in comparing health-care systems cross-culturally concern the importance of historical background, cultural beliefs, economic structure, and even geographic characteristics in accounting for system differences. Yet there are some similarities that emerge, and many will continue in the future. Although there are variations in the structure of service delivery, in the relative importance given to primary care as against high-technology medicine, and in the mechanism of financing, there is one common theme. All health-care systems have to face the tension between the extent of coverage and cost containment. This tension is unlikely to diminish in the face of new technological discoveries, which are usually costly while they extend life or its quality. One additional fact that received little attention in the various reviews of health care systems throughout the world is the rapidly increasing percentage of elderly in both developing and developed countries. Persons of advanced years account for one-third of all health-care costs, at least in industrialized societies. If there is any convergence between systems cross-culturally, it will be not only in problems of coverage and cost but also in finding ways to provide adequate care for the growing numbers of the aged.

BIBLIOGRAPHY

Aaron, H. J., and W. B. Schwartz 1984 *The Painful Prescription: Rationing Hospital Care.* Washington, D.C.: The Brookings Institution.

Abu-Zeid, H. A., and W. B. Daum 1985 "Health Services Utilization and Cost in Ismailia, Egypt." *Social Science and Medicine* 21:451–461.

Anderson, O. W. 1989 "Issues in the Health Services of the United States." In M. G. Field, ed., *Success and Crisis in National Health System: A Comparative Approach.* New York: Routledge.

Andes, N. 1989 "Socioeconomic, Medical Care, and Public Health Contexts Affecting Infant Mortality: A Study of Community Level Differentiation in Peru." *Journal of Health and Social Behavior* 30:386–397.

Anyinam, C. A. 1989 "The Social Costs of the International Monetary Fund's Adjustment Programs for Poverty: The Case of Health Care Development in Ghana." *International Journal of Health Services* 19:531–547.

Cho, S. 1989 "The Emergence of a Health Insurance System in a Developing Country: The Case of South Korea." *Journal of Health and Social Behavior* 30:467–471.

Davis, C. M. 1989 "The Soviet Health System: A National Health Service in a Socialist Society." In M. G. Field, ed., *Success and Crisis in National Health Systems: A Comparative Approach.* New York: Routledge.

de Brun, S., and R. H. Elling 1987 "Cuba and the Philippines: Contrasting Cases in World-System Analysis." *International Journal of Health Services* 17:681–701.

de Miguel, J. M., and M. F. Guillen 1989 "The Health System in Spain." In M. G. Field, ed., *Success and Crisis in National Health System: A Comparative Approach.* New York: Routledge.

Elling, R. H. 1980 *Cross-National Study of Health Systems: Political Economies and Health Care.* New Brunswick, N.J.: Transaction Books.

Field, M. G. 1967 *Soviet Socialized Medicine: An Introduction.* New York: Free Press.

Gill, D. G. 1980 *The British National Health Service: A Sociologist's Perspective.* Publication no. 80-2054. Washington, D.C.: U.S. Department of Health and Human Services, National Institute of Health.

Haug, M. R. 1976 "Erosion of Professional Authority: A Cross-Cultural Inquiry in the Case of the Physician." *Milbank Memorial Quarterly* 54:83–106.

Hsiao, W. C. 1984 "Transformation of Health Care in China." *The New England Journal of Medicine* 310:932–936.

Kohn, R., and K. L. White (eds.) 1976 *Health Care: An International Study.* London: Oxford University Press.

Krause, E. A. 1988 "Doctors, Partitocrazia, and the Italian State." *The Milbank Quarterly* 66 (Supp. 2) 148–166.

Lehmann, P., F. Gutzwiller, and J. F. Martin 1989 "The Swiss Health System: The Paradox of Ungovernability and Efficacy." In M. G. Field, ed., *Success and Crisis in National Health Systems: A Comparative Approach.* New York: Routledge.

Light, D. W. 1986 "Comparing Health Care Systems: Lessons from East and West Germany." In P. Conrad and R. Kern, eds., *The Sociology of Health and Illness: Critical Perspectives.* 2d ed. New York: St. Martin's Press.

Mechanic, D., and A. Kleinman 1980 "Ambulatory Medical Care in the People's Republic of China: An Exploratory Study." *American Journal of Public Health* 70:62–66.

Parmelee, D. E. 1989 "Yugoslavia: Health Care under Self-Managing Socialism." In M. G. Field, ed., *Success and Crisis in National Health Systems: A Comparative Approach.* New York: Routledge.

Powell, M., and M. Anesaki 1990 *Health Care in Japan.* New York: Routledge.

Quah, S. R. 1989 "The Social Position and Internal Organization of the Medical Profession in the Third World: The Case of Singapore." *Journal of Health and Social Behavior* 30:450–466.

Raffel, M. W. 1989 "New Zealand Health Services." In M. G. Field, ed., *Success and Crisis in National Health Systems: A Comparative Approach.* New York: Routledge.

Rees, S. J., and L. Gibbons 1986 *The Brutal Game: Patients and the Doctors' Dispute.* North Ryde, NSW Australia: Angus and Robertson Publishers.

Roemer, M. I. 1977 *Comparative National Policies on Health Care.* New York: Marcel Decker.

Scarpaci, J. L. 1985 "Restructuring Health Care Financing in Chile." *Social Science and Medicine* 21:415–431.

Sidel, R. and V. W. Sidel 1982 *The Health of China.* Boston: Beacon Press.

Sokolowka, M., and A. Rychard 1989 "Alternatives in the Health Area: Poland in Comparative Perspective." In M. L Kohn, ed., *Cross-National Research in Sociology.* Newbury Park, Calif.: Sage.

Steslicke, W. E. 1989 "Health Care and the Japanese State." In M. G. Field, ed., *Success and Crisis in National Health Systems: A Comparative Approach.* New York: Routledge.

Subedi, J. 1989 "Modern Health Services and Health Care Behavior: A Survey in Kathmandu, Nepal." *Journal of Health and Social Behavior* 30:412–420.

Ubell, R. N. 1983 "High-Tech Medicine in the Caribbean: Twenty-five years of Cuban Health Care." *The New England Journal of Medicine* 309:1468–1472.

– MARIE R. HAUG

COMPLEX ORGANIZATIONS

Organizations, as a class, are socially constructed innovations, deliberately designed as solutions to problems. Although some forms of organization, such as churches and armies, have been around for centuries, only since the Industrial Revolution have complex organizations assumed the form people take for granted today. Because they are shaped by the contexts, or environments, in which they are established, contemporary organizations reflect the impact of their historical origins in societies characterized by growing affluence and conflicts over the control and distribution of wealth. Organizations come in a bewildering variety of forms because they have been explicitly created to deal with a wide range of problems and because they have emerged under widely varying environmental conditions.

Definitions of Organizations

What are complex organizations? A simple definition is that organizations are goal-directed, boundary-maintaining, socially constructed systems of human activity. Some definitions add other criteria such as deliberateness of design, existence of status structures, patterned understandings between participants, orientation to an environment, possession of a technical system for accomplishing tasks, and substitutability of personnel (Scott 1987).

Goal orientation and deliberate design of activity systems are distinctive features discriminating between organizations and other collectivities such as families and small groups. Organizations are purposive systems in which members behave as if their organizations have goals, although individual participants may personally feel indifferent toward those goals or even alienated from their organizations. Concerted collective action toward an apparent common purpose also distinguishes organizations from such social units as friendship circles, audiences, and mass publics. Because many organizational forms are now institutionalized in modern societies, people readily turn to them or construct them when a task or objective exceeds their own personal abilities and resources (Meyer and Rowan 1977; Zucker 1988).

Organizations have activity systems, or technologies, for accomplishing work, which can include processing raw materials, information, or people. Activity systems consist of bounded sets of interdependent role behaviors; the nature of the interdependencies is often contingent upon the techniques used.

Other key elements of organizations, such as socially constructed boundaries, are shared with other types of collectivities. The establishment of an "organization" implies a distinction between members and nonmembers, thus marking off organizations from their environments. Maintaining this distinction requires boundary-maintenance activity because boundaries may be permeable, and, thus, some organizations establish an authoritative process to enforce membership distinctions. For example, businesses have human resource management departments that select, socialize, and monitor employees, and voluntary associations have membership committees that perform similar functions. Distinctive symbols of membership may include unique modes of dress and special vocabularies.

Organizations, with few exceptions, are incomplete social systems that depend on interchanges with their environments. Pertinent features of the environment include technical elements directly tied to the accomplishment of work, such as information and other resources, and cultural or institutional elements shared with the wider society such as rules, understandings, and meanings about organizations (Meyer and Scott 1983).

Goal setting by owners or leaders thus must take into account the sometimes contrary preferences of other organizations, as activity systems are fueled by resources obtained from outsiders. For example, participants must be enticed or coerced into contributing to the organization's activities. Businesses pay people to work for them, and nonprofit organizations may offer more intangible benefits such as sociable occasions. Because organizations are not self-sufficient, they are subject to uncertainties and may be vulnerable to exploitation or external control by the outsiders on whom they depend (Pfeffer and Salancik 1978). Contemporary research often focuses on how these external dependencies are managed by organizations.

Most organizations are fairly vulnerable to environmental forces and must adapt to them or disband.

Within organizations, goal attainment and boundary maintenance manifest themselves as issues of coordination and control, as authorities construct arrangements for allocating resources or integrating work flows. These internal structures affect the perceived meaning and satisfaction of individual participants by, for example, differentially allocating power and affecting the characteristics of jobs. Control structures, which shape the way participants are directed, evaluated, and rewarded, are constrained by participants' multiple external social roles, some complementing, but others conflicting with, organizational roles. Over the past few decades, organizational sociology has gradually expanded its scope to include more of the external uncertainties associated with organizational life.

Importance of Organizations

Why are complex organizations important? Organizations, which produce goods, deliver services, maintain order, and challenge the established order, are the fundamental building blocks of modern societies and the basic vehicles through which collective action is undertaken. The prominence of organizations in contemporary society is apparent when we consider some consequences of their actions.

Organizations coordinate the actions of people in pursuit of activities too broad in scope to be accomplished by individuals alone. Railroads were the first large corporations in the United States, arising because the passage of long-distance shipments could not be effectively coordinated by many small, autonomous merchants and traders. In the twentieth century, the production of mass-market consumption goods such as automobiles and electric appliances has been made possible by the rise of large, vertically integrated manufacturing firms. Similarly, in the public sector, the implementation of government social policies has necessitated the development of large government agencies that process thousands of cases on a universalistic, impersonal basis.

The concentration of power in organizations contributes not only to the attainment of large-scale goals in modern societies but also to some major social problems. Hazardous waste contamination in the so-called Love Canal episode in Buffalo, New York, was a result of the careless disposal of unwanted hazardous materials by large chemical manufacturers. Less dramatic, but still illustrative of the capacity of organizations to do harm and good, are accounts of unsafe consumer products and the relative collapse of the savings and loan industry in the late 1980s.

Increasingly, major tasks in society are addressed, not by single organizations, but by sets of interdependent organizations. The National Cooperative Research Act of 1984 allowed businesses that normally compete with each other to establish research-and-development consortia for conducting research on processes or products that benefit an entire industry. Interorganizational arrangements among hospitals, doctors, and university laboratories have been created by the National Cancer Institute to coordinate cancer research and treatment.

Organizational Demographics

The number of organizations in industrial societies is very large. Over five million businesses with at least one employee existed in the United States in 1990, and there were thousands of governmental, nonprofit, membership, and voluntary associations. Social scientists have developed various schemes to describe the diversity of organizations. For example, the Standard Industrial Classification (Office of Management and Budget 1972) sorts establishments by their products and the processes used to make them. Organizations can also be classified according to their goals, the social functions they serve (Parsons 1960), and the prime beneficiaries of organizational actions: owners, members, clients, or the general public (Blau and Scott 1962). Another classification contrasts generalist and specialist organizations and hypothesizes that each type thrives in a different kind of environment (Hannan and Freeman 1989).

Business organizations are highly stratified by size, and large firms have more resources with which to resist and counter environmental pressures. The vast majority of organizations are small, however. Most business establishments employ fewer than one hundred workers, and typical voluntary associations have fewer than fifty members. Thus, most organizations are fairly vulnerable to environmental forces and must adapt to them or disband. A representative sample of organizations would yield predominantly small ones, rather than organizations as large as International Business Machines (IBM), General Motors, or Exxon.

Even though most organizations are small, their numbers are often counterbalanced by the extreme wealth and power of the handful of truly enormous organizations. In the United States, more than 50 percent of the civilian labor force is employed by only 2 percent of employing units, and, in manufacturing, the top 200 firms control about 60 percent of all assets (Useem 1984). About 50 percent of all banking assets are controlled by thirty out of 14,000 banks, and eight out of approximately 1,800 insurance companies hold half of the assets in that industry (Kerbo 1983). Some sociologists have argued that large organizations are so effective at neutralizing competitive forces that their survival is never in jeopardy (Perrow 1986).

Populations of organizations in modern societies are constantly undergoing processes of expansion, contraction, and change. Some organizations are founded in a flash of creative energy and then disbanded almost immediately, whereas others emerge slowly and last for decades. Some organizations adapt readily to every environmental challenge, whereas others succumb to the first traumatic event they face. Sociologists have turned their attention to these vital events surrounding the reproduction and renewal of organizational populations, focusing on three processes: foundings, transformations, and disbandings (Aldrich 1979; Hannan and Freeman 1989).

New organizations are established fairly frequently, although systematic data on founding rates are available only for businesses. Studies in the United States and other Western industrialized nations show that about ten businesses are founded per year for every one hundred businesses active at the start of the year. Explanations for variations in rates of organizational foundings have stressed the characteristics of opportunity structures, organizing capacities of groups, and strategies adopted by entrepreneurs as they take account of opportunities and resources available to them (Aldrich and Wiedenmayer 1991).

Societal demands for special-purpose organizations increased with urbanization and with economic, political, and social differentiation, while the resources required to construct organizations grew more abundant with the development of a money economy and the spread of literacy (Stinchcombe 1965). The spread of facilitative legal, political, and other institutions also played a major role by creating a stable, predictable context within which entrepreneurs could look forward to appropriating the gains from organizational foundings. Occasional periods of political upheaval and revolution stimulate foundings by freeing resources from previous uses, and thus massive changes are likely to occur in the organizational populations of Eastern Europe in the 1990s.

Transformations occur when existing organizations adapt their structures to changing conditions. The issue of how frequently and under what conditions organizations change has provoked some of the most spirited debates in organizational sociology. Strategic choice theorists have argued for managerial autonomy and adaptability, whereas ecological and institutional theorists have tended to stress organizational inertia and dependence. Recent research has moved away from polarizing debates and reframed the question of transformation, asking about the conditions under which organizations change and whether changes occur more frequently in core or peripheral features (Singh and Lumsden 1990).

During the 1980s growing awareness of techniques for performing dynamic analyses produced some useful studies such as those on diversification, top executive changes, and changes in corporate form (Fligstein 1991). These studies tell us that changes *do* occur, although they do not report whether rates of change go up or down over an organization's life cycle. Most of these studies are of the very largest business firms, for which data are publicly available, and not of representative samples.

If all newly founded organizations lived forever, the study of organizational change would be confined to issues of founding, adaptation, and inertia. Research has shown that organizations disband at a fairly high rate, however, and a sizable literature has grown up on organizational mortality (Carroll 1984; Singh 1990). Organizations can cease to exist as separate entities in two ways: by completely dissolving, the process by which the vast majority of organizations disband, or by becoming part of a different entity through merger or acquisition.

Age and size are the strongest predictors of how long an organization will survive. Young organizations disband at a substantially higher rate than older ones, a conservative estimate being that only half of new organizations survive more than five years (Birch 1987). Internally, new organizations depend upon the cooperation of strangers, who must be taught new routines, some of which are unique to particular organizations (Stinchcombe 1965). Externally, new organizations must find niches in potentially hostile environments, overcoming competitors and establishing their legitimacy with potential members, customers, suppliers, and others. Survival beyond infancy is easier when an organization adopts a form that has already been institutionalized and is widely regarded as legitimate and proper (Zucker 1988).

Sources of Internal Diversity Among Organizations

All models of organizations as coherent entities can be reduced to two basic views. The systemic view sees organizations as social systems, sustained by the roles allocated to their participants, whereas the associative perspective treats organizations as associations of self-interested parties, sustained by the rewards the participants derive from their association with the organizations (Swanson 1971). These two views each have a venerable heritage in the social sciences. Despite subtle variations, all perspectives on organizations ultimately use one or both of these models.

Differentiation of social organization is a centrifugal force threatening the coherence of social units.

Institutional, functionalist, and ecological perspectives rely on a systemic model, viewing organizations as relatively coherent, stable entities. Such models emphasize the activity systems in organizations that are deliberately designed to accomplish specific goals. Formal structures of organizations, including division of labor, authority relationships, and prescribed communication channels, are treated as fulfilling a purposeful design. For example, an institutional approach emphasizes member socialization and other processes that make the transmission of shared meanings easier. Ecological models usually treat organizations as units that are being selected for or against by their environments and, thus, assume that organizations cohere as units.

Interpretive and more microanalytic views rely heavily on an associative model, leading to the expectation that organizations are constantly at risk of dissolution (March and Olsen 1976). For example, in the interpretive view, the reproduction of organizational structure depends on participants resubscribing to, or continually negotiating, a shared understanding of what they jointly are doing. Some cultural theories of organization emphasize the different, conflicting views that coexist within one organization (Martin and Meyerson 1988).

Views of organizations as marketplaces of incentives (Dow 1988), bundles of transactions (Williamson 1981), or arenas of class conflict (Clegg 1989) are in harmony with the associative view, insofar as they focus on actors' contributions to sustaining interaction. Indeed, organizational economics views organizations primarily as mechanisms for mediating exchanges among individuals, arguing that they arise only when market-based mechanisms have proven inadequate (Williamson 1981).

These complementary views of organizations, the associative and the systemic, highlight the sources of two fundamental problems of social organization, those of differentiation and integration. Some differentiation occurs through the division of labor among different roles and subunits; for example, employees may be divided into departments such as sales, finance, and manufacturing. Differentiation pressures also arise because participants sometimes bring widely varying expectations to the same organization. Differentiation is thus a centrifugal force threatening the coherence of social units. Integration, in contrast, refers to procedures for maintaining coherence, as diverse roles are linked and activities coordinated to sustain an organization as a coherent entity. Examples of integrative processes include the holding of weekly departmental meetings or the circulation of interoffice memos.

Differentiation increases organizational complexity because it increases the extent and nature of specialization (Blau 1972). Complexity increases with the number of different components and may be horizontal (tasks spread over many roles or units), vertical (many levels in a hierarchy of authority), or spatial (many operating sites). Complexity also increases when tasks are grouped by product or market (soap, paper products, or foods) or by function (finance, production, or marketing).

There are problems of coordination for any activity system, but especially for a complex one. Many concepts used to describe organizational structure involve alternative processes employed in attempts to achieve integration. One scheme, for example, identified five coordinating mechanisms: direct supervision, formalization, and three forms of standardization (Mintzberg 1983).

With direct supervision, or simple control, decision making is highly centralized: Persons at the top of a hierarchy make decisions that lower-level personnel simply carry out. This coordination pattern was prevalent in preindustrial organizations, and today it is especially likely within small organizations (Edwards 1979).

Formalization, sometimes termed *bureaucratic control,* achieves coordination through rules and procedures. Examples include rules for arriving at work on time, for processing orders, for assembling and packaging products, and for conducting screening interviews for clients. A formalized organization may appear decentralized, since few explicit commands are given and lower-level participants have freedom in making decisions within the rules. The rules may, however, be so restrictive as to leave little room for discretion.

Coordination can also be attained through standardizing work processes, skills, or outputs to create technical control. With standardized work processes, coordination is built into machinery, as in an assembly line. Most discretion is eliminated by the design of the technical system, and what remains is centralized in the upper echelons.

Standardization of skills involves considerable training and indoctrination of personnel, so that participants carry out organizational policies with minimal oversight. Organizations employing large numbers of professionals are likely to rely on this coordination strategy (Von Glinow 1988). Professionalized participants enjoy considerable autonomy in making decisions, but their prior socialization determines most decision premises for them.

By producing products with standard properties, subunits of an organization are able to work independently of one another; if they use each other's outputs, the standards tell them what to anticipate. For example, large clothing firms produce massive runs of identical garments, and, thus, the various departments within firms know precisely what to expect from one another as they follow daily routines.

Conclusion

Complex organizations are the building blocks of industrial societies, enabling people to accomplish tasks that are otherwise beyond their individual competencies. Organizations also help create and sustain structures of opportunities and constraints that affect nearly all aspects of societies. Sociologists and other social scientists are grappling with a variety of complementary and conflicting perspectives on organizations, ranging from microanalytic interpretive views to macroevolutionary institutional and ecological views. Regardless of perspective, research on organizations has shown its capacity to interest, inform, and provoke us as sociologists investigate these social constructions that figure so prominently in our lives.

[See also Bureaucracy; Voluntary Associations.]

BIBLIOGRAPHY

Aldrich, Howard E. 1979 *Organizations and Environments.* Englewood Cliffs, N.J.: Prentice-Hall.

———, and Gabriele Wiedenmayer 1991 "From Traits to Rates: An Ecological Perspective on Organizational Foundings." In Jerome Katz and Robert Brockhaus, eds., *Advances in Entrepreneurship, Firm Emergence, and Growth,* vol. 1. Greenwich, Conn.: JAI.

Birch, David 1987 *Job Creation in America.* New York: Free Press.

Blau, Peter M. 1972 "Interdependence and Hierarchy in Organizations." *Social Science Research* 1:1–24.

———, and W. Richard Scott 1962 *Formal Organizations.* San Francisco: Chandler.

Carroll, Glenn R. 1984 "Organizational Ecology" In Ralph H. Turner and James F. Short, Jr., eds., *Annual Review of Sociology,* vol. 10. Palo Alto, Calif.: Annual Reviews.

Clegg, Stewart 1989 "Radical Revisions: Power, Discipline and Organizations." *Organization Studies* 10:97–115.

Dow, Gregory K. 1988 "Configurational and Coactivational Views of Organizational Structure." *Academy of Management Review* 13:53–64.

Edwards, Richard C. 1979 *Contested Terrain: The Transformation of the Workplace in the Twentieth Century.* New York: Basic Books.

Fligstein, Neil 1991 *The Transformation of Corporate Control.* Cambridge, Mass.: Harvard University Press.

Grimm, W. T. 1989 *Mergerstat Review 1988.* Chicago: Grimm.

Hannan, Michael T., and John H. Freeman 1989 *Organizational Ecology.* Cambridge, Mass.: Harvard University Press.

Kerbo, Harold 1983 *Social Stratification and Inequality.* New York: McGraw-Hill.

March, James G., and Johan P. Olsen 1976 *Ambiguity and Choice in Organizations.* Bergen, Norway: Universitetsforlaget.

Martin, Joanne, and Debra Meyerson 1988 "Organizational Cultures and the Denial, Channeling, and Acknowledgment of Ambiguity." In Louis R. Pondy, Richard Boland, Jr., and Howard Thomas, eds., *Managing Ambiguity and Change.* New York: Wiley.

Meyer, John W., and Brian Rowan 1977 "Institutionalized Organizations: Formal Structure as Myth and Ceremony." *American Journal of Sociology* 83:340–363.

Meyer, John W., and W. Richard Scott 1983 *Organizational Environments: Ritual and Rationality.* Beverly Hills, Calif.: Sage.

Mintzberg, Henry 1983 *Structure in Fives: Designing Effective Organizations.* Englewood Cliffs, N.J.: Prentice-Hall.

Office of Management and Budget, Statistical Policy Division 1972 *Standard Industrial Classification Manual.* Washington, D.C.: U.S. Government Printing Office.

Parsons, Talcott 1960 *Structure and Process in Modern Societies.* New York: Free Press.

Perrow, Charles 1986 *Complex Organizations.* New York: Scott, Foresman.

Pfeffer, Jeffrey, and Gerald R. Salancik 1978 *The External Control of Organizations.* New York: Harper and Row.

Scott, W. Richard 1987 *Organizations: Rational, Natural, and Open Systems.* Englewood Cliffs, N.J.: Prentice-Hall.

Singh, Jitendra (ed.) 1990 *Organizational Evolution.* Beverly Hills, Calif.: Sage.

———, and Charles Lumsden 1990 "Theory and Research in Organizational Ecology." In W. Richard Scott and Judith Blake, eds., *Annual Review of Sociology,* vol. 16. Palo Alto, Calif.: Annual Reviews.

Small Business Administration 1986 *The State of Small Business.* Washington, D.C.: U.S. Government Printing Office.

Stinchcombe, Arthur 1965 "Social Structure and Organizations." In J. G. March, ed., *Handbook of Organizations.* Chicago: Rand McNally.

Swanson, Guy E. 1971 "An Organizational Analysis of Collectivities." *American Sociological Review* 36:607–614.

Useem, Michael 1984 *The Inner Circle.* New York: Oxford University Press.

Von Glinow, Mary Ann 1988 *The New Professionals: Managing Today's High-Tech Employees.* Cambridge, Mass.: Ballinger.

Williamson, Oliver 1981 "The Economics of Organization: The Transaction Cost Approach." *American Journal of Sociology* 87:548–577.

Zucker, Lynne G. (ed.) 1988 *Institutional Patterns and Organizations: Culture and Environment.* Cambridge, Mass.: Ballinger.

– HOWARD E. ALDRICH
PETER V. MARSDEN

COUNTERCULTURES

The enclaves in which people of the modern era live no longer resemble the small, integrated, and homogeneous communities of earlier times; rather, these have been replaced by large societies that are complex and diverse in their composition. The United States, a prime exemplar, is composed of multiple smaller groups holding characteristics, beliefs, customs, and interests that vary from the rest of society. While there are many cultural universals binding such groups to the mainstream, they also exhibit significant cultural diversity. Some of these groups display no clear boundaries demarcating them from the rest of society and fail to achieve any degree of permanence. Yet those that do, and that also share a distinctive set of norms, values, and behavior setting them off from the dominant culture, are considered *subcultures.* Subcultures can be organized around age, ethnicity, occupation, social class, religion, or life-style and usually contain specific knowledge, expressions, ways of dressing, and systems of stratification that serve and guide members. Distinctive subcultures within the United States include jazz musicians, gangs, Chicanos, homosexuals, college athletes, and drug dealers. While it was once hypothesized that these subcultures would merge together in a melting pot incorporating a mix of the remnants of former subcultures, more recent trends suggest that they resist total assimilation and retain their cultural diversity and distinct identity (Irwin 1970).

Countercultures, through their oppositional culture, attempt to reorganize drastically the normative bases of social order.

Some subcultures diverge from the dominant culture without morally rejecting the norms and values with which they differ. Others are more adamant in their condemnation, clearly conflicting with or opposing features of the larger society. Milton Yinger first proposed, in 1960, to call these groups *contracultures,* envisioning them as a subset of all subcultures: those having an element of conflict with dominant norms, values, or both (Yinger 1960). Indeed, the feature he identified as most compelling about a contraculture is its specific organization in opposition to some cultural belief(s) or expression(s). Contracultures often arise, he noted, where there are conflicts of standards or values between subcultural groups and the larger society. Factors strengthening the conflict then strengthen the contracultural response. Contracultural members, especially from such groups as delinquent gangs, may be driven by their experiences of frustration, deprivation, or discrimination within society.

Yinger's conceptualization, although abstract and academic at first, came to enjoy widespread popularity and fruition with the advent of the 1960s and the student movement. Here was the kind of contraculture he had forecast, and his ideas were widely applied to the trends of the time, albeit under another label. Most analysts of contracultures preferred the term *counterculture,* and this soon overtook its predecessor as the predominant expression. In 1969 Theodore Roszak published his *The Making of a Counter Culture,* claiming that a large group of young people (ages fifteen to thirty) had arisen who adamantly rejected the technological and scientific outlook characteristic of Western industrialized culture, replacing this, instead, with a humanistic/mysticist alternative. Keniston (1971) described this counterculture as composed of distinct subgroups (radicals, dropouts, hippies, drug users, communards) rising from the most privileged children of the world's wealthiest nation. Douglas (1970) also discussed the social, political, and economic background to this movement and its roots in members' entrenchment in the welfare state and the existing youth and student cultures. While this movement was clearly political as well, Douglas outlined some of its social dimensions, including its rejection of the workaday world and its idealization of leisure, feeling, openness, and antimaterialism. Flacks (1971) and Davis (1971) followed with descriptions of the counterculture's overarching life-styles, values, political beliefs, and ideologies. Turner (1976), Adler (1972), and Erikson (1968) explored the social psychological implications of this counterculture, positing, respectively, a transformation in the self from "institution" to "impulse," the rise of an antinomian personality, where individuals oppose the obligatoriness of the moral law, and the formation of the "negative identity." Rothchild and Wolf (1976) documented the vast extension of counter-cultural outposts around the country and their innovations in child rearing. Reich (1970) emphatically stated that this counterculture was being reinforced by merging with nonstudent youth, educated labor, and the women's movement, already effecting a major transformation in Western laws, institutions, and social structure. There was strong belief that this movement would significantly and permanently alter both society and its consciousness (Wuthnow 1976). After researching one commune in depth, Berger (1981) later mused about the survival of the counterculture, acknowledging its failure to meet earlier expectations, yet examining how its ideals and values became incorporated into the mainstream culture (cf. Spates 1976).

Other subcultural analysts noted more broadly that these groups are typically popular among youth, who have the least investment in the existing culture, and that, lacking power within society, they are likely to feel the forces of social control swiftly moving against them, from the mass media to police action. Countercultures were further differentiated from subcultures by the fact that their particular norms and values were not well integrated into the dominant culture, these being generally known only among group members.

Yinger reclaimed theoretical command of the countercultural concept with his reflective expansions on the term in a presidential address for the American Sociological Association (Yinger 1977) and a book that serves as the definitive statement on the topic (1982). He asserted the fundamental import of studying these sharp contradictions to the dominant norms and values of a society as a means of gaining insight into social order. Countercultures, through their oppositional culture (polarity, reversal, inversion, and diametric opposition), attempt to reorganize drastically the normative bases of social order. These alternatives may range from rejecting a norm or value entirely to exaggerating its emphasis in their construction of countervalues. As a result, some countercultures fade rapidly while others are lasting, and some have no significant impact on the larger society while parts of others become incorporated into the broader cultural value system. Examples of countercultural groups would include the 1960s student counterculture (in both its political and social dimensions); youth gangs (especially delinquent groups); motorcycle gangs (such as the Hell's Angels); revolutionary groups (the Weathermen of the Students for a Democratic Society, or the Black Panthers); terrorist organizations (such as the Symbionese Liberation Army); extremist racist groups (the Ku Klux Klan, the skinheads, the

Aryan Nation); survivalists; punkers; bohemian Beats, and some extremist religious sects (such as the Amish and the Hare Krishnas).

Varieties of Countercultures

Yinger believed that countercultural groups could take several forms. The *radical activist* counterculture "preaches, creates, or demands new obligations" (Yinger 1977, p. 838). They are intimately involved with the larger culture in their attempts to transform it. Members of the *communitarian utopian* counterculture live as ascetics, withdrawing into an isolated community forged under the guidelines of their new values. *Mystical* countercultures search for the truth and for themselves, turning inward toward consciousness to realize their values. Theirs is more a disregard of society than an effort to change it. These three forms are not necessarily intended to describe particular groups. Rather, they are ideal types, offered to shed insight into characteristics or tendencies groups may combine or approximate in their formation. Hippie communities or bohemian Beat groups combined the mystical and utopian features of countercultures in their withdrawal from conventional society and their search for a higher transcendence. Revolutionary youth gangs, such as the 1960s radicals, the Hell's Angels, and the punkers, fuse the mystical search for new experiences and insights (often through drug use) with an activist attack on the dominant culture and its institutional expressions. Survivalists, Amish, and Hare Krishnas fuse the radical critique of conventional values and life-styles with a withdrawal into an isolated and protected community.

Countercultures can also be differentiated by their primary breaks with the dominant culture. Some take odds with its *epistemology,* or the way society contends that it knows the truth. Hippies and other mystics, for example, have tended to seek insight in homespun wisdom, meditation, sensory deprivation, drugs, or direct experience with the cosmos, rejecting the cold rationality of science and technology. Others assert an alternative system of *ethics,* arguing about the values pursued in defining the good or striving for the good life. Some,

Studying counterculture groups, such as these punk rockers of the 1980s, provides insights into social order because these groups display sharp contradictions to the dominant norms and values of a society. (Nik Wheeler/Corbis)

like skinheads or KKK members, may be quite conservative in their definition of the good life; others are libertarian, advocating for people to "do their own thing." Third, countercultures offer alternative *aesthetic standards* by which fashion, taste, and beauty are to be judged. Punk or acid rock musical movements, performance or postmodernist art movements, and bohemian or hippie fashion movements were all aesthetic statements that incorporated a radical rejection of the standards of conventional taste and its connection to conventional values. Thus, entire countercultural movements may be based on their advocacy of these competing beliefs.

Countercultures and Social Change

Due to their intense opposition to the dominant culture, countercultures are variously regarded as "engines of social change, symbols and effects of change, or mere faddist epiphenomena" (Yinger 1982, p. 285). Examining these in reverse order, countercultures are often considered *mutations* of the normative social order, encompassing such drastic life-style changes that they invoke deep ambivalence and persecution. Most major countercultural mutations appear in the form of religious movements. Other countercultures arise out of underlying or developing societal stresses: rapid political or economic change; demographic transformations in the population (age, gender, location); a swift influx of new ideas; drastic escalation or diminishment of hopes or aspirations; weakening of ties to primary support circles (families, neighborhoods, work groups); and the erosion of meaning in the deepest symbols and rituals of society. These factors are then augmented by communication among people sharing such experiences or beliefs, leading them to coalesce into normatively and ideologically integrated groups. Countercultures can also precipitate social change if the norms and values they champion are incorporated into the mainstream. In commenting on the 1960s student movement, Chief Justice Warren Burger of the United States Supreme Court stated that "the turbulent American youth, whose disorderly acts [I] once 'resented,' actually had pointed the way to higher spiritual values" (cited in Yinger 1977, p. 848). Lasting influence may not always result from major countercultural movements, as witnessed by the rapid erosion in influence of Mao's cultural revolution after his death, yet it is possible. This occurs through a cultural dialectic, wherein each normative system, containing within it the seeds of its own contradiction, gives rise to the oppositional values of a counterculture that are ultimately incorporated into its future synthesis.

Counterculture Case Studies

While the student movement of the 1960s was undoubtedly the largest and most influential counterculture to arise in the United States, a review of three more contemporary countercultures may yield further insight into the parameters and character of these movements. Let us focus briefly on the Hare Krishnas, punks, and survivalists.

The Hare Krishna movement, also known as the International Society for Krishna Consciousness (ISKCON), is one of the new religious movements that became popular in the United States during the great "cult" period of the 1970s (Judah 1974; Rochford 1985). Its rise after the decline of the 1960s student movement is not coincidental, for many people who were former hippies or who were influenced by or seeking the ideals and values of the 1960s turned toward new religions (Tipton 1982) in search of the same features of community, idealism, antimaterialism, mysticism, transcendence to a higher plane, and "a spiritual way of life, which stands outside the traditional institutions found in America" (Rochford 1985, p. 44). Its primary values conflicting with mainstream culture include the rejection of (1) material success through competitive labor; (2) education to promote that end; (3) possessions for sense gratification; (4) authority favoring the status quo; (5) imperialistic aggression; and (6) the hypocrisy of racial discrimination (Judah 1974, p. 16). After the death of its American spiritual master, Srila Prabhupada, in 1977, however, the movement peaked and became more commercialized, transferring its emphasis from self-expression and uniqueness to survival, thereby becoming more of a mass phenomena.

In contrast to the religious and value components of the Hare Krishnas' rejection of mainstream culture, the punk or punk rock counterculture of the late 1970s and early 1980s was more of a style movement (Hebdige 1981). As Fox (1987, p. 349) has noted, "The punks created a new aesthetic that revealed their lack of hope, cynicism, and rejection of societal norms." This was expressed in both their appearance and their life-style. The punk belief system was antiestablishment and anarchistic, celebrating chaos, cynicism, and distrust of authority. Punks disdained the conventional system, with its bureaucracies, power structures, and competition for scarce goods (Fox 1987). Members lived outside the system, unemployed, in old abandoned houses or with friends, and engaged in heavy use of nihilistic drugs such as heroin and glue. Hard-core commitment was usually associated with semipermanent alteration of members' appearance through tattoos, shaven heads, or Mohawk hairstyles (Brake 1985). The musical scene associated with punks was contrary to established tastes as well and often involved self-abandonment characterized by "crash dancing" (Street 1986).

In contrast to the hippies, Krishnas, and punks, the survivalist counterculture was grounded in exaggeration of right-wing beliefs and values. While the former groups preached love, survivalists centered themselves on hate. Formed out of extremist coalition splinter groups such as neo-Nazis, Klansmen, John Birchers, fundamentalist Mormon Freemen, the White Aryan Resistance, and tax protesters from Posse Comitatus, survivalists drew on long-standing convictions that an international conspiracy of Jews was taking over everything from banking, real estate, and the press to the Soviet Politburo and that the white race was being "mongrelized" by civil-rights legislation. A cleansing nuclear war or act of God, with "secular" assistance, would soon bring the Armageddon, eradicating the "Beast" in their midst (Coates 1987). Members thus set about producing and distributing survivalist literature, stockpiling machine guns, fuel, food, and medical supplies on remote farms and in underground bunkers, joining survivalist retreat groups, and attending survivalist training courses (Peterson 1984). Within their retreat communities they rejected the rationalization, technologization, secularization, and commodification of society, creating an environment of creative self-expression where an individual could accomplish meaningful work with a few simple tools. In their withdrawn communities and utopian future scenario, men would reclaim their roles as heads of the family; women would regain mastery over crafts and nurturance. Theirs is thus a celebration of fantasy and irrationality (Mitchell 1991, n.d.). Yet while they isolate themselves in countercultures peopled by like-minded individuals, they try to influence mainstream society through activism in radical right-wing politics as well. Their actions and beliefs, although rejecting the directions and trends in contemporary society, arise out of and represent frustrations felt by embattled segments of the moral majority.

Countercultures thus stand on the periphery of culture, spawned by and spawning social trends and changes in their opposition. As Yinger (1977, p. 850) has noted, "Every society gets the countercultures it deserves, for they do not simply contradict, they also express the situation from which they emerge. . . . Countercultures borrow from the dominant culture even as they oppose it."

[See also Alternative Life-Styles; Social Movements; Student Movements.]

BIBLIOGRAPHY

Adler, Nathan 1972 *The Underground Stream: New Life Styles and the Antinomian Personality.* New York: Harper.

Berger, Bennett 1981 *The Survival of a Counterculture.* Berkeley: University of California Press.

Brake, Michael 1985 *Comparative Youth Culture: The Sociology of Youth Culture and Subcultures in America, Britain, and Canada.* London: Routledge.

Coates, James 1987 *Armed and Dangerous.* New York: Hill and Wang.

Davis, Fred 1971 *On Youth Subcultures: The Hippie Variant.* New York: General Learning Press.

Douglas, Jack D. 1970 *Youth in Turmoil.* Chevy Chase, Md.: National Institute of Mental Health.

Erikson, Erik 1968 *Identity: Youth and Crisis.* New York: W. W. Norton.

Flacks, Richard 1971 *Youth and Social Change.* Chicago: Markham.

Fox, Kathryn J. 1987 "Real Punks and Pretenders: The Social Organization of a Counterculture." *Journal of Contemporary Ethnography* 16:344–370.

Hebdige, Dick 1981 *Subcultures: The Meaning of Style.* New York: Methuen.

Irwin, John 1970 "Notes on the Present Status of the Concept Subculture." In D. O. Arnold, ed., *The Sociology of Subcultures.* Berkeley: Glendessary Press.

Judah, J. Stillson 1974 *Hare Krishna and the Counterculture.* New York: Wiley.

Keniston, Kenneth 1971 *Youth and Dissent: The Rise of a New Opposition.* New York: Harcourt Brace Jovanovich.

Mitchell, Richard n.d. "Dancing at Armageddon: Doomsday and Survivalists in America." Unpublished paper, Oregon State University.

——— 1991 "Secrecy and Disclosure in Fieldwork." In W. Shaffir and R. Stebbins, eds., *Experiencing Fieldwork.* Newbury Park, Calif.: Sage.

Peterson, Richard G. 1984 "Preparing for Apocalypse: Survivalist Strategies." *Free Inquiry in Creative Sociology* 12:44–46.

Reich, Charles A. 1970 *The Greening of America.* New York: Random House.

Rochford, E. Burke 1985 *Hare Krishna in America.* New Brunswick, N.J.: Rutgers University Press.

Roszak, Theodore 1969 *The Making of a Counter Culture.* New York: Doubleday.

Rothchild, John, and Susan Berns Wolf 1976 *The Children of the Counter-Culture.* New York: Doubleday.

Spates, James L. 1976 "Counterculture and Dominant Culture Values: A Cross-National Analysis of the Underground Press and Dominant Culture Magazines." *American Sociological Review* 41:868–883.

Street, J. 1986 *Rebel Rock: The Politics of Popular Music.* Oxford: Basil Blackwell.

Tipton, Steven M. 1982 *Getting Saved from the Sixties.* Berkeley: University of California Press.

Turner, Ralph 1976 "The Real Self: From Institution to Impulse." *American Journal of Sociology* 81:989–1,016.

Wuthnow, Robert 1976 *The Consciousness Revolution.* Berkeley: University of California Press.

Yinger, J. Milton 1960 "Contraculture and Subculture." *American Sociological Review* 25:625–635.
——— 1977 "Countercultures and Social Change." *American Sociological Review* 42:833–853.
——— 1982 *Countercultures.* New York: Free Press.

– PATRICIA A. ADLER
PETER ADLER

COURTSHIP

Given the centrality of the family institution in society, and the role of courtship in the family formation process, it is not surprising that the study of courtship has received attention from several disciplines. Anthropologists have described practices in primitive and other societies, historians have traced courtship patterns in America from colonial to contemporary times, psychologists and social psychologists have examined intra- and interpersonal components of relationships, and sociologists have developed research-based theories explaining the process of mate selection and have investigated its dynamics. Here, some attention will be given to each of these approaches, along the way selectively noting scholars who have made major contributions.

Historically, according to Rothman, the term "*courtship* applied to situations where the intention to marry was explicit (if not formally—and mutually—stated). *Courting* was the broader term used to describe socializing between unmarried men and women" (Rothman 1984, p. 23, italics in original).

Dating is a twentieth-century term for a primarily recreational aspect of courting.

Scholars have disagreed as to whether dating—a twentieth-century term for a primarily recreational aspect of courting—should be considered a part of courtship since, according to Waller (1938) and others, dating may be merely thrill seeking and exploitative and not marriage-oriented (see Gordon 1981 for an opposing view). However, wooing (that is, seeking favor, affection, love, or any of these) may be integral to courtship but need not result in marriage. For present purposes, then, courtship will be understood in its broadest sense—as a continuum from casual to serious. Thus, "the unattached flirt, the engaged college seniors, the eighth-grade 'steadies,' and the mismatched couple on a blind date are all engaging in courtship" (Bailey 1988, p. 6).

Queen, Habenstein, and Quadagno's (1985) classic text provides much of the basis for the following brief and highly generalized overview of some mate-selection patterns unlike those found in contemporary America. Some of these systems involve little or no courtship. For example, among the ancient Chinese, Hebrews, and Romans, marriage was arranged by male heads of kin groups. Among the ancient Greeks and until recently among the Chinese, many brides and grooms did not meet until their wedding day. Around the turn of the century, infant marriages were the rule among the Toda of south India, and the bride was deflowered at about age ten by a male who was not of her clan and not her husband. In medieval England, contrary to the literature of chivalry, love had little to do with mate selection in any social class because marriages were arranged by lords or parents with primary regard to the acquisition of property.

In societies where romantic love is not a basis for mate choice, such sentiments are seen as dangerous to the formation and stability of desirable marital unions—those that maintain stratification systems (see Goode 1969). Queen, Habenstein, and Quadagno (1985) describe still other mate-selection patterns that do involve courtship and some form of love, including the systems found on Israeli kibbutzim at midcentury, among ethnic immigrant groups in the United States, and among American blacks during slavery (see also Ramu 1989). Since the turn of the century, however, and especially since the 1920s, courtship in Western societies has been participant-run and based on romantic love. In the United States today, it is not uncommon for a couple to meet, woo, and wed almost without the knowledge of their respective kin. "Compared with other cultures, ours offers a wide range of choices and a minimum of control" (Queen, Habenstein, and Quadango 1985, pp. 8–9).

In colonial America, practices differed somewhat between the North and South. In the North, mate choice was participant-run, but a suitor's father had control over the timing of marriage because he might delay the release of an adequate section of family land to his son while his labor was needed. Conjugal (not romantic) love was the sine qua non of marriage, and couples came to know and trust one another during often lengthy courtships. In the South, a custom of chivalry developed, closely guarding the purity of (at least upper class) women but condoning promiscuity among men. Parental consent was required for the beginning of courtship and for marriage, and open bargaining about property arrangements was commonplace. Unlike the colonial north, where marriage was considered a civil ceremony, in most parts of the South, Anglican church ministers were required to officiate at weddings. In both regions, banns were published prior to weddings.

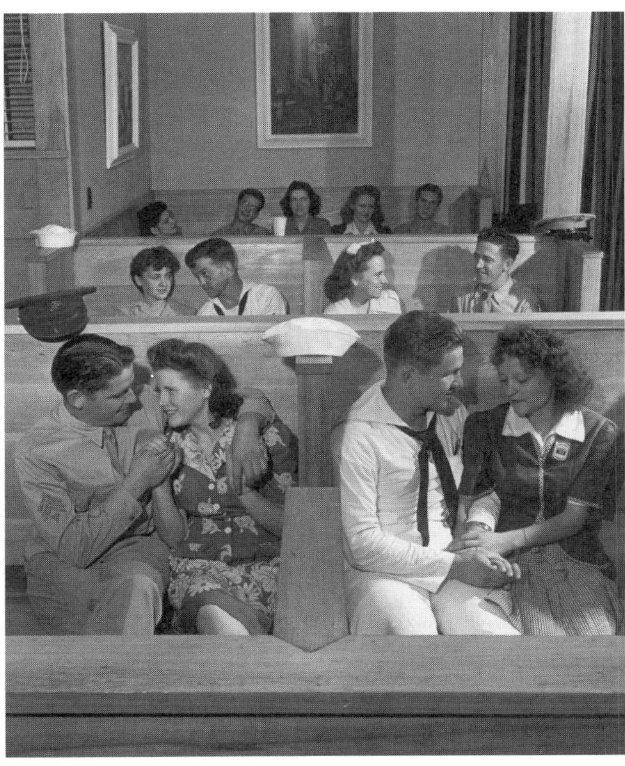

Dating in twentieth-century culture is often a recreational aspect of courting and is not always intended to result in marriage. (Corbis-Bettmann)

During the 1800s, mate choice became more autonomous with the growth of cities and the spread of industrial employment. Choices were affected less by wealth than by personal qualities—especially morality, spirituality, and "character." Wooing was rather formal, with each participant carefully evaluating the qualities of the other. Courtship tended to be exclusive and directed toward marriage.

Then, from about 1900 to World War II, there was much "playing the field" (casual dating), gradually more exclusive dating (going steady), engagement, and, finally, wedding—a relatively fixed sequence. Following World War II, stages were typically marked by symbols (e.g., wearing a fraternity pin, then an engagement ring), each stage implying increased commitment between the partners. By the 1950s, a separate youth culture had developed. Ages at first marriage declined dramatically, and dating started earlier than ever before. The sexual exploration that had previously been part of the last stage of courtship now occurred earlier, even in very young couples.

During the 1960s, a time of "sexual revolution," nonmarital cohabitation increased in acceptability—not substituting for marriage but perhaps delaying it. In the postwar period and since, among the young especially, demands for both freedom and dependency (e.g., the right to sexual freedom without assuming responsibility for its multifaceted consequences) have been relatively widespread (Queen, Habenstein, and Quadango 1985, p. 271). Concurrently, rates of non-marital pregnancy rose dramatically.

In general, every society attempts to control sexual activity among unmarried (and married) persons, but the forms of control (e.g., chaperonage) and the degree of enforcement have varied. Virginity, especially in women, is highly prized and guarded in some cultures but has no special value in others. Similarly, all societies attempt to constrain the pool of those eligible to marry, but the precise constraints have differed from society to society and from time to time. Typically, blood kin and relatives by marriage (and in some cases baptismal relatives such as godparents) are delimited to greater or lesser degrees from the eligibility pool.

Where male elders have arranged marriages for their offspring (generally in ascription-based societies), the accumulation of family power and prestige has been of primary concern, with dowries, bride prices, or both figuring importantly in prenuptial arrangements. In participant-run mate selection (generally in achievement-oriented societies), the power and prestige of a dating partner (although defined in terms other than land, cattle, and the like) is still valuable. Good looks in women (however defined), for instance, are a status symbol for men, and conspicuous consumption in men (cars, clothing, and spending habits) provides status for women. Thus, within the field of eligibles is a smaller field of desirables. Unfortunately, the qualities that are valued in dates (from among whom a mate may ultimately be chosen) are not necessarily those one would want in a spouse.

Even in participant-run "free choice" systems, there is a tendency toward homogamy in the selection of courtship partners, whether conscious or not. To the extent that a society becomes more varied in its mix of persons within residential, educational, religious, or work-related clusterings, the tendency toward heterogamy increases—that is, the fields of eligibles and desirables come to be more broadly defined. Heterogeneity leads to a prediction of "universal availability" (Farber 1964) as the salience of social categories declines. For example, interracial relationships, once unthinkable (e.g., in the American colonial South), increased with urbanization, industrialization, and a general movement toward educational and income equality.

Social class endogamy, however, is the general preference, although women are encouraged with varying degrees of subtlety to "marry up," and a dating differential exists such that men tend to court women who are slightly younger, physically smaller, and somewhat less well educated or affluent than themselves.

Contemporary courtship, marked as it is by freedom of choice, has been likened to a market in which the buyer must be wary and in which there is no necessary truth in advertising. Persons compete, given their own assets, for the best marital catch or the most status-conferring date. Waller and Hill (1951) warned about the exploitative potential in both casual and serious courtship, and, indeed, critics of conventional dating have decried it as a sexist bargaining arrangement in which men are exploited for money and women for sexual favors. The superficiality of dating, its commercialization, the deceit involved (given contradictory motives), and the high levels of anxiety produced by fears of rejection (especially in men) are additional drawbacks. Since status differentials still characterize the sexes, dating may also be seen as a contest in which a struggle for power and control between partners is part of the game. Thus, courtship's emphasis on individualism, freedom, commercialism, competitive spirit, and success reflects the larger social system within which it functions. One may well ask whether such a system prepares participants in any sense for marriage, which requires cooperation and compromise for its survival.

Efforts to predict who marries whom and why, to delineate the courtship process itself, or both, have interested a number of scholars. Based on a large body of theoretical and empirical work, Adams (1979) developed a propositional theory to explain how courtship moves from initial acquaintance toward (or away from) marriage in an achievement-oriented society. The propositions, in slightly modified language, are as follows:

1. Proximity, which facilitates contact, is a precondition for courtship and marriage.
2. As time passes, marriage is increasingly more likely to be with a currently propinquitous than with a formerly propinquitous partner.
3. Propinquity increases the likelihood that one will meet, be attracted to, and marry someone of the same social categories as himself or herself.
4. Early attraction is a result of immediate stimuli such as physical attractiveness, valued surface behaviors, and similar interests.
5. The more favorable the reactions of significant others to an early relationship, the more likely the relationship will progress beyond the early attraction stage.
6. The more positive the reaction of the partners to self-disclosures, the better the rapport between the pair.
7. The better the rapport between the pair, the more likely the relationship will be perpetuated beyond the early attraction stage.
8. The greater the value compatibility-consensus between partners, the more likely that the relationship will progress to a deeper level of attraction.
9. The greater the similarity in physical attractiveness between the partners, the more likely that the relationship will progress to a deeper level of attraction.
10. The more the partners' personalities are similar, the more likely that the relationship will progress to a deeper level of attraction.
11. The more salient the categorical homogeneity of the partners, the more likely that the relationship will progress to a deeper level of attraction.
12. The more salient the categorical heterogeneity of the partners, the more likely that the relationship will terminate either before or after reaching a deeper level of attraction.
13. The greater the unfavorable parental intrusion, the more likely that a relationship will terminate either before or after reaching a deeper level of attraction.
14. An alternative attraction to the current partner may arise at any stage of a couple's relationship. The stronger that alternative attraction to either partner, the greater the likelihood that the original couple's relationship will terminate.
15. The greater the role compatibility of couple members, the more likely that the relationship will be perpetuated.
16. The greater the empathy between couple members, the more likely that the relationship will be perpetuated.
17. The more each of the partners defines the other as "right" or "the best I can get," the less likely it is that the relationship will terminate short of marriage.
18. The more a relationship moves to the level of pair communality, the less likely it is that it will terminate short of marriage.
19. The more a relationship moves through a series of formal and informal escalators, the less likely it is to terminate short of marriage. (Adams 1979, pp. 260–267)

Adams (1979) provides some caveats about these propositions. First, some factors (such as a partner's good looks) have greater salience for men than for women, while some (such as a partner's empathic capacity) have greater salience for women than for men. Second, some factors such as parental interference may have different outcomes in the long run compared to the short run. Third, the timing of courtship may bring different considerations into play, e.g., courtship in later life such as following divorce or widowhood, when children from previous marriages must be considered (see Bulcroft and O'Connor 1986). Finally, social class factors may affect the predictive value of the propositions. Bernard (1964) distinguished between parallel and interactional marriages—parallel (or traditional) arrangements are more often found in the working class and among certain ethnic groups, while interactional (or equalitarian) arrangements are more likely to characterize the middle class. Thus, the kind of marriage one anticipates may influence the mate-selection process. (See also Aronson 1972 for specifications of the conditions under which various interpersonal attraction predictors such as propinquity and similar interests operate.)

Further, as courtship has moved away from the fixed-stages sequence of development, it may be best viewed through a circular-causal model (Stephen 1985), in which progress is strongly influenced by communication within the couple, leading to increased (or decreased) movement toward marriage.

The timing of marriage may be influenced by such factors as meaningful employment opportunities for women (which may diminish their motivation to marry), the increasing acceptability of nonmarital cohabitation and adult singlehood (see Stein 1981), and the effects of nonmarital pregnancy or of various intolerable conditions in the family of origin (Adams 1979).

Regarding premarital factors that contribute to later marital adjustment, no scholar has presented evidence to refute Kirkpatrick's ([1955] 1963) conclusions: happiness of parents' marriage; adequate length of courtship; adequate sex information in childhood; a happy childhood including a harmonious relationship with parents; approval of the courtship relationship by significant others; good premarital adjustment of the couple and strong motivation to marry; homogamy along age, racial-ethnic, and religious lines; and later age (late twenties) at marriage.

In his review of mate-selection scholarship from the 1970s, Murstein (1980) predicted that there would be less focus in the future on such "old standby" variables as race, class, and religion and more on the dynamic aspects of courtship. Murstein was correct. What follows is an attempt to identify some of the major themes that have interested students of courtship phenomena in recent years.

Studies focused on the effects of cohabitation on subsequent marital happiness find that living with someone unmarried has little or no positive effect.

With regard to cohabitation, early studies included efforts to identify its types, both structural and motivational. Later studies focused on the effects of cohabitation on subsequent marital happiness and satisfaction, finding, almost uniformly, that living with someone unmarried has little or no positive effect. Some studies find a negative effect on marital adjustment, partly attributable to the qualities of persons who choose this still nonconventional arrangement (but see Popenoe 1987 for a different view of cohabitation in a setting where it is more normative).

As rates of sexual activity outside of marriage rose, and as sex (especially since the advent of the birth control pill in the 1960s) was disengaged to some extent from procreation, research and theoretical interest focused on changes in sexual behavior and values. (See Schur 1988 for a highly negative view of the "Americanization" of sex.) Also on the negative side of the ledger, there is concern about the spread of sexually transmitted diseases and on factors related to the use (or nonuse) of "safe" sexual practices. Research continues to examine variations in premarital sexual activity rates and their effects.

The study of courtship processes has become part of the broader study of "close" or "intimate" relationships (see Brehm 1985) as practices have changed from stylized conventional dating to the more informal "hanging out" and "partying," and from the-man-always-pays norm to sharing expenses. In part, this follows from a weakening of the normative imperative to marry (Thornton 1989) and in part from a trend toward more egalitarian relationships between the sexes. However, in almost all research, male/female similarities and differences continue to form part of data analysis.

Considerable research interest has been devoted to identifying the components of conventional masculinity and femininity and their effects and on resistance to change in these stereotypes—for example, because of ongoing conventional socialization practices and, as communications experts have documented, because of the effects of various media portrayals supporting the status quo ante. Scholars have also noted the greater likelihood of relational success among androgynous than among conventionally masculine men and feminine women (Cancian 1986).

Barriers to understanding between the sexes have been investigated, including the effects of stereotyping (noted above), and research has extended to the study of "taboo" conversational topics in courtship, degrees and forms of honesty and deception, communication style differences between men and women, and methods of conflict resolution that enhance relationship survival or presage breakup. Interest in failed relationships has attempted to identify factors at both individual and dyadic levels that might have predicted which pairings would last and which would not.

Early-encounter studies have examined the efficacy (or lack of it) of "opening lines," of flirtation patterns leading to meetings, and of "scripts" for early dates and their persistence across social time. In ongoing relationships, scholars have investigated the positive and negative effects of outside influences such as parental and peer pressures, and the parts played by same- and cross-sex friends. Other topics of concern have included barriers to the development of trust and the effects of its loss, the meanings of commitment, and the effects of self-disclosure, self-esteem, self-awareness, and jealousy on close relationships.

Recent years have witnessed a virtual explosion in the study of love—attempts to identify its forms, its properties, its distribution of types across women and men, and the effects of all of these, especially in terms of romantic love. Interestingly, and again on the negative side, a number of studies of courtship violence have shown relatively high rates of this kind of activity but also reveal that a sizeable minority of those who have experienced violence in a close relationship identify it with a loving motive. This seemingly odd justification is readily explained by the practice of parents, when using violence against their children, of indicating that they do it "out of love." Thus, the lesson (or the rationalization) is learned early. Other negative aspects of courtship include the study of "mind games" and other facets of competition between partners, sexual aggression including date rape, and the effects of contrasts between ideal images and courtship realities.

As courtship itself has expanded, researchers have taken interest in an expanded range of relationship types (Buunk and van Driel 1989). For example, the romantic involvements between lesbian women and between gay men have been studied and compared with those between heterosexual partners. A predictable area for future study is the recently legalized status of relationships between same-sex partners.

Other relatively recent innovations such as video- and computer-matching and personal advertisements in print media have also captured researchers' attention. Another fairly recent development is the increased use of prenuptial agreements, and scholars may be expected to pursue the study of their impact on relationships. To a lesser extent, older lines of research have continued to probe the purported decline of or changes in the double standard, the "principle of least interest" (Waller 1938) as related to changes in gender roles, the dimensions of intimacy (including the crucial component of communication), motivators toward marriage and toward single adult status, and on desired traits in partners as these may differ (or not) between dates and mates. Interrelationships between variables have also received wider attention.

As society grows more complex and as the rate of change seems increasingly rapid, confusion over the mate-selection process appears to be rife. A recent study of college student dating shows that these young adults have questions about virtually every aspect of the process and the choices they make (Laner 1989). High divorce rates in recent years have produced a backlash of insecurity as the marriage decision approaches. This is reflected in the frequently voiced question, "How can I be *sure* of making the right choice in a partner?" Sociologists and scholars in related disciplines continue to study a growing set of factors that shed light on the answer.

[See also Alternative Life-Styles; Love; Mate Selection Theories.]

BIBLIOGRAPHY

Adams, Bert N. 1979 "Mate Selection in the United States: A Theoretical Summarization." In W. R. Burr, R. Hill, F. I. Nye, and I. L. Reiss, eds., *Contemporary Theories about the Family.* New York: Free Press.

Aronson, Elliot 1972 *The Social Animal.* New York: Viking.

Bailey, Beth L. 1988 *From Front Porch to Back Seat: Courtship in Twentieth-Century America.* Baltimore: Johns Hopkins University Press.

Bernard, Jessie 1964 "The Adjustments of Married Mates." In H. T. Christensen, ed., *The Handbook of Marriage and the Family.* Chicago: Rand McNally.

Brehm, Sharon S. 1985 *Intimate Relationships.* New York: Random House.

Bulcroft, Kris, and Margaret O'Connor 1986 "The Importance of Dating Relationships on Quality of Life for Older Persons." *Family Relations* 35:397–401.

Buunk, Bram P., and Barry van Driel 1989 *Variant Lifestyles and Relationships.* Newbury Park, Calif.: Sage.

Cancian, Francesca 1986 "The Feminization of Love." *Signs* 11:692–709.

Farber, Bernard 1964 *Family Organization and Interaction.* San Francisco: Chandler.

Goode, William J. 1969 "The Theoretical Importance of Love." *American Sociological Review* 34:38–47.

Gordon, Michael 1981 "Was Waller Ever Right? The Rating and Dating Complex Reconsidered." *Journal of Marriage and the Family* 43:67–76.

Kirkpatrick, Clifford [1955] 1963 *The Family as Process and Institution,* 2nd ed. New York: Ronald.

Laner, Mary R. 1989 *Dating: Delights, Discontents, and Dilemmas.* Salem, Wisc.: Sheffield.

Murstein, Bernard I. 1980 "Mate Selection in the 1970s." *Journal of Marriage and the Family* 42:777–792.

Popenoe, David 1987 "Beyond the Nuclear Family, A Statistical Portrait of the Changing Family in Sweden." *Journal of Marriage and the Family* 49:173–183.

Queen, Stuart A., Robert W. Habenstein, and Jill S. Quadagno 1985 *The Family in Various Cultures,* 5th ed. New York: Harper and Row.

Ramu, G. N. 1989 "Patterns of Mate Selection." In K. Ishwaran, ed., *Family and Marriage: Cross-Cultural Perspectives.* Toronto: Wall and Thompson.

Rothman, Ellen K. 1984 *Hands and Hearts: A History of Courtship in America.* New York: Basic Books.

Schur, Edwin M. 1988 *The Americanization of Sex.* Philadelphia: Temple University Press.

Stein, Peter J. (ed.) 1981 *Single Life: Unmarried Adults in Social Context.* New York: St Martin's.

Stephen, Timothy D. 1985 "Fixed-Sequence and Circular-Causal Models of Relationship Development: Divergent Views on the Role of Communication in Intimacy." *Journal of Marriage and the Family* 47:955–963.

Thornton, Arland 1989 "Changing Attitudes toward Family Issues in the United States." *Journal of Marriage and the Family* 51:873–893.

Waller, Willard 1938 "The Rating and Dating Complex." *American Sociological Review* 2:727–734.

Waller, Willard, and Reuben Hill 1951 *The Family: A Dynamic Interpretation,* rev. ed. New York: Dryden.

– MARY RIEGE LANER

COURT SYSTEMS OF THE UNITED STATES

The American court system is composed of several jurisdictional and hierarchical structures. While these structures are somewhat complex, they delineate the fundamental ways in which courts are organized.

The first and most important distinction is between state and federal courts. All fifty states and the District of Columbia have their own independent court systems for the adjudication of state cases, over which they have jurisdiction. In addition, the United States as a whole has a federal court system, which is completely separate from the state systems in its jurisdictional boundaries and hierarchical structure. Superimposed on this federal-state stratification of courts are still other methods by which courts are organized. Specifically, within both the federal and state systems, there are courts whose subject matter jurisdiction is limited to certain types of cases. For example, there are special bankruptcy courts in the federal system, while many states have courts exclusively for juvenile offenders.

Turning first to the separate hierarchies within the various court systems, it is important to note that each state has a system of lower courts and higher courts (e.g., trial courts and appellate courts), as does the United States. Moreover, the hierarchy may differ within those systems depending on the subject matter of the case. For example, Texas has a separate appellate court for criminal cases; in the federal system, while most courts of appeals are regional, one such court hears appeals from all federal trial courts when the substantive issue at hand is a patent matter. Finally, there is a certain amount of interaction between the state and federal courts. Not only does the jurisdiction of lower state and federal courts sometimes overlap, but the U.S. Supreme Court, under certain circumstances, has the authority to review the ruling of a state supreme court.

The Federal System

In Article III of the Constitution, the Framers established the U.S. Supreme Court and authorized Congress to create lower federal courts. In the Judiciary Act of 1789, Congress established the federal district courts as the trial courts and the circuit courts of appeal to review the decisions of the lower trial courts. The district courts are the general courts of original jurisdiction in the federal system. Congress has divided the nation into ninety-four federal districts, each with its own district court (28 U.S.C. § 81–131). Every state has at least one federal district within its boundaries; some of the larger states contain as many as four federal districts. The number of federal district court judges appointed to serve in each district depends on the caseload in the district. For example, the district of Wyoming has two district court judges, while the Southern District of New York has twenty-seven (28 U.S.C. § 133). In 1988, a total of 284,219 cases were commenced in federal district courts nationwide (Administrative Office of the United States Courts 1988, pp. 8, 14).

Continuing up the hierarchy, above the district courts in the federal system are the courts of appeals. In general, cases appealed from the ninety-four federal district courts are reviewed by one of the courts of appeals. Congress has created thirteen circuits, each with its own court of appeals. Twelve of the circuits are territorial; that is, each encompasses one or more of the ninety-four districts. For example, the Seventh Circuit hears appeals from the federal trial courts of Illinois, Indiana, and Wisconsin. Thus, a litigant wishing to challenge a decision of the federal district court for the Southern District of Indiana would appeal to the Court of Appeals for the Seventh Circuit. The thirteenth court of appeals is the Federal Circuit, created in 1982; the Federal Circuit is unique in that it has nationwide appellate jurisdiction over certain specialized areas of federal law including customs, international trade, patent, and trademark cases (28 U.S.C. § 1295).

Whereas cases in the district courts are heard by a single trial judge, cases before the courts of appeals are heard by a panel of three circuit court judges. In 1988, a total of 37,524 appeals were commenced before the thirteen federal courts of appeals (Administrative Office of the United States Courts 1988, p. 2).

The highest court in the federal system is, of course, the U.S. Supreme Court. The Supreme Court reviews decisions of the courts of appeals, and in some cases it reviews the decisions of the district courts. Unlike the federal courts of appeals, the Supreme Court has complete discretion as to which cases it will hear. That is, litigants seeking to challenge a lower court decision have no right to be heard by the Supreme Court. Rather, they must petition the Court for a "writ of certiorari"; their case will be heard only if the Supreme Court decides to grant the petition (28 U.S.C. §§ 1254, 1257). Because of the flood of litigants seeking Supreme Court review, the Court grants only a small percentage of the petitions for writs of certiorari it receives. In certain rare cases, the Supreme Court does have original jurisdiction, such as when one state sues another state (Art. III).

In addition to the three levels of federal courts discussed above, there are a number of specialized courts in the federal system. These courts hear cases involving special areas of federal law, cases whose volume or complexity would place too great a burden on the federal district courts. Examples of these courts are the United States Bankruptcy Courts, the United States Tax Court, and the United States Claims Court.

The creation of these specialized courts by Congress brings to light the distinction between so-called constitutional and legislative courts in the federal system. Article III of the Constitution mandates that "the judicial Power of the United States shall be vested in one supreme Court, and in such inferior Courts as the Congress may from time to time ordain and establish." Article III also provides that judges of both the Supreme Court and the lower courts "shall hold their Offices during good Behaviour," which effectively grants them life tenure. In addition, Article III prohibits Congress from diminishing the compensation of these judges while they are in office.

The purpose of these provisions was to ensure that federal judges are insulated from political pressure exercised by the other branches of government as well as the public. In *The Federalist* No. 78, Alexander Hamilton referred to the "good behavior" provision as "the best expedient in any government, to secure a steady, upright and impartial administration of laws" (Wills 1982, p. 393). Indeed, Hamilton considered the permanency of judicial office as "the citadel of the public justice and the public security" (Wills 1982, p. 394). Hamilton went on to note that, besides life tenure, "nothing can contribute more to the independence of the judges than a fixed provision for their support," because "a power over a man's subsistence amounts to a power over his will" (Wills 1982, p. 400).

In creating specialized courts, Congress decided not to imbue the judges of these courts with the protections of Article III.

Interestingly, in creating the specialized courts delimited above (e.g., the United States Claims Court), Congress decided not to imbue the judges of these courts with the protections of Article III. There are any number of reasons Congress may have wished to avoid creating more Article III judges. By not doing so, Congress retains greater flexibility to adjust its response to whatever problem it seeks to address by creating the court. Importantly, because Congress created these specialized courts under its Article I rather than its Article III authority, these courts are known as "legislative" or "Article I" courts.

The authority of a non-Article III court to exercise judicial power presents a complicated issue of constitutional law. Alexander Hamilton's remarks notwithstanding, Justice Sandra Day O'Connor once noted with regards to a majority opinion that "an absolute construction of Article III is not possible" and that "the Court has long recognized that Congress is not barred from acting pursuant to its powers under Article I to vest decisionmaking authority in tribunals that lack the attributes of Article III courts" (*Thomas* v. *Union Carbide Agricultural Products Co.* 1985, p. 583). However, the scope of this congressional authority has never clearly been defined. Several commentators have suggested that current Supreme Court jurisprudence indicates that the validity of laws that give legislative courts the authority to adjudicate cases arising under federal law depends on a balancing of the concerns that prompted Congress to create the court against the Article III values of judicial independence (Bator, Mishkin, Meltzer and Shapiro 1988, p. 470).

The State Systems

Turning now to the state court systems, all fifty states and the District of Columbia have their own court systems. Each state has trial courts that serve as the general courts of original jurisdiction for the state. In addition, many states have intermediate appellate courts as well as a supreme court, paralleling the hierarchical structure of the federal system. A number of smaller states (such as Iowa and Rhode Island) have only two levels of courts, with no intermediary review between the lower courts and the highest court. In many states, judges at all levels of the state court system are elected by the public. These judges, much like the legislators and the governor, serve fixed terms. This practice is in striking contrast to the federal system, in which all Article III judges are appointed for life terms. A few states follow the federal model in this regard (New Jersey, for example), but they are the exception rather than the rule.

As in the federal court system, many states additionally have specialized courts that have particular subject matter jurisdiction over particular types of cases. For example, a number of states have special courts for juvenile proceedings, family law matters, and probate cases.

Interaction of the Federal and State Systems

As noted previously, every federal district overlaps geographically with at least one state (if one includes the District of Columbia). Not surprisingly, there is a considerable amount of interaction between the state and federal courts. To understand this interaction, one must first consider the comparative jurisdictions of the two court systems.

The jurisdiction of federal courts can be divided into two broad categories: "federal question" jurisdiction and "diversity" jurisdiction. The first of these two categories is derived from the language of Article III of the Constitution, which states that federal courts may be given jurisdiction over cases "arising under this Constitution, the Laws of the United States, and Treaties made, or which shall be made, under their authority." For the federal court to have jurisdiction, the federal question must be "substantial"; as a result, federal courts lack jurisdiction if the federal claim upon which the plaintiff (the complaining party) bases jurisdiction is obviously frivolous or without merit (Wright, Miller, and Cooper 1984, vol. 13b, p. 68).

Most federal question jurisdiction is based on federal statutory law. Congress does not have the authority to pass whatever laws it pleases; Congress may legislate only according to the specific mandates of authority prescribed in the Constitution. However, these provisions have been read quite liberally, such that federal law now encompasses a very broad range of activity in both the areas of civil and criminal law. To illustrate, the modern federal criminal laws proscribing illegal drug possession and distribution are based on Congress's power to regulate interstate commerce (Abrams 1986, p. 342). Not surprisingly, federal law often regulates the same conduct as does state law. For example, the federal narcotics laws noted above overlap substantially with many state laws. As a result, almost all drug trafficking cases can be prosecuted in either federal or state court. The decision whether to proceed federally or in the state rests with the prosecutor to whom the case is presented.

In many cases, plaintiffs in civil cases will seek to advance both federal and state claims. For example, a plaintiff who feels that her patent has been infringed may couple a federal patent infringement claim with a state unfair competition claim. To accommodate these situations, federal courts have developed a doctrine known as "pendent jurisdiction." Under this doctrine, a federal court may hear a state law claim if it derives from the same "common nucleus of operative fact" as the federal claim (*United Mine Workers* v. *Gibbs* 1966, p. 725).

The second category of federal court jurisdiction is "diversity" jurisdiction. As with federal question jurisdiction, diversity jurisdiction has its origins in Article III of the Constitution. That provision contains a clause giving Congress the power to vest jurisdiction in the federal courts over cases that involve a dispute between citizens of different states or between a citizen of a state and an alien. Although there is some debate over the intent of the Framers in enshrining federal diversity jurisdiction in the Constitution, the traditional explanation emphasizes a fear that state courts would be prejudiced against out-of-state litigants (Wright, Miller, and Cooper 1984, vol. 13b, p. 338). Under current law, federal courts may hear diversity cases only if the amount in controversy exceeds $50,000 (28 U.S.C. § 1332).

In contrast to this limited federal jurisdiction, state courts have much broader authority to hear disputes. Naturally, state courts have subject matter jurisdiction over all claims based on state law. In addition, state courts have jurisdiction over many federal law claims, except where Congress has given exclusive jurisdiction to the federal courts (bankruptcy, for example).

The subject matter of the lawsuit is not, however, the only consideration in establishing whether a state court has jurisdiction over a dispute. State courts are limited in their ability to exercise personal jurisdiction over litigants who are not in-state residents. In other words, a California court does not automatically have jurisdiction over a defendant who resides in Oklahoma. The United States Supreme Court has held that for a state court to have jurisdiction over individuals (or corporations) who are not residents, the individual must have some "minimum contacts" with that state (*International Shoe Co.* v. *State of Washington* 1945, p. 316). This requirement will not be satisfied unless the defendant "purposely avails" himself of the "privilege of conducting activities within the forum state" (*Hanson* v. *Denckla* 1958, p. 253). In other words, there must be evidence of some purposeful act by the defendant, which makes it foreseeable that he could be subject to suit in the forum state (Friedenthal, Kane, and Miller 1985, p. 132). In the final analysis, federal and state courts often have overlapping original jurisdiction. This interaction extends to the appellate review process, although in a limited manner. The United States Supreme Court is the ultimate arbiter of federal law; similarly, the highest court in a state has the final word as to that state's law. To illustrate, if a litigant loses an appeal on a state law claim in the Virginia Supreme Court, that litigant has no recourse to the United States Supreme Court. On the other hand, if the litigant's claim was based on federal law, he can appeal the Virginia Supreme Court's decision to the United States Supreme Court. The analysis becomes more complex when the litigant's appeal is based on both federal and state law. The established rule provides that if the judgment of the state court is based on a nonfederal ground that is "independent of the federal ground and adequate to support the judgment," the United States Supreme Court has no jurisdiction to hear an appeal of the state court decision (*Fox Film Corp.* v. *Muller* 1935, p. 210). This "independent and adequate state ground" requirement has proven to be quite difficult in its application (Bator, Mishkin, Meltzer, and Shapiro 1988, p. 536). To elaborate, state courts are often ambiguous as to the grounds for their decisions in cases with both federal and state law issues. In these situations, the U.S. Supreme Court has ruled that unless it is clear from the face of the state court opinion that the decision rests on an independent and adequate state ground, the U.S. Supreme Court has jurisdiction over the case (*Michigan* v. *Long* 1983, p. 1042).

It is appropriate to examine the different major actors who operate within court systems. As discussed previously, judges in the federal system are appointed for life terms by the President with the advice and consent of the United States Senate; state court judges are generally elected, rather than appointed, for a specific rather than a life term. This distinction holds true for prosecutors. In the federal system, there is a chief prosecutor in each of the federal districts. These prosecutors are known as United States Attorneys; they are appointed by the President, with the advice and consent of the United States Senate. United States Attorneys are in the executive branch of government; as such, they are in a completely distinct hierarchical structure than are federal judges, who are located in the judicial branch. Unlike judges, U.S. Attorneys are under the supervision of the Attorney General of the United States and ultimately the President.

In state systems, the chief prosecutors are almost always elected by the public to fixed terms. They typically are referred to as "district attorneys," and they usually serve a county, local district, or other political subdivision of the state. Similar to the federal system, each state also has an attorney general; unlike the Attorney General for the United States who is appointed by the President, state attorneys general are usually elected to serve as the chief law enforcement officer in the state.

Private attorneys, both publicly and privately compensated, often practice in both the federal and the state court systems. However, all fifty states and the federal courts regulate separately the attorneys who practice within their respective court systems. As a result, an attorney who wishes to argue a case in a Vermont state court must be admitted to the Vermont bar; attorneys wishing to appear in federal court must be members of the federal bar.

Finally, in both the federal and state systems there are probation officers. Probation officers serve as an arm of the court and play a crucial role in the criminal justice arena. The primary task of probation officers is to monitor the behavior of convicted offenders who are placed on probation or some form of supervised release. In addition, probation officers act as independent fact finders for judges; in this regard they often play a key role at sentencing. This is especially true in the federal system, where probation officers' calculations of the appropriate sentencing range under the new federal guidelines are referred to by judges in determining sentences.

[See also Criminal Sanctions, Criminology; Law and Legal Systems.]

BIBLIOGRAPHY

Books

Abrams, Norman 1986 *Federal Criminal Law and Its Enforcement* St. Paul, Minn.: West.

Administrative Office of the United States Courts 1988 *Annual Report of the Administrative Office of the United States Courts 1988.* Washington, D.C.: U.S. Government Printing Office.

Bator, Paul M., Paul J. Mishkin, Daniel J. Meltzer, and David L. Shapiro 1984 *Hart and Weschler's The Federal Courts and the Federal System,* 3rd ed. Westbury, N.Y.: Foundation Press.

Friedenthal, Jack H., Mary Kay Kane, and Arthur R. Miller 1985 *Civil Procedure.* St. Paul, Minn.: West.

Wills, Garry (ed.) 1982 *The Federalist Papers.* New York: Bantam Books.

Wright, Charles A., Arthur R. Miller, and Edward H. Cooper 1984 *Federal Practice and Procedure.* 2d ed. Vols. 13, 13b. St. Paul, Minn.: West.

Cases

Fox Film Corp. v. *Muller,* 296 U.S. 207 (1935).

Hanson v. *Denckla,* 357 U.S. 235 (1958).

Michigan v. *Long,* 463 U.S. 1032 (1983).

International Shoe Company v. *State of Washington,* 326 U.S. 310 (1945).

Thomas v. *Union Carbide Agricultural Products Co.,* 473 U.S. 568 (1985).

United Mine Workers v. *Gibbs,* 383 U.S. 715 (1966).

Statutes

28 U.S.C.A. §§ 81–131, 133 (West 1968 & Supp. 1990).

28 U.S.C.A. §§ 1254, 1257 (West 1966 & Supp. 1990).

28 U.S.C.A. § 1295 (West 1966 & Supp. 1990).

28 U.S.C.A § 1332 (West 1966 & Supp. 1990).

– ILENE H. NAGEL
NICOLAS D. MANSFIELD

CRIME DETERRENCE

Attempts to prevent and control crime have employed three principal techniques, each based on a particular view of the causes of crime and the nature of the criminal. *Incapacitation* seeks to control crime by making it physically impossible for an offender to commit a crime (Cohen 1983). Imprisonment, castration of rapists, and execution are each a form of incapacitation. Policies based on incapacitation assume offenders behave reflexively and impulsively, paying little attention to the consequences of their actions. *Deterrence* attempts to prevent crime by threatening potential offenders with legal punishment. Policies based on deterrence assume offenders are sensitive to incentives and deliberately choose to commit crime because the rewards outweigh the costs (Becker 1968). *Rehabilitation* attempts to control crime through reeducating or resocializing offenders and by treating rather than punishing them (Cullen and Gilbert 1982). Policies based on rehabilitation can be compatible with either of the above conceptions of the offender.

Criminal justice policies of modern societies generally reflect belief in deterrence and view criminals as freely choosing actors. While deterrence had long been a major goal of punishment, in eighteenth-century Europe it came to form the centerpiece of the movement for legal and penal reform. In an age when the death penalty was widely available but relatively infrequently employed, reformers such as Cesare Beccaria and Jeremy Bentham argued that the severity of punishments should vary according to the gravity of the crime; that is, that punishments be both harsh enough to counterbalance the gains from crime and moderate enough that judges, juries, and prosecutors would be prepared to carry them out. Potential offenders would be convinced of the credibility of punishment and thereby be deterred (Beccaria 1977).

The central tenet of deterrence—that the avoidance of pain is a primary motivation for behavior—corresponds to common sense and experience. Many can think of times they have complied with a law only because of the anticipated or actual presence of a police officer. The crime waves that accompany police strikes further illustrate the limits of voluntary conformity (Russell 1975). These are real-world examples of *general deterrence,* or the inhibiting effect of the threat of punishment on potential offenders. Almost any criminal justice system can be said to have some general deterrent effect on crime. However, there have also been questions raised about the extensiveness of deterrence. Most people are aware that many of those punished by the criminal justice system continue to engage in crime. Such high rates of recidivism testify to the limits of *specific deterrence,* or the inhibiting effect of punishment on the punished person's subsequent behavior (Martinson 1974).

Not even the strongest advocates of deterrence argue that *absolute deterrence*—the complete prevention of crime through threatened or actual legal punishment—is possible. Instead, most policies and public debates focus on *partial deterrence,* the reduction in crime from its level were there no punishment, or *marginal deterrence,* the reduction in crime from increasing the punishment by some increment (Zimring and Hawkins 1973). The widely acknowledged limits to absolute deterrence have also shaped the questions addressed by researchers. Rather than asking whether deterrence works, most research examines under what conditions, for what types of persons, behaviors, or both, and through what characteristics of punishment deterrence is likely to work.

When the certainty of punishment is increased, the court and penal systems can become overloaded. This may reduce the deterrent effect of punishments.

Three deterrent characteristics of punishment—its certainty, severity, and celerity (speed)—are generally acknowledged as significant, with certainty considered to be the most important of these (Gibbs 1975). These three aspects of punishment often influence one another and interact to produce complex effects on criminal behavior. For example, even the most horrendous punishment is unlikely to deter if there is almost no probability of its occurrence; that is, extremely high severity accompanied by low certainty limits the deterrent effect of a penalty. Alternatively, when the certainty of punishment is increased—for example, through more efficient policing—the court and penal systems can become overloaded. This may reduce the speed, severity, and hence the deterrent effect of punishments.

Despite the formative role deterrence has played in policies of crime prevention and control, it has been systematically studied only in recent decades. Much has been learned about the potential for controlling crime through the threat of legal punishments, although the complexities associated with answering even basic questions about deterrence have also been highlighted. Perhaps the most common question asked by policy makers and the public is whether a change in a law or its enforcement will affect the crime rate. That is, how much partial, general deterrence will result if sentences for crimes are lengthened or arrest rates are increased?

Research has taken two approaches to answering this question. In one, geographical areas that differ in their legal penalties (e.g., cities, states, countries) are compared to see if these differences are reflected in their crime rates. Some of the earliest research on deterrence used this technique to examine the deterrent effect of the death penalty (Sellin 1959). Since then, a number of such *cross-sectional* studies have used official statistics to study the relationship between punishment and major forms of crime. A second technique involves comparing the crime rates in a single jurisdiction before and after changes in legislation or enforcement practices. This *time-series* approach has been used, for example, to assemble a large body of data on changes in drinking and driving laws and their enforcement (Ross 1984). An important insight from this research is that the deterrent effect of enhanced legal threats may wear off over time.

Both of these techniques are examples of *aggregate-level* analyses, in which group characteristics, rather than perceptions and behaviors of individuals, are studied. Much aggregate-level research has found a deterrent effect for the certainty of punishment by demonstrating, for example, that the higher the likelihood of arrest (or imprisonment) in an area the lower its crime rate (Gibbs 1986). In contrast to the certainty of punishment, the severity of punishment (e.g., prison sentence length) appears to have either weak or no deterrent effects in aggregate-level research.

These conclusions must be interpreted with caution, however. Critics have questioned whether an aggregate approach can accurately estimate deterrent effects for a number of reasons (Blumstein, Cohen, and Nagin 1978). Aggregate-level studies rely on official data on crime and punishment, which can distort estimates of the true incidence of criminal behavior and the true probability of punishment. In addition, it can be difficult to determine whether a relationship between punishment and crime is, in fact, due to the effect of the former on the latter (a deterrent effect). Crime rates may decrease as punishment becomes more certain or severe because more criminals are incapacitated for longer periods of time, not because potential offenders are deterred by threats of punishment. Furthermore, in cross-sectional studies, it may be impossible to rule out the possibility that differences in crime rates lead to differences in the certainty or severity of punishment rather than vice versa. For example, if areas with very low crime rates can expend more resources on capturing each criminal, low crime rates could raise the certainty of punishment. Finally, in both aggregate cross-sectional and time-series studies, it is unlikely that all of the factors that might influence the rates of both crime and punishment will be taken into account. Unless they are, estimates of the deterrent effect of punishment will be inaccurate.

Other disadvantages of aggregate-level research concern the absence of information on individuals and the situations in which they make decisions about crime. Because aggregate-level research does not examine the perceptions and behaviors of individuals, it ignores the crucial psychological processes in deterrence. There is no way to determine if the people who are most fearful of punishment are those least likely to engage in crime. Aggregate-level research does not reveal whether certain types of people are more likely to be deterred than others or *how* threats of punishment act to deter crime. Is it because people fear the experience of being arrested, tried, convicted, and jailed? Is it because they fear they will lose their friends, family, and job opportunities? Is it because the existence of certain and severe punishments teaches and reaffirms the morality of conforming behavior?

These types of questions, which could be crucial to formulating effective crime control policies, can best be addressed through *individual-level* research. Individual-level research collects information on people's perceptions or experiences of legal punishments and on their criminal behavior. Because it can study both those who have actually experienced punishment and those who have only anticipated it, individual-level research provides insights into both specific and general deterrence. Three types of individual-level research have contributed to our knowledge about deterrence in recent years: *perceptual studies, field experiments, and observational studies.*

Perceptual studies ask people to estimate their chances of being punished (certainty) if they committed a crime and the undesirability of the punishment (severity) they would receive. People are also asked either to estimate their chances of engaging in crime or report their actual criminal activity. In addition, they may be asked to indicate what it is they fear about the possibility of punishment. The most valid of these studies interview people first about their perceptions of punishment and then, typically months later, about their criminal activity; this ensures that the perceptions came before the behavior rather than vice versa (Williams and Hawkins 1986).

As in aggregate-level research, evidence from perceptual research is mixed. Among conventional people, the fear of informal consequences of punishment—the loss of family, friends, or reputation—has much more influence on behavior than does the fear of arrest or imprisonment (Tittle 1980). In other words, the perceived threat of legal punishment does appear to have some general deterrent effect, but its effect is largely indirect, rather than directly due to legal reactions. For those who have committed crimes and been punished, their estimates of the likelihood of further punishment appear to matter little for their behavior; instead, they place much more weight on expectations of criminal opportunities and rewards (Piliavin et al. 1986). Hence, perceptual studies provide little evidence of either a general or a specific deterrent effect of legal punishment per se. The more general consequences of legal punishment, however, appear to encourage conformity within the conventional population.

In observational research, people are observed and talked to in their natural surroundings, typically over an extended time. This method is useful for understanding how decisions about crime are made in situations influenced by multiple factors such as peer pressure, group allegiances, and immediate personal needs. These factors appear to affect perceptions of the certainty and severity of punishment and the influence of these perceptions on criminal behavior—though not necessarily as deterrence would predict. For example, legal threats can strengthen the solidarity of a criminal group, and this increased solidarity may increase the likelihood that group members will commit crime. Observational research has shown how threats of legal punishment influence decisions to commit crime in complex and competing ways, in part depending on informal, interpersonal pressures in the particular situation (Ekland-Olsen, Lieb, and Zurcher 1984).

Legal threats can strengthen the solidarity of a criminal group, and this increased solidarity may increase the likelihood that group members will commit crime.

Because of ethical and practical constraints, field experiments that subject individuals to different types of legal punishments are rare. However, field experiments provide some of the most useful information on deterrence because they examine crime and punishment as they occur in real life. An example is a study of the deterrent effect of arrest on wife abusers (Sherman and Berk 1984). In it, police randomly chose one of three methods of responding when faced with a misdemeanor case of wife assault: They either arrested the suspect, provided advice and mediation, or ordered the suspect to leave for eight hours. The original study found that those who were less likely to abuse their wives again were those who were arrested rather than those subject to the other two treatments. Apparently, then, criminal justice sanctions can have a specific deterrent effect for some types of offenders.

Deterrence will likely remain one of the primary methods of crime prevention and control, despite contradictory evidence on its effectiveness. Clearly, threats of legal punishment can affect criminal decisions in a variety of ways—sometimes directly and indirectly to deter crime, sometimes indirectly to increase the likelihood of crime. Research indicates that potential offenders are not irrational but instead weigh the rewards or costs of crime in predictable, if not always perfectly logical, ways. Finally, it appears that decisions about crime are often influenced by considerations not related to the law—for example, group pressures or moral inhibitions. These considerations may, however, depend on legal prohibitions. All of these have produced new insights into why so many crime prevention and control policies have failed and have suggested ways to make them more effective.

[See also Criminal Sanctions; Criminology.]

BIBLIOGRAPHY

Beccaria, Cesare 1977 *On Crimes and Punishments,* 6th ed., trans. Henry Paolucci. Indianapolis: Bobbs-Merrill.

Becker, Gary S. 1968 "Crime and Punishment: An Economic Analysis." *Journal of Political Economy* 78:189–217.

Blumstein, Alfred, Jacqueline Cohen, and Daniel Nagin 1978 *Deterrence and Incapacitation Estimating the Effects of Criminal Sanctions on Crime Rates.* Washington, D.C.: National Academy of Science.

Cohen, Jacqueline 1983 *Incapacitating Criminals: Recent Research Findings.* Washington D.C.: National Institute of Justice.

Cullen, Francis, and Karen Gilbert 1982 *Reaffirming Rehabilitation.* Cincinnati, Ohio: Anderson.

Ekland-Olsen, Sheldon, John Leib, and Louis Zurcher 1984 "The Paradoxical Impact of Criminal Sanctions: Some Microstructural Findings." *Law and Society Review* 18:159–178.

Gibbs, Jack 1975 *Crime, Punishment, and Deterrence.* New York: Elsevier.

——— 1986 "Deterrence Theory and Research." In Gary Melton, ed., *Law as a Behavioral Instrument.* Lincoln: University of Nebraska Press.

Martinson, Robert 1974 "What Works? Questions and Answers About Prison Reform." *Public Interest* 35:22–54.

Piliavin, Irving, Rosemary Gartner, Craig Thornton, and Ross L. Matsueda 1986 "Crime, Deterrence, and Rational Choice." *American Sociological Review* 51:101–119.

Ross, H. Laurence 1984 *Deterring the Drinking Driver: Legal Policy and Social Control.* Lexington, Mass.: Lexington Books.

Russell, Francis 1975 *A City in Terror, 1919: The Boston Police Strike.* New York: Viking.

Sellin, Thorsten 1959 *The Death Penalty.* Philadelphia: American Law Institute.

Sherman, Lawrence, and Richard A. Berk 1984 "The Specific Deterrent Effects of Arrest for Domestic Assault." *American Sociological Review* 49:261–272.

Tittle, Charles R. 1980 *Sanctions and Social Deviance.* New York: Praeger.

Williams, Kirk R., and Richard Hawkins 1986 "Perceptual Research on General Deterrence: A Critical Review." *Law and Society Review* 20:545–572.

Zimring, Frank E., and Gordon Hawkins 1973 *Deterrence: The Legal Threat in Crime Control.* Chicago: University of Chicago Press.

– ROSEMARY I. GARTNER

CRIME RATES

In their generic form, crime rates are simple calculations that relate the number of crimes that occur during a given time period in a geographical area to the population base from which the crimes emanate. For instance, equation 1 produces a crude crime rate:

$$\frac{\text{Number of Crimes}}{\text{Population}} \times K = \text{Crude Crime Rate} \qquad (1)$$

where *K* is a constant. When expressing crime rates for large populations (e.g., cities or countries) the constant, *K*, is usually 100,000. The expression indicates the number of crimes committed in a given time period for every 100,000 people living in the geographic area.

If it were possible to generate a number representing all crimes that occur in the United States in a year, that number would be the numerator and the United States population would be the denominator. A crude crime rate is the result of dividing one by the other and multiplying by 100,000. Unfortunately, no number representing all crime that occurs in the United States for any given period of time can be calculated.

The most widely cited number representing crime in the United States is generated from official police reports about crime. "Crime rate" most often refers to the "official crime rate," which is based on police reports of crime. Ultimately these data are compiled by the Federal Bureau of Investigation (FBI) and published in its annual report, *Crime in the United States.*

Accurate crime rates are important because they are used for many purposes: as indicators of the amount of crime in society; as an indicator of trends (increasing or decreasing) of crime in society; by local authorities to allocate law enforcement resources; by politicians to allocate money to law enforcement agencies; and by social scientists to test theories about crime.

Official Crime Rates

In the 1920s the International Association of Chiefs of Police developed a system for producing uniform police statistics. In 1929 their plan was complete and became the basis for the uniform crime reporting program used in the United States. The object of the system was to produce reliable national statistics about crime. The *Uniform Crime Reporting* (UCR) Program, in place since 1930, remained relatively unchanged through the late 1980s (U.S. Department of Justice 1988a).

One problem in getting national data on crime is that the definition of specific crimes vary in each state. The UCR developed standardized definitions of offenses without reference to local statutes used by local officials to record offenses. No matter which jurisdiction is involved, offenses can be classified in a way that is consistent with UCR definitions (U.S. Department of Justice 1988a).

In its current form the UCR is managed by the FBI and relies on over 16,000 city, county, and state law enforcement agencies voluntarily to report data on crime that comes to their attention. The FBI compiles and publishes these reports and makes available a separate data set for homicide offenses. The original Committee on Uniform Crime Records evaluated various crimes on the basis of their seriousness, frequency of occurrence, pervasiveness in all geographic areas of the country, and likelihood of being reported to law enforcement. On those bases, a compilation of eight "index" crimes is used to gauge fluctuations in overall volume and rate of crime for the country and its regions. The "crime index" includes: murder and nonnegligent manslaughter, forcible rape, robbery, aggravated assault, burglary, larceny-theft, motor vehicle theft. In 1979 arson was added as an index offense and the new list became known as the modified crime index.

Based on records of all reports of crime received from victims, officers who discover infractions, or other sources, law enforcement agencies across the country tabulate the number of crime index offenses during each month and forward that information to the FBI. It is these data that become the national crime statistics. Complaints determined to be false through investigation are eliminated from an agency's count. The number of "actual offenses" (the number of reported offenses minus those eliminated as false) are recorded regardless of whether an arrest is made, stolen property is recovered, or prosecution is undertaken (U.S. Department of Justice 1988a).

Crime rates for the United States are generated by adding together the number of index offenses known to the police in a given year and reported to the FBI, dividing by an estimate of the U.S. population for that year and multiplying by 100,000 (U.S. Department of Justice 1988a). For instance, the index crime rate calculation for 1996 is shown in equation 2.

$$\frac{13{,}473{,}600}{265{,}284{,}000} \times 100{,}000 = 5{,}078.9 \qquad (2)$$

There were 13,473,600 index crimes recorded by the FBI. The population estimate for 1996 was 265,284,000. For every 100,000 people living in the United States in 1996 there were 5,079 index crimes reported and recorded. This is a decrease of 6.7 percent since 1992, and a decrease of 0.3 percent since 1987 (Uniform Crime Reports, 1996).

The UCR is meant to gauge fluctuations in crime in the United States by using serious crimes as an indicator of criminal activity. Its success, to some extent, depends on the reportability of the crimes in the index. One of the reasons that the eight crimes designated as index offenses were chosen to represent fluctuations in crime rates is that they are relatively well-reported crimes. But the National Crime Survey and other victimization studies have demonstrated that even for these very serious crimes a high proportion go unreported (the two exceptions being motor vehicle theft and homicide). Crime reporting by the public varies both by seriousness of the event and by the type of crime itself. Forcible rape, one of the most serious crimes against the person, has a relatively low reporting rate due to expected reactions of police, embarrassment, the victim's relation to the offender, and other factors (O'Brien 1985). On the other hand, motor vehicle theft, a much less serious property crime, is highly reported because usually victims can collect their insurance only after they report the crime. With these and a few other exceptions, the more serious the crime, the higher the likelihood of a report being filed. When no report is filed or if the police have not discovered the crime, then for statistical purposes no crime has taken place. There will be no number in the crime index to show that a crime was committed.

Forcible rape, one of the most serious crimes against the person, has a relatively low crime reporting rate.

Crime also fluctuates by local assignment of police to particular duty (initially raising arrest rates but ultimately lowering arrest rates in the area), and by systematic variations in the way local enforcement agencies record crime, by the degree of professionalism of the force, and by the population to police ratio (O'Brien 1985). Coupled with these issues is the degree of discretion exercised by police. The more discretion exercised, the less likely some crimes are to become statistics. Finally, political pressure to raise or lower the crime rate has at times had an effect on crimes reported at the local level and, in turn, to the FBI. In sum, a variety of variables determines whether or not a criminal event becomes a criminal statistic. Many studies have shown that a large portion of even serious crime does not appear in national criminal statistics. However, the precise impact of local variations in reporting has not been quantitatively assessed and the UCR program does use data quality control measures in an attempt to rectify excessive deviations.

Compounding the problems associated with crimes that do not become known to the police are problem associated with the UCR scoring rules themselves. For instance, when several crimes occur in one incident, only the most serious crime is recorded in the national statistics (the hierarchy rule). In addition, crimes against the person are counted as one crime per victim, while for crimes against property (robbery, burglary, larceny-theft, motor vehicle theft) one offense per distinct operation or attempt is counted. When the two are combined, different units of count have been aggregated.

The UCR is designed to gauge the extent of shifts in serious crimes occurring in the United States. The flaws in the system (under-reporting and the problems associated with the reporting rules) may mean that the program is not accomplishing its goals well. On the other hand, while the results of victimization studies show much more crime, at least some studies have indicated a high correlation with UCR reflections of crime trends.

Despite criticisms levelled at the UCR, the crime index has been used for decades as the basis for policy decisions and comparisons between jurisdictions. In an effort to take advantage of automated law enforcement record keeping, respond to increased demand for refined crime data, rectify some of the program defects and to improve the quality of data generated nationally, the FBI in 1984 began efforts to redesign the UCR. The new version is called the *National Incident-Based Recording System* (NIBRS).

The major differences between the UCR and NIBRS lie in the structure of the data sets generated by the two systems. The new data set allows more sophisticated data manipulations. Most of the general methods for collecting, scoring, and reporting UCR data remain applicable in the NIBRS. Hence, the proportion of all serious crime occurring that become national crime statistics will change only as a result of the change in the hierarchy rule (see below) and changes in police procedures.

In contrast to the UCR summary procedures, NIBRS data are incident based. For each incident the system will attempt to collect information about fifty-two data elements regarding the offense, property characteristics, victim characteristics and offender/arrestee characteristics. Most of the data elements will be new to national crime reporting, and the overall data set will be much richer than the UCR summary information. While the UCR crime index included eight crimes, NIBRS "group A" offenses consist of twenty-two crime categories composed of forty-six offenses. The twenty-two categories include both incidents and arrests and serve as the basis for crime rate calculations (U.S. Department of Justice 1988b).

The following categories make up the list of group A offenses: arson, assault (aggravated, simple, intimidation), bribery, burglary/breaking and entering, counterfeiting/forgery, destruction/damage/vandalism of property, drug/narcotic offenses, embezzlement, extortion/blackmail, fraud offenses, gambling offenses, homicide offenses (murder, nonnegligent homicide, negligent manslaughter, justifiable homicide), kidnapping/abduction, larceny/theft offenses, motor vehicle theft, pornography/obscene material, prostitution offenses, robbery, sex offenses (forcible rape, forcible sodomy, sexual assault with an object, forcible fondling), nonforcible sex offenses (incest, statutory rape), stolen property, and weapon law violations. Other offense data are collected as part of "group B" offenses. These include bad checks, curfew, disorderly conduct, driving under the influence, drunkenness, family offenses (nonviolent), liquor law violations, peeping Tom, runaway, trespass of real property, and all other offenses.

There are no immediate plans to change the crime index as a measure of national fluctuations. For the time being, reports of both the index of crime, "group A" and "group B" criminality will be published.

The overall crime rate in Canada cannot be compared with that of the U.S. crime index rate because the Canadian rates take into account much more crime.

It is clear that NIBRS represents vast improvements in the types of data collected. The data provide the possibility of constructing victim and offender profiles, of examining victim/offender relationships, and for studying many more demographic correlates of crime. Further, the new system overcomes criticisms of the hierarchy rule (the new system records all incidents) and offense scoring becomes automated.

Group A crimes reflect increases and new interest in particular types of crime. For instance, group A crimes include white collar crimes that are of concern and consequence because of relatively recent awareness of political criminality. The inclusion of drugs reflects the massive problem faced by this country with regard to drug use and importation. On the other hand, group A crimes include many crimes (white collar and drugs included) with dismal reporting histories. Some of the crimes vary substantially by region of the country and valid data will be extremely difficult to obtain. The inclusion of these crimes may detract from the system's stated purpose of serving as a gauge of crime and criminal behavior in the nation.

While NIBRS addresses some of the criticisms of the old UCR, it does not ensure higher rates of reporting, improve differences in reporting due to differing police practices, or address regional variation due to differences in laws and reporting practices. No doubt the new system, when it is in place, will provide more information, but only time will tell if the quality of data improves along with the quantity.

During the time taken by agencies to obtain data processing and other facilities necessary to join NIBRS, the old UCR will continue. For some time to come the two systems will operate jointly, and data from the new system will be used to create the summary information needed to ensure that national data can be published. The new system began in ten states in 1989. In 1997, ten states were certified to submit to NIBRS and an additional 24 states were in various stages of testing the system. Crime rates may seem easy to calculate, but in fact many variables enter into that final number that represents crime in any society. These rates must be used with caution because of the many factors that influence them.

International Comparisons

While it is problematic to make comparisons between jurisdictions within the United States, international comparisons are even more difficult. Not only do laws differ substantially, but recording systems often bear no resemblance to one another. Table 1 offers an example of problems in trying to make international comparisons even when the basic information is relatively good. The table presents the best available data about homicide in each country and it is tempting to draw conclusions from the comparative homicide rates. For statistical purposes, however, each country defines homicide slightly differently. In the United States these data include murder, manslaughter (negligent manslaughter and attempted murder and manslaughter are not included); in the United Kingdom the data include murder, attempted murder, threat or conspiracy to murder, manslaughter and infanticide (child destruction is not included); in the Federal Republic of Germany the data are for murder, manslaughter, "murder on demand," and infanticide; France includes murder, manslaughter, parricide (parent killing) infanticide, and poisoning; Japan includes murder, manslaughter, and robbery causing death (attempts *are* included) (Ministry of Justice 1989). Japan's data may also include preparation for commission of a homicide and participation in suicide although it excludes assaults leading to homicide (U.S. Department of Justice 1988c); homicide in Canada is first and second degree murder, manslaughter and infanticide; homicide in the USSR is undefined by the source from which the data were derived. Hence, no

TABLE 1

HOMICIDE BY COUNTRIES, 1986 (NUMBER AND RATE PER 100,000)

	U.S.A.	U.K.	F.R.G.	France	Canada	Japan
Number	20,613	2,160	2,728	2,413	569	1,744
Rate	8.6	4.3	4.5	4.4	2.2	1.4

Sources: Ministry of Justice 1989; Statistics Canada 1989; Eklof 1990.

two countries' data are the same and some of the differences, particularly the inclusion or exclusion of attempts, involve major substantive differences. Nonetheless, as gross comparisons, these data for homicide are better than for any other crimes. In making international comparisons, probably the best technique is to use multiple sources of data on the same crimes when such information is available. For example, the Department of Justice had some success in comparing various types of crime across nations using World Health Organization, United Nations and Interpol data (U.S. Department of Justice 1988c).

Most international crime comparisons are possible only when one fully grasps the system of reporting, definitions of crime and peculiarities of the systems discussed. A few specific examples complete this introduction to crime rates.

Canada's Uniform Crime Reporting system was modeled on the UCR of the United States but Canada did not start using it until 1962. Because Canada has a single criminal law for the whole country, it has encountered fewer problems of comparability than the U.S. Nonetheless, the Canadian UCR has faced criticisms on virtually identical grounds to those levelled at the U.S. UCR (Silverman, Teevan, and Sacco 1991). Rather than being compiled by a police agency, the Canadian UCR is the responsibility of the Canadian Centre for Justice Statistics, Statistics Canada. Police reporting to that agency is not voluntary; it is mandated by law.

A major element differentiating Canada's UCR from the U.S. UCR is that Canada does not use a crime index to calculate its crime rate. Crime rate is calculated on the basis of all criminal code violations. Hence, overall crime rate cannot be compared with that of the U.S. crime index rate because the Canadian rates take into account much more crime. In 1988 the crime rate for Canada was 9,233 per 100,000 (estimated population, 25,911,800; criminal code violations, 2,392,419).

It is possible to compare crime rates for individual crimes if care is taken to ensure that the categories being used are similar. For instance, it is fairly common to compare Canada's assault rate with that of the United States. The surprising, but incorrect finding is that Canada apparently has a higher assault rate. While the two reporting systems refer to "assault," the U.S. category includes only aggravated assault while the Canadian system counts both aggravated and simple assaults. This example typifies the dangers of international comparisons.

Homicide data are more comparable. The legal definitions are similar if not identical and the reporting is equally reliable in the two countries. Over many years Canada has consistently had a rate of homicide between one-third and one-fourth that of the United States.

In the early 1990s Canada will switch to an incident based reporting system. Like the U.S. system, it will eliminate many of the problems of the old UCR by expanding the data elements to be included, but it will retain problems associated with initial reporting of crime (coverage). The new Canadian system should be in place by 1992. Because of the uniformity of Canada's criminal law and the attention Canada is giving to implementing the new system, it should generate some of the best official criminal statistics in the world.

In delimiting its crime trends since 1946, Japan reports all offenses including "traffic professional negligence," which the United States would not consider either an index offense or a "group A" offense in NIBRS. Crime rate comparisons with Japan are difficult because of legal definitions and law enforcement emphasis. Given Japan's tendency to include all penal code offenses in calculations, it is, in fact, easier to compare overall Japanese statistics with Canadian statistics. Eliminating the traffic offenses, Japan reports a rate of 1,291 penal offenses per 100,000 for 1987. Hence, Japan's total crime rate is one-fourth the U.S. index rate and one-seventh of the total Canadian rate. The Japanese crime rate declined between the mid-1940s and the mid-1970s (from a high of 2,000 to a low of 1,091). Since that time there has been a slight rise (Ministry of Justice 1989).

While both organized crime gangs and drugs are considered to be major problems in Japan, these issues bear little resemblance in substance or quantity to the same issues in the United States. To understand the absolute rate of crime, crime reporting, and crime trends in Japan, it is necessary to attempt to understand the forces that generate the crime, the informal ways of handling crime, and the law enforcement focus in the country. It has been suggested that the amount of crime that occurs in Japan is far greater than officially recorded crime.

International comparisons often require more than looking at the numbers produced by the statistical agencies of the countries. The bases for calculations, counting methods, legal definitions, as well as political motives and cultural differences in dealing with crime all must be taken into account.

[See also Criminology; Juvenile Delinquency and Juvenile Crime.]

BIBLIOGRAPHY

The Current Digest of the Soviet Press 1989 "State and Law" 41 (2):23–24.

——— 1990a "Fight Crime Don't Fear Statistics." 42 (2):31–32.

——— 1990b "Bakatin Reports on Organized Crime." 42 (8):17–20.

——— 1990c "Bakatin Gives Details on Crime 'Crisis.' " 42 (16):11–12.

Eklof, B. 1990 "Trapped in a Mine Cave-In? The Soviet People Today." *Arts and Sciences* 13:6–10.

Ministry of Justice 1989 *Summary of the White Paper on Crime, 1988.* Tokyo: Research and Training Institute, Government of Japan.

Moscow News 1990 "Narcotics, Narcomania, Narcobusiness." 24:15.

O'Brien, Robert M. 1985. *Crime and Victimization Data,* vol. 4. Law and Criminal Justice Series. Beverly Hills, Calif.: Sage.

Silverman, R. A., J. Teevan, V. Sacco (eds.) 1991 *Crime in Canadian Society,* 4th ed. Toronto: Butterworths.

Statistics Canada 1989 *Canadian Crime Statistics 1988.* Ottawa: Minister of Supply and Services.

U.S. Department of Justice 1988a *Crime in the United States: Uniform Crime Reports, 1987.* Washington, D.C.: U.S. Government Printing Office.

——— 1988b *National Incident-Based Reporting System,* vol. 1, *Data Collection Guidelines.* Washington, D.C.: U.S. Government Printing Office.

——— 1988c *International Crime Statistics.* Bureau of Justice Statistics Special Report. Washington, D.C.: U.S. Department of Justice.

——— 1990 *Crime in the United States: Uniform Crime Reports, 1989.* Washington, D.C.: U.S. Government Printing Office.

– ROBERT A. SILVERMAN

CRIME, THEORIES OF

Most accounts of the rise of criminological inquiry indicate that it had its beginnings in mid-nineteenth-century developments in Europe, including the work of Cesare Lombroso, an Italian prison physician, who argued that many criminals are atavists, that is, biological throwbacks to a human type, *homo delinquens,* that allegedly existed prior to the appearance of *homo sapiens.* Since the time of Lombroso and other early figures in criminology, the field has grown markedly, both in terms of the variety of scholars who have tried to uncover the causes of crime and also in terms of the diverse theories that have been produced by these persons (Vold and Bernard 1986). Currently, criminological theorizing and research is engaged in by legal theorists, psychologists, economists, geographers, and representatives of other scholarly fields as well, but the largest share of work has been carried on by sociologists. Thus, criminology is frequently identified as a subfield of sociology (Gibbons 1979).

Crime and criminal behavior are defined or identified by the criminal laws of nations, states, and local jurisdictions. Acts that are not prohibited or required by the criminal law are not crimes, however much they may offend some members of the community. Also, the reach of the criminal law in modern societies is very broad, involving a wide range of behavioral acts that vary not only in form but in severity as well. The criminal laws of various states and nations prohibit morally repugnant acts such as murder or incest, but they also prohibit less serious offenses such as vandalism, petty theft, and myriad other acts. No wonder, then, that there are a large number of theories of crime, given the varieties of behavior that are defined as criminal and the differing perspectives from which the phenomenon of crime has been addressed.

Persons of all ages violate criminal laws, although a number of forms of criminality are most frequent among persons in their teens or early twenties. Except for "status offense" violations such as running away, truancy, and the like, which apply only to juveniles (usually defined as persons under eighteen years of age), juvenile delinquency and adult criminality are defined by the same body of criminal statutes. However, criminologists have usually constructed theories about delinquency separate from explanations of adult criminality. Although many theories of delinquency closely resemble those dealing with adult crime, some of the former are not paralleled by theories of adult criminality. In the discussion to follow, most attention is upon explanatory arguments about adult lawbreaking, but some mention is also made of causal arguments about juvenile crime.

Criminological Questions and Causal Theories

There are two basic forms taken by most theories of crime: Some center on the explanation of crime patterns and crime rates, or what might be termed "crime in the aggregate," while others are pitched at the individual level and endeavor to identify factors that account for the involvement or noninvolvement of specific individuals in lawbreaking conduct (Gibbons 1987, pp. 35–38; Sutherland and Cressey 1978, pp. 62–63).

These are related but analytically separate questions about crime causation. As Edwin Sutherland and Donald Cressey (1978, pp. 62–63) have argued, an adequate account of criminality should contain two distinct but consistent aspects: "First, there will be a statement that explains the statistical distribution of criminal behavior in time and space (epidemiology). . . . Second, there will be a statement that identifies the process or processes by which persons come to exhibit criminal behavior."

Statistical distributions of criminal behavior in time and space are usually portrayed in the form of crime rates of one kind or another. One of the most familiar of these is the "index crime rate" reported annually for cities, states, and other jurisdictions by the Federal Bureau of Investigation. The index crime rate involves the number of reported cases of murder, nonnegligent manslaughter, forcible rape, aggravated assault, robbery, larceny, burglary, and auto theft per jurisdiction, expressed as a rate per 100,000 persons in that jurisdiction's population.

Many crime rate patterns are well known, including relatively high rates of violence in the United States compared to other nations, state-by-state variations in forcible rape rates, regional variations in homicide and other crimes within the United States, and so forth. Criminologists have also developed a number of theories or explanations for these crime rate variations. One case in point is Larry Baron and Murray Straus's (1987) investigation of rape rates for the fifty American states, in which the authors examined the influence of state-to-state variations in gender inequality, social disorganization (high divorce rates, low church attendance, and the like), pornography readership, and "cultural spillover" (authorized paddling of school children, etc.) on forcible rape.

Crime rates are important social indicators that reflect the quality of life in different areas. Additionally, theories such as the one by Baron and Straus, linking various social factors to those rates, provide considerable insight into the causes of lawbreaking. But, it is well to keep in mind that crime rates are the summary expression of illegal acts of individuals. Much of the time, the precise number of offenders who have carried out the reported offenses is unknown because individual law violators engage in varying numbers of crimes per year. But even so, crime rates summarize the illegal actions of individuals. Accordingly, theories of crime must ultimately deal with the processes by which these specific persons come to exhibit criminal behavior.

In practice, criminological theories that focus on crime rates and patterns often have had relatively little to say about the causes of individual behavior. For example, variations in income inequality from one place to another have been identified by criminologists as being related to rates of predatory property crime such as burglary, automobile theft, and larceny. Many of the studies that have reported this finding have had little to say about how income inequality, defined as the unequal distribution of income among an entire population of an area or locale, affects individuals. In short, explanations of crime rate variations often do not indicate how the explanatory variables they identify "get inside the heads of offenders," so to speak.

Although criminological theories about crime rates and crime patterns have often been developed independently of theories relating to the processes by which specific persons come to exhibit criminal conduct, valid theories of these processes should have implications for the task of understanding the realities of criminal conduct. For example, if variations in gender inequality and levels of pornography readership are related to rates of forcible rape, it may be that individuals who carry out sexual assaults also believe that discrimination against women is legitimate and are avid readers of pornography. In the same way, if income inequality bears some consistent relationship to rates of predatory crime, it may also be that individual predators express relatively strong feelings of "relative deprivation," that is, perceptions of economic disadvantage. However, some additional factors may also have to be identified that determine which of the persons who feel relatively deprived become involved in illegal conduct and which do not.

Perspectives, Theories, and Hypotheses

A number of arguments about crime patterns and the processes through which individuals get involved in lawbreaking are examined below. Before moving to these specific theories, however, two other general observations are in order. First, in criminology, as in sociology more generally, there is considerable disagreement regarding the nature of perspectives, theories, and hypotheses. *Theories* are often described as sets of concepts, along with interconnected propositions that link the concepts together into an "explanatory package"; *perspectives* are identified as broader and less systematically organized arguments; and *hypotheses* are specific research propositions derived from theories. In practice, however, many causal explanations that have been described as theories are incomplete and also conceptually imprecise. Jack Gibbs (1985) has labeled such theories as being in "the discursive mode" rather than as formal theories. According to Gibbs, because most criminological theories are discursive, precise predictions from them are not possible, nor is it possible to subject predictions to empirical test, that is, to validation through research.

Many criminological theories involve vague concepts, faulty underlying logic, and other problems. At the same time, it is possible to identify a number of general theoretical perspectives in criminology and to differentiate these from relatively formalized and precise theories. For example, many criminologists contend that American society is "criminogenic" because it involves social and economic features that appear to contribute heavily to criminality. However, this is a general perspective rather than a theory of crime in that it does not identify the full range of factors that contribute to lawbreaking, and it also lacks a set of explicit and interrelated propositions. By contrast, the income inequality argument more clearly qualifies as a causal theory, as does the formulation that links gender inequality, pornography readership, and certain other influences to forcible rape.

Many criminologists contend that American society is "criminogenic" because it involves social and economic features that appear to contribute heavily to criminality.

A few other comments are in order on theoretical perspectives in criminology. During most of the developmental history of criminology in the United States, from the early 1900s to the present, sociological criminologists voiced support for the criminogenic culture thesis that directs attention to social-structural factors thought to be responsible for criminality. Thus, this view might also be referred to as "mainstream criminology." Most criminologists have linked lawbreaking to major "rents and tears" in societal structure at the same time that most of them have also assumed that these crime-producing features can be remedied or lessened through social and economic reforms of one kind or another (Gibbons 1979, 1987).

In the 1970s, a markedly different perspective competed for attention. Variously referred to as "radical-Marxist," "critical," or "new" criminology, it asserted that the causes of crime arise out of societal characteristics that are inherent in corporate capitalism (Gibbons 1987, pp. 125–144; Chambliss 1975; Quinney 1974, 1977). According to radical-Marxist criminologists, criminal laws are created to serve the interests of the capitalist ruling class. In turn, the system of corporate capitalism over which the ruling class presides depends for its survival on the exploitation of the resources and people of other countries and the economic oppression of citizens within capitalist nations. These conditions create economic strains for many persons, contribute to the deterioration of family life, and in other ways drive many individuals into desperate acts of lawbreaking.

The radical-Marxist perspective received considerable attention in the 1970s. Those who criticized it claimed that it presented a one-dimensional, oversimplified account of the social sources of criminality. For example, while some criminal laws favor the interests of the owners of capital, many others serve broader social interests. Similarly, while some forms of crime may be related to economic problems, others are not.

A major trend in criminological investigations in recent years has been away from broad mainstream and radical perspectives and toward relatively detailed theories specific to one or another form of crime, such as the argument by Baron and Straus (1987) that links gender inequality, pornography, and social disorganization. Regarding radical-Marxist viewpoints, the delinquency theory of Mark Colvin and John Pauly (1983), centered on serious forms of juvenile misconduct, is another example of the movement away from global formulations to more specific ones. Colvin and Pauly argued that the employer-employee relationships to which lower class workers are subjected are coercive. In turn, the coercive social environment in which workers exist leads to punitive and repressive child-rearing practices on their part, alienating children from their parents. Those youngsters who have poor affectional ties to their parents also become disinterested in activities deemed important to children, activities, for instance, such as doing well in school. Finally, children who are on poor terms with their parents and who are alienated from school become prime candidates for involvement in delinquency, particularly of a serious and repetitive form.

Forms of Crime and Types of Offenders

One central problem that quickly comes to the fore when theorizing turns to particular forms of criminality is the classificatory one. The legal codes of the various states and of the federal government include hundreds of specific offenses, but the explanatory task is to develop a relatively small set of theories to make sense of this diverse collection of illegal activities. Accordingly, criminologists have tried to amalgamate these diverse offenses into a smaller number of sociologically meaningful groupings or crime forms (Farr and Gibbons 1990). Some criminologists have singled out crude property crime, consisting of larceny, burglary, robbery, and kindred offenses, as one type of crime; others have placed homicide and assaultive acts into a crime type; while still others have treated forcible rape and other sexual offenses as another broad form of lawbreaking. Then, too, "white-collar" or organizational crime has often been singled out as a crime pattern (Sutherland 1949; Schrager and Short 1978; Coleman 1987). "Organized crime" is still another type that has received a good deal of criminological attention. Some persons have also drawn attention to a collection of offenses that receive little visibility in the media and elsewhere and have termed these "folk crime" (Ross 1960–1961, 1973) or "mundane crime" (Gibbons 1983). Finally, "political crime" has been identified as a major pattern of lawbreaking (Turk 1982).

Although these groupings identify forms of lawbreaking that differ from each other in important ways, it is also true that they are relatively crude in form in that the underlying dimensions or variables on which they are based are not clearly spelled out. Further, there is disagreement among criminologists as to the specific crimes that should be identified as instances of white-collar crime, mundane crime, or some other category.

Criminologists have also developed systems for sorting individual offenders into behavioral types (Gibbons 1965). Although related to crime classification efforts, categorization of lawbreakers into types is a separate form of activity. While it may be possible to identify groupings such as predatory property crime, it may not be true that individual offenders specialize only in that form of criminality, hence it may be incorrect to speak of "predatory offenders" as a type of criminal. Most offender classification systems have been deficient in one respect or another (Gibbons 1985), but the most serious flaw is that these categorizations are oversimplified. Researchers have discovered that many offenders engage in a diverse collection of offenses over their criminal "careers" rather than being crime specialists such as "burglars," "robbers," or "drug dealers" (Chaiken and Chaiken 1982).

Theories of Crime

The number of theories regarding particular forms of crime is extensive, thus they cannot all be reviewed here. A sampling of some of the more important ones would include the "routine activities" explanation of predatory property crime. Lawrence E. Cohen and Marcus Felson (1979) have contended that predatory property crime involves three major elements: the supply of motivated offenders, the supply of suitable targets, and the absence of capable guardians. In other words, these crimes are carried out by persons with criminal motives, but the incidence of such offenses also depends upon the number of opportunities to burglarize homes or to rob persons. Also, the number of burglaries from one community to another is influenced by the degree to which residents in local areas act as capable guardians by maintaining surveillance over homes in their neighborhoods or by taking other crime-control steps. This theory contends that crime opportunities have increased in the United States in recent decades at the same time that capable guardianship has declined, due principally to changes in employment patterns. In particular, the number of families in which both adult members work during the day has grown markedly, as has the number of employed, single-parent families. Finally, research evidence lends considerable support to this theory (Cohen and Felson 1979).

Another related theory regarding predatory offenses centers on income inequality, defined as the degree to which the total income of a group, such as the residents of a particular city, is distributed unevenly, with a small portion of the group having control over a large portion of the total income (Braithwaite 1979; Carroll and Jackson 1983).

Research evidence indicates that income inequality is related to predatory property crime. Further, Leo Carroll and Pamela Irving Jackson (1983) have argued that the routine activities and income inequality arguments are interrelated. They have suggested that the labor market trends identified in the former have lead both to increased crime opportunities, declines in guardianship, and heightened levels of income inequality.

Theories of Criminal Behavior

While theories about crime patterns and rates have been developed principally by sociological criminologists, representatives of a number of disciplines have endeavored to identify factors and processes that explain the involvement or noninvolvement of specific individuals in lawbreaking. Three basic perspectives can be noted: the biogenic, psychogenic, and sociogenic approaches. *Biogenic views* attribute the genesis or causes of lawbreaking to constitutional and hereditary factors, while *psychogenic perspectives* often contend that lawbreakers exhibit personality problems to which their illegal conduct is a response. By contrast, sociologists have most often advanced *sociogenic theories* arguing that criminal behavior is learned in a socialization process by individuals who are neither biologically nor psychologically flawed. Also, some persons have constructed theories that combine or integrate elements of these three approaches, an important one being James Q. Wilson and Richard J. Herrnstein's (1985) argument that the behavior of criminals has genetic and constitutional roots and that offenders tend to be more mesomorphic in body build, less intelligent, and more burdened with personality defects than their noncriminal peers. Wilson and Herrnstein also contend that various social factors such as unemployment, community influences, and the like play some part in criminality.

Three generalizations can be made about biological theories: First, conclusive evidence supporting these arguments has not yet been produced; second, biological factors cannot be ruled out on the basis of the empirical evidence currently on hand; and third, if biological factors are involved in criminality, they probably are intertwined with social and psychological influences (Trasler 1987; Fishbein 1990).

Edwin H. Sutherland's theory of differential association (Sutherland and Cressey 1978, pp. 80–98) has been the most influential sociological theory about the processes through which persons come to engage in criminality. Sutherland maintained that criminal behavior, including techniques of committing crime and attitudes favorable to lawbreaking activity, is learned in association with other persons. Many of the associations of persons involve face-to-face contact, but criminal conduct definitions can also be acquired indirectly from reference groups, that is, from persons who are important to individuals but with whom they do not directly associate. Sutherland also contended that associations vary in frequency, duration, priority, and intensity. The first three of these conditions are relatively self-evident, while intensity has to do with the personal meaning or significance to individuals of particular social ties.

The core of Sutherland's theory is that before persons engage in lawbreaking, they go through a learning process through which they acquire what he called "definitions favorable to the violation of law," which can be interpreted as motivation to engage in criminality. A radically different theory, directed mainly at explanation of juvenile delinquency, has been put forth by Travis Hirschi (1969). Hirschi has argued that if, through faulty socialization, individuals fail to become bonded to others (that is, if they do not develop positive attachments to adult persons such as parents or teachers), they will then be unlikely to refrain from misbehavior. The emphasis in this theory is on the failure to acquire nondelinquent sentiments rather than on the learning of antisocial ones. In Hirschi's view, delinquency is the result of defective socialization rather than of socialization patterns through which criminal attitudes are learned.

The research evidence that has been produced on delinquents indicates that Hirschi's control theory has merit, particularly as an explanation for relatively petty delinquency and for misconduct on the part of juvenile females (Gibbons and Krohn 1991, pp. 101–105). It is also true, however, that Hirschi's control theory has not been widely adopted as an explanation for adult criminality.

Returning to Sutherland's learning theory and other sociological theories, many of these arguments have asserted or implied that personality differences among individuals are not associated with criminal or delinquent behavior (Sutherland and Cressey 1978). According to Sutherland and Cressey, "No consistent, statistically significant differences between personality traits of delinquents and personality traits of nondelinquents have been found. The explanation of criminal behavior, apparently, must be found in social interaction" (1978, p. 176).

It may be that lawbreaking is often related to psychic needs of individuals.

Sutherland and Cressey were not alone in rejecting personality factors as important in lawbreaking. Several reviews of the evidence, particularly findings having to do with the alleged role of personality defects in criminality, have turned up little or no support for this thesis (Schuessler and Cressey 1950; Waldo and Dinitz 1967; Tennebaum 1977). However, some psychologists have argued that even though the theory that criminality is due to marked personality defects on the part of lawbreakers lacks support, it is nonetheless true that individual differences in the form of personality patterns must be incorporated into criminological theories (Andrews and Wormith 1989). And, in the opinion of a number of sociological criminologists, the argument that individual differences make a difference, both in accounting for criminality and conformity, is persuasive (Gibbons 1989). Personality dynamics play a part in the behavior patterns that individuals exhibit, thus such concepts as role and status are often not able entirely to account for the behavior of individuals. It may be that lawbreaking is often related to psychic needs of individuals as well as to economic pressures and the like that play upon them. On this point, Jack Katz (1988) has explored the personal meanings of homicidal acts, shoplifting, and a number of other kinds of criminality to the persons who are engaged in these acts.

A final word: Further theoretical investigation and research probing the interconnections between biological, psychological, and social factors in criminal conduct remain major pieces of unfinished business in the criminological enterprise.

[See also Criminology; Juvenile Delinquency Theories.]

BIBLIOGRAPHY

Andrews, D. A., and J. Stephen Wormith 1989 "Personality and Crime: Knowledge Destruction and Construction." *Justice Quarterly* 6:289–309.

Baron, Larry, and Murray A. Straus 1987 "Four Theories of Rape: A Macrosociological Analysis." *Social Problems* 34:467–489.

Braithwaite, John 1979 *Inequality, Crime and Public Policy.* London: Routledge and Kegan Paul.

Carroll, Leo, and Pamela Irving Jackson 1983 "Inequality, Opportunity, and Crime Rates in Central Cities." *Criminology* 21:178–194.

Chaiken, Jan, and Marcia Chaiken 1982 *Varieties of Criminal Behavior.* Santa Monica, Calif.: Rand.

Chambliss, William 1975 "Toward a Political Economy of Crime." *Theory and Society* 2:148–155.

Cohen, Lawrence E., and Marcus Felson 1979 "Social Change and Crime Rate Trends: A Routine Activities Approach." *American Sociological Review* 44:588–607.

Coleman, James W. 1987 "Toward an Integrated Theory of White-Collar Crime." *American Journal of Sociology* 93:406–439.

Colvin, Mark, and John Pauly 1983 "A Critique of Criminology: Toward an Integrated Structural-Marxist Theory of Delinquency Production." *American Journal of Sociology* 89:513–551.

Cressey, Donald R. 1972 *Criminal Organization.* New York: Harper and Row.

Farr, Kathryn Ann, and Don C. Gibbons 1990 "Observations on the Development of Crime Categories." *International Journal of Offender Therapy and Comparative Criminology* 34.

Fishbein, Diana H. 1990 "Biological Perspectives in Criminology." *Criminology* 28:27–72.

Gibbons, Don C. 1965 *Changing the Lawbreaker.* Englewood Cliffs, N.J.: Prentice-Hall.

——— 1979 *The Criminological Enterprise.* Englewood Cliffs, N.J.: Prentice-Hall.

——— 1983 "Mundane Crime." *Crime and Delinquency* 29:213–227.

——— 1985 "The Assumption of the Efficacy of Middle-Range Explanations: Typologies." In R. F. Meier, ed., *Theoretical Methods in Criminology.* Beverly Hills, Calif.: Sage.

——— 1987 *Society, Crime, and Criminal Behavior,* 5th ed. Englewood Cliffs, N.J.: Prentice-Hall.

——— 1989 "Comment-Personality and Crime: Non-Issues, Real Issues, and a Theory and Research Agenda." *Justice Quarterly* 6:311–323.

———, and Marvin D. Krohn 1991 *Delinquent Behavior,* 5th ed. Englewood Cliffs, N.J.: Prentice-Hall.

Gibbs, Jack P. 1985 "The Methodology of Theory Construction in Criminology." In R. F. Meier, ed., *Theoretical Methods in Criminology.* Beverly Hills, Calif.: Sage.

Greenberg, David F. 1976 "On One-Dimensional Criminology." *Theory and Society* 3:610–621.

Hirschi, Travis 1969 *Causes of Delinquency.* Berkeley: University of California Press.

Katz, Jack 1988 *Seductions of Crime.* New York: Basic Books.

Quinney, Richard 1974 *Critique of Legal Order.* Boston: Little, Brown.

——— 1977 *Class, State, and Crime.* New York: McKay.

Ross, H. Laurence 1960–61. "Traffic Law Violation: A Folk Crime." *Social Problems* 9:231–241.

——— 1973 "Folk Crime Revisited." *Criminology* 11:41–85.

Schrager, Laura Shill, and James F. Short, Jr. 1978 "Toward a Sociology of Organizational Crime." *Social Problems* 25:407–419.

Schuessler, Karl F., and Donald R. Cressey 1950 "Personality Characteristics of Criminals." *American Journal of Sociology* 55:476–484.

Sutherland, Edwin H. 1949 *White Collar Crime.* New York: Dryden.

———, and Donald R. Cressey 1978 *Criminology,* 10th ed. Philadelphia: Lippincott.

Tennebaum, D. J. 1977 "Personality and Criminality: A Summary and Implications of the Literature." *Journal of Criminal Justice* 5:225–235.

Trasler, Gordon 1987 "Biogenetic Factors." In Herbert C. Quay, ed., *Handbook of Juvenile Delinquency.* New York: Wiley.

Turk, Austin T. 1982 *Political Criminality.* Beverly Hills, Calif.: Sage.

Vold, George B., and Thomas J. Bernard 1986 *Theoretical Criminology,* 3rd ed. New York: Oxford.

Waldo, Gordon P., and Simon Dinitz 1967 "Personality Attributes of the Criminal: An Analysis of Research Studies, 1950-1965." *Journal of Research in Crime and Delinquency* 4:185–202.

Wilson, James Q., and Richard J. Herrnstein 1985 *Crime and Human Nature.* New York: Simon and Schuster.

– DON C. GIBBONS

CRIMINAL AND DELINQUENT SUBCULTURES

The notion of a subculture is that it is derivative of, but different from, some larger referential culture. The term is used loosely to denote shared systems of norms, values, or interests that set apart some individuals, groups, or other aggregation of people from larger societies and from broader cultural systems. Common examples include youth subcultures, ethnic subcultures, regional subcultures, subcultures associated with particular occupations, and subcultures that develop among people who share special interests such as bird-watching, stamp collecting, or a criminal or delinquent behavior pattern.

Neither membership in a particular category (age, ethnicity, place of residence, occupation) nor behavior (bird-watching, stamp collecting, crime, or delinquency) is sufficient to define a subculture, however. The critical elements are, rather, (1) the degree to which values, norms, and identities associated with membership in a category or with types of behavior are shared, and (2) the nature of relationships, within some larger cultural system, between those who share these elements and those who do not.

In these terms, criminal or delinquent subcultures denote systems of norms, values, or interests that support criminal or delinquent behavior. The many behaviors specified in law as criminal or delinquent are associated with many criminal and delinquent subcultures. The norms, values, or interests of these subcultures may support particular criminal acts, a limited set of such acts (as, for example, a subculture of pickpockets or safe crackers), or they may be even broader in scope. Donald R. Cressey argues that "subcultural definitions of appropriate behavior pertain to very specific kinds of offenses rather than to crime in general" (1983, p. 587). This is especially true of "professional criminals," who take pride in their craft, organize themselves for the safe and efficient performance of the crimes in which they specialize, and generally avoid other types of criminal involvement that might bring them to the attention of the authorities (see Sutherland 1937). Not all criminal subcultures are this specific, however. Some are more opportunistic, embracing several types of criminal behavior as opportunities arise. So it is with delinquent subcultures, where narrow specialization is rare.

While delinquent subcultures typically are associated with a broad range of illegal behaviors, among delinquent groups and subcultures there is great variation in the nature and strength of group norms, values, and interests. Moreover, the extent to which delinquent behavior is attributable to group norms, values, or special interests is problematic. Much delinquent behavior of highly delinquent gangs, for example, results from the operation of group processes rather than group norms per se (see Short 1990). The normative properties of groups vary greatly, but even the most delinquent gang devotes relatively little of its group life in the pursuit of delinquent behaviors. Further, when gangs do participate in delinquent episodes, some members of the gang typically do not become involved. Why this should be the case is an important feature of delinquent subcultures.

For analytical purposes it is important to distinguish between subcultures and the particular groups and individuals who carry them, that is, the individuals and groups who share the norms, values, and interests of the subculture. While members of a delinquent gang may be the sole carriers of a particular subculture, some subcultures are shared by many gangs. Conflict subcultures, for example, are shared by rival fighting gangs among whom individual and group status involves values related to the defense of "turf" (territory) and "rep" (reputation) and norms supportive of these values. Subcultures oriented to theft and other forms of property crime vary in the extent to which they are associated with particular groups. Some types of property crimes require organization and coordination of activities in order to be successful. Some also necessarily involve the efforts of others, such as "fences," in addition to members of a criminally organized gang (see Klockars 1974). Others, such as mugging and other types of robbery, may be carried out by individual offenders, who nevertheless share a subculture supportive of such behavior. Most drug-using subcultures tend to be less oriented toward particular groups than are conflict subcultures because the subcultural orientation is toward drug consumption, and this orientation can be shared with other drug users in many types of group situations. To the extent that a subculture is oriented to experiences associated with a particular group, however, a drug-using subculture may also be unique to that group.

Cultures, subcultures, and the groups associated with them overlap, often in multiple and complex ways. To speak of youth culture, for example, is to denote a subculture of a larger adult-dominated and institutionally defined culture. Similarly, delinquent subcultures contain elements of both youth and adult cultures. Williams's (1989) lower class, minority "cocaine kids," for example, were entrepreneurial, worked long hours, and maintained self-discipline—all important elements in the achievement ideology of the American Dream. Most saw their involvement in the drug trade as a way to get started in legitimate business or to pursue other conventional goals, and a few succeeded at least temporarily in doing so. The criminal subculture with which they identified shared a symbiotic relationship with their customers (including many middle and upper class persons), who shared subcultural values approving drug use but who were not full participants in the subculture of drug distribution. For these young people drug dealing was a way to "be somebody" and to acquire such things as jewelry, clothing, and cars—the symbols of wealth, power, and respect.

The nature of relationships between delinquent subcultures and larger cultural systems is further illustrated by Mercer Sullivan's study of Brooklyn gangs, among whom the "cultural meaning of crime is constructed in . . . interaction out of materials supplied from two sources: the local area in which they spend their time almost totally unsupervised and undirected by adults, and the consumerist youth culture promoted in the mass media" (1989, p. 249). The research literature on criminal and delinquent subcultures is devoted largely to describing and accounting for these types of varied and complex relationships.

Theory and Research

Despite efforts to define the concept of subculture—and related concepts—more precisely and to describe and account for the empirical reality represented by these concepts, no general theory of subcultures has emerged (see Yinger 1960; 1977). Instead, research has continued to reveal enormous variation in what are termed subcultures, and theory has proceeded by illustration and analogy, with little progress in measurement or formal theoretical development. Despite this scientifically primitive situation, principles of sub-cultural formation have been identified, and knowledge of it has advanced.

It is a "fundamental law of sociology and anthropology," notes Daniel Glaser, that "social separation produces cultural differentiation" (1971, p. 90). More formally, and more cautiously, social separation is a necessary but not sufficient condition for the formation of subcultures. To the extent that groups or categories of persons are socially separated from one another, subcultural formation is likely to occur.

Albert Cohen argues that a "crucial" (perhaps "necessary") "condition for the emergence of new cultural forms is the existence, in effective interaction with one another, of a number of actors with similar problems of adjustment" (1955, p. 59). While the notion of "similar problems of adjustment" can be interpreted to include problems faced by quite conventional people with special interests who find themselves "in the same boat" with others who have these same interests (let us say, bird-watchers), this condition seems especially appropriate to subcultures that embrace vandalism, "hell raising," and other types of nonutilitarian delinquent behavior, as Cohen intended. Observing that this type of behavior occurs most frequently among working-class boys, Cohen hypothesized that this type of delinquent subculture was formed in reaction to status problems experienced by working-class boys in middle class institutions such as schools. Many working-class boys are inadequately prepared for either the educational demands or the discipline of formal education, and they are evaluated poorly in terms of this "middle class measuring rod." Working-class girls are less pressured in these terms, Cohen argued, because they are judged according to criteria associated with traditional female roles, and they are subject to closer controls in the family.

The solution to their status problems, for some working-class boys, according to Cohen's theory, is to reject the performance and status criteria of middle class institutions, in effect turning middle class values upside down. The theory thus seeks to account for the highly expressive and hedonistic quality of much delinquency and for the malicious and negativistic quality of vandalism.

Cohen did not attempt to account for the delinquent behavior of particular individuals or for the behavior of all working-class boys. Most of the latter do not become delinquent—at least not seriously so. They choose instead—or are channeled into—alternative adaptations such as the essentially nondelinquent "corner boys" or the high-achieving "college boys" described by William Foote Whyte (1943).

While the forces propelling youngsters into alternative adaptations such as these are not completely understood, many working-class and lower class boys and girls are devalued in middle class institutional contexts. Their marginality sets the stage for subcultural adaptations. Delinquents and criminals occupy even more marginal positions. This is particularly true of persistent delinquents and criminals who commit serious crimes, in contrast to those who only rarely transgress the law and with little consequence. When marginality is reinforced by labeling, stigmatization, or prejudicial treatment in schools and job markets, "problems of adjustment" magnify. The common ecological location of many delinquents, in the inner city slums of large cities, and their coming together in schools, provides the setting for "effective interaction." The result often is the formation of youth gangs, the most common organizational form taken by delinquent subcultures (see Thrasher 1927; Short 1990).

When marginality is reinforced by labeling, stigmatization, or prejudicial treatment in schools and job markets, "problems of adjustment" magnify.

While there is no universally agreed-upon definition of youth gangs, for theoretical purposes it is useful to define them as groups whose members meet together with some regularity over time and whose membership is selected on the basis of group-defined criteria and according to group-defined organizational characteristics. Most importantly, they are not adult-sponsored groups. The nature of relationships between young people and conventional adults is the most critical difference between gangs and other youth groups (see Schwartz 1987). Gang members are less closely tied to conventional institutions and therefore less constrained by institutional controls than are non-gang youth. Group processes of status achievement, allocation, and defense are more likely to result in delinquent behavior among gangs than among adult-sponsored groups.

How Do Criminal and Delinquent Subcultures Get Started?

Cressey notes that "delinquent and criminal subcultures have long been present in industrialized societies" (1983, p. 585). Herman and Julia Schwendinger (1985) trace the origins of adolescent subcultures, including delinquent varieties, to social changes associated with the advent of sixteenth-century capitalism in Western Europe. Vast changes in traditional economic and social relationships, which changes were associated with capitalism and the Industrial Revolution, left in their wake large numbers of unemployed persons, disrupting communities, families, and other primordial groups. Cut adrift from traditional crafts and communities, thousands roamed the countryside, subsisting as best they could off the land or by victimizing travelers. The "dangerous classes" eventually settled in cities, again to survive by whatever means were available, including crime. Criminal subcultures and organizational networks often developed under these circumstances.

The Schwendingers emphasize the importance for criminal subcultural formation of capitalist values and their accompanying norms/and interests—individualism and competitiveness, acquisitiveness and exploitativeness—and the relationship between capitalism and emerging nation-states of the period.

While many of the facts upon which this Marxist interpretation is based are generally accepted, careful historical analysis of economic and political systems and their consequences cautions against any simple or straightforward interpretation (see Chirot 1985). The connection between global phenomena and crime and delinquency always is mediated by historical, cultural, and local circumstances—by the historically concrete (see Tilly 1981).

In contrast to this account of the origins of Western European youth cultures, Ko-lin Chin (1990) traces the development of Chinese youth gangs in the United States to ancient secret society traditions, specifically to more recent Triad societies that formed in the late seventeenth century in China, and their counterpart tongs in the United States. Formed initially as political groups representing "ousted Chinese officials and the alienated poor" (p. 9), these groups initially stressed patriotism, righteousness, and brotherhood as primary values. Their secret nature was conducive to clandestine activities such as gambling, prostitution, and running opium dens. Competition among Triad societies in these areas often led to violence. Failure to achieve political power led to their further transformation into criminal organizations involved in extortion, robbery, drug trafficking, and other serious crimes.

The first Chinese street gangs in the United States did not form until the late 1950s, but their numbers increased dramatically during the following decade, when changed immigration laws permitted more Chinese to enter the country. Conflict between foreign- and American-born youths led to the emergence of several gangs. From the beginning, many Chinese youth gangs have been associated in a variety of ways with established adult secret societies in this country, in Hong Kong and Taiwan, or in all three places. Others, particularly in New York City, emerged from American youth culture in response to conflicts with other racial and ethnic groups. Some evolved into seriously delinquent gangs. Chin attributes this development to alienating problems experienced by immigrant Chinese youth in their families, schools, and communities, in dramatic contrast to their high-achieving, American-born counterparts. The existence of "Triad-influenced" tong organizations has been critical to the types of gangs that have emerged in Chinese communities and to the nature of their criminal activities, however.

While the origins of delinquent subcultures may reside in antiquity, the formation and evolution of modern variations of them thus can be explained in terms of more immediate macro-level developments. Some of these relate primarily to the ongoing activities and interests of gang members rather than to racial or ethnic changes, or to sweeping social changes. The nature of these influences is illustrated by a drug-using group studied by James Short, Fred Strodtbeck, and their associates (Short and Strodtbeck 1965; Short 1990). This gang was observed as it developed its own unique subculture. The subculture of the "Pill Poppers," as they became known to the research team, evolved from their relationship with a larger, conflict-oriented gang of which they had previously been a part. The Pill Poppers' preoccupation with drugs and their refusal to participate in the more bellicose activities of the larger gang led to their withdrawal and increasing isolation, by mutual agreement. The researchers were able to observe the evolution of this subculture, which was characterized by normative approval of drug consumption, a high value on "getting high," and mutual interest in the "crazy" things that happened to them when they were under the influence of drugs. The latter, in particular, became legendary within the group, being told and retold with nostalgia and humor when members of the gang were together. Short and Strodtbeck contrasted the subculture of this gang with that of other gangs that participated in a conflict subculture.

Levels of Explanation of Criminal and Delinquent Subcultures

These theories of criminal and delinquent subcultures are macro-level theories. Their purpose is to explain what it is about political, economic, and other social systems that explains the emergence and the social distribution of these phenomena. Other theories at this level focus on the impact of local and broader community opportunities on delinquent subcultures and on youth subcultures generally. Cloward and Ohlin (1960) relate varieties of delinquent subcultures to the availability of legitimate and illegitimate economic opportunities in local communities. Schwartz (1987) stresses the importance of local community youth-adult authority relationships in determining the nature of youth subcultures, including the extent and the nature of delinquent activities associated with them. Sullivan (1989) relates gang adaptations to more global economic developments such as the transfer of manufacturing jobs from the United States to other countries and an increasingly segmented labor market, which has resulted in the concentration of low-wage and surplus labor in inner-city minority communities (see also Hagedorn 1987).

Wilson (1987) argues that an important consequence of these economic changes is the emergence of a permanent underclass of the "truly disadvantaged." Research on delinquent subcultures supports this argument and documents significant changes in gang membership. Because fewer good jobs are available to poor, minority young men, more gang members continue their association with gangs as they enter adulthood. In the past, gang members typically "grew out of" the gang to take jobs, get married, and often to become associated with adult social clubs in stable, ethnically based communities. These options have become less viable among the poor of all races, but minorities have increasingly become the truly disadvantaged. Gang organization has been affected by this change, as older members assume or continue leadership roles. The result often has been that gang involvement in criminal activities has become more sophisticated and instrumental, and younger members have been exploited in criminal enterprise. Relationships between young people and conventional adults also suffer, as older, stable role models and monitors of youthful behavior are replaced by young adult, often criminal, role models for the young (see Anderson 1990).

Sullivan's study of groups of young males in three Brooklyn communities—black, predominantly Latino, and white—is particularly significant in this regard. The young men in Hamilton Park, the white group, were able to find better jobs than were the others at all ages. More important, because "they had become more fa-

These members of a Los Angeles gang known as the Crips represent a change in gang activity whereby minority youths continue gang membership into adulthood because they lack access to viable mainstream options. (Daniel Lainé/Corbis)

miliar with the discipline of the workplace," as they grew older they were able to secure better-quality jobs and to hold on to them, more so than were the minority youth. Familiarity with the discipline of the workplace is a type of human capital that was made possible by an important type of social capital—the superior personal networks that the Hamilton Park youth shared with the adult community (Sullivan 1989, pp. 105, 226). The minority youth were disadvantaged, with respect to both human and social capital, in the family and in other ways (see Coleman 1988).

Familiarity with the discipline of the workplace is an important type of human capital.

Human and social capital are individual characteristics determined largely by social experience. All macro-level theories make certain assumptions about the individual level of explanation. The most prominent of these assumptions is that individuals learn subcultural norms, values, and the behaviors they encourage in interaction with others in their environment. The general processes of learning have been well established by research and theory (see Bandura 1986; Eron 1987). The child's most important learning experiences take place in the family, but other influences quickly assert themselves, especially as children associate with age and gender peers. With the beginning of adolescence the latter become especially powerful, as young people experience important biological and social changes. It is at this point that youth subcultures become especially significant.

Subcultures are dynamic and ever changing, influenced by both external and internal forces and processes. Substantial knowledge gaps exist at each level of explanation. Gaps between macro-and individual-level explanations result in large part from the fact that these levels ask different questions and explain different aspects of subcultures and behavior. As noted above, macro-level explanations ask why it is that subcultures and behaviors are distributed as they are in social and cultural systems and why they occur as they do in some times and places. Explanation at this level focuses on differences in rates of subcultural phenomena, while the individual level focuses on individuals—their biological and psychological makeup and their social experiences.

Precisely how these levels of explanation relate to each other is not well understood. Group processes such as those noted above help to inform the nature of the relationship, however. By documenting the ongoing interaction among gang members and between gang members and others, this micro-level explanation reveals group processes that are consistent with what is known at the individual and macro levels of explanation. Both intragang and intergang fighting often serve group purposes, as for example by demonstrating personal qualities that are highly valued by the gang or by reinforcing group solidarity (see Miller, Geertz, and Cutter 1961; Jansyn 1966). Gang conflict often occurs when a gang believes its "rep," its "turf," or its resources (for example, its share of a drug market) are threatened by another gang. Threats to individual or group status often result in violent or other types of criminal behavior (Short 1990).

Conclusion

No general theory of criminal or delinquent subcultures has been entirely successful. The rich research materials that have accumulated suggest two conclusions, however: (1) there is a great variety of such adaptive phenomena and (2) these phenomena are of an ever-changing nature. Because they both effect social change and adapt to it, subcultures—including criminal and delinquent subcultures—continue to be important theoretically, empirically, and practically, that is, as a matter of social policy.

[See also Crime, Theories of; Criminology; Juvenile Delinquency and Juvenile Crime; Juvenile Delinquency, Theories of.]

BIBLIOGRAPHY

Anderson, Elijah 1990 *Streetwise: Race, Class, and Change in an Urban Community.* Chicago: University of Chicago Press.

Bandura, Albert 1986 *Social Foundations of Thought and Action: A Social Cognitive Theory.* Englewood Cliffs, N.J.: Prentice-Hall.

Chin, Ko-lin 1990 *Chinese Subculture and Criminality: Nontraditional Crime Groups in America.* Westport, Conn.: Greenwood Press.

Chirot, Daniel 1985 "The Rise of the West." *American Sociological Review* 50:181–195.

Cloward, Richard A., and Lloyd E. Ohlin 1960 *Delinquency and Opportunity: A Theory of Delinquent Gangs.* New York: Free Press.

Cohen, Albert K. 1955 *Delinquent Boys: The Culture of the Gang.* New York: Free Press.

Coleman, James S. 1988 "Social Capital in the Creation of Human Capital." *American Journal of Sociology* 94 (Suppl.): S95–S120.

Cressey, Donald R. 1983 "Delinquent and Criminal Subcultures." In S. E. Kadish, ed., *Encyclopedia of Crime and Justice.* New York: Free Press.

Eron, Leonard D. 1987 "The Development of Aggressive Behavior from the Perspective of a Developing Behaviorism." *American Psychologist* 42:435–442.

Fagan, Jeffrey 1990 "Social Processes of Delinquency and Drug Use among Urban Gangs." In C. Ronald Huff, ed., *Gangs in America.* Newbury Park, Calif.: Sage.

Glaser, Daniel 1971 *Social Deviance.* Chicago: Markham.

Hagedorn John M., with Perry Macon 1987 *People and Folk: Gangs, Crime, and the Underclass in a Rustbelt City.* Chicago: Lake View Press.

Jansyn, Leon R. 1966 "Solidarity and Delinquency in a Street-Corner Group." *American Sociological Review* 31:600–614.

Johnson, Bruce D., Terry, Williams, Kojo A. Dei, and Harry Sanabria 1990 "Drug Abuse in the Inner City: Impact on Hard-Drug Users and the Community." In Michael Tonry and James Q. Wilson, eds., *Drugs and Crime.* Chicago: University of Chicago Press.

Klockars, Carl B. 1974 *The Professional Fence.* New York: Free Press.

Miller, Walter B. 1958 "Lower Class Culture as a Generating Milieu of Gang Delinquency." *Journal of Social Issues* 14:5–19.

Miller, Walter B., Hildred Geertz, Henry S. G. Cutter 1961 "Aggression in a Boys' Street-Corner Group." *Psychiatry* 24:283–298.

Schwartz, Gary 1987 *Beyond Conformity or Rebellion: Youth and Authority in America.* Chicago: University of Chicago Press.

Schwendinger, Herman, and Julia Siegel Schwendinger 1985 *Adolescent Subcultures and Delinquency.* New York: Praeger.

Short, James F. 1990 *Delinquency and Society.* Englewood Cliffs, NJ.: Prentice-Hall.

———, and Fred L. Strodtbeck 1965 *Group Process and Gang Delinquency.* Chicago: University of Chicago Press.

Sullivan, Mercer L. 1989 *"Getting Paid": Youth Crime and Work in the Inner City.* Ithaca, N.Y.: Cornell University Press.

Sutherland, Edwin H. 1937 *The Professional Thief.* Chicago: University of Chicago Press.

Thrasher, Frederic M. 1927 *The Gang: A Study of 1,313 Gangs in Chicago.* Chicago: University of Chicago Press.

Tilly, Charles 1981 *As Sociology Meets History.* New York: Academic Press.

Vigil, James Diego 1988 *Barrio Gangs.* Austin: University of Texas Press.

Whyte, William Foote 1943 *Street Corner Society.* Chicago: University of Chicago Press.

Williams, Terry 1989 *The Cocaine Kids: The Inside Story of a Teenage Drug Ring.* Menlo Park, Calif.: Addison-Wesley.

Wilson, William Julius 1987 *The Truly Disadvantaged: The Inner City, the Underclass, and Public Policy.* Chicago: University of Chicago Press.

Yinger, Milton 1960 "Contraculture and Subculture." *American Sociological Review* 23:625–635.

——— 1977 "Countercultures and Social Change." *American Sociological Review* 42:833–853.

– JAMES F. SHORT, JR.

CRIMINALIZATION OF DEVIANCE

A 1985 household survey dealing with drug abuse revealed that 22 percent of persons eighteen to twenty-five, 17 percent of persons twenty-six to thirty-four, and 2 percent of persons thirty-five years or older had smoked marijuana within the last thirty days (U.S. Department of Health and Human Services 1988). The same survey showed that a majority of persons eighteen to thirty-four had smoked marijuana at least once during their lifetimes. Rather than containing an overwhelming majority who believe that smoking marijuana is wrong and just a sprinkling of individuals who believe that it is legitimate, American society is polarized into first, a large group, probably a majority, who consider smoking marijuana wrong and second, a smaller group (but a substantial proportion of young adults) who consider marijuana harmless and who are indignant at societal interference. A nonconformist is immensely strengthened by having even one ally, as the social psychologist Solomon Asch demonstrated in laboratory experiments (Asch 1955). Unfortunately, contemporary societies, being large and heterogeneous, are likely to provide allies for behavior that the majority condemns.

Yet moral polarization does not characterize American society on every issue. Consensus exists that persons who smell bad and persons who force others to participate unwillingly in sexual relations are reprehensible. Body odor and rape seem an incongruous combination. What they have in common is that both are deviant, which means that they are strongly disapproved by the overwhelming majority of Americans. Where they differ is that only one (rape) is a statutory crime that can result in police arrest, a court trial, and a prison sentence. The other, body odor, although deviant, is not criminalized. When deviance is criminalized, the organized collectivity channels the indignant response of individuals, as the following true story illustrates:

> In March, 1983, a 21-year-old woman, new to a Portuguese neighborhood in New Bedford, Massachusetts, stopped into Big Dan's Tavern for cigarettes and a drink at 9 P.M. on a Sunday evening. She emerged after midnight, screaming for help, bruised, her clothes partially torn off. She told the police that she had been hoisted onto the pool table held there against her will, and raped repeatedly by a group of men. The patrons of the bar stood watching, taunting her, and cheering on the rapists. A week later 2,500 silent protestors marched through New Bedford carrying lighted candles and banners with the words, "Rape Is Not a Spectator Sport." The march, which drew support from women's groups throughout the Northeast, was covered both by TV and the print media. (Toby 1988)

In this case, what was alleged to have occurred in the tavern simultaneously aroused both police intervention and widespread public indignation. That indignation was sufficient to pressure the owners of Big Dan's tavern to give up their liquor license and to close down. On the legal level, the rapists were tried, convicted, and sent to prison. Some sociologists argue that when sufficient consensus exists about the wrongfulness of an act, the act gets criminalized. This is usually the case but not always. Despite consensus that failing to bathe for three months is reprehensible, body odor has not been criminalized. And acts *have* become criminalized, for example, patent infringement and other white-collar crimes, but these do not arouse much public indignation. In short, the relationship between what is deviant and what is criminal is complicated.

For a clue to an explanation of how and why deviance gets criminalized, note how difficult it is for members of a society to know with certainty what is deviant. Conceptually, deviance refers to the purposive evasion or defiance of a normative consensus. Defiant deviance is fairly obvious. If Joe, a high school student, is asked a question in class by his English teacher pertaining to the lesson, and he replies, "I won't tell you, asshole," most Americans would probably agree that he is violating the role expectations for high school students in this society. Evasive deviance is less confrontational, albeit more common than defiant deviance, and therefore more ambiguous. If Joe never does the assigned homework or frequently comes late without a good explanation, many Americans would agree that he is not doing what he is supposed to do, although the point at which he steps over the line into outright deviance is fuzzy. Both evasive and defiant deviance require other members of the society to make a judgment that indignation is the appropriate response to the behavior in question. Such a judgment is difficult to make in a heterogeneous society because members of the society cannot be sure how closely other people share their values.

The social response to an act that is on the borderline between deviance and acceptability is unpredictable. This unpredictability may restrain onlookers from taking action.

To be sure, the individual knows from living in a society what sorts of behavior will trigger indignant reactions, but not with great confidence. The issue is blurred by subgroup variation and because norms change with the passage of time. Bathing suits that were entirely proper in 1990 in the United States would have been scandalous in 1920. A survey might find that a large percentage of the population disapproves now of nudity on a public beach. The survey cannot reveal for how long the population will continue to disapprove of public nudity. Nor can the survey help much with the crucial problem of deciding how large a proportion of the population disapproves strongly enough to justify categorizing public nudity as "deviant."

In short, whether a normative consensus has been violated depends, first, on whether a consensus exists at all; to determine this, individual normative judgments must somehow be aggregated, say, by conducting a survey that would enable a representative sample of the population to express reactions to various kinds of behavior. Ideally, these responses differ only by degree, but in a large society there are often qualitatively different conceptions of right and wrong.

In practice, then, in modern society neither the potential perpetrator nor the onlooker can be certain what is deviant. Consequently the social response to an act that is on the borderline between deviance and acceptability is unpredictable. This unpredictability may tempt the individual to engage in behavior he would not engage in if he knew that the response would be widespread disapproval. It may also restrain onlookers from taking action—or at least expressing disapproval—against persons violating the informal rules.

What Crime Involves: A Collective Response

Crime is clearer. The ordinary citizen may not know precisely which acts are illegal in a particular jurisdiction. But a definite answer is possible. A lawyer familiar with the criminal code of the State of New Jersey can explain exactly what has to be proved in order to convict a person of drunken driving in New Jersey. The codification of an act as criminal does not depend on its intrinsic danger to the society but on what societal leaders perceive as dangerous. For example, Cuba has the following provision in its criminal code:

> Article 108. (1) There will be a sanction of deprivation of freedom of from one to eight years imposed on anyone who:
>
> (a) incites against the social order, international solidarity or the socialist State by means of oral or written propaganda, or in any other form;
>
> (b) makes, distributes or possesses propaganda of the character mentioned in the preceding clause.
>
> (2) Anyone who spreads false news or malicious predictions liable to cause alarm or discontent in the population, or public disorder, is subject to a sanction of from one to four years imprisonment.
>
> (3) If the mass media are used for the execution of the actions described in the previous paragraphs, the sanction will be deprivation of freedom from seven to fifteen years. (Ripoll 1985, p. 20)

In other words, mere possession of a mimeograph machine in Cuba is a very serious crime because Fidel Castro considers the dissemination of critical ideas a threat to his "socialist State," and in Cuba Castro's opinions are literally law. Hence, possession of a mimeograph machine is a punishable offense. Members of Jehovah's Witnesses who used mimeograph machines to reproduce religious tracts have been given long prison sentences. On the other hand, reproducing religious tracts may not arouse indignation in the Cuban population. If so, it is not deviant.

In California or New Jersey, as in Cuba, a crime is behavior punishable by the state. But the difference is that in the fifty states, as in all democratic societies, the legislators and judges who enact and interpret criminal laws do not simply codify their own moral sentiments; they criminalize behavior in response to influences brought to bear on them by members of their constituencies. True, women, children, members of ethnic and racial minorities, and the poorly educated may not have as much political input as affluent, middle-aged, white male professionals. But less influence does not mean they don't count. In a dictatorship, on the other hand, the political process is closed; few people count when it comes to deciding what is a crime.

Why Deviance is Criminalized

Criminalization, solves the problem of predictability of response by transferring the obligation to respond to deviance from the individual members of society to agents of the state (the police). But criminalization creates a new problem: Which members of society are able to persuade the state to enforce *their* moral sentiments? In short, criminalization means that the social control of deviance is politicized. In every society, deviant acts get criminalized in the course of a political process. Generally, the political leadership of a society criminalizes an act when it becomes persuaded that without criminalization the deviant contagion will spread, thereby undermining social order. The leaders may be wrong. Fidel Castro might be able to retain control even if Cubans were allowed access to mimeograph machines and word processors. Nevertheless, leaders decide on crimes based on their perception of what is a threat to the collectivity. According to legal scholars (Packer 1968), the tendency in politically organized societies is to overcriminalize, that is, to involve the state excessively in the punishment of deviance. Political authorities find it difficult to resist the temptation to perceive threats in what may only be harmless diversity and to attempt to stamp it out by state punishment.

Sociology's labeling perspective on deviance (Becker 1963; Lemert 1983) goes further; it suggests that overcriminalization may *increase* deviance by changing the self-concept of the stigmatized individual. Thus, pinning the official label of "criminal" on someone may amplify criminal tendencies. At its most extreme, this point of view denies the desirability of *any* kind of criminalization: "The task [of radical reform] is to create a society in which the facts of human diversity, whether personal, organic, or social, are not subject to the power to criminalize" (Taylor, Walton, and Young 1973, p. 282).

The absence of criminal law—and consequently of state-imposed sanctions for violations—is no threat to small primitive communities: Informal social controls can be counted on to prevent most deviance and to punish what deviance cannot be prevented. In heterogeneous modern societies, however, the lack of some criminalization would make moral unity difficult to achieve. When Emile Durkheim spoke of the collective conscience of a society, he was writing metaphorically; he knew that he was abstracting from the differing consciences of thousands of individuals. Nevertheless, the criminal law serves to resolve these differences and achieve a contrived—and indeed precarious—moral unity. In democratic societies, the unity is achieved by political compromise. In authoritarian or totalitarian societies the power wielders unify the society by imposing their own values on the population at large. In both cases law is a unifying force; large societies could not function without a legal system because universalistic rules, including the rules of the criminal law, meld in this way ethnic, regional, and class versions of what is deviant (Parsons 1977, pp. 138–139).

The Consequences of Criminalization

The unifying effect of the criminal law has unintended consequences. One major consequence is the development of a large bureaucracy devoted to enforcing criminal laws: police, judges, prosecutors, jailors, probation officers, parole officers, prison guards, and assorted professionals like psychologists and social workers who attempt to rehabilitate convicted offenders. Ideally, these employees of the state should perform their roles dispassionately, not favoring some accused persons or discriminating against others. In practice, however, members of the criminal justice bureaucracy bring to their jobs the parochial sentiments of their social groups as well as a personal interest in financial gain or professional advancement. This helps to explain why police are often more enthusiastic about enforcing some criminal laws than they are about enforcing others.

Another consequence of criminalization is that the criminal law, being universal in its reach, cannot make allowance for subgroup variation in sentiments about what is right and what is wrong. Thus, some people are imprisoned for behavior that neither they nor members of their social group regard as reprehensible, as in Northern Ireland where members of the Irish Republican Army convicted of assassinating British soldiers consider themselves political prisoners. They have gone on hunger strikes—in some cases to the point of death—rather than wear the prison uniform of ordinary criminals.

Conclusion

The more heterogeneous the culture and the more swiftly its norms are changing, the less consensus about right and wrong exists within the society. In the United States, moral values differ to some extent in various regions, occupations, religions, social classes, and ethnic groups. This sociocultural value pluralism means that it is difficult to identify behavior that everyone considers deviant. It is much easier to identify crime, which is codified in politically organized societies. The criminalization of deviance makes it clear when collective reprisals will be taken against those who violate rules.

Deviance exists in smaller social systems, too: in families, universities, corporations. In addition to being subjected to the informal disapproval of other members of these collectivities, the deviant in the family, the university, or the work organization can be subjected to formally organized sanctioning procedures like a disciplinary hearing at a university. However, the worst sanction that these nonsocietal social systems can visit upon deviants is expulsion. A university cannot imprison a student who cheats on a final exam. Even in the larger society, however, not all deviance is criminalized, sometimes for cultural reasons as in American refusal to criminalize the expression of political dissent, but also for pragmatic reasons as in the American failure to criminalize body odor, lying to one's friends, or smoking in church.

[See also Criminology; Deviance; Deviance Theories.]

BIBLIOGRAPHY

Asch, Solomon E. 1955 "Opinions and Social Pressure." *Scientific American* 193, November.

Becker, Howard S. 1963 *Outsiders: Studies in the Sociology of Deviance.* New York: Free Press.

Lemert, Edwin M. 1983 "Deviance." In Sanford H. Kadish, ed., *Encyclopedia of Crime and Justice.* New York: Free Press.

Packer, Herbert L. 1968 *The Limits of the Criminal Sanction.* Stanford, Calif.: Stanford University Press.

Parsons, Talcott 1977 *The Evolution of Societies.* Englewood Cliffs, N.J.: Prentice-Hall.

Ripoll, Carlos 1985 *Harnessing the Intellectual: Censoring Writers and Artists in Today's Cuba.* Washington, D.C.: Cuban American National Foundation.

Taylor, Ian, Paul Walton, and Jock Young 1973 *The New Criminology.* London: Routledge and Kegan Paul.

Toby, Jackson 1988 "Should Film Makers Never Choose Myth over Fact?" *Los Angeles Times,* December 18.

U.S. Department of Health and Human Services, National Institute of Drug Abuse 1988 *National Household Survey on Drug Abuse: Main Findings 1985.* Washington, D.C.: U.S. Government Printing Office.

– JACKSON TOBY

CRIMINAL SANCTIONS

Criminal sanctions are the penalties imposed by a legally constituted authority on violators of the criminal laws. These penalties vary widely in form, including corporal and capital punishment, imprisonment, exile, fine, probationary supervision, or community service. Underlying these various forms is a common denominator of stigma, which is not inherent in other deprivations of resources and freedom imposed by the state (Feinberg 1970). This stigma arises from the nature of crime being in principle an offense committed against the community as a whole rather than a wrong committed by one individual against another. Traditionally, this stigma entailed permanent civil disabilities in public employment, child custody, voting, and other rights (Burton, Cullen, and Travis 1987). Because criminal sanctions are so consequential, societies that emphasize the value of individualism tend to elaborate due process in criminal prosecutions more than for any other exercise of state power.

The criminal sanction is a legal category, not a primitive term in social theory. Consequently, instead of developing a general theory of penality, sociology has developed a plurality of inquiries into the social organizational antecedents and consequences of variations in the form and frequency of criminal sanctions. For social theory, the significance of the criminal sanction arises from its position as a critical nexus between the individual and society, exposing the nature of social solidarity (Durkheim [1893] 1950), political power (Foucault 1979), or class relations (Rusche and Kirchheimer [1939] 1968). This article delineates the distinctive agenda of sociological studies of the criminal sanction and then outlines some major lines of empirical study of the criminal sanction's impact on society and the variations in its forms.

Sociological Perspectives on Criminal Sanction

Several disciplines examine the relationships between the criminal sanction and social organization. The applied field of *penology* compares the effectiveness of sanction policies, isolating these pragmatic concerns from their political, economic, and social contexts. Alternatively, *moral philosophy* begins with value premises and seeks to evaluate the justification for imposing criminal sanctions. Consider, for instance, the use of the criminal sanction to rehabilitate offenders, Penologists evaluate rehabilitation in terms of the impact alternative treatments produce on the recidivism rate (e.g., Martinson 1974). Moral philosophers assess rehabilitation in light of general principles of social justice (e.g., Fogel 1975).

Sociologists, in contrast, seek to explain variations in the adoption of the rehabilitation rationale for punishment as a function of variations in such aspects of social structure as the nature of class relationships and state power (e.g., Humphries and Greenberg 1981). While policy and moral implications are incorporated in such work, they do not, as in the case of the other two disciplines, constitute the core of the analysis. More central to the sociological enterprise is some form of empirical analysis that tests theoretical generalizations about sanctions and structures. From this perspective sociologists have produced a variety of analyses of the societal consequences and antecedents of variation in criminal sanctions, a sample of which will now be reviewed.

Consequences of Enforcing Criminal Sanctions

Research on the consequences of enforcing criminal sanctions was initially framed by the utilitarian doctrine of *deterrence:* Crime varies inversely with the certainty, severity, and celerity of the criminal sanction. Several traditions in sociology posit an antithesis to deterrence theory, namely, that criminal sanctions amplify deviance. Amplification may result from imposing on rulebreakers an identity change and opportunity costs (cf. Thomas and Bishop 1984) or, in the case of capital punishment, from reinforcing the social climate of violence (Bowers 1984, pp. 271–335). While several isolated observations support both deterrence and amplification hypotheses, the conditions under which these effects hold remains to be theoretically specified.

Crime varies inversely with the certainty, severity, and celerity of the criminal sanction.

Extant empirical research estimates the effects on crime of marginal changes in the severity or certainty of punishment. Much of this work is based on correlations between aggregate rates of crime and punishment using, for example, interstate variations in crime and imprisonment rates. This evidence suggests that (1) the risk of criminal sanctions deters more strongly than severity of punishment; (2) the effects are neither strong nor consistent; and (3) other social influences create an observed relationship between crime rates and sanction levels. Increasingly sophisticated multivariate research designs have not noticeably reduced the sharpness of debate over the magnitude of deterrence effects (for review of this literature see Beyleveld 1980).

This continuing debate is fed in part by reliance upon aggregate social indicator research beset by various methodological barriers. For example, the deterrence hypothesis predicts that crime rates will decrease as sanction levels increase, but the same correlation will arise from an overloading of the criminal justice system. As the number of cases increase, crime control organizations with fixed budgets can arrest, prosecute, and punish proportionately fewer offenders.

Because the aggregate measures of risk are far removed from individual decision making, researchers have investigated variations in levels of the punishment's publicity (Bailey and Peterson 1989) or the effectiveness of social networks in transmitting information about punishments to potential offenders (Ekland-Olson, Lieb, and Zurcher 1984). Alternatively, survey research may measure more directly the subjective response to the threat of sanctions by having respondents report their perceptions of the risk and severity of sanctions along with confessions of past or intended law breaking. Although these studies often confirm deterrence theory's predictions, the results are open to reservations about the representativeness of samples (Piliavin et al. 1986) and the ability of respondents to report accurately their decision making (Paternoster et al. 1982).

An alternative mode of support for deterrence effects appears in one of the rare field experiments on sanctioning. Sherman and Berk (1984) assigned domestic violence cases randomly to four alternative police responses. Consistent with deterrence theory, they found that arrest produced the greatest reduction in subsequent levels of domestic violence. Questions, particularly about the external validity of these results, have stimulated an ongoing program of replication studies. While sociologists were once inclined to favor labeling over deterrence theories on a priori moral grounds, current thinking views the issue as open and resolvable only by innovative research designs.

Consequences of Enacting Criminal Sanctions: Legal Impact Studies

A separate literature examines the related issue of the social impact of imposing criminal sanctions on categories of conduct rather than on individual malefactors. This research is dominated by historical case studies from which investigators seek to extract generalizations about the consequences of criminalization or decriminalization. Unfortunately, such generalizations are not easily excavated from this evidence. For example, Prohibition (1919–1933) is popularly perceived to exemplify the failure of criminalization to change social patterns of drug use. Even assuming this assessment is accurate, the generalization is readily countered by the roughly contemporaneous Harrison Narcotic Act (1914), which appears to have altered dramatically the social class distribution of opiate abuse (Conrad and Schneider 1980, pp. 121–130).

Legal impact research tends to support labeling over deterrence theory; it suggests that if criminal sanctions have any impact at all, it is to exacerbate the problems they are designed to solve at considerable cost in law-enforcement resources. These conflicting conclusions result in part from differences in the crimes studied. Where deterrence research concentrates on common-law crimes of predation and violence, much of the legal impact research has been concerned with "victimless crimes" of abortion, alcohol and drug use, gambling, homosexuality, pornography, and prostitution; all entail strong public demands being regulated by laws resting on contested morality.

Research on the social impact of criminalization tends to be policy relevant, issue specific, and atheoretical. Research has grown primarily through the exploration of new arenas of application for criminal sanctions, such as pornography (Downs 1989) and drunk driving (Gusfield 1980). Consequently, debates over the consequences of legal change, such as decriminalization of narcotics, rely on precedents and analogies to assess the consequences of legal change, such as decriminalization of narcotics, rely on precedents and analogies to assess the consequences of decriminalization on rates of use and viability of alternative modes of social control (e.g., Nadelmann 1989).

Antecedents of Criminal Sanction

While the consequences of criminal sanctions are important for both social theory and social policy, sociological research has equally been concerned with understanding the social structural antecedents of criminal sanctions. It is convenient to classify these concerns into issues of qualitative versus quantitative variation.

QUALITATIVE VARIATIONS IN SANCTIONS. The forms that criminal sanctions take have been extensively investigated. The past two centuries of Western criminal law have been marked by a series of reforms, including the abolition of corporal and capital punishment, the rise of the penitentiary, and probation. Sociological accounts of these developments have emphasized their relationships to concomitant changes in the nature of economic production (Rusche and Kirchheimer [1939] 1968; Humphries and Greenberg 1981), social organization (Erikson 1966), state formation (Hamilton and Sutton 1989), and cultural values (Spierenburg 1984). These varying accounts continue to stimulate a wide range of work concerned with historical origins and subsequent trajectories of the forms of the criminal sanction (for overview, see Garland 1990).

QUANTITATIVE VARIATIONS IN SANCTIONS. Social structure influences not only the form of the criminal sanction but the rate at which it is imposed. Because discretionary decision making plays a key role in selecting lawbreakers for criminal sanctioning, status characteristics may influence the selection of law violators for sanctioning and the nature of the sanction imposed on them. Among the factors that influence discretion, sociological research has given special attention to labor markets. While unemployment may increase crime and thus increase punishment, its effect on sanctions may also be direct. Unemployment levels may lead judges, for example, to impose prison sentences rather than probation because the employed run a lower risk of future lawbreaking (for an overview, see Melossi 1989).

Distinct albeit related factors prominent in the research are race and gender. The research strategy here has been to estimate the effect of extralegal characteristics on sanctions net of crime. This problem corresponds to that in labor-market research on occupational attainment, which attempts to estimate the effects of ascribed characteristics apart from job-related inputs of minorities. Estimates of race and gender effects on sentencing are much more mixed (Wilbanks 1987 offers a comprehensive albeit controversial summary of the work on race; on gender, see Daly 1989). Perhaps the most important development sociologically in this research is a recognition that discrimination itself is a variable with social organizational antecedents. While traditional research sought to document the simple presence of discrimination, the new approach seeks to explain its variability. Closely related is the research concerned with the impact of sentencing reforms designed to reduce discretion in the application of sanctions (Cohen and Tonry 1983). Again, results are mixed, and it may be too soon to obtain a coherent reading of the impact of these reforms.

Future of the Criminal Sanction

Orwell's nightmare of expanding state repression is well represented in current theory of the "carceral society" (Foucault 1979) and the "maximum security society" (Marx 1988). Forecasting trends in phenomena still only vaguely understood is a risky enterprise. The dramatic expansion of the U.S. prison population in the 1980s may reflect less of a change in the structural propensity to punish than it represents the growth of the age population at risk and changing age-specific propensities to engage in imprisonable offenses.

Observers who point to indicators of increasing state coercion seldom take into account the concomitant expansion in recent years of due process in criminal procedure and the growing body of legal constraints on the treatment of prison inmates (Bottoms 1983). While conservatives have lamented the constraints on crime control created by this expansion of constitutional restraints, the impact of these reforms has yet to be assessed beyond isolated empirical case studies of how particular Supreme Court decisions alter police (mal)practice. Furthermore, some analysts point to the ways in which extension of the criminal sanction into new areas such as juvenile offenses entails expansion of procedural protections (Feld 1984).

By domesticating the criminal sanction, reforms may have stimulated the development for more subtle and pervasive forms of social control.

The various limitations of the criminal sanction (due-process requirements, level of the burden of proof) may have stimulated the growth of medical controls (Kittrie 1971; Conrad and Schneider 1980) and administrative law and its variants (Freiberg and O'Malley 1984). It is important in thinking about the future of the criminal sanction to extend our vision beyond its familiar forms. These new forms of state control circumvent the constraints that render the criminal sanction especially difficult to apply in victimless, corporate, and organized crimes. By domesticating the criminal sanction, reforms may have stimulated the development for more subtle and pervasive forms of social control.

Such developments are not novel. Indeed, the ambiguities of the legal definition of criminal sanction suggested at the start of this article reflect the extent to which criminal sanctions are the outcome of social organizational processes rather than logical deductions from coherent and consistent principles of law. Some understanding of that process is the promise of sociological investigation of the criminal sanction.

[See also Crime Deterrence, Probation and Parole.]

BIBLIOGRAPHY

Bailey, William C., and Ruth D. Peterson 1989 "Murder and Capital Punishment: A Monthly Time-Series Analysis of Execution Publicity." *American Sociological Review* 54:722–743.

Beyleveld, Deryek 1980 *Bibliography on General Deterrence.* Hampshire, England: Saxon House.

Bottoms, Anthony E. 1983 "Neglected Features of Contemporary Penal Systems." In David Garland and Peter Young, eds., *The Power to Punish Contemporary Penality and Social Analysis.* Atlantic Highlands, N.J.: Humanities Press.

Bowers, William J. 1984 *Legal Homicide: Death as Punishment in America, 1824–1982.* Boston: Northeastern University Press.

Burton, Velmer S., Francis T. Cullen, and Lawrence F. Travis III 1987 "The Collateral Consequences of a Felony Conviction: A National Study of State Statutes." *Federal Probation* 51:52–60.

Cohen, Jacqueline, and Michael Tonry 1983 "Sentencing Reforms and Their Impacts." In Alfred Blumstein, Jacqueline Coyen, Susan E. Martin, and Michael H. Tonry, eds., *Research in Sentencing: The Search for Reform,* vol. 2. Washington, D.C.: National Academy Press.

Conrad, Peter, and Joseph V. Schneider 1980 *Deviance and Medicalization: From Badness to Sickness.* St. Louis: Mosby.

Daly, Kathleen 1989 "Neither Conflict nor Labeling nor Paternalism Will Suffice: Intersections of Race, Ethnicity, Gender, and Family in Criminal Court Decisions." *Crime and Delinquency* 35:136–168.

Downs, Donald A. 1989 *The New Politics of Pornography.* Chicago: University of Chicago Press.

Durkheim, Emile (1893) 1950 *The Rules of Sociological Method.* New York: Free Press.

Ekland-Olson, Sheldon, John Lieb, and Louis Zurcher 1984 "The Paradoxical Impact of Criminal Sanctions: Some Microstructural Findings." *Law and Society Review* 18:159–178.

Erikson, Kai T. 1966 *Wayward Puritans: A Study in the Sociology of Deviance.* New York: Wiley.

Feinberg, Joel 1970 "The Expressive Function of Punishment." In *Doing and Deserving: Essays in the Theory of Responsibility.* Princeton, N.J.: Princeton University Press.

Feld, Barry 1984 "Criminalizing Juvenile Justice: Rules of Procedure for Juvenile Court." *Minnesota Law Review* 69:141–276.

Fogel, David 1975 *We Are the Living Proof: The Justice Model of Corrections.* Cincinnati, Ohio: W. H. Anderson.

Foucault, Michel 1979 *Discipline and Punish.* New York: Vintage.

Freiberg, Arie, and Pat O'Malley 1984 "State Intervention and the Civil Offense." *Law and Society Review* 18:373–394.

Garland, David 1990 *Punishment and Modern Society: A Study in Social Theory.* Chicago: University of Chicago Press.

Gusfield, Joseph 1980 *The Culture of Public Problems: Drunk-Driving and the Symbolic Order.* Chicago: University of Chicago Press.

Hamilton, Gary G., and John R. Sutton 1989 "The Problem of Control in the Weak State: Domination in the United States, 1880–1920." *Theory and Society* 18:1–46.

Humphries, Drew, and David Greenberg 1981 "The Dialectics of Crime Control." In David Greenberg, ed., *Crime and Capitalism.* Palo Alto, Calif.: Mayfield.

Kittrie, Nicholas N. 1971 *The Right to Be Different: Deviance and Enforced Therapy.* Baltimore: Johns Hopkins University Press.

Martinson, Robert 1974 "What Works? Questions and Answers About Prison Reform." *Public Interest* 35:22–54.

Marx, Gary 1988 *Undercover: Police Surveillance in America.* Berkeley: University of California Press.

Melossi, Dario 1989 "Fifty Years Later: *Punishment and Social Structure* in Comparative Analysis." *Contemporary Crises* 13:311–326.

Nadelmann, Ethan A. 1989 "Drug Prohibition in the United States: Costs, Consequences, and Alternatives." *Science* 245:939–947.

Paternoster, Raymond, Linda Saltzman, Theorodre Chiricos, and Gordon Waldo 1982 "Perceived Risk and Deterrence: Methodological Artifacts in Perceptual Deterrence Research." *Journal of Criminal Law and Criminology* 73:1238–1258.

Piliavin, Irving, Rosemary Gartner, Craig Thornton, and Ross L. Matsueda 1986 "Crime, Deterrence, and Rational Choice." *American Sociological Review* 51:101–119.

Rusche, Georg, and Otto Kirchheimer (1939) 1968 *Punishment and Social Structure.* New York: Russell and Russell.

Sherman, Lawrence, and Richard A. Berk 1984 "The Specific Deterrent Effect of Arrest for Domestic Assault." *American Sociological Review* 49:261–272.

Spierenburg, Pieter 1984 *The Spectacle of Suffering: Executions and the Evolution of Repression: From a Preindustrial Metropolis to the European Experience.* Cambridge: Cambridge University Press.

Thomas, Charles W., and Donna M. Bishop 1984 "The Effect of Formal and Informal Sanctions on Delinquency: A Longitudinal Comparison of Labeling and Deterrence Theories." *Journal of Criminal Law and Criminology* 75:1222–1245.

Wilbanks, William 1987 *The Myth of a Racist Criminal Justice System.* Monterey, Calif.: Brooks-Cole.

– JAMES INVERARITY

CROWDS AND RIOTS

Crowds are a ubiquitous feature of everyday life. People have long assembled collectively to observe, to celebrate, and to protest various happenings in their everyday lives, be they natural events, such as a solar eclipse, or the result of human contrivance, such as the introduction of machinery into the production process. The historical record is replete with examples of crowds functioning as important textual markers, helping to shape and define a particular event, as well as strategic precipitants and carriers of the events themselves. The storming of the Bastille and the sit-ins and marches associated with the civil rights movement are examples of crowds functioning as both important markers and carriers of some larger historical happening. Not all crowds function so significantly, of course. Most are mere sideshows to the flow of history. Nonetheless, the collective assemblages or gatherings called crowds are ongoing features of the social world and, as a consequence, have long been the object of theorizing and inquiry, ranging from the psychologistic renderings of Gustave LeBon (1895) and Sigmund Freud (1921) to the more sociological accounts of Neil Smelser (1963) and Ralph Turner and Lewis Killian (1987) to the highly systematic and empirically grounded observations of Clark McPhail and his associates (1983, 1991).

Crowds have traditionally been analyzed as a variant of the broader category of social phenomena called collective behavior. Broadly conceived, collective behavior refers to group problem-solving behavior that encompasses crowds, mass phenomena, issue-specific publics, and social movements. More narrowly, collective behavior refers to "two or more persons engaged in one or more behaviors (e.g., orientation, locomotion, gesticulation, tactile manipulation, and/or vocalization) that can be judged common or convergent on one or more dimensions (e.g., direction, velocity tempo, and/or substantive content)" (McPhail and Wohlstein 1983, pp. 580–581). Implicit in both conceptions is a continuum on which collective behavior can vary in terms of the extent to which its participants are in close proximity or diffused in time and space. Instances of collective behavior in which individuals are in close physical proximity, such that they can monitor one another by being visible to, or within earshot of, one another, are constitutive of crowds. Examples include protest demonstrations, victory celebrations, riots, and the dispersal processes associated with flight from burning buildings. In contrast are forms of collective behavior that occur among individuals who are not physically proximate but who still share a common focus of attention and engage in some parallel or common behaviors without developing the debate characteristic of the public or the organization of social movements, and who are linked together by social networks, the media, or both. Examples of this form of collective behavior, referred to as diffuse collective behavior (Turner and Killian 1987) or the mass (Lofland 1981), include fads and crazes, deviant epidemics, mass hysteria, and collective blaming. Although crowds and diffuse collective behavior are not mutually exclusive phenomena, they are analytically distinct and tend to generate somewhat different literatures—thus, the focus on crowds in this selection.

Understanding crowds and the kindred collective phenomenon called "riots" requires consideration of four questions: (1) How do these forms of collective behavior differ from the crowd forms typically associated with everyday behavior, such as audiences and queues? (2) What are the distinctive features of crowds as collective behavior? (3) What are the conditions underlying the emergence of crowds? and (4) What accounts for the coordination of crowd behavior?

Distinguishing Between the Crowds of Collective Behavior and Everyday Behavior

There has been increasing recognition of the continuity between collective behavior and everyday behavior, yet the existence of collective behavior as an area of sociological analysis rests in part on the assumption of significant differences between collective behavior and everyday institutionalized behavior. In the case of crowds, those commonly associated with everyday life, such as at sports events and holiday parades, tend to be highly conventionalized in at least two or three ways. Such gatherings are recurrent affairs that are scheduled for a definite place at a definite time; they are calendarized both temporally and spatially. Second, associated behaviors and emotional states are typically routinized in the sense that they are normatively regularized and anticipated. And third, they tend to be sponsored and orchestrated by the state, a community, or a societal institution, as in the case of most holiday parades and electoral political rallies. Accordingly, they are typically socially approved affairs that function to reaffirm rather than challenge some institutional arrangement or the larger social order itself.

In contrast, crowds commonly associated with collective behavior, such as protest demonstrations, victory celebrations, and riots, usually challenge or disrupt the existing order. This is due in part to the fact that these crowds are neither temporally nor spatially routinized. Instead, as David Snow and his colleagues (1981) have noted, they are more likely to be unscheduled and staged in spatial areas (streets, parks, malls) or physical structures (office buildings, theaters, lunch counters) that were designed for institutionalized, everyday behavior rather than contentious or celebratory crowds. Such crowd activities are also extrainstitutional, and thus unconventional, in the sense that they are frequently based on normative guidelines that are emergent and ephemeral rather than enduring (Turner and Killian 1987), on the appropriation and redefinition of existing networks or social relationships (Weller and (Quarantelli 1973), or on both.

Crowd behavior has long been described as "extraordinary" in the sense that its occurrence indicates that something unusual is happening. Precisely what it is

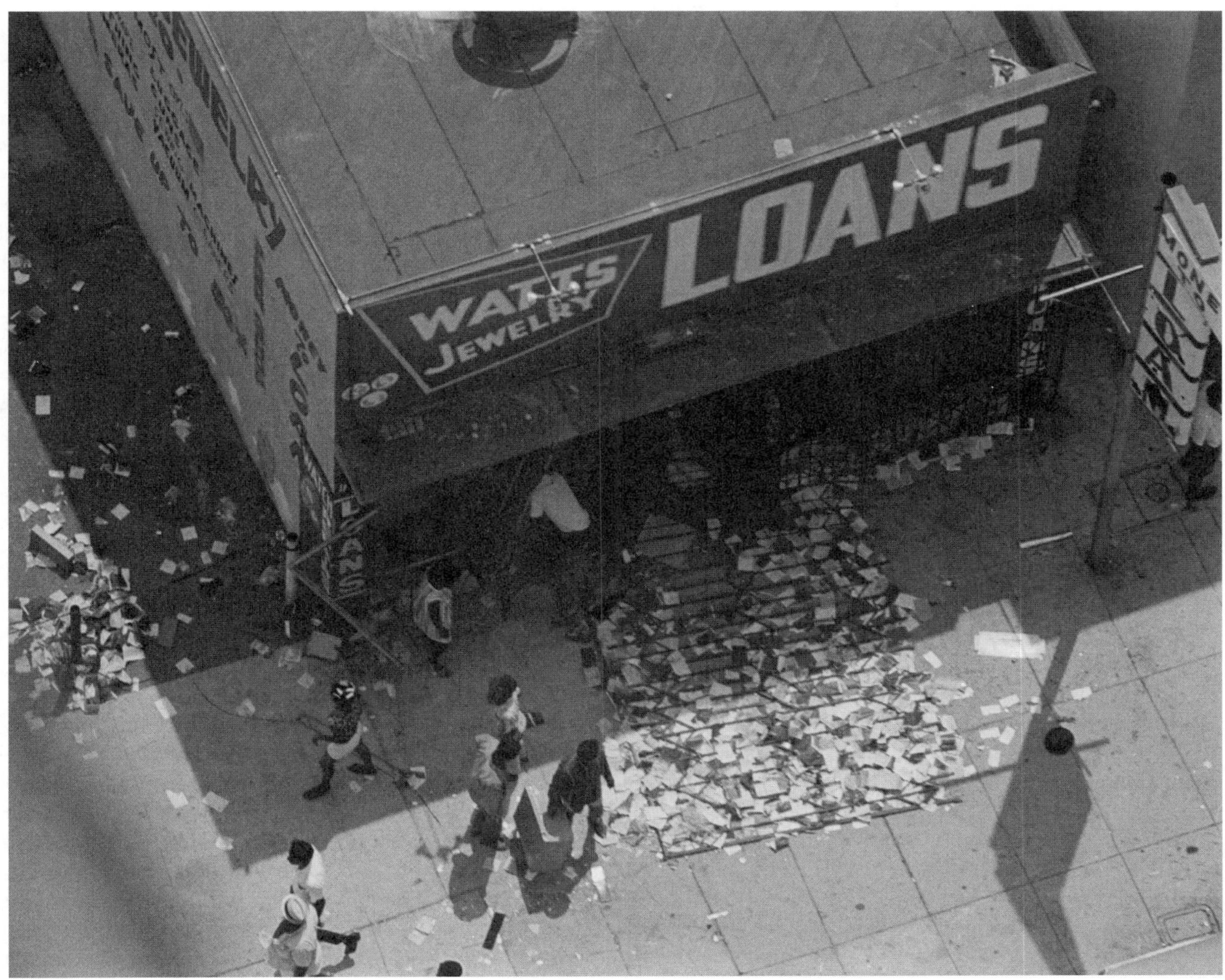

Study of crowd behavior shows it to be patterned and collective rather than random and individualistic, even in such events as the Los Angeles riot of 1965. (UPI/Corbis-Bettmann)

that gives rise to the sense that something "outside the ordinary" is occurring is rarely specified unambiguously, however. John Lofland (1981) suggests that it is increased levels of emotional arousal, but such arousal is not peculiar to crowd episodes. The conceptualization offered here suggests several possibilities: It is the appropriation and use of spatial areas, physical structures, or social networks and relations for purposes other than those for which they were intended or designed that indicates something extraordinary is happening.

Characteristic Features of Crowds

Crowds have been portrayed historically and journalistically as if they are monolithic entities characterized by participant and behavioral homogeneity. Turner and Killian (1972) called this image into question, referring to it as "the illusion of unanimity," but not until the recent turn toward more systematic empirical examination of crowds was it firmly established that crowd behaviors are typically quite varied and highly differentiated, and that crowd participants are generally quite heterogeneous in terms of orientation and behavior.

VARIATION IN CROWD BEHAVIORS. Based on extensive field observation of crowds, Sam Wright (1978) differentiated between two broad categories of crowd behaviors: crowd activities and task activities. "Crowd activities" refers to the redundant behavior seemingly common to all incidents of crowd behavior, such as assemblage, milling, and divergence. In their overview of empirical research on behaviors within crowds, McPhail and Wohlstein (1983) include collective locomotion, collective orientation, collective gesticulation, and collective vocalization among the types of crowd behaviors "repeatedly observed across a variety of gatherings, demonstrations, and some riots" (p. 595).

Taking these observations together, one can identify the following "crowd activities" (Wright 1978) or "elementary forms" of crowd behavior (McPhail and Wohlstein 1983): assemblage/convergence; milling; collective orientation (e.g., common or convergent gaze, focus, or attention); collective locomotion (e.g., common or convergent movement or surges); collective gesticulation (e.g., common or convergent nonverbal signaling); collective vocalization (e.g., chanting, singing, booing, cheering); and divergence/dispersal. Given the recurrent and seemingly universal character of these basic crowd behaviors, it is clear that they do not distinguish between types of crowds, that is, between demonstrations, celebrations, and riots.

To get at the variation in types of crowds, attention must be turned to what Wright conceptualized as "task activities" (1978). These refer to joint activities that are particular to and necessary for the attainment of a specific goal or the resolution of a specific problem. It is these goal-directed and problem-oriented activities that constitute the primary object of attention and thus help give meaning to the larger collective episode. Examples of task activities include parading or mass marching, mass assembly with speech making, picketing, proselytizing, temporary occupation of premises, lynching, taunting and harassment, property destruction, looting, and sniping.

The massed march and mass assembly are both collective task activities specific to the twentieth century.

Several caveats should be kept in mind with respect to crowd task activities. First, any listing of task activities is unlikely to be exhaustive, because they vary historically and culturally. Charles Tilly's (1978) concept of "repertories of collective action" underscores this variation. Tilly has stressed that, while there are innumerable ways in which people could pursue collective ends, alternatives are in fact limited by sociohistorical forces. His research suggests, for example, that the massed march, mass assembly, and temporary occupation of premises are all collective task activities specific to the twentieth century.

Second, crowd task activities are not mutually exclusive but are typically combined in an interactive fashion during the history of a crowd episode. The mass assembly, for example, is often preceded by the massed march, and property destruction and looting often occur together. Indeed, whether a crowd episode is constitutive of a protest demonstration, a celebration, or a riot depends, in part, on the particular configuration of task activities and, in part, on who or what is the object of protest, celebration, or violence. Both of these points can be illustrated with riots. It is generally agreed that riots involve some level of collective violence against persons or property, but that not all incidents of collective violence are equally likely to be labeled riots. Collective violence against the state or its social control agents is more likely to be labeled riotous, for example, than violence perpetrated by the police against protesting demonstrators. Traditionally, what gets defined as a riot involves interpretive discretion, particularly by the state. But even when there is agreement about what constitutes a riot, distinctions are often made between types of riots, as evidenced by Morris Janowitz's (1979) distinction between communal riots (interracial clashes) and commodity riots (extensive looting), and Gary

Marx's (1972) distinction between "protest riots" and "issueless riots."

Following from these observations is a final caveat: The task activities associated with any given crowd episode vary in the degree to which they are the focus of attention. Not all are equally attended to by spectators, social control agents, or the media. Consequently, task activities can be classified according to the amount of attention they receive. One that is the major focus of attention and thus provides the phenomenal basis for defining the episode constitutes "the main task activity," whereas those subordinate to the main task activity are "subordinate or side activities." The major task activity is on center stage. In contrast, the remaining task activities are side-shows, occasioned by and often parasitic to the focal activity. Examples of subordinate task activity include counterdemonstrations, media work, and peace marshaling.

VARIATION IN PARTICIPATION UNITS. Just as more recent empirical research on crowds has discerned considerable heterogeneity in behavior, so there is corresponding variation in terms of participants. Some are engaged in various task activities, some are observing, and still others are involved in the containment and control of the other participants and their interactions. Indeed, most of the individuals who make up a crowd fall into one of three categories of actors: task performers, spectators or bystanders, and social control agents. Task performers include the individuals performing both main and subordinate tasks. In the case of an antiwar march, for example, the main task performers would include the protesting marchers, with counterdemonstrators, peace marshals, and the press or media constituting the subordinate task performers.

Spectators, who constitute the second set of actors relevant to most instances of crowd behavior, have been differentiated into proximal and distal groupings according to proximity to the collective encounter and the nature of their response. Proximal spectators, who are physically co-present and can thus monitor firsthand the activities of task performers, have generally been treated as relatively passive and nonessential elements of crowd behavior. However, research on a series of victory celebrations shows that some spectators do not merely respond passively to the main task performance and accept the activity as given, but can actively influence the character of the activity as well (Snow, Zurcher, and Peters 1981). Accordingly, proximal spectators can vary in terms of whether they are passive or animated and aggressive. "Distal spectators" refers to individuals who take note of episodes of crowd behavior even though they are not physically present during the episodes themselves. Also referred to as "bystander publics" (Turner and Killian 1987), they indirectly monitor an instance of crowd behavior and respond to it, either favorably or unfavorably, by registering their respective views with the media, and community officials. Although distal spectators may not affect the course of a single episode of crowd behavior, they can clearly have an impact on the career and character of a series of interconnected crowd episodes.

Social control agents, consisting primarily of police officers and military personnel, constitute the final set of participants relevant to most instances of crowd behavior. Since they are the guardians of public order, their primary aim with respect to crowds is to maintain that order by controlling crowd behavior both spatially and temporally or by suppressing its occurrence. Given this aim, social control agents can clearly have a significant impact on the course and character of crowd behavior. This is evident in most protest demonstrations and victory celebrations, but it is particularly clear in the case of riots, which are often triggered by overzealous police activity and often involve considerable interpersonal violence perpetrated by the police. The urban riots of the 1960s in the United States illustrate both tendencies (Bergesen 1980; Kerner 1968).

Although there is no consensual taxonomy of crowd behaviors and interacting participation units, the foregoing observations indicate that behavioral and participant heterogeneity are characteristic features of most crowd episodes. In turn, the research on which these observations are based lays to rest the traditional image of crowds as monolithic entities composed of like-minded people engaged in undifferentiated behavior.

Conditions of Emergence

Under what conditions do individuals come together collectively to engage in crowd task activities constitutive of protest or celebration, and why do these occurrences sometimes turn violent or riotous? Three sets of interacting conditions are discernible in the literature: (1) conditions of conduciveness; (2) situational precipitants or strains; and (3) conditions for mobilization.

CONDITIONS OF CONDUCIVENESS. The concept of conduciveness directs attention to structural and cultural factors that make crowd behavior physically and socially possible (Smelser 1963). Conditions of conduciveness constitute the raw material for crowd behavior and include three sets of factors: ecological, technological, and social control. Ecological factors affect the arrangement and distribution of people in space so as to facilitate interaction and communication. One such factor found to be particularly conducive is the existence of large, spatially concentrated populations. The vast majority of campus protest demonstrations in the 1960s occurred on large universities, for example. Similarly, the urban riots of the 1960s typically occurred in densely populated residential areas, where there were large, easily mobilizable black populations. Seymour Spilerman's (1976) aggregate-level research on ghetto riots found an almost linear relationship between the size of a city's black population and the likelihood and number of disorders experienced, thus suggesting that there was a threshold population size below which riots were unlikely. Taken together, such findings provide strong support for the hypothesis that, all other things being equal, the greater the population density, the greater the likelihood of crowd behavior.

The heightened prospect of interpersonal interaction and communication associated with population concentration can also be facilitated by the diffusion of communication technology, namely telephone, radio, and television. But neither the diffusion of such technology nor population density guarantee the emergence of crowd behavior in the absence of a system of social control that allows for freedom of assembly and speech. It has been found repeatedly that incidence of public protest against the state diminishes considerably in political systems that prohibit and deal harshly with such crowd behavior, whereas the development of a more permissive attitude toward public protest and a corresponding relaxation of measures of social control is frequently conducive to the development of protest behavior. The proliferation of public protest throughout Eastern Europe, including the former Soviet Union, in 1989 and 1990 is illustrative of this principle; so is Bert Useem and Peter Kimball's (1989) research on prison riots, which reveals that they are sparked in part by erosion of prison security systems and the increased physical vulnerability of those systems.

PRECIPITATING EVENTS AND CONDITIONS. However conducive conditions might be for crowd behavior, it will not occur in the absence of some precipitating event or condition. Although the specific precipitants underlying the emergence of crowd behavior may be quite varied, most are variants of two generic conditions: (1) ambiguity; and (2) grievances against the state or some governmental, administrative entity.

Ambiguity is generated by the disruption or breakdown of everyday routines or expectancies, and has long been linked theoretically to the emergence of crowd behavior (Johnson and Feinberg 1990; Turner and Killian 1987). Evidence of its empirical linkage to the emergence of crowd behavior is abundant, as with the materialization of crowds of onlookers at the scene of accidents and fires; the celebrations that sometimes follow high-stakes, unanticipated athletic victories; the collective revelry sometimes associated with disruption of interdependent networks of institutionalized roles, as in the case of power blackouts and police strikes; and prison riots that frequently follow on the heels of unanticipated change in administrative personnel, procedures, and control.

The existence of grievances against the state or some governmental, administrative unit is equally facilitative of crowd behavior, particularly of the protest variety. Such grievances are typically associated with the existence of economic and political inequities that are perceived as unjust or political decisions and policies that are seen as morally bankrupt or advantaging some interests to the exclusion of others. Examples of protest crowds triggered in part by such grievances include the hostile gatherings of hungry citizens and displaced workers in industrializing Europe; the striking crowds of workers associated with the labor movement; and the mass demonstrations (marching, rallying, picketing, vigiling) associated with the civil rights, student, antiwar, and women's movements of the 1960s and 1970s.

Interpersonal violence most often results from the dynamic interaction of protestors and police.

Crowd violence—"riotous" task activities such as property destruction, looting, fighting, and sniping—has been an occasional corollary of protest crowds, but it is not peculiar to such crowds. Moreover, the occurrence of crowd violence, whether in association with protest demonstrations or celebrations, is relatively infrequent in comparison to other crowd behaviors (Eisinger 1973; Gamson 1975; Lewis 1982). When it does occur, however, there are two discernible tendencies: Interpersonal violence most often results from the dynamic interaction of protestors and police (Kritzer 1977; MacCannell 1973); and property violence, as in the case of riot looting, tends to be selective and semiorganized rather than random and chaotic (Berk and Aldrich 1972; Quarantelli and Dynes 1968).

CONDITIONS FOR MOBILIZATION. A precipitating condition coupled with a high degree of conduciveness is rarely sufficient to produce an instance of crowd behavior. In addition, people have to be assembled or brought into contact with one another, and attention must be focused on the accomplishment of some task. On some occasions in everyday life the condition of assemblage is already met, as in the case of the pedestrian crowd and conventional audience. More often than not, however, protest crowds, large-scale victory celebrations, and riots do not grow out of conventional gatherings but require the rapid convergence of people in time and space. McPhail and Miller (1973) found this assembling process to be contingent on the receipt of assembling instructions; ready access, either by foot or by other transportation, to the scene of the action; schedule congruence; and relatively free or discretionary time. It can also be facilitated by life-style circumstances and social networks. Again, the inner-city riots of the 1960s are a case in point. They typically occurred on weekday evenings or weekends in the summer, times when people were at home, were more readily available to receive instructions, and had ample discretionary time (Kerner 1968).

The focusing of attention typically occurs through some "keynoting" or "framing" process whereby the interpretive gesture or utterance of one or more individuals provides a resonant account or stimulus for action. It can occur spontaneously, as when someone yells "Cops!" or "Fire!"; it can be an unintended consequence of media broadcasts; or it can be the product of prior planning, thus implying the operation of a social movement.

Coordination of Crowd Behavior

Examination of protest demonstrations, celebratory crowds, and riots reveals in each case that the behaviors in question are patterned and collective rather than random and individualistic. Identification of the sources of coordination has thus been one of the central tasks confronting students of crowd behavior.

Earlier theorists attributed the coordination either to the rapid spread of emotional states and behavior in a contagion-like manner due to the presumably heightened suggestibility of crowd members (LeBon [1895] 1960; Blumer 1951) or to the convergence of individuals who are predisposed to behave in a similar fashion because of common dispositions or background characteristics (Allport 1924; Dollard et al. 1939). Both views are empirically off the mark. They assume a uniformity of action that glosses the existence of various categories of actors, variation in their behaviors, ongoing interaction among them, and the role this interaction plays in determining the direction and character of crowd behavior. These oversights are primarily due to the perceptual trap of taking the behaviors of the most conspicuous element of the episode—the main task performers—as typifying all categories of actors, thus giving rise to the previously mentioned "illusion of unanimity" (Turner and Killian 1987).

A more modern variant of the convergence argument attributes coordination to a rational calculus in which individuals reach parallel assessments regarding the benefits of engaging in a particular task activity (Berk 1974; Granovetter 1978). Blending elements of this logic with strands of theorizing seemingly borrowed from LeBon and Freud, James Coleman (1990) argues that crowd behavior occurs when individuals make a unilateral transfer of control over their actions. Such accounts are no less troublesome than the earlier ones in that they remain highly individualistic and psychologistic, ignoring the extent to which crowd behavior is the product of collective decision making involving the "framing" and "reframing" of probable costs and benefits and the extent to which this collective decision making frequently has a history involving prior negotiation between various sets of crowd participants.

A sociologically more palatable view holds that crowd behavior is coordinated by definition of the situation that functions in normative fashion by encouraging behavior in accordance with the definition. The collective definition may be situationally emergent (Turner and Killian 1987) or preestablished by prior negotiation among the relevant sets of actors (Snow and Anderson 1985). When one or more sets of actors cease to adjust their behaviors to this normative understanding, violence is more likely, especially if the police seek to reestablish normative control, and the episode is likely to be labeled as riotous or moblike.

Today it is generally conceded that most instances of crowd behavior are normatively regulated, but the dynamics underlying the emergence of such regulations are still not well understood empirically. Consequently, there is growing re-march interest in detailing the interactional dynamics underlying the process by which coordinating understandings emerge and change. Distinctive to this research is the view that social interaction among relevant sets of actors, rather than the background characteristics and cognitive states of individuals, holds the key to understanding the course and character of crowd behavior.

BIBLIOGRAPHY

Allport, Floyd H. 1924 *Social Psychology.* Boston: Houghton Mifflin.

Bergesen, Albert 1980 "Official Violence During the Watts, Newark, and Detroit Race Riots of the 1960s." In Pat Lauderdale, ed., *A Political Analysis of Deviance.* Minneapolis: University Minnesota Press.

Berk, Richard 1974 "A Gaming Approach to Crowd Behavior." *American Sociological Review* 39:355–373.

———, and Howard Aldrich 1972 "Patterns of Vandalism During Civil Disorders as an Indicator of Selection of Targets." *American Sociological Review* 37:533–547.

Blumer, Herbert 1951 "Collective Behavior." In Alfred McClung Lee, ed., *Principles of Sociology.* New York: Barnes and Noble.

Coleman, James S. 1990 *Foundations of Social Theory.* Cambridge: Harvard University Press.

Dollard, John, Leonard Doob, Neal Miller, Herbert Mowrer, and Robert Sears 1939 *Frustration and Aggression.* New Haven, Conn.: Yale University Press.

Eisinger, Peter 1973 "The Conditions of Protest Behavior in American Cities." *American Political Science Review* 67:11–28.

Freud, Sigmund 1921 *Group Psychology and Analysis of the Ego.* London: International Psychoanalytical Press.

Gamson, William 1975 *The Strategy of Social Protest.* Homewood, Ill.: Dorsey.

Granovetter, Mark 1978 "Threshold Models of Collective Behavior." *American Journal of Sociology* 83:1420–1443.

Janowitz, Morris 1979 "Collective Racial Violence: A Contemporary History." In Hugh Davis Graham and Ted Gurr, eds., *Violence in America: Historical and Comparative Perspectives,* rev. Beverly Hills, Calif.: Sage.

Johnson, Norris R., and William E. Feinberg 1990 "Ambiguity and Crowds: Results from a Computer Simulation Model." *Research in Social Movements, Conflict and Change* 12:35–66.

Kerner, Otto 1968 *Report of the National Advisory Commission on Civil Disorders.* New York: E. P. Dutton.

Kritzer, Herbert M. 1977 "Political Protest and Political Violence: A Nonrecursive Causal Model." *Social Forces* 55:630–640.

LeBon, Gustave (1895) 1960 *The Crowd: A Study of the Popular Mind.* New York: Viking Press.

Lewis, Jerry 1982 "Fan Violence: An American Social Problem" *Research on Social Problems and Public Policy* 2:175–206.

Lofland, John 1981 "Collective Behavior: The Elementary Forms." In Morris Rosenberg and Ralph Turner, eds., *Social Psychology.* New York: Basic Books.

MacCannell, Dean 1973 "Nonviolent Action as Theater." Nonviolent Action Research Project Series No. 10, Haverford College Center for Nonviolent Conflict Resolution, Haverford, Pa.

Marx, Gary 1972 "Issueless Riots." In James F. Short and Marvin E. Wolfgang, eds., *Collective Violence.* Chicago: Aldine-Atherton.

McPhail, Clark 1991 *The Myth of the Madding Crowd.* New York: Aldine de Gruyter.

McPhail, Clark, and David L. Miller 1973 "The Assembling Process: A Theoretical and Empirical Examination." *American Sociological Review* 38:721–735.

McPhail, Clark, and Ronald T. Wohlstein 1983 "Individual and Collective Behaviors Within Gatherings, Demonstrations, and Riots." *Annual Review of Sociology* 9:579–600.

Quarantelli, Enrico L., and Russell Dynes 1968 "Looting in Civil Disorders: An Index of Social Change." In Louis Masotti and Don R. Bowen, eds., *Riots and Rebellion.* Beverly Hills, Calif.: Sage.

Smelser, Neil 1963 *Theory of Collective Behavior.* New York: Free Press.

Snow, David A., and Leon Anderson 1985 "Field Methods and Conceptual Advances in Crowd Research." Paper presented at Conference on Research Methods in Collective Behavior and Social Movements, Collective Behavior/Social Movements Section of the American Sociological Association, Bowling Green State University.

Snow, David A., Louis A. Zurcher, and Robert Peters 1981 "Victory Celebrations as Theater: A Dramaturgical Approach to Crowd Behavior." *Symbolic Interaction* 4:21–42.

Spilerman, Seymour 1976 "Structural Characteristics of Cities and the Severity of Racial Disorders." *American Sociological Review* 35:627–649.

Tilly, Charles 1978 *From Mobilization to Revolution.* Reading, Mass.: Addison-Wesley.

Tuner, Ralph H., and Lewis Killian 1987 *Collective Behavior.* Englewood Cliffs, N.J.: Prentice-Hall.

Useem, Bert, and Peter Kimball 1989 *States of Siege: U.S. Prison Riots 1971–1986.* New York: Oxford University Press.

Weller, Jack, and Enrico L. Quarantelli 1973 "Neglected Characteristics of Collective Behavior." *American Journal of Sociology* 79:665–685.

Wright, Sam 1978 *Crowds and Riots: A Study in Social Organization.* Beverly Hills, Calif.: Sage.

– DAVID A. SNOW
RONNELLE PAULSEN

CULTS

As a sociological term, cults has three related but conceptually distinct meanings (Roberts 1984, pp. 241–247). Its oldest meaning developed through attempts to typologize religious groups as churches, denominations, sects, or cults. Howard Becker used the term cult to describe a loose association of people who hold eclectic religious views (Becker 1932) and built on Ernst Troeltsch's identification of "mysticism" as a loosely knit association whose participants emphasized the value of "a purely personal and inward experience" (Troeltsch 1911, p. 993; see also Mann 1955). Meredith McGuire refined the typology by distinguishing between organizational characteristics and the religious orientation of members. The organizational characteristics of cults include ideological toleration of other groups despite their own tension with society, and the religious orientation of cult members includes the compartmentalization of religion into particular aspects of life while questing after higher levels of "awareness" (McGuire 1987, pp. 117–125).

Cults are cultural innovations.

The second meaning of the term *cult* specifically depends on whether a new group's theological ideas and related practices have ideational precedent within its culture (Stark and Bainbridge 1985, pp. 26–37). Both sects and cults exist in relatively high tension with society, but sects are schismatic movements that borrow heavily from their parent groups' doctrines and practices, while cults "do not have a prior tie with another established religious body in the society in question" (Stark and Bainbridge 1985, p. 25). Cults, therefore, are cultural innovations, and as such they appear in three forms, differing in their degrees of organization, especially concerning the manner in which leaders relate to members. "Audience cults" have "virtually no aspects of formal organization" concerning either formal membership or the conveyance of ideology, and leaders disseminate their information in loosely structured situations such as lectures or private readings of occult books. "Client cults" often exhibit considerable organization "among those [leaders] offering the cult service," but the partakers of the message are little organized (as is the case with alternative healing organizations [Stark and Bainbridge 1985, p. 26]). Finally, cult movements have formal structures in which followers or members operate under leaders' directives, although the degree of members' participation varies from relatively weak to complete immersion (Stark and Bainbridge 1985, p. 29). Moreover, cult movements offer members the widest degree of general supernatural promises about salvation or deliverance, much like major, traditional religions (Stark and Bainbridge 1985, p. 30).

Third, "cult" carries pejorative connotations as an exploitative group that demands unreasonable obligations from group members, usually under the direction of a manipulative charismatic leader and at the expense of members' former family and friends. "Cults" in this sense appear in the fields of religion, politics, psychotherapy and personal development, health, science, and economics, all of them sharing a fundamental characteristic of ideologies. Their adherents are unable publicly to express doubts about the groups' fundamental assumptions (see Feuer 1975, pp. 104–105). Although few sociologists use "cults" in this manner (partly in reaction to its negative tone), the term has entered popular vocabulary with these inferences.

Cults in this third sense have spurred considerable public debate, especially after the Charles Manson murders (1969), the Patti Hearst kidnapping story (1974), and the Jonestown murder/suicides (1978) (Hall 1987). Numerous "anticult" or "countercult" organizations of varying size, complexity, and activity emerged in the United States during early 1972 (Shupe and Bromley 1980, p. 90; Shupe and Bromley 1984), followed by similar organizations in other Western countries (see Beckford 1985). These oppositional groups, some of which have evolved into organizations that still are active in the 1990s, initially were comprised largely of relatives with family members involved in various alternative religions, along with some clergy and professionals from the mental health field. Countercult organizations served both as support groups for relatives and former members and as vocal critics of many cult activ-

In popular vocabulary, the term "cult" refers to an exploitative group that demands excessive devotion from members, usually in obedience to a charismatic leader. The Unification Church, whose leader performs mass wedding ceremonies of members, fits that definition. (UPI/Corbis-Bettmann)

ities and practices. Adopting and later modifying a "brainwashing" and "coercive persuasion" model that initially researchers used to explain ideological reversals among captives in various communist indoctrination programs during the 1950s (Lifton 1961; Ofshe and Singer 1986), many relatives argued that family members had to be removed from the groups (by force if necessary) and "deprogrammed" from their "totalistic" views. Consequently, an intense social debate ensued between the "cults" (or as they preferred to call themselves, the "new religions") and their opponents, with each side attempting to damage the public image of their enemies while at the same time presenting themselves in a favorable light (Kent 1990).

BIBLIOGRAPHY

Becker, Howard 1932 *Systematic Sociology.* New York: Wiley

Beckford, James A. 1985 *Cult Controversies.* London: Tavistock.

Bromley, David G., and Phillip E. Hammond (eds.) 1987 *The Future of New Religious Movements.* Macon, Ga.: Mercer University Press.

Choquette, Diane, comp. 1985 *New Religious Movements in the United States and Canada: A Critical Assessment and Anotated Bibliography.* Westport, Conn.: Greenwood Press.

Feuer, Lewis S. 1975 *Ideology and the Ideologists.* New York: Harper and Row.

Hall, John R. 1987 *Gone from the Promised Land: Jonestown in American Cultural History.* New Brunswick, N.J.: Transaction Books.

Jacobs, Janet 1989 *Divine Disenchantment.* Bloomington and Indianapolis: Indiana University Press.

Kent, Stephen A. 1990 "Deviance Labelling and Normative Strategies in the Canadian 'New Religions/Countercult' Debate." *Canadian Journal of Sociology* 15:393–416.

Lifton, Robert J. 1961 *Thought Reform and the Psychology of Totalism.* New York: W. W. Norton.

McGuire, Meredith B. 1987 *Religion: The Social Context,* 2nd ed. Belmont, Calif.: Wadsworth.

Mann, W. E. 1955 *Sect, Cult and Church in Alberta.* Toronto: University of Toronto Press.

Melton, J. Gordon 1986 *Biographical Dictionary of American Cult and Sect Leaders.* New York: Garland.

——— 1987 *The Encyclopedia of American Religions.* Detroit: Gale Research.

Ofshe, Richard, and Margaret T. Singer 1986 "Attacks on Peripheral Versus Central Elements of Self and the Impact of Thought Reforming Techniques." *The Cultic Studies Journal* 3:3–24.

Robbins, Thomas 1988 *Cults, Converts and Charisma.* Beverly Hills, Calif.: Sage.

Roberts, Keith A. 1984 *Religion in Sociological Perspective.* Homewood, Ill.: Dorsey.

Saliba, John A. 1987 *Psychiatry and the Cults: An Annotated Bibliography.* New York: Garland.

Shupe, Anson D., Jr., and David G. Bromley 1980 *The New Vigilantes: Deprogrammers, Anti-Cultists, and the New Religions.* Beverly Hills, Calif.: Sage.

——— 1984 *The Anti-Cult Movement in America: A Bibliography and Historical Survey.* New York: Garland.

Stark, Rodney, and William Sims Bainbridge 1985 *The Future of Religion.* Berkeley: University of California Press.

Troeltsch, Ernst 1911 *The Social Teachings of the Christian Churches,* 2 vols., trans 1931 by Olive Wyon. London: George Allen and Unwin.

Zald, Mayer N., and John D. McCarthy 1987 "Religious Groups as Crucibles of Social Movements." In *Social Movements in an Organizational Society,* ed. by Mayer N. Zald and John D. McCarthy. New Brunswick, N.J.: Transaction Books.

– STEPHEN A. KENT

CULTURE

To produce a definition of culture, one can examine the concept in the abstract, that is, explore the concept theoretically from a variety of standpoints and then justify the definition that emerges through deductive logic. Or one can explore how the concept is used in practice, that is, describe how sociologists, both individually and collectively, define culture in the research process and analyze how they inductively construct a shared definition. This article takes the latter collective-inductive approach to defining culture. Such an approach is inherently sociological and does not presume to produce a definition for the field, rather it seeks to document how successful participants in the field have been in producing a shared definition for themselves. To produce such a "working" definition of culture, one starts by examining the social science roots and current status of the sociology of culture.

The focus on culture in sociology has flourished over the past fifteen years, as evidenced by the fact that the Culture Section in the American Sociological Association has become one of the largest and is still one of the fastest-growing sections in the discipline. The growth of interest in culture is also nicely documented by the number of recent review articles (e.g., Peterson 1990, 1989, 1979; Wuthnow and Witten 1988; Blau 1988; Mukerji and Schudson 1986). As is clear from the reviews, interest in cultural analysis has grown significantly. The focus on culture in all spheres of research has increased tremendously, and culture is now readily accepted as a level of explanation in its own right. Even in traditionally materialist-oriented research arenas, such as stratification and Marxist studies, cultural activities and interests are not treated as subordinate to economic explanations in current research (e.g., Bourdieu 1984; Williams 1977, 1981). Cultural studies and analysis have become one of the most fertile areas in sociology.

The rapid growth in the focus on culture and cultural explanations has produced some definitional boundary problems. The term *culture* has been used in contemporary sociological research to describe everything from elite artistic activities (Becker 1982) to the values, styles, and ideology of day-to-day conduct (Swidler 1986). Included among the current "mixed bag" of research that takes place under the auspices of the sociology of culture is work in science (Latour 1987; Star 1989), religion (Neitz 1987), law (Katz 1988), media and popular culture (Gitlin 1985; Chambers 1986), and work organization (Lincoln and Kalleberg 1990). With such an extensive variety in the empirical focus of cultural studies, the question for many participants in the field is how to translate this eclecticism into a coherent research field. This goal has not yet been reached, but while a coherent concept of culture is still evolving and the boundaries of the current sociology of culture research community are still fluid and expanding, it is possible to explore how different types of researchers in the social sciences, both currently and historically, have approached the concept of culture. In this inventory process, a better understanding of the concept of culture will emerge, that is, what different researchers believe the concept of culture includes, what the concept excludes, and how the distinction between categories has been made. This article will provide a historical overview of the two major debates on the appropriate focus and limitations of the definition of culture, and then turn to the contemporary social context in an effort to clarify the issues underlying the current concept of culture.

The Culture-Social Structure Debate

From the turn of the century until the 1950s, the definition of culture was embroiled in a dialogue that sought to distinguish the concepts of culture and social structure. This distinction was a major bone of contention among social scientists, most noticeably among anthropologists divided between the cultural and social traditions of anthropology. Researchers in the cultural or ethnological tradition, such as Franz Boas (1896/1940), Bronislaw Malinowski (1927, 1931), Margaret Mead (1928, 1935), Alfred Kroeber (1923/1948, 1952), and Ruth Benedict (1934) felt culture was the central concept in social science. "Culturalists" maintained that culture is primary in guiding all patterns of behavior, including who interacts with whom, and should therefore be given priority in theories about the organization of society. This position was countered by researchers in the structural tradition, such as A. R. Radcliffe-Brown ([1952] 1961) and E. E. Evans-Pritchard (1937, 1940) from the British school of social anthropology, and Claude Levi-Strauss ([1953] 1963) in French structuralism. "Structuralists" contended that social structure was the primary focus of social science and should be given priority in theories about society because social structure (e.g., kinship) determines patterns of social interaction and thought. Both schools had influential and large numbers of adherents.

The culturalists took a holistic approach to the concept of culture. Stemming from Edward Tylor's classic definition, culture was ". . . that complex whole which includes knowledge, belief, art, morals, law, custom, and any other capabilities and habits acquired by man as a member of society" ([1871] 1924, p. 1). This definition leaves little out, but the orientation of the late nineteenth century intended the concept of culture to be as inclusive as possible. Culture is what distinguishes man as a species from other species. Therefore culture consists of all that is produced by human collectivities, that is, all of social life. The focus here stems from the "nature" vs. "nurture" disputes common during this period. Anything that differentiates man's accomplishments from biological and evolutionary origins was relevant to the concept of culture. That includes religion as well as kinship structures, language as well as nation-states.

"Culturalists" maintained that culture is primary in guiding all patterns of behavior.

Following Boas, the study of culture was used to examine different types of society. All societies have cultures, and variations in cultural patterns helped further the argument that culture, not nature, played the most significant role in governing human behavior. In addition, the cultural variances observed in different societies helped break down the nineteenth-century anthropological notions of "the psychic unity of mankind, the unity of human history, and the unity of culture" (Singer 1968, p. 527). The pluralistic and relativistic approaches to culture that followed emphasized a more limited, localized conception. Culture was what produced a distinctive identity for a society, socializing members for greater internal homogeneity and identifying outsiders. Culture is thus created as differentiating concept, providing recognition factors for internal cohesion and external discrimination.

Although this tradition of ethnographic research on culture tended to be internal and localized, what is termed an "emic" approach in cognitive anthropology (Goodenough 1956), by the 1940s there emerged a strong desire among many anthropologists to develop a comparative "etic" approach to culture, that is, construct a generalized theory of cultural patterns. In the comparison of hundreds of ethnographies written in this period, A. L. Kroeber and Clyde Kluckhohn sought to build such a general definition of culture. They wrote,

> Culture consists of patterns, explicit and implicit, of and for behavior acquired and transmitted by symbols, constituting the distinctive achievement of human groups, including their embodiments in artifacts; the essential core of culture consists of traditional (i.e., historically derived and selected) ideas and especially their attached values; culture systems may, on the one hand, be considered as products of action, on the other as conditioning elements of further action ([1952] 1963, p. 181).

Milton Singer (1968) characterized this "pattern theory" definition as a condensation of what most American anthropologists in the 1940s and 1950s called culture. It includes behavior, cultural objects, and cognitive predispositions as part of the concept, thus emphasizing that culture is both a product of social action and a process that guides future action. The pattern theory stated simply that behavior follows a relatively stable routine, from the simplest levels of custom in dress and diet to more complex levels of organization in political, economic, and religious life. The persistence of specific patterns is variable in different arenas and different societies, but larger configurations tend to be more stable, changing incrementally unless redirected by external forces. In addition, the theory emphasized that the culture from any given society can be formally described, that is, it can be placed in formal categories representing different spheres of social life to facilitate comparison between societies. As such, universal patterns of culture can be constructed.

In comparison, anthropological structuralists in this period conceive of culture less comprehensively. The structuralist concept of culture is made distinct through emphasis on a new concept of social structure. Largely through the efforts of Radcliffe-Brown, a theory emerges that argues social structure is more appropriately represented by a network or system of social relations than a set of norms. The structuralist argument is intended to clarify how actors in a society actively produce and are socially produced by their cultural context. By distinguishing the actors and interaction in a social system from the behavioral norms, structuralists seek to establish a referent for social structure that is analytically independent of the culture and artifacts produced in that system. The production of culture is thus grounded clearly in an interactional framework. Norms of interaction are also produced by interacting participants, but the question of causal primacy between culture and social structure can be considered separately. The initial effort here is simply not to reify the origins of culture.

The exact relationship of culture and social structure, however, becomes the central issue of the structuralist/culturalist debate. For example, how to identify the boundaries of a society one is researching is problematic when the society is not an isolate. Structuralists tend to give social relations, that is, the extent of a network, priority in identifying boundaries, while culturalists focus on the extent of particular types of cultural knowledge or practices. Since both elements are obviously operating interdependently, the efforts to disentangle these concepts make little headway. The arguments to establish causal priority for one concept vis-à-vis the other settle into a fairly predictable exchange. Structuralists base their priority claims on the fact that the interaction of actors in a society is empirically preliminary to the development and application of cultural elements. Culturalists respond that interaction itself is at least partially a cultural phenomenon, and that in most complex societies cultural patterns have been well established prior to ongoing social relationships.

By the late 1950s, the concept of culture was becoming increasingly important to sociologists. To help resolve the now tired debate over cultural and structural foci and precedence, A. L. Kroeber and Talcott Parsons publish a report in the *American Sociological Review* titled "The Concepts of Culture and Social System" (1958), which seeks to establish some ground rules for differentiating the two concepts. At least for sociologists, many of whom identify explicitly with the structural-functional theories of the anthropological structuralists, acknowledgment of a separate social system component that delimits the scope of culture is not difficult. More difficult is ascertaining where the appropriate limits for the concept of culture lie within this domain. Kroeber and Parsons suggest restricting the usage of culture to, "transmitted and created content and patterns of values, ideas, and other symbolic-meaningful systems as factors in the shaping of human behavior and the artifacts produced behavior" (1958, p. 583). This definition emphasizes the predispositional aspect of a cultural referent, limiting the scope of culture to a cognitive perspective, and concentrates on a carefully worded description of "symbolic-meaningful systems" as the appropriate referent for culture. While no longer the omnibus conception of a traditional, Tylor-derived approach, this type of cultural analysis is still potentially applicable to any realm of social activity.

The High-Mass Culture Debate

In the 1950s and early 1960s, the concept of culture becomes enmeshed in a new debate that like the previously documented dialogue has both influential and significant numbers of participants on each side of the dispute. Sociologists, however, are more central to the discussion, pitting those who support a broadly conceived, anthropological interpretation of culture that places both commonplace and elite activities in the same category, against a humanities oriented conception of culture that equates the identification of cultural activity with a value statement. This debate attempts to do two things: to classify different types of cultural activity, and to distinguish a purely descriptive approach to the concept of culture from an axiological approach that defines culture through an evaluative process.

That an axiological approach to culture can be considered legitimate by a "scientific" enterprise is perhaps surprising to contemporary sociologists entrenched in the positivistic interpretation of science, yet a central issue for many sociologists in this period was how and whether to approach questions of moral values. For example, the critical theorist Leo Lowenthal (1950) characterized this period of social science as "applied asceticism" and stated that the moral or aesthetic evaluation of cultural products and activities is not only sociologically possible, but also should be a useful tool in the sociological analysis of cultural differentiation.

The legitimacy of mass culture is a matter of ideology, one that positions the elitist minority versus the growing democratization of culture.

These evaluative questions certainly play a part in the analysis of "mass culture," a term that the critic Dwight McDonald explains is used to identify articles of culture that are produced for mass consumption, "like chewing gum" (McDonald 1953, p. 59). A number of commentators, including both sociologists and humanists, observe the growth of mass culture production in the post World War II United States with a mixture of distaste and alarm. The concern of McDonald and critics like him is the decline of intrinsic value in cultural artifacts, a decline in quality that stems from, or is at least attributed to, a combination of economic and social factors associated with the growth of capitalism. For example, mass culture critics argue that the unchecked growth of capitalism in the production and distribution phases of culture industries leads to a "massification" of consumption patterns. Formerly localized, highly differentiated, and competitive markets become dominated by a single corporate actor who merges different sectors of the consumer landscape and monopolizes production resources and distribution outlets. Within these giant culture industry organizations the demand for greater efficiency and the vertical integration of production lead to a bureaucratically focused standardization of output. Both processes function to stamp out cultural difference and create greater homogeneity in moral and aesthetic values, all at the lowest common denominator.

Regardless of the causes of the mass culture phenomenon, the critics of mass culture believe it to be a potentially revolutionary force that will transform the values of society. One critic states that "mass culture is a dynamic, revolutionary force, breaking down the old barriers of class, tradition, taste, and dissolving all cultural distinctions. It mixes and scrambles everything together, producing what might be called homogenized culture, . . . It thus destroys all values, since value judgements imply discrimination" (McDonald 1953, p. 62).

In launching this attack, mass culture opponents see themselves as the saviors of a "true" or "high" culture (e.g., McDonald, Greenberg, Berelson, and Howe; see Rosenberg and White 1957). They argue that the consumption of mass culture undermines the very existence of legitimate high culture, that is, the elite arts and folk cultures. Without the ability to differentiate between increasingly blurred lines of cultural production, the average consumer turns toward mass culture due to its immediate accessibility. Further, simply through its creation, mass culture devalues elite art and folk cultures by borrowing the themes and devices of different cultural traditions and converting them into mechanical, formulaic systems (Greenberg 1946). Thus critics of mass culture argue that it is critical for the health of society to discriminate between types of culture.

Defenders of mass culture, or at least those who feel the attack on mass culture is too extreme, respond that mass culture critics seek to limit the production and appreciation of culture to an elitist minority. They contend that the elitist criticism of culture is ethnocentric and that not only is mass, popular, or public culture more diverse than given credit for (e.g., Lang 1956; Kracauer 1949), but also the benefits of mass cultural participation far outweigh the limitations of a mass media distribution system (White 1956; Seldes 1956). Post-World War II America experienced an economic boom that sent its citizens searching for a variety of new cultural outlets. The increase in cultural participation certainly included what some critics might call "vulgar" activities, but it also included a tremendous increase in audiences for the arts across the board. Essentially, mass culture defenders assert that the argument over the legitimacy of mass culture comes down to a matter of ideology, one that positions the elitist minority versus the growing democratization of culture.

To extricate themselves from this axiological conundrum, many sociologists of culture retreated from a morally evaluative stance to a normative one. As presented by Gertrude Jaeger and Philip Selznick (1964), the normative sociological approach to culture, while still evaluative, seeks to combine anthropological and humanist conceptions of culture through a diagnostic analysis of cultural experience. The emphasis here is on elaborating the nature of "symbolically meaningful" experiences, the same focus for culture that Kroeber and Parsons (1958) take in their differentiation of culture and social system. To do this, Jaeger and Selznick adopt a pragmatist perspective (Dewey 1958) that accords symbolic status to cultural objects or events through a social signification process. Interacting individuals create symbols through the communication of meaningful experience, using both denotative and connotative processes. By creating symbols, interacting individuals create culture. Thus the definition of culture becomes: "Culture consists of everything that is produced by, and is capable of sustaining, shared symbolic experience" (Jaeger and Selznick 1964, p. 663).

In establishing this sociological definition of culture emphasizing the shared symbolic experience, Jaeger and Selznick also seek to maintain a humanist-oriented capability to distinguish between high and mass culture without marginalizing the focus on high culture. Following Dewey, they argue that the experience of art takes place on a continuum of cultural experience that differs in intensity from ordinary symbolic activities, but has essentially the same basis for the appreciation of meaning. Art or high culture is simply a more "effective" symbol, combining "economy of statement with richness of expression" (Jaeger and Selznick 1964, p. 664). As such, art, like all culture, is identified through the normative evaluation of experience.

In sum, the high culture-mass culture debate shifted the focus on the concept of culture from a question of appropriate scope to a question of appropriate values. From a functionalist point of view, the health of a society's culture is not simply an issue of what type of values are advocated, but of how culture serves a moral and integrative function. Yet the mass culture critique was often unable to distinguish the cultural values of elite intellectuals from the effect of these values on society. To escape from this ethnocentric quagmire, contemporary sociologists have generally turned away from an evaluative position toward culture.

The Contemporary Debate on Culture

As mentioned at the beginning, the contemporary approach to culture in sociology is eclectic. Despite the elaborate historical lineage of the concept, there is no current, widely accepted, composite resolution of the definition of culture. Instead, culture is still defined through an extensive variety of perspectives, sanctioning a broad, historically validated range of options. While the omnibus definition from the cultural anthropology tradition has been generally relegated to introductory texts, and the elitist attack on mass culture has been largely replaced by an anti-ethnocentric, relativist position open to a wide spectrum of symbolic arenas and perspectives, many of the elements of these old debates still appear in new cultural analyses.

For example, as categorized by Richard Peterson introducing a recent review of new cultural studies (Peterson 1990), culture tends to be used two ways in sociological research; as a "code of conduct embedded in or constitutive of social life," and as "the symbolic products of group activity" (Peterson 1990, p. 498). The first approach is clearly indebted to the traditional cultural anthropology approach and indeed is used to characterize social units ranging from whole societies (e.g., Bellah et al. 1985) and extensive youth cohorts (e.g., Hebdige 1979; Willis 1977) to smaller communities organizing collective activities (e.g., see Fine 1987 on Little League baseball; Latour and Woolgar 1979 on science). The second approach takes the more limited focus of culture as symbols and symbol-making and emphasizes the meaning and social effect of specific forms of cultural expression. The range of potential application, however, is as expansive as the general approach and includes the moral discourse on the abortion issue (Luker 1984), the politics and aesthetics of the theater audience (Griswold 1986), and the motivational and ideological context of organizational or work cultures (Burawoy 1979; Fantasia 1988).

From the above array, it is clear that the contemporary concept of culture in sociology does not exclude any particular empirical forms of activity, except perhaps through an emphasis on shared or collective practices, thus discounting purely individual foci. All collective social practices are potentially symbolic and therefore potentially cultural. The question is to what degree the participants in any particular area treat their own or others' activities as symbolic. Certain areas of social practice, such as the arts and religion, are more overtly symbolic than others, such as work and the economy. But an argument could be made that this distinction is merely a matter of emphasis by individual actors and that there is nothing inherently noncultural about utilitarian activities.

Along these lines, recently in order to establish more intelligible parameters in the sociology of culture, some participants in the field have argued that the concept of culture should be centered around traditional substantive foci such as art, science, religion, and popular culture. The centering of the sociology of culture as a substantive focus might serve research coherence, but the expanding application of cultural analysis to nontraditional fields suggests that to many sociologists, culture is more an explanatory perspective than an area of study. As such, future limitations on the focus of culture will likely be conceptual, not empirical. The contemporary emphasis on culture as symbols and symbol-making activity represents such a "working" focus.

In sum, there is a new appreciation of the salience of culture as an explanatory perspective in contemporary sociological research. Whether it involves the convention setting influence of art worlds, the moral authority of organizational cultures, or the facilitation of class privileges through habitus, the concept of culture is used to explain behavior and social structure from a distinct and powerful perspective. The future elaboration of this perspective in sociology looks very promising.

BIBLIOGRAPHY

Becker, Howard S. 1982 *Art Worlds.* Berkeley: University of California Press.

Bellah, Robert, Richard Madsen, William Sullivan, Ann Swidler, and Steven Tipton 1985 *Habits of the Heart.* Berkeley: University of California Press.

Benedict, Ruth 1934 *Patterns of Culture.* Boston: Houghton Mifflin.

Blau, Judith 1988 "Study of the Arts: A Reappraisal." *Annual Review of Sociology* 14:269–292.

Boas, Franz (1896) 1940 "The Limitations of the Comparative Method of Anthropology." Reprinted in Boas, *Race, Language, and Culture.* New York: Macmillan.

Bourdieu, Pierre 1984 *Distinction.* Cambridge, Mass.: Harvard University Press.

Burawoy, Michael 1979 *Manufacturing Consent.* Chicago: University of Chicago Press.

Chambers, Iain 1986 *Popular Culture.* London: Methuen.

Dewey, John 1958 *Art as Experience.* New York: Capricorn Books.

Evans-Pritchard, E. E. 1937 *Witchcraft, Oracles and Magic Among the Azande.* Oxford: Clarendon Press.

——— 1940 *The Nuer.* London: Oxford University Press.

Fantasia, Rick 1988 *Cultures of Solidarity.* Berkeley: University of California Press.

Fine, Gary 1987 *With the Boys.* Chicago: University of Chicago Press.

Gitlin, Todd 1985 *Inside Prime Time.* New York: Pantheon.

Goodenough, Ward 1956 "Componential Analysis and the Study of Meaning." *Language* 32:22–37.

Greenberg, Clement 1946 "Avant-Garde and Kitsch." *The Partisan Reader* 378–389.

Griswold, Wendy 1986 *Renaissance Revivals.* Chicago: University of Chicago Press.

Hebdige, Dick 1979 *Subculture: The Meaning of Style.* London: Routledge.

Jaeger, Gertrude, and Philip Selznick 1964 "A Normative Theory of Culture." *American Sociological Review* 29:653–669.

Katz, Jack 1988 *Seductions of Crime: Moral and Sensual Attractions of Doing Evil.* New York: Basic Books.

Kracauer, Siegfried 1949 "National Types as Hollywood Presents Them." *Public Opinion Quarterly* 13:53–72.

Kroeber, Alfred (1923) 1948. *Anthropology.* New York: Harcourt.

——— 1952 *The Nature of Culture.* Chicago: University of Chicago Press.

———, and Clyde Kluckhohn (1952) 1963 *Culture: A Critical Review of Concepts and Definitions.* New York: Vintage Books.

———, and Talcott Parsons 1958 "The Concepts of Culture and Social System." *American Sociological Review* 23:582–583.

Lang, Kurt 1957 "Mass Appeal and Minority Tastes." In Bernard Rosenberg and David Manning White, eds., *Mass Culture.* New York: Free Press.

Latour, Bruno 1987 *Science in Action: How to follow Scientists and Engineers Through Society.* Cambridge, Mass.: Harvard University Press.

———, and Steve Woolgar 1979 *Laboratory Life.* Beverly Hills, Calif.: Sage.

Levi-Strauss, Claude (1953) 1963 *Structural Anthropology.* New York: Basic Books.

Lincoln, James, and Arne Kalleberg 1990 *Culture, Control, and Commitment: A Study of Work Organization and Work Attitudes in the United States and Japan.* Cambridge: Cambridge University Press.

Lowenthal, Leo 1950 "Historical Perspectives of Popular Culture." *American Journal of Sociology* 55:323–332.

Luker, Kristen 1984 *Abortion and the Politics of Motherhood.* Berkeley: University of California Press.

McDonald, Dwight 1953 "A Theory of Mass Culture." *Diogenes* 3:1–17.

Malinowski, Bronislaw 1927 *Sex and Repression in Savage Society.* London: Routledge.

——— 1931 "Culture." *Encyclopedia of the Social Sciences* 4:621–646.

Mead, Margaret 1928 *Coming of Age in Samoa.* New York: Morrow.

——— 1935 *Sex and Temperament in Three Primitive Societies.* New York: Morrow.

Mukerji, Chandra, and Michael Schudson 1986 "Popular Culture." *Annual Review of Sociology* 12:47–66.

Neitz, Mary Jo 1987 *Charisma and Community: A Study of Religious Commitment Within the Charismatic Renewal.* New Brunswick, N.J.: Transaction Books.

Peterson, Richard 1979 "Revitalizing the Culture Concept." *Annual Review of Sociology* 5:137–166.

——— 1989 "La Sociologie de l'art et de la culture aux Etats-Unis." *L'Année sociologique* 39:153–179.

——— 1990 "Symbols and Social Life: The Growth of Cultural Studies." *Contemporary Sociology* 19:498–500.

Radcliffe-Brown, A. R. (1952) 1961 *Structure and Function in Primitive Society: Essays and Addresses.* New York: Free Press.

Rosenberg, Bernard, and David Manning White (eds.) 1957 *Mass Culture.* New York: Free Press.

Seldes, Gilbert 1957 "The Public Arts." In Bernard Rosenberg and David Manning White, eds., *Mass Culture.* New York: Free Press.

Singer, Milton 1968 "Culture: The Concept of Culture." In David L. Sills, ed., *International Encyclopedia of the Social Sciences.* New York: Macmillan and Free Press.

Star, Susan Leigh 1989 *Regions of the Mind: Brain Research and the Quest for Scientific Certainty.* Stanford, Calif.: Stanford University Press.

Swidler, Ann 1986 "Culture in Action." *American Sociological Review* 51:273–286.

Tylor, Edward (1871) 1924 *Primitive Culture.* Gloucester, Mass.: Smith.

White, David M. 1957 "Mass Culture in America: Another Point of View." In Bernard Rosenberg and David Manning White, eds., *Mass Culture.* New York: Free Press.

Williams, Raymond 1977 *Marxism and Literature.* Oxford: Oxford University Press.

——— 1981 *The Sociology of Culture.* New York: Schocken Books.

Willis, Paul 1977 *Learning to Labor.* New York: Columbia University Press.

Wuthnow, Robert, and Marsha Witten 1988 "New Directions in the Study of Culture." *Annual Review of Sociology* 14:49–67.

– SAMUEL GILMORE

DEATH AND DYING

In the 1930s a U.S. encyclopedic entry on this topic might well have focused on the economic plight of the bereaved family (Eliot 1932). In the 1950s the focus might have been on the high cost of dying and the commercialization of funerals (Bowman 1959). Twenty years later, it could have shifted to the social implications of relaxing the taboo on death (Riley 1970). This article will (1) review what sociologists have learned to date and (2) predict that the main focus of sociological interest over the proximate future will be on the process of dying. Two trends make this prediction plausible. Greater longevity dictates that most deaths will continue to occur in the later years of life, and continuing use of life-sustaining technologies dictate that the circumstances of dying will be increasingly controllable and negotiable.

General Background

There is today no well-developed sociology of "death and dying." The phrase was first celebrated in 1969 in the title of a psychologically oriented best-seller (Kübler-Ross). Sociologists tended to be critical but recognized the appeal of the subject matter. During the subsequent decade a spate of popular literature appeared, but no major sociological work (Charmaz 1986). One sociologist termed the literature of that modern-day "discovery" of death as "a collective bustle" and summarized the ideas as "the happy death movement" (Lofland 1978).

A scattered body of sociological knowledge, however, tells us that death, in all known societies, imposes imperatives. A corpse must be looked after; property must be reallocated; vacated roles must be reassigned; the solidarity of the deceased's group must be reaffirmed (Blauner 1966; Riley 1968). A volume by Kearl (1989) makes notable contributions to the sociological perspective, relating death and dying to politics, the military, religion, war, and popular culture. Throughout this literature death is typically viewed as a transition, as a *rite de passage.*

Several threads running through the research literature also tell us that death and dying can be thought about and talked about quite openly in American society; various "arrangements" are increasingly being negotiated prior to death; dying persons are generally more concerned about their survivors than they are about themselves; dying individuals are able to exercise a significant degree of control over the timing of their deaths; tensions often exist between the requirements of formal care and the wishes of dying patients; and similar tensions almost always exist between formal and informal caregivers—between hospital bureaucracies and those significant others who are soon to be bereaved (Glaser and Strauss 1965, 1968; Riley 1983; Kalish 1985b).

NO SYSTEMATIC SOCIOLOGY. Despite this background of knowledge and research, death has received surprisingly little systematic attention from sociologists. There are only two indexed references in the 1988 *Handbook of Sociology* (Smelser 1988): one to poverty resulting from death of breadwinners, the other to the role of death in popular religion. The *Encyclopedia of the Social Sciences* (Sills 1968) contains two entries, both on the social meanings of death. Furthermore, sociologists have failed to generate any overarching theory, although there have been many attempts.

Several kernels illustrate the range of these theoretical efforts. Talcott Parsons (1963) related the changing meanings of death to basic social values; Karl Mannheim (1928, 1952) used mortality to explain social change; Renée Fox (1980, 1981) finds that "life and death are coming to be viewed less as absolute . . . entities . . . and more as different points on a meta-spectrum . . . a new theodicity." Dorothy and David Counts (1985) specify the role of death in the various social transformations from preliterate to modern societies; Paul Baker (1990), following Warner (1959) and others, is beginning to elaborate the long-recognized theory that images of the dead exert profound influences on the living; Victor Marshall is engaged in a sustained effort—both theoretical and empirical—to link aging and dying. His basic postulate is that "awareness of finitude" operates as a trigger that permits socialization to death (Marshall 1980; Marshall and Levy 1990).

Topical Sociological Findings

A review of the empirical literature tells us that sociological research on death has been largely topical, ranging from a taboo on death to suicide.

A TABOO ON DEATH. In contemporary American society, death has, until recently, been viewed as a taboo topic. By the early 1960s, however, a national survey reported that the great majority of Americans (85 percent) are quite realistic and consider it important to "try to make some plans about death" and to talk about it with those closest to them (Riley 1970). Recent studies have shown that bereavement practices, once highly socially structured, are becoming increasingly varied and individually therapeutic; dying is feared primarily because it eliminates the opportunities for self-fulfillment; and active adaptations to death increase as one approaches the end of the life course (the making of wills, leaving instructions, negotiating interpersonal conflicts, etc.).

Dying is feared primarily because it eliminates the opportunities for self-fulfillment.

SOCIAL ORGANIZATION OF DEATH. Most deaths in the United States occur in hospitals. Two aspects have been studied sociologically. First, a detailed account of the social organization of death in a public hospital focuses on the corpse. According to the rules, the body must be washed, cataloged, and ticketed. Dignity and bureaucratic efficiency are at odds (Sudnow 1967). A contrasting account of public and private rules governing disposition of the body in contemporary Ireland is even more sociological in emphasis (Prior 1989). Second, the caring issue has been studied more as a social problem. The dying person has often been treated according to rigid rules, and selfhood is put at risk in a hospital setting that is essentially dedicated to efficiency. Changes, however, have been noted, stressing the need for caring attitudes (Kalish 1985b).

HOSPICE CARE. The major contemporary response to care of the dying in the United States is found in programs of hospice care. While its definitive sociological significance is still to be documented, several studies have noted that the hospice team "mediates between the families and formal institutions that constitute the social organization of death and dying" (Marshall and Levy 1990; Levy 1982).

THE FUNERAL. Sociologists have studied the funeral mainly as a social institution. A massive cross-cultural study attests to its worldwide function in marking a major social transition (Haben-stein and Lamers 1963). Although Durkheim had emphasized its ceremonial role in facilitating social regrouping, later sociologists have shown that elaborate and extravagant funeral rites are more reflective of commercial interests than of human grief or mourning (Parsons and Lidz 1967).

BEREAVEMENT. A now classic study (Eliot 1932) of the bereaved family stimulated a large literature that documents the general proposition that survivors—particularly significant others—require various types of social supports to "get through" the period of intense personal grief and the more publicly expressed mourning. In today's societies, the time devoted to bereavement activities generally becomes shorter (Pratt 1981). This is consistent with Parsons' position that in societies characterized by an "active" orientation, the bereaved are expected to carry out their grief work quickly and privately.

WIDOWHOOD. It is estimated that by the year 2000 there will be sixty-five men for every 100 women over age sixty-five and that most of the women will be widows. Many studies (e.g., Lopata 1973, 1979) have detailed the negative aspects of widowhood: loneliness, poor health, loss of personal identity, anxiety about the future. A somewhat different picture has emerged from an analysis of data (Hyman 1983) from the General Social Surveys. Samples of widows (who were not interviewed as widows) were compared with control samples of married and divorced women. Although somewhat controversial, this study reported that widowhood does not produce the negative and enduring consequences that the earlier studies had documented.

SOCIAL STRESSORS AND DEATH. Sociologists have investigated many social "causes" of death: individually experienced stressors such as retirement and bereavement, and collectively experienced stressors such as economic depressions, wars, and technological revolutions. By and large all such studies have been inconclusive. For example, the hypothesis that a bereaved spouse is at higher risk of death (that death causes death) has been widely investigated but with no conclusive results, although recent and as yet unpublished research suggests that bereavement may have a negative mortality effect for older spouses. Retirees in some longitudinal studies have been shown to experience excess mortality, whereas other investigations have reported opposite results. (Retirement is a complex process, not a simple or single event.) In an era in which nursing homes play an important role in the lives of many older people, the consequences of residential relocation have come under critical scrutiny. Several studies have reported that the "warehousing" of the frail elderly results in increased mortality, while in other studies feelings of security in the new "home" are reported to enhance both a sense of well-being and lower mortality. (Obviously the nursing home population is far from homogeneous.) Similar caveats apply to macro-level studies that attempt to relate economic and technological change to trends in mortality. Recent advances in mathematical modeling and the increasing availability of relevant data sets make this problem an attractive area for continuing sociological research (Riley 1983).

SUICIDE. Durkheim's studies of suicide spawned a wide, diverse, and sometimes confusing research literature. In most such studies social integration is the operative concept. If the theoretical relationship is believed to be relatively unambiguous, the empirical relationship is far from tidy. For example, war has been found to heighten integration, both economic and political, but it also diminishes the availability of beverage alcohol, which, in turn, reduces suicides triggered by alcohol consumption (Wasserman 1989). Various other types of intervening variables have been studied (e.g., "suggestion") (Phillips 1974).

Focus on Dying

Apart from suicide, it is a sociological truism that individuals are often socially motivated to try to influence the time of their own deaths. Several studies, for example, have tested the hypothesis of a "death dip"—that social events of significance are preceded by lower than expected mortality (Phillips and Feldman 1973). These studies rest on Durkheim's insight that if some are so detached from society that they commit suicide, others may be so attached to society that they postpone their deaths in order to participate in events in which they are involved (Phillips and Smith 1990). The same hypothesis has been extended to studies of a "birthday dip" in which the event is more personal and local in its significance for death (Phillips 1972). Along similar lines, several sociological investigations have explored the proposition that some people die socially before they die biologically. These studies center on the notion of levels of "awareness" of death (Glaser and Strauss 1965). When both the dying person and his significant others are cognizant of death as a soon-to-be-experienced event, an ensuing "open" awareness may enable them to negotiate various aspects of the final phase of life. Further research on "dying trajectories" involves certainties and uncertainties as to the time of death (Glaser and Strauss 1968).

Recently, this question has been asked: Does the individual, in a society deeply committed to the preser-

The funeral marks a major social transition among cultures worldwide. This Christian ceremony is typical of American bereavement practices. (Eldad Rafaeli/Corbis)

vation of life, have a "right" to die? The U.S. Supreme Court has answered this in the affirmative but with limitations. The issue has become one of the most profound, complex, and pressing questions of our time. It involves the "rights" and wishes of the dying person; the "rights" and responsibilities of his or her survivors; the "rights" and obligations of attending physicians; and the "rights" and constraints of the law. And the human side of the issue is producing a tidal wave of public interest: television documentaries, opinion surveys, radio talk shows. The issue is openly debated in leading medical journals, which now carry editorials on euthanasia—an unthinkable topic only a few years ago. It is altering age-old hospital rules in which resuscitation orders were written on blackboards, then quickly erased. A major book proposes rationing medical resources (Callahan 1987). Radical movements have sprung up that advocate active euthanasia. The mounting costs of the last days of life have been dramatized. All this ferment reflects powerful ideas that potentially fuel social change (M. W. Riley 1978).

NEW NORMS FOR DYING. Demography dictates that a substantial proportion of the 5,500 or so deaths that occur each day in the United States will be at the later years of life, but medical technology now offers options as to timing. The period of dying can be lengthened or shortened. Sociology has identified three elements in the process of dying: (1) depending on the "level of awareness," the dying person is able to "negotiate" to some degree both the course of dying and the consequences of death (Glaser and Strauss 1965); (2) depending on "awareness of finitude," dying persons are able to be socialized to death and to prepare themselves for it (Marshall 1980); (3) depending on the quality of care, both the physical pain of dying and the psychosocial pain of separation and loss can be mitigated (Kalish 1985a; Levy forthcoming; Bass 1985).

Depending on the "level of awareness," the dying person is able to "negotiate" both the course of dying and the consequences of death.

Today, moreover, the problems and dilemmas inherent in the "management" of death have captured both popular and scientific attention. The reality of the extreme case is starkly clear. Many dying persons have given written or oral instructions that they do not want to go on living under certain conditions, often specified in "living wills." Similarly, many kin of nonsentient or hopelessly ill and suffering persons may not want to have the lives of such patients prolonged. In both instances doctors and lawyers play ambiguous but critical roles. It is, however, the "negotiation" that is of sociological interest. Norms designed to reduce the perplexities in wrenching decisions or to reassure the decision makers (including dying persons) are generally lacking. The need for relevant norms governing "the dying process" has been noted (Riley and Riley 1986), and the main considerations have been specified (Logue 1989). The U.S. Office of Technology Assessment (1987) and the Hastings Center (1987) have issued medical and ethical guidelines, respectively, on the use of life-sustaining procedures. In the 1970s sociologists developed research models for studying the social aspects of heroic operations and the treatment of nonsalvageable terminal patients (Fox and Swazey 1974; Crane 1975). Yet models necessary to the formation of norms capable of handling the "rights" and wishes of the various parties to the process of dying are still clearly needed. Today such models are yet to be developed, although human "rights" are being recognized as basic components in the development of social theory (Coleman 1990).

While a sociology of "dying" is yet to be developed, at least three aspects of norms and "rights" governing the dying process have been identified: timing and level of awareness, socialization to death, and quality of care. These suggest for sociological research a demanding agenda that should carry well into the twenty-first century.

[See also Long-Term Care; Social Gerontology; Widowhood.]

BIBLIOGRAPHY

Baker, Paul M. 1990 "Socialization After Death: The Might of the Living Dead." In Beth Hess and Elizabeth Markson, eds., *Growing Old in America.* New Brunswick, N.J.: Transaction Books.

Bass, David M. 1985 "The Hospice Ideology and Success of Hospice Care." *Research on Aging* 7:1.

Blauner, Robert 1966 "Death and Social Structure." *Psychiatry* 29:378–394.

Bowman, L. 1959 *The American Funeral: A Study in Guilt, Extravagance, and Sublimity.* Washington, D.C.: Public Affairs Press.

Callahan, Daniel 1987 *Setting Limits: Medical Goals in an Aging Society.* New York: Simon and Schuster.

Charmaz, K. C. 1986 *Social Reality of Death.* Reading, Mass.: Addison-Wesley.

Coleman, James P. 1990 *Foundations of Special Theory.* Cambridge, Mass.: Harvard University Press.

Counts, D. A., and D. C. Counts 1985 *Aging and Its Transformations: Moving Toward Death in Pacific Societies.* Lanham, MD.: University Press of America.

Crane, D. 1975 *The Sanctity of Social Life: Physicians' Treatment of Critically Ill Patients.* New York: Russell Sage Foundation.

Eliot, T. 1932. "The Bereaved Family." Special issue, *The Annals* 160.

Fox, R. C. 1980 "The Social Meaning of Death." *The Annals* 447.

——— 1981 "The Sting of Death in American Society." *Social Service Review* March: 42–59.

———, and T. P. Swazey 1974 *The Courage to Fail: A Social View of Organ Transplantation and Dialysis.* Chicago: University of Chicago Press.

Glaser, B. G., and A. L. Strauss 1965 *Awareness of Dying.* Chicago: Aldine.

——— 1968 *Time for Dying.* Chicago: Aldine.

Habenstein, R. W. 1968 "The Social Organization of Death." In D. L. Sills, ed. *International Encyclopedia of the Social Sciences.* New York: Macmillan and Free Press.

———, and M. W. Lamers 1963 *Funeral Customs the World Over.* Milwaukee, Wisc.: Bulfin.

Hastings Center, The 1987 *Guidelines on the Termination of Life-Sustaining Treatment and the Care of the Dying.* Bloomington: Indiana University Press.

Hyman, H. H. 1983 *Of Time and Widowhood: Nationwide Studies of Enduring Effects.* Durham, N.C.: Duke University Press.

Kalish, R. A. 1985a *Death, Grief and Caring Relationships.* Monterey, Calif.: Brooks/Cole.

——— 1985b "The Social Context of Death and Dying." In R. H. Binstock and E. Shanas, eds., *Handbook of Aging and the Social Sciences.* New York: Van Nostrand Reinhold.

Kearl, Michael C. 1989 *Endings: A Sociology of Death and Dying.* Oxford, Eng.: Oxford University Press.

Kübler-Ross, E. 1969 *On Death and Dying.* New York: Macmillan.

Levine, S., and N. A. Scotch 1970 "Dying as an Emergent Social Problem." In O. G. Brim, Jr., et al., eds., *The Dying Patient.* New York: Russell Sage Foundation.

Levy, Judith A. 1982 "The Staging of Negotiations Between Hospice and Medical Institutions." *Urban Life* 11.

——— Forthcoming "Hospice in an Aging Society." *Journal of Aging Studies.*

Lofland, L. 1978 *The Craft of Dying: The Modern Face of Death.* Beverly Hills, Calif.: Sage Publications.

Logue, B. 1989 *Death Control and the Elderly: The Growing Acceptability of Euthanasia.* Providence, R.I.: Population Studies and Training Center, Brown University.

Lopata, H. Z. 1973 *Widowhood in an American City.* Cambridge, Mass.: Schenkman.

——— 1979 *Women as Widows: Support Systems.* New York: Elsevier.

Mannheim, K. (1928) 1952 "The Problem of Generations." In P. Keeskemeti, ed., *Essays in Sociological Knowledge.* London: Routledge and Kegan Paul.

Marshall, V. W. 1980 *Last Chapters: A Sociology of Aging and Dying.* Belmont, Calif.: Wordsworth.

———, and J. A. Levy 1990 "Aging and Dying." In R. H. Binstock and L. George, eds., *Handbook of Aging and the Social Sciences,* 3rd ed. San Diego, Calif.: Academic Press.

Parsons, T. 1963 "Death in American Society: A Brief Working Paper." *American Behavioral Scientist.*

———, and V. W. Lidz 1967 "Death in American Society." In E. S. Shneidman, ed., *Essays in Self-Destruction.* New York: Science House.

Phillips, D. P. 1972 "Deathday and Birthday: An Unexpected Connection." In J. Tanur, ed., *Statistics: Guide to the Unknown.* San Francisco: Holden-Day.

——— 1974 "The Influence of Suggestion on Suicide: Substantive and Theoretical Implications of the Werther Effect." *American Sociological Review* 39:340–354.

———, and L. L. Carstensen 1986 "Clustering of Teenage Suicides After Television Stories About Suicide." *New England Journal of Medicine* 315 (11).

———, and K. A. Feldman 1973 "A Dip in Deaths Before Ceremonial Occasions: Some New Relationships Between Integration and Mortality." *American Sociological Review* 38:678–696.

———, and D. G. Smith 1990 "Postponement of Death Until Symbolically Meaningful Occasions." *Journal of the American Medical Association* 203 (14).

Pratt, L. V. 1981 "Business Temporal Norms and Bereavement Behavior." *American Sociological Review* 4:317–333.

Prior, Lindsay 1989 *The Social Organization of Death: Medical Discourses and Social Practices in Belfast.* New York: St. Martin's Press.

Riley, J. W., Jr. 1968 "Death and Bereavement." In D. L. Sills, ed., *International Encyclopedia of the Social Sciences.* New York: Macmillan and Free Press.

——— 1970 "What People Think About Death." In O. G. Brim, Jr., et al., eds., *The Dying Patient.* New York: Russell Sage Foundation.

——— 1983 "Dying and the Meanings of Death: Sociological Inquiries." *Annual Review of Sociology* 9:191–216.

Riley, M. W. 1978 "Aging, Social Change and the Power of Ideas." *Daedalus* 107:39–52.

———, A. Foner, and J. Waring 1988 "Sociology of Age." In N. J. Smelser, ed., *Handbook of Sociology.* Newbury Park, Calif.: Sage Publications.

———, and J. W. Riley, Jr. 1986 "Longevity and Social Structure: The Added Years," *Daedalus* 115:51–75.

Sills, David L. (ed.) 1968 *International Encyclopedia of the Social Sciences.* New York: Macmillan and Free Press.

Smelser, Neil J. (ed). 1988 *Handbook of Sociology.* Newbury Park, Calif.: Sage Publications.

Stroebe, W., and M. E. Stroebe 1987 *Bereavement and Health: The Psychological and Physical Consequences of Partner Loss.* Cambridge: Cambridge University Press.

Sudnow, D. 1967 *Passing On: The Social Organization of Dying.* Englewood Cliffs, N.J.: Prentice-Hall.

U.S. Congress, Office of Technology Assessment 1987 *Life-Sustaining Technologies and the Elderly.* Washington, D.C.: U.S. Government Printing Office.

Warner, W. L. 1959 *The Living and the Dead.* New Haven, Conn.: Yale University Press.

Wasserman, I. M. 1989 "The Effects of War and Alcohol Consumption Patterns on Suicide: United States (1910–1953)." *Social Forces* 66:513–533.

– JOHN W. RILEY, JR.

DECOLONIZATION

Decolonization refers to a polity's movement from a status of political dependence or subordination to a status of formal autonomy or sovereignty. In modern usage, it is generally assumed that the imperial or metropolitan center is physically separated from the dependency and that the two areas are made up of racially distinct populations. The term is almost always used to refer specifically to the disintegration of Western overseas empires and their replacement by sovereign states in the Americas, Asia, and Africa.

There are several routes by which decolonization can take place. Most frequently, the dependency becomes a new sovereign state, a political entity recognized in the international arena as independent of other states and as possessing final jurisdiction over a defined territory and population. Less often, decolonization may occur through the dependency's full incorporation into an existing polity, such that it is no longer separate and subordinate.

It is often unclear when (or whether) decolonization has occurred.

It is often unclear when (or whether) decolonization has occurred. Puerto Rico's relation to the United States can be described as one of colonial dependency or as free association. In the 1960s, Portugal claimed to have no colonies, only overseas territories that had been formally incorporated into a unitary Portuguese state (Nogueira 1963). And where political relations are not contested, the absence of overt conflict makes it difficult to know when sovereignty has been achieved. For example, arguments can be made for dating Canadian independence at 1867, 1919, 1926, or 1931.

This article will briefly review the pattern of decolonization in the modern Western experience and outline some central arguments about causes and consequences.

Historical Overview

Virtually all of the decolonization of Western overseas empires occurred in two historical eras (Bergesen and Schoenberg 1980). The major American colonies became independent during the late eighteenth and early nineteenth centuries. The mid-twentieth century witnessed a more rapid and complete wave of decolonization worldwide (Strang 1990). The types of colonies in existence in each period and the nature of the decolonization process vary greatly across the two periods (Fieldhouse 1966).

The first wave of decolonization began with the independence of Britain's thirteen Continental colonies as the United States of America. The French Revolution touched off a slave uprising that led ultimately to the independence of the French colony of Saint Domingue as Haiti. Portuguese Brazil and Spanish Central and South America became independent after the Napoleonic Wars, which had cut Latin America off from the Iberian peninsula.

While the first period of decolonization was limited to the Americas, twentieth-century decolonization was global in scope. It included the independence of most of the Indian subcontinent, Southeast Asia and Australasia, the Middle East, Africa, and the Caribbean. Between the world wars, some of Britain's settler colonies and a number of loosely held protectorates became fully sovereign. Soon after World War II, the major Asian colonies—India, Indonesia, Indochina, and the Philippines—achieved independence. The pace of change rapidly accelerated during the 1960s, which saw the decolonization of nearly all of Africa. By the 1980s nearly all major colonies had become independent or had been fully incorporated into sovereign states.

One fundamental difference between the two eras of decolonization has to do with who sought independence. Early American decolonizations were creole revolutions, as the descendants of European settlers sought political autonomy from the "mother country." The American Revolution and the Spanish Wars for Independence were political but not social revolutions. Slave revolt in Haiti provided the sole instance of destruction of settler rule (to the horror of rebels and loyalists elsewhere).

By contrast, twentieth-century decolonization was generally rooted in indigenous rather than creole movements for independence, as decolonization came to mean freedom from racially alien rule. After World War II, settler minorities generally opposed decolonization, since national independence spelled an end to their privileged economic, political, and social position. Only in South Africa did a racist minority regime survive decolonization.

A second basic difference between the first and second periods of decolonization lies in the degree of violence involved. Early decolonization in the Americas was won through military combat between settler and imperial forces. Wars for independence raged in Britain's thirteen Continental colonies, in Spanish Central and South America, and in Haiti. Only in Portuguese Brazil was independence achieved without a fight, largely because Brazil was several times richer and more populous than Portugal.

During the twentieth century, colonies like Indochina, Indonesia, Algeria, and Angola won their independence after protracted military struggle. But these were the exceptions to the rule. Most colonies became independent with little or no organized violence between the imperial state and colonial nationalists. In much of Africa, imperial powers virtually abandoned colonies at the first sign of popular opposition to the colonial regime. By the mid-1960s, decolonization had become a rather routine activity for many imperial powers, often achieved through institutionalized expressions of popular will (such as plebiscites).

Causes of Decolonization

A variety of arguments have been developed about factors contributing to decolonization. While most arguments have dealt with a single dependency or empire, there have been a number of recent efforts to develop explicitly comparative analyses (see Emerson 1960; Grimal 1978; Lang 1975; Smith 1978; Bergesen and Schoenberg 1980; Albertini 1982; Anderson 1983; Holland 1985; Boswell 1989; and Strang 1990).

Decolonization is often seen as the result of structural change in the dependency itself. Settler colonies are thought to undergo a natural process of maturation, well expressed in the physiocratic maxim that colonies are like fruit that fall from the tree when they are ripe. Indigenous populations are also importantly affected by contact with Western economic and political structures.

In both kinds of colonies, the specific condition that seems to precipitate decolonization is the emergence of peripheral nationalism. Settler colonies generally began as economic corporations chartered by European states. Non-Western peoples were generally tribal or segmental societies prior to colonization, and imperial structures were fundamentally dependent on the collaboration of indigenous elites (Robinson 1972). Decolonization required a new vision of the colonial dependency as a national society (Diamond 1958; Anderson 1983).

Colonial powers contributed unintentionally to the formulation of a national vision. They did so partly by spurring the rise of new social groups—indigenous bourgeois, landless workers, civil servants, teachers—who proved to be the carriers of colonial nationalism and independence. Perhaps most important, contact with the colonial power exposed indigenous groups to the notions and institutions of the Western nation-state while simultaneously denying them participation rights. Settlers, of course, carried notions of these rights with them (see Bailyn 1967 and Greene 1986 on the ideological origins of the American Revolution). Under these conditions, nationalism was a weapon easily turned on its creators (Emerson 1960).

While pressures for decolonization invariably stem from the dependency itself, the response of the metropolitan power plays a crucial role in the outcome. The classic contrast in imperial policy is between British "association" and French "assimilation" (though parallel contrasts between the imperial policies of the United States and Portugal are even more striking). The British empire was administratively structured around indirect rule and local autonomy, which permitted considerable flexibility in the imperial reaction to pressures for decolonization. By contrast, the French aimed at the assimilation of their colonies into a unitary republic, which led to firmer resistance to decolonization.

In some instances, the metropolitan state was simply unable to suppress pressures for decolonization, despite a full-fledged military commitment to do so. Early American decolonization nearly always had this character. In the twentieth century, the major imperial states emerged from World War II as second-rate powers. At critical junctures, these states found themselves unable to project sufficient military power abroad to control events: the British in Suez, the French in Indochina and Algeria, the Dutch in Indonesia.

Finally, several systemic factors or processes may be linked to decolonization. One is the presence of a state that is economically and politically dominant on the world stage. It has been argued that such a "hegemonic" state tends to create a global free-market system rather than paying the overhead costs of empire (Krasner 1976; Bergesen and Schoenberg 1980; Boswell 1989). This argument has much in common with Gallagher and Robinson's (1953) notion of an "imperialism of free trade," which is preferable to direct administration. Both Britain and the United States favored decolonization during their periods of global hegemony.

The contagiousness of independence is most apparent in the rapidity with which decolonization swept across Africa.

A second systemic factor is the contagiousness of decolonization. The American Revolution served as a model for insurrection in both Haiti and Latin America. After World War II, the independence of India, Indochina, and Indonesia had a substantial impact on colonized peoples everywhere. The contagiousness of independence is most apparent in the rapidity with which decolonization swept across Africa, where thirty-three colonies became independent between 1957 and 1966.

Finally, the content of global political understandings and discourse plays a critical role in decolonization (Strang 1990). After 1945, the two superpowers were ideologically opposed to colonialism, though each accused the other of imperialism. Even the major imperial powers (Great Britain, France, the Netherlands) found it difficult to reconcile colonial possessions with the political ideas and institutions of the national polity. As a result, the rationale of colonialism crumbled under pressure, with imperialism being formally denounced by the United Nations in 1960.

These understandings lend great political importance to the distinction between a dependency and a territory integrated into the nation-state. A sharp distinction is generally drawn between the overseas empires of European states and "internal colonies" such as Wales and Scotland. While the empirical basis for such a distinction is shaky, it has real implications. Identification as a colonial dependency greatly increases the chances of mobilizing internal and external support for indigenous nationalism; it also vastly reduces the compulsion that the metropolitan state can legitimately bring to bear.

Consequences of Decolonization

The issue that dominates most discussion of decolonization concerns its implications for more general notions of international domination or exploitation. Dependency-world systems theorists view decolonization as producing change in the form but not the content of core-periphery relations (Chase-Dunn and Rubinson 1979). The argument is that contact between more and less developed economies reinforces the differential between them, even in the absence of explicit political controls. Dependence on foreign capital has been argued to slow long-term economic growth (Bornschier, Chase-Dunn, and Rubinson 1978) and more generally to shape the political and economic structure of the dependent society (Amin 1973; Cardoso and Faletto 1979).

On the other hand, it seems clear that decolonization involves a fundamental shift in the structures regulating international exchange, especially in the post-World War II era. Contemporary states are armed with widely accepted rights to control economic activity within their boundaries, including rights to nationalize foreign-owned industries and renegotiate contracts with multinational corporations (Krasner 1978; Lipson 1985). Third-world nations mobilize visibly around these rights (Krasner 1985), and the negative impact of economic dependency seems to decrease when the peripheral state is strong (Delacroix and Ragin 1981).

While notions of dependency and neocolonialism are the subject of vigorous debate, the most straightforward consequence of decolonization is its central role in expanding the originally Western, and now global, interstate system. Most of the present members of the United Nations became sovereign through decolonization. And historically, the political units emerging from decolonization have been strikingly stable. Few ex-dependencies have been recolonized or annexed or have merged or dissolved (Jackson and Rosberg 1982; Strang 1991). Against much expectation, decolonization has produced states that appear to be relatively permanent elements of the international economic and political order.

[See also Imperialism and Colonialism; Industrialization in Less Developed Countries.]

BIBLIOGRAPHY

Albertini, Rudolf von 1982 *Decolonization: The Administration and Future of the Colonies 1919–1960.* New York: Holmes and Meier.

Amin, Samir 1973 *Neo-Colonialism in West Africa.* London: Monthly Review Press.

Anderson, Benedict 1983 *Imagined Communities: Reflections on the Origins and Spread of Nationalism.* London: Verso.

Bailyn, Bernard 1967 *The Ideological Origins of the American Revolution.* Cambridge, Mass.: Harvard University Press.

Bergesen, Albert, and Ronald Schoenberg 1980 "The Long Waves of Colonial Expansion and Contraction 1415–1970." In A. Bergesen, ed., *Studies of the Modern World System.* New York. Academic Press.

Bornschier, Volker, Christopher Chase-Dunn, and Richard Rubinson 1978 "Cross-National Evidence of the Effects of Foreign Investment and Aid on Economic Growth and Inequality: A Survey of Findings and a Reanalysis." *American Journal of Sociology* 84:651–683.

Boswell, Terry 1989 "Colonial Empires and the Capitalist World-Economy: A Time Series Analysis of Colonization, 1640–1960." *American Sociological Review* 54:180–196.

Cardoso, Fernando H., and Enzo Faletto 1979 *Dependency and Development in Latin America.* Berkeley: University of California Press.

Chase-Dunn, Christopher, and Richard Rubinson 1979 "Toward a Structural Perspective on the World-System." *Politics and Society* 7:453–476.

Delacroix, Jacques, and Charles C. Ragin 1981 "Structural Blockage: A Cross-National Study of Economic Dependency, State Efficacy, and Underdevelopment." *American Journal of Sociology* 86:1,311–1,347.

Diamond, Sigmund 1958 "From Organization to Society." *American Journal of Sociology* 63:457–475.

Emerson, Rupert 1960 *From Empire to Nation.* Cambridge, Mass.: Harvard University Press.

Fieldhouse, David K. 1966 *The Colonial Empires.* New York: Dell.

Gallagher, John, and Ronald Robinson 1953 "The Imperialism of Free Trade." *Economic History Review,* 2nd. ser., 6:1–15.

Greene, Jack P. 1986 *Peripheries and Center: Constitutional Development in the Extended Polities of the British Empire and the United States 1607–1788.* Athens: University of Georgia Press.

Grimal, Henri 1978 *Decolonization.* London: Routledge and Kegan Paul.

Holland, R. F. 1985 *European Decolonization 1918–1981.* New York: St. Martin's Press.

Jackson, Robert, and Carl Rosberg 1982 "Why Africa's Weak States Persist: The Empirical and the Juridical in Statehood." *World Politics* 35:1–24.

Krasner, Stephen D. 1976 "State Power and the Structure of International Trade." *World Politics* 28:317–343.

——— 1978 *Defending the National Interest.* Princeton, N.J.: Princeton University Press.

——— 1985 *Structural Conflict.* Berkeley: University of California Press.

Lang, James 1975 *Conquest and Commerce: Spain and England in the Americas.* New York: Academic Press.

Lipson, Charles 1985 *Standing Guard: Protecting Foreign Capital in the Nineteenth and Twentieth Centuries.* Berkeley: University of California Press.

Nogueira, Franco 1963 *The United Nations and Portugal: A Study of Anti-Colonialism.* London: Sidgwick and Jackson.

Robinson, Ronald 1972 "Non-European Foundations of European Imperialism: Sketch for a Theory of Collaboration." In R. Owen and B. Sutcliffe, eds., *Studies in the Theory of Imperialism.* Bristol: G. B. Longman.

Smith, Tony 1978 "A Comparative Study of French and British Decolonization." *Comparative Studies in Society and History* 20:70–102.

Strang, David 1990 "From Dependency to Sovereignty: An Event History Analysis of Decolonization." *American Sociological Review* 55:846–860.

——— 1991 "Anomaly and Commonplace in European Political Expansion: Realist and Institutional Accounts." *International Organization* 45:142–161.

– DAVID STRANG

DEMOCRACY

Democracy is one of the most studied and disputed topics in the social sciences. It has drawn such attention because it has come to be a value with considerable legitimacy, shared by many individuals worldwide. As a result, considerable resources have been devoted to understanding the sources, effects, strengths, and weaknesses of democracy. In developing an understanding of this research on democracy it is best to begin by explicitly considering how democracy is defined.

What constitutes a minimum level of control over decision making by members for a system to be thought of as democratic?

At the core of most discussions of democracy is the common view that democracy is a method of governance or decision making for groups, organizations, or governments in which the members of a group, organization, or polity participate, directly or indirectly, in the decision making of that entity. Further, members participate in decision making to such an extent that they are considered to govern or control that group, organization, or polity. In short, democracy is a system of governance in which members control group decision making.

Yet such a definition leaves considerable room for contention. Two central issues are most often examined: What does, or should, constitute a minimum level of control over decision making by members for a system to be thought of as democratic? Who are, or should, be considered members of the polity? The fact that these issues are matters not only of empirical observation but also of moral and political philosophy makes the analysis of democracy particularly difficult.

Three factors add to the difficulty of approaching democracy as a field of research in the social sciences. First, theoretical and normative definitions are often not fully specified in the analysis of democracy. This in turn can lead to considerable confusion. Democratic systems of governance can be characterized by many attributes—frequency of member participation, the form of member participation, and so forth. Evaluating the extent to which a particular system of governance is democratic, then, involves making decisions about which attributes are essential to a democratic system. Where a definition is not fully examined, the question of whether a political regime is or is not democratic often leads to conflating theoretical definition and empirical analysis (Macpherson 1962).

A second factor increasing the difficulty of this subject matter is that democracy is a system of governance found in many different kinds of collectivities, including states, formal organizations, and informal groups. It is thus necessary to be cautious in applying models, findings, and relationships that hold in the analysis of democracy for one unit of analysis to other units of analysis. It is not sufficient, for example, to assume that what causes democratic regimes to be effective at a nation-state level also functions in a similar manner in formal organizations.

Finally, democracy is a complex subject because democracy is more than just an outcome variable. Social scientists are interested in democracy not just for its own sake but also because it is thought to be associated with other critical issues, including the efficiency or effectiveness of organizations and nation-states, levels of income inequality and social stratification, and individual liberty.

While the difficulties of this subject can be daunting, much innovative work has been done in this field. It is best to begin in laying out the state of knowledge regarding democracy with the range of theoretical conceptions of democracy that predominate. Sociologists have in this regard relied heavily on ideas and arguments advanced by "democratic theorists," scholars who have concentrated on the moral basis of systems of governance. The first theoretical and definitional issue is: Who is or should be members or citizens of a democratic polity? Most systems commonly thought to be democratic have through the ages excluded some portion of those subject to the will of the democracy from participation in the decision-making process. Such exclusion has occurred on the basis of race, sex, income, relationship to property, criminal status, mental health, religion, age, and other characteristics. While use of many of these categories as a justification for excluding individuals from participation has declined in recent times, others remain, and there is continuing disagreement about the moral and political bases for excluding or including specific groups. Guest workers in Western Europe, for example, are subject to the action of the state on a long-term basis and yet remain excluded from full political participation in those states (Brubaker 1989). At the level of the organization, the movement toward increasing the power of corporate "stakeholders" over decision making by large business corporations is another example. Several theorists have argued that where the lives of individuals are influenced by the decisions of large business corporations, even though those individuals are neither employees, contractors, or shareholders, they should have a say in those key decisions (Nader and Green 1976). This movement is in part motivated and legitimated by democratic claims that value individuals having a say in decisions that affect their lives.

The second and more fundamental definitional issue concerns what should constitute the form of influence and participation that individuals have in decision making in a democratic system. A traditional view has long been that a representative system is appropriate for allowing participation in decision making. Representative democracy is that form of governance in which members of the organization or polity exercise their control over the organization through the regular election of members of a decision-making body. For example, the United States is a representative democracy in which citizens directly elect senators and representatives to the federal Congress, which in turn makes political decisions about the actions of the federal government. Theorists since the Enlightenment have argued that representative democracy is an appropriate means for conveying participation in decision making in large-size organizations, where individuals are thought not to be able to participate in all decisions (Hobbes 1986; Rousseau 1968; Locke 1980; Mill 1958).

Representative democracy has been attacked by critics who argue that in such democracies influence is exercised over the decision-making process in the government or organization not just through voting but also through the exertion of undue influence in the process of choosing representatives, and through extra-electoral influence over representatives themselves. Hence, these critics argue, it is futile to argue that some government or organization is fully democratic simply because voting is the key procedural element in the decision-making process, when "undue" influence can be exercised, either by swaying votes; through various forms of media or propaganda; or, at the level of the representatives themselves, through postelectoral influence over legislative activity. Such arguments are also raised in the context of democracy in formal organizations, as when larger stockholders or a board of directors and management may be able to influence the decision-making process through control over access to critical information. Indeed, early American legislators sought to reduce this tendency toward oligarchy in business corporations by specifying, in corporate charters, restrictions that limited the maximum number of votes that any single shareholder could control.

A second criticism of representative democracy as a form of governance concerns the problem of oligarchical tendencies on the part of the representatives themselves. First articulated by Mosca, the argument reached its fullest form in the work of Robert Michels (Mosca 1939). The argument is that in any large organization (and hence in any nation-state) a democratic system of governance inevitably leads to the rise of an oligarchy, and worse, to an oligarchy whose leaders have interests that differ from those of the ordinary citizens or members. Oligarchy arises because the organization needs experienced, skilled leaders. Experience in leadership, however, also tends to give leaders access to key organizational resources that are valuable in returning that leadership to office. And as leaders remain in office over an extended time, their interests and attitudes are likely to diverge from those of members, in part because leaders start to have different life chances from the members of organizations. Hence Michels, while arguing that formal organization is necessary for social life, and especially for politics, also believes that democracy in such organization is essentially impossible (Michels 1966).

Joseph Schumpeter and Robert Dahl have defended democratic systems in response to these critiques, and they have done so in part by reconsidering theoretical conceptions of democracy. For them, a key element in determining whether a system is democratic is the extent to which that system remains open to nonelectoral forms of influence by interest groups. The forms of influence and participation that constitute and define the presence of a democratic system are not limited to participation via the immediate electoral system but also include influence and participation external to the electoral system, such as lobbying and mobilization of protest. If a variety of interest groups are able to exercise power and influence in the system through a variety of means, then the system, with all its flaws, can be considered democratic (Schumpeter 1976; Dahl 1961). This view responds to both criticisms of representative government: extra-electoral influence becomes valued, because it is a means of democratic influence open to all interests; and organized extra-electoral influence becomes valued, even if oligarchical, because the multiplicity of interests reduces the costs of oligarchy.

One weakness of the pluralist view of democracy is that not all groups in society may be able effectively to form organizations to defend their interests. Mancur Olson has argued that because of problems associated with the distribution of collective goods, collective actors may not arise to represent groups with large numbers of members. The core of his argument is that if such interest-based organizations representing large numbers of individuals are to be created and maintained, special incentives must be made available to attract members to these groups. Groups representing weak and powerless individuals may be unable to supply such special incentives. Olson's challenge to the likelihood of individuals forming groups under these circumstances is one that sociologists have focused attention on for some time (Olson 1971). Recent work by Pam Oliver and others suggests that social movements are more likely to be formed as interest groups grow in size (Oliver and Marwell 1988). These criticisms of Olson's analysis of the collective action problem may actually serve to strengthen the pluralist account of democracy.

Yet many theorists remain critical of the pluralist account (Domhoff 1967). As a response to the pluralist arguments, many researchers again returned in the 1970s and 1980s to the question of what democracy should mean. The argument is both that greater participation in decision making is possible than is usually the practice, and that the purpose of democracy as a system of governance has been misconstrued. Rather than just being about democratic control of decision making, theorists such as Finley and Pateman, in examining both the classical Greek case and the neoclassical theory of democracy, argue that democratic systems are also about creating educated members, who are better able to comprehend the decision-making process. As members participate in decision making, they learn more about the criteria that need to be used in

The United States is a representative democracy in which citizens can directly elect members of decision-making bodies. (Philip Gould/Corbis)

effective decision making and thus become even better at evaluating the choice of representatives in a representative democracy (Finley 1985; Pateman 1970). Sociologists also moved to consider empirical examples of organizations more oriented toward participatory management. Burawoy and Kanter, for example, have attempted to show that democratic systems of management are more broadly possible than had previously been expected, although the conditions under which such systems of decision making can be created and maintained remain under debate (Burawoy 1979; Kanter 1984).

Not all groups in society may be able effectively to form organizations to defend their interests.

These issues, concerning the nature, purposes, and limits of democratic control, form the center of social science treatments of democracy. Yet democracy is also an important topic because it is associated with other issues.

One such central issue has been a focus of research since de Tocqueville and has to do with the relationship between democracy and equality. More recently, research has been centered around this specific question: Does democracy promote or retard income inequality in nation-states? Key research has been performed in this area by Parkin and by Bollen. This is an extremely contentious issue, and is as yet not fully resolved (Parkin 1976; Bollen 1985). A second such question, often raised in the context of formal organizations, is the relationship between democracy and effectiveness. Put more pointedly: Can democratic organizations be effective? This question has been raised for both political organizations and economic organizations (Lenin 1932; Piven and Cloward 1977; Blumberg 1968). As yet there seems to be no definitive answer, and the issue certainly merits more attention. Finally, an important question is: What are the conditions under which democracy arises and fails in nation-states? Also under considerable debate, some of the most interesting work in modern sociology is related to this issue (Moore 1966; Skocpol 1979; Hannan and Carroll 1981).

While these research questions have dominated sociological research about democracy in recent years, other questions deserve attention. For example, the relationship between democracy and individual liberty has not attracted much current sociological attention, yet has been a central concern ever since theorists first turned their attention to the subject (Burke 1987). Further, questions such as those asked above might also be examined more thoroughly at different levels of analysis. For example: What are the sources of democratic governance in formal organizations? And what are the sources of the effectiveness of democratic government in nation-states? These and other questions suggest that considerable research remains to be done on democracy, one of the most important subjects in sociology.

[See also Capitalism.]

BIBLIOGRAPHY

Blumberg, Paul 1968 *Industrial Democracy: The Sociology of Participation.* New York: Schocken Books.

Bollen, Kenneth A., and Robert W. Jackman 1985 "Political Democracy." *American Sociological Review* 50:438–457.

Brubaker, William Rogers 1989 *Immigration and the Politics of Citizenship in Europe and North America.* Lanham, Md.: University Press of America; German Marshall Fund of the United States.

Burawoy, Michael 1979 *Manufacturing Consent.* Chicago: University of Chicago Press.

Burke, Edmund 1987 *Reflections on the Revolution in France.* Indianapolis: Hackett Publishers.

Dahl, Robert A. 1961 *Who Governs?* New Haven, Conn.: Yale University Press.

——— 1989 *Democracy and Its Critics.* New Haven, Conn.: Yale University Press.

Domhoff, G. William 1967 *Who Rules America?* Englewood Cliffs, N.J.: Prentice-Hall.

Finley, M. I. 1985 *Democracy: Ancient and Modern.* London: Hogarth Press.

Hannan, Michael T., and Glenn R. Carroll 1981 "Dynamics of Formal Political Structure: An Event-History Analysis." *American Sociological Review* 46:19–35.

Hobbes, Thomas 1986 *Leviathan.* Hammondsworth, Eng.: Penguin.

Kanter, Rosabeth M. 1984 *The Change Masters.* New York: Simon and Schuster.

Lenin V. I. 1932 *State and Revolution.* New York: International Publishers.

Lipset, Seymour Martin, Martin A. Trow, and James S. Coleman 1959 *Union Democracy.* New York: Free Press.

Locke, John 1980 *Second Treatise of Government.* Indianapolis: Hackett Publishers.

Macpherson, C. B. 1962 *The Political Theory of Possessive Individualism: Hobbes to Locke.* Oxford: Clarendon Press.

Michels, Robert 1966 *Political Parties.* New York: The Free Press.

Mill, John Stuart 1958 *Considerations on Representative Government.* New York: Liberal Arts Press.

Moore, Barrington 1966 *The Social Origins of Dictatorship and Democracy.* Boston: Beacon Press.

Mosca, Gaetano 1938 *The Ruling Class (Elementi di Science Politica).* New York: McGraw-Hill.

Nader, Ralph, and Mark Green 1976 *Taming the Giant Corporation.* New York: W. W. Norton.

Oliver, Pamela E., and Gerald Marwell 1988 "The Paradox of Group Size in Collective Action." *American Sociological Review* 53:2–8.

Olson, Mancur 1971 *The Logic of Collective Action.* Cambridge, Mass.: Harvard University Press.

Parkin, Frank 1976 *Class Inequality and Political Order.* New York: Praeger Publishers.

Pateman, Carole 1970 *Participation and Democratic Theory.* Cambridge, Eng.: Cambridge University Press.

Piven, Frances Fox, and Richard Cloward 1977 *Poor People's Movements.* New York: Pantheon.

Rothschild-Whitt, Joyce, and A. Whitt 1986 *Work Without Bosses: Conditions and Dilemmas of Organizational Democracy in Grassroots Cooperatives.* New York: Cambridge University Press.

Rousseau, Jean-Jacques 1968 *The Social Contract.* Baltimore: Penguin.

Schumpeter, Joseph A. 1976 *Capitalism, Socialism, and Democracy.* New York: Harper and Row.

Skocpol, Theda 1979 *States and Social Revolution.* Cambridge, Eng.: Cambridge University Press.

Tocqueville, Alexis de 1969 *Democracy in America,* ed. J. P. Jayer. Garden City, N.Y.: Anchor Books.

– ANDREW L. CREIGHTON

DEVIANCE

The word *deviance*—today a familiar member of both professional and lay vocabularies—entered the English language only in the early 1940s in *Webster's Ninth Collegiate Dictionary,* quite possibly as an invention of sociologists. What is now known as the study of deviance, a vibrant branch of sociology that attracts large numbers of students and researchers, dates from that period. The background to this linguistic addition reveals much about the modern study of deviant behavior.

There has always been a need in sociology to distinguish crime from the deviance that runs counter to local moral norms but that is not virtually or actually a violation of criminal law. Depending on the community, noncriminal deviance may consist of, among other acts, nudism, mental disorder, religious aberration, living on skid row, certain political belief systems, excessive gambling and consumption of alcohol, and certain sexual and drug use patterns. Where they are not considered criminal or otherwise a significant threat, these acts have in common their tolerance by much of the local population. When they are ostensibly illegal, tolerance is evident in the systematic failure to apply the law, because it is vague, difficult to enforce, or of low police priority (Stebbins 1988, pp. 3–4).

From approximately 1880 to 1940, sociologists held a patently moralistic view of deviance, both criminal and noncriminal, referring to it in such loaded terms as "social pathology," "antisociality," and "social problems" (Lemert 1951, p. 3; Giddings 1896, p. 72). In the 1930s, during the rise of so-called scientific sociology and its value-neutrality, sustaining a censorious outlook on tolerable, noncriminal deviance became increasingly untenable. It is likely, too, that the range of tolerated acts and beliefs had expanded as a result of urbanization (Karp et al. 1977, chap. 5).

Whether by design or by accident, scientific language in the area began to change, moving first to the cold, unemotional notion of statistical deviation from the average. Robert K. Merton (1938), in what is possibly the first exposition of modern deviance theory, discussed "deviate conduct," "deviate behavior," and "deviation from normal behavior." Shortly thereafter, Merl E. Bonney (1941) described and analyzed a variety of "social deviates."

By the end of the 1940s, the statistical model had lost its appeal. Merton (1949), as part of the first revision of his 1938 statement, replaced the earlier terminology with "deviant" and "deviant behavior." Two years later, Edwin M. Lemert (1951) had partially made the same transition, writing both about deviation and about deviants and deviant behavior.

Why this second change? One can only speculate, but it is possible that Merton sensed the inherent inadequacy of the statistical model: Most deviance, whether criminal or noncriminal, is categorical rather than continuous—that is, for sociologists and the lay public alike, being deviant is a matter of identity, of being or not being homeless, alcoholic, mentally disordered, or politically radical. The statistical model assumes a continuum, as found in the measurement of intelligence or eyesight. At any rate, by the early 1950s sociology had arrived at a valid, nonjudgmental conception of what was once known as antisociality or social pathology. The modern speciality of the sociology of deviance had been launched.

Anomie and Labeling

Although they had important precursors, Merton and Lemert are commonly seen as the fathers of the two main approaches to the study of deviance: anomie and labeling. These two men and their contributions remain prominent to this day. Labeling theory still guides most research and theorizing in this area, whereas anomie is presented in textbooks as an important, albeit partial, explanation of deviance, and one that has engendered little research of late.

Merton's main precursor was Emile Durkheim, who developed (in French) the concept of anomie to help explain his findings on suicide (Durkheim 1951). Merton reworked his ideas into an explanation of deviance in general. We draw here from Merton's second and final revision of his 1938 statement (Merton 1957). The theoretical elaborations made to it by others are mentioned to the extent that they are still regarded as important.

The word *anomie* is conventionally translated into English as "normlessness." Unfortunately, the translation is woefully inadequate and therefore an impediment to understanding Merton's ideas (not to mention those of Durkheim). According to the French dictionary *Le Petit Robert 1* (1989 update), anomie is the absence of social and legal organization. An anomic society is hardly normless; it is in the course of reorganization, where old norms (values, relations, etc.) no longer apply and new norms (values, relations, etc.) are emerging.

Merton noted that "strain" sometimes develops between the cultural structure and the social structure of the society—that is, there is a discrepancy between the social organization and goals of the society and the capacities of many of its members to reach the goals. Though he believed his theory applied to other culturally accepted goals as well, Merton (1957, p. 181) limited his analysis to the pursuit of success goals of a materialistic nature. This orientation, he said, was particularly characteristic of American society. Although he never clarified what he meant by the "social structure" or "capacity" or "institutionalized means" by which these goals are reached, it is evident that he was referring to occupational roles.

Merton recognized that a disturbance in the equilibrium of society can lead to deviance. He believed that this disturbance stems from the pursuit of goals that lie beyond personal economic means. For those affected in this manner, society is anomic.

Where the rebellion is small and concentrated among those with little power, subgroups may form that develop into an integrated society in their own right.

Merton suggested that people adapt to anomie in one of five "modes." An adaptation is deviant when it is expressed in behavior that departs from cultural goals or institutional means of reaching those goals or both. Table 1 depicts the five modes of adaptation identified by Merton and how they relate as deviance or conformity to the goals and means. The first of these modes, *conformity,* plays a negligible role in the theory. It is not deviance. It is most prevalent when the society is stable, when there is little or no anomie.

As the strain between cultural structure and social structure increases—as anomie increases—additional (deviant) adaptations are made by some members of the community—that is, most people continue to conform in these circumstances, but the number grows of those who do not. *Innovation* is the deviant adaptation springing from the acceptance of cultural goals and the rejection of institutionalized means of attaining them. People are most likely to make innovations in a society where success goals are ideally open to all members, but in actuality are restricted or even completely closed to some of them. The incentives for success are provided by the established values of the culture. Yet certain barriers are present, such as educational requirements, monetary resources, and family background, which block achievements. In this situation, says Merton, pressure increases for the use of illegitimate means. This mode of adaptation, when implemented in response to monetary goals, typically manifests itself as crime or vice, particularly among those in the manual labor and lower white-collar occupations.

TABLE 1

A TYPOLOGY OF MODES OF INDIVIDUAL ADAPTATION

Modes of Adaptation	Cultural Goals	Institutionalized Means
Conformity	+	+
Innovation	+	–
Ritualism	–	+
Retreatism	–	–
Rebellion	±	±

\+ = acceptance
– = rejection
± = rejection followed by acceptance of new goals and means
Source: Adapted from Merton 1957, p. 140.

When an individual scales down or even abandons a culturally approved goal but continues to abide almost compulsively by the means of attaining that goal, he or she has employed *ritualism* as an adaptation to anomie. By diluting achievement goals to manageable size, this person gains security, whereas high ambitions invite possible frustration and failure. The rulebound bureaucrat was the principal example used by Merton. He observed that this sort of adaptation is most likely to occur in lower-middle-class settings where conformity is a strong motive and where social climbing is less likely to be successful than in other parts of the middle class.

Merton believed that *retreatism,* the mode of adaptation where both cultural goals and means of attainment are rejected, is probably the least common of the five modes. Some of the behavior of psychotics, pariahs, tramps, chronic drunkards, and drug addicts can be interpreted as retreatist. Originally, both the goals and the means were internalized, but these individuals found the way to them blocked. Internalization of conventional values prevents the active innovation of illegitimate means or goals. Instead, the individual only abandons the legitimate means and goals and retreats in a deviant manner. Although such deviants may have contact with others who share their proclivities, Merton held that this adaptation is essentially private. One noteworthy, albeit generally nondeviant, variation of retreatism is found in apathy, indifference, cynicism, and disenchantment.

The final mode of adaptation, *rebellion,* consists of the rejection of established goals and means of the society for those of a new social system. Where the rebellion is small and concentrated among those with little power, subgroups may form that, although isolated from the rest of the community, develop into an integrated society in their own right—for instance, a religious commune. Still, a rebellion involving a substantial number of the members of a society can culminate in a full-scale revolution. The final result here is modification of the established cultural and social structures.

Richard A. Cloward (1959) extended Merton's theory by adding several propositions about the illegitimate opportunities open to those seeking a deviant adaptation to anomie. It was evident to him that there are variations in the availability of illegitimate means, just as Merton had observed a similar variation in legitimate means. This availability of illegitimate means is controlled by the same criteria that control the availability of conventional means. Both are limited and both are differentially open to people in the society according to their positions in the social structure.

Cloward is more specific in his definition of means than Merton. The term "means" implies two things: "First, that there are appropriate environments for the acquisition of the values and skills associated with the performance of a particular role; and second, that the individual has opportunities to discharge the role once he has been prepared. The term, therefore, subsumes both *learning structures and opportunity structures*" (1959, p. 168; emphasis in original). Some people encounter learning and opportunity structures that lead to deviance, whereas others do not. This contingency is partly explained by Edwin H. Sutherland's theory of differential association (Sutherland and Cressey 1978, pp. 80–82)—that is, youth selectively associate with other youth. If they choose to interact with those who are deviant, the first often learn to enjoy the deviance of the second.

Anomie theory offers a causal explanation of deviance, both criminal and noncriminal. Its focus is chiefly on the macrosociological antecedents leading to the initial act or acts of deviance. Thanks to Cloward's insertion of the principle of differential association, the theory now helps explain a variety of forms of deviance at the interactive level as well as at the structural-cultural level.

The enthusiasm for research using the anomie perspective that prevailed in the 1950s and 1960s waned thereafter. Although it had not been empirically rejected, it had also not been supported. Fault lay in part with the abstractness of Merton's formulation, which impeded testing. The most studied area of deviance was juvenile delinquency, which, however, tended to rely on official arrest rates. Such data suggest that crime rates are highest for youth from lower socioeconomic backgrounds, even though it is now evident that similar proportions of youth are delinquent in every social class (Schwendinger and Schwendinger 1985, pp. 181–183). Marshall B. Clinard (1964, pp. 55–56) has compiled a more specific list of weaknesses of anomie theory as it bears on deviance.

Labeling Theory

Behind the scenes and out of the spotlight on anomie, labeling theory, or societal reaction theory, was developing quietly, awaiting its ultimate place onstage. Lemert's most immediate precursor was Frank Tannenbaum (1938), who, concerned with crime, observed that the acts of juvenile delinquents are seen as evil in the wider community. This image eventually spreads to the delinquents themselves; they, too, are seen as evil. As the community comes to define delinquents as evil, juvenile delinquents definitions of themselves change accordingly. The result is a sort of self-fulfilling prophecy: "The process of making the criminal, therefore, is a process of tagging, defining, identifying, segregating, describing, emphasizing, making conscious and self-conscious; it becomes a way of stimulating, suggesting, emphasizing, and evoking the very traits that are complained of" (Tannenbaum 1938, pp. 19–20).

The study of deviance had to wait thirteen years for a more complete statement of this process. At that time Lemert (1951) published his "theory of sociopathic behavior" and later its elaborations (Lemert 1972). Although the complete theory is considerably more detailed and complex, the following summary communicates its essentials:

> People and groups are differentiated in various ways, some of which are deviant and which bring them penalties, rejection, and segregation. Penalties, rejection, and segregation are aspects of a community, or societal reaction against the deviance. This reaction affects the initial process of differentiation by sometimes increasing and other times decreasing the tendency to deviate. Accordingly, deviance can be studied from both a col-

lective perspective (society, community) and an individual perspective (paraphrased from Lemert 1951, p. 22).

There are three important aspects to this theory that receive a great deal of further elaboration in Lemert's book. The first of these, the process of *differentiation,* refers to the fact that these people differ or deviate from average characteristics of the populations in which they are found and in which they interact. The second is the *societal reaction,* which refers to both the expressive reactions of others (moral indignation) toward deviance and the action directed toward its control. Of course, this depends on the deviant individual or class of individuals being sufficiently visible to react toward. *Individuation,* the third aspect of the theory, refers to the manifestation of the causes of deviance in the individual deviant and to how he or she comes to terms with the deviance.

This framework is then given a more substantive form by being incorporated into a body of postulates:

1. There are modalities in human behavior and clusters of deviations from these modalities that can be identified and described for situations specified in time and space.
2. Behavioral deviations are a function of culture conflict, and such conflict is expressed through social organization.
3. There are societal reactions to deviations ranging from strong approval through indifference to strong disapproval.
4. Sociopathic behavior is deviation that is effectively disapproved.
5. The deviant person is one whose role, status, function, and self-definition are importantly shaped by how much deviation he engages in, by the degree of its social visibility, by the particular exposure he has to the societal reaction, and by the nature and strength of the societal reaction.
6. There are patterns of restriction and freedom in the social participation of deviants that are related directly to their status, role, and self-definitions. The biological strictures upon social participation of deviants are directly significant in comparatively few cases.
7. Deviants are individuated with respect to their vulnerability to the societal reaction because: (a) the person is a dynamic agent and (b) there is a structuring to each personality that acts as a set of limits within which the societal reaction operates (Lemert 1951, pp. 22–23).

The process of individuation has become the core of modern labeling theory. Individuation can be best understood by looking at the events and processes associated with *primary deviation* and *secondary deviation.* The first of these refers to deviant behavior that is normalized by the deviant person—that is, deviance remains primary or symptomatic and situational as long as it is rationalized or otherwise dealt with as part of a socially accepted role (Lemert 1972). This may be done through normalization, where the deviance is perceived by the individual as a normal variation or merely a minor problem of everyday living. Or it may be done in a way that does not seriously impede the basic accommodation that deviants make to get along with other people.

Secondary deviation refers to the responses that people make to problems created by the societal reaction to their deviance. These problems are those that are generated by social control mechanisms, punishment, stigmatization, segregation, and the like. They are of exceptional importance to the individual in that they alter his or her personality. The secondary deviant is a person whose life and identity are organized around the facts of deviance.

Lemert expresses the relationship between primary and secondary deviation in the following way:

> The sequence of interaction leading to secondary deviation is roughly as follows. (1) primary deviation; (2) social penalties, (3) further primary deviation; (4) stronger penalties and rejections; (5) further deviation, perhaps with hostilities and resentment beginning to focus upon those doing the penalizing; (6) crisis reached in the tolerance quotient, expressed in formal action by the community stigmatizing the deviant; (7) strengthening of the deviant conduct as a reaction to the stigmatizing and penalties; (8) ultimate acceptance of deviant social status and efforts at adjustment on the basis of the associated role (Lemert 1951, p. 77).

This relationship between primary and secondary deviation can, with little difficulty, be incorporated into the idea of a deviant career.

Howard S. Becker (1963) pioneered the application of concept of career to deviant behavior. A *career,* whether in deviance or an occupation, is the passage of the typical individual through recognized stages in one or more related identities. Careers are further comprised of the adjustments to and interpretations of the contingencies and turning points encountered at each stage.

False accusation of deviant behavior can, under certain circumstances, lead to a subsequent deviant career.

Objectively, the initial act of deviance launches the individual's deviant career. However, career turning points, including this one, depend on the actor's recognition and interpretation of them before they can be seen by that actor as part of a career. This is usually evident only in retrospect, after he or she has spent a certain amount of time in the identity with which the career is associated. Thus, upon reflection, the first remembered act of homosexuality, the first interest in communist literature, or the first drag on a marijuana cigarette constitutes the inception of the person's deviant career. This may or may not be the initial instance of deviance from a more objective point of view. This act and those further acts of primary deviation that may or may not follow are the results of many factors—social, cultural, psychological, and physiological—and their many combinations. Of course, any discussion of deviance should not overlook the possibility of false accusation of deviant behavior, an event that can also, under certain circumstances, lead to a subsequent deviant career.

Becker (1963, p. 23) identified three types of deviants. There are *secret deviants,* whose behavior is not known beyond themselves and perhaps a few others. The *falsely accused deviants,* whether this attitude is in fact valid or not, believe in their own innocence. These deviants are also discovered deviants in the sense that they have been apprehended for or suspected of deviant behavior. Finally, there are the *pure deviants,* who are also discovered deviants, since they have behaved in an aberrant way, know it, and have been apprehended for or suspected of such activity by the larger community.

Another key idea in labeling theory is Becker's concept of the *moral entrepreneur.* Groups of rule makers, rule enforcers, and ordinary nondeviant members of the community may join hands in this capacity. Such people, be they crusading individuals or change-oriented organizations, create moral norms on their own initiative and subsequently enforce them against those who disapprove of the new rules and deviate from them.

The prototype of the rule creator, says Becker, is the "crusading reformer" whose dissatisfaction with existing rules is acute. This individual campaigns for changes in the moral norms (e.g., to add new laws or procedures, to rescind old ones) or for changes in attitudes; both are designed to produce what he or she considers proper behavior. Society is replete with past and present crusaders. Groups and individuals have tried to eliminate drug abuse, discourage alcohol consumption, reduce the availability of pornography, and stop the exploitation of women in the workplace. Organizations have been formed to stress the need for mental health and for protection against breaking and entering.

It is no accident, then, that the least influential members of society (i.e., the poor, powerless ethnic groups) are most often disproportionately caught in the web of social control and labeled deviant. In other words, deviance is created by society. For moral entrepreneurs the infraction of moral norms constitutes deviance. Moral entrepreneurs also apply these norms to particular people, thereby *labeling* them as deviants of some sort. As Becker (1963, p. 9) points out, "The deviant is one to whom that label has successfully been applied; deviant behavior is behavior that people so label." Lest this statement seem restrictive, it should be added that secret deviants are deviant, too. They have simply not been discovered and publicly labeled as such.

Labeling theory complements anomie theory to the extent that the former focuses on the deviant career and the processes and conditions that commit a person to many years of deviance. The labeling approach offers less insight into why deviants start their careers than into why they continue or fail to continue beyond the initial acts of deviance. Despite Lemert's (1951, pp. 22–23) early interests in differentiation, culture conflict, and social organization and Becker's interest in moral entrepreneurs, labeling theory has developed into a predominantly social psychological explanation of continued deviance.

Other Approaches

Labeling theory is not without its problems and hence its critics. According to Barry Glassner (1982), the problems have been analyzed from three principal perspectives: neo-Marxist, empiricalist, and phenomenological. Each critique forms the nucleus of still another approach to the study of deviance.

The principal neo-Marxist objection to labeling theory is that it fails to relate crime and other forms of deviance to the larger society. It fails to account for historical and contemporary political and economic interests. After all, deviant acts and careers do take place within such a context. Neo-Marxists also hold that labeling theorists overlook the division between the powerful and the powerless in explaining deviance. Powerful members of society also violate laws and other norms, even while making some of them in their role as moral entrepreneurs.

The concept of the moral entrepreneur and the categories of secret and falsely accused deviants suggest, however, that labeling theorists have some understanding of the power differences in society. Perhaps the fairest criticism is that they have failed to go as far as they could in linking power to such concepts as labeling, deviant career, and agents of social control. Still, the observation that labeling theory overlooks the larger social context of deviance is apt. It exposes the predominantly social-psychological character of the perspective.

The empiricalists find several research weaknesses in labeling theory and its empirical support. Glassner (1982) discusses three of these. First, labeling theorists are said to examine only, or chiefly, formally labeled deviants—those who have been officially identified as having deviated (charged and convicted or examined and hospitalized). It is true that labeling theorists have frequently preferred a narrow conception of the labeling process. Such an approach opens these theorists to the criticism that labeling makes no difference. Yet some deviants—for example, religious fanatics or occultists—are deviant even though they rarely if ever gain official recognition as such.

Second, the empiricalists argue that labeling as a cause of deviance is inadequately conceptualized. This is a misunderstanding. As this article points out, labels are seen by labeling theorists as interpretations rather than causes. The label of deviant is a career contingency, an event, a process, or a situation interpreted by the deviant as having a significant impact on his or her moral career.

Third, the empiricalists claim that labeling theory lacks testable propositions. Consequently, data in this area can be explained in many different ways. Glassner notes that the empiricalists assert that tests by quantitative, statistical means are the only definitive way of confirming propositions. Labeling theorists defend their approach by arguing that qualitative methods, particularly participant observation, are more appropriate for the study of interaction, labeling, career, and self-conception. These phenomena rest on definitions of situations, images of self and others, negotiations of reality, and similar processes that are difficult to measure and therefore hard to quantify. Nevertheless, qualitative research often proceeds from the intense examination of individual groups and cases. Such studies are arduous and time-consuming, with the result that there are relatively few of them. There is only suggestive, yet-to-be confirmed evidence for many of the propositions in labeling theory.

Glassner calls those who follow the writings of Alfred Schutz "phenomenologists." Their chief concern with labeling theory is its tendency to neglect this question: How do people make sense of their social world? The people of interest to phenomenologists are not always deviant, however. Rather, phenomenologists are interested in how agents of social control and ordinary citizens make sense of deviants and deviant acts. Labeling theorists are accused of ignoring the ways in which the conventional world identifies and classifies morally offensive people and behaviors. The important data for the phenomenologists are the clues people use to identify kinds of deviants and deviant acts. People use this knowledge to determine such conclusions as guilt or innocence.

For example, Peter McHugh (1970) observed that for an act to be defined as deviant, it must be seen by ordinary members of the community as one of a set of alternative acts available to the offender—that is, the act, in their view, must not have been coerced, accidental, or miraculous. Moreover, to be deviant it must have been perpetrated by someone who knew what he or she was doing, who knew that he or she was violating a moral rule of the community. David Sudnow (1965) demonstrated how crimes in the American criminal justice system come to be defined as "normal" by the public defender. The category of normal crime enables the public defender to represent the accused person more efficiently than if the crime is exceptional in some significant way and thereby fails to fit established procedure. A crime is normal when it is seen by criminal justice personnel as having, among other characteristics, the following: (1) The focus is on types of offenses rather than on the individual offender. (2) The public defender tries to call attention to aspects of the crime that are familiar to the community at that moment in its history. (3) The act was committed in a geographical location known for this kind of behavior. In short, studying such processes shows how people construct special social realities—the realities of who did what to whom, at what time, and at what place.

To some extent, labeling theorists are guilty as charged. Although there are occasional hints of phenomenological thinking in the literature, there has been, until recently, a tendency to rely heavily on official definitions, or labels of what and who is deviant. But even official definitions and their applications are informed by common sense. They, too, warrant phenomenological analysis.

Conclusion

At present these critiques have done little more than point out weaknesses in the labeling perspective. Andrew T. Scull (1988, pp. 684–685) describes the predicament now faced by the sociology of deviance: None of the new approaches has "succeeded in establishing an alternative orientation to the field that commands wide assent. The study of deviance is thus in a state of profound epistemological and theoretical confusion . . . with few signs that the intellectual crisis will soon be resolved."

[See also Criminalization of Deviance; Deviance Theories; Legislation of Morality.]

BIBLIOGRAPHY

Becker, Howard S. 1963 *Outsiders.* New York: Free Press.

Bonney, Merl E. 1941 "Parents as the Makers of Social Deviates." *Social Forces* 20:77–87.

Clinard, Marshall B. 1964 *Anomie and Deviant Behavior.* New York: Free Press.
Cloward, Richard A. 1959 "Illegitimate Means, Anomie, and Deviant Behavior." *American Sociological Review* 24:164–176.
Durkheim, Emile 1951 *Suicide,* trans. John Spaulding and George Simpson; originally published in 1897. New York: Free Press.
Giddings, Franklin 1896 *Principles of Sociology.* New York: Macmillan.
Glassner, Barry 1982 "Labeling Theory." In M. M. Rosenberg, R. A. Stebbins, and A. Turowetz, eds., *The Sociology of Deviance.* New York: St. Martin's Press.
Karp, David A., Gregory P. Stone, and William C. Yoels 1977 *Being Urban.* Lexington, Mass.: D. C. Heath.
Lemert, Edwin M. 1951 *Social Pathology.* New York: McGraw-Hill.
——— 1972 *Human Deviance, Social Problems, and Social Control,* 2nd ed. Englewood Cliffs, NJ.: Prentice-Hall.
McHugh, Peter 1970 "A Common-Sense Conception of Deviance." In Jack D. Douglas, ed., *Deviance and Respectability: The Social Construction of Moral Meanings.* New York: Basic Books.
Merton, Robert K. 1938 "Social Structure and Anomie." *American Sociological Review* 3:672–682.
——— 1949 "Social Structure and Anomie: Revisions and Extensions." In R. N. Anshen, ed., *The Family.* New York: Harper & Brothers.
——— 1957 *Social Theory and Social Structure,* rev. ed. New York: Free Press.
Schwendinger, Herman, and Julia S. Schwendinger 1985 *Adolescent Subcultures and Delinquency.* New York: Praeger.
Scull, Andrew T. 1988 "Deviance and Social Control." In N. J. Smelser, ed., *Handbook of Sociology.* Newbury Park, Calif.: Sage Publications.
Stebbins, Robert A. 1988 *Deviance: Tolerable Differences.* Toronto: McGraw-Hill Ryerson.
Sudnow, David 1965 "Normal Crimes: Sociological Features of the Penal Code in a Public Defender Office." *Social Problems* 12:255–276.
Sutherland, Edwin H., and David R. Cressey 1978 *Principles of Criminology,* 10th ed. Philadelphia: Lippincott.
Tannenbaum, Frank 1938 *Crime and the Community.* New York: Columbia University Press.

– ROBERT A. STEBBINS

DEVIANCE THEORIES

Since its inception as a discipline, sociology has studied the causes of deviant behavior, examining why some persons conform to social rules and expectations and others do not. Typically, sociological theories of deviance reason that characteristics of individuals and the social areas in which they live assist in explaining the commission of deviant acts. These theories are important to understanding the roots of social problems such as crime, violence, and mental illness and to explaining how those problems may be remedied. By specifying the causes of deviance, the theories reveal how aspects of the social environment influence the behavior of individuals and groups. Further, the theories suggest how changes in these influences may yield changes in problematic behaviors.

Despite their importance, deviance theories disagree about the precise causes of deviant acts. Some look to the structure of society and groups or geographic areas within society, explaining deviance in terms of broad social conditions in which deviance is most likely to flourish. Others explain deviant behavior using the characteristics of individuals, focusing on those characteristics that are most highly associated with learning deviant acts. Other theories view deviance as a social status conferred by one group or person on others, a status that is imposed by persons or groups in power in order to protect their positions of power. These theories explain deviance in terms of differentials in power between individuals or groups.

Deviance is a social status that is imposed on others by persons or groups in power in order to protect their positions of power.

This article reviews the major sociological theories of deviance. It offers an overview of each theory, summarizing its explanation of deviant behavior. Before reviewing the theories, however, it may prove useful to describe two different dimensions of theory that will structure our discussion. The first of these, the *level of explanation,* refers to the scope of the theory and whether it focuses on the behavior and characteristics of individuals or on the characteristics of social aggregates such as neighborhoods, cities, or other social areas. *Micro-level* theories stress the individual, generally explaining deviant acts in terms of personal characteristics of individuals or the immediate social context in which deviant acts occur. In contrast, *macro-level* theories focus on social aggregates or groups, looking to the structural characteristics of areas in explaining the origins of deviance, particularly rates of deviance among those groups.

Theories of deviance also vary in relation to a second dimension, *causal focus.* This dimension divides theories into two groups, those that explain the social origins of norm violations and those explaining societal reactions to deviance. *Social origin* theories focus on the causes of norm violations. Typically, these theories identify aspects of the social environment that trigger norm violations, social conditions in which the violations are most likely to occur. In contrast, *social reaction* theories argue that deviance is often a matter of social construction, a status imposed by one person or group on others and a status that ultimately may influence the subse-

quent behavior of the designated deviant. Social reaction theories argue that some individuals and groups may be designated or labeled as deviant and that the process of labeling may trap or engulf those individuals or groups in a deviant social role.

These two dimensions offer a fourfold scheme for classifying types of deviance theories. The first type, macro-level origin theories, focuses on the causes of norm violations associated with broad, structural conditions in the society. These theories generally examine the influences of such structural characteristics of populations or communities as the concentration of poverty, levels of community integration, or the density and age distribution of the population on areal rates of deviance.

Second, micro-level origin theories focus on the characteristics of the deviant and his or her immediate social environment. These theories typically examine the relationship between a person's involvement in deviance and such characteristics as the influences of peers and significant others as well as people's emotional stakes in conformity, their beliefs about the propriety of deviance and conformity, and their perceptions of the threat of punishments for deviant acts.

A third type of theories may be termed micro-level reaction theories. These accord importance to those aspects of interpersonal reactions that may seriously stigmatize or label the deviant and thereby reinforce her or his deviant social status. According to these theories, reactions to deviance may have the unintended effect of increasing the likelihood of subsequent deviant behavior.

Finally, macro-level reaction theories emphasize broad structural conditions in society that are associated with the designation of entire groups or segments of the society as deviant. These theories tend to stress the importance of structural characteristics of populations, groups, or geographic areas, such as degrees of economic inequality or concentration of political power within communities or the larger society. According to macro-level reaction theories, powerful groups impose the status of deviant as a mechanism for controlling those groups that represent the greatest political, economic, or social threat to their position of power.

The rest of this article is divided into sections corresponding to each of these "types" of deviance theory. The article concludes with a discussion of new directions for theory—the development of explanations that cut across and integrate different theory types and the elaboration of existing theories through greater specification of the conditions under which those theories apply.

Macro-Level Origins of Deviance

Theories of the macro-level origins of deviance look to the broad, structural characteristics of society, and groups within society, to explain deviant behavior. Typically, these theories examine one of three aspects of social structure. The *first* is the pervasiveness and consequences of poverty in modern American society. Robert Merton's (1938) writing on American social structure and Richard Cloward and Lloyd Ohlin's (1960) subsequent work on urban gangs laid the theoretical foundation for this perspective. Reasoning that pervasive materialism in American culture creates unattainable aspirations for many segments of the population, Merton (1964) and others argued that there exists an environmental state of "strain" among the poor. The limited availability of legitimate opportunities for attaining material wealth forces the poor to adapt through deviance, either by achieving wealth through illegitimate means or by rejecting materialistic aspirations and withdrawing from society altogether.

According to this reasoning, deviance is a byproduct of poverty and a mechanism through which the poor may attain wealth, albeit illegitimately. Thus, "strain" theories of deviance interpret behaviors such as illegal drug selling, prostitution, and armed robbery as innovative adaptations to blocked opportunities for legitimate economic or occupational success. Similarly, the theories interpret violent crimes in terms of the frustrations of poverty, as acts of aggression triggered by those frustrations (Blau and Blau 1982). Much of the current research in this tradition is examining the exact mechanisms by which poverty and economic inequality influence rates of deviant behavior.

The second set of macro-level origins theories examine the role of culture in deviant behavior. Although not ignoring structural forces such as poverty in shaping deviance, this class of theories reasons that there may exist cultures within the larger culture that endorse or reinforce deviant values, deviant subcultures that produce higher rates of deviance among those segments of the population sharing subcultural values.

Subcultural explanations have their origin in two distinct sociological traditions. The first is writing on the properties of delinquent gangs that identifies a distinct lower-class culture of gang members that encourages aggression, thrill seeking, and antisocial behavior (e.g., Miller 1958). The second is writing on cultural conflict that recognizes that within complex societies there will occur contradictions between the conduct norms of different groups. Thorsten Sellin (1938) suggested that in heterogeneous societies several different subcultures may emerge, each with its own set of conduct norms. According to Sellin, the laws and norms applied to the entire society do not necessarily reflect cultural consensus but rather the values and beliefs of the dominant social groups.

Subcultural theories emerging from these two traditions argue that deviance is the product of a cohesive set of values and norms that favors deviant behavior and is endorsed by a segment of the general population. Perhaps most prominent among the theories is Marvin Wolfgang and Franco Ferracuti's (1967) writing on subcultures of criminal violence. Wolfgang and Ferracuti reasoned that there may exist a distinct set of beliefs and expectations within the society, a subculture, that promotes and encourages violent interactions. According to Wolfgang and Ferracuti, this violent subculture is pervasive among blacks in the United States and may explain extremely high rates of criminal homicide among young black males.

Although Wolfgang and Ferracuti offer little material specifying the subculture's precise causes, or empirical evidence demonstrating the pervasiveness of subcultural beliefs, other writers have extended the theory, exploring the relationship between beliefs favoring violence and such factors as the structure of poverty in the United States (Curtis 1975; Messner 1983), the history of racial oppression of blacks (Silberman 1980), and ties to the rural South and a southern culture of violence (Gastil 1971; Erlanger 1974). Even these writers, however, offer little empirical evidence of violent subcultures within U.S. society.

Rates of deviance will be high in densely populated areas because social controls in the form of parental supervision are either weak or entirely absent.

A third class of theories about the macro-level origins of deviance began with the work of sociologists at the University of Chicago in 1920s. Unlike strain and subcultural theories, these stress the importance of the social integration of neighborhoods and communities—the degree to which neighborhoods are stable and are characterized by a homogeneous set of beliefs and values—as a force influencing rates of deviant behavior. As levels of integration increase, rates of deviance decrease. Based in the early work of sociologists such as Clifford Shaw and Henry McKay, the theories point to the structure of social controls in neighborhoods, arguing that neighborhoods lacking social controls are "disorganized," that is, areas in which there is a virtual vacuum of social norms. It is in this normative vacuum that deviance flourishes. Therefore, these theories view deviance as a property of areas or locations rather than specific groups of people.

Early writers in the "disorganization" tradition identified industrialization and urbanization as the causes of disorganized communities and neighborhoods. Witnessing immense growth in cities such as Chicago, these writers argued that industrial and urban expansion create zones of disorganization within cities. Property owners move from the residential pockets on the edge of business and industrial areas and allow buildings to deteriorate in anticipation of the expansion of business and industry. This process of natural succession and change in cities disrupts traditional mechanisms of social control in neighborhoods. As property owners leave transitional areas, more mobile and diverse groups enter. But the added mobility and diversity of these groups translate into fewer primary relationships—families and extended kinship and friendship networks. And as the number of primary relationships declines, so will informal social controls in neighborhoods. Hence, rates of deviance will rise.

Recent writing from this perspective looks closely at the mechanisms by which specific places in urban areas become the spawning grounds for deviant acts (Bursik and Webb 1982; Bursik 1984; and others). For example, Rodney Stark (1987) argues that high levels of population density are associated with particularly low levels of supervision of children. With little supervision, children perform poorly in school and are much less likely to develop "stakes in conformity" —that is, emotional and psychological investments in academic achievement and other conforming behaviors. Without such stakes, children and adolescents are much more likely to turn to deviant alternatives. Thus, according to Stark, rates of deviance will be high in densely populated areas because social controls in the form of parental supervision are either weak or entirely absent.

Similarly, Robert Crutchfield (1989) argues that the structure of work opportunities in areas may have the same effect. Areas characterized primarily by secondary sector work opportunities—low pay, few career opportunities, and high employee turnover—may tend to attract and retain persons with few stakes in conventional behavior—a "situation of company" in which deviance is likely to flourish.

In sum, theories of the macro-level origins of deviance argue that many of the causes of deviance may be found in the characteristics of groups within society, or in the characteristics of geographic areas and communities. They offer explanations of group and areal differences in deviance—for example, why some cities have relatively higher rates of crime than others or why blacks have higher rates of serious interpersonal violence than other ethnic groups. These theories make no attempt to explain the behavior of individuals or the occurrence of individual deviant acts. Indeed, they reason that deviance is best understood as a property of an area, community, or group, regardless of the individuals living in the area or community, or the individuals comprising the group.

Micro-Level Origins of Deviance

Many explanations of deviance argue that its causes are rooted in the background or personal circumstances of the individual. Micro-level origins theories have developed over the past fifty years, identifying mechanisms by which ordinarily conforming individuals may become deviant. These theories assume the existence of a homogeneous, pervasive set of norms in society and proceed to explain why persons or entire groups of persons violate the norms. There exist two important traditions within this category of theories. The first tradition involves social learning theories—explanations that focus on the mechanisms through which people learn the techniques and attitudes favorable to committing deviant acts. The second tradition involves social control theories—explanations that emphasize factors in the social environment that regulate the behavior of individuals, thereby preventing the occurrence of deviant acts.

Edwin Sutherland's (1947) theory of differential association laid the foundation for learning theories. At the heart of this theory is the assumption that deviant behavior, like all other behaviors, is learned. Further, this learning occurs within intimate social groups—networks of family members and close friends. Therefore, according to these theories individuals learn deviance from persons closet to them. Sutherland specified a process of *differential association,* reasoning that people become deviant in association with deviant others. People learn from others the techniques of committing deviant acts and attitudes favorable to the commission of those acts. Moreover, Sutherland reasoned that people vary in their degree of association with deviant others; those regularly exposed to close friends and family members who hold beliefs favoring deviance and who commit deviant acts would be much more likely than others to develop those same beliefs and commit deviant acts.

Sutherland's ideas about learning processes have played a lasting role in micro-level deviance theories. Central to his perspective is the view that beliefs and values favoring deviance are a primary cause of deviant behavior. Robert Burgess and Ronald Akers (1966) and subsequently Akers (1985) extended Sutherland's ideas, integrating them with principles of operant conditioning. Reasoning that learning processes may best be understood in terms of the concrete rewards and punishments given for behavior, Burgess and Akers argue that deviance is learned through associations with others and through a system of rewards and punishments, imposed by close friends and relatives, for participation in deviant acts. Subsequent empirical studies offer compelling support for elements of learning theory (Matsueda 1982; Akers et al. 1979; Matsueda and Heimer 1987).

Some examples may be useful at this point. According to the theory of differential association, juveniles develop beliefs favorable to the commission of delinquent acts and knowledge about the techniques of committing deviant acts from their closest friends, typically their peers. Thus, sufficient exposure to peers endorsing beliefs favoring deviance who also have knowledge about the commission of deviant acts will cause the otherwise conforming juvenile to commit such acts. Therefore, if adolescent peer influences encourage smoking, drinking alcohol, and other forms of drug abuse—and exposure to these influences occurs frequently, over a long period of time, and involves relationships that are important to the conforming adolescent—then he or she is likely to develop beliefs and values favorable to committing these acts. Once those beliefs and values develop, he or she is likely to commit the acts.

The second class of micro-level origins theories, control theories, explores the causes of deviance from an altogether different perspective. Control theories take for granted the existence of a cohesive set of norms shared by most persons in the society and reason that most persons want to and will typically conform to these prevailing social norms. The emphasis in these theories, unlike learning theories, is on the factors that bond individuals to conforming life-styles. The bonds act as social and psychological constraints on the individual, binding persons to normative conformity (Toby 1957; Hirschi 1969). People deviate from norms when these bonds to conventional life-styles are weak, and hence, when they have little restraining influence over the individual. Among control theorists, Travis Hirschi (1969) has made the greatest contributions to our knowledge about bonding processes and deviant behavior. Writing on the causes of delinquency, he argued that four aspects of bonding are especially relevant to control theory; emotional attachments to conforming others, psychological commitments to conformity, involvements in conventional activities, and beliefs consistent with conformity to prevailing norms.

Among the most important of the bonding elements are emotional attachments individuals may have to conforming others and commitments to conformity—psychological investments or stakes people hold in a conforming life-style. Those having weak attachments—that is, people who are insensitive to the opinions of conforming others—and who have few stakes in conformity, in the form of commitments to occupation or career and education, are much more likely than others to deviate (see, e.g., Paternoster et al. 1983; Thornberry and Christenson 1984; Liska and Reed 1985). In effect, these individuals are "free" from the constraints that ordinarily bond people to normative conformity. Conversely, individuals concerned about the opinions of conforming others and who have heavy psychological investments in work or school will see the potential consequences of deviant acts—rejection by friends or loss of job—as threatening or costly, and consequently will refrain from those acts.

Most recently, Michael Gottfredson, in conjunction with Hirschi, has developed a general theory of crime that builds on and extends the basic assumptions of control theory (Hirschi and Gottfredson 1987; Gottfredson and Hirschi 1990). Arguing that all people are inherently self-interested, pursuing enhancement of personal pleasure and avoiding pain, Gottfredson and Hirschi suggest that most crimes, and for that matter most deviant acts, are the result of choices to maximize pleasure and/or minimize pain. Crimes occur when opportunities to maximize personal pleasure are high and when the certainty of painful consequences is low. Further, people who pursue short-term gratification with little consideration for the long-term consequences of their actions are most prone to criminal behavior. In terms of classical control theory, these are individuals who have weak bonds to conformity or who disregard or ignore the potentially painful consequences of their actions. They are "relatively unable to or unwilling to delay gratification; they are indifferent to punishment and the interests of others" (Hirschi and Gottfredson 1987, pp. 959–960).

A related concern is the role of sanctions in preventing deviant acts. Control theorists like Hirschi reason that most people are utilitarian in their judgments about deviant acts, and thus evaluate carefully the risks associated with each act. Control theories typically maintain that the threat of sanctions actually prevents deviant acts when the risks outweigh the gains. Much of the most recent writing on sanctions and their effects has stressed the importance of perceptual processes in decisions to commit deviant acts (Gibbs 1975, 1977; Tittle 1980; Paternoster et al. 1982, 1983; Piliavin et al 1986; Matsueda, Piliavin, and Gartner 1988). At the heart of this perspective is the reasoning that individuals perceiving the threat of sanctions as high are much more likely to refrain from deviance than those perceiving the threat as low, regardless of the actual level of sanction threat.

In sum, micro-level origins theories look to those aspects of the individual's social environment influencing her or his likelihood of deviance. Learning theories stress the importance of deviant peers and other significant individuals, and their impact on attitudes and behaviors favorable to the commission of deviant acts. These theories assume that the social environment acts as an agent of change, transforming otherwise conforming individuals into deviants through peer influences. People exposed to deviant others frequently and sufficiently, like persons exposed to a contagious disease who become ill, will become deviant themselves. Control theories avoid this "contagion" model, viewing the social environment as a composite of controls and restraints cementing the individual to a conforming life-style. Deviance occurs when elements of the bond—aspects of social control—are weak or broken, thereby freeing the individual to violate social norms. Sanctions and the threat of sanctions are particularly important to control theories, a central part of the calculus that rational actors use in choosing to commit or refrain from committing deviant acts.

Micro-Level Reactions to Deviance

Unlike micro-level origin theories, micro-level reaction theories make no assumptions about the existence of a homogeneous, pervasive set of norms in society. These theories take an altogether different approach to explaining deviant behavior, viewing deviance as a matter of definition, a social status imposed by individuals or groups on others. Most argue that there exists no single pervasive set of norms in society and that deviant behavior may best be understood in terms of norms and their enforcement. These theories typically stress the importance of labeling processes—the mechanisms by which acts become defined or labeled as "deviant"—and the consequences of labeling for the person so labeled. Many of these theories are concerned with the development of deviant life-styles or careers, long-term commitments to deviant action.

Labeling forces the individual into a deviant social role.

One of the most important writers in this tradition is Howard Becker (1963). Becker argues that deviance is not a property inherent in any particular form of behavior but rather a property conferred on those behaviors by audiences witnessing them. Becker (1963, p. 9) notes that "deviance is *not* a quality of the act the person commits, but rather a consequence of the application by others of rules and sanctions to an 'offender.' The deviant is one to whom that label has successfully been applied; deviant behavior is behavior that people so label." Thus, Becker and others in this tradition orient the study of deviance on rules and sanctions, and the application of labels. Their primary concern is the social construction of deviance—that is, how some behaviors and classes of people come to be defined as "deviant" by others observing and judging the behavior.

Equally important is the work of Edwin Lemert (1951). Stressing the importance of labeling to subsequent deviant behavior, he argued that repetitive deviance may arise from social reactions to initial deviant acts. According to Lemert (1951, p. 287), deviance may often involve instances where "a person begins to employ his deviant behavior . . . as a means of defense, attack or adjustment to the . . . problems created by the consequent social reactions to him." Therefore, a cause of deviant careers is negative social labeling; instances where reactions to initial deviant acts are harsh and reinforce a "deviant" self-definition. Such labeling forces the individual into a deviant social role, organizing his or her identity around a pattern of deviance that structures a way of life and perpetuates deviant behavior (Becker 1963; Schur 1971, 1985).

Perhaps the most significant developments in this tradition have contributed to knowledge about the causes of mental illness. Proponents of micro-level reaction theories argue that the label "mentally ill" can be so stigmatizing to those labeled, especially when mental-health professionals impose the label, that they experience difficulty returning to nondeviant social roles. As a result, the labeling process may actually exacerbate mental disorders. Former mental patients may find themselves victims of discrimination at work, in personal relationships, or in other social spheres (Scheff 1966). This discrimination, and the widespread belief that others devalue and discriminate against mental patients, may lead to self-devaluation and fear of social rejection by others (Link 1982, 1987). In some instances, this devaluation and fear may be associated with demoralization of the patient, loss of employment and personal income, and the persistence of mental disorders following treatment (Link 1987).

Hence, micro-level reaction theories reason that deviant behavior is rooted in the process by which persons define and label the behavior of others as deviant. The theories offer explanations of individual differences in deviance, stressing the importance of audience reactions to initial deviant acts. However, these theories make no attempt to explain the origins of the initial acts (Scheff, 1966). Rather, they are concerned primarily with the development and persistence of deviant careers.

Macro-Level Reactions to Deviance

The final class of theories looks to the structure of economic and political power in society as a cause of deviant behavior. Macro-level reaction theories—either Marxist or other conflict theories—view deviance as a status imposed by dominant social classes to control and regulate populations that threaten political and economic hegemony. Like micro-level reaction theories, these theories view deviance as a social construction and accord greatest importance to the mechanisms by which society defines and controls entire classes of behavior and people as deviant in order to mediate the threat. However, these theories reason that the institutional control of deviants has integral ties to economic and political order in society.

Marxist theories stress the importance of the economic structure of society and begin with the assumption that the dominant norms in capitalist societies reflect the interests of the powerful economic class, the owners of business. But contemporary Marxist writers (Quinney 1970, 1974, 1980; Spitzer 1975; Young 1983) also argue that modern capitalist societies are characterized by large "problem populations"—people who have become displaced from the work force and alienated from the society. Generally, the problem populations include racial and ethnic minorities, the chronically unemployed, and the extremely impoverished. They are a burden to the society and particularly to the capitalist class because they create a form of social expense that must be carefully controlled if the economic order is to be preserved.

Marxist theories reason that economic elites use institutions such as the legal, mental-health, and welfare systems to control and manage society's problem populations. In effect, these institutions define and process society's problem populations as deviant in order to ensure effective management and control. In societies or communities characterized by rigid economic stratification, elites are likely to impose formal social controls in order to preserve the prevailing economic order.

Conflict theories stress the importance of the political structure of society and focus on the degree of threat to the hegemony of political elites, arguing that elites employ formal social controls to regulate threats to political and social order (Turk 1976; Chambliss 1978; Chambliss and Mankoff 1976). According to these theories, threat varies in relation to the size of the problem population, with large problem populations substantially more threatening to political elites than small populations. Thus, elites in societies and communities in which those problem populations are large and perceived as especially threatening are more likely to process members of the problem populations as deviants than in areas where such populations are small.

Much of the recent writing in this tradition has addressed the differential processing of people defined as deviant. Typically, this writing has taken two forms. The first involves revisionist histories linking the development of prisons, mental asylums, and other institutions of social control to structural changes in U.S. and European societies. These histories demonstrate that those institutions often target the poor and chronically unemployed independent of their involvement in crime and other deviant acts, and thereby protect and serve the interests of dominant economic and political groups (Scull 1978; Rafter 1985).

A second and more extensive literature includes empirical studies of racial and ethnic disparities in criminal punishments. Among the most important of these studies is Martha Myers and Suzette Talarico's (1987) analysis of the social and structural contexts that foster racial and ethnic disparities in the sentencing of criminal offenders. Myers and Talarico's research, and other studies examining the linkages between community social structure and differential processing (Myers 1987, 1990; Peterson and Hagan 1984; Bridges, Crutchfield, and Simpson 1987; Bridges and Crutchfield 1988), demonstrate the vulnerability of minorities to differential processing during historical periods and in areas in which they are perceived by whites as serious threats to political and social order. In effect, minorities accused of crimes during these periods and in these geographic areas are perceived as threats to white hegemony, and therefore become legitimate targets for social control.

Thus, macro-level reaction theories view deviance as a by-product of inequality in modern society, a social status imposed by powerful groups on those who are less powerful. Unlike micro-level reaction theories, these theories focus on the forms of inequality in society and how entire groups within the society are managed and controlled as deviants by apparatuses of the state. Like those theories, however, macro-level reaction theories make little or no attempt to explain the origins of deviant acts, claiming instead that the status of "deviant" is, in large part, a social construction designed primarily to protect the interests of the most powerful social groups. The primary concern of these theories is explicating the linkages between inequality in society and inequality in the labeling and processing of deviants.

New Theoretical Directions

A recurring issue in the study of deviance is the contradictory nature of many deviance theories. The theories often begin with significantly different assumptions about the nature of human behavior and end with significantly different conclusions about the causes of deviant acts. Some scholars maintain that the oppositional nature of these theories—the theories are developed and based on systematic rejection of other theories (Hirschi 1989)—tends toward clarity and internal consistency in reasoning about the causes of deviance. However, other scholars argue that this oppositional nature is intellectually divisive—acceptance of one theory precludes acceptance of another—and "has made the field seem fragmented, if not in disarray" (Liska, Krohn, and Messner 1989, p. 1).

A related and equally troublesome problem is the contradictory nature of much of the scientific evidence supporting deviance theories. For each theory, there exists a literature of studies that supports and a literature that refutes major arguments of the theory. And although nearly every theory of deviance may receive empirical confirmation at some level, virtually no theory of deviance is sufficiently comprehensive to withstand empirical falsification at some other level. The difficult task for sociologists is discerning whether and under what circumstances negative findings should be treated as negating a particular theory (Walker and Cohen 1985).

"Urbanness" may constitute a condition that activates theories linking poverty to deviance.

In recent years, these two problems have renewed sociologists' interest in deviance theory and, at the same time, suggested new directions for the development of theory. The oppositional nature of theories has quite recently spawned interest in theoretical integration. Many scholars are dissatisfied with classical theories, arguing that their predictive power is exceedingly low (see Elliott 1985; Liska, Krohn, and Messner 1989). Limited to a few key explanatory variables, any one theory can explain only a limited range and amount of deviant behavior. And because most scholars reason that the causes of deviance are multiple and quite complex, most also contend that it may be "necessary to combine different theories to capture the entire range of causal variables" (Liska, Krohn, and Messner 1989, p, 4).

Because it combines the elements of different theories, the new theory will have greater explanatory power than theories from which it was derived. However, meaningful integration of deviance theories will require much more than the simple combination of variables. Scholars must first reconcile the oppositional aspects of theories, including many of their underlying assumptions about society, the motivations of human behavior, and the causes of deviant acts. For example, learning theories focus heavily on the motivations for deviance, stressing the importance of beliefs and values that "turn" the individual to deviant acts. In contrast, control theories accord little importance to such motivations, examining instead those aspects of the social environment that constrain people from committing deviant acts. Reconciling such differences is never an easy task, and in some instances may be impossible (Hirschi 1979).

The problem of contradictory evidence suggests a related but different direction for deviance theory. Theories may vary significantly in the conditions—termed *scope conditions*—under which they apply (Walker and Cohen 1985; Tittle 1975; Tittle and Curran 1988). Under some scope conditions, theories may find extensive empirical support, and under others virtually none. For instance, macro-level origin theories concerned with the frustrating effects of poverty on deviance may have greater applicability to people living in densely populated urban areas than those living in rural areas. The frustrations of urban poverty may be much more extreme than in rural areas, even though the actual levels of poverty may be the same. As a result, the frustrations of urban poverty may be more likely to cause deviant adaptations in the form of violent crime, drug abuse, and vice than those of rural poverty. In this instance, "urbanness" may constitute a condition that activates strain theories linking poverty to deviance. Obviously, the same theories simply may not apply in rural areas or under other conditions.

Effective development of deviance theory will require much greater attention to the specification of such scope conditions. Rather than combining causal variables from different theories as integrationists would recommend, this approach to theory development encourages scholars to explore more fully the strengths and limitations of their own theories. This approach will require more complete elaboration of extant theory, explicitly specifying those circumstances under which each theory may be meaningfully tested and thus falsified. The result will be a greater specification of each theory's contribution to explanations of deviant behavior.

These two directions have clear and very different implications for the development of deviance theory. Theoretical integration offers overarching models of deviant behavior that cut across classical theories, combining different levels of explanation and causal focuses. If fundamental differences between theories can be reconciled, integration is promising. The specification of scope conditions offers greater clarification of existing theories, identifying those conditions under which each theory most effectively applies. Although this direction promises no general theories of deviance, it offers the hope of more meaningful and useful explanations of deviant behavior.

[See also Deviance; Legislation of Morality.]

BIBLIOGRAPHY

Akers, Ronald L. 1985 *Deviant Behavior: A Social Learning Approach* Belmont, Calif.: Wadsworth.

———, Marvin D. Krohn, Lonn Lanza-Kaduce, and Marcia Radosevich 1979 "Social Learning and Deviant Behavior: A Specific Test of a General Theory." *American Sociological Review* 44:636–655.

Becker, Howard 1963 *The Outsiders.* Chicago: University of Chicago Press.

Blau, Judith, and Peter Blau 1982 "Metropolitan Structure and Violent Crime." *American Sociological Review* 47:114–128.

Bridges, George S., and Robert D. Crutchfield 1988 "Law, Social Standing and Racial Disparities in Imprisonment." *Social Forces* 66:699–724.

———, and Edith Simpson 1987 "Crime, Social Structure and Criminal Punishment" *Social Problems* 34:344–361.

Bursik, Robert J., and J. Webb 1982 "Community Change and Ecological Studies of Delinquency." *American Jurnal of Sociology* 88:24–42.

Bursik, Robert J. 1984 "Urban Dynamics and Ecological Studies of Delinquency." *Social Forces* 63:393–413.

Burgess, Robert L., and Ronald Akers 1966 "A Differential Association-Reinforcement Theory of Criminal Behavior." *Social Problems* 14:128–147.

Chambliss, William 1978 *On the Take.* Bloomington: Indiana University Press.

———, and Milton Mankoff 1976 *Whose Law, What, Order?* New York: Wiley.

Cloward, Richard 1959 "Illegitimate Means, Anomie and Deviant Behavior." *American Sociological Review* 24:164–176.

———, and Lloyd E. Ohlin 1960 *Delinquency and Opportunity.* New York: Free Press.

Crutchfield, Robert D. 1989 "Labor Stratification and Violent Crime." *Social Forces* 68:489–513.

Curtis, Lynn 1975 *Violence, Race and Culture.* Lexington, Mass.: Heath.

Elliott, Delbert 1985 "The Assumption That Theories Can Be Combined with Increased Explanatory Power: Theoretical Integrations." In Robert F. Meier, ed., *Theoretical Methods in Criminology.* Beverly Hills, Calif.: Sage.

Erlanger, Howard 1974 "The Empirical Status of the Subculture of Violence Thesis." *Social Problems* 22:280–292.

Gastil, Raymond 1971 "Homicide and a Regional Culture of Violence." *American Sociological Review* 36:412–427.

Gibbs, Jack P. 1975 *Crime, Punishment and Deterrence.* New York: Elsevier.

——— 1977 "Social Control, Deterrence, and Perspectives on Social Order." *Social Forces* 62:359–374.

Gottfredson, Michael R., and Travis Hirschi 1990 *A General Theory of Crime.* Palo Alto, Calif.: Stanford University Press.

Hirschi, Travis 1969 *Causes of Delinquency.* Berkeley: University of California Press.

——— 1979 "Separate and Unequal Is Better." *Journal of Research in Crime and Delinquency* 16:34–37.

——— 1989 "Exploring Alternatives to Integrated Theory." In Steven F. Messner, Marvin D. Krohn, and Allen E. Lisca, eds., *Theoretical Integration in the Study of Deviance and Crime Problems and Prospects.* Albany, N.Y.: SUNY Press.

———, and Michael R. Gottfredson 1987 "Causes of White Collar Crime." *Criminology* 25:949–974.

Lemert, Edwin 1951 *Social Pathology.* New York: McGraw-Hill.

Link, Bruce 1982 "Mental Patient Status, Work and Income: An Examination of the Effects of a Psychiatric Label." *American Sociological Review* 47:202–215.

——— 1987 "Understanding Labeling Effects in the Area of Mental Disorders: An Assessment of the Effects of Expectations of Rejection." *American Sociological Review* 52:96–112.

Liska, Allen, and Mark Reed 1985 "Ties to Conventional Institutions and Delinquency." *American Sociological Review* 50:547–560.

Liska, Allen E., Marvin D. Krohn, and Steven F. Messner 1989 "Strategies and Requisites for Theoretical Integration in the Study of Deviance and Crime." In Steven F. Messner, Marvin D. Krohn, and Allen E. Liska, eds., *Theoretical Integration in the Study of Deviance and Crime: Problems and Prospects.* Albany, N.Y.: SUNY Press.

Matsueda, Ross L. 1982 "Testing Control Theory and Differential Association: A Causal Modeling Approach." *American Sociological Review* 47:36–58.

———, and Karen Heimer 1987 "Race, Family Structure and Delinquency: A Test of Differential Association and Social Control Theories." *American Sociological Review* 52:826–840.

———, Irving Piliavin, and Rosemary Gartner 1988 "Ethical Assumptions versus Empirical Research." *American Sociological Review* 53:305–307.

Merton, Robert K. 1938 "Social Structure and Anomie." *American Sociological Review* 3:672–682.

——— 1964 *Social Theory and Social Structure.* New York: Free Press.

Messner, Steven F. 1983 "Regional and Racial Effects on the Urban Homicide Rate: The Subculture of Violence Revisited." *American Journal of Sociology* 88:997–1,007.

Miller, Walter B. 1958 "Lower Class Culture as a Generating Milieu of Gang Delinquency." *Journal of Social Issues* 14:5–19.

Myers, Martha 1987 "Economic Inequality and Discrimination in Sentencing." *Social Forces* 65:746–766.

——— 1990 "Economic Threat and Racial Disparities in Incarceration: The Case of Postbellum Georgia." *Criminology* 28(4):627–656.

———, and Suzette Talarico 1987 *Social Contexts of Criminal Sentencing.* New York: Springer-Verlag.

Paternoster, Raymond L., Linda Saltzman, Gordon P. Waldo, and Theodore Chiricos 1982 "Perceived Risk and Deterrence: Methodological Artifacts in Deterrence Research." *Journal of Criminal Law and Criminology* 73:1,243–1,255.

——— 1983 "Perceived Risk and Social Control." *Journal of Criminal Law and Criminology* 74:457–480.

Peterson, Ruth D., and John Hagan 1984 "Changing Conceptions of Race: Toward an Account of Anomalous Findings of Sentencing Research." *American Sociological Review* 49:56–70.

Piliavin, Irving, Rosemary Gartner, Craig Thornton, and Ross L. Matsueda 1986 "Crime, Deterrence and Rational Choice." *American Sociological Review* 51:101–120.

Quinney, Richard 1970 *The Social Reality of Crime.* Boston: Little, Brown.

——— 1974 *Critique of Legal Order.* Boston: Little, Brown.

——— 1980 *Class, State and Crime.* New York: Longman.

Rafter, Nicole Hahn 1985 *Partial Justice: Women in State Prisons, 1800–1935.* Boston: Northeastern University Press.

Scheff, Thomas 1966 *Being Mentally Ill.* Chicago: Aldine.

Schur, Edwin 1971 *Labelling Deviant Behavior.* New York: Harper and Row.

——— 1985 *Labelling Women Deviant: Gender, Stigma and Social Control.* New York: Harper and Row.

Scull, Andrew T. 1978 *Museums of Madness.* London: Heinemann.

Sellin, Thorsten 1938 *Culture, Conflict and Crime.* New York: Social Science Research Council.

Shaw, Clifford 1930 *The Jack-Roller.* Chicago: University of Chicago Press.

Shaw, Clifford, and Henry McKay 1942 *Juvenile Delinquency and Urban Areas.* Chicago: University of Chicago Press.

Silberman, Charles 1980 *Criminal Justice, Criminal Violence.* New York: Vintage.

Spitzer, Steven 1975 "Toward a Marxian Theory of Deviance." *Social Problems* 22:638–651.

Stark, Rodney 1987 "Deviant Places: A Theory of the Ecology of Crime." *Criminology* 25:893–910.

Sutherland, Edwin H. 1947 *Principles of Criminology,* 4th ed. Philadelphia: Lippincott.

Thornberry, Terence P., and R. L Christenson 1984 "Unemployment and Criminal Involvement: An Investigation of Reciprocal Causal Structures." *American Sociological Review* 49:398–411.

Tittle, Charles R. 1975 "Deterrents or Labelling?" *Social Forces* 53:399–410.

——— 1980 *Sanctions and Social Deviance.* New York: Praeger.

———, and Barbara A. Curran 1988 "Contingencies for Dispositional Disparities in Juvenile Justice." *Social Forces* 67:23–58.

Toby, Jackson 1957 "Social Disorganization and Stakes in Conformity: Complementary Factors in the Predatory Behavior of Hoodlums." *Journal of Criminal Law and Criminology and Police Science* 48:12–17.

Turk, Austin T. 1976 "Law as a Weapon in Social Conflict." *Social Problems* 23:276–291.

Walker, Howard, and Bernard P. Cohen 1985 "Scope Statements." *American Sociological Review* 50:288–301.

Wolfgang, Marvin L, and Franco Ferracuti 1967 *The Subculture of Violence: Towards an Integrated Theory in Criminology.* London: Tavistock.

Young, Peter 1983 "Sociology, the State and Penal Relations." In David Garland and Peter Young, eds., *The Power to Punish.* London: Heinemann.

– GEORGE S. BRIDGES

DISABILITY RIGHTS MOVEMENT

The disability rights movement comprises a number of related but distinct social movements advocating civil rights for an estimated 43 million U.S. citizens with physical, sensory, psychological, or cognitive disabilities that affect their daily activities. Emerging after World War II, these movements replaced a medical model of disability with a minority-group model. The medical model defined disability as physical, psychosocial, and vocational limitation resulting from illness or injury. Locating the problem within individuals, it prescribed the solution as treatment to cure or at least correct individual functioning. The minority model asserted that limitations in social and vocational functioning were not the exclusive and inevitable result of bodily impairment but were also a product of the inadequacies in the architectural and social environment. Thus, for example, paralyzed legs did not inevitably cause limitations in mobility, but the absence of ramps did. The new model saw devaluation of disabled persons as producing socioeconomic discrimination.

Chicago's "ugly" law, prohibited "diseased, maimed, mutilated, or . . . deformed" persons from appearing in public.

The disability rights movements arose in response to a historic legacy of discrimination and segregation. In the late nineteenth and early twentieth centuries, most professionals in medicine, social services, and education increasingly attributed a lack of moral and emotional self-control to the "defective classes," which included virtually anyone with a disability, blaming them for the poverty, vice, crime, and dislocations of the new industrial order. People with mental retardation, epilepsy, or cerebral palsy were often permanently institutionalized as a danger to society. Others with physical disabilities were at times segregated by such ordinances as Chicago's "ugly" law, which prohibited "diseased, maimed, mutilated, or . . . deformed" persons from appearing in public. Reacting to an emerging deaf subculture, an "oralist" movement began in the 1880s to oppose sign language and insist that deaf people learn speech and speech-reading. Led by Alexander Graham Bell, it took over much of deaf education and sought to disperse the deaf community. Eugenicists pressed for the sterilization of people with various disabilities, and by 1931 more than half the states had adopted sterilization laws, and thousands of people were sterilized. Meanwhile, contemporary welfare policy defined disability as the incapacity for productive labor and, in effect, incompetency to manage one's life, and thus brought many disabled people under permanent medical and social-service supervision and relegated them to a stigmatized and segregated economic dependency.

Beginning during World War I some professionals avowed continuing faith in treatment and training. Special education of disabled children and medical-vocational rehabilitation of disabled adults sought to correct the functional limitations that allegedly prevented social integration. People with physical and sensory disabilities were imbued with an ethos of individualistic striving known as "overcoming," with President Franklin D. Roosevelt as the prime example during the 1930s and early 1940s. Mentally handicapped people, however, were still often institutionalized or subjected to social control in the community. After 1945 the disability rights movements developed in opposition to these ideologies and practices. Parents' groups lobbied in state legislatures and in Congress for the right of disabled children to a "free and appropriate" public education in "the least restrictive environment"—integration to the maximum extent. These principles were embodied in the Education for All Handicapped Children Act of 1975. Other parents' groups and reform-minded professionals promoted deinstitutionalization and community-based group homes for developmentally disabled persons.

Beginning in the late 1960s deaf advocates redefined deafness as a linguistic difference and demanded their rights to sign language and cultural self-determination. Their efforts culminated in the March 1988 "Deaf President Now" campaign at Gallaudet University, when a student strike at that university for deaf people, supported by the deaf community, won its demand for selection of a deaf educator to head the university. Meanwhile, physically disabled activists launched an independent-living movement for self-directed, community-based living. They also claimed the right of equal access to public transit and public accommodations. Through lobbying and demonstrations they won passage and increasing enforcement of accessibility statutes. The organized blind movement, long the most politically effective disability movement, lobbied successfully for both access (the right to use white canes and guide dogs in public places) and policies to advance economic well-being (through tax exemptions, for example).

All these efforts reflected an emerging minority consciousness documented in a 1986 opinion survey of disabled adults: 54 percent of those aged eighteen to forty-four identified disabled people as a minority group that faced discrimination. The movement thus demanded federal protection against discrimination in education, jobs, public accommodations, and government-funded activities. Antidiscrimination and the right of equal access were the basis of fifty federal laws that began with the Architectural Barriers Act of 1968 and culminated in the Americans with Disabilities Act of 1990. These statutes adopted the disability rights movements' major contribution to U.S. civil rights theory—the concept of equal access. Adaptive devices, assistive services, and architectural modifications (for example, Braille markings, sign-language interpreters, and ramps) had been considered special benefits to those who were fundamentally dependent. Equal access moved beyond such social welfare notions by viewing these provisions as reasonable accommodations for different ways of functioning. Traditional civil rights theory sometimes allowed differential treatment of a minority as a temporary remedy to achieve equality. Disability rights ideology argued that for persons with disabilities, permanent differential treatment in the form of accessibility and reasonable accommodations was legitimate because it was necessary to achieve and maintain equal access and thus equal opportunity for full participation in society.

– PAUL K. LONGMORE

A number of federal laws formalized the concept of equal access for United States citizens with disabilities. Consequently, efforts to provide access have spread even to such places as this tourist train in Colorado. (Lowell Georgia/Corbis)

DISASTER RESEARCH

Descriptions of calamities go as far back as the earliest human writings, but systematic empirical studies and theoretical treatises on social aspects of disasters have appeared only in the twentieth century. The first publications in both cases were produced by sociologists. Samuel Prince (1920) wrote a doctoral dissertation in sociology at Columbia University that examined the social change consequences of a munitions ship explosion in the harbor of Halifax, Canada. Two decades later, Pitirim Sorokin (1942) wrote *Man and Society in Calamity,* which mostly speculated on how war, revolution, famine, and pestilence might affect the mental processes, behavior, social organizational, and cultural life of involved populations.

However, there was no building on these pioneering efforts, and it was not until the early 1950s that disaster studies started to show any continuity and the accumulation of a knowledge base. Military interest in possible American civilian reactions to post-World War II threats from nuclear and biological warfare led to support of academic research on peacetime disasters, with the key project being done in 1950–1954 by the National Opinion Research Center (NORC) at the university of Chicago. This project, in intent multidisciplinary, came to be dominated by sociologists, as were other studies at about the same time at the University of Oklahoma, Michigan State University, and the University of Texas. The NORC study not only promoted field research as the major way of studying behavior but also brought sociological ideas from collective behavior and notions of organizational structure and functions into the thinking of disaster researchers (Quarantelli and Dynes 1977; Dynes 1988).

While the military interest quickly waned, research in the area obtained a strategic point of salience and support when the U.S. National Academy of Sciences created the Disaster Research Group (DRG) in the late 1950s. Operationally run by sociologists using the NORC work as a prototype, the DRG supported field research of others in addition to conducting its own studies (Fritz 1961). When DRG was phased out in 1963, the Disaster Research Center (DRC) was established at Ohio State University. DRC helped the field of study to become institutionalized by its continuous existence to the present day (having moved to the University of Delaware in 1985) and by the training of dozens of graduate students, the building of the largest specialized library in the world on social aspects of disasters, the production of over five hundred publications, the continual and conscious opening up to a sociological perspective of new disaster research topics, the setting up of an interactive computer net of researchers in the area, and an intentional effort to help create domestic and international networks and critical masses of disaster researchers (Quarantelli and Dynes 1977; Kreps 1984).

The sociological work in disasters was joined in the late 1960s by geographers with interest in natural hazards, and in the 1980s by risk analysts especially concerned with technological threats (Perrow 1984; Short 1984). The initial focus by sociologists on emergency time behavior also broadened to include studies on mitigation and prevention as well as recovery and reconstruction. More important, in the 1980s disaster research spread around the world and led to the development of a critical mass of researchers that culminated in 1986 in the establishment within the International Sociological Association of the Research Committee on Disasters, with membership in over thirty countries; its own professional journal, *International Journal of Mass Emergencies and Disasters;* and a newsletter, *Unscheduled Events.* Sociologists are particularly prominent in current research in China, Germany, Italy, Japan, and Sweden as well as in the United States.

Conceptualization of "Disaster"

Conceptualizations and definitions of "disaster" have slowly evolved from acceptance of everyday usages of the term, through a focus on social aspects, to attempts to set forth more sociological characterizations. The earliest definitions equated disasters with features of physical agents and made distinctions between "acts of God" and "technological" agents. This was followed by notions that disasters were phenomena that resulted in significant disruptions of social life, which, however, might not involve a physical agent of any kind (e.g., a rumor that a dam had burst could evoke the same kind of evacuation behavior, etc., that an actual event would). More recently disasters have been seen not only as social constructions of reality by responders, but also as the political definitions of certain socially disruptive crises in social systems. Other researchers equate disasters with occasions where the demand for emergency actions by community organizations exceeds their capabilities for response. Finally, more recent conceptions of disasters see them as overt manifestations of latent societal vulnerabilities, basically of weaknesses in social structures or systems (Quarantelli 1987; Kreps 1989a; Schorr 1987).

Given these variants about the concept, it is not surprising that no one formulation is totally accepted within the disaster research community. However, there would be considerable agreement that the following would constitute the dimensions involved in using the term "disaster" as a sensitizing concept. Disasters are relatively sudden occasions when, because of perceived threats, the routines of the collective social units involved are seriously disrupted and when unplanned courses of action have to be undertaken to cope with the crisis. The notion of relatively sudden occasions indicates that disasters have unexpected life histories that can be designated in social space and time. Disasters involve perceptions of dangers and risks to valued social objects, especially people and property. The idea of disruption of routines indicates that everyday adjustive social mechanisms cannot cope with the perceived threats. Disasters necessitate the emergence of new behaviors not in the standard repertoire of the endangered collectivity, a community, which is usually the lowest social-level entity accepted by researchers as being able to have a disaster (Kreps 1989b).

The notion of "relatively sudden occasions" indicates that disasters have unexpected life histories that can be designated in social space and time.

In the process of refining the concept, sociologists have almost totally abandoned the distinction between "natural" and "technological" disasters; any disaster is seen as inherently social in nature, whether this be origin, manifestation, or consequences. However, there is lack of consensus on whether social happenings involving intentional, deliberate human actions to produce social disruptions, such as occur in riots, civil disturbances, terrorist attacks, product tampering or sabotage, or wars, should be considered disasters. The majority who oppose their inclusion argue that conflict situations are inherently different in their social intentions and goals. They note that in disaster occasions there is no conscious attempt to bring about negative effects as there is in conflict situations (Quarantelli 1987). However, there is general agreement that both conflict- and consensus-type emergencies are part of a more general category of collective stress situations, as first suggested by Allan Barton (1970).

Major Research Findings

While the research efforts have been uneven, much has been learned about the behavior of individuals, organizations, communities, and societies in the pre-, trans-, and postimpact time periods (Kreps 1984, 1985; Drabek 1986).

PREIMPACT BEHAVIOR. *Individuals.* Most individuals show little concern about disasters before they happen, even in risk-prone areas. Citizens tend to see disaster planning as primarily a moral rather than a legal responsibility of the government. Exceptions to these passive attitudes occur where there is much recurrent experience of disasters, as occurs in some developing countries, where disaster subcultures (institutionalized expectations) have developed and where potential disaster settings, such as at hazardous-waste sites, are the focus of attention of citizen groups.

Organizations. Except for some disaster-oriented groups such as police and fire departments, there usually is little organizational planning for disasters. Even agencies that plan tend to think of disasters as extensions of everyday emergencies and fail, according to researchers, to recognize the qualitative as well as quantitative differences between routine crises and disaster occasions. These involve the fact that in disasters the involved organizations have to quickly relate to more and different groups than normal, adjust to losing part of their autonomy to overall coordinating groups, apply different performance standards and criteria, operate within a closer-than-usual public and private interface, and function when their own facilities and operations may be directly impacted by the disaster agent.

Communities. Usually low priority is given to preparing localities for disasters, and when there is some effort it is almost always independent of general community development and planning. This reflects the reactive rather than the proactive orientation of most politicians and bureaucrats and the fact that the issue of planning very seldom becomes a matter of broad community interests, as would be indicated by mass media focus, discussions in the political arena, or interest groups. Efforts to initiate general overall disaster preparedness often are hindered by prior organizational and community conflicts, cleavages, and disputes.

Societies. Generally disaster planning does not rank very high on the agenda of most societies. However, increasingly there are exceptions in developing countries when major recurrent disasters have major impact on the gross national product and on developmental programs. Also, certain catastrophes such as a Bhopal or Chernobyl can become symbolic occasions that lend impetus to instituting preparedness measures for specific disaster agents. Increasingly, too, attention to national-level disaster planning has increased as citizens in recent times have come to expect their governments to provide more security in general for the population.

TRANSEMERGENCY PERIOD BEHAVIOR. *Individuals.* When disasters occur, individuals generally react very well. They are not paralyzed by a threat but actively seek relevant information and attempt to do what they can in the emergency. Victims, while usually very frightened, not only act positively but also show little deviant behavior; they extremely seldom break in panic flight; they do not act irrationally, especially from their perspective; and they very rarely engage in antisocial activities, although stories of such contrary behavior as looting may circulate very widely. Prosocial behavior especially comes to the fore, with the initial search and rescue being undertaken quickly and mostly by survivors in the immediate area. Most immediate needs, such as emergency housing, are met by family and friends rather than by official relief agencies. Family and household relationships are very important in affecting immediate reactions to disasters, such as whether evacuation will occur or whether warnings will be taken seriously.

Organizations. While there are many organizational problems in coping with the emergency time period demands of a disaster, these difficulties are often not the expected ones. Often it is assumed that if there has been organizational disaster planning, there will be successful crisis or emergency management; but apart from the possibility of planning being poor in the first place, planning is not management, and the former does not always translate well into the latter in community disasters. There typically are problems in intra- and interorganizational information flow, and in communication between and to organizations and the general public. Groups initially often have to struggle with major gaps in knowledge about the impact of a disaster. There can be organizational problems in the exercise of authority and decision making. These can stem from losses of higher-echelon personnel because of overwork, conflict regarding authority over new disaster tasks, and clashes over organizational jurisdictional differences. Generally there is much decentralization of organizational response, which in most cases is highly functional. Organizations operating with a command and control model of response do not do well at emergency times. Often, too, problems created by new disaster tasks and by the magnitude of a disaster impact strain organizational relationships.

Communities. The greater the disaster, the more there will be the emergence of new and adaptive community structures and functions, especially emergent groups. The greater the disaster, the more organized improvisations of all kinds appear, accompanied by pluralistic decision making. While functional in some ways, the mass convergence of outside personnel and resources on

impacted communities creates major coordination problems.

Societies. Few societies ignore major disasters, but this does occur, especially in the case of slow and diffuse occurrences such as droughts and famines, and especially if they primarily affect subgroups not in the mainstream of a developing country. In responding to domestic disasters, societies typically provide massive help to impacted areas, even using help from outside enemies. Increasingly, most societies, including governmental officials at all levels, obtain their view of their disasters from mass media accounts; this also affects what is often remembered about the occasions.

POSTIMPACT BEHAVIOR. *Individuals.* While the experience of a major disaster is a memorable one from a social-psychological point of view, there do not appear to be many lasting negative behavioral consequences. Disasters very seldom produce any new psychoses or severe mental illnesses. They do often, but not always, generate subclinical, short-lived, and self-remitting surface reactions, such as loss of appetite, sleeplessness, and anxiety. More common are many problems in living that stem more from inefficient and ineffective relief and recovery efforts of helping organizations than from the direct physical impact of disasters. In some cases, the experience of undergoing a disaster results in positive self-images and closer social ties among victims. Overall, there is little personal learning as a result of undergoing a single disaster.

Organizations. Organizational change, whether for planning for disasters or for other purposes, in the postimpact period is not common and is selective at best. Most modifications are simply accelerations of changes already planned or under way. Much postimpact discussion of how to improve disaster planning seldom gets translated into concrete action (unlike civil distur-

These rescuers of an earthquake victim are behaving typically of individuals in a disaster situation, reacting swiftly and helpfully. (UPI/Corbis-Bettmann)

bances, which at least in American society in the 1960s led to many changes in organizations). However, overall, both in the United States and elsewhere, there has been in recent decades the growth of small, locally based, formal social groups primarily concerned with emergency time disaster planning and management.

Communities. There are selective longer-run outcomes and changes in communities that have been impacted by disasters. There can be acceleration of some ongoing and functional community trends (e.g., in local governmental arrangements and power structures), and generation of some limited new patterns (e.g., in providing local mental-health services or some mitigation measures such as regulations for floodproofing). On the other hand, particularly as the result of rehousing and rebuilding patterns, there can be magnifications of preimpact community conflicts as well as generation of new ones; some of the latter is manifested in blame assignation, which, however, tends to deflect attention away from social structural flaws to a mass-media-influenced search for individual scapegoats. It is also being recognized after disasters that changes in technology that create diffuse networks and systems, such as among lifeline organizations, are increasingly creating the need for regional rather than just community-based disaster planning.

Societies. In developed societies, there are few long-run negative consequences of disaster losses, whether of people or of property, since such effects are absorbed by the larger system. In developing societies and very small countries, this is not necessarily true. Nevertheless, change or improvement in national disaster planning often does not occur; cases such as after the 1985 Mexico City earthquake, when an unusual set of circumstances existed, including a "political will" to do something, constitute the exception. But increasingly, in the aftermath of major disasters, to the extent that planning is instituted or improved, it is being linked to developmental planning, a move strongly supported by international agencies such as the World Bank.

The Future

There is a dialectical process at work: There will be more and worse disasters at the same time that there will be more and better planning. Why more and worse disasters? Risks and threats to human beings and their society are increasing. Traditional natural-disaster agents such as earthquakes and floods will simply have more people on whom to impact as the result of normal population growth and higher, denser concentration of inhabitants in risk-prone localities such as flood-plains or hurricane-vulnerable shorelines that otherwise are attractive for human occupancy. There is an escalating increase in certain kinds of technological accidents and mishaps in the chemical, nuclear, and hazardous-waste areas that are new in that they were almost unknown before World War II. Technological advances can create risks and complexities to old threats, such as when fires are prevented in high-rise buildings by constructing them with highly toxic materials, or when removal of hazardous substances from solid sewage waste generates products that contain dangerous viruses and gases. New versions of old threats are also appearing, such as the increasing probability of urban rather than rural droughts, or the potential large-scale collapse of the infrastructure of older metropolitan area lifeline systems. Finally, there is the continual development of newer kinds of risks ranging from the AIDS epidemic to the biological threats inherent in genetic engineering to the crises that will be generated as the world increasingly becomes dependent on computers that are bound to fail at some key point, with drastic consequences for social systems. In addition, the newer threats are frequently dangerous at places and times distant from their initial source or origin, as dramatized by the Chernobyl nuclear radiation fallout and some problems regarding hazardous-waste sites (Quarantelli 1987).

On the other hand, increasing concern and attention is being paid to disaster planning of all kinds. The future augurs well for more and better planning. Citizens almost everywhere are coming to expect that their governments will take steps to protect them against disasters; this is often actualized in planning for emergency preparedness and response. Whereas two decades ago a number of societies had no preimpact disaster planning of any kind, this is no longer the case. A symbolic manifestation of this trend has been the proclamation by the United Nations of the 1990s as the Decade for Natural-Disaster Reduction. This international attention will undoubtedly accelerate efforts at planning for better prevention of, preparation for, response to, and recovery from disasters; an activity in which there is reason to believe that social scientists, especially sociologists, will have an important role.

Relationship to Sociology

Although this is not true everywhere, sociologists have been increasingly accepted as having an important contribution to make to disaster planning. In part this stems from the fact that in many countries they have played the lead role among social scientists in undertaking disaster studies. While many reasons account for this, probably the crucial factor has been that much in general sociology can be used in doing research in this area.

There has been a close relationship between disaster studies and sociology from the earliest days of work in the area (Killian 1952; Form and Nosow 1958). In part this is because sociologists, being among the leading pioneers and researchers in this area, have tended to use what they could from their discipline. Thus, sociology has contributed to the research techniques used (e.g., field studies and open-ended interviewing), the research methodology utilized (e.g., the "grounded theory" approach and the employment of inductive analytical models), the theoretical ideas utilized (e.g., the notion of emergence from collective-behavior thinking and the idea of informal and formal structures of organizations), and the general perspectives used (e.g., that there can be latent as well as dysfunctional aspects of any behavior and that societies and communities have a social history that is not easily set aside). In a recent volume entitled *Sociology of Disasters: Contributions of Sociology to Disaster Research* (Dynes, De Marchi, and Pelanda 1987), these and other contributions to disaster theory, disaster research methods, disaster models, and disaster concepts are set forth in considerable detail (see also Wright and Rossi 1981).

There is a dialectical process working: There will be more and worse disasters at the same time that there will be more and better planning.

The relationship has not been one-sided, since disaster research has also contributed to sociology. The field of collective behavior has probably been most influenced, but there have been significant contributions to the study of formal organizations, social roles, social problems, organizational and social change, mass communications, the urban community, and medical sociology (Dynes and Quarantelli 1968; Dynes 1974; Quarantelli 1978; Wright and Rossi 1981; Kreps 1984; Quarantelli 1989). A recent symposium on social structure and disaster, coattended by disaster researchers and prominent sociological theorists, attempted to examine how disaster studies not only are informed by but also could inform sociological theory; the proceedings have been published in *Social Structure and Disaster* (Kreps 1989b).

[See also Technological Risks and Society.]

BIBLIOGRAPHY

Barton, Allan 1970 *Communities in Disaster: A Sociological Analysis.* Garden City, N.Y.: Anchor Books.

Drabek, Thomas 1986 *Human System Responses to Disasters: An Inventory of Sociological Findings.* New York: Springer-Verlag.

Dynes, R. R. 1974 *Organized Behavior in Disasters.* Newark, Del.: Disaster Research Center, University of Delaware.

——— (ed.) 1988 "Disaster Classics Special Issue." *International Journal of Mass Emergencies and Disasters* 6:209–395.

———, B. De Marchi, and C. Pelanda (eds.) 1987 *Sociology of Disaster: Contributions of Sociology to Disaster Research.* Milan: Franco Angeli.

———, and E. L. Quarantelli 1968 "Group Behavior Under Stress: A Required Convergence of Organizational and Collective Behavior Perspectives." *Sociology and Social Research* 52:416–429.

Form, William, and Sigmund Nosow 1958 *Community in Disaster.* New York: Harper and Row.

Fritz, Charles 1961 "Disaster." In Robert Merton and Robert Nisbet, eds., *Contemporary Social Problems.* New York: Harcourt, Brace and World.

Killian, Lewis 1952 "The Significance of Multiple Group Membership in Disaster Study." *American Journal of Sociology* 57:309–314.

Kreps, Gary 1984 "Sociological Inquiry and Disaster Research." *Annual Review of Sociology* 10:309–333.

——— 1985 "Disaster and the Social Order." *Sociological Theory* 3:49–65.

——— (ed.) 1989a "The Boundaries of Disaster Research: Taxonomy and Comparative Study Special Issue." *International Journal of Mass Emergencies and Disasters* 7:213–431.

———1989b *Social Structure and Disaster.* Newark, Del.: University of Delaware Press.

Perrow, Charles 1984 *Normal Accidents: Living with High-Risk Technologies.* New York: Basic Books.

Prince, Samuel 1920 *Catastrophe and Social Change.* New York: Columbia University Press.

Quarantelli, E. L. (ed.) 1978 *Disasters: Theory and Research.* Beverly Hills, Calif.: Sage Publications.

——— 1987 "What Should We Study? Questions and Suggestions for Researchers About the Concept of Disasters." *International Journal of Mass Emergencies and Disasters* 5:7–32.

——— 1989 "The Social Science Study of Disasters and Mass Communication." In L. Walters, L. Wilkins, and T. Walters, eds., *Bad Tidings: Communication and Catastrophe.* Hillsdale, N. J.: Lawrence Erlbaum.

———, and R. R. Dynes 1977 "Response to Social Crises and Disasters." *Annual Review of Sociology* 3:23–49.

Schorr, J. 1987 "Some Contributions of German *Katastrophensoziologie* to the Sociology of Disaster." *International Journal of Mass Emergencies and Disasters* 5:115–135.

Short, James F. 1984 "The Social Fabric at Risk: Toward the Social Transformation of Risk Analysis." *American Sociological Review* 49:711–725.

Sorokin, Pitirim 1942 *Man and Society in Calamity.* New York: E. P. Dutton.

Wright, James, and Peter Rossi (eds.) 1981 *Social Science and Natural Hazards.* Cambridge, Mass.: Abt Books.

– ENRICO L. QUARANTELLI

DISCRIMINATION

Discrimination, in its sociological meaning, involves highly complex social processes. The term derives from the Latin *discriminatio,* which means to perceive distinctions among phenomena or to be selective in one's judgment. Cognitive psychology retains the first of these meanings, popular usage the second. Individual behavior that limits the opportunities of a particular group is encompassed in many sociological considerations of discrimination. But exclusively individualistic approaches are too narrow for robust sociological treatment. Instead, most sociologists understand discrimination not as isolated individual acts but as "a system of social relations" (Antonovsky 1960, p. 81) that produce intergroup inequities in social outcomes.

This definitional expansion transforms "discrimination" into a truly sociological concept. But in its breadth, the sociological definition leaves room for ambiguity and controversy. Obstacles to consensus on a more precise definition stem from two sources—one empirical, the other ideological and political. First, deficiencies in analysis and evidence limit our ability to trace thoroughly the dynamic web of effects produced by discrimination. Second, because social discrimination is contrary to professed American values and law, a judgment that unequal outcomes reflect discrimination is a call for costly remedies. Variable willingness to bear those social costs contributes to dissension about the extent of discrimination.

The broadest sociological definitions of discrimination assume that racial minorities, women, and other historical targets have no inherent characteristics warranting inferior social outcomes. Thus, all inequality is seen as a legacy of discrimination, whether proximal or distal, and as a social injustice to be remedied.

By contrast, political conservatives favor a far narrower definition, one that limits the concept's scope by including only actions *intended* to restrict a group's chances. For solid conceptual reasons, sociologists have seldom followed suit (but see Burkey 1978, p. 79). First, an intentionality criterion returns the concept to the realm of psychology and deflects attention from restraining social structure. Second, the difficulty in ascertaining intentions creates insuperable obstacles to thorough documentation of discrimination.

Most important, their understanding of intricate societal patterns sensitizes sociologists to the fact that disadvantage accruing from intentional discrimination typically cumulates, extends far beyond the original injury, and long outlives the deliberate perpetration. Many sociologists distinguish between *direct* and *indirect* discrimination (Pettigrew 1985). Direct discrimination occurs at points where inequality is generated, often intentionally. When decisions are based explicitly on race, discrimination is direct. Indirect discrimination is the perpetuation or magnification of the original injury. It occurs when the inequitable results of direct discrimination are used as a basis for later decisions ("past-in-present discrimination") or decisions in linked institutions ("side-effect discrimination"; Feagin and Feagin 1986). In other words, discrimination is indirect when an ostensibly nonracial criterion serves as a *proxy* for race in determining social outcomes.

To illustrate with respect to wages, direct discrimination exists when equally qualified blacks and whites or men and women are paid at different rates for the same work. Indirect discrimination exists when the two groups are paid unequally because prior discrimination in employment, education, or housing created apparent differences in qualifications or channeled the groups into better- and worse-paying jobs. This direct versus indirect distinction resembles the legal distinction between disparate treatment and disparate impact. While intentional direct discrimination may have triggered the causal chain, the original injury is often perpetuated and magnified by unwitting social actors. The application of intentionality criteria would deny that the continuing disadvantage is a legacy of discrimination.

A half-century ago, Williams restricted the concept differently. "Discrimination may be said to exist to the degree that individuals of a given group who are otherwise *formally qualified* are not treated in conformity with these nominally *universal institutionalized codes*" (Williams 1947, p. 39, emphasis added). Antonovsky (1960, p. 81) used a related qualification: Discrimination is "the effective injurious treatment of persons on grounds *rationally irrelevant* to the situation" (emphasis added). Economists use starker terms. For Becker (1968, p. 81), economic discrimination occurs "against members of a group whenever their earnings fall short of the amount *'warranted' by their abilities*" (emphasis added).

Two problems arise with these definitions. First, the assessment of "abilities" and the determination of what treatment is "rationally" relevant or "warranted" is no easy task. Critical examination of common practice has uncovered many instances where formal qualifications and "nominally universal institutionalized codes" proved *not* to provide a logical basis for distinctions. Recent employment testing litigation demonstrates that when hiring criteria once legitimized by tradition or "logic" are put to scientific test, they often fail to predict job performance in the assumed fashion. Analogous fallacies have been identified in the conventional wisdom guiding admission to advanced education. Hence, nominally universalistic standards may provide an imperfect or altogether illogical basis for decision making. If such misguided selection procedures also work to the disadvantage of historical victims of discrimination, these practices should not be protected from the charge of discrimination by their universalistic facade.

The second problem with these definitions is that they ignore another, prevalent form of indirect discrimination. Even where nominally universalistic standards do serve some legitimate social function such as selecting satisfactory workers, adverse impact of these standards on those who bear the cumulated disadvantage of historical discrimination cannot be disregarded.

The intricacy of discrimination and unresolved issues about its definition impede easy application of social science methods to inform institutional policy. Apparently rigorous quantitative analyses often only camouflage the crucial issues, as critical examination of wage differential decompositions reveals.

Through their interpretation of findings, researchers consciously or unwittingly shape their own answers: Any appearance of scientific certitude is an illusion.

Assessments of discrimination, produced by decomposing gross race or gender differences in such social outcomes as wages, are common in sociology (e.g., Corcoran and Duncan 1978; Farley 1984; Featherman and Hauser 1976; Johnson and Sell 1976) as well as economics (e.g., Oaxaca 1973). One segment of the intergroup differential is defined by its empirical linkage to "qualifications" and other factors deemed legitimate determinants of social rewards. The second, residual segment not demonstrably linked to "legitimate" determinants of the outcomes is sometimes labeled the measure of "proximal" or "direct" discrimination but more often is presented simply as the estimate of discrimination. However, in the absence of better information than usually available and greater agreement on what constitutes discrimination, no *unique* estimate is possible. Through their choice of control variables to index "legitimate" determinants of social outcomes and their interpretation of findings, researchers consciously or unwittingly shape their own answers: Any appearance of scientific certitude is an illusion. For example, estimates of the proportion of the gender earnings gap caused by discrimination in the United States range from Sanborn's (1969) 10 percent or less to Blinder's (1973) 100 percent. Predictably, each has been challenged (Bergman and Adelman 1973; Rosensweig and Morgan 1976).

A close look at one application of the decompositional approach, a recent analysis of sex differentials in faculty salaries at a large public university, illustrates the difficulty of separating "legitimate" wage differentials from inequity (Taylor 1988). About 90 percent of a $10,000 sex difference in faculty salaries was empirically linked to three factors widely considered legitimate determinants of faculty pay: academic rank, age, and discipline. Women tend to hold lower academic rank, to be younger, and more often than men to be affiliated with poorly paid disciplines. Insofar as women's lower salaries are linked to rank, age, and discipline, is the salary differential free from any legacy of sex discrimination? Conventional wage differential decompositions imply an unequivocal yes. If a simple answer is given, it surely should be no. But in truth, when policymakers ask for dollar estimates of inequity, or specifically for inequity that the institution is obliged to remedy, the answers are neither unequivocal nor simple.

If the university's promotion system has operated fairly, a sex gap reflecting differences in rank may be warranted. If sex bias has existed in the university's promotion system, depressing the average academic rank of women faculty, the resulting deficit in women's salaries reflects indirect discrimination; attention should then be directed to the offending promotion processes. However, direct salary adjustments may also be in order, because sex bias in promotions makes the link between rank and salary itself look unreasonable. Unlike many embodiments of indirect discrimination, inequitable depression of women's ranks would not necessarily lessen their actual contributions to the faculty, just their status. Application of a universalistic salary determination standard based on rank would then stand as an impediment to the very goal it was intended to promote—the matching of rewards to contributions.

Salary differences tied to the age differential of female and male faculty also raise troublesome questions. If the relative youth of women faculty reflects lower retention and higher turnover as a result of discriminatory review processes or generally inhospitable conditions, salary differentials tied to age differences are again textbook examples of indirect discrimination. The evidence would signal a need for institutional efforts to improve the retention of women faculty. But here it is not clear that salary adjustments are warranted: Because faculty contributions may be a function of experience, application of the universalistic age criterion is arguably reasonable. Any sex gap in salary tied to age differentials could, then, be both a legacy of discrimination and a reasonable conditioning of rewards on contributions. The age-linked salary differential plot grows even thicker when it is recognized that affirmative action efforts often meet with greatest success in recruiting junior candidates. Thus, without supplementary data, it is not even clear whether an age-linked sex gap in salary reflects continuing institutional discrimination or affirmative hiring.

Sex differences in salary associated with discipline present even more complicated interpretational problems. Women and men are distributed across academic disciplines in a fashion that mirrors the sex distribution across occupations. And disciplinary differences in average salary likewise mirror wage differentials across occupations. But are these patterns simply a matter of sex differences in preferences or abilities, with no implication of discrimination? Or are women steered away or outright excluded from lucrative fields, so that sex differentials in salary linked to disciplinary affiliation represent an indirect effect of discrimination in training, recruitment, and hiring? Or does the pattern of occupational wage differentials mirrored in disciplinary differences represent direct discrimination, an influence of sex composition per se on occupational wage structures (England et al. 1988)? In the latter case, assignment of responsibility for remedy presents particular problems. The university, like any other single employer, is simultaneously vulnerable to competitive forces of the wider labor market and a constituent element of that wider market. Defiance of the market by a single organization is costly; adherence by all organizations to the broader occupational wage structure perpetuates sex inequity.

The faculty salary study considered here did not examine the role of scientific "productivity" in relation to salary differentials. But the inclusion of productivity measures among the control variables would raise another difficult issue involving feedback effects and reciprocal causation. There is evidence that on standard "productivity" measures, women faculty average lower scores than men (Fox 1991). Thus, many institutional studies of salary differentials would probably find some segment of the male-female salary gap linked to productivity differences. Fox's research demonstrates, however, that sex differences in scientific productivity reflect contrasting levels of resources that institutions provide to male and female faculty. Like age and rank, the sex difference in productivity may itself be a product of institutional discrimination; by implication, salary differentials based on these male-female productivity differences represent indirect discrimination. The new ingredient here is that institutional shaping of productivity is subtle. Scientific productivity is ordinarily seen as an outgrowth of talent and effort, not potentially sex-biased institutional resource allocation. Thus, credible documentation of this process of indirect discrimination is a greater challenge for researchers.

Critical reflection on this sample decomposition of a sex differential in faculty salaries has highlighted a set of interrelated points about the complex nature of discrimination and unresolved issues of remedy.

1. In American society today, the injuries of indirect discrimination are often far more extensive than those of direct discrimination.
2. Apparently reasonable universalistic principles may on closer examination be unnecessary or even dysfunctional. Scrutiny of employment criteria prompted by the Supreme Court's 1971 *Griggs* v. *Duke Power Co.* decision has provided useful models for challenging nominally universalistic standards. Where it is possible to substitute standards that do as well or better at screening or evaluation without adversely affecting historical targets of discrimination, there are gains for all involved.
3. When legacies of discrimination take the form of qualifications that may well be reasonable prerequisites for social rewards, as with experience and salary, more extensive remedies are needed. For example, where training deficits impair employability, or inadequate preparation impedes admission to higher education, attention should be given to the earlier schooling processes that generated these deficiencies. This form of remedy aids future generations. In the meantime, compensatory training can reduce the liabilities of those who have already fallen victim to inferior schools.
4. Microcosms cannot escape the discriminatory impact of the societal macrocosm. Just as salary differences across academic disciplines reflect general occupational wage structures, institutions are often both prey to and participant in broader social forces. Narrow, legalistic approaches to the assignment of remedy are inadequate for addressing this dynamic of discrimination.
5. Empirical research on group discrimination must mirror the phenomenon in its variety and complexity. The regression decomposition approach described here has proven useful, but we have noted its limitations. Regression analyses could provide more pertinent information if based on fuller structural equation models that acknowledge reciprocal causation. Most important, if the aim is to guide policy, a framework considerably more complex than the dichotomous discrimination-or-not approach is required. But the sociological arsenal of methods offers other promising approaches. Research that traces the actual processes of institutional discrimination is essential (e.g., Braddock, Crain, and McPartland 1984; Braddock and McPartland 1987; Braddock and McPartland 1989). Also needed is attention to victims' perceptions of discrimination processes and investigation of the changes generated by antidiscrimination efforts.

Finally, a comprehensive understanding of societal discrimination must encompass these two propositions.

1. The long-lasting character of discrimination means that the effects typically outlive the initiators of discriminatory practices. Apart from its importance to the law, this feature of modern discrimination has critical implications for sociological theory. Discrimination is fundamentally normative; its structural web operates in large part independent of the dominant group's present "tastes," attitudes, or awareness. Hence, models based primarily on individual prejudice or "rationality," whether psychological or economic, will uniformly understate and oversimplify the phenomenon.
2. Discrimination is typically cumulative, compounding, and self-perpetuating. For example, an array of research on black Americans has demonstrated that neighborhood racial segregation leads to educational disadvantages, thus to occupational disadvantage, and thus to income

deficits (Pettigrew 1979; 1985). To be effective, structural remedies must reverse this "vicious cycle" of discrimination (Myrdal 1944).

Seen in sociological perspective, then, discrimination is considerably more intricate and entrenched than commonly thought. The complexity of discrimination presents major challenges to social scientific attempts to trace its impact. This complexity also makes impossible any one-to-one correspondence between perpetration and responsibility for remedy. Broad social programs will be necessary if the full legacy of discrimination is finally to be erased.

[See also Affirmative Action; Comparable Worth; Equality of Opportunity; Prejudice; Race; Segregation and Desegregation.]

BIBLIOGRAPHY

Antonovsky, A. 1960 "The Social Meaning of Discrimination." *Phylon* (11):81–95.

Becker, G. 1968 "Economic Discrimination." In D. L. Sills, ed., *International Encyclopedia of the Social Sciences.* New York: Macmillan.

Bergman, B. R., and I. Adelman 1973 "The 1973 Report of the President's Council of Economic Advisors: The Economic Role of Women." *American Economic Review* (63):509–514.

Blinder, A. S. 1973 "Wage Discrimination: Reduced Form and Structural Estimates." *Journal of Human Resources* (8):463–455.

Braddock, J. H., II, R. L. Crain, and J. M. McPartland 1984 "A Long-Term View of Racial Desegregation: Some Recent Studies of Graduates as Adults." *Phi Delta Kappan* (66):259–264.

Braddock, J. H., II, and J. M. McPartland 1987 "How Minorities Continue to Be Excluded from Equal Employment Opportunities: Research on Labor Market and Institutional Barriers." *Journal of Social Issues* (43):5–39.

——— 1989 "Social Psychological Processes That Perpetuate Racial Segregation: The Relationship between School and Employment Desegregation." *Journal of Black Studies* (19):267–289.

Burkey, R. 1978 *Ethnic and Racial Groups: The Dynamics of Dominance.* Menlo Park, Calif.: Cummings.

Corcoran, M., and G. J. Duncan 1978 "Work History, Labor Force Attachment, and Earning Differences between Races and Sexes." *Journal of Human Resources* (14):3–20.

England, P., G. Farkas, B. Kilbourne, and T. Dou 1988 "Explaining Occupational Sex Segregation and Wages: Findings from a Model with Fixed Effects." *American Sociological Review* (53):544–558.

Farley, R. 1984 *Blacks and Whites: Narrowing the Gap?* Cambridge, Mass.: Harvard University Press.

Feagin, J. R., and C. B. Feagin 1986 *Discrimination American Style: Institutional Racism and Sexism.* Malabar, Fla.: Krieger.

Featherman, D. L., and R. M. Hauser 1976 "Changes in the Socioeconomic Stratification of the Races, 1962–1973." *American Journal of Sociology* (82):621–652.

Fox, M. F. 1991 "Gender, Environmental Milieux, and Productivity in Science." In J. Cole, H. Zuckerman, and J. Bruer, eds., *The Outer Circle: Women in the Scientific Community.* New York: W. W. Norton.

Johnson, M., and R. Sell 1976 "The Cost of Being Black: A 1970 Update." *American Journal of Sociology* (82):183–190.

Myrdal, G. 1944 *An American Dilemma.* New York: Harper and Row.

Oaxaca, R. 1973 "Male-Female Wage Differentials in Urban Labor Markets." *International Economic Review* (14):693–709.

Pettigrew, T. F. 1979 "Racial Change and Social Policy." *Annals of the American Association of Political and Social Science* (441):114–131.

——— 1985 "New Black-White Patterns: How Best to Conceptualize Them?" In R. Turner, ed., *Annual Review of Sociology, 1985.* Palo Alto, Calif.: Annual Reviews.

Rosensweig, M. R., and J. Morgan 1976 "Wage Discrimination: A Comment." *Journal of Human Resources* (11):3–7.

Sanborn, H. 1969 "Pay Differences between Men and Women." *Industrial and Labor Relations Review* (17):534–550.

Taylor, M. C. 1988 "Estimating Race and Sex Inequity in Wages: Substantive Implications of Methodological Choices." Paper presented at the 1989 Research Conference of the Association for Public Policy Analysis and Management, Seattle, Washington, October 29, 1988.

Williams, R. M., Jr. 1947 *The Reduction of Intergroup Tensions.* New York: Social Science Research Council.

– THOMAS F. PETTIGREW
MARYLEE C. TAYLOR

DIVORCE

Divorce is of sociological significance for several reasons. To begin, divorce rates are often seen as indicators of the health of the institution of marriage. When divorce rates rise or fall, many sociologists have been inclined to view these changes as indicating something about the aggregate quality of marriages or, alternatively, the stability of social systems.

Viewed from another perspective, divorce interests sociologists as one of several important transitions in the life course of individuals. The adults and children who experience divorce have been studied to understand both the causes and consequences. From this perspective, a divorce is an event in the biography of family members, much as other life course transitions (remarriage, childbirth, retirement).

Sociological interest in divorce also focuses on the macrosocial events associated with it. Divorce figures prominently in any sociological analysis of industrialization, poverty, educational attainment, conflict resolution, or law.

At least one-half of all recent marriages will end in divorce.

For sociologists, divorce may characterize an individual, a family, a region, a subgroup, a historical period, or an entire social system. It may be studied as either cause or consequence of other phenomena. Still, the overriding concern of almost all research on this topic in the twentieth century has been the increase in divorce over time. This century began with very little divorce. It draws to a close with divorce being as common as its absence in the lives of recently married couples. Although marital instability has not increased significantly since 1980, present rates are at an all-time high. Recent estimates based on national surveys are that at least one-half of all recent marriages will end in divorce (assuming there is no significant drop in rates of marital disruption; Martin and Bumpass 1989). Understanding the increase in divorce has been the larger sociological endeavor—regardless of the particular sociological perspective employed. A historical account of trends is necessary before considering contemporary issues associated with divorce.

A Brief Historical Record of Divorce in America

THE COLONIAL PERIOD. Divorce was not legal in any but the New England settlements. The Church of England allowed for legal separations (*a mensa et thoro*) but not for divorce. The New England Puritans who first landed at Plymouth in 1621, however, were disenchanted with this, as well as many other Anglican doctrines. Divorce was permitted on the grounds of adultery or seven-year desertion as early as 1639 in Plymouth. Other New England colonies followed similar guidelines. Divorce governed by rudimentary codified law was effected by legislative decree. Individual petitions for divorce were debated in colonial legislatures and were effected by bills to dissolve a particular marriage. Still, though legal, divorce was very rare. During the seventeenth century, there were fifty-four petitions for divorce in Massachusetts, of which forty-four were successful (Phillips 1988, p. 138). The middle colonies provided annulments or divorces for serious matrimonial offenses such as prolonged absence or bigamy. The southern colonies afforded no provisions for divorce whatsoever.

POST-REVOLUTIONARY WAR. Immediately after the Revolutionary War, without British legal impediments to divorce, the states began discussion of laws allowing divorce. In New England and middle states divorce became the province of state courts, while in the more restrictive southern states it was more often a legislative matter. By the turn of the nineteenth century, almost all states had enacted some form of divorce legislation. And by the middle of the century, even southern states were operating within a judicial divorce system.

The shift to judicial divorce is significant. By removing divorce deliberations from legislatures, states were forced to establish grounds that justified a divorce. Such clauses reflected the prevailing sentiments governing normative marriage—they indicated what was expected of marriage at the time. And by investing judges with the authority to interpret and adjudicate, such changes significantly liberalized the availability of divorce. Northern and southern states permitted divorces for specific offenses such as adultery, desertion, bigamy, and, increasingly with time, cruelty. In the newer frontier western states, grounds resembled those of the East plus "any other cause for which the court shall deem it proper that the divorce shall be granted" (Phillips 1988, p. 453).

Throughout the nineteenth century, there was a gradual liberalization of divorce laws in the United States and a corresponding increase in divorce as well. Where divorces totaled a few hundred at the beginning of the nineteenth century, the numbers grew exponentially as the century wore on; 7,380 divorces in 1860, 10,962 in 1870, 19,663 in 1880, 33,461 in 1890, and 55,751 in 1900 (U.S. Bureau of the Census 1975). These figures assume greater significance when growth in population is removed from them. Whereas the divorce rate (number of divorces per 1,000 marriages) was 1.2 in 1869, it had climbed to 4.0 by 1900. In short, the increase in divorce outstripped the increase in population several times.

A number of factors have been identified as causes of such dramatic increases. In part, these can be described as social changes that made marriage less essential. The growth of wage labor in the nineteenth century afforded women an alternative to economic dependence on a husband. In an economy dominated by individuals rather than families, marriage was simply less essential. Life as a single individual gradually lost its stigma (New England settlements had forbidden solitary dwelling, while southern communities had taxed it heavily).

More important, however, were fundamental shifts in the meaning of marriage. Divorce codes reflected the growing belief that marriages should be imbued with heavy doses of affection and equality. Divorce grounds of cruelty or lack of support indicate that marriage was increasingly viewed as a partnership. Where a century earlier men had been granted greater discretion in their personal lives, latter-nineteenth-century morality attacked such double standards. Men were not necessarily less culpable than women for their vices. Victorian morality stressed the highest standards of sexual behavior for *both* husbands and wives. Changing divorce codes coincided with the passage of laws restricting husbands' unilateral control over their wives' property. The passage of married women's property acts throughout the nation in the latter nineteenth century acknowledged married women's claims to property brought to or acquired in marriage. By 1887, thirty-three states and the District of Columbia gave married women control over their property and earnings (Degler 1980, p. 332).

Divorce codes including omnibus grounds such as "cruelty" (which could justify a divorce from a drunkard husband, for example) may be viewed as reflecting a Victorian American belief that women were morally sensitive and fragile and in need of protection (Phillips 1988, p. 500). More particularly, the growing use of offenses against the intimate and emotional aspects of marriage reflected a growing belief that such things constituted matrimonial essentials.

THE TWENTIETH CENTURY. The first half of this century was a continuation of trends established in the late nineteenth century. Gradually increasing divorce rates were interrupted by two world wars and the Great Depression. During each war and during the depression, divorce rates dropped. After each, rates soared before falling to levels somewhat higher than that which preceded these events. Sociological explanations for these trends focus on women's employment opportunities. Women's labor force participation permits the termination of intolerable unions. The separations, hastily timed marriages, and sexual misalliances characteristic of wartime were also undoubtedly factors in the postwar divorce rates. Further, the increases in divorce following these difficult times may be seen, in part, as a delayed reaction. Once the depression or war was over, the reservoir of impending divorces broke. And finally, postwar optimism and affluence may have contributed to an unwillingness to sustain an unhappy marriage.

With the exception of the peculiar 1950s, the trend for the second half of the 1900s has been a regular and exponential growth in divorce.

The second half of the century has witnessed even more dramatic increases in divorce. With the exception of the peculiar 1950s, the trend for the second half of the 1900s has been a regular and exponential growth in divorce.

Though specific explanations for the increase in divorces during the twentieth century vary, several themes may be noted. First, marriage this century has lost much of its central economic and social significance—especially for women. For example, divorce was undoubtedly inhibited by the fact that prior to the twentieth century, custody of children was uniformly awarded to fathers (since they were legally responsible for financial support). With the acceptance in the early 1900s of Freudian ideas of psychosexual development and similar ideas about intellectual and cognitive growth, the so-called Tender Years Doctrine became accepted practice in courts, which then awarded custody to mothers as regularly as they had once done to fathers. And as it became more commonplace, remarriage began to lose some of its stigma. All these changes made it possible for women to divorce their husbands if they wished. But why did so many wish to obtain divorces?

The simplest explanation is that more divorce is a consequence of higher and higher expectations of marriage. More and more grounds for divorce are developed as there are higher and higher expectations for what a marriage should be. In the nineteenth century, drunkenness, cruelty, and failure to provide were added to more traditional grounds of adultery and desertion. In the early twentieth century, cruelty was continually redefined to include not only physical but mental cruelty as well.

The postwar surges in divorce created sufficient numbers of divorced persons that the practice lost much of its stigma. Add to this the widespread employment of women since the mid 1960s, and increase in divorce becomes more understandable. When women are employed, there is less constraint on them to remain in a marriage. But there is also less constraint on their husbands, who will not be required to support their employed ex-wives after a divorce.

In the last twenty years, divorce has been fundamentally redefined. No-fault divorce laws passed since the early 1970s have defined as unacceptable those marriages in which couples are "incompatible" or have "irreconcilable differences," or those that are "irretrievably broken." The nonadversarial grounds for divorce are now almost entirely based on the failures of emotional essentials. Emotional marital breakdown may have been a feature of large numbers of marriages in earlier historical periods. Only now, however, is such a situation viewed as solely sufficient grounds for terminating the marriage.

Divorce in the West

Any theory of divorce must be able to account for the broad similarities in trends throughout the Western world during the twentieth century. These similarities exist despite notable differences in national economies, state forms of government, and the role of the church. The trends are well known. There was very little divorce until the end of the nineteenth century, a slow but constant growth in divorce rates through the first half of the twentieth century (interrupted by two world wars and an international economic depression), and significant increases in divorce rates since the 1960s. The twentieth century, in short, is when most significant changes in divorce rates occurred. And the changes noted in America were seen in most other Western nations.

Between World Wars I and II, widespread changes in divorce laws reflected changing beliefs about matrimony and its essentials. The strains of war and the associated problems that produced more divorces made the practice more conspicuous and consequently more acceptible. There is no doubt one cause of divorce is divorce. When obscure, the practice was stigmatized and there was little to counter stereotypes associated with its practice. When divorce became more commonplace, it lost some of its stigma.

Social changes pertaining to women's roles are a large part of the story of divorce during the postwar era. One sign of these changes was the growth, throughout the

Laws allowing divorce on grounds of cruelty reflected the nineteenth-century development of the belief that emotional aspects of marriage are important. (Corbis-Bettmann)

West, in women's labor force participation. But the most conspicuous symbol of the changing role of women was the passage of suffrage legislation throughout the Western world. Before 1914, women were permitted to vote only in New Zealand, Australia, Finland, Norway, and eleven western U.S. states. In the United States, women were enfranchised in 1920. In Britain, Sweden, Germany, and many other European countries, suffrage passed soon after World War I.

Divorce laws, similarly, were altered between the wars in accordance with changing views of marriage and the role of women. The British Parliament enacted divorce reform in 1937 by significantly extending the grounds for divorce (including "cruelty") and granting women new options for filing for divorce. Scotland reformed its divorce laws in 1938 by extending grounds for divorce to include failures of emotional essentials—cruelty and habitual drunkenness, for example. In 1930, the Canadian Parliament for the first time empowered judicial magistrates to grant divorce rather than requiring legislative decrees. And the Spanish divorce law of 1932 was the most liberal in contemporary Europe—providing divorce by mutual consent (Phillips 1988, p. 539). Even Nazi Germany permitted no-fault divorce by 1938 (though divorce law was aimed at increasing the number of Aryan children born).

Following World War II, divorce rates throughout the Western world stabilized after an initial increase. The low divorce rates, high fertility, and lower age at marriage that characterized all Western nations after World War II are trends that have not been adequately explained. Whether these trends reflected the consequences of war, the effects of having grown up during the worldwide depression, or a short-term rise in social conservatism is now debated. Regardless of the cause, the decade of the 1950s is universally regarded as a temporary aberration in otherwise long-term and continuous twentieth-century trends. Not until the 1960s were there additional significant changes in divorce laws or divorce rates.

The 1960s were years of significant social change in almost all Western nations. The demographic consequences of high fertility during the 1950s became most apparent in the large and vocal youth movements challenging conventional sexual and marital norms, censorship, the war in Vietnam, and educational policies. Challenges to institutional authority were commonplace. Divorce laws were not immune to the general liberalization. "Between 1960 and 1986 divorce policy in almost all the countries of the West was either completely revised or substantially reformed" (Phillips 1988, p. 562). Most such reforms occurred in the late 1960s to the late 1970s. Unlike earlier divorce law reforms, those during the post-World War II era did not extend the grounds for divorce so much as they redefined the jurisdiction over it. The passage of no-fault divorce laws signaled a profound shift in the way divorce was to be handled.

Most significantly, divorce became the prerogative of the married couple with little involvement of the state. No-fault divorce does not require either spouse to be guilty of an offense. Instead, it focuses on the breakdown of the emotional relationship between the spouses. These statutes typically require a period of time during which the spouses do not live together. Beyond that, evidence must be adduced to substantiate one or both spouses' claim that the marriage is irretrievably broken. The significance of no-fault divorce lies entirely in the fact that decisions about divorce are no longer the prerogative of the state or church but rather of the married couple.

The passage of no-fault divorce laws in the West is properly viewed as a response to changing behaviors and attitudes. Indeed, social science research has shown that divorce rates began to increase significantly prior to passage of such laws and did not change any more dramatically afterward (Stetson and Wright 1975).

The changes in divorce law and actual divorce behaviors in the West are a reflection of the redefinition of marriage. The economic constraints that once held spouses together have been replaced by more vulnerable and fragile emotional bonds. The availability of gainful employment for women makes marriage less essential and divorce more possible. Indeed, the significant changes in women's social positions and the corresponding changes in normative expectations (i.e., gender) have been the subject of significant sociological research. These changes are recognized as fundamentally altering almost all social institutions. Marriage is no exception.

The redefinition of marriage in the latter twentieth century throughout the West reflects the profound changes in relationships between men and women that have occurred. No longer an economic institution, marriage is now defined by its emotional significance. Love and companionship are not incidentals of the institution. Rather, they are essentials. Meeting these high expectations may be difficult. But sustaining them is certainly more so.

Taken together, the changes in the second half of this century may be summarized as redefining the meaning of marriage. Children are not economic assets. Spouses are not economic necessities. Marriage is a conjugal arrangement where the primary emphasis is on the relationship between husband and wife. The reasons for divorce are direct consequences of the reasons for marriage. As one changes so does the other. Since it is more difficult to accomplish and sustain matrimonial essentials, it is easier to terminate the legal framework surrounding them. Divorce is less costly (both financially, legally, and reputationally) as marriage is more so (in terms of the investments required to accomplish what is expected of it).

Correlates of Divorce

Sociologists have documented a number of demographic and personal characteristics that correlate with the probability of divorce. These include early age at marriage, premarital births, divorce from a previous marriage, and low educational attainments. Social class is inversely related to divorce, yet wives' employment significantly increases divorce probabilities (see Huber and Spitze 1988 for a review).

Race correlates with divorce—even after controls are imposed for socioeconomic correlates of race—with black individuals having divorce rates approximately twice those of whites. However, such differences associated with race are recent in origin. Not until the late 1950s did significant differences between blacks and whites emerge in divorce, separation, and other marital statuses. Such recency has been taken to suggest that the differences stem from the contemporary rather than historical circumstances. As Cherlin suggests, the recent changes in black Americans' family situations "represent the response of the poorest, most disadvantaged segment of the black population to the social and economic conditions they have faced in our cities over the past few decades" (Cherlin 1981, p. 108). Such an interpretation is consistent with research showing that marriage plays a less significant role in the transition to adulthood for young American women—especially so for black women (Bennett, Bloom, and Craig 1989).

Consequences of Divorce

FOR CHILDREN. A central concern of much of the recent research on divorce is how children fare. The answer to this question depends largely on which aspects of children's lives are studied. When attention is focused on children's personal adjustment (self-control, leadership, responsibility, independence, achievement orientation, aggressiveness, and gender-role orientation), the conclusion from research done over the past ten years seems to be that there is an initial deleterious effect—especially for young boys. However, within two or three years, children who have experienced divorce seem to do as well as those who have not (Demo and Acock 1988). This optimistic conclusion is drawn, almost entirely, from cross-sectional studies, often surveys of individuals.

Longitudinal research is now beginning to offer a decidedly less sanguine view of the consequences of divorce for children. Long-term psychological consequences have been described in dramatic terms for children followed a decade after their parents' marriages ended in divorce:

> The cumulative effect of the failing marriage and divorce rose to a crescendo as each child entered young adulthood. It was here, as these young men and women faced the developmental task of establishing love and intimacy, that they most felt the lack of a template for a loving, enduring, and moral relationship between a man and a woman. It was here that anxiety carried over from divorced family relationships threatened to bar the young people's ability to create new, enduring families of their own. The new families that are formed appear vulnerable to the effects of divorce. (Wallerstein and Blakeslee 1989, pp. 297–298)

Sociological longitudinal research on the inter-generational effects of divorce provides even stronger evidence of the negative consequences of divorce. In their socioeconomic attainments, children who experienced their parents' divorce average one to two fewer years of educational attainment than children from intact homes (Krein and Beller 1988; Hetherington, Camara, and Featherman 1983). Such effects are found even after rigorous controls are imposed for such things as race, sex, years since the divorce, age at time of divorce, parental income, parental education, number of siblings, region of residence, educational materials in the home, or the number of years spent in the single-parent family. There are comparable effects of divorce on occupational prestige, income and earnings, and unemployment (Nock 1988).

White women who spent some childhood time in a single-parent family as a result of divorce are 164 percent more likely to have premarital births.

White women who spent some childhood time in a single-parent family as a result of divorce are 53 percent more likely to have teenage marriages, 111 percent more likely to have teenage births, 164 percent more likely to have premarital births, and 92 percent more likely to experience marital disruptions than are daughters who grew up in two-parent families. The effects for black women are similar, though smaller. Controls for a wide range of background factors have little effect on the negative consequences of divorce. Further, remarriage does not remove these effects of divorce. And there is no difference between those who lived with their fathers and those who lived with mothers after divorce. Experiencing parents' divorce has the same (statistical) consequences as being born to a never-married mother (McLanahan and Bumpass 1988).

Such large and consistent negative effects have eluded simple explanation. Undoubtedly much of the divorce experience is associated with the altered family structure produced—in 90 percent of all cases a single-mother family. Such a structure is lacking in adult role models, in parental supervision, and in hierarchy. On this last dimension, research has shown that divorced women and their children are closer (less distinguished by generational distinctions) to one another than is true in intact families. Parent and child are drawn together more as peers, both struggling to keep the family going. The excessive demands on single parents force them to depend on their children in ways that parents in intact families do not, leading to a more reciprocal dependency relationship (Weiss 1975, 1976). Single mothers are "likely to rely on their children for emotional support and assistance with the practical problems of daily life" (Hetherington, Camara, and Featherman 1983, p. 218). In matters of discipline, single mothers have been found to rely on restrictive (authoritarian as opposed to authoritative) disciplinary methods—restricting the child's freedom and relying on negative sanctions—a pattern psychologists believe reflects a lack of authority on the part of the parent (Hetherington 1972). Whatever else it implies, the lack of generational boundaries means a less hierarchical family and less authoritative generational distinctions.

The institutional contexts within which achievement occurs, however, are decidedly hierarchical in nature. Education, the economy, and occupations are typically bureaucratic structures in which an individual is categorically subordinate to a superior—an arrangement Goffman described as an "echelon authority structure" (1961, p. 42). The nuclear family has been described as producing in children the skills and attitudes necessary for competition within such echelon authority structures. "There is a significant correspondence between the authority relationships in capitalist production and family childrearing. . . . The hierarchical division of labor (in the economy) is merely reflected in family life" (Bowles and Gintis 1976, pp. 144–147). The relative absence of clear subordinate-superordinate relationships in single-parent families has been argued to socialize children inadequately or place them in a disadvantageous position when and if they find themselves in hierarchical organizations.

FOR ADULTS. A wide range of psychological problems have been noted among divorcing and recently divorced adults. A divorce occasions changes in most every aspect of adult life—residence, friendship networks, economic situation, and parental roles. Marriage in America makes significant contributions to individual well-being. Thus, regardless of the quality of the marriage that ends, emotional distress is a near-universal experience for those who divorce (Weiss 1979). Anxiety, anger, and fear are dominant psychological themes immediately before and after divorce. At least for a year or two after divorce, men and women report psychosomatic symptoms of headaches, loss of appetite, overeating, drinking too much, trembling, smoking more, sleeping problems, and nervousness (Group for the Advancement of Psychiatry 1980).

Immediately after a divorce, women suffer an average 30 to 40 percent decline in their overall standards of living.

The emotional problems occasioned by divorce are accompanied by major changes in economic situations, as well, especially for women. The vast majority of those involved in divorce experience a significant decline in their immediate standard of living. This problem is especially acute for women who—in almost 90 percent of cases—assume custody of children. Immediately after a divorce, women suffer an average 30 to 40 percent decline in their overall standards of living (Peterson 1989). Either in anticipation of or as a consequence of divorce, there is typically an increase in divorced women's labor force participation. Analyzing national longitudinal data, Peterson estimates that one year before the divorce decree (when most divorcing individuals are separated), women's average standard of living (total family income divided by the poverty threshold for a family of a particular size) is 70 percent of its level in the previous year. As a consequence of increased hours worked, the standard of living increases one year after divorce, and by five or six years after divorce "the standard of living of divorced women is about 85 percent of what it had been before separation" (1989, p. 48). Women who have not been employed during their marriages, however, are particularly hard-hit, the majority ending up in poverty.

Child support from fathers is not a solution to the economic problems for two reasons. First, about one-quarter of women due child support receive none. Another one-quarter receive less than the court-ordered amount. In 1985, the average amount of child support received by divorced mothers was $2,538 per year (U.S. Bureau of the Census 1989b). About 13.5 million or 88 percent of the 15.3 million children in single-parent families in 1988 were living with the mother; their average (mean) family income was $11,989, compared with $34,919 for those in single-father situations and $40,067 for children in households where both parents were present (U.S. Bureau of the Census 1989a). Families headed by single mothers are the most likely to be in poverty. In 1987, one-half of all single-mother families were in poverty (compared to fewer than 8 percent of two-parent families). Analyzing national longitudinal data, Greg Duncan concluded that changes in family status—especially divorce and remarriage—are the most important causes of change in family economic well-being and poverty among women and children (Duncan 1984).

Single-parent families in America have grown dramatically as a result of increasing divorce rates. And even though most divorced persons remarry, Bumpass has shown that the average duration of marital separation experienced by children under age eighteen was 6.3 years for whites and 7.5 years for blacks. In fact, 38 percent of white and 73 percent of black children are still in a single-parent family ten years after the marital disruption—a reflection of blacks' lower propensity to remarry and their longer intervals between divorce and remarriage (Bumpass 1984). The role of divorce in the formation of single-parent families differs by race. Among all single-parent white families, 17 percent are maintained by never-married mothers, 42 percent by divorced mothers. Among blacks, the comparable percentages are 54 and 16. Divorce is the primary route to single parenthood for white mothers, whereas out-of-wedlock childbearing is for black mothers (U.S. Bureau of the Census 1989b, p. 14).

Families headed by single women are the poorest of all major demographic groups regardless of how poverty is measured. Combined with frequent changes in residence and in employment following divorce, children and mothers in such households experience significant instabilities—a fact reflected in the higher rates of mental health problems among such women (Garfinkel and McLanahan 1986, pp. 11–17).

Conclusion

High rates of remarriage following divorce clearly indicate that marital disruption does not signify a rejection of marriage. There is no evidence of widespread abandonment of conjugal life by Americans. Admittedly, marriage rates have dropped in recent years. However, such changes are best seen to be the result of higher educational attainments, occupational commitments, and lower fertility expectations, not a rejection of marriage per se. Rather, increasing divorce rates reflect the fact that marriage is increasingly evaluated as an entirely emotional relationship between two persons. Marital breakdown, or the failure of marriage to fulfill emotional expectations, has come increasingly to be a cause for divorce. Since the 1970s, our laws have explicitly recognized this as justification for terminating a marriage—the best evidence we have that love and emotional closeness are the *sine qua non* of modern American marriage. Contemporary divorce rates thus signal a growing unwillingness to tolerate an unsatisfying emotional conjugal relationship.

The consequences of divorce for children are difficult to disentangle from the predictable changes in household structure. Whether the long-term consequences are produced by the single-parent situation typically experienced for five to ten years, or from the other circumstances surrounding divorce, is not clear. It is quite apparent, however, that divorce occasions significant instabilities in children's and mothers' lives.

Our knowledge about the consequences of divorce for individuals is limited at this time by the absence of controlled studies that compare the divorced to the nondivorced. Virtually all research done to date follows the lives of divorced individuals without comparing them to a comparable group of individuals who have not divorced. A related concern is whether the consequences of divorce reflect the experience itself or whether they reflect various selection effects. That is, are people who divorce different from others to begin with? Are their experiences the results of their divorce or of antecedent factors?

When half of all marriages are predicted to end in divorce, it is clear that martial disruption is a conspicuous feature of our family and kinship system. Divorce creates new varieties of kin not heretofore incorporated in our dominant institutions. The rights and obligations attached to such kinship positions as that of spouse of the noncustodial father are ambiguous—itself a source of problems. The social institution of the family is redefined continuously as a consequence of divorce. Entering marriage, for example, is less commonly the beginning of adult responsibilities. Ending marriage is less commonly the consequence of death. Parents are not necessarily co-residents with their children. And new categories of "quasi" kin are invented to accommodate the complex connections among previously married spouses and their new spouses and children. In many ways, divorce itself has become a dominant institution in American society. It is, however, significantly less structured by consensual normative beliefs than the family institutions to which it is allied.

[See also Marriage; Marriage and Divorce Rates; Remarriage.]

BIBLIOGRAPHY

Bennett, Neil G., David E. Bloom, and Patricia H. Craig 1989 "The Divergence of Black and White Marriage Patterns." *American Journal of Sociology* 95:692–772.

Bowles, Samuel, and Herbert Gintis 1976 *Schooling in Capitalist America.* New York: Basic Books.

Bumpass, Larry L. 1984 "Children and Marital Disruption: A Replication and Update." *Demography* 21:71–82.

Cherlin, Andrew J. 1981 *Marriage, Divorce, and Remarriage.* Cambridge, Mass.: Harvard University Press.

Degler, Carl N. 1980 *At Odds: Women and the Family in America from the Revolution to the Present.* New York: Oxford University Press.

Demo, David H., and Alan C. Acock 1988 "The Impact of Divorce on Children." *Journal of Marriage and the Family* 50:619–648.

Duncan, Greg J. 1984 *Years of Poverty, Years of Plenty.* Ann Arbor: University of Michigan, Institute for Social Research.

Garfinkel, Irwin, and Sara S. McLanahan 1986 *Single Mothers and Their Children.* Washington, D.C.: The Urban Institute Press.

Goffman, Erving 1961 *Asylums.* New York: Anchor.

Group for the Advancement of Psychiatry 1980 *Divorce, Child Custody, and the Family.* San Francisco: Jossey-Bass.

Hetherington, E. Mavis 1972 "Effects of Paternal Absence on Personality Development in Adolescent Daughters." *Development Psychology* 7:313–326.

Hetherington, E. M., K. A. Camara, and D.L. Featherman 1983 "Achievement and Intellectual Functioning of Children in One Parent Households." In J. T. Spence, ed., *Achievement and Achievement Motives.* San Francisco: W. H. Freeman.

Huber, Joan, and Glenna Spitze 1988 "Trends in Family Sociology." In N. J. Smelser, ed., *Handbook of Sociology.* Beverly Hills, Calif.: Sage.

Krein, Sheila F., and Andrea H. Beller 1988 "Educational Attainment of Children from Single-Parent Families: Differences by Exposure, Gender, and Race." *Demography* 25:221–234.

Martin, Teresa C., and Larry L. Bumpass 1989 "Recent Trends in Marital Disruption." *Demography* 26:37–51.

McLanahan, Sara S., and Larry Bumpass 1988 "Intergenerational Consequences of Family Disruption." *American Journal of Sociology* 94:130–152.

Nock, Steven L. 1988 "The Family and Hierarchy." *Journal of Marriage and the Family* 50:957–966.

Peterson, Richard R. 1989 *Women, Work, and Divorce.* Albany: State University of New York Press.

Phillips, Roderick 1988 *Putting Asunder: A History of Divorce in Western Society.* New York: Cambridge University Press.

Stetson, Dorothy M., and Gerald C. Wright, Jr. 1975 "The Effects of Law on Divorce in American States." *Journal of Marriage and the Family* 37:537–547.

U.S. Bureau of the Census 1975 *Historical Statistics of the United States: Colonial Times to 1970. Part I.* Washington, D.C.: U.S. Government Printing Office.

——— 1989a "Child Support and Alimony: 1985." *Current Population Reports.* Series P-23, No. 154. Washington, D.C.: U.S. Government Posting Office.

——— 1989b "Studies in Marriage and the Family." Current Population Reports, Series P-23, No. 162. Washington, D.C.: U.S. Government Posting Office.

Wallerstein, Judith S., and Sandra Blakeslee 1989 *Second Chances: Men, Women, and Children a Decade After Divorce.* New York: Ticknor and Fields.

Weiss, Robert 1975 *Marital Separation.* New York: Basic Books.

——— 1976 "The Emotional Impact of Marital Separation." *Journal of Social Issues* 32:135–145.

——— 1979 *Going It Alone: The Family Life and Social Situation of the Single Parent.* New York: Basic Books.

– STEVEN L. NOCK

DRUG ABUSE

Drug abuse is the use of an illicit drug, such as heroin, or the use of a licit substance, such as barbiturates, outside of medical supervision. The substance is taken to modify or maintain a mood and may be potentially harmful to the person or to society. *Abuse* is a term that has been developed and widely used in the United States; *drug dependence* is frequently employed in other countries.

Dependence is defined as a state, psychic and sometimes also physical, characterized by a compulsion to take a drug either continually or periodically, to experience its psychic effects, or to avoid the discomfort of its absence. A person may be dependent on a stimulant (e.g., cocaine), a depressant (e.g., heroin), or a hallucinogen (e.g., LSD). It is more useful to speak of "hard" and "soft" use of drugs than of "hard" or "soft" drugs.

"Addiction" characterizes many people's reactions to opioids, barbiturates, and alcohol. It includes three dimensions: tolerance, or the body's need for increasing doses of the drug; withdrawal, or a predictable physical response when the product is not available; and habituation, or a psychological need for the drug. In some contexts, "addiction" is used to communicate loss of control because of drug use.

There is a perennial debate over whether the drug problem is or ought to be considered a crime or a disease. The U.S. Supreme Court (*Robinson* v. *California,* 1972) has classified narcotic addiction as a disease that a person cannot control and for which a penalty would represent cruel and unusual punishment. Creation of the National Institute on Drug Abuse in 1973 represented the federal government's formal recognition of drug abuse as a health problem. However, possession or sale of specific substances is handled by the criminal justice system.

The United Nations has a system for coordinating world licit production of opiates, although there has always been illicit production in countries like Turkey, Mexico, and Laos. Most countries, including the United States, subscribe to the 1961 Single Convention on Narcotic Drugs, which deals with opiates, cocaine, and marijuana. In 1971, the Convention on Psychotropic Substances established international controls on amphetamines, barbiturates, and other sedatives and some tranquilizers. The international controls regulate the amount of each medicinally important substance that may be grown or manufactured, in accordance with the world medical requirements for the substance.

There are federal and state laws prohibiting the possession or sale of a wide range of substances and providing prison sentences, fines, or both for violation of the laws. The Drug Enforcement Administration classifies mood-modifying substances into five schedules, with schedule I having the least medical utility and being the most dangerous (e.g., heroin) and schedule V the most medically useful and least subject to abuse (e.g., cold medications that include codeine). Schedule II includes licit substances that may be abused, such as tranquilizers and cocaine. State laws generally are similar to federal laws in terms of the control of mood-modifying substances. Typically, federal agents pursue larger traffickers, and state authorities prosecute lesser distributors and users.

How many drug abusers are there? Each country would answer this question differently, in terms of the substances involved and the frequency of their use. Someone who has only taken a drug once, or is an occasional social-recreational user, is a different kind of user from a person who ingests a substance daily. A person who smokes marijuana is considered differently from one who injects cocaine intravenously. A controlled user who is functioning effectively in a noncriminal setting would be perceived differently from a compulsive user who is heavily involved in a criminal subculture.

The level of drug use is higher in the United States than in any other industrial nation. More than one-half of American youth try an illicit drug before they finish high school. An estimated 14.5 million Americans used a drug illicitly in the month prior to a national household survey in 1988. At least one million persons are regular and heavy dysfunctional users of heroin or cocaine. Males are substantially more likely than females to use illegal drugs. Young adults are the age group most likely to use mood-modifying drugs. Drug use is now pervasive in all socioeconomic groups, although cocaine users are most heavily concentrated in urban minority areas.

Overall, drug use has been declining since approximately 1985. The announcement of a national war on drugs, coordinated by a cabinet-level executive in 1989, was typical of previous government responses to a drug problem in that it began after the problem had peaked.

From 1918 through the 1930s, the typical narcotic addict was a white itinerant farm worker in the South.

Americans have been taking drugs to modify moods since the Civil War. Until the early twentieth century, many women used opiates that were significant ingredients in patent medicines. When the Harrison Act was passed in 1914, possession of narcotic drugs without a doctor's prescription became illegal. From 1918 through the 1930s, the typical narcotic addict was a white itinerant farm worker in the South.

The modern drug problem began to take shape in the late 1940s, when several large cities reported an epidemic of heroin use among male minority teenagers. This epidemic continued until 1964, when middle class youths became involved. It continued to attract new users steadily until 1974. In the late 1960s, substantial numbers of American military personnel in Vietnam became regular users of the high-quality inexpensive heroin available there. In order to cope with these and other drug problems, President Nixon, in 1971, appointed a Commission on Marijuana and Drug Abuse (1973), the report of which still influences current policy.

Marijuana, which became illegal in 1937, rapidly became a favorite among minorities, musicians, and a number of other groups. In the 1960s, it became popular with high school and college students as a symbol of generational conflict, and its use expanded until 1975.

Powdered cocaine had been a moderately popular drug, the use of which was restricted by its high cost, since the 1950s. By 1985, in the form of "crack" crystals, which were smoked in a special pipe, it became the drug of choice among urban minorities, especially young people. As a result of the epidemic of crack use, drug abuse had become the country's most important social problem by 1990.

The amount of crime in which drug abusers engage in order to get money for drugs is a major contributor to the salience of the drug problem. A number of studies have quantified the relationship between crime and drugs. Over an eleven-year period in Baltimore, a sample of 243 male addicts averaged over 2,000 offenses per person. They engaged in six times more criminal activity when addicted than when they were not on drugs. The measure of "crime-days per week at risk" is

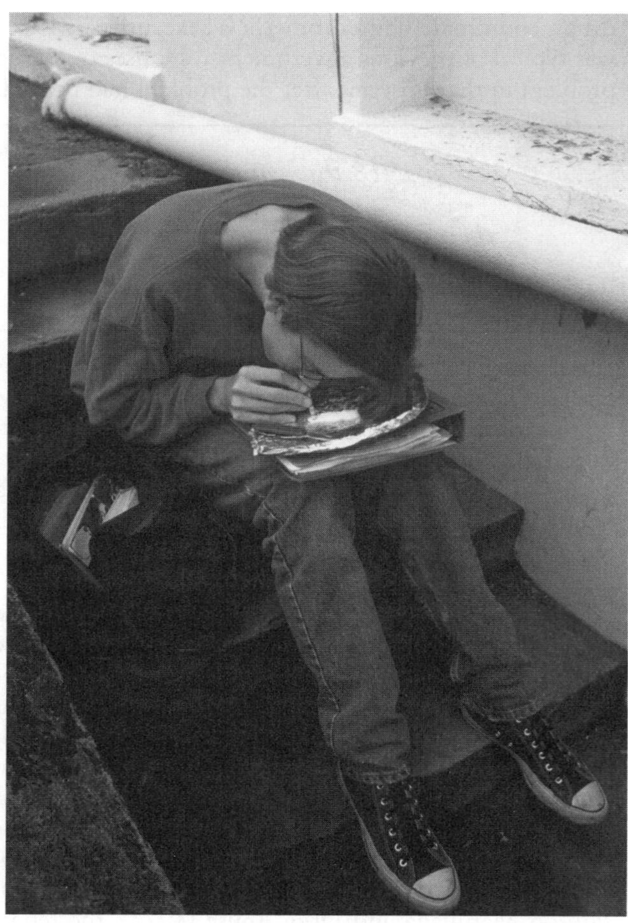

Cocaine use became epidemic in the Untied States in the mid-1980s. (James Marshall/Corbis)

used to identify a day in which at least one crime is committed (Winick 1983).

Criminal activity by drug abusers has been classified into a variety of "hustles" (Hanson et al. 1985). They may be opportunistic, such as stealing; skilled, such as picking pockets; or drug-related, such as selling drugs. The likelihood that any specific crime of a drug user will result in arrest is very slight. An increase in the price of illegal drugs leads to an increase in the crime rate; a 10 percent increase in illegal drug prices is associated with a 1.1 percent increase in the crime rate.

In order to estimate the proportion of criminals who are drug abusers, a program of urine testing of samples of men and women arrested for all offenses in twenty-one cities has been conducted (National Institute of Justice 1990). The range of positive tests was from 53 to 84 percent for males and 42 to 90 percent for females, with cocaine the most frequently detected drug for both men and women. Thus, the overwhelming majority of arrested persons, at least in the early 1990s, has consisted of users of illegal drugs.

Prior to the 1960s, drug users tended to prefer and use one substance such as marijuana, heroin, or amphetamines. Beginning in the late 1960s, polydependence became the norm. A drug-dependent person might have a specific drug of choice but typically would use other substances, depending on the drug's availability, the individual's access to money, police action, the setting, and similar factors. A large proportion and perhaps even a majority of drug-dependent persons would use alcohol to reinforce or ease the effect of other drugs or instead of other drugs. Polydependent users typically use substances that are chemically analogous to each other or are cross-tolerant, so that a barbiturate user may take alcohol, since the two substances are both depressants.

The drug of choice changes from year to year and from region to region, depending on price, availability, law enforcement efforts, fads, and socioeconomic status of the users. A drug may become less popular but still remain available in a community and reemerge in the future. Thus, heroin was supplanted by cocaine in many urban areas in the mid-1980s but began reemerging as a preferred drug by 1990. Mood-modifying drugs do not vanish completely but enjoy cycles of popularity and unpopularity.

Individuals progress through identifiable developmental stages in the use of licit and illicit drugs from adolescence through young adulthood, when the period of risk for initiation into drugs usually terminates. In men, alcohol precedes marijuana; alcohol and marijuana precede other illicit drugs; alcohol, cigarettes, and marijuana precede prescribed psychoactive drugs. In women, either alcohol or cigarettes precede marijuana; alcohol, cigarettes, and marijuana precede other illicit drugs; alcohol and either cigarettes or marijuana precede prescribed psychoactive drugs (Yamaguchi and Kandel 1984).

A considerable number of drug abusers stop taking drugs, on a permanent basis, often without experiencing treatment. This process of "maturing out," analogous to what happens to delinquents, involves an interaction between individual factors and the environment (Winick 1979). The self-limiting nature of much drug abuse has been a contributor to some sociologists' urging that legislation of drug use be adopted as a national policy. Others argue that legalization or decriminalization pose many problems, but they are less serious than the huge costs and uncertain outcome of current policy, which is to punish and eliminate illegal drug use (Reinarman and Levine 1989).

Recent American policy has been what may be characterized as liberal hard-line. It is liberal in that drug abusers are encouraged to seek treatment, for which there is considerable federal and state funding. It is hard-line in that there is vigorous law enforcement, which receives the bulk of the available funding, and because prevention programs actively discourage young people from beginning or continuing drug use. This policy has been dominant since the report of the President's Commission on Marijuana and Drug Abuse.

American policy views all drugs of abuse as undesirable and is directed at eliminating such use. The policy is based on the concept that any drug can be a gateway to a more dangerous substance so that the use of all such substances is discouraged. Eleven states have decriminalized possession of small quantities of marijuana for personal use, with no significant accompanying increase in the use of other mood-modifying drugs. On the federal level, however, there is consistent opposition to any attempt to liberalize the laws against possession of marijuana.

Drug control programs have never been able to have a significant impact on the problem.

Community programs to cope with drug abuse typically have three components: interdiction and control of the supply, prevention and education, and treatment. The policy of the federal and local governments has always been to concentrate primarily on control by attempting to interdict supply and arrest sellers and users. Treatment is a secondary priority, and prevention has been a minimal goal. Drug control programs have never been able to have a significant impact on the problem; treatment approaches are able to engage only a small proportion of abusers and cannot be targeted to specific clients with significant accuracy; and prevention efforts have not been conducted for long enough to have established their efficacy.

There are three major kinds of treatment: pharmacotherapy, therapeutic communities, and outpatient counseling. Most pharmacotherapy consists of methadone maintenance for heroin users, replacing heroin with methadone, a longer-acting opiate that does not give a "high" and enables the patient to function. Therapeutic communities, such as Daytop and Phoenix House, usually require twelve to eighteen months of residence in a total institution with rigid rules of progression through several (usually three or four) stages. Therapeutic communities treat users of all kinds of drugs, and the reasons for their success have been studied by some prominent sociologists (Volkman and Cressey 1963).

Outpatient counseling, also used for all kinds of drug users, probably accounts for approximately three-fifths of all treatment, pharmacotherapy represents approximately three-tenths, and residential programs service one-tenth of the users. Drug dependence is a chronic relapsing condition, so that it is common for a person to revert to drug use after treatment.

During the 1980s, it became clear that acquired immunodeficiency syndrome (AIDS) was transmitted to many people by the use of previously contaminated needles in intravenous injection of various drugs, especially heroin. In cities like New York, two-thirds of AIDS cases result from use of contaminated needles, mostly by heterosexuals. Nationally, approximately one-fourth to one-third of AIDS cases can be attributed to drug abusers' use of contaminated needles.

Sociologists' interest in drug abuse has been increasing because of a growing recognition of the significant role of culture and social structure in the genesis and continuation of drug abuse. Sociologists are actively involved in evaluating the effectiveness of treatment and prevention programs, in estimating the impact and costs of current policies, in conducting cross-cultural investigations, and in conducting surveys and ethnographic studies of epidemiology. Sociologists have also addressed the issue of national policy toward the drug abuse problem (Winick 1974).

[See also Alcohol; Criminalization of Deviance.]

BIBLIOGRAPHY

Commission on Marijuana and Drug Abuse 1973 *Final Report.* Washington, D.C.: U.S. Government Printing Office.

Hanson, B., G. Beschner, J. M. Walters, and E. Bovelle 1985 *Life with Heroin: Voices from the Inner City.* Lexington, Mass.: Lexington Books.

National Institute of Justice 1990 *Drug Use Forecasting.* Washington, D.C.: U.S. Department of Justice.

Reinarman, C., and H. G. Levine 1989 "Crack in Context: Politics and Media in the Making of a Drug Scare." *Contemporary Drug Problems* 18:535–577.

Volkman, R., and D. R. Cressey 1963 "Differential Association and the Rehabilitation of Drug Addicts." *American Journal of Sociology* 69:129–142.

Winick, C. 1979 "The Drug Offender." In H. Toch, ed., *Psychology of Crime and Criminal Justice.* New York: Holt, Rinehart and Winston.

——— 1983 "Addicts and Alcoholics as Victimizers." In D. E. J. MacNamara and A. Karmen, eds., *Deviants: Victims or Victimizers?* Beverly Hills, Calif.: Sage Publications.

——— (ed.) 1974 *Sociological Aspects of Drug Dependence.* Cleveland: CRC Press.

Yamaguchi, K., and D. B. Kandel 1984 "Patterns of Drug Use from Adolescence to Young Adulthood: II. Sequences of Progression." *American Journal of Public Health* 74:668–672.

– CHARLES WINICK

E

EDUCATIONAL ORGANIZATION

Education and schooling are not synonymous. Education is the more encompassing concept, referring to the general process by which a social group—whether an entire society or just a family—transmits attitudes, beliefs, behaviors, and skills to its members. Within these broad boundaries, education greatly varies, with educational scholars typically distinguishing three general types: formal education, nonformal education, and informal education. These different kinds of education can be distinguished according to where they take place, the characteristics of teachers, the methods of instruction, and what is learned.

Informal education takes such forms as family child rearing, peer group socialization, and learning on one's own such skills as auto repair and guitar playing. It takes place in the context of everyday, intimate relationships, with teachers being family members or friends and learning occurring through observation and imitation ("hands on"). Formal education or schooling, meanwhile, takes place outside the family in institutions that specialize in education and that we call schools. Instruction is led by teachers who are not students' intimates, whose principal occupation is education, and who stress learning through verbal and written description and guided inquiry rather than through observation and imitation. Nonformal education, finally, includes on-the-job training, agricultural extension programs, and family planning outreach programs. It differs from informal education in that it takes place outside the family, but it also differs from formal education in that it does not take place in schools and its aims are more specific and short-term.

Virtually all societies utilize all three forms of education, but they differ in the relative predominance of these forms. In nonindustrialized societies, informal education dominates, with formal and nonformal education only marginally present. But in highly industrialized societies such as the United States, formal education rivals, if not exceeds, nonformal and informal education in its importance and its use of society's resources. Despite a common emphasis on formal education, the United States is quite different from other advanced industrial societies in how its school system is organized. Six divergences stand out (Dougherty and Hammack 1990, chap. 3).

First, the American school system is much larger. This is a product not just of the United States' large population but also of the fact that its schools enroll a far larger proportion of students, particularly among those above the age of compulsory school attendance. For example, in 1982, college students represented 5.3 percent of the entire U.S. population, while the comparable percentage was 2.3 in West Germany, 2.2 in France, 2.0 in Japan and the Soviet Union, and 1.6 in the United Kingdom.

Second, the American school system is far less centralized than the school systems of most advanced industrial societies (Hopper 1977). Most other industrial societies largely vest control of their school systems in a national ministry of education that finances the schools and sets basic rules for curriculum, admission, and graduation and for teacher education, hiring, and promotion. Such a pattern of strong national centralization, with minimal local voice, can be seen in Japan, France, Italy, and the Soviet Union (Ignas and Corsini 1981; King 1979). In the United States, meanwhile, the states have constitutional sovereignty over education and, furthermore, allow local districts great power over the day-to-day functioning of the schools (Campbell et al. 1985; Wirt and Kirst 1989). This decentralization of authority is enhanced by the fact that American schools receive most of their funds not from the national government but from state and local sources.

Because of its greater decentralization, the American school system is less homogeneous across different regions of the country than are the school systems in other advanced industrial societies. In comparison to French students living in different regions of their country, American students living in different states encounter greater differences in how much is spent on their education, how educated their teachers are, and what education they are provided.

A third distinctive feature of the American school system is that it is much less driven by examination requirements than are many other school systems. In good part because the American system is much less centralized, it does not have the system of nationwide exams that are present in most other advanced societies and that powerfully mold students' educational careers. In most other countries, exams taken before high school determine the kind of high school one can attend, and exams taken at the end of high school determine whether one can go on to higher education and what kind of college one can attend. As a result, exam taking assumes a critical and hellish importance in such countries as Japan, France, Germany, and England. In the United States, however, one can still get into college without doing well on the Scholastic Aptitude Test (SAT) or American College Test (ACT) or even taking them at all. However, the American exemption from the "examination hell" may be disappearing as states and local school districts increasingly require students to pass a minimum competency test to receive a high school diploma or enter college.

Exam taking assumes a critical and hellish importance in such countries as Japan, France, Germany, and England.

While the American school system is less centralized and therefore less homogeneous across regions than the systems in most other industrial societies, it is also *more* homogeneous *within the same district.* This is the fourth major difference among industrial societies. The United States has long enrolled its students in "comprehensive" schools: that is, institutions that offer both academic and vocational subjects. Most other advanced industrial societies traditionally have had strongly differentiated secondary and postsecondary educational systems. Until recently, many students have enrolled in specialized high schools, whether vocational schools or elite academic high schools (the English grammar school, the French lycée, and the German gymnasium). In turn, higher education in most advanced societies has been strongly divided between academically oriented universities and less prestigious, vocationally oriented technical and teacher-training institutions. This curricular division has tended to coincide with social class divisions. The elite academic secondary schools and the universities have long drawn disproportionately from the upper class and upper middle class. Meanwhile, lower-middle-class and working-class students have gone to vocational schools and low-prestige comprehensive schools and, if they reached higher education, technical and teacher-training colleges. In the United States, meanwhile, students of all classes attend comprehensive schools and colleges because of the relatively small number of exclusively vocational or academic schools and colleges.

But if American schools in the same district evidence great homogeneity, this is purchased in good part through greater heterogeneity *within* those schools. This is the fifth difference between American schools and those of other countries. Unlike Japanese and French schools, American schools group students within schools according to apparent ability and interests—and, as a result, social class and ethnicity (Ignas and Corsini 1981; King 1979).

The sixth and final divergence is that U.S. schools typically take on far more tasks than is typical in other societies. Americans expect schools to address such problems as poor driving, drug abuse, sexual ignorance, and poor nutrition at home.

A closer examination of how U.S. schools are controlled is merited, for this is one of the more striking ways that they deviate from schools in other societies. In fact, the structure of control in U.S. schools produces recurrent political conflicts that tend to be unique to the United States.

A variety of entities sponsor education in the United States. The most prominent are governmental bodies. At the elementary and secondary school level, local school districts operate three-quarters of all schools. The nongovernmental patrons include religious bodies (above all the Catholic church) and independent nonprofit organizations. At the postsecondary level, governmental bodies sponsor 45 percent of all colleges and universities in the United States; these 1,500 public colleges account for three-quarters of all college enrollments. The biggest actors are state governments, followed by local governments and, far back in the distance, the federal government. The remaining 1,800 colleges are private, owned either by nonsectarian, nonprofit boards (25 percent), religious groups—especially the Protestant denominations (24 percent), or profit-making corporations (7 percent) (Dougherty and Hammack 1990, chap. 3).

Schools are controlled by four different mechanisms: bureaucracy, profession, politics, and markets. Schools are bureaucratic organizations because they serve explicit goals and are composed of a variety of people who do specialized work and whose efforts need to be coordinated. Formal rules specify which jobs are to be done within the organization, and there are explicit differences in the authority of members according to their places in the school's hierarchy (Bidwell 1965; Corwin 1970). School boards, central school district officials, and state education authorities decide what the curriculum will include, what books to use, and what objectives they should strive to achieve. These goals and the means to achieve them descend to school-level principals and curriculum leaders and then to individual classroom teachers.

But schools are only partially bureaucratic organizations. Even as they aim to control teachers, they also have to give them considerable autonomy. Boards of education often have no clear consensus on what the goals of education should be or how to achieve them. The technology of teaching is relatively primitive, without "magic bullets" or drugs that can "heal" the patients or eradicate ignorance. Hence, school administrators often leave many decisions about the techniques and at times the very goals of education to teachers. Therefore, teachers often have great autonomy in the classroom. It is this autonomy that makes them professionals. But teaching is unlike other professions in that success is more problematic. Its technology is less certain in its result, in good part because it demands the active participation of the client. To be successful, teachers must successfully motivate students to value school achievement and to conform to the essential requirements of the classroom (Metz 1978; Meyer and Rowan 1978).

Schools are also governed by external political control. As noted earlier, the decentralized nature of the American school affords the opportunity for diverse groups to influence educational policy. One of these, of course, is voters. All adults can elect representatives to public school boards. In fact, citizens can even govern them directly, voting on school budgets, tax rates, and bond issues. In addition, organized interest groups—ranging from business to religious groups—influence school decisions through lobbying and their ability to shape the agenda for school policymaking (Campbell et al. 1985; Wirt and Kirst 1989).

Finally, schools are governed by market mechanisms. This is particularly obvious in the case of private schools, which do not have a guaranteed clientele and must recruit students every year. But public schools also face market forces because parents who are unhappy with their local schools may move to another neighborhood, leaving schools with fewer students and lower state aid. These market forces within public education have increased with recent efforts to increase parental choice within and even between districts: magnet schools, schools within schools, and voucher plans (Chubb and Moe 1990; Metz 1986; Spicer and Hill 1990).

The combination of bureaucratic, professional, political, and market controls makes schools unique organizations, with distinctive and recurrent tensions. A clash between bureaucracy and professionalism can be seen in the current conflict between those reformers calling for tighter administrative regulation of teachers' work and other reformers defending teachers' autonomy as professionals and intellectuals (Apple 1986; Aronowitz and Giroux 1985). In turn, those defending teachers' professional autonomy have also found themselves in conflict with groups calling for increased local community control. Schools are not only workplaces for teachers but also places where communities try to pass on their ways of life to their children. Professionalization threatens community control by shifting authority from lay people to educational experts, who do not necessarily have the promotion of local community values as their top priority. Our tradition of local control of public schools is inherently suspicious of educational decisions being made by officials who are not directly accountable to local citizens and taxpayers.

Another clash has come from the efforts of state bureaucratic authorities to eliminate local variation in school spending, curriculum, facilities, and outcomes. This effort has been actively resisted by local communities, teachers, and administrators. There have been great fights over school consolidation, school spending, and textbook content in recent decades (Peshkin 1978).

Finally, a clash between market and other forms of regulation is much in the news with the debate between those calling for greater parental choice (in order to increase competition between schools and thus force improvement) and those fearing that this will result in public schools becoming even more segregated by race and social class and less able to provide equal opportunity (Chubb and Moe 1990; Spicer and Hill 1990).

This concern about segregation is merited, given that American schools already differ greatly among themselves in student body composition: that is, in the social class, race, and ethnic distribution of their students (Dougherty and Hammack 1990, Chapter 3). Because of racial, ethnic, and economic segregation in residence patterns, as well as overt discrimination in drawing district boundaries, schools are often dominated by one social group and are thus segregated. From the Supreme Court's *Brown* v. *Board of Education of Topeka, Kansas* (1954) decision onward, civil rights rulings have altered this pattern somewhat. Yet the student composition of many schools still does not reflect the diversity of a community's population of young people.

In the case of higher education, one finds that as one moves from universities to four-year colleges to two-year colleges, the proportion of students who are male, white, upper class, or academically high performing drops. In addition, some colleges serve the needs of distinct populations of students: for example, the nearly 200 single-sex colleges and nearly 100 all-black colleges (U.S. National Center for Education Statistics 1985; Rudolph 1962; Solomon 1985).

Schools also differ among themselves in the programs they offer. While most elementary and secondary schools offer fairly similar programs, they often differ in how they package the common curriculum. High schools, especially, may emphasize a particular vocational connection to their curriculum—for example, by offering preparation for health or business careers.

Colleges also differ in their offerings. Universities offer doctoral and professional programs and produce a large number of graduates with doctorates or medical or dental degrees. "Comprehensive" institutions offer diverse undergraduate curricula and some graduate programs. "General baccalaureate" or "liberal arts" colleges emphasize undergraduate education and have very few, if any, graduate programs. "Specialized" colleges emphasize one field, such as engineering or the arts, offering either a baccalaureate or postbaccalaureate training. The nearly 1,300 "two-year colleges" specialize in subbaccalaureate degrees such as associate of arts and various kinds of vocational certificates in areas like dental assisting or auto repair (Brint and Karabel 1989; Cohen and Brawer 1989; Dougherty 1988). (The number of two-year institutions would be far greater if we were to include the many for-profit postsecondary schools, numbering 7,645 in 1986, that offer technical and vocational training.)

Special education programs have become ghettos for nonwhite and working-class students.

But if schools differ mightily between themselves, they are also as strongly or more strongly differentiated internally. Two students in the same school may experience educational environments as varied as those experienced by two students at different schools. One of the most important differentiations takes the form of "ability grouping" or tracking in elementary and secondary schooling. This pervasive practice involves breaking students up into different classes or groups within classes, ostensibly on the basis of academic aptitude, and teaching them different material or the same material but at different paces. This differentiation of students is said to be based mainly on test scores, but in actuality other factors also play an important role, such as students' interests, the number of students in the class, and the distribution of student ability. Hence, curriculum or instructional groups are often rather heterogeneous in test scores and only partially approach being ability groups. Many scholars argue that curriculum grouping plays a key role in producing class and race differences in educational attainment, because students differing in social class and race tend to be assigned to different tracks and because tracking has a significant impact on educational attainment, independent of the characteristics of students (Barr and Dreeben 1983; Dreeben and Gamoran 1986; Peterson, Wilkinson, and Hallinan 1984; and Rosenbaum 1980).

Elementary and secondary schools also engage in curriculum grouping in the form of special education, gifted education, and bilingual education. These programs have become targets of considerable criticism in recent years. The term *special education* applies to programs for those who have academic, physical, or emotional difficulties that require special educational provision. In recent years, however, many observers have argued that special education programs have become ghettos for nonwhite and working-class students, because they more often receive lower test scores than white or middle- and upper-class students. Gifted education, conversely, has become a reserve for white and, increasingly, Asian students. Gifted education has been developed ostensibly to meet the needs of students of such unusual ability that they require a specially enriched education. Many critics argue, however, that these programs have become devices for keeping white students in urban public schools by offering the prospect of largely white or Asian classmates. Bilingual education, finally, enrolls students whose native language is not English. These students are instructed in both English and their native language for the first few years so that they can keep pace academically with native students. In recent years, however, many have argued that these programs prevent assimilation into American culture (Dougherty and Hammack 1990, chap. 8).

Colleges and universities also engage in curriculum grouping in the form of different majors. These constitute different environments that result in different educational and occupational outcomes for students. However, this curricular differentiation has not been considered as problematic as elementary and secondary tracking, because it occurs at a higher level and involves greater student choice.

This article has traced a complex pattern of repeated differentiation in order to elucidate how education is organized. This complex structure produces certain recurrent tensions that repeatedly break into educational politics.

[See also Socialization.]

BIBLIOGRAPHY

Apple, Michael 1986 *Teachers and Texts.* New York: Routledge, Chapman and Hall.

Aronowitz, Stanley, and Henry Giroux 1985 *Education under Siege.* South Hadley, Mass.: Bergin and Garvey.

Barr, Rebecca, and Robert Dreeben 1983 *How Schools Work.* Chicago: University of Chicago Press.

Bidwell, Charles 1965 "The School as a Formal Organization." In James G. March, ed., *Handbook of Organizations.* Chicago: Rand McNally.

Brint, Steven, and Jerome Karabel 1989 *The Diverted Dream.* New York: Oxford University Press.

Campbell, Roald F., Luvern L. Cunningham; Raphael O. Nystrand, and Michael D. Usdan 1985 *Organization and Control of American Schools,* 5th ed. Columbus, Ohio: Merrill.

Chubb, John E., and Terry Moe 1990 *Politics, Markets, and America's Schools.* Washington, D.C.: Brookings Institution.

Cohen, Arthur M., and Florence Brawer 1989 *The American Community College,* 2nd ed. San Francisco: Jossey-Bass.

Corwin, Ronald 1970 *Militant Professionalism: A Study of Organizational Conflict in High Schools.* New York: Appleton-Century-Crofts.

Dougherty, Kevin J. 1988 "The Politics of Community College Expansion." *American Journal of Education* 96:351–393.

———, and Floyd M. Hammack (eds.) 1990 *Education and Society.* San Diego: Harcourt Brace Jovanovich.

Dreeben, Robert, and Adam Gamoran 1986 "Race, Instruction, and Learning." *American Sociological Review* 51:660–669.

Hopper, Earl 1977 "A Typology for the Classification of Educational Systems." In Jerome Karabel and A. H. Halsey, eds., *Power and Ideology in Education.* New York: Oxford University Press.

Ignas, Edward, and Raymond Corsini (eds.) 1981 *Comparative Educational Systems.* Itasca, Ill.: F. E. Peacock.

King, Edmund 1979 *Other Schools and Ours,* 5th ed. New York: Oxford University Press.

Metz, Mary Haywood 1978 *Classrooms and Corridors.* Berkeley: University of California Press.

——— 1986 *Different by Design: Politics, Purpose, and Practice in Three Magnet Schools.* New York: Routledge, Chapman and Hall.

Meyer, John, and Brian Rowan 1978 "The Structure of Educational Organizations." In Marshall W. Meyer and Associates, *Environments and Organizations.* San Francisco: Jossey-Bass.

Peshkin, Alan 1978 *Growing Up American.* Chicago: University of Chicago Press.

Peterson, Penelope, Louise Cherry Wilkinson, and Maureen Hallinan (eds.) 1984 *The Social Context of Instruction.* New York: Academic Press.

Rosenbaum, James 1980 "Social Implications of Educational Grouping." In David Berliner, ed., *Review of Research in Education.* Washington, D.C.: American Educational Research Association.

Rudolph, Frederick 1962 *The American College and University.* New York: Vintage.

Solomon, Barbara Miller 1985 *In the Company of Educated Women.* New Haven: Yale University Press.

Spicer, Michael W., and Edward W. Hill 1990 "Evaluating Parental Choice in Public Education." *American Journal of Education* 98:97–113.

U.S. National Center for Education Statistics 1985 *Traditionally Black Institutions of Higher Education: Their Development and Status, 1860–1982.* Washington, D.C.: U.S. National Center for Education Statistics.

Wirt, Frederick, and Michael Kirst 1989 *Schools in Conflict,* 2nd ed. San Francisco: McCutchan.

– KEVIN DOUGHERTY
FLOYD M. HAMMACK

EDUCATION AND MOBILITY

The role of education in relation to social mobility and reproduction has long been debated between those who emphasize its contribution to social mobility and those who focus on its contribution to social reproduction. In order to understand this debate, it is useful to review the key concepts and theoretical perspectives before considering the empirical evidence and then offering a resolution.

Social stratification refers to the class or status hierarchy in society and the inequality in social rewards between people who belong to different classes or have different status. *Class* is the term preferred by theorists who view the social order as consisting of distinctive economic groupings struggling to maximize their interests vis-a-vis each other, while *status* is preferred by theorists who perceive a continuing distribution of socioeconomic variation without clear-cut divisions and conflict. *Social mobility* is the movement from one class or status to another. The emphasis here, as with most studies of social mobility, is on *intergenerational mobility.* Intergenerational mobility refers to the change in class or status from parents to their adult children. An example of intergenerational mobility is when the daughter or the son of peasants becomes a doctor. In contrast, when the offspring of peasants ends up being a peasant, it is an example of *social reproduction.*

The social class or status positions that individuals occupy in society are usually attributed to both *ascriptive* and *achievement* processes. These are generally viewed as opposite or contradictory processes involving either ascribed characteristics based on biological factors and family of origin or achieved characteristics based on individual traits and behaviors. Stratification systems that emphasize ascriptive characteristics for class or status placement are defined as "closed" and lead to status inheritance or class reproduction. Those stratification systems that emphasize achieved characteristics are defined as "open" and are expected to lead to social mobility.

The opposing positions are formalized in the functionalist and conflict theories of social stratification. With respect to the role of education in producing social mobility, functionalists argue that different social roles require different skills and abilities and, if society is to function effectively, they must be filled by individuals possessing the appropriate skills and abilities (Davis and Moore 1945). The positions most valued by society are usually the most critical for societal functioning and the most demanding of individual skills and ability. In order to encourage individuals to invest the time and effort for training and to attract the best qualified individuals, these positions have to be accompanied by higher social and economic rewards. Education is widely viewed as both developing and reflecting individual skills and abilities and is therefore used as a means of social selection. Thus, education enhances social mobility by providing for social selection based on achieved rather than ascribed characteristics of individuals.

Conflict theorists start with the premise that society consists of different groups with conflicting interest, and they argue that stratification exists because groups that acquired power, wealth, and prestige want to maintain and enhance their position at the expense of less privileged groups. In respect to education, most conflict theorists agree that schools help to reproduce and legitimize the stratification system by portraying attainment as an achieved individual characteristic, while in fact they select and process individuals on the basis of ascriptive characteristics (Bowles and Gintis 1976; Willis 1977; Bourdieu 1977).

Empirical research on the role of education in the process of social mobility or reproduction has produced conflicting evidence. The argument of mobility through education as suggested by functional theories depends on the validity of two general conditions: (1) educational attainment must be used as a criterion of eventual social class or status position; and (2) the level of educational attainment of individuals must not be influenced by the level of their family's class or status. Boudon (1976) calls these two conditions necessary for social mobility "meritocracy" and "equality of educational opportunity" respectively. It is important to note that social mobility exists only if both conditions are met and that each of them alone is a necessary but insufficient condition for social mobility.

Many studies have tested empirically the meritocracy hypothesis, and almost all have found a significant relationship between educational and later socioeconomic attainments (Blau and Duncan 1967; Sewell, Haller, and Portes 1969; Duncan, Featherman, and Duncan 1972; Jencks et al. 1972). Indeed, most studies in the United States have found educational attainment to be among the most important determinants of occupational and status attainment, although the findings regarding its relationship with income are not as conclusive (Jencks et al. 1972). In short, the meritocracy condition is well supported by empirical evidence.

The tremendous expansion of education in the last century left the opportunities for social mobility essentially unchanged.

However, other studies of social mobility found that employing meritocracy in the allocation of occupational and social status has not resulted in substantial increases in social mobility (Boudon 1974; Collins 1979). Boudon, using data from Western industrialized countries, and Collins, analyzing data from the United States, found that the tremendous expansion of education in the last century left the opportunities for social mobility essentially unchanged. It did expand the educational attainment of many social groups, but, as the educational attainment of individuals from lower socioeconomic strata increased, individuals from higher strata acquired even more education, thus shifting the overall educational attainment of the population upward but keeping in tact the stratification of educational attainment (Boudon 1974; Collins 1979). Given that meritocracy in the allocation of social positions exists, these findings suggest the lack of equality of educational opportunity.

In relation to the latter, the functionalist position is that schools do provide equality of opportunity. For empirical support, they point to the numerous empirical studies suggesting that the process of educational attainment is an achievement process. The best-known model of educational and status attainment in the United States, known as the Wisconsin Model, describes the process as one whereby individual and background characteristics are translated into differential status attainment only after they have been transformed into individual performance and psychological variables (Sewell, Haller, and Portes 1969; Sewell, Haller, and Ohlendorf 1970). Although this model has been criticized for excluding social constraints and related structural variables (see Kerckoff 1976), its explanatory power remains strong, and it has withstood a number of replications (Alexander, Eckland, and Griffin 1978; Jencks, Crouse, and Mueser 1983). Indeed, most of the research on the social selection process that followed the Wisconsin Model has shown that schools select, process, and reward students based on individual traits and achievements such as aspirations and ability and that educational attainment in turn is the major determinant of occupational status attainment.

Conflict theorists and researchers, by contrast, have not been very successful in describing and explaining a social selection process that leads to social reproduction. The explanations and the evidence as to why individuals from higher social strata acquire consistently better education have not been able to dispute or account for the fact that the educational selection process is ostensibly an "achievement" process. In general, the argument from a conflict perspective is that structural limitations imposed on the schooling of some groups restrict their educational success, thus helping to reproduce the educational and social hierarchies.

Some structural limitations on both the quality and quantity of educational opportunity of children from low socioeconomic strata do indeed exist. Differential quality and quantity of schooling may have been especially influential in the past, but it still exists today. Some of the best schools at all educational levels in the United States are private, with high tuition, and obviously not all social groups have equal access to or success in these institutions. Also, fewer institutions, especially at the postprimary levels, are available in rural or low income areas. Nonetheless, the impact of variation in quality and quantity of schooling has been reduced over the years, and evidence does not indicate it as a major determinant of educational attainment. For example, the well-publicized report *Equality of Educational Opportunity* (Coleman et al. 1966) found that differences between public schools had no significant effect on student performance. In general, even though some relevant quality differences between schools may still exist today, this structural variable is a relatively weak factor in explaining differential educational attainment.

Other structural variables, such as curriculum tracking (Alexander, Cook, and McDill 1978), and differential treatment by teachers and counselors (Rist 1970; Karabel 1972) also have been found to exert significant influence on educational attainment. In addition, researchers have found that cultural differences linked to differential social origin are also responsible for the unequal educational attainment of students from different social groups (Bourdieu 1977; Bourdieu and Passeron 1977; DiMaggio 1982). Overall, however, structural limitations and cultural deficiencies account for only a small amount of attainment differences as compared to the individual achievement variables.

Summarizing the findings on equality of educational opportunity and meritocracy presents a paradoxical picture of social stratification and leaves the issue of social mobility through education largely unresolved: Status attainment research has shown that educational and status attainment is a meritocratic process based on individual achievement variables, but it has not explained the relatively low social mobility rates. Critical research, on the other hand, has shown reproduction of social status, but it has not been able to unseat the equality of opportunity thesis resting on the association of individual achievement with educational status attainment.

This apparent paradox may be due in part to the fact that research on educational and social stratification in the last few decades has been dominated by the ascription-achievement controversy without necessarily examining the relationship between this controversy and the broader mobility-reproduction debate. The underlying assumption of this focus seems to have been that achievement leads to mobility and ascription leads to reproduction. But however important achievement and ascription may be, they do not address the same issues as mobility and reproduction. A way out of this impasse may be to challenge the assumed correspondence between what we traditionally consider individual achievements on the one hand and social mobility on the other. There is no reason to assume that an empirical finding of schooling as an achievement process is necessarily incompatible with a theoretical argument of schooling as a process of reproduction. As long as individual qualities and achievements are determined by the social origin of the student, educational systems can promote not only social reproduction and individual achievement but social reproduction *through* achievement (Katsillis and Rubinson 1990).

One of the most consistent findings of the research on educational and status attainment is that the socioeconomic status of the family influences the whole educational process, including many, if not all, individual student achievements and abilities that lead to socioeconomic status attainment. Thus, once the assumption that achievement implies social status or class mobility is abandoned, there is no contradiction between the findings of status attainment research that indicate an achievement-oriented educational selection system and the findings of critical research that schools reproduce social status or class inequalities.

This, of course, poses some interesting questions, especially in relation to the meaning and the role of equality of educational opportunity as we understand it today: Does a process that transforms family status inequality into differential individual achievements or qualities and, subsequently, into unequal educational attainment constitute equality of educational opportunity? If it does not, what constitutes equality of educational opportunity, and how is it attained? We may have to rethink the whole process of equality of opportunity before we are able to provide satisfactory answers to the question of education and social mobility.

[See also Equality of Opportunity; Social Mobility; Social Stratification.]

BIBLIOGRAPHY

Alexander, K. L., M. A. Cook, and E. L. McDill 1978 "Curriculum Tracking and Educational Stratification: Some Further Evidence." *American Sociological Review* 43:47–66.

———, B. K. Eckland, and L. J. Griffin 1978 "The Wisconsin Model of Socioeconomic Attainment: A Replication." *American Journal of Sociology* 81:324–342.

Blau, P. M., and O. D. Duncan 1967 *The American Occupational Structure.* New York: Wiley.

Bourdieu, P. 1977 "Cultural Reproduction and Social Reproduction." In J. Karabel and A. H. Halsey, eds., *Power and Ideology in Education.* New York: Oxford University Press.

———, and J. C. Passeron 1977 *Reproduction in Education, Society, and Culture.* Beverly Hills, Calif.: Sage Publications.

Bowles, S., and H. Gintis 1976 *Schooling in Capitalist America.* New York: Basic Books.

Coleman, J. S., E. Q. Campbell, C. J. Hobson, J. McPartland, A. M. Mood, F. D. Weinfall, and R. L. York 1966 *The Equality of Educational Opportunity.* Washington, D.C.: U.S. Department of Health, Education, and Welfare.

Davis, K. and W. Moore 1945 "Some Principles of Stratification." *American Sociological Review* 10:242–249.

DiMaggio, P. 1982 "Cultural Capital and School Success: The Impact of Status Culture Participation on the Grades of U.S. High School Students." *American Sociological Review* 47:189–201.

Duncan, O. D., D. L. Featherman, and B. Duncan 1972 *Socioeconomic Background and Achievement.* New York: Seminar Press.

Jencks, C., J. Crouse, and P. Mueser 1983 "The Wisconsin Model of Status Attainment: A National Replication with Improved Measures of Ability and Aspirations." *Sociology of Education* 56:3–19.

Jencks, C., M. Smith, H. Acland, J. M. Bane, D. Cohen, H. Gintis, B. Heyns, and S. Michelson 1972 *Inequality: A Reassessment of Family and Schooling in America.* New York: Basic Books.

Karabel, J. 1972 "Community Colleges and Social Stratification." *Harvard Educational Review* 42:521–562.

———, and A. H. Halsey (eds.) 1977 *Power and Ideology in Education.* New York: Oxford University Press.

Katsillis, J., and R. Rubinson 1990 "Cultural Capital, Student Achievement, and Educational Reproduction: The Case of Greece." *American Sociological Review* 55:270–279.

Kerckhoff, A. C. 1976 "The Status Attainment Process: Socialization or Allocation?" *Social Forces* 52:368–381.

Rist, R. C. 1970 "Student Social Class and Teacher Expectations: The Self-Fulfilling Prophecy in Ghetto Education." *Harvard Educational Review* 40:411–451.

Sewell, W. H., A. O. Haller, and G. W. Ohlendorf 1970 "The Educational and Early Occupational Status Attainment Process: Replications and Revisions." *American Sociological Review* 34:1,014–1,027.

Sewell, W. H., A. O. Haller, and A. Portes 1969 "The Educational and Early Occupational Status Attainment Process." *American Sociological Review* 34:82–92.

Willis, P. 1977 *Learning to Labor.* New York: Columbia University Press.

– JOHN KATSILLIS
J. MICHAEL ARMER

ENVIRONMENTAL MOVEMENT

The publication in 1962 of Rachel Carson's *Silent Spring* is one of the markers of the beginning of the environmental movement in the United States. The best-selling book sounded this tocsin to the world: "As man proceeds toward his announced goal of the conquest of nature, he has written a depressing record of destruction, directed not only against the earth he inhabits but against the life that shares it with him." Carson established beyond a doubt that chemicals in the air and water, especially DDT, were killing "birds, mammals, fishes, and indeed practically every form of wildlife." Out of the shock engendered by Carson's book grew a new sensibility about and a dedication to saving and protecting the environment. An older form of environmentalism, usually called conservationism, had existed for decades and was associated with John Muir, Aldo Leopold, William O. Douglas, Howard Zahnister, and David Brower, among others, but the effort that emerged in the 1960s was the first concerted, populous, vocal, active, and influential movement, and several new organizations were established, such as the Environmental Defense Fund, the Natural Resources Defense Council, Environmental Action, Friends of the Earth, and the Clearwater Project. The decade ended with Earth Day 1970, an outpouring of environmental sentiment involving an estimated 20 million people that, according to its chief organizer, Senator Gaylord Nelson of Wisconsin, sent "a big message to the politicians—a message to tell them to wake up and do something."

The election of Ronald Reagan as president in 1980 and the effect of the conservative agenda he supported temporarily checked the momentum of the environmental movement.

In the 1970s pollution became a major concern for the American public. Congress passed three amendments to the Clean Air Act of 1970—the Water Quality Act, the Solid Waste Disposal Act, and the Wilderness Act—the last to keep 9 million acres of public land pristine. The most significant act, the National Environmental Protection Act of 1970, was given its impetus and power by public enthusiasm and created the Environmental Protection Agency. The EPA became the largest regulatory body ever established in the federal government. The act also created the environmental impact statement, which requires federal agencies to assess the environmental consequences of all projects and transformed the way the United States built, planned, moved, and thought.

The growing acceptance of the nation's environmental crisis—and of the human as an endangered species—became evident in the 1970s in an array of popular works with titles like *The Last Days of Mankind, The Death of Tomorrow, Terracide, The Doomsday Syndrome, This Endangered Planet,* and *The Limits to Growth.* There was widespread media coverage of such events as the North Sea oil blowout in 1977, the revelation in 1978 that the houses along Love Canal in Buffalo, N.Y., were built on contaminated soil, the accident at the Three Mile Island nuclear power plant in Pennsylvania in 1979, and the EPA disclosure in 1979 that 50,000 sites in the United States were dangerously toxic. Membership in environmental groups increased dramatically; the National Audubon Society (founded 1905) tripled its membership in the 1970s to 400,000, the National Wildlife Federation (1936) membership reached 818,000, and that of the Sierra Club (1892) rose to 165,000. New groups appeared everywhere: Greenpeace (1971), the Trust for Public Land (1972), the Cousteau Society (1973), Worldwatch Institute (1975), and Sea Shepherd (1977). Environmental organizations began to exercise their political influence in Washington, where many of them established their headquarters, moving with increasingly sophisticated tactics to get Congress to pass no fewer than eighteen far-ranging environmental laws, from the Pesticide Control Act of 1972 and the Endangered Species Act of 1973 to the Federal Land Policy Act of 1976 and the Ocean Dumping Act of 1977.

The election of Ronald Reagan as president in 1980 and the effect of the conservative agenda he supported temporarily checked the momentum of the environmental movement. The real strength of the movement became apparent when it resisted the administration and continued to operate effectively. The national environmental groups, most headquartered in Washington, expanded memberships and staffs: the National Wildlife Federation, the Sierra Club, and the Wilderness Society were sufficiently influential to earn designation by the *National Journal* as three of the most effective lobbying groups in Washington. At the same time, local grass-roots organizations mushroomed, and by 1987 there were an estimated 25 million environmental activists across the country. A Harris poll reported in 1985 that 80 percent of the U.S. public supported environmental laws and regulations.

A more radical strain of environmentalism developed in the 1980s, one that scorned the environmental lobbying organizations and was committed to direct action, sometimes even illegal action. Earth First!, established in 1980 by people frustrated with the failures and compromises of the mainstream groups, was the most prominent of these new groups, with seventy-five chapters and half a million members. The group engaged in demonstrations, guerilla theater, media stunts, and, most notorious, "ecotage," the sabotage of equipment used for clearcutting, road-building, and dam construction. Other radical groups developed around such new ideas as bioregionalism, ecofeminism, and deep ecology (a philosophy espousing the equality and the right of all species to life and denouncing the anthropocentrism of most of the traditional environmental movement).

By the 1990s the effect and importance of environmentalism was a fact of life in the United States. Congressional action included the passage of amendments to the Clean Water Act, first passed in 1960, Resource Conservation and Recovery Act of 1976, the Safe Drinking Water Act of 1974, and the Coastal Zone Management Act of 1972 and appropriating enough funds to allow the EPA to implement all its regulations. On the electoral front, environmentalists selected and supported candidates at all levels; both the League of Conservation Voters, formed in 1980, and a variety of environmental political action committees disbursed funds, organized campaigns, canvassed membership lists, and advised candidates. The election in 1992 of Vice President Al Gore, an avowed and committed environmentalist, seemed to signal the effectiveness of this strategy.

By 1992, thirty years after it had begun, the environmental movement constituted the most powerful

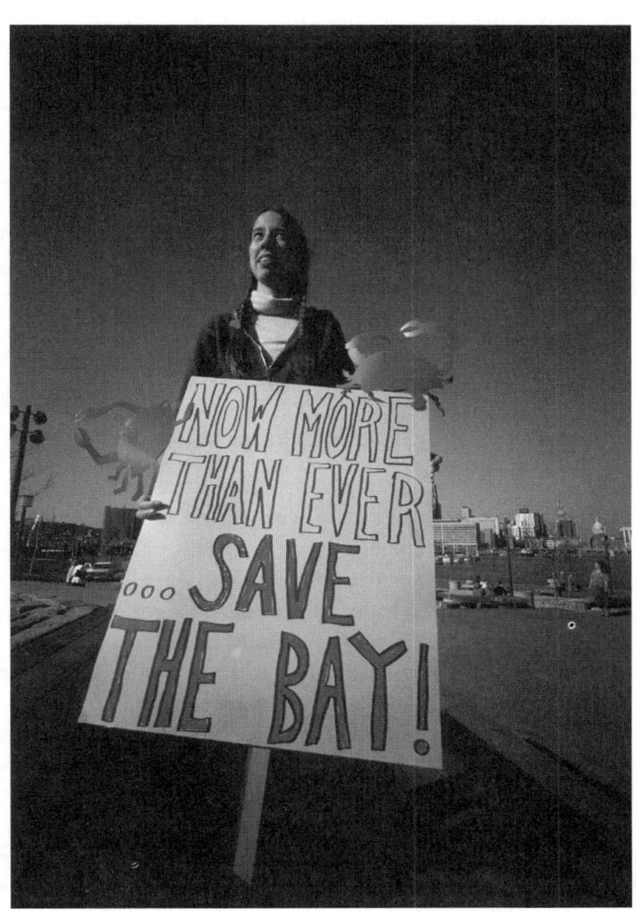

The environmental movement in the United States began in the 1960s, developing into a powerful force for social change by the 1990s. (Lowell Georgia/Corbis)

and successful social change movement since the nineteenth-century abolitionists. Membership in the largest national organizations was about 20 million (the largest, the National Wildlife Federation, had 5.6 million), and three-fourths of the American public described themselves as environmentalists. Spending on environmental causes was estimated at $2.5 billion in 1991, and the budgets of the leading organizations were $600 million. Earth Day 1990 was celebrated by an estimated 100 million people in 140 countries, including 25 million in the United States, with a fervor that led the *New York Times* to call environmentalism "a modern secular religion." An array of laws at the federal level ensured that environmental causes would remain embedded in national public policy, with the government's regulatory tasks estimated to cost society $125 billion each year. Despite this apparent success, however, the environment in the United States and around the world had not improved substantially and had declined in many areas. The WorldWatch Institute reported in 1993 that there was not a single life-support system on the planet that was not strained and threatened. In 1992 more than half the U.S. population lived in counties with polluted air. Five tons of carbon per person were poured into the air, more than 170,000 lakes and millions of acres of forests were acidified, 90 percent of the garbage went unrecycled, 95 percent of the worst toxic waste sites were untreated, topsoil was lost at a rate of 3 billion tons a year, and water was depleted and polluted annually at the rate of 10 billion gallons. The biosphere itself was an endangered species, and all the considerable efforts at saving it were failing.

– KIRKPATRICK SALE

EQUALITY OF OPPORTUNITY

Equality of opportunity refers to the fairness of processes through which individuals with different backgrounds or from different social groups reach particular outcomes, such as educational or occupational goals. Sociologists have developed several alternative approaches to defining and assessing equality of opportunity in each outcome domain, including residual differences after relevant qualifications are taken into account, process differences in the variables linking individual attributes to outcomes, and structural differences in the barriers encountered in preparing for, learning about, or obtaining particular educational or occupational achievements. Each approach has advantages and disadvantages for particular scientific, policy, and practical purposes.

Residual Differences in Equality of Opportunity

Equality of opportunity is usually judged with reference to major social groupings, such as race, sex, or socioeconomic status. The issue is whether individuals from major population subgroups have the same chances to achieve educational or occupational success, assuming that they possess the same distributions of personal attributes to qualify for success. Because any initial average outcome gaps between subgroups can be due to unequal possession of relevant qualifications, as well as to unfair access to the opportunities that link qualifications to achievements, it is necessary to take into account differences in personal qualifications before deciding that unequal opportunities exist.

Researchers have frequently tested for inequalities of opportunity by estimating the residual gap between the educational or occupational success of selected race, sex, or social class groups after individual differences in relevant credentials or competencies and educational or labor market locations have been statistically controlled for. The usual methodology is to estimate a prediction equation or to use other methods of standardization for selected individual resource variables that permit a researcher to compare the actual group difference in an educational or occupational outcome with the residual gap that would be expected if one group's productivity resources were replaced by the average resources of the other group (Farley and Allen 1987, chap. 11). For example, the actual average difference in annual earnings of African-American and white workers in the North would be compared against the residual earnings gap when one assumes that African-American workers' resources (such as education and labor market experience) deliver the same rate of return in earnings as that experienced by white workers. Some problems are inherent in this approach, including the risk of overestimating the residual gap if some important qualification variables are omitted or poorly measured, and the chance of underestimating the residual gap when some groups are deprived of relevant qualifications due to earlier unequal opportunities not reflected in the estimation methodology. Nevertheless, several important residual race, sex, or social class gaps have been identified for various important educational and occupational outcomes. However, these gaps are often associated with some subgroups but not others, and some gaps have been changing more rapidly than others in recent years.

Numerous national and regional studies have been conducted since the 1960s to estimate the inequality of job opportunities, including research that examines residual subgroup differences in unemployment rates, occupational distributions, and dollar returns from holding a job. Studies of race, sex, and social class residual gaps in earnings and income of employed workers have been particularly noteworthy, with more than twenty-five major national studies having been published since 1965 (Farley and Allen 1987).

The research on earnings gaps that estimates the "cost of being black" due to inequality of job opportunities has contrasted the experiences of male and female workers and reported the continuing but declining significance of race. After taking into account differences in educational attainment, age or years of potential labor market experience, hours of work, and regional location, large residual gaps in earnings are found between male African-American and white workers, with African-Americans earning 10 to 20 percent less than comparable whites in various regions and at various educational levels. Women continue to earn much less than men of the same race with similar educational credentials, but the residual race gap for women is no longer the same as reported for men. In 1960, African-American women earned less than white women at all educational levels except college graduate, but this gap had been eliminated or reversed by 1980, when college-educated African-American women actually reported greater earnings, largely because of greater hours of employment. The residual race gap in earnings for employed workers also appeared to grow somewhat smaller for men between 1960 and the 1980s, but still remains between 10 and 15 percent at all educational levels.

At the same time, evidence is mounting that race gaps in rates of unemployment are significant and have been growing worse since the 1960s for African-American men in most age and education categories; they are especially severe for unmarried young African-American men in the North who have limited educational attainments (Jaynes and Williams 1989, ch. 6; Farley and Allen 1987, chaps. 8–11).

Top-ability students are only half as likely to attend college if they came from the lowest quarter, rather than the highest quarter, in socioeconomic status.

Inequalities of educational opportunity have been examined by estimating residual race, sex, or social class gaps in outcomes net of initial resources, especially for college enrollment and completion rates. Among the earliest evidence of a social class gap in college attendance net of academic ability is data from the 1960s showing that even after controlling on standardized test performance, students from lower categories of socioeconomic status are much less likely to enter college within five years of high school graduation. The talent loss due to unequal social class background was estimated to be 50 percent of top-ability students who do not enter college from the lowest socioeconomic quartile, compared with a loss of only 5 percent of high-ability students from the highest socioeconomic quartile (U.S. Department of Health, Education and Welfare 1969). The importance of social class factors for educational equity was reinforced by extensive research on Wisconsin high school students that included measures of race as well as student achievement on standardized tests. Social class disparities in educational attainment net of academic ability were again in evidence, as it was reported that top-ability students are only half as likely to attend college or to graduate from college if they came from the lowest quarter, rather than the highest quarter, in socioeconomic status (Sewell and Hauser 1980). These studies also estimated that observed African-American-white differences in years of educational attainment can largely be accounted for by social class differences between the racial groups.

Other race differences in educational outcomes are not so well explained by socioeconomic status alone, including differences in students' achievement test performance and choice of major fields of study, whereas race contrasts in labor market discrimination, residential segregation, and the quality of schooling available to African-Americans are often weakly related to social class differences but strongly related to student motivation and performance in school (Jaynes and Williams 1989).

Process Differences in Opportunities

Another approach to assessing equality of opportunity is to compare the attainment processes that link personal resources or investments to educational or occupational achievements for different social groups. Opportunities can be defined as unequal when the major avenues to advancement used by one group are not as effective for another. Researchers have frequently reported attainment process differences in the degree to which various population subgroups have been able to capitalize on advantages of family background or have experienced a high rate of return on investments in building relevant competencies or credentials. Some of this work has been criticized for possible shortcomings of methodology and interpretation.

Studies of social group differences in an attainment process are important because they help to estimate the long-run prospects for closing existing achievement gaps (Featherman and Hauser 1978, chap. 6). The prospects are positive if each subgroup has access to an attainment process that will translate improvements of personal and family resources into achievement outcomes, especially when programs and policies are available for investments in upgrading resources of groups that at present are weak. But if some groups are lagging in relevant skills and credentials, and are exposed only to attainment processes that provide poor returns in comparison with other groups, then the prospects are dim for closing existing gaps.

Studies of general social mobility processes have identified the special problems of African-American males in translating any advantages from the family of origin into attainments in their own adult lives. For the white male population in this country, clear intergenerational processes have been evidenced in which sons can build upon a middle- or upper-class family background, as shown by the strong relationship between father's and son's occupational status for whites over many recent decades. In contrast, through the 1960s, African-American males have not been as able to capitalize on any family advantages in building their occupational careers, as shown by the weak relationship for intergenerational mobility and the frequency with which substantial proportions of African-American males from nonmanual or white-collar households are downwardly mobile and unable to benefit from their family advantages. There is some indication that since the 1970s race differences for males in the opportunities to benefit from any inheritance of family social class advantages have closed (Featherman and Hauser 1978; Farley and Allen 1987).

Race differences in the processes of school effects on achievement have been reported in two national studies by the sociologist James S. Coleman and his research coworkers. In a 1966 national study of public schools, differences in school resources and learning environments were found to have larger average effects on African-American students' achievement than on white students' achievement (Coleman et al. 1966). The result was interpreted as a differential sensitivity of disadvantaged students to school improvements, because these students from poor families relied more on good schools for their development of academic skills. A similar race difference in educational processes was found in the 1980s with national data from public and private high schools (Coleman and Hoffer 1987). African-Americans, Latinos, and students from low socioeconomic backgrounds were found to do better in Catholic schools than in public high schools, in terms of both higher test scores and lower dropout rates. It was argued that these students especially benefited from the greater academic demands that can be enforced by the sense of community established by Catholic schools, which compensates for family disadvantages of many of these students. Again, minority and disadvantaged students were found to be more responsive to changes in school environments that have effects on high school students' achievement and completion rates. Other researchers have questioned the recent results on the grounds that key student/family self-selection variables were not controlled in the analyses of public-Catholic school differences and that the sizes of the race interaction effects were not impressive by conventional statistical standards (Alexander and Pallas 1985; McPartland and McDill 1982).

Research has indicated that race inequalities are currently much less evident in educational attainment processes than in occupational attainment processes. Analyses using appropriate statistical tests of the processes that yield important educational achievements—such as additional years of schooling and scholastic outcomes including grades and test scores—have found great similarities between African-Americans and whites (Gottfredson 1981; Wolfle 1985; Pallas 1987). Thus, not only have African-American–white differences in the frequency of high school graduation and college education been diminishing, the processes that link social background and school input variations to educational achievements have become very similar for African-Americans and whites. At the same time, race gaps in school test scores have been closing more slowly, and serious disparities persist in the level of financing and concentration of single-race and disadvantaged student bodies in schools attended by racial minorities, even though education attainment processes would translate improvements of such inputs into attainments for African-Americans (Jaynes and Williams 1989).

However, major race and sex differences continue in the occupational domain regarding both the processes of attainment and the gaps in achievement. Labor market disparities by race and sex are much more apparent than differences in educational opportunities, but the disparities are exhibited in complex patterns or processes according to individuals' social class position, labor market location, career stage, and other factors (Jaynes and Williams 1989; Featherman and Hauser 1978; Farley and Allen 1987; Wilson 1987). The chances are equally good for African-Americans and whites of each sex who are highly educated to gain entry to good jobs, but advancement opportunities to higher positions at later career stages are more likely to be missed by African-Americans. At the same time, African-American male workers with less advanced credentials are much more likely to have periods of unemployment or reduced hours, and to be paid less when employed, than white males with equivalent years of schooling. The greatest race discrepancies are observed for poorly educated young African-American males, who are much more likely than comparable whites to be unemployed, to have dropped out of the labor force, or to report no annual earnings. William J. Wilson has developed a theory of the "declining significance of race" that considers the growing social class gaps within the African-American population in occupational success, as well as the special difficulties faced by poorly educated African-American males in urban racial ghettos, whom he views as "the truly disadvantaged" (Wilson 1987).

Structural Barriers to Educational Opportunities

While careful studies of residual differences and attainment process differences can document the existence of unequal opportunities, other research is required on specific interactions and practices in schools or labor markets to understand the actual barriers that unfairly inhibit individuals because of their sex, race, or social class position. For education, research on differential access to specific components of schooling, studies of tracking and grouping policies in elementary and secondary schools, and examinations of financial aid practices in higher education have identified some specific structural barriers in educational opportunities.

A landmark study was conducted in response to a congressional request under the 1964 Civil Rights Act and published in 1966 with the title *Equality of Educational Opportunity* (EEO). Also known as the "Coleman Report," after the sociologist James S. Coleman, who directed the research, EEO was both influential and controversial for the way it examined educational opportunities and for its major findings (Coleman et al. 1966). Based on a large national survey of students and schools at both elementary and secondary levels, EEO collected the most comprehensive data available at that time on equity issues in education. It was not satisfied to compare only the average school input resources experienced by different race and ethnic groups—such as textbooks, libraries and laboratories, per-pupil expenditures, teacher qualifications, or class size. EEO also considered race and ethnic differences on student outcomes as measured by standardized tests in major subjects, and asked how different school components contributed to student learning, in order to weigh inequalities of school inputs by their importance for student outcomes. The simultaneous examination of school inputs, student outcomes, and their relationships to one another had not been attempted before in assessing equity issues, and the published results have been a continuing source of reanalysis and reinterpretation.

EEO did find large differences in test scores between white and most racial and ethnic minority groups that existed from the time students began school and were not reduced, on the average, as students moved from grade 1 to grade 12. These differences in student outcomes could not be explained by variations in the school input factors measured by the EEO surveys, because within each region no great disparities of school inputs appeared for different racial and ethnic groups, and these factors did not relate strongly to student outcomes in any case after family background and social class factors were statistically controlled. In fact, when school factors were combined into three clusters for analysis—(a) instructional materials and resources, (b) teacher and staff characteristics, and (c) student body composition—the most important component in accounting for variations in student test scores net of family background was the attributes of fellow students. Thus, the large observed group differences in student outcomes were not found to be accounted for by existing variations in conventional school and teacher components, although attending a school with fellow students who were college bound did seem to make a positive contribution to the learning environment.

Subsequent investigations have confirmed the general picture drawn by EEO of an educational system that does little to reduce the large racial and ethnic differences in academic test scores with which students begin elementary grades (Mosteller and Moynihan 1972; Jencks et al. 1972). But specific limitations of EEO data prevented researchers from identifying factors within schools and classrooms that have potential for improving educational opportunities, and other conditions that have likely consequences on equality of opportunities have changed since the 1960s.

School-level barriers to equal educational opportunities have worsened since the 1960s.

EEO data did not measure within-school differences in educational resources and learning environments, and consequently was unable to analyze major barriers to equal opportunities from specific internal school practices, such as tracking and ability grouping. Other research has shown that when students are tracked into separate programs or separate courses according to their earlier test scores or grades, those in the lower-level groups are likely to encounter serious barriers to their educational growth and progress. Lower tracks and lower-level courses have been shown to offer weaker educational resources, such as fewer expert teachers and poorer educational climates with lower academic expectations, that can lead to lower average student achievement test scores and decreased probabilities of completing high school and continuing education in college (Oakes 1985; Gamoran 1986; Hallinan 1988). Tracking is now seen as a major barrier to equal educational opportunities because tracking and ability grouping are very common practices in American schools, and minorities and socioeconomically disadvantaged students are much more likely to be assigned to the lower-level programs and courses within their schools (Bowles and Gintis 1976; Oakes 1985; Braddock 1990).

Moreover, the educational resources available at the school level are thought to be more unequal for minorities and disadvantaged students at the present time than they were found to be in the 1966 EEO assessments (Smith and O'Day 1991). Since the 1960s, demographic trends have created greater concentrations of poverty in large urban schools, and changes in funding support for public education in central city districts have reduced those districts' relative ability to purchase adequate classroom supplies and materials, and to recruit and retain highly qualified teachers. Consequently, school-level barriers to equal educational opportunities have worsened since the 1960s, because the changing urban demographics and negative fiscal trends have dramatically altered the student body composition and the quality of the teaching staff that the EEO study found to be the most important factors of a good school.

Barriers have been identified in college educational opportunities, which also may have gotten worse, especially for African-American males, in recent years. Minorities have long been underrepresented as students at four-year colleges, in scientific major fields, and in obtaining advanced degrees (ISEP 1976; Thomas 1986; Trent and Braddock 1987). Some of these gaps had been closing through the 1970s, but since that time, uniform progress is no longer evident and some actual downturns in minority enrollments and attainments have been recorded (Jaynes and Williams 1989). African-American and Latino students often encounter special problems in pursuing college programs because of insufficient social and academic support on campus or of inadequate prior educational experiences (Green 1989). Recent reversals in minority enrollments have been explained by increasing tensions related to race and ethnicity on some college campuses and to changes from grants to loans in many financial assistance programs which poor students are less likely to receive or use (Blackwell 1990).

Structural Barriers to Occupational Opportunities

To help account for residual sex or race gaps in job success and in the career attainment process, research has identified specific structural barriers to sex equality and to racial equality in occupational opportunities.

Studies of the large average earnings differences between men and women workers show that very large gaps remain after statistically controlling on individual differences in input variables such as education and experience, but these gaps are substantially reduced by adding measures of each person's occupation or occupational group. This result indicates that sex gaps in earnings have much of their source in the extreme job segregation by sex in the American labor market—many occupations are primarily filled by women or primarily filled by men—and the wage levels are much lower for "female" occupations (Treiman and Hartmann 1981). Since fully two-thirds of men and women would have to change jobs to achieve similar representation of each sex across occupations, full enforcement of antidiscrimination laws against unequal pay for men and women in the same occupation can achieve only modest improvements in wage differentials by sex. Other suggested approaches to reducing sex segregation of jobs and associated wage gaps—such as enriching the socialization experiences toward a wider range of career exposures for children and youth of both sexes, or incorporating policies of "comparable worth" that establish wage rates by job features, irrespective of sex or race of incumbents (Hartmann 1985; Marini 1989)—have not yet made large inroads.

To specify how occupational opportunities continue to be unequal for racial or ethnic minorities, research has identified structural barriers at each stage of the occupational career process. Barriers can appear at the job candidate stage, when employers are recruiting the pool of candidates for job openings; at the job entry stage, when an individual is actually selected to fill a vacancy; and at the job promotion stage, when transfers are made within a firm to fill spots at higher levels (Braddock and McPartland 1987; Feagin and Feagin 1978; Marini 1989).

At the job candidate stage, qualified minorities of either sex may fail to learn about many desirable job openings because they are excluded from useful social networks that provide others with information about and contacts for particular employment opportunities. Employers find job candidates more frequently from walk-ins and friends of current employees (the result of informal social networks) than any other recruitment means for lower- and middle-level jobs. The social contacts used by many minorities are racially segregated networks that on the average are not as well tied to good job information as the social networks available to whites. This barrier to equal opportunities at the job candidate stage is partially kept in place by the continued racial segregation of the schools and neighborhoods that create many social networks, and by the underrepresentation of minorities in the upper levels of firms, where informal information for friends and relatives about job openings is often best acquired (Rossi, Berk, and Eidson 1974; Crain 1970).

At the job entry stage, otherwise qualified minorities are often not selected because of barriers of statistical discrimination and information bias. Employers who do not wish to invest much to obtain extensive information about job applicants will often use a group identifier, such as sex or race, in hiring decisions when they believe that traits on which subgroups may differ statistically predict job performance. For example, such "statistical discrimination" can occur when an employer selects a white over a minority applicant for a job requiring good academic skills, based on a belief in average racial group differences on academic test scores rather than on actual individual candidates' differences in academic skills shown on tests administered or obtained by the employer during the screening process (Thurow 1975; Bielby and Baron 1986; Braddock et al. 1986).

Even when qualification data from individuals are relied upon in hiring decisions, other barriers to equal opportunities occur due to "information bias" of data on minority candidates. References and recommendations from school or employment officials for African-American applicants may be viewed as less credible by white employers who are less familiar with an African-American school, a member of the African-American clergy, or an African-American firm, or who may be more wary of information provided by minority sponsors due to stigmas or stereotypes attached to these sources. Similarly, minority job applicants who grow up in communities that have high youth unemployment rates will be less able to satisfy prospective employers' interests in previous employment experiences and references (Braddock and McPartland 1987).

The average pay differential between African-American and white workers is less for jobs filled from inside a firm than for jobs filled from outside.

At the job promotion stage, minorities may face unfair barriers due to internal recruitment methods or because they are poorly positioned within internal labor markets. However, findings from a national study indicate the potential benefits to minorities of seeking internal promotions: The average pay differential between African-American and white workers is less for jobs filled from inside a firm than for jobs filled from outside for individuals of the same sex and education level, suggesting that unfair selection is reduced when employers process information on applicants' actual job performance within their firm. On the other hand, the same study showed that unless an internal vacancy is widely advertised within a firm, whites are more likely to be sought out for available promotions (Braddock and McPartland 1987). Moreover, research has shown that minorities are less likely to have entered a firm on a career ladder that ordinarily leads to promotion opportunities, so they may never be eligible to compete for advancement through an internal labor market (Rosenfield 1980).

Policies and Practices

Governments and courts have established policies and practices in recent decades that are intended to eliminate race and sex discrimination and to ensure equality of opportunity. These range from the 1954 Supreme Court decision against segregated schools to the civil rights legislation of the 1960s and the executive orders to establish affirmative action guidelines in employment (Jaynes and Williams 1989; Burstein 1985).

Although it is difficult to distinguish the effects of one governmental action from those of another in improving the life chances of women and minorities, clear advances have been made that can be attributed to the combined impacts of various public policies for equal rights. For example, from 1970 to 1990 the race gaps in academic test scores of schoolchildren decreased between 25 and 50 percent for different age groups (Smith and O'Day 1991). Reductions in the race gaps in terms of years of school completed have been dramatic, especially among female students. Greater equity is also evident in some labor market behaviors, including the distribution of occupations by race within sex groups. On the other hand, racial improvements are not so evident in employment rates and income levels of adult males, and extensive racial segregation of housing and schooling remains a dominant feature of American life (Jaynes and Williams 1989). Still, progress in equal opportunities for sex and race groups clearly has been coincident with the major thrusts of legislation and court decisions to foster civil rights.

Controversy continues to accompany further efforts to sustain current policies and to institute new practices for equal opportunities. The differences are most evident on whether outcome-based policies are required to overcome systemic barriers—for instance, affirmative action programs that use guidelines and timetables—or whether efforts should concentrate only on intentional discrimination or on specific aspects of the processes that inhibit equal rights (Levinger 1987).

[See also Affirmative Action; Discrimination; Education and Mobility; Ethnicity; Social Mobility; Race.]

BIBLIOGRAPHY

Alexander, Karl A., and Aaron M. Pallas 1985 "School Sector and Cognitive Performance." *Sociology of Education* 58:115–127.

Bean, Frank D., and Marta Tienda 1987 *The Hispanic Population of the United States.* New York: Russell Sage Foundation.

Bielby, William T., and James N. Baron 1986 "Men and Women at Work: Sex Segregation and Statistical Discrimination." *American Journal of Sociology* 91:759–799.

Blackwell, James E. 1990 "Current Issues Affecting Blacks and Hispanics in the Educational Pipeline." In Gail E. Thomas, ed., *U.S. Race Relations in the 1980s and 1990s.* New York: Hemisphere.

Blau, Peter M., and Otis D. Duncan 1967 *The American Occupational Structure.* New York: Wiley.

Bowles, Samuel, and Herbert Gintis 1976 *Schooling in Capitalist America.* New York: Basic Books.

Braddock, Jomills H., II 1990 *Tracking: Implications for Student Race-Ethnic Subgroups.* Report No. 2. Center for Research on Effective Schooling for Disadvantaged Students, The Johns Hopkins University, Baltimore, Md.

———, and James M. McPartland 1987 "How Minorities Continue to Be Excluded from Equal Employment Opportunities: Research on Labor Market and Institutional Barriers." *Journal of Social Issues* 43 (1):5–39.

———, et al. 1986 "Applicant Race and Job Placement Decisions: A National Survey Experiment." *International Journal of Sociology and Social Policy* 6:3–24.

Burstein, Paul 1985 *Discrimination, Jobs and Politics: The Struggle for Equal Employment Opportunity in the United States Since the New Deal.* Chicago: University of Chicago Press.

Coleman, James S. 1968 "The Concept of Equality of Educational Opportunity." *Harvard Educational Review* 38:7–22.

———, and Thomas Hoffer 1987 *Public and Private High Schools.* New York: Basic Books.

——— et al. 1966 *Equality of Educational Opportunity.* Washington, D.C.: U.S. Government Printing Office.

Crain, Robert L. 1970 "School Integration and Occupational Achievement of Negroes." *American Journal of Sociology* 75:593–606.

Duncan, Otis D. 1969 "Inheritance of Poverty or Inheritance of Race?" In Daniel P. Moynihan, ed., *Understanding Poverty.* New York: Basic Books.

Farley, Reynolds, and Walter R. Allen 1987 *The Color Line and the Quality of Life in America.* New York: Russell Sage Foundation.

Feagin, J. R., and C. B. Feagin 1978 *Discrimination American Style: Institutional Racism and Sexism.* Englewood Cliffs, N.J.: Prentice-Hall.

Featherman, David L., and Robert M. Hauser 1978 *Opportunity and Change.* New York: Academic Press.

Gamoran, Adam 1986 "Instructional and Institutional Effects of Ability Grouping." *Sociology of Education* 59:185–198.

Gottfredson, Denise C. 1981 "Black-White Differences in the Educational Attainment Process: What Have We Learned?" *American Sociological Review* 46:542–557.

Granovetter, Mark S. 1974 *Getting a Job: A Study of Contacts and Careers.* Cambridge, Mass.: Harvard University Press.

Green, Madeleine F. 1989 *Minorities on Campus: A Handbook for Enhancing Diversity.* Washington, D.C.: American Council on Education.

Hallinan, Maureen T. 1988 "Equality of Educational Opportunity." *Annual Review of Sociology* 14:249–268.

Hartmann, Heidi I. (ed.) 1985 *Comparable Worth: New Directions for Research.* Washington, D.C.: National Academy Press.

Institute for the Study of Educational Policy. 1976 *Equal Educational Opportunity for Blacks in U.S. Higher Education: An Assessment.* Washington, D.C.: Howard University Press.

Jaynes, Gerald David, and Robin M. Williams, Jr. (eds.) 1989 *A Common Destiny: Blacks and American Society.* Washington, D.C.: National Academy Press.

Jencks, Christopher, et al. 1972 *Inequality: A Reassessment of the Effect of Family and Schooling in America.* New York: Basic Books.

——— 1979 *Who Gets Ahead? The Determinants of Economic Success in America.* New York: Basic Books.

Levinger, George (ed.) 1987 "Black Employment Opportunities: Macro and Micro Perspectives." *Journal of Social Issues* 43:1–156.

Marini, Margaret Mooney 1989 "Sex Differences in Earnings in the United States." *Annual Review of Sociology* 15:343–380.

McPartland, James M., and Edward L. McDill 1982 "Control and Differentiation in the Structure of American Education." *Sociology of Education* 55:65–76.

Mosteller, Frederick, and Daniel P. Moynihan (eds.) 1972 *On Equality of Educational Opportunity.* New York: Random House.

Oakes, Jeannie 1985 *Keeping Track.* New Haven, Conn.: Yale University Press.

Pallas, Aaron M. 1987 "Black-White Differences in Adolescent Educational Outcomes." Paper prepared for Committee on the Status of Black Americans. Washington, D.C.: National Research Council.

Reskin, Barbara F. (ed.) 1984 *Sex Segregation in the Workplace.* Washington, D.C.: National Academy Press.

Rosenbaum, James E., Takehiko Kariya, Rick Settersten, and Tony Marier 1990 "Market and Network Theories of the Transition from High School to Work: Their Application to Industrialized Societies." *Annual Review of Sociology* 16:263–299.

Rosenfield, Rachel A. 1980 "Race and Sex Differences in Career Dynamics." *American Sociological Review* 45:583–609.

Rossi, Peter H., Richard A. Berk, and Betty K. Eidson 1974 *The Roots of Urban Discontent: Public Policy, Municipal Institutions and the Ghetto.* New York: Wiley.

Sewell, William H., and Robert M. Hauser 1980 "The Wisconsin Longitudinal Study of Social and Psychological Factors in Aspirations and Achievements." In Alan C. Kerckhoff, ed., *Research in Sociology of Education and Socialization,* Vol. I. Greenwich, Conn.: JAI Press.

Smith, Marshall S., and Jennifer O'Day 1991 "Educational Equality: 1966 and Now." In Deborah Verstegen, ed., *Spheres of Justice in American Schools.* New York: Harper Business.

Thomas, Gail E. 1986 *The Access and Success of Blacks and Hispanics in U.S. Graduate and Professional Education.* Working Paper, Office of Scientific and Engineering Personnel, National Research Council. Washington, D.C.: National Academy Press.

Thurow, Lester 1975 *Generating Inequality.* New York: Basic Books.

Treiman, Donald J., and Heidi I. Hartmann (eds.) 1981 *Women, Work and Wages: Equal Pay for Jobs of Equal Value.* Washington, D.C.: National Academy Press.

Treiman, Donald J., Heidi I. Hartmann, and Patricia A. Roos, 1984 "Assessing Pay Discrimination Using National Data." In Helen Remick, ed., *Comparable Worth and Wage Discrimination.* Philadelphia: Temple University Press.

Trent, William T., and Jomills Henry Braddock II 1987 "Trends in Black Enrollment and Degree Attainment." In John B. Williams, ed., *Title VI Regulation of Higher Education: Problems and Progress.* New York: Teachers College Press.

U.S. Department of Health, Education and Welfare 1969 *Toward a Social Report.* Washington, D.C.: U.S. Government Printing Office.

Wilson, William Julius 1980 *The Declining Significance of Race: Blacks and Changing American Institutions,* 2nd ed. Chicago: University of Chicago Press.

——— 1987 *The Truly Disadvantaged: The Inner City, the Underclass and Public Policy.* Chicago: University of Chicago Press.

Wolfle, Lee M. 1985 "Postsecondary Educational Attainment Among Whites and Blacks." *American Educational Research Journal* 22:501–525.

– JOMILLS HENRY BRADDOCK II
JAMES M. MCPARTLAND

ETHNICITY

Ethnicity is a salient feature of numerous societies throughout the world. Few societies are ethnically homogeneous, even when they proclaim themselves to be. Consequently, ethnicity has been a preoccupation of sociologists since the early days of the discipline (although more so in the United States than elsewhere).

Yet there is not complete agreement on how the subject should be defined. In the past, it was common to highlight cultural difference as an essential feature of ethnic distinctiveness (see van den Berghe 1967). Recently, this has been deemphasized on the grounds that cultural differences may vary from one setting to another and from one historical period to another. Following an approach attributed to Barth (1969), recent definitions have therefore focused on the existence of a recognized social boundary. Perhaps the most useful definition is still the classic one of Max Weber ([1922] 1968, p. 389): An ethnic group is one whose members "entertain a subjective belief in their common descent because of similarities of physical type or of customs or both, or because of memories of colonization and migration." Weber adds insightfully, "it does not matter whether or not an objective blood relationship exists."

Despite definitional disagreements, a number of characteristics are generally recognized as hallmarks of ethnicity; not all of them will be present in every case, but many will be. They include features shared by group members, such as the same or similar geographic origin, language, religion, foods, traditions, folklore, music, and residential patterns. Also typical are: special political concerns, particularly with regard to a homeland; institutions (e.g., social clubs) to serve the group; and a consciousness of kind or a sense of distinctiveness from others (for the full listing, see Thernstrom, Orlov, and Handlin 1980, p. vi).

There is further disagreement over whether race should be viewed as a form of ethnicity. In this context, "race" should not be understood as a bundle of genetically determined traits that generate of themselves social differences—a view that has been repudiated by the vast majority of social scientists—but as a kind of social classification used by members of a society. Some scholars distinguish between ethnicity and race. For example, van den Berghe (1967) defines race as a social classification based on putative physical traits, and ethnicity as a classification based on cultural ones. But more commonly, race is seen as a variant of ethnicity: A racial group is, then, an ethnic group whose members are believed, by others if not also by themselves, to be physiologically distinctive. This is the approach adopted in this article.

Sociologists recognize that the imprint of history on the contemporary ethnic relations of any society is deep, and this gives rise to another distinction that is potentially central to any discussion of ethnicity. It pertains to the mode of entry of a group into a society and has been formulated by Lieberson (1961) in terms of the situation that obtains just after contact between an indigenous group and one migrating into an area. One possibility is that the migrant group dominates, typically through conquest (often aided by the introduction of new diseases). This is exemplified in the contacts between indigenes and European settlers in Australia and the United States. The other is that the indigenous group dominates, as occurred during the century of mass immigration (1830–1930) into the United States. The crux of the matter here is whether a group is incorporated into a society through force or through more or less voluntary migration. Lieberson argues that a group's mode of entry is fateful for its trajectory of development in a society, and this is amply borne out in the literature on ethnicity.

Ethnicity has also been viewed as "primordial."

Stated in very broad terms, three approaches dominate the sociological study of ethnicity (see Sakong 1990). One, the *assimilation* perspective, focuses on social processes and outcomes that tend to dissolve ethnic distinctions, leading to the assimilation of one ethnic group by another or by the larger society. The second approach could be labeled as *stratification.* As the name implies, it is concerned with the origins and consequences of inequalities of various kinds among ethnic groups. The third approach focuses on *ethnic group resources.* Its domain encompasses such processes as mobilization and solidarity, by which the members of ethnic groups attempt to use their ethnicity to compete successfully with others.

No one of these three approaches could be described as preeminent, and each is a major presence in contemporary research on ethnicity. Other approaches are possible but are not as theoretically and empirically developed as these three. One other possibility seeks a basis for ethnicity in sociobiology, viewing ethnicity as a form of genetic nepotism, a generalization of the presumably universal tendency among animals to favor kin. Van den Berghe (1981) has been an exponent of such an approach, but as yet no body of evidence has been developed to distinguish it from more sociological approaches; other sociologists have not followed his lead. Ethnicity has also been viewed as "primordial," deriving from deeply seated human impulses and needs that are not eradicated by modernization (Isaacs 1975). But this viewpoint has not led to sociologically interesting research, and it has lacked exponents in recent decades. The newest attempt stems from "rational choice theory" (Banton 1983; Hechter 1987) and seeks to explain ethnic phenomena in terms of the efforts of individuals to maximize their advantages (or, in technical language, utilities). The use of rational choice theory is still too novel to draw up a meaningful balance sheet.

The assimilation approach has deep roots in classical social theory as well as in American sociology, where it is often traced to Robert E. Park's 1926 formulation of a race relations cycle of "contacts, competition, accommodation, and eventual assimilation" (Park 1950, p. 150) The canonical statement of the assimilation approach is by Gordon (1964). Although Gordon was addressing the role of ethnicity in the United States, his formulation is so general that it can be readily applied to other societies. At the heart of his contribution is the recognition that assimilation is a multidimensional concept. He distinguished, in fact, among seven types of assimilation, but the critical distinction lies between two: *acculturation* and *structural* (or social) *assimilation.* Acculturation means the adaptation by an ethnic group of the cultural patterns of the surrounding society (recognizing that these patterns may themselves be changed by the group's presence). Such acculturation encompasses not only external cultural traits, such as dress and language, but also internal ones, such as beliefs and values. Gordon (1964, p. 77) theorized that acculturation is typically the first of the types of assimilation to occur and that the stage of " 'acculturation only' may continue indefinitely"—hence the importance of the second assimilation type, structural assimilation. Structural assimilation is defined by Gordon to mean the entry of an ethnic group's members into close, or primary, relationships with members of the dominant group (or, at least, with ethnic outsiders). The cardinal hypothesis in Gordon's scheme is that structural assimilation is the key that unlocks all other types: "Once structural assimilation has occurred . . . all of the other types of assimilation will naturally follow" (Gordon 1964, p. 81). Once structural assimilation occurs, the way is open to widespread intermarriage, an abating of prejudice and discrimination, and the full participation of ethnic-group members in the life of a society.

Gordon discussed certain models or theories of the assimilation process (they might also be described as ideologies because of their value-laden character). Although these were again developed for the U.S. context, Gordon's discussion is so lucid that the models have passed into more general application. One is labeled "Anglo-conformity" by Gordon, and it describes an assimilation that is limited to acculturation to the behavior and values of the core ethnic group, taken in the American context to be Protestants with ancestry from the British Isles. A second model is that of the "melting pot." It envisions an assimilation process that operates on cultural and structural planes. One outcome is a culture that contains contributions from numerous ethnic groups and is adopted by their members. A parallel outcome on a structural plane is a pattern of widespread marriage across ethnic lines, in which the members of all ethnic groups participate, leading ultimately to population made up of individuals of quite intermixed ancestry. The melting pot idea corresponds with some popular notions about U.S. society, but so does the last model explicated by Gordon—namely, "cultural pluralism." Cultural pluralism corresponds with a situation in which ethnic groups remain socially differentiated, often with their own institutions and high rates of in-group marriage, and retain some culturally distinctive features. It is, in fact, an apt description of many societies throughout the world.

Urban ecology, dating back to the origins of the Chicago School of American Sociology, is quite compatible with the assimilation approach. The core tenets of this tradition, as updated in the model of *spatial assimilation* (Massey 1985), are that residential mobility follows from the acculturation and socioeconomic mobility of ethnic-group members and that residential mobility is an intermediate step on the way to more complete (i.e., structural) assimilation. The model envisions an early stage of residential segregation, as the members of ethnic groups—typically, immigrants and their children—are concentrated in urban enclaves, which frequently result from the displacement of other groups. But as the members of an ethnic group acculturate and establish themselves in the labor markets of the host society, they attempt to leave behind less successful coethnics and to convert socioeconomic and assimilation progress into residential gain by "purchasing" residence in places with greater advantages and amenities. This process implies, on the one hand, a tendency toward dispersion of an ethnic group, opening the way for increased contact with members of ethnic majority, and, on the other hand, greater resemblance in terms of residential characteristics between successful ethnic-group members and their peers from the majority. This model has been applied to immigrant groups in six different societies by Massey (1985).

The assimilation perspective has been successfully applied to American ethnic groups derived from European immigration (although the ultimate assimilation of these groups is still debated). In a review of the evidence, Hirschman (1983) documents the abating of ethnic differences in the white population in terms of socioeconomic achievement, residential location, and intermarriage. To cite some representative research findings, Lieberson and Waters (1988, chap. 5), comparing the occupations of European-ancestry men in 1900 and 1980, find a marked decline in occupational concentrations, although these still show traces of the patterns of the past. These authors and Alba (1990) also demonstrate the great extent to which interethnic marriage now takes place within the white population: Three of every four marriages in this group involve some degree of ethnic boundary crossing.

Much of the evidence on assimilation and ethnic change is derived from cross-sectional studies rather than those over time; the latter are difficult to conduct because of the limited availability of comparable data from different time points. Cross-sectional analyses involve some dissection of an ethnic group into parts expected to display a trajectory of change. One basis for such a dissection is generational groups. *Generation* here refers to distance in descent from the point of entry into a society. (By convention, generations are numbered with immigrants as the "first," so that their children are the "second," their grandchildren are the "third," etc.) Generally speaking, later generations are expected to be more assimilated than earlier ones. Another basis for dissection is *birth cohorts,* defined as groups born during the same period. Cohort differences can provide insight into historical changes in a group's position. Both kinds of differences have been used to study ethnic changes in the United States (for an application of the generational method, see Neidert and Farley 1985; for the cohort method, see Alba 1988).

The second major approach to the study of ethnicity and race, labeled above as "stratification," is considerably less unified than the assimilation approach, encompassing quite diverse theoretical underpinnings and research findings. Yet there are some common threads throughout. One is an assumption that ethnic groups generally are hierarchically ordered: There is typically a dominant or *superordinate* group, which is often described as the *majority* group (even though in some societies, such as South Africa, it may be a numerical minority of the population). There are also *subordinate* groups, often called *minorities* (although they may be numerical majorities). Second, these groups are assumed to be in conflict over scarce resources, which may relate to power, favorable occupational position, educational opportunity, and so forth. In this conflict, the dominant group employs a variety of strategies to defend or enhance its position, while minority groups seek to challenge it. Often, the focus of the stratification approach is on the mechanisms that help preserve ethnic inequalities, although there has also been some attention to the means that enable minorities successfully to challenge entrenched inequality.

Despite a secular decline in prejudiced attitudes and beliefs, there has been little increase in support for government policies that implement principles of racial equality.

One tradition in ethnic stratification research has looked to mechanisms of inequality that are rooted in ideologies, in belief systems that are then manifested in the outlooks and behavior of individuals. This is, in fact, a common meaning for the word *racism.* A long-standing research concern has been with *prejudice,* which is generally defined as a fixed set of opinions and attitudes, usually unfavorable, about the members of a group (Allport 1954). Prejudice is frequently an outgrowth of *ethnocentrism,* the tendency to value positively one's own group and denigrate others. It can lead to *discrimination,* which is a behavior: the denial of equal treatment to a group's members, exemplified by the refusal to sell homes in certain neighborhoods to minority group members. The investigation of prejudice was one of the early testing grounds for survey research. In the United States, this research uncovered a dimension of *social distance,* expressing the specific gradations of social intimacy the majority is willing to tolerate with the members of various ethnic groups (Bogardus 1928). Recent research has revealed a paradoxical set of changes: on the one hand, a secular decline in prejudiced attitudes and beliefs, most notably those held by whites toward blacks; on the other, little increase in support for government policies that implement principles of racial equality (Schuman, Steeh, and Bobo 1985).

However persuasive as explanatory factors prejudice and discrimination may appear to the lay person, sociologists have in recent decades more and more neglected them in favor of *institutional* or *structural* mechanisms of inequality. One reason for this shift has been skepticism that prejudice and discrimination by themselves are adequate to account for the depth and durability of racial and ethnic cleavages in industrial societies, especially since these factors have seemed to decline in tandem with rising educational levels. (However, the emphasis on structural mechanisms can itself be faulted for neglecting the ideological component in racism.)

One expression of the focus on structural factors has been the notion of *institutional racism* (Blauner 1972). According to this notion, inequality among racial and ethnic groups depends not so much on individual acts of discrimination as it does on the workings of such institutions as the schools and the police, which process and sort individuals according to their racial and ethnic origins and ultimately impose very different outcomes on them. An assumption of this approach is that this sort of discrimination can occur on a wide scale without equally widespread prejudice. Indeed, it may even be possible without any discriminatory intent on the part of individuals in authority. An example would be educational tracking systems that sort students according to racial background based on culturally and socially biased cues that are presumed by teachers and administrators to be related to intellectual ability. Studies deriving from the notion of institutional racism have in fact provided some compelling analyses of the perpetuation of inequalities (on education, see Persell 1977), although they also can easily descend into controversy, as when any unequal outcome is declared to indicate the operation of racism.

A major theme in the stratification approach is the often complicated relationship or interaction between ethnicity and social class. In treating this theme, one viewpoint is that ethnicity is, to some degree at least, a manifestation of deeply rooted class dynamics. This has led to analyses that emphasize the economic and material foundations of what appear superficially to be cultural and ethnic distinctions. Analyses of this type have sometimes been inspired by Marxism, but they are hardly limited to Marxists. For example, Herbert Gans ([1962] 1982), in an influential analysis of second-generation Italians in a Boston neighborhood, argued that many of their distinctive traits could be understood as a function of their working-class position, which was not greatly changed from the situation of their southern Italian ancestors. In a related vein, Steinberg (1981) argues that cultural explanations of ethnic inequalities, which impute "undesirable" characteristics to some groups and "desirable" ones to others, are often rationalizations of economic privilege.

It is sometimes argued that inequalities that once rested on an ethnic basis now rest primarily on one of class. An important, if controversial, instance is Wilson's (1978, 1987) claim of a "declining significance of race" for American blacks. One part of Wilson's argument focuses on an increasing socioeconomic split within the black population. This is held to result from the increasing opportunities available to young, well-educated African-Americans since the 1960s. However, while improvements have been registered for a minority of the group, the lot of the black poor has not improved—it has even worsened. Wilson describes their situation as one of an *underclass,* which he defines in terms of isolation from the mainstream economy and society. His explanations for the emergence of the underclass are structural, not individualistic, and include: the spatial concentration of the black poor in rundown urban neighborhoods, which have been stripped of their institutional fabric and middle-class residents; and the exodus of suitable job opportunities from central cities to suburbs and Sunbelt areas. This interpretation gives insight into the emergence of deviant characteristics in these ghettoes, such as high rates of out-of-wedlock births.

An economic approach has also been used to explain ethnic conflict, which is seen as an outgrowth of the conflicting material interests of different ethnic groups. An exemplar is provided by the theory of the ethnically *split labor market* (Bonacich 1972). Such a labor market develops when two ethnically different groups of workers compete (or could compete) for the same jobs *at different costs to employers.* It is typical in such situations for the higher priced group of workers to have the same ethnic origins as employers and therefore for the lower priced group to be ethnically different from both. Nevertheless, it is in the interest of employers to substitute lower priced workers for higher priced ones wherever possible, despite the ethnic ties they share with the latter. Intense ethnic conflict can therefore develop between the two groups of workers, as the higher priced group seeks to eliminate the threat to its interests. Two strategies may be employed: exclusion of the lower priced group (for example, through legal restrictions on the immigration of its members); or creation of a caste system (i.e., the limitation of the lower priced group to a separate sphere of undesirable jobs). Split labor market theory has been applied to black–white relations in South Africa and the United States.

Yet, even in terms of a strictly economic approach, the precise genesis of the conflict between different ethnic groups of workers is open to question, and the theory of *segmented labor markets* gives another picture (Piore 1979). This theory divides the economies and labor markets of advanced capitalist societies into a primary sector, which combines relatively secure, well-paid jobs with decent working conditions and the opportunity for advancement, and a secondary sector, made up of insecure, dead-end jobs at low wages. Regardless of their class position, workers from the dominant group prefer to avoid jobs in the secondary sector and usually can manage to do so. Even unemployment may not be sufficient to force them into the secondary sector because the benefits and resources available to most members of the dominant group, such as relatively generous unemployment compensation and seniority rights, enable them to wait out periodic unemployment. Hence, there is a need for another supply of workers, typically drawn from minorities and immigrants, who have no alternative but to accept employment in the secondary sector. Immigrants, in fact, are often willing to take these jobs because, as sojourners, the social stigma attached to the work is less meaningful for them than for the native born. In contrast to the theory of the split labor market, which takes the existence of an ethnic difference among workers as a given, segmented labor market theory explains why ethnic differences, especially between natives and immigrants, are so prevalent and persistent in the industrial societies of the West.

Domination in Northern Ireland encompasses more than social class privilege and gives even working-class members of the Protestant group a sense of status and superiority.

An economic explanation of ethnic differences is sometimes placed in a context of worldwide colonialism and capitalist exploitation (Rex 1981). Indeed, ethnic inequalities *within* a society are sometimes seen as the consequence of international relations between colonizers and the colonized. The notion that subordinate groups form economically exploited *internal colonies* in Western societies is an important expression of this (Blauner 1972). This notion is compatible with a hypothesis of a *cultural division of labor,* according to which positions in the socioeconomic order are assigned on the basis of cultural markers and hence ethnic origin (Hechter 1975).

The stratification approach need not focus exclusively on socioeconomic differences. Some scholars, in fact, prefer to see inequalities of power as more fundamental (Horowitz 1985; Stone 1985). This is a very general perspective on ethnic stratification and is quite compatible with such fundamental notions as dominant and subordinate groups. According to it, social class relations are but one instance, no matter how important, of the institutionalized inequalities between ethnic groups. Equally important, ethnic dominance cannot be reduced to, or explained solely in terms of, social class mechanisms. (An implication is that class analysis of ethnic relations can be reductionist, an attempt to explain away ethnicity's causal independence.) Thus, the antagonism and sectarian violence between Catholics and Protestants in Northern Ireland is not comprehensible solely in the terms of a social class analysis, even though aggregate class differences between the groups exist as a result of centuries-long Protestant domination. This domination, the legacy of colonial treatment of Ireland by the British, is manifest in a number of areas—in separate residential neighborhoods and schools, in social relations between members of the two groups, and in the political system. In short, domination encompasses much more than social class privilege and gives even working-class members of the Protestant group a sense of status and superiority.

Distinguishing empirically between ethnic stratification based on power and that rooted in economic structure has proven difficult. In one attempt, Blalock (1967) has formulated a *power threat hypothesis,* to be contrasted with one derived from economic competition between groups. These two hypotheses can be tested in the relationship between discrimination and the size of a minority group. In particular, threats to the power of the dominant group are expected to result in discrimination that rises sharply with increases in the size of a minority; the same is not true for economic competition. So far, this test has been applied mainly to the American South.

Theories concerning power differentials among ethnic groups border on the final major approach to the study of ethnicity, with its focus on ethnic group resources (a term borrowed for this context from Light and Bonacich 1988 and Sakong 1990). This approach, like the stratification approach, takes its point of departure from the inequalities among groups. However, its vision is less one of the domination of some groups over others than it is of a more balanced competition, which is affected by characteristics of the groups, such as their numbers, their solidarity, and their ability to form separate ethnic subeconomies. Such characteristics can give the group and its members relative advantages or disadvantages in this competition. Insofar as advantages are conferred, there may be incentives for individuals to maintain their attachments to a group rather than to assimilate. In a sense, theories of ethnic group resources can be seen as counterarguments to assimilation theories.

This is certainly clear in Glazer and Moynihan's (1970) politically based explanation for the continuing importance of ethnicity in the United States. These authors acknowledge that immigrant cultures fade quickly under the impact of the assimilation process; assimilation is accomplished to this degree. However, ethnicity comes to coincide with differences in American circumstances, such as residential and occupational concentrations, which are similarly affected by government policies and actions. Hence, ethnicity takes on importance in the political sphere: Ethnic groups become "interest groups," reflecting the interests of many similarly situated individuals. This role breathes new life into what might otherwise languish as an Old World social form. Glazer and Moynihan give many examples of the working of such interest groups in New York City.

Others have argued that ethnicity has become "politicized" in many contemporary societies, including many industrialized ones, and this leads to an unanticipated ethnic "resurgence." Bell (1975) states one basis for this point of view, claiming that politics is increasingly replacing the market as the chief instrument of distribution and that politics recognizes only group claims, thus enhancing ethnicity's political import. Horowitz (1985), on the other hand, sees the ethnic political conflict characterizing many third world nations as originating in part in colonial policies and then intensified by the anxieties of groups over their status in the post-colonial order. On a different note, Nielsen (1985) contends that ethnicity offers a wider basis for political recruitment than the chief alternative, social class.

Students of ethnic politicization have focused especially on the phenomenon of ethnic mobilization, which is epitomized in separatist movements in modern states as in Brittany and Quebec (Olzak 1983). Mobilization can be regarded as one manifestation of ethnic solidarity, a core concept in the literature on ethnicity. *Solidary* ethnic groups can be defined as self-conscious communities whose members interact with each other to achieve common purposes, and *mobilization* occurs when members take some collective action to advance these purposes. Recent research on ethnic movements appears to demonstrate that they are not generally interpretable in modern polities as the vestiges of traditional loyalties that have yet to be submerged by the modernization processes attendant upon development; rather, such movements can be outcomes of these processes and thus increase as economic development proceeds. The specific causes of this linkage are disputed, however (Olzak 1983).

Culture is another domain in which the search for group resources has been carried out. The group resources approach is compatible with the cultural pluralist description of society, described earlier. More commonly in the past than today, the relative success of ethnic groups has been explained in terms of cultural traits. Quite often, the advantages these give have been analyzed in social psychological terms. A well-known attempt along these lines was that of Rosen (1959), who matched American ethnic groups against the profile of the "achievement syndrome," a configuration of values that is presumed to predispose individuals to success. Included are an orientation to the future rather than the past and a downplaying of fatalism. In Rosen's analysis, the presence or absence of these traits in the culture of a group was explained according to the group's history and experience and frequently in terms of the culture of the society from which it came.

This sort of analysis, presuming stable cultural traits and rooting socioeconomic success in social-psychological prerequisites, has fallen into disfavor of late. In fact, it is often seen as more popular myth than social science (Steinberg 1981). Cultural explanations, however, are not limited to the social-psychological realm. As one example, Light (1972) has devised an intriguing partial explanation for the entrepreneurial proclivities of different groups—in terms of the extent to which their cultures sponsor mechanisms that generate capital for the start-up of small businesses. Light argues that the business success of some Asian groups can be understood in part as an outcome of the rotating credit association, a traditional social form imported from their home societies. Nevertheless, sociologists recently have stressed the malleability of culture and have tended to view it more as an adaptation to, and hence outcome of, socioeconomic position than as a cause of it. Consequently, cultural interpretations currently play only a minor role in the study of ethnicity. This may be a neglect engendered by cyclical intellectual fashion. In the future, they may loom larger.

A final theory that fits under the group resources umbrella focuses on the ability of some ethnic groups to form separate economic sectors, which can shelter ethnic entrepreneurs and workers from the disadvantages they would face in the mainstream economy. In the guise of *ethnic enclave* theory, this set of ideas recently has been highly developed by Portes and various colleagues (e.g., Portes and Bach 1985), although its intellectual ancestry is considerably older. Examining the trajectories of recent, non-European immigrant groups in the United States, Portes and his coauthors argue that the mode of economic incorporation is fateful for the group. The members of immigrant groups that lack an independent economic base have little alternative but to offer their labor power in the mainstream economy, where they typically find themselves disadvantaged by language, by foreign educational backgrounds, and by their ethnic ancestry itself. The story can be quite different for the members of groups that are able to establish their own niches, or ethnic enclaves, in the economy. (Portes and Bach 1985 cite Cubans as a case in point.) These groups, which typically contain a high-status stratum composed of individuals with professional occupations, capital, or both, are able to establish networks of businesses in specific industrial sectors. The success of these businesses is predicated upon ethnic loyalty to some degree. Where suppliers and purchasers of materials for production (in, say, the garment industry) share the same ethnic background, an advantage based on ethnicity is created, for suppliers have a guaranteed outlet for their product and purchasers a guaranteed source, and perhaps credit, to satisfy their production needs. Where workers and bosses share the same ethnicity, a further advantage may exist. Workers may be willing to work longer hours or for lower wages, thus enhancing the profitability of a business, because they are able to work in a culturally familiar environment (usually speaking their mother tongue, for example). Workers may also have the opportunity to learn about running a business, and some eventually graduate to become entrepreneurs themselves.

Once established, an enclave economy offers an alternative to assimilation into the mainstream economy. This is evident in two ways. First, participants in the enclave economy receive income returns on their education and other human capital equivalent to those obtained by participants in the mainstream economy. There is, then, no economic loss associated with the enclave. Second, because ethnic solidarity is the linchpin of the enclave, the formation of an enclave economy in turn fosters the perpetuation of solidarity and its cultural and social underpinnings. Thus, an enclave economy creates countercurrents to the general tide of assimilation.

Despite its attractiveness on theoretical grounds, the implications of the enclave economy are disputed. One criticism is that such an economy offers few benefits for workers; the economic gains accrue to ethnic entrepreneurs (Sanders and Nee 1987). Another is that the success of the enclave depends on very low-cost *female* labor and thus on gender exploitation (Zhou and Logan 1989). If true, both criticisms suggest that the enclave as a positive alternative to the mainstream, and thus the incentives to resist assimilation, may be overstated. What is clear is that more research is needed to clarify both the conditions under which an enclave economy will prosper and its ramifications for an ethnic group.

The literature on ethnicity remains unsettled in its theoretical core. The persistence—perhaps even the resurgence—of ethnic difference and conflict in societies throughout the world has attracted much attention from sociologists and other social scientists. But the paradoxes associated with ethnicity, evidenced in the United States by the assimilation of some groups and the continued separateness and even subordination of others, have yet to be resolved. They remain fruitful for sociology, nevertheless: The study of ethnicity has produced some of the discipline's most striking findings and, no doubt, will continue to do so.

[See also Culture; Discrimination; Nationalism; Social Mobility; Social Stratification.]

BIBLIOGRAPHY

Alba, Richard 1988 "Cohorts and the Dynamics of Ethnic Change." In Matilda White Riley, Bettina Huber, and Beth Hess, eds., *Social Structures and Human Lives.* Newbury Park, Calif.: Sage.

——— 1990 *Ethnic Identity: The Transformation of White America.* New Haven, Conn.: Yale University Press.

Allport, Gordon 1954 *The Nature of Prejudice.* New York: Addison-Wesley.

Banton, Michael 1983 *Racial and Ethnic Competition.* Cambridge: Cambridge University Press.

Barth, Frederik 1969 "Introduction." In Frederik Barth, ed., *Ethnic Groups and Boundaries.* Boston: Little, Brown.

Bell, Daniel 1975 "Ethnicity and Social Change." In Nathan Glazer and Daniel P. Moynihan, eds. *Ethnicity: Theory and Experience.* Cambridge, Mass.: Harvard University Press.

Blalock, Hubert 1967 *Toward a Theory of Minority-Group Relations.* New York: Capricorn.

Blauner, Robert 1972 *Racial Oppression in America.* New York: Harper and Row.

Bogardus, Emory 1928 *Immigration and Race Attitudes.* Boston: D. C. Heath.

Bonacich, Edna 1972. "A Theory of Ethnic Antagonism: The Split Labor Market." *American Sociological Review* 37:547–559.

Gans, Herbert (1962) 1982 *The Urban Villagers: Group and Class in the Life of Italian Americans.* New York: Free Press.

Glazer, Nathan, and Daniel Patrick Moynihan 1970 *Beyond the Melting Pot: The Negroes, Puerto Ricans, Jews, Italians, and Irish of New York City,* 2nd ed. Cambridge, Mass.: MIT Press.

Gordon, Milton 1964 *Assimilation in American Life.* New York: Oxford University Press.

Hechter, Michael 1975 *Internal Colonialism: The Celtic Fringe and British National Development.* Berkeley: University of California Press.

——— 1987 *Principles of Group Solidarity.* Berkeley: University of California Press.

Hirschman, Charles 1983 "America's Melting Pot Reconsidered." *Annual Review of Sociology* 9:397–423.

Horowitz, Donald 1985 *Ethnic Groups in Conflict.* Berkeley: University of California Press.

Isaacs, Harold 1975 "Basic Group Identity: The Idols of the Tribe." In Nathan Glazer and Daniel P. Moynihan, eds., *Ethnicity: Theory and Experience.* Cambridge, Mass.: Harvard University Press.

Lieberson, Stanley 1961 "A Societal Theory of Race and Ethnic Relations." *American Sociological Review* 26:902–910.

———, and Mary Waters 1988 *From Many Strands: Ethnic and Racial Groups in Contemporary America.* New York: Russell Sage Foundation.

Light, Ivan 1972 *Ethnic Enterprise in America: Business and Welfare Among Chinese, Japanese, and Blacks.* Berkeley: University of California Press.

———, and Edna Bonacich 1988 *Immigrant Entrepreneurs: Koreans in Los Angeles, 1965–1982.* Berkeley: University of California Press.

Massey, Douglas 1985 "Ethnic Residential Segregation: A Theoretical Synthesis and Empirical Review." *Sociology and Social Research* 69:315–350.

Neidert, Lisa, and Reynolds Farley 1985 "Assimilation in the United States: An Analysis of Ethnic and Generation Differences in Status and Achievement." *American Sociological Review* 50:840–850.

Nielsen, François 1985 "Toward a Theory of Ethnic Solidarity in Modern Societies." *American Sociological Review* 133–149.

Olzak, Susan 1983 "Contemporary Ethnic Mobilization." *Annual Review of Sociology* 9:355–374.

Park, Robert E. 1950 *Race and Culture.* New York: Free Press.

Persell, Caroline 1977 *Education and Inequality: The Roots of Stratification in America's Schools.* New York: Free Press.

Piore, Michael 1979 *Birds of Passage: Migrant Labor and Industrial Societies.* New York: Cambridge University Press.

Portes, Alejandro, and Robert Bach 1985 *Latin Journey: Cuban and Mexican Immigrants in the United States.* Berkeley: University of California Press.

Rex, John 1981 "A Working Paradigm for Race Relations Research." *Ethnic and Racial Studies* 4:1–25.

Rosen, Bernard 1959 "Race, Ethnicity, and the Achievement Syndrome." *American Sociological Review* 24:47–60.

Sakong, MyungDuk 1990 "Rethinking the Impact of the Enclave: A Comparative Analysis of Korean Americans' Economic and Residential Adaptation." Ph.D. diss., State University of New York, Albany.

Sanders, Jimy, and Victor Nee 1987 "Limits of Ethnic Solidarity in the Enclave Economy." *American Sociological Review* 52:745–767.

Schuman, Howard, Charlotte Steeh, and Lawrence Bobo 1985 *Racial Attitudes in America: Trends and Interpretations.* Cambridge, Mass.: Harvard University Press.

Steinberg, Stephen 1981 *The Ethnic Myth: Race, Ethnicity, and Class in America.* New York: Atheneum.

Stone, John 1985 *Racial Conflict in Contemporary Society.* London: Fontana Press/Collins.

Thernstrom, Stephan, Ann Orlov, and Oscar Handlin 1980 *Harvard Encyclopedia of American Ethnic Groups.* Cambridge, Mass.: Harvard University Press.

van den Berghe, Pierre 1967 *Race and Racism: A Comparative Perspective.* New York: Wiley.

——— 1981 *The Ethnic Phenomenon.* New York: Elsevier.

Weber, Max [1922] 1968 *Economy and Society.* New York: Bedminster Press.

Wilson, William J. 1978 *The Declining Significance of Race: Blacks and Changing American Institutions.* Chicago: University of Chicago Press.

——— 1987 *The Truly Disadvantaged: The Inner City, the Underclass, and Public Policy.* Chicago: University of Chicago Press.

Zhou, Min, and John Logan 1989 "Returns on Human Capital in Ethnic Enclaves: New York City's Chinatown." *American Sociological Review* 54:809–820.

– RICHARD D. ALBA

EVOLUTION: BIOLOGICAL, SOCIAL, CULTURAL

The diverse forms of life on earth have apparently emerged from a common source through a process of evolution that has the following characteristics:

1. The course of evolution does not always proceed along a straight path, for example, from simple to complex forms. Instead, it can meander like a stream, directed largely by environmental circumstances, and occasionally it appears to reverse direction in certain respects. Our own distant ancestors, for instance, became adapted to life in the trees, but our more recent ancestors readapted to living on the ground. When the course of evolution does reverse direction, it generally does so with respect to comparatively few features only; a complex evolutionary development never comes close to being totally reversed. Thus, we humans retain various characteristics evolved earlier in connection with life in the trees: stereoscopic vision, visual acuity, reduced sense of smell, hands adapted for grasping, and so forth.

2. Different groups of organisms sometimes evolve in similar directions in certain respects when exposed to similar environmental conditions. Thus, whales—descendants of mammals that lived on land—acquired fishlike shapes when they adapted to life in the water.

3. However, parallelism in evolutionary development generally remains limited: Different evolutionary lines do not come close to "merging." Whales, even though living in the ocean and acquiring fishlike shapes, retain basic anatomical and physiological features of mammals, quite different from those of fish.

The life-cycle of an individual human involves fixed stages (infancy, childhood, adolescence, adulthood, old age) that represent an unfolding of innate potentialities, that millions of people pass through, and that culminate in inevitable death. The evolution of a new biological species, by contrast, is a unique historical development involving movement in directions shaped primarily in response to environmental pressures, without any inevitable "death" or other predetermined end.

A "Lamarckian" evolutionary process (named, somewhat inappropriately, after Jean Baptiste Lamarck, 1744–1829) would involve inheritance of acquired characteristics. Thus, if evolution followed the Lamarckian pattern, giraffes might have acquired their long necks because in each generation necks were stretched (perhaps to obtain food high up in trees or to detect approaching enemies) and because the effect of each generation's stretching tended to be inherited by the generation that followed. However, Lamarckian ideas were found to be invalid long ago.

The course of evolution

does not always proceed along a straight path.

Instead, it can meander like a stream,

and occasionally it appears to reverse direction.

An alternative approach developed by Charles Darwin (1859) and others does not assume that acquired characteristics (such as effects of neck-stretching) are inherited. Rather, it assumes (1) random or randomlike variation among the offspring in each generation (with some giraffes happening by chance to have longer necks than others); (2) natural selection, involving tendencies for certain variants (longer-necked giraffes) to survive and reproduce more than others; and (3) preservation through inheritance of the effects of natural selection (longer-necked giraffes tending to have similarly long-necked offspring, although—as suggested above—there would still be some random variation among these offspring with respect to neck length).

Darwinian ideas challenged traditional Christian religious beliefs by suggesting (1) that humans are descended from more primitive creatures and, ultimately, from elementary life forms; (2) that our evolution was basically an unplanned outcome of diverse environmental pressures rather than something planned in advance; and (3) that the earth is old enough for evolutionary processes to have had time to produce the variety and complexity of life forms that we actually find. Although still resisted today by many on religious grounds, Darwinian theory ultimately came to be generally accepted by biologists, with important modifications and certain disagreements about details, and in combination with new knowledge in other areas of biology and other scientific disciplines that was not available to Darwin (see Gould 1982; Mayr 1982, pp. 299–627; and Stebbins and Ayala 1985).

In the late nineteenth and early twentieth centuries, evolutionary concepts and associated slogans such as "survival of the fittest" came to provide a rationale for a "social Darwinist" social policy. Various business, political, ideological, and military leaders in several countries, along with some scholars in several disciplines (including the sociologists Herbert Spencer and William Graham Sumner), emphasized the importance of the struggle for survival in maintaining a hardy population and a vigorous society and opposed social welfare measures that they thought would encourage "unfit" people to reproduce. Supporters of this approach differed among themselves in several ways: Some emphasized individual struggle, others group (e.g., racial or national) struggle; some emphasized nonviolent means (e.g., economic competition); and others emphasized armed conflict (see Hofstadter 1955).

The emergence of evolutionary theory in biology was also accompanied by the emergence of theories about human societal change that came to be called "evolutionary," although this label may be misleading. The idea that human society evolves from simple beginnings through comparatively fixed stages came to be commonly accepted in the nineteenth century, although different theorists had different conceptions of what these stages were. Examples include analyses of transitions from theological to metaphysical and then "positivistic" thought styles (Comte 1875); from savagery to barbarism and finally to civilization (Morgan 1877); from tribalism to slavery, feudalism, capitalism, and then communism (Marx and Engels 1947, first published 1846); and from simple to compounded, doubly compounded, and then triply compounded societies (Spencer 1967, first published 1885–1886).

When societies, cultures, or civilizations are said to pass from childhood to adulthood and then to old age, or are said to grow and then decline, there is an analogy not with the evolution of a species but rather with the human life-cycle, as illustrated in the works of Oswald Spengler and Arnold J. Toynbee. Nineteenth-century "social-evolutionary" theories departed from the life-cycle model in that they did not involve the idea of decline or old age followed by death as the end point of a cycle. Quite the opposite: The trends they described tended to culminate in triumphant achievements: "positivism" (Comte), "civilization" (Morgan), "communism" (Marx and Engels), and societies "compounded" many times (Spencer). In this one respect, but only in this respect, these theories resembled the bioevolutionary model: Biological species do not have to become extinct—even though many of them actually do—in the same sense in which individuals have to die. However, these theories nevertheless reflect a life-cycle model insofar as they involve one society after another following essentially the same pattern of development, just as one infant after another follows the same general route to adulthood. And, they do not appear to involve, in any major way, the evolutionary mechanisms of random variation and selection. In fact, they are primarily theories of progress, not of evolution in any sense that biologists would recognize, regardless of the "evolutionary" label commonly attached to them (Nisbet 1969).

The social-evolutionary idea fell into disfavor around the turn of the century but was revived several decades later, for example, with Talcott Parsons's analysis of primitive, intermediate, and modern societies (1977), and Lenski and Lenski's (1982) analysis of transitions from hunting-and-gathering to horticultural, agrarian, and industrial societies. Although based on more accurate and more extensive facts than were available in the nineteenth century, the newer social-evolutionary schemes are nevertheless fundamentally similar to their nineteenth-century predecessors in that they present various societies as passing through specific stages in a predominantly unidirectional pattern—which, as noted above, represents a sharp divergence from the bioevolutionary model. This is not necessarily a defect: The development of new types of society simply may not be a process to which concepts of a bioevolutionary sort are fully applicable.

Such concepts are more readily applicable to the development of culture, especially in the areas of science (Hull 1988) and technology (Basalla 1988) in which the cumulative character of culture is most strongly manifested. Competing scientific hypotheses are the "randomlike variations" in science as an evolutionary process; research results that evaluate such hypotheses select some of them for survival and others for extinction; and the knowledge that constitutes the outcome of this process in any given generation of scientists is "inherited" by subsequent generations through textbooks, teaching, and research publications. In technological evolution, positive selection (i.e., acceptance) of variations (innovations) depends not only on research results (i.e., on how well they "work") but also on costs, competitive pressures, compatibility with prevailing culture, and other factors.

The bioevolutionary model is not useful when applied to social or cultural changes that are cyclical, easily reversed, or primarily planned, innately determined, or repetitive. It may be usefully applied when a complex transformation that would be hard to repeat or reverse occurs gradually without being planned, through environmentally determined selections from among divergent alternative directions of change (see Campbell 1965; Richter 1982, pp. 19–34).

[See also Culture.]

BIBLIOGRAPHY

Basalla, George 1988 *The Evolution of Technology.* New York: Cambridge University Press.

Campbell, Donald T. 1965 "Variation and Selective Retention in Socio-Cultural Evolution." In Herbert R. Barringer, George I. Blanksten, and Raymond W. Mack, eds., *Social Change in Developing Areas.* Cambridge, Mass.: Schenkman.

Comte, Auguste 1875 *The Positive Philosophy,* 2nd ed. Harriet Martineau, trans. and cond. London: Trubner.

Darwin, Charles 1859 *On the Origin of Species.* London: Murray.

Gould, Stephen Jay 1982 "Darwinism and the Expansion of Evolutionary Theory." *Science* 216:380–387.

Hofstadter, Richard 1955 *Social Darwinism in American Thought.* Boston: Beacon Press.

Hull, David L. 1988 *Science as a Process.* Chicago: University of Chicago Press.

Lenski, Gerhard, and Jean Lenski 1982 *Human Societies: An Introduction to Macrosociology.* New York: McGraw-Hill.

Marx, Karl, and Friedrich Engels 1947 *The German Ideology.* New York: International Publishers.

Mayr, Ernst 1982 *The Growth of Biological Thought.* Cambridge, Mass.: Harvard University Press, Belknap Press.

Morgan, Lewis H. 1877 *Ancient Society.* Chicago: Charles H. Kerr.

Nisbet, Robert A. 1969 *Social Change and History.* London: Oxford University Press.

Parsons, Talcott 1977 *The Evolution of Societies,* ed. Jackson Toby. Englewood Cliffs, N.J.: Prentice-Hall.

Richter, Maurice N., Jr. 1982 *Technology and Social Complexity.* Albany: State University of New York Press.

Spencer, Herbert 1967 *The Evolution of Society,* ed. Robert L Carneiro. Chicago: University of Chicago Press. Excerpted from *Principles of Sociology,* vols. 1 and 2, rev. ed. London: Williams and Margate, 1885–1886.

Stebbins, G. Ledyard, and Francisco J. Ayala 1985 "The Evolution of Darwinism." *Scientific American* 253:72–82.

– MAURICE N. RICHTER, JR.

F

FAMILY AND POPULATION POLICY IN LESS DEVELOPED COUNTRIES

The term *family policy* is defined variously, with little consensus about its precise referent other than involving the government's orientation or actions toward "the family" (itself an ill-defined term). For example, in a review of usages, Kamerman and Kahn (1978, pp. 3–8) suggest that "family policy" is used in three distinct ways. In the first usage, the term refers to a field of planning or activity in which certain objectives for the family are defined, and programs or regulations intended to achieve these objectives are created. In the second usage, goals for the family are used as a rationale or rationalization for other, possibly less legitimate, objectives—for example, as a way of increasing or reducing the supply of female workers to the labor market. In the third usage, objectives for the family are used as a criterion by which to evaluate all social policy choices—that is, a government's family policy becomes a yardstick against which military, land use, housing, educational, welfare, and other social policies are measured. There do not appear to be societies where this last usage holds true, but some social policy specialists advocate that it be established, for example, by requiring "family impact statements" whenever social programs are proposed (Kamerman and Kahn 1978, p. 2).

Kamerman and Kahn suggest that family policy ultimately refers to "everything that government does to and for the family" (1978, p. 3) or, more specifically, to "deliberate actions taken [by government] toward the family, such as day care, child welfare, family counseling, family planning, income maintenance, some tax benefits, and some housing policies" (p. 3). They make a distinction between *explicit* family policy, that is, "programs and policies which deliberately do things to and for the family" (p. 3), in some cases guided by specific and explicit overarching goals for the family and in other cases without such goals, and *implicit* family policy, consisting of governmental "actions and policies not specifically or primarily addressed to the family, but which have indirect consequences" (p. 3). An example of the latter is policy to improve literacy by creating a mass public educational system, a development that has been argued to bring about such changes as reductions in average family size (Caldwell 1980) and improvement in the status of women (Mason 1984).

In other usages, "policy" refers to a set of goals for the family and is distinguished from the laws, regulations, and programs that are used to implement the policy or that are evaluated in terms of it. This last usage is less confusing than the usages in which goals and actions are lumped together, so long as it is recognized that implicit family policies can be inferred only by analyzing governmental actions. In these terms, then, *a family policy is a set of explicit or implicit governmental goals for various aspects of family composition or functioning,* goals that are implemented or inferable through the government's regulatory, distributive, or redistributive actions. Common arenas of government action through which explicit family policies are implemented (or implicit policies are inferred) include (1) the enactment or enforcement of family-related laws; (2) the creation of taxation policies affecting family composition or functioning; and (3) the implementation or encouragement of social service programs that influence the family.

Often all three mechanisms will be used to achieve the same goal. For example, a division of labor between spouses in which the wife specializes in domestic chores and child care while the husband provides the household's income may be reinforced through family law (such as making a woman's failure to provide domestic services or a man's failure to provide income, but not the reverse, grounds for divorce; Weitzman 1981, pp. 1–134); through taxation policy (for instance, not taxing a wife's earnings if they are small, as is done in Japan); and through the provision of particular social services (such as public assistance payments for women with dependent children and no husband, but not for men with dependent children and no wife).

Population policies are distinct from family policy because they are oriented toward achieving particular demographic goals rather than particular goals for the family per se. Especially common in today's less developed countries are policies designed to reduce the population growth rate by reducing the birth rate (United Nations 1990), and policies that seek to change the geographic distribution of the population by encouraging or discouraging migration into and out of particular areas of a country (United Nations 1981). Because these demographic outcomes arise from the accumulated decisions of individual family units, however, many population policies are also family policies, at least implicitly. For example, policies designed to reduce the average number of children that couples bear not only may affect family size (itself important as an aspect of the family) but also may reduce the older generation's authority over offspring or increase the wife's autonomy from the control of her husband or mother-in-law. Confusion between population and family policies often arises because the chief population policy in less-developed countries since the 1960s has been to encourage "family planning," a term referring to actions that limit or space births. This phrase dominates public discourse; the phrase *family policy* is rarely heard. The focus of this essay is family policy. Population policies are touched on here insofar as they involve goals for the family.

In every known society, the family/kinship system is a critical social institution, not least because it regulates resource use and allocation, and ensures the continuity of society by rearing the new generation. The composition and functioning of families are governed by moral precepts and social norms. While not all of these regulate behavior strictly (as do, for example, incest taboos), they are strongly felt by most of the population. For this reason, the conduct of family life (for example, the distribution of property among children, or the distribution of rights to children's loyalty and labor among adult family members) is rarely a matter of moral or emotional neutrality, both at the mass level and in government. In this sense, every known society has an "unconscious" family policy consisting of its values and norms about the formation of family units and the conduct of family life.

Some countries have explicit goals to "strengthen" the family, while in others, the goal has clearly been to weaken it.

The universality of strong moral codes concerning the family does not, however, result in the universal existence of explicit government family policies. Among less developed countries today there is great variation in the extent to which explicit family policies can be found (United Nations 1987). Almost all countries have laws intended to regulate important aspects of family life, such as marriage, divorce, and inheritance; but while some have explicit goals for the family—as implied, for example, by the statement in the Philippines' constitution that "the State shall strengthen the family as a basic social institution" (Romero 1983, p. 413)—others have no such goals and no explicit policies beyond those embodied in the law (United Nations 1987).

One reason for this variation among countries is that explicit policies are often enacted in order to bring about change in the family, a goal that not all governments share. The desire to change traditional family morality has often motivated the enactment of laws on marriage, divorce, dowry, women's family rights, and other aspects of family behavior. For example, in the decade after independence, the government of India sought to change a number of traditional aspects of the Hindu family system by enacting legislation that outlawed polygyny, made remarriage legally possible for Hindu women, gave married daughters a right to their father's estate, and proscribed dowry (Sethi and Sibia 1987). The desire to reduce population growth by regulating age at marriage and, hence, marital childbearing underlies family legislation in some countries—for example, China during the 1970s, when the later-longer-fewer policy was introduced (the three words refer to marriage, interbirth intervals, and children, respectively; Greenhalgh 1990).

Variation among countries in family policy occurs not only because of variation in government attitudes toward family change but also because of variation in internal conflicts over the family. Even where government statements suggest consensus on family issues, considerable discord often exists within the population. For example, the above statement from the Philippines' constitution of 1986 reflects not consensus but conflict between Roman Catholic conservative groups and more liberal elements of Filipino society (Philippine Population Journal 1986). While most governments favor social change, not all sectors of society share that view or agree about the desirable direction of change. Conflict about social change in general, and about the family in particular, is often found between social classes, between groups with varying degrees of exposure to Western or other "outside" cultures, and especially among the ethnic and religious groups that were artifically aggregated into nation-states during the colonial or postcolonial period in many regions of the world.

Whether less developed countries adopt explicit family policies may also reflect the strength of the state and the extent of its struggle to wrest control from local organizations (Migdal 1988). Especially where large kinship groups, such as clans or lineages, have formed the traditional basis of social control, the creation of the modern state may be perceived by leaders to require the curtailment of the power of family groups and, hence, a change in the way that families are formed and function. The state's attempt to gain control through family change may be exacerbated by ethnic heterogeneity in family systems within the society (see Shah 1989 on India). The ongoing contest between traditional and "modern" elements, and between societies and states, can be observed in many settings, though with important variations. In much of Africa, states are attempting to meld diverse tribal systems of custom and law. Church influence (as in the Philippines), the adoption of Western values, and the general extent of centralized planning in the government are other factors that may motivate the creation of an explicit family policy and that help to explain variation among countries in the existence of such policy.

In addition to variation among countries in their adoption of explicit family policies is variation in the content of family policy, both explicit and implicit. For example, some countries have explicit goals to "strengthen" the family, while in others, the goal has clearly been to weaken it (as in China in the two decades following the establishment of the People's Republic [Greenhalgh 1990] or Iran prior to the 1979 revolution). Despite this variation across countries in the content of family policy, however, certain concerns about family-related issues are shared by a number of today's less-developed countries' governments. Demographic problems that many of these countries face are one source of shared concern. Paramount among these is rapid population growth, a concern that has motivated a variety of family-oriented laws and programs, including raising the minimum legal age for marriage in order to reduce the reproductive span during which women are exposed to regular sexual activity (Piepmeier and Hellyer 1977), providing family planning services to married couples, and, in countries such as Singapore and China, offering incentives and disincentives for childbearing that involve the provision or withholding of housing, paid maternity leave, and medical or educational services (Quah 1990; Greenhalgh 1990).

Another demographic problem faced by many less developed countries that influences family policy is the lengthening of adolescence and the attendant development of an independent youth culture caused by declining ages at puberty and rising ages at marriage (United Nations 1989). A number of less developed countries' governments, especially in Asia, have established sex education or "family life education" policies and programs oriented toward the adolescent population, in part in response to the growing youth culture and extension of adolescence, and in part as a way of maintaining government family planning programs in the face of increasingly low levels of marital fertility (Xenos 1990). States have increasingly differentiated youth from adults in their constitutions (Boli-Bennett and Meyer 1978), and youth policies are an increasingly important element of family policy (see Central Committee on Youth 1988; Paxman 1984).

Nations such as China have enacted programs to slow their rapid population growth. This Chinese couple with one child stands near a sign promoting the goal of one child per family. (Owen Franken/Corbis)

Still another emerging demographic problem that is influencing family policy in many less-developed countries is the proportionate growth of the aged population that invariably occurs when birth rates fall. How a growing population of the aged is to be cared for, and whether the family or the state should provide this care, are topics receiving increasing attention in the less-developed countries that have experienced a decline in the birth rate. In some countries, policies are being considered to keep this burden within families rather than making it a government responsibility (Martin 1988).

In addition to common areas of concern caused by demographic trends are areas of concern that reflect the global movement toward equal rights for oppressed groups (including those based on gender and age) and fundamentalist countermovements, especially those associated with Islam. Many less developed countries' governments have moved to grant women equal (or more equal) rights with men, a change that invariably has affected family policy. In many countries, legislation outlawing bigamy or polygyny, the dowry, exclusive property inheritance by males, the prohibition of remarriage for women, men's exclusive right to initiate divorce, and the control of married women's property and earnings by husbands or fathers has been enacted. The passage of such laws has by no means guaranteed their enforcement or the population's compliance with them (see Sethi and Sibia 1987 for evidence of this in India), and in some countries, in response to fundamentalist movements, a trend toward reducing women's family rights can be found (as in Iran and Pakistan). But the point is that many governments have been motivated to alter the legal arrangements surrounding family relationships by the desire to change women's rights vis-à-vis men.

Rising divorce rates and the accompanying perception of family "breakdown" is another concern affecting family policy in less developed countries. Although divorce rates have fallen in some countries where they were traditionally high (such as Malaysia and Indonesia), other countries that historically had little divorce have seen an increase. As in the West, this has often led to concern about the breakdown of traditional family arrangements, especially those involving the care of children. Traditional and contemporary patterns vary widely across world regions, with high rates of out-of-wedlock childbearing and child rearing having existed in some areas for a century or more (such as the Caribbean); nor are responses to this problem uniform. Nevertheless, if divorce rates continue to rise, it seems likely that less developed countries' governments will enact new legislation and programs touching on this problem.

In discussing family policy it is important to recognize that the object of this policy—the family—is a diverse entity, both within and between countries. The bounded, economically independent conjugal unit consisting of husband, wife, and dependent children that is often thought of as constituting "the" family in the West is not recognized as a meaningful unit in some traditional cultures, especially in sub-Saharan Africa. In that part of the world, the lineage, the mother-child unit, or the sibling group often is the important unit within which the economic, social, political, and child-rearing work of the family takes place (Goody 1972). Family systems vary enormously within the Third World—for example, the ideal of the patrilineal, patrilocal "grand family" found in China and India is largely absent in Southeast Asia, where a far more "conjugalized" system tends to dominate (Xenos 1988)—and family policy often varies according to the nature of the ideal family system. For example, in Japan, where the ideal of a patrilateral stem family in which the eldest son remains in the parental home has dominated for a century or more (Ueno 1987), it is not surprising that the government continues to emphasize the family as the most desirable source of care for the aged.

Recognition of important variation in what constitutes "the" family raises an important issue: the strain in many countries between an imported, Westernized vision of the family that is supported by the government, and the traditional family forms supported at the grass roots. In many less developed countries, the government vision of the family may result from the colonial experience (although in some instances, such as India, the colonial power has been more laissez faire about native family forms than the postindependence government), or it may reflect the exposure of the urban elite to Western society, or the perceived consonance between a more Westernized family system and other governmental goals, such as economic development or undermining the power of large kin groups. Where political struggle focuses on family policy, the underlying issue that is often at stake involves alternative definitions of the family. The proponents of these alternative definitions often are distinguished by elite versus mass background, as well as by membership in different elites.

Social policy in developing countries has been much influenced by emerging global viewpoints and by the sanction given to them by international organizations. For example, various arms of the United Nations offer explicit recommendations on a range of policies, including those on education, family health, women's labor force participation, and the family (United Nations 1987). Moreover, such recommendations are closely tied to the system of international aid. An important outcome has been the development of consistent systems for collecting social data and monitoring social change. There is a remarkable homogeneity across less developed countries in the types of data available to inform national debate on family and other social policies that has resulted from the effort of international agencies to ensure uniform social statistics.

[See also Family Planning; Population.]

BIBLIOGRAPHY

Boli-Bennett, John, and John W. Meyer 1978 "The Ideology of Childhood and the State: Rules Distinguishing Children in National Constitutions, 1870–1970." *American Sociological Review* 43:797–812.

Caldwell, John C. 1980 "Mass Education as a Determinant of the Timing of Fertility Decline." *Population and Development Review* 6 (June):225–255.

Central Committee on Youth 1988 *Report on Youth Policy.* Hong Kong: Central Committee on Youth.

Goody, Jack 1972 "The Evolution of the Family." In P. Laslett and R. Wall, eds., *Household and Family in Past Time.* Cambridge: Cambridge University Press.

Greenhalgh, Susan 1990 *State-Society Links: Political Dimensions of Population Policies and Programs, with Special Reference to China.* Research Division Working Papers, no. 18. New York: Population Council.

Kamerman, Sheila B., and Alfred J. Kahn, (eds.) 1978 *Family Policy: Government and Families in Fourteen Countries.* New York: Columbia University Press.

Martin, Linda G. 1988 "The Aging of Asia." *Journal of Gerontology* 43, no. 4:S99-S113.

Mason, Karen Oppenheim 1984 *The Status of Women: A Review of Its Relationships to Fertility and Mortality.* New York: Rockefeller Foundation.

Midgal, Joel S. 1988 *Strong Societies and Weak States: State-Society Relations and State Capabilities in the Third World.* Princeton, N.J.: Princeton University Press.

Paxman, John M. 1984 *Law, Policy and Adolescent Fertility: An International Overview.* London: International Planned Parenthood Federation.

Philippine Population Journal 1986 "Proceedings of the Constitutional Commission on the Family, 1986 (Part 1)." *Philippine Population Journal,* 2, nos. 1–4:135–156.

Piepmeier, Katherine B., and Elizabeth Hellyer 1977 "Minimum Age at Marriage: 20 Years of Legal Reform." *People* 4, no. 3 [data chart].

Quah, Stella R. 1990 "The Social Significance of Marriage and Parenthood in Singapore: Policy and Trends." In S. R. Quah, ed., *The Family as an Asset: An International Perspective on Marriage, Parenthood and Social Policy.* Singapore: Times Academic Press.

Romero, Flerida Ruth P. 1983 "New Policy Directions in Philippine Family Law." *Philippine Journal of Public Administration* 27 (October):412–417.

Sethi, Raj Mohini, and Kiran Sibia 1987 "Women and Hindu Personal Laws: A Socio-Legal Analysis." *Journal of Sociological Studies* 6 (January):101–113.

Shah, A. M. 1989 "Parameters of Family Policy in India." *Economic and Political Weekly,* March 11, pp. 513–516.

Ueno, Chizuko 1987 "The Position of Japanese Women Reconsidered." *Current Anthropology* 28 (August–October):S75–S84.

United Nations 1981 *Population Distribution Policies in Development Planning.* New York: United Nations, Department of International Economic and Social Affairs.

——— 1987 *The Family.* No. 3: *National Family Policies: Their Relationship to the Role of the Family in the Development Process.* New York: United Nations, Department of International Economic and Social Affairs.

——— 1989 *Adolescent Reproductive Behaviour: Evidence from Developing Countries,* vol. II. New York: United Nations, Department of International Economic and Social Affairs.

——— 1990 *World Population Trends and Policies: 1989 Monitoring Report.* New York: United Nations, Department of International Economic and Social Affairs.

Weitzman, Lenore J. 1981 *The Marriage Contract: Spouses, Lovers, and the Law.* New York: Free Press.

Xenos, Peter 1988 "Family Theory and the Southeast Asian Family." Paper prepared for the IUSSP/NIRA Seminar on Theories of Family Change, Tokyo, November 29–December 2, 1988.

——— 1990 "Youth, Sexuality and Public Policy in Asia: A Research Perspective." In S. R. Quah, ed., *The Family as an Asset: An International Perspective on Marriage, Parenthood and Social Policy.* Singapore: Times Academic Press.

– KAREN OPPENHEIM MASON
PETER XENOS

FAMILY PLANNING

Most people want to have children at some time in their lives. Americans generally want two children, and, on average, women have 1.8 births over their lifetime. In order to limit lifetime births to such a small number, family planning or fertility control is a necessity; couples must either abstain from intercourse, have high levels of contraceptive use, or resort to abortion. Indeed, sexually active women from ages fifteen to forty-four would average eighteen births if they used no contraception and no induced abortion. This chapter summarizes information regarding sexual activity, the timing of desired pregnancies and births, infertility, the risk of unintended pregnancy, contraceptive use, and levels of pregnancy, birth, and abortion in the United States.

Comparison with Other Western, Industrialized Countries

We are similar to women and men in most other developed countries in both the desire for small families and the achievement of low birth or fertility rates, but we have a relatively high pregnancy rate and high abortion rate. American women average 2.6 pregnancies (not including those that end in miscarriage) and have 0.8 abortions. Table 1 gives data for the nine Western, developed countries that have complete and recent data on pregnancy and the planning status of pregnancies, summarized into estimates of the average number of pregnancies, births, and abortions a woman in each of the countries would have over her reproductive life (i.e., between the ages of fifteen and forty-four). Although

Sexually active women from ages fifteen to forty-four would average eighteen births if they used no contraception and no induced abortion.

there is variation between countries, the range of difference in pregnancy rates in developed countries is quite small. Total pregnancy rates differ by less than one per woman, and the total fertility rates differ by only

TABLE 1

TOTAL PREGNANCY RATES,* BY PLANNING STATUS AND BY OUTCOME, AND RELATIVE LEVEL OF CONTRACEPTIVE USE AMONG WOMEN AGES FIFTEEN TO FORTY-FOUR, IN SELECTED COUNTRIES, 1977–1985

		Planning status		Outcome		Contraceptive	
Country	Total pregnancy rate	Total planned pregnancy rate	Total unplanned pregnancy rate	Total fertility rate	Total abortion rate	Any method	Effective method
Belgium	2.00	1.17	0.83	1.71	0.29	H	M
Canada	2.03	1.24	0.79	1.67	0.36	H	H
Denmark	2.50	1.32	1.18	1.75	0.75	M	M
Finland	2.09	1.03	1.06	1.63	0.46	H	M
France	2.53	1.18	1.35	1.87	0.66	H	M
Netherlands	1.65	1.37	0.28	1.47	0.18	H	H
Sweden	2.19	1.39	0.80	1.62	0.57	M	M
Great Britain	1.98	1.35	0.63	1.68	0.30	H	H
United States	2.56	1.25	1.31	1.80	0.76	L	M

* Pregnancies ending in miscarriage are not included.
Note: L-low; M-moderate; H-high.
Source: Jones et al. 1989. Tables 2.1, 2.2, 2.5, and Appendix B.

0.4 births per woman across the nine countries. Compared with the other countries, however, the United States falls at the high end of each measure. France and Denmark also have relatively high rates; the lowest pregnancy, birth, and abortion rates are in the Netherlands.

The greatest difference between the United States and other countries is in the rate of unplanned pregnancies. Slightly more than one-half of all pregnancies in the United States are unintended, for a total unplanned pregnancy rate of 1.3 per woman. This is similar to the rate in France but substantially higher than other countries, especially Canada, the Netherlands, Sweden, and Great Britain, where the average unplanned pregnancy rate is 0.8 per woman or less. Relative rankings of the nine countries in Table 1 by the level of contraceptive use shows that the three countries with high use of methods considered the most effective—sterilization, oral contraceptives, and the intrauterine contraceptive device (IUD)—have the lowest levels of unplanned pregnancy. Denmark, France, and the United States, which have the highest levels of unplanned pregnancy and abortion, all fall in the moderate level of effective contraceptive use rankings.

Exposure To Risk of Pregnancy

Most Americans begin to have intercourse during their late adolescence and continue to be sexually active throughout their reproductive lives. In 1988, one-half of all men in the United States had had intercourse by age 16.5, and, by age 17.4, one-half of all women had had sex. Table 2 shows information for women by age groups. The proportion who never had intercourse decreases quickly from 47 percent of teens ages fifteen to nineteen to 1 to 2 percent of all women ages thirty to forty-four. About 7 percent of women in each group have had intercourse but are not currently in a relationship (i.e., they have not had sex within the last three months). Some 6 percent of women ages fifteen to forty-four are infertile or noncontraceptively sterile because of illness, surgery (that was not for contraceptive purposes), menopause, or some other reason. The proportion that is infertile increases steadily with age, from 1 to 2 percent of women under age thirty to about 20 percent of those ages forty to forty-four. Many of these women want to have a child or another child, especially those in their mid-twenties to early thirties. The proportion of women who are pregnant, postpartum, or trying to become pregnant (and not known to be infertile) is highest among women ages twenty to thirty-four.

Women who are at risk for an unintended pregnancy account for two-thirds of all women ages fifteen to forty-four at any point in time. Women at risk are those who are currently in a sexual relationship, are fertile, and wish to avoid becoming pregnant. The proportion at risk of unintended pregnancy increases from 41 percent of teenagers to 72 to 75 percent of all women ages twenty-five to forty-four. Women who are currently

TABLE 2

PERCENTAGE DISTRIBUTION OF WOMEN AGES FIFTEEN TO FORTY-FOUR ACCORDING TO EXPOSURE TO THE RISK OF UNINTENDED PREGNANCY, BY AGE, 1995

Risk Status	Total	15–19	20–24	25–29	30–34	35–39	40–44
Total	100.0	100.0	100.0	100.0	100.0	100.0	100.0
Not at risk	30.0	63.1	30.2	25.7	22.3	21.7	22.3
Surgically and non-contraceptively sterilized	4.3	0.8	0.6	1.3	2.9	7.4	11.5
Pregnant/Postpartum/Trying	8.6	5.4	10.7	14.5	11.8	6.7	2.6
Infrequent intercourse	6.2	7.1	6.8	5.7	4.9	6.2	6.8
Never had intercourse	10.9	49.8	12.1	4.2	2.7	1.4	1.4
At risk	70.0	36.9	69.8	74.3	77.7	78.3	77.7

Source: Abma JC, Chandra A, Mosher WD, Peterson L, Piccinino L. "Fertility, Family Planning, and Women's Health: New Data from the 1995 National Survey of Family Growth." National Center for Health Statistics. Vital Health Stat 23(19), 1997.

married or cohabiting are most likely to be at risk for unintended pregnancy—79 percent of them are at risk, compared with 63 percent of formerly married women and 49 percent of never-married women not currently in union. The most common reason some married and cohabiting women are not at risk of unintended pregnancy is that they are pregnant, postpartum, or trying to become pregnant. Among women who never have been married, no intercourse or infrequent intercourse are the most common reasons. Among never-married women who have had intercourse, the proportion at risk of unintended pregnancy is almost as high as among women currently in union—74 percent.

Contraceptive Use

Women and men in the United States have a variety of contraceptive methods available to them, although fewer than couples in some other countries. Surgical contraceptive sterilization is available for both women and men. Physician visits and prescriptions are required for oral contraceptives, the IUD, the diaphragm, contraceptive implants, and the contraceptive cap. Other methods—condoms and spermicidal foam, cream, jelly, and film—can be purchased over the counter in pharmacies or other stores. Instruction in periodic abstinence is available from physicians and other family planning providers as well as through classes where only that method is taught.

Nine in ten women ages fifteen to forty-four in 1988 who were classified as being at risk of unintended pregnancy were using a contraceptive method, as shown in Table 3. Thirty-five percent relied on contraceptive sterilization of themselves or their partner, 55 percent used reversible methods, and 10 percent were currently using no contraceptive, even though they were at risk of unintended pregnancy.

Patterns of use differ by age. Younger women at risk of unintended pregnancy are most likely to be using no method of contraception. Twenty-one percent use no method, compared to 6 to 8 percent of women at risk ages thirty to forty-four. The proportion using reversible methods declines with age. Oral contraceptives are the most commonly used method among women ages fifteen to twenty-nine. About one in five women—and 28 percent of teens—at risk of unintended pregnancy rely on the condom, diaphragm, or a spermicidal method for contraception, methods that reduce the risk of both pregnancy and sexually transmitted disease. As women become older and complete their families, male and female contraceptive sterilization become increasingly common, rising steeply from 6 percent of women at risk ages twenty to twenty-four to 21 percent of women in their late twenties and to over 60 percent of those ages thirty-five to forty-four. Among women in their twenties, female sterilization is about three times more common than vasectomy. The margin narrows among older women to slightly more than two times more common.

Among women in their twenties, female sterilization is about three times more common than vasectomy.

The proportion of women at risk of unintended pregnancy who use no contraceptive method is highest among never-married women who are not in a cohabiting union, 20 percent as compared to 6 percent of those who are currently married or in a cohabiting union, and 12 percent of formerly married women. Sterilization is the most frequently used method among

TABLE 3

PERCENTAGE DISTRIBUTION OF WOMEN AT RISK OF UNINTENDED PREGNANCY ACCORDING TO CONTRACEPTIVE METHOD USED, BY AGE, 1995

Contraceptive method	Total	15–19	20–24	25–29	30–34	35–39	40–44
Total	100.0	100.0	100.0	100.0	100.0	100.0	100.0
Sterilization							
Female	17.8	0.1	2.5	11.8	21.4	29.8	35.6
Male	7.0	—	0.7	3.1	7.6	13.6	14.5
Reversible methods							
Pill	17.3	13.0	33.1	27.0	20.7	8.1	4.2
Implant	0.9	0.8	2.4	1.4	0.5	0.2	0.1
Injectable	1.9	2.9	3.9	2.9	1.3	0.8	0.2
IUD	0.5	—	0.2	0.5	0.6	0.7	0.9
Diaphragm	1.2	0.0	0.4	0.6	1.7	2.2	1.9
Condom	13.1	10.9	16.7	16.8	13.4	12.3	8.8
Female condom	0.0	—	0.1	—	—	—	—
Periodic abstinence	1.5	0.4	0.6	1.2	2.3	2.1	1.8
Natural family planning	0.2	—	0.1	0.2	0.3	0.4	0.2
Withdrawal	2.0	1.2	2.0	2.6	2.1	2.3	1.4
Other methods*	1.0	0.3	0.0	1.2	1.3	0.9	1.8
No method+	35.8	70.2	36.6	30.7	27.3	27.1	28.5

* Includes morning-after pill, foam, cervical cap, Today™ sponge, suppository, jelly or cream (without diaphragm), and other methods not shown separately.

+ Includes categories not shown separately: "sterile, nonsurgical—male"; "sterile, surgical—male"; "sterile, unknown—male."

Source: Abma JC, Chandra A, Mosher WD, Peterson L, Piccinino L. "Fertility, Family Planning, and Women's Health: New Data from the 1995 National Survey of Family Growth." National Center for Health Statistics. Vital Health Stat 23(19), 1997.

women who are currently married or cohabiting (44 percent) as well as formerly married women who are not currently in a union (49 percent). The pill is the most commonly used method among never-married women (47 percent). One in five women at risk who are not currently in a union use methods that also help protect against sexually transmitted disease—11 percent of the formerly married and 23 percent of never-married women.

Poorer women (those with family incomes less than 200 percent of the federal poverty level) at risk of unintended pregnancy are almost twice as likely to be using no contraceptive method as higher income women, 15 versus 8 percent. At each age, they are less likely to rely on reversible methods and more likely to rely on sterilization than higher income women. Eleven percent of poor women at risk ages twenty to twenty-four and 33 percent of those ages twenty-five to twenty-nine use sterilization as their method, compared with 2 and 15 percent of higher income women in these age groups. Poor women relying on sterilization are much more likely than higher income women to have been sterilized themselves rather than have a partner who has a vasectomy. Female sterilization accounts for 85 percent of all contraceptive sterilization among poor women, compared with 63 percent among those with higher incomes.

Contraceptive Service Provision

About 45,000 general and family practitioners in the United States (84 percent of those providing office-based patient care) and essentially all 23,000 obstetrician-gynecologists provide reversible contraceptive services. Obstetrician-gynecologists serve more than two-thirds of all women visiting private physicians for reversible contraception. Services are also provided at 5,100 family planning clinic sites. Prescriptive and nonprescriptive supplies can be obtained from the more than 58,000 pharmacies in the country.

Women strongly prefer private physicians for family planning care because they are seen as providing more personal and higher quality care. Sixty-nine percent of women making a medical visit for reversible contraceptives go to a private physician, and the others obtain services from family planning clinics. Family planning clinics were set up, most with federal funding, to provide care to those who could not afford services from private physicians or who cannot use private physicians for other reasons. In the mid-1980s, for example, an initial contraceptive visit with a general or family practitioner cost about $39, while a visit to an obstetrician-gynecologist cost $66; an annual supply of oral contraceptives cost $169. Fewer than one in five health insurance participants are covered for routine family planning visits, and contraceptive supplies are often also considered to be preventive care and not covered. Only one-half of the physicians providing reversible contraceptive care will accept Medicaid, the federal and state program paying for medical care for very poor people, and no more than 15 percent will provide services at reduced fees for women who cannot afford their charge. In addition, only 65 percent of the physicians will provide contraception to unemancipated minors without parental consent.

In almost all family planning clinics, on the other hand, minors are offered confidential services, Medicaid is accepted, and the cost of services depends on a patient's income. Family planning clinics are run by public health departments (serving 40 percent of all clients), Planned Parenthood agencies (28 percent), hospitals (11 percent), and other organizations such as neighborhood health centers, women's health centers, and other community-based groups (21 percent). They tend to be situated in lower income areas of communities and often operate only a few times a week in a medical facility used for other services as well. Poor women are more likely than others to depend on clinics for care. Fifty-seven percent of women under the federal poverty level who make a medical visit for reversible contraception go to a family planning clinic; another 14 percent go to private physicians who are paid through Medicaid. Lower income women who go to clinics instead of private physicians do so primarily because they cannot afford private physicians' fees or because the clinic will accept Medicaid. One-half of all teens who make a medical visit go to clinics. Adolescents who go to clinics do so because of the free or low-cost services and because they are afraid a private physician will tell their parents about their contraceptive use. In addition, some women, especially teenagers who have never been to a physician on their own, go to clinics because they do not know a private physician who would serve them. Clinic patients usually shift to private physicians when their incomes rise and as they become older or when they become pregnant and must look elsewhere for obstetric care.

About 80 percent of female sterilizations are done by obstetrician-gynecologists. Almost all (94 percent) obstetrician-gynecologists and 18 percent of the general and family practitioners in office-based private practice perform female sterilizations. About one-half of all vasectomies are done by urologists, 89 percent of whom (6,000) perform the operation. In addition, one-half of the general surgeons (12,000) and 26 percent of general and family practitioners (14,000) do vasectomies. About one-fifth of family planning agencies offer female or male sterilization services, but they are not offered at all clinic sites in an agency, and patients are often referred for the surgery to a private physician who is paid under contract from the agency. Eighty-three percent of private physicians performing tubal sterilizations and 95 percent of vasectomy providers place some conditions on whom they will serve. The most common are spousal consent (50 and 79 percent of providers, respectively), minimum age (47 and 40 percent), and waiting periods (39 and 44 percent). Where there is an age limit, the average minimum age for tubal ligation is set at twenty-three years and, for vasectomy, at twenty-five years. Thirty percent of providers require that the woman or man have at least one child. Only 22 percent of private physicians performing tubal ligations and 51 percent of those doing vasectomies will accept Medicaid; 4 and 12 percent, respectively, will reduce their fees for women and men who cannot afford them.

Most tubal ligations are done in a hospital; 52 percent are performed on an inpatient basis, 41 percent take place in hospitals on an outpatient basis, and most of the others occur in ambulatory nonhospital clinics. Most vasectomies occur in physicians' offices (64 percent); 23 percent are performed on an outpatient basis in a hospital facility, and only 8 percent are done on an inpatient basis. In 1983, the most recent year for which data are available, physician and hospital charges for an inpatient or outpatient tubal ligation averaged $1,300, and the fee for an office vasectomy was $240.

Attitudes About Contraceptive Methods

Women are most likely to have favorable attitudes about oral contraceptives (77 percent of women ages fifteen to forty-four), the condom (61 percent), vasectomy (61 percent), and female sterilization (57 percent). Fewer than one-third have favorable opinions of other available methods. Among those currently using a method, at least eight in ten have a favorable opinion of the one they are using. Almost nine in ten women relying on sterilization have a favorable opinion of it, but one-quarter say they would like more children, and one in ten would like it reversed. It is not clear to what extent this reflects actual dissatisfaction with sterilization or with their being in a situation in which they feel they cannot have more children.

The reason most often given by those at risk of unintended pregnancy for not using a contraceptive method is concern about side effects and health risks.

The reason most often given by those at risk of unintended pregnancy for not using a contraceptive method or for using the condom, diaphragm, or spermicides is concern about side effects and health risks.

The condom and spermicidal methods are being used increasingly for protection against sexually transmitted disease as well as for pregnancy protection. Thirteen percent of all women ages fifteen to forty-four in 1988 who had ever had intercourse were using condoms (12 percent) or spermicides (1 percent) to prevent STDs. About one-third were seeking to prevent both pregnancy and STDs; the others were using these methods only to prevent STDs. Women using oral contraceptives, the IUD, and sterilization do so primarily because of concerns about the effectiveness of other methods and because other methods interfere with intercourse and can be inconvenient to use.

Fears of health risks from contraceptives, especially oral contraceptives, are common in the United States, even though this method is most favorably rated. Three-quarters of adult women and two-thirds of men think using the pill represents substantial risks, primarily from cancer and from blood clots. Extensive medical studies show that, except for women with risky behavior such as heavy smoking or with preexisting health conditions, using oral contraceptives or any other method is safer than using no contraceptive at all if women are at risk of unintended pregnancy. Some of the health risk comes from use of the method itself and some from pregnancies that occur to contraceptive users. If those pregnancies end in abortion rather than in birth, the health risks are substantially lowered.

Contraceptive Effectiveness

Pregnancies occur to couples using contraceptive methods for two reasons—because of the inadequacy of the method itself or because it was not used correctly or consistently. It is not possible to measure the theoretical success or failure (the method effectiveness) of a contraceptive independent from what happens when it is actually used. Studies instead measure the use effectiveness, which relates to the experience of an actual group of users. Failure rates differ by method, with some consistently showing higher effectiveness than others; rates also differ by sociodemographic subgroup within study populations. Clinical studies of specially selected and followed patients tend to show lower failure rates than when methods are used by the general population.

Table 4 shows estimates of what the method failure rates of the most commonly used reversible contraceptive methods might be, along with the rates actually observed across age, race, and marital status subgroups of women in the United States. In each case, the observed rates are substantially higher than the estimated method failure rates, and, for most methods, the difference between the lowest and highest subgroup rates is quite wide. The lowest failure rates are achieved with oral contraceptives, while spermicidal methods have the highest failure rates. In general, women who are young, unmarried, poor, and nonwhite have higher failure rates. The differences in failure rates between methods and between subgroups are much greater than what any difference in method effectiveness or in the biology of women would cause and are assumed primarily to reflect differences in the correctness and consistency of method use.

Unintended Pregnancy and Abortion

Of the 110 pregnancies each year per 1,000 women ages fifteen to forty-four in the United States, 48 are intended; of these, 40 end in births and 8 end in miscarriage. The peak ages of intended pregnancy in the United States are the twenties, when about 8 percent of all sexually active women have planned pregnancies each year.

Over one-half of all pregnancies in the United States are unintended, that is, they occur to women who want to have a baby later but not now (generally called "mistimed") or to women who did not want to have any children in the future (called "unwanted"). An estimated 56 percent of all pregnancies are unintended, and 6 percent of women ages fifteen to forty-four have an unintended pregnancy each year. Of the 110 total pregnancies per 1,000 women ages fifteen to forty-four, 27 are unintended pregnancies that end in birth, 27 end in abortion, and 8 are unintended pregnancies that end in miscarriage. Forty percent of all births are unintended, 28 percent are mistimed, and 12 percent were reported by the mother as having been unwanted.

The proportion of pregnancies that are unintended is highest among adolescents—81 percent. Among every 1,000 women ages fifteen to nineteen, 127 become pregnant each year, 102 of them unintentionally. Almost as many unintended pregnancies among adolescent women end in birth (forty-three per 1,000) as end in abortion (forty-six per 1,000), and thirteen per 1,000 end in miscarriage. Because only slightly more than one-half of all women ages fifteen to nineteen have had intercourse, rates among all teenagers understate the frequency of pregnancy. Among those who have ever had intercourse, 24 percent become pregnant each year; 20 percent of those who have had sex have an unintended pregnancy annually.

The proportion of pregnancies that are unintended varies widely by age. It decreases from eight in ten of the pregnancies to adolescents to four in ten among women ages thirty to thirty-four and then rises again to almost eight in ten among women ages forty to forty-four. The proportion of unintended pregnancies that end in abortion varies little by age up to age thirty-five,

TABLE 4

ESTIMATED PERCENTAGE OF WOMEN WHO EXPERIENCE A CONTRACEPTIVE FAILURE DURING THE FIRST TWELVE MONTHS OF USE GIVEN PERFECT USE, AND OBSERVED FAILURE RATES BY METHOD ACROSS AGE, RACE, AND MARITAL STATUS GROUPS

		Observed rates		
Method	**Perfect Use**	**All Users**	**Lowest**	**Highest**
Oral contraceptives*	0.1–0.5	6.2	1.9	18.1
Condom	2.0	14.2	3.3	36.3
Diaphragm	3.0	15.6	10.3	57.0
Periodic Abstinence*	2.0–10.0	16.2	6.2	34.1
Spermicide*	3.0–8.0	26.3	9.1	38.7

* Rate varies by type of method or formulation used.

Source: E. F. Jones and J. D. Forrest 1989 "Contraceptive Failure in the United States: Revised Estimates from the 1982 National Survey of Family Growth." *Family Planning Perspectives* 21:3, 103.

from 47 to 51 percent. More unintended pregnancies to older women, however, end in abortion—55 percent of those to women ages thirty-five to thirty-nine and 59 percent of unintended pregnancies to women ages forty to forty-four.

One-quarter of all pregnancies in the United States end in induced abortion. Because of the high level of unintended pregnancy in the United States, each year almost 3 percent of all women ages fifteen to forty-four have an abortion. At current levels of abortion, it is estimated that almost one-half of all women will have at least one abortion in their lifetime and that many will have more than one.

Approximately 2,600 facilities provide abortion services in the United States. Hospitals represent 40 percent of all abortion providers, even though only about one in five short-term general hospitals provides abortion services. Four percent of abortion service facilities are private physician offices serving fewer than 400 women a year for abortion. Hospitals and private physician facilities serve relatively small numbers of women and account for only 10 and 4 percent of all patients, respectively. Nonhospital clinics serve 86 percent of women having abortions. Almost all abortions are provided as ambulatory procedures, even if done in a hospital. Abortion services in the United States are heavily concentrated in larger metropolitan areas of the country. In 1988, 90 percent of all providers, which performed 98 percent of all abortions, were located in metropolitan areas. Thirty-one percent of women of reproductive age live in counties where there are no abortion providers, and 42 percent live where there are no providers serving at least 400 abortion patients per year. Facilities set limits on the maximum gestation at which they will provide abortion services; 57 percent perform them only at twelve or fewer weeks since the last menstrual period, and 76 percent only do so at sixteen weeks or less. Some states require that unemancipated minors notify or obtain consent from a parent or parents before they may have an abortion or that they obtain a court ruling that they are sufficiently mature to make the decision themselves or that having an abortion is better for them than giving birth. In addition, some facilities, especially hospitals, require parental consent or notification for abortion services provided to young adolescents. Funding for abortion for women covered by Medicaid is restricted to abortions for the purpose of preserving a woman's health or to abortions to women in the few states that provide state funds for abortion services.

Because of the uneven distribution of abortion services around the country, about 40 percent of women who have abortions obtain them from providers in another county or state. There are no data on what proportion of women giving birth wanted to have an abortion and would have done so if services were more accessible. One-half of all abortions are performed within eight weeks of the woman's last menstrual period, and 91 percent are performed within twelve weeks. Four percent occur at sixteen or more weeks since the last menstrual period and 1 percent at twenty-one weeks or more. About one-quarter of those having abortions at sixteen or more weeks said the chief reason for not having had the abortion earlier was difficulty making arrangements, especially obtaining money for the abortion quickly enough. As of mid-1985, the average cost for a nonhospital abortion at ten weeks' gestation with local anesthesia was $238. Abortions performed later in gestation or using general anesthesia are more expensive, and the cost of hospital abortions, even those done on an outpatient basis, are more than double the average nonhospital cost.

Links Between Contraceptive Use and Unintended Pregnancy

Women who are using no contraceptive method account for about 10 percent of women at risk of unintended pregnancy, but, because they are more likely to become pregnant than those using a method, they account for the majority of unplanned pregnancies, an estimated 57 percent. Significant reductions in unintended pregnancy and abortion could occur with decreased levels of sexual activity, with increased contraceptive use, with more effective use of existing methods, and with the development and marketing of additional methods. It has been estimated that eliminating nonuse could result in a 57 percent reduction in the level of unintended pregnancy and a 48 percent reduction in abortion.

[See also Birth and Death Rates; Family Size.]

BIBLIOGRAPHY

Forrest, Jacqueline Darroch, Rachel Benson Gold, and Asta-Maria Kenney 1989 *The Need, Availability, and Financing of Reproductive Health Services.* New York: Alan Guttmacher Institute.

Harlap, Susan, Kathryn L. Kost, and Jacqueline Darroch Forrest 1991 *Preventing Pregnancy, Protecting Health: A New Look at Birth Control Choices in the United States.* New York: Alan Guttmacher Institute.

Henshaw, Stanley, and Jennifer Van Vort (eds.) 1991 *Abortion Services in the United States, Each State and Metropolitan Area, 1987–1988.* New York: Alan Guttmacher Institute.

Jones, Elise F., Jacqueline Darroch Forrest, Stanley K. Henshaw, Jane Silverman, and Aida Torres 1989 *Pregnancy, Contraception, and Family Planning Services in Industrialized Countries.* New Haven, Conn.: Yale University Press.

Mastroianni, Luigi, Jr., Peter J. Donaldson, and Thomas T. Kane (eds.) 1990 *Developing New Contraceptives: Obstacles and Opportunities.* Washington, D.C.: National Academy Press.

Pratt, William F., William D. Mosher, Christine A. Bachrach, and Marjorie C. Horn 1984 "Understanding U.S. Fertility: Findings from the National Survey of Family Growth, Cycle III." *Population Bulletin* 39.

– JACQUELINE DARROCH FORREST

FAMILY ROLES

For a family to survive and function well, an optimal division of labor among adult family members is necessary. This labor includes not only such tangible work as housework, child care, and making a living, but also such intangibles as making decisions for the family and helping to maintain the happiness and psychological well-being of its members. How these tasks are divided among family members is, to a great extent, prescribed by the social norms of the society in which the family resides. These patterns of the division of labor are called *family roles.* Thus, family roles may be defined as "prescriptions for interpersonal behavior associated with one's position in the family" (Heiss 1976, p. 3). Put another way, family roles are socially constructed "beliefs or expectations that [family members] ought or ought not to behave in certain ways" (Burr, Leigh, Day, and Constantine 1979, p. 54).

Attempts to describe observed differences between the family roles of husbands and wives led to the concept of "instrumental" and "expressive" roles. Earlier research on small groups had shown that when a group was given a task to solve, two leaders tended to emerge (Bales 1958). The first leader was the one who talked most during the discussion, expressed many opinions, and gave out information. This person might have contributed a great deal to solving the task, but she or he usually was not the one most liked by other group members. The other leader was the one who showed solidarity and agreement more than did the others and tried to release tension among group members. This second leader was most liked by the others. These two leaders were called the "instrumental leader" and the "expressive leader," respectively. Because this instrumental–expressive differentiation occurs in most task-solving groups, particularly after the group has worked together for some time, it was assumed that this role differentiation was universal to all small groups, including the family. Because a husband "must provide for his family" and is "responsible for the support of his wife and children" (Zelditch 1955, p. 339), the instrumental role was attributed to the husband and the expressive one to the wife.

As dual-income couples have become the majority in the United States and other industrialized countries, the instrumental–expressive role differentiation of husbands and wives has lost some, but not all, of its validity. Child care, which requires affectionate and emotional interactions with children, is still assumed more by the wife than by the husband. Major financial decisions, such as whether or where to move or whether to buy a house, are still made by the husband in many families. This differentiation, however, may not be solely the result of husband–wife role differentiations but rather the result of more specific attributes of each spouse in realms outside family, such as employment status, income, and occupation.

The provider–homemaker dichotomy is another way of explaining the difference in family roles. Goods and services necessary to family life are produced or obtained through the enactment of the "provider" role, while the same goods and services are maintained or converted for family use by someone acting as the "homemaker." Thus, these two roles complement each other (Slocum and Nye 1976). Until recently, family labor was divided into these two roles in middle class American families: market labor by the husband as provider and household labor by the wife as homemaker. This provider–homemaker role differentiation, however, is far from universal. This pattern became typical only after the family's place of production and place of consumption became separated: The home became the site of family consumption, and the farm, factory, or office became the place of production. Furthermore, in traditional agricultural families, this provider-homemaker role differentiation was never as well established as one might think. In most farming families, husbands and wives worked very much together in the field, particularly during the harvest.

It has been argued that husbands do not assume the homemaking role to the extent that wives assume the provider role.

In contemporary American society, the distinction between these two roles has become less clear because more than half of all married women now are gainfully employed. In a family of an early industrialized society, the husband exchanged his earned money and social status for different but complementary resources—time, energy, and skill at household work—provided by the wife. In many contemporary families, however, the resources exchanged between husband and wife are the same: Monetary resources and household work are provided by both spouses. Recent research has found that the husband's share of the household work increases when his wife is gainfully employed, when she has a large income, or both (Kamo 1988). In other words, the husband's contribution in household labor (traditionally part of the homemaker role) is associated with his wife's contribution in market labor (traditionally part of the provider role). Nevertheless, it also has been found that the husband's contribution to the household work is not nearly as large as the wife's, even when they have provided roughly the same income (Kamo 1988). This suggests that the differentiation of provider–homemaker roles is not a simple function of both spouses' work status. It has been argued that husbands do not assume the homemaking role to the extent that wives assume the provider role. Alternatively, some scholars argue that, even though both spouses are gainfully employed, the wife may not be assuming the duty of providing for the family and that the husband may not be relinquishing his provider-role responsibilities (Perry-Jenkins 1988). The spouses' expectations of the roles and behaviors associated with each gender then become crucial in explaining the role differentiation in contemporary societies.

The importance of the spouses' gender-role attitudes to their household division of labor has been widely demonstrated (Coverman 1985; Bird, Bird, and Scruggs 1984). Those who believe in traditional gender-role differentiation share household work accordingly, regardless of how much income each generates or whether or not both are employed. Nevertheless, the relationship between one's attitude toward provider–homemaker roles and one's enactment of those roles is not perfect. Specifically, although both husbands and wives say they support sharing the provider and homemaker roles equally, their actual behavior indicates otherwise.

In some societies, individual behaviors are strictly prescribed by traditions and rules, and so are family roles. In many early industrialized societies, for example, there were inviolable rules about the roles individuals played within the family. In nineteenth-century rural France, family roles were rigid, and sanctions for deviating from them were harsh. A husband had to maintain authority at home, and if his wife battered him in a fight, he was ridiculed in a community ceremony, called "charivari," by being mounted backward on top of a donkey, with the donkey's tail in his hands (Segalen 1983). The same punishment was used for an adulterous couple, indicating the seriousness with which violation of certain family roles was regarded. Also ridiculed were "feminized" husbands who stayed home cooking meals, which was considered to be strictly the wife's role.

Comparative and historical analyses of family roles suggest that rigid family roles may be accounted for by the strength of social norms based on tradition and culture and by the social structure of a given society. Where sanctions for deviating from family roles are weak, such as in contemporary America, family behaviors become more spontaneous and innovative. In other words, although family roles used to be universally determined in traditional societies, in contemporary society family roles are more flexible and determined by specific family situations. The behavior expected of certain family members is determined more by such specific attributes as personality, individual preference, work status, and income rather than by the universal status of being a husband or a wife.

The family roles of a given society are closely related to that society's more general gender roles, which include behaviors expected in other areas such as education, politics, and community involvement. Likewise, an individual's attitude toward family roles is closely related to his or her gender-role attitude. Family roles, therefore, are a link between the behavior of family members and their status in the larger society. The latter includes whether they are employed, in what type of work, how much they earn, and what roles they play in their community. When several groups are compared, either cross-culturally or within a society, the general status of men and women in the society will have a direct relationship to what is expected of a husband or a wife. Through careful examination of family roles and behaviors—even those as basic as the domestic division of labor—we may reach a better understanding of the human behaviors in the family, in the work place, and in the community.

[See also Alternative Life-Styles; American Families.]

BIBLIOGRAPHY

Bales, Robert F. 1958 "Task Roles and Social Roles in Problem-Solving Groups." In E. E. Maccoby, T. M. Newcomb, and E. L. Hartley, eds., *Readings in Social Psychology,* 3rd ed. New York: Holt.

Bird, Gloria W., Gerald A. Bird, and Marguerite Scruggs 1984 "Determinants of Family Task Sharing: A Study of Husbands and Wives." *Journal of Marriage and the Family* 46:345–355.

Burr, Wesley R., Geoffrey K. Leigh, Randall D. Day, and John Constantine 1979 "Symbolic Interaction and the Family." In W. Burr, R. Hill, F. I. Nye, and I. Reiss, eds., *Contemporary Theories about the Family.* New York: Free Press.

Coverman, Shelley 1985 "Explaining Husband's Participation in Domestic Labor." *Sociological Quarterly* 26:81–97.

Heiss, Jerold 1976 "An Introduction to the Elements of Role Theory." In J. Heiss, ed., *Family Roles and Interaction: An Anthology.* Chicago: Rand McNally.

Kamo, Yoshinori 1988 "Determinants of Household Labor: Resources, Power, and Ideology." *Journal of Family Issues* 9:177–200.

Perry-Jenkins, Maureen 1988 "Future Directions for Research on Dual-Earner Families: A Young Professional's Perspective." *Family Relations* 37:226–228.

Segalen, Martine 1983 *Love and Power in the Peasant Family: Rural France in the Nineteenth Century,* trans. Sarah Matthews. Chicago: University of Chicago Press.

Slocum, Walter L., and F. Ivan Nye 1976 "Provider and Housekeeper Roles." In F. Ivan Nye, ed., *Role Structure and Analysis of the Family.* Beverly Hills, Calif.: Sage Publications.

Zelditch, Morris, Jr. 1955 "Role Differentiation in the Nuclear Family: A Comparative Study." In Talcott Parsons and Robert F. Bales, eds., *Family, Socialization, and Interaction Process.* New York: Free Press.

– YOSHINORI KAMO

FAMILY SIZE

Family size may be considered from two perspectives. At the individual (micro) level, it defines one aspect of an individual's family background or environment. As such, it represents a potential influence on the development and accomplishments of family members. At the societal (macro) level, family size is an indicator of societal structure that may vary over time, with concomitant implications for individual development and social relations in different cohorts. In this essay, consideration is given to both aspects of family size, as it is reflected in sociological theory and research.

While the term *family size* is sometimes used to represent the total number of individuals comprising a family unit, Treas (1981) argues convincingly for decomposing the concept into two components: numbers of children and numbers of adults in the household. This distinction is important, as observed patterns of change in overall family size may be attributable to one component or the other, as may effects of overall family size. In the present discussion, family size is defined in terms of the number of children in the household.

A further distinction is made between family size in the parental and filial households, sometimes referred to as the family of origin (or orientation) and the family of procreation. Some use the term *sibship size* to refer to the number of children in an individual's parental family (Blake 1989; Ryder 1986). However, the two are not directly comparable: mean family size takes into account those families which have no children, while mean sibship size is necessarily restricted to families with children.

Family size can also be differentiated from fertility, which reflects the aggregate numbers of births relative to the numbers of women in the population, without regard for the distribution of those births across family units. Fertility and family size are both important characteristics of cohorts; however, for assessing relationships at the individual level, family size or sibship size is the more meaningful construct (Ryder 1986).

The subsequent sections address the following aspects of family size: demographic trends in family size, antecedents and correlates of family size, and implications of sibship size and family size for child and adult members of the family.

Demographic Trends

The twentieth century has witnessed substantial change in both fertility and family size (as indicated by the number of children in the household), with the overall trend being toward smaller families. Such trends can be examined through comparisons of fertility rates and mean family size, and also through investigation of parity distributions—that is, the numbers of families with zero, one, two (and so on) children.

Drawing on fertility tables compiled by the National Center for Health Statistics, Ryder (1986) presents time-series data for successive cohorts of women in the

United States born between 1867 and 1955 (and who would thus be bearing children between approximately 1885 and 1975) that show the following general trends in fertility and family size:

1. Total fertility declined by 52 percent in the period being considered, from 4.00 for women born in 1867–1870 to 1.92 for women born in 1951–1955. A similar rate of decline occurred in marital fertility.
2. This decline was punctuated by a temporary upsurge in fertility for women born in 1916–1940, who were bearing children during the two decades following World War II (the "babyboom" years).
3. Variation in fertility rates increased for cohorts through 1910, and since then has consistently decreased, suggesting that in recent years there have been fewer women bearing no children or large numbers of children and an increasing concentration of families of moderate size.
4. Family size (the mean number of children in the family) decreased by 61 percent, from a high of 7.3 for women born in 1867–1870 to 2.8 for women born in 1951–1955.

It thus appears that during the period under consideration, mean family size decreased at an even faster rate than fertility. Further, the increased fertility during the "babyboom" years appears to have been offset by reduced variation in fertility for those cohorts of women, with the result that mean family size held relatively constant during that period, then continued its pattern of decline.

Treas (1981) examined changes in family size between 1955 and 1978 for whites and for non-whites, using data from the March Current Population Surveys. Throughout the period, nonwhites consistently had larger families than did whites: In 1955 the mean number of children was 1.26 in white families and 1.80 in nonwhite families; in 1978 the corresponding figures were 1.04 and 1.56. During this period Treas found similar patterns of increases in family size through the 1960s, followed by decreasing family size in the 1970s, for both groups. However, the shifts were considerably more pronounced among nonwhite families.

Data obtained from the U.S. census on the distribution of family sizes (parity distributions) provide further insight on the trend toward smaller families. During the years between 1970 and 1988 the proportion of families with no children under eighteen increased substantially, from 44 percent to 51 percent, while the proportion of families with one child or two children increased only slightly (from 18 percent to 21 percent, and from 17 percent to 18 percent, respectively). However, the proportion of families with three or more children decreased markedly, from 20 percent to 10 percent during this period. Among black and Hispanic families, the increase in families with no children was not as pronounced as among white families, but the increases in families with one or two children were greater, as were the decreases in families with three or more children (U.S. Bureau of the Census 1990, p. 51).

Further insight into the decline in family size is provided by investigations of parity progression, or the probability of having (or intending to have) an additional child at each parity level. Decomposing his time-series data into parity progressions, Ryder (1986) reports that the "babyboom" was the result of an increase in progression from parities one and two, but that progression from parities three and higher have shown consistent declines. Similarly, data on intended parities show that the proportions intending progression from parity one have increased over time, while the intended progression ratios for parity three and higher have declined.

Other data on ideal, or normative, family sizes support this pattern of increasing concentration of smaller families. West and Morgan (1987) cite historical data showing that fertility norms have fluctuated in parallel with fertility rates and family sizes: During the 1930s and early 1940s two- and three-child families were preferred. During the post-World War II era three- and four-child families became the ideal, but in the late 1960s preferences reverted to the two- or three-child family. They further report that, among a sample of contemporary adults, a significant majority (64.8 percent) view the two-child family as ideal; that belief was surprisingly consistent across various subgroups defined by current family size, marital status, race, and religion.

At the same time that families have tended to become smaller on average, there has been increased variability in the timing of childbearing. One trend that has been widely noted has been the increase in childbearing among teenagers, particularly among lower SES, nonwhite, and less academically able youth (Card and Wise 1978). At the same time, there has been an increase in the proportion of women who delay childbearing until their early and mid thirties or who remain childless (Bloom and Trussell 1984). As will be discussed below, the timing of the first birth has implications for the eventual family size, and thus for the development and accomplishment of family members.

In sum, in the United States there appears to have been a strong shift toward smaller families, with the ideal being a two- or three-child family. A similar trend toward smaller families is found in other developed countries, while in developing countries families are more likely to be larger (Lopreato and Yu 1988). One exception to this generalization concerns countries, such as the Peoples Republic of China, that are trying to implement a policy of restricting families to one child. However, while the policy appears to have led to lower mean family sizes, numerous families have continued to have two or more children, and a preferred family size of two continues to be the mode (Whyte and Gu 1987).

Antecedents and Correlates of Family Size

Determinants of family size have been investigated at both the societal and the individual level. At the societal level, researchers have sought to account for differences in fertility and family size over time or between societies. Easterlin (1980) advanced a theory to account for changes in fertility and family size over time, as a function of individuals' economic resources and aspirations. He attributes the "babyboom" surge in fertility and family size to the generation of young men following World War II who experienced high wages, as a result of the expanding economy, and had relatively low material aspirations, as a result of being raised during the Depression. Conversely, the "babyboom" generation confronted increased competition for jobs, which, combined with higher aspirations, led to the "babybust" of the 1970s and 1980s. One implication of Easterlin's theory is that smaller birth cohorts are likely to experience more favorable labor markets, resulting in higher fertility.

Female labor force participation and fertility are negatively correlated.

A variation of this theory is presented by Devaney (1983), who argues that the decline in fertility observed during the 1960s and 1970s can be attributed to increases in female wages and female employment, which in turn served to depress fertility, rather than to conscious decisions to limit fertility in the face of disadvantageous economic conditions. Her analyses, based on national fertility data and data on female labor force participation rates and male and female earnings, suggest that (1) female labor force participation and fertility are highly and negatively correlated, and (2) that female wage rates are the dominant factor in explaining recent variations in fertility and female employment. While this model differs from Easterlin's in terms of the process by which economic factors are thought to influence fertility, they are similar in viewing fertility as a response to economic market conditions.

Studies of developing countries have focused on several sociocultural as well as socioeconomic factors associated with fertility and family size: modernization (Levy 1985), contraceptive use and family planning programs (Koenig, Phillips, Simmons, and Khan 1987), and cultural attitudes and values, such as the perceived old-age security value of children (Rani 1986) or the view of children as risk insurance (Robinson 1986).

At the individual level, researchers have examined the extent to which fertility and family size may vary depending on individuals' family backgrounds, social and psychological characteristics, or economic status. Inverse relationships between social class and family size have been documented in a number of data sets: Individuals from larger families tend to have less-well-educated fathers who have lower-status occupations. Also, farm background is associated with larger family sizes (Blake 1989).

Parents' sibship size (the number of siblings that each parent had) is a second major determinant of family size: Women and men from larger families are more likely to have larger families (Ben-Porath 1975; Thornton 1980). This gives rise to an apparent paradox: While there is an overall trend toward small families, a high proportion of children come from larger families (Blake 1989). This paradox arises from the distinction noted above between cohort fertility rates, which are based on all women or all families, and children's sibship sizes, which are necessarily limited to women or families who have had children.

Retherford and Sewell (1988) investigated the relationship between intelligence and family size in their analysis of data from the Wisconsin Longitudinal Study of the High School Class of 1957, finding that the overall relationship between IQ and family size was negative for both sexes. However, the relationship proved to be much stronger for females, who showed consistent declines in family size as IQ increased. Among men the relationship was less consistent. Retherford and Sewell also reviewed the results of other, earlier studies, noting that the negative relationship between IQ and family size appears to have become more pronounced in the post-"babyboom" cohorts.

Additional factors associated with family size pertain primarily to family and achievement-related characteristics of the mother: More education, later age at marriage, longer interval between marriage and the birth of the first child, and employment status are all associated with smaller families—that is, fewer children (Wagner, Schubert, and Schubert 1985). Family configuration has also been found to be associated with increased family size, with the probability of having an additional child being higher in families with all children of the same sex (Gualtieri and Hicks 1986). Also, only children are disproportionately likely to come from broken families (Blake 1989).

The interaction between wives' employment and childbearing has been a topic of much study, as women have increasingly entered or remained in the work force, but the results obtained are inconsistent. Waite and Stolzenberg (1976) found a significant negative relationship between wife's work and family size. However, based on analyses of longitudinal data that allowed for the study of recursive processes as well as inclusion of several additional measures, Bagozzi and Van Loo (1988) found no causal relationships between wife's employment and family size, and suggested that both labor force participation and family size are code-termined by the wife's achievement motivation, sex role norms, and perceived value of children.

Oropesa (1985) used data from the NORC General Social Surveys to test the hypotheses represented in Easterlin's model at the micro level, using relative affluence as the predictor and expected family size as the outcome of interest. He found that relative affluence is more likely to be associated with expected births for women than for men, and that the effects are stronger with regard to expected births in the short term than with total expected family size.

The research cited above focuses on static determinants of childbearing and family size. However, some investigators have examined fertility and childbearing decisions as a dynamic process, influenced by life situation and life events, that may change over time, as well as by relatively fixed individual characteristics. One line of investigation has focused on timing of first birth as a determinant of eventual family size. Card and Wise (1978) and Hofferth and Moore (1979) demonstrated that early first births are associated with larger families; Bloom and Trussell (1984) similarly demonstrated that delayed childbearing is associated with smaller average family sizes, as well as with childlessness.

A second line of research has investigated the relationships between parity level and fertility decisions. Udry (1983) examined the relative influence of initial fertility plans and intervening life events (such as births during the interval, change in household income, change in education, female work status, change in marital satisfaction) on couple's fertility decisions at different parity levels. He found that including intervening events in the analyses improved the prediction of both fertility plans and, especially, actual fertility behavior, providing support for a sequential model of fertility decision making. White and Kim (1987) investigated whether the determinants of fertility choices vary by parity, and found a nonlinear relationship between fertility determinants and childbearing, especially with regard to factors related to women's roles. Both sex-role traditionalism and achievement in nonfamily roles were associated with a higher probability of having a child at parity zero or one, but a lower probability of having a child among women at higher parities. These findings are somewhat contrary to those based on cross-sectional analyses of family size, suggesting the importance of taking parity level into account in such investigations.

Implications of Family Size

The effects of sibship/family size and family composition on children and on adults has long been a topic of popular interest, and in recent years has become the focus of a considerable body of sociological and psychological inquiry. In particular, attention has been directed to effects of sibship size on children's cognitive development, physical and social-psychological development, educational attainment, and socioeconomic attainment and mobility. Consideration is also given to effects of family size on parents and on family well-being.

COGNITIVE DEVELOPMENT. Interest in the relationship between sibship size and intelligence dates back to Anne Anastasi's (1956) review, which found an inverse relationship between the two. Subsequent empirical studies, in the United States as well as in Europe, using various measures of ability and controlling for family background characteristics, have confirmed this finding (Belmont and Marolla 1973; Breland 1974; Claudy, Gross, and Strause 1974). Blake (1989) provides a comprehensive review of this literature, including a discussion of limitations and weaknesses in the prior studies.

Only children present a special case. Numerous studies have reported that only children do not perform as well on intelligence measures as do children from two-child families. Indeed, in the Belmont and Marolla study (1973), only children were found to be lower in intelligence than first-borns in families up to size four, and lower than second-borns in families up to size three. Claudy et al. (1974) obtained similar results after controlling for differences in SES. However, when differences in family composition were taken into account by restricting the sample to only children in two-parent families, the differences between only children and first-born children in larger families became nonsignificant (Claudy, Farrell, and Dayton 1979).

In an effort to account for the observed relationships between sibship size and intellectual ability, Zajonc (1976) introduced the "confluence model," which postulates that the intellectual environment in the home, defined by the combined intellectual levels of the parents and children, accounts for the observed relationships. According to his theory, the intellectual level is at its peak in families with two adults and no children; as the number of children in the home increases, the intellectual environment afforded to any individual child is effectively diluted. There are two implications of the "confluence model": Children from smaller families should show higher intelligence, and children born earlier in families should show higher intelligence. While the former hypothesis has been supported by a number of empirical studies, the latter did not account for the findings pertaining to only children. In response, Zajonc expanded the confluence model, postulating that younger siblings provide an opportunity for teaching, thus enriching the intellectual experience of older children; the lower intellectual performance of only children is attributed to the fact that they cannot avail themselves of this opportunity. While the confluence model has generated considerable discussion and debate, particularly regarding possible interactions between family size and birth order, and with family SES (see, for example, Steelman 1985; Zajonc 1986), a systematic test of the model remains to be conducted.

Blake (1989) identifies two limitations in the previous work: lack of differentiation of various kinds of intellectual ability (such as verbal and nonverbal) and potential interactions with SES. She finds that the inverse relationship between sibship size and intelligence holds for measures of verbal skill, but not for measures of nonverbal ability, and that the verbal ability deficits observed among children in large families are not limited to those from more disadvantaged backgrounds.

PHYSICAL AND SOCIAL-PSYCHOLOGICAL DEVELOPMENT. Compared with other outcome measures, relatively little attention has been given to the study of sibship size effects on children's physical and social-psychological development. Mednick, Baker, and Hocevar (1985) and Wagner et al. (1985) provide brief reviews of this literature. Family size has been found to be inversely related to children's height and weight; it is also positively correlated with morbidity and mortality. With regard to social-psychological development, children from larger families have been found to have poorer self-concepts, value conformity and self-control rather than independence and self-expression, and to show a greater tendency toward antisocial behavior. They are also less likely to be interested in white-collar occupations.

Blake (1989) investigated the relationship between sibship size and educational expectations, using data from three different cohorts of youth, and found that young people from smaller families, as well as from higher-status families, tend to have higher educational goals. These effects, however, are mediated through ability and grades, and through parents' expectations.

EDUCATIONAL ATTAINMENT. Blake's (1989) book, *Family Size and Achievement,* provides the most comprehensive assessment to date of this area. Two sets of questions are addressed: First, does sibship size affect educational expectations and attainment, and if so, where in the educational process? Second, what is the relative importance of sibship size, relative to other measures of family background?

With regard to the first question, sibship size does appear to have a substantial effect on educational attainment. Individuals from small families had approximately two additional years of schooling, relative to their peers from larger families—net of differences attributable to parental characteristics. The greatest impact on education occurred at the high school level, with individuals from larger families more likely to drop out of high school.

With regard to the second question, relative to other background variables in the analysis, sibship size was consistently second in importance for years of schooling, behind father's education. However, the negative effects of large families were somewhat mitigated by high parental SES and by membership in certain religious or ethnic groups. Similarly, the effects of parental SES were somewhat mitigated for youth in small families.

Some have argued that sibship size is simply a proxy for otherwise unmeasured characteristics of parents' family background, and does not exert any independent effect on education in its own right. To address this concern, Blake (1989) examined the extent to which children from different-sized families have different home environments that might, in turn, influence educational attainment. In particular, attention was given to characteristics of the home setting (such as time spent reading newspapers, reading books, watching television) and to parental behaviors directed toward the child (such as encouragement, correction, goal setting). Children from smaller families were more likely to spend time in intellectual and cultural pursuits, to spend time playing alone, to have been read to as children, and to have had music or dance lessons. However, no significant differences were found in parental values for their children or in parenting style after parents' education and SES were taken into account. Thus, while there appear to be differences in the home environments afforded to children in smaller versus larger families, these differences do not appear to be attributable to differences in parental values or parenting style.

SOCIOECONOMIC ATTAINMENT AND MOBILITY. A long tradition of research has addressed the question of how family background conditions or constrains individuals' socioeconomic attainment and social mobility. While primary consideration has been given to the impact of family social resources (father's education and occupation) on children's attainment, sibship size also was found to be related to occupational attainment

(Blau and Duncan 1967). Among both women and men, those from larger families were more likely to have lower-status jobs and lower earnings, even after adjusting for differences in fathers' SES and educational attainment, both of which are correlated with family size. Among women, the effect of sibship size on earnings was stronger than the effect of father's occupation (Featherman and Hauser 1976). Using path analysis to model both indirect and direct relationships, however, Duncan, Featherman, and Duncan (1972) found that the negative effect of sibship size on men's occupational status could be accounted for primarily by the effect of sibship size on educational attainment. This finding lends some support to arguments that larger families result in a dilution of family economic resources, thus constraining the opportunities available to children.

PARENTS' ECONOMIC WELL-BEING. Duncan et al. (1972) examined the impact of family size (as contrasted with sibship size) as a contingency in men's socioeconomic attainment, finding a slight and negative effect on occupational status but a positive effect on earnings, net of other background variables. Studies that included women found evidence of reciprocal relationships between family size and labor force participation, which in turn affected women's career attainment (Waite and Stolzenberg, 1976). However, as noted previously, Bagozzi and Van Loo (1988) suggested that women's work and family size are not causally related but are mutually dependent on other, achievement-related characteristics of the wife.

Relationships have been reported between the timing of childbearing and subsequent economic well-being. Card and Wise (1978) found that teenage parents of both sexes tended to have less education, lower job prestige, and lower earnings, relative to later childbearers, net of differences in background characteristics. Investigating this relationship in greater depth, Hofferth and Moore (1979) found that the effects of early childbearing on women's subsequent earnings were primarily attributable to the larger family sizes of these women, and the consequent implications for (less) work experience. However, they also found that early childbearing was less of a handicap for black women, due to weaker relationships between early childbearing and subsequent education and employment. Hofferth (1984) found that among women aged sixty or over, the number of children per se was not related to measures of economic well-being, but that the timing of childbearing was: Those who delayed the first birth until after age thirty had higher family incomes and higher standards of living than did women whose first child was born before age thirty. This relationship was most pronounced among delayed childbearers who had small families, suggesting an interaction between timing of childbearing and family size.

Massagli (1987) has argued for a life cycle model of the process of stratification that incorporates information on family size in both the parental and the filial generations. He hypothesizes that sibship size does not affect socioeconomic attainment directly but, rather, is related to the timing of early life cycle transitions and to marital fertility; the observed negative effects of sibship size on attainment are attributed to the product of the relationship with life cycle transitions and marital fertility and the negative effect of marital fertility on attainment.

Parents in larger families have also been found to have poorer marital relations.

PARENTAL ATTITUDES AND WELL-BEING. Wagner et al. (1985) review a number of studies of effects of family size on parental attitudes and parental health. They find that parental attitudes and treatment of children vary with family size: Larger families are more family centered, with a greater role played by fathers; at the same time, parents in larger families tend to be more authoritarian, and more inclined to treat all children alike. Parents in larger families have also been found to have poorer marital relations. Finally, men and women who have many children are at greater risk of hypertension and other physical ailments.

In sum, sibship size and family size both appear to exert significant influence on the children and on the parents. Sibship size is closely related to family socioeconomic background, however, which is also a major influence on children's development and attainment. As a result, care must be taken to differentiate between effects of sibship size per se and effects of socioeconomic background. Similarly, family size among adults (the number of children they have) is highly correlated with socioeconomic status, intelligence, and other characteristics; again, it is important to consider the effects of family size net of these other factors. In many instances, the effects of sibship size and family size appear to be indirect. For example, sibship size is highly correlated with educational attainment, and thus with subsequent occupational attainment. Similarly, among adults, family size is correlated with employment, and thus with socioeconomic attainment. Finally, family size is often closely related to other characteristics of the family: Among children, it may be related to birth order, and among parents, it may be related to the timing of childbearing. Understanding these indirect as well as direct relationships yields a better understanding of the ways in which, and the extent to which, sibship size and family size may affect the lives of children and adults.

[See also Family Planning.]

BIBLIOGRAPHY

Anastasi, A. 1956 "Intelligence and Family Size." *Psychological Bulletin* 53:187–209.

Bagozzi, Richard P., and M. Frances Van Loo 1988 "An Investigation of the Relationship Between Work and Family Size Decisions over Time." *Multivariate Behavioral Research* 23:3–34.

Belmont, L., and F. A. Marolla 1973 "Birth Order, Family Size, and Intelligence." *Science* 182:1096–1101.

Ben-Porath, Y. 1975 "First-Generation Effects on Second-Generation Fertility." *Demography* 12:397–405.

Blake, Judith 1986 "Number of Siblings, Family Background, and the Process of Educational Attainment." *Social Biology* 33:5–21.

——— 1989 *Family Size and Achievement.* Berkeley: University of California Press.

Blau, Peter M., and Otis D. Duncan 1967 *The American Occupational Structure.* New York: Free Press.

Bloom, David E., and James Trussell 1984 "What Are the Determinants of Delayed Childbearing and Permanent Childlessness in the United States?" *Demography* 21:591–611.

Breland, H. M. 1974 "Birth Order, Family Configuration, and Verbal Achievement." *Child Development* 45:1011–1019.

Card, Josefina J., and Lauress L. Wise 1978 "Teenage Mothers and Teenage Fathers: The Impact of Early Childbearing on the Parents' Personal and Professional Lives." *Family Planning Perspectives* 10:199–205.

Claudy, John G., William S. Farrell, Jr., and Charles W. Dayton 1979 "The Consequences of Being an Only Child: An Analysis of Project TALENT Data." Final report. Palo Alto, Calif.: American Institutes for Research.

Claudy, John G., David E. Gross, and Rebecca D. Strause 1974 "Two Population Studies: I. Family Size, Birth Order, and Characteristics of Young Adults, and II. A Study of Married Couples in Knox County, Tennessee." Final report. Palo Alto, Calif.: American Institutes for Research.

Devaney, Barbara 1983 "An Analysis of Variations in U.S. Fertility and Female Labor Force Participation Trends." *Demography* 20:147–161.

Duncan, Otis D., David L. Featherman, and Beverly Duncan 1972 *Socioeconomic Background and Achievement.* New York: Seminar Press.

Easterlin, Richard A. 1980 *Birth and Fortune.* New York: Basic Books.

Featherman, David L., and Robert M. Hauser 1976 "Sexual Inequalities and Socioeconomic Achievement." *American Sociological Review* 41:462–483.

Gualtieri, C. Thomas, and Robert E. Hicks 1986 "Family Configuration and Family Size." *Social Biology* 33:146–147.

Hofferth, Sandra L. 1984 "Long-Term Economic Consequences for Women of Delayed Childbearing and Reduced Family Size." *Demography* 21:141–155.

———, and Kristin A. Moore 1979 "Early Childbearing and Later Economic Well Being." *American Sociological Review* 44:784–815.

Koenig, Michael A., James F. Phillips, Ruth S. Simmons, and Mehrab A. Khan 1987 "Trends in Family Size Preferences and Contraceptive Use in Matlab, Bangladesh." *Studies in Family Planning* 18:117–127.

Levy, Victor 1985 "Cropping Pattern, Mechanization, Child Labor, and Fertility Behavior in a Farming Economy: Rural Egypt." *Economic Development and Cultural Change* 33:777–791.

Lopreato, Joseph, and Mai-yu Yu 1988 "Human Fertility and Fitness Optimization." *Ethology and Sociobiology* 9:269–289.

Massagli, Michael P. 1987 "Effects of Family Size on the Process of Stratification: A Structural Equation Model for White Couples in the U.S. in 1962 and 1973." In *Research in Social Stratification and Mobility,* vol. 6, Robert V. Robinson, ed. Greenwich, Conn.: JAI Press.

Mednick, Birgitte R., Robert L. Baker, and Dennis Hocevar 1985 "Family Size and Birth Order Correlates of Intellectual, Psychosocial, and Physical Growth." *Merrill-Palmer Quarterly* 31:67–84.

Oropesa, R. S. 1985 "Subject Relative Affluence and Expected Family Size." *Sociology and Social Research* 69:501–515.

Rani, Usha D. 1986 "Old Age Security Value of Children and Fertility in Relation to Social Policy." Paper presented at the annual meeting of the International Sociological Association.

Retherford, Robert D., and William H. Sewell 1988 "Intelligence and Family Size Reconsidered." *Social Biology* 35:1–40.

Robinson, W. C. 1986 "High Fertility as Risk-Insurance." *Population Studies* 40:289–298.

Ryder, Norman B. 1986 "Observations on the History of Cohort Fertility in the United States." *Population and Development Review* 12:617–643.

Steelman, Lala C. 1985 "A Tale of Two Variables: A Review of the Intellectual Consequences of Sibship Size and Birth Order." *Review of Educational Research* 55:353–386.

Thornton, A. 1980 "The Influence of First Generation Fertility and Economic Status on Second Generation Fertility." *Population and Environment* 3:51–72.

Treas, Judith 1981 "Postwar Trends in Family Size." *Demography* 18:321–334.

Udry, J. Richard 1983 "Do Couples Make Fertility Plans One Birth at a Time?" *Demography* 20:117–128.

U.S. Bureau of the Census 1990 *Statistical Abstract of the United States: 1990.* Washington, D.C.: U.S. Government Printing Office.

Wagner, Mazie E., Herman J. P. Schubert, and Daniel S. P. Schubert 1985 "Family Size Effects: A Review." *Journal of Genetic Psychology* 146:65–78.

Waite, Linda J., and Ross M. Stolzenberg 1976 "Intended Childbearing and Labor Force Participation of Young Women: Insights from Nonrecursive Models." *American Sociological Review,* 41:235–252.

West, Kirsten K., and Leslie A. Morgan 1987 "Public Perceptions of the Ideal Number of Children for Contemporary Families." *Population and Environment* 9:160–171.

White, Lynn K., and Hyunju Kim 1987 "The Family-Building Process: Childbearing Choices by Parity." *Journal of Marriage and the Family* 49:271–279.

Whyte, Martin K., and S. Z. Gu 1987 "Popular Response to China's Fertility Transition." *Population and Development Review* 13:471–494.

Zajonc, Robert B. 1976 "Family Configuration and Intelligence." *Science* 192:227–236.

——— 1986 "Family Factors and Intellectual Test Performance: A Reply to Steelman." *Review of Educational Research* 56:365–371.

– LAURI STEEL

FAMILY VIOLENCE

Physical violence of all types, from slaps to murder, probably occurs more frequently in the family than in any other setting or group except the armed services in time of war or riot. This article summarizes the incidence rates and examines reasons for the high rates, with emphasis on the characteristics of the family as a social institution and on social inequality.

Physical violence is defined as an act carried out with the intention or perceived intention of causing physical pain or injury to another person (Gelles and Straus 1979). For certain purposes, the term *assault* is preferable because much intra-family violence is a statutory crime. However, not all violence is criminal. Hitting a misbehaving child is legal and expected in all but a few countries. Hitting an "errant wife" was legal under the common law in the United States until the 1870s (Calvert 1974).

Child abuse was not regarded as a widespread social problem by sociologists, family therapists, or the public until the 1960s (Nelson 1984; Pfohl 1977), and wife beating not until the 1970s. The subsequent emergence of public concern and research on these and other aspects of family violence reflects major social changes, including the following:

1. The social activism of the 1960s, which sought to aid oppressed groups of all types, was extended to this aspect of the oppression of children and women.
2. The rising homicide and assault rate, violent political and social protest and assassinations, terrorist activity, and the Vietnam war sensitized people to violence.
3. Disenchantment with the family in the 1960s and early 1970s facilitated perceiving negative features of family life, including violence.
4. The growth of paid employment by married women provided the economic means for them no longer to tolerate the abuse that had long been the lot of women.
5. The reemerged women's movement made battering a central issue in the mid 1970s and gave it wide publicity.
6. The creation by the women's movement of a new social institution—shelters for battered women—did more than provide material assistance. Shelters were ideologically important because they concretized and publicized a phenomenon that had previously been ignored.
7. Changes in theoretical perspectives in sociology put the consensus model of society under attack by conflict theory. The inevitability of conflict in all human groups, including the family, was recognized, along with the possibility of violent conflict.

Prevalence of Family Violence

HOMICIDE. In the United States, about one-quarter of all murders involve family members (Straus 1986). In other industrialized countries the percentage is much higher, for example, 48 percent in Canada and 67 percent in Denmark (Straus 1987). These high percentages occur because Canada and Denmark have *low* homicide rates. The few family homicides that occur are a large proportion of the low overall rate. This suggests that when homicide has been almost eliminated in a society such as Denmark, the family is the setting in which it is most likely to persist.

OFFICIAL STATISTICS ON CHILD ABUSE AND SPOUSE ABUSE. National statistics on child abuse cases reported to welfare authorities in the United States have been published since 1976. In that year 669,000 cases were reported, of which about one-quarter (167,000) were physical abuse (American Association for the Protection of Children 1986). These statistics vastly underestimate the actual extent of child abuse. Many times more children are severely beaten each year but do not come to public attention. Officially reported cases grew by about 10 percent per year during the period 1976–1985, for a total increase of about 300 percent. However, rather than an increase, historical and survey evidence suggests that the true incidence of child physical abuse has been slowly decreasing since the late seventeenth century (Radbill 1987; Straus and Gelles 1986). The growth in officially known cases from 1976 to 1985 did not occur because more children were assaulted but because the child abuse education campaigns and the social changes listed earlier led the public and professionals to report cases that in previous times would have been ignored.

Most cases of violence between spouses do not come to the attention of the police

There are no official statistics for the United States on violence between spouses because the Uniform Crime Reporting System used by almost all police departments does not classify assaults on the basis of relationship between victim and offender. Even if such data were gathered, only a small fraction of the cases would be included because most do not come to the attention of the police (Kaufman Kantor and Straus 1990). A similar problem makes the U.S. National Crime Survey (Gaquin 1977–1978; U.S. Department of Justice 1980) vastly underestimate the incidence of wife beating. The public tends to consider assault by a spouse as a "family problem" rather than a "crime" and rarely informs the survey interviewer of such events.

THE NATIONAL FAMILY VIOLENCE SURVEYS. National surveys of U.S. families were conducted in 1975 and 1985 to secure a better estimate of the incidence and prevalence of family violence. These surveys were made possible by the development of the "Conflict Tactics Scales" to measure family violence (Straus 1979, 1990). The following rates are based on the 6,002 families in the 1985 study (Straus and Gelles 1986, 1990). The resulting annual incidence rates are many times greater than rates based on cases known to child welfare professionals, the police, shelters, or the National Crime Survey, but are still believed to be lower-bound estimates.

Sixteen percent of the couples surveyed reported one or more incidents involving physical violence during 1985. Attacks by husbands on wives that were serious enough to warrant the term "wife beating" (because they involved punching, biting, kicking, choking, etc.) were reported for 3.2 percent of wives, resulting in a lower-bound estimate of 1.7 million beaten women in 1985. The 1975 and 1985 National Family Violence Surveys, and all other studies of marital violence that do not use samples selected from the clientele of shelters and similar agencies, find that women assault their husbands at about the same rate as men assault their wives (Straus 1990); however, men are injured at only one-seventh the rate of injury to women (Stets and Straus 1990; Straus 1990).

The most violent role within the family is that of parent, because almost all parents use physical punishment. Over one-fifth of the parents of infants in the 1985 National Family Violence Survey reported hitting their child that year. Over 90 percent of parents of three-year-old children used physical punishment. The figure decreased steadily from age five on, but one-third of parents of children fifteen to seventeen years old reported hitting the child that year.

Child abuse is more difficult to operationalize than *physical punishment* because the line differentiating *abuse* from *physical punishment* is to a considerable extent a matter of social norms. Two different rates, based on different normative assumptions, were therefore computed from the National Family Violence Survey data. The first rate indicates the percentage of children who were kicked, bitten, punched, beaten, scalded, or attacked with a knife or gun. This resulted in a child abuse rate of 2.4 percent, and a lower-bound estimate of 1.5 million U.S. children abused in 1985. Hitting children with an object such as a stick or a belt was not included in the first rate because the courts and much of the general public continue to uphold its legality. However, the proportion of the public who accept such acts as legitimate physical punishment seems to be decreasing. Consequently, a second rate, which classifies hitting a child with an object as abusive, was computed. This resulted in a rate of 11 percent and an estimate of more than 6.9 million U.S. children physically abused in 1985. The first of these two estimates is about six times greater than the number of cases reported to protective service agencies in 1985, and the second of the estimates is twenty-seven times greater.

Intrafamily relationships between children are extremely violent. But, like violence of parents, it is not perceived as such because there is an implicit normative tolerance. Almost all young children hit a sibling, and more than 20 percent hit a parent. Even in their late teens (age fifteen to seventeen) the rate of violence between siblings is enormous: More than two-thirds of that age group hit a sibling during the year of the survey.

Comparison of the two National Family Violence Surveys found a substantial reduction in the rates of child abuse and wife beating (Straus and Gelles 1986), reflecting a centuries-long trend. Nevertheless, the rates just reported show that American society still has a long way to go before a typical citizen is as safe in his or her own home as on the streets or in the workplace.

Explanations of Family Violence

HIGH LEVEL OF FAMILY CONFLICT. A characteristic of the family that helps accounts for the high rate of violence is its inherently high level of conflict. One reason for high conflict is that, as in other primary groups, family members are concerned with "the whole person." Consequently, there are more issues over which conflict can occur than in nonprimary relationships. Moreover, when conflict does occur, the deep commitment makes arguments emotionally charged. A disagreement about music with colleagues at work is unlikely to have the same emotional intensity as when children favor rock and parents favor Bach. The likelihood of conflicts is further multiplied because families usually consist of both males and females and parents and children, thus juxtaposing differences in the orientations and interests of different genders and generations. The family is the prime locus of the "battle of the sexes" and the "generation gap."

NORMS TOLERATING OR REQUIRING VIOLENCE. Although conflict is endemic in families, it is not the only group or institution with a high level of conflict. Conflict is also high in academic departments and congressional committees, yet physical violence is practically nonexistent in those groups. Additional factors are needed to explain why violence is so much more frequent in the family than in other groups. One of these is the existence of cultural norms that tolerate or require violence. The clearest example is the right and obligation of parents to use physical force to train, protect, and control a child. Eighty-four percent of Americans believe "It is sometimes necessary to discipline a child with a good hard spanking" (Lehman 1989). These norms contrast with those prevailing within other institutions. Even prison authorities are no longer permitted to use corporal punishment.

Similar norms apply to husband–wife relations. However, they are implicit and taken for granted, and therefore largely unrecognized. Just as parenthood gives the right to hit, so the marriage license is also a hitting license (Greenblat 1983; Straus 1976). As with other licenses, rules govern its use. Slapping a spouse, for example, is tolerable if the spouse is perceived to be engaged in a serious wrong and "won't listen to reason." Many of the men and women interviewed by Gelles (1974, p. 58) expressed this normative principle with such phrases as "I asked for it" or "She needed to be brought to her senses."

The common law right of a husband to "physically chastise an errant wife" was recognized by U.S. courts until the late nineteenth century (Calvert 1974). Informally, it lived on in the behavior of the public, the police, and the courts, and continues to do so. Under pressure from the women's movement, this is changing, but slowly. There have been major reforms in police and court procedures (Lerman 1981; Sherman and Cohn 1989), but the public and many police officers continue to believe that "it's their own business" if spouses are violent to each other, provided the blow is not severe enough to cause an injury that requires medical treatment, whereas they would not tolerate a similar pattern of assault in an office, factory, or church. Only a very small percent of men in the 1985 National Family Violence Survey believed that a legal sanction would be likely if they assaulted their wife (Carmody and Williams 1987). Of the more than six hundred women in this survey who were assaulted by their husbands, the police were involved in only 6.7% of the incidents and an arrest was made in only five cases (Kaufman Kantor and Straus 1990). The probability of legal sanction for assaulting a wife is even less than the .008 indicated by those five cases, because two-thirds of the six hundred women were assaulted more than once during the year of the survey.

FAMILY SOCIALIZATION IN VIOLENCE. In a certain sense it begs the question to attribute the high rate of family violence to norms that tolerate, permit, or require violence because it does not explain why the norms for families are different from those for other social groups or institutions. There are a number of reasons, but one of the most fundamental is that the family is the setting in which physical violence is first experienced, and in which the normative legitimacy of violence is learned. Learning about violence begins with physical punishment, which, as noted above, is experienced by over 90 percent of American children. Physical punishment is used to teach that certain types of behavior are not condoned, but simultaneously, social learning processes teach the legitimacy of and behavioral script for violence.

From the earliest level of psychosocial development, children learn that those to whom they are most closely bonded are also those who hit.

The first step in the process is the association of love with violence. Since physical punishment begins in infancy, parents are the first, and usually the only, ones to hit an infant. From the earliest level of psychosocial development, children learn that those to whom they are most closely bonded are also those who hit. Second, since physical punishment is used to train the child in morally correct behavior or to teach about danger to be avoided, it establishes the normative legitimacy of hitting other family members. Third, physical punishment teaches the cultural script for use of violence. For example, parents often refrain from hitting until their anger or frustration reaches a certain point. The child therefore learns that anger and frustration justify the use of physical force.

As a result of these social learning processes, use of violence becomes internalized and generalized to other social relationships, especially such intimate relationships as husband and wife and parent and child. Both National Family Violence Surveys found that the more physical punishment experienced as a child, the higher the probability of hitting a spouse (Straus 1983; 1991; Straus, Gelles, and Steinmetz 1980). Many children do not even need to extrapolate from physical punishment of children to other relationships because they directly observe role models of physical violence between their parents.

GENDER INEQUALITY. Despite egalitarian rhetoric and the trend toward a more egalitarian family structure, male dominance in the family and in other spheres remains an important cause of family violence (Straus 1976). Most Americans continue to think of the husband as the "head of the family," and many believe that status gives him the right to have the final say. This sets the stage for violence because force is ultimately necessary to back up the right to have the final say (Goode 1971).

Numerous structural patterns sustain the system of male dominance: The income of women employed full-time is about a third lower than the income of men, and money is a source of power. Men tend to marry women who are younger, shorter, and less well educated; and age, physical size, and education form a basis for exercising power. Thus, the typical marriage begins with an advantage to the man. If the initial advantage changes or is challenged, many men feel morally justified in using their greater size and strength to maintain the right to have the final say, which they perceive to have been agreed on at the time of the marriage (LaRossa 1980). As a result, male-dominant marriages have been found to have the highest rate of wife beating (Coleman and Straus 1986; Straus, Gelles, and Steinmetz 1980), and societies in which male-dominant marriages prevail have higher rates of marital violence than more egalitarian societies (Levinson 1989; Straus 1977).

The privileged economic position of men also helps to explain why beaten wives so often stay with an assaulting husband (Kalmuss and Straus 1983). As recently as the 1980 U.S. census, about half of all married women with children had no earned income of their own. The other half earned only about half of the male wage. When marriages end, children stay with the mother in about 90 percent of the cases. Child support payments are typically inadequate and typically not made after a year or two. No-fault divorce has worked to the economic disadvantage of women (Weitzman 1986). Consequently, many women stay in violent marriages because the alternative is bringing up their children in poverty.

OTHER FACTORS. Many other factors contribute to the high rate of intrafamily violence in the United States, even though they do not explain why the family is, on the average, more violent than other groups. Space permits only some of these to be identified briefly.

The empirical evidence shows that the greater the number of stressful events experienced by a family, the higher the rate of marital violence and child abuse (Makepeace 1983; Straus 1980; Straus and Kaufman Kantor 1987). In addition to specific stressful events that impinge on families, chronic stresses, such as marital conflict and poverty, are also strongly associated with child abuse and spouse abuse.

Almost all studies that have investigated this issue find a strong association between drinking and family violence (Coleman and Straus 1983; Kaufman Kantor and Straus 1987). However, even though heavy drinkers have two to three times the violence rate of abstainers, most heavy drinkers do *not* engage in spouse abuse or child abuse (Kaufman Kantor and Straus 1987).

The higher the level of nonfamily violence in a society, the higher the rate of child abuse and spouse abuse (Levinson 1989; Straus 1977). The nonfamily violence can be in the form of violent crime or socially legitimate violence such as warfare. The carryover of violent behavior from one sphere of life to another may be strongest when the societal violence is "legitimate violence" rather than "criminal violence," because most individual acts of violence are carried out to correct some perceived wrong. Archer and Gartner (1984) and Huggins and Straus (1980) found that war is associated with an increase in interpersonal violence. Straus constructed an index to measure differences between the states of the United States in the extent to which violence was used or supported for socially legitimate purposes such as corporal punishment in the schools, or expenditure per capita on the National Guard (Baron and Straus 1989). The higher the score of a state on this Legitimate Violence Index, the higher the rate of *criminal* violence such as homicide (Baron and Straus 1988) and rape (Baron and Straus 1989).

Family violence occurs at all social levels, but it is more prevalent at the lowest socioeconomic level and among disadvantaged minorities. Socioeconomic group differences in physical punishment of children or slapping of spouses are relatively small, but the more severe the violence, the greater the socioeconomic difference. Thus, punching, biting, choking, attacking with weapons, and killing of family members occur much more often among the most disadvantaged sectors of society (Straus, Gelles, and Steinmetz 1980; Bachman, Linsky, and Straus 1988).

THE OVERALL PATTERN. No single factor, such as male dominance or growing up in a violent family, has been shown to account for more than a small percentage of the incidence of child abuse or spouse abuse. However, a study of the potential effect of twenty-five such "risk factors" found that in families where only one or two of the factors existed, there were no incidents of wife beating during the year studied. On the other hand, wife beating occurred in 70 percent of the families with twelve or more of the twenty-five factors (Straus, Gelles, and Steinmetz 1980, p. 203). Similar results were found for child abuse. Thus, the key to unraveling the paradox of family violence appears to lie in understanding the interplay of numerous causal factors.

The Future

During the period 1965 to 1985, the age-old phenomena of child abuse and wife beating underwent an evolution from "private trouble" to "social problem"—and in the case of wife beating, to a statutory crime. Every state in the United States now employs large numbers of "child protective service" workers, and there are national and local voluntary groups devoted to prevention and treatment of child abuse. There are about a thousand shelters for battered women, whereas none existed in 1973. There are growing numbers of counseling programs for batterers and of family dispute mediation programs. Criminal prosecution of violent husbands, although still the exception, is increasing.

Child protective services, shelters for battered women, and treatment programs for wife beaters are essential services. However, the root causes of child abuse and spouse abuse lie in the characteristics of the family and of other social institutions. Consequently, social services for abused children, shelters, counseling, and prosecution are unlikely to have a major or lasting effect unless there are also changes in those institutional characteristics. The changes must address the pervasive inequality between men and women within the family and in society at large; the high incidence of normatively legitimate violence, ranging from the almost universal practice of physical punishment to capital punishment, and bombing countries engaged in "state terrorism"; social norms tolerating violence between spouses; and the stress and frustration experienced by the millions living in poverty and under racial oppression.

[See also Incest; Sexual Violence and Abuse.]

BIBLIOGRAPHY

American Association for the Protection of Children 1986 *Highlights of Official Child Neglect and Abuse Reporting 1984.* Denver: The Association.

Archer, Dane, and Rosemary Gartner 1984 *Violence and Crime in Cross-National Perspective.* New Haven, Conn.: Yale University Press.

Bachman, Ronet, Arnold S. Linsky, and Murray A. Straus 1988 "Homicide of Family Members, Acquaintances, and Strangers, and State-to-State Differences in Social Stress, Social Control and Social Norms." Paper presented at the meeting of the American Sociological Association; Atlanta. Durham: Family Research Laboratory, University of New Hampshire.

Baron, Larry, and Murray A. Straus 1988 "Cultural and Economic Sources of Homicide in the United States." *The Sociological Quarterly* 29:371–390.

——— 1989 *Four Theories of Rape in American Society: A State Level Analysis.* New Haven, Conn.: Yale University Press.

Calvert, Robert 1974 "Criminal and Civil Liability in Husband–Wife Assaults." In Suzanne K. Steinmetz and Murray A. Straus, eds., *Violence in the Family.* New York: Harper and Row.

Carmody, Diane C., and Kirk R. Williams 1987 "Wife Assault and Perceptions of Sanctions." *Violence and Victims* 2:25–38.

Coleman, Diane H., and Murray A. Straus 1983 "Alcohol Abuse and Family Violence." In E. Gottheil, K. A. Druley, T. E. Skolada, and H. M. Waxman, eds., *Alcohol, Drug Abuse and Aggression.* Springfield, Ill.: C. C. Thomas.

——— 1986 "Marital Power, Conflict, and Violence in a Nationally Representative Sample of American Couples." *Violence and Victims* 1:141–157.

Gaquin, Deirdre A. 1977–1978 "Spouse Abuse: Data from the National Crime Survey." *Victimology* 2:632–643.

Gelles, Richard J. 1974 *The Violent Home: A Study of Physical Aggression Between Husbands and Wives.* Beverly Hills, Calif.: Sage.

Gelles, Richard J., and Murray A. Straus 1979 "Determinants of Violence in the Family: Toward a Theoretical Integration." In W. R. Burr, R. Hill, F. I. Nye, and I. L. Reiss, eds., *Contemporary Theories About the Family.* New York: Free Press.

Goode, William J. 1974 "Force and Violence in the Family." In Suzanne K. Steinmetz and Murray A. Straus, eds., *Violence in the Family.* New York: Harper and Row.

Greenblat, Cathy S. 1983 "A Hit Is a Hit Is a Hit . . . or Is It? Approval and Tolerance of the Use of Physical Force by Spouses." In David Finkelhor, Richard J. Gelles, Gerald T. Hotaling, and Murray A. Straus, eds., *The Dark Side of Families.* Beverly Hills, Calif.: Sage.

Huggins, Martha D., and Murray A. Straus 1980 "Violence and the Social Structure as Reflected in Children's Books From 1850 to 1970." In Murray A. Straus and Gerald T. Hotaling, eds., *The Social Causes of Husband–Wife Violence.* Minneapolis: University of Minnesota Press.

Kalmuss, Debra S., and Murray A. Straus 1983 "Feminist, Political, and Economic Determinants of Wife Abuse Services in American States." In David Finkelhor, Richard J. Gelles, Gerald T. Hotaling, and Murray A. Straus, eds., *Issues and The Dark Side of Families.* Beverly Hills, Calif.: Sage.

Kaufman Kantor, Glenda, and Murray A. Straus 1987 "The 'Drunken Bum' Theory of Wife Beating." *Social Problems* 34:213–230.

——— 1990 "Response of Victims and the Police to Assaults on Wives." In Murray A. Straus and Richard J. Gelles, eds., *Physical Violence in American Families: Risk Factors and Adaptations to Violence in 8,145 Families.* New Brunswick, N.J.: Transaction Books.

LaRossa, Ralph E. 1980 "And We Haven't Had Any Problem Since: Conjugal Violence and the Politics of Marriage." In Murray A. Straus and Gerald T. Hotaling, eds., *The Social Causes of Husband–Wife Violence.* Minneapolis: University of Minnesota.

Lehman, Betsy A. 1989 "Spanking Teaches the Wrong Lesson." *Boston Globe,* March 13, p. 27.

Lerman, Lisa 1981 *Prosecution of Spouse Abuse: Innovations in Criminal Justice Response.* Washington, D.C.: Center for Women Policy Studies.

Levinson, David 1989 *Family Violence in Cross-Cultural Perspective.* Newbury Park, Calif.: Sage.

Makepeace, James M. 1983 "Life Events Stress and Courtship Violence." *Family Relations* 32:101–109.

Nelson, Barbara J. 1984 *Making an Issue of Child Abuse: Political Agenda Setting for Social Problems.* Chicago: University of Chicago Press.

Pfohl, Stephen J. 1977 "The Discovery of Child Abuse." *Social Problems* 24 (February):310–323.

Radbill, Samuel X. 1987 "A History of Child Abuse and Infanticide." In Ray E. Helfer and C. Henry Kempe, eds., *The Battered Child,* 4th ed. Chicago: University of Chicago Press.

Sherman, Lawrence W., and Ellen G. Cohn 1989 "The Impact of Research on Legal Policy: The Minneapolis Domestic Violence Experiment." *Law and Society Review* 23, no. 1:117–144.

Stets, Jan E., and Murray A. Straus 1990 "Gender Differences in Reporting Marital Violence and Its Medical and Psychological Consequences." In Murray A. Straus and Richard J. Gelles, eds., *Physical Violence in American Families: Risk Factors and Adaptations to Violence in 8,145 Families.* New Brunswick, N.J.: Transaction Books.

Straus, Murray A. 1976 "Sexual Inequality, Cultural Norms, and Wife-Beating." In E. C. Viano, ed., *Victims and Society.* Washington, D. C.: Visage Press. Also in *Victimology* 1 (Spring

1976):54–76; and in J. R. Chapman and M. Gates, eds., *Women into Wives: The Legal and Economic Impact of Marriage.* Sage Yearbook in Women Policy Studies, Vol 2. Beverly Hills, Calif.: Sage, 1977.

——— 1977 "Societal Morphogenesis and Intrafamily Violence in Cross-Cultural Perspective." *Annals of the New York Academy of Sciences* 285:719–730.

——— 1979 "Measuring Intrafamily Conflict and Violence: The Conflict Tactics (CT) Scale." *Journal of Marriage and the Family* 41:75–88.

——— 1980 "Social Stress and Marital Violence in a National Sample of American Families." In F. Wright, C. Bahn, and R. Rieber, eds., *Forensic Psychology and Psychiatry.* New York: New York Academy of Sciences. *Annals of the New York Academy of Sciences,* 347.

——— 1983 "Ordinary Violence Versus Child Abuse and Wife Beating: What Do They Have in Common?" In David Finkelhor, Gerald T. Hotaling, Richard J. Gelles, and Murray A. Straus, eds., *The Dark Side of Families: Issues and Controversies in the Study of Family Violence.* Beverly Hills, Calif.: Sage.

——— 1986 "Domestic Violence and Homicide Antecedents." *Bulletin of the New York Academy of Medicine* 62, no. 5:446–465.

——— 1987 "Primary Group Characteristics and Intra-family Homicide." Paper presented at the Third National Conference for Family Violence Researchers, Family Research Laboratory, University of New Hampshire, Durham.

——— 1989 "Assaults by Wives on Husbands: Implications for Primary Prevention of Marital Violence." Paper presented at 1989 meeting of the American Society of Criminology, Reno, Nev. Durham: Family Research Laboratory, University of New Hampshire.

——— 1990 "The Conflict Tactics Scale and Its Critics: An Evaluation and New Data on Validity and Reliability." In Murray A. Straus and Richard J. Gelles, eds., *Physical Violence in American Families: Risk Factors and Adaptations to Violence in 8,145 Families.* New Brunswick, N.J.: Transaction Books.

——— 1991 "Discipline and Deviance: Physical Punishment of Children and Violence and Other Crime in Adulthood." *Social Problems* 38, no. 2.

Straus, Murray A., and Richard J. Gelles 1986 "Societal Change and Change in Family Violence from 1975 to 1985 as Revealed by Two National Surveys." *Journal of Marriage and the Family* 48:465–479.

———, eds. 1990 *Physical Violence in American Families: Risk Factors and Adaptations to Violence in 8,145 Families.* New Brunswick, N.J.: Transaction Books.

Straus, Murray A., Richard J. Gelles, and Suzanne K. Steinmetz 1980 *Behind Closed Doors: Violence in the American Family.* New York: Doubleday/Anchor.

Straus, Murray A., and Glenda Kaufman Kantor 1987 "Stress and Physical Child Abuse." In Ray E. Helfer and C. Henry Kempe, eds., *The Battered Child,* 4th ed. Chicago: University of Chicago Press.

U.S. Department of Justice 1980 *Intimate Victims: A Study of Violence Among Friends and Relatives. A National Crime Survey Report.* Washington, D.C.: Bureau of Justice Statistics.

Weitzman, Lenore J. 1986 *The Divorce Revolution.* New York: Free Press.

– MURRAY A. STRAUS

FEMININITY/MASCULINITY

Femininity and masculinity (*gender*), in a social or psychological sense, are distinguished from male and female (*sex*), in a biological sense (Lindsey 1990). The focus of this article is on the former. Conceptions of the nature of femininity and masculinity are varied and have changed over the past several decades (Maccoby 1987). In discussing the nature of femininity/masculinity, researchers have referred variously to gender-related dispositions, traits, and temperaments, to gender roles, and to gender identities. Often they use these terms almost interchangeably. There is a general belief that biological sex, gender roles, and masculine and feminine psychological characteristics and gender identities are all tightly interrelated (Spence and Helmreich 1978). Whether or not this interrelationship is true, however, it is necessary to keep the concepts distinct and not confuse them. What is true with respect to one (for example, gender identities) may not be true with respect to another (for example, gender roles).

Gender identity refers to the way in which people view themselves along feminine/masculine lines. There are two parts to this. The first is basic gender identification or the cognitive knowledge that one is male or female. By the age of two, most children have established their basic gender identification (Money and Ehrhardt 1972). The second is gender-role identity or the nature of the view of the self as a male or female in society (Kagan 1964). For example, a person may know himself to be a male (basic gender identification) but view himself as somewhat feminine (gender-role identity). Gender-role identity, in this sense, develops more slowly over time as the result of socialization (Kagan 1964; Smith and Lloyd 1978).

Gender role refers to the ways in which males and females behave (or are expected to behave) in society. In the United States, for example, males traditionally are expected to behave in a logical, competitive, and ambitious way, while females traditionally are expected to behave in a gentle, sensitive, and warm manner (Broverman et al. 1972).

Gender-related personality traits and temperaments refer to the underlying dispositions and emotional characteristics distinguishing males from females. Temperament and personality dispositions are thought by some researchers to underlie the observable differences between the behavior of men and women. Early research addressed issues of sex differences in temperament with a concern that such differences may be innate (cf. Mead 1935). While the issue of innate differences is not dead (Money 1987), most current research and thinking about issues of femininity/masculinity in the social and behavioral sciences bypass questions of innate sex differences in temperaments and traits. Instead, such research examines how men and women are socialized to be different (learned gender-related traits).

Innate Temperament

Gender-role differentiation is fairly universal across societies. Men and women are assigned different behaviors, tasks, rights, obligations, privileges, and resources. In Western culture (stereotypically), men are aggressive, competitive, and instrumentally oriented, while women are passive, cooperative, and expressive. Early thinking often assumed that this division was based on underlying innate differences in traits, characteristics, and temperaments of males and females. Measures of femininity/masculinity might be used to diagnose problems of basic gender identification.

The 1935 study Sex and Temperament in Three Primitive Societies *concluded that there are no necessary differences in traits and temperaments between the sexes.*

Margaret Mead addressed the issue of sex differences in temperament in her 1935 study *Sex and Temperament in Three Primitive Societies.* This study concludes that there are no necessary differences in traits and temperaments between the sexes. Observed differences in temperament between men and women are not a function of their biological differences. Rather, they result from differences in socialization and the cultural expectations held for each sex.

Mead came to this conclusion because the three societies she studied showed patterns of temperament that varied greatly from our own. Among the Arapesh, both males and females display what we would consider a "feminine" temperament (passive, cooperative, and expressive). Among the Mundugamor, both males and females display what we would consider a "masculine" temperament (active, competitive, and instrumental). Finally, among the Tchambuli men and women display temperaments that are different from each other but opposite to our own pattern. In that society, men are emotional and expressive, while women are active and instrumental.

Mead's study caused people to rethink the nature of femininity/masculinity. Different gender-related traits, temperaments, roles, and identities could no longer be tied inextricably to biological sex. Since Mead's study, the nature-nurture issue has been examined extensively and with much controversy, but no firm conclusions are yet clear (Maccoby and Jacklin 1974). While there may be small sex differences in temperament at birth (and the evidence on this is not consistent), there is far more variability within each sex group (Spence and Helmreich 1978). Further, the pressures of socialization and learning far outweigh the impact of possible innate sex differences in temperament.

Behaviors, Personality Traits, and Roles

The high degree of variability in temperament within each sex group, and the strong trends toward behaviorism in the 1950s and 1960s, led many researchers to examine observable, behavioral differences between men and women and to pay less attention to questions of innate temperament. Two approaches to the study of such behavioral differences developed during this time, each based within an academic discipline. On the one hand, psychologists understood the differences in behavior between men and women to be the result of differences in conditioning and socialization. They believed personality traits developed from socialization and then instigated behavior. Sociologists, on the other hand, viewed behavior less as the result of individual motivation and instigation and more as the result of society organizing and shaping individuals into various roles. For them the question was how society formed and organized masculine and feminine gender roles. However, since both roles and personality traits are inferences made from observed behavior, researchers tend often to be confused about what is being studied (Locksley and Colten 1979).

On the sociological side, Parsons and Bales (1955), in a merger of grand social theorizing and careful observation of moment-to-moment behaviors of individuals interacting in groups, proposed a model of leadership-role differentiation. The idea was that in any group, including the family, there were two basic issues with which a group needs to deal. One concerns satisfying the group's need to perform instrumental tasks and attain its goals. The other centers on the need of the group to maintain the emotional and expressive bonds among its members. Parsons and Bales suggested that the pursuit of the group's instrumental tasks and goals by some individuals often disrupts the social bonds. This makes it very difficult for these same individuals to pursue the emotional and expressive needs of the group. As a result, other individuals play the expressive role, which results in a division of labor. One person becomes the instrumental, task-oriented leader, and another becomes the social-emotional, expressive leader in a group (Bales and Slater 1955).

The parallel between these instrumental and expressive leadership roles and the masculine and feminine gender roles in American society was not unnoticed. The gender-role division was said to grow out of the functioning of the nuclear family (cf. Parsons 1955; Zelditch 1955). Gender roles, within the functionalist framework of Parsons and Bales, are the result of inevitable social forces at play in groups, organizations, and societies (Bales and Slater 1955), not differences in the personality traits of males and females. The ideologically conservative justification of the status quo (male dominance) implied by this functionalist theory has been noted (Lindsey 1990). However, there is nothing in the theory that forces a sex link to the instrumental and expressive dimensions. The question of what makes instrumental activity be male sex-linked and expressive activity be female sex-linked has never been answered fully. By focusing on behaviors, however, one is not tied inevitably to that sex link.

On the psychological side, Bakan (1966), again noting the wide variability of "masculine" and "feminine" tendencies in all people, suggested that persons have both male (agency) and female (communion) tendencies or traits. He further suggested that culture and socialization mold the particular combination of these personality traits in individuals. Based on this reasoning, both Bem (1974) and Spence, Helmreich, and Stapp (1974) developed scales to measure separately these masculine and feminine personality traits in both males and females. In each case, the characteristics or behaviors that are included in the scales are those that are positively valued for either sex but are more "appropriate" for either males (M scales) or females (F scales). "Appropriate," of course, is judged relative to the norms and standards of the culture.

For the Bem scale, descriptions for the masculine scale include, for example, "acts as leader," "makes decisions easily," and "willing to take risks." Descriptions for the feminine scale include "affectionate," "gentle," and "sensitive to the needs of others." For the Spence, Helmreich, Stapp scales, masculinity was measured with bipolar items like "very independent" (vs. "not at all independent") and "can make decisions easily" (vs. "has difficulty making decisions"). Femininity was measured with items such as "very emotional" (vs. "not at all emotional") and "very helpful to others" (vs. "not at all helpful to others"). In addition to the masculinity and femininity scales, Spence, Helmreich, and Stapp developed a third scale, which they labeled MF. This scale had bipolar items that were "appropriate" for males on one end of the continuum, and "appropriate" for females on the other end of the continuum. For example, "very submissive" (vs. "very dominant") and "feelings not easily hurt" (vs. "feelings easily hurt") are typical items.

With separate measures of masculinity and femininity, it is possible to ask about the relationship between them. When this relationship was examined, it was found that the two scales were not strongly negatively related, as would be expected if a masculine gender role were the opposite of a feminine gender role. Instead, the two ratings were relatively uncorrelated (Bem 1974; Spence and Helmreich 1978). People had all combinations of scores in relatively equal proportions. People who combined high scores on masculinity with high scores on femininity were said to be *androgynous* with respect to their gender roles (Bem 1977; Spence and Helmreich 1978). The other classifications were *masculine* (high M and low F scores), *feminine* (high F and low M scores), and *undifferentiated* (low M and low F scores) gender roles. Those classified as masculine or feminine are either sex typed (gender appropriate) or cross sex typed (gender inappropriate).

These measures of masculinity, femininity, and androgyny were usually interpreted in terms of individual personality characteristics and orientations rather than as gender-role performances, though this was not uniformly true. Additionally, the measures were often vaguely thought of as measures of gender self-concept (since they were obtained by respondents providing self-descriptions using the scales). The language of many research reports is confusing on this conceptual issue (Locksley and Colten 1979).

Once these M and F scales were developed to measure masculinity and femininity, a great deal of research ensued. Studies found that sex-typed individuals were more likely to choose behaviors that are consistent with their own gender than androgynous or cross sex-typed individuals (Bem and Lenney 1976; Helmreich, Spence, and Holahan 1979). They also avoided gender-inappropriate activities (Bem, Martyna, and Watson 1976). On the other hand, several studies have found that androgynous people who combine masculine and feminine characteristics are more adaptable, flexible, and mentally healthy (Bem 1975; Helmreich, Spence, and Holahan 1979). They also have higher self-esteem (Spence and Helmreich 1978), although this finding is somewhat problematic since the measures of masculinity and femininity contain traits that are desirable for anyone in our society (Bem 1974; Spence and Helmreich 1978).

Gender-Role Identities and Self-Concepts

Masculinity and femininity, considered as desirable personality characteristics for men and women, respectively, are labels provided by the researcher. Masculinity and femininity may also be considered as part of the self-descriptions or self-concepts that men and women apply to themselves and, as such, are also a source of motivation for action (Foote 1951; Burke 1980). In this latter sense, it is possible to speak of gender-role identities.

Gender-role identities are the self-meanings of masculinity or femininity one has as a male or female member of society and are inherently derived from and tied to social structure. Masculinity and femininity, considered as personality traits as in the last section, are individual attributes that are neither a source of motivation nor necessarily tied to social structure. The self-meaning of one's gender-role identity helps to form the self-concept, which is understood as the hierarchical organization of a set of role identities ordered by centrality or salience (McCall and Simmons 1978, Stryker 1968). Role identities are the meanings of the self-in-role as an object to the self (Burke and Tully 1977). In this sense, gender identities would consist of the self-relevant meanings of being a male or a female in society. These self-meanings are formed in social situations and are based on a role's similarities and differences with counterroles (Lindesmith and Strauss 1956; Turner 1968). Because there are only two gender roles, the meanings of masculine and feminine in this context necessarily contrast. For gender identities, masculinity and femininity would be based on the similarities and differences between the male role and the female role in society. To be a male (masculine) is not to be a female (feminine) and vice versa (Storms 1979).

Starting from an interactionist theoretical position, Burke and Tully (1977) used the semantic differential (Osgood, Succi, and Tannenbaum 1957) to develop procedures for measuring self-meanings based on (1) differences between either actual or stereotypical meanings of target roles and counterroles, and (2) views of the self in relation to these differences. Using this procedure, they then examined the gender-related self-meanings (gender identities) of a large sample of middle school girls and boys. The items that defined gender for these children included, for example, "soft" (vs. "hard"), "weak" (vs. "strong"), and "emotional" (vs. "not emotional"). The gender-identity scores for both boys and girls were approximately normally distributed along the masculine-feminine dimension. About 18 percent of the sample consisted of individuals who had a gender identity that was closer to the modal identity of the opposite sex.

Burke and Tully (1977) found that the children with cross-sex identities (boys who thought of themselves in ways similar to the way most girls thought of themselves, and vice versa) were more likely than children with gender-appropriate identities (1) to have engaged in gender-inappropriate behavior; (2) to have been warned about engaging in gender-inappropriate behavior; and (3) to have been called names like "tomboy," "sissy," or "homo." Finally, they found that boys and girls with cross-sex gender identities were more likely to have low self-esteem.

In other studies using the Burke-Tully measure, gender identity was found to be related to a variety of behaviors from performance in school to abuse in dating relationships. Among middle school children, boys and girls with a more feminine gender identity had higher marks than those with a more masculine gender identity. This was true independent of the child's sex, race, grade, subject area, or sex of teacher (Burke 1989). Among college students, males and females with a more feminine gender identity were more likely to inflict and to sustain both physical and sexual abuse in dating relationships (Burke, Stets, and Pirog-Good 1988). In each case, the behaviors were consistent with the relationship orientation and emotional expressiveness of the cultural definitions of gender-role performance.

Among middle school children, boys and girls with a more feminine gender identity have higher marks than those with a more masculine gender identity.

Because masculinity and femininity using the Burke-Tully measure are on opposite sides of a single scale, and one's gender identity is the location of the self somewhere along this dimension, it is conceptually impossible to be both masculine and feminine in one's gender identity. Androgyny, thus, cannot be a combination of masculinity and femininity as in the Spence, Helmreich, and Stapp measure or in the Bem measure. Instead, androgyny is defined by Burke (1980) as the range or span of the gender scale across which an individual is comfortable interacting in situations. The link between this definition of androgyny and notions of flexibility, openness, and so forth is quite clear. Additionally, such a conception prevents contamination of the concept of androgyny with self-esteem or social desirability, from which the Bem scale suffers.

Basic Issues and Open Questions

The biggest issue that has plagued social scientists in defining the concepts of masculinity, femininity, and androgyny has been the variety of conceptions and confusions that exist in the literature. Future research and discussion must be more careful to distinguish between masculine and feminine as applied to gender identities, gender roles, personality traits resulting from socialization practices, and genetic dispositions. Had such clarity of reference been maintained in the past, the debate between the bipolar and the dualistic conceptions of masculinity and femininity, for example, would likely not have arisen. When we distinguish between identities (bipolar distinctions between two groups) and roles (a dualistic mix of instrumental and expressive behaviors), it is clear that there is no debate. Each view is appropriate in the correct context (Spence and Helmreich 1978).

Another issue is the nature-nurture question. This is basically a false distinction, and researchers today are less prone to waste time with it. There is no way that nature and nurture can be separated one from the other. Genetic, biological differences play themselves out in a social world; social factors work with the genetic and biological beings that we are. On the other hand, the issue captures people's imagination as they ask questions like that raised by Margaret Mead (1949, p. 13) "In educating women like men, have we done something disastrous to both men and women alike, or have we only taken one further step in the recurrent task of building more and better on our original human nature?" The answer, of course, depends upon values, not upon science.

Finally, as was pointed out, the different bases of masculinity and femininity (genes, traits, roles, and identities), while not the same, are all interrelated. There is clearly some general phenomenon underlying all of this, and it needs to be understood. A first attempt at such an understanding lies in the concept of gender schema. A schema is a cognitive structure that organizes and guides an individual's perception. Bem (1981) introduced the idea or theory of a gender schema that sorts persons, attributes, and behaviors into masculine and feminine categories. She suggests that gender schema are supplied by culture as fundamental ways of dealing with information. Sex typing derives, in part, from gender-schematic processing of information on the basis of sex-linked associations derived from our culture. While it is clear that gender identities are built upon the gender schema supplied by society, it is less clear how that same gender schema colors all perceptions of social and physical reality, politicizing and polarizing the world into masculine and feminine. How and why this is the case needs to be understood.

[See also Gender; Sex Differences.]

The question of whether certain gender-related traits, roles, and identities can be strictly tied to biological sex has provided for endless debate. These female bodybuilders are engaged in an activity that challenges many gender definitions. (David Reed/Corbis)

BIBLIOGRAPHY

Bakan, David 1966 *The Duality of Human Existence.* Chicago: Rand McNally.

Bales, Robert F., and Philip E. Slater 1955 "Role Differentiation in Small Decision-Making Groups." In Talcott Parsons and Robert F. Bales, eds., *Family, Socialization and Interaction Process.* New York: Free Press.

Bem, Sandra L. 1974 "The Measurement of Psychological Androgyny." *Journal of Consulting and Clinical Psychology* 42:155–162.

——— 1975 "Sex-Role Adaptability: One Consequence of Psychological Androgyny." *Journal of Personality and Social Psychology* 31:634–643.

——— 1977 "On the Utility of Alternate Procedures for Assessing Psychological Androgyny." *Journal of Consulting and Clinical Psychology* 45:196–205.

——— 1981 "Gender Schema Theory: A Cognitive Account of Sex Typing." *Psychological Review* 88:354–364.

———, and E. Lenney 1976 "Sex Typing and the Avoidance of Cross-Sex Behavior." *Journal of Personality and Social Psychology* 33:48–54.

———, W. Martyna, and C. Watson 1976 "Sex Typing and Androgyny:Further Exploration of the Expressive Domain." *Journal of Personality and Social Psychology* 34:1016–1023.

Broverman, I. K, et al. 1972 "Sex-Role Stereotypes: A Current Appraisal." *Journal of Social Issues* 28:59–78.

Burke, Peter J. 1980 "The Self: Measurement Implications from a Symbolic Interactionist Perspective." *Social Psychology Quarterly* 43:18–29.

——— 1989 "Gender Identity, Sex and School Performance." *Social Psychology Quarterly* 52:159–169.

———, Jan E. Stets, and Maureen Pirog-Good 1988 "Gender Identity, Self-Esteem, and Physical and Sexual Abuse in Dating Relationships." *Social Psychology Quarterly* 51:272–285.

———, and Judy Tully 1977 "The Measurement of Role/Identity." *Social Forces* 55:880–897.

Foote, Nelson N. 1951 "Identification as the Basis for a Theory of Motivation." *American Sociological Review* 26:14–21.

Helmreich, Robert L., Janet T. Spence, and Carole K. Holahan 1979 "Psychological Androgyny and Sex-role Flexibility: A Test of Two Hypotheses." *Journal of Personality and Social Psychology* 37:1631–1644.

Hull, Jay G., and Alan S. Levy 1979 "The Organizational Functions of Self: An Alternative to the Duval and Wicklund Model of Self-Awareness." *Journal of Personality and Social Psychology* 37:756–768.

Kagan, Jerome 1964 "Acquisition and Significance of Sex Typing and Sex Role Identity." In Martin L. Hoffman and Lois W. Hoffman, eds., *Review of Child Development Research,* vol. 1. New York: Russell Sage Foundation.

Lindesmith, Alfred R., and Anselm L. Strauss 1956 *Social Psychology.* New York: Holt, Rinehart and Winston.

Lindsey, Linda L. 1990 *Gender Roles. A Sociological Perspective.* Englewood Cliffs, NJ.: Prentice-Hall.

Locksley, Anne, and Mary Ellen Colten 1979 "Psychological Androgyny: A Case of Mistaken Identity?" *Journal of Personality and Social Psychology* 37:1017–1031.

McCall, George J., and J. L Simmons 1978 *Identities and Interactions,* rev. ed. New York: Free Press.

Maccoby, Eleanor E. 1987 "The Varied Meanings of 'Masculine' and 'Feminine'." In June M. Reinisch, Leonard A. Rosenblum, and Stephanie A. Saunders, eds., *Masculinity/Femininity: Basic Perspectives.* New York: Oxford University Press.

———, and Carol N. Jacklin 1974 *The Psychology of Sex Differences.* Stanford, Calif.: Stanford University Press.

Mead, Margaret 1935 *Sex and Temperament in Three Primitive Societies.* New York: Dell Publishing.

——— 1949 *Male and Female: A Study of the Sexes in a Changing World.* New York: Dell Publishing.

Money, John 1987 "Propaedeutics of Diecious G-I/R: Theoretical Foundations for Understanding Dimorphic Gender-Identity/Role." In June M. Reinisch, Leonard A. Rosenblum, and Stephanie A. Saunders, eds., *Masculinity/Femininity: Basic Perspectives.* New York: Oxford University Press.

———, and A. E. Ehrhardt 1972 *Man and Woman, Boy and Girl.* Baltimore: Johns Hopkins University Press.

Osgood, Charles E., George J. Succi, and Percy H. Tannenbaum 1957 *The Measurement of Meaning.* Urbana: University, of Illinois Press.

Parsons, Talcott 1955 "Family Structure and the Socialization of the Child." In Talcott Parsons and Robert F. Bales, eds., *Family, Socialization and Interaction Process.* New York: Free Press.

———, and Robert F. Bales 1955 *Family, Socialization and Interaction Process.* New York: Free Press.

Smith, Caroline, and Barbara Lloyd 1978 "Maternal Behavior and Perceived Sex of Infant: Revisited." *Child Development* 49:1263–1265.

Spence, Janet T., and Robert L. Helmreich 1978 *Masculinity and Femininity: Their Psychological Dimensions Correlates, and Antecedents.* Austin: University of Texas Press.

Spence, Janet T., Robert L. Helmreich, and J. Stapp 1974 "The Personal Attributes Questionnaire: A Measure of Sex-Role Stereotypes and Masculinity-Femininity." *JSAS Catalogue of Selected Documents in Psychology* 4:127.

Storms, Michael D. 1979 "Sex Role Identity and Its Relationships to Sex Role Attitudes and Sex Role Stereotypes." *Journal of Personality and Social Psychology* 37:1779–1789.

Stryker, Sheldon 1968 "Identity Salience and Role Performance." *Journal of Marriage and the Family* 4:558–564.

Turner, Ralph 1968 "The Self-Conception in Social Interaction." In C. Gorden and K.J. Gergen, eds., *The Self in Social Interaction.* New York: Wiley.

Zelditch, Morris, Jr. 1955 "Role Differentiation in the Nuclear Family: A Comparative Study." In Talcott Parsons and Robert F. Bales, eds., *Family, Socialization and Interaction Process.* New York: Free Press.

– PETER J. BURKE

FILIAL RESPONSIBILITY

The term *filial responsibility* denotes the "responsibility for parents exercised by children. The term emphasizes duty rather than satisfaction and is usually connected with protection, care, or financial support" (Schorr 1980, p. 1). Although there is popular belief that the obligation of children to care for their parents has origins in antiquity which are based on widely held moral beliefs, both historical and sociological evidence suggests that neither element of this belief is true (Finch 1989; Schorr 1980).

Historical Patterns of Support

One source of the persistent belief in both the historical existence of filial responsibility and its moral derivation stems from an equally persistent belief that there was a time in the past when "the family" had a stronger sense of responsibility toward looking after its aging members (Finch 1989). However, a consistent literature on the history of families and demographic trends has emerged that refutes this belief (Laslett 1972). Central to this literature is an understanding of the effects of the demographic transition, medical advances, and changes in social and health practices that have resulted in a significant increase in the numbers of persons living into old age. Together these factors have resulted in dramatic changes in the population structure of modern societies wherein the aging segments account for a significantly higher proportion of the population than ever before. Put simply, until recent history only an extremely small segment of the population survived into an extended and dependent old age (Anderson 1980; Johansson 1977).

Furthermore, as a result of the nature of the preindustrial economy, those persons who did survive into old age were not dependent upon the goodwill or a sense of obligation on the part of their children to assure their financial support. In preindustrial economies both land and businesses that served as the family's source of sustenance were owned by the older generation and passed down to the younger generation only after the older's death. Hence, it was not the older generation who was dependent upon the younger generation; rather, it was the younger generation who was dependent upon the older generation for housing and income. What care may have been provided to parents was therefore not necessarily based on a sense of moral obligation but stemmed from economic necessity (Demos 1978; Schorr 1980).

The shift to an industrial economy changed the financial base of the family and introduced the possibility of children's independent access to financial resources.

As long as this economic basis for support existed, there was no need for filial responsibility laws (Schorr 1980; Finch 1989). Only with the introduction of an industrial economy that provided a means for children to leave the parental home and obtain an income was there a need for the community to regulate filial responsibility. Finch (1989, p. 84) notes:

> Much of the historical evidence . . . suggests that under the harsh conditions of poverty which prevailed for most people in the early industrial period, family relationships necessarily were highly instrumental, with support being offered only if there was . . . hope of mutual benefit precisely because anything else would have been an unaffordable luxury.

The shift to an industrial economy changed the financial base of the family and introduced the possibility of children's independent access to financial resources. This shift effectively emphasized the possibility of elders becoming destitute (Bulcroft et al. 1989).

Legal Mandates

Crowther (1982) argues that the legal mandate for filial responsibility which began with the Elizabethan poor laws originated in the need to keep down public expenditure. The poor laws established for the first time in history that the community would help an indigent parent only after the means of his or her child or children had been exhausted (Schorr 1980). The poor laws were not simply laws about poverty; they were laws to govern the lower class in order to keep down public expenditure. This motivation continues to underlie current laws and practices concerning the care of the elderly in both England and the United States, even when legal support for family responsibilities has been presented as a moral matter (Abel 1987; Finch 1989). Despite the moral rhetoric in which filial responsibility laws are often couched, these laws, which currently exist in some form in thirty states, emerged not as a result of moral values but in response to a threat of a growing financial burden that dependent elders posed to an industrial society (Bulcroft et al. 1989).

Perhaps this absence of a moral basis for filial responsibility laws accounts for the inconsistency among states in the statement of filial responsibility and its capricious enforcement (Bulcroft et al. 1989). Filial responsibility laws are variously located in domestic statutes, poor laws, penal codes, and human resource laws. Among the state laws there are variations in the specificity as to which members of the family are responsible and the conditions under which they are responsible. A consistent order does exist, however, that places responsibility first on spouses, second on parents, and third on children. For the most part filial responsibility as incorporated in laws is limited to financial support; and, for the most part, these laws have gone unenforced. Clearly such laws do not account for the prevalence of children as caregivers either in historical or in modern times.

Attitudes Toward Filial Responsibilities

Just as the discrepancy between the existence of filial responsibility laws and the lack of their enforcement suggests an equivocal attitude toward children's responsibilities, so results of surveys of attitudes about filial responsibility have been inconsistent. Surveys generally yield respectable percentages of responses favoring filial responsibility as long as the question is limited to ethical and general terms (Schorr 1980). However, when the question is reframed to introduce an individual's own responsibility or to force a choice between the child and other sources of support, a majority of aged persons opposed filial responsibility (Schorr 1980; Sussman 1976). Generally there has been a movement toward acceptance of the government or insurance programs as the source for financial support of the elderly. This trend is witnessed by the introduction of Social Security and Supplemental Security Income. Similarly, adult children and their parents express a preference for independent living arrangements for the two generations.

Current practices of filial responsibility correspond to these expressed preferences. For most families, the flow of financial support between generations is primarily from the older generation to the younger generation and the two generations reside in separate housing units (Sussman 1976; Mindel and Wright 1982). Furthermore, when parents and adult children live together, it is usually as a result of the needs of the younger generation or the mutual benefits for both generations. The situation of a parent moving into the home of an adult child is relatively rare and is usually associated with a need for personal care rather than for housing.

Personal Care

The most significant change in family roles and filial responsibility practices in recent history has been the assumption by large numbers of adult children of responsibility for the welfare and direct care of their parents. Although the motives that prompt adult children to care for their frail parents are not well understood, the predominance of adult children among informal caregivers is undisputed when all types and levels of assistance are considered (Stone 1987). The prevalence of children as sources of emotional support, assistance with transportation and banking matters, and help with household chores and activities of daily living has been widely documented (Brody 1985; Shanas 1979b).

There is, however, a significant difference between sons and daughters in their caregiving activities and experience. Almost uniformly studies have shown that greater numbers of daughters than of sons assist their parents with a wide range of tasks, and that daughters' predominance is especially strong with respect to direct personal assistance to their impaired parents (Horowitz 1985b; Stone et al. 1987). Daughters are more likely to provide assistance to their parents, and there is a substantial difference in the way in which sons and daughters engage in and are affected by the caregiving role. As a rule, daughters are more likely than sons to help elders with household chores, especially food preparation and laundry, as well as with personal care tasks that require "hands-on" care and daily assistance (Horowitz 1985a; Montgomery and Kamo 1989). In contrast, sons are more likely to perform home repair and maintenance tasks (Coward 1987; Stoller 1990). Indicative of the different types of tasks that sons and daughters tend to assume, daughters spend more hours each week in parent care (Montgomery and Kamo, 1989).

Caregiving Roles

The difference in the types of tasks that sons and daughters perform is related to the types of caregiving roles that the two sexes tend to assume. Daughters are not only more likely to engage in caregiving tasks but also are more likely to assume the role of primary caregiver (Abel 1987; Montgomery and Kamo 1989; Stoller 1990). As such, they are more likely to provide "routine" care over longer periods of time (Matthews and Rosner 1988; Montgomery and Kamo 1989; Stoller 1990). Sons, in contrast, assume supportive roles that require commitments over shorter periods of time and tend to be peripheral helpers within a caregiving network rather than the central actors.

Numerous explanations have been advanced to account for the observed divergence of caregiving behaviors between sons and daughters. Most of these explanations center on differences in male and female roles and differences in power within the family and within society in general (see Finley 1989). However, there is little evidence to support any of the hypothesized explanations, and none of them account for the persistence of parent care activities.

Affection and Obligation

The relatively recent emergence of the parent care role as it exists in the United States today is most often attributed to the unprecedented size of the elderly population, especially that segment requiring assistance with household and personal tasks (Stone et al. 1987). Yet the physically determined needs of parents for assistance do not fully account for the now widely documented willingness of adult children to assume caregiving roles to meet these needs (Brody 1985; Stone 1987). The persistence of these parent care activities, despite the absence of legal or economic imperatives, has often led researchers and policymakers to focus on affection as the primary source for these filial responsibility practices (Jarrett 1985). Numerous studies have noted the relationship between affection and the felt obligation to provide for parent care (Horowitz 1985b), as well as the importance of attitudes of obligation as correlates of contact with and assistance to parents (Walker et al. 1990).

For many children, affection may influence the way in which responsibilities are experienced, but these children frequently provide care simply because parents need it.

However, there is a growing literature that questions the importance of "affection" as the primary force underlying filial responsibility and/or the performance of caregiving tasks (Jarrett 1985). Repeatedly it has been shown that there can be emotional closeness between parent and child without contact or aid being given (Shanas 1979a; Walker et al. 1989). At the same time, it has been demonstrated that children who do not feel great affection for their parents are still able and willing to provide needed assistance (Walker et al. 1989, 1990). Furthermore, there is growing evidence that caregiving is governed by a plurality of motives that encompass both affection and obligation (Walker et al. 1989, 1990). For many children, affection may influence the way in which responsibilities are experienced, but these children frequently provide care simply because parents need it (Leigh 1982) or because children perceive few alternatives (Brody 1985; Birkel and Jones 1989).

Social Policy as a Source

It has been suggested that the lack of alternatives for parent care is due to existing social policy that incorporates assumptions about filial responsibility although it does not necessarily explicitly legislate this responsibility (Abel 1987; Finch 1989; Montgomery and Borgatta 1987). Specifically, as implemented and practiced, policies and programs concerned with services for the elderly in both England and the United States reflect the belief that there is a latent willingness, presumably based upon a residual sense of responsibility that can be activated. This assumption is reinforced in reality by rationing the use of scarce public services and concentrating them upon people who have no relatives providing informal care. It is also evidenced in debates among policymakers and policy analysts regarding the appropriate role of the family in the care of the elderly (Maroney 1980; Callahan et al. 1980).

Taken together, the evidence regarding filial responsibility suggests trends in laws and practice that reflect a decline in expectation for financial support of the elderly while at the same time there is a continued and growing expectation for children, especially daughters, to support parents in more direct ways (Finch 1989). Also, there is an indication that filial responsibility, as practiced in terms of both financial and direct care, stems largely from necessity and is created by social policies and practices that tend to invoke a questionable or mythical moral basis for such responsibility.

[See also Intergenerational Relations.]

BIBLIOGRAPHY

Abel, E. K. 1987 *Love Is Not Enough.* Washington, D.C.: American Public Health Association.

Anderson, M. 1980 *Approaches to the History of the Western Family 1500–1914.* London: Macmillan.

Birkel, R., and C. J. Jones 1989 "A Comparison of the Caregiving Network of Dependent Elderly Individuals Who Are Lucid and Those Who Are Demented." *The Gerontologist* 29, no. 114–119.

Brody, E. M. 1985 "Parent Care as a Normative Family Stress." *The Gerontologist* 25, no. 1:19–29.

Bulcroft, K. J. Van Leynseele, and E. F. Borgatta 1989 "Filial Responsibility Laws." *Research on Aging* 11, no. 3:374–393.

Callahan, J. J., Jr., L. D. Diamond, J. Z. Giele, and R. Morris 1980 "Responsibility of the Family for Their Severely Disabled Elders." *Health Care Financing Review,* 1 (Winter):29–48.

Coward, R. T. 1987 "Factors Associated with the Configuration of the Helping Networks of Noninstitutionalized Elders." *Journal of Gerontological Social Work* 10:113–132.

Crowther, M. A. 1982 "Family Responsibility and State Responsibility in Britain Before the Welfare State." *Historical Journal* 25, no. 1:131–145.

Demos, J. 1978 "Old Age in Early New England." In J. Demos and S. Boocock, eds., *Turning Points.* Chicago: University of Chicago Press.

Finch, J. 1989 *Family Obligations and Social Change.* Cambridge: Polity Press and Basil Blackwell.

Finley, N. J. 1989 "Theories of Family Labor as Applied to Gender Differences in Caregiving for Elderly Parents." *Journal of Marriage and the Family* 51, no. 1:79–86.

Gilligan, C. 1982 *In a Different Voice.* Cambridge, Mass.: Harvard University Press.

Horowitz, A. 1985a "Family Caregiving to the Frail Elderly." *Annual Review of Gerontology and Geriatrics* 6:194–246.

——— 1985b "Sons and Daughters as Caregivers to Older Parents: Differences in Role Performance and Consequences." *The Gerontologist* 25, no. 6:612–617.

Jarrett, W. H. 1985 "Caregiving Within Kinship Systems: Is Affection Really Necessary?" *The Gerontologist* 25, no. 1:5–10.

Johansson, S. R. 1977 "Sex and Death in Victorian England: An Examination of Age- and Sex-Specific Death Rates 1840–1910." In M. Vicinus, ed., *A Widening Sphere: Changing Roles of Victorian Women.* London: Methuen.

Laslett, P. 1972 "Introduction: The History of the Family." In P. Laslett and R. Wall, eds., *Household and Family in the Past Time.* Cambridge: Cambridge University Press.

Leigh, G. K. 1982 "Kinship Interaction over the Family Life Span." *Journal of Marriage and the Family* 44, no. 1:197–208.

Maroney, R. M. 1980 *Families, Social Services and Social Policy: The Issue of Shared Responsibility.* Washington, D.C.: Department of Health and Human Services, U.S. Government Printing Office.

Matthews, S. H., and T. T. Rosner 1988 "Shared Filial Responsibility: The Family as the Primary Caregiver." *Journal of Marriage and the Family* 50:185–195.

Mindel, C. H., and R. Wright, Jr. 1982 "Satisfaction in Multigenerational Households." *Journal of Gerontology* 37, no. 4:483–489.

Montgomery, R. J. V., and Edgar F. Borgatta 1987 "Aging Policy and Societal Values." In Borgatta and Montgomery, eds., *Critical Issues in Aging Policy: Linking Research and Values.* Newbury Park, Calif.: Sage.

Montgomery, R. J. V., and Y. Kamo 1989 "Parent Care by Sons and Daughters." In J. A. Mancini, ed., *Aging Parents and Adult Children.* Lexington, Mass.: Lexington Books/D. C. Heath.

Schorr, A. L. 1980 *Thy Father and Thy Mother . . . A Second Look at Filial Responsibility and Family Policy.* Social Security Administration Publication No. 13–11953. Washington, D.C.: U.S. Government Printing Office.

Shanas, E. 1979 "The Family as a Social Support System in Old Age." *The Gerontologist* 19, no. 2:169–174.

Stoller, E. P. 1990 "Males as Helpers: The Role of Sons, Relatives, and Friends." *The Gerontologist* 30, no. 2:228–235.

Stone, R. 1987 *Exploding the Myths: Caregiving in America.* Select Committee on Aging, House of Representatives, Publication No. 99–611. Washington, D.C.: U.S. Government Printing Office.

———, G. Cafferata, and J. Sangl 1987 "Caregivers of the Frail Elderly: A National Profile." *The Gerontolgist* 27:616–626.

Sussman, M. 1976 "The Family Life of Old People." In R. H. Binstock and E. Shanas, eds., *Handbook of Aging and the Social Sciences.* New York: Van Nostrand Reinhold.

Walker, A. J., C. C. Pratt, H. Y. Shin, and L. L. Jones 1989 "Why Daughters Care: Perspectives of Mothers and Daughters in a Caregiving Situation." In J. A. Mancini, ed., *Aging Parents and Adult Children.* Lexington, Mass.: Lexington Books/D. C. Heath.

———, 1990 "Motives for Parental Caregiving and Relationship Quality." *Family Relations* 39, no. 1:51–56.

– RHONDA J. V. MONTGOMERY

G

GAY AND LESBIAN MOVEMENT

The gay and lesbian movement in the United States refers to organized efforts to fight prejudice, discrimination, and persecution resulting from the classification of homosexuality as sin, crime, or illness. While its proponents disagree about the origins of homosexuality (whether inborn or acquired), they are united around the concept of homosexuality as a component of personal and political identity. Although historians often date the movement's origin from the June 1969 riot at the Stonewall Inn, a gay bar in New York City where patrons fought with police, the movement's origins can be traced to World War II and earlier. Gay and lesbian subcultures were present in American cities for most of the twentieth century. During World War II, however, military deployment offered homosexuals greater opportunities to meet each other, increasing the size and visibility of these subcultures and reinforcing the concept of homosexual community. Both abroad and at home lesbians benefited from the greater freedom women in general were experiencing (mobility, different work, wearing slacks), as new standards for acceptable female behavior more closely matched their own. Nonetheless, the greater visibility of homosexuals coincided with use of psychiatry in the military services to define gay people as unfit for service and encouraged the belief that homosexuality is a mental illness.

Many persons seen as gay lost their jobs, some were imprisoned, and others were subjected to "therapies" ranging from shock treatment to castration.

In the 1950s anticommunists associated homosexuality with political danger, arguing that gay people were mentally or emotionally unstable and therefore security risks; others simply equated homosexuality with communism. Many persons seen as gay lost their jobs, some were imprisoned, and others were subjected to "therapies" ranging from shock treatment to castration. In this atmosphere arose the homophile movement embodied in the Mattachine Society, founded in 1950–1951, and the Daughters of Bilitis, founded in 1955, the first sustained homosexual organizations in the United States. (The earliest known group, the Chicago Society for Human Rights, lasted only a few months in 1924–1925.) Both groups sought to unite homosexuals around social and political goals and by the late 1950s emphasized accommodation to heterosexual (straight) society while seeking support from the legal and medical professions. At the same time, other gay men and lesbians continued to develop roles by which to define themselves in relation to each other and to straight society. Butch-femme roles became prominent among working-class lesbians, and many gay men continued to dress in drag (female attire).

Homosexual organizations experienced the same tensions that characterized other movements. Coalitions such as the East Coast Homophile Organizations (ECHO) and the North American Conference of Homophile Organizations (NACHO) broadened the movement by the mid-1960s, while such groups as the Society for Individual Rights (SIR) and dissenters within older organizations advocated a more assertive stance. In the wake of the Stonewall riot, "gay liberation" built upon the growing sense of identity within the general climate of revolution. From civil rights and the New Left came tactics and ideas, while feminism and sexual liberation shared many goals and strategies with gay liberationists. The phrases "gay power" and "gay pride" emerged, and political organizing was revitalized. According to historian John D'Emilio, the two features of gay liberation were "coming out" (publicly declaring oneself a homosexual) and the development of lesbian feminism and a lesbian liberation movement. The Gay Liberation Front (GLF) represented a rejection of what liberationists saw as the homophile movement's overreliance on experts and assimilation. Out of the GLF came the Gay Activists Alliance, a less radical group devoted to reform within, which produced the National Gay Task Force (later the National Gay and Lesbian Task Force).

In the 1970s the new activism reached into higher education in the form of the Gay Academic Union, caucuses within academic organizations, student groups, and the first gay and lesbian studies courses. The concept of a gay community became important socially and politically. Bars continued as the primary locus of the movement, while symbols, styles of dress, newspapers, fiction, and even music and humor arose as part of an open gay-lesbian movement. Gay-pride parades were opportunities to unite publicly. Gay and lesbian activists scored several victories. The American Psychiatric Association removed homosexuality from its diagnostic manual and a few communities adopted antidiscrimination laws. Harvey Milk, an openly gay San Francisco supervisor, was murdered in 1978 along with Mayor George Moscone, and the light sentence given the man convicted of both shootings galvanized gay communities.

In the 1980s two factors brought setbacks for the movement, the AIDS epidemic and the hostility of conservative Christian groups, but visibility continued as the main strategy of gays and lesbians. A few entertainment and sports figures came out (movie star Rock Hudson, who died of AIDS, tennis champion Martina Navratilova, country singer k. d. lang). Gay advocates such as the Gay and Lesbian Alliance Against Defamation (GLAAD) monitored the media for tone and content, while others formed direct-action groups, such as ACT UP (AIDS Coalition to Unleash Power) and Queer Nation. After 1990 the movement focused increasingly on fighting the ban on homosexuals in the military, continuing the struggle for equal legal treatment, and promoting the idea of gay people as an economic as well as political force. In 1987 and 1993 gay people participated in marches on Washington to protest government support of discrimination in such areas as employment, housing, health care and insurance, parental rights, and adoption.

– VICKI L. EAKLOR

GENDER

Despite the enormous weight of scientific evidence that differences between women and men are deceptive (Epstein 1988), societies continue to create and maintain these differences (Hess 1990). In an effort to analyze the processes of differentiation, as well as to trace their effects and perhaps derive some policies with which to modify them, sociologists have been wrestling with the conceptualization of gender (Lorber and Farrell 1991).

Gender is the organized pattern of social relations between women and men, not only in face-to-face interaction and within the family but also in the major

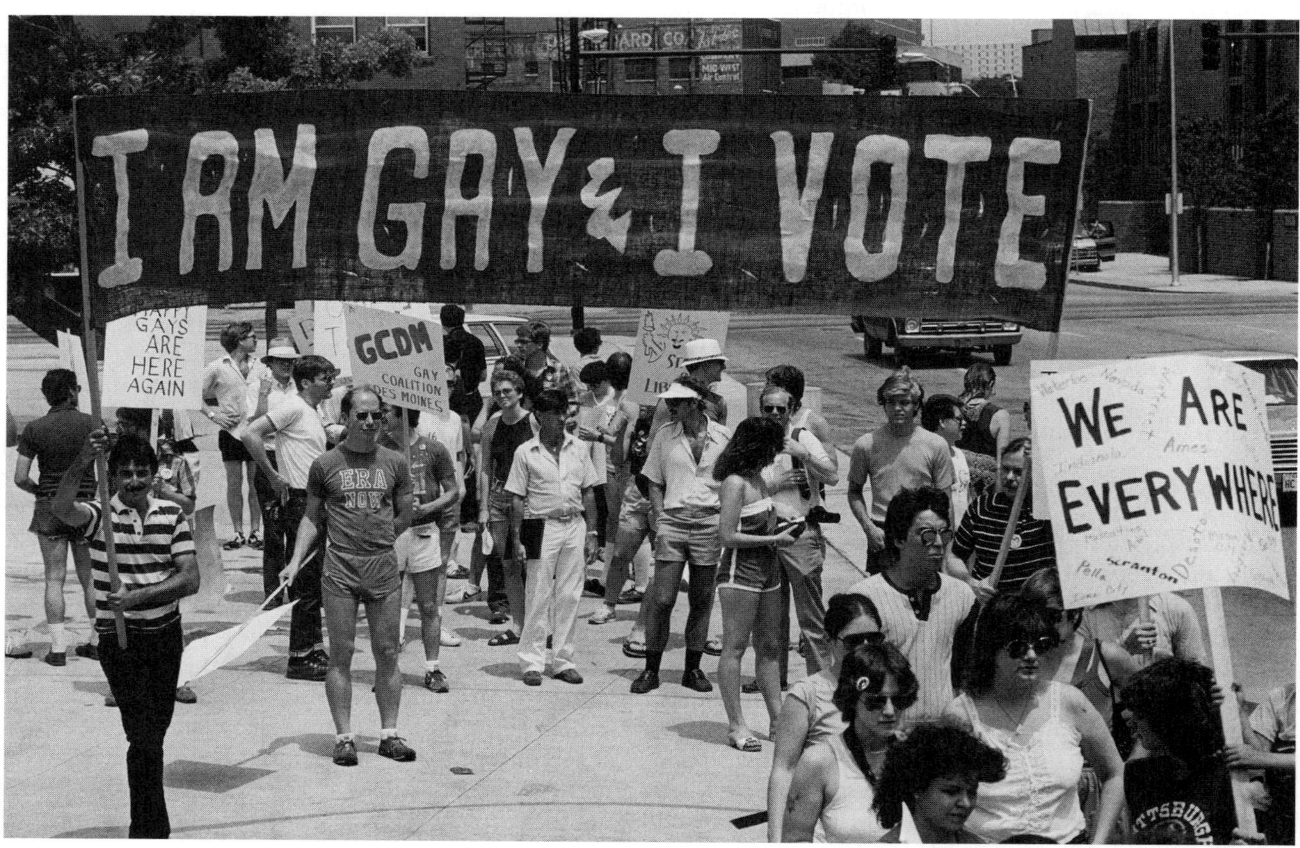

Gays and lesbians by the 1990s openly exercised their power as a political and economic force. (UPI/Corbis-Bettmann)

institutions of society, such as social class, the hierarchies of large-scale organizations, and the occupational structure (Acker 1988, 1990; Reskin 1988). In order to sustain these patterns, women and men need to be demonstrably different—they have to be perceived as clearly separable.

The social reproduction of gender in individuals sustains the gendered societal structure; as individuals act out the expectations of their gender status in face-to-face interaction, they are constructing gender and, at the same time, gendered systems of dominance and power (West and Zimmerman 1987). In most societies, women and men are not only perceived as different but are also differently evaluated, and these supposed differences in characteristics and capabilities justify the power differences between them. As Joan Wallach Scott (1988) says, "Gender is a constitutive element of social relationships based on perceived differences between the sexes, and gender is a primary way of signifying relationships of power" (p. 42).

Gender is so pervasive that, in our society, we assume it is bred into our genes. Given our naturalistic orientation, it is hard to believe that gender is constantly created and recreated out of human interaction, out of social life, and at the same time is the texture and order of that social life. Gender signs and signals are so ubiquitous that we usually fail to notice them. If we meet someone whose gender signals are ambiguous, however, and we cannot tell whether the person is a woman or a man, we are uncomfortable until we have successfully placed that person in some gender category (Devor 1990). In our society, the category can be transvestite (someone who dresses in sex-inappropriate clothing) or transsexual (someone who has had a sex-change operation); these categories confine the ambiguity without disturbing the gender dichotomy. There could be no cross-dressing if there were no distinction between what women and men should wear, and so, underneath the inappropriate clothing, the transvestite is still, we believe, a woman or a man. Actually, the transvestite is a biological female masquerading as a man or a biological male masquerading as a woman. A female-to-male or male-to-female transsexual has traversed the boundaries of gender but has ended up securely in a conventional category, the status of man or woman.

In most instances, a glance places a person in a gender category; the interaction can then proceed along lines established for people of the same or different gender, depending on the context and on other status markers, such as age, race, education, occupational position, religion. Deeply embedded in these established, taken-for-granted rules of everyday interaction are signifiers of power. In "doing gender," as West and Zimmerman (1987) point out, "men are also doing dominance and women are doing deference" (p. 146).

In all societies, the belief that women and men are inherently different provides the moral justification for allocating certain kinds of work to women and to men, and for relegating the rearing of children to women. Religion, language, education, and culture (both popular and high) teach and reinforce the society's values for women and men. The result is a gendered moral order. The acceptance of the legitimacy of this moral order by those who have lesser access to the rewards of the society (property, power, and prestige) makes the dominant moral order hegemonic.

Most analyses of gender and authority try to separate gender effects from standards of competence, demonstrated leadership, or value to the group. Legitimacy—the right to compete for or be appointed to positions of power and prestige—may be used as an intervening variable to see if the same standards apply to women and men (Ridgeway 1988). Only when women and men have the same right to compete are the same standards applied to both, evenhandedly. But where does legitimacy—the sense of the right to a position of authority—come from? Situational theorists argue that it comes from what people in face-to-face interaction bring to the encounter and also, if the dyad or group meets regularly, from the norms and expectations they build up (Stewart 1988; Wagner 1988). Under certain conditions, the group experience can counteract the effect of stereotyped expectations of women and men and even carry over into different groups (Pugh and Wahrman 1983). Given enough such counteractions, new expectations of the leadership potential of women may attain legitimacy.

However, it is difficult to separate gender, competence, leadership, power, and legitimacy. Whether the candidate for leadership is a woman or a man influences the assessment of that person's competence, potential for leadership, and right to a high-status position of power. Gender is not *added* to task-oriented and expressive behaviors; they are *defined by* gender, as in "men are rational; women are emotional" (Hochschild 1983). More research is needed on the conservatism and malleability of gendered status expectations in face-to-face encounters.

Similarly, social institutions and their established positions are so gendered (doctors and nurses, teachers and supervisors, priests and nuns) that when gender boundaries are broken, the prevailing gender dichotomy remains (references to a president, police officer, fire fighter, Supreme Court Justice need to be qualified when the incumbent is a woman; nurse, kindergarten teacher, social worker, secretary need a qualifier when referring to a man). Work and family, the main institutions of most societies, are almost completely gendered. With little rationale or uniformity from society to society, occupations, professions, and jobs within occupations and professions are divided into women's work and men's work (Roos 1985). In the family, all the main kin statuses are gendered, as signified by their names (mother, father, daughter, son, sister, brother, aunt, uncle), although lesser relationships may not be (cousin, stepchild). Here, too, gender is built into the structure of the institution and also played out in its practices, particularly the division of household labor (Berk 1985). Research examining the processes that build gender into paid work and work for the family would be more useful at this point than further studies of what kinds of jobs women and men are tracked into and what kinds of household labor each does.

Finally, gender is not just one among many elements in the stratification systems of complex societies; wherever there is unequal distribution of society's rewards, the lesser distribution of property, power, and prestige to women is considered perfectly equable. Within classes and within racial ethnic groups, whether the group's share of valued resources is larger or smaller, if there are any valued resources at all to be distributed, men monopolize them (Almquist 1987). Gender equality exists under conditions of scarce resources and no permanent property or privileges, as in gathering-hunting societies and in slums, barrios, and ghettos. In the worst human conditions—slavery, concentration camps—women suffer more than men do because they are subject to sexual exploitation and violence from the men in power.

Violence against women is a prevalent form of gendered social control that is ambiguously sanctioned.

In complex societies, the dominant social group or groups use agencies of social control (government, law, education, medicine, the military, religion) to reinforce the moral order and repress or minimize the effects of resistance and rebellion against the gendered social order. Women's responsibility for reproduction and child rearing justifies men's control over their sexuality in societies in which descent comes through the male line; in matrilineal societies, women have greater sexual freedom. The use of violence (rape and battering) against women is considered an illegitimate means of social control in societies ruled by law; nonetheless, violence against women is a prevalent form of gendered social control that is ambiguously sanctioned (Connell 1987; MacKinnon 1989). In all societies, women are encouraged or coerced into having children or not having them, depending on the needs of the group for current or future workers, and also for future mothers and future soldiers. To the extent that women are coerced into having or not having children by state policy, that policy becomes an additional form of gendered social control (Jenson 1986).

In sum, gender patterns face-to-face interaction; structures work, family, and other social institutions; determines the distribution of scarce and valued resources as well as life chances; and provides the moral legitimacy that keeps most women and men from questioning, challenging, and, to a great extent, even thinking about why these things are the way they are.

Doing Research on Gender

There have been many studies comparing women and men, but few analyzing gender itself. First, the concept is usually sex, not gender—that is, an assumed biological "fact" and not a social construction. Also, there is almost no recognition that both sex, as a social category, and gender, as a social construction, are problematic. That there are two sexes or two genders is taken as a given (Kessler and McKenna 1978); furthermore, it is assumed that any interviewer can recognize which of the two the respondent is. If a respondent claims to be a woman, it is assumed that a "normal, natural woman" is meant, but the person could instead be a permanent transvestite or a transsexual or someone in transition. It is also assumed that no one ever lies about it.

So sex and gender are twofold variables in most research—and assumed to be the cause, a prior condition, and not an effect. Another assumption is that men and women are so different they can be put into discrete categories. The researcher then usually goes on to see what difference sex, or gender, makes to the variation in the topic under study (attitudes, or voting behavior, or capacity for various kinds of work, for nurturance, etc.). If differences are found, they are taken to be the result of whatever is different about those in the category, males and females, or men or women, which is a tautology, since the researcher had to start out with the assumption of difference in order to put women and men in different categories in the first place. If differences are not found, it is concluded that sex or gender is not salient to this particular variable, without really disturbing the overall belief that women and men are, basically, different.

Another way of studying gender is to take the point of view of the subject. For the most part, in sociology today, such research is done by women about women (Smith 1987), although there have also been fine studies of men's lives (Brod 1987; Kimmel and Messner 1989). Taking the standpoint of the subject allows for insightful understanding of the perspectives of others, and others' experiences and the meanings of those experiences produce rich and complex data. The problem is that women and men vary by race and ethnicity, social class, language, culture, religion, and politics, by where they were born and where they live at the time of the research, and by sexual practices. So who can take whose standpoint, and what group of women or men can be taken as representative of "woman" or "man"?

In either quantitative or qualitative research, it might be useful to consider the components of gender when designing the research. Gender is not a unitary essence but has many components (cf. West and Zimmerman 1987) that link up as follows:

Sex—actual combination of genes and genitalia; prenatal, adolescent, and adult hormonal input; and procreative capacity (*assumed* to be congruous with one another and with sex category assignment);

Sex category—assignment at birth based on appearance of genitalia;

Sex-gender identity—sense of gendered self as a member of a sex category, sense of female or male body, socially contextualized;

Gender as process—learning, being taught, picking up cues, enacting behavior already learned to be gender-appropriate (or inappropriate if rebelling, testing), "doing gender" as a member of a sex category; and

Gender as status and structure—the individual's gender status as part of the society's structure of prescribed gender relations, especially patterns of dominance and subordination, and the gendered division of labor in the home and at paid work.

In any research on gender, the design should specify which components are being examined and should be careful to confine comparisons to the same component. That is, if women's and men's statuses are the subject of study, their sex category should not be the basis for comparison, since a transsexual has a woman's gender status but was not assigned to the sex category female at birth. The cause or the effect of gender status, therefore, cannot be reduced to biological sex.

If gender as process is the research question, it would be useful to compare the socialization of those who were assigned the sex category female, were brought up as girls, and took on the adult status of woman, with those who took on the adult status of man (for example, passed for men so they could work as men or had sex-change surgery). Similarly, one could compare subjects who were assigned the category male, were brought up as boys, and took on the adult status of man, with those who took on the adult status of woman (permanent transvestites and transsexuals). Then all of these groups could be compared with one another. In this design, there are *four to six* genders, not two.

Research on the intersection of gender status and gendered social institutions has compared women who have gender-inappropriate careers with men in the same occupation to see whether the processes that led to their occupational choices and to their achievements are similar or different (Epstein 1981; Kanter 1977; Lorber 1984). What is needed is more research that compares men in gender-inappropriate family roles with women, such as Beer's study of "house-husbands" (1982) and Risman's study of single fathers (1987).

The Intersection of Gender, Race, and Social Class

Gender has a material base in the production of food and the reproduction of children. Gender patterns and orders economic production and social reproduction, creating cooperation, reciprocal exchange, and competition for scarce resources, bonds of trust and loyalty, and also conflict. For individuals, gender, race, and social class greatly affect opportunities for a good education, well-paying jobs, and positions of authority. For the society as a whole, gender, race or ethnicity, and social class are the main building blocks of the stratification system that structures the distribution of power, prestige, and property.

The outcome of these patterns is often inferior status for all women (Chafetz 1984) and oppression for the women of the most disadvantaged races and classes, particularly in developing countries (Benéria and Stimpson 1987; Brydon and Chant 1989; Leacock and Safa 1986; Mies, Bennholdt-Thomsen, and von Werlhof 1988; Nash and Fernández-Kelly 1983). In the United States, black working-class women are subject to discrimination by white men and white women and may also suffer from sexist attitudes of black men (Hooks 1984). Similar patterns occur among Asian Americans (Chow 1987) and Hispanic Americans (Garcia 1989). Much more work is needed at this point on the intersection of gender, race, and class, particularly in family structure (Zinn 1990), and further work needs to be done on the articulation of work for the family and work for pay along the lines of Hartsock's *Money, Sex, and Power* (1983) and Sokoloff's *Between Money and Love* (1980).

Although there are many past and present instances of subversion and rebellion on the part of women and men of all groups to the strictures of gender, race, and class, societies and communities that have tried to become egalitarian have never seriously restructured the gendered division of work or family roles (Agassi 1989;

Chafetz and Dworkin 1986). Nor have they tried to structure a society where women and men, defined as different, are equal (Lapidus 1978; Stacey 1983). To do so would entail scrupulously monitoring women's and men's rights, responsibilities, and rewards to make sure neither group becomes dominant (Chafetz 1990).

The question of social orders without gender, or with significantly different gender patterns, has been explored in science fiction (LeGuin 1969; Piercy 1976), but has not been extensively discussed in social theory (Lorber 1986). While such "thought experiments" might be seen as fanciful, they would challenge the underlying assumption of most current sociological theory and research that gender and sex are interchangeable and that these variables are dichotomies.

[See also Comparable Worth; Sex Differences; Socialization.]

BIBLIOGRAPHY

Acker, Joan 1988 "Class, Gender, and the Relations of Distribution." *Signs* 13:473–497.

——— 1990 "Hierarchies, Jobs, and Bodies: A Theory of Gendered Organizations." *Gender & Society* 4:139–158.

Agassi, Judith Buber 1989 "Theories of Gender Equality: Lessons from the Kibbutz." *Gender & Society* 3:160–186.

Almquist, Elizabeth M. 1987 "Labor Market Gendered Inequality in Minority Groups." *Gender & Society* 1:400–414.

Beer, William R. 1982 *Househusbands*. New York: Praeger.

Benéria, Lourdes R., and Catherine R. Stimpson (eds.) 1987 *Women, Households, and the Economy*. New Brunswick, N.J.: Rutgers University Press.

Berk, Sarah Fenstermaker 1985 *The Gender Factory*. New York: Plenum.

Brod, Harry (ed.) 1987 *The Making of Masculinities*. Boston: Allen and Unwin.

Brydon, Lynne, and Sylvia Chant 1989 *Women in the Third World*. New Brunswick, N.J.: Rutgers University Press.

Chafetz, Janet Saltzman 1984 *Sex and Advantage*. Totowa, N.J.: Rowman & Allenheld.

——— 1990 *Gender Equity*. Newbury Park, Calif.: Sage.

———, and Anthony Gary Dworkin 1986 *Female Revolt*. Totowa, N.J.: Rowman & Allenheld.

Chow, Esther Ngan-Ling 1987 "The Development of Feminist Consciousness among Asian American Women." *Gender & Society* 1:284–299.

Connell, Robert W. 1987 *Gender and Power*. Stanford, Calif.: Stanford University Press.

Devor, Holly 1990 *Gender Blending*. Bloomington: Indiana University Press.

Epstein, Cynthia Fuchs 1981 *Women in Law*. New York: Basic Books.

——— 1988 *Deceptive Distinctions: Sex, Gender and the Social Order*. New Haven, Conn.: Yale University Press.

Garcia, Alma M. 1989 "Chicana Feminist Discourse: 1970–1980." *Gender & Society* 3:217–238.

Hartsock, Nancy C. M. 1983 *Money, Sex, and Power: Toward a Feminist Historical Materialism*. New York: Longman.

Hess, Beth B. 1990 "Beyond Dichotomy: Drawing Distinctions and Embracing Differences." *Sociological Forum* 5:75–93.

Hochschild, Arlie Russell 1983 *The Managed Heart*. Berkeley: University of California Press.

Hooks, Bell 1984 *Feminist Theory: From Margin to Center*. Boston: South End Press.

Jenson, Jane 1986 "Gender and Reproduction: or, Babies and the State." *Studies in Political Economy* 20:9–46.

Kanter, Rosabeth Moss 1977 *Men and Women of the Corporation*. New York: Basic Books.

Kessler, Suzanne J., and Wendy McKenna 1978 *Gender: An Ethnomethodological Approach*. Chicago: University of Chicago Press.

Kimmel, Michael S., and Michael M. Messner (eds.) 1989 *Men's Lives*. New York: Macmillan.

Lapidus, Gail Warshofsky 1978 *Women in Soviet Society*. Berkeley: University of California Press.

Leacock, Eleanor, and Helen I. Safa 1986 *Women's Work: Development and the Division of Labor by Gender*. South Hadley, Mass.: Bergin and Garvey.

LeGuin, Ursula K. 1969 *The Left Hand of Darkness*. New York: Ace.

Lorber, Judith 1984 *Women Physicians: Careers, Status, and Power*. New York and London: Tavistock.

——— 1986 "Dismantling Noah's Ark." *Sex Roles* 14:567–580.

———, and Susan A. Farrell (eds.) 1991 *The Social Construction of Gender*. Newbury Park, Calif.: Sage.

MacKinnon, Catharine A. 1989 *Toward a Feminist Theory of the State*. Cambridge, Mass.: Harvard University Press.

Mies, Maria, Veronika Bennholdt-Thomsen, and Claudia von Werlhof 1988 *Women: The Last Colony*. London: Zed Books.

Nash, June, and Patricia Fernández-Kelly (eds.) 1983 *Women, Men, and the International Division of Labor*. Albany: State University of New York Press.

Piercy, Marge 1976 *Woman on the Edge of Time*. New York: Fawcett Crest.

Pugh, M. D., and Ralph Wahrman 1983 "Neutralizing Sexism in Mixed-Sex Groups: Do Women Have to Be Better Than Men?" *American Journal of Sociology* 88:746–762.

Reskin, Barbara 1988 "Bringing the Men Back In: Sex Differentiation and the Devaluation of Women's Work." *Gender & Society* 2:58–81.

Ridgeway, Cecilia L. 1988 "Gender Differences in Task Groups: A Status and Legitimacy Account." In Murray Webster, Jr., and Martha Foschi, eds., *Status Generalization: New Theory and Research*. Stanford, Calif.: Stanford University Press.

Risman, Barbara J. 1987 "Intimate Relationships from a Microstructural Perspective: Men Who Mother." *Gender & Society* 1:6–32.

Roos, Patricia A. 1985 *Gender and Work: A Comparative Analysis of Industrial Societies*. Albany: State University of New York Press.

Scott, Joan Wallach 1988 *Gender and the Politics of History*. New York: Columbia University Press.

Smith, Dorothy E. 1987 *The Everyday World as Problematic*. Toronto: University of Toronto Press.

Sokoloff, Natalie J. 1980 *Between Money and Love*. New York: Praeger.

Stacey, Judith 1983 *Patriarchy and Socialist Revolution in China*. Berkeley: California University Press.

Stewart, Penni 1988 "Women and Men in Groups: A Status Characteristics Approach to Interaction." In Murray Webster, Jr., and Martha Foschi, eds., *Status Generalization: New Theory and Research*. Stanford, Calif.: Stanford University Press.

Wagner, David G. 1988 "Gender Inequalities in Groups: A Situational Approach." In Murray Webster, Jr., and Martha Foschi, eds., *Status Generalization: New Theory and Research*. Stanford, Calif.: Stanford University Press.

West, Candace, and Don Zimmerman 1987 "Doing Gender." *Gender & Society* 1:125–151.

Zinn, Maxine Baca 1990 "Family, Feminism, and Race in America." *Gender & Society* 4:68–82.

– JUDITH LORBER

GENOCIDE

The adoption in December 1948 of the United Nations Convention for the Prevention and Punishment of the Crime of Genocide held out promise of revolutionary change in the internal relations of groups within member states and in the international relations of the states themselves. But in fact the United Nations convention has contributed little to the eradication of genocide, described in the convention as an odious scourge that has inflicted great losses on humanity throughout all periods of history.

In antiquity the annihilation of peoples was common, whether as punishment for resistance, as incidental to conquest, or as a means of spreading terror.

Indeed, the recognition of genocide as a crime under international law is a recent development. In antiquity the annihilation of peoples was common enough, whether as punishment for resistance, as incidental to conquest, or as a means of spreading terror. The deity or deities might be participants, thereby sanctifying the destruction. In Europe, during the Middle Ages and later, religious conflict or challenge often resulted in the eradication of dissident sects, and pogroms were associated with periods of religious effervescence, such as the Crusades and Easter, or disaster such as famine or the Black Death.

The current rejection of genocide is a product of the Enlightenment, the influence of the natural law of human rights, the acceptance of humanitarian intervention in the internal affairs of states for the protection of persecuted minorities, the humanitarian conventions regulating warfare, and above all the revulsion against the systematic annihilation of victim peoples by Nazi Germany.

Definition

The free creation of definitions greatly impedes the comparative study of genocide. Yet a curious anomaly is that, notwithstanding this diversity, scholars working on genocide as a general phenomenon agree appreciably on their selection of case studies.

The definitions derive from the perspectives of different disciplines and under the influence of varied ideological commitments, theoretical or ethnocentric. If the emphasis is on the broad category of massacres, then an arbitrary element may enter into the selection of types of massacres deemed to constitute genocide. The scope of genocide may be extended to the one-sided mass murder of any group or fantasized social category. Or the definition may be based on the recognition of the central role of the state in most genocides, which are then viewed as state crimes, with special concern for the types of states that have engaged in genocide. Ethnocentric perspectives are associated, for example, with an excluding emphasis on the genocide perpetrated against one's own group, as in the Holocaust of Jews, and a diminished significance attached to the genocides perpetrated against other groups.

The United Nations convention defines genocide as follows:

> any of the following acts committed with intent to destroy, in whole or in part, a national, ethnical, racial or religious group, as such:
>
> (a) killing members of the group;
>
> (b) causing serious bodily or mental harm to members of the group;
>
> (c) deliberately inflicting on the group conditions of life calculated to bring about its physical destruction in whole or in part;
>
> (d) imposing measures intended to prevent births within the group;
>
> (e) forcibly transferring children of the group to another group.

This definition has the advantage of being the internationally accepted legal definition, incorporated in a convention that provides some mechanisms for punishment and prevention. It represents, moreover, a crystallization of the varied national and historical experiences and cultural perspectives of the participants in the debates on the convention, and it has now been ratified by over 100 states, though with reservations by a number of signatories.

As is to be expected in a definition arrived at on the basis of consensus and compromise, there are many defects in the final text. The phrase "in whole or in part" is imprecise, and "in part" will be interpreted here to signify an appreciable part of the victimized group. "As such," which qualifies the intent to destroy, replaces an original formulation specifying motive but gives rise to varied interpretations. The present discussion does not view motivation as a legal requisite for commission of the crime, however significant in other respects. The phrase "as such" is here interpreted to signify that the criterion for selection of the victims is membership of the targeted group. And finally, the acts specified as constituting the crime are of very different orders, but they are drawn together as expressions of the intent to destroy.

Selecting from the United Nations convention, the definition of genocide may be summarized as the deliberate destruction of a racial, ethnic, national, or religious group, in whole or appreciable part, by killing members of the group or imposing conditions inimical to survival. This links genocide to central concerns in the social sciences—namely the relations between racial, ethnic, national, and religious groups, illuminating these relations by examining them in the extremes of annihilatory violence and directing attention to the processes of polarization.

These skulls silently testify to the genocide practiced by the Khmer Rouge regime that tortured and executed tens of thousands of Cambodian people for their real or perceived political beliefs. (Kevin R. Morris/Corbis)

Typologies

Genocide is not a uniform phenomenon, save at a high level of abstraction, and its manifestations are quite varied. Typologies may be derived inter alia from motivations, objectives, or, if the emphasis is on genocide as a crime committed by states, the nature of the state.

A primary distinction must be drawn between "domestic" genocides, based on internal divisions within a society, and genocide in the course of international war, though bearing in mind that wars may be the occasion for domestic genocides, as in the Turkish genocide of Armenians in World War I and the Nazi Holocaust of Jews, Gypsies, and other groups in World War II. Moreover, the global competition between the superpowers, the so-called cold war, has been waged appreciably by intervention of the superpowers or their surrogates in the domestic conflicts of other states, thereby raising the level of annihilatory violence. The following typology of domestic genocides is based on a classification of the victims in their varied societal contexts. The first two categories may be viewed as perpetually at risk.

Small indigenous groups, often hunters and gatherers, are particularly vulnerable if they inhabit areas with exploitable resources. These are the so-called victims of progress, threatened by settlers, multinational corporations, or governmental agencies.

The second groups are often described as "middleman minorities," engaged in trade or other desirable occupations and usually of a culture and religion different from the dominant groups. Assaults on these groups are relatively unpredictable because the groups are in effect hostages to the fortunes of the host society.

The major sources of domestic genocides are the struggles by racial, ethnic, or religious groups for power, greater autonomy, secession, or more equal participation and freedom from discrimination.

Domestic genocides are phenomena of plural societies. These societies comprise different racial, ethnic, national, or religious groups within a single polity but maintain well-defined divisions between the constituent units; these divisions result from the superimposition of differences—for example, in culture, occupations, political rights, and spatial distribution of the constituent units. By reason of this superimposition, conflicts readily move from one social sector to another, thereby reverberating throughout the society and sometimes escalating to indiscriminate massacre and a point of no return. The processes of polarization in these societies are well known and readily predictable, having been studied in many societies: Algeria, Burundi, German

South-West Africa (the Hereros), northern Nigeria, Rwanda, the Sudan, the Ukraine (the "Man-Made Famine of 1932–33"), and Zanzibar.

Many genocides have been committed in the creation of plural societies by colonization and later struggles for decolonization.

Theories

Apart from theories of the plural society, which are illuminating for the analysis of domestic genocides, there are more general theories, derived from conceptions of human nature and the social conditions predisposing groups to genocide.

Two antithetical views of the biological nature of human beings or of their personality structure, as molded by the advance of civilization, have been influential in the analysis of genocide. The first, as, for example, in the works of Lorenz (1977) and Koestler (1978), emphasizes human destructiveness in human nature. Since this is presumably a constant, and since many societies have lived for long periods of time in peaceful relations with other societies and with their own inhabitants, it is clear that, even accepting the premise, analysis must be directed to the preconditions that precipitate genocide, such as the responses to the crises of traumatic events.

By contrast, a widely accepted theory postulates dehumanization of the victims, as in the animal or evolutionary analogies of colonization, or the demonization of Jews, as a necessary condition for genocide. This presupposes powerful inhibitions in human society against the mass murder of one's own kind, but it is hardly consistent with the evidence of the vast destruction of human lives in the two world wars of the twentieth century, contemporary genocides, the institutionalization of torture in many societies as a routine instrument of government, and the frequent reports of the joyous abandon of perpetrators in the annihilation of their victims.

An alternate thesis, the brutalization of the perpetrators, with its consequent detachment from empathy with the victims is certainly a major predisposing condition. In societies with highly developed technologies and bureaucracies, this brutalized detachment is promoted by distancing individuals from the killing fields, facilitating the participation of genteel strata.

Contemporary developments as manifested in the Nazi genocide and in nuclearism encourage the development of a new genocidal class, the "killing professionals," analyzed by Lifton and Markusen (1990). However, direct participation in the killing fields is by no means excluded, many Nazi doctors having applied their medical skills, with greater facility and assurance of success, to the annihilation of their helpless victims.

Functional theories, frustration and aggression, Malthusian restraints on population growth, and the expendability of redundant populations are all invoked in theories explaining genocide. The complexity of genocide, and its varied manifestations, certainly call for eclectic interdisciplinary approaches, with particular attention to predisposing conditions and processes.

Some sacred texts can readily be interpreted as legitimizing and, indeed, sanctifying genocide. Secular ideologies often serve the same function.

Ideologies, in a broad societal context of other predisposing conditions, are often a significant element in genocide, contributing to motivation or serving as justification. Differences in religion are a common element in genocide, even when the conflicts do not relate to issues of doctrine or ritual and sectarian challenge. Some sacred texts can readily be interpreted as legitimizing and, indeed, sanctifying genocide, these warrants for genocide entering as predisposing conditions. Secular ideologies, with comparable Manichean perspectives, often serve the same function.

Nuclearism and the Threat of Omnicide

At the level of process, movement along the continuum of destruction facilitates genocide in the domestic conflicts between racial, ethnic, and religious groups. The same process has also been significant in the threat to the survival of our species by nuclearism.

The habituation to mass killings in the world wars of the twentieth century, the progressive abolition of the distinction between civilians and combatants in the bombing of London, Coventry, Liverpool, and Rotterdam, and more particularly in the pattern bombings of Dresden and Hamburg and the fire bombing of Tokyo, heralded the advent of nuclearism. The atomic holocausts of Hiroshima and Nagasaki represent the most significant movement on the continuum of destruction toward total war and the rejection of humanitarian rules of war, preparing the way for the proliferation of increasingly sophisticated and annihilatory nuclear weapons. Nuclear bombs, warheads, and missiles are weapons of indiscriminate effect—genocidal weapons par excellence.

Nuclearism has produced an ultimate absurdity, analyzed by Lifton and Markusen (1990), which greatly magnifies the nuclear threat. Incredibly, we rely for protection on the proliferation of the very weapons that threaten our survival, enhancing their lethal power by the continuous invention of technological improvements, and we seek prevention in deterrence, which to be realistic implies a readiness to engage in nuclear war.

The movement toward nuclearism appears to have a momentum of its own, propelled by the involvement of leading scientists seeking to control the elemental forces of nature, and the competitive interests of giant bureaucracies and great industrial empires. Perhaps the reconciliation in the early 1990s between the superpowers holds promise for the future. This reconciliation has initiated a reversal of the superpowers' race to deploy more powerful weapons. But in the meantime, nuclear technology has proliferated beyond the superpowers' borders, and this still poses a threat to the survival of our species.

Nuclearism has produced an ultimate absurdity: we rely for protection on the proliferation of the very weapons that threaten our survival.

Lifton and Markusen seek a long-term solution in the development of "species consciousness," defined as "an expansion of collective awareness, an altered sense of self that embraces our reality as members of a single species" (1990, p. 255). It is the theoretical antithesis of the genocidal mentality activating genocide and nuclearism.

Prevention

Meanwhile, domestic genocides continue, seemingly unabated. Development projects still routinely threaten the survival of small indigenous groups. Conflicts between racial, ethnic, and religious groups take their deadly toll of lives. Starvation, a traditional weapon in forcing submission, is deployed, as in the Sudan, Somalia, and Eritrea, even when relief aid is immediately available. And there are grounds for anticipating a mounting wave of genocide as a result of the increasing pressure of population on resources, the ready availability of more lethal weapons in a vigorous national and international arms trade, and the seeming condonation implicit in the failure of preventive measures.

The United Nations convention relied appreciably on punishment as a deterrent. But to be effective, provision should have been made for universal jurisdiction, as in the crimes of piracy or the forging of currency. Instead, jurisdiction is vested in a competent tribunal of the state in which the act was committed or in an international penal tribunal whose jurisdiction has been accepted. Because no such tribunal has been established, or seems likely to be established, and because domestic genocides are generally committed by or with the complicity of governments, there is an implicit absurdity in vesting jurisdiction in the offending governments. It is only when the government has been overthrown that punitive action might be instituted, and even then the former leaders are likely to find sanctuary in other countries.

This same characteristic of genocide as primarily a government crime inhibits preventive action in the United Nations. Contracting parties to the convention may bring complaints of genocide to the International Court of Justice, but no such complaint has ever been filed, and a well-prepared initiative charging genocide by the Khmer Rouge in Cambodia foundered because no state was willing to sponsor the action. And in deliberations within the United Nations, regional and ideological alliances and calculations of national self-interest protect offending states.

Nevertheless, preventive action can be effective in the early stages of genocidal conflict, when the many infringements of human rights provide opportunities for applying restraint and alerting international opinion. And other intergovernmental forums, such as the European Assembly and Parliament, provide more favorable milieus for preventive action.

States, and particularly wealthy donor states, can apply diplomatic, trade, and other sanctions. But much of the initiative has come from the many nongovernmental organizations that have proliferated in recent years to compensate for the inadequacies of intergovernmental institutions. Their continued active involvement remains an indispensable prerequisite for effective preventive action.

[See also International Law; Race; War.]

BIBLIOGRAPHY

Becker, Elizabeth 1986 *When the War Was Over: The Voices of Cambodia's Revolution and Its People.* New York: Simon and Schuster.

Chaliand, Gerard, and Yves Ternon 1983 *The Armenians: From Genocide to Resistance.* London: Zed Press.

Chalk, Frank, and Kurt Jonassohn 1990 *The History and Sociology of Genocide.* New Haven, Conn.: Yale University Press.

Charney, Israel 1984 *Toward the Understanding and Prevention of Genocide.* Boulder, Colo.: Westview Press.

Charney, Israel (ed.) 1988 *Genocide: A Critical Bibliographic Review.* New York: Facts on File.

Dadrian, Vahakn N. 1989 "Genocide as a Problem of National and International Law: The World War I Armenian Case and Its Contemporary Legal Ramifications." *Yale Journal of International Law* 14:221–334.

Davis, Shelton H. 1977 *Victims of the Miracle: Development and the Indians of Brazil.* Cambridge: Cambridge University Press.

Drechsler, Horst 1980 *"Let Us Die Fighting": The Struggle of the Herero and the Nama against German Imperialism.* London: Zed Press.

Fein, Helen 1979 *Accounting for Genocide: National Responses and Jewish Victimization during the Holocaust.* New York: Free Press.

Grosser, Alfred 1989 *Le Crime et la mémoire.* Paris: Flammarion.

Hirsch, Herbert, and Roger Smith 1990 "The Language of Extermination." In Israel Charney, ed., *Genocide: A Critical Bibliographic Review.* New York: Facts on File.

Hovannisian, Richard G. (ed.) 1986 *The Armenian Genocide in Perspective.* New Brunswick, N.J.: Transaction Books.

Koestler, Arthur 1978 *Janus: A Summing Up.* London: Hutchinson.

Kuper, Leo 1981 *Genocide: Its Political Use in the Twentieth Century.* New Haven, Conn.: Yale University Press.

——— 1985 *The Prevention of Genocide.* New Haven, Conn.: Yale University Press.

Lemarchand, René, and David Martin 1974 *Selective Genocide in Burundi.* Report No. 20. London: Minority Rights Group.

Lemkin, Raphael 1944 *Axis Rule in Occupied Europe.* Washington, D.C.: Carnegie Endowment.

Lifton, Robert J. 1986 *The Nazi Doctors: Medical Killing and the Psychology of Genocide.* New York: Basic Books.

———, and Erik Markusen 1990 *The Genocidal Mentality: Nazi Holocaust and Nuclear Threat.* New York: Basic Books.

Lorenz, Konrad 1977. *On Aggression.* New York: Harcourt, Brace, and World.

Melson, Robert 1982 "A Theoretical Inquiry into the Armenian Massacres of 1894–1895." *Comparative Studies in Society and History* 2:481–509.

Staub, Ervin 1989 *The Roots of Evil: The Origins of Genocide and Other Group Violence.* Cambridge: Cambridge University Press.

Walliman, Isidor, and Michael N. Dobkowski (eds.) 1987 *Genocide and the Modern Age: Etiology and Case Studies of Mass Death.* New York: Greenwood Press.

– LEO KUPER

GOVERNMENT REGULATION

Government regulation is part of a larger area of study encompassing state policymaking and administration. Along with political scientists, economists, legal scholars, and historians, sociologists studying regulation contribute to an interdisciplinary growth industry. There is no uniformly agreed-upon concept of regulation that separates it from other kinds of government activity. Mitnick (1980, pp. 3–19) offers a good overview of concepts of regulation. Narrow definitions typically focus on government action affecting private business by policing market entry and exit, rate or price, and profit structures and competitive environment. Some narrow definitions confine regulatory activity to that undertaken by administrative agencies. Law enforcement by courts is excluded, no matter what its object. On the other hand, the broadest definitions conceptualize regulation as government action affecting private businesses or private citizens. "Regulation" thus becomes virtually coterminous with all government policymaking and administration, whether by legislatures, administrative agencies, or courts.

Sabatier (1975) has offered a useful definition of regulation in between these two extremes. The definition is based on the goals and content of government policy, not on the means of enforcement, and it highlights the distinction between government policing of behavior and government allocation of goods and services. Distributive (e.g., defense contracts) and redistributive (e.g., the income tax, social welfare legislation) policies allocate goods and services. Government policing is self-regulatory if it polices behavior to the benefit of the group whose behavior is policed; it is regulatory if it "seek[s] to change the behavior of some actors in order to benefit others" (Sabatier 1975, p. 307). Antipollution, antidiscrimination, consumer protection, occupational safety and health, and antitrust are examples of regulatory policies. Sociologists often distinguish between economic and social regulation. Whereas economic regulation controls market activities—for example, entry and exit or price controls—social regulation controls aspects of production—for example, occupational safety and health standards and pollution control (e.g., Szasz 1986). The term *social regulation* also is used to signal regulation that directly affects people rather, or more than, markets (Mitnick 1980, p. 15).

Regulation is dynamic. It is "an ongoing process or relation" (Mitnick 1980, p. 6) between regulator and regulated parties. Because of the nature of the legal system in the United States, regulation tends to involve the issuance and application of legal rules (Sabatier 1975, p. 307). For example, Congress has legislated federal statutes to promote competitive markets, to prevent race and gender discrimination in employment, and to increase workplace safety. These laws have been interpreted and enforced by the appropriate federal administrative agencies and by the federal courts. Federal regulatory agencies include the Interstate Commerce Commission (ICC), Federal Trade Commission (FTC), Federal Communications Commission (FCC), Securities and Exchange Commission (SEC), Equal Employment Opportunity Commission (EEOC), National Labor Relations Board (NLRB), Environmental Protection Agency (EPA), Food and Drug Administration (FDA), and Occupational Safety and Health Administration (OSHA). (See Wilson 1980b; Derthick and Quirk 1985 for case studies of many of these agencies.)

Consistent with the U.S. emphasis on legal rules as mechanisms to constrain or implement regulation, institutional forms used to reach regulatory goals are varied. Breyer (1982) provides an overview of the ideal-typical workings of various regulatory forms, including cost-of-service rate-making (e.g., public utility regulation), standard setting (e.g., administrative rule making and enforcement by the EPA and OSHA), and individualized screening (e.g., the FDA regulations pursuant to which direct food additives can be marketed). Mitnick (1980) also provides an overview of regulatory forms and contrasts regulation by directive (e.g., administrative and adjudicative rule making) with regulation by incentive (e.g., tax incentives, effluent charges, and subsidies).

Theories of Regulation

There are various general theoretical approaches to regulation. Most are concerned with regulatory origins or processes, but often they also address questions of impact, at least implicitly. Mitnick (1980) and Moe (1987) provide detailed exposition and evaluation of theories of regulation. All are theories of "interest." Marver Bernstein's classic life-cycle theory (see Mitnick 1980, pp. 45–50) argues that regulatory agencies designed in the public interest become captured by the powerful private interests they are designed to regulate. The diffuse majority favoring regulation loses interest once the initial statute is legislated, leaving the agency with few political resources to confront strong, well-organized regulatory parties with a large stake in agency outcomes.

Arguing that regulatory agencies are not simply captured by private interests but are designed from the beginning to do their bidding, Stigler (1971) and others have developed the economic theory of regulation. This theory assumes that all actors behave rationally in their self-interest and so try to use government to achieve their own ends. But economic interest does not necessarily result in effective mobilization of resources. Because "there is a mobilization bias in favor of small groups, particularly those having one or more members with sizeable individual stakes in political outcomes" (Moe 1987, pp. 274–75), concentrated business interests have great advantages over diffuse groups in mobilizing for regulatory legislation. When costs of regulation fall upon a concentrated group (e.g., a particular industry such as railroads or airlines) and benefits on a diffuse one (e.g., consumers) "capture" will result. Similarly, when benefits fall upon a concentrated group and costs on a diffuse one, regulation will be designed to benefit regulated parties.

The economic theory of regulation does not always predict capture. Generally, regulatory policies result from a chain of control running from economic groups to politicians to bureaucrats and reflect the underlying balance of power among economic groups, whatever that balance may be. Considering different distributions of regulatory costs relative to regulatory benefits, Wilson (1980a, pp. 364–72) sketches four different political scenarios for the origins of regulation. Exemplified by the origin and operation of the Civil Aeronautics Board, "client politics" is consistent with Stigler's prediction that regulation reflects the regulated industry's desires. Client politics results when costs are widely distributed and benefits are concentrated. When both costs and benefits are narrowly concentrated, both sides have strong incentives to organize and exert influence, so "interest group politics" results. Wilson views passage of the Commerce Act in 1886 as a product of conflict over rate regulation, in which interest group participants included railroads, farmers, and shippers. When both costs and benefits are widely distributed, interest groups have little incentive to form around regulatory issues because none can expect to capture most of the benefits or to avoid most of the costs. "Majoritarian politics," in which the mobilization of popular opinion is likely to play an important role, governs passage of such legislation. "Entrepreneurial politics" characterize the dynamics of mobilization around policies that offer widely distributed benefits but narrowly concentrated costs. Here, although policy opponents benefit from the mobilization bias of small numbers and have strong incentives to organize, a "policy entrepreneur" can "mobilize latent public sentiment . . . [and] put the opponents" on the defensive (Wilson 1980a, p. 370). For Wilson, antipollution laws enforced by the EPA exemplify entrepreneurial politics. Although the traditional economic theory of regulation predicts ultimate capture of agencies created by entrepreneurial politics, Sabatier (1975) argues that such agencies can avoid capture by concentrated business interests if they actively develop a supportive constituency able to monitor regulatory policy effectively.

Regulatory policies result from a chain of control running from economic groups to bureaucrats and reflect the underlying balance of power among economic groups.

Economic theories of regulation have much to say about the political dynamics of social groups seeking and resisting regulation, but they do not attend to political and regulatory institutions. In contrast, the positive theory of institutions "traces the congressional and bureaucratic linkages by which interests are translated into public policy" (Moe 1987, p. 279). It argues that political institutions and rules of the game matter. Although political actors try to create rules that lead to outcomes they favor, institutionalized rules may well be out of sync with underlying economic interests. Whether congressional regulatory policies reflect any given economic interest depends on the distribution of that interest across congressional districts, the location of Congress members who support that interest on particular committees with particular prerogatives and jurisdictions, and the rules of the congressional game.

The positive theory of institutions ordinarily begins with and focuses on the self-interest of actors in Congress and the regulatory agencies rather than of actors outside these political and regulatory institutions. It argues that legislative choice of regulatory forms as well as of regulatory content can be modeled as a function of the costs and benefits to legislators of selecting particular regulatory strategies (see, e.g., Fiorina 1982). These costs and benefits are a function of the distribution of economic interests across districts and the political-institutional rules of the game. In general, electoral incentives prevent members of Congress from placing high priority on controlling administrative agencies. The principal–agent models of control employed by the positive theory of institutions "suggest . . . that even when legislators do have incentives to control agencies toward specific ends, they are likely to meet with some measure of failure, owing to . . . conflicts of interest, information asymmetries, and opportunities for bureaucratic 'shirking'" (Moe 1987, p. 281). Game-theoretic models of regulatory enforcement developed in this theory indicate ample opportunity for the capture of regulators by regulated parties (Ayres and Braithwaite 1989). However, where some forms of capture are economically undesirable, others are economically (Pareto) efficient.

Other theoretical perspectives used by sociologists to study regulation include various forms of neo-Marxist political economy or class theory (see Levine 1988; Yeager 1990) and the political-institutional view developed by Theda Skocpol and others (Weir, Orloff, and Skocpol 1988). Where the former parallels the economic theory of regulation in focusing on the organization and mobilization of nongovernmental actors—specifically classes and segments of classes—in support of their interests, the latter parallels the positive theory of institutions in stressing the import of political structures and rules of the game. But in contrast to economic and positive theories, which largely model comparative statics (Moe 1987), class and political-institutional theories focus on historical dynamics.

Political institutionalists stress, for example, the importance of feedback from prior to current regulatory policies and of political learning by government actors. Class theorists stress how regulatory enforcement and cycles of regulation and deregulation evolve over time in response both to the structural constraints of a capitalist economy and to active struggles over regulation by classes and class segments. For example, Yeager (1990) argues that because government depends on tax revenues from the private accumulation of capital, it tends to resolve conflict conservatively over such negative consequences of production as air and water pollution, so as not to threaten economic growth. Many aspects of regulatory processes make it likely that laws passed against powerful economic actors will be limited in impact or will have unintended effects that exacerbate the problems that initially caused regulation.

The effectiveness of regulatory statutes may be limited by implementation decisions relying on cost–benefit considerations because ordinarily costs are more easily determined than benefits and because cost–benefit analyses assert the primacy of private production. Moreover, government relies upon signals from private business to gauge when regulation is preventing adequate economic growth. Limited effectiveness of regulation also results from enforcement procedures tilted in favor of regulated parties that have the technical and financial resources needed to negotiate with agency officials. Corporate organizational forms encourage regulatory leniency and negotiations regarding compliance; corporate officials are seldom prosecuted for criminal violations because the corporate form makes it difficult to locate individual culpability. Because courts emphasize proper legal reasoning when reviewing agency decisions, regulatory agencies may focus on procedure rather than substance. This too tilts enforcement toward the interests of regulated parties. Finally, because no unit of government has complete control over any given policy from legislation through funding and implementation, parties bearing the cost of regulation need thwart regulation at only one point in the process, while supporters of regulation must promote it effectively at all points. In implementation, advocates of tough enforcement are likely to lose to more resource-rich segments of business seeking to limit regulation (Yeager 1990).

Notwithstanding forces that load regulatory processes in favor of the regulated business community and particularly the larger, more powerful corporations at the expense of smaller firms, consumers, environmentalists, and labor, class theorists also see limits on regulatory leniency and on the success of deregulatory movements by business. For example, Yeager (1990) argues that antipollution enforcement biased toward large corporations dominating the U.S. economy will reproduce both the dominance of this business segment and large-scale pollution. Economic growth facilitated by lenient enforcement is accompanied by technological development that fosters both higher pollution risks and greater capacity to detect pollution. Regulatory ineffectiveness may lead to a loss of legitimacy for government as the public responds to higher risk and to perceived governmental failure by pressuring for additional antipollution efforts.

Finally, although the concept of interest is central to theories of regulation, sociologists studying regulation are sensitive to the causal role of norms and ideas as well as of economic and political interests. Ayres and Braithwaite (1989) have approached the problem of regulatory capture with a synthesis of economic interest and socialization mechanisms. Seeking a social framework to facilitate economically efficient forms of capture while deterring inefficient capture, they point to benefits obtainable if all participants in regulatory processes that empower public interest groups adhere to a culture of regulatory reasonableness. For example, social and self-disapproval sanctions in a regulatory ethic that is firm but reasonable will inhibit regulators from capitulation to law evasion by industry and from punitive enforcement when industry is complying with regulatory law. Yeager (1990) views limits on regulatory law as a function of prevailing systems of cultural belief as well as of class and group relations. Notions of regulatory responsiveness and reasonableness are negotiated in enforcement interactions between regulators and regulated parties within an overall cultural framework that attributes moral ambivalence rather than unqualified harm to regulated conduct. This facilitates adoption of a technical orientation to solving "noncompliance" problems rather than of a more punitive approach. Because the regulation of business has to be constantly justified within U.S. culture, administering regulation itself becomes morally ambivalent. This also contributes to less aggressive enforcement.

Empirical Studies of Regulation

Empirical research on regulation includes studies of regulatory origins (e.g., Sanders 1981; 1986; Steinberg 1982), processes (e.g., Moe 1987; Yeager 1990), and impact (e.g., Beller 1982; Mendeloff 1979). There also are studies of deregulation (e.g., Derthick and Quirk 1985; Szasz 1986). Studies of processes look at the evolution of regulatory forms (e.g., Stryker 1989; 1990) as well as of the substance of regulatory rules (Melnick 1983; McCammon 1990). Researchers employ a variety of methodologies, from quantitative assessment of causes and consequences of regulation (e.g., Steinberg 1982; Mendeloff 1979) or models of regulatory processes (e.g., Yeager 1990) to qualitative, historical, and comparative accounts of regulatory evolution (e.g., Sanders 1981; Stryker 1990; Moe 1987). It is difficult to generalize about findings from empirical studies of regulation. It is clear, however, that (1) no general theory or perspective on regulation enjoys unqualified support when stacked up against the variety and complexity of actual regulatory experiences; and (2) all theories have something to offer the empirical analyst.

Political structures and rules of the game matter because they are the mechanisms through which groups must translate their interests into regulatory policy.

First, economic interests and resources are major, but they are not the sole, determining factor of the dynamics of political struggles over regulatory origins and administration (Sanders 1986; Stryker 1989; 1990; Yeager 1990; Szasz 1986; Moe 1987). Political structures and rules of the game matter because they are the mechanisms through which economic and social actors must translate their interests into regulatory policy (Moe 1987). But for legislative, administrative, and judicial participants in policy processes, these institutional mechanisms also create independent interests in, and resources for, regulatory policy-making. Sanders (1981) shows that the regulation of natural gas has been a function of four sets of regionally based economic interests, including gas producer regions of the United States and gas deficit consumer regions, as well as of electoral rules and structures. Regulatory outcomes have resulted from a dynamic relationship among political actors who reflect the changing market positions of their constituents. "The potential for sectional conflict is exacerbated by the territorial basis of elections, the weakness of the party system, and a federal structure that not only encloses different political cultures and legal systems, but also supports fifty sets of elected officials sensitive to encroachments on their respective turfs" (Sanders 1981, p. 196). Current regulatory structures and policies do have feedback effects constraining and providing opportunities for subsequent regulatory policies as well as for subsequent action by parties with interests at stake in regulation (see, e.g., Sanders 1981; Steinberg 1982; Stryker 1990).

Second, the legal structures and culture through which most regulation is administered in the United States significantly shape regulatory processes and outcomes. For example, Melnick (1983) shows how the narrow, highly structured, reactive, and adversarial legal processes through which antipollution enforcement takes place in the United States have led to court decisions that simultaneously extend the scope of EPA programs and lessen agency resources for achieving antipollution goals. Appellate judges tend to promote stringent antipollution standards because they are removed from local concerns and are likely to be inspired by broad public goals. In a different institutional location, trial judges observe the impact on local businesses and citizens of imposing strict regulation. Their flexibility in response to the perceived harm of strict regulation generates an equity-balancing enforcement that counteracts what is accomplished in standard setting.

Third, regulatory implementation is influenced by internal agency politics as well as by the agency's external environment. For example, Stryker (1989; 1990) has shown how, in conjunction with class and political-institutional factors, intra-NLRB conflict between agency economists and lawyers over the proper administrative use of social science caused Congress to abolish the NLRB's economic research unit. Katzmann (1980) has indicated how internal jockeying by economists within the FTC changed enforcement priorities and outcomes through the 1970s.

Fourth, regulation often has unintended effects. Yeager (1990) shows how EPA sanctioning decisions and processes, while rational in the face of economic, political, and legal constraints on the agency, reproduce private sector inequality by favoring large corporations that have financial and technical resources. Large companies have greater access to agency proceedings than do small companies. Agency proceedings often change antipollution requirements in favor of regulated firms so that ultimately large corporations have fewer pollution violations. In decisions to apply the harshest sanctions—criminal and civil prosecutions—the EPA may well avoid tangling with the most resource-rich firms, for fear of losing in court. Melnick (1983, p. 354) indicates a similar dynamic. Ostensibly neutral procedures, then, create inequitable law application and also may help reproduce the problems that led to the initial antipollution legislation.

Fifth, although capture of administrative agencies by regulated parties can and does occur (see Sabatier 1975; Sanders 1981), it need not. Enactment of regulatory legislation also can lead to cycles of aggressive enforcement alternating with periods of capture or, similarly, to enforcement that oscillates between or among the interests at stake in regulation or between periods of regulation and deregulation. For example, over time, FTC enforcement has alternated between favoring big or small business and core or peripheral economic regions of the country (Stryker 1990). Sanders' (1981) study of natural gas regulation shows that initial federal legislation mixed the goals of consumer protection and of industry promotion. Federal Power Commission interaction with its environment did not result in stable capture by gas producers but rather in oscillation between "capture" by gas consumers and capture by gas producers. Clearly, consumers, labor, and other subordinate groups can and have benefited from regulation (see, e.g., Steinberg 1982; Sanders 1981; Stryker 1989). But the political economy of capitalism also sets structural and cultural limits to these benefits (Szasz 1986; McCammon 1990; Yeager 1990).

A major challenge to theories and empirical research in the future is to model the historical dynamics of various types of regulation. Ideally, the juxtaposition of abstract theory and concrete, historical research can lead to integrated theories of regulatory origins, processes, and impact. Such theories must be sensitive to economic and organizational interests and resources, to political structures and rules, and to regulatory cultures. They also must be sensitive to periods or cycles in which different economic or institutional arrangements, incentives, and constraints operate and to feedback effects from past to future regulatory policies and processes.

[See also Bureaucracy.]

BIBLIOGRAPHY

Ayres, Ian, and John Braithwaite 1989 "Tripartism, Empowerment, and Game-Theoretic Notions of Regulatory Capture." American Bar Foundation Working Paper 8902. Chicago: American Bar Foundation.

Beller, Andrea H. 1982 "Occupational Segregation by Sex: Determinants and Changes." *Journal of Human Resources* 17:371–392.

Breyer, Stephen 1982 *Regulation and Its Reform.* Cambridge, Mass.: Harvard University Press.

Derthick, Martha, and Paul Quirk 1985 *The Politics of Deregulation.* Washington D.C.: Brookings Institution.

Fiorina, Morris P. 1982 "Legislative Choice of Regulatory Forms: Legal Process or Administrative Process?" *Public Choice* 39:33–66.

Katzmann, Robert A. 1980 *Regulatory Bureaucracy: The Federal Trade Commission and Antitrust Policy.* Cambridge, Mass.: MIT Press.

Levine, Rhonda 1988 *Class Struggle and the New Deal: Industrial Labor, Industrial Capital, and the State.* Lawrence: University of Kansas Press.

McCammon, Holly J. 1990 "Legal Limits on Labor Militancy: U.S. Labor Law and the Right to Strike since the New Deal." *Social Problems* 37:206–229.

Melnick, R. Shep 1983 *Regulation and the Courts: The Case of the Clean Air Act.* Washington D.C.: Brookings Institution.

Mendeloff, John 1979 *Regulating Safety: An Economic and Political Analysis of Occupational Safety and Health Policy.* Cambridge, Mass.: MIT Press.

Mitnick, Barry M. 1980 *The Political Economy of Regulation: Creating, Designing and Removing Regulatory Forms.* New York: Columbia University Press.

Moe, Terry 1987 "Interests, Institutions, and Positive Theory: The Politics of the NLRB." *Studies in American Political Development* 2:236–299.

Sabatier, Paul 1975 "Social Movements and Regulatory Agencies: Toward a More Adequate—and Less Pessimistic—Theory of 'Clientele Capture'." *Policy Sciences* 6:301–342.

Sanders, M. Elizabeth 1981 *The Regulation of Natural Gas: Policy and Politics, 1938–78.* Philadelphia: Temple University Press.

——— 1986 "Industrial Concentration, Sectional Competition, and Antitrust Politics in America, 1880–1980." *Studies in American Political Development* 1:142–214.

Steinberg, Ronnie 1982 *Wages and Hours: Labor and Reform in Twentieth-Century America.* New Brunswick, N.J.: Rutgers University Press.

Stigler, George 1971 "The Theory of Economic Regulation." *Bell Journal of Economic and Management Science* 2:3–21.

Stryker, Robin 1989 "Limits on Technocratization of the Law: The Elimination of the National Labor Relations Board's Division of Economic Research." *American Sociological Review* 54:341–358.

——— 1990 "A Tale of Two Agencies: Class, Political-Institutional, and Organizational Factors Affecting State Reliance on Social Science." *Politics and Society* 18:101–141.

Szasz, Andrew 1986 "The Reversal of Federal Policy Toward Worker Safety and Health." *Science and Society* 50:25–51.

Weir, Margaret, Ann Shola Orloff, and Theda Skocpol 1988 "Understanding American Social Politics." In M. Weir, A. Orloff, and T. Skocpol, eds., *The Politics of Social Policy in the United States.* Princeton, N.J.: Princeton University Press.

Wilson, James Q. 1980a "The Politics of Regulation." In J. Q. Wilson, ed., *The Politics of Regulation.* New York: Basic Books.

———, ed. 1980b *The Politics of Regulation.* New York: Basic Books.

Yeager, Peter 1990 *The Limits of Law: The Public Regulation of Private Pollution.* Cambridge: Cambridge University Press.

– ROBIN STRYKER

GROUP PROBLEM SOLVING

From the early 1900s social psychologists have been interested in the effect of the presence of other persons on an individual's behavior in problem solving and in other forms of activity. By the 1920s experiments were performed to observe problem solving in groups (Hare 1976, pp. 384–395). The comparison of the individual problem solver with a group has continued through the present day since there are economic and social costs in maintaining a group to solve problems. Thus, the question remains, for what types of problems are individuals best able to find a solution and for what types is it best to have a group? In answer to this question, a summary of research comparing individuals and groups will be presented first, followed by a comparison of different types of groups (Hare 1976, chaps 14, 15; Hare et al. 1991, chaps 8, 11, 12).

Individual Versus Group

For many group tasks an individual is first required to reach an individual decision or perform some individual activity before sharing or combining the individual product with that of other group members to form a group decision or a group product. Thus, the first phase of a group task is often carried out by individuals in a group situation. Any effect of the presence of other persons on an individual's activity becomes important at this time. A person performing an individual task in the presence of others may do less well, as well, or better than when performing alone. Zajonc (1965) hypothesized that, when subjects are aroused by the presence of others, well-learned or easy (hence dominant) responses would be enhanced by the presence of others, while performance on novel, poorly learned, or complex tasks would deteriorate because the dominant response would be to make errors. Arousal may be increased because of a drive based on survival, or knowledge that others may reward or punish behavior, or because the others distract the subject's attention and it becomes necessary to deal with both the task and the distraction. The performance of an individual in the presence of others is lower if the others interfere with the activity in some way and higher if the others provide high-performance role models.

For research comparing the productivity of an individual with that of a group, the task has to be one that is capable of being performed by an individual. There would be no contest if the task required a set of actions, to be performed simultaneously, that would be impossible for an individual. Thus, we should not be surprised to find that, for these types of problem-solving situations, an individual can be just as effective as a group.

When individuals are compared with groups on the same task, groups are generally found to be better than the average individual but seldom better than the best (Hill 1982). The productivity of the group tends to be less than that of the same number of individuals if no division of labor is required, if there are problems of control, or if the group develops a norm against high productivity. In terms of the number of individual hours required for a task, an individual is usually more productive than a group. When groups appear to be better than individuals, part of the group effect is simply having a larger number of persons to remember facts, identify objects, or produce ideas, especially for tasks requiring low levels of creativity. The average of a number of judgments is usually more accurate than that of a single individual. In addition, the result of a group decision by majority opinion may be more accurate than that of the average of the same number of individuals because the majority decision will not include deviant opinions that would be included in the average.

The fact that groups do better than individuals on difficult and complex tasks, requiring high levels of creativity, may result from having at least one skilled problem solver in the group (Laughlin and Futoran 1985). This is especially true for puzzles for which the correct answer is obvious once one person discovers it. Thus, "truth" wins the decision. Groups may do less well if the type of feedback they are given makes it difficult to locate their errors.

Individuals' productivity in groups may be lower if they engage in "social loafing" and put in less effort than they would in doing the same task on their own (Latané, Williams, and Harkins 1979). This is more likely to happen if there is shared responsibility for the outcome, if the individuals believe their efforts are dispensable or cannot be identified, or if their motivation is low. These effects are more likely to result with tasks requiring low levels of creativity.

The group process called "brainstorming" was developed as a method of enhancing creativity in a group by having individuals generate ideas without criticism from other group members. However, as with other tasks, sets of individuals working alone produce more ideas than the same number of persons working in a group (Street 1974). Part of the problem in groups is a "production block" that results when group members use valuable time as they take turns talking (Diehl and Stroebe 1987). For both individuals and groups it is easier to produce ideas if there is no limit on their practical usefulness.

Several systems have been suggested to take advantage of the problem-solving abilities of a number of individuals without having them participate in a group discussion. In these "nominal" groups individual judgments are combined by some system of averaging (Rohrbaugh 1981).

Some research continues to explore the possibility that individuals will make more "risky" decisions when they participate in group discussion. However, the body of research indicates that the factors that influence "choice" in a group are the same as those that influence any other type of behavior, namely attributes of the situation, the group, and the individual (Isenberg 1986). Individual choice shift as a result of group discussion is influenced by social comparison and persuasive argumentation. The process of social comparison appears to involve an exaggerated perception of the group norm on the part of individual members or a shift to a position more extreme than the group norms (overconformity). Group members are also found to be sensitive to the number of arguments in a particular direction as well as to the novelty and persuasiveness of the arguments. Some norms and arguments may be sex- or personality-linked and thus only have an effect in particular contexts or with particular tasks.

Group Versus Group

Productive groups have a commitment to a clear goal and a combination of personalities, skills, structure, role assignment, morale, and problem-solving experience that is appropriate for the task (McGrath 1984). Although competition between members may result in higher total output, it may also result in lower member satisfaction. However, if the group members are interdependent, and some cooperation is necessary, then competition will lower efficiency (Rosenbaum et al. 1980).

Groups composed of individuals whose personality traits enable them to take initiative, act independently, and act compatibly with other members will be more productive. When possible, group members will develop a group structure that is compatible with their personalities. For example, members who value authority will create a bureaucratic structure, and those who value intimate relations will create a collaborative structure (Friedlander and Green 1977). When a structure is imposed on a group, productivity will be higher when the structure fits the personality characteristics.

High cohesiveness in a group, measured by members' desire to belong to the group, is associated with high productivity.

High cohesiveness, measured by members' desire to belong to the group, is associated with high productivity. In sports groups, group success leads to a further increase in cohesiveness.

For a discussion task, a five-member group is optimal (Bales 1954; Yetton and Bottger 1983). In general, groups will be less efficient if they have either fewer or more members than those actually required for the task.

Productivity is increased if group members have appropriate information, adequate time for task completion, and a communication network that allows for maximum communication. It usually helps to have a leader designated to coordinate group activity, unless group members are accustomed to sharing the coordination functions. Training for the group task, feedback about the performance, or previous experience with the same task results in improved performance.

A variety of decision-making rules have been suggested for increasing group efficiency. All have the effect of leading members to a more systematic consideration of the facts and members' abilities. For example, Janis (1982) has labeled as "group think" defective policy planning by political decision-making groups. This phenomenon can be avoided if measures are taken to ensure that all negative information is thoroughly considered and group members are given a second chance to express doubts. As a safeguard, more than one set of members and experts may be asked to reach a decision, and the results could be compared.

A decision-making rule that calls for a majority agreement and one that requires unanimity (all members have, or at least agree to, the same opinion) usually result in the same decision. However, a decision made by consensus (members unite in their support of a decision after considering the needs and interests of the individual members) has been viewed as superior to majority rule in terms of decision quality, valuing of all members, and conflict resolution, although a decision may take longer to reach (Hare 1982, pp. 146–154).

Research on the decisions of juries has been conducted using simulations (Tindale and Davis 1985). In much of the research no actual interaction between the "jurors" occurs. Typically a court case is compiled with variations in the sex or apparent guilt of the accused. Subjects are then asked to give their verdicts. Aside from the facts that the decision is about another human being, leading to more sympathy for the defendant of one's own sex, and a greater certainty of guilt and willingness to convict if the subject has had actual jury experience, the results of simulated jury deliberations are similar to those of other task groups. It is easier for a jury to reach a decision under a majority decision rule than one requiring a unanimous decision, although under the majority rule there may be a dissatisfied minority. After deliberation, individuals' opinions may become polarized. The initial distribution of opinions among the members of a jury is a good predictor of the final outcome.

As noted in the comparison of individual and group decisions, when the cost of bringing group members together is high, a decision method that combines individual opinions statistically may produce satisfactory solutions. Even without a conscious decision rule, when the answer to a problem is immediately evident, once it has been proposed by one member, the answer will be accepted by the group (the case where "truth wins"). In laboratory groups, when no decision rule is specified, members seem to use an "equi-probability" scheme in which each strategy advocated by a member has an equal probability of being selected (Davis, Hornik, and Hornseth 1970). Group members also try to be fair, allowing most members to reach their own level of aspiration. Resulting decisions are often the median of the individual opinions.

Group success tends to be attributed to the skill and effort of the members. Opposing teams or other external features are likely to be blamed for failure.

For additional reviews of the literature on group problem solving, see Brandstätter, Davis, and Stocker-Kreichgauer (1982); Davis and Stasson (1988); Kaplan (1989); McGrath (1984); McGrath and Kravitz (1982); and Silver, Cohen, and Rainwater (1988).

BIBLIOGRAPHY

Bales, Robert F. 1954 "In Conference." *Harvard Business Review* 32:44–50.

Brandstätter, Hermann, James H. Davis, and Gisela Stocker-Kreichgauer, eds. 1982 *Group Decision Making.* London: Academic Press.

Davis, James H., John Hornik, and John P. Hornseth 1970 "Group Decision Schemes and Strategy Preferences in a Sequential Response Task." *Journal of Personality and Social Psychology* 15:397–408.

Davis, James H., and Mark F. Stasson 1988 "Small Group Performance: Present Research Trends." *Advances in Group Processes* 5:245–277.

Diehl, Michael, and Wolfgang Stroebe 1987 "Productivity Loss in Brainstorming Groups: Toward the Solution of a Riddle." *Journal of Personality and Social Psychology* 53:497–509.

Friedlander, Frank, and P. Toni Green 1977 "Life Styles and Conflict-Coping Structures." *Group and Organization Studies* 2:101–112.

Hare, A. Paul 1976 *Handbook of Small Group Research.* New York: Free Press.

——— 1982 *Creativity in Small Groups.* Beverly Hills, Calif.: Sage.

———, Herbert H. Blumberg, Martin F. Davies, and M. Valerie Kent 1991 *Small Group Research: A Handbook.* Norwood, N.J.: Ablex Publishing Co.

Hill, Gayle W. 1982 "Group Versus Individual Performance: Are *N* + 1 Heads Better Than One?" *Psychological Bulletin* 91:517–539.

Isenberg, Daniel J. 1986 "Group Polarization: A Critical Review and Meta-Analysis." *Journal of Personality and Social Psychology* 50:1,141–1,151.

Janis, Irving L. 1982 *Groupthink: Psychological Studies of Policy Decisions and Fiascos.* Boston: Houghton Mifflin.

Kaplan, Martin F. 1989 "Task, Situational, and Personal Determinants of Influence Process in Group Decision Making." *Advances in Group Processes* 6:87–105.

Latané, Bibb, Kipling Williams, and Stephen Harkins 1979 "Social Loafing." *Psychology Today* October, pp. 104–110.

Laughlin, Patrick R., and Gail C. Futoran 1985 "Collective Induction: Social Combination and Sequential Transition." *Journal of Personality and Social Psychology* 48:608–613.

McGrath, Joseph E. 1984 *Groups: Interaction and Performance.* Englewood Cliffs, N.J.: Prentice-Hall.

———, and David A. Kravitz 1982 "Group Research." *Annual Review of Psychology* 33:195–230.

Rohrbaugh, John 1981 "Improving the Quality of Group Judgment: Social Judgment Analysis and the Nominal Group Technique." *Organizational Behavior and Human Performance* 28:272–288.

Rosenbaum, Milton E., Danny L. Moore, John L. Cotton, Michael S. Cook, Rex A. Hieser, M. Nicki Shovar, and Morris J. Gray 1980 "Group Productivity and Process: Pure and Mixed Reward Structures and Task Interdependence." *Journal of Personality and Social Psychology* 39:626–642.

Silver, Steven D., Bernard P. Cohen, and Julie Rainwater 1988 "Group Structure and Information Exchange in Innovative Problem Solving." *Advances in Group Processes* 5:169–194.

Street, Warren R. 1974 "Brainstorming by Individuals, Coacting and Interacting Groups." *Journal of Applied Psychology* 59:433–436.

Tindale, R. Scott, and James H. Davis 1985 "Individual and Group Reward Allocation Decisions in Two Situational Contexts: Effects of Relative Need and Performance." *Journal of Personality and Social Psychology* 48:1148–1161.

Yetton, Philip, and Preston Bottger 1983 "The Relationships Among Group Size, Member Ability, Social Decision Schemes, and Performance." *Organizational Behavior and Human Performance* 32:145–159.

Zajonc, Robert B. 1965 "Social Facilitation." *Science* 149:269–274.

– A. PAUL HARE

HEALTH AND ILLNESS BEHAVIOR

Health behavior usually refers to preventive orientations and the positive steps people take to enhance their physical well-being and vitality. Traditionally, work in health behavior has focused on the use of preventive services such as immunizations, medical checkups, hypertensive screening, and prophylactic dentistry (Becker 1974). It also includes research on such behaviors as cigarette smoking, substance abuse, nutritional practices, and exercise.

The conventional approach to health behavior has been limited, focusing on the origins of particular behaviors damaging to health and strategies to modify them. The most widely used general model—the health belief model—conceptualizes preventive health action within a psychological cost-benefit analysis (Rosenstock 1974). Behavior change is seen as following motives that are salient and perceived as yielding valuable benefits in situations where people have conflicting motives. An important component of the model involves cues to action, since an activating stimulus often appears to be necessary in the initiation of a new behavioral sequence. Over the years, this model has been expanded (Becker and Maiman 1983), but it serves more as an organizing framework for study of preventive health behavior than as a successful predictive model. Most studies applying the model achieve only modest success in prediction.

Efforts to develop a general theory are limited by the fact that behavior conducive to health derives from diverse and sometimes conflicting motives. The correlations among varying positive health practices tend to be modest, although there are clusters of behaviors (such as smoking, marijuana use, and alcohol consumption) that are somewhat more highly intercorrelated (Mechanic 1979; Langlie 1977). Nevertheless, there is no simple identifiable positive health orientation that can serve as a basis for promoting risk aversion and health maintenance.

The lack of such a general orientation results because most behaviors with important implications for health arise from motives not related to health and are significantly programmed into the daily patterns and institutional life of communities and families (Mechanic 1990). Health-protective behaviors that are consequences of accepted, everyday, conventional activities require neither conscious motivation nor special efforts to be sustained. The favorable health experience of Mormons, for example, is a product of their belief systems and patterns of activity reinforced by the way of life of this cultural community (Mechanic 1990).

One implication is that promoting health is more a matter of changing culture and social structure than of modifying personal motives or intentions. Patterns of behavior that depend on sustained conscious motivation are less stable than those that are a natural consequence of the accepted norms and understandings within a community. Expectations not only affect the prevalence of varying behaviors but also establish constraints on the acquired behaviors of children and adolescents. Changes in the last decade in the social constraints on smoking, and the growing unacceptability of smoking in varying social contexts, may have more significance than any program to change personal behavior.

Although there is no evidence for a unitary health orientation, some social factors, particularly socioeconomic status (SES), predict good outcomes across a wide range of health indicators (Bunker, Gomby, and Kehrer 1989). Persons of higher SES have less morbidity and lower mortality, are less likely to smoke and abuse drugs, more readily seek and use preventive health opportunities, and are more interested in health and acquire more information about it. Across nations, education is the most powerful predictor of health outcomes, particularly maternal education—a factor crucial for the reduction of infant mortality and maintenance of child health (Caldwell 1986). The precise ways in which SES affects these outcomes are not understood, although there are many plausible hypotheses. Beyond the income advantages and related opportunities that education commonly brings, schooling also enhances knowledge, self-concept, sense of control, personal autonomy, and social participation. Education is also the single best predictor of "psychological modernity," an orientation conducive to family planning, health, and social involvement (Inkeles 1983; Inkeles and Smith 1974).

A variety of behaviors noxious to health (smoking, drug use, and drinking) develop or increase during adolescence and young adulthood. However, young people who have a good relationship with their parents and who are attuned to parent-oriented values as measured by school performance, attending religious services, and having meals with parents do relatively well across a variety of health measures (Hansell and Mechanic 1990). In contrast, high engagement with peer-oriented social activities is associated with increases in behavior associated with health risk.

Individuals tend to assess their health holistically in terms of vitality and capacity to perform their social activities and roles.

Individuals' appraisals of their health depend as much on their global sense of well-being as they do on specific patterns of illness (Mechanic 1978). Studies of perceptions of health show that they are independently influenced both by the prevalence of symptoms and illness conditions and by the person's psychological well-being (Tessler and Mechanic 1978). Individuals tend to assess their health holistically in terms of vitality and capacity to perform their social activities and roles. Psychological distress often diminishes vitality and functioning as much as serious medical conditions. The RAND Medical Outcomes Study found that depressive symptoms were more disabling than many chronic physical conditions that physicians view as extremely serious (Wells et al. 1989). Several longitudinal studies of the elderly have found that subjective self-assessments of health predict future mortality after taking account of known risk factors and socio-demographic measures. Such self-assessments prospectively predict longevity better than physician assessment (Kaplan and Camacho 1983; Mossey and Shapiro 1982).

An important issue is how sense of well-being becomes incorporated into people's judgments of their physical health. One approach is to study health appraisals among children and adolescents who have little serious illness. A recent prospective study found that adolescents who were more competent and more engaged in age-related activities as measured by school performance and participation in sports and other exercise rated their health more highly (Mechanic and Hansell 1987). Adolescents' health assessments are shaped by their overall sense of functioning, and they do not seem to differentiate among physical and psychological aspects of well-being in making general assessments of how they feel. These findings may help explain the common inclination of adults to express general malaise and psychosocial problems through physical complaints.

The study of illness behavior, in contrast to health behavior, is concerned with the way people monitor their bodies, define and interpret bodily indications, make decisions about needed treatment, and use informal and formal sources of care (Mechanic 1986). Illness behavior begins prior to the use of services and shapes decisions about whether to seek care and what pathways to follow.

A wide range of factors affects the appraisal of symptoms and response to perceived illness (McHugh and Vallis 1986). Sickness is an accepted role in society, bringing sympathetic attention and legitimate release from expected performance (Parsons 1951). Determinations of illness may involve intense negotiations about individuals' claims that, when legitimized, may justify failure to meet expectations or allow escape from onerous obligations (Mechanic 1978). In some situations the sick role becomes a point of tension and conflict between the claimant, who seeks legitimation of sickness with its special privileges, and other interested parties including families, employers, and welfare administrators, who may seek to limit release from social obligations or diminish special privileges granted to the sick and disabled (Field 1957). Most illness situations are neither problematic nor sources of conflict, but the contested cases make evident the social assumptions and expectations around which illness is organized.

Like other behavior, illness behavior is learned through socialization in families and peer groups and through exposure to the mass media and education. There is great diversity of attitudes, beliefs, knowledge, and behavior all of which affect the definitions of problematic symptoms, the meanings and causal attributions that explain them, socially anticipated responses, and the definition of appropriate remedies and sources of care. Motivation and learning affect the initial recognition of symptoms, reactions to pain, the extent of stoicism and hypochondriasis, the readiness to seek release from work, school, and other obligations and to seek help (Mechanic 1978).

Processes of symptom appraisal are influenced by the manner in which symptoms occur and their characteristics, by knowledge, and by past experiences with illness (Mechanic 1972; Leventhal 1986). Some symptoms are so painful and incapacitating that they inevitably lead to intervention without significant inquiry. Others are so familiar and generally understood as self-limited that they also are dealt with routinely. Many symptoms, however, are neither familiar nor easily understood, resulting in a process of interpretation within the context of personality, situational cues and stressors, and environmental influences. Only a small proportion of symptoms leads to formal consultation or care. The vast majority are denied, normalized, or evaluated as having little significance.

In situations where there are no obvious explanations for the occurrence of symptoms, individuals seek meanings for changes in their feeling states. The commonsense theories they apply may either be idiosyncratic or drawn from socially prevalent conventional explanations such as stress, lack of sleep, overwork, and overeating. These lay explanations are influential on subsequent behavior such as care-seeking and use of medication (Kleinman 1980; Leventhal, Meyer, and Nerenz 1980; Leventhal, Prohaska, and Hirschman 1985). For example, it is commonly believed that stress increases blood pressure and that relaxation reduces it. Most individuals, however, cannot assess whether their blood pressure is high or low on the basis of available cues, yet many believe they can. Persons with hypertension, an asymptomatic condition, commonly use self-assessments of their stress levels or relaxation as an indicator of their blood pressure levels and adjust their medication accordingly, despite medical advice to the contrary (Leventhal, Prohaska, and Hirschman 1985). Similarly, many patients with limited understanding of the biological processes through which drugs such as antibiotics or antidepressants act increase or decrease medication in relation to changes in how they feel and environmental cues.

In short, illness appraisal is a two-step process (Mechanic 1972). In the initial step, persons monitor their bodies to assess the location, duration, intensity, and persistence of discomfort. In the second stage, which may occur almost concurrently, they seek explanations for perceived changes. If an obvious explanation is not available, or is disconfirmed by further checking, individuals look to their environment for new cues and explanations. These interpretations, in light of knowledge and other beliefs, may then play a role in the formal initiation of care.

Persons seeking medical care commonly express their distress and lowered sense of well-being through many diffuse physical complaints such as fatigue, insomnia, and aches and pains in different bodily systems, a process referred to as somatization (Kleinman 1986). Although much of the existing literature focuses on somatization as a problematic process, it is by far the predominant pattern for expressing distress. Until the last forty or fifty years it was uncommon to conceptualize distress in psychological terms, and even now such expressions are used primarily among well-educated populations receptive to psychological interpretations. General distress has both physical and psychological concomitants; the language that people use to characterize distress depends on the cultural context, the perceived appropriateness of psychological complaints, and the stigma attached to emotional disorder.

There is controversy as to whether psychological idioms are inaccessible to many people due to cultural factors or limited schooling, or whether somatization represents a choice among alternative idioms because such presentations are seen as more consistent with the medical care context. Rates of reported depression in Chinese cultures, for example, are extremely low, although "neurasthenia" is a common diagnosis in Chinese medical care settings (Kleinman 1986). Psychiatrists in China routinely view neurasthenia as a "disorder of brain function involving asthenia of cerebral cortical activity," but alternatively the symptoms reported are strikingly similar to the physical manifestations of depressive disorders more commonly seen in Western countries. It remains unclear whether these diagnoses characterize the same underlying disorders that are expressed differently in varying cultural groups or whether they are fundamentally different. This debate shares common features with the discussion of gender differences in the prevalence of psychiatric disorder. While depression is seen more commonly among women, men have higher rates of antisocial behavior and substance abuse. Researchers differ on whether these are fundamentally different disorders or alternative manifestations of common underlying difficulties. The debate is difficult to resolve because it reflects two fundamentally different models of the nature of illness itself. Within one perspective depression reflects a discrete underlying disorder, while in the other it is simply one alternative adaptive pattern (Mechanic 1989).

The social complexity of the relationships between illness and illness behavior are illustrated by a prospective study of Chinese patients diagnosed as neurasthenic who also met the criteria for a diagnosis of major depression consistent with American diagnostic standards. Kleinman (1986) treated these patients with antidepressant drugs but found on follow-up that while a majority showed significant improvements in clinical psychiatric symptoms, they continued to be impaired, to function badly, and to seek help for their condition. They also remained skeptical of the drug treatment they received. Kleinman links these responses to the patients' needs for the medical legitimation of their "illness" to explain past failures and to justify continuing difficulties in meeting social expectations.

Certification of illness becomes a public issue when physicians have moral and legal authority to define illness and disability and to sanction the sick role. Such influence is found in certifying justified absenteeism for employers, in litigation, and in decisions on eligibility in insurance and disability entitlement programs. Efforts are often made to maintain the illusion that these are objective decisions based solely on medical expertise and clinical experience, but judgments often depend on who the physician represents. The state or other formal organizations may thus attempt to control physicians by limiting their discretion, as happened in the Soviet Union when physicians were viewed as allowing people excuses to escape work too easily (Field 1957), or by taking physicians acting as patients' agents out of the decision-making loop as in the American disability determination system. The need for bureaucratic control tends to be refocused on the new alternative decision-makers as evidenced by the continuing efforts of the Social Security Administration to constrain the decisions of state agencies and administrative law judges (Osterweis, Kleinman, and Mechanic 1987). In short, the definition of illness and disability is the "rope" in a tug of war in which competing parties seek determinations in their own interest.

The definition of illness and disability is the "rope" in a tug of war in which competing parties seek determinations in their own interest.

The study of illness behavior has many applications in research, clinical care, public health, and social policy (Mechanic 1986). Such patterns of behavior substantially affect pathways into care and selectively shape the samples studied in clinical contexts. Failure to understand these selection effects and how they operate lead to erroneous conclusions about the nature of basic disease processes. A common error is to attribute to the etiology of the illness influences triggering use of services, a problem that plagues much research on stress and illness. At the clinical level, awareness of how people construe illness, present symptoms, and respond to care can improve understanding and communication and help health professionals to guide more effectively the treatment regimen. Much of illness behavior, as illustrated, is an alternative to other types of coping and environmental mastery. Increasing evidence suggests that a personal sense of control (Rodin 1986) and self-esteem (Mechanic 1980) contribute to physical vitality and satisfaction and promote health. These areas of concern are important for the public health agenda.

Health and illness behavior studies make clear that the forces affecting health and treatment outcomes transcend medical care and the transactions that take place between doctor and patient. In recent decades there have been increasing tendencies toward the medicalization of social problems and a failure to address the complicated longitudinal needs of patients with serious chronic illness and disabilities. Moreover, the problems of managing the frailties of old age, characterized by a combination of medical, instrumental, and psychosocial needs, increasingly challenge the operating assumptions of treatment focused on narrow definitions of disease and care. Studies of illness behavior teach the importance of moving beyond initial complaints and narrow definitions of problems and examining the broad context of individuals' lives and the factors that affect social function and quality of life. They point to the diverse adaptations among persons with comparable physical debility and potential. They reinforce the need to take account of the environmental and social context of people's lives, their potential assets, and their disease. A medical care system, responsive to these broad concerns, would be better prepared for the impending health care challenges of the 1990s.

[See also Health Promotion; Mental Health; Mental Illness and Mental Disorders.]

BIBLIOGRAPHY

Becker, Marshall (ed.) 1974 *The Health Belief Model and Personal Health Behavior.* Thorofare, N.J.: Slack.

———, and Lois Maiman 1983 "Models of Health-Related Behavior." In D. Mechanic, ed., *Handbook of Health, Health Care and the Health Professions.* New York: Free Press.

Bunker, John, Deanna Gomby, and Barbara Kehrer (eds.) 1989 *Pathways to Health: The Role of Social Factors.* Menlo Park, Calif.: Kaiser Family Foundation.

Caldwell, John 1986 "Routes to Low Mortality in Poor Countries." *Population and Development Review* 12:171–220.

Field, Mark G. 1957 *Doctor and Patient in Soviet Russia.* Cambridge, Mass.: Harvard University Press.

Hansell, Stephen, and David Mechanic 1990 "Parent and Peer Effects on Adolescent Health Behavior." In Klaus Hurrelman and Friedrich Losel, eds., *Health Hazards in Adolescence.* New York: De Gruyter.

Inkeles, Alex 1983 *Exploring Individual Modernity.* New York: Columbia University Press.

———, and D. H. Smith 1974 *Becoming Modern: Individual Change in Six Developing Countries.* Cambridge, Mass.: Harvard University Press.

Kaplan, George, and Terry Camacho 1983 "Perceived Health and Mortality: A Nine-Year Follow-Up of the Human Population Laboratory Cohort." *American Journal of Epidemiology* 117:292–304.

Kleinman, Arthur 1980 *Patients and Healers in the Context of Culture.* Berkeley: University of California Press.

——— 1986 *Social Origins of Distress and Disease: Depression, Neurasthenia, and Pain in Modern China.* New Haven: Yale University Press.

Langlie, Jean 1977 "Social Networks, Health Beliefs, and Preventive Health Behavior." *Journal of Health and Social Behavior* 18:244–260.

Leventhal, Howard 1986 "Symptom Reporting: A Focus on Process." In Sean McHugh and T. Michael Vallis, eds., *Illness Behavior: A Multidisciplinary Model.* New York: Plenum.

———, Daniel Meyer, and David Nerenz 1980 "The Common-Sense Representation of Illness Danger." In Stanley Rachman, ed., *Contributions to Medical Psychology.* New York: Pergamon.

———, Thomas Prohaska, and Robert Hirschman 1985 "Preventive Health Behavior across the Life Span." In James Rosen and Laura Solomon, eds., *Prevention in Health Psychology.* Hanover: University Press of New England.

McHugh, Sean, and T. Michael Vailis (eds.) 1986 *Illness Behavior: A Multidisciplinary Model.* New York: Plenum.

Mechanic, David 1972 "Social Psychologic Factors Affecting the Presentation of Bodily Complaints." *The New England Journal of Medicine* 286:1132–1139.

——— 1978 *Medical Sociology.* 2nd ed. New York: Free Press.

——— 1979 "The Stability of Health and Illness Behavior: Results from a Sixteen-Year Follow-Up." *American Journal of Public Health* 69:1142–1145.

——— 1980 "Education, Parental Interest, and Health Perceptions and Behavior." *Inquiry* 17:331–338.

——— 1985 "Health and Illness Behavior." In J. M. Last and Maxcy-Rosenau, eds., *Preventive Medicine and Public Health.* 12th ed. New York: Appleton-Century Crofts.

——— 1986 "Illness Behavior: An Overview." In S. McHugh and T. M. Vallis, eds., *Illness Behavior: A Multidisciplinary Model.* New York: Plenum.

——— 1989 *Mental Health and Social Policy.* 3rd ed. Englewood Cliffs, N.J.: Prentice-Hall.

——— 1990 "Promoting Health." *Society* 27(2):16–22.

Mechanic, David, and Stephen Hansell 1987 "Adolescent Competence, Psychological Well-Being and Self-Assessed Physical Health." *Journal of Health and Social Behavior* 28:364–374.

Mossey, Jane, and Evelyn Shapiro 1982 "Self-Rated Health: A Predictor of Mortality among the Elderly." *American Journal of Public Health* 72:800–808.

Osterweis, Marian, Arthur Kleinman, and David Mechanic (eds.) 1987 *Pain and Disability: Clinical, Behavioral and Public Policy Perspectives.* Washington, D.C.: National Academy Press.

Parsons, Talcott 1951 *The Social System.* New York: Free Press.

Rodin, Judith 1986 "Aging and Health: Effects of the Sense of Control." *Science* 233:1,271–1,276.

Rosenstock, Irwin 1974 "The Health Belief Model and Preventive Health Behavior." In Marshall Becker, ed., *The Health Belief Model and Personal Health Behavior.* Thorofare, N.J.: Slack.

Tessler, Richard, and David Mechanic 1978 "Psychological Distress and Perceived Health Status." *Journal of Health and Social Behavior* 19:254–262.

Wells, Kenneth, Anita Stewart, Ron D. Hays, Audrey Burnam, William Rogers, Marcia Daniels, Sandra Berry, Sheldon Greenfield, and John Ware 1989 "The Functioning and Well-Being of Depressed Patients: Results from the Medical Outcomes Study." *Journal of the American Medical Association* 262:914–919.

– DAVID MECHANIC

HEALTH AND THE LIFE COURSE

Health and *the life course* are two broad concepts of interest to sociologists. Each of these concepts must be nominally defined.

Conceptions of Health

Health can be conceptualized in three major ways: the medical model (or physical definition); the functional model (or social definition); and the psychological model (or the subjective evaluation of health; Liang 1986). In the medical model, health is defined as the absence of disease. The presence of any disease condition is determined by reports from the patient, observations by health practitioners, or medical tests. The social definition of health is derived from Parsons's (1951) work and refers to an individual's ability to perform roles, that is, to function socially. Illness or impairment is a function of reduced capacity to perform expected roles, commonly measured in terms of activities of daily living (ADLs—eating, dressing, bathing, walking, grooming, etc.). The psychological model, or the subjective evaluation of health, is often based on the response to a single question asking one to rate one's health on a scale from poor to excellent. The definition of health used by the World Health Organization since 1946 reflects this multidimensional perspective: "a state of complete physical, mental, and social well-being and not merely the absence of disease or infirmity."

It has been suggested (e.g., Schroots 1988) that a distinction be made between *disease* and *illness.* It is argued that disease refers to an objective diagnosis of a disorder, while illness refers to the presence of a disease plus the individual's perception of and response to the disease. Thus, one may have a disease, but as long as one does not acknowledge it and behave accordingly (e.g., take medicine), one will perceive oneself as healthy (Birren and Zarit 1985).

A distinction should also be made between *acute* and *chronic* conditions. These two types of health conditions are differentially related to older and younger age groups (discussed more below). That is, there is a morbidity shift from acute to chronic diseases as an individual ages. In addition, Western societies experienced a dramatic shift from infectious diseases (a form of acute condition) to chronic, degenerative diseases in the late nineteenth century and the first half of the twentieth century.

Conceptions of the Life Course

The life course is a progression through time (Clausen 1986), in particular, social time. Social time is a set of norms governing life transitions for particular social groups. These transitions may vary from one group to another (e.g., working class versus middle class) and from one historical period to another. The life course approach focuses on "age related transitions that are *socially created, socially recognized,* and *shared*" (Hagestad and Neugarten 1985, p. 35). Historical time plays a key role in life course analysis because of the emphasis on social time and social transitions (Elder 1977; Hareven 1978). Changes that take place in society lead to a restructuring of individual life courses. Thus, life courses will vary from one cohort (generation) to the next.

The life course perspective should be differentiated from the lifespan perspective or other developmental models of psychology. In these latter approaches the focus is on the individual, especially on personality, cognition, and other intrapsychic phenomena (George 1982). In these developmental approaches, change results from within the individual, and this change is universal—it is a function of human nature. Typically, developmental changes are linked to chronological age, with little or no reference to the social context or the sociohistorical or individual-historical context. The life course perspective, in contrast, focuses on transitions when the "social persona" (Hagestad and Neugarten 1985, p. 35) undergoes change.

Conceptions of Aging

In order to understand health and the life course it is also important to understand the aging process. Aging is best understood in a life course perspective. Persons do not suddenly become old at age sixty or sixty-five or at retirement. Aging is the result of a lifetime of social, behavioral, and biological processes interacting with one another. While genetics may play a part in predisposing individuals to certain diseases or impairments, length and quality of life have been found to be highly dependent on behaviors, life-styles, and health-related attitudes (e.g., Haug and Ory 1987).

A distinction is often made between primary and secondary aging (see Schroots 1988). Primary aging, or normal aging, refers to the steady declines in functioning in the absence of disease or despite good health. Secondary aging, or pathological aging, refers to the declines that are due to illnesses associated with age but not to aging itself. This suggests that secondary aging can be reversed, at least in principle (Kohn 1985).

Variations in Health and Life Expectancy

The largest cause of death in America for people under age forty-five is accidents and adverse effects (National Center for Health Statistics 1989). For people five to fourteen years of age and twenty-five to forty-four years of age, malignant neoplasms (tumors) rank second as a cause of death. For persons fifteen to twenty-four years of age, homicide, followed closely by suicide, are the next leading causes of death.

For adults ages sixty-five and over the causes of death are quite different. Cardiovascular disease, malignant neoplasms, cerebrovascular disease, and influenza and pneumonia are the most common causes of death (Schroots 1988; White et al. 1986). Older persons, too, are more likely to suffer from chronic, and often limiting, conditions. Most common among these are arthritis, hypertension, hearing impairments, heart conditions, chronic sinusitis, visual impairments, and orthopedic impairments (e.g., back). Interestingly, these same conditions are among the most commonly mentioned by persons ages forty-five to sixty-four, though their prevalence is generally considerably less than that of persons sixty-five and older.

At the turn of the century, life expectancy for a person sixty-five years of age was almost twelve years. By 1978, life expectancy for a sixty-five-year-old was fourteen years for males and eighteen years for females. Many of the improvements in life expectancy came about before large-scale immunization programs. These programs largely affected the health of those born during the 1940s and 1950s. These programs have, however, reduced infant mortality and reduced the likelihood of certain debilitating diseases (e.g., polio).

The chance of surviving to old age with few functional disabilities is strongly related to socioeconomic position, educational level, and race (Berkman 1988). People in lower classes and with less education have higher mortality risk and have higher incidence and prevalence of diseases and injuries. They have more hospitalizations, disability days, and functional limitations.

Life expectancy also varies by social class. At age twenty-five life expectancy, for those with four or fewer years of education, is forty-four years for men and almost forty-seven years for women. For men and women with some college education, life expectancy is forty-seven years and fifty-six years respectively. After age sixty-five, however, this relationship becomes less clear-cut, suggesting that for older cohorts a different set of factors is involved.

Issues and Implications

Differences in health conditions by age raise at least two issues regarding the analysis and understanding of health. First, it has been suggested that in trying to understand health and health behavior of the elderly, especially as our models become more complex, the *individual* is the critical unit of analysis (Wolinsky and Arnold 1988). That is, we must focus on individual differentiation over the life course. Aging is a highly individual process, resulting from large inter- and intra-individual differences in health and functioning.

The second issue concerns the extent to which many processes thought to be life course processes may in fact be cohort differences (see Dannefer 1988). An assumption is often made that the heterogeneity within older cohorts is an intracohort, life course process: Age peers become increasingly dissimilar as they grow older. This conclusion is, however, often based on cross-sectional data and may lead to a life course fallacy. Age differences may reduce to cohort differences. If each succeeding cohort becomes more homogeneous, older cohorts will display greater heterogeneity compared to younger cohorts. Evidence suggests that for several cohort characteristics this may be the case. For example, there has been increasing standardization of years of education, age of labor-force entry and exit, age at first marriage, number of children, and so on. Thus, younger age groups would exhibit less diversity than older cohorts.

Some deterioration of health appears to be the result of an accumulation of life experiences and behaviors.

Not all health deterioration is a normal process of aging. Some of it appears to be the result of an accumulation of life experiences and behaviors. Many of the experiences and behaviors are different for older and younger cohorts, suggesting that an understanding of factors affecting health for older cohorts may not hold for younger cohorts as they age.

Two possible scenarios exist. One is that older people in the future will experience less morbidity than today's elderly, even though later life will be longer. That is, they will be older longer, sick for a very short period of time, and then die. An alternative situation is one in which elderly live longer and are sick or impaired for many of those years. That is, they will be sick for an extensive period of their later life. Given the fact that more people are living longer, the general expectation is that the demand for health care by elderly will be greater in the future. The extent of the demand will depend, in part, on which of these two scenarios is closer to the truth. The conservative approach, and the one generally adopted, is that estimates of tomorrow's needs for care are based on data from today's elderly. However, a life course perspective might yield quite a different picture because the life experiences, behaviors, and health attitudes of today's elderly may be quite different from those of younger cohorts, tomorrow's elderly.

[See also Health and Illness Behavior; Life Course; Life Expectancy; Social Gerontology.]

BIBLIOGRAPHY

Berkman, Lisa F. 1988 "The Changing and Heterogeneous Nature of Aging and Longevity: A Social and Biomedical Perspective." In G. L. Maddox and M. P. Lawton, eds., *Varieties of Aging.* Vol. 8 of *Annual Review of Gerontology and Geriatrics.* New York: Springer.

Birren, James E., and Judy M. Zarit 1985 "Concepts of Health, Behavior, and Aging." In J. E. Birren and J. Livingston, eds., *Cognition, Stress and Aging.* Englewood Cliffs, N.J.: Prentice-Hall.

Clausen, John A. 1986 *The Life Course: A Sociological Perspective.* Englewood Cliffs, N.J.: Prentice-Hall.

Dannefer, Dale 1988 "Differential Gerontology and the Stratified Life Course: Conceptual and Methodological Issues." In G. L. Maddox and M. P. Lawton, eds., *Varieties of Aging.* Vol. 8 of *Annual Review of Gerontology and Geriatrics.* New York: Springer.

Elder, Glen H., Jr. 1977 "Family History and the Life Course." *Journal of Family History* 2:279–304.

George, Linda K. 1982 "Models of Transitions in Middle and Later Life." *Annals of the Academy of Political and Social Science* 464:22–37.

Hagestad, Gunhild O., and Bernice L. Neugarten 1985 "Age and the Life Course." In R. H. Binstock and E. Shanas, eds., *Handbook of Aging and the Social Sciences.* New York: Van Nostrand Reinhold Company.

Hareven, T. K. 1978 *Transitions: The Family and the Life Course in Historical Perspective.* New York: Academic Press.

Haug, Marie R., and Marcia G. Ory 1987 "Issues in Elderly Patient–Provider Interactions." *Research on Aging* 9:3–44.

Kohn, R. R. 1985 "Aging and Age-Related Diseases: Normal Processes." In H. A. Johnson, ed., *Relations between Normal Aging and Disease.* New York: Raven Press.

Liang, Jersey 1986 "Self-Reported Physical Health among Aged Adults." *Journal of Gerontology* 41:248–260.

National Center for Health Statistics 1989 "Advance Report of Final Mortality Statistics, 1987." *Monthly Vital Statistics Report.* Vol. 38 No. 5, Supp. Hyattsville, Md.: Public Health Service.

Parsons, Talcott 1951 *The Social System.* New York: Free Press.

Schroots, Johannes J. F. 1988 "Current Perspectives on Aging, Health, and Behavior." In J. J. F. Schroots, J. E. Birren, and A. Svanborg, eds., *Health and Aging: Perspectives and Prospects.* New York: Springer.

White, Lon R., William S. Cartwright, Jean Cornoni-Huntley, and Dwight B. Brock 1986. "Geriatric Epidemiology." In C. Eisdorfer, ed., *Annual Review of Gerontology and Geriatrics,* Vol. 6. New York: Springer.

Wolinsky, Fredric D., and Connie Lea Arnold 1988 "A Different Perspective on Health and Health Services Utilization." In G. L. Maddox and M. P. Lawton, eds., *Varieties of Aging.* Vol. 8 of *Annual Review of Gerontology and Geriatrics.* New York: Springer.

– DONALD E. STULL

HEALTH PROMOTION

Health promotion and disease prevention are vital activities that help a society maintain a well-functioning, long-lived population. This statement may appear obvious, but an examination of health-relevant knowledge, attitudes, or behaviors shows that health promotion and disease prevention play only small roles in the U.S. health care system. The basic principles of health promotion receive little attention in medical textbooks or in the journals that physicians regularly read. Furthermore, little funding has been forthcoming for these activities.

The U.S. health care system revolves around treatment and attempts to cure existing health problems. A vast biomedical, surgical, pharmaceutical, mechanical, and human technology has emerged. This technological armamentarium is primarily devoted to medical treatment of injury and disease, and physicians frequently use this technology when taking heroic measures to save lives. Unfortunately, most of the rescued individuals have not experienced wellness programs nor other organized health promotion efforts that might have prevented their health problems from developing or from reaching the stage where massive intervention was required.

The field of health promotion may become increasingly important as society acknowledges the rapidly rising cost of maintaining our medical technology. Many influential people are concerned about the economic burden and are beginning to call for health promotion programs in worksites and elsewhere. It is noteworthy that the "ounce of prevention" philosophy is increasingly espoused. There is greater willingness to accept the notion that health promotion activities are worthwhile.

The Goals of Health Promotion

The federal government has spearheaded efforts to focus the nation's attention on health promotion as a meaningful medical goal. The U.S. Public Health Service (1989) believes that the health and well-being of the U.S. population can be significantly improved by the year 2000 by engaging in specific health promotion activities. This body has defined five national health promotion goals for the new century. These are:

1. Reducing infant mortality to no more than seven deaths per 1,000 live births (the present rate is ten per 1,000).
2. Increasing life expectancy at birth to at least seventy-eight years (currently seventy-five).
3. Reducing the proportion of people disabled by chronic conditions to no more than 6 percent of the population (current chronic disease disability rates are 9 percent).
4. Increasing years of healthy life (quality-adjusted life years) to at least sixty-five (estimated to be sixty years in 1987).
5. Decreasing the disparity in life expectancy between white and minority populations to no more than four years (in 1990 there was a six-year gap).

To achieve these goals the U.S. Public Health Service targeted seven areas: nutrition; physical activity and fitness; tobacco use; alcohol and drug use; sexual behavior; violent/abusive behavior; and vitality and independence of older people. Education and interventions in these areas can significantly reduce the illness burden and greatly enhance the health of the public.

It is noteworthy that the U.S. Public Health Service has singled out violent and abusive behavior. Social scientists have long regarded violence as a social problem. Yet, in a broader context, violence-induced problems not only threaten human life, dignity, and the social order but pose serious strain to our health care resources. Victims of violent and abusive behavior crowd hospital emergency rooms. Many require lifelong treatment for injuries they have sustained.

Health Promotion Activities

Health promotion activities incorporate health education, health screening, an active surveillance system for present and potential health problems, preventive services, and medical care for serious and minor health problems. Some health promotion activities are directed at the physical environment (e.g., pollution control), others are focused on the social environment (e.g., stress-reduction clinics), still others relate to human biology or human behavior (e.g., immunization and anti-smoking campaigns). It is believed that health promotion is best accomplished by a lifetime health monitoring program.

Most experts conclude that health promotion activities involve the primary, secondary, and tertiary prevention of disease. These terms are used in relationship to the stage of illness. *Primary prevention* applies to the period prior to the onset of a disease. Thus, health promotion is directed toward those persons without disease manifestations and includes activities that will help individuals to maintain a healthy, well-functioning body. In contrast, *secondary* and *tertiary prevention* occur after a disease has been detected. These health promotion efforts are directed at individuals who are already afflicted with a condition, and they consist of interventions that can slow the progress of disease. Thus, secondary and tertiary prevention actually fall under the sphere of medical treatment for disease.

Primary prevention is defined as actions that avert the occurrence of disease, injury, or defects. The aim of primary prevention is to maintain health by eliminating the factors that cause disease or can cause a departure from health. Hence, a disease or illness never manifests itself because the individual has either avoided exposure or has engaged in activities that retard the onset of a condition. An example is a society's efforts to prevent polio by immunization. Another example is increased regulation of smoking in public places; doing so can help prevent major lung and heart diseases.

Activities under the rubric of primary prevention include educational efforts addressed toward the reduction of chronic disease. Five chronic illnesses account for most of the deaths, hospital care, and disability of

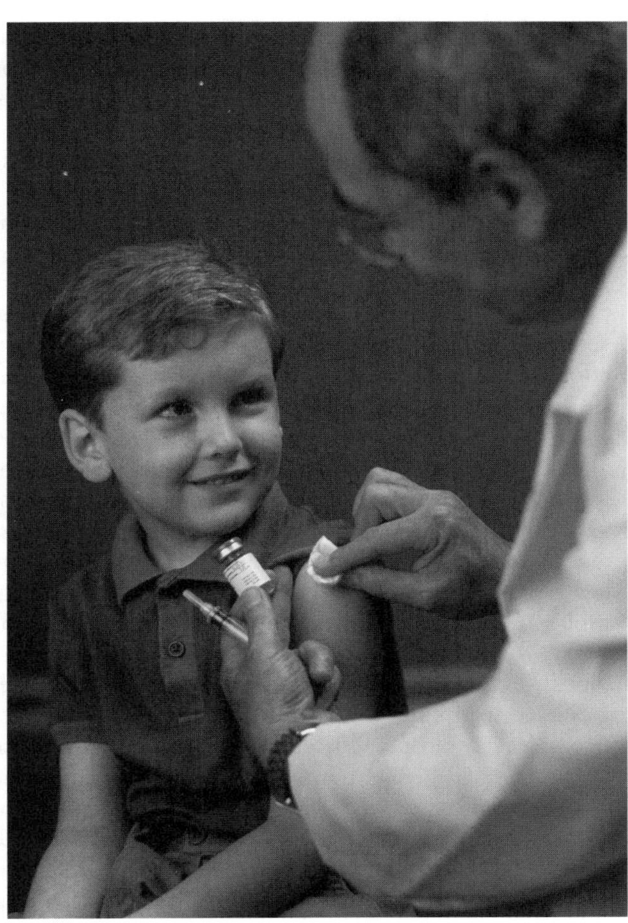

The vaccination of children against serious diseases is an example of primary prevention, in which disease, injury, or defects are actively averted. (Bob Krist/Corbis)

the U.S. population. These illnesses are: arthritis, hypertension, heart disease, bronchitis, and diabetes. The problem increases in magnitude as persons age. There is a significant increase in chronic disease after the sixth decade, and arthritis, hypertension, and heart disease rates are at least ten times as high for persons over sixty-five as for their counterparts who are less than forty-five years old.

If the progress of chronic disease is traced, it becomes obvious that chronic conditions are readily amenable to preventive action. Fries and Crapo (1986) illustrated the typical decline from specific chronic diseases over a fifty-year period. The conditions they traced all had behavioral etiologies associated with lifestyle, habits, and health-risk behaviors. The problems actually began when individuals were in their twenties, as optimal physiological response was altered. By the time people were in their forties there were subclinical manifestations of the disease, and by age fifty the threshold stage had been reached. As people reached their sixties the severe phase of chronic disease was reached, and in the seventies there was endstage disease that could cause death.

The development of heart disease provides a good example of this process. While most individuals do not develop major heart conditions before age sixty-five, after this time the disease is very prevalent (there are over four million heart patients aged sixty-five or older). For most of these individuals the disease process began decades before. At age twenty, elevated cholesterol readings might have been detected; small plaques may have been discernible on an arteriogram at age thirty and would have been much more visible at age forty. If the patient reported leg pain when exercising as he or she reached their fifties, physicians may have detected the threshold phase of the disease. This may have progressed to angina pectoris around age sixty. Finally, as the person reached his or her seventies, a heart attack would be the likely outcome.

Primary prevention of heart disease and most other chronic conditions begins with risk-factor reduction. Health promotion efforts that involve eliminating or reducing cardiac risk behaviors can lessen the likelihood of heart disease. The major cardiovascular risk factors are cigarette smoking, high blood pressure (hypertension), obesity, physical deconditioning, high lipid count (dyslipidemia), heredity, and impaired glucose tolerance. Most of these also constitute risk for cerebrovascular and diabetic disease. Yet all of the above, with the exception of the hereditary factor, are modifiable (Kannel et al. 1987; Herd et al. 1987). Persons who change their behaviors with regard to even one of these significantly decrease their risk of developing heart disease. They are also much less likely to die from a heart condition. Typical risk-reduction instruction for heart disease emphasizes no smoking, weight control, dietary change, exercising, and regular blood pressure and urine tests.

Secondary prevention contrasts with primary prevention because it involves control of a condition observed by medical practitioners. The aims of secondary prevention are to ensure early detection of conditions, followed by prompt treatment. Efforts toward halting, slowing, or possibly reversing the progression of a condition are given major attention.

One important tool for persons involved in secondary prevention is health screening. Procedures to screen individuals include blood pressure tests, chest X-rays, Pap smears, glaucoma, hearing, and similar tests, as well as thorough investigations of urine and blood. Electrocardiograms, breast examinations, and dental examinations are often included in screening efforts. These secondary prevention efforts can be widespread, involving community agencies and the public health sector; they can be limited to the workplace; or they can be restricted to physicians and allied health professionals using their clinical practice sites.

While most individuals do not develop major heart conditions before age sixty-five, after this time the disease is very prevalent.

These procedures are immensely valuable. They are considered to be the best means for postponing disability and preventing chronic conditions from progressing to dangerous clinical thresholds. For example, urine testing that detects diabetes early in the course of the disease can prevent the development of impaired circulation; this testing can, in turn, prevent amputation of limbs. These procedures can also enhance the quality of life of the ailing person. Blindness and deterioration of vision can be prevented if diabetes is treated promptly with dietary modification, medication regimes, or both so the individual can retain sight indefinitely. Not only can secondary prevention efforts forestall further development of the disease and improve life quality, but they can prevent premature death.

Unfortunately, secondary prevention procedures are used less than is optimal or even desirable. In a recent survey of physicians, office practices regarding early cancer detection were investigated. Data showed that internists offered their patients the most opportunity for standard cancer detection tests (Pap tests, chest X-rays, mammograms, stool blood determinations, and prostate, breast, digital rectal, and proctoscopic examinations), but that fewer than half of all physicians surveyed indicated they would schedule proctoscopic exams and chest X-rays for asymptomatic patients with no personal history of cancer (American Cancer Society 1990).

Tertiary prevention refers to medical interventions that prevent disability associated with bodily deterioration from a well-established disease. The aim of tertiary intervention is to provide good health care to an individual. This is likely to halt the downward trajectory of a serious illness while reducing the likelihood of preventable complications. Thus, effective medical treatment of disease and injury represent tertiary prevention efforts.

In the United States, tertiary prevention practices illustrate our most successful health promotion efforts. They reflect the vast technological armamentarium available to our health care system. Breakthrough medical interventions have resulted. Unfortunately, this type of prevention is responsible for much of the accelerating cost of health care.

Cardiovascular disease is again the example of the use of tertiary prevention practices. In the 1980s, mortality from heart conditions declined steadily (National Center for Health Statistics 1986). While some have argued that this resulted from better dietary practices (primary prevention) and hypertension screening (secondary prevention), many experts believe that tertiary prevention efforts are responsible. They cite medical advances including the following: (1) the introduction of new categories of heart drugs that prevent cardiac deterioration and, in some instances, actually dissolve the blood clot associated with a heart attack; (2) the massive use of surgical interventions such as coronary artery bypass graft surgery, which replaces diseased arteries to the heart so that blood flow is increased; (3) semisurgical procedures such as coronary angioplasty, involving temporary insertion of a "balloon" device to remove arterial blockages; and (4) newer medical management strategies used in the hospital setting. In addition, the practice of heart transplantation is used increasingly. These practices have given many thousands of persons the chance to enjoy life with less pain and fewer limitations and to survive longer. Yet, as has been found for all tertiary prevention practices, there is only so much that can be accomplished because the person's body has been ridden with heart and circulatory disease for many years and has typically suffered anatomical and physiological decline. Furthermore, when the cost of providing these interventions is calculated, it is clear that tertiary prevention is not the best societal focus.

Health Promotion Barriers

Some health promotion activities are popular and widely used while others are not. Most people agree that health promotion is a worthwhile goal, but not all concur with the U.S. Public Health Service that it should be a societal priority. Especially as defined in the five goals for the nation presented earlier, there is little consensus on whether these defined areas should be emphasized. There is even less consensus on what specific activities should receive greater support, on where the responsibility lies for health promotion, or on how to pay for these efforts.

Health promotion activities do not typically include all seven areas denoted by the U.S. Public Health Service. For example, nutrition, physical activity and fitness, tobacco use, alcohol and drug use, sexual behavior, violent/abusive behavior, and vitality and independence of older people do not receive equal attention. There are educational programs to impart the dangers of smoking to the public, yet efforts to prevent sexually transmitted disease were rarely noticed until the AIDS epidemic, and few pregnant women besides those receiving regular prenatal care are instructed about alcohol and drug use during pregnancy. Even in the area of nutrition, many of the health education efforts have been fad-related. As calcium or fat ingestion practices become popular, materials are circulated that provide information about their proper use. However, many people have not been exposed to the health risks of poor and unbalanced diets. Similarly, the risks associated with poor or inappropriate exercise are not well understood. Exercise is often neglected in educational efforts or may be misrepresented. A large proportion of health education material advises the public to "get more exercise." However, the American Heart Association guidelines on exercise for a "healthy heart" (National Heart, Lung, and Blood Institute 1988) are not known to most people. They have not been exposed to material about specifically beneficial types of exercise (aerobic), nor do they have adequate information about the frequency or duration of exercise.

The responsibility for health promotion has been alternatively assigned to public agencies, the health care system, health professionals, and individuals. Each, in turn, has been considered to be the major player.

Many people believe that the individual has sole responsibility for his or her health status. If someone is to remain healthy, or even to avoid death from a condition, it is that person who must act in a health-promoting manner. The failure of individuals to exert control over their health behaviors is often cited as a major contributor to our disease rates. One article (Rastam, Luepker, and Pirie 1988) showed that only 57 percent of persons identified as having elevated cholesterol levels during public screening programs actually visited a physician after being notified. This type of report is often used to promulgate the notion that people do not care enough about their health to take appropriate action.

Physicians are often held responsible for health promotion. According to this view, the physician must take the initiative, advise patients of their personal risk, and propose means of risk reduction. Data are cited that indicate few patients (especially the aged) are given adequate information by their doctor.

The health care system and public agencies are often considered responsible. According to this view, the Surgeon General of the United States, the U.S. Public Health Service, the National Institutes of Health, and other governmental agencies bear the responsibility for a healthy public. It is considered to be the job of these agencies to provide health information and health screening to the public at large. Furthermore, the government is expected to fund preventive services so that all persons can have financial access to this care.

Clearly, the patient, his or her physician, the health care system, and the public sector all have roles to play. Health promotion must represent a combined effort. Schools, workplaces, and local agencies must impart information about health maintenance and health risks; health providers must advise at-risk people that they are likely candidates for a particular disease; private and public health facilities must be available to screen and provide treatment; there must be a means for payment for the health care or advice received; individuals must comply with the advice and health-promoting behaviors that have been proposed.

Conclusions

Health promotion is an often-used term. The principle appeals to most people, but it is not a widely supported activity. Our society has traditionally focused on providing a wide range of medical treatment services rather than on educational and applied efforts to prevent the development of deteriorating diseases and injuries. Furthermore, there is little consensus about what should constitute a health promotion program or what primary, secondary, or tertiary activities this type of program requires to reach health-promotion and disease-prevention goals. Yet without a widespread program, little control can be exerted over the human, social, and financial cost of illness. For this or any society to maintain the health and vitality of its citizens; for reduction of the illness burden to both the population and society; for greater longevity, health promotion must be a societal priority.

[See also Health and Illness Behavior; Health Services Utilization.]

BIBLIOGRAPHY

American Cancer Society 1990 "1989 Survey of Physicians' Attitudes and Practices in Early Cancer Detection." *Ca-A Cancer Journal for Clinicians* 40:77–101.

Fries, James F., and Lawrence M. Crapo 1986 "The Elimination of Premature Disease." In Ken Dychtwald, ed., *Wellness and Health Promotion for the Elderly.* Rockville, Md.: Aspen.

Herd, J. Alan, Alastair J. J. Wood, James Blumenthal, James E. Daugherty, and Raymond Harris 1987 "Medical Therapy in the Elderly." *Journal of the American College of Cardiology* 10:29–34.

Kannel, William B., Joseph T. Doyle, Roy J. Shephard, Jeremiah Stamler, and Pantel S. Vokonas 1987 "Prevention of Cardiovascular Disease in the Elderly." *Journal of the American College of Cardiology* 10A:25–28.

National Center for Health Statistics 1986 "Current Estimates from the National Health Interview Survey, United States, 1984." *Vital and Health Statistics.* Series 10, No.156. DHHS Pub. No.

(PHS) 86–1584. Public Health Service. Washington, D.C.: U.S. Government Printing Office.

National Heart, Lung, and Blood Institute 1988 *Blood Pressure Month Information Kit.* Washington, D.C.: NHLBI Information Center.

Rastam, Lennart, Russell V. Luepker, and Phyllis L. Pirie 1988 "Effect of Screening and Referral on Follow-up and Treatment of High Blood Cholesterol Levels." *American Journal of Preventive Medicine* 4:244–248.

U.S. Public Health Service 1989 *Promoting Health/Preventing Disease: Year 2000 Objectives for the Nation.* Draft for Public Review and Comment. Washington, D.C.: U.S. Department of Health and Human Services.

– ROSALIE F. YOUNG

HEALTH SERVICES UTILIZATION

The study of the use of health services is at the center of the field of medical sociology. In part, this is because, either directly or indirectly, all facets of medical care have to take into account the quantity and types of services that community members utilize (Freeman et al. 1987). In part, it is related to the intellectual attraction of the area for persons of different conceptual and methodological leanings. To estimate and explain the use of health services, it is necessary to draw upon the full range of available micro- and macrosociological knowledge and to use the entire spectrum of research methodologies (Freeman and Levine 1989).

A Microperspective

Health and illness remain social concepts even in today's medical care world, where the extensive training given to physicians and other providers and the widespread use of high technology have increased the validity and reliability of diagnoses (Parsons 1951). Persons with the same biomedical conditions and manifesting the same symptoms differ considerably in their self-evaluations of health status, in their willingness to comply with suggested regimens to prevent more serious conditions and to improve their health status, and in their competence to deal with providers and health care organizations.

Health and illness remain social concepts in today's medical care world.

Likewise, individual medical providers vary greatly in their identification of persons as sick or well, in the treatments they prescribe, and in the ways they relate to patients. Because of these well-documented findings, there has been extensive sociopsychological research on the provision and utilization of health services (Andersen, Kravits, and Anderson 1976).

Perhaps the most researched area, in which considerable work goes on now, is how to encourage persons to participate in preventive programs (Becker and Rosenstock 1989). While perhaps not health services in the strict sense, current efforts to modify diet and increase exercise are seen as means to reduce illness and disease. But it goes beyond that, ranging from following generally regarded frequencies of visits to providers, depending upon health status, age, sex, and other characteristics, to practicing safe sex in the face of the AIDS epidemic and the number of seropositive persons in the community. Thus, there is extensive interest in a "health belief model" and in "social power" strategies for modifying health care behavior (Becker and Joseph 1988).

Of course, microdimensions are not independent of macro ones. This is illustrated by the well-known concept of the *sick role* discussed by Parsons (1951) several decades ago. He observed that the sick role was a means for persons to minimize their participation in instrumental roles normatively expected of them. Similarly, public health efforts to minimize the AIDS epidemic depend upon developing efficacious programs for reducing unsafe sex and eliminating needle sharing.

A Macroperspective

Understanding the utilization of health services, however, requires bringing in social structural and organizational dimensions as well. Although a persistent area of sociological study, interest in the relations between structural and organizational arrangements for care and the quantity, types, and quality of health care utilized has increased markedly in recent years because of the spiraling costs of health services for everyone (Shortell and Kaluzny 1987).

Health insurance now represents a major economic burden for even reasonably well-to-do families and their employers, and public medical care costs are a significant tax burden for community members. As a consequence, new forms of medical care organizations have emerged, and they have been the focus of intensive study (Freeman et al. 1990).

A frequently encountered type is the *staff model* health maintenance organization (HMO), where primary-care physicians may practice on a salary and the focus is on prevention and early detection, in order to minimize expensive inpatient and high-tech services. They operate on a capitation basis, with employers or individuals paying a fee to cover all or almost all of their health care costs (Luft 1983).

Unfortunately, not all such HMOs have prospered, because of the failure to manage them properly, the extensiveness of the services provided, or the selection of such settings by persons requiring extensive care. Other common options are *preferred provider organizations* (PPOs), in which groups of primary-care physicians, who may be salaried or may work for fees, provide routine care but refer out patients for specialty services. Some of these PPOs permit patients to choose their own specialists, although they are usually required to pay part of the medical care costs if they do so. There are a number of variant models of *managed care,* as well as physicians who arrange with insurance carriers to provide care under a variety of different fiscal arrangements. Each innovation in the way health care is delivered affects the utilization of services, creating literally endless opportunities for research. So, too, does the emergence of new disorders and the redefinition of the social dimensions of others. AIDS and the HIV virus are a clear example of the former; the medical ramifications of domestic violence and the abuse of family members by each other, of the latter.

But there are other reasons for organizational change in medicine. For example, organizational arrangements are a major factor in the training of health providers and, thus, in the types of patients who utilize their services (Ludmerer 1985). Fledgling providers select and are selected differently, depending upon organizational features of settings; receive quite different substantive educations once there; and have their career trajectories determined to a large degree by the sites in which they have been trained. The patients of a doctor with an MD from Harvard, a residency at Johns Hopkins, and a practice that is teaching-hospital based receive markedly different care than the patients of a doctor who went to a foreign medical school, interned at a community hospital for one year, and maintains a solo practice in a small-sized community.

At the same time, there are some research concerns that have persisted since sociologists began to study medical care and the utilization of services. Since their beginnings, hospitals have been class structured, ranging from "charity hospitals" for the impoverished to "doctors' hospitals" for the rich. Utilization of health services still varies, depending upon access to hospitals and health care providers (Iglehart 1985). Access to care today continues to differ, depending upon the social characteristics of patients. Health insurance coverage, furthermore, is a major determinant of the type, quantity, and quality of care that a patient receives.

Moreover, the organizational arrangements under which medical care is provided are major determinants of the extent and nature of health services that community members receive. This is the case for both ambulatory and hospital care, whether one takes a national perspective and pursues research opportunities in a single nation or an international one and undertakes comparative investigations.

AMBULATORY CARE. At one time the image of the solo practitioner traveling to the patient's bedside and diagnosing and treating with the few instruments and medicines contained in his black bag was rooted in fact. Most doctors were generalists and had limited technical training. There was only a small number of specialists to call upon for consultation, and few tests were available to help confirm diagnoses. Further, there were marked variations in the quantity and quality of care received by different income groups. For the most part, costs of doctors' visits and prescriptions were borne by individual patients, and differences in access to care were much greater than now (Mechanic and Aiken 1989).

Current concern centers on the problems of too many physicians being trained in many specialties, excess use of technology, and overtreatment of patients.

Today, of course, ambulatory care is delivered primarily by providers who undergo extensive training, have a broad array of technology to employ in making diagnoses, and frequently refer patients to superspecialists for both diagnostic procedures and treatment (Aiken and Freeman 1980). Indeed, current concern centers on the problems of too many physicians being trained in many specialties, excess use of technology, and overtreatment of patients. In part, present concerns are stimulated by the intense interest in cost containment; in part, by skepticism that high-tech "modern medicine" necessarily benefits patients from either a medical care or psychological standpoint.

The differentials in care related to socioeconomic characteristics may have narrowed, but there are still major barriers to care faced by many of the poor in the United States, in some of the other industrialized countries, and in all of the less-developed ones. For example, it is advisable that adult women have regular breast examinations including mammograms. Most middle-income women with health insurance in the United States have no economic barriers to receiving what is now a well-established preventive procedure, one that results in early detection of cancer and reduced mortality. At the same time, Medicaid, the federal-state program that provides health care for many poor women, in many states does not include mandatory payment for mammograms or many other preventive services. Moreover, emergency rooms staffed primarily by students and physicians-in-training become the site of care for many of the poor, particularly the uninsured. In contrast, the insured, economically fortunate, community members are treated by highly trained and experienced primary-care physicians who often refer patients to their super-specialist colleagues for consultations and nonroutine treatment.

Variations in ambulatory care have received extensive sociological study. It is a much more complicated area for research than it may seem at first glance. A major reason is the difficulty of differentiating and measuring *need* and *demand*. Ideally, the former concept would be reserved for the care required from a medical perspective; and the latter, for what the patient wishes to receive.

But, as noted in the discussion of the microdimension, need generally has its social components as well as biomedical ones and patients are rarely autonomous in their search for health care. For example, on the one hand, a somewhat compulsive person with hypertension can be taught to take her or his blood pressure weekly and, if compliant about taking the medication, need see her or his physician every six months (although she may demand to do so much more often). On the other, a person unwilling to regularly take her or his blood pressure and medicine may need to see a provider monthly, although such patients only demand care when they manifest disabling symptoms.

The concept of access is used to differentiate the use of health services over time and, more important, between groups such as the insured and the uninsured, Anglos and Hispanics and Afro-Americans, and rural and urban dwellers. These community and national studies are posited on the position that, given equity in access, if anything, there should be higher use of services among economically and socially disfranchised groups. This view is held because of the association identified early in the history of social medicine between poor health and disadvantageous quality of life. Thus, the health care utilization of the advantaged groups is used as the "gold standard." While it is difficult to develop ways of measuring need, particularly on large samples and without extensive medical examinations, there are continuing efforts to develop proxies for it that are useful in epidemiological research and surveys on use of health services (McKinlay, McKinlay, and Beaglehole 1989). In part this is because of the intrinsic interest in social structural differences in access; in part, because advocates of disadvantaged groups legally and politically bring pressure to remedy the lack of services of these groups, compared with the more economically fortunate and better insured in the population.

INSTITUTIONAL CARE. Ambulatory care is simple to study and understand, compared with the institutional care of patients. The settings providing inpatient care range from small homelike places providing convalescent care to huge, bureaucratic organizations with thousands of patients and employees, complex vertical and horizontal structures, and all of the organizational features of large conglomerates (American Hospital Association 1986). Indeed, some are just that, for national profit and nonprofit multihospital corporations are publicly held and truly "big business."

In all medical institutions, however, the services available and received by patients are determined only in part by the resolution of need and demand differences and the likelihood that they will benefit the recipients. Other determinants include the costs of care; the probability of reimbursement; the risks of malpractice and other legal actions; the extent to which the mission of the institution is patient care, compared with teaching students and young doctors and doing research; and the likelihood that the actions taken will enhance the power and standing of individual providers and the institution as a whole.

All of the determinants just mentioned, individually and collectively, have been the subject of sociological studies using every conceptual framework imaginable and just about all research methodologies. Because of the variations in types of health services provided and the differences in settings, sociologists often specialize in subareas, for example, in the study of the use of services and the impact of the organizations on them among persons with psychiatric illnesses, acute and chronic physical health conditions, and so on.

Moreover, the research undertaken is often not purely sociological. To research problems of institutional care (and only to a slightly lesser extent, ambulatory care) in these times one needs to consider the economics of medical care and a host of management and human resource problems. In fact, some researchers become so multidisciplinarily oriented that they lose their identity as sociologists and become health services researchers (Freeman 1988). But they, as well as their peers who maintain their disciplinary identity, are assured of continued opportunities for research, for the gaps and differentials in use of health services undoubtedly will continue to confront persons in all communities and every nation.

BIBLIOGRAPHY

Aiken, Linda H., and Howard E. Freeman 1980 "Medical Sociology and Science and Technology in Medicine." In P. T. Durbin, ed.,

A Guide to the Culture of Science, Technology and Medicine. New York: Free Press.

American Hospital Association 1986 *Hospital Statistics 1986.* Chicago: American Hospital Association.

Andersen, R., J. Kravits, and O. W. Anderson 1976 *Two Decades of Health Services: Social Survey Trends in Use and Expenditure.* Cambridge, Mass.: Ballinger.

Becker, M. H., and J. G. Joseph 1988 "AIDS and Behavioral Change to Reduce Risk: A Review." *American Journal of Public Health* 78:394–410.

Becker, Marshall H., and Irwin M. Rosenstock 1989 "Health Promotion, Disease Prevention, and Program Retention." In H. E. Freeman and S. Levine, eds., *Handbook of Medical Sociology,* 4th ed. Englewood Cliffs, N.J.: Prentice-Hall.

Freeman, Howard E. 1988 "Medical Sociology." In E. Borgatta and K. Cook, eds., *The Future of Sociology.* Beverly Hills, Calif.: Sage.

Freeman, Howard E., Linda H. Aiken, Robert J. Blendon, and Christopher R. Corey 1990 "Uninsured Working-Age Adults: Characteristics and Consequences." *Health Services Research* 24(6):811–823.

Freeman, Howard E., Robert J. Blendon, Linda H. Aiken, Seymour Sudman, Connie F. Mullinix, and Christopher R. Corey 1987 "Americans Report on Their Access to Health Care." *Health Affairs* 6(1):6–18.

Freeman, Howard E., and Sol Levine 1989 *Handbook of Medical Sociology,* 4th ed. Englewood Cliffs, N.J.: Prentice-Hall.

Iglehart, J. W. 1985 "Medical Care of the Poor: A Growing Problem." *New England Journal of Medicine* 313:59–63.

Ludmerer, Kenneth 1985 *Learning to Heal: The Development of American Medical Education.* New York: Basic Books.

Luft, Harold S. 1983 "Health Maintenance Organizations." In D. Mechanic, ed., *Handbook of Health, Health Care and the Health Professions.* New York: Free Press.

McKinlay, John B., Sonja M. McKinlay, and Robert Beaglehole 1989 "Trends in Death and Disease and the Contribution of Medical Measures." In H. E. Freeman and S. Levine, eds., *Handbook of Medical Sociology,* 4th ed. Englewood Cliffs, N.J.: Prentice-Hall.

Mechanic, David, and Linda H. Aiken 1989 "Access to Health Care and Use of Medical Care Services." In H. E. Freeman and S. Levine, eds., *Handbook of Medical Sociology,* 4th ed. Englewood Cliffs, N.J.: Prentice-Hall.

Parsons, Talcott 1951 "Illness and the Role of the Physician: A Sociological Perspective." *American Journal of Orthopsychiatry* 21:452–460.

Shortell, Stephen M., and Arnold D. Kaluzny 1987 "Organization Theory and Health Care Management." In S. M. Shortell and A. D. Kaluzny, eds., *Health Care Management.* New York: John Wiley.

– HOWARD E. FREEMAN

HETEROSEXUAL BEHAVIOR PATTERNS

Social science researchers have learned a great deal about human sexual behavior since Alfred Kinsey and his colleagues conducted their pioneering studies on male and female sexuality in the late 1940s and early 1950s (Kinsey et al. 1953; Kinsey, Pomeroy, and Martin 1948). However, much of what has been learned has focused on sexuality issues within a "social problems" context. Relatively little attention has been devoted to studying the expression of sexuality in noncontroversial, everyday life circumstances. Moreover, research typically has been conducted in a manner consistent with popular culture's image that individuals' sexuality reflects their innate biological and psychological traits (see Stein 1989 for a review of the major theoretical models guiding sex research, and for contemporary sociological theoretical statements on sexuality see Reiss 1986; Simon and Gagnon 1986).

The politics of sex research has clearly thwarted researchers' efforts to overcome the sharpest criticism of Kinsey's earlier work—biased sampling (see Callero and Howard 1989). Even the contemporary political climate, at least in the final decision-making stages, has impeded the scientific objective of developing a reliable, systematic understanding of individuals' sexual attitudes and behaviors. For example, during 1989 the U.S. House Appropriations Committee deleted $11 million from the 1990 fiscal appropriations bill for the Departments of Labor, Health and Human Services, Education and Related Agencies which had been targeted for a national survey of 20,000 Americans' sexual attitudes and behaviors. Similarly, Britain's former Prime Minister Margaret Thatcher canceled in the same year Britain's largest national sex survey, $1.2 million and 20,000 respondents, before it was fielded.

Data on sexuality issues remain quite limited and are restricted typically to descriptive questions about age at first intercourse and frequency of sexual relations.

Thus, nationally representative data on sexuality issues remain quite limited and are restricted typically to descriptive questions about age at first intercourse and frequency of sexual relations. Consequently, our knowledge about the more diverse and dynamic aspects of sexual experience is based on research with varying degrees of generalizability and scientific rigor. In general, sex researchers are probably challenged more by issues related to response bias, sample representativeness, measurement, and ethics than most social scientists because of the sensitive nature of sexuality. With these methodological issues in mind (see Bentler and Abramson 1980; Jayne 1986; Kelley 1986), and given this chapter's space limitations, this review assesses the available research on *heterosexual behavior* within the United States (individual chapters in this volume address homosexuality and lesbianism). The brevity of this chapter precludes reviewing the plethora of literature on individuals' subjective perceptions about sexuality. Although this discussion is not meant to be exhaustive, it does take into account four basic and interrelated features of sexuality: (1) its varied meaning throughout the life course; (2) the consensual and coercive contexts within which sex occurs; (3) the gendered aspects of its expression; and (4) the relationship between the HIV epidemic and sexual behavior. Finally, while this chapter reviews primarily social scientific literature, a number of authors have published books in the popular press—some of which have received considerable attention by the lay population—based on empirical findings often derived from self-selected samples of persons who returned magazine surveys (see Kelley 1990 for a review of these works).

Childhood Sexual Behavior

Anthropological research has shown quite clearly that, while individuals in Western cultures tend to view children as asexual, children are viewed as being capable of sexual activity within many nonindustrialized, non-Western countries (Ford and Beach 1951). Parents in these non-Western countries may sometimes tolerate and even encourage their children to pursue heterosexual behaviors (including intercourse), homosexual behaviors (e.g., fellatio), or both. In some societies mothers actually masturbate their children in order to soothe them. Given the Western view of children, it should not be surprising that little social science research has been conducted on childhood sexuality in the United States. Available research does indicate that boys are much more likely to masturbate and to do so at younger ages than are girls. For example, Hunt (1974) found that 63 percent of boys and 33 percent of girls in his nonrepresentative urban sample could recall having an orgasm while masturbating before the age of thirteen. Boys also appear to participate throughout childhood in both heterosexual and homosexual play activities that have sexual overtones (e.g., "doctor and nurse"). These activities typically include some element of exhibition, exploration, and experimentation.

Thorne and Lurias' (1986) participant observation study of nine- to eleven-year-old boys and girls within a school context provides fresh insights into studying childhood sexuality. Although this study does not address sexual behavior as defined in conventional "adult" terms, it is nevertheless an important contribution because it clarifies how children structure their social worlds in response to gender and sexuality issues. In the process, these authors assess the ways in which children structure their behavior by drawing upon and employing sexual meanings in their gender-differentiated environments. It seems reasonable to argue that these processes are likely to influence children's sexual behaviors later on in life as well.

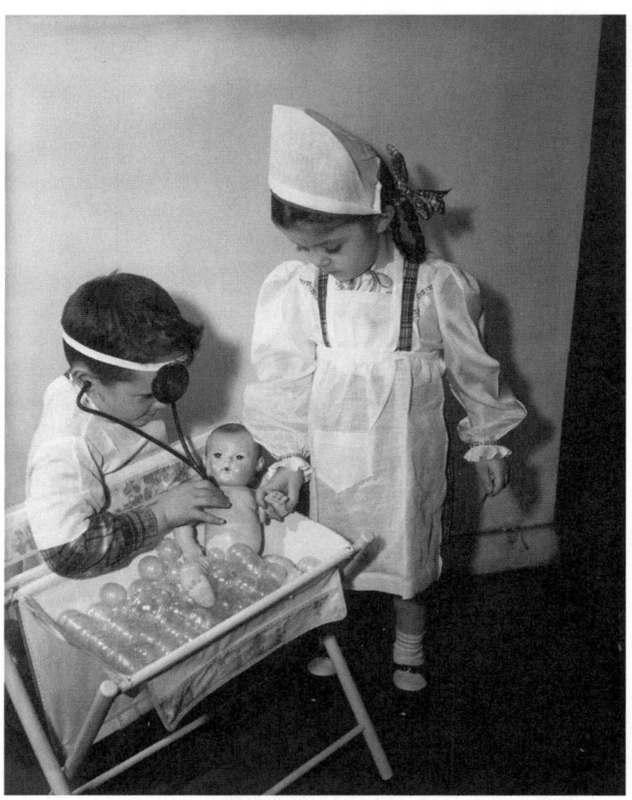

It is common for children to engage in play activities that include exploration and experimentation that sometimes has heterosexual or homosexual overtones. (UPI/Corbis-Bettmann)

Adolescent and Young Adult Sexual Behavior

In contrast to the small amount of research on childhood sexuality, an expansive body of literature on adolescent sexual behavior has emerged during the past two decades (see Hofferth 1987; Marsiglio 1988; Walsh 1989). Much of this research has used one of several national data sets to document and examine rates and trends for age at first intercourse, with particular attention given to racial patterns. Overall, the bulk of the evidence suggests that there was a sizable increase in the rate of sexual activity among teenage females during the 1970s, although this increase appears to have leveled off during the 1980s. Rates among black and white females converged during this period. Sexual activity rates among comparably aged males have also increased and have always been higher than those for females. While the rates for females and males converged during this period, some evidence suggests that this trend may have peaked.

One study that employed data from three separate national surveys compared the retrospective reports of females living in metropolitan areas at age fourteen who had been born between 1959 and 1963 and found that between 10.2 and 19 percent of whites had become sexually active before the age of sixteen and between 54.2 and 56.9 percent had had intercourse before their nineteenth birthday (Kahn, Kalsbeek, and Hofferth 1988). Meanwhile, the comparable range of percentages for black females was 18 to 42.3 and 73.4 to 85.5. Another study compared two separate national samples of metropolitan males born between 1959 and 1963 with those born between 1969 and 1973 and found that the more recent cohort was significantly more likely to initiate sex at younger ages (Sonenstein, Pleck, and Ku 1989). Whereas 55.7 and 77.5 percent of seventeen- and nineteen-year-old males from the older cohort were sexually active, 71.9 and 87.8 percent of the seventeen- and nineteen-year-olds in the more recent cohort of teenage males had already had intercourse.

Attempts to explain why youth initiate sex have focused primarily on the direct and indirect influence of sociodemographic, social psychological, and biological factors. In her review of research on sexual initiation, Hofferth (1987) posits a model that assesses the impact of both biological and psychosocial factors. Most of the research designs are not ideal for concluding a causal relationship between beliefs, attitudes, or values and sexual behavior because these variables tend to be measured simultaneously. Despite this methodological shortcoming, Hofferth identifies a number of factors that appear to be related positively (in a multivariate context) to the probability of individuals initiating intercourse at a young age: being black, living in a poverty area, having weak religious beliefs, attending a segregated school (for blacks), attending an integrated school (for whites), lower parental education, having a mother who was sexually active at a young age, living in a single parent household, having more siblings, and having a low level of academic achievement.

In addition to these social variables, Udry (1988) and his associates have employed biosocial models to conduct a series of novel studies of the sexual behavior of school-age youth in a southern public school setting. This research provides preliminary evidence that adolescents' sexuality (both attitudes and behavior) is related to hormonal factors and that models that posit an interaction between hormones and social variables may explain sexual behavior more fully than sociological models alone. While some sociologists have criticized this research because of the importance it places on the biological substratum, others have advocated the merits of developing biosocial models that take into account the complex interrelationship between the pubertal process, sexual identity development, sexual behavior, and societal norms.

While most research has focused on sexual intercourse, a number of studies of adolescent and college populations have examined issues related to other types of sex acts and the sequencing of petting behaviors. Researchers have shown, for example, that the prevalence of oral sex has grown tremendously during this century. Kinsey's data revealed that very few college women born between 1910 and 1935 performed fellatio (11 percent) or received cunnilingus (12 percent). More recent studies in California and North Carolina suggest that between one-third and one-half of adolescents fifteen to eighteen have engaged in oral sex (Hass 1979; Newcomer and Udry 1985), while nonrepresentative studies of college students in the United States and Canada indicate that between 32 and 86 percent of females have administered oral sex and between 44 and 68 percent say they have received it (Herold and Way 1983; Young 1980). Furthermore, Kinsey's data suggested that oral sex was primarily experienced only among those who also had experienced coitus (only 5 percent of male and female virgins reported performing it), but more recent research indicates that a sizable minority of youth are experiencing oral sex while they are still technically "virgins."

One recent fourteen-year study of three cohorts of women at the same Northeastern private university concluded that college women had not changed their sexual practices in terms of the frequency with which they engaged in fellatio, cunnilingus, and anal intercourse (Debuono et al. 1990). However, female students in 1989 were at least twice as likely to report using condoms "always or almost always" than their counterparts were in 1986. Another survey of college students at Rhode Island University in 1986 (Carroll 1988) found that 40 percent reported that their concern over AIDS had altered their sexual behavior. Among those sexually active, 54 percent had changed their behavior with 30 percent reporting that they exercised greater discretion when selecting partners—although this did *not* mean that they were more likely to enter an exclusive relationship, nor did it mean that they reduced coital frequency. Fifteen percent of the nonactive students said they had not engaged in sexual intercourse because of their concerns about AIDS.

Although researchers have used college populations to examine different aspects of young adults' sexual behavior, relatively little research has considered the sexual behavior of young and middle-aged heterosexual single adults, especially those not enrolled in college. One recent exception to this pattern that also dealt with the issue of HIV infection is the controversial epidemiological study by Masters, Kolodny, and Johnson (1988), which received extensive media coverage. Their study was based on a nonrandomly selected sample of 800 sexually active, self-identified heterosexuals, twenty-one to forty years of age, who had not had a blood transfusion or injected illegal drugs since 1977. Respondents were enrolled from one of four cities (Atlanta, Los Angeles, New York, and St. Louis), with half (200 men and 200 women) reporting that they had had at least six sexual partners during each of the preceding five years and the other half reporting that they were in a monogamous relationship for at least five years. The authors' major conclusion was that public health officials had grossly underestimated the incidence and spread of HIV. The authors contended that in the heterosexual population this rate would continue to climb because the most sexually active persons were insensitive to the possibility of HIV infection; none of the men and only 3 percent of the women reported using condoms regularly during the preceding year.

Sexually Coercive Behavior

Although most sexual interaction involves consenting partners, some does not. In response to the feminist movement, scholars increasingly have focused on the power dimension of sexuality by documenting and explaining the various forms of coercive sexuality (i.e., sexual relations that occur because of the threat or actual use of physical force or other controlling behaviors) and other exploitative forms of sexuality (for a macrosociological perspective on rape, see Baron and Straus 1987). The scientific rigor of research in this area has improved over the years, but questions concerning the validity of data persist, given the moral and criminal nature of these issues.

It is exceedingly difficult to estimate the prevalence of the various forms of coercive sexuality because the Uniform Crime Reports are widely believed to underreport the true rate of sex crimes, and anonymous, self-report surveys vary widely in their sampling techniques and findings. Nevertheless, Grauerholz and Solomon's (1989) succinct review of research in this area suggests that a large proportion of the U.S. population has or will experience coercive sexual relations at one time or another, either as a victim, a perpetrator, or both. Researchers' estimates of the pervasiveness of incest may vary the most. Whereas some researchers have observed that about 1 percent of U.S. females have been incest victims (Kempe and Kempe 1984), others have reported much higher figures. For example, Russell (1984) found that 16 percent of her large household sample of women eighteen years of age and older in San Francisco had experienced incest before age eighteen, and 20 percent of Finkelhor's (1979) predominantly white, middle class, New England college student sample who were raised primarily in nonmetropolitan areas reported having been an incest victim. While females are more likely to be the victims of coercive and exploitative sexuality, studies also indicate that many young boys are victimized in this manner (Finkelhor 1979; Moore, Nord, and Peterson 1989).

Mary Koss and her colleagues (Koss et al. 1985; Koss et al. 1988), using a recent national survey of college students, found that 38 percent of female college students reported sexual victimization that met the legal criterion for rape or attempted rape, and 7.7 percent of males actually admitted they had either raped or attempted to rape at least one woman since their fourteenth birthday, a finding supported by other studies (Mosher and Anderson 1986; Rapaport and Burkhart 1984). Using data from the 1987 wave of the National Survey of Children, Moore, Nord, and Peterson (1989) also found that about 7 percent of U.S. adults aged eighteen to twenty-two (females being more likely than males) confirmed that they had had sex against their will or had been raped at least on one occasion. Other researchers have reported that between 10 and 12 percent of women report having been raped by dates and between 8 and 14 percent of wives report that their husbands have sexually assaulted or raped them (Finkelhor and Yllo 1985; Russell and Howell 1982).

Having documented that coercive sexuality is quite prevalent, the question remains: Why do many men, and some women, coerce others to have sex with them? Some theorists argue that males are more likely to engage in various forms of coercive sexuality if they have strong ties to a peer group that supports sexually aggressive behavior. Compared to their less stereotypically masculine counterparts, men studied in the research noted above who possess strong "macho" personality characteristics and hold rigid, conservative views of sex-role stereotypes are more likely to report that they have used physical force and threats to have sex and that they would probably use physical force to obtain sex if they could be assured that they would not be prosecuted. Other theorists have argued that a small percentage of women may even facilitate different forms of coercive sexuality by playing sexually receptive or seductive roles. Not surprisingly, it is common for rapists to believe, or at least report, that their victims were willing participants who actually enjoyed themselves while being raped—even though these perceptions are clearly *incon-*

sistent with rape victims' own accounts (Scully and Marolla 1984).

While the several forms of coercive sexuality share a number of common themes, such as the objectification of women, individual factors and circumstances may be more or less significant in accounting for why particular types of coercive sexuality occur. One of the important factors that seems to distinguish the typical stranger or the acquaintance rapist from the "average" date rapist is the former's greater tendency to have been sexually or physically abused by his parents or others. Date rape incidences tend to involve partners who knew one another and had established at least a modicum of interpersonal trust by making a commitment to spend some time together. The dynamic nature of interaction episodes that typify date rapes, and the fact that at least one of the persons often has been influenced by drugs, alcohol, or both, can obscure participants' intentions and behavior. Furthermore, the more that individuals' sexual scripting is influenced by traditional gender-role socialization, the more likely coercive sexuality will occur because of sexual miscommunication and males' reliance on coping strategies that emphasize dominance and aggression. Many males assume that women will tend to offer token resistance to their sexual advances in order to create an impression that they are not sexually "promiscuous" (Check and Malamuth 1983). Indeed, one study of 610 female undergraduates revealed that almost 40 percent had engaged in this type of token resistance at least once (Muehlenhard and Hoolabaugh 1988). While these patterns should not be used to justify date rape in any way, it should come as no surprise that some males grossly distort the consensual petting that generally precedes date rape as a woman's way of acknowledging her willingness to engage in more intimate forms of sexual interaction—even if this means that in some cases males will be required to pursue it forcefully. Finally, while there are many factors related to fathers' incestuous behavior, one of the more frequently noted arguments underscores the common pattern whereby a father pursues sexual and emotional intimacy with his female children (usually a series of episodes over time with the eldest female child) in order to compensate for his unfulfilling relationship with the adult female, who generally has withdrawn from her roles as mother and wife (partner).

Pornography represents the final factor we discuss that may be related to coercive sexuality. Edward Donnenstein and N. Malamuth have conducted an ambitious series of social psychological experimental studies to examine the relationship between viewing pornographic materials (especially versions that depict male aggression toward women) and various forms of coercive sexuality. Donnenstein and Linz (1986, p. 212) conclude their review of the research that addresses the question of whether pornography influences men's attitudes and behaviors toward women by arguing that "there is no evidence for any 'harm'-related effects from sexually explicit materials. But research may support potential harmful effects from aggressive materials. Aggressive images are the issue, not sexual images."

Many males assume that women will offer token resistance to their sexual advances in order to create an impression that they are not sexually "promiscuous."

From a feminist perspective, instances of coercive sexuality all involve a critical power or control dimension; however, the issue of sexual discretion and availability must also be discussed in relation to many instances of coercive sexuality, especially date and marital rape. By definition, men can only engage in coercive sexuality with women if women do not want to have sex in a given instance. Unfortunately, data are not available that would enable a reliable analysis of historical trends to determine the ways and extent to which the change in norms regarding the sexual double standard, which was brought about by the women's movement, have altered rates (either increased or decreased) for different forms of coercive sexuality.

Prostitution

Contemporary sociological research on prostitution has typically involved small-scale, convenience samples. Unfortunately, Kinsey's nonrepresentative data, which are more than forty years old, are probably the best available data on clients of prostitutes. Gagnon (1977) suggested that the six most common reasons men visit prostitutes include: (1) sex without negotiation; (2) involvement without commitment; (3) sex for eroticism and variety; (4) a form of socializing; (5) sex away from home; and (6) sex for those who fear rejection most.

Many commentators have indicated that rates of prostitution, a form of commercialized sex that had in the past provided men with sexual opportunities in a less sexually open society, have decreased drastically since World War II. Kinsey reported that prior to the war between 60 and 70 percent of adult men had visited a prostitute and about 15 to 20 percent used them regularly. Some sociologists believed that prostitution served a useful societal function in that it provided men with a convenient sexual outlet, which in turn minimized the numbers of sexual transgressions against "respectable" women. One reason males may be using prostitutes less often during recent decades is that they can obtain sex more easily now and women appear to be more inclined to engage in sexual activities (e.g., oral-genital sex) that they previously had found less appealing. In addition, anecdotal and journalistic accounts suggest that some men today are avoiding prostitutes because they fear they would be exposed to the AIDS (HIV) virus.

Elderly Sexual Behavior

Although the proportion of the U.S. population over fifty continues to grow, research addressing the relationship between aging and sexuality, and in particular the sexual behavior of the elderly population (sixty-five and older), is still quite limited due to its frequent use of small, nonrepresentative samples, its cross-sectional research designs, and its narrow, youth-oriented definitions of sexuality as coitus. Consequently, generalizations are difficult to make, and most of the research on elderly persons' sexual behavior deals with the physiological and psychological aspects of this phenomenon. Several reviews of sexuality among the elderly currently exist (Ludeman 1981; Riportella-Muller 1989; Starr 1985).

Two of the more frequently cited studies of aging and sexuality issues include the Starr-Weiner Report (1981) and the second Duke Longitudinal Study (George and Weiler 1981), neither of which were based on random sampling techniques. The former included 800 sociodemographically diverse participants in senior centers, while the latter included a panel design of men and women health-insurance program participants, who were forty-six to seventy-one years of age at the first observation period in 1969 and were followed for six years ($n = 348$ for those enrolled in all four data collection points). Seventy-five percent of the respondents in the first study reported that sex felt as good or better than when they were younger. Results from an analysis restricted to the 278 *married* respondents who had been retained throughout the Duke study revealed that patterns of sexual interest and activity remained fairly stable over time, men reported higher levels of sexual interest and activity than their female age peers, and younger cohorts of respondents reported higher levels of sexual interest and activity.

Compared to earlier studies (e.g., the Kinsey reports), the Starr-Weiner and Duke studies as well as more recent ones have found higher levels of sexual activity among older persons. Accordingly, Riportella-Muller (1989, p. 214) concluded that "for those elderly who remain sexually active and have a regular partner, the rate of decline is not as great as formerly believed." However, many older persons do not remain sexually active. Indeed, George and Weiler (1981) found, using data from the second Duke study, that of those who were at least fifty-six years of age at the first observation date, 21 percent of men and 39 percent of women reported six years later that they had either abstained from sexual relations throughout the study or were currently inactive.

In a recent study using data from a nationally representative household sample, Marsiglio and Donnelly (forthcoming) found that about 53 percent of all married persons sixty years of age and older reported having coitus within the past month with 65 percent of those sixty to sixty-five years old being sexually active compared to 44 percent of those sixty-six or older. Among those who had been coitally active during the past month, the overall mean frequency for coitus was 4.3 times. In a multivariate context, persons were most likely to have had coitus during the past month if they were younger, married to a spouse who self-reported his or her health status as favorable, and had a higher sense of self-worth and competency. Surprisingly, when an interaction term was used to compare husbands and wives, no significant differences were observed in the way their partner's health status was related to their coital behavior, although other research has found that both husbands and wives report that males' attitudes or physical condition tends to be the principal reason why they have curtailed or ceased to have sexual relations. Meanwhile, other research indicates that being widowed is the most frequently cited reason for not being sexually active among older women overall. While data on persons who are institutionalized are scarce, it appears as though their sexual activity levels are rather low.

Being without a spouse does not necessarily mean that older persons will be sexually inactive.

Being without a spouse does not necessarily mean that older persons will be sexually inactive. Brecher (1984) reported, for example, that among unmarried persons sixty years of age and older, about 75 percent of men and 50 percent of women were sexually active. These findings are reinforced by Starr and Weiner's (1981) finding that 70 percent of their respondents over sixty were sexually active, although only 47 percent were married. Finally, masturbation is another option used by some elderly to express their sexuality, presumably in a nonsocial setting. A few studies have found that about one-third of women and slightly less than one-half of men over seventy report masturbating.

Conclusion

This brief review has documented the extensive efforts of social scientists during recent decades to enhance our understanding of human sexual behavior. Indeed, our knowledge of sexual behavior has increased dramatically since the days of Kinsey's early studies. This review also serves as a reminder, however, that our knowledge about human sexual behavior, in some areas more so than others, remains quite limited. Moreover, our knowledge is a function of both moral and political decisions. Just as social scientists can largely be held accountable for any shortcomings associated with the prevailing theoretical approaches to sexuality issues, the larger society and its institutionalized mechanisms for providing research support, are responsible in various ways for impeding the research community's efforts to understand sexual behavior. Because sexual activity tends to be a highly private social experience, social scientists' incremental advances in documenting and explaining it are linked inevitably to the lay population's commitment to this type of research endeavor.

[See also Courtship; Sexual Behavior and Marriage; Sexual Orientation; Sexual Violence and Abuse.]

BIBLIOGRAPHY

Baron, Larry, and Murray A. Straus 1987 "Four Theories of Rape: A Macrosociological Analysis." *Social Problems* 34:467–489.

Bentler, P. M., and P. R. Abramson 1980 "Methodological Issues in Sex Research: An Overview." In R. Green and J. Weiner, eds., *Methodological Issues in Sex Research.* Rockville, Md.: National Institute of Mental Health, U.S. Department of Health and Human Services.

Brecher, Edward 1984 *Love, Sex, and Aging: A Consumer Union Report.* Mount Vernon, N.Y.: Consumers Union.

Callero, Peter L, and Judith A. Howard 1989 "Biases of the Scientific Discourse on Human Sexuality: Toward a Sociology of Sexuality." In Kathleen McKinney and Susan Sprecher, eds., *Human Sexuality: The Societal and Interpersonal Context.* Norwood, N.J.: Ablex.

Carrol, Leo 1988 "Concern with AIDS and the Sexual Behavior of College Students." *Journal of Marriage and the Family* 50:405–411.

Check, J. V. P., and N. M. Malamuth 1983 "Sex Role Stereotyping and Reactions to Depictions of Stranger vs. Acquaintance Rape." *Journal of Personality and Social Psychology* 45:344–356.

Debuono, Barbara A., Stephen H. Zinner, Maxim Daamen, and William M. McCormack 1990 *The New England Journal of Medicine* 322:821–825.

Donnenstein, E., and D. Linz 1986 "Mass Media Sexual Violence and Male Viewers." *American Behavioral Scientist* 29:601–618.

Finkelhor, D. 1979 *Sexually Victimized Children.* New York: Free Press.

———, and K. Yllo 1985 *License to Rape.* New York: Holt, Rinehart and Winston.

Ford, Clellan, and F. Beach 1951 *Patterns of Sexual Behavior.* New York: Harper.

Gagnon, John 1977 *Human Sexualities.* Glenview, Ill.: Scott, Foresman.

George, L. K., and S. J. Weiler 1981 "Sexuality in Middle and Late Life." *Archives of General Psychiatry* 38:919–923.

Grauerholz, Elizabeth, and Jennifer Crew Solomon 1989 "Sexual Coercion: Power and Violence." In Kathleen McKinney and Susan Sprecher, eds., *Human Sexuality: The Societal and Interpersonal Context.* Norwood, N.J.: Ablex.

Hass, W. 1979 *Teenage Sexuality.* New York. Macmillan.

Herold, W., and L. Way 1983 "Oral-Genital Sexual Behavior in a Sample of University Females." *The Journal of Sex Research* 19:327–338.

Hofferth, Sandra L. 1987 "Factors Affecting Initiation of Sexual Intercourse." In Sandra L. Hofferth and Cheryl D. Hayes, eds., *Risking the Future: Adolescent Sexuality, Pregnancy, and Childbearing.* Washington, D.C.: National Academy Press.

Hunt, M. 1974 *Sexual Behavior in the 1970s.* Chicago: Playboy Press.

Jayne, C. E. 1986 "Methodology on Sex Research in 1986: An Editor's Commentary." *The Journal of Sex Research* 22:1–5.

Kahn, Joan R., William D. Kalsbeek, and Sandra L. Hofferth 1988 "National Estimates of Teenage Sexual Activity: Evaluating the Comparability of Three National Surveys." *Demography* 25:189–204.

Kelley, Gary F. 1990 *Sexuality Today: The Human Perspective.* Guilford, Conn.: Dushkin Publishing.

Kelley, K. 1986 "Integrating Sex Research." In D. Bryne and K. Kelley, eds., *Alternative Approaches to the Study of Sexual Behavior.* Hillsdale, N.J.: Erlbaum.

Kempe, R. S., and H. Kempe 1984 *The Common Secret: Sexual Abuse of Children and Adolescents.* New York: Freeman and Co.

Kinsey, Alfred C., Wardell Pomeroy, and Clyde Martin 1948 *Sexual Behavior in the Human Male.* Philadelphia: Saunders.

Kinsey, Alfred C., Wardell Pomeroy, Clyde Martin, and Paul Gebhard 1953 *Sexual Behavior in the Human Female.* Philadelphia: Saunders.

Koss, Mary, Thomas E. Dinero, Cynthia A. Seibel, and Susan L. Cox 1988 "Stranger and Acquaintance Rape: Are There Differences in the Victim's Experience?" *Psychology of Women Quarterly* 12:1–23.

Koss, Mary, Kenneth E. Leonard, Dana A. Beezley, and Cheryl J. Oros 1985 "Nonstranger Sexual Aggression: A Discriminant Analysis of the Psychological Characteristics of Undetected Offenders." *Sex Roles* 12:981–992.

Ludeman, Kate 1981 "The Sexuality of the Older Person: Review of the Literature." *Gerontologist* 21:203–208.

Marsiglio, William 1988 "Adolescent Male Sexuality and Heterosexual Masculinity: A Conceptual Model and Review." *Journal of Adolescent Research* 3:285–303.

———, and Denise Donnelly forthcoming "Sexual Intercourse in Later Life: A National Study of Married Persons." *Journal of Gerontology.*

Masters, William H., V. E. Johnson, and R. C. Kolodny 1988 *Crisis: Heterosexual Behavior in the Age of AIDS.* New York: Grove Press.

Moore, Kristin Anderson, Christine Winquist Nord, and James L. Peterson 1989 "Nonvoluntary Sexual Activity among Adolescents." *Family Planning Perspectives* 21:110–114.

Mosher, D. L., and R. D. Anderson 1986 "Macho Personality, Sexual Aggression, and Reactions to Guided Imagery of Realistic Rape." *Journal of Research in Personality* 20:77–94.

Muehlenhard, C. L., and L. C. Hollabaugh 1988 "Do Women Sometimes Say No When They Mean Yes: The Prevalence and Correlates of Women's Token Resistance to Sex." *Journal of Personality and Social Psychology* 54:872–879.

Newcomer, S., and J. Udry 1985 "Oral Sex in an Adolescent Population." *Archives of Sexual Behavior* 14:41–46.

Rapaport, K., and B. R. Burkhart 1984 "Personality and Attitudinal Correlates of Sexual Coercive College Males." *Journal of Abnormal Personality* 93:216–221.

Reiss, Ira L. 1986 *Journey into Sexuality: An Exploratory Voyage.* Englewood Cliffs, N.J.: Prentice-Hall.

Riportella-Muller, Roberta 1989 "Sexuality in the Elderly: A Review." In Kathleen McKinney and Susan Sprecher, eds., *Human Sexuality: The Societal and Interpersonal Context.* Norwood, N.J.: Ablex.

Russell, D. E. 1984 *Sexual Exploitation.* Beverly Hills, Calif.: Sage.

Russell, D. E. H., and N. Howell 1982 *Rape in Marriage.* New York: Macmillan.

Scully, D., and J. Marolla 1984 "Convicted Rapists' Vocabulary of Motive: Excuses and Justifications." *Social Problems* 31:530–544.

Simon, William, and John H. Gagnon 1986 "Sexual Scripts: Permanence and Change." *Archives of Sexual Behavior* 15:97–120.

Sonenstein, Freya, Joseph Pleck, and Leighton C. Ku 1989 "Sexual Activity, Condom Use and AIDS Awareness Among Adolescent Males." *Family Planning Perspectives* 21:152–158.

Starr, Bernard D. 1985 "Sexuality and Aging." *Annual Review of Gerontology and Geriatrics* 5:97–126.

———, and Marcella B. Weiner 1981 *The Starr-Weiner Report on Sex and Sexuality in the Mature Years.* Briarcliff Manor, N.Y.: Stein & Day.

Stein, Arlene 1989 "Three Models of Sexuality: Drives, Identities, and Practices." *Sociological Theory* 7:1–13.

Thorne, Barrie, and Zella Luria 1986 "Sexuality and Gender in Children's Daily Worlds." *Social Problems* 33:176–190.

Udry, J. Richard 1988 "Biological Predispositions and Social Control in Adolescent Sexual Behavior." *American Sociological Review* 53:709–722.

Walsh, Robert H. 1989 "Premarital Sex among Teenagers and Young Adults." In Kathleen McKinney and Susan Sprecher, eds., *Human Sexuality: The Societal and Interpersonal Context.* Norwood, N.J.: Ablex.

Young, M. 1980 "Attitudes and Behaviors of College Students Relative to Oral-Genital Sexuality." *Archives of Sexual Behavior* 9:61–67.

– WILLIAM MARSIGLIO
JOHN H. SCANZONI

HISPANIC-AMERICAN STUDIES

Despite their common linguistic heritage, Hispanic-Americans are a heterogeneous and rapidly growing population that includes no less than twenty-three distinct national identities and combines recent immigrants with groups whose ancestors predated the formation of the United States as we know it today. In 1989 the U.S. Census Bureau estimated the Hispanic population at 20.1 million, with nearly two-thirds (63 percent) of Mexican origin, while 12 percent traced their origins to Puerto Rico, 5 percent to Cuba, and 13 percent to other Central and South American nations. An additional 8 percent of Hispanics were of unspecified national origin, which includes mixed Spanish-speaking nationalities, Spaniards, and "Hispanos," the descendants of the original Spanish settlers in what came to be known as Colorado and New Mexico.

The two largest groups also have the oldest established communities in the United States, but the Cuban presence is clearly evident in southern Florida and selected neighborhoods of various northeastern and midwestern cities. Furthermore, the late 1970s and 1980s witnessed the proliferation of Central and South American ethnic neighborhoods in various cities across the United States but especially the major cities of southern California, Texas, New York, Florida, and Illinois. Although small Cuban and Puerto Rican communities can be traced back to the turn of the century and before, these settlements were tiny and geographically contained compared to the Mexican presence in the Southwest.

Social science interest in Hispanic-Americans has increased greatly since 1960, and the scope of topics investigated has expanded accordingly. Whereas studies conducted during the 1960s and through the mid-1970s tended to focus on one highly localized population, the 1980s witnessed a proliferation of designs that compared group experiences. This shift in the research agenda brought into focus the theme of diversity and inequality among national origin groups. Beyond cultural, generational, and socioeconomic heterogeneity as a defining feature of Hispanic-Americans, two additional themes stand out in recent writings about this population. One concerns the rate of growth and persisting residential concentration, and the second, which is related to the first, concerns their long-term prospects for social integration. As one of the most rapidly growing minority populations in the United States, the growing Hispanic presence has raised fears about the potential "Latinization" or "Hispanicization" of the United States. Such nativist sentiments are particularly evident in areas where Hispanics are highly concentrated.

Larger numbers are not likely to be the most decisive force shaping the Hispanic imprint on the U.S. ethnic landscape, for size does not automatically confer power. As numbers increase, politics also become increasingly important in determining the social and economic destiny of Hispanic origin groups. To evaluate the likely imprint of Hispanics in the United States, the following article summarizes several themes that have unfolded in the sociological literature on Hispanic-Americans. These include: the changing social and demographic composition of the population; the origin of current ethnic labels; the roots of diversification; and the political implications of recent social and economic trends. A concluding section summarizes key lessons from existing studies and identifies areas for further investigation.

Recent Demographic and Socioeconomic Trends

Until World War II, virtually all people currently classified as Hispanics were of Mexican origin, but after the war this picture changed radically with the advent of heavy migration from Puerto Rico to the Northeast and the arrival of thousands of Cubans in south Florida and the Northeast following the 1959 Cuban Revolution. Although immigration has figured prominently in the growth of the Hispanic population since 1941, its influence on demographic growth has been especially pronounced since 1965. In 1960 the Hispanic population was just under seven million; but by 1980 the population had doubled, and it had tripled by 1990! The significance of this growth—phenomenal by any standard—is accentuated when evaluated against evidence that the growth rate of the non-Hispanic white population has slowed. Hence, by 1989 approximately 8 percent of the U.S. population was Hispanic, compared with 4 percent in 1960.

Consistent with the theme of increasing differentiation along national-origin lines, growth rates differed among the major nationality groups. Owing to continued high fertility and heavy immigration during the 1980s, the Mexican share of the total rose from 60 to 63 percent, while the Puerto Rican share declined from 14 to 12 percent. This decline resulted from lower fertility and the absence of a strong net in-migration flow from the island. Furthermore, as immigration from Central and South America continued, these groups increased their shares of the Hispanic population from 7 to 12 percent. This increase in population shares was also accompanied by changes in the country-of-origin composition. By 1980 over one in three Hispanics from Central America and the Caribbean traced their origins to the Dominican Republic, compared to less than one in five two decades earlier. When military and political events in Central America escalated during the 1980s, the presence of immigrants from El Salvador, Guatemala, and Nicaragua also began to rise. However, the future prospects of these flows remain highly uncertain.

The visibility of distinct Hispanic communities is heightened by persisting regional concentration along national origin lines. Two states—California and Texas—housed half of all Hispanics in 1989, with Mexicans and Central Americans disproportionately concentrated in these states. Despite some tendency toward residential dispersion, Puerto Ricans remain concentrated in the Northeast—predominantly in the large cities of New York and New Jersey—while Cubans have become bimodally distributed in south Florida and large northeastern cities (Bean and Tienda 1987). Residential segregation compounds geographic concentration further by spatially isolating some Hispanics—particularly those of low socioeconomic status and recent immigrant groups—from non-Hispanic whites. This segregation reinforces the cultural distinctiveness of Hispanics in regions where visible communities have been established.

The diverse immigration histories and settlement patterns of Mexicans, Puerto Ricans, and Cubans manifest themselves in distinct subpopulations with clearly discernible social and economic profiles.

A social and economic profile of the Hispanic population since 1960 provides signals of optimism and pessimism about the long-term economic prospects of distinct nationality groups. Trends in educational attainment are quite revealing in themselves and in terms of their implications for labor-market prospects. On the one hand, from 1960 to 1988 Hispanics witnessed an unmistakable improvement in their educational achievement. On the other hand, high school noncompletion rates remain disturbingly high for Mexicans and Puerto Ricans—the two groups with the longest history in the United States. That Cubans outperform these two groups undermines simplistic explanations that immigration and language are the reasons for the continued educational underachievement of Mexicans and Puerto Ricans.

These educational disadvantages carry into the labor market. Since 1960 the labor-force standing of Puerto Rican men and women has deteriorated, while Cubans have become virtually indistinguishable from non-Hispanic whites in terms of participation rates, unemployment rates, and occupational profiles. Mexicans stand somewhere between these extremes, with greater success than Puerto Ricans in securing employment. However, Mexicans are more highly represented among the working poor than are whites. Puerto Rican men witnessed unusually high rates of labor-force withdrawal during the 1970s, and their labor-force behavior has converged with that of economically disadvantaged blacks (Tienda 1989). Numerous explanations have been provided for the deteriorating labor-market position of Puerto Ricans, including the unusually sharp decline of manufacturing jobs in the Northeast; the decline of union jobs in which Puerto Ricans traditionally concentrated; increased labor-market competition with Colombian and Dominican immigrants; and the placement of Puerto Rican workers at the bottom of a labor queue. However, empirical tests of these working hypotheses—all of which have merit—have not been forthcoming.

Less debatable than the causes of weakened labor-market position are its economic consequences. During the 1970s median family incomes of blacks and whites respectively increased 8 and 6 percent in real terms, compared with increases of 18 and 20 percent enjoyed by Mexicans and Cubans. However, during this same decade, family incomes of Puerto Ricans and Central and South Americans weathered real declines of about 4 to 6 percent (Tienda and Jensen 1988). For the latter, this decline can be traced to changes in the class composition of recent immigrants coupled with deleterious effects of the recession of the early 1980s. Again, the reasons for the decline in Puerto Rican incomes are more perplexing and in any event must be associated with the weakened labor-market standing of this group. It is also unclear why the deleterious effects of recessions take their heaviest toll on minority groups, but this phenomenon is consistent with the premises of queuing theory, which claims that groups at the bottom of a status hierarchy will benefit most from economic expansion and lose most from economic contraction (Lieberson 1980). The merits of this perspective have yet to be explored systematically with Hispanic groups.

Ethnic Labels Amidst Diversity

Ethnic labels are partly imposed by the host society and partly taken by immigrant groups who wish to preserve their national identity. The labels *Spanish Origin* and *Hispanic* originally were coined as terms of convenience for official reporting purposes. Essentially these labels serve as an umbrella to identify persons of Latin American origin who reside in the United States. Before the mid-1960s, Hispanics were unfamiliar to most observers outside the Southwest, where persons of Mexican ancestry were well represented, and the Northeast, where Puerto Rican communities began to flourish after

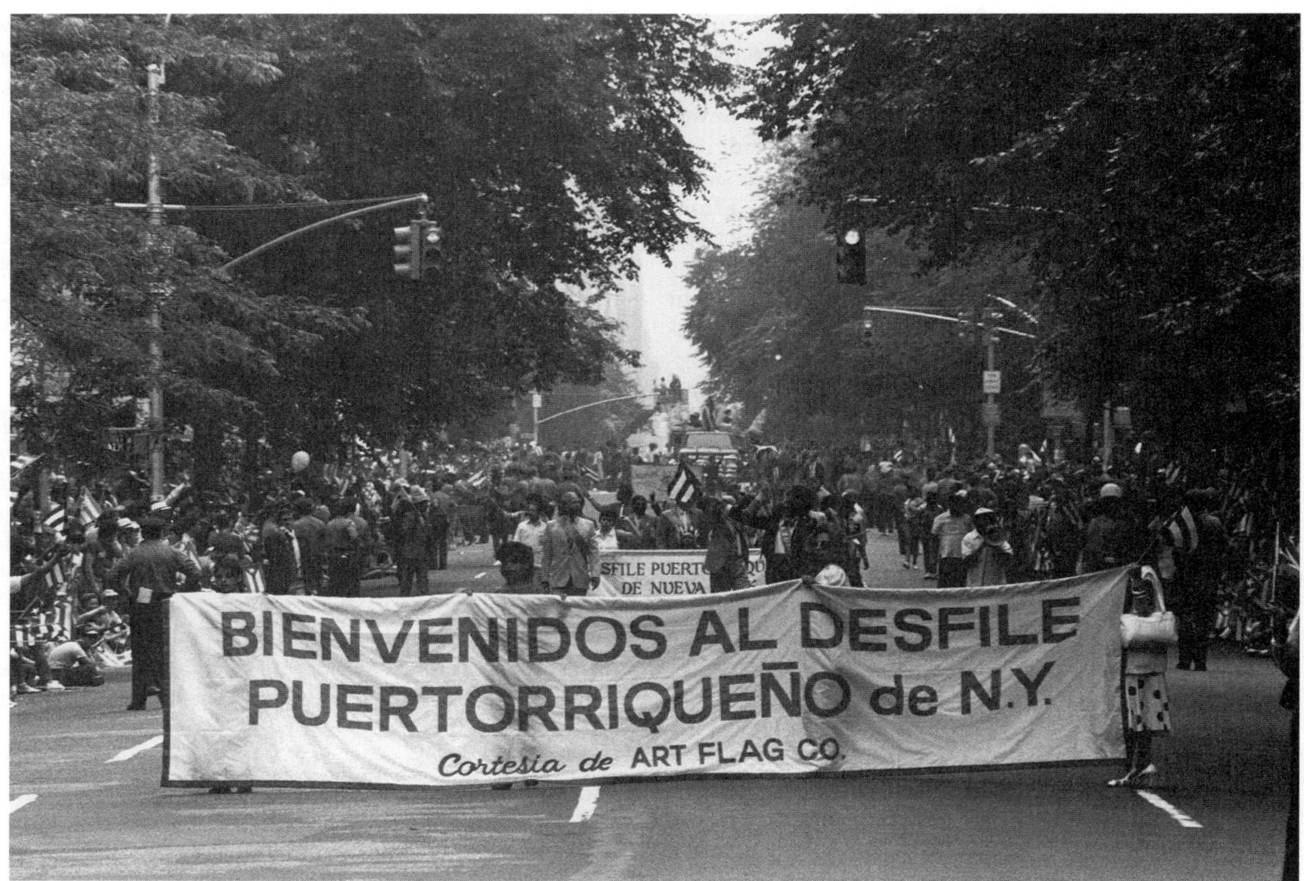

A strong Puerto Rican presence in the Northeastern United States can be seen in such events as this Puerto Rican Day parade in New York City. Immigrants from Mexico, Puerto Rico, and Cuba make up a large percentage of Hispanic-Americans. (Owen Franken/Corbis)

World War II. Therefore, until 1960 the "Spanish-surname" concept was adequate for identifying persons of Mexican origin residing in the Southwest, and "Puerto Rican stock" was used to identify persons who resided in the Northeast (predominantly New York) and who were born in or whose parents were born in Puerto Rico. However, with increasing intermarriage and residential dispersion, these concepts became progressively less useful to identify persons from Mexico and Puerto Rico. Furthermore, the influx of immigrants from Central and South America and the Spanish-speaking Caribbean into areas traditionally inhabited by Mexicans and Puerto Ricans required labels that could better represent the growing diversity along national origin lines.

In recognition of the growing residential and marital heterogeneity of the Spanish-speaking population, in 1970 the U.S. Census Bureau adopted the "Spanish Origin concept," which was based on self-identification and could be administered to the U.S. population on a national level (Bean and Tienda 1987). And in 1980 the term *Hispanic* accompanied *Spanish Origin* on the census schedule to identify persons from Latin America. However, through the 1980s the term *Latino* came into popular use as an alternative to *Hispanic.* As a symbol of self-determination and self-definition, it is the label preferred by many ethnic scholars—second, of course, to specific national identities. The label *Hispanic* was used in the 1990 census to identify persons from Latin America (except Brazil) and Spain, or whose ancestors were traced to these countries, but whether the label *Latino* will appear in the census of 2000 remains to be seen.

Despite their popular use and administrative legitimacy, generic terms such as *Latino* or *Hispanic* are less precise ethnic labels than Puerto Rican, Venezuelan, Cuban, or Mexican. In fact, the considerable socioeconomic and generational diversity of Hispanic-Americans undermines the value of a common ethnic label—except for administrative efficiency. The diverse immigration histories and settlement patterns of Mexicans, Puerto Ricans, Cubans, and persons from Central and South America manifest themselves in distinct subpopulations with clearly discernible social and economic profiles and with apparently unequal opportunities to succeed. Not surprisingly, diversity along national origin lines became a major intellectual theme in the scholarly writings about Hispanics during the mid- to late 1980s.

The Roots of Diversity

The cultural and socioeconomic heterogeneity of Hispanic-Americans can be traced to the diverse modes of incorporation into the United States. Nelson and Tienda (1985) proposed a framework for conceptualizing the emergence, consolidation, and persistence of distinct Hispanic ethnicities. They identified three domains of immigrant incorporation that are pertinent for understanding socioeconomic stratification of Hispanics: (1) the mode of entry, namely whether groups were colonized or migrated voluntarily; (2) the mode of integration, that is, the climate of reception at the time of mass entrance to the host society; and (3) the reaffirmation of national origin. The latter emphasizes the distinction between the cultural or symbolic content of Hispanic origin and the economic consequences of ethnicity that result in the formation of minority groups. This distinction between the economic and the cultural underpinnings of Hispanic national origins is pertinent for theorizing about the long-term integration prospects of Hispanics.

Along these three domains of ethnic incorporation, the major national origin groups exhibit considerable diversity. For example, the origin of the Mexican and Puerto Rican communities can be traced to annexation, although the timing and particulars of both cases were quite distinct. The annexation of Mexican territory resulted from a political settlement subsequent to military struggle and was followed by massive and voluntary wage-labor migration throughout the twentieth century, but particularly after 1960. The Puerto Rican annexation will remain an incomplete process until statehood or independence is achieved, but, like the Mexican experience, it was characterized by a massive wage-labor flow well after Puerto Rico was officially made a Commonwealth of the United States.

These distinct modes of incorporation are sharpened by the Cuban experience, whose socioeconomic success is as striking as the socioeconomic failure of Puerto Ricans. The Cuban community was established by political events that eventuated in the creation of a wave of political refugees who were themselves differentiated by social classes. The so-called golden exile cohort, which virtually gutted the Cuban middle class, was followed by the exodus of skilled and semiskilled workers who made up the vast majority of Cuban emigres. Although the distinction between political and economic migrants is murky, unlike wage-labor migrants, political refugees commanded immediate acceptance from the host society, however symbolic in character. Hence, the Cuban experience also stands in sharp contrast to that of recent political refugees from Central America (Guatemala and El Salvador, primarily) whose refugee story is one of clandestine entry and extended legal and political struggles for recognition. These groups have yet to be officially recognized as political refugees.

Immigration from Central and South America has continued to diversify not only the country-of-origin composition of the Hispanic population but also the socioeconomic position of the various groups. However, the future role of immigration in stratifying the Hispanic population is highly uncertain, as these depend both on changes in U.S. foreign policy toward Central and South America and on revisions in immigration policy concerning the disposition of undocumented aliens and quotas on future admissions. Nonetheless, a comparison of wage-labor migration histories of Hispanics clearly illustrates how diverse modes of entry and integration fueled the diversification of Hispanic-Americans.

Ethnic reaffirmation and consolidation can best be understood as immigrant minority communities define themselves vis-a-vis the host society. For groups who were relatively successful in adapting to the host society, such as Cubans, national heritage acquired a highly symbolic character, used for economic relationships when expedient and downplayed otherwise. Alternatively, for immigrants destined to become minorities, class position and national origin become inextricably linked when social opportunities are limited or blocked altogether, as seems to have occurred for Mexicans and especially Puerto Ricans, or when illegal status forces many underground, as occurred among large segments of the Dominican, Colombian, and Mexican labor pools. Thus, the distinction between symbolic ethnicity and minority status revolves around the degree of choice groups have in controlling their socioeconomic destiny (Gans 1979; Vincent 1974). This distinction is pertinent for understanding the increasing socioeconomic and demographic heterogeneity among Hispanic-Americans.

Integration Prospects

The changing demography of Hispanics has direct implications for the integration of Hispanic immigrant minority groups. First, the rapid growth and residential concentration of the groups raise questions about the prospects for assimilation of Hispanics. Second, the rising salience of immigration as a component of demographic growth serves to revitalize Hispanic cultures even as earlier arrivals are culturally assimilated, while also reactivating nativist sentiments when economic opportunities shrink and Hispanic immigrants are seen to be in competition for jobs.

Puerto Ricans are U.S. citizens by definition and enjoy most of the privileges that citizenship confers, while Mexicans who enter legally must wait at least five years to apply for citizenship. Those who enter illegally continue to have an uncertain status in the United States. That Puerto Ricans have been less successful economically than Mexicans places in question the significance of citizenship as a requisite for socioeconomic integration. The newest wage-labor migrants—Colombians, Dominicans, and some Central Americans—seem to be faring better than Puerto Ricans, posing yet another challenge to conventional understandings about immigrant assimilation processes, but it is too early to determine their placement in the ethnic queue because the process of assignment appears to be quite fluid. Furthermore, the growing number of illegals among these groups could undermine their political leverage over the short to medium term.

Some observers interpret the rise and proliferation of ethnic neighborhoods as evidence of limited integration prospects, irrespective of whether the segregation is voluntary or involuntary.

Although it is difficult to predict the long-term integration prospects of any group, the diversity of the Hispanic experience complicates this task further because of the uncertain future of immigration and the state of the economy and because the political participation of Hispanics traditionally has been low. While the spatial concentration of Hispanics allows native languages to flourish and under some circumstances promotes ethnic enterprises, some observers interpret the rise and proliferation of ethnic neighborhoods as evidence of limited integration prospects, irrespective of whether the segregation is voluntary or involuntary. An alternative interpretation of rising residential segregation among Hispanics is that of ethnic resilience. This perspective maintains that in the face of interethnic tension and economic adversity, individuals rely on their ethnic compatriots for social supports and hence promote solidarity along ethnic lines. One implication of this view is that ethnic resilience is the *consequence* rather than the *cause* of unequal integration prospects, and their tendency to elaborate ethnic ties reflects their tentative acceptance by the dominant society. As such, ethnic traits become enduring rather than transitional features of Hispanic neighborhoods (Portes and Bach 1980).

A similar debate over the integration prospects of Hispanics clouds the issue of Spanish retention, which is politically significant because it provides a ready target for policies designed to assimilate linguistically diverse populations and because Spanish retention is a ready scapegoat for the poor educational achievement of Mexicans and Puerto Ricans. While there exists considerable controversy about the socioeconomic consequences of bilingualism, the preponderance of research shows that Spanish retention and bilingualism per se are not the sources of Hispanic underachievement. Rather, the failure to acquire proficiency in English is the source of underachievement. In support of the distinction between bilingualism and lack of proficiency in English, there is some evidence that bilingualism may be an asset, albeit only among the middle classes who are able to convert this skill to social and financial resources (Lopez 1976; Tienda 1982). The failure of many Hispanics to achieve proficiency in English certainly limits their economic opportunities, but it is facile to equate lack of proficiency in English with bilingualism, which does not preclude proficiency in English.

Finally, the socioeconomic prospects of the Hispanic population depend on whether and how groups from specific localities or national origin groups mobilize themselves to serve ethnic interests. The record on Hispanic political participation shows great room for improvement. Obviously, Hispanics do not represent a unified political force nationally, and the fragility of their coalitions could easily be undermined by the trend toward greater socioeconomic inequality. Furthermore, greater numbers are insufficient to guarantee increased representation, particularly for a population with a large number of persons under voting age, coupled with low rates of naturalization and, among eligible voters, a dismal record at the polls. That voter turnout also varies by national origin will further divide the fragile Hispanic political alliances, such as the Hispanic Caucus, by splitting the Hispanic vote along class and party lines.

Summary

Several lessons can be culled from the scholarly literature and public discourse over the social and economic future of Hispanic-Americans. One is that generic labels, like *Hispanic* and *Latino,* are not useful for portraying the heterogeneous socioeconomic integration experiences of the Hispanic national origin groups. A second major lesson is that the evolving differentials in economic standing of Hispanic national origin groups are rooted in the distinct *modes of incorporation* of each group, which in turn have profound implications for integration prospects. A third major lesson, which is related to the second, is that the socioeconomic imprint of Hispanic-Americans will be as varied as the population itself. Changes in immigrant composition and residential segregation will play decisive parts in determining how Hispanics shape the ethnic landscape of the United States into the twenty-first century.

The nagging question is: Why does there persist a close association between Hispanic national origin and low social standing? On this matter there is much debate, but both sides accord great emphasis to the role of immigration in deciding the socioeconomic destiny of Hispanic-Americans. One interpretation—the replenishment argument—emphasizes how immigration continues to diversify the composition of the population by introducing new arrivals on the lower steps of a social escalator, while earlier arrivals experience gradual improvements in their economic and social statuses. Consistent with the predictions of classical assimilation theory, this view implies that observed differences in socioeconomic standing among Hispanics will disappear with time, irrespective of country of origin or period of arrival. Lending support to this prediction is a growing body of evidence showing that later arrivals fare better in the U.S. labor market and social institutions than do earlier arrivals.

Despite some compelling aspects of the replenishment argument, it falls short of accounting for the limited social mobility of Mexicans and Puerto Ricans, the two groups with the longest exposure to U.S. institutions and traditions. These experiences challenge the replenishment argument and place greater emphasis on the complex set of circumstances that define distinct modes of incorporation for the major national origin groups and entry cohorts. The structural interpretation emphasizes the role of unique historical circumstances under which each national origin group established its presence in the United States and acknowledges that social opportunities depend greatly on the state of the economy and public receptiveness toward new arrivals.

Unfortunately, it is too early to evaluate the relative merits of the two hypotheses, especially in the absence of longitudinal data required to trace socioeconomic trajectories of successive generations. That the future of immigration (its volume, source countries, and composition) is highly indeterminate further aggravates the difficulties of assessing these hypotheses. Of course, the greatest uncertainty about immigration concerns the flow of illegal migrants—both in terms of its volume and source countries. Finally, the socioeconomic fate of Hispanic-Americans as a whole and as separate national origin groups will depend also on the extent to which Hispanic elected and appointed officials use ethnicity as a criterion for defining their political agendas. The 1990s will be pivotal in resolving these uncertainties.

[See also Discrimination; Ethnicity.]

BIBLIOGRAPHY

Bean, Frank D., and Marta Tienda 1987 *The Hispanic Population of the United States.* New York: Russell Sage Foundation.

Gans, Herbert J. 1979 "Symbolic Ethnicity: The Future of Ethnic Groups and Cultures in America." *Ethnic and Racial Studies* 2:1–19.

Lieberson, Stanley 1980 *A Piece of the Pie.* Berkeley: University of California Press.

Lopez, David E. 1976 "The Social Consequences of Home/School Bilingualism." *Social Problems* 24:234–246.

Nelson, Candace, and Marta Tienda 1985 "The Structuring of Hispanic Ethnicity: Historical and Contemporary Perspectives." *Ethnic and Racial Studies* 8:49–74.

Portes, Alejandro, and Robert L. Bach 1980 *Latin Journey.* Berkeley: University of California Press.

Southwest Voter Research Notes 1989 Vol. 3, No. 2. October.

Tienda, Marta 1982 "Sex, Ethnicity, and Chicano Status Attainment." *International Migration Review* 16:435–472.

——— 1989 "Puerto Ricans and the Underclass Debate." *Annals of the American Academy of Political and Social Sciences* 501:105–119.

———, and Leif I. Jensen 1988 "Poverty and Minorities: A Quarter-Century Profile of Color and Socioeconomic Disadvantage." In Gary D. Sandefur and Marta Tienda, eds., *Divided Opportunities.* New York: Plenum Press.

Vincent, Joan 1974 "The Structuring of Ethnicity." *Human Organization* 33:375–379.

– MARTA TIENDA

HOMELESSNESS

Literal homelessness—lacking permanent housing of one's own—is a condition that has been present throughout human history. It has always been dangerous as well, given the necessity of shelter for survival. Nevertheless, the routine occurrence of homelessness in the past probably prevented the problem from generating any extraordinary degree of collective concern. Members of premodern societies often experienced losses or disruptions of residence as a result of food scarcity, natural disaster, epidemic disease, warfare, and other environmental and self-inflicted circumstances. Such forces contributed to the likelihood, if not the expectation, that most people would be homeless at some point in the life cycle.

Ironically, now that homelessness is relatively rare in Western societies, it has achieved a special notoriety. When shelter security becomes the norm, the significance of housing evolves beyond the purely functional. Homes, like jobs, constitute master statuses, anchoring their occupants in the stratification system. Hence, being without a home portends a more general and threatening *disaffiliation,* defined as "a detachment from society characterized by the absence or attenuation of the affiliative bonds that link settled persons to a network of interconnected social structures" (Caplow, Bahr, and Sternberg 1968, p. 494). This is the broadest meaning associated with the concept of homelessness, at the opposite end of the continuum from its literal definition.

Homelessness, broadly construed, began to assume major proportions as a social problem in the United States near the end of the nineteenth century. Over the several preceding decades, urban homeless populations had emerged in response to a series of events at the national level, including Civil War displacement; the arrival of impoverished European immigrants; seasonal employment patterns in agriculture, construction, and the extractive industries; and severe economic setbacks in the early 1870s and 1890s (Hoch 1987; Rooney 1970). As a temporary remedy, downtown warehouses and old hotels were converted into inexpensive, dormitory-style lodging facilities. The proximity of the lodging facilities to one another, along with the distinctive mix of service and recreational establishments growing up around them, served to concentrate the homeless physically in areas that came to be known as *skid rows* (supposedly named for a "skid road" in Seattle used to slide logs downhill).

The homeless concentrated in areas that came to be known as skid rows, *named for a "skid road" in Seattle used to slide logs downhill.*

The manpower needs created by World War I drained skid row districts of their inhabitants, but a pool of footloose veterans replenished them at war's end. An even greater surge in homelessness—one extending well beyond the boundaries of skid row—was soon sparked by the Great Depression. The widespread hardship of the period forced previously domiciled individuals into a migrant life-style, and shantytowns (dubbed "Hoovervilles") sprang up in urban and rural settings alike. These new manifestations of homelessness in turn stimulated the first generation of sustained research on the subject among sociologists. Anderson (1940), Sutherland and Locke (1936), and other scholars conducted studies of different segments of the homeless population as part of the Depression-era relief effort.

A second generation of research started in the 1950s. Large-scale single-city surveys—many of which were funded by urban renewal agencies—informed the debate over what to do about skid row areas (Bahr and Caplow 1974; Bogue 1963). Demographic data obtained during the surveys showed homeless respondents to be predominantly male, white, single, older, and of local origins. The surveys also lent credibility to the popular image of the homeless as deviant "outsiders." Depending upon the city under examination, between one-fourth and one-half reportedly were problem drinkers, a higher percentage had spent time in jail or prison, most were unable or unwilling to hold down steady employment, many suffered from poor health, and few were enmeshed in supportive social networks. This negative image based on the survey findings was countered by a parallel body of ethnographic evidence. Field observers like Wallace (1965) portrayed the homeless of skid row in subcultural terms, as a cohesive group with their own language, norms, and status hierarchy. Participation in the subculture was believed to help members cope with a problem more serious than their presumed deviance: extreme poverty.

In the 1970s, almost a century after skid row first appeared as a recognizable entity in the American city, its demise seemed imminent. Urban renewal and redevelopment projects had eliminated much of the infrastructure of skid row while a slackening demand for short-term unskilled labor was eroding one of the few legitimate economic roles the area could claim to play. Consequently, several investigators predicted skid row's disappearance and, by implication, the decline of the U.S. homeless population (Bahr 1967; Lee 1980). Yet within a decade of such forecasts, homelessness had resurfaced as an important national issue. During the 1980s media coverage of the so-called *new homeless* increased dramatically, and federal legislation (most notably the McKinney Act) was formulated to address their plight. The amount of social scientific inquiry rose as well. Indeed, over the past eight years the outpouring of scholarly monographs on the topic may have surpassed that of any prior generation of research.

Despite this renewed interest, what is known about contemporary homelessness remains limited, for several reasons. Unlike most groups surveyed by sociologists, the homeless are not easily reached at residential addresses or telephone numbers. The demolition of skid row districts in general and of single-room-occupancy (SRO) hotels in particular has intensified the difficulties involved in finding homeless people, pushing a higher percentage of them onto the streets and into more dispersed locations. Those referred to as the *doubled up*, who stay on an irregular basis with settled relatives or friends, are virtually inaccessible to investigators. Even among the homeless who can be found, participation rates fall far short of perfect. Some individuals have always been too suspicious and others too incoherent to take part in an interview, and their numbers may be increasing.

Finally, the political context surrounding the latest wave of research magnifies the significance of each methodological obstacle just identified. Because the homelessness issue has been transformed into a referendum on the ability of the state to meet its citizens' needs, liberals and conservatives both use the slightest technical shortcoming as ammunition with which to attack any study unfavorable to their own position. Thus, apparently straightforward "facts" about homelessness—and there are few of these to begin with—become matters open to debate.

Data on the size of the national homeless population illustrate the uncertain nature of the existing knowledge base. According to an early assertion by advocates, the number of homeless in the United States as of 1982 stood at 2.2 million, or approximately 1 percent of the total population of the country (Hombs and Snyder 1982). However, only two years later the U.S. Department of Housing and Urban Development (1984) compiled a series of point estimates, extrapolated from street counts and surveys of informants and shelter operators, that yielded a "most reliable" range of 250,000 to 350,000. More recently, an Urban Institute study has arrived at a figure—500,000 to 600,000 homeless nationwide on a single day—that falls between the advocate and HUD extremes (Burt and Cohen 1989). Whatever its true size, the homeless population is thought to have grown rapidly over the past decade, by as much as 25 percent annually in some places. That growth rate could be inflated, though, given the relative stability documented in one of the few large cities (Nashville, Tennessee) for which longitudinal observations are available (Lee 1989).

While definitional differences underlie much of the disagreement over the magnitude of the homeless population, generalizations about its composition have been complicated by (1) the selective emphasis of many inquiries on atypical "slices" of the whole (homeless veterans, the mentally ill, etc.), and (2) real variation in the characteristics of the homeless across communities. Contrary to media reports and popular perceptions that suffer from such distorting influences, the modal homeless individual is still an unattached white male with local roots, similar in fundamental ways to his skid row counterpart of two decades ago. Yet there clearly have been striking compositional shifts during the intervening period. Blacks and other minorities, rarely found on skid row, are now overrepresented among the homeless, and women, children, young adults, and high school graduates constitute larger segments of the population both absolutely and proportionally than they once did (Momeni 1989; Rossi 1989; Wright 1989). Family groupings, usually headed by the mother alone, have become more common as well. Taking these elements of demographic continuity and change together, perhaps the safest conclusion to be drawn is that a trend toward greater diversity distinguishes the new homelessness from the old.

The same conclusion applies fairly well with respect to deviant characteristics. Alcoholism, which previously constituted the most noticeable form of deviance among the homeless, is now rivaled by other kinds of substance abuse, and mental illness has surpassed physical illness as an object of public concern. Beyond a rough consensus regarding the greater variety of such problems in the current homeless population, little of a definitive nature is known about them. For example, a recent review of nine studies cited mental illness prevalence rates that run from a low of one-tenth to a high of one-half of all homeless (U.S. General Accounting Office 1988), and occasional reports suggest that as many as 90 percent are at least mildly clinically impaired. This wide range leaves room for opposing arguments: on the one hand, that pervasive mental illness is the principal cause of contemporary homelessness (Bassuk 1984; Eagle and Caton 1990); on the other, that its presumed causal role represents a stereotypic "myth" created by the visibility of a small minority of disturbed folk (Snow, Baker, and Anderson 1986).

Even if the extent of mental illness has been exaggerated, there can be no doubt that the general well-being of the homeless remains low. This is hardly surprising in light of the stresses that accompany life on the street. The absence of shelter exposes homeless persons to the weather, criminal victimization, and other threatening conditions. They have trouble fulfilling basic needs that most Americans take for granted, such as finding work, obtaining nutritionally adequate meals, getting around town, washing clothes, storing belongings, and locating toilet and bathing facilities. Fortunately, the percentage of the homeless who have to confront these difficulties over an extended period appears to be smaller today than in the past. Results from several local surveys suggest that the median episode of homelessness lasts between six months and one year (Rossi 1989, pp. 94–95; U.S. Department of Housing and Urban Development 1984). Some people, of course, still experience the longer-duration bouts common in the skid row era; as many as 10 percent may be homeless for five continuous years or more.

Several factors make it difficult to study the number and nature of the homeless population in the United States. Consequently, estimates of the number of homeless people vary widely, and policymakers dispute the magnitude of the problem. (Richard T. Nowitz/Corbis)

Whether temporarily or chronically homeless, few choose to be in that state. But if choice can be ruled out, what forces do account for the new homelessness? Among the numerous answers elicited by this question so far, two general classes are discernible. *Structural* explanations treat homelessness as a consequence of societal trends, including changes in the economy (a decline in limited-skill jobs, deindustrialization), mental health policy (deinstitutionalization), and welfare provision (shrinkage of the social service "safety net"). Arguably, the availability of affordable housing has received the most attention of any structural factor. The thrust of the housing thesis is that government action, a supply-demand "squeeze," inner-city revitalization, and related events have not only priced many low-income households out of rental status but have also eliminated a key fallback option historically open to them: SRO units in downtown residential hotels (Hoch and Slayton 1989; Ringheim 1990; Wright and Lam 1987). With the depletion of the SRO stock, displacement from other sectors of the housing market may lead directly to a homeless outcome.

In contrast to the structural approach, *individualistic* explanations posit traits or attributes internal to the person as the main causes of homelessness. Older thinking about the inherent immorality and wanderlust of skid row denizens has given way to revisionist claims that the primary antecedents are deficits in talent or motivation (Main 1983; McMurry 1988) or the debilitating effects of mental illness. Interestingly, many scholars who subscribe to some version of the individualistic view have had to invoke associated structural trends—deinstitutionalization in the case of mental illness, for example—in order to explain the size and compositional changes that have occurred in the homeless population in recent years.

The tendency to draw on both individualistic and structural perspectives has grown more pronounced with the realization that a theory of homelessness, like that of any social phenomenon, can never be fully satisfying when cast in exclusively micro- or macro-level terms. To date, the work of Rossi (1989) offers the most compelling cross-level synthesis. He contends that structural changes have put everyone in extreme poverty at higher risk of becoming homeless, especially those poor people who exhibit an "accumulation of disabilities," such as drug abuse, bad health, unemployment, and a criminal record. Being "disabled" forces one to rely on a network of friends and family for support, often over prolonged periods. If the strain placed on this support network is too great and it collapses, homelessness is the likely result.

Though Rossi's central idea—that structural factors and individual problems combine to make certain segments of the poor more vulnerable to homelessness than others—seems reasonable to social scientists, it could prove less acceptable to members of the general public. In fact, based on previous research into public beliefs about the causes of poverty (Kluegel and Smith 1986), most Americans might be expected to hold the homeless responsible for their lot. However, the small amount of evidence that bears directly on this expectation contradicts rather than confirms it. Findings from a local survey, supplemented with data from a national opinion poll, indicate that (1) more people blame homelessness on structural variables and bad luck than on individualistic causes, and (2) many hold a mixture of structural and individualistic beliefs, consistent with the complex roots of the condition (Lee, Jones, and Lewis 1990).

The relative frequency of the two types of beliefs is a matter of substantial political significance, since the study just cited shows that each type implies a distinctive set of policy attitudes. As a rule, members of the public who believe in structural causes consider homelessness a very important problem, feel that the response to it has been inadequate, and endorse a variety of ameliorative proposals, including a tax increase and government-subsidized housing. This policy orientation stands at odds with that for individualistic believers, who tend to devalue homelessness as an issue and favor restrictive measures (vagrancy enforcement, access limitation, etc.) over service provision. Regardless of which orientation ultimately registers the greatest impact on policymaking, the sharp contrast between them says much about how homelessness has managed to stay near the top of the U.S. domestic social agenda for the past decade.

The United Nations' designation of 1987 as the "Year of Shelter for the Homeless" attests that homelessness has been an international concern as well. The situation is particularly acute in the developing countries of the Third World, where rapid population growth outstrips the expansion of the housing stock by a wide margin (Burns and Grebler 1977). Compounding the growth-housing mismatch are prevailing patterns of spatial redistribution: rural-to-urban migration streams have created huge pools of homeless people in tenements, in squatter communities, and on the streets of many large cities. Besides such demographic trends, periodic events of the kind that once created literal homelessness in premodern societies—drought, food shortages, war, and the like—still contribute to the problem today outside the West. Sadly, the prospects for effective intervention must be judged slim in the face of the financial debts, service demands, and other burdens under which Third World governments operate. Possibly because these burdens are so overwhelming, homelessness—while important—has yet to achieve dominant-issue standing. As one informed observer put the matter, "neither the resources to address the plight of the homeless nor the degree of aroused public sympathy present in the United States are in evidence in the developing world" (Knight 1987, p. 268). However, that is the sector of the world in which a vast majority of all homeless persons will continue to live for the foreseeable future.

More people blame homelessness on bad luck than on individualistic causes.

[See also Income Distribution in the United States; Poverty.]

BIBLIOGRAPHY

Anderson, Nels 1940 *Men on the Move.* Chicago: University of Chicago Press.

Bahr, Howard M. 1967 "The Gradual Disappearance of Skid Row." *Social Problems* 15:41–45.

———, and Theodore Caplow 1974 *Old Men Drunk and Sober.* New York: New York University Press.

Bassuk, Ellen L. 1984 "The Homelessness Problem." *Scientific American* 251:40–45.

Bogue, Donald J. 1963 *Skid Row in American Cities.* Chicago: Community and Family Study Center, University of Chicago.

Burns, Leland S., and Leo Grebler 1977 *The Housing of Nations.* London: Macmillan.

Burt, Martha R., and Barbara E. Cohen 1989 *America's Homeless: Numbers, Characteristics, and the Programs That Serve Them.* Washington, D.C.: Urban Institute.

Caplow, Theodore, Howard M. Bahr, and David Sternberg 1968 "Homelessness." In David L. Sills, ed., *International Encyclopedia of the Social Sciences,* Vol. 6. New York: Macmillan.

Eagle, Paula F., and Carol L. M. Caton 1990 "Homelessness and Mental Illness." In Carol L. M. Caton, ed., *Homeless in America.* New York: Oxford University Press.

Hoch, Charles 1987 "A Brief History of the Homeless Problem in the United States." In Richard D. Bingham, Roy E. Green, and Sammis B. White, eds., *The Homeless in Contemporary Society.* Newbury Park, Calif.: Sage.

Hoch, Charles, and Robert A. Slayton 1989 *New Homeless and Old: Community and the Skid Row Hotel.* Philadelphia: Temple University Press.

Hombs, Mary E., and Mitch Snyder 1982 *Homelessness in America: A Forced March to Nowhere.* Washington, D.C.: Community for Creative Non-Violence.

Kluegel, James R., and Eliot R. Smith 1986 *Beliefs About Inequality: Americans' Views of What Is and What Ought to Be.* New York: Aldine de Gruyter.

Knight, Rudolph H. 1987 "Homelessness: An American Problem?" In Richard D. Bingham, Roy E. Green, and Sammis B. White, eds., *The Homeless in Contemporary Society.* Newbury Park, Calif.: Sage.

Lee, Barrett A. 1980 "The Disappearance of Skid Row: Some Ecological Evidence." *Urban Affairs Quarterly* 16:81–107.

——— 1989 "Stability and Change in an Urban Homeless Population." *Demography* 26:323–334.

———, Sue Hinze Jones, and David W. Lewis 1990 "Public Beliefs About the Causes of Homelessness." *Social Forces* 69:253–265.

Main, Thomas J. 1983 "The Homeless of New York." *Public Interest* 72:3–28.

McMurry, Dan 1988 "Hard Living on Easy Street." *Chronicles* 12 (8):15–19.

Momeni, Jamshid A. (ed.) 1989 *Homelessness in the United States, Volume I: State Surveys.* New York: Greenwood.

Ringheim, Karin 1990 *At Risk of Homelessness: The Roles of Income and Rent.* New York: Praeger.

Rooney, James F. 1970 "Societal Forces and the Unattached Male: An Historical Review." In Howard M. Bahr, ed., *Disaffiliated Man: Essays and Bibliography on Skid Row, Vagrancy, and Outsiders.* Toronto: University of Toronto Press.

Rossi, Peter H. 1989 *Down and Out in America: The Origins of Homelessness.* Chicago: University of Chicago Press.

Snow, David A., Susan G. Baker, and Leon Anderson 1986 "The Myth of Pervasive Mental Illness among the Homeless." *Social Problems* 33:407–423.

Sutherland, Edwin H., and Harvey J. Locke 1936 *Twenty Thousand Homeless Men.* Chicago: J. B. Lippincott.

U.S. Department of Housing and Urban Development 1984 *A Report to the Secretary on the Homeless and Emergency Shelters.* Washington, D.C.: Office of Policy Development and Research, U.S. Department of Housing and Urban Development.

U.S. General Accounting Office 1988 *Homeless Mentally Ill: Problems and Options in Estimating Numbers and Trends.* Washington, D.C.: Program Evaluation and Methodology Division, U.S. General Accounting Office.

Wallace, Samuel E. 1965 *Skid Row as a Way of Life.* Totowa, N.J.: Bedminster.

Wright, James D. 1989 *Address Unknown: The Homeless in America.* New York: Aldine de Gruyter.

———, and Julie A. Lam 1987 "Homelessness and the Low Income Housing Supply." *Social Policy* 17:48–53.

– BARRETT A. LEE

HUMAN ECOLOGY AND THE ENVIRONMENT

The term *ecology* comes from the Greek word *oikos* (house) and, significantly, has the same Greek root as the word *economics,* from *oikonomas* (household manager). Ernst Haeckel, the German biologist who coined the word *ecology* in 1868, viewed ecology as a body of knowledge concerning the economy of nature, highlighting its roots in economics and evolutionary theory. He defined ecology as the study of all those complex interrelations referred to by Darwin as the conditions of the struggle for existence.

Ecologists like to look at the environment as an ecosystem of interlocking relationships and exchanges that constitute the web of life. Populations of organisms occupying the same environment (habitat) are said to constitute a community. Together, the communities and their abiotic environments constitute an ecosystem. The various ecosystems taken together constitute the ecosphere, the largest ecological unit. Living organisms exist in the much narrower range of the biosphere, which is said to extend a few hundred feet above the land or under the sea. On its fragile film of air, water, and soil, all life is said to depend. For the sociologist, the most important ecological concepts are diversity and dominance, competition and cooperation, succession and adaptation, evolution and expansion, and carrying capacity and the balance of nature. Over the years, three distinct approaches have come to characterize the field of human ecology.

Conventional Human Ecology

The Chicago sociologists Louis Wirth, Robert Ezra Park, Ernest W. Burgess, and Roderick McKenzie are recognized as the founders of the human ecological approach in sociology. In the early decades of the twentieth century, American cities were passing through a period of great turbulence due to the effects of rapid industrialization and urbanization. The urban world, with its fierce competition for territory and survival, appeared to mirror the very life-world studied by the plant ecologists. In their search for the principles of order, the human ecologists started looking at the process of city development in terms of the process of "succession," which involved an orderly sequence of invasions and displacements leading to a climax or equilibrium state. In their hands, human ecology became synonymous with the ecology of space. Park and Burgess identified the "natural areas" of land use, which come into existence without a preconceived design. Quite influential and popular for a while was the "Burgess Hypothesis" regarding the spatial order of the city as a series of concentric zones emanating from the central business district. However, Hawley (1984) has pointed out that with urban characteristics now diffused throughout society, one in effect deals with a system of cities in which the urban hierarchy is cast in terms of functional rather than spatial relations.

Park (1936) identified the problematics of human ecology as the investigation of the processes by which biotic balance and social equilibrium are maintained by the interaction of the three factors constituting what he termed the "social complex" (population, technological culture [artifact], and nonmaterial culture [custom and belief]) with the fourth, natural resources of the habitat. Essentially the same factors reappear as the four POET variables (population, organization, environment, and technology) in Otis Dudley Duncan's Ecological Complex, indicating its point of contact with the early human ecology (Duncan 1964). In any case, it was McKenzie who, by shifting attention from spatial relations to the analysis of sustenance relations, provided the thread of continuity between the two approaches. His student Amos Hawley, who has been the "exemplar" of conventional human ecology since the 1940s, defines it as the attempt to deal holistically with the phenomenon of organization.

Hawley (1986) views the ecosystem as the adaptive mechanism that emerges out of the interaction of population, organization, and the environment. Organization is the adaptive form that enables a population to act as a unit. The process of system adaptation involves members in relations of interdependence to secure sustenance from the environment. Growth is the development of the system's inner potential to the maximum size and complexity afforded by the existing technology for transportation and communication. Evolution is the creation of higher potential for resumption of system development through the incorporation of new information that enhances the capacity for the movement of people, materials, and messages. In this manner, the system moves from simple to more complex forms.

Through the use of the ecological concept of "expansion," Hawley (1979) has applied his framework to account for the growth phases that intervene between stages of development. The evolution of a system takes place when its scale and complexity do not go hand in hand. Thus, an imbalance between population and the carrying capacity of the environment may create external pressures for branching off into colonies and establishing niches in a new environment. However, when complexity and scale do advance together, the normal condition for growth or expansion arises from the colonization process itself. Hawley identifies the technology of movement as the most critical variable. It determines accessibility and, therefore, governs the spread of settlements, changes in hierarchy and division of labor, and the creation of interaction networks among the settlements. According to Hawley, the process can work on any scale and is limited only by the level of technological development of communication and transportation.

Hawley (1979) points out that while expansionism in the past relied on political domination, its modern variant aims at structural convergence along economic and cultural axes to obviate the need for direct rule by the center. In this way, free trade and "resocialization" of cultures and whole populations into standardized organizational forms and procedures create a far more efficient and cost-effective global reach. At the same time, as polities try to bring larger portions of system territories under their jurisdictions, the management of scale becomes highly problematical. Lacking a single supranational polity, the international pecking order is then subject to increasing instability, challenge, and change.

The system tends to return to scale as the costs of administration mount. This results in decentralization and some local autonomy. But improvements in technology of movement start the growth process all over again. The picture thus is that of a global system thoroughly interlinked by transportation and communication networks. Hawley (1979, p. 29) believes that the growth of social systems has now reached a point at which the evolutionary model has lost its usefulness in explaining cumulative change. However, since a single world order has only a small tolerance for errors, this situation harbors the grave danger that a fatal error may destroy the whole system.

The real irony of this relentless global expansion elaborated by Hawley lies, however, in the coexistence of extreme opulence and affluence of the few with stark poverty and misery of the majority at home and abroad. The large metropolitan centers provide a very poor quality of life. The very scale of urban decay underscores the huge problems facing the city—congestion, polluted air, untreated sewage, high crime rates, dilapidated housing, domestic violence, and broken lives. One therefore needs to ask: What prospect does this scale and level of complexity hold for the future?

Over sixty thousand synthetic chemicals are now on the market, of which a sizable number contaminate the environment and pose health hazards.

Industrial and industrializing nations are now beset with more or less the same devastating problems of air, land, and water pollution and environmental destruction. Large numbers of lakes and rivers that were not naturally eutrophic have now become so as a result of pollution and chemical runoffs. In the United States, Love Canal and Times Beach, Missouri, made headlines in the 1980s as much as Chernobyl did in 1986 in the Soviet Union. Sulfur dioxide emissions from industrial and power plants cause acid rain that inflicts irreparable damage on buildings, monuments, marine life, trees, and plants. Over sixty thousand synthetic chemicals are now on the market, of which a sizable number contaminate the environment and pose health hazards. Over half a million tons of toxic wastes are produced each year in the United States, where the five-year cost of cleaning the nuclear waste, which remains dangerously radioactive for thousands of years, may well exceed thirty billion dollars. The soil and the lake water and groundwater near nuclear power and weapons plants are heavily contaminated with such toxins as mercury, arsenic, and many types of solvents, and with deadly radioactive materials such as plutonium, tritium, and strontium-90. The contamination is so bad in eight states that huge tracts of land are said to be totally unfit for human habitation and pose serious health hazards for the surrounding communities.

The environmental destruction is far more serious and widespread in Eastern Europe and Russia. These countries are the site of some of the world's worst pollution. Lakes and rivers are dead or dying. Water is so contaminated in some areas that it is undrinkable. Chemical runoff and sewage and wastewater dumping have created serious groundwater contamination. Lignite (brown coal), the major source of energy for industry and homes in some of these nations, is responsible for heavy concentration of sulfur dioxide and dust in the air that has caused serious respiratory problems and additional health damage. The haze-covered cities are an environmental disaster. As a result, environment and politics are becoming an explosive mix and the source of action and instability in the region (French 1990, p. 9). Zhores Medvedev believes Russia is losing its forests at the same rate as rain forests are being destroyed in Brazil. Between 1960 and 1989, it lost more land through land and environmental degradation than the combined total cultivable area in Belgium and Ireland. Besides the effects of Chernobyl and other major nuclear disasters, it lost more agricultural land and pastureland to radioactive contamination than the total cultivated acreage in Switzerland (Medvedev 1990, p. 28). Experts fear that from twenty-five thousand to seventy-five thousand persons in Russia and Europe may die prematurely from cancer and other effects of the radiation fallout from Chernobyl, history's worst nuclear disaster. A quarter to a third of the forests in eastern Europe show signs of dying from air pollution. These environmental problems are thus not only transboundary, they also cut across ideological labels.

In non-Western nations, a million people suffer acute poisoning and twenty thousand persons die every year from pesticides. Pesticides are a major source of environmental and health problems in the United States as well. But the United States alone exports over half a billion pounds of pesticides that are restricted or banned for domestic use. The ecology, natural environment, and resources of these non-Western nations are being destroyed and contaminated at a frightening rate. Irreversible damage is being done by large-scale destruction of rain forests and the intensive use of marginal lands and by the imbalances that result from population pressures and the practices of multinational firms and national elites. Desertification now threatens a third of the earth's land surface. Poverty, hunger, starvation, famine, and death are endemic throughout much of the world.

Environmental Sociology and the New Human Ecology

The mounting public concern during the 1970s about fuel shortages, oil spills, nuclear powerplant accidents, acid rain, dying lakes, urban smog, famine and death in the Sahel, rain forest destruction, and the like made social scientists realize that overexploitation of the ecosystem may destroy the very basis of our planetary survival. Many environmentalists blamed the dominant social paradigm of industrial societies for the destruction of the fragile balance among the components of the ecological complex.

The antiecological worldview of the dominant social paradigm, which was shaped by the experience of a seemingly limitless frontier and of extraordinary abundance, is said to be a major reason for the neglect of the physical environment by American sociologists. Another reason is related to the Durkheimian emphasis on explaining social facts by other social facts. Together with the general aversion of sociologists to any form of determinism, these reasons ruled out the due consideration of environmental factors even by human ecologists (Freudenberg and Gramling 1989). William Catton and Riley Dunlap (1978) point out that the exaggerated emphasis by conventional human ecologists on culture, science, and technology as "exceptional" human achievements has led to the illusion that humans are "exempt" from bioecological constraints to which all species are subject. This awareness has led Catton and Dunlap to develop the fields of new human ecology (Buttel 1987) and "environmental sociology" to deal with the reciprocal interaction between human activities and the physical environment. They believe that the POET model, broadened to include the role of human agency and culture, provides a useful analytical framework for grounding environmental sociology in the ecological perspective. In addition, they have identified the important subfield of the sociology of environmental issues, which is concerned with the study of the environmental movement, wildland recreation, and resource management problems and the like, but mainly within the sociological tradition.

In a comprehensive review of the new field, Buttel (1987) has made two essential points. He argues that both the cleavage between the conventional and the new human ecology, and the conflict-versus-consensus cleavage of mainline sociology, continue to be important. Buttel would also like to shift the focus of environmental sociology from the imbalance of population and resources, emphasized by Catton, to the reality of the unequal distribution of these resources. Allan Schnaiberg's idea of the "treadmill of production" (1980), which emerges from a dialectical relationship between economic growth and ecological structures, points to the need for focusing on production institutions as the primary determinants of economic expansion and for incorporating a conflict dimension in environmental analysis. Buttel's own work in environmental sociology draws upon the "political economy tradition" of the neo-Marxists and the neo-Weberians. Catton's major contributions, on the other hand, are in the neo-Malthusian tradition.

Thus, while the problem of order created by the harsh realities of industrial life and expansionism defined the central problematics of sociology and conventional human ecology, the problem of survival now defines the central problematics of environmental sociology and the new human ecology: to the earlier question of how social order is possible is now added the more urgent concern with survival itself.

The Political Economy Approach

A "new urban sociology" conflict paradigm in the political economy tradition has been put forward by M. Gottdiener and Joe Feagin (1988) as an alternative to the conventional and the new human ecology paradigms. Societies, in their view, are neither mere population aggregates nor unified biotic communities, but are specified by their mode of production. Crisis tendencies and profit generation constitute the core of societal development, which is dominated by the capital accumulation process. Thus, to take one example, conventional human ecologists like to regard central-city restructuring as a consequence of adaptation to increasing population size and the growing complexity of social organization. They then relate these changes to the size of the metropolitan hinterland. The new urban paradigm, on the other hand, emphasizes the impact of a global economy, the multinational corporations, the shift to functional specialization in world-system financial and administrative activities, the constant subsidization by the state, the efforts of pro-growth coalitions, and changes in labor force requirements leading to some renovation and central city gentrification. The following are some of the basic questions that the new urban sociology paradigm seeks to answer: What is the character of power and inequality? How do they relate to "ecological" patterns? How do production and reproduction processes of capital accumulation, as well as the processes of crisis adjustment, manifest themselves in sociospatial organization?

Relation Between Population and the Environment

For human ecology, the most salient aspect of the population-environment relationship is the way it affects human survival and the quality of human life. Under the impact of the interlocking crisis of overpopulation, resource depletion, and environmental degradation, issues of sustainability and survival have come to occupy center stage. Corresponding to the main approaches in human ecology, three broad positions may be identified for discussion: the pro-growth (expansionist), the neo-Malthusian, and the political economy perspectives. The discussion of these positions is followed by a consideration of the Brundtland Report, issued by the World Commission on Environment and Development, and of the traditional-Gandhian view of the ecological crisis. Extended treatment of the issues involved may be found in Catton (1980), Schnaiberg (1980), Humphrey and Buttel (1982), Redclift (1987), Mellos (1988), and de la Court (1990).

THE PRO-GROWTH (EXPANSIONIST) PERSPECTIVE. In expansionist thinking, scale, complexity, and acceleration—that is, the constant broadening of the limits of the maximum permitted by prevailing circumstances—mark the human-environment encounter. The basic conviction is that man through his unaided reason can comprehend and control the processes of the world. This is the meaning of Hawley's apparently guarded conviction that evolution as a mode of change has disappeared from human social systems (1979, p. 29)—that is, that by grasping the very mainspring of evolution, man has already seized "the tiller of the world," in the words of Teilhard de Chardin. In responding to the concern of the neo-Malthusians about population outrunning resources, Hawley (1986, pp. 110–112), points to the inherently expansive nature of populations, technology, and organization, which through resource substitutions, intensive use and exploitation of land and resources, and the exploration and discovery of new frontiers and new resources, can allay concerns regarding environmental finitude. In his view, the problem of food and resource shortages is really rooted in poverty rather than in resource scarcity. In short, Hawley believes that industrial systems have no known upper limits on either the number of specializations or the size of the populations that can be supported. Similar pro-growth sentiments are expressed by other expansionist thinkers.

Some believe that the world would drown in its own filth if most of the people in the world were to live at Western standards.

While Colin Clark directly links population numbers to power, Herman Kahn (1974) views population increase as a necessary stimulus to economic growth and believes the earth can easily support fifteen billion people at twenty thousand dollars per capita for a millennium. In fact, he believes that the wider the gap between the rich and the poor, the more the riches will percolate downward. In any case, he is unconvinced that the rich would agree to part with their income to ensure a more equitable distribution of wealth. Roger Revelle (1974) believes the earth can actually support nearly thirty times the present population in terms of food supplies, and that it would take almost 150 years to hit that mark. While economic development is necessary to provide people with the basis to control their fertility, Revelle is certain the world would drown in its own filth if most of the people in the world were to live at Western standards. Finally, the postindustrial sociologist Daniel Bell (1977) is convinced that economic growth is necessary to reduce the gap between the rich and the poor nations. He has little doubt that the "super-productivity society," with less than 4 percent of its labor force devoted to agriculture, could feed the whole population of the United States, and most of the world as well. In his opinion, pollution exists because the market principle has never been applied to the use of collective goods. Actually, Bell suggests that the government itself could utilize the market to demand a public accounting from all parties on issues of public interest, levy effluent charges for pollutants, and bring effective compliance through the price mechanism.

However, while corporations have shown greater sensitivity and self-regulation, there is evidence that the attempts to enforce the "polluter pays" principle are likely to be resisted or the costs passed on to the public. The negative impact of governmental policies that alleviate energy and resource scarcities is more likely to be felt at the lower socioeconomic levels (Morrison 1978). Dunlap (1979) presents evidence to show that the effects of pollution and the costs of cleaning the environment are borne disproportionately by the poor and may actually serve to reinforce class inequalities.

THE NEO-MALTHUSIAN PERSPECTIVE. The neo-Malthusian perspective is based on the well-known Malthusian law of a geometric increase in population far outstripping the arithmetic increase in food supplies in the absence of constraints. The disparity between the two growth rates poses a perpetual threat to the human prospect and serves as a natural brake on unlimited population increase by triggering war, widespread famine, disease, and death. In place of these harsh "positive checks," Malthus (1766–1834) wished to substitute the "preventive check" of "moral restraint," not the artificial methods of birth control and abortion. The crucial linking concept between population and environment is the biological concept of "carrying capacity." The carrying capacity for humans is the maximum population that can be supported indefinitely by a particular environment under exploitation by specified technology and organization (Catton 1978, p. 231). With each technological breakthrough, humans have so far been able to raise their carrying capacity through extending their territorial and environmental reach, which now goes to the ends of the globe. A more or less stable population of five hundred million in 1650 jumped to a billion in 1850. In 1930, it was two billion; and in 1975, four billion. Now humans number 5.2 billion, with prospects of the earth's population doubling about once every thirty years. Three-fourths of the earth's inhabitants live in non-Western nations. The 1990 U.S. population of 250 million is expected to jump to 300 million in 30 years.

Compounding the environmental effects of the poverty-stricken and "food hungry" populations of the world are the impacts of massive consumption and pollution of the "energy hungry" nations (Miller 1972, p. 117). The latter rise sharply with even a slight growth in population of Western nations, where one-quarter of the world's population is responsible for over 85 percent of worldwide consumption of natural resources and the environmental sinks. Within the United States a bare 6 percent of the world's population consumes over half of the world's nonrenewable resources and over a third of all the raw materials produced. Miller (1972, p. 122) believes that the real threat to our life-support system, therefore, comes not from the poor but from the affluent megaconsumers and megapolluters who occupy more space, consume more of natural resources, disturb the ecology more, and directly and indirectly pollute the land, air, and water with ever-increasing amounts of thermal, chemical, and radioactive wastes. While the Club of Rome (Meadows et al. 1972) and the other neo-Malthusians give a grace period of thirty or so years, Catton believes we have already overshot the maximum carrying capacity, and are now on a catastrophic downward crash course. In any case, he is convinced that our best bet would be to act *as if* a crash were imminent and to take advance measures to minimize its impact.

However, these premises of Malthusian theory have not stood the test of time. The social and economic forces unleashed by the Industrial Revolution not only telescoped the doubling of human population within a shorter time span, they also brought about ever-rising material standards of living due to astronomical increases in the scale and speed of agricultural and industrial production in the advanced nations. Worldwide, the annual rate of population growth fell to 1.8 percent in 1990, and is expected to stabilize around 1.5 percent by the year 2000. Annual food production in the developing countries is increasing by 4.4 percent, over twice the rate of population growth. What has caused the huge increase in numbers in poor nations is the fact that while the birthrate has declined, the death rate has gone down as well. In Western nations, on the other hand, fertility rates registered a dramatic decline between the two world wars, boomed thereafter to everybody's disbelief, and have again hit such low levels that population replacement has become a major concern for many industrial nations. The Western nations are thus said to have completed a "demographic transition." In the initial stage, population is kept stable as high birthrates are balanced by high death rates due to the operation of the Malthusian positive checks. In the second stage, population increases rapidly as death rates decline but birthrates soar due to an increase in food supply and improved health care. In the third stage, birthrates decline more rapidly than death rates due to the use of family planning and birth control measures. Finally, low birthrates and low death rates lead to a stabilization of the population at a lower level. A decline in fertility rates to a level below replacement (1.3 per woman) in industrialized countries such as Germany and Denmark is said to constitute the current "second demographic transition." France and the Soviet Union have officially encouraged childbearing to counter falling birthrates. Thus, in the present era, the challenges and opportunities opened up by declining fertility rates and record food surpluses have totally eclipsed the Malthusian specter for the rich nations while again casting its shadow on the poor. In any case, population is but one factor, albeit a most significant one, in the complex interaction between social structure and the environment.

To revert to the neo-Malthusian argument: The tragedy of numbers is compounded by the "free rider," who derives personal benefits from the collective efforts of others, and the more serious "tragedy of the commons" (Hardin 1966), where each herdsman will add cattle without limit, ignoring the costs imposed on the others and must, therefore, degrade the land held in common. Hardin believes that the administrative system, supported by a common standard of judgment and having access to "mutual coercion mutually agreed upon," can avoid the collective tragedy. However, unless the users jointly own the commons and exercise joint control over the resources and their use, Hardin's cure may place them at the mercy of the custodians, leaving them worse off individually and collectively. The threat of imminent ethnocide facing the remaining native populations is a case in point.

On the other hand, the "development" of poor nations has created a new set of claimants for the resources needed to maintain the high material standard of living of affluent nations. As the poor nations begin to assert control over their own resources, try to set terms of their exchange, or resist outside pressures to transform them into "environmental preserves" or the "global commons," the prospects of conflict, particularly over critical mineral and energy resources, are greatly magnified. Amartya Sen (1981) has looked at the famine situation as essentially a "crisis of entitlement," not so much because there is lack of food but because the many are denied any claims to it because of their lowly position in society. In the West, the entitlement revolution has entailed huge welfare expenditures, which could be financed either by economic growth or by direct redistribution of income (Bell 1977, p. 20). For Bell and the neo-Malthusians, the latter is out of the question. There is thus a natural progression from Hardin's "commons" view to his "lifeboat ethics." While he admits it is possible to significantly increase food supply to match the demand, he is convinced that every Indian life saved would only diminish the quality of life of those aboard the "lifeboat" and of their descendants. The situation, he feels, demands a world authority to take control of reproduction and resource use. In a piece published in 1969 in the *Stanford Alumni Almanac,* and appropriately titled "The Immorality of Being Softhearted," Hardin is quite clear that food would be the worst thing to send to the poor. Nothing short of the final solution will do. "Atomic bombs would be kinder. For a few moments the misery would be acute, but it would soon come to an end for most of the people, leaving a very few survivors to suffer thereafter." These solutions, which bring about decimation of entire populations, have been called ecofascist. Such sentiments are by no means uncommon among the neo-Malthusians.

The "tragedy of the commons" is really the tragedy of individualism from which all constraints of private and common morality have been removed. However, others have been quick to point to the equal or far greater extent of environment pollution and ecological destruction in socialist countries as one more evidence of the inevitable convergence of capitalism and socialism! Many environmental problems are clearly transideological and transnational. Acid rain, oil spills, destruction of the ozone layer, threat of global warming—all call for common responsibility and joint regulation. Ironically, it appears that the expressed concern about the destruction of the global commons through overpopulation or industrial pollution is seldom matched by a parallel commitment by powerful nations to preserve or clean up the environment or provide support for international population control efforts. Instead, one witnesses a mad scramble to divide up the remaining oceanic and other planetary resources without regard to equity, ecology, or environment. As a result, the air and the oceans, as well as the forests and lands of other nations, are being overexploited or used as garbage and toxic dumps with impunity.

The concern about the destruction of the global commons is seldom matched by a parallel commitment by powerful nations to clean up the environment.

Of no small consequence globally is the environmental impact of waste, widespread corruption at all levels, hoarding and price-fixing, and poor storage, distribution, and transportation networks. B. B. Vohra, a top Indian government official, has pointed out how "formidable mafias based on a triangular alliance between the corrupt bureaucrat, the corrupt politician and the corrupt businessman emerged in all [Indian] States and became a most powerful threat to the conservation of the country's tree cover" (1985, p. 50). When one adds to this list the role of political and economic elites and multinational corporations, and of huge debts, huge dams, and huge arms stockpiles, it becomes clear that povery, hunger, malnutrition, and starvation may have far more to do with political, cultural, and socioeconomic components of food shortages than with sheer numbers alone. This is not to underestimate the immensity of the population problem or to minimize the difficulty of its solution.

THE POLITICAL ECONOMY PERSPECTIVE. Barry Commoner (1974) faults socialist as much as capitalist economic theories for neglecting the biosphere as a major factor of production, but regards both poverty and growth of population as outcomes of colonial exploitation. The world, he believes, has enough food and resources to support nearly twice its present population. The problem, in his view, is a result of gross distributive imbalances between the rich and the poor, and requires a massive redistribution of wealth and resources to abolish poverty and raise standards of living in order to wipe out the root cause of overpopulation. The alternative to this humane solution is the unsavory one of genocide or natural destruction.

A study of environmental destruction in southern Honduras by Susan Stonich (1989) illustrates the power of a perspective that combines the concerns of political economy, ecology, and demography. Her conclusion is that environmental degradation arises from fundamental social structure and is intricately connected to problems of land tenure, unemployment, poverty, and demography. She identifies political and economic factors and export-promotion policies of international lending institutions and aid agencies as the key elements of a development policy for the whole of Central America that is likely to lead to destruction of the remaining tropical forests, worsen poverty and malnutrition, and increase inequality and conflicts within and between nations. Government policies encourage commercial agriculture for earning foreign exchange in the face of mounting external debt, which rose by 170 percent in just seven years to cover three-fourths of the 1986 gross national product. The expansion of export-oriented agriculture and the integration of resource-poor rural households into the capitalist sector, often by ruthless and violent means, concentrates highest population densities in the most marginal highland areas and encourages intensive land-use and adaptive strategies that accelerate ecological decline. Between 1952 and 1974, as a result of changes in land-use patterns, forest land declined by over two-fifths and the area in fallow by three-fifths. In the same period, food crop production was reduced drastically while the pasture area rose by more than half regionally and by over 150 percent in the highlands, where the number of cattle rose by about 70 percent. By 1974, a third of all rural families were landless; two-fifths were below the subsistence level in 1979.

The result has been the evolution of a class of rich peasants raising export-oriented cattle and cash crops, a class of land-poor and landless peasants and wage laborers, and a class of middlemen operatives who serve as transportation links in an expanding regional and national network. The whole socioeconomic structure has a most deleterious effect on the regional ecology and environment. These patterns are being repeated all over Africa and Asia. Even the "green revolution" provides only a temporary respite. Its recurrent and increasing high capital requirements for seed, fertilizer, insecticide, water, land, and machinery wipe out the small farmers and landless laborers. It destroys peasant agriculture, exposes the monocultures to destruction by disease and pests, magnifies inequality, and sows the seeds of social instability and rural strife. To those who subscribe to the political economy perspective, the biological explanation thus appears to be too simplistic. It overlooks the social context of development and land distribution within which worldwide destruction of traditional agriculture and the rain forests is now occurring.

In sum, these considerations bring out the fact that debates surrounding resource distributions and the control of population and consumption patterns are neither entirely scientific nor purely ecologically inspired. As Barry Commoner (1974) points out, they are political value positions. Will the changes come voluntarily, or will they involve totalitarian nightmares? "Sustainable development" and "traditional ecology" hold out two contrasting possibilities for the future.

The Brundtland Report

At the heart of the 1987 Brundtland Report of the World Commission on Environment and Development is the idea of "sustainable development" that has become the rallying point for diverse agendas linking poverty, underdevelopment, and overpopulation to environmental degradation and "environmental security." The report defines sustainable development as "development which meets the needs of the present without compromising the ability of future generations to meet their own needs." Its popularity lies in its ability to accommodate the opposing idea of limits to growth within the context of economic expansion, but with a new twist. As pointed out by Gro Brundtland (1989), the "central pivot" of the notion of sustainable development remains "progress, growth, the generation of wealth, and the use of resources." The imposition of limits on consumption is then justified in order to protect the resource base of the environment both locally and globally. At the same time, continuous economic growth is held essential to meeting the needs of the world's neediest. In fact, the Brundtland Report indicates that "a five- to tenfold increase in world industrial output can be anticipated by the time world population stabilizes sometime in the next century."

Sustainable development is also seen as a strategy to enhance global security by reducing the threat posed by conflict and violence in an inequitable and resource-hungry world. To this end, it promotes a commitment to multilateralism, with a call for strong international institutions to ward off the new threats to security and for the collective management of global interdependence (Brundtland 1989, p. 14). As a result, the interests of economic growth and the environment are seen as mutually reinforcing rather than contradictory (Arnold 1989, p. 22). The Brundtland Report (1987) duly notes that ecology and economy "are becoming ever more interwoven—locally, regionally, nationally, and globally—into a seamless net of causes and effects." The 1990 Worldwatch Institute Report predicts that the world will have a sustainable society by the year 2030 (Brown et al. 1990, p. 175). Meanwhile, the challenge, as Arnold states, is to ensure that the sustainability vision "is not trivialized or, worse, used as one more way to legitimize the exploitation of the weak and vulnerable in the name of global interest and solidarity."

To its credit, the Brundtland Report singled out some forms of economic growth that destroy resources and the environment. The present one-trillion-dollar expenditure on armaments, for example, constitutes "more than the total income of the poorest half of humanity." According to the 1990 United Nations estimates, military expenditures in developing countries, which account for 75 percent of the arms trade, have multiplied by seven times since 1965 to almost two hundred billion dollars, compared with a doubling by the industrialized countries. In addition, burgeoning debt, adverse trade policies, and internal instability constitute the overwhelming obstacles to sustained development. With Africa's total debt approaching two hundred billion dollars (half of its overall gross national product and three to four times its annual income from exports), average debt repayments amount to more than half the export income. The debt burden forces the African nations to concentrate on monocrop export agriculture to the detriment of food crop production, and pushes hungry and landless farmers and nomads to marginal lands that they overgraze and overexploit in order to survive. However, with respect to fixing the responsibility for deforestation, the Brundtland Report appears to be of two minds (de la Court 1990). In asserting that to "most farmers, especially the poor ones, wood is a 'free good' until the last available tree is cut down," the report partly sides with the "tragedy of the commons" argument, accusing the poor farmers of being "both victims and agents of destruction." On the other hand, it also points to a different cause: "The fuelwood crisis and deforestation—although related—are not the same problems. Wood fuels destined for urban and industrial consumers do tend to come from the forests. But only a small proportion of that used by the rural poor comes from forests. Even in these cases, villagers rarely chop down trees; most collect dead branches or cut them from trees" (quoted in de la Court 1990, p. 68).

Traditional Ecology and the Environment

Patterns of human social organization and technology use reflect the vision a people have of themselves and of their place in the universe. According to Karl Polanyi (1974), the question of how to organize human life in a machine society confronts us with a new urgency: "Behind the fading fabric of competitive capitalism there looms the portent of an industrial civilization with its paralyzing division of labor, standardization of life, supremacy of mechanism over organism, and organization over spontaneity. Science itself is haunted by insanity. This is the abiding concern" (p. 213–214). Bell (1976) has made the critical point that while the dominant nineteenth-century view of society as an interrelated web, a structured whole unified by some inner principle, still rules Marxist and functionalist thought, it is no longer applicable. On the contrary, society today is composed of three distinct realms—the techno-economic structure, the polity, and the culture—each obedient to a different axial (governing) principle, having different rhythms of change, and each following different norms that legitimate different and even contradictory types of behavior. The discordances between these realms are responsible for various contradictions within society. Bell has proposed the creation of a "public household" to overcome the disjunctions between the family, the economy, and the state through the use of modified market mechanisms to further social goals. At the same time, he is convinced that the crisis is a spiritual one of belief and meaning. "But today what is there left in the past to destroy, and who has the hope for a future to come? . . . What holds one to reality, if one's secular system of meanings proves to be an illusion?" he asks (1976, p. 29). His answer is the return in Western society of some conception of religion to restore the continuity of generations and provide a ground for humility and care for others. The task is truly formidable, for as he admits, "such a continuity cannot be manufactured, nor a cultural revolution engineered" (1976, p. 30).

It is doubtful that the problems of order created by the "normal" but dangerous disrelation between the life-sustaining (ecology–economy) and order-maintaining (sociopolitical) systems of contemporary society can be corrected by the creation of a miracle hybrid "public household," protected and nurtured by the polity and the household to serve the interests of the techno-economic structure, and by the side-door entry of the "religious" to provide for the integrative and "higher"-order needs of a socially disjointed and spiritually vacuous society. Even the frantic use of a "holistic" ecological approach is bound to fail if its actual goal is somehow to dominate or hold on desperately to a sundered reality in which everything is so hopelessly *dis*-related to everything else. The high-powered techno-economic structure, driven by the insatiable demand for energy, resources, and markets, is inherently antiecological. Its immensity of scale and utilitarian thrust not only destroy traditional socioeconomic structures but also set in motion irreversible and ecologically damaging global processes whose attempted solutions greatly magnify the problems. Marston Bates states that humans now truly constitute a new geological force. While the West is involved in a massive effort to take over the life-support systems of the earth, it is clear that a dependent part cannot grow infinitely at the expense of the others, or usurp the whole for its own purposes within conditions of environmental finitude.

A. K. Saran (1978) does not doubt in the least that the ecological crisis is a self-inflicted one, because an entropic environmental system and an infinitely expanding economy and technology are mutually incompatible. Furthermore, he points out that in the modern, historicist, horizontal framework of thought governed by a demiurgic anthropology, there can only be a technological solution to the problem of order in the sociopolitical realm. Ideally, it would require the destruction of this cosmos and the reconstruction of a new heaven, a new earth, "for if it were of a lesser order, a fundamental alteration of the nature of earth and sky could release forces and generate possibilities that must necessarily prove beyond the powers of the supposed masters of the earth to control. . . . For not having the power to reverse processes once started, [they] become their victims at the next stage" (Saran 1978, pp. 25, 31).

The attempt to appropriate Mother Earth or other symbols may be ideologically seductive but is both scientifically irrelevant and spiritually vacuous.

Saran's main argument is that since the modern system excludes a truly vertical dimension, it has absolutely no authoritative foundation. It does not provide a coherent worldview or the proper regulative principle to satisfy the needs of the different orders in a unitive way. Where centricity and true hierarchy have been rejected, a piecemeal approach will be relied on in the interest of the strong to deal with the consequences of a discordant and disharmonious order. In addition to generating tremendous violence, universal disorder, and planetary destruction in the desperate attempt to hold the parts together under its hegemony, such an approach is bound to fail. Since the symbolic is not an integral part of the modern literal consciousness, the attempt to appropriate Mother Earth or other symbols, such as that by the proponents of Gaia, may be ideologically seductive but is both scientifically irrelevant and spiritually vacuous. Since evolution has been the master concept to organize and rearrange the world in human terms, the ontology of modern science is necessarily anthropocentric. Saran's conclusion, therefore, is that there can be no ecological science unless it is grounded in traditional cosmology.

In a study of the Tukano Indians of the northwest Amazon, G. Reichel-Dolmatoff shows how aboriginal cosmologies, myths, and rituals

> . . . represent in all respects a set of ecological principles . . . that formulate a system of social and economic rules that have a highly adaptive value in the continuous endeavor to maintain a viable equilibrium between the resources of the environment and the demands of society. (1977, p. 5)
>
> The cosmological myths which express the Tukano world-view do not describe Man's Place in Nature in terms of dominion, or mastery over a subordinate environment, nor do they in any way express the notion of what some of us might call a sense of "harmony with nature". Nature, in their view, is not a physical entity apart from man and, therefore, he cannot confront it or oppose it or harmonize with it as a separate entity. Occasionally man can unbalance it by his personal malfunctioning as a component, but he never stands apart from it. Man is taken to be a part of a set of supra-individual systems which—be they biological or cultural—transcend our individual lives and within which survival and maintenance of a certain quality of life are possible only if all other life forms too are allowed to evolve according to their specific needs, as stated in cosmological myths and traditions. (1977, p. 11)
>
> . . . This cosmological model . . . constitutes a religious proposition which is ultimately connected with the social and economic organization of the group. In this way, the general balance of energy flow becomes a religious objective in which native ecological concepts play a dominant organizational role. To understand the structure and functioning of the ecosystem becomes therefore a vital task to the Tukano. (1977, p. 6)

However, modernity in its essence has been totally destructive of the traditional vision of human nature, our proper place in the "web of life," and our conception of the ultimate good. Polanyi points out how with the modern separation of "economy" as the realm of hunger and gain, our

> animal dependence upon food has been bared and the naked fear of starvation permitted to run loose. Our humiliating enslavement to the "material", which all human culture is designed to mitigate, was deliberately made more rigorous. This is the root of the "sickness" of an acquisitive society that Tawney warned of. . . . [T]he task of adapting life in such surroundings to the requirements of human existence must be resolved if man is to continue on earth. (1974, p. 219)

The post-World War II creation of the global economy through the idea of "development" is the other half of the story. As pointed out by Wolfgang Sachs, and in line with Hawley's observation, the concept of development provided the United States with the vision of a new global order in which the former colonies were held together not through political domination but through economic interdependence. But

> [t]o define the economic exploitation of the land and its treasures as "development" was a heritage of the productivist arrogance of the 19th century. Through the trick of a biological metaphor, a simple economic activity turns into a natural and evolutionary process. [Soon] traditions, hierarchies, mental habits—the whole texture of societies—were all dissolved in the planner's mechanistic models . . . patterned on the American way of life. (Sachs 1990, p. 42)

However, even after nearly two decades of development work, the results were far from heartening. Instead of declining, inequality, poverty, unemployment, hunger, and squalor actually increased manyfold in all "developing" countries.

To summarize: While the expansionist vision ties ecology, economy, and polity together, and the neo-Malthusians add biology to the list, it is in "sustainable development" that all these orders are firmly knit together—but at a price. The paradoxical nature of the term *sustainable development* arises from the fact that it attempts to combine the contradictory notions of limits to growth and active growth promotion. However, if the key to maintaining ecological integrity is economic self-sufficiency and production for use, then the problem today is surely one of the inhuman scale of enterprise based on the "techniques of degradation" (Marcel 1962, p. 70), which serve nothing higher than human self-interest, and of the concept of man as an economically rather than a spiritually determined nature (Coomaraswamy 1946, p. 2).

Roy Rappaport (1976) has documented how the Maring of New Guinea support as many as two hundred people per square mile by cultivating nearly forty-five acres of cleared forest at a time, without damaging the environment. But then they look at the world through very different eyes!

The Environmental Movement

Sociologists have paid significant attention to the study of the nature and dynamics of the environmental movement, which by the early 1980s involved over 3,000 organizations in the United States alone, though only about 250 operated on the national or multistate level (Humphrey and Buttel 1982).

The overriding emphasis of the environmental movement has been reformist. Concern with conservation and efficiency in resource and energy use, rather than with reallocating the production surplus among social classes, has dominated its agenda. Thus, the radical challenge to the dominant high-technology "treadmill of production," and the "softening" of the resource perspective of environmentalism by the emergence of equity concerns surrounding the new "appropriate technology" and "deep ecology" movements (Morrison 1980), have remained largely rhetorical, even as the focus on efficient resource use in production has made common cause between their membership and elite interests. Schnaiberg (1983), however, sees no upswelling of such redistributive politics in the near future.

One of the major research contributions has been the finding that public concern with the environment follows the same issue-attention cycle that is characteristic of most social movements. Thus, a review of current research by Dunlap (1986) revealed that public concern with environmental quality, which rose sharply in the latter half of the 1960s but peaked by 1970, declined throughout the 1970s, then rose again in force in the 1980s. As a result of Earth Day, and the intense national and global publicity and debate on environmental issues, such as global warming and the unprecedented "environmental terrorism" in the Gulf region, public concern is at an all-time high in this United Nations "Decade of the Environment."

Environmental sociologists have explored the charge of "elitism" leveled against the environmental movement. A review by Morrison and Dunlap (1986) points out that the class composition of the environmentalists is similar to that of participants in other mass movements, that their ideological commitments range from the cause of the privileged to the problems of the poor, and that reforms do appear to have had a somewhat disproportionate negative impact at the lower end of the socioeconomic scale. Research in this and other areas is summarized in Buttel (1987).

The United Nations' 1972 Stockholm Conference marks a watershed in the history of global action to protect the environment.

Overall, while the environmental movement has had a significant worldwide impact on the way people and politicians look at the environment and its problems, this change has not yet been translated into comprehensive and effective policies to promote and protect environmental interests. Internationally, the United Nations' 1972 Stockholm Conference marks a watershed in the history of global action to protect the environment. It led to the formation of the United Nations Environment Programme and to various important declarations, protocols, and treaties on deforestation, desertification, management of oceanic and other common resources, transboundary pollution, global climatic change, international legal and regulatory mechanisms to ensure compliance, and the like (Leonard 1990). A concise and comprehensive history of the birth and growth, and the philosophy, of the global environmental movement is given in Sinh (1985). Sinh also has outlined the agenda to harness the tremendous potential power of people's elected representatives in the service of the environment. The 1992 global conference on the environment to be held in Brazil will review two decades of progress since Stockholm, and is likely to bring the deeply divergent views of the North and the South on the environment into sharper focus.

A Proactive Environmental Sociology

The newly emerging concern with human ecology and the environment has moved into the mainstream of public life as a major national and international concern. This provides important opportunities for environmental sociologists to contribute to the understanding and solution of these problems. Constance Holden (1989) has highlighted the report of the National Academy of Sciences that outlines an agenda for both micro and macro social scientific studies of "anthropogenic" stresses on the resources and the environment in the north circumpolar region, which has general application. The fragile arctic region has a great wealth of natural resources. It comprises one-tenth of the global area and has eight million people, of whom a quarter are natives. The report placed major emphasis on interdisciplinary studies, particularly those linking the social and physical sciences and basic and applied research. It emphasized the need for drawing on native knowledge and put urgent priority on issues such as cultural survival and the allocation of scarce resources. It also asked the social scientists to come up with models generalizable to other areas.

An interesting insight concerns how each of the several identities of the Arctic (e.g., as homeland for the natives, as a "colony" exploited for its natural resources, and as the last wilderness) results in a distinctive approach to the human–environment relationships. "These approaches have come increasingly into conflict as subsistence hunters and commercial interests vie for limited stocks of fish and game; communities are shaken by boom and bust cycles in scrambles for mineral resources; and rapid modernization has inflicted trauma on native cultures" (Holden 1989, p. 83). The committee identified three areas of interest to the social scientist. In the area of human–environment relationships, there is need for studies on conflict resolution to strike a balance between commercial needs and the interests of subsistence hunters, sportsmen, and conservation. The second area pertains to community viability, for which a systematic approach is needed to help develop physical and social services infrastructure to meet the special climatic needs of the region. A final area pertains to the study of the impact of rapid social change (single-industry cash economy, the snowmobile revolution), which is exacting a heavy price from the local inhabitants in terms of higher rates of alcoholism, suicide, stress, loneliness, accidents, and violence.

The commitment to protect growth or a certain way of life has led conventional human ecologists and the neo-Malthusians to disregard the minimum well-being or sheer survival of the rest of humankind. In fact, Hawley (1986, p. 127) admits that while "competition," resulting from demand exceeding the carrying capacity, may account for the exclusion of some contestants from access to their share of a limited resource, it does not shed "any light on what happens to the excluded members of a population after their exclusion." This serious neglect of the concern for the underdog and the undermined is matched by the self-admitted tendency of the human ecologists "not [to] confront policy matters directly" (Hawley 1986, p. 127).

Edgar Borgatta (1989) has sought to develop an important field called "proactive sociology," with a view to closing the wide gap between sociological theory and practice and to save sociology from sheer irrelevance. Sociological approaches, even when application-oriented, have been largely timid, inactive, or merely reactive. Rather than waiting to study only the aftereffects of "all in the path"—the Three Mile Island radiation leak or the *Exxon Valdez* oil spill—or stepping in at the end of the "issue-attention" cycle, when the problem is historically interesting but socially irrelevant, a proactive sociology will concern itself with the dynamics out of which problems arise, anticipating potential problem areas and their alternative solutions as the means to translate desired values into effective policy. This will involve identifying possible futures and the consequences of action or inaction for their attainment, a policy dimension ignored by sociologists, despite their belief that this may make all the difference in a fast-changing and turbulent world in which the ability to handle and manage change requires the ability to anticipate change and to adapt social structures to changing requirements. To this end, the sociologist needs to ask if what he or she is doing will make an impact and be useful to society. The fundamental assumption here is that if we know something about the impact of social structure on behavior, we should be able to propose models for changes in social structures that will effectively implement values which have priority status in society (Borgatta 1989, p. 15). Sociologists are then obligated to "address societal values more directly by providing alternate models of potential changes and exploring the consequences these changes may produce if identified values are implemented" (Borgatta and Hatch 1984, p. 354).

Following this lead, a "proactive environmental sociology" would broaden the scope of the "sociology of environmental issues" by focusing specifically on the changes that are required to effectively implement stated values (equity, social justice, "future generations," conservation, sharing the global commons, clean and healthy environment, changes in life-styles and consumption patterns, and the like), and by exploring the possible consequences of these changes. Thus, David Mahar, an adviser to the World Bank, has argued that blaming peasant colonists for deforestation is "tantamount to blaming the victim" for "misguided public policies" that promote road building, official colonization of the forest, and extensive livestock development, and that "purposely or inadvertently encourage rapid depletion of the forest." This definition of the situation led Mahar to propose an "alternative development model" that would put government action on hold so that, based on land-use surveys, "(l)ands found to have limited agricultural potential—virtually whole of *terra firme* [sic] of Amazonia—would be held in perpetuity as forest reserves. . . ." These and other unconventional conclusions are stated by Mahar as his own and carry the disclaimer that they do not necessarily represent the views and policies of the World Bank itself (cited in Hildyard 1989).

This example also brings out Borgatta's point that a proactive stance may involve the espousing of unpopular positions. It may lead a proactive environmental sociologist to examine the role of established institutions and values (crass individualism and the impact of "anthropocentric," "cowboy," "superpower," and "sustained development" approaches to the use of finite resources and a fragile environment, corporate nonaccountability and the global impact of multinationals, the state, and the like) in order to facilitate the creation of environmentally sustainable social structures that implement stated values. On this basis, a systematic concern with the application of knowledge would lead to a "proactive environmental sociology" that would prompt the sociologist to formulate alternative policies with respect to the set of environmental values or goals that are to be implemented (cf. Borgatta and Cook 1984, p. 17). This will also ensure that the applied aspects of "environmental sociology" will flourish within the discipline and not become detached from sociology, as has been the fate of industrial sociology and many other areas in the past (Borgatta 1989).

Overview

Environmental sociologists have complained of the lack of a unifying focus within the field, and have noted its specialized, fragmented, and dualistic tendencies, which hinder concept and theory development (Buttel 1987, p. 466). This should be a cause for serious concern insofar as the new human ecology is supposed to provide a holistic, integrated understanding of human–environment interactions. In addition to the problems surrounding functionalist as well as Marxist categories and assumptions is the difficulty of adapting bioecological concepts to the human context. Notions such as ecosystem, niche, succession, climax communities, balance of nature, even evolution, have no clear social referents and pose formidable problems of inappropriate or illegitimate transferral of concepts. Thus, while one finds constant reference to urban or social "ecosystems" in the literature, the wide-ranging, even global, energy-exchange patterns make the boundaries so diffuse that it becomes impossible to locate an urban *ecosystem* in time and space, at least in biological terms (Young 1983, p. 195). Or, if humans are defined as niche dwellers, the term *niche,* "if adopted directly from biology would produce only one worldwide niche for the entire global species, a result that would render the concept useless. How can the species problem be overcome in adapting such a concept to human ecology?" (Young 1983, p. 795).

Terms such as *the environment* are not easy to define or conceptualize; nor are ecological chain reactions, multiple causal paths, and feedback mechanisms in complex ecosystems easy to delineate. In recognition of the substantial difference between human and bioecological orders, some human ecologists, such as Hawley, have moved away from bioecological models. Thus, Hawley is highly critical of the neo-Malthusian application of the "carrying capacity" notion, on the ground that "while the argument may be suitable for plants and animals, its transfer to the human species is highly questionable" (1986, p. 53). While still shying away from assigning a critical role to human agency, or even a policymaking role to the human ecologist, Hawley has nonetheless broadened the scope of his theory by incorporating culture and norms as ecosystem variables. Rappaport has raised more basic objections: To treat the components of the environment as if they were mere resources is to view them exclusively in economic terms and invite "the use and abuse of biological systems of all classes and the neglect of moral and aesthetic considerations in general. Whatever may be meant by the phrase 'quality of life,' exploitation does not enhance it" (1978, pp. 266–267).

Pollution, "resource" depletion, and the diminution of the quality of life are tied to the voracious appetites of industrial metabolisms.

Human ecologists, in general, have not dealt adequately with such concerns nor with the problems of power, domination, and the role of the state and of "values" in human–environmental relationships. At a minimum, one needs to know the role of the state in the regulation, maintenance, expansion, suppression, and "resocialization" of peoples and societies. If ecosystems are constituted of interdependent parts, one needs to know the nature of the reciprocal relationships among the parts and among the parts and the ecosystem. Rappaport (1978) has drawn attention to the maladaptive tendency of subsystems to become increasingly powerful and to dominate and use the larger system for their own benefit, to the detriment of the general interest and the adaptive flexibility of the system. He mentions the dominating positions occupied by huge corporations and the "military industrial complex" as examples. More broadly, Rappaport ties pollution, "resource" depletion, and the diminution of the quality of life and the destruction of its meanings to the scale of modern societies and the voracious appetites of their industrial metabolisms. Thus, while he does not deny that population increase may have a negative impact on the quality of life, he has little doubt that the real cause of ecosystem destruction and the deterioration of the quality of life is to be found in the way societies are organized, not in their population trends. If that is so, what alternative do humans have?

Within the human ecological perspectives, environmental problems are seen as arising either from the unplanned nature of growth and expansionism, and its attendant externalities and "commons" tragedies, and growth and market restrictions (the pro-growth, expansionist perspective), or as a result of the excess of population over the carrying capacity of the environment (the neo-Malthusian perspective). To restore ecological balance and environmental health, human ecologists place their faith in value consensus, rational planning, systems theory, computer models, economic growth, trickle-downs, market mechanisms, technological fixes (the pro-growth perspective) or in limits to growth, sustainable development, sticks and carrots, benign neglect, the triage, die-offs, outright compulsion, even genocide (the neo-Malthusian perspective). Within the political economy perspective, on the other hand, the emphasis is on internal contradictions, uneven development, center–periphery relations, capitalist exploitation, the role of multinationals and the state, trade imbalances, and the treadmill of production. To ensure environmental protection, distribution, social justice, and equality, the proposals from a political economy standpoint range from social revolution, conflict, and confrontation to social welfarism and mixed economies.

The political economy perspective is critical of the basic assumption of the Chicago ecologists that changes in population, organization, and the technologies of movement explain expansionary movements and territorial arrangements. By allowing planners to alter spatial forms to dissipate class conflict and social unrest, Smith (1979, p. 255) believes, the perspective becomes a powerful depoliticizing weapon in their hands. He favors "client-centered" planning, which does not assume that "physical structure determines social structure," but holds that both are shaped by the economic and political structures of society which provide selective access to opportunities, and further discriminatory patterns of land use and investment. Smith, therefore, offers "conflictual planning" on behalf of the poor and the powerless, to call attention to the hidden social costs of development and to increase the political costs of pursuing repressive policies disguised as rationally planned allocational, locational, and investment choices. This approach poses three basic questions: "Whose values, interests, and social actions will determine the purpose, pace, and direction of historical change? Can the costs and benefits of historical change be distributed fairly? Can the changes that do occur further the cause of social justice?" (Smith 1979, p. 288).

Schnaiberg (1980) has identified three responses to the contradiction between production expansion and ecological limits: (1) the expansionist, which will be temporary, increasingly unequal, environmentally stressful, and authoritarian; (2) the business-as-usual, which will be unstable, socially regressive, unequal, and of limited environmental value; (3) the ecological, involving appropriate technology, reduced consumption, and reduced inequality, which will be the most durable but also the most socially disruptive and the least desirable. William Ophuls (1977) has called for a rejection of Alexander Hamilton's ruling vision of power in order to realize the Jeffersonian vision of republican simplicity. Schnaiberg's own preference, short of a social revolution, is for a mixed social democratic system like Sweden's, with some production expansion and improved welfare distribution under close state supervision.

However, this solution does not quite address the critical concerns of the environment or the needs of three-fourths of humanity. It presents to the world the antiecological model of the "treadmill of production" under a more benign form. The common problem, as Hilary French (1990) points out in a Worldwatch paper on environmental reconstruction in socialist nations, is that of finding the proper balance between sufficiency and excess, which he says will be as difficult for the socialist countries as it has been for the West. He is afraid that under the impact of powerful forces, the socialist countries may end up repeating some of the West's errors. In this context, he points out how the president of the Czech Republic, Vaclav Havel, has identified "the omnipresent dictatorship of consumption, production, advertising, commerce, and consumer culture" as the common enemy. Nancy Anderson, the well-known New England environmental educator and activist, blames uncontrolled greed for the frightening global environmental degradation and for overpowering our sense of responsibility to future generations.

Gandhi, aware both of the fatal attraction and the destructive potential of wanton materialism, saw it as constituting the gravest threat to human freedom, survival, and environmental security. He therefore opted for a simple, nonexploitative, and ecologically sustainable social order. Such a decentralized social order, based on truth and nonviolence, is to be governed by the metaphysically determined optimum levels of wants, technology, and resource use fitted to the requirements of the human scale. In the interim, he demanded that the rich become trustees of the poor in order to serve justice, to mitigate the negative impacts of the differentials of wealth and power, and to avoid class conflicts. His radical vision of a normal social order, nowhere realized as yet, provides a useful yardstick for measuring how ecologically sound and environmentally sustainable a society is in its actual operation (Saran 1977; see also Bharadwaj 1984). Noting that the world has enough for everyone's needs but not for everyone's greed, Gandhi was convinced that such a social order would come about

> only if the means of production of the elementary necessaries of life remain in the control of the masses. These should be freely available to all as God's air and water are or ought to be; they should not be made a vehicle of traffic for the exploitation of others. Their monopolization by any country, nation or group of persons would be unjust. The neglect of this simple principle is the cause of the destitution that we witness today not only in this unhappy land but in other parts of the world too. (quoted in Sinha 1976, p. 81)

From this point of view, while there is little disagreement that overpopulation aggravates environmental and other problems, the attempts to eradicate the root causes of social instability, inequality, and poverty are bound to be far more effective in the long run than the impressive but partially effective approaches to population control. Brian Tokar (1988) has pointed out that, historically, rapid increases in population occur when people become dislocated from their traditional land base and become less secure about their personal and family survival. On the other hand, populations become stable when the future is secure, the infant mortality rate is low, social choices for women are expanding, and parents are not worried about who will support them in their old age.

How to effect the radical changes required to restore the proper ecological balance and preserve the biocultural integrity and diversity of the global "household," but "without the most fantastic 'bust' of all time" (Ehrlich 1968, p. 169), is the formidable challenge and the urgent task facing humankind. This will involve a redirection of the vast, creative human energies away from a self-defeating and ecodestructive expansionist and wasteful orientation, and their rechanneling into the life-giving and life-promoting forms of human action and human social organization.

[See also Population; Technological Risks and Society.]

BIBLIOGRAPHY

Arnold, Steven H. 1989 "Sustainable Development: A Solution to the Development Puzzle." *Development, Journal of SID* 2/3:21–24.

Bell, Daniel 1976 *The Cultural Contradictions of Capitalism.* New York: Basic Books.

——— 1977 "Are There 'Social Limits' to Growth?" In Kenneth D. Wilson, ed., *Prospects for Growth: Changing Expectations for the Future.* New York: Praeger.

Bharadwaj, L. K. 1984 "The Contribution of Gandhian Thinking to the Understanding of the World Crisis." *Revue internationale de sociologie* 20:65–99.

Borgatta, Edgar F. 1989 "Towards a Proactive Sociology." Paper presented at the 29th International Congress of the International Institute of Sociology, Rome.

———, and Karen S. Cook 1988 "Sociology and Its Future." In Edgar F. Borgatta and Karen S. Cook, eds., *The Future of Sociology.* Newbury Park, Calif.: Sage.

———, and Laurie Russell Hatch 1988 "Social Stratification." In Edgar F. Borgatta and Karen S. Cook, eds., *The Future of Sociology.* Newbury Park, Calif.: Sage.

Brown, Lester R., Christopher Flavin, and Sandra Postel 1990 "Picturing a Sustainable Society." In Lester R. Brown and associates, *State of the World 1990: A Worldwatch Institute Report on Progress Toward a Sustainable Society.* New York: W. W. Norton.

Brundtland, Gro Harlem 1989 "Sustainable Development: An Overview." *Development, Journal of SID* 2/3:13–14.

Buttel, Frederick H. 1987 "New Directions in Environmental Sociology." *Annual Review of Sociology* 13:465–488.

Catton, William R., Jr. 1978 "Carrying Capacity, Overshoot, and the Quality of Life." In J. Milton Yinger and Stephen J. Cutler, eds., *Major Social Issues: A Multidisciplinary View.* New York: Free Press.

——— 1980 *Overshoot.* Urbana: University of Illinois Press.

———, and Riley E. Dunlap 1978 "Environmental Sociology: A New Paradigm." *American Sociologist* 13:41–49.

Commoner, Barry 1974 "Interview on Growth." In Willem L. Oltmans, ed., *On Growth: The Crisis of Exploding Population and Resource Depletion.* New York: Capricorn Books.

Coomaraswamy, A. K. 1946 *The Religious Basis of the Forms of Indian Society.* New York: Orientalia.

de la Court, Thijs 1990 *Beyond Brundtland: Green Developments in the 1990s.* New York: New Horizon Press.

Duncan, Otis Dudley 1964 "Social Organization and the Ecosystem." In Robert E. L. Faris, ed., *Handbook of Modern Sociology.* Chicago: Rand McNally.

Dunlap, Riley E. 1979 "Environmental Sociology." *Annual Review of Sociology* 5:243–273.

——— 1986 "Two Decades of Public Concern for Environmental Quality: Up, Down and Up Again." Paper presented at the Annual Meetings of the American Sociological Association, New York.

Ehrlich, Paul R. 1968 *The Population Bomb.* New York: Ballantine Books.

French, Hilary F. 1990 *Green Revolutions: Environmental Reconstruction in Eastern Europe and the Soviet Union.* Worldwatch Paper 99:1–62. Washington, D.C.: Worldwatch Institute.

Freudenberg, William R., and Robert Gramling 1989 "The Emergence of Environmental Sociology: Contributions of Riley E. Dunlap and William R. Catton, Jr." *Sociological Inquiry* 59:439–452.

Gottdiener, M., and Joe R. Feagin 1988 "The Paradigm Shift in Urban Sociology." *Urban Affairs Quarterly* 24:163–187.

Hardin, Garrett 1968 "The Tragedy of the Commons." *Science* 162:1243–1248.

Hawley, Amos H. 1979 "Cumulative Change in Theory and in History." In Amos H. Hawley, ed., *Societal Growth: Processes and Implications.* New York: Free Press.

——— 1984 "Sociological Human Ecology: Past, Present, and Future." In Michael Micklin and Harvey M. Choldin, eds., *Sociological Human Ecology: Contemporary Issues and Applications.* Boulder, Colo.: Westview.

——— 1986 *Human Ecology: A Theoretical Essay.* Chicago: University of Chicago Press.

Hildyard, Nicholas B. 1989 "Adios Amazonia? A Report from Altimira Gathering." *The Ecologist* 19:53–67.

Holden, Constance 1989 "Environment, Culture, and Change in the Arctic." *Science* 243:883.

Humphrey, Craig R., and Frederick H. Buttel 1982 *Environment, Energy, and Society.* Belmont, Calif.: Wadsworth.

Kahn, Herman 1974 "Interview on Growth." In Willem L. Oltmans, ed., *On Growth: The Crisis of Exploding Population and Resource Depletion.* New York: Capricorn Books.

Leonard, Pamela 1990 *Effective Global Environmental Protection: World Federalist Proposals to Strengthen the Role of the United Nations.* Washington, D.C.: World Federalist Association. (In collaboration with Walter Hoffman.)

Meadows, Donella, Dennis Meadows, Jorgen Randers, and William Behrens 1972 *The Limits to Growth: A Report for the Club of Rome's Project on the Predicament of Mankind.* New York: Universe Books.

Medvedev, Zhores A. 1990 "The Environmental Destruction of the Soviet Union." *The Ecologist* 20:27–29.

Mellos, Koula 1988 *Perspectives on Ecology: A Critical Essay.* New York: St. Martin's.

Micklin, Michael, and Harvey M. Choldin (eds.) 1984 *Sociological Human Ecology: Contemporary Issues and Applications.* Boulder, Colo.: Westview.

Miller, G. Tyler, Jr. 1972 *Replenish the Earth: A Primer in Human Ecology.* Belmont, Calif.: Wadsworth.

Morrison, Denton E. 1976 "Growth, Environment, Equity and Scarcity." *Social Science Quarterly* 57:292–306.

——— 1978 "Equity Impacts of Some Major Energy Alternatives." In Seymour Warkov, ed., *Energy Policy in the United States: Social and Behavioral Dimensions.* New York: Praeger.

——— 1980 "The Soft, Cutting Edge of Environmentalism: Why and How the Appropriate Technology Notion Is Changing the Movement." *Natural Resources Journal* 20:275–298.

———, and Riley E. Dunlap 1986 "Environmentalism and Elitism: A Conceptual and Empirical Analysis." *Environmental Management* 10:581–589.

Ophuls, William 1977 "Buddhist Politics: In Politics as in Economics, 'Small Is Beautiful.' " *The Ecologist* 7:82–87.

Park, Robert E. 1936 "Human Ecology." *American Journal of Sociology* 42:1–15.

Polanyi, Karl 1974 "Our Obsolete Market Mentality." *The Ecologist* 4:213–220. Reprint of 1947 article.

Rappaport, Roy A. 1976 "Forests and Man." *The Ecologist* 6:240–246.

——— 1978 "Biology, Meaning, and the Quality of Life." In J. Milton Yinger and Stephen J. Cutler, eds., *Major Social Issues: A Multidisciplinary View.* New York: Free Press.

Redclift, Michael 1987 *Sustainable Development: Exploring the Contradiction.* New York: Methuen.

Reichel-Dolmatoff, G. 1977 "Cosmology as Ecological Analysis: A View from the Rain Forest." *The Ecologist* 7:4–11.

Revelle, Roger 1974 "Interview on Growth." In Willem L. Oltmans, ed., *On Growth: The Crisis of Exploding Population and Resource Depletion.* New York: Capricorn Books.

Sachs, Wolfgang 1990 "On the Archeology of the Development Idea." *The Ecologist* 20:42–43.

Saran, A. K. 1977 *Gandhi and the Concept of Politics: Toward a Normal Civilization.* New Delhi: Nehru Memorial Museum and Library.

——— 1978 "The Traditional Vision of Man." UNESCO Seminar, Hyderabad, India. Mimeo.

Schnaiberg, Allan 1980 *The Environment: From Surplus to Scarcity.* New York: Oxford University Press.

——— 1983 "Redistributive Goals Versus Distributive Politics: Social Equity Limits in Environmental and Appropriate Technology Movements." *Sociological Inquiry* 53:200–219.

Sen, Amartya K. 1981 *Poverty and Famines: An Essay on Entitlement and Deprivation.* Oxford: Clarendon Press.

Sinh, Digvijay 1985 *The Eco-Vote: People's Representatives and Global Environment.* New Delhi: Prentice-Hall of India.

Sinha, Radha 1976 *Food and Poverty: The Political Economy of Confrontation.* London: Croom Helm Ltd.

Smith, Michael P. 1979 *The City and Social Theory.* New York: St. Martin's.

Stonich, Susan C. 1989 "The Dynamics of Social Processes and Environmental Destruction: A Central American Case Study." *Population and Development Review* 15:269–296.

Tokar, Brian 1988 "Social Ecology, Deep Ecology and the Future of Green Political Thought." *The Ecologist* 18:132–141.

Vohra, B. B. 1985 "Why India's Forests Have Been Cut Down." *The Ecologist* 15:50–51.

World Commission on Environment and Development 1987 *Our Common Future.* New York: Oxford University Press (The Brundtland Report).

Young, Gerald (ed.) 1983 *Origins of Human Ecology.* Stroudsburg, Pa.: Hutchinson Ross.

– LAKSHMI K. BHARADWAJ

HUMAN NATURE

Debates over the nature of human nature have characterized social theory since it emerged in the Renaissance. As Thomas Sowell has argued, these debates generally take two forms: the optimistic and the pessimistic (Sowell 1987). The former position, associated with Rousseau and anarchists such as William Goodwin, holds that humans are essentially good, but they are turned bad by the institutions of their society. The latter position is rooted in the assumption that humans are fundamentally egoistic and selfish, thereby requiring either a strong state to regulate them or, in a less pessimistic account, an institution like the market to guide their affairs toward an optimal result.

The plasticity of human experience has become the dominant way of thinking about human nature.

For sociologists, neither position became the dominant way of thinking about human nature; instead, the plasticity of human experience was emphasized. Durkheim (1973) wrote the most important defense of a pluralistic approach to the subject, one that remains unsurpassed to this day in its clarity of presentation. Human nature was dualistic, he argued, speaking to the needs of both body and soul, the sacred and the profane, the emotional and the cognitive, and other such dualities. We are, in short, what we make ourselves. This version of a flexible approach to human nature would come to characterize contemporary theorists such as Parsons, who spoke of "much discussed 'plasticity' of the human organism, its capacity to learn any one of a large number of alternative patterns of behavior instead of being bound by its generic constitution to a very limited range of alternatives" (1951, p. 32).

In current sociological debates, the plasticity of human nature is emphasized by the general term *social construction.* If one argues that we ought to speak of gender roles rather than sex roles—the former is recognized to be the product of how people arrange their cultural rules, whereas the latter is understood to be fixed biologically—one is making a case for plasticity (Epstein 1988). Indeed, given the importance of feminism in contemporary theory, which tends to argue that "nothing about the body, including women's reproductive organs, determines univocally how social divisions will be shaped" (Scott 1988, p. 2), the strength of a plasticity approach to human nature is probably stronger than ever before.

Current research in many areas of sociology is premised on a social construction approach. Work stimulated by ethnomethodology is one clear case. In contrast to a Chomskian understanding of language as originating in rules hard-wired in the brain, the tradition of conversation analysis examines how human beings in real conversation twist and shape their utterances to account for context and nuance (Schegloff and Sacks 1979; Scheff 1986). Moreover, since the language we use is a reflection of the way we think, it is possible to argue that the mind itself is socially constructed, that the a priori nature of the way we think is relatively minimal (Coulter 1979). Accounts of sociological practice based on the assumption of plasticity do not end there. It has been argued that homosexuality is not driven by biological destiny but is a socially constructed phenomenon (Greenberg 1988). Morality, as well, can be understood as socially constructed (Wolfe 1989). Underlying a wide variety of approaches to sociology—from symbolic interactionism to social problems—is an underlying premise that human nature is not driven by any one thing.

The only dissent from a general consensus over human nature's plasticity is rational choice theory. At least among economists who believe that economic methodologies can be used to study social institutions such as the family, there is a belief that "human behavior is not compartmentalized, sometimes based on maximizing, sometimes not, sometimes motivated by stable preferences, sometimes by volatile ones, sometimes resulting in an optimal accumulation, sometimes not" (Becker 1976, p. 14). Yet there are many versions of rational choice theory; at least one of them, that associated with Jon Elster, is committed to methodological individualism, but is also willing to concede the existence of a "multiple self" (Elster 1986). It is far more common in contemporary sociology to speak of egoism and altruism as existing in some kind of unstable combination rather than giving the priority totally to one or the other (Etzioni 1988).

Arguments about human nature, in turn, are related to the philosophical anthropology that shaped so much social theory. It has been a consistent theme of the sociological enterprise to argue that humans are different from other species. From the emphasis on *homo faber* in Marx and Engels through Weber's notions about the advantages of culture to Mead's account of why dogs and other animals are incapable of exchanging significant symbols, humans have been understood to possess unique characteristics that determine the organization of their society. Twentieth-century theorists such as Arnold Gehlen or Helmuth Plessner carried forward this tradition and are increasingly translated and read (for an overview, see Honneth and Joas 1988). Even Niklas Luhmann, whose work is heavily influenced by biology and cybernetics, can still claim that "the decisive advantage of human interaction over animal interaction stems from this elemental achievement of language" (1982, p. 72).

The most important shift in philosophical anthropology in recent years is a shift from an essentially materialist understanding of human capacities to an essentially mental one. Powers of interpretation and narrative, it has been argued, constitute the essential features of the human self (Taylor 1989). Just as an argument about the plasticity of human nature enables sociology to avoid reduction into psychological categories, an emphasis on the interpretive powers of humans prevents a reduction of sociology to sociobiology and other basically algorithmic ways of thinking about evolution.

As with the issue of plasticity, not all sociologists agree either that there are specific human characteristics or that, if there are, they ought to be understood as primarily mental and interpretive. Sociobiologists argue that not only are humans driven by their genetic structure more than they would like to believe, but other animals also possess cultural skills. There is therefore no fundamental difference between human and nonhuman species, merely points along a continuum (Lumsden and Wilson 1981). Both sociologists and anthropologists, consequently, have argued for the use of sociobiological approaches in the social sciences (Lopreato 1984; Wozniak 1984; Rindos 1986), although there are also critics who question such an enterprise (Blute 1987).

Another challenge to the anthropocentric view that social scientists have taken toward humans has arisen with cognitive science and artificial intelligence. Whereas classical sociological theory compared humans to other animal species, we can now compare them to machines. Computers, after all, process information just as human brains do, use language to communicate, reason, and can, especially in new approaches to artificial intelligence called connectionist, learn from their mistakes. There are, consequently, some efforts to apply artificial intelligence to sociology as there are efforts to use the insights of sociobiology (Gilbert and Heath 1986), although here, again, there are strong critical voices (Wolgar 1985; Wolfe 1991). In the more recent work of Luhmann, as well as in the writings of some other theorists, emphasis is placed on information science, systems theory, even thermodynamics, all of which are approaches based on a denial that human systems require special ways of understanding that are different from other systems (Luhmann 1989; Beniger 1986; Bailey 1990).

In spite of efforts to develop sociological theory on the basis of algorithmic self-reproducing systems, it is unlikely that assumptions about the unique, interpretative, meaning-producing capacities of humans will be seriously challenged. It is the capacity to recognize the contexts in which messages are transmitted and thereby to interpret those messages that make human mental capacities distinct from any organism, whether natural or artificial, that is preprogrammed to follow explicit instructions. One reason humans are able to recognize contexts is precisely the plasticity of their mental capacities. The plastic theory of human nature, in short, overlaps with an emphasis on philosophical anthropology to produce an understanding of human behavior that does not follow already-existing rules so much as it alters and bends rules as it goes along.

Both understandings of human nature and accounts of specifically human capacities will be relevant to future efforts in sociological theory to reconcile micro and macro approaches. Although there has been a good deal of effort to establish a micro-macro link (Alexander et al. 1987), the more interesting question may turn out not to be not whether it can be done but whether (and how) it ought to be done. Systems theory and the information sciences provide a relatively easy way to make a link between parts and wholes: each part is understood to have as little autonomy as possible so that the system as a whole can function autonomously with respect to other systems. The micro, like a bit of information in a computer program, would be structured to be as dumb as possible so that the macro system itself can be intelligent. Nonhuman enterprises—computers on the one hand and the structure of DNA in other animal species on the other—show that there is a major bridge between the macro and the micro. But the cost of constructing that bridge is the denial of the autonomy of the parts, a high cost for humans to pay.

But conceptions of human beings as preprogrammed rule followers are not the only way to conceptualize micro sociological processes. The traditions of ethnomethodology and symbolic interactionism, which are more compatible with notions emphasizing the plasticity of human nature, imagine the human parts of any social system as engaged in a constant process of renegotiating the rules that govern the system. When the micro is understood as plastic, the macro can be understood as capable of existing even in imperfect, entropy-producing states of disorder. Indeed, for human systems, as opposed to those of machines and other species, disorder is the norm, integration the exception. If there is going to be a micro-macro link in sociology, it may well come about not by denying human plasticity and uniqueness, but rather by accounting for the particular and special property humans possess of having no fixed nature but a repertoire of social practices that in turn make human society different from any other kind of system.

[See also Evolution: Biological, Social, Cultural; Intelligence; Sex Differences.]

BIBLIOGRAPHY

Alexander, Jeffrey C., Bernhard Giesen, Richard Münch, and Neil J. Smelser 1987 *The Macro-Micro Link.* Berkeley: University of California Press.

Bailey, Kenneth D. 1990 *Social Entropy Theory.* Albany: State University of New York Press.

Becker, Gary 1976 *The Economic Approach to Human Behavior.* Chicago: University of Chicago Press.

Beniger, James R. 1986 *The Control Revolution: Technological and Economic Origins of the Information Society.* Cambridge, Mass.: Harvard University Press.

Blute, Marion 1987 "Biologists on Sociocultural Evolution: A Critical Analysis." *Sociological Theory* 5:185–193.

Coulter, Jeff 1979 *The Social Construction of Mind.* London: Macmillan.

Durkheim, Emile 1973 "The Dualism of Human Nature and Its Social Conditions." In Robert N. Bellah, ed., *Emile Durkheim on Morality and Society: Selected Writings.* Chicago: University of Chicago Press.

Elster, Jon (ed.) 1986 *The Multiple Self.* Cambridge: Cambridge University Press.

Epstein, Cynthia 1988 *Deceptive Distinctions: Sex, Gender, and the Social Order.* New Haven, Conn.: Yale University Press.

Etzioni, Amitai 1988 *The Moral Dimension.* New York: Free Press.

Gilbert, C. Nigel, and Christian Heath (eds.) *Social Action and Artificial Intelligence: Surrey Conferences on Sociological Theory and Method 3.* Aldershot, England: Gower.

Greenberg, David 1988 *The Construction of Homosexuality.* Chicago: University of Chicago Press.

Honneth, Axel, and Hans Joas 1988 *Social Action and Human Nature.* Cambridge: Cambridge University Press.

Lopreato, Joseph 1984 *Human Nature and Biocultural Evolution.* Boston: Allen and Unwin.

Luhmann, Niklas 1982 *The Differentiation of Society,* trans. Stephen Holmes and Charles Larmore. New York: Columbia University Press.

——— 1989 *Ecological Communication,* trans. John Bednarz. Chicago: University of Chicago Press.

Lumsden, Charles J., and Edward O. Wilson 1981 *Genes, Mind, and Culture: The Coevolutionary Process.* Cambridge, Mass.: Harvard University Press.

Parsons, Talcott 1951 *The Social System.* New York: Free Press.

Rindos, David 1986 "The Evolution of the Capacity for Culture: Sociobiology, Structuralism, and Cultural Selectiveness." *Current Anthropology* 27:315–332.

Scheff, Thomas J. 1986 "Micro-Linguistics and Social Structure: A Theory of Social Action." *Sociological Theory* 4:71–83.

Schegloff, Emmanuel, and Harvey Sacks 1979 "Opening Up Closings." In Ray Turner, ed., *Ethnomethodology: Selected Readings.* Baltimore: Penguin.

Scott, Joan Wallach 1988 *Gender and the Politics of History.* New York: Columbia University Press.

Sowell, Thomas 1987 *A Conflict of Visions.* New York: William Morrow.

Taylor, Charles 1989 *Sources of the Self: The Making of the Modern Identity.* Cambridge, Mass.: Harvard University Press.

Wolfe, Alan 1989 *Whose Keeper?: Social Science and Moral Obligation.* Berkeley: University of California Press.

——— 1991 "Mind, Self, Society, and Computer: Artificial Intelligence and the Sociology of Mind." *American Journal of Sociology* 96:1073–1096.

Woolger, Steve 1985 "Why Not a Sociology of Machines?: The Case of Sociology and Artificial Intelligence." *Sociology* 19:557–572.

Wozniak, Paul R. 1984 "Making Sociobiological Sense out of Sociology." *Sociological Quarterly* 25:191–204.

– ALAN WOLFE

HUMAN RIGHTS MOVEMENT

The atrocities committed during World War II provided the catalyst for the developments in human rights law that characterized the second half of the twentieth century. Although there is no precise agreement on the content of human rights, three substantive areas have been recognized—individual rights, economic and social rights, and collective rights. A major innovation of the approach to human rights has been the recognition that rights are interdependent and that all persons are entitled not only to traditional civil and political rights but to economic, social, and cultural rights. The international community has also recognized that the observance of human rights by countries for their own nationals is a matter of international concern.

Human rights were central in the planning and drafting of the United Nations Charter (1945), which reaffirms the faith of the world's peoples in "fundamental human rights, in the dignity and worth of the human person, in the equal rights of men and women and of nations large and small." Chapter I, article I, specifies that one of the purposes of the United Nations is to "achieve international co-operation in . . . promoting and encouraging respect for human rights and for fundamental freedoms for all without distinction as to race, sex, language or religion." Through the charter, the United Nations is required to promote the observance of human rights, and all member states are pledged to cooperate in the achievement of this goal. Despite strong human rights provisions, the charter includes no codification or enumeration of rights. The Commission on Human Rights was created to draft such a list. As chair of the first Human Rights Committee, Eleanor Roosevelt was instrumental in securing the Universal Declaration of Human Rights, adopted without dissent by the General Assembly in 1948. The declaration was not intended to be a legally binding document but was, as stated in its preamble, a "common standard of achievement for all people and all nations." Its importance, however, cannot be overestimated. It has been characterized as similar to the Magna Carta, its provisions have been incorporated in the constitutions of many countries, and many of its articles have been accepted as international law. As a statement of goals and principles the declaration was a major step. Its thirty articles spell out basic civil, political, economic, social, and cultural rights: freedom of religion, expression, and assembly; freedom from arbitrary arrests or ex post facto laws; and equal protection under the law. It also recognizes a right to work, to education, and to a standard of living adequate to health and well-being.

To achieve the rights contained in the Universal Declaration, two multilateral conventions, one on civil and political rights, the other on social and economic rights, were drafted by the Human Rights Committee in 1954 and approved by the General Assembly in 1966. These conventions are legally binding on the nations that ratify them and subject those nations to the enforcement procedures set forth. The International Covenant on Civil and Political Rights, ratified by the United States in 1992 and by 114 other countries, not only encompasses most of the rights contained in the U.S. Bill of Rights but provides for the right to self-determination, the right to dispose of property, the right to nationality at birth, the right to move freely within a country, and the right to leave a country. It prohibits slavery; forced or compulsory labor; unlawful interference with privacy, family, or honor and reputation; propaganda for war; and advocacy of national, racial, or religious hatred that constitutes incitement to discrimination, hostility, or violence. The International Covenant on Economic, Social and Cultural Rights, ratified by more than 118 states, excluding the United States, protects the right to work and just and favorable conditions of work, including fair wages and equal remuneration for work of equal value; the right to social security and an adequate standard of living; the right to the highest attainable standard of physical and mental health; the right to education; and the right to take part in cultural life and to enjoy the benefits of scientific progress.

Numerous human rights conventions have been widely ratified, including the Convention on the Prevention and Punishment of the Crime of Genocide, the Convention on the Elimination of All Forms of Racial Discrimination, the Convention on the Elimination of All Forms of Discrimination Against Women, the Convention on the Elimination of Torture, and the Convention on Rights of the Child. Despite the proliferation of instruments and conventions that define and seek to protect human rights, a fundamental weakness of the system is a lack of effective enforcement mechanisms. Typically, nations that have ratified the conventions are required to report on their progress toward fulfilling their commitments. Unless a state, through a separate agreement, allows an individual to bring a complaint against the state, the individual has no recourse for relief from human rights abuses in an international forum. Nevertheless, respect for human rights is espoused by virtually all nations, has become an important foreign policy issue, and influences the activities of such organizations as the International Monetary Fund and the World Bank.

Women are particularly vulnerable to religious extremism and to certain traditional and customary practices, such as dowry and genital mutilation.

In the second half of the twentieth century, human rights of specific groups, such as women, minorities, indigenous peoples, and children, were addressed by the international community. Human rights of women are particularly and systematically abused through gender-based violence, sexual exploitation, harassment, and international trafficking in women. As a group, women are particularly vulnerable to religious extremism and to certain traditional and customary practices, such as dowry and genital mutilation. In addition, during armed conflicts, women are often systematically subjected to rape and prostitution. In 1994, the United Nations took a significant step toward addressing this serious human rights violation by adopting the Declaration on the Elimination of Violence Against Women, which urges nations to combat violence perpetrated against women not only by the state but by individuals (including domestic violence).

In 1993 the World Conference on Human Rights sponsored by the United Nations was held in Vienna. Nearly every country sent an official delegation to the conference. The Vienna Declaration reaffirmed the universality of human rights despite the efforts of some countries, notably China, to assert that human rights are not universal but culturally based. It affirmed that all human rights are interdependent and that civil and political rights must be linked with economic and social rights. An important result of the conference was the recognition of women's rights as human rights and the emphasis on rights of minority and indigenous peoples. The Vienna Declaration affirmed that the human rights of women and girls are an inalienable, integral, and indivisible part of universal human rights and urged full and equal participation of women; the eradication of all forms of discrimination on grounds of sex became a priority objective of the international community.

A significant development in the late twentieth century was the emphasis on democracy as a human right. After the demise of the Soviet Union and the political upheavals accompanied by the overthrow of dictators, there were greater freedoms and choices for many oppressed peoples. Democracy based on the freely expressed will and choice of peoples to determine their political, economic, social, and cultural systems was recognized as an important aspect of human rights law. The Vienna Declaration of 1993 and other human rights instruments affirm that democracy, development and respect for human rights, and fundamental freedoms are interdependent and reinforce each other.

The U.S. position on human rights is ambiguous. The Constitution and the Bill of Rights are based on the liberal tradition articulated by the philosopher John Locke and recognize that the individual possesses certain inalienable rights that the government may not trample on. They protect civil and political rights but not economic and social rights. Individual rights are protected from government infringement and increase individual liberty. They do not allow an individual to make claims upon the government for economic or social rights, such as subsistence and housing. Attempts through litigation to secure constitutional protection for economic and social rights, such as the right to an education or to a minimum standard of living, have failed. In practice, however, free education is provided to all, and government entitlement programs, such as social security and welfare, have been a part of U.S. law for several decades.

Despite its relatively good record with respect to observance and protection of human rights, until 1986 the United States was not a party to any of the major human rights conventions. Objections were generally based on legal grounds related to, for example, federalism. The ratification in 1992 by the United States of the Covenant on Civil and Political Rights indicated a change in U.S. policy in this area. The United States continued to monitor human rights abuses throughout the world, by linking a nation's observance of human rights to the granting of some economic or strategic benefit or to most-favored-nation trade status. For example, the former Soviet Union was subjected to economic pressure because of its policy on emigration.

Despite the advances in the development and acceptance of human rights as an integral part of international law, abuses of human rights continued. Amnesty International, a leading organization in monitoring human rights abuses, reported a lack of consistent commitment to human rights among 161 governments surveyed, although no nation was prepared to admit abuses of the rights of its own nationals. The international community, through the United Nations, has been effective in setting human rights norms and securing their acceptance. The challenge for the future is to achieve these norms worldwide.

– ELIZABETH F. DEFEIS

I

ILLEGITIMACY

Until the 1960s, it was widely assumed that marriage was a universal or nearly universal institution for licensing parenthood. Marriage assigned paternity rights to fathers (and their families) and guaranteed social recognition and economic support to mothers and their offspring. According to Malinowski (1930), who first articulated "the principle of legitimacy," and to Davis (1939, 1949), who extended Malinowski's theory into sociology, marriage provides the added benefit to children of connecting them to a wider network of adults who have a stake in their long-term development.

This functional explanation for the universality of marriage as a mechanism for legitimating parenthood became a source of intense debate in anthropology and sociology during the 1960s. Evidence accumulated from cross-cultural investigations showed considerable variation in marriage forms and differing levels of commitment to the norm of legitimacy (Bell and Vogel 1968; Blake 1961; Goode 1961; Coser 1964). More recently, historical evidence indicates that the institution of marriage was not firmly in place in parts of Western Europe until the end of the Middle Ages (Laslett 1972; Gillis 1985).

When "giving a name" to children offers few material, social, or cultural benefits, the norms upholding marriage will become attenuated.

The accumulation of contradictory data led Goode (1960, 1971) to modify Malinowski's theory to take account of high rates of informal unions and nonmarital childbearing in many New World nations and among dispossessed cultural minorities. Goode (1971) argued that the norm of legitimacy was likely to be enforced only when fathers possessed wealth and property or when their potential economic investment in child rearing was high. Therefore, he predicted that when "giving a name" to children offers few material, social, or cultural benefits, the norms upholding marriage will become attenuated.

So vast have been the changes in the perceived benefits of marriage since the 1960s in the United States and most Western nations that even Goode's modification of Malinowski's theory of legitimacy now seems to be in doubt (Davis 1985; Popenoe 1988; Cherlin and Furstenberg 1988). Indeed, the term *illegitimacy* has fallen into disfavor precisely *because* it implies inferior status to children born out of wedlock. The nuclear unit (biological parents and their offspring)—once regarded as the cornerstone of our kinship system—remains the modal family form, but it no longer represents the exclusive cultural ideal, as was the case in the mid-1960s. The incentives for marriage in the event of premarital pregnancy have declined, and the sanctions against remaining single have diminished (Cherlin 1988; Bane and Jargowsky 1988; Thornton 1989).

Trends in Nonmarital Childbearing

Premarital pregnancy has never been rare in the United States or in most Western European nations (Vinovskis 1988; Smith 1978; Goode 1961). Apparently the tolerance for pregnancy before marriage has varied over time and varies geographically at any given time. Throughout the first half of the twentieth century, premarital pregnancy almost always led to hasty marriages rather than out-of-wedlock births—even for very young women (Vincent 1961; O'Connell and Moore 1981). Rates of nonmarital childbearing were actually higher in the middle of the nineteenth century in England, Wales, and probably the United States (Clague and Ventura 1968) than a century later. In 1940, illegitimacy was uncommon in the United States, at least among whites. Nonmarital births were estimated at about 3.6 per 1,000 unmarried white women, while the comparable rate for nonwhites was 35.6. For all age groups, and among whites and nonwhites alike, a spectacular rise occurred over the next two decades (Clague and Ventura 1968; Cutright 1972).

In the 1960s and 1970s, nonmarital childbearing rates continued to increase for younger women, albeit at a slower pace, while for women in their late twenties and thirties rates temporarily declined. Then, in the late 1970s, nonmarital childbearing rose again for all age groups and among both whites and African-Americans. Current levels in the United States are unprecedented. Moreover, since rates of marriage and marital childbearing have fallen precipitously since the 1960s, the ratio of total births to single women has shot up (Centers for Disease Control and Prevention; Monthly Vital Statistics Report; Vol. 45, No. 11, Supplement; June

10, 1997). Nearly a third of all births (32.2 percent) in 1995 occurred out of wedlock, more than seven times the proportion in 1955 (4.5 percent) and more than twice that in 1975 (14.3 percent). The declining connection between marriage and parenthood is evident among all age groups but is especially pronounced among women in their teens and early twenties. Nearly two-thirds of births to teens and close to one-third of all births to women ages twenty to twenty-four occurred out of wedlock. Virtually all younger blacks who had children in 1988 (over 90 percent) were unmarried, while half of white teens and a quarter of women twenty to twenty-four were single.

Nonmarital childbearing was initially defined as a problem among teenagers and black women (Furstenberg 1991). But these recent trends strongly suggest that the disintegration of the norm of legitimacy has spread to all segments of the population. First the link between marriage and sexual initiation dissolved, and now the link between marriage and parenthood has become weak. Whether this trend is temporary or a more permanent feature of the Western family system is not known. But public opinion data suggest that a high proportion of the population finds single parenthood acceptable. A Roper study (Virginia Slims American Women's Opinion Poll 1985) revealed that 49 percent of women agreed that "There was no reason why single women should not have children and raise them if they want to."

Nonmarital childbearing became more socially acceptable by the latter quarter of the 1900s. This trend included such women as this 44-year-old who planned and chose to raise her child as a single parent. (Laura Dwight/Corbis)

Citing similar attitudinal evidence from the National Survey of Families and Households in 1987–1988, Bumpass (1990) concludes that there has been an "erosion of norms" proscribing non-marital childbearing. He concludes that this behavior is not so much motivated by the desire to have children out of wedlock as it is by the reduced commitment to marriage and the limited sanctions forbidding nonmarital childbearing. Bumpass argues that much of the nonmarital childbearing is unplanned and ill-timed.

The Consequences of Nonmarital Childbearing

Although extensive research exists on the economic, social, and psychological sequelae of single parenthood for adults and children, relatively little of this research distinguishes between the consequences of marital disruption and non-marriage (Garfinkel and McLanahan 1986; Furstenberg 1989; Furstenberg and Cherlin 1991). A substantial literature exists on the consequences of nonmarital childbearing, but it is almost entirely restricted to teenage childbearers (Hofferth and Hayes 1987; Chilman 1983; Moore, Simms, and Betsey 1986; Miller and Moore 1990). It is difficult, then, to sort out the separate effects of premature parenthood, marital disruption, and out-of-wedlock childbearing on parents and their offspring.

Nonmarital childbearing most certainly places mothers and their children at risk of long-term economic disadvantage (McLanahan and Booth 1989). Out-of-wedlock childbearing increases the odds of going on welfare and of long-term welfare dependency (Duncan and Hoffman 1990). The link between nonmarital childbearing and poverty can probably be traced to two separate sources. The first is "selective recruitment," that is, women who bear children out of wedlock have poor economic prospects before they become pregnant, and their willingness to bear a child out of wedlock may also reflect the bleak future prospects of many unmarried pregnant women, especially younger women (Hayes 1987; Hogan and Kitagawa 1985; Geronimus 1987; Furstenberg 1990). But it is also likely that out-of-wedlock childbearing—particularly when it occurs early in life—directly contributes to economic vulnerability because it reduces educational attainment and limits a young woman's prospects of entering a stable union (Hofferth and Hayes 1987; Trussell 1988; Furstenberg 1991).

If nonmarital childbearing increases the risk of lengthy periods of poverty for women and their children, it is also likely that it restricts the opportunities for intra- and intergenerational mobility of families formed as single-parent units. Growing up in poverty restricts access to health, high-quality schools, and community resources that may promote success in later life (Ellwood 1988; Wilson 1987). Apart from the risks associated with poverty, some studies have shown that growing up in a single-parent family may put children at greater risk because they receive less parental supervision and support (McLanahan and Booth 1989; Dornbush 1989). As yet, however, researchers have not carefully distinguished between the separate sources of disadvantage that may be tied to nonmarital childbearing: economic disadvantage (that could restrict social opportunities or increase social isolation) and psychological disadvantage (that could foster poor parenting practices or limit family support).

Even though nonmarital childbearing may put children at risk of long-term disadvantage, it is also possible that over time the advantages conferred by marriage may be decreasing in those segments of the population that experience extremely high rates of marital disruption (Bumpass 1990). Moreover, the social and legal stigmata once associated with nonmarital childbearing have all but disappeared in the United States and many other Western nations (Glendon 1989). Over time, then, the hazards associated with nonmarital childbearing (compared with ill-timed marital childbearing) for women and their children could be declining (Dechter and Furstenberg 1990).

Nonmarital Childbearing and Public Policy

Growing rates of nonmarital childbearing in the United States and many Western nations suggest the possibility that the pattern of childbearing before marriage or between marriages may be spreading upward into the middle class. In Scandinavia, where marriage has declined most dramatically, it is difficult to discern whether formal matrimony is being replaced by a de facto system of informal marriage (Hoem and Hoem 1988). If this were to happen, the impact on the kinship system or the circumstances of children might not be as dramatic as some have speculated. But if the institution of marriage is in serious decline, then we may be in the midst of a major transformation in the Western family.

The weakening of marriage has created confusion and dispute over parenting rights and responsibilities. A growing body of evidence indicates that most nonresidential biological fathers, especially those who never marry, typically become disengaged from their children (Furstenberg and Nord 1985; Setzer, Schaeffer, and Charng 1989; Teachman 1990). Most are unwilling or unable to pay regular child support, and relatively few have constant relationships with their children. Instead, the costs of child rearing have been largely assumed by mothers and their families, aided by public assistance. A minority of fathers do manage to fulfill economic and social obligations, and some argue that many others would do so if they had the means and social support for continuing a relationship with their children (Smollar and Ooms 1987). Some researchers observe that the role of biological fathers is often assumed by surrogates, who may come to assume some or most paternal responsibilities (Mott 1990). In short, it is possible that social parenthood is becoming more important than biological parenthood.

Nevertheless, the uncertain relationship between biological fathers and their children has created a demand for public policies to shore up the family system. Widespread disagreement exists over specific policies for readdressing current problems. Advocates who accept the current reality of high levels of nonmarriage and marital instability propose more generous economic allowances and extensive social support to women and their children to offset the limited economic role of men in disadvantaged families (Ellwood 1988). Critics of this approach contend that such policies may further erode the marriage system (Vinovskis and Chase-Lansdale 1988). Yet few realistic measures have been advanced for strengthening the institution of marriage (Furstenberg and Cherlin 1991).

One policy—enforcement of child support—has attracted broad public support. A series of legislative initiatives culminating in the Family Support Act of 1988 has increased the role of federal and state governments in collecting child support from absent parents (typically fathers) and standardizing levels of child support. Some states, notably Wisconsin and New York, have designed but not yet implemented measures for creating a child support assurance system that will guarantee payments to single mothers and their children. It is too early to tell whether these sweeping measures will succeed in strengthening the economic contributions of fathers who live apart from their children. And, if it does, will greater economic support by absent parents reinforce social and psychological bonds to their children (Furstenberg 1989; Garfinkel and McLanahan 1991).

As for the future of marriage, few, if any, sociologists and demographers are predicting a return to the status quo or a restoration of the norm of legitimacy. Short of a strong ideological swing favoring marriage and condemning non-marital sexual activity and childbearing, it is difficult to foresee a sharp reversal in present trends (Blankenhorn, Bayme, and Elshtain 1990). Predicting the future, however, has never been a strong point of demographic and sociological research.

More fathers would fulfill economic and social obligations with their children if they had the means and social support for continuing a relationship with them.

[See also Deviance.]

BIBLIOGRAPHY

Bane, M. J., and P. A. Jargowsky 1988 "The Links Between Government Policy and Family Structure: What Matters and What Doesn't." In A. Cherlin, ed., *The Changing American Family and Public Policy.* Washington, D.C.: Urban Institute Press.

Bell, N. W., and E. F. Vogel (eds.) 1968 *A Modern Introduction to the Family.* New York: Free Press.

Blake, J. 1961 *Family Structure in Jamaica.* New York: Free Press.

Blankenhorn, D., S. Bayme, and J. B. Elshtain 1990 *Rebuilding the Nest.* Milwaukee, Wisc.: Family Service America.

Bumpass, L. 1990 "What's Happening to the Family? Interactions Between Demographic and Institutional Change." *Demography* 27:483–498.

Cherlin, A. 1988 "The Weakening Link Between Marriage and the Care of Children." *Family Planning Perspectives* 20:302–306.

———, and F. F. Furstenberg, Jr. 1988 "The Changing European Family: Lessons for the American Reader." *Journal of Family Issues* 9:291–297.

Chilman, C. S. 1983 *Adolescent Sexuality in a Changing American Society: Social and Psychological Perspectives for the Human Services Professions.* New York: Wiley.

Clague, A. J., and S. J. Ventura 1968 *Trends in Illegitimacy: United States 1940–1965.* Vital and Health Statistics, Public Health Service Publication no. 1000, ser. 21, no. 15. Washington, D.C.: U.S. Government Printing Office.

Coser, R. L. (ed.) 1964 *The Family: Its Structures and Functions.* New York: St. Martin's Press.

Cutright, P. 1972 "Illegitimacy in the United States, 1920–1968." In C. Westoff and R. Parks, eds., *Demographic and Social Aspects of Population Growth.* Washington, D.C.: U.S. Government Printing Office.

Davis, K. 1939 "Illegitimacy and the Social Structure." *American Journal of Sociology* 45:215–233.

——— 1949 *Human Society.* New York: Macmillan.

——— 1985 *Contemporary Marriage: Comparative Perspectives on a Changing Institution.* New York: Russell Sage Foundation.

Dechter, A., and F. F. Furstenberg, Jr. 1990 "The Changing Consequences of Adolescent Childbearing: A Comparison of Fertility and Marriage Patterns Across Cohorts." Paper presented at the annual meetings of the American Sociological Association, Washington, D.C., August.

Dornbush, S. M. 1989 "The Sociology of Adolescence." *Annual Review of Sociology* 15:233–259.

Duncan, G. J., and S. D. Hoffman 1990 "Teenage Welfare Receipt and Subsequent Dependence Among Black Adolescent Mothers." *Family Planning Perspectives* 22:219–223.

Ellwood, D. T. 1988 *Poor Support.* New York: Basic Books.

Furstenberg, F. F., Jr. 1988 "Bringing Back the Shotgun Wedding." *Public Interest* 90:121–127.

——— 1989 "Supporting Fathers: Implications of the Family Support Act for Men." Paper presented at the forum on the Family Support Act sponsored by the Foundation for Child Development, Washington, D.C., November.

——— 1990 "Coming of Age in a Changing Family System." In S. Feldman and G. Elliott, eds., *At the Threshold: The Developing Adolescent.* Cambridge, Mass.: Harvard University Press.

——— 1991 "As the Pendulum Swings: Teenage Childbearing and Social Concern." *Family Relations.*

———, and A. Cherlin 1991 *Divided Families: What Happens to Children When Their Parents Part.* Cambridge, Mass.: Harvard University Press.

———, and C. W. Nord 1985 "Parenting Apart: Patterns of Childbearing After Divorce." *Journal of Marriage and the Family* 47:898–904.

Garfinkel, I., and S. McLanahan 1986 *Single Mothers and Their Children.* Washington, D.C.: Urban Institute Press.

——— 1990 "The Effects of the Child Support Provisions of the Family Support Act of 1988 on Child Well-Being." *Policy Review* 9:205–234.

Geronimus, A. T. 1987 "On Teenage Childbearing in the United States." *Population and Development Review* 13:245–279.

Gillis, J. R. 1985 *For Better, for Worse: British Marriages 1600 to the Present.* New York: Oxford University Press.

Glendon, M. A. 1989 *The Transformation of Family Law.* Chicago: University of Chicago Press.

Goode, W. J. 1960 "A Deviant Case: Illegitimacy in the Caribbean." *American Sociological Review* 25:21–30.

——— 1961 "Illegitimacy, Anomie, and Cultural Penetration." *American Sociological Review* 26:319–325.

——— 1971 "Family Disorganization." In R. K. Merton and R. Nisbet, eds., *Contemporary Social Problems,* 3rd ed. New York: Harcourt Brace Jovanovich.

Hayes, C. D. 1987 *Risking the Future,* Vol. 1. Washington, D.C.: National Academy Press.

Hoem, B., and J. M. Hoem 1988 "The Swedish Family: Aspects of Contemporary Developments." *Journal of Family Issues* 9:397–424.

Hofferth, S. L., and C. D. Hayes 1987 *Risking the Future,* Vol. 2. Washington, D.C.: National Academy Press.

Hogan, D. P., and E. Kitagawa 1985 "The Impact of Social Status, Family Structure, and Neighborhood on the Family Structure of Black Adolescents." *American Journal of Sociology* 90:825–855.

Laslett, P. 1972 "Introduction: The History of the Family." In P. Laslett and R. Wall, eds., *Household and Family in Past Time.* Oxford: Oxford University Press.

McLanahan, S., and K. Booth 1989 "Mother-Only Families: Problems, Prospects, and Politics." *Journal of Marriage and the Family* 51:557–580.

Malinowski, B. 1930 "Parenthood, the Basis of Social Structure." In R. L. Coser, ed., *The Family: Its Structures and Functions.* New York: St. Martin's Press.

Miller, B. C., and K. A. Moore 1990 "Adolescent Sexual Behavior, Pregnancy, and Parenting." *Journal of Marriage and the Family* 52, no. 4:1025–1044.

Moore, K. A., M. C. Simms, and C. L. Betsey 1986 *Choice and Circumstance: Racial Differences in Adolescent Sexuality and Fertility.* New Brunswick, N.J.: Transaction Books.

Mott, F. 1990 "When Is Father Really Gone? Paternal–Child Contact in Father-Absent Homes." *Demography* 27:499–517.

National Center for Health Statistics 1990 *Advance Report of Final Natality Statistics, 1988.* Supp. to *Monthly Vital Statistics Report* 39, no. 4. Hyattsville, Md.: U.S. Public Health Service.

O'Connell, M., and M. J. Moore 1981 "The Legitimacy Status of First Births to U.S. Women Aged 15–24, 1939–1978." In F. F. Furstenberg, Jr., R. Lincoln, and J. Menken, eds., *Teenage Sexuality, Pregnancy, and Childbearing.* Philadelphia: University of Pennsylvania Press.

Popenoe, D. 1988 *Disturbing the Nest.* New York: Aldine De Gruyter.

Setzer, J. A., N. C. Schaeffer, and H. Charng 1989 "Family Ties After Divorce: The Relationship Between Visiting and Paying Child Support." *Journal of Marriage and the Family* 51:1013–1032.

Smith, D. S. 1978 "The Dating of the American Sexual Revolution: Evidence and Interpretation." In M. Gordon, ed., *The American Family in Social-Historical Perspective.* New York: St. Martin's Press.

Smollar, J., and T. Ooms 1987 *Young Unwed Fathers: Research Review, Policy Dilemmas, and Options.* Washington, D.C.: Maximus, Inc.

Teachman, J. D. 1990 "Still Fathers? The Reorganization of Parental Obligations Following Divorce." Paper presented at the Albany Conference on Demographic Perspectives on the American Family: Patterns and Prospects, April.

Thornton, A. 1989 "Changing Attitudes Towards Family Issues in the United States." *Journal of Marriage and the Family* 51:873–893.

Trussell, J. 1988 "Teenage Pregnancy in the United States." *Family Planning Perspectives* 20:262–272.

Vincent, C. E. 1961 *Unmarried Mothers.* New York: Free Press.

Vinovskis, M. 1988 *An "Epidemic" of Adolescent Pregnancy? Some Historical and Policy Considerations.* New York: Oxford University Press.

———, and P. L. Chase-Lansdale 1987 "Should We Discourage Teenage Marriage?" *Public Interest* 87:23–37.

Virginia Slims American Women's Public Opinion Poll 1985 A study conducted by The Roper Organization, Inc.

Wilson, W. J. 1987 *The Truly Disadvantaged.* Chicago: University of Chicago Press.

– FRANK F. FURSTENBERG, JR.

IMPERIALISM AND COLONIALISM

Imperialism is among the most overused and contested terms in our political vocabulary, so much so that Hancock was led to brand it "a word for the illiterates of social science" (1950, p. 17). Viewed more hopefully, the study of imperialism seems dogged by two conceptual problems: the centrality of politics versus that of economics, and the awkward relationship between *imperialism* and *empire.*

Imperialism was first used in the 1830s to recall Napoleonic ambitions. It gained its classic meaning around the turn of the century as a description of the feverish colonial expansion of Britain, France, Germany, Russia, the United States, and Italy. But the term is seldom confined to formal colonial expansion; in particular, the continuing dependence of much of the third world on Western states and multinational corporations is often understood as neocolonialism or neoimperialism (Nkrumah 1966; Magdoff 1969).

Attempts to distill these diverse usages generally define imperialism as the construction and maintenance of relationships of domination between political communities. Such relations are often seen as explicitly political, either in the narrow sense of direct administrative control or more broadly as formal or informal control over state policy. Economic conceptions of imperialism sometimes develop an analogue to these notions, where relations of economic control or exploitation replace political domination.

This usage should be distinguished from the equation of imperialism with particular modes of production or types of economic systems. Lenin's statement that "imperialism is the monopoly stage of capitalism" ([1917] 1939, p. 88) may be understood as such a definition. This usage fundamentally changes the terms of debate in ways that the extension from "political" to "political and/or economic" do not. Arrighi, among others, argues that Lenin is better understood as formulating a substantive proposition; he suggests the interpretation "imperialism, or the tendency to war between capitalist countries, is a necessary consequence of the transformation of capitalism into monopoly or finance capital" (1978, p. 14).

Even when imperialism is equated with the establishment and maintenance of political domination, an awkward relationship between *imperialism* and *empire* persists. Classically, empire refers to the great agrarian bureaucracies that dominated antiquity, from the Aztec to the Chinese, from ancient Sumer to Imperial Rome. It is not clear how much these structures have in common with the overseas colonial empires of Western states, much less with contemporary structures of dependence on foreign investment. For instance, while agrarian bureaucracies involved ethnic divisions, these separated classes (most importantly the ruling warrior class from others) rather than political communities or nations (Gellner 1983).

A second historical use of *empire* is the medieval image of a temporal parallel to the Roman church (Folz 1969; Guenee 1985). Rather than an alien and illegitimate structure, empire was seen as a political order unifying the Christian world. Revived by Charlemagne, the notion of a universal polity lived on, in an increasingly ghostly fashion, through the Holy Roman Empire. It receded into the background as a real political force with the construction of absolutist states and was lost as a compelling image with the rise of the nation-state.

In contrast to these historical understandings of empire, modern conceptions of imperialism rest on the notion that popular sovereignty forms the basis of political community. Only with the notion of popular sovereignty does domination refer to relationships between rather than within communities. If the criteria that the United Nations uses to identify colonialism today were applied before 1700, for example, all territories would be parts of empires and all peoples would be dependent subjects. It is thus no accident that the notion of imperialism arose with the nation-state; it connotes the expansionary drive of a community that is internally organized around (the myth of) popular sovereignty.

Some authors have used *colonialism* to refer to the construction and maintenance of colonies in a literal sense, groups of people who emigrate to form new societies in new lands. But today colonialism is generally synonymous with imperialism, though it has the specific connotation of Western domination over non-Western peoples.

Western Political Expansion

While different theoretical analyses of imperialism often seek to understand different sets of events, they generally overlap in attending to the formation of Western colonial empires. This essay will thus briefly review the history of Western expansion and then consider some of the major arguments about the sources of imperialism.

Less than 50 years after the voyages of Columbus, Spanish conquistadores had laid waste to the Aztec empire and were sending riches back to Spain.

Western overseas expansion can be described crudely as occurring in two stages, the colonial and the imperial. In the fifteenth and sixteenth centuries, sea-going powers constructed networks of colonial enclaves along the route to the East Indies. Less than half a century after the voyages of Columbus, Spanish conquistadores had laid waste to the Incan and Aztec empires and were sending gold and silver back to Spain. In the following two centuries, Spain, Portugal, Great Britain, France, and the Netherlands colonized virtually the whole of the Caribbean, Central and South America, and the North Atlantic seaboard. The colonial period per se came to a close with the decolonization of the Americas between 1776 and 1830, leaving Western states in control of vastly diminished overseas possessions.

The second period of expansion, one of imperial rather than colonial expansion, began after an interregnum marked by British naval hegemony. In the three decades after 1880, a scramble for territory partitioned Africa, Southeast Asia, and the Pacific between Great Britain, France, Germany, Belgium, and Portugal, while the United States annexed the remains of the Spanish Empire. None of this expansion involved much metropolitan emigration; colonial officials, traders, planters, and missionaries formed a thin veneer on indigenous societies. These empires disintegrated as quickly as they were formed, as almost all Western dependencies became recognized sovereign states in the decades following World War II.

When examining the political structures of imperial rule, it is important to consider both metropolitan and indigenous traditions. Colonies tended to be formally organized along metropolitan lines (Fieldhouse 1966). Settler colonies mirrored domestic political structures quite directly (Lang 1975), while nonsettler colonies recall metropolitan structures in a more abstract fashion. For example, the British tried to fashion systems of local rule (Lugard [1922] 1965) while the French strove to create a unified, centralized administration. But the superficiality of most imperial rule led to great variation in actual administrative arrangements. Even empires whose guiding rationale was assimilation (the French and the Portuguese) depended heavily on indigenous authorities and traditions.

Overseas colonies also varied greatly in their economic relationship to the metropolis. Only a few colonies were the source of great riches for the metropolitan economy: most prominently, the American settler colonies, British India, and the Dutch East Indies (Indonesia). Others had a largely strategic value; much of the British empire, for instance, was acquired in the effort to maintain lines of communication to India. The great majority of colonies acquired after 1880 had rather little importance for the metropolis, either as markets for imperial products or as sources of raw materials (Fieldhouse 1973).

Theories of Imperialism

The starting point for modern theories of imperialism is John Hobson's *Imperialism: A Study* ([1902] 1965). A liberal critic of the Boer War, Hobson saw imperial expansion as a search for new outlets for investment. He found the roots of this search in the surplus capital amassed by increasingly monopolistic corporate trusts. Hobson viewed imperial expansion as costly for the nation as a whole and sought to expose the special interests promoting imperialism. He also contended that capital surpluses could be consumed domestically by equalizing the distribution of income.

Lenin's *Imperialism: The Highest Stage of Capitalism* ([1917] 1939) provides the most influential statement of an economic analysis of imperialism. Lenin agreed with Hobson that imperialism flowed from the need to invest outside the domestic economy, drawing explicitly on Hilferding's ([1910] 1981) analysis of finance capital as a stage of capitalism. He was concerned to show that imperialism was a necessary rather than an avoidable result of the dynamics of capitalism (in contrast to Hobson's anticipation of Keynes) and that the expansionary impulse could not be globally coordinated (versus Kautsky's notion of an ultra-imperialism). Lenin argued that the unevenness of development makes imperialist war inevitable, as "late starters" demand their own place in the sun.

More contemporary writers like Baran and Sweezy (1966), Frank (1967), and Wallerstein (1974) draw upon both the Marxist tradition and Latin American theories of *dependencia* to suggest an alternative economic analysis of imperialism. They argue that international economic relations involve a net transfer of capital from the "periphery" to the "core" of the economic system and point to the continuities in this process from early colonial expansion to contemporary neoimperialism. This is in sharp contrast with the Leninist tradition, which argues that imperialism develops the productive powers of noncapitalist societies and emphasizes the special affinity of imperialism and monopoly capital.

Others writers consider political ambitions or relationships to be the taproot of imperialism. Schumpeter (1951) turned the Marxist perspective on its head. He noted that the characteristic motif of the ancient empires is military expansion for its own sake. Schumpeter argued that imperialism appears as an atavistic trait in the landed aristocracy of modern societies, and stresses the mismatch between the social psychology of the warrior and the industrious, calculating spirit of capitalism.

Other analyses focusing on political processes emphasize the anarchical structure of the Western state system (Cohen 1973; Waltz 1979). In the absence of an enforceable legal order, states are forced to expand when they can or decline relative to more aggressive states. This perspective explains European imperialism in the nineteenth century as the product of increasing levels of international competition and conflict.

Whether economic or political, most analyses of imperialism find its sources in the logic of the West, ignoring indigenous peoples in the process. Some recent work, led by the historians John Gallagher and Ronald Robinson, has sought to redress this imbalance. Their seminal essay "The Imperialism of Free Trade" (1953) emphasizes the continuity in British policy between the informal imperialism of the mid-eighteenth century and the rush for colonies after 1880. In *Africa and the Victorians,* Robinson, Gallagher, and Denny (1961) argued that it was largely change in the periphery, particularly increasing resistance to Western influence, that led Western powers to replace informal domination with formal empire. In later work, Robinson (1972) has emphasized the other side of the coin—the extent to which Western imperialism was dependent on local collaboration.

The theoretical approaches reviewed above differ partly because they seek to explain somewhat different, though overlapping, events. Different theoretical aims make the study of imperialism a contested and messy business; they also point to the importance of the debate. Whether as the last stage of capitalism, the workings of an anarchical state system, or the evolving relationship between Europeans and the rest of the world, imperialism seems crucial to the violence and the dynamism of the twentieth century.

[See also Decolonialization.]

BIBLIOGRAPHY

Arrighi, Giovanni 1978 *The Geometry of Imperialism.* London: New Left Books.

Baran, Paul, and Paul Sweezy 1966 *Monopoly Capital.* New York: Monthly Review Press.

Cohen, Benjamin J. 1973 *The Question of Imperialism.* New York: Basic Books.

Fieldhouse, David K. 1966 *The Colonial Empires.* New York: Dell.

——— 1973 *Economics and Empire, 1830–1914.* Ithaca, N.Y.: Cornell University Press.

Folz, Robert 1969 *The Concept of Empire in Western Europe from the Fifth to the Fourteenth Century.* London: Arnold.

Frank, Andre Gunder 1967 *Capitalism and Underdevelopment in Latin America.* New York: Monthly Review Press.

Gallagher, John, and Ronald Robinson 1953 "The Imperialism of Free Trade." *Economic History Review* S5:1–15.

Gellner, Ernest 1983 *Nations and Nationalism.* Oxford: Basil Blackwell.

Guenee, Bernard 1985 *States and Rulers in Later Medieval Europe.* Oxford: Basil Blackwell.

Hancock, William K. 1950. *The Wealth of Colonies.* Cambridge: Cambridge University Press.

Hilferding, Rudolf (1910) 1981 *Finance Capital.* London: Routledge and Kegan Paul.

Hobson, John A. (1902) 1965 *Imperialism: A Study.* New York: Allen and Unwin.
Lang, James 1975 *Conquest and Commerce: Spain and England in the Americas.* New York: Academic Press.
Lenin, Vladimir Ilich (1917) 1939 *Imperialism: The Highest Stage of Capitalism.* London: International Publishers.
Lugard, Frederick J. D. (1922) 1965 *The Dual Mandate in British Tropical Africa.* 5th ed. London: Cass.
Magdoff, Harry 1969 *Age of Imperialism.* New York: Monthly Review Press.
Nkrumah, Kwame 1966 *Neo-Colonialism: The Last Stage of Imperialism.* London: International Publishers.
Robinson, Ronald 1972 "Non-European Foundations of European Imperialism: Sketch for a Theory of Collaboration." In Roger Owen and Bob Sutcliffe, eds., *Studies in the Theory of Imperialism.* Bristol: G. B. Longman.
———, John Gallagher, and Alice Denny 1961 *Africa and the Victorians: The Official Mind of Imperialism.* London: St. Martin's Press.
Schumpeter, Joseph 1951 "The Sociology of Imperialism." In Schumpeter, *Imperialism and Social Classes.* New York: Kelley.
Wallerstein, Immanuel 1974, 1980, 1989 *The Modern World-System.* 3 vols. Cambridge: Cambridge University Press.
Waltz, Kenneth 1979 *Theory of International Politics.* Reading, Mass.: Addison-Wesley.
Weber, Max 1958 *The Protestant Ethic and the Spirit of Capitalism.* New York: Scribners.

– DAVID STRANG

INCEST

Incest is illicit sex or marriage between persons socially or legally defined as related too closely to one another. All societies have rules regarding incest. Incest is conceptualized in four ways: as a proscribed or prescribed marriage form; as a taboo; as prohibited coitus; and as child abuse. The first three conceptualizations are most closely related to early scholars (mid-1800s to mid-1900s), who tended to overlap them. The last conceptualization has become prominent more recently.

Incest-as-marriage rules are usually proscriptive ("Thou shalt not"). Prescriptive ("Thou shalt") incestuous marriage rules have been documented for royalty in Old Iran and ancient Egypt and for Mormons in the United States (Lester 1972). That some groups proscribe while others prescribe incestuous marriages has caused some to be skeptical of many theories about incest, especially theories that assume that incest avoidance is natural, close inbreeding is genetically disadvantageous, or that there is an incest taboo.

John F. McLennan ([1865] 1876), a lawyer, coined the terms *endogamy* (within-the-group marriage) and *exogamy* (outside-the-group marriage). He defined incest as endogamy. Based on his analyses of marriage in Ireland, Australia, ancient Greece, and other societies, he concluded that rules proscribing endogamy evolved as a group survival mechanism. He reasoned that as members of one tribe or group married into others, "blood ties" emerged. These blood ties encouraged reciprocity between groups and cooperation and harmony within groups. Anthropologist Lewis Henry Morgan agreed with McLennan's definition of incest as endogamy and with McLennan's assumption that proscribing incest promoted both exogamy and group survival. Morgan assumed, however, that incest originally became prohibited due to the presumed deleterious effects of inbreeding. Tylor (1889) elaborated on McLennan's notion of exchange and reciprocity among exogamous groups. He noted that men made political alliances with men in other groups by exchanging women in marriage. The common thread among these theories is the focus upon incest rules as social organizational principles. A shared weakness is the reliance upon analyses of primitive or premodern groups. These inclinations are also found in varying degrees in writings by Sir James Frazer, Herbert Spencer, Brenda Seligman, Robert Briffault, Bronislaw Malinowski, George Murdock, and Claude Lévi-Strauss. Many of these and other writers also fail to differentiate between incest rules and exogamy rules. What one group calls incestuous marriage may not biologically be such. Likewise, some groups' exogamy rules permit biologically incestuous marriage. Recognizing that incest rules are socially defined, Sumner (in his famous tome *Folkways*) countered Morgan and presaged today's sociobiologists. He argued that incest rules should be modified as researchers gathered genetic evidence that dispelled fallacious beliefs that all incestuous matings are deleterious.

Sociologist Emile Durkheim's *Incest: The Nature and Origin of the Taboo* ([1898] 1963) is an infrequently cited magnum opus. Based on ethnographic research in Australia, this book emphasized and illustrated the social and moral origins of incest taboos. Durkheim noted the ways in which prohibitions against incest and penalties for rule violations organize social groups internally. Cooperation and alliances with other groups via exogamy are consequently prompted. Durkheim contends that the incest taboo has a religious origin. It is derived from the clan's sentiments surrounding blood, specifically menstrual blood. While blood is taboo in a general way, contact with the blood of the clan is taboo in specific ways. Durkheim reasoned that menstrual blood represents a flowing away of the clan's life blood. The taboo against blood is thus associated with women of the clan. This renders women taboo for and inferior to men of the same clan. The taboo relates to intercourse in general and to marriage in particular. Blood and incest are presumed to be related such that a man violating the taboo is seen as a murderer.

Durkheim contended that the origin of the taboo is lost to the consciousness of clans over time but that the taboo itself is replaced by a generalized repugnance of incest. This repugnance prompts men to exchange women with other groups, thus facilitating political alliances between men of different groups. In addition, in his *The Division of Labor in Society* (1893), Durkheim posited that when incest loses its religiously based criminal status, prohibitions against it are or will be codified into law. Prefiguring more recent research on incest as child abuse, Durkheim noted also that incest violations are most likely to occur in families in which members do not feel morally obligated to be dutiful to one another and to practice moral restraint ([1898] 1963, p. 102).

Freud posited that in the original family there was a jealous and violent father who engaged his daughters in incest.

Sigmund Freud focused on the incest taboo ([1913] 1950) and infantile sexuality ([1905] 1962). Through his tale of the primal horde, Freud posited that in the original family there was a jealous and violent father who engaged his daughters in incest. The jealous brothers banded together, killed, and ate the father. Horrified by their deeds, the brothers made incest taboo. For Freud, this (the moment when humans made incest rules) was when humans became social. He assumed that very young (Oedipal) children sexually desire their opposite-sex parent. Little boys then suffer from castration anxiety, fearing that the father will become aware of their desires and punish them. While little girls see their mothers as inferior to men, they also know them to be more powerful than they. Thus, little girls resignedly align themselves with their mothers, repress their incestuous impulses, and experience penis envy.

Even though Freud's theories were based on conjecture and focused on the bourgeois nuclear family of his day, they have nonetheless influenced many social scientists, including French anthropologist Jean Claude Lévi-Strauss ([1949] 1969) and American sociologist Talcott Parsons (1954). Lévi-Strauss agreed with Freud that humans became social with the creation of incest rules. Borrowing from the emphasis on the exchange of women, found in the works of Durkheim and Marcel Mauss, and Durkheim's assumption that women of a clan become the symbol (totem) for the clan, Lévi-Strauss posited that exogamy represents a special form of alliance-creating reciprocity. Since incest involves sexuality, incest rules and the exchange of women represent a unique social connection between the biological and the cultural. Although frequently lauded by social scientists, the work of Lévi-Strauss adds little to previous theories about incest.

Parsons incorporated Freud's theory of infantile sexuality into his structural-functionalist view of the American nuclear family. Like functionalists before him, he assumed that incest rules exist to prevent role confusion within the nuclear family and to encourage alliances with other families. He contended that the mother was to exploit her son's Oedipal desires as if she had him on a rope. At earlier ages she was to pull him toward her, encouraging heterosexuality. At later ages she was to push him away, encouraging him to establish relationships with nonrelated females. Tugging and pulling on the rope were also designed to assist the son in internalizing society's incest rules and guide him in creating his own nuclear family.

Parsons assumed that little girls also experience an erotic attachment to their mothers. He argued that as the mother severed this attachment, it was her responsibility to instill in the daughter an aversion to father–daughter and brother–sister incest. Failure to do this would result in family disorganization and in the daughter's inability to become a normatively functioning adult. Parsons contended that incest aversion would be realized if the mother kept the erotic bond with her husband intact. Parsons's analysis has thus assisted in perpetuating what child abuse researchers have sought to eradicate: placing blame on mothers when fathers incestuously abuse their daughters (see Finkelhor 1984; Vander Mey and Neff 1986; Russell 1986).

Psychologist Edward Westermarck (1891) contended that family and clan members develop a sexual aversion to one another due to the dulling effects of daily interaction and the sharing of mundane tasks. This aversion prompts the development of laws and customs proscribing incest among persons with a shared ancestor and set of obligations based on clan membership. Westermarck noted that failure to develop this aversion and the propensity to violate incest laws were due to alcoholism, membership in the lower social classes, inability to control the sex drive, lack of alternative sexual outlets, social and geographic isolation, and failure to have developed normative, family-like feelings of duty. Variations on Westermarck's thesis appear in writings today. Some focus on a learned aversion that Oedipal children develop as their fantasies cannot be realized, due to their lack of full sexual maturation. Westermarck's thesis is weak because if there were a natural aversion to incest, then laws prohibiting it would be unnecessary. Furthermore, a growing body of literature suggests that persons who share mundane tasks and interact daily do not develop a sexual aversion to one another (see Vander Mey and Neff 1986).

Sociobiologists (e.g., Parker 1976; van den Berghe 1980) variously incorporate Freudian theses, Westermarck's thesis, and the assumption that human social behavior follows a fitness maxim such that a group establishes prescriptive or proscriptive incest rules that enhance a group's survival to its genetic advantage. Sociobiologists typically use the functionalist assumption that incest rules regulate the internal dynamics of the procreating group and encourage affiliation with other nuclear groups. Violations of incest rules are assumed to be caused by the factors identified by Westermarck. Many sociobiologists link intercourse directly to procreation. This is not always true of adult–adult intercourse. The assumption has no merit when one tries to explain why adult–child and child–child intercourse occurs. Equally problematic is the frequent reliance on the rules proscribing incest among royals. Dismissed is the role that ethnocentrism plays in such rules. Finally, serious questions arise when research on primates, birds, or other nonhumans is extrapolated to human social behavior and organization.

Of current concern is incest as a serious and severe type of child abuse. As child abuse, incest is any form of sexual touching, talking, or attempted or actual intercourse between an adult and a child or between two children when the perpetrator is significantly older than the victim or forces the victim to engage in actions against his or her will. The perpetrator and victim are related either by consanguinity or affinity. Incest is abuse because it harms the victim and violates the child's basic human rights. Its negative effects linger throughout victims' lives (Russell 1986). That the sexual victimization of children is nothing new, but rather ancient, is well documented (Rush 1980; deMause 1982). Public recognition of incest as child abuse, however, has its roots in research and public discourse of roughly the past fifteen years.

Had Freud not abandoned his first psychoanalytical paper, "The Aetiology of Hysteria" ([1896] 1946), he could have been heralded as the savior of children. In this paper he described incest and other sexual abuse experienced by eighteen patients when they were children. He linked his adult patients' problems to their experiences of childhood sexual trauma. However, when his paper was coldly received and then ignored by senior psychologists, and Freud faced professional ostracization, he dismissed these findings (see Jurjevich 1974; Masson 1984). He reasoned that his patients were incorrectly recalling masturbatory childhood fantasies of sexual encounters with adults (Freud [1905] 1962). Freud then associated adult neurosis and hysteria with unfulfilled childhood incest fantasies.

Freud's revamped theories quickly became popular. Several writers then recounted case studies of children who had experienced sex with an adult. The children were described as seductive and provocative. They were not seen as victims; rather, they were seen as sexual initiators (see Vander Mey and Neff 1986). Although Swedish sociologist Svend Riemer (1940) and American sociologist S. Kirson Weinberg (1955) tried to bring attention to incest as a form of family deviance that sometimes resulted in harm to victims, Freudian theory held fast until the late 1960s. The "discovery" of child abuse, in conjunction with the civil rights movement, the anti-Vietnam War movement, and the resurgence of the women's rights movement, refocused attention such that the physical abuse of children and rape of women became seen as serious wrongs inflicted on other humans and as special types of social problems. Since that time, theories and research have explored in great detail why and how incestuous abuse occurs and its lasting negative effects. Laws protecting children against such abuse have been improved. These laws mandate that treatment services be available for victims, perpetrators, and families (Fraser 1987). They also stipulate penalties (fines, imprisonment) for convicted abusers. These operate on a sliding scale, with harsher penalties applied to cases in which the victim is very young or has suffered serious physical or psychological trauma due to the abuse. Some cases are handled in family courts. Others, especially those involving serious harm to the child, are heard in criminal courts. Although variable in scope, laws in European nations prohibit and punish incestuous child abuse (Doek 1987). As with statutes in the United States, applicable penalties often depend on the victim-perpetrator relationship, the age of the victim, and the seriousness of harm to the victim. And, as in the United States, these laws are still inadequate. However, efforts to refine legal statutes and penalties continue. Refinement is needed, for instance, for statutes that designate only men as perpetrators and only females as victims. Laws are also needed that specifically define and punish child–child incestuous abuse.

Feminists focus on father–daughter incest. They refer to it as rape to emphasize the specific type of abuse that it is. The term *rape* also illustrates the point that if an adult male forced another person to engage in intercourse with him, he would be arrested for the very serious crime of rape. However, if he rapes his own child, it is called incest, which is often seen as a disgusting, private, family problem (Brownmiller 1975).

Feminists see incest as commonplace, originating in and perpetuated by patriarchy (Rush 1980). A general feminist approach to father–daughter incest incorporates a discussion of the sex-role socialization of males and the male-as-superior patriarchal ideology as causal factors in incest. The contention is that females ultimately are rendered second class citizens, the property of men, and sexual outlets for men (see Rush 1980). Problems with a general feminist perspective on incest include a focus limited to father–daughter incest, the monocausal linkage of patriarchy to incest, the portrayal of all incest perpetrators as male and all incest victims as female, and the oversimplified view of male sex-role socialization (Vander Mey, 1991).

Incest perpetrators are not usually sexually deprived.

American feminist sociologist Diana Russell (1986) extends and refines the general feminist approach to incest. She argues that males are socialized to sexualize the power given them by virtue of the fact that they are male. This includes sexualizing the power they have over their own children. Moreover, Russell recognizes that mothers and children can be incest perpetrators. She advocates androgynous socialization of children, more equality between men and women, and more public awareness of the harsh realities of incestuous abuse.

Welsh psychologist Neil Frude (1982) relied upon existing empirical and clinical research to articulate a five-factor explanatory model of father–daughter incest. These five factors are: sexual need (of the perpetrator); attractive partner; opportunity; disinhibition; and sexual behavior. A strength of Frude's model is the attention paid to the intertwisting of sex and power. Weaknesses include the fact that incest perpetrators are not usually sexually deprived, victim attractiveness is often irrelevant, and families are not usually closed systems today. American sociologist David Finkelhor (1984) offers a somewhat similar model, although it differs from Frude's model in that Finkelhor pays keen attention to the myriad ways in which larger social forces and cultural ideology are related to child sexual abuse. Finkelhor's model has the added strength of being applicable to several types of incest and other sexual abuse.

American sociologists Brenda Vander Mey and Ronald Neff (1986) have constructed a research-based ecological model of father–daughter incest. They begin with the assumption that there is no incest taboo. Rather, there are rules proscribing adult–child incest. They contend that characteristics of the society, the neighborhood, the family and the marital dyad, and the father–daughter dyad differentially affect the probability that a daughter will be sexually abused by her father. These levels of influence interact in complicated ways. Father–daughter incest is associated with male dominance in society and in the family, residence in a violent neighborhood, social isolation of the family, family disorganization, and a father's lack of empathy for his wife and children. Mitigating factors decreasing the likelihood of incest include a father's conformity to rules against incest, sex education of the daughter, and media announcements of adult–child incest as wrong and illegal. This model is strong in its reliance on research and theoretical principles. Although this model is limited to father–daughter incest, it does provide information that can assist in identifying children at risk for incestuous abuse. Vander Mey (1991) suggests, however, that a general systems model be constructed that taps factors correlated with a range of incestuous abuse.

Incestuous abuse is seen as an international social problem today. At least four journals frequently carry the latest research on this topic. These are: *Child Abuse and Neglect; Journal of Family Violence; The Journal of Interpersonal Violence;* and *The Journal of Child Sexual Abuse.*

[See also Sexual Violence and Abuse.]

BIBLIOGRAPHY

Brownmiller, Susan 1975 *Against Our Will: Men, Women and Rape.* New York: Simon and Schuster.

deMause, Lloyd 1982 *Foundations of Psychohistory.* New York: Creative Roots.

Doek, Jack E. 1987 "Sexual Abuse of Children: An Examination of European Criminal Law." In P. B. Mrazek and C. H. Kempe, eds., *Sexually Abused Children and Their Families.* New York: Pergamon.

Durkheim, Emile (1893) 1963 *The Division of Labor in Society,* trans. G. Simpson. New York: Free Press.

———(1898) 1963 *Incest: The Nature and Origin of the Taboo.* A. Ellis, trans. New York: Lyle Stuart.

Finkelhor, David 1984 *Child Sexual Abuse: New Research and Theory.* New York: Free Press.

Fraser, Brian G. 1987 "Sexual Child Abuse: The Legislation and the Law in the United States." In P. B. Mrazek and C. H. Kempe, eds., *Sexually Abused Children and Their Families.* New York. Pergamon.

Freud, Sigmund (1896) 1946 "The Aetiology of Hysteria." In E. Jones, ed., and J. Riviere, trans. *Collected Papers.* New York: The International Psycho-Analytical Press.

———(1905) 1962 "My Views on the Part Played by Sexuality in the Aetiology of the Neurosis." In P. Reiff, ed., *Sexuality and the Psychology of Love.* New York: Collier Books.

———(1913) 1950 *Totem and Taboo.* J. Strachey, trans. New York: Norton.

Frude, Neil 1982 "The Sexual Nature of Sexual Abuse: A Review of the Literature." *Child Abuse and Neglect* 6:211–223.

Jurjevich, Ratibor-Ray M. 1974 *The Hoax of Freudism: A Study of Brainwashing the American Professionals and Laymen.* Philadelphia: Dorance.

Lester, David 1972 "Incest." *The Journal of Sex Research* 8:268–285.

Lévi-Strauss, Jean Claude (1949) 1969 *The Elementary Structure of Kinship.* J. H. Bell, J. R. von Sturmer, and R. Needham, trans. Boston: Beacon Press.

Masson, Jeffrey M. 1984 *The Assault on Truth: Freud's Suppression of the Seduction Theory.* New York: Farrar, Straus, and Giroux.

McLennan, John F. (1865) 1876 *Primitive Marriage: An Inquiry into the Origin of the Form of Capture in Marriage Ceremonies.* London: Bernard Quaritch.

Parker, Seymour 1976 "The Precultural Basis of the Incest Taboo: Toward a Biosocial Perspective." *American Anthropologist* 78:285–305.

Parsons, Talcott 1954 "The Incest Taboo in Relation to Social Structure and the Socialization of the Child." *British Journal of Sociology* 5:101–117.

Riemer, Svend 1940 "A Research Note on Incest." *American Journal of Sociology* 45:566–575.

Rush, Florence 1980 *The Best Kept Secret: Sexual Abuse of Children.* New York: McGraw-Hill.

Russell, Diana E. H. 1986 *The Secret Trauma: Incest in the Lives of Girls and Women.* New York: Basic Books.

Tylor, Edward B. 1889 "On the Method of Investigating the Development of Institutions; Applied to Laws of Marriage and Descent." *Journal of the Royal Anthropological Institute* 18:245–269.

van den Berghe, Pierre 1980 "Incest and Exogamy: A Sociobiological Reconsideration." *Ethology and Sociobiology.* 1:151–162.

Vander Mey, Brenda J. 1991 "Theories of Incest." In W. O'Donohue and J. Geer, eds., *The Sexual Abuse of Children: Research, Theory, and Therapy.* Hillsdale, NJ.: Erlbaum.

———, and Ronald L. Neff 1986 *Incest as Child Abuse: Research and Applications.* New York: Praeger.

Weinberg, S. Kirson 1955 *Incest Behavior.* New York: Citadel Press.

Westermarck, Edward (1891) 1922 *The History of Human Marriage.* New York: Allerton.

— BRENDA J. VANDER MEY

INCOME DISTRIBUTION IN THE UNITED STATES

The United States today is characterized by both an increasing concentration of wealth and widespread poverty. These trends, however, are somewhat obscured if one looks at only the information on yearly money income reported by American householders and families. This entry examines trends from 1960 to 1990 as well as the most recent Bureau of the Census data on all three topics: income distribution, wealth, and poverty.

Income Distribution

Data on money income are published each year by the Bureau of the Census, based on information from approximately 55,000 households scientifically selected to represent the entire nation. Respondents are asked about all sources of money income for the preceding year, including wages, Social Security benefits, welfare payments, workers' compensation, returns on investments, and pensions. Although the reported amounts tend to be somewhat lower than the aggregate estimates derived from tax records, these data are considered to be as refined as can be expected for such a major undertaking.

HOUSEHOLD INCOME. In 1993, when the median yearly money income of all American households was $31,241, 14.2 percent of households had incomes of under $10,000, in contrast to 5.8 percent reporting incomes of $100,000 or more. Compared with similar data from 1968, adjusted for inflation (so that the median in 1968 was only $900 lower than in 1988), these numbers indicate that the proportion of households at the top earnings level had more than quadrupled (up from 1.3 percent), while the percent in the lowest level had declined somewhat (from 18.8 percent).

The largest percentage decline, however, occurred in the middle of the income distribution, among households reporting money incomes between $25,000 and $35,000: from 20.6 percent in 1968 to 14.7 percent in 1993. Overall, the proportion of households with incomes between $15,000 and $50,000 had declined from almost 60 percent in 1968 to 47.9 percent in 1993, leading many scholars to refer to the "disappearing middle" in the American income spectrum.

Because "households" can be composed of one person, often a young person beginning worklife or an older individual living on a limited income, household income is typically lower than that for "families," which consist of at least two persons related by blood, marriage, or adoption. Therefore, it is important to examine family income in order to test the disappearing middle thesis.

FAMILY INCOME. As expected, the proportion of families at the bottom of the distribution in 1993 was smaller than for households—only 9.6 percent below $10,000—while the percentage at the top was somewhat higher—almost 3 percent. But in comparison with 1968, there was only a slight increase in the proportion at the bottom, while those with incomes of $75,000 and over had more than doubled. In addition, the percentage in the middle, between $25,000 and $50,000, declined from over 44 percent of all families in 1968 to almost 32.7 percent in 1993. In other words, there was a clear upward thrust in the distribution of family income in the United States from 1968 to 1993. In this sense, it can be claimed that, in terms of money income, American families are, on average, better off in 1990 than they were in the late 1960s. Such aggregate numbers, however, hide important differences by race and Hispanic origin among families and households.

SUBGROUP DIFFERENCES. For example, while only 7.3 percent of white families had money incomes below $10,000 in 1993, 25.8 percent of black families and 17.9 percent of Hispanic-origin families fell into that category, reflecting the higher proportion of single-parent families within these two populations. Comparable percentages for households were 12.2 percent for white but nearly one-third for black and close to one-fifth for households headed by a person of Hispanic origin.

In general, also, family and household incomes vary systematically by region of the country (highest in the Northeast and lowest in the South), by age of householder (highest for those ages forty-five to fifty-four, lowest for those fifteen to twenty-four), by number of wage earners, and by sex of householder. Incomes of female householders, in all regions, at all ages, and in all racial-ethnic categories, are typically less than half the income for married-couple units or even those occupied by a male householder, no wife present. For example, the 1993 median money income for all married-couple families was $43,005 in contrast to $17,443 for a family with a female householder, no husband present. Most of this income differential reflects variation in labor force participation rates, but even when women are employed full-time year-round, their median income in 1993 was $26,165, compared to $39,806 for a full-time, year-round male worker.

At the other end of the income distribution, households and families classified as white are three times more likely than those headed by blacks or Hispanics to report money incomes in excess of $100,000. Although the proportion of all units at the top income level has more than doubled over the past two decades, this does not mean that the wealth of the nation is more evenly distributed than in the past.

Wealth

While measuring income is fraught with difficulties, including underreporting, it is relatively straightforward when compared to measuring net wealth: the total value of all assets owned by a family, household, or person, less what is owed. Such assets include investment portfolios, bank accounts, real estate, homes and their furnishings, insurance policies and annuities, pension equity, real estate, vehicles, and the contents of safe deposit boxes. Total assets, minus debts, equals net worth.

The first systematic study of American wealthholding was conducted by the Federal Reserve Board (FRB) in 1963–1964. At that time, researchers found that the top 0.5 percent of households (the "super rich") owned 25 percent of the total net assets of the nation. The next 0.5 percent ("very rich") accounted for an additional 7 percent, and the 9 percent of households composing the plain "rich" owned 33 percent, leaving approximately 35 percent of the total net assets of the United States to the remaining 90 percent of the population.

Although comparable data were not gathered for the next twenty years, there was scattered evidence from the Internal Revenue Service's estate tax records to suggest that the share of assets owned by the super rich had declined between 1965 and 1976 to a low of 14.4 percent. This drop was due in part to an extended stock market slump and in part to changes in tax policies as well as to the growth of social welfare programs, including Aid to Families with Dependent Children, liberalization of Social Security benefits, and the introduction of Medicare/Medicaid, all of which tended to shift income from the more affluent to the more needy.

When the Internal Revenue Service withdrew access to its estate tax records from researchers in 1976, reliable data on wealth were difficult to obtain. This situation changed in 1983 and 1984 when two separate surveys of wealthholding were conducted, one by the Bureau of the Census and one by the Federal Reserve Board, designed to be comparable to its 1963 study. The U.S. Bureau of the Census (1986) survey of 26,000 living units, selected for representativeness, asked about household wealth and asset ownership, including bank accounts, investments, pensions, real estate, vehicles, and business ownership.

Wealth today is more concentrated than it was in the 1960s and the steepest rise occurred in the 1980s during the Reagan administration.

Unfortunately, the Census Bureau's random sample contained very few living units at the top of the asset scale, so it is difficult to generalize about the very rich and super rich from these data. In contrast, the Federal Reserve Board study, while relatively small—a basic random sample of 3,800 living units—was augmented with an additional 435 high-asset households (Avery and Elliehausen 1986). The FRB also gathered information on a broader range of assets than did the Bureau of the Census. In addition, the FRB data have been reexamined by researchers from the University of Michigan in an analysis prepared for the Joint Economic Committee of the U.S. Congress (1986); this analysis also permits direct comparison with the 1963 study. For these reasons, we believe that the FRB data are the more accurate indicators of the distribution of wealth in the United States at the end of the 1980s.

The major finding is that between 1976 and 1983 the downward trend of asset ownership by the super rich was dramatically reversed. From owning less than 15 percent of the net wealth of the nation in 1976, the super rich accounted for a full 35 percent just six years later. In large part, this increase reflected changing stock market values, but it was also reinforced by Reagan administration policies on taxes and welfare that shifted wealth from the poor to the affluent.

The top 1 percent of American wealthholders—the super rich and the very rich—today own more than 40 percent of the net assets of the country, and the top 10 percent own 72 percent of the total wealth. When compared to the 1963 data, it is clear that wealth today is more concentrated than it was in the 1960s and that the steepest rise occurred in the 1980s. To the extent that we have comparable data, wealth in America today is more concentrated than at any time since 1927, before the stock market crash and the Great Depression, when the share of net assets owned by the super rich also exceeded 30 percent of the total.

Even in the depths of the Great Depression, the share of net assets owned by the super rich did not fall below 25 percent. This was also the time when one-third of the nation could be described as ill-fed, ill-housed, ill-clothed, and jobless in a society without an extensive public social welfare system.

Poverty

The one-third of the nation deprived of adequate income, food, and housing in 1930 was not very different in size or background characteristics from those who were counted as poor in the late 1950s. Despite the introduction of Social Security for the retired, disabled, and dependents of deceased workers, and the other programs of the New Deal designed to minimize the effects of poverty, 22.4 percent of the American population was classified as poor in 1959. Their plight evoked images of the impoverished of the Great Depression: old people, rural Yankee families of Appalachia, unemployed white working men, grim-faced farmers, and possibly a dignified black couple. Faced with such daunting numbers, it became necessary to set standards of eligibility for the array of welfare programs that had gradually been introduced and expanded since the 1930s.

DEFINING POVERTY. By 1964, the Social Security Administration had devised a method for defining poverty. Back in 1955, the Department of Agriculture had discovered that families of three or more persons spent one-third of their income on food. As the Department of Agriculture had also computed the price of the least expensive nutritionally adequate food plan, the Social Security Administration simply multiplied the cost of that food basket by three, and with a few corrections for family size, rural or urban residence, and age and sex of householder, arrived at a dollar figure that demarcated the poor from the non-poor. Households with income over that line were officially not poor; those that fell below the threshold became officially poor.

The value of the economy food plan is adjusted each year to the cost-of-living index, but the basic formula remains unchanged even though housing costs now outstrip the proportion of income spent on food. There have been changes in the index, such as no longer distinguishing rural from urban (the rural threshold was lower, presumably because country folk could grow some of their own food), or male from female heads of household (the latter were assumed to need less food than the former). Only size of household and age of householder have been retained in the calculations.

In 1990, the poverty threshold for a single person was approximately $5,500, slightly higher if under age sixty-five, and somewhat lower if over age sixty-five, on the assumption that older people eat less than younger ones. The poverty line for a two-person family was slightly over $7,000 and that for a family of four was about $11,500. These are the dollar values deemed adequate to house, feed, and clothe members of a household. Those with money income above the threshold are no longer eligible for additional benefits, including both income support (Aid to Families with Dependent Children, Supplemental Security Income) and in-kind programs (e.g., food stamps, Medicaid, housing subsidies). As low as these amounts may seem, there was a concerted effort during the Reagan administration to recalculate "income" to include the dollar value of in-kind benefits, which would have reduced the poverty rate by 25 to 30 percent, without any additional assistance to the poor. Although this new number continues to be included in Census Bureau publications (e.g., 1990c), the official poverty level remains calculated on the basis of income received or earned.

The poverty *rate,* then, represents the proportion of individuals, families, or households whose income falls below the threshold. Throughout the early 1960s, between 22 and 19 percent of all Americans were officially classified as poor. Programs introduced in the Johnson administration's War on Poverty helped to bring this figure down to slightly over 11 percent in the early 1970s. The poverty rate remained under 12 percent until the 1980s, when the recession of 1982–83, combined with Reagan administration cutbacks in social welfare programs, raised the poverty rate to 15.2 percent, before slowly declining to its current 13 percent.

WHO ARE THE POOR? Poverty, however, is not evenly distributed among Americans. Although 65 percent of the poverty population in 1988 was white, this represents only 10 percent of all American whites. In contrast, 31.6 percent of blacks and 26.8 percent of persons of Hispanic origin had incomes below the poverty line in 1988, as did 20 percent of persons of "other races" (Asian, American Indian). Married couples fared much better than did unrelated individuals or persons in female-headed households, regardless of race or ethnicity, but, compared to whites, smaller proportions of American blacks and Hispanics live in married-couple families. At the extremes, while under 5 percent of white married couples fell below the poverty line, 56.3 percent of families headed by a black woman were so classified. Today, close to one-half of all black children and 40 percent of children of Hispanic origin will spend part of their lives in households below the poverty level, compared to 15 percent of children in white families.

In terms of age, one of every five American children is poor, in contrast to one in ten adults ages eighteen to sixty-four. Among the elderly (age sixty-five and over), 12 percent live in poverty, slightly below the national rate. This was not always so. Indeed, the high proportion of older people living in poverty was a major impetus for the social welfare reforms of the 1930s and the 1960s. Because the elderly could be perceived as "deserving" poor, it was possible to create a voting constituency favorable to such initiatives during both periods. Amendments to the Social Security Act in 1965 and 1972 broadened coverage, extended benefits, and initiated the Medicare program for reimbursing limited health care costs. As a consequence, poverty among the elderly declined from a post-Depression high of 35.2 percent in 1959 to its current 12 percent, but there are signs that housing and medical costs are once more outstripping the income resources of many elderly, especially for the very old, the frail, and the widowed—the vast majority of whom are women.

Indeed, it appears that poverty has increasingly become a problem for women of all ages, particularly those who are not married: teenage mothers, displaced homemakers, divorcees in general, and frail elderly widows. But the "feminization of poverty" (Pearce 1978) since 1970 is only partly due to an increase in female householders. Wives of the unemployed or of low earners also suffer. The basic causes of poverty in the United

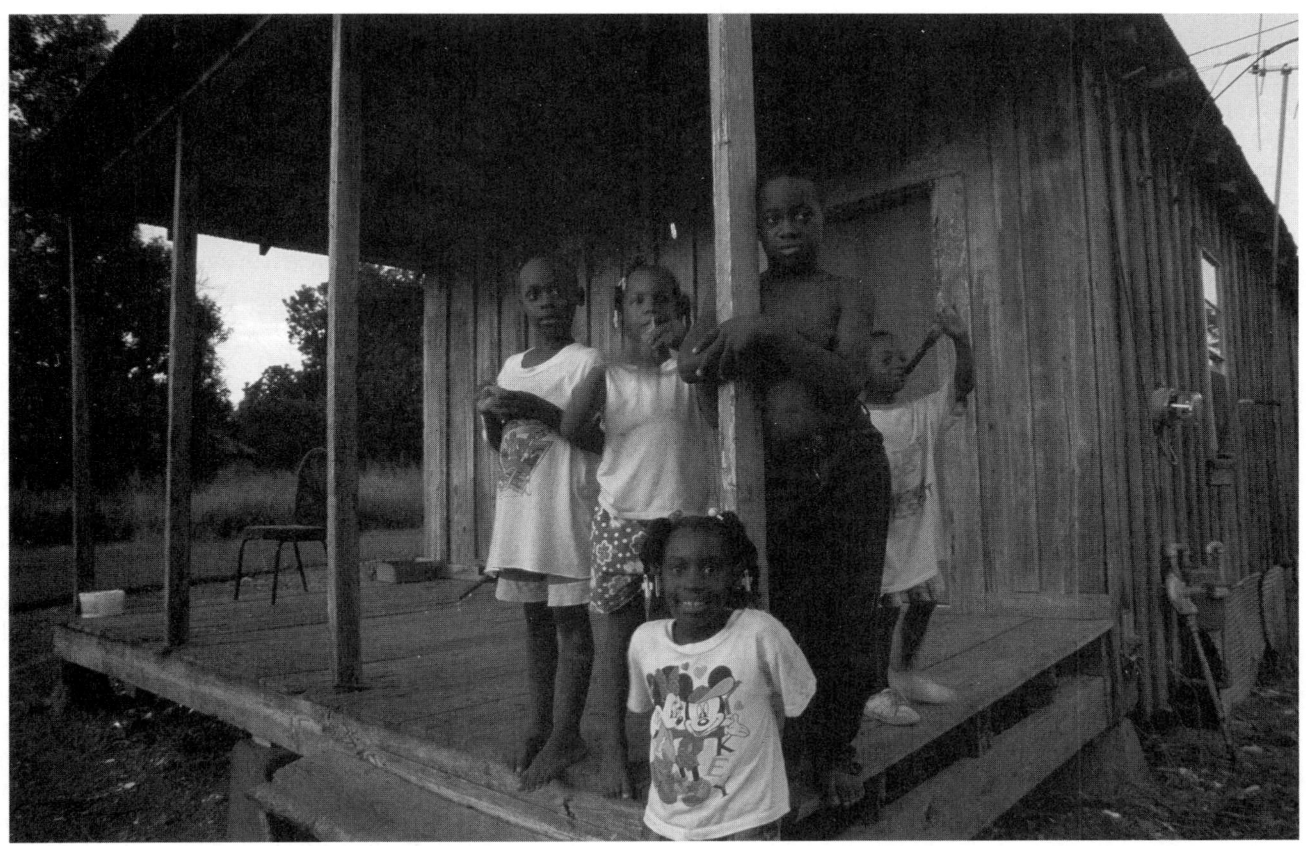

Poverty strikes Americans unevenly. About 32 percent of blacks and 27 percent of Hispanics lived in poverty in 1988 as opposed to 10 percent of whites. One in five American children were poor, in contrast to one in ten adults ages eighteen to sixty-four. (Kevin Fleming/© Corbis)

States today are low wages and limited employment opportunities for large numbers of men and women, especially racial-ethnic minorities; cutbacks in social welfare programs at all levels of government; and a decline in average earnings among young families in general, but most particularly for those headed by high school dropouts. People who work full-time, year-round at the minimum wage still fall below the poverty threshold for a family of three.

THE NEAR POOR. In addition to those who fall below the official poverty level, millions of other individuals and families float precariously above that dollar threshold. The Bureau of the Census also counts individuals and families whose income is 125 percent of the poverty line—the "near poor." Including the near poor would have raised the 1988 poverty rate for families to over 14.5 percent and to almost 41 percent for female householders. In addition, the Bureau of the Census estimates that another 5 to 6 percent of Americans have been lifted above the poverty line by virtue of Social Security benefits to retired workers, survivors of deceased workers, and the disabled.

It appears, then, that poverty and near poverty are widespread, touching the lives of one in four Americans. The line between official poverty and nonpoverty is very thin, and individuals and families tend to slip under it and rise again with changes in employment, health, and marital status. That is, contrary to popular opinion, the poverty population is not characterized by long-term welfare dependency. Fewer than 10 percent remain on the welfare rolls for a decade or more, primarily women who entered the system as very young unwed mothers and who have been unable to develop job skills or find employment that pays enough to lift the family out of poverty. For most others, poverty and nonpoverty are temporary states. An extended illness, divorce, and job loss will plunge the unit below the threshold; remarriage, employment, and recovery from illness pulls the unit above the line (Duncan et al. 1984; Ruggles 1988; U.S. Bureau of the Census 1990a, 1990b).

Also contrary to public opinion, there is no evidence that poor women have children in order to increase their welfare benefits, or that variations in benefit levels affect the formation of single-parent families (Ellwood 1988). The prevalence of female householders among blacks is due primarily to a shortage of marriageable men. Young black males are disproportionately victims of homicide and accidental deaths; many are imprisoned; and large numbers are unemployed or underemployed.

Finally, living in poverty is a troubled existence. The poor are more likely than the nonpoor to be ill, to be without adequate health care, to feel emotional anguish, to be victims of crime, to fail in marriage, and to see their children suffer from malnutrition, crippling disease, and early death. In addition, as the stock of low-income rental or subsidized housing steadily diminished throughout the 1980s—due to the phasing out of federal programs combined with owners' decisions to convert much of this housing to condominiums—many of the poor and near poor entered the ranks of America's homeless. What remained of federal housing assistance under the Reagan administration was tainted by graft and political favoritism.

If there is a "culture of poverty," it is a normal response to the unchanging conditions that create and maintain impoverishment.

If there is a "culture of poverty" characterized by the intergenerational transmission of maladaptive attitudes toward work and marriage, as conservative critics of the welfare system claim (Lewis 1961; Murray 1984), sociologists tend to explain the persistence of such behaviors as normal responses to the unchanging structural conditions that create and maintain impoverishment—low wages, uncertain employment, inadequate housing and health care, failing schools, an indifferent public, and an often hostile government. Anyone living under these circumstances would most likely respond in similar ways. That is, rather than explaining social patterns by reference to the characteristics of individuals, sociologists examine the contexts in which that behavior takes place.

Future Trends

Will the context for the distribution of income in the United States undergo change in the near future? There does not appear to be any major thrust toward revising the tax structure, to make the system more progressive, that is, to tax higher incomes at significantly higher rates. Indeed, quite the contrary appears to be the case at the state and local level, where the trend has been away from relatively progressive income taxes toward property and sales taxes that apply the same rate to all payers.

Nor does there appear to be much public sentiment toward raising welfare benefits in order to lift households over the poverty threshold. In general, eligibility rules and procedures tend to be more punitive than meliorative, so that large numbers of people eligible for in-kind benefits are not enrolled. The most recent attempts to reduce long-term welfare dependency involve state-sponsored "workfare" programs whereby single mothers are trained for entry into the labor force. During the training period and for some time afterward, the family continues to receive income assistance, Medicaid coverage, and child care. To date, workfare has not had a major impact on the poverty rate, in large part because the jobs for which the women are being trained do not raise their income sufficiently to compensate for the loss of health care coverage.

Behind the American public's resistance to changes in either the tax structure or the welfare system is a set of deeply ingrained attitudes about wealth and poverty. Based on the set of values often referred to as the "work ethic," these attitudes and beliefs have been central to the development of capitalism: work as a "calling" (sacred task); success as a sign of personal virtue; failure as a signal of moral flaw; and each person's responsibility for her or his conduct in this world. From this perspective, Americans tend to see success and failure as individually determined. Thus, poverty is thought to be due to laziness, lack of talent, or loose morals, rather than being linked to societal factors such as changes in the occupational structure, the flight of jobs and capital from central cities, and the subsequent deterioration of housing and schools (Feagin 1986). Conversely, the successful are thought to be endowed with special gifts of talent and virtue, including a willingness to work hard.

There are also indications that it will be harder than in the past to generate a collective commitment to alleviate poverty. America's poor today are different from the impoverished of the 1930s and even the late 1950s: less likely to be white, to be married, or to be male. The sympathy that is so readily evoked by the plight of an unemployed coal miner and his family is rarely extended to the dark-skinned inner city unwed mother who actually has fewer children on average than Appalachian whites.

Therefore, unless there is a major shift in values and political leadership, it is unlikely that there will be any marked reversal of current trends in the distribution of income, wealth, and poverty in the United States through the remainder of this century. Wealth will continue to become concentrated, even as the proportion of high wealthholders increases. The middle of the income distribution will continue to shrink, albeit slowly. And one in four Americans, and a higher proportion of children, will continue to live in or near poverty.

Comparative Perspectives

Any discussion of wealth, poverty, and the distribution of income within a population must take into account the vast differences between modern industrial societies and the less developed nations. Poor people in high-income societies are rarely as deprived of the basic necessities of survival as are most people in the third world, where income inequality is typically higher than in industrial societies (World Bank 1989). But Americans do not compare themselves to Sudanese; rather, they measure their circumstances against those of other Americans to whom they feel similar. It is a sense of relative rather than absolute deprivation that tends to fuel hostility, violence, indifference, or withdrawal into a world of drug-induced oblivion.

Yet, comparing only modern industrial societies, there is evidence that the extent of poverty and associated social problems—for example, single-parent families, teenage pregnancy, homicide, substance abuse, homelessness, infant mortality, violent crime—is greater in the United States than in other Western democracies. This is so largely because the United States has the least extensive social welfare system of any modern state. Alone among its industrialized peers, the United States is without a comprehensive family policy, lacks a national health insurance system, and emphasizes limitations rather than entitlements to benefit programs. As a consequence, there are few institutionalized mechanisms, other than Social Security, for the redistribution of income that narrow the gap between the very rich and very poor or that substantially reduce both the likelihood and impact of poverty. In the absence of a revitalization of a sense of collective responsibility, income inequality will continue to characterize the United States.

[See also Homelessness; Poverty; Social Stratification.]

BIBLIOGRAPHY

Avery, Robert B., and Gregory E. Elliehausen 1986 "Financial Characteristics of High-Income Families." *Federal Reserve Bulletin* 72:163–176.

Duncan, Greg J., Richard D. Coe, Mary E. Corcoran, Martha S. Hill, Saul D. Hoffman, and James N. Morgan 1984 *Years of Poverty, Years of Plenty: The Changing Economic Fortunes of American Workers and Families.* Ann Arbor: Institute for Social Research, University of Michigan.

Ellwood, David T. 1988 *Poor Support: Poverty in the American Family.* New York: Basic Books.

Feagin, Joe R. 1986 *Social Problems: A Critical Power-Conflict Perspective,* 2nd ed. Englewood Cliffs, N.J.: Prentice-Hall.

Lewis, Oscar 1961 *Children of Sanchez.* New York: Random House.

Murray, Charles 1984 *Losing Ground.* New York: Basic Books.

Pearce, Diana 1978 "The Feminization of Poverty: Women, Work, and Welfare." *Urban and Social Change Review* February:1–17.

Ruggles, Patricia 1988 *Short Term Fluctuations in Income and Their Relationship to the Characteristics of the Low Income Population.* Survey of Income and Program Participation Working Paper No. 8802. Bureau of the Census. Washington, D.C.: U.S. Government Printing Office.

U.S. Bureau of the Census 1986 *Household Wealth and Asset Ownership: 1984.* Current Population Reports, Series P-70, No. 7. Washington, D.C.: U.S. Government Printing Office.

——— 1989 *Money Income and Poverty Status in the United States: 1988 (Advance Data from the March 1989 Current Population Survey).* Current Population Reports, Series P-60, No. 166. Washington, D.C.: U.S. Government Printing Office.

——— 1990a *Transitions in Income and Poverty Status: 1985–1986.* Current Population Reports, Series P-70, No. 18. Washington, D.C.: U.S. Government Printing Office.

——— 1990b *Trends in Income, by Selected Characteristics: 1947 to 1988.* Current Population Reports, Series P-60, No. 167. Washington, D.C.: U.S. Government Printing Office.

——— 1990c *Measuring the Effect of Benefits and Taxes on Income and Poverty: 1989.* Current Population Reports, Series P-60, No. 169-RD. Washington, D.C.: U.S. Government Printing Office.

U.S. Congress 1986 *The Concentration of Wealth in the United States: Trends in the Distribution of Wealth Among American Families.* Washington, D.C.: Joint Economic Committee.

World Bank 1989 *World Development Report 1989.* New York: Oxford University Press.

– BETH B. HESS

INDIVIDUALISM

Individualism is a doctrine concerning both the composition of human society and the constitution of sociocultural actors. The term was invented in the 1820s, apparently, in France (Swart 1962). Its first appearance in English dates from the 1835 translation of Alexis de Tocqueville's study of the United States (Tocqueville [1850] 1969). The basic notion conveyed by the newly coined word, that the individual is sovereign vis-à-vis society, was intensely controversial, for it symbolized the death of one established order and the rise of another. As an early French critic saw it, individualism "destroys the very idea of obedience and of duty, thereby destroying both power and law," leaving nothing "but a terrifying confusion of interests, passions and diverse opinions" (cited in Lukes 1973, p. 6).

Individualism should be distinguished from historically specific constitutions of the individuality of human beings. The word *individual,* used to discriminate a particular human being from collectivities *(family, state),* had been in circulation for centuries prior to Tocqueville, and individualizations had been practiced under one description or another long before that, at least as evidenced in the oldest surviving texts of human history. However, premodern constitutions of individuality did not become the focus of a distinctive doctrine called individualism. That development came in response to the profound changes of social structure and consciousness that had been slowly accumulating during the seventeenth and eighteenth centuries. In the transformation from a medieval to a modern world, new transparencies of meaning evolved, among the most important a particular conception of *the individual.* The enormous power of that conception is reflected in the fact that people of modern society have generally had no doubt as to what an individual *is.* The reference has been self-evident because the object referred to, an *individual,* has been self-evident, pregiven, natural.

The basic notion that the individual is sovereign vis-à-vis society was intensely controversial.

But one must remember that *the individual* is a construct. Like all constructs, it is historically variable. The meaning of individualism's individual was formed under specific historical circumstances that, in practice as well as ideology, increasingly prized values of rational calculation, mastery, and experimentation; deliberate efforts toward betterment of the human condition; and a universalism anchored in the conviction that human nature is basically the same everywhere at all times and that rationality is singular in number. These commitments were manifested in the doctrine of individualism (as indeed in the formation of the modern social sciences). By the time of Tocqueville and the newly coined word, individualism's individual had become integral to much of the practical consciousness of modern society. Human beings were being objectified as instances of *the individual,* that is, as instances of a particular kind of individuality.

The forces created during that formative period wrought great changes in the fabric of society, many of which continue to reverberate. Of course, as historical circumstances have changed, both the individual of individualism and the constitution of individuality have changed. Nonetheless, a certain transparency of meaning remains today in our practical consciousness of the individual, and it is still informed by a doctrine of individualism. Thus, when a sociologist today says that "a natural unit of observation is the individual" (Coleman 1990, p. 1), he or she can safely assume that most readers will know exactly what is meant.

The remainder of this article offers cursory accounts of (1) the development of individualism during the seventeenth, eighteenth, and nineteenth centuries; (2) the recent shifts of emphasis in individualism's conception of the individual; and (3) some current issues and concerns. More extended treatments can be found in Macpherson (1962); Lukes (1973); Abercrombie, Hill, and Turner (1986); and Heller, Sosna, and Wellbery (1986), among others.

The Self-Representing Individual

Although elements of individualism can be seen in expressions of practical affairs as early as during the twelfth-century renaissance, (Macfarlane 1978; Ullmann 1966), the first more or less systematic statement of the doctrine came during the 1600s. Scholars such as René Descartes, Thomas Hobbes, and John Locke believed that, to understand a whole (e.g., society), one had first to understand the parts of which it was composed. In the case of society, those "parts," the building blocks of a society, were instances of the individual. Although disagreeing on various specific issues—for example, whether human agency is distinct from a natural world of causal necessity (Descartes) or a product of that causal necessity (Hobbes)—these seventeenth-century scholars displayed remarkable confidence in their understanding of the individual as a presocial atom. Their individual was a highly abstract being, squatting outside the world.

In the premodern order of European society, social relations had been organic, corporate, and mainly determined by family lineage and other group-based traits. Sovereignty was a complex relation of duty, responsibility, and charity, focused on a specific location in the hierarchical order of organic community. Certainly members of the community were individualized, but the distinction was constituted primarily by their positions in the hierarchical order. It is clear from surviving documents of the twelfth century, for example, that one individual knight was discriminable from any other in ways that we would describe as "personality." With rare exception, however, that discrimination was local. Otherwise, knights were discriminable mainly by pedigree, lines of fealty, and quality of chivalry. Individuals could rise (and fall) through gradations of rank, but vertical movement was first within the family or household group. A knight who aspired to still higher standing had first to be retained in another, more powerful, family.

In the new order, in contrast, social relations were conceived as contractual rather than organic, based on achieved traits (rather than on traits fixed at birth or by family lineage) of individuals free of the constraints of community. City life was once again the center of gravity in territorial organization, having displaced the manorial system. The new individual was conceived as a wholly separate entity of self-identical integrity, a "bare individual" who could freely consent to enter into concert with other equivalently constituted individuals, each propelled by self-interest. This was, as Macpherson (1962) describes it, the advent of "possessive individualism," and it correlated well with the developing motivations of capitalism.

By the end of the eighteenth century, individualism had attained mature statement in treatises by David Hume, Adam Smith, and Immanuel Kant, among others. This mature statement, worked out in the context of rapidly changing politico-economic institutions, emphasized the centrality of a *self-representing individual.* The chief claim—that "every individual appears as the autonomous subject of his [or her, but primarily his] decisions and actions" (Goldmann [1968] 1973, p. 20)—served as linchpin to formalized explanations of the political and economic rights of members of society, especially the propertied members. Expressions of the chief claim in moral and legal rights of the individual became enshrined in newly invented traditions, in legitimizing principles such as *popular sovereignty* and *inalienable rights,* and in documents of public culture such as the Declaration of the Rights of Man and the U.S. Constitution (Hobsbawm and Ranger 1983; Morgan 1988). The prayerful injunction "God bless the squire and his relations and keep us in our proper stations" had been replaced by the almost wholly secular "*I* pledge allegiance to the flag" (i.e., to an abstract sign). Although the claim of autonomy emphasized the universality of rights and the particularity of the *I,* the practical emphasis on a self-representing individual was formulated in politico-economic terms that "necessitated" elaborate definitions and procedures for the defense of "property rights" long before equivalent attention would be given to, say, "rights of the handicapped."

Much like the individual of organic community, the self-representing individual is a substantial presence, manifest as the embodiment of a uniform human nature and, as such, is the bearer of various traits, dispositions, and affirmations. However, the site of the self-representing individual's capacity for agency and potential for autonomy is neither the community nor the accumulated traits, dispositions, and affirmations. Rather, it is deeply interior to what became a new *inner nature* of being human. Beneath the faculty of reason, beneath all feeling and emotion and belief, there is *the will.* Emile Durkheim ([1914] 1973) described it as the egoistic will of the individual pole of *homo duplex;* for George Herbert Mead (1934) it was "the principle of action." But before either of those sociologists, the master theorizer of the self-representing individual, Kant, had formulated the basic principle as the pure functioning of the I through time. Only because I can unite a variety of given representations of objects in *one* consciousness, Kant ([1787] 1929, B133) argued, is it possible for me to "represent to myself the *identity of consciousness*" throughout those representations. In other words, the very possibility of knowledge of the external world is dependent on the temporal continuity of the I. The individual is absolute proprietor of this pure functionality, this willing of the I as basic principle of action; the individual owes absolutely nothing to society for it.

By conceiving the essential core of human individuality as a deeply interiorized, radically isolated, pure functionality, connections between the individual and the substantive traits that she or he bears become arbitrary. The individual is formally free to exercise a choice of which traits to bear, free to be mobile geographically, socially, culturally, personally. Ascriptive traits (e.g., sex, skin color) are devalued in favor of achieved traits, and one set of achieved traits can always be exchanged for yet another set. This principle of freely exchangeable traits, an aspiration directing progress toward *the good society,* depended on new means of socialization (or internalization of norms) to ensure sufficient regularity in the processes of exchange. Indeed, the self-representing individual was central to a distinctive regimen of behavior, a new practical meaning of *discipline* (Foucault [1975] 1977). As the doctrine of individualism expressed it, the contractual, associative forms of social relation, though looser fitting in their constraints than the old organic community, were complemented by the figure of *the self-made man* who had internalized all the norms of rectitude and propriety so nicely as to merit life in an unprecedentedly free society. When reality failed the image, there were courts and legal actions for deciding conflicts of interest and the clash of individuals' rights. Notably, not a single book on the law of torts had been published in English by the mid-1800s; the explosive growth of tort law and third-party rules was only beginning (Friedman 1985, pp. 53–54).

The doctrine of individualism provided a set of answers to questions that were foundational to sociology.

Because the doctrine of individualism provided a set of answers to questions that were foundational to sociology (as to the social sciences in general)—What is the individual? How is society possible? and others—virtually every topic subsequently addressed by sociology has in one way or another involved aspects of individualism. Given the composition of individualism's self-representing individual, the most prominent issues have often centered on questions of relationship between the rise of individualism and the development of new forms of politico-economic organization as manifested in capitalism, bureaucracy, and the modern state. Indeed, that relationship was the focus of one of the great controversies occupying many early sociologists (Abercrombie et al. 1986). Hardly anyone doubted the existence or importance of a relationship. Rather, the debates were about such issues as causal direction (which caused which?), periodizations (e.g., when did capitalism begin?), and whether ideas or material conditions (each category conceived as devoid of the other) were the primary motive force. In many respects the debates were a continuation of the struggles they were about.

Other, more specific topics addressed by sociologists have also involved aspects of the rise of individualism. Several have already been mentioned (e.g., a new regime of discipline). Additional examples are the development of sectarian (as opposed to churchly) religions, followed by an even more highly privatized mystical-religious consciousness of the isolated individual; changes in domestic architecture, such as greater emphasis on individualized spaces for privacy and functionally specialized rooms; changes in table manners, rules of courtesy, and other refinements of taste; emergence of a *confessional self* and practices of diary keeping; increased emphasis on romantic love (affective individualism) in mate selection; new forms of literary discourse such as the novel and the autobiography; and the rise of professionalism (see Abercrombie et al. 1986; Perrot [1987] 1990).

The Self-Expressing Individual

The figure of the self-representing individual proved to be unstable, even as the meaning of representation gradually changed. This was mainly because the same factors that had produced this version of individualism's individual also led to dissolution of the transparent sign. For example, whereas clothing, manners, bodily comportment, and similar traits had been, in the old order, reliable signs (representations) of a person's rank or station in life, the sign became increasingly arbitrary in its relationship to ground. This loosening of the sign, together with a proliferation of signs in exchange, led to a new universalism of *the empty sign.* The prototype was money and the commodity form: Devoid of intrinsic value and capable of representing everything, it represents nothing in particular. As one scholar described the process, borrowing a clause from Karl Marx, "all that is solid melts into air" (Berman 1983).

At the same time, the rhetoric of transhistorical forms of value (e.g., the commodity, inalienable rights) allows for an enormous amount of individual variation in the sociocultural conditions under which that rhetoric can succeed. Individualism's emphasis on the bare individual was being increasingly generalized, further reducing the import of group-based relations and traits. In the mid-1800s, for instance, the distinction between public affairs and private matters was drawn at the door of home and family. Family life provided the chief "haven" of organic relations, nurturant domesticity, and refuge from the trials of work and politics. But soon the haven itself became a site of struggle toward still greater individuation. Of the many factors contributing to this rebellion against the traditional restraints of family, one of the most important was a new culture of sexuality, which manifested a more general and growing concern for the interior interests and needs of the individual.

Precedent for this concern can be seen in Kant's conception of the self-representing individual (because of the transcendental I, every individual has in common the potential for *self-actualization*), as well as in romanticist movements of the early 1800s. However, the creation of a new "inner discourse of the individual" has been mostly a twentieth-century phenomenon. The psychology of Sigmund Freud and his disciples formed part of that development, certainly; but another part was formed by the conception of a new "social citizenship" (Marshall 1964), which emphasized an individual's right to social welfare in addition to the earlier mandates of political and economic rights. A new figure of individualism's individual gradually emerged, the *self-expressing individual.*

The individualism of the self-representing individual promoted the idea that all interests are ultimately interests of the bare individual. The new version of individualism both extends and modifies that idea. Whereas the self-representing individual puts a premium on self-control and hard work, the self-expressing individual generalizes the value of *freedom of choice* from politico-economic exchange relations to matters of personal life-style and consumption preferences (Inglehart 1990). The central claim holds that "each person has a unique core of feeling and intuition that should unfold or be expressed if individuality is to be realized" (Bellah, Madsen, Sullivan, Swidler, and Tipton 1985, p. 336), and each person has the right to develop his or her unique capacities for self-expression. A recent change in divorce law partly illustrates the import of that claim. Prior to the 1960s one of the few organic relations still surviving in modern society was the marital bond; few conditions were deemed grave enough to have legal standing as grounds for breaking it. With the invention of *no fault divorce* (relatively noncontroversial legislation that spread rapidly from state to state; Jacob 1988), the marital relation became a civil contract much like any other, and a spouse's freedom to choose divorce in the interest of satisfying unfulfilled needs of self-expression gained recognition.

Not only does individualism's self-expressing individual remain a trait-bearing substantial entity, but also the variety of bearable traits is greatly expanded by the shift in emphasis from self-control to self-expression through life-style experimentation. Moreover, this shift in emphasis is accompanied by the stipulation that only those traits that an individual can freely choose to assume, and then jettison, should be relevant criteria by which to discriminate and evaluate individuals. Criteria falling outside the bounds of individual choice (*immutable* traits, whether biologic or sociocultural) are deemed to be both irrelevant and, increasingly, violations of an individual's rights. In conjunction with the *entitlements* logic of social citizenship, this stipulation of a radically individualistic freedom of reversible choice has been linked to the emergence of a generalized expectation of "total justice" (Friedman 1985).

The self-expressing individual would "transcend" domination by concentrating on rights to free expression.

By the same token, the doctrine of individualism has always contained a large fictive component. Long after the doctrine proclaimed the sovereignty of the bare individual, for example, the actual individuality of human beings continued to be heavily marked by ascriptive traits (e.g., gender, race) and by sociocultural inheritances from one's parents. The shift to an expressive individualism reflects efforts to situate the agency of a free individual outside the separately conceived domain of relations of domination. Rather than attempt to change those relations, the self-expressing individual would "transcend" them by concentrating on a logic of rights pertaining to the free expression of individual will in a domain of "personal culture" (Marcuse [1937] 1968).

Fictions can be productive in various ways, however. The fictions of individualism have often been made taskmasters, as women, African-Americans, the handicapped, and other human beings discriminated primarily by ascriptive or group-based criteria have struggled to make reality conform to doctrinal image.

Some Current Issues

Because individualism has been one of the professional ideologies of the social sciences *(methodological individualism),* a perennial issue concerns the proper structure of explanation, specifically whether explanation of any sociocultural phenomenon must ultimately refer to facts about individuals and, if so, what precisely that means (Lukes 1973, pp. 110–122). No one denies that collectivities are composed of individuals. But that truism does not settle how *composition* is to be understood or what constitutes the individual. In short, the allegedly methodological issue involves a number of conceptual issues, including several located at the intersection between individualism's individual and historical variations in the actual constitution of individuality (Heller et al. 1986). The doctrine of individualism has consistently conceptualized the individual as a distinct and self-contained agent who acts within, yet separate from, a constraining social structure. Rather than being an ensemble of social relations, individualism's individual is the substantial atom out of which any possible social relations are composed. This has certain implications for the empirical field.

Some sociologists contend, for example, that individualism's self-expressing individual is an accurate depiction of contemporary reconstitutions of individuality and that, in this new form of the individual, the substance of selfhood, an individual's self-identical integrity, is being evacuated. Bellah et al. indict the emergence of "a language of radical individual autonomy" in which people "cannot think about themselves or others except as arbitrary centers of volition" (1985, p. 81). Others argue that the emphasis on individual autonomy and separation is an expression of masculine, patriarchal values, as contrasted with feminine values of social attachment (Gilligan 1982, pp. 22–23). Still others see the development of an entirely new "order of simulacra" (Baudrillard [1976] 1983), in which simulation or the simulacrum (representation) substitutes for and then vanquishes the real (e.g., television images establish the parameters of reality). The alleged result is a collapse of "the social" into the indifference of "the masses," who no longer care to discriminate among "messages" (beyond their entertainment effects) because one simulation is as good as another.

Contentious issues surround people's sense of entitlement and the array of legal rights claimed on behalf of individual choice.

Equally contentious issues surround the evident growth in people's sense of entitlement and in the array of legal rights claimed and often won on behalf of *individual choice.* Individualism's figure of the self-expressing individual is held by some to be the harbinger of a new age of democracy, by others the confirmation of a continuing trend toward greater atomization (Friedman 1985). Both assessments point to the emergence of a *rights industry* that promotes the invention of new categories of legal right pertaining to everything from the guaranteed freedom to experiment with unconventional life-styles without risk of discrimination or retribution, to the rights of animals both individually and as a species (Norton 1987), to the possibility of endowing genes with *subjectlike powers* and, thus, legal standing (Oyama 1985, p. 79). Some critics contend that the expansion of concern for increasingly particularized and "arbitrary" individual choices comes at the expense of diminished concern for social outcomes. "Unless people regain the sense that the practices of society represent some sort of natural order instead of a set of arbitrary choices, they cannot hope to escape from the dilemma of unjustified power" (Unger 1976, p. 240). The conviction recalls that of the early French critic quoted in the initial paragraph.

[See also Capitalism; Democracy.]

BIBLIOGRAPHY

Abercrombie, Nicholas, Stephen Hill, and Bryan S. Turner 1986 *Sovereign Individuals of Capitalism.* London: Allen and Unwin.

Baudrillard, Jean (1976) 1983 *In the Shadow of the Silent Majorities.* New York: Semiotext(e).

Bellah, Robert N., Richard Madsen, William M. Sullivan, Ann Swidler, and Steven M. Tipton 1985 *Habits of the Heart.* Berkeley, Calif.: University of California Press.

Berman, Marshall 1983 *All That Is Solid Melts into Air.* London: Verso.

Coleman, James S. 1990 *Foundations of Social Theory.* Cambridge, Mass.: Harvard University Press.

Durkheim, Emile (1914) 1973 "The Dualism of Human Nature and Its Social Conditions." In Robert Bellah, ed., *Emile Durkheim on Morality and Society.* Chicago: University of Chicago Press.

Foucault, Michel (1975) 1977 *Discipline and Punish,* Alan Sheridan, trans. New York: Pantheon.

Friedman, Lawrence 1985 *Total Justice.* New York: Russell Sage Foundation.

Gilligan, Carol 1982 *In a Different Voice.* Cambridge, Mass.: Harvard University Press.

Goldmann, Lucien (1968) 1973 *Philosophy of the Enlightenment,* Henry Maas, trans. Cambridge, Mass.: MIT Press.

Heller, Thomas C., Morton Sosna, and David E. Wellbery 1986 *Reconstructing Individualism.* Stanford, Calif.: Stanford University Press.

Hobsbawm, Eric, and Terence Ranger (eds.) 1983 *The Invention of Tradition* Cambridge: Cambridge University Press.

Inglehart, Ronald 1990 *Cultural Shift in Advanced Industrial Society.* Princeton, N.J.: Princeton University Press.

Jacob, Herbert 1988 *Silent Revolution.* Chicago: University of Chicago Press.

Kant, Immanuel (1787) 1929 *The Critique of Pure Reason,* 2nd ed., trans. Norman Kemp Smith. London: Macmillan.

Lukes, Steven 1973 *Individualism.* Oxford: Basil Blackwell.

Macfarlane, Alan 1978 *The Origins of English Individualism.* Oxford: Basil Blackwell.

Macpherson, C. B. 1962 *The Political Theory of Possessive Individualism.* Oxford: Oxford University Press.

Marcuse, Herbert [1937] 1968 "The Affirmative Character of Culture." In *Negations,* Jeremy J. Shapiro, trans. Boston: Beacon.

Marshall, T. H. 1964 *Class, Citizenship, and Social Development.* New York: Doubleday.

Mead, George Herbert 1934 *Mind, Self, and Society,* ed. Charles W. Morris. Chicago: University of Chicago Press.

Morgan, Edmund S. 1988 *Inventing the People.* New York: Norton.

Norton, Bryan G. 1987 *Why Preserve Natural Variety?* Princeton, N.J.: Princeton University Press.

Oyama, Susan 1985 *The Ontogeny of Information.* Cambridge: Cambridge University Press.

Perrot, Michelle (ed.) (1987) 1990 *A History of Private Life,* vol. 4, Arthur Goldhammer, trans. Cambridge, Mass.: Harvard University Press.

Swart, Koenraad W. 1962 "Individualism' in the Mid-Nineteenth Century (1826–1860)." *Journal of the History of Ideas* 23:77–90.

Tocqueville, Alexis de (1850) 1969. *Democracy in America,* 13th ed., J. P. Mayer, ed. George Lawrence, trans. New York: Doubleday.

Ullmann, Walter 1966 *The Individual and Society in the Middle Ages.* Baltimore: Johns Hopkins University Press.

Unger, Roberto Mangabeira 1976 *Law in Modern Society.* New York: Free Press.

– LAWRENCE HAZELRIGG

INDUSTRIALIZATION IN LESS DEVELOPED COUNTRIES

In the two hundred years since the Industrial Revolution in England, the process of industrialization has had perhaps more impact on all the nations of the world than any other complex set of forces. This process has not been uniformly introduced in all countries, nor has it occurred at the same time or at the same rate. Despite the common features of industrialization, these differences in its introduction and adoption have produced inequities among nations and among people on a scale never before experienced.

In describing various countries and regions of the world, certain terms have been adopted, first by official agencies such as the United Nations and national governments, and then more generally by scholars, journalists, and those interested in making sense out of international relations. According to a now commonly used United Nations classification, *more developed countries* (MDCs) comprise all of Europe, North America (excluding Mexico), Japan, Australia, New Zealand, and the former USSR; *less developed countries* (LDCs) constitute the remainder. This classification mirrors the famous "North–South divide" coined by former chancellor Willy Brandt (1980) in his commission's report to the World Bank. Also, MDCs were equated with the capitalist Western nations (First World countries) and the communist Eastern-bloc countries (Second World), while the LDCs constituted the remaining nonaligned countries of the Third World (Crow and Thomas 1983, p. 8).

In some cases, the underlying variable upon which these distinctions are made is economic, in other cases it is political, and in still others it is unspecified. However, generally speaking, MDCs are "rich" and LDCs are "poor." In 1986, the per capita gross national product among all MDCs was US$10,700, while in the LDCs it was only US$640, or almost seventeen times less *(1988 World Population Data Sheet).* The major explanation for this vast discrepancy is that MDCs are fully industrialized whereas LDCs are not.

Industrialization Defined

Industrialization is a complex process comprised of a number of interrelated dimensions. Historically, it represents a transition from an economy based on agriculture to one in which manufacturing represents the principal means of subsistence. Consequently, two dimensions of industrialization are the work that people do for a living (economic activity) and the actual goods they produce (economic output). Other dimensions include the manner in which economic activity is organized (organization), the energy or power source used (mechanization), and the systematic methods and innovative practices employed to accomplish work (technology). Table 1 specifies these dimensions and also lists indicators commonly used to measure them.

TABLE 1

DIMENSIONS AND MEASURES OF INDUSTRIALIZATION

1. *Economic Activity*
   a. Percentage of labor force in manufacturing
   b. Percentage of labor force in industry
2. *Economic Output*
   a. Manufacturing as a percentage of gross domestic product
   b. Industry as a percentage of gross domestic product
   c. Gross output per employee in manufacturing
   d. Earnings per employee in manufacturing
3. *Organization*
   a. Wage and salary earners as a percentage of the labor force
   b. Number of manufacturing establishments employing fifty or more workers per capita
4. *Mechanization*
   a. Commercial energy consumption per capita
   b. Total cost of fuels and purchased electrical energy per employee in manufacturing
5. *Technology*
   a. Percentage of professional and technical workers in labor force
   b. Registered patents in force per capita
   c. Registered industrial designs in force per capita

According to these indicators, MDCs are fully industrialized. On average, close to one-third of the labor forces in these countries are employed in industry; manufacturing makes up approximately one-quarter of the gross domestic product; the overwhelming majority of workers are employees of organizations; commercial energy consumption is high (over 4,500 kilograms of oil equivalent per capita); and professional and technical workers comprise 15 percent of the work force (Hedley forthcoming). Furthermore, virtually all of the registered patents and industrial designs in force are held in the MDCs (Kurian 1984, pp. 217–219). Industrial activity and the services associated with it constitute the major driving force and source of income in these industrially developed countries.

In contrast, none of the LDCs is fully industrialized, as measured by these five dimensions of industrialization. Whereas manufacturing accounts for a significant proportion of many of these countries' total output, most do not achieve industrial status on any of the other dimensions. Manufacture in these countries is accomplished largely by traditional methods that have varied little over successive generations. Consequently, although manufacturing, or the transformation of raw materials into finished goods, is indeed an essential component of industrialization, there is considerably more to the process. Because industrialization is multidimensional, it therefore cannot be measured by only one indicator.

In general, LDCs may be classified into three major groups according to how industrialized they are. The first and smallest group, referred to in the literature as *newly industrializing countries* (NICs), contains the most industrialized, in that they achieve industrial status on at least two of the dimensions listed in Table 1. According to Frederick Clairmonte and John Cavanagh (1984, p. 84), just four of these NICs, all situated in east Asia (Taiwan, South Korea, Hong Kong, and Singapore), accounted for over half of the total industrial exports of all developing countries in 1980. Other important NICs, most notably Brazil and Mexico, are located in Latin America. Although China and, to a lesser degree, India (because of their huge population bases) contribute significantly to the manufactured exports of LDCs (World Bank 1987, pp. 228–229), they have not developed their industrial infrastructures to the same extent as these NICs and, therefore, do not belong in the most industrialized group of LDCs.

A subgroup of NICs are the high-income, oil-exporting nations (e.g., United Arab Emirates, Kuwait, Saudi Arabia, and Libya). While they do not have large manufacturing bases, they do have significant proportions of their labor forces involved in industry (oil exploration and refining), a substantial component of professional and technical workers (many of them imported), and high per capita commercial energy consumption (World Bank 1987). Consequently, although they are concentrated in just one industry, they are more industrialized than most other LDCs, according to the criteria specified in Table 1. As a result of their petrodollars, they have acquired an industrial infrastructure that in other countries has taken decades upon decades to establish.

The second, very large, group of LDCs in terms of industrialization are those countries with a traditionally strong manufacturing base that also have a substantial agricultural component. Their economies straddle the agricultural and industrial modes of production. China and India are in this group, as are most of the non-European countries that form the Mediterranean basin. The goods that these LDCs predominantly manufacture (e.g., apparel, footware, textiles, and consumer electronics) are essential to their own domestic markets and, because they are labor intensive, also compete very well in the international marketplace. In addition, they export natural resources and agricultural products. Other countries included in this semi-industrial group of LDCs are most of the nations in South America, as well as many in south and east Asia.

The third and final group of LDCs are not industrialized on any of the five dimensions listed in Table 1. On average, fewer than 10 percent of their labor forces are employed in industry; anywhere from 60 to over 90 percent work in agriculture. Manufacturing contributes less than one-tenth to their national products; the bulk of income derives from natural resources, and cash crops grown exclusively for export. Per capita gross national product is very low, usually below US400 (World Bank 1987). Most of these nonindustrial LDCs are located in Africa and Asia.

Approximately one-quarter of the world is fully industrialized.

Of these three groups of LDCs, the semi-industrial cluster of nations is by far the largest, constituting just over half the world's population. China and India alone make up two-thirds of this group. The second largest group, ranging between 10 and 15 percent of the world total, is the nonindustrial countries, and NICs, including high-income oil exporters, comprise less than 10 percent. Thus, approximately one-quarter of the world is fully industrialized, another 10 percent are industrializing, half are semi-industrial, and the remaining 15 percent are nonindustrial.

Correlates of Industrialization

Research has demonstrated that industrialization is directly related to national and individual income, urbanization, the development of an infrastructure (e.g., communication and transportation networks, education, and health and welfare programs), and the overall quality of life (Hedley forthcoming). For example, concerning income, in 1850 when the Industrial Revolution was well under way, per capita income in the industrialized MDCs was 70 percent higher than in the nonindustrialized LDCs (Murdoch 1980, p. 246). However, one hundred years later the difference had grown to over 2000 percent, and by 1980, just thirty years later, the average citizen in the MDCs was earning almost 4000 percent, or 40 times, more than her or his counterpart in the LDCs. Per capita income in the LDCs was US$245, while in the MDCs it was US$9,648 (Seligson 1984). For a variety of reasons, the direct relationship between industrialization and income is increasing.

In a comprehensive, worldwide study of 124 countries, Richard Estes (1988) examined the relationship between national economic development and the "capacity of nations to provide for the basic social and material needs of their populations." From 1970 to 1983, he measured the progress of these nations using thirty-six indicators grouped into ten dimensions of national well-being. Table 2 presents his detailed and exhaustive list of measures. To determine the effect of national development on these indicators of progress, Estes classified nations into four major groups: (1) twenty-four First World countries; (2) eight Second World countries; (3) sixty-seven Third World countries; and (4) twenty-five Fourth World countries (i.e., the least developed Third World countries officially "designated by the United Nations as LDCs . . . targeted for priority international development assistance"). Thus, the first two categories represent MDCs and the latter two are LDCs (the Fourth World countries correspond approximately to the nonindustrial nations described earlier).

From the scores on each of the ten dimensions, or subindexes, Estes constructed a cumulative Index of Social Progress for each country, which ranged between −8 (Ethiopia) and +208 (Denmark). Table 3 presents the values on this index for each of the group of countries mentioned, first in 1970 and then in 1983. The extreme differences in total scores between MDCs and LDCs are indicative of how poorly off people living in less developed countries are, relative to their fellow hu-

TABLE 2

INDEX OF SOCIAL PROGRESS INDICATORS BY SUBINDEX

1. *Education Subindex*
   - School enrollment ratio, first level (+)*
   - Pupil–Teacher ratio, first level (−)
   - Percent adult illiteracy (−)
   - Percent GNP in education (+)
2. *Health Status Subindex*
   - Male life expectancy at 1 year (+)
   - Rate of infant mortality (−)
   - Population in thousands per physician (−)
   - Per capital daily calorie supply (+)
3. *Women Status Subindex*
   - Percent eligible girls in first level schools (+)
   - Percent adult female illiteracy (−)
   - Length of time legislation in effect protecting legal rights of women (+)
4. *Defense Effort Subindex*
   - Military expenditures as percent of GNP (−)
5. *Economic Subindex*
   - Per capita gross national product (+)
   - GNP per capita annual growth rate (+)
   - Average annual rate of inflation (−)
   - Per capita food production index (+)
   - External public debt as percent of GNP (−)
6. *Demography Subindex*
   - Total population (−)
   - Crude birth rate (−)
   - Crude death rate (−)
   - Rate of population increase (−)
   - Percent of population under 15 years (−)
7. *Geography Subindex*
   - Percent arable land mass (+)
   - Natural disaster vulnerability index (−)
   - Average death rate from natural disasters (−)
8. *Political Participation Subindex*
   - Violations of political rights index (−)
   - Violations of civil liberties index (−)
   - Composite violations of human freedoms (−)
9. *Cultural Diversity Subindex*
   - Largest percent sharing same mother tongue (+)
   - Largest percent sharing same religious beliefs (+)
   - Largest percent with same racial/ethnic origin (+)
10. *Welfare Effort Subindex*
    - Years since first law:
      - Old age, invalidity, death (+)
      - Sickness and maternity (+)
      - Work injury (+)
      - Unemployment (+)
      - Family allowance (+)

* The sign specifies the direction of "progress."

Source: Richard J. Estes, *Trends in World Social Development: The Social Progress of Nations, 1970 to 1987.* (New York: Praeger, 1988), pp. 2–3.

TABLE 3

INDEX OF SOCIAL PROGRESS BY DEVELOPMENTAL STATUS OF COUNTRY, 1970 AND 1983

Developmental Status of Country	Number of Countries	Year 1970	Year 1983	Percentage Change 1970–1983
First World	24	163	172	+ 5.5
Second World	8	158	142	−10.1
Third World	67	87	91	+ 4.6
Fourth World	25	45	43	− 4.4

Source: Adapted from Richard J. Estes, *Trends in World Social Development: The Social Progress of Nations, 1970–1987.* (New York: Praeger, 1988), pp. 40–41.

man beings in the more prosperous, developed nations. With the exception of the defense, geography, and cultural diversity subindexes, LDCs at best score only half as well as MDCs in providing for the basic needs of their citizens, and in the most disadvantaged, Fourth World, countries, the differences are even greater.

With respect to changes in the Index of Social Progress over the fourteen-year period represented in Table 3, the developed market economies of the First World registered the greatest advance. Thus, even in this brief interval, the evidence indicates that the gap between MDCs and LDCs is increasing. The least developed Fourth World countries actually declined from what little "progress" they had initially achieved. As Estes (1988, p. 43) states, "Increased militarism and internal political oppression—coupled with *decreased* government expenditures for health, education, fertility control and related programs—are only suggestive of the high level of 'mal-development' that characterizes current social trends."

As indicated, there is a strong direct relationship between industrialization and economic development, and as Estes's research demonstrates, this relationship impinges directly upon the quality of life of people everywhere. Unfortunately for the vast majority of the world's citizens, their circumstances do not even approximate those structural features of society that most people in the more developed countries have largely come to take for granted (see Table 2).

Paths of Development

Various schemes, proposals, and strategies have been suggested whereby LDCs can begin to share the same advantages as those presently enjoyed by MDCs. For example, two World Bank commissions under the direction of the former prime minister of Canada, Lester Pearson (1969), and the ex-chancellor of West Germany, Willy Brandt (1980), have made recommendations concerning such things as the institution of a modified and more equitable world financial structure, the liberalization of international trading policy, an increase in agricultural and energy production, and the establishment of a more workable international negotiating process. Similarly, the LDCs themselves have made proposals regarding what has come to be known as the New International Economic Order (see Tinbergen 1976). In a slightly different vein, the World Commission on Environment and Development (1987) has presented various options and strategies whereby economic development can occur in ecologically sound ways.

Generally, there are two dominant strategies of economic development: inwardly focused import substitution and outwardly oriented export promotion (see Balassa 1981, pp. 1–26). Countries employing import substitution attempt to industrialize by manufacturing for their own domestic markets the majority of those products they have normally been importing. According to this strategy, these countries become not only industrialized but also economically self-sufficient, thus diminishing their heavy reliance upon MDCs for expensive manufactured imports. India and many Latin American countries have established economies that are illustrative of this approach. On the other hand, countries emphasizing export promotion concentrate on those goods, both primary and manufactured, that have traditionally contributed to their economies and that, therefore, can earn export income. Successful pursuit of this strategy results in more profitable manufactured goods making up an increasing share of total exports, and consequently, there occurs both industrial and economic development. The four east Asian NICs mentioned exemplify this approach.

While the viability of either of these strategies obviously depends upon many factors (e.g., size of domestic market, natural resources, education and skills of the labor force, presence and type of foreign investment, and sociopolitical conditions), the evidence to date favors the outward orientation as the preferred path of development (see Syrquin and Chenery 1989). According to the World Bank (1987, pp. 92–94), "Outward orientation encourages efficient firms and discourages inefficient ones. And by creating a more competitive environment for both the private and public sectors, it also promotes higher productivity and hence faster economic growth."

India and many Latin American countries have established economies that are economically self-sufficient, thus diminishing their reliance upon more developed countries for expensive manufactured imports.

Although there are monumental barriers to industrialization and economic development for the LDCs, they can be overcome (see Hedley 1985). To the extent that nothing is done, and the gap between the rich and the poor continues to widen, dire predictions have been made as to possible consequences. In fact, there is already an increase in world disorder. Manifestations of this deterioration include multiplying acts of terrorism and civil disobedience, illegal migration, increased crime, widespread famine, and internal disputes that escalate into international conflicts. Further instability may be introduced through large-scale default on debt repayment, expropriation and curtailment of the activities of transnational corporations, formation of cartels among LDCs to limit the supply of necessary goods to the developed nations, breakdown of international bodies and diplomatic communication, and finally, revolution and war.

To the extent that the now industrialized countries are not cognizant of the difficulties faced by the LDCs and do not act to ameliorate them, the rich nations along with the poor will suffer the calamitous consequences. As Lester Pearson prophesied, "Before long, in our affluent, industrial, computerized jet society, we shall feel the wrath of the wretched people of the world. There will be no peace" (cited in Tinbergen 1976, p. 59).

BIBLIOGRAPHY

Balassa, Bela 1981 *The Newly Industrializing Countries in the World Economy.* New York: Pergamon.

Brandt Report 1980 *North–South: A Program for Survival. Report of the Independent Commission on International Development Issues.* Cambridge, Mass.: MIT Press.

Clairmonte, Frederick F., and John H. Cavanagh 1984 "Transnational Corporations and Global Markets: Changing Power Relations." In Pradip K. Ghosh, ed., *Multi-national Corporations and Third World Development,* pp. 47–91. Westport, Conn.: Greenwood.

Crow, Ben, and Alan Thomas 1983 *Third World Atlas.* Milton Keynes, U.K.: Open University Press.

Estes, Richard J. 1988 *Trends in World Social Development: The Social Progress of Nations, 1970–1987.* New York: Praeger.

Hedley, R. Alan 1985 "Narrowing the Gap between the Rich and the Poor Nations: A Modest Proposal." *Transnational Perspectives* 11(2–3):23–27.

——— Forthcoming *Making a Living: Technology, Industry, and Change.* New York: Harper Collins.

Kurian, George T. 1984 *The New Book of World Rankings.* New York: Facts on File.

Murdoch, William W. 1980 *The Poverty of Nations: The Political Economy of Hunger and Population.* Baltimore: Johns Hopkins University Press.

Pearson Report 1969 *Partners in Development: Report of the Commission on International Development.* New York: Praeger.

Seligson, Mitchell A. 1984 "The Dual Gaps: An Overview of Theory and Research." In Mitchell A. Seligson, ed., *The Gap between Rich and Poor: Contending Perspectives on the Political Economy of Development,* pp. 3–7. Boulder, Colo.: Westview.

Syrquin, Moshe, and Hollis Chenery 1989 "Three Decades of Industrialization." *World Bank Economic Review* 3(2):145–181.

Tinbergen, Jan 1976 *Reshaping the International Order.* New York: Dutton.

World Bank 1987 *World Development Report 1987.* New York: Oxford University Press.

World Commission on Environment and Development 1987 *Our Common Future.* Oxford: Oxford University Press.

1988 World Population Data Sheet 1988 Washington, D.C.: Population Reference Bureau.

– R. ALAN HEDLEY

INFANT AND CHILD MORTALITY

The term *mortality* refers to the rate at which death occurs to members of a population. It is measured not by a count of deaths but by quotients that relate deaths to the size of the population in which those deaths occur. The most common measure of infant mortality is the infant mortality rate, the ratio of deaths that occur to children below age one in a particular year to births that occur in that year. This ratio is an excellent approximation to the probability that a newborn child will die before his or her first birthday.

The age referent for "child mortality" is less clear-cut. Among demographers, the term is used most frequently to refer to the probability that a newborn child will die before his or her fifth birthday. Obviously, such a measure of child mortality reflects infant mortality as well. The first five years of life are among the ages of highest mortality, matched in most populations only by the very old ages. In contrast, ages five to fifteen are usually the ages of lowest mortality.

Knowledge about levels of infant and child mortality is drawn from many sources. For prehistoric populations, the only evidence is derived from skeletal remains, which are not thought to provide a reliable account because of the fragility of infant skeletons and uncertainties about burial practices. After writing skills were developed, burial inscriptions and genealogies offered new sources of information. However, these records are also thought to be unreliable because infants and very young children would not have achieved the social significance that is typical of adults. Therefore, it is less likely that their deaths would be recorded.

It is only with the advent of modern vital statistics in eighteenth- and nineteenth-century Europe that a clear picture emerges about levels of infant and child mortality. For the earlier period, which covers the vast fraction of human evolution, the most that can be said is that infant and child mortality were undoubtedly very high by modern standards. It is likely that 20 percent to 30 percent of newborns died before their first birthday, and 30 percent to 60 percent before their fifth (Acsadi and Nemeskeri 1970).

There are reasons to believe that infant and child mortality rose when people settled in agricultural communities, and remained higher than had been typical in nomadic groups. Settlement in larger and denser communities allowed some bacterial and viral diseases, such as measles and smallpox, to be sustained from year to year by virtue of the larger number of new victims who could be attacked each year and who could pass the disease on to others who had not acquired immunities (Cockburn 1963). This speculation, which has a sound theoretical basis, has been supported by observations of contemporary nomadic groups (Howell 1979) and of low-density populations into which new diseases are introduced (McNeil 1976; Cockburn 1963).

When vital statistics on births and deaths first became available for European populations, they revealed very high levels of infant and child mortality. Sweden, the first country to have complete national data, had an infant mortality rate of 18 percent to 23 percent over the period 1778–1832 and a probability of dying before age five of about 30 percent (Keyfitz and Flieger 1968). Substantial annual fluctuations in these indexes were evident, reflecting both the natural cycle of diseases and epidemics and variations in the adequacy of annual harvests.

As other nations developed their systems of vital registration, Sweden was found to have one of the lowest infant and child mortality levels in Europe, probably owing to its rural character, low density, and mild summers. Southern and Eastern Europe had exceptionally high infant mortality, with European Russia having an infant mortality rate of 27.7 percent as late as 1896–1897. Some of the high infant mortality in Eastern Europe has been traced to its unusually short periods of breast-feeding, undoubtedly the most important health protection that could be offered an infant before the twentieth century.

High infant mortality was not confined to the poorer lands of Eastern and Southern Europe. England, the home of the industrial revolution and by 1900 one of the three richest countries in the world in terms of per capita income, had an infant mortality rate of 16 percent in 1901. Moreover, the rate had improved little since vital statistics became available in 1836. Data on infant mortality by area within England suggested that the most important source of variation was size and density of an area, rather than its economic circumstances (Woods 1985). It seems likely that the fall of infant mortality during the nineteenth century had been impeded by the rapid urbanization of the British population. Sweden, where urbanization was much less advanced, showed a slow and irregular improvement in infant mortality during the nineteenth century.

Previous theories of disease causation stressed the maintenance of balance among bodily "humours" and the importance of foul-smelling atmospheric contaminants as sources of disease.

A new era in infant and child mortality was ushered in around 1880 in most of the now-industrialized world. Rates of improvement were much faster than they had been, and backsliding became infrequent. These countries have now achieved infant mortality rates on the order of 1 percent, with relatively little international variation. Most of the improvement occurred in the period 1880–1930. The most likely cause of the accelerated decline during this period was a revolution in bacteriology. The germ theory of disease was empirically validated in the 1870s and 1880s and led to a much clearer understanding of the nature of most of the diseases that were killing children. Previous theories of disease causation had stressed the maintenance of balance among bodily "humours" and the importance of foul-smelling atmospheric contaminants, derived from such sources as decaying vegetation, slaughter-houses, and sewers, as sources of disease. Before the germ theory, the role of contagious mechanisms was clearly recognized only for such spectacularly episodic diseases as cholera and typhus.

The ascendance of the germ theory was not instantaneous, and it met with resistance in many quarters, including physicians wedded to old practices. But by 1910 it had clearly become the dominant view among public health authorities who were responsible for making environmental improvements that reduced the incidence of disease. Bacterial counts rather than odor became the dominant criterion for water quality, and water supplies were improved in nearly all municipalities. Equally important for child survival were governmentally mandated improvements in the cleanliness of milk supplies, a process that began later and extended into the 1930s. An excellent review of these and other developments in the United States is provided in Ravenel (1921). The fact that infant and child mortality declined much faster in urban than in rural areas, which had much weaker public health programs, is additional evidence of the importance of public intervention in speeding health advances (Davis 1973).

Individual parents concerned with the survival of their children also had new and improved strategies for use in the home. The germ theory stimulated such practices as sterilization of bottles and milk, washing of hands, and isolation of sick family members. Information about the value of these practices was disseminated through many routes by public authorities. In the United States, the Children's Bureau, founded in 1912, was an especially effective agent of change. One of its publications, *Infant Care,* became the largest-selling publication in the history of the U.S. Government Printing Office (Ewbank and Preston 1990).

Physicians and drugs probably played a minor role in the modernization of infant and child mortality, a position supported most forcefully by Thomas McKeown (1976) with reference to England and Wales. Until the advent of sulfa drugs and antibiotics in the late 1930s and 1940s—by which time infant mortality rates had fallen by two-thirds—physicians had few drugs that could arrest the progress of disease. The main progress appears to have been made in the area of prevention rather than cure, and it was the combination of public authorities and parents that proved most effective in this arena. McKeown himself stresses the importance of improvements in the quantity of food available. But this explanation appears seriously inadequate both in England (Szreter 1988) and in the United States (Preston and Haines 1991).

That advances in lowering levels of infant and child mortality did not rely heavily on improved standards of living is also suggested by the experiences of the developing countries of Asia, Africa, and Latin America. The United Nations (1989) estimated that the average infant mortality rate for the developing world was 8.9 percent in 1980–1985, a rate that would have been the envy of England and Wales or the United States in 1900, even though they were already much richer countries than the typical developing country today.

Data on infant and child mortality in developing countries are much less adequate than in the industrialized world. A few nations in Latin America and East Asia have good systems of vital statistics, and India has useful vital data for a representative sample of its population. However, information for most countries is derived from questions asked of women on censuses or surveys about the number of children they have borne and the number of them who have survived.

The data that are available suggest that infant and child mortality during the twentieth century started from a substantially higher level and declined even faster than in developed countries. Data for rural China in the 1920s indicate a probability of dying before age five of about 38 percent, and Chilean data suggest a level of 40 percent in 1920 (Hill 1991). These countries had levels of about 3.9 percent and 2.3 percent, respectively, in the 1980s.

The sources of declining child mortality in developing countries are probably much the same as in developed countries. In particular, public health programs appear to have been successful in many areas. Their most spectacular successes probably pertain to antimalarial programs, where mosquito control could increase survival dramatically in a very short period. Many such programs were deployed in the 1945–1955 period, some under the instigation of international agencies and foundations (Preston 1980). Antibiotics and drug therapy probably played a larger role in the mortality decline in developing countries, in part because little improvement had occurred before their advent. Immunization has also been a potent weapon in the decline in child mortality in developing counties.

Differentials in Infant and Child Mortality

Many studies have examined differences in infant and child mortality among social groups within the same population. These can be summarized by saying that geographic location was a decisive factor in child mortality during the period 1600–1900 and that social location has become the dominant factor during the twentieth century. Before there was a clear understanding of the nature of infectious diseases, they made very heavy inroads among all social groups, rich and poor alike. Richer groups were somewhat better protected than poorer ones, probably because of better nutrition and more spacious housing. But where one lived—especially the population density in one's area—seemed to be a more important factor. Larger cities suffered higher child mortality than small towns, which in turn had higher mortality than rural areas (Weber 1899). These residential differences are manifest in occupational differences as well. In the United States in the 1890s, children of farmers had 15 percent lower child mortality than children of professionals. Size of place was the single most important correlate of child mortality (Preston and Haines 1991).

In the course of the twentieth century, urban-rural differences narrowed to insignificance, while social class differences in child mortality tended to widen. The largest data series pertains to England and Wales, where the Registrar General defines social class in terms of father's occupational group. Pamuk (1988) has shown that social class differences in infant mortality widened in England and Wales between 1921 and 1971, despite the 1947 introduction of the British Health Service, which tended to equalize access to medical care. One may speculate that as environmental conditions improved, especially in cities, individual differences in resources and information acquired greater latitude in influencing child mortality.

In developing countries, existing data series fail to show that cities have had substantially worse child mortality conditions than rural areas. In fact, larger cities at present tend to have lower child mortality than rural areas. It is likely that this reversal of the patterns that were displayed earlier in the developed world is a reflection of the concentration of health services in cities. It also reflects the higher educational attainments of urban residents.

A large United Nations study investigated recent patterns of social and residential differences in child mortality in fifteen developing countries. The variable that emerged as most persistently and strongly related to child mortality was the mother's education (United Nations 1985). Each additional year of schooling for the mother reduced child mortality levels by about 6 percent on average. This influence was much stronger than that pertaining to the father's education or occupation, even though these variables would typically be more closely associated with a household's economic circumstances.

Caldwell (1990) argues that the strength of association between mother's education and child mortality in part reflects the fact that schooling elevates a woman's position in the home. It also exposes her to Western ideas and values and helps to break traditional, sometimes fatalistic, approaches to household management and interpersonal relations. Clelland and van Ginneken (1988) present evidence that in a number of countries better-educated mothers are more likely to use the preventative or curative services offered by modern medicine.

Since death is a biological event, social and economic influences on infant and child mortality must work through intervening biological mechanisms. Probably the most important of these mechanisms in the United States at present is birth weight (Institute of Medicine 1985). Very-low-birth-weight babies are at much higher risk of death, despite technological advances that have sharply improved their survival chances. Many of the other biomedical influences on infant mortality, such as the widely observed U-shaped relationships between infant mortality and age of mother or birth order of child, are primarily reflections of birth-weight differences.

The distribution of birth weights also helps to explain why the United States ranks only fifteenth to twentieth in the world in infant survival. Its set of infant mortality rates *at a particular birth weight* is about the lowest in the world. But it has a substantially higher fraction of births at very low weights. Why birth weights are lower in the United States is not clearly understood but may reflect poorer standards of prenatal care and weaker social support, including marital support, for mothers.

[See also Birth and Death Rates; Health Promotion.]

BIBLIOGRAPHY

Acsadi, G., and J. Nemeskeri 1970 *History of Human Life Span and Mortality.* Budapest: Akad. Kiado.

Caldwell, J. 1990 "Cultural and Social Factors Influencing Mortality Levels in Developing Countries." *Annals of the American Academy of Political and Social Science* 510:44–59.

Clelland, J. G., and J. K. van Ginneken 1988 "Maternal Education and Child Survival in Developing Countries: The Search for Pathways of Influence." *Social Science and Medicine* 27:1357–1368.

Cockburn, A. 1963 *The Evolution and Eradication of Infectious Diseases.* Baltimore: Johns Hopkins University Press.

Davis, K. 1973 "Cities and Mortality." International Union for the Scientific Study of Population. *International Population Conference: Liège, 1973* 3:259–282. Liège: IUSSP.

Ewbank, D., and S. H. Preston 1990 "Personal Health Behavior and the Decline in Infant and Child Mortality: The United States, 1900–30." In J. Caldwell, ed., *What We Know About the Health Transition.* Canberra: Australia National University Press.

Hill, K. 1991 "The Decline of Childhood Mortality." Manuscript, Department of Population Dynamics, The Johns Hopkins University.

Howell, N. 1979 *The Demography of Dobe! Kung.* New York: Academic Press.

Institute of Medicine 1985 *Preventing Low Birthweight.* Washington, D.C.: National Academy of Sciences Press.

Keyfitz, N., and W. Flieger 1968 *World Population: An Analysis of Vital Data.* Chicago: University of Chicago Press.

McKeown, T. 1976 *The Modern Rise of Population.* New York: Academic Press.

McNeil, W. 1976 *Plagues and People.* Garden City, NY: Anchor Press.

Pamuk, E. 1988 "Social Class Inequality in Infant Mortality in England and Wales from 1921 to 1980." *European Journal of Population* 4:1–21.

Preston, S. H. 1980 "Causes and Consequences of Mortality Declines in Less Developed Countries During the Twentieth Century." In R. A. Easterlin, ed., *Population and Economic Change in Developing Countries.* Conference Report 30, Universities-National Bureau Committee for Economic Research. Chicago: University of Chicago Press.

———, and M. Haines 1991 *Fatal Years: Child Mortality in Late Nineteenth Century America.* Princeton, NJ.: Princeton University Press.

Ravenel, M. P. (ed.) 1921 *A Half Century of Public Health.* New York: American Public Health Association.

Szreter, S. 1988 "The Importance of Social Intervention in Britain's Mortality Decline c. 1850–1914: A Reinterpretation of the Role of Public Health." *Social History of Medicine* 1:1–37.

United Nations 1985 *Socioeconomic Differentials in Child Mortality in Developing Countries.* New York: United Nations.

——— 1989 *World Population Prospects, 1988.* New York: United Nations.

Weber, Adna F. 1899 *The Growth of Cities in the 19th Century: A Study in Statistics.* New York: Macmillan.

Woods, R. 1985 "The Effects of Population Redistribution on the Level of Mortality in Nineteenth-Century England and Wales." *Journal of Economic History* 45 (3):645–651.

– SAMUEL H. PRESTON

INFORMATION SOCIETY

The increased reliance on activities directly associated with the production, distribution, and utilization of information has led to the characterization of many of the advanced countries of the world as information societies. The term *information society* and similar concepts such as information age and knowledge economy describe a society in which there is great dependence on use of information technologies to produce all manners of goods and services. In contrast to the industrial society, which relied on internal combustion engines to augment the physical labor of humans, the information society relies on computer technologies to augment their mental labor.

Trends in labor force composition both define and measure the extent to which a nation can be described as an information society. Machlup (1962) was perhaps the first to describe U.S. society in these terms. He estimated in 1958 that nearly one-third of the labor force worked in information industries such as communications, computers, education, and information services, and accounted for 29 percent of the gross national product (GNP). Using a slightly different methodology, Porat (1977) estimated that information activities had risen to just under half of the U.S. GNP by 1967.

Advances in the capabilities of information technologies to process large quantities of information quickly have been a crucial factor in the development of the information society. These technologies are of two types, computing power and transmission capability (Mayo 1985). Development of inexpensive silicon integrated circuits containing as many as a million transistors on a single chip by the mid-1980s made it possible to pack tremendous information processing power into very little space. Desktop microcomputers now have processing power comparable to the largest mainframe computers of the previous decade. Corresponding breakthroughs have occurred in photonics as a result of the development of laser technology and ultrapure glass fiber. The result of these developments is the ability to transmit enormous quantities of information long distances on tiny optic fibers without amplification. Efforts to connect much of the world with fiber optics are now proceeding at a very rapid pace. The practical effect of these and related advancements such as facsimile and satellite transmission technologies will be to make computers even more commonplace and easy to use, and to make communications among them equally commonplace and inexpensive. Thus, the information society must now be considered in the early stages of its existence.

James Beniger (1986) views the information society as long in its development as a result of a crisis of control evoked by the industrial revolution in the late 1800s. Industrialization speeded up material processing systems. However, innovations in information processing and communications lagged behind innovations in the use of energy to increase productivity of manufacturing and transportation systems. Development of the telegraph, telephone, radio, television, modern printing presses, and postal delivery systems all represented innovations important to the resolution of the control crisis, which required replacement of the traditional bureaucratic means of control that had been depended on for centuries before.

An entirely new stage in the development of the information society has been realized through recent advances in microprocessing technology, and the convergence of mass media telecommunications and computers into a single infrastructure of societal control (Beniger 1986). An important factor in this convergence is digitalization of all information so the distinctions between types of information such as words, numbers, and pictures become blurred and communications between persons and machines become impossible. Therefore, it is concluded by Beniger that digitalization allows the transformation of information into a generalized medium for processing and exchange by the social system, much as common currency and exchange rates, centuries ago, did the same for the economic systems of the world (1986).

An important attribute of the information society is the search for improvements in productivity primarily through the substitution of information for energy, labor, and physical materials. In practical terms, this means such things as supplying workers with computerized workstations that are networked to other workstations, utilizing computer software to retool equipment in distant locations, and sending facsimile or computer transmissions, which eliminates physical delivery of messages; these improvements make organizational production, distribution, and management decisions more efficient. One indicator of the extent to which industries in a developing information society seek productivity improvements through the use of information equipment is that in 1984 40 percent of all U.S. investment in durable equipment was spent on the purchase of computers and communication equipment, up from only 10 percent in 1960 (U.S. Congress 1988). The use and impact of these technologies are pervasive, influencing nearly all institutions, from those in education to those in the political realm (Weinberg 1990).

An important attribute of the information society is the search for improvements in productivity through the substitution of information for energy, labor, and physical materials.

The implications of living in a fully developed information society are many (Dillman 1985). Chief among them is the breaking down of geographic barriers, whereby businesses are more connected to other businesses and consumers in other countries than they are to those in their own nation, thus providing a basis for the development of the global economy. Information technologies provide the potential for overcoming remoteness. They may also result in a dramatic modification of the relationship between worker and workplace, as technologies facilitate telecommuting from one's home as a means of dealing both with urban congestion and rural isolation. Such technologies also provide a basis for forming new groups and maintaining group identities that geographic separation heretofore made impossible. The emergence of global networks of information also puts pressure on all societies to conform to emergent international norms of openness and accountability (Weinberg 1990).

The information society differs significantly from the mass society with which it is sometimes contrasted (Dillman 1985). Whereas the latter emphasizes one-way communication, large-scale mass production of products and ideas, and the creation of uniformity, the information society emphasizes two-way communication, batch or even single-unit production, and development of a pluralism of interests. The information society can be considered an extension of the postindustrial society concept described by Daniel Bell (1973), with more recognition being given to the role of information technologies as the major driving force in transforming societal organization.

Quite different views exist about the possible effects of the development of a full-fledged information society. One view is that it will empower workers, providing direct access to opportunities unavailable to them in an industrial society except by high organizational position and proximity to centralized positions of power. For example, Harlan Cleveland (1985) describes information as being fundamentally different than the resources for which it is being substituted, for example, not being used up by one who consumes it and hence making its use possible by others. It is also easily transportable from one point to another. Cleveland projects that the information society will force dramatic changes in long-standing hierarchic forms of social organization, terminating many existing taken-for-granted hierarchies based on control, secrecy, ownership, early access, and geography. A similar view is provided by Masuda (1985), writing in a Japanese context, who envisions the development of participatory democracies, the eradication of educational gaps between urban and rural areas, and the elimination of a centralized class-based society.

A more pessimistic view of the consequences of knowledge becoming the key source of productivity is offered by Castells (1989). Fundamentally, the new information infrastructure that connects virtually all points of the globe to all others allows for great flexibility in all aspects of production consumption, distribution, and management. To take advantage of the efficiencies offered by full utilization of information technologies, organizations plan their operations around the dynamics of their information-generating units, and not around a limited geographic space. Individual nations lose the ability to control corporations. Information technologies, therefore, become instrumental in the implementation of fundamental processes of capitalist restructuring. Efforts are made to increase the rate of profits by substituting machines for workers, and the decentralization of production threatens the position of labor unions. In contrast to the view offered by Cleveland, the stateless nature of the corporation is seen as contributing to an international hierarchical functional structure in which the historic division between intellectual and manual labor is taken to an extreme. The consequences for social organization are to dissolve localities as functioning social systems and to supersede societies.

There is little doubt that the development of a full-fledged information society can produce dramatic changes in existing social structures and relationships. However, it remains to be seen whether the nature of those impacts will be primarily determined by the structural requirements of the new technologies as they seek to fulfill their development potential, or whether their impact will be primarily influenced by necessary adaptation to other forces of social change.

[See also Mass Media Research.]

BIBLIOGRAPHY

Bell, Daniel 1973 *The Coming of Post-Industrial Society: A Venture in Social Forecasting.* New York: Basic Books.

Beniger, James R. 1986 *The Control Revolution: Technological and Economic Origins of the Information Society.* Cambridge, Mass.: Harvard University Press.

Castells, Manuel 1989 *The Informational City.* Cambridge: Basil Blackwell.

Cleveland, Harlan 1985 "The Twilight of Hierarchy: Speculations on the Global Information Society." *Public Administration Review* 45:185–196.

Dillman, Don A. 1985 "The Social Impacts of Information Technologies in Rural North America." *Rural Sociology* 50:1–26.

Machlup, Fritz 1962 *The Production and Distribution of Knowledge in the United States.* Princeton, N.J.: Princeton University Press.

Masuda, Yoneji 1981 *The Information Society as Post-Industrial Society.* Tokyo: Institute for the Information Society; Bethesda, Md.: World Future Society.

Mayo, John S. 1985 "The Evolution of Information Technologies." In Bruce R. Guile, ed., *Information Technologies and Social Transformation.* Washington, D.C.: National Academy of Engineering, National Academy Press.

Porat, M. U., et al. 1977 *The Information Economy.* OT Special Publication 77-12. Washington, D.C.: U.S. Department of Commerce.

U.S. Congress, Office of Technology Assessment 1988 *Technology and the American Transition: Choices for the Future.* OTA-TET-2A3. Washington, D.C.: U.S. Government Printing Office.

Weinberg, Nathan 1990 *Computers in the Information Society.* Boulder, Colo.: Westview Press.

– DON A. DILLMAN

INTELLIGENCE

Intelligence is a hypothetical concept, or latent variable, on which individuals differ or vary from each other. The concept of intelligence is not itself directly observable or measurable. Intelligence, an abstract continuum, is distinct from its nonabstract presumed indicators or measures; "intelligence" (concept) is distinct from "intelligence test" (indicator). The accuracy of the indicator—that is, its validity and reliability—is a matter of how accurately it measures observable phenomena presumed to reflect differing amounts of intelligence. The IQ or "intelligence quotient" is thus an operational, observable, presumed indicator of the concept, intelligence, and not the concept itself.

Various definitions of intelligence have appeared since the idea of a unitary coordinating "mental" faculty was used by the ancient Greek philosophers. The principal formulation of the modern notion of intelligence as some kind of mental capacity began in 1850 with Herbert Spencer and Sir Francis Galton. Since then, definitions of intelligence have varied but generally involve a notion of "potential," "ability," or "capacity" as distinct from actual achievement, attainment, or accomplishment. It is a cognitive disposition as distinct from an affect or emotion. Researchers have defined intelligence as "the ability to carry on abstract thinking" (Terman 1916, inventor in 1916 of the still popular Stanford-Binet IQ test); "innate general cognitive ability" (Burt 1972); and "the ability to adapt to the environment" (Thorndike 1905). Some have distinguished two kinds or "dimensions" of intelligence: certain given characteristics of the individual's nervous system (called "fluid" intelligence by R. B. Cattell) versus intelligence acquired through learning, experience, education, and social environment (called "crystallized" intelligence by Cattell).

The development of psychological testing for intelligence began in the early 1900s with A. Binet in France, who invented the notion of IQ as the ratio (quotient) of mental age to chronological age; J. M. Cattell in the United States; and C. Spearman and C. L. Burt in England. This inaugurated the continuing controversy of whether intelligence is reducible to some common set of highly correlated abilities or capacities (the unidimensional theory) or whether it is a matter of several, or many, relatively uncorrelated or independent (nonoverlapping) abilities or capacities (the multidimensional theory).

Measurement

Measurement accuracy—or, conversely, measurement error—is the degree to which presumed indicators of intelligence (intelligence tests such as the Stanford-Binet or the Wechsler Adult Intelligence Scales [WAIS], or the "ability" portion, as distinct from the achievement sections, of the popular Scholastic Aptitude Test [SAT]) accurately reflect or measure the extent to which an individual possesses intellectual ability. The degree of measurement accuracy is called the validity and reliability of the indicator(s). Validity is the degree to which the score on an indicator reflects the unknown, unobserved score on the concept "intelligence." Reliability refers to the stability or consistency of an indicator across, for example, different times (test-retest reliability), different forms or wordings of the same test (equivalent forms reliability), or different researchers. Hence, measurement accuracy (and its complement, measurement error) is the relationship or "epistemic" correlation between indicator and concept. Since the true score on the concept is not directly observable or measurable, validity is assessed indirectly, as by observing the relationships among several presumed indicators themselves.

A closely allied issue of measurement is whether the concept intelligence is unidimensional or multidimensional. In 1904 Spearman maintained that there was a statistical dimension or factor (called simply *g*) for "general intelligence," and that this factor accounted for, and correlated very highly with, specific separate abilities or performances on tests. This view—that intelligence is fundamentally reducible to one basic, though general, master capacity—is still somewhat popular today. This would mean that persons who score high on one type of ability (say, mathematics) would tend to score high on certain other abilities as well (such as reading comprehension, vocabulary, verbal analogies, and so on); and that persons who score low on one ability would also tend to score low on others. In fact, modern-day factor analysis, a set of techniques for assessing the extent to which many indicators may be parsimoniously accounted for by their relationship to (correlations with) a fewer number of variables called factors, began with Spearman's analyses.

This unidimensional formulation was challenged by L. L. Thurstone's multidimensional principle, which argued that intelligence consists of six or seven largely uncorrelated or nonoverlapping skills or capacities, called "primary abilities," such as spatial, quantitative, verbal, and inductive. Today, the multidimensional view of intelligence predominates over the strict unidimensional view, and it is argued that intelligence probably reflects both some unidimensionality as well as quite a bit of multidimensionality.

Is creativity a separate trait itself or does it bear some relationship or overlap to general intelligence?

From 1960 to about 1975, important contributions to the multidimensional view were made by J. P. Guilford, who theorized that intelligence was so multidimensional that it could be broken down into as many as 120 specific abilities. A number of these abilities encompass what has come to be called creative intelligence. While the unidimensional view stressed individual abilities at inductive and also deductive reasoning, creative intelligence stresses "divergent" reasoning, or the ability to draw new and unanticipated conclusions or inferences. Debates in the professional literature now center on the question of whether creativity is a separate trait itself or whether it bears some relationship or overlap to unidimensional general intelligence. Some studies have shown significant correlation or overlap between general intelligence and creativity; others have shown little or no overlap and have concluded that the two are quite independent. It has been noted, however, that while measures of general intelligence correlate moderately to strongly with creativity for individuals in the low to normal ranges on both, the two types of abilities differ markedly and are virtually independent at the extreme upper ranges, namely among uniquely gifted individuals. Finally, a recent multidimensional formulation is that of H. Gardner, who posits seven independent abilities: logical–mathematical, linguistic, spatial, musical, interpersonal, intrapersonal, and body-kinesthetic.

Reliability of measures of intelligence has been assessed mainly by examining how stable one's intelligence scores for different types of abilities remain as a function of increasing age. Most studies show moderate to high correlations (of about 0.70) between IQ at age five and IQ during the late teenage years. The famous and long-term (forty-year) "studies of genius" by Terman, carried out on a large sample (1,528 persons initially) from the mid-1920s through the mid-1960s, demonstrated that high-IQ individuals consistently remain high in IQ from childhood right on through the retirement years. Other studies show only slightly less stability over such long periods of time for individuals who are in the normal (90–110) IQ range. Finally, studies of problem-solving ability show that it tends to decline relatively little before old age but that the speed of solving unfamiliar problems tends to decline with age.

Attempts to alter or increase IQ by means of specific coaching or environment-manipulation programs have met with some limited success. In general, such attempts to increase IQ are more successful for individuals in the normal ranges of IQ than for individuals who score either very high or very low in IQ. Programs geared to specific abilities (as increasing math skills) are more likely to result in an increase in that particular ability rather than in other abilities not addressed by the program. Recent evidence shows that such attempts to increase IQ among black and Hispanic youths can result in gains of up to 20 IQ points and that such gains do persist at least for several years. Finally, studies of the effect of coaching to increase SAT scores show that after removing the effect of test experience—that is, subtracting out the average difference between first and subsequent test scores for matched control, individuals who have not had an intervening coaching seminar—(most people score higher the second time they take the SAT than on their first attempt), some increase in SAT scores results, depending on the length and type of coaching program. There is no evidence that coaching has differing effects on males versus females, or upon white, black, or Asian groups.

Validity of measures of intelligence has been most often assessed through what is called predictive, or criterion, validation—finding the degree of relationship (size and direction of correlation and of slope) between some measure of intelligence, taken at one point in time, and some other "criterion" measure taken later, such as grades obtained later on in college or the type of occupation chosen after graduation. The higher the correlation or slope or both between test score and criterion, the higher the predictive validity of the test.

In general, studies show that predictive validity is better at the extremes (for those scoring either very high or very low on the test) than for individuals within the normal range. Oden's forty-year follow-up analysis of the Terman gifted group showed that individuals scoring 140 or higher on the Stanford-Binet IQ test when they were in their teens were 40 years later disproportionately more likely to have graduated from college (71 percent of the males and 67 percent of the females in the sample had graduated from college, with 40 percent and 24 percent respectively having gotten advanced graduate or professional degrees). Similarly, high proportions of both men (47 percent) and women (64 percent) became professionals. These predictions were not perfect, however. A small percentage of individuals dropped out of high school or college; some were unsuccessful at their chosen profession or remained unemployed; and a few committed suicide. These numbers were small. The entire sample was white, largely of middle class origins, and from urban California. Thus, no conclusions can be drawn regarding race, socioeconomic, or regional differences.

Group and Cultural Differences

Predictive validity has been assessed in many studies for different racial and ethnic groups (white, black, Hispanic, Asian). It is generally found that whites tend to score *on the average* about one standard deviation higher than blacks and Hispanics on IQ tests (about 15 IQ points higher) and on ability tests such as the SAT (about 50 to 100 SAT points higher, on a scale of 200 to 800). Since the 1980s, Asians have scored on the average slightly higher than or the same as whites on the quantitative portions of such tests, and either the same as or somewhat lower than whites on the verbal portions.

These average differences are regarded as being environmental in origin, reflecting group differences in education, socioeconomic status, childhood socialization, language, nutrition, and cultural advantages. There is no evidence whatever that such *between-group* differences are in any way genetic in origin. (*Within-group* differences in IQ that may be genetic in origin are discussed below under "Nature versus Nurture.")

Average differences in test scores reflect not only differences in social environment, but they may reflect lack of equivalence between groups in the predictive validities of the test. A test may be more predictively valid for one group than for another; namely, a test may have less measurement error for one group than for another. This is determined by assessing the relationship between the test score (X) at one point in time and some criterion measure (Y) such as college grades at a later point in time for the two groups being compared. Equivalent slopes and correlations for two groups would be interpreted as equal predictive validity for the two groups. Higher correlation or slope means higher predictive validity; lower correlation or slope means lower predictive validity. Different slopes or correlations for two groups would be evidence that the test (X) is not as valid for one group as for the other and that the test does not predict as well for one group as for the other.

A large number of studies show roughly equivalent test-to-grade predictions for whites and blacks. Such studies show that test scores and grades are moderately correlated for whites, correlating in some studies as low as 0.15 and in other studies up to about 0.60, with an average correlation of about 0.35, and with the correlations for blacks falling in the same range. This evidence suggests that one can, to a modest extent, predict later grades (such as first-year college grades) from ability test scores (SAT scores) and that these predictions are roughly the same for whites and blacks.

However, a significant number of studies (about one-fourth of those done) show some differences in either slope or correlation or both for whites compared to blacks and Hispanics, with the slopes and correlations being greater for whites, with blacks and Hispanics being roughly the same. This means that, at least for these studies, the test is less predictively valid for blacks and Hispanics than for whites. This is evidence for relatively more measurement error (thus measurement bias) in the case of blacks and Hispanics. Considerably less data are available on Asians; some studies show equal predictive validities, a few show less, and very few show slightly higher predictive validities for some Asian groups.

Apart from the question of validity, average differences in the test score itself exist on the basis of race and ethnicity, of socioeconomic status (social class and the linguistic and cultural differences associated with class differences), and of gender.

In almost every multiracial nation in the world, race differences are strongly confounded with social class differences. Thus, it is difficult to separate the effects of race on IQ from the effects of social class. In studies of race differences in intelligence in countries where white culture is the dominant culture, as in the United States, it has been consistently found that groups classified as Negro, black, or colored are disproportionately represented among the lower classes, and they also score lower on intelligence tests than those classified as white. These are *average* differences, as the distributions of scores for the two groups overlap considerably. In most cases, individuals were tested by white examiners, and there is evidence that one performs somewhat better on a test when examiner and examinee are of the same race.

There is some evidence that gender bias in certain test questions is present and may account for a portion of the gender difference in test scores.

In the United States, studies over the years have consistently found that Northern blacks, on average, score higher on IQ tests than Southern blacks. In some cases Northern blacks have scored higher, on average, than Southern whites. These differences reflect the differences in both socioeconomic status as well as region. Comparing whites and blacks of the same socioeconomic status and the same region lessens their average differences in IQ scores considerably. The differences between blacks and whites are further reduced when linguistic and cultural biases are removed from the tests. Similar findings are obtained in comparisons of whites and Hispanics. With regard to the relative effects of race versus class, in studies in which children of different races have been matched by socioeconomic status of their families (by parental occupation, education, income, and neighborhood), social class shows a stronger relative effect than race. Thus, average differences in IQ by class for individuals of the same race exceed average differences by race for individuals of the same social class.

Gender differences in intelligence, like race differences, are confounded by the differences in social status that men and women occupy in society. In all known societies, gender is correlated with social status; in the vast majority of societies and particularly the United States, women have been traditionally forced to occupy lower average social and economic status than men. Hence, like the minority-to-white comparison, the female-to-male comparison reveals some differences in IQ, with females scoring less on abilities defined as valuable (such as quantitative ability) by society. It used to be thought that the variability in IQ scores is greater among men than among women, with proportionately more men than women in both the gifted as well as the severely retarded range. More recent studies have shown this not to be the case and that with adequate sampling designs (absent in many past studies) the extremes of the distribution are equal for males and for females, as are the middle ranges. While recent studies show average IQ scores to be roughly equal for males and females, differences do arise on specific abilities: Men score higher, on average, in numerical reasoning, gross motor skills, spatial perception, and mechanical aptitude; women score higher, on average, in perception of detail, verbal facility, and memory. These average differences may reflect differences between the sexes in childhood socialization and differences in societal expectations or norms pertaining to men and women. Finally, there is some limited evidence that sex-typing (gender bias) in certain test questions, even in the quantitative sections, is present and thus may account for a portion of the gender difference.

Nature Versus Nurture

Since the mid-nineteenth century a controversy has raged in the social, behavioral, and natural sciences: Are human differences in intelligence influenced more by biological heredity (nature), by social environment (nurture), or primarily by combinations (interactions) of both? The contemporary approach to the issue has been to attempt to estimate empirically what is called the broad heritability coefficent (h^2), defined as the proportion of the total differences (total variance) in intelligence in a population that is causally attributable to genetic factors. Equivalently, it is the proportion of variance in intelligence that is accounted for by the genetic similarity between pairs of biological relatives. Consequently, if heritability in a population is 30 percent, then statistically speaking 30 percent of the differences in intelligence among individuals in that population are due to genetic factors, assuming that intelligence is validly and reliably measured. A 30 percent heritability would mean that 70 percent of the differences in intelligence in the population would be due to environment or to combinations or interactions, or to the covariance, of genes and environment.

The environment includes a large range of variables such as education, social class, cultural advantages or disadvantages, childhood socialization, nutrition, and many others. The heritability coefficient is not a characteristic of a single individual but of a specific population being studied at the time. Virtually all heritability estimates to date are based on white populations. The heritability estimate is not generalizable from one population to another; thus, for example, heritability estimates on whites cannot be generalized to blacks or any other racial or ethnic group. Nor can the heritability coefficient be used to draw conclusions about between-group average differences. Heritability has been variously estimated to be as low as 20 percent and as high as 80 percent, depending on the methodological accuracy of the study, the statistical assumptions used, types of biological relatives studied, and a host of other things. Some argue convincingly that heritability is impossible to estimate in any reliable way. The most recent reliable studies tend to center on a heritability of 40 to 50 percent.

How then is the heritability of intelligence actually calculated or estimated? One must first assume that IQ score validly measures intelligence, a conclusion that, as already noted, is subject to controversy. Assuming that IQ score measures at least some aspects of intelligence validly, then heritability is estimated by comparing pairs of individuals of varying degrees of biological relatedness: If any pair of individuals who are biologically related to each other are also similar in IQ, and if individuals who are more highly related biologically are also more similar in IQ, then, assuming equal environmental similarities for the different types of pairs, genes are hypothesized to be a cause of their IQ similarity.

Identical (monozygotic) twins are genetically identical to each other; they are genetic clones of one another. It is noted that identical twins raised together in the same family are very similar in IQ and in other traits suspected of high genetic causation, such as height. Their average IQ pair correlation is about 0.90, which is very high. This correlation reflects both their genetic similarity and their environmental similarity, since they were raised together. Pairs of fraternal (dizygotic) twins are less related biologically and, like ordinary brothers and sisters, share on the average half of their genes in common. Their similarity in IQ is about 0.60 in correlation. Ordinary siblings (brothers and sisters) correlate about 0.50 in their IQs, thus showing the effects of their lower environmental similarity in relation to the fraternal twin pairs. Pairs of first cousins are even less in biological overlap, and they correlate still less in IQ, at about 0.15. Finally, pairs of unrelated individuals picked at random do not correlate at all in IQ (the pair correlation is zero). In general, then, the closer the biological overlap of pairs of persons, the more similar they are in IQ, thus suggesting that genetic similarity is at least partly responsible for the similarity in IQ.

Such comparisons, however, do not rule out the effect of environment. Identical twin pairs raised together have very similar environments in addition to their identical genes; thus, environmental similarity could also be a cause of their similarity in IQ. By similar reasoning, fraternal twins are less similar to each other genetically, but also less similar environmentally, than are identical twin pairs. For example, it has been shown that fraternal twin pairs are less likely to play together, study together, and are treated less similarly by parents and teachers, than are identical twin pairs. Hence, the lower environmental similarity could be a cause of their lower similarity in IQ. Consequently, the effects of both genetic similarity and environmental similarity are confounded and entangled in such comparisons.

There have been four procedures used to attempt to disentangle the effects of environmental similarity from the effects of genetic similarity for pairs of relatives. The first of these is widely regarded as the best single-kinship procedure for estimating heritability: the study of identical twins who have been raised separately. In such instances, if the twins were separated virtually at birth (because of the death of a parent or other family problems) and raised in randomly differing environments and scattered over a wide range of environments, then any remaining similarity in their IQs would be caused genetically, since all they have in common would be their genes (and since the effects of prenatal environment are assumed to be slight). Also, with these givens, the magnitude of the resulting IQ correlation is a direct estimate of the magnitude of the heritability of IQ.

Given the extreme rarity of separated identical twins, there have been only four studies to date of pairs of separated identical twins (Newman, Freeman, and Holzinger 1937; Bouchard et al. 1990; Shields 1962; Juel-Nielsen 1965; a fifth study, Burt 1957, 1972 has been thoroughly discredited as having fabricated and falsified data on twins). These studies find the IQ similarity (correlation) of separated twins to be between 0.62 and 0.77. This would suggest strong genetic causation for the IQ similarity.

Methodological critics, however, discovered that quite a few of the twin pairs in three out of these four studies were not actually raised separately but were instead raised in different branches of the same family, or were separated not at birth but later during the teenage years, or were raised in social environments that were very similar in many respects. In quite a few cases the twins had actually attended the same schools for the same number of years before being tested for IQ. When the truly separated twins are singled out for analysis, their pair correlation, and thus the heritability estimate, falls to 0.30 or 0.40.

The second procedure for estimating IQ heritability, less methodologically pure than studying separated identical twins, is to compare the IQ correlation of identical twins raised together to that for fraternal twins raised together. When this is done, heritability estimates in the range of 0.50 to 0.60 are obtained. For this procedure to be valid, one must assume that identical twins raised together are no more similar in their environments than are fraternal twins raised together, a questionable assumption.

A third procedure is the converse of the first: the study of unrelated pairs of individuals adopted into the same family. Whereas identical twins raised separately provide pairs with perfect genetic similarity and dissimilar environments, the study of adopted unrelated pairs raised together provides us with the study of high similarity in family environment but zero genetic similarity. Hence, any IQ similarity for such pairs is entirely due to environment (and only family environment, not nonfamily environment). Such studies estimate environmental effects to be around 0.30, and thus heritability would be no more than 0.70.

A fourth procedure, the most up to date, called the multikin method, in effect averages the results for many kinships together. The procedure solves algebraically for the value of the heritability coefficient by utilizing an overidentified least-squares solution system for several simultaneous equations, where one equation is stated for each type of kinship (relative) such as identical twins raised together; identical twins apart; fraternal twins together; siblings together; parent-offspring pairs; cousins raised together; pairs of adopted children; and parent-adopted pairs. In such analyses, a number of (often implausible) assumptions must be made, such as zero measurement error, no sample bias, equal (or estimated) environmental similarity, no gene-by-environment interaction, and others. One such analysis found that the best-fitting set of equations yielded a heritability estimate of 0.51. Similar multikin analyses that include a direct estimate of environmental similarity for certain pairs of relatives yield somewhat lower heritability estimates, at about 0.40.

Considering all four methodologies, and granting for the moment all the necessary statistical assumptions (many of which are implausible), a tentative estimate of (broad) heritability of intelligence for Western white populations would be between 0.40 and 0.50, or 40 to 50 percent.

Conclusion

How is the study and measurement of intelligence important to sociology and the social sciences? What are the uses of intelligence measurement?

First, the study of intelligence involves a large number of disciplines and fields. For example, the relative effects of nature (genes) and nurture (social environment), and their interaction upon intelligence, is multidisciplinary and is analyzed and debated in the professional literature in biology (particularly population genetics), sociology, psychology, economics, and education.

Second, the history of the measurement of intelligence has been very closely tied to the development of empirical measurement in general in the social and behavioral sciences, and certainly in sociology. Developments in measurement theory, the distinction between concepts and indicators, and the development of techniques to assess validity and reliability of indicators—including recent work in multi-indicator models—has grown partly, though significantly, out of the study of the measurement of intelligence.

Third, among all the subspecialties in the discipline of sociology, the Sociology of Education has probably employed the concept and measurement of intelligence most productively. Intelligence has been used in at least three ways: (1) as an effect (as, when considering the relative effects of nature versus the effects of early home environment, schooling, and other environmental variables); (2) as a cause (a considerable amount of research in the sociology of education has evaluated the effects, or lack thereof, of measured intelligence upon performance in school, upon occupational achievement and earnings in later life, and also upon such phenomena as criminality); (3) as a control variable whose relative effects are analyzed in combination with other variables. For example, an important body of literature in status attainment has shown that when the effects of schooling, intelligence, and home environment upon later occupational achievement are analyzed, then the effects of schooling may be less than the combined effects of intelligence and home environment. Similarly, there are studies that show that the effects of teacher expectations upon student performance in the classroom are present in addition to (but not in place of) the effects of measured intelligence upon performance in the classroom.

[See also Sex Differences; Socialization.]

BIBLIOGRAPHY

Bouchard, T. J., Jr., and M. McGue 1981 "Familial Studies of Intelligence: A Review." *Science* 212:1055–1058.

———, et al 1990. "Sources of Human Psychological Differences: The Minnesota Study of Twins Reared Apart." *Science* 250:223–228.

Burt, C. 1957 "The Relative Influence of Heredity and Environment on Assessments of Intelligence." *British Journal of Statistical Psychology* 10:99–104.

——— 1972 "Inheritance of General Intelligence." *American Psychologist* 27:175–190.

Chipmer, H. M., M. J. Rovine, and R. Plomin 1990 "LISREL Modeling: Genetic and Environmental Influences on IQ Revisited." *Intelligence* 14:11–29.

Dorfman, D. D. 1978 "The Cyril Burt Question: New Findings." *Science* 201:1177–1186.

Goldberger, A. S. 1978a "Heritability." Social Systems Research Institute, University of Wisconsin, Madison. Typescript. (Revised version of paper presented at Newmarch Lectures in Economic Statistics at University College London, June 6 and 7, 1978.)

——— 1978b "Pitfalls in the Resolution of IQ Inheritance." In N. E. Morton and C. S. Chung, eds., *Genetic Epidemiology.* New York: Academic Press.

Guilford, J. P. 1968 "The Structure of Intelligence." In D. K. Whitla, ed., *Handbook of Measurement and Assessment in the Behavioral Sciences.* Boston: Addison-Wesley.

Hearnshaw, L. S. 1979 *Cyril Burt, Psychologist.* Ithaca, N.Y.: Cornell University Press.

Jencks, C., et al. 1972 *Inequality: A Reassessment of the Effect of Family and Schooling in America.* New York: Basic Books.

Jensen, A. R. 1967 "Estimation of the Limits of Heritability Traits by Comparison of Monozygotic and Dizygotic Twins." *Proceedings of the National Academy of Sciences* 58:149–156.

——— 1969 "How Much Can We Boost IQ and Scholastic Achievement?" *Harvard Educational Review* 39:1–123.

——— 1980 *Bias in Mental Testing.* New York: Free Press.

Juel-Nielsen, N. 1965 "Individual and Environment: A Psychiatric-Psychological Investigation of Monozygous Twins Reared Apart." *Acta Psychiatrica et Neurologica Scandinavica,* Monograph supp. 183.

Kamin, L. J. 1974 *The Science and Politics of IQ.* Potomac, Md.: Lawrence Erlbaum Associates.

Morton, N. E., and C. S. Chung (eds.) 1978 *Genetic Epidemiology.* New York: Academic Press.

———, and D. C. Rao 1978 "Quantitative Inheritance in Man." *Yearbook of Physical Anthropology* 21:12–41.

Newman, H. H., F. N. Freeman, and K. J. Holzinger 1937 *Twins: A Study of Heredity and Environment.* Chicago: University of Chicago Press.

Oden, M. H. 1968 "The Fulfillment of Promise: 40-year Follow-up of the Terman Gifted Group." *Genetic Psychology Monographs* 77:3–93.

Plomin, R., J. C. DeFries, and J. C. Loehlin 1977 "Genotype–Environment Interaction and Correlation in the Analysis of Human Behavior." *Psychological Bulletin* 84:309–322.

Shields, J. 1962 *Monozygotic Twins Brought Up Apart and Brought Up Together.* London: Oxford University Press.

Taylor, H. F. 1980 *The IQ Game: A Methodological Inquiry into the Heredity-Environment Controversy,* New Brunswick, N.J.: Rutgers University Press.

——— 1981 "Biases in *Bias in Mental Testing.*" *Contemporary Sociology* 10:172–174.

——— 1992 "Group Differences and the Methodology of Standardized Testing." In J. H. Stanfield, ed., *Methods in Race and Ethnic Relations Research.* Beverly Hills, Calif.: Sage.

Terman, L. M. 1916 *The Measurement of Intelligence.* Boston: Houghton Mifflin.

Thorndike, E. L. 1905 "Measurement of Twins." *Journal of Philosophy, Psychology, and Scientific Method* 2:547–553.

– HOWARD F. TAYLOR

INTERGENERATIONAL RELATIONS

Throughout recorded history, much concern has been expressed about relations among the generations. Historians have identified changing patterns of relationships between the old and the young, pointing out that in some epochs veneration of the aged was common, while in other eras, the aged were more likely to be held up to scorn and ridicule. In contemporary American society, these contrasts are more muted, and themes of both consensus and conflict are present.

Sociologists have explored intergenerational relations extensively, using both macrosociological and microsociological approaches. Scholars who have taken a macrosociological approach have examined the discontinuity caused by the succession of different groups of individuals who were born during the same time period and who therefore age together (Foner 1986). Sociologists refer to such groups as *cohorts.* Many important questions have been raised regarding relations among cohorts, including: How do people differ as a result of membership in a specific cohort? How and why do cohorts come into conflict with one another? Does a "generation gap" exist?

Merely by belonging to a given generation, people will show certain similarities, as they are endowed with "a common location in the historical process."

In contrast, sociologists who have taken a microsociological approach have focused on intergenerational relations within families. These scholars have examined the content and quality of relationships among family members in different generations, posing such questions as: How much contact do adult children have with their parents? What kinds of exchanges occur between older and younger generations? What is the role of grandparents in families? Under what circumstances does conflict among the generations in families occur? It is essential to study both levels and to draw connections between them.

Macrosociological Perspectives

MANNHEIM'S VIEW OF GENERATIONS. Karl Mannheim provided one of the most enduring analyses of relations between cohorts (Mannheim, however, used the term *generation* instead of the contemporary sociological term *cohort,* used here). Mannheim argued that the individuals born into a given cohort experience the same set of sociopolitical events that occur while they are growing up; this sets them off as a special social group. Merely by their location in a given cohort, members will show certain similarities, as they are endowed with "a common location in the historical process" (Mannheim 1952, p. 290).

Thus, position within a cohort—like position within the socioeconomic structure—limits members to a narrow range of possible experiences and predisposes them to characteristic modes of thought. These differences can lead to conflict between the cohorts, as younger cohorts try to impose their views on society. The older cohort, on the other hand, has a major stake in preserving the existing social order. The interaction between these divergent cohort groups, according to Mannheim, is a critically important aspect of human social life.

To be sure, Mannheim did not compare belonging to a cohort with belonging to a more concrete group—such as a family—in that a cohort lacks a clear organizational framework. Further, he noted that there can be differences within cohorts. That is, within the same cohort, subgroups (in Mannheim's terms, *generational units*) can form, and these subgroups differ from each other and may even be antagonistic toward one another. Nevertheless, Mannheim viewed location in a cohort as a powerful influence on people's lives, analogous to class position. This concern with the continual succession of cohorts, and with its effects on social life, has found its clearest contemporary expression in age stratification theory.

AGE STRATIFICATION THEORY. Age stratification theory begins with the fundamental assumption that in order to understand intercohort relations, we need to see society as *stratified* according to age. Consistent with Mannheim, this view holds that society is divided into a hierarchy of socially recognized age strata. Each stratum consists of members who are similar in age and whose behavior is governed by the same set of norms for behavior appropriate for their age group. Further, members of various age strata differ in their abilities to obtain and control social resources. For example, young people in most societies have less power and fewer resources than do middle-aged adults.

The duties, obligations, and privileges associated with age strata vary according to individual attributes, but they are always influenced by the structural aspect of age. Thus, in a society various cohorts may have greatly divergent views on filial responsibility, expectations for independence of children, and other values.

Sociologists see such differences among cohorts as the basis for possible conflict of interest in society. In fact, conflict regarding continuity and discontinuity has been a major theme in macrosociological approaches to relations between age groups. As Bengtson (1989, p. 26) notes, members of the older cohort desire continuity: They want to transmit to younger cohorts "what is best in their own lives." Correspondingly, they fear discontinuity: that young people will choose to live by very different sets of values. What has come to be known as the "problem of generations" reflects "the tension between continuity and change, affirmation and innovation, in the human social order over time" (Bengtson 1989, p. 26).

As an example, an age stratification perspective on intergenerational relations can be applied to the politi-

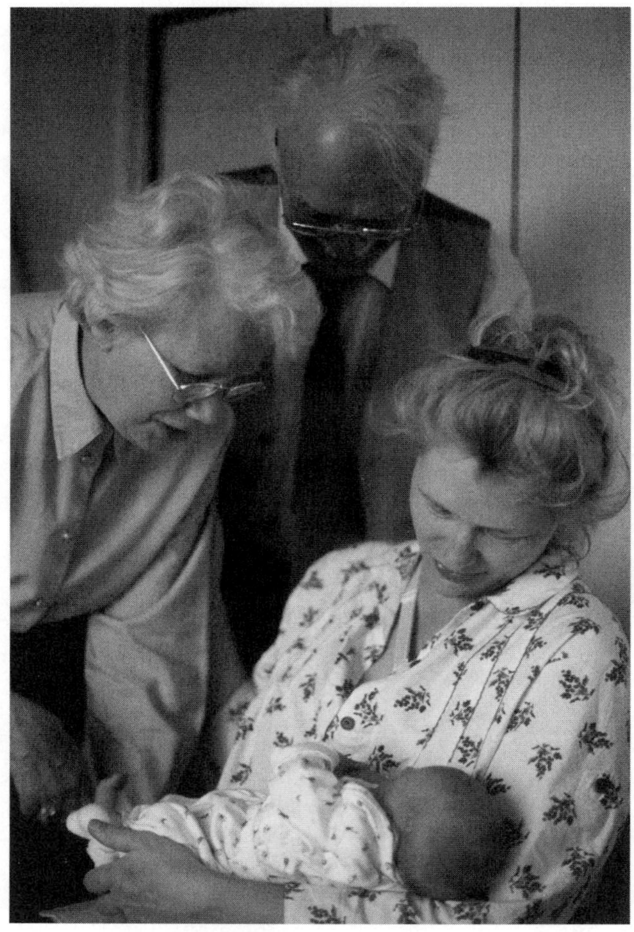

Intergenerational relations involve passing along values from one generation to the next. (Owen Franken/Corbis)

cal realm. When the age stratification system is viewed as analogous to other stratification systems (e.g., class or gender), it follows that group solidarity can develop within each age cohort and that conflict—both overt conflict and conflict of interests—may occur between two different cohorts.

On a basic level, members of older and younger cohorts find different political issues more salient; for example, the elderly are more likely to focus on old-age pensions and health benefits, while the young are concerned with issues such as educational loans or the military draft (Riley, Foner, and Waring 1988). Divergences in political ideology among older and younger cohorts have been examined, with the fairly consistent finding that the current aged cohort is generally more conservative than younger cohorts. (However, these cross-sectional differences do not highlight the fact that people change their political attitudes over time, in line with changes in the society as a whole.)

Do divergent interests and attitudes result in age-related collective political action? Sociologists have examined whether the aged constitute a self-defined political group that sets its agenda against those of other age strata. On the whole, it is not clear that a voting block can be organized around old-age interests, as political differences vary greatly within the cohort. Further, the elderly are a heterogeneous group. There are differences in socioeconomic status and racial and ethnic background within the aged cohort. In addition, the interests of the "young-old" (sixty-five to seventy-five) may differ from the "old-old" (over seventy-five), with the former more concerned with retirement issues, income maintenance, and leisure opportunities, and the latter interested more heavily in funding for medical services and long-term care. The overall evidence shows that the aged are willing to act together on some issues (like Social Security) but not on others.

A recent political development, however, may create more polarization among cohorts and thus lead to an upswing in age-based politics. This is the rising concern over "generational equity." Streib and Binstock (1988) have summarized the issue in the following way. The elderly in developed nations were seen as a disadvantaged group from the 1950s to the early 1970s. They were portrayed as having low economic and social status, compared with younger persons. By the late 1970s, however, some scholarly and popular literature began to assert that old people had in fact overbenefited, and the elderly came to be seen as potentially burdensome economically to younger generations.

The older generation has at times been viewed as a scapegoat for a number of problems (Binstock 1983). In particular, the elderly have come to be seen as demanding resources for themselves and thus depriving children of quality schooling, health care, and other services. Organizations have arisen whose goal is to advocate the interests of the young at the expense of the older cohort. These groups have the expressed goal of establishing "generational equity" by transferring resources back to the young.

In the face of such attacks, it is conceivable that the elderly will begin to coalesce into a more unified generational unit. In response to these claims, however, there has developed a counter-movement that encourages cooperation among advocates for youth *and* the elderly. On the level of practice, this interest has led to the development of intergenerational programs that bring old and young together.

The macrosociological approach provides important insights into intergenerational relations and has obvious relevance for public policy on aging issues. It is equally critical, however, to examine intergenerational relations on the micro-social level.

Macrosociological Approaches: A Focus on the Family

In recent years, many sociologists have focused on the smaller world of the family in an attempt to understand intergenerational relations. The family resembles the larger society in that it is the locus of both intergenerational consensus and conflict. There is considerable family solidarity, indicated by feelings of affection and attachment that result from a shared history and close contact (Bengtson, Rosenthal, and Burton 1988), as well as inequalities of power and social resources. The twin themes of solidarity and conflict are evident throughout sociological research on the topic.

Studies of the effects of gender consistently demonstrate stronger affectional ties between mothers and daughters than between any other combination.

The way in which these themes are worked out in families is affected by dramatic changes in the age structure of American society. In particular, average lifespan has increased, which means that family members will spend more time than ever before occupying intergenerational family roles. Further, increased life expectancy leads to a greater likelihood that families will spend longer periods of time caring for disabled elderly relatives.

Societal changes have also increased the complexity of intergenerational relations. For example, the high divorce rate found in contemporary American society raises the likelihood that adult children will return to their parents' homes, often bringing their own young children with them. Women's unprecedented participation in the labor force and their return to college in great numbers may also affect intergenerational relations. To be sure, the acquisition of these nonfamilial roles provides new and enriching opportunities for women; however, it may alter the time that has traditionally been devoted to "kinkeeping" between the generations.

It is possible to comment on only a few major themes in this review. The most widely studied area is that of parent–child relations in later life, including patterns of intergenerational contact and factors that affect the quality of adult child–elderly parent relationships. Two additional issues are relations with grandparents in the family and the importance of changing dependencies among the generations over the life course.

CONTACT BETWEEN PARENTS AND CHILDREN. A major concern of researchers has been to understand patterns of contact between adult children and older parents. Research on this issue has gone through two major phases. First, there was a period in which the nuclear family was held to be isolated. This view was based in part on Talcott Parson's analyses of family relations, which held that modernization had brought about the decline of the extended family (DeWit and Frankel 1988). During this period, it was widely believed that because of the geographic mobility of children, families abandoned their elderly relatives. This view also held that most elderly persons rarely saw their children and that family members no longer provided care for older relatives (Shanas 1979).

In the second phase, many prominent researchers devoted considerable effort to demonstrating that this view is inaccurate. Investigators such as Ethel Shanas, Marvin Sussman, and Eugene Litwak, as well as later researchers, clearly established that older persons have frequent contact with family members and that few are totally isolated from kin. Further, most aged family members are involved in a network of emotionally and instrumentally supportive relationships.

A major factor in determining the frequency of contact is physical proximity. Numerous studies have found that the frequency of intergenerational contact is greatly affected by geographical distance between households, with more distant children interacting less often with parents. However, it is clear that many geographically distant children nevertheless continue to interact to a significant degree with parents (DeWit and Frankel 1988). Further, several studies have found that some parents and children are able to maintain close ties despite being separated by great distances. Thus, it appears that distance is only one of several variables that are important in determining the quality of parent–child relationships.

QUALITY OF PARENT—CHILD RELATIONSHIPS. Researchers have moved beyond simply establishing patterns of contact to examining factors that affect the quality of parent–child relations in later life. A number of factors appear to have an impact on relationship quality.

Increased parental dependency is frequently cited as a factor that negatively affects the quality of aged parent–adult child relations. Studies have highlighted imbalanced exchanges and perceptions of inequity between the generations as major causes of family disharmony. For example, several investigations have suggested that an increase in parents' dependence upon their adult children may reduce positive feelings between the generations. Other studies have found that adult children's feelings of closeness and attachment are reduced when parents' health declines. As parents' health deteriorates, adult children are likely to need to increase their levels of support to previously independent parents, as well as to accept a lessening or termination of the parents' provision of support—thus disrupting the previously established flow of support between the generations.

A second factor affecting parent–child relations is *gender.* Studies of the effects of gender consistently demonstrate stronger affectional ties between mothers and daughters than between any other combination (Rossi and Rossi 1990). Mothers report more positive affect with adult daughters than with sons and are more likely to rely on daughters than on sons as confidants and comforters. Daughters in turn report greater feelings of closeness to mothers and are more likely to turn to them as confidants than to fathers.

Third, the *age of the child* affects relationships with parents. Theories of adult development and intergenerational relations lead to the expectation that a child's age will be negatively related to parent–child conflict and positively related to closeness. This literature suggests that maturational changes are likely to reduce differences between parents and adult children, thus minimizing the bases for conflict between them. For example, Bengtson (1979) suggests that, as children mature, their orientations become more similar to those of their parents. Similarly, Hagestad (1987) posits both that differences between parents and children become muted across time and that there is greater tolerance for differences that remain. A variety of empirical findings support these assertions.

Fourth, changes in the degree of *status similarity* between adult children and their parents may affect their relationship. In particular, many studies have found a consistent pattern of increased closeness in intergenerational relations when children begin to share a larger number of adult statuses with their parents (Adams 1968; Young and Willmott 1957). For example, the mother–daughter relationship appears to assume greater importance from the daughters' perspective when they themselves become mothers (Fischer 1986). Conversely, decreases in status similarity may negatively affect adult child–parent relations. For example, the status dissimilarity that develops when daughters surpass their mothers educationally may have particular potential for creating difficulties between the generations (Suitor 1987).

The role of grandparent is not clearly defined in American society, and the expectations, privileges, and obligations are ambiguous.

GRANDPARENTHOOD. In recent years, sociologists have shown increasing interest in studying the role of grandparents in families. The demographic shifts noted above have brought about changes in the nature of grandparenthood in several ways. First, more people now survive to become grandparents than ever before. Second, the entry into grandparenthood is likely to occur in midlife, rather than in old age; thus, the duration of grandparenthood may extend to four decades or more. Third, the role of grandparent is not clearly defined in American society, and the normative expectations, privileges, and obligations are ambiguous (Hagestad 1985).

Studies have uncovered several consistent findings about grandparenthood. Contrary to popular stereotypes, most grandparents do not wish to take on a parental role toward their grandchildren. Rather, they generally prefer a more distant role in the grandchildren's lives. Nevertheless, grandparents are also a critical resource for families in times of trouble, as studies of divorce and teenage parenting make clear (Troll 1985).

Perhaps the most consistent finding in over twenty-five years of research is diversity in grandparenting styles. A number of typologies have been identified that array grandparents along a continuum from intense involvement and assumption of parental responsibilities, on the one hand, to relative alienation from grandchildren on the other (Neugarten and Weinstein 1964).

The most ambitious study to date used a representative survey to examine styles of grandparenting and to uncover factors that determine the adoption of a particular style (Cherlin and Furstenberg 1986). Andrew Cherlin and Frank Furstenberg were able to identify five basic grandparenting styles. *Detached* grandparents have little contact with their grandchildren. *Passive* grandparents visit somewhat more frequently but carefully maintain a distance from their grandchildren's lives. *Supportive* grandparents have more contact and focus on providing services to the grandchildren. *Authoritative* grandparents exert parent-like influence to a relatively great degree. Finally, *influential* grandparents combine involvement both in the provision of services and in adopting a parental role.

Cherlin and Furstenberg found that geographical distance was the most critical factor in determining which style of grandparenting developed. Detached grandparents were much more likely to live far away, while the most involved grandparents lived in close proximity to the grandchildren. Further, grandparents practiced "selective investment" in their grandchildren. They had more intense relationships with some grandchildren and more distant relationships with others. Other studies have affirmed this finding and have also pointed to the importance of gender: Grandmothers tend to have closer relationships with grandchildren than grandfathers do.

Research interest has also highlighted the effects of children's marital disruption on the relationship between grandparents and grandchildren. Despite suggestions in the popular media that relations between grandchildren and grandparents are damaged when adult children divorce, studies have shown that this is not necessarily the case. Cherlin and Furstenberg (1986) found that "custodial grandparents" (that is, those whose adult children were awarded custody of the grandchildren) tended to maintain very close ties with their grandchildren, while "noncustodial grandparents" were less likely to maintain such ties. Since custody of minor children continues to be awarded more frequently to mothers than to fathers, this means that ties with maternal grandparents are more likely to be maintained or strengthened following a divorce, while ties with paternal grandparents are more vulnerable—particularly in terms of frequency of interaction.

CHANGING DEPENDENCIES. Social scientists have convincingly demonstrated that children and parents continue to depend on one another for both emotional and instrumental support throughout the life course (Hill 1970). The literature on intergenerational relations, however, has focused more heavily on children's support to elderly parents than on the reverse. Thus, before turning to a brief discussion of the issue of caregiving to the elderly, it is important to emphasize the *reciprocal* nature of intergenerational assistance.

Sussman (1985) has provided a model of parent–child relations across the lifespan that emphasizes the cyclical shift in relations with parents. In the beginning, parents provide a substantial amount of assistance to their offspring, even into the children's early married life. Then, as children become more independent—and possibly move away—there is a decrease in intergenerational helping. Finally, as elderly parents begin to decline in health, they come to depend more heavily on their children. This cyclical view of support is important in that it stresses patterns of *mutual* aid between the generations (see also Rossi and Rossi 1990). Further, it should be noted that it is usually only very late in the life course that children's provision of support exceeds that of parents, and even then only when parents become frail and disabled.

In the past decade, several hundred articles have been published examining the experiences of families at this stage of the life course. Research has documented the strains experienced by middle-aged children when parents become dependent, including practical problems of managing competing demands on their time and energy, as well as emotional stress, increased social isolation, guilt, and feelings of inadequacy.

Besides establishing both the prevalence of support for aged parents and problems in providing care, researchers have attempted to determine who is most likely both to become a caregiver and to experience the greatest stress from caregiving. Two of the most consistent findings involve the issues of gender and the relationship to the elderly person. First, women are substantially more likely to become caregivers than are men, and they experience much greater stress and disruption in their daily lives from caregiving (Horowitz 1985). Second, when the elderly person is married, it is the spouse who almost always becomes the primary caregiver. Thus, adult children generally become caregivers only when the care recipient's spouse is not available to occupy this status. Further, spouses appear to experience greater physical and financial strain than do adult child caregivers (Cantor 1983).

Although research has focused on the detrimental consequences of caregiving, recent evidence suggests that most caregivers can also identify positive consequences of caregiving. These positive aspects usually involve feelings of gratification derived from helping someone they love, and fulfilling expectations of filial responsibility. Thus, the issue of changing dependencies in later life reflects the twin themes of consensus and conflict evident throughout theory and research on intergenerational relations.

[See also Filial Responsibility; Parental Roles; Social Mobility.]

BIBLIOGRAPHY

Adams, Bert N. 1968 *Kinship in an Urban Setting.* Chicago: Markham.

Bengtson, Vern L. 1979 "Research Perspectives on Intergenerational Interaction." In Pauline K. Ragan, ed., *Aging Parents.* Los Angeles: University of Southern California Press.

——— 1989 "The Problem of Generations: Age Group Contrasts, Continuities, and Social Change." In V. L. Bengtson and K. W. Schaie, eds., *The Course of Later Life: Research and Reflections.* New York: Springer.

———, Carolyn Rosenthal, and Linda Burton 1988 "Families and Aging: Diversity and Heterogeneity." In R. H. Binstock and L. K. George, eds., *Handbook of Aging and the Social Sciences,* 3d ed. San Diego: Academic Press.

Binstock, R. H. 1983 "The Aged as Scapegoat." *Gerontologist* 23:136–143.

Cantor, Majorie 1983 "Strain among Caregivers: A Study of Experience in the United States." *Gerontologist* 23:597–604.

Cherlin, Andrew J., and Frank F. Furstenberg, Jr. 1986 *The New American Grandparent: A Place in the Family, A Life Apart.* New York: Basic Books.

DeWit, David J., and B. Gail Frankel 1988 "Geographic Distance and Intergenerational Contact: A Critical Assessment and Review of the Literature." *Journal of Aging Studies* 2:25–43.

Fischer, Lucy Rose 1986 *Linked Lives: Adult Daughters and Their Mothers.* New York: Harper and Row.

Foner, Anne 1986 *Aging and Old Age: New Perspectives.* Englewood Cliffs, N.J.: Prentice-Hall.

Hagestad, Gunhild O. 1985 "Continuity and Connectedness." In V. L. Bengtson and J. F. Robertson, eds., *Grandparenthood.* Newbury Park, Calif.: Sage.

——— 1987 "Dimensions of Time and the Family." *American Behavioral Scientist* 29:679–694.

Hill, Reuben 1970 *Family Development in Three Generations.* Cambridge, Mass.: Schenkman.

Horowitz, Amy 1985 "Family Caregiving to the Frail Elderly." In C. Eisdorfer et al., eds., *Annual Review of Gerontology and Geriatrics.* New York: Springer.

Johnson, Elizabeth S. " 'Good' Relationships between Older Mothers and Their Daughters: A Causal Model." *Gerontologist* 18:301–306.

Mannheim, Karl 1952 *Essays on the Sociology of Knowledge,* Paul Kecskemeti, trans. London: Routledge and Kegan Paul.

Neugarten, Bernice L., and K. K. Weinstein 1964 "The Changing American Grandparent." *Journal of Marriage and the Family* 26:199–204.

Riley, Matilda White, Anne Foner, and Joan Waring 1988 "Sociology of Age." In *Handbook of Sociology.* Newbury Park, Calif.: Sage.

Rossi, Alice S., and Peter H. Rossi 1990 *Of Human Bonding: Parent–Child Relations across the Life Course.* New York: Aldine de Gruyter.

Shanas, Ethel 1979 "Social Myth as Hypothesis: The Case of the Family Relations of Old People." *Gerontologist* 19:3–9.

Streib, Gordon, and Robert H. Binstock 1988 "Aging and the Social Sciences: Changes in the Field." In R. H. Binstock and L K. George, eds., *Handbook of Aging and the Social Sciences.* 3d ed. San Diego: Academic Press.

Suitor, J. Jill 1987 "Mother–Daughter Relations When Married Daughters Return to School: Effects of Status Similarity." *Journal of Marriage and the Family* 49:435–444.

Sussman, Marvin 1985 "The Family Life of Older People." In R. H. Binstock and E. Shanas, eds., *Handbook of Aging and the Social Sciences.* New York: Van Nostrand Reinhold.

Troll, Lillian E. 1985 "The Contingencies of Grandparenting." In V. L. Bengtson and J. F. Robertson, eds., *Grandparenthood.* Newbury Park, Calif.: Sage.

Young, Michael, and Peter Willmott 1957 *Family and Kinship in East London.* London: Routledge and Kegan Paul.

– KARL PILLEMER
J. JILL SUITOR

INTERMARRIAGE

Intermarriage among people of different races, religion, nationality, and ethnicity would be a subject of little concern in many societies (Degler 1971). That should be expected of a culturally diverse society such as the United States. Indeed, the United States is the most racially and culturally diverse nation in the Western, industrialized world. The heterogeneous composition of the United States should lend itself to a high degree of tolerance and acceptance of diversity in marriage patterns among its constituent groups (Spickard 1989). As of the 1990s, intermarriage rates among populations defined as ethnic minorities in the United States are practically normative (U.S. Bureau of the Census 1985). Only between blacks and whites has intermarriage remained such a rare practice as to continue to be regarded as socially deviant behavior. For that reason, our discussion of intermarriage will focus largely on those two groups.

Slavery had its greatest impact on interracial relations of the Africans brought to the United States. Most of the slaves who came in the beginning were males. The number of black females was not equal to that of males until 1840. As a result, the number of sexual relations between black slaves and indentured white women was fairly high. Some of these interracial relationships were more than casual contacts and ended in marriage. The intermarriage rate between male slaves and free white women increased to the extent that laws against them were passed as a prohibitive measure. Before the alarm over the rate of intermarriages, male slaves were encouraged to marry white women, thereby increasing the property of the slavemaster since the children from such unions were also slaves (Jordan 1968).

The end of slavery did not give the black woman any right to sexual integrity.

The end of slavery did not give the black woman any right to sexual integrity. What slavery began, racism and economic exploitation continued to impose on the sexual lives of black women. In the postbellum South, black women were still at the mercy of the carnal desires of white men. According to historians, black women were forced to give up their bodies like animals to white men at random. Many have noted that many Southern white men had their first sexual experience with black women. In some cases the use of black women as sexual objects served to maintain the double standard of sexual conduct in the white South. Many white men did not have sexual relations with white women until they married. Some Southern white men were known to joke that until they married they did not know that white women were capable of sexual intercourse (Cash 1960; Dollard 1957).

It was the protection of the sexual purity of the white women that partially justified the establishment of racially segregated institutions in the South. The Southern white man assumed that black men have a strong desire for intermarriage and that white women would be open to proposals from black men if they were not guarded from even meeting with them on an equal level. As Bernard (1966, p. 75) writes, "The white world's insistence on keeping Negro men walled up in the concentration camp (of the ghetto) was motivated in large part by its fear of black male sexuality."

The taboo on intermarriage is mostly centered on black men and white women. One reason for this is that white men and black women have engaged in coitus since the first black female slaves entered this country. Some black slave women were forced to engage in sexual relations with their white masters; others did so out of desire. Children resulting from these interracial sexual unions are always considered black, and the prevalent miscegenation of black women and white men has produced a much lighter-skinned American black than their African ancestor.

Traditionally, white fear of interracial relations has focused on the desire to avoid mongrelization of the races. Such a fear lacks any scientific basis since many authorities on the subject of racial types seriously question that a pure race ever existed on this planet. Most authorities note it is an actual fact that the whole population of the world is hybrid and becoming increasingly so. At any rate, the rate of miscegenation in the past almost certainly casts doubt on any pure race theory for the United States (Day 1972).

Since the interracial taboo is mostly centered on black men and white women, it is not strange that these two groups may have a certain curiosity about each other. Inflaming this curiosity are the sexual stereotypes mutually held by blacks and whites about each other as sexual partners. Just as these sexual stereotypes may stimulate the curiosity of white women, the black male may be equally attracted by the concept of sacred white womanhood applied to all white women. Especially in the South, the penalties for a black man having sex with a white female were extremely severe. Her status as forbidden fruit could only add to the natural attraction that most men feel toward the opposite sex. What is taken for granted by most white men became a forbidden pleasure to black males.

Regardless of the social taboos, intermarriage does take place between the races—most noticeably in the North. Despite the problems inherent in interracial marriages, such unions appear to be increasing. The U.S. Supreme Court ruling of 1967 that all laws prohibiting marriage between members of different races are unconstitutional, along with the status gains for blacks in the 1960s, influenced this increase. It has also been noted that most partners in this type of marriage are in the same educational brackets as their spouses. Little research is available on the success of interracial marriages. Authorities who have studied the subject generally have concluded these marriages have a fairly good chance of survival. The external pressures faced by interracial couples are often great but do not appear to be overwhelming (Cretser and Leon 1982).

Contemporary Black and White Marriage

The 1970s and 1980s witnessed a significant increase in interracial dating and marriage. Among the reasons for this change in black–white dating and marriage was the desegregation of the public school system, the work force, and other social settings. In those integrated settings, blacks and whites met as equals. There were, of course, other factors such as the liberation of many white youth from parental control and the racist values parents conveyed to them (Staples 1981).

This country's history is replete with acts of terror and intimidation of interracial couples who violated the society's taboos on miscegenation.

Many black women are gravitating toward white men because of the shortage of black males and their disenchantment with those they are able to meet. In a similar vein some white men are dissatisfied with white females and their increasing and vociferous demands for sex-role parity. At the same time there is a slight but noticeable decrease in black male–white female unions. A possible reason is that they are no longer as fashionable as they were in the 1960s and 1970s. Also, much of their attraction to each other was based on the historical lack of access to each other and the stereotype of black men as superstuds and white women as forbidden fruit (Staples 1981). Once they had extensive interaction, the myths were exploded and the attraction consequently diminished (Hernton 1965).

We should be fairly clear that there are relatively normal reasons for interracial attractions and matings. At the same time it would be naive to assume that special factors are not behind them in a society that is stratified by race. Given the persistence of racism as a pervasive force, many interracial marriages face rough going. In addition to the normal problems of working out a satisfactory marital relationship, interracial couples must cope with social ostracism and isolation. A recent phenomenon has been the increasing hostility toward such unions by the black community, which has forced some interracial couples into a marginal existence (Hare and Hare 1984). Such pressures cause the interracial marriage rate to remain very low.

There are many factors and problems associated with interracial dating. Because of the unique and historical relationships between the races, such interracial dating practices often have a different motivation and character than the same behavior between members of the same race (Beigel 1966). Heer (1974) used an analysis of census data to interpret the changes in interracial marriages in the period between 1960 and 1970. Among his major findings was the shift of such marriages from the South to the North, an increase in black husband–white wife unions, and a fairly high rate of dissolution of such marriages.

If blacks are asked if they have ever dated a member of another race, two types of responses emerge. One group is so strongly opposed to it that they give a strident No. The other group has engaged in mixed dating and is quite defensive about it. Some of the latter group think it is a hostile, even stupid, question and assumes there is something strange about people who date across the color line. Whether strange or not, it is undeniable that interracial dating is a controversial activity (Staples 1981). Male–female relationships without the racial element are a controversial topic, and race has historically been a volatile and emotional issue. It is a fact that the scars of nearly 400 years of the worst human bondage known are not healed, and disapproval by many black and white people of interracial love affairs is one of the wounds.

Intermarriage is certainly nothing new in the United States. Its meaning and dynamics have, however, changed over the 400 years since blacks entered this country. In the era before slavery black male and white female indentured servants often mated with each other. During the period of black bondage, most mixed sexual unions took place between white men and female slaves, often involving coercion by the white partner. A similar pattern of miscegenation occurred after slavery, with a white man and a black woman as the typical duo. When blacks moved to larger cities outside the South, the black male–white female pairing became more common. As is commonly known, legal unions between the races was prohibited by law in many states until 1967. Legal prohibitions were not the only deterrent to such biracial unions. This country's history is replete with acts of terror and intimidation of interracial couples who violated the society's taboos on miscegenation. While blacks and whites came together in love and marriage over the years, it was generally at a high cost ranging from death to social ostracism (Stember 1976).

Around 1968 society witnessed the first significant increase in interracial dating. This was the year that blacks entered predominantly white college campuses in comparatively large numbers. Contemporaneous with this event was the sexual and psychological liberation of white women. While white society disapproved of all biracial dating, the strongest taboo was on the black male–white female bond. Hence, they became the dominant figures in the increments of biracial dating. The college campus became an ideal laboratory for experiments in interracial affairs. Young white women, who were not as racist as their parents, were liberated from parental and community control. Their student cohorts were more accepting or indifferent to their dating across racial lines. One study revealed that as many as 45 percent of the white female students had dated interracially (Willie and Levy 1972). There were, of course, regional differences: While 20 percent of all Americans had dated outside their race, the South had the lowest incidence of biracial dating (10 percent), while the West and young people had the highest rate (one out of three; Downs 1971).

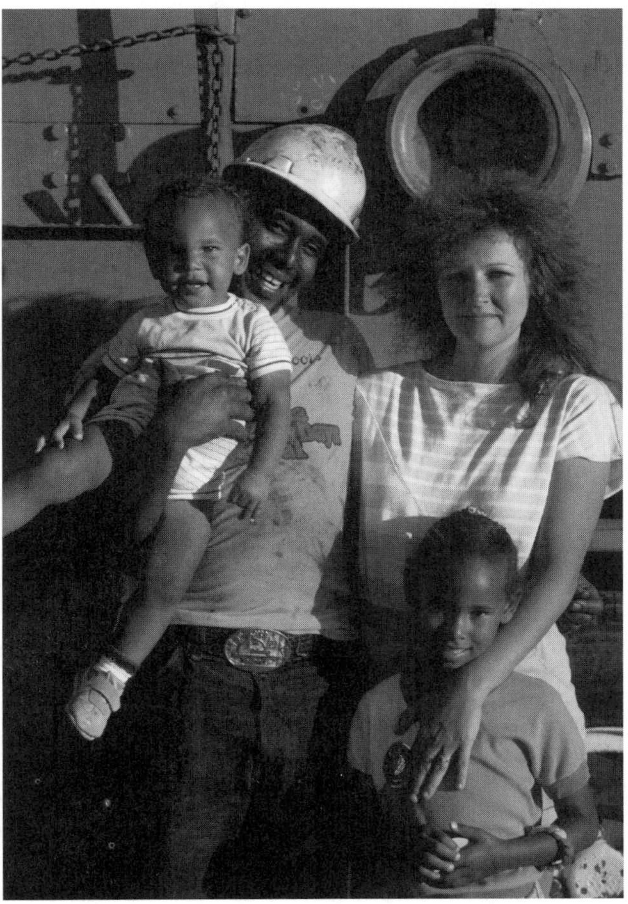

Intermarriage between blacks and whites has taken place throughout American history, but was legally prohibited until 1967 in many states. From the 1960s onward, social disapproval of interracial dating declined, and the number of intermarriages increased. (Kit Kittle/Corbis)

Those changes in interracial dating practices coincided with the civil rights movement and a greater white acceptance of blacks as racial equals. Moreover, in the university setting the blacks and whites who dated were peers. They had similar educational backgrounds, interests, and values. Along with increments in racial unions came what appeared to be a change in public attitudes toward biracial couples. A 1985 poll indicated that only a minority of white Americans would not accept their child's marrying outside his or her race (Schuman, Steel, and Bobo 1985). This poll result could be misleading. Many people tend to give the liberal answer they think is proper or expected when asked about controversial issues such as interracial marriage. However, when confronted with the issue on a very personal level, their response is likely to be much different. Whether parents approve or not, it is clear that biracial matches have become part of the changing American scene. Mixed couples can be observed daily in the cities of the deep South and are commonplace in such liberal bastions as New York, Boston, and San Francisco; and parental approval is irrelevant to a number of black and white singles who have deviated from other norms related to sexual orientation, sex roles, sexual behaviors, marriage, and the like.

Factors in Interracial Marriages

The increase in interracial dating has resulted in an increase in interracial marriages. Using selective data, Heer (1974) found definite evidence of an upward trend in the percentage of blacks marrying whites. The interracial marriage rate was particularly high in those areas where residential segregation by race was low and where there are minimal status differences between the white and black population. However, Heer also discovered that marriages between black men and white women are much more common than those between white men and black women. In the western region, for example, the interracial marriage rate of black men is 12.3 percent and of black women 3.1 percent (Tucker and Mitchell-Kernan 1990).

Other factors may propel people into an interracial marriage. Some students of the subject assert that uneven sex ratios are a basic cause. Wherever a group in nearness to another group has an imbalance in sex ratio, there is a greater likelihood of intermarriage. If the groups have a relatively well-balanced distribution of the sexes, members will marry more within their own group (Guttentag and Secord 1983; Parkman and Sawyer 1967).

People may marry "their own kind" for the weirdest reasons, yet these reasons do not make the marriage suspect.

In interracial marriages, one always looks for ulterior motives. It is said that people marry interracially because of rebellion against their parents, sexual curiosity, and other psychological reasons. But many marriages that are homogeneous take place for the same reasons. There are all kinds of unconscious variances that attract individuals in many marriages. Thus, people may marry "their own kind" for the weirdest reasons, yet these reasons do not make each marriage suspect. Perhaps the imputation of ulterior motives to interracial couples says more about the individual making these interpretations and about the society we live in than about the couple who intermarry.

While the proportion of western black men dating interracially is much higher than black women, the difference is not so great when it comes to interracial marriages nationally. While black women are deprived of many dates by white women, the vast majority of black males are still available to them for marriage. Moreover, a great number of black women marry white men. The percentage of dating relationships between black women and white men that result in marriage may be even greater than the corresponding percentage for black men and white women.

In the past, many of the black men who married white women were of a higher social status than their wives. In fact, this marrying down was so common that sociologists formulated a theory about it. They hypothesized that the black groom was trading his class advantage for the racial caste advantage of the white bride (Davis 1941; Merton 1941). But contemporary interracial marriages are more likely to involve spouses from the same social class. Furthermore, when intermarriages involved members of different social classes, there was a pronounced tendency for black women to marry up rather than to marry down (Heer 1974; Monahan 1976).

Consequently, one reason that black women marry white men is to increase their station in life. Of course, this is true of many marriages. One exception, however, is black female entertainers. Because they are closely associated with white males in the course of their jobs, many of them form interracial unions. Most of the celebrated cases in recent years have involved famous black women who married white men not equally famous or wealthy.

While the motivation for an interracial marriage may or may not differ from that of intraracial marriages, there are problems that are unique to interracial marriages. When researchers studied interracially married couples they discovered that courtship in most cases had been carried on clandestinely and, further, that many of them were isolated from their families following the marriage. The white families, in particular, frequently refused to have anything to do with children who entered into interracial marriages (Golden 1954; Porterfield 1982; Spickard 1989).

Other outstanding social problems encountered by the couples centered on such factors as housing, occupation, and relationships with family and peers. Several of the spouses lost their jobs because of intermarriage, while others felt it necessary to conceal their marriages from their employers. The children born of such marriages identified themselves with and were accepted by the black community. In sum, the couples had to rely upon themselves and their own power of determination to continue the marriage (Wilkinson 1975).

As for the sociocultural factors that promote or deter interracial marriages, several explanations have been put forth to explain the variation in intermarriage patterns in the United States. Tucker and Mitchell-Kernan (1990) hypothesized that certain environments are more racially tolerant of intermarriage than are others. Their hypothesis is based on the findings from U.S. census data showing interracial marriage rates highest in the West and lowest in the South (U.S. Bureau of the Census 1985). Similar to their explanation is the argument by Blau and Schwartz (1984) that the larger the group size as a proportion of the population, the less likely it is that members will marry outside their group. Second, they suggested that the more heterogeneous an area's population, the more likely it is that people will marry outside their group. Both the aforementioned propositions imply that intermarriage is a function of environmental forces, not individual motivations.

Summary

Interracial mating is a subject fraught with controversy. Those who oppose it often combine a hostility toward racial equality with invidious assessments of the private thoughts and lives of interracial couples. Many men and women mate for no more complex reasons than meeting, liking each other as individuals, and choosing to transcend the societal barriers to their relationship. Only in societies similar to the one in the United States does a biracial union take on any greater significance. For centuries, Latin American nations have undergone such a fusion of the races that only nationality, language, and religion remain as sources of identity. But the painful history of race relations in North America militates against the natural mixing of individuals from different races. Instead of regarding interracial dating and marriage as a matter of personal choice, many minorities have taken up the call for racial purity so common to their white-supremacy adversaries of the past.

Despite the opposition to biracial unions, they will continue to increase, among both men and women, as long as the social forces that set intermarriage in motion are extant. There is, for example, the class factor. As long as middle-class blacks occupy token positions in the upper reaches of the job hierarchy, most of the people they meet in their occupational world will be white. Considering the fact that the job setting is the paramount place for meeting mates, it is only natural that many blacks will date and marry whites. Those whites will be the people they most often encounter and with whom they share common values, interests, and lifestyles. Almost twenty-five years ago, E. Franklin Frazier (1957, p. 335) predicted:

> The increasing mobility of both white and colored people will not only provide a first-hand knowledge of each for the other but will encourage a certain cosmopolitanism. That means there will be a growing number of marginal people who will break away from their cultural roots. These marginal people will help create not only an international community but an international society. In becoming free from their local attachments and provincial outlook, they will lose at the same time their racial prejudices, which were a product of their isolation. Many of these marginal people will form interracial marriages because they are more likely to find suitable marriage partners in the cosmopolitan circles than within their native countries.

Not all blacks who consort with nonblacks will do so for noble motives. Because blacks tend to stereotype each other in negative terms, many will cross the color line to find what they believe is "absent" in their own race. However, many of the alleged advantages of the white female actually result from her longer tenure and security in her class position. It is easier, for instance, to enact the traditional female role when the men in your class and race can fulfill the normative masculine role, and few black males have been allowed that opportunity in a racially stratified society.

The wave of the future, however, does not seem to be the black male–white female dyad. Increasingly, black women are dating and marrying white males. The attention of society in general and black women in particular has focused on black men and white women, and the fact that the most common interracial pairs in the 1960s were black women and white men has been overlooked. Some studies reveal that as many as 49 percent of black women have dated white men. As black women ascend in the middle class world, they, too, will mate on the basis of proximity and class interests. Previously, fewer black women engaged in interracial mating because white males were not interested in them, at least not for marriage. As racial barriers drop in the society in general, especially among the middle classes, the opportunity structure will increase for black women, and the outcome will be the same for them as for black men. Whether their biracial unions will be any more durable may depend primarily on the trajectory of social forces in the society at large.

[See also Courtship; Discrimination; Ethnicity; Mate Selection Theories; Race.]

BIBLIOGRAPHY

Beigel, Hugo G. 1966 "Problems and Motives in Interracial Relationships." *Journal of Sex Research* 2:185–205.

Bernard, Jessie 1966 *Marriage and Family among Negroes.* Englewood Cliffs, N.J.: Prentice-Hall.

Blau, Peter, and Joseph E. Schwartz 1984 *Crosscutting Social Circles: Testing a Macrostructural Theory of Intergroup Relations.* Orlando, Fla.: Academic Press.

Cash, W.J. 1960 *The Mind of the South.* New York: Vintage.

Cretser, Gary, and Joseph Leon 1982 *Intermarriage in the United States.* New York: Haworth Press.

Davis, Kingsley 1941 "Intermarriage in Caste Societies." *American Anthropologist* 43:376–395.

Day, Beth 1972 *Sexual Life between Blacks and Whites: The Roots of Racism.* New York: World Publishing.

Degler, Carl N. 1971 *Neither Black nor White.* New York: Macmillan.

Dollard, John 1957 *Caste and Class in a Southern Town.* Garden City, N.Y.: Doubleday.

Downs, Joan 1971 "Black/White Dating." *Life,* 28 May, 56–61.

Frazier, E. Franklin 1957 *Race and Cultural Contacts in the Modern World.* New York: Alfred A. Knopf.

Golden, Joseph 1954 "Patterns of Negro–White Intermarriage." *American Sociological Review* 19:144–147.

Guttentag, Marcia, and Paul F. Secord 1983 *Too Many Women? The Sex Ratio Question.* Beverly Hills, Calif.: Sage.

Hare, Nathan, and Julia Hare 1984 *The Endangered Black Family.* San Francisco: Black Think Tank.

Heer, David 1974 "The Prevalence of Black-White Marriage in the United States, 1960 and 1970." *Journal of Marriage and the Family* 36:246–258.

Hernton, Calvin 1965 *Sex and Racism in America.* New York: Doubleday.

Jordan, Winthrop D. 1968 *White Over Black: American Attitudes toward the Negro 1550–1812.* Chapel Hill: University of North Carolina Press.

Merton, Robert 1941 "Intermarriage and Social Structure: Fact and Theory." *Psychiatry* 4:361–374.

Monahan, Thomas P. 1976 "The Occupational Class of Couples Entering Into Interracial Marriages." *Journal of Comparative Family Studies* 7:175–192.

Parkman, Margaret A., and Jack Sawyer 1967 "Dimensions of Ethnic Intermarriage in Hawaii." *American Sociological Review* 32:593–608.

Porterfield, Ernest 1982 "Black-American Intermarriage in the United States." In Gary A. Cretser and Joseph J. Leon, eds., *Intermarriage in the United States.* New York: Haworth Press.

Schuman, Howard, Charlotte Steel, and Lawrence Bobo 1985 *Racial Attitudes in America.* Cambridge, Mass.: Harvard University Press.

Spickard, Paul R. 1989 *Mixed Blood: Intermarriage and Ethnic Identity in Twentieth-Century America.* Madison: University of Wisconsin Press.

Staples, Robert 1981 *The World of Black Singles: Changing Patterns of Male/Female Relations.* Westport, Conn.: Greenwood Press.

Stember, Charles Herbert 1976 *Sexual Racism.* New York: Elsevier.

Tucker, M. Belinda, and Claudia Mitchell-Kernan 1990 "New Trends in Black American Interracial Marriage: The Social Structural Context." *Journal of Marriage and the Family* 52:209–218.

U.S. Bureau of the Census 1985 *Census of the Population, 1980.* Vol. 2, *Marital Characteristics.* Washington, D.C.: U.S. Government Printing Office.

Wilkinson, Doris Y. 1975 *Black Male/White Female: Perspectives on Interracial Marriage and Courtship.* Cambridge, Mass.: Schenkman.

Willie, Charles V., and Joan D. Levy 1972 "Black Is Lonely." *Psychology Today,* March, 76–86.

— ROBERT STAPLES

INTERNAL MIGRATION

Migration is the relatively permanent movement of individuals or groups over varying distances to change places of residence; permanence and distance are its major defining dimensions. Internal migration occurs within the boundaries of a given country. Migration is a type of geographic mobility status.

Definitions

The following definitions are standard in the field of social demography (Bogue 1985):

Mobility Status. A classification of the population based on a comparison between the place of residence (destination) of each individual in a census enumeration or survey and the place of residence (origin) at some specified earlier date. Mobility status in terms of the distance of the move falls into four main categories: nonmovers, local movers, intrastate migrants, and interstate migrants. They may be looked at more specifically in the list below:

1. *Nonmovers* or nonmobile persons live in the same house at the time of the census as at the date of origin.
2. *Movers* or mobile persons live in a different house and are further classified as to where they were living at the earlier date.
   a. *Local movers* are mobile persons who live in the same county at census time as at the date of origin.
   b. *Migrants* are mobile persons who live in a different county at census time than at the date of origin. Migrants may be further subclassified:
      1. *Intrastate migrants* live in a different county but within the same state.
      2. *Interstate migrants* live in a different state.
      3. *Interregional migrants* live in a different geographic division or census geographic region; they are also interstate migrants.

Mobility Interval. The lapsed time between the date specified for previous residence and the date of enumeration is usually either one year or five years. Recent census enumerations specify five years, and the Current Population Surveys have specified intervals of one, two, three, four, and five years.

Metropolitan Mobility. A system of subdividing mobile persons into categories by place of residence at the beginning and the end of the mobility interval and according to standard metropolitan statistical areas (SMSAs) is as follows:

1. Within the same SMSA
2. Between SMSAs
3. From outside SMSAs to SMSAs
4. From SMSAs to outside SMSAs
5. Outside SMSAs at both dates

Mobility Rates. The number of persons in a specified mobility status per one hundred or per one thousand population of the area in which they resided at the end of the mobility interval is a mobility rate. Such rates may refer to any of the categories of nonmobile or mobile persons specified above. Mobility rates may be specific for age, race, sex, or other traits. The denominator may also be the origin date or the midpoint of the migration interval.

Migration Flows. The key distinction is that either the origin or the destination is unknown. There are two types of flows:

1. *In-migration* is comprised of migrants arriving at a particular place of destination, with no reference to the place of origin. In-flows could also arrive at a specified type of place, such as central cities or metropolitan areas.
2. *Out-migration* is comprised of migrants departing from a particular area, with no reference to the place of destination. Out-flows may also depart from specified types of places, such as places outside SMSAs or suburban metropolitan rings of SMSAs.

Migration Streams. These connect an origin to a destination. There are three types of migration streams:

1. *Specific streams.* Streams that connect particular places within a category, such as streams between specific cities, counties, states, or regions. This is the major use of the term.
2. *Typological streams.* Streams that connect types of places, such as streams between all central cities and suburbs in a state or the nation.
3. *Counterstreams.* When a stream between two places endures, it usually generates a counterstream, a smaller stream in the opposite direction. The stream and counterstream are referred to as an exchange.

Net Migration. This is the difference obtained when the number of out-migrants is subtracted from the number of in-migrants in a particular place or type of place. A location that experiences a loss of population through migration is said to have a negative net migration; one that gains population through migration has a positive net migration. Because of its birth and death rates, an area may have a negative net migration and continue to have a growing population. There is no such thing as a net migrant, however.

Return Migration. The census contains an item that identifies the state of birth. Return migrants are those persons who return to their state of birth during the mobility interval.

Migration Research

Net migration rates before 1940 were estimated using a survival-rate method, adding births and subtracting deaths and attributing most of the resulting decade population change to migration (Bogue and Beale 1961). The 1940 census was the first to include a mobility item. It asked where persons lived five years before. In 1950, after World War II, there was so much population movement that a one-year interval was substituted in the census. In 1960 the five-year mobility interval was restored and has been retained in subsequent decades. Because of these measurement changes, the 1960 and 1970 censuses were the first from which decade changes could be derived. Thus, several landmark studies appeared in the 1960s, breaking new ground and setting patterns for future migration research (Long 1988). Henry S. Shryock's (1964) work showed the importance of studying gross migration flows, in addition to the prevailing dependence on net migration. Ira S. Lowry (1966) introduced econometric modeling to migration research. Finally, Lansing and Mueller (1967) helped introduce survey approaches to analyzing internal migration.

U.S. Mobility

Americans are unusually mobile (Bogue 1985). Only Canada and Australia have populations as mobile as that of the United States. In a single year 17 percent of U.S. inhabitants move from one domicile to another, and about 6 percent change their county of residence. At current mobility rates average Americans live at fourteen different addresses during their lifetimes. Of these thirteen moves, three are as a dependent moving with parents and ten are on their own volition. People who have lived their entire lives at the same address account for no more than 2 percent or 3 percent of the adult population. Perhaps no more than 10 percent to 15 percent of people spend their entire lives in their county of birth.

When the five-year mobility interval is used, the mobility rates are not five times as large as those for a single year because persons who move several times within the interval are counted only once. Nearly one-half of the population is mobile over a five-year period, and more than one-fifth are migrants. Since 1980 there appears to have been no diminution in the tendency to migrate, but there has been an apparent reduction in local mobility.

One can discover contradictory findings in the mobility literature. These contradictions are often due to the data bases being analyzed (Long 1988). Some data bases use mortgage data, leaving out renters; others, such as the Annual Housing Survey, use households; and some, such as most census publications, use individuals as their units of analysis, each data base giving somewhat different results. In addition, some data sources offer little information on the characteristics of migrants. The individual master file of the Internal Revenue Service includes state and county migration data but includes no personal characteristics, and several large moving companies provide data on their customers, also without personal characteristics (Kahley 1990).

REASONS FOR MIGRATION. Migration may occur in response to changing economic, social, or political conditions. *Push factors* are conditions in the sending population that impel or stimulate migration. Conditions that attract in-migrants are classified as *pull factors* (Ravenstein 1889; Lee 1966).

Declining economic opportunities, political instability, or the weakening of place ties may stimulate out-migration. Expanding economic opportunities, potential for advancement, the presence of family members and friends, or previous vacationing or residential experience tend to attract migrants. Not surprisingly, rural communities with high birthrates and regions with limited opportunities are areas of high outmigration, whereas urban, industrial regions and communities with expanding opportunities tend to have high in-migration (Prehn 1986).

Only Canada and Australia have populations as mobile as that of the United States.

Labor-force migration is viewed as an equilibrating mechanism that redistributes population as local economies rise and fall relative to one another. It contributes to economic expansion in the receiving population. Nonlabor-force migration responds more to amenity and social network factors, previous experience, and cost of living, but not to economic opportunities.

Wilbur Zelinski (1971) proposed a macro-level three-stage model of national internal migration. First, with the onset of modernization, the overall level of migration increases, primarily in the form of rural-to-urban moves. Second, as industrialization and modernization spread to more regions, migration may continue to increase because improved transportation and communication increase the availability of information and decrease the uncertainty of moving. Interurban moves become more important and eventually become the majority of all moves. Finally, at advanced stages, when level-of-living differences among areas have diminished, there may be more urban-to-rural movement and more "consumer-oriented" migration toward warm climates or locations with other amenities (Long 1988).

DIFFERENTIAL MIGRATION. What population characteristics predict migration? Characteristics that indicate less entanglement with social obligations, greater need for employment, and higher job skills are good predictors. Men are more mobile with respect to residence than women, although the difference is small. The single migrate at higher rates than the married. For several decades, blacks have been more mobile than whites. However, in 1980 whites migrated at higher rates than blacks, although blacks continued to be more mobile locally. Hispanics migrated internally at a rate between those of the black and the white populations. Persons with higher levels of education are more likely to migrate than those who are less well educated.

AGE AND MOBILITY. The shape of the age profile of migrants in the United States has been consistent for decades, changing only gradually over time. The younger children are, the more likely they are to migrate. The migration rate of children bottoms out in the early teens and does not increase rapidly until the late teens. More than one-third of Americans in their young adult years, ages twenty to twenty-four, the peak migration years during the life course, moved at least once between 1982 and 1983, and nearly one-half of this mobility was migratory. Not surprisingly, this age corresponds with college graduation and marriage for many. The increasing age of children in the home, particularly once they begin their formal schooling, dampens the attractiveness of migration for their parents. The age-specific migration rate declines slowly at first, then more steeply until age thirty-five, after which it slowly declines throughout the middle years to a life-course low point just before the retirement years. The retirement migration hump between ages sixty and seventy is small by comparison to the early adulthood migration bulge. The final increase in age-specific migration rises at the end of life and is related largely to health issues. The elderly as a broad age category are only about one-half as mobile as the general population.

Migration and Regional Redistribution of Population

Three large interregional flows of internal migration have been occurring in the United States for many decades.

WESTWARD MOVEMENT. For a long time, there has been a high-volume flow of persons into the Pacific region, principally California, as well as a high-volume flow into the mountainous southwestern states. The 1970–1980 decade had a higher volume of westward movement than any previous decade. Mountain states that previously had been suffering losses all made positive gains, and Colorado, Nevada, and Arizona continued the large gains of the previous decade.

NORTHWARD MOVEMENT FROM THE SOUTH. The southern region lost population heavily between the close of the Civil War and 1950. A very large share of the migrating population was absorbed by industrial centers in the Northeast and East-North-Central regions. Both white and black migrants have flowed along these channels in great numbers. Some southern states, however, particularly Florida and Texas, were exceptions. Between 1970 and 1980 the net outflow from the South completely disappeared. Those who leave the South prefer the West rather than the North as a destination, and in-migrants to the South currently balance the out-migrants. Every state in the Northeast and North-Central regions suffered a net migration loss during the decade, resulting in a major regional migration turnaround (Bogue 1985).

THE SOUTHWARD MOVEMENT TO THE GULF COAST AND THE SOUTHERN ATLANTIC SEABOARD. The entire Gulf Coast, from the mouth of the Rio Grande in Texas across the coastal portions of lower Louisiana, Mississippi, and Alabama, and on to include all of Florida, has undergone a much more rapid and intensive economic development than the southern and southeastern parts of the United States lying away from the coast. Although this trend is a very old one, it accelerated rapidly in the 1970s.

As of 1980 there were only two regional migration streams instead of three: movement toward the South and Southwest, and movement toward the West. The Northeast and the North-Central region are the sources from which these migrants come (Bogue 1985).

One of the macro-level processes that affects geographic mobility in our time is metropolitan deconcentration. Many nonmetropolitan counties in the United States experienced a slowing of population decline in the 1960s, and in the 1970s their net migration rates climbed above the break-even point, signaling a genuine and widespread "rural-urban turnaround." Older people seem to have been in the vanguard of migration to nonmetropolitan counties; the turnaround for them happened in the 1960s rather than the 1970s. This reversal of a long-term trend of rural-to-urban migration has been of great interest to demographers. Mounting evidence now indicates that although deconcentration continues in nonmetropolitan America for the population as a whole, metropolitan counties by the late 1980s were outgrowing nonmetropolitan ones (Long and DeAre 1988).

Retirement Migration

Demography has tended traditionally to focus on youthful migration, and labor-force migration in particular. Increasing attention, however, is being given to nonlabor-force-motivated migration, particularly to the migration of persons of retirement age (Longino 1990). For the elderly, interstate flows are highly channelized—that is, half of the interstate migrants, regardless of their origin, flow into only seven of the fifty states. Florida dominates the scene, having received about one-quarter of all interstate migrants aged sixty or over in the five years preceding the 1960, 1970, and 1980 censuses. Although Florida, California, and Arizona have different major recruitment areas, they are the only states that attract several unusually large streams from outside their regions. Florida draws primarily from east of the Mississippi River, and Arizona and California draw from west of it. Among the elderly, the special characteristics of the destination tend to be more important than the distance. Warm climate, economic growth, and lower cost of living are still important causal factors.

Distance selectivity of elderly migration has been studied. Local movers are generally not as economically and socially well off as nonmovers, and migrants are more so. Interstate migrants tend to have the most positive characteristics.

Permanence is an important but difficult dimension of migration to study. The census assumes that one's "usual place of residence" is not temporary. In reality, however, much of the migration among older people may be temporary. Further study needs to develop a serious research literature on nonpermanent migration. So far, studies of elderly seasonal migrants have shown them to be relatively advantaged, attracted by nonlabor-force issues such as climate, cost of living, and the locations of family members and friends.

Metropolitan-to-metropolitan migration predominates among the elderly. Metropolitan-to-nonmetropolitan migrants, especially those moving longer distances, tend to have more income, to be married, and to live in their own homes. A higher proportion of nonmetro-to-metro migrants is older, widowed, and living dependently, especially with their children.

The cycle of migration for a job when one is young, and returning to one's roots after retirement, has been an appealing notion to theorists. Andrei Rogers (1990), however, recently demonstrated that elderly persons are not any more likely to return home than are the nonelderly; the probabilities of return migration by the elderly are lower than those of the general population even after controlling for the different mobility levels of the two populations. There is wide state variability, however. The southeastern region is unusually attractive to older return migrants, and return migration is uncommonly high among older blacks moving into that region.

International Comparisons of Internal Migration

There is little research comparing countries on internal migration because measures, data sources, and units of analysis differ widely among countries. Consequently, international organizations have not published compendiums of national comparative data on migration as they have on fertility and mortality. In addition, internal migration is conceived differently in certain types of cultures. In some small countries or where there is little new housing stock, residential movement is very limited. Further, in countries where, for historical reasons, transportation routes primarily connect the peripheral towns to a central national capital, migration is also limited. However, in countries such as the United States, with widely dispersed regional centers and major cities, internal migration is amplified and culturally expected.

Some tentative generalizations can be drawn from existing studies that compare internal migration in the United States with that of other countries (Long 1988). The U.S. national average for moves is higher than that of most other countries because (1) cities in the South and West are growing; (2) a relatively large minority of people who repeatedly move elevates the U.S. averages for lifetime moves above that for most other countries; and (3) during the past two decades the baby-boom generation in the United States has moved through the life-cycle stages that have the highest rates of geographic mobility.

Comparative studies have also given attention to older migrants, although their mobility rates are lower than for the young. Rogers (1989) argued that as the populations of industrialized nations age, the internal migration patterns of elderly persons will change. Elderly migration levels are low in countries in the first stage of this population transition. In the second stage of the transition, large, long-distance flows to particular principal destination regions appear. The third stage continues to exhibit large numbers of elderly migrants, but their moves now include a significant number of short-distance moves to more dispersed inland regions. Rogers and his colleagues (1990) argue from comparative data that England is in the third stage, the United States is transitioning between the second and the third, Italy is well into the second, and Japan is in the first stage.

Elderly persons are not any more likely to return home than are the nonelderly.

Since 1970, for most developed countries, population aging has brought declining national rates of internal migration (Long 1988). For the United States, the decline appears to be greater for local moves than for long-distance movement. Urbanization was the dominant redistribution trend in the 1950s in fourteen European countries studied by Fielding (1989). The relationship between net migration and settlement size began to break down, however, in the 1960s—first in the countries of northwestern Europe in the mid-1960s, then in the countries and regions of the southern and Western European periphery through the 1960s, and in the case of Spain, into the 1970s. By the 1970s, most of the countries of Western Europe were recording counterurbanization, where the net flow was away from cities and toward smaller settlements. That counterurbanization became less dominant in the early 1980s but was not replaced by urbanization. Only in West Germany and Italy did the counterurbanization relationship persist. The United States experienced a similar pattern of long-term urbanization, reversed in the 1970s and then nearly reversed again in the 1980s (Frey 1990).

Why it is Difficult to Predict Future Migration

There are several trends that could potentially reduce migration, some only in the short run. These demographic, economic, and social trends might have countervailing effects on recent and future levels of interstate migration (Long 1988). First, a generally slower economic growth in the late 1970s compared with the 1960s may have dampened interstate migration, particularly among the young. Second, the increased labor-force participation of women increased the number of dual-career households. Dual career households tend to have lower rates of long-distance migration. Third, housing conditions in the 1970s may have depressed interstate migration when a potential increase in salary was exceeded by the cost of a much more expensive mortgage at the new location. Fourth, migrants were more likely to move to smaller, cleaner cities with lower crime rates during the 1970s. These migrants may be less likely than others to make a second move.

In contrast, other trends could increase migration rates (Long 1988). First, the age composition has shifted. There were more persons in the twenty-to-thirty age range in the 1980s, the prime mobility age sector. The baby-boom generation is actually less likely to make long moves, on average. However, in the short run the incidence of migration increased anyway, because of their large numbers. In the long run, as baby boomers leave their prime mobility years, their aging will likely dampen the incidence of moving. Second, the rising level of education may increase migration: Each new cohort of adults has a higher level of education than their seniors. Third is household change: Married couples are increasingly likely to divorce, a situation favoring migration, but at the same time there are more dual-career couples in the population, which favors nonmobility.

[See also Population; Retirement.]

BIBLIOGRAPHY

Bogue, Donald J. 1985 *The Population of the United States: Historical Trends and Future Projections.* New York: Free Press.

———, and Calvin L. Beale 1961 *Economic Areas of the United States.* New York: Free Press.

Fielding, A. J. 1989 "Migration and Urbanization in Western Europe since 1950." *The Geographical Journal* 155:60–69.

Frey, William H. 1990 "Metropolitan America: Beyond the Transition." *Population Bulletin* 45:1–51.

Kahley, William J. 1990 "Measuring Interstate Migration." *Economic Review* 75 (2):26–40.

Lansing, John B., and Eva Mueller 1967 *The Geographic Mobility of Labor.* Ann Arbor: Institute for Social Research, University of Michigan.

Lee, Everett S. 1966 "A Theory of Migration." *Demography* 3:47–57.

Long, Larry H. 1988 *Migration and Residential Mobility in the United States.* New York: Russell Sage Foundation.

———, and D. DeAre 1988 "U.S. Population Redistribution: A Perspective on the Nonmetropolitan Turnaround." *Population and Development Review* 14: 433–450.

Longino, Charles F., Jr. 1990 "Geographic Distribution and Migration." In R. H. Binstock and L. K. George, eds., *Handbook of Aging and the Social Sciences,* 3rd ed. San Diego, Calif.: Academic Press.

Lowry, Ira S. 1966 *Migration and Metropolitan Growth: Two Analytic Models.* San Francisco: Chandler.

Prehn, John W. 1986 "Migration." *The Encyclopedic Dictionary of Sociology,* 3rd ed. Guilford, Conn.: Dushkin.

Ravenstein, E. G. 1889 "The Laws of Migration." *Journal of the Royal Statistical Society* 52:245–301.

Rogers, Andrei 1989 "The Elderly Mobility Transition: Growth, Concentration and Tempo." *Rasearch on Aging* 11:3–32.

——— 1990 "Return Migration to Region of Birth Among Retirement-Age Persons in the United States." *Journal of Gerontology: Social Sciences* 45:S128–S134.

———, John F. Watkins, and Jennifer A. Woodward 1990 "Interregional Elderly Migration and Population Redistribution in Four Industrialized Countries: A Comparative Analysis." *Research on Aging* 12:251–293.

Shryock, Henry S. 1964 *Population Mobility within the United States.* Chicago: Community and Family Study Center, University of Chicago.

Zelinski, Wilbur 1971 "The Hypothesis of the Mobility Transition." *Geographical Review* 61:219–249.

– CHARLES F. LONGINO, JR.

INTERNATIONAL LAW

International law is the system of rules and principles governing relations at the interstate level. It originally developed in response to the needs of states but in recent times has grown to include international organizations and, to some extent, individuals.

International law as a systematic body of rules began in Europe in the seventeenth century. Before then, and from earliest history, rules existed governing the interrelations of various groups of people (Nussbaum 1958). But the rules were systematized in Europe only when the contacts among peoples became regular and frequent and the idea of a single ruler for all known society foundered. That occurred with the collapse of the Holy Roman Empire during the Thirty Years War (1618–1648). The state system developed in its place, characterized by a number of kingdoms and principalities, each equal to the others, sovereign within its own borders, and subject to no outside sovereign. Hugo Grotius, a Dutchman who lived during this time, wrote a seminal book, *De Jure Belli ác Pacis* (1620–1625), describing legal rules, derived from natural law, by which these states could achieve peaceful coexistence and, when they failed, how they could conduct their wars with some semblance of humanity. His book popularized international law, and he is generally considered the founder of international law.

The rules and principles Grotius described reflected the characteristics of states. The fundamental notion that states were sovereign and equal became a principle of international law. And because the rulers of states respected that principle as law, they were less likely to wage war or to annex their neighbors. International law helped create the success of the state system and in turn reflected the features of the system.

Grotius derived his rules from natural law, thus suggesting that nature was superior to states. By the nineteenth century, however, theorists abandoned natural law as a source of international law. Instead, they looked at the behavior of the states themselves as the source of international law. International lawyers became positivists, and the state became for international law the ultimate political entity. The rules of international law could guide and could set out regular procedures to ensure the smooth and peaceful conduct of international relations, but they permitted states wide prerogatives. Governments acquiesced in international legal rules because their states benefited from an orderly system of international relations in which they gave up few of the attributes of absolute sovereignty. For example, the rules did not speak to what states did internally, no matter how egregious. Individuals were not considered subjects of international law. Nor did the rules restrain states from the use of force. International law described permissible uses of force, but states could in effect use force whenever they chose.

By the twentieth century pressures for change began to develop. Technological advances in war and communications accounted for movements aimed at restraining states in their use of force and abuse of human beings. People such as Elihu Root, U.S. Secretary of State in Theodore Roosevelt's administration, wanted international law to provide the vehicle for restraint. Governments started experimenting with dispute settlement through arbitration and courts. They formed the League of Nations to help them control states' uses of force. International law and international institutions were being substituted for unbridled state sovereignty. The concept was a radical departure from the past and came about only over the course of half a century and two world wars.

After World War II, governments were willing in theory to contemplate real restraints on their ultimate sovereign prerogatives. The United Nations was created as an entity under international law. Its charter committed states to uphold human rights, to cooperate in solving world problems, to abandon the use of force, and to follow the commands of the organization itself. The idea was to lessen state sovereignty for the good of the whole world community. Thus, the state began to lose its place as the ultimate political entity almost exactly 300 years after its rise.

Certain international legal norms are now theoretically superior to the wills of the states. In other words, a certain amount of natural law now characterizes the system again. In addition, the state is making way for other types of political institutions such as regional arrangements, although if the state should ever become finally obsolete so will international law. The current form of international law and many of its rules and principles presuppose a system of coequal entities without a single sovereign.

While the state system remains intact, however, international law has taken on an increasingly important role in governing the relations of states in an interdependent, technologically linked world. It does this even though international law has never had the institutions typical of domestic law: a legislature for making law, an executive to enforce it, and a judiciary to adjudicate and interpret it. In some respects international law still functions as it did in the nineteenth century because the system benefits the state. Nevertheless, law does get made, enforced, and adjudicated, and social movements are at work putting demands on states to form and live by new norms of international law.

The Nuremberg and Japanese (shown here) War Crimes Trials broke new ground in international law by holding that individuals had rights and responsibilities beyond the laws of their own nations. (Hulton-Deutsch Collection/Corbis)

Because of the informal condition in which international law exists, however, some legal thinkers argue it is not law at all but rather moral precepts or mere guidelines. Most prominent of these thinkers was John Austin, who described law as a series of commands backed by sanctions. International law has no overarching authority to issue commands, and the sanctions are irregular. But Austin's criticism depends on his definition of law. If law is defined as behavior or behavioral restraint induced by a sense of obligation, international law, in its sphere, is law. Positivist international lawyers also point out that in the end the states acknowledge that international law is law, and that is the relevant indicator.

International legal rules have two basic sources: custom and treaty. Rules of customary international law are created through practices that states engage in because they believe they have a legal obligation to do so. Treaties are the explicit agreements states make with each other to be bound. As the need for international law has grown, states have relied on treaties as a law-making vehicle more and more. The general multilateral treaty has become a common form of law making for important international concerns. For almost ten years nearly every state of the world attended a conference to negotiate a comprehensive treaty on the law of the sea. Because so many states attended and the treaty was so long in the making, the treaty began to take on the characteristics of customary international law, irrespective of its status as a treaty.

When no rule of custom can be found and no treaty exists, international courts have in some disputes turned to a third source of law—general principles of law. These are principles commonly found in domestic legal systems and can serve to fill any gaps in international law, which suffers from its ad hoc law-making process. Theorists consider general principles a subsidiary source of international law because general principles are not made in a positive sense by all the states of the system, and they may be applied to a state that did not wish to be bound by them. Custom and treaty, however, generally allow states to opt out of a rule, thus reflecting the traditional view that the states are superior to the system of law. In the last thirty years, however, states have accepted that certain principles cannot be derogated from because they are considered peremptory norms or *jus cogens.* Examples of such norms are the prohibitions on genocide, the slave trade, and the use of force to advance a state's political agenda. With the concept of *jus cogens,* international law has again taken on some elements of natural law.

Jus cogens also exemplifies the extent to which international law has overcome cultural relativity. As new states emerged in the 1960s, scholars from these states questioned whether international law should be binding on them since it was a European product that had aided in perpetuating colonialism. These criticisms have faded, however, because it became clear that international law also created the thing desired most by newly independent countries—statehood. Moreover, because international law is made by states, the new majority could begin to re-create international law. The process of international law has succeeded to the point of bringing states together in accepting that certain principles are overriding, despite the particular value systems of individual states.

Like the law-making system, the law-adjudicating system in international law depends on states volunteering to use it. The system does have courts, in particular, the International Court of Justice. But no state needs to subject itself to the court unless it wishes to do so. The court does have limited compulsory jurisdiction in the case of states that agree to submit cases to it in advance of disputes arising. Nicaragua brought a case against the United States under such an agreement in 1986. States can also agree on an ad hoc basis to submit disputes to arbitral tribunals. The vast majority of international law is adjudicated informally, however. If a state violates international law, such as when Iraq invaded Kuwait in 1990, most states in the system will pronounce their views regarding the legality of the action. Assessing these evaluations leads to conclusions regarding lawfulness. Thus, states make and adjudicate the law themselves.

States also enforce international law themselves. International law is notorious for being poorly enforced. In fact, however, most international law is in fact observed most of the time. Because the states must agree to the law, they tend to make only the laws they want and are willing to live by. Otherwise they opt out of the rules, as the United States has done for some of the new law of the sea. Law is not so well observed, however, in those areas that make headlines—war, human rights, terrorism—which perhaps accounts for international law's poor reputation for enforcement.

When a rule of international law is violated, the state that is harmed is allowed to take action against the perpetrator. For example, if a fishing treaty between state A and state B is violated because state A's fishermen overfish in state B's waters, state B might be entitled to terminate the treaty and prevent future fishing by state A. This system works to some extent, but states have tried to improve on it in recent decades by, first, giving the United Nations and, in particular, the Security Council authority to police some violations of international law and to expand the ability of domestic institutions in enforcing international law by expanding the concept of universal jurisdiction.

The Security Council has authority to maintain peace. In article 42 of the U.N. Charter, it is given the power to call on member states to contribute troops to fight at the direction of the council. The idea comes very close to having an international police force. It has only been used once, however—in Korea in the 1950s. Other attempts were stymied by the cold war antagonism of the United States and the Soviet Union, each of which had a veto over invocation of article 42. As a sort of substitute, the Secretary General has regularly sent troops, contributed voluntarily by U.N. members, to serve a peacekeeping role. Peacekeeping troops are not supposed to take enforcement action. But enforcement action may be a possibility again with the end of the cold war. Following Iraq's invasion of Kuwait in 1990, the council ordered worldwide economic sanctions and permitted the use of force, both to enforce the sanctions and to push Iraqi troops out of Kuwait.

Custom and treaty generally allow states to opt out of a rule, reflecting the traditional view that the states are superior to the law.

Another solution to enforcement has been the widening of universal jurisdiction. To prevent states from interfering in each other's affairs, international law contains principles of jurisdiction defining when and where a state may enforce rules of domestic or international law. In some instances any state may take action. This concept of universal jurisdiction is as old as international law. It was originally developed to handle the problem of piracy. Pirates are defined as persons who commit crimes for profit on the high seas. Generally they do not fly any state's flag, and they act outside the territorial jurisdiction of any state. Typically, the state where the act took place or the state of the pirate's nationality would have jurisdiction, but those categories often do not exist for pirates. The state of the victim might have jurisdiction, but the international system developed the rule that any state may board a vessel that fails to fly a flag and that any state may arrest, try, and punish pirates.

After World War II, universal jurisdiction was expanded to include the concept of crimes against humanity. The victorious allied powers tried German and Japanese individuals, holding them personally responsible for human rights abuses, characterized as crimes against humanity and thus crimes for which any state in the world could take jurisdiction. The Nuremburg and Japanese War Crimes Trials broke new ground in international law by holding that individuals had rights and responsibilities not only under their nation's law but under international law and by expanding the scope of a state's jurisdiction.

Individual responsibility and expanded state jurisdiction are being included today in a variety of treaties, especially related to human rights, narcotics, and terrorism. Customary international law now permits universal jurisdiction over persons who have committed genocide or war crimes. The International Court of Justice has also suggested that important human rights may be enforced by any state regardless of its connection with the violation because the obligation to respect human rights is an obligation owed to all people; it is a right *erga omnes.*

International law will need these improvements in enforcement. The scope of questions now covered by international law grows annually with the increasing interdependence of the world and the technological advances that bring peoples into conflicting contact. The need to protect the global environment is the newest challenge for international law. States may soon decide they need an international organization to regulate the world trading system. The problems of development, health, communications, education, population, and use of space on earth and in outer space are all new problems in need of attention. Add to them the old problems of war, territorial disputes, governing international organizations, treaties, dispute resolution, refugees, human rights, diplomatic immunity, law of the sea, air space, recognition of new states, and so on, and the growing importance of international law becomes apparent. International law will continue to serve as a means of conducting smooth international relations, its traditional role, but it will also continue to assume new importance as a means of solving problems. In order to achieve this, however, international law must improve its institutions and be accepted by more states, whose own sovereignty will diminish as international law advances.

[See also Genocide; Law and Legal Systems; War.]

BIBLIOGRAPHY

Brownlie, Ian 1990 *Principles of Public International Law.* Oxford: Clarendon Press.

Janis, Mark 1988 *An Introduction to International Law.* Boston: Little, Brown.

Max Planck Institute for Comparative Public Law and International Law 1981 *Encyclopedia of Public International Law.* New York: North-Holland.

Nussbaum, Arthur 1958 *A Concise History of the Law of Nations.* New York: Macmillan.

Parry, Clive, and John Grant 1988 *Encyclopedic Dictionary of International Law.* New York: Ocean Publications.

Stone, Julius 1983 "A Sociologial Perspective on International Law." In R. St. J. McDonald and D. M. Johnston, eds., *The Structure and Process of International Law: Essays in Legal Philosophy Doctrine and Theory.* The Hague: Martinus Nijhoff.

– MARY ELLEN O'CONNELL

INTERNATIONAL MIGRATION

International migration is a term used to refer to change of usual residence between nations. The number of international migrants is always very much less than the total number of persons traveling across international frontiers, because the overwhelming majority of such travelers do not intend to change their usual residence. International migration is contrasted with *internal migration,* which refers to a change of usual residence within a nation. The term *immigration* is used to denote the flow of persons establishing a usual residence in a given nation whose last residence was in some other nation. The term *emigration* is used to denote the flow of persons relinquishing a usual residence in a given nation to establish residence in some other nation. Net international migration denotes the difference between the number of persons immigrating to a given nation in a given period and the number emigrating from that nation in the same period.

Immigratory and emigratory events constitute two of the four components of national population change; the other two components are births and deaths. For most nations, population change is determined predominantly by the balance of births and deaths (natural increase). However, for a few nations in certain periods, the net international immigration has also been an important component of the total population change.

In determining the number of persons who have changed residence among nations, national statistical agencies must specify the meaning of a change in usual residence. The United Nations suggests (1978, p. 57) that international movements with an intended stay of more than one year be classified as international migration. Unfortunately, there is considerable lack of uniformity among nations with respect to how international migration is defined. For example, according to data of the Mexican government, some 46,000 Mexicans emigrated to the United States in 1973; according to data of the United States government, the number of permanent legal immigrants from Mexico was about 72,000 (United Nations 1978, pp. 605–623). Also, many governments, including the United States, collect data on immigration but not on emigration. Finally, all data on immigration published by governments refer to legal immigration only. Data on illegal or undocumented immigration cannot be tabulated.

Certain terms useful for the study of either international or internal migration will now be explained. A *migration stream* is defined as the total number of migratory events from Place A to Place B during a given time. The *counterstream* is defined as the total number of migratory events from Place B to Place A. The sum of events in the stream and counterstream is termed the *gross interchange* between A and B. The *effectiveness of* migration is defined as the ratio of the net migration between A and B and the gross interchange between the two places. The effectiveness of migration can therefore vary from a low of 0 to a high of 1. For most pairs of geographic units the effectiveness of migration tends to be much closer to 0 than to 1.

Petersen (1975, pp. 321–324) makes very useful distinctions among the concepts of free, impelled, and forced migrations. In free migration the will of the migrant is the main factor. In impelled migration the will of the migrant is subordinated to the will of other persons. In forced migration the will of other persons is paramount, and the will of the migrant is of no weight at all. Another useful term is *return migration,* defined as migration back to a place in which one had formerly resided. *Chain migration* (MacDonald and MacDonald 1964) is also a frequently used concept. It refers to the common pattern whereby a given individual migrates to a particular destination in which he or she already has kin or friends who have previously migrated from his or her own area of origin.

Migration Differentials

It is universally observed that the propensity for international migration is strongest among young adults. Other differentials in migration tend to be limited to particular cultures or locales. Because the highest propensity for international migration is among young adults, the contribution of international migration to population change is often considerably greater than the net international migration by itself. This is because the birth rate for migrants is higher than for the total population, and the death rate is lower.

Determinants of the Volume of International Migration

Demographers analyze the determinants of the volume of a migratory stream into two components. The first concerns the specific propensity to migrate for individuals of each given type. The second concerns the number of individuals of each given type. The volume of a migratory stream can be calculated as the sum of the products obtained by multiplying the specific propensity to migrate for individuals of each given type by the number of individuals of that type.

The determinants of the propensity to migrate may conveniently be analyzed in terms of a preference system, a price system, and the total amount of resources available for all goals (Heer 1975, pp. 94–96). The preference system describes the relative attractiveness of various places as goals for potential migrants, compared to other goals that their resources would allow them to pursue. An area's attractiveness is the balance between the positive and negative values that it offers.

Among the most important of the positive values is the prospect of a better-paying job. Other positive values achieved by migration include the chance to live in a more favorable climate, freedom from persecution, opportunity for marriage, and continuation of marital ties. In the case of forced migration, the positive value achieved is simply to save one's own life.

However, international migration also creates negative values. A major disincentive to migration is that it involves a disruption of interpersonal relationships with kin and old friends. Chain migration is so attractive precisely because it mitigates the disruption of such relationships (Massey, Alarcon, Durand, and Gonzalez 1987). Other negative values created by international migration are the necessity to learn new customs and, often, a new language. Laws restraining legal entry or departure are also, of course, very important deterrents to international migration and will be discussed later in more detail.

The price system describes the costs in money, energy, and time, which cannot be used in the pursuit of other goals, imposed by a given migration decision. Since the cost of international migration generally varies in direct proportion to the distance traveled, the number of immigrants to a given place tends to vary inversely with the distance.

The total resources available for all goals also affects the decision to migrate. If the only drawback to migration is the expense of the move, an increase in monetary income should increase the probability of migration.

Major Streams of International Migration

Certain major streams of international migration deserve mention, either because they have had important historical consequences or because they otherwise exemplify unusual patterns. One of the earliest streams of international migration with historical significance was the westward movement of nomadic tribes in Europe and Central Asia at the time of the fall of the Roman Empire. The many tribes that moved westward during this period included those speaking Celtic, Germanic, and Ural-Altaic languages. As the easternmost tribes moved westward, they pushed forward the tribes in front of them. One suggested explanation for this extensive migration is that the grasslands of Central Asia had become desiccated. A second possibility is that an expanding Chinese Empire disrupted the life of the nomadic tribes near its borders and, thus, provoked the movement of all the other tribes (Bury 1928; Huntington 1924; Teggart 1939).

The European and African migrations to North America, South America, and Oceania have probably had more important historical consequences than any other migratory stream. This flow began slowly after Columbus's voyage to America in 1492. It has been estimated that over sixty million Europeans left for overseas points in the centuries since then. However, net migration was lower, since many of those leaving Europe later returned (United Nations 1953, pp. 98–102). The migration from Africa to the New World was almost wholely a forced migration of slaves. The first slaves were brought to the colony of Virginia in 1619, and the slave trade in the United States was not legally ended until 1808. During the period of slave trade, about 400,000 Africans were brought to the United States (U.S. Bureau of the Census 1909, p. 36). The impact of the migration of slaves is revealed by the fact that, in 1790, 20 percent of the four million persons in the United States were black.

Perhaps the world's largest gross interchange in a short time took place in India and Pakistan following the 1947 partition of British India.

The emigration from Puerto Rico to the mainland United States, of major magnitude in the years following World War II, is of interest because it exemplifies an extremely high rate. According to the 1970 Census of the United States, the combined total of the population of Puerto Rico and of persons in the United States of Puerto Rican birth or parentage was about 4.1 million, of which around 1.4 million were in the United States. Thus 33.9 percent of all Puerto Ricans were on the mainland (U.S. Bureau of the Census 1971, p. 48; 1973, p. 1).

Immigration into Israel following World War II is likewise noteworthy because it exemplifies an extremely high rate. In 1948, when independence was established, the total population of Israel was 650,000; by 1961, after the influx of more than 1 million immigrants, it had risen to 2.2 million (Bouscaren 1963, pp. 89–90; United Nations 1966, p. 113).

Perhaps the world's largest gross interchange in a short time took place in India and Pakistan following the 1947 partition of British India and the establishment of these two areas as independent states. This migration is also of interest because it was impelled rather than free. In the face of violence, Hindus and Sikhs in Pakistan moved to India and Muslims in India moved to Pakistan. From 1947 through 1950, ten million persons migrated from Pakistan to India and 7.5 million from India to Pakistan (Spate 1957, p. 119).

The two most recent major streams of international migration exemplify what has been termed *labor migration.* The first stream was the large-scale migration of workers into the prosperous nations of northern and western Europe from poorer nations in the Mediterranean region such as Italy, Spain, Portugal, Yugoslavia, Greece, Turkey, Algeria, and Morocco. This stream began around 1960 and ended in 1973, following the sudden elevation of petroleum prices by the Organization of Petroleum Exporting Countries (OPEC). The proportion of the total population that was foreign increased substantially in all of the northwest European nations. For example, from 1960 to 1970, the foreign population of the German Federal Republic increased from 1 percent to 5 percent and that of Switzerland from 9 percent to 16 percent (Van de Kaa 1987, p. 42). The second major stream has been the large-scale migration of workers into the major oil-producing nations in the Persian Gulf region out of such nations as Jordan, Egypt, Yemen, Pakistan, and India. For example, from 1957 through 1975, 70 percent to 75 percent of the total labor force in Kuwait consisted of foreigners (Birks and Sinclair 1981, p. 459).

Consequences of International Migration

One may examine the possible consequences of international migration for the individual, the area of net emigration, the area of net immigration, and the larger social system, which includes areas of net emigration and net immigration. The discussion must be in part speculative, since knowledge about these topics is incomplete.

Before a move, an immigrant will have anticipated a net balance of favorable consequences. Sometimes, however, reality will fall short of expectations, and dissatisfaction will provoke the immigrant to either return to her or his nation of origin or, on occasion, move on to some other nation.

Net emigration may have several important consequences for an area. By relieving population pressure, it may cause the average level of wage and salary income to rise. Remittances from emigrants may also be helpful. On the other hand, net emigration may cause the value of land and real estate to decline. Moreover, areas of net emigration suffer the loss of investments made to raise and educate children who spend their productive years elsewhere. This loss is particularly large when the individual receives a higher education prior to emigration. Such a loss is termed *brain drain.* Finally, since emigration rates are selective by age, nations with substantial net emigration may have relatively few young adults relative to the number of children and the aged.

Net immigration may also have important consequences. If the area is definitely underpopulated, the resultant population increase may help the nation to achieve economies of scale (reduction in the cost of goods obtainable by increasing the scale of production and marketing) and, thus, raise the general standard of living. Under other circumstances, net immigration may result in some decline in average wage and salary income. In either case, a net flow of immigrants tends to raise the price of land and real estate. Furthermore, in general, net immigration increases the proportion of young adults in the total population. Dependent on their composition, immigrants may receive either more or less in government benefits than the amount of their tax payments. Finally, net immigration may make the population more heterogeneous with respect to race, religion, or language.

For the system comprising the nations of both net inflow and net outflow, the direct effect of international migration is of course to promote a redistribution of population. If migrants have been responsive to differences in job opportunities, this redistribution may further the economic development of the total system. Moreover, a substantial amount of international migration responsive to job opportunities might also induce a decline in the degree to which there is economic inequality among nations. Unrestricted international migration might make the poor nations richer and the rich nations less prosperous. However, there is substantial disagreement among scholars as to what the effect of unrestricted immigration from the poor nations might be on the prosperity of the rich nations such as the United States. Julian Simon (1984) believes that net immigration to the United States will serve to increase its average income. Kingsley Davis, on the other hand, takes a much more pessimistic view (1981, pp. 428–429).

Legislation Affecting Immigration and Emigration

National laws concerning immigration have varied from almost complete prohibition to positive encouragement. Laws restricting emigration are now relatively rare but have been of important consequence in modern times for at least one nation, Russia.

In the seventeenth and eighteenth centuries a mercantilist ideology, which saw a large population as the key to national wealth and power, encouraged many of the governments of Europe to attempt to prohibit emigration and to encourage immigration. In the late seventeenth century, the French minister Colbert enacted legislation prescribing the death penalty for persons attempting to emigrate or helping others to emigrate, except to a French colony. In 1721, Prussia passed a similar law. Moreover, the Prussian emperor Frederick the Great invested state funds in subsidizing the settlement of immigrants. In Russia both Tsar Peter and Tsarina Catherine subsidized colonists from abroad, mostly from Germany (Glass 1940, pp. 94–96).

The nineteenth century, influenced by the economic doctrines of laissez faire, was the great period of unrestricted international migration. During this century the European governments freely permitted emigration, and the newly independent United States of America welcomed millions of immigrants.

After World War I, the United States government took a more active role in restricting international immigration. The major events in this connection were changes in immigration law in 1921 and 1924 that greatly restricted the number of immigrants to the United States, establishing a quota for each of the countries outside the Western Hemisphere. Furthermore, each of the nations of northwestern Europe was given a much larger quota relative to its population than those of southern or eastern Europe. This was done even though, in the immediately preceding years, rates of immigration from southern and eastern Europe had been much higher than those from northwestern Europe. The justification made at the time for the quota differentials was the presumed greater ease with which immigrants from northwestern Europe could assimilate themselves (Eckerson 1966, pp. 4–14).

By the 1960s, a changing climate of opinion with respect to the inferiority or superiority of different ethnic groups made it possible for President Kennedy to advocate the abolition of the discriminatory national-origins quota system, and a law accomplishing this was enacted in 1965 under the Johnson administration. The 1965 law called for the abolition of the national-origins quota system as of July 1, 1968, but, nevertheless, imposed an overall annual quota of 170,000 immigrants from outside the Western Hemisphere and 120,000 from within it (exclusive of immediate relatives of U.S. citizens). This legislation granted preference to persons with relatives already in the United States, to persons with needed occupational skills, and to refugees. Additional legislation passed in 1976 abandoned the separate quotas for the two hemispheres and imposed a 20,000 limit on quota immigrants from any nation in the Western Hemisphere (the 20,000 limit had previously been in existence only for Eastern Hemisphere nations). The major effect of the 1976 legislation was to make it more difficult for Mexicans legally to enter the United States.

Formerly, Canada and Australia subsidized immigrants from European nations while placing severe restrictions on the immigration of nonwhites.

Some nations, while placing severe restrictions on immigrants in general, have made use of positive inducements to encourage immigration from selected nations or groups. Currently the best example of such legislation is that of Israel, which has committed itself to encouraging the immigration of Jews from anywhere in the world. Formerly, Canada and Australia also exemplified such policies of selective encouragement. Each of these nations subsidized immigrants from European nations while placing severe restrictions on the immigration of nonwhites (Bouscaren 1963, pp. 105–108, 141–144; Petersen 1964, pp. 301–322).

The United States, Australia, Canada, and Israel have laws that allow immigrants permanent residence leading to citizenship. In recent decades, other nations, particularly in northwestern Europe and in the Persian Gulf, have had policies that encouraged only labor migration, that is, migration of workers, mostly male, who were supposed to return to their native countries following a fixed term. In the case of the European nations at least, these policies had unintended results. The contract workers were allowed to extend their stays beyond the times originally set for them to leave. Finally, they were allowed to bring their dependents to live with them. Hence, they became permanent immigrants even though this was not the result intended by original policy (United Nations 1982).

In many nations of the world, particularly in the United States, a major phenomenon is the existence of illegal, or undocumented, immigrants. A necessary condition for the existence of illegal immigration is a lack of congruence between the laws regulating the supply of legal immigrant opportunities and the demand for them. For example, the demand to immigrate to the United States from a particular nation should be a reflection of that nation's population size and the average propensity to immigrate to the United States if there were no legal restrictions. Accordingly, nations with large population size are likely to have more immigrant demand than nations with small populations; yet all nations, without regard to population size, have the same 20,000 person annual quota. Furthermore, national differences in individual propensity to immigrate to the United States should be a function of such variables as the difference in standard of living compared with that of the United States, proximity to the United States, degree of similarity with the language and culture of the United States, and prior existence of immigrants that allows for chain migration. Given Mexico's population size and presumed high average propensity for immigration to the United States, one can easily explain why a very large proportion of all undocumented persons in the United States are from that nation (Heer 1990).

Rising concern over the extent of undocumented immigration into the United States led the U.S. Congress to enact the Immigration Reform and Control Act of 1986. The intent of the legislation was to eliminate the presence of undocumented aliens in the United States either by legalizing their status or by forcing them to leave the country. This act had two key provisions. The first was the imposition of sanctions upon employers who knowingly employed illegal aliens. The second was the provision of a process whereby undocumented persons who had lived in the United States continuously since January 1, 1982, or had worked in U.S. agriculture for ninety days in the period from May 1985 to May 1986 were allowed to become temporary legal residents. After a short time, they would be allowed to become permanent legal residents. The success of employer sanctions is problematic because sanctions can be applied only if the employer knowingly hires illegal aliens and because it is relatively easy for an undocumented person to present to the potential employer either fake documents or the documents of some other legally resident person. On the other hand, over three million persons applied for legalization of status after the act was passed, among whom about 2.3 million were from Mexico (U.S. Immigration and Naturalization Service 1990).

In 1989 more than three-quarters of the world's 5.2 billion persons lived in one of the less developed nations. The annual rate of natural increase in these nations was around 2.1 percent; in the developed nations it was only 0.6 percent. In the developed nations per capita gross national product was $12,070; in the less developed nations, only $670 (Population Reference Bureau 1989). These facts imply a strongly increasing demand for immigration to the developed nations from the less developed. Given the current barriers to legal immigration imposed by the developed nations, undocumented immigration will be of increasing prevalence unless the governments of the developed nations take extraordinary measures to curb it.

[See also Ethnicity; Population.]

BIBLIOGRAPHY

Birks, John, and Clive A. Sinclair 1981 "Demographic Settling amongst Migrant Workers." In *International Population Conference, Manila 1981,* vol. 2, pp. 449–469. Liège, Belgium: International Union for the Scientific Study of Population.

Bouscaren, Anthony T. 1963 *International Migration Since 1945.* New York: Praeger.

Bury, B. 1928 *The Invasion of Europe by the Barbarians.* London: Macmillan.

Davis, Kingsley 1981 "Emerging Issues in International Migration." In *International Population Conference, Manila 1981,* Vol. 2, pp. 419–429. Liège, Belgium: International Union for the Scientific Study of Population.

Eckerson, Helen F. 1966 "Immigration and National Origins." *Annals of the American Academy of Political and Social Science* 367:4–14.

Glass, David V. 1940 *Population Policies and Movements in Europe.* Oxford: Clarendon Press.

Heer, David M. 1975 *Society and Population,* 2nd ed. Englewood Cliffs, N.J.: Prentice-Hall.

——— 1990 *Undocumented Mexicans in the United States.* New York: Cambridge University Press.

Huntington, Ellsworth 1924 *Civilization and Climate.* New Haven, Conn.: Yale University Press.

MacDonald, John S., and Leatrice D. MacDonald 1964 "Chain Migration, Ethnic Neighborhood Formation, and Social Networks." *Milbank Memorial Fund Quarterly* 52:82–97.

Massey, Douglas, Rafael Alarcon, Jorge Durand, and Humberto Gonzalez 1987 *Return to Aztlan: The Social Process of International Migration from Western Mexico.* Berkeley, Calif.: University of California Press.

Petersen, William 1964 *The Politics of Population.* Garden City, N.Y.: Doubleday.

——— 1975 *Population,* 3rd ed. New York: Macmillan.

Population Reference Bureau 1989 *World Population Data Sheet.* Washington, D.C.: Population Reference Bureau.

Simon, Julian 1984 "Immigrants, Taxes, and Welfare in the United States." *Population and Development Review* 10:55–69.

Spate, O. H. K. 1957 *India and Pakistan: A General and Regional Geography.* New York: Dutton.

Teggart, Frederick J. 1939 *Rome and China: A Study of Correlations in Historical Events.* Berkeley, Calif.: University of California Press.

United Nations 1953 *The Determinants and Consequences of Population Trends.* New York: United Nations.

——— 1966 *United Nations Demographic Yearbook, 1965.* New York: United Nations.

——— 1978 *United Nations Demographic Yearbook, 1977.* New York: United Nations.

——— 1982 *International Migration Policies and Programmes: A World Survey.* New York: United Nations.

U.S. Bureau of the Census 1909 *A Century of Population Growth in the United States: 1790–1900.* Washington, D.C.: U.S. Government Printing Office.

——— 1971 *U.S. Census of Population: 1970.* Final Report PC(1)-A1. Washington, D.C.: U.S. Government Printing Office.

——— 1973 *U.S. Census of Population: 1970.* Final Report PC(2)1E. Washington, D.C.: U.S. Government Printing Office.

U.S. Immigration and Naturalization Service 1990 *Provisional Legalization Application Statistics, January 9, 1990.* Washington, D.C.: U.S. Immigration and Naturalization Service.

Van de Kaa, Dirk J. 1987 "Europe's Second Demographic Transition." *Population Bulletin* 42:1–59.

– DAVID M. HEER

INTERPERSONAL ATTRACTION

Everyone meets many people. With some there is a natural fit; with others there isn't. Liking a person is quite different from liking chocolate, or liking to ski. Liking someone implies feelings of warmth, intimacy, and consideration and a desire for time spent together. Interpersonal attraction plays a large part in the formation of all relationships except for those into which a person is born, that is, all nonascriptive relationships. Everyone uses tactics that are expected to recruit potential partners; the specific tactics used in presenting oneself, as well as the characteristics for which an individual looks in others, will vary depending upon whether what is sought is friendship or love or a good working partner (McCall 1974, p. 392). Even though liking someone is based on many factors that can't always be defined, a person does know upon meeting someone whether he or she is in fact liked. This perceived liking in turn draws us toward the other (Sprecher and Hatfield 1982, p. 79). Men and women operate differently in the area of choosing people as being attractive. For example, men are more inclined to reject a person who disagrees with them than are women, and more likely to choose the same type of person as a friend and as a marriage partner (Lindzay and Aronson 1969, p. 97).

First impressions don't necessarily last. Nisbett, reanalyzing Newcomb's data in 1989, found that people's liking of other people after sixteen weeks' acquaintance was not predicted very well by their initial liking of these others after one week's acquaintance (Nisbett and Smith 1989, p. 72).

Theoretical Explanations of Interpersonal Attraction

Homans, working from the perspective of exchange theory, states that people consider the rewards versus the costs of any potential relationship (Lindzay and Aronson 1969, p. 83) and are attracted to those people who provide the most reward at the least cost. From this perspective, the ideal relationship is one in which both participants have equal costs and rewards, so that neither feels cheated or exploited. Newcomb asserts that frequency of interaction is an important determinant of attraction, a view known as the *propinquity perspective.* The basic assumption is that the more frequently one interacts with others, the more attractive they become. It is expected that frequency of interaction will lead to increasing similarity of beliefs and values and that this *assumed similarity* will in turn lead to increased attraction. This perspective ignores the possibility that getting to know a person better may actually reveal many differences (Lindzay and Aronson 1969, pp. 94–95). Despite the idea's appeal to common sense, there is little evidence of increasing reciprocity of interpersonal attraction over time (Kenny and LaVoie 1982, p. 54).

Despite the folk wisdom that opposites attract, similarity is more powerful than complementarity.

People do prefer those who are similar in background, interests, and values. They want to talk about things that interest them and do things familiar to them. A person who can provide social support by having similar beliefs and values is a likely potential friend. Despite the folk wisdom that opposites attract, similarity is more powerful than complementarity. The exceptions are those with strong needs on either end of the dominance–submission continuum or the nurturance–succorance continuum (Argyle 1969, p. 213); when strong needs exist in these areas, complementarity is more powerful.

Forming Relationships

First meetings proceed cautiously. In every cultural group there are conventions about how long the preliminaries must last. These conventions vary depending upon the age and gender of the participants, as well as where the meeting takes place.

In general, encounters that grow into close social relationships have the following characteristics: (1) a smooth pattern of interaction develops; (2) role relationships are clear, with participants agreeing on the definition of the situation and its rules and accepting the self-image presented by the other; (3) each comes to see the other and the link between them as special; (4) as trust grows, disclosure grows (Argyle 1969, pp. 207–208). The goals of the encounter determine the interpersonal attraction tactics used. For example, when characteristics of potential dating partners were varied along two dimensions, physical attractiveness and personality desirability, undergraduate males chose physical attractiveness as the deciding variable (Glick 1985, p. 561). Therefore, a female hoping for a date would find that increasing physical attractiveness would be more effective than showing what a nice personality she had.

In a culture that, like the United States, values openness, psychological awareness, and emotional vulnerability, self-disclosure increases likability. Those who disclose little are less apt to be found attractive by others (Montgomery 1986, p. 143).

Playing and Working Together

Competition has an interesting relationship with interpersonal attraction. Rees found that during intragroup competition, football players reported the most liking and respect for those who played their own position yet outperformed them (Rees and Segal 1984, p. 329). Riskin also found that males, when given background data indicating both the degree of competitiveness and the degree of work mastery in target males, rated the most competitive as most attractive, as long as they were also seen as having ability. In addition, these competitive males were assumed by the male subjects to be more attractive to women (Riskin and Wilson 1982, pp. 449–450). Numerous studies have shown that emergent leaders are given high interpersonal-attraction ratings by both sexes.

The workplace provides a setting where qualities of competitiveness, ability, and leadership are displayed. It might be assumed that this leads to the formation of romantic attachments. Though this does in fact occur, the work setting also provides for additional complexity in the handling of personal attraction. Attraction and intimacy must be seen in the context of outsiders' view of the relationship. Attempts must be made to balance the demands of the job and those of the relationship. Role relationships within the workplace are expected to contain a degree of distance that is at odds with the demands of "getting closer." Despite these problems, people do get romantically involved with co-workers. One study of 295 adults (average age: thirty-two) revealed that 84 had been involved in a romantic relationship with someone at work and 123 had been aware of a romance in their workplace. Such relationships are more likely to occur in less formal organizations, especially those that are very small or very large. The person most likely to enter into such a relationship is a female who is young, new, and of low rank (Dillard and Witteman 1985, p. 113).

Friendship

Being perceived as friendly, pleasant, polite, and easy to talk to increases a person's ability to attract potential friends. If in addition similar values, interests, and backgrounds are present, the likelihood of friendship is even greater (Johnsons 1989, p. 387). In ongoing relationships friendship has nothing to do with the participants' rating of each other's physical appearance. Nevertheless, at the initial meeting stage a person judged as being too physically attractive will be avoided. In one study, sixty undergraduate males were shown a male target population (previously rated from 1 to 5 by a male and female sample) and were asked who among this group they would like to meet. The most attractive were chosen less frequently; they were judged to be more egocentric and less kind. It was the moderately attractive who were seen as being the type of person most of the subjects would like to meet. Explaining these findings in terms of exchange theory, one would say that most people rate themselves as bringing moderate attractiveness to a relationship and feel that extreme attractiveness throws off the equality (Gailucci 1984).

Though it is often assumed that young people do not see older people as potential friends, a review of forty research reports reveals that perceived agreement in attitudes tends to neutralize young adults' general perception of older adults as unattractive. Elders may perceive young people as attractive or unattractive, but they still prefer to associate with individuals who are middle-aged or older (Webb, Delaney, and Young 1989).

Sexual Attraction and Romantic Relationships

While males and females alike differ in their ability to distinguish between friendly and sexually interested behavior, males are more likely to see sexual intent where females see only friendly behavior. When shown videotapes of five couples, each showing a male and a female behaving in either a friendly or a sexually interested way, males consistently saw more sexual intent (Shotland and Craig 1988, pp. 66–73).

Men and women also differ as to the relative importance of physical features and personal qualities in determining the choice of romantic partners. Even though both sexes rated personal qualities as being more important than physical features, males placed greater emphasis on the physical than did women (Nevid 1984). Despite this, there seems to be a point at which attempting to increase physical appeal by dressing to reveal the body has a negative effect on one's appeal as a marital partner. Hill reports that when male and female models wore very tight clothes that displayed a great deal of skin, they were rated as being very attractive as potential sex partners but their marital potential was lowered. High-status dressing had the opposite effect for both males and females: Ratings of physical, dating, sexual, and marital attractiveness all increased as the status of clothing increased (Hill, Nocks, and Gardner 1987, p. 144).

A shared sense of humor is another important component of loving and liking. When a humor test comprising cartoons, comic strips, and jokes was given to thirty college couples, along with a test that measured how much the partners loved and liked each other, a strong correlation between shared humor and a predisposition to marry was found (Murstein and Brust 1985). It can probably be assumed that the shared humor comes before the relationship, as well as serving as a factor that enhances it.

Trying to Attract Others

Though different factors come into play when one is evaluating someone as a potential friend or a potential work partner or a potential romantic partner, there seem to be inferred qualities that make a stranger appear to be likable or not likable. One study found that when videotapes of women were shown to males and females to judge, those most often chosen were apt to be described as sociable, cheerful, and positive emotionally; the underchosen were more apt to be described as negative and moody (Hewitt and Goldman 1982).

In personal ads, it is interesting to note that the richer a man claims to be, the younger, taller, and prettier a woman he wants.

A modern form of presentation of self that tells quite a bit about what people feel makes them appear attractive is the personal ad. No longer are these dismissed as being for the desperate; rather, they are seen as just another way to introduce oneself. A study of the responses to different sets of physical characteristics referred to in ads showed that tall men and thin women received the greatest number of responses (Lynn and Shurgot 1984, p. 351). In these ads it can also be seen that people present themselves as happy, able, capable, and very successful. It is interesting to note that the richer a man claims to be, the younger, taller, and prettier a woman he wants. The younger and prettier a woman presents herself as being, the more successful a man she wishes to meet.

[See also Courtship: Exchange Theory; Love; Mate Selection Theories; Personal Relationships; Social Psychology.]

BIBLIOGRAPHY

Argyle, Michael 1969 *Social Interaction.* Chicago: Aldine.

Dillard, James P., and Hal Witteman 1985 "Romantic Relationships at Work. Organizational and Personal Influences." *Human Communication Research* 12:99–116.

Gailucci, N. 1984 "Effects of Men's Physical Attractiveness on Interpersonal Attraction." *Psychological Reports* 55:935–938.

Glick, Peter 1985 "Orientations Toward Relationships: Choosing a Situation in Which to Begin a Relationship." *Journal of Experimental Social Psychology* 21:544–562.

Hewitt, J., and Morton Goldman 1982 "Traits Attributed to Over- and Under-Chosen Women." *Psychological Reports* 5:431–439.

Hill, Elizabeth, Elaine Nocks, and Lucinda Gardner 1987 "Physical Attractiveness: Manipulation by Physique and Status Displays." *Ethnology and Sociobiology* 8:143–154.

Johnsons, Martin R. 1989 "Variables Associated with Friendship in an Adult Population." *Journal of Social Psychology* 129:379–390.

Kenny, David A., and Lawrence LaVoie 1982 "Reciprocity of Interpersonal Attraction: A Confirmed Hypothesis." *Social Psychology Quarterly* 45:54–58.

Lindzay, Gardner, and Elliot Aronson 1969 *The Handbook of Social Psychology,* Vol. 3. Reading, Mass.: Addison Wesley.

Lynn, Michael, and Barbara A. Shurgot 1984 "Responses to Lonely Hearts Advertisements: Effects of Reported Physical Attractiveness, Physique, and Coloration." *Personality and Social Psychology Bulletin* 10:349–357.

McCall, George J. 1974 "A Symbolic Interactionist Approach to Attraction." In T. L. Huston, ed., *Foundations of Interpersonal Attraction.* New York: Academic Press.

Montgomery, Barbara 1986 "Interpersonal Attraction as a Function of Open Communication and Gender." *Communication Research Reports* 3:140–145.

Murstein, Bernard I., and Robert G. Brust 1985 "Humor and Interpersonal Attraction." *Journal of Personality Assessment* 49:637–640.

Nevid, Jeffrey F. 1984 "Sex Differences in Factors of Romantic Attraction." *Sex-Roles* 11:401–411.

Nisbett, Richard E., and Michael Smith 1989 "Predicting Interpersonal Attraction from Small Samples: A Re-analysis of Newcomb's Acquaintance Study." *Social Cognition* 7:67–73.

Rees, C. Roger, and Mady-Wechsler Segal 1984 "Intragroup Competition, Equity and Interpersonal Attraction." *Social Psychology Quarterly* 47:328–336.

Riskin, John, and David Wilson 1982 "Interpersonal Attraction for the Competitive Person: Unscrambling the Competition Paradox." *Journal of Applied Social Psychology* 12:444–452.

Shotland, R., and Jane Craig 1988 "Can Men and Women Differentiate Between Friendly and Sexually Interested Behavior?" *Social Psychology Quarterly* 51:66–73.

Sprecher, Susan, and Elaine Hatfield 1982 "Self-Esteem and Romantic Attraction: Four Experiments." *Recherches de Psychologie Sociale* 4:61–81.

Webb, Lynn, Judith Delaney, and Lorraine Young 1989 "Age, Interpersonal Attraction and Social Interaction: A Review and Assessment." *Research on Aging* 11:107–123.

— ARDYTH STIMSON

INTERPERSONAL POWER

In its broadest sense, interpersonal power refers to any cause of any change in the behavior of one actor, B, which can be attributed to the effect of another actor, A. It sometimes refers to the capacity to cause such change (Weber [1918] 1968), sometimes to actual use of that capacity (Simon 1953; Dahl 1957), but always to overcoming the "resistance" of B (Weber [1918] 1968), hence causing B to do something B would not otherwise do (Dahl 1957). Interpersonal power is therefore the power of one individual "over" another as opposed to an individual's power to do something, the capacity of an actor to attain some goal (as in Russell 1938). "Power over" always implies a relation between two actors rather than referring to an attribute of an actor. It is sometimes thought of as "micro" power and contrasts with "power to," which is attributed to collectives (Hawley 1963; Parsons 1963) and is thought of as "systemic" or "macro" power.

Adequate description of a power relation will typically refer to: (1) the *bases* of power (the bases of A's power over B are the resources that are possessed by A that are instrumental to the goals of B); (2) the *means* of power (the ways in which A uses these resources to change the behavior of B); (3) the *strength* of power (the costs to B if B does not comply with demands by A); (4) the *costs* of power (the costs of A of having to exercise power over B); (5) the *amount* of power (the extent to which A is able to get B to do something that B would not otherwise have done); (6) the *scope* of power (the acts with respect to which the amount of A's power over B is greater than zero); and (7) the *domain* of power (the persons over whom the amount of A's power is greater than zero). However, there is a great deal of disagreement over which of these constitute power and what kinds of bases, means, costs, and particularly compliance the word covers.

Concepts of Power

In his work on power, Simon (1953) treats the effects rather than the causes of power and covers by the one word a whole family of concepts describing the effects of all the human causes of human conduct. Force, power, influence, authority, and manipulation all have a strong family resemblance to each other, and Dahl (1957), March (1955), and Simon (1953) have all treated them as one process. But French and Raven (1959) have pointed out important ways in which the dynamics of different kinds of power differ, and March (1966) has shown compellingly that treating them all as one unitary process leads only to a dead end.

Force, power, influence, authority, and manipulation all have a strong resemblance to each other.

The laws of *force,* for example, differ in a fundamental way from the laws governing power. In using force, A does not require B to choose between compliance or noncompliance. A kills B, imprisons B, drags B, wrestles B to the ground, but does not require choice by B. Threat of force requires a choice, but threat of force is a different process (Goode 1972). A threat may be futile if B has decided to die for a cause; the threat may not accomplish its purpose. Actual force will accomplish its purpose whether B chooses to comply or not. It simply removes B as a factor opposed to A's wishes.

Like force, *manipulation* does not require that B choose between complying or not complying with the wishes of A. A may control B by controlling the information at B's disposal, by preventing certain choices being open to B, or by activating motives of B known to lead B to do what A wants. In some sense, B may be said to make choices (hence the difference from force), but A does not require B to choose between compliance and noncompliance. A controls the conditions that govern how B analyzes the choice to be made.

Although there are more than one narrow senses of the term *power,* all are distinguished from force and manipulation by the fact that power involves a choice by B between compliance and noncompliance. But this is true also of influence and authority. What distinguishes power is that it involves external sanctions. In Blau (1964) B is coerced to do something, X, by threat of a penalty for noncompliance. In Festinger (1953), B is induced to do X by a promise of reward for compliance or coerced to do X by threat of a penalty for noncompliance. Both rewards and penalties are external to the actor. They make no internal change, no change in the actor's state of mind. B does not change views privately, even if B conforms publicly. *Influence,* on the other hand, persuades B that X is right according to B's own interests, hence B complies privately as well as publicly. Compliance is willing in the case of influence, "forced" (Festinger 1953) in the case of power. If compliance were not observable to A, B would still comply in the case of influence but would not in the case of power. Hence, power is highly dependent on observability, but influence is not (French and Raven 1959).

Authority differs from both: It refers to a claim by A, accepted by B, that A has a legitimate right to expect compliance by B, even if compliance runs counter to B's own preferences (Barnard 1938). It differs from influence because whether B likes or does not like X is irrelevant. It differs from power in that B is expected to comply (and, if B accepts A's authority, does comply) because it is right, not because it is expedient. If B accepts A's legitimate authority, then B complies with A's commands whether compliance is observable to A or not. Furthermore, the power that legitimate authority makes possible has different effects because it is legitimate. Power exercised outside the scope of legitimate authority creates "reactance" (Brehm 1966), but power exercised inside the scope of legitimate authority does not (French and Raven 1959).

French and Raven (1959) also distinguish reward from punishment power and hence inducement from coercion. Coercion causes reactance; inducement does not. But they are so indissolubly connected that it becomes difficult to treat them as distinct processes. A reward foregone is a cost, and a penalty foregone is a reward. Hence, withholding a reward is equivalent to imposing a penalty, and withholding a penalty is equivalent to giving a reward. In order to distinguish the two, one would have to be able to separate giving something from withholding something. This might be possible in principle, but not in the case of power. Power depends on the contingency of sanctions; that is, A must be able to give *or* withhold something, depending on whether B does not comply. It is difficult to have one without the other. Thus, probably the most satisfactory concept of interpersonal power is Festinger's forced compliance (1953), compliance that is public but not private, caused either by threat of penalty or promise of reward.

This still leaves the question of whether power is potential or actual. Weber ([1918]: 1968) emphasized the capacity of one actor to overcome the resistance of another whether or not the capacity is actually used. Simon (1953) and Dahl (1957) have objected to making inferences from a potential that might or might not actually be used. Research in fact consistently shows that not all potential power is used (see below), and Dahl in particular has argued that power has an effect only if used. On the other hand, Friedrich (1937) has argued that B might comply with the preferences of A because of anticipated reward or punishment, even if A says or does nothing that overtly demands compliance by B. Bachrach and Baratz (1962) go further and argue that certain kinds of acts that involve B doing nothing (nondecisions) occur without B even needing to know what A will do, simply because B knows what A *could* do. Both arguments imply that sheer existence of potential power has an effect whether used or not. The effect does not even have to be intended.

Not only can potential power have an effect without being used, "use" of power occurs without necessarily being intended.

The issue of intentionality is another of the disputed questions in conceptualizing power, but not only can potential power have an effect without being used, there are even theories, such as Cartwright (1959) and Emerson (1962; 1972), in which "use" of power occurs without necessarily being intended by anyone.

The dispute over potential versus actual power refers more to causes, the dispute over broad versus narrow concepts of power more to effects. Thus, another ambiguity of power is whether one is referring to causes, effects, or the process relating the two.

The Causal Approach to Power

As process, power most typically refers to an exchange of "resources" (characteristics or objects instrumental to the attainment of goals). The only exception is the "causal" approach to power. Simon (1953) pointed out the similarity between the concept of "power over" and causality, leading to a long-standing tradition in which the former is defined in terms of the latter (as in Dahl 1957; Nagel 1975). But this led to so many difficulties that March (1966) concluded that the concept of power was superfluous. Although Nagel (1975) attempted to give the concept more explanatory power by narrowing it (to the effects of A's preferences on B), this led to little further advance, possibly because causal modeling gives one little insight into the process relating causes to effects.

But "process" theories themselves divide into four types: field theory; rational choice or decision, theories of exchange; behavioral exchange theory; and a neo-Weberian "resistance" theory of exchange.

The Field Theory of Power

In field theory, power is the ability to activate forces in the life space of another in the direction of X (Cartwright 1959). The capacity to activate such forces depends on the motive base of B, thought of as a tension system, which, when activated by A, produces a vectored force that reduces the tension. Thus, power depends on the needs of B as much as on the wishes of A. It was this approach that gave rise to the concept of a "resource": Transferable resources give rise to power. But use of power by A faces not only opposing forces leading B away from X but also resistance due to the exercise of power itself. (This resistance was later termed *reactance* by Brehm 1966 to distinguish it from resistance due to B's dislike of doing X itself.) A's "control" over B is the outcome of the opposing forces acting on B. Thus, the outcome of the reduction of tension in the force field is distinguished from A's power in a manner corresponding to the distinction between actual versus potential power. In field theory, therefore, success—that is, actual compliance by B—is not the measure of A's power since there are many forces other than A affecting B's behavior.

Field theory, like the causal approach to power, treats the whole family of power concepts as power, excluding only physical force. But research in this tradition was much concerned with differences between different types of power, including reward power, punishment power, expert power, legitimate power, and referent power (power arising from B's attraction to A, which causes a desire to be similar to A). It was found that both reward and punishment power depend on A's ability to observe B's behavior, while the other forms of power do not. Coercion increased but reward decreased reactance. Legitimacy normatively constrained power so that using it outside its legitimate scope reduced its effect. Use of coercion when it is legitimate decreased reactance, while use of rewards when they are not legitimate increased reactance (French and Raven 1959). Because of reactance, use of coercion depends on restraints that prevent B from leaving the field.

Exchange Theories of Power

The most important difference between field theory and exchange theories is that in the latter alternatives become the most important factor in the analysis of power. The reason is that, assuming voluntary relations, an actor may do things which she or he would prefer not to do because they are nevertheless preferable to any available alternative. Thus, an abused wife may not leave her husband because separation or divorce are either even less desirable or even more costly. But exchange theories themselves come in three somewhat distinct forms: rational choice, or decision theory; behavioral exchange theory; and resistance theory.

RATIONAL CHOICE THEORIES OF EXCHANGE AND POWER. Thibaut and Kelley (1959) offer perhaps the earliest rational choice model of the exchange process applied to power. They treat all interaction by analogy to the exchange of goods and services, each actor's participation in exchange being determined by choice among alternatives, the outcomes of which are characterized by their rewards and costs. Rewards are simply the positive values, costs the negative values, associated with the consequences of choosing an alternative. The value that results from the algebraic sum of rewards and costs is the payoff for a given act. Given interaction between two actors, A and B, payoffs are a joint function of the choices made by each. A matrix of joint payoffs for alternative actions by A and B formulates the conditions determining interaction between the two, in particular whether a relation forms and persists. Thibaut and Kelley treat payoffs in terms of their subjective value for the actors, hence in terms of their "utility" (although they do not use the term). In general, actors are assumed to maximize utility and continue in a relation only if for each actor a course of action is better than the best available alternative.

Thibaut and Kelley deal largely with stable relations rather than with particular acts. Power in a relation arises out of the "dependence" of the actors on each other. It can take either (or both) of two forms: A may be able to control the outcomes of B independently of any act by B, hence control B's fate, or A may be able to make rewards and costs contingent on B's behavior, hence control B's behavior. But an important principle of the theory is that control of an individual's fate can be converted into behavioral control.

There are many variants of the decision-theoretic approach to exchange, each differing with respect to how they treat the choice that underlies it. Value can be treated as objective (for example, in monetary terms) or subjective (for example, in terms of the meaning of money to the actor). The latter gives rise to a utility theory, such as in Thibaut and Kelley (1959) Blau (1964), and Bacharach and Lawler (1981). The relation between choice of an alternative and its outcome can be treated deterministically (as is true of all three of the utility theories just cited) or probabilistically. If value is treated objectively and outcomes probabilistically, one has an *expected utility* theory as in Harsanyi (1962). Among probabilistic theories, probability itself can be treated objectively or subjectively: In March (1955) the probabilities are objective, in Nagel (1968) and Tedeschi, Schlenker, and Bonoma (1975) they are subjective. In the latter case one has a *subjective expected utility* theory. In all these variants of decision theory, the central axiom is that the actor maximizes whatever the theory's criterion of choice.

Despite the variations among these theories, in general they predict that, given a conflict of interest, A is more likely to use power when more is at stake, when the cost of exercising power is less, when the likelihood of compliance is greater, and when there are fewer alternative means of obtaining compliance. The costs of exercising power include the relative depletion of A's stock of resources, the likelihood of retaliation, and the effect of reactance on subsequent relations with B. In general, the evidence supports these predictions, although "use" sometimes refers to whether or not A prefers to impose his or her will on B, sometimes to whether or not, if A does have such a preference, it is accomplished by manipulating rewards and punishments rather than by other means, and sometimes to whether or not A's behavior is overt and explicit, communicating threats or promises, or is covert. Rational choice theories also will in general predict that B is more likely to comply with A's preferences the larger the reward-attached to compliance, the larger the penalty attached to noncompliance, the greater the credibility is of A's promises of reward or threat of penalty, and the fewer the alternatives available to B. Again, the evidence largely supports these predictions. But it is well to keep in mind that with respect to both use and compliance, the evidence deals largely with voluntary relations.

Unlike other decision theories, subjective expected utility theory (especially Nagel 1968) makes use of Friedrich's (1937) "law of anticipated reactions," in which compliance occurs without directives, threats, or promises by A. In the case of punishment, not only is there no visible exercise of power by A, but compliance by B may appear to be willing because there is no visible resistance. In addition, if one takes into account that the law of anticipated reactions can be applied to A as well as to B, A may know in advance that B will comply and therefore know that it is unnecessary visibly to exercise power in order to achieve A's objective (Samuel and Zelditch 1989).

Rational choice theories predict that B is more likely to comply with A's preferences the larger the reward attached to compliance.

Bacharach and Lawler (1981) have pointed out that even though relative power in a relation is necessarily zero-sum, meaning that a gain by one actor implies loss by the other, relative power can be distinguished from absolute power, the sheer quantity of resources controlled by an actor. Hence, relative power can be distinguished from total power, the sum of the resources possessed by A and B. Total power, unlike relative power, is a variable that can increase for both actors at the same time. Bacharach and Lawler argue that total power has an effect independent of relative power, especially on the use of punitive power capabilities. Given a conflict of interest, if punitive power is an available tactic, the likelihood of its use by the more powerful actor increases as his or her relative power increases but decreases as total power increases.

Thibaut and Kelley note that all these ideas are more useful as the pattern of exchange becomes more stable, hence, the focus of exchange theory is often not only on the fact that power is relational, which is true even at the level of a unit act, but on the structure of relations arising from enduring patterns of repeated exchanges. The most influential theory of this kind has been Emerson's theory of power–dependence relations (1962; 1972). Though it originally grew out of Thibaut and Kelley, this theory has come to be associated more recently with behavioral exchange theory, a theory originating in the work of Homans.

BEHAVIORAL EXCHANGE THEORY. Homans (1961) behaviorized exchange theory by transforming rewards and costs into reinforcement contingencies and the process of exchange into mutual operant conditioning. Many fundamental concepts of decision theory, however, survive in behavioral exchange theory. Choices are determined by maximizing profit, which is the difference between rewards and costs. Costs in Homans take a form more like costs in economics than in Thibaut and Kelley, becoming opportunity costs, that is, profit foregone by choosing X over not-X. But, as in Thibaut and Kelley, exchange occurs at a point at which for both actors exchange is more profitable than each actor's best available alternative. Thus, A uses power in Homans—where "use" means attempts to direct the behavior of another—when it is more profitable than any alternative available to A, and B complies when compliance is more profitable than noncompliance. Homans, however, gives more emphasis than does Thibaut and Kelley to the effect of satiation on the value of a reward: Accumulation of rewards brings diminishing returns. Hence, poor actors are more responsive than are rich ones to offers of any given level of reward for doing an otherwise undesired act.

Emerson's power–dependence theory, perhaps the most influential theory of interpersonal power, was originally a utility theory of relations like Thibaut and Kelley's (Emerson 1962). But Emerson (1972) followed Homans in behaviorizing exchange theory, except that, unlike Homans, Emerson again dealt with relations rather than acts. Power–dependence theory is formulated in terms of two actors whose social relations entail ties of mutual dependence. "Power" is the amount of B's resistance that can be overcome by A: It is potential rather than actual power that is used to describe the relation. Power is a function of dependence, which arises from the control by one actor of resources on which another depends for achieving his or her goals. Dependence varies directly with an actor's motivational investment in goals but inversely with the availability of alternative sources of resources outside the relation. The "power advantage" of one actor over another is a function of the net balance of each one's dependence on the other. If net balance is zero, power is equal, or "balanced." A relatively unique feature of Emerson's theory is that balanced power is assumed to be stable, while imbalance creates pressures to change the power relation in the direction of balance. There are four kinds of balancing operations. B may (1) reduce motivational investment in the goals mediated by A, withdrawing from the relation; (2) increase the number of alternative sources of the resource (extend networks); (3) increase A's motivational investment in goals mediated by B (for example, by offering status to A); or (4) deny to A alternative sources of resources mediated by B (coalition formation). Attention to these operations leads one to distinguish use of power from change of power—increasing or decreasing dependence in the relation. These assumptions about balance have had a major impact on the study of organizations (beginning with Thompson 1967), but other exchange theories have tended to reject the balance assumption, especially Blau (1964), who instead treats the balance mechanisms as means by which A maintains or increases power over B.

"Use" in power–dependence theory comes to mean something quite different from what it means in decision or field-theoretic formulations: It refers now to asymmetries in the outcomes of exchange. It is assumed that use of power, in the more usual sense, increases until an equilibrium is reached, at which point the less powerful actor is receiving no more benefits than the best alternative source could provide. While power imbalance does in fact increase asymmetry of exchange, it has been consistently found that use is suboptimal. It is constrained in part by search costs (Molm 1987b) and in part by commitment to the other and concern for equity (Cook and Emerson 1978). Furthermore, use of punishment power depends not only on punishment capability but also on reward capability: Those weaker in reward power are, other things being equal, more likely to use punishment power (Molm 1987a).

The most significant development in the behavioral exchange theory of power has been its extension to networks of dyadic relations. Interpersonal power is not necessarily confined to a dyadic relation, as Coleman has shown (Coleman 1973). But except for Coleman, interpersonal power has usually been treated as dyadic. More complex structures are possible, however, by connecting dyads into networks (Emerson 1972). Study of such networks has rapidly developed as a central preoccupation of research on interpersonal power, especially preoccupation with the question of determinants of power at a position within a network. Most of this research has been concerned with negatively connected networks. A negative connection is one such that exchange in one relation decreases the value of exchange in another, while a positive connection increases its value. Thus, if A must choose which of two offers of exchange to accept from two others, B and C, AB is negatively connected to AC because choice of AB excludes exchange between A and C. Subsequent research has concentrated on the effects of varying structures of negatively connected networks. Centrality of a position turns out not to predict asymmetry of exchange very well, hence, much theory and research has been directed at discovering what alternative concept of power of a position does predict asymmetry of exchange. Cook and Emerson (1978) proposed "vulnerability" as an alternative and defined it as the effect that removing a position would have on the total quantity of resources available for exchange in a network. An intuitively appealing concept, this idea works well for many networks, though Markovsky, Miller, and Patton (1988) have objected that there are certain structures for which it does not accurately predict asymmetries. Their alternative conception derives from resistance theory.

RESISTANCE THEORY. Willer's (1981) resistance theory objects to the importance of satiation in behavioral exchange theory and as an alternative goes back to Weber's concept of power as overcoming resistance. Willer conceives of interaction as exchange of sanctions. The value of a sanction is a function of its objective value multiplied by its quantity, but value is not itself a function of quantity, hence, there is no satiation effect. Willer focuses instead on the "preference alteration state" of the actor (P_A), consequent on sanctions, and defines resistance as the ratio of two differences: the best possible outcome minus the value of P_A is divided by P_A minus the worst possible outcome B will accept, called P_A at confrontation. Exchange occurs at equiresistance.

Willer's resistance theory objects to the importance of satiation and conceives of interaction as exchange of sanctions.

The emphasis on resistance leads the theory to incorporate coercion and conflict more easily within the same framework as voluntary exchange. But in addition it leads to a different understanding of power at a position in a network. As in Cook and Emerson (1978), power at a position depends on alternatives, but Markovsky, Miller, and Patton (1988) propose a graph-theoretic index of power based on Willer's concept of exclusion. The difference between the two is that in Markovsky, Miller, and Patton exclusion is relative to the number of exchanges sought, while in Cook and Emerson actors seek to make a single exchange at a given point in time. It is "advantageous" in resistance theory to be connected to positions that have few alternatives relative to the number of exchanges sought and disadvantageous to be connected to positions that have many alternatives relative to the number sought. In negatively connected networks, an odd number of positions is advantageous, an even number disadvantageous. The ratio of advantageous to disadvantageous paths leading out from a point in a network (counting overlapping paths only once) gives the graph-theoretic index of power at that point in the network. The logic of the argument can be extended to inclusion as well as to exclusion. An inclusive connection is one such that exchange in one cannot occur until exchange in another also occurs. Inclusive relations, for example, increase the power of peripheral positions in a network.

BIBLIOGRAPHY

Bacharach, Samuel B., and Edward J. Lawler 1981 *Bargaining: Power, Tactics, and Outcomes.* San Francisco: Jossey-Bass.

Bachrach, Peter, and Morton S. Baratz 1963 "Decisions and Nondecisions: An Analytical Framework." *American Political Science Review* 57:632–642.

Barnard, Chester I. 1938 *The Functions of the Executive.* Cambridge, Mass.: Harvard University Press.

Blau, Peter M. 1964 *Exchange and Power in Social Life.* New York: Wiley.

Brehm, Jack W. 1966 *A Theory of Psychological Reactance.* New York: Academic Press.

Cartwright, Dorwin 1959 "A Field Theoretical Conception of Power." In Dorwin Cartwright, ed., *Studies in Social Power.* Ann Arbor: University of Michigan Press.

Coleman, James S. 1973 *The Mathematics of Collective Action.* Chicago: Aldine.

Cook, Karen S., and Richard M. Emerson 1978 "Power, Equity, and Commitment in Exchange Networks." *American Sociological Review* 43:721–739.

Dahl, Robert A. 1957 "The Concept of Power." *Behavioral Science* 2:201–215.

Emerson, Richard M. 1962 "Power–Dependence Relations." *American Sociological Review* 27:31–41.

——— 1972 "Exchange Theory." In Joseph Berger, Morris Zelditch, and Bo Anderson, eds., *Sociological Theories in Progress,* vol. 2. Boston: Houghton Mifflin.

Festinger, Leon 1953 "An Analysis of Compliant Behavior." In Musafir Sherif and Milbourne O. Wilson, eds., *Group Relations at the Crossroads.* New York: Harper.

French, John R. P., and Bertram Raven 1959 "The Bases of Social Power." In Dorwin Cartwright, ed., *Studies in Social Power.* Ann Arbor: University of Michigan Press.

Friedrich, Carl J. 1937 *Constitutional Government and Politics: Nature and Development.* New York: Harper and Bros.

Goode, William J. 1972 "The Place of Force in Human Society." *American Sociological Review* 37:507–519.

Harsanyi, John C. 1962 "Measurement of Social Power, Opportunity Costs, and the Theory of Two-Person Bargaining Games." *Behavioral Science* 7:67–80.

Hawley, Amos 1963 "Community Power and Urban Renewal Success." *American Journal of Sociology* 68:422–431.

Homans, George C. 1961 *Social Behavior: Its Elementary Forms.* New York: Harcourt Brace Jovanovich.

March, James G. 1955 "An Introduction to the Theory and Measurement of Influence." *American Political Science Review* 49:431–451.

——— 1966 "The Power of Power." In David Easton, ed., *Varieties of Political Theory.* Englewood Cliffs, N.J.: Prentice-Hall.

Markovsky, Barry, David Willer, and Travis Patton 1988 "Power Relations in Exchange Networks." *American Sociological Review* 53:220–236.

Molm, Linda 1987a "Extending Power-Dependence Theory: Power Processes and Negative Outcomes." In Edward J. Lawler and Barry Markovsky, eds., *Advances in Group Processes: Theory and Research,* vol. 4. Greenwich, Conn.: JAI Press.

——— 1987b "Linking Power Structure and Power Use." In Karen S. Cook, ed., *Social Exchange Theory.* Newbury Park, Calif.: Sage.

Nagel, Jack H. 1968 "Some Questions about the Concept of Power." *Behavioral Science* 13:129–137.

——— 1975 *The Descriptive Analysis of Power.* New Haven, Conn.: Yale University Press.

Parsons, Talcott 1963 "On the Concept of Political Power." *Proceedings of the American Philosophical Society* 107, no. 3:232–262.

Russell, Bertrand R. 1938 *Power: A New Social Analysis.* London: Allen and Unwin.

Samuel, Yitzhak, and Morris Zelditch, Jr. 1989 "Expectations, Shared Awareness, and Power." In Joseph Berger, Morris Zelditch, Jr., and Bo Anderson, eds., *Sociological Theories in Progress: New Formulations.* Newbury Park, Calif.: Sage.

Simon, Herbert 1953 "Notes on the Observation and Measurement of Political Power." *Journal of Politics* 15:500–516.

Tedeschi, James T., Barry R. Schlenker, and Thomas V. Bonoma 1973 *Conflict, Power, and Games.* Chicago: Aldine.

Thibaut, John W., and Harold H. Kelley 1959 *The Social Psychology of Groups.* New York: Wiley.

Thompson, James D. 1967 *Organizations in Action.* New York: McGraw-Hill.

Weber, Max (1918) 1968 *Economy and Society.* Guenther Roth and Claus Wittich, eds.; trans. by Ephraim Fischoff et al. New York: Bedminster Press.

Willer, David 1981 "Quantity and Network Structure." In David Willer and Bo Anderson, eds., *Networks, Exchange, and Coercion.* New York: Elsevier/Greenwood.

– MORRIS ZELDITCH, JR.

INVENTIONS

Sociologists have studied independent inventors, industrial research laboratories, the process of technological innovation, the effects of technology on society, and the influence of social factors on technological development, yet the sociology of invention largely remains to be synthesized, or invented, from the above elements and related themes. Indeed, one common notion of invention is that it is the putting together of elements of existing technology in a new format to solve a problem. The sociological perspective views invention as a series of incremental improvements to a technical process rather than as a single great innovation (Gilfillan 1970). For example, the diesel engine has been shown to be the result of such an extended process of invention by many persons rather than the sole accomplishment of the individual who was given eponymous recognition.

Even the notion of a succession of individual inventors working to improve a technology has been revised in light of the scale of cooperative effort required in many technical fields. Under contemporary conditions of technical complexity, invention has been professionalized and bureaucratized in R&D laboratories. In the late nineteenth century, United States corporations such as General Electric established laboratories, often headed by scientists drawn from universities, to improve existing products and develop areas of research likely to lead to new products. Under these conditions, development of new devices is a group effort or even a combination of a coordinated effort and a competitive race among several groups to achieve the desired goal. Kidder (1981) depicts the internal struggle between two branches of a computer corporation to invent its next product and the network of competitive and cooperative relationships within one of the groups.

In the late nineteenth century Edison noted that his backers expected a return within three years, a time frame that has not changed appreciably.

Application of theory to making new devices has become a technique of organized invention. World War II successes in developing radar, the proximity fuse, and the atomic bomb exemplified the ability of large-scale, well-organized, and well-funded programs to invent toward a goal, combining theoretical understanding with trial-and-error approaches. These successes lent support to an even stronger version of the relationship between theory and invention: the notion of a unidirectional flow from basic to applied research to technological development as expressed by Vannevar Bush in his postwar manifesto for government support of science, *The Endless Frontier.* The premise was that scientists, well funded and allowed to follow their research instincts wherever they led them, would, as a by-product of their unfettered investigations, produce useful innovations. There are certainly significant examples of new technologies, such as lasers, emerging from the "meandering stream" of basic research. Nevertheless, the exigencies of international economic competition have led to a call for "directed basic research" in which exploration is targeted to specific economic and technological goals, such as the development of materials with novel properties.

While the sociology of invention is often presumed to be solely about the creation of physical artifacts to solve problems, it is also recognized that there are social inventions. Organizational and attitudinal innovations are deliberately sought to solve problems. For example, the "quality circle" bringing together workers and managers to solve industrial production problems across hierarchical lines and the "T" group for exploration and resolution of group process issues can be viewed as social inventions, as can "matrix organization" and bureaucracy itself.

Extending the sociology of invention to the realm of the social would seem to include all efforts at planned social change. However, even if the definition is limited to the creation of physical artifacts, the role of the social in facilitating or retarding technological innovation is a large one. Among the social elements identified in this process are the roles of:

Social movements in calling attention to a problem area and creating support for work on technical solutions, such as rocketry in early twentieth-century Germany (Bainbridge 1983) and birth control in the United States

Economic concentrations of power, such as oligopolistic and monopolistic corporations, in settling on an existing technology, such as the automobile industry and its commitment to the internal combustion engine to the virtual exclusion of electric or other alternatives, and electric lamp producers as manufacturers of incandescent bulbs who, for a time, ignored or deliberately blocked the introduction of fluorescent lighting until a new company eventually succeeded in bringing it to market (Bright 1947).

Governments also play an important role in shaping the development of technologies to achieve public policy goals. For example, the United States Army subsidized the development of the transistor through its procurement policy of purchasing large numbers of the devices during the 1950s in order to miniaturize battlefield communications equipment. The existence of a customer willing to pay high prices encouraged new firms to enter the industry (Etzkowitz 1984). Production in larger quantities led to improvements in the technology, and lower prices resulted in civilian uses, first in hearing aids and portable radios and then in an ever increasing number of consumer electronic devices. Indeed, a probabilistic relationship called "the learning curve" has been identified in which an increase in the scale of production of a device, with a concomitant lowering of its cost, brings with it a speeding of the process of invention (Nelson 1962). In the 1970s a proposal made in response to the energy crisis—to have the army purchase a large number of solar cells to meet its needs for electricity production and thereby induce a learning curve for that technology—failed through lack of sufficient political support. More recently, government environmental regulations have induced a wave of technological innovations in the steel and coal industries, relatively stagnant technical areas in the United States, that not only have reduced pollution but also have resulted in more efficient production processes.

The ability to attract a source of capital, whether public or private, is crucial to sustaining the process of invention. In 1869 Thomas Edison, a budding inventor of telegraphic devices, moved from Boston, then the technological center of the United States, to New York, its financial center. He also oriented his inventing skills to meeting the need of the financial industry for improved communication, thereby improving his chances of gaining financial support.

Availability of venture capital has been found to be a crucial determinant of technological innovation. Given that a new device or process has been invented outside of an existing firm, or even within a firm that does not perceive it as relevant to its business, what happens next? Often nothing, unless people and resources can be brought together to mount an effort to introduce the invention into use. Entrepreneurship and invention, and organizational and technical innovation, are inevitably intertwined. In the course of such ventures, inventors and scientists sometimes become businesspersons. The success of individual firms and the growth of groups of related technical firms in areas such as Silicon Valley in California and along Route 128 near Boston have become the basis of strategies for regional economic development elsewhere. Contemporary state government efforts to encourage technological innovation typically include a component to provide capital for new technical firms as part of their repertoire of initiatives (Etzkowitz 1990).

Time as well as money is a factor in the process of invention, and the two are often related. The ability to collapse the time frame necessary to make an invention allows increased access to funds under conditions of strict time limitations for return of capital on invest-

Thomas Edison, a prolific American inventor, succeeded in part because he understood the demands of the market. As a young inventor he moved to New York, the nation's financial center, and worked to meet technological needs of the financial industry. (Corbis-Bettmann)

ment. In the late nineteenth century Edison noted that his backers expected a return within three years, a time frame that has not changed appreciably in the United States to this day. He successfully attempted to speed up the pace of invention to meet this requirement. Conversely, the availability of capital for long-term investment in Japan allows the support of longer-term programs of technological innovation. Similarly, when a Swiss firm with a longer time frame than United States stockholders typically allow purchased an interest in Genentech, a United States biotechnology company, the firm was able to continue research programs that it was about to eliminate. These instances illustrate the conditions of temporal and financial exigency under which invention often takes place.

Beyond the role of social factors in shaping the course of technological development is the question of the extent to which physical artifacts are an embodiment of social structures. Nuclear reactors have been found to require a bureaucratic form of organization to operate and control (Winner 1986). Other technologies, such as computers and solar cells, are variable in scale, and social impetuses can lead to a line of inventions emphasizing one characteristic or another, such as centralization of control in mainframe computers or decentralization in personal computers (Etzkowitz 1991). Nonetheless, some social structures have been viewed as a result of the invention and introduction of particular physical artifacts, such as the growth of dispersed suburbs following from the mass production of automobiles. The ubiquity of these connections between physical devices and social structures suggests that it is problematic to meaningfully view these two spheres in isolation from each other (Collins 1987).

Finally, there is the issue of the relationship of science to technology. One view is that although invention was formerly an untutored occupation, evolving independently of science, it has now been incorporated into science. A long-term relationship has been noted in which basic understanding of physical phenomena later results in practical devices that utilize earlier discoveries. For example, Marconi's patent application of 1896 for a long-range radio transmitter was "the technological embodiment of Maxwell's theory of the electromagnetic field, stated thirty years earlier (Aitken 1976, p. 209). A major scientific advance in the understanding of a physical phenomenon had been translated into a working device. Typically, each phase was conducted by different persons, with different professional outlooks and goals: discovery and theoretical advance versus commercial and military use.

More recently these processes have been collapsed into each other, sometimes with the same individuals involved in each phase. For example, the first successful insertion of foreign DNA into a host microorganism in 1973 was quickly followed, from 1976 on, by the founding of small entrepreneurial firms to make industrial applications of this new genetic technique in the production of new drugs and chemicals (Office of Technology Assessment 1984). Herbert Boyer, a university professor who was a leading figure in developing these gene-splicing techniques was also a cofounder of Genentech, a company organized to develop pharmaceutical and other products using those techniques. Other molecular biologists with university appointments soon participated in organizing their own companies. Subsequent academic research in this field has been carried out with the knowledge that commercial implications are an imminent possibility, and an increasing number of researchers and universities actively seek out the industrial potential of research (Etzkowitz 1990).

Another view is that technological innovation still largely proceeds on an alternative path to science and is also an independent sphere out of which scientific discoveries can flow. Invention is based on solving problems in industry, often by trial-and-error, "cut-and-try" methods. A theoretical understanding is worked out, if at all, after a working device is created. The invention of the transistor is often viewed as the classic example of the use of theory to aid in the invention of a device, but even in this instance the starting point was a commercial need to develop a more efficient alternative to existing mechanical switching devices for telephones. Solid-state physics was focused upon by researchers at Bell Laboratories as an area likely to produce a new type of switching device, and further pursuit of fundamental research on the solid state eventually led to the invention of the transistor.

On the other hand, the ovonic effect in polycrystalline silicon is an example of the development of theory following from the invention of a device. Stanford Ovshinsky, a self-taught expert on materials who formerly worked in the auto industry, found a way to line up molecules of silicon so that he could produce solar cells that generate electricity more simply and potentially more cheaply than do conventional methods. This new form of silicon, at first dismissed by professionally trained scientists, was later accepted when one of them developed a theoretical explanation for the property that Ovshinsky had obtained.

The relationship among science, applied research, and industrial problem solving are reconciled in a multidirectional model of technological innovation in which they are viewed as alternative, mutually influencing sources of invention. Projects often viewed as exemplifying the application of basic science to development of a device, such as the World War II United States effort to build an atomic bomb, also relied on "cut-and-try" techniques as well as on guidelines derived from theory. For example, in an effort to devise a fine-screen filter device to produce purified uranium, scientists accompanied by army officers went to a printing plant and attempted to adapt its sophisticated lithography equipment to solve the problem. Edison's collection and testing of a range of materials to produce an effective electric lamp filament is a classic example of the systematic use of this method. However, Edison, who is often viewed as the prototypical "trial-and-error" inventor, also had trained scientists on the staff of his "invention factory" and used a repertoire of electrical components with known properties to build devices to solve different problems.

Efforts to balance and integrate these apparently divergent approaches can be found in university research centers in the United States. They are often funded by a multiplicity of sources with different goals, from the most basic to the highly applied. To meet the needs of their sponsors and achieve their own intellectual goals, researchers attempt in the course of the same project to reconcile different goals by, for example, at one and the same time producing methods to analyze mortgage securities for the financial industry while advancing the theory of parallel processing in computer science (Etzkowitz 1991b). Thus, science and invention increasingly become organizationally and intellectually intertwined in government, industry, and university laboratories.

[See also Technology and Society.]

BIBLIOGRAPHY

Aitken, Hugh 1976 *Syntony and Spark: The Origins of Radio.* New York: Wiley.

Bainbridge, William 1983 *The Spaceflight Revolution.* New York: Wiley.

Bijker, Wiebe, Thomas P. Hughes, and Trevor Pinch 1987 *The Social Construction of Technological Systems.* Cambridge, Mass.: MIT Press.

Bright, Arthur 1947 *The Electric Lamp Industry: Technological Change and Economic Development from 1800 to 1947.* New York: McGraw-Hill.

Collins, Randall 1987 "A Theory of Technology." In Collins, *Weberian Sociological Theory.* Cambridge: Cambridge University Press.

Etzkowitz, Henry 1984 "Solar Versus Nuclear Energy: Autonomous or Dependent Technology?" *Social Problems* (April):418–434.

——— 1990 "The Capitalization of Knowledge." *Theory and Society* 19:107–121.

——— 1991a "Technology and Social Change: Alternative Paths." In Henry Etzkowitz and Ronald Glassman, eds., *The Renascence of Sociological Theory.* Itasca, Ill.: Peacock.

——— 1991b "Regional Industrial and Science Policy in the United States." *Science and Technology Policy* (April).

Gilfillan, S. C. 1970 (1935) *The Sociology of Invention.* Cambridge, Mass.: MIT Press.

Kidder, Tracy 1981 *The Soul of a New Machine.* Boston: Little, Brown.

Nelson, Richard 1962 "The Link Between Science and Invention: The Case of the Transistor." In Nelson, *The Rate and Direction of Inventive Activity.* Princeton, N.J.: National Bureau of Economic Research.

Office of Technology Assessment 1984 *Commercial Biotechnology: An International Analysis.* Washington D.C.: Office of Science and Technology.

Whalley, Peter 1986 *The Social Production of Technical Work.* Albany, N.Y.: SUNY Press.

Winner, Langdon 1986 *The Whale and the Reactor: The Search for Limits in an Age of High Technology.* Chicago: University of Chicago Press.

– HENRY ETZKOWITZ

J

JUVENILE DELINQUENCY AND JUVENILE CRIME

The year 1990 apparently witnessed the growth and spread of street crime in America with a parallel growth in the fear of youth gangs. Youth violence seemed to grow in many cities in 1990: Boston, Philadelphia, Washington, Richmond, Los Angeles, Phoenix, New York, and others. The year ended with a public shootout by warring gangs at a theater showing *Godfather III.* The parks are places where muggings, as well as "wildings" (gang rapes and violent attacks on women, especially) can take place. No wonder the year ended on a dismal note.

In a comment made in 1959, but which is still relevant to those who are intrigued, frightened, or perplexed by the "heedlessness" of today's youth, Teeters and Matza stated: "It has always been popular for each generation to believe its children were the worst, the most lawless and the most unruly" (p. 200). We are also reminded by them that "Sir Walter Scott in 1812 deplored the insecurity of Edinburgh where groups of boys between 12 and 20 years scoured streets and knocked down and robbed all who came in their way" (p. 200). Apropos of delinquency, such remarks underscore the relativity of opinions and the brevity of trends. They also remind us that while juvenile delinquency is a relatively new legal category that subjects children to court authority, it is also a timeless and ubiquitous part of life. As such, I shall consider here some of the varieties of modern data on juvenile misconduct.

The term "modern" underscores the fact (emphasized by writers such as Gibbons and Krohn [1991], Empey [1982], and Short [1990]) that "juvenile delinquency" is a relatively recent social construction. It grew out of legal and humanitarian concern for the well-being of children and was designed to allow children to be handled outside the criminal law. The first juvenile court, established in Cook County, Illinois, in 1899, was designed to meet the special needs of children at a time of great industrialization in the United States. The data of delinquency, however, are not limited to the legal status of "juvenile delinquent," because sociologists are just as interested in unofficial as in official acts of delinquency. More specifically, it is well known that much of the behavior defined by law as delinquent is not detected, not reported, or not acted on by legal agents of control.

Moreover, different jurisdictions have different legal definitions of delinquency. Within the United States, for example, while the statistics defining delinquency are similar in the fifty states and District of Columbia with respect to age and type of offense requiring juvenile court control, there are more differences than similarities. First, the laws vary in terms of the age limits of juvenile court jurisdiction; thirty-one states and the District of Columbia set seventeen years of age as the upper age limit, twelve states set sixteen years, six set fifteen years, and one sets eighteen years. Moreover, in many states the delinquency laws empower the juvenile court to remand youths under the maximum juvenile court age to criminal courts. In such cases, the offenses are often those for which adults may be arrested: index crimes (see below). In addition, some states have passed legislation that requires certain cases, such as homicides, or youths charged with serious offenses, to be dealt with by the criminal court. In these cases, the juvenile acquires the legal status of criminal. Finally, it should be noted that all American state jurisdictions contain an omnibus clause or provision, referred to as status offenses, that awards the court jurisdiction over youths who have behaved in ways not forbidden by criminal law. While these provisions differ from state to state, it is of interest to note a few examples of these conditions. They include engaging in indecent behavior, knowingly associating with vicious or immoral persons, growing up in idleness or crime, being incorrigible, and wandering in the streets at night. Critics note that these behavior categories are so vaguely defined that nearly all youngsters could be subjected to them.

Such different procedures and practices caution us against making easy generalizations both within and between countries when examining official data. Indeed, other shortcomings likewise warn against drawing firm conclusions when unofficial data are examined. Although methodological shortcomings may exist in the study of delinquency, there may be advantages in utilizing all the data of delinquency (official and unofficial) in pursuit of its understanding. Thus, the study of official delinquency data places much of the focus on the actions of official agents of control (the police, the courts), while the study of unofficial—including hidden—delinquency often allows students to examine the processes leading to the behavior. Moreover, as Vold and Bernard (1986) and others have noted, unofficial data, especially self-reports, frequently focus on trivial offenses, while the more serious offenses often do not appear in self-reports but in reports of official agencies.

In sum, our concern here will be to discuss those topics of delinquency which are of the greatest concern: the frequency, the severity, and the duration of delinquency, from both individual and aggregate perspectives. These will devote some attention to trends. In the following section, the focus is on the extent of delinquent behavior.

Extent of and Trends in Delinquency

In addressing the matter of the extent of delinquency, it is important to note the admonitions of Empey and Erickson (1966), Hirschi (1969), Matza (1964), and others that delinquency is not only transient but also widespread. Many juveniles engage in delinquency only occasionally, and some engage in it more frequently. Gibbons and Krohn (1991) call delinquency "a sometime thing," while Matza describes the process of drifting into and out of delinquency. Moreover, it should be kept in mind that some acts of delinquency are serious acts of criminality and others are petty, trivial acts. As we consider both official and unofficial data on juvenile delinquency and juvenile crime, we will encounter these various clarifying factors.

OFFICIAL DELINQUENCY. The most serious crimes committed by youth and adults in the United States are referred to as index crimes and are compiled by the FBI, based on reports of approximately sixteen thousand law enforcement agencies throughout the country. These index crimes, reported in Uniform Crime Reports, are divided into two major types: violent (homicide, rape, robbery, and aggravated assault) and property (burglary, larceny-theft, motor vehicle theft, and arson). Nonindex offenses are those considered to be relatively petty, such as liquor law violations, disorderly conduct, and sex offenses (except forcible rape, prostitution, and commercialized vice).

Index crimes are reported annually by the FBI and sometimes as estimates for the United States as a whole from a sample of reporting agencies. In 1996, the FBI's Uniform Crime Reports indicated that of all arrests in the United States that year, approximately 19 percent were of youths under eighteen years of age; 18.7 percent of the arrests for violent crime in 1996 (murder and manslaughter, forcible rape, robbery, and aggravated assault) were of persons under eighteen years of age.

One of the most striking facts about officially recorded delinquency is that it has increased in recent years in the United States. For the period between 1987 and 1996, there was a 35.4 percent increase in the total number of arrests of persons under eighteen. Consistent with and extending the latter data, the subsequent Uniform Crime Report presents data showing that while total arrests increased by over 16.3 percent between 1987 and 1996, arrests of persons under eighteen years of age increased by 35.4 percent. This increase in arrests of youths under eighteen must be interpreted with caution. During the period 1980–1989, the percent change in number of persons under eighteen who were arrested actually showed a decline, but a small one of 7 percent.

Underscoring this caution is the fact that while the Uniform Crime Report shows a decline in index arrests for urban, suburban, and rural youth alike for the period 1979–1988, the number of index arrests increased substantially across these residential categories between 1965 and 1977. Peter and Lucille Kratcoski, in viewing this dramatic change, suggest that it could be due to "movement of the 'baby-boom' segment of the population through the high offense years during the mid-70s followed by a reduction in the under-18 population since 1978" (1990, p. 15). Gibbons and Krohn (1991) also suggest that such trends may be due to shifts within the delinquency-eligible youth group. Further, the latter authors suggest that such trends may reflect increased or decreased concern about youthful misconduct.

Consistent with the decreasing trend in juvenile arrests is the fact that the numbers of youngsters who have been sent to juvenile courts (that is, officially processed) have decreased since 1975. Index and nonindex delinquency cases referred to courts in 1985 numbered 534,000, while court status offense cases in the same year numbered some 88,000, about one-sixth of the delinquency cases, according to the U.S. Department of Justice. Status offenses in 1985 were fairly equally apportioned among the four categories of runaway, ungovernability, liquor law, and truancy violations. Among the delinquency cases referred to juvenile courts in 1985, 9.1 percent involved index crimes of violence, 42.6 percent involved index property crimes, and over 48 percent involved nonindex delinquency. Considering delinquent cases (violations of criminal statutes) and status cases together for 1984, Gibbons and Krohn (1991) indicate that less than 5 percent of the youth population appeared in juvenile courts in 1984. This figure includes both petitioned (officially processed) and nonpetitioned cases.

A notable exception to the decline in arrests and court referrals of persons under eighteen years of age is the increase in murder and nonnegligent manslaughter. More specifically, the Uniform Crime Report shows that between 1980 and 1989 there was an increase from 1,189 to 1,733 cases of murder and nonnegligent manslaughter by the under-eighteen group, an increase of over 45 percent. Indeed, there was a general increase in index crimes of violence for the under-eighteen group of 5.7 percent for that period. Forcible rape showed an increase of 22.8 percent, and aggravated assault increased by 33.7 percent. Only robbery showed a decline, of 21.1 percent. The data for 1990 will, no doubt, exaggerate these trends, given the substance of preliminary reports in the media.

COHORT STUDY. One of the first longitudinal studies of delinquency was conducted by Wolfgang, Figlio, and Sellin (1972) in Philadelphia. They traced the police contacts of all boys born in 1945 who lived in the city between their tenth and eighteenth birthdays. One of their aims was to trace the volume and frequency of delinquent careers up to age eighteen in a cohort of 9,945. They found that 35 percent of these boys (3,475) were involved with the police at least once during the time between their tenth and eighteenth birthdays. Of these 3,475 boys with police contacts, 54 percent were repeaters. The total number of delinquent events (offenses) for the 3,475 delinquent boys

Facilities for delinquent juveniles, separate from those of adult criminals, grew from humanitarian interests in the well-being of young criminals. (Hulton-Deutsch Collection/Corbis)

amounted to 10,214 through age seventeen. Thus, it is clear that the number of offenses far outnumbers the number of offenders found in the cohort. One must note, then, that longitudinal study of delinquents yields data with important differences from those obtained when cross-sectional studies of persons arrested are conducted. Examples of other longitudinal studies include the Provo Study, the Cambridge-Somerville Study, the Vocational High Study, and, in Britain, the National Survey of Health and Development.

SELF-REPORTS: OFFENDER REPORTS AND VICTIM REPORTS. Official reports of crime and juvenile delinquency have been criticized for years because they are widely believed to underreport the volume of offenses. Moreover, there was considerable belief, especially among those with a conflict perspective, that official reports underreported middle-class crime and delinquency. In an effort to detect "hidden" delinquency, sociologists developed a technique designed to produce a more accurate picture. The technique used by Short and Nye (1958), in a number of studies of hidden delinquency, consisted of having juveniles in a school or other population complete questionnaires and reveal the extent to which they engaged in law-violating behavior. They found that delinquency was widespread throughout the juvenile population. Subsequently, Williams and Gold (1972) and Empey and Erickson (1966) embarked on studies employing self-reports. These writers found that 88 percent and 92 percent of their study groups, respectively, had engaged in violations. Hindelang, Hirschi, and Weis (1981) present a similar volume of law-violating behavior in their Seattle study. Criticisms of the self-report method followed many of these studies, centering on issues of respondent misrepresentation, respondent recall, and weaknesses of study groups. A major criticism (by Nettler [1984], for example) was that self-reports elicited minor or petty infractions for the most part. Because of its obvious utility, the self-report technique has been greatly improved in recent years, becoming an important, if not the dominant, method of measurement in studies focusing on the extent and cause of delinquency.

A number of students of delinquency agree that many of the improvements in self-report studies have been contributed by Delbert Elliott and his colleagues (Regoli and Hewitt [1991]; Gibbons and Krohn [1991]; Bartol and Bartol [1989]). Elliott and his colleagues have initiated a panel design that employs periodic interviews instead of questionnaires. The study, called the National Youth Survey (NYS), utilizes a national probability sample of 1,726 adolescents aged eleven to seventeen in 1976 and covers over one hundred cities and towns in the United States. In contrast with earlier self-report studies, Elliott asks his respondents about a full range of activities designed to get at serious as well as minor infractions. In addition, his respondents are asked whether they were caught when engaging in delinquent and criminal activities.

Over eighteen percent of the arrests for violent crime in 1996 were of persons under eighteen years of age.

Another attempt to ascertain the volume of delinquency in the United States is represented by the National Crime Survey (NCS). This survey, an effort to ascertain the extent of victimization in the population of the United States, was begun in 1973 after an initial study sponsored by the President's Commission on Law Enforcement and Administration of Justice in 1967. Interviews are conducted semiannually by the Bureau of the Census in a large national sample of sixty thousand households (Bartol and Bartol 1989). The survey was intended to supplement the Uniform Crime Report (UCR) data and measures the extent to which persons and households are victims of rape, robbery, assault, burglary, motor vehicle theft, and larceny. Binder, Geis, and Bruce note that one of the major findings of the 1967 study of victims by the President's Commission was the revelation that "actual crime was several times that indicated in the UCR" (1988, p. 34). In the current victim interviews, if the respondent has been victimized, he or she will be asked questions about characteristics of both victim and offender, including victim perceptions of the offender. Binder and his colleagues warn about the difficulty of age discrimination by the victim under stress and suggest that this method cannot be relied on too heavily in measuring delinquency.

Nevertheless, Laub (1983) has found NCS data useful in addressing the issue of the extent and change in delinquency volume. In an analysis of NCS data obtained between 1973 and 1980, he found no increase in juvenile crime over those years. He further noted that data from the National Center for Juvenile Justice supported this conclusion. It would seem, then, that NCS data, UCR data, and juvenile court data are in some agreement that delinquency has not increased recently, contrary to much public opinion. While self-report data indicate that violations are consistently widespread in American society, it is important to note that these reports involve primarily minor violations. Indeed, to the extent that almost everyone engages in minor violations, it may make sense to focus primarily on serious violations. Nettler (1984), noting that self-report studies find a large number of minor infractions, suggested that such violators are best described as lying on a continuum rather than as "delinquent" or "nondelinquent." The cohort studies by Wolfgang and his colleagues (1972) showed that serious violations involved only a small proportion of the study groups.

Factors Related to Delinquency

AGE AND GENDER. In the United States, in Britain, and in other countries of Europe where delinquency is recognized and studied, there is general agreement that it peaks in adolescence (ages fifteen to eighteen) rather than in childhood. (This is not to say, however, that delinquency is not on the increase among younger children. A study by the FBI in 1990 found that the arrest rate for rape among males twelve years and under has more than tripled since 1970. [Boston Globe, January 14, 1991, p. 25]). The UCR shows that 19 percent of all arrests in 1996 involved persons under eighteen years of age. This age group produced 30.9 percent of arrests for index crimes, however. Male arrests peaked at age eighteen (5.0 percent of all male arrests), followed by ages seventeen and nineteen (4.7 percent of arrests). Considering arrests of females under eighteen, the peak age was sixteen (5.2 percent of all female arrests), followed by age fifteen (5.1 percent). Earlier studies and analyses by Empey and Erickson (1966), by Wolfgang (1983), and by Braithwaite (1981) are consistent with this picture, with sixteen years being the peak year for juvenile misconduct.

It has consistently been found that males outnumber females in UCR arrest data. Thus, in 1996, males were arrested almost three times more frequently than females, among those under eighteen. For those under eighteen in 1996, males outnumbered females 5.6 to one in arrests for violent offenses. However, James Short (1990) points out that lately the gender ratio has declined substantially. Recent UCR trends suggest that Short may be correct when considering serious violations among those under eighteen. Thus, between 1987 and 1996 violent crime increased by 52.7 percent for males under eighteen and by 118.1 percent for comparable females. Considering all arrests for males and females under eighteen, males showed an increase of 30.2 percent between 1987 and 1996, while females showed an increase of 53 percent for the same period. This could be indicative of major changes to come.

Perhaps Hagan's power-control theory is relevant here. Hagan et al. (1987) suggest that child-rearing styles in the home (the power structure) are determined in part by the nature of the parents' occupations. The two main types of child-rearing styles are patriarchal and egalitarian. In occupations the two types are command (managerial) and obey (subject to others' authority). In the egalitarian family where both parents work in authority positions, the mother's authority means she has a substantial amount of power in the home, and this leads to the daughters' having increased freedom relative to sons. This situation is reversed in patriarchal families, controlled by fathers and sons. In the egalitarian family, the adolescent daughter has an increased willingness to take risks. Hagan assumes that willingness to take risks is a fundamental requirement for delinquency. He also predicts that female delinquency will be high in mother-only homes. The absence of a father leaves a void in male power, allowing the adolescent girl more freedom, greater risk taking, and an increased tendency to deviate. The theory needs to be tested more fully.

With respect to self-reports, the reports of the NYS suggest that age was not related to involvement in delinquent acts. Although males admitted to more infractions than did females, the differences are much less pronounced than those seen in the UCRs. Again, it should be emphasized that efforts are being made to enhance the ability of self-report studies to elicit information on more serious infractions.

RACE AND CLASS. UCRs for 1985 and 1989 present data on arrests by race in the United States. Among persons arrested and under eighteen years of age, blacks showed an increase from 23 percent in 1985 to 28 percent in 1989, while whites showed a decrease from 75 percent to 70 percent. The remainder of the arrests by race were attributed to Native Americans, Asians, Pacific Islanders, and Alaskan Natives. The proportion of index violent crime for blacks under eighteen increased from 52 percent in 1985 to 53 percent in 1989, while the comparable proportions for whites were 46 percent and 45 percent. Meriting considerable concern are the figures for murder and nonnegligent homicide. Here, blacks under eighteen accounted for 51 and 61 percent, respectively, of these crimes in 1985 and 1989; whites accounted for 48 and 37 percent during the same two years. This increase in the proportion of murder and nonnegligent manslaughter accounted for by blacks under eighteen is accompanied by the fact that the number of such crimes doubled for blacks and increased by 30 percent for whites during the five-year period. Aggravated assaults also increased substantially during this period for both whites and blacks under eighteen. Some consolation, perhaps, may be taken from the fact that among those under eighteen, the number of forcible rapes declined among blacks and showed a 1 percent increase for whites between 1985 and 1989. Among this age group property crimes showed a fair decline for whites and remained almost the same for blacks.

The dramatic overall increase in crimes of violence in recent years brings to mind Jackson Toby's (1967) classic work on delinquency in affluent society, as well as Durkheim's (1951) discussion of rising expectations in his theory of anomie. In Toby's case, he was trying to account for the rise in theft crimes in a variety of countries. He took special note of adolescent crime in industrial countries like Japan, Sweden, and Great Britain, but also included developing countries such as Nigeria and India in his analysis. Toby suggested that the resentment of poverty is likely to be greater among the relatively poor in an affluent society than among the poor in a poor society. He suggests, however, that envy is at work not only in the more affluent societies like Japan but also in countries with rising standards of living, such as India and Nigeria. Moreover, Toby suggests that not only adults but also the young are subject to rising expectations. It may be that relative deprivation can account for at least some of the rise in youth violence in the United States. Toby's work also suggests that the presence of such envy could be heightened where the inhibiting effect of schools or families is missing in either affluent or developing societies. Here Toby's thesis greatly resembles control theory. The increase in single-parent families among blacks, persisting educational inequalities for blacks, and chronic employment problems for black youth may tend to lessen social controls and could be factors in the greater increase in violence among them.

Social class has been, by far, the most controversial of all the factors studied in connection with juvenile delinquency. The argument seems to revolve around both method and theory. Some argue about the impact of social class, others debate the measurement of social class, and a few argue about both. In recent years, several writers have attempted to review the research on class and delinquency or crime. Tittle and his associates (1978), noting that nearly every sociological theory of crime or delinquency had class as a key factor, reviewed thirty-five such studies. Their findings suggested to Tittle and his colleagues that the class and crime-delinquency connection might be a "myth" because the relationship could not be confirmed empirically.

Subsequently, John Braithwaite (1981) criticized Tittle's study not only as incomplete but also as having come to the wrong conclusions. He reviewed fifty-three studies that used official data and forty-seven studies that used self-reports in the study of delinquency. Braithwaite forcefully argues that the class-crime relationship is no myth. Of the studies using official records, Braithwaite found that the vast majority (forty-four) showed lower-class juveniles to have substantially higher offense rates than middle-class juveniles. Of the forty-seven self-report studies, he concluded that eighteen found lower-class juveniles reported higher levels of delinquent behavior, seven reported qualified support for the relationship, and twenty-two found no relationship. Braithwaite is critical of self-report studies when (1) they do not closely examine the lowest group on the social class continuum (the lumpenproletariat) and (2) they do not include serious offenses and chronicity in their data gathering. While the argument may continue, Braithwaite and others seem to be less critical of self-report studies when they correct these apparent shortcomings.

In the egalitarian family, the adolescent daughter has an increased willingness to take risks.

Apparently the work of Elliott and Ageton (1980) has done much to defuse this issue. They found, for example, that the relationship between class and self-reported delinquency is totally a consequence of the difference between the lowest class group and the rest of the sample, with no difference between the working and middle classes. Recent writers like Messner and Krohn (1990), Hagan and Palloni (1990), and Colvin and Pauly (1983) have apparently profited from these debates; their work shows an inclination to refine the "objective" measure of class, using insights from conflict theory as they formulate explanations of delinquency. Indeed, it is safe to say that social class is alive and well, but it is more broadly conceptualized now; many of the new theories include patterns of child rearing, job experiences, and family structure that are incorporated into the framework of a more radical neo-Marxist perspective. The effort by sociologists in the United States and in other countries to better understand juvenile delinquency appears to be entering a new and more urgent phase.

[See also Crime, Theories of; Criminal and Delinquent Subcultures; Criminology; Juvenile Delinquency, Theories of; Socialization.]

BIBLIOGRAPHY

Ageton, Suzanne, and Delbert Elliott 1978 *The Incidence of Delinquent Behavior in a National Probability Sample of Adolescents.* Boulder, Colo.: Behavioral Research Institute.

Bartol, Curt, and Anne Bartol 1989 *Juvenile Delinquency: A System Approach.* Englewood Cliffs, N.J.: Prentice-Hall.

Binder, Arnold, Gilbert Geis, and Dickson Bruce 1988 *Juvenile Delinquency: Historical, Cultural, Legal Perspectives.* New York: Macmillan.

Braithwaite, John 1981 "The Myth of Social Class and Criminality Reconsidered." *American Sociological Review* 46:36–57.

——— 1989 *Crime, Shame, and Reintegration.* Cambridge: Cambridge University Press.

Colvin, Mark, and John Pauly 1983 "A Critique of Criminology: Toward an Integrated Structural-Marxist Theory of Delinquency Production." *American Journal of Sociology* 89:513–551.

Durkheim, Emile 1951 *Suicide,* J. A. Spaulding and George Simpson, trans. New York: Free Press.

Elliott, Delbert, and Suzanne Ageton 1980 "Reconciling Race and Class Differences in Self-Reported and Official Estimates of Delinquency." *American Sociological Review* 45:95–110.

Empey, Lamar T. 1982 *American Delinquency,* rev. ed. Homewood, Ill.: Dorsey.

———, and Maynard Erickson 1966 "Hidden Delinquency and Social Status." *Social Forces* 44:546–554.

Gibbons, Don, and Marvin Krohn 1991 *Delinquent Behavior,* 5th ed. Englewood Cliffs, NJ.: Prentice-Hall.

Hagan, John, and Alberto Palloni 1990 "The Social Reproduction of a Criminal Class in Working-Class London, Circa 1950–1980." *American Journal of Sociology* 96:265–299.

———, J. Simpson, and A. R. Gillis 1987 "Class in the Household: A Power-Control Theory of Gender and Delinquency." *American Journal of Sociology* 92:788–816.

Hindelang, M. J., Travis Hirschi, and Joseph Weis 1981 *Measuring Delinquency.* Beverly Hills, Calif.: Sage.

Hirschi, T. 1969 *Causes of Delinquency.* Berkeley: University of California Press.

Kratcoski, Peter, and Lucille Dunn Kratcoski 1990 *Juvenile Delinquency,* 3rd ed. Englewood Cliffs, NJ.: Prentice-Hall.

Laub, John 1983 "Trends in Serious Juvenile Crime." *Criminal Justice and Behavior* 10:485–506.

Matza, David 1964 *Delinquency and Drift.* New York: Wiley.

McCord, William, Joan McCord, and Irving Zola 1959 *Origins of Crime: A New Evaluation of the Cambridge-Somerville Study.* New York: Columbia University Press.

Messner, Steven, and Marvin Krohn 1990 "Class, Compliance Structures, and Delinquency: Assessing Integrated Structural-Marxist Theory." *American Journal of Sociology* 96:300–328.

Nettler, Gwynn 1984 *Explaining Crime,* 3rd ed. New York: McGraw-Hill.

Regoli, Robert, and John Hewitt 1991 *Delinquency in Society.* New York: McGraw-Hill.

Short, James 1990 *Delinquency in Society.* Englewood Cliffs, N.J.: Prentice-Hall.

———, and F. Ivan Nye 1958 "Extent of Unrecorded Juvenile Delinquency: Tentative Conclusions." *Journal of Criminal Law, Criminology and Police Science* 49:296–302.

Teele, James E. (ed.) 1970 *Juvenile Delinquency: A Reader.* Itasca, Ill.: Peacock.

Teeters, Negley, and David Matza 1959 "The Extent of Delinquency in the United States." *Journal of Negro Education* 28:200–213.

Tittle, Charles R., Wayne Villemez, and Douglas Smith 1978 "The Myth of Social Class and Criminality: An Empirical Assessment of the Empirical Evidence." *American Sociological Review* 43:643–656.

Toby, Jackson 1967 "Affluence and Adolescent Crime." In *1967 President's Commission on Law Enforcement and Administration of Justice: Task-Force Report on Juvenile Delinquency and Youth Crime.* Washington, D.C.: U.S. Government Printing Office. Reprinted in James E. Teele, ed., *Juvenile Delinquency: A Reader.* Itasca, Ill.: Peacock, 1970.

U.S. Department of Justice 1984 *Juvenile Court Statistics.* Washington, D.C.: U.S. Department of Justice.

——— 1988 *Crime in the United States.* Washington, D.C.: U.S. Department of Justice.

——— 1989 *Crime in the United States.* Washington, D.C.: U.S. Department of Justice.

Vold, George, and Thomas Bernard 1986 *Theoretical Criminology.* New York: Oxford University Press.

Williams, Jay, and Martin Gold 1972 "From Delinquent Behavior to Official Delinquency." *Social Problems* 20:209–229.

Wilmott, Peter 1966 *Adolescent Boys in East London.* London: Routledge and Kegan Paul.

Wolfgang, Marvin 1983 "Delinquency in Two Birth Cohorts." *American Behavioral Scientist* 27:75–86.

———, Robert Figlio, and Thorsten Sellin 1972 *Delinquency in a Birth Cohort.* Chicago: University of Chicago Press.

– JAMES E. TEELE

JUVENILE DELINQUENCY, THEORIES OF

The topic of juvenile delinquency is a fertile area for construction of sociological theory. Three major sociological traditions, including structural functionalism, symbolic interactionism, and conflict theory, contribute to the explanation of delinquency. Much of the work in this area seeks to explain why officially recorded delinquency is concentrated in the lower class, or in what is today more often called the underclass. This entry considers the most prominent theories of delinquency under the theoretical rubrics noted above.

Structural Functionalism and Delinquency

Structural-functional theories regard delinquent behavior as the consequence of strains or breakdowns in the social processes that produce conformity. These theories focus on institutions, such as the family and school, that socialize individuals to conform their behavior to values of the surrounding society and on the ways in which these institutions can fail in this task. Wide agreement or consensus is assumed about which behaviors are valued and disvalued in society. The question structural-functional theories try to answer is, why do many individuals during their adolescence behave in ways that challenge this consensus? That is, why do many adolescents violate behavioral norms that nearly all of us are assumed to hold in common?

ANOMIE THEORY. The roots of functional theory are found in Durkheim's notion of *anomie* ([1897] 1951). To Durkheim, this term meant an absence of social regulation, or normlessness. Merton (1938, 1957) revived the concept to describe the consequences of a faulty relationship between goals and the legitimate means of attaining them. Merton emphasized two features of social and cultural structure: culturally defined goals (such as monetary success) and the acceptable means (such as education) to their achievement. Merton argued that in our society success goals are widely shared, while the means of or opportunities for attaining them are not.

Merton's theory is used to explain not only why individual adolescents become delinquents but also why some classes are characterized by more delinquency than others. Since members of the lower- or underclass are assumed to be most affected by the disparity between the goals and the means of attaining success, this class is expected to have a higher rate of delinquent behavior. Merton outlined a number of ways individuals adapt when faced with inadequate means of attaining their goals. Among these, *innovation* involves substituting illegitimate for legitimate means to goal attainment; it is the resort to this adaptation that is thought to account for much theft among adolescents from the underclass.

SUBCULTURAL THEORY. Group-based adaptations to the failure to attain success goals involve the *delinquent subculture.* Cohen (1955) suggests that children of the underclass, and potential members of a delinquent subculture, first experience a failure to achieve when they enter school. When assessed against a "middle class measuring rod," these children are often found lacking. A result is a growing sense of "status frustration." Underclass children are simply not prepared by their earliest experiences to satisfy middle class expectations. The delinquent subculture therefore emerges as an alternative set of criteria or values that underclass adolescents can meet.

Cohen argues that these subcultural values represent a complete repudiation of middle class standards; the delinquent subculture expresses contempt for a middle class life-style by making its opposite a criterion of prestige. The result, according to Cohen, is a delinquent subculture that is "nonutilitarian, malicious, and negativistic"—an inversion of middle class values. Yet this is only one possible type of subcultural reaction to the frustration of failure. As we see next, many subcultural responses are elaborated in the theoretical tradition of structural functionalism.

DIFFERENTIAL OPPORTUNITY THEORY. Cloward and Ohlin (1960) argue that to understand the different forms that delinquent and ultimately criminal behavior can take, we must consider the different types of illegitimate opportunities available to those who seek a way out of the underclass and where these opportunities lead. Different types of community settings produce different subcultural responses. Cloward and Ohlin suggest that three types of responses predominate, each one leading to its own respective subculture: a stable criminal subculture, a conflict subculture, and a retreatist subculture.

The *stable criminal subculture* offers, as its name suggests, the most promising (albeit still illegitimate) prospects for upward economic mobility. According to Cloward and Ohlin, this subculture can emerge only when there is some coordination between those in legitimate and in illegitimate roles—for example, between politicians or police and the underworld. One pictures the old-style political machine, with protection provided for preferred types of illegal enterprise. Only in such circumstances can stable patterns be established, allowing opportunities for advancement from adolescent to adult levels of the criminal underworld. When legitimate and illegitimate opportunity structures are linked in this way, the streets become safe for crime, and reliable upward mobility routes can emerge for aspiring criminals.

Violence and conflict, on the other hand, disrupt both legitimate and illegitimate enterprise. When both types of enterprises coexist, violence is restrained. However, in the "disorganized slum," where these spheres of activity are not linked, violence can reign uncontrolled. Cloward and Ohlin see these types of communities as producing a *conflict subculture.* A result of this disorganization is the prevalence of adolescent street gangs and their violent activities, making the streets unsafe for more profitable crime.

The earliest North American efforts to explain delinquency saw entire neighborhoods as lacking the cohesion and constraint that could prevent crime and delinquency.

The *retreatist subculture* includes adolescents who fail in their efforts in both the legitimate and illegitimate opportunity structures. These "double failures" are destined for drug abuse and other forms of escape.

Cloward and Ohlin's theory played a role in encouraging the Kennedy and Johnson administrations of the 1960s to organize the American War on Poverty, which attempted to open up legitimate opportunities for youth and minorities in the underclass (see Moynihan 1969). However, another important variant of structural-functional theory argued that the most important cause of delinquency was not a strain between goals and means but rather a relative absence of goals, values, commitments, and other sources of social control.

SOCIAL DISORGANIZATION THEORY. The earliest North American efforts to explain crime and delinquency in terms of social control focused on the absence of social bonds at the community level. Entire neighborhoods were seen as being socially disorganized, as lacking the cohesion and constraint that could prevent crime and delinquency. This work began in the late 1920s, when Clifford Shaw and Henry McKay (1931, 1942) sought to identify areas of Chicago that were experiencing social disorganization. They explored the process that characterized these communities. What they found were indications of what they assumed to be social disorganization—truancy, tuberculosis, infant mortality, mental disorder, economic dependency, adult crime, and juvenile delinquency. In Chicago, the rates of these conditions were highest in the slums near the city center; they diminished in areas farther away from the center. Since these problems were assumed to be contrary to the shared values of area inhabitants, they were taken as indications that these areas were unable to realize the goals of their residents. In other words, they were taken as indicators of social disorganization.

Shaw and McKay also attempted to determine the sorts of community characteristics that were correlated with delinquency so that they could infer from these characteristics what the central components of social disorganization were and how they caused delinquency. Three types of correlates were identified: the economic status of the community, the mobility of community residents, and community heterogeneity. The implication was that poverty, high residential mobility, and ethnic heterogeneity led to a weakening of social bonds or controls and, in turn, to high rates of delinquency. All of this was being said of the neighborhoods Shaw and McKay studied; it was left to later theories to spell out the meaning of weakened neighborhood bonds or controls for individuals.

CONTROL THEORY. At the level of individuals, to have neither goals nor means is to be uncommitted and thus uncontrolled. Hirschi (1969) has argued that the absence of control is all that really is required to explain much delinquent behavior. There are other types of controls (besides *commitment* to conformity) that may also operate: *involvement* in school and other activities; *attachments* to friends, school, and family; and *belief* in various types of values and principles. Hirschi argues that delinquent behavior is inversely related to the presence of these controls. Alternatively, as these controls accumulate, so too does conformity. According to control theory, the more committed, attached, involved, and believing individuals are, the greater is their bond to society. Again, Hirschi's point is that no special strain between goals and means is necessarily required to produce delinquent behavior; all that is required is the elimination of the constraining elements of the social bond.

In each of the theories that we have considered thus far, values or beliefs play some role in causing delinquency. It is argued that the presence of success goals or values without the means to obtain them can produce deviant behavior, as can the absence of these goals or values in the first place. It is an emphasis on these values, and the role of the school and family in transmitting them, that ties the structural-functional theories together.

Symbolic Interactionism and Delinquency

Symbolic-interactionist theories of delinquency are concerned less with values than with the way in which social meanings and definitions can help produce delinquent behavior. The assumption, of course, is that these meanings and definitions, these symbolic variations, affect behavior. Early versions of symbolic-interactionist theories focused on how adolescents acquired these meanings and definitions from others, especially peers; more recently, theorists have focused on the role of official control agencies, especially the police and courts, in imposing these meanings and definitions on adolescents. The significance of this difference in focus will become apparent as we consider the development of the symbolic-interactionist tradition.

DIFFERENTIAL ASSOCIATION THEORY. Edwin Sutherland (1939; 1949) anticipated an emphasis of the symbolic-interactionist perspective with his early use of the concept of *differential association.* This concept referred not only to associations among people but also, and perhaps even more importantly, to associations among ideas. Sutherland's purpose was to develop a general theory that explained delinquency as well as adult criminality. He argued that people violate laws only when they define such behavior as acceptable and that there is an explicit connection between people and their ideas (that is, definitions). So, for example, delinquent behavior is "learned in association with those who define such behavior favorably and in isolation from those who define it unfavorably," and this behavior occurs when "the weight of the favorable definitions exceeds the weight of the unfavorable definitions."

Although Sutherland intended his theory to be general and explicitly to include the explanation of delinquency, his best-known applications of the theory were in his famous studies of professional theft and white-collar crime. Nonetheless, Sutherland's emphasis on white-collar illegality was important for the study of delinquency because it stressed the ubiquity of criminality, and, as we see next, it helped to mitigate delinquency theory's preoccupation with underclass delinquency.

NEUTRALIZATION THEORY. While most of the theories we have considered to this point portray the delinquent, especially the underclass delinquent, as markedly different from "the rest of us," Sykes and Matza

(1957, 1961) follow Sutherland's lead in suggesting that the similarities actually outnumber the differences. Their argument is based in part on the observation that underclass delinquents, like white-collar criminals, usually exhibit guilt or shame when detected violating the law.

Sutherland had argued that individuals become white-collar criminals because they are immersed with their colleagues in a business ideology that defines illegal business practices as acceptable. Sykes and Matza (1957) argue that the delinquent, much like the white-collar criminal, drifts into a deviant life-style through a subtle process of justification. "We call these justifications of deviant behavior techniques of neutralization," they write, "and we believe these techniques make up a crucial component of Sutherland's definitions favorable to the violation of law" (p. 667).

Sykes and Matza list four of these *neutralization techniques:* denial of responsibility (e.g., blaming a bad upbringing), denial of injury (e.g., claiming that the victim deserved it), condemnation of the condemners (e.g., calling their condemnation discriminatory), and an appeal to higher loyalties (e.g., citing loyalty to friends or family as the cause of the behavior). Sykes and Matza's point is that delinquency in the underclass, as elsewhere, is facilitated by this kind of thinking. A question lingered, however: Why are these delinquencies of the underclass more frequently made the subjects of official condemnation?

LABELING THEORY. Franklin Tannenbaum (1938) anticipated a theoretical answer to this question. He pointed out that some aspects of juvenile delinquency—the play, adventure, and excitement—are a normal part of teenage street life and that, later in their lives, many nostalgically identify these activities as an important part of their adolescence. But others see such activities as a nuisance or as threatening, so they summon the police.

Tannenbaum's concern is that police intervention begins a process of change in the way the individuals and their activities are perceived. He suggests that there is a gradual shift from defining specific acts as evil to defining the individual as evil. Tannenbaum sees the individual's first contact with the law as the most consequential, referring to this event as a "dramatization of evil" that separates the child from his or her peers for specialized treatment. Tannenbaum goes on to argue that this dramatization may play a greater role in creating the criminal than any other experience. The problem is that individuals thus singled out may begin to think of themselves as the type of people who do such things—that is, as delinquents. From this viewpoint, efforts to reform or deter delinquent behavior create more problems than they solve. "The way out," Tannenbaum argues, "is through a refusal to dramatize the evil." He implies that the less said or done about delinquency the better.

Sociologists have expanded Tannenbaum's perspective into what is often called a labeling, or societal reactions, theory of delinquency and other kinds of deviance. For example, Lemert (1967) suggests the terms *primary deviance* and *secondary deviance* to distinguish between acts that occur before and after the societal response. Acts of primary deviance are those that precede a social or legal response. They may be incidental or even random aspects of an individual's general behavior. The important point is that these initial acts have little impact on the individual's self-concept. Acts of secondary deviance, on the other hand, follow the societal response and involve a transformation of the individual's self-concept, "altering the psychic structure, producing specialized organization of social roles and self-regarding attitudes." From this point on, the individual takes on more and more of the "deviant" aspects of his or her new role (Becker 1963, 1964). The societal response has, from this viewpoint, succeeded only in confirming the individual in a deviant role: for example, by potentially making adolescent delinquents into adult criminals through the punitive reactions of the police, courts, and others.

Not only the actor but also reactors participate in creating the meanings and definitions that generate delinquency.

In the end, symbolic interactionists do not insist that all or even most delinquent behavior is caused by officially imposed labels. Being labeled delinquent is thought, rather, to create special problems for the adolescents involved, often increasing the likelihood that this and related kinds of delinquent behavior will be repeated. The point is that not only the actor but also reactors participate in creating the meanings and definitions that generate delinquency. The symbolic interactionists note that the poor are more likely than the rich to get caught up in this process. This point is further emphasized in conflict theories.

Conflict Theory and Delinquency

The most distinctive features of conflict theories include attention to the role of power relations and economic contradictions in generating delinquency and reactions to it. For example, conflict theories have focused on the role of dominant societal groups in imposing legal labels on members of subordinate societal groups (Turk 1969). The fact that subcultural groups typically are also subordinate groups ties this work to earlier theoretical traditions discussed above.

AN EARLY GROUP-CONFLICT THEORY. George Vold (1958) was the first North American sociologist to write explicitly about a group-conflict theory of delinquency. He began with the assumption that criminality involves both human behavior (acts) and the judgments or definitions (laws, customs, or mores) of others as to whether specific behaviors are appropriate and acceptable or inappropriate and disreputable. Of the two components, Vold regarded judgments and definitions as more significant. His salient interest was in how groups impose their value judgments by defining the behaviors of others as illegal.

Vold regarded delinquency as a "minority group" behavior. For example, he argues that "the juvenile gang . . . is nearly always a 'minority group', out of sympathy with and in more or less direct opposition to the rules and regulations of the dominant majority, that is, the established world of adult values and powers" (p. 211). In this struggle, the police are seen as representing and defending the values of the adult world, while the gang seeks the symbolic and material advantages not permitted it under the adult code. At root, Vold argues, the problem is one of intergenerational value conflict, with adults prevailing through their control of the legal process.

A THEORY OF LEGAL BUREAUCRACY. According to this viewpoint, determining which groups in society will experience more delinquency than others may be largely a matter of deciding which laws will be enforced. Chambliss and Seidman (1971) observe that in modern, complex, stratified societies such as our own, we assign the task of resolving such issues to bureaucratically structured agencies such as the police. The result is to mobilize what might be called the primary principle of legal bureaucracy. According to this principle, laws will be enforced when enforcement serves the interests of social control agencies and their officials; and laws will not be enforced when enforcement is likely to cause organizational strain. In other words, the primary principle of legal bureaucracy involves maximizing organizational gains while minimizing organizational strains.

Chambliss and Seidman conclude that a consequence of this principle is to bring into operation a "rule of law," whereby "discretion at every level . . . will be so exercised as to bring mainly those who are politically powerless (e.g., the poor) into the purview of the law" (p. 268). Theoretical work of this kind coincided with important research on the policing of juveniles (e.g., Reiss 1971). According to the conflict theorists, poor minority youth appear disproportionately in our delinquency statistics more because of class bias and police and court prejudice than because of actual behavioral differences.

RECENT STRUCTURAL THEORIES. Some recent theories of delinquency have combined conflict theory's structural focus on power relations with etiological questions about sources of delinquent behavior as well as reactions to it. Thus Spitzer (1975) begins the formulation of a Marxian theory of delinquency (and deviance more generally) with the observation, "We must not only ask why specific members of the underclass are selected for official processing, but also why they behave as they do" (p. 640).

A recent effort to answer behavioral questions with insights from conflict theory is an "integrated structural-Marxist theory" proposed by Colvin and Pauly (1983). This theory integrates elements of control theory and Marxian theory. The theory is comprehensive, and only some of its most striking features can be outlined here. These features include a Marxian focus on working class parents' experiences of coerciveness in the workplace, which Colvin and Pauly suggest lead to coerciveness in parenting, including parental violence toward children. In turn, Colvin and Pauly argue that such children are more likely to be placed in coercive control structures at school and to enter into alliances with alienated peers. All of these experiences make delinquent behavior more likely, including the violent and instrumental kinds of delinquent behavior that may be precursors of adult criminality.

Power-control theory is another recent structural formulation (Hagan 1989) that attempts to explain large and persistent gender differences in delinquency by taking power relations into account. Power relations in the family are the starting point of this theory. The cornerstone of the theory is the observation that, especially in more patriarchal families, mothers more than fathers are involved in controlling daughters more than sons. A result of this intensified mother–daughter relationship is that daughters become less inclined to take what they perceive as greater risks of involvement in delinquency. Police and other processing agencies act on stereotypes that extend these gender differences in officially recorded delinquency. Power-control theory generally predicts that in more patriarchal families, sons will be subjected to less maternal control, develop stronger preferences for risk taking, be more delinquent, and more often be officially labeled for being so.

These structural approaches illustrate a trend toward theoretical integration in this tradition and elsewhere in the study of delinquency (Messner, Krohn, and Liska 1989). These integrations involve theories that are often thought to be in apposition if not opposition to one another. One of the distinctive features of sociological theories of delinquency is the richness of their diversity, and it is not yet clear whether diversity or integration will provide the greater source of theoretical and empirical advancement in years to come.

[See also Crime, Theories of; Criminology; Juvenile Delinquency and Juvenile Crime.]

BIBLIOGRAPHY

Becker, Howard 1963 *Outsiders: Studies in the Sociology of Deviance.* New York: Free Press.

——— 1964 *The Other Side: Perspectives on Deviance.* New York: Free Press.

Chambliss, William, and Robert Seidman 1971 *Law, Order and Power.* Reading, Mass.: Addison-Wesley.

Cloward, Richard, and Lloyd Ohlin 1960 *Delinquency and Opportunity: A Theory of Delinquent Gangs.* New York: Free Press.

Cohen, Albert 1955 *Delinquent Boys.* New York: Free Press.

Colvin, Mark, and John Pauly 1983 "A Critique of Criminology: Toward an Integrated Structural-Marxist Theory of Delinquency Production." *American Journal of Sociology* 89 (3):512–552.

Durkheim, Emile 1951 (1897) *Suicide,* trans. John Spaulding and George Simpson. New York: Free Press.

Hagan, John 1989 *Structural Criminology.* New Brunswick, N.J.: Rutgers University Press.

Hirschi, Travis 1969 *Causes of Delinquency.* Berkeley: University of California Press.

Lemert, Edwin 1967 *Human Deviance, Social Problems and Social Control.* Englewood Cliffs, N.J.: Prentice-Hall.

Merton, Robert 1938 "Social Structure and Anomie." *American Sociological Review* 3:672–682.

——— 1957 *Social Theory and Social Structure.* New York: Free Press.

Messner, Steven, Marvin Krohn, and Allen Liska 1989 *Theoretical Integration in the Study of Deviance and Crime: Problems and Prospects.* Albany: State University of New York Press.

Moynihan, Daniel P. 1969 *Maximum Feasible Misunderstanding.* New York: Free Press.

Reiss, Albert 1971 *The Police and the Public.* New Haven, Conn.: Yale University Press.

Shaw, Clifford, and Henry McKay 1931 *Social Factors in Juvenile Delinquency.* Washington, D.C.: National Commission of Law Observance and Enforcement.

——— 1942 *Juvenile Delinquency and Urban Areas.* Chicago: University of Chicago Press.

Spitzer, Steven 1975 "Toward a Marxian Theory of Deviance." *Social Problems* 22:638–651.

Sutherland, Edwin 1939 *Principles of Criminology.* Philadelphia: Lippincott.

——— 1949 *White Collar Crime.* New York: Dryden.

Sykes, Gresham, and David Matza 1957 "Techniques of Neutralization: A Theory of Delinquency." *American Sociological Review* 26:664–670.

——— 1961 "Juvenile Delinquency and Subterranean Values." *American Sociological Review* 26:712–719.

Tannenbaum, Frank 1938 *Crime and the Community.* Boston: Ginn.

Turk, Austin 1969 *Criminality and the Legal Order.* Chicago: Rand McNally.

Vold, George 1958 *Theoretical Criminology.* New York: Oxford University Press.

– JOHN HAGAN

K

KINSHIP SYSTEMS AND FAMILY TYPES

Kinship systems are mechanisms that link conjugal families (and individuals not living in families) in ways that affect the integration of the general social structure and enhance the ability of the society to reproduce itself in an orderly fashion. Kinship performs these social functions in two ways. First, through relationships defined by blood ties and marriage, kinship systems make possible ready-made *contemporaneous networks* of social ties sustained during the lifetimes of related persons and, second, they enable the *temporal continuity* of identifiable family connections over generations, despite the limited lifespan of a family's members. Variations in norms governing the structure of contemporaneous networks and the modes of temporal continuity compose the basis for the typologies of kinship systems described in this article.

In conceptualizing connections between kinship systems and family types, social scientists have applied either of two approaches. Some have developed typologies from historical analyses (and evolutionary schemes) that depict the transition of Western societies from ancient or medieval origins to modern civilizations. Other social scientists construct typologies that cut across diverse historical periods. Each historical era then constitutes a unique medium in which the structural typologies are expressed.

Modernity, Family Patterns, and Kinship Systems

There are at least three ways to develop historical typologies related to kinship and family. One way is to hypothesize a linear historical progression, which includes a family type existing at the beginning point in time, a particular historical process that will act upon the family and kinship structures (e.g., urbanization or industrialization), and a logical outcome at the end of the process. A second approach builds upon the above approach by positing a transitional family type that emerges during the historical process and gives way in the final stages of the process to another family type. A third approach is to devise a family type based upon a configuration of attributes peculiar to a particular historical era (e.g., the Victorian family, the American colonial family) and implies that any historical era represents a unique convergence of diverse factors.

BIPOLAR TYPOLOGIES. By and large, sociologists have drawn a connection between kinship and family on the basis of a distinction between traditionalism and modernity. Generally, this distinction draws upon Henry Maine's (1885) depiction of the transformation of social relations in early societies. Maine argued that social relations changed from those based on ascriptive status (deriving from birth) to relations created and sustained through voluntary contractual arrangements. Maine's theory has evoked a series of typologies that, in large measure, refine the status–contract distinction. For instance, an ideal type developed by Ferdinand Tönnies ([1887] 1957) has provided a backdrop for later typologies. The Tönnies typology itself refers to a shift from *Gemeinschaft* (community) as a form of social organization based upon an existential will (*Wesserville*), which is suited to feudalism and peasant society, to *Gesellschaft* (society) as a social form based upon rational will (*Kurwille*), which fits an urban environment under modern capitalism. Contemporary family typologies, in building upon Tönnies's conceptual scheme, portray a weakening of kinship obligations and constraints.

Basic changes in kinship are initiated by a shift in the relative importance of men and women to the economic life of the society.

One position, rooted in George P. Murdock's (1949) analysis of cross-cultural archives, has resulted in the main sequence theory of social change in kinship structure (Naroll, 1970). Main sequence theory pertains to the way differential gender contributions to production of material resources affects the use of kindred as human resources/property. This theory holds that basic changes in kinship are initiated by a shift in the relative importance of men and women to the economic life of the society. First, there is a modification in the economic division of labor by gender. (For example, in hoe cultures, women tend to do the farming; when plows are introduced, men become the farmers.) Second, the shift in sexual division of labor generates a change in married couples' choices of residence, the major alternatives being near the husband's relatives (patrilocal), the wife's (matrilocal), or anywhere the couple desires. (Plow cultures tend toward patrilocal residence.) Third, the change in choice of residential site affects the line of descent and inheritance favored in the kinship system: the husband's side (patrilineal), the wife's (matrilineal), or both sides (bilateral). (Plow cultures show a greater inclination toward patrilineality than do hoe cultures.) Fourth, the transfer to lineage affiliation generates a change in kinship terminology, particularly in ways that show tribal or clan membership, or, in modern societies, the dissolution of larger kinship structures. As applied to the emergence of modernity, main sequence theory predicts a continual emancipation from kinship constraints. An increase in the proportion of women in the labor force will produce a trend toward neolocal residence, which in turn will lead to increased emphasis upon bilaterality, weakening sibling ties and obligations to both sides of the extended family, and in the long run to changes in kin terminology and identity (e.g., voluntarism in choice of surnames).

In a variation of main sequence theory, urban sociologists such as Wirth (1956) and Burgess, Locke, and Thomas (1963) wrote on the effects of transferring the economic base of societies from the land to urban centers. The theme of their work is to be found in the German proverb "Stadt Luft macht frei" ("city air makes one free"). For example, Burgess, Locke, and Thomas described a progression from what they named the institutional family to the companionship family. In this conceptualization, the institutional family, embedded in a larger kinship group, is characterized by patriarchy, clearly defined division of household labor by sex, and high fertility. Its unity is derived mainly from external constraints—social mores, religious authority, fixity in location, position in the social structure, and the value of familism (i.e., values giving priority to the collective welfare of the family over that of individual members). Burgess, Locke, and Thomas regarded the institutional family as an adaptation to relatively immobile, rural, agricultural societies and believed its way of life was fixed over time. By way of contrast, urban society, which is characterized by mobility, anonymity, and change, makes inoperative the social control mechanisms developed to maintain stable, rural societies. With the withering of these external controls on rural family life, Burgess, Locke, and Thomas proposed that the companionship family is bound together by internal forces—mutual affection, egalitarianism, a sense of belonging, common interests—and affords freedom from the demands of traditional family and kinship ties.

Unlike the urban sociologists, structural functionalists such as Talcott Parsons (1954) place considerable emphasis on the interaction of subsystems in the larger social system. In part, structural functionalists are concerned with economic and kinship factors in structuring nuclear family relationships. Parsons describes American kinship as "a 'conjugal' system in that it is made up *exclusively* of interlocking conjugal families" (1954, p. 180) and is multilineal (i.e., bilateral) in descent. Parsons associates kinship solidarity with unilineal descent, that is, with a "structural bias in favor of solidarity with the ascendant and descendant families in any one line of descent" (1954, p. 184). The absence of such bias in the American descent system, Parsons suggests, is in large measure responsible for "the structural isolation of the individual conjugal family." The importance Parsons attributes to unilineality as a factor in facilitating strong dependence upon kin ties is exemplified by his highlighting two exceptions to the structural isolation of the conjugal family in America—the upper class elements, whose status depends on the continuity of their patrilineages' solidarity, and the lower class elements, in which there is "a strong tendency to instability of marriage and a 'mother-centered' type of family structure" (Parsons 1954, p. 185). However, Parsons regards the urban middle classes as characterizing "the focal American type of kinship." Since in the middle classes the residence of the conjugal family typically is neolocal, and the conjugal family is economically independent of "the family of orientation of either spouse," the role of the conjugal family in U.S. society can be, for theoretical purposes, understood as master of its own destiny, rid of the impediments of extended-family ties.

In reaction to those sociologists who see modernity as inimical to bonds of kinship, other social scientists (e.g., Adams [1968]; Firth, Hubert, and Forge [1969]; Litwak [1985]; Mogey [1976]; Shanas et al. [1968]; and Sussman [1959]) turn their attention to the attenuated functions of kinship in contemporary society. Just as Goode (1963) notes a "fit" between the needs of modern capitalist society for a socially and geographically highly mobile population and the flexibility of the isolated conjugal family system, the revisionists indicate a similar fit between the existence of a highly mobile population and the presence of kin who give emergency aid and social support to relatives. The revisionists shift our attention away from constraints imposed by kinship loyalties and obligations and direct it instead to sources of services, goods, and emotional support that cannot readily be supplied by bureaucracies, markets, or other agencies. In his typology, Litwak (1960a and 1960b) distinguishes the isolated nuclear family (without kinship resources) from the traditional extended family (implying a hierarchy of authority), on the one hand, and from the modified extended family (which consists of a network of related but autonomous nuclear families), on the other. Although the revisionists have not destroyed the foundation of the bipolar family typologies, they do focus on a previously neglected area of analysis.

THREE-STAGE TYPOLOGIES. Some modernization typologies introduce a third, transitional stage between traditional and modern kinship and family structures. These typologies accept the position that initially there is an emancipation from traditional kinship constraints and obligations, but they also propose that at some point new values of modernity emerge to fill the vacuum left by the dissipation of the old kinship constraints. For example, building on the work of LePlay, Zimmerman and Frampton (1966) offer a scheme of transformation in which families change from a patriarchal form to a stem-family structure and thence to an unstable type. Zimmerman and Frampton begin with the premise that each social organization derives its "essential character" from a triad of "imperishable institutions"—family, religion, and property. However, in their view, "familism is necessary in all complete social organization to a degree more imperative than the need for property" (1966, p. 14). Zimmerman and Frampton regard the patriarchal family as the most familistic form. The patriarchal type is rooted in idealistic religion and is characterized by a common household of a patriarch and his married sons and their families, wherein the property is held in the name of the "house," with the father as trustee. They identify the patriarchal form as having been prevalent among agriculturists in the Orient, in rural Russia, and among Slavonic peasants.

With urbanization and industrialization, however, the unstable family becomes predominant. Zimmerman and Frampton associate the unstable family with ma-

Modern middle-class American families tend to be economically independent of extended family ties. (Joseph Sohm; ChromoSohm Inc./Corbis)

terialism and individualism and the resulting atomization of social life. Individuals are "freed from all obligations toward their parents and relatives" (1966, p. 15), and the identity of each conjugal family as a social unit ends with the death of the parents and the dispersal of the children.

The stem family represents a transitional state between the patriarchal and unstable forms. The stem family extends branches into urban centers while retaining its roots in the ancestral lands. As a result, the stem family provides a balance between the security of the traditional influences and resources of the "house" and the freedom and resources of the cities. (However, historical researchers yield less idyllic descriptions of the stem family than the Zimmerman and Frampton portrait. See Berkner 1972.)

A less romantic depiction of a transitional family type is drawn by Lawrence Stone (1975) in his typology of the English family's movement from feudalism to modernity. Stone posits the existence of a dual historical process. He places the decline of the importance of kin ties in the context of the emergence of a powerful, centralized state, and he then regards the rise of the modern family as an ideological emergence accompanying the development of capitalism.

According to Stone's typology, feudal England emphasized (1) kin-group responsibility for crimes and treasonable acts of members and (2) the institution of cousinship with its broad obligations. As political and economic power moved away from the traditional, landed elite to the state and the entrepreneurial class, the common law of the courts no longer recognized criminal and civil deviance as a kin-group responsibility, and cousinship lost its effectiveness. To fill the vacuum left by the decline of kinship as a factor in one's destiny, the relatively denuded conjugal family had to take over the task of guiding the destiny for its members. Consequently, by the sixteenth century, as an intermediate step toward the modern family, there was a trend toward authoritarianism in husband–wife interaction, and family governance took the form of patriarchy.

Stone (1975, p. 15) suggests that it was not until the eighteenth century that the spread of individualism and utilitarianism gave rise to a more companionate and egalitarian family structure. This last family form has been designated by Alan Macfarlane (1986) as the Malthusian marriage system, in which (1) marriage is seen as ultimately the bride's and groom's concern rather than that of the kin group; (2) marital interaction is supposed to be primarily companionate; and (3) love is supposed to be a precursor of marriage. Functionally, the Malthusian system yields relatively fewer children—by choice—than earlier family forms.

THE PROBLEM OF STRUCTURE IN MODERNITY TYPOLOGIES. Typologies depicting historical transformations in family and kinship place much emphasis on the "fit" between the needs of modern industrial society and the presence of the conjugal family type (Parsons 1954; Litwak 1960a; 1960b). Despite this conjecture, Parsons (1954, p. 184) suggests that in Western society an "essentially open system" of kinship, with its "primary stress upon the conjugal family" and its lack of larger kin structures, has existed for centuries, long before the modern period. Like Macfarlane (1986), Parsons dates its establishment in late medieval times "when the kinship terminology of the European languages took shape." Moreover, Goode's (1963) analysis of family trends in eleven societies indicates that acceptance of modern, conjugal family ideology may precede economic and industrial development rather than come as a subsequent adaptation. Such findings cast doubt on the validity of the dichotomy between traditional societies and modernity as providing a theoretical basis for the typologies discussed above.

Parsons argues that (1) there is an incompatibility between corporate kinship and multilineal systems, and (2) in large measure, this incompatibility accounts for the prevalence of highly adaptable, structurally independent conjugal households in modern societies. However, findings by Davenport (1959), Mitchell (1963), Pehrson (1957), Peranio (1961), and others that corporate structures of kinship (such as clans) do exist in some multilineal kinship systems undercut Parsons's argument that such structures are to be found only in unilineal systems. Nevertheless, if multilateral kinship systems can accommodate corporate structures, then they can also include other kinship elements that sustain loyalties to descent groups and facilitate segmentation of the society.

THE PROBLEM OF CONNECTING KINSHIP AND FAMILY IN MODERNITY TYPOLOGIES. Revisionists of the isolated conjugal family position have presented considerable evidence of residual elements of kinship ties in contemporary society. However, they do not adequately explain the connections between types of kinship systems and variation in performance of family functions in different parts of the social structure. Their main concern is with changes in kinship and family, changes that are consistent with the general loosening of tradition in modern society. But their focus on emancipation from tradition diverts their attention (1) from the influence of emerging ethnic, religious, or class interests upon patterns of integration of family networks in the larger social structure, and (2) from the temporal dimensions of kinship, which go beyond living kin to departed ancestors and generations yet to come.

Additionally, given the fact that the family-kinship typologies described above have their roots in the distinction between tradition and modernity, they overlook those nonindustrial, primarily nonurban societies in which families approach the companionship model as well as those ethnic and religious segments of industrial, primarily urban societies where strong familistic tendencies persist. Except for Stone (1975) and Zimmerman and Frampton (1966), these typologies are based on the concept of emancipation from tradition, and they do not deal explicitly with the emergence of new family values (other than flexibility and freedom). Most of all, their emphasis on emancipation from the constraints of tradition precludes their explaining why cohesive forces of family and kinship may remain strong (or increase in strength) in the face of an economic and social environment that is hostile to stable family life. (Exceptions are Sennett [1970] and Harris and Rosser [1983].)

A Transhistorical Typology of Kinship and Family Systems

For well over a millennium, church intellectuals have been aware of variations in marital selection and their implications for family structure and kinship ties as well as for social structure. Early in the fifth century, in his *De Civitate Dei (City of God),* Saint Augustine of Hippo (1966, vol. 4, pp. 503–505) noted that in early biblical times demographic insufficiencies made it necessary for Jews to practice kinship endogamy. However, he proposed that marrying close relatives, and thereby creating multiple family ties with the same people, restricted the potential expanse of social circles that could be tied into a coherent community. Kinship endogamy tends to divide societies into segments. On the other hand, marrying persons from previously unrelated families would "serve to weld social life securely" by binding diverse peoples into an extensive web of relationships. Later, in the twelfth century, Gratian suggested that God commanded the Hebrews to select relatives as mates "because the salvation of man was realized in the pure Jewish race" but that the Christian faith, which could be readily spread through teaching, made kinship endogamy obsolete (Chodorow 1972, p. 74).

Gratian's argument suggests that the differences between Judaic and Christian marriage systems have broad implications for contemporaneous functions of kinship as well as for temporal functions, connecting past and future generations. The discussion that follows presents a kinship and family typology derived ultimately from Augustine's and Gratian's depictions of marriage systems as well as from issues pertaining to descent. This typology involves theoretical concerns drawn from sociology and anthropology.

CONTEMPORANEOUS AND TEMPORAL FUNCTIONS OF KINSHIP SYSTEMS. Both marriage systems and descent rules affect the character of links between contemporaneous networks of families. A major controversy that at one time occupied many social anthropologists was whether marriage systems (i.e., marital alliances between groups) are more fundamental in generating forms of social organization than are descent rules or vice versa. At stake in the controversy was the issue of whether the social solidarity undergirding descent rules is more fundamental than the ideas of reciprocity and exchange involved in marriage systems. In the end, Africanists favored descent rules, while Asianists leaned toward marital alliances. In their assessment of the controversy, Buchler and Selby (1968) found evidence for the validity of both views.

However, despite the chicken-and-egg character of the controversy, the alliance–descent issue highlights the contradictory nature of kinship structure. This contradiction is depicted in the opposing views of structuralists such as Claude Levi-Strauss (1969), who supports the alliance position, and functionalists such as Meyer Fortes (1969), who argues for the descent position.

To alliance theorists, marriage is essentially a mode of exchange whose primary reason for existence is to inhibit conflict in society.

Alliance theories of kinship systems identify the primary function of kinship as the integration of networks of related families into the contemporaneous social fabric. Alliance adherents begin with marriage as the central element in structuring the way kinship operates. To alliance theorists, the significance of marriage lies in the idea that marriage is essentially a mode of exchange whose primary reason for existence is to inhibit conflict in society. In their view, kin groups exist as organized entities to effect marital exchanges. According to Lévi-Strauss, the leading figure in alliance theory, "exchange in human society is a universal means of ensuring the interlocking of its constituent parts" (1963, p. 2). In unilineal systems, women are exchanged for equivalent valuable property, services, or both; in bilateral systems (which by their nature become multilateral in the long run), commitments to each other's relatives are exchanged. In bilateral kinship, bride and groom are of presumably equivalent value. Thus, in general, alliance theorists regard descent groupings primarily as a necessary ingredient for sustaining the marriage exchange system over the generations.

The descent theory of kinship systems rests on the assumption that the continued welfare of kindred over the generations is the primary function of kinship. In particular, Fortes regards "filiation"—being ascribed the status of a child of one's parents, with all the lifetime rights and obligations attached to that status (1969, p. 108)—as the "crucial relationships of intergenerational continuity and social reproduction" (pp. 255–256). He proposes that, as a concomitant of filiation, "the model relationship of kinship amity is fraternity, that is sibling unity, equality, and solidarity" (p. 241), and he provides a biblical example of the tie between David and Jonathan. But he also notes that "the Euro-American kinship institutions and values of Anglo-Saxon origin are imbued with the same notion of binding force of kinship amity" (p. 242), and he cites the mother–daughter relationship in England (in research findings by Young and Willmott [1957]) as exemplifying that same moral code of diffuse but demanding reciprocal obligations.

On the one hand, alliance theory postulates that the basic drive in kinship organization is derived externally, from the kind of alliances appropriate to the structure of power in the community. Collectively, marital alliances create between families a network of links that integrate them in reference to overarching religious, economic, and political institutions. On the other hand, descent theory ascribes the bases of organization to internal demands, structural factors in the persistence of the kindred: rules governing residential location, division of labor and authority among members, and the various economic and political functions to be performed by the kinship system (Buchler and Selby 1968, p. 129).

Given the contradiction in the impulse for kinship organization, there is an apparent "impasse between the alliance and filiation point of view" (Buchler and Selby 1968, p. 141). What appears to be at issue is the depiction of the kinds of reciprocity norms that define the character of kinship. Descent theory presumes that an axiom of amity (i.e., prescriptive altruism or general reciprocity) is basic to the coherence of kin groups; alliance theory holds that balanced reciprocity (i.e., the rightness of exchanges for overt self-interest, opportunistic individualism, or noumenal norms) is in the final analysis the glue that integrates families and kin groups into a coherent whole.

The contradiction is apparent in many ways. For example, in biblical references and religious writings, the Ten Commandments enjoin one to honor parents and, conversely, to "cleave" to one's spouse and maintain peace in the household. In terms of kinds of reciprocity, one commandment involves unconditional giving or honoring, while the other concerns maintaining domestic peace (implying fair give-and-take).

Similarly, contemporary writers on marriage generally find the concept of balanced reciprocity appropriate in describing the quality of husband–wife ties. For example, Walster and Walster (1978) report that marriages work best when both husband and wife (as well as lovers) believe that each is receiving a fair exchange for what he or she offers in the relationship. Moreover, in their review of research on the quality of marriage, Lewis and Spanier (1982) note the importance of the symmetry of exchange in establishing and maintaining strong marital ties. However, in the socialization of children and in the allocation of resources, the rule of amity (or prescriptive altruism) is supposed to prevail. For example, parents are ordinarily expected to make "sacrifices" for their children when necessary; to do otherwise is to be a "bad" parent. In the American court system, the general rule for the disposition of children in cases of divorce, child neglect or abuse, or adoption is that the court should base its decision on the welfare of the child rather than on the interests of the parents or other parties.

To some extent, the descent–marriage contradiction can be obscured by compartmentalizing marital, parental, and filial conduct and by dividing responsibilities of husband and wife. However, conflicts in norms for dealing with family members and kindred may occur for several reasons, but they occur principally because of scarcities of time and resources required to carry out duties and obligations in the face of a wide range of simultaneous and conflicting demands. Since the resulting dilemmas are widespread in the society, there is a need for a general rule. Because contradictory alliance and descent impulses are operative, each group is pushed to establish a coherent kinship scheme that gives priority to one impulse over the other or at least establishes some form of compromise between them.

There is evidence that rules governing marital functions conflict with those pertaining to descent functions, paralleling the alliance-descent controversy in kinship systems. Where descent functions are given precedence in family organization, marital functions are subordinated (and vice versa). Examples of this inverse relationship are (1) if husband–wife unity is central, then the unity between siblings is peripheral (and the reverse), and (2) if marriage between close affines is forbidden, first-cousin marriage is permitted (and vice versa). These examples are discussed in the sections that follow.

MARITAL UNITY VERSUS UNITY OF THE SIBLING GROUP. Comparisons between societies indicate that ties between siblings have an inverse relationship to husband–wife ties. Where descent is valued over alliance or marriage in kinship relations, brother–sister bonds are particularly close (Parsons 1954), while the husband–wife relationship is relatively distant. In such family systems (whether or not its therapeutic implications are true), parents are expected to remain together for the sake of the children, and this expectation expresses the priority of descent over marital ties. Conversely, in family systems where the marriage function is more valued, the husband–wife relationship is intense (e.g., the importance of the give-and-take of love and of companionship for marriage) and the brother–sister relationship is competitive, distant, or both and the incest taboo justifies their apartness (see Lopata [1973] on widows and their brothers). In societies where priority is given to marital bonds over descent ties, the presence of children is of less importance in dissolving an unhappy marriage, and there is greater ambiguity about what is best for the children. The mere fact that the strength of brother–sister ties and that of marital ties vary inversely in different societies lends support to the proposition that there is a contradiction in the family system between its marital functions and its descent functions.

AFFINES AND COUSINS IN AMERICAN MARRIAGE LAW. The opposition between marital and descent functions in the family is also illustrated by the inverse relationship in American law of marriages considered to be incestuous: As a general tendency, states that *forbid* second marriages between a person and certain affines (such as that person's parents-in-law and sons- or daughters-in-law) *allow* first cousins to marry, while those that *permit* marriage between close affines *forbid* first-cousin marriage (Farber 1968, pp. 27–28). If the preferred function of marriage is to reinforce close consanguineous kinship ties, then this pattern of marital prohibitions signals a subordination of affinal bonds to those of consanguinity. Marrying into the family of the former spouse will not reinforce any of the other existing bonds of consanguinity. Consequently, although first-cousin marriage is to be permitted in order to reinforce intimate kinship ties, marriage with close affines should be avoided. However, if marriage is considered to be primarily a mechanism for creating new bonds between previously unrelated families, then a second marriage into the same family merely serves to maintain the affinal bonds initiated in the first marriage.

SOCIAL STRUCTURE AND KINSHIP SYSTEMS. The presence of contradictory impulses in organizing kinship ties produces a predicament in establishing priorities between them. This contradiction evokes a question: Which circumstances lead some societies (and ethnic and religious subgroups) to give priority to descent and others to favor alliance assumptions in their kinship and family organization (Farber 1975)? In their analyses of the relationship between kinship organization and social structure, both Paige (1974) and Swanson (1969) distinguish between societies that feature the legitimacy of special interests—factionalism—in organizing social life and those that feature the importance of common interests—communalism—as an organizing theme.

Factions are a means for gathering forces and mobilizing members for conflict or competition with other factions. They emerge as a reaction to perceived danger to their well-being from other groups (cf. Douglas 1966). Factions emerge where either (1) special interest groups vie for superiority over other groups for access to power, wealth, or some other property, or (2) groups sense a danger to their continued autonomous existence as an ethnic or religious entity.

In kinship organization, the mobilization of property and of members in factionalism involves generating norms to facilitate the pulling inward of human, symbolic, and material resources. (Consequently, this type of kinship organization, associated with factionalist social structure, can be called *centripetal.*) This centripetal tendency permits each kin group to separate itself from competing groups. As a result, kin groups favor norms strengthening *descent* relationships over norms facilitating new alliances with other groups through marriage. Insofar as descent group norms are rooted in the axiom of amity, one would expect centripetal kinship organization to feature the norm of prescriptive altruism over balanced reciprocities in kinship and family relations (see Farber 1975).

In traditional Judaism, whatever Jewish mothers did for their children was accompanied by a flow of language, consisting of rich, colorful expressive words and phrases.

Jewish family norms provide some insight into the relationship between centripetal kinship systems and the application of the axiom of amity. In its basic ideology and in the code of laws supporting that ideology, Judaism assigns a major significance to the concept of nurturance (Farber 1984). Since nurturance is a central feature of maternal giving, it can be regarded as a metaphor for the axiom of amity. The *Code of Jewish Law (Shulkhan Arukh)* offers numerous instances that signify the place of nurturance in Judaism (Ganzfried 1963).

For example, the code sublimates feeding and eating into sacred, ritualistic acts. The act of eating is invested with holiness, to be enjoyed in abundance, particularly on feast days and the Sabbath. A connection is made in the code between providing food and giving gifts and charity. It proposes that festive occasions are also times for charity to the needy and for sending gifts. In addition to drawing a connection between food and charity, the code applies the metaphor of the parent–child relationship to charity giving and assigns a priority to family in its general concept of nurturance: First parents, then offspring, and "other kinsmen take precedence over strangers" (Ganzfried 1963, chap. 34). The injunction to nurture children involves an emphasis not only on food but on other aspects as well (for example, an exaggerated emphasis on elaborated linguistic codes for use in childrearing). Zena Smith Blau (1974, p. 175) writes that "whatever Jewish mothers did for their children—and they did a great deal—was accompanied by a flow of language, consisting of rich, colorful expressive words and phrases." The aim of socialization is presumably to turn the child into a *Mensch*—to transform the child from a receiver of nurture to a giver of nurture (Zborowski and Herzog 1952, p. 335). Hence, in traditional Judaism, the concept of nurturance seems to tie together the kinship emphasis on descent and the axiom of amity in organizing family relationships.

As opposed to factionalism, communalism implies a situation in which special interests are subordinated to common concerns of diverse groups. In stateless societies, these common concerns may well emerge from economic interdependence or the presence of a common enemy. In societies with a centralized government, the state presumably symbolizes a concern for the common welfare of the populace. Other unifying concerns may exist as well, for example, the presence of a universal church (as opposed to competing sects and denominations), nationalism (as opposed to ethnic self-determination), a centralized bureaucracy or market (as opposed to regional competition for dominance), and so on. The common concerns would best be served if members of kin groups were to be dispersed by marriage to previously unrelated people living throughout the society. This dispersal would maximize the number of diverse kin groups with which any family is connected, and it would thereby scatter kinship loyalties, obligations, and property as widely as possible. (Consequently, this kind of kinship system, associated with communalism, can be called *centrifugal.*)

In contrast to the centripetal system, the centrifugal system subordinates kinship ties to conjugal family ties and extends marital prohibitions widely in order to inhibit marriages that would merely reinforce existing consanguineous ties. According to the theory outlined above, in centrifugal kinship systems, in which marriage functions are given priority over descent functions, the appropriate norm for defining family interaction is balanced reciprocity—exchange rather than the axiom of amity.

In the United States, although the centrifugal kinship system appears in a wide range of socioeconomic, religious, and ethnic groups, it is found disproportionately at lower socioeconomic levels, where families seek improved integration into the larger society (Farber 1981).

The application of balanced exchange as a norm in family and kinship is exemplified in a study of poor families by Carol Stack (1974). She describes the prevalence of "swapping" as a named, bartering norm governing both ties between kin and between family members in their struggle for survival. Stack notes that "reciprocal obligations last as long as both participants are mutually satisfied" and that they continue such exchange relationships as long as they can "draw upon the credit they accumulate with others through swapping" (p. 41). Indeed, according to Stack, "those actively involved in domestic networks swap goods and services on a daily, practically an hourly, basis" (p. 35). But this exchange does not constitute a playing out of the axiom of amity since "the obligation to repay carries kin and community sanctions" (p. 34) and it extends beyond family and kin to friends. Although swapping may involve some element of trust, it exists to ensure exchanges in the lean times that predictably recur in domestic networks that are too marginal in resources to be magnanimous. It pays to create numerous bartering arrangements rather than to accumulate obligations within a very small network of intimate kin. Thus, in its own way, swapping mimics the proliferation of networks of previously unrelated families characteristic of centrifugal kinship systems.

RELATED TRANSHISTORICAL TYPOLOGIES. Variations on issues pertinent to the structural contradiction typology have been developed in other transhistorical schemes associated with the role of marriage and descent systems in organizing family and kinship systems. For instance, Guichard (1977) distinguishes between Eastern/Islamic and Western/Christian kinship systems. According to his typology, in the Eastern system, (1) descent is patrilineal; (2) marital ties are weak and polygyny and easy divorce are permitted; (3) close ties exist between kin related through male lineage groups; (4) strong preference is given to endogamy within patrilineages; and (5) the sexes are segregated and women are relatively secluded within the home. In contrast, in the Western system, (1) kinship is bilineal or bilateral/multilateral, with ties to the maternal family considered important and with an emphasis on affinal connections as well; (2) marital bonds are the dominant unifying feature in family and kinship, with monogamy as prescribed and with extended kin ties as weak; (3) kin ties are defined according to individual connections rather than by lineage groups, with an emphasis upon the ascending line rather than the descending line and with little importance attached to lineal continuity or solidarity; (4) kinship exogamy is prescribed, with endogamy permitted primarily for economic reasons; and (5) interaction between the sexes occurs in a wide range of circumstances.

In his reaction to Guichard, Goody (1983) revives the anthropological controversy between alliance theory and descent theory. Goody criticizes Guichard for basing his typology upon marital norms (i.e., the endogamy-exogamy distinction) and suggests that by not starting with descent factors (i.e., inheritance practices), Guichard has overlooked a more fundamental distinction—that between kinship systems in which property is passed from one generation to the next through both sexes (by means of inheritance and dowry) and those systems in which property is transmitted unisexually (usually through males). Goody contends that passing property down unisexually encourages the development of corporate kinship groups (e.g., African systems). However, the use of bilateral devolution discourages such corporate structures, and Goody places both Eastern and Western systems in Guichard's dichotomy in the bilateral category. He faults Guichard for overstating the existence of corporate structures in Eastern kinship and proposes that Guichard's Western type represents merely a later historical development away from its roots in the Eastern system. Goody sees the primary problem of explaining the character of family and kinship in Western society as one of discerning how European societies shifted from preferred kinship endogamy (e.g., first-cousin marriage) to prescribed exogamy.

In his analysis of European kinship, Goody considers the changes introduced by the Christian (i.e., Roman Catholic) church from its beginnings to the late medieval period. He interprets the shift from kinship endogamy to exogamy mainly as a strategic move by the church to gain control over the lives of its members. As part of this effort, it had to wrest access to resources (especially productive land) from enduring control by family and kin. As a result, church laws evolved favoring those norms that might enhance allegiance to the church and weaken competition from the family and the state. In consequence, the church favored: (1) the use of testation permitting bequests to the church; (2) the prescription of kinship exogamy as a means for inhibiting both the reinforcement of close kin ties and the passing down of resources exclusively within lineages; (3) the requirement of the consent of both bride and groom in marriage; (4) late marriage as a means for weakening family control over mate selection; (5) prohibition of divorce even for childless couples; and so on.

The ban on divorce in Roman Catholicism was devised primarily to encourage bequeathing estates to the church in case of childlessness.

Goody seems to overstate his case in trying to interpret the shifts in kinship in ways that are consistent with his basic typology. For example, in giving primacy to inheritance patterns, Goody asserts that the ban on divorce in Roman Catholicism was devised primarily to encourage bequeathing estates to the church in case of childlessness. But, in fact, when there were no children, bequests usually were made "to brothers and sisters and to nieces and nephews" (Sheehan 1963, p. 75). Moreover, Goody's explanation of the ban ignores the widespread practice of bequeathing a portion of one's estate to the church even when one left a widow, children, or both. Michael Sheehan (1963, p. 298) reports that these bequests were made for the good of the soul. "Among the Anglo-Saxons, bequests to the parish church became so general that they were eventually required by law." This practice was not restricted to England. According to Sheehan, "Christians in the Mediterranean basin had developed the practice of bequeathing part of their estate in alms" (p. 303). Thus, church heirship in medieval Christian Europe was tied to repentance regardless of the existence of familial beneficiaries. Since church acquisition did not have to depend on bequests from childless couples, it is unlikely that the ban on divorce derives primarily from the desire of the church for additional benefices.

In addition, Goody dismisses the intermittent presence of kinship endogamy in medieval Europe as opportunistic deviations from the moral injunctions of the church. Yet, as Duby (1977) indicates, in medieval Europe the ebb and flow in kinship endogamy was tied to the amount of emphasis given to strengthening lines of descent. For example, Duby notes that in northern France, from before the tenth century to about the middle of the eleventh century, there was little utilization of the concept of lineage and only vague awareness of genealogy and knowledge about ancestors. Prior to that time, even members of the aristocracy considered their family to consist of "a horizontal grouping" of neighbors and kin "whose bonds were as much the result of marriage alliances as of blood" (Duby 1977, p. 147). Then, beginning with the tenth century, there was a change in ideas and norms regarding kinship—a conscious strengthening of lineage by controlling marriage, which frequently took place between close relatives (despite impediments in canon law [Canon Law Society 1983]). To summarize, Goody's argument is that medieval deviation from canon law consisted of opportunistic economic decisions and did not derive from a different set of norms. But Duby describes the coordination of kinship endogamy with the emerging notion of the legitimacy of lineage—a complex of ideas that requires a consensus among the kin in order to be effective. Hence, it appears that the change in marriage rules and in the significance of lineage signaled more than ad hoc departures from church law.

There is still another reason for questioning Goody's conclusions: Goody makes the point that through bequests the Catholic church became the largest landowner in Europe. In his focus upon the growth of exogamy as a consequence of devolution of estates to both sexes, he has overlooked the church's own involvement as a major heir in the inheritance system. Particularly in the light of the church's view that ties through faith are equivalent to blood ties, the church is identified with spiritual kinship (Goody 1983, pp. 194ff). However, if it is legitimate to consider the church as an heir on par with familial heirs, then the system becomes one of *trilateral* devolution—sons, daughters, *and* the church. In that case, the European system differs markedly from the Eastern kinship system described by Guichard. Indeed, in contrast to Judaism and Islam, Christianity, at least until the end of the medieval period, saw family and kinship ties as *competitive* with church interests and the strategies the church applied to weaken these ties altered both the marriage and the inheritance systems. The data imply that, despite their contradictory implications, both the marriage or alliance component and the descent component should be addressed as equal factors in organizing family life.

A task that remains is to integrate typologies of the emergence of modern kinship systems with transhistorical, structural typologies.

[See also Alternative Life-Styles; American Families; Family and Household Structure; Family Roles.]

BIBLIOGRAPHY

Adams, Bert N. 1968 *Kinship in an Urban Setting.* Chicago: Markham.

Augustine, Saint 1966 *The City of God against the Pagans.* Cambridge, Mass.: Harvard University Press.

Berkner, Lutz 1972 "The Stem Family and the Developmental Cycle of a Peasant Household: An Eighteenth-Century Example." *American Historical Review* 77:398–418.

Blau, Zena Smith 1974 "The Strategy of the Jewish Mother." In Marshall Sklare, ed., *The Jew in American Society.* New York: Behrman House.

Bott, Elizabeth 1972 *Family and Social Network.* New York: Free Press.

Buchler, Ira R., and Henry A. Selby 1968 *Kinship and Social Organization.* New York: Macmillan.

Burgess, Ernest W., Harvey J. Locke, and Mary Margaret Thomas 1963 *The Family: From Institution to Companionship.* New York: American Book Company.

Canon Law Society of Great Britain and Ireland 1983 *The Code of Canon Law.* London: Collins Liturgical Publications.

Chodorow, Stanley 1972 *Christian Political Theory and Church Politics in the Mid-Twelfth Century.* Berkeley: University of California Press.

Davenport, W. 1959 "Nonunilinear Descent and Descent Groups." *American Anthropologist* 61:557–572.

Douglas, Mary 1966 *Purity and Danger.* London: Routledge and Kegan Paul.

Duby, Georges 1977 *The Chivalrous Society.* London: Edward Arnold.

Farber, Bernard 1968 *Comparative Kinship Systems.* New York: Wiley.

——— 1975 "Bilateral Kinship: Centripetal and Centrifugal Types of Organization." *Journal of Marriage and the Family* 37:871–888.

——— 1981. *Conceptions of Kinship.* New York: Elsevier.

——— 1984. "Anatomy of Nurturance: A Structural Analysis of the Contemporary Jewish Family." Paper presented at Workshop on Theory Construction and Research Methodology, National Council on Family Relations, San Francisco, October.

Firth, Raymond, Jane Hubert, and Anthony Forge 1969 *Families and Their Relatives.* New York: Humanities Press.

Fortes, Meyer 1969 *Kinship and Social Order.* Chicago: Aldine.

Ganzfried, Solomon 1963 *Code of Jewish Law (Kitzur Shulkhan Arukh),* rev., annot. ed. New York: Hebrew Publishing Company.

Goode, William J. 1963 *World Revolution and Family Patterns.* New York: Free Press.

Goody, Jack 1983 *The Development of the Family and Marriage in Europe.* New York: Cambridge University Press.

Guichard, P. 1977 *Structures sociales 'orientales' et 'occidentales' dans l'Espagne musulmane.* Paris: Mouton.

Harris, C. C., and Colin Rosser 1983 *The Family and Social Change.* Boston: Routledge and Kegan Paul.

Lévi-Strauss, Claude 1963 *Structural Anthropology.* New York: Basic Books.

——— 1969 *The Elementary Structures of Kinship.* Boston: Beacon Press.

Lewis, Robert A., and Graham B. Spanier 1982 "Marital Quality, Marital Stability and Social Exchange." In F. Ivan Nye, ed., *Family Relationships: Rewards and Costs.* Beverly Hills, Calif.: Sage.

Litwak, Eugene 1960a "Occupational Mobility and Extended Family Cohesion." *American Sociological Review* 25:9–21.

——— 1960b "Geographical Mobility and Extended Family Cohesion." *American Sociological Review* 25:385–394.

——— 1985 *Helping the Elderly: The Complementary Roles of Informal Networks and Formal Systems.* New York: Guilford Press.

Lopata, Helena Znaniecki 1973 *Widowhood in an American City.* Cambridge, Mass.: General Learning Press.

Macfarlane, Alan 1986 *Marriage and Love in England: Modes of Reproduction* 1300–1840. New York: Basil Blackwell.

Maine, Henry S. 1885 *Ancient Law.* New York: Henry Holt.

Mitchell, William E. 1963 "Theoretical Problems in the Concept of the Kindred." *American Anthropologist* 65:343–354.

Mogey, John 1976 "Content of Relations with Relatives." In J. Caisenier, ed., *The Family Life Cycle in European Societies.* Paris: Mouton.

Murdock, George Peter 1949 *Social Structure.* New York: Macmillan.

Naroll, Rauol 1970 "What Have We Learned from Cross-Cultural Surveys?" *American Anthropologist* 75:1227–1288.

Paige, Jeffery M. 1974 "Kinship and Polity in Stateless Societies." *American Journal of Sociology* 80:301–320.

Parsons, Talcott 1954 "The Kinship System of the Contemporary United States." In Talcott Parsons, ed., *Essays in Sociological Theory.* New York: Free Press.

Pehrson, R. N. 1957 *The Bilateral Network of Social Relations in Konkama Lapp District.* Bloomington: Indiana University Research Center in Anthropology, Folklore, and Linguistics.

Peranio, R. 1961 "Descent, Descent Line, and Descent Group in Cognatic Social Systems." In V. E. Garfield, ed., *Proceedings of the Annual Meeting of the American Ethnological Association.* Seattle: University of Washington Press.

Sennett, Richard 1970 *Families Against the City: Middle Class Homes of Industrial Chicago, 1872–1890.* Cambridge, Mass.: Harvard University Press.

Shanas, Ethel, Peter Townsend, Dorothy Wedderburn, Henning Friis, Paul Milhøj, and Jan Stehouwer 1968 *Old People in Three Industrial Countries.* New York: Atherton Press.

Sheehan, Michael M. 1963 *The Will in Medieval England: From the Conversion of the Anglo-Saxons to the End of the Thirteenth Century.* Toronto: Pontifical Institute of Medieval Studies.

Stack, Carol B. 1974 *All Our Kin.* New York: Harper Colophon Books.

Stone, Lawrence 1975 "Rise of the Nuclear Family in Early Modern England: The Patriarchal Stage." In Charles E. Rosenberg, ed., *The Family in History.* Philadelphia: University of Pennsylvania Press.

Sussman, Marvin 1959 "The Isolated Nuclear Family: Fact or Fiction?" *Social Problems* 6:333–340.

Swanson, Guy E. 1969 *Rules of Descent: Studies in the Sociology of Parentage.* Anthropological Papers, no. 39. Ann Arbor: Museum of Anthropology, University of Michigan.

Tönnies, Ferdinand [1887] 1957. *Community and Society.* East Lansing: Michigan State University Press.

Walster, Elaine, and G. William Walster 1978 *A New Look at Love.* Reading, Mass.: Addison-Wesley.

Wirth, Louis 1956 *Community Life and Social Policy.* Chicago: University of Chicago Press.

Young, Michael, and Peter Willmott 1957 *Family and Kinship in East London.* London: Routledge and Kegan Paul.

Zborowski, Mark, and Elizabeth Herzog 1952 *Life Is with People: The Culture of the Stetl.* New York: Shocken Books.

Zimmerman, Carle C., and Merle E. Frampton 1966 "Theories of Frederic LePlay." In Bernard Farber, ed., *Kinship and Family Organization.* New York: Wiley.

— BERNARD FARBER

L

LABOR FORCE

Although labor force concepts were originally designed to study economic activity and guide government policies, economic activities are a form of *social* behavior, with numerous social determinants and consequences. Hence labor force behavior has been the subject of a substantial body of sociological research.

Measurement

The U.S. Bureau of the Census developed the labor force concept to measure the number of working-age people who were economically active during a particular time: the calendar week preceding the sample interview (Cain 1979; U.S. Department of Labor 1982). It has two components: (1) *the employed,* those who, during the reference week, did any work at all as paid employees, self-employed, or unpaid family workers working at least fifteen hours in a family-operated enterprise. Included also are those who were employed but on vacation, home sick, or not on the job for various other reasons, and (2) *the unemployed,* those who were not employed during the reference week but were available for work and had actively sought employment sometime within the preceding four-week period. All those who are neither employed or unemployed are defined as being out of the labor force and primarily include students, housewives, the retired, and the disabled. Since the size of the population affects the number of people who work, labor force measures are usually expressed in ratio form. The *labor force participation rate* is the percentage of the total working-age *population* that is in the labor force, whereas the *unemployment rate* is the percentage of the *labor force* that is unemployed. To compare particular subgroups in the population, analysts compute group-specific measures such as the percentage of all women, versus men, who are in the labor force or the percentage of black, versus white, labor force members who are unemployed.

The Census Bureau developed the labor force concepts during the Great Depression of the 1930s in response to the government's difficulty in charting the severity of unemployment during that crisis. Prior to 1940, measures of economic activity were only collected at the time of the decennial censuses, making it impossible to track business-cycle fluctuations in unemployment; for example, most of the Great Depression came between the 1930 and 1940 censuses. Hence, to provide ongoing unemployment data, the Census Bureau initiated the monthly Current Population Survey in the 1940s.

A second problem was the ambiguity of the previously used measure of economic activity, the *gainful worker concept,* which was designed to ascertain individuals' usual occupations, if they had them, rather than whether they were actually working at any given time (Durand 1948; Hauser 1949). In fact, census enumerators were often specifically instructed to record an occupation, even if the individual were currently unemployed, thus *over*stating the number employed. On the other hand, some kinds of employment were often *under*estimated because people who considered their market work to be secondary to their other activities, such as taking care of the home and children or going to school, were less likely to report themselves as employed in response to a question on their usual occupation. Such misreporting was unlikely with the labor force measure, since most people could remember whether they had worked at all the previous week or, if not, whether they had been looking for a job. Information on occupation and on other important characteristics of their employment, such as hours worked, was then obtained separately in response to additional questions.

While labor force concepts are relatively unambiguous measures of economic activity, they too exhibit problems. A general concern is the adequacy of the unemployment measure. The extent of unemployment may be understated if persistently unemployed persons eventually give up trying and drop out of the labor force. The Census Bureau has therefore included additional questions to try to ascertain the number of such "discouraged workers" (Cain 1979). The work of Clifford Clogg and Teresa Sullivan extends this approach to address the larger question of "*under*employment" (Sullivan 1978; Clogg and Sullivan 1983). They have developed and applied a variety of indicators of underemployment, in order to achieve a more extensive assessment of the problem. In addition to the usual unemployment rate and estimates of discouraged workers, they use three other indicators: a measure of involuntary part-time work (due to economic factors); low work-related income relative to the poverty level, and a measure of the proportion of workers who are "overeducated" ("mismatched") for the jobs they hold. The "adequately employed" are all those who are not underemployed in any one of these five categories. Their results indicate that underemployment is more common among the young and the old and appears to have increased in recent years. While several of the indices, particularly the mismatch measure, are somewhat controversial (Keyfitz 1981), their work represents an important innovation in the multidimensional measurement of underemployment.

Full-time homemakers are never counted as employed, although they usually put in long hours producing goods and services for their families.

A major characteristic of the labor force concept is that it is a measure of market-oriented economic activities. People are only considered employed if they work for pay (or in the production of goods or services for sale). Yet there is a considerable amount of economic production for home consumption. Hence, labor force status per se is an imperfect indicator of whether an individual is economically productive; for example, full-time homemakers are never counted as employed, although they usually put in long hours producing goods and services for their families. However, if the market-oriented nature of the measure is kept in mind, this limitation is not too serious in a modern industrial society. Increases in married women's labor force participation can then be interpreted as indicating their growing participation in the market sector of the economy, usually in addition to their home productive activities, although working wives do less housework than nonworking (Vanek 1974; Berardo, Shihan, and Leslie 1987).

More serious problems arise in comparing societies at different levels of economic development (Moore 1953). Preindustrial subsistence economies produce few goods or services for a market. As societies develop economically, an increasing proportion of labor is sold in the marketplace, and the goods and services families consume are also increasingly purchased, rather than home-produced. It is often difficult to undertake a meaningful comparison of labor force or unemployment rates among such different economies. The measurement of agricultural employment, especially that of women and youth, can be particularly problematic in countries with a large subsistence sector, and measurement inconsistencies are common (Dixon 1982). Moreover, *unemployment,* especially in rural areas, is often manifested as *under*employment, and its extensiveness is difficult to determine.

Determinants and Consequences of Labor Force Changes

The size and rate of growth of the labor force is dependent on three factors.

1. *The size and rate of population growth.* A large and/or rapidly growing population produces a large and/or growing labor force.

2. *The propensity of the population to enter the labor force and how this varies among population subgroups.* Age and sex, and what these signify biologically and socially, are the major reasons for varying propensities. Infants and young children do not work but, generally starting in adolescence, labor force participation increases with age, peaking for those in their late thirties and early forties and starting an accelerating decline thereafter. Married women, particularly mothers of young children, have historically had lower labor force participation rates than adult males, although this is much less so now than in the past (U.S. Department of Labor 1988).

3. *The composition of the population.* Since different population segments have different work propensities, the composition of the population affects the overall proportions in the labor force. Sharp *short*-run fluctuations in the U.S. birth rate have led to corresponding variations in the relative size of the working-age population. After sixteen–eighteen years, baby booms greatly increase the number of new labor force entrants, while baby busts reduce it. However, the overall *long*-run declines in U.S. fertility, combined with declines in mortality among the elderly, have increased the relative number of elderly in the population, an age group with low work propensities. On the other hand, foreign migration to the United States somewhat counteracts the effects of an aging population, since it has historically been disproportionately composed of young working-age adults drawn to the United States by job opportunities.

One long-term trend in labor force participation in the United States has been the decline in employment of older males, primarily due to the earlier retirement made possible by the institution and spread of the social security system, combined with the greater availability of disability benefits and pensions. The employment of young males has also decreased, due to more extended schooling, although offset somewhat by a rise in student employment (U.S. Department of Labor 1988). However, the most substantial postwar change in employment behavior has been the enormous increase in married-women's labor force participation. While paid employment used to be generally limited to the period between school and marriage, since the 1940s married women's employment has become so prevalent that, by 1996, between 65 percent and 73 percent of those in the 20–44 age groups were in the labor force. Moreover, almost 63 percent of married mothers of children under age six were also in the labor force (U.S. Census Bureau; Labor Force, Employment and Earnings; 1998).

There are several reasons for this rapid rise in women's employment in addition to the impetus provided by rapid economic growth. The bureaucratization of government and industry has raised the demand for clerical workers. Population growth, prosperity, and rising living standards have greatly expanded the consumption of services. This, in turn, has raised the demand for salespeople, or those in the helping professions such as teachers and social workers, and nurses and others in health-related occupations. Since the great majority of young, single, out-of-school women work, the result of this increasing demand has been a strong and continuing demand for a previously underutilized source of female labor: married women (Oppenheimer 1970).

For their part, married women often had several major reasons for wanting to work: the need, early in marriage, to help set up a new household and perhaps save money for a down payment on a house; the desire to save for the children's schooling; the couple's desire to achieve a high level of living. In addition, a woman's desire for greater personal economic security has also probably been an important factor. Trends in the cost of living have also increased the need to raise family income to achieve and maintain a high living standard (Oppenheimer 1982).

The effects of changing labor force behavior are not limited to the economic realm. A number of sociologists, as well as economists, have argued that it has also had an important impact on marriage and the family. Since the late 1960s the average age at marriage has risen substantially, after having declined through most of the twentieth century; nonmarital cohabitation has become increasingly prevalent; and marital instability has accelerated its long-term upward trend, after a sharp reversal in the early post-World War II period. Two competing employment-related explanations for these trends are currently under debate. In one, the argument is that married women's rapidly rising labor force participation has increased their economic independence from males (Becker 1981; Espenshade 1985; Goldscheider and Waite 1986; Farley 1988). The result is a decreasing desire on the part of women to remain in an unhappy marriage or even to marry at all. In addition, since women's traditional time-and energy-consuming familial roles of childbearing and child rearing compete with the pursuit of individual career goals, more women are either forgoing childbearing entirely or settling for one or two children at most.

The extensiveness of the changes in women's employment qualifies this factor as one potentially important reason for the recent trends in marriage and family behavior. However, it is well known that marriage formation and marital stability are also related to *men's* employment characteristics (Goldscheider and Waite 1986; Teachman, Polonko, and Leigh 1987; Ross and Sawhill 1975; Cherlin 1979). Moreover, research in both sociology and economics indicates that men's labor market position, especially *young* men's, has also changed substantially since the late 1960s. Particularly important has been the marked decline in the earnings position of young men relative to that of prime working-age males (Easterlin 1987; Oppenheimer 1988). The reason for this, Richard Easterlin hypothesizes, is that the prolonged postwar baby boom led to a lengthy period during which relatively large birth cohorts were crowding the labor market, and the resulting increase in competition for good jobs reduced the relative economic position of the young, at least temporarily. This led, in turn, Easterlin argues, to delayed marriage, lower fertility, and more unstable marriages. However, the small baby-bust cohorts (the result of the long-term declines in fertility since the late 1950s) have only recently started entering the labor market and, according to Easterlin, their small size should lead to an improvement in the relative economic position of the young, facilitating earlier marriage and providing greater economic security to marriages already formed.

Tests of Easterlin's hypothesis have had mixed results, some positive and some negative (MacDonald and Rindfuss 1981; Devaney 1983). One important problem is that marriage and fertility behavior seem to fluctuate more in response to historical factors such as wars, business cycles, and social changes than to a cohort phenomenon such as group size (Rodgers and Thornton 1985; Smith 1981). For example, marriage delays increased during the 1980s, even though the relative size of cohorts entering the labor market had started to decline (U.S. Department of Commerce 1989a). There are also reasons to believe that the poor relative economic position of young males may never entirely reverse itself, despite shifts in relative cohort size. Rising educational attainment postpones young men's transition to their adult occupational careers, reducing their relative economic position in youth, although it may improve in maturity (Oppenheimer 1982). In addition, there is evidence that the structure of the American economy has been shifting in recent years. There has been a decline in manufacturing employment, particularly in the well-paid, durable-goods industries, accompanied by a substantial rise in the absolute and relative importance of employment in service industries (Urquhart 1984). Part of this reflects an expansion of jobs in low-paying service industries such as fast food and other retail trade industries, but there has also been an expansion in technical service jobs at various levels, most of which require a relatively well-educated labor supply. The result seems to be a worsening of the relative economic position of less-educated workers, particularly those who have not completed high school (Markey 1988).

William Julius Wilson (1987) has elaborated this argument to explain the particularly sharp decline in marriage formation among blacks, combined with the rapid increase in marital instability and the resultant rise in female-headed families. His hypothesis is that, because of the suburbanization of manufacturing and the growth of information-processing industries in large central cities, less educated, central-city blacks are increasingly isolated from good blue-collar jobs, resulting in a sharp rise in black unemployment rates and a decline in labor force participation, as well as the growth of criminal behavior. In short, an urban ghetto underclass with poor long-term economic prospects has been created. The consequence, Wilson argues, is a decline in the relative supply of "eligible" (i.e., nonincarcerated and employed) males for black women to marry.

Two back-to-back recessions in the 1980s exacerbated the economic problems of young black men, especially since recessions selectively affect the young and minorities most heavily.

Critics of Wilson's thesis, have argued, however, that central-city labor markets are not really isolated and that the black labor market disadvantage exists regardless of location (Ellwood 1986). Moreover, the work of Robert Mare and Christopher Winship (1984) indicates that at least some of the decline in black youth employment is the result of an increase in delayed labor force entry by more employable black males, due to rising school enrollment and military service. In addition, whatever the reasons for the shifts in these males' relative economic position, two back-to-back recessions in the 1980s exacerbated these problems, especially since recessions selectively affect the young and minorities most heavily, that is, those with less job security. Other critics have argued that increases in delayed marriage and marital instability are not limited to the "underclass" populations Wilson is describing (Farley 1988). However, this may simply reflect the fact that young men *in general* have recently experienced a deterioration in their labor market position, a deterioration that has been, however, particularly acute among blacks.

This article has reviewed the history of labor force measures, as well as several important current issues in labor force analysis. First, the study of the labor force reveals the changing significance of work in the lives of different segments of the population. Second, since economic behavior affects other social systems such as the family and stratification systems, labor force analysis will continue to be an essential field for sociological analysis.

[See also Occupational and Career Mobility; Work and Occupations.]

BIBLIOGRAPHY

Becker, Gary S. 1981 *A Treatise on the Family.* Cambridge, Mass.: Harvard University Press.

Berardo, Donna Hodgkins, Constance L. Shehan, and Gerald R. Leslie 1987 "A Residue of Tradition: Jobs, Careers, and Spouses' Time in Housework." *Journal of Marriage and the Family* 49:381–390.

Cain, Glenn C. 1979 "Labor Force Concepts and Definitions in View of Their Purposes." *Concepts and Data Needs—Appendix Vol. 1.* Washington, D.C.: National Commission on Employment and Unemployment Statistics.

Cherlin, Andrew J. 1979 "Work Life and Marital Dissolution." In George Levinger and Oliver C. Moles, eds., *Divorce and Separation: Contexts, Causes and Consequences.* New York: Basic Books.

Clogg, Clifford C., and Teresa A. Sullivan 1983 "Labor Force Composition and Underemployment Trends, 1969–1980." *Social Indicators Research* 12:117–152.

Devaney, Barbara 1983 "An Analysis of Variations in U.S. Fertility and Female Labor Force Participation Trends." *Demography* 20:147–142.

Dixon, Ruth B. 1982 "Women in Agriculture: Counting the Labor Force in Developing Countries." *Population and Development Review* 8:539–561.

Durand, John D. 1948 *The Labor Force in the United States, 1890–1960.* New York: Social Science Research Council.

Easterlin, Richard A. 1987 *Birth and Fortune.* Chicago: University of Chicago Press.

Ellwood, David T. 1986 "The Spatial Mismatch Hypothesis: Are There Teenage Jobs Missing in the Ghetto?" In Richard B. Freeman and Harry J. Holzer, eds., *The Black Youth Employment Crisis.* Chicago: University of Chicago Press.

Espenshade, Thomas J. 1985 "Marriage Trends in America: Estimates, Implications, and Underlying Causes." *Population and Development Review* 11:193–245.

Farley, Reynolds 1988 "After the Starting Line: Blacks and Women in an Uphill Race." *Demography* 25:477–495.

Goldscheider, Frances Kobrin, and Linda J. Waite 1986 "Sex Differences in the Entry into Marriage." *American Journal of Sociology* 92:91–109.

Hauser, Philip M. 1949 "The Labor Force and Gainful Workers: Concept, Measurement and Comparability." *American Journal of Sociology* 54:338–355.

Keyfitz, Nathan 1981 "Review of Measuring Underemployment, by C. C. Clogg." *American Journal of Sociology* 86:1163–1165.

MacDonald, Maurice M., and Ronald R. Rindfuss 1981 "Earnings, Relative Income, and Family Formation." *Demography* 18:123–136.

Mare, Robert D., and Christopher Winship 1984 "The Paradox of Lessening Racial Inequality and Joblessness among Black Youth: Enrollment, Enlistment, and Employment, 1964–1981." *American Sociological Review* 49:39–55.

Markey, James P. 1988 "The Labor Market Problems of Today's High School Dropouts." *Monthly Labor Review* 111:36–43.

Moore, Wilbert E. 1953 "The Exportability of the Labor Force Concept." *American Sociological Review* 18:68–72.

Oppenheimer, Valerie Kincade 1970 *The Female Labor Force in the United States: Demographic and Economic Factors Governing Its Growth and Changing Composition* (Population Monograph Series, No. 5). Berkeley, Calif.: University of California, Institute of International Studies.

——— 1982 *Work and the Family: A Study in Social Demography.* New York: Academic Press.

——— 1988 "A Theory of Marriage Timing." *American Journal of Sociology* 94:563–591.

Rodgers, Willard, and Arland Thornton 1985 "Changing Patterns of First Marriage in the United States." *Demography* 22:265–279.

Ross, Heather L., and Isabel V. Sawhill 1975 *Time of Transition: The Growth of Families Headed by Women.* Washington, D.C.: Urban Institute.

Smith, D. P. 1981 "A Reconsideration of Easterlin Cycles." *Population Studies* 35:247–264.

Sullivan, Teresa A. 1978 *Marginal Workers, Marginal Jobs: The Underutilization of American Workers.* Austin, Tex.: University of Texas Press.

Teachman, Jay D., Karen A. Polonko, and Geoffrey K. Leigh 1987 "Marital Timing: Race and Sex Comparisons." *Social Forces* 66:239–268.

U.S. Department of Commerce, Bureau of the Census 1989a "Marital Status and Living Arrangements: March 1989." *Current Population Reports* (P-20, No. 445).

U.S. Department of Commerce, Bureau of the Census 1989b *Statistical Abstract of the United States: 1989.* Washington, D.C.: U.S. Government Printing Office.

U.S. Department of Labor, Bureau of Labor Statistics 1982 *BLS Handbook of Methods,* Vol 1. Washington, D.C.: U.S. Government Printing Office.

U.S. Department of Labor, Bureau of Labor Statistics 1988 *Labor Force Statistics Derived from the Current Population Survey* (Bulletin 2307). Washington: U.S. Government Printing Office.

Urquhart, Michael 1984 "The Employment Shift to Services: Where Did It Come From?" *Monthly Labor Review* 107:15–22.

Vanek, Joan 1974 "Time Spent in Housework." *Scientific American* 231:116–120.

Wilson, William Julius 1987 *The Truly Disadvantaged.* Chicago: University of Chicago Press.

– VALERIE KINCADE OPPENHEIMER

LABOR MOVEMENTS AND UNIONS

Broadly defined, labor movements consist of collective actions, mainly on the part of wage workers in market societies, to improve their economic, social, and political positions in society. The main organizational forms of movements are labor unions and political parties. Others include producer and consumer cooperatives, credit unions, newspapers, and educational, welfare, cultural, and recreational facilities.

From the inception of the discipline, sociologists have studied labor movements and unions, but their scholarly production has been modest. The *American Journal of Sociology, American Sociological Review,* and *Social Forces,* in 195 accumulated years of publication, offered only fifty articles whose titles reveal a focus on labor movements and unions. Although Europeans produced more studies than American sociologists, labor economists and social historians have contributed even more. Sociologists have conspicuously neglected collective bargaining, mediation, and arbitration. Yet they have contributed to knowledge about labor movements and unions while attacking related problems in such central areas of the discipline as social stratification (e.g., working-class formation, income inequality), organizations (union leadership turnover), race and gender relations (discrimination in unions), politics (party preferences of unionists), and industry (shop-floor life, the labor process). Students of social movements, with some notable exceptions (Lipset 1971; Tilly 1978; Jenkins 1985), have also neglected labor movements and unions. Yet when sociological contributions are added to the sociologically oriented work of labor economists and historians, a sizable literature becomes available.

Social Origins of the Labor Movement

The labor movement and unions began to emerge with the Industrial Revolution and free labor markets in eighteenth-century England. Scholars agree that labor unions do not trace their origins to medieval guilds. Master-owners dominated guilds, which were status groups, while propertyless journeymen created mutual aid and protective societies to buffer the vicissitudes of a free market. Later, workers created temporary organizations to withhold their labor from employers, control production, and protect their wages. Eventually the organizations became permanent. They sought to control the supply of local labor, the training of workers, and the conditions of work in local factories (Jackson 1984). As product markets grew and spread and unions responded by creating new local unions, the movement became larger, more formalized, and more diversified. Thus, individual unions organized themselves around occupational, industrial, regional, religious, and other lines (Sturmthal 1974).

Since this organizational fragmentation exposed unions to changing business strategies, labor leaders realized that they needed a united movement to respond to threats wherever they might occur. However, the vision of a united movement always remained difficult to realize because individual unions and sets of unions hesitated to sacrifice their special interests for the undefined well-being of the movement. Many scholars have mistakenly confused the growth of the labor movement with the formation of the working class, or proletariat. Although the two phenomena are related, they vary enormously in time and place. When labor movements first emerged, they were not class movements. Rather, they were efforts on the part of the minority of skilled workers to protect their traditional privileges (Calhoun 1982). When unions later expanded to include all workers, then wage, status, and influence distinctions based on skill typically persisted (Form 1985, p. 96). In contrast, the appearance of a cohesive class movement involved a much more complex process; the building of ties between a stratified labor movement, nonunionized workers, and parties (Tilly 1978; Katznelson and Zolberg 1986).

Both the character and strength of labor movements must be understood in the context of the societies in which they arise and especially in the context of labor's relationship to capital and the state. Some scholars maintain that autonomous labor movements and unions survive only in capitalist democratic industrial societies. When membership is compulsory, when unions embrace the entire labor force, and when unions are subsumed under totalitarian political institutions, they lack the strength and independence to pursue the special interests of workers (Sturmthal 1968).

Types of Labor Movements

Labor movements can be subsumed under five types, according to their relationships to government and the broader society. Three types include the majority of movements. In the first, or independent, type such as the United States, the labor movement and its unions are independent of all major institutions, economic, political, and religious. Although American labor seeks political influence, it is a voluntary part of a multiclass coalition in the Democratic party and, as a special interest group, has limited representation in government. In the second, or social, democratic type such as European capitalistic democracies, the labor movement has formal social legitimacy and, being a dominant player in a socialist, labor, or social democratic party, it sometimes shares in the control of the government. In the third, or party-incorporated, type, found in some developing societies with mixed economies such as Mexico, labor movements are formally part of a coalition of a permanent ruling party. This incorporation places some restrictions on labor's economic, political, and governmental independence. The fourth and fifth types of labor movements have even less independence. In the enterprise unions of Japan and Korea, the labor movement consists mainly of unions that have consultative roles in individual enterprises. The national bonds of these unions are weak and loose. Finally, in totalitarian countries, labor movements and their unions have displayed the least independence because they have been subjected to strong party and governmental controls.

In the first, or independent, type, labor unions most closely conform to the characteristics of genuine social movements because they exist in a turbulent economic and political environment, must mobilize resources, and adapt creatively or decline or die (Tilly 1978). In the second, or social democratic, type, as in Britain, the labor movement is institutionally tied to a dominant party and to a political program that attracts other segments of society. Here labor shares some attributes of a social movement because it must adapt to a changing economy and constantly seek the support of other interests in its quest for a party majority and a share of governmental power (Bauman 1972). Enterprise-based labor movements and movements embedded in permanent ruling parties and governments display very few attributes of social movements.

American Exceptionalism

Scholars have long tried to explain why labor movements in most of the advanced industrial democracies became attached to labor or socialist parties and why the United States is an exception (Sombart 1906). Despite some irreconcilable theories, some consensus has emerged. Most scholars agree that European societies have longer and stronger links to past institutions. Where landed aristocrats, business, military, and religious elites cohesively resisted the incorporation of workers in the polity, class-oriented parties tended to appear. They sought to obtain voting rights for workers with the eventual aim of securing governmental protection for unions and providing them with benefits that could not be wrested from employers through collective bargaining. Moreover, in such exclusionary class environments, unions not only supported class parties but also developed separate institutions tuned to their interests such as intellectual elites, cooperatives, newspapers, banks, schools, and recreational clubs. In Europe, in response to a threatening, all-embracing, Marxist labor movement, churches created Christian labor unions and parties and extended their schools, hospitals, newspapers, and clubs to envelop workers in a class-inclusive organizational system (Knapp 1976).

The labor movement in the United States faced a different environment. The absence of traditional exclusionary aristocratic, military, and religious elites had the effect of dampening the class sentiments of workers. Early extension of suffrage to all adult males removed that objective as a rallying goal of unions. The rapid expansion of industry into new areas, high rates of immigration and internal migration, and ethnic and religious diversity in the labor force undermined workplace bonds. Moreover, an aggressive capitalist class, not bound by traditions of obligation toward subordinates, successfully convinced legislatures to erect a legal and judicial framework that favored property rights over organizational rights. Labor movements did develop in the late nineteenth and early twentieth centuries that sought to organize workers politically (Knights of Labor, International Workers of the World) and, for a few years, the Socialist party won notable local victories. But the American presidential system, the decentralized state structure, the constitutional barriers to the federal government's making national economic policy, and the electoral college system undermined third-party movements (Lipset 1977).

These circumstances created an American labor movement that has traditionally focused on wage bargaining and working conditions. Without the leverage of a strong pro-labor party in office, the movement's fortunes were exposed to economic vicissitudes and business onslaughts. Thus, American unions experienced membership growth before and during World Wars I and II, periods of relative prosperity and governmental tolerance. Membership, as a percentage of the labor force, declined rapidly in the depressions after World War I, slowly after World War II, and rapidly during the economic recessions of the 1970s and 1980s. The slower pace of the post-World War II decline reflected changes in labor's political environment during the Great Depression.

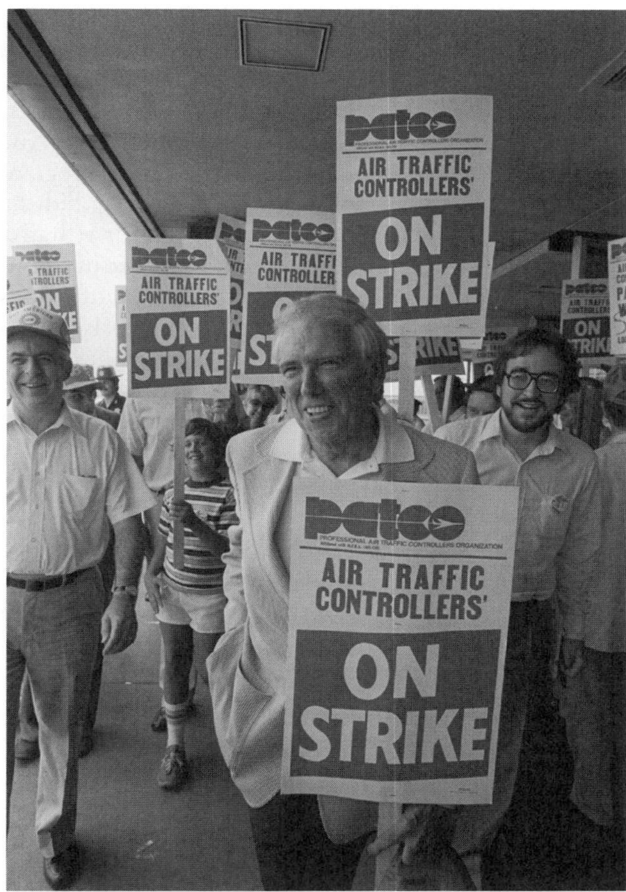

The American labor movement has traditionally focused on bargaining for improved wages and working conditions. (UPI/Corbis-Bettmann)

Possible Convergence of Labor Movements

A combination of events moved American unions toward the European social democratic pattern, and events in Europe moved its labor movements toward the American pattern. During the crisis of the Great Depression in the United States, the Democratic party came to power with the backing of urban industrial workers. It quickly designed a program whose purpose was to increase labor's purchasing power, to reduce price competition, and to restore economic order. The National Industrial Recovery Act (1934) and the subsequent National Labor Relations Act (1935) gave unions legal protection to grow (Skocpol 1980). Meanwhile, a militant union drive greatly augmented the membership. Eager to protect and extend its gains, a split but grateful labor movement, swollen with new unskilled members in the Committee for Industrial Organization, abandoned its traditional nonpartisan political stand and backed the Democratic party. After World War II, both the Congress of Industrial Organizations and the American Federation of Labor formed political units to mobilize voters to keep the Democratic party in power. To most intents and purposes, these units became part of the Democratic electoral machine. This marriage of Labor and the Party and the commitment of both to the welfare state led some scholars to conclude that the American labor movement was no longer exceptional because it had helped create a welfare state similar to those forged by the social democratic parties in Europe (Greenstone 1977).

This claim appears farfetched because neither the American labor movement nor the Democratic party ever embraced socialism. Yet it is possible for nations to achieve some socialist reforms without adopting socialism. Also, it is possible for social democratic parties to avoid nationalizing industries once they are in office. Zygmunt Bauman (1972) early pointed out that the Labour Party in Britain and social democratic parties elsewhere had to deemphasize their socialist programs in order to come to power. And, where they did, nationalization of the economy was partial or tentative. Parties had to compromise on public ownership of industry in order to secure the votes of middle-class groups that embraced some social welfare goals of labor parties but not socialism. Once in power, social democratic parties had to make many concessions to intellectuals and legislators, as well as to business, military, religious, and other groups. Moreover, even in cases where the majority of the labor force was unionized, large minorities of workers and their unions also opposed socialization. In short, the conservative forces in social democratic parties and the associated labor movements pushed both of them toward the American pattern.

Without the leverage of a strong pro-labor party in office, the movement's fortunes in the United States were exposed to economic vicissitudes and business onslaughts.

Recent evidence suggests that the third type of labor movement, those part of a coalition of a permanent ruling party, are beginning to show signs of independence. They are carrying out strikes, forming independent partylike structures, and searching for coalitions with other interest groups. And even enterprise unions in Japan show signs of independence.

If present trends continue, perhaps the long-term evolutionary trend of labor movements will be toward parallel convergence. Sufficient research is not available to uncover all of the causes of this plausible trend, but at least three conditions seem to be involved. First, if governments create organizations that have the appearance of labor movements and expect workers to participate in elections, conferences, and other union-like activities, appearances of independence eventually become actualized under turbulent conditions. Thus, in Japan, enterprise bargaining and the participation of workers in union affairs are beginning to show Western patterns of independence and conflict (Okochi, Karsh, and Levine 1974; Kuruvilla et al. 1990). Second, this process is speeded up when external political and economic crises destabilize traditional authority patterns in industry. Thus, during the economic and political turbulence in Mexico and the Soviet Union of the late 1980s, party unions usurped the authority of management over working conditions, wage determination, and political choice. Third, as economies develop more complex industrial and occupational systems, managers find it increasingly difficult to exert overall control. Bodies that resemble labor unions then begin to confront authorities and press for worker rights. In situations such as existed in Poland in the late 1980s, unions, with the help of clergy, intellectuals, farmers, and others, defied central authority, formed independent parties, and pushed for a decentralized social order. This may produce a labor relations system akin to those in Western capitalist democracies.

Democracy or Oligarchy in the Labor Movement

Unlike most institutions, the labor movement everywhere claims to be democratic in its ideology and structure. Union officers are leaders of the membership and, whether elected or appointed, should represent its interests. Sociologists have long pondered whether democratic movements that develop large and complex organizations can avoid the rigid bureaucracy and stratification so characteristic of other institutions.

The most famous exponent of the position that democratic organizations evolve into oligarchies was Robert Michels (1911), who studied the socialist party in pre-World War I Germany. He held that its officers became a self-perpetuating elite. They controlled communication with the membership, appointed their staffs and successors, and pursued their self-interests. Subsequent case studies of labor unions challenged Michels's thesis. In a detailed analysis of the International Typographical Unions, Seymour Martin Lipset, Martin A. Trow, and James A. Coleman (1956) found that its party system fostered electoral competition, officer turnover, and member involvement in union affairs. J. David Edelstein and Malcolm Warner's (1979) study of fifty-one international unions showed that the extent of officer turnover varied with certain constitutional provisions such as frequency of elections, percentage of officers elected, and frequency of conventions. Daniel B. Cornfield (1989) found that substantial ethnic turnover among officers of the United Furniture Workers of America resulted from the external changes in the economy, the regional dispersal of the industry, political disputes among the officers, ethnic tolerance among the members, and a tradition of membership union involvement. Most of these case studies focused on relatively small unions whose members were rather homogeneous in their skills and earnings.

These challenges to Michels reveal some conditions that facilitate leadership turnover. Importantly, they do not reveal the extent to which these conditions prevail in the universe of unions and in labor movements as a whole. Nor do they reveal the conditions that strengthen oligarchy. Compared with other organizations, turnover among top officers of most large unions is low. It is probably even lower in the national and international associations of unions. And when the labor movement is defined to include labor political parties, oligarchic tendencies may be even larger.

Unfortunately, very few scholars have examined organizational cleavages and stratification tendencies within labor movements over their entire histories. In a rare study, Bauman (1972) demonstrated that cleavages along skill lines persisted during the entire growth of the British labor movement. Skilled workers formed societies at the beginning of the Industrial Revolution. From 1850 to 1890, they formed craft unions that sought and obtained legitimacy, and between 1890 and 1924, they became an elite sector of a mass union movement. They still maintained their identity in the large industrial unions that appeared. With the development of the Liberal, and later the Labour parties, trade union leaders gradually became subordinated to university-trained, middle-class intellectuals who dominated the Party, its seats in Parliament, and its government positions. Herman Bensen (1986) argues that this pattern applies equally well to the American labor movement. Finally, Alain Touraine (1986) notes that everywhere labor union involvement in political parties and governments increases occupational stratification, magnifies the distance between unions and their parties, and subordinates union interests to workers' goals. Apparently, increasing size and organizational complexity of the labor movement is accompanied by increasing stratification and an increasingly unresponsive bureaucracy. This kind of evidence supports Michels's original argument.

Conclusions

American sociological research has fluctuated with the fortunes of the labor movement. As union membership and power grew, research increased, hitting its apogee in the 1950s and 1960s. As membership began to fall, research slackened. Yet labor's problems always offered new research opportunities. Today, scholars should analyze why some labor movements decline while others stabilize or grow. Most current explanations of labor's decline in the United States are inadequate. Thus, the economy's shift from manufacturing to services does not account for the decline because Lipset (1986, p. 426), dean of sociological research on American labor, shows that in eleven capitalist democracies industrial shifts do not vary with level of unionization. Michael Goldfield's (1987) study of labor's decline in the United States supports Lipset's position. After Goldfield eliminated changes in the economy and changes in industrial and occupational composition of the labor force as possible causes, he demonstrated that a sustained employer drive slowly succeeded in shifting the decisions of the National Labor Relations Board against organized labor. He and Richard B. Freeman and James L. Medoff (1984) also show that the impressive growth of white-collar unions demonstrates that unions can grow despite employer resistance. Moreover, some of the membership decline also results from spending less money on organizing drives.

Sociologists have neglected other research areas such as collective bargaining, perhaps because these areas call for an intimate understanding of labor-management interaction. While sociologists have improved their theory and statistics, they have neglected field studies on how unions actually work (see Freeman and Medoff 1984). For example, the surge in statistical studies on income discrimination in the 1970s (see Berg 1981) has provided many data on the amount of discrimination but little on the informal bargaining processes that protect or eradicate it. The tradition of case studies that characterized the 1950s (e.g., Seidman et al. 1958) needs to be revived. Nowhere is this need more urgent than in the study of union politics at the local, state, and national levels. Field studies should examine labor's relations with the Democratic party and state legislatures.

The changing world economy also raises challenging research questions. Movement toward a global economy and large tariff-free trade zones, such as the European Union, eventually will force unions of different nations to coordinate their collective bargaining and political strategies, lest they be weakened by the flexible investment strategies of multinational firms. How will this be done and what will be the effects? The movement of some managed economies of underdeveloped nations toward freer markets suggests that their unions will have to engage in true collective bargaining. And they will have to consider how their behavior will affect prices, profits, and societal stability. How will this transition be made? The global trend toward greater union participation in economic decisions at the enterprise level calls for comparative analysis. Paradoxically, collective bargaining will become increasingly complex and politicized as more of the world moves toward a freer market economy. This will increase the organizational complexity and internal stratification of labor, reviving Michels's concern about oligarchy.

If the labor movement is going to survive, especially in the United States, it must increase the loyalty and involvement of its members, as well as its societal political influence. These mandates will pull labor leadership in two directions. First, at the level of the workplace, members measure union performance in terms of their earnings improvements and the quality of work life. Although the two goals are related, American unions have traditionally handled them separately. To make progress on these two fronts, labor must press for greater participation in the economic and organizational management of the enterprise. Fierce resistance is inevitable. Second, to regain political influence, as it must or continue to decline, labor must forge stronger and more lasting bonds with Hispanics, African-Americans, women, the elderly, and other nonunionized groups. Again, paradoxically, the labor movement will become stronger the more it stresses the well-being of other less fortunate groups in society (Form 1990). The labor movement will surely survive, but, in so doing, it will have to create innovative solutions to two evolutionary dilemmas: increasing membership loyalty in the face of increasing organizational complexity, and increasing public acceptance while improving the well-being of its members.

Collective bargaining will become increasingly complex and politicized as more of the world moves toward a freer market economy.

[See also Labor Force; Social Movements.]

BIBLIOGRAPHY

Bauman, Zygmunt 1972 *Between Class and Elite.* Manchester, England: Manchester University Press.

Benson, Herman 1986 "The Fight for Union Democracy." In Seymour Martin Lipset, ed., *Unions in Transition.* San Francisco: Institute for Contemporary Studies.

Berg, Ivar (ed.) 1981 *Sociological Perspectives on Labor Markets.* New York: Academic Press.

Calhoun, Craig 1982 *The Question of Class Struggle.* Chicago: University of Chicago Press.

Cornfield, Daniel B. 1989 *Becoming a Mighty Voice: Conflict and Change in the United Furniture Workers of America.* New York: Russell Sage Foundation.

Edelstein, J. David, and Malcolm Warner 1979 *Comparative Union Democracy.* New Brunswick, N.J.: Transaction Press.

Form, William 1985 *Divided We Stand: Working-Class Stratification in America.* Urbana: University of Illinois Press.

——— 1990 "Organized Labor and the Welfare State." In Kai Erikson and Stephen P. Vallas, eds., *The Nature of Work.* New Haven, Conn.: Yale University Press.

Freeman, Richard B., and James L. Medoff 1984 *What Do Unions Do?* New York: Basic Books.

Goldfield, Michael 1987 *The Decline of Organized Labor in the United States.* Chicago: University of Chicago Press.

Greenstone, J. David 1977 *Labor in American Politics.* Chicago: University of Chicago Press.

Jackson, Kenneth Robert 1984 *The Formation of Craft Markets.* Orlando, Fla.: Academic Press.

Jenkins, J. Craig 1985 *The Politics of Insurgency: The Farm Worker Movement in the 1960s.* New York: Columbia University Press.

Katznelson, Ira, and Aristide R. Zolberg (eds.) 1986 *Working-Class Formation: Nineteenth Century Patterns in Europe and the United States.* Princeton, N.J.: Princeton University Press.

Knapp, Vincent J. 1976 *Europe in the Era of Social Transformation: 1700–Present.* Englewood Cliffs, N.J.: Prentice-Hall.

Kuruvilla, Sarosh, Daniel G. Gallagher, Jack Fiorito, and Mitsuru Wakabayashi 1990 "Union Participation in Japan: Do Western Theories Apply?" *Industrial and Labor Relations Review* 43:366–373.

Lipset, Seymour Martin 1971 *Agrarian Socialism: The Cooperative Commonwealth Movement in Saskatchewan.* Berkeley: University of California Press.

——— 1977. "Why No Socialism in the United States." In Seweryn Bialer and Sophis Sluzar, eds., *Sources of Contemporary Radicalism.* Boulder, Colo.: Westview Press.

——— 1986 "North American Labor Movements: A Comparative Perspective." In Seymour Martin Lipset, ed., *Unions in Transition: Entering the Second Century.*" San Francisco: Institute for Contemporary Studies.

———, Martin A. Trow, and James A. Coleman 1956 *Union Democracy.* New York: Free Press.

Michels, Robert (1911) 1959 *Political Parties.* New York: Dover.

Okochi, Kazuo, Bernard Karsh, and Solomon B. Levine, eds. 1974 *Workers and Employers in Japan: The Japanese Employment Relations System.* Princeton, N.J.: Princeton University Press.

Seidman, Joel, Jack London, Bernard Karsh, and Daisy L. Tagliacozzo 1958 *The Worker Views His Union.* Chicago: University of Chicago Press.

Skocpol, Theda 1980 "Political Response to Capitalist Crisis." *Politics and Society* 10:155–201.

Sombart, Werner 1906 *Warum gibt es in den Vereinigten Staaten keinen Socialismus.* Tübingen: Mohr.

Sturmthel, Adolph F. 1968 "Labor Unions: Labor Movements and Collective Bargaining in Europe." In David L. Sills, ed., *International Encyclopedia of the Social Sciences,* Vol. 8. New York: Macmillan and Free Press.

——— 1974 "Trade Unionism." In *Encyclopedia Britannica,* Vol. 5. Chicago: William Benton.

Tilly, Charles 1978 *From Moblization to Revolution.* Reading, Mass.: Addison-Wesley.

Touraine, Alain 1987 "Unionism as a Social Movement." In Seymour Martin Lipset, ed., *Unions in Transition.* San Francisco: Institute for Contemporary Studies.

– WILLIAM FORM

LAW AND LEGAL SYSTEMS

Law is surprisingly difficult to define. Perhaps the best-known definition within the sociology of law community is that of Max Weber. "An order will be called *law* if it is externally guaranteed by the probability that coercion (physical or psychological), to bring about conformity or avenge violation, will be applied by a *staff* of people holding themselves specially ready for that purpose" (1954, p. 5). Similar definitions include Donald Black's terse statement that "Law is governmental social control" (Black, 1976, p. 2). While these types of definitions have sometimes been attacked as employing a Westernized conception, appropriate for developed states but inappropriate for other societies, Hoebel advances a similar definition of law in all societies: "The really fundamental *sine qua non* of law in any society—primitive or civilized—is the legitimate use of physical coercion by a socially authorized agent" (Hoebel 1954, p. 26).

Definitions such as these are perhaps more interesting for what they exclude than for what they include. Weber and Hoebel attempt to draw a line where the boundary between law and something else is fuzziest. By including the term *legitimate,* Hoebel's definition is intended to distinguish law from the brute exercise of force. The leader of a criminal gang who forces people to give him money may be doing many things, but he is not enforcing the law. He is not a socially authorized agent, and his use of force is not legitimate. Legitimacy itself is a slippery concept, and disagreements about when it is present give rise to questions such as whether the Nazis governed under the rule of law.

The inclusion of coercion and specialized agents of enforcement in both Weber's and Hoebel's definitions is meant to distinguish law from customs or norms, the breach of which either is not sanctioned or is sanctioned only by members of the group against which the breach occurred. The internal rules (norms and customs) governing a family's life or an organization's life are not law unless they are reinstitutionalized, that is, unless they are "restated in such a way that they can be applied by an institution designed (or at very least, utilized) specifically for that purpose" (Bohannan 1965, p. 36).

The boundary maintenance functions of definitions such as those of Weber, Hoebel, and Bohannan undoubtedly have their place, but law's empire is so large that the border skirmishes occurring out on its frontiers have limited influence on our shared understanding of the words *law* and *legal system.* Wherever it occurs, law is a body of rules that speak to how people should behave in society (substantive law) and how the legal system itself should proceed (adjective law). The volume and complexity of rules may be expected to parallel the size and complexity of the society of which they are a part. But broad categories of substantive law—tort, property, criminal law—apparently exist in all legal orders, as do the fundamentals of adjective law—procedure and evidence.

Moreover, by restricting the term *law* to rules enforced by specialized legal staffs, these definitions exclude much of what the legal sociologist will find interesting. There is "law-stuff" everywhere. Families and organizations do generate rules and do coerce or induce compliance. These groups constitute what Moore (1973) calls "semiautonomous fields." Not only are the rules of these organizations interesting in their own right, the interaction of these rules and the state rules we call law helps to shape the fundamental choice between avoidance and compliance that is faced by all to whom rules are addressed. We will be well served if we follow Griffiths' (1984) advice and view "legalness" as a variable rather than thinking of "law" as a special, definable species of social control. The complex body of substantive and adjective rules at different levels comprise a legal system.

Legal Systems

The comparative study of law might trace its roots to Aristotle's comparison of Greek city-state constitutions. A more recent example is Montesquieu, who, in *The Spirit of the Laws* (1748 [1962]), attempted to explain legal diversity in terms of various factors in the social setting. Interspersed between these efforts were comparisons of canon law with Roman law in Europe and with the common law in England. Despite these precursors, the modern study of comparative legal systems became a topic of sustained academic interest only during the last 100 to 150 years.

The history of comparative law is set forth in a number of works, including Zweigert and Kotz (1987) and David and Brierley (1985). The present essay discusses a small part of this history, focusing on what Zweigert and Kotz call scientific or theoretical comparative law rather than legislative comparative law, in which foreign laws are examined and invoked in the process of drafting new nation-state laws.

Early theoretical efforts, exemplified by Maine's *Ancient Law* ([1861] 1963), adopted evolutionary theories of legal development. In Maine's famous formulation, legal systems, following changes in social arrangements, move from *status* wherein one's rights and duties were determined by one's social niche (the law of feudalism) to *contract,* wherein ones rights and duties were determined by oneself and the contracts one entered into (eventually the law of capitalism).

A second well-known developmental theory of changes in legal systems is that of Durkheim ([1893] 1964). A societal movement from mechanical to organic solidarity is accompanied by a movement from repressive law (law that punishes those who violate a shared moral understanding) to restitutive law (law that attempts to facilitate cooperation and to return people to a status quo ante when rule violations occur).

From the sociological point of view, perhaps the most important contributor to the early development of comparative law was that preeminent lawyer-social scientist, Max Weber. Weber's contribution was in three parts. First, he developed the device of an ideal type, a stylized construct that represents the perfect example of a phenomenon. The ideal type acts as a yardstick against which we might measure actual legal systems. Second, using ideal types, he provided a typology of legal systems classified by the formality and the rationality of their decision-making processes. Ideally, legal systems could be thought of as formal or substantive, rational or irrational. A legal system is formal to the extent that the norms it applies are intrinsic to the system itself. Substantive law, as the term was used earlier, should not be confused with the substantive dimension of Weber's typology. A legal system is substantive in Weber's sense to the extent that the source of the norms it applies is extrinsic to the legal system. For example, a legal system would be substantive if a court resolved disputes by reference to a religious rather than a legal code.

A legal system is rational if it yields results that are predictable from the facts of cases; that is, case outcomes are determined by the reasoned analysis of action in light of a given set of norms. A legal system is irrational when outcomes are not predictable in this way. Basically, a legal system is rational to the extent that similar cases are decided similarly.

A formally irrational legal system exists when judgments follow consultation of an oracle or trial by ordeal.

A formally irrational system exists when the legal order produces results unconstrained by reason. Classic examples are judgments following consultation of an oracle or trial by ordeal. Substantive irrationality exists when lawmakers and finders do not resort to some dominant general norms but, instead, act arbitrarily or decide upon the basis of an emotional evaluation of a particular case. Weber apparently had in mind the justice dispensed by the Khadi, a Moslem judge who, at least as Weber saw him, sat in the marketplace and rendered judgment by making a free and idiosyncratic evaluation of the particular merits of each case.

A substantively rational legal system exists when lawmakers and finders follow a consistent set of principles derived from some source other than the legal system itself. Again, Weber thought that Moslem law tended toward this type insofar as it tried to implement the thoughts and commands of the Prophet.

Western legal systems, especially those of civil law countries such as France and Germany, most nearly approximated the formally rational ideal, a legal system where the generality of legal rules is high and where the legal rules are highly differentiated from other social norms.

The relationship between formal and substantive law is obviously more complex than can be reflected in these four Weberian types. For example, legal systems may be procedurally quite formal while incorporating substantive norms rooted in nonlegal institutions. Moreover, rational systems may incorporate potentially irrational components, as when the final judgment in a case is left to a lay jury. Nevertheless, as ideal types Weber's categories help to locate idealized Western law in a wider universe of possible legal systems.

The importance of Weber's categories, like those of Maine, resides in large part in his efforts to link types of rationality with different types of societies and different ways of organizing legal systems. He associated an irrational legal order with domination by a charismatic leader. Formal rationality, on the other hand, accompanies the rise of the bureaucratic style of organization. Weber regarded logically formal rationality as the most "advanced" kind of legal ordering and as particularly hospitable to the growth of the capitalist state.

Weber's third contribution to comparative legal studies was his insight that the nature of a society's legal system is shaped by the kinds of individuals who dominate it. On the European continent, in the absence of a powerful central court, domination fell into the hands of the university law faculties who strove, through the promulgation and interpretation of authoritative texts, to create and understand the legal system as a general and autonomous set of rules. The common law in England, on the other hand, grew under the tutelage of a small elite judiciary and accompanying centralized bar, more concerned with pronouncing rules for the settlement of disputes than in developing generalized rules of law (Weber 1954). In time, the differences in the legal systems created by these different sets of *honoratiores* helped to spur interest in comparative legal systems.

Overall, Weber's contribution was part of a general movement away from comparing the legal codes of various societies and toward a comparison of the legal solutions that "are given to the same actual problems by the legal systems of different countries seen as a complete whole" (Zweigert and Kotz 1987, p. 60, quoting Rabel). From this perspective, legal systems confront similar problems, and if we examine the whole system we will uncover fundamental differences and similarities in their various solutions. The effort to uncover these similarities and differences has taken several different paths.

MACROCOMPARISONS. One path has involved attempts to develop macrocomparisons of entire legal systems. This effort has resulted in a number of taxonomies of legal systems in which the laws of nations are grouped by what are commonly called "legal families." The criteria for classification and the ultimate categories of family types have varied from scholar to scholar. Among the factors that have been used are historical tradition, the sources of law, the conceptual structure of law, and the social objectives of law. Socialist writers have traditionally focused on the relationship of law to underlying economic relations and a society's history of class conflict (Szabo and Peteri 1977; Eorsi 1979), although more recent efforts paint a much more complex picture that threatens some of the presumed differences between socialist and "capitalist" law (Sypnowich 1990). David (1950) and David and Brierley (1985) base their classification on ideology (resulting from philosophical, political, and economic factors) and legal technique. Zweigert and Kotz (1987, p. 69) base their classification on a multiple set of criteria they call the "style" of law. Legal style includes: historical background and development, predominant modes of thought in legal matters (contrasting the use of abstract legal norms in civil law versus the narrow, reasoning by analogy typical of the common law), distinctive concepts (such as the trust in the common law and the abuse of right in civil law), the source of law (statutory or case law), and ideology (e.g., the ideology of socialist and Western legal families).

Given the wide variety of criteria used by various scholars, perhaps it is surprising that the resulting "families" tend to be quite similar. To provide but one example, Zweigert and Kotz (1987) divide the world into the following eight families: (1) Romanistic family (e.g., France); (2) Germanic family (e.g., Germany); (3) Nordic family (e.g., Sweden); (4) common law family (e.g., England); (5) socialist family (e.g., Soviet Union); (6) Far Eastern family (e.g., China); (7) Islamic systems; and (8) Hindu law. While some taxonomies may have fewer civil law divisions, this set of categories shares with many others a Eurocentric emphasis and a resulting inability easily to fit non-European legal systems into the taxonomy (see Ehrmann 1976; David and Brierley 1985), although the rise of non-Western societies such as Japan should help to redress this imbalance in time (see Institute of Comparative Law, Waseda University 1988).

The Eurocentric and Western emphasis is not simply a matter of greater particularity in describing differences between the legal traditions of Europe. It is also reflected in the concepts used to make distinctions. The categories of the various typologies are based primarily on a comparison of private law rather than on public or constitutional law and on substantive law rather than on adjective law. A different focus may lead to different family configurations. For example, American and German constitutional law are in some ways more similar to each other than to French or English constitutional law. The focus on private substantive law has the additional result that it overemphasizes legal doctrine while underemphasizing the degree to which legal systems are a product of the surrounding society. The consequence is to understate similarities in Western legal arrangements that may be captured by the idea of a legal culture.

One alternative designed to avoid this tendency is found in Merryman's (1969) concept of legal traditions. Legal traditions are

> a set of deeply rooted, historically conditioned attitudes about the nature of law, about the role of law in the society and the polity, about the proper organization and operation of a legal system, and about the way law is or should be made, applied, studied, perfected, and taught. The legal tradition relates the legal system to the culture of which it is a partial expression. (Merryman 1969, p. 2)

From this perspective the Western legal tradition usefully may be compared and contrasted to legal systems in other cultures (Barton et al. 1983).

A second alternative to the "legal families" approach are taxonomies that are not based on differences in substantive law. One recent example, closer to the Weberian heritage, is that of Damaska (1986). Like Weber, Damaska uses two dimensions to develop ideal-typical legal orders. The first dimension divides legal orders into activist and reactive systems of justice. Activist states attempt to use law to manage society, whereas reactive states attempt only to provide a legal framework for social interaction. At the heart of the image of law of the activist state is the state decree, spelling out programs, assigning tasks, and distributing welfare to citizens. At the heart of the reactive state are devices facilitating agreement, contracts, and pacts. While it might be thought that this dimension is designed primarily to distinguish capitalist and socialist legal orders, Damaska observes that not all types of socialist models follow the state socialism that once dominated the Soviet Union and Eastern Europe. Yugoslavian self-management concepts spoke to this reactive tradition in socialism. Likewise, capitalist societies exhibit considerable differences in their commitment to an activist state.

Damaska's second dimension divides legal orders into hierarchical and coordinate systems of judicial organization. In the hierarchical ideal officials are professionals who are arranged in a strict hierarchy and who employ special, technical standards of decision making. The coordinate ideal describes a more amorphous machine in which legal functionaries are amateurs who are arranged in relationships of relatively equal authority and who do justice based on prevailing ethical, political, or religious norms. Weber's vision of the Moslem Khadi applying substantive (religious) law would appear to describe this type of legal order.

There are other strong parallels between Damaska's and Weber's ideal types. Their categories are less obviously Eurocentric and, more important, employ a set of concepts that facilitate an understanding of ways in which the relationship between the state and society is mediated through law. Both analyses are inclined toward a functional approach. Rather than beginning with individual legal histories and doctrines and grouping them into families, this approach begins with a set of problems—how to mediate the relationship of the state and society and how to organize the structure of the legal honoratiores—and arranges legal systems according to how they address these problems.

Damaska's distinction between the hierarchical and coordinate ideal and Weber's distinction between formal and substantive rationality direct our attention to a central issue concerning law—the degree to which different legal systems are autonomous. An autonomous legal system is independent of other sources of power and authority in social life; its legal outcomes are influenced only by preestablished, status-neutral rules of the legal system; the actions and actors brought to the legal system are dealt with only after their dispute is translated into a set of legal categories (debtor-unsecured creditor, lessor-lessee); parties come to law with equal competence. An extreme version of legal autonomy is a legal system that is autopoietic. An autopoietic system, like a living organism, produces and reproduces its own elements by the interaction of its elements (Teubner 1988). Legal autonomy and even legal autopoiesis are best thought of as variables, other important ways in which we may distinguish legal systems. Using Damaska's typology, we might expect that legal systems that reflect the hierarchical ideal will be more likely to exhibit some of the features of greater autonomy.

MICROCOMPARISONS. Microcomparisons of legal systems are concerned with the details of specific legal rules and institutions rather than with entire legal systems (Rheinstein 1968). The functional approach is even more pronounced at this level. Scholars often begin with a specific social problem and seek to discover the various ways in which legal systems solve it, or they begin with a specific legal institution and examine how it operates in various systems. For example, Shapiro (1981) makes a comparative analysis of the court as an institution in common law, civil law, imperial Chinese, and Islamic legal systems.

The most valuable work done at this level has been that of legal anthropologists. By examining the dispute-processing activities of African, Latin American, and Asian legal tribunals they have provided new insights into the connection between a society's social relationships and the way in which it processes disputes. Ethnographies by Gluckman (1967), Gulliver (1963), Nader (1969) and others exposed a general pattern wherein tribunals confronted with disputes among individuals who are in multiplex and enduring relationships are more likely to widen the range of relevant evidence and to search for outcomes that allow flexibility, compromise, and integration. Tribunals confronted with disputes among individuals who are in one-dimensional and episodic relationships are more likely to narrow the range of relevant evidence and to provide binary outcomes where one side clearly wins and the other loses.

Legal ethnographies have also supported the earlier observation based on macrocomparisons that the organization of courts and judges plays a role in determining styles of dispute processing. Fallers (1969), for instance, found that the Soga, a society in many ways very similar to the Barotse studied by Gluckman, tended to craft decisions that were narrower and that resulted in "legalistic" rulings. His explanation was that the "judiciary" in the two societies differed in at least one key respect. The Soga courts were more purely "judicial" bodies without administrative and executive functions. A specialized legal staff was more likely to issue narrower opinions. Moreover, because binary outcomes result in a judgment to be enforced against a losing party, the availability of a coercive judicial apparatus may facilitate this type of dispute resolution (Lempert and Sanders 1986).

Perhaps because of the seminal work by Llewellyn and Hoebel (1941) on the Cheyenne, the work of legal anthropologists, more than most macro approaches to the study of legal systems, builds on the sociological jurisprudence and the legal realist traditions (Pound 1911–12; Oliphant 1928; Llewellyn 1930; Arnold 1935). It is concerned with the law in action, with the actual experience of the legal staff and the disputants. As a consequence, legal anthropology has had a substantial influence on the sociological study of disputing and what has come to be called alternative dispute resolution in Western societies (Greenhouse 1986; Abel 1981).

Nearly all existing legal systems are, to a greater or lesser extent, externally imposed, and therefore all legal systems are layered.

Recently, anthropologists have come to appreciate the degree to which African and other consensual legal systems are themselves partly the outgrowth of colonial experience and of the distribution of power in society (Starr and Collier 1989). This observation underlines a more general point that has been noted by macro and micro scholars alike. Nearly all existing legal systems are, to a greater or lesser extent, externally imposed, and therefore all legal systems are layered. In many societies layering occurs because of the existence of a federal system creating an internal hierarchy of rules, some of which are imposed from above. Layered legal systems also occur when nations such as Turkey (the Swiss code) or Japan (the German code) shop abroad and adopt the laws of another nation as the basic framework for substantial parts of their own legal systems. In some situations the imposition is done wholesale and involuntarily, as when colonial powers impose a legal system. The result can be considerable social dislocation (Burman and Harrell-Bond 1979). In time, multiple layers may exist, as in Japan, where indigenous law has been overlaid by both the adopted German code and American constitutional law concepts imposed after World War II.

In each of these situations a society's legal system is unlikely to fit easily within any of the legal families. For instance, a society may borrow another's substantive and adjective law for commercial law purposes but retain the existing law of domestic relations. Frequently, such societies are said to have a "dual legal system." However, to the degree that this phrase describes a situation where two equal systems stand side by side and rarely interact, it fails to capture the rich variety of hierarchical structures in layered systems. An important task for the students of legal systems is to understand the process by which individuals and groups use law at different levels and in so doing transform both.

Indeed, the existence of a global economic order promotes some similarities in all laws governing economic transactions. Islamic law has been compelled to create a number of legal devices and fictions designed to avoid direct confrontation with several teachings of the Koran, such as the prohibition against charging interest that would make participation in a modern economic order difficult (David and Brierley 1985, p. 469).

A number of additional global issues also create pressures toward the creation of transnational legal arrangements. These include transnational crime, ethnic and racial conflict, world population and migration patterns, labor flows, and, perhaps most significant, environmental regulation. Common legal structures created to address these issues and demands that nation-state legal systems enact and enforce appropriate compliance mechanisms may lead to the rebirth of the ideal of international legal unification that was popular at the beginning of the century. As can be seen in the European example, such unification inevitably involves some imposition of law.

Because pressures to build a more complex body of transnational law coincide with the diminution of differences in Western legal systems, over the next few decades one of the most interesting issues in the study of legal systems will involve movements toward and resistance to a transnational legal order premised on the hegemony of Western legal systems and Western legal concepts. The future task of comparative law is to understand the processes of borrowing, imposition, and resistance, both among nations and between levels of legal systems.

[See also Court Systems of the United States.]

BIBLIOGRAPHY

Abel, Richard 1981 *The Politics of Informal Justice,* 2 vols. New York: Academic Press.

Arnold, Thurmond 1935 *The Symbols of Government.* New Haven, Conn.: Yale University Press.

Barton, John, James Gibbs, Victor Li, and John Merryman 1983 *Law in Radically Different Cultures.* St. Paul, Minn.: West Publishing Co.

Black, Donald 1976 *The Behavior of Law.* New York: Academic Press.

Bohannan, Paul 1965 "The Differing Realms of the Law." *American Anthropologist* 67 (6, pt. 2): 133–142.

Burman, Sandra, and Barbara Harrell-Bond, eds. 1979 *The Imposition of Law.* New York: Academic Press.

Damaska, Mirjan 1986 *The Faces of Justice and State Authority: A Comparative Approach to the Legal Process.* New Haven, Conn.: Yale University Press.

David, René 1950 *Traité élémentaire de droit civil comparé.* Paris: Librairie Générale de Droit et de Juris prudence.

———, and John Brierley 1985 *Major Legal Systems in the World Today.* London: Stevens and Sons.

Durkheim, Emile (1893) 1964 *The Division of Labor in Society.* New York: Free Press.

Ehrmann, Henry 1976 *Comparative Legal Cultures.* Englewood Cliffs, N.J.: Prentice-Hall.

Eorsi, Gy 1979 *Comparative Civil Law.* Budapest: Akademiai Kiado.

Fallers, Lloyd 1969 *Law Without Precedent: Legal Ideas in Action in the Courts of Colonial Busoga.* Chicago: University of Chicago Press.

Gluckman, Max 1967 *The Judicial Process among the Barotse of Northern Rhodesia.* Manchester, England: Manchester University Press.

Greenhouse, Carol 1986 *Praying for Justice.* Ithaca, N.Y.: Cornell University Press.

Griffiths, John 1984 "The Division of Labor in Social Control." In Donald Black, ed., *Toward a General Theory of Social Control.* New York: Academic Press.

Gulliver, P. M. 1963 *Social Control in an African Society: A Study of the Arusha.* London: Routledge and Kegan Paul.

Hoebel, E. Adamson 1954 *The Law of Primitive Man.* Cambridge, Mass.: Harvard University Press.

Institute of Comparative Law, Waseda University, ed. 1988 *Law in East and West.* Tokyo: Waseda University Press.

Lempert, Richard, and Joseph Sanders 1986 *An Invitation to Law and Social Science.* Philadelphia: University of Pennsylvania Press.

Llewellyn, Karl 1930 "A Realistic Jurisprudence: The Next Step." *Columbia Law Review* 30:431–465.

———, and E. Adamson Hoebel 1941 *The Cheyenne Way: Conflict and Case Law in Primitive Society.* Norman: University of Oklahoma Press.

Maine, Henry (1861) 1963 *Ancient Law: Its Connection with the Early History of Society and Its Relation to Modern Ideas.* Boston: Beacon Press.

Merryman, John Henry 1969 *The Civil Law Tradition: An Introduction to the Legal Systems of Western Europe and Latin America.* Stanford, Calif.: Stanford University Press.

Montesquieu (1748) 1962 *The Spirit of the Laws,* 2 vols. New York: Hafner.

Moore, Sally Falk 1973 "Law and Social Change: The Semi-Autonomous Social Field as an Appropriate Subject of Study." *Law and Society Review* 7:719–746.

Nader, Laura 1969 "Styles of Court Procedure: To Make the Balance." In Laura Nader, ed., *Law in Culture and Society.* Chicago: Aldine.

Oliphant, Herman 1928 "A Return to *Stare Decisis.*" *American Bar Association Journal* 14:71, 159.

Pound, Roscoe 1911–12 "The Scope and Purpose of Sociological Jurisprudence." Parts 1, 2, and 3. *Harvard Law Review* 24:591–619; 25:140–168; 25:489–516.

Rheinstein, Max 1968 "Legal Systems." In David L. Sills, ed., *International Encyclopedia of the Social Sciences,* Vol. 9. pp. 204–210. New York: Macmillan.

Shapiro, Martin 1981 *Courts: A Comparative and Political Analysis.* Chicago: University of Chicago Press.

Starr, June, and Jane Collier (eds). 1989 *History and Power in the Study of Law: New Directions in Legal Anthropology.* Ithaca, N.Y.: Cornell University Press.

Sypnowich, Christine 1990 *The Concept of Socialist Law.* Oxford: Clarendon Press.

Szabo, I., and Z. Peteri (eds.) 1977 *A Socialist Approach to Comparative Law.* Leyden, The Netherlands: A. W. Sijthoff.

Teubner, Gunther (ed.) 1988 *Autopoietic Law: A New Approach to Law and Society.* Berlin: Walter de Gruyter.

Weber, Max 1954 *On Law in Economy and Society.* New York: Simon and Schuster.

Zweigert, Konrad, and Hein Kotz 1987 *Introduction to Comparative Law.* Vol. 1, The Framework. Oxford: Clarendon Press.

– JOSEPH SANDERS

LAW AND SOCIETY

The concepts of *law* and *society* refer to macrostructural phenomena. Is there a macro-oriented theory of law and society or a macro sociolegal theory to guide this field? As an interdisciplinary endeavor, the sociology of law relies upon, or is influenced by, the intellectual assumptions and propositions of general sociology and legal theory. This article will therefore consider the relationship of this field to both parent disciplines.

Relationship to General Sociology

It is no exaggeration to state that the field of sociology lacks a systematically developed and precise theory of society. Although interest in macrosociological theory building has been in evidence for the past two decades, particularly among those concerned with comparative sociology (Eisenstadt and Curelaru 1977), no such theory has yet been developed in sufficient detail and precision to guide empirical research. This is not to deny the fact that such macrotheorists as Marx, Durkheim, Weber, and Parsons have exerted a pervasive influence on various specialties within sociology, including the relationship between law and society.

MARX. Marx conceived of law as a component of the "superstructure" of a capitalist society. As an epiphenomenon of the superstructure, it provides a rationale or ideology for preserving the existing class relations in a capitalist economy. Concepts of property and contract, for example, become instrumentalities for maintaining and reproducing class hegemony. In other words, legal concepts and doctrines reinforce the position of the ruling class and, at the same time, become the constituents of the "false consciousness" from which the working class suffers. Implicit in this theory of law as a weapon wielded by the state in a capitalist society against the working class is the assumption that if private property were abolished and a classless socialist society were ushered in, the state would "wither away" and, with it, law would "wither away" as well.

Marx conceived of law as a component of the "superstructure" of a capitalist society.

As usually formulated, the Marxian theory of law and society is not empirically verifiable. It does not follow, however, that this theory is devoid of any empirical implications. Questions can be raised—and have been raised—concerning class bias in the adjudication of civil and criminal cases, in the emergence of significant legal norms—for example, those regarding inheritance—and in the recurrent failure of agrarian reform laws. Likewise, it is possible to investigate a proposition counter to the Marxian thesis, namely, that the passage of laws in a capitalist state can potentially diminish the power of the ruling class vis-a-vis the working class. A case in point is the enactment of the National Labor Relations Act of 1935 in the United States, which institutionalized the rights of employees to unionize and to engage in collective bargaining with employers. Research questions such as those cited above would test the validity of some propositions derivable from the Marxian theory of law and society.

DURKHEIM. Turning to Durkheim's contribution to this field, one of necessity reverts to his *Division of Labor in Society* (1933), in which he argued that in societies characterized by "mechanical solidarity" there is a predominance of repressive laws, whereas in societies characterized by "organic solidarity" there is a predominance of restitutive laws. A number of social scientists have subjected Durkheim's thesis to empirical tests and have found it wanting (Schwartz and Miller 1964). It is a testament, however, to the intriguing character of Durkheim's thesis that it continues to evoke the interest of researchers (Baxi 1974; Schwartz 1974; Sheleff 1975). A more general formulation of Durkheim's thesis would be that societies differing along various dimensions of societal development—of which the division of labor is but one—will exhibit systematic differences in their legal systems (Evan 1968).

In the course of developing his thesis that the division of labor is the principal source of social solidarity, Durkheim formulated his seminal idea of an "index" (Durkheim 1933, pp. 64–65). Apart from his fame as the "father of modern sociology," Durkheim is the originator of the concept of an "index", that is, an indirect and "external" measure of a complex dimension of social structure such as social solidarity. That he developed the concept of an index in connection with "juridical rules" and types of laws is of particular interest to sociologists of law and legal scholars. Under the circumstances, it is indeed surprising that to date, with few exceptions (Evan 1965, 1968, 1980; Merryman, Clark, and Friedman 1979; Lidz 1979), this facet of Durkheim's work has been neglected. The concept of a "legal index" or a "legal indicator" merits systematic attention if we are to become more precise in our understanding of the role of law in social change.

WEBER. In comparison with the work of Durkheim and Marx, Weber's contributions to the sociology of law are appreciably more diverse and complex. Embedded in an intricate mosaic of ideal types and comparative and historical data on the emergence of legal rationality in Western civilization and on the role of law in the origins of capitalism (Weber 1950; Rheinstein 1954; Trubek 1972; Collins 1980), Weber's welter of legal conceptualizations poses a difficult challenge to the empirically oriented researcher. For example, his famous typology of lawmaking and lawfinding suggests possible research leads for comparative and historical analysis. Rheinstein, who edited and translated Weber's work on the sociology of law, lucidly summarizes his typology in the following manner:

1. irrational, i.e., not guided by general rules
   a. formal: guided by means which are beyond the control of reason (ordeal, oracle, etc.)
   b. substantive: guided by reaction to the individual case
2. rational, i.e., guided by general rules
   a. substantive: guided by the principles of an ideological system other than that of the law itself (ethics, religion, power, politics, etc.)
   b. formal:
      (1) extrinsically, i.e., ascribing significance to external acts observable by the senses
      (2) logically, i.e., expressing its rules by the use of abstract concepts created by legal thought itself and conceived of as constituting a complete system.

(Rheinstein 1954, p. 1)

Assuming that the meaning of each of these ideal type categories can be clarified and that legal indicators can be developed for each of the types, a comparative study could be undertaken to explore differences in lawmaking and in lawfinding of such major legal systems as common law, civil law, socialist law, and Moslem law. Equally challenging would be a study of long-term trends within each of these legal systems. The findings of such an inquiry would shed light on the occurrence of the evolutionary stages postulated by Weber:

> The general development of law and procedure may be viewed as passing through the following stages: first, charismatic legal revelation through "law prophets"; second, empirical creation and finding of law by legal honoratiores; . . . third, imposition of law by secular or theocratic powers; fourth and finally, systematic elaboration of law and professionalized administration of justice by persons who have received their legal training in a learned and formally logical manner. (Rheinstein 1954, p. 303)

Another significant thesis in Weber's corpus of writings on law is the innovative role he attributes to "legal honoratiores" or "legal notables" (Bendix 1960). Is Weber's thesis more valid for civil law systems, with its heavy immersion in Roman law, than it is for common law, let alone for socialist law or Moslem law? Once again it would be necessary to develop appropriate legal indicators to measure the degree to which legal notables—lawyers, judges, and high-level civil servants—introduce new rules and new interpretations of existing legal norms in the course of administering justice.

PARSONS. For decades, Parsons was the leading macrosociological theorist in the United States, making singular contributions to structural functionalism and to a general theory of action. Focusing on the action of social systems, Parsons developed a "four-function paradigm." According to Parsons, every society faces four subsystem problems: adaptation, goal attainment, integration, and pattern maintenance or latency (AGIL). The societal subsystems associated with these four functional problems are, respectively, the economy, the polity, law, and religion and education.

Parsons treats law as a rational legal system consisting of a set of prescriptions, proscriptions, and permissions.

Following Weber, Parsons treats law as a rational legal system consisting of a set of prescriptions, proscriptions, and permissions. The legal system, especially in highly differentiated modern societies, performs the functions of a "generalized mechanism of social control" (Parsons 1962). This function is performed vis-à-vis the economy, the polity, and pattern maintenance or latency. The net effect of the pervasive normative regulation is the integration of society. As Parsons puts it: "The legal system . . . broadly constitutes what is probably the single most important institutional key to understanding . . . problems of societal integration" (Parsons 1978, p. 52).

With his four-function paradigm, Parsons addresses the nexus between law and society with the aid of "generalized media of interchange." The economy in a developed and differentiated society uses the medium of money for transactions. Functionally analogous media of exchange operate in each of the other subsystems—power in the polity, value commitment in pattern maintenance, and influence in law.

Suggestive as Parsons's framework is for understanding interinstitutional relations, the generalized media of interchange have not, as yet, been operationalized so as to explain how the legal system interacts with other societal subsystems. In other words, since Parsons has not explicated specific linkages between the legal and nonlegal subsystems, it is difficult to discern what hypotheses can be tested against any body of data. Hence, a reasonable conclusion is that Parsons's macrosociological theory, in its present form, is actually a metatheory.

The foregoing review of some sociological theories of law and society raises two common themes: (1) each of the theorists endeavored to comprehend the macrostructural relationships between law and other institutional systems of a society, and (2) if the hypotheses implicit in these theories are to be empirically tested, systematic attention would have to be devoted to the development of a body of legal indicators. The current generation of sociologists of law has yet to face up to the problems engendered by both of these themes.

Relationship to Legal Theory

Is the relationship between the sociology of law and the field of legal theory any less problematic than it is with general sociology? On its face, the question should be answered in the affirmative because the sociologist of law must take some of the legal scholars' subjects as objects of inquiry. In actuality, because of the traditions of legal scholarship, legal scholars do not generally provide an analytical basis for sociological research. Legal scholarship tends to be preoccupied with legal rules, legal principles, and their application to a multitude of specific conflict situations. As a consequence, the scholarly literature—apart from being intellectually insular—is almost entirely verbal and idiographic, with virtually no interest in a *nomothetic,* let alone *quantitative,* analysis of legal phenomena. Furthermore, there is a high degree of specialization within legal scholarship such that most scholars tend to devote their entire careers to a particular body of law, be it labor law, criminal law, contract law, family law, and so forth, in their own country. Those scholars specializing in comparative law are inclined to study a particular specialty, for example, family law, by comparing case studies from two or more countries (Glendon 1975). Relatively few legal scholars seek to study the legal system of an entire society, such as the work of Hazard (1977) and Berman (1963) on the Soviet legal system. And fewer still have had the temerity to undertake systematic comparisons of total legal systems or families of legal systems, as exemplified in the work of David and Brierly (1968) and Wigmore (1928); and those who do make no effort to relate characteristics of total legal systems to the social-structural attributes of the societies in which they are embedded.

Surveying current legal theory, three distinct theoretical perspectives can be discerned: the theory of legal autonomy, critical legal studies, and autopoietic law. Each of these perspectives will be briefly reviewed and appraised for their implications for a theory of law and society.

LEGAL AUTONOMY. Traditional conceptions of the legal order and "sources of law" are based on two assumptions, the first being that the law is a "seamless web," a relatively "closed system." Whatever processes of change occur in the law are generated from within the legal system, not from without. In other words, processes of change are immanent or endogenous and are not externally induced. The second assumption is that the legal system is, by definition, autonomous from other systems or institutions of a society. Therefore, it is unnecessary to inquire into how the legal system interacts with other subsystems of a society or into what degree of autonomy a given legal system actually has from other societal subsystems.

Perhaps the most quintessential articulation of the theory of legal autonomy in recent years can be found in the work of Watson, a renowned legal historian and comparative law scholar. Watson has repeated his thesis of legal autonomy in a number of monographs and articles (Watson 1974, 1978, 1981, 1983, 1985, 1987). He contends that the growth and evolution of the law is determined largely by an autonomous legal tradition, which exists and operates outside the sphere of societal needs.

> To a large extent law possesses a life and vitality of its own; that is, no extremely close, natural or inevitable relationship exists between law, legal structures, institutions and rules on the one hand and the needs and desires and political economy of the ruling elite or of the members of the particular society on the other hand. If there was such a close relationship, legal rules, institutions and structures would transplant only with great difficulty, and their power of survival would be severely limited. (Watson 1978, pp. 314–315)

> Law is largely autonomous and not shaped by societal needs; though legal institutions will not exist without corresponding social institutions, law evolves from the legal tradition. (Watson 1985, p. 119).

Unlike the Marxist view of law, Watson's is that the law does not advance the interests of the ruling class; instead, it reflects the "culture" of the legal elite. He bolsters his provocative thesis with a study of legal borrowing, which he refers to as "legal transplants" (1974). The fact that the individual statutes, legal doctrines, and entire codes have been borrowed by countries differing in cultural, political, economic, and other respects provides evidence, according to Watson, in support of his thesis of legal autonomy.

The concept of "legal transplant" has a naturalistic ring to it as though it occurs independent of any human agency. In point of fact, however, elites—legal and nonlegal—often act as "culture carriers" or intermediaries between societies involved in a legal transplant. Legal scholars who are associated with political elites may be instrumental in effecting a legal transplant. Moreover, many instances of legal borrowing involve the "imposition" of a foreign body of law by a colonial power (Burman and Harrell-Bond 1979). Hence, it is a mistake to describe and analyze the diffusion of law as if it were devoid of human agency. If human volition is involved, it is indeed questionable whether the borrowed legal elements do not perform a societal function—at the very least on behalf of the legal elite.

CRITICAL LEGAL STUDIES. Unlike Watson's internalist focus on the legal system and its autonomous development, the critical legal studies (CLS) movement appears to pursue a dual strategy: externalist as well as internalist. CLS is externalist in its critique of the social order and of the values dominating judicial decision making. It is internalist in its fundamental critique of traditional jurisprudence and legal reasoning.

The critical legal studies (CLS) movement appears to pursue a dual strategy: externalist as well as internalist.

The CLS movement emerged in the late 1970s in American law schools. It brought together a diverse group of scholars with a left-of-center ideology concerned about inequality and injustice in American society. Although lacking any consensus regarding societal transformation, CLS scholars sought to identify the impact of society's dominant interests on the legal process and the impact of social and political values on legal decision making.

In his introduction to a volume of essays by CLS authors, David Kairys discusses the "basic elements" of the legal theory of this movement. Three of these elements are externalist in nature:

> We place fundamental importance on democracy, by which we mean popular participation in the decisions that shape our society and affect our lives. . . . We reject the common characterization of the law and the state as neutral, value-free arbiters, independent of and unaffected by social and economic relations, political forces, and cultural phenomena. The law's ultimate mechanism for control and enforcement is institutional violence, but it protects the dominant system of social and power relations against political and ideological as well as physical challenges. (Kairys 1982, pp. 3–5)

These three externalist principles of the CLS movement have a familiar ring to them; namely, they are reminiscent of criticisms leveled by Marxists and neo-Marxists against the legal order of capitalist societies.

By far the most distinctive contribution of the CLS movement has been its elaborate internalist critique of legal reasoning and legal process. As Kairys puts it:

> We reject . . . the notion that a distinctly legal mode of reasoning or analysis characterizes the legal process or even exists. . . . There is no legal reasoning in the sense of a legal methodology or process for reaching particular, correct results. There is a distinctly legal and quite elaborate system of discourse and body of knowledge, replete with its own language and conventions of argumentation, logic, and even manners. In some ways these aspects of the law are so distinct and all-embracing as to amount to a separate culture; and for many lawyers the courthouse, the law firm, the language, the style, become a way of life. But in terms of a method or process for decision making—for determining correct rules, facts, or results—the law provides only a wide and conflicting variety of stylized rationalizations from which courts pick and choose. Social and political judgments about the substance, parties, and context of a case guide such choices, even when they are not the explicit or conscious basis of decision. (Kairys 1982, p. 3)

Not only do critical legal scholars reject the notion of legal reasoning, they also reject other idealized components constituting a "legal system," in particular, that law is a body of doctrine, that the doctrine reflects a coherent view of relations between persons and the nature of society, and that social behavior reflects norms generated by the legal system (Trubek 1984, p. 577).

The general conclusion CLS writers draw from "unmasking" the legal system, "trashing" mainstream jurisprudence, and "deconstructing" legal scholarship (Barkan 1987) is that "law is simply politics by other means" (Kairys 1982, p. 17). Such a conclusion, on its face, does not hold out any promise for developing a new, let alone heuristic, approach to a theory of law and society. On the contrary, its antipositivism combined with its search for a transformative political agenda has prompted CLS writers to view with increasing skepticism the sociology of law and research into the relationship between law and society (Trubek and Esser 1989).

AUTOPOIETIC LAW. Similar in some respects to Watson's theory of legal autonomy, but fundamentally different from the theory of the CLS movement, autopoietic law claims to be a challenging new theory of law and society (Teubner 1988a). For the past few years several continental social theorists, who are also legal scholars, have enthusiastically developed and propagated the theory of autopoietic law. A complex cluster of ideas, this theory is derived from the work of two biologists, Maturana and Varela (Varela 1979; Maturana and Varela 1980).

Autopoietic law claims to be a challenging new theory of law and society.

In the course of their biological research, Maturana and Varela arrived at some methodological realizations that led them to generalize about the nature of living systems. Maturana coined the term *autopoiesis* to capture this new "scientific epistemology" (Maturana and Varela 1980, p. xvii). "This was a word without a history, a word that could directly mean what takes place in the dynamics of the autonomy proper to living systems." Conceptualizing living systems as machines. Maturana and Varela present the following rather complex and abstract definition:

> Autopoietic machines are homeostatic machines. Their peculiarity, however, does not lie in this but in the fundamental variable which they maintain constant . . . an autopoietic machine continuously generates and specifies its own organization through its operation as a system of production of its own components, and does this in an endless turnover of components under conditions of continuous perturbations and compensation of perturbations. (Maturana and Varela 1980, pp. 78–79)

Another definition of autopoiesis is presented by Zeleny, one of the early advocates of this new theory:

> An *autopoietic system* is a distinguishable complex of component-producing processes and their resulting components, bounded as an autonomous unity within its environment, and characterized by a particular kind of relation among its components, and component-producing processes: the components, through their interaction, recursively generate, maintain, and recover *the same* complex of processes which produced them. (Zeleny 1980, p. 4)

Clearly, these definitions and postulates are rather obscure and high-level generalizations that, from a general systems theory perspective (Bertalanffy 1968), are questionable. Especially suspect is the assertion that autopoietic systems do not have inputs and outputs. The authors introduce further complexity by postulating second- and third-order autopoietic systems, which occur when autopoietic systems interact with one another and, in turn, generate a new autopoietic system (Maturana and Varela 1980, pp. 107–111). Toward the end of their provocative monograph, Maturana and Varela raise the question of whether the dynamics of human societies are determined by the autopoiesis of its components. Failing to agree on the answer to this question, the authors postpone further discussion (Maturana and Varela 1980, p. 118). Zeleny, however, hastens to answer this question and introduces the notion of "social autopoiesis" to convey that human societies are autopoietic (Zeleny 1980, p. 3).

Luhmann, an outstanding German theorist and jurist, has also gravitated to the theory of autopoiesis. According to Luhmann, "social systems can be regarded as special kinds of autopoietic systems" (1988b, p. 15). Influenced in part by Parsons and general systems theory, Luhmann applied some systems concepts in analyzing social structures (1982). In the conclusion to the second edition of his book *A Sociological Theory of Law* (1985), Luhmann briefly refers to new developments in general systems theory that warrant the application of autopoiesis to the legal system. Instead of maintaining the dichotomy between closed and open systems theory, articulated by Bertalanffy, Boulding, and Rapoport (Buckley 1968), Luhmann seeks to integrate the open and closed system perspectives. In the process he conceptualizes the legal system as self-referential, self-reproducing, "normatively closed," and "cognitively open"—a theme he has pursued in a number of essays (1985, 1986, 1988c).

This formulation is, to say the least, ambiguous. Given normative closure, how does the learning of the system's environmental changes, expectations, or demands get transmitted to the legal system? Further complicating the problem is Luhmann's theory of a functionally differentiated modern society in which all subsystems—including the legal system—tend to be differentiated as self-referential systems, thereby reaching high levels of autonomy (Luhmann 1982). Although Luhmann has explicitly addressed the issue of integrating the closed and open system perspectives of general systems theory, it is by no means evident from his many publications how this is achieved.

Another prominent contributor to autopoietic law is the jurist and sociologist of law Gunther Teubner. In numerous publications, Teubner discusses the theory of autopoiesis and its implications for reflexive law, legal autonomy, and evolutionary theory (Teubner 1983a, 1983b, 1988a, 1988b). One essay, "Evolution of Autopoietic Law" (1988a), raises two general issues: the prerequisites of autopoietic closure of a legal system, and legal evolution after a legal system achieves autopoietic closure. With respect to the first issue, Teubner applies the concept of *hypercycle,* which he has borrowed from others but which he does not explicitly define. Another of his essays (Teubner 1988b) reveals how Teubner is using this concept. For Teubner, all self-referential systems involve, by definition, "circularity" or "recursivity" (1988b, p. 57). Legal systems are preeminently self-referential in the course of producing legal acts or legal decisions. However, if they are to achieve autopoietic autonomy their cyclically constituted system components must become interlinked in a "hypercycle," "i.e., the additional cyclical linkage of cyclically constituted units" (Teubner 1988b, p. 55). The legal system components—as conceptualized by Teubner, "element, structure, process, identity boundary, environment, performance, function" (1988b, p. 55)—are general terms not readily susceptible to the construction of legal indicators.

The second question Teubner addresses, legal evolution after a legal system has attained autopoietic closure, poses a similar problem. The universal evolutionary functions of variation, selection, and retention manifest themselves in the form of legal mechanisms.

> In the legal system, normative structures take over variation, institutional structures (especially procedures) take over selection and doctrinal structures take over retention. (Teubner 1988a, p. 228)

Since Teubner subscribes to Luhmann's theory of a functionally differentiated social system, with each subsystem undergoing autopoietic development, he confronts the problem of intersubsystem relations as regards evolution. This leads him to introduce the intriguing concept of *co-evolution.*

> The environmental reference in evolution however is produced not in the direct, causal production of legal developments, but in processes of co-evolution. The thesis is as follows: In co-evolutionary processes it is not only the autopoiesis of the legal system which has a selective effect on the development of its own structures; the autopoiesis of other subsystems and that of society also affects—in any case in a much more mediatory and indirect way—the selection of legal changes. (Teubner 1988a, pp. 235–236)

Given the postulate of "autopoietic closure," it is not clear by what mechanisms nonlegal subsystems of a society affect the evolution of the legal system and how they "co-evolve." Once again, we confront the unsolved problem in the theory of autopoiesis of integrating the closed and open systems perspectives. Nevertheless, Teubner, with the help of the concept of co-evolution, has drawn our attention to a critical problem even if one remains skeptical of his proposition that "the historical relationship of 'law and society' must, in my view, be defined as a co-evolution of structurally coupled autopoietic systems" (Teubner 1988a, p. 218).

At least three additional questions about autopoietic law can be raised. Luhmann's theory of a functionally differentiated society in which all subsystems are autopoietic raises anew Durkheim's problem of social integration. The centrifugal forces in such a society would very likely threaten its viability. Such a societal theory implies a highly decentralized social system with a weak state and a passive legal system. Does Luhmann really think any modern society approximates his model of a functionally differentiated society?

A problem is the ethnocentrism of social scientists writing against the background of highly developed Western societies where law enjoys a substantial level of functional autonomy.

A related problem is the implicit ethnocentrism of social scientists writing against the background of highly developed Western societies where law enjoys a substantial level of functional autonomy, which, however, is by no means equivalent to autopoietic closure. In developing societies and in socialist countries, many of which are developing societies as well, this is hardly the case. In these types of societies legal systems tend to be subordinated to political, economic, or military institutions. In other words, the legal systems are decidedly *allopoietic.* To characterize the subsystems of such societies as *autopoietic* is to distort social reality.

A third problem with the theory of autopoietic law is its reliance on the "positivity" of law. This fails to consider a secular legal trend of great import for the future of humankind, namely, the faltering efforts—initiated by Grotius in the seventeenth century—to develop a body of international law. By what mechanisms can autopoietic legal systems incorporate international legal norms? Because of the focus on "positivized" law untainted by political, religious, and other institutional values, autopoietic legal systems would have a difficult time accommodating themselves to the growing corpus of international law.

Stimulating as is the development of the theory of legal autopoiesis, it does not appear to fulfill the requirements for a fruitful theory of law and society (Blankenburg 1983). In its present formulation, autopoietic law is a provocative metatheory. If any of its adherents succeed in deriving empirical propositions from this metatheory (Blankenburg 1983), subject them to an empirical test, and confirm them, they will be instrumental in bringing about a paradigm shift in the sociology of law.

The classical and contemporary theories of law and society, reviewed above, all fall short in providing precise and operational guidelines for uncovering the linkages over time between legal and nonlegal institutions in different societies. Thus, the search for a scientific macro sociolegal theory will continue. To further the search for such a theory, a social-structural model will now be outlined.

A Social-Structural Model

A social-structural model begins with a theoretical amalgam of concepts from systems theory with Parsons' four structural components of social systems: values, norms, roles, and collectivities (Parsons 1961, pp. 41–44; Evan 1975, pp. 387–388). Any subsystem or institution of a societal system, whether it be a legal system, a family system, an economic system, a religious system, or any other system, can be decomposed into four structural elements: values, norms, roles, and organizations. The first two elements relate to a cultural or normative level of analysis and the last two to a social-structural level of analysis. Interactions between two or more subsystems of a society are mediated by cultural as well as by social-structural elements. As Parsons has observed, law is a generalized mechanism for regulating behavior in the several subsystems of a society (Parsons 1962, p. 57). At the normative level of analysis, law entails a "double institutionalization" of the values and norms embedded in other subsystems of a society (Bohannan 1968). In performing this reinforcement function, law develops "cultural linkages" with other subsystems, thus contributing to the degree of normative integration that exists in a society. As disputes are adjudicated and new legal norms are enacted, a value from one or more of the nonlegal subsystems is tapped. These values provide an implicit or explicit justification for legal decision making.

Parsons's constituents of social structure (values, norms, roles, and organizations) are nested elements, as in a Chinese box, with values incorporated in norms, both of these elements contained in roles, and all three elements constituting organizations. When values, norms, roles, and organizations are aggregated we have a new formulation, different from Parsons's AGIL paradigm, of the sociological concept of an institution. An institution of a society is composed of a configuration of values, norms, roles, and organizations. This definition is applicable to all social institutions, whether economic, political, religious, familial, educational, scientific, technological, or legal. In turn, the social structure of a society is a composite of these and other institutions.

Of fundamental importance to the field of the sociology of law is the question of how the legal institution is related to each of the nonlegal institutions. A preliminary answer to this question will be set forth in a model diagramming eight types of interactions or linkages between legal and nonlegal institutions (see Figure 1).

On the left-hand side of the diagram are a set of six nonlegal institutions, each of which is composed of values, norms, roles, and organizations. If the norms comprising the nonlegal institutions are sufficiently institutionalized, they can have a direct regulatory impact on legal personnel as well on the citizenry (interaction 4, "Single institutionalization"). On the other hand, according to Bohannan (1968), if the norms of the nonlegal institutions are not sufficiently strong to regulate the behavior of the citizenry, a process of "double institutionalization" (interaction 1) occurs whereby the legal system converts nonlegal institutional norms into legal norms. This effect can be seen in the rise in the Colonial period of "blue laws," which were needed to give legal reinforcement to the religious norms that held the Sabbath to be sacred (Evan 1980, pp. 517–518, 530–532). In addition, the legal system can introduce a norm that is not a component of any of the nonlegal institutions. In other words, the legal system can introduce an innovative norm (interaction 2) that does not have a counterpart in any of the nonlegal institutions (Bohannan 1968). An example of such an innovation is "no-fault" divorce (Weitzman 1985; Jacob 1988).

The legal system's regulatory impact (interaction 3) may succeed or fail with legal personnel, with the citizenry, or with both. Depending on whether legal personnel faithfully implement the law, and the citizenry

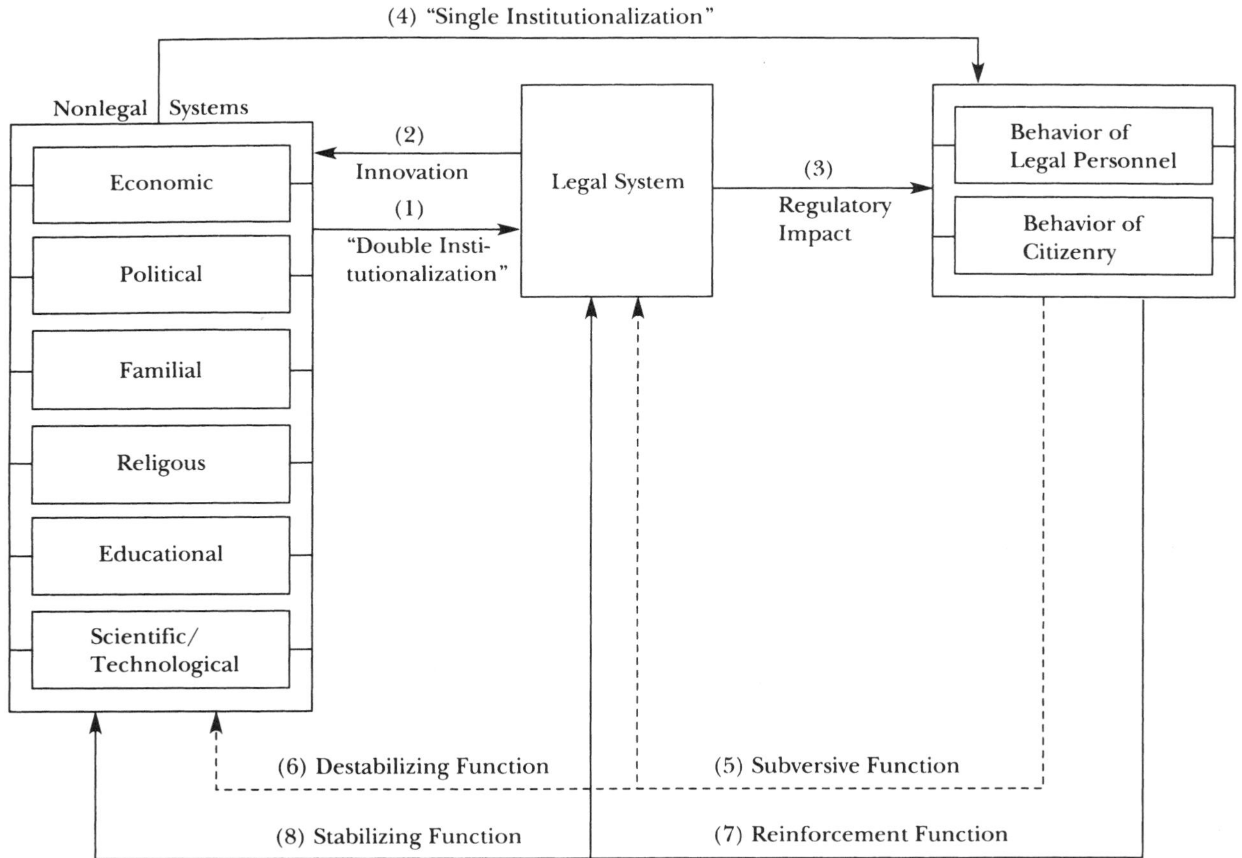

Figure 1. A Social-Structural Model of the Interactions of Legal and Nonlegal Institutions.

faithfully complies with the law, the effect on the legal system can be reinforcing (interaction 7) or subversive (interaction 5), and the effect on nonlegal institutions can be stabilizing (interaction 9) or destabilizing (interaction 6).

In systems-theoretic terms, the values of a society may be viewed as goal parameters in comparison with which the performance of a legal system may be objectively assessed. The inability of a legal system to develop "feedback loops" and "closed loop systems" to monitor and assess the efficacy of its outputs makes the legal system vulnerable to various types of failures. Instead of generating "negative feedback," that is, self-corrective measures, when legal personnel or rank-and-file citizens fail to comply with the law, the system generates detrimental "positive feedback" (Laszlo, Levine, and Milsum 1974).

Conclusion

What are some implications of this social-structural model? In the first place, the legal system is not viewed as only an immanently developing set of legal rules, principles, or doctrines insulated from other subsystems of society, as expressed by Watson and to some extent by Luhmann and Teubner. Second, the personnel of the legal system, whether judges, lawyers, prosecutors, or administrative agency officials, activate legal rules, principles, or doctrines in the course of performing their roles within the legal system. Third, formally organized collectivities, be they courts, legislatures, law-enforcement organizations, or administrative agencies, perform the various functions of a legal system. Fourth, in performing these functions, the formally organized collectivities comprising a legal system interact with individuals and organizations representing interests embedded in the nonlegal subsystems of a society. In other words, each of the society's institutions or subsystems—legal and nonlegal—has the same structural elements: values, norms, roles, and organizations. Interinstitutional interactions involve an effort at coupling these structural elements across institutional boundaries. A major challenge to the sociologists of law is to discover the diverse couplings or linkages—cultural and social-structural—between the legal system and the nonlegal systems in terms of the four constituent structural elements. Another challenge is to ascertain the impact of these linkages on the behavior of legal personnel and on the behavior of the citizenry, on the one hand, and to measure the impact of "double institutionalization" on societal goals, on the other.

A serendipitous outcome of this model is that it suggests a definition of law and society or the sociology of law, that is, that the sociology of law deals primarily with at least eight interactions or linkages identified in Figure 1. Whether researchers accept this definition will be determined by its heuristic value, namely, whether it generates empirical research concerning the eight linkages.

[See also Law and Legal Systems.]

BIBLIOGRAPHY

Barkan, Steven M. 1987 "Deconstructing Legal Research: A Law Librarian's Commentary on Critical Legal Studies." *Law Library Journal* 79:617–637.

Baxi, U. 1974 "Comment—Durkheim and Legal Evolution: Some Problems of Disproof." *Law and Society Review* 8:645–651.

Bendix, Reinhard 1960 *Max Weber: An Intellectual Portrait.* New York: Doubleday.

Berman, Harold J. 1963 *Justice in the U.S.S.R: An Interpretation of the Soviet Law.* Cambridge, Mass.: Harvard University Press.

Bertalanffy, Ludwig von 1968 *General System Theory.* New York: G. Braziller.

Blankenburg, Erhard 1983 "The Poverty of Evolutionism: A Critique of Teubner's Case for 'Reflexive Law.' " *Law and Society Review* 18:273–289.

Bohannan, Paul 1968 "Law and Legal Institutions." In David L. Sills, ed. *International Encyclopedia of the Social Sciences.* New York: Macmillan and Free Press.

Buckley, Walter (ed.) 1968 *Modern Systems Research for the Behavioral Scientist.* Chicago: Aldine.

Burman, Sandra, and Barbara E. Harrell-Bond (eds.) 1979 *The Imposition of Law.* New York: Academic Press.

Collins, Randall 1980 "Weber's Last Theory of Capitalism: A Systemization." *American Sociological Review* 45:925–942.

David, Rene, and John E. C. Brierley 1968 *Major Legal Systems in the World Today.* London: Free Press and Collier-Macmillan Ltd.

Durkheim, Emile 1933 *The Division of Labor in Society.* New York: Free Press.

Eisenstadt, S. N., and M. Curelaru 1977 "Macro-Sociology: Theory, Analysis and Comparative Studies." *Current Sociology* 25:1–112.

Evan, William M. 1965 "Toward A Sociological Almanac of Legal Systems." *International Social Science Journal* 17:335–338.

——— 1968 "A Data Archive of Legal Systems: A Cross-National Analysis of Sample Data." *European Journal of Sociology* 9:113–125.

——— 1975 "The International Sociological Association and the Internationalization of Sociology." *International Social Science Journal* 27:385–393.

——— 1980 *The Sociology of Law.* New York: Free Press.

Glendon, Mary Ann 1975 "Power and Authority in the Family: New Legal Patterns as Reflections of Changing Ideologies." *American Journal of Comparative Law* 23:1–33.

Hazard, John N. 1977 *Soviet Legal System: Fundamental Principles and Historical Commentary.* 3rd ed. Dobbs Ferry, N.Y.: Oceana Press.

Jacob, Herbert 1988 *Silent Revolution: The Transformation of Divorce Law in the United States.* Chicago: University of Chicago Press.

Kairys, David, ed. 1982 *The Politics of Law.* New York: Pantheon.

Laszlo, C. A., M. D. Levine, and J. H. Milsum 1974 "A General Systems Framework for Social Systems." *Behavioral Science* 19:79–92.

Lidz, Victor 1979 "The Law as Index, Phenomenon, and Element: Conceptual Steps Towards a General Sociology of Law." *Sociological Inquiry* 49:5–25.

Luhmann, Niklas 1982 *The Differentiation of Society.* New York: Columbia University Press.

——— 1985 *A Sociological Theory of Law.* Elizabeth King and Martin Albrow, trans. London: Routledge and Kegan Paul.

——— 1986 "The Self-Reproduction of Law and Its Limits." In Gunther Teubner, ed., *Dilemmas of Law in the Welfare State.* Berlin: Walter de Gruyter.

——— 1988a "The Sociological Observation of the Theory and Practice of Law." In Alberto Febrajo, ed., *European Yearbook in the Sociology of Law.* Milan: Giuffre Publisher.

——— 1988b "The Unity of Legal Systems." In Gunther Teubner, ed., *Autopoietic Law: A New Approach to Law and Society.* Berlin: Walter de Gruyter.

——— 1988c "Closure and Openness: On Reality in the World of Law." In Gunther Teubner, ed., *Autopoietic Law: A New Approach to Law and Society.* Berlin: Walter de Gruyter.

Maturana, Humberto R., and Francisco J. Varela 1980 *Autopoiesis and Cognition.* Dordrecht, The Netherlands: D. Reidel Publishing Co.

Merryman, John Henry, David S. Clark, and Lawrence M. Friedman 1979 *Law and Social Change in Mediterranean Europe and Latin America.* Stanford, Calif.: Stanford Law School.

Parsons, Talcott 1961 "An Outline of the Social System." In Talcott Parsons, Edward Shils, Kasper D. Naegele, and Jesse R. Pitts, eds., *Theories of Society.* New York: Free Press.

——— 1962 "The Law and Social Control." In William M. Evan, ed., *Law and Sociology.* New York: Free Press.

——— 1978 "Law as an Intellectual Stepchild." In Harry M. Johnson, ed., *Social System and Legal Process.* San Francisco: Jossey-Bass.

Rheinstein, Max (ed.) 1954 *Max Weber on Law in Economy and Society.* Cambridge, Mass.: Harvard University Press.

Schwartz, R. D. 1974 "Legal Evolution and the Durkheim Hypothesis: A Reply to Professor Baxi." *Law and Society Review* 8:653–668.

Schwartz, R. D., and J. C. Miller 1964 "Legal Evolution and Social Complexity." *American Journal of Sociology* 70:159–169.

Sheleff, L. S. 1975 "From Restitutive Law to Repressive Law: Durkheim's *The Division of Labor in Society* Revisited." *European Journal of Sociology* 16:16–45.

Teubner, Gunther 1983a "Substantive and Reflexive Elements in Modern Law." *Law and Society Review* 17:239–285.

——— 1983b "Autopoiesis in Law and Society: A Rejoinder to Blankenburg." *Law and Society Review* 18:291–301.

——— 1988a *Autopoietic Law: A New Approach to Law and Society.* Berlin: Walter de Gruyter.

——— 1988b "Hypercycle in Law and Organization: The Relationship Between Self-Observation, Self-Constitution, and Autopoiesis." In Alberto Febrajo, ed., *European Yearbook in the Sociology of Law.* Milan: Giuffre Publisher.

Trubek, David M. 1972 "Max Weber on Law and the Rise of Capitalism." *Wisconsin Law Review* 730:720–753.

——— 1984 "Where the Action Is: Critical Legal Studies of Empiricism." *Stanford Law Review* 36:575.

———, and John Esser 1989 " 'Critical Empiricism' in American Legal Studies: Paradox, Program, or Pandora's Box?" *Law and Social Inquiry* 14:3–52.

Varela, Francisco J. 1979 *The Principle of Autonomy.* New York: North-Holland.

Watson, Alan 1974 *Legal Transplants: An Approach to Comparative Law.* Charlottesville: University of Virginia Press.

——— 1978 "Comparative Law and Legal Change." *Cambridge Law Journal* 37:313–336.

——— 1981 *The Making of the Civil Law.* Cambridge, Mass.: Harvard University Press.

——— 1983 "Legal Change, Sources of Law, and Legal Culture." *University of Pennsylvania Law Review* 131:1,121–1,157.

——— 1985 *The Evolution of Law.* Baltimore: Johns Hopkins University Press.

——— 1987 "Legal Evolution and Legislation." *Brigham Young University Law Review* 1987:353–379.

Weber, Max 1950 *General Economic History.* New York: Free Press.

Weitzman, Lenore J. 1985 *The Divorce Revolution: The Unexpected Social and Economic Consequences for Women and Children in America.* New York: Free Press.

Wigmore, John Henry 1928 *A Panorama of the World's Legal Systems.* 3 vols. St. Paul, Minn.: West Publishing Co.

Zeleny, Milan 1980 *Autopoiesis, Dissipative Structures, and Spontaneous Social Orders.* Boulder, Colo.: Westview Press, for the American Association for the Advancement of Sciences.

– WILLIAM M. EVAN

LEADERSHIP

Leadership is a concept most often used in the study of small groups or complex organizations. It refers to a set of social processes: directing the productive activities of a group, defending the group against external threat, maintaining group cohesion, and so forth. It may also refer to individuals performing leadership roles, as when reference is made to "the leadership" of a group or organization. There are often multiple leadership roles within a single group, and different situations often make different types of leaders more effective.

Contrary to popular belief, most leaders are not all-powerful individuals with the freedom to do whatever they like.

Max Weber noted that there are three types of "legitimate authority" in social and economic organizations. The first rests on charismatic qualities of the leader as an individual, the second involves patriarchal or traditional principles, and the third is leadership by formal rules, or bureaucratic authority. Many sociologists agree with Weber's hypothesis that modern societies stress bureaucratic leadership.

Small group theory and research suggest strongly that all social groups have two distinctive leadership positions. The task leader is responsible for organization and direction. The social leader deals with group solidarity or morale.

This distinction between the task leader and the social leader is based on functionalist theory. Most empirical studies show this pattern of dual leadership. Research also supports the principle that the two roles are incompatible: Different individuals usually occupy the two roles.

Contrary to popular belief, most leaders are not all-powerful individuals with the freedom to do whatever they like. They are subject to stronger expectations than other group members. They are often considered role models, and if leaders fail in their roles, they are subject to serious sanctions by the group or organization. If the group does not succeed in attaining its goals, the leader is blamed or replaced. Thus, leadership is clearly a two-way social process.

Leadership in Small Groups

Much of the current theory and research on leadership in small groups is based on the work by Robert F. Bales and Philip E. Slater (1955), who hypothesized that all social systems have functional needs for two types of leadership roles: a task leader and a social-emotional leader.

The task (or instrumental) leadership role deals with problems of defining the task, suggesting solutions, and moving the group toward achievement of the goals of production, efficiency, and so forth. The person occupying this role dominates the group's activity, especially in the early stages of the problem-solving process. A strong correlation has been found between how much an individual talks and that individual's ratings as a task leader by observers or group members.

The social-emotional (or expressive) leader occupies a less visible role in most groups, but this role seems equally essential to the effective functioning of the group. When the task leader dominates the group discussion, suggests solutions, and criticizes others' contributions, the social-emotional leader acts as a buffer and helps to maintain group cohesion. This function is most obvious in the later stages of the problem-solving process: When a solution has been reached, the social-emotional leader often wraps up the discussion by making jokes, complimenting the task leader, and so forth.

Individual Characteristics and Leadership

Most individuals occupying leadership roles exhibit traits such as intelligence, dominance, extroversion, and talkativeness. However, the sociological perspective argues that leaders are made, not born. This approach downplays the impact of personality traits on the emergence of leadership. Situational factors, the type of task, and social characteristics appear to have more significant effects on the selection of specific individuals for leadership roles.

Studies of informal groups with no designated leader reveal that socially significant factors such as gender, age, race, education, and occupation all affect the choice of leader by group members. *Expectation states theory* calls these factors "diffuse status characteristics" because they are associated with very general expectations about abilities and status. When the wider society gives lower status to females, the young, nonwhites, and those with lower levels of education and occupation, such statuses will usually be carried into the group's structure and result in those types of persons being chosen less often as leaders. However, there are usually some "task-relevant characteristics" that are equally important in leadership emergence: For example, a group member who is an experienced computer programmer will naturally receive more votes as leader if the task is something related to computers.

Leadership Styles and Situational Factors

Leadership roles are heavily influenced by the type of task, by the communication patterns imposed by spatial or technological factors, and by group size.

Generalizations about leadership are made risky by the diversity of tasks groups face. Another way to put this is that different types of groups give rise to different types of leadership structures. For example, when a task is simple and can be divided among all group members, the leader will act as a coordinator or chair rather than as an active director or "head."

Fiedler (1967) proposed a "contingency model of leadership effectiveness," which has received considerable support from empirical research. Fiedler argues that leaders who stress task completion rather than group morale will be most effective in situations when the task is complex and leader-follower relationships are strained. In other words, authoritarian task leaders and democratic social-emotional leaders will be successful in different situations.

Many studies show that leaders, formal and informal, are the center of group attention. Laboratory research on seating arrangements and communication networks reveal that task leaders emerge from more visible or central positions (e.g., at the head of the table). Naturalistic studies also show that leaders actively choose to take prominent positions within the group.

The size of the group has a pronounced effect on leadership structures. Georg Simmel (1950, pp. 87–104) noted the "significance of numbers for social life" long ago, pointing out the increased need for coordination as group size increases. Large informal groups, and all complex organizations, exhibit multiple levels of leadership.

Leadership in Formal Organizations

Bureaucracies and formal organizations require effective leadership, in part because of their sheer size and diversity. Sociologists such as Max Weber and Simmel both wrote about this need for a hierarchy of authority.

Early empirical research tested the differences between "human relations" and "scientific management" styles of leadership. In the former, the social-emotional needs of individuals are considered by supervisors in an attempt to encourage productivity and lessen turnover. The latter approach stresses tasks, efficiency, and authority. Subsequent theory and research on management styles has generally paralleled the work on small groups, showing that the nature of the task, the characteristics of the group members, and the type of leadership are all important factors in determining effectiveness.

There is a continuing concern for the important question: How much impact do leaders actually have on their organization? The best conclusion at this stage of knowledge is that some factors create more favorable opportunities for leaders. When the environment is supportive, and the organization is not already highly structured, effective leadership may emerge. Of course, because of the great difficulty in conducting experimental research on complex organizations, much of the evidence for this conclusion remains anecdotal.

Decision making is another facet of leadership. Executives are hired to make decisions for the organization, but sociologists have found that effective organizations usually require some degree of participative decision making. It appears that even if no objective criterion of success is available, when members of an organization are involved in the process, they tend to evaluate the decision (and the formal leader) as being satisfactory. However, as noted above, when the group clearly fails to achieve its goals, the leader is often replaced.

Leadership in Social Movements

The sociological study of social movements and politics seems a natural arena for the analysis of leadership, but in fact research is quite sparse.

Conflict-oriented sociologists consider leadership as essential to political mobilization. Without effective leadership, social movements may remain nothing more than mobs. At the same time, authoritarian leadership is often viewed as a damaging source of within-group inequality and divisiveness in democratic movements. Robert Michels's (1959) "iron law of oligarchy" captures this dilemma and argues that every human organization will create its own potentially oppressive leaders.

This makes the legitimation of leadership essential in democracies. One way to limit the concentration of power, or its abuse, is to establish a set of written rules that apply to any individual who occupies an influential position. Frequent changes in leadership are not usually desirable or possible, and so the group must follow this bureaucratic route.

Weber pointed out that the followers of charismatic leaders who want to perpetuate the movement when the leader dies face the opposite problem. The charisma of the individual must be transformed into a combination of traditional and legitimate authority. He called this the "routinization of charisma."

BIBLIOGRAPHY

Bales, Robert F., and Philip E. Slater 1955 "Role Differentiation." In T. Parsons and R. F. Bales, eds., *Family, Socialization, and Interaction Process.* Glencoe, Ill.: Free Press.

Bass, Bernard M. 1960 *Leadership, Psychology, and Organizational Behavior.* New York: Harper.

Borgatta, Edgar F., Carl S. Couch, and Robert F. Bales 1954 "Some Findings Relevant to the Great Man Theory of Leadership." *American Sociological Review* 19:755–759.

Fiedler, Fred E. 1967 *A Theory of Leadership Effectiveness.* New York: McGraw-Hill.

Gibb, Cecil A. 1969 *Leadership: Selected Readings.* Baltimore: Penguin.

Hare, A. P. 1976 "Leadership." In A. Paul Hare, ed. *Handbook of Small Group Research.* 2d ed. New York: Free Press.

Michels, Robert 1959 *Political Parties: A Sociological Study of the Oligarchical Tendencies of Modern Democracy.* New York: Dover.

Simmel, Georg 1950 "Quantitative Aspects of the Group." In *The Sociology of Georg Simmel,* trans. Kurt H. Wolff. New York: Free Press.

Stogdill, R. 1974 *Handbook of Leadership.* New York: Free Press.

Tannenbaum, Arnold S. 1968 "Leadership: Sociological Aspects." In David L. Sills, ed., *International Encyclopedia of the Social Sciences.* New York: Macmillan and Free Press.

Weber, Max 1962 "The Three Types of Legitimate Rule." In Amitai Etzioni, ed., *Complex Organizations: A Sociological Reader.* New York: Holt, Rinehart, and Winston.

— PAUL MORGAN BAKER

LEGISLATION OF MORALITY

In *The Division of Labor in Society* ([1893] 1984), Emile Durkheim advanced the idea that the distinctive sociological feature of crime is society's reaction to it. Durkheim was writing at a time when Lombroso's view on the heritability of criminality dominated scientific and popular opinion. Science sought the etiology of crime

> *The temperance movements were a form of status politics designed to reaffirm the prestige of a life-style.*

in the biology of the criminal, in *atavism*—crime viewed as a reversion to primitive, ancestral characteristics. From this perspective, the harmfulness of criminality was taken for granted. Given his more comparative and anthropological outlook, Durkheim rejected the idea that crime was condemned by society because of its harmful consequences or because the deviant act was in itself evil. For Durkheim, many things that attracted the severest reprimands of society were objectively quite harmless, such as the neglect of the food taboos or the neglect of religious observance. In his view, the major issue was the integrative function of law, not the individual sources of deviance. Indeed, in *Suicide* ([1897] 1951) he characterized individual acts of despair as expressions of social structural pathologies. He also noted that the integrative function of law extracted far more from the condemnation of the lower class thief than from the middle class embezzler—even though the latter's financial gain was greater and the social consequences of his acts much more adverse. From these observations Durkheim concluded that the societal reactions to crime and deviance were not based on rational models of the incapacitation or deterrence of the offender. In contrast to such utilitarian thinking, the societal reaction to crime was marked by an impassioned moral condemnation. This common feeling of moral outrage was a mark of the collective consciousness of society, particularly in highly cohesive, simple, or "tribal" societies. The condemnation of crime exercised the collective outlook, and it reinforced the group's collective beliefs and values. In short, the criminal was a scapegoat, and if he did not exist in fact, given his functional importance, he could be invented.

With the advance of more competitive and technologically sophisticated societies, the division of labor resulted in a partitioning of the collective consciousness across various elements of society and resulted in the rise of legal codes with less appetite for vengeance and with a greater investment in the reconciliation of competing interests. Hence, for Durkheim, punitive criminal law was the hallmark of primitive societies, which enjoyed a "mechanical" division of labor (i.e., a ho-

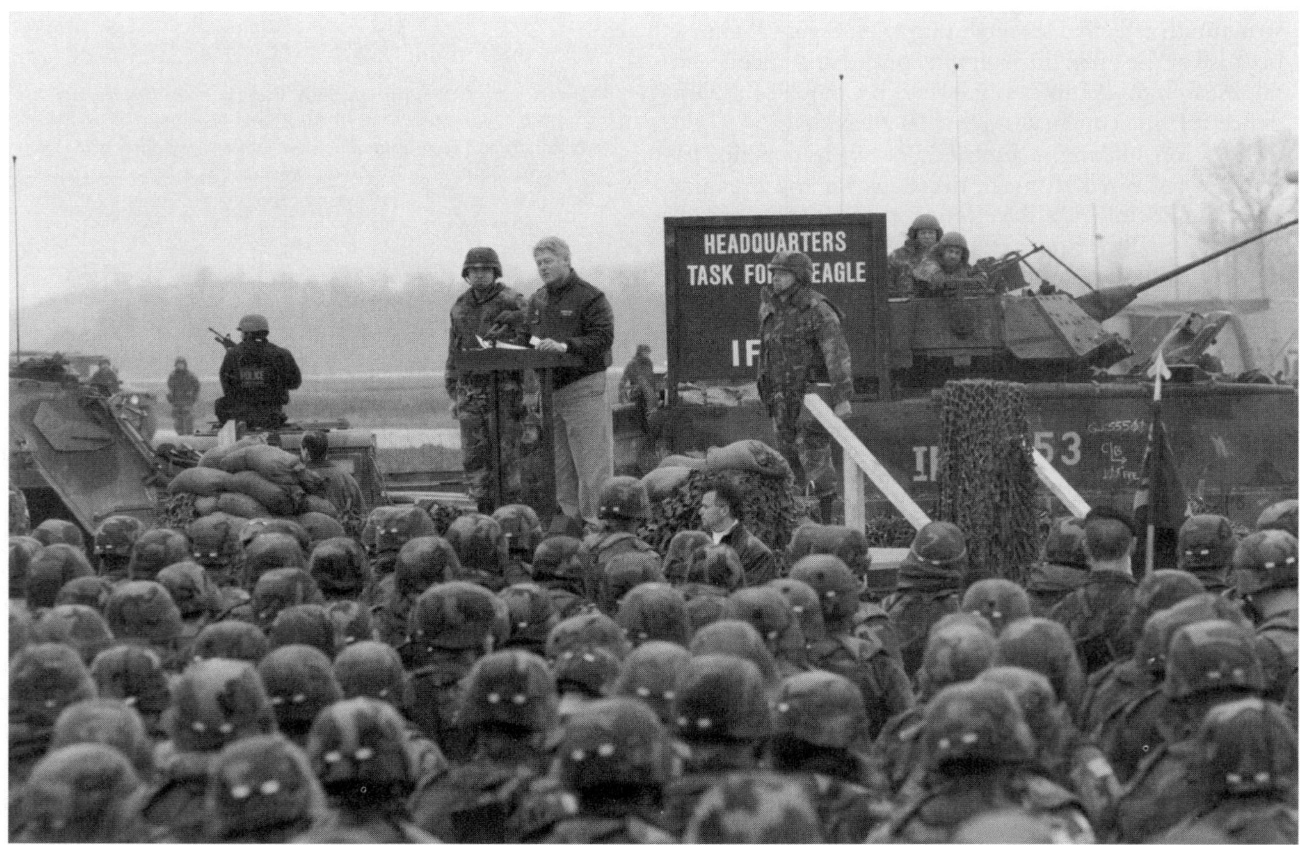

The legitimization of leadership is essential in a democracy in order to prevent weak leadership on one extreme or authoritarian leadership on the other. (Emmanuel Ortiz/Corbis)

mogeneity of work functions), while reconciliatory civil law characterized advanced societies with an "organic" division of labor (i.e., a diverse but mutually dependent specialization of tasks). The former societies were characterized by brutal executions, the latter by written contracts.

Other nineteenth-century authorities tackled the role of law in society. Marx and Engels shared Durkheim's insight that the thing that needed explaining was not why people break laws—the problem of criminology—but why people make laws—the problem of the sociology of law (Cain and Hunt 1979). In their view, law was primarily an instrument of control and a source of both mystification and legitimation. As the urban merchant classes expanded their private estates into the countryside, these classes employed laws to transform the existing common rights of the rural peasants to the harvest of the forest—to deer, fish, pasture, firewood, and so forth—into crimes of theft from private property (Thompson 1975). In addition, the rise of capitalist agriculture, which was associated with the international trade in wool, cleared the British and European common lands of subsistent peasant farmers. Under contract law, the disenfranchised peasants became independent juridical subjects, able to engage in agreements to sell their labor for wages in the cities, although the urban working classes, having been displaced from subsistence on rural estates, had little choice, aside from starvation, but to work in factories.

Durkheim's position on law as an expression of the collective consciousness and Marx and Engel's views on law as an instrument of control continue to exert influence on contemporary thinking about law and morality. Where Durkheim treated the law as an expression of general social consciousness, Marx and Engels viewed it as an expression of a class consciousness, although, to be fair, Durkheim's model of collective consciousness held for a sort of mythic primitive society—akin to Hobbes on the "natural" state of man confronting the war of all against all or akin to Veblen or Freud's primal horde. In each case, the ideal type was an imaginative, indeed a fictional, reconstruction of human origins. The division of consciousness by class would have been possible for Durkheim in advanced societies—even if it constituted a state that he classified in *The Division of Labor in Society* as "abnormal" and even if it was the sort of awareness he wanted to overcome through the "corporations" that cut across class divisions and that Durkheim speculated might form the political nucleus of a future society.

In North America, sociological theories about the legislation of morality took a distinctive turn with investigations of "moral panics," "victimless crimes," and "moral entrepreneurs"—all of which figured importantly in the labeling theories of the 1960s. The studies investigated distinctively morally charged issues and stressed the influence of both social movements and the mass media in the construction of the criminal law. By way of example, Sutherland (1950) examined the role of "moral crusaders" in the context of the sexual psychopathy laws that were enacted in 1937 and thereafter in eleven northern states, California, and the District of Columbia. These laws provided for indefinite incarceration in hospitals for the criminally insane for anyone pronounced by a psychiatrist to be a sexual psychopath. Retrospectively, this diagnosis is not based on a discernible medical disease. In fact, many psychiatric categories are only labels for things we do not like. Nonetheless, a wide series of jurisdictions, with one eye to reforming sexual deviants, enacted laws based on this "disease."

There was a threefold process underlying the creation of these laws. First, the laws were enacted after a state of fear and hysteria following newspaper accounts of several sex crimes committed coincidentally in quick succession. In these states there was a rush to buy guns, guard dogs, and locks and chains, reflecting widespread evidence of public fears. Second, these fears were fueled by news coverage of related sex crimes in other areas and other times in history and of sex-related behaviors and morality (including questions regarding striptease) and by letters to newspaper editors and statements made by public figures. The third phase was the creation of committees to study "the facts" of the sex crimes and "the facts" of sexual psychopathology. These committees, though initially struck on the basis of collective terror, persisted long after the fear and news stories subsided. They resulted in a presentation of briefs to legislative bodies, particularly by a new class of medical experts—psychiatrists. The community hysteria was legitimated by the identification of the crimes as a form of disease by the psychiatric professionals. The legislatures responded to public fears by passing laws to control the offending parties, in this instance by making sexual psychopaths subject to incarceration under psychiatric supervision.

A second important illustration is the history of the American prohibition movement, reported in the classic sociological study by Joseph Gusfield—*Symbolic Crusade* (1963). From 1919 to 1933 an amendment to the American Constitution outlawed the manufacture and sale of alcoholic beverages. The law was passed after decades of lobbying by members of the numerous "temperance movements," who originated predominantly from fundamentalist Protestant stock, largely from rural areas, and initially of middle class background. They were the upholders of the Protestant ethic and valued hard work, self-reliance, and sobriety.

Gusfield argues that as America industrialized during the nineteenth century, the traditional rural settlers experienced a loss of social status compared to the new urban classes and experienced a challenge to their traditional values as urban development introduced increasingly nontraditional immigrants. The temperance movements were a form of status politics designed to reaffirm the prestige of a life-style. In the early period (1825–1875) the temperance movements pursued their objective through education, persuasion, and the reform of social conditions that caused excessive drinking. With increasing urbanization and greater European immigration, however, the tactics changed from a policy of socialization to one of coercive reform. The temperance movement became a prohibition movement. And when conservative forces came to dominate the political scene in America following World War I, the value of sobriety was to be achieved coercively—by outlawing booze. In Canada prohibition was approved in a national plebiscite in 1898 and enabled by federal law in 1916. The federal law allowed provinces to implement their own legislation, and all but Quebec outlawed booze, although booze continued to be manufactured for export—usually illicitly to the United States—and was available in Canada by prescription in pharmacies. The Canadian experiment in forced temperance ended in the mid-1920s, and the United States repealed prohibition in 1933.

Gusfield's work is important for several reasons. It stressed the idea that legislation was "symbolic"—that it reflected the values of distinctive social groups and that such groups struggled to have their views insinuated into state legislation. Unlike Marx, who viewed political struggle as class politics, Gusfield stressed "status" politics—the advancement of group respectability or status by seeking to have the group values enshrined in law. Gusfield further implied that laws, particularly in the field of "victimless crimes," were symbolic in another sense. Instrumentally, prohibition was a terrible failure. It created huge markets for organized crime, and liquor consumption appears to have proceeded in spite of the law. Hence, the condemnation of insobriety was merely ritualistic (i.e., symbolic) because it did not extirpate drunkenness nor seriously inhibit liquor consumption. Similar arguments have been raised regarding the criminalization of narcotics, prostitution, and pornography—classical "victimless crimes," the markets for which thrive on a demand that seems little impeded by legal proscription.

The labeling theories of the 1960s developed the Durkheimian emphasis on the importance of societal reaction to crime (Kitsuse 1962; Lemert 1967) and identified some of the processes by which conduct was successfully labeled as criminal or how it successfully evaded such a label (Becker 1963). Theorists explored the self-fulfilling prophecies of deviant labels and the role of stigma in stabilizing rejected identities (Goffman 1961, 1963). The role of moral entrepreneurs was identified; these Weberian charismatics personified the struggle against evil and expedited legal change by campaigning in the media on the dire consequences of everything from dance halls to crime comics to television violence and marijuana use. Research on societal reaction proliferated. Studies focused on the manufacture of mental illness (Scheff 1966; Szasz 1961, 1970), the creation of witchcraft as a form of labeling (Erikson 1966; Currie 1968), the selective policing and the resulting social construction of delinquents (Cicourel 1968), the political hysteria that underlay political show trials (O'Connor 1972), the role of hysterical stereotypes in the criminalization of narcotics (Cook 1969; Lindesmith 1965), and the mythification of the Hell's Angels in the popular press (Thompson 1966).

The studies of this period had an insurgent flavor and a barely concealed contempt for legal structures and institutions that drew the line between conformity and deviance in an arbitrary fashion. This was particularly true in the context of legislation outlawing "victimless crimes." John Stuart Mill had established the ideological pedigree of this critique when he suggested that the democratic state's sole justification for limiting the freedom of an individual was that the person's behavior was harmful to others. Legal critics in the 1960s and 1970s objected to the extension of the law to cover vices and immoral activities since the participants in these acts, it was argued, were autonomous beings who had chosen them voluntarily and so were mischaracterized as either criminals or victims. The argument was that participants were not criminals since their behavior was not harmful to others, and they were not victims since their fates were chosen voluntarily (Schur 1965). Since these activities flowed from free choice in democratic states, how could they have been made unlawful? The answer lay in the fact that conservative forces led by moral entrepreneurs had stampeded democratic governments through wild allegations that the activities in question were so harmful that they struck at the very fabric of society and that however voluntary or self-inflicted the corruption, its control and eradication was justified for the sake of society itself. More recent studies have taken a different turn. Studies of the law-and-order campaigns associated with the resurgency of political conservatism have led sociologists to ask different sorts of questions.

Where Gusfield stressed that legislation might take on a symbolic aspect that reflects the interests of discrete social groups, recent work suggests that laws may *mystify* the social conditions that give rise to them and consequently may result in social control that is sought for altogether different reasons than the ones identified in the legislation. Taylor (1982) argues that many crime waves, moral panics, and anticrime campaigns are orchestrated in response to basic social conflicts and shifting economic realities and that they function to misdirect our attention away from social contradictions. Three noted British investigations lend support to this view. Hall et al. (1978) argue that the moral panic in British papers over street mugging in the early 1970s that resulted in calls for tougher jail sentences and more law and order in England mystified a basic structural shift in employment patterns that occurred during attempts to dismantle the British welfare state. In the late 1960s and early 1970s there was a conservative political movement in both America and Great Britain to curb state investments in public welfare—to "downsize" governments and to privatize public institutions. There was a certain amount of conscious political resistance in the labor movement and in socialist political quarters. However, the control culture succeeded in redefining the political resistance into an issue of individual lawlessness that required tougher policing, particularly of those persons who experienced the greatest amount of social dislocation as a result of fiscal restraint—poor youth, minority groups, and immigrants. The reports of street "muggings" imparted to England the imagery of lawlessness from the American ghetto, creating the impression that there were dramatic increases in street crime, that the crimes were disturbingly "un-British," and that they were symptomatic of a wider threat to Great Britain's collective security as witnessed by violence in industrial disputes (fights at picket lines) and misconduct among soccer fans.

Having defined the problem as individual lawlessness, the conservative solution of more law and order, greater investment in policing, longer jail sentences, and so forth, occluded the problem of youthful unemployment that *resulted* from conservative fiscal policies and that contributed to theft and other petty rackets in the first place. In this interpretation, moral panics have a material foundation in everyday experience, but where the earlier labeling theorists viewed the panics as *causes* of legal change, the British theorists suggest that panic was the *result* of social change. Sensationalism over crime in the popular media legitimates the introduction of coercive legislation that frequently suspends normal democratic liberties and replaces parsimonious forms of control with more punitive measures. In the case reported by Hall et al. (1978), penalties for petty street crimes increased dramatically as the public, the judiciary, and the politicians were treated to hysterical excesses in the popular press of violent youth running amok.

A similar structural argument is advanced by Stanley Cohen in *Folk Devils and Moral Panics* (1972). This study examines the role of the media in the re-creation of the "mods" and "rockers." There have been a series of distinct trends in youth culture in both America and Great Britain over the last four or five decades—the zoot suiters, the Teddy Boys, the beats, the skin heads and punks, the soccer hooligans, and the motorcycle rebels—all of whom expressed antiauthoritarianism and youthful rebellion. What seems to have set off the postwar youth cultures was society's relative affluence, which created conditions for distinctive consumption patterns supporting unique fashion styles, musical tastes, and recreational opportunities. The mods and rockers were motorcycle-riding youth groups who appeared in the British seaside resorts in the middle 1960s. As Hunter Thompson discovered in his study (1966) of the California Hell's Angels, the British newspapers made a feast of the mods' antics, typically exaggerating and reporting spuriously on their activities. Cohen (1972) stresses that the function of the news hysteria was to create a kind of rogue's gallery of folk devils—vivid, even fearsome images that registered collective fears about the youth, their mobility, and their independence, which served as collective reminders of what youth should not be.

Moral panics are orchestrated when individuals feel compelled by their sense of the collective consciousness to repair a breach in the ideological fabric of society.

In this approach, moral panics are an ongoing, recurrent, and predictable aspect of the popular culture. From this perspective, they are not considered the handiwork of individual moralists who may or may not decide for personal reasons to pursue a moral campaign. Moral panics are orchestrated when individuals feel compelled by their sense of the collective consciousness to repair a breach in the ideological fabric of society. Typically, such persons are affiliated with institutions that have a long-standing investment in moral control—church organizations, community groups, political parties, and so forth—or who occupy roles as self-appointed arbiters in democratic societies—academic experts, professional journalists, and publishers.

Also, moral panics and the legislative changes they engender track important shifts in social structure fairly closely. This is the conclusion of Pearson's *Hooligan: A History of Respectable Fears* (1983). Pearson reports that the current "public" appetite for law and order, for stiffer justice, and for a return to the past are recurrent themes in Western history. The historical perspective suggests that the feelings that, from the perspective of crime and delinquency, things are at an unprecedented nadir, that the present conduct of society compares poorly with the way things were in a previous golden age, that the family is falling apart, and that the popular entertainments of the lower classes are criminogenic, are recurrent in every major period of British history from the 1750s to the present. Over time, the rhetoric of decline has an uncanny similarity. Pearson's point is that crime fears or moral panics occur when the legitimacy of state control over the working class is somehow challenged or brought into question. In the nineteenth century the British working class was only partially integrated into the political process. Consequently, their consent to government—which was dominated by the propertied classes—was usually testy. In the 1840s in particular, there is an apprehension in philanthropical writings about the working class "dodgers," bold, independent delinquents viewed as potential revolutionaries who might fuel the Chartist movement and overthrow the private ownership of property. In this context, philanthropists prescribed education and policing to create internal restraints in the interest of protecting property.

From this perspective, class tensions were misinterpreted in the public press and by middle class politicians as "rising crime and delinquency," and the middle class solutions were recurrently more "law and order" on the one hand and education on the other—that is, more police repression and control, a return to birching, a removal of the un-British elements of the population, a repudiation of meretricious American culture, and a return to the tranquility of the golden age when people knew their place.

It is difficult to give an overall assessment of how the processes of legislating morality discovered in the labeling period in America can be integrated with the class

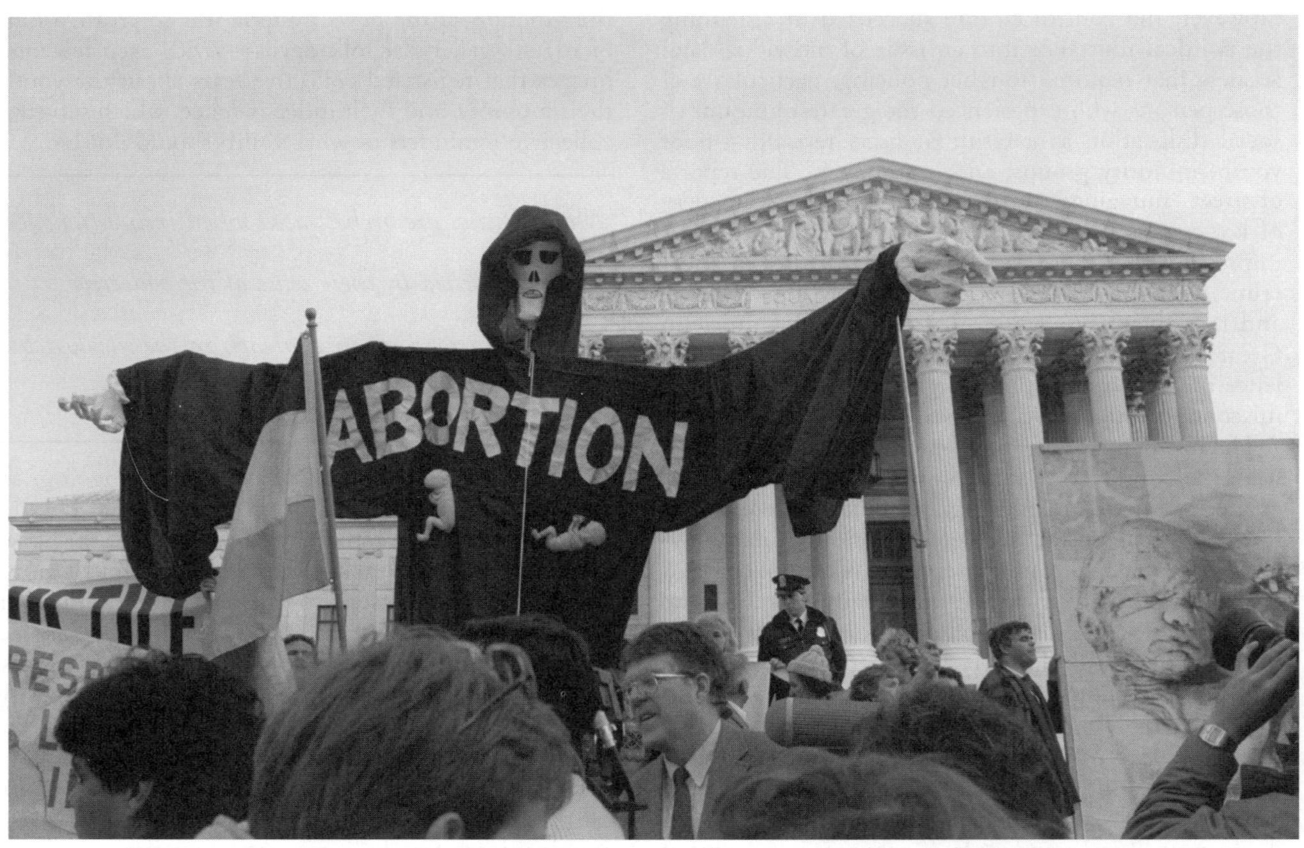

Public preoccupation with the legality of abortion represents deeper concerns about social structural transformations occurring in modern culture. (UPI/Corbis-Bettmann)

conflict approaches stressed in the recent British studies. Certainly, there is no reason to believe that the class antagonisms that characterize British society are as developed in North America, nor that these would be a monolithic source of legal change. On the other hand, there is also no reason that the search for systematic sources of moral panics as effects of social change could not be undertaken in North American studies. Since the early 1980s it has become clear that the preoccupation with abortion, pornography, the funding of AIDS research, gay bashing, and the Equal Rights Amendment in U.S. public discourses is related to important trends in family composition and female labor force participation. For the traditionally minded, the suppression of access to abortion, pornography, and the ERA, as well as lethargy in dealing with AIDS, all seems to be an attempt to turn the clock back toward patriarchal families. For more progressive feminists, access to abortion on demand, suppression of degrading pornography, and the confrontation of the epidemics of sexual and physical violence against women and children are essential ideological matters for the insurance of greater female social and economic advancement. In both cases, the public imagery of epidemics of fetal massacres on the one hand, and epidemics of incest and female abuse on the other, are not the products of idiosyncratic moral campaigns but arise in the context of profound social structural transformations—suggesting the need to develop a convergence of theories of symbolic interests and structural shifts that have developed independently to date.

[See also Deviance.]

BIBLIOGRAPHY

Becker, Howard S. 1963 *Outsiders.* New York: Free Press.

Cain, M., and A. Hunt 1979 *Marx and Engels on Law.* New York: Academic Press.

Cicourel, Aaron 1968 *The Social Organization of Juvenile Justice.* London: Heinemann.

Cohen, Stanley 1972 *Folk Devils and Moral Panics.* Oxford: Basil Blackwell.

Cook, S. 1969 "Canadian Narcotics Legislation 1908–1923: A Conflict Approach." *Canadian Review of Sociology and Anthropology* 6:36–46.

Currie, Elliott P. 1968 "Crimes Without Criminals: Witchcraft and Its Control in Renaissance Europe." *Law and Society Review* 3(1):7–32.

Durkheim, Emile (1893) 1984 *The Division of Labor in Society.* New York: Free Press.

——— (1897) 1951 *Suicide.* New York: Free Press.

Erikson, Kai T. 1966 *Wayward Puritans.* New York: Wiley.

Goffman, Erving 1961 *Asylums.* New York: Doubleday/Anchor.

——— 1963 *Stigma.* Englewood Cliffs, N.J.: Prentice-Hall.

Gusfield, Joseph R. 1963 *Symbolic Crusade: Status Politics and the American Temperance Movement.* Urbana: University of Illinois Press.

Hall, S., C. Critcher, T. Jefferson, J. Clarke, and B. Roberts 1978 *Policing the Crisis: Mugging, the State, and Law and Order.* London: Macmillan.

Kitsuse, John I. 1962 "Societal Response to Deviance: Social Problems of Theory and Method." *Social Problems* 9:247–256.

Lemert, Edwin 1967 "The Concept of Secondary Deviation." In E. Lemert, ed., *Human Deviance, Social Problems, and Social Control.* Englewood Cliffs, N.J.: Prentice-Hall.

Lindesmith, A. 1965 *The Addict and the Law.* Bloomington: Indiana University Press.

O'Connor, Walter D. 1972 "The Manufacture of Deviance: The Case of the Soviet Purge, 1936–1938." *American Sociological Review* 37:403–413.

Pearson, Geoffrey 1983 *Hooligan: A History of Respectable Fears.* London: Macmillan.

Scheff, Thomas 1966 *Being Mentally Ill.* Chicago: AVC.

Schur, Edwin 1965 *Crimes without Victims.* Englewood Cliffs, N.J.: Prentice-Hall.

Sutherland, Edwin 1950 "The Diffusion of Sexual Psychopath Laws." *American Journal of Sociology* 56:142–148.

Szasz, Thomas 1961 *The Myth of Mental Illness.* New York: Heuber-Harper.

——— 1970 *The Manufacture of Madness.* New York: Harper and Row.

Taylor, Ian 1982 "Moral Enterprise, Moral Panic, and Law-and-Order Campaigns." In M. M. Rosenberg, R. A. Stebbins, and A. Turowitz, eds., *The Sociology of Deviance.* New York: St. Martin's Press.

Thompson, E. P. 1975 *Whigs and Hunters.* Harmondsworth, England: Penguin.

Thompson, Hunter S. 1966 *Hell's Angels.* New York: Random House.

– AUGUSTINE BRANNIGAN

LEISURE

Since 1930 the sociology of leisure in North America and Europe has not developed in a linear or cumulative fashion. Rather, research agendas, the accepted premises for research and theory, and the "common wisdom" of the field have been revised and challenged. Change did not come in one great overturning but in a sequence of revisions. A dialectical model seems to be most appropriate for following the sequence. Through the 1950s, there was an accepted consensus as to both issues and premises. This consensus was eroded as well as challenged by new research. The "revised consensus" expanded agendas for both research and theory without completely overturning earlier developments.

Currently, a more critical antithesis has emerged to subject the second consensus to a more thoroughgoing revision. The sources of this antithesis have included conflict or neo-Marxist theory, gender-focused critiques, non-Western perspectives, and various post-structural analytical approaches. Critiques are associated with concepts such as hegemony and power, commodification, gender and patriarchical structures, imperialism, world views, ideologies, and existential action.

Now a central question concerns the kind of synthesis that will be developed in the ongoing process.

The dialectical sequence provides a dynamic framework for a review of central areas in the study of leisure. Although many issues and lines of research can be identified, four have consistently been most salient. In a highly abbreviated form, we will summarize the dialectics of theory and research in relation to (1) work and time, (2) family and community, (3) aging and the life course, and (4) the nature of leisure.

Work and Time

LEISURE AND WORK DOMAINS. When sociologists turned their attention to leisure in the 1960s, three perspectives were adopted. The first, based on earlier community studies, approached leisure as a dimension of the social organization of the community (Lundberg, Komarovsky, and McInerney 1934; Dumazedier 1967). The second, exemplified by work that David Riesman initiated at the University of Chicago, viewed leisure as social action that created its own worlds of meaning. The third, the one that came to shape domain assumption and research agendas, emerged from the sociology of work. Its fundamental premise was that economic institutions are central to the society and that economic roles are the primary determinants of other roles. Leisure was assumed especially to be secondary and derivative. As a consequence, various theorists proposed models of how leisure's role was determined by work. Some modeled leisure as similar to work ("spillover" or identity), others as contrasting with work (compensation), and still others as separate from work (Wilensky 1960; Parker 1971). The bias, however, was clearly toward some kind of determination rather than toward segmentation.

As research proceeded, the "long arm of the job" was found to be both shorter and less powerful than expected as only limited, modest, and sometimes inconsistent relationships were found between leisure styles and occupational level and type (Wilson 1980). In a fuller perspective, on the other hand, it was evident that economic roles are determinative of the social context of adult lives—schedules, control of resources, autonomy, and other basic conditions (Blauner 1964). Leisure is part of the reward structure of a social system with differential access to resources based largely on socioeconomic position.

A second revision of the common wisdom concerned time available for leisure. The long-term reduction in the average number of hours in the work week from as high as eighty in the early days of the Industrial Revolution to about forty in the post-World War II period, along with the five-day work week and paid vacations for many workers, had led to an unquestioned assurance that more and more leisure time would be the product of increased economic productivity. In the 1970s, however, the declining rate of the decrease in hours worked per week, moving toward stability, produced a revised consensus suggesting segmented time scarcity and a variety of social timetables.

A next challenge to the early common wisdom was a recognition of leisure as a dimension of life with its own meaning and integrity. Leisure is more than leftover and derivative time; it has its own place in the rhythm and flow of life. First, leisure came to be defined more as activity than as empty time. Among the themes emerging were relative freedom of choice, distinction from the obligations of other roles, and the variety of meanings and aims that might be sought in such activity. Just as important as the revised definition, however, was the identification of leisure as something more than a derivation of work. Social life could not be characterized as work versus leisure but consisted of multiple sets of intersecting roles. Leisure, although having a particular relationship with the bonding of family and other immediate communities (Cheek and Burch 1976), had multiple contexts, connections, and meanings (Kelly 1981).

THE CHALLENGE OF CRITICAL THEORY. The domain assumptions of functional sociology have been challenged by critical analyses with roots in neo-Marxist cultural studies (Clarke and Critcher 1985), by historical study that focuses on power and the struggles of the working class, and by social construction approaches that take into account the interpretive activity of social actors (Rojek 1985).

The central theme of the critical challenge is social control by ruling elites. Leisure is seen as a critical element in the hegemony of ruling elites in a capitalist society. In order to assure compliance in the workplace, the political arena, and in the marketplace, leisure has emerged as central to the capitalist reward and control system. Leisure is, from this critical perspective, a market-mediated instrument that binds workers to the production process and to roles that support the reproduction of the capital-dominated social system. Leisure is defined as a commodity that must be earned and is indissolubly connected to what can be purchased and possessed.

A number of themes are gathered in this critique. The power to enforce compliance is masked behind an ideology in which "freedom" comes to be defined as purchasing power in the marketplace of leisure. Such "commodity fetishism" (Marx 1970) of attachment to things defines life and leisure in terms of possessions. Social status is symbolized by leisure display (Veblen

[1899] 1953). Absorption in mass media legitimates consumption-oriented values and world views (Habermas 1975). What appear to be varying styles of leisure reflect the profoundly different conditions of work, family, and leisure assigned by class, gender, and race (Clarke and Critcher 1985).

A PROSPECTIVE SYNTHESIS. The fundamental presupposition of any sociology of leisure is that leisure is a thoroughly social phenomenon, a product of the social system, and a phenomenon of the culture. Leisure is not separate and secondary but embedded in the institutional structures, social times, and power allocations of the society. In a complex social system, both individual self-determination and institutional control differ by economic and social position. Leisure is not segmented but woven into the system. Out of the current dialectic between the original consensus and the critique, a number of issues call for attention.

The first agenda is to move beyond ideologies to examine the lived conditions of poor, excluded, and disinherited children, women, and men. Their struggles for life in the present and for a future are reflected in what they do to express themselves, create community, fill ordinary hours and days, and seek new possibilities.

The second issue is to identify the ways in which economic roles provide contexts, resources, limitations, and orientations for other areas of life—family and community as well as leisure. The question is not the simple determination of life and leisure by work but how determinative definitions of both the self and society are learned in a power-differentiated social context.

The third issue is one of meanings. Purchasing is not necessarily commodification, and owning is not fetishism. What are the commitments, symbols, meanings, self-definitions, and world views that are the cognitive context of decisions and actions? What are the meanings and outcomes of leisure-related spending, media use, packaged entertainment, and images of pleasure? Possession may be a way of life or an instrument of activity. Does leisure, in fact, reflect a culture of possession? Or is there a deep paradox between alienation and creation that permeates the entire society?

The fourth issue concerns time. If we discard misleading models about average work weeks, what are the actual patterns and varieties of time structure and allocation? How do these patterns and possibilities vary by economic role, gender, life course, family conditions, ethnicity and race, location, and other placement factors? Time remains a basic resource for leisure, one that not only varies widely but is one index of the possibility of self-determination.

Family and Community

LEISURE AS A CONTEXT FOR FAMILY BONDING. If leisure is not just activity determined by and complementary to work, does leisure have some other critical relationship to the social system? The evident connection is, of course, to family and other immediate communities (Roberts 1970). Most leisure is in or around the home. The most common leisure companions are family and other close friends and intimates.

The primary function of leisure is to provide a context for social bonding, especially that of family and ethnic community.

The basis of the first consensus was the series of community studies beginning in the 1930s (Lundberg, Komarovsky, and McInerney 1934; Lynd and Lynd 1956). Leisure was found to be a web of ordinary activity, mostly social interaction and tied to the institutions of the community, from the family outward to status-based organizations. From this perspective, the later work of Cheek and Burch (1976) argued that the primary function of leisure is to provide a context for social bonding, especially that of family and ethnic community.

An anomaly in family leisure began a revision to the first consensus. The family context was reaffirmed and the centrality of the family to leisure supported (Kelly 1983). However, despite the traditional focus on freedom as the primary defining theme of leisure, activity with major components of obligation was found to be most important to most adults. The major theme was that leisure was closely tied to central roles, not separate from them.

Leisure, then, is bound to both the roles and the developmental requirements of life (Rapoport and Rapoport 1976). In fact, from this perspective it may be quite central to life, not residual or secondary at all. It is a primary setting for social bonding and expression as well as for human development. The implied issue, on the other hand, is the consequences for the nature of freedom and choice in leisure. No activity embedded in primary role relationships can ever be free of accompanying obligations and responsibilities (Kelly 1987a, Chapter 6). Leisure might be more central, but it is also less pure and simple.

POWER AND SELF-DETERMINATION IN LEISURE ROLES. First, there is the challenge posed by changing family patterns now that an unbroken marriage and family through the life course has become a minority probability. The most radical response and antithesis, however, begins with the suggestion that leisure, like other areas of life, has roles. That is, the expectations and power differentials that characterize family, work, and community roles are found in leisure as well. Currently the most salient source of this challenging antithesis is the focus on gender, especially from a feminist perspective (Henderson et al. 1989).

The critique calls for sociologists to go beneath the rhetoric of freedom and self-expression to the realities of lives with limited power of self-determination. From this perspective, the history of the culture is characterized by male domination of women in profound and multifaceted ways that permeate every aspect of life (Deem 1986). Not only have women been repressed in where they are permitted to go and what they are allowed to do in leisure, but even in the home women's leisure is fundamentally different from that of men. It is usually women who are expected to do the work that makes "family leisure" possible. It is the "hidden work" of women that offers relative freedom to much of the leisure of men and children.

What, then, is the meaning of freedom and self-determination for any subordinate population segment? What about the poor, the racially and ethnically excluded, those cut off from opportunity in abandoned urban areas, and even many of the old? The resources of time, money, access, and autonomy are evidently unevenly distributed in any society.

In this antithesis, the connections of leisure to nonwork roles and resources, especially family and community, and the positive evaluation of how leisure contributes to development through the life course are brought up against a critical model of society. Leisure may indeed be indissolubly tied to family and community, but in ways that reflect social divisions and dominations as well as expressive action.

LEISURE'S IMMEDIATE CONTEXT: THE NEW AGENDA. Leisure takes place in its small worlds but also in the larger scale of the society. Further, its actualization is in the midst of real life. Research may be based on premises of systemic integration and the benefits of leisure as well as challenged by critiques reflecting ideologies of subjugation and alienation. A new agenda for research, however informed, should be directed toward the actual lived conditions of decisions, actions, relationships, and roles. In such an agenda related to community and family, several themes are highlighted by critiques of the common wisdom.

First, the realities of leisure as a struggle for action and self-determination in the midst of acute differences in power and access to resources will receive more attention. Especially gender, race, and poverty will reconstitute research strategies and frames past the easy assumptions that leisure is equally free and beneficial for all. The realities of family instability and crisis as well as of community divisions and conflicts will be taken into account as the immediate communities of leisure are reformulated.

Second, underlying the new agenda is the theme of differential power, not only power to command resources but to determine the course of one's life and what is required of others. In the action of leisure, there is both a relative openness for action and modes of repression that stimulate submission *and* resistance.

Third, the danger of leisure becoming increasingly privatized, bound only to immediate communities and the small worlds of personal life construction, is a perspective that runs counter to the functional view of leisure as a context for social bonding. There may be a negative side to a focus on the family basis of leisure activity and meanings. As technologies increasingly make the home a center of varied entertainment, leisure could become more and more cut off from larger communities.

In general, leisure is surely not peripheral to the central concerns and relationships of life. That, however, does not lead simply to bonding without domination, to development without alienation, or to intimacy without conflict.

Aging and the Life Course

CONTINUITY AND CHANGE IN THE LIFE COURSE. The earliest consensus was simply that age indexed many kinds of leisure engagement. In a simple model, age was even referred to as a cause of decreased rates of participation. It was assumed that something decremental happened to people as they aged. The rates of decline varied according to activity: rapid for sports, especially team sports; more gradual for travel and community involvement. Attention given to those in their later years, generally in their sixties and seventies but sometimes fifties as well, suggested that such "disengagement" might even be functional. Perhaps older people needed to consolidate their activity and recognize their limitations.

The revised consensus began by recasting age as an index of multiple related changes rather than as an independent variable. Further, the revised framework became the life course rather than linear age (Neugarten 1968). A number of themes emerged.

First, in the Kansas City study of adult life, normative disengagement was replaced with activity (Havighurst 1961). Rather than needing or wishing to withdraw from activity, older people were found to revise their patterns and commitments in ways that fit their later life roles and opportunities. Leisure was conceptualized as multidimensional in meaning as well as in forms. More recently, this approach has led to a discovery of the "active old," those before and in retirement who adopt life styles of engagement in a variety of leisure activities and relationships. Further, such engagement has been found consistently to be a major factor in life satisfaction (Cutler and Hendricks 1990).

Second, the model of inevitable decrement was challenged by research that failed to measure high correlations between age and functional ability. Rather, a model of aging that stressed *continuity* rather than loss and change was applied to leisure as well as to other aspects of life (Atchley 1989). A return to earlier socialization studies provided a base for a revised model that identified lines of commitment rather than age-graded discontinuity. The "core" of daily accessible activity and interaction remains especially central to time allocation through the life course (Kelly 1983).

Third, the life course also provided a perspective in which intersecting work, leisure, and family roles and opportunities were related to developmental changes (Rapoport and Rapoport 1976). Leisure is not a list of activities dwindling with age but a social environment in which many critical issues of life may be worked out. Developing sexual identity for teens, expressing intimacy for those exploring and consolidating family commitments, reconstituting social contexts after mid-life disruptions, and ensuring social integration in later years are all central requirements of the life course that are developed in leisure. Not only interests but also significant identities are often found in leisure as well as in family and work (Gordon, Gaitz, and Scott 1976).

In the revised consensus, then, the life course with its interwoven work, family, and community roles was accepted as a valuable framework for analyzing both the continuities and changes of leisure. Leisure was seen as tied not only to role sequences but also to developmental preoccupations. The life course was found to incorporate revisions and reorientations rather than to consist of an inevitable downhill slide measured by participation rates in selected recreational pursuits.

AN INTEGRATED VIEW OF LIFE AND LEISURE. The regular and predictable transitions of the life course model, however, seem to gloss over many of the realities of contemporary life. A majority of adults in their middle or later years have experienced at least one disrupting trauma in health, work, or family that has required a fundamental reconstituting of roles and orientations (Kelly 1987b). Further, conditions are not the same for all persons in a social system. Race, gender, class, and ethnicity designate different life chances.

In this perspective of continuity and change in a metaphor of life as journey, a number of issues call for attention. First, salient differences in life conditions are more than variations in starting points for the journey. Rather, deprivation and denial are cumulative in ways that affect every dimension of life. Second, individuals come to define themselves in the actual circumstances of life, not in an abstracted concept. Identities, the concepts of the self that are central to what we believe is possible and probable in our lives, are developed in the realities of the life course. And, third, the structures of the society, including access to institutional power, provide forceful contexts of opportunity and denial that shape both direction and resources for the journey.

In this revised life course approach, leisure remains as a significant dimension, tied to family, work, education, community, and other elements of life. Changes in one may affect all the others. Leisure, then, is distinct from the product orientation of work and the intimate bonding of the family and yet connected to both.

LEISURE AND THE LIFE COURSE: NEW AGENDAS. From the perspective of the life course, research focusing on leisure now requires several revised issues, and among the most significant are the following.

First, leisure is woven through the life course. It is existential in a developmental sense. That is, leisure is action that involves *becoming,* action in which the actor becomes something more than before.

Second, the developmental orientation of some leisure is highlighted by this perspective that recognizes lines of action as well as singular events and episodes. What has been termed "serious leisure" by Stebbins (1979) is activity in which there is considerable personal investment in skills and often in equipment and organization. Such investment places serious leisure in a central position in identity formation and expression. Leisure identities may provide continuity through the transitions and traumas of the life course. Yet, how women and men define themselves and take action toward redefinition has been a subject of speculation more than research.

Third, what is the place of leisure in the schema of life investments and commitments? Further, how do those investments differ according to the life conditions of men and women as they make their way through the shifting expectations and possibilities of the life course? Gallier (1988) presents a model of the life course that emphasizes disruptions rather than linear progress. In an irregular life journey, work, family, and leisure may rise and fall both in salience and in the "chunks" of time they are allocated. Gallier proposes that education, production, and leisure become themes woven through life rather than discrete sequential periods.

The Nature of Leisure

As already suggested, perspectives on the nature of leisure have changed in the modern period of scholarly attention from the 1930s to the present. The change is not self-contained but reflects shifts in theoretical paradigms and draws from other disciplines, especially that of social psychology.

LEISURE AS FREE TIME AND MEANING. Despite repeated references to Greek roots and especially Aristotle, the first accepted operational definition of leisure was that of time. Leisure did not require that all other role obligations be completed but that the use of the time be more by choice than requirement. How choice was to be measured was seldom addressed. Concurrently, international "time-budget" research quantified leisure as one type of activity that could be identified by its form (Szalai 1974). Leisure was assumed to be clearly distinguished from work, required maintenance, and family responsibilities.

The first consensus, although persisting in many research designs, did not endure long without amendment. To begin with, it was obvious that any activity might be required, an extension of work or other roles. Further, even terms as simple as *choice* or *discretionary* implied that the actor's definition of the situation might be crucial.

In the 1970s, the field claimed more attention from psychologists who focused on attitudes rather than activities. Leisure was said to be defined by attitudes or a "state of mind" that included elements such as perceived freedom, intrinsic motivation, and a concentration on the experience rather than external ends (Neulinger 1974). Attention was directed toward meanings, but wholly in the actor rather than in definitions of the social context. Such psychological approaches were one salient influence on sociologists who added at least three dimensions to the earlier consensus regarding time and activity.

First, in the 1950s, the Kansas City research (Havighurst 1961) and the community studies tied leisure to social roles. The satisfactions one anticipated in an activity involved meanings and relationships one brought to the action context as well as what occurred in the time frame.

Second, the immediate experience might be the critical focus for leisure, but it occurs in particular environments that involve social learning, acquired skills and orientations (Csikszentmihalyi 1981), and interaction with components imported from other role relationships (Cheek and Burch 1976). Freedom is or is not perceived in actual circumstances.

Third, although the dimension of freedom recurs in the literature, studies of experiences and activity engagements found that leisure seldom is monodimensional. The meanings, outcomes, motivations, and experiences themselves are multifaceted (Havighurst 1961; Kelly 1978).

In the revised approaches, then, leisure is a more complex phenomenon than either the earlier sociologists or psychologists proposed. In fact, the consensus broke down under the weight of multiple approaches that ranged from individualistic psychology to functional sociology, from presumably self-evident quantities of time to interpretive self-definitions and lines of action, and from discrete self-presentations (Goffman 1967) to actions embedded in life course role sequences (Rapoport and Rapoport 1976).

REVOLT AGAINST THE ABSTRACT. Antithetical themes came from several directions. First, which is fundamental to accounting for life in society, the interpretive acts of the individual or the social context in which the action takes place (Giddens 1979)? Further, since the forms and symbols by which action is directed are learned and reinforced in the society, can action be prior to the context? The nature of leisure, then, is neither a contextual act nor a determined social role. Rather, it is actualized in processual action (Rojek 1990). And this process has continuities that extend beyond the immediate to personal development and the creation of significant communities (Kelly 1981).

Leisure is not entirely a free, creative, and community-building activity. It may also be, perhaps at the same time, stultifying and alienating.

Second, a number of critical analysts have raised questions about the positive cast usually given to leisure. Such positive approaches seem to presuppose resources, options, perspectives, and self-determination that are in fact unequally distributed in societies (Clarke and Critcher 1986). Do the unemployed and the poor have enough resources for discretion and choice to be meaningful concepts? Do histories of subjugation and life-defining limits for women in male-dominated societies make assumptions of self-determining action a sham? Such opportunity differences are most substantive in a market system of buying, renting, or otherwise acquiring resources. The real contexts of leisure are not voids of time and space but are extensions of the structures of the society and ideologies of the culture.

Third, a consequence of this distorted and constricted context of leisure is alienation. Leisure is not entirely a free, creative, authentic, and community-building activity. It may also be, perhaps at the same time, stultifying and alienating. It may separate rather than unite, narrow rather than expand, and entrap rather than free. It may, in short, be negative as well as positive. It is not a rarefied ideal or a perfect experience. It is real life, often involving struggle and conflict as well as development and expression.

The dialectic between expression and oppression that characterizes the rest of life in society is the reality of leisure as well. Being role-based in a stratified society means being limited, directed, and excluded. The contexts of any experience, however free and exhilerating, are the real culture and social system. The multiple meanings of leisure include separation as well as community, determination as well as creation, and routine as well as expression. The former simplicity of leisure as essentially a "good thing" becomes alloyed by situating it in the real society with all its forces, pressures, and conflicts.

LEISURE AS A DIMENSION OF LIFE. The question is, then, what does such extension and critique do to any conceptualization of the nature of leisure? Leisure encompasses both the existential and the social. It has myriad forms, locales, social settings, and outcomes. Leisure is neither separated from social roles nor wholly determined by them. Leisure has developed amid conflict as well as amid social consensus, in division as well as in integration, with control as well as with freedom. It may involve acquiescence as well as resistance, alienation as well as authenticity, and preoccupation with self as well as commitment to community. Leisure, then, is multidimensional and cannot be characterized by any single or simple element.

A further issue is whether leisure is really a domain of life at all. Is leisure clearly distinguished from work, family, community, church, and school, or is it a dimension of action and interaction within them all? In the childhood and adolescent periods, leisure is a social space for the exploration and development of sexual identities as well as for working out the issues of peer identification and independence from parents and the past. It also stresses the theme of expression that is central to developing a sense of selfhood, of personal identity among emerging social roles. In the early adult period, leisure adds the dimension of bonding to intimate others, especially in the formation and consolidation of the family. In later years, leisure has meanings tied to integration with significant other persons and to maintaining a sense of ability when some work and community roles are lost. Leisure, then, might be conceptualized as being woven into the intersecting role sequences of the life course rather than being a segregated realm of activity. Productivity is not limited to work, bonding to the family, learning and development to education, or expression to leisure. Production, bonding and community, learning and development, and relative freedom and self-authenticating experience may all be found in any domain of life.

Yet, there must also be distinguishing elements of leisure, or it disappears into the ongoing round of life. Further, those elements should be significant in relation to central issues of life such as production and work, love and community, sexuality and gender, learning and development, emotion and involvement. It should connect with the lived conditions of ordinary life rather than be an esoteric and precious idea to be actualized only in rare and elite conditions.

Leisure, then, may be more a dimension than a domain, more a theme than an identifiable realm (Kelly 1987a). That dimension is characterized by three elements: First, it is action in the inclusive sense of doing something, of intentioned and deliberate act. Such action is existential in producing an outcome with meaning to the actor. Second, this action is focused on the experience more than on the result. It is done primarily because of what occurs in the defined time and space. And, third, leisure as a dimension of life is characterized by freedom more than by necessity. It is not required by any role, coercive power, or repressive ideology. Leisure is not detached from its social and cultural contexts but is a dimension of relatively self-determined act within such contexts. Its meaning is not in its products as much as in the experience, not in its forms as much as in its expression.

The sociology of leisure, then, is not a closed book or a finalized product. Rather, central issues are currently being raised that promise to reform the field in its premises as well as conclusions. No common wisdom will go unchallenged, no consensus remain unchanged, and no theoretical formulation be above conflict. Yet every challenge, conflict, and developing synthesis provides a new basis for at least one conclusion: Leisure is a significant dimension of life that calls for both disciplined and innovative attention.

[See also Life Course.]

BIBLIOGRAPHY

Atchley, Robert 1989 "A Continuity Theory of Normal Aging." *Gerontologist* 29:183–190.

Blauner, Robert 1964 *Alienation and Freedom: The Factory Worker and His Industry.* Chicago: University of Chicago Press.

Cheek, Neil, and William Burch 1976 *The Social Organization of Leisure in Human Society.* New York: Harper and Row.

Clarke, John, and Charles Critcher 1985 *The Devil Makes Work: Leisure in Capitalist Britain.* Champaign: University of Illinois Press.

Csikszentmihalyi, Mihaly 1981 "Leisure and Socialization." *Social Forces* 60:332–340.

Cutler, Stephen, and Jon Hendricks 1990 "Leisure and Time Use across the Life Course." In R. Binstock and L. George, eds.,

Handbook of Aging and the Social Sciences. 3rd ed. New York: Academic Press.

Deem, Rosemary 1986 *All Work and No Play: The Sociology of Women and Leisure.* Milton Keynes, UK: Open University Press.

Dumazedier, Joffre 1967 *Toward a Society of Leisure.* New York: Free Press.

Gallier, Xavier 1988 *La deuxieme carrière: Âges, emplois, retraite.* Paris: Éditions du Seuil.

Giddens, Anthony 1979 *Central Problems in Social Theory: Action, Structure, and Contradiction in Social Analysis.* Berkeley: University of California Press.

Goffman, Erving 1967 *Interaction Ritual.* New York: Anchor Books.

Gordon, Chad, C. Gaitz, and J. Scott 1976 "Leisure and Lives: Personal Expressivity across the Life Span." In R. Binstock and E. Shanas, *Handbook of Aging and the Social Sciences.* New York: Van Nostrand Reinhold.

Habermas, Jurgen 1975 *Legitimation Crisis.* Boston: Beacon Press.

Havighurst, Robert 1961 "The Nature and Values of Meaningful Free-Time Activity." In R. Kleemeier, ed., *Aging and Leisure.* New York: Oxford University Press.

Henderson, Karla, M. Deborah Bialeschki, Susan M. Shaw, and Valeria J. Freysinger 1989 *A Leisure of One's Own.* State College, Pa.: Venture Publishing.

Kelly, John R. 1978 "Situational and Social Factors in Leisure Decisions." *Pacific Sociological Review* 21:313–330.

——— 1981 "Leisure Interaction and the Social Dialectic." *Social Forces* 60:304–322.

——— 1983 *Leisure Identities and Interactions.* London: Allen and Unwin.

——— 1987a *Freedom to Be: A New Sociology of Leisure.* New York: Macmillan.

——— 1987b *Peoria Winter: Styles and Resources in Later Life.* Lexington, Mass.: Lexington Books.

Lundberg, George, Mirra Komarovsky, and M. McInerney 1934 *Leisure: a Suburban Study.* New York: Columbia University Press.

Lynd, Helen, and Robert Lynd 1956 *Middletown.* New York: Harcourt Brace.

Marx, Karl 1970 *The Economic and Philosophical Manuscripts of 1844.* M. Milligan, trans. London: Lawrence and Wishart.

Neugarten, Bernice 1968 *Middle Age and Aging.* Chicago: University of Chicago Press.

Neulinger, John 1974 *The Psychology of Leisure.* Springfield, Ill.: C. C. Thomas.

Parker, Stanley 1971 *The Future of Work and Leisure.* New York: Praeger.

Rapoport, Rhona, and Robert Rapoport 1976 *Leisure and the Family Life Cycle.* London: Routledge and Kegan Paul.

Roberts, Kenneth 1970 *Leisure.* London: Longmans.

Rojek, Chris 1985 *Capitalism and Leisure Theory.* London: Tavistock.

——— 1990 "Leisure and Recreation Theory." In E. Jackson and T. Burton, eds., *Understanding Leisure and Recreation.* State College, Pa.: Venture Publishing.

Stebbins, Robert 1979 *Amateurs: On the Margin between Work and Leisure.* Beverly Hills, Calif.: Sage.

Szalai, Alexander 1974 *The Use of Time: Daily Activities of Urban and Suburban Populations in Twelve Countries.* The Hague: Mouton.

Veblen, Thorstein [1899] 1953 *The Theory of the Leisure Class.* New York: New American Library.

Wilensky, Harold 1960 "Work, Careers, and Social Integration." *International Social Science Journal* 12:543–560.

Wilson, John 1980 "Sociology of Leisure." *Annual Review of Sociology* 6:21–40.

– JOHN R. KELLY

LIBERALISM/CONSERVATISM

"Is (or was) Blank a liberal?" The precise reply to this question inevitably begins with a throat-clearing preface such as, "It all depends on the period you have in mind—and the place. Are you speaking of someone in nineteenth-century England, the United States during the Franklin Roosevelt New Deal days, contemporary Great Britain, continental Europe, or contemporary U.S.A.?"

For Americans nurtured on the "liberal" tradition of Franklin Delano Roosevelt and the Democratic party, the significance of the *L* word was quite clear. The private business establishment, left to its own devices, had brought about the economic collapse of 1929. "Rugged individualism" had demonstrated its inadequacies even for many rugged individualists themselves. Almost two-thirds of a century after that collapse, the Great American Depression still retains the power to evoke terrifying memories of mass unemployment, bank failures, small business bankruptcies, soup kitchens, and popular ditties like "Brother can you spare a dime?" These were all nostalgic but chilling reminiscences of the desolation to which "nonliberal," or "conservative," social, economic, and political policies had led. There seems to persist an enormous reluctance to release this era and its memories to the historians as just another noteworthy episode in American history like the War of 1812 or the Panic of 1873.

For other Americans, some of whom matured perhaps too rapidly during the late 1960s and whose memories were filled with visions of the war in Vietnam, the battles for Civil Rights, and the turmoil in urban ghettos, things were much less clear. Stalwarts of liberalism like Hubert Humphrey (senator, vice president, and unsuccessful Democratic candidate for President) seemed to become part of the very establishment toward which hostility was directed. Government, instead of representing a liberating force, increasingly was seen as the source of existing difficulties. Liberalism, for many, was no longer the solution; it had become part of the problem.

Liberalism has often been identified with the struggle to free individuals from the confining embraces of other persons, institutions, or even habitual ways of behaving. It is seen by its advocates as a liberating orientation. Thoughts that, in various times and places, have been called liberal, all seem to have as their common denominator this fundamental notion of freedom for individual human beings.

It was during the period between the Reformation and the French Revolution that a new social class emerged. Political control by a landowning aristocracy was challenged by this new class whose power lay only in the control of movable capital. It consisted of such people as bankers, traders, and manufacturers. Science began to replace religion as the source of ultimate authority; contract replaced status as the legal foundation of society. The ideas of individual initiative and individual control became the basis for a new philosophy: liberalism (Laski 1962, p. 11).

During the period between the Reformation and the French Revolution, the ideas of individual initiative and control became the basis for a new philosophy: liberalism.

Liberalism began as the champion of freedom and the foe of privilege derived from inherited class position. But freedom was not fought for on behalf of everyone in society. The constituency of liberalism consisted of those who had property to defend. Its supporters sought to limit the range of political authority and tried to develop a system of fundamental rights not subject to invasion by the state (Laski 1962, p. 13). Most of the population (e.g., factory and agricultural workers) were not initially included in the concerns of liberalism. But redefinitions of governmental concerns and authority inevitably had consequences for all members of society. Thoughtful economists and others soon realized this.

Thus, from the perspective of the closing years of twentieth-century America, it is easy to forget that classical economists like Adam Smith and David Ricardo, far from being simply reflex ideologists for the business establishment, were deeply concerned about liberty for individuals and saw their classical economic doctrines as the best way to insure it. In this sense, many contemporary Americans could legitimately view them as representatives of the liberal, rather than the conservative, genre. The *free enterprise* game was originally a liberal game.

For many participants in this great game of free enterprise, it became increasingly more obvious that the game was "fixed," that somehow participants did not emerge with either their liberty or their pocketbooks intact. To insure even a modicum of freedom and liberty for individuals, it became necessary to provide them with a helping hand from a source outside the marketplace. This source, a powerful and beneficent outsider, the national government, could help monitor the rules and to some extent the play of the economic game. It *could* provide, for heavy losers or potential losers, social benefits in the form of such consolations as unemployment insurance, old age pensions, insured bank accounts, and coordinated measures to combat environmental pollution. It *could* help protect consumers from the harmful effects of adulterated food and drug products; it *could* protect workers from the hazards of unregulated workplaces. In short the liberal ethos in twentieth-century America incorporated as one of its tenets reliance on government action to protect the liberty of individuals.

The conservative ethos, on the other hand, during the same period has been characterized by a hands-off posture with respect to many aspects of government policy. This constitutes a fascinating reversal of traditional conservatism. The shades of Edmund Burke and other historical conservative spirits might well cringe at the characterization of their philosophy as "less government."

For some observers, this liberal-conservative contrast seems to be based on different psychological sets, or frames, of mind. Thus, we have been told that liberals are more hospitable to change, more willing to reexamine institutions and established practices in the light of new problems and needs. From this perspective, conservatives are those who appeal to the experience of the past but do not learn from it. Liberals are presented as being less reverent of the status quo, more venturesome in the realm of ideas, and much more optimistic about the possibilities available through exploration and discovery (Girvetz 1966).

Willingness to change becomes meaningful only when viewed against the nature of the status quo. When "liberal" governments adopt measures to provide for persons who are aged, ill, unemployed, or handicapped (as they have in some Scandinavian countries), to be "liberal" may mean to *retain* the status quo. To eliminate the measures—to engage in change—may be precisely what Western conservatives might demand.

For many observers of the dramatic events occurring at the end of the 1980s and in the early 1990s in Eastern Europe, members of communist parties who struggled to maintain their power in government were labeled "conservatives." Those fighting for *free enterprise* and other capitalist-like changes were called "liberal reformers." Communists for many years had been viewed by Western conservatives as the ultimate enemy; liberals were characteristically referred to by many of these conservatives as thinly disguised "Reds." In a dramatic and even comic reversal, dedicated Stalinists were now described as "conservatives."

At one time or another a wide variety of ideas have been called conservative. There have been efforts, however, to reduce the essence of these ideas to a limited number of more or less well defined notions. Clinton Rossiter and Russell Kirk, two ardent defenders of the conservative faith, once prepared a summary that received widespread approval. Although not all conservatives would necessarily agree with everything appearing in their summary, "it would be exceedingly difficult to find a conservative who did not agree with a good deal of what Professors Kirk and Rossiter impute to their tradition" (Witonski 1971, pp. 34–35).

The imputation begins with an assumption about the more or less immutable character of human nature. Behind the curtain of civilized behavior there exists, in human beings, wickedness, unreason, and an urge to engage in violence. In addition, a great deal of emphasis is placed upon the conviction that people are not naturally equal in most qualities of mind, body, and spirit. Liberty is more important than social equality. This leads to the conclusion that society must always have its classes. It is futile to level or eliminate them. Accordingly, societies will always require ruling aristocracies; efforts to have majority rule will lead to errors and potential tyranny.

Human beings, this conservative ethos insists, are not born with rights. These are earned as a result of duties performed. Service, effort, obedience, cultivation of virtue and self-restraint are the price of rights. Of primary importance to liberty, order, and progress, is the institution of private property. Inherited institutions, values, symbols, and rituals are indispensable and even sacred. Human reason is subject to error and severely limited; the surest guide to wisdom and virtue is historical experience.

Beyond this, fundamental to conservatism is the belief that all political problems are fundamentally religious in nature. Narrow rationality cannot, in itself, satisfy human needs. Both society and conscience are ruled by divine intent. Conservatives, it is asserted, have an affection for the traditional life; others (presumably liberals) favor narrow uniformity, egalitarianism, and pursuit of utilitarian goals. The only true equality is moral equality; civilized society requires orders and classes. Property and freedom are inseparable. If property is separated from private possession, liberty disappears.

This basic conservative creed goes on to say that human beings have anarchic impulses and are governed more by emotion than by reason. It therefore becomes necessary to place controls on human appetite. The correct method of accomplishing this is through tradition and sound "prejudice."

Finally, the proper instrument for social change is Providence. Some change is necessary from time to time to conserve society. It is like the perpetual renewal of the human body. But this change must always be accomplished slowly and with an awareness of the direction in which Providence is moving social forces (Witonski 1971, pp. 32–34).

Undergirding the entire structure of this conservative doctrine is a more or less explicit version of the *chain of being.* This metaphor is designed to express the enormous extent, variety, order, and unity of "God's Creation." The chain stretches from the foot of God's throne to the meanest of inanimate objects. Every speck of creation is a link in this chain, and every link except those at the two extremities is simultaneously bigger and smaller than another; there can be no gap (Tillyard 1959). The classic examination of the history of this idea was written by Arthur S. Lovejoy (1960).

Every category of things excels at *something.* Plants are higher than stones, but stones are stronger and more durable. Animals ("beasts") are above plants, but plants can assimilate nourishment better. Human beings are above beasts but inferior to them in physical energy and desires.

All this suggests a sort of interdependency among all objects and living creatures. Central to the idea of the chain is the concept that every object, animal or person, is part of an all-encompassing whole. Basic to the metaphor is an implicit, if not always explicit, view of the universe as an organism (strong traces of this continue to be found in some formulations of contemporary systems theory).

Pushed to its logical conclusion, this suggests that all creatures and objects are equally important. Every existing part of the cosmic organism might well be seen as necessary (perhaps in some unknown way) for the survival of the whole. This, in turn implies that, although they do different things, all human beings, for example, are equally necessary. This logic could lead to dangerous subversive doctrines about social equality. Another feature was required to make the chain-of-being notion acceptable to those searching for reasons to justify existing inequalities in human societies. This was found in the *primacy doctrine,* the idea that, within each category of objects and creatures, there is one above the others, a *primate.* The eagle is first among birds; the whale or dolphin, among "fishes"; the rose, among flowers; the fire, among elements; the lion or elephant, among beasts; and, naturally, the emperor, among men (Tillyard 1959, pp. 29–30).

More recently, the distinguished conservative sociologist Robert Nisbet has insisted that conservatism is simply one of three major political ideologies of the eighteenth and nineteenth centuries. The other two are *liberalism* and *socialism.* Interestingly, an ideology for him, in addition to having a "reasonably" coherent body of ideas, has a *power base* that makes possible a victory for the body of ideas. It extends over a period of time and has "major" advocates or spokespersons as well as a "respectable" degree of institutionalization and charismatic figures. For conservatism, these figures would include people like Edmund Burke, Benjamin Disraeli, and Winston Churchill. Liberals have their own counterparts to these. The philosophical substance of conservatism dates from 1790 with the publication of Edmund Burke's *Reflections on the Revolution in France* (Nisbet 1986; Burke 1855).

There is a fascinating contradiction to be found in conservative doctrine. Methodologically, Nisbet offers it as a champion of historical method. This he approves of as an alternative to the liberal utilitarianism of Jeremy Bentham that is "soulless," "mechanical," and even "inhuman." Bentham's doctrine idolizes pure reason, but human beings require a different mode of thought, one based on feelings, emotions, and long experience, as well as on pure logic.

In attacking liberal utilitarianism, Nisbet is attacking a doctrine essentially abandoned by twentieth-century American liberals. Sociologist L. T. Hobhouse must be credited with having made the most serious effort to reformulate liberal doctrine.

Utilitarianism, as fashioned by Jeremy Bentham and his followers, was the visible core of nineteenth-century liberalism. It has been defined as "nothing but an attempt to apply the principles of Newton to the affairs of politics and morals" (Halevy 1972, p. 6). The principle of utility, the notion that every possible action of human beings is either taken or not depending upon whether it is seen as resulting in either pleasure or pain, was the basis for an "objective science" of behavior modeled on the physical sciences. As such, in common with other alleged sciences, it was perhaps congenitally soulless, somewhat mechanical, and potentially inhuman. Using a "rational" (but not empirically derived) model, it announced that, by pursuing his or her own pleasure and avoiding pain, each person would maximize happiness for everyone. Society was simply a collection of separate individuals operating in their individual self-interests. Government action, or "interference," constituted a disservice to these individuals and should be rejected on "scientific" grounds.

Hobhouse took issue with this view but modestly presented John Stuart Mill as the transition figure between the old and new liberalisms. Mill, reared on Benthamite doctrine, continually brought it into contact with fresh experience and new trains of thought. As a result, Mill is, "the easiest person in the world to convict of inconsistency, incompleteness, and lack of rounded system. Hence also his work will survive the death of many consistent, complete, and perfectly rounded systems" (Hobhouse 1964, p. 58).

Hobhouse noted that, although the life of society is, ultimately, the life of individuals as they act upon each other, the lives of individuals would be quite different if they were separated from society. He stressed the fact that collective social action does not necessarily involve coercion or restraint. The state is simply one of many forms of human association, a form to which individuals owe much more of their personal security and freedom than most people recognize. "The value of a site in London," he pointed out, "is something due essentially to London, not to the landlord. More accurately, a part of it is due to London, a part to the British empire, a part, perhaps we should say, to Western civilization" (Hobhouse 1964, p. 100). "Democracy," he tells us, "is not founded merely on the right or the private interest of the individual. . . . It is founded equally on the function of the individual as a member of the community" (Hobhouse 1964, p. 116).

Collective social action does not necessarily involve coercion or restraint.

In sum, Hobhouse helped provide a theoretic basis for a twentieth-century liberalism severed from the constricted framework of its origins and aimed at the liberation of *all* members of society. It continues to be very much concerned with feelings, emotions, and historical experience. Twentieth-century *conservatism* assumed the mantle of rigid utilitarianism shorn of its humanistic aspirations.

The contradictions in conservative doctrine become even more apparent when the matter of prejudice is considered. As Nisbet explains it, prejudice has its own intrinsic wisdom anterior to intellect. It can be readily applied in emergencies and does not leave one indecisive at the moment of decision. It sums up in an individual mind tradition's authority and wisdom (Nisbet 1986, p. 29).

This seems to epitomize the "mechanical" thought attributed to utilitarian or enlightenment liberals. Prejudice, in these terms, is, in effect, a mode of preprogrammed decision making. It insists upon shackling the human mind when confronted with new or unforeseen situations. It demands that such situations be dealt with through the use of what may well be outdated modes of thought, with strategies that were perhaps once useful but have lost their relevance. It denies a role for human creativity.

It is but a step from this doctrine to the prejudice castigated by civil rights activists and others. We meet a man whose skin is black or yellow; we meet a woman whose features tell us she is Jewish. We have preprogrammed responses to each of these, based on the "wisdom" of tradition, informing us that they, in various ways, are inferior creatures who must be dealt with accordingly.

The feudal origins of conservative doctrine are seen most clearly in its adamant stand on the issue of inheritance and property. Not only does it fight all efforts to loosen property from family groups by means of taxation, it fights all other efforts to redistribute wealth, ranging from special entitlements to affirmative action programs. It insists upon the indestructibility of existing hierarchical structures in society, seeing all efforts to modify them as attacks on cultural and psychological diversity.

Further complicating the distinction between liberalism and conservatism has been what some might refer to as a fringe movement within conservatism, called *neoconservatism.*

One explanation for the emergence of this phenomenon begins by noting that in the mid-1960s American universities, as well as literature and art in general, had become increasingly radicalized. Some cold war liberals, others who were uncomfortable with black power politics, and some critics of the counterculture disengaged themselves from liberalism. Prominent names in this group include Irving Kristol, Norman Podhoretz, and sociologists Seymour Martin Lipset, Nathan Glazer, Daniel Bell, and James Coleman. Some of these continue to reject the label but "it is as though by some invisible hand their writings and lectures gave help to the conservative cause when it was needed" (Nisbet 1986, p. 101).

Periodicals most strongly identified with neoconservatism are *The Public Interest* and *Commentary.* Neoconservatives have had close ties with the Scaife, Smith Richardson, John M. Olin, and other foundations. They have appeared as resident scholars and trustees of think tanks like the Hoover Institution, The Heritage Foundation, and the American Enterprise Institute (Gottfried and Fleming 1988, p. 73).

Unlike more traditional conservatives, neoconservatives are not irrevocably opposed to some possible versions of a welfare state. They do not depend upon historical methodology; on the contrary, they seem to show a marked preference for quantification.

Thus, the difference between contemporary liberalism and conservatism is apparently not to be found in issues of methodology, personality, or individual items of public policy. Yet there seems to remain an ineradicable core of difference. Ultimately this must be sought in the structure of material interests on the one hand and values on the other.

Historically, conservative doctrine was formulated as an intellectual defense of feudal property rights against the onslaughts of an emerging, business-oriented, industrializing bourgeoisie. Liberalism, with its early defense of individualism, championed the enemies of conservative doctrine and properly (from its perspective) fought against dominance by a central governing authority. Subsequently (as in the case of New Deal liberalism), it discovered that the logic of unhampered individualism led to serious economic difficulties for large numbers of the population. Experiments with varieties of the welfare state since the days of Bismarck probably can all be traced in considerable measure to the fear of more drastic consequences that might follow any effort to persist in an uncontrolled laissez-faire economy.

Government-sponsored lotteries hold out the hope of dramatic changes in class position.

In the contemporary world complexity has become compounded. It has probably always been the case that some people refuse to act in accordance with their own more or less self-evident material interests. These days, however, the arts of propaganda and advertising have been raised to a level of effective applied science. It is difficult for many to recognize exactly where their own self-interest lies. Beyond this, numerous techniques have been developed with the practical effect of inducing many to adopt positions in marked contrast to their own existing material interests. Government-sponsored lotteries hold out the hope of dramatic changes in class position. Tales of fabulous profits to be made in real estate or the stock market induce many to identify with the interests toward which they aspire rather than with those they hold and are likely to retain.

This is not the only source of confusion. Although many intellectuals, as well as others, having "made it," subsequently become concerned with the maintenance of an order that has been good to them (Coser 1977), there are many others who, despite coming from very well-to-do backgrounds, maintain values consistent with economic deprivation. There are indeed generous souls as well as villains to be found among adherents of both liberalism and conservatism.

The shape of values is by no means always coterminous with the shape of existing material interests. Labels like liberalism and conservatism are uncertain predictors of specific actions, as are existing material interests. A variety of social forms, or structures, can be used to serve either selfish or communally oriented values. It is these values that are ultimately more reliable auguries.

In recent years there have been efforts to develop more useful theoretical frameworks for conceptualizing value configurations and more empirically based social policy alternatives. For example, Amitai Etzioni has elaborated an "I-We" paradigm as a substitute for both "unfettered" individualism and organismic views of society (Etzioni 1988). S. M. Miller and his colleagues eschew the *liberal* label in favor of *progressive,* a term less saddled with conflicting conceptual baggage. They have provided an agenda for social policy issues requiring considerable rethinking by those unwilling to accept either contemporary conservative and neoconservative doctrine or traditional socialist formulations (Ansara and Miller 1986).

It is clear that serious linguistic difficulties serve to exacerbate the problem of distinguishing clearly between liberalism and conservatism. Each term tends to represent a generic symbol for a range of widely diversified issues, values, and interests. Surrogate expressions are used extensively in popular speech to convey either finer shades of meaning or degrees of opprobrium.

For conservatives these expressions may include "right-wing crazies," "extreme right," "right-wing," "supply-siders," "libertarians," "filthy rich," "Republicans," and others. In contemporary America, portions of the conservative spectrum voice strong opinions not only on economic issues but also on such "social" issues as pornography, abortion, and affirmative action, although opinion on these issues is by no means unanimous. Traditional conservatism would, of course, back state-supported cultural standards in speech, art, literature, and entertainment. Nineteenth-century liberalism would oppose these in the name of individual "rights." Is abortion a woman's "right" or is it an "offense" against society? Many conservatives might define it as an offense; others might well define it as a right—a traditional liberal position.

Among liberals, surrogate expressions in use include "Red," "parlor-pink," "left-liberal," "bleeding heart," "tax and spender," "Democrat," and "Progressive." The liberal spectrum tends to support rights of women to have abortions or, more generally, to maintain control over their own bodies. It opposes abrogation of rights of self-expression through pornography legislation, cen-

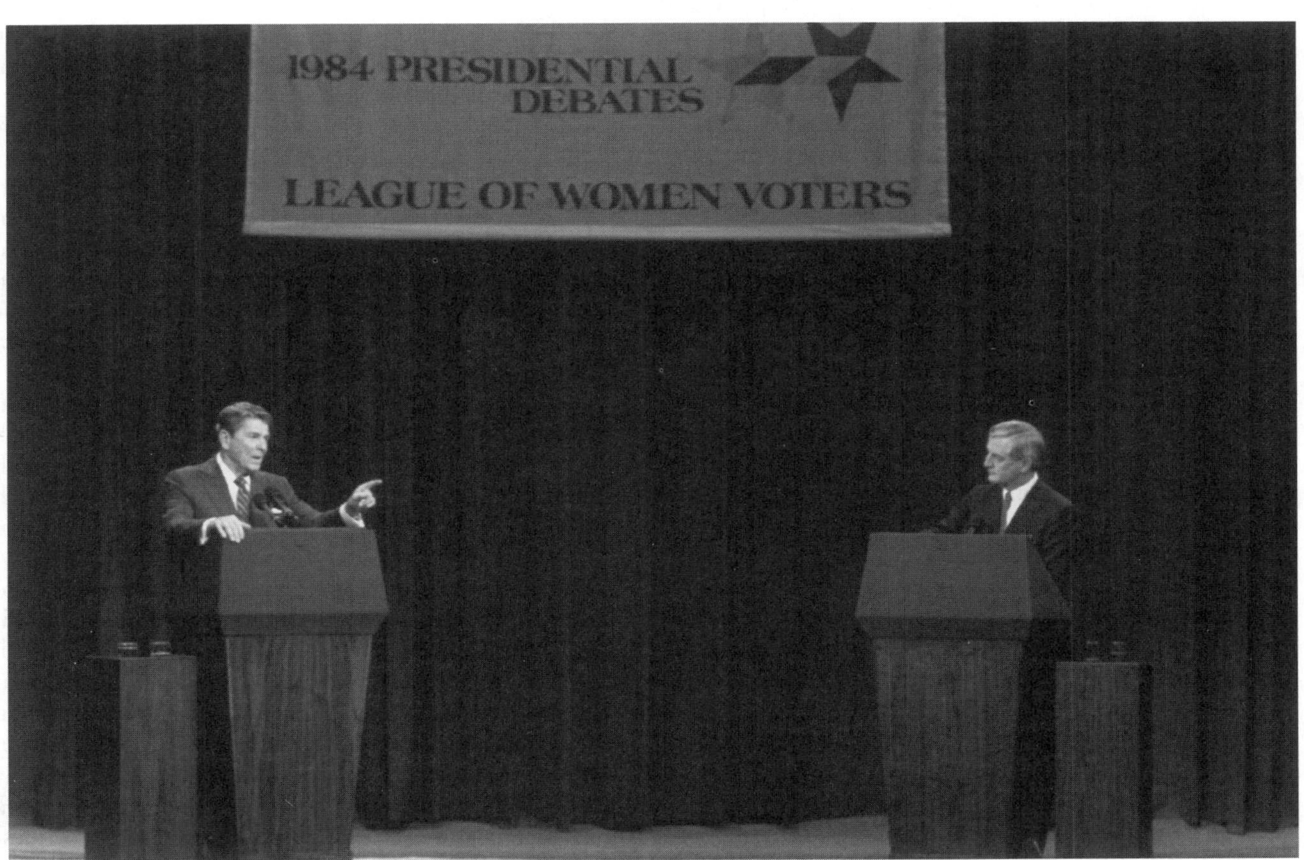

People often label Republicans as conservative and Democrats as liberals, but these terms are generic and fail to account for the unique political views of individuals. (Ronald Reagan Library/Corbis)

sorship, or other efforts to monitor art, literature, theatre, and other communication vehicles. On the other hand, American liberals favor limitations on the asserted "rights" of corporations or individual business persons to discriminate in employment, housing, and other areas on the basis of skin color, age, religion, or physical disability—property rights that many conservatives insist are inviolable.

As one might expect, survey researchers have made and continue to make strong efforts to detect empirical differences between persons who are called or who call themselves liberal or conservative. Data from a variety of survey research studies indicate that, despite the existence of important philosophical differences between liberals and conservatives, changing social and economic conditions have at times compelled them to alter their positions on certain economic, social, and political issues without altering their underlying philosophies (McCloskey and Zaller 1984, p. 191). In general, these studies seem to confirm stereotypical images of both liberals and conservatives.

Liberals show a marked preference for social progress and human betterment, especially for the poor and powerless. Some believe personal happiness and success depend heavily upon institutional arrangements. Most liberals are "inveterate reformers"; they continually look for ways to improve the human condition by remodeling social, economic, and political institutions. Underlying this pursuit of change, social reform, and benevolence is faith in the potential perfectability of human beings and their capacity to manage their own affairs in a responsible and reasoned fashion.

Conservatives have a different notion of what constitutes the good society and how it can be achieved. Survey research data show that they have a more pessimistic view of human nature and its perfectability. They feel that people need strong leaders, firm laws and institutions, and strict moral codes to keep their appetites under control. Firm adherence to conventional norms and practices is essential for human well-being. They believe that those who fail in life must bear primary responsibility for its consequences. They are far less likely than liberals to support movements that have as their objectives the eradication of poverty, the better treatment of oppressed minorities, or the alleviation of social distress generally. They maintain that these movements, by disrupting existing institutions, do more harm than good (McCloskey and Zaller 1984, pp. 190–191).

Conventional public opinion polling techniques encounter increasing difficulties in this area. Thus, one study examined a hypothesized inverse relationship between socioeconomic status and conservatism on a wide range of so-called social issues. (Many observers felt that, during the 1970s and 1980s, as well as during the late 1960s, the main support for liberal and left political parties in the United States and other Western industrialized countries came from youthful members of the upper or middle strata.) It found that, in practice, many issues defied a neat separation of interests and values or of economic versus social arenas. Many social issues such as environmental protection, nuclear power, defense spending, and race or gender problems have an economic dimension, to the extent that they influence opportunities for jobs or profits. Conversely, government domestic spending, a classic economic issue, may have a social dimension if it is seen as involving welfare or aid to minorities. No consistent relationship between socioeconomic status and conservatism was found, with one exception. Liberalism on social issues tends to increase with education, but even here the relationship varies considerably from issue to issue. The authors suggest that lack of a consistent relationship reflects both the diversity of social issues and the fuzziness of the social/economic distinction (Himmelstein and McCrae 1988).

Another study examined what appeared to be an anomaly in this area. It postulated that high socioeconomic status remains one of the best predictors of Republican party support and conservative attitudes in the United States, that Republicans are wealthier, more educated, and hold higher status jobs than Democrats and independents. Jewish liberalism, however, confounds this general relationship. American Jews are generally wealthier, better educated, and hold higher status jobs than average Americans but continue to be the most liberal white ethnic group in the United States (Lerner, Nagai, and Rothman 1989, p. 330).

The emergence of a small cadre of Jewish neoconservative intellectuals has raised questions about Jewish liberalism. A sample of Jewish elites was compared with their Gentile counterparts. The study found that Jewish elites continue to be more liberal. Despite a plethora of competing explanations, the study concludes that Jewish liberalism is a product of a family tradition of liberalism that developed in response to European conditions. Specifically, the authors suggest that the Jewish elites inherited a tradition of responding in particular ways to felt marginality. This raises the question as to whether a realignment might occur when this cohort of American Jews loses its prominence and is replaced by a cohort with different patterns of socialization. In a concluding footnote, the authors raise the open question of whether events in the Middle East and the emergence in the Democratic party of an increasingly powerful African-American presence less supportive of Israel can transform the liberalism of American Jews (Lerner, Nagai, and Rothman 1989).

A study of public opinion on nuclear power concludes that assessing public opinion through responses to survey questions with fixed categories presents serious difficulties. It compares these difficulties with those arising from the effort to "impose elite dichotomies such as 'liberal' and 'conservative' on a mass public whose beliefs are not organized by such dimensions" (Gamson and Modigliani 1989, p. 36).

Perhaps the more general difficulty is not to be found solely in the insufficiency of measuring instruments but in the increasingly more truncated vistas of the "mass publics." Fundamental philosophical positions and value orientations seem to have become increasingly more obscured by the exigencies of short-range decision making.

In societies where immediate job opportunities, social pressures, and short-range profits have serious implications not only for the quality of life but also for existence itself, it is scarcely surprising to find that many public issues and even individual values are filtered through the prisms of short-run individual economic concerns and ethnic identification. Manipulating perceptions of vital interests through sophisticated media technology does much to resolve the recurrent riddle, "Is Blank a liberal—or a conservative?"

[See also Attitudes; Public Opinion; Voting Behavior.]

BIBLIOGRAPHY

Ansara, Michael, and S. M. Miller 1986 "Opening Up of Progressive Thought." *Social Policy* 17:3–10.

Burke, Edmund 1855 "Reflections on the Revolution in France." In *Works,* Vol. 1. New York: Harper.

Coser, Lewis A. "Introduction." In Coser, Lewis A., and Irving Howe, eds. 1977 *The New Conservatives: A Critique from the Left.* New York: Meridian.

Etzioni, Amatai 1988 *The Moral Dimension: Toward a New Economics.* New York: Free Press.

Gamson, William A., and Andre Modigliani 1989 "Media Discourse and Public Opinion on Nuclear Power: A Constructionist Approach." *American Journal of Sociology* 95:1–37.

Girvetz, Harry K. 1966 *The Evolution of Liberalism.* New York: Collier.

Gottfried, Paul, and Thomas Fleming 1988 *The Conservative Movement.* Boston: Twayne.

Halevy, Elie (1928) 1972 *The Growth of Philosophic Radicalism,* trans. Mary Morris. London: Faber and Faber.

Himmelstein, Jerome L., and James A. McRae, Jr. 1988 "Social Issues and Socioeconomic Status." *Public Opinion Quarterly* 52:492–512.

Hobhouse, L. T. (1911) 1964 *Liberalism.* New York: Oxford University Press.

Laski, Harold J. (1936) 1962 *The Rise of European Liberalism.* New York: Barnes & Noble.

Lerner, Robert, Althea K. Nagai, and Stanley Rothman 1989 "Marginality and Liberalism Among Jewish Elites." *Public Opinion Quarterly* 53:330–352.

Lovejoy, Arthur 1960 *The Great Chain of Being: A Study of the History of an Idea.* New York: Meridian.

McCloskey, Herbert, and John Zaller 1984 *The American Ethos: Public Attitudes Toward Capitalism and Democracy.* (A Twentieth Century Fund Report) Cambridge, Mass.: Harvard University Press.

Nisbet, Robert 1986 *Conservatism.* Minneapolis: University of Minnesota Press.

Tillyard, E. M. W. 1959 *The Elizabethan World Picture.* New York: Vintage.

Witonski, Peter (ed.) 1971 *The Wisdom of Conservatives,* vol. 1. New York: Arlington.

— ROBERT BOGUSLAW

LIFE COURSE

The study of lives represents an enduring interest of the social sciences and reflects important social changes over the twentieth century. Most notably, developments after World War II called for new ways of thinking about lives, society, and their connection. Launched in the 1920s and 1930s, pioneering longitudinal studies of children in the United States became studies of the young adult in post-war America, thereby focusing attention on trajectories that extend across specific life stages. In addition, the changing demography of society assigned greater significance to problems of aging and study of them. Insights regarding old age directed inquiry to earlier phases of life and to the process by which life patterns are shaped by a changing society.

The life course represents a concept and a theoretical perspective. As a concept, it refers to age-graded life patterns embedded in social institutions and subject to historical change. The life course consists of interlocking trajectories or pathways across the lifespan that are marked by sequences of social transitions. As a theoretical orientation, the life course has established a common field of inquiry by providing a framework that guides research in terms of problem identification and formulation, variable selection and rationales, and strategies of design and analysis.

Conceptual Distinctions

A number of concepts have been applied interchangeably to studies of life patterns (life course, life cycle, lifespan, and life history), but each makes a distinctive contribution that deserves notice in mapping the conceptual domain. The *life course* is defined by trajectories that extend across much of the life course, such as family and work; and by short-term changes or transitions, such as leaving home, getting a full-time job, and marrying (Elder 1985). Transitions are always embedded in trajectories and social arrangements that give them distinctive meaning, such as loss of a job for the young adult and the middle-aged. Interlocking trajectories and their transitions structure the individual life course, since movement across life stages entails the concurrent assumption of multiple roles. Major transitions in the life course typically involve multiple life changes, from entry into the diverse roles of adulthood (Modell 1989) to later-life changes in work, residence, and family (Hareven 1978). These transitions may also entail a sequence of phases or choice points. The transition to unwed motherhood thus involves premarital sexual experience followed by decisions not to have an abortion, not to give the child up for adoption, and not to marry the father (Furstenberg 1976). Causal influences vary across the choice points.

The social meanings of age give structure to the life course through age norms and sanctions, social timetables for the occurrence and order of events, generalized age grades (childhood, adolescence, etc.), and age hierarchies in organizational settings. In theory, a normative concept of social time specifies an appropriate time or age for marriage, childbearing, and retirement (Neugarten and Datan 1973; Lawrence 1984). Differential timing orders events (as when marriage occurs before the first child's birth) and determines the duration of waiting time between one event and the next. Empirical findings are beginning to cumulate on event timing, sequences, and durations, although the knowledge base is thin on causal mechanisms (Hogan and Astone 1986). Beyond these social distinctions, age has historical significance for the life course by locating people in historical context according to birth cohorts.

Within the life course of each generation, unexpected and involuntary events occur through life changes in related generations.

Family transitions invariably place the life course in a broader matrix of kinship relationships, one that extends beyond the boundaries of the immediate family to in-laws, parents, and grandparents. Within the life course of each generation, unexpected and involuntary events occur through life changes in related generations. Thus a fifty-year-old woman becomes a grandmother when her daughter has a first baby, and parents lose their status as son and daughter when their own parents die. Among dual-earner couples, the timing of retirement has become a family contingency as couples work out an appropriate course of action for each partner and their relationship (O'Rand, Henretta, and Krecker 1991). Synchronization of lives is central to life-course planning in families. As in the case of social age, the road map of marriage, kinship, and the generations tells family members where they have been, are, and will be.

The *life-cycle* concept is frequently used to describe a sequence of life events from birth to death, though its more precise meaning refers to a sequence of parenthood stages over the life course, from birth of the children through their departure from the home to their own childbearing (O'Rand and Krecker 1990). This sequence, it should be noted, refers to a reproductive process in human populations. Within a life cycle of generational succession, newborns are socialized to maturity, give birth to the next generation, grow old, and die. The cycle is repeated from one generation to the next, though *only* within the framework of a population. Some people do not have children and consequently are not part of an intergenerational life cycle.

The life cycle is commonly known in terms of the family cycle, a set of ordered stages of parenthood defined primarily by variations in family composition and size (Hill 1970; Elder 1977). Major transition points include marriage, birth of the first and last child, the children's transitions in school, departure of the eldest and youngest child from the home, and marital dissolution through the death of one spouse. The stages are not defined in terms of age, as a rule, and typically follow a preferred script of a marriage that bears children and survives to old age, an increasingly rare specimen in contemporary society. Moreover, as Rindfuss, Swicegood, and Rosenfeld (1987, p. 27) conclude, "understanding the nature and importance of sequence in the life course requires analyzing what the roles themselves mean and how they are causally linked." This meaning derives in large measure from knowledge of the duration and timing of events. Thus, a rapid sequence of births produces a very different family dynamic in terms of demands and pressures from that of widely dispersed births. A mother's life stage, whether she is in late adolescence or her mid-thirties, also has obvious relevance to the meaning of a birth sequence.

Lifespan specifies the temporal scope of inquiry and specialization, as in lifespan sociology or psychology. A lifespan study extends across a substantial period of life and generally links behavior in two or more life stages. Instead of limiting research to social and developmental processes within a specific life stage, a lifespan design favors studies of antecedents and consequences. Any coverage of lifespan issues necessarily brings up the meaning of *life stage.* Sociologists tend to focus on the social life course, in which life stage refers to either socially defined positions, such as the age of adolescence, or to analytically defined positions, such as the career stage of men or women at age forty. Thus, men who differ in age when they encounter work-life misfortune may be said to occupy different life stages at the time.

Developmental stages and trajectories are the foci of lifespan psychology. Examples include Erik Erikson's (1963) psychosocial stages, such as the stage of generativity. Lifespan psychology gained coherence and visibility through a series of conferences at the University of West Virginia beginning in the late 1960s (Baltes and Reese 1984). The approach is defined by a concern with the description and explanation of age-related biological and behavioral changes from birth to death. In terms of stage and rate of advance, social and developmental trajectories may show varying degrees of correspondence, such as a physical rate of maturation that does not match the athletic demands of a student's role.

Life history commonly refers to a lifetime chronology of events and activities that typically and variably combine data records on education, work life, family, and residence. These records may be generated by obtaining information from archival materials or from interviews with a respondent, as in the use of a life calendar or age-event matrix (Freedman et al. 1988). Life calendars record the age (year and month) at which transitions occur in each activity domain, and thus depict an unfolding life course in ways uniquely suited to event-history analyses and the assessment of time-varying causal influences (Featherman 1986; Mayer and Tuma 1990). Life history also refers to self-reported narrations of life, as in Thomas and Znaniecki's famous life history of Wladek in *The Polish Peasant in Europe and America* (1918–1920). Whether self-reported or collected by a research staff, life histories are products of data collection in the form of time-ordered events or accounts.

All the concepts above have a place in studies of the life course. Contemporary inquiry extends across the lifespan and frequently draws upon the life records and life cycles of successive generations. The life course takes the form of a multidimensional and intergenerational concept; a moving set of interlocking trajectories and transitions, such as work, marriage, and being parents. Within this context, misfortune and opportunity are *intergenerational* as well as life problems. Failed marriages and work lives frequently lead adult offspring back to the parental household and alter the parents' life plans for their later years. Conversely, economic setbacks and marital dissolution among the parents of adolescents may impede the children's transition to adulthood by postponing higher education and marriage. Each generation is bound to fateful decisions and events in the other's life course.

As implied by relations among these concepts, age and kinship distinctions inform a common theoretical orientation on the life course, one that defines this topic as a field of inquiry, identifies key problems, and structures research through concepts and models. The age-graded life course, timetables, and birth cohorts are central to the sociology of age and the life course. From the field of kinship comes life cycle, generation or generational position, lineage, and family time (Hagestad 1990).

In a family timetable of four generations, the number and configuration of the generations can vary sharply across a single lifespan. Consider a person born during World War I who became one of several great-grandchildren of a woman in her nineties. Three higher stations in the generational series are occupied: the parent, grandparent, and great-grandparent generations. This hierarchy continues until the great-grandmother dies, in the child's sixth year. By the time the child enters middle school, both grandparents on both sides of the family have died, producing a two-generation structure. Changes of this sort in generational position have consequences for self-identity, inter-generational obligations, and social support, but the full significance depends on the individual's historical context and life stage.

The recent convergence of age and kinship distinctions is most readily seen by describing an early phase of life study, before World War II, and comparing developments at that time with those observed since the 1960s.

Life Course Study in Historical Context

The study of lives has known two eras of distinctive vitality: the phase before 1940, which is most closely identified with the early Chicago school of sociology (1915–1935), and the decades since 1960. The first era viewed lives from a kinship perspective and neglected variations in life patterns. At a time of rapid demographic and social change, studies in the second era discovered the complexity of lives and articulated for the first time a framework linking social history and social structure in the life course.

ERA I: THE GENERATIONS AND LIVES. The first wave of research interest in the life course accompanied the sociological study of problems in a rapidly changing society—waves of immigrants to cities, high rates of delinquency, and other forms of social pathology. Following the example set by Thomas and Znaniecki ([1918–1920] 1974), researchers began to use life records to study lives in changing times. Thomas (Volkart 1951, p. 593) urged that research take full advantage of the "longitudinal approach to life history." Studies, he argued, should investigate "many types of individuals with regard to their experiences and various past periods of life in different situations" and follow "groups of individuals into the future, getting a continuous record of experiences as they occur."

Thomas's approach to this record of experience had much to do with kinship and the generations and very little to do with the meanings of age, whether social or historical. The sequence of generations in *The Polish Peasant* is only loosely placed in historical time and context. Indeed, the age range of members of a particular generation may exceed thirty years. People of similar age frequently occupy very different generational positions, such as parent and grandparent. Moreover, the ages and years of emigration are not reported so that we do not know precisely when people left their homes and communities for urban destinations. From the standpoint of this study and others from that period, the sociology of age had not as yet informed the conceptual framework of life-course research.

A number of longitudinal studies launched with children born in the 1920s or earlier seemed to follow Thomas's recommendation for this type of research design. Most prominent in this effort are the Lewis Terman study of gifted Californians born between 1904 and 1920, the Oakland Growth Study of persons born in 1920 and 1921, and the Berkeley Guidance and Growth Studies of children who were born in 1928 and 1929 (see Eichorn et al. 1981). These studies were not designed to track the developmental course of children into the adult years, but they eventually did so, with data collection continuing well into the 1980s and thus capturing the later years of the respondents' lives. However, it is notable that early uses of the data did not examine the age-graded life course and its developmental effects, nor did this research explore the implications of historical change in this rapidly changing part of the twentieth century. These emphases emerged after 1960 and soon encouraged uses of the archival data that linked human development and lives to aspects of a changing society. Life patterns and the historical record were no longer unrelated fields of inquiry.

ERA II: THE DISCOVERY OF VARIABILITY IN LIVES. A major advance in life-course theory came from the generalized recognition of variability in lives by social scientists—notably Bernice Neugarten, Norman Ryder, and Matilda Riley—who were studying development, aging, and cohorts during the 1960s. There are three dimensions of this new consciousness. First, research began to report a wide variability of age patterns in lives. Contrary to modal views of *age patterns* in cultures (Eisenstadt 1956; cf. Kertzer and Keith 1984), people of the same age do not march in concert across major events of the life course; rather, they vary in pace and sequencing, and this variation has real consequences for people and society (Hogan 1981). Second, *kinship and family* emerged as a primary source of variation and regulation in life trajectories. Lives are lived inter-dependently among members of family and kin units. Third, the new work on aging underscored the role of *historical change* as a source of life-course variation (Baltes and Reese 1984). Important methodological issues stemmed from this recognition. If social change and aging are interrelated, then research must disentangle the different sources of age-related behavior change over the life course.

Social timing and life-course variations. During the late 1950s and early 1960s, a research program led by Bernice Neugarten (Neugarten and Datan 1973) developed a normative perspective on the life course that featured the concept of normative timetables and individual deviations from such expectations. The timetable of the life course refers to social age, as defined by people's expectations of norms regarding events. In theory, age expectations specify appropriate times for major transitions. There is an appropriate time for entering school, leaving home, getting married, having children, and retiring. Generally, departures from the usual timetable entail social and psychological consequences, from informal sanctions to lost opportunities and life-course disorder. Ever since this pioneering work and the growth of social demography, the study of differential timing and order among events has been one of the most active domains in life-course research. However, we still lack knowledge of age expectations in large populations concerning events in the life course. Study of the *normative* foundation of the life course deserves far more attention than it has received to date.

People of the same age do not march in concert across major events of the life course; rather, they vary in pace and sequencing.

Neugarten addressed her work on the normative timetable to the individual life course, though her thinking prompted consideration of the interlocking transitions of family members. One of the clearest examples of this phenomenon comes from a study of female lineages in a black community of Los Angeles (Burton and Bengtson 1985). The birth of a child to the teenage daughter of a young mother created a large disparity between age and kinship status, between being young and facing the prospects of grandparental obligations. Four out of five mothers of young mothers actually refused to accept these new child-care obligations, shifting the burden up the generational ladder to the great-grandmother, who in many cases was carrying a heavy load. By comparison, the women who became grandmothers in their late forties or so were eager for the new role; in this lineage, a timely transition to motherhood by the daughter meant her own mother's timely transition to grandmotherhood.

The most significant integration of age and kinship distinctions among contemporary studies of the life course is found in *Of Human Bonding* (Rossi and Rossi 1990). Using a three-generation sample in the Boston region, the study investigates the interlocking nature of the life course within family systems, with particular focus on the relation between individual aging and kin-defined relationships across the lifespan. Most of the study centers on the formation, maintenance, and expression of parent-child ties, as indexed by affective closeness, association, and value consensus. Using contemporaneous and retrospective data, the study first charts patterns of aging, expressed in age concepts of self, level of energy, and goals; then examines types of kin obligations over the life course and their correlates; and concludes with a thorough study of developmental and social factors in parent-child solidarity. Among their numerous results, the authors find that affective closeness between adult children and their parents varies according to the quality of family life in childhood, the degree of shared values in adulthood, and the aging experience of the parents (good health, etc.).

Clearly, much has been achieved in conceptual models of the life course since the 1960s, but these models refer mainly to the life course worked out by the individual *within* a social system of institutionalized pathways—the life course as constructed by the individual in terms established by the larger society. Mayer (1986, p. 166) had these terms in mind when he identified key societal mechanisms "which impose order and constraints on lives," including institutional careers, the cumulative effects of delayed transitions, the collective conditions associated with particular cohorts (historical circumstances, etc.), and state intervention and regulation. The growth of the state in social regulation counters the potential fragmentation of increasing institutional differentiation. At the individual level "the state legalizes, defines, and standardizes most points of entry and exit: into and out of employment, into and out of marital status, into and out of sickness and disability, into and out of formal education. In doing so, the state turns these transitions into strongly demarcated public events and acts as a gatekeeper and sorter" (Mayer 1986, p. 167). These are elements of what Buchmann (1989, p. 28) properly calls "the public life course."

Social change and lives. Though studies of social change and life patterns had been conducted up to the 1960s as if they had little in common, this assumption was challenged by Norman Ryder's (1965) concept of the interaction of social and life history. He proposed the term *cohort* as a concept for studying the life course. With its "life stage principle," Ryder's essay provided a useful point of departure toward understanding the interplay between social change and the life patterns of age cohorts: The impact of a historical event on the life course reflects the life stage at which the change was experienced. Differences in life stage offer insight into the adaptive resources, options, and meanings that become potential elements in relating social change and life outcomes.

Ryder's essay on the bond between age and time brought more sophisticated awareness to connections between historical and individual life time and, in doing so, generated fresh insights concerning the temporal aspects of lives. Once individuals are placed in historical context, the personal impact of historical conditions must be considered. The publication of *Aging and Society* (Riley, Johnson, and Foner 1972) strengthened this sensitivity to the historical setting of birth cohorts and brought historical differentiation to notions of the age-graded life course. By relating birth cohorts and age divisions in the social structure, this volume highlights important differences between these modes of age differentiation. For example, birth cohorts do not possess the social and cultural meanings of normatively defined age divisions, and their age spans (from one year to fifteen or more) vary greatly according to historical conditions and the requirements of research. These variations raise unexplored questions concerning the interaction of historical change, cohorts, and prescribed age divisions in life patterns.

Genuine empirical study of historical influences on life patterns gained encouragement from a vigorous new wave of research that used archival data to construct life courses and life-styles in past time. For example, a sociological study of historical influences on the life course tested Ryder's life-stage principle by tracing the effects of drastic income loss in the Great Depression on the family and individual experience of two birth cohorts, one with birthdates at the beginning of the 1920s and the other with birthdates between 1928 and 1929 (Elder 1974; 1979). Consistent with the life-stage hypothesis, the younger children were more strongly influenced by family hardship than the older children, with impairment most evident in the lives of the younger boys. Though diminishing in strength over time, the difference persisted up to the middle years in work life, family relationships, and psychological functioning.

This depression study illustrates one of the ways lives can be influenced by social change: a *cohort effect.* Historical influence takes the form of a cohort effect when social change differentiates the life patterns of successive cohorts, such as the older and younger children from the 1920s. History also takes the form of a *period effect* when the influence of a social change is relatively uniform across successive birth cohorts. Secular trends in the scheduling of marriages and first births across the twentieth century are largely an expression of massive period effects. A third type of effect occurs through *maturation* or *aging.*

Unfortunately, efforts to partition the variance according to these effects have not advanced knowledge on social change in lives. Too often research does not address questions that specify a type of social change or the process by which it alters the life course. Instead, questions assign environmental change to an error term or compare multiple cohorts as a test of the generalization boundaries of behavioral outcomes. Even when history is substantively important, it may be operationalized as a period or cohort effect that provides no clue as to the precise nature of the influence. In addition, cohort comparisons restrict what is learned about the effects of social change by obscuring variations within successive cohorts. As the Great Depression study makes clear, the economic decline was not uniformly experienced by families, and not all subgroups of children were affected by family hardship in the same way. Experiential variations by subgroups within specific cohorts represent a significant conceptual distinction, as Mannheim's writings (1928) on generation units imply.

By the 1990s, the life course had become a general theoretical framework for the study of lives, human development, and aging *in a changing society.* Rapid change drew attention to historical influences and prompted the new sociological literatures on age and kinship to fashion concepts of a life course embedded in social institutions and subject to historical changes and the choices-cum-actions of individuals. This development is coupled with the continued growth of longitudinal studies and the emergence of new methodologies for the collection and analysis of the life-history data that represent time, process, and context (Freedman et al. 1988; Mayer and Tuma 1990). However, much work remains in relating lives to their changing society, a point stressed by the central themes of promising research in life-course study.

Promise and Challenge: Central Themes

Despite promising cross-level developments in life-course research, most studies continue to follow one of two tracks, the macroscopic or microscopic. Explanations for life-course change often draw upon a mix of cultural, demographic, and economic factors at the macro level, but they seldom relate these structures to patterns of individual behavior. This limitation may reflect the task of linking social change and lives—a challenging venture because so little theory extends across levels and provides guidelines for causal chains. Theories are available on the macro and micro level, but one finds little guidance of this kind in connecting levels. The major challenges for life-course studies are to account for the process by which social structures and changes make a difference in life patterns, and to explain continuity and change in observed effects across the life course. Both types of accounts or explanations entail linkages in the overlapping regions of different conceptual systems, such as the individual and the interactional context and the relation between this setting and the large-scale social organization.

Empirical research has identified five mechanisms that portray some ways in which changing times affect life patterns: control cycles, situational imperatives, the accentuation principle, the life-stage distinction, and a concept of interdependent lives (Elder and Caspi 1990). The first three concern the relative fit between a changing environment and the life course, whether compatible or not. The life-stage notion, from the work of Norman Ryder (1965), refers to the individual's location within the life course when major social change occurs, such as childhood, late adolescence, or old age. The concept of interdependent lives relates all people to significant others who mediate the influence of social change.

An account of historical influence at a point in time does not explain why the effect persists in some cases and fades in others over the individual life course, as in the case of American children who grew up in the Great Depression (Elder 1974). Keeping this distinction in mind, the following discussion begins with mechanisms linking social change and life patterns, then turns to processes that account for continuity and change of influences across the life course.

Rapid social change produces a disparity between claims and the resources to achieve them, resulting in a corresponding loss of control, followed by efforts to regain control, through adaptations of one kind or another. *Control cycles,* then, refer to equilibrating processes in which losing control prompts efforts to restore control. Families in the Great Depression regained a measure of control over their situations through expenditure reductions and multiple earners (Elder 1974). Families and individuals constructed and reworked their life course through adaptations of this kind.

The influence of a social change depends in part on the behavioral requirements or demands of the new situation, called the *situational imperatives.* A long-term research program directed by Kohn and Schooler (Kohn 1969; Kohn and Schooler 1983) shows that the behavioral imperatives of work shape how men and women think and function. The most powerful imperative is occupational self-direction or autonomy; the greater the self-direction, the more workers deal with substantively complex, nonroutinized tasks that entail minimal supervision. Self-directed workers also seek out jobs that allow them substantial control. Demotions or de-skilling would lower such control and could initiate efforts to regain it through exploration of other job possibilities.

Very rarely does catastrophic social change produce catastrophic alterations in personality.

Life-course choices and behavioral adaptations are shaped by the imperatives of the new situation, and by the resources or dispositions people bring to it. *Accentuation* refers to the process by which the new situation heightens selected attributes. Explosive men become more explosive, and weak family relationships shatter under stress. To illustrate this dynamic, consider a study of personality under social catastrophe (Allport, Bruner, and Jandorf 1941). After analyzing personal documents on ninety individuals who experienced the Nazi revolution of the 1930s, the investigators observe that "very rarely does catastrophic social change produce catastrophic alterations in personality" (p. 7). On the contrary, the basic structure of personality persists despite the upset and upheaval in the total life space. Moreover, "where change does take place, it seems invariably to accentuate trends clearly present in the pre-crisis personality" (p. 8).

The *life-stage principle* supplements the accentuation dynamic by claiming that an individual's life stage at the point of social change determines whether and how the person will be influenced by the change. Children born in 1920 and 1928–1929 are cases in point. On the basis of the life-stage principle, there is reason to expect more adverse effects of family hardship among the younger children, and the results generally affirm this conclusion for boys (Elder 1979).

From a general perspective, social change is expressed in lives through the experience of others, and this experience of *interdependent lives* (as in families, etc.) represents a primary means by which large-scale social changes affect the life course. For example, McAdam's (1989) study of adults who participated in a civil rights project during the Mississippi summer of 1964 found that organizational and social ties helped to sustain activist politics and its influence on their marital and occupational choices. This interpretation leads to questions concerning the mechanisms through which such ties facilitate continuity in political behavior. What is it about friendship continuity that sustains political continuity from adolescence to the middle years?

Caspi and Bem (1990) identify three types of interaction between person and environment over the life span—proactive, reactive, and evocative—that have particular relevance to the likelihood and nature of life-course continuity and change. *Proactive* interaction applies most directly to McAdam's finding and refers to the process by which people select rewarding or compatible environments, as in mate selection. Studies suggest that the personal stability of men and women across the life course is partly due to the stabilizing influences of marital partners and friends with whom they have much in common (Caspi and Bem 1990). This dynamic applies to the remarkable political stability of women who attended Bennington College in the 1930s and were studied by Theodore Newcomb (Alwin, Cohen, and Newcomb 1991). Conversely, social discontinuity between childhood and adult friends is a potential factor in behavioral change over this part of the life course. Sampson and Laub's (1990) follow-up of a low-income sample of delinquents and controls provides some evidence along this line. They found that adult bonds to conventional figures and lines of activity defined a route of escape from delinquency for a substantial number of the men. The puzzle is how such bonds are formed among young men with a history of antisocial behavior.

Reactive interaction refers to a situation in which different individuals encounter the same objective environment but interpret and respond to it differently. Different adaptations thereby construct different life trajectories and entail the possibility of increasing individual differences up to old age.

Evocative interaction refers to the reciprocal intermingling of behavior and personal attributes in social relationships. An individual's personality elicits distinctive responses from others, a process exemplified by affirmative responses to personal competence (Clausen 1991) and the destabilizing effects of personal irritability and explosiveness. When ill-tempered, hostile adults evoke similar behavior from others, they may learn this definition of the other (reactive interaction) and in turn become more inclined to respond explosively to any evidence of personal threat.

In summary, the flourishing area of life-course studies owes much to the general recognition that any effort to make sense of individual behavior should be informed by knowledge of (1) how lives and societal change are reciprocally linked and (2) how early events and influences persist and fade across the life course in a changing world. These lines of inquiry are interrelated in a number of respects. The impact of an ever-changing environment is central to an understanding of life-course continuity and change, whereas knowledge of such continuity enables us to interpret the full meaning of historical effects in human lives.

The two tasks also have in common the challenge of building conceptual bridges in largely uncharted territory that extends across multiple levels of analysis. At present, the wealth of theories on the macro and micro levels is not matched by theories that specify chains of influence between different levels. Little is known about the downward causation process in connecting macro change in social institutions and environments to the micro experience of individuals. Most studies of human lives continue to follow one of two tracks, the individual or the macroscopic level, although the most important future advances will be made by research that takes seriously the multiple-level, embedded, and dynamic features of the life course.

[See also Health and the Life Course; Social Gerontology.]

BIBLIOGRAPHY

Allport, Gordon W., J. S. Bruner, and E. M. Jandorf 1941 "Personality under Social Catastrophe: Ninety Life-Histories of the Nazi Revolution." *Character and Personality* 10:1–22.

Alwin, Duane F., Ronald L. Cohen, and Theodore M. Newcomb 1991 *Aging, Personality, and Social Change: Attitude Persistence and Change over the Life-Span.* Madison: University of Wisconsin Press.

Baltes, Paul B., and Hayne W. Reese 1984 "The Life-Span Perspective in Developmental Psychology." In Marc H. Bornstein and Michael E. Lamb, eds., *Developmental Psychology: An Advanced Textbook.* Hillsdale, N.J.: Erlbaum.

Buchmann, Marlis 1989 *The Script of Life in Modern Society: Entry into Adulthood in a Changing World.* Chicago: University of Chicago Press.

Burton, Linda M., and Vern L. Bengtson 1985 "Black Grandmothers: Issues of Timing and Continuity of Roles." In Vern L. Bengtson and Joan F. Robertson, eds., *Grandparenthood.* Beverly Hills, Calif.: Sage.

Caspi, Avshalom, and Daryl J. Bem 1990 "Personality Continuity and Change across the Life Course." In Lawrence A. Pervin, ed., *Handbook of Personality: Theory and Research.* New York: Guilford Press.

Clausen, John A 1991 "Adolescent Competence and the Shaping of the Life Course." *The American Journal of Sociology* 96:805–842.

Eichorn, Dorothy H., John A. Clausen, Norma Haan, Marjorie Honzik, and Paul H. Mussen (eds.) 1981 *Present and Past in Middle Life.* New York: Academic Press.

Eisenstadt, S. N. 1956 *From Generation to Generation: Age Groups and Social Structure.* Glencoe, Ill.: Free Press.

Elder, Glen H., Jr. 1974 *Children of the Great Depression: Social Change in Life Experience.* Chicago: University of Chicago Press.

——— 1977 "Family History and the Life Course." *Journal of Family History* 2:279–304.

——— 1979 "Historical Changes in Life Patterns and Personality." In Paul B. Baltes and Otis G. Brim, Jr., eds., *Life-Span Development and Behavior,* Vol. 2. New York: Academic Press.

——— 1985 "Perspectives on the Life Course." In Glen H. Elder, Jr., ed., *Life Course Dynamics: Trajectories and Transitions, 1968–1980.* Ithaca, N.Y.: Cornell University Press.

———, and Avshalom Caspi 1990 "Studying Lives in a Changing Society: Sociological and Personological Explorations." In A. I. Rabin, Robert A. Zucker, R. Emmons, and Susan Frank, eds., *Studying Persons and Lives.* New York: Springer.

Erikson, Erik H. (1950) 1963 *Childhood and Society,* 2d ed., rev. and enl. New York: Norton.

Featherman, David L. 1986 "Biography, Society, and History: Individual Development as a Population Process." In Aage B. Sorensen, Franz E. Weinert, and Lonnie R. Sherrod, eds., *Human Development and the Life Course: Multidisciplinary Perspectives.* Hillsdale, N.J.: Erlbaum.

Freedman, Deborah, Arland Thornton, Donald Camburn, Duane Alwin, and Linda Young-DeMarco 1988 "The Life History Calendar: A Technique for Collecting Retrospective Data." *Sociological Methodology* 18:37–68.

Furstenberg, Frank F., Jr. 1976 *Unplanned Parenthood: The Social Consequences of Childbearing.* New York: Free Press.

Hagestad, Gunhild O. 1990 "Social Perspectives on the Life Course." In Robert H. Binstock and Linda K. George, eds., *Handbook of Aging and the Social Sciences,* 3d ed. New York: Academic Press.

Hareven, Tamara K. (ed.) 1978 *Transitions: The Family and the Life Course in Historical Perspective.* New York: Academic Press.

Hill, Reuben 1970 *Family Development in Three Generations.* Cambridge, Mass: Schenkman.

Hogan, Dennis P. 1981 *Transitions and Social Change: The Early Lives of American Men.* New York: Academic Press.

———, and Nan Marie Astone 1986. "The Transition to Adulthood." *Annual Review of Sociology* 12:109–130.

Kertzer, David I., and Jennie Keith (eds.) 1984 *Age and Anthropological Theory.* Ithaca, N.Y.: Cornell University Press.

Kohn, Melvin L. (1969) 1977 *Class and Conformity: A Study in Values, with a Reassessment.,* 2d ed. Chicago: University of Chicago Press.

———, and Carmi Schooler. 1983. *Work and Personality: An Inquiry into the Impact of Social Stratification.* Norwood, N.J.: Ablex.

Lawrence, Barbara S. 1984 "Age Grading: The Implicit Organizational Timetable." *Journal of Occupational Behavior* 5:23–35.

Mannheim, Karl [1928] 1952 "The Problem of Generations." In *Essays on the Sociology of Knowledge,* trans. Paul Kecskemeti. London: Routledge and Kegan Paul.

Mayer, Karl Ulrich 1986 "Structural Constraints on the Life Course." *Human Development* 29:163–170.

——— and Nancy Brandon Tuma (eds.) 1990 *Event History Analysis in Life Course Research.* Madison: University of Wisconsin Press.

McAdam, Doug 1989 "The Biographical Consequences of Activism." *American Sociological Review* 54: 744–760.

Modell, John 1989 *Into One's Own: From Youth to Adulthood in the United States, 1920–1975.* Berkeley: University of California Press.

Neugarten, Bernice L., and Nancy Datan 1973 "Sociological Perspectives on the Life Cycle." In Paul B. Baltes and K. Warner

Schaie, eds., *Life-Span Developmental Psychology: Personality and Socialization.* New York: Academic Press.

O'Rand, Angela M., John C. Henretta, and Margaret L. Krecker 1991 "Family Pathways to Retirement: Early and Late Life Family Effects on Couples' Work Exit Patterns." In Maximiliane Szinovacz, D. Ekerdt, and Barbara H. Vinick, eds., *Families and Retirement: Conceptual and Methodological Issues.* Newbury Park, Calif.: Sage.

———, and Margaret L. Krecker 1990 "Concepts of the Life Cycle: Their History, Meanings, and Uses in the Social Sciences." *Annual Review of Sociology* 16:241–262.

Riley, Matilda W., Marilyn Johnson, and Anne Foner 1972 *Aging and Society.* Vol. 3, *A Sociology of Age Stratification.* New York: Russell Sage Foundation.

Rindfuss, Ronald R., C. Gray Swicegood, and Rachel A. Rosenfeld 1987 "Disorder in the Life Course: How Common and Does It Matter?" *American Sociological Review* 52:785–801.

Rossi, Alice S., and Peter H. Rossi. 1990. *Of Human Bonding: Parent-Child Relations across the Life Course.* New York: A. de Gruyter.

Ryder, Norman B. 1965 "The Cohort as a Concept in the Study of Social Change." *American Sociological Review* 30:843–861.

Sampson, Robert J., and John H. Laub 1990 "Crime and Deviance over the Life Course: The Salience of Adult Social Bonds." *American Sociological Review* 55:609–627.

Thomas, William I, and Florian Znaniecki [1918–1920] 1974 *The Polish Peasant in Europe and America.* 2 vols. New York: Octagon.

Volkart, Edmund Howell 1951 *Social Behavior and Personality: Contributions of W. I. Thomas to Theory and Social Research.* New York: Social Science Research Council.

– GLEN H. ELDER, JR.

LIFE EXPECTANCY

Life expectancy (or the expectation of life) is the average length of life remaining to be lived by a population at a given age. It is computed in the process of building a life table and can be computed for any age in the life table. Life expectancy at birth is the most commonly presented value because it provides a succinct indicator of mortality that reflects mortality conditions across the age range and is unaffected by the age structure of the actual population and thus can be compared across populations. The symbol used to represent life expectancy is $\mathring{e}_x$ where x represents an exact age.

Life Expectancy in the United States

In 1994, life expectancy at birth, $\mathring{e}_0$, in the United States was 75.7 years; at age 65, $\mathring{e}_{65}$ was 17.4 years; and at age 85, $\mathring{e}_{85}$ was 6.1 years (National Center for Health Statistics). These figures can be interpreted to mean that if a baby born in 1995 were exposed to the mortality conditions existing at each age of the life span in 1995, the baby with an average length life would live 75.8 years.

Period and Cohort Values

The 1989 U.S. life table is a period life table, based on cross-sectional data collected over a year; thus, this life table indicates the mortality experience of a hypothetical cohort. No actual cohort ever experiences the mortality in a period or cross-sectional life table; rather, the table indicates mortality conditions if the mortality levels of each age group at the period of time used as a reference were experienced by the hypothetical cohort. Because mortality has been falling over time, period life tables for a cohort's year of birth have indicated an average expected length of life that is lower than that actually achieved by the cohort. For instance, in 1900 the cross-sectional life table for the United States showed expectations of life of forty-six for males and forty-nine for females. On the basis of actual experience to date, the 1900 birth cohort is expected to average a length of life of fifty-two years for males and fifty-eight years for females (Faber and Wade 1983).

Generation or cohort life tables, like that described for the 1900 birth cohort, based on the experience of an actual cohort, are sometimes constructed, and these indicate the average length of life actually lived after specific ages for a real cohort. The major difficulty in building cohort life tables is obtaining population and death data for a cohort from birth until the last survivors have died—over a 100-year period.

A person who has already reached older adulthood on average will die at an age that exceeds life expectancy at birth by a significant amount.

A mistaken notion held by many people is that life expectancy at birth is a good indicator of the age at which an older individual will die. This notion has undoubtedly led to some poor planning for old age because a person who has already reached older adulthood on average will die at an age that exceeds life expectancy at birth by a significant amount. Expectation of life in 1994 was 17.4 years for sixty-five-year-olds, 11.0 for seventy-five-year-olds, and 6.1 for eighty-five-year-olds. With this number of years remaining to be lived on average, sixty-five-year-olds should expect to live to eighty-two on average. Those who live to seventy-five should expect to live to almost eighty-six, and those who live to eighty-five can expect to live to ninety-one on average. While expectation of life decreases as age increases, the expected age at death increases for those who survive.

Changes in Life Expectancy Over Time

As noted above, life expectancy has been increasing over time. This has probably been going on since some time in the last half of the nineteenth century, although reliable data for large sections of the country are not available to track the increase before 1900. In 1900, life expectancy at birth for both sexes was 47.3 years (U.S. Bureau of the Census 1975). This indicates an increase in life expectancy between 1900 and 1994 of 28.4 years. Most of this increase in life expectancy since 1900 is due to declines in mortality among infants and children. These mortality declines were due primarily to the diminishing force of infectious and parasitic diseases, which were the most important causes of death among children.

Because life expectancy was low in the past, people often hold the mistaken notion that very few people ever reached old age under high mortality conditions. Yin and Shine (1985) have demonstrated that this mistaken notion is so prevalent that it has been commonly incorporated into gerontology textbooks. The fact is that even under conditions of low life expectancy, once childhood is survived, the chances of living to old age are quite high. This is indicated by the fact that life expectancy at the older years has not increased over time nearly as much as life expectancy at birth. For instance, while life expectancy at birth has increased almost thirty years since 1900, life expectancy for white males at age forty has increased only 8.3 years between 1900 and 1994, from 27.7 years to 36 years; at age seventy, the increase for males has been slightly less than three years, from 9.0 to 11.8 (U.S. Bureau of the Census 1975; National Center for Health Statistics 1990b).

It should be noted, however, that in recent years the pace of improvement in life expectancy at the oldest ages has increased. In 1970 expectation of life for white males at age seventy was 10.5 years, indicating an improvement of 1.5 years in the seventy years between 1900 and 1970. Between 1970 and 1994, the increase was 2 years—a 25 percent greater improvement than during the first seven decades of the century. This reflects the new era of mortality decline where decreases in mortality are due to decreased mortality from chronic conditions and are concentrated among the old.

Calculation of Life Expectancy

These observations about changes in life expectancy should make clear that life expectancy at birth is heavily weighted by mortality conditions at the youngest ages. A brief explanation of how life expectancy is calculated demonstrates why this is the case.

Life expectancy, or $\mathring{e}_x$, is computed from the T_x and l_x columns of the life table: $\mathring{e}_x = T_x / l_x$. T_x is the total number of years lived by the life table population after reaching age x, and l_x is the number of people surviving to exact age x in the life table population. To use a simplistic illustration, if mortality is reduced by a child surviving death early in the first year of life and then living to be seventy-five, approximately seventy-five years would be added to the total number of years lived by the population. On the other hand, if mortality declines because a person survives death at age seventy-five and then dies at eighty, only five years will be added to the total number of years lived. Thus, changes in mortality at the youngest ages have added the most to life expectancy in the past.

The United States ranks quite low in life expectancy among developed countries and relative to its income level.

A number of authors have studied the relationships between changes in age-specific mortality and life expectancy. Vaupel (1986) concludes that a reduction in the force of mortality of 1 percent at all ages would not produce as much gain in life expectancy today as it did in 1900. This is because we have already made so much progress in lowering infant and child mortality. Vaupel also shows that as mortality moves to lower levels, more progress is made in increasing life expectancy from mortality declines at older ages rather than at younger ages. At the level of mortality now experienced in the United States, much of the future increase in life expectancy will come from mortality declines occurring at ages over sixty-five. This is true because of previous success in reducing mortality at earlier ages to such low levels.

Differentials in Life Expectancy

There are large differentials in life expectancy among demographic and socioeconomic groups in the United States. Males have lower life expectancies than females throughout the age range. Males' lower chances for a longer life are thought to result from a combination of biological differences and life-style factors. In 1994, life expectancy at birth was 73.3 for males and 79.3 for females (National Center for Health Statistics). By age fifty, the difference is narrowed to 4.5 years with a life expectancy of 27.2 for men and 31.0 for women. At age eighty-five, men can expect to live another 5.2 years, while women can expect to live 6.4 years.

There is also a significant difference in life expectancy between whites and blacks in the United States. This is assumed to result from the differences in socioeconomic status and accompanying life circumstances that exist between blacks and whites. In 1994, life expectancy at birth was 79.6 and 73.3 for white women and men respectively, and only 73.9 and 64.9 for black women and men. At age sixty-five, white life expectancy was about 17 years; while for blacks of that age, it was approximately 15 years. At the oldest ages, a crossover in mortality occurs, and black life expectancy exceeds white life expectancy. In 1987 this was true at ages above eighty-three. The crossover shows up repeatedly in comparisons of black and white mortality in the United States and has been attributed to the "survival of the fittest" among the black population (Manton and Stallard 1981). Recently, however, some doubt has been raised as to whether the crossover is real or is a statistical artifact resulting from age misstatement by older blacks in both the census and vital records of deaths (Coale and Kisker 1986). Interestingly, Hispanics appear to have life expectancy values that are similar to non-Hispanic whites (Schoen and Nelson 1981).

International Differences

The life expectancy of a country is related to its level of socioeconomic development. Most countries that are classified as "more developed" have higher levels of life expectancy at birth than most of the countries classified as "developing"; however, within each of these groups of countries there is quite a bit of variability in life expectancy. While the United States has a high level of life expectancy compared to that of the developing countries of the world, the United States ranks quite low in life expectancy among developed countries and relative to its income level. A recent United Nations listing of the developed countries by level of life expectancy at birth ranks U.S. males as fifteenth and U.S. females as eighth (United Nations 1982). The countries with higher life expectancy for women include Japan and the Scandinavian countries. For men, most European countries including some in southern Europe have higher life expectancies at birth than the United States. The low ranking of the United States is attributed, in part, to the inequities in mortality among subgroups of the population, especially the high level among blacks, and also to the high level of violent deaths. In recent years Japan has become the world leader in life expectancy at birth, with values of $\mathring{e}_0$ of 76.4 for men and 82.9 for women in 1995 (Ogawa). These values exceed 1994 U.S. values by 3.1 years for men and 3.3 years for women. The success of the Japanese in raising their levels of life expectancy has been due to large declines in mortality from cerebrovascular disease and maintenance of low levels of heart disease relative to other developed countries (Yanagishita and Guralnik 1988).

Related Concepts

There are some concepts that are related to life expectancy and sometimes confused with life expectancy. One is *lifespan.* The lifespan of a species is the age to which the longest-lived members survive. The lifespan of humans is thought to be approximately 115 years. Reports of longer-lived humans, while widely circulated, have not been documented. Current thinking is that while life expectancy has increased dramatically over the last century, the lifespan of humans has not changed over time; however, this does not mean it will never change. If future discoveries enable us to retard the aging process, it may be possible to lengthen the human lifespan in the future.

The lifespan of a species is the age to which the longest-lived members survive. The lifespan of humans is thought to be about 115 years. (Kit Kittle/Corbis)

Life endurancy is another related concept that is computed from the life table. This is the age at which a specified proportion of the life table entry cohort is still alive. For instance, in 1990 the age at which ten percent of the life table population remains alive is expected to be ninety years for men and ninety-six years for women. Life endurancy has been increasing over time and is expected to continue to change with changes in survival rates. In 1900 the 10-percent survival age was eighty-one for men and eighty-two for women (Faber and Wade 1983).

Finally, *total life expectancy* at any age is the sum of two parts: *active life expectancy* and *inactive life expectancy.* Active life expectancy has been interpreted by some to mean average length of life free of dependency on others for the performance of basic activities necessary to living, such as eating, bathing, getting in and out of bed, and so forth (Katz et al. 1985; Rogers, Rogers, and Belanger 1989). Others have interpreted active life expectancy as average length of life free from a disability that causes a person to alter his or her normal activity (Wilkins and Adams 1983; Bebbington 1988; Crimmins, Saito, and Ingegneri 1989; Colvez et al. 1986). Crimmins, Saito, and Ingegneri (1989) estimated that active life expectancy or disability-free life expectancy at birth in the United States in 1980 was 55.5 years for men and 60.4 years for women. The difference between blacks and whites in disability-free life expectancy at birth was even greater than the difference in total life expectancy. In 1980 black disability-free life expectancy was 49.1 years, while that for whites was 56.2 years.

Interest in active life expectancy has grown recently as people have recognized that gains in total life expectancy today may not mean the same thing as in the past. Past gains in life expectancy came about largely because fewer people died of infectious diseases, either because they did not get the diseases or they received treatment that prevented death. People thus saved from death were generally free of the disease. Under these circumstances gains in life expectancy were accompanied by better health in the population surviving. Now, with gains in life expectancy being made because of declining death rates from chronic diseases especially among the old, it is not clear that the surviving population is a healthier population. This is because generally there is no cure for the chronic diseases, and their development has not been prevented. People are being saved from death, but they live with disease. This is the basis for questioning whether the additions to life expectancy are healthy or unhealthy years. Studies that have addressed the issue of changes in active life expectancy over time have reported that while life expectancy has definitely increased in recent years, active life expectancy has not increased (Wilkins and Adams 1983; Crimmins, Saito, and Ingegneri 1989).

[See also Birth and Death Rates.]

BIBLIOGRAPHY

Bebbington, A. C. 1988 "The Expectation of Life Without Disability in England and Wales." *Social Science and Medicine* 27:321–326.

Coale, A. J., and E. E. Kisker 1986 "Mortality Crossovers: Reality or Bad Data?" *Population Studies* 40:389–401.

Colvez, A., J. M. Robine, D. Bucquet, F. Hatton, B. Morel, and S. Lelaidier. "L'espérance de vie sans incapacité en France en 1982." *Population* 41:1,025–1,042.

Crimmins, E. M., Y. Saito, and D. Ingegneri 1989 "Changes in Life Expectancy and Disability-Free Life Expectancy in the United States." *Population and Development Review* 15:235–267.

Faber, J., and A. Wade 1983 *Life Tables for the United States: 1900–2050.* Actuarial Study No. 89. Baltimore: U.S. Department of Health and Human Services, Social Security Administration, Office of the Actuary.

Katz, S., L. Branch, M. Branson, J. Papsidero, J. Beck, and D. S. Greer 1985 "Active Life Expectancy." *New England Journal of Medicine* 309:1,218–1,224.

Manton, K. G., and E. Stallard 1981 "Methods for Evaluating the Heterogeneity of Aging Processes in Human Populations Using Vital Statistics Data: Explaining the Black/White Mortality Crossover by a Model of Mortality Selection." *Human Biology* 53:47–67.

National Center for Health Statistics 1990a "Annual Summary of Births, Marriages, Divorces, and Deaths: United States, 1989." *Monthly Vital Statistics Report.* 38(13). Hyattsville, Md.: U.S. Public Health Service.

——— 1990b *Vital Statistics of the United States, 1987.* Vol. 2, *Mortality,* Part A. Washington, D.C.: U.S. Public Health Service.

Ogawa, N. 1989 "Population Aging and Its Impact Upon Health Resource Requirements at Government and Familial Levels in Japan," *Aging and Society* 9:383–405.

Rogers, R., A. Rogers, and A. Belanger 1989 "Active Life among the Elderly in the United States: Multistate Life Table Estimates and Population Projections." *The Milbank Quarterly* 67:370–411.

Schoen, R., and V. Nelson 1981 "Mortality by Cause among Spanish Surnamed Californians, 1969–1971." *Social Science Quarterly* 62:259–274.

United Nations 1982 *Levels and Trends of Mortality since 1950.* New York: United Nations.

U.S. Bureau of the Census 1975 *Historical Statistics of the U.S., Colonial Times to 1970, Bicentennial Edition,* Part 2. Washington, D.C.: U.S. Government Printing Office.

Vaupel, J. 1986 "How Change in Age-Specific Mortality Affects Life Expectancy." *Population Studies* 40:147–157.

Wilkins, R. and O. Adams 1983 "Health Expectancy in Canada, Late 1970's: Demographic, Regional, and Social Dimensions." *American Journal of Public Health* 73:1073–1080.

Yanagishita, M. and J. Guralnik 1988 "Changing Mortality Patterns That Led Life Expectancy in Japan to Surpass Sweden's: 1972–1982." *Demography* 25:611–624.

Yin, P., and M. Shine 1985 "Misinterpretations of Increases in Life Expectancy in Gerontology Textbooks." *The Gerontologist* 25:78–82.

– EILEEN M. CRIMMINS

LIFE-STYLES AND HEALTH

Life-styles are a major determinant of who shall live shall live and who shall die (Fuchs 1974). Mechanic (1978, p. 164) argues that the concept of life-styles refers to a diverse set of variables, including nutrition, housing, health attitudes and beliefs, risk-taking behavior, health behavior and habits, and preventive health behavior.

Establishing the causal linkage between life-styles and health is not a simple task. Variables included in life-styles interact with each other (Mechanic 1978), making it difficult to separate out their unique contributions to health and illness. There is a need to adjust for confounding variables such as race, gender, education, and psychological distress.

In addition, there are problems in specifying the nature of the etiological relationship between life-styles and disease. Not every person who engages in an unhealthy life-style will die prematurely. For example, some heavy smokers do not develop lung cancer. Genetic predisposition, co-morbidities, other health habits, and access to adequate medical care are factors that may intervene in the relationship between host and disease.

The most convincing models of the relationship between life-styles and health are those built on triangulated evidence from animal, clinical, and epidemiological studies. As an example, consider the link between tobacco use and cancer. In experimental animal studies, one group of animals is exposed to tobacco smoke while the control group is not. If the experimental group has a higher incidence of cancer than the control group, the study provides evidence to link smoking with cancer. Another strategy involves clinical studies. Lung tissue of smokers is compared with lung tissue of nonsmokers. If more smokers than nonsmokers show cancerous cells in the lung tissue, this provides additional data to con-

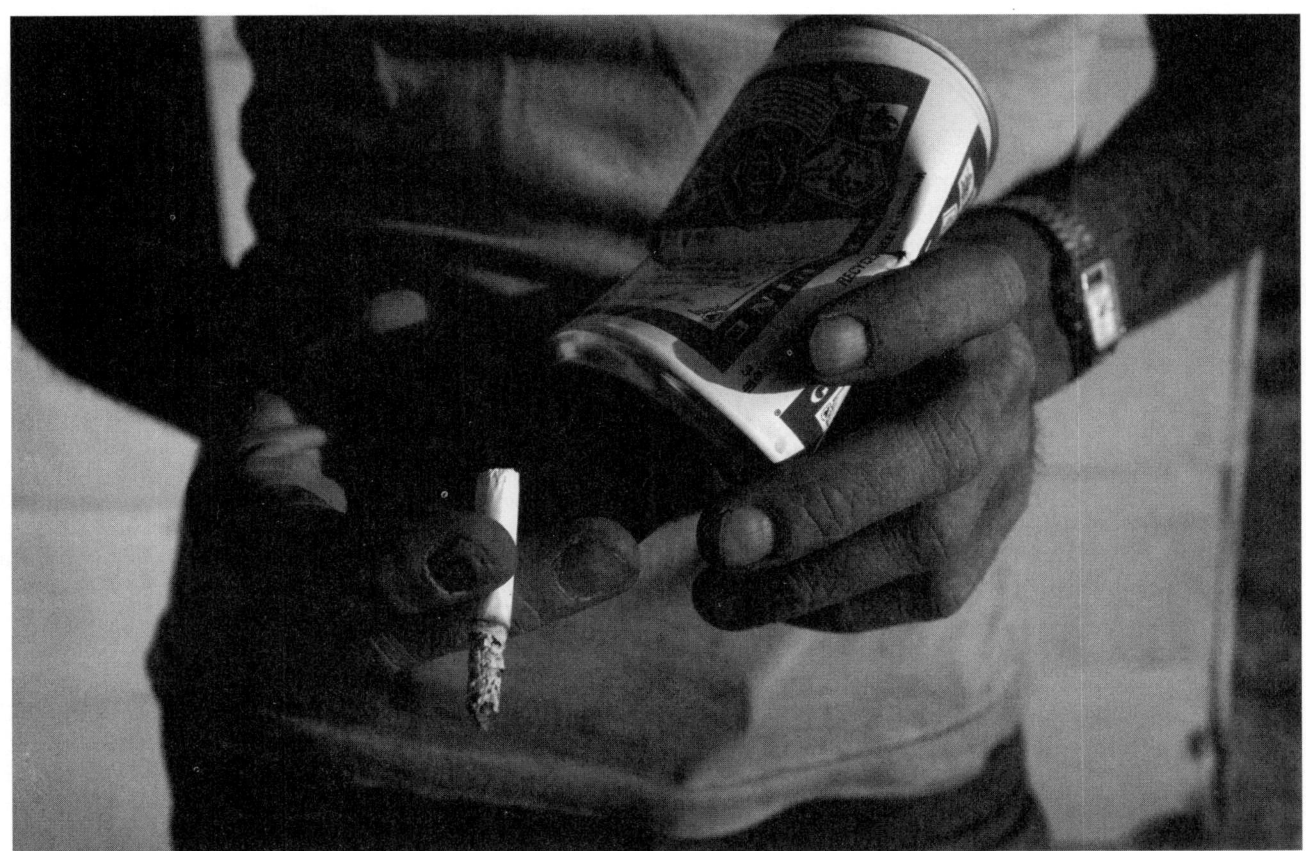

Alcohol and tobacco use are two life-style choices that can negatively impact a person's health and longevity. (Kit Kittle/Corbis)

firm that smoking causes lung cancer. A final strategy uses epidemiological methods. In prospective studies, separate groups of smokers and nonsmokers are followed over time to establish the risk of developing cancer. If, all else being equal, members of the smoking group develop more cases of cancer, the causal relationship between smoking and cancer is confirmed.

With these methodological issues in mind, three behaviors are selected to illustrate how life-styles impact on health: tobacco use, alcohol consumption, and diet. For these three variables there are extensive animal, clinical, and epidemiological data to support the causal relationship between each agent and disease. Illustrations are provided to indicate how healthy habits can reduce mortality rates.

Tobacco Use

Tobacco use has been defined as the most important single preventable cause of disease and death in society. It is responsible for more than one of every six deaths in the United States. Tobacco use kills more than 400,000 Americans annually (Centers for Disease Control 1998). According to Warner, "Thirty percent of all cancer deaths are attributable to smoking, as are 21% of all coronary heart disease deaths, 18% of stroke deaths, and 82% of deaths from chronic obstructive pulmonary disease."

Careful epidemiological studies have determined that tobacco use causes lung, laryngeal, lip, and esophageal cancer. Tobacco use is also associated with coronary artery disease, chronic bronchitis, cerebrovascular disease, emphysema, and low birth weight (Office of Smoking and Health 1989). In addition, smoking has been linked to cancer of the cervix, pancreas, and liver. There is new evidence that women who smoke at the time of conception have an increased risk for an ectopic pregnancy (Chow et al. 1988; Coste, Job-Spira, and Fernandez 1991).

Children exposed to parental smoking have a greater risk for wheezy bronchitis.

Passive smoking is also associated with increased rates of illness (Center for Disease Control 1988). Increased risks for lung cancer and heart disease are reported for nonsmokers who live with smokers (Sandler et al. 1989). Children exposed to parental smoking have a greater risk for wheezy bronchitis (Neuspiel et al. 1989).

Alcohol

The National Institute on Alcohol Abuse and Alcoholism (1990) estimates that alcohol use is responsible for 100,000 deaths each year in this country. Forty-one percent of the motor vehicle fatalities in 1996 were alcohol related (National Highway Traffic Safety Administration 1996). Alcohol has frequently been implicated in suicides, falls, drownings, and fires and burns.

From 10 to 20 percent of heavy drinkers develop cirrhosis of the liver, which was the ninth leading cause of death in the United States in 1994 (Grant, Dufour, and Harford). The liver is the primary site of alcohol metabolism, and drinkers are at risk for other forms of liver disease, including alcoholic hepatitis and cancer.

Chronic alcohol consumption may cause damage to the heart muscle, heart arrhythmias, and hypertension. There is suggestive evidence that alcohol may relate to ischemic heart disease and cerebrovascular illness (Moore and Pearson 1986). Alcohol abuse is also a risk factor for cancer of the liver, breast, esophagus, nasopharynx, and larynx (Driver and Swann 1987; Freudenheim and Graham 1989). NIAAA concludes: "The range of medical consequences of alcohol abuse is both immense and complex—virtually no part of the body is spared the effects of excessive alcohol consumption" (1990, p. 127).

Alcohol also functions as a teratogen, producing defects in the human fetus in utero. The possible effects of alcohol on the fetus include gross morphological defects and cognitive/behavioral dysfunctions. Fetal alcohol syndrome is the most severe consequence of the mother's heavy drinking during pregnancy and is characterized by craniofacial anomalies, mental retardation, central nervous system dysfunction, and growth retardation (Jones and Smith 1973; Rosett 1980; Abel and Sokol 1986). Fetal alcohol syndrome is one of the leading preventable causes of birth defects.

Diet

Dietary factors have been linked to mortality from cardiovascular disease and cancer. It is estimated that diet contributes to up to one-third of cardiovascular deaths (Milio 1986) and up to 35 percent of all deaths from cancer (Doll and Peto 1981).

Among men, diet-related cancer occurs in the colon or rectum and the prostate. Among women, cancer of the breast, colon/rectum, and uterine corpus have been found to be related to diet (Schatzkin, Baranovsky, and Kessler 1988). Diets with high levels of saturated fats are related to cancer of the colon and rectum. Further, there is evidence that a high-vegetable-fiber diet may help to prevent colon cancer. Fat intake may be related to breast cancer, although the evidence is conflicting. There are some data to support the hypothesis that fat intake increases the risk of lung cancer (controlling for smoking levels), prostate cancer, and bladder cancer (Freudenheim and Graham 1989).

The relationship between diet and coronary heart disease is well established (Fraser 1968). Dietary practices that increase the levels of serum lipids and lipoproteins increase the rate of coronary heart disease. Individuals whose diets are high in saturated fats and cholesterol have a higher risk for myocardial infarction. There is some recent evidence that oatmeal and oat bran may reduce cholesterol levels, which in turn may lower the risk of heart disease (Humble 1991).

Healthy Habits

The Alameda County Study (Berkman and Breslow 1983) illustrates how healthy habits may increase life expectancy. The authors followed 4,700 persons for nine years and found that five health practices prolonged life expectancy: never smoking, exercising regularly, drinking alcohol in moderation, being of average weight for height, and sleeping seven or eight hours a day. Women who engaged in all these healthy practices had an adjusted mortality rate of 3.9/100 compared with 11.9/100 for women who engaged in none to two of these practices. The comparable rates for men were 5.8/100 and 16.0/100. These differences persisted after controlling for perceived health status, socioeconomic factors, and psychological characteristics. These healthy practices lowered the mortality rate for heart disease, cancer, and cerebrovascular disease.

Three examples were selected to illustrate the role of life-styles in health. There are other lifestyle components that are related to health which are beyond the scope of this chapter. For example, stressful life-styles have been linked to mental illness, gastrointestinal disorders, and heart disease. Regular use of seat belts reduces the likelihood of death or injury in automobile accidents. Proper dental hygiene decreases the rate of dental caries. Childhood immunizations prevent measles, mumps, and polio.

It must be emphasized that while a healthy life-style may be a necessary condition for longevity, it is not a sufficient condition. Many variables interact with life-styles to protect against disease and death. For example, evidence is mounting that genetics has a very important role in the risk for heart disease and cancer. Thus, the models predicting who shall live and who shall die involve complicated interactions of health practices, genetic risk, sociodemographic characteristics, and so on. Nonetheless, individuals who abstain from smoking, drink alcohol in moderation, and watch dietary fat and cholesterol intake have a better chance of survival than those who do not.

[See also Alcohol; Drug Abuse; Health and the Life Course; Health Promotion.]

BIBLIOGRAPHY

Abel, Ernest L., and Robert J. Sokol 1986 "Fetal Alcohol Syndrome Is Now Leading Cause of Mental Retardation." *Lancet* ii:1222.

Berkman, Lisa F., and Lester Breslow 1983 *Health and Ways of Living. The Alameda County Study.* New York: Oxford University Press.

Center for Disease Control 1988 "Passive Smoking: Beliefs, Attitudes, and Exposures, United States, 1986." *Morbidity Mortality Weekly Review* 37:239–241.

Chow, W. H., J. R. Daling, N. S. Weiss, and L. F. Voigt 1988 "Smoking and Tubal Pregnancy." *Obstetrics and Gynecology* 71:167–170.

Coste, Joel, Nadine Job-Spira, and Herve Fernandez 1991 "Increased Risk of Ectopic Pregnancy with Maternal Cigarette Smoking." *American Journal of Public Health* 81:199–201.

Doll, R., and R. Peto 1981 "The Causes of Cancer: Quantitative Estimates of Avoidable Risks of Cancer in the U.S. Today." *Journal of the National Cancer Institute* 66:1193–1308.

Driver, H. E., and P. F. Swann 1987 "Alcohol and Cancer (Review)." *Anticancer Research* 7:309–320.

Fraser, G. 1968 *Preventive Cardiology.* New York: Oxford University Press.

Freudenheim, Jo L., and Saxon Graham 1989 "Toward a Dietary Prevention of Cancer." *Epidemiologic Reviews* 11:229–235.

Fuchs, Victor 1974 *Who Shall Live? Health Economics and Social Change.* New York: Basic Books.

Grant, B. F., M. C. Dufour, and T. C. Harford 1988 "Epidemiology of Alcoholic Liver Disease." *Seminars in Liver Disease* 8:12–25.

Humble, Charles G. 1991 "Oats and Cholesterol: The Prospects for Prevention of Heart Disease." *American Journal of Public Health* 81:159–160.

Jones, K. L., and A. W. Smith 1973 "Recognition of the Fetal Alcohol Syndrome in Early Infancy." *Lancet* i:1267–1271.

Mechanic, David 1978 *Medical Sociology,* 2nd ed. New York: Free Press.

Milio, N. 1986 *Promoting Health Through Public Policy.* Ottawa: Canadian Public Health Association.

Moore, R. D., and T. A. Pearson 1986 "Moderate Alcohol Consumption and Coronary Artery Disease: A Review." *Medicine* 65:242–267.

National Highway Traffic Safety Administration, National Center for Statistics 1988 *Drunk Driving Facts.* Washington, D.C.: NHTSA.

National Institute on Alcohol Abuse and Alcoholism 1990 *Seventh Special Report to the U.S. Congress on Alcohol and Health.* DHHS Pub. no. (ADM) 90-1656. Rockville, Md.: U.S. Department of Health and Human Services.

Neuspiel, Daniel R., David Rush, Neville R. Butler, Jean Golding, Polly Bijur, and Matthew Kurzon 1989 "Parental Smoking and Post-Infancy Wheezing in Children: A Prospective Cohort Study." *American Journal of Public Health* 79:168–171.

Office of Smoking and Health 1989 *Reducing the Health Consequences of Smoking: 25 Years of Progress. A Report to the Surgeon General.* DHHS Pub. no. (CDC) 89-8411. Washington, D.C.: U.S. Department of Health and Human Services.

Rosett, Henry L. 1980 "A Clinical Perspective of the Fetal Alcohol Syndrome." *Alcoholism* (New York) 4:119–122.

Sandler, Dale P., George W. Comstock, Knud J. Helsing, and David L. Shore 1989 "Deaths from All Causes in Non-Smokers Who

Lived with Smokers." *American Journal of Public Health* 79:163–167.

Schatzkin, Arthur, Anne Baranovsky, and Larry G. Kessler 1988 "Diet and Cancer: Evidence from Associations of Multiple Primary Cancers in the SEER Program." Cancer 62:1451–1457.

Warner, Kenneth E. 1989 "Smoking and Health: A 25-Year Perspective." *American Journal of Public Health* 79:141–143.

– JANET HANKIN

LONG-TERM CARE

Long-term care consists of a range of health, supportive personal care, and social services delivered over a sustained period to individuals who lack some capacity for self-care (Kane and Kane 1987). It includes services for persons with chronic physical or mental illness, mental retardation, or other severe disabling conditions. Long-term care is distinct from acute care in that its purpose is maintenance and custodial rather than curative. It entails, primarily, low-level technology that is provided by low-paid paraprofessionals or family members; and, notably, its costs are paid for by individuals or welfare programs, rather than by traditional insurance mechanisms.

Need for Long-Term Care

Major demographic, social, and health changes resulting in large and growing numbers of older, disabled persons have led to a corresponding increase in the need for long-term care. Improved standards of living and medical advances in the prevention and control of infectious diseases have enabled increasing proportions of the population to live longer. The elderly population as a whole has grown twice as fast as the total population since the 1970s, and this growth has been most rapid for the group over the age of eighty-five (Ferraro and Wan 1990; Longino 1990). Because the incidence of chronic illness increases with age, this growth in the aged population has resulted in a significant increase in the number of persons with chronic disabilities that are the primary determinants of need for long-term care (Senate Committee on Aging 1988). The extent of an individual's disability is most often measured by assessing functional ability, using one of a variety of measures of activities of daily living (ADL) or instrumental activities of daily living (IADL) (see Kane and Kane 1981). It is important to note that while the prevalence of functional disability is higher among the oldest old, the actual number of disabled persons is largest among the younger old (Macken 1986).

Recent research suggests that the chances of going through life without disability may be declining in measurable ways (McKinlay et al. 1989). Despite some debate about the compression of morbidity (Fries 1980; Schneider and Brody 1983), some researchers present an overall picture of increasing disability that counters the hopeful view of increased life expectancy and the compression of morbidity (Brody et al. 1987). Together, these trends have led to large and increasing numbers of elderly needing long-term care.

Despite frequent references to the long-term care "system," there is little systematic about long-term care. It varies from state to state and from community to community in composition, organization, eligibility criteria, and financing mechanisms. Among the formal services that have been included are nursing homes, home care, adult day care, respite care, a variety of sheltered housing options, senior centers, congregate dining, and home-delivered meals.

Long-Term Care Providers and Services

NURSING HOMES. Although the majority of long-term care is provided by informal sources, nursing homes are the bulwark of the current formal long-term care system and the service that has the highest costs. Factors associated with nursing home placement include age, sex, and marital status. The need for nursing home care increases with age. The percentage of nursing home residents per thousand is thirteen times higher for men eighty-five and over than for men sixty-five to seventy-four, and eighteen times higher for women eighty-five and over than for women sixty-five to seventy-four (Ferraro and Wan 1990). The large majority of nursing home patients are female and unmarried.

FAMILY CARE. The majority of long-term care takes place within the home, and the bulk of this care comes from relatives, friends, and neighbors. And as is true with the nursing home population, age is associated with functional dependencies among the elderly living in the community. The oldest old are much more likely to be living in the community with functional dependencies than are the younger old, and they are more likely to have multiple assistance needs.

Informal sources provide assistance with a wide range of tasks, including help with banking and legal matters, help with transportation, and assistance with household tasks and personal care. A sizable literature has developed which indicates that the type, intensity, and duration of caregiving varies by the relationship and proximity of the potential caregiver to the receiver (Stone et al. 1987; Montgomery 1991b).

There is a consensus within the literature that a hierarchy exists for designating the informal source of care and for types of care provided (Cantor 1980). When they are available, spouses provide care. When there is no spouse, daughters step in, followed by daughters-in-law, sons, and then more distant relatives. Spouses are likely to provide all types of care when care is needed, including personal care. Daughters and daughters-in-law also provide personal care, although less frequently than do spouses. In contrast, sons, more distant relatives, and friends are more likely to play a backup role, helping with emergencies and limited-time tasks (Gurland et al. 1978; Montgomery 1991b).

A huge literature has emerged that has documented the social, psychological, and physical costs of this informal care (Montgomery 1985; George and Gwyther 1986), and has contributed to the focus on formal support services as a means to augment or replace informal support. The most commonly used community formal support services are home care and adult day care (Benjamin 1991).

HOME CARE. Home care, like long-term care, is difficult to define because it encompasses a wide range of specific services. Home care is used to refer to in-home health and supportive services that include professional, paraprofessional, post-acute, and long-term care in a recipient's home (Benjamin 1991; Kane and Kane 1987). At one end of the continuum of cost and skills, these include physician and nursing services, and at the other end of the continuum, they include housekeeper and chore services (Kane and Kane 1987).

ADULT DAY CARE. Although nursing home care, informal care, and home care are the most common sources of long-term care, three other types of services are often considered to be part of long-term care. These are sheltered care, adult day care, and respite services. Adult day care is a community-based, therapeutically oriented program that provides health, social, and rehabilitative services to frail older persons in a congregate setting during daytime hours. Day care centers vary in emphasis from those that focus on rehabilitation and follow a medical model to those that focus on maintenance and follow a social model. A wide range of services can be offered through such programs, including physical therapy, health maintenance programs, assistance with daily activities, and social and recreational activities.

Unfortunately, many day care centers struggle to keep their census up and their doors open because there are few sources of third-party payment for adult day care and many potential clients cannot afford it. In the design and delivery of their services, adult day care centers focus on the impaired older person. Their goals include the maintenance of maximum functioning in their clients and the improvement of their quality of life. One of the main purposes of day care centers, however, is to benefit family members who are providing the majority of care for these impaired elders, by providing family members a break from their daily caregiving tasks. As such, adult day care has become one of the primary sources of respite care.

RESPITE CARE. Like most other long-term care services, respite care can entail a wide range of services. In addition to adult day care, respite services have included nursing home services, home care services, and stays in hospitals. The unique aspect of respite is not the specific service that is offered but the purpose for which the service is offered, which is to provide a break for the primary caregiver of an impaired elder. Research focused on long-term care and families has consistently reported that respite services, particularly in-home services, have emerged as the type of support most frequently desired by family members (Montgomery 1991a). However, due to lack of funding by third-party sources, it remains a service that is not widely available. More troubling is the past research which shows that respite services frequently go unused when they are available, a fact that has prompted researchers to begin investigating factors affecting utilization (Montgomery 1991a; Lawton 1989).

The deep ambivalence that Americans have felt about poverty is reflected in the fact that Medicare only provides for for acute care needs of the elderly.

SHELTERED CARE. Although the bricks-and-mortar part of housing falls outside long-term care per se, Kane and Kane (1987) argue that housing policy can provide a framework for effective long-term care delivery and that many housing arrangements can directly or indirectly provide services, such as congregate meals and social programs, which can be considered aspects of long-term care. Federal housing for the elderly, congregate care settings, board and care housing, shared housing, and life care communities have been developed as means to ensure long-term care. Although there has been evidence that such housing improves the ability of functionally impaired persons to live independently, these housing options are not widely available nor is there a consistent means of financing such housing for low-income, impaired older persons.

Long-Term Care as a Public Issue

Long-term care has become a salient and publicly debated issue primarily because the growing numbers of persons needing care and the rapidly rising costs of health care have created a burden for both the public purse and individual resources (Kane and Kane 1987; Estes and Lee 1985). Because funding of long-term care has been limited, decentralized, categorical, and linked with welfare programs, the heavy burdens of long-term care have touched not only the poor but also millions of middle-income families and individuals. For these persons the high cost of caring for a chronically or acutely ill elderly person can lead to impoverishment and the necessity of relying on public resources (Estes and Lee 1985). Hence, the focus of public debate has been the primary dilemma of long-term care—to identify an affordable and equitable means to provide care.

BIOMEDICAL BIAS. To a large extent, the long-term care dilemma has emerged as a consequence of three distinct but related value conflicts. First, long-term care has suffered because there is a biomedical bias among providers and policymakers (Estes and Lee 1985). In accord with the medical model, legitimate health care needs are those which require technical and medical care that will lead to cures or rehabilitations. The social and custodial needs of patients are given low priority. This bias toward medical care in the allocation of resources has resulted in the "medicalization" of services, as exemplified in the high proportion of publicly financed health expenditures allocated to hospital and physician coverage, as opposed to community, in-home, and other social services (Estes and Lee 1985).

This bias toward medical care in the allocation of public resources is also reflected in the two separate mechanisms that currently finance the majority of care for the elderly (Meyer and Quadagno 1990). Medicare, which is the primary source for financing acute medical care, is a universal health program; Medicaid, which is the primary source for financing long-term care, is a means-tested program for the impoverished. Furthermore, Medicare is a centralized federal mechanism for paying for acute care needs, while Medicaid is a decentralized, federal/state mechanism that varies across states in terms of eligibility, coverage, and benefits (Ferraro and Wan 1990). These differences in funding mechanisms have contributed to the low priority given to long-term care by physicians and hospitals because it is not economically rewarding for health care professionals to provide services to Medicaid beneficiaries.

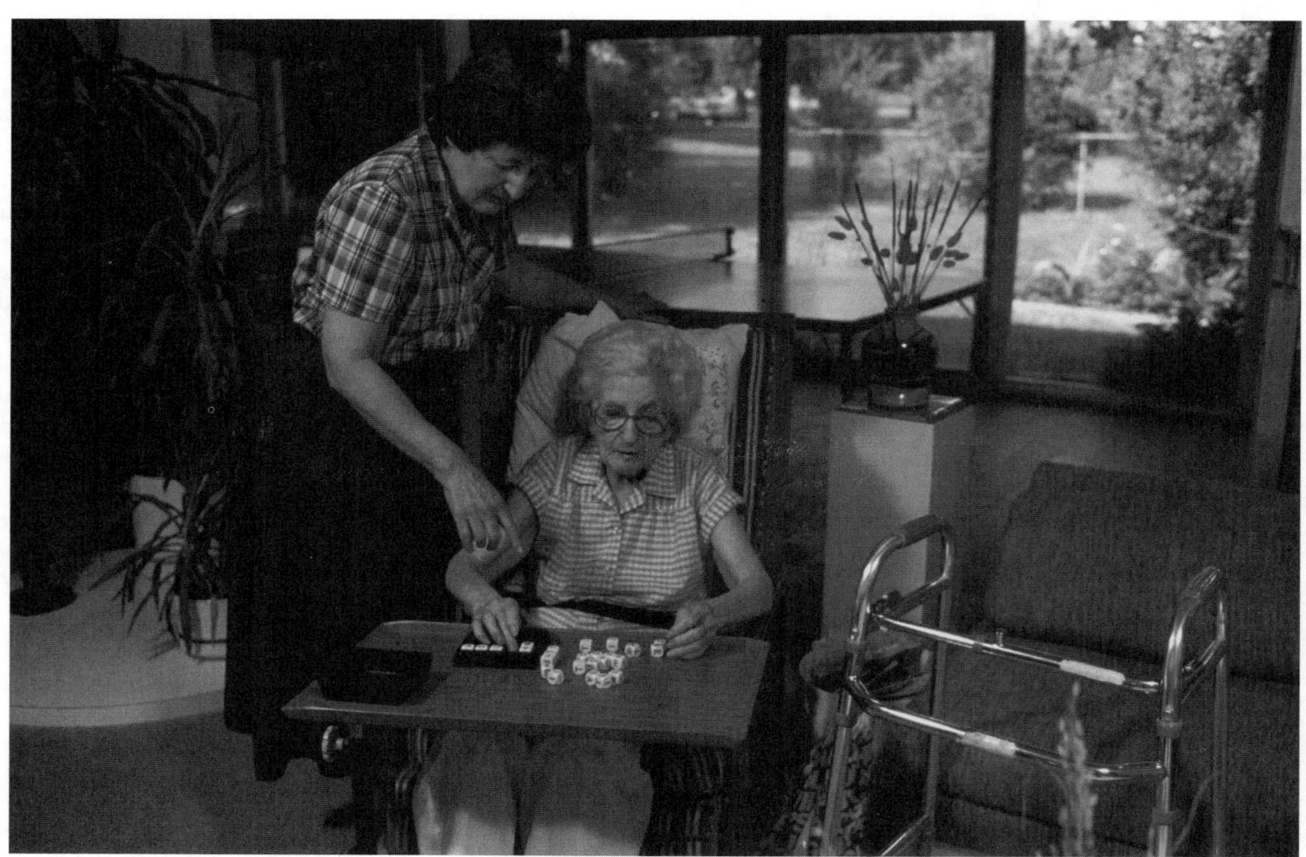

Home care refers to in-home health and supportive services that include professional, paraprofessional, post-acute, and long-term care in a recipient's home. (David H. Wells/Corbis)

CRITERIA FOR ELIGIBILITY. The dual basis for financing long-term care versus acute care reflects the second conflict that underlies the long-term care policy dilemma, the criteria of eligibility for benefits. Specifically, long-term care policy reflects an ambivalence toward the belief that age is a legitimate criterion for defining need (Meyers and Quadagno 1990). A historical review of policy development indicates that both the Medicare Act and the Medicaid legislation are grounded in welfare policy that has been strongly influenced by the Elizabethan poor laws, which were created to assist only the deserving poor and to discourage the undeserving poor from seeking help (Meyer and Quadagno 1990). The difference between the two programs rests in the definition of *deserving.* The Medicare program, with its emphasis on acute care, treats age as a legitimate criterion for determining *deserving.* Marmor (1970, p. 15) notes that the Medicare Act of 1965 defined the aged as both "needy and deserving through no fault of their own because they had less income and greater medical needs." However, the deep ambivalence that Americans have long felt about poverty is reflected in the fact that the Medicare Act provides for universal entitlement for the elderly only for acute care needs. The long-term care needs of disabled elderly, which are primarily social service needs, are financed through Medicaid, a means-tested program that defines need based on income and disability rather than on age. As such, long-term care policy is the stepchild of traditional welfare policy, which has been developed and instituted by state and local government to deal with the poor. The goal of this public policy has been to manage the care of the poor in the most efficient and least costly way, rather than to redress the underlying social causes of dependency (Estes and Lee 1985).

FAMILY RESPONSIBILITY. The third value conflict that contributes to policy debates and the dilemma of providing adequate long-term care also has its roots in the Elizabethan poor laws. This conflict concerns the appropriate role of family members in providing long-term care. At issue is the relative responsibility of the state versus that of the family. Although social historians have documented the economic basis for family responsibility in the past, there is a widely held public belief that family responsibility for the care of the elderly is a moral obligation (Schorr 1980). In part, this belief has emerged because the Elizabethan poor laws, which specifically designated the family members as the parties having the first line of responsibility for the care of dependent members, have been the model for modern welfare laws. These laws were created to protect the public purse after industrialization freed individuals to earn a living apart from family-owned land and businesses, creating the possibility that older persons could become dependent on the community for care.

Despite this economic basis for the creation of the Elizabethan poor laws and modern derivatives in welfare and long-term care legislation, the reasons for enacting them have often been couched in moral language, creating and reinforcing a common belief about the moral basis of family responsibility (Schorr 1980). The presence of this belief, combined with the reality that the majority of long-term care is provided by family members, has led to policy debates about the appropriate role of the family, and to the implementation of programs and practices aimed at retaining and/or supporting families as the primary sources of long-term care (Borgatta and Montgomery 1987).

Together these three value conflicts have created the context within which long-term care policy and practices have been debated and legislation has been formulated and reformulated. As a result, long-term care policy has evolved in a piecemeal, crisis-oriented manner that has perpetuated an uncoordinated set of services with fragmented funding. The three value conflicts have also been the context within which research and demonstration programs have been implemented to address the long-term care dilemma. These demonstrations and policy changes have usually been aimed at constraining costs of long-term care for the public purse by substituting low-cost services for higher-cost services, restricting access to services, and/or shifting responsibility for care to the family. The most notable experiments have been the national channeling demonstration of the 1980s, the establishment of social/health maintenance organizations; the imposition of a prospective payment system (diagnostic-related groups) in 1983; and the passage (1988) and repeal (1989) of the Medicare catastrophic coverage. Additionally, numerous programs introducing respite care, support groups, and education programs for family caregivers have been designed and tested (Montgomery 1991a). Unfortunately, none of these experiments has led to a solution of the long-term care dilemma, which will continue to be a major policy issue until the basic value conflicts are addressed more directly.

[See also Death and Dying; Health and the Life Course; Social Gerontology.]

BIBLIOGRAPHY

Benjamin, A. E. 1991 (Forthcoming) "In-Home Health and Supportive Services for Older Persons: Background and Perspective." In M. Ory and A. Duncker, eds., *In-Home Health and Supportive Services for Older People.* Newbury Park, Calif.: Sage.

Borgatta, E. F., and R. J. V. Montgomery 1987 "Aging Policy and Societal Values." In E. F. Borgatta and R. J. V. Montgomery, eds., *Critical Issues in Aging Policy: Linking Research and Values.* Newbury Park, Calif.: Sage.

Brody, J., D. Brock, and T. F. Williams 1987 "Trends in the Health of the Elderly Population." *Annual Review of Public Health* 8:211–234.

Cantor, M. H. 1980 "The Informal Support System: Its Relevance in the Lives of the Elderly." In E. F. Borgatta and N. G. McCluskey, eds., *Aging and Society: Current Research and Policy Perspectives.* Beverly Hills, Calif.: Sage.

Conrad, K. J., P. Hanrahan, and S. L. Hughes 1990 "Survey of Adult Day Care in the United States." *Research on Aging* 12, no. 1:36–56.

Estes, C. L., and P. R. Lee 1985 "Social, Political, and Economic Background of Long Term Care Policy." In C. Harrington, R. J. Newcomer, and C. L. Estes, eds., *Long Term Care of the Elderly: Public Policy Issues.* Beverly Hills, Calif.: Sage.

Ferraro, K. F., and T. T. H. Wan 1990 "Health Needs and Services for Older Adults: Evaluating Policies for an Aging Society." In S. M. Stahl, ed., *The Legacy of Longevity.* Newbury Park, Calif.: Sage.

Fries, J. F. 1980 "Aging, Natural Death, and the Compression of Morbidity." *New England Journal of Medicine* 303:130–135.

George, L. K., and L. P. Gwyther 1986 "Caregiver Well-being: A Multidimensional Examination of Family Caregivers." *The Gerontologist* 26, no. 3:253–259.

Gurland, B., L. Dean, R. Guland, and D. Cook 1978 "Personal Time Dependency in the Elderly of New York City: Findings from the U.S.-U.K. Cross-National Geriatric Community Study." New York: Community Council of Greater New York.

Kane, R. A., and R. L. Kane 1981 *Assessing the Elderly: A Practical Guide to Measurement.* Lexington, Mass.: D. C. Health.

——— 1987 *Long-Term Care: Principles, Programs and Policies.* New York: Springer.

LaPlante, M. P. 1989 "Disability in Basic Life Activities Across the Life Span." *Disability Statistics Report* 1:1–42.

Lawton, M. P. 1989 "A Controlled Study of Respite Service for Caregivers of Alzheimer's Patients." *The Gerontologist* 29, no. 1:8–16.

Liang, J., and E. J. Tu 1986 "Estimating Lifetime Risk of Nursing Home Residency: A Further Note." *The Gerontologist* 26, no. 5:560–563.

Longino, C. 1990 "The Relative Contributions of Gender, Social Class, and Advancing Age to Health." In S. M. Stahl, ed., *The Legacy of Longevity.* Newbury Park, Calif.: Sage.

Macken, C. L. 1986 "A Profile of Functionally Impaired Elderly Persons Living in the Community." *Health Care Financing Review* 7:33–49.

Marmor, T. 1970 *The Politics of Medicare.* New York: Aldine.

McAuley, W. J., S. S. Travis, and M. Safewright 1990 "The Relationship Between Formal and Informal Health Care Services for the Elderly." In S. M. Stahl, ed., *The Legacy of Longevity.* Newbury Park, Calif.: Sage.

McKinlay, J., S. McKinlay, and R. Beaglehole 1989 "Trends in Death and Disease in the Contribution of Medical Measures." In H. Freeman and S. Levin, eds., *Handbook of Medical Sociology.* Englewood Cliffs., N.J.: Prentice-Hall.

Meyer, M. H., and J. Quadagno 1990 "The Dilemma of Poverty-Based Long-Term Care." In S. M. Stahl, ed., *The Legacy of Longevity.* Newbury Park, Calif.: Sage.

Montgomery, R. J. V. 1984 "Barriers to the Design and Delivery of Family Support Services." Paper presented to Conference on Families at Interage, September.

——— 1985 "Measurement and the Analysis of Burden." *Research on Aging* 7, no. 1:137–152.

——— 1991a "Examining Respite: Its Promise and Limits." In M. Ory and A. Duncker, eds., *In-Home Health and Supportive Services for Older People.* Newbury Park, Calif.: Sage.

——— 1991b "Gender Differences in Patterns of Child-Parent Caregiving Relationships." In J. W. Dwyer and R. T. Coward, eds., *Gender and Family Care of the Elderly.* Newbury Park, Calif.: Sage.

Schneider, E. L., and Jacob A. Brody 1983 "Aging, Natural Death, and the Compression of Morbidity: Another View." *New England Journal of Medicine* 309, no. 14:854–856.

Schorr, A. L. 1980 *Thy Father and Thy Mother . . . a Second Look at Filial Responsibility and Family Policy.* No. 13-11953. Social Security Administration. Washington, D.C.: U.S. Government Printing Office.

Senate Committee on Aging 1988 *Developments in Aging, 1987,* Vol. III, *Long Term Care Challenge.* Washington, D.C.: U.S. Government Printing Office.

Soldo, B. J. 1982 "Effects of Number and Sex of Adult Children on LTC Service Use Patterns." Paper prepared for the annual meeting of the Gerontological Society of America, November.

——— 1984 "Supply of Informal Care Services: Variation and Effects on Service Utilization Patterns." In W. Scanlon, ed., *Project to Analyze Existing Long-Term Care Data,* vol. 3. Washington, D.C.: The Urban Institute.

——— 1985 "In-Home Services for the Dependent Elderly: Determinants of Current Use and Implications for Future Demand." *Research on Aging* 7, no. 2:281–304.

Soldo, B., and K. Manton 1985 "Health Status and Service Needs of the Oldest Old: Current Patterns and Future Trends." *Milbank Memorial Fund Quarterly* 63:286–319.

Stone, R. 1986 "Aging in the Eighties, Age 65 Years and Over—Use of Community Services." NCHS Advance Data, no. 124. Hyattsville, Md.: National Center for Health Statistics.

———, G. Cafferata, and J. Sangl 1987 "Caregivers of the Frail Elderly: A National Profile." *The Gerontologist* 27:616–626.

Vincente, L. 1979 "The Risk of Institutionalization Before Death." *The Gerontologist* 19:361–367.

Weissert, W. G., T. Wan, B. Livieratos, and S. Katz 1980 "Effects and Costs of Day-Care Services for the Chronically Ill." *Medical Care* 18:567–584.

– RHONDA J. V. MONTGOMERY

LOVE

Sociologists agree that love is one of the most elusive concepts to deal with from a scientific point of view. Indeed, they often point out that poets, novelists, and musical composers are much more adept at producing eloquent expressions about this pervasive sentiment. Dictionary definitions are of limited use in categorizing the essential ingredients of love, except to connote its many variations as an attitude, an emotion, or a behavior. No one definition can capture all the dimensions of love, which can involve a wide range of elements such as romantic obsession, sexuality, caring, even irrationality. Part of the difficulty is that individuals and their cultures define love very differently, depending on particular relationships and circumstances. The love of an infant, for example, is not the same as that felt toward a parent, a spouse, a relative, a friend, or a lover.

Conceptions of love have varied from one culture to another, from one historical era to another (Murstein 1974; Hunt 1959). The range of psychological, social, and cultural meanings attached to love would, therefore, appear to be limitless. However, we experience and express love mostly according to the culture and subcultures in which we have formed our sentiments. The formation of these sentiments begins very early and evolves through the physical and emotional attachments that characterize the parent-child relationship. While idiosyncratic patterns exist, love scripts by and large reflect the influence of cultural conditioning. In short, love is largely a learned response.

We experience and express love mostly according to the culture and subcultures in which we have formed our sentiments.

Cultural norms are internalized and program us to fall in love with specific types of people, within certain social contexts, to the exclusion of others. However, love is not necessarily related to marriage. There is a saying, for example, that in the West one falls in love and then gets married, whereas in the East one marries and then falls in love. In some societies arranged marriages were and still are contracted. The emotional intensity a couple feels toward each other is given little or no consideration. Instead, emphasis is given to the sociopolitical implications of the marital alliance for the families and kinship groups involved.

In the United States, on the other hand, love is viewed as an important condition to marriage. We are generally suspicious of anyone who would marry for any other reason. We are not comfortable with the idea that in some cultures a man marries his mother's brother's daughter because that is the prescribed pattern. Even among our upper classes, where concern over protecting family resources leads to a greater emphasis on such practical considerations in mate selection, couples are expected to espouse mutual love as the basis for their marriage, else their motives become suspect. Marital alliances concocted primarily to preserve or enhance family wealth often receive a cynical response from the public at large.

Families recognize that courtship and mate selection merge not only two individuals but also two different kinship lines, which in turn may affect their socioeconomic and political stature. Consequently, families invest considerable energy and resources to control love (Goode 1959). Several mechanisms to accomplish this have been identified, including the direct control provided by (1) child marriages, in which betrothal may occur before puberty or even before the child is born; (2) defining the pool of eligibles, that is, delineating whom one can and cannot marry; (3) physical or social isolation to limit the probabilities of contact; and (4) various indirect controls such as moving to preferred residential neighborhoods, enrolling children in appropriate schools, joining select organizations, or attending certain churches. The latter mechanism is most characteristic of Western societies.

In American society a *romantic love complex* exists, and this complex posits love as a central prerequisite to marriage. The basic components of this complex are assimilated through the mass media—through romantic stories in novels, magazines, television, and movies. In this way we are psychologically prepared to fall in love. The major characteristics of romantic love include romantic democracy; that is, cultural differences between couples are minimized or ignored because "love and love alone" is sufficient. Indeed, it involves the notion that romantic love thrives on such differences. Romantic love also includes romantic intensity; that is, people are expected to fall in love instantly (love at first sight) and deeply, with great emotional attachment. Finally, romantic love includes romantic monopoly in that once the "bolt from the blue" strikes, the couple presume exclusive emotional and social rights to each other, in perpetuity (Merrill 1959). A person experiencing the full thrust of this complex is supposedly consumed by constant thoughts about the beloved, a longing to spend all one's time with that person, a sad pining in the beloved's absence, and a feeling that life would not be worth living without him or her (Tennov 1980).

There is disagreement as to the extent to which people adhere to the tenets of the romantic love complex and whether it actually influences mate selection. Sociologists have generally viewed it as a poor basis for the establishment of permanent unions inasmuch as it involves an element of capricious choice based upon an unpredictable emotion. Moreover, romantic love is not completely rational. Part of its credo is that there is one and only one true love or ideal mate. Yet we know that people fall in and out of love several times in a lifetime.

People caught up in the romantic complex often idealize their partners. Some argue that this process of idealization, in which a distorted positive picture of the love partner is constructed, results from the blockage of sexual impulses by cultural prohibitions. If this were true, then one would expect a liberalization of our sexual mores to be accompanied by a decline in romanticism. However, this does not appear to have happened, at least in Western societies. What does happen is that the elements of the romantic love complex, including the idealized picture of the partner, are modified to fit the reality of that person that emerges through close and intimate interaction over time. Couples unable to make this accommodation are apt to suffer disillusionment, and their marriages may encounter persistent difficulties. For marriage to succeed, the overromanticized notions and idealizations of romantic love must eventually be replaced by *conjugal love,* which is based upon habits, common interests, mutual acceptance, and mature companionship derived from a shared history.

Sexual impulses and romantic love are often directed at the same person, but they are not the same. People are known to pursue sexual encounters in the absence of any romantic feelings. One is derived from our biological heritage, and the other is a learned cultural pattern. They bear a relationship to one another, however, in that romance often encompasses sexually motivated behavior plus a cluster of cultural expectations (Merrill 1959).

There appear to be gender differences with respect to love and loving. It is generally assumed that such differences reflect culturally defined sex roles. Women have been stereotypically portrayed as starry-eyed romantics, while men are viewed as exploitative realists. However, research shows that men fall in love more quickly than women do and with less deliberation, score higher on scales of romanticism, express stronger romantic attitudes, and suffer greater emotional stress when relationships are terminated. Because women may have potentially more to lose from a social and economic standpoint, they tend to be more prudent or discriminating in establishing and maintaining love relationships (Hochschild 1983). They are more apt to take into account practical considerations regarding mate selection. Hence, in comparison to men, women are more likely to terminate relationships and more easily to disengage emotionally when couples break up (Rubin 1973).

This actor and actress portray Romeo and Juliet, two of Western culture's icons of romantic love. Such tales promote the concept of romantic love, which is generally not considered a stable basis for long-term commitment. (Hulton-Deutsch Collection/Corbis)

Social scientists have explored the sequences through which the dimensions of love relationships develop and have constructed numerous typologies of love. They have also detected and described a number of styles of loving (Kemper 1988; Lasswell and Lasswell 1980). Love is said to begin typically with physical symptoms—palpitations of the heart, rapid breathing, sweating, and so on. At this stage the symptoms are essentially similar to those associated with other emotions such as fear. Next the person proceeds to label this arousal as a love response. This labeling process gains impetus from social pressures and cultural dictates, which prod one to define the experience as love and to follow its ritualistic patterns.

The optimum conditions for love to flourish require that the couple be equally involved in and committed to each other and the relationship. Where there is unequal involvement, the person with the strongest commitment may be vulnerable to exploitation. This is known as the *principle of least interest,* in which the partner with the least interest has the most control. Few relationships that are based on this principle can endure.

[See also Courtship; Interpersonal Attraction; Mate Selection Theories.]

BIBLIOGRAPHY

Goode, William J. 1959 "The Theoretical Importance of Love." *American Sociological Review* 24:38–47.

Hochschild, Arlie R. 1983 *The Managed Heart.* Berkeley: University of California Press.

Hunt, Morton 1959 *The Natural History of Love.* New York: Alfred A. Knopf.

Kemper, Theodore 1988 "Love and Like and Love and *Love.*" In David Franks, ed., *The Sociology of Emotions.* Greenwich, Conn.: JAI Press.

Lasswell, Marcia, and Norman M. Lasswell 1980 *Styles of Loving.* New York: Doubleday.

Merrill, Francis E. 1959 *Courtship and Marriage.* New York: Holt-Dryden.

Murstein, Bernard I. 1974 *Love, Sex, and Marriage Through the Ages.* New York: Springer.

Rubin, Zick 1973 *Loving and Liking.* New York: Holt, Rinehart and Winston.

Schwartz, Gary, Don Mertem, Fran Beham, and Allyne Rosenthal 1980 *Love and Commitment.* Beverly Hills, Calif.: Sage.

Tennov, Dorothy 1980 *Love and Limerence: The Experience of Being in Love.* New York: Stein and Day.

– FELIX M. BERARDO

M

MARITAL ADJUSTMENT

Marital adjustment has long been a popular topic in studies of the family, probably because the concept is believed to be closely related to the stability of a given marriage. Well-adjusted marriages are expected to last for a long time, while poorly adjusted ones end in divorce. Simple as it seems, the notion of marital adjustment is difficult to conceptualize and difficult to measure through empirical research. After more than half a century of conceptualization about and research on marital adjustment, the best that can be said may be that there is disagreement among scholars about the concept, the term, and its value. In fact, several scientists have proposed abandoning entirely the concept of marital adjustment and its etymological relatives (Lively 1969; Donohue and Ryder 1982; Trost 1985).

Conceptual Issues

Scientists have long been interested in understanding which factors contribute to success in marriage and which to failure. As early as the 1920s, Gilbert Hamilton (1929) conducted research on marital satisfaction by using thirteen clusters of questions. In 1939, Ernest Burgess and Leonard Cottrell published *Predicting Success or Failure in Marriage,* in which they systematically discussed marital adjustment. They defined the adjustment as "the integration of the couple in a union in which the two personalities are not merely merged, or submerged, but interact to complement each other for mutual satisfaction and the achievement of common objectives" (p. 10).

Researchers have not agreed upon the use of the term itself. To describe the seemingly same phenomenon, some have used the terms *marital quality, marital satisfaction,* and *marital happiness.* Robert Lewis and Graham Spanier, for example, have defined marital quality as "a subjective evaluation of a married couple's relationship" (Lewis and Spanier 1979, p. 269)—a concept virtually identical to that of marital adjustment. There have been numerous definitions of marital adjustment or quality (Spanier and Cole 1976), and it may not be fruitful to attempt to define the concept in a sentence or two. Rather, the following description of the factors that constitute marital adjustment or quality may prove more meaningful.

Since Burgess and Cottrell's formulation, scientists have examined extensively the factors constituting marital adjustment. Although there has been no consensus among researchers, factors constituting marital adjustment include *agreement, cohesion, satisfaction, affection,* and *tension.* Agreement between spouses on important matters is critical to a well-adjusted marriage. Though minor differences may broaden their perspectives, major differences between the spouses in matters such as philosophy of life, political orientations, and attitudes toward gender roles are detrimental to marital adjustment. In addition, agreement on specific decisions about family matters must be reached in good accord. Marital cohesion refers to both spouses' commitment to the marriage and the companionship experienced in it. In a well-adjusted marriage, both spouses try to make sure that their marriage will be successful. They also share common interests and joint activities. In a well-adjusted marriage, both spouses must be satisfied and happy with the marriage. Unhappy but long-lasting marriages are not well-adjusted ones. Spouses in well-adjusted marriages share affection, and it is demonstrated as affectionate behavior. Finally, the degree of tension in a well-adjusted marriage is minimal, and when it arises it is resolved amicably, probably in discussion, and the level of tension and anxiety is usually low.

On the basis of a psychological theory of well-being, it has been suggested that marital adjustment or quality has two conceptually distinct factors, marital happiness (or interaction) and marital problems (or instability), and that we should treat these dimensions separately rather than combine them in the concept of marital adjustment or quality (Orden and Bradburn 1968). This position was later supported by a refined statistical analysis (Johnson et al. 1986).

The core component of marital adjustment is marital satisfaction, and it has been extensively studied as a stand-alone concept. As such, it deserves separate consideration. Marital satisfaction has been defined as "the subjective feelings of happiness, satisfaction, and pleasure experienced by a spouse when considering all current aspects of his marriage. This variable is conceived as a continuum running from much satisfaction to much dissatisfaction. Marital satisfaction is clearly an attitudinal variable and, thus, is a property of individual spouses" (Hawkins 1968, p. 648). Again, scientists disagree about the definition. Some scholars conceptualize satisfaction rather as "the amount of congruence between the expectations a person has and the rewards the person actually receives" (Burr et al. 1979, p. 67). Because marital satisfaction is influenced not only by the congruence between expectations and rewards but also by other factors, the former definition is broader than the latter and thus is adopted here.

There are two kinds of marital satisfaction in a marriage, the husband's and the wife's, and they are conceptually distinct.

Although many scientists treat marital satisfaction as a factor of marital adjustment, there exists a possibly major difference between these two concepts about the unit of analysis. Because satisfaction is a subjective property of an actor, there are two kinds of marital satisfaction in a marriage, the husband's and the wife's, and they are conceptually distinct. As Jessie Bernard (1972) stated, there are always two marriages in a family: the husband's marriage and the wife's marriage. Then, do these two marital satisfactions go hand in hand, or are they independent of each other? Research has produced mixed findings. In general, the more satisfied one spouse is with the marriage, the more satisfied is the other, but the correlation between the husband's and the wife's marital satisfactions is far from perfect (Spanier and Cole 1976). Marital adjustment or quality, on the other hand, can be either an individual or dyadic property. When we say "a well-adjusted marriage," we refer to the dyad, while when we say, "She is well adjusted to her marriage," we refer to the individual. No one has proposed valid measurement techniques for examining marital adjustment as a dyadic property, although some observational methods might be considered.

Another difference between marital satisfaction and marital adjustment is that while the former is a static product, the latter can be a dynamic process. In fact, marital adjustment is sometimes defined as a dynamic process, and marital satisfaction is listed as one of the outcomes of the adjustment process (Spanier and Cole 1976, pp. 127–28). It also has been proposed that marital adjustment be defined as a dynamic process and yet be measured as a state at a given point in time, a "snapshot" conception (Spanier and Cole 1976). Nevertheless, this connotation of dynamic process in the term *adjustment* has been criticized (Trost 1985) as a confusion of its meaning because no measure of "adjustment" involves dynamic change, such as negotiation between the spouses.

Without agreeing on which term to use nor on its definition, researchers have tried for decades to measure marital adjustment, quality, or satisfaction. Burgess and Cottrell (1939) created one of the first measures of marital adjustment from twenty-seven questions pertaining to five subareas (agreement, common interests and joint activities, affection and mutual confidences, complaints, and feelings of being lonely, miserable, and irritable). Along with numerous attempts at measuring marital adjustment, Locke and Wallace (1959) modified Burgess and Cottrell's measure and called it the Marital Adjustment Test. Based on factor analysis, the test consists of fifteen questions ranging from the respondent's overall happiness in the marriage, the degree of agreement between the spouses in various matters, how they resolved conflicts, and the number of shared activities, to the fulfillment of their expectations about the marriage. This measure was widely used until a new measure, the Dyadic Adjustment Scale, was proposed (Spanier 1976). It is composed of thirty-two questions and four subscales: dyadic satisfaction, dyadic cohesion, dyadic consensus, and affectional expression. This scale has been used most widely in the last decade.

All of the above measures have been criticized as lacking a criterion against which the individual items are validated (Norton 1983; Fincham and Bradbury 1987). It has been argued that only global and evaluative items, rather than content-specific and descriptive ones, should be included in marital adjustment or quality measures because the conceptual domain of the latter is not clear. What constitutes a well-adjusted marriage may differ from one couple to another as well as cross-culturally and historically. Whether spouses kiss each other or not every day, for example, may be an indicator of a well-adjusted marriage in the contemporary United States but not in some other countries. Thus, marital adjustment or quality should be measured by the spouses' evaluation of the marriage as a whole rather than by its specific components. Instead of "How often do you and your husband (wife) agree on religious matters?" (a content-specific description), it is argued that such questions as, "All things considered, how satisfied are you with your marriage?" or, "How satisfied are you with your husband (wife) as a spouse?" (a global evaluation) should be used. By the same reasoning, the Kansas Marital Satisfaction Scale (KMS) has been proposed. This test includes only three questions: "How satisfied are you with your (a) marriage; (b) husband (wife) as a spouse; and (c) relationship with your husband (wife)?" (Schumm et al. 1986).

Traditional indices also have been criticized for their lack of theoretical basis and the imposition of what constitutes a "successful marriage." On the basis of exchange theory, Ronald Sabatelli (1984) developed the Marital Comparison Level Index (MCLI), which measures marital satisfaction by the degree to which respondents feel that the outcomes derived from their marriages compare with their expectations. Thirty-six items pertaining to such aspects of marriage as affection, commitment, fairness, and agreement were originally included, and thirty-two items were retained in the final measure. Because this measure is embedded in the tradition of exchange theory, it has strength in its validity.

Predicting Marital Adjustment

How is the marital adjustment of a given couple predicted? According to Lewis and Spanier's (1979) comprehensive work, three major factors predict marital quality: social and personal resources, satisfaction with life-style, and rewards from spousal interaction.

In general, the more social and personal resources a husband and wife have, the better adjusted their marriage is. Findings that spouses coming from similar racial, religious, or socioeconomic backgrounds are better adjusted to their marriages are synthesized by this general proposition. Material and nonmaterial properties of the spouses enhance their marital adjustment. Examples include emotional and physical health, socioeconomic resources such as education and social class, personal resources such as interpersonal skills and positive self-concepts, and knowledge they had of each other before getting married. It was also found that good relationships with and support from parents, friends, and significant others contribute to a better adjusted marriage.

The second major factor in predicting marital adjustment is satisfaction with life-style. It has been found that material resources such as family income positively affect both spouses' marital adjustment. Both the husband's and the wife's satisfaction with their jobs enhances better adjusted marriages. Furthermore, the husband's satisfaction with his wife's work status also affects marital adjustment. The wife's employment itself has been found both instrumental and detrimental to the husbands' marital satisfaction (Fendrich 1984). This is because the effect of the wife's employment is mediated by both spouses' attitudes about her employment. When the wife is in the labor force, and her husband supports it, marital adjustment could be enhanced. On the other hand, if the wife is unwilling to be employed, or is employed against her husband's wishes, this can negatively affect their marital adjustment. Marital adjustment is also affected by the spouses' satisfaction with their household composition and by how well the couple is embedded in the community.

Parents' marital satisfaction was found to be a function of the presence, density, and ages of children (Rollins and Galligan 1978). Spouses (particularly wives) who had children were less satisfied with their marriages, particularly when many children were born soon after marriage at short intervals (high density). The generally negative effects of children on marital satisfaction and marital adjustment could be synthesized under this more general proposition about satisfaction with life-style.

It has been consistently found that marital satisfaction plotted against the couple's family life-cycle stages forms a U-shaped curve (Rollins and Cannon 1974). Both spouses' marital satisfaction is highest right after they marry, hits the lowest point when the oldest child is a teenager, and gradually bounces back after all children leave home. This pattern has been interpreted to be a result of role strain or role conflict between the spousal, parental, and work roles of the spouses. Unlike the honeymoon and empty-nest stages, having children at home imposes the demand of being a parent in addition to being a husband or wife and a worker. When limited time and energy cause these roles to conflict with each other, the spouses feel strain, which results in poor marital adjustment. Along this line of reasoning, Wesley Burr et al. (1979) proposed that marital satisfaction is influenced by the qualities of the individual's role enactment as a spouse and of the spouse's role enactment. They argue further, from the symbolic-interactionist perspective, that the relationship between marital role enactment and marital satisfaction is mediated by the importance placed on spousal role expectations.

As seen above, the concept of family life cycle seems to have some explanatory power for marital satisfaction. Researchers and theorists have found, however, that family life cycle is multidimensional and conceptually unclear. Once a relationship between a particular stage in the family life cycle and marital satisfaction is identified, further variables must be added to explain that relationship, variables such as the wife's employment status, disposable income, and role strain between spousal and parental roles (Schumm and Bugaighis 1986). Furthermore, the proportion of variance in marital satisfaction "explained" by the family's position in its life cycle is small, typically less than 10 percent (Rollins and Cannon 1974). Thus, some scholars conclude that family life cycle has no more explanatory value than does marriage or age cohorts (Spanier and Lewis 1980).

The last major factor in predicting marital adjustment is the reward obtained from spousal interaction. On the basis of exchange theory, Lewis and Spanier summarize past findings that "the greater the rewards from spousal interaction, the greater the marital quality" (Lewis and Spanier 1979, p. 282). Rewards from spousal interaction include value consensus, a positive evaluation of oneself by the spouse, and one's positive regard for things such as the physical, mental, and sexual attractiveness of the spouse. Other rewards from spousal interaction include such aspects of emotional gratification as the expression of affection, respect and encouragement between the spouses, love and sexual gratification, and egalitarian relationships. Married couples with more effective communication, expressed in more self-disclosure, frequent successful communication, and understanding and empathy, are better adjusted to their marriages. Complementarity in the spouses' roles and needs, similarity in personality traits, and sexual compatibility all enhance marital adjustment. Finally, frequent interaction between the spouses leads to a better adjusted marriage. The lack of spousal conflict or tensions should be added to the list of rewards from spousal interactions.

Symbolic interactionists also argue that relative deprivation of the spouses affects their marital satisfaction: If, after considering all aspects of the marriage, spouses believe themselves to be as well off as their reference group, they will be satisfied with their marriages. If they think they are better off or worse off than others who are married, they will be more or less satisfied with their marriages, respectively (Burr et al. 1979).

Consequences of Marital Adjustment: Marital Stability

Does marital adjustment affect the stability of the marriage? Does a better adjusted marriage last longer than a poorly adjusted one? The answer is generally yes, but this is not always the case. Some well-adjusted marriages end in divorce, and many poorly adjusted marriages endure. As for the latter, John Cuber and Peggy Harroff (1968) conducted research on people whose marriages "lasted ten years or more and who said that they have never seriously considered divorce or separation" (p. 43). They claim that not all the spouses in these marriages are happy and that there are five types of long-lasting marriages. In a "conflict-habituated marriage," the husband and the wife always quarrel. In a "passive-congenial marriage," the husband and the wife take each other for granted without zest, while "devitalized marriages" started as loving but have degenerated to passive-congenial marriages. In a "vital marriage," spouses together enjoy such things as hobbies, careers, or community services, while in a "total marriage," spouses do almost everything together. It should be noted that even conflict-habituated or devitalized marriages can last as long as vital or total marriages. For people in passive-congenial marriages, the conception and the reality of marriage are devoid of romance and are different from other people's.

In a "passive-congenial marriage," the husband and the wife take each other for granted without zest.

What then determines the stability of marriage and how the marital adjustment affects it? It is proposed that although marital adjustment leads to marital stability, two factors intervene: alternative attractions and external pressures to remain married (Lewis and Spanier 1979). People who have both real and perceived alternatives to poorly adjusted marriages—another romantic relationship or a successful career—may choose divorce. A person in a poorly adjusted marriage may remain in it if there is no viable alternative, if a divorce is unaffordable or would bring an intolerable stigma, or if the person is exceptionally tolerant of conflict and disharmony in the marriage. Nevertheless, it should be emphasized that even though marital stability is affected by alternative attractions and external pressures, marital adjustment is the single most important factor in predicting marital stability.

[See also Divorce; Family Roles; Interpersonal Attraction; Marriage.]

BIBLIOGRAPHY

Bernard, Jessie 1972 *The Future of Marriage.* New York: World Publishing.

Burgess, Ernest W., and Leonard Cottrell, Jr. 1939 *Predicting Success or Failure in Marriage.* New York: Prentice-Hall.

Burr, Wesley R., Geoffrey K. Leigh, Randall D. Day, and John Constantine 1979 "Symbolic Interaction and the Family." In W. Burr, R. Hill, F. I. Nye, and I. Reiss, eds., *Contemporary Theories about the Family.* New York: Free Press.

Cuber, John F., and Peggy B. Harroff 1968 *The Significant Americans: A Study of Sexual Behavior Among the Affluent.* Baltimore: Penguin Books.

Donohue, Kevin C., and Robert G. Ryder 1982 "A Methodological Note on Marital Satisfaction and Social Variables." *Journal of Marriage and the Family* 44:743–747.

Fendrich, Michael 1984 "Wives' Employment and Husbands' Distress: A Meta-analysis and a Replication." *Journal of Marriage and the Family* 46:871–879.

Fincham, Frank D., and Thomas N. Bradbury 1987 "The Assessment of Marital Quality: A Reevaluation." *Journal of Marriage and the Family* 49:797–809.

Hamilton, Gilbert V. 1929 *A Research in Marriage.* New York: A. and C. Boni.

Hawkins, James L. 1968 "Associations Between Companionship, Hostility, and Marital Satisfaction." *Journal of Marriage and the Family* 30:647–650.

Johnson, David R., Lynn K. White, John N. Edwards, and Alan Booth 1986 "Dimensions of Marital Quality: Toward Methodological and Conceptual Refinement." *Journal of Family Issues* 7:31–49.

Lewis, Robert A., and Graham B. Spanier 1979 "Theorizing about the Quality and Stability of Marriage." In W. Burr, R. Hill, F. I. Nye, and I. Reiss, eds., *Contemporary Theories about the Family.* New York: Free Press.

Lively, E. L. 1969 "Toward Concept Clarification: The Case of Marital Interaction." *Journal of Marriage and the Family* 31:108–114.

Locke, Harvey J., and Karl M. Wallace 1959 "Short Marital-Adjustment and Prediction Tests: Their Reliability and Validity." *Marriage and Family Living* 21:251–255.

Norton, Robert 1983 "Measuring Marital Quality: A Critical Look at the Dependent Variable." *Journal of Marriage and the Family* 45:141–151.

Orden, Susan R., and Norman M. Bradburn 1968 "Dimensions of Marriage Happiness." *American Journal of Sociology* 73:715–731.

Rollins, Boyd C., and Kenneth L. Cannon 1974 "Marital Satisfaction over the Family Life Cycle: A Reevaluation." *Journal of Marriage and the Family* 36:271–282.

Rollins, Boyd C., and Richard Galligan 1978 "The Developing Child and Marital Satisfaction of Parents." In R. M. Lerner and G. B. Spanier, eds., *Child Influences on Marital and Family Interaction.* New York: Academic Press.

Sabatelli, Ronald M. 1984 "The Marital Comparison Level Index: A Measure for Assessing Outcomes Relative to Expectations." *Journal of Marriage and the Family* 46:651–662.

Schumm, Walter R., and Margaret A. Bugaighis 1986 "Marital Quality over the Marital Career: Alternative Explanations." *Journal of Marriage and the Family* 48:165–168.

Schumm, Walter R., Lois A. Paff-Bergen, Ruth C. Hatch, Felix C. Obiorah, Janette M. Copeland, Lori D. Meens, and Margaret A. Bugaighis 1986 "Concurrent and Discriminant Validity of the Kansas Marital Satisfaction Scale." *Journal of Marriage and the Family* 48:381–387.

Spanier, Graham B. 1976 "Measuring Dyadic Adjustment: New Scales for Assessing the Quality of Marriage and Similar Dyads." *Journal of Marriage and the Family* 38:15–28.

———, and Charles L. Cole 1976 "Toward Clarification and Investigation of Marital Adjustment." *International Journal of Sociology of the Family* 6:121–146.

———, and Robert A. Lewis 1980 "Marital Quality: A Review of the Seventies." *Journal of Marriage and the Family* 42:825–839.

Trost, Jan E. 1985 "Abandon Adjustment!" *Journal of Marriage and the Family* 47:1,072–1,073.

– YOSHINORI KAMO

MARRIAGE

The current low rates of marriage and remarriage and the high incidence of divorce in the United States are the bases of deep concern about the future of marriage and the family. Some have used these data to argue the demise of the family in the Western world (Popenoe 1988). Others see such changes as normal shifts and adjustments to societal changes (Bane 1976). Whatever the forecast, there is no question that the institution of marriage is currently less stable than it has been in previous generations. This chapter explores the nature of modern marriage and considers some of the reasons for its vulnerability.

Marriage can be conceptualized in three ways: as an institution (a set of patterned, repeated, expected behaviors and relationships that are organized and endure over time); a rite/ritual (whereby the married status is achieved); and a process (a phenomenon marked by gradual changes that lead to ultimate dissolution through separation, divorce, or death). In the discussion that follows we examine each of these conceptualizations of marriage, with the greatest attention given to marriage as a process.

Marriage As Institution

From a societal level of analysis the institution of marriage represents all the behaviors, norms, roles, expectations, and values that are associated with the legal union of a man and woman. It is the institution in society in which a man and woman are joined in a special kind of social and legal dependence to found and maintain a family. For most people becoming married and having children are the principal life events that pass an individual into mature adulthood. Marriage is considered to represent a lifelong commitment by two people to each other and is signified by a contract sanctioned by the state (and for many people, by God). It thus involves legal rights, responsibilities, and duties that are enforced by both secular and sacred laws. As a legal contract ratified by the state, marriage can be dissolved only with state permission.

Marriage is at the center of the kinship system. New spouses are tied inextricably to members of the kin network. The nature of these ties or obligations differs in different cultures. In many societies almost all social relationships are based on or mediated by kin, who also may serve as allies in times of danger, be responsible for the transference of property, or are turned to in times of economic hardship (Lee 1982). In the United States, kin responsibilities rarely extend beyond the nuclear family (parents and children). With the possible exception of caring for elderly parents, and even here norms have not yet been developed (Lang and Brody 1983), there are no normative obligations an individual is expected to fulfill for sisters or brothers, not to mention uncles, aunts, and cousins. Associated with few obligations and responsibilities is greater autonomy and independence of one's kin.

In most societies the distribution of power in marriage is given through tradition and law to the male—that is, patriarchy is the rule as well as the practice. For many contemporary Americans the ideal is to develop an egalitarian power structure, but a number of underlying conditions discourage attaining this goal. These deterrents include the tendency for males to have greater income, higher status jobs, and, until recently, higher educational levels than women. In addition, the tradition that women have primary responsibility for child rearing tends to increase their dependency on males.

Historically, the institution of marriage has fulfilled several unique functions for the larger society. It has served as an economic alliance between two families, as the means for legitimizing sexual relations, and as the basis for legitimizing parenthood and offspring. In present-day America the primary functions of marriage appear to be limited to the legitimization of parenthood (Davis 1949; Reiss and Lee 1988) and the nurturance of family members (Lasch 1977). Recently, standards have changed and sexual relations outside of marriage have become increasingly accepted for unmarried people. Most services that were once performed by members of a family for other members can now be purchased in the marketplace, and other social institutions have taken over roles that once were assigned primarily to the family. Even illegitimacy is not as negatively sanctioned as in the past. The fact that marriage no longer serves all the unique functions it once did is one reason that some scholars have questioned the vitality of the institution.

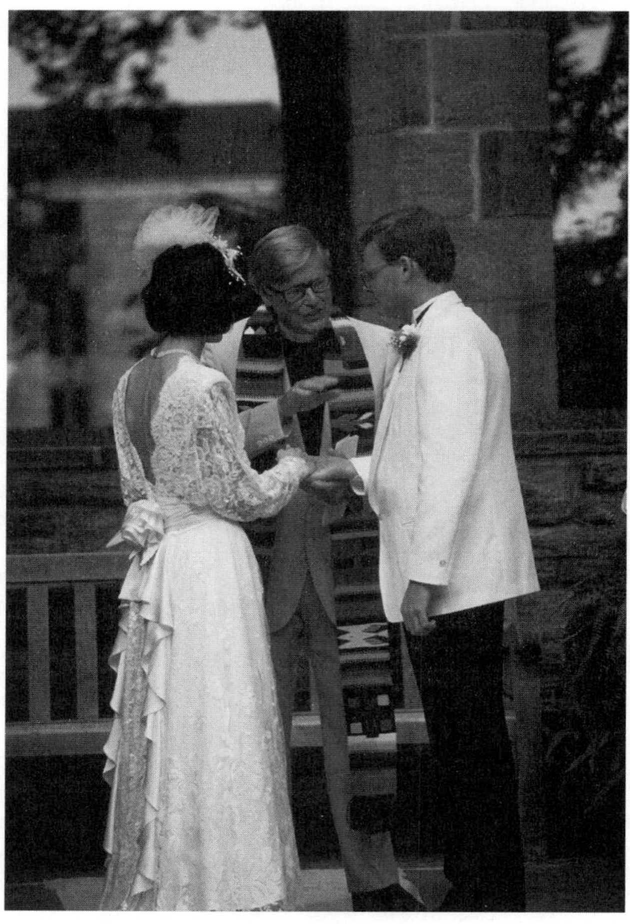

Various elements of a wedding serve to link a couple to the larger social group. (Kit Kittle/Corbis)

Marriage As Rite/Ritual

Not a great deal of sociological attention has been given to the study of marriage as a rite/ritual that transfers status. Philip Slater, in a seminal piece written in 1963, discussed the significance of the marriage ceremony as a social mechanism that underscores the dependency of the married couple and links the new spouses to the larger social group. Slater claims that various elements associated with the wedding (e.g., bridal shower, bachelor party) help create the impression that the couple is indebted to their peers and family members who organize these events. He writes,

> . . . family and friends [are] vying with one another in claiming responsibility for having "brought them together" in the first place. This impression of societal initiative is augmented by the fact that the bride's father "gives the bride away." The retention of this ancient custom in modern times serves explicitly to deny the possibility that the couple might unite quite on their own. In other words, the marriage ritual is designed to make it appear as if somehow the idea of the dyadic union sprang from the community, and not from the dyad itself (Slater 1963, p. 355).

Slater describes the ways in which rite and ceremony focus attention on loyalties and obligations owed others: "The ceremony has the effect of concentrating the attention of both individuals on every OTHER affectional tie either one has ever contracted" (Slater 1963, p. 354). The intrusion of the community into the couple's relationship at the moment of unity serves to inhibit husband and wife from withdrawing completely into an intimate unit isolated from (and hence not contributing to) the larger social group.

Martin Whyte (1990) ascertained the lack of information on marriage rituals and conducted a study to help fill this gap. He found that since 1925, wedding rituals (bridal shower, bachelor party, honeymoon, wedding reception, church wedding) have not only persisted but also have increased in terms of the number of people who incorporate them into their marriage plans. Weddings also are larger in scale in terms of cost, number of guests, whether a reception is held, etc. Like

Slater, Martin links marriage rituals to the larger social fabric and argues that an elaborate wedding serves several functions. It

> serves notice that the couple is entering into a new set of roles and obligations associated with marriage, it mobilizes community support behind their new status, it enables the families involved to display their status to the surrounding community, and it makes it easier for newly marrying couples to establish an independent household (p. 63).

Marriage As Process

Of the three ways in which marriage is conceptualized—institution, rite/ritual, and process—most scholarly attention has focused on process. Here the emphasis is on the interpersonal relationship. Changes in this relationship over the course of the marriage have attracted the interest of most investigators. Key issues studied by researchers include the establishment of communication, affection, power, and decision-making patterns; development of a marital division of labor; and learning spousal roles. The conditions under which these develop and change (e.g., social class level, age at marriage, presence of children) and the outcomes of being married that derive from them (e.g., degree of satisfaction with the relationship) are also studied. For illustrative purposes, the remainder of this article will highlight one of these components, marital communication, and one outcome variable, marital quality. We also address different experiences of marriage based on sex of spouse: "his" and "her" marriage.

THE PROCESS OF COMMUNICATION. The perception of "a failure to communicate" is a problem that prompts many spouses to seek marital counseling. The ability to share feelings, thoughts, and information is a measure of the degree of intimacy between two people, and frustration follows from an inability or an unwillingness to talk and listen (Klagsbrun 1986). However, when the quality of communication is high, marital satisfaction and happiness also are high (Holman and Brock 1986; Gottman and Porterfield 1981; Lewis and Spanier 1979).

The role of communication in fostering a satisfactory marital relationship is more important now than in earlier times because the expectations and demands of marriage have changed. As noted above, marriage in America is less dependent on and affected by an extended kin network than on the spousal relationship. One of the principal functions of contemporary marriage is the nurturance of family members. Perhaps because this function and the therapeutic and leisure roles that help fulfill it in marriage are preeminent, "greater demands are placed on each spouse's ability to communicate" (Fitzpatrick 1988, p. 2). The communication of positive affect, and its converse, emotional withdrawal, may well be the essence/antithesis of nurturance. Bloom, Niles, and Tatcher (1985) suggest that one important characteristic of marital dissatisfaction is the expectation that marriage is a "source of interpersonal nurturance and individual gratification and growth" (p. 371), an expectation that is very hard to fulfill.

The marriage ceremony underscores the dependency of the married couple and links the new spouses to the larger social group.

In the 1990s many studies focused on the role of communication in differentiating distressed from nondistressed marriages (Noller and Fitzpatrick 1990). The findings from this body of research suggest that there are clear communication differences between spouses in happy and in unhappy marriages. Patricia Noller and Mary Anne Fitzpatrick (1990) reviewed this literature, and their findings can be summarized as follows: couples in distressed marriages report less satisfaction with the social-emotional aspects of marriage, develop more destructive communication patterns (i.e., a greater expression of negative feelings, including anger, contempt, sadness, fear, and disgust), and seek to avoid conflict more often than nondistressed couples. Nevertheless, couples in distressed marriages report more frequent conflict and spend more time in conflict. In addition, gender differences in communication are intensified in distressed marriages. For example, husbands have a more difficult time interpreting wives' messages. Wives in general express both negative and positive feelings more directly and are more critical. Spouses in unhappy marriages appear to be unaware that they misunderstand one another. Generally, happily married couples are more likely to engage in positive communication behaviors (agreement, approval, assent, and the use of humor and laughter), while unhappy couples command, disagree, criticize, put down, and excuse more.

Communication patterns may be class-linked. Working-class wives in particular complain that their husbands are emotionally withdrawn and inexpressive (Komarovsky 1962; Rubin 1976). Olsen and his colleagues (1979) assign communication a strategic role in marital/family adaptability. In their conceptualization of marital/family functioning, communication is the process that moves couples along the dimensions of cohesion and adaptability. In another study the absence of good communication skills was associated with conjugal violence (Walker 1979).

Differences between the sexes have been reported in most studies that examine marital communication. The general emphasis of these findings is that males appear less able to communicate verbally and to discuss emotional issues. However, communication is not the only aspect of marriage where sex differences have been reported. Other components of marriage also are experienced differently, depending on the sex of spouse. The following paragraphs report some of these.

SEX DIFFERENCES. In *The Future of Marriage* (1972), Jessie Bernard pointed out that marriage does not hold the same meanings for wives as for husbands, nor do wives hold the same expectations for marriage as do husbands. These sex differences (originally noted but not fully developed by Emile Durkheim in 1897 in *Le Suicide*) have been observed and examined by many others since Bernard's publication (Larson 1988; Stinnett 1971; Feldman 1982). For example, researchers report differences between husbands and wives in responses to perceptions of marital problems, reasons for divorce (Levinger 1966; Fulton 1979), and differences in perceived marital quality; wives consistently experience/perceive lower quality than husbands. Wives are viewed as the partner who undergoes the most change (adjustment) in marriage (Luckey 1960). They are more susceptible to influence within the marriage (Bernard 1982), and they undergo greater value change than husbands (Barry 1970; Burgess and Wallin 1953; Sanders and Suls 1982).

Sex differences in marriage are socially defined and prescribed (Lee 1982). One consequence of these social definitions is that sex differences get built into marital roles and the division of labor within marriage. For example, it has been observed that wives do more housework (Atkinson and Huston 1984) and child care (McHale and Huston 1984) than husbands. Even wives who work in the paid labor force spend twice as many hours per week in family work as husbands (Benin and Agostinelli 1988). Wives are assigned or tend to assume the role of family kinkeeper (Adams 1968; Rosenthal 1985). To the extent that husbands and wives experience different marriages, wives are thought to be disadvantaged by their greater dependence, secondary status, and the uneven distribution of family responsibilities associated with marriage (Baca Zinn and Eitzen 1990).

All of these factors are assumed to affect the quality of marriage—one of the most studied aspects of marriage (Adams 1988; Berardo 1990). It will be the subject of our final discussion.

MARITAL QUALITY. Marital quality may be the "weather vane" by which spouses gauge the success of their relationship. (The reader should be sure to differentiate the concept of marital quality from two other closely related concepts: family quality, and the quality of life in general, called global life satisfaction in the literature. Studies show that people clearly differentiate among these three dimensions of well-being [Ishii-Kuntz and Ihinger-Tallman 1991].)

Marriage begins with a commitment, a promise to maintain an intimate relationship over a lifetime. Few couples clearly understand the difficulties involved in adhering to this commitment or the problems they may encounter over the course of their lives together. More people seek psychological help for marital difficulties than for any other type of problem (Fincham and Bradbury 1987; Veroff, Kulka, and Douvan 1981). For a large number of spouses, the problems become so severe that they renege on their commitment and dissolve the marriage.

A recent review of the determinants of divorce lists the following problems as major factors that lead to the dissolution of marriage: "alcoholism and drug abuse, infidelity, incompatibility, physical and emotional abuse, disagreements about gender roles, sexual incompatibility, and financial problems" (White 1990, p. 908). Underlying these behaviors appears to be the general problem of communication. In their study of divorce, Gay Kitson and Marvin Sussman (1982) reported lack of communication/understanding to be the most common reason given by both husbands and wives concerning why their marriage broke up. The types of problems responsible for divorce have not changed much over time. Older studies list nonsupport, financial problems, adultery, cruelty, drinking, physical and verbal abuse, neglect, lack of love, in-laws, and sexual incompatibility as reasons for divorce (Goode 1956; Harmsworth and Minnis 1955; Levinger 1966).

Not all unhappy marriages end in divorce. Many factors bar couples from dissolving their marriage, even under conditions of extreme dissatisfaction. Some factors that act as barriers to marital dissolution are strong religious beliefs, pressure from family or friends to remain together, and the lack of perceived attractive alternatives to the marriage (Levinger 1965; Lewis and Spanier 1979).

One empirical finding that continues to be reaffirmed in studies of marital quality is that the quality of marriage declines over time, beginning with the birth of the first child (Pineo 1961). Consequently, the transition to parenthood and its effect on the marital relationship has generated a great deal of research attention (Cowen and Cowen 1989; LaRossa and LaRossa 1981;

Ruble, Fleming, Hackel, and Stangor 1988; Ryder 1973). The general finding is that marital quality decreases after the birth of a child, and this change is more pronounced for mothers than for fathers. Two reasons generally proposed to account for this decline are that the amount of time couples have to spend together decreases after the birth of a child, and sex role patterns become more traditional (McHale and Huston 1985).

In an attempt to disentangle the duration of marriage and parenthood dimensions, White and Booth (1985) compared couples who became new parents with nonparent couples over a period of several years and found a decline in marital quality regardless of whether the couple had a child. A longitudinal study conducted by Belsky and Rovine (1990) confirmed the significant declines in marital quality over time reported in so many other studies. They also found the reported gender differences. However, their analysis also focused on change scores for individual couples. They reported that while some couples' marital quality declined, this was not true for all couples—it improved or remained unchanged for others. Thus, rather than assume that quality decline is an inevitable consequence of marriage, there is a need to examine why and how some couples successfully avoid this deterioration process. The authors called for the investigation of individual differences among couples rather than continuing to examine the generally well-established finding that marital quality declines after children enter the family and remains low during the child-rearing stages of the family life cycle.

Many students of the family have found it useful to consider marital development over the years as analogous to a career that progresses through stages of the family life cycle (Duvall and Hill 1948; Aldous 1978). This allows for considering changes in the marital relationship that occur because of spouses' aging, duration of marriage, and the aging of children. In addition to changes in marital quality, other factors have been examined, such as differences in the course of a marriage when age at first marriage varies (e.g., marriage entered into at age nineteen as opposed to midthirties), varied duration of child-bearing (few vs. many years), varied number of children (small family vs. large), and the ways in which consumer decisions change over the course of marriage (Aldous 1990).

Conclusion

If the vitality of marriage is measured by the extent to which men and women enter marriage, then some pessimism about its future is warranted. Marriage rates are currently lower than during the early Depression years of 1930–1932—which were the lowest in our nation's recent history (Sweet and Bumpass 1987). One conclusion that might be drawn from reading the accumulated literature on marriage, especially the writings that discuss the inequities of men and women within marriage, increasing incidence of marital dissolution, cohabitation as a substitute for marriage, and the postponement of marriage, is that the institution is in serious trouble. These changes have been interpreted as occurring as part of a larger societal shift in values and orientations (Glick 1989) that leans toward valuing adults over children and toward individualism over familism (Glenn 1987; White 1987; see the entire December 1987 issue of *Journal of Family Issues,* devoted to the state of the American family). Supporting this perspective are the data on increased marital happiness among childless couples and lower birth rates among married couples.

Is every era judged to be worse than previous ones when social institutions are scrutinized?

Yet every era has had those who write of the vulnerability of marriage and family. For example, in 1920 Edward Alsworth Ross wrote, ". . . we find the family now less stable than it has been at any time since the beginning of the Christian era" (1920, p. 586). Is every era judged to be worse than previous ones when social institutions are scrutinized? More optimistic scholars look at the declining first-marriage rate and interpret it as a "deferral syndrome" rather than as an outright rejection of the institution (Glick 1989; Teachman, Polonko, and Scanzoni 1987). This is because, in spite of declines in the overall rate, the historical 8 percent to 10 percent of never-married in the population has remained constant; almost 90 percent of all women in the United States eventually marry at least once in their lifetime (Norton and Moorman 1987). Also, projections that about two-thirds of all first marriages in the United States will end in divorce (Martin and Bumpass 1989) do not deter people from marrying. In spite of the high divorce rate, an increased tolerance for singleness as a way of life, and a growing acceptance of cohabitation, the majority of Americans continue to marry. Unhappy couples divorce, but most remarry. Marriage is still seen as a source of personal happiness (Campbell, Converse, and Rogers 1976; Kilbourne, Howell, and England 1990).

More fundamentally, marriage rates and the dynamics of marital relationships tend to reflect conditions in the larger society. What appears clear, at least for Americans, is that they turn to marriage as a source of sustenance and support in a society where, collectively, citizens seem to have abrogated responsibility for the care and nurturance of each other. Perhaps it is not surprising that divorce rates are high, given the demands and expectations placed on modern marriages.

[See also Alternate Life-Styles; Courtship; Family Roles; Heterosexual Behavior Patterns; Intermarriage; Marital Adjustment; Remarriage; Sexual Behavior and Marriage.]

BIBLIOGRAPHY

Adams, Bert N. 1968 *Kinship in an Urban Setting.* Chicago: Markham.

——— 1988 "Fifty Years of Family Research: What Does it Mean?" *Journal of Marriage and the Family* 50:5–17.

Aldous, Joan 1978 *Family Careers: Developmental Changes in Families.* New York: Wiley.

——— 1990 "Family Development and the Life Course: Two Perspectives on Family Change." *Journal of Marriage and the Family* 52:571–583.

Atkinson, Jean, and Ted L. Huston 1984 "Sex Role Orientation and Division of Labor Early in Marriage." *Journal of Personality and Social Psychology* 41:330–345.

Baca Zinn, Maxine, and D. Stanley Eitzen 1990 *Diversity in Families,* 2nd ed. New York: Harper & Row.

Bane, Mary Jo 1976 *Here to Stay: American Families in the Twentieth Century.* New York: Basic Books.

Barry, W. A. 1970 "Marriage Research and Conflict: An Integrative Review." *Psychological Bulletin* 73:41–54.

Belsky, Jay, and Michael Rovine 1990 "Patterns of Marital Change Across the Transition to Parenthood: Pregnancy to Three Years Postpartum." *Journal of Marriage and the Family* 52:5–19.

Benin, Mary H., and Joan Agostinelli 1988 "Husbands' and Wives' Satisfaction with the Division of Labor." *Journal of Marriage and the Family* 50:349–361.

Berardo, Felix M. 1990 "Trends and Directions in Family Research in the 1980s." *Journal of Marriage and the Family* 52:809–817.

Bernard, Jessie 1972 *The Future of Marriage.* New York: Bantam Books.

——— 1982 *The Future of Marriage,* 1982 ed. New Haven, Conn.: Yale University Press.

Bloom, Bernard L., Robert L. Niles, and Anna M. Tatcher 1985 "Sources of Marital Dissatisfaction Among Newly Separated Persons." *Journal of Family Issues* 6:359–373.

Burgess, Ernest, and Paul Wallin 1953 *Engagement and Marriage.* Philadelphia: Lippincott.

Campbell, Angus, Philip E. Converse, and Willard Rogers 1976 *The Quality of American Life.* New York: Russell Sage Foundation.

Cowen, Phillip, and C. Cowen 1989 "Changes in Marriage During the Transition to Parenthood: Must We Blame the Baby?" In G. Michaels and W. Goldberg, eds., *The Transition to Parenthood: Current Theory and Research.* New York: Cambridge University Press.

Davis, Kingsley 1949 *Human Society.* New York: Macmillan.

Durkheim, Emile 1897 *Le Suicide.* Paris: F. Alcan.

Duvall, Evelyn M., and Reuben Hill 1948 "Report of the Committee on the Dynamics of Family Interaction." Paper delivered at the National Conference on Family Life, Washington, DC.

Feldman, L. B. 1982 "Sex Roles and Family Dynamics." In F. Walsh, ed., *Normal Family Processes.* New York: Guilford.

Fincham, Frank D., and Thomas N. Bradbury 1987 "The Assessment of Marital Quality: A Reevaluation." *Journal of Marriage and the Family* 49:797–809.

Fitzpatrick, Mary Anne 1988 "Approaches to Marital Interaction." In P. Noller and M. A. Fitzpatrick, eds., *Perspectives on Marital Interaction.* Clevedon, Eng.: Multilingual Matters, Ltd.

Fulton, Julie 1979 "Parental Reports of Children's Post-Divorce Adjustment." *Journal of Social Issues* 35:126–139.

Glenn, Norval D. 1987 "Tentatively Concerned View of American Marriage." *Journal of Family Issues* 8:350–354.

Glick, Paul C. 1989 "The Family Life Cycle and Social Change." *Family Relations* 38:123–129.

Goode, William J. 1956 *After Divorce.* New York: Free Press.

Gottman, John M., and Albert L. Porterfield 1981 "Communicative Competence in the Nonverbal Behavior of Married Couples." *Journal of Marriage and the Family* 43:817–824.

Harmsworth, Harry C., and Mhyra S. Minnis 1955 "Nonstatutory Causes of Divorce: The Lawyer's Point of View." *Marriage and Family Living* 17:316–321.

Holman, Thomas B., and Gregory W. Brock 1986 "Implications for Therapy in the Study of Communication and Marital Quality." *Family Perspectives* 20:85–94.

Ishii-Kuntz, Masako, and Marilyn Ihinger-Tallman 1991 "The Subjective Well-Being of Parents." *Journal of Family Issues* 12:58–68.

Kilbourne, Barbara S., Frank Howell, and Paul England 1990 "Measurement Model for Subjective Marital Solidarity: Invariance Across Time, Gender and Life Cycle Stage." *Social Science Research* 19:62–81.

Kitson, Gay C., and Marvin B. Sussman 1982 "Marital Complaints, Demographic Characteristics and Symptoms of Mental Distress in Divorce." *Journal of Marriage and the Family* 44:87–102.

Klagsbrun, Francine 1986 *Married People.* New York: Bantam Books.

Komarovsky, Mirra 1962 *Blue-Collar Marriage.* New York: Vintage Books.

LaRossa, Ralph, and M. LaRossa 1981 *Transition to Parenthood.* Beverly Hills, Calif.: Sage Publications.

Lang, Abigail M., and Elaine M. Brody 1983 "Characteristics of Middle-aged Daughters and Help to Their Elderly Mothers." *Journal of Marriage and the Family* 45:193–202.

Larson, Jeffery H. 1988 "The Marriage Quiz: College Students' Beliefs in Selected Myths About Marriage." *Family Relations* 37:3–11.

Lasch, Christopher 1977 *Haven in a Heartless World.* New York: Basic Books.

Lee, Gary 1982 *Family Structure and Interaction: Comparative Analysis.* Minneapolis: University of Minnesota Press.

Levinger, George 1965 "Marital Cohesiveness and Dissolution: An Integrative Review." *Journal of Marriage and the Family* 27:19–28.

——— 1966 "Sources of Marital Dissatisfaction Among Applicants for Divorce." *American Journal of Orthopsychiatry* 36:803–807.

Lewis, Robert A., and Graham B. Spanier 1979 "Theorizing About the Quality and Stability of Marriage." In W. R. Burr, R. Hill, R. I. Nye, and I. L. Reiss, eds., *Contemporary Theories About the Family,* Vol 1. New York: Free Press.

Luckey, Eleanore B. 1960 "Marital Satisfaction and Congruent Self-Spouse Concepts." *Social Forces* 39:153–157.

McHale, Susan M., and Ted L. Huston 1984 "Men and Women as Parents: Sex Role Orientations, Employment, and Parental Roles." *Child Development* 55:1349–1361.

——— 1985 "The Effect of the Transition to Parenthood on the Marriage Relationship." *Journal of Family Issues* 6:409–433.

Martin, Teresa C., and Larry L. Bumpass 1989 "Recent Trends in Marital Disruption." *Demography* 26:37–51.

Noller, Patricia, and Mary Anne Fitzpatrick 1990 "Marital Communication in the Eighties." *Journal of Marriage and the Family* 52:832–843.

Norton, A. J., and J. E. Moorman 1987 "Current Trends in Marriage and Divorce Among American Women." *Journal of Marriage and the Family* 49:3–14.

Olsen, David H., D. Sprenkle, and C. Russell 1979 "Circumplex Model of Marital and Family Systems I: Cohesion and Adaptability Dimensions, Family Types and Clinical Applications." *Family Process* 18:3–28.

Pineo, Peter C. 1961 "Disenchantment in the Later Years of Marriage." *Marriage and Family Living* 23:3–11.

Popenoe, David 1988 *Disturbing the Nest: Family Change and Decline in Modern Societies.* New York: Aldine de Gruyter.

Reiss, Ira L., and Gary R. Lee 1988 *Family Systems in America.* New York: Holt, Rinehart, and Winston.

Rosenthal, Carolyn 1985 "Kinkeeping in the Familial Division of Labor." *Journal of Marriage and the Family* 47:965–974.

Ross, Edward Alsworth 1920 *The Principles of Sociology.* New York: Century Co.

Rubin, Lillian 1976 *Worlds of Pain: Life in the Working Class Family.* New York: Basic Books.

Ruble, Diane, A. Fleming, L. Hackel, and C. Stangor 1988 "Changes in the Marital Relationship During the Transition to First-Time Motherhood: Effects of Violated Expectations Concerning Division of Labor." *Journal of Personality and Social Psychology* 55:78–87.

Ryder, Robert 1973 "Longitudinal Data Relating Marital Satisfaction and Having a Child." *Journal of Marriage and the Family* 35:604–607.

Sanders, Glenn S., and Jerry Suls 1982 "Social Comparison, Competition and Marriage." *Journal of Marriage and the Family* 44:721–730.

Slater, Philip 1963 "On Social Regression." *American Sociological Review* 28:339–364.

Stinnett, Nick 1971 "An Investigation of Selected Attitudes of College Students Toward Marriage." *Journal of Home Economics* 63:33–37.

Sweet, James A., and Larry L. Bumpass 1987 *American Families and Households.* New York: Russell Sage Foundation.

Teachman, Jay D., D. Polonko, and John Scanzoni 1987 "Demography of the Family." In Marvin B. Sussman and Suzanne K. Steinmetz, eds., *Handbook of Marriage and the Family.* New York: Plenum Press.

Veroff, Joseph, Richard Kulka, and Elizabeth Douvan 1981 *Mental Health in America: Patterns of Help-Seeking from 1957 to 1976.* New York: Basic Books.

Walker, Lenore E. 1979 *The Battered Woman.* New York: Harper and Row.

White, Lynn K. 1987 "Freedom Versus Constraint: The New Synthesis." *Journal of Family Issues* 8:468–470.

——— 1990 "Determinants of Divorce: Review of Research in the Eighties." *Journal of Marriage and the Family* 52:904–912.

———, and Alan Booth 1985 "The Transition to Parenthood and Marital Quality." *Journal of Family Issues* 6:435–449.

Whyte, Martin K. 1990 *Dating, Mating, and Marriage.* New York: Aldine de Gruyter.

– MARILYN IHINGER-TALLMAN

MARRIAGE AND DIVORCE RATES

Marriage and divorce rates are measures of the propensity for the population of a given area to become married or divorced during a given year. Some of the rates are quite simple, and others are progressively more refined. The simple ones are called *crude rates* and are expressed in terms of the number of marriages or divorces per 1,000 persons of all ages in the area at the middle of the year. These are the only marriage and divorce rates available for every state in the United States. They have the weakness of including in the base not only young children but also elderly persons, who are unlikely to marry or become divorced. But the wide fluctuations in crude rates over time are obviously associated with changes in the economic, political, and social climate.

Women who first marry after they reach their thirties are more likely to have stable marriages than those who marry in their twenties.

More refined rates will be discussed below, but the following illustrative crude rates of marriage for the United States will demonstrate the readily identifiable consequences of recent historical turning points or periods (National Center for Health Statistics 1990a, 1990b).

Between 1940 and 1946 the crude marriage rate for the United States went up sharply, from 12.1 per 1,000 to 16.4 per 1,000, or by 36 percent, showing the effects of depressed economic conditions before, and disarmament after, World War II.

Between 1946 and 1956 the rate went down rapidly to 9.5 per 1,000, or by 42 percent, as the baby boom peaked. The unprecedented increase in the number of young children was included in the base of the rate, and this helped to lower the rate.

Between 1956 and 1964 the rate declined farther to 9.0 per 1,000, or by 5 percent, as the baby boom ended and the Vietnam War had begun. Between 1964 and 1972 the rate went up moderately to a peak of 10.9 per 1,000, or by 21 percent, as the Vietnam War ended and many returning war veterans married.

Between 1972 and 1989 the rate declined irregularly to 9.7 per 1,000, or by 11 percent, because of developments that will be discussed below.

Refined marriage rates show the propensity to marry for adults who are eligible to marry. They exclude from the base all persons who are too young to marry and may also limit the base to an age range within which most marriages occur. Thus, vital statistics annual reports regularly present crude marriage rates for the entire United States, for regions, and for individual states;

and historical series on marriage rates for unmarried women under forty-five years of age are presented only for the United States as a whole (National Center for Health Statistics 1990b). More detailed characteristics of brides and grooms are published only for the entire United States. The conventional practice of basing these rates on the number of women rather than all adults has the advantage of making the level of the rates correspond approximately to the number of couples who are marrying. Moreover, the patterns of changes in rates over time are generally the same for men and women.

Changes over time in the tendency for adults to marry are more meaningful and may fluctuate more widely if they are reported in refined rather than crude rates. To illustrate, the crude marriage rate declined between 1972 and 1995 from 10.9 per 1,000 population to 8.9, or by 20 percent, while the refined rate (marriages per 1,000 women fifteen to forty-four years old) declined from 141.3 to 83.0, or by 41 percent. A change that appeared relatively small when measured crudely turned out to double when based on a more relevant segment of the population. Persons who want to have others believe that the change was small may cite the crude rates, and persons who want to demonstrate that the marital situation was deteriorating rapidly may cite the refined rates. But persons interested in making a balanced presentation may choose to cite both types of results and explain the differences between them.

Still greater refinement can be achieved by computing marriage rates according to such key variables as age groups and previous marital status. Examples appear in table 1 and figures 1 and 3 for the United States from 1971 to 1987. Table 1 and figure 1 show first marriage rates by age for the only marital status category of eligible persons, namely, never-married adults (women) fifteen years old and over. Figure 2 shows divorce rates by age for married women, and figure 3 shows remarriage rates by age for divorced women. The low remarriage rates for widows are not shown here but are treated briefly elsewhere in the article. Rates of separation because of marital discord are also not presented here: Separated adults are still legally married and are therefore included in the base of divorce rates.

The marriage and divorce rates in table 1 were based on data from annual reports published by the National Center for Health Statistics (NCHS). These reports contain information, obtained from central offices, of vital statistics in the states that are in the Marriage Registration Area (MRA) and the Divorce Registration Area (DRA). In 1990 the District of Columbia and all but eight states were in the MRA, while the District of Columbia and only thirty-one states were in the DRA. Funding for the central offices is determined by each state's legislature. But for states not in the MRA or DRA the NCHS requests the numbers of marriages and divorces from local offices where marriage and divorce certificates are issued. The reports on divorce include the small number of annulments and dissolutions of marriage. Bases for the marriage and divorce rates in table 1 were obtained from special tabulations made by the U.S. Bureau of the Census from Current Population Survey data. These are tabulations of adults in MRA and DRA states and classified by marital status, age, and sex. Because not all the population of the United States is included in the MRA and DRA, the detailed marriage and divorce statistics published by the NCHS constitute approximations of the marital situation in the country as a whole. This article contains much numerical information that was published in one or more of the three NCHS reports listed among the references.

First Marriage Rates by Age

Illustrations of first marriage rates appear in table 1. For the United States, the first marriage rates per 1,000 never-married women fifteen years old and over were 93 in 1971 and 59 in 1987. (When this article was prepared, the most recent years for which detailed marriage and divorce rates had been published was 1987. In effect, 9.3 percent of the never-married women in 1971, and 5.9 percent in 1987, became married for the first time.) For men, the corresponding rates were 68 in 1971 and 49 in 1987.

First marriage rates tend to decline with age, and the rates for most of the age groups shown in table 1 were declining over time. The rates for the age groups under twenty years of age were the highest, but they dropped so sharply that they were only about one-third as high in 1987 as they had been in 1971. At the oldest ages, the change appears to have been slight. Obviously, the propensity to marry was falling far more abruptly among the young than among the older singles, probably in reaction to the suddenly changing cultural climate.

The generally downward trend in the marriage rate for each young age group was especially rapid during the early 1970s. By 1975, the veterans of the Vietnam War had already entered delayed marriages, and the upsurge in cohabitation outside marriage was only beginning to depress the first marriage rate. During the 1980s the slight upturn in the first marriage rate for women over thirty years of age probably reflected an increase in marriages among women who had delayed marrying for the purposes of obtaining a higher education and becoming established in the work-place. Research has produced evidence that women who marry for the first time

TABLE 1

FIRST MARRIAGE RATES PER 1,000 NEVER-MARRIED WOMEN, DIVORCE RATES PER 1,000 MARRIED WOMEN, AND REMARRIAGE RATES PER 1,000 DIVORCED WOMEN BY AGE: UNITED STATES, 1970 TO 1987

Age (years)	1970[a]	1975	1980[b]	1983	1985	1987
First Marriage Rate						
15 or over	93	76	68	64	62	59
15 to 17	36	29	22	16	13	12
18 to 19	150	115	92	73	67	58
20 to 24	198	144	122	107	102	98
25 to 29	131	115	104	105	104	105
30 to 34	75	62	60	61	66	69
35 to 39	48	36	33	38	37	42
40 to 44	27	26	22	22	24	22
45 to 64	10	9	8	8	11	10
65 or over	1	1	1	1	1	1
Divorce Rate						
15 or over	14	NA	20	19	19	19
15 to 19	27	NA	42	48	48	50
20 to 24	33	NA	47	43	47	46
25 to 29	26	NA	38	36	36	34
30 to 34	19	NA	29	28	29	27
35 to 44	11	NA	24	25	22	22
45 to 54	5	NA	10	11	11	11
55 to 64	3	NA	4	4	4	4
Remarriage Rate						
15 or over	133	117	104	92	82	81
20 to 24	420	301	301	240	264	248
25 to 29	277	235	209	204	184	183
30 to 34	196	173	146	145	128	137
35 to 39	147	117	108	99	97	92
40 to 44	98	91	69	67	63	69
45 to 64	47	40	35	31	36	37
65 or over	9	9	7	5	5	5

[a] First marriage and remarriage rates for 1971.
[b] First marriage and remarriage rates for 1979.
Source: National Center for Health Statistics, 1990b and 1990c.

after they reach their thirties are more likely to have stable marriages than those who marry in their twenties (Norton and Moorman 1987). Although first marriage rates among adults in their forties are relatively low, they are by no means negligible.

As first marriage rates declined between the mid-1960s and the late 1980s, the median age at first marriage rose at an unprecedented pace over this short period of time. According to vital statistics, the median age at first marriage for women went up from 20.3 years in 1963 to 24 in 1990; for men it went up from 22.5 years to 25.9 years. As age at first marriage increased, the distribution of ages at first marriage also increased (Wilson and London).

One of the consequences of the great delay of first marriage has been a very sharp rise in premarital pregnancy. Only 5 percent of births in 1960 occurred to unmarried mothers, but this increased to 32.6 percent in 1994. Research by Bumpass and McLanahan (1989) showed that one-half of nonmarital births during the late 1980s were first births, and about one-third occurred to teenagers. Moreover, about one-tenth of brides were pregnant at first marriage. Thus, about one-third of the births during the late 1980s were conceived before marriage.

As the first marriage rate declined, the proportion of all marriages that were primary marriages (first for bride and groom) also declined. In 1970, two-thirds (68 percent) were primary marriages, but by 1987 the proportion was barely over one-half (54 percent). Meantime, marriages of divorced brides to divorced grooms nearly doubled, from 11 percent to 19 percent, while mar-

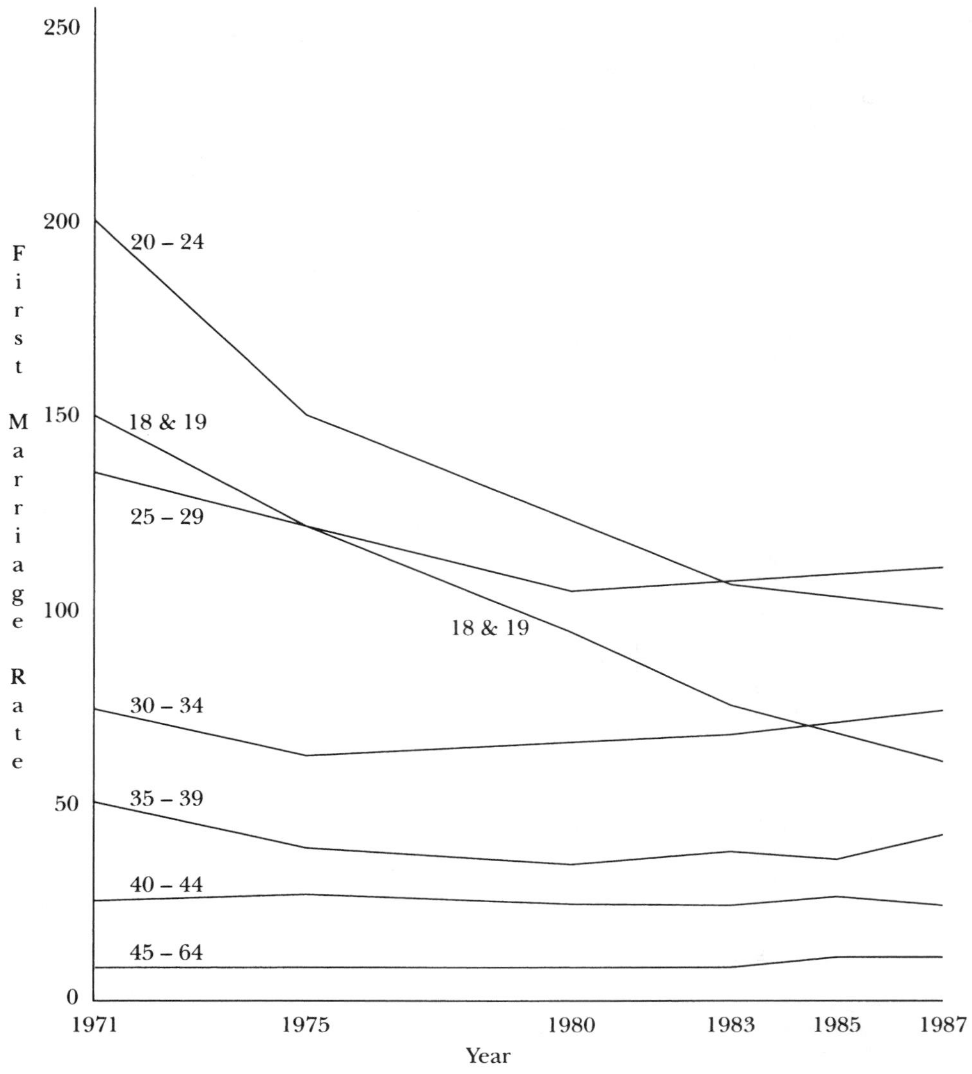

Figure 1. First marriage rate per 1,000 never-married women, by age: United States, 1971–1987.

riages of widows to widowers went down from 2 percent to 1 percent.

Men and women, regardless of previous marital status, tend to marry someone whose age is similar to their own. But men who enter first marriage when they are older than the average age of men at marriage have a reasonable likelihood of marrying a woman who has been divorced.

Procedures have been developed for projecting the proportion of adults of a certain age who are likely to enter first marriage sometime during their lives. This measure is, in effect, "a lifetime first marriage rate." One of these procedures was used by Schoen et al. (1985) to find that about 94 percent of men born in the years 1948 to 1950 and who survived to age fifteen were expected to marry eventually; for women, it was 95 percent. Their projections for those born in 1980 were significantly lower, 89 percent for men and 91 percent for women. Despite the implied decline, a level of nine-tenths of the young adults deciding to marry at least once is still high by world standards.

Divorce Rates by Age

The NCHS publishes annual reports that show the number of divorces occurring among persons in their first marriage, their second marriage, and their third or subsequent marriage (National Center for Health Statistics 1990c). But the required bases for computing

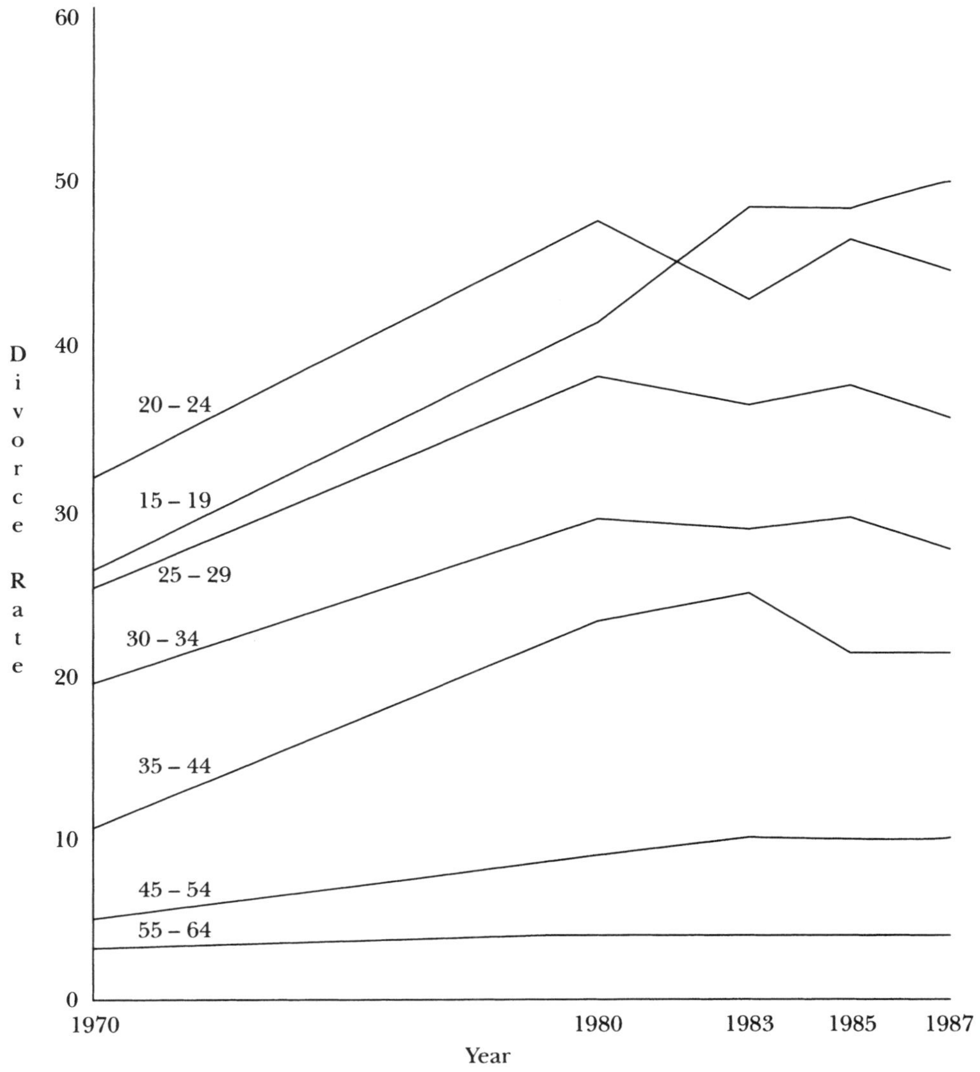

Figure 2. Divorce rate per 1,000 married women, by age: United States, 1970–1987.

first divorce rates and redivorce rates are not available. During the 1980s, about three-fourths of the divorces were obtained by adults in their first marriage, about one-fifth by those in their second marriage, and one-twentieth by those who had been married at least three times.

The divorce rates in table 1 provide illustrations of the magnitude of the rates for the period 1970 to 1987. The divorce rate per 1,000 married women was 14 in 1970 and 19 in 1987. Corresponding rates for men were the same. The rate reached a peak of 20 in 1980, nearly half again as high as in 1970, and declined slightly to 19 in 1987, a level still well above that in 1970.

The divorce rate for married women rose dramatically in every age group during the 1970s and changed relatively little from then through the 1980s. In January 1973 the Vietnam War ended, and at that time the norms regarding the sanctity of marriage were being revised. The advantages of a permanent marriage were being weighed against the alternatives, including freedom from a seriously unsatisfactory marital bond and the prospect of experimenting with cohabitation outside marriage or living alone without any marital entanglements.

Married women under twenty-five years of age have consistently high divorce rates resulting largely from adjustment difficulties associated with early first marriage.

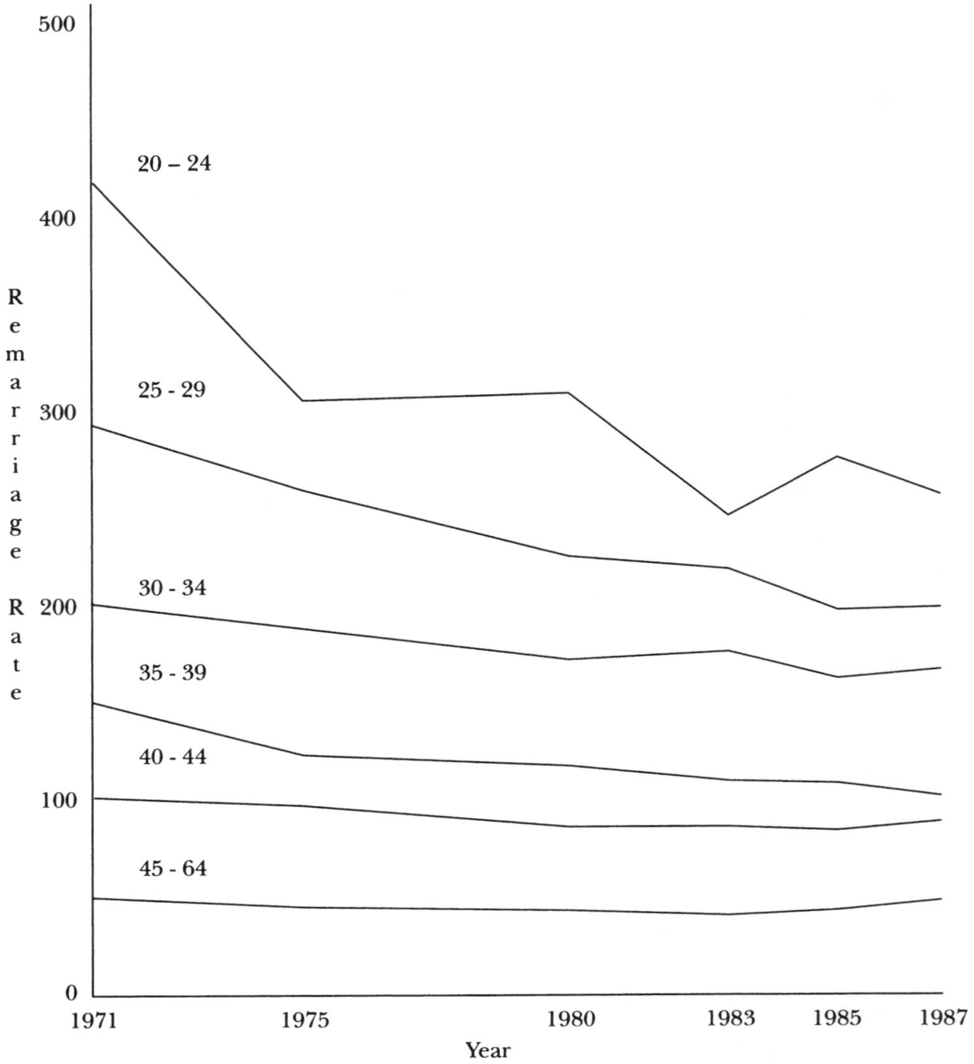

Figure 3. Remarriage rate per 1,000 divorced women, by age: United States, 1971–1987.

Noteworthy in this context is the finding that 30 percent of the women entering a first marriage in 1980 were in their teens, while 40 percent of those obtaining a divorce had entered their marriage while teenagers.

More divorces during the 1980s were occurring to married adults twenty-five to thirty-four years of age than to those in any other ten-year age group. A related study by Norton and Moorman (1987) concluded that women in their late thirties in 1985 were likely to have higher lifetime divorce rates (55 percent) than those either ten years older or ten years younger. This cohort was born during the vanguard of the baby boom and became the trend setter for higher divorce rates. The lower rate for those ten years younger may reflect their concern caused by the adjustment problems of their older divorced siblings or friends.

Married women over forty-five years of age have quite low divorce rates. Most of their marriages must still be reasonably satisfactory, or not sufficiently unsatisfactory to persuade them to face the disadvantages that are often associated with becoming divorced. Yet, the forces that raised the divorce rate for younger women greatly after 1970 also made the small rate for the older women increase by one-fourth during the 1970s and remain at about the same level through the 1980s.

The median duration of marriage before divorce has been seven years for several decades. This finding is not proof of a seven-year itch. In fact, the median varies widely according to previous marital status from eight years for first marriages to six years for second marriages and four years for third and subsequent marriages. The number of divorces reaches a peak during the third year of marriage and declines during each succeeding year of marriage.

Among separating couples, the wife usually files the petition for divorce. However, between 1975 and 1987, the proportion of husband petitioners increased from 29.4 percent to 32.7 percent, and the small proportion of divorces in which both the husband and the wife were petitioners more than doubled, from 2.8 percent to 6.5 percent. These changes occurred while the feminist movement was becoming increasingly diffused and the birth rate was declining, with the consequence that only about one-half (52 percent) of the divorces in 1987 involved children under eighteen years of age and one-fourth (29 percent) involved only one child. It is not surprising that nine-tenths of children under eighteen living with a divorced parent live with their mother, far more often in families with smaller average incomes than those living with divorced fathers.

Although only about one-tenth of the adults in the United States in 1988 were divorced (7.4 percent) or separated (2.4 percent), the lifetime experience of married persons with these types of marital disruption is far greater. Based on adjustments for underreporting of divorce data from the Current Population Survey and for underrepresentation of divorce from vital statistics in the MRA, Martin and Bumpass (1989) have concluded that two-thirds of current marriages are likely to end in separation or divorce.

Remarriage Rates by Age

Annual remarriage rates published by NCHS include separate rates for remarriages after divorce and after widowhood as well as for all remarriages. In this article attention is concentrated on remarriages after divorce, which constitute about nine-tenths of all remarriages. As mentioned above, the remarriage rate after divorce is a measure of the number of divorced women who marry in a given year per 1,000 divorced women at the middle of the year. For example, table 1 shows that the remarriage rate after divorce for the United States was 133 in 1970 and 81 in 1987. Therefore, about 13 percent of the divorced women in 1970 became remarried in that year, as compared with 8 percent in 1987, only three-fifths as much as in 1970.

Divorced men have far higher remarriage rates than divorced women (in 1987, 116 versus 81). This situation and women's greater longevity largely account for the number of divorced women fifty-five years old and over in 1988 being one and one-half times the number of divorced men of that age (U.S. Bureau of the Census 1989).

Like first marriage rates, remarriage rates tend to decline with age, and the rate for each age group declined after 1970. The especially sharp drop during the first half of the 1970s for women under forty years of age resulted from the compounding effect of a rapid increase in divorce and a rapid decline in remarriage during that period.

A large majority of divorced persons eventually remarry. In 1980, among persons sixty-five to seventy-four years old, 84 percent of the men and 77 percent of the women who had been divorced had remarried (U.S. Bureau of the Census 1989). But because of the declining remarriage rates, a projection based on information from the National Survey of Families and Households conducted in 1987 and 1988 shows that 72 percent of the recently separated persons are likely eventually to remarry (Bumpass, Sweet, and Martin 1989). About 6 percent of those who become separated never become divorced and therefore are not eligible for remarriage. Two-thirds of the remarriages in recent years occurred to women who entered first marriages as teenagers, according to the same study. Moreover, the rate of remarriage declines as the number of young children increases. Among married parents of young children with one or both parents remarried, about one-third of the children were born after the remarriage, and the others are stepchildren with the usually accompanying adjustment problems (Glick and Lin 1987).

In a given year about two of every three adults who marry are marrying for the first time, but this includes those marrying after widowhood as well as divorce. Among those who remarry after divorce, about three-fourths have been married only once, one-fifth have been married twice, and one-twentieth three or more times. Some couples who remarry had been married to each other previously. According to unpublished data from the National Survey of Families and Households, this occurred in about 3.3 percent of all marriages and closer to 5 percent for those in the age range when most remarriages after divorce occur.

Men are older than women, on the average, when they marry for the first time or when they remarry. Moreover, the gap is considerably wider at remarriage than at first marriage, but it narrowed somewhat between 1970 and 1987. Thus, successive marriages have been happening at older ages but with shorter intervals between them. In this context, the wider gap at remarriage than at first marriage may be less socially significant than an identical gap would have been at first marriage.

A woman in her second marriage is likely to be married to a man who is about ten years older than her first husband when she married him. Therefore, her second husband was probably more advanced in his occupation than her first husband was when she married him. But research has established that her first husband was probably about as far advanced ten years after her first marriage as her second husband was when she married him (Jacobs and Furstenberger 1986).

Other Marriage and Divorce Rates

Another rate that differs from the rates shown in table 1 is the *total marriage rate.* This rate is intended to show the number of marriages that a group of 1,000 men and women would have if they experienced in their lives the age-sex marriage rates observed in a given year (National Center for Health Statistics 1990b). It is therefore a hypothetical rate analogous to a total fertility rate. The NCHS publishes both total first marriage rates and total remarriage rates annually. Each of the two rates uses as the base the total population in each age group without regard to previous marital status.

The total first marriage rate for the United States in 1987 implied that only 69 percent of men and 70 percent of women would eventually marry. The corresponding remarriage rates were 45 percent for men and 41 percent for women. Because both rates are based on the population regardless of marital status, they are additive. Therefore, the (combined) total marriage rate for 1987 implied that men are likely to have 1.14 marriages during their lifetime and women 1.11. These results may seem low because of the assumptions involved. For instance, if currently about 90 percent of every 100 adults marry, if one-half of the first marriages end in divorce, and if 70 percent of the divorced persons remarry, this would mean that 100 young adults in the 1990s are likely to have 90 first marriages and 32 second marriages after divorce ($.90 + .90 \times .50 \times .70$). In addition, many will redivorce and remarry again, and others will become widowed and remarry. Thus, realistically, the average young adult in the 1990s who marries is likely to have more than 1.1 marriages.

Remarriage among widowed adults is not featured in this article. However, the remarriage rate per 1,000 widows declined from 6 in 1982 to 5 in 1987, while the rate for widowers declined from 32 to 26. The remarriage rate for widowers is much higher than the rate for widows because about one-half of them marry widows, who out-number them five to one (U.S. Bureau of the Census 1989). Of all men and women who married in 1987, 68 percent had never previously married, 29 percent were divorced, and only 3 percent were widowed.

Divorce rates per 1,000 involving children under eighteen are published annually by NCHS. In 1990, the rate was 17, implying that 1.7 percent of the children under eighteen years of age in the United States were involved in parental divorces in that year. This finding implies further that, if the same rate continued for eighteen years, 30.6 percent of the children would likely experience parental divorce before they reached eighteen years of age. Data from the U.S. Bureau of Census used by Norton and Glick (1986) put the estimate at 40 percent. They also estimated that about an additional 20 percent of children become members of one-parent families because of premarital birth, parental separation that does not end in divorce, or death of a parent. Therefore, about 60 percent of the children born in the 1980s may expect to spend a significant amount of time in a one-parent family before they become eighteen years of age.

Marriage rates vary among countries as a reflection of dissimilar social, demographic, and economic conditions. An analysis of marriage rates in fifteen developed countries revealed that between 1965 and 1980 the rate per 1,000 unmarried women declined in all but two of the countries (Glick 1989). The marriage rates in English-speaking countries and Israel were above the average for the entire group, but the rates were below the average in the Germanic, French, and Scandinavian countries. A special reason for the differences was the extent to which cohabitation had been accepted as at least a temporary alternative to marriage. The generally downward trend among the marriage rates shows that the changing social conditions related to the propensity toward marriage have become widely diffused.

High divorce rates tend to be associated with high marriage rates in English-speaking countries.

Divorce rates per 1,000 married women in almost all of the fifteen countries went up between 1965 and 1980 and doubled in the majority of them. Most of the countries with divorce rates above the overall average were English speaking. High divorce rates tended to be associated with high marriage rates because remarriages after divorce make an important contribution to the level of the marriage rates per 1,000 unmarried women.

Remarriage rates have been falling in most of the fifteen countries. In Canada a part of the decline between 1965 and 1980 was attributed to a change in the divorce laws and an increase in the delay of remarriage. The remarriage rate in New Zealand actually rose slightly in the context of a baby boom and an increase in immigration of young adults with subsequent high divorce rates. Countries with the highest remarriage rates were English speaking, and those with the lowest were Scandinavian, French, and certain other European countries where cohabitation outside marriage had risen sharply.

Variation in the level of marriage and divorce rates among the American regions and states can be documented only by the use of crude rates. The Northeast and Midwest had consistently lower marriage rates than the South and West. The general pattern is similar for divorce rates. Some of the variations in the rates by states result from differences in the strictness of residence requirements for obtaining a marriage or divorce license. About seven of every eight marriages occur in the state where both the bride and the groom have their usual residence.

Selected Variables Related to Marriage and Divorce

Annual marriage and divorce rates are not presented in the NCHS reports by education and race of those involved. However, the reports do show distributions of first marriages and remarriages by several categories of education and race. The 1987 report documents that those marrying for the first time had more education, on the average, than those who were remarrying. Information from the 1980 census showed that women twenty-five to thirty-four years of age who had exactly four years of college training had distinctly the largest proportion with intact first marriages; those with graduate school training had a somewhat smaller proportion; and those with an incomplete college education had a smaller proportion than those in any other education category (U.S. Bureau of Census 1985).

The 1987 report on marriage provided evidence that white adults tend to marry at a younger age than black adults. The difference was two years for both brides and grooms at first marriage and two years at remarriage after divorce. Information for 1988 from the U.S. Bureau of the Census (1989) indicated that 18 percent of black adults had not married by the time they were forty years old, as compared with 8 percent for white adults of the same age. The pressure to marry and to remain married evidently tends to be less for black adults than white adults.

Interracial marriage occurs between a small but socially significant proportion of those who marry. In 1987, 2 percent of black brides married white grooms, and 6 percent of black grooms married white brides. Also, nearly 2 percent of black women obtaining divorces were married to white men, and more than 4 percent of black men obtaining divorces were married to white women. Thus, among those who intermarried, the marriages of black men to white women tend to be more stable than marriages of white men to black women.

Cohabitation outside marriage increased dramatically from only one-half million heterosexual couples in 1970 to 2.6 million in 1988, with about one million of their households maintained by the woman. This numerical growth occurred primarily among adults below middle age and has contributed importantly to the decline in marriage rates as well as to the increase in the number of separated persons. According to the 1987–1988 National Survey of Families and Households, "almost half of the persons in their early thirties and half of the recently married have cohabited" (Bumpass and Sweet 1989, p. 615). In order to provide some balance on the issue, Thornton (1985, p. 497) has concluded that "even though cohabitation will be experienced by many, most people will continue to spend substantially more time in marital unions than in cohabiting unions."

The health of adults is related to marital selection and marital stability, but NCHS does not provide marriage and divorce rates by the health status of those involved. The center does, however, publish current information on several indicators of the health condition of adults by marital status. Nearly all of the indicators confirm that people with more signs of good health are likely to marry and remain married or to remarry after marital dissolution (Wilson and Schoenborn 1989). Parental divorce tends to be related to health problems of children but largely through the custodial parents' loss of income and time to spend with the children after divorce (Mauldon 1988). And stress prior to an event such as divorce or premarital breakup may actually reduce the impact of the life transition (Wheaton 1990).

Current trends in marriage and divorce rates do not necessarily indicate whether the rates will tend to stabilize at or near their 1990 levels, to resume their movement in historical directions, or to continue fluctuating in response to future social developments. A few more decades of observing the impact of past changes in marriage and divorce rates on the persons involved may be necessary before a definitive evaluation can be made concerning the longtime effect of these changes on family and child welfare.

[See also: Divorce; Marriage; Remarriage.]

BIBLIOGRAPHY

Bumpass, Larry, and Sara McLanahan 1989 "Unmarried Motherhood: Recent Trends, Composition, and Black-White Differences." *Demography* 26:279–286.

Bumpass, Larry, and James A. Sweet 1989 "National Estimates of Cohabitation." *Demography* 26:615–625.

Bumpass, Larry, James A. Sweet, and Teresa Castro Martin 1989 "Changing Patterns of Remarriage." Working Paper 89-02. Madison: Center for Demography and Ecology, University of Wisconsin.

Glick, Paul C. 1989 "The Family of Today and Tomorrow." In K. Ishwaran, ed., *Family and Marriage: Cross-Cultural Perspectives.* Toronto: Wall and Thompson.

Glick, Paul C., and Sung-Ling Lin 1987 "Remarriage after Divorce: Recent Changes and Demographic Variations." *Sociological Perspectives* 30:162–179.

Jacobs, Jerry A., and Frank F. Furstenberg, Jr. 1986 "Changing Place: Conjugal Careers and Women's Marital Stability." *Social Forces* 63:714–732.

Lin, Sung-Ling 1987 "Marital Selection and Child-Bearing and Companionship Functions of Marriage and Remarriage." Ph.D. diss., Arizona State University, Tempe.

Martin, Teresa Castro, and Larry L. Bumpass 1989 "Recent Trends in Marital Disruption." *Demography* 26:37–51.

Mauldon, Jane 1988 "The Effect of Marital Disruption on Children's Health." Paper presented at the Population Association of America meeting, New Orleans.

National Center for Health Statistics 1990a "Births, Marriages, Divorces, and Deaths for 1989." *Monthly Vital Statistics Report* 38, no. 12.

——— 1990b "Advance Report of Final Marriage Statistics, 1987." *Monthly Vital Statistics Report* 38, no. 12, Supplement.

——— 1990c "Advance Report of Final Divorce Statistics, 1987." *Monthly Vital Statistics Report* 38, no. 12, Supplement 2.

Norton, Arthur J., and Paul C. Glick 1986 "One-Parent Families: A Social and Economic Profile." *Family Relations* 35:9–17.

Norton, Arthur J., and Jeanne E. Moorman 1987 "Current Trends in Marriage and Divorce among American Women." *Journal of Marriage and the Family* 49:3–14.

Schoen, Robert, William Urton, Karen Woodrow, and John Baj 1985 "Marriage and Divorce in Twentieth-Century American Cohorts." *Demography* 22:101–114.

Thornton, Arland 1988 "Cohabitation and Marriage in the 1980s." *Demography* 25:492–508.

U.S. Bureau of the Census 1985 *1980 Census of Population: Marital Characteristics.* Washington, D.C.: U.S. Government Printing Office.

——— 1989 "Marital Status and Living Arrangements: March 1988." *Current Population Reports* P-20, no. 433. Washington, D.C.: U.S. Government Printing Office.

Wheaton, Blair 1990 "Life Transitions, Role Histories, and Mental Health." *American Sociological Review* 55:209–223.

Wilson, Barbara F., and Kathryn A. London 1987 "Going to the Chapel." *American Demographics* 9:26–31.

Wilson, Barbara F, and Charlotte Schoenborn 1989 "A Healthy Marriage." *American Demographics* 11:40–43.

– PAUL C. GLICK

MASS MEDIA RESEARCH

The interest of sociologists in mass communication was stimulated by developments in technology allowing the reproduction and speedy transmission of messages. It began with the rise of the popular press, followed by the invention of film, sound broadcasting, and the audiovisual. As a result, all of us live in a world of media-constructed images that, presumably, significantly influence what we think and how we partition our attention, time, and other scarce resources. So pervasive has been the media presence that issues relating to these influences have also drawn the attention of researchers from disciplines other than sociology.

It is to Harold Lasswell (1947), an empirically oriented political scientist, that the social science community owes a succinct formula that lays out the major elements within the field of communication research: *Who* says *what* to *whom* and with what *effect?* The term *how* has since been added to identify the particular channel (face-to-face, print, electronic, etc.) through which communication takes place. Only some channels lend themselves to *mass* communication, which can be defined, in the terms of the above formula, as the transmission by professional communicators (who) of a continuous flow of a uniform content (what) by means of a complex apparatus (how) to a large, heterogeneous, and geographically dispersed audience (to whom).

The physical or electronic transmission of message content does not in itself suffice for communication.

Not included in this definition of mass communication are its effects or, more broadly speaking, its consequences, toward which most of the sociological research effort has been directed. The physical or electronic transmission of message content does not in itself suffice for communication, which is indisputably social in that it consists of a meeting of minds in the sense of mutual accommodation. Yet the nature and extent of effects have been, over the years, the central problem of sociological interest in media research.

Media effects have been studied on three levels: the atomistic, the aggregate, and the societal. Effects on the atomistic level involve the cognitive processes and behavioral responses of *individuals* who make up the various mass audiences. By contrast, aggregate measures take into account only *distributions* that produce changes in averages usually expressed as net effects. Consequences for society have more to do with the political, cultural, and other *institutional* changes that represent cumulative adaptations over time to the dominance of a particular mass medium. Inferences based on the observation of effects on one level when ascribed to effects on a different level have often turned out to be invalid.

The Atomistic Level

Much of the research effort has been a response to the operational needs of communicators and propogandists, or of those who wished to defend the public against what was perceived as the pernicious influence of the media. The basic problem has been that of precisely pinpointing effects: What were the characteristics of the potential audience? Who among them was susceptible? What were the determinants of their reactions?

To answer these and similar questions, audience research has typically focused on the situations in which mass communications are received and on the habits and cognitive processes that underlie the responses of individuals either to specific media messages or some significant part of the media fare. The responses under scrutiny have ranged from the arousal of interest, gains in knowledge, the recognition of dangers, changes of opinion, and other attitudinal measures to such behavioral indicators as consumer purchases, electoral decisions, and the "elevation" of cultural taste.

Precisely because of its focus on the individual, this line of research tends to stress the diversity of ways in which individuals relate to media content. First of all, audiences are found to be stratified by education, interest, taste, leisure habits, and so forth, with people at different levels paying attention to different media offerings. The observation that some content had only minimal audience penetration helped explain why some information campaigns failed. Consistent patterns of exposure to different kinds of content further suggested that members of the mass audience, by and large, found what suited their needs and interests.

Second, even common exposure turns out to be a less strong predictor of response than expected. Not everyone understands or understands fully, and reactions are affected by the preconceptions with which people approach the content, by preconceptions rooted in past socialization experience but also reflecting the perspective of groups with which they are associated or identify themselves. Audiences are obstinate and people have options in how they orient themselves to any particular set of messages. They can ignore, misunderstand, accept, find fault with, or be entertained by the same content. In other words, there is no assurance that anyone other than those, for whatever reason, already so disposed will accept the facts, adopt the opinion, or carry out the actions suggested by the mass communicator (Schramm 1973).

This downplaying of the importance of content elements by a methodical partitioning of the mass audience received systematic formulation in the "minimal effects" theorem, derived from Joseph Klapper's review (1960) of certain empirical research findings of studies conducted mostly during the 1940s and 1950s. He generalized that certain factors, such as audience characteristics and a pluralistic media structure, which mediated between content and response, worked primarily in the service of reinforcement of prior attitudes. Changes triggered by exposure were pretty much limited to people whose situations already impelled them to move in that direction. Klapper did, however, acknowledge the power of mass communication to move people on matters with which they were unfamiliar and concerning which they had no distinct views of ingrained habits.

Strong evidence in favor of not-so-minimal effects has come from observations made in the laboratory, especially through the series of experimental studies on children, reported in *Television and Social Behavior,* conducted under the auspices of the U.S. Surgeon General (Murray and Rubinstein 1972). After exposure to programs that included "violent" behavior, subjects often engaged in similar behavior during their play and they were more likely than subjects not so exposed to commit other violent acts.

Still, experiments are generally set up to maximize the possibility of demonstrating direct effects. Thus, in this instance, children, especially young children, would be inclined to model their own behavior on what they see. Moreover, such findings of short-term effects observed in a play situation have to be considered within the context of the whole socialization experience over many years. Longitudinal studies and experimental studies of older children in a more natural setting have yielded results that are more ambiguous (Milavsky et al. 1982). Laboratories do not fully replicate communication situations of real life (Milgram 1973).

But the challenges posed by experimental studies have to be faced. Casual but repeated exposure to televised messages results in incidental learning. Content gradually intrudes into our consciousness until we associate a product with a particular brand name; issues dominating the news become the criteria by which we measure the effectiveness of a political leadership. Insofar as the various mass media sources transmit similar content and play on similar themes, such limited effects, if they are cumulative, can produce shifts of landslide proportions.

Aggregate Effects

Because the responses of persons are so diverse, the effect of communication en masse has to be conveyed in some kind of summary measure—as an average, a trend, a general movement. From this perspective, the magnitude of the shift in the responses of individuals, or whether this represents reinforcement or a reversal, matters less than the overall picture.

How differently effect can appear when viewed from different perspectives may be illustrated by reference to studies of innovations (Rogers 1971). Detailed documentation of the process by which they are adopted and spread suggests that early adopters (also called influentials or opinion leaders, depending on context) are more cosmopolitan in their orientation and hence more attuned to certain media messages. They select from the total stream the ones that best meet their needs and interests. Others will adopt an innovation only after its success has been demonstrated or, if that is precluded—as it would be in most political decisions—out of trust in the expertise of the pacesetters. One can account for the different behavior of leaders and followers in such situations—that is, why one moves ahead and the other is content to wait—in terms of personal characteristics and social relationships. Aggregate effects, on the other hand, have to do with whether or not there has been a general movement toward acceptance or rejection of the innovation.

The most direct measures of aggregate effects are to be found in two-variable relationships, with one variable functioning as an indicator of media presence and the other representing the response. Many such combinations are possible. One can use media penetration (e.g., newspaper circulation or the proportion of homes with a television set) or content characteristics (e.g., the number of violent acts in children's programs, editorial endorsements, or issues emphasized in the news). This rules out media behavior, which is voluntary, and may reflect the influence of still other, often unmeasured, variables that also account for the presumed effect.

As the age of television dawned, opportunities for "controlled" observation—comparing two matched areas, one receiving television and the other not yet within reach of the broadcast signal—were never fully exploited. Rarely did findings about the advent of television go beyond documenting the rather obvious fact that television viewing cut into the use of some other media, especially radio and to a lesser degree movie attendance and children's comic book reading. Nor were the consequences of this reallocation of time at all clear. A study of children in "Teletown" and "Radiotown," the latter community still without television but comparable in other respects, concluded that "before television, many children [had gone] through the same type of change as today from fantasy-seeking media behavior toward reality-seeking media behavior" (Schramm, Lyle, and Parker 1961).

Evidence of this kind is similarly lacking on matters relating to citizen participation among adults. Systematic comparisons between the turnout and overall responsiveness to "party" issues during the 1952 presidential election in counties with high TV-penetration and low TV-penetration revealed no consistent differences, probably because other media were already saturated enough with campaign material to have produced a high level of interest. Situations subject to such "ceiling" effects prevent further movement in response to the presence of a new medium.

Variations in content, when they occur, have offered far more opportunities for controlled observations, many of which have challenged the conventional wisdom. That voters on the west coast of the United States would be dissuaded from voting in the presidential election once television, based on early returns, had declared a winner seemed only logical. Yet studies showed that westerners continued to cast ballots in roughly the same proportions as their compatriots in states where polls had already closed. In voting, they were evidently moved by considerations other than practical utility and by other competing media messages. Whatever the effects of such broadcast returns on the decision to vote or not to vote, they have been too small to measure with any precision. As regards editorial endorsements, where the range of variations is greater, research has shown that such support gives candidates for minor offices, many of whom are only names on a ballot, an incremental but nevertheless distinct advantage over other minor candidates on the same slate.

Correlations that pair a media variable with some measure of response always imply change over time. The alternative is to study change in response to events as they are being communicated via the mass media: a televised speech by a political leader, the announcement of an unexpected reversal of government policy, news of foreign crisis, or simply the flow of information about economic conditions and problems facing the country.

Polls before and after an appropriately timed speech have documented the power of a head of state to move opinion through appeals directed to the public. Speeches can create greater awareness. They are designed to focus attention on those issues and actions from which the politician stands to benefit. The effectiveness of such media events is apt to be greatest when an issue is just surfacing. Leaders also have the ability to make news. Even without an undisputed success, their public appearances, diligently reported by the news media, are used to dramatize their own role in promoting solutions to matters believed to be of general concern.

Careful analysis of the impact of many such events over the years again challenges the conventional wisdom. Neither speeches nor foreign travel by American presidents over nine administrations have, by themselves or in combination, *uniformly* shored up public support. Public response to these events has been highly dependent on the political context—that is, whether they coincided with other events that tended to enhance the president's standing or whether his administration was plagued by intractable problems, such as public concern about a declining economy, an indignation over American hostages whose release it could not effect, or revelations of governmental wrongdoing such as those that surfaced during Watergate and led to the resignation of Richard Nixon (Lang and Lang 1984).

Mass communication influences not so much what *people think but what they think* about.

What stands out in a long line of studies is the general correspondence over time between the overall amount of attention a topic, issue, or personality enjoys in the media and the awareness, interest in, and concern about these. Mass communication influences not so much *what* people think (opinion) but what they think *about* (recognition). Insofar as there is enough common emphasis, the media perform an "agenda-setting" function (Iyengar and Kinder 1987). Collectively, they define the terms of public debate. Media attention also confers status on some of the many voices clamoring to be recognized.

This simple formulation, which has been a central focus of effects research in political communication for some years, attributes to the media at one and the same time too much and too little influence. On the one hand, the media do not, all on their own, dictate or control the political agenda. Neither public awareness nor recognition of a problem is sufficient to stir a controversy on which people take sides. On the other hand, access to the media is a major resource for the advocates of particular policies. Concerns become issues through discussion in which political leaders, government officials, news and commentary in the press, and the voices of citizens reciprocally influence one another in a process more aptly characterized as "agenda building" (Lang and Lang 1984).

The Systemic Perspective

The dissemination of content via the mass communication system occurs in a highly selective fashion. Some information is privileged; other information is available only to those with the interest and resources to pay for it. The upshot of all the efforts to direct communication flow is a repertoire of images of events and ongoing social activities. Media organizations are themselves producers of content. The mass communications through which the world is brought into focus are, in the broadest sense, cultural creations that incorporate the perspectives of the producers and of others whose views have to be taken into account. This influence of the communication system on the content, intended or not, is a source of bias often unrecognized by those responsible for it.

One has to differentiate between two sources of bias: technological and social. Technological bias stems from the physical characteristics of the medium. Harold Innis (1951), the Canadian institutional economist, distinguished between bias toward space and bias toward time. Paper, he averred, because of its light weight, was easily transported but also perishable, and so supported the development of centralized administration. The uniformity thus imposed over a given area (space) was usually at the expense of continuity (time). A more flexible medium could adapt to an oral tradition that favored spontaneous cooperation among autonomous units. There are indeed signs that cheaper and smaller electronic devices may be radically increasing the control individuals have over the information available to them and what to do with it (Beniger 1986).

Applied mechanistically, without regard to who is in control, these categories lead to a simple-minded media determinism. Social bias has to do with how the capabilities intrinsic to the dominant medium are exploited. Television may not have had any demonstrable effect on voter turnout. But a nonpartisan political coverage, designed not to offend, was not only implicit in the economic logic of aiming for the largest possible audience but was reinforced by the regulatory system. The fact that a well-financed candidate could buy nearly unlimited time to air well-targeted political messages may not, in and of itself, have caused the decline of party machines but it certainly contributed to it. Television has helped to make the nominating process far more open to "outsiders" without a firm following among party regulars. And nominating conventions in which political bosses once traded votes were transformed into showpieces, played for a national audience as the curtain raiser for the campaign.

More generally, its penetration into the spheres of other institutions—political, cultural, educational, and so on—is what makes mass communication a potentially powerful influence on the societal level. It hardly matters whether the media are viewed as a resource or as a threat. The publicity generated through mass communication brings the norms of the larger society to bear on actions that once might have been considered privileged or at least shielded from public scrutiny. Conversely, the competition for visibility is an inducement for elite institutions to adopt at least some of the conventions of the media culture.

There remains the question of who sets these norms and standards. Some scholars have argued that repeated exposure to a sanitized media culture results in "mainstreaming." Accordingly, all but a few of the diverse currents that feed into the kaleidoscope of minority cultures receive little or no recognition. Lacking an effective institutional representation, they are more readily marginalized. Content analyses of character portrayal and the values espoused by heroes in the popular entertainment fare have lent some support to the charge of "mainstreaming." Despite the premium on novelty, most media organizations are inclined not to stray too far from what is popularly accepted but will, on the other hand, eagerly imitate any demonstrated success.

The representation of political views is similarly constrained. Despite the independence of the press and a few celebrated instances where a few persistent journalists initiated an inquiry, the more typical pattern is to wait until political actors have highlighted a problem. Usually, it is they, rather than the press, who define the terms of controversies over policy. And, to paraphrase W. Lance Bennett (1988), when the institutional voices speaking in protest are stilled, all but the more radical media are inclined to drop the issue as well. Discussion and diversity exist but usually within self-imposed limits.

It should be clear that major media organizations, though important players, are less than fully separate from other establishments. Their influence on events is greatest when they act in conjunction with other agencies.

[See also: Information Society; Public Opinion.]

BIBLIOGRAPHY

Beniger, James R. 1986 *The Control Revolution: Technological and Economic Origins of the Information Society.* Cambridge, Mass.: Harvard University Press.

Bennett, W. Lance 1988 *News: The Politics of Illusion.* New York: Longman.

Innis, Harold A. 1951 *The Bias of Communication.* Toronto: University of Toronto Press.

Iyengar, Shanto, and Donald R. Kinder 1987 *News That Matters: Television and Public Opinion.* Chicago: University of Chicago Press.

Klapper, Joseph T. 1960 *The Effects of Mass Communication.* New York: Free Press.

Lang, Gladys Engel, and Kurt Lang 1984 *Politics and Television Re-Viewed.* Beverly Hills, Calif.: Sage.

Lasswell, Harold D. 1947 "The Structure and Function of Communication in Society." In L. Bryson, ed., *The Communication of Ideas.* New York: Harper.

Milavsky, J. Ronald, Horst Stipp, Ronald C. Kessler, and William S. Rubens 1982 *Television and Aggression: A Panel Study.* New York: Academic.

Milgram, Stanley 1973 *Television and Anti-Social Behavior: A Field Experiment.* New York: Academic.

Murray, John P., and Eli A. Rubinstein 1972 *Television and Social Behavior: Reports and Papers,* 5 vols. Washington, D.C.: National Institute for Mental Health.

Rogers, Everett M. 1971 *Communication of Innovations: A Cross-Cultural Approach.* New York: Free Press.

Schramm, Wilbur 1973 *Men, Women, Messages and Media.* New York: Harper and Row.

———, Jack Lyle, and Edwin B. Parker 1961 *Television in the Lives of Our Children.* Stanford, Calif.: Stanford University Press.

– GLADYS ENGEL LANG
KURT LANG

MATE SELECTION THEORIES

Social scientists who study the family have long been interested in the question, "Who marries whom?" On one level, the study of mate selection is conducted from the perspective of family as a social institution. Emphasis is placed on the customs that regulate choice of mates. A counterperspective views the family as an association. This perspective centers instead on the couple and attempts to understand the process of marital dyad formation. Both of these perspectives generate an abundance of knowledge concerning mate selection. Beginning primarily in the 1920s, theoretical and empirical work in the area of mate selection has made great advances in answering the fundamental question, "Who marries whom?"

Institutional Perspectives on Mate Selection

Anthropologists have studied kinship structures as they relate to mate selection in arranged marriage systems. Sociological inquiry that sees the family as a social institution in the context of the larger society focuses instead on the evolution of courtship systems as societies modernize. In this respect, it is important to note the contributions of scholars such as Bernard Murstein (1974, 1976) who have pointed out the importance of cultural and historical effects on courtship systems that lead to marriage.

Historical evidence suggests that as a society modernizes, changes in the courtship system reflect a movement toward autonomous courtship systems. Thus, parentally arranged marriages diminish in industrialized cultures because arranged marriages are found in societies in which strong extended kinship ties exist or where the marriage has great significance for the family and community in terms of resources or status allocation. As societies modernize, arranged marriages are supplanted by an autonomous courtship system in which free choice of mate is the preferred form. These autonomous courtship systems are also referred to as "love" marriages, since the prerequisite for selection of a mate has shifted from the need to consolidate economic resources to that of individual choice based on love. Of course, family sociologists are quick to point out that the term *love marriage* is somewhat of a misnomer because many other factors operate in the mate selection process.

Correlates of Mate Selection

Family social scientists have tried to understand the human mate selection process by using a variety of data sources and theoretical perspectives. The most global or macro-level approaches have made use of vital statistics such as census data or marriage license applications to study the factors that predict mate selection. Attention has been placed on social and cultural background characteristics such as age, social class, race, religion, and educational level.

Norms of endogamy require that people marry those belonging to the same group. While some of these norms have been formalized, such as in U.S. laws that prohibited blacks and whites from marrying, most of the norms operate informally. Thus, analysis of vital statistics on marriage patterns in the United States shows that much similarity exists between marital partners in age, race, social class, religion, and educational level. Although there seems to be more tolerance for exogamous marriages, those marriages occurring between dissimilar partners, the data show that age between partners is similar, with men being about two years older than their wives. Interracial marriage is still rare, with less than 2 percent of all marriages occurring between persons of different races (U.S. Bureau of the Census 1986). Mate selection in the social classes also follows the norm of endogamy, with the upper class being the most restrictive in terms of marriage patterns. Thus, the Cinderella story is more of a fantasy than a reality, and self-help books entitled *How to Marry a Rich Man (Woman)* have little basis in fact.

Those who live geographically proximate to each other are more likely to meet and marry. Put simply, "Cupid's wings are best suited for short flights."

Census data indicate that the most educationally homogamous marriages occur between individuals with a high school education. In other words, similarity in level of educational attainment was the most pronounced for couples who had not completed college degrees. But as men's educational levels increase, the tendency is for these men to marry women who have less education (Rawlings 1978). The norms have consistently reinforced the notion that women should not have educational levels much more advanced than their husbands'. The general belief that educationally hypergamous marriages (wife has less education than her husband) are more stable and compatible unions than educationally hypogamous (wife has more education than her husband) has empirical support (Houseknech and Macke 1981; Jaco and Shepard 1975).

Again, the effects of industrialization can be seen in mate selection patterns as they relate to endogamy. The likelihood of marrying across social class, ethnic, and religious boundaries is strongly affected by how homogeneous (similar) the population is (Blau, Blum, and Schwartz 1982). In large cities where the opportunity structures are more heterogeneous (diverse), rates of intermarriage are higher, while in the small rural communities that contain homogeneous populations, the norm of endogamy is even more pronounced.

The factors that operate in the selection process of a mate also function in conjunction with opportunity structures that affect the potential for social interaction. The evidence suggests that propinquity is an important factor in determining who marries whom. Thus, those who live geographically proximate to each other are more likely to meet and marry. Early work by Bossard (1932) shows that at the time of the marriage license application, about 25 percent of all couples live within two city blocks of each other. Bossard's Law, derived from his empirical findings, states, "the proportion of marriages decreases steadily and markedly as the distance between the consenting parties increases." Or, put more simply, "Cupid's wings are best suited for short flights." Of course, current American society has changed since the time Bossard studied mate selection patterns in Philadelphia, and there is a tendency to think that as society becomes more mobile propinquity plays less of a role in the choice of a mate. Propinquitous mate selection does not mean nonmobility, however. It is simply the case that the influence of propinquity shifts as the individual geographically shifts. Thus, one is more likely to marry someone who is currently near than someone previously propinquitous. The overriding effect of propinquity is that people of similar backgrounds will meet and marry because residential homogamy remains a dominant feature of American society.

One interesting area of research that often goes overlooked in discussions of the correlates of mate selection concerns homogamy of physical attractiveness. Based on the equity theory of physical attractiveness, one would expect that persons who are similar in physical attractiveness levels would marry. Many experimental designs have been conducted to test the effects of physical attractiveness on attraction to a potential dating partner. In general, the experimental conditions have yielded the findings that the more highly attractive individuals are the most desired as a dating partner. But studies of couples actually involved in selecting a mate or who are already married support the notion that individuals who are similar in attractiveness level marry. Thus, while attractiveness is a socially valued characteristic in choice of a mate, the norms of social exchange dictate that we select a partner who is similar in attractiveness and is thus attainable. It is only when other highly valued factors such as wealth, wit, or intelligence compensate for deficits in attractiveness that inequity of physical attractiveness in mate selection might occur.

In conclusion, the correlates of mate selection have been widely studied, beginning in the 1920s. But within the past decade emphases have shifted in the studies of mate selection to the examination of the dyadic processes involved. Researchers generally concur that the factors of endogamy, propinquity, and equity of physical attractiveness continue to operate in very important ways, but attention has been expanded to examination of courtship cohabitation and the process of mate selection.

Need Complementarity

While earlier work on the correlates of mate selection focused on homogamy of background characteristics, the work of Winch (1958) set the stage for further investigation into the hypothesis that "opposites attract," that is, that persons of dissimilar values or personality traits would marry. While value theorists speculated that similarity of values and personality would lead to great affiliation and propensity to marry, Winch posited that persons select mates whose personality traits are complementary (opposite) to their own. Inherent in Winch's theoretical work is the notion that certain specific trait combinations will be gratifying to the individuals involved. For example, a submissive person would find it gratifying or reciprocal to interact with a mate who had a dominant personality. Winch developed twelve such paired complementary personality traits, such as dominant-submissive and nurturant-receptive, for empirical testing using a very small sample of recently married couples. In Winch's work, as well as the work of others, the notion that complementarity of traits was the basis for marriage was not supported by the data.

Although empirical support for need complementarity is lacking, the concept remains viable in the study of mate selection. The appeal of the concept rests in its psychological origins, as work prior to Winch's focused primarily on structural and normative influences in mate selection. The work of Winch set the stage for research commencing in the 1960s that began to examine the processes of mate selection on the dyadic level.

Process Theories of Mate Selection

The process of selecting a mate received considerable attention beginning in the 1970s. The basic form these theories take follows the "filter theory" of Kerckoff and Davis (1962). Kerckoff and Davis found empirical support that individuals, having met through the channels of propinquity and endogamy, proceed through a series of stages or steps in the development of the relationship. According to their theory, social status variables such as social class and race operate early on in the relationship to bring people together. The next stage involved the consensus of values, during which time the couple determines the degree of similarity in their value orientations. Couples who share similar values are likely to continue to the third stage, need complementarity. However, the data collected by Kerckoff and Davis offered only weak support for need complementarity as part of the process of mate selection.

Development of process theories of mate selection continued into the 1970s and is exemplified in the work of Reiss (1960), Murstein (1974, 1976), Lewis (1973), and Centers (1975). While these theoretical perspectives differ in terms of the order and nature of the stages, they have much in common. Melding these theories of mate selection, the following assumptions can be made concerning the stages of dyad formation that lead to marriage:

1. There are predictable trajectories or stages of dyadic interaction that lead to marriage.
2. The social and cultural background of the couple provides the context for the interpersonal processes.
3. Value similarity leads to rapport in communication, self-disclosure, and the development of trust.
4. Attraction and interaction depend on the exchange value of the assets and liabilities that the individuals bring to the relationship.
5. There may be conditional factors such as age, gender, or marital history that influence the order, duration of the stages, or probability of the relationship ending in marriage.

All the studies of the mate selection process have struggled with methodological difficulties. Most studies have relied on small, volunteer samples of couples. Most have used college-age, never-married couples. And, finally, most studies have made extensive use of retrospection in assessing the process of dyad formation rather than collecting longitudinal data. These methodological difficulties may, in part, account for the recent decline in the number of studies examining the process of mate selection.

Furthermore, these stages in the mate selection process may or may not result in marriage, but the primary focus of the research is on relationships that endure or terminate in marriage. Therefore, relatively little is known about the mate selection process as it pertains to rejection of a potential mate or how such terminations of relationships affect subsequent mate selection processes.

Many of the theories have also overlooked the influence of peer groups and family members in the mate selection process. The theoretical and empirical inquiry that has paid attention to peer and kin influences is restricted to studies of dating. Unfortunately, studies of dating and studies of mate selection have not been sufficiently integrated to provide the field with adequate data concerning the interrelationships between dating and mate selection processes.

Yet another area of research that has the potential for contributing to further understanding of the mate selection process is the study of romantic love. Process theories of mate selection seldom examine love as the basis, or even as a stage, in the development of a heterosexual relationship. While there is a large body of empirical and theoretical work on romantic love, the studies of love have been treated as conceptually quite distinct from the research on mate selection. Contrary to popular opinion, the relationship between love and marriage is not well understood.

Future Directions

As the family system changes in American society, the direction of research on mate selection also shifts. As more couples delay first marriage, examination of courtship cohabitation becomes more salient. Future studies of courtship cohabitation will most likely examine the association between increasing rates of cohabitation and decreasing rates of marriage. On the individual level, the effects of the cohabitation experience on the decision to marry also warrant attention.

Research is just beginning on the mate selection process of remarriage (Bulcroft et al. 1989; Rodgers and Conrad 1986; Spanier and Glick 1980). While some factors that predict first marriage (such as endogamy and propinquity) may remain constant in remarriage, other factors may come into play in remarriage. For example, age homogeneity may be less of a factor in remarriage because the pool of eligible mates is affected by sex ratio imbalance. The exchange relationship in the mate selection process also differs in remarriage because the presence of children, prior marital history, and the economic liabilities of child support or alimony bring new dimensions when considering remarriage. Of particular interest are barriers to remarriage in the middle and later years of the life cycle: Cohabitation or serious dating might offer more long-term rewards to the couple than legal marriage might provide. Thus, the strong profamilial norms that encourage the younger members of society to marry dissipate at mid- and later life. Low rates of remarriage for those individuals over the age of fifty indicate, in part, that societal pressure to marry is greatly reduced.

Lastly, it has generally been assumed that homogeneity of background characteristics leads to similarity of values, shared marital role expectations, rapport, and intimacy in the process of mate selection. But due to changing gender-role expectations, this assumption may no longer be valid. As a result, more attention needs to be given to the process of role negotiation as part of the mate selection process.

In summary, studies of mate selection began with understanding the correlates of mate selection. Social scientists began by studying demographic data on homogamy in religion, social class, age, and other factors as these variables related to who married whom. For a brief period from the 1960s through the early 1980s, attention was turned to theories and data that examined the process of mate selection. Current research has not abandoned the study of the correlates and theories of mate selection, but as the nature of the family system changes, researchers have begun to consider that the generalizability of theories and findings may be limited when trying to explain mate selection at a point later than young adulthood.

[See also: Courtship; Interpersonal Attraction; Love.]

BIBLIOGRAPHY

Blau, Peter, Terry Blum, and Joseph Schwartz 1982 "Heterogeneity and Intermarriage." *American Sociological Review* 47:45–62.

Bossard, James 1932 "Residential Propinquity as a Factor in Marriage Selection." *American Journal of Sociology* 38:219–224.

Bulcroft, Kris, Richard Bulcroft, Laurie Hatch, and Edgar F. Borgatta 1989 "Antecedents and Consequences of Remarriage in Later Life." *Research on Aging* 11:82–106.

Centers, Richard 1975 *Sexual Attraction and Love: An Instrumental Theory.* Springfield, Ill.: C. C. Thomas.

Houseknech, Sharon, and Ann Macke 1981 "Combining Marriage and Career: The Marital Adjustment of Professional Women." *Journal of Marriage and the Family* 43:651–661.

Jaco, Daniel, and Jon Shepard 1975 "Demographic Homogeneity and Spousal Consensus: A Methodological Perspective." *Journal of Marriage and the Family* 37:161–169.

Kerckoff, Alan, and Keith Davis 1962 "Value Consensus and Need Complementarity in Mate Selection." *American Sociological Review* 27:295–303.

Lewis, Robert 1973 "A Longitudinal Test of a Developmental Framework for Premarital Dyadic Formation." *Journal of Marriage and the Family* 35:16–27.

——— 1974 *Love, Sex, and Marriage through the Ages.* New York: Springer.

——— 1976 *Who Will Marry Whom? Theories and Research in Marital Choice.* New York: Springer.

Rawlings, Stephen 1978 *Perspectives on American Husbands and Wives.* Current Population Reports, Ser. P-23, No. 77. Washington, D.C.: U.S. Bureau of the Census.

Reiss, Ira 1960 "Toward a Sociology of the Heterosexual Love Relationship." *Marriage and Family Living* 22:139–145.

Rodgers, Roy, and Linda Conrad 1986 "Courtship for Remarriage: Influences on Family Reorganization after Divorce." *Journal of Marriage and the Family* 48:767–775.

Spanier, Graham, and Paul Glick 1980 "Paths to Remarriage." *Journal of Divorce* 3:283–298.

U.S. Bureau of the Census 1986 *Statistical Abstract of the United States.* Washington, D.C.: U.S. Government Printing Office.

Winch, Robert 1958 *Mate Selection: A Study of Complementary Needs.* New York: Harper and Row.

– KRIS BULCROFT

MENTAL HEALTH

The concept of positive mental health was developed by Jahoda (1958), who argues that the notion of mental health can be viewed as an enduring personality characteristic or as a less permanent function of personality and the social situation (Jahoda 1958). This article summarizes Jahoda's approach to mental health, reviews other discussions of the concept, describes a challenge to the assumption that mental health requires the accurate perception of reality, and concludes with a discussion of the value assumptions inherent in the concept.

In her classic book *Current Concepts of Positive Mental Health,* Jahoda (1958) identified the following six approaches to the definition of mental health, which are described in detail below: (1) attitude toward own self; (2) growth, development, and self-actualization; (3) integration; (4) autonomy; (5) perception of reality; and (6) environmental mastery.

1. Acceptance of self, self-confidence, and self-reliance characterize the mentally healthy person. An important attribute of mental health includes the understanding of one's strengths and weaknesses, coupled with the conviction that one's positive characteristics outweigh the negative traits. Independence, initiative, and self-esteem are other indicators of mental health.

2. The realization of one's potential is the underlying assumption of this dimension of mental health. Maslow (1954) explains that self-actualization is a motive that encourages the person to maximize capabilities and talents. It is hypothesized that growth motivation is positively related to mental health. Rather than meeting basic human needs, self-actualization implies movement toward higher goals. This dimension of mental health also implies an investment in living, a concern with other people and one's environment rather than a primary focus on satisfying one's own needs (Jahoda 1958).

3. The mentally healthy person has a balance of psychic forces, a unifying outlook on life, and resistance to stress (Jahoda 1958). Psychoanalysts view integration as the balance of the id, the ego, and the superego. This balance is viewed as changeable, with flexibility as the desired end result. It is also suggested that mental health implies integration at the cognitive level, which implies a unifying philosophy of life that shapes feelings and behaviors. Finally, resistance to stress characterizes the integrated person. The mentally healthy person can adapt to stress without deteriorating. Everyone, it is argued, experiences anxiety when encountering a stressful situation. A mentally healthy response to anxiety and stress implies some tolerance of tension, ambiguity, and frustration.

A mentally healthy response to anxiety and stress implies some tolerance of tension, ambiguity, and frustration.

4. Autonomy implies self-determination and independence in the decision-making process. The concept suggests that the mentally healthy person is self-directed and self-controlled. The individual acts independently of the outside world; behavior is not dictated by environmental circumstances.

Jahoda points out that some authors interpret autonomy quite differently. Autonomy may be defined as having freedom of choice. An autonomous person freely chooses whether to conform to society's norms. This perspective implies that the person is not independent of the environment but has free choice to decide how to respond to demands made by society.

5. "As a rule, the perception of reality is called mentally healthy when what the individual sees corresponds to what is actually there" (Jahoda 1958, p. 49). Mentally healthy reality perception includes perception free from need distortion. A mentally healthy person views the world without distortions, fitting the perception to objective cues that are present, and does not reject evidence because it does not fit his or her wishes or needs.

Jahoda also argues that this dimension of mental health implies the ability to perceive others in an empathetic manner. This social sensitivity enables a healthy person to put himself or herself in another person's place and anticipate that person's behavior in a given social situation.

6. Mastery of the environment implies achieving success in some social roles as well as appropriate function in those roles. Mental health also includes the ability to

have positive affective relationships and adequate interpersonal relations. The social roles involved in environmental mastery may include sexual partner, parent, and worker. Environmental mastery suggests the ability to adapt, adjust, and solve problems in an efficient manner.

Other Definitions of Mental Health

Jourard and Landsman (1980, p. 131) propose similar criteria for mental health: positive self-regard, ability to care about others, ability to care about the natural world, openness to new ideas and to people, creativity, ability to work productively, ability to love, and realistic perception of self.

Jensen and Bergin (1988) conducted a nationwide survey of 425 professional therapists (clinical psychologists, marriage and family therapists, social workers, and psychiatrists) to determine values associated with mental health. Eight themes were identified as important for a positive, mentally healthy life-style: (1) competent perception and expression of feelings (sensitivity, honesty, openness with others); (2) freedom/autonomy/responsibility (self-control, appropriate feelings of guilt, responsibility for one's actions, increasing one's alternatives at a choice point); (3) integration, coping, and work (effective coping strategies, work satisfaction, striving to achieve); (4) self-awareness/growth (awareness of potential, self-discipline); (5) human relatedness/interpersonal and family commitment (ability to give and receive affection, faithfulness in marriage, commitment to family needs, self-sacrifice); (6) self-maintenance/physical fitness (healthful habits, self-discipline in use of alcohol, drugs, tobacco); (7) mature values (purpose for living, having principles and ideals); and (8) forgiveness (making restitution, forgiving others) (Jensen and Bergin 1988, p. 293). They found a high level of consensus among the practitioners. Many of these values are consistent with the six approaches identified by Jahoda in 1958.

Illusions and Mental Health

One of these approaches to mental health has been questioned (Snyder 1989). Is accurate reality perception the hallmark of mental health? For most people, reality negotiation is a mentally healthy process. Taylor and Brown (1988, p. 193) explain that "certain illusions may be adaptive for mental health and well being."

According to Taylor and Brown (1988), mentally healthy persons have an unrealistic positive self-evaluation. Normal individuals are more aware of their strengths and less aware of their weaknesses. Mentally healthy persons perceive themselves as better than the average person and view themselves in a more positive light than others see them (Taylor and Brown 1988).

Another illusion of the mentally healthy person is an exaggerated sense of self-control. Taylor and Brown (1988) cite evidence that depressed individuals are more likely to have realistic perceptions of personal control than are nondepressed persons. Positive illusions of personal control over the environment, self-worth, and hopefulness about the future imply mental health and enable people to function in an adaptive manner.

Taylor and Brown (1988) suggest that illusions can promote several criteria of mental health, including happiness or contentment, the ability to care for others, and the capacity for intellectually creative and productive work. While mentally healthy people learn from negative experiences, their illusions help them to cope with stresses and strains (Taylor et al. 1989).

Taylor and Brown (1988, p. 204) conclude that "the mentally healthy person appears to have the enviable capacity to distort reality in a direction that enhances self-esteem, maintains beliefs in personal efficacy, and promotes an optimistic view of the future."

The Role of Underlying Value Assumptions

Jahoda (1980) argues that the definition of mental health depends upon underlying value assumptions. The definition of what is mentally healthy varies across societies. In addition, there may be variance across social groups within one society (e.g., social class, gender, race, ethnicity).

Mentally healthy persons perceive themselves as better than the average person and view themselves in a more positive light than others see them.

For example, there is evidence that there are different standards of mental health for men and women. Broverman et al. (1981) report sex role stereotypes in the clinical judgments of mental health among seventy-nine psychotherapists. The respondents were asked to identify the characteristics that portrayed healthy, mature, and socially competent adults. Broverman et al. (1981, p. 92) found "that healthy women differ from healthy men by being more submissive; less independent; less adventurous; more easily influenced; less aggressive; less competitive."

Finally, according to Jahoda (1988), the definition of mental health is also influenced by the following four assumptions: (1) the criteria for judging health and illness are debatable; (2) mental illness and mental health cannot be defined by the absence of the other; (3) there are degrees of mental health; and (4) a low level of mental health is not synonymous with mental illness. While there is continued debate on how to characterize the mentally healthy person, researchers agree that mental health is more than the absence of mental illness; it represents the enhancement of human potential.

[See also Health Promotion; Mental Illness and Mental Disorder.]

BIBLIOGRAPHY

Broverman, Inge K., et al. 1981 "Sex-Role Stereotypes and Clinical Judgments of Mental Health." In Elizabeth Howell and Majorie Bayes, eds., *Women and Mental Health.* New York: Basic Books.

Jahoda, Marie 1958 *Current Concepts of Positive Mental Health.* New York: Basic Books.

———1980 *Current Concepts of Positive Mental Health,* rev. ed. New York: Arno Press.

———1988 "Economic Recession and Mental Health: Some Conceptual Issues." *Journal of Social Issues* 44:13–23.

Jensen, Jay P., and Allen E. Bergin 1988 "Mental Health Values of Professional Therapists: A National Interdisciplinary Survey." *Professional Psychology: Research and Practice* 19:290–297.

Jourard, S. M., and T. Landsman 1980 *Healthy Personality: An Approach from the Viewpoint of Humanistic Psychology,* 4th ed. New York: Macmillan.

Maslow, Abraham H. 1954 *Motivation and Personality.* New York: Harper and Row.

Snyder, C. R. 1989 "Reality Negotiation: From Excuses to Hope and Beyond." *Journal of Social and Clinical Psychology* 8:130–157.

Taylor, Shelley, and Jonathan Brown 1988 "Illusion and Well Being: A Social Psychological Perspective on Mental Health." *Psychological Bulletin* 103:193–210.

Taylor, Shelley, et al. 1989 "Maintaining Positive Illusions in the Face of Negative Information: Getting the Facts Without Letting Them Get to You." *Journal of Social and Clinical Psychology* 8:114–129.

— JANET HANKIN

MENTAL ILLNESS AND MENTAL DISORDERS

After years of empirical research and theoretical activity, social scientists still do not agree about what mental illness actually is, let alone about what its primary causes are or about the efficacy of various treatments. Sociologists disagree about whether or not mental disorder is truly a disease that fits a medical model of health and illness. They disagree about the relative importance of genetics, personality characteristics, and stress in the onset and course of psychiatric impairment. Nevertheless, sociologists do agree that definitions of mental illness are shaped by the historical, cultural, and interpersonal contexts within which they occur. The significance of any particular set of psychological or behavioral symptoms to a diagnosis of mental disorder lies as much with the audience as with the actor. Given this understanding of mental illness, sociologists are as interested in understanding the consequences of being labeled mentally ill as they are in understanding the causes. Sociologists do, indeed, study the social distribution and determinants of mental disorder. However, they also study social reactions to mental illness and the mentally ill and investigate the ways in which mental-health professionals and institutions can come to serve as agents of social control.

Classification and Diagnosis

Although psychiatrists themselves have difficulty defining mental illness, the official system for classifying and diagnosing mental disorder in the United States is produced by the American Psychiatric Association (APA). It is known as the *Diagnostic and Statistical Manual of Mental Disorders* (DSM) and was first published in 1952. In its earliest form, DSM-I included a list of sixty separate mental illnesses. By the second edition in 1968, psychiatric definitions of mental illness had changed so markedly that 145 different types of mental disorder were included. Despite the attempt in DSM-II to define more precisely the parameters of mental illness, critics from both within and without psychiatry pointed out that psychiatric diagnoses were extremely unreliable. When different psychiatrists independently used DSM-II to diagnose the same patients, they did so with substantially different results. Studies conducted during the 1960s and 1970s indicated that there was poor agreement about what disease classification was appropriate for any given patient; studies also found that clinicians had difficulty discriminating normal persons from mental patients and that they frequently disagreed about prognosis and the clinical significance of particular symptom patterns (Loring and Powell 1988; Townsend 1980).

After years of debate, some of which was quite heated, the APA published a third edition of DSM in 1980. Mental disorder was defined in DSM-III as "a clinically significant behavioral or psychological syndrome or pattern that occurs in an individual that is typically associated with either a painful symptom (distress) or impairment in one or more areas of functioning (disability)" (American Psychiatric Association 1980, p. 6). DSM-III took a purely descriptive approach to diagnosis; diagnostic criteria, including a list of essential and associated features, were outlined for each disorder, but virtually no attempt was made to explain the etiology of either symptoms or illnesses. Revised again in 1987, DSM-IIIR contains over 200 mental diagnoses, including such disorders as nicotine dependence, caffeine intoxication, and hypoactive sexual desire disorder. DSM-IV was published in 1994.

The use of DSM-III and DSM-IV criteria has vastly improved the overall reliability of psychiatric diagnoses, thereby enabling psychiatry to meet one of the major criticisms of the medical model of mental disorder. The inclusion of more and more categories of illness in each succeeding version of DSM has led to more precise and consequently more reliable diagnoses. However, some scholars have argued that this expansion of mental diagnoses has less to do with problems of disease classification than it does with "problems" in third-party reimbursement (Mirowsky and Ross 1989). Each increase in the number of disorders listed in DSM has increased the scope of psychiatric practice. As the number of patients with recognized illnesses increases, so too does the amount of compensation that psychiatrists receive from insurance companies.

Even the firmest supporters of DSM-IV recognize that the classification of mental disorder is influenced by nonmedical considerations. In order to reduce their payment liabilities, insurance companies have lobbied the APA to reduce the number of diagnoses; changes in public attitudes toward sexual preference issues led, in 1974, to dropping homosexuality from the list of mental disorders; veterans' groups successfully pressed for the inclusion of posttraumatic stress syndrome (Scott 1990); feminists have successfully protested against the male bias implicit in such diagnoses as "gender-identity disorder," a label often attached to girls who liked to play boys' games and with boys' toys. In sum, there is a less than perfect correspondence between some disease-producing entity or syndrome and the diagnosis of a psychiatric disorder; psychiatric diagnosis is based partly in the reality of disordered behavior and emotional pain and partly in the evaluations that society makes of that behavior and pain. Thus, the questions about the validity of psychiatric diagnosis are as troubling for DSM-IV as they were for DSM-I. As one observer has noted, "We have learned how to make reliable diagnoses, but we still have no adequate criterion of their validity" (Kendell 1988, p. 374). Given the problems that scholars have in defining mental disorder, and given the validity problems that ensue, it is not surprising that epidemiologists have used a number of different strategies to estimate rates of psychiatric impairment. These different research methodologies often have led to quite different interpretations of the role of social factors in the etiology of mental illness.

Measurement

The earliest sociological research on mental disorder relied on data from individuals receiving psychiatric care. In a classic epidemiological study, Faris and Dunham (1939) reviewed the records of all patients admitted to Chicago's public and private mental hospitals between 1922 and 1934. They found that admission rates for psychosis were highest among individuals living in the inner city. Several years later, researchers used a similar design to study the social class distribution of mental disorder in New Haven. In contrast to the Chicago study, which focused only on individuals who had been hospitalized, Hollingshead and Redlich (1958) included individuals receiving outpatient care from private psychiatrists in their study. Results from the New Haven study confirmed the earlier findings; the lower the social class, the higher the rate of mental disorder. More recent studies have also used information on treated populations. Studies of patient populations provide useful information, to be sure; findings shed light on the social factors that influence the course of mental-health treatment. Individuals receiving treatment for mental disorder, however, are not a random subset of the population of individuals experiencing psychological distress. Everybody who has potentially diagnosable mental disorder does not receive treatment. Furthermore, pathways to mental-health care may be systematically different for individuals with different social characteristics. Consequently, research based on treated rates of mental disorder seriously underestimates the true rate of mental illness in a population; it also may confuse the effects on psychiatric treatment of variables such as social class, gender, place of residence, or age with the impact of those same variables on the development of psychiatric impairment.

An alternative strategy for studying the epidemiology of mental disorder is the community survey. Early studies, such as the midtown Manhattan study (Srole et al. 1962), used symptom checklists with large random samples to estimate the amount of psychiatric impairment in the general population. Although such studies provided less biased estimates of the prevalence of psychological distress than did research on patient populations, they were subject to a different set of criticisms. The most serious limitation of the early community studies was that they used impairment scales that measured global mental health. Not only did the scales fail to distinguish different types of disorders, they confounded symptoms of physical and psychological disorder (Crandall and Dohrenwend 1967), measured relatively minor forms of psychiatric impairment, and frequently failed to identify the most serious forms of mental illness (Dohrenwend and Crandall 1970). Since it was not clear what relationship psychological symptom scales bore to cases of actual psychiatric disorder, it was also not clear how results from these studies contributed to an understanding of the social causes of mental illness.

Recent advances have solved some of the problems of the early global impairment scales; the development of symptom scales that measure specific forms of psychiatric impairment has done much to improve the reliability and validity of community survey research. The CES-D, for instance, is a twenty-item scale designed to measure depression. Weissman et al. (1977) report that the CES-D accurately distinguishes clinical from normal populations and depression from other psychiatric diagnoses. In addition, methods have now been developed to provide reliable psychiatric diagnoses of community respondents. Probably the most widely used diagnostic instrument of this sort was developed by a team of researchers at Washington University as part of the National Institute of Mental Health (NIMH) Division of Biometry and Epidemiology's Catchment Area Program. Called the Diagnostic Interview Schedule (DIS), the instrument can be administered by nonpsychiatrists doing interviews with the general population. Using DSM-IV criteria, it provides both current and lifetime diagnoses for thirty-six adult psychiatric disorders. Enormous amounts of time and money have been devoted to the development of the DIS, and research that makes use of it promises to provide a vital link between studies of clinical and community populations. (See Weiss-man, Myers, and Ross 1986 for an excellent review and critique of the DIS and other measures used in community mental health research.) Nevertheless, even instruments like the DIS have shortcomings.

Research based on treated rates of mental disorder seriously underestimates the true rate of mental illness in a population.

Mirowsky and Ross (1989) challenged the DIS and DSM-III on the grounds that psychiatric diagnosis is a weak form of measurement and that it is of questionable validity. These authors claim that psychiatric disorders are dimensional, not categoric. By collapsing a pattern of symptoms into a single diagnostic case, valuable information is lost about the nature of the disorder. As a result, the causes of mental, emotional, and behavioral problems are obscured. Mirowsky and Ross go on to suggest that the reliance on diagnosis does not give a true, that is, a valid picture of psychiatric distress. Instead, psychiatrists use diagnosis because it allows them to receive payment from insurance companies who will pay only for cases and because it establishes mental distress as a problem that can be treated only by a physician. Although their criticisms are harsh, these authors reestablish the important distinction between the social construction of psychiatric diagnoses and the social causes of psychological pain. It is the latter issue, however, that most sociological research has addressed.

The Epidemiology of Mental Disorder

SOCIOECONOMIC STATUS. The inverse relationship between socioeconomic status and mental disorder is now so well established that it has almost acquired the status of a sociological law. The relationship is surprisingly robust; it holds for most forms of mental disorder, no matter how socioeconomic status is measured, and for both patient populations and community samples. The inverse relationship is strongest and most consistent for schizophrenia, personality disorders, and organic syndromes. Findings for the major affective disorders are somewhat less consistent. Studies based on hospital populations (Goodman et al. 1983; Ortega and Rushing 1983) tend to report weak to moderate inverse relationships between social class and the incidence of major affective disorders such as manic depression; lifetime prevalence studies, however, often indicate a positive class gradient (Weissman and Myers 1978). Evidence on the class distribution of minor depression is more clear-cut, with studies almost universally showing higher levels of depressive symptomatology among the lower strata. Similarly, research consistently shows that the highest general levels of distress are also found among those with the lowest income, education, or occupational status.

There are two general qualifications to the pattern outlined above. First, even though socioeconomic status is negatively associated with most types of mental disorder, the relationship is probably not linear. Extremely high rates of disorder are typically found in the lowest stratum. Higher strata do have progressively lower rates, but variation is considerably less between them than between the lowest and the next-to-lowest tier. Some scholars have claimed, therefore, that serious mental illness is primarily an underclass phenomenon. Second, the inverse relationship between social class and mental disorder is probably stronger in urban than in rural areas and in the United States than in other societies. (For a comprehensive review of this literature, see Ortega and Corzine 1990.)

Most, if not all, of the major sociological theories of mental illness begin with the empirical observation that psychological disorder is most prevalent among those individuals with the fewest resources and the least social power. Until recently, researchers focused almost exclusively on one dimension of inequality—social class. Indeed, the dominant paradigms in the sociology of mental health have derived primarily from the attempt to explain this relationship; hypotheses regarding the effects of gender, age, or marital status on psychological distress are often simple elaborations of models derived from the study of social class and mental disorder. Three general models of the relationship between social resources and mental illness have been suggested. These are (1) the "social causation" hypothesis; (2) the "social selection" or "drift" hypothesis; and (3) the "labeling" or "societal reaction" approach.

SOCIAL CAUSATION. *Social causation* is a general term, used to encompass a number of specific theories about the class-linked causes of mental disorder. Perhaps the most common version of social causation explains the higher rates of mental disorder among the lowest socioeconomic strata in terms of greater exposure to stress. According to this perspective, members of the lower class experience more stressful life events and more chronic strains. In addition, they are more likely to experience physical hazards in the environment, blocked aspirations, and status frustration (Kleiner and Parker 1963). Taken together, these stresses produce elevated rates of psychiatric impairment. In another version of social causation, scholars have argued that class differences in coping resources and coping styles are at least as important in the etiology of mental disorder as are class differences in exposure to stress (Pearlin and Schooler 1978). In this view, poverty increases the likelihood of mental illness because it (1) disrupts precisely those social networks that might effectively buffer the effects of stressful events and (2) inhibits the development of an active, flexible approach to dealing with problems. For both social and psychological reasons, then, the lower classes make use of less effective coping strategies. Finally, part of the class difference in mental disorder, especially in rates of treated disorder, may stem from class differences in attitudes toward mental illness and psychiatric care. Because of more negative attitudes toward mental illness and because of inadequate access to appropriate psychiatric care, the lower classes may be more seriously ill when they first come in contact with the mental-health-care system, and thus they may be more likely to be hospitalized (Gove and Howell 1974; Rushing and Ortega 1979).

SOCIAL SELECTION AND DRIFT. This perspective implies that, rather than causing mental disorder, low socioeconomic status is a *result* of psychological impairment. Two mobility processes can be involved. According to the drift hypothesis, the onset of mental disorder adversely affects an individual's ability to hold a job and generate income. As a result of psychological disorder, then, individuals experience downward intragenerational mobility and physical relocation to less socially desirable neighborhoods. Social selection, on the other hand, occurs when premorbid characteristics of the mentally disordered individual prevent him or her from attaining as high a social status as would be expected of similar individuals in the general population. Here, the focus is on intergenerational mobility (Eaton 1980; Ortega and Corzine 1991).

LABELING OR SOCIETAL REACTION. Based on the work of Thomas Scheff (1966), this approach holds that much of the class difference in mental disorder stems not from any real difference in mental illness but rather from a tendency to diagnose or label a disproportionate number of lower class individuals as psychologically impaired. According to Scheff, the process works as follows. Psychiatric symptoms have many different causes, and many people experience them. Only a few individuals, however, are ever labeled as mentally ill. Those who are are drawn from the ranks of those least able to resist the imputation of deviance. Once an individual is identified as mentally ill, a number of forces work to reinforce and solidify a mentally ill self-identity. Once labeled, individuals are encouraged by family and mental-health professionals to acknowledge their illness. They are rewarded for behaving as "good" patients should, a task made easier by virtue of the fact that individuals learn the stereotypes of mental illness in early childhood. When individuals are discharged from the mental hospital, or otherwise terminate treatment, they may be rejected by others. This rejection has psychological consequences that simply reinforce a mentally ill identity. The process is self-fulfilling, leading Scheff to conclude that attachment of the mentally ill label is the single most important factor in the development of chronic mental disorder.

AN ASSESSMENT. After years of often acrimonious debate, the search for unitary explanations of the mental-disorder-to-social-class relationship has largely been abandoned. Sociologists seldom claim that mental illness derives only from medical factors, is caused only by features of the social environment, or stems purely from societal reaction. Most scholars now believe that different types of disorders require different types of explanations. Genetic and other biomedical factors are clearly involved in the etiology of organic brain syndromes, schizophrenia, and some forms of depression. However, genetics, brain chemistry, and other medical factors do not provide the entire answer since, even among identical twins, concordance rates for mental illness fall only in the range of 30 to 50 percent. Thus, the causes of mental disorder must also be sought in the social environment. Research does suggest a modest relationship between the social stressors attendant to lower class status and the onset of some forms of mental disorder. The evidence is clearest, however, for relatively minor forms of depression or psychological distress. For the more severe forms of mental illness, the drift and selection hypothesis appears to have the most empirical support. Although labeling is not the only cause of chronic mental illness, it is clear that the mental illness label does have negative consequences; the actual status of ex-mental patient, coupled with the ex-patient's expectation of rejection by others, adversely affects earnings and work status (Link 1987). Thus, labeling may be one of the processes through which drift occurs. As researchers refine the measurement of mental illness and more clearly delineate the processes of social causation, drift, and labeling, it is likely that further theoretical convergences will be identified.

GENDER. It is not yet clear whether there are significant gender differences in overall rates of mental illness. There is little doubt, however, that certain types of disorders occur more frequently among women than among men. Most research reports that women are more likely to suffer from major and minor depression and anxiety than are men (Fox 1980; Weissman and Klerman 1977). Men, however, are usually found to have higher rates of antisocial personality disorders (Dohrenwend and Dohrenwend 1976). The sex ratio for some forms of mental disorder may be age-dependent; males have higher rates of schizophrenia prior to adolescence, and females have higher rates in later adulthood (Loring and Powell 1988). Studies also find that male-female differences in levels of depression are most pronounced among young adults (Dean and Ensel 1983). Furthermore, gender effects appear to interact with those of marital, occupational, and parental roles.

Small children can simultaneously increase their mothers' life satisfaction and their overall levels of distress.

Scholars continue to disagree about the precise form of the interaction effects of gender and marital status on mental illness. Virtually all studies report that gender differences are most pronounced among married persons; married women consistently show higher levels of depression and anxiety than married men. Evidence on the unmarried, however, is mixed. Research based on treated populations often finds higher rates of disorder among single men. Studies based on community samples more frequently report higher distress levels among unmarried women. The interaction between gender and marital status is further complicated by the presence of children, work outside the home, or both.

Some research on married persons finds that gender differences are reduced when both husbands and wives are employed. Studies comparing groups of women often find that employment has modest, positive effects on mental health. However, other studies report no difference between employed women and housewives, and a few report that married, full-time homemakers with children have fewer worries and more life satisfaction (Veroff, Douvan, and Kulka 1981). These apparently contradictory findings stem, in part, from the different measures of mental health and illness used. It is possible, for instance, that small children can simultaneously increase their mothers' life satisfaction and their overall levels of distress. However, two substantive factors also appear to be involved. First, it is the demands created by children and employment, rather than parental or employment status per se, that cause elevated levels of distress among married women (Rosenfield 1989). The level of demands varies, of course, depending upon the level of male responsibility for child care and housework. Second, employment decreases gender differences in distress only when it is consistent with both the husband's and the wife's desires. Married men's distress levels may, in fact, surpass married women's when wives work but their husbands prefer them not to (Ross, Mirowsky, and Huber 1983).

As is true for social class, explanations for gender differences of mental disorder fall into three broad classes: social causation, social selection, and labeling. Because of the consistency of gender effects (at least for depression and anxiety) and improvements in the reliability of psychiatric diagnoses, most recent work has focused on the ways in which the social and psychological correlates of male and female roles cause variation in rates of mental disorder. Some have argued that differences in sex-role socialization make females more likely to direct frustration inward, toward themselves, rather than toward others, as males might. Thus, women are more likely to develop intropunitive disorders, whereas men are more likely to behave in antisocial ways (Loring and Powell 1988). Others have argued that women are more attached to others and are more sensitive to their needs than are men. As a result, women's mental health is influenced by their own experiences, and, in contrast to men, women are also more psychologically vulnerable to the stresses or losses of loved ones (Kessler and McLeod 1984). According to this perspective, women experience more stressful events and are more psychologically reactive to them than are men. Other explanations—for both direct and interactive effects—of gender on mental illness have focused on male-female differences in power, resources, demands, and personal control. Insofar as employment increases women's power and resources, it is likely to have positive effects on mental health. Well-educated employed women have fewer mental symptoms than nonworking women; among working- and lower class women, however, employment may actually increase anxiety and depression because it elevates demands at the same time that it produces only marginal increases in resources (Sales and Hanson Frieze 1984). Since employed women generally retain full responsibility for children, the demands of caring for children, particularly those under the age of six, exacerbate work-related stress. Thus, male-female differences in power and resources produce differences in the ability to control demands. Gender differences in control, in turn, shape perceptions of personal mastery; personal mastery is the psychological mechanism that connects gender differences in resources and demands to gender differences in mental illness (Rosenfield 1989).

The social selection perspective is valid only for explaining male-female differences in the relationship between marital status and mental disorder. The argument is that mental illness is more likely to select men out of marriage than women. (See Rushing 1979 for a related discussion.) According to this perspective, male forms of mental disorder—psychosis and antisocial personality, for example—prevent impaired men from satisfactorily discharging the traditional male obligation to be a good economic provider, making them ineligible as marriage partners. In contrast, female forms of psychiatric impairment may go undetected for long periods of time and may not seriously interfere with a woman's ability to fulfill the traditional housekeeping role. Thus, the higher rates of female disorder among the married are simply an artifact of the differing probabilities of marriage for mentally disordered men and women.

The labeling explanation for male-female differences in psychiatric impairment begins by challenging the notion that women actually experience more mental symptoms and disorders than men do. Labeling theorists argue that women are overdiagnosed and overmedicated because of biases on the part of predominantly male psychiatrists and because of the male biases inherent in psychiatric nomenclature. Coupled with the greater willingness of females to admit their problems and to seek help for them, these biases simply produce the illusion that women are more likely to be disordered than men. Scholars using the labeling-societal reaction-critical perspective argue that the effects of gender biases are not benign and that they have consequences at two levels. First, individual women are unlikely to receive appropriate services for their real mental-health problems. Second, and at a societal level, critics argue that psychiatry simply legitimates traditional gender roles, thereby buttressing the status quo (Chesler 1973).

A THEORETICAL ASSESSMENT. With the development of DSM-IV and with increases in the number of female mental-health professionals, concern over the issues raised by labeling theorists has died down. Trusting that the most blatant instances of sexism have been eliminated, researchers have turned their attention toward specifying the social psychological dynamics of the gender–mental-health equation; considerable progress has been made in elucidating the circumstances under which women are most likely to experience symptoms of mental disorder. Nevertheless, it may be premature to close the question of gender bias in psychiatric diagnosis. In one study, male clinicians appeared to overestimate the prevalence of depressive disorders among women, a tendency that is certainly consistent with gender stereotypes. In the same study, black males were most likely to be diagnosed as paranoid schizophrenics, a view consistent with both gender and racial stereotypes. The advances of DSM-III notwithstanding, the authors of this study concluded that sex and race of client and psychiatrist continue to influence diagnosis even when psychiatric criteria appear to be clear-cut (Loring and Powell 1988).

AGE. Among adults, and with the exception of some types of organic brain syndromes, rates of mental illness decrease with age. Rates of schizophrenia, manic disorder, drug addiction, and antisocial personality all peak between the ages of twenty-five and forty-four (Robins et al. 1984). Furthermore, older persons with serious mental disorders are likely to have had their first psychiatric episode in young or middle adulthood. At least 90 percent of older schizophrenics experienced the onset of the disorder in earlier life. Similarly, about two-thirds of older alcholics have a long history of alcohol abuse or dependence (Hinrichsen 1990). Depression is the disorder most likely to occur among the elderly, and a substantial proportion of older community residents do report some of its symptoms. Nevertheless, relatively few of these individuals meet criteria for clinical depression (Blazer, Hughes, and George 1987), and rates of major depression are lower among older adults than in younger age groups. Some older persons, however, are more vulnerable to depression than others. As is true throughout the life cycle, women, individuals with health problems, the unmarried, and those with lower socioeconomic status are at greater risk of depression in late life than their peers. Estimating the true prevalence of depression among the elderly is especially problematic because its symptoms are frequently confused with those of dementia or other forms of organic brain disorder.

According to some estimates, two to four million older Americans suffer some form of chronic organic brain disorder. Of these, roughly half are diagnosed with Alzheimer's, a disease that involves an irreversible, progressive deterioration of the brain. Approximately half of all nursing home residents are estimated to suffer from some form of dementia. Because there is no known treatment for most of these disorders, older mental patients receive little psychiatric care. Critics suggest, however, that many older persons are improperly diagnosed with chronic brain syndromes. A sizable minority may actually be depressed; others may have treatable forms of dementia caused by medications, infection, metabolic disturbances, alcohol, or brain tumors. In many instances, then, the stereotype that senility is a concomitant of the aging process prevents appropriate diagnosis, intervention, and treatment.

Most explanations of the age–mental-health relationship have focused on specific age groups. Clinicians suggest, for instance, that anxiety and depression in middle age are a consequence of hormonal change or of changes in family and occupational roles. The personality disorders of young adulthood are often explained in terms of the stresses produced by the transition from adolescence to full adult roles. Among the elderly, explanations have focused on either organic or environmental factors. The chronic brain syndromes have recognized organic causes. Although neither is a normal part of the aging process, the two major causes of these disorders are the deterioration of the brain tissue, associated with Alzheimer's disease, and cerebral arteriosclerosis. However, environmental factors also contribute to the onset of the brain syndromes. They do so, in part, by increasing the likelihood of stroke or heart attack. In contrast, functional disorders, such as depression, personality disorders, and anxiety, depend more directly upon environmental factors. Some types of depression appear to have a genetic component, but the genetic link appears to be stronger in early than in late-onset cases. Individuals who have their first episode of clinical depression prior to the age of fifty, for instance, are more likely to have relatives with depression than those who became depressed in later years (Hinrichsen 1990). Consequently, losses typical of late life, losses of health, occupation, income, and loved ones, appear to be the primary causes of mental-health problems among older adults.

Clearly, no single theory can adequately explain the etiology of mental disorder; at each stage of the life cycle, variables that are relevant to the onset of one type of disorder may be insignificant in the onset of other illnesses. Similarly, no single variable or set of variables is likely to explain age differences in overall rates of mental disorder. Nevertheless, efforts are under way to systematically explain the inverse relationship between age and functional psychiatric impairment. Gove and his associates have suggested that psychological distress decreases with age because individuals are able, over time, to find and settle into an appropriate social niche; as individuals move through life, they become less emotional and self-absorbed, function more effectively in their selected roles, and generally become more content with themselves and with others. As a result, rates of mental disorder decrease from late adolescence through late life (Gove 1985; Gove, Ortega, and Style 1989).

Studies that explicitly compare rural and urban communities generally find that rates of psychosis are higher in rural communities.

PLACE OF RESIDENCE. Sociologists have commonly assumed that rates of mental disorder are higher in urban than in rural areas. However, this assumption is based more on the antiurban bias of much sociological theory than it is on empirical research. In a thoughtful and systematic review, Wagenfeld (1982) has argued that there is little evidence in the mental-health literature to suggest the superiority of rural life. In several of the rural community studies Wagenfield cites, researchers report a "probable" case rate for depression and anxiety of 12 to 20 percent. Studies that explicitly compare rural and urban communities generally find that rates of psychosis are higher in rural communities and that rates of depression are somewhat higher in urban areas. Differences in case definition and diagnosis, differences in how rural place of residence is defined and measured, and differences in the time period during which studies were conducted make it difficult to assess whether rural communities have significantly higher overall rates of pathology than urban areas. Results are sufficient, however, to suggest that rural life is not as blissful as it is often claimed to be. Recent declines in the rural economy, the out-migration of the young and upwardly mobile, and the relative paucity of mental-health services are likely to be major contributing factors in the etiology of rural mental-health problems.

OTHER FACTORS. Epidemiologists have also explored the relationships between the incidence or prevalence of mental disorder and such variables as race and ethnicity, migration, social mobility, and marital status. In each case, results generally support the view that individuals with the fewest resources—both social and economic—are most likely to experience psychiatric impairment. However, most research has adopted a rather static view; few studies have assessed the extent to which relationships between each of these variables and mental disorder have changed over time. Given the significant change in the mental-health professions over the last decades, this is a striking omission.

An Agenda for Future Research

Since the early 1960s, psychiatric sociology has undergone enormous change. During the 1960s and 1970s, much of the literature was sharply critical of psychiatry and of medical models of madness. Although sociologists were divided about the relative importance of labeling processes in the etiology of mental illness, most agreed that psychiatric diagnoses were unreliable and were influenced by social status and social resources, that long-term institutionalization had detrimental effects, and that at least some patients were hospitalized inappropriately. Such criticisms provided one impetus for the substantial change that took place in psychiatric care during this same period. Laws were changed to make involuntary commitment more difficult; steps were taken to deinstitutionalize many mental patients; and a major effort was made to improve the reliability of mental diagnoses. By the time DSM-III was published in 1980, the most flagrant abuses and the sharpest criticisms of psychiatry seemed to have disappeared. Throughout the 1980s, sociologists returned to a medical model of impairment, and research focused on delineating the linkage between social variables, such as gender, age, race, social class, or place of residence, and specific diagnoses. Indeed, the psychiatric view of mental disorder is so well established in sociology that the growing literature on homelessness has generally accepted the assertion of mental-health professionals that most of the homeless are simply individuals who have fallen through the cracks of the mental-health-care system. (For one notable exception, see Snow, Baker, and Anderson 1986.) It is surprising that sociologists have been so uncritical in their acceptance of this position; it is also surprising that they have been so ready to accept the view that mental illness is primarily a problem of brain chemistry, genetics, and so forth and that it can be treated just like any other disease. It is certainly true that enormous strides have been made in the diagnosis and treatment of mental disorder. It is also true that biomedical factors are certainly involved in the etiology of some types of mental illness. Sociologists must, therefore, continue their efforts to develop a model of mental disorder that integrates medical, psychological, and social factors.

As some critics point out, however, the current emphasis on diagnoses and cases of mental disorder has limitations. Acceptance of the psychiatric view of mental disorder and acceptance of the policy implications of that view are not yet firmly grounded in empirical research. Independent of the field trials used in their formulation, few studies to date have assessed the reliability of DSM-IV (Mirowsky and Ross 1989); even fewer have assessed the extent to which changes in psychiatric diagnosis or changes in the civil rights guarantees of mental patients have affected the delivery and quality of mental-health services. It is far from clear, for instance, that lower class women are any more likely to receive appropriate care in 1990 than they were in 1950 or 1960. It is unclear whether urban-rural differences in rates of mental disorder have changed over time and, if so, to what extent changes in diagnostic systems or service availability are implicated. It is also far from clear that deinstitutionalization of the mentally ill is the primary cause of homelessness in America; it is empirically no less plausible that the economic dislocations of the 1980s are the root causes of homelessness, in both rural and urban communities. Research in the 1990s must adopt a more dynamic or process view of mental-health issues. The consequences of changes in psychiatric diagnosis, of the increased reliance on drug therapies, of changes in mental-health law and policy, and in the availability of mental-health services must be assessed. Changes in the practice of mental-health care must be linked to changes in the composition of the pool of "potential clients" and to issues regarding the development of gender, age, class, and culturally appropriate care.

[See also Mental Health.]

BIBLIOGRAPHY

American Psychiatric Association 1980 *Diagnostic and Statistical Manual of Mental Disorders III.* Washington, D.C.: American Psychiatric Association.

Blazer, Dan, Dana C. Hughes, and Linda K. George 1987 "The Epidemiology of Depression in an Elderly Community Population." *Gerontologist* 27:281–287.

Chesler, Phyllis 1973 *Women and Madness.* New York: Avon Books.

Crandall, D. L., and B. P. Dohrenwend 1967 "Some Relations among Psychiatric Symptoms, Organic Illness, and Social Class." *American Journal of Psychiatry* 123:1,527–1,538.

Dean, Alfred, and Walter M. Ensel 1983 "Socially Structured Depression in Men and Women." In James Greenley, ed., *Research in Community Mental Health,* Vol. 3. Greenwich, Conn.: JAI.

Dohrenwend, Bruce P., and D. L. Crandall 1970 "Psychiatric Symptoms in Community, Clinic, and Mental Hospital Groups." *American Journal of Psychiatry* 126:1,611–1,621.

———, and Barbara Snell Dohrenwend 1976 "Sex Differences in Psychiatric Disorder." *American Journal of Sociology* 81:1,447–1,459.

Eaton, William W. 1980 *The Sociology of Mental Disorders.* New York: Praeger.

Faris, Robert E., and H. Warren Dunham 1939 *Mental Disorders in Urban Areas.* Chicago: University of Chicago Press.

Fox, John W. 1980 "Gove's Specific Sex-Role Theory of Mental Illness: A Research Note." *Journal of Health and Social Behavior* 21:260–267.

Goodman, A. B., C. Siegel, T. J. Craig, and S. P. Lin 1983 "The Relationship between Socioeconomic Class and Prevalence of Schizophrenia." *American Journal of Psychiatry* 140:166–170.

Gove, Walter R. 1985 "The Effect of Age and Gender on Deviant Behavior: A Biopsychosocial Perspective." In Alice S. Rossi, ed., *Gender and the Life Course.* New York: Aldine.

———, and Patrick Howell 1974 "Individual Resources and Mental Hospitalization: A Comparison and Evaluation of the Societal Reaction and Psychiatric Perspectives." *American Sociological Review* 39:86–100.

———, Suzanne T. Ortega, and Carolyn Briggs Style 1989 "The Maturational and Role Perspectives on Aging and Self through the Adult Years: An Empirical Evaluation." *American Journal of Sociology* 94:1,117–1,145.

Hinrichsen, Gregory A. 1990 *Mental Health Problems and Older Adults.* Santa Barbara: ABC-CLIO.

Hollingshead, A. B., and F. C. Redlich 1958 *Social Class and Mental Illness.* New York: Wiley.

Kendell, R. E. 1988 "What Is a Case? Food for Thought for Epidemiologists." *Archives of General Psychiatry* 45:374–376.

Kessler, Ronald C., and Jane D. McLeod 1984 "Sex Differences in Vulnerability to Undesirable Life Events." *American Sociological Review* 49:620–631.

Kleiner, R. J., and S. Parker 1963 "Goal-Striving, Social Status, and Mental Disorder." *American Sociological Review* 28:129–203.

Link, Bruce 1987 "Understanding Labeling Effects in the Area of Mental Disorders: An Assessment of Expectations of Rejection." *American Sociological Review* 52:96–112.

Loring, Marti, and Brian Powell 1988 "Gender, Race, and DSM-III: A Study of the Objectivity of Psychiatric Behavior." *Journal of Health and Social Behavior* 29:1–22.

Mirowsky, John, and Catherine E. Ross 1989 "Psychiatric Diagnosis as Reified Measurement." *Journal of Health and Social Behavior* 30:11–25.

Ortega, Suzanne T., and Jay Corzine 1990 "Socioeconomic Status and Mental Disorders." In James Greenley, ed., *Research in Community and Mental Health,* Vol. 6. Greenwich, Conn.: JAI.

———, and William A. Rushing 1983 "Interpretation of the Relationship between Socioeconomic Status and Mental Disorder: A Question of the Measure of SES." In James Greenley, ed., *Research in Community and Mental Health,* Vol. 3. Greenwich, Conn.: JAI.

Pearlin, Leonard, and Carmi Schooler 1978 "The Structure of Coping." *Journal of Health and Social Behavior* 19:2–21.

Robins, L. N., J. E. Helzer, M. M. Weissman, H. Orvaschel, E. Gruenberg, J. D. Burke, Jr., and D. A. Regier 1984 "Lifetime Prevalence of Specific Psychiatric Disorders in Three Sites." *Archives of General Psychiatry* 41:949–958.

Rosenfield, Sarah 1989 "The Effects of Women's Employment: Personal Control and Sex Differences in Mental Health." *Journal of Health and Social Behavior* 30:77–91.

Ross, Catherine E., John Mirowsky, and Joan Huber 1983 "Dividing Work, Sharing Work, and In-Between: Marriage Patterns and Depression." *American Sociological Review* 48:809–823.

Rushing, William A. 1979 "The Functional Importance of Sex Roles and Sex-Related Behavior in Societal Reactions to Residual Deviants." *Journal of Health and Social Behavior* 20:208–217.

———, and Suzanne T. Ortega 1979 "Socioeconomic Status and Mental Disorder: New Evidence and a Sociomedical Formulation." *American Journal of Sociology* 84:1,175–1,200.

Sales, Esther, and Irene Hanson Frieze 1984 "Women and Work: Implications for Mental Health." In L. E. Walker, ed., *Women and Mental Health Policy.* Beverly Hills, Calif.: Sage.

Scheff, Thomas J. 1966 *Being Mentally Ill: A Sociological Theory.* Chicago: Aldine.

Scott, Wilbur J. 1990 "PTSD in DSM-III: A Case in the Politics of Diagnosis and Disease." *Social Problems* 37:294–310.

Snow, David, Susan Baker, and Leon Anderson 1986 "The Myth of Pervasive Mental Illness among the Homeless." *Social Problems* 33:407–423.

Srole, L., T. S. Langner, S. T. Michel, M. D. Opler, and T. C. Rennie 1962 *Mental Health in the Metropolis: The Midtown Manhattan Study.* New York: McGraw-Hill.

Townsend, John M. 1980 "Psychiatry versus Societal Reaction: A Critical Analysis." *Journal of Health and Social Behavior* 21:268–278.

Veroff, Joseph, Elizabeth Douvan, and Richard A. Kulka 1981 *The Inner American.* New York: Basic Books.

Wagenfeld, Morton O. 1982 "Psychopathology in Rural Areas: Issues and Evidence." In P. A. Keller and J. D. Murray, eds., *Handbook of Rural Community Mental Health.* New York: Human Sciences Press.

Weissman, Myrna M., and Gerald L. Klerman 1977 "Sex Differences and the Epidemiology of Depression." *Archives of General Psychiatry* 34:98–111.

———, and Jerome K. Myers 1978 "Affective Disorders in a U.S. Urban Community." *Archives of General Psychiatry* 35:1,304–1,311.

———, Jerome K. Myers, and Catherine E. Ross 1986 "Community Studies in Psychiatric Epidemiology: An Introduction." In M. M. Weissman, J. K. Myers, and C. E. Ross, eds., *Community Surveys of Psychiatric Disorders.* New Brunswick, N.J.:Rutgers University Press.

———, D. Scholomskas, M. Pottenger, B. Prusoff, and B. Locke 1977 "Assessing Depressive Symptoms in Five Psychiatric Populations: A Validation Study." *American Journal of Epidemiology* 106:203–214.

– SUZANNE T. ORTEGA

MILITARY SOCIOLOGY

Military sociology has been a relatively obscure field in American sociology. Few sociologists conduct research and write on military topics, and few university departments offer courses of study in this field. To the layperson this circumstance may seem rather myopic, given the sheer size and complexity of the military enterprise and the impact that its products—war and peace—have on individual societies and on the world order as a whole. Some might wonder how sociologists can comprehend the structure and processes of human society without full attention to this major institution. The Persian Gulf War of 1991 is a vivid reminder that military institutions and operations are of importance to most societies.

There is no single reason for this lack of emphasis. One reason, of course, is ideological aversion to military matters. Most sociologists fall on the liberal-left side of the political spectrum, but the same might be said of other social and behavioral scientists who do the bulk of the research on defense-related social issues. Another reason may be that the access and support necessary for most military research requires policy relevance, which defines it as "applied" and therefore of less interest to many sociologists. Unlike other social sciences, sociology has not developed a sizeable cadre of practitioners who conduct research or policy studies in those non-academic settings where most military research takes place.

There are notable exceptions. One is the classic work by Samuel Stouffer and colleagues during World War II, *The American Soldier* (Stouffer et al. 1949). Its studies of cohesion, morale, and race relations among combat units made critical contributions to both sociological theory and military personnel policies. The work of Morris Janowitz on organizational and occupational changes in the military is also a significant exception to the rule (Janowitz 1960). Charles Moskos at Northwestern University and David and Mady Segal at the University of Maryland are upholding this tradition today, and their universities are among the few that offer courses on military sociology.

In recent years most of the studies that could be classified as military sociology have been carried out in private research institutes and companies or in military agencies, such as the Rand Corporation, the Brookings Institute, the Human Resources Research Organization (HumRRO), the Army Research Institute, and the Office of the Secretary of Defense. Study teams are generally interdisciplinary, with the fields of psychology, economics, political science, and management frequently represented. While these studies have a sociological complexion, they are not limited to sociological concepts or theory, and they usually have a military policy focus.

Much of the published work in this field consists of reports from these various organizations and agencies. No journal is devoted specifically to military sociology, although there is an American Sociological Association Section on Peace and War. *Armed Forces and Society* is an interdisciplinary journal that focuses on social-science topics in the military, and *Military Psychology*, published by the Division on Military Psychology of the American Psychological Association, also covers topics of sociological interest.

This review will emphasize contemporary issues and studies in military sociology, most of which focus on the American military. For reviews that include historical perspectives the reader is referred elsewhere (David R. Segal 1989; Segal and Segal 1991).

The Basis of Service

Without question the most significant issue in American military sociology since World War II is the shift from conscription to voluntary service in 1973. Indeed, many contemporary issues in military sociology—social representation, national service, race, and gender—flow directly or indirectly from this change in the basis of service.

The most significant issue in American military sociology since World War II is the shift from conscription to voluntary service in 1973.

The notion of voluntary service is not new; indeed, compulsory military service has been the exception rather than the rule in the history of most Western societies, although the meaning of "involuntary" and the nature of service has changed over time. Until the Civil War, U.S. military manpower was raised through state militias, which technically encompassed all "able-bodied men" and hence might be thought of as involuntary. But the raising and maintenance of militia was left to the discretion and policies of individual states, and they varied greatly in their representation and effectiveness. Although the desirability and feasibility of national conscription has been debated since the beginning of American history, until 1948 it was employed only during the Civil War and during World Wars I and II. At all other times enlistment was voluntary (Lee and Parker 1977).

The peacetime conscription adopted in 1948 was a significant and historic departure for U.S. military policy. It was prompted by a combination of factors, including Cold War tensions with the Soviet Union, the critical role being played by the United States in defense alliances, and a perception that America had been inadequately prepared for World War II. These conditions led to proposals for a large standing or "active duty" military force that most believed could not be maintained by voluntary methods. The policy was supported by the American public at that time, and it was consistent with the long-standing value that all "able-bodied men" should serve their country.

The end of the peacetime draft occurred in 1973 at the end of the Vietnam War. The debate over draft policies had been intensifying during the 1960s, particularly over the issue of equity. Given the growth in the American youth population (from the post-World War II babyboom), not all men were needed for the military, and a succession of draft-exemption policies—college, occupational, marriage—fueled the debate over the fairness and equity of the draft. Not only were all able-bodied men not serving, those exempted from service tended to be from more affluent classes. In an attempt to solve the equity problem, nearly all exemptions were eliminated during the late 1960s, and a national lottery system was eventually adopted in 1969. These changes did not quell the debate, however; indeed, they probably doomed the draft, since they coincided with one of the most unpopular and unsuccessful of undeclared wars in America's history. Ending exemptions for college students at a time when college students were leading the Vietnam antiwar movement simply fanned the flames of opposition.

On the other side, most defense and military leaders, including many in Congress, initially opposed ending the draft. The conditions leading to a large peacetime military force (over two million active-duty personnel) were unchanged and were not under debate. If such a large force was maintained by voluntary means, it was argued, it would be (1) a mercenary force lacking patriotic motivation and might be either adventuresome or ineffective in large-scale combat; (2) socially unrepresentative, thereby placing the burden of combat on minorities, the poor, and the uneducated; and (3) costly and unaffordable (Segal 1989).

The shift to voluntary service followed definitive recommendations from a presidential commission, known as the Gates Commission, which concluded that a large peacetime force could be adequately maintained with an all-voluntary force (AVF), provided that basic pay was increased to be competitive with comparable civilian jobs. The commission argued that paying enlisted personnel below-market wages was not only unfair but entailed "opportunity" costs in the form of lost productivity of persons who are compelled to work at jobs they would not voluntarily perform. If military pay and benefits were competitive, the commission's studies concluded, a volunteer force would be socially representative and would be as effective as a drafted force. Although some attention was given the social costs of the draft, there is little question that economic analysis and arguments formed the central basis of the commission's report (President's Commission 1970).

The All-Volunteer Force

The AVF seemed to work well for the first several years, and the dire predictions of those who opposed ending the draft did not materialize. Enlistment requirements were met, and neither quality nor representation differed much from draft-era enlistments. It appeared that the predictions of the Gates Commission would be validated (Cooper 1977).

During the late 1970s, however, this positive picture changed. Military pay and benefits did not keep up with the civilian sector, and Vietnam antiwar attitudes among youth contributed to a generally negative image of the military. Enlistments began to decline, and increasing numbers were recruited from lower education and aptitude categories. To make matters worse, a misnorming error was discovered in the military aptitude test, and the quality of personnel was even lower than had been thought. By 1980 the Army was particularly affected, with enlistments falling significantly below requirements and with the proportion of lowest-aptitude recruits—those reading at fourth-and fifth-grade levels—reaching 50 percent (Eitelberg 1988).

Some claimed that the Gates Commission had been wrong after all and called for a return to the draft. Others, including a Secretary of the Army, proposed eliminating the aptitude and education standards that had been used since the draft era, arguing that they were not important for military job performance and were potentially discriminatory. Yet others argued that both the AVF and quality standards could be maintained but only by increasing pay and benefits to enable competition with the civilian sector. Critical to this third argument were policy studies led by the Rand Corporation showing a relationship between aptitudes and military job performance and the feasibility of economic incentives for enlistment (Armor et al. 1982; Polich, Dertouzos, and Press 1986)

Substantial increases in pay and other benefits in the early 1980s, as well as changes in recruiting techniques including advertising, had a dramatic impact on recruiting success. By 1986 all military services, including the Army, were not only meeting requirement quotas but were setting new records in the quality of personnel, surpassing even the draft years in the proportion of recruits with high school diplomas and with higher aptitudes. Most military leaders, many of whom had been skeptical about ending the draft, became strong supporters of the AVF and claimed that morale and skills were at all-time highs and discipline problems were at all-time lows. Although this success did require significant increases in the military personnel budget, both the Congress and the public seemed prepared to pay this cost (Bowman, Little, and Sicilia 1986).

The one argument against voluntary service that had never been tested empirically was the combat effectiveness of a market-motivated military. The dramatic success of American forces in the 1991 Persian Gulf war put an end to any doubt about the ability of a volunteer military to operate successfully. Although high-technology weapons systems received much of the publicity during the war, most military leaders gave equal credit to the skill and motivation of their troops.

National Service

The increasing success and acceptance of a voluntary military did not end the debate over alternative bases of service. The reasons are numerous, including concern over a shrinking youth population, doubts that a voluntary force can recruit sufficient quality and remain socially representative, and beliefs that it will ultimately be too costly. But the larger issue in this debate involves a clash of fundamental values: whether defense of country should be motivated by monetary incentives or the obligation of citizenry. A major figure in this ideological discussion is Charles Moskos, who describes the change from the draft to the AVF as a transition from "citizen soldier" to "economic man" (Moskos 1988a).

Although few policy leaders call for a return to a draft, there have been serious proposals for a national service policy. Most current national service proposals envisage a program whereby young people devote one or two years to either civilian or military service; they would receive only subsistence wages during their service but at the end would receive a voucher that could be used for college, job training, or home purchase. Most proponents of national service make an argument similar to the "able-bodied men" thesis of the classic militia model. That is, all citizens in a democracy should be willing to serve their country in some fashion, unmotivated primarily by economic gain. Although early proposals for national service envisaged universal military duty, more recent proposals for national service include voluntarism, civilian settings, and monetary incentives—although some see their potential for becoming universal (see Moskos in Evers 1990).

Most military and defense policy leaders who oppose national service argue that the voluntary military is working well and that national service is unnecessary for the purpose of the armed forces. The common refrain would be, "If it isn't broken, don't fix it!" Indeed, some argue that a program for short-term enlistments with subsistence pay plus benefit vouchers would be more costly than current policies because of training costs and the loss of high-quality recruits who would be willing to serve longer terms (Bandow 1988).

Interestingly, while the roots of national service stem from ideologies holding the obligations of citizenship above economic self-interest, all serious national service proposals embrace the key market and economic concepts of the AVF—voluntarism and financial incentives. As long as the voluntary military remains representative, effective, and popular, the debate on national service will generally boil down to costs and affordability as opposed to differences over more fundamental values.

Social Representation and Race

The social representation of the American military has been a long-standing issue, predating the debate over the draft and the AVF. It was an issue in the Vietnam War, when some alleged that blacks were overrepresented in combat forces; it was an issue during the draft and AVF debate; and it has remained an issue during the AVF years and in the debates over national service. It was raised once again during the Persian Gulf War, when some black leaders including Jesse Jackson criticized the Department of Defense for the overrepresentation of minorities and the poor in the troops serving in the Gulf.

The experience of the Persian Gulf War, where women in noncombat jobs were killed, injured, and captured while on duty, confirms the risks of noncombat jobs.

There are three basic policy questions at stake in the issue of representation. The first and most fundamental question concerns the equity of a military force, or the extent to which the burden of service and risk is borne by all segments of the citizenry. Since a military force has the job of defending the national interests of an entire country, with potential exposure to high risk of death or injury, many national value systems hold that this obligation should be shared uniformly by all citizens, or at least all "able-bodied men." Placing this burden unequally upon certain socioeconomic or racial groups not only violates the canons of fairness in democratic societies but also potentially undermines troop morale and motivation if they perceive the disproportion as unfair (Congressional Budget Office 1989).

A second question involves the impact of social representation on the effectiveness of the armed forces.

Since most military leaders believe that the quality of a military force (in other words, its educational and aptitude levels) affects its combat effectiveness, an unrepresentative force might be less effective than a representative force. Although the AVF attained its quality goals during the 1980s, it has not always done so. There has also been continuing concern that the AVF does not include the same proportion of highest-aptitude recruits (above the 35th percentile) as during the draft era. Although the proportion of high-aptitude enlistees has never been large, as in most work forces they occupy a disproportionate share of critical technical and supervisory jobs.

Finally, social representation is sometimes raised as a requirement for a military force's responsiveness to civilian control as well as for its respect for American democratic values and institutions. A military force that overrepresents particular social strata or groups (not necessarily lower strata) might place parochial interests or values over the interests and values of the society as a whole. A force drawn proportionately from all major sectors of a society—regions, races, social classes—is viewed as one most likely to respect and advance the shared values and goals of the total society.

While the issue of representation is not unique to a voluntary military, it has been especially prominent during the AVF era and remains a major argument for proponents of a draft or national service. The most frequent concern has been the overrepresentation of blacks and lower socioeconomic groups. Given the early experience with the AVF, this concern is not without some justification, although the situation improved considerably during the 1980s.

Table 1 shows the percentage of black recruits for several fiscal years: 1973, the last year of the draft; 1979, the highest level of black representation during the AVF era; 1983, the lowest level of black representation during the 1980s; and 1989. Even during the draft years, black representation exceeded the black proportion of the youth population, due in part to higher voluntary enlistment and—prior to the Vietnam War—college exemption policies that applied disproportionately to white youth. But the proportion of black recruits increased dramatically during the 1970s, declined during the 1980s, and increased to 22 percent by 1989.

Socioeconomic representation generally parallels the trends for race, which is not surprising, given the correlation between race and socioeconomic variables. Recruits as a whole come from families with somewhat less education and lower economic levels than the total youth population. In 1989, 19 percent of recruits came from college graduate families and 79 percent from families that owned their homes, compared to 26 percent and 84 percent, respectively, for the general youth population.

Nonetheless, recruits have higher educational and aptitude levels than the youth population because of enlistment eligibility requirements. In 1989, military recruits had reading scores at the 11.2 grade level and 96 percent were high school graduates, compared to reading scores at the 9.4 grade level and 82 percent graduates, respectively, for the youth population. Thus, while the American enlisted forces somewhat underrepresent whites and higher socioeconomic levels, they overrepresent youth with higher personal education and aptitude levels. This means that the current social representation may raise an equity question but not necessarily an effectiveness issue.

It should not be inferred from these data that blacks and the poor are at greater risk of death or injury from combat. In fact, blacks and whites in the enlisted active-duty force are about equally represented in combat jobs such as infantry, gun crews, and combat ships. On the other hand, a higher proportion of blacks occupy administrative, clerical, and supply jobs, while a higher proportion of whites occupy electronic and mechanical repair jobs.

Some argue that these differences in representation present a policy problem, although there is no consensus on what, if anything, should be done about it. Given the AVF experience, it is unclear how a voluntary national service would alter these outcomes, and there are no serious proposals at this time to return to a peacetime draft or compulsory national service. There has been at least one concrete proposal that the Department of Defense adopt limitations or quotas for minority enlistments, but such a practice could be viewed as discriminatory (Walters 1991). The higher black representation reflects a more positive view of the military and a higher demand for military careers among the black population, and any attempt to restrict black enlistments could be legitimately viewed as a denial of equal opportunity to the black community.

Women in the Military

Another topic that has received considerable attention from military sociologists since the advent of the AVF is the role of women in the military. Until 1967 women's participation in the military was limited to 2 percent by law, and most military jobs were closed to women. Even after this restriction was lifted by Congress, the representation of women did not change until the AVF policy and the opening of more noncombat jobs to women. From 1973 to 1980 the percentage of women enlistees increased from about 5 percent to about 14 percent and then stabilized. By 1989 women

TABLE 1

PERCENTAGE OF BLACK RECRUITS, ACTIVE FORCES

Fiscal Year	Army	Navy	Marine Corps	Air Force	Total Active Forces	Total U.S. population, ages 18–24
1973	19	11	22	14	17	12
1979	37	16	28	17	26	13
1983	22	14	17	14	18	14
1989	26	22	18	12	22	14

Source: Office of the Assistant Secretary of Defense (1990, p. 19).

composed about 11 percent of the active enlisted force and 12 percent of the active officer force. This representation is highest among all NATO countries (Office of the Assistant Secretary of Defense 1990; Stanley and Segal 1988).

The growing participation of women in the military reflects both the need for manpower in the AVF era as well as the increased concern for equity in the treatment of men and women in the workplace. Although all military services recruited more women to help alleviate shortfalls during the 1970s, the Department of Defense has also been pressured by Congress and various interest and advisory groups to enlarge the opportunities for women (Segal 1982).

The changing role of women in the military has been accompanied by controversy and debates over a number of issues that remain unresolved. They include the role of women in combat, the provisions for career development within the military job structure, and the problem of sexual harassment. All of these issues were reviewed in a recent Task Force on Women in the Military (Department of Defense 1988).

The most controversial of these issues is the ongoing dialogue on women in combat. While the arguments against women in combat include physical and emotional differences and the potential negative impact on unit cohesion and morale, the overriding reason is one of basic values: Most military leaders and Congress reflect the general public's view that women should be protected from the high risk of death, injury, or capture in combat jobs. Proponents of women in combat counter that (1) women should be judged individually and not as a group for their physical and emotional suitability for combat; (2) the experience of women in noncombatant units has shown no serious adverse impacts on cohesion or morale; and (3) women currently serve in jobs and units that are exposed to increased risks of death, injury, or capture, thereby rendering the moral argument moot and in conflict with current policies (Segal 1982).

Although combatant jobs generally entail the highest risks, it is true that women now serve in many jobs close to or actually in the combat theater, particularly in the Army and Air Force, where risks are substantial due to the technological and doctrinal changes of modern warfare. The experience of the Persian Gulf War, where women were killed, injured, and captured while on duty, confirms the risks of noncombat jobs.

The problem of career development is closely related to the issue of combat job restrictions, particularly for women officers. In many military career fields, career progression and promotion to senior officer status require leadership experience in various kinds of units and positions. Since many types of units are closed to women because of combat restrictions, these requirements are frequently hard to meet, given the number of women competing for promotion. The problem has been especially acute in the surface ship portion of the Navy, where career progression requires a ship command position but where few ships are open to women. As a result of the 1988 Task Force on Women in the Military a number of "combat logistics" ships—which were not actual combatants—were opened to women, thereby enhancing the career progression of women officers in the surface ship Navy.

The concern about sexual harassment is not unique to the military; it has been and continues to be an issue in all mixed-gender work forces. It may be more acute in settings like the military, a traditional male institution, where women compose a relatively small minority of personnel. Very little was known about the extent of sexual harassment in the military until 1988, when the 1988 Task Force on Women in the Military recommended a comprehensive survey of all active-duty personnel. The results indicated rather serious levels of sexual harassment: 5 percent of women reported actual or attempted rape or sexual assault from someone at work during the previous year, 15 percent experienced pressure for sexual favors, 38 percent experienced unwanted touching or cornering, and even higher rates were reported for a variety of other less serious actions (looks, gestures, teasing, jokes). All together, 64 percent of women experienced some form of sexual harassment during a one-year period. About 20 percent of the perpetrators were immediate supervisors, 20 percent were from other higher-ranking persons, and about 50 percent were coworkers (Martindale 1990).

These rates are considerably higher than rates found in a similar survey of federal civilian employees in 1987. The causes of these high rates of harassment are unknown at the present time, but it may be associated in part with the relatively recent increases of women in a traditional male workplace. Another factor may be the attitudes and actions of military leaders and supervisors. Only about half of the women responding believe that the senior leadership of their service and their installation make "honest and reasonable" attempts to prevent sexual harassment, and only 60 percent say their immediate supervisor does so. Whether or not these rates reflect the actual prevention activities of military leaders, there is a perception among many women that not much is being done to stop sexual harassment.

Other Issues

There are a number of other topics that are studied by military sociologists or that raise important sociological issues. While they have not received the same degree of attention as the topics reviewed above, they deserve mention.

SOCIOLOGY OF COMBAT. A major focus of *The American Soldier* studies during World War II, the sociology of combat deals with the social processes involved in combat units, such as unit cohesion and morale, leader-troop relations, and the motivation for combat. Recent works include studies of the "fragging" incidents in the Vietnam War and the role of ideology in combat motivation (Moskos 1988b) and unit rotation policies in the Army (Segal 1989).

FAMILY ISSUES. The proportion of military personnel who are married increased from 38 percent in 1953

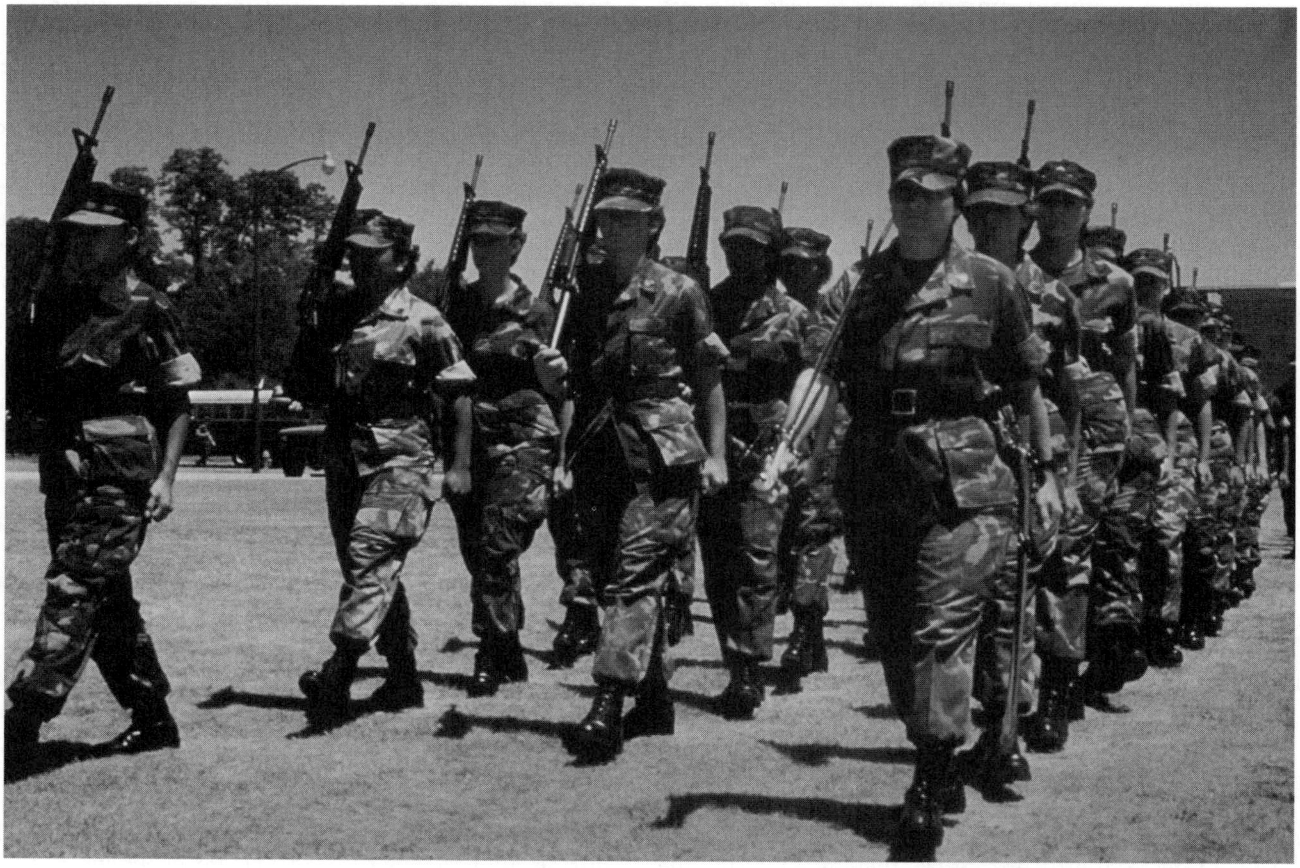

The increased presence of women in the military has raised controversy over the issues of women in combat, career development for women, and the problem of sexual harassment. (U.S. Department of Defense/Corbis)

to 61 percent by 1980. The active force also has a higher proportion of career personnel than the draft-era forces (50 percent compared to 25 percent), which means more families and family concerns. Much of the increase in military benefits are related to families—housing improvements, medical insurance, overseas schools, child care. Family policy issues include the role and rights of spouses (especially officer spouses) and the issue of child care when single-parent members are deployed in a conflict (Segal 1986; Stanley, Segal, and Laughton 1990).

THE MILITARY AS WELFARE. Somewhat at odds with the social representation issue, some argue that the military should provide opportunity for educational and occupational advancement to the less advantaged in society. The most dramatic example was Project 100,000 begun in 1966 as part of President Johnson's War on Poverty, whereby 300,000 men (mostly black) who did not meet education and aptitude requirements were offered enlistments. According to recent follow-up studies of this group as well as a group of low-aptitude recruits who entered the AVF during the misnorming era, military training and experience do not appear to offer advantages when compared to civilian experiences (Segal 1989; Laurence and Ramsberger 1991)

MILITARY SOCIAL ORGANIZATION. Given changes in military organization at several levels—from draft to AVF, from combat-intensive jobs to technical and support jobs, and from leadership to rational management—some have argued that the military is changing from an institution or "calling" legitimized by normative values to an occupation legitimized by a market orientation (Moskos and Wood 1988). While some of these changes apply to the military as well as to many other American institutions, others suggest that the role of institutional values and traditions is still a dominant characteristic of the American military (Segal 1989).

WAR AND PEACE. The most profound impacts of national security policies and their associated military forces are on the relations between whole societies. There is very little serious sociological work at this level, although some of the issues would seem to be fairly critical for sociological theory (e.g., the effectiveness of deterrence policies during the cold war; the role and effects of military alliances; the consequences of war for societal changes). One of the few sociological discussions of these broader issues is found in Segal (1989).

COMPARATIVE PERSPECTIVES. As in many other fields of sociology, comparative studies of socio-military issues across nations are relatively scarce. Exceptions are some comparative studies of whether the military is an institution or an occupation (Moskos and Wood 1988) and of women in military forces (Stanley and Segal 1988).

Conclusion

Although military sociology may have few practitioners, it is not a small field. It should be clear from this review that the types of military issues that are or can be addressed by social scientists have important ramifications for military policy as well as for the development of sociology as a discipline. On the one hand, sociological concepts and perspectives have contributed to rationalizing the basis of service, studying the problems of social representation, and improving the role of women in the military. On the other hand, studies of the structure and processes of military institutions and conflicts can enhance sociological understanding and insights about important forms of social behavior, thereby contributing ultimately to advances in social theory.

[See also Gender; Peace; War.]

BIBLIOGRAPHY

Armor, D. J., R. L. Fernandez, Kathy Bers, and Donna Schwarzbach 1982 *Recruit Aptitudes and Army Job Performance.* R-2874-MRAL. Santa Monica, Calif.: Rand Corporation.

Bandow, D. 1988 "An Involuntary Military: Paying More for Less." In Lee Austin, ed., *The Anthropo Factor in Warfare: Conscripts, Volunteers, and Reserves.* Washington, D. C.: National Defense University.

Bowman, W., R. Little, and G. T. Sicilia 1986 *The All-Volunteer Force after a Decade.* Washington, D.C.: Pergamon-Brassey's.

Congressional Budget Office 1989 *Social Representation in the U.S. Military.* Washington, D.C.: Congress of the United States.

Cooper, Richard V. L. 1977 *Military Manpower and the All-Volunteer Force.* R-1450-ARPA. Santa Monica, Calif.: Rand Corporation.

Department of Defense 1988 *Report of the Task Force on Women in the Military.* Washington, D.C.: Office of the Assistant Secretary of Defense.

Eitelberg, Mark J. 1988 *Manpower for Military Occupations.* Alexandria, Va.: HumRRO.

Evers, Williamson M. 1990 *National Service, Pro and Con.* Stanford, Calif.: Hoover Institution Press.

Janowitz, Morris 1960 *The Professional Soldier.* Glencoe, Ill.: Free Press.

Laurence, J. H., and P. F. Ramsberger 1991 *Low-Aptitude Men in the Military: Who Profits, Who Pays?* Alexandria, Va.: HumRRO.

Lee, G. C. and G. Y. Parker 1977 *Ending the Draft: The Story of the All-Volunteer Force.* FR-PO-77-1. Alexandria, Va.: HumRRO.

Martindale, Melanie 1990 *Sexual Harassment in the Military: 1988.* Arlington, Va.: Defense Manpower Data Center.

Moskos, Charles C. 1988a *A Call to Civic Service.* New York: Free Press.

——— 1988b *Soldiers and Sociology.* Alexandria, Va.: U.S. Army Research Institute for the Behavioral and Social Sciences.

———, and F. R. Wood 1988 *The Military: More Than Just a Job?* Washington, D.C.: Pergamon-Brassey's.

Office of the Assistant Secretary of Defense 1990 *Population Representation in the Military Services.* Washington, D.C.: U.S. Government Printing Office.

Polich, J. M., J. N. Dertouzos, and S. J. Press 1986 *The Enlistment Bonus Experiment.* R-3353-FMP. Santa Monica, Calif.: The Rand Corporation.

President's Commission 1970 *Report of the President's Commission on an All Volunteer Force.* Washington, D.C.: U.S. Government Printing Office.

Segal, David R. 1989 *Recruiting for Uncle Sam.* Lawrence: University Press of Kansas.

———, and M. W. Segal 1991 "Sociology, Military." *International Military and Defense Encyclopedia.* New York: Macmillan.

Segal, Mady Wechsler 1982 "The Argument for Female Combatants." In Nancy Loring Goldman, ed., *Female Soldiers: Combatants or Noncombatants?* Westport, Conn.: Greenwood Press.

——— 1983 "Women's Roles in the U.S. Armed Forces." In Robert K. Fullinwinder, ed., *Conscripts and Volunteers.* Totowa, N.J.: Rowman and Allanheld.

——— 1986 "The Military and the Family as Greedy Institutions." *Armed Forces and Society* 13:9–38.

Stanley, J., M. W. Segal, and C. J. Laughton 1990 "Grass Roots Family Action and Military Policy Responses." In R. S. Hanks and M. B. Sussman, eds., *Corporations, Businesses, and Families.* New York: The Haworth Press.

Stanley, S. C., and M. W. Segal 1988 "Military Women in NATO: An Update." *Armed Forces and Society* 14:559–585.

Stouffer, S. A., et al. 1949 *The American Soldier.* Princeton: Princeton University Press.

Walters, Ronald 1991 *African-American Participation in the All Volunteer Force.* Testimony before the Committee on Armed Services, U.S. House of Representatives, March 4, 1991.

– DAVID J. ARMOR

MONEY

Sociologists treat money paradoxically: On the one hand, money is considered a central element of modern society, and yet it remains an unanalyzed sociological category. In classic interpretations of the development of the modern world, money occupies a pivotal place. As "the most abstract and 'impersonal' element that exists in human life" (Weber [1946] 1971, p. 331), it was assumed that money spearheaded the process of rationalization. For Georg Simmel and Karl Marx, money revolutionized more than economic exchange: It fundamentally transformed the basis of all social relations by turning personal bonds into calculative instrumental ties.

But by defining money as a purely objective and uniform medium of exchange, classical social theory eclipsed money's sociological significance. If indeed money was unconstrained by subjective meanings and independent from social relations, there was little left of sociological interest. As a result, economists took over the study of money: There is no systematic sociology of money. Significantly, the *International Encyclopedia of the Social Sciences* devotes over thirty pages to money but not one to its social characteristics. There are essays on the economic effect of money, on quantity theory, on velocity of circulation, and on monetary reform, but nothing on money as a "réalité sociale," using Simiand's apt term (1934).

The sociological invisibility of money is hard to pierce. For instance, the current resurgence of interest in economic sociology has led to a serious revamping of the neoclassical economic model of the market (see, e.g., Granovetter 1985; White 1988; Swedberg 1990). Yet the sociology of markets has not extended into a sociology of money. Or consider the recent literature on the culture of consumption, which boldly reverses our understanding of modern commodities. The new revisionist approach uncovers the symbolic meanings of what money buys, but, curiously, the cultural "freedom" of money itself is never directly challenged (see, e.g., Appadurai 1986; Bronner 1989).

A sociology of money must thus dismantle a powerful and stubborn utilitarian paradigm of a single, neutral, and rationalizing market money. It must show that money is a meaningful, socially constructed currency, continually shaped and redefined by different networks of social relations and varying systems of meanings. There is some evidence that the sociological conversion of money has begun (Turner 1986; Zelizer 1989). And in anthropology, psychology, political science, and history there are also scattered indications that the economic model of money is starting to lose its hold. The following two sections will first discuss the classic approach to money and then propose the basis for a sociology of money.

Market Money: A Utilitarian Approach to Money

Many eighteenth-century thinkers saw the monetization of the economy as compatible with or even complementary to the maintenance of a morally coherent social life (see Hirschman 1977; Silver 1990). But the transformative powers of money captured the imagination of nineteenth- and early twentieth-century social theorists. Money turned the world, observed Simmel ([1908] 1950, p. 412), into an "arithmetic problem." On purely technical grounds, the possibility of money accounting was essential for the development of impersonal rational economic markets. But traditional social thinkers argued that the effects of money transcended the market: More significantly, money became the catalyst for the generalized instrumentalism of modern social life. As Simmel ([1900] 1978, p. 346) observed: "The complete heartlessness of money is reflected in our social culture, which is itself determined by money."

The task of social theory was thus to explain the uncontested revolutionary power of money. Presumably, it came from money's complete indifference to values. Money was perceived as the prototype of an instrumental, calculating approach; in Simmel's ([1900] 1978, p.

211) words, money was "the purest reification of means." Unlike any other known product, money was the absolute negation of quality. With money, only quantity mattered. That "uncompromising objectivity" allowed it to function as a "technically perfect" medium of modern economic exchange. Free from subjective restrictions, indifferent to "particular interests, origins, or relations," money's liquidity and divisibility were infinite, making it "absolutely interchangeable" (Simmel [1900] 1978, pp. 373, 128, 441). Noneconomic restrictions in the use of money were unequivocally dismissed as residual atavisms. As money became nothing but "mere money," its freedom was apparently unassailable and its uses unlimited. With money, all qualitative distinctions between goods were equally convertible into an arithmetically calculable "system of numbers" (Simmel [1900] 1978, p. 444).

"The complete heartlessness of money is reflected in our social culture, which is itself determined by money."

This objectification of modern life had a dual effect. On the one hand, Simmel argued that a money economy broke the personal bondage of traditional arrangements by allowing every individual the freedom of selecting the terms and partners of economic exchange. But the quantifying alchemy of money had a more ominous chemistry. In an early essay, Marx ([1844] 1964, p. 169) had warned that the transformational powers of money subverted reality: "Confounding and compounding . . . all natural and human qualities . . . [money] serves to exchange every property for every other, even contradictory, property and object: it is the fraternization of impossibilities." As the ultimate objectifier, money not only obliterated all subjective connections between objects and individuals but also reduced personal relations to the "cash nexus." Half a century later, Simmel ([1908] 1950, p. 414) confirmed Marx's diagnosis, dubbing money a "frightful leveler" that perverted the uniqueness of personal and social values. And Max Weber ([1946] 1971, p. 331) pointed to the fundamental antagonism between a rational money economy and a "religious ethic of brotherliness."

The prevailing classic interpretation of money thus absolutized a model of market money, shaped by the following five assumptions:

1. The functions and characteristics of money are defined strictly in economic terms. As a qualityless, absolutely homogeneous, infinitely divisible, liquid object, money is a matchless tool for market exchange.
2. All monies are the same in modern society. Differences can exist in the quantity of money but not in its meaning. Thus, there is only one kind of money—market money.
3. A sharp dichotomy is established between money and nonpecuniary values. Money in modern society is defined as essentially profane and utilitarian in contrast to noninstrumental values. Money is qualitatively neutral; personal, social, and sacred values are qualitatively distinct, unexchangeable, and indivisible.
4. Monetary concerns are seen as constantly enlarging, quantifying, and often corrupting all areas of life. As an abstract medium of exchange, money has not only the freedom but also the power to draw an increasing number of goods and services into the web of the market. Money is thus the vehicle for an inevitable commodification of society.
5. The power of money to transform nonpecuniary values is unquestioned, while the reciprocal transformation of money by values or social relations is seldom conceptualized or else is explicitly rejected.

As the classic view reasons, the monetization of the economy made a significant difference to the organization of social life. For example, it facilitated the multiplication of economic partners and promoted a rational division of labor. But a link is missing from the traditional approach to money. Impressed by the fungible, impersonal characteristics of money, classic theorists emphasized its instrumental rationality and apparently unlimited capacity to transform products, relationships, and sometimes even emotions into an abstract and objective numerical equivalent. But money is neither culturally neutral nor socially anonymous. It may well "corrupt" values and social ties into numbers, but values and social relations reciprocally corrupt money by investing it with meaning and social patterns.

Toward a Sociology of Money

The utilitarian model has had a remarkable grip on theorizing about money. Coleman (1990, pp. 119–131), for example, builds an extremely sophisticated analysis of social exchange yet continues to treat money as the ultimate impersonal common denominator. Even when analysts recognize the symbolic dimension of modern money, they stop short of fully transcending the utilitarian framework. Parsons (1971a, p. 241; 1971b, pp. 26–27), for instance, explicitly and forcefully called for a "sociology of money" that would treat money as one of the various generalized symbolic media of social interchange, along with political power, influence, and value commitments. In contrast to Marx's ([1858–1859] 1973, p. 222) definition of money as the "material representative of wealth," in Parsons's media theory, money was a shared symbolic language; not a commodity, but a signifier, devoid of use-value. Yet Parsons restricts the symbolism of money to the economic sphere. Money, Parsons (1967, p. 358) contends, is the "symbolic 'embodiment' of economic value, of what economists in a technical sense call 'utility'." Consequently, Parsons's media theory left uncharted the symbolic meaning of money outside the market: money's cultural and social significance beyond utility. Giddens (1990) complains that Parsons incorrectly equates power, language, and money, whereas for Giddens money has a distinctly different relationship to social life. As a "symbolic token," money, in Giddens's analysis, serves as a key example of the "disembedding mechanisms associated with modernity," by which he means the " 'lifting out' of social relations from local contexts of interaction and their restructuring across indefinite spans of time-space" (1990, pp. 22, 25, 21). Giddens's interpretation still ignores the fact that despite the transferability of money, people make every effort to embed it in particular times, places, meanings, and social relations.

Anthropologists provide some intriguing insights into the extraeconomic, symbolic meaning of money, but only with regards to primitive money. For instance, ethnographic studies show that in certain primitive communities, money attains special qualities and distinct values independent of quantity. How much money is less important than *which* money. Multiple currencies, or "special-purpose" money, using Polanyi's (1957, pp. 264–266) term, have sometimes coexisted in one and the same village, each currency having a specified, restricted use (for purchasing only certain goods or services), special modes of allocation and forms of exchange (see, e.g., Bohannan 1959), and, sometimes, designated users.

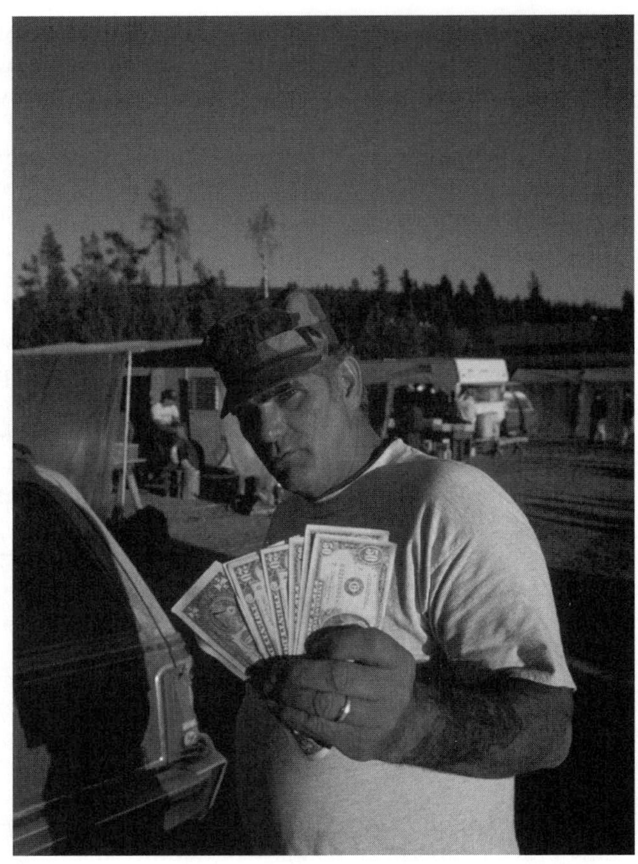

In addition to serving as a medium of exchange, money functions as a social marker that can be used to acquire status. (Dan Lamont/ Corbis)

These special moneys, which Douglas (1967) has perceptively identified as a sort of primitive coupon system, control exchange by rationing and restricting the use and allocation of currency. In the process, money sometimes performs economic functions serving as media of exchange, but it also functions as a social and sacred "marker," used to acquire or amend status, or to celebrate ritual events. The point is that primitive money is transformable, from fungible to nonfungible, from profane to sacred.

But what about modern money? Has modernization indeed stripped money of its cultural meaning? Influenced by economic models, most interpretations establish a sharp dichotomy between primitive, restricted "special-purpose" money and modern "all-purpose" money, which, as a single currency, unburdened by ritual or social controls, can function effectively as a universal medium of exchange. Curiously, when it comes to modern money, even anthropologists seem to surrender their formidable analytical tools. For instance, twenty years ago, Douglas (1967), in an important essay, suggested that modern money may not be unrestricted and "free" after all. Her evidence, however, is puzzlingly limited. Modern money, argues Douglas (1967, p. 139), is controlled and rationed in two situations: in international exchange and at the purely individual personal level, where "many of us try to primitivize our money . . . by placing restrictions at source, by earmarking monetary instruments of certain kinds for certain purposes."

Modern money, however, is marked by more than individual whim or by the different material form of currencies. As François Simiand, one of Durkheim's students, argued (1934), the extra-economic, social basis of money remains as powerful in modern economic systems as it was in primitive and ancient societies. Indeed, Simiand (1934) warned against an orthodox rationalist approach that mistakenly ignores the persistent symbolic, sacred, and even magical significance of modern money. In recent work sociologists, as well as anthropologists, psychologists, historians, and political scientists have finally heeded the warning, proposing long overdue alternatives to the standard utilitarian model of money.

Impatient with their former theoretical blinders, some anthropologists are now claiming modern money for their disciplinary terrain, casting off the fallacy of a single, culturally neutral currency. An important recent collection of essays demonstrates the heterogeneity of money, showing how the multiple symbolic meanings of modern money are shaped by the cultural matrix (Parry and Bloch 1989; see also Lederer 1988). And in psychology, new studies reject the notion that money is psychologically general, maintaining that instead money involves "multiple symbolizations" (Lea, Tarpey, and Webley 1987, p. 335). An exciting literature on "mental accounting" challenges the economists' assumption of fungibility by showing the ways individuals distinguish between kinds of money. For instance, they treat a windfall income much differently from a bonus or an inheritance, even when the sums involved are identical (see, e.g., Thaler 1990; Kahneman and Tversky 1982; for a historian's critique of the economic model of money, see Reddy 1987, and for a political scientist's perspective, Lane 1990).

A sociological accounting of money goes even further. Anthropologists reveal the multiple symbolic representations of modern money in societies outside the centers of capitalism, and psychologists explore individually or household-based differentiations between monies. A sociological model, on the other hand, must show how, even in the most advanced capitalist societies, different networks of social relations and meaning systems mark modern money, introducing controls, restrictions, and distinctions that are as influential as the rationing of primitive money. Special money in the modern world may not be as visibly identifiable as the shells, coins, brass rods, or stones of primitive communities, but its invisible boundaries emerge from sets of historically varying formal and informal rules that regulate its uses, allocation, sources, and quantity. How else, for instance, do we distinguish a bribe from a tribute or a donation, a wage from an honorarium, or an allowance from a salary? How do we identify ransom, bonuses, tips, damages, or premiums? True, there are quantitative differences between these various payments. But surely, the special vocabulary conveys much more than diverse amounts. Detached from its qualitative differences, the world of money becomes undecipherable.

The sociological model of money thus challenges the traditional utilitarian model of market money by introducing different fundamental assumptions in the understanding of money:

1. While money does serve as a key rational tool of the modern economic market, it also exists outside the sphere of the market and is profoundly shaped by different networks of social relations and varying systems of meaning.
2. Money is not a single phenomenon. There are a plurality of different kinds of monies; each special money is shaped by a particular set of cultural and social factors and is thus qualitatively distinct. Market money does not escape extraeconomic influences but is in fact one type of special money, subject to particular social and cultural influences.
3. The classic economic inventory of money's functions and attributes, based on the assumption of a single general-purpose type of money, is thus unsuitably narrow. By focusing exclusively on money as a market phenomenon, it fails to capture the very complex range of characteristics of money as a social medium. A different, more inclusive coding is necessary, for certain monies can be indivisible (or divisible but not in mathematically predictable portions), nonfungible, nonportable, deeply subjective, and therefore qualitatively heterogeneous.
4. The assumed dichotomy between a utilitarian money and nonpecuniary values is false, for money under certain circumstances may be as singular and unexchangeable as the most personal or unique object.
5. Given the assumptions above, the alleged freedom and unchecked power of money become untenable assumptions. Culture and social structure set inevitable limits to the monetization process by introducing profound controls and restrictions on the flow and liquidity of money. Extraeconomic factors systematically constrain and shape (a) the uses of money, earmarking, for instance, certain monies for specified uses; (b) the users of money, designating different people to handle specified monies; (c) the allocation system of each particular money; (d) the control of different monies; and (e) the sources of money, linking different sources to specified uses.

Exploring the quality of multiple monies does not deny money's quantifiable and instrumental characteristics but moves beyond them; it suggests very different theoretical and empirical questions from those derived from a purely economic model of market money. In fact, a utilitarian theory of money had a straightforward task: explaining how money homogenized and commoditized modern social life. Its critics have a much more complex empirical agenda. The illusion of a fully commoditized world must be rectified by showing how different social relations and systems of meanings actively create and shape a plurality of qualitatively distinct kinds of money. Specifically, a sociological theory of money must come to grips with the remarkably different ways in which people identify, classify, interpret, organize, and use money.

Consider for instance the family economy. Domestic money—which includes wife's money, husband's money, and children's money—is a special category of money. Its meanings, uses, allocation, and even quantity are partly determined by considerations of economic efficiency, but domestic money is equally shaped by ideas about family life, by power relationships, age, gender, and social class (Zelizer 1989; Pahl 1989). For instance, a wife's pin money—regardless of the amount involved—was traditionally reserved for special purchases such as clothing or vacations and kept apart from the "real" money earned by her husband. Or consider the case of gift money. When money circulates among friends or kin as a personal gift for ritual events such as weddings, christenings, bar mitzvahs, or Christmas, it is reshaped into a sentimental currency expressing care and affection. It matters who gives it, when it is given, how it is presented, and how spent. Within formal institutions, money is again redefined this time partly by bureaucratic legislation (Goffman 1961).

These cases are not anomalies or exceptions to value-free market money but typical examples of money's heterogeneity in modern society. In fact, money used for rational instrumental exchanges is simply another socially created currency, not free from social constraints, but subject to particular networks of social relations and its own set of values and norms. A sociological theory of money must explain the sources and patterns of variation between multiple monies. How, for instance, do personal monies, such as domestic and gift monies, which emerge from the social interaction of intimates, differ from the imposed institutional money of inmates? How does the social status of transactors affect the circulation of monies? What determines the relative rigidity or permeability of boundaries between monies? And what are the patterns of conversions between them?

Detached from its qualitative differences, the world of money becomes undecipherable.

Developing a sociological model of multiple monies forms part of a broader challenge to neoclassical economic theory. It offers an alternative approach not only to the study of money but to all other aspects of economic life, including the market. In the long run, a proper sociological understanding of multiple monies should challenge and renew explanation of large-scale economic change and variation. It should illuminate such phenomena as aggregate expenditures on consumer durables, rates of saving, response to inflation, income redistribution, and a wide range of other phenomena in which individual consumer actions make a large macroeconomic difference. In the sociological model, economic processes of exchange and consumption are defined as one special category of social relations, much like kinship or religion. Thus, economic phenomena such as money, although partly autonomous, intertwine with historically variable systems of meanings and structures of social relations.

BIBLIOGRAPHY

Appadurai, Arjun (ed.) 1986 *The Social Life of Things.* Cambridge: Cambridge University Press.

Bohannan, Paul 1959 "The Impact of Money on an African Subsistence Economy." *Journal of Economic History* 19:491–503.

Bronner, Simon J. (ed.) 1989 *Consuming Visions.* New York: Norton.

Coleman, James 1990 *Foundations of Social Theory.* Cambridge, Mass.: Harvard University Press.

Douglas, Mary 1967 "Primitive Rationing." In Raymond Firth, ed., *Themes in Economic Anthropology.* London: Tavistock.

Giddens, Anthony 1990 *The Consequences of Modernity.* Stanford, Calif.: Stanford University Press.

Goffman, Erving 1961 *Asylums.* New York: Anchor.

Granovetter, Mark 1985 "Economic Action and Social Structure: The Problem of Embeddedness." *American Journal of Sociology* 91:481–510.

Hirschman, Albert O. 1977 *The Passions and the Interests.* Princeton, N.J.: Princeton University Press.

Kahneman, Daniel, and Amos Tversky 1982 "The Psychology of Preferences." *Scientific American* 246 (January): 160–173.

Lane, Robert E. 1990 "Money Symbolism and Economic Rationality." Paper presented at the Second Annual Meeting of the Society for the Advancement of Socio-Economics, Washington, D.C., March.

Lea, Stephen E. G., Roger Tarpy, and Paul Webley 1987 *The Individual in the Economy.* New York: Cambridge University Press.

Lederer, Rena 1988 "Pearlshells In and As Mendi History." Paper presented at the 1988 meetings of the American Anthropological Association, Phoenix, Ariz., November.

Marx, Karl (1844) 1964 "The Power of Money in Bourgeois Society." *The Economic and Philosophic Manuscripts of 1844.* New York: International Publishers.

——— (1858–1859) 1973 *Grundrisse.* New York: Vintage.

Pahl, Jan 1989 *Money and Marriage.* New York: St. Martin's Press.

Parry, J., and M. Bloch (eds.) 1989 *Money and the Morality of Exchange.* Cambridge: Cambridge University Press.

Parsons, Talcott 1967 "On the Concept of Influence." In *Sociological Theory and Modern Society.* New York: Free Press.

——— 1971a "Higher Education as a Theoretical Focus." In Herman Turk and Richard L. Simpson, eds., *Institutions and Social Exchange.* New York: Bobbs-Merrill.

——— 1971b "Levels of Organization and the Mediation of Social Interaction." In Herman Turk and Richard L. Simpson, eds., *Institutions and Social Exchange.* New York: Bobbs-Merrill.

Polanyi, Karl 1957 "The Economy as an Instituted Process." In Karl Polanyi, Conrad M. Arensberg, and Harry W. Pearson, eds., *Trade and Market in the Early Empires.* New York: Free Press.

Reddy, William 1987 *Money and Liberty in Modern Europe.* New York: Cambridge University Press.

Silver, Allan 1990 "Friendship in Commercial Society: Eighteenth-Century Social Theory and Modern Sociology." *American Journal of Sociology* 95:1,474–1,504.

Simiand, François 1934 "La monnaie, réalité sociale." *Annales sociologiques,* ser. D, pp. 1–86.

Simmel, Georg (1900) 1978 *The Philosophy of Money,* trans. Tom Bottomore and David Frisby. London: Routledge and Kegan Paul.

——— (1908) 1950 *The Sociology of Georg Simmel,* ed. Kurt H. Wolf. New York: Free Press.

Swedberg, Richard 1990 *Economics and Sociology.* Princeton, N.J.: Princeton University Press.

Thaler, Richard H. 1990 "Anomalies: Saving, Fungibility, and Mental Accounts." *Journal of Economic Perspectives* 4:193–205.

Turner, Bryan S. 1986 "Simmel, Rationalisation, and the Sociology of Money." *The Sociological Review* 34:93–114.

Weber, Max (1946) 1971 "Religious Rejections of the World and Their Directions." In H. H. Gerth and C. Wright Mills, eds., *From Max Weber: Essays in Sociology.* New York: Oxford University Press.

White, Harrison C. 1988 "Varieties of Markets." In Barry Wellman and S. D. Berkowitz, eds., *Social Structure: A Network Approach.* Cambridge, Mass.: Harvard University Press.

Zelizer, Viviana 1989 "The Social Meaning of Money: 'Special Monies'." *American Journal of Sociology* 95:342–377.

– VIVIANA ZELIZER

MORAL DEVELOPMENT

Morality refers to a set of values that have to do with "how humans cooperate and coordinate their activities in the service of furthering human welfare, and how they adjudicate conflict among individual interests" (Rest 1986, p. 3). Moral behavior is any course of action that serves these functions in a given situation, and moral judgment is the cognitive process by which one determines which particular behavior is morally appropriate.

Moral judgment is but one component of the process that leads to the actual performance of moral behavior. Rest (1986) identifies three other components, specifically (1) a sensitivity to what kinds of behavior are possible in a given situation and how they would affect the interested parties, (2) giving priority to behaving morally as opposed to responding to other personal values (e.g., professional success) that may conflict, and (3) the ability to follow through with the course of action that has been identified as moral.

However, research on moral development over the past thirty-five years has focused primarily on the development of moral judgment. This is due in large part to the influence of psychologists Lawrence Kohlberg (1969, 1971, 1976) and Jean Piaget ([1932] 1948). Both theorists maintained that moral behavior largely depends upon how one perceives the social world and oneself in relation to it. They therefore emphasized the cognitive component as critical to understanding moral development. Furthermore, they viewed moral decision making as a rational process and thus linked the development of moral judgment to the development of rational functioning.

Theoretical Foundation

Kohlberg built on Piaget's theory of cognitive development to hypothesize a sequence of six specific stages of moral judgment in individual development. This theory of moral development is based on a fundamental idea from Piaget that the way people think about the physical and social world is the result of an "interactional" process between the human organism's innate tendencies and influences from the environment.

This "cognitive-developmental" approach is thus distinguished from both maturational and environmental theories of development. Maturational theories (Gesell 1956) maintain that patterns of behavior express the organism's inherent tendencies. Development is seen as the natural unfolding of a process determined by hereditary factors. In contrast, environmental theories argue that behavior is determined primarily by external influences. From this point of view, behavior is not innately patterned but is essentially learned, whether as a result of conditioning processes that associate the behavior with particular stimuli, rewards, and punishment, or as a result of observing (and subsequently modeling) the behavior of others.

Social learning theory (Bandura 1977) has produced considerable research on how observational learning explains a variety of behaviors relevant to morality, including prosocial behavior (e.g., sharing, cooperation), aggression, resistance to temptation, and delayed gratification. More recent developments have pursued the question of how individuals exert control over their behavior, thus providing some balance to the theory's focus on environmental influences. Bandura's (1982) self-efficacy theory, for example, emphasizes the individual's expectations as important to the successful performance of a behavior. However, social learning theory has not addressed moral action and moral character in terms of a broad developmental course (Musser and Leone 1986).

Cognitive-developmental theory, on the other hand, focuses on the developmental process by which people come to understand and organize, or "cognitively structure," their experience. It attempts to resolve the "nature-nurture" controversy by emphasizing the development of these cognitive structures as the result of the interaction between organismic tendencies and influences from the outside world. While particular ways of understanding experience may reflect innate tendencies, they develop in response to the individual's specific experiences with the environment.

Thus, development is not seen as primarily maturational, because experience is necessary for cognitive structure to take shape. Also, the rate at which development occurs can be influenced by the individual's experience. However, neither is development thought to be primarily determined by the environment. Rather, cognitive-developmentalists argue that, because the underlying thought organization at each stage is qualitatively different, cognitive development is more than the progressively greater acquisition of information. Furthermore, at any given stage, the current cognitive structure can influence how the world is perceived. Thus, cognitive structure is seen to be "the result of an interaction between certain organismic structuring tendencies and the structure of the outside world, rather than reflecting either one directly" (Kohlberg 1969, p. 352).

The Doctrine of Cognitive Stages

Piaget's theory of cognitive development maintains that cognitive structures are periodically transformed or restructured as they become unable to account for (or assimilate) new information from the external world adequately. These periods of restructuring result in new ways of understanding that are different from the earlier mental structures as well as from those to be developed later. This allows for the differentiation of distinct cognitive stages, each identifiable by a characteristic approach to processing and organizing one's experience of external reality.

Only a minority of adults recognize that social rules have been established for the larger purpose of serving universal moral principles.

Piaget (1960) identified four main characteristics of cognitive stages. Kohlberg (1969) maintains that these characteristics accurately describe his stages of moral development.

1. Stages refer to distinct *qualitative differences* in the way a person thinks about an experience or solves a problem. Although the focus of attention may be the same, the mode of thinking about it is very different.

2. The progression of stages follows an *invariant sequence* in the development of individuals. That is, the order in which the stages occur is universal for all human organisms. It is possible that the speed or timing at which one progresses through the stages may vary with individual or cultural environments—or even that development may stop at one point or another. However, a given stage cannot be followed by any other stage than the one that is next in the sequence. Conversely, the earlier stage must first be achieved before its inadequacies become apparent and the subsequent transformation to the next stage can occur.

3. The characteristic mode of thinking represents a *structured whole.* Specific cognitive responses to specific tasks depend upon the overall organizational framework within which one processes information. It is this underlying cognitive structure that produces a logical consistency to one's responses. Thus, the stage is not identified by specific responses to specific stimuli but by the pattern in one's responses that indicate a particular underlying cognitive structure.

4. The sequence of stages is *hierarchical.* At each stage, the underlying structure represents a more integrated and complex organizational system that adequately accounts for information that created discrepancies within the previous structure. For example, children in the preoperational period of cognitive development cannot understand that equally sized balls of clay formed into two different shapes still have an equal amount of clay. However, children who have achieved concrete operational thinking understand the principle of conservation and thus recognize that the amount of clay remains the same (is conserved) for both pieces, even though they have changed in shape (Piaget and Inhelder 1969). Thus, the underlying cognitive structure of concrete operational thinking differentiates between amount and shape and integrates the information to achieve a more complex understanding of the phenomenon. It is thus logically superior to preoperational thinking. That the later stages in cognitive development are also more comprehensive and advanced in this way produces a hierarchical element to the sequence. Thus the stages of cognitive development are not just different but also hierarchical in the sense that they provide a progressively more differentiated and integrated—and hence more adaptive—understanding of one's interaction with the environment.

Kohlberg's Stages of Moral Development

Kohlberg's six stages of moral reasoning are divided into three levels, each consisting of two stages. The three levels are differentiated according to what serves as the basis for the person's moral judgment, particularly with regard to the significance given the prevailing, or "conventional," social expectations and authority. Briefly, the "preconventional" level, which is the level of most children under nine years old, is prior to the individual's achieving a full understanding of what is expected or required socially. The "conventional" level, which characterizes most adolescents and adults, refers to an understanding of the social conventions and a belief in conforming to and maintaining the established social order. The "postconventional" level is reached only by a minority of adults who understand and generally accept the social rules and expectations but who recognize that these have been established for the larger purpose of serving universal moral principles. Should the social conventions conflict with these principles, then moral judgment at this level will support the principles at the expense of the conventions.

Within each level, the second stage is a more advanced form than the first. More specifically, the preconventional level refers to judgment based not so much on a sense of what is right and wrong but on the physical consequences that any given act will have for the self. Accordingly, at the first stage within this level, characterized by the *punishment and obedience* orientation, the child will make judgments on the basis of avoiding trouble. This includes obeying authorities to avoid punishment.

At Stage 2, in what is still the preconventional level, the individual has a sense of the needs of others but still makes judgments to serve the self's practical interests. This is called the *instrumental* orientation. Although the person is beginning to understand that social interaction involves reciprocity and exchange among participants, moral judgment is still determined by the significance that the action has for oneself. Thus a child may share candy to get some ice cream.

Next is the conventional level, wherein moral judgment is determined by what is considered "good" according to conventional standards. At this level, the individual has an understanding of what kind of behavior is expected. The first stage at this level (Stage 3) is characterized by the *good boy/nice girl* orientation. Judgment as to what is right is based on living up to the expectations of others. It involves a trust in established authority and conformity for the sake of approval.

At Stage 4, the orientation is toward doing one's duty. This is called the *law and order* orientation. The individual personally subscribes to the existing social order and thus believes that obeying authority and maintaining the social order are good values in their own right. Whereas behaving according to the typical moral conventions is desirable at Stage 3 because it produces approval from others, at Stage 4 the individual has successfully "internalized" these conventions, so that proper behavior is rewarding because it reinforces one's sense of doing one's duty and therefore produces self-approval.

At the postconventional level, one's understanding of what is right and wrong is based on one's personal values and a sense of shared rights and responsibilities. Morality is no longer determined simply by social definition, but rather by rational considerations. Stage 5 is characterized by the *social contract* orientation, which recognizes that conventions are determined by social consensus and serve a social function. There is an emphasis on utilitarian agreements as to what will serve the most good for the most people. Here the person recognizes that rules or expectations are essentially arbitrary. The focus on agreement or contract produces an emphasis on what is legal and on operating "within the system" to achieve one's goals.

Stage 6, however, places the responsibility of a given moral decision firmly on the shoulders of the individual. The basis for moral judgment is found in *universal ethical principles* rather than socially established rules or expectations. One is guided by one's own conscience and recognizes the logical superiority of principles such as respect for human dignity. At Stage 6, it is thus possible to adopt a position that is in conflict with the prevailing social order and maintain this position as morally correct.

Measuring Moral Judgment

Kohlberg's procedure for assessing moral judgment involves presenting the subject with a hypothetical "dilemma" that requires the subject to make a moral choice. The most famous example refers to "Heinz," a man whose wife is dying of cancer. The woman could possibly be saved by a new drug, but the druggist who discovered it is charging an exorbitant amount of money for it, ten times what it costs him to make it. Heinz tried but could not raise enough money. Should he steal the drug?

Because Kohlberg's scheme emphasizes cognitive structure, an individual's stage of moral development is indicated not by the actual behavior that is advocated but rather by the pattern of reasoning behind the decision. Thus, two people may arrive at the same decision (e.g., that Heinz should steal the drug to save the life of his dying wife) but for two entirely different reasons. An individual at the preconventional Stage 2, operating within the instrumental orientation, might recommend stealing the drug because any jail term would be short and worth saving his wife. An individual at the postconventional Stage 6 might also recommend stealing the drug but with a different understanding of the dilemma: Although stealing would violate the law, it would uphold the higher principle of valuing human life and allow Heinz to maintain his self-respect.

The difference between the actual behavioral content of a decision and the underlying cognitive structure responsible for making the decision is also illustrated when two people arrive at different decisions but for similar reasons. Thus, the decision not to steal the drug because Heinz would go to jail and probably not be released until after his wife died is also Stage 2 thinking. Even though the ultimate decision advocates the opposite behavior of what was indicated above, it is similarly based on the consideration of what would be most instrumental to Heinz's own self-interest. On the other hand, an individual at Stage 6 might recommend not stealing the drug because, although other people would not blame Heinz if he stole it, he would nonetheless violate his own standard of honesty and lose his self-respect.

Because the stage of moral development is demonstrated not by the behavioral content but by the form of the moral judgment, subjects are allowed to respond freely to these moral dilemmas and asked to explain and justify their answers. The interviewer can probe with specific questions to elicit more information on the basis for the subject's decision. Interviewers are trained to collect relevant information without directing the subject's response.

Subjects' answers are then transcribed and coded for stage of moral development. Kohlberg identified twenty-five aspects of moral judgment, basic moral concepts that refer to such matters as rules, conscience, one's own welfare, the welfare of others, duty, punishment, reciprocity, and motives. Each of the twenty-five aspects was defined differently for each of the six stages of moral development. Originally, Kohlberg used an aspect-scoring system, whereby every statement made by the subject was coded for aspect and rated as to stage ("sentence scoring"). The subject's usage of any given stage of moral reasoning was indicated by the percentage of his or her statements that was attributed to that stage. Aspect scoring also included an overall "story rating," whereby a single stage was assigned to the subject's total response.

Coding difficulties led to the abandonment of the aspect-scoring system. Because the unit of analysis for sentence scoring was so small, coding often became dependent upon the specific content and choice of words and did not lend itself to identifying the general cognitive structure underlying the statement. Conversely, whereas story rating referred to the total response as the unit of analysis, it created some uncertainty when the subject's answer included conflicting themes.

Kohlberg and his colleagues recognized these scoring difficulties and devoted considerable attention to developing a more reliable and valid scoring system. This led to "standardized issue scoring," which relies on the use of a standardized interview format. The subject is presented with three standard dilemmas, and the interviewer probes for only two issues that are specified for each dilemma (e.g., life and punishment in the Heinz dilemma). Scoring of the subject's responses refers to a manual that describes the patterns of reasoning for Stages 1–5 on each issue (Colby et al. 1987). Stage 6 was dropped from the coding procedure, due to its empirically low incidence, but retained as a theoretical construct. Because the focus of the new scoring system is directed more toward the abstract mode of reasoning, the unit of analysis is thus considered larger and less concrete than the single sentence. However, because this approach focuses on specifically identified issues, norms, and elements, it is considered more precise than the global story rating. Despite the qualitative nature of this approach and its potential vulnerability to rater bias, its developers report that long-term study of its inter-rater reliability, test-retest reliability, internal consistency, and validity has produced favorable results (Colby and Kohlberg 1987).

Validity has been a major concern regarding the Moral Judgment Interview. Kurtines and Grief (1974) criticized the low utility of moral judgment scores for predicting moral action. Other questions have been raised about the validity of the data collected, even for purposes of assessing moral judgment. For one, the representativeness of the "classical" dilemmas used in this research has been criticized, in terms of both their addressing hypothetical—as opposed to real-life—circumstances and their reference to a limited domain of moral issues (e.g., property, punishment). A related matter is whether responses are affected by characteristics (e.g., gender) of the story's protagonist. Also, the effect of differences in interviewing style, as interviewers interact with subjects and probe for further information, needs to be considered. Of particular importance is this method's dependence on the subject's verbal expression and articulation skills for the information that is collected. To the extent that the rating might be affected by either the amount of information that is provided or the manner in which it is expressed, the validity of the scoring system is called into question. (See Modgil and Modgil 1986 for discussion of these issues.)

An alternative to Kohlberg's Moral Judgment Interview is the Defining Issues Test (DIT; Rest 1986). This is a standardized questionnaire that presents a set of six moral dilemmas and, for each dilemma, specifically identifies twelve issues that could be considered in deciding upon a course of action. The subject's task is to indicate, on a five-point scale, how important each issue is to deciding what ought to be done in the given situation. The subject also ranks the four most important issues.

Here, the term *issue* is used differently than it is in Kohlberg's new scoring procedure. The items are prototypical statements designed to represent considerations (e.g., "whether a community's laws are going to be upheld") that are characteristic of specific stages of moral reasoning as they are described in Kohlberg's theory. The importance assigned by the subject to items that represent a particular stage is taken to indicate the extent to which the subject's moral judgment is characterized by that stage's mode of thinking.

There are advantages and disadvantages to the DIT compared with the open-ended interview. Whereas the interview is helpful for originally identifying the considerations that may be relevant to resolving a moral dilemma, the DIT provides a more systematic assessment of the relative importance of such considerations. In the open-ended interview, it is never clear whether a specific concern is not identified because it is not important or because the subject failed to articulate it. Similarly, interviews are less comparable to the extent that subjects do not all address the same issues. These problems are avoided by the more structured DIT because the task requires the subject only to recognize what is important rather than to identify and articulate it spontaneously. However, because recognition is an easier task than spontaneous production, it tends to allow higher-level responses. Another important difference is that the DIT measures the maturity of moral judgment as a continuous variable rather than in terms of the step-by-step sequence of cognitive-developmental stages. Researchers must be aware of such differences when interpreting results.

Theoretical Criticisms

Besides the methodological problems discussed above, Kohlberg's theory of moral development has been criticized on a number of points. The major criticisms include the following:

1. The sequence of stages is more representative of Western culture and thus not universal or invariant across all cultures. Moreover, it is culturally biased in that it maintains the ideals of Western liberalism as the highest form of moral reasoning.

2. Like many theories of personality development, Kohlberg's theory fails to describe accurately the development of women but provides a much better understanding of male development. This is a specific variation of the first criticism, suggesting that the theory itself reflects the sexism of Western culture.

3. Kohlberg's theory fails to describe adult development adequately. In particular, its emphasis on abstract principles fails to recognize how adult moral judgment is more responsive to the specific practical matters of everyday, real-life contexts. Also, its emphasis on cognitive structure fails to recognize that changes in the content of moral reflection may be the most important aspect of adult moral development.

CULTURAL BIAS. A cornerstone of cognitive-developmental theory is that of invariant sequence, the notion that the given developmental progression is universal for all human beings within all cultures. Because the conceptual organization of any given stage is considered logically necessary before the cognitive structure of the next stage can develop, each stage is said to have logical priority to subsequent stages. Shweder and LeVine (1975) take issue with both the notion of logical priority and the doctrine of invariant sequence, although they do not address the development of moral judgment per se. Specifically, they analyze dream concepts among children from the Hausa culture in Nigeria and conclude that there are multiple sequences by which such concepts develop.

Shweder (1982) follows up this initial skepticism with a fuller critique of what he sees as Kohlberg's failure to recognize cultural conceptions of morality as relative to one another. He disagrees with the assertion that there is a rational basis upon which morality can be constructed objectively. Rather, he argues that the post-conventional morality that Kohlberg maintains as rationally superior is simply an example of American ideology.

Specific moral dilemmas used in the testing situation may not have the same meaning for people of different cultures.

Similarly, others (Broughton 1986; Simpson 1974; Sullivan 1977) argue that Kohlberg's theory is necessarily culture-bound, reflective of the Western society from which it originates. Simpson suggests that the specific moral dilemmas used in the testing situation may not have the same meaning for people of different cultures and thus the scoring system may not adequately detect legitimate cultural variations in moral structures. Thus, he maintains that the claims to universality are not valid. Sullivan goes even further to suggest that Stage 6 reasoning is so rooted in the philosophical rationale for current Western society that it serves to defend the status quo. In so doing, it distracts attention from the injustices of such societies.

In a response to the charge of cultural bias, Kohlberg, Levine, and Hewer (1983) acknowledge the influence of Western liberal ideology on the theory. They agree there is a need to be more sensitive to cultural differences in the meaning attributed not only to the various elements of the research protocol but, consequently, also to the responses of the subjects themselves. However, they defend the claim to universality for the six-stage sequence of moral development and maintain that empirical research using the scientific method will help to determine to what extent this position is tenable.

They also maintain that, while it is appropriate to remain impartial in the study of moral judgment, this does not make it necessary to deny the relative value of certain moral positions. They assert that some positions are rationally superior to others. They thus continue to subscribe to the ideal that any given moral conflict can be brought to resolution through rational discourse.

Kohlberg's position on invariant sequence has been supported by a number of cross-cultural studies, although postconventional reasoning (Stages 5 and 6) may occur less frequently in nonurbanized cultures (Snarey 1985). However, in a sample of subjects from India, Vasudev and Hummel (1987) not only found the stage of moral development to be significantly related to age, but also found postconventional thinking to occur among a substantial proportion of adults. Concluding that commonalities exist across cultures, Vasudev and Hummel also suggest there is cultural diversity in the way moral principles are expressed, interpreted, and adapted to real life.

GENDER BIAS. Carol Gilligan (1982) argues that the major theories of personality development describe males more accurately than females. She includes Kohlberg's theory in this assessment and points to the prevalence of all-male samples in his early research as a partial explanation. Gilligan contrasts two moral orientations. The first is the morality of justice, which focuses on fairness, rights, and rules for the resolution of disputes. The second is the morality of care, which focuses on relationships, a sensitivity to the needs of others, and a responsibility for others. Gilligan asserts that the orientation towards morality as justice is more characteristic of males and, conversely, the morality of care and responsibility is especially relevant to females. To the extent that Piaget, Freud, and Kohlberg each address morality as justice, they more accurately represent male moral development but inadequately represent female moral development.

Gilligan argues that women are more likely to rely on the orientation of care to frame personal moral dilemmas. Furthermore, whereas the morality of care focuses on interpersonal relationship, it resembles the Stage 3 emphasis on satisfying the expectations of others. Gilligan believes this resemblance results in a high number of female responses being misrepresented with Stage 3 ratings.

Gilligan thus argues that Kohlberg's theory and scoring system are biased to favor men. However, Walker (1984), after systematically reviewing empirical studies that used Kohlberg's method, concludes that men do not score higher than women when samples are controlled for education, socioeconomic status, and occupation. Similarly, Thoma (1986) reports that sex differences on the Defining Issues Test actually favor women but that the differences are trivial.

Kohlberg, Levine, and Hewer (1983) address Gilligan's criticisms and agree that the care orientation is not fully assessed by their measurement but disagree that this leads to a biased downscoring of females. They suggest that care and justice may develop together and that Stage 6 nonetheless represents a mature integration of the care and justice moralities. (See also Vasudev 1988.)

ADULT DEVELOPMENT. A third major issue concerning Kohlberg's theory is whether or not it accurately addresses continued adult development. This issue reflects a more general concern in lifespan developmental psychology regarding the applicability (or inapplicability) of Piaget's model for cognitive development beyond adolescence (Commons, Richards, and Armon 1984). Murphy and Gilligan (1980) provide evidence that college and postcollege subjects not only indicated a greater tendency to appreciate the importance of specific contexts in real-life dilemmas but also indicated a slight tendency to regress from Stage 5 moral reasoning on the classical dilemmas. They suggest that a more mature recognition of the significance of contextual particulars leads one to question the validity of abstract moral principles (hence the regressed score). This argument is consistent with other work suggesting that adult development is marked by a greater appreciation of the practical realities of day-to-day living (Denney and Palmer 1981; Labouvie-Vief 1984; Perry 1970).

Finally, Gibbs (1979) argues that adult development is characterized more by increased reflection on such existential matters as meaning, identity, and commitment than by any structural change in the way one thinks. He suggests that Kohlberg's postconventional stages are not structural advances over the earlier stages but would be more appropriately described in terms of existential development. In response, Kohlberg, Levine, and Hewer (1983) maintain that Stage 5 represents a legitimate cognitive structure. However, they acknowledge the possibility of further nonstructural development in the adult years with regard to both specific contextual relativity and existential reflection. They suggest that such development could be described in terms of "soft" stages that do not strictly satisfy Piaget's formal criteria for cognitive stages.

In spite of the formidable criticisms that have been levied against it, Kohlberg's theory of moral development remains the centerpiece to which all other work in this area is addressed, whether as an elaboration or as a refutation. At the very least, Kohlberg has formulated a particular sequence of moral reasoning that adequately represents the prevalent sequence of development in traditional Western society. To that extent, it serves as a model, not only for building educational devices (see Modgil and Modgil 1986; Nucci 1989;

Power, Higgins, and Kohlberg 1989), but also for comparing possible alternatives. Whether or not this sequence is in fact universal or relative to the particular culture—or a particular socialization process within one's culture—is a debate that continues. Nonetheless, the scheme remains the prototype upon which further work in this area is likely to be based.

[See also Socialization.]

BIBLIOGRAPHY

Bandura, Albert 1977 *Social Learning Theory.* Englewood Cliffs, N.J.: Prentice-Hall.

——— 1982 "Self-Efficacy Mechanism in Human Agency." *American Psychologist* 37:122–147.

Broughton, John M. 1986 "The Genesis of Moral Domination." In S. Modgil and C. Modgil, eds., *Lawrence Kohlberg: Consensus and Controversy.* Philadelphia: Falmer Press.

Colby, Anne, and Lawrence Kohlberg 1987 *The Measurement of Moral Judgment,* vol. 1, *Theoretical Foundations and Research Validation.* New York: Cambridge University Press.

———, Lawrence Kohlberg, Alexandra Hewer, Daniel Candee, John C. Gibbs, and Clark Power 1987 *The Measurement of Moral Judgment,* vol. 2, *Standard Issue Scoring Manual.* New York: Cambridge University Press.

Commons, Michael L., Francis A. Richards, and Cheryl Armon (eds.) 1984 *Beyond Formal Operations: Late Adolescent and Adult Cognitive Development.* New York: Praeger.

Denney, Nancy W., and Ann M. Palmer 1981 "Adult Age Differences on Traditional and Practical Problem-Solving Measures." *Journal of Gerontology* 36:323–328.

Gesell, Arnold 1956 *Youth: The Years from Ten to Sixteen.* New York: Harper and Row.

Gibbs, John C. 1979 "Kohlberg's Moral Stage Theory: A Piagetian Revision." *Human Development* 22: 89–112.

Gilligan, Carol 1982 *In a Different Voice: Psychological Theory and Women's Development.* Cambridge, Mass.: Harvard University Press.

Kohlberg, Lawrence 1969 "Stage and Sequence: The Cognitive-Developmental Approach to Socialization." In D. Goslin, ed., *Handbook of Socialization Theory and Research.* Chicago: Rand McNally.

——— 1971 "From *Is* to *Ought:* How to Commit the Naturalistic Fallacy and Get Away with It in the Study of Moral Development." In T. Mischel, ed., *Cognitive Development and Epistemology.* New York: Academic Press.

——— 1976 "Moral Stages and Moralization: The Cognitive Developmental Approach." In T. Lickona, ed., *Moral Development and Behavior: Theory, Research, and Social Issues.* New York: Holt, Rinehart, and Winston.

———, Charles Levine, and Alexandra Hewer 1983 *Moral Stages: A Current Formulation and a Response to Critics.* Basel, Switzerland: Karger.

Kurtines, William, and Esther B. Grief 1974 "The Development of Moral Thought: Review and Evaluation of Kohlberg's Approach." *Psychological Bulletin* 81:453–470.

Labouvie-Vief, Gisela 1984 "Culture, Language, and Mature Rationality." In K. McCluskey and H. W. Reese, eds., *Life-Span Developmental Psychology: Historical and Generational Effects.* New York: Academic Press.

Modgil, Sohan, and Celia Modgil 1986 *Lawrence Kohlberg: Consensus and Controversy.* Philadelphia: Falmer Press.

Murphy, John M., and Carol Gilligan 1980 "Moral Development in Late Adolescence and Adulthood: A Critique and Reconstruction of Kohlberg's Theory." *Human Development* 23:77–104.

Musser, Lynn M., and Christopher Leone 1986 "Moral Character: A Social Learning Perspective." In R. T. Knowles and G. F. McLean, eds., *Psychological Foundations of Moral Education and Character Development: An Integrated Theory of Moral Development.* Lanham, Md.: University Press of America.

Nucci, Larry P. (ed.) 1989 *Moral Development and Character Education: A Dialogue.* Berkeley, Calif.: McCutchan.

Perry, William G., Jr. 1970 *Forms of Intellectual and Ethical Development in the College Years.* New York: Holt, Rinehart, and Winston.

Piaget, Jean [1932] 1948 *The Moral Judgment of the Child.* Glencoe, Ill.: Free Press.

——— 1960 "The General Problems of the Psychobiological Development of the Child." In J. M. Tanner and B. Inhelder, eds., *Discussions on Child Development: Proceedings of the World Health Organization Study Group on the Psychobiological Development of the Child.* New York: International Universities Press.

———, and Barbara Inhelder 1969 *The Psychology of the Child.* New York: Basic Books.

Power, Clark F., Ann Higgins, and Lawrence Kohlberg 1989 *Lawrence Kohlberg's Approach to Moral Education.* New York: Columbia University Press.

Rest, James R. 1986 *Moral Development: Advances in Research and Theory.* New York: Praeger.

Shweder, Richard 1982 "Review of Lawrence Kohlberg's Essays in Moral Development, Vol. 1, The Philosophy of Moral Development: Liberalism as Destiny." *Contemporary Psychology* 27:421–424.

———, and Robert A. LeVine 1975 "Dream Concepts of Hausa Children: A Critique of the 'Doctrine of Invariant Sequence' in Cognitive Development." *Ethos* 3:209–230.

Simpson, Elizabeth L. 1974 "Moral Development Research: A Case Study of Scientific Cultural Bias." *Human Development* 17:81–106.

Snarey, John R. 1985 "Cross-Cultural Universality of Social-Moral Development: A Critical Review of Kohlbergian Research." *Psychological Bulletin* 97:202–232.

Sullivan, Edmund V. 1977 "A Study of Kohlberg's Structural Theory of Moral Development: A Critique of Liberal Social Science Ideology." *Human Development* 20:352–376.

Thoma, Stephen J. 1986 "Estimating Gender Differences in the Comprehension and Preference of Moral Issues." *Developmental Review* 6:165–180.

Vasudev, Jyotsna 1988 "Sex Differences in Morality and Moral Orientation: A Discussion of the Gilligan and Attanucci Study." *Merrill-Palmer Quarterly* 34:239–244.

———, and Hummel, Raymond C. 1987 "Moral Stage Sequence and Principled Reasoning in an Indian Sample." *Human Development* 30:105–118.

Walker, Lawrence J. 1984 "Sex Differences in the Development of Moral Reasoning: A Critical Review of the Literature." *Child Development* 55:677–691.

– THOMAS J. FIGURSKI

MULTICULTURALISM

In the 1990s multiculturalism dominated interpretive and curricular debates about history in schools and universities. The idea responds in part to the diversity of students, especially in urban areas, increasingly from African-, Hispanic-, and Asian-American backgrounds. Taken together, minority groups are nearing a majority in such major cities as New York and Los Angeles and in states including California, Texas, Florida, and New York. By the year 2000 non-European ethnic minorities are expected to make up one-fourth of the nation's population. State and federal education officials, test designers, and educational publishers are concerned by these changes. Since demonstrations at Stanford University in 1988, educators on campuses across the country have debated the extent to which a history curriculum should be Eurocentric, that is, be based on classical Western texts, take a triumphal view of national settlement or expansion by Europeans, or emphasize the history of U.S. political and economic elites. Some multiculturalists claim that white Americans of European heritage have unjustly tried to impose ethnocentric values on nonwhite Americans. They hold that the school-based imposition of Western history, literature, ideas, institutions, and values on children of non-European backgrounds is unjust and culturally biased. Other scholars assert that the nation's political institutions, language, cultural ideals, and economic system derive mainly from Europe, notably from England.

Multiculturalism emphasizes the recognition and study of national diversity, especially along lines of ethnicity and gender. Both pluralists and group separatists claim its philosophical foundations: Multiculturalism may acknowledge qualities of U.S. culture and politics that transcend group differences, or it may contend that racial, ethnic, sexual, religious, and other human characteristics create "separate realities" and "multiple cultural perspectives" of learning. Many multiculturalists reject the idea of a common culture, including older ethnic melting-pot ideals and the idea of pluralism. The multicultural concept is often linked to self-esteem training used to advance the self-image of minorities and women. Some educators envision multiculturalism as a tool to change the educational environment so that students from various groups and social classes will experience equal educational opportunity. According to a 1991 New York City Board of Education declaration, "Multicultural education is an interdisciplinary approach to education designed to foster intergroup knowledge and understanding, to engender greater self-esteem within the entire school community, and to equip students to function effectively in a global society." Some philosophers distinguish between multiculturalism and pluralism in that the former "repudiates the idea of national identity and the emotion of national pride." They worry that such a repudiation, if standard in history and government, invites social fragmentation and civil disorder, whereby students will identify with groups rather than through bonds of citizenship, language, and law.

– GILBERT T. SEWALL

N

NATIONALISM

Nationalism has been defined in a variety of ways at different levels of analysis (e.g., Kohn 1955, 1968; Symmons-Symonolewicz 1970; Kamenka 1973; Plamenatz 1973; Snyder 1984; Smith, 1976, 1981). The concept combines a sense of identification with a people, an ideology of common history and destiny, and a social movement addressed to shared objectives. This definition raises questions about what differentiates a people or a nation from others, the nature of identification, the conditions under which nationalist ideologies develop, and the course and aims of nationalist movements.

Historically the term *nationalism* was applied to attempts to follow early European models "to make the boundaries of the state and those of the nation coincide" (Minogue 1967), that is, to create loyalty to a nation-state (Kohn 1968). It was also applied to struggles, proliferating after World War II, to gain independence from colonial domination and join the community of sovereign states. More recently, however, analysts have found the confusion between the concepts of state and nation to be a hindrance to understanding contemporary nationalism. Only rarely, if at all, do the boundaries of a state coincide with those of a nation. By *nation* we mean an ethnic group that (1) shares one or more identifying characteristics, such as language, religion, racial background, culture, and/or territory; and (2) is politically mobilized and/or amenable to such mobilization. Thus, *nationalism* should be distinguished from *patriotism,* in that the identification and loyalty in the former is to an ethnic group or nation, and in the latter to the state.

Identification

Debates centering on the intrinsic nature of collective ethnic identification feature variations on two general themes—primordial and structural. Implied in the primordial perspective is a deemphasis on an instrumental view of ethnic ties. Rather, these ties are seen as ends in themselves shaped by forces other than material self-interest; they are persistent and resist the homogenization predicted by convergence and modernization theorists. The essence of these ties "is a psychological bond that joins a people and differentiates it in the subconscious conviction of its members from all other people in the most vital way" (Connor 1978, quoted in Stack 1986, pp. 3, 4). These bonds stem from "immediate contiguity and kin connection mainly, but beyond them . . . from being born into a particular religious community, speaking a particular language, or even a dialect of a language, and following particular social practice" (Geertz 1963, pp. 14, 15). To structuralists, "ethnic identity results instead from objective intergroup differences in the distribution of economic resources and authority" (Hechter 1986, p. 109). Implied here is rational choice and self-interest, that ethnic ties are means to certain ends, and that the boundaries of ethnic groups are changeable.

Communication is subject not only to commonality of language and cultural background but also to available means.

Neither primordialists nor structuralists would deny the obvious variations in the intensity of identification and in the potential for nationalist movements cross-culturally and over time. Several factors are expected to contribute to these variations. Among the more important of these factors is coterminality of characteristics. In most instances multiple characteristics are involved in distinguishing among ethnic groups—in an overlapping manner at times and coterminously at others. The United States offers an example of overlapping identities where people from different racial backgrounds share the same religious orientations, people with different religious orientation share a common language, and there is no territorial exclusiveness. This overlap in ethnic identification is credited in part with lowering intergroup tensions (Williams 1947). At the other extreme are peoples in southern Sudan, Tibet, and other places for whom all or a combination of racial, religious, linguistic, cultural, and territorial maps largely coincide. The greater the number of factors that coincide, the greater the gulf or "social fault" among ethnic groups along which nationalist sentiments and tensions are likely to intensify.

In addition to differentiating attributes and geographic distributions, a number of features of the social structure contribute heavily to variance in intensity and patterns of nationalism. Hechter (1986) suggests two types of such factors. One is the institutionalization of ethnic differences in legal and normative rules, especially those which govern property and civil rights, as was the case of South Africa. The other is differentiation in positions in the division of labor that shape "specialization experiences as well as material interests." Deutsch (1966) offers another factor in nationalism, attributing membership in a people essentially to a "wide complementarity of social communication" that "consists in the ability to communicate more effectively, and over a wide range of subjects, with members of one large group than with outsiders." Communication is subject not only to commonality of language and cultural background but also to available means. These include networks of social relations as well as the ever-advancing technological means of mass communications.

Nationalism

In addition to identification and "consciousness of kind," nationalism involves ideology and mobilization for social movement and political action. The ideology stems from identification, the sense of uniqueness of group origin, history, culture, collective authority, and destiny (Smith 1981). Political mobilization and the course of nationalist movements are greatly influenced by a host of internal and external factors. Important among the internal factors are uneven economic conditions and disparities along cultural lines in control of resources, access to goods, and distribution of positions in the occupational structure. The collective perception of an ethnic group of its deprivation or exploitation may challenge not only the legitimacy of the regime but also of the state itself. The theme of "relative deprivation" has been central to explanations of political violence (e.g., Gurr 1970).

The political system allocates power and authority. An uneven distribution among ethnic groups can be the direct result of exclusionary rules and practices or the indirect result of socioeconomic disparities. Whatever the reason, a cultural distribution of power is as evocative of a nationalist sense of deprivation as a cultural distribution of resources. The close relationship between power and resources led Lasswell (1936) to observe that politics is "Who gets What, When, and How."

Applying a developmental perspective, Huntington (1968) connects political stability/instability to the balance between "institutionalization" and "participation." This line of reasoning suggests to some analysts (e.g., Sanders 1981) a linear relationship between political development and political instability—in this case arising from nationalism, which is credited with having been the most prevalent reason for state-level violence (Said and Simmons 1976). Support for such a pattern of relationships derives also from the expectation that the national integration and political assimilation characteristic of developed societies contribute to a shift from culturally based to functionally based cleavages. The net result is a reduction in the prevalence and intensity of ethnic mobilization in the more politically developed countries. However, clearly implied in Huntington's discussion of relations between demand for participation and institutional capacity is a balance at low levels in the least developed countries and at high levels in the developed ones. Imbalances can be expected at early and middle stages of development, which suggests a curvilinear pattern.

There is no unanimity on the relationships between development and nationalism. This is understandable in view of the complexity of both phenomena and the

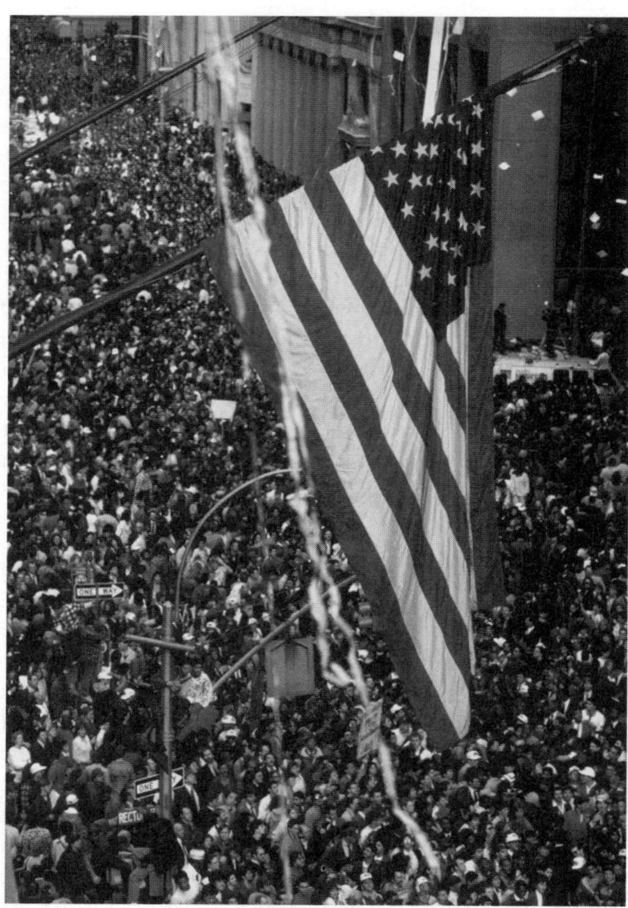

Nationalism differs from patriotism in that the identification and loyalty of the nationalist is to an ethnic group or nation while the patriot is loyal to the state. (Joseph Sohm; ChromoSohm Inc./Corbis)

current state of research. An important voice on these relationships is that of Walker Connor (e.g., 1972), who contends that modernization, the spread of education, and improved means of mass communication are responsible for a resurgence in ethnic nationalism. Juan Linz observes that "in the modern world the aim seems to be to build nations rather than states, a task that is probably beyond the capacity of any state that has not achieved the characteristics of a nation-state before the era of nationalism" (1978, p. 62). The distinction between "level" and "process" of modernization and development is useful in understanding the rise in nationalist sentiments. As Smith has noted, "Perhaps, then, it is not the fact of economic progress or decline that is relevant to ethnic revival, but simply economic change per se. Most change today is painful and uprooting" (1981, p. 34). Tensions, strains, and dislocations associated with change in the structure and distribution of power—political change—are no less painful or uprooting. Attempts by central governments to secularize and to shift loyalties from ethnic groups to the state underlie much of contemporary, nationalism.

The rise of nationalism and the forms and directions it takes are significantly influenced by forces external to the respective states—regional and global socioeconomic and political conditions, and the spread of ideologies. The power vacuum created by the liquidation of colonialism after World War II tended to be filled by the newly created states. Regional power struggles, territorial disputes, economic competition, and ideological differences have left many regions of the world fraught with turmoil. Since cultural pluralism is characteristic of most, if not all, of the new states, ethnic nationalism often figures prominently in regional conflicts—as a cause at times, and as a consequence at others. The regional dynamics of ethnonationalism can take many forms.

The phenomenal advancements in means of communication and transportation have enormously increased the intensity and scope of global relations. Four features of these relations are particularly relevant to nationalism. First is the spread of ideologies related to human rights and the right to self-determination. Reports of abuses of these rights are communicated in a rapid, if not an instant, manner. They galvanize global public opinion and prod governments to intercede. Rapid communication also brings to ethnic communities the successes of others who are engaged in struggles or have succeeded in attaining varying measures of autonomy. Second is the presence of world forums to address these issues and bring to bear the weight of the global community, such as the United Nations General Assembly, the Security Council, the International Court of Justice, and other governmental and nongovernmental organizations. Third is the increasing globalization of the economy, which makes it possible for small sociopolitical units to find multilateral niches, thereby reducing dependency on bilateral economic relations with either former colonial powers or states from which they have seceded. Fourth is the geopolitical relations among the superpowers. They have frequently supported different sides of conflicts within pluralistic societies, either directly or through proxies. It is interesting to note that, in the past, both the United States and the Soviet Union took positions in support of the doctrine of "self determination." (President Wilson was a staunch spokesman for the principle during and after World War I. Around the same time, "at the Seventh All Russian Democratic Labor Party Conference of May 12, 1917 . . . in a resolution drafted by Lenin, the conference unequivocally endorsed the right of all of the nations forming part of Russia freely to secede and form independent states" [Connor 1984].) In contemporary global relations both nations show less commitment to the principle. Their approaches to nationalism are shaped by strategic and economic interests, tempered by the balance of force that can be brought to the situation. The ebb and flow of relations among superpowers exert considerable influence on ethnonationalism.

Nationalist Movements

The literature offers two perspectives in explaining the formation of social movements—collective behavior and resource mobilization. In the former, social movements are viewed as responses to a rise in grievances and the actors are seen as "arational" if not "irrational"; in the latter they are considered as goal-oriented, rational responses dependent on organization and mobilization of resources (Jenkins 1983). Debates concerning the strengths and limitations of these two perspectives are yet to be settled. Important to a discussion of nationalism, however, is that literature on social movements, especially on resource mobilization, is primarily Western in conceptualization and empirical foundations. Significant in this respect are differences in aims that guide social movements. More common to Western societies is "changing some elements of the social structure and/or reward distribution of a society" (McCarthy and Zald 1977, pp. 1217, 1218), compared with nationalist movements that press for autonomy, if not for secession. The first type of movement seeks change through influencing political institutions, the legitimacy of which is not in question. Nationalist movements, on the other hand, often challenge, if not outright reject, the legitimacy of the state. This is not to cast doubt on the applicability of theories of social movements to ethnic nationalism but, rather, to point out that the influence of differences among societies in levels of development, political institutions, types of regimes, and movements' aims has not been adequately explored (see McCarthy and Zald 1977; Tilly 1978; Jenkins 1983).

In the following paragraphs we shall outline some of the important features of nationalist movements and the processes of mobilization. More specifically, we shall consider the role of grievance, resources, repertoires of expression, and aims.

The role of grievances remains unresolved. While traditional analysis places grievances stemming from structural strains associated with social change at the root of movements (e.g., Smelser 1962; Gurr 1970; Gusfield 1970), resource mobilization proponents favor structural "causal" explanations (e.g., Tilly 1978). Some feel discontent is ubiquitous and therefore, by itself, cannot explain the emergence of social movements. McCarthy and Zald go even further: "For some purposes, grievances and discontent may be defined, created and manipulated by issue entrepreneurs and organizations" (1977, p. 1215). In line with this perspective is Smith's (1981) account of "ethnic revival." He maintains that the unique and distinguishing rationale of an ethnic group is the emphasis on group belonging and group uniqueness that links successive generations of the group with specific origins and history. Driving the engines of "historicism" and "nationalism" are discontented intellectuals, educators, and professional intelligentsia. Blocked mobility, opposition, and repression by traditional authorities, and frustrated expectations concerning recognition, especially on the part of Third World intellectuals, are factors in the radicalization of these groups, which then turn to historicism and inward to their ethnic communities (Smith 1981).

In explaining the spread of "value-oriented movements," Smelser (1962) refers to "structural conduciveness." Two elements of conduciveness are highly applicable to ethnonationalist movements. One is "the availability of means to express grievances" during troubled or uncertain times in order to redress problems. The other relates to the importance of communication in "disseminating a generalized belief"—a position consistent with that of Deutsch and Connor cited earlier.

Attempts to explain nationalist movements must account for the mobilization of resources. McCarthy and Zald outline five central considerations: (1) "aggregation of resources (money and labor)"; (2) the form of organization these resources entail; (3) involvement of individuals and organizations outside the movement; (4) the flow of resources to and from the movement; and (5) "the importance of costs and rewards in explaining individual and organizational involvement" (1977, p. 1216).

The prevailing patterns of social relations are expected to influence the potential for, and forms of, organizations and mobilization. Tilly (1978) maintains that combined strength in identification and interpersonal bonds lead to high levels of organization and to greater possibilities for mobilization. In a similar vein Oberschall (1973) offers a classification for patterns of organization. Along one dimension—relations within collectivities—he identifies three types: "communal," "associational," and "weakly [organized] or unorganized." Mobilization, which is facilitated by communal and associational forms, is rendered difficult by the weakly organized and unorganized structures. Along another dimension Oberschall distinguishes between "vertical" and "horizontal" relations to other collectives and segments of society. Social and political bonds across classes and collectivities can influence mobilization; however, the direction of influence can be expected to vary depending on the type of movement. For example, Oberschall observes: "If in a stratified society there exist [*sic*] strong vertical social and political bonds between upper and lower classes, mobilization into protest movements among lower classes is not likely to take place" (1973, p. 120). While this may be the case in regard to class conflicts, vertical bonds within an ethnic group can significantly facilitate mobilization.

If strong social and political bonds exist between upper and lower classes, mobilization into protest movements among lower classes is not likely to take place.

Strength in family and kinship relations underlies Tilly's networks of interpersonal bonds and Oberschall's communal organization. Houseknecht sees strength here as referring "to the extent to which family/kinship obligations and rights take precedence over their nonkinship counterparts" (1990, p. 1). She outlines important ways in which kinship relates to ethnic identification, nationalism, and the organization of movements. Early socialization builds identification with an ethnic culture and commitment to its values and norms, which continue to be strengthened and enforced through kinship ties. Commonality in cultural background facilitates social communication, and the networks of kinship ties are readily available channels for the mobilization of human and material resources. Furthermore, the traditional authority structure afforded by strong family and kinship systems provides protection in resisting pressures applied by the state's central authorities.

While informal networks of kinship and interpersonal relations are important to nationalist movements, the role of formal organizations cannot be overstated. As pointed out by McCarthy and Zald (1977), a social movement may include more than one organization; and all organizations in a movement compose a "social movement industry." Competition over resources can arise between a movement industry and other commitments, as well as among organizations within the same movement industry. The latter form of competition is common to nationalist movements. This frequently encourages the involvement of neighboring states or major powers, and often leads to internal conflicts within movements.

These lines of reasoning concerning the role of kinship and interpersonal relations bring up the unresolved debate over the relative effectiveness of bureaucratic centralized movement organizations compared with those of an informal decentralized nature. While some argue that "a formalized structure with a clear division of labor maximizes mobilization by transforming diffuse commitments into clearly defined roles and . . . centralized decision making," others maintain that "decentralized movements with a minimum division of labor and integrated by informal networks and an overarching ideology are more effective" (Jenkins 1983, p. 539).

Why would individuals and organizations contribute their labor and resources to ethnonationalist movements? To primordialists, the answer is that they do so in order to preserve cultural integrity and a way of life, to maintain group solidarity and social bonds, and to advance the cause of a community from which a sense of security and pride is derived. These are valued ends in themselves. To collective behavior theorists, the answer is in the collective mood, social contagion, and the state of mind that are engendered in response to the perception of grievances. To structuralists and resource mobilization proponents, the answer lies in rational collective action and the pursuit of interests.

The vested interests of other states are usually rooted in resources, trade, security, geopolitical advantage, and/or ideology. While the large states "are likely to intervene for instrumental reasons," the small ones "are more likely to intervene for affective reasons" (Heraclides 1990, p. 377). Regional and global influences may strengthen the state's means of control and repression, contribute to the movement's resources and sanctuary, and/or raise awareness and help mobilize regional and global public opinion. These interests and their expression, directly or through international organizations, expand or inhibit opportunities for nationalist movements.

Opportunities for mobilization are also enhanced by the quality of leadership and its effectiveness in articulating the interests of the group. Smelser explains that the significance of charismatic leadership to value-oriented movements, in such forms as "the dreamer prophet of the cult, the nationalist crusader, and the totalitarian demagogue," is compatible with the character of these movements in certain phases of their development. He goes on to point out, however, that "Insofar as a value-oriented movement receives material from outside sources, and insofar as it inherits an organizational structure, the need for charismatic leadership lessens" (1962, pp. 355, 356). Useful here are categories identified by Hermann (1986) to analyze political leaders. Particularly important are such contextual factors as to whom the leaders are accountable, forms of interaction with followers, the constraints defined by constituents' beliefs and norms, the strength and nature of opposition, and available resources.

Repertoires of expression of ethnic nationalist movements vary along a wide spectrum that includes interest articulation, passive resistance, demonstrations and riots, sabotage, terrorist acts, and internal wars. Patterns of expression are shaped by the style of leadership, the level of organization, and resources. They are also influenced by the reactions of the state as well as by external forces. These expressions represent events in the life history of movements. The points at which these movements begin and end are generally difficult, if not impossible, to ascertain. Thus, what might be referred to as beginnings or outcomes may well represent only arbitrarily defined points in a process.

Ethnic movements differ in aims and strategies. Smith identifies six types:

> 1. Isolation. . . . was the most common strategy for smaller ethnic communities in the past. The ethnic community chooses to stay aloof from society as a whole.
>
> 2. Accommodation. Here the ethnic community aims to adjust to its host society by encouraging its members to participate in the social and political life of the society and its state. Often, individual members try to assimilate to the host society, or at least become acculturated, for individual advancement.
>
> 3. Communalism. . . . is simply a more dynamic and active form of accommodation. . . . The aim is communal control over communal affairs in those geographical areas where the ethnic community forms a demographic majority.

4. Autonomism. There are . . . various forms and degrees of autonomy. . . . Cultural autonomy implies full control by representatives of the ethnic community over every aspect of its cultural life, notably education, the press and mass media, and the courts. Political autonomy or "home rule" extends this to cover every aspect of social, political, and economic life, except for foreign affairs and defense. Ideally, autonomists demand a federal state structure, and this strategy is really only open to communities with a secure regional base.

5. Separatism. This is the classic political goal of ethnonational self-determination. . . . In each case, the aim is to secede and form one's own sovereign state, with little or no connection with former rulers.

6. Irredentism. Here an ethnic community, whose members are divided and fragmented in separate states, seeks reunification and recovery of the "lost" or "unredeemed" territories occupied by its members. In general, this is only possible where the ethnic community has its membership living in adjoining states or areas. (1981, pp. 15–17)

Seeking independent rule, as in secessionist or separatist movements, poses the most serious threat to the state. Such movements challenge not only the legitimacy of the government or regime but also the integrity of the state itself.

It is reasonable to expect that factors shaping the intensity of nationalist movements will, in turn, influence the formation of secessionist goals. Territorial coterminality with lines of ethnic identification is a strong contributor, with distance from the ruling center adding to the potential for secessionist claims (Young 1975; Islam 1985; Pankhurst 1988). Timing seems to be important to the rise of such claims as well as to their success. Based on the experiences of several African countries, Young (1975) points out that time is conducive when polity in the parent state falls into disrepute, calling its legitimacy into question because of mismanagement, corruption, and discrimination. He also concludes that times of cataclysmic events in the lives of states offer opportunities for secessionist claims because of the fluidity these events engender, the options they open, and the push for choices to be made. Young cites other antecedents that provide a basis for solidarity and mobilization, such as regional differentials in concentration of wealth and representation in power positions, and at least the minimum political resources to make independent status possible even when economic sacrifice is required. To this list of contributing factors, Islam (1985) adds the magnitude of suffering, the impact of the secession of a region on the rest of the country, whether the seceding region represents a majority or a minority of the population, and the involvement of outside powers.

International relations—regional and global—also influence secessionist movements. The spread of the ideology of minority rights and self-determination plays a special role. In a comparative analysis Sigler (1983) concludes: " There is historical weight to the charge that minority rights is a guise for separatist sentiment" (p. 188). He maintains that the "concept of minority rights briefly blossomed under the minorities treaties system" that followed from the Treaty of Versailles. The system was to protect the rights of minorities in many countries, mostly in Europe, after World War I. It gave jurisdiction to the Permanent Court of International Justice, but litigations became protracted and difficult to adjudicate, thus severely limiting the court's role. It gave power to the Council of the League of Nations to intervene but did not guarantee that disciplinary actions could be carried out against states for infractions. Mutual reinforcement of the system of states as a basis for international relations restrained the various states from interfering in each other's internal affairs. "The collapse of the minorities treaties system . . . has encouraged minority separatist movements. . . . In the absence of a strong international system for the protection of minority rights, resort to separatist politics may have become more prevalent" (Sigler 1983, p. 190). This reinforces Smelser's ideas about structural conduciveness mentioned earlier.

There is historical weight to the charge that minority rights is a guise for separatist sentiment.

If the odds facing secessionists are great, those facing irredentists are much greater. By definition, irredentism involves multiple secessions, which means contending with the forces of more than one state. An exception is when an ethnic group in one state seeks to attach itself to a neighboring state that includes parts of the same group. This tactic is used by some secessionists to obtain external support (Young 1975).

Reactions of the State

Actions by the authorities and the means of control they employ are largely shaped by the objectives of nationalist movements and greatly affect their course. When perceived as threats to the stability of state and government, they are usually met with repression. However, nationalist movements that remain clandestine and limited under conditions of severe repression tend to gather momentum and erupt into open expression when a new regime reduces coercion. Recent events in the Soviet Union and other countries illustrate the point.

Repression is not the only means used by states in responding to threats of ethnonationalism. Some states, such as the People's Republic of China, adopt population redistribution policies aimed at diluting the coterminality of ethnicity with territory. Language policies in education are also used to increase homogenization. Central governments in some pluralist states adopt redistributive policies in regard to resources to assist economic development in lagging regions. Yugoslavia offers good examples of redistributive policies and their effects.

Other means in the state's arsenal are arrangements for power sharing in governance and mechanisms for conflict regulation. Nordlinger (1972) outlines six such mechanisms: (1) a stable governing coalition of political parties involving all major conflict groups; (2) proportional distribution of elective and appointive positions; (3) mutual veto by which government decisions must be acceptable to major conflict organizations; (4) purposive depoliticization in which leaders of conflict groups agree to keep government out of policy areas that impinge upon the various segments' values and interests; (5) regulation by compromise over conflictual issues; and (6) one group granting concessions to another as a way of managing conflicts. He also sees four motives for leaders to engage in conflict regulation: (1) external threats or pressure; (2) negative effects on the economic well-being of the groups involved; (3) aversion to risking violence and human suffering that might result from unregulated conflicts; and (4) the protection of leaders' own power positions.

Lijphart (1977) places equal emphasis on leaders "whose cooperative attitudes and behavior are needed to counteract the centrifugal tendencies inherent in plural societies" (p. 1). The forms he outlines for "consociational" democracies overlap in many ways with Nordlinger's mechanisms for conflict regulation. One important difference, however, is Lijphart's inclusion of "segmental autonomy," that is, federalism. Nordlinger specifically excluded federalism as a mechanism for regulating conflicts because he saw in it a recipe for a breakup of the state.

In conclusion, it can be said that the pervasiveness of nationalism should be self-evident. The socioeconomic, political, and other human costs are frequently staggering. As a major feature of social structure, ethnicity is of central theoretical importance. However, many (and often large) gaps in the state of knowledge exist, both in theory and in accumulated data. There are basically three shortcomings in the literature that account for this. First are conceptual and theoretical limitations, especially at the intermediate levels of abstraction that connect abstract explanatory schemes—of which a notable few exist—with concrete events. Second is that the preponderance of empirical work in this area is in the form of case studies that are mostly historical. They offer uniformity neither in concepts nor in evidence. The third problem with literature on ethnic nationalism is its fragmentation. A coherent picture must draw upon concepts and propositions from a number of traditions. And there are many overriding concepts with which to assemble frameworks to advance theory and to guide the collection of evidence. While they are difficult to plan and execute, there is compelling need for comparative studies to advance understanding of the underlying principles. Clear understanding of nationalism, and of the processes involved, is essential to evolving appropriate educational, policy, constitutional, and other legal means for accommodating cultural diversity.

[See also Ethnicity; Social Movements.]

BIBLIOGRAPHY

Connor, Walker 1972 "Nation-Building or Nation-Destroying?" *World Politics* 24:319–355.

——— 1978 "A Nation Is a Nation, Is a State, Is an Ethnic Group, Is a. . . ." *Ethnic and Racial Studies* 1, no. 4:377–400.

——— 1984 *The National Question in Marxist-Leninist Theory and Strategy.* Princeton, N.J.: Princeton University Press.

Deutsch, Karl W. 1984 *Nationalism and Social Communication.* Cambridge, Mass.: MIT Press.

Geertz, Clifford 1963 "The Integrative Revolution: Primordial Sentiments and Civil Politics in the New States." In Clifford Geertz, ed., *Old Societies and New States: The Quest for Modernity in Asia and Africa.* New York: The Free Press.

Gurr, Ted Robert 1970 *Why Men Rebel.* Princeton, NJ.: Princeton University Press.

Gusfield, Joseph R. 1970 "Introduction: A Definition of the Subject." In Joseph R. Gusfield, ed., *Protest, Reform, and Revolt: A Reader in Social Movements.* New York: Wiley.

Hechter, Michael 1986 "Theories of Ethnic Relations." In John F. Stack, Jr., ed., *The Primordial Challenge: Ethnicity in the Contemporary World.* New York: Greenwood Press.

Heraclides, Alexis 1990 "Secessionist Minorities and External Involvement." *International Organization* 44, no. 3 (Summer): 341–378.

Hermann, Margaret G. 1986 "Ingredients of Leadership." In Margaret G. Hermann, ed., *Political Psychology: Contemporary Problems and Issues.* San Francisco: Jossey-Bass.

Houseknecht, Sharon K. 1990 "The Role of Family and Kinship in Ethnic Nationalist Movements." Columbus: Mershon Center, Ohio State University. Mimeograph.

Huntington, Samual P. 1968 *Political Order in Changing Societies.* New Haven: Yale University Press.

Islam, Rafiqul 1985 "Secessionist Self-Determination: Some Lessons from Katanga, Biafra and Bangladesh." *Journal of Peace Research* 22, no. 3:211–221.

Jenkins, J. Craig 1983 "Resource Mobilization Theory and the Study of Social Movements." *Annual Review of Sociology* 9:527–553.

Kamenka, Eugene (ed.) 1973 *Nationalism, the Nature and Evolution of an Idea.* London: Edward Arnold.
Kohn, Hans 1955 *Nationalism.* Princeton, N.J.: D. Van Nostrand.
——— 1968 "Nationalism." In David L. Sills, ed., *International Encyclopedia of the Social Sciences,* vol. 11, Macmillan and Free Press.
Lasswell, Harold D. 1936 *Politics: Who Gets What, When, How.* New York: McGraw-Hill.
Lijphart, Arend 1977 *Democracy in Plural Societies: A Comparative Exploration.* New Haven: Yale University Press.
Linz, Juan J. 1978 "The Breakdown of Democratic Regimes: Crisis Breakdown and Reequilibrium." In Juan J. Linz and Alfred Stepan, eds., *The Breakdown of Democratic Regimes.* Baltimore: Johns Hopkins University Press.
McCarthy, John D., and Mayer N. Zald 1977 "Resource Mobilization and Social Movements: A Partial Theory." *American Journal of Sociology* 82:1212–1241.
Minogue, K. R. 1967 *Nationalism.* New York: Basic Books.
Nordlinger, Eric 1972 *Conflict Regulation in Divided Societies.* Cambridge, Mass.: Center for International Affairs, Harvard University.
Oberschall, A. 1973 *Social Conflict and Social Movements.* Englewood Cliffs, NJ.: Prentice-Hall.
Pankhurst, Jerry G. 1988 "Muslims in Communist Nations: The Cases of Albania, Bulgaria, Yugoslavia, and the Soviet Union." In Anson Shupe and Jeffery Hadden, eds., *The Politics of Religion and Social Change: Religion and Political Order,* vol. 2. New York: Paragon House.
Plamenatz, John P. 1973 "Two Types of Nationalism." In Eugene Kamenka, ed., *Nationalism, the Nature and Evolution of an Idea.* London: Edward Arnold.
Said, Abdul, and Luis Simmons 1976 *Ethnicity in the International Context.* New Brunswick, NJ.: Transaction Books.
Sanders, David 1981 *Patterns of Political Instability.* London: Macmillan.
Sigler, Jay A. 1983 *Minority Rights: A Comparative Analysis.* Westport, Conn.: Greenwood Press.
Smelser, Neal 1962 *Theory of Collective Behavior.* New York: Free Press.
Smith, Anthony D. 1976 "Introduction: The Formation of Nationalist Movements." In Anthony D. Smith, ed., *Nationalist Movements.* London: Macmillan.
——— 1981 *The Ethnic Revival.* Cambridge: Cambridge University Press.
Snyder, Louis L. 1984 *Macro-Nationalism: A History of the Pan-Movements.* Westport, Conn.: Greenwood Press.
Stack, John F., Jr. 1986 "Ethnic Mobilization in World Politics: The Primordial Perspective." In John F. Stack, Jr., ed., *The Primordial Challenge.* New York: Greenwood Press.
Symmons-Symonolewicz, Konstantin 1970 *Nationalist Movements: A Comparative View.* Meadville, Pa.: Maplewood Press.
Tilly, Charles 1978 *From Mobilization to Revolution.* Reading, Mass.: Addison-Wesley.
Williams, Robin M., Jr. 1947 *The Reduction of Intergroup Tensions.* New York: Social Science Research Council.
Young, M. Crawford 1975 "Nationalism and Separatism in Africa." In Martin Kilson, ed., *New States in the Modern World.* Cambridge, Mass.: Harvard University Press.

– SAAD Z. NAGI

NEW AGE MOVEMENT

The New Age movement is an international social movement that began in the late 1960s when Eastern religions became popular in the United States. It combined earlier metaphysical beliefs such as Swedenborgianism, mesmerism, transcendentalism, and theosophy. As expressed by Baba Ram Dass (born Richard Alpert), its first recognized national exponent, the New Age movement believes in the totality of the human body, mind, and spirit. The movement may be defined by its experience of transformation through rebirthing, meditation, possessing a crystal, or receiving a healing. Projecting from the concept of personal transformation, New Agers envision a new era that will witness a universal religion placing emphasis on mystical self-knowledge and belief in a pantheistic god as the ultimate unifying principle. The New Age movement is perhaps best known for its emphasis on holistic health, which emphasizes the need to treat patients as persons and offers alternative methods of curing, including chronobiological diet, naturopathy, vegetarianism, and a belief in the healing process of crystals and their vibrations, which restore the balance of bodily energy. New Age techniques include reflexology, which involves foot massage; acupuncture; herbalism; shiatsu, a form of massage; and Rolfing, a technique named after Ida P. Rolf, the originator of structural integration, in which deep massage aims to create a structurally well-balanced human being. Music is also used as therapy and as a form of meditation. While the term "New Age music" in the mid-1990s was a marketing slogan that included almost any type of music, true New Age music carries no message and has no specific form because its major use is as background for meditation.

– JOHN J. BYRNE

OCCUPATIONAL AND CAREER MOBILITY

Occupational and career mobility in adulthood is often referred to as intragenerational social mobility. It involves change in an individual's position in the labor market over the adult life course. Change is studied with respect to both type of work and the rewards derived from work. The term *career* refers to an individual's job history. Empirical *regularity* in the careers of individuals in the labor force defines what we call a "career line" or "job trajectory," since a work history common to a portion of the labor force reflects the existence of structurally determined linkages among jobs in the economy. Jobs are located in particular firms, whereas occupations and industries encompass jobs in many firms. An individual may remain in the same occupation or industry but change firms and jobs within the same firm any number of times. Since the process of job change does not necessarily involve a change of occupation or industry, but a change of occupation or industry always involves a job change, the process of job change provides a more detailed account of career movement. Changes in the rewards derived from work usually accompany job changes but can also occur during the course of tenure in a job.

Occupational and career mobility in adulthood is often referred to as intragenerational social mobility.

Research on intragenerational mobility has focused on the labor force as a whole and on employees in particular occupations and firms. Research on the labor force as a whole has usually considered change in occupation and industry, as measured for detailed categories or more aggregated groupings that define broad occupational and industrial groups. It has also considered change in the rewards derived from work, focusing primarily on occupational prestige and earnings. Research on particular occupations and firms has usually focused on job status and authority changes within organizational hierarchies and on changes in work rewards.

Early work on intragenerational mobility involved the mathematical modeling of transition probabilities, usually among a few, highly aggregated categories (see Mayer 1972 for a review). This work used Markov models and semi-Markov models to analyze transition probabilities in a sequence under the assumption that the job category an individual will occupy in the future depends only on the job category occupied in the present and not on job categories occupied previously. Although there is empirical support for this assumption in some studies (see, e.g., White 1970; March and March 1977), it has not been found to be broadly applicable. In semi-Markov models transition probabilities are permitted to vary with time and for subgroups of the population. These models capture declines in mobility with age or duration of stay and allow for the fact that some individuals are more likely to move than others. There is evidence to indicate that mobility is an exponentially declining function of time (Mayer 1972) and that some individuals become "movers" while others become "stayers" (Blumen, Kogan, and McCarthy 1955).

Later analyses have considered more refined models of job change, focusing on job shifts as elementary acts in the mobility process. Job shifts also occur at a decreasing rate with time, and the rate of mobility varies with characteristics of the individual, the job, and the environment (Sørensen 1975b; Felmlee 1982; Rosenbaum 1984). Change in the rewards derived from work usually accompanies a job shift (Sørensen 1974, 1975a; Rosenbaum 1984) but may also occur during the course of a job. For the labor force as a whole, occupational prestige and earnings increase over the adult working life. The shape of these trajectories tends to be concave downward—with a rise early in the career, a plateau during the middle years, and a slight decline as the end of the work career approaches. Status and earnings trajectories have the same form, but the former is flatter (Mincer 1974; Rosenfeld 1980). There is also variation in the shape of these trajectories for those in different career lines (Spilerman 1986).

Given the heterogeneity of career lines and the important role that age, or duration since career entry, plays in shaping career lines, there have been attempts to study the path of careers in recent years. For example, mobility not only declines sharply with age, but job changes that occur later in an individual's work life tend to involve jobs requiring skills that are more similar than those that occur earlier in the work life (Spenner, Otto, and Call 1982). There is also evidence that early career experiences have an important effect on later career outcomes. This evidence indicates not only that those entering *different* career lines, who receive different rewards at career entry, can expect different career outcomes (Sewell and Hauser 1975; Marini 1980; Spenner, Otto, and Call 1982), but also that early experiences *within* a career line can condition subsequent progression and the level of reward attained relative to others who enter the same career line (Rosenbaum 1984). The career lines most often studied have been trajectories within institutional structures, but there have also been attempts to describe career lines that cross institutional boundaries (Spilerman 1977; Spenner, Otto, and Call 1982).

Labor Market Structure

The concept of "career line" or "job trajectory" derives from the view that the labor market is structured in a way that makes some types of job changes more likely than others. Early work on career mobility ignored this structural differentiation, estimating the overall (linear) relationship between the status and earnings of an individual's first job and the status and earnings of a job held later in the career (Blau and Duncan 1967; Coleman et al. 1972; Jencks et al. 1972; Sewell and Hauser 1975; Marini 1980). Jobs resembling each other in status, pay, and working conditions, however, are sometimes part of a career line and sometimes not, and even if part of a career line can be attached to *different* career lines. Jobs providing similar current rewards may therefore not offer the same prospects for future mobility.

Since career lines are rooted in labor market structure, their existence demonstrates that intragenerational mobility is influenced by the structure of the labor market, as well as the demography of the labor force and individual characteristics that affect movement within segments of the labor market. If jobs have entry requirements and confer rewards, the structure of jobs plays a critical role in establishing the link between the attributes of individuals and work rewards. Recognition that the labor market is structured in a way that produces segmentation among career lines has led to attempts not only to describe career lines but to identify the forces shaping them.

During the 1940s and 1950s, institutional economists called for an understanding of well-defined systems of jobs and firms, drawing a distinction between internal and external labor markets. For example, Dunlop (1957) argued that within a firm there are groups of jobs, or "job clusters," each of which is linked together by technology, the administrative organization of the production process, and the social customs of the work community. A job cluster usually contains one or more key jobs and a group of associated jobs, and the wage rates for the key jobs mediate the effects of labor market influences, including union and government wage policies, and forces in the market for products on the wage structure of the firm. The distinction between internal and external labor markets was later reintroduced by Doeringer and Piore (1971), who discussed what they called a "mobility cluster." The central idea was that administrative rules and procedures tend to set up separate markets for those already hired (an internal labor market) and those seeking employment (an external labor market). A firm hires workers from the outside labor market into "entry jobs," and other jobs are filled internally as workers progress on well-defined career ladders by acquiring job-related skills, many of which are firm-specific. Thus, firms make investments in individuals, and these investments segment the work force with respect to advancement opportunity.

Administrative rules and procedures tend to set up separate markets for those already hired (an internal labor market) and those seeking employment (an external labor market).

The concept of the internal labor market was developed further in what was first called *dual* and then *segmented* labor market theory (Gordon 1972; Kalleberg and Sørensen 1979). This theory draws a distinction between primary and secondary jobs, arguing that the internal labor market is only one kind of work setting. *Primary* jobs emphasize long-term attachment between workers and firms and offer built-in career ladders and promotion opportunities, whereas *secondary* jobs do not offer these advantages. The distinction between primary and secondary jobs may occur within the same firm or between firms, since primary jobs are considered more likely to be found in oligopolistic, unionized industries, and secondary jobs in competitive industries.

Dual and other segmented labor market theories came under attack as being too crude to meaningfully characterize the multiple dimensions on which labor markets vary. Attempts to measure labor market segmentation by crude topologies, including industrial and occupational categories, were also criticized (Baron and Bielby 1980; Hodson and Kaufman 1982). Because there is extensive heterogeneity within industrial and occupational categories, and there is no way to link them to the kinds of job clusters hypothesized to exist, more disaggregated analyses of jobs and firms were argued to be needed. Many subsequent analyses have focused on particular bureaucracies or firms.

Attempting to develop a systematic conceptual scheme for studying labor market segmentation, Althauser and Kalleberg (1981 p. 130) argued that "the concept of an internal labor market should include any cluster of jobs, regardless of occupational titles, or employing organizations, that have three basic structural features: (a) a job ladder, with (b) entry only at the bottom, and (c) movement up this ladder, which is associated with a progressive development of knowledge and skill." Based on four possible pairings of type of control and prospects for advancement, they differentiated four types of labor market structures: (1) firm internal labor markets, which are internal labor markets controlled by firms; (2) occupational internal labor markets, which are internal labor markets controlled by occupational incumbents; (3) firm labor markets, which provide firm-specific security without advancement prospects; and (4) occupational labor markets, which provide occupational security without advancement prospects. Within an occupation or firm, there may be multiple job ladders that vary in length. Advancement prospects depend on the length of job ladders and the interconnections between them (Rosenbaum 1984; Baron, Davis-Blake, and Biebly 1986; DiPrete 1989). In an analysis of the U.S. federal civil service, for instance, DiPrete (1989) found a two-tiered job ladder system for clerical and administrative work.

Although there is general agreement that the technical character of work influences organizational development, existing variation in personnel structures, especially cross-nationally, indicates that the technical character of work alone does not determine job ladders and career lines. These are affected by the historical circumstances surrounding an organization's founding, including the gender, racial, and ethnic composition of the work force, market conditions that affect the rate of employment growth, and the negotiating strength of various bargaining units. A number of specific explanations have been advanced for the emergence of distinct labor market segments. Becker (1964) noted that when workers receive firm-specific training, it is in the interest of employers to bind them to the firm with promises of promotion, salary increases, and employment security. A related explanation that has received substantial empirical support is that internal labor markets result from employers' needs for renewable supplies of otherwise scarce, highly skilled workers. This explanation is linked to explanations emphasizing firm-specific skills and on-the-job training, since firm-specific skills are, by definition, not available on the external market and on-the-job training often produces firm-specific skills or skills that are scarce on the external market. Another explanation, offered by Bulow and Summers (1986), is that job hierarchies offering promotion prospects and wage increases are an important means of motivating workers when individual performance is not easily monitored.

The emergence and spread of internal labor markets has also been seen as related to the development of personnel departments, formalized rules, and the rise of bureaucratic control. There is some empirical support for this view, but at least some internal labor markets preceded the emergence of these bureaucratic control systems and rules (Althauser 1989). Spilerman (1986) has noted that workers have an interest in barring lateral entry and in having high-level positions filled through promotion. Workers may also wish to limit employer discretion by having decisions about promotion and layoff tied to seniority. These worker interests cause labor unions to work to create more widespread job hierarchies and promotion. Because firms characterized by high profit levels, oligopolistic pricing, and large organizational size can better afford to create internal labor markets, these firms have been argued to be more likely to do so; however, there is evidence that internal labor markets are not merely a derivative feature of core-economy organization (Althauser 1989).

Because mobility depends on the availability of positions, the shape of organizational hierarchies constrains the probability of career advancement. Most organizational hierarchies are pyramidal, with many more low-level than high-level positions. The average employee's advancement therefore must slow down over time. Aggregate age-promotion curves appear to be described by an exponential-decline function where the highest promotion changes occur at the outset, declines are a fixed proportion of an individual's current chances, and promotion chances become increasingly rare but not impossible. In short, promotion favors youth, declines gradually, but does not disappear for older workers. In keeping with human capital theory, there may also be chances for an increase in promotion during the initial career years, when most of the on-the-job training occurs.

Career lines not only involve substantial movement between job ladders within firms but often cross firm and industry boundaries rather than remaining within them. For example, it has been estimated that only somewhat over a quarter of U.S. workers are continuously employed by the same employer for twenty years or more (Hall 1982). In some careers, such as the salaried professions, crafts, and "secondary" labor market positions, firm and industry are not a locus of career line structure. Nevertheless, moves between firms and industries often occur between related positions so that labor market segmentation emerges even without institutional barriers.

Because the availability of vacancies in organizational hierarchies affects career advancement, promotion is affected by demographic factors such as cohort size and the rate of exit from positions (Stewman and Konda 1983). It is also affected by organizational growth and contraction that result in the creation and termination of jobs. This change in the actual structure of jobs occurs in response to social and economic influences, including technological development.

Worker Characteristics

Given the structure of the labor market, particularly the local labor market where most job search occurs, entry into a career line is affected by worker characteristics, such as job-related credentials (e.g., education, intelligence, physical attributes), job preferences, and access to resources (e.g., information, material support, sponsorship by influential others). In some career lines worker characteristics at entry may also influence career progression, whereas in others such characteristics may have little effect after access to a career line is obtained. If worker characteristics at entry continue to have an effect, they may do so in part because they influence subsequent on-the-job training and performance.

Promotion is affected by demographic factors such as cohort size and the rate of exit from positions.

Human capital theory has been advanced by economists to explain change in work rewards. In human capital theory, workers are seen as rational actors who make investments in their productive capacities to maximize lifetime income (Becker 1964; Mincen 1974). The investments usually studied are education and on-the-job training, although the theory applies to other investments, such as effort, job search, geographic mobility, and health. It is assumed that labor markets offer open opportunity and that earnings growth is a function of how hard individuals work and the ability, education, and training they possess. Individuals can increase their productivity not only through formal education but by learning on the job. On-the-job training occurs in formal training programs provided by employers or as a result of informal instruction by supervisors and coworkers and simply by doing the job. Time away from the job, in contrast, can lead to skill depreciation. Because investments in education and training are costly, workers concentrate their investments in the early part of their careers, sacrificing immediate earnings for better long-term career prospects.

Although worker qualifications that may affect productivity are associated with advancement, these associations are consistent with explanations other than that afforded by human capital theory. As many critics have pointed out, the assumption that worker characteristics such as formal education, labor market experience, and interruptions in employment reflect differences in productivity has not been adequately tested. These variables are assumed to reflect productivity, but they may reflect other influences. For instance, formal education may be used by employers as a credential for screening workers and may affect wages because it affects access to jobs (Spence 1974). Labor market experience may affect wages because it is a proxy for seniority so that wages rise with seniority and job tenure regardless of productivity. For women, labor market experience may be an outcome rather than a determinant of career mobility if entry into career lines offering little opportunity for advancement affects labor force participation.

Although information on the actual productivity of workers is difficult to obtain, evidence on the relationships of worker characteristics such as formal education and labor market experience to productivity within occupations suggests that although these variables have some bearing on productivity, their effects on career advancement are largely independent of productivity (Horowitz and Sherman 1980; Medoff and Abraham 1980, 1981; Maranto and Rodgers 1984). Moreover, much variability is seen across occupations and work contexts in the extent to which education and work experience affect either productivity or earnings (Horowitz and Sherman 1980; Spilerman 1986). Evidence also contradicts the "tradeoff hypothesis"—that individuals sacrifice earnings at the beginning of their careers for better long-term career prospects. Individuals with lower earnings early in their careers actually have lower rather than higher job status and earnings later.

Recently, new explanations of the relationships of education and experience to career advancement have been surfacing. Some economists now attribute the relationship between experience and earnings to the desire of employers, especially those who make large investments in screening and training employees, to retain workers and motivate high performance over time (Lazear 1981; Lazear and Rosen 1981; Bulow and Summers 1986). Promotions and wage increases are seen as a means of eliciting effort from workers when the monitoring of their efforts and outputs is prohibitively expensive. These new explanations deviate from the view that labor is paid its marginal product in each short period, assuming that workers are paid their marginal product over the life cycle or in some cases in excess of their marginal product. So far, none of these explanations has an empirical basis, and, as single-factor explanations, they are unlikely to account for the diverse compensation schemes observed across occupations and work settings (Talbert and Bose 1977; Spilerman 1986).

Sociologists view the relationships of education and experience to career advancement as influenced primarily by the organizational, and even the broader societal, context in which the administrative arrangements that govern salary advancement and promotions arise. Spilerman (1986) has suggested that education and experience bear weaker relationships to earnings and promotion when organizational rules rigidly prescribe the temporal paths of earnings and occupational advancement. These rigid schedules are usually found in workplaces where the majority of workers are engaged in a very few career lines, or where multiple career lines exist, but there is little opportunity for transferring among them. Such schedules often result from unionization, since labor unions seek to standardize work arrangements. Even the effects of education and experience that exist under this type of personnel system vary across cities in ways suggesting an influence of general societal beliefs that educated and experienced workers should be paid more. Because such beliefs do not specify how much more, compensation schedules vary widely. Education and experience appear to bear stronger relationships to earnings in large nonunionized organizations that encompass many occupational specialties. However, even in these organizations, societal notions of equity and custom may affect wage structures. In Japan, for example, both seniority and family size are major determinants of salary in large companies (Dore 1973).

Sociological accounts differ from economic explanations in recognizing that the rewards of work derive from job occupancy and that a relatively enduring structure of jobs determines the relationships of individual effort, ability, and performance to work rewards. In the sociological view, jobs are assigned wage rates via processes operating at the societal and organizational levels, and the mechanisms that match individuals to jobs produce associations between individual effort, ability, and training, on the one hand, and work rewards, on the other. Jobs differ in the routes by which they are entered and in the extent to which performance can affect work rewards.

Within the organizational hierarchies of firms and occupations, patterned relationships among jobs produce job ladders and career lines composed of multiple job ladders. To the extent that upward mobility is possible and the shape of the hierarchy is pyramidal, workers entering a career line are in competition with others at the same level for advancement to the next highest level. Because jobs at the next level are filled from those occupying positions in the level below, entry to a job ladder and performance at each step on the ladder affect ultimate career attainments. Rosenbaum (1984) describes the process by which a cohort of employees is progressively differentiated throughout their careers in a series of implicit competitions as being like a tournament. Selections among the members of a cohort occur continually as careers unfold, and each selection affects the opportunity to advance further. Over time, career histories come to differ in the timing and occurrence of advancement, and factors affecting performance and selection early in the career have more important effects because more of the future remains to be determined.

What influences advancement is not the attributes of individuals per se, but their attributes in relation to organizational positions. Organizations define the criteria by which ability is identified and to the extent that ability is not tied to those criteria, it will not be recognized and rewarded. If individuals of limited ability are able by chance or other more calculated means to meet the criteria by which ability is identified, they will be assumed to have ability by an inference process in which the direction of causality is reversed. An important consequence of this system is that factors affecting access to positions, of which ability is only one, and factors affecting performance in accordance with organizationally recognized criteria, including the willingness to conform to organizational goals and practices, have an important influence on long-term career outcomes.

Job structure mediates the relationship of characteristics such as gender, race, and ethnicity to job rewards.

Given the importance of the structure of jobs in mediating the relationship between individual attributes such as education and experience and job rewards, it is not surprising that these attributes have little direct effect on rewards within job status categories. However, they have an important effect on careers via their influence on access to positions in the structure of jobs. Education is a major determinant of access to job ladders and career lines, and movement within these produces relationships between education and experience and work rewards. The organizational hierarchies to which college graduates, especially those from preferred colleges, have access increase the effects of college on career attainments over time. These hierarchies are moved through via experience. The job structure also mediates the relationship of ascriptive characteristics such as gender, race, and ethnicity to job rewards, where these characteristics become a basis for the differentiation of job ladders and career lines, as well as a basis for access to the jobs within them (Spilerman 1977; DiPrete 1989; Marini 1989).

Selection by Employers

Movement within a career line is affected not only by the characteristics of workers but by the characteristics and actions of those empowered by employers to make hiring and promotion decisions. Evaluation of performance and ability is usually based on incomplete information. In many jobs performance is difficult to assess, and ability is even harder to assess because it is inferred from performance. In addition, human perceptive capabilities are limited and variable. As a result, employers tend to rely on readily available information, or "signals," such as the amount of education attained, where it is attained, the amount and types of prior job experience, observable personal attributes, and evidence of past performance such as the rate of career advancement and prior job status and earnings. The criteria on which individuals are evaluated are therefore often superficial, and having the resources (i.e., money, knowledge, and skill) to identify the way the evaluation process works and acquire an appropriate set of signals plays an important role in career advancement. Because of the difficulty of obtaining information, employers are also susceptible to employee attempts to supply and manipulate information about themselves as well as others.

Another influence on the evaluation of ability and performance is attitudes and beliefs previously acquired by those with decision-making authority. Information is unconsciously filtered and interpreted through that cognitive lens. The effect of prior attitudes and beliefs is evident in the prejudice and stereotyping triggered by ascriptive characteristics such as gender, race, and ethnicity (Hamilton 1981; Marini 1989), which have been a focus of theories of discrimination in the labor market (see, e.g., Blau 1984).

In addition to the difficulties that arise in assessing performance and ability, personal relationships and political coalitions influence mobility. There is growing evidence that personal contacts and relationships constitute important sources of information and influence in gaining access to jobs (Granovetter 1984). An employee's position in workplace political coalitions can also affect career advancement.

[See also Labor Force; Professions; Work and Occupations.]

BIBLIOGRAPHY

Althauser, Robert P. 1989 "Internal Labor Markets." *Annual Review of Sociology* 15:143–161.

———, and Arne L. Kalleberg 1981 "Firms, Occupations and the Structure of Labor Markets: A Conceptual Analysis." In I. Berg, ed., *Sociological Perspectives on Labor Markets.* New York: Academic.

Baron, James N., and William T. Bielby 1980 "Bringing the Firms Back In: Stratification, Segmentation, and the Organization of Work." *American Sociological Review* 45:737–765.

Baron, James N., Alison Davis-Blake, and William T. Biebly 1986 "The Structure of Opportunity: How Promotion Ladders Vary within and among Organizations." *Administrative Science Quarterly* 31:248–273.

Becker, Gary S. 1964 *Human Capital.* New York: National Bureau of Economic Research.

Blau, Francine D. 1984 "Discrimination against Women: Theory and Evidence." In W. Darity, Jr., ed., *Labor Economics: Modern Views.* Boston: Kluwer-Nijhoff.

Blau, Peter M., and Otis Dudly Duncan 1967 *The American Occupational Structure.* New York: Wiley.

Blumen, Isadore, M. Kogan, and P. J. McCarthy 1955 *The Industrial Mobility of Labor as a Probability Process. Cornell Studies in Industrial and Labor Relations,* vol. 6. Ithaca: New York State School of Industrial and Labor Relations, Cornell University.

Bulow, J. I., and Larry H. Summers 1986 "A Theory of Dual Labor Markets with Application to Industrial Policy, Discrimination, and Keynesian Unemployment." *Journal of Labor Economics* 4:376–414.

Coleman, James S., Zahava D. Blum, Aage B. Sørensen, and Peter H. Rossi 1972 "White and Black Careers during the First Decade of Labor Force Experience. I. Occupational Status." *Social Science Research* 1:243–270.

DiPrete, Thomas A. 1989 *The Bureaucratic Labor Market.* New York: Plenum.

Doeringer, Peter B., and M. J. Plore 1971 *Internal Labor Markets and Manpower Analysis.* Lexington, Mass.: Heath.

Dore, Ronald P. 1973 *British Factory—Japanese Factory.* Berkeley: University of California Press.

Dunlop, John 1957 "The Task of Contemporary Wage Theory." In G. W. Taylor and F. C. Pierson, eds., *New Concepts in Wage Determination.* New York: McGraw-Hill.

Felmlee, Diane H. 1982 "Women's Job Mobility Processes within and between Employers." *American Journal of Sociology* 80:44–57.

Gordon, David M. 1972 *Theories of Poverty and Underemployment.* Lexington, Mass.: Heath.

Granovetter, Mark 1984 *Getting a Job: A Study of Contacts and Careers.* Cambridge, Mass.: Harvard University Press.

Hall, Robert E. 1982 "The Importance of Lifetime Jobs in the U.S. Economy." *American Economic Review* 72:716–724.

Hamilton, David L. 1981 *Cognitive Processes in Stereotyping and Intergroup Behavior.* Hillsdale, N.J.: Erlbaum.

Hodson, Randy, and Robert Kaufman 1982 "Economic Dualism: A Critical Review." *American Sociological Review* 47:727–739.

Horowitz, Stanley A., and Allan Sherman 1980 "A Direct Measure of the Relationship between Human Capital and Productivity." *Journal of Human Resources* 15:67–76.

Jencks, Christopher, M. Smith, H. Ackland, M. Bane, D. Cohen, H. Gintis, B. Heyns, and S. Michelson 1972 *Inequality: A Reassessment of the Effect of Family and Schooling in America.* New York: Basic Books.

Kalleberg, Arne, and Aage B. Sørensen 1979 "The Sociology of Labor Markets." *Annual Review of Sociology* 5:351–379.

Lazear, Edward P. 1981 "Agency, Earnings Profiles, Productivity, and Hours Restrictions." *American Economic Review* 71:606–620.

———, and S. Rosen 1981 "Rank-order Tournaments as Optimum Labor Contracts." *Journal of Political Economy* 89:841–864.

Maranto, Cheryl L., and Robert C. Rodgers 1984 "Does Work Experience Increase Productivity? A Test of the On-the-job Training Hypothesis." *Journal of Human Resources* 19:341–357.

March, James C., and James G. March 1977 "Almost Random Careers: The Wisconsin School of Superintendency, 1940–1972." *Administrative Science Quarterly* 22:377–409.

Marini, Margaret Mooney 1980 "Sex Differences in the Process of Occupational Attainment: A Closer Look." *Social Science Research* 9:307–361.

——— 1989 "Sex Differences in Earnings in the United States." *Annual Review of Sociology* 15:343–380.

Mayer, Thomas 1972 "Models in Intragenerational Mobility." In J. Berger, M. Zelditch, Jr., and B. Anderson, eds., *Sociological Theories in Progress,* vol. 2. Boston: Houghton Mifflin.

Medoff, James L., and Katherine G. Abraham 1980 "Experience, Performance, and Earnings." *Quarterly Journal of Economy* 95:703–736.

——— 1981 "Are Those Paid More Really More Productive? The Case of Experience." *Journal of Human Resources* 16:186–216.

Mincer, Jacob 1974 *Schooling, Experience, and Earnings.* New York: National Bureau of Economic Research.

Rosenbaum, James E. 1984 *Career Mobility in a Corporate Hierarchy.* New York: Academic.

Rosenfeld, Rachel A. 1980 "Race and Sex Differences in Career Dynamics." *American Sociological Review* 45:583–609.

Sewell, William H. and Robert M. Hauser 1975 *Education, Occupation, and Earnings.* New York: Academic.

Sørensen, Aage B. 1974 "A Model for Occupational Careers." *American Journal of Sociology* 80:44–57.

——— 1975a "Growth in Occupational Achievement: Social Mobility or Investment in Human Capital." In K. L. Land and S. Spilerman, eds., *Social Indicator Models.* New York: Russell Sage Foundation.

——— 1975b "The Structure of Intragenerational Mobility." *American Sociological Review* 40:456–471.

Spence, Michael A. 1974 *Market Signaling.* Cambridge: Harvard University Press.

Spenner, Kenneth I., Luther B. Otto, and Vaughn R. A. Call 1982 *Career Lines and Careers.* Lexington, Mass.: Lexington Books.

Spilerman, Seymour 1977 "Careers, Labor Market Structure, and Socioeconomic Achievement." *American Journal of Sociology* 83:551–593.

——— 1986 "Organizational Rules and the Features of Work Careers." *Research in Social Stratification and Mobility* 5:41–102.

Stewman, Shelby, and S. L. Konda 1983 "Careers and Organizational Labor Markets: Demographic Models of Organizational Behavior." *American Journal of Sociology* 88:637–685.

Stiglitz, Joseph E. 1973 "Approaches to the Economics of Discrimination." *American Economic Review* 63:287–295.

Talbert, Joan, and Christine E. Bose 1977 "Wage Attainment Processes: The Retail Clerk Case." *American Journal of Sociology* 83:403–424.

White, Harrison C. 1970 *Chains of Opportunity.* Cambridge: Harvard University Press.

– MARGARET MOONEY MARINI

ORGANIZED CRIME

Organized crime is considered one of the most serious forms of crime for two reasons: (1) It is so often lucrative and successful; and (2) it is so difficult to counteract. In the broadest terms, organized crime can be viewed as any form of group conduct designed to take advantage of criminal opportunities, whether on a one-time or a recurring basis. More commonly, the label *organized crime* has more restricted usage.

Having coconspirators increases the visibility of criminal conduct, the risks of apprehension, and, upon apprehension, the risk of betrayal.

It should not be a surprise to find criminals associating for the purpose of committing crime. The achievement of goals through cooperative efforts is a common element of contemporary life. Association with other criminals creates an interesting dilemma for the individual criminal. Having coconspirators increases the visibility of criminal conduct, the risks of apprehension, and, upon apprehension, the risk of betrayal. On the other hand, some types of criminal opportunities can be exploited only through group behavior. Offenders who fail to join with others may thereby limit their rewards from criminal conduct. For organized crime to persist, it must function both to overcome the risks of associating with others and result in positive benefits and increased rewards for those who participate.

No one knows how much organized crime is committed every year. Rather than being measured in numbers of events, the significance of organized crime is generally recorded in the dollar volume of activities. Some have argued that revenue estimates for organized crime are advanced more in the interest of drama than of accuracy, but the estimates are nonetheless staggering. For example, annual revenue from the sale of drugs is placed in the $40 to $60 billion range, and annual revenue from illicit gambling operations, at $20 to $40 billion.

Organized crime is unlikely to be reflected in official crime statistics for three reasons: first, crime statistics record information about individual criminal events rather than about the individuals or groups committing them; second, many of the activities of organized crime groups involve so-called victimless crimes where no report of a crime is made; and third, persons who are victimized by organized crime groups may be unlikely or unwilling to come forward and report their victimization.

Organized crime is best understood by examining the nature of ongoing criminal organizations, their activities, and societal response to the behavior of these organizations. A secondary use of the term, referring to criminal support systems that aid all offenders, is also briefly noted.

Ongoing Criminal Organizations

Organized crime usually refers to the activities of stable groups or gangs that commit crimes on an ongoing basis. While not all group crime is properly labeled "organized crime," there exists no standard definition of the term. Instead, the phenomenon has been variously described as "a cancerous growth on American society" (Andreoli 1976, p. 21); "one of the queer ladders of social mobility" (Bell 1970, p. 166); "a society that seeks to operate outside the control of the American people and its governments" (President's Commission 1967, p. 1); and "the product of a self-perpetuating criminal conspiracy to wring exorbitant profits from our society by any means" (Salerno and Tompkins 1969, p. 303).

Scholars have identified the following as elements that characterize all groups labeled as organized crime: a hierarchical organizational structure, dominated by a strong leader; a territorial imperative, exhibited in attempts to monopolize all lucrative criminal opportunities within a geographic area; a predilection to violence both to enforce internal norms and to advance economic objectives; and a desire to influence the social response to criminal conduct, as demonstrated in significant investments in public corruption. Cressey (1969) identified these latter two characteristics—the "element of enforcement" and the "element of corruption"—as the essential features of organized crime.

In the United States, organized crime has been personified in ethnically based criminal organizations and, in particular, the twenty-four fictive "families" believed to make up the American Mafia. Joseph Valachi, in testimony before the United States Senate in 1963, revealed a sordid and secret world in which he claimed these criminal organizations operated and prospered.

While some scholars pointed to inconsistencies in Valachi's statements, and other criminals would later question the depth of his experience and knowledge, his testimony spawned a series of books and movies that placed Italian criminal organizations in the forefront of the public's consciousness with respect to organized crime.

The term *mafia* (with either upper- or lower-case letters) is used variously to apply to a secret criminal organization or to a life-style and philosophy that developed in sixteenth- and seventeenth-century southern Italy and Sicily in opposition to a series of foreign rulers who dominated the area. The life-style combines the idea of manliness in the face of adversity with an antagonism to authority and a closeness and reliance on family and clan.

Smith (1975) argues that applying the "mafia" label to Italian criminal organizations in the United States was both fateful and calculated. It was fateful because it imbued these organizations with international connections that there was little evidence they had. This may in turn have helped these organizations consolidate and solidify their power, in competition with other ethnic (primarily Irish) criminal organizations that were actually more prevalent in the early decades of the twentieth century. Use of the label was calculated in that it gave Italian criminal organizations a subversive and sinister character designed to ensure public support for extraordinary law enforcement efforts to eradicate these groups.

Overlooked in much of the attention paid to Mafia "families" was the fact that bands of brigands and smugglers, displaying many of the same organizational attributes as "mafia," were well established in Elizabethan England; that criminal organizations linked to a life-style based on the primacy of male-dominated families and the concept of dignity and manliness are common in Central and Latin America; and that criminal societies and associations have been successful vehicles for social mobility in many cultures, for example, the Chinese Triads or the Japanese Yakuza.

Also overlooked were some significant changes occurring during the late 1960s and early 1970s in the major cities in which the Mafia "families" were believed to operate. These changes signaled what Ianni (1974) called "ethnic succession" in organized crime: That is, as the populations of inner cities came to be dominated by racial minorities, so too were the ranks of those running criminal organizations. This gave rise to law enforcement characterizations of such groups as the "Mexican Mafia" or the "Black Mafia," not because of their associations with Mafia "families" but as a shorthand way of communicating their organizational style and methods of operating.

By the 1980s, the term *organized crime* had lost its ethnic distinction. Instead, the label started being applied to many more criminal associations, from motorcycle and prison gangs to terrorist groups to some juvenile gangs. Observed in all these groups were the organizational characteristics that had first been identified as distinctive of Mafia "families."

Activities of Organized Crime Groups

The activities in which organized crime groups are involved constitute another distinctive hallmark. Broadly defined, the term *organized crime* can be used to describe the activities of a band of pickpockets, a gang of train robbers, or a cartel of drug smugglers. Practically speaking, however, use of the term is somewhat more restrictive.

Commentators, scholars, and lawmakers generally use the term when referring to criminal conspiracies of an entrepreneurial nature—in particular, enterprises focused in black-market goods and services. Black markets are those in which contraband or illegal goods and services are exchanged. In this more restrictive use of the term, the activities of drug smugglers would be included while the conduct of pickpockets or train robbers would not.

These latter groups, and others involved in various forms of theft and extortion, commit what are best termed *predatory crimes.* As such, they are generally regarded as social pariahs. Society and the forces of social control will actively seek to root out such groups and bring them to justice. This is despite the fact that such groups may display a highly evolved organizational structure, a strong sense of territory, and a tendency toward violence.

Contrast this with groups engaged in entrepreneurial conduct. These groups supply the society with goods and services that are illegal but in demand. While some in society may still view these criminals as social pariahs, many in society will not. Instead, the criminal group establishes patron-business relationships with criminal and noncriminal clients alike. The forces of social control are not so bent on eradicating these groups because of the widespread social support they garner. This support, when added to the profits reaped as criminal entrepreneurs, creates both the means and the conditions for corruption.

If any one activity can be considered the incubator for organized crime in the United States, it would be the distribution and sale of illegal alcohol during Prohibition. The period of Prohibition (1920–1933) took a widely used and highly desired commodity and made it illegal; it also created the opportunity for a number of predatory criminal gangs to evolve as entrepreneurs. These entrepreneurs then developed important client

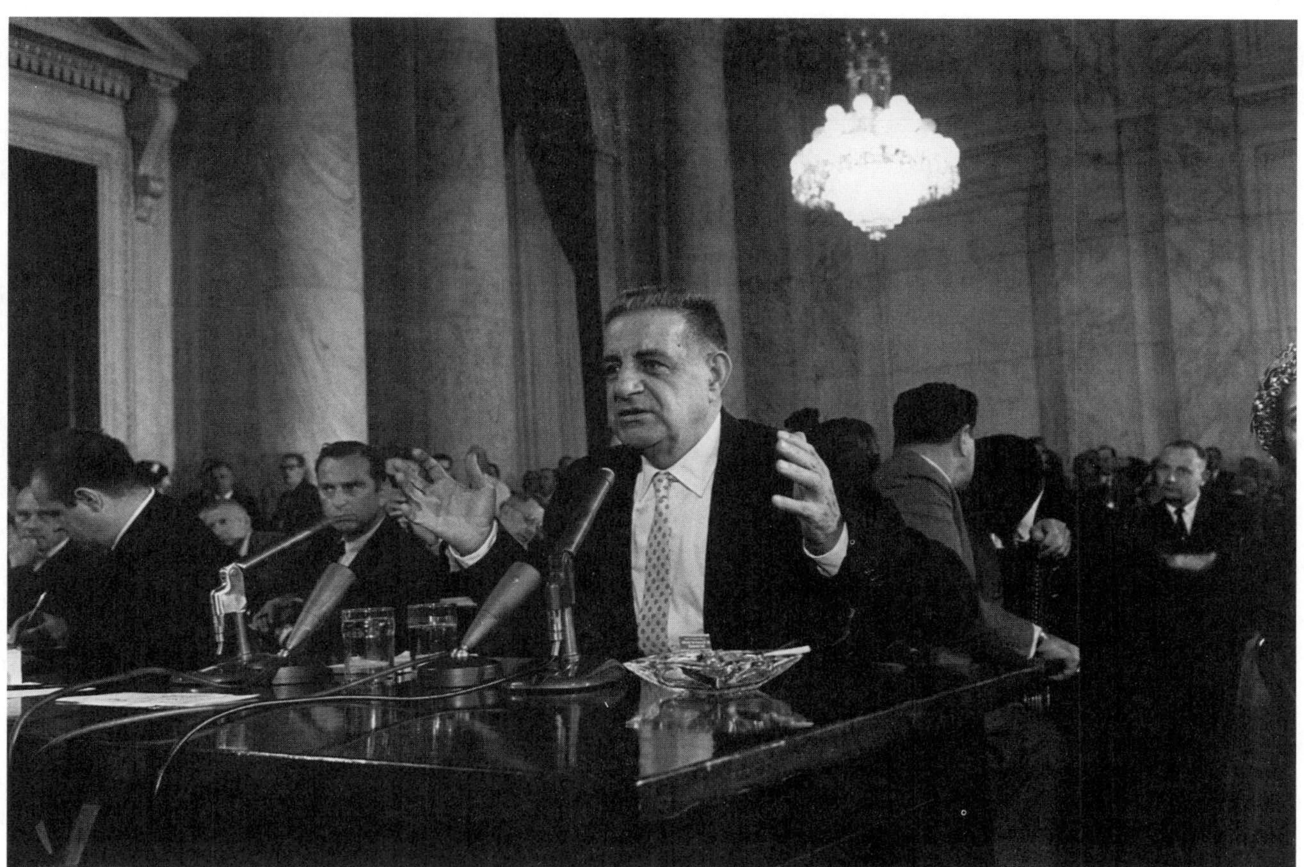

Joseph Valachi, a former Mafia member, testified before the United States Senate in 1963, revealing a significant amount of information about organized crime in the United States. (Library of Congress/Corbis)

and business relationships and emerged from Prohibition as wealthy and somewhat more respectable members of their communities.

Gambling and other vices have similar social support profiles. Purveyors of these services are widely perceived as engaged in victimless crimes, that is, black-market transactions involving willing buyers and sellers. Their activities, while morally unacceptable to many, arouse little social concern.

Societal ambivalence becomes even more pronounced where gray-market goods and services are involved. These are situations where legal goods or services are being provided in an illicit manner or to persons ineligible to receive them. Abuses of wartime rations is a good example of a gray-market situation, as is the negotiation of so-called sweetheart labor contracts or the illegal disposal of hazardous waste.

Criminal groups involved in gray-market activities are very tightly meshed in the economic and social fabric of the legitimate community. The persona of such groups is more likely to be legal than illegal, and the capacity of their members to become closely affiliated with persons of power and authority is likely to be great. Public corruption becomes not only likely but inevitable.

By the 1980s, the term organized crime *had lost its ethnic distinction. Instead, the label started being applied to many more criminal associations.*

Combined with the characteristics that groups of criminals exhibit, the activities in which they engage are also likely to define such groups as organized crime. Some commentators feel it is impossible to separate a group's character from the nature of the crimes it commits. To this way of thinking, selling drugs requires a certain level of organization, but it is impossible to tell whether a group has evolved an organizational style in order to sell drugs or began to sell drugs as a consequence of its organizational capacity.

What is clear is that the capacity to exploit one type of criminal opportunity can be parlayed into other legal and illegal endeavors. Similarly, profits from organized crime activities can permit individual criminals to climb that "queer ladder of social mobility" that wealth creates.

Society and Organized Crime Groups

The final aspect of organized crime that distinguishes it from other forms of crime is its relationship with the society in which it operates. Organized crime is the one form of crime that assesses criminal opportunities in light of the probable social response as well as the possible economic and social rewards.

Cressey (1969) identified this capacity of organized crime as a "strategic planning" capability. Using this capability, organized crime groups choose "safe crime": where there is high social tolerance or at least ambivalence toward the conduct; where the chances of apprehension are therefore not great; where, even if apprehended, the chances of conviction are small; and where, even if convicted, the likelihood of serious consequences is also small.

In this assessment, society's attitudes toward various criminal activities become a key determinant in the nature of organized crime activities that will be displayed. Society's attitudes, as embodied in the criminal law, become even more significant.

Packer (1969) argued that in black- and gray-market situations, the criminal law may actually serve as a protective tariff. As such, the law limits the entry of entrepreneurs into the proscribed marketplace while guaranteeing, for those who do enter the market, exorbitant profits. The theory of deterrence does not work in such markets because as the sanction increases so do the likely rewards.

A similar analysis by Smith (1978) suggests that the law operates in many marketplaces to segment generic demand, labeling some legal and some illegal. By so doing, the law does not reduce demand; what it does is change the dynamics of the market, creating the "domain" or market share of organized crime. In this sense, it is society—through its legislative enactments—that generates and structures the dynamics of organized crime opportunities.

Social institutions also play a role in structuring the nature and success of organized crime. The nature of government and the underpinnings of justice systems loom large in determining how organized crime groups will operate and succeed. Anglo-American legal systems, founded on the principle of individual responsibility for criminal acts, deal at best ineptly with group crime. When faced with more sophisticated criminal conspiracies, they appear to falter.

Where criminal organizations are armed with investments in public corruption, justice systems will not operate properly. Where government operates ineffectively or unfairly, the black market will flourish. Where there is the tendency to proscribe what cannot be controlled, criminal organizations will reap social support and financial rewards.

Criminal Support Systems

A secondary use of the term *organized crime* refers to support systems that aid the criminal activities of all offenders. The typical list of support systems includes the tipster, the fix, the fence, and the corrupt public official. Each of these mechanisms serves to reduce the risks of criminal conduct or to lessen its consequences.

For example, tipsters function to provide criminals with information critical to committing a crime, such as the internal security schedule for a building or the timing of valuable cargo shipments. By doing so, they reduce the uncertainties the offenders face and enhance the chances for success. As a reward, tipsters receive a percentage of the "take," or proceeds of the crime.

The fix arranges for special disposition of a criminal's case, once it is in the justice system. This might mean seeing that paperwork is lost, or that a light sentence is imposed. Usually, the fix operates with the aid of corrupt public officials who are in a position to accomplish the required improper acts.

The fence serves as the market for stolen property, transforming it into cash or drugs for thieves. In the role of middleman, the fence determines what thieves steal, how much they are paid to do so, and, consequently, how often they steal. Fences provide structure and stability to a wide range of offenders. Like other criminal support systems, they impose organization on the activities of criminal groups and individual criminals.

Not all criminals can access the services of criminal support systems. These mechanisms will not act to serve the notorious or the psychotic. In this way, criminal elites are established and preserved. For those who use these support systems, crime is organized, the justice system is predictable, and success is likely.

There was a time when the "criminal underworld" was a physical place, a true sanctuary to hide and protect criminals. Now the underworld exists as a communication system, an important dimension of which involves support systems that can aid and protect offenders. The manner in which these systems function provides stability and organization to the underworld.

Summary

Organized crime refers primarily to the broad range of activities undertaken by permanent criminal organizations having the following characteristics: a hierarchical organizational structure; a territorial imperative; a predilection for violence; and the capacity and funds to corrupt public officials.

These groups tend to locate in gray or black markets where they establish patron-client relationships with much of society. The funds they earn as entrepreneurs, combined with social support for their activities, permit them to influence the social response to their acts. They may become upwardly mobile as a result of investing their profits in both legal and illegal endeavors.

Organized crime also refers to criminal support systems such as the tipster, the fix, the fence, and the corrupt official, who impose organization and stability in the underworld.

[See also Criminology.]

BIBLIOGRAPHY

Abadinsky, Howard 1981 *Organized Crime.* Boston: Allyn and Bacon.

Anderson, Annelise Graebner 1979 *The Business of Organized Crime.* Stanford, Calif.: Hoover Institution Press.

Andreoli, P. D. 1976 "Organized Crime Enterprises—Legal." In S. A. Yefsky, ed., *Law Enforcement Science and Technology: Proceedings of the First National Conference on Law Enforcement Science and Technology.* Chicago: IITRI.

Bell, Daniel 1970 "Crime as an American Way of Life." In M. E. Wolfgang, L. Savitz, and N. Johnson, eds., *The Sociology of Crime and Delinquency.* New York: Wiley.

Chambliss, William J. 1978 *On the Take: From Petty Crooks to Presidents.* Bloomington: Indiana University Press.

Cressey, Donald R. 1969 *Theft of the Nation: The Structure and Operations of Organized Crime in America.* New York: Harper and Row.

Homer, Frederic D. 1974 *Guns and Garlic: Myths and Realities of Organized Crime.* West Lafayette, Ind.: Purdue University Press.

Ianni, Francis A. J. 1974 *Black Mafia: Ethnic Succession in Organized Crime.* New York: Simon and Schuster.

Kwitny, Jonathan 1979 *Vicious Circles: The Mafia in the Marketplace.* New York: Morton.

Maas, Peter 1968 *The Valachi Papers.* New York: Putnam.

Packer, Herbert L. 1969 *The Limits of the Criminal Sanction.* Stanford, Calif.: Stanford University Press.

President's Commission on Law Enforcement and the Administration of Justice 1967 *Task Force Report: Organized Crime.* Washington, D.C.: U.S. Government Printing Office.

Robertson, Frank 1977 *Triangle of Death: The Inside Story of the Triads—The Chinese Mafia.* London: Routledge and Kegan Paul.

Salerno, Ralph, and John S. Tompkins 1969 *The Crime Confederation: Cosa Nostra and Allied Operations in Organized Crime.* Garden City, N.Y.: Doubleday.

Smith, Dwight C., Jr. 1975 *The Mafia Mystique.* New York: Basic Books.

——— 1978 "Organized Crime and Entrepreneurship." *International Journal of Criminology and Penology* 6:161–177.

Walsh, Marilyn E. 1977 *The Fence: A New Look at the World of Property Theft.* Westport, Conn.: Greenwood Press.

– MARILYN E. WALSH

P

PARENTAL ROLES

In the closing years of the twentieth century, most adults still become parents. The ages at which they start having children, as well as the number of children they have, differ significantly from earlier generations, as do the social and economic conditions of parenthood.

In this article, several major aspects of parenthood in the contemporary United States are discussed. First, several demographic patterns associated with parenting are reviewed. Second, the rewards and costs associated with parenting are examined. Third, changes in the responsibilities of parents, as defined by social perceptions of the nature of childhood, are discussed. In this section, special attention is given to gender and social class differences in parenting styles. The fourth section examines the impact of the first child's birth on the parents. The paper closes with a discussion of parent-child relations in later life.

Demographic Trends in Parenting

One of the most dramatic changes in the nature of parenthood has been the decline in the average number of births to each woman. Over the past 200 years, this number has decreased from seven births per woman, on the average, to less than two. This downward trend has not been steady or consistent. During some periods, such as the Great Depression of the 1930s, the rate of decline was much more pronounced, while at other times, most notably during the post-World War II baby-boom, the number of births per woman actually increased. In 1936, the middle of the depression, American women were giving birth to two children, on the average, while in 1957, the number reached 3.6 births per woman. Today, the average number of births each woman has is slightly under two. There are, however, racial and socioeconomic differences in fertility. In the United States, white women have the fewest number of births, followed by black and Hispanic women (Zinn and Eitzen 1990, p. 290).

Race and ethnicity differences in fertility can be explained largely in terms of socioeconomic factors. Blacks and Hispanics in the United States tend to be disproportionately poor, uneducated, and underemployed. Such persons are likely to place a high value on childbearing and to believe in traditional gender roles. For people with limited occupational options, childbearing and child rearing may offer rewards that are lacking in employment. Moreover, high fertility may be viewed by people of lower socioeconomic status as one way of lifting the family out of poverty insofar as it may increase the family's likelihood of having at least one child of superior talent or ability in some area. In addition, people of lower socioeconomic status tend to marry earlier than those of higher status and thus have a longer marital childbearing period. Finally, affiliation with the Roman Catholic church, which has a restrictive policy toward fertility control, may be responsible for the higher fertility rate among Hispanic women (Zinn and Eitzen 1990, p. 295).

One of the most dramatic changes in the nature of parenthood has been the decline in the average number of births to each woman.

Why has the average number of births per woman decreased over the past 200 years? One major reason for the current low fertility rates is that women are marrying at a later age than during the babyboom years. As a result, the number of marital childbearing years is lower and the number of children that can be born is also lower. The relatively high divorce rate has had a similar effect on fertility. Another major reason for the low fertility rate is the high female labor force participation rate. Child-rearing duties decrease the amount of time and energy mothers can devote to their jobs; therefore, women who are career oriented often choose to forgo childbearing altogether or to limit the number of children they have. A final factor that has reduced the average number of births per woman is the legalization of abortion. Currently, 30 percent of all pregnancies that do not end in stillbirth or miscarriage are aborted (Zinn and Eitzen 1990, pp. 290–291).

These social changes have been reflected not only in a reduction in the average number of children born per woman but also in the age at which women begin to have children. In the past twenty years, more and more couples are postponing parenting. In 1970, women under age twenty-five accounted for four out of every five first births that were occurring. By the late 1980s, women of this age accounted for only one out of every two first births. More women were waiting to have their first babies until their late twenties, thirties, and even forties (U.S. Bureau of the Census 1988, p. 3).

Another significant change in fertility is the increase in births to unmarried women. Over 20 percent of all births in the United States today are to unwed mothers. The rate is higher among blacks than it is among whites. Nearly 60 percent of all black babies are born to unmarried mothers (U.S. Bureau of the Census 1989).

As a consequence of the high out-of-wedlock birth rate and the high divorce rate, an increasing number of women are engaging in solo parenting. About one-fourth of all American families with children have only one parent (U.S. Bureau of the Census 1988). Some experts predict that two out of every three white children and nine out of ten black children born in 1980 will be living in a single-parent household by age eighteen (Brophy 1986). Children spend between six and eight years, on the average, living in a single-parent home (Hofferth 1985). Most tend to have little contact with their nonresidential parent. In fact, one study revealed that about two out of every five children of divorce had no contact with their fathers in over five years. Some did not even know whether their fathers were still living (Furstenberg and Nord 1982).

Single-parent families headed by women have many special problems, not the least of which is limited economic resources. The average income of such families is only one-third that of families with two parents (Johnson 1980). Nearly one-half of female-headed families live below the poverty level (Payton 1982). A major contributing factor to this "feminization of poverty" is the fact that not all noncustodial fathers are ordered by the courts to pay child support after divorce, and, of those who are, less than half actually pay the full amount (Weitzman 1985).

Economic need has led to a dramatic increase in the employment of mothers, married as well as divorced. In 1960, fewer than one in every five mothers of preschool children was employed. Today, well over 60 percent are employed (U.S. Bureau of the Census 1989). The increased demand for substitute child care has become one of the most pressing social problems in the 1990s.

The Childbearing Decision: The Rewards and Costs of Parenting

Since individuals are now better able to control their reproductive functions due to advances in contraceptive technology and access to legal abortion, it is important to examine why the majority of adults still choose to become parents. For most people, becoming a parent involves a decision-making process in which the anticipated rewards and costs of parenting are weighed. One major influence on this choice is societal pressure. The United States is often referred to as "pronatalist," which means that dominant values and attitudes promote and encourage childbearing.

Studies of the value of children to their parents have identified many major rewards that child rearing provides (Hoffman and Hoffman 1973; Hoffman and Manis 1979). In one national study (Hoffman and Manis 1979), respondents were asked to identify the advantages and disadvantages of having children. One major type of reward provided by children is self-preservation and family continuity. The birth of children ensures that the father's family name will continue into the future, at least for one more generation, and it may give the parents a sense of immortality, a feeling that part of them will survive after death. Moreover, in earlier historical periods, children were valued in large part because their labor could greatly enhance a family's economic survival. Today, children continue to have economic value for some parents who view them as a type of old age insurance. A small minority of parents, typically those from rural areas, also see children's ability to participate in household labor as a valuable asset. Children may also enable a family to maintain control over property or a family-owned or operated farm or business. For most families, though, children may be more of an economic liability than a benefit. Their primary value to their parents is emotional and symbolic. Understanding the nonmaterial benefits of child rearing helps in understanding why most people choose to become parents when they are no longer forced to do so by biological necessity.

One major type of nonmaterial reward provided by children is self-enhancement. Becoming a parent leads to a change in social identity. It bestows adult status, which carries with it implications of maturity and stability. In fact, for many people, parenthood is *the* event that gives a sense of feeling like an adult (Hoffman and Manis 1979). Having children may also produce a sense of achievement, not only for the physical fact of conception but also for the challenges of raising a child. Moreover, many parents also feel a sense of accomplishment through their children's achievements. Finally, during the child-rearing years, the legitimate authority that is attached to the parent role, as well as the resulting power and influence parents have over their children's lives, may be self-enhancing, especially to parents who lack such influence and control in other aspects of their lives.

The most frequently mentioned reward of child rearing is the provision of primary group ties and affection. Children are expected to help prevent loneliness and to provide love and companionship. These rewards may be particularly important to blue-collar couples, insofar as their marriages may not provide adequate companionship and affection (Rainwater 1960).

The stimulation and fun that child rearing provides are also identified as rewards of the parent role. The presence of a new baby in the home is an immediate source of novelty. As they grow and mature, children continue to provide new experiences for their parents.

Finally, many people regard childbearing as a sacred duty and may feel that by becoming parents they are fulfilling a divine commandment (Scanzoni and Scanzoni 1988). Moreover, the physical and symbolic sacrifices involved in child rearing are perceived by some as a sign that parents are more virtuous and altruistic than childless adults.

There are also costs, financial and socio-emotional, associated with parenting. Over the years, economists have estimated the direct (e.g., food, clothing, shelter, medical and dental care, toys, recreation, leisure, and education) and indirect costs (e.g., foregone savings and investments, lower standards of living, loss of potential income for parents who leave the labor market to care for the child) of child rearing. In 1985, raising a child, including sending her or him to a state university for four years, cost parents $232,000 (Belkin 1985). While couples may be aware of the magnitude of financial costs associated with child rearing, most are not deterred by their awareness (Hoffman and Manis 1979). Economic considerations play only a small role in the decision to become a parent (Blake 1979).

The presence of children may also be costly to adults through the restriction of their activities and the resulting loss of freedom. Parents are responsible for the mental, emotional, physical, spiritual, and social development of their offspring. Obviously, such responsibility may consume much of the parents' time and attention and may require a readjustment of lifestyle to take the children's needs and activities into account. Consequently, parenting may have negative effects on marriage. Studies have shown that the birth of children may hurt a couple's affectional and sexual relationship, due largely to frequent interruptions, a loss of privacy, and increased demands on time and energy (Glenn and McLanahan 1982; Hoffman and Levant 1985; Miller and Sollie 1980). The birth of children often results in role segregation, which means that spouses engage in fewer joint activities as they attempt to fulfill their parental responsibilities.

Our society, however, is very effective in over-emphasizing the positive outcomes of parenting while downplaying the negative. Some scholars have concluded that it is necessary for every society to do this in order to ensure that adults do not try to avoid taking on these difficult but essential societal functions (LeMasters and DeFrain 1983; LeMasters 1970). The set of folk beliefs that depict children as fun, cute, clean, healthy, and intelligent, and child rearing as easy and enjoyable are not always supported by facts. Indeed, most studies reveal that adults believe these overly positive depictions of children and child rearing only until they become parents and reality sets in (LaRossa and LaRossa 1981).

Largely as a result of powerful pronatalist forces, then, most adults choose to have children. Throughout this century, the proportion of childless marriages ranged from 5 to 10 percent. The rates have doubled in the past twenty years, however, and some experts are predicting that between 25 and 30 percent of American women now in their late twenties and early thirties will remain childless throughout their lives (Bloom and Bennett 1986).

Prior to the seventeenth century, parental love was rarely identified by child-rearing experts as a critical factor in the development of a child.

For the small minority of persons who are voluntarily child-free, the anticipated costs of having children outweigh the anticipated rewards. Adults who choose to remain childless may believe that having children would interfere with their ability to achieve in their careers or in other types of public service. They may feel that caring for children would drain away the time and energy that could be devoted to other highly valued pursuits. Another important consideration for such adults is the expectation that the commitment to parenthood would reduce the time available to commit to the marital relationship. To voluntarily childless couples, marriage is the primary source of affection and sense of belonging. Children are not needed to provide such rewards. Finally, voluntarily childless couples may believe that children would create a monotonous routine and reduce the time and money available for valuable adult activities (Veevers 1979; 1980).

The Responsibilities of Parents

For most of human history, simple physical survival of children was the dominant issue in child rearing (Skolnick 1987). Prior to the seventeenth century, parental love was rarely identified by child-rearing experts as a critical factor in the development of a child. Parents provided physical care, consistent discipline, and a model for proper behavior (Kagan 1977). Today, parents are responsible not only for the child's physical well being but also for his or her psychological adjustment. Often, flaws in a person's adjustment are traced to a lack of parental love or some other parental shortcoming (Skolnick 1987).

Ideas about ideal parental behavior have varied in conjunction with conceptions of children's needs. Today, Americans assume that children have a distinct nature that distinguishes them from adults. While adults work, assume responsibility, act in a controlled and rational manner, think abstractly, and seek and maintain sexual relationships, children play and forgo assumption of responsibility, act in an irrational and emotional manner, think in concrete terms, and are asexual creatures (Benedict 1938). As a result of children's undeveloped state, parents are assigned responsibility for protecting, providing, and psychologically shaping them.

The concept of childhood as a separate developmental stage of life is a relatively modern invention. In premodern societies a different concept of childhood dominated. Children were seen as "miniature" adults (Aries 1962). As such, they participated fully in the adult world. For instance, in preindustrial Europe, children were involved in various occupations such as farming, baking, shoemaking, the law, business, pharmacy, administration, and the clergy. School was part of the adult world, as well, and was not age-graded. Students made their own rules and were unsupervised by adults. They could enter college at the age of nine or ten, completing their studies at age thirteen. In fact, children could be found in all places where adults regularly spent their time—at work, in the army, and in taverns and houses of ill repute.

A similar process occurred in the emergence of adolescence as a distinct stage of development in Western societies. Although Americans think of the period between puberty and the assumption of adult roles, which lasts anywhere from ten to fifteen years, as a biologically determined stage, it is, in reality, a social invention. In some societies, contrary to our own, puberty leads directly from childhood to adulthood. Adolescence was not established as a distinct stage of social development in our society until the early 1900s, after industrialization had reduced the significance of the family as the unit of economic production, compulsory education was institutionalized, and child labor laws removed children from the work force (Skolnick 1987, p. 350). The teenage years became a time of occupational choice and preparation rather than a period of apprenticeship in the occupation of one's parents. Thus, the period of children's dependence on their parents increased further.

There is some reason to believe that this period of preadulthood is being lengthened even further. Keniston (1971) proclaimed the existence of a "youth" stage between adolescence and adulthood and that this stage was emerging because rapid social change was making it increasingly difficult for young people to establish their own independent identity. Indeed, during the 1980s, more and more young people past the conventional age of independence were still living in their parents' home (Glick and Lin 1986). Nearly two-thirds of the young men and about half of the young women between the ages of eighteen and twenty-four were living with their parents in the mid-1980s. This suggests that parents may continue to feel responsibility for their children into the third decade of their children's lives.

THE MOTHER ROLE. To many people, parenting is synonymous with mothering, and mothering is believed by many to be an instinct found in all women. While scientists have yet to find an instinctual motive for motherhood among humans, they have demonstrated a strong learned need among women to have children. Most women, given the choice to become a mother, would choose to do so and most women who are already mothers would choose the role again (Genevie and Margolies 1987).

The belief that motherhood is necessary for women's fulfillment and for the normal healthy development of children has waxed and waned throughout our history, largely in response to economic conditions. When women's labor is not needed outside the home, the mother role is glorified and exalted; when women's labor is essential to the economy, the importance of the mother child bond is downplayed (Margolis 1984). Earlier in our history, when our economy was agrarian, parenting was more of a joint venture. Child rearing was shared among a larger number of adults and the mother-child bond was not regarded as primary. Only after industrialization and urbanization changed the nature of work and family life did the role of mother in child development become preeminent. As will be discussed below, similar changes are under way in regard to the father role.

THE FATHER ROLE. While the verb *to mother* is used to refer to the nurturance and care given to children, usually by women, the verb *to father* has a much more restricted meaning. To many, this simply refers to the male role in procreation. The responsibilities attached to the father role have traditionally been economic. To be a good father, a man had to be a good provider. Participation in the daily custodial care of the child was not expected, nor was companionship or nurturance. In recent decades, with the entrance of large numbers of mothers into the labor force, the expectations attached

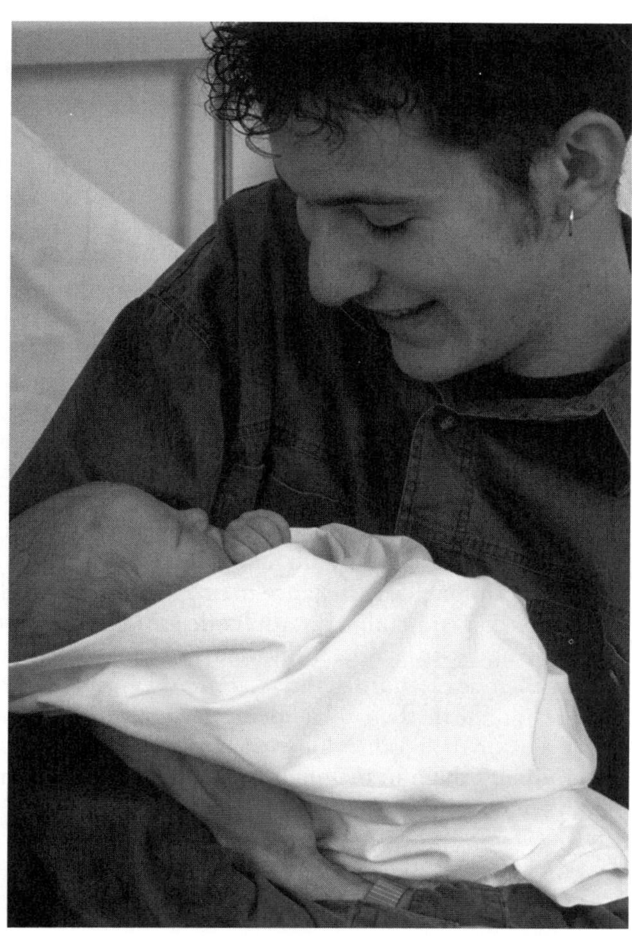

Although fathers traditionally maintained economic responsibilities for children, by the late 1900s, fathers sought to participate more fully in daily care and nurturance of their children. (Jennie Woodcock; Reflections Photolibrary/Corbis)

to the father role are beginning to change. Men can no longer be good fathers simply by being good providers. They must also participate more fully in the daily care of their children and in the socialization process (Pleck 1979).

It appears that these expectations are being reflected in changed behavior (Pruett 1987). More men are attending child birth education classes with their wives and are present at the births of their children (Bigner 1979). Additionally, reports of the average amount of time men spend with their children has increased since the early 1970s, from thirty-eight seconds per day with infants in the early 1970s (Rebelsky and Hanks 1971) to eight minutes per weekday in the mid-1980s (Fischman 1986). These changes provide support to studies that have shown that men are psychologically capable of participating in all parenting behaviors (except for gestation and lactation, which they are biologically incapable of performing; Fein 1980). Perhaps the most telling evidence of the extent to which Americans' ideas about the father role have changed since the 1940s can be found in the expert advice on parenting. In the first edition of his classic book, *Baby and Child Care,* published in 1945, Dr. Benjamin Spock reminded fathers that they need not be as involved in child care as mothers, at most "preparing a formula on Sundays." By the 1980s, Dr. Spock admonished fathers to take on half of all child care and housework tasks (Spock and Rothenberg 1985).

SOCIAL CLASS VARIATIONS IN PARENTAL VALUES. As noted above, ideas about the proper role of parents have varied historically. Sociologists have also identified significant variation in child-rearing attitudes by social class (Kohn 1969). The values parents attempt to convey to their children are learned through personal experience in the occupational world. Because jobs differ significantly in many ways, workers learn different ways of coping on the job to ensure success in the work world. When these behaviors bring occupational success to workers, they attempt to apply similar traits to other areas of their lives. Higher status jobs permit, even require, self-direction. They encourage flexibility, creativity, and decision making. People who hold these jobs come to value these traits and attempt to instill them in their children with the hope that they will bring them success. Lower status jobs, on the other hand, rarely provide opportunities for self-direction and require conformity to authority. Thus, lower class and working-class parents believe that the most important trait they can teach their children is obedience and conformity.

Parental disciplinary tactics reflect these values. While both middle class and working-class parents emphasize behavior control in their approach to child rearing, they look for the source of this control in different places. Middle class parents expect their children to be self-directed, to have inner control, whereas lower and working-class parents expect their children to be obedient to external sources of control. As a result, working-class parents will punish any disobedient acts, whereas middle class parents will punish only those disobedient acts that they view as having violent intent. These findings apply to mothers as well as to fathers and to black parents as well as to white parents (Scanzoni 1977). At one point, scholars believed that lower class parents were simply more likely than middle class parents to use physical punishment (Kerckhoff 1972, p. 42). A closer reexamination of the evidence has called this conclusion into question (Pearlin 1972; Straus 1971). The major difference seems to be the conditions under which parents will use physical punishment, not how likely they are to use it (Kohn 1969).

Transition to Parenthood

Some sociological studies have found that many couples experience the birth of their first child as a crisis (LeMasters 1957; Dyer 1964). The changes brought about by the addition of a baby to a household are indeed extensive. Occupational commitments, particularly of the mother, may be reduced, and family economics must be reorganized as spending increases and earnings are reduced. Household space must be reallocated to accommodate the infant's lifestyle. The parents' time and attention must be redirected toward the infant. Relationships with kin, neighbors, and friends must be redefined to include the baby's schedule. The marital relationship itself may be disrupted due to the enormous demands for time, energy, and attention made by the baby. As a result, new mothers frequently report unexpected fatigue, confinement to the home and a sharp reduction in social contacts, and loss of satisfaction that accompanied outside employment. New fathers feel added economic pressure and a general disenchantment with the parent role (LaRossa and LaRossa 1981).

The severity of the crisis experienced by new parents may be related to the degree to which the parents had romanticized parenthood.

The severity of the crisis experienced by new parents does not seem to be related to the quality of the marital relationship before the birth of the child or to the degree to which the child was planned and wanted. Instead, it may be the degree to which the parents had romanticized parenthood in conjunction with their lack of preparation for the role that leads to a feeling of crisis. As a result of the tremendous changes brought about by the presence of children and the burdens associated with child rearing, marital satisfaction appears to decline sharply around the time of the first child's birth and to remain low until children leave the home (Rollins and Cannon 1974).

There is some indication that the transition to parenthood is more difficult for middle class couples than it is for blue-collar couples. The reasons for this are many. Working-class women may place a greater intrinsic value in child rearing, may have fewer alternative sources of gratification outside the family, may have more experience in caring for children, may have fewer conflicting demands from occupational aspirations, and may have had less companionate, less satisfying marital relationships prior to the arrival of children. Thus, for these couples, the birth of the first child may offer more rewards than it produces costs.

Parenting in the Later Years of Life

Research has demonstrated that the rewards of parenting persist through life (Long and Mancini 1989). Feelings of continued attachment to their children help to minimize elderly parents' sense of isolation and loneliness. Believing that their children would take care of their needs, regardless of the time, energy, or money involved, helps to build a sense of security in old age and is important in day-to-day survival. However, opportunities to continue to provide nurturance to their children are also highly valued by elderly parents. Their contributions to their adult children occur in many forms, from financial assistance to help with housework and care of grandchildren. Adults derive a great sense of pride and satisfaction from their parental role, even when their sons and daughters are middle-aged adults with children of their own. Being recognized by their children for their value and competence in the role of parent helps them to maintain high levels of self-esteem (Long and Mancini 1989).

[See also American Families; Family Roles; Socialization.]

BIBLIOGRAPHY

Aries, Phillipe 1962 *Centuries of Childhood: A Social History of Family Life.* New York: Alfred A. Knopf.

Belkin, Lisa 1985 "Parents Weigh the Costs of Children." *New York Times* May 23.

Benedict, Ruth 1938 "Continuities and Discontinuities in Cultural Conditioning." *Psychiatry* 1:161–167.

Bigner, Jerry 1979 *Parent-Child Relations: An Introduction to Parenting.* New York: Macmillan.

Blake, Judith 1979 "Is Zero Preferred? American Attitudes Toward Childlessness in the 1970s." *Journal of Marriage and the Family* 41:245–257.

Bloom, David, and Neil Bennett 1986 "Childless Couples." *American Demographics* 8:23–25, 54–55.

Brophy, Beth 1986 "Children Under Stress." *U.S. News and World Report* October 27, pp. 58–63.

Clemens, Audra, and Leland Axelson 1985 "The Not-So-Empty Nest: The Return of the Fledgling Adult." *Family Relations* 34:259–264.

Dyer, Everett 1964 "Parenthood as Crisis." *Marriage and Family Living* 25:196–201.

Fein, Robert 1980 "Research on Fathering." In Arlene Skolnick and Jerome Skolnick, eds., *The Family in Transition.* Boston: Little, Brown.

Fischman, Joshua 1986 "The Children's Hours." *Psychology Today,* October 10.

Furstenburg, Frank, and Christine Nord 1982 "Parenting Apart: Patterns of Childrearing After Marital Disruption." *Journal of Marriage and the Family* 47:893–904.

Genevie, Lou, and Eva Margolies 1987 *The Motherhood Report: How Women Feel About Being Mothers.* New York: Macmillan.

Glenn, Norvall, and Sara McLanahan 1982 "Children and Marital Happiness: A Further Specification of the Relationship." *Journal of Marriage and the Family* 44:64–72.

Glick, Paul, and Sung-Ling Lin 1986 "More Young Adults Are Living with Their Parents: Who Are They?" *Journal of Marriage and the Family* 48:107–112.

Hofferth, Sandra 1985 "Updating Children's Life Course." *Journal of Marriage and the Family* 47:93–115.

Hoffman, Lois, and Martin Hoffman 1973 "The Value of Children to Parents." In James T. Fawcett, ed., *Psychological Perspectives on Population.* New York: Basic Books.

Hoffman, Lois, and Jean Manis 1979 "The Value of Children in the United States: A New Approach to the Study of Fertility." *Journal of Marriage and the Family* 41:583–596.

Hoffman, Susan, and R. F. Levant 1985 "A Comparison of Child-Free and Child-Anticipated Married Couples." *Family Relations* 34:197–203.

Johnson, Beverly 1980 "Single Parent Families." *Family Economics Review* (Summer–Fall):22–27.

Kagan, Jerome 1977 "The Child in the Family." *Daedalus* 106:33–56.

Keniston, Kenneth 1971 "Psychosocial Development and Historical Change." *Journal of Interdisciplinary History* 2:329–345.

Kerckhoff, Alan 1972 *Socialization and Social Class.* Englewood Cliffs, NJ.: Prentice-Hall.

Kohn, Melvin 1969 *Class and Conformity: A Study in Values.* Homewood, Ill.: Dorsey.

LaRossa, Ralph, and Maureen LaRossa 1981 *Transition to Parenthood: How Infants Change Families.* Beverly Hills, Calif.: Sage.

LeMasters, E. E. 1957 "Parenthood as Crisis." *Marriage and Family Living* 19:352–355.

——— 1970 *Parents in Modern America: A Sociological Analysis.* Homewood, Ill.: Dorsey.

———, and John DeFrain 1983 *Parents in Contemporary America.* Homewood, Ill.: Dorsey.

Long, Janie, and Jay Mancini 1989 "The Parental Role and Parent-Child Relationship Provisions." In Jay Mancini, ed., *Adult Parents and Adult Children.* Lexington, Mass.: Lexington Books.

Margolis, Maxine 1984 *Mothers and Such: Views of American Women and Why They Changed.* Berkeley: University of California Press.

Miller, Brent, and D. Sollie 1980 "Normal Stresses during the Transition to Parenthood." *Family Relations* 29:459–465.

Payton, Isabelle 1982 "Single-Parent Households: An Alternative Approach." *Family Economics Review* (Winter):11–16.

Pearlin, Leonard 1972 *Class Context and Family Relations: A Cross-National Study.* Boston: Little, Brown.

Pleck, Joseph 1979 "Men's Family Work: Three Perspectives and Some New Data." *Family Coordinator* 28:481–489.

Pruett, Kyle 1987 *The Nurturing Father: Journey Toward the Complete Man.* New York: Warner Books.

Rainwater, Lee 1960 *And the Poor Get Children.* Chicago: Quadrangle.

Rebelsky, F., and C. Hanks 1971 "Fathers' Verbal Interactions with Infants in the First Three Months of Life." *Child Development* 42:63–68.

Rollins, Boyd, and Kenneth Cannon 1974 "Marital Satisfaction over the Family Life Cycle: A Reevaluation." *Journal of Marriage and the Family* 36:271–282.

Rossi, Alice 1984 "Gender and Parenthood." *American Sociological Review* 49:1–19.

Scanzoni, John 1977 *The Black Family in Modern Society: Patterns of Stability and Security.* Chicago: University of Chicago Press.

Scanzoni, Letha, and John Scanzoni 1988 *Men, Women, and Change: A Sociology of Marriage and Family.* New York: McGraw-Hill.

Skolnick, Arlene 1987 *The Intimate Environment: Exploring Marriage and the Family.* Boston: Little, Brown.

Spock, Benjamin 1945 *Baby and Child Care.* New York: Pocket Books.

———, and Michael Rothenberg 1985 *Dr. Spock's Baby and Child Care.* New York: Pocket Books.

Straus, Murray 1971 "Some Social Antecedents of Physical Punishment: A Linkage Theory Interpretation." *Journal of Marriage and the Family* 33:658–663.

U.S. Bureau of the Census 1988 "Households, Families, Marital Status and Living Arrangements: March 1988." *Current Population Reports,* Series P-20, no. 432. Washington, D.C.: U.S. Government Printing Office.

——— 1989 "Fertility of American Women: June 1988." *Current Population Reports,* Series P-20, No. 436. Washington, D.C.: U.S. Government Printing Office.

——— 1989 *Statistical Abstract of the United States, 1989.* Washington, D.C.: U.S. Government Printing Office.

Veevers, Jean 1979 "Voluntary Childlessness: A Review of Issues and Evidence." *Marriage and Family Review* 2:1–26.

——— 1980 *Childless by Choice.* Toronto: Butterworths. Weitzman, Lenore 1985 *The Divorce Revolution.* New York: Free Press.

Zinn, Maxine Baca, and D. Stanley Eitzen 1990 *Diversity in Families,* 2nd ed. New York: Harper and Row.

– CONSTANCE L. SHEHAN

PATIENTS' RIGHTS MOVEMENT

The patients' rights movement was an outgrowth of the movement for individual rights of the 1960s and 1970s that gave rise to the idea of a set of rights for protection of medical patients and succeeded in having those rights enacted into law in many states. Although medical and hospital patients in most states were beneficiaries of common-law rights well before the 1960s, these protections were limited to the right not be treated without consent, the confidentiality of statements made to a physician during treatment, the right to damages in event of malpractice, and, to some extent, the confidentiality of a patient's hospital records. An advance in patients' rights occurred in 1973 when the American Hospital Association (AHA) approved a bill of rights for adoption by member hospitals. It promised patients considerate and respectful care, the right to know hospital rules and regulations relating to patient conduct, the right to know the identity of the physician in charge of care, sufficient information to enable patients to make informed decisions with respect to their treatment, the right to obtain information concerning diagnosis and treatment as well as prognosis if medically advisable, the right not to be a subject of experiment, the confidentiality of clinical records, and the right to receive an explanation of the hospital bill.

Although the AHA represented almost all of the 5,300 nonprofit, general, and investor-owned hospitals in the United States in the 1990s, the bill of rights adopted by most of the association's members was of little or no legal value because it was voluntary. Nonetheless, it established public awareness of patients' rights and set the stage for a second advance that took place between 1975 and 1985, when one-third of the states enacted patients' rights statutes. Although these statutes varied, they all incorporated the AHA pledges and generally went beyond them to guarantee the right to prompt emergency attention, the right to examine one's clinical chart during the course of treatment and to obtain a copy of it, the right (within limits) to privacy during the hospital stay, the right to receive an itemized bill, and the right to receive information about financial assistance and free care. The most important aspect of these statutes was that they were enforceable. California, Colorado, Illinois, Maryland, Massachusetts, Michigan, Minnesota, New York, Pennsylvania, and Rhode Island were some of the states that enacted statutes. In most instances the statutes were also applied to nursing homes. The right to refuse treatment extended to psychiatric patients if they were competent. By the 1990s federal law required hospitals and nursing homes to advise patients of their right to refuse care and their right to execute living wills or to name proxies if they become unable to make life-and-death treatment decisions.

– JACK HANDLER

PEACE

The study of peace is not a tidy, well-ordered field, but it is flourishing. In recent decades, work in peace research, peace studies, peace science, conflict resolution, and nonviolent action has expanded greatly in the United States, Europe, and many other parts of the world. The work has been truly global and interdisciplinary, but this article emphasizes recent writing by U.S. sociologists and other social scientists drawing from sociological theory and research.

The concept of peace is a matter of controversy. Some writers use the term in distinction to war; this is *negative peace,* defined as the absence of direct physical violence. Other writers stress *positive peace;* this may entail integrative and cooperative relations, or the absence of great inequalities in the life chances of different populations. Some writers' conception of peace includes relations among all kinds of groups and between individuals, as well as between countries; others define peace in terms of global actors in a world system.

This article is about international peace, but it also considers peace processes among various social units and levels. Reflecting considerable consensus in the field, we examine the social conditions fostering integration, equity, and mutual security, not merely the absence of war. Not focusing on the causes of war, reviewed elsewhere in this volume, we discuss sociological work regarding: (1) *peacebuilding,* creating conditions that prevent the emergence of violent conflicts; (2) *peacemaking,* developing processes that contribute to the deescalation and settlement of conflicts; and (3) *peacekeeping,* creating conditions for maintaining and expanding nonviolent relations and equitable outcomes.

As for any conflict, important factors shaping developments at each of those stages of international struggles arise from three major sources: (1) within one of the primary adversaries; (2) in the relationship between them; and (3) in the social system of which they are a part (Kriesberg 1982). Analysts tend to stress one or another of these sources, and each will be discussed as it relates to peacebuilding, peacemaking, and peacekeeping.

A final introductory observation: Much of the sociological work concerning peace follows traditional directions, analyzing empirical data about when and how actions contributing to peace have occurred. Some of it takes a critical stance, examining the social conditions and processes that produce wars and other forms of violent international struggle and stressing factors that are not conventionally used to account for and justify the struggles. Finally, still other writing is more policy- and futurist-oriented, emphasizing possibilities for fostering peace.

Peacebuilding

Considerable research and theorizing have been done about the conditions within societies that generate international conflicts and wars. Unmasking those conditions is sometimes expected to lead to changing them and thus building peace. Following in the tradition of C. Wright Mills, one subject of such work is the military-industrial complex. The assumption of much of this work is that preparing to fight a war, even if justified in terms of defense or to deter war, has a dynamic of its own. Consequently, it becomes disproportionate to the goals sought, generates mutual mistrust, and hence increases the likelihood of war. The dynamic is driven by military, industrial, and political elites with a vested interest in maintaining high military expenditures. Popular support for this military preparedness is mobilized, and people in mass societies are particularly vulnerable to appeals for national solidarity against a terrible external threat.

Illustrative works include Sanders's (1983) study of the Committee on the Present Danger, which effectively pressured the U.S. government in the mid-1970s to increase weapons development and procurement; and Wolfe's (1979) analysis of the domestic coalitions, which explained the changing perceptions of a Soviet threat. The end of the Cold War is providing additional kinds of evidence about the significance of internal factors within both the American and Soviet societies for sustaining the cold war between them.

Influenced by the feminist tradition, attention is now being given to the importance of gender socialization as a domestic factor affecting peace-building. Men tend to view social relations in a more adversarial and competitive way than do women, who tend to emphasize integrative relations. This is manifested, too, in different conceptions of war, peace, and security and in gender differences in supporting reliance on military versus noncoercive means of conducting international relations (Boulding 1977; Northrup 1990). Societal differences in the socialization of men and women then would help explain differing national predispositions toward fighting and the use of violence.

The way in which language is used to frame conflict and means of waging struggles is also a matter of considerable recent attention. Discourses of the mass media and of films have been analyzed as sources for overreliance on violence and the threat of violence in conducting conflicts (Gibson 1989). Such work also illuminates the processes of dehumanization in social conflicts that supports the disproportional character of much conflict escalation and intractability.

The role of social structure and culture in setting the style of conducting conflicts is a matter of great significance. Attention has been given to the repertoire of methods to conduct conflicts. Information about effective nonviolent ways of settling conflicts may become peacebuilding methods added to a society's repertoire.

In addition to internal conditions, we note two of the several aspects of relations between global actors that affect the likelihood that those actors will conduct their relations peacefully. One longstanding area of work has been the effects of integration between societies, including the exchange of peoples, goods, and ideas. On the whole, research supports the generalization that such integration enhances mutual security and reduces the chances of waging wars or threatening each other's security. Increased integration not only creates greater bonds of mutual identity and interest but also improves communication and exchanges that parties will regard as equitable.

Recent work has given particular attention to alternatives to traditional reliance on military threat as a means of sustaining security. Sharp's (1973, 1990) studies of nonviolent action as a means of achieving social change and of defending a society against aggression are increasingly significant as the Cold War ends. The development of nonviolent or civilian-based defense clearly is less threatening and therefore less provocative in intersocietal relations.

Finally, the global system within which adversaries interact also affects the likelihood that their relations will be peaceful. In this context, the concepts of positive peace and structural violence are particularly significant. Unlike personal violence, structural violence is indirect. It refers to the "avoidable denial of what is needed to satisfy fundamental needs" (Galtung 1980, p. 67). Thus, structural conditions may damage and cut short people's lives by restrictions of human rights or by malnutrition and illness while other people using conventionally available knowledge do not suffer the same deprivations. Such inequities are built into many social systems and into the global order and constitute negative peace. This has been an influential idea and has stimulated a variety of studies, particularly regarding conditions in the Third World.

Public opinion and organized public pressure have influenced governments on foreign policy issues, often in the direction of peacemaking.

Another area of considerable sociological work pertains to the expansion in number, size, and scope of international nongovernmental organizations (NGOs). Many kinds of transnational organizations perform activities and are arenas for interactions that supplement or even compete with states and international governmental organizations. NGOs include multinational corporations, religious and ideological organizations, professional and trade associations, trade union federations, and ethnically based associations. These groupings provide important bases of identity and action that crosscut country borders (Angell 1969; Evan 1981; Boulding 1988).

International and supranational governmental organizations have also been examined by sociologists. They have sought to understand the conditions in which such institutions emerge and survive and serve as agencies to prevent conflicts from arising and escalating to violence (Etzioni 1965).

Peacemaking

Recent work has focused particularly on the ways in which the escalation of conflicts is limited, how transitions occur toward deescalation, and how negotiations end conflicts. Domestic, relational, and contextual factors all contribute to such peacemaking, as discussed next.

Among domestic conditions, sociological work gives attention to popular forces that pressure governments to move toward an accommodation with adversaries. This interest combines with the recent growth in theory and research about social movements to generate considerable work on peace movements (Lofland and Marullo 1990). For example, McCrea and Markle (1989) analyzed the nuclear freeze campaign of the early 1980s as well as earlier campaigns against nuclear weapons. There is a variety of evidence that at least within the United States and Western Europe, public opinion and organized public pressure have influenced governments on foreign policy issues, often in the direction of peacemaking.

Research has drawn from and contributes to studies of conflict resolution and negotiation. This work focuses on unilateral, conciliatory gestures and other initiatives in deescalating conflicts, on managing crises and transforming intractable conflicts into negotiable problems, and on strategies and techniques for negotiating mutually acceptable agreements (Patchen 1988; Kriesberg 1988).

Finally, sociological attention is given to the role of nonofficial groups that serve as links and channels of communication between adversaries (Schwartz 1989). Sometimes based in one camp, they provide some mediating services in deescalating a protracted conflict, acting as quasi-mediators.

This is closely related to aspects of the global context that may advance peacemaking. Sociologists have contributed to understanding, for example, the possible roles of mediation in conflict deescalation and resolution. Practice and analysis pertain to getting parties to the negotiating table, facilitating meetings, creating new options, and building support for agreements (Burton 1990; Laue, Burde, Potapchuk, and Salkoff 1988).

Although much of this attention has been focused on nonofficial and informal mediation, the roles of governmental actors, often with great resources, and of international governmental organizations are also being examined (e.g., Rubin 1981).

Peacekeeping

Sustaining cease-fires, settlements about disputes, and peace agreements, as well as general accommodations between former adversaries are all part of peacekeeping. The development of vested interests within each society for the maintenance of peace is similar to the domestic processes and conditions related to peacebuilding discussed earlier and will not be further elaborated on here.

Peacekeeping between adversaries is being changed by new conceptions of security. Led by work done in Western Europe, many analysts stress the reality that seeking security by threatening the security of others is inadequate, and this perspective has fostered examining new ways of achieving mutual security. In addition, the very concept of security has been broadened to include more than state security by military means. For example, threats to life and well-being arising from environmental developments and global inequities, as well as changes in the means by which security is attained, are receiving new attention (Stephenson 1988).

Seeking security by threatening the security of others is inadequate, and this perspective has fostered examining new ways of achieving mutual security.

The international system includes international governmental organizations that have played important roles in peacekeeping, as have individual governments and ad hoc multinational groups. Sociologists have studied the working of such peacekeeping forces and the impact of that experience on the soldiers so involved (Moskos 1976).

Conclusions

Sociological students of peace have generally sought to be relevant for policy as well as theory. For U.S. analysts this generally meant focusing on the U.S.-Soviet conflict and the threat of nuclear war (Gamson 1990). One important task now is to assess different explanations for the end of the Cold War. To what extent do the analysts who emphasized the unrealistic nature of the Cold War and the positive contributions of official and popular peacemaking efforts convincingly explain the transformation, or to what extent are those who stressed the primacy of coercion and military threat vindicated?

The Cold War served as the paradigm-setting conflict in recent peace research. Its end gives new significance to other enduring conflicts and issues as well as to emerging challenges to peace. The United States is now the single military and economic superpower; its role as a guarantor of peace and as a threat to peace will need to be examined intensively. This examination, in the new global context, will provide new tests for old ideas.

Long-standing sociological interest in community, tradition, and collective identity will be helpful in understanding the impact of the new prominence of ethnic and nationalist conflicts, and the reduced prominence of unversalistic ideological struggles. These newly significant conflicts will also seem to be more realistically grounded struggles over territory and authority than was the U.S.-Soviet rivalry.

Other conflicts evoke global identifications and perspectives. They entail common interests as well as conflicting ones. The conflicts pertain to environmental challenges, economic development, and human rights. In these struggles, nonstate actors are increasingly important, and the sociological attention to such movements and NGOs is therefore especially relevant.

Finally, the rapidly changing nature of world conflicts means that new perspectives for analysis and for policy will be pitted against each other. The ideas of conflict resolution, of framing and reframing conflicts, and of participation by non-governmental forces and actors across the world in the construction of peace will take on increased importance.

[See also Military Sociology; Religion, Politics, and War; War.]

BIBLIOGRAPHY

Angell, Robert C. 1969 *Peace on the March: Transnational Participation.* New York: Van Nostrand Reinhold.

Boulding, Elise 1977 *Women in the Twentieth Century World.* New York: Sage.

——— 1988 *Building a Global Civic Culture.* New York: Teachers College Press.

Burton, John 1990 *Conflict: Resolution and Provention.* New York: St. Martin's Press.

Etzioni, Amitai 1965 *Political Unification.* New York: Holt, Rinehart and Winston.

Evan, William M. (ed.) 1981 *Knowledge and Power in a Global Society.* Beverly Hills, Calif.: Sage.

Galtung, Johan 1980 *The True Worlds: A Transnational Perspective.* New York: Free Press.

Gamson, William A. 1990 "Sociology and Nuclear War." In H. Gans, ed., *Sociology in America.* Beverly Hills, Calif.: Sage.

———, and André Modigliani 1971 *Untangling the Cold War. A Strategy for Testing Rival Theories.* Boston: Little, Brown.

Gibson, James William 1989 "American Paramilitary Culture and the Reconstitution of the Vietnam War." In J. Walsh and J. Aulich, eds., *Vietnam Images: War and Representation.* New York: St. Martin's Press.

Kriesberg, Louis 1982 *Social Conflicts,* 2nd ed. Englewood Cliffs, NJ.: Prentice-Hall.

——— 1988 "Strategies of Negotiating Agreements: U.S.-Soviet and Arab-Israeli Cases." *Negotiation Journal* 4:19–29.

Laue, James H., Sharon Burde, William Potapchuk, and Miranda Salkoff 1988 "Getting to the Table: Three Paths." *Mediation Quarterly* 20:7–21.

Lofland, John, and Sam Marullo (eds.) 1990 *Peace Movement Dynamics.* New Brunswick, NJ.: Rutgers University Press.

McCrea, Frances B., and Gerald E. Markle 1989 *Minutes to Midnight.* Newbury Park, Calif.: Sage.

Moskos, Charles C., Jr. 1976 *Peace Soldiers: The Sociology of a United Nations Military Force.* Chicago: University of Chicago Press.

Northrup, Terrell A. 1990 "Personal Security, Political Security: The Relationship Between Conceptions of Gender, War, and Peace." In L. Kriesberg, ed., *Research in Social Movements, Conflicts and Change,* vol. 12. Greenwich, Conn.: JAI Publications.

Patchen, Martin 1988 *Resolving Disputes Between Nations: Coercion or Conciliation?* Durham, N.C.: Duke University Press.

Rubin, Jeffrey Z. 1981 *Dynamics of Third Party Intervention: Kissinger in the Middle East.* New York: Praeger.

Sanders, Jerry W. 1983 *Peddlers of Crisis.* Boston: South End Press.

Schwartz, Richard D. 1989 "Arab-Jewish Dialogue in the United States: Toward Track II Tractability." In L. Kriesberg, T. A. Northrup, and S. J. Thorson, eds., *Intractable Conflicts and Their Transformation.* Syracuse, N.Y.: Syracuse University Press.

Sharp, Gene 1973 *The Politics of Nonviolent Action.* Boston: Porter Sargent.

——— 1990 *Civilian-Based Defense.* Princeton, NJ.: Princeton University Press.

Stephenson, Carolyn M. 1988 "The Need for Alternative Forms of Security: Crises and Opportunities." *Alternatives: Social Transformation and Humane Governance* 13:55–76.

Wolfe, Alan 1979 *The Rise and Fall of the "Soviet Threat": Domestic Sources of the Cold War Consensus.* Washington, D.C.: Institute for Policy Studies.

– LOUIS KRIESBERG

PEACE MOVEMENTS

U.S. citizens take part in peace movements for a variety of reasons. Some limit their commitment to specific antiwar activities, particularly during military conflicts. Others champion internationalism, supporting worldwide peace organizations. Many are pacifists, religious or secular. Some believe that large standing armies pose a threat to liberty and democracy. Many link peace to such other interests as feminism, socialism, civil rights, or environmentalism. With the end of the Vietnam War in 1975 the broad coalition of peace activists who had come together to protest the longest conflict in U.S. history broke down once again into smaller groups addressing a range of concerns.

Protests against the nuclear arms race, which had been a focus of peace groups since the 1950s, intensified in the 1980s in response to the Ronald Reagan administration's buildup of the U.S. nuclear arsenal. In the early 1980s the nonviolent Livermore Action Group sought to close the Lawrence Livermore National Laboratory in California, which produced nuclear weapons. Such actions reinforced the wider nuclear freeze campaign, a movement that in November 1982 led to the largest voter referendum on any issue in U.S. history. More than 11.5 million Americans, 60 percent of those voting on the freeze issue, supported the measure. The freeze issue appeared on the ballot in states and localities across the country. Twelve state legislatures, 321 city councils, 10 national labor unions and international bodies endorsed the effort by the United States and Soviet Union to ban mutually the testing, production, and deployment of nuclear weapons. One result of the movement was the Intermediate-Range Nuclear Forces (INF) Treaty of 1988 with the Soviet Union.

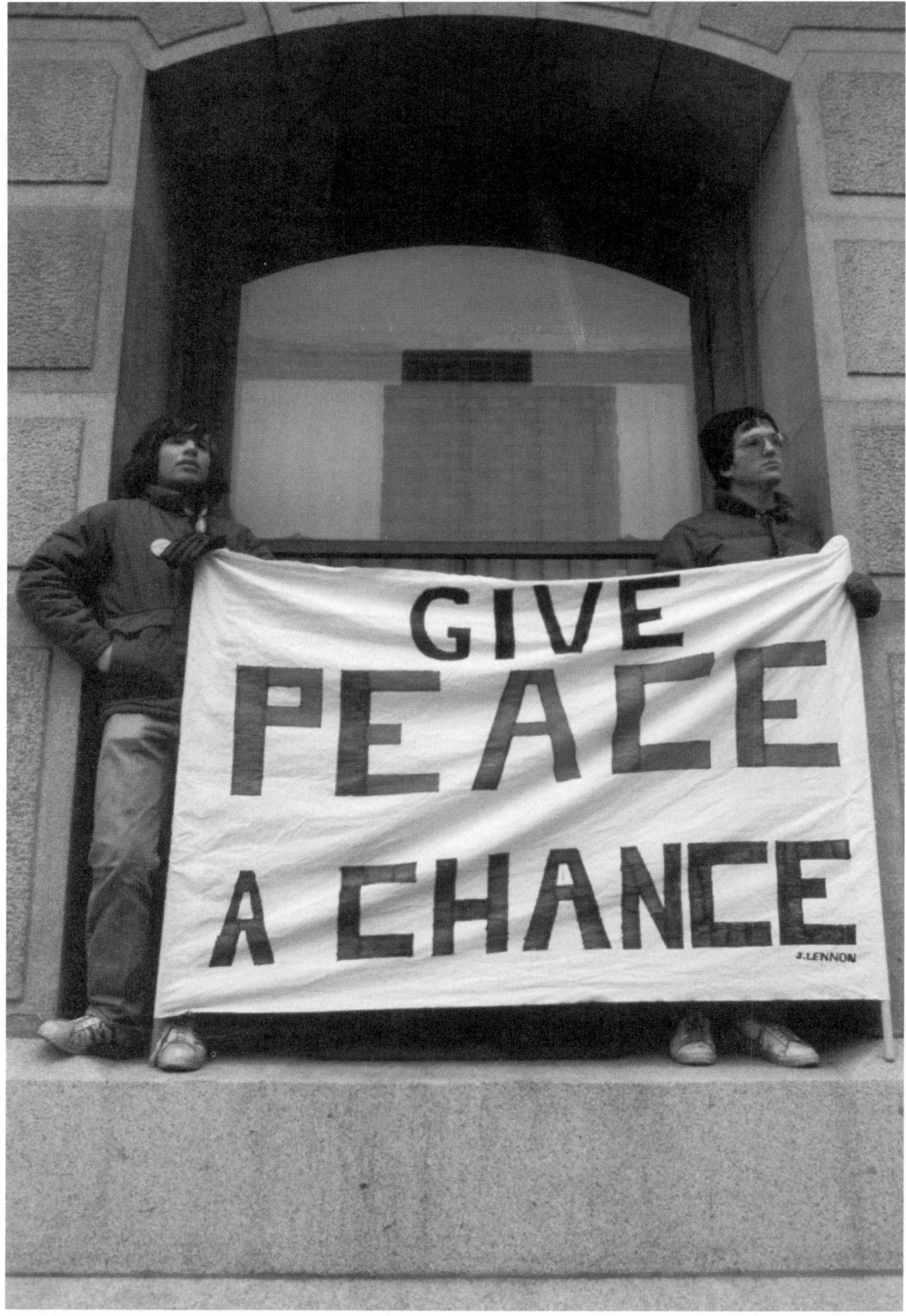

Peace demonstrators criticized American military interventions in other nations, which they denounced for perpetuating the maintenance of a large military budget at the expense of domestic social aid. (Leif Skoogfors/Corbis)

Activists also linked the huge U.S. military budget with neglect of such human needs as education, health care, and housing for the poor, which led to ambitious campaigns against such costly projects as the B-1 bomber, the MX missile system, and the Strategic Defense Initiative ("Star Wars"). Peace groups were critical of U.S. military interventions in Grenada (1983) and Panama (1989), and to a lesser extent, in Somalia (1992), challenging the morality as well as the effectiveness of using military means to achieve political, economic, or even humanitarian ends. Although the brief Gulf War of 1991 elicited overwhelming public support in favor of halting Iraq's aggression against Kuwait, many peace activists criticized the George Bush administration for engaging in a war they believed was more about U.S. dependency on Middle East oil than about freedom for the citizens of Kuwait. Elsewhere, protests were aimed at the Reagan administration for its support of the Contras seeking to overthrow the Sandinista government in Nicaragua, where in 1990 U.S. peace organizations monitored free elections.

A unique aspect of the peace movement since the 1970s has been the surge of feminist involvement. Awareness generated by the 1975–1985 United Nations Decade for Women resulted in international networks concerned with global issues of war, economic crises, and the rights of women. In 1980 and 1981 women encircled the Pentagon to oppose war. New York State in 1983 witnessed the massive Women's Encampment for the Future of Peace and Justice sited next to the Seneca Army Depot, a nuclear weapons storage facility. The 1987 Mother's Day action at the Department of Energy's nuclear test site near Las Vegas enlisted thousands of women from throughout the country. As in the past, peace movements appealed most to middle-income women, clergymen, educators, college students and people in their twenties, and some business leaders. Geographically, their centers of strength were in college towns, the large metropolitan areas of the Northeast and Midwest, and along the West Coast.

– CHARLES F. HOWLETT

PERSONAL RELATIONSHIPS

Personal relationships permeate the social environment. People have relatives, friends, parents, siblings, spouses, and/or children to whom they are more or less obligated, more or less committed, and more or less close. These relationships involve sentiments, values, shared activities, public declarations of commitment, and exchanges of information, thoughts, feelings, and services. Paradoxically, these relationships also involve issues of conflict and power.

Much attention has been directed toward the study of personal relationships in recent years. The argument has even been made that personal relationships should be a separate discipline (Kelley 1986). However, this argument overlooks the fact that some aspects of personal relationships, such as marriage and courtship, have a long history of sociological research and study (see, e.g., Waller 1938; Simmel 1950). The following essay argues that personal relationships are sociologically relevant because they create social structure and are affected by that structure. After contrasting primary relationships with secondary relationships, key theories and examples of research findings are presented. Throughout the essay a special emphasis is placed on friendship and its characteristics as an important type of personal relationship. Finally, the essay considers the absence of personal relationships by looking at research on loneliness and concludes by examining possibilities for future research.

Relationships exist along a continuum, moving from the most impersonal to the most intimate.

Relationships exist along a continuum, moving from the most impersonal (secondary relationships) to the most intimate (primary relationships). Secondary relationships are formal and, often, instrumental in nature. People at this end of the continuum respond to each other on the basis of their statuses or roles rather than considering the unique and personal characteristics of the individual. Secondary relationships may be of short duration with little or no intimacy. Examples of secondary relationships include coworkers or sales clerk and customer. Primary relationships, however, are informal, enduring, and expressive, involving intimate interactions over a period of time. Primary relationships need not be sexually intimate. As Simmel suggests, "it is by no means only erotic relations which attain a special, significant timbre, beyond their describable content and value, through the notion that an experience like theirs never existed before" (1950, p. 125). Examples of primary relationships include spouses and friends. Of course, secondary relationships can move toward primary relationships by becoming closer and more intimate; and primary relationships can move toward secondary relationships by becoming less close and less intimate (as in the case of a divorced couple, for example). Personal relationships are, therefore, primary relationships. As McCall (1970) suggests, however, personal relationships are probably best conceived as a combination of both secondary and primary relationships.

It has been observed that strong, intimate bonds tend to confine people to limited social circles, limiting relationships to in-group associations and fragmenting society. Nevertheless, weak social bonds between people integrate society by establishing, intergroup relationships (Blau 1977; Granovetter 1973). Couple and kinship relationships are strong bonds constraining individual behavior through their obligatory nature. In addition, kinship bonds are also strong due to their ascribed status. A marriage, by its very nature (e.g., exclusivity, commitment, social sanctions), is a strong bond that hinders the individual's participation in other relationships. Friendship can have varying degrees of closeness and intimacy, but it is neither obligatory nor ascribed (at least in Western society). Therefore, friendship (except perhaps for best-friendship) is a weaker bond than marriage and, as such, encourages intergroup relationships, thus creating community.

The most intimate type of primary relationship is marriage. It is characterized by ceremony, legal recognition, and normative expectations of mutual loyalty and obligation. Cohabitation, which since the late 1970s has become increasingly common (Bumpass 1990), is a personal relationship of importance and interest equal to marriage. Since some have argued that cohabitation is a stage leading to marriage (Blumstein and Schwartz 1983; Bumpass 1990), the study of cohabitation can answer questions about the process by which some relationships move from less committed to more committed and why some relationships do not make that transition. In addition, Blumstein and Kollock (1988) argue that it is useful to compare cohabiting couples with married couples because they are comparable on all structural variables, except for the institutionalized nature of marriage.

Some researchers have considered the distinction between secondary and primary friendships. Friendship, like marriage and cohabitation, is expressive, focusing on the unique characteristics of the individuals involved. Of course, friends may use friends in an instrumental way. This is permissible as long as it is understood that the friend is not a friend solely because of his/her usefulness (Allan 1979). For example, Kurth (1970) examined the difference between friendships and friendly relations. According to Kurth, friendly relations lack a sense of uniqueness about the individuals involved, there is little intimacy, and there are few obligations. As friendly relations take on these characteristics of personal uniqueness, intimacy, and obligations, they move toward primary relationships, either of friendship or courtship. Using a structural approach, Kurth further argues that some relationships are constrained from forming due to three important variables: age, gender, and marital status. Friendships form between those of the same age, same gender, and same marital status. Research supports the idea that same-sex friendship is the norm (Rose 1985; Bell 1981; Allan 1979; Booth and Hess 1974). Researchers have also found evidence for general equality between friends due to similarities in age, social class, and marital status (Bell 1981; Allan 1979). However, important empirical questions follow. For example, to what extent is friendship inhibited on the basis of these factors? To what degree are friendships exploitative when they cross the barriers of age, gender, and marital status?

Waller's (1938) principle of least interest may explain why some relationships continue and others do not. According to this principle, the individual with the least interest in continuing the relationship has the most power. Personal relationships, therefore, may become exploitative to the extent that those with more interest in the relationship, and therefore less power, are unable to negotiate fair exchanges (Kurth 1970). Ironically, power issues operate alongside the notion of reciprocity. Gouldner (1960) reasons that reciprocity is a norm with two aspects. First, a friend should repay a favor received; and second, a friend should not do harm to a person who has given a favor.

Two important theories are exchange theory and equity theory.

Two important theories are exchange theory and equity theory. Exchange theory, as developed by Thibaut and Kelley (1959), attempts to account for much of the variability in personal relationships by a cost/reward analysis. All social relationships incur both costs and rewards for the individuals. Often a person must decide between one relationship and another on the basis of an analysis of cost and reward (Kelley 1979). This analysis occurs at two levels. At the comparison level the individual evaluates costs and rewards within the relationship based on his/her own standards. At the comparison level for alternatives, the individual evaluates the costs and rewards based on the possibility of alternative relationships. Consequently, whether the relationship continues depends on the cost/reward analysis. Equity or fairness within the relationship is theoretically important (Walster et al. 1978; Kelley 1986). Researchers have found that personal relationships that are equitable are more satisfying to the individuals involved. In a study of lesbian couples by Caldwell and Peplau

(1984), satisfaction with the relationship was related to equity.

A zero-sum view of social involvements holds that increased involvement in one relationship demands decreased involvement in other relationships (Johnson and Leslie 1982). When the individual assumes a new role—that of a spouse, for example—all other role identities must be reprioritized because of the costs incurred with the new role. Therefore, the dyadic withdrawal hypothesis proposes that as a couple move closer together, their social network decreases (Burgess and Huston 1979). For example, Johnson and Leslie (1982), in a study of 419 college students, found that the number of friends reported by couples decreased, according to the stage of the couple relationship, from occasional dating to marriage. The reasons given by the authors for this finding is the exclusive nature of the couple relationship, the requirement of long-term commitment, and the increasing time requirement of the relationship.

Two models of personal relationships have been developed to capture the diversity of relationships. The first is Backman's (1981) four-stage theory of relationship development. The first stage describes the movement from no contact to unilateral awareness. In this stage physical proximity is essential. The second stage focuses on the processes of first impressions and sorting on the basis of similarities, physical attractiveness, and self-presentation. Obviously, most of the important work regarding interpersonal attraction occurs in this stage. The third stage involves the development of interdependence and role negotiation in which self-disclosure, exchanges, and attribution are central. The last stage concerns those processes that lead either to maintenance or to dissolution of the relationship. The last two stages are important to both exchange and equity theorists. The advantage of this model is that the focus remains on the dyad. It is also a process model, as opposed to a structural model.

The second model is by Blumstein and Kollock (1988), who identified five key characteristics or dimensions of personal relationships: (1) whether the relationship is kinship based, (2) whether the relationship has a sexual-romantic aspect, (3) whether the individuals live together, (4) whether the relationship is hierarchical or egalitarian, and (5) whether it is a cross-sex or same-sex relationship. Using this model, personal relationships can then be classified on each dimension. For example, individuals in a marriage are nonkin, sexual-romantic, cohabiting, and cross-sex. Since the authors argue that researchers need to take a comparative approach in analyzing relationships, one could compare marriages as described above with commuter marriages (in which individuals do not cohabit) to determine the differences between the two types of marriage. Such a study would be complicated, however, by the fact that in any marriage relationships are more or less egalitarian, more or less hierarchical.

The absence of personal relationships often creates a condition identified as loneliness. Loneliness can be conceived as the absence of a relationship with another and, therefore, "represents a very specific relation to society" (Simmel 1950, p. 120). This area has experienced much recent attention, primarily from psychologists (see, e.g., Hojat and Crandall 1989), coinciding with growth of interest in personal relationships (Perlman 1989). What is the societal significance of loneliness? How is it experienced differently by gender? by class? by race? Research has shown that loneliness is experienced disproportionately by the elderly, suggesting that the study of personal relationships in relation to the life course is important. Theoretically the sociologist needs to be concerned with loneliness because it fragments society and weakens controls on behavior (see Hirschi 1969 for a discussion on control theory).

Several studies on friendship have indicated that the life cycle is an important factor in predicting the friendship patterns of couples. Reisman (1981) found that friends dominate the lives of single, young adults and the elderly but decrease in importance during the child-bearing and career-building years, a finding also observed by Rubin (1985) and Fischer and Oliker (1983). It is unlikely that life stage is important only in friendships.

The following excerpt captures the importance of personal relationships in a commonsense yet elegant manner:

> Man is gifted with reason; he is life being aware of itself; he has awareness of himself, of his fellow man, of his past, and of the possibilities of his future. This awareness of himself as a separate entity, the awareness of his own short life span, of the fact that without his will he is born and against his will he dies, that he will die before those whom he loves, or they before him, the awareness of his aloneness and separateness, of his helplessness before the forces of nature and of society, all this makes his separate, disunited existence an unbearable prison. He would become insane could he not liberate himself from this prison and reach out, unite himself in some form or other with men, with the world outside. (Erich Fromm, *The Art of Loving,* pp. 6–7.)

One way in which knowledge regarding personal relationships can be advanced is by studying other societies in order to understand the ways in which personal relationships vary depending on societal norms. As Brain (1976) found, friendships vary cross-culturally, with other cultures having more norms regarding appropriate friendship behavior. He concludes that in Western societies friendship is often disposable. This, however, may be more often the case for friendly relations (secondary relationships) than for friendships (primary relationships).

Knowledge regarding personal relationships can be advanced by studying other societies to understand the ways relationships vary depending on societal norms.

This essay has briefly reviewed the general area of personal relationships, distinguishing between primary and secondary relationships. A special emphasis was placed on friendship as a type of primary relationship. In addition, key theories and models were presented. One question remains, however: Should personal relationships be a separate discipline? The answer here is no. Sociologists need to reclaim the study of relationships precisely because they are central to people's lives and form the basis for society. The study of the dyad in sociology has a long history, from Cooley (1902) to Waller (1938) to Simmel (1950). Sociologists need to be concerned with the subject matter because it focuses on the most fundamental of all social groups, the dyad, rather than on the individual.

[See also Interpersonal Power.]

BIBLIOGRAPHY

Allan, G. A. 1979 *A Sociology of Friendship and Kinship.* London: George Allen and Unwin.

Backman, C. W. 1981 "Attraction in Interpersonal Relationships." In M. Rosenberg and R. H. Turner, eds., *Social Psychology: Sociological Perspectives.* New York: Basic Books.

Bell, R. R. 1981 *Worlds of Friendship.* Beverly Hills, Calif.: Sage.

Blau, P. 1977 *Inequality and Heterogeneity.* New York: Free Press.

Blumstein, P., and P. Kollock 1988 "Personal Relationships." *Annual Review of Sociology* 14:467–490.

Blumstein, P., and P. Schwartz 1983 *American Couples.* New York: Morrow.

Booth, A., and E. Hess 1974 "Cross-Sex Friendships." *Journal of Marriage and the Family* 36:38–47.

Brain, R. 1976 *Friends and Lovers.* New York: Basic Books.

Brown, R. 1965 *Social Psychology.* New York: Free Press.

Bumpass, L. L. 1990 "What's Happening to Family? Interactions Between Demographic and Institutional Change." *Demography* 27, no. 4:483–496.

Burgess, R. L., and T. L. Huston 1979 *Social Exchange in Developing Relationships.* New York: Academic Press.

Caldwell, M. A., and L. A. Peplau 1984. "The Balance of Power in Lesbian Relationships." *Sex Roles* 10, no. 7/8:587–599.

Cooley, C. H. 1902 *Human Nature and the Social Order.* New York: Scribners.

Fischer, C. S., and S. J. Oliker 1983 "A Research Note on Friendship, Gender, and the Life Cycle." *Social Forces* 62, no. 1:124–133.

Gouldner, A. W. 1960 "The Norm of Reciprocity: A Preliminary Statement." *American Sociological Review* 25, no. 2:161–178.

Granovetter, M. S. 1973 "The Strength of Weak Ties." *American Journal of Sociology* 78, no. 6:1360–1380.

Hirschi, T. 1969 *Causes of Delinquency.* Berkeley: University of California Press.

Hojat, M., and R. Crandall (eds.) 1989 *Loneliness: Theory, Research and Applications.* Newbury Park, Calif.: Sage.

Johnson, M. P., and L. Leslie 1982 "Couple Involvement and Network Structure: A Test of the Dyadic Withdrawal Hypothesis." *Social Psychology Quarterly* 45, no. 1:34–43.

Kelley, H. H. 1979 *Personal Relationships: Their Structures and Processes.* Hillsdale, N.J.: Erlbaum.

——— 1986 "Personal Relationships: Their Nature and Significance." In R. Gilmour and S. Duck, eds., *The Emerging Field of Personal Relationships.* Hillsdale, N.J.: Erlbaum.

Kurth, S. B. 1970 "Friendship and Friendly Relations." In G. McCall, ed., *Social Relationships.* Chicago: Aldine.

McCall, G. 1970 "The Social Organization of Relationships." In G. McCall, ed., *Social Relationships.* Chicago: Aldine.

Perlman, D. 1989 "Further Reflections on the Present State of Loneliness Research." In M. Hojat and R. Crandall, eds., *Loneliness: Theory, Research and Applications.* Newbury Park, Calif.: Sage.

Reisman, J. M. 1981 "Adult Friendships." In S. Duck and R. Gilmour, eds., *Personal Relationships,* vol. 2. New York: Academic Press.

Rose, S. M. 1985 "Same- and Cross-Sex Friendships and the Psychology of Homosociality." *Sex Roles* 12:73–74.

Rubin, L. 1985 *Just Friends: The Role of Friendship in Our Lives.* New York: Harper and Row.

Simmel, G. 1950 *The Sociology of Georg Simmel,* K. H. Wolff, ed. and trans. New York: Free Press.

Thibaut, J., and H. H. Kelley 1959 *The Social Psychology of Groups.* New York: Wiley.

Waller, W. 1938 *The Family: A Dynamic Interpretation.* New York: Dryden.

Walster, E., G. W. Walster, and E. Berscheid 1978 *Equity: Theory and Research.* Boston: Allyn and Bacon.

– KATHLEEN A. WARNER

POLICE

For modern sociology the core problem of police has been, and continues to be, the extrication of the concept *police* from the forms and institutions in which it has been realized and the symbols and concealments in which it has been wrapped. Doing so is essential to the interpretive understanding of the idea of police and is prerequisite to mature answers to the question of what policing means, has meant, and can mean. In one form or another it is the project that has occupied sociologists of police since the early 1960s, and although there is occasional overlap and interchange, attention to it is primarily what distinguishes contributions to the sociology of police from scholarly efforts in the study of police administration, jurisprudence, criminalistics, and police science.

The Police: A Sociological Definition

By the end of the 1960s a small number of now-classic empirical studies of police had made it apparent that conventional understandings of the idea of police were fundamentally and irreparably flawed. In the face of large-scale studies by Reiss (1971) and Black (1971) which showed that the model tour of duty of a patrol officer in the high-crime areas of the nation's largest cities did not involve the arrest of a single person, it became impossible for sociologists to continue to speak of police as "law enforcers" or of their work as "law enforcement." Likewise, both Skolnick's *Justice Without Trial* (1966) and Wilson's *Varieties of Police Behavior* (1968) illustrated dramatic differences in the way police were organized and the relationships they elected to enjoy with courts and law. Similarly, early studies of both the exercise of patrol officer discretion (Bittner 1967a, 1967b) and requests for police service (Cumming et al. 1965; Bercal 1970) cast substantial doubt on the notion that a substantial, much less a defining, activity of police was "fighting crime."

POLICE ROLE AND FUNCTIONS. The task of extricating the concept of police from these common misconceptions was assumed by Egon Bittner in his *The Functions of Police in Modern Society* (1970). A fundamental theme of Bittner's work was that to define police as "law enforcers," "peacekeepers," "agents of social control," "officers of the court," or, indeed, in any terms that suppose what police should do, confuses police role and function. Throughout history, in this country and in others, police have performed all sorts of functions. In fact, the functions, both manifest and latent, which police have performed are so numerous and so contradictory that any attempt to define police in terms of the functions they are supposed to perform or the ends they are supposed to achieve is doomed to failure.

FORCE AS THE CORE OF THE POLICE ROLE. Sociologically, policing cannot be defined in terms of its ends; it must be defined in terms of its means. In *Functions* Bittner advanced an approach to understanding the role of the police that was based on the single means which was common to all police, irrespective of the ends to which they aspired or were employed. The means Bittner found to define police was a right to use coercive force. Police, said Bittner, are "a mechanism for the distribution of non-negotiably coercive force" (1971). No police had ever existed, nor is it possible to conceive of an entity that could be called police ever existing, that did not claim the right to use coercive force.

Sociologically, Bittner's formulation had three major virtues. First, it was universal. It was applicable to police everywhere and at all times, police as diverse as the sheriff's posse of the old West, the London bobby, the FBI, or the police of Hitler's Third Reich or Castro's Cuba. Second, it was politically and morally neutral. It could be used to refer to police whose behavior was exemplary as readily as it could be applied to police whose behavior was appalling. And, third, it made it possible to make explicit and to probe in systematic ways a host of questions about the role of police that could not previously be explored because they had been concealed in the confusion between role and function: Why do all modern societies, from the most totalitarian and most tyrannical to the most open and democratic, have police? What does having police make available to society that no other institution can supply? What functions are appropriate to assign to police and what are best left to other institutions?

Why do all modern societies, from the most totalitarian and most tyrannical to the most open and democratic, have police?

These questions are of such enormous consequence and so fundamental to an understanding of the role of the police that it is difficult to conceive of a sociology of police existing prior to their recognition.

WHY POLICE? If police are a "mechanism for the distribution of non-negotiably coercive force," why should all modern societies find it necessary to create and sustain such a mechanism? What does having such a mechanism make available to modern societies that no other institution can provide?

Bittner's answer is that no other institution has the special competence required to attend to "situations which ought not to be happening and about which something ought to be done NOW!" (1974; p. 30). The critical word in Bittner's careful formulation of the role of the police is "now." What the right to distribute coercive force gives to police is the ability to resolve situations that cannot await a later resolution. The crucial element is time. Turning off a fire hydrant against the wishes of inner-city street bathers, preventing the escape of a serial murderer, halting the escalation of a domestic dispute, or moving back the curious at the scene of a fire so that emergency equipment can pass—these and hundreds of other tasks fall to police because their capacity to use force may be required to achieve them "now."

This view of police radically inverts some conventional conceptions. While popular opinion holds that police acquire their right to use coercive force from their duty to enforce the law, the sociology of police holds that police acquire the duty to enforce the law because doing so may require them to invoke their right to use coercive force. Similarly, focus by police on the crimes and misdemeanors of the poor and humble, and their relative lack of attention to white-collar and corporate offenders, is often promoted as reflecting a class or race bias in institutions of social control. While not denying that such biases can exist and do sometimes influence the direction of police attention, if such biases were eliminated entirely, the distribution of police effort and attention would undoubtedly remain unchanged. It would remain unchanged because the special competence of police, their right to use coercive force, is essential in enforcement efforts in which offenders are likely to physically resist or to flee. In white-collar and corporate crime investigations, the special competence of lawyers and accountants is essential, while the special competence of police is largely unnecessary.

Institutional Forms

Although all modern societies have found it necessary to create and maintain some form of police, it is obvious that any institution which bears the right to use coercive force is extraordinarily dangerous and highly subject to abuse and corruption. The danger of the institution of police would appear to be magnified when it gains a monopoly or a near monopoly on the right to use coercive force and those who exercise that monopoly are almost exclusively direct and full-time employees of the state. Appearances and dangers notwithstanding, these are nevertheless the major terms of the institutional arrangement of police in every modern democracy. Some comment on the sociology of this institutional uniformity may be helpful.

AVOCATIONAL POLICING. For most of human history most policing has been done by individuals, groups, associations, and organizations in the private sector. This type of private-sector policing, done by citizens not as a job but as an avocation, may be classified into at least three types, each of which offered a somewhat different kind of motivation to private citizens for doing it (Klockars 1985). Historically, the most common type is *obligatory avocational policing.* Under its terms private citizens are compelled to police by the threat of some kind of punishment if they fail to do so. In American police history the sheriff's posse is perhaps the most familiar variety of this type of policing. The English systems of frank-pledge (Morris 1910) and parish constable (Webb and Webb 1906) were also of this type.

A second type of private-sector policing, *voluntary avocational policing,* is done by private citizens not because they are obliged by a threat of punishment but because they, for their own reasons, want to do it. The most familiar American example of this type of policing is vigilante groups, over three hundred of which are known to have operated throughout the United States up to the end of the nineteenth century (Brown 1975).

A third type, *entrepreneurial avocational policing,* includes private citizens who as English thief takers, American bounty hunters, French agents provocateurs, and miscellaneous paid informants police on a per-head, per-crime basis for money.

The institutional history of these avocational forms of policing is thoroughly disappointing, and modern societies have largely abandoned these ways of getting police work done. The central flaw in all systems of obligatory avocational policing is that as the work of policing becomes more difficult or demanding, obligatory avocational policing takes on the character of forced labor. Motivated only by the threat of punishment, those who do it become unwilling and resistant, a situation offering no one any reason to learn or cultivate the skill to do it well. All forms of voluntary avocational policing suffer from the exact opposite problem. Voluntary avocational police, vigilantes and the like, typically approach their work with passion. The problem is that because the passionate motives of voluntary avocational police are their own, it is almost impossible to control who and where and what form of police work they do and on whom they do it. Finally, the experience with entrepreneurial forms of avocational policing—thief takers, bounty hunters, and paid informants—has been the most disappointing of all. The abuse and corruption of entrepreneurial avocational police has demonstrated unequivocally that greed is too narrow a basis on which to build a police system.

Sociologically, the shortcoming of all forms of avocational policing is that none of them offers adequate means of controlling the police. This observation leads directly to the question of why one might have reason to suspect that a full-time, paid police should be easier to control than its avocational precedents. What new means of control is created by establishing a full-time, paid, police vocation?

The answer to this problem is that only when policing becomes a full-time, paid occupation is it possible to dismiss, to *fire,* any particular person who makes his or her living doing it. The state can only hire entrepreneurial avocational police, bounty hunters, paid informants, and thief takers; it cannot fire them. Vigilantes are driven by their own motives and cannot be discharged from them. Obligatory avocational police are threatened with punishment if they don't work; most would love to be sacked. Because the option to fire, to take police officers' jobs away from them, is the only essential means of controlling police work that separates the police vocation from all avocational arrangements for policing, how that option is used will, more than anything else, determine the shape and substance of the police vocation.

THE POLICE VOCATION. The English, who in 1829 created the first modern police, were intimately familiar with the shortcomings of all forms of avocational policing. They had, in fact, resisted the creation of a paid, full-time police for more than a century, out of fear that such an institution would be used as a weapon of political oppression by the administrative branch of government. To allay the fears that the "New Police" would become such a weapon, the architects of the first modern police, Home Secretary Robert Peel and the first commissioners of the New Police, Richard Mayne and Charles Rowan, imposed three major political controls on them. Peel, Mayne, and Rowan insisted that the New Police of London would be unarmed, uniformed, and confined to preventive patrol. Each of these features shaped in profound ways the institution of the New Police and, in turn, the police of the United States and other Western democracies that explicitly copied the English model.

UNARMED. Politically, the virtue of an unarmed police is that its strength can be gauged as a rough equivalent of its numbers. Weapons serve as multipliers of the strength of individuals and can increase the coercive capacity of individuals to levels that are incalculable. One person with a rifle can dominate a dozen citizens; with a machine gun, hundreds; with a nuclear missile, thousands. One person with a police truncheon is only slightly stronger than another, and that advantage can be quickly eliminated by the other's picking up a stick or a stone. In 1829 the individual strength of the three thousand-constable, unarmed New Police offered little to fear to London's 1.3 million citizens.

While this political virtue of an unarmed police helped overcome resistance to the establishment of the institution, the long-run sociological virtue of an un-

For much of history, private-sector policing served to maintain order. However, in the mid-1800s, England developed the first modern police force in which officers are agents of the state. The United States and other Western democracies have followed this model. (Morton Beebe-S.F./Corbis)

armed police proved far more important. Policing is, by definition, a coercive enterprise. Police must, on occasion, compel compliance from persons who would do otherwise. Force is, however, not the only means to compel compliance. Sociologically, at least three other bases for control are possible: authority, power, and persuasion.

Unarmed and outnumbered, the New Police "bobby" could not hope to police effectively on the basis of force. Peel, Mayne, and Rowan knew that if the New Police were to coerce successfully, they would have to do so on the basis of popular respect for the authority and power of the institution of which they were a part. The respect owed each constable was not owed to an individual but to a single, uniform temperament, code of conduct, style of work, and standard of behavior that every constable was expected to embody.

In order to achieve this uniformity of temperament, style, conduct, and behavior, the architects of the New Police employed the option to dismiss with a passion. "Between 1830 and 1838, to hold the ranks of the New Police of London at a level of 3300 men required nearly 5000 dismissals and 6000 resignations, most of the latter not being altogether voluntary" (Lee 1971; p. 240). During the first eight years of its organization, every position on the entire force was fired or forced to resign more than three times over!

What prevented the effective use of the firing option by early American police administrators was that police positions were patronage appointments of municipal politicians.

Unlike their earlier London counterparts, the new American police were undisciplined by the firing option. What prevented the effective use of the firing option by early American police administrators was that police positions were, by and large, patronage appointments of municipal politicians. In New York, for example, the first chief of police did not have the right to fire any officer under his command. So while London bobbies were being dismissed for showing up late to work or behaving discourteously toward citizens, American police were assaulting superior officers, taking bribes, refusing to go on patrol, extorting money from prisoners, and releasing prisoners from the custody of other officers.

In New York, Boston, Chicago, and other American cities the modern police began, in imitation of London's bobbies, as unarmed forces; but, being corrupt, undisciplined, and disobedient, they could not inspire respect for either their power or their authority. In controlling citizens they had no option but to rely on their capacity to use force. The difficulty with doing so unarmed is that someone armed with a multiplier of strength can always prove to be stronger. Gradually, against orders, American police armed themselves, at first with the quiet complicity of superior officers and later, as the practice became widespread, in open defiance of departmental regulations. Eventually, in an effort to control the types of weapons their officers carried, the first municipal police agencies began issuing standard service revolvers.

The long-run sociological consequence of arming the American police can be understood only by appreciating how it shaped American police officers' sense of the source of their capacity to control the citizens with whom they dealt. While the London bobbies drew their capacity for control from the profoundly social power and authority of the institution of which they were a part, American police officers understood their capacities for control to spring largely from their own personal, individual strength, multiplied if necessary by the weapon they carried on their hips. This understanding of the source of their capacity for control led American police officers to see the work they did and the choices they made in everyday policing to be largely matters of their individual discretion. Thus, the truly long-run sociological effect of the arming of the American police has been to drive discretionary decision making to the lowest and least public levels of American police agencies. Today how an American police officer handles a drunk, a domestic disturbance, an unruly juvenile, a marijuana smoker, or a belligerent motorist is largely a reflection not of law or agency policy but of that particular officer's personal style. This is not to say that law or agency policy cannot have influence over how officers handle these types of incidents. However, one of the major lessons of recent attempts by sociologists to measure the impact of changes in law or police policy in both domestic violence and drunken driving enforcement is that officers can resist those changes vigorously when the new law or policy goes against their views of proper police response (see Dunford et al. 1990; Mastrofski et al. 1988).

UNIFORMED. Politically, the requirement that police be uniformed is a guarantee that they will not be used as spies; that they will be given information only when their identity as police is known; that those who give them information, at least when they do so in public, are likely to be noticed doing so; and that they can be held accountable, as agents of the state, for their behavior. The English, who had long experience with uniformed employees of many types, understood these political virtues of the uniform completely. In fact, an incident in 1833 in which a police sergeant assumed an ununiformed undercover role resulted in such a scandal that it nearly forced the abolition of the New Police.

By contrast, the early American understanding of the uniform was totally different. Initially it was seen to be a sign of undemocratic superiority. Later it was criticized by officers themselves as a demeaning costume and resisted on those grounds. For twelve years, despite regulations that required them to do so, early New York policemen successfully refused to wear uniforms. In 1856 a compromise was reached by allowing officers in each political ward to decide on the color and style they liked best.

Despite the early resistance to the uniform and the lack of appreciation for its political virtues, American police eventually became a uniformed force. But while the London bobby's uniform was explicitly designed to have a certain "homey" quality and reflect restraint, the modern American police officer's uniform is festooned with the forceful tools of the police trade. The gun, ammunition, nightstick, blackjack, handcuffs, and Mace, all tightly holstered in shiny black leather and set off with chromium buckles, snaps, badges, stars, flags, ribbons, patches, and insignia, suggest a decidedly military bearing. The impression intended is clearly one not of restraint but of the capacity to overcome the most fearsome of enemies by force.

THE MILITARY ANALOGY AND THE WAR ON CRIME. To understand the sociology of the American police uniform, it is necessary to see in it a reflection of a major reform movement in the history of the American police. Around 1890 American police administrators began to speak about the agencies they administered as if they were domestic armies engaged in a war on crime (Fogelson 1977).

The analogy was powerful and simple. It drew upon three compelling sources. First, it sought to connect police with the victories and heroes of the military and to dissociate them from the corruption and incompetence of municipal politics. Second, it evoked a sense of urgency and emergency in calls for additional resources. From the turn of the century to the present day, the war on crime has proved a useful device for getting municipal governments and taxpayers to part with money for police salaries and equipment. And, third and most important, the war on crime and the military analogy sought to create a relationship between police administrators and politicians at the municipal level that was similar to the relationship enjoyed by military generals and politicians at the national level. At the national level Americans have always conceded that the decision on whether to fight a war was a politicians' decision, but how that war was to be fought and the day-to-day discipline of the troops was best left to the generals. By getting the public and the politicians to accept these terms of the police-politics relationship, the early police administrators found a way to wrest from the hands of politicians the tool they needed to discipline their troops: the option to fire disobedient officers.

The uniform of the war-ready American police officer is testimony to the fact that since the 1940s, American police administrators have won the battle to conceive of police as engaged in a war on crime. And in doing so they have gained control of the option to fire for administrative purposes. However, the cost of that victory has been enormous.

A major problem is the idea of a war on crime and the expectation police have promoted that they can, in some sense, fight or win it. In point of fact, a war on crime is something police can neither fight nor win for some fundamental sociological reasons. It is simply not within the capacity of police to change those things—unemployment, the age distribution of the population, moral education, civil liberties, ambition and the social and economic opportunities to realize it—that influence the amount and type of crime in any society. These are the major social correlates of crime, and despite presentments to the contrary, police are but a small tail on a gigantic social kite. Moreover, any kind of real "war on crime" is something that no democratic society would be prepared to let its police fight. No democratic society would be able to tolerate the kinds of abuses to the civil liberties of innocent citizens that fighting any real "war" on crime would necessarily involve. It is a major contribution of the sociology of police since the 1960s to demonstrate that almost nothing police do can be shown to have any substantial effect on reducing crime.

The problems of policing in the name of crime when one cannot do much of anything about it are enormous. It is not uncommon for patrol officers to see their employers as hypocritical promoters of a crime-fighting image that is far removed from what they know to be the reality of everyday police work. They may seek to explain what they know to be their failure to do much about crime in terms of the lack of courage of their chief, the incompetence of police administration, or sinister political forces seeking to "handcuff" the police. They often close off what they regard as the disappointing reality of what they do in cynicism, secrecy, and silence—the "blue curtain," the occupational culture of policing.

Equally problematic as a spoil of the early chiefs' victory in their war on crime is the quasi-military police administrative structure. Although once heralded as a model of efficiency, it is now regarded as an organizationally primitive mode of management. It works, to the extent that it works, by creating hundreds and sometimes even thousands of rules and by punishing departures from those rules severely. The central failing of such an administrative model is that it rests on the unwarranted assumption that employees will not discover that the best way to avoid punishment for doing something wrong is to do as little as possible. The administration can, in turn, respond by setting quotas for the minimum amount of work it will tolerate from employees before it moves to punish them, but if it does so, that minimal amount of work is, by and large, all it will get.

PREVENTIVE PATROL. The third major mechanism with which architects of the New Police sought to neutralize their political uses was to confine police to preventive patrol. This restriction was understood to have the effect of limiting the uniformed, patrolling constable to two relatively apolitical types of interventions: situations in which constables would be called upon for help by persons who approached them on the street and situations that, from the street, constables could see required their attention. These political virtues of patrol impressed the architects of the New Police, particularly Sir Richard Mayne. Mayne postponed the formation of any detective unit in the New Police until 1842, and for his 40 years as commissioner held its ranks to fewer than 15 detectives in a force of more than 3,500.

In the early American experience uniformed patrol served the principal purpose of imposing some semblance of order on unruly officers. Patrol offered some semblance of assurance that officers could be found at least somewhere near the area to which they were assigned. And while American police created detective forces almost immediately after they were organized, patrol has become in the United States, as in Britain and other modern democracies, the major means of getting police work done.

Sociologically, patrol has had tremendous consequences for the form and substance of policing. It has, for example, been extraordinarily amenable to the three most profound technological developments of the past century: the automobile, the telephone, and the wireless radio. And while there is no evidence that increasing or decreasing the amount of patrol has any influence whatsoever on the crime rate, each of these technological developments has made police patrol more convenient and attractive to citizens who wish to call for police service. It is not an exaggeration to say that the vast majority of the activity of most modern police agencies is driven by a need to manage citizen demand for patrol service.

In recent years, attempts to manage this demand have taken many forms. Among the most common are the creation of computer-aided dispatch systems that prioritize the order in which patrol officers are assigned to complaints and increasingly stringent policies governing the types of problems for which police will provide assistance. Also increasingly common are attempts to handle complaints that merely require a written report, by taking that report over the telephone or having the complainant complete a mail-in form. In no small part, such efforts at eliminating unnecessary police response and making necessary police response efficient have produced some of the increasing cost for police labor.

Reorienting Policing

Despite efforts at prioritization, limitation of direct police response, and development of alternative ways of registering citizen complaints, demand for police service continues to grow. And despite the fact that individual citizens appear to want this form of police service more than any other, some contemporary approaches suggest that the entire idea of "dial-a-cop," "incident-driven" policing requires reconsideration. Two such approaches, "community-oriented policing" (Skolnick and Bayley 1986) and "problem-oriented policing" (Goldstein 1979, 1990), have been advanced as the next generation of "reform" movements in American policing (Greene and Mastrofski 1988).

The vast majority of the activity of most modern police agencies is driven by a need to manage citizen demand for patrol service.

As theories of police reform, both "problem-oriented" and "community-oriented" policing are grounded in the suspicion that the traditional police response of dispatching patrol officers in quick response to citizen complaints does little to correct the underlying problem that produced the complaint. To some degree at least, this suspicion is confirmed by studies which tend to show that a fairly small number of addresses tend to generate disproportionate numbers of calls for police service, and that patrol officers commonly return to such "hot spots" again and again to attend to similar problems (Sherman et al. 1989).

Both problem-oriented and community-oriented policing offer strategies to deal with such problems that go beyond merely dispatching an officer to the scene. Problem-oriented policing offers a generic, four-step, problem-solving strategy—scanning, analysis, response, and assessment—that police can use to identify problems and experiment with solutions. Community-oriented policing, by contrast, does not offer a mechanism for problem analysis and solution. It is, however, committed to a general strategy that calls for cooperative, police-community efforts in problem solving. In such efforts it encourages the employment of a variety of police tactics—foot patrol, storefront police stations, neighborhood watch programs—that tend to involve citizens directly in the police mission.

While both approaches to reorienting policing have been heralded as revolutionary in their implications for the future of policing, both confront some major obstacles to their realization. The first is that neither problem-oriented nor community-oriented police efforts have been able to reduce the demand for traditional patrol response. Unless that demand is reduced or police resources are increased to allow it to be satisfied along with nontraditional approaches, the community- and problem-oriented policing approaches will most likely be relegated, at best, to a secondary, peripheral role.

The second problem confronting both community- and problem-oriented policing stems from the definition of police and the role appropriate to it in a modern democratic society. The special competence of police is their capacity to use force, and for that reason all modern societies find it necessary and appropriate to have them attend to situations that cannot await a later resolution. Reactive, incident-driven, dial-a-cop patrol is a highly popular, extremely efficient, and, as near as possible, politically neutral means of delivering that special competence. To expand the police role to include responsibility for solving the root problems of neighborhoods and communities is an admirable aspiration. But it is a responsibility that seems to go beyond the special competence of police and to require, more appropriately, the special competence of other institutions.

[See also Criminal Sanctions; Criminology.]

BIBLIOGRAPHY

Bercal, T. E. 1970 "Calls for Police Assistance: Consumer Demand for Governmental Service." *American Behavioral Scientist* 13, no. 2 (May–August):221–238.

Bittner, E. 1967a "Police Discretion in Apprehension of Mentally Ill Persons." *Social Problems* 14 (Winter):278–292.

——— 1967b "The Police on Skid Row: A Study of Peace Keeping." *American Sociological Review* 32 (October):699–715.

——— 1970 *The Functions of Police in Modern Society.* Washington, D.C.: U.S. Government Printing Office.

——— 1974 "Florence Nightingale in Pursuit of Willie Sutton: A Theory of Police." In H. Jacob, ed., *The Potential for Reform of Criminal Justice.* Beverly Hills, Calif.: Sage.

Black, D. 1971 "The Social Organization of Arrest." *Stanford Law Review* 23 (June):1087–1111.

Brown, R. M. 1975 *Strain of Violence: Historical Studies of American Violence and Vigilantism.* Oxford: Oxford University Press.

Cumming, E., I. Cumming, and L. Edell 1965 "Policeman as Philosopher, Guide, and Friend." *Social Forces* 12, no. 3:276–286.

Dunford, F. W., D. Huizinga, and D. S. Elliott 1990 "The Role of Arrest in Domestic Assault: The Omaha Police Experiment." *Criminology* 28, no. 2:183–206.

Fogelson, R. 1977 *Big City Police.* Cambridge, Mass.: Harvard University Press.

Goldstein, H. 1979 "Improving Policing: A Problem-Oriented Approach." *Crime and Delinquency* 25 (April):236–258.

——— 1990 *Problem-Oriented Policing.* New York: McGraw-Hill.

Greene, J., and S. Mastrofski 1988 *Community Policing: Rhetoric or Reality.* New York: Praeger.

Klockars, C. B. 1985 *The Idea of Police.* Beverly Hills, Calif.: Sage.

Lee, M. 1971 *A History of Police in England.* Montclair, N.J.: Patterson Smith.

Mastrofski, S., R. R. Ritti, and D. Hoffmaster 1988 "Organizational Determinants of Police Discretion: The Case of Drunk Driving." *Journal of Criminal Justice* 15:387–402.

Morris, W. A. 1910 *The Frankpledge System.* New York: Longmans, Green and Co.

Reiss, A. J., Jr. 1971 *Police and the Public.* New Haven, Conn.: Yale University Press.

Sherman, L. W., P. Gartin, and M. E. Buerger 1989 "Hot Spots of Predatory Crime: Routine Activities and the Criminology of Place." *Criminology* 27:27–55.

Skolnick, J. K. 1966 *Justice Without Trial.* New York: John Wiley.

———, and D. Bayley 1986 *The New Blue Line.* New York: Free Press.

Webb, S., and B. Webb 1906 *English Local Government from the Revolution to the Municipal Corporations Act: The Parish and the County.* New York: Longmans, Green and Co.

Wilson, J. Q. 1968 *Varieties of Police Behavior: The Management of Law and Order in Eight Communities.* Cambridge, Mass.: Harvard University Press.

– CARL B. KLOCKARS

POLITICAL CRIME

Political crime has been more often an object of partisan assertion than of independent research. Passions are easily aroused, facts are difficult to establish. Nevertheless, a growing number of studies have contributed to (1) articulating the issues in defining political criminality; (2) describing instances and patterns of resistance to political-legal authority; (3) cataloging and analyzing governmental efforts to prevent and counter such challenges; and (4) proposing research agendas.

The Problem of Definition

Political criminality may be narrowly or broadly defined, with greater or lesser regard for definitions offered by laws and interpretations by authorities. Moreover, the values and politics of observers frequently influence their conceptions of what and who is politically criminal. The resulting mélange of definitions has led Kittrie and Wedlock (1986, p. xlii) to conclude pessimistically, "It may be that an objective and neutral definition of political crime is impossible, because the term seems to involve relativistic relationships between the motives and acts of individuals and the perspectives of government toward their conduct and allegiances." However, an alternative view is implicit in their understanding of political criminality as perceptual and relational, defined in interaction between opposing parties.

Whose perceptions decide what is to be called political crime? Apart from partisan and subjective answers, the empirical reality of political criminality is that it is defined by those with enough power to impose their perceptions. Insofar as a political authority structure has been established, one may argue that the dominant parties within it by definition have the power to define criminality (Turk 1982a, pp. 11–68, 1984, pp. 119–121; see also Ingraham 1979, pp. 13, 19). However, this view leaves unsettled the question of how authorities themselves may be defined as political criminals.

The most common resolution is to expand the definition to include anyone who commits extralegal acts defending or attacking an authority structure. For example, Roebuck and Weeber (1978, pp. 16–17) consider political crime to be any illegal or disapproved act committed by "government or capitalistic agents" or by "the people against the government." This very subjective definition (disapproved by whom?) leaves one unable to distinguish either between acts against and on behalf of authority or between legal and nonlegal behavior. A more promising approach is to recognize that criminality may be defined at different levels of political organization—international as well as national. To the extent that sanctions are likely to be applied to offenders, the Universal Declaration of Human Rights, formally accepted by nearly all members of the United Nations (Henkin 1989, p. 13), may eventually serve to define political crime by national and international elites as well as their challengers. Within nations, acts by local authorities may be effectively treated as political crimes (subversive of the authority structure) by national elites, as in the U.S. federal government's historic crackdown on southern state and local violations of constitutionally guaranteed civil rights.

Another question is whether political criminality is to be defined only as behavior. While one may agree that only specified harmful acts *should* be punishable, the historical fact is that in addition to offending behavior, nonbehavioral attributes such as ethnicity and class background have frequently been used by antagonists as criteria of intolerable political deviance. Moreover, imputed as well as observed deviations or threats have been used. Anticipation as well as reaction are involved in the identification of political criminality. In sum, political criminality is most realistically defined as whatever is treated as such by specified actors (usually governments, dominant groups, or their agents) in particular historical situations.

Resisting Authority

Resistance to political authority may be more or less deliberate, organized, or planned. The appearance or potential of resistance may be sufficient for authorities to act against perceived challengers. Resisters may be engaged in activities ranging from merely disrespectful comments to the most violent assaults, from spontaneous eruptions to carefully orchestrated attacks, from individually motivated acts to organized strategies of rebellion. Acts of resistance may be categorized as evasion, dissent, disobedience, or violence.

Resisters may simply evade the orders and demands of the powerful. Avoiding masters, bosses, tax collectors, and military conscription has generally been safer than explicit defiance—because open defiance tends to force authorities to respond, while tacit evasion is more easily ignored or minimized.

The right to speak out against authority is enshrined in many legal traditions but in practice is limited by the varying tolerance of authorities and people—decidedly lower in wartime and economic hard times. After centuries of attempting to deter such offenses as seditious libel and treasonous utterances, more democratic governments have de facto concluded that the effort is incompatible with the concept of free speech (Law Commission 1977; Stone 1983; Hurst 1983; cf. Franks 1989). However, other labels may be invoked to authorize punishing those whose dissent is especially galling, especially when authorities feel particularly threatened. U.S. Senator Joseph McCarthy, for instance, achieved the lasting notoriety of "McCarthyism" by freewheeling accusations of "subversion" against a wide spectrum of targets—from known communists to President Eisenhower.

Dissenting is one thing, actually disobeying rules and commands is another. Lower class people have historically suffered many demonstrations of their vulnerability, so have characteristically been less likely than higher class people either to dissent or to disobey overtly (Turk 1982a, pp. 69–114). On the other hand, dissenting or disobedient higher class, especially youthful, resisters have typically been subjected to less punitive treatment. For instance, sentences of Vietnam draft resisters decreased in response to the political repercussions of imprisoning growing numbers of higher class young men

(Hagan and Bernstein 1979). Not surprisingly, civil disobedience has been more likely to be a higher class than a lower class mode of resistance—that is, a tactic of those whose backgrounds encourage them to believe, perhaps erroneously, in their own significance and efficacy and in legal rights and protections.

Not surprisingly, civil disobedience has been more likely to be a higher class than a lower class mode of resistance.

Violent resistance by individuals and small organizations seldom threatens authority structures directly, but does indirectly weaken them in that authorities facing or fearing violence typically adopt extralegal and repressive control measures—which contradict beliefs in legal restraints on governmental power. The more actually and ideologically democratic the political order, the greater the contradiction—which is associated with the greater vulnerability of democratic than despotic regimes to terrorism (Turk 1982b, p. 127).

Political offenders have commonly been viewed as morally or mentally defective. However, even the most violent assassins and terrorists appear unlikely to exhibit psychopathology (Turk 1983, 1984, p. 123; cf. Schafer 1974). The effort to understand political resisters begins in recognizing that they may vary enormously in political consciousness and motivation, organizational involvement, and readiness to commit violent acts, in addition to other characteristics, such as class origins. Distinctions must be made among deliberate political actors, emotional reactors to climates of political instability and violence, and apolitical opportunists such as ordinary criminals who merely seek to profit from their contacts with resistance figures and movements.

Asserting Authority

Political dominance is defended legally and often extralegally at all institutional levels. The highest and broadest level is typified by national (and increasingly international) policies of insulation, sanctioning, and persuasion designed to ensure that potential resisters lack the opportunities, resources, and will to challenge authority (Gamson 1968). More specifically focused on controlling resistance is political policing—the organized effort to gather relevant intelligence, manipulate channels of communication, neutralize opposition, and deter challenges.

Because the value of information can never be fully anticipated, intelligence-gathering is inherently limitless. Advancing technologies of surveillance and analysis enable ever more extensive and intensive monitoring of human behavior and relationships. The distinction between public and private is increasingly dubious in both law and practice. Recurring legislative and judicial efforts to impose legal restraints have occasionally slowed but never stopped the trend (Marx 1988).

Authorities have never been entirely comfortable with the ideal of free and open communications. Even where that ideal has been most firmly asserted in law, in practice the right to disseminate critical information and ideas has been limited (Kittrie and Wedlock 1986, passim). Openly or subtly, communications favoring the status quo have been facilitated, while dissent has been inhibited to a greater or lesser degree.

When resistance is encountered, some blend of enclosure and terror tactics is used—that is, methods designed not only to suppress resistance but also to convince offenders that apprehension is inevitable and punishment unbearably severe. Psychological as well as physical coercion is accomplished by subjecting targets to sanctions varying from character assassination to torture and extermination. International covenants notwithstanding, torture and other violations of human rights continue throughout the world (Amnesty International 1984). Clearly, authorities facing serious challenges are unlikely to be restrained by legal or other norms.

The ultimate goal of political policing is general deterrence. Insofar as the subject population does not knowingly and willingly accept the political order, fear and ignorance may still ensure acquiescence. Surveillance, censorship, and neutralization are designed not only to repress political deviance but also to discourage any inclination to question the social order. But intimidation must be supplemented by persuasion if superior power is to be legitimated—transformed into authority. A classic technique is the political trial, in which legal formalities are used to portray the accused as a threat to society, to convey the impression that political policing is legally restrained, and to reinforce the sense that political dominance is both right and irresistible (Kirchheimer 1961; Christenson 1986).

Research Agendas

Studies of political criminality have raised far more questions than they have answered. In the future, not isolated, small-scale investigations but ongoing research programs are essential if the quest for systematic explanations of political criminality is to be successful. Such programs will necessarily be multilevel, integrating research on the political socialization of individuals, the radicalization of defenders as well as challengers of authority, the interaction of resistance and policing strategies, and the conditions under which the political organization of social life is relatively viable (low rates of both resistance and repression).

The viability of a political authority structure can in principle be objectively defined: The probability of its survival increases or decreases. Accordingly, research can identify progressive actions (increase viability) and destructive actions (decrease viability) by anyone involved in political conflict. Turk (1982a, pp. 181–191) hypothesizes that random violence, economic exploitation, and weakening social bonds are destructive, while nonviolent actions increasing the life chances of everyone instead of only some people are likely to be progressive.

[See also Criminology; White-Collar Crime.]

BIBLIOGRAPHY

Amnesty International 1984 *Torture in the Eighties.* London: Amnesty International Publications.

Christenson, Ron 1986 *Political Trials: Gordian Knots in the Law.* New Brunswick, N.J.: Transaction Books.

Franks, C. E. S., ed. 1989 *Dissent and the State.* Toronto: Oxford University Press.

Gamson, William A. 1968 *Power and Discontent.* Homewood, Ill.: Dorsey Press.

Hagan, John, and Ilene Bernstein 1979 "Conflict in Context: The Sanctioning of Draft Resisters, 1963–76." *Social Problems* 27:109–122.

Henkin, Louis 1989 "The Universality of the Concept of Human Rights." *Annals of the American Academy of Political and Social Science* 506:10–16.

Hurst, James Willard 1983 "Treason." In Sanford H. Kadish, ed., *Encyclopedia of Crime and Justice,* vol. 4. New York: Free Press.

Ingraham, Barton L. 1979 *Political Crime in Europe. A Comparative Study of France, Germany and England.* Berkeley: University of California Press.

Kirchheimer, Otto 1961 *Political Justice: The Use of Legal Procedure for Political Ends.* Princeton, N.J.: Princeton University Press.

Kittrie, Nicholas N., and Eldon D. Wedlock, Jr. (eds.) 1986 *The Tree of Liberty: A Documentary History of Rebellion and Political Crime in America.* Baltimore: Johns Hopkins University Press.

Law Commission 1977 *Codification of the Criminal Law: Treason, Sedition, and Allied Offences.* Working Paper 72. London: Her Majesty's Stationery Office.

Marx, Gary T. 1988 *Undercover: Police Surveillance in America.* Berkeley: University of California Press.

Roebuck, Julian, and Stanley C. Weeber 1978 *Political Crime in the United States: Analyzing Crime by and against Government.* New York: Praeger.

Schafer, Stephen 1974 *The Political Criminal: The Problem of Morality and Crime.* New York: Macmillan.

Stone, Geoffrey R. 1983 "Sedition." In Sanford H. Kadish, ed., *Encyclopedia of Crime and Justice,* vol. 4. New York: Free Press.

Turk, Austin T. 1982a *Political Criminality: The Defiance and Defense of Authority.* Newbury Park, Calif.: Sage.

——— 1982b "Social Dynamics of Terrorism." *Annals of the American Academy of Political and Social Science* 463:119–128.

——— 1983 "Assassination." In Sanford H. Kadish, ed., *Encyclopedia of Crime and Justice,* vol. 1. New York: Free Press.

——— 1984 "Political Crime." In Robert F. Meier, ed., *Major Forms of Crime.* Newbury Park, Calif.: Sage.

– AUSTIN T. TURK

POPULAR CULTURE

Since the 1960s, studies of popular culture in the United States have proliferated and a range of novel arguments have been proposed, linking patterns of popular culture production and consumption to systems of stratification and power. Before the 1960s in Europe, Roland Barthes ([1957] 1972) and Fernand Braudel ([1949] 1966) championed (for quite different reasons) increased attention to everyday culture and its social significance, and members of the Frankfurt school emigrating to the United States brought new theories of mass culture to American academics (Rosenberg and White 1957; Lowenthal 1961), but American scholars still did not generally see any value in studying popular culture.

Beginning in the mid-1960s, as the American middle class began to be targeted by the mass media as the desired audience, more American educators started to show more interest in media-based popular culture, even though in much of academia, studying popular culture was either declassé or taboo (Ross 1989). A few hardy souls from sociology and literary criticism looked at popular culture as a realm of interesting fads and fashions, ephemeral cultural forms that plummeted through modern urban life with regularity, gave rise to much cultural entrepreneurship, and left ordinary citizens running to keep up with what was "happening." Sociologists found it a bit easier to justify ongoing attention to these social ephemera because of the established tradition in sociology of examining urban and suburban communities and their cultures (Park 1955; Lynd and Lynd 1929). By the mid-1960s a quite active community of scholars around Bowling Green University proliferated empirical and descriptive accounts of everything from fast-food restaurants to rock and roll (Keil 1966; Nye 1972; Cawelti 1972; Browne 1982). At roughly the same time, a small group of literary scholars drew on long standing literary interest in the voices of the people in literature (Shiach 1989, chaps. 2 and 4), and argued that to understand contemporary uses of language, one had to study commercial language in popular culture (McQuade and Atwan 1974). This work did not have much success in changing either sociology or literature. In sociology, it was eclipsed conceptually by sociological work that linked patterns of popular culture to systems of institutional control (Cantor 1971; Denisoff 1974; Hirsh 1972). This work had greater legitimacy because it addressed the organizations' literature, but it also reinforced the sense that the study of popular culture was not really important enough to stand on its own.

By the end of the 1960s, as the political climate shifted, radical scholars began to champion studies of popular culture either to understand the world of "the people" (disregarded by elites) or to account for the political passivity of the working class and poor. They tried to resuscitate questions about elite distaste for popular culture itself and its relation to systems of social control. These questions gave popular culture new importance, not as an aesthetic or commercial system but as a political actor in systems of stratification and power (Schiller 1969; Guback 1969; Aronowitz 1973; Gans 1974).

This legacy has been carried into present-day popular culture research as it has spread through sociology, literature, anthropology, history, and cultural studies. Ongoing fascination with "politics from below" has made this subfield a conceptually complex and politically "left" branch of cultural studies, not concerned so much with the moral fabric of society or the ideational sources of its integration (subjects derived from the Weberian tradition of cultural studies), but rather with the use of culture to exert or avoid systematic domination from above.

Some have perceived mass culture as aesthetically and politically debilitating.

Many contemporary attempts to explain patterns of cultural domination through popular culture are indebted to (and in different ways critical of) the work on mass culture and consciousness begun by the Frankfurt school. Members of the Frankfurt Institute of Social Research originally organized themselves to examine the philosophical underpinnings of Marxism, but when Hitler came to power, since most of the leading members of the group were Jewish, this project was disrupted and many figures came to the United States. The work on mass culture that developed from this group was (not surprisingly) devoted to understanding the success of Nazism by dissecting and analyzing the psychological and political effects of mass society (Jay 1973). Members of the Frankfurt school perceived mass culture as aesthetically and politically debilitating, reducing the capacities of audiences to think critically and functioning as an ideological tool to manipulate the political sentiments of the mass public. They argued that in modern industrial societies, the pursuit of economic and scientific rationality provided an impoverished environment for human life. The realm of culture, which might have provided respite from the drudgery of everyday life, was itself being industrialized, yielding a commercial mass culture that atomized audiences and lulled them with emotionally unsatisfactory conventionality. This world of commodities only added to the dissatisfactions that deflected people from their desires. The dulling of their senses made them politically passive and their emotional discontent made them easy targets for propaganda that addressed their powerful inner feelings. This combination, according to theory, was what made the propaganda in Nazi Germany so effective (Horkheimer and Adorno 1972).

During the 1960s, critical theory, as the work of the Frankfurt school came to be known, continued in U.S. intellectual circles to be used to explain the political conservatism of the working class, but it was also taken up in the student movement as a critique of commercial mass culture that justified the efforts by flower children to create radical social change through cultural experimentation. The problem was that, for the latter purpose, critical theory was too deterministic to have much room for human agency, including cultural strategies for change. Constructivist models from the sociology of culture could be and were used to explain how ordinary people could break the hold of political institutions over their imaginations (Blumer 1969; Goffman 1959; Berger and Luckmann 1966; Schutz 1967; Becker 1963), but they did not explain how ideological control of populations by elites could work. The insights of the Italian communist political writer Antonio Gramsci (1971) about hegemony seemed a better scheme for explaining both the role of ideology in systems of power and the constructed nature of social reality. According to Gramsci, elites maintained their power and legitimacy by creating hegemonic definitions of reality that were accepted as common sense by the population. By subscribing to these views, nonelites collaborated in their own oppression. Gramsci's work, available in English translations and popularized in the academic community in the 1970s, gave the study of culture and power in the English-speaking world new direction.

By the 1970s, much innovative work on popular culture was coming out of Great Britain. The British school of cultural studies drew attention to the role of nonelites in systems of power, but it focused more on working-class culture—particularly its role as a crucible for cultural resistance, innovation, and change. This school had its roots in the work of E. P. Thompson (1963) and Raymond Williams (1961; 1977; 1980). These authors began from the premise that the working class is not just defined by relations of production, but a self-consciousness bred in a class-based way of life. The working class has its own history and traditions that give its members distinct values and a complex relation to societal level systems of power. In their own cultural enclaves, class members are active producers of their own political institutions and popular entertainments (and through them defined social realities). So while the public culture of Western industrialized societies may be dominated by elites who control the mass media and who try to use cultural systems for exerting power, their hegemonic control is circumscribed by the cultures of subordinated groups. The realm of popular culture, in this tradition, is an arena of conflict in which cultural identity, authority, and autonomy are contested. Social rifts are made manifest in the multiplicity of points of view that enter into the public sphere along with the hegemonic messages of much mass culture (Curran, Gurevitch, and Woolacott 1979; Hall and Whannel 1965).

While early British cultural studies paid greatest attention to working-class culture, the ideas about cultural resistance were easily transferred to the analysis of other subordinated groups such as women, youth, and minorities. This broader approach to cultures of resistance gave birth to the kind of subcultural analysis conducted, for example, by Dick Hebdige (1979). He argues that innovations in youth culture come from marginalized working-class youths rebelling against both their parents and hegemonic culture. New developments in music and dress are culled from the cultural possibilities made available in mass society, both in commercial commodities and local cultures. These cultural resources are mixed and reassembled to create new subcultural styles. Much innovation of this sort comes from minority communities and is picked up by middle-class kids in part because it is so offensive to their parents. The irony, of course, is that if they make these styles popular, they end up making them part of the world of mass culture, economic mainstays of the entertainment industry.

One of the most interesting literatures spawned in America by this British school comes from historians looking to the realm of popular culture to try to understand class, gender, and ethnic relations in the United States. Roy Rosenzweig (1983), Kathy Peiss (1985), and George Lipsitz (1990) look at how class, gender, and ethnic culture are sustained and dissolved over time in patterns of resistance, co-optation, mutual influence, and change. They identify ways that residues of older cultural traditions both resist and are incorporated into the cultural mainstream, and how different groups have absorbed and used elements of both traditional and mass culture to fashion distinct identities and ways of life.

Rosenzweig (1983), studying the white working class in nineteenth-century America, treats popular culture as a site of resistance to work discipline in the factory. The division of life into periods of work and leisure for workers in this period was not, to Rosenzweig, the articulation of two spheres of activity, but a political division that was part of a struggle over control of time by workers.

Peiss (1985) looks at women workers in nineteenth-century cities. She demonstrates that young working women used their new economic independence to resist the constraints of the family as well as of the factory. They were able to develop new styles of dress, dancing, and play, but could not free themselves from their highly structured gender relations.

Lipsitz (1990) looks at how ethnic and class cultures have been sustained and dissolved in the late twentieth century in the United States. He sees popular culture forming a kind of popular memory, obscuring and yet reviving the U.S. working class's immigrant past and ethnic complexity. Centralized mass media such as television have helped to create and record the decline of immigrant identity under the force of consumerism. In contrast, more participatory cultural forms like street dancing and parading during Mardi Gras and some popular music forms have allowed ethnic groups to play their identities and create an urban mixed culture that simultaneously embraces and rejects traditional ethnic identity.

Another direction in the analysis of class and culture has been developed by Pierre Bourdieu (1984) and his colleagues in France. They have been looking for the mechanisms by which domination has been sustained across generations. If social constructivists are right and social life must necessarily be "created" by each new generation, then social *stability* over time needs theoretical explanation. To Bourdieu, culture is a main source of class stability. He argues that each rank has its own kind of cultural tastes, some systems of taste constituting cultural capital that can be exchanged for economic capital. People at the top of the hierarchy have a class culture with a high amount of cultural capital. They teach this culture to their children and thereby give them an economic edge. This kind of elite culture is also taught in school, but kids from less affluent backgrounds often resist learning it. This cultural resistance by the working class is not a victory for Bourdieu; rather, it is a trap for reproducing the class system.

Bourdieu's theory of cultural and social stratification is interestingly unlike most models found in the United States and Britain because it has no special place for a homogenizing mass culture. Bourdieu argues that members of different social ranks may see the same films (or other forms of mass culture), but they see them in different ways and they like or dislike them for different reasons. Elite culture is more abstract and formal than working-class culture, so elite filmgoers pay more attention to film language while nonelites care more about plots and stars. These differences in cultural consumption are more significant to Bourdieu than differences of cultural production (mass versus handmade culture) because elites identify with formal approaches to culture and prefer to associate with (and hire) those who share their views.

Scholars in both Britain and the United States have been profoundly influenced by Bourdieu. Paul DiMaggio (1982), in a study of the Boston Symphony and its development in the nineteenth century, paid attention to the differentiation of tastes and social ranks at issue when concerts for elite audiences were purged of popular songs and were used to define a special repertoire of classical music. This happened when the symphony was established as an elite musical institution and drove out competing musical organizations that had more "democratic" tastes. DiMaggio argues that this cultural differentiation took place when immigrant groups grew dramatically in Boston and took over local politics there. The superiority of traditional elites was no longer visible in the public sphere, but it remained central to the economy. The creation of cultural institutions identifying this elite with elevated tastes helped to make class power visible and to sustain it over time by giving upper-class Bostonians a distinctive culture.

In Britain, Paul Willis (1977) has confirmed Bourdieu's perceptions about class reproduction through his study of the education of working-class youths. He argues that distaste for the "elevated" values of the school among working-class youths is expressed in school by resistance to lessons. This resistance does not have the optimistic possibilities found in the theories of Williams (1977) or Hebdige (1979), but results in class reproduction. Working-class youths, in eschewing elite cultural values, end up reproducing their own domination

Mass participation in cultural events such as Mardi Gras in New Orleans allows ethnic groups to display their identities while also creating a mixed urban culture. (Philip Gould/Corbis)

within the class system. MacLeod (1987) in the United States finds much the same thing, although he focuses on differences between blacks and whites. Members of gangs from both ethnic communities who lived in the same housing project found difficulty escaping their social rank because of difficulties at school. The blacks believed that by going to school they could achieve mobility, while the white kids did not. Still, both groups were kept in their "places" by a lack of cultural capital.

Since the end of the 1970s, there has been a growing literature, stimulated by the women's movement, on gender stratification and popular culture. The bulk of it addresses two media—novels and film—because of the centrality of women to the economic development of these two areas of popular entertainment. As Ann Douglas (1977) pointed out in her seminal and controversial book, *Feminization of American Culture,* women readers and women writers helped to establish this form of popular novel writing in the United States during the nineteenth century. Sentimental novels were tailored to the domesticated women in the period, who had to stay home and devote their attention to familial relations and child rearing. The novels focused on interpersonal relations and problems of individuals' morals (as opposed to large issues of morality)—just the kind of thing that both fit and justified middle-class women's highly circumscribed lives. Douglas decries the role of women writers in shaping this disempowering literature for women and praises in contrast more "masculine" and male writings from the period (hence generating much controversy about her easy acceptance of the literary canon). Most important for students of popular culture, she argues that the sentimental novels were models of mass culture that have been used ever since in romance novels and soap operas.

Through romance novels, women claimed their reading time as their own, and used it to withdraw from the uninterrupted flow of demands on their attention.

Janice Radway (1984) questioned this easy dismissal of romance novels, and went out to study in a quasi-ethnographic fashion the readers of contemporary romance novels to see how they were affected by their reading. She found that the novels had more mixed effects than Douglas supposed. While they taught traditional gender relations (including male violence toward women), they also celebrated the gentler side of men and (more important) were used by women readers as a reason to deflect demands on their time by husbands and children. Women claimed their reading time as their own, and used it to withdraw temporarily from the uninterrupted flow of demands on their attention.

Gaye Tuchman's (1989) book provides some interesting history that serves as a vantage point from which to view the controversy between Douglas and Radway. She shows how around the turn of the century, publishing houses began to reject the women novelists and their sentimental novels and to favor male novelists. Publishers were central to the switch to the canons of modernism, and the "expulsion" of women from the profession of novel writing. Women readers still constituted the major market for novels, but their market had become so lucrative that high status male poets, who had eschewed the novel before, began to be interested in it. Once this occurred, their tastes were taken as authoritative and the novel was quickly placed in their hands. Tuchman makes clear that changes in taste like this were neither arbitrary nor grounded purely in aesthetics; they were the result of economic changes in the literary market, institutional decisions about how to address them, and institutional trivialization of women and their culture.

The attention to gender and film has been inspired not by the importance of the female audience or the centrality of women to the film industry (the opposite is the case), but rather the importance of actresses, of the faces and bodies of film stars, to the commercial and cultural success of the industry. When feminist studies of film began in the 1970s, most of the work was on the exploitation of the female body in films by male filmmakers and for a male audience. This kind of analysis stressed how commercial films used male-centered notions of sexuality and power, presenting women in films as objects of desire and/or violence (Weibel 1977; Tuchman, Daniels, and Benet 1978). In the 1980s, researchers turned away from the study of film production and toward analyses of film language and film consumption to construct a psychology of film watching (Modleski 1982; Mulvey 1989). Much of this literature focuses on the voyeuristic pleasure film watching provides men by allowing them to gaze at women's bodies while sitting in a dark theater where the female objects of the gaze cannot look back. Scholars in this tradition examine in shot-by-shot detail how men and women are differentially presented on film: men are generally in medium shots, carrying the action of films, while women stand in the background (or are dissected in close-ups to appear as faces or other body parts, available to the male gaze). Because this type of analysis seems to prove so decisively that films are constructed for a male audience, recent feminists have wondered why women seem to find so much pleasure going to the movies. How could women look at other women through the male gaze without feeling alienated or demeaned? One answer is that some films contain strong and interesting female characters who address issues of concern to female audiences. Another is that interpretations of films are not overwhelmingly determined by the filmmaker's point of view (or a male gaze). Drawing on reader response theory, Nancy Chodorow's (1978) ideas about female psychology, Carol Gilligan's (1982) ideas about female reasoning, Lacanian psychology, and post-structuralist views of the politics of interpretation (Eagleton 1983), a new psychology of film reading is looking at how audiences (particularly women) construct meaningful messages from film texts (Mulvey 1985, 1989; Erens 1979).

In the 1980s, two opposite developments in culture theory have emerged from renewed attention (in post-structuralism in general and in the film theory described above) to the multivocality of texts and the proliferation of meanings through multiple readings. The upbeat one emphasizes the liberatory nature of culture, and is related to: (1) the poststructuralist argument that asserting alternative interpretations undermines the authority of canonical readings; (2) feminist versions of reader response theory that contend that how you use culture is central to what it is; and (3) the idea from the British school of cultural studies that competing social voices enter into the public sphere and are available for readers/audiences to find. Advocates of this position claim that efforts at social control through culture do not work very well because, in their own life worlds, people use the cultural resources around them in their own ways. These new constructivists—for example, Robert Bellah (Bellah et al. 1985) Ann Swidler (1986), Joseph Gusfield (1989), and Michael Schudson (1989)—are much like Goffman (1959) and earlier symbolic interactionists who presented everyday life as a cultural achievement, but they see the construction of meaning in everyday life (in an optimistic reversal of Foucault and other poststructuralists) as a healthy exercise of power as well as symbolic manipulation (Foucault 1970, 1975, 1979; Jameson 1984; Zukin 1988).

This optimistic view of the proliferation of meanings in everyday life is countered by students of postmodernism who derive from structuralism and poststructuralism an interest in the languages of culture and see in modern urban society a loss of meaning resulting from the multiplication of signs and their decontextualization/reappropriation. They argue that commercial culture has such a need to assign meaning to objects (in order to make sense of their consumption and use) that signs are proliferated, reappropriated, mixed, and reused until they lose their meaning. For example, as famous paintings are used to sell cosmetics, images of the Old West are used to signify the solidity of banks, and bits and pieces of past architecture are mixed to construct a new built environment, history is made meaningless. The play with signs goes on without serious thought to what this does to human life. The result is (to postmodernists) an overwhelming alienation. Cultural production and counterproduction, the argument goes, may reduce hegemony by undermining attempts to define "common sense," and may give people pleasure through the free play of signs, but they provide only an illusion of freedom, and breed alienation. This view of modern urban life contains some of the unremitting pessimism of the Frankfurt school, but it is tied to a view of cultural decentralization that is at odds with traditional critical theory.

The diverse approaches to popular culture that have developed since the 1960s seem to have produced a proliferation of meanings for popular culture itself, but the result has not been alienation. Popular culture research has gained an analytic richness that it lacked when few scholars dared or cared to approach it. Conflicting theoretical views about what makes popular culture significant may make it more difficult to define and characterize (much less understand) popular culture. The theories often begin from quite different assumptions about the sources of structure and agency in human life. But they share a common origin in the critique of culture as a source of social control, and they remain committed to the view that through the study of popular culture one can learn something about the worlds of nonelites and their relations to systems of power. All the debates consider how groups come to understand the world they live in, and how those understandings subordinate or alienate them (on the one hand) or liberate them to make meaningful lives, in spite of efforts by others to control them. This heritage is clear, and gives both meaning and direction to popular culture studies.

[See also Mass Media Research; Social Movements.]

BIBLIOGRAPHY

Aronowitz, Stanley 1973 *False Promises.* New York: McGraw-Hill.

Barthes, Roland (1957) 1972 *Mythologies.* New York: Hill and Wang.

Becker, Howard 1963 *Outsiders: Studies in the Sociology of Deviance.* New York: Free Press.

Bellah, Robert N., et al. 1985 *Habits of the Heart.* Berkeley: University of California Press.

Berger, Peter, and T. Luckmann 1966 *Social Construction of Reality.* Garden City, N.Y.: Doubleday.

Blumer, Herbert 1969 *Symbolic Interactionism: Perspective and Method.* Berkeley: University of California Press.

Bourdieu, Pierre 1984 *Distinction: A Social Critique of the Judgment of Taste.* Cambridge, Mass.: Harvard University Press.

Braudel, Fernand (1949) 1966 *The Mediterranean and the Mediterranean World in the Age of Phillip II.* New York: Harper.

Browne, Ray 1982 *Objects of Special Devotion.* Bowling Green, Ohio: Popular Press.

Cantor, Muriel 1971 *The Hollywood Producer.* New York: Basic Books.

Cawelti, J. G. 1972 *The Six-Gun Mystique.* Bowling Green, Ohio: Popular Press.

Chodorow, Nancy 1978 *Reproduction of Mothering.* Berkeley: University of California Press.

Curran, James, Michael Gurevitch, and Janet Woolacott 1979 *Mass Communication and Society.* New York: Russell Sage Foundation.

Denisoff, Serge 1974 *Solid Gold: The Popular Record Industry.* New Brunswick, N.J.: Transaction Books.

DiMaggio, Paul 1982 "Cultural Entrepreneurship in Nineteenth-Century Boston: The Creation of an Organizational Base for High Culture in America." *Media, Culture and Society* 4:33–50.

Douglas, Ann 1977 *Feminization of American Culture.* New York: Knopf.

Eagleton, Terry 1983 *Literary Theory.* Minneapolis: University of Minnesota Press.

Erens, P. 1979 *Sexual Stratagems.* New York: Horizon.

Foucault, Michel 1970 *The Order of Things.* New York: Random House.

——— 1975 "What is an Author?" *Partisan Review* 4:603–614.

——— 1979 *Discipline and Punish.* New York: Vintage.

Gans, Herbert 1974 *Popular Culture and High Culture.* New York: Basic Books.

Gilligan, Carol 1982 *In a Different Voice.* Cambridge, Mass.: Harvard University Press.

Goffman, Erving 1959 *Presentation of Self in Everyday Life.* Garden City, N.Y.: Anchor.

Gramsci, Antonio 1971 *Selections from the Prison Notebooks.* New York: International Publishers.

Guback, Thomas 1969 *The International Film Industry: Western Europe and America Since 1945.* Bloomington: Indiana University Press.

Gusfield, Joseph 1989 *On Symbols and Society.* Chicago: University of Chicago Press.

Hall, Stuart, and Paddy Whannel 1965 *The Popular Arts.* New York: Pantheon.

Hebdige, Dick 1979 *Subculture: The Meaning of Style.* New York: Methuen.

Hirsh, Paul 1972 "Processing Fads and Fashions: An Organization-Set Analysis of Cultural Industry Systems." *American Journal of Sociology* 77:639–659.

Horkheimer, Max, and Theodor Adorno (1944) 1972 *Dialectic of Enlightenment,* New York: Seabury.

Jameson, Frederic 1984 "Postmodernism, of the Cultural Logic of Late Capitalism." *New Left Review* 146:53–93.

Jay, Martin 1973 *The Dialectical Imagination: A History of the Frankfurt School and the Institute of Social Research 1923–50.* Boston: Little, Brown.

Keil, C. 1966 *Urban Blues.* Chicago: University of Chicago Press.

Lipsitz, George 1990 *Time Passages.* Minneapolis: University of Minnesota Press.

Lowenthal, Leo 1961 *Literature, Popular Culture and Society.* Englewood Cliffs, N.J.: Prentice-Hall.

Lynd, Robert and H. Lynd 1929 *Middletown.* New York: Harcourt, Brace, and World.

MacLeod, Jay 1987 *Ain't No Making It.* Boulder, Colo.: Westview Press.

McQuade, Donald, and Robert Atwan 1974 *Popular Writing in America.* New York: Oxford University Press.

Modleski, Tania 1982 *Loving with a Vengeance.* Hamden, Conn.: Archon Books.

Mulvey, Laura 1985 "Film and Visual Pleasure." In G. Mast and M. Cohen, eds., *Film Theory and Criticism.* New York: Oxford University Press.

——— 1989 *Visual and Other Pleasures.* Bloomington: Indiana University Press.

Nye, R. B. 1972 *New Dimensions in Popular Culture.* Bowling Green, Ohio: Popular Press.

Park, Robert 1955 *Society.* New York: Free Press.

Peiss, Kathy 1985 *Cheap Amusements: Working Women and Leisure in New York City, 1880 to 1920.* Philadelphia: Temple University Press.

Radway, Janice 1984 *Reading the Romance.* Chapel Hill: University of North Carolina Press.

Rosenberg, Bernard, and David Manning White 1957 *Mass Culture.* New York: Free Press.

Rosenzweig, Roy 1983 *Eight Hours for What We Will: Workers and Leisure in an Industrial City, 1870–1920.* Cambridge and New York: Cambridge University Press.

Ross, Andrew 1989 *No Respect: Intellectuals and Popular Culture.* New York: Routledge and Kegan Paul.

Schiller, Herbert 1969 *Mass Communication and American Empire.* New York: Kelly.

Schudson, Michael 1989 "How Culture Works." *Theory and Society.* 18:153–180.

Schutz, Alfred 1967 *Collected Papers.* Vol. 3, *The Problem of Social Reality.* The Hague: Martinus Nijhoff.

Shiach, Morag 1989 *Discourse an Popular Culture.* Stanford, Stanford University Press.

Swidler, Ann 1986 "Culture in Action: Symbols and Strategies." *American Sociological Review* 51:273–286.

Thompson, E. P. 1963 *The Making of the English Working Class.* New York: Vintage.

Tuchman, Gaye 1989 *Edging Women Out.* New Haven, Conn.: Yale University Press.

———, Arlene Daniels, and James Benet 1978 *Hearth and Home.* New York: Oxford University Press.

Weibel, Kathryn 1977 *Mirror, Mirror.* Garden City, N.Y.: Anchor.

Williams, Raymond 1961 *The Long Revolution.* New York: Columbia University Press.

——— 1977 *Marxism and Literature.* Oxford: Oxford University Press.

——— 1980 *Problems in Materialism and Culture.* London: Verso.

Willis, Paul 1977 *Learning to Labor.* New York: Columbia University Press.

Zukin, Sharon 1988 "The Post-Modern Debate over Urban Form." *Theory, Culture and Society* 5:431–446.

– CHANDRA MUKERJI

POPULATION

Because "population" is such a comprehensive term, the study of human populations might seem to include all the activities of the social sciences and many of the life sciences. In practice, however, the topic more modestly refers to the number and composition of various social groupings and to the dynamics of change in these characteristics. It extends to the determinants and consequences of levels, differentials, and changes in fertility, mortality, and spatial distribution. Within the social sciences, population study has a broad concern with the cultural, social, economic, and psychological causes and consequences of these characteristics (see Hauser and Duncan 1959; Coleman and Schofield 1986; Stycos 1987; Namboodiri 1988). Within sociology, the main concern is with linkages between social institutions and the dynamics of population change and equilibrium (see Taeuber, Bumpass, and Sweet 1978). Demography, an important component of population study, focuses on data collection, measurement, and description (for an inventory of demographic methods, see Shryock and Siegel 1971).

Overview of Population History

In the course of providing an overview of major changes in population characteristics, it is possible to indicate some of the linkages between social life and these characteristics. (For a more detailed discussion see, for example, Wrigley 1969 and Petersen 1975.)

During Neolithic times, hunting and gathering groups probably consisted of only a few dozen individuals. Based on the carrying capacity of that technology and the area believed to have been populated, it is estimated that in about 8000 to 6000 B.C. the population of the world was only five million to ten million (Yaukey 1985, p. 38). Probably about half of all children died before age five. Mainly because of the high mortality of infants and children, life expectancy was probably only about twenty years, although some adults would have survived to advanced ages. Maternal mortality was also high, probably resulting in considerably shorter life expectancy for females than for males (United Nations 1973, p. 115). In such a setting, which until recently has been observable in certain remote locations, the social consequences of these fundamental demographic facts would have been enormous. Many of our current social values and institutions have their roots in this kind of harsh environment.

Death was sudden, random, and frequent—about five times as common, in a population of a given size, as it would be in a developed country today. A major function of religion was to enable people to interpret death as a part of the life course and to surround it with rituals. New births to offset these deaths were essential for the survival of a group. There can be no doubt that many groups, of various sizes, failed in this effort, but the survivors were our ancestors. Children were important to the micro economy of the household and community from an early age; young adults were crucial for the survival of older adults. Practices and institutions to encourage fertility—of humans, as well as of the environment of plants and animals—were essential. Marital unions of some type would have been virtually universal and would have begun at an early age. It is likely that unions would have been arranged by the parents, partly because they occurred at such early ages, as well as because of the social advantages of arranged marriages for strengthening an intergenerational network of social obligations. Thus a case can be made that the social institutions of religion, marriage, and the extended family, among others, had some of their original impetus in the extremely high mortality of human prehistory and the consequent imperative for high fertility and child survivorship.

One of the most remarkable functions of social institutions is that they provide valves or mechanisms by which population size can be regulated to be compatible with the prevailing environmental circumstances and level of technology (Davis 1963). As just mentioned, high mortality must be accompanied by comparably high fertility if a population is to sustain itself. For the most part, it is the level of mortality that drives the level of fertility, through various intervening mechanisms, although mortality (e.g., infanticide) has sometimes served as a means of population control. Therefore social regulation of population size usually takes the form of increasing or decreasing the average number of births per woman.

A major function of religion was to enable people to interpret death as a part of the life course and to surround it with rituals.

Humans have a much greater capacity to reproduce than is often recognized, and even in situations of very high mortality and fertility there is usually an untapped potential for even higher fertility. There are well-documented populations in which the average woman who survives the childbearing ages has ten to eleven children after age twenty, and it is estimated that the average after age fifteen could be as high as sixteen children under some circumstances. (Of course, if maternal mortality is high, many women will not survive the childbearing years.) The potential supply of births is adequate to balance even the most severe conditions; if it were not, the species would not have survived.

Over the long run, there has been a general pattern of increased life expectancy with two major transitions.

The transition from hunting and gathering to settled agriculture and larger human settlements produced a net increase in life expectancy, although with some shifts in causes of death. Larger settlements have a higher incidence of infectious diseases because of inadequate sanitation and sources of clean drinking water. The second major transition began in the seventeenth century with industrialization and the progressive reduction of deaths from infectious diseases and will be discussed in the next section.

Fluctuations in mortality due to transitory influences have been superimposed on these two main transitions (Tilly 1978; Wrigley and Schofield 1981). Some of the short-term increases in mortality, due to wars, famines, and epidemics, have been devastating; for example, the Black Death in fourteenth-century Europe eliminated more than one third of the population in several areas.

Trends and fluctuations in mortality have direct consequences for population size and indirect consequences for reproduction, through socially sanctioned regulatory mechanisms. Consider, for example, the transition to agriculture and larger settlements. Mortality fell and population size increased, so that at the beginning of the Christian era, the world population is estimated to have been about three hundred million. However, at some point a new equilibrium was achieved, with relative stability at the higher size. The increase in carrying capacity with a new technology and social organization probably had its principal effect on reproduction at the household level (Laslett and Wall 1972; Goody 1976, 1983). If territory for new settlements is absent or inaccessible, too many children will result in too much division of land and property. Some kind of limitation on reproduction will result.

The most important social mechanism or lever for regulating fertility has probably been limitation of exposure to the risk of conception—in short, regulation of sexual activity. Thus, in preindustrial Europe, the age at marriage was high—on average, in the mid-twenties. The motivation for delaying marriage and the formation of new households probably arose at the micro level, because the parental generation had limited land to pass to their children. Marriage and childbearing were deferred until a viable household could be established. These micro-level motives led to a general consensus that marriage at later ages was preferable. Associated with late age at marriage were voluntary rather than arranged marriages, and apprenticeships or domestic service for many young people. Alternatives to married life developed—for example, in celibate religious communities. These behaviors can be viewed as mechanisms for fertility limitation, even though they certainly had other functions as well. Within marriage there was probably very little use, or even knowledge, of contraception.

Similarly, the response to short-term increases in mortality, when they occurred, was to increase the prevalence of marriage and to reduce the mean age at marriage. Again, these motivations operated primarily at the micro level, in the sense that when mortality rose, there were increased opportunities for land division and settlement, and new households could be formed more quickly.

This has been an effort to characterize population growth and homeostasis in the broadest terms, up to the beginning of the industrial era in the West. Because of limited space, this description has glossed over enormous differences worldwide in the patterns of reproduction and social structure and their linkages. There have been several ethnographic and historical analyses of these variations (see, e.g., Hanley and Wolf 1985).

Mortality Decline

The declines in mortality and fertility, and the rapid increase in population over the past three centuries, are described as the demographic transition. This topic is discussed elsewhere and will treated here only briefly.

The transformation of mortality from a common event, occurring most often to children, to a relatively rare event, occurring most often to the elderly, arose from a confluence of technological and social developments. Most important among these was the control of infectious diseases spread by microorganisms in the air and water. An improved understanding of the etiology of these diseases, together with technical capacity and political support for public health measures, led to childhood vaccinations, clean drinking water, and improved sanitation (McKeown 1976). Standards of personal hygiene and cleanliness of clothing improved. There is little evidence that improvements in diet were important, and curative (as contrasted with preventive) medicine played a relatively small role in the main part of the transformation.

In developed countries, the infant mortality rate has steadily fallen from about 250 deaths (in the first year of life) per 1,000 births to a present level of less than 10 per 1,000 (Mosley and Chen 1984). One consequence of a decline in the risk of infant and child deaths is to increase the sense of parental control over reproduction. It is more rational to develop notions of desired numbers of children when the survivorship of children is less random. Similarly, as survivorship improves, it is more rational to invest in children's future by providing them with formal education. The value of children—to their parents and to the larger society—increases as child mortality falls and life expectancy improves (see, e.g., Easterlin 1976).

The increase in life expectancy, currently about seventy-three years in the developed countries, has also resulted in a rise in the mean age of the population, in a substantial increase in the proportion who are elderly or retired, and in a shift to causes of death associated with old age. These trends have broad social implications—for example for the employment of and advancement opportunities for young people, the resilience of political structures, and the support of retirement programs and medical care for the elderly.

Fewer births per woman, together with the now negligible rates of maternal mortality in developed countries, have resulted in a substantially greater life expectancy for women than for men. The differential, now about seven years, works against the typically earlier age at marriage for women than for men. Although at birth there are about 104 males for every 100 females, there are progressively more females, per male, for every age after about age thirty in the United States. Thus the elderly population consists disproportionately of women, and women typically experience much longer periods of widowhood and living alone than men do.

In today's developing countries, the pace of mortality decline has been much more rapid than it was in the developed countries, because an accumulation of Western public health measures could be introduced nearly simultaneously. Most of the decline has occurred since World War II and the ensuing independence of most of these countries from colonial powers, but some of it can be traced back to earlier decades of the twentieth century. The rapidity of the mortality decline and its largely exogenous nature have been factors in the delay of a subsequent fertility decline in many cases (see Preston 1978).

Fertility Decline

The lag between the decline in mortality and the decline in fertility resulted in substantial population growth in the West. In Europe, the onset of substantial reductions in fertility occurred first in France early in the nineteenth century, and last in Ireland early in the twentieth century. In the earliest cases, it can be argued that the onset of fertility control coincided with mortality decline rather than following it. In the United States as in Britain, 1880 is regarded as a watershed year for widespread initiation of contraception.

With no exceptions, from the cases of France through Ireland, the initiation and the bulk of the modern fertility declines occurred as a result of contraception rather than delayed marriage, and in contexts in which contraception was publicly regarded as immoral, supplies and information were illegal, and methods were primitive by today's standards. Substantial proportions of married couples actually had no children or only one child, but the main reduction came about through the truncation or termination of family formation after some point. As a generalization, births were not intentionally spaced or postponed; rather, attempts were made to terminate childbearing at some earlier parity than would have been the case without intervention. The main contraceptive method was withdrawal (coitus interruptus). Abstinence was probably not infrequently used as a last resort. Rhythm may have been used, but probably incorrectly; douching was common but is now known to be ineffective. Sterilization was not available, although it is likely that a high proportion of hysterectomies served the same function. Condoms were not widely available until the twentieth century.

In Pakistan, it is held that the number of births is in the hands of Allah, and there is virtually no effective use of contraception.

It is clear that the motivation to control fertility was both powerful and personal. It is unfortunate that it is so difficult at this distance to reconstruct the specific strategies that were employed, patterns of communication between couples, and sources of information. However, at least two generalizations can be made. One is that the practice of contraception required an ideational justification, to the effect that individual couples have a personal right to control their family size. From a modern perspective it is easy to overlook the fundamental role of this concept. It is not just a coincidence that France was the first country to experience contraception on a wide scale and was also the home of the Enlightenment and was the first European country to experience a fundamental political revolution. Intervention to prevent a birth rests on the premise that it is legitimate for an individual—or a couple—to make critical choices affecting personal welfare. Contraception can be viewed as the ultimate micro-level manifestation of a macro-level value for personal freedom, even in the face of strong pronatalist positions by both church and state.

A secondary condition for contraceptive use in the West appears to have been some degree of local development, as evidenced by higher literacy and a higher standard of living. Historical research continues into the importance of specific factors such as the relative status of women, the transition to a wage-earning class, local industrialization, improvements in Social Security and public welfare, and so on. (For more details on specific countries see, e.g., Ryder 1969; Livi Bacci 1977; Teitelbaum 1984. For a general discussion of these factors in Europe, see van de Walle and Knodel 1980. For theoretical discussions see Caldwell 1976 and 1978.)

In the economically less developed countries, one to two generations of reduced mortality combined with a traditional high level of fertility have resulted in annual growth rates often over 3 percent. However, beginning in the late 1960s, some Asian countries, particularly Taiwan and South Korea, began to experience rapid declines in fertility. At present these countries have reached approximate equilibrium between fertility and mortality rates, although they continue to grow because of their youthful age distributions. About a decade later, Thailand and Indonesia and several Latin American countries such as Colombia and Mexico showed rapid reductions in their fertility rates. At present, dramatic fertility declines are under way in most countries outside of Africa, South Asia (excluding Sri Lanka and the Indian state of Tamil Nadu, which have experienced significant declines), and the Islamic Middle East. The declines are due in small part to delayed marriage, but for the most part to use of contraception—primarily sterilization, and secondarily reversible methods such as intrauterine devices (see Bulatao and Lee 1983; Cleland and Hobcraft 1985).

The conditions for these fertility declines show both similarities and differences from the Western declines. It appears critical to have the concept that it is appropriate to intervene in the procreative process. In Pakistan, for example, it is commonly held that the number of births, as well as their gender and survivorship, is in the hands of Allah, and there is virtually no effective use of contraception. Contraception tends to be found where the concepts of political and economic self-determination are better established, particularly among women.

In contrast with the Western experience, however, it also appears critical to have institutional support for contraception. The countries that have shown the clearest declines in fertility have had national family planning programs and visible support for these programs at the highest levels of the government. The most effective programs have integrated family planning services into a general program of maternal and child health (see Lapham and Mauldin 1987).

The consequences of population growth for economic development have been much debated (Simon 1977; Birdsall 1980). There are many cases, such as Japan and South Korea, in which rapid economic expansion occurred simultaneously with rapid increases in population. Virtually all such cases, however, were transitional, and the fertility of those countries is currently at the replacement level.

A growing population has a young age distribution, with many new entrants to the labor force and relatively few old people in need of pensions and health care. These factors may stimulate economic growth, but they must be balanced against the costs of supporting and educating large numbers of children. In several countries, such as the Philippines, the economy is unable to employ large cohorts of young people satisfactorily, especially those who are better educated, and they emigrate in large numbers. In addition, household welfare can be adversely affected by large numbers of children, even in situations of economic expansion at the macro level. The consequences of rapid growth extend beyond the economy and into the areas of health, social welfare, political stability, and the environment.

Changes in Population Distribution

Superimposed on the major trends in population size described above, there have been enormous changes in geographical distribution. Many of the social problems attributed to rapid population growth are more accurately diagnosed as consequences of increasing concentration. Urban areas, in particular the megalopolises of developing countries such as Mexico City, Buenos Aires, and New Delhi, have been growing during the twentieth century at more than twice the rate of the countries in which they are located. This growth has exacerbated the problems of inadequate housing, sanitation, transportation, schooling, unemployment, and the crime associated with urban life. On the other hand, cities are centers of concentration of economic, intellectual, and political life (see Hawley 1981).

The growth of cities has resulted in part from the excess of births over deaths in rural areas. Individuals have been displaced from these areas, which cannot absorb them, and have moved to cities, which are perceived to have better economic opportunities. Often that perception is incorrect. With a few exceptions, such as Pakistan, fertility is lower in cities than in rural areas.

A second major type of population redistribution in recent centuries has, of course, been across national borders. Movement to the Americas was greatest during the half-century between 1880 and 1930, and continues to the present. There are many streams of both short-term and long-term international migration, for example out of South and Southeast Asia and into the Middle East, Europe, and North America, and from Africa into Europe and North America, and the economies of several sending countries are strengthened by monthly remittances from their emigrants (United Nations 1979).

Population of the United States

The United States had a population of approximately 250 million at the time of the 1990 census and a growth rate of about 1 percent annually, roughly one-fifth of which is due to immigration and four-fifths to natural increase. Fertility is slightly below replacement level, but there are more births than deaths because of the large size of the babyboom cohort, born from the late 1940s through the early 1960s. Age-specific fertility rates are increasing for women in their thirties, mainly because of postponed first and second births rather than from higher-order births. Rates have been declining for women below age twenty but are still higher than in most other developed countries.

Perhaps the most serious issues related to fertility are the large numbers of unplanned births to young women and the high numbers of abortions—about two for every five births—that could have been averted by contraception. Few developed countries have a range of contraceptive methods as limited as the United States. As mentioned earlier, most of the fertility decline in the West occurred while contraception was considered immoral and was explicitly illegal. Although contraception and even abortion are now legal, deep cultural ambiguities remain in the linkage between sexuality and procreation. A litigious environment has inhibited the development of new contraceptives by American pharmaceutical companies, or the marketing of new contraceptives developed elsewhere, and the U.S. government plays a minimal role in such development.

Life expectancy in 1987 in years was 72.2 for white males, 78.9 for white females, 67.3 for nonwhite males, and 75.2 for nonwhite females (National Center for Health Statistics 1989). Although life expectancy is increasing for both males and females, the female advantage is also increasing. The greatest improvements in mortality are in the highest age groups. Because of increases in the number of elderly and projected changes in the age distribution of the labor force, the age at

Mexico City is a huge megalopolis that has experienced a growth rate of more than twice that of Mexico itself. The city struggles to meet residents' needs for housing, sanitation, transportation, and school. However, the city is also a vibrant center of economic, political, and intellectual achievement. (Sergio Dorantes/© Corbis)

receipt of full Social Security benefits is scheduled to increase gradually, from sixty-five to sixty-six by the year 2009 and to sixty-seven by the year 2027 (Binstock and George 1990).

Life expectancy for black males is currently falling, due mainly to deaths by homicides to black males in their twenties and a greater prevalence of cardiovascular disease among blacks (Keith and Smith 1988). Infant mortality rates for nonwhite babies are increasing, due to low birth weights and inadequate prenatal care. These reversals of earlier long-term improvements are indicators of worsening conditions among poorer Americans.

Future Population

The overriding concern of world population policy at present is the achievement of a new equilibrium between fertility and mortality so that growth will be slowed or stopped. At the present rate of growth, about 2 percent annually, the world population of about five and a third billion (in 1990) will double in about thirty-five years (see United Nations 1988 for a range of projections). Even if reproduction immediately came into balance with mortality, in the sense that each woman had a little more than two births (and the net reproduction rate were 1.0), the momentum due to the youthful age distribution of the population would produce an excess of births over deaths (i.e., growth) for nearly half a century. Under optimistic projections, it is expected that by the year 2025 the world population will be eight and a half billion. This projected growth will occur almost entirely in the less developed countries (World Bank 1990).

The net reproduction rate is currently less than 1.0 (that is, fertility is below the long-term level needed to balance mortality) in virtually all of the more developed countries. The quarter of the world's population that resides in those countries will increase scarcely at all, and much of that growth will be the result of immigration from developing countries. It is projected that the median age in Europe may rise to the mid-forties. Policies directed at increasing fertility in European countries have met with little success (see Calot and Blayo 1982; van de Kaa 1987).

In urban settings with a high standard of living, children lose much of their earlier value as a source of economic activity, household wealth, and security in old age. They become increasingly expensive in terms of direct costs such as clothing, housing, and education, and in terms of opportunity costs such as forgone labor force activity by the mother.

In brief, there are probably two main reasons why fertility has not declined even further in the developed countries. One is the adherence to a powerful norm for two children that was consolidated around the middle of the twentieth century. Surveys show an overwhelming preference for exactly two children—preferably one boy and one girl—with little flexibility either above or below that number. Actual childbearing often departs from the norm, more commonly by being below two children, so that fertility is below replacement.

Second, children provide parents with a primary social group. There is no longer an expectation that they will provide support in old age, nor an important concern with carrying on the family name, but children do provide psychic and social rewards. To bear children is to emulate the behavior of one's parents and to replicate the family of orientation.

Surveys show an overwhelming preference for exactly two children.

Although the world as a whole is far indeed from experiencing a decline in population, and European demographers have been concerned for decades about the specter of national declines, the low reproductivity of some countries and subpopulations raises questions of more than intellectual interest about the future mechanisms for restraining an indefinite decline in fertility. This is not to argue that some decline in population or changes in the balance of national populations would be undesirable, but simply to speculate on the long-term scenario (see Teitelbaum and Winter 1985; Davis, Bernstam, and Ricardo-Campbell 1986).

Major reductions in fertility in the past have been the result of delayed marriage and contraception and have been motivated at the level of the household. Maintenance of equilibrium in the future will require an increase in desired family size and less use of contraception. The norm for two children is pervasive, but norms are also fragile and largely reflect recent and current behavior. As increasing numbers of women opt for no children or only one, it is possible that the widespread preference for two will weaken. The other influence mentioned above, the desire for a primary group analogous to the family of orientation, could be satisfied with a single child rather than two. Indeed, this has been demonstrated in the surprisingly general acceptance of the one-child policy in urban China. For these reasons, it is easier to project a continued decline in fertility, rather than a significant upturn, in the absence of major changes or interventions in the micro economy of the household.

[See also Life Expectancy.]

BIBLIOGRAPHY

Binstock, Robert H., and Linda K. George (eds.) 1990 *Handbook of Aging and the Social Sciences.* London: Academic Press.

Birdsall, Nancy 1980 "Population Growth and Poverty in the Developing World." *Population Bulletin* 35 (5).

Bogue, Donald J. 1985 *The Population of the United States: Historical Trends and Future Projections.* New York: Free Press.

Bulatao, Rodolfo, and Ronald D. Lee 1983 *Determinants of Fertility in Developing Countries.* New York: Academic Press.

Caldwell, John G. 1976 "Toward a Restatement of Demographic Transition Theory." *Population and Development Review* 2:321–366.

——— 1978 "A Theory of Fertility: From High Plateau to Destabilization." *Population and Development Review* 4:553–577.

Calot, G., and Chantal Blayo 1982 "The Recent Course of Fertility in Western Europe." *Population Studies* 36:349–372.

Cleland, John, and John Hobcraft, eds. 1985 *Reproductive Change in Developing Countries.* Oxford: Oxford University Press.

Coleman, David, and Roger Schofield, eds. 1986 *The State of Population Theory.* Oxford: Basil Blackwell.

Davis, Kingsley 1963 "The Theory of Change and Response in Modern Demographic History." *Population Index* 29:345–366.

———, Mikhail S. Bernstam, and Rita Ricardo-Campbell, eds. 1986 *Below-Replacement Fertility in Industrial Societies: Causes, Consequences, Policies. Population and Development Review,* a supplement to Vol. 12.

Easterlin, Richard A. 1976 "The Conflict Between Resources and Aspirations." *Population and Development Review* 2:417–425.

Goody, Jack 1976 *Production and Reproduction.* Cambridge: Cambridge University Press.

——— 1983 *The Development of the Family and Marriage in Europe.* Cambridge: Cambridge University Press.

Hanley, Susan B., and Arthur P. Wolf (eds.) 1985 *Family and Population in East Asian History.* Stanford, Calif.: Stanford University Press.

Hauser, Philip M., and Otis Dudley Duncan (eds.) 1959 *The Study of Population.* Chicago: University of Chicago Press.

Hawley, Amos H. 1981 *Urban Society.* New York: Wiley.

Keith, Verna M., and David P. Smith 1988 "The Current Differential in Black and White Life Expectancy." *Demography* 25:625–632.

Lapham, Robert J., and W. Parker Mauldin 1987 "The Effects of Family Planning on Fertility: Research Findings." In R. J. Lapham and G. B. Simmons, eds., *Organizing for Effective Family Planning Programs.* Washington, D.C.: National Academy Press.

Laslett, Peter, and Richard Wall (eds.) 1972 *Household and Family in Past Time.* Cambridge: Cambridge University Press.

Lieberson, Stanley, and Mary C. Waters 1988 *Ethnic and Racial Groups in Contemporary America.* New York: Russell Sage Foundation.

Livi Bacci, M. 1977 A *History of Italian Fertility.* Princeton, N.J.: Princeton University Press.

McKeown, Thomas 1976 *The Modern Rise of Population.* New York: Academic Press.

Mosley, W. Henry, and Lincoln C. Chen (eds.) 1984 *Child Survival: Strategies for Research. Population and Development Review,* a supplement to Vol. 10.

Namboodiri, Krishnan 1988 "Ecological Demography: Its Place in Sociology." *American Sociological Review* 53:619–633.

National Center for Health Statistics 1989 *Monthly Vital Statistics Report* 38 (5).

Petersen, William 1975 *Population.* New York: Macmillan.

Preston, Samuel H. 1978 *Mortality Patterns in National Populations.* New York: Academic Press.

Ryder, Norman B. 1969 "The Emergence of a Modern Fertility Pattern: United States 1917–1966." In S. J. Behrman, ed., *Family Planning: A World View.* Ann Arbor: University of Michigan Press.

Shryock, Henry S., and Jacob S. Siegel 1971 *The Methods and Materials of Demography.* Washington, D.C.: U.S. Bureau of the Census.

Simon, Julian 1977 *The Economics of Population Growth.* Princeton, N.J.: Princeton University Press.

Stycos, J. Mayonne (ed.) 1987 *Demography as an Interdiscipline.* Special issue of *Sociological Forum* 2 (4).

Sweet, James A., and Larry L. Bumpass 1988 *American Families and Households.* New York: Russell Sage Foundation.

Taeuber, Karl E., Larry L. Bumpass, and James A. Sweet (eds.) 1978 *Social Demography.* New York: Academic Press.

Teitelbaum, Michael S. 1984 *The British Fertility Decline: Demographic Transition in the Crucible of the Industrial Revolution.* Princeton, N.J.: Princeton University Press.

———, and Jay M. Winter 1985 *The Fear of Population Decline.* San Diego, Calif.: Academic Press.

Tilly, Charles (ed.) 1978 *Historical Studies of Changing Fertility.* Princeton, N.J.: Princeton University Press.

United Nations 1973 *The Determinants and Consequences of Population Trends: New Summary of Findings on Interaction of Demographic, Economic and Social Factors,* vol. 1. *Population Studies* 50. New York.

——— 1979 *Trends and Characteristics of International Migration Since 1950.* New York.

——— 1988 *World Demographic Estimates and Projections, 1950–2025.* New York.

Van de Kaa, Dirk J. 1987 "Europe's Second Demographic Transition." *Population Bulletin* 42 (1).

Van de Walle, Etienne, and John Knodel 1980 "Europe's Fertility Transition: New Evidence and Lessons for Today's Developing World." *Population Bulletin* 34 (6).

World Bank 1990 *World Development Report 1990.* Washington, D.C.: Oxford University Press.

Wrigley, E. A. 1969 *Population and History.* New York: McGraw-Hill.

———, and R. S. Schofield 1981 *The Population History of England 1541–1871: A Reconstruction.* London: Edward Arnold.

Yaukey, David 1985 *Demography: The Study of Human Population.* New York: St. Martin's.

– THOMAS W. PULLUM

PORNOGRAPHY

Sexually explicit material—a live show, book, magazine, movie, play, videotape, photograph, sculpture, painting, or song lyric—is popularly termed *pornography,* but the term is usually defined as content that violates the laws against obscenity. Pornographic material is prosecuted in accordance with the laws against obscenity.

The U.S. Supreme Court has ruled that in order to be considered obscene, material must meet three criteria: It is patently offensive, it appeals to the prurient interest of the average adult applying contemporary community standards, and it lacks literary, artistic, political, or scientific value (*Miller* v. *California* 1973). "Community" refers not to a national but to a local community, which may be a county, state, or several counties, depending on the jurisdiction.

Sociological research on sexually explicit materials, much of it conducted under the auspices of the President's Commission on Obscenity and Pornography (1971), has established that there is no special demographic subgroup that uses such materials; the content appears to have no long-term negative effects; the materials have little effect on the incidence of sex offenses, except perhaps to lead to a decline in some offenses; satiation occurs after intensive exposure to sexually explicit media; and women can be as responsive as men to sexually oriented material. The commission, headed by a law school dean, commissioned a substantial body of research on pornography.

The promulgation in 1968 of the movie rating system gave respectability to X-rated movies, some of which starred mainstream actors

X-rated videotapes, which represent perhaps one-sixth of the stock of videotape stores, account for almost two-fifths of the rentals at the stores. This interest of Americans in sexually explicit materials began to emerge in the early 1970s as the result of a number of factors: the availability of inexpensive super-8 film projectors and ten- to twelve-minute cartridges of explicit "loop" materials; a series of liberal U.S. Supreme Court decisions in the 1960s declaring a number of movies and novels not to be obscene; the promulgation in 1968 of the movie rating system, which gave respectability to X-rated movies, some of which starred mainstream actors (e.g., Marlon Brando in *Last Tango in Paris* in 1973) or won Best Picture Academy Awards (e.g., *Midnight Cowboy* in 1969); and a general loosening of sexual attitudes (Winick 1977).

In the 1980s, a major institutional spur to increasing audiences for explicit materials was the Federal Communications Commission's decision not to regulate cable television. As a result, in dozens of American cities, cable television nightly presents all kinds of sexual representations. As the audiences for such materials increase, it becomes less likely that the adults who compose the audiences, and who also may function as jurors who may try obscenity cases, will convict a film, book, or magazine.

The Attorney General's Committee on Obscenity and Pornography (1985), headed by a prosecutor, conducted public hearings and recommended stricter enforcement of the existing laws against pornography. Federal and state laws against pornography are essentially similar, and the decision on jurisdiction or venue is often made on the relative expectations of the prosecutors about where a conviction is most likely.

Pornography involving children is illegal and is not commercially available. Materials combining sex and violence are also not generally sold in the United States. Even the most hard core materials tend to have relatively conventional content. There appears to be no relationship between pornography and prostitution; consumers of pornography are unlikely to be customers of prostitutes because of differences in the nature of the gratifications provided by the two activities.

The President's Commission on Obscenity and Pornography recommended, in the absence of any data demonstrating negative long-term effects of sexually explicit materials, that such materials should be legally available to adults but not to children. Similar recommendations were subsequently made in every country that has conducted a systematic study, including England, Sweden, Norway, Denmark, Israel, and Germany.

Long-term follow-up studies of the effects of legalization of explicit print (1967) and pictorial (1968) media in Denmark have concluded that there were no negative consequences and that there may have been some positive consequences. One major finding of the Danish experience was the public's loss of interest in the materials, soon after they became available, because the materials' novelty had ceased to be a contributor to their attractiveness (Kutchinsky 1985).

Surveys have generally found community attitudes toward sexually explicit materials to be accepting and positive, even in traditionally conservative areas like the South and Midwest. Some communities have established specific zoning regulations for the concentration of movies, bookstores, and other licit sexually oriented businesses in designated "adult entertainment" areas. Such segregation, as in Boston and Detroit, makes it easier for the motivated consumer to shop for "adult" materials and makes it less likely that a nonconsumer will be offended by an unexpected encounter with a movie marquee or bookstore window.

Beginning in the 1980s, the great increase in videocassette recorder (VCR) use made it easier for an adult to view sexually explicit materials inexpensively and conveniently at home. In response to this huge market, there was an explosion of the number of commercially prepared, sexually explicit, X-rated videotapes—to as many as 4,000 new titles a year by 1990.

Research has identified a number of functions served by sexually explicit materials: They provide fantasy, information, sexual stimulation, and reassurance about one's body and about specific practices; they ease anxiety; they serve as items for those interested in collecting materials or following the careers of specific performers; they facilitate communication about sex as a result of desensitization; they encourage communication between sexual partners; and they provide a socially acceptable substitute for masturbation and for acting out of socially harmful sexual acts (Winick 1971).

Sociological investigations of pornography include studies of users of pornography and of organizations of the adult entertainment industry, surveys of the general public's attitudes toward the materials, studies of the career lines of performers and personalities, investigations of pornography's relationship to incidence of criminal activity, analyses of the effects of court decisions, and discussions of the content of pornographic material.

[See also Deviance; Legislation of Morality.]

BIBLIOGRAPHY

Attorney General's Committee on Obscenity and Pornography 1985 *Final Report.* Washington, D.C.: U.S. Government Printing Office.

Kutchinsky, B. 1985 "Pornography and Its Effects in Denmark and the United States." *Comparative Social Research* 8:301–330.

President's Commission on Obscenity and Pornography 1971 *Final Report.* Washington, D.C.: U.S. Government Printing Office.

Winick, C. 1971 "A Study of Consumers of Explicitly Sexual Materials: Some Functions Served by Adult Movies." In *President's Commission on Obscenity and Pornography, Technical Report,* Volume IV. Washington, D.C.: U.S. Government Printing Office.

——— 1977 "From Deviant to Normative." In E. Sagarin, ed., *Deviance and Social Change.* Beverly Hills, Calif.: Sage Publications.

– CHARLES WINICK

POVERTY

Concerning poverty, scholarly as well as ideological debate has long centered on the most elementary questions: What is poverty? How can it be measured? What causes it? Is it a natural phenomenon or a symptom of a poorly ordered society? Although answers exist for all of these questions, no definitive answer exists for any one of them; nor can there ever be, for the questions are not purely demographic but moral, ethical, and political as well. Poverty is a concept, not a fact, and must be understood as such. If no definitive answers are possible, this does not mean that all other answers are thereby equal, since many may be based on ignorant assumptions and ill-formed judgments. Sociologists involved in poverty research seek to be sure that all understand the meaning and consequences of various points of view and that both theoretical and policy research are based soundly, on clear definitions and reliable data.

Even the definition of poverty is problematic. The word derives from the French *pauvre* (meaning "poor"), and means simply the state of lacking material possessions, of having little or no means to support oneself. All would agree that anyone lacking the means necessary to remain alive is in poverty, but beyond that there is little agreement. Some scholars and policy makers would draw the poverty line at the bare subsistence level, as did Rowntree (1902): "the minimum necessaries for the maintenance of merely physical efficiency." Others argue for definitions that include persons whose level of living is above subsistence but who have inadequate means; among those holding to the latter, further arguments concern the definition of adequacy. Social science cannot resolve the most basic arguments. For example, the level of living implied by the poverty threshold in the United States would be seen as desirable and unattainable in many other countries, yet few would suggest that poverty in the United States be defined by such outside standards. Sociologists can evaluate the demographic and economic assumptions underlying standards of poverty, but not the standards themselves.

Conceptions of Poverty

Poverty can be defined in absolute or relative terms. The subsistence line is a good example of an absolute definition. A criterion based on some arbitrary formula, such that poverty equals some fraction of the median income or below, is a good example of a relative definition. In all industrial societies an absolute definition will result in far fewer persons officially in poverty than will a relative definition, creating natural political pressure for absolute definitions (e.g., a study in 1976 revealed that if poverty was defined as 50 percent of the median income, data on income distributions would show that an unchanging 19 percent of the population would have been poor for almost the previous two decades; see U.S. Department of Health, Education, and Welfare 1976). Beyond that, there are valid arguments for both types of definitions. There is evidence that most people see poverty in relative terms rather than as an absolute standard (Rainwater 1974; Kilpatrick 1973). That is, popular conceptions of what level of living constitutes poverty have been found to change as general affluence goes up and down. Advocates of relative measures point out that any absolute measure is arbitrary and thus meaningless. A reasonable definition of the poor, they argue, should be one that demarcates the lower tail of the income distribution as the poor, whatever the absolute metric represented by that tail, for those persons will be poor by the standards of that time and place. As the average level of income rises and falls, what is seen as poverty will, and should, change.

Advocates of absolute measures of poverty do not deny that poverty is intimately tied to distributional inequality, but they argue that relative definitions are too vague for policy purposes. An absolute standard, defined on some concrete level of living, is a goal that can possibly be attained. Once it is attained, a new goal could be set. Eliminating poverty as defined by relative standards is a far more difficult goal, both practically and politically. Marshall (1981, p. 52) noted: "the question of what range of inequality is acceptable above the 'poverty line' can only marginally, if at all, be affected by or affect the decision of where that line should be drawn."

Poverty, in the extreme Calvinist viewpoint, is largely a consequence of vice and can even be regarded as just punishment from a righteous God.

Relative versus absolute poverty is a distributional distinction, but there are other important ones as well. A social distinction, and one with considerable political import, is that usually made between the deserving poor and the undeserving poor. In their brief summary of the historical origins of this distinction, Morris and Williamson (1986, pp. 6–12) maintain that it became significant in the fourteenth century, when, for a variety of reasons (the decline of feudalism, the rise of a market economy with concomitant periodic labor dislocations, bubonic plague-induced regional labor shortages), the poor became geographically mobile for the first time. Before that, the local Catholic parish, with its "blessed are the poor" theology, was the primary caretaker of the indigent. Mobility caused an increase in the number of able-bodied individuals needing temporary assistance, and troubles arising from their presence contributed to a growing antipathy toward the able-bodied poor. Feagin (1975, Chapter 2) locates the origins of negative attitudes toward the poor in the Protestant Reformation. Under Protestantism, he notes, the "work ethic"—the ideology of individualism—became a central tenet of the Western belief system. Poverty, in the extreme Calvinist version of this viewpoint, is largely a consequence of laziness and vice and can even be regarded as just punishment from a righteous God. The rise of Puritan thought contributed to the increasing disfavor with which the unemployed and destitute were regarded. It became a matter of faith that poverty was individually caused and must thereby be individually cured. These ideas became secularized, and programs to aid the poor thereafter focused on curing the individual faults that led to poverty—potential problems in the structure of society that caused unemployment and underemployment were not to be scrutinized in search of a solution. The notion of poverty continues to be in flux. As Marshall (1981) noted, the concept has been with us since antiquity, but its meaning has not been constant through the ages.

Theory and Policy

The epitome of the individual viewpoint in the social sciences was the once-dominant "culture of poverty" explanation for destitution. Oscar Lewis (1961; 1966) is usually credited with this idea, which sees poverty not only as economic deprivation, or the absence of something, but also as a way of life, the presence of specific subcultural values and attitudes passed down from generation to generation. Lewis saw the structure of life among the poor as functional, a set of coping mechanisms without which the poor could not survive their harsh circumstances. But there were negative consequences of the value system as well, he noted. Family life was disorganized, there was an absence of childhood as a prolonged life-cycle stage, a proliferation of consensual marriages, and a very high incidence of spouse and child abandonment—all of which left individuals unprepared and unable to take advantage of opportunities. Exacerbating the problem, the poor were divorced from participation in and integration into the major institutions of society, leading to constant hostility, suspicion, and apathy. Many have maintained that the culture of poverty viewpoint dovetailed perfectly into a politically liberal view of the world. It blamed the poor as a group for their poverty but held no single person individually responsible, nor did it blame the structure of the economy or the society. This view of the poor led to antipoverty policies directed at changing the attitudes and values of those in poverty so that they could "break out" of the dysfunctional cultural traits they had inherited. It led political liberals and radicals to attempt to "organize the poor." Political conservatives transformed the explanation into one that held the poor more culpable individually and the problem into one that was intractable—"benign neglect" being then the only sensible solution (Banfield 1958; 1970; Katz 1989).

There are many problems with the culture of poverty explanation. Most serious was the fact that the cultural scenario simply does not fit. Only a minority of the poor are poor throughout their lives; most move in and out of poverty. Also, a substantial proportion of those in poverty are either women with children who fell into poverty when abandoned by a spouse, or the elderly who became poor when their worklife ended—neither event could be explained by the culture of the class of destination. Many studies falsified specific aspects of the culture of poverty thesis (for a review see Katz 1989, pp. 41 ff.), and Rodman's (1971) influential notion of the "lower-class value stretch" offered an alternative explanation. Rodman argued that the poor actually share mainstream values but must "stretch" them to fit their circumstances. Remove the poverty, and they fit neatly into the dominant culture, Rodman believed. Furthermore, attempts to alter their "culture" are unnecessary and meaningless, since "culture" is not the problem.

Nonetheless, the culture of poverty thesis was (and to some extent still is) a very popular explanation for poverty. This is probably so, in part, because it fits so well the individualistic biases of the majority of Americans. Surveys of attitudes toward poverty have shown that most people prefer "individualistic" explanations of poverty, those that place the responsibility for poverty primarily on the poor themselves. A minority of Americans have subscribed to "structural" explanations that blame external social and economic factors, and in the early 1970s this minority consisted largely of the young, the less educated, lower income groups, nonwhites, and Jews (Feagin 1975, p. 98).

One of the most influential recent works on poverty policy has been that of Murray (1984). Murray argued that the viewpoint that individuals ultimately caused their own poverty changed in the 1960s to the viewpoint that the structure of society was ultimately responsible. This alteration in the intellectual consensus, which freed the poor from responsibility for their poverty, was fatally misguided, he argues, and caused great damage to the poor. Despite enormously increased expenditures on social welfare from 1965 on, he maintains, progress against poverty ceased at that point. In the face of steadily improving economic conditions, the period 1965 to 1980 was marked by increases in poverty, family breakdown, crime, and voluntary unemployment. Murray argues that this occurred precisely because of the increased expenditures on social welfare, not despite them. Work incentive declined during these years because of government policies that rewarded lack of employment and nonintact family structure. It is a standard economic principle that any activity that is subsidized will tend to increase. Murray's arguments have had policy impact but have been subject to extensive criticism by students of the field.

As evidence of the disincentive to work brought about by social welfare payments, Murray cites the Negative Income Tax (NIT) experiments. These were large social experiments designed to assess the effects of a guaranteed income. The first NIT experiment was a four-year study in New Jersey from the late 1960s to the early 1970s. In this study, 1,375 intact "permanently poor" families were selected, and 725 of them were assigned to one of eight NIT plans. It was found that the reduction in labor market activity for males caused by a guaranteed income was not significant but that there were some reductions for females (5 to 10 percent of activity), most of which could be explained by the substitution of labor market activity for increased child care (home employment). In a larger NIT study conducted throughout the 1970s, the Seattle-Denver Income Maintenance Experiment (usually referred to in the literature as the SIME-DIME study), much larger work disincentives were found, about 10 percent for men, 20 percent for their spouses, and up to 30 percent for women heading single-family households (see Haveman 1987, Chapter 9, for an excellent summary of the many NIT experiments). Murray offered these findings as evidence that existing welfare programs contributed to poverty by creating work disincentives. Cain (1985) pointed out that the experiments provided much higher benefits than existing welfare programs and also noted that, given the low pay for women at that level, the 20 percent reduction for wives would have a trivial effect on family income. If it resulted in a proportionate substitution of work at home, the reduction could actually lead to an improvement in the lives of the poor. Commentators have presented arguments against almost every point made by Murray, insisting that either his measures or interpretations are wrong. For example, Murray's measure of economic growth, the GNP, did increase throughout the 1970s, but real wages declined, and inflation and unemployment increased—poverty was not increasing during good times, as he argues. His other assertions have been similarly challenged (see McLanahan et al. 1985 and Katz 1989, Chapter 4, for summaries), but the broad viewpoint his work represents remains important in policy deliberations.

Measures of Poverty

In the United States, official poverty estimates are based on the Orshansky Index. The index is named for Mollie Orshansky of the Social Security Administration, who first proposed it (Orshansky 1965). It is an absolute poverty measure based on the calculated cost of food sufficient for an adequate nutritional level and on the assumption that people must spend one-third of their after-tax income on food. Thus, the poverty level is theoretically three times the annual cost of a nutritionally adequate "market basket." This cost was refined by stratifying poor families by size, composition, and farm or nonfarm residence and creating different income cutoffs for poverty for families of differing types. Originally there were 124 income cutoff points, but by 1980 the separate thresholds for farm families and female-headed households had been eliminated and the number of thresholds reduced to forty-eight. Since 1969 the poverty line has been updated regularly using the consumer price index to adjust for increased costs. The original index was based on the least costly of four nutritionally adequate food plans developed by the Department of Agriculture. Since a 1955 Department of Agriculture survey of food consumption patterns had determined that families of three or more spent approximately one-third of their income on food, the original poverty index was simply triple the average cost of the economy food plan. This index was altered for smaller families to compensate for their higher fixed costs and for farm families to compensate for their lower costs (the farm threshold began as 70 percent of the nonfarm for an equivalent household and was raised to 85 percent in 1969). Originally, the poverty index was adjusted yearly by taking into account the cost of the food items in the Department of Agriculture economy budget, but, this changed in 1969 to a simple consumer price index adjustment (U.S. Bureau of the Census 1982).

Over the years there have been many criticisms of the official poverty measure and its assumptions (for summaries and extended discussion see U.S. Department of Health, Education, and Welfare 1976; Haveman 1987). The first set of problems, some argue, comes from the fact that the very basis of the measure is flawed. The economy food budget at the measure's core is derived from an outdated survey that may not reflect changes in tastes and options. Further, the multiplication of food costs by three is only appropriate for some types of families; other types must spend greater or lesser proportions on food. Some estimates indicate that the poor spend one-half or more of their income on food; the more well-to-do spend one-third or less. And, even if the multiplier was correct, the original Department of Agriculture survey discovered it for post-tax income; in the poverty measure it is applied to pre-tax income, though the poor pay little in taxes. Other problems-often cited include the fact that the "economy budget" assumes sufficient knowledge for wise shopping—a dubious assumption for the poor—and the fact that the poor are often locked into paying much higher prices than average because of a lack of transportation. An additional problem is that the poverty thresholds are not updated by using changes in the actual price of food but instead by changes in the consumer price index, which includes changes in the price of many other items such as clothing, shelter, transportation, fuel, medical fees, recreation, furniture, appliances, personal services, and many other items probably irrelevant to the expenses of the poor. Findings are mixed, but it is generally agreed that the losses in purchasing power suffered by the poor in inflationary periods is understated by the consumer price index (see Oster, Lake, and Oksman-1978, p. 25). A second set of problems derives from the fact that the definition is based on income only. Both in-kind transfers and assets are excluded. Excluding in-kind transfers means that government-provided food, shelter, or medical care is not counted. Excluding assets means that a wealthy family with little current taxable or reportable income might be counted as poor.

Demography of Poverty

In 1987 the average poverty threshold for a family of four was $11,611 per year (all figures in this paragraph are from U.S. Bureau of the Census 1989; 1990). This means the assumed annual cost of an adequate diet for four persons was $3,870.33, or about 88 cents per meal per person. For a single person the poverty threshold was $5,778 and the food allowance $1.76 per meal. In 1986 the same poverty threshold was $11,203, allowing 85 cents per meal, and in 1988 it had risen to $12,091, or 92 cents per meal. In the United States in 1987 there were 32,341,000 persons below the poverty threshold, or 13.4 percent of the population. In 1988 there were 31,878,000, or 13.1 percent, almost one-half million fewer persons below official poverty than the year before. These figures underestimate official poverty somewhat since they are based on the Current Population Survey, which is primarily a household survey and thus does not count the homeless not in shelters. The decline from 1987 to 1988 in the number in poverty is part of a long-term trend. In 1960 there were eight million more—39,851,000 persons—who by today's guidelines would have been counted as officially in poverty, representing 22.2 percent of the population. By the official, absolute standard, poverty has greatly decreased since the early 1960s, both in terms of the actual number of persons below the threshold and, even more dramatically, in terms of the percentage of the population in poverty (U.S. Bureau of the Census 1989). This decrease was actually over two decades, since the number in poverty in 1970 had declined to only 25,420,000, or 12.6 percent of the population, and the number and percentage have risen since then, but never back as high as the 1960 levels. Poverty is not evenly spread over the population. Of those below the official poverty level in 1988, 57.1 percent were female, 29.6 percent were black, and 16.9 percent were Hispanic. Female-headed families with children were disproportionately poor. In 1988, 38.2 percent of all such white families were in poverty, and 56.3 percent of all such black families were in poverty (this is a gender phenomenon, not a single-parent one, since in 1988 only 18 percent of male-headed single-parent families were below the poverty threshold). The age composition of the poor population has changed. In 1968, 38.6 percent of those in poverty were of working age (eighteen to sixty-four), while twenty years later 49.6 percent of those in poverty were of working age. From 1968 to 1988 the proportion of the poor population over sixty-five declined from 18.2 percent to 10.9 percent, and the proportion that were children under eighteen declined from 43.1 percent to 39.5 percent. A higher percentage of working-age poor is seen by some as a sign of worse times. It almost certainly reflects not only economic downturns but also in part ideological biases toward helping the presumedly able-bodied poor; most antipoverty programs have been specifically aimed at the old or the young.

The number of extremely poor people has more than doubled since 1970, while the population has increased by only 20 percent.

Despite extensive debate about the policy implications of various definitions of poverty, one can have confidence that the poor are being counted with considerable precision. More than one generation of social scientists has contributed to the refinement of the measures of poverty, and existing statistical series are based on data collected by the U.S. Bureau of the Census—an organization whose technical competence is unparalleled. Nonetheless, there is one group, the extremely poor, whose numbers are in doubt. All current measurement relies on the household unit and assumes some standard type of domicile. As Rossi (1989, p. 73) puts it, "our national unemployment and poverty statistics pertain only to that portion of the domiciled population that lives in conventional housing." An extremely poor person living, perhaps temporarily, in a household where other adults had sufficient income would not be counted in poverty. Even more important, the literally homeless who live on the street, and those whose homes consist of hotels, motels, rooming houses, or shelters are not counted at all in the yearly Current Population Survey (the decennial census does attempt to count those in temporary quarters, but the 1990 census was the first even to attempt to count those housed in unconventional ways or not at all). The studies of Rossi and his colleagues indicate that the number of extremely poor people in the United States (those whose income is less than two-thirds of the poverty level) is somewhere between 4 and 7 million. The number of literally homeless poor people, those who do not figure into the official poverty counts, must be estimated. The best available estimate is that they number between 250,000 and 350,000, about 5 to 8 percent of the extremely poor population (Rossi 1989). The number of extremely poor people has more than doubled since 1970, while the population has increased by only 20 percent (Rossi 1989, p. 78). The extremely poor are at considerable risk of becoming literally homeless. When they do so, they will disappear from official statistics (just as the unemployed cease being officially unemployed soon after they run out of benefits and/or give up the search for work). To see that official statistics remain reliable in the face of increasing extreme poverty is the most recent methodological challenge in the field.

The study of poverty is a difficult field and is not properly a purely sociological endeavor. As even this brief overview shows, a thorough understanding requires the combined talents of sociologists, economists, demographers, political scientists, historians, and philosophers. All of these fields have contributed to our understanding of the phenomenon.

[See also Homelessness; Income Distribution in the United States; Social Mobility; Social Stratification.]

BIBLIOGRAPHY

Banfield, Edward C. 1958 *The Moral Basis of a Backward Society.* New York: Free Press.

——— 1970 *The Unheavenly City.* Boston: Little, Brown.

Cain, Glen 1985 "Comments on Murray's Analysis of the Impact of the War on Poverty on the Labor Market Behavior of the Poor." In Sara McLanahan, et al. *Losing Ground: A Critique.* Special Report no. 38. Madison: University of Wisconsin, Institute for Research on Poverty.

Feagin, Joe R. 1975 *Subordinating the Poor: Welfare and American Beliefs.* Englewood Cliffs, N.J.: Prentice-Hall.

Haveman, Robert H. 1987 *Poverty Policy and Poverty Research: The Great Society and the Social Sciences.* Madison: University of Wisconsin Press.

Katz, Michael B. 1989 *The Undeserving Poor: From the War on Poverty to the War on Welfare.* New York: Pantheon Books.

Kilpatrick, R. W. 1973 "The Income Elasticity of the Poverty Line." *Review of Economics and Statistics* 55:327–332.

Lewis, Oscar 1961 *The Children of Sanchez.* New York: Random House.

——— 1966 *La Vida: A Puerto Rican Family in the Culture of Poverty—San Juan and New York.* New York: Random House.

Marshall, T. H. 1981 *The Right to Welfare and Other Essays.* New York: Free Press.

McLanahan, Sara, et al. 1985 *Losing Ground: A Critique.* Special Report no. 38. Madison: University of Wisconsin, Institute for Research on Poverty.

Morris, Michael, and John B. Williamson 1986 *Poverty and Public Policy: An Analysis of Federal Intervention Efforts.* Westport, Conn.: Greenwood Press.

Murray, Charles 1984 *Losing Ground: American Social Policy, 1950–1980.* New York: Basic Books.

Orshansky, Mollie 1965 "Counting the Poor: Another Look at the Poverty Profile." *Social Security Bulletin* 28(1):3–29.

Oster, Sharon M., Elizabeth E. Lake, and Conchita Gene Oksman 1978 *The Definition and Measurement of Poverty.* Boulder, Colo.: Westview Press.

Rainwater, Lee 1974 *What Money Buys: Inequality and the Social Meaning of Income.* New York: Basic Books.

Rodman, Hyman 1971 *Lower-Class Families: The Culture of Poverty in Negro Trinidad.* London: Oxford University Press.

Rossi, Peter H. 1989 *Down and Out in America: The Origins of Homelessness.* Chicago: University of Chicago Press.

Rowntree, B. S. 1902 *Poverty: A Study of Town Life.* London: Macmillan.

U.S. Bureau of the Census 1982 "Changes in the Definition of Poverty." *Current Population Reports.* Series P-60, no. 133. Washington, D.C.: U.S. Government Printing Office.

——— 1989 "Poverty in the United States: 1987." *Current Population Reports.* Series P-60, no. 163. Washington, D.C.: U.S. Government Printing Office.

——— 1989b "Money Income and Poverty Status in the United States: 1988." *Current Population Reports.* Series P-60, no. 166. Washington, D.C.: U.S. Government Printing Office.

——— 1990 "Measuring the Effect of Benefits and Taxes on Income and Poverty: 1989." *Current Population Reports.* Series P-60, no. 169-RD. Washington, D.C.: U.S. Government Printing Office.

U.S. Department of Health, Education, and Welfare 1976 *The Measure of Poverty: A Report to Congress as Mandated by the Education Amendments of 1974.* Washington, D.C.: U.S. Government Printing Office.

— WAYNE J. VILLEMEZ

PREJUDICE

Gordon Allport, in his classic, *The Nature of Prejudice,* defined prejudice as "an antipathy based upon a faulty and inflexible generalization" (1954, p. 9). This phrasing neatly captures the notion that both inaccurate beliefs and negative feelings are implicated in prejudice. To these "cognitive" and "affective" dimensions of prejudice, some analysts add "conative," referring to action orientation (Klineberg 1972) and prescription (Harding et al. 1969). Allport's circumspection on the conative implications of prejudice—he said prejudice "may be felt or expressed" (1954, p. 9)—foreshadowed our growing understanding that the correspondence of behavior with cognitions and feelings is uncertain and a research issue in its own right (Schuman and Johnson 1976).

Racial and ethnic prejudice was Allport's primary interest. Emerging social issues have brought expanded attention to other forms of prejudice—against women, the elderly, handicapped persons, AIDS patients, and others. This discussion will focus on racial prejudice among white Americans, in the expectation that parallels and points of contrast will continue to make race relations research relevant to other forms of prejudice.

Trends and Patterns

For many years, derogatory stereotypes, blatant aversion to interracial contact, and opposition in principle to racial equality were seen as the central manifestations of race prejudice, virtually defining the social science view of the problem. Indicators of these beliefs and feelings show a clear positive trend (Jaynes and Williams 1989; Schuman, Steeh, and Bobo 1985). White Americans who believed in the innate intellectual inferiority of blacks declined from 53 percent in 1942 to about 20 percent in the 1960s, when the question was discontinued in major national surveys. The percentage of whites who said it wouldn't make any difference to them if a Negro of equal social status moved into their block rose from 36 percent to 85 percent between 1942 and 1972. White opinion that blacks should have "as good a chance as white people to get any kind of job" climbed from 45 percent in 1944 to 97 percent in 1972. Smith and Sheatsley sum up this picture without equivocation: "Looking over this forty-year span, we are struck by the steady, massive growth in racial tolerance" (1984, p. 14).

Recurrent outbursts of overt racial hostility serve as unfortunate reminders that some white Americans still cling to blatant prejudice. More importantly, even the majority of whites, those on whom Smith and Sheatsley focused, appear unambiguously tolerant only if attention is confined to such traditional survey indicators as those described above. A confluence of developments has broadened the study of race prejudice and transformed our understanding of white racial attitudes. First, evidence of widespread, subtle prejudice has been revealed in research using disguised, "nonreactive" methods. Second, "social cognition" scholarship, prominent in the psychological wing of social psychology, has been powerfully applied to intergroup relations. Third, evolution of the struggle for racial equality in the United States has shifted attention to a new domain of racial policy-related beliefs and feelings. These perspectives provide ample evidence that white racial prejudice is not a thing of the past but exists today in complex forms that have yet to be thoroughly charted.

EVIDENCE FROM "NONREACTIVE" STUDIES. Given the clear dominance of "liberal" racial norms evidenced in public opinion data, it might be expected that needs for social acceptability and self-esteem would lead many whites to withhold evidence of negative racial feelings and cognitions whenever possible. Disguised, "nonreactive" research (Webb et al. 1981) provides substantial evidence that, indeed, traditional survey approaches underestimate negative racial feeling. Field experiments reveal that whites often provide less help to victims who are black (Crosby, Bromley, and Saxe 1980), sometimes redefining the situation so as to justify their lack of response (Gaertner 1976). Such elements of nonverbal behavior as voice tone (Weitz 1972) and seating proximity (Word, Zanna, and Cooper 1974) have been found to reveal negative racial feelings and avoidance. Reaction time studies suggest the existence of a subtle form of stereotyping, not derogating blacks, but reserving positive characteristics for whites (Dovidio, Mann, and Gaertner 1989). Thus, accumulating evidence reveals that "microaggressions" (Pettigrew 1989) often accompany self-portrayals of liberalism.

SOCIAL COGNITION PERSPECTIVES. In recognizing aspects of prejudice as predictable outgrowths of "natural" cognitive processes, Allport (1954) was ahead of his time. The current wave of social cognition research on intergroup relations was set in motion by Tajfel (1969), who demonstrated that mere categorization—of physical objects or of people—encourages exaggerated perception of intragroup homogeneity and intergroup difference. Even in "minimal groups" arbitrarily created in psychology laboratories, these effects of social categorization are often accompanied by outgroup discrimination (Brewer 1979; Hamilton 1979). Accumulating evidence of the negative consequences of ingroup-outgroup categorization has spurred research aimed at identifying conditions of intergroup contact that are likely to decrease category salience and promote "individuation" or "decategorization" (Brewer and Miller 1988; Wilder 1978) or at least to reduce the negativity of outgroup stereotypes (Rothbart and John 1985; Wilder 1984).

The study of attributional processes (Heider 1958; Jones and Davis 1965) also has been usefully applied to intergroup relations, calling attention to such issues as whether whites believe that black economic hardship results from discrimination or lack of effort. Research evidence has linked stereotypic thinking to attributions of outgroup behavior (Hamilton 1979). Specific predictions are developed in Pettigrew's (1979) discussion of the "ultimate attributional error," the tendency to hold outgroups personally responsible for their failures but to "discount" their responsibility for successes, attributing successes to such factors as luck or unfair advantage.

THE EXPANDED RACIAL ATTITUDE DOMAIN. Over the past twenty-five years, evolution in the struggle for racial equality has brought new complexity to the public debate about racial issues. Notions that barriers to black equality consist solely of white hostility and aversion or formal denial of rights now appear naive. Advocates insist that structural barriers far more complex and pervasive than formal denial of access prevent actual equality of opportunity and desegregation, making questions about acceptance by white individuals a moot point for millions of black Americans.

Asked about specific policies and programs designed to increase racial equality, white Americans show substantially less support than they voice for racial equality in principle.

In the current era of U.S. race relations, traditional manifestations of race prejudice recede in relevance, and different forms of race-related belief and feeling take center stage—reactions to agitation for change, recognition and interpretation of continuing inequality, support for proposed remedies. By all indications, such white "perceptions, explanations, and prescriptions" (Apostle et al. 1983, p. 18) show far less consensus and support for racial change than appeared in traditional race survey data. Asked about specific policies and programs designed to increase racial equality—fair housing guarantees, school desegregation plans, affirmative action in hiring and college admission—white Americans show substantially less support than they voice for racial equality in principle (Schuman, Steeh, and Bobo 1985). In the minds of many white Americans, recent black gains and benefits of affirmative action are exaggerated, and remaining inequality is underestimated (Kluegel and Smith 1982). There is substantial white resentment of black activism and perceived progress (Bobo 1988a; Schuman, Steeh, and Bobo 1985).

The influence of attribution research in social psychology and earlier societal analyses (Ryan 1971; Feagin 1975) is reflected in a remarkable convergence of recent scholarly opinion that explanations are at the heart of the matter. The research evidence tells a clear story: Whites explain the economic plight of black Americans more often as the result of such "individualistic" factors as lack of motivation than as the result of such "structural" factors as discrimination (Apostle et al. 1983; Kluegel and Smith 1986; Sniderman and Hagen 1985). Furthermore, individualistic attributions are linked to a variety of policy-relevant beliefs and opinions including opposition to affirmative action (Kluegel and Smith 1983; 1986).

Characterizations of White Racial Attitudes

Efforts to characterize the complex pattern of racial attitudes held by white Americans emphasize an array of themes:

1. *Natural cognitive processing.* As noted earlier, social cognition analyses claim that a substantial part of the race prejudice once thought to have sociocultural or psychodynamic roots actually stems from ordinary cognitive processing, particularly categorization (Hamilton 1979). Social cognition portrayals have become somewhat more eclectic in recent years, allowing motivational and social influences (Hamilton and Trolier 1986; Fiske 1987), but there remains a tone of contrast between cognitive explanations and what Tajfel called "blood and guts" notions (1969, p. 80).

2. *Strain between individualism and egalitarianism.* Current racial policy issues are said to pull whites between two cherished American values, individualism and egalitarianism (Lipset and Schneider 1978). *Qualified* support for social programs exists, in this view, because egalitarian sentiments prevail only until a proposal challenges individualistic values.

3. *Ambivalence.* Adding psychodynamic flavor to the idea of a strain between individualism and egalitarianism, some analysts describe current white feelings as an ambivalence that produces an unpredictable mix of amplified positive and negative responses (Katz, Wackenhut, and Hass 1986).

4. *Aversive racism.* A desire to avoid interracial contact, muted negative feelings, and egalitarian self-concepts are the mix Kovel (1970) characterized as aversive racism. Aversive racism leads one to avoid positive interracial behavior when the situation can be defined to permit it and to express negative feelings when there are ostensible nonracial justifications (Gaertner 1976; Gaertner and Dovidio 1986).

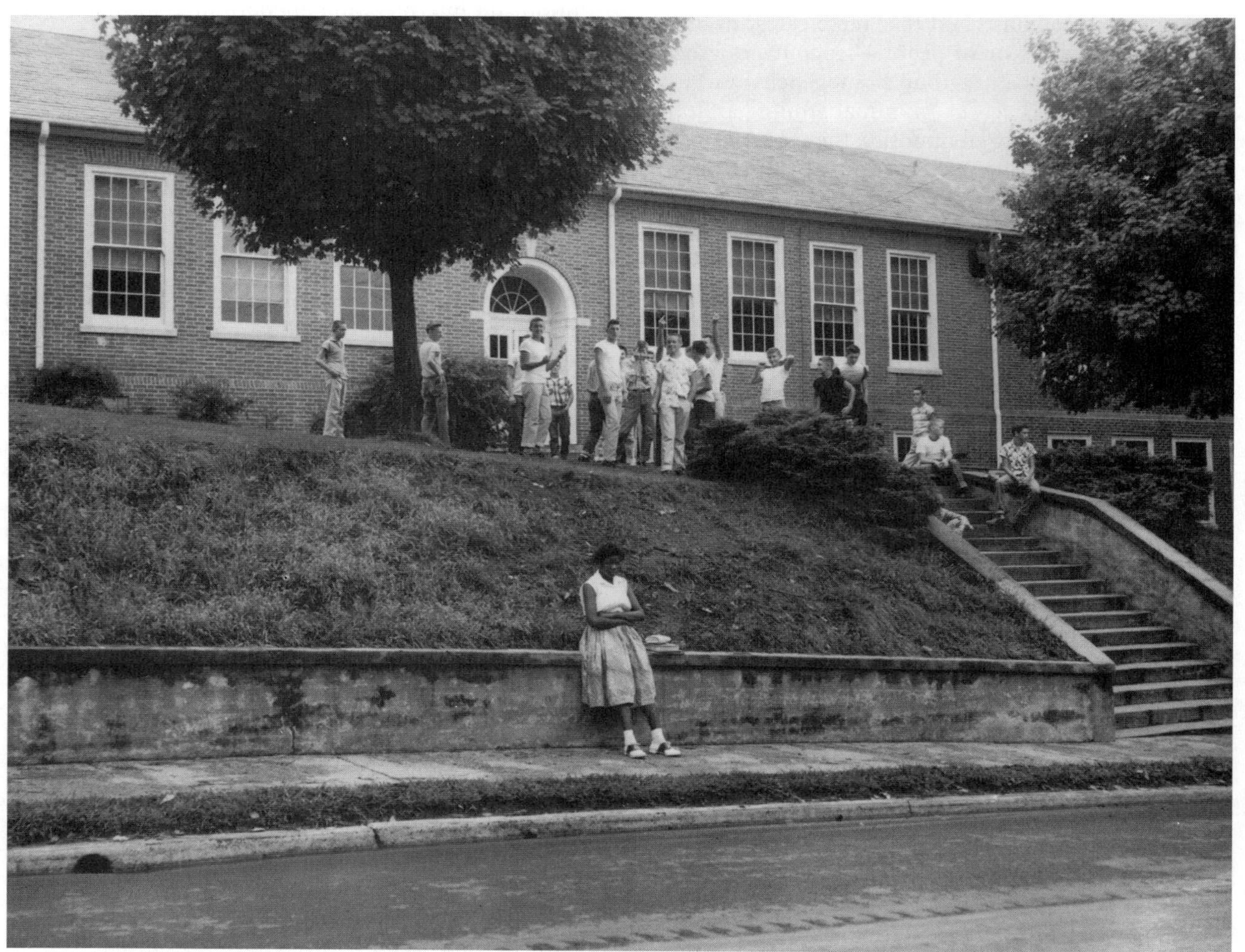

In the mid-1900s, American Southern whites tried to keep blacks out of their schools. Sociologists call this behavior aversive racism, in which individuals or groups desire to avoid contact with those of another race. (UPI/Corbis-Bettmann)

5. *Self-interest.* Collective self-interest is sometimes identified as the primary basis of whites' interracial beliefs and feelings (Jackman and Muha 1984; Wellman 1977). If zero-sum assumptions prevail, redistribution in favor of blacks will be seen as a losing proposition to whites. Self-interest is at the heart of what Bobo (1988b) calls an "ideology of bounded racial change": white acceptance of racial change ends when the changes are perceived to threaten the well-being of whites.

6. *Symbolic or modern racism.* Anti-black affect instilled by childhood socialization and the sense that racial change threatens fondly held individualistic values, not self-interest, constitute Sears's (1988) "symbolic" racism. "Modern" racism contains the added ingredient of denying continuing racial inequality (McConahay 1986).

7. *Dominant stratification ideology.* A belief that opportunity is plentiful and equally distributed, and thus that effort is economically rewarded and economic failure is deserved, compose the "dominant stratification ideology" (Huber and Form 1973; Kluegel and Smith 1986). Although personal status and strands of American "social liberalism" also play a role, unyielding adherence to this American "dominant ideology" is portrayed as a major impediment to public support for redistributional claims in general and to calls for racial change in particular (Kluegel and Smith 1986). On a foundation of ignorance resulting from social segregation, whites' own experiences of economic success work to prevent recognition of the continuing barriers to full opportunity for black Americans (Kluegel 1985).

Prescriptions for Modern Prejudice

When the lessons from cognitive social psychology are counterposed with those from other perspectives on modern race prejudice, an apparent dilemma is revealed. Though social cognition findings indicate that category salience can promote stereotype change under some circumstances (Cook 1984; Pettigrew and Martin 1987; Rothbart and John 1985), much of the cognitive literature insists that categorization is a central contributor to race prejudice and negative race relations: Color-consciousness is often portrayed as an evil, color-blindness as the ideal. From other scholars of modern prejudice, the analysis and prescription are nearly a mirror image of this view. Color-blindness is said to impede forthright problem solving in desegregated institutions (Schofield 1986); to represent ignorance of the structural barriers faced by black Americans (Kluegel 1985); and to be used as a weapon by those opposing black claims of collective rights (Jackman and Muha 1984; Omi and Winant 1986). The solution implied or stated by these analysts is for whites to adopt a color-consciousness that fully acknowledges the historical impact of racial subordination and the continuing liabilities of direct and indirect discrimination. The two streams of advice present this challenge: How to promote in the white public a racial understanding that avoids the psychological liabilities of ingroup and outgroup categorization while acknowledging the full sociological implications of the past and continuing color line.

[See also Attitudes; Discrimination; Race; Segregation and Desegregation.]

BIBLIOGRAPHY

Allport, Gordon 1954 *The Nature of Prejudice.* Cambridge, Mass.: Addison-Wesley.

Apostle, Richard A., Charles Y. Glock, Thomas Piazza, and Marijean Suelzle 1983 *The Anatomy of Racial Attitudes.* Berkeley: University of California Press.

Bobo, Lawrence 1988a "Attitudes Toward the Black Political Movement: Trends, Meaning, and Effects on Racial Policy Preferences." *Social Psychology Quarterly* 51:287–302.

——— 1988b "Group Conflict, Prejudice, and the Paradox of Contemporary Racial Attitudes." In Phyllis A. Katz and Dalmas A. Taylor, eds., *Eliminating Racism.* New York: Plenum Press.

Brewer, Marilynn B. 1979 "Ingroup Bias in the Minimal Intergroup Situation: A Cognitive-Motivational Analysis." *Psychological Bulletin* 86:307–324.

Brewer, Marilynn B., and Norman Miller 1988 "Contact and Cooperation: When Do They Work?" In Phyllis A. Katz and Dalmas A. Taylor, eds., *Eliminating Racism.* New York: Plenum Press.

Cook, Stuart W. 1984 "Cooperative Interaction in Multiethnic Contexts." In Norman Miller and Marilynn B. Brewer, eds., *Groups in Contact: The Psychology of Desegregation.* New York: Academic Press.

Crosby, Faye J., Stephanie Bromley, and Leonard Saxe 1980 "Recent Unobtrusive Studies of Black and White Discrimination and Prejudice: A Literature Review." *Psychological Bulletin* 87:546–563.

Dovidio, John F., Jeffrey Mann, and Samuel L. Gaertner 1989 "Resistance to Affirmative Action: The Implications of Aversive Racism." In Faye J. Crosby and Fletcher A. Blanchard, eds., *Affirmative Action in Perspective.* New York: Springer-Verlag.

Feagin, Joe R. 1975 *Subordinating the Poor.* Englewood Cliffs, N.J.: Prentice-Hall.

Fiske, Susan T. 1987 "On the Road: Comment on the Cognitive Stereotyping Literature in Pettigrew and Martin." *Journal of Social Issues* 43:113–118.

Gaertner, Samuel L. 1976 "Nonreactive Measures in Racial Attitude Research: A Focus on 'Liberals'." In Phyllis A. Katz, ed., *Toward the Elimination of Racism.* New York: Pergamon.

Gaertner, Samuel L., and John F. Dovidio 1986 "The Aversive Form of Racism." In John F. Dovidio and Samuel L. Gaertner, eds., *Prejudice, Discrimination, and Racism.* Orlando, Fla.: Academic Press.

Hamilton, David A., and Tina K. Trolier 1986 "Stereotypes and Stereotyping: An Overview of the Cognitive Approach." In Phyllis A. Katz and Dalmas A. Taylor, eds., *Eliminating Racism.* New York: Plenum Press.

Hamilton, David L. 1979 "A Cognitive-Attributional Analysis of Stereotyping." In Leonard Berkowitz, ed., *Advances in Experimental Social Psychology.* Vol. 12. New York: Academic Press.

Harding, John, Harold Proshansky, Bernard Kutner, and Isador Chein 1969 "Prejudice and Intergroup Relations." In Gardner Lindzey and Elliot Aronson, eds., *Handbook of Social Psychology.* 2d ed. Reading, Mass.: Addison-Wesley.

Heider, Fritz 1958 *The Psychology of Interpersonal Relations.* New York: Wiley.

Huber, Joan, and William H. Form 1973 *Income and Ideology.* New York: Free Press.

Jackman, Mary R., and Michael J. Muha 1984 "Education and Intergroup Attitudes: Moral Enlightenment, Superficial Democratic Commitment, or Ideological Refinement?" *American Sociological Review* 49:751–769.

Jaynes, David Gerald, and Robin M. Williams, Jr. 1989 *A Common Destiny: Blacks and American Society.* Washington, D.C.: National Academy Press.

Jones, Edward E., and Keith E. Davis 1965 "From Acts to Dispositions: The Attribution Process in Perception Perception." In Leonard Berkowitz, ed., *Advances in Experimental Social Psychology.* Vol. 2. New York: Academic Press.

Katz, Irwin, Joyce Wackenhut, and R. Glen Hass 1986 "Racial Ambivalence, Value Duality, and Behavior." In John F. Dovidio and Samuel L. Gaertner, eds., *Prejudice, Discrimination, and Racism.* Orlando, Fla.: Academic Press.

Klineberg, Otto 1972 "Prejudice: The Concept." In David L. Sills, ed., *International Encyclopedia of the Social Sciences.* New York: Macmillan and Free Press.

Kluegel, James R. 1985 "If There Isn't a Problem, You Don't Need a Solution." *American Behavioral Scientist* 28:761–784.

———, and Eliot R. Smith 1982 "Whites' Beliefs about Blacks' Opportunity." *American Sociological Review* 47:518–532.

——— 1983 "Affirmative Action Attitudes: Effects of Self-Interest, Racial Affect, and Stratification Beliefs on Whites' Views." *Social Forces* 61:797–824.

——— 1986 *Beliefs about Inequality: Americans' Views of What Is and What Ought to Be.* New York: Aldine de Gruyter.

Kovel, Joel 1970 *White Racism: A Psychohistory.* New York: Pantheon.

Lipset, Seymour Martin, and William Schneider 1978 "The Bakke Case: How Would It Be Decided at the Bar of Public Opinion?" *Public Opinion* 1:38–44.

McConahay, John B. 1986 "Modern Racism, Ambivalence, and the Modern Racism Scale." In John F. Dovidio and Samuel L. Gaertner, eds., *Prejudice, Discrimination, and Racism.* Orlando, Fla.: Academic Press.

Omi, Michael, and Howard Winant 1986 *Racial Formation in the United States from the 1960s to the 1980s.* New York: Routledge and Kegan Paul.

Pettigrew, Thomas F. 1979 "The Ultimate Attribution Error: Extending Allport's Cognitive Analysis of Prejudice." *Personality and Social Psychology Bulletin* 5:461–476.

——— 1989 "The Nature of Modern Racism." *Revue internationale de psychologie sociale* 2:291–305.

———, and Joanne Martin 1987 "Shaping the Organizational Context for Black American Inclusion." *Journal of Social Issues* 43:41–78.

Rothbart, Myron, and Oliver P. John 1985 "Social Categorization and Behavioral Episodes: A Cognitive Analysis of the Effects of Intergroup Contact." *Journal of Social Issues* 41:81–104.

Ryan, William 1971 *Blaming the Victim.* New York: Vintage.

Schofield, Janet Ward 1986 "Causes and Consequences of the Colorblind Perspective." In John F. Dovidio and Samuel L. Gaertner, eds., *Prejudice, Discrimination, and Racism.* Orlando, Fla.: Academic Press.

Schuman, Howard, and Michael P. Johnson 1976 "Attitudes and Behavior." *Annual Review of Sociology* 2:161–207.

Schuman, Howard, Charlotte Steeh, and Lawrence Bobo 1985 *Racial Attitudes in America: Trends and Interpretations.* Cambridge: Mass.: Harvard University

Sears, David O. 1988 "Symbolic Racism." In Phyllis A. Katz and Dalmas A. Taylor, eds., *Eliminating Racism.* New York: Plenum Press.

Smith, Thomas W., and Paul B. Sheatsley 1984 "American Attitudes toward Race Relations." *Public Opinion* 6:14–15, 50–53.

Sniderman, Paul M., with Michael Gray Hagen 1985 *Race and Inequality: A Study in American Values.* Chatham, N.J.: Chatham House Publishers.

Tajfel, Henri 1969 "Cognitive Aspects of Prejudice." *Journal of Social Issues.* 4:79–97.

Webb, Eugene J., Donald T. Campbell, Richard D. Schwartz, Lee Sechrest, and J. B. Grove 1981 *Nonreactive Measures in the Social Sciences.* 2nd ed. Boston: Houghton Mifflin.

Weitz, Shirley 1972 "Attitude, Voice, and Behavior: A Repressed Affect Model of Interracial Interaction." *Journal of Personality and Social Psychology* 32:857–864.

Wellman, David T. 1977 *Portraits of White Racism.* New York: Oxford University Press.

Wilder, David A. 1978 "Reduction of Intergroup Discrimination through Individuation of the Out-Group." *Journal of Personality and Social Psychology* 36:1,361–1,374.

——— 1984 "Intergroup Contact: The Typical Member and the Exception to the Rule." *Journal of Experimental Social Psychology* 20:177–194.

Word, Carl O., Mark P. Zanna, and Joel Cooper 1974 "The Nonverbal Mediation of Self-Fulfilling Prophecies in Interracial Interaction." *Journal of Experimental Social Psychology* 10:109–120.

– MARYLEE C. TAYLOR
THOMAS F. PETTIGREW

PRISONS AND PRISON REFORM MOVEMENT

Since the 1970s the goal of U.S. prisons has changed from rehabilitation to punishment. Most efforts at prison reform before that decade had been to introduce presumably better methods of turning criminals into good citizens. Beginning in the first quarter of the nineteenth century, reformers have debated the merits of the Pennsylvania (solitary confinement) and Auburn (separate and silent) systems, both designed for rehabilitation, but by the 1970s a number of academic studies concluded that none of the programs for rehabilitation had been successful. The studies came at a time when the national political climate was becoming conservative, with an emphasis on punishing rather than reforming criminals. A radical prisoners movement combined with academic studies and political conservatism to discredit rehabilitation.

Inspired by the civil rights movement and aided by the greater willingness of courts to intervene in supporting rights of prisoners, prisoners had become politically active beginning in the late 1960s. They protested against what they saw as the unfairness of indeterminate sentences, which were a part of the emphasis on rehabilitation. Convicts served unequal amounts of time for similar crimes, depending on the judgment of "experts" as to whether they had reformed. Activists believed that the length of time served should be proportionate to the seriousness of the crime. Court decisions supporting religious freedom in prison for Black Muslims and the rights of prisoners to sue prison officials led to increased activism in the 1970s, as well as frequent resentment on the part of many prison officials and guards who felt they were losing authority and respect. Prison demonstrations and rebellions of this period were not just about better physical conditions but also about greater rights for prisoners. Events at California's Soledad prison in 1969–1970 led to the organization of supporters outside the prison, the Soledad Brothers Defense Fund. Lists of demands at Soledad were echoed by inmates at California's Folsom Prison later in 1970, and at New York's Attica in 1971. Soledad, Folsom, and Attica became symbols of a movement that activists, outside prisons as well as inside, believed would radically change the nature of prisons in the United States.

The concept of prisoner rehabilitation formed the basis for indeterminate sentencing, allowing early releases for good behavior. However, prisoners' rights activists viewed uneven sentences for similar crimes as unfair. By the late 1980s, mandatory sentencing became common. (Michael S. Yamashita/Corbis)

Prisons did change but not in the direction desired by activists. An ironic effect of prisoner opposition to indeterminate sentences provided support for a conservative movement to "get tough" on criminals. By the end of the 1970s both the activist movement and the goal of rehabilitation had greatly weakened. The 1980 riot in the New Mexico State Penitentiary at Santa Fe contrasted with the Attica riot of 1971. Both were bloody, but at Attica most of the killing was done by officers of the law, whereas at Santa Fe prisoners tortured and killed other prisoners. The Santa Fe riot symbolized the end of hopes for prisoner activism. Mandatory sentencing became the norm in many states, and in 1987 guidelines for mandatory sentences for federal crimes were approved by the House of Representatives. Sentencing guidelines were not implemented in support of prisoners' rights but were part of the movement toward making prisons simply places of punishment.

The more punitive approach to imprisonment did not reduce the national crime rate, but it had noticeable effects upon rates of imprisonment. Rates remained steady during the 1960s but rose sharply in the early 1970s. The United States had about three times as many inmates in the 1990s (almost 800,000) as in the 1970s and more prisoners per capita than any other industrial democracy. For every 100,000 people, the United States has 300 in prison. Canada has the next highest rate, at 100 per 100,000, while that of the Netherlands is the lowest, fewer than 50 per 100,000.

Rates of imprisonment are not inevitable consequences of natural forces but the results of policy. They explain historical changes in imprisonment rates in Great Britain and the United States in terms of changes in policies in both countries. Punitive policies in Great Britain resulted in a rapid rise in the rate of imprisonment in the nineteenth century until about 1878. After that time different policies resulted in decreasing rates until about 1930, when they began to rise again. U.S. policies since the 1980s have resulted both in an extraordinarily high rate of imprisonment and serious levels of overcrowding. While there is general agreement that overcrowded prisons are inhumane and dangerous, there is little agreement about what ought to be done. Public opinion in the 1990s continued to support stiff sentences for individuals convicted of serious crimes but opposed tax increases to construct more prisons. Legislators responded by passing punitive laws but refused to appropriate funds and legislate taxes necessary to support these laws humanely.

– RICHARD W. MOODEY

PROBATION AND PAROLE

The criminal justice system is the primary institution responsible for the formal social control of criminal deviance. Those who violate the criminal law are subject to a variety of sanctions, ranging from the reprimand of a police officer to execution by hanging. Most offenders are not apprehended, and among those who are arrested many are not prosecuted nor convicted of a crime. For offenders who are found guilty, either by trial or more often by negotiated guilty plea, the sentence handed down by the court typically mandates correctional supervision, usually either some form of probation or incarceration with early release to some form of parole.

Even though probation and parole have been integral components of corrections since the nineteenth century, the differences between them are not always clear. Both are postconviction alternatives to incarceration that include supervision in the community by a probation or parole officer, who, depending on the jurisdiction, may be the same person. They are conditional releases to the community that are contingent on compliance with stipulated conditions, which if violated, may lead to revocation. Many probation and parole programs are similar (e.g., intensive supervision) or they share clientele. Last, as alternatives to incarceration, both are less expensive, less punitive, and probably more effective strategies of crime control.

Probation was instituted as an alternative to incarceration at a time when jail and prison overcrowding became a critical management and humanitarian issue.

The major difference between probation and parole is that probationers are sentenced directly to community supervision without being incarcerated, while parolees serve part of their sentence incarcerated before they are released to parole. Parole is a conditional release from confinement, whereas probation is a conditional suspension of a sentence to confinement. In both cases, a new crime or technical violation of conditions may lead to enhanced restrictions or incarceration. A general definition of *probation* is the conditional supervised release of a convicted offender into the community in lieu of incarceration (Allen et al. 1985). *Parole* is the conditional supervised release of an incarcerated offender into the community after serving part of the sentence in confinement (Clear and Cole 1986).

Probation

Before informal probation was created in Boston in 1841 by philanthropist John Augustus, and the first statewide probation law was enacted in Massachusetts in 1978, convicted offenders were typically fined or imprisoned, often serving their full sentence. Probation was instituted as an alternative to incarceration at a time when jail and prison overcrowding became a critical management and humanitarian issue. Probation was considered a front-end sentencing solution to overcrowding, intended specifically for less serious, first-time, and juvenile offenders amenable to "rehabilitation."

Over the years, rehabilitation has remained the primary goal of probation, and to this end, probation facilitates behavioral reform in a variety of ways. First, the often negative practical and symbolic consequences of the stigma of being an "ex-con" are neutralized. As less notorious and visible "probationers," the label will have less deleterious effects on the rehabilitative process. Second, the contaminating effects of imprisonment are avoided. This is particularly important for the less experienced offender, who may learn more about crime from more sophisticated, and sometimes predatory, inmates. The "pains of imprisonment" also produce anger, resentment, hostility, cynicism, and many other dysfunctional attitudes and feelings that make it more difficult to reform. Third, probation supports the existing social integration of the offender in the free community of noncriminals, including family, neighbors, employers and co-workers, friends, teachers and classmates, and others who are critical to the informal social control of crime. The offender released from incarceration will have the more difficult task of "reintegration." Fourth, the rehabilitative programs and services available to probationers are generally less coercive and more varied, flexible, and effective than those provided for prisoners. Fifth, the implied trust in leaving an offender in the community to demonstrate the ability to conform reinforces a positive attribution of self and expectations of appropriate behavior. Probation is more likely than incarceration to contribute to a self-fulfilling prophecy of rehabilitation.

Secondary goals of probation are more punitive. Probation is a penal sanction by virtue of the restrictions placed on the freedom of the offender. The conditions range from very lenient (e.g., weekly phone contact with a probation officer) to very punitive (e.g., twenty-four-hour home confinement), depending on the nature of the offense and offender characteristics. The goal of crime control can also be addressed by enhanced monitoring of probationers' compliance with the terms of probation, particularly their whereabouts. This can be accomplished by increasing the number and duration of meaningful (namely, face-to-face) contacts between probationer and probation officer, in the department's office, at home, at work, in a residential or nonresidential program facility, or anywhere else in the community. More comprehensive control is possible with electronic monitoring devices; for example, transmitter anklets can verify the location of a probationer within, or outside of, a stipulated free movement area. The goal of deterrence is served to the extent that rehabilitation and punishment succeed in preventing probationers from committing more crimes and returning to the criminal justice system. Finally, justice is achieved when probation is the appropriate sentence for the offense and offender, and its application is equitable and uniform across race, sex, and socioeconomic status categories (McAnany, Thomson, and Fogel 1984).

The decision to grant probation is the product of a complex organization of legal actors, sentencing procedures, decision criteria, and system capacity. The decision may be initiated by the prosecutor, who negotiates a guilty plea in exchange for a recommendation to the judge that the defendant be sentenced to probation. Or it may await conviction at trial. In either case, a presentence investigation report prepared by a probation officer may support the recommendation by providing background information on the offender and an assessment of the public risks and prospects for probation success.

There are intense organizational pressures to minimize the number of trials and to divert convicted offenders from incarceration: There are huge case backlogs in the courts (Meeker and Pontell 1985) and tremendous overcrowding in jails and prisons, as evidenced by the almost forty states in 1988 that were under court order to reduce inmate populations in order to meet a variety of correctional standards (Petersilia 1987). Incredibly, it has been estimated that more than 90 percent of convictions for felonies are the result of negotiated guilty pleas (McDonald 1985), and a high percentage of those receive probation since, by state, from 25 to 70 percent of convicted felons are sentenced to probation (Petersilia 1985). It is clearly in the personal and organizational interests of the defendant, prosecutor, judge, and even the jailer and prison superintendent to support "copping" a plea for probation.

Whether the conviction is negotiated or decided at trial, the judge sentences the offender, within the constraints imposed by the sentencing model and guidelines used in the jurisdiction. Most states use indeterminate sentencing, where judges have substantial discretion in rendering sentences and parole authorities are responsible for release decisions of incarcerated offenders. The trend is toward determinate sentencing, where judges and parole boards have much less influence on sentence and release decisions. In both models, probation is a widely used sentencing option, especially for less serious offenders but even for many serious offenders: Nationally, as high as 20 percent of violent offenders receive probation, including 13 percent of defendants convicted of rape and 9 percent of those convicted of homicide (Lisefski and Manson 1988).

Despite the confluence of the trend toward determinate sentencing, more pervasive justice model practices in corrections, and increased public pressure to be more punitive with criminals, there are relatively more offenders on probation than incarcerated or on parole than there were two decades ago (Petersilia et al. 1985). More serious offenders are being incarcerated for more fixed sentences, but the concomitant institutional overcrowding has produced a greater utilization of probation, as well as a variety of types of probation designed to meet the needs of both less serious and middle-range offenders, who in the past would have been more likely to be incarcerated. In addition to "standard probation," characterized by assignment to a probation officer with a caseload of as many as two hundred probationers and nominal contact, supervision, and rehabilitative services, a whole range of "intermediate sanctions" has been created that includes programs that are typically more punitive, restrictive, intensive, and effective than standard probation (Petersilia 1987; Morris and Tonry 1990). Judges now have a diversity of probation alternatives at sentencing: intensive supervised probation, home confinement, electronic monitoring, residential centers (halfway houses), and split sentences (jail/probation). These alternatives are often combined and coupled with other probation conditions that require restitution to victims, employment or education, payment of program costs, random urinalysis, specialized treatment or classes (e.g., Alcoholics Anonymous), or community service. Many of the intermediate sanctions are also used in the supervision of parolees.

Parole

Like probation, parole in the United States was created to relieve the serious overcrowding problem in prisons at the beginning of the nineteenth century. Years before informal probation began, some prison wardens and correctional administrators were releasing prisoners before their full sentence was served. They were either released outright, much as if they had received a pardon, or were monitored informally by the police. Based on the European correctional innovations of "good time" and "ticket of leave," formal parole emerged toward the end of the nineteenth century, with the first indeterminate sentencing law passed in 1876 in New York (Champion 1990).

Nationally, as high as 20 percent of violent offenders receive probation.

Until Maine abolished parole in 1976, all states had indeterminate sentencing and parole authorities. In general, within these systems a prisoner earns good time by productive participation in institutional programs and good conduct. The accumulated good time is subtracted from the sentence to determine the time incarcerated. This decision is typically made by a parole board, which is often a group of political appointees from a variety of occupations and constituencies. The offender is then released (or awarded a leave) to the supervision of a parole officer. If an offender does not commit a new crime or violate the conditions upon which release to parole is contingent, he or she can complete the remainder of the sentence as a parolee, to the time of discharge and freedom.

The goals of parole are anchored in indeterminate sentencing and the tenets of the rehabilitative ideal. It is assumed that offenders are amenable to reformation, through both the rehabilitation provided by the prison's treatment, educational, and vocational programs and the reintegration back into the free world facilitated by the transitional programs and services of parole. These twin primary goals of "rehabilitation" and "reintegration" drive the decisions and actions of the parole system. Parole is granted when the prisoner is considered ready for release, based on behavior during confinement, the extent to which rehabilitation is evident, and the apparent risk to public safety. In practice, many offenders spend a relatively small proportion of their sentence incarcerated; for instance, a convicted murderer with a life sentence may "do hard time" for as few as, say, ten years and serve the rest of the sentence on parole. Parole is revoked, or modified, when there are indications that reintegration is in jeopardy or unlikely, owing to violation of parole conditions. A new crime, in particular, but even a technical violation may be sufficient for the parole board to reincarcerate a parolee. The parole board also has the discretionary authority to set dates for parole hearings, fix minimum terms and release dates, determine good time credits, and specify parole conditions and requirements.

Like probation, the secondary goals of parole include punishment, crime control, and deterrence. After all, parole is a part of the penal sanction defined by the sentence to imprisonment, and, depending on the type of parole and stipulated conditions, the parole experience can be very restrictive and quasi-custodial. Effective rehabilitation, supervision, and monitoring of parolees should also produce deterrent effects—the combination of reformation and punishment should prevent future criminal conduct among parolees.

Unfortunately, by the mid-1970s, evidence had accumulated that suggested that parole was not an especially effective crime control strategy (Martinson 1974), and the shift away from the rehabilitative ideal to a more punitive justice philosophy (von Hirsch 1976) began in earnest. About one-third of states have returned to some form of determinate sentencing, and more are likely to follow. The discretionary power of judges in rendering sentences and of parole boards in implementing them has been abridged, in order to make decisions more rational and fair by linking them to the severity of the offense rather than the characteristics of the offender. Offenders are now more likely to be serving sentences in confinement—since 1980, the rate of incarceration has increased by 76 percent (Bureau of Justice Statistics 1989). They are also less likely to be placed on parole by a paroling authority—between 1977 and 1987, releases from imprisonment decided by parole boards dropped from about 70 percent to 40 percent of all releases, while mandatory releases increased from roughly 5 percent to 30 percent of the total (Hester 1988). With determinate sentencing, many states simply do not have paroling authorities or parole supervision in the community.

These changes have also affected the types of parole that are still available in a majority of states. Although many parole and probation programs are similar, the usually more serious offenses and criminal histories of parolees and the shift toward more punitive correctional systems have led to a hardening of the conditions of (cf. U.S. Sentencing Commission 1987) and less utilization of "standard parole" and a greater emphasis on protecting public safety by extending custody from the institution to the community. The goals of rehabilitation and reintegration have become less important, while crime control and deterrence have become more important. Consequently, there is greater reliance on transitional programs that maximize monitoring and supervision, while providing opportunities and services (e.g., employment, school, counseling, drug treatment) intended to facilitate reentry into the community and desistance from crime during parole and, ultimately, after discharge from correctional supervision. These programs are more intensive and custodial, often involving residential placement in a halfway house, intensive parole supervision, or home confinement with electronic monitoring. From these community bases, parolees may participate in work or school releases, home furloughs, counseling, religious services, and a variety of other reintegrative activities.

Although parole is not used to the extent that it was before the advent of determinate sentencing, and there are those who believe that it should be abolished in all states, some research suggests that determinate sentencing is no more a panacea than prior correctional reforms. There may be a leveling of sentencing disparities, and more offenders are being incarcerated. But they, on the average, are doing less time and, after release, may be as likely to be reconvicted and reincarcerated (Covey and Mande 1985).

Research

While the research evidence on the efficacy of determinate sentencing may be sketchy, there are many studies of other issues in probation and parole that have produced more substantive results. Social scientific research on probation and parole has tended to revolve around a set of related issues that are common to both: program effectiveness, recidivism, and classification and prediction. The overriding empirical and policy question is "What works?" Attempts to address the question vary in rigor and quality, and the answers are neither direct nor simple.

There are innumerable studies of program effectiveness, most of them not producing useful, much less compelling, evidence of program success or failure. For example, many studies conclude that a probation program is successful because 30 percent of participants recidivate or that a parole program is successful because 40 percent of participants recidivate. There are serious problems with those kinds of studies. First, they do not compare the program being evaluated with others, either with other probation or parole programs, or across correctional alternatives (e.g., release, probation, incarceration, and parole).

Second, without comparison groups, one can only evaluate program effectiveness in relation to some standard of success. But preordained acceptable levels of recidivism are determined normatively, not empirically. Normative criteria of success cannot be applied uniformly across the incredible variation in probation and parole programs. For instance, some probation programs, because of the very low risk participants, should probably generate recidivism rates that are closer to 5 percent than 30 percent.

Third, recidivism is often not defined or measured adequately. Generically, recidivism has come to mean "reoffending," particularly by offenders who have had contact with the criminal justice system, as measured typically by rearrest, reconviction, reincarceration, or some variation or combination thereof. But what does a probationer or parolee relapse to, and what is the most appropriate and accurate measure? The answers are complicated by the fact that probation and parole can be revoked if an offender commits a crime that becomes known to criminal justice authorities or by a noncriminal violation of release conditions (a "technical violation"). Paradoxically, practically all studies ignore the substantial amount of successful criminal behavior that remains hidden from officials, but many use both revocation criteria as measures of recidivism. Which measure is used can dramatically affect judgments about program effectiveness. Evaluations of three intensive probation supervision programs show that technical violations, as compared to new crimes, account for the majority of revocations. The revocation rates due to technical violations for these programs were 56 percent, 70 percent, and 85 percent, respectively. However, if the technical violations are not counted in the recidivism rates, the rates drop to 7 percent, 8 percent, and 5 percent, respectively (Petersilia 1987). Depending on program objectives, recidivism, no matter how measured, may not be the only or most appropriate criterion of program effectiveness. It may also be useful to assess relative costs and savings, impacts on jail and prison overcrowding, effects on public perceptions of safety, performance at school or in the workplace, changes in offenders' attitudes and self-concept, and so on.

More rigorous studies utilize comparison groups in order to assess the relative effectiveness of different correctional strategies. A typical study compares the recidivism rates of various combinations of offenders on probation, incarcerated, and on parole, and concludes that probationers are least likely and ex-prisoners are most likely to recidivate. Of course, one would predict those results based on the differences between the groups in their risk to recidivate. The selection biases of the court place the least serious, low-risk offenders on probation and the most serious, high-risk offenders in institutions. The observed differences in recidivism do not reflect the relative effectiveness of the programs, but the original differences in the recidivism risks of the comparison groups.

Some studies attempt to produce more comparable groups by using more objective probation and parole prediction instruments to classify and then compare offenders by level of recidivism risk across programs. That is, they try to improve comparability by "matching" offenders within the different program groups. For example, a study of the relative effectiveness of standard probation, intensive supervision probation, and incarceration with parole classified offenders within each group into low-, medium-, high-, and maximum-risk levels. Comparisons of recidivism, measured by rearrest, reconviction, and reincarceration, across the three program alternatives for each of the four categories of offenders (namely, least likely to most likely to recidivate) show that parole is least effective in preventing recidivism at all levels of recidivism risk. But the differences between standard and intensive probation are not as consistent: no matter how recidivism is measured, the rate is higher among intensive supervision probationers who are low- and high-risk offenders; among medium-risk offenders, it varies by the measure of recidivism; and for maximum-risk probationers, there seems to be little difference in the effectiveness of standard or intensive supervision, except for the somewhat higher reincarceration rate among intensive supervision probationers (Erwin 1986).

Evaluations of three intensive probation supervision programs show that technical violations, as compared to new crimes, account for the majority of revocations.

The equivocal findings of this and many similar studies reflect the difficulty in predicting recidivism risk with any degree of accuracy. The most comprehensive and statistically sophisticated techniques (e.g., cluster analyses, linear models, complex contingency tables) are not much more accurate than bivariate tabular procedures developed seventy years ago by Ernest Burgess. And no technique is able to predict recidivism with higher than 70 percent accuracy, with most slightly better than chance (Blumstein et al. 1986). Therefore, it is virtually impossible to make groups comparable on the basis of recidivism risk, or any other prediction criteria, which compromises the validity of the findings regarding differential program effectiveness.

The mixed results probably also reflect the paradox of intensive supervision programs in general: Increasing supervision and monitoring may increase, rather than decrease, the probability of recidivism. The offender is at greater risk to recidivate, simply because there is a better chance that unacceptable conduct will be observed. However, depending on the declared program goals, this may indicate success rather than failure: If intensive supervision probation and parole are intended to enhance crime control and public safety, rather than to rehabilitate, higher rates of recidivism may demonstrate program effectiveness (Gottfredson and Gottfredson 1988).

Research on probation and parole effectiveness cannot produce compelling findings from studies that depend on comparisons of typically noncomparable groups. What is necessary are "equivalent" groups that are created through random assignment within experiments. Unfortunately, experimental designs are usually more expensive and more difficult to implement and complete in natural settings. Consequently, they are extremely rare in research on probation and parole. For instance, there are more than one hundred studies of the effectiveness of intensive probation supervision, but none have an experimental design with random assignment to program conditions (Petersilia 1987). There are some current efforts to implement studies of probation and parole that have experimental designs, but if the objective is to produce valid and useful knowledge on "what works," there must be a greater commitment on the part of the criminal justice system, funding agencies, and the social science research community.

[See also Court Systems of the United States; Criminal Sanctions; Criminology.]

BIBLIOGRAPHY

Allen, Harry E., Chris Eskridge, Edward Latessa, and Gennaro Vito 1985 *Probation and Parole in America.* New York: Free Press.

Blumstein, Alfred, Jacqueline Cohen, Jeffrey Roth, and Christy Visher, (eds.) 1986 *Criminal Careers and "Career Criminals."* Washington, D.C.: National Academy Press.

Bureau of Justice Statistics 1989 *Prisoners in 1988* (bulletin). Washington, D.C.: U.S. Department of Justice.

Champion, Dean J. 1990 *Probation and Parole in the United States.* Columbus, Ohio: Merrill.

Clear, Todd, and George F. Cole 1986 *American Corrections.* Belmont, Calif.: Brooks/Cole.

Covey, Herbert C., and Mary Mande 1985 "Determinate Sentencing in Colorado." *Justice Quarterly* 2:259–270.

Erwin, Billie S. 1986 "Turning Up the Heat on Probationers in Georgia." *Federal Probation* 50:17–24.

Gottfredson, Michael, and Don M. Gottfredson 1988 *Decision Making in Criminal Justice.* New York: Plenum.

Hester, Thomas 1988 *Probation and Parole, 1987.* Washington, D.C.: U.S. Department of Justice.

Lisefski, Edward, and Donald Manson 1988 *Tracking Offenders.* Washington, D.C.: U.S. Department of Justice.

Martinson, Robert 1974 "What Works? Questions and Answers About Prison Reform." *Public Interest* 35:22–54.

McAnany, Patrick D., Doug Thomson, and David Fogel (eds.) 1984 *Probation and Justice: Reconsideration of a Mission.* Cambridge, Mass.: Oelgeschlager, Gunn and Hain.

McDonald, William F. 1985 *Plea Bargaining: Critical Issues and Common Practices.* Washington, D.C.: U.S. Department of Justice.

Meeker, James, and Henry M. Pontell 1985 "Court Caseloads, Plea Bargains, and Criminal Sanctions: The Effects of Section 17 P.C. in California." *Criminology* 23:119–143.

Morris, Norval, and Michael Tonry 1990 *Between Prison and Probation: Intermediate Punishments in a Rational Sentencing System.* New York: Oxford.

Petersilia, Joan 1985 *Probation and Felony Offenders.* Washington, D.C.: U.S. Department of Justice.

——— 1987 *Expanding Options for Criminal Sentencing.* Santa Monica, Calif.: Rand.

———, Susan Turner, James Kahan, and Joyce Peterson 1985 *Granting Felons Probation: Public Risks and Alternatives.* Santa Monica, Calif.: Rand.

U.S. Sentencing Commission 1987 *United States Sentencing Commission Guidelines Manual.* Washington, D.C.: U.S. Sentencing Commission.

Von Hirsch, Andrew 1976 *Doing Justice.* New York: Hill and Wang.

– JOSEPH G. WEIS

PROFESSIONS

The idea of a "profession" did not exist in ancient times. Although there were people who did what is currently denoted as professional work, these "professionals" often labored in dependent positions. For example, physicians in the Roman Empire were slaves in wealthy households, and architects worked as salaried public employees. These "professionals" also had little education. Lawyers in ancient Greece were merely friends of the litigants who spoke before a gathering of their peers. Neither lawyers nor physicians received formal training (Carr-Saunders and Wilson 1933).

By medieval times, the three classic professions—medicine, law, and the clergy (which included university teaching)—began to approximate more closely the modern conception of a profession. With the development of universities, then under religious auspices, would-be professionals completed lengthy training in their chosen fields. They also began to constitute a new class of intellectuals. As society increasingly secularized, the professions emerged from under religious control and began to organize professional associations. By the eighteenth century they had achieved independent status.

In the nineteenth century, middle-class occupations such as dentistry, architecture, and engineering began to professionalize, aspiring to the gentlemanly status of the classic, learned professions (Dingwall and Lewis 1983). "Gentlemanly" was the appropriate description, since the majority of professionals were men. It was not until the 1970s that women began to make significant inroads into these occupations, and even today men predominate in the status professions.

In the nineteenth and early twentieth centuries, professionalism developed in concert with the increasing division of labor and rationalization characteristic of industrializing Europe and the United States. As competitors in market economies, occupational incumbents sought to professionalize to improve their status. In addition, they wanted to better their economic positions by securing occupational niches for their services (Ritzer and Walczak 1986). In the United States, at least, universities played the key role of transferring both the technical know-how and the culture of professionalism to new generations of professional aspirants (Bledstein 1976).

Which Occupations are Professions?

Today the term *profession* includes a range of occupations arrayed along a continuum of high to medium levels of prestige. First, at the high end of the continuum are the classic, or "status," professions of medicine, law, clergy, and university teaching. Incumbents in these occupations usually receive high incomes, exercise job autonomy, and receive deference from the public and those lower in the status hierarchy. They are also typically male—in 1988, women's representation among college and university teachers, physicians, lawyers, and the clergy were 38, 20, 19, and 9 percent, respectively (U.S. Bureau of Labor Statistics 1989).

Second, somewhat lower on the continuum are the "newer" professions such as dentistry, engineering, accounting, and architecture, which also command respect and relatively high salaries. Men also predominate in these occupations—in 1988, 9, 7, and 15 percent of dentists, engineers, and architects were women. Only in accounting have women made significant inroads—by 1988, nearly half of all accountants and auditors were women. This feminization is attributable largely to that occupation's dramatic occupational growth in the 1970s (Reskin and Roos 1990).

Third, still lower on the professional continuum are the marginal professions (e.g., pharmacy, chiropractic) and the semiprofessions (e.g., nursing, public school teaching, librarianship). These occupations exhibit some characteristics of the classic professions but have not acquired full professional status. They have been unable to professionalize fully because of opposition from established professions and an inability to convince the public that they command unique expertise. As a consequence, they are less prestigious and are paid less than incumbents in either the classic or new professions. Moreover, because they concentrate in bureaucratic settings, incumbents in these occupations exercise less job autonomy than higher-status professionals. An important feature of the marginal and semiprofessions is that the former are predominantly male (in 1988, 32 percent of pharmacists were female), the latter predominantly female (women composed 95, 73, and 85 percent of nurses, public school teachers, and librarians, respectively).

Finally, while not professionals per se, paraprofessionals work with, but as subordinates to, members of the other professions. They are generally technicians associated with various professional occupations. Paralegals, for example, work closely with lawyers, and physicians delegate certain tasks and responsibilities to physicians' assistants. As in the semiprofessions, women tend to predominate in paraprofessional occupations.

The Process of Professionalization

Given the stratification of the U.S. occupational structure, it is clear why workers desire to professionalize. Professionalization brings higher income, higher prestige, and greater job autonomy. It also protects incumbents from competition. The "process of professionalization" posits a common sequence of development that occupations undergo. Some scholars accept Harold Wilensky's (1964) depiction of this process. First, people begin to work full time at a specific set of tasks that will form the new occupation's core jurisdiction. Second, those in the occupation establish a university-affiliated training program, and some incumbents undertake the responsibility for training new generations of practitioners. Third, practitioners and teachers combine to form a professional association that identifies the occupation's core tasks and makes claims regarding skill jurisdiction. Fourth, occupational incumbents seek to protect their jurisdictional claims by political means. Professionals lobby for legal protection, in the form of licensing and certification requirements, to generate labor market shelters that ensure their monopoly of skills. Finally, incumbents develop a formal code of ethics that embodies rules to protect clients, eliminate the unqualified, and spell out the occupation's service ideal.

Approaches to the Study of the Professions

What distinguishes the professions from other occupations? Theoretical approaches in studying this question have changed over time and remain in flux. Scholars have also developed new methods to address these questions.

THE TRAIT APPROACH. After World War II, the trait approach was the dominant one in scholarship on the professions (Freidson 1986). Scholars—mostly American academics—tried to define the professions by generating an exhaustive list of characteristics. These traits, scholars hoped, would distinguish professions from nonprofessions and higher-status professions from those of lower status. The main method used was the case study. Scholars carefully scrutinized particular occupations to determine how well they approximated an ideal-typical profession.

Professionals are experts, possessing abstract knowledge and skills that set them apart from ordinary people.

Theorists posited that four major criteria, or traits, existed in the ideal-typical profession (Hodson and Sullivan 1990). First, professions have esoteric knowledge. Professionals are experts, possessing abstract knowledge and skills that set them apart from ordinary people. Second, because of their unique expertise, professionals are able to exercise autonomy on the job. Codes of ethics help to ensure autonomy from outside control by permitting professionals to police misconduct internally. Third, their esoteric knowledge allows professionals to claim authority over their clients and subordinate occupational groups. Finally, the professions are altruistic, that is, service- rather than profit-oriented. Underlying these four traits is a fifth characteristic—the public must recognize the occupation as a profession. Regardless of an occupation's *claim* of unique expertise, if the public does not view the occupation's knowledge as abstract, it is difficult for those working in it to claim professional status and the perquisites that accompany it.

Scholars used these criteria to differentiate among the professions, most particularly in comparing the female semiprofessions to the typically male status professions. While the semiprofessions have a body of knowledge, they lack a monopoly over that knowledge. They also have a difficult time convincing the public that their skills are professional. The public is less likely to recognize their expertise (e.g., teaching children, servicing library patrons) as particularly esoteric. Semiprofessionals typically work in bureaucratic settings and, as a consequence, are subject to heteronomy, or supervision by organizational superiors and professional colleagues. Thus, semiprofessionals can make only limited claims to autonomy.

THE POWER APPROACH. In the 1960s, scholars in the United States and Great Britain began to criticize the trait approach for being static and ideological. Power theorists also shifted to historical methods to understand the sources of professional power. These scholars argued that occupations we view as professions do not necessarily exhibit the requisite traits. Rather, incumbents in these occupations simply have the power to convince the public that they possess these traits. Power thus became the operative word, supplanting expertise as the mechanism whereby professionals achieve market control and prestige. Power theorists viewed the professions as monopolistic organizations intent on gaining and retaining professional control and ensuring their status in the stratification system. Eliot Freidson (1986), for example, described his early work as focusing on the political and cultural influences of the professions and as depicting how professions establish protected labor markets for their services. Magali Sarfatti Larson (1977) argued that the professions are market organizations in the capitalist economy, explicitly seeking to dominate the market for their expertise.

For these theorists, the so-called objective characteristics of the trait approach are ideological attempts to preserve the professions' status and privilege (Freidson 1986). For example, they posited that, rather than being truly altruistic, the professions create the myth of service orientation to gain public goodwill, enhance their status, and minimize external control. In addition, they contended that professionals abuse their autonomy by failing to police themselves—incompetent doctors and lawyers fleece the public with little fear of reprisal from their peers. Finally, the professional's authority over clients has also declined in recent years as the public has become more active in activities seen as the province of professionals (e.g., getting second opinions on medical recommendations and becoming more educated consumers regarding medical and legal issues).

The historical battles between physicians, on the one hand, and pharmacists and chiropractors on the other, illustrate how an established profession exercises power against competing occupations (Starr 1982). When the pharmacists' traditional task of compounding drugs shifted to pharmaceutical companies, they lost their diagnostic expertise (and hence monopoly over their knowledge). With respect to chiropractors, the American Medical Association has lobbied to keep this occupation from threatening their jurisdictional claims by restricting access through licensing laws or blocking reimbursement from private insurance companies. As a consequence, pharmacy and chiropractic remain marginal to the established professions and have not achieved full professional status.

What enables professions to wield power? According to power theorists, the major sources for professional power are indeterminacy and uncertainty (Ritzer and Walczak 1986). Those professions that have achieved and maintained power are those whose tasks cannot be broken down or otherwise routinized (indeterminacy). Similarly, those that deal with areas of uncertainty are also likely to preserve their power. As Wilensky (1964) described it, professional knowledge involves a "tacit" dimension, in Polanyi's (1967) terminology. Their lengthy training and years of practical application ensure that physicians "know" what treatments to use for which symptoms. Similarly, lawyers "know" what legal strategies work best, given the particulars of the cases they take to court. Reading a textbook or consulting computerized data bases is not equivalent to tacit knowledge. This kind of knowledge—expertise refined by years of experience—is not easily routinized. Physicians and lawyers also deal with areas of high uncertainty for their clients, the former with physical health and the latter with legal affairs. Clients need these professionals to translate medical and legal jargon into everyday language they can more readily understand.

THE SYSTEM OF PROFESSIONS. Andrew Abbott's (1988) theory of professions critiques previous approaches, especially the notion that professions undergo a common process of development. Employing historical and comparative methods, Abbott provides a wealth of evidence that the history of the professions is much more complicated than that suggested by a linear process of professionalization. Rather than a history of professions that established systems of control (e.g., schools, professional associations, licensing and certification), Abbott's account is of interprofessional competitions, squabbles over jurisdictions, and professional births and deaths.

Physicians consolidated their control over medical jurisdictions by successfully pressing for legislation to outlaw midwives.

Abbott's contention is that professionalization must be seen as part of a larger "system of professions." Professions make up an interdependent system, and understanding modern professions entails articulating their histories of conflict with other professions. Thus, comprehending the realities of modern medicine, for example, depends more on an investigation of its historical conflicts with closely related professions such as psychiatry and chiropractic than on the particulars of medieval or nineteenth-century medicine.

Recognizing the interdependence of professions is important because it clarifies that professions emerge, grow, change, and die within the historical context of competition with other professions. Interprofessional competition means that occupations compete over closely related jurisdictions. Jurisdictional disputes arise out of one of the characteristics peculiar to the professions—abstract knowledge. Professionals can use their abstract knowledge to define a core set of tasks (their jurisdiction), defend that jurisdiction from others, or appropriate the tasks of others. When any of these events occur, or when some outside force such as technology impinges on how professionals perform their jobs, the changes reverberate throughout the system. The professions reequilibrate, with some occupations accepting a subordinate or advisory role, some agreeing to split jurisdictions or clients, and others exiting the professions altogether.

Sex Differences in the Professions

As noted, women heavily concentrate in the semiprofessions (as nurses, public school teachers, and librarians) and men in the higher-status professions (as physicians, lawyers, and engineers). Incumbents in the former earn less and exercise less autonomy than workers in the latter. As in the entire labor force, the professions are thus highly segregated by sex.

Even within the higher-prestige professions, women work in different, lower-paying, and less-prestigious jobs than men. Women lawyers, for example, work in government jobs, in research rather than litigation, and in certain specialties such as trust and estates; women physicians are more likely than men to specialize in pediatrics and to work in health maintenance organizations (HMOs); female clergy specialize in music or education (Reskin and Phipps 1988).

Part of the reason for this differential job distribution by sex has to do with a characteristic unique to the professions. The high level of uncertainty inherent in prestigious professional jobs means that employers are careful to choose recruits who "fit in" with those already on the job. Thus, as Rosabeth Moss Kanter (1977) suggested, employers tend to recruit people much like themselves, a process she calls "homosocial reproduction." The predominance of males in the status professions thus ensures the perpetuation of sex segregation.

Organizations that employ professionals tend to diverge enough from the ideal-typical bureaucracy to protect professional privilege.

Other factors reducing women's access to high-status professions are entrance restrictions such as certification and licensing. Physicians, for example, consolidated their control over medical jurisdictions by successfully pressing for legislation to outlaw midwives and prohibit the licensing of those trained at "irregular" schools, activities that disproportionately affected women. In 1872, the Supreme Court restricted women's ability to practice law, arguing that "the natural and proper timidity and delicacy which belongs to the female sex unfits it for many of the occupations of civil life" (Reskin and Phipps 1988). Professionals, most of whom were males, were thus able to establish labor market shelters to protect themselves from competition from women as well as other "undesirables."

But what of the present day? Since 1970, women have made inroads into some of the professions, including occupations such as medicine, law, and pharmacy. Indications are, however, that internal differentiation within the professions perpetuates occupational segregation by sex (Reskin and Roos 1990). For example, Polly Phipps (1990) found that women's representation in pharmacy nearly tripled (from 12 to 32 percent) between 1970 and 1988. Phipps also noted, however, that women pharmacists concentrate in the lower-paying hospital sector, while men predominate in the higher-paying retail sector. Similar ghettoization exists in other professions that are admitting more women.

The Changing Professions

Some view the future of the professions as bleak, pointing to ongoing proletarianization or deprofessionalization as eliminating the professions' unique traits. The proletarianization thesis argues that an increasing division of labor and bureaucratization within the professions are routinizing knowledge and transferring authority from professionals to organizational superiors. The deprofessionalization thesis documents declines in the professions' monopolistic control over their knowledge, their exercise of autonomy on the job, their ability to protect their jurisdiction from encroachments, and the public's deference to professional authority (Ritzer and Walczak 1986).

Some occupations, of course, have deprofessionalized. As noted, as pharmaceutical companies increasingly absorbed the compounding of drugs, and as chains replaced independent pharmacies, pharmacists lost some of their autonomy and monopoly of their knowledge to physicians. Taking a broad view of the professions, however, Freidson (1984) provided evidence that the presumed incompatibility between bureaucratization and professionalization is overstated. Working in organizations, he argued, has been the norm for most professions from their inception, with engineers the most obvious example. In addition, organizations that employ professionals tend to diverge enough from the ideal-typical bureaucracy to protect professional privilege. For example, professionals in organizations often exercise a lot of autonomy, working under senior members of their own profession rather than nonprofessional managers. Freidson thus portrays organizations as accommodating professionals.

Freidson (1984) also found no evidence that the prestige of the professions as a whole has declined. Nor did he find that public trust in professionals has deteriorated relative to other American institutions. Thus, when viewed as a set of occupations, he argued that the professions have not deteriorated in status. Moreover, the professions' continuing ability to erect labor market barriers to competition is important evidence of their enduring power. Professionals today continue to remain strong enough to exert their will against others lower in the occupational hierarchy. Professional privilege thus remains intact in the American occupational structure.

[See also Work and Occupations.]

BIBLIOGRAPHY

Abbott, Andrew 1988 *The System of Professions: An Essay on the Division of Expert Labor.* Chicago: University of Chicago Press.

Bledstein, Burton J. 1976 *The Culture of Professionalism: The Middle Class and the Development of Higher Education in America.* New York: W. W. Norton.

Carr-Saunders, A. M., and P. A. Wilson 1933 "Professions." In Edwin R. A. Seligman and Alvin Johnson, eds., *Encyclopaedia of the Social Sciences.* New York: Macmillan.

Dingwall, Robert, and Philip Lewis 1983 *The Sociology of the Professions: Lawyers, Doctors and Others.* London: Macmillan.

Freidson, Eliot 1984 "The Changing Nature of Professional Control." *Annual Review of Sociology* 10:1–20.

——— 1986 *Professional Powers: A Study of the Institutionalization of Formal Knowledge.* Chicago: University of Chicago Press.

Hodson, Randy, and Teresa A. Sullivan 1990 *The Social Organization of Work.* Belmont, Calif.: Wadsworth.

Kanter, Rosabeth Moss 1977 *Men and Women of the Corporation.* New York: Harper and Row.

Larson, Magali Sarfatti 1977 *The Rise of Professionalism: A Sociological Analysis.* Berkeley: University of California Press.

Phipps, Polly A. 1990 "Industrial and Occupational Change in Pharmacy: Prescription for Feminization." In Barbara F. Reskin and Patricia A. Roos, *Job Queues, Gender Queues: Explaining Women's Inroads into Male Occupations.* Philadelphia, Pa.: Temple University Press.

Polanyi, Michael 1967 *The Tacit Dimension.* Garden City, N.Y.: Anchor Books.

Reskin, Barbara F., and Polly A. Phipps 1988 "Women in Male-Dominated Professional and Managerial Occupations." In Ann H. Stromberg and Shirley Harkess, eds., *Women Working: Theories and Facts in Perspective.* Mountain View, Calif.: Mayfield.

Reskin, Barbara F., and Patricia A. Roos 1990 *Job Queues, Gender Queues. Explaining Women's Inroads into Male Occupations.* Philadelphia: Temple University Press.

Ritzer, George, and David Walczak 1986 *Working: Conflict and Change.* 3rd ed. Englewood Cliffs, N.J.: Prentice-Hall.

Starr, Paul 1982 *The Social Transformation of American Medicine: The Rise of a Sovereign Profession and the Making of a Vast Industry.* New York: Basic Books.

U.S. Bureau of Labor Statistics 1989 *Employment and Earnings,* Vol. 36 (January). Washington, D.C.: U.S. Government Printing Office.

Wilensky, Harold L. 1964 "The Professionalization of Everyone?" *American Journal of Sociology* 70:137–158.

– PATRICIA A. ROOS

PROSTITUTION

Prostitution is the granting of nonmarital sexual access for remuneration that provides part or all of the prostitute's livelihood. Most prostitution involves a woman who services male clients; perhaps 5 percent involves males servicing other males in the United States.

There is a prostitution subculture that involves pimps and a range of intermediaries such as convention personnel, bartenders, taxi drivers, and hotel bellhops. The pimp is a confidante, protector, and manager who usually gets all of the woman's earnings. The intermediaries, who steer the client to the woman, typically receive

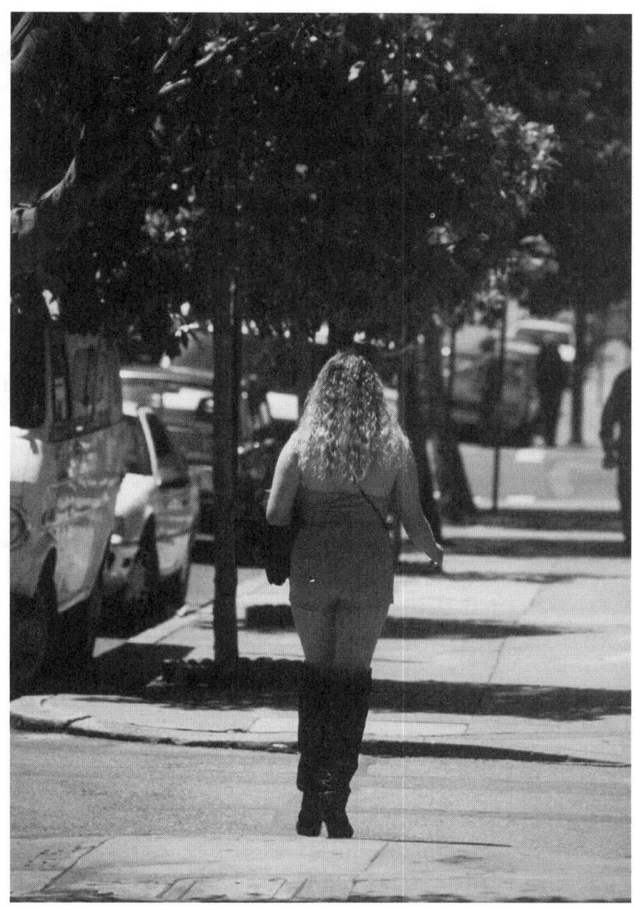

Prostitution is illegal in each of the fifty United States, although Nevada allows its counties to choose legalization. (Robert Holmes/Corbis)

around 40 percent of her charge to the client. If the woman works out of a call house, the madam receives half of the payment. If the woman works in a brothel, the madam also gets half.

A brothel is an apartment or house where there is a manager and a number of prostitutes on duty so that the customer can choose one and go to a room for the sexual activity. The brothel, also called a whorehouse or bawdy house and formerly concentrated in specific areas called red light districts, exists today on a limited basis. It used to be the most frequent American format for prostitution until World War II, when the large number of young men away from home led to concern about the many brothels that opened near the training camps but that were soon closed by new federal laws. The brothels have largely been supplanted by hotels, bars, streetwalking, and quasi-legal activities like escort services and massage parlors.

Call girls are at the apex of prestige of prostitution; streetwalkers are at the bottom. Women are relatively unlikely to move from one type or format of prostitution to another. Prostitution is one occupation in which age is negatively correlated with success because of the extent to which youth is prized by customers.

A variety of positive social functions has been cited for prostitution. It has been said to provide a sexual outlet for male immigrants or males who do not marry, to offer a form of sexual initiation for young men, to make available sexual satisfaction for handicapped men and others with exotic tastes that cannot be satisfied conventionally, to encourage marital stability by providing outlets for husbands with unusual sexual requirements that cannot be satisfied in the home, to meet fantasy needs of men and provide an activity that is collateral to gambling and spectator athletics (Winick and Kinsie 1972).

Beginning in the 1960s, some feminist writers began discussing prostitution as an ultimate degradation and symbol of men's exploitation of women. Other feminists saw prostitutes as the only honest women because they charge for their services rather than submit to a marriage contract that forces them to work for life without pay.

Half the states have a "customer amendment" that considers a patron as guilty of a crime as the prostitute. However, the law against patrons is seldom implemented. Laws against prostitutes are themselves implemented inconsistently and are not assigned a high priority in most communities by prosecutors, police, or citizens. If prostitutes are arrested, they are likely to be given a small fine, serve a short prison term, or both.

The United Nations (1968) treaty on prostitution prohibited government licensing of prostitution and recommended that houses of prostitution be closed. It prohibited exploitation of prostitutes by third persons, recommended a program of rehabilitation of prostitutes, and emphasized the need for each country to follow a flexible course because of cultural traditions. Probably a majority of the countries in the world are following the United Nations treaty recommendations. The United States, which did not ratify the treaty, is unique in that its prohibitionist approach punishes both prostitutes and clients.

Some women may have become prostitutes in order to get money for illegal drugs, and others began using drugs after entering the occupation, as one way of coping with their work. Prostitutes' drug use has become a social issue because of the extent to which intravenous drug users are implicated in the spread of AIDS as a result of sharing infected needles. Non-drug using prostitutes have not been significant contributors to venereal disease because they generally examine clients' genitalia, take prophylactic doses of drugs like penicillin, and use condoms, even when providing oral sex. In general, prostitutes do not represent a significant contributor to AIDS and other sexually transmitted diseases.

The Dutch government requires prostitutes to pay income taxes and makes social services available to them.

Most countries are ambivalent about prostitution and are unable to resolve the differences between its seeming ubiquity and the norms against it. A few countries, like the Netherlands, have made prostitution a legal occupation; the government requires prostitutes to pay income taxes and makes social services available to them. Most Western countries, like England, permit prostitution so long as it does not represent a public nuisance such as aggressive street soliciting.

When sexual attitudes became more liberal in the 1960s, there was speculation that prostitution would decline. However, it did not decline and actually developed new formats. In recent years, there has been an increase in the number of women working as part-time prostitutes. Unless prostitution assumes the kind of salience as a public issue that it had early in the twentieth century, when it was known as "the master problem" or "the social evil," it is unlikely to attract the kind of legislative and political attention that will lead to significant changes in policy.

Sociologists have studied the subculture and social structure of prostitution, methods of induction into the occupation, prostitution's different formats, trends in customers and services, relations to patterns of sexual behavior in the larger society, and indirect cooperation by structural arrangements within the community (Frey, Reichert, and Russell 1981).

[See also Deviance; Heterosexual Behavior Patterns; Legislation of Morality.]

BIBLIOGRAPHY

Frey, J. H., L. R. Reichert, and K. V. Russell 1981 "Prostitution, Business, and Police: The Maintenance of an Illegal Economy." *The Police Journal* 54:239–249.

Goldstein, P. 1979 *Prostitution and Drugs.* Lexington, Mass.: Lexington Books.

United Nations 1968 *Study on Traffic in Persons and Prostitution.* New York: United Nations.

Winick, C., and P. M. Kinsie 1972 *The Lively Commerce: Prostitution in the United States.* New York: New American Library.

– CHARLES WINICK

PROTEST MOVEMENTS

Protest movements have been of high interest to sociological research since the inception of the discipline in the early nineteenth century, during the periods of great industrial and urban development in Europe and North America. During massive changes in the economic structure and mass rural-to-urban and cross-national migration, a variety of protest movements developed, and they caught the attention of Comte, Le Bon, Weber, and other early sociological analysts. In the United States the first widely used introductory sociology textbook, developed by Chicago School sociologists Park and Burgess (1921), was organized around the concept of collective behavior, with protest movements occupying a substantive part of the text.

Such movements have generally been seen as an interim form of collective challenge to some aspect of the social status quo. The protest continuum ranges from localized groups and crowds that organize around specific and short-term delimited grievances to mass protest movements about social conditions and perceived injustices. These mass protests are designed to generate comprehensive and fundamental changes in a society and sometimes across societies (Heberle 1968, p. 439; Turner and Killian 1986, p. 401). More so than localized acting crowds and less so than systemic social movements, protest movements encompass mass behavior that extends beyond a localized situation, and they have the potential of generating social movements when a variety of conducive conditions exist (Gusfield 1968; Smelser 1962; Tilly 1978).

The twentieth century has been characterized by a wide variety of protest movements. In the United States, industrial labor protests were common for the first third of the century, as were anti-immigration protests. The suffragette movement early in the century was a precursor to the women's movement for equal treatment and opportunity in the latter third of the century; the civil rights movement, led by blacks in the 1950s and 1960s, precipitated countermovements (another characteristic of protest movements) including the White Citizens' Council protests and the reemergence of the Ku Klux Klan. Poor people in Chile, El Salvador, Nicaragua, and other Latin American countries have protested the privileges of an elite economic class as vestiges of an unproductive and rigid class colonial structure. Such protest movements have also occurred in Africa, the Middle East, and Asia.

A common thread through the wide variety of protest movements is their political nature. In various ways governmental authority is challenged, changed, supported, or resisted in specific protest movements. To advance their prospects for success, protest movement leaders often engage in coalition politics with more powerful individuals and groups who, for their own interests and values, support the challenge raised by the movement (Piven and Cloward 1977; Rustin 1965). When protest movements succeed in generating sufficient public support to secure all or most of their goals, governments may offer policy legitimization of the movement as a means of adapting to or modifying a movement's challenge to the state of pre-movement affairs.

Such political legitimation has taken a variety of forms. The labor protest movements culminated in the passage of the National Labor Relations Act of 1935, which legitimized labor-management collective bargaining agreements. The suffragette movement resulted in passage of the Nineteenth Amendment to the Constitution, guaranteeing that the right to vote in the United States could not be denied or abridged on account of sex. The civil rights movement attained support with passage of the comprehensive Civil Rights Act of 1964 and the Economic Opportunity Act and Elementary and Secondary Education Act, both in 1965.

Success of these and other movements is often tempered by countermovements, participants of which perceive their relative positions and interests to be threatened. For instance, the women's movement experienced a series of challenges from those, often from fundamentalist religious groups, adhering to patriarchy (a male-dominated hierarchy). As a consequence, women's progress was slowed in winning various forms of equal treatment and opportunity in economic, political, and social areas of life, and the U.S. Congress failed to pass the Equal Rights Amendment.

More generally, after passage of civil rights legislation in the mid-1960s, a series of protest movements within the Democratic and, more extensively, the Republican parties resulted in growing administrative, legislative, and judicial resistance to equality in educational, occupational, and housing opportunities. The counter-movement result has been a reentrenchment of a long-established economic structure of racism and low income class rigidity that functions independently of personalized racist feelings and beliefs (Wilson 1987, pp. 11–12). A reflection of such counter-movement pressure is the growth in perception among white males that affirmative action educational and occupational policies directed toward racial and ethnic minorities and women constitute a form of reverse or "affirmative discrimination" (Glazer 1975).

Countermovements have generated their own countermovements, known as counter-counter protest movements. This variation of Hegelian dialectic does not result in a return to whatever constituted premovement normalcy; in conventional political terms the results are more conservative, reactionary, liberal, or radical than what existed before the protest movement. These terms may apply to the participants of a specific protest movement as well as to established authorities. Further, while a predominant orientation may exist among protest activists and another among established authorities, in complex, mass modern societies, values and political orientations are usually contending among protestors and their supporters and among established authorities and their supporters, against whom the protest is directed (Mueller and Judd 1981).

The U.S. civil rights movement can be viewed in historical terms, if not in contemporary political terms, as a primarily conservative movement. The predominant aim of activists and organizations was to allow blacks and other minorities to break into the political and economic system rather than to break the established system. In contrast, the late 1980s' and early 1990s' liberal to radical protest movements in Poland, Hungary, Rumania, and other Eastern European countries aimed to break the system of exclusive communist political and economic domination.

In the United States, protest ideologies are largely reminiscent of established, liberal democratic political ideals. This is evidenced in the way protest groups adopt language from the Declaration of Independence to fit their purposes. For example, the Black Panthers, popularly perceived as a radical group, adopted a statement of purpose that held, "We hold these truths to be self-evident, that all black and white [*sic*] men are created equal and endowed by their creator with certain unalienable rights." Similarly, the National Organization for Women inserted into their declaration of purposes the wording that "men and women" were created equal.

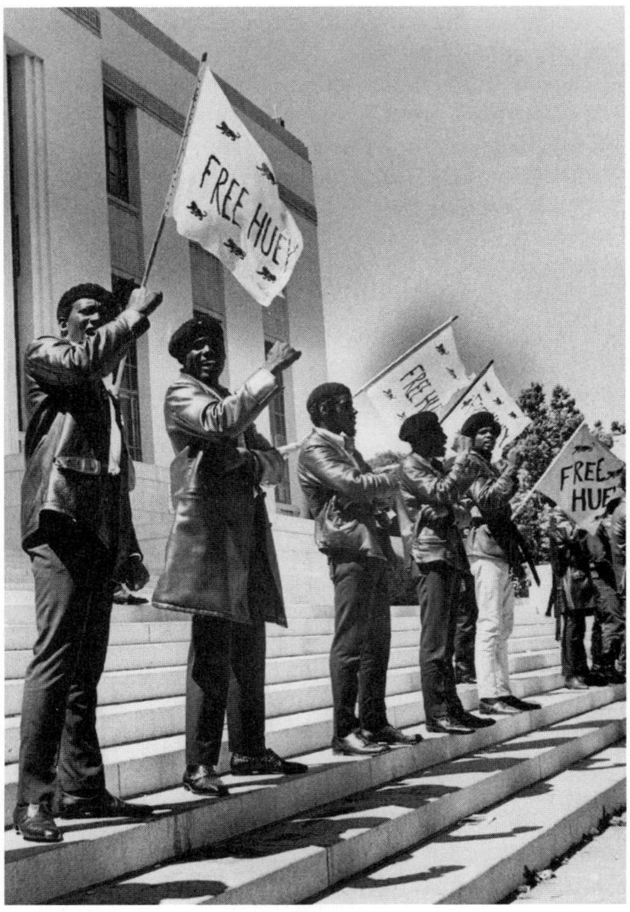

American protest groups, such as the Black Panthers shown here, often adopt language from the Declaration of Independence to fit their purposes. The Panthers declared "that all black and white men are created equal." (UPI/Corbis-Bettmann)

Protest movements attain mixed and sometimes changed results. These results occur because of institutional inertia (certain things have been done certain ways over a long period of time) and because of countermovements within institutional centers such as schools, businesses, and local, state, and national government offices. In the United States, reactions to the civil rights movement have resulted in private and public attitudes and behaviors that have combined to disadvantage more severely low income racial and ethnic minorities (Bonacich 1988). It is also the case that despite all the countermovement resistance to educational, economic, and political advances for minority status groups, census bureau reports document a growing number and proportion of blacks, women, and other minority status group members moving into educational institutions, occupational settings, and political positions from which they were formerly excluded *de jure* or *de facto* (e.g., see U.S. Bureau of the Census 1983; 1984).

Examples from history and other cultures demonstrate the mixed potential and results of protest movements. The German Nazi protest movement in the 1920s illustrated that a movement could be radical *and* reactionary, in that case toward further destabilization of the Weimar Republic's democratic government, which was perceived as being decreasingly effective and legitimate by growing sectors of the German public (Shirer 1960). After the Nazis succeeded in countering various democratic and communist protest movements, Germany saw a more comprehensive institutionalization of Nazi ideological and authoritarian control during the 1930s. More recently, in 1989, the Chinese student democratic protest movement in Tiananmen Square resulted in a government-sponsored countermovement that physically shattered the student protest and resulted in a system of political, economic, and educational controls that were more comprehensively rigid than those that existed before the protest movement.

It is evident that there is a wide range of protest participants and of protest methods employed. The characteristics of protest participants and the methods they employ have been central concerns of research on such movements.

Protest Participants and Methods of Protest

If protest participants could alleviate their grievances or sense of injustice individually, there would be no likely motivation for them to become active in a protest movement. Protest participants thus have two central characteristics: (1) they have insufficient influence to gain a desired change in their circumstances, and (2) they seek active association with relatively like-minded persons to gain relief from their aggrieved state.

These two characteristics can be seen among protest participants over time and in different locales. In the 1960s civil rights movements in the United States, leading activists—including blacks, Hispanics, Native Americans, and women—expressed a strong sense of unequal treatment and opportunity while associating with and supporting activists to achieve equal opportunities in schools, jobs, elected offices, and other social settings, College students, the most active participants in the civil rights movement, could not generally be characterized in these minority status terms. Yet, they were not yet an established part of the economic and political order being challenged and were in a position to be critical of that order (Lipset 1971). Other participant supporters such as labor unions, selected corporate leaders, and religiously motivated persons often saw protest related change needed in terms of their own long-term interests and worked either to help the civil rights movement succeed or to preempt or co-opt it (Gamson 1975, pp. 28–31). The broad political support base for the comprehensive 1964 Civil Rights Act had all these protest movement participant elements.

The individuals who are most likely to initiate and support a protest movement tend to be those with long-developed grievances within a society. A case in point is Solidarity, the labor group that precipitated the successful 1980s protest movement against communist rule in Poland and that helped precipitate other successful Eastern European protest movements. The initial work stoppage, instrumental in offering a political challenge to Polish and Soviet Marxist authority, occurred at the Lenin Shipyard in Gdansk, a center of Cassubian ethnic residence. For a long time Cassubians have held a minority status in Polish society (Lorentz 1935). As the protest movement proceeded to secure broad-based support among Polish citizens, it was no accident that Cassubians, who have experienced prejudice and discrimination beyond communist rule in Poland, would be at the forefront. It is also not surprising that Solidarity was led by a Cassub, Lech Walesa. It is also noteworthy that the protest movement received strong support from another Cassub, Pope John Paul II, whose original name of Karol Wojtyla ends with a Cassubian "a" rather than the more typical Polish "ski."

In the United States, the civil rights movement was manifestly initiated and led by blacks (Morris 1984). Jews, who have experienced more prejudice and discrimination than most other whites in American society, where they constitute less than 3 percent of the population, composed the largest group of whites in the movement. In the Congress of Racial Equality (CORE), one of the leading mass civil rights protest organizations, almost one-half of the white participants identified themselves as Jewish or as secularists whose parents were Jewish (Bell 1968).

The methods employed by protest participants and leaders tend to reflect a lack of institutionalized power. When such institutionalized power is available, it can be exercised to redress grievances without resorting to mass protests. Within democratic political processes in the United States and in other democratic societies, much organized protest on such issues as trade policies, road construction and placement, and taxation can be viewed in more normative, adaptive terms.

When such normative activities do not result in a resolution of grievances, the potential for a protest movement increases. In such a context, legitimized guarantees of the right to protest, as embedded in the U. S. Constitution's First Amendment guarantee of the right to assemble and petition for redress of grievances, do not preclude protest strategies that go beyond legal or normative boundaries of protest behavior.

Methods of protest are related to prospects of success and levels of frustration. When a protest movement or a countermovement has broad public support and is likely to receive a positive response from targeted authorities, protest activities are likely to be peaceful and accepted by such authorities. Such is the case with prochoice protests on the abortion issue, protests for clean air, and protests in support of Jewish and other minority religious status groups in the Soviet Union. All these protest activities have relatively broad American support, even when they experience a minority activist opposition.

It is also not surprising that Solidarity was led by a Cassub, Lech Walesa, and received strong support from another Cassub, Pope John Paul II.

A variety of nonlegitimate strategies are used when protest movements address issues and involve participants with relatively little public support and active opposition. One such nonlegitimate strategy is Ghandi's nonviolent confrontation. Adapted by Martin Luther King, Jr., and most other black civil rights protest leaders in the 1950s and early 1960s, the strategy of nonviolence was designed to call general public attention in a nonthreatening manner to perceived injustices experienced by blacks. With such techniques as sit-ins at racially segregated lunch counters and boycotts of segregated public buses, this nonviolent method generates conflict by breaking down established social practices. The aim of such nonviolent methods is to advance conflict resolution by negotiating a change in practices that produced the protest. The most famous case is perhaps the 1955 Montgomery, Alabama, bus boycott, which was one of several major precipitants of the national black-led civil rights movement (Mauss 1975, p. 520; Morris 1984).

Other, violent, forms of protest include both planned strategies and unplanned spontaneous crowd action. In either case such activity tends to be perceived by authorities and their supporters as disorderly and lawless mob behavior. Masses of protest participants are likely to be drawn to violent action when the general perception (or emergent norm) (Turner and Killian 1986, pp. 21–25) develops that redress of felt grievances cannot be achieved either in normal conditions before protest or by peaceful means. The history of violent protest is a long one and includes the forcible occupation of farms and fields by landless French peasants in the eighteenth century, American attacks on British possessions and military posts prior to the Declaration of Independence, and bread riots by Russian urban dwellers in World War I (Graham and Gurr 1969).

Violent protests usually concern specific issues such as taxes, conscription into the military, and food shortages, issues that are confined to particular situations and times. Although these types of protests do not evolve into major social movements, they have had severe and immediate consequences, as in 1863, during the Civil War, when Irish Catholics protested what they perceived as the unfair nature of the military draft in New York City. These protests left several hundred dead. Likewise, college students in the late 1960s and early 1970s revolted against the draft during the unpopular Vietnam War, and these revolts included loss of human life.

Unplanned violence may also be a form of protest. As reported by the National Advisory Commission on Civil Disorders and other research on over two dozen urban racial riots in the 1960s in the United States, these riots, which resulted in over a hundred deaths and over $100 million in property damage, were disorganized extensions of the black civil rights movement (National Advisory Commission on Civil Disorders 1968; Fogelson 1971). These violent events closely fit Davies's (1974) J-curve thesis, which argues that rising expectations, produced by legal successes in the mid-1960s by the black civil rights movement, were frustrated by the declining urban ghetto environments and growing Vietnam War tensions, both of which were related to the fact that large numbers of blacks were being drafted while most white college students were exempted.

Overall, protest movements are more frequent in societies that legitimize the right of protest. In such societies, social conflict generated by protest movements is often functional in resolving conflict over issues between challenging and target groups (Coser 1956). Still, urban and campus riots of the 1960s illustrate that formal rights of protest do not preclude democratic authorities and their public supporters from responding with police force or from beginning a countermovement. Authoritarian societies may experience fewer protest movements, but when they do occur, such movements are far more likely to be intense and to have the potential for massive social movements designed to transform the society. This could be seen in widely disparate societies including most Eastern European nations and the Soviet Union, El Salvador, Nicaragua, Namibia, South Africa, Iran, and mainland China.

Consequences of Protest Movements

Given the long and continuing history of protest movements, there has been growing interest in the long-term consequences of such movements. Some assessments concentrate on historical, comparative analysis such as Snyder and Tilly's (1972) analysis of French collective violence in response to government-sponsored repression between 1830 and 1968, or Bohstedt and Williams' (1988) analysis of the diffusion of riotous protests in Devonshire, England, between 1766 and 1801. Other studies of long-term consequences make empirical assessments of the aftermath of more contemporary protest movements. Examples include Gordon's (1983) community-based assessment of black and white leadership accommodation in the decade following the Detroit race riots of 1967 and Morris's (1980) assessment of the decade-long impact on national public values of the environmental movement of the late 1960s.

The need for more short- and long-term assessment of the consequences of protest movements is evident in reviews of past movements. William Gamson's consideration of fifty-three protest movements in the United States between the 1830s and 1930s illustrates the need. Gamson categorized each movement's own specific goals in one of four ways: co-opted, preempted, full response success, or collapsed failure (Gamson 1975, pp. 145–153). Gamson assessed each protest movement's success in achieving its goals during its own period of organized activity: For instance, Gamson assessed such groups as the German American Bund (1936–1943), the American Proportional Representation League (1893–1932), and the Dairymen's League (1907–1920).

Of the fifty-three identified protest movements, twenty-two, the largest single proportion, were categorized as being collapsed failures, twenty as achieving full response success, six as being preempted, and five as being co-opted. Protest movements categorized as collapsed failures and full response successes demonstrate the need for assessment of protest movements long beyond their activist periods. Listed under collapsed failures were major long-term successful movements including the abolitionist North Carolina Manumission Society (1816–1834) and the American Anti-Slavery Society (1833–1840). In contrast, among full response success movements was the American Committee for the Outlawry of War (1921–1929), a major force in the achievement of the international Kellogg-Briand Pact of 1928, which outlawed war between nations, a short-lived success that for most of the rest of the twentieth century proved a grand failure.

Successful or unsuccessful in the short or long term, protest movements are periodically a part of social change at local, national, and global levels and in situational, institutional, and cross-cultural concerns. In the United States and other modern mass urban societies, protest movements are becoming more professionalized and are mobilizing more resources to more effectively challenge entrenched interests (McCarthy and Zald 1973). Modern communication systems, international economic interdependence, and economical movement of masses of people over great distances assure that protest movements of the future will increasingly be characterized by a combination of ideas, people, and organization across all of these areas of social life.

[See also Segregation and Desegregation; Social Movements; Student Movements.]

BIBLIOGRAPHY

Bell, Inge Powell 1968 *CORE and the Strategy of Non-Violence.* New York: Random House.

Bohstedt, John, and Dale E. Williams 1988 "The Diffusion of Riots: The Patterns of 1766, 1795, and 1801 in Devonshire." *Journal of Interdisciplinary History* 19 (no. 1):1–24.

Bonacich, Edna 1988 "Sociology of Race Relations in the United States." In E. F. Borgatta and K. S. Cook, eds., *The Future of Sociology.* Beverly Hills, Calif.: Sage.

Coser, Lewis 1956 *The Functions of Social Conflict.* New York: Free Press.

Davies, James C. 1974 "The J-Curve and Power Struggle Theories of Collective Violence." *American Sociological Review* 39:607–612.

Fogelson, Robert 1971 *Violence as Protest: A Study of Riots.* New York: Anchor.

Glazer, Nathan 1975 *Affirmative Discrimination.* Cambridge, Mass.: Harvard University Press.

Gamson, William A. 1975 *The Strategy of Social Protest.* Homewood, Ill.: Dorsey.

Gordon, Leonard 1983 "Aftermath of a Race Riot: The Emergent Norm Process Among Black and White Community Leaders." *Sociological Perspectives* 26:115–135.

Graham, Hugh D., and Ted Gurr (eds.) 1969 *The History of Violence in America: Report of the National Commission on the Causes and Prevention of Violence.* New York: Bantam.

Gusfield, Joseph R. 1968 "The Study of Social Movements." In D. L. Sills, ed., *International Encyclopedia of the Social Sciences.* New York: Macmillan and Free Press.

Heberle, Rudolf 1968 "Types and Functions of Social Movements." In D. L. Sills, ed., *International Encyclopedia of the Social Sciences.* New York: Macmillan and Free Press.

Lipset, Seymour M. 1971 *Rebellion in the University.* Boston: Little, Brown.

Lorentz, Frederick 1935 *The Cassubian Civilization.* London: Faber and Faber.

Mauss, Armand L. 1975 *Social Problems as Social Movements.* New York: J. B. Lippincott.

McCarthy, John, and Mayer Zald 1973 *The Trend of Social Movements in America: Professionalization and Resource Mobilization.* Morristown, N.J.: General Learning.

Morris, Aldon D. 1984 *The Origins of the Civil Rights Movement: Black Communities Organizing for Change.* New York: Free Press.

Morris, Denton 1980 "The Soft Cutting Edge of Environmentalism: Why and How the Appropriate Technology Notion Is Changing the Movement." *Natural Resources Journal* 20:275–298.

Mueller, Carol, and Charles Judd 1981 "Belief Consensus and Belief Constraint." *Social Forces* 60:182–187.

National Advisory Commission on Civil Disorder 1968 *Report of the National Advisory Commission on Civil Disorders.* New York: Bantam.

Park, Robert E., and Ernest W. Burgess 1921 *Introduction to the Science of Sociology.* Chicago: University of Chicago Press.

Piven, Frances Fox, and Richard A. Cloward 1977 *Poor People's Movements: Why They Succeed, How They Fail.* New York: Vintage.

Rustin, Bayard 1965 "From Protest to Politics: The Future of the Civil Rights Movement." *A Commentary* Reprint. New York: Institute of Human Relations.

Shirer, William 1960 *The Rise and Fall of the Third Reich.* New York: Simon and Schuster.

Smelser, Neil J. 1962 *Theory of Collective Behavior.* New York: Free Press.

Snyder, David, and Charles Tilly 1972 "Hardship and Collective Violence in France: 1830 to 1960." *American Sociological Review* 37:520–532.

Tilly, Charles 1978 *From Mobilization to Rebellion.* Reading, Mass. Addison-Wesley.

Turner, Ralph, and Lewis M. Killian 1986 *Collective Behavior.* 3rd ed. Englewood Cliffs, N.J.: Prentice-Hall.

U.S. Bureau of the Census 1983 *Handbook of Labor Statistics.* Washington, D.C.: U.S. Government Printing Office.

——— 1984 *Employment and Earnings.* Washington, D.C.: U.S. Government Printing Office.

Wilson, William J. 1987 *The Truly Disadvantaged: The Inner City, the Underclass, and Public Policy.* Chicago: University of Chicago Press.

– LEONARD GORDON

PUBLIC OPINION

Public opinion is characterized, on the one hand, by its form as elementary collective behavior (Blumer 1972) and, on the other, by its function as a means of social control (Ross 1901). It comes into play in problematical situations characterized by some degree of normative ambiguity in one of several senses: The situation is novel and unprecedented, so that persons cannot cope by falling back on generally accepted codes of conduct; people actively disagree over the appropriate way of coping with the situation; or existing practices have been challenged by a dissident group. In the extreme case, controversy over what should be done can heat up to a point where order gives way to violent intragroup conflict or revolution.

Interest in public opinion is historically linked to the rise of popular government. Although rulers have always had to display some minimum sensitivity to the needs and demands of their subjects, they felt little need, unlike most of today's governments that must face voters in mandated elections, to anticipate their constituents' reactions to events that were yet to occur or to policies still to be implemented. But public opinion operates equally outside the relationship of citizens to the state. Its influence is felt throughout civil society, where on many matters, including personal taste in dress, music, or house furnishings, people remain sensitive to the changing opinions of peers and neighbors. They court approval by showing themselves in step with the times.

Opinions have behind them neither the sanctity of tradition nor the sanctions of law. Their only force is agreement, and people can change their minds. Labeling something as "opinion" implies a certain willingness to acknowledge the validity of contrary views, which opens the issue to discussion. Those involved to the degree that their attention is focused on the issue and they are ready to take sides make up a public. It usually expands in size as an issue heats up, to contract again as the focus shifts to new problems. There are in fact as many publics as there are issues.

In the center of early sociological studies of public opinion was the question of competence. Analysts sought to distinguish conceptually between the reasoned opinions developed in discussion and the nondebatable demands voiced by the greatly feared "mob" acting under the sway of emotion. But two works, one in Germany and one in America, coincidentally published the same year, analyzed the problem in structural terms. Tönnies (1922) pointed to the press and to associations who usurped for themselves the role of articulating public opinion. To Lippmann (1922) the notion that ordinary citizens—even the most well-educated among them—had the time and incentive to acquire the expertise necessary to grasp the complex problems of the day in sufficient detail to direct the course of events was a false ideal. Drawing on a wide range of literature, he showed how the public saw the world in stereotypes fed to them by the press. Whenever the public attempted to intervene in the policy process, he argued, it was inevitably as the dupe or unconscious ally of special interests. The role of the public was necessarily limited to identifying the problems and areas in need of remedial action of some sort and to deciding which party, institution, or agency should be trusted to work out solutions. Mostly he saw the public as a potentially effective "reserve force" to be mobilized in support of the procedural norms of democracy.

The list of social scientists echoing these skeptical views about "rule by public opinion" under modern conditions includes Mannheim (1940), Schumpeter (1942), Schattschneider (1960), Bogart (1972), and most recently Ginsberg (1986). "The paradox of mass politics," writes Neuman (1986, p. 3), "is the gap between the expectation of an informed citizenry put forward by democratic theory and the discomforting reality revealed by systematic survey interviewing." Where pluralists see a public made up of many competing interests, each with its own leadership, Neuman sees only three: a tiny percentage of sophisticated citizens with some input into policy; uninterested and inactive know-nothings, who make up roughly one-fifth; and a large middle mass that votes largely out of a sense of duty but with only a very limited understanding of the issues their vote is meant to decide. The discrepancy from the ideal, which appears over and over again in public opinion polls, cannot be discounted as attributable to flaws in techniques.

Polls do, of course, vary in quality. The reliability and validity of any particular survey as a measure of public opinion hinges on three general factors: who is interviewed, the situation in which the interview takes place, and the questions asked. Insofar as elections are opportunities for the public to go on record with its "opinion," the utility of polling as a research tool can be ascertained by comparing pre-election readings with the actual vote count.

We will never see again the wildly incorrect 1936 forecast by the Literary Digest *that Roosevelt, who won by a landslide, would lose the election.*

The two fiascoes in polling history have been painstakingly diagnosed. We will never see again the wildly incorrect 1936 forecast by the *Literary Digest* that Roosevelt, who won by a landslide, would lose the presidential election. Poll-takers learned the hard way not to rely solely on sample size, and to shed the commonsense belief that larger automatically means better. The *Digest* poll was based on 2.3 million returns from over ten million straw ballots mailed to persons drawn from automobile registration lists and telephone books. Owners of cars and telephones were somewhat less supportive of Roosevelt than those too poor to own either or both such conveniences. A second, actually more important, source of bias was the large number of Republicans, compared with Democrats, motivated to respond by using the straw ballot to register a protest against the party in power.

When in 1948 the public pollsters, despite more skillfully designed samples and more sophisticated methods, nevertheless wrongly predicted the defeat of incumbent Harry Truman, this became the occasion for one of the most extensive inquiries into polling practices by a committee of the Social Science Research Council (Mosteller et al. 1949). Its report stressed the importance of samples based on random selection that would give every voter the same chance of being contacted, an objective often difficult to implement. Polling techniques have come a long way since, but, as an investigation by Crespi (1988) of the factors associated with accurate prediction in 430 pre-election polls during the 1980s showed, the extra effort invested in callbacks still pays off in greater accuracy. Persons missed because they are hard to get hold of or refuse to answer often differ from the rest in ways difficult to estimate.

As to the interview situation, answering the questions of a poll-taker is hardly the same as casting a vote, all the more so when the election is months away. The large margins by which Truman had been trailing in the early fall of 1948 caused several pollsters to cease polling weeks before voting day. Thus, they never registered the strong Democratic rally that occurred toward the end of the campaign. Crespi's more recent tabulations show that proximity to the election remains a major determinant of the accuracy in pre-election polls. Much depends on how far in advance people first make up their minds, on the firmness of their convictions, and on the influence of such major events as occur during the election campaign. Responses to polls taken too early may be artifacts of the interview situation. These non-attitudes, as they are called, are an especially dangerous contaminant in low-turnout elections with little-known candidates and in referendums on questions beyond the understanding of most voters.

The problems encountered in election research, where the issue boils down to a choice between two leading candidates, are more elusive when there is no outside standard against which to validate the opinions voiced in the interview. Poll-takers have long learned to omit from their tabulations of pre-election surveys anyone identified as a likely nonvoter. Similar "filters" are used to eliminate the responses of people questioned about matters of little concern to them, to which they have given no thought, and of which they may not even have been aware except for the question having been put to them. Respondents who admit to being unfamiliar with or unconcerned about an issue are asked no further questions about it. This still leaves those reluctant to make such an admission. One survey that deliberately inserted a question about a nonexistent act allegedly under consideration in Congress had significant minorities respond that they had heard of it, with some going on to fabricate an opinion about it.

Measures of public opinion based on a single question can be misleading. They take no account of the complexities of the underlying issue. Thus, a poll taken in 1971, when concern over American involvement in Vietnam was higher than over any other issue on the public agenda, put the following direct question to respondents: "Do you favor or oppose the withdrawal of all American troops from Vietnam by the end of the year?" The result: Two out of three respondents replied that they favored withdrawal. On another question in the same survey about whether they favored withdrawing all troops "regardless of how the war was going," they split with a bare plurality of 44 percent against, 41 percent in favor. Does the 22-point difference between the 66 percent found in favor on the first question and the 44 percent on the second identify a group ready to take back an off-the-cuff answer because of the reminder of possible consequences? Or were they confident that South Vietnam would not fall, in which event the contingency incorporated into the second question was purely hypothetical and had no practical relevance for them? There is still a third possibility: Were they afraid to admit to the interviewer that they did not care whether or not America was forced to withdraw in defeat?

Polls on the Vietnam war exemplify how responses to differently phrased questions can give contradictory readings of where the public actually stands on a complex policy question. Thus, at the same time majorities declared their support for both immediate withdrawal and stepping up the air war on North Vietnam. Many people who thought Vietnam a mistake nevertheless remained steadfast backers of Johnson's Vietnam policy. Nor were self-styled "doves" necessarily in sympathy with student protesters. One needs a series of probing questions to assess what is on people's minds.

There are alternatives to the survey, but these, too, require caution. Letters, telegrams, and phone calls to political leaders may reflect nothing more than the effort of a well-organized minority. On the other hand, a rise in the number who refuse draft calls or desert from the armed forces, a change in the incidence of certain crimes, or the number of demonstrations, strikes, and other forms of protest can be important clues—not necessarily to general opinion but at least to what the groups most affected by some problem may be unwilling to settle for (Tilly 1978).

Studies of public opinion have to contend with a broad range of beliefs. Located at one extreme are the more stable political allegiances; at the other, the often fluctuating "gut" responses to whatever happens to be current. Specific opinions, as Converse (1964) showed through surveys taken during the early 1960s, do not form clearly defined ideological clusters; the relation of each opinion to others is rather loose.

Other more general ideas that underlie the legitimacy of the political system have greater stability insofar as they build on childhood experience within the family, where children tend to adopt the views of their parents. Early views are then elaborated or modified, as the children grow up, by sustained contact with other major institutions like school or church and, to some extent (especially during major catastrophes affecting the country or its leaders), by the news media (Renshaw 1977). The content of the political culture assimilated differs from milieu to milieu.

Controversy is likely to arise during crises that highlight the endemic cleavages related to position in social structure and in historical time. The activation of old loyalties causes public opinion to divide in predictable ways—by region, race, religion, ethnicity, class background, educational experiences, and so forth. If the cleavage is deep enough, issues stand a good chance of escalating into coercive conflict. The more powerful groups will dominate.

Yet changes in basic attitudes do occur, though slowly, partly through replacement and partly through the diffusion of new experience. Differential birth rates, migration, social mobility, and the metabolic succession of generations are processes that disturb the existing balance without any change on the individual level and despite evidence of political continuity between parents and offspring. Distinct intergenerational differences are believed to develop in response to certain critical experiences, like the encounter, early in adulthood before one's outlook has fully crystallized, with general poverty and war, or participation in social struggles.

Attitudes on race are a good example of how diffusion and replacement operate in conjunction with each other. Surveys taken over time show a distinct movement toward greater racial tolerance (Schuman and Bobo 1985). All groups moved in the same direction, even if at greatly different speeds. The young showed the way, often with tacit support of sympathetic parents not yet themselves prepared to issue a radical challenge to segregation. Rising levels of education and replacement of the more conservative account for part of the shift, while people in regions where segregationist practices were most firmly entrenched changed more rapidly than the rest of the country, once the full force of public opinion had been brought to bear on them.

The day-to-day shifts in public opinion on matters great and small are more subject to influence by the media of mass communication, the great force toward homogenization that helped intransigent Southerners opposed to racial desegregation to see themselves as the rest of the country saw them. More generally, the news of major events gives the public a common focus. By highlighting a problem or giving space and air time to some political figure to do so, the media collectively define the public agenda (agenda setting). Their treatment of the principal actors, of the causes and consequences of the problems, has a distinct influence on the terms on which the issue is debated (agenda building). This role is well documented in case studies of Watergate (Lang and Lang 1983) and of child abuse as an emergent social problem (Nelson 1984).

Media power is nevertheless limited (Paletz and Entman 1981). Some problems, like corruption in high places or a bad turn in foreign relations, about which no one would know unless alerted, depend more on media recognition than do inflation or shortages, which directly impinge on nearly everyone, or grievances anchored in group experience. The latter will not go away for mere lack of mention. Moreover, media managers are less than fully independent. They have to accommodate other actors intent on publicizing only those issues (or aspects of issues) that work in their favor. This is where the highly developed art of news management comes into play. Whoever succeeds in controlling the coverage gains. Public discussion and, indirectly, public opinion have come to be governed by media strategies aimed less at persuading opponents than at neutralizing them.

Most of the public is not issue-oriented but reacts to the general image of presidential performance.

Shifts in attention cause revaluation. The measures most consistently used for tracking public opinion are the presidential approval ratings. Incoming presidents typically stand high in the polls. On the assumption that the public reacts primarily to policy issues, Mueller (1973) attributes the progressive erosion of popularity to a coalition of minorities: Each decision the president makes will antagonize some constituency. In fact, most of the public is not issue-oriented but reacts to the general image of presidential performance. "Good" news of any kind tends to bolster that image, with one major exception. A national crisis generally sets in motion a rally to the flag. Oppositional voices are stilled, at least temporarily, in a show of patriotic unity.

As to the effects of such opinions, at least two presidents have been driven from office when confronted with clear erosion of public support. Following the all too evident failure of his Vietnam policy, Lyndon B. Johnson declared himself out of the race for reelection, even though as a sitting president he would have been assured renomination as the standard bearer of his party (Schandler 1977). Richard M. Nixon made several concessions and ultimately bowed to public opinion in releasing the tapes with the incriminating evidence that made his impeachment and removal from office, subsequent to a Senate trial, a near certain probability (Lang and Lang 1983).

Popularity is an obvious asset, not only for a president but for anyone aspiring to influence. Social control often works subtly to discourage those who feel out of step from asserting themselves as confidently and forcefully as they might otherwise. They may actually lapse into silence and, however reluctantly, go along with the apparent majority. Noelle-Neumann (1984) refers to the process underlying such bandwagon effects as a "spiral of silence," which further strengthens the already dominant opinion. There is no question about the effectiveness of such silencing. The control of public opinion by totalitarian regimes depends to a large extent on their control over the conversational channels through which ideologically deviant tendencies may spread. In societies governed by the norm of free discussion, all but the most intransigent will recognize when an issue has been settled to a point where further debate becomes superfluous. Likewise, the need to display unity in a crisis or moral fervor, whipped up in crusades against alleged internal enemies, is apt to keep discussion within acceptable bounds. Leaders become cautious and dissidents lie low. Whether such spirals generally operate in ways described by Noelle-Neumann (1984) remains questionable.

Whether elected or not, the leaders of major institutions have proved distinctly sensitive to trends in public opinion that bear on their policies or measures under consideration. Congress, understandably, keeps its finger on the public pulse. Lacking evidence of majority support, members have been inclined to wait, watching to see which way the public tilts. In the controversy over Roosevelt's plan to pack the Supreme Court as well as the one over Nixon's complicity in Watergate, opinion was moved by events, including events generated by the debate. On civil rights, major legislation was passed only after mass demonstration and media attention to discriminatory practices had created public concern and support for the principle had reached or exceeded the two-thirds mark. Laws subsequent to the initial path-breaking legislation could then be enacted without direct pressure from below. But none of these things could have been achieved without effective political leadership.

Legal decisions, at least in principle, are seen as insulated from the direct pressure of public opinion. Yet even the U.S. Supreme Court, the most august of all judicial bodies, so Marshall (1989) concludes, has been an essentially majoritarian institution. Of 142 decisions from the mid-1930s to the mid-1980s for which there were comparable opinion data, over four-fifths turned out to be consistent with expressed public preferences. The linkage, strongest in times of crisis, may be explained by the court's sensitivity to legislative and executive concerns incorporating public opinion rather than as a direct response to public pressure.

It is on questions relating to the constitutional rights of dissident minorities that the court has most consistently set itself against majority opinion. Other countermajoritarian opinions have either articulated a rising trend, strengthened by the voice of the court, or been modified by later decisions that, in an apparent response to public opinion, carved out exceptions and introduced qualifications to the broad rule laid down during the original case. By and large, opinions with majority support are less likely to be reversed by subsequent courts.

Although many measures cast doubt on the public's qualifications, political leaders do experience constraints, even when dealing with the more obscure issues usually cleared through networks known mostly to insiders. The prudent ones are forever listening and managing appearances. Rarely does the public become aroused by some all too apparent failure, a scandal, or some official act involving its own interest. It is on these occasions that the power of the public as a "reserve force," wisely or otherwise, is felt most directly.

[See also Attitudes; Mass Media Research.]

BIBLIOGRAPHY

Blumer, Herbert 1972 "Outline of Collective Behavior." In Robert R. Evans, ed., *Readings in Collective Behavior.* Chicago: Rand McNally.

Bogart, Leo 1972 *Polls and the Awareness of Public Opinion.* New York: Wiley.

Converse, Philip E. 1964 "The Nature of Belief Systems in Mass Publics." In David Apter, ed., *Ideology and Discontent.* New York: Free Press.

Crespi, Irving 1988 *Pre-Election Polling; Sources of Accuracy and Error.* New York: Russell Sage.

Ginsberg, Benjamin 1986 *The Captive Public: How Mass Opinion Promotes State Power.* New York: Basic Books.

Lang, Gladys Engel, and Kurt Lang 1983 *The Battle for Public Opinion: The President, the Press, and the Polls during Watergate.* New York: Columbia University Press.

Lippmann, Walter 1922 *Public Opinion.* New York: Macmillan.

Mannheim, Karl 1940 *Man and Society in an Age of Reconstruction.* New York: Harcourt, Brace.

Marshall, Thomas 1989 *Public Opinion and the Supreme Court.* Boston: Unwin Hyman.

Mosteller, Frederick, Herbert Hyman, Philip J. McCarthy, Eli S. Marks, and David B. Truman 1949 *The Preelection Polls of 1948,* Bulletin no. 68. New York: Social Science Research Council.

Mueller, John E. 1973 *War, Presidents, and Public Opinion.* New York: Wiley.

Nelson, Barbara 1984 *Making an Issue of Child Abuse: Agenda Setting for Social Problems.* Chicago: University of Chicago Press.

Neuman, W. Russell 1986 *The Paradox of Mass Politics: Knowledge and Opinion in the American Electorate.* Cambridge, Mass.: Harvard University Press.

Noelle-Neumann, Elisabeth 1984 *The Spiral of Silence.* Chicago: University of Chicago Press.

Paletz, David L., and Robert F. Entman 1981 *Media Power Politics.* New York: Free Press.

Renshaw, Stanley A., ed. 1977 *A Handbook of Political Socialization.* New York: Free Press.

Ross, Edward A. 1901 *Social Control: A Survey of the Social Foundations of Order.* New York: Macmillan.

Schandler, Herbert J. 1977 *The Unmaking of a President: Lyndon B. Johnson and Vietnam.* Princeton: Princeton University Press.

Schattschneider, E. E. 1960 *The Semisovereign People: A Realist's View of Democracy in America.* Hinsdale, Ill.: Dryden Press.

Schuman, Howard, and Lawrence Bobo 1985 *Racial Attitudes: Trends and Interpretations.* Cambridge, Mass.: Harvard University Press.

Schumpeter, Joseph A. 1942 *Capitalism, Socialism, and Democracy.* New York: Harper and Row.

Sigel, Roberta S. (ed.) 1989 *Political Learning in Adulthood: A Sourcebook of Theory and Research.* Chicago: University of Chicago Press.

Tilly, Charles 1978 *From Mobilization to Revolution.* New York: Random House.

Tönnies, Ferdinand 1922 *Kritik der öffentlichen Meinung.* Berlin: Springer.

– KURT LANG

QUALITY OF LIFE

Although the concept of quality of life (QL) is not new, quality of life as an area of research and scholarship dates back only to the 1960s. Schuessler and Fisher (1985) recently noted that President Eisenhower's 1960 Commission on National Goals and Bauer's book on social indicators (1966) are often credited as providing the impetus for the development of QL as an area of research. Campbell (1981) suggested that the 1960s were favorable times for the development of QL research because of the emergence then of a concern that people must examine the quality of their lives and must do so in an environment that goes beyond providing material goods to foster individual happiness. Campbell quotes President Johnson, who stated in 1964:

> The task of the Great Society is to ensure our people the environment, the capacities, and the social structures which will give them a meaningful chance to pursue their individual happiness. Thus the Great Society is concerned not with how much, but with how good—not with the quantity of goods but with the quality of their lives. (Campbell 1981, p. 4)

Schuessler and Fisher (1985) note that the Russell Sage Foundation promoted QL and research on social indicators in the 1960s and 1970s and that the Institute for Social Research at the University of Michigan and the National Opinion Research Center at the University of Chicago have conducted QL research since the late 1960s. Despite the high volume of QL research during the 1960s and 1970s, it was not until 1979 that "Quality of Life" became an index entry in *Sociological Abstracts.*

The emerging QL research in the 1970s provided a departure from previous work that focused on objective indicators, primarily economic in nature, of individual well-being. The book *The Quality of American Life: Perceptions, Evaluations, and Satisfactions,* written by Campbell, Converse, and Rodgers in 1976, particularly promoted the use of subjective or psychological indicators of well-being. The work reported was founded on the conviction that the relationship between objective and subjective well-being indicators was weak and poorly understood. Moreover, the rising affluence of the post-World War II era had been accompanied by steady increases in social problems afflicting American society as well as other Western societies.

The year 1976 also saw the publication of another major work focusing on subjective indicators of well-being. *Social Indicators of Well-Being: Americans' Perceptions of Life Quality* by Andrews and Withy (1976) reported findings from interviews with representative samples of more than 5,000 Americans. The interviews focused on satisfaction with the quality of various life domains. A more recent volume, titled *Research on the Quality of Life,* edited by Frank Andrews (1986), brought together a variety of papers originating at a symposium honoring the memory of Angus Campbell, one of the founders of the Institute for Social Research. And, although this volume included important papers on cross-national differences in life satisfaction and papers on blacks and Hispanics, a number of the papers had no direct relationship to QL research. Rockwell (1989) noted that a useful focus of the field was lost in this volume, the focus on subjective indicators of the quality of life. Andrews also noted that support for large-scale, wide-ranging surveys become increasingly difficult in the 1980s in the United States, resulting in a lack of replication of the national surveys conducted in the previous decade by the Institute for Social Research.

Parallel to the large national surveys of subjective well-being during the 1970s, there was a proliferation of studies focusing on the subjective well-being of the elderly. In a useful article, Larson (1978) reviewed three decades of research that focused on the psychological well-being of older people. Perhaps no other area of research in the emerging field of gerontology had received as much attention during the 1960s and 1970s as the area of life satisfaction, morale, mental health, and psychological well-being in general. Much of this research was spurred by the lively debate over the merits of disengagement theory (proposed by Cumming and Henry 1961) and activity theory (identified with various authors, including Havighurst, Neugarten, and Tobin 1968; Maddox 1968, 1970) in predicting "successful aging." Gerontological work in the 1980s showed a marked decline in the number of articles predicting life satisfaction and morale and an increase in articles focusing on specific dimensions of psychological well-being, such as depression and psychological distress, as well as articles focusing on the prediction of physical health outcomes (Markides 1989).

The relative decline in research on the subjective quality of life of Americans in general as well as the subjective well-being of the elderly observed in the 1980s was accompanied by a marked increase in QL research in medicine. In 1989, for example, the *Journal of the American Medical Association* published three major articles on quality of life (Stewart et al. 1989; Tarlov et al. 1989; Wells et al. 1989) of various kinds of patients. In contrast, not a single paper focusing on quality of life was published in the *American Sociological Review* in the same year. A careful examination of the 1990 program of the annual meeting of the American Sociological Association revealed no sessions or papers focusing directly on QL research.

Within medicine, there has been particular interest in studying the quality of life of cancer patients. Before 1970, cancer research focused almost exclusively on survival and its extension. With extended survival from cancer becoming the rule, research has given increasing attention to the quality of life of the surviving patients afflicted with cancer or patients treated for cancer. In 1987, for example, a volume entitled *The Quality of Life of Cancer Patients* was published. The volume, edited by Aaronson and Beckman (1987), contains papers from researchers in a number of European countries as well as the United States.

Another parallel to this work has been the recent focus on active life expectancy. The work has gone beyond predicting extension of life in general to investigating the extent to which recent extensions of life expectancy have been accompanied by extensions of "active" life.

Definitions of Quality of Life

As seen in the previous section, there has been a movement in recent decades away from objective, quantitative research toward subjective, qualitative assessments of QL in sociology and other fields. But even within these broad approaches to QL, there appears to be little agreement about an appropriate definition of QL.

Some writings include under QL research the social indicators movement. Land (1971) noted that in the early years of the movement, the most popular definition of social indicators was given in *Toward a Social Report* (U.S. Department of Health, Education, and Welfare 1969, p. 97):

> A social indicator . . . may be defined to be a statistic of direct normative interest which facilitates concise, comprehensive and balanced judgments about the condition of a major aspect of a society. It is in all cases a direct measure of welfare and is subject to the interpretation that, if it changes, in the "right" direction, while other things remain equal, things have gotten better, or people are "better off." Thus statistics on the number of doctors or policemen could not be social indicators whereas figures on health or crime rates could be.

Land criticized the above definition and proposed a broader one that treats social indicators as both "outputs" and "inputs" in "a sociological model of a social system or some segment thereof" (1971; p. 324). Thus, for example, the number of doctors is essential to understanding the health of the population, as are other factors. Land's definition has been largely accepted by the social indicators movement (Mukherjee 1989; p. 53).

This entry gives only limited attention to social indicators. Yet the term is often used interchangeably with QL, at least with respect to what Mukherjee (1989; p. 49) calls "need-based" quality of life research. Moreover, the journal *Social Indicators Research* is subtitled *An International Journal of Quality of Life Measurement.*

In his book *The Quality of Life Valuation in Social Research,* Mukherjee notes that QL researchers employ several dichotomies such as "quantity" and "quality," "behavior" and "perception," and "objective" and "subjective" indicators. He argues:

> Economists and planners . . . are almost exclusively concerned with behavioural research on the basis of quantitative variables to improve the quality of life of the people. In that context, they ignore qualitative variations in the appraisal of a better quality of life or treat these variations as introducing a classificatory . . . distinction in the field of enquiry. They also equate the individual-wise subjective perception of reality to a group-wise "objective" perception by experts. Their appraisal of social reality in this manner leads them to formulate what the people *need* in order to improve their quality of life. (Mukherjee 1989, pp. 37–38)

This need-based approach to QL research is not limited to the work of economists and planners. For example, as mentioned above, the social indicators movement is largely need-based research.

Need-based research has been criticized on a variety of grounds. Michalos argues:

> The existence of a great gap between Maslow-type needs and specific items of actions in the world is one reason why the attempt to develop indicators from needs does not seem worthwhile. . . . Indeed, contrary

> to those who think we might be able to construct a theory of value based on needs. I am sure that the logic of the situation is just the reverse. Values are prior to needs and required for their definition. To see that this is so, consider what one means to say about something when one says that it is needed. At the very least it is assumed that if someone needs something, that person would suffer from some form of *deterioration* in its absence. (Michalos 1974, p. 125)

This argument favors a "want-based" approach to QL research that focuses on people's perceptions, expectations, aspirations, and achievement orientations (Mukherjee 1989; p. 44). Bharadwaj and Wilkening argue, for example:

> The recognition that the economic health of a nation is not synonymous with individual satisfaction and well-being had led to the development of social indicators to assess individual quality of life. . . . The new emphasis is on the monitoring of change in goals, values, attitudes and satisfaction that affect individual lives and nations. The overall thrust appears to be "the development of a set of 'dependent variables'." (Bharadwaj and Wilkening 1980, p. 377)

Similarly, in describing the results of their research, Campbell, Converse, and Rogers argue:

> The research with which this book is concerned derives from the conviction that the relationship between objective conditions and psychological states is very imperfect and that in order to know the quality of life experience it will be necessary to go directly to the individual himself for his description of how his life feels to him. (Campbell, Converse, and Rogers 1976, p. 4)

From this kind of perspective, quality of life typically involves "a sense of achievement in one's work, an appreciation of beauty in nature and the arts, a feeling of identification with one's community, a sense of fulfillment of one's potential" (Campbell, Converse, and Rogers 1976, p. 1).

The "dependent variables" of this research tend to be items or scales measuring satisfactions or happiness. Milbrath (1978, p. 36), for example, argues: "I have come to the conclusion that the only defensible definition of quality of life is a general feeling of happiness." And even though such global evaluations have been common, much of the research has focused on describing and explaining satisfactions with various life "domains" such as work, family, housing, and so forth.

In discussing subjective indicators of QL, Land noted the difficulties in relating them to objective indicators. He noted, for example, that while income levels tend to be associated with satisfactions and happiness within given countries and at given times, "higher per capita levels of national income do not produce higher average levels of national satisfaction over time or cross sectionally" (1983, p. 5). He goes on to suggest that from the standpoint of generating theory of social change, it is not clear that satisfaction indexes are the most desirable subjective indicators as opposed to values, aspirations, or expectations, nor is it clear that satisfaction indexes provide an unambiguous criterion for the formulation of public policy. He notes, for example, that research by Andrews and Withy (1976), among others, has found that areas most critical to individual satisfactions do not seem very amenable to public policy interventions.

Measuring Quality of Life

The broadest and most commonly employed distinction in measures of QL is between objective and subjective measures. Among the former are indicators such as per capita income, average calorie consumption, percent of adult illiteracy, quality of air, average daily temperature, crime rates, life expectancy, and a myriad of other indicators that are best seen as causes of quality of life.

While income levels tend to be associated with happiness, higher per capita levels of national income do not produce higher average levels of national satisfaction.

Any one of the above has shortcomings. For example, GNP per capita has been acknowledged to suffer from many well-known limitations, including that it may not capture the spending power of the masses but rather that of a small minority (Mukherjee 1989, p. 42). To overcome the limitations of single indicators, researchers have proposed a number of composite indexes such as the Physical Quality of Life Index (PQLI; see Morris 1977) that includes, among other variables, life expectancy at birth, infant mortality, and literacy. The purpose of the PQLI was to rank countries by physical well-being. Yet it has limitations, as its proponent acknowledges, including that "it is based on the assumption that the needs and desires of individuals initially and at the most basic level are for larger life expectancy, reduced illness, and greater opportunity" (Morris 1977, p. 147).

Another composite index of objective indicators of QL is the Index of Social Progress (ISP) proposed originally by Estes (1984) and revised more recently by the same author (Estes 1988). The latest version (ISP83) consists of thirty-six indicators and is divided into ten subindexes covering "education, health status, status of women, defense effort, economic, demographic, political participation, cultural diversity and welfare effort" (Estes 1988, p. 1). A number of equally important indicators are not included because reliable data are not available on the 124 nations studied (e.g., crime rates, suicide rates, maldistribution of wealth). Estes goes on to acknowledge further the index's limitations as a measure of quality of life:

> [The ISP is not] a tool that attempts to assess personal happiness, satisfaction with life, or the degree of personal "fulfillment" experienced by individuals living in particular nations. Rather, the ISP measures the changing capacity of nations to provide for the basic social and material needs of their populations as a whole. . . . Consequently, the ISP should be regarded as a quantitative measure of national human welfare, and is not to be construed as a tool that can be used to assess directly varying degrees of personal fulfillment. (Estes 1988, p. 4)

There has also been a lively interest in developing indexes consisting of objective indicators to rank quality of life of American cities. Liu (1976), for example, utilized 1970 U.S. Census data covering five major domains of quality of life: economic, environmental, health and education, political, and social. Weighting was employed to create an overall index as well as domain-specific subindexes. Other similar indexes were offered by J. Wilson (1967), Smith (1972), Boyer and Savageau (1981), Rosen (1979), and Berger, Blomquist, and Waldner (1987). Such rankings of cities typically elicit national attention and often surprise individuals about how high or low their community ranks. Rankings also do not often correlate with each other. For example, Berger, Blomquist, and Waldner (1987) found that their revealed-preference ranking had a correlation of −0.075 with those proposed by Boyer and Savageau (1981) and a correlation of 0.048 with Liu's (1976) rankings.

There have been numerous subjective measures of QL, with most relating to happiness or life satisfaction. Some measures are global in the sense that they aim at capturing happiness or satisfaction with life as a whole, while others pertain to happiness or satisfaction with certain life-domains.

The studies by Andrews and Withy (1976) and Campbell, Converse, and Rogers (1976) included measures of both domain-specific and global life satisfaction and employed the former as predictors of the latter. In general, they found that the best predictors of global satisfaction are marriage and family life, leisure activities, work and finances, housing, the community, and friendships.

Well before these landmark studies, W. Wilson (1967) reviewed prior literature on subjective well-being and concluded that the "happy person emerges as a young, healthy, well-educated, well-paid, extroverted, optimistic, worry-free, religious, married person with high self-esteem, high job morale, modest aspirations, of either sex and of a wide range of intelligence" (1967, p. 294). He also concluded that little progress had been made in understanding happiness since the time of the Greek philosophers.

Diener (1984) noted that between W. Wilson's 1967 article and 1984, over 700 studies on subjective well-being had been published. In general, Wilson's conclusions regarding predictors of well-being appeared supported by the literature, including that little theoretical progress had been made in the field since the ancient Greeks.

This voluminous literature on subjective well-being has employed a variety of single-item and multiple-item measures of happiness and life satisfaction. Among the best-known single-item measures are: Cantril's (1965) "self-anchoring ladder," which asks respondents to place themselves on a nine-rung ladder ranging from "best possible for you" to "worst possible for you"; Gurin, Veroff, and Feld's (1960) item, "Taking all things together, how would you say things are these days?", with possible response choices being "very happy," "pretty happy," and "not too happy"; and Andrews and Withy's (1976) item, "How do you feel about how happy you are?", with seven choices ranging from "delighted" to "terrible."

A problem with single-item measures is that because internal reliability estimates cannot be computed, the only way of assessing their reliability is through temporal correlation, which makes it difficult to separate measurement error from true change. However, convergence with other measures of well-being has suggested that these single-item measures enjoy moderate levels of validity. They do suffer from other limitations, however, such as positive skewness, acquiescence, and inability to capture the various dimensions of well-being (Diener 1984).

There have also been a variety of multi-item scales employed. Some of the best-known general scales include: the Affect Balance Scale (Bradburn 1969), which consists of items capturing positive and negative well-being, the two being relatively independent of each other, and Campbell, Converse, and Rogers's (1976) Index of General Affect, which asks respondents to describe their present lives using semantic differential scales (miserable-enjoyable, hard-easy, boring-interesting, useless-worthwhile, lonely-friendly, discouraging-hopeful, empty-full, disappointing-rewarding, and doesn't give me a chance-brings out the best in me).

Although happiness and satisfaction are often used interchangeably, many writers believe they are distinct measures of well-being. George, for example, suggests that "happiness refers to an affective assessment of quality of life," while "life satisfaction refers to an assessment of the overall conditions of life, as derived from a comparison of one's aspirations to one's actual achievements" (1981, p. 351). Campbell, Converse, and Rogers (1976) prefer satisfaction measures over happiness measures because they are more sensitive to intervention. While happiness tends to be transitory and volatile, life satisfaction changes gradually and systematically in response to changing life conditions (see also Stull 1987). Satisfaction scales have been particularly popular in gerontology.

Quality of Life in the Elderly

An area in which lively interest has been shown in subjective indicators of QL has been the emerging field of gerontology. As mentioned earlier, use of subjective measures of well-being was particularly high during the 1960s and 1970s, when social gerontologists were occupied with assessing the merits of disengagement and activity theories. In the late 1970s, Larson (1978) reviewed three decades of research and concluded that the most consistent predictors of subjective well-being are self-reports of health.

Although gerontological studies have employed general well-being measures (e.g., the Affect Balance Scale), they have also employed scales specifically developed for use with older people. The two best known are the Life Satisfaction Index A (Neugarten, Havighurst, and Tobin 1961) and the Philadelphia Geriatric Morale Scale (Lawton 1975). The Life Satisfaction Index A consists of twenty items, with which respondents agree or disagree. A combined life satisfaction score is obtained by summing scores on all twenty items. Because the index covers a variety of areas, including happiness, satisfaction, and "activation level" (see Cherlin and Reeder 1975), the combined score confounds separate dimensions of well-being (Stull 1987). The Philadelphia Geriatric Center Morale Scale (PGCMS) originally consisted of twenty-two items (Lawton 1972), and the revised version consisted of seventeen items (Lawton 1975). Factor analyses with the latter have produced three dimensions: Agitation, Attitude toward Own Aging, and Lonely Dissatisfaction. The scale has problems similar to those of the Life Satisfaction Index, such as the confounding of satisfaction and happiness. The two scales are in many ways similar (in fact, they share some items) and have been found to be highly intercorrelated ($r = 0.76$; see Lohman 1977).

Liang (1985) attempted to integrate the Life Satisfaction Index A and the Affect Balance Scale by selecting seven items from the former and eight from the latter. His analysis yielded four factors (congruence, happiness, positive affect, and negative affect) that correspond to dimensions of well-being discussed by Lawton (1983). However, Liang acknowledged a gap between the operationalization of well-being and its theoretical operationalization: "Most instruments were developed with only a general conceptual definition, and the sampling of the item domain is usually based on intuition, experience, and empirical experimentation" (Liang 1985, p. 553).

After reviewing the voluminous literature on subjective well-being among the elderly, Gubrium and Lynott (1983) concluded that it was time to "rethink life satisfaction" in old age. One of their key concerns was that the dominant measures employed tended to dwell on the earlier years of people's lives and have less relevance for their current circumstances. In addition, "current measures do not allow for co-equal dialogue between subject and researcher about the content of items and responses" (Gubrium and Lynott 1983, p. 37).

Possibly because of these and other conceptual and methodological problems in subjective well-being measures, we have seen a substantial decline in published studies in major journals aiming at predicting life satisfaction, morale, and related concepts during the 1980s. Social gerontologists have instead concentrated on predicting more narrow dimensions of well-being, such as psychological distress and depression, and are increasingly employing a life course perspective that involves examination of main and interactive effects of stress, social support, and related factors (e.g., George 1989). Measures of depression and psychological distress are being employed more frequently, perhaps because they are perceived as more amenable to intervention than are measures of life satisfaction and morale. Other measures of well-being that are more amenable to intervention are various indicators of physical health that are also increasingly being studied from a life course perspective (Markides and Cooper 1989).

Studies of the Quality of Life of Patients

Perhaps the most activity in the area of quality of life is currently found in medicine, much of it conducted by behavioral and social scientists. Interest in QL after medical treatments is based on the realization that chronic diseases cannot be cured, and, therefore, the goal of much therapy becomes to limit the effects of illness so that patients may live productive, comfortable, and satisfying lives. Traditionally, success of medical treatment was evaluated in terms of lengthening lives and post-treatment complications. However, there has been a realization that medical and surgical treatments may extend survival but often reduce quality of life (Eisman 1981).

There has been a realization that medical and surgical treatments may extend survival but often reduce quality of life.

Hollandsworth (1988) reviewed studies evaluating the impact of medical treatment on QL during the period 1980 to 1984 and compared his results with those of studies conducted during 1975 to 1979 (Najman and Levine 1981). Hollandsworth's (1988) comparison revealed a marked increase between the two time periods in both quantity and quality of studies. Although recent studies tended to be more sophisticated, the majority nevertheless relied on convenience samples. One marked improvement in the recent research is the increase in use of subjective measures of quality of life, with 60 percent of the recent studies employing at least one such measure, compared to only around 10 percent in the earlier period.

Another interesting outcome of Hollandsworth's (1988) analysis was the increase over time in the proportion of studies that do not report favorable outcomes. Studies published in the late 1970s were almost unanimous in claiming favorable outcomes of treatment, but this optimism must be tempered by the many methodological limitations of these studies (Najman and Levine 1981). Of the more sophisticated studies published from 1980 to 1984, almost one-half reported either negative outcomes or at least mixed results. In fact, it appeared that the probability of reporting negative outcomes (or lack of positive results) tended to be correlated with the methodological sophistication of the studies (Hollandsworth 1988).

The impact of a variety of medical treatments have been examined, including cardiovascular therapies (e.g., Jenkins et al. 1983; Wenger et al. 1984), end-stage renal disease (e.g., Evans et al. 1985), and chronic obstructive pulmonary disease (e.g., McSweeney et al. 1982). However, by far the most frequently studied area is that relating to outcomes of cancer treatment (see Aaronson 1989; Aaronson and Beckman 1987; Cella and Cherin 1988). Aaronson (1989, p. 69) noted that while "there is no universally accepted definition of the quality of life concept, in oncology it is most often used to describe such aspects of health status as physical symptoms, daily activity level, psychological well-being, and social functioning." This increasing use of subjective QL indicators is becoming an integral part of evaluation in clinical cancer research, but a major challenge facing researchers is the development of measures capturing all dimensions of QL while meeting rigorous standards of reliability and validity (Aaronson 1988).

An overview of the literature on medical treatment outcomes does indeed reveal increasing use of subjective quality of life measures. As in the broader QL field, many studies tend to employ single-item global indicators capturing life satisfaction or happiness. However, an increasing number of studies are employing general multiple-item measures discussed earlier, such as the Affect Balance Scale and the Life Satisfaction Index Z. Other scales capturing more specific and narrow dimensions of QL include measures of mood, anxiety, self-concept, and depression (Hollandsworth 1988) as well as more comprehensive instruments that capture physical, emotional, and social functioning, such as the McMaster Health Index Questionnaire (Chambers et al. 1982).

Conclusion

This brief and selective overview of the field of quality of life indicates a variety of perspectives employed within sociology and related fields. In fact, it may be said that there is more interest in QL outside of the mainstream of sociology, as, for example, in the area of medical treatment. While much of the pioneer work and large-scale national studies in the 1970s were conducted by sociologists, research on quality of life remains very much outside the mainstream of sociology. For example, Schuessler and Fisher's (1985) review uncovered only one article (Gerson 1976) explicitly on quality of life published in the *American Sociological Review* way back in 1976.

This overview also reveals some patterns and trends in QL research in the last three decades. First, there have been two broad approaches, one focusing on objective indicators and one focusing on subjective indicators. Related dichotomies noted by Mukherjee (1989) include quantity versus quality and behavior versus perception. It is clear that there has been a trend away from relying simply on objective indicators to relying increasingly on people's subjective reports about the quality of their lives. Objective measures have been the domain primarily of the social indicators movement, with subjective approaches to QL increasingly perceived as the domain of QL research (Mukherjee 1989).

Within the subjective QL approach, we also see a trend away from single-item indicators capturing global happiness and life satisfaction to multiple-item scales such as the Affect Balance Scale and the Life Satisfaction Index Z. At the same time, there have been attempts to measure subjective quality of life in specific life domains. And, there has been continuing interest by sociologists, economists, and others (including popular magazines) to rank urban areas according to a variety of QL indicators.

During the 1960s and 1970s a great deal of subjective QL research was conducted by social and behavioral gerontologists, who used measures of life satisfaction and morale as indicators of successful aging. For a number of reasons, gerontologists began abandoning research on life satisfaction and morale in favor of measures more amenable to intervention, such as measures of psychological distress, depression, and physical health function. Perhaps the most exciting research on QL currently being conducted is in the area of medical treatment outcomes, particularly cancer treatment.

It is becoming increasingly difficult to obtain funding to conduct large-scale national surveys of subjective quality of life such as those conducted during the 1970s. The future of QL research is uncertain, at least as a broad unified field of inquiry. Studies ranking urban areas are likely to continue, if anything because of the immediate and broad appeal they elicit. It is also safe to predict that the concept of quality of life will continue to have some appeal in social gerontology. The most exciting work may well take place in the area of medical intervention outcomes. Sociologists and other behavioral scientists are increasingly conducting research related to medicine, and much of this research relates to quality of life. It is becoming apparent that medical interventions (as well as other factors) are enabling us to live longer, but it is not clear that the added years of life are "quality" years. There will be increasing interest in finding ways to improve the quality of the added years, and sociologists have an opportunity and responsibility to help find ways of accomplishing that.

[See also Attitudes; Health and Illness Behavior; Mental Health; Social Gerontology.]

BIBLIOGRAPHY

Aaronson, Neil K. 1989 "Quality of Life: What Is It? How Should It Be Measured?" *Oncology* 2:69–74.

———, and J. H. Beckman (eds.) 1987 *The Quality of Life of Cancer Patients.* New York: Raven.

Andrews, Frank M. (ed.) 1986 *Research on the Quality of Life.* Ann Arbor: University of Michigan, Institute for Social Research.

———, and Stephen B. Withey 1976 *Social Indicators of Well-Being: Americans' Perceptions of Life Quality.* New York: Plenum.

Bauer, Raymond A. (ed.) 1966 *Social Indicators.* Cambridge, Mass.: MIT Press.

Berger, Mark C., Glenn C. Blomquist, and Werner Waldner 1987 "A Revealed-Preference Ranking of Quality of Life for Metropolitan Areas." *Social Science Quarterly* 68:761–778.

Bharadwaj, Lakshmi K., and E. A. Wilkening 1980 "Life Domain Satisfactions and Personal Social Integration." *Social Indicators Research* 7:337–351.

Boyer, Rick, and D. Savageau 1981 *Places Rated Almanac.* Chicago: Rand McNally.

Bradburn, Norman 1969 *The Structure of Psychological Well-Being.* Chicago: Aldine.

Campbell, Angus 1981 *The Sense of Well-Being in America: Recent Patterns and Trends.* New York: McGraw-Hill.

———, Phillip Converse, and Willard L. Rogers 1976 *The Quality of American Life: Perceptions, Evaluations, and Satisfactions.* New York: Russell Sage Foundation.

Cantril, Hadley 1965 *The Pattern of Human Concerns.* New Brunswick, N.J.: Rutgers University Press.

Cella, David F., and E. A. Cherin 1988 "Quality of Life during and after Cancer Treatment." *Comprehensive Therapy* 14:69–75.

Chambers, Larry W., Lorry A. MacDonald, Peter Tugwell, W. Watson Buchanan, and Gunnar Kraag 1982 "The McMaster Health Index Questionnaire as a Measure of Quality of Life for Patients with Rheumatoid Disease." *Journal of Rheumatology* 9:780–784.

Cherlin, Andy, and Leo G. Reeder 1975 "The Dimensions of Psychological Well-Being. A Critical Review." *Sociological Methods and Research* 4:189–214.

Cumming, Elaine, and William E. Henry 1961 *Growing Old: The Process of Disengagement.* New York: Basic Books.

Diener, Ed 1984 "Subjective Well-Being." *Psychological Bulletin* 95:542–575.

Eisman, B. 1981 "The Second Dimension." *Archives of Surgery* 116:11–13.

Estes, Richard J. 1984 *The Social Progress of Nations.* New York: Praeger.

——— 1988 *Trends in World Social Development: The Social Progress of Nations. 1970–1987.* New York: Praeger.

Evans, R. W., D. L. Manninen, L. P. Garrison, L. G. Hart, C. R. Blagg, R. A. Gutman, A. R. Hull, and E. G. Lowrie 1985 "The Quality of Life of Patients with End-Stage Renal Disease." *New England Journal of Medicine* 312:553–559.

George, Linda K. 1981 "Subjective Well-Being: Conceptual and Methodological Issues." *Annual Review of Gerontology and Geriatrics* 2:345–382.

——— 1989 "Stress, Social Support, and Depression over the Life Course." In Kyriakos S. Markides and Cary L. Cooper, eds., *Aging, Stress and Health.* Chichester, United Kingdom: Wiley.

Gerson, Elihu M. 1976 "On 'Quality of Life'." *American Sociological Review* 41:793–806.

Gubrium, Jaber F., and Robert J. Lynott 1983 "Rethinking Life Satisfaction." *Human Organization* 42:30–38.

Gurin, Gerald, J. Veroff, and S. Feld 1960 *Americans View Their Mental Health.* New York: Basic Books.

Havighurst, Robert J., Bernice Neugarten, and Sheldon S. Tobin 1968 "Disengagement and Patterns of Aging." In Bernice L. Neugarten, ed., *Middle-Age and Aging.* Chicago: University of Chicago Press.

Hollandsworth, James G. 1988 "Evaluating the Impact of Medical Treatment on the Quality of Life: A Five-Year Update." *Social Science and Medicine* 26:425–434.

Jenkins, C. David, Babette A. Stanton, J. A. Savageau, P. Denlinger, and M. D. Klein 1983 "Coronary Artery Bypass Surgery: Physical, Psychological, Social, and Economic Outcomes of Six Months Later." *Journal of the American Medical Association* 250:782–88.

Land, Kenneth C. 1971 "On the Definition of Social Indicators." *American Sociologist* 6:322–325.

——— 1983 "Social Indicators." *Annual Review of Sociology* 9:1–26.

Larson, Reed 1978 "Thirty Years of Research on Subjective Well-Being of Older Americans." *Journal of Gerontology* 33:109–125.

Lawton, M. Powell 1972 "The Dimensions of Morale." In Donald Kent, Robert Kastenbaum, and Sylvia Sherwood, eds., *Research, Planning, and Action for the Elderly.* New York: Behavioral Publications.

——— 1975 "The Philadelphia Geriatric Center Morale Scale: A Revision." *Journal of Gerontology* 30:85–89.

——— 1983 "The Varieties of Well-Being." *Experimental Aging Research* 9:65–72.

Liang, Jersey 1985 "A Structural Integration of the Affect Balance Scale and the Life Satisfaction Index A." *Journal of Gerontology* 40:552–561.

Liu, Ben-Cheih 1976 *Quality of Life Indicators in U.S. Metropolitan Areas.* New York: Praeger.

Lohman, Nancy 1977 "Correlations of Life Satisfaction, Morale, and Adjustment Measures." *Journal of Gerontology* 32:73–75.

McSweeney, A. J., I. Grant, R. K. Heaton, K. Adams, and R. M. Timms 1982 "Life Quality of Patients with Chronic Obstructive Pulmonary Disease." *Archives of Internal Medicine* 142:473–478.

Maddox, George L. 1968 "Persistence of Life Styles among the Elderly: A Longitudinal Study of Patterns of Social Activity in Relation to Life Satisfaction." In Bernice L. Neugarten, ed., *Middle-Age and Aging.* Chicago: University of Chicago Press.

——— 1970 "Themes and Issues in Sociological Theories of Aging." *Human Development* 13:17–27.

Markides, Kyriakos S. 1989 "Aging, Gender, Race/Ethnicity, Class, and Health: A Conceptual Overview." In K. S. Markides, ed., *Aging and Health: Perspectives on Gender, Race, Ethnicity, and Class.* Newbury Park, Calif.: Sage.

———, and Cary L. Cooper (eds.) 1989 *Aging, Stress, and Health.* Chichester, United Kingdom: Wiley.

Michalos, Alex C. 1974 "Strategies for Reducing Information Overload in Social Reports." *Social Indicators Research* 8:385–422.

Milbrath, L. W. 1978 "Indicators of Environmental Quality." In UNESCO, ed., *Indicators of Environmental Quality and Quality of Life.* UNESCO Reports and Papers in the Social Sciences, No. 38. Paris: UNESCO.

Morris, David M. 1977 "A Physical Quality of Life Index (PQLI)." In J. W. Sewell, ed., *The United States and the World Development Agenda 1977.* New York: Praeger.

Mukherjee, Ramkrishna 1989 *The Quality of Life Valuation in Social Research.* New Delhi: Sage Publications.

Najman, J. M., and Sol Levine 1981 "Evaluating the Impact of Medical Care and Technologies on the Quality of Life: A Review and Critique." *Social Science and Medicine* 15(F):107–115.

Neugarten, Bernice L., Robert J. Havighurst, and Sheldon S. Tobin 1961 "The Measurement of Life Satisfaction." *Journal of Gerontology* 16:134–143.

Rockwell, R. C. 1989 Review of *Research on Quality of Life,* ed. F. M. Andrews. In *Social Forces* 67:824–826.

Rosen, Sherwin 1979 "Wage-Based Indexes of Urban Quality of Life." In Peter Mieszkowski and Mahlon Straszheim, eds., *Current Issues in Urban Economics.* Baltimore: Johns Hopkins University Press.

Schuessler, Karl F., and G. A. Fisher 1985 "Quality of Life Research in Sociology." *Annual Reviews of Sociology* 11:129–149.

Smith, David M. 1972 "Towards a Geography of Social Well-Being: Inter-State Variations in the United States." *Antipode Monographs in Social Geography* 1:17–46.

Stewart, Anita L., S. Greenfield, R. D. Hays, K. Wells, W. H. Rogers, S. D. Berry, E. A. McGlynn, and J. E. Ware 1989 "Functional Status and Well-Being of Patients with Chronic Conditions: Results from the Medical Outcomes Study." *Journal of the American Medical Association* 262:907–913.

Stull, Donald E. 1987 "Conceptualization and Measurement of Well-Being: Implications for Policy Evaluation." In Edgar F. Borgatta and Rhonda J. V. Montgomery, eds., *Critical Issues in Aging Policy.* Newbury Park, Calif.: Sage.

Tarlov, Alvin R., J. E. Ware, S. Greenfield, E. C. Nelson, E. Perrin, and M. Zubkoff 1989 "The Medical Outcomes Study: An Application for Monitoring the Results of Medical Care." *Journal of the American Medical Association* 262:925–930.

U.S. Department of Health, Education, and Welfare 1969 *Toward a Social Report.* Washington, D.C.: U.S. Government Printing Office.

Wells, Kenneth B., A. Stewart, R. D. Hays, M. A. Burnam, W. Rogers, M. Daniels, S. Greenfield, and J. Ware 1989 "The Functioning and Well-Being of Depressed Patients." *Journal of the American Medical Association* 262:914–919.

Wenger, Nanette K., Margaret E. Mattson, Curt D. Furberg, and Jack Elinson (eds.) 1984 *Assessment of Quality of Life in Clinical Trials of Cardiovascular Therapies.* New York: Le Jacq Publishing.

Wilson, John O. 1967 *Quality of Life in the United States: An Excursion into the New Frontier of Socioeconomic Indicators.* Kansas City, Mo.: Midwest Research Institute.

Wilson, Warner 1967 "Correlates of Avowed Happiness." *Psychological Bulletin* 67:294–306.

– KYRIAKOS S. MARKIDES

R

RACE

The study of race and race relations has long been a central concern of sociologists. The assignment of individuals to racial categories profoundly affects the quality and even the length of their lives. These assignments are ostensibly made on the basis of biological criteria, such as skin color, hair texture, and facial features. Yet the biological meaning of race is so unclear that some social scientists argue that *race,* as a biological phenomenon, does not exist. Others take the less extreme position that while different races exist, extensive interbreeding in many societies has produced large numbers of people of mixed ancestry. The assignment of these people to racial categories depends on social, rather than on biological, criteria. Thus the social consequences of biologically inherited traits is the fundamental issue of the sociological study of race.

Biological Conceptions of Race

While the terms *race* and *ethnicity* are often used interchangeably, it is more precise to see race as a special case of ethnicity (van den Berghe 1981). *Ethnic groups* are extended kinship groups; that is, membership in an ethnic group is based on common ancestry. Members of ethnic groups also share a common culture: language, religion, and styles of dress and cooking are cultural markers that identify individuals as members of a given ethnic group. Furthermore, members of ethnic groups generally marry within their group, a practice known as endogamy, which tends to preserve the distinctiveness of the group and prevents its assimilation into other groups. Finally, shared ancestry and cultural heritage produce a sense of solidarity among ethnic group members; they identify themselves as members of the group and are so identified by others.

Endogamy tends to preserve the distinctiveness of the group and prevents its assimilation into other groups.

For most of human history, ethnic groups living in close proximity did not differ significantly in physical appearance. Thus the observable biological differences associated with race were not used as ethnic markers, and interracial antagonisms were unknown. The rapid, long-distance migration required to bring members of different racial groups together is a comparatively recent phenomenon that was accelerated by trade and the large-scale European exploration and colonial expansion of the sixteenth through the nineteenth centuries (van den Berghe 1981). It was also during this period that Western science assumed a central role in the attempt to understand the natural and social worlds. Thus, as Europeans became aware of peoples who differed from them in culture and appearance, the concept of race entered the popular and scientific vocabularies as a means of classifying previously unknown groups.

Not content merely to classify people into racial groups, nineteenth- and early twentieth-century scientists attempted to uncover differences between groups. Darwin's theory of evolution, which holds that species are engaged in a struggle for existence in which only the fittest will survive, was gaining widespread acceptance during this period. Herbert Spencer, William Graham Sumner, and other early social theorists extended this evolutionary argument, suggesting that different social groups, including races, were at different stages of evolution; the more advanced groups were destined to dominate groups less "fit." This idea, called social Darwinism (which Darwin himself did not support), provided justification for imperialism by the British and others, and for America's treatment of its racial minorities.

Building on the notion that some races were at a more-advanced stage of evolution than others, a number of scientists tried to measure differences between the races, especially in the area of intelligence. The first intelligence test was developed by Alfred Binet and Theodore Simon in 1905. Modified versions of this test were administered to approximately one million American soldiers in World War I, and the results were used to argue that there were large, genetically determined differences in intelligence between blacks and whites. Such a conclusion implied that blacks could not benefit from education to the extent that whites could; these findings were then used as a justification for the inferior education made available to blacks.

Binet himself rejected the notion that intelligence was a fixed quantity determined by heredity, or that intelligence could be measured with the kind of precision claimed by other intelligence testers, especially in the United States. Furthermore, other scholars demonstrated that the tests were heavily biased against members of certain ethnic, class, and cultural groups, including blacks. While the *average* scores of blacks have tended to fall below the average scores of whites, greater variation occurs within each group than between the two groups; that is, many blacks outscore many whites. Since these tests measure academic achievement and middle-class cultural knowledge, rather than potential, the impoverished backgrounds and substandard educations of some blacks offer reasonable explanations for their lower average scores. Research has repeatedly failed to demonstrate that racial groups differ in terms of their innate capacity for learning. Today, therefore, the vast majority of social scientists reject the idea that any one race is superior in intelligence or any other ability, at least to the extent that such abilities are determined by heredity. (For an interesting account of the race-intelligence controversy, see Gould 1981; Montagu 1975.)

Controversy continues however on the subject of race itself. In the nineteenth century the concept was defined quite loosely, and the idea was widely held that people of similar appearance but different nationalities constituted different races. As recently as World War II it was not uncommon to hear people speak of the "British race," the "Jewish race," and so on. Some physical anthropologists narrowed the concept to include three main groups: the Negroid, Caucasoid, and Mongoloid races. Others argue that human populations have always exhibited some degree of interbreeding; that this has greatly increased during the last few centuries, producing large groups of people who defy such racial classification. "Pure races" have probably never existed, and certainly do not exist now. According to this argument, race is a cultural myth, a label that has no biological

The racial categories of white, black, and Hispanic have been commonly used. However, the biological grounds for these categories have become less clear as the study of genetics has progressed. Some scientists have asserted that race as a biological phenomenon does not exist. (Owen Franken/ Corbis)

basis but is attached to groups in order to buttress invidious social distinctions (Lieberman 1975).

Social Conceptions of Race

Two conclusions may be drawn from the above discussion of biological conceptions of race. First, if one follows common practice and assigns individuals to one of three main "racial" groups, no evidence exists that those groups differ in the distribution of intelligence or other innate abilities. Second, the biological meaning of race, and racial categorization, is unclear. Human beings can be classified in any number of ways, according to shoe size, forearm length, and so on, ad infinitum. While race may be of little or no biological significance, it does have tremendous social significance. Racial distinctions are meaningful because we *attach* meaning to them, and the consequences vary from prejudice and discrimination to slavery and genocide.

Since people believe that racial differences are significant, and behave accordingly, those differences become significant. Hitler, for example, believed that Jews constituted a distinct and inferior race, and the consequences of his belief were very real for millions of Jews. Thus the major questions confronting sociologists who study race relations concern the social consequences of racial categorization. To what degree are different racial and ethnic groups incorporated into the larger society? How can we account for variations in the economic, political, legal, and social statuses of different groups?

American sociologists have found their own society to be a natural laboratory for the study of these issues. The United States has a wide variety of racial and ethnic groups, and some of these have fitted more successfully into American society than have others. Within any group there is substantial variation in economic achievement; still, considered as groups, Jews and Japanese have been more successful in America than have blacks and Mexicans. One explanation for these differences that has found some acceptance both within and outside scientific circles is that the cultures and values of these groups differ. Some groups' values are believed to be more conducive to success than others. Jews, for example, have traditionally valued scholarship and business acumen; as a result they have worked hard in the face of discrimination, educated their children, and pulled themselves up from poverty. African Americans, by contrast, allegedly lacked these values; the result is their continued concentration in the poor and working classes.

Most sociologists reject this argument, which Stephen Steinberg (1981) refers to as the "ethnic myth." Steinberg argues that this line of reasoning is simply a new form of social Darwinism, in which the fittest *cultures* survive. A closer look at the experiences of immigrants in America (including African Americans) reveals that not all immigrant groups start at the bottom; some groups arrive with the skills necessary to compete in the American labor market while others do not. Furthermore, the skills possessed by some groups are in high demand in the United States, while other groups find fewer opportunities. Thus Steinberg argues that the success of an immigrant group depends on the occupational structure of its country of origin, the group's place in that structure, and the occupational structure of the new country.

Steinberg uses the case of American Jews to support his argument. In terms of education, occupation, and income, Jews have been highly successful. In 1971, 36 percent of the adult Jewish population had graduated from college, compared with 11 percent of non-Jews. Seventy percent of Jews were in business or the professions, compared with roughly a third of non-Jews. The median family income of Jews in 1971 was fourteen thousand dollars, approximately 30 percent more than the average American family. It is possible to overstate Jewish success, since many Jews are still poor or working-class; middle-class Jews are concentrated in small business and the professions and are nearly absent from corporate hierarchies. Furthermore, Jews have experienced a great deal of economic and social discrimination. Nevertheless, compared with other ethnic and racial groups in America, they have been quite successful.

This success, Steinberg argues, is attributable in part to the origins of Jewish immigrants, most of whom came from Russia and Eastern Europe, and arrived in the United States in the late nineteenth and early twentieth centuries. Since Jews in Eastern Europe could not own land, they tended to live in cities; even those who lived in rural areas were mostly merchants and traders, rather than farmers. The urban concentration and above-average literacy rates of Jews affected their occupational distribution: in 1897, 70 percent of Russian Jews worked as artisans or in manufacturing or commerce; even unskilled Jews worked in industrial occupations. Of the immigrants who arrived in America between 1899 and 1910, 67 percent of Jews were skilled workers, compared with 49 percent of English immigrants, 15 percent of Italians, and 6 percent of Poles.

Furthermore, Jewish immigrants were disproportionately represented in the garment industry, which was growing at two to three times the rate of other American industries. Jobs in the garment industry were better paid than other industrial jobs, and Jews, with their higher skill level, tended to have the better-paid jobs within the industry. The garment industry also offered unusual opportunities for individual entrepreneurship, since little capital was required to start a small clothing business.

In sum, Jewish immigrants did well in America because they brought industrial skills to an industrializing country. Although the majority of Jewish immigrants arrived with little money and encountered widespread discrimination, American industry could not afford to exclude them completely. Steinberg concludes that while a case can be made that Jews have traditionally valued educational and occupational achievement, and that this contributed to their success, Jews do not hold a monopoly on these values. Furthermore, if they had encountered an occupational structure that offered no hope for the fulfillment of these aspirations, Jews would have scaled their goals down accordingly.

Jewish immigrants did well in America because they brought industrial skills to an industrializing country.

The inability of other racial and ethnic groups to match the success achieved by Jewish Americans has also been attributed to the cultures and values of those groups. Glazer and Moynihan (1970), for example, blame the persistent poverty of blacks on "the home and family and community . . . It is there that the heritage of two hundred years of slavery and a hundred years of discrimination is concentrated; and it is there that we find the serious obstacles to the ability to make use of a free educational system to advance into higher occupations and to eliminate the massive social problems that afflict colored Americans and the city" (pp. 49, 50). Yet, as Gutman (1976) has shown, the black family emerged from slavery relatively strong and began to exhibit signs of instability only when blacks became concentrated in urban ghettos. Furthermore, for generations after emancipation, blacks faced extreme educational and employment discrimination; the notion that a free educational system provided a smooth path to the higher occupations is simply inconsistent with blacks' experience in America.

Most sociologists tend, like Steinberg, to locate the cause of blacks' poverty relative to white immigrant groups in the structure of opportunity that awaited them after slavery. The South was an economically backward region where blacks remained tied to the land and subject to conditions that were in many cases worse than those they had known under slavery. The vast majority of white immigrants settled in the North, where industry provided jobs and taxpaying workers provided schools. The more agricultural South had fewer educational opportunities to offer blacks or whites. Immediately after the Civil War, when they were provided access to education, blacks flocked to southern schools. This opportunity was short-lived, however, since the scarcity of educational resources made it advantageous for whites to appropriate the blacks' share for themselves, a temptation they did not resist.

By the time large numbers of blacks migrated north, the period of industrial expansion that had provided so many jobs for immigrants was drawing to a close. Moreover, the newly freed slaves did not have industrial skills and were barred from industrial occupations. Given the generations of social, economic, political, and legal discrimination that followed, and the fact that blacks did take advantage of the opportunities that presented themselves, it is unnecessary to call on "inferior values" to explain the difference in achievement between American blacks and white immigrants to the United States. (For a historical account of the struggle of blacks in the postbellum South and North, as well as that of nonwhites in South Africa, see Frederickson 1981; for a comparison of the conditions faced by U.S. blacks and white immigrants, and the effects of these differences on each group's success, see Lieberson 1980.)

Conclusions

Ever since Darwin proposed that the evolutionary process of natural selection ensures that only the fittest species survive, social science has been bedeviled by the notion that some human groups, especially races, are more biologically or culturally fit than others. This extension of Darwin's principle to competition for survival *within* the human species, especially when applied to modern industrial societies, cannot withstand close scrutiny. While differences in pigmentation, the distribution of body fat, height, and so on, may have been important earlier in human history they are hardly relevant in today's school or workplace.

Furthermore, cultural differences between groups can be identified, and these differences may have economic consequences, but they are more likely to reflect a group's historical experiences than the value its members attach to economic success. Thus, the current trend in sociology is to explain differences in the success of racial and ethnic groups in terms of the economic and political resources possessed by those groups, and by the groups with whom they are in competition and conflict.

One reason for the longevity of the biological and cultural forms of social Darwinism may be that for many years most natural and social scientists have been white, and middle-class to upper-class. While the objective search for truth is the goal of the scientific enterprise, race is an emotionally and ideologically loaded concept, and even the most sincere humanitarians have been led to faulty conclusions by their own biases. The greatest prospect for the advancement of the scientific study of race, then, is the recruitment of new scholars with a wide diversity of backgrounds, from both within and outside the United States. This increasing diversity will ensure that the exchange of ideas so necessary to scientific inquiry will be more balanced and less subject to bias than it has been in the past.

[See also Ethnicity; Intelligence.]

BIBLIOGRAPHY

Frederickson, George M. 1981 *White Supremacy.* New York: Oxford University Press.

Glazer, Nathan, and Daniel Patrick Moynihan 1970 *Beyond the Melting Pot.* Cambridge, Mass. MIT Press.

Gould, Stephen Jay 1981 *The Mismeasure of Man.* New York: Norton.

Gutman, Herbert 1976 *The Black Family in Slavery and Freedom.* New York: Pantheon.

Lieberman, Leonard 1975 "The Debate over Race: A Study in the Sociology of Knowledge." In Ashley Montagu, ed., *Race and IQ.* New York: Oxford University Press.

Lieberson, Stanley 1980 *A Piece of the Pie: Blacks and White Immigrants Since 1880.* Berkeley: University of California Press.

Montagu, Ashley (ed.) 1975 *Race and IQ.* New York: Oxford University Press.

Steinberg, Stephen 1981 *The Ethnic Myth.* New York: Atheneum.

van den Berghe, Pierre L. 1981 *The Ethnic Phenomenon.* New York: Praeger.

– SUSAN R. PITCHFORD

RELIGION, POLITICS, AND WAR

The outcome and settlement of World War II made the independent sovereign nation-state the dominant system of action for managing and governing populations (Nettl and Robertson 1968; Meyer 1980). The most important factors affecting the likelihood that religion has a role in the political affairs of a nation-state are: (1) the religious traditions that are present in a nation-state's population and (2) a nation-state's institutional and social organization.

The symbols, myths, and ideology of a religious tradition are a cultural resource that may affect politics. Whether a religious tradition has the capacity to affect politics depends on the ethical and doctrinal components of its symbols, myths, and ideology. Ethics and doctrines vary in terms of orientation to the affairs of the everyday world, the extent to which adherents are expected to express their beliefs in the practical affairs of a society, and whether claims are made on politically controlled social and economic resources. Differences on those dimensions determine the likelihood that a religious tradition encourages political action. For example, within Protestant Christian traditions in the United States, Pentecostals emphasize individual religious experience and behavior, while many mainline denominations tend to stress social action and reform (Roof and McKinney 1987; Poloma 1989). Pentecostals are less likely to be involved in politics than members of mainline Protestant denominations. Some religious traditions (for example, Theravada Buddhism) value withdrawal from the everyday world as a path to enlightenment and salvation (Gombrich 1988). Others, such as Calvinistic Protestantism, stress the methodical performance of ordinary tasks and jobs (including political roles) as a religious duty and calling (Poggi 1983). Adherents of world-rejecting traditions are less likely to be involved in politics than followers of world-affirming traditions.

Claims on the resources of a society are a major focus of political action. By rejecting in principle the authority of any state and, thereby, the mechanisms of resource distribution that are embedded in governments, some religious traditions exclude themselves from ordinary politics. Jehovah's Witnesses fit into this category (Stroup 1945). On the other hand, subject to constitutional and other constraints that may be imposed by national regimes, the Roman Catholic Church has an interest in obtaining resources that are distributed through state action, thereby implicating itself in politics.

Whether religion becomes a force in the internal factional politics of a nation-state depends in part upon the extent of religious diversity in a population in addition to predisposing ethical or doctrinal factors. Religious diversity alone, however, is seldom a direct cause of political action and conflict. Religion in combination with other properties of a nation-state's population provides a basis for politics that can be affected by religious differences. Those properties include differences in language, race, patterns of settlement, and class. Religiously inspired political tension and conflict can occur where religious differences are correlated with differences in language and other social characteristics (Eversley 1989). If religious differences are only weakly related to other significant divisions in a population, it is unlikely that religion will be implicated in the internal politics of a nation-state (cf. Lipset 1960).

Secular ideological alternatives to religion—communism, for example—can also be a basis for population diversity and political conflict (O'Toole 1977). Major intranational conflicts in the twentieth century that pitted secular and religious forces or their representatives against one another include the Spanish Civil

War (1936–1939) and the movement to democratize Poland at the end of the cold war. Controversies over abortion, censorship, and sexual orientation frequently involve clashes between the adherents of secular and religious ideologies (Simpson 1983; Luker 1984).

Variation in the religious characteristics of populations and their relationships with language, race, class, and patterns of settlement provide clues regarding the likelihood that a population's capacity for religiously based politics will be manifested in action. A population's characteristics that enhance or discourage a tie between religion and politics, however, should always be considered in the context of the institutional and social organization of nation-states. Institutional and social organization influence the likelihood that population characteristics that enhance or inhibit religiously based politics will be expressed in action.

Economic, political, and cultural spheres of action including religion constitute the institutional sectors of the nation-state. Nation-states vary according to the extent to which their institutional sectors are intertwined or stand as differentiated and autonomous sources of action (cf. Luhmann 1982). Those differences affect the forms that religiously based conflict and politics may take.

The relationship between the religious and the political institutions of a nation-state can be classified in terms of three models: (1) the theocratic/caesaropapist model; (2) the two-powers model; (3) the strict-separation model. The theocratic/caesaropapist model assumes an identity of interests and an interpretive unity in religious and political fields of action. At the limit no distinction is made between religious and political or military acts. Politics is an explicit expression of the divine will, and war is holy. Supreme authority in both religious and political matters lies in either a lay ruler (caesaropapism) or clergy, priests, or other religious officials (theocracy).

Historically, caesaropapism is identified with the Christian rulers of the Roman Empire (313–395) and the Byzantine Empire (330–1453; Walker 1959). Today, theocracy is best exemplified within Islam, whose founder, Muhammad (570–632), was both the secular and religious leader of his followers. His cultural legacy, normative Islam, makes no distinction, in principle, between the political and religious institutions of a society (Cragg and Speight 1988). The Republic of Iran is a contemporary example of a theocracy where Islamic law and ethics are established and public officials tend to be religiously qualified persons (Akhavi 1986).

While the theocratic/caesaropapist model is usually found where a single religious ideology dominates, the form of the model may also apply in the case of dominant secular ideologies. Thus, under communism as advocated by Lenin, no distinction was made between a political and an ideological ("religious") act. Positions of power were occupied by Communist party members, and, in principle, there were no ideological differences across the institutional sectors of a society or between those in responsible positions. One had to be ideologically qualified in order to occupy an office (Tucker 1975).

Unlike theocracy or caesaropapism, the two-powers model assumes the differentiation of religious and political action and the distinct authority of both secular rulers and religious functionaries in their respective domains of action. The origin of the model can be traced to the exile of the ancient Hebrews in Babylon following the conquest of the Kingdom of Judah in the sixth century B.C. (Zeitlin 1984). There, under foreign domination, religious observance was adapted and elaborated without the support of a Hebrew state and in the absence of worship in the Temple. The idea that religion could be independent of protective state power entered history. Following a strand of its Hebrew roots, early Christianity recognized the authority of the state while asserting the autonomy of its own spiritual sphere of action, a notion summed up in the saying attributed to Jesus: "Render therefore to Caesar the things that are Caesar's and to God the things that are God's." Although Christianity became the official religion of the Roman Empire in the fourth century under Constantine the Great, the Western Christian notion of separate spiritual and temporal realms of power expressed in distinct but complementary organizational milieux persisted and proved to be a basis for accommodation and conflict throughout European history (Walker 1959).

Under the two-powers model the religious and political spheres have separate and, in principle, equal standing in a society. A common arrangement is church establishment where the state recognizes the preeminence of a particular religious tradition and grants a religious monopoly and material support in return for the recognition of its authority and legitimacy by the established religion. In that circumstance jurisdictional conflicts over control of resources and authority can arise. Where the state enforces a religious monopoly, religiously based conflict and politics are likely to involve matters related to dissent from the established religion.

In contrast to both the theocratic/caesaropapist and two-powers models, the model of strict separation eliminates all ties between religious and political institutions. The model can be traced to the Anabaptist movement in sixteenth-century Europe, which viewed the church as a community of the redeemed and the state as an institution with no competence in matters of faith and conscience (Littel 1958). Church and state operate with distinct and different interpretive modes and logics and do not exchange resources. Religious adherence is voluntary, and legal barriers may be erected to prevent one sector from intruding on the other. Where the strict-separation model holds, religious belief and practice may become a private, individual matter without reference to arenas of public action (Luckmann 1967; Neuhaus 1984). In that circumstance religiously inspired politics is likely to involve conflict over church-state boundaries and safeguards that protect religious freedom.

In modernized nation-states elements from the three models may be mixed together. Thus, features of both the two-powers and strict-separation models are found in Western nation-states where an established church exists—Sweden and the United Kingdom, for example—and the voluntary principle of membership is recognized through official toleration of all religions (Martin 1978). No effective limitations are placed on religious freedom. Modern Japan combines elements of a modified theocratic/caesaropapist model with the strict-separation model. Although he is no longer revered as a divine ruler, the emperor of Japan is honored as the symbolically dominant spirit of the nation in a society where eclectic patterns of religious observance are not unusual and no formal or legal constraints are placed on religious practice (Kitagawa 1987).

The institutional arrangements in a nation-state underwrite preferred modes of patterned action. Those arrangements receive empirical specificity in social organization where action is realized. The state-society relationship is the most important social feature affecting the form and expression of religion in the public arena.

While nation-states are formally similar (all are units with sovereign territorial jurisdiction and a governing apparatus), there is considerable variation in the state-society relationship. Civil society—a sector of public

Emperor Hirohito (right) fulfilled his role as the symbolically dominant spirit of Japan in greeting President Ronald Reagan (left) when Reagan visited Japan. (Wally McNamee/Corbis)

action separate from the domains of the state and the church—developed in the West in the eighteenth century (Poggi 1978). The extent to which civil society is a source of authoritative action, however, is not uniform across nation-states (Swanson 1967; 1971).

Where private interests have no public significance or legitimacy or are proscribed as a basis for action, the state does not (or will not) factor those interests into its actions. The one-party states of Eastern Europe that arose in the aftermath of World War II exemplified that pattern. All public actions were, in principle, the actions of agents of the state, and no public legitimacy was accorded actions not explicitly defined by the state as legitimate. In Poland, Czechoslovakia, and Hungary the Roman Catholic church played an important role in democratizing those countries by supporting and promoting the emergence of civil society as a source of action and meaning independent of the state (Michel 1990).

In the United States, religious interest groups enter the arena of party politics on an ad hoc basis.

Where civil society is a source of authoritative action, organized private interests can penetrate the state. The party politics of stable Western democracies exemplify that pattern. Religious interests may be expressed in the normal course of politics (Clark 1945). If religious differences are highly correlated with other differences in a population, such as language, patterns of settlement, and so forth, it is likely that religiously based political parties will be among those contesting the right to govern a nation-state, as in the Netherlands and Switzerland (McRae 1974). If religious differences are not highly correlated with many other significant cleavages in a population, then major national political parties will not be organized around religious traditions. The United States is a case in point. There, religious interest groups enter the arena of party politics on an ad hoc basis, but the major parties are not organized around religious or well-defined and articulated ideological traditions as some parties are, for example, in Germany (Martin 1978).

While religion may affect the internal politics of nation-states under the conditions outlined above, it is also the case that religion can be implicated in conflicts between nation-states or between nationalities within states. Such conflicts now occur in a world made into a single place by technological, economic, and social developments (Meyer 1980; Wallerstein 1983; Robertson and Chirico 1985). Increasingly, what is done in one locale can have significant effects on what happens elsewhere in the world within a short time span and despite great geographic distances, national boundaries, and differences in language, culture, local political traditions, and economic development. In that circumstance, communications media construct a global arena of events where the identities of nation-states and nationalities are at stake.

In the global arena religion may be an ingredient in the formation and projection of a national identity. Some nations project an identity that is founded on religion, for example, Iran. In other cases, groups or movements may seek to redefine the image of a nation-state in terms of a religious or ideological tradition (Liebman and Wuthnow 1983; Liebman and Don-Yehiya 1984). Some nation-states project an explicitly secular image (France) or an atheistic image (Albania).

The images that nations or contending groups within nations project into the global arena either coincide or are in conflict with an emergent set of global cultural norms that have a structural base in various transnational cultural, scientific, and educational organizations and in such bodies as the United Nations. Global cultural norms include: (1) respect for the principle of national sovereignty and self-determination; (2) respect for human rights; (3) adherence to the notion that the nation-state should be progressive in its orientation to its citizens and underwrite and promote their economic and social welfare; (4) respect for the environment; (5) the recognition of science as the universal mode of knowledge construction (Thomas and Meyer 1984).

The norms of global culture are invoked in the arena of global events, where they may be reinforced or contradicted and opposed by religious groups following the doctrines and ethics of their traditions. If nation-states or nationalities project and defend an image based on religious absolutes, conflict with the norms of global culture and other religious traditions is inevitable. Whether such conflicts rise to the level of armed aggression between nation-states or groups within nation-states depends on many contingencies including the economic, political, and military capacity to wage war in a given circumstance. Whatever the case, the potency of religion as a factor in national identity formation underscores its importance as one enduring source of conflict in the global arena (Swatos 1989).

[See also Sociology of Religion; War.]

BIBLIOGRAPHY

Akhavi, Shahrough 1986 "State Formation and Consolidation in Twentieth-Century Iran: The Reza Shah Period and the Islamic Republic." In A. Banuazizi and M. Weiner, eds., *The State, Reli-*

gion, and Ethnic Politics: Afghanistan, Iran, and Pakistan.* Syracuse, N.Y.: Syracuse University Press.

Clark, S. D. 1945 "The Religious Sect in Canadian Politics." *American Journal of Sociology* 51:207–216.

Cragg, Kenneth, and R. Marston Speight 1988 *The House of Islam.* Belmont, Calif.: Wadsworth.

Eversley, David 1989 *Religion and Employment in Northern Ireland.* London: Sage Publications.

Gombrich, Richard F. 1988 *Theravada Buddhism.* London: Routledge Chapman Hall.

Kitagawa, Joseph M. 1987 *On Understanding Japanese Religion.* Princeton, N.J.: Princeton University Press.

Liebman, Charles S., and Eliezer Don-Yehiya 1984 *Religion and Politics in Israel.* Bloomington: Indiana University Press.

Liebman, Robert C., and Robert Wuthnow 1983 *The New Christian Right.* New York: Aldine.

Lipset, Seymour Martin 1960 *Political Man.* Garden City, N.Y.: Doubleday.

Littel, Franklin H. 1958 *The Anabaptist View of the Church.* Boston: Starr King Press.

Luckmann, Thomas 1967 *The Invisible Religion.* London: Macmillan.

Luhmann, Niklas 1982 *The Differentiation of Society.* New York: Columbia University Press.

Luker, Kristin 1984 *Abortion and the Politics of Motherhood.* Berkeley: University of California Press.

Martin, David 1978 *A General Theory of Secularization.* New York: Harper and Row.

McRae, Kenneth D. (ed.) 1974 *Consociational Democracy.* Toronto: McClelland and Stewart.

Meyer, John W. 1980 "The World Polity and the Authority of the Nation-State." In A. J. Bergesen, ed., *Studies of the Modern World-System.* New York: Academic Press.

Michel, Patrick 1990 *Politics and Religion in Eastern Europe.* Cambridge, England: Polity Press.

Nettl, J. P., and Roland Robertson 1968 *International Systems and the Modernization of Societies.* New York: Basic Books.

Neuhaus, Richard John 1984 *The Naked Public Square: Religion and Democracy in America.* Grand Rapids, Mich.: Eerdmans.

O'Toole, Roger 1977 *The Precipitous Path.* Toronto: Martin.

Poggi, Gianfranco 1978 *The Development of the Modern State.* Stanford, Calif.: Stanford University Press.

——— 1983 *Calvinism and the Capitalist Spirit.* Amherst: University of Massachusetts Press.

Poloma, Margaret M. 1989 *The Assemblies of God at the Crossroads.* Knoxville: University of Tennessee Press.

Robertson, Roland, and JoAnn Chirico 1985 "Humanity, Globalization, and Worldwide Religious Resurgence." *Sociological Analysis* 46:219–242.

Roof, Wade Clark, and William McKinney 1987 *American Mainline Religion.* New Brunswick, N.J.: Rutgers University Press.

Simpson, John H. 1983 "Moral Issues and Status Politics." In Robert C. Liebman and Robert Wuthnow, eds., *The New Christian Right.* New York: Aldine.

Stroup, Herbert H. 1945 *The Jehovah's Witnesses.* New York: Columbia University Press.

Swanson, Guy E. 1967 *Religion and Regime.* Ann Arbor: University of Michigan Press.

——— 1971 "An Organizational Analysis of Collectivities." *American Sociological Review* 36:607–623.

Swatos, William H., Jr. (ed.) 1989 *Religious Politics in Global and Comparative Perspective.* Westport, Conn.: Greenwood Press.

Thomas, George M., and John W. Meyer 1984 "The Expansion of the State." In R. H. Turner and J. F. Short, Jr., eds., *Annual Review of Sociology.* Vol. 10. Palo Alto, Calif.: Annual Reviews.

Tucker, Robert, ed. 1975 *The Lenin Anthology.* New York: W. W. Norton.

Walker, Williston 1959 *A History of the Christian Church.* New York: Charles Scribner's Sons.

Wallerstein, Immanuel 1983 *Historical Capitalism.* London: Verso.

Zeitlin, Irving M. 1984 *Ancient Judaism.* Cambridge, England: Polity Press.

— JOHN H. SIMPSON

RELIGIOUS FUNDAMENTALISM

Fundamentalism has four distinct meanings. These different meanings are often intermingled in both mass media and scholarly usage, with the result of considerable confusion and misunderstanding of the phenomenon. Significant theological (Barr 1977; Sandeen 1970) and historical (Marsden 1980) literatures are available on fundamentalism, but neither a theoretical nor an empirical sociological literature is well developed. This article identifies the four distinct meanings of fundamentalism, locates each in historical context, and then concludes with a brief discussion of the utility of the concept for comparative sociological research.

First, fundamentalism refers to a Christian *theological* movement that experienced its greatest strength in the first quarter of the twentieth century; it was concerned with defending the faith against an internal movement seeking to make changes to accommodate Protestant Christianity to the modern world. As a theological movement, fundamentalism sought to purge the teachings of "modernism" from churches and theological schools. Modernist teachings emerged during the late nineteenth century as a means of accommodating Christian doctrine to the evidence and teachings of science (Hutchinson 1976).

The most basic teaching of fundamentalism is that the scriptures are inerrant—that is, literally true (Scofield 1945). Closely related is the doctrine of *millenarianism,* which prophesies the imminent return of Christ. In the early days of the fundamentalist movement, these theological battles were waged in the leading theological seminaries of the nation (e.g., Princeton Theological Seminary).

An important development in this struggle was the publication, between 1910 and 1915, of a series of twelve books that sought to defend and reaffirm "fundamental" Christian principles in the face of the teachings of liberal scholars who did not believe that the Bible should be understood as literal truth. Leading scholars from the United States and England contributed articles to the books, titled *The Fundamentals.* Published by two wealthy Christian brothers, Lyman and Milton Steward, *The Fundamentals* were distributed gratis to over a quarter-million clergy, seminary students, and teachers throughout the United States. These tracts provided the inspiration for the name of the movement, but the term *fundamentalism* was not coined until 1920 by a Baptist newspaper editor, Curtis Lee Laws (Marsden 1980, p. 159).

Defense of the faith against the encroachment of modernist theological teachings was at the core of the fundamentalist movement. But fundamentalism was profoundly influenced by the *holiness* movement, which was just as concerned with correct behavior as fundamentalism was with correct belief. The personal piety and renunciation of "worldly" vices of the holiness movement was combined with the combative spirit of theological fundamentalism to produce a *political fundamentalism,* the second distinct kind of fundamentalism.

The first wave of political fundamentalism was a short-lived but vigorous conservative movement with several agendas, including temperance and anticommunism. The critical and ultimately fatal crusade of the fundamentalist movement occurred in the arena of public education policy. Charles Darwin's theory of evolution, which had gained popularity among scientists and teachers, was clearly incompatible with a literal reading of the Bible. Among other incompatible passages, the Genesis story of creation in the Bible states that the earth and all that dwells therein were created in six days. The fundamentalists launched a campaign to prohibit the teaching of Darwinism in public schools, a campaign that initially met with considerable success.

The struggle came to a climax in 1925 in one of the most celebrated trials of the twentieth century. John Scopes, a substitute biology teacher, was charged with violating a Tennessee state law that prohibited the teaching of evolution. Dubbed "the Monkey Trial," this epochal event drew two of America's greatest trial lawyers to the tiny town of Dayton, Tennessee. For the prosecution was William Jennings Bryan, brilliant orator, three times presidential nominee of the Democratic Party, and the unchallenged leader of the fundamentalist political movement. Scopes was defended by Clarence Darrow, a bitter foe of organized religion who was believed by many to be the outstanding trial lawyer in the nation (Stone 1941). Darrow gained prominence as a defender of labor unions and in litigation against monopolistic corporations.

The highlight of the trial came when, in a surprise move, Darrow called Bryan as a witness. While Bryan claimed to have been a scholar of the Bible for fifty years, his ability to defend some of the finer points and implications of fundamentalist theology proved wanting. In the end, his testimony was a debacle for the prosecution. George Marsden, the premier historian of fundamentalism, described the scene thus: "Bryan did not know how Eve could be created from Adam's rib, where Cain got his wife, or where the great fish came from that swallowed Jonah. He said that he had never contemplated what would happen if the earth stopped its rotation so that the sun would 'stand still' " (Marsden 1980, p. 186).

The trial was quintessentially a confrontation between the emerging modern world and the forces of traditionalism. The drama was played out on the turf of traditionalism—a sleepy, small town in Tennessee—but it was communicated to the world by journalists who were sages of the new modern order. The fundamentalists were portrayed as fossilized relics from an era long past. Darrow himself portrayed the trial as a struggle of modern liberal culture against "bigots and ignoramuses" (Marsden 1980, p. 187). John Scopes was convicted, but that fact seemed inconsequential. The forces of modernity and tradition had met face to face, and modernity triumphed. William Jennings Bryan collapsed and died a few days after the trial without ever leaving Dayton, Tennessee. In popular myth, Bryan died of a broken heart. Bryan had planned a national campaign to compel schools across the nation to teach evolution as a theory, not a scientific fact (Stone 1941, p. 464). There was no one else of Bryan's stature to pick up the cause. The first wave of political fundamentalism died when Bryan was unable to defend its theological underpinnings.

The third distinct meaning of fundamentalism emerges from a melding of the two movements to create a popular caricature of small-town Americans as culturally unenlightened religious fanatics. H. L. Mencken (1919–1927) and Sinclair Lewis (1927), writing in the second and third decades of this century, set the tone and style of a genre of lambasting literature that subsequent generations of writers have admired and sought to emulate. Fundamentalists were portrayed as backwater fools preyed on by hypocritical evangelists, but most certainly a withering species destined to disappear from the modern world. They could be meddlesome and annoying, but they were not viewed as politically dangerous. In time they would most certainly die off, even in the rural hinterlands of America.

The Scopes trial clearly marked the demise of the first wave of political fundamentalism. Fundamentalists in the major Protestant denominations did lose ground to the modernists, but biblical fundamentalism did not so much wane as it passed from high public visibility. A number of leaders bolted from mainline Protestant churches and formed new denominations and seminaries. But out of the limelight of the press and mainstream culture, fundamentalism did not wither as had been forecast. Rather, it continued to grow, particularly in the Midwest and South (Carpenter 1984a). Fundamentalists also were schism-prone, so that none of the scores of groups developed into large new denominations, such as occurred with the Baptists and Methodists in the nineteenth century (Finke and Stark forthcoming). This, too, served to diminish the fundamentalists' visibility.

An important development occurred during the 1940s when fundamentalism effectively divided into two camps. The first, which was more insular and combative toward the larger culture, joined with Carl McIntire to create the American Council of Christian Churches (ACCC). McIntire was militantly antimodernist, and he viewed the ACCC as an instrument for doing battle with the liberal Federal Council of Churches (FCC), which in 1950 became the National Council of Churches. There was yet another large contingent of fundamentalists who were neither with the militant McIntire contingent nor the modernist tradition aligned with the FCC. In 1942 this second group of fundamentalists founded the National Association of Evangelicals (NAE). Theologically the NAE might have considered themselves neofundamentalists, but they recognized the negative cultural stereotype associated with fundamentalism. The use of the term *evangelical* was a reappropriation of a term that most Protestant groups used to describe themselves before the modernist-fundamentalist schism. It was more respectable and, clearly, the members of the NAE wanted to put some

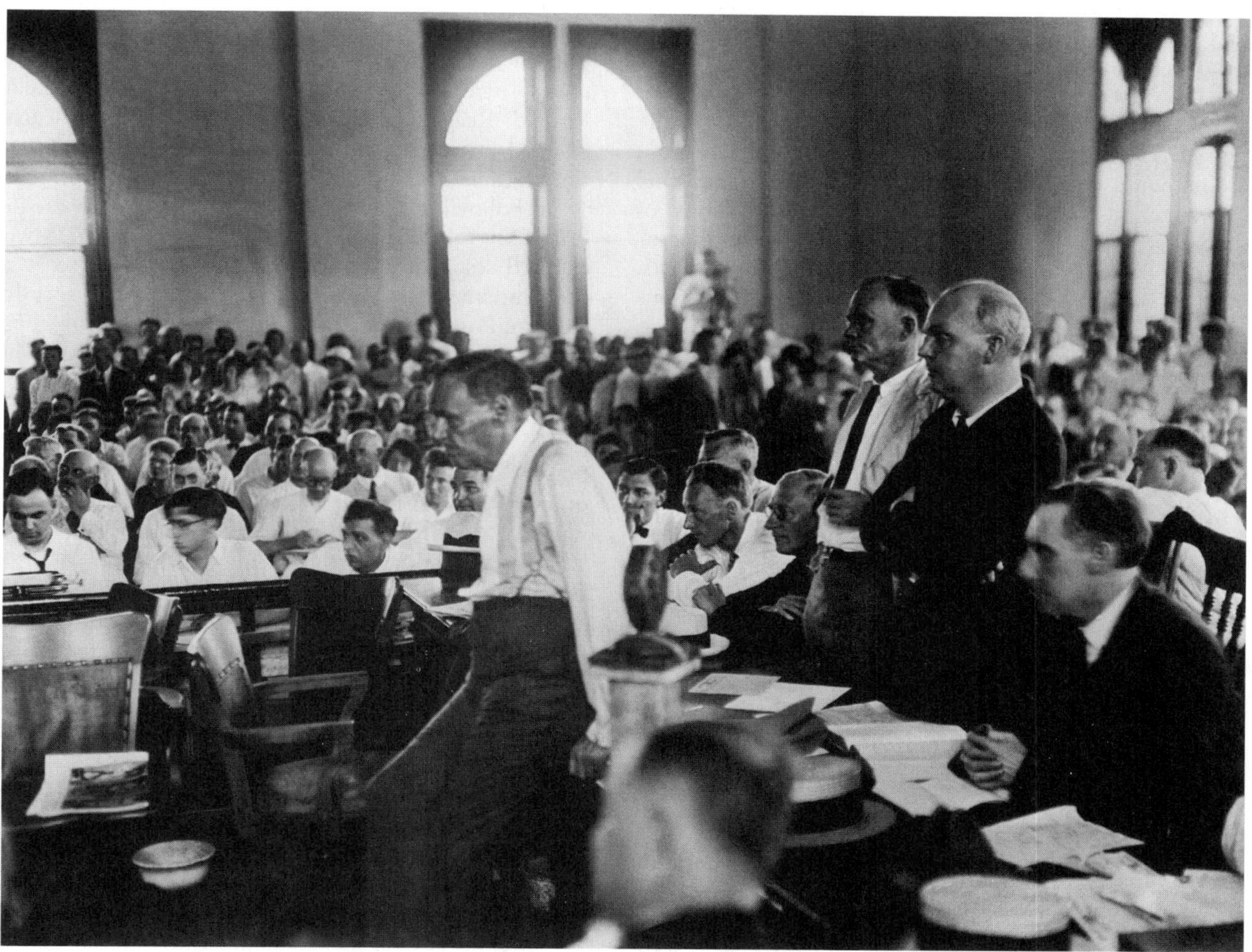

The first wave of political fundamentalism faded after the famous Scopes trial in which Clarence Darrow (leaning back on table) defended John T. Scopes (standing with arms crossed) against charges of teaching evolution in school. Although Scopes was convicted, Darrow presented compelling arguments against the Biblical view of creation that received widespread attention. (Corbis-Bettmann)

distance between themselves and other fundamentalists who had joined forces with Carl McIntire. But theologically the NEA was not much different from the fundamentalist movement of the early part of the century (Marsden 1987).

The label "evangelical" has served to mainstream millions of Christians whose theological beliefs are hardly discernible from those who are identified as fundamentalists.

Publicly NAE leaders stressed their desire to emphasize the positive aspects of their beliefs in contrast to the highly negative and combative posture of the ACCC toward both theological modernism and political liberalism (Carpenter 1984b, p. 12). Some of the leaders of the NAE later admitted that the reappropriation of the name "evangelical" was a strategy to escape the negative cultural stereotypes against fundamentalism. Whether a self-conscious strategy or not, the label "evangelical" has served to mainstream millions of Christians whose theological beliefs are hardly discernible from those who are identified as fundamentalists. Billy Graham, perhaps the most respected religious leader of the second half of the twentieth century, is considered an evangelical. Theologically speaking, his basic beliefs are virtually indistinguishable from those of fundamentalist Jerry Falwell or the leadership of the Southern Baptist Convention, which staged a takeover of the Southern Baptist denomination during the 1980s.

Notwithstanding an underlying core of basic beliefs, fundamentalism in the United States is highly varied in terms of social organization, nuances of belief, and social class backgrounds. To the general public, however, fundamentalists are known in terms of the caricature that is the legacy of the Scopes trial debacle—people who are narrow-minded, bigoted toward persons different from their own kind, obscurantist, sectarian, and hostile to the modern world. The mass media dredge up enough examples of people exhibiting these traits to keep the stereotype alive (Hadden and Shupe 1990).

From the 1930s forward there have been periodic flurries of right-wing political activity led by preachers and laypersons who have been labeled fundamentalists. During the Depression William Dudley Pelley, Gerald B. Winrod, and Gerald L. K. Smith led movements that blended religion with anti-Semitism (Ribuffo 1983). For many decades from the 1940s forward, Carl McIntire was a strident anti-Catholic propagandist. Frederick C. Schwarz, Billy James Hargis, and Edgar Bundy were among the most visible anticommunist crusaders of the post-World War II era (Forster and Epstein 1964). Liberal political pundits and scholars have always viewed these groups with mixed feelings. Some have unequivocally looked on them with great alarm (e.g. Clabaugh 1974), and that sense of alarm has always been greatest during periods when their movements were highly visible. Outside of periods of high visibility, the general consensus of scholars is that the fundamentalist right embodies doctrines and attracts an element that is on the fringe of the mainstream of American politics. While perhaps repugnant to the liberal ethos, they have not been widely perceived as a serious threat to democratic institutions.

In 1979 Jerry Falwell, a fundamentalist television preacher, founded a political organization named the Moral Majority. Initially the media paid little attention, but when Falwell and his fellow right-wing fundamentalists organized to help elect presidential candidate Ronald Reagan, interest picked up. When Reagan reached out and embraced the fundamentalists, attention escalated (Hadden and Swann 1981, pp. 130–133). Following the Reagan victory, along with the defeat of several ranking senators and congressmen, Falwell claimed responsibility. Pollster Lou Harris agreed that the fundamentalist vote was the margin of victory for Reagan. Postelection analysis did not support this claim (Hadden and Swann 1981), but the high media profile of Falwell and his fellow televangelists gave fundamentalism its highest public profile since the 1920s.

This most recent wave of concern about the political power of fundamentalists might have blown over quickly were it not for the timing of this development with the rise of the Islamic imam Ayatollah Khomeini, who led a revolution that deposed the shah of Iran; shortly thereafter, Khomeini's followers held sixty-two Americans hostage for fourteen months. Political analysts concerned with the power of the fundamentalists in America were soon comparing the religious right in America with the followers of Ayatollah Khomeini and other radical Muslim factions in the Middle East. From these comparisons was born the concept "Islamic fundamentalism." This linkage was quickly followed by the labeling of selected politically active religious groups around the world as "fundamentalist."

Thus was born the concept *global fundamentalism,* the fourth distinct meaning of fundamentalism. During the 1980s the idea of global fundamentalism became widely accepted by the mass media and scholars alike. But like previous uses of the term, global fundamentalism has suffered from lack of systematic conceptualization and consistent application. The global application of the concept thus has many of the same underlying presuppositions of the popular caricature of fundamentalism in U.S. Protestantism. It is an uncomplimentary epithet for religious groups that are viewed as out of sync with the modern world. Fundamentalism, whether the American variety or of some other culture and faith, is characterized by blind adherence to a religious dogma or leader and zealous rejection of the modern world. It is also widely assumed that fundamentalists are contemptuous of democratic institutions.

Inconsistencies in the application of the concept were readily available. Perhaps this is nowhere so apparent as with discussions of the Afghan Muslim guerrillas who fought the Soviet army to a standoff during the 1980s. Both theologically and politically the Afghan rebels were unmistakably Islamic fundamentalists, but they were almost never so identified in the Western press. Rather, these Afghans are almost always referred to as the *mujaheddin,* usually with positive references such as courage, bravery, and freedom fighters. But seldom did anyone mention that *mujaheddin* means, literally, one who fights a *jihad* or holy war. This and other instances of inconsistent application suggest that the concept of fundamentalism is reserved for religious zealots who are disapproved.

In sum, both popular and scholarly use of the concept of fundamentalism during the twentieth century has had a strong ideological bias. This bias has carried over to the creation of the notion of global fundamentalism. Given this history, it might be proposed that fundamentalism has not been a concept of great utility for sociological analysis and thus its use should be discouraged. In support of this proposition can be added the observation that social scientists have not developed any instruments that have been widely used to measure fundamentalism. Such a proposal may be premature.

Even though popular use of the concept of global fundamentalism had tended to connote the same stereotypical content as the term has conveyed when applied to Protestant fundamentalists in the United States, the suggestion that the phenomenon might exist across cultures and world religions invites comparative analysis that was lacking when the concept was restricted to American Protestantism. By the late 1980s serious comparative analysis of fundamentalism had begun (e.g., Caplan 1987; Lawrence 1989).

Comparative sociological inquiry suggests that the characterization of fundamentalism as an unenlightened backwater form of resistance to modernization involves a misplaced emphasis. The forces of tradition have always resisted innovation. Bruce Lawrence, along with others, argues that fundamentalism is a product of modernity and thus is a phenomenon that did not exist prior to modernity, and "because modernity is global, so is fundamentalism" (Lawrence 1989, p. 3). In a similar argument, Anson Shupe and Jeffrey K. Hadden contend that "fundamentalism is a truly modern phenomenon—modern in the sense that the movement is always seeking original solutions to new, pressing problems" (Shupe and Hadden 1989, p. 112). Shupe and Hadden note that *secularization,* the cognitive counterpart to modernization, has progressively compartmentalized religion from and defined it as irrelevant to other institutional spheres. Fundamentalism may be viewed as a proclamation of reclaimed authority of a sacred tradition that is to be reinstated as an antidote for a society that has strayed from its cultural moorings. Sociologically speaking, fundamentalism involves (1) a refutation of the radical differentiation of the sacred and the secular that has evolved with modernization, and (2) a plan to dedifferentiate this institutional bifurcation and thus bring religion back to center stage as an important factor of interest in public policy decisions.

The characterization of fundamentalism as an unenlightened backwater form of resistance to modernization involves a misplaced emphasis.

So conceived, fundamentalism is not antimodern. Fundamentalists, for example, are typically not against the use of modern technology, but rather certain applications of it. Further, they have proven themselves to be particularly adept at utilizing technology, particularly communications technology, to their own ends. From the invention of radio to the development of syndicated television broadcasting, fundamentalists have dominated the use of the airwaves for religious broadcasting in the United States. They have also succeeded in developing a significant global presence. In terms of sheer volume, the four major international religious broadcasting organizations transmit more hours per week in more languages than the BBC, Radio Moscow, and the Voice of America together (Hadden 1990, p. 162).

Fundamentalism is clearly an assault on the cognitive components of modernization. Insofar as the process of modernization is not globally uniform, the development of fundamentalism may be expected to manifest a different character in different cultures. The most ambitious comparative study of fundamentalism to date was launched in 1987 by the American Academy of Arts and Sciences with a substantial grant from the John D. and Catherine T. MacArthur Foundation. Over a period of five years the Fundamentalism Project brought together scholars of religion from around the world to prepare studies of groups that have been identified as fundamentalist. This project has encouraged a large number of scholars to study the phenomenon seriously. In addition, the published papers from the project will provide a rich source of original studies for comparative and synthesizing work.

[See also Religious Movement.]

BIBLIOGRAPHY

Barr, James 1977 *Fundamentalism.* Philadelphia: Westminster Press.

Caplan, Lionel, ed. 1987 *Studies in Religious Fundamentalism.* Albany: State University of New York Press.

Carpenter, Joel A. 1984a "The Renewal of American Fundamentalism, 1930–1945," Baltimore: Ph.D. diss., The Johns Hopkins University.

——— 1984b "From Fundamentalism to the New Evangelical Coalition." In George Marsden, ed., *Evangelicalism and Modern America.* Grand Rapids, Mich.: Eerdmans.

Clabaugh, Gary K. 1974 *Thunder on the Right: The Protestant Fundamentalists.* Chicago: Nelson-Hall.

Finke, Roger, and Rodney Stark (Forthcoming) *The Churching of America: 1776–1990.* New Brunswick, N.J.: Rutgers University Press.

Forster, Arnold, and Benjamin R. Epstein 1964 *Danger on the Right.* New York: Random House.

Hadden, Jeffrey K. 1990 "Precursors to the Globalization of American Televangelism." *Social Compass* 37:161–167.

———, and Anson Shupe 1990 "Elmer Gantry: Exemplar of American Televangelism." In Robert Abelman and Stewart M. Hoover, eds., *Religious Television: Controversies and Conclusions.* Norwood, N.J.: Ablex.

———, and Charles E. Swann 1981 *Prime Time Preachers.* Reading, Mass.: Addison-Wesley.

Hutchinson, William R. 1976 *The Modernist Impulse in American Protestantism.* Cambridge, Mass.: Harvard University Press.

Lawrence, Bruce B. 1989 *Defenders of God.* San Francisco: Harper and Row.

Lewis, Sinclair 1927 *Elmer Gantry.* New York: Harcourt, Brace.

Marsden, George M. 1980 *Fundamentalism and American Culture.* New York: Oxford University Press.

——— 1987 *Reforming Fundamentalism.* Grand Rapids, Mich.: Eerdmans.

Marty, Martin E., and R. Scott Appleby (eds.) 1991 *Fundamentalism Observed.* The Fundamentalism Project, vol. 1. Chicago: University of Chicago Press.

Mencken, Henry Louis 1919–1927 *Prejudices,* 6 vols. New York: Alfred A. Knopf.

Ribuffo, Leo P. 1983 *The Old Christian Right.* Philadelphia: Temple University Press.

Sandeen, Ernest R. 1970 *The Roots of Fundamentalism: British and American Millenarianism 1800–1930.* Chicago: University of Chicago Press.

Scofield, Cyrus Ingerson 1945 *The Scofield Reference Bible.* New York: Oxford University Press.

Shupe, Anson, and Jeffrey K. Hadden 1989 "Is There Such a Thing as Global Fundamentalism?" In Jeffrey K. Hadden and Anson Shupe, eds., *Secularization and Fundamentalism Reconsidered.* Religion and the Political Order, vol. 3. New York: Paragon House.

Stone, Irving 1941 *Clarence Darrow for the Defense.* Garden City, N.Y.: Doubleday, Doran.

– JEFFREY K. HADDEN

[See also Religious Movements.]

RELIGIOUS MOVEMENTS

Most people do not perceive of religious beliefs as changing very much over the centuries. Religions, after all, are engaged in the propagation of eternal truths. And whereas religious organizations may change, that process is perceived to occur only very slowly.

Contrary to these popular perceptions, both religious beliefs and religious organizations are dynamic, ever-changing phenomena. Changes in the beliefs and structure of religions reflect adaptations, accommodations, and innovations to continuously changing cultural, political, and economic environments. Without more or less constant change, religions become irrelevant to their environments and simply become defunct.

Some changes in religious organizations occur as the result of decisions by leaders empowered to do so. Some changes in beliefs occur so slowly that adherents and leaders alike hardly notice. But much change occurs as the result of movements. *Religious movements* may be understood as a subcategory of *social movements*—that is, organized efforts to cause or prevent change. There are three discrete types or categories of religious movements. First, *endogenous religious movements* constitute efforts to change the internal character of the religion. Second, *exogenous religious movements* attempt to alter the environment in which the religion resides. Third, *generative religious movements* seek to introduce new religions into the culture or environment.

Religions consist of beliefs, symbols, practices, and organizations. *Endogenous movements* seek to change one or more of these aspects of a religion (Stark and Bainbridge 1985, p. 23). Some endogenous movements have had monumental impact on both history and culture—for example, the great schism that split Christianity into Western Catholicism and Eastern Orthodoxy in the eleventh century; and the Reformation, which developed in the sixteenth century and which split Protestantism from Roman Catholicism. Other movements, while important to the participants, have been of little cultural significance.

Endogenous movements frequently result in a schism—the division of the religious organization into two or more independent parts (Stark and Bainbridge 1987, p. 128). Protestantism has been particularly schism-prone. J. Gordon Melton (1989) has identified more than 750 Protestant groups in North America alone. New religious groups formed through the process of schism are known as *sects.* Sectarian movements tend to be led by laity or lower-echelon clergy. Many religious movements result in reform rather than schism. Reform is a more likely outcome when movements are initiated by the religious leaders, or when the religious hierarchy responds to and co-opts grassroots demands for change.

The Second Vatican Council (1962–1965) was called by Pope John XXIII in response to strong internal pressures to modernize the Roman Catholic Church and improve relations with other faiths. The Council produced many wide-sweeping changes in the Catholic church. In addition, it spawned many other religious movements within the Catholic church (e.g., liberation theology, the women's ordination movement, and movements for greater lay participation). A second important hierarchically initiated movement of the twentieth century was the Protestant ecumenical movement. After several centuries of denominational proliferation, the second half of the twentieth century has witnessed a powerful ecumenical movement that has resulted in the union of diverse Protestant traditions.

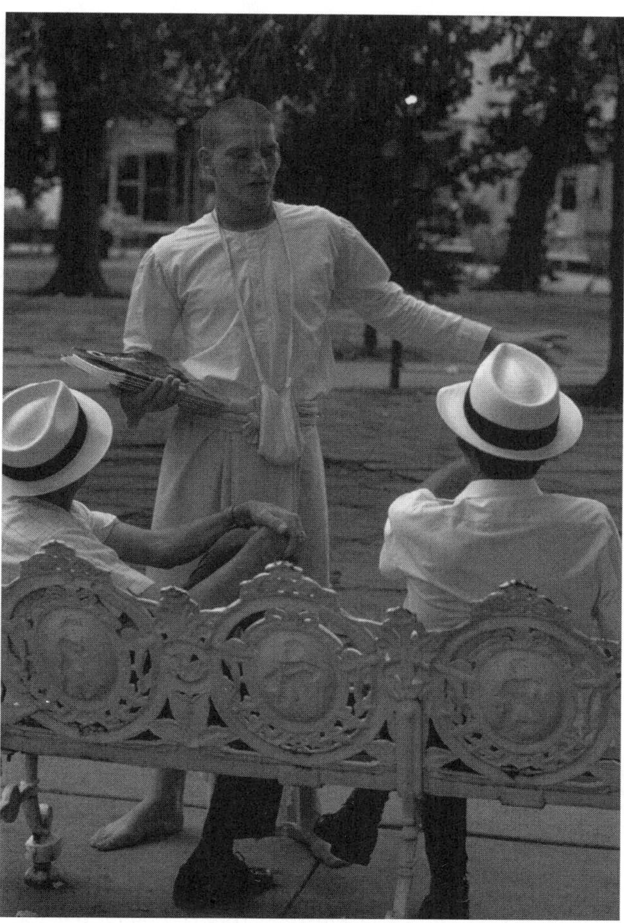

Hare Krishnas first appeared in the United States in the 1960s, but their beliefs are traceable to Hindu religious practices dating from the sixteenth century. (Adam Woolfitt/Corbis)

Exogenous movements constitute a second general type of religious movement. They are concerned with changing some aspect of the environment in which a religious organization exists. Religious organizations bring to the environments in which they exist the interests of (1) survival; (2) economics; (3) status; and (4) ideology (Hadden 1980). As long as these interests are secure, the religious organization may be said to exist in equilibrium or harmony with its environment. But when any of these interests are threatened, or the leadership of the religious organization seeks to enhance or expand its interests, religious movements may ensue. Often, exogenous religious movements are indistinguishable from social movements and, indeed, are frequently pursued in coalition with secular social movement organizations.

The very essence of religious organizations is that they carry cultural values, ideals, customs, and laws that claim transcendental character. When religious leaders engage in exogenous religious movements, they almost always draw on these transcendental principles to legitimate their cause. The claim that movement objectives are part of a divine plan, or that God is on the side of the movement, may serve as a powerful motivation for adherents of the faith to participate. Witness, for example, the many occasions during the 1980s when Islamic leaders exhorted their followers to engage in *jihad* (holy war).

In addition to legitimating religious movements with transcendental principles, religious leaders are often enlisted by secular social movement leaders to legitimate their movements. As a general proposition, religious leaders are specialists in the legitimation of social movement causes.

The civil-rights movement in the United States was substantially a religious movement. It was led by black ministers, activities were organized in black churches, funds were raised in liberal white churches, white clergy bolstered the troops who marched and picketed, and idealistic black and white youth—motivated by their religious traditions—participated in civil-rights campaigns and projects. The strength of the movement came not only from the broad base of religious participation but also from the ability of the leaders to legitimate the movement constantly in terms of sacred religious principles. For example, civil-rights leaders repeatedly quoted the passage in the Declaration of Independence that acknowledges the role of the Creator in human rights: "We hold these Truths to be self-evident, that all Men are created equal, that they are endowed by their Creator with certain unalienable Rights, that among these are Life, Liberty, and the Pursuit of Happiness . . ."

The Solidarity labor movement in Poland, which was the first major social movement that led to the collapse of communism in Eastern Europe, sought and received legitimacy from the Catholic church. Not only in Poland but also throughout Eastern Europe, religious traditions were deeply involved in the movement for liberation from communism (Echikson 1990).

Not all exogenous religious movements are movements of liberation. Around the globe religious groups call on divine providence to help them in struggles against other religions, ethnic rivals, and unsympathetic governments.

There are literally hundreds of these movements around the globe in various stages of ascendancy or abatement. In predominantly Hindu India, Muslims in the northern province of Kashmir seek independence or union with Pakistan, while Sikhs in the nearby province of Punjab have for many years waged a bloody confrontation with the government for independence. In Sri Lanka, just off India's southern shores, Tamils, members of a Hindu sect, seek an independent state in a nation that is predominantly Buddhist. In Northern Ireland, Protestants and Catholics have experienced periodic conflict since Protestant settlers arrived in the middle of the seventeenth century, but since 1968 the two rivals have been locked in a high level of tension punctuated with intermittent outbursts of violence (Bruce 1986, p. 412).

The third type of religious movement is *generative*—a deliberate effort to produce a new religious movement. New religions are introduced to a culture either externally by missionaries or are products of innovation (invention) by members of the culture. Whereas schismatic movements produce variations on an existing religion within a culture, new religions are novel to the host culture (Stark and Bainbridge 1987, p. 157). Sociological scholars refer to these new religions as *cults.*

New religions are not necessarily newly created. Hare Krishnas, adorned in saffron robes and chanting on street corners, first appeared in the United States during the mid-1960s. The Krishnas brought Hindu beliefs and practices that were clearly novel to North America, but they were first practiced in India in the sixteenth century (Rochford 1985, p. 11). In contrast, the Reverend Sun Myung Moon, a Korean and founder of the Unification Church, created a religion that involved a blending of significantly reconstructed Christian beliefs along with important elements of eastern religions. In still another example, L. Ron Hubbard, a science fiction writer, published a book in 1950 titled *Dianetics,* which outlined psychotherapeutic or mental-health techniques. The book became a best seller, and in 1954 Hubbard founded the Church of Scientology.

In these three groups we have examples of the importation of an old religion based on sacred texts of Hinduism (Hare Krishnaism), a newly created religion based on reported revelation from the God of the monotheistic traditions of Judaism and Christianity (Unificationism), as well as an indigenous religion based on techniques of modern psychotherapy (Scientology). All are new and novel to North American culture.

The late 1960s and early 1970s produced a flurry of new religious movements in the United States. The youth counterculture of the 1960s provided a receptive environment for new religions. Equally important, the repeal of the Oriental Exclusion Acts in 1965 paved the way for many Eastern gurus to come to the United States as missionaries of their faiths (Melton and Moore 1982, p. 9). While not nearly as extensive, this activity can be compared to that of the Christian missionaries who flocked to Africa and Asia during the late nineteenth and early twentieth centuries to seek converts to their faith.

This period of rapid cult formation was not particularly unique. The nineteenth century, for example, produced a large number of cults and sectarian movements in the United States. Christian Science, Mormonism, Seventh-day Adventism, the Jehovah's Witness movement, and Theosophy are but a few examples of groups emerging in that time frame that remain viable in the late twentieth century.

Significant social-science literature exists on all three types of religious movements: endogenous, exogenous, and generative. The focus of inquiry has shifted significantly over time, and the discipline of the investigators has influenced the selection of questions addressed.

Over time, sects institutionalize and gradually become more like the churches from which they earlier broke.

During the formative years of sociology much attention was devoted to discerning how new religions arise and evolve (Glock 1973, pp. 207–208). Max Weber (1958) and Ernst Troeltsch (1960) conceptualized what is known as the "sect-church" theory. Sects develop as a result of dissent within churches, which break away and form sects. Over time, sects institutionalize and gradually become more like the churches they earlier broke from, even as new sects are being formed. H. Richard Niebuhr (1929) postulated that sects recruit disproportionately from "the disinherited" or economically deprived classes. Benton Johnson (1961) argued that sectarian groups socialize their members to the dominant middle-class values of society.

Until the mid-1960s, much of the sociological literature focused on what has here been identified as endogenous movements. Much of this literature concerned questions relating to the formation of religious movements. Most explanations could be classified as theories of (1) deprivation (socioeconomic and other); (2) social dislocation; or (3) socioeconomic change (McGuire 1981, p. 121).

Historical work has focused on exogenous and generative movements, although this literature supports much sociological work that concludes that religious groups emerge on the fringe of society. Norman Cohn's monumental work *The Pursuit of the Millennium* concludes that revolutionary millenarian movements during the eleventh and sixteenth centuries drew their strength from groups on the margin of society. By marginal Cohn means persons who are not just poor but who also have no "recognized place in society [or] regular institutionalized methods of voicing their grievances or pressing their claims" (1970, p. 282).

Anthropological literature focuses on generative movements. The question that has dominated their inquiry was inherited from the evolutionary agenda of Social Darwinism in the late nineteenth century: What are the origins of religion? New religions, they conclude, emerge during periods of rapid social change, disorganization, and dislocation (Hine 1974, p. 646). In anthropological literature, this cultural strain is most often identified as the result of the invasion of an indigenous culture by a militarily advanced culture—the typical pattern of conquest and colonization by European cultures from the late fifteenth century forward.

The new religions are variously identified as "cargo cults," "messianic movements," "nativistic movements," and "revitalization movements." Anthropological literature postulates that new religions emerge as a means of dealing with cultural stress. Weston La Barre (1972) generalizes from the scores of ethnographic studies of anthropologists to locate the origins of all religions in cultural crisis. Vittorio Lanternari, surveying anthropological and historical literature on new religions that emerge as a result of intercultural conflict, concludes that these religions "tend to seek salvation by immediate action through militant struggle or through direct and determined opposition to the foreign forces" (1965, p. 247).

Psychological literature has been much less concerned with religious movements. Following the logic of Sigmund Freud's cultural bias against religion, some psychologists have identified the leaders of religious movements as psychopathological and their followers as psychologically defective. This literature has not been particularly productive of insights about religious movements (see Saliba 1987, pp. xvii–xxxix; Anthony 1990).

The ferment of generative religious movements in the wake of the youth counterculture of the late 1960s stimulated a tremendous volume of sociological inquiry (Bromley and Hadden forthcoming). In terms of sheer volume, research and theorizing about "new religious movements" eclipsed all other subtopics of inquiry in the social scientific study of religion during the 1970s and 1980s. In addition to new conceptual perspectives on how religious groups form (Stark and Bainbridge 1987; Stark 1987), studies have examined (1) the organizational development of new religions (Robbins 1988); (2) the structural and social-psychological dynamics of affiliation (Snow and Machalek 1984) and disaffiliation (Bromley 1988); and (3) the persistence of intragroup conflict between new and established religious traditions (Shupe, Bromley, and Oliver 1984).

BIBLIOGRAPHY

Anthony, Dick 1990 "Religious Movements and Brainwashing Litigation." In Thomas Robbins and Dick Anthony, eds., *In Gods We Trust,* 2nd ed. New Brunswick, N.J.: Transaction Books.

Bromley, David G. (ed.) 1988 *Falling from Faith: Causes and Consequences of Religious Apostasy.* Newbury Park, Calif.: Sage.

———, and Jeffrey K. Hadden (eds.) Forthcoming *Handbook of Cults and Sects in America,* 2 vols. Greewich, Conn.: JAI Press.

Bruce, Steve 1986 "Protestantism and Politics in Scotland and Ulster." In Jeffrey K. Hadden and Anson Shupe, eds., *Prophetic Religions and Politics.* Religion and the Political Order, vol 1. New York: Paragon House.

Cohn, Norman 1970 *The Pursuit of the Millennium.* New York: Oxford University Press.

Echikson, William 1990 *Lighting The Night: Revolution in Eastern Europe.* New York: William Morrow.

Glock, Charles Y. 1973 "On the Origin and Evolution of Religious Groups." In Charles Y. Glock, ed., *Religion in Sociological Perspective.* Belmont, Calif.: Wadsworth.

Hadden, Jeffrey K. 1980 "Religion and the Construction of Social Problems." *Sociological Analysis* 41:99–108.

Hine, Virginia H. 1974 "The Deprivation and Disorganization Theories of Social Movements." In Irving I. Zaretsky and Mark P. Leone, eds., *Religious Movements in Contemporary America.* Princeton, N.J.: Princeton University Press.

Johnson, Benton 1961 "Do Holiness Sects Socialize in Dominant Values?" *Social Forces* 39:309–316.

La Barre, Weston 1972 *The Ghost Dance.* New York: Delta.

Lanternari, Vittorio 1965 *The Religions of the Oppressed.* New York: Mentor Books.

McGuire, Meredith B. 1981 *Religion: The Social Context.* Belmont, Calif.: Wadsworth.

Melton, J. Gordon 1989 *The Encyclopedia of American Religions,* 3rd ed. Detroit, Mich.: Gale Research.

Melton, J. Gordon, and Robert L. Moore 1982 *The Cult Experience.* New York: Pilgrim Press.

Niebuhr, H. Richard 1957 *The Social Sources of Denominationalism.* Cleveland, Ohio: Meridian Books.

Robbins, Thomas 1988 *Cults, Converts and Charisma.* Newbury Park, Calif.: Sage.

Rochford, E. Burke, Jr. 1985 *Hare Krishna in America.* New Brunswick, N.J.: Rutgers University Press.

Saliba, John A. 1987 *Psychiatry and the Cults: An Annotated Bibliography.* New York: Garland.

Shupe, Anson D., Jr., David G. Bromley, and Donna L. Oliver 1984 *The Anti-Cult Movement in America.* New York: Garland.

Snow, David A., and Richard Machalek 1984 "The Sociology of Conversion." In Ralph H. Turner and James F. Short, Jr., eds., *Annual Review of Sociology,* vol. 10. Palo Alto, Calif.: Annual Reviews.

Stark, Rodney 1987 "How New Religions Succeed: A Theoretical Model." In David G. Bromley and Phillip E. Hammond, eds., *The Future of New Religious Movements.* Macon, Georgia: Mercer University Press.

———, and William Sims Bainbridge 1985 *The Future of Religion.* Berkeley, Calif.: University of California Press.

——— 1987 *A Theory of Religion.* New York: Peter Lang.

Troeltsch, Ernst 1960 *The Social Teachings of Christian Churches,* 2 vols. New York: Harper & Row.

Wallace, Anthony F. C. 1966 *Religion: An Anthropological View.* New York: Random House.

Weber, Max 1958 "The Social Psychology of the World's Religions." In H. H. Gerth and C. Wright Mills, eds. and trans., *From Max Weber: Essays in Sociology.* New York: Oxford University Press.

– JEFFREY K. HADDEN

RELIGIOUS ORGANIZATIONS

The social organization of religion in the United States is diverse and complex. Most religious organizations are local churches (congregations, parishes, synagogues) tied to national religious bodies (usually referred to as denominations). According to the *Yearbook of American and Canadian Churches,* there are almost 350,000 churches in 219 denominations in the United States. The membership reported by these churches equals almost 59 percent of the U.S. population (Jacquet 1989). The largest denominations are the Roman Catholic Church (53,496,862 members in 1988), the Southern Baptist Convention (14,722,617 members), and the United Methodist Church (9,124,575 members). Most denominations are quite small. In all, the twenty-three denominations with membership in excess of one million members account for more than 127,000,000 members—about 90 percent of all church members in the United States. In contrast, the 108 denominations with fewer than 25,000 members account for about 730,000 members, about 0.5 percent of church members (above figures calculated from information in Jacquet 1989).

Local churches typically hold worship services at least once a week and also have educational activities, especially for children and youth. Most churches organize various groups within the church to accomplish particular tasks (for example, missions, evangelism, or community action) or for the association of persons with common interests, for instance, women, youth, or senior citizens. Women's groups are especially active. Moreover, churches often serve as community centers providing space for meetings of all sorts of neighborhood and community organizations.

Most religious organizations are local churches tied to national religious bodies.

Local churches usually have a pastor (priest, rabbi) and a lay governing board. There is great variation from denomination to denomination on the authority of lay boards, and, within denominations, there is variation from church to church in informal power. Research has shown that control by inner circles of informal leaders is likely to emerge when formal mechanisms of control and official leaders are not performing effectively (Hougland and Wood 1979).

The degree to which the denomination exercises control over the local church depends in large part upon the polity, or political structure, of the denomination. Students of religious organizations place denominations in three categories according to polity. Congregational polity is the weakest. In this polity the local church owns its own property and hires and fires its own pastor. In contrast, in a hierarchical (often episcopal) polity the national (or regional) body holds title to the property and controls the placement of pastors. An in-between category is often called presbyterial. There are a number of correlates of polity. For example, denominations with strong polities were more active supporters of the civil-rights movement and more aggressively pressed for the integration of their churches (Wood 1981).

Though the organization of Jewish synagogues is similar to that of many Protestant churches, the Jewish perspective on religious organization is somewhat different. In 1987 the officials of the congregational organizations of the Orthodox, Conservative, and Reform branches of Judaism reported 3,750,000 persons associated with their synagogues and temples. However, there are approximately six million Jews in the United States considered an ethnic, social, and religious community (Jacquet 1989, pp. 243–244). Daniel Elazar stresses that Jews see no meaningful line of separation between "churchly" purposes and other communal needs, hence Jewish organizations are not neatly divided into religious and nonreligious ones. "It is *not simply* association with a *synagogue* that enables a Jew to become part of the organized Jewish community. Affiliation with *any of a whole range of organizations,* ranging from clearly philanthropic groups to 'secularist' cultural societies, offers the same option" (Elazar 1980, p. 131). Elazar argues that local Jewish federations for welfare, educational, and cultural activities should be seen as religious organizations (p. 133).

Religious Organizations in Sociological Context

Religious organizations provide patterns for the interaction of religious individuals. Social forces change these patterns, but in turn the collective action of religious people influences society. Sociologists looking at religious organizations have been interested especially in their importance as plausibility structures that foster specific beliefs and values (Berger 1967) and as structures of action that mobilize people to seek social change.

Until the 1970s the sociological approach to religious organizations was guided primarily by the church–sect typology. This theoretical framework helped to explain the number and variety of religious bodies and differences in their behaviors by reference to the social class of their adherents. Max Weber distinguished between a church, a continuously operating rational, compulsory association that claims a monopolistic authority, and a sect, "a voluntary association [that] admits only persons with specific religious qualifications" (Weber 1978, p. 56). One becomes a member of the church by birth, but a "sect . . . makes membership conditional upon a contractual entry into some particular congregation" (p. 456). Weber's student, Ernst Troeltsch (1961), developed a typology from these concepts, and some variation of the church–sect typology has been used repeatedly in studying U.S. religious organizations.

In the Weberian tradition, H. Richard Niebuhr stressed the sociological sources of sect formation and the way in which social forces tended to turn sects into churches. He argued that sects originate "in the religious revolts of the poor, of those who were without effective representation in church or state" and who employed a democratic, associational pattern in pursuing their dissent because it was the only way open to them. Niebuhr observed that the pure sectarian character of organization seldom lasts more than one generation. As children are born to the voluntary members of the first generation,

> the sect must take on the character of an educational and disciplinary institution, with the purpose of bringing the new generation into conformity with ideals and customs which have become traditional. Rarely does a second generation hold the convictions it has inherited with a fervor equal to that of its fathers, who fashioned these convictions in the heat of conflict and at the risk of martyrdom. As generation succeeds generation, the isolation of the community from the world becomes more difficult. Furthermore, wealth frequently increases when the sect subjects itself to the discipline of asceticism in work and expenditure; with the increase of wealth the possibilities for culture also become more numerous and involvement in the economic life of the nation as a whole can less easily be limited. (Niebuhr 1954, pp. 19–20)

Nancy Ammerman's work continues the research tradition that relates the evolution of churches to social class backgrounds. Ammerman traces the rise of fundamentalism in the Southern Baptist Convention to the erosion of cultural support for traditional beliefs. She found that fundamentalism decreased with increased levels of education and with increased levels of income. But "many at the edges of this transition are likely to respond by embracing fundamentalist beliefs more vigorously than ever (Ammerman 1986, p. 487).

H. Richard Niebuhr argued that sects originate "in the religious revolts of the poor, of those who were without effective representation in church or state."

According to James Beckford, "The question of the degree to which any particular organisation was church-like or sect-like was taken seriously for what it implied about that organisation's capacity to survive in the modern world" (Beckford 1984, p. 85). The church–sect theorizing was dominated by considerations of rationalization and compromise. Beckford detected a shift in the focus of sociologists studying religious organizations in the 1970s toward "the capacity of religious organisations to foster a sense of personal authenticity, conviction and self-identity" (p. 85). The 1970s saw a great many studies about recruitment and mobilization by religious organizations. Many of these studies focused on the growth and decline of traditional organizations, but many others dealt with religious movements that were new, or at least new upon the U.S. scene. Beckford refers to a number of authors who have found that cult-like formations are appropriate to an age marked by rationalization, bureaucratization, and privatization. That is, small groups of people cultivating esoteric religion in private are flexible and adaptable to the conditions of highly mobile and rapidly changing societies. Some of these scholars have linked cults' ability to inspire and mobilize their members to their distinctive forms of organization.

In recent years more emphasis is placed on applying general organization theory to religious organizations. Many recent studies of religious organizations are characterized by an open systems approach, which views organizations as adaptive organisms in a threatening environment (Scherer 1980). The questions of adaptability to the modern world and that of inspiration and mobilization of followers come together in studies of the Roman Catholic Church. Seidler and Meyer (1989) examine that denomination's accommodations to the modern world, many of which involve important structural changes, such as priest's councils, and other changes that allowed both priests and lay people to have more say in the operation of the church.

A relatively new theoretical perspective within the sociology of organizations and social movements—resource mobilization—has illuminated much of the current scene of new religious movements. Bromley and Shupe (1979) did a detailed resource mobilization analysis of the Unification Church. They argue that one key element in the church's establishment in the United States was the development of mobile fund-raising teams.

Current Issues

A more varied theoretical approach to religious organizations has allowed scholars to focus on different kinds of issues. A major concern has been the decline of the liberal mainline denominations and the significance of that decline (Roof and McKinney 1987; Hoge and Roozen 1979). The liberal mainline churches in the United States share with other churches in a vast mobilization of voluntary time and money in activities caring for individuals such as the poor, the sick, and the elderly. Churches are particularly effective at such mobilization because they instill philanthropic values and present information and opportunities for philanthropic activities in face-to-face settings such as worship services and Sunday School classes. The liberal churches have played the additional role of implementing socially liberal policies, that is, policies designed to change the structure of society so that, for example, income as well as opportunities for individual achievement are more widely distributed throughout society. The liberal social agenda also includes sharp criticism of the U.S. government's role as promoter of U.S. business interests abroad. Mobilizing individuals and groups to press for the acceptance and implementation of a liberal social agenda may be these churches' most significant contribution to U.S. society (Wood 1990).

Religious organizations also play an important role in the process of consensus formation in our society. Amitai Etzioni (1968) argues that a healthy society is one in which the relationship between citizens and national leaders is mediated by a large network of groups and organizations where multiple perspectives are reduced toward consensus. The effect of any direct appeal by national leaders or by mass media campaigns to individual citizens is determined largely by the multiple membership of the citizens in groups and organizations. This mediation protects against mass emotional manipulation. At the national level the many "legislatures" within the major religious bodies in this country are of enormous importance in shaping the working consensus that enables both the formulation and the implementation of national policies. The representative selection procedures for national meetings and the deliberative consensus formation processes typical of the major denominations are an important contribution to informed public opinion in U.S. society.

Liberal mainline churches in the United States share with other churches in a vast mobilization of voluntary time and money.

At the local level, meetings of the congregation or its committees provide a forum in which differing opinions can be expressed in a context of mutual respect. Knoke and Wood (1981) show that a wide variety of nonreligious social influence associations did not attract people with views as diverse as those in the church. They suggest that "the goals of these organizations are fairly clear to members before they join. Members know what they are getting into. And in most of these organizations, policy-dissatisfied members probably do not feel the social pressure to remain in the organization comparable to that felt by dissatisfied church members" (p. 103). Churches' multiple goals and the emotional and value ties provide holding power that keeps members with different views together in the same church. Voluntary associations in which individuals can debate the critical issues face to face encourage individuals to act out their selfless values rather than their selfish interests and provide a bulwark against the manipulation of the public by computer-generated direct mailings and mass media campaigns for a particular group's vested interest in ideology, money, or power.

Other Religious Organizations

Wuthnow (1988) has described the rise of numerous special purpose organizations that are rooted in religion and draw legitimation and resources from the more traditional religious organizations but with the objective of achieving a quite specific purpose. These organizations provide new options for religious people in addition to participation in local churches. A wide variety of purposes are pursued, including the advancement of nuclear disarmament and meeting the spiritual needs of senior citizens. Wuthnow suggests that "as far as the society as a whole is concerned, these organizations may be the ones that increasingly define the public role of American religion. Rather than religion's weight being felt through the pressure of denominations, it may be exercised through the more focused efforts of the hundreds of special purpose groups now in operation" (1988, p. 121). Though these special purpose groups are in many ways a revitalizing influence on traditional religious organizations (denominations and local churches), they may have important sociological implications for them. For example, while the traditional organizations have often held together people of diverse social backgrounds, special purpose groups may have a tendency toward homogeneity.

There are also a number of important umbrella organizations, such as the National Council of Churches and the National Association of Evangelicals, that facilitate the cooperation of sets of denominations. The National Council of Churches was particularly important in mobilizing a segment of the church population into the civil rights movement (Wood 1972). There has also been a growth of community councils of churches.

In the news in recent years there have been a number of religious organizations that are unrelated either to the Judeo–Christian heritage or to immigrant groups. They draw their adherents largely from the broad center of the U.S. middle class. Ellwood and Partin (1988) discuss more than forty of these groups. None of them is very large and in the majority most of their members remain affiliated for less than a year. Perhaps their greatest importance from the sociological perspective is that they introduce new organizational models into the U.S. scene.

The Future

New immigrant people are bringing their religions. Islam in particular is growing rapidly. People in the United States may have to start thinking of themselves as a Protestant, Catholic, Jewish, Islamic nation. According to one source, in 1973 there were fifteen or twenty local centers of Muslim worship in the United States; by 1980 Muslim centers were reported in all of the 300 largest cities in the United States. Two million adherents were reported in 1980; six million were reported in 1989. Most Islamic organizations in the United States are local centers (variously called Islamic Society, Islamic Center, or Muslim Mosque). These organizations provide a place of worship and a center for other religious, social, and educational activities. Islam does not have an organized hierarchy, but several regional and national groups help to coordinate the work of local groups and promote unity among them (Jacquet 1989). If, as Elazar (1980) contends, many Jewish organizations in addition to the synagogue play a religious role, in Islam it appears that the religious centers play many roles in addition to the religious one. Perhaps this is always the case with the churches of recent immigrants.

Stark and Bainbridge (1985) think that traditionally organized religion may decline drastically as more and more people pursue individualistic "careers" of going from one self-enhancement group to another. If they are correct, any societal influence of religious organizations would be felt more through influence on individuals than through collective action of large religious bodies. However, there is much evidence that the traditional structure of religious organization in the United States will persist.

BIBLIOGRAPHY

Ammerman, Nancy T. 1986 "The New South and the New Baptists." *The Christian Century* May 14, pp. 486–488.

Beckford, James A. 1984 "Religious Organisation: A Survey of Some Recent Publications." *Archives de Sciences Sociales des Religions* 57:83–102.

Berger, Peter L. 1967 *The Sacred Canopy.* Garden City, N.Y.: Doubleday.

Bromley, David G., and Anson D. Shupe, Jr. 1979 *"Moonies" in America: Cult, Church, and Crusade.* Beverly Hills, Calif.: Sage.

Elazar, Daniel J. 1980 "Patterns of Jewish Organization in the United States." In Ross P. Scherer, ed., *American Denominational Organization.* Pasadena, Calif.: William Carey Library.

Ellwood, Robert S., and Harry B. Partin 1988 *Religious and Spiritual Groups in Modern America.* Englewood Cliffs, N.J.: Prentice-Hall.

Etzioni, Amitai 1968 *The Active Society.* New York: Free Press.

Hoge, Dean R., and David A. Roozen 1979 *Understanding Church Growth and Decline: 1950–1978.* New York: Pilgrim Press.

Hougland, James G., Jr., and James R. Wood 1979 " 'Inner Circles' in Local Churches: An Application of Thompson's Theory." *Sociological Analysis* 40:226–239.

Jacquet, Constant H., Jr. (ed.) 1989 *Yearbook of American and Canadian Churches.* Nashville, Tenn.: Abingdon Press.

Knoke, David, and James R. Wood 1981 *Organized for Action: Commitment in Voluntary Associations.* New Brunswick, N.J.: Rutgers University Press.

Niebuhr, H. Richard 1954 *The Social Sources of Denominationalism.* Hamden, Conn.: Shoe String Press.

Roof, Wade Clark, and William McKinney 1987 *American Mainline Religion: Its Changing Shape and Future.* New Brunswick, N.J.: Rutgers University Press.

Scherer, Ross P. 1980 *American Denominational Organization.* Pasadena, Calif.: William Carey Library.

Seidler, John, and Katherine Meyer 1989 *Conflict and Change in the Catholic Church.* New Brunswick, N.J.: Rutgers University Press.

Stark, Rodney, and William S. Bainbridge 1985 *The Future of Religion: Secularization, Revival, and Cult Formation.* Berkeley: University of California Press.

Troeltsch, Ernst 1961 *The Social Teachings of the Christian Churches.* New York: Harper and Row.

Weber, Max 1978 *Economy and Society.* Berkeley: University of California Press.

Wood, James R. 1972 "Unanticipated Consequences of Organizational Coalitions: Ecumenical Cooperation and Civil Rights Policy." *Social Forces* 50:512–521.

——— 1981 *Leadership in Voluntary Organizations: The Controversy over Social Action in Protestant Churches.* New Brunswick, N.J.: Rutgers University Press.

——— 1990 "Liberal Protestant Social Action in a Period of Decline." In Robert Wuthnow and Virginia A. Hodgkinson, eds., *Faith and Philanthropy in America: Exploring the Role of Religion in America's Voluntary Sector.* San Francisco: Jossey-Bass.

Wuthnow, Robert 1988 *The Restructuring of American Religion: Society and Faith since World War II.* Princeton, N.J.: Princeton University Press.

– JAMES R. WOOD

RELIGIOUS ORIENTATIONS

Sociologists generally conceive of religion as a system of symbols that evokes a sense of holistic or transcendent meaning (Bellah 1970, p. 16; Geertz 1973, pp. 90–125). This definition reflects sociology's claim that symbols are essential to the human capacity to experience and interpret reality (Berger and Luckmann 1966). Symbols are acts, objects, utterances, or events that stand for something—that is, that give meaning to something by connecting it to something else. Symbols give order and meaning to life. Without them, life would be experienced as senseless and chaotic. Indeed, research suggests that individuals are able to experience and understand only those aspects of their worlds for which they have symbols (Farb 1973).

Sociologists' emphasis on holistic or transcendent meaning as the defining feature of religion arises from their view that meaning is always contextual (Langer 1951). The meaning of a particular word depends on the other words that form its immediate context. For example, the word "courts" means one thing if it appears with the word "tennis," but something different when the words "justice" or "dating" are present. Similarly, in their daily lives people give meaning to their activities by associating them with various frames of reference. Hitting a tennis ball has meaning, for example, because it is associated with the rules of the game of tennis. Each frame of reference, moreover, has meaning because it can be placed within a more encompassing symbolic context (tennis, say, within the context of physical exercise and health). But if each symbolic framework requires a broader framework to have meaning, then, some form of holistic or transcendent symbol system that embraces all of life must be present. These are what sociologists call religious orientations or religious systems (Berger 1967; Roberts 1984).

The questions that typically invoke religious symbols involve the quest to make life itself meaningful. Such questions arise at the extremities of human existence: Where did I come from? Why am I here? What happens when I die? These questions, framed at the individual level, may also be asked about the collectivity to which one belongs or about humanity in general: How did our tribe originate? Where is humanity headed? Other questions focus on the absolutes or landmarks that make life recognizable in its most basic sense: What is beauty? What is truth? How can we know truth? What is essential about the human condition? There are also questions that arise because the events they deal with make no sense to us on the surface: Why must I die? Why is there suffering in the world? What is the reason for evil?

Transcendent symbol systems address these questions at a variety of levels. Elaborate philosophical and theological doctrines sometimes supply rational answers that satisfy canons of logic and empirical evidence. In daily life these questions are more likely to be addressed through narratives, proverbs, and maxims, and ikonic representations rich with experiential connotations. Religious orientations are likely to be structured less by abstract deductive reasoning than by parables that raise questions but leave open precise answers, by personal stories that link experience with wider realities, and by creeds and images that have acquired meaning through long histories of interpretation in human communities (Greeley 1982, pp. 53–70).

Like other symbol systems, religious orientations are thought to be the products of social interaction. Although the role of such factors as divine revelation cannot be ruled out, sociologists focus on the ways in which symbols come to have meaning through the interaction of individuals and groups in human communities. Sometimes these communities invent collective symbols to articulate powerful experiences they may have undergone. More commonly, communities borrow symbols available within their cultural traditions, but then adapt these symbols to their own use, giving them new meanings and interpretations. Communities also underwrite the plausibility of religious belief systems (Berger 1967, p. 45). They do so by providing evidence that such beliefs are not the product of individual imaginations alone, by encouraging the public expression of beliefs, and by creating occasions on which beliefs may be enacted and predictions fulfilled. Without the ongoing interaction of people in communities, it is doubtful whether belief systems could long be sustained. Research has also demonstrated that personal religious orientations are more likely to have behavioral consequences if these orientations are supported by communities of like-minded individuals (Roof 1978).

Communities borrow symbols available within their cultural traditions, but then adapt these symbols to their own use, giving them new meanings and interpretations.

In defining religion as a symbol system that deals with ultimate questions, sociologists assume that humans have the capacity to question their experience and a desire to make sense of their worlds. Whether all people pursue this desire with equal intensity is more doubtful. It is possible, for example, to explain a plane crash by observing that a rivet came loose. It is also possible to let the incident raise questions about the meaning of pain, the frailty of human existence, or the meaning and purpose of one's own life. How much the quest for holistic meaning and transcendence enters into people's lives is, therefore, a matter of variation. Studies indicate that most people say they have thought about the meaning and purpose of life, but individuals vary in the extent to which they have been troubled by this issue. They also vary in the amount of explicit attention they have devoted to it and in their views about the possibility of arriving at definite answers (Stark and Glock 1968, p. 77). Agnosticism, for example, is a religious orientation that grants the importance of ultimate questions about meaning and purpose but denies the possibility of finding answers to these questions.

The kinds of symbols that come into play in relation to such questions are also matters of variation. While all such symbol systems may perform functionally similar roles, it is useful to distinguish them substantively. These substantive distinctions are usually the basis on which religious orientations are delineated in popular discourse. At the broadest level, sociologists distinguish theistic meaning systems, which recognize the existence of a God or divine being, from atheistic systems, which do not acknowledge a divine being (Glock and Stark 1965, pp. 3–17). Christianity is an example of the former; Marxism, of the latter. Insofar as it addresses the same higher-order questions about the meaning of life, Marxism would be considered functionally similar to Christianity. But this does not mean that Marxism necessarily functions this way. Just as one might study Marxism to derive economic principles, so one might study Christianity simply as an example of literature. In neither case would it be appropriate to say that a religious orientation is at work. Only as they function to evoke holistic meaning and transcendence do symbol systems become religious orientations.

The distinction between theistic and atheistic meaning systems is useful when the relevant concept is the presence or absence of a divine entity. But this distinction may be less useful in other contexts. For example, contemporary discussions in theology and in science sometimes distinguish religious orientations on the basis of whether they posit a reality that is humanly knowable or ultimately mysterious, whether reality is empirical or includes a supraempirical dimension, or whether being implies something that is not being itself but the ground of being. In these debates the boundary between varieties of ultimate meaning systems is often ambiguous.

In contemporary societies religious orientations are often distinguished in popular belief according to the dominant force or power that people perceive as governing their lives (Wuthnow 1976). Some people may conceive of this force as God; others, as luck or fate. Natural or human causes may also be considered dominant; for example, the force of heredity, of scientific law, society, or individual willpower. Whether a part of elaborate philosophical systems or simple pieces of folk wisdom, such understandings help people to make sense of their lives by identifying the causal agents that control human events.

Sociologists have insisted that religious orientations become important to the study of human behavior insofar as these orientations are internalized as part of the individual's worldview. A worldview can be defined as a person's guiding outlook on life. The essential aspects of a religious orientation are the person's beliefs and assumptions about the meaning of life and such matters as the existence and nature of God, goodness and evil, life beyond death, truth, and the human condition. These beliefs and assumptions help the individual make sense of life cognitively. They also have an emotional dimension, perhaps including a feeling of awe, reverence, fear, or peace, comfort, and security. In addition, they are regarded as behavioral predispositions that lead to various actions, such as participation in worship, prayer, or ethical decisions (Spilka, Hood, and Gorsuch 1985).

The importance of religious orientations for ethical decisions has been of long-standing interest to sociologists. In the classical work of Max Weber (1963), religious orientations were conceived of as symbolic frameworks that made sense of the world, in part, by providing explanations for the existence of evil (also known as theodicies). Some religious orientations, for example, explained evil as a struggle between God and the devil, others saw evil as part of a cycle of regeneration and renewal, while still others attributed evil to the workings of an all-powerful but inscrutable deity. The implications for ethical action derived from the prescriptions for salvation implied by these different conceptions of evil. In one tradition, for example, people might be expected to pray and meditate in order to escape from the cycle of evil and regeneration; in another tradition, they might be expected to do good deeds as a way of siding with the forces of good against those of evil.

Much of the research by sociologists on religious orientations has dealt with their subjective aspects (Blasi and Cuneo 1986). Assuming that the important feature of symbolism is its meaning, researchers have tried to discover what religious symbols mean to individuals. Efforts have been made to tap the deeper predispositions presumed to underlie such religious expressions as prayer and worship, to say how deeply implanted the religious impulse is, and to classify varieties of religious outlooks and experiences.

Recent developments in sociological theory have resulted in some rethinking of this emphasis on subjective religiosity. Current research is beginning to focus more on the observable manifestations of religious symbolism itself, rather than claiming to know what lies beneath the surface in the subjective consciousness of the individual (Wuthnow 1987). Discourse, language, gesture, and ritual have become more important in their own right (Tipton 1982). The contrast between this and the earlier approach can be illustrated by comparing two statements: "I believe God exists" and "God speaks to us through the Word." A subjective approach would treat both statements as manifestations of some inner conviction of the individual. The more recent approach would pay closer attention to the language itself, noting, for example, the more personalized style of the first statement and the collective reference contained in the second.

The value of the more recent approach is that it recognizes the public or social dimension of religious orientations. Observers may not know what goes on in the dark recesses of the believer's soul. But if that person tells a story, or participates in worship, the researcher can then study the observable manifestations of that person's faith.

To account for variations in religious orientations sociologists usually look at the social conditions to which people are exposed. They assume that most people do not make up their own religions from scratch. Rather, they borrow from the various symbol systems that are available in their environment. The most significant borrowing occurs in early childhood. Family is thus an important factor, and it, in turn, is influenced by broader conditions such as social class, levels of education, race and ethnicity, and exposure to regional subcultures.

A generation ago, sociologists often held the view that scientific generalizations could be made about the relationships between social factors and religious orientations. For example, much work was inspired by the hypothesis that theistic religious orientations were more common among persons with lower levels of education than among persons in better-educated social strata. Another common hypothesis suggested that religious orientations were likely to be associated with various kinds of social deprivation, since the deprived would presumably seek solace in otherworldly beliefs. Empirical studies have found some support for such hypotheses. But the ability to make generalizations has remained limited. Different relationships seem to be present in different communities and in different time periods.

More attention has turned in recent years, therefore, toward describing the rich and complex processes by which religious orientations and social environments intermingle. In one setting people without college educations may turn to religious views that shield them from the uncertainties of science and other modern ideas. In another setting people with high levels of education may also turn to religion, but do so in a way that combines ideas from science and Scripture or that focuses on the therapeutic needs of people working in the professions. In both settings, religious orientations provide answers to ultimate questions. But the composition of these orientations reflects ideas present in the different social settings.

An earlier generation of social theorists also sought to explain the variations in religious orientations in ways that often reduced them to little more than the byproducts of social or psychological needs. Sociologists following in the tradition of Karl Marx, for example, regarded religion merely as a reflection of class struggles, while some following Emile Durkheim viewed it as a reflection of the corporate authority of society (Swanson 1960, 1967). The reductionism in these approaches consisted not only of regarding social structure as more basic than religion but also of implying that religion would gradually disappear as people became more aware of its origins (Fenton 1970). Recent work is decidedly less reductionistic in its assumptions about religion. It still assumes that religion fulfills human needs and that it is influenced by social conditions, but regards religion as a more active contributor to human experience and considers its future more viable.

In addition to the more general social conditions that may influence the religious orientations of individuals, sociologists have also been particularly interested in the institutions that devote specific energies to the promulgation of religious orientations. These institutions supply the resources needed for religious orientations to be perpetuated. Leadership, producers of religious knowledge, specialists in the dissemination of such knowledge, organizational skills, physical facilities, and financial resources are all required for religious orientations to be maintained over time. Religious institutions must compete with other institutions, such as governments, businesses, and families, for these resources.

In most modern societies competition is also present among the adherents of various religious orientations (Wuthnow 1988a). When such competition has been recognized either governmentally or culturally, we say that a condition of religious pluralism exists (Silk 1988). Pluralism often becomes a kind of religious orientation itself, imposing norms of civility and tolerance on particularistic religious traditions. When multiple religious orientations are forced to compete with one another, the plausibility of any one such tradition may be diminished as a result of believers' seeing others who hold views different from their own. At the same time, pluralism appears to contribute to the overall vitality of religious orientations in a society by encouraging competition among them for adherents and by giving believers more options from which to choose (Christiano 1987).

Most people do not make up their own religions from scratch. Rather, they borrow from the various symbol systems that are available in their environment.

It has been common in the past for individuals to choose one particular religious orientation with which to identify. Often these orientations have been defined by religious institutions, such as the Roman Catholic church, or by denominational organizations, such as the Presbyterian or Methodist churches (Greeley 1972). Increasingly, however, it appears that individuals in modern societies are exposed to a variety of religious institutions and orientations. As a result, they may pick and choose particular elements from several different faiths and traditions. Their religious orientation therefore takes on a more personalized character (Bellah et al. 1985, pp. 219–249; Roof and McKinney 1987, pp. 40–71).

Although some individuals work out highly coherent religious orientations that have internal consistency and integrity, it appears that the more common result of living in religiously pluralistic settings is a form of personalized eclecticism. People become heteroglossic—that is, they gain the capacity to speak with many religious voices. Their religious orientations may not provide a guiding philosophy of life that maintains an orderly view of the world. Rather, religious orientations become tool kits (Swidler 1987) assembled from a variety of personal experiences, social contacts, books, sermons, and other cultural repertoires, and from which the individual is able to draw as he or she is confronted with the challenges of life.

At present, research studies indicate that large proportions of the population in societies like the United States hold theistic religious orientations (Wuthnow 1988b). In other societies where religious institutions have had fewer resources in the past, such orientations are less common. In all societies, though, theistic orientations are confronted by the humanistic orientations promulgated by secular institutions. The outcome appears to involve a balance between pressures to adapt, on the one hand, and tendencies by religious adherents to resist these pressures, on the other hand (Hammond 1985; Beckford 1989). Much of the struggle depends on the ability of religious leaders to articulate visions that grow out of particular confessional traditions in ways that appeal to the universalistic norms governing wider social audiences.

Although religious orientations have become more diverse and eclectic as a result of cultural contact and mass communication, evidence also suggests that in some societies a basic polarization has emerged between those whose orientation involves traditionalistic, fundamentalistic, or conservative norms, on one side, and those whose orientation involves progressive, modernistic, or liberal norms, on the other side (Wuthnow 1988b). Conservatives are characterized by adherence to the authority of traditional scriptural texts, while liberals emphasize more the relativity of these texts and the need for reason and experience in interpreting them. Liberal religious orientations have been nurtured by relativistic views in higher education, in the professions, and in the mass media in market-oriented societies, but conservative orientations have grown as well, not only in reaction to liberalism, but also as a result of conservatives gaining educational or political advantages and seizing on opportunities created by the ill effects of rapid societal change (Ammerman 1987; Hunter 1987). Whereas earlier discussions predicted the demise of fundamentalist religious orientations, current studies are more concerned with the ongoing tensions between fundamentalist and more liberal or more humanistic religious orientations.

BIBLIOGRAPHY

Ammerman, Nancy Tatom 1987 *Bible Believers: Fundamentalists in the Modern World.* New Brunswick, N.J.: Rutgers University Press.

Beckford, James A. 1989 *Religion and Advanced Industrial Society.* London: Unwin Hyman.

Bellah, Robert N. 1970 *Beyond Belief: Essays on Religion in a Post-Traditional World.* New York: Harper and Row.

———, Richard Madsen, William M. Sullivan, Ann Swidler, and Steven M. Tipton 1985 *Habits of the Heart: Individualism and Commitment in American Life.* Berkeley: University of California Press.

Berger, Peter L. 1967 *The Sacred Canopy: Elements of a Sociological Theory of Religion.* Garden City, N.Y.: Doubleday.

———, and Thomas Luckmann 1966 *The Social Construction of Reality: A Treatise in the Sociology of Knowledge.* Garden City, N.Y.: Doubleday.

Blasi, Anthony J., and Michael W. Cuneo 1986 *Issues in the Sociology of Religion: A Bibliography.* New York: Garland.

Christiano, Kevin J. 1987 *Religious Diversity and Social Change: American Cities, 1890–1906.* Cambridge: Cambridge University Press.

Farb, Peter 1973 *Word Play.* New York: Bantam.

Fenton, John Y. 1970. "Reductionism in the Study of Religion." *Soundings* 53:61–76.

Geertz, Clifford 1973 *The Interpretation of Cultures.* New York: Harper and Row.

Glock, Charles Y., and Rodney Stark 1965 *Religion and Society in Tension.* Chicago: Rand McNally.

Greeley, Andrew M. 1972 *The Denominational Society: A Sociological Approach to Religion in America.* Glenview, Ill.: Scott Foresman.

——— 1982 *Religion: A Secular Theory.* New York: Free Press.

Hammond, Phillip E. (ed.) 1985 *The Sacred in a Secular Age.* Berkeley: University of California Press.

Hunter, James Davison 1987 *Evangelicalism: The Coming Generation.* Chicago: University of Chicago Press.

Langer, Susanne K. 1951 *Philosophy in a New Key.* New York: Mentor.

Roberts, Keith A. 1984 *Religion in Sociological Perspective.* Belmont, Calif.: Wadsworth.

Roof, Wade Clark 1978 *Community and Commitment: Religious Plausibility in a Liberal Protestant Church.* New York: Elsevier.

———, and William McKinney 1987 *American Mainline Religion: Its Changing Shape and Future.* New Brunswick, N.J.: Rutgers University Press.

Silk, Mark 1988 *Spiritual Politics: Religion and America Since World War II.* New York: Simon and Schuster.

Spilka, Bernard, Ralph W. Hood, Jr., and Richard L. Gorsuch 1985 *The Psychology of Religion: An Empirical Approach.* Englewood Cliffs, N.J.: Prentice-Hall.

Stark, Rodney, and Charles Y. Glock 1968 *American Piety: The Nature of Religious Commitment.* Berkeley: University of California Press.

Swanson, Guy E. 1960 *The Birth of the Gods: The Origin of Primitive Beliefs.* Ann Arbor: University of Michigan Press.

——— 1967 *Religion and Regime: A Sociological Account of the Reformation.* Ann Arbor: University of Michigan Press.

Swidler, Ann 1987 "Culture in Action: Symbols and Strategies." *American Sociological Review* 51:273–286.

Tipton, Steven M. 1982 *Getting Saved from the Sixties: Moral Meaning in Conversion and Cultural Change.* Berkeley: University of California Press.

Weber, Max 1963 *The Sociology of Religion.* Boston: Beacon.

Wuthnow, Robert 1976 *The Consciousness Reformation.* Berkeley: University of California Press.

——— 1987 *Meaning and Moral Order: Explorations in Cultural Analysis.* Berkeley: University of California Press.

——— 1988a "Sociology of Religion." In Neil J. Smelser, ed., *Handbook of Sociology.* Beverly Hills, Calif.: Sage.

——— 1988b *The Restructuring of American Religion: Society and Faith Since World War II.* Princeton, N.J.: Princeton University Press.

– ROBERT WUTHNOW

RETIREMENT

Retirement is primarily a twentieth-century phenomenon that developed through a convergence of public and private employment policies, a restructuring of the life span relative to work activity, and a redefinition of the terms of monetary compensation for work performed. It may be tempting to view retirement as the "natural" development of a social institution matched to the needs of older people experiencing declines in capacity and competency. But the invention of a distinctive status called *retirement* was not simply a response to the phenomenon of human aging. Rather, in reconciling a transformed economy to an aging population with an increasing amount of surplus labor, an explicit policy of job distribution was produced. Retirement policies incorporated age as a characteristic that served as both a qualifying and an exclusionary principle for work and income. The fact that these policies were age-based can be linked to the social production of age as a valid predictor of individual capacity and potential, a production that had ideological roots in the science and larger culture of the time.

Historical Developments

While *retirement contracts* existed in traditional Europe (Gaunt 1987) and colonial America (Fischer 1977), Plakans (1989) argues that this preindustrial retirement was a more gradual transition that allowed the head of a household to transfer legal title to an heir in exchange for some combination of monetary payments, material provisions, and services as stipulated by the aged person or couple. These contracts were typical of agrarian economies in which land was the main factor in production; they represented the final step in a long and sometimes elaborate process of property transfer. These "stepping down" practices were therefore most immediately linked to inheritance patterns; they could be used to ensure that family control of the land was maintained (Sorensen 1989).

Between 1790 and 1820, American legislatures introduced policies of mandatory retirement for certain categories of public officials. By the late 1800s, the majority of businesses still had no formal policies of fixed-age retirement; however, most used informal policies to eliminate older workers from their labor forces (Fischer 1977). This decline in the demand for older workers can be linked to changes in the structure of American capitalism. During the late 1800s the structure of American capitalism began to change from small-producer, competitive capitalism to large-scale corporate capitalism (Sklar 1988). Part of this reconstruction involved attempts to rationalize age relations in the workplace, a process that was embedded in a more general disenchantment with older workers and a devaluation of their skills. Indeed, the employment rates for men aged sixty-five and over showed a steady decline during this period, from 80.6 percent in 1870 to 60.2 percent in 1920 (Graebner 1980). According to Graebner's analysis, retirement became the impersonal and egalitarian method adopted by both public and private employers for dealing with superannuated workers. It allowed employers to routinize the dismissal of older workers, thereby restructuring the age composition of their work forces in a way they believed would enhance efficiency, a belief supported by the principles of scientific management. Pension plans legitimized this process and, at the same time, served as an effective labor control device.

The first pension plan (1875) is credited to the American Express Company, but benefits were restricted to permanently incapacitated workers who were

Retirement is a twentieth-century concept resulting from changes among several factors, including employment policies, lifespan, and monetary compensation for worth. (Stephanie Maze/Corbis)

at least sixty-five years old with a minimum of twenty years of service (Schulz 1976). In 1920, the first general piece of retirement legislation, the Civil Service Retirement Act, provided pension coverage for federal civilian employees. One year later, the Revenue Act of 1921 encouraged businesses to implement private plans by exempting both the income of pension and profit-sharing trusts and the employer contributions to these trusts from income-tax liability. Nevertheless, coverage remained concentrated in a few industries, and 85 percent of the work force continued to be without pension coverage (Schulz 1976).

The first pension plan (1875) is credited to the American Express Company.

By the 1930s, the question of how to solve the problem of superannuated workers was coupled with the more general problem of managing surplus labor. The changing technology of the workplace, the speeding up and mechanization that were part of the transformation of the labor process, the subsequent increase in worker productivity, and the growing recognition of the cyclical crises inherent in industrial capitalism broadened the concern beyond that of simple superannuation to that of job distribution and consumption capacity.

The Great Depression of the 1930s greatly exacerbated the growing problem of old-age poverty and unemployment. By 1935 unemployment rates among those sixty-five and older were well over 50 percent (Holzman 1963). Even those with pension benefits did not escape poverty; trade union plans were collapsing, and state and local governments were decreasing or discontinuing pension payments (Olsen 1982). Legislative proposals for alleviating some of these problems included the Townsend Plan and the Lundeen Bill. The Townsend Plan proposed a flat $200 monthly pension for older Americans; recipients had to spend the pension within thirty days. The Lundeen Bill proposed benefits at the level of prevailing local wages for all unemployed workers aged eighteen and older (including the elderly) until suitable employment was located (Olsen 1982). Neither of these plans was directly related to a retirement transition. The Townsend Plan would grant equal benefits to all nonemployed persons over age sixty. The Lundeen Bill focused more on job creation for workers of all ages than on limiting labor supply through age exclusions.

In 1934, President Franklin Roosevelt appointed the Committee on Economic Security (CES) to develop legislation to address the problems of old-age poverty and unemployment. The Social Security Act of 1935 offered a solution that based benefits on the level of worker contributions to a general trust fund. Upon their retirement, covered workers (primarily those in manufacturing) could draw retirement benefits, assuming they met the age and work eligibility requirements.

For the CES, retirement referred to complete withdrawal from the labor force. As stated by Barbara Armstrong, an original member of the CES, "Retirement means that you've stopped working for pay." According to Armstrong, the option facing the Roosevelt administration pitted older workers against younger workers (Graebner 1980, p. 186). Retirement would reduce unemployment by moving older workers out of the labor force, allowing industries characterized by surplus labor to transfer jobs from older to younger workers. The federal government could facilitate this process by shifting the focus of older workers' financial dependency from the wage contract to a federal income maintenance program. In that sense, the Social Security Act of 1935 established what was primarily a program of old-age relief; its limited coverage and low benefit levels precluded its serving as an effective instrument of retirement. However, in establishing a measure of income support for retired older workers, the act reinforced the view that in the competition for jobs, age was a legitimate criterion, and youth had the "higher claim" (Graebner 1980). Ironically, the mobilization for World War II created job opportunities for older workers, as it did for women. Even though these opportunities proved temporary, they called into question the connection between retirement and superannuation, a connection that was asserted more emphatically when the supply of labor exceeded the demand.

During the next several decades, considerable growth in private pension plans occurred; coverage increased from 4 million workers in the late 1930s to 10 million workers in 1950 and 20 million workers in 1960. The expansion was spurred by a number of factors including the desire of firms to encourage loyalty and reduce turnover, favorable tax treatment, and the 1949 Supreme Court decision to uphold a National Labor Relations Board ruling that pensions were appropriate issues of negotiation through collective bargaining (Schulz 1976). During this same period, an increasing number of occupations were included under the umbrella of Social Security, and Congress continued to raise benefits in response to changes in the cost of living, although actual benefit levels remained relatively low (Derthick 1979).

Retirement Research

Early research on retirement was centrally concerned with the question of voluntarism in the retirement transition, as well as with the financial, social, and psychological consequences of leaving the labor force. Even though the expansion of both public and private pensions had improved the economic situation of older people in retirement, poverty rates among the elderly were still high. By 1960, 35.2 percent of persons aged sixty-five and over were below the poverty line, compared with 22.4 percent of the general population. Poverty was the norm for older white women and older blacks, although, among blacks, the risk of poverty was not as greatly exacerbated by age (U.S. Bureau of the Census 1987).

During the 1950s, the Social Security Administration began studying the characteristics of newly entitled beneficiaries. Initial reports stated that early retirement occurred primarily because of poor health and difficulties with finding and keeping jobs; the availability of Social Security retirement benefits played a secondary role (Wentworth 1945; Stecker 1955). Although these studies relied on beneficiary-reported reasons for retirement, a measurement strategy that was criticized because of its susceptibility to social desirability bias, their findings cannot be totally discounted. Retirement in the 1950s was not a financially attractive status for many older workers. Given that retirement income programs offered "fixed" benefits (benefits that remained nominally the same but, with inflation, declined in real terms), the financial security of middle- and working-class retirees was in jeopardy.

During the 1950s, retirement grew as a social phenomenon. Insurance companies led the way in developing "retirement preparation" programs, as researchers attempted to define strategies for "successful aging." In 1961, Cumming and Henry argued that disengagement, the gradual relinquishment of social roles and positions of authority and responsibility, was a natural process of aging that served positive functions for both the individual and society. By extension, retirement from the labor force was a process older workers should not resist. This perspective contrasted sharply with the tenets of activity theory, which held that successful aging resulted from remaining active and involved in social networks.

In an era of postwar prosperity, retirement came to be viewed as a "period of potential enjoyment and creature experience which accrues as a social reward for a life-time of labor" (Donahue, Orbach, and Pollak 1960, p. 361). Researchers investigating the effect of retirement on life satisfaction found that "retirement does not cause a sudden deterioration in psychological health as [had] been asserted by other writers" (Streib and Schneider 1971). Rather than rejecting the idea of retirement, the policy concerns advanced by advocacy groups for the elderly emphasized the conditions of retirement, in particular the adequacy of retirement income. Mandatory retirement had not yet become an issue (Achenbaum 1983). Instead, the trend was in the direction of earlier retirement, that is, before the age of sixty-five. In 1956, women, and in 1962, men, were allowed to retire at age sixty-two by accepting actuarially reduced Social Security benefits.

During the mid-1960s, in the context of Lyndon Johnson's War on Poverty, the issue of poverty of the elderly again captured the attention of elected officials. In the Older Americans Act of 1965, Congress established a "new social contract for the aged" (Achenbaum 1983, p. 95) by specifying a series of objectives that, if met, would significantly improve the quality of life enjoyed by older people. Among these objectives was the entitlement of older people to "equal opportunity to the full and free enjoyment of . . . an adequate income in retirement in accordance with the American standard of living . . . [and] retirement in health, honor, and dignity" (U.S. Department of Health, Education, and Welfare 1976).

It was during Richard Nixon's presidency that the era of modern retirement was inaugurated (Myles 1988). Whereas earlier amendments to the Social Security Act had brought more and more workers into the system, they had not significantly improved the level of retirement benefits (Munnell 1977). The presumption that Social Security benefits should serve as retirement income supplements rather than as the primary source of income had not been challenged. But the persistently high rates of old-age poverty lent credence to the charge that benefits were inadequate. During the decade following passage of the Older Americans Act, benefits increased five times and, in 1972, were indexed relative to changes in the consumer price index. Both the "real" level of benefits and the replacement rate of benefits to previous earnings were improved. These enhancements in the "retirement wage" allowed workers to maintain their standard of living across the retirement transition and helped redefine retirement as a legitimate nonwork status that average-income workers could afford to enter voluntarily (Myles 1988). During the decade of the 1970s, private pension plans were also being reorganized. In 1974, passage of the Employee Retirement Income Security Act regularized vesting plans and provided workers with some protection against benefit loss (Schulz 1976). Private-sector initiatives aimed at inducing early retirement were also becoming more common (Barfield and Morgan 1969). Until the 1970s, workers choosing early retirement virtually always accepted reduced benefits. During the 1970s, however, private plans began providing early retirement benefits greater than their actuarial equivalent (Schulz 1976).

The parallel changes in labor force participation rates and in poverty rates among the elderly are noteworthy. During the 1970s, labor force participation rates for older men dropped significantly, especially among early retirement-aged workers. For men aged 55 to 64, rates dropped from 83 percent in 1970 to 75.6 percent in 1975 and 72.1 percent in 1980 (U.S. Department of Labor 1983). In addition, at the beginning of the decade, 24.6 percent of those aged 65 and older were living below the poverty line, twice the 12.1 percent that characterized the general population. By the end of the decade, the poverty rate among the elderly had dropped to 15.2 percent, compared with an overall poverty rate of 11.7.

Until the 1970s, workers choosing early retirement virtually always accepted reduced benefits.

During the 1970s and 1980s, retirement research produced a fairly consistent picture of the retirement process. Most of this research was being conducted by economists and sociologists. These studies concentrated on workers' circumstances at the time of their retirements rather than on post hoc explanations that retirees offered for their behavior, an analytic design facilitated by federally funded longitudinal surveys such as the Retirement History Surveys and the National Longitudinal Survey of Older Men (NLS), both of which began in the mid to late 1960s.

Economists typically conceptualized retirement as an individual decision based in utility theory and the underlying assumption that equates choice with revealed preference. Individuals attempt to maximize pleasure and minimize discomfort; therefore, they "choose" to retire when the "benefits" of entering retirement exceed the "costs." Clark and Barker (1981) argue that increased wealth may make work less attractive and that variation in retirement behavior can be explained by individual differences in personal characteristics, in preferences for work versus leisure, and in work opportunities. These econometric studies frequently focused on establishing the determinants of early retirement. They consistently documented the importance of retirement income in retirement decision making: eligibility for benefits (both Social Security and private pension benefits), benefit amount, and financial consequences of postponing retirement benefits. Health limitations also continued to reliably predict early retirement (Bowen and Finegan 1969), and several studies (e.g., Quinn 1977) reported that the availability of retirement income, especially Social Security benefits, had a stronger effect on health-impaired workers than on healthy workers.

Sociologists have largely shared an individualistic orientation to retirement decision making, but they have also introduced structural features of older workers' situations into models of retirement behavior. A central argument in this literature derives from traditional theories of stratification and stresses the importance of occupational structure in shaping behavioral contingencies. Workers in different structural locations face different opportunities/constraints on their behaviors (Hardy 1985). Some positions (e.g., unionized manufacturing) are structured in ways that protect older workers through seniority systems; at the same time, they encourage early retirement by providing pension plans that make retirement financially feasible, especially for workers with many years of continuous service, and by socializing workers to the benefits of early retirement. However, older workers are also vulnerable to plant closings and job dislocations that accompany mergers, downsizing, and cutbacks in government spending (Schulz 1976). This perspective does not argue that all workers in similar circumstances behave in the same way. But it does suggest that the likelihood of certain outcomes (as referenced by the incidence of certain behaviors) varies across structural contexts, thereby producing different "normative patterns" of retirement. In this perspective, retirement is embedded in work careers, with late-career behaviors being at least partially contingent on earlier career opportunities. In addition, retirement behavior is embedded in more general macroeconomic conditions. Rates of unemployment, changes in both private and public pension policies, and the age structure of the population are all involved in defining the supply-and-demand relations for labor and, ultimately, in the encouragement or discouragement of retirement.

By the time of the 1978 amendments to the Age Discrimination and Employment Act that raised allowable mandatory retirement from age sixty-five to seventy in most occupations and removed it completely in federal civil service, retirement studies were reporting that mandatory retirement policies play only a minor role in the process of labor force withdrawal among older workers (Burkhauser and Quinn 1983), a factor that may be due, at least in part, to the increasing orientation of larger firms toward retirement incentives rather than compulsory terminations. In a 1966 survey of industrial firms in the United States with fifty or more employees, Slavick (1966) found that mandatory policies were more common in large firms and firms that offered private pensions. Though only a minority of firms enforced mandatory retirement, approximately half of wage-and-salary workers were believed to be subject to these policies. Although the number of potential "forced" retirements was quite large, the actual number of workers whose retirements appeared to be the result of mandatory retirement was quite small: Parnes and Less (1985) reported that fewer than 5 percent of the retired men in the NLS were forced out through mandatory plans.

Changing Definitions of Retirement

As the incidence and study of retirement increased, so did the ambiguity of the concept. Armstrong's definition of "no longer working for pay" was being replaced by a variety of definitions that revolved around factors other than work activity per se. In general, these definitions differ in the way they frame the transition that is central to retirement. Whereas Armstrong's definition focused on the worker's exit from the labor force, other definitions are oriented toward transitions out of career employment or full-time work or changes in major income sources (the receipt of retirement pension benefits) or in identity structures (e.g., through self-identification as a retiree). As definitions of retirement shifted toward pensions and the inclusion of part-time workers (Atchley 1982), the concerns of government turned toward the escalating cost of retirement and the advisability of delaying it.

A more recent refinement in using labor force participation as the criterion for retirement has been to distinguish among subcategories of nonparticipation, that is, differentiating the retired from the disabled older worker. Studies invoking this distinction document different patterns of withdrawal by occupational category. Professionals, managers, and salesmen tend to delay retirement, whereas skilled and semiskilled blue-collar workers move more rapidly into retirement; clerical workers move more quickly into both retirement and disability statuses, and service workers experience relatively high rates of disability and death out of employment (Hayward, Hardy, and Grady 1989).

Older, discouraged workers have received less attention. The official category of discouraged workers is a relatively recent creation of the Bureau of Labor Statistics denoting former workers who would like to work but are not seeking employment because they believe either that no jobs are available or that their skills or their age make them unhirable. The discouraged worker hypothesis, that older workers leave the labor force after unsuccessful job searches, suggests that labor force exits should be responsive to changes in levels of unemployment. Bowen and Finegan (1969) demonstrate that the responsiveness of labor force participation to changes in unemployment increases with age for both men and married women, and Rosenblum (1975) argues that workers aged fifty-five or older had the highest rates of discouragement.

All of these developments in defining retirement have expanded and refined the status beyond that of a single category of older nonworkers. Studies that distinguish retirees from older disabled workers reflect the change in the social definition of what it means to be retired. Whereas earlier views defined retirement as a status for people who couldn't work because of illness or couldn't find work, retirement gradually became redefined as a distinct life stage devoted to the enjoyment of leisure activities before the onset of disabling health conditions (Atchley 1985). Definitions that allowed retirees to also be workers became more common as the propensity for older workers to maintain marginal attachments to the labor force through temporary or part-time work increased. More recent studies (e.g., Beck 1984) have reported that a significant minority of those who leave the labor force reenter at a later time. For some, retirement is a partial or temporary status rather than a complete and final exit.

Issues of Gender and Race

The development of retirement policy has been predominantly male-centered. The structure of "retirement wages" has been oriented to the work careers of men, predominantly white men. The original Social Security program excluded industries in which women and blacks were concentrated. Although later amendments eventually covered these categories of workers, the benefit structure continued to reward long and continuous attachment to the labor force and penalize workers for extended or frequent absences from the labor force, regardless of the reasons for these absences. The temporal organization of women's lives relative to work and family activities has important ramifications for their retirement. Women whose work careers are interrupted by years of childbearing and child rearing may find it difficult to retire, since they are "off schedule" in the accumulation of retirement income (O'Rand and Henretta 1982a, 1982b).

African-Americans are more likely to exit from the labor force through disability and also more likely to continue to work intermittently after retirement. However, Gibson (1987) argues that disability is simply another pathway to retirement for older African-Americans, one that offers financial advantages. The work patterns of African-Americans also present special challenges to retirement researchers. In youth, as well as in old age, work patterns among them can appear sporadic, a factor that creates ambiguity in determining the exact timing of retirement (Gibson 1987; Jackson and Gibson 1985). In addition, work histories characterized by frequent spells of unemployment, illness, or temporary disability are linked to lower average retirement benefits.

The career disadvantages of women and African-Americans translate into higher poverty rates for these groups. Married women who qualify for Social Security benefits in their own right frequently find it to their advantage to claim dependents' benefits based on their husbands' work histories (Quadagno 1988). Benefit structures in private pension plans are also weighted in favor of long-tenured employees, both in eligibility requirements and benefit amounts. A study by the U.S. Bureau of Labor Statistics reported that 26.7 percent of the sampled plans required thirty years of service for normal retirement benefits (Bell and Marclay 1987).

For some, retirement is a partial or temporary status rather than a complete and final exit.

Dramatic changes in women's work patterns during this century have made the gendered structure of retirement income programs a source of increasing concern. Whereas the labor force participation rates of U.S. men have shown steady decline, the rates for women have held steadier in both the 55–64 and 65 and older age ranges (Treas 1981). The studies addressing the retirement determinants for older women workers suggest that women's plans are strongly influenced by their own eligibility for Social Security and, when applicable, private pensions (Shaw 1984). They also appear more likely to retire early or late, rather than at the conventional age of 65, and more likely to retire for health reasons (Atchley 1982).

The increasing rates of labor force participation among married women have led some researchers to argue that retirement should be viewed as a joint decision. In fact, there is evidence to suggest that couples may prefer to retire at the same time; however, wives who are younger than their husbands tend to continue working after their husbands retire (Henretta and O'Rand 1980).

International Comparisons

Discussion of the connection between the development of retirement as a labor force policy and the changes in economic and political organization occurring within the last century need not be limited to a case study of the United States. A comparison across nations can provide valuable insight into the retirement process by showing how different societies regulate the relationship between age and labor markets. Cross-national comparisons indicate that the age of retirement has been declining dramatically in many industrialized nations (Guillemard 1985; Meyer and Featherman 1989). Pampel (1985) reports that, among advanced industrial nations, a pattern of low labor force participation among aged males is related to the level of industrialization and population aging. Mirkin (1987) notes that, among countries of Western Europe and North America, the broadening of eligibility for retirement and disability programs is a favored policy for alleviating unemployment. Although the United States has recently modified public retirement policy in an effort to encourage workers to postpone retirement, early retirement policies in Europe have been more pervasive, a difference he attributes to the greater severity of unemployment problems in Western Europe and the difference in the pace of population aging. In apparent contrast with the experiences of Western Europe, Canada, and the United States, labor force participation rates in Japan appear relatively high (Organization for Economic Co-operation and Development [OECD] 1988). However, in making comparisons on the basis of rates of labor force participation, it is important to take into account national differences in census procedures, how the labor forces are defined, and what types of activities constitute work (Holden 1978). In addition, labor force participation rates do not measure partial retirement. However, because countries differ in the paths workers take to retirement, using pension receipt as an indicator is also flawed. In Germany and France, for example, disability benefits and intermediate unemployment benefits also provide access to early retirement.

Though there is little variation among industrialized nations in the legal retirement age, nations appear to be on different trajectories with regard to retirement policy. In 1983 in the United States, amendments to the Social Security Act legislated a gradual increase in the age of full entitlement. In 1982 France lowered its legal retirement age to sixty. Whereas recent debate in the United States has centered on the financial burdens of supporting a growing population of retirees and the desirability of reversing the trend toward early retirement, Guillemard notes that, in France, "old age is seen as a time in life when work is illegitimate" (Guillemard 1983, p. 88). In trying to understand the difference between these two views, it is necessary to consider more than the characteristics of older workers and retirees; it is necessary to consider how the rights and privileges of different age groups are constructed relative to each other.

[See also Labor Force; Social Gerontology; Social Security Systems.]

BIBLIOGRAPHY

Achenbaum, W. Andrew 1983 *Shades of Gray: Old Age, American Values, and Federal Policies since 1920.* Boston: Little, Brown.

Atchley, Robert 1982 "Retirement: Leaving the World of Work." *Annals of the Academy of Political and Social Science* 464:120–131.

——— 1985 *Social Forces and Aging.* Belmont, Calif: Wadsworth.

Barfield, Richard E., and James N. Morgan 1969 *Early Retirement: The Decision and the Experience.* Ann Arbor, Mich.: University of Michigan Press.

Beck, Scott 1985 "Determinants of Labor Force Activity Among Retired Men." *Research on Aging* 7(2):251–280.

Bell, Donald, and William Marclay 1987 "Retirement Eligibility and Pension Trends." *Monthly Labor Review* April:18–25.

Bowen, William G., and T. Aldrich Finegan 1969 *The Economics of Labor Force Participation.* Princeton, N.J.: Princeton University Press.

Burkhauser, Richard V., and Joseph F. Quinn 1983 "Is Mandatory Retirement Overrated? Evidence from the 1970s." *Journal of Human Resources* 18(3):337–358.

Clark, Robert, and David T. Barker 1981 *Reversing the Trend toward Early Retirement.* Washington, D.C.: American Enterprise Institute.

Cumming, Elaine, and William E. Henry 1961 *Growing Old: The Process of Disengagement.* New York: Basic Books.

Derthick, Martha 1979 *Policymaking for Social Security.* Washington, D.C.: Brookings Institution.

Donahue, Wilma, Harold Orbach, and Otto Pollak 1960 "Retirement: The Emerging Social Pattern." In Clark Tibbitts, ed., *Handbook of Social Gerontology.* Chicago: University of Chicago Press.

Fischer, David H. 1977 *Growing Old in America.* New York: Oxford University Press.

Gaunt, David 1987 "Rural Household Organization and Inheritance in Northern Europe." *Journal of Family History* 2:121–141.

Gibson, Rose 1987 "Reconceptualizing Retirement for Black Americans." *Gerontologist* 27(6):691–698.

Graebner, William 1980 *A History of Retirement: The Meaning and Function of an American Institution, 1885–1978.* New Haven, Conn.: Yale University Press.

Guillemard, Anne-Marie 1983 "The Making of Old Age Policy in France: Points of Debate, Issues at Stake, Underlying Social Relations." In Anne-Marie Guillemard, ed., *Old Age and the Welfare State.* Beverly Hills, Calif.: Sage.

——— 1985 "The Social Dynamics of Early Withdrawal from the Labor Force in France." *Aging and Society* 5(4):381–412.

Hardy, Melissa A. 1985 "Occupational Structures and Retirement." In Zena Blau, ed., *Current Perspectives on Aging and the Life Cycle.* Greenwich, Conn.: JAI Press.

Hayward, Mark D., Melissa A. Hardy, and William R. Grady 1989 "Labor Force Withdrawal Patterns among Older Men in the United States." *Social Science Quarterly* 70(2):425–448.

Henretta, John, and Angela O'Rand 1980 "Labor Force Participation Patterns of Older Married Women." *Social Security Bulletin* 43:10–16.

Holden, Karen C. 1978 "Comparability of the Measured Labor Force of Older Women in Japan and the United States." *Journal of Gerontology* 33(3):422–426.

Holzman, Abraham 1963 *The Townsend Movement: A Political Study.* New York: Bookman.

Jackson, James, and Rose Gibson 1985 "Work and Retirement Among the Black Elderly." In Zena Blau, ed., *Current Perspectives On Aging and the Life Cycle.* Greenwich, Conn.: JAI Press.

Mayer, Karl Ulrich, and David L. Featherman 1989 "Methodological Problems in Cross-National Research on Retirement." In David Kertzer and K. Warner Schaie, eds., *Age Structuring in Comparative Perspective.* Hillsdale, N.J.: Erlbaum.

Mirkin, Barry 1987 "Early Retirement as a Labor Force Policy: An International Overview." *Monthly Labor Review* March:19–33.

Munnell, Alicia H. 1977 *The Future of Social Security.* Washington, D.C.: Brookings Institution.

Myles, John 1988 "Postwar Capitalism and the Extension of Social Security into a Retirement Wage." In Margaret Weir, Ann Orloff, and Theda Skocpol, eds., *The Politics of Social Policy in the United States.* Princeton, N.J.: Princeton University Press.

Olsen, Laura Katz 1982 *The Political Economy of Aging: The State, Private Power, and Social Welfare.* New York: Columbia University Press.

O'Rand, Angela, and John Henretta. 1982a. "Delayed Career Entry, Industrial Pension Structure and Retirement in a Cohort of Unmarried Women." *American Sociological Review* 47:365–373.

——— 1982b. "Women at Middle Age: Developmental Transitions." *Annals of the Political and Social Sciences,* 464:57–64.

Organisation for Economic Co-operation and Development 1988 *Aging Populations: The Social Policy Implications.* Paris: OECD.

Pampel, Fred 1985. "Determinants of Labor Force Participation Rates of Aged Males in Developed and Developing Nations, 1965–1975." In Zena Blau, ed., *Current Perspectives on Aging and the Life Cycle.* Greenwich, Conn.: JAI Press.

Parnes, Herbert S., and Lawrence J. Less 1985 "The Volume and Pattern of Retirements, 1966–1981." In Herbert S. Parnes, et al., eds., *Retirement Among American Men.* Lexington, Mass.: D. C. Heath.

Plakans, Andrejs 1989 "Stepping Down in Former Times: A Comparative Assessment of Retirement in Traditional Europe." In David Kertzer and K. Warner Schaie, eds., *Age Structuring in Comparative Perspective,* Hillsdale, N.J.: Erlbaum.

Quadagno, Jill 1988 "Women's Access to Pensions and the Structure of Eligibility Rules: Systems of Production and Reproduction." *Sociological Quarterly* 29(4):541–558.

Quinn, Joseph 1977 "Microeconomic Determinants of Early Retirement: A Cross Sectional View of White Married Men." *Journal of Human Resources* 12:329–346.

Rosenblum, Marc 1975 "The Last Push: From Discouraged Worker to Involuntary Retirement." *Industrial Gerontology* 2:14–22.

Schulz, James H. 1976 *The Economics of Aging.* Belmont, Calif.: Wadsworth.

Shaw, Lois 1984 "Retirement Plans of Middle-Aged Women." *Gerontologist* 24(2):154–159.

Sklar, Martin J. 1988 *The Corporate Reconstruction of American Capitalism, 1890–1916.* New York: Cambridge University Press.

Slavick, Fred 1966 *Compulsory and Flexible Retirement in the American Economy.* Binghamton, N.Y.: Hall.

Sorensen, Aage B. 1989 "Old Age, Retirement, and Inheritance." In David Kertzer and K. Warner Schaie, eds., *Age Structuring in Comparative Perspective.* Hillsdale, N.J.: Erlbaum.

Stecker, Margaret 1955 "Why Do Beneficiaries Retire? Who Among Them Return to Work?" *Social Security Bulletin* 18:3.

Streib, Gordon F., and Clement Schneider 1971 *Retirement in American Society.* Ithaca, N.Y.: Cornell University Press.

Treas, Judith 1981 "Women's Employment and Its Implications for the Status of the Elderly in the Future." In Sara B. Keisler, James N. Morgan, and Valerie Oppenheimer, eds., *Aging, Social Change.* New York: Academic Press.

U.S. Bureau of the Census. 1987. *Statistical Abstract of the United States 1986.* Washington, D.C.: U.S. Government Printing Office.

U.S. Department of Health, Education, and Welfare 1976 *Older Americans' Act of 1965, as Amended and Related Acts, Bicentennial Compilation, March 1976.* Washington, D.C.: Office of Human Development, Administration on Aging.

U.S. Department of Labor, Bureau of Labor Statistics 1983 Current Population Reports, Series P-60, No. 148. Washington, D.C.: U.S. Government Printing Office.

Wentworth, Edna C. 1945 "Why Beneficiaries Retire." *Social Security Bulletin* 8:16–20.

– MELISSA HARDY

REVOLUTIONS

Revolutions are rapid, fundamental transformations of a society's socioeconomic and political structures (Huntington 1968). Social revolutions differ from other forms of social transformation, such as rebellions, coups d'état, and political revolutions. *Rebellions* involve the revolt of society's subordinate classes—peasants, artisans, workers—but do not produce enduring structural changes. *Coups d'état* forcibly replace the leadership of states but do not alter state structures. *Political revolutions* transform state structures but leave social structures largely intact. What is distinctive to social revolutions is that basic changes in social structures and political structures occur in a mutually reinforcing fashion (Skocpol 1979).

Recent sociological work on revolutions recognizes their importance to the making of the modem world order and the opportunities revolutions offer for building theories of social and political change. These opportunities were most emphatically embraced by Marx, who placed the study and the project of revolution at the center of his lifework. Virtually all theories of revolution since Marx share his concern with three separate yet interrelated phenomena: (1) the social conditions that lead to revolution or its absence; (2) the character of participation in revolutions; and (3) the outcomes of revolutions (see Tucker 1978). This review compares Marx's analysis with significant contemporary interpretations in order to examine how events after his death have changed theories of revolution and to consider how much Marx's legacy might endure in future work.

First, Marx understood modern revolutions to be byproducts of the historical emergence of capitalism. Revolutionary situations emerged when contradictions between the forces of production (how the means of existence are produced) and the relations of production (how labor's product is distributed) within an existing mode of production reached their limits. These contradictions were evident in the crises of overproduction that well up from time to time in capitalist economies. Revolutions brought the resolution of crises by serving as bridges between successive modes of production, enabling the ascent of capitalism over feudalism and, later, the replacement of capitalism by socialism.

Second, Marx held that revolutions were accomplished through class struggle. Revolutionary situations intensified conflict between the existing dominant class and the economically ascendant class. Under feudalism class conflict pitted the aristocracy against the ascendant bourgeoisie. Under capitalism the differing situations of segments of society determined their revolutionary tendency. Some classes, such as the petite bourgeoisie, would become stakeholders in capitalism and allies of the dominant bourgeoisie. Others, such as the peasantry, that did not fully participate in wage labor and lacked internal solidarity, would stay on the sidelines. The industrial proletariat would be the midwife of socialist revolution, for wage labor's concentration in cities would generate collective consciousness of the proletariat's exploitation by the bourgeoisie. Class consciousness was a necessary (though not a sufficient) condition for revolution.

Third, Marx believed that revolutions so thoroughly transformed class relations that they put in place new conditions enabling further economic advance. Revolutions were locomotives of history that brought in train new structures of state administration, property holding, and political ideology. Reinforcing the fundamental changes in class relations, these transformations culminated the transition from one mode of production to another.

In sum, Marx's theory identified the conditions that spawn revolutionary situations, the classes that would make revolutions, and the outcomes of revolutions. How well has Marx's analysis served later generations of scholars and revolutionaries? Many of the sociopolitical transformations since his death were unanticipated by Marx. In light of these events, contemporary sociologists have reconsidered his thinking.

Consider first the social conditions making for revolution or its absence. Social revolutions are rare. Modern capitalist societies have experienced deep economic crises that intensified class conflicts and gave the appearance of revolutionary situations, but they have skirted actual revolution. Capitalist economies have great staying power, and reform rather than revolution is the rule in advanced nations. Indeed, the great revolutions of France, Russia, and China, and those in Third World states such as Cuba, Vietnam, and Nicaragua, have occurred in predominantly agrarian economies where capitalist relations of production were only moderately developed. The 1917 Russian Revolution stands as proof of Lenin's claim that revolution was possible in Russia despite its failure to develop a fully capitalist economy in the manner of Western European states.

Rather than growing from contradictions between the forces and the relations of production, revolutionary situations arise in political crises occasioned by international competitive pressures. States with relatively backward economies are vulnerable to military defeats, as occurred in Russia in 1917, and to financial crises like that of 1789 France after a century of costly struggle with Britain. Countries that are disadvantaged within the international states system are most at risk to externally induced crises and to the possibility of social revolution.

A state's vulnerability to crisis, however, depends fundamentally on its relationship to elites, whether nobles, landlords, or religious authorities. State managers are forever caught in the cross pressures between attempts to meet international competitive challenges by increasing revenues and resistance by angry elites to resource extraction. States that are weakly bureaucratized, where elites control high offices and key military posts, cannot act autonomously. When powerful elites can paralyze the state's resource accumulation, severe conflicts occur, as in the English, French, and Chinese revolutions (Goldstone 1986).

However, externally induced crises may initiate an "elite revolution," as occurred in Japan's 1868 Meiji restoration and Ataturk's 1919 revolution in Turkey. In such regimes a bureaucratic elite of civil and military officials emerged that lacked large landholdings or ties to merchants and landlords. In the face of Western military threats to national sovereignty and, consequently, to their own power and status, these elites seized control of the state apparatus. With the aim of resolving economic and military difficulties, they transformed existing sociopolitical structures through land reform, leveling of status distinctions, and rapid industrialization

The 1979 overthrow of the Shah of Iran resulted from an urban revolution that met little resistance from powerful military forces. (UPI/Corbis-Bettmann)

(Trimberger 1978). These transformative episodes, sometimes called "revolutions from above," are distinguished by the absence of popular revolts "from below."

Neopatrimonial regimes are highly vulnerable to revolutionary overthrow (Eisenstadt 1978). Examples include pre-1911 Mexico, pre-1959 Cuba, pre-1979 Nicaragua, and pre-1979 Iran. Centered on the personal decisions of a dictator, these regimes operate through extensive patronage networks rather than a bureaucratized civil service and professional military. Their exclusionary politics makes reform nearly impossible and, in the event of a withdrawal of support by stronger states, invites challenges that may overwhelm corrupt armed forces.

In contrast, revolution is unlikely in open, participatory regimes typical of modern capitalist democracies. By enfranchising new groups, these systems successfully incorporate challengers. By redistributing wealth and opportunity, they are able to mute class antagonisms.

In sum, contradictions between the state apparatus and the dominant classes have been crucial to the onset of revolutionary situations. State bureaucrats are caught in the cross pressures between meeting the challenges of the international states system and yielding to the competing claims of elites. Consequently state structures differ in their vulnerability to political crises.

Consider next the character of participation in revolutions. Challengers of Marx's voluntarist theory assert that no successful social revolution has been made by a self-consciously revolutionary movement. They allow that revolutionaries do guide the course of revolutions, but assert that they do not create revolutionary situations, which emerge from externally induced political crises. These theorists also offer a different reading of the roles of social classes in revolutions. Urban workers, favored by Marx's theory, played important parts in revolutions. However, their numbers were small and their contribution was less crucial than that of peasants, who comprised the vast bulk of producers. When political crises immobilized armies and weakened supervision, they opened the way for peasant revolts that provided the "dynamite" to bring down old regimes (Moore 1966). Revolts against the landed upper classes made it impossible to continue existing agrarian class relations and thereby reduced the prospects for liberalism or counterrevolution. It was the conjunction of political crisis and peasant insurrection that brought about the fundamental transformations identified with social revolution (Skocpol 1979).

But peasants often do not act alone. A key difference between earlier and twentieth-century revolutions is the greater importance of coalitions in the latter (Tilly 1978). Peasants in France and Russia lived in solitary and relatively autonomous villages that afforded them the solidarity and tactical space for revolt (Wolf 1969). Elsewhere, professional revolutionaries provided leadership and ideologies that cemented disparate local groups into potent national movements. The success of their efforts depended in part on the breadth of the coalition they were able to realize among peasants, landless and migrant laborers, rural artisans, and sometimes landlords (Goodwin and Skocpol 1989).

Urban groups have played crucial parts in Third World revolutions. In Cuba and Nicaragua students, professionals, clerics, and merchants joined workers and peasants in coalitions that toppled dictatorical regimes. The 1979 overthrow of the Shah of Iran resulted from an urban revolution that met little resistance from powerful military forces (Farhi 1990).

Finally, revolutionary leaderships have not come from among those who controlled the means of production nor from the ranks of a risen proletariat. Rather, marginal political elites were most likely to consolidate power, for they were both skilled in the running of state organizations and tied by identity and livelihood to the aggrandizement of national welfare and prestige. Their role is clearest in revolutions from above but is no less prominent in social revolutions.

Consider, last, the outcomes of revolutions. For Marx revolutions were bridges between successive modes of production. Bourgeois revolutions marked the transition from feudalism to capitalism; socialist revolutions, the transition from capitalism to communism, history's final stage. Once completed, socialist revolution would open the way to the end of class struggle and the disappearance of state power.

Capitalist economies have great staying power, and reform rather than revolution is the rule in advanced nations.

That revolutions transform social and political institutions is undeniable, but the mechanisms of transformation are open to question. In all historically successful revolutions, the resultant sociopolitical transformations were accomplished by new state structures. The state did *not* wither away.

Moreover, the new states were more centralized and bureaucratized. Liberal parliamentary regimes appeared in the early phases of the French and Russian revolutions. However, these gave way in the face of counterrevolutionary threats and international pressures that were met with rationalized state institutions. Revolutionary events in the twentieth century also make clear that the completion and political consolidation of social revolutions depend on the openings offered by military conflicts and the international balance of power. Liberal parliamentary regimes have met similar fates in successful twentieth-century revolutions.

Through the centralization of political power, what changed most in revolutions was the mode of social control of the lower strata. All revolutions ended in the consolidation of new mass-mobilizing state organizations through which peasants and urban workers were for the first time directly incorporated into national economies and politics. National liberation movements in Asia and Africa combined aspirations for independence and for incorporation in a fashion similar to these newly formed revolutionary states.

Finally, much as revolutionary situations are in part determined by world historical events like wars and depressions, revolutionary outcomes transform the structure of the international states system and of world markets. Revolutions break old alliances and create new ones. They launch new programs of agricultural and industrial production. Past revolutions stand as models for present and future revolutions. In all these ways revolutions shape the possibilities for revolution and reform in the modern world order.

Sociologists who study revolutions have been engaged in a project of revision. Informed by recent sociopolitical transformations and new research on past revolutions, their work questions and qualifies much of Marx's analysis. It considers revolutions in the context of the world economy and the international states system. It places the relations between states and social classes in a new light. And it examines how transformations in the recent or distant past weigh on the course of revolutionary events. But, on balance, it largely confirms and continues the main thrust of Marx's method, notably his focus on actors embedded in concrete organizational settings within historically specific circumstances. This view, rather than a focus on the alternatives of personality, collective mentality, or system dysfunction, distinguishes the sociology of revolution. It owes much to Marx's legacy.

BIBLIOGRAPHY

Eisenstadt, S. N. 1978 *Revolution and the Transformation of Societies.* New York: Free Press.

Farhi, Farideh 1990 *States and Urban-Based Revolutions: Iran and Nicaragua.* Urbana: University of Illinois Press.

Goldstone, Jack A. 1986 "The Comparative and Historical Study of Revolutions." In J. A. Goldstone, ed., *Revolutions.* San Diego: Harcourt Brace Jovanovich.

Goodwin, Jeff, and Theda Skocpol 1989 "Explaining Revolutions in the Contemporary Third World." *Politics & Society* 17:489–509.

Huntington, Samuel P. 1968 *Political Order in Changing Societies.* New Haven: Yale University Press.

Moore, Barrington, Jr. 1966 *Social Origins of Dictatorship and Democracy.* Boston: Beacon Press.

Skocpol, Theda 1979 *States and Social Revolutions.* New York: Cambridge University Press.

Tilly, Charles 1978 *From Mobilization to Revolution.* Reading, Mass.: Addison-Wesley.

Trimberger, Ellen Kay 1978 *Revolution from Above: Military Bureaucrats and Development in Japan, Turkey, Egypt, and Peru.* New Brunswick, N.J.: Transaction Books.

Tucker, Robert (ed.) 1978 *The Marx-Engels Reader.* New York: Norton.

Wolf, Eric R. 1969 *Peasant Wars of the Twentieth Century.* New York: Harper and Row.

– ROBERT C. LIEBMAN

S

SEGREGATION AND DESEGREGATION

In the early years of the American colonies and the new republic of the United States, segregation was not only impractical but undesirable. To benefit from slavery, slave masters had to manage and control slaves. They therefore had to work with them. Not all slaves were field hands or agricultural workers; some were domestic servants, which meant that the slave master and mistress had to share their private quarters with slaves. Thus, many white Americans, especially Southerners in the pre–Civil War South, accepted daily, intimate, personal, primary face-to-face contact with slaves as a necessity. They insisted, however, that all such contacts reflect proper social distance: Slaves were always to be subservient; behavioral assimilation was allowed only to a point; slaves were supposed to know dominant-group culture, use it when and where appropriate, yet always recognize that they were not the equals of their masters. Although structural assimilation was occurring at a primary level, it was not among equals.

With the Emancipation Proclamation of 1863 and the ratification of the Thirteenth Amendment in 1865, some Americans seriously considered the idea of separating blacks and whites. As some blacks emigrated to poor urban areas in the South, and as their numbers increased, some whites recognized that blacks were becoming a threat to the hard-won victories of higher priced white labor (Bonacich 1972). They recognized that the former mechanisms of deference and social distance would no longer allow whites to maintain the subordination of black men and women. And so they insisted on a system of separation. It was not enough to separate residentially; it was necessary to establish a caste system that would deny blacks access to most jobs, social and governmental services, schools and colleges, public accommodations, and the right to vote.

In both the South and the North, segregation was practiced long before it became embodied in law. It was a Supreme Court decision, however, that in 1896 established segregation as the law of the land. It was through the medium of statutes, therefore, that domination was ultimately exercised. In other words, it was the polity, not the economy, that suppressed the competition of black urban laborers and that established this shift from paternalistic to competitive race relations (Scott 1977; van den Berghe 1967).

Segregationist laws were passed as early as 1875 in Tennessee; they rapidly advanced throughout the South and by the 1880s blacks were separated on all modes of transportation (Franklin 1947). Very soon, however, the Civil Rights Act of 1875, which guaranteed black Americans all the privileges and rights of citizenship, became an impediment to the policy of segregation. But the impediment was removed in 1883 when the Supreme Court declared the Civil Rights Act of 1875 unconstitutional. Soon after the High Court's decision, black Americans were banned in certain Southern venues, from hotels and other places of public accommodation—restaurants, theaters, and places of public amusement. As the process continued, by 1885 most Southern states had enacted laws requiring separate schools for blacks and for whites. Finally, on May 18, 1896, the Supreme Court in its infamous *Plessy* v. *Ferguson* decision made segregation the law of the land (Kromkowski 1991). Both the North and the South were elated, but the implication of the decision and the way it was to be implemented would be considerably different in these two regions. As a result, the consequences and effects of segregation in the South would be different from those in the North.

If segregation had not legitimated the rights of Southern whites to degrade and control blacks, blacks might have seen opportunities for independent growth in segregation. Segregation in the South meant biracialism, and biracialism meant the creation of black institutions, institutions that were to some extent administered and controlled by blacks. Although most blacks in the South worked for whites, they did not have to depend on them for all their basic services. They had separate schools, hospitals, and churches. Most blacks in the South became sharecroppers, working rented land. The land meant debt to the sharecropper on one hand, but it also meant a certain amount of daily independence, on the other. It is conceivable, therefore, that under a more positive set of circumstances blacks could have focused on the "equal requirement" of the *Plessy* "separate but equal" decision. But because segregation became the detested symbol of injustice, Southern blacks insisted on destroying it.

As blacks struggled against segregation they were beaten and murdered. Law enforcement participated in these affronts either by refusing to protect black people or by becoming the perpetrators of violence. Such actions reinforced the view in the minds of Southern blacks that segregation was the symbol of black inferiority. As blacks struggled to defend themselves they learned that sheriffs and law enforcement officials, mayors, governors, the FBI, the federal government, the Attorney General of the United States, and even the president participated in one way or another in the maintenance of a system of segregation that declared black people inferior.

Because the major problem in the North was not segregation, the strategies of Southern blacks were inappropriate for the problems of Northern blacks.

Although Southern blacks were eventually successful in destroying the system of segregation in the South, blacks in the North, where the *Plessy* decision had been implemented differently, often failed. Because the major problem in the North was not segregation, the strategies of Southern blacks were inappropriate for the problems of Northern blacks and those who moved north. Desegregationist strategies were designed for problems like residential segregation but not for problems like poverty and differential access to occupational opportunities. This is why the Southern Christian Leadership Conference left the urban slums of Chicago, where the real problems were, and attacked the issue of segregated housing in Cicero, Illinois, which for blacks during this period of their history was irrelevant and insignificant.

Although Southern whites insisted on black inferiority, one should not assume that they therefore wanted to dispose of blacks. They needed blacks for at least two reasons: first, to establish their alleged superiority and, second, to exploit black labor. Blacks had been their slaves, had worked their fields, had stablized and maintained their households, and had been a source of wealth and sometimes even pleasure. Many Southern whites had even developed a degree of affection for blacks.

Northern whites were quite different in this regard. Some knew the value of black Americans, but their major goal was to make certain that blacks and whites remained apart. A biracial system was not required because occupational and economic discrimination kept blacks and whites apart. And, when and where necessary, whites would use restrictive real estate clauses to keep the races separate. Whites in the North wanted blacks to stay completely to themselves unless there was some need for their labor. With the exception of hiring black women, whites did not really want to make much competitive use of black labor. It seems that Northern whites wanted blacks to disappear, and so they pretended they did not exist.

In the South, segregationist policies eventually led to a biracial system that produced unanticipated consequences. It actually laid the groundwork for the development of a black middle class composed of clergy, college administrators and professors, medical doctors, journalists, school teachers, artisans, and skilled craftspeople, all of whom had learned to be independent in their respective institutional settings. They were the decision makers and leaders of their people. They would train the new teachers, the new professionals, even a new business elite. Their protégés would become the new entrepreneurs and open businesses of various kinds—barbershops, beauty shops, grocery stores, restaurants, and nightclubs. They would establish black banks, publish black newspapers, and establish professional societies. Many of the college graduates would become ministers and establish their own churches. In time all of these professionals would combine their resources and expertise and, using their two institutional bases, the school and the church, would lead a struggle against the very system that made their existence possible, the system of segregation. In the South segregation did not mean separation only. It meant the right of whites to degrade blacks, to treat blacks unjustly, and mostly to keep blacks in an inferior condition.

Eventually the black church, a product of segregation and discrimination, would become the institutional base for the fight against segregation and discrimination. Not only did the black church provide the leadership, it also provided the following. However, since black churches had existed for decades, and their congregations were ready for change for decades, why did the "movement" take until 1955 to start? A critical component is the size of the black middle and skilled-worker classes. In the mid-to-late 1950s these two classes constituted approximately 39 percent of the black community, a larger percentage than before. World War II had been a major period of opportunity for these people, and as a result they garnered more resources and began to expect more from the system. In short, they experienced a revolution of rising expectations. They had become intolerant of abuse and of insults to their dignity. They were in need of a social movement.

Desegregation: The Civil-Rights Movement

The impetus for the civil-rights movement, the movement to desegregate the South, actually began before Mrs. Rosa Parks's heroic refusal in 1955 to give up her bus seat to a white person. The initial stimulus was the

May 17, 1954, decision of the Supreme Court, in *Brown* v. *Board of Education* (1954), that the 1896 *Plessy* decision was unconstitutional. Black soldiers returning from World War II and the burgeoning black middle class heralded the decision and proclaimed that the *Brown* decision must usher in "a new order of things."

No sooner had the decision been made, however, than the nation was shocked by the grizzly murder of a young teenager, Emmett Till, in Sumner, Mississippi. The murder dramatized the fact that no change in the law would change the customs of Southern whites, and the case demonstrated how circumstances of blacks in the South were radically different from those in the North. According to Emmett Till's uncle, Emmett had been bragging to some black youngsters outside a rural store. He claimed to have white friends, even white girlfriends, in Chicago and showed photographs of his friends. Emmett had just arrived in Sumner, and was trying to impress these young boys, to gain their friendships. One of the boys apparently said to Emmett, "I bet you won't go into that store and say something to that white lady." Till accepted the challenge, went in, purchased some candy, and in leaving said "'bye, baby." Late the same night two or more white men knocked at the door of Emmett's grandfather, Mose Wright, and took the boy away in a car. When Emmett Till was found, he had been mutilated and beaten beyond recognition, with a bullet hole through his temple. The picture of Emmett Till's disfigured body was published in *Jet* magazine by Johnson Publications, a black publishing firm. Black people throughout the nation saw the picture. Till's mother insisted on an open casket. Two men were charged with the murder, but both were found not guilty. Passionately, black people recognized that a change in the law was not enough. More had to be done.

Emmett Till was a Northern urban kid who had grown up and apparently gone to school with some liberal whites, and although the commingling of whites and blacks in the North could lead to violence, in some circles it was tolerated. Because the issue in the North was residential separation, it was easy for a black person to find himself in a predominantly black school, though generally there were at least a few white students. More important, however, was the fact that the overwhelming majority of the teachers were white (Jones 1985, p. 180). These teachers and other professionals usually lived outside the school district in which they taught. Although they insisted that black schoolchildren should obey them, they did not insist that blacks should act subservient and inferior. As teachers they were proud of their successful black students. Northern blacks thus developed self-esteem, a sense of "somebodyness," a belief that they were the equals of others. This attitude was reinforced in black urban enclaves. In the South, however, every contact a black person had with a white person required a demonstration of black inferiority, even fear. The idea of being equal to whites was generally unthinkable, that is, if the idea was to be put into action. Northern blacks were always warned by their relatives when they went to the South that the rules were quite different there—that not obeying them could place everybody in jeopardy and could even lead to the loss of life.

Emmett Till was a tough urban kid, not unlike many of the gang members of the 1990s, and the fact that he was not afraid of his captors and refused to stop fighting back made them angrier. He obviously did not know that what he did in the North could get him killed in the South. He either had not been warned, or he did not heed the warning.

Emmett Till's murder and the injustice of the final verdict produced mounting frustration. Thus, on December 1, 1955, Mrs. Rosa Parks told a bus driver who asked her to give her seat to a white person, which was the law, that she would not. This galvanized the entire black population of Montgomery, Alabama. The black community organized a bus boycott, and soon the buses were empty. The leadership was surprised (Raines 1977). Black people were fed up. They had always been angered by such demands and customs, but as Christians they had been taught to accept them and hope for change. By now, however, former soldiers and their families who had been patriotic and who had sacrificed during World War II had become intolerant. Segregation did not mean biracialism to them. Instead it meant abuse and insult. A social movement had started.

Soon a brilliant young black Baptist minister would join the movement, and even though only twenty-six years of age he would become the leader. That leader, Martin Luther King, Jr., defined the enemy as segregation. Segregation, King insisted, "scars the soul of the segregated. . . . It not only harms one physically, but injures one spiritually." It is a system, asserted King, that "forever stares the segregated in the face saying you are less than, you are not equal to." Segregation denies a human being the right to express his or her true essence; therefore, it must be destroyed. King declared that nonviolence would be the movement's strategy and philosophy. Nevertheless, violence erupted immediately. Whites were resisting, but the Montgomery Improvement Association won its victory when the Supreme Court declared segregated busing unconstitutional. King and his leadership cadre immediately set about the task of desegregating other public facilities in Montgomery. The movement had begun, and from this point on other struggles would erupt spontaneously across the South. All of them devoted themselves to desegregation.

As black college students observed the activities of Dr. King and his organization, the Southern Christian Leadership Conference (SCLC), they decided to continue the process of desegregation. Dr. King was desegregating downtown department stores in Montgomery; they would desegregate lunch counters. It was the custom in the South not to serve blacks at lunch counters in the various dime stores, especially the Woolworth's chain. So on November 1, 1960, four students from the local black college took seats at the lunch counter in Greensboro, North Carolina. They asked to be served, and when the management refused they resolved to stay. After a day or two violence began. A group of young white toughs and some older adults began to pull them out of their seats and beat them. The police were called in but refused to arrest the perpetrators of the violence. Instead they arrested the victims, those who were involved peacefully in what became known as the sit-ins. As a result of the police actions, Southern blacks noted again that not only were the citizens of the South opposed to their rights, but so were the public officials. Segregation had to be destroyed "lock, stock, and barrel, top to bottom, left to right" (Carmichael 1971), because it even corrupted public officials and officers of the law, whose sworn duty it was to protect the citizenry. From this point on segregation was the enemy, and going to jail to end it became a badge of honor.

The issue of segregation on buses involving interstate travel remained a problem even after the Montgomery victory. Therefore it was not long before groups of Freedom Riders were mobilized to test the Supreme Court decision's relevance to interstate travel. The Freedom Riders included blacks and whites, a fact that should not be forgotten. In some instances whites actually outnumbered blacks. The Freedom Rides began in May 1961 and were immediately confronted with violence. Buses were bombed. Freedom Riders were beaten unmercifully at most destinations. Some were permanently disabled. The perpetrators were indiscriminate: They beat blacks and whites. In fact, their hatred seemed greater for whites—"Nigger lovers," they were called—than for blacks. The Freedom Riders expected to be protected by the FBI, but J. Edgar Hoover, the director, made it clear that his agency had no intention of protecting these agitators. The failure of the federal government to uphold the law, in this instance, finally communicated to black people and some whites that the existence of segregation had corrupted not just local public officials but even officials of the federal government. The fight had to begin at the top.

The next major chapter in the effort to desegregate the South took place in Albany, Georgia, in 1961. Failing in their desegregation efforts there, King and the SCLC launched a new project to protest segregated lunch counters in downtown Birmingham, Alabama. King was jailed. While in jail, he wrote his philosophically brilliant "Letter from a Birmingham Jail." Although Birmingham's white business leaders agreed on a desegregation plan, King's motel was still bombed. Medgar Evers was shot to death in neighboring Jackson, Mississippi, and four young children were murdered in the bombing of the Sixteenth Street Baptist Church in Birmingham. Blacks learned that even if they could get local public officials and businessmen to change segregationist policies, some Southern whites, perhaps even the majority, would not accept change. They also learned that among the majority there were those that were willing to use violence. Blacks had to have protection from some other source.

In 1964 the Student Nonviolent Coordinating Committee (SNCC) began its Freedom Summers Project in Mississippi. Mississippi was considered by blacks to be the most dangerous state in the South, and it lived up to its reputation. On Sunday, August 4, 1964, Mississippi claimed three lives, those of James Chaney, Michael Swerner, and Andrew Goodman—the two latter were white. All three were members of SNCC's Freedom Summer Project. Their only offense was that they had volunteered to teach black youth, work with the rural poor, and register blacks to vote. If it was not apparent during the Freedom Rides, it was now apparent that Southern whites would kill anybody, whites included, who opposed their way of life. Blacks now had a growing collection of concerned Northern whites. Swerner's wife commented that it was unfortunate, but apparently whites had to die before other, complacent whites would listen. The parents of the two young white students, Swerner and Goodman, talked about the martyrdom of their children. They were proud but grief-stricken. They insisted that the monstrous evil of segregation must be destroyed. Black members of the Congress on Racial Equality (CORE) and SNCC were furious. Some of them had been personal friends of James Chaney, who was black. They passionately blamed the governor of the state and the federal government for what happened in Philadelphia, Mississippi, during the summer of 1964. As a result of these murders by law enforcement authorities, SNCC and the SCLC decided to march from Selma to Montgomery. Near the end of their march, however, as they approached the Edmond Pettus Bridge, they were attacked by mounted sheriff's officers wielding clubs. They were beaten indiscriminately, men and women, young adults and children.

In sum, the central focus of black struggle in the South from 1955 to 1965 was desegregation. Blacks insisted on desegregating public transportation facilities, public eating establishments, public water fountains, public bathrooms, and public institutions of higher education. As a result of their sacrifices during this decade black Southerners had learned that desegregation required changes in the law at the national level. A civil-rights bill was therefore required. It also required a willingness on the part of government officials to protect and defend the rights of black Americans.

It was not long after Selma that Watts, an urban ethnic enclave near Los Angeles, blew up in the race riots of 1965. Stores were torched and looted. Surveying the destruction in Watts, Dr. King and the SCLC decided that it was time to take their movement to the North. What they were not aware of was that their desegregation strategies would not solve the problems of Northern blacks, because the central problem for this group was not segregation. To understand this we need to contrast the evolution of the black middle class in the South with that in the North.

Desegregation Versus Integration

A biracial system similar to the South never surfaced in the American North. As a result blacks there depended almost completely on whites for employment. Northern whites, furthermore, had not come to depend on black labor, with the possible exception of domestic labor. Domestic labor, however, did not produce wealth; it was a symbol of surplus wealth. In addition, Northern whites wanted to remain physically (residentially) separated from blacks and whites did not feel any need to employ them. With the influx of European immigrants, Northern whites preferred to hire the sons and daughters of Europe rather than the emancipated slaves of the South (Blauner 1972; Jones 1985). In fact, from the turn of the century to the beginning of World War II, Northern blacks never established a foothold in the

School bussing became a strategy in the 1970s to integrate schools and allow black students the same educational opportunities as white students. Because neighborhoods tend to separate racially, white and black students are bussed to other areas to integrate schools. (UPI/Corbis-Bettmann)

manufacturing industries of the North (Jones 1985). Indeed, according to Blauner, in those ancillary industries such as meat packing where blacks gained a foothold, they were actually displaced by European immigrants.

Given this background, the black middle class developed differently in the North than in the South. At first the Northern middle class was a status category more than a class and was composed primarily of the biracial offspring of blacks and whites (then called mulattoes). Generally, they had disdain for the new black immigrants, who were darker, usually rural, and less "cultured" (i.e., less civilized). As a "class" the mulattoes tended to have reasonably good relationships with upper middle class whites. Often, they had white clients, lived in white neighborhoods, and attended white schools and churches (Landry 1987). They did not serve the black community. By 1915 they would be replaced by a new and different Northern black middle class. And as the black population increased, this new black middle class began to serve the black community. They opened their own businesses: Beauty parlors, grocery stores, barbershops, cleaners, funeral parlors, and restaurants proliferated. With the exception of the black church, none of these businesses was associated with a large institutional base like the black schools in the South. The majority of teachers who taught black students in the North were white, whether the schools were in adjacent white or black communities (Jones 1985, p. 180).

In this context it is surprising that the issue of desegregating Northern schools came up. If black students were not learning in schools and were not learning from white teachers, then it seems reasonable to ask whether the white teachers should have been viewed as the problem. But, instead, it was the fact that black students were not learning in an environment with other blacks that was defined as the problem. This meant that integrationists believed that black pupils could learn only when they were in a setting where there were white pupils, and that blacks do not develop adequately and perform productively when they are in predominantly black settings.

In the North, the issue was to integrate everything, but especially the schools. Perhaps this whole issue turns on the matter of law. *Plessy* v. *Ferguson* was a constitutional and therefore a national issue, but it had to be implemented by a proliferation of local statutes. This had occurred in the South but not generally in the North. In the North, therefore, it was assumed necessary only to change customs and normative patterns of behavior, and the way to do this was thought to be by integration. Even though black businesses proliferated from 1915 to 1945 in Northern black communities, black people remained dependent on white businesses for both services and jobs, just as they were dependent on white teachers for their education (Landry 1987). The problem for the black middle class in the North, then, was different from that for the black middle class in the South. And the leadership of the civil-rights movement knew it. At one point Dr. King said that "the struggles of the past decade were not national in scope; they were Southern; they were specifically designed to change life in the South" (1968, p. 70).

The Freedom Riders expected protection from the FBI, but J. Edgar Hoover made it clear that his agency had no intention of protecting these agitators.

Northern blacks had only been segregated (*de facto*) residentially. Otherwise they could ride public transportation and eat at many of the major restaurants, although it was understood that some owners would discourage blacks from coming by being discourteous. The major concern of Northern middle class blacks, therefore, was not formal desegregation but rather discrimination and unequal access. They insisted that they should get the same quality of goods or service for their money. They also insisted on greater job opportunities. They rejected the idea of caste barriers in employment. They insisted on fair evaluation for good performance. And they insisted that promotions be tied fairly to evaluation, irrespective of race. They rejected job ceilings and the idea of determining job status on the basis of race. These kinds of problems could not be solved by civil rights marches. They could not be solved simply by changing the law. Such changes would help, perhaps, but what was required was to get the federal government to establish civil-rights policies that would declare such acts as violations of the law and then, and even more important, connect these policies to some kind of enforcement device so that private corporations and governmental agencies would comply with the law. This is exactly what the Civil Rights Act of 1964 did.

The Failure of Integration: The Urban Poor

Soon after the Civil Rights Act was passed by Congress and signed by President Lyndon B. Johnson, Executive Orders 11246 and 11375 were issued. These executive orders led to the policy of affirmative action (Black 1981). Affirmative action policies essentially required that all city, state, or federal agencies, as well as any private corporation that contracted with the federal government, make every reasonable attempt to increase the proportion of minority workers in their work force. Affirmative action was to be a device to address the effects of past discrimination. It did not take long to realize, however, that mostly middle class blacks were benefiting from affirmative-action policies (Wilson 1987). The reason for this was twofold. First, middle class blacks were the only ones who had competitive resources (such as skills they had acquired from higher education), who owned businesses, or who had parents who as a result of their professional status (i.e., doctors, dentists, ministers, etc.) were able to provide a competitive advantage for their children. Second, the American economy underwent structural changes that created more opportunities for professional, technical, human service, and clerical staff. As these opportunities increased, affirmative-action policies increased the likelihood that some of these jobs would go to black Americans. It was not long, however, before it also became apparent that neither affirmative-action policies nor the structural shift in the economy would aid black Americans who were poor and unskilled. In fact, as the economy shifted from a majority of manufacturing industries to a majority of service industries, a segmented labor market developed. A segmented labor market is one that provides differential rates of mobility for differing class segments of the same group (Wilson 1978; 1981; 1987).

It is not surprising then that when Mayor Richard Daly of Chicago and Martin Luther King, Jr., met early in 1966, and King complained about the slum housing of poor blacks in that city, Daly responded, "How do you expect me to solve the problems of poverty and joblessness overnight?" King had no answer. He would quickly leave Chicago and the North after unsuccessful attempts both to help the impoverished and to desegregate Cicero, Illinois. It is to Dr. King's credit, however, that he recognized that the problems of the poor had not been solved and that a Poor People's Campaign was required.

Oblivious to the needs of the poor in the black community, Northern blacks who had turned a desegregationist movement into an integrationist movement (those that Sowell [1984] incorrectly labels as people with a civil-rights vision) pursued integration with a vengeance. When the Civil Rights Act of 1964 became the law of the land, affirmative action was to be its guiding policy and equal opportunity and equal access the measure of fairness. It was not long, however, before civil-rights advocates recognized that something was amiss, not only for the Northern black poor but also for the middle class. For example, although data from the 1970 census show that black male college graduates in 1969 received a slightly higher average income than comparable whites, other data demonstrate that the majority of black college students do not graduate from college. In fact, when Fleming (1985) researched this issue and compared the performance of black colleges with limited resources to predominantly white urban universities with considerably more resources that attract black students with higher SAT scores, she found that the black colleges produced more intellectual and psychosocial development among black students than did the white colleges. Further, she found that typically white colleges produced "academic deterioration" among black students and concluded that better facilities and more institutional resources do not necessarily translate into a higher quality college or university education (Fleming 1985, p. 186). She added that similar findings have been reported in desegregated or so-called integrated public schools (Knowles 1962).

The fact is that, whether or not schools are integrated, the situation confronting black children in most Northern and Southern public schools is catastrophic. Indeed, for the most part integration has failed black children. Once they enter school they fall quickly behind their white counterparts on most measures of intelligence and scholastic achievement (Coleman 1966; Denton 1981). In fact, the longer black children remain in school the further they fall behind. Denton (1981) reports that, compared to white children, black children are three times as likely to be labeled mentally retarded, twice as likely to be suspended for discipline and attendance problems, and twice as likely to drop out of high school (White 1984, pp. 102–103). Black students who remain in school on average are two to three years below grade level in all of the basics—reading, writing, and arithmetic. These kinds of problems compound in later life such that black students have only "half as much of a chance as a white child of finishing college and becoming a professional person," twice as much chance of being unemployed, a one in ten chance of getting in trouble with the law, (and, if these students are young males, they have a one in four chance of involvement with the criminal justice system); finally, as they age, black students have a life expectancy that is five years shorter than white adults (White 1984, p. 103). Integration in this context has led to less growth and, even worse, the actual deterioration of the academic potential of black students in institutions of higher education. In those situations where deterioration does not actually occur, stagnation does (Black 1981). Wilson (1981, 1987) examined the combined indicators of unemployment rates, labor-force participation rates, employment–population ratios, and work experience and concluded that not only do these indicators reveal a disturbing picture of joblessness, but they also indicate that a growing percentage of young black males are not marriageable, that is, they cannot contribute to the support of a family. Examining rates of teenage pregnancy, crime and violence, especially homicide, and increases in substance abuse, Wilson argues that many of these young men are more likely to become predators than responsible workers.

Further, according to Wilson, poverty has compounded in black urban ethnic enclaves. He demonstrated that there had been a significant increase in what he called extreme poverty areas (i.e., areas with a poverty rate of at least 40 percent) in the black urban ethnic enclave. Wilson contrasted the growth of these areas with low poverty areas (census tracts with a poverty rate of at least 20 percent) and high poverty areas (with a poverty rate of at least 30 percent). The number of extreme poverty areas, he emphasized, increased by a staggering 161 percent.

Wilson also demonstrated that the black community is losing its vertical class integration. Middle-class and stable working-class black families are choosing to live in the suburbs, and as they do the institutions they used to support and nourish decline in importance and eventually pass away.

For the most part integration has failed black children.

The eventual demise of urban ethnic enclaves has been experienced by all ethnic groups in America; for Europeans the process has taken from four to six generations. For blacks the process began in the late 1960s and for many the early 1970s. Of course resistance existed for residential integration, as mirrored in the hostility that exploded in Cicero, Illinois, in the 1960s. Nor is resistance to residential integration infrequent in the 1990s. If it was not a significant issue for most Northern blacks in the 1960s, it is one now in the 1990s. Although blacks residing in white suburbs are often racially harassed, residential integration is gaining momentum, according to Wilson, even as some whites move out of suburbia to exurbia or back to the city.

It should be noted, however, that the process of ethnic enclave decline for blacks is fundamentally different from that for European ethnics. Europeans settled in urban areas at a time when urban job opportunities were increasing. Most of the jobs were in manufacturing and did not require skilled labor. And since Europeans were preferred over blacks the sheer numbers of jobs allowed them to lift a whole mass of people out of squalor. As economic stability increased, European ethnics began the process of preparing themselves for increased mobility within the American occupational structure. To do this, education was critical—educational institutions are essentially preparatory institutions. In sum, occupational and economic success for European ethnics required a stable economic base first, education second, and occupational success third (Greeley 1976). The circumstances for black Americans (a sizable segment of whom were denied stable employment opportunities in the North) were totally different. For those who were already in the North when European ethnics were reaping the benefits of full employment, the denial of job opportunities undermined their ability to establish a stable economic base. And for those who would come later, when manufacturing jobs were actually diminishing rather than increasing, there would be nothing but long-term unemployment. These groups would eventually form the black underclass as one generation of unemployed workers would quickly give rise to another. European ethnics were described by the sociologists of the 1920s and 1930s as socially disorganized (Thomas and Zananiecki 1927). Their communities were plagued by crime, delinquency, gangs, prostitution, and filth, but the availability of employment opportunities allowed many to "lift themselves up by their own bootstraps."

The jobs that are available to blacks now because of the growth in the service sector of the American economy are jobs that require considerable education and training, and so black urban ethnic enclaves are likely to undergo a different kind of transformation than the European ethnic enclaves of the early 1900s. The middle class will be increasingly siphoned off from such enclaves, leaving behind a large residue of the most despondent and dependent, the most impoverished, the most violent, and the most criminal elements. Without new institutions to play the role of surrogate parents, without some kind of mandatory civilian social service corps, blacks in these communities may become a permanent underclass. A residue was also left behind by European ethnics, but it was much smaller and therefore much less problematic. As the black middle class leaves, it leaves its ethnic community devoid of the leadership or resources needed to regain its health. And as the numbers of female-headed families increase, the middle class will eventually have left the majority of black people behind. Integration, then, has undermined the health and the integrity of the black community.

Surprisingly, given this set of circumstances, Wilson's proposed solution jettisons race as a pivotal factor. The solution, he proposed, requires jobs, training programs, residential relocation, a child-care strategy, a child-support assurance program, a family-allowance program, a tight labor market, fiscal and monetary policies to stimulate noninflationary growth, and an increase in the competitiveness of American goods on both the domestic and international markets. Race-specific strategies, he has warned, will not solve the problems. They also run the risk of losing the support of political officials and the American public. But much of what Wilson has suggested would increase the rate of integration in America and would therefore undermine black ethnic enclaves even more.

The counterposition is now being proffered by many people, organizations, and school systems throughout the United States. This can be seen in the proliferation of segregated black programs where black youngsters are being taught only by black teachers. In this context, race clearly is the critical issue. Gender, however, has also become an issue. In many of these schools black males insist that only they can do the job. Since black women have had to bear the burden of rearing the children alone for so long, there is no doubt but that they can use some help. One critical problem remains for people of this persuasion, however, and that is the continuing trend of black middle-class and stable working-class flight. Can the black community stem the tide? It is not suggested here that the black middle class can solve the problem alone but rather that they must provide the leadership, as they have in the segregated black institutions of the South, and that government must pay for it. Can the exodus be diminished? Only time will tell. If the history of European ethnic enclaves is at all indicative, it would appear that as those who are able to compete are accepted in the broader society, ethnicity for some blacks then may become like ethnicity for most European ethnics, symbolic (Gans 1979). If this occurs, then the problems of the truly disadvantaged will not be solved by the black middle class, and therefore Wilson's proposed nonracial solution may indeed be the only answer.

[See also Apartheid; Discrimination; Equality of Opportunity; Ethnicity; Prejudice; Race; Segregation and Desegregation; Slavery and Involuntary Servitude.]

BIBLIOGRAPHY

Adam, Herbert 1971 *Modernizing Racial Domination: The Dynamics of South African Politics.* Berkeley: University of California Press.

Black, Albert N., Jr. 1977 "Racism Has Not Declined, It Has Just Changed Form." *Umojo* 1, no. 3 (fall).

——— 1981 "Affirmative Action and the Black Academic Situation." *Western Journal of Black Studies* 5:87–94.

Blauner, Robert 1972 *Racial Oppression in America.* New York: Harper and Row.

Blumer, Herbert 1965 "Industrialization and Race Relations." In G. Hunter, ed., *Industrialization and Race Relations: A Symposium.* New York: Oxford University Press.

Bonacich, Edna 1972 "A Theory of Ethnic Antagonism: The Split Labor Market." *American Sociological Review* 37 (October):547–559.

Coleman, James S. 1966 *Equality of Educational Opportunity.* Washington, D.C.: U.S. Government Printing Office.

Denton, Herbert 1981 "Future Still Bleak for Black Children, Lobbying Group's Statistics Show." *Los Angeles Times,* January 14(1A):4.

Exum, William H. 1983 "Climbing the Crystal Stair: Values, Affirmative Action, and Minority Faculty." *Social Problems* 30:383–399.

Fleming, Jacqueline 1985 *Blacks in College.* San Francisco: Jossey-Bass.

Franklin, John Hope 1947 *From Slavery to Freedom: A History of Negro Americans,* 4th ed. New York: Alfred A. Knopf.

Gans, Herbert 1979 "Symbolic Ethnicity: The Future of Ethnic Groups and Culture in America." *Ethnic and Racial Studies* 2, no. 1.

Gordon, Milton M. 1961 "Assimilation in America: Theory and Reality." *Daedalus* 90, no. 2:263–285.

Greeley, Andrew M. 1976 "The Ethnic Miracle." *The Public Interest* 45 (fall):20–36.

Gutman, H. G. 1976 *The Black Family in Slavery and Freedom, 1750–1925.* New York: Pantheon.

Jones, Jacqueline 1985 *Labor of Love, Labor of Sorrow: Black Women, Work and the Family, From Slavery to the Present.* New York: Vintage.

King, Martin Luther, Jr. 1968 *Where Do We Go From Here: Chaos or Community?* Boston: Beacon Press.

Knowles, L. W. 1962 "Part 1, Kentucky." In United States Commission on Civil Rights, *Civil Rights USA: Public Schools, Southern States.* Washington, D.C.: U.S. Government Printing Office.

Krombowski, John A. (ed.) 1991 *Annual Edition: Race and Ethnic Relations, 91 to 92.* Guilford, Conn.: Dushkin.

Landry, Bart 1987 *The New Black Middle Class.* Berkeley: University of California Press.

Raines, Howell 1977 *My Soul Is Rested.* New York: Penguin.

Scott, Joseph W. 1977 "Afro-Americans as a Political Class: Towards Conceptual Clarity." *Sociological Focus* 10, no. 4:383–395.

Sowell, Thomas 1984 *Civil Rights: Rhetoric or Reality?* New York: Morrow.

Thomas, William I., and Florian Zananiecki 1927 *The Polish Peasant in Europe and America.* New York: Alfred A. Knopf.

van den Berghe, Pierre L. 1967 *Race and Racism: A Comparative Perspective.* New York: Wiley.

White, Joseph 1984 *The Psychology of Blacks: An Afro-American Perspective* Englewood Cliffs, N.J.: Prentice-Hall.

Wilson, William J. 1978 "The Declining Significance of Race: Revisited but Not Revised." *Society,* vol. 15.

——— 1981 "The Black Community in the 1980s: Questions of Race, Class, and Public Policy." *Annals of the American Academy of Political and Social Science,* vol. 454.

——— 1987 *The Truly Disadvantaged: The Inner City, Underclass, and Public Policy.* Chicago: University of Chicago Press.

– ALBERT N. BLACK, JR.

SELF-HELP MOVEMENT

The self-help movement is a vast collection of mostly small, local groups of people loosely linked through national newsletters or associations. These groups seek to reach, through mutual support, such goals as physical, mental, and spiritual enhancement; the ability to cope with loss or social stigma; upgrading occupational status; improving interpersonal relations; and achieving competence in specialized activities. Although physicians, social workers, therapists, clergy, and other professionals often initially form and convene self-help groups, their continued involvement is usually limited. Groups have not been the only vehicle through which self-help activities have been undertaken. With the development and growth in popularity of videocassettes and personal computers, along with books, magazines, and recordings, entrepreneurs have created a huge and thriving industry of self-help materials that consumers can use by themselves. This trend appears to have diminished the need for groups, making self-help less a grass-roots social movement and more a vast sea of isolated individuals seeking personal change.

– NORMAN GEVITZ

SEX DIFFERENCES

"Sex differences" is the traditional rubric for considering variations between women and men. The use of the term *sex* reflects the basis of selection, dividing women and men into two groups on the basis of their unique biological features. The term *differences* derives from the tradition of differential psychology, in which distinct groups of people (defined by either natural categories such as sex or constructed categories such as socioeconomic class) are compared in terms of some outcome.

Both terms have been criticized. To many people, references to sex differences imply a biological determinism that ignores the role of socialization and context. The more contemporary usage of "gender" directs attention to the social meanings assigned to the categories of male and female. In neither case, however, is it necessary to assume a particular causal factor for an observed pattern of differences. The term "differences" raises questions as well. An emphasis on the term "differences" can suggest that differences are the norm and similarities the exception. More appropriately, one makes comparisons to see if there are similarities or differences.

Comparisons between women and men, whatever the rubric used to characterize the investigation, pervade the social science literature. Literally thousands of studies exist, analyzing sex-related patterns in physical performance, cognitive abilities, personality traits, moral reasoning, social interaction, occupational choice, sexual behavior, and almost any other domain of human activity that one can imagine. To learn how these behaviors emerge, developmental psychologists explore the ways in which specific socialization practices contribute to observed differences in girls and boys and, by extension, women and men. Sociologists direct their attention to structural features that shape the roles of women and men in organizational settings, family units, and labor markets. All of these analyses contribute to our understanding of gender.

Not all of these topics can be discussed here. Nor will this discussion deal with sexual behavior or the biological differences related to sexuality. Here the focus is on sex differences in two general domains: cognitive abilities and social behaviors. Within those domains, the most well documented areas take precedence. In most cases this means that a large set of studies have been analyzed using meta-analysis, a statistical technique that enables researchers to combine results across studies. Chance findings are discarded through this procedure, and a more accurate picture of the stability and reliability of a particular sex difference emerges (cf. Ashmore, 1990; Hyde & Linn 1986).

Sex Differences in Cognitive Abilities

The question of who is smarter has fascinated social scientists for decades. In the late nineteenth century, many psychologists and physiologists devoted themselves to measuring the size of male and female brains. Their biases often intruded, and conclusions about sex differences were frequently in error (Shields 1975; Rosenberg 1982). In the early twentieth century, pencil-and-paper intelligence tests replaced tape measures and scales as a way of assessing mental capacity. In developing these intelligence tests, investigators concluded that there were no significant differences between males and females in intellectual ability. Thus the Stanford-Binet IQ test, for example, shows no systematic sex differences. More specific cognitive abilities, however, continued to intrigue researchers interested in possible sex differences. Three specific areas of investigation are mathematical abilities, spatial skills, and verbal abilities.

Males and females differ in their performance on tests of mathematical skill. The difference is small, however, accounting for only 1 percent of the variance in scores across assorted tasks and age groups (Hyde 1981). Furthermore, the difference is smaller now than it was some years ago (Rosenthal and Rubin 1982). Sex differences are greater among selected samples of mathematically talented youth tested on the mathematics section of the Scholastic Aptitude Test (Benbow 1988; Benbow and Stanley 1980). Overall, the average scores of 12- and 13-year-old boys are higher than those of girls in these samples; the variability in the boys' scores is also greater. As a result, in the upper 3 percent of the distribution defined as mathematically precocious, boys outnumber girls in ratios that sometimes are quite dramatic. Yet it must be remembered that these are very specifically selected groups, of a particular age performing a particular task. They are not a random sample of the general population.

Spatial ability is another type of cognitive skill. One reason for an interest in this skill is its possible link to mathematical aptitude and scientific achievement (which is not at all certain, however). Investigators studying spatial skill discovered that there are several kinds of spatial skills, not necessarily related very closely to another. Three specific categories are mental rotation, spatial perception, and spatial visualization (Linn and Petersen 1985, 1986). Sex differences favoring men are largest in the first of these categories, which refers to people's ability to visualize the rotation of a three-dimensional object. Spatial perception, which for example, involves determining the true vertical plane when one is seated in a tilted chair, shows a smaller but still significant male advantage. The third category, exemplified by the Embedded Figures Task, which requires people to find a simple shape embedded in a complex pattern of shapes, yields no sex differences. Thus, sex differences in this domain are quite task-specific.

Many people think that women excel in verbal abilities. In fact, there are no substantial differences between women and men (Hyde and Linn 1988). They are equivalent on verbal ability in general and in most more specific types of verbal ability such as vocabulary, verbal analogies, and reading comprehension. The one possible exception is speech production, as indexed by the quality of speech, where women show a slight superiority. Age has no effect on these patterns. More interesting is the influence of time. As in the case of mathematical ability, recent studies are much less likely to find a sex difference than are earlier studies.

It is one thing to find a difference between males and females in some area of cognitive performance. More difficult is the task of explaining why observed differences occur. Investigators invoke both biological and experiential factors and debate which cause is most likely. At the same time, many reported sex differences change significantly over relatively short periods of time. Thus, whatever their origin, most of these abilities are rather easily modified by experience. Experience with spatial activities plays a demonstrable role in one's level of spatial skills, for example. Similarly, specific training programs designed to improve spatial skills are equally effective for women and men (Baenninger and Newcombe 1989). Goals, values, and the expectations of others also affect a person's performance in cognitive domains. Gender-stereotyped beliefs of parents, for example, predict students' performance in mathematics courses. Parents who believe that girls are inferior in mathematical ability are more likely to have daughters who do poorly in mathematics. The value that students themselves place on the particular cognitive ability also influences their performance (Eccles 1985).

How general are any of these cognitive skills? Within a general domain, such as spatial ability, quite different patterns sometimes emerge. Changing the content of the question, from mechanics to health care, for example, can alter the performance of women and men. Thus, although many of these tests show sex differences, generalizations should be made very cautiously. Publicity about sex differences often obscures these distinctions.

Sex Differences in Social Behaviors

Conclusions regarding sex differences in cognitive abilities are not simple. Yet the picture for social behaviors is even more complex. The presence or absence of a sex difference in social behavior depends heavily on the situation, and the parameters of social situations are far more numerous and less easily catalogued than task characteristics. Thus, simple "more or less" statements almost always require qualification.

Sex differences are larger for physical aggression than for psychological or verbal aggression.

Aggression is an area in which simple statements are often made. It is true that men are more aggressive than women. However, the difference is only moderate in size, amounting to half of a standard deviation or less (Eagly 1987; Hyde 1986). Sex differences are larger for physical aggression than for psychological or verbal aggression. Differences are also more pronounced for younger children than for adults, suggesting that societal norms and socialization pressures play a large role in aggression.

Some other areas for male–female comparisons include nonverbal communication, social influence, group interaction, and leadership behaviors. Extensive observations suggest that women are more skilled and more involved in interpersonal communication than are men. The difference is particularly strong in nonverbal forms of communication. In transmitting messages nonverbally, women do a better job than men do. They code their intended messages more efficiently and they transmit them to partners more effectively. They also smile significantly more when talking to others, and they spend more time gazing at their conversational partners (Hall and Halberstadt 1986). Yet, even though sex differences are stronger in this area than elsewhere, many modifying conditions exist. Differences are larger in laboratory studies than in natural settings, for example, and are greater when the context is social than impersonal.

Social influence is a general term referring to reactions such as conforming to the pressures of group opinion or responding favorably to persuasive messages. Overall, women are more easily influenced than men. This difference is most evident in a group setting in which there are pressures to go along with other group members, and it is much less evident when people are responding to a written message or a persuasive television commercial. Differences between women and men are more pronounced when other people are present, suggesting the influence of gender-linked social norms. Outside of the research laboratory, power differences in role relationships, for example between a male supervisor and a female secretary, undoubtedly exacerbate these sex differences in social influence (Eagly 1987).

Group interactions also foster sex differences on some occasions. Men tend to focus more on the goal-directed, task features of a situation, whereas women contribute to the socioemotional climate. This pattern is particularly likely when the topic of discussion is a neutral one. When women and men have different amounts of knowledge or experience in a topic area, task-related behaviors are more likely to come from whichever sex is more familiar with the topic of discussion. Sex differences in group interaction are most likely when it is unclear how competent other group members are. In such circumstances, gender acts as an implied status characteristic, and men are assumed to have greater competence than women. Specific information about the competence of members counteracts these stereotypes and, in turn, eliminates sex differences in group interaction. For similar reasons, men are more likely to emerge as leaders in initially leaderless groups. Men are most likely to be chosen as leaders when the group is focused on a specific task and when social interaction needs are minimal (Eagly and Karau forthcoming). Again, we see how the assumptions about gender can create sex differences in behavior.

How large are any of these sex differences? If one uses occupational segregation or division of labor as the reference point, the differences in cognitive abilities and social behaviors are really quite small. By themselves, they can hardly explain the occupational and economic disparities between women and men (cf., Hess and Ferree 1987). Some differences are larger than others, of course. Performance on mental rotation tasks, for example, shows a relatively large sex difference. Differences in aggression, gazing behaviors, and some mathematics skills are somewhat smaller. For smiling, social influence, and leadership emergence, the differences are smaller still. In many other areas of social and cognitive behavior, men and women do not differ at all. Questions of sex differences, as suggested earlier, sometimes mask sex similarities.

Contextual Influences on Sex-Related Patterns

Summarizing the differences between women and men is not an easy task, once one leaves the obvious biological domains. Both task characteristics and social context are influential, creating sex differences or making them disappear. As Deaux and Major (1987) suggest, the basic repertoires of women and men are quite similar, particularly when it comes to social behaviors. Both women and men know how to be aggressive, how to be helpful, how to smile, and how to be rude. What they actually do is determined less by differential abilities than by the context in which they are acting. Attitudes and actions of others affect what people do. Societal norms and expectations are also influential. So, too, do people alter their own behavior from one situation to another, depending on their goals and objectives.

Comparisons of women and men cannot be analyzed in a vacuum, independent of their social context. Even in the area of cognitive abilities, the differences between women and men have shifted over time. Now there are fewer differences than there were twenty years ago. In considering context, it is also important to recognize that most research has been done in the United States. Sex differences observed here may not be true in other countries or even in less frequently studied subcultures within the United States.

No doubt people will continue to ask how men and women differ. But the answers will never be simple ones. Nor can observed differences between the sexes be used as a simple explanation for the broader gender roles of women and men. Indeed, the causal direction may be just the reverse: Accepted roles may channel men and women into different patterns of behavior. Whatever the patterns observed, most sex differences will continue to reflect a gendered environment and be subject to further change.

[See also Gender; Intelligence; Socialization.]

BIBLIOGRAPHY

Ashmore, R. D. 1990 "Sex, Gender, and the Individual." In L. A. Pervin, ed., *Handbook of Personality Theory and Research.* New York: Guilford Press.

Baenninger, M., and N. Newcombe 1989 "The Role of Experience in Spatial Test Performance: A Meta-analysis." *Sex Roles* 20:327–344.

Benbow, C. P. 1988 "Sex Differences in Mathematical Reasoning Ability in Intellectually Talented Pre-adolescents: Their Nature, Effects, and Possible Causes." *Behavioral and Brain Sciences* 11:169–232.

———, and J. C. Stanley 1980 "Sex Differences in Mathematics Ability: Fact or Artifact?" *Science* 210:1,262–1,264.

Deaux, K., and B. Major 1987 "Putting Gender into Context: An Interactive Model of Gender-Related Behavior." *Psychological Review* 94:369–389.

Eagly, A. E. 1987 *Sex Differences in Social Behavior: A Social Role Interpretation.* Hillsdale, N.J.: Erlbaum.

———, and S. J. Karau (Forthcoming). "Gender and the Emergence of Leaders: A Meta-analysis." *Journal of Personality and Social Psychology.*

Eccles, J. E. 1985 "Sex Differences in Achievement Patterns." In T. B. Sonderegger, ed., *Psychology and Gender. Nebraska Symposium on Motivation, 1984.* Lincoln, Nebr.: University of Nebraska Press.

Hall, J. A., and A. G. Halberstadt 1986 "Smiling and Gazing." In J. S. Hyde and M. C. Linn, eds., *The Psychology of Gender. Advances through Meta-Analysis,* pp. 136–158. Baltimore: Johns Hopkins University Press.

Hess, B., and M. Ferree eds. 1987 *Analyzing Gender: A Handbook of Social Science Research.* Newbury Park, Calif.: Sage.

Hyde, J. S. 1981 "How Large Are Cognitive Gender Differences? A Meta-analysis Using ω^2 and *d.*" *American Psychologist* 36:892–901.

——— 1986 "Gender Differences in Aggression." In J. S. Hyde and M. C. Linn, eds., *The Psychology of Gender: Advances through Meta-Analysis,* pp. 51–66. Baltimore: Johns Hopkins University Press.

———, and M. C. Linn (eds.) 1986 *The Psychology of Gender: Advances through Meta-Analysis.* Baltimore: Johns Hopkins University Press.

——— 1988 "Gender Differences in Verbal Ability: A Meta-analysis." *Psychological Bulletin* 10:53–69.

Linn, M. C., and A. C. Petersen 1985 "Emergence and Characterization of Sex Differences in Spatial Ability: A Meta-analysis." *Child Development* 56:1,479–1,498.

——— 1986 "A Meta-analysis of Gender Differences in Spatial Ability: Implications for Mathematics and Science Achievement." In J. S. Hyde and M. C. Linn, eds., *The Psychology of Gender: Advances through Meta-Analysis.* Baltimore: Johns Hopkins University Press.

Rosenberg, R. 1982 *Beyond Separate Spheres: Intellectual Roots of Modern Feminism.* New Haven, Conn.: Yale University Press.

Rosenthal, R., and D. B. Rubin 1982 "Further Meta-analytic Procedures for Assessing Cognitive Gender Differences." *Journal of Educational Psychology* 74:708–712.

Shields, S. A. 1975 "Functionalism, Darwinism, and the Psychology of Women: A Study in Social Myth." *American Psychologist* 30:739–754.

– KAY DEAUX

SEXUAL BEHAVIOR AND MARRIAGE

A particular view of sexuality, derived from a synthesis of Freudian and functionalist elements, has dominated sociology for most of its history. Sex was said to be a powerful biological drive, exceedingly difficult to harness, and capable of being extraordinarily disruptive for society. The family was said to function as the major social control mechanism of sexuality, both in terms of adult needs and in terms of the production and care of the outcomes of sex, namely children (Davis 1976). From a theoretical standpoint, the family has been viewed as the more general and more significant phenomenon, subsuming beneath it numerous issues, including sexuality. Given the decline of functionalism in mainstream sociology, alternative models have appeared describing the connections between sex and society in dialectic terms (Scanzoni et al. 1989; Stein, 1989). Our purpose here is to focus on the literature describing the socially legitimate and nonlegitimate connections between sex and marriage and to do so in the context of these two competing theoretical paradigms.

In 1964 Ehrmann observed that family sociologists had relegated the study of sex to a status peripheral to their major concern with "marital adjustment, happiness," and the like. Sexual satisfaction was conceptualized as one of the several correlates of "adjustment." If we use Booth's (1990) review of 1980s family sociology as an indicator, it appears that in thirty years the study of sexuality has not advanced beyond its peripheral status. In spite of significant societal changes in sexual phenomena, no review essay systematically addressed connections between those phenomena and changes in families.

Since the incidence of nonmarital sex has increased substantially without accompanying chaos, some analysts allege that they have discovered the positive *functions of nonmarital sex.*

Why the peripheral status of sexuality? Max Weber (Collins 1986) and Murdock (1949) both argued that marriage rests on twin interdependencies: economic and sexual. With the movement of women into paid labor, economic interdependence has gotten attention, although prior to this movement economics was also relatively peripheral. Most U.S. sociologists avoided the issue of how persons and groups (re)create marriage. Instead, working from organicist assumptions, they assumed marriage to be a "natural given" requisite for the survival of society. The organicism that has pervaded family sociology for a century led researchers to ignore the issue of "marriage construction" and to focus instead on how marriages could thrive and thus benefit society. They argued that a major function of marriage for society was to control both sexuality and childbearing (Davis 1976). To achieve control, dominant norms prescribed chastity prior to the wedding and fidelity afterwards. Children presumably learned these norms and later conformed accordingly.

Prior to the 1960s researchers paid scant attention to violations of the chastity norm and even less to deviance from the fidelity norm, although Kinsey (a zoologist) et al. (1948, 1953) had documented a surprising amount of nonconformity on both counts. Assuming conformity to be the predominant pattern, most sociologists continued to describe how sexual satisfaction contributed to marital quality. Nevertheless, evidence of increasing deviance from the chastity norm forced researchers to take notice, although, as Ehrmann (1964) observed, their major concern was the potential dysfunctions of premarital sex for marriage and society. Davis (1976), for example, used terms such as *anomie* and *disorganization* to describe "contemporary sexual behavior" in the forms of "illicit pregnancy . . . abortions . . . venereal disease." Ironically, since the incidence of nonmarital sex has increased substantially without accompanying chaos, some analysts now allege that they have discovered the *positive* functions of nonmarital sex. Having sex before marriage, they say, enables persons to sort out sexual "incompatibles," thus increasing the likelihood of stability. Hence, even though one might wonder whether nonmarital sex is getting out of control, we are assured such worry is groundless because sex is "subordinate to the family" (Davis 1976, p. 226). Davis asserts (and Sprey 1986 concurs) that societies allow sex to interfere with the engendering and enhancement of children *only to a limited degree.* By making marital sex "normatively superior" to all forms of nonmarital sex, these forms are structurally constrained in their potential threats to marriage. Hence, in functionalist thought, sex is secondary because it is analyzed in terms of its functions and dysfunctions for the larger whole of marriage—the whole being much more significant than any of its parts.

This reasoning is particularly pertinent to extramarital sex relations because Davis (1976, p. 242), following Malinowski (1930), argues that most civilizations and tribes have been much more rigid in their proscriptions of extra- than of premarital sex, especially for women. Although some explicit arguments have been made asserting the functions of extramarital coitus (EMC) for (open) marriage (Smith and Smith 1974), most sociologists accept tacitly the functionalist reasoning that EMC violations ultimately reinforce the "normative superiority" of marriage. Davis (1976, p. 243) maintains that media-reported EMC violations "arouse sensational attention . . . for they represent both a suspension of the rule and provision of opportunities." In that regard, Sponaugle (1989) documents recent instances of public figures whose professional lives have been severely discredited because of media reports of their EMC violations (Gary Hart, Ted Kennedy, Wilbur Mills, Robert Baumann, Jimmy Baker, Jimmy Swaggart, and so on). Furthermore, observes Sponaugle, EMC is "one of the most common themes" in both literary fiction and nonfiction—the latter including accounts of the EMC behaviors of figures such as Franklin Roosevelt and John Kennedy. Finally, newspapers, magazines, drama, cinema, TV, music, and humorists also make EMC "a mainstay topic."

Although in 1976 Davis (p. 243) contended that media attention to EMC extended "far beyond . . . [its] numerical significance" in the population, by 1989 Sponaugle asserted that millions of persons engage in EMC at some point in their lives and that millions more are indirectly affected by those EMC behaviors. Using conservative estimates from the literature that 50 percent of ever-married males and 30 percent of ever-married females have engaged in EMC, and using as a base 1986 census figures for the ever- or currently married, Sponaugle calculates that "at least 52,000,000 Americans eighteen and older have been engaged in . . . [EMC] at least once while married." Second, to that number Sponaugle adds the so-far undocumented (but "substantial") numbers of never-married persons who have had coitus with married persons (Richardson 1986). Finally, he says that if we add to that figure persons *indirectly* affected by EMC ("spouses, children, parents, siblings, other relatives, friends, and colleagues"), the sum represents a majority of citizens (Sponaugle 1989, p. 189). Moreover, in European societies such as the Netherlands, EMC violations are apparently even more common than they are in the United States, and attitudes toward it are more tolerant (Buunk 1983, p. 314). In addition, countries having the strictest proscriptions and most severe penalties against EMC (e.g., Islamic and Roman Catholic) are known for widespread EMC deviation by males (W. J. Goode 1963). Finally, in view of increases in heterosexual cohabitators (characterized by similar monogamy norms) throughout Western societies, and in view of evidence (Blumstein and Schwartz 1983) that they are no more monogamous than marrieds, we may expand significantly the proportion of the population affected by violations of exclusivity norms.

How is it that such a ubiquitous rule coexists alongside such widespread deviation? How valid is functionalist reasoning that, by tacitly allowing elasticity in the rule, societies actually reinforce the uniqueness of marriage? Is Davis correct in asserting that EMC violations occur because of the "very intensity" of the rule (rules are made to be broken, and the more powerful the rule the greater the challenge to break it)? Although Sponaugle does not address these conceptual issues, he does review the empirical literature on *attitudes* toward EMC in the United States. He reports that although EMC attitudes have been investigated since the 1920s, the research has been of "poor quality" (p. 192). Most of the research is devoted to accounting for variation in indicators such as the following: "What is your opinion about a *married* person having sexual relations with someone *other* than the marriage partner? Is it always wrong, almost always wrong, wrong only sometimes, or not wrong at all?" In 1985, the percentages of a national sample of Americans choosing these four categories were 73.7, 13.4, 8.4, and 2.8, respectively (National Opinion Research Center 1986). (The remainder said "don't know" or did not answer.) This type of item is said to measure the respondent's belief in the appropriateness of EMC in terms of *general* societal norms. Separate "self-focused" indicators measure how appropriate the respondent perceives EMC is for himself or herself.

Sponaugle (1989, p. 205) summarizes eighteen "independent variables" shown by the literature to be related to the *approval* of EMC. These include approval of premarital coitus, lower marital satisfaction, years of schooling, less religiosity, larger community size, perceived opportunity for EMC, diffuse intimacy conception ("defined as the degree to which an individual focuses his or her satisfaction of intimacy needs on more than just his or her mate," Sponaugle, p. 197), male gender, premarital sexual activity, endorsement of gender equality, sociopolitical liberalism, younger age, being unmarried, being child free, less satisfaction with marital sex, autonomy of heterosexual interaction, marital power, and sexual pleasure emphasis.

Love, like sex, requires social control lest it disrupt social order.

What has been the underlying theoretical rationale for this type of research? From a functionalist perspective, variation in EMC attitudes is an indicator of the degree of social control of sexuality. Discovering the conditions under which persons approve or disapprove of EMC indicates the extent to which persons subjectively conform to dominant norms. As long as functionalist thought pervaded studies of marriage, it made sense to concentrate on EMC attitudes.

However, Stein (1989, p. 11) reports that recent theory on sexuality has moved beyond functionalist notions of " 'social control' to . . . [focus on] 'social change'. Individuals came to be seen as playing a greater part in shaping sexual behavior through social learning and daily situational interaction." Importantly, Stein indicates that "the theory of sexuality implicit in this latter paradigm differed from . . . [functionalism because] there is no natural sexual impulse which must be repressed in order for society to function smoothly." Her critique (1989, p. 12) of the functionalist alignment between marriage and sex is a modern statement of the question posed above by Weber and by Murdock: How do persons and groups struggle at both the micro and macro levels in order to create arrangements that facilitate their goals regarding sex? That these goals are as much *political* as they are personal is witnessed by ongoing struggles between New Right and progressive interest groups.

This fresh theory of sexuality turns the century-old functionalist alignment between marriage and sex on its head. Instead of marriage being viewed as conceptually more significant than sex, sexual interdependence occupies a conceptually prior position. Contemporary analysts no longer view "the sex drive as an object of regulation" (Davis 1976, p. 223) in the interests of social equilibrium. Stein argues instead that goals regarding sexuality are socially constructed. Consequently, rather than focusing either on the functions of sex for marital quality or on social control in the form of variation in EMC attitudes, the research emphasis shifts to (among other issues) the dialectics involved in creating and maintaining varied social expressions of sexual interdependencies. These expressions—whether marriage, cohabitation, or partners living in separate households—are subsumed by what Scanzoni et al. (1989) describe as the "sexually bonded primary relationship" (SBPR). Since SBPR partners are engaged in ongoing dialectics regarding a wide range of issues, their relationship is in continual development (Scanzoni and Marsiglio [a, b]).

One of the implications of this approach is that coitus with someone other than one's legal (or nonlegal) partner is no longer explored from a functionalist perspective. A more conceptually fruitful approach would, for instance, be to examine conditions and consequences of persons in SBPRs having multiple sexual relationships in which marital status is, to be sure, a crucial variable. Underlying that issue is the social organization of the SBPR: What is it about the SBPR that makes multiple relationships a scientific issue as well as a trigger for media sensationalism? Some clues emerge from the recently developing "sociology of emotions" literature. Several analysts, including Collins (1981), argue that in addition to the cognitive and normative dimensions that preoccupied functionalists, emotions play an important part in shaping and in changing social organization at all levels of society. Thoits (1989, p. 318) defines emotions as "culturally delineated *types* of feelings or affects. . . . Emotions involve: (a) appraisals of a situational stimulus or context, (b) changes in physiological or bodily sensations, (c) the free or inhibited display of expressive gestures, and (d) a cultural label applied to specific constellations of one or more of the first three components."

In a recent anthology exploring love, no essay systematically examined the love–marriage connection, although all contributors acknowledged that, among other things, love is a powerful emotion (Sternberg and Barnes 1988). Likewise, in family sociology, little attention was paid to the theoretical connections between love and marriage. The most systematic treatment was W. J. Goode's (1959) functionalist argument that love, like sex, requires social control lest it disrupt social order. Peele (1988) and Berscheid (1988) contend that love tends to be correlated with another variable that is, among other things, also a powerful emotion—jealousy for one's sexual "property." Jealousy has received even less attention than love in the marriage literature (White and Mullen 1989). But if we draw on Thoits's definition of emotions, we can conceptualize jealousy as an "independent" variable that is at least as powerful as normative elements in circumscribing the SBPR as well as in accounting for persons' strong reactions to multiple sexual partnerships (MSP).

Besides love and jealousy, Katz (1988) identifies a third pertinent emotional dimension. In his review of Katz, E. Goode (1990) suggests that deviance in general (including "adultery," p. 8), "is the existential pursuit of passion, a 'lucid' enterprise . . . a fevered out-of-one's head experience, a world of beauty all its own, accessible only to the . . . daring members of a soulful elite" (p. 7). If for want of a better label we call this the "heady experience" dimension, we may ask how all three emotions, alongside cognitive elements, help us grasp the complex intertwinings of sex and social relationships.

Sociologists are beginning to appreciate the complexities inherent in multiple sexual relationships—complexities that writers have wrestled with since the Old Testament.

Cognitive elements circumscribing the SBPR include the all-important *definition of the situation*—a person perceives that she or he is or is not sexually interdependent with another—and these elements include norms prescribing meanings and degrees of sexual exclusivity. Simultaneously, *emotional* elements include the degree of jealousy felt for that sexual interdependence. Scanzoni et al. (1989) suggest that the SBPR, like all forms of social organization, passes through at least three phases of structuring or development—formation, maintenance and change (MC), and dissolution. Persons A and B may experience coitus but feel no jealousy (or love), nor define themselves as being sexually interdependent. If A and B subsequently define themselves as sexually interdependent, then they can be said to have entered an MC phase; moreover, there is very likely a high correlation between that definition and the rapid emergence of feelings of jealousy. Simultaneously, A or B may also be in a previously existing SBPR that may or may not include marriage, and that person may or may not reveal this to the other.

The 1980s saw several authors analyze multiple sexual relationships from a "woman's" or "feminist" perspective. (No comparable work examined them from a male perspective.) Among these, Lawson (1989) approached "adultery" from an essentially functionalist position, whereas Atwater (1982) approached the "extramarital connection" in terms of what Stein identified as choice and personal control. During 1974 and 1975, Atwater interviewed fifty self-selected women who had recently been or were then in an SBPR with one person while married to another person. Atwater begins her report by describing the several steps in the process of "getting involved." Step one is *preinvolvement.* Its first aspect is degree of premarital sexual activity. Atwater states that her respondents' premarital sexual behavior was high (80 percent) for that era. This indicates, she says, that her respondents had been actively engaging in sexual choices for a large portion of their lives. She calls the second aspect of preinvolvement "first opportunities." She reports that although all her respondents chose to "resume sexual monogamy at marriage," most women, regardless of marital status, receive subtle sexual invitations and sometimes outright propositions from men. Atwater indicates that her respondents "felt they did not suggest or invite" male overtures and were ill-prepared for this type of struggle. However, that kind of dialectic had an effect on the women's own development: They first had to come to terms with the unexpected reality that, contrary to folklore, being married does not (as Farber noted in 1964) exclude one from the "market." Second, they had to cultivate (or revive) skills necessary to resist unwanted overtures. Atwater identifies the existence of a role model (friend or kin who had "done it") as the third aspect. A fourth aspect (often overlapping with the third) is discussing MSP with a friend; and fifth is a period of serious reflection regarding potential sexual involvement. According to Atwater, these women did not merely "drift into 'affairs' " or become "spontaneously" swept away.

Atwater's step two, or *involvement,* describes the processes of entry into formation of an SBPR alongside marriage (p. 40). First she identifies situations such as work that supply the context for "repeated exposure" to another, and this repeated exposure "introduces a note of 'gradualism' which serves to ease the transition to extramarital involvement." Second, Atwater addresses the issue of emotions and concludes that women in her sample did not feel "in love" prior to first coitus, nor did they consider love a requisite for it. They did, however, report that the other person was a friend or that they "liked" him. Nonetheless, many women (and men) in an SBPR have experienced the phenomena described so far but chose not to have coitus with the other person. Hence, to account for choice, Atwater reports that, in line with the literature, she found that the third and crucial element precipitating coitus subsumes a complex combination of current marital dissatisfaction and "personal needs for growth, knowledge, and sex" (p. 43). In some cases, there was very little dissatisfaction but extremely high personal needs.

Step three is *extramarital sex* or entry into a phase of maintenance/change. Atwater (p. 35) notes that the question of precisely when this occurs rests with a person's own definition—especially in light of evidence since Kinsey that a certain proportion of married women, in addition to those acknowledging coitus, admit extramarital "petting." Nevertheless, for Atwater's respondents, "genital intercourse" (p. 35) appeared to be the Rubicon. Previously, they had been "just friends" with the other person (even if they had petted); now they became lovers as well. In interpreting their pleasurable reactions to what for most of her respondents was their first extramarital coitus, Atwater asserts that her evidence "contradicts traditional myths that women can achieve sexual satisfaction only in marriage, and that guilt will ruin any sex that violates the marriage bed. . . . The extra sex is often equally as good or better than marital sex." In addition, Atwater identifies a second reaction: "a sense of learning, self-recognition, and self-discovery" (p. 47).

Step four is *afterwards* and explores women's emotions about being in a second SBPR. Atwater reports (p. 51) that although guilt did not undermine pleasure, nevertheless many of her respondents felt it very keenly. Richardson's (1986, 1988) studies of single women's relationships with married men suggest that secrecy is a major guilt-precipitating element in any covert multiple partner situation, and Atwater (p. 79) reports a similar finding. Although guilt among Atwater's respondents was assuaged by the presence of a " 'peculiarly modern type of justification, namely, *self-fulfillment*' " (p. 51), they were well aware that their choices to exercise personal control are labeled as deviant. Their choices clash with the efforts of others (their husbands in particular) to exercise control over them via negative sanctions. Secrecy is a means to avoid those sanctions and the overt clashes that accompany them. Secrecy also postpones facing the *currently* unwanted choice between husband and lover (pp. 79–80).

It was beyond the scope of Atwater's investigation to detail the conditions under which women in her sample might move from either formation or maintenance/change into a dissolution phase of their nonlegal SBPR. Similarly, her main task was not to focus on the conditions under which some of the women separated from or remained with their husbands, nor to investigate whether a woman eventually did or did not marry a man with whom she had been covertly sexual. Nor did she explicitly address feelings of jealousy among her respondents. Nevertheless, her data and their interpretation are a prime example of the dialectic approach to sexuality described by Stein. Women *and* men are viewed as struggling for a wide range of personal (and political) goals. Dominant norms structuring marriage have limited women's goal attainment, most fundamentally in terms of their self-fulfillment *and not merely via the economic marketplace.* Waller (1938) was among the first to argue that the double standard allows men to enhance self-fulfillment through deviant sexual adventures.

Atwater (pp. 57ff) argues that a vital component of self-fulfillment among her respondents was the quest for *emotional intimacy,* defined by one as "the closeness and the ability to communicate with a male." Lacking intimacy with their husbands, respondents were seeking it with other men. At the same time, Atwater suggests a second component in the quest for fulfillment, namely, Katz's "heady experience" described above. The descriptions of their deviance provided by several of Atwater's respondents (pp. 60–63) are strongly analogous to experiential descriptions supplied by Katz's respondents of their deviance: "It was an ego trip"; "It was fun. . . . There's something very therapeutic about spending a couple of hours in a hotel room in the middle of business day"; "I get a kick out of the relationship. It's a thrill for me . . . the thrill of being with a man who wants me as a woman, in a sexy way." This latter respondent connects her heady experience with intimacy: "If I hadn't gotten involved with him, I wouldn't have known him as well."

Modell (1989) describes younger persons over the past fifty years as "innovators" because they have created whole new sets of norms and behaviors regarding nonmarital sex. Atwater's argument is that younger married women (and men) are also creating new sets of norms and behaviors regarding sex and social relationships (SBPRs) *including marriage.* Her pivotal point is that as women are increasingly freed from economic dependence on men, women as well as men become freer to seek higher levels of emotional intimacy and "heady experience." She emphasizes that these goals "contrast with the traditional male emphasis on physical satisfaction" and conquest (Atwater 1982, p. 191). She implies that with persons seeking intimacy and experience, the norm is being created that if multiple sexual relationships enhance those goals, then persons may justify those relationships. Consequently, says Atwater (p. 204), we may expect that the incidence of multiple sexual relationships is likely to increase in the future.

Research Directions

Lawson (1989, p. 309) predicts the future very differently: "There will . . . be less rather than more adultery . . . because . . . people will not stay married long enough to see it increase." Testing these alternative predictions involves a host of complex issues. For example, if and when a person is becoming preinvolved or involved she or he must face the issues of secrecy and guilt. It is those issues that most complicate Atwater's notion of emerging patterns. Formerly, secrecy was synonymous with "cheating." During the past two decades, proponents of "swinging" and other forms of "open" sexual patterns argued that openness eliminates cheating. However, observers such as Weis (1983) find no evidence to support either widespread creation of norms supporting openness or reduced inclinations toward sexual jealousy. To test Atwater, one must examine the degree to which persons now relabel secrecy to be what Becker (1960) called a "hedge" on their prior relationship. To what extent is the hedge justified in terms of intimacy and heady experience, thus muting the cheating label and minimizing guilt? Moreover, what part do a person's perceptions of another's jealousy play in researching the conditions under which secrecy is or is not being widely redefined as a mechanism to prolong one person's prior relationship until hard choices must be made?

These kinds of questions require a research design in which couples are followed over time and that describes the gradual development of persons and the structuring of their relationships.

First, among those already in an SBPR (whether legal or not), what are the conditions under which a person might enter a formation phase with a particular "prospect," i.e., someone with whom a person feels she or he might potentially establish an additional SBPR? What are the conditions under which the prospect becomes a sexual partner, that is, the person actually crosses into a maintenance/change phase of an additional SBPR? For instance, was the person in a dissolution phase of the relationship with his or her prior partner? Once SBPR multiplicity occurs, what are the consequences for the person's relationship with the prior partner? What are the conditions under which the person continues it, or else terminates sexual interdependence with the prior partner? If the person is residing with and/or is married to the prior partner, how are those two variables connected with the person's choices? These choices began with the allowance of a prospect and later a partner and thus multiplicity; and now entail wrestling with whether or not to continue that multiplicity.

Second, if relationship phases are so crucial, how may we describe them and account for movement across them? We might say that a formation phase is characterized by a person's discovery of high levels of intimacy and heady experience with another. An MC phase is characterized by the hope that these exchanges will continue and perhaps increase. A dissolution phase is characterized by the dimunition of these exchanges and uncertainty that they can or will expand. Third, Atwater (p. 193) argues that negotiation dynamics and their outcomes are strongly associated with intimacy, heady experience, and thus relationship phase. Once in an ongoing MC phase, the dialectics that the couple experience pertaining to day-to-day as well as to long-range matters keenly influence both kinds of benefits (Scanzoni et al. 1989) and thus through them affect the probability of seeking those benefits elsewhere.

In sum, sociologists are beginning to appreciate the complexities inherent in multiple sexual relationships—complexities that writers have wrestled with since the Old Testament (Heller 1984). A simple dichotomy between marital and extramarital sex reveals little about the emerging world scene in which women's historic economic dependence on men is being eroded at the same time that both genders are enlarging their mutual expectations for intimacy and experience. Added to those divergent trajectories are the constants of jealousy, distaste for secrecy, and the importance of hedging one's bets. The resulting sum of empirical complexities challenge sociologists to devise conceptual models in which "control of sex" is replaced by the "dialectics of sex."

[See also Alternative Life-Styles; Heterosexual Behavior Patterns.]

BIBLIOGRAPHY

Atwater, Lynn 1982 *The Extramarital Connection.* New York: Irvington.

Becker, Howard S. 1960 "Notes on the Concept of Commitment." *American Journal of Sociology* 66:32–40.

Berscheid, Ellen 1988 "Some Comments on Love's Anatomy: Or, Whatever Happened to Old-Fashioned Lust?" In Robert J. Sternberg and Michael L. Barnes, eds., *The Psychology of Love.* New Haven: Yale University Press.

Blumstein, Philip, and Pepper Schwartz 1983 *American Couples: Money, Work, and Sex.* New York: Morrow.

Booth, Alan (ed.) 1990 "Decade Review of the 1980s." *Journal of Marriage and Family* 52.

Buunk, Bram 1983 "Alternative Lifestyles from an International Perspective: A Trans-Atlantic Comparison." In Eleanor D. Macklin and Roger H. Rubin, eds., *Contemporary Families and Alternative Lifestyles.* Beverly Hills, Calif.: Sage.

Collins, Randall 1981 "On the Microfoundations of Macrosociology." *American Journal of Sociology* 86:984–1,014.

——— 1986 *Weberian Sociological Theory.* New York: Cambridge University Press.

Davis, Kingsley 1976 "Sexual Behavior." In Robert Merton and Robert Nisbet, eds., *Contemporary Social Problems.* New York: Harcourt Brace Jovanovich.

Ehrman, Winston 1964 "Marital and Nonmarital Sexual Behavior." In Harold T. Christensen, ed., *Handbook of Marriage and Family.* Chicago: Rand McNally.

Farber, Bernard 1964 *Family Organization and Interaction.* San Francisco: Chandler.

Goode, Erich 1990 "Crime Can Be Fun: The Deviant Experience." *Contemporary Sociology* 19:5–12.

Goode, William J. 1959 "The Theoretical Importance of Love." *American Sociological Review* 24:38–47.

——— 1963 *World Revolution and Family Patterns.* New York: Free Press.

Heller, Joseph. 1984. *God Knows.* New York: Knopf.

Katz, Jack 1988 *Seductions of Crime: Moral and Sensual Attractions of Doing Evil.* New York: Basic Books.

Kinsey, Alfred C., Wardell Pomeroy, and Clyde Martin 1948 *Sexual Behavior in the Human Male.* Philadelphia: Saunders.

——— 1953 *Sexual Behavior in the Human Female.* Philadelphia: Saunders.

Lawson, Annette 1989 *Adultery: An Analysis of Love and Betrayal.* New York: Basic Books.

Malinowski, Bronislaw 1930 "Parenthood: The Basis of Social Structure." In V. F. Calverton and S. D. Schmalhausen, eds., *The New Generation.* New York: McCauley.

Modell, John 1989 *Into One's Own: From Youth to Adulthood in the United States, 1920–1975.* Berkeley: University of California Press.

Murdock, George P. 1949 *Social Structure.* New York: Macmillan.

National Opinion Research Center 1986 *General Social Surveys, 1972–1986; Cumulative Codebooks.* Chicago: University of Chicago, NORC.

Peele, Stanton 1988 "Fools for Love: The Romantic Ideal, Psychological Theory, and Addictive Love." In Robert J. Sternberg and Michael L. Barnes, eds., *The Psychology of Love.* New Haven, Conn.: Yale University Press.

Richardson, Laurel 1986 *The New Other Woman: Contemporary Single Women in Affairs with Married Men.* New York: Free Press.

——— 1988 "Secrecy and Status: The Social Construction of Forbidden Relationships." *American Sociological Review* 53:209–219.

Scanzoni, John, Karen Polonko, Jay Teachman, Linda Thompson 1989 *The Sexual Bond: Rethinking Families and Close Relationships.* Newbury Park, Calif.: Sage.

Scanzoni, John, and William Marsiglio (Forthcoming) (a) "Marriage and Sex as Social Constructs: Conceptual Issues and Research Questions." *Marriage and Family Review.*

———(Forthcoming) (b) "The Social Organization of Primary Relations: Toward a Recasting of the Institution of Families."

Smith, James R., and Lynn G. Smith, eds. 1974 *Beyond Monogamy: Recent Studies of Sexual Alternatives in Marriage.* Baltimore: Johns Hopkins University Press.

Sponaugle, George C. 1989 "Attitudes toward Extramarital Relations." In Kathleen McKinney and Susan Sprecher, eds., *Human Sexuality: The Societal and Interpersonal Context.* Norwood, N.J.: Ablex.

Sprey, Jetse 1986 "A Reply to Kersti Yllo." *Journal of Marriage and Family* 48:887.

Stein, Arlene 1989 "Three Models of Sexuality: Drives, Identities, and Practices." *Sociological Theory* 7:1–13.

Sternberg, Robert J., and Michael L. Barnes (eds.) 1988 *The Psychology of Love.* New Haven, Conn.: Yale University Press.

Thoits, Peggy A. 1989 "The Sociology of Emotions." In Richard Scott and Judith Blake, eds., *Annual Review of Sociology,* Vol. 15. Palo Alto: Annual Reviews, Inc.

Waller, Willard 1938 *The Family: A Dynamic Interpretation.* New York: Dryden.

Weis, David L. 1983 " 'Open' Marriage and Multilateral Relationships: The Emergence of Nonexclusive Models of the Marriage Relationship." In Eleanor D. Macklin and Roger H. Rubin, eds., *Contemporary Families and Alternative Lifestyles.* Newbury Park, Calif.: Sage.

White, Gregory L., and Paul E. Mullen 1989 *Jealousy: Theory, Research, and Clinical Strategies.* New York: Guilford.

– JOHN SCANZONI
WILLIAM MARSIGLIO

SEXUALLY TRANSMITTED DISEASES

Until the 1980s, social science research on sexually transmitted diseases (STDs) has been focused primarily on the history of various pestilences, the epidemiology of these diseases, and the description of mass disaster (Brandt 1985; Aral and Holmes 1989). The topic commonly considered was syphillis, long the most identified and feared of the STDs. Historians and anthropologists have written numerous treatises on its origin and the social consequences of its introduction into isolated, tribal, or Third World societies (Wood 1978; Crosby 1969; Hart 1978). More recently, the consequences of other STDs have been studied, especially as a sequela of prostitution (Kalm 1985; Porde 1981; Poherat, Rothenberg, and Bross 1981).

When awareness of the "sexual revolution" finally sank in enough to get social scientists and epidemiologists thinking about the effects of STDs on less traditionally sexually active parties than prostitutes and their clients, the literature turned to the newly sexually active and therefore newly vulnerable teenagers (Washington, Sweet, and Shafer 1985; Zelnik and Kanter 1980) and to other young people involved in premarital sex (McCormack et al. 1985; O'Reilly and Aral 1985). The intensification of discussion and research on STDs, however, came only with the medical community's horrified acknowledgment that the newest STD to become epidemiologically important was also the deadliest, and that *social,* not just biological, information was essential in order to combat it.

When AIDS (acquired immune deficiency syndrome) first began to be discussed in the late 1970s—long before it was given its current appellation—the medical community was already alarmed at its mystery and virulence (Aral and Holmes 1989). But unhappily it took years before extraordinary measures, such as institutes devoted to AIDS research, were hurried into being. Journalists like Randy Shilts persuasively argue that the lack of a three-alarm reaction right from the start was due to the fact that the early victims were homosexual men and not Legionnaires or Girl Scouts (Shilts 1987). While at least the basic facts of AIDS—for example, that in the United States homosexual men are disproportionately infected, along with people who mix blood during exchange of hypodermic needles—are inescapable in today's media, the sharing of information in the early 1980s was abysmally inadequate, and myth and rumor educated more people than did either social or medical research.

With the fine accuracy of hindsight, it is clear that sociologists should have immediately looked at the sociocultural histories of recent sexual behavior in sectors of homosexual and heterosexual life and used this information to help study disease transmission—indeed, even to predict the eventual holocaust. But no one was proactive, and it took years for a pertinent literature to emerge. The exceptions to this rule were a small group of social researchers at the Centers for Disease Control, whose work was restricted to STD-related topics, and a few epidemiologists studying the social location of this disease in the gay male world (Aral and Holmes 1990) and in Africa. Otherwise, the analysis of AIDS remained mostly ghettoized in medical literatures until the mid-1980s.

Finally, the combination of organized gay activism and public alarm made more research money available and launched a flood of AIDS research. Indeed, interest in sex research in general, previously an area treated like a poor and unwelcome relative, received more credibility and funding—though not enough to allow a national probability study on sex behaviors to get funded. A large, approved study to be funded by the National Institutes of Health was stopped in 1990 after Senator Jesse Helms convinced the U.S. Senate that Americans should not be exposed to "dirty" questions. Nonetheless, research on sexuality, especially on STDs and on sexuality and STDs among gay men, found funds—and larger, more diverse, professional audiences. Before AIDS prevalence among gay men was well understood or publicized, research was describing how great numbers of anonymous sexual contacts in gay bars, baths, and parks happened and how such activity set the stage for infection (Darrow 1979; Ross 1984; Klovdahl 1985). By the mid-1980s research attention had become ratcheted on how gay and other sexual cultures exposed people to AIDS.

As AIDS gained its terrible momentum, a smaller preceding and parallel literature on herpes, mostly focused on the stigma of having the disease and/or its impact on subsequent behavior, paled in importance. Still, this research provides for interesting comparisons between herpes sufferers and HIV-positive persons. For example, a study of 1,016 college students found that 2.6 percent of them had had herpes; 89 percent of these students informed partners, and 65 percent looked for similarly infected partners; most did not opt for sexual abstinence (Mirotznik et al. 1987). These responses can be compared with those given when the stakes became deadlier.

Current AIDS literature centers on two main questions: (1) who is at risk and why; and (2) risk-reduction factors, including education.

Who is at Risk and Why

While more heterosexual men and women have contracted the disease in Africa and worldwide and the World Health Organization projects that by the year 2000, up to 90 percent of all HIV infections in the world will be transmitted heterosexually, most of the AIDS literature in the United States is primarily on homosexual men and secondarily on intravenous-drug users (Aral and Holmes 1991). Research established that transmission of body fluids, semen and especially blood, made infection possible, though not 100 percent predictable (Aral and Holmes 1990; Winkelstein et al. 1987). Many researchers are interested in rates and ratios of both heterosexual and homosexual anal sex, since it is believed that the abrasion of skin during anal intercourse creates an opportunity of infection from HIV-laced blood or semen (Voeller 1989; Sion et al. 1988). The interaction of co-factors in transmission is, however, still far from an uncontroversial topic (Peterman and Curran 1986), especially since researchers disagree or demur as to what is risk-related.

Most researchers include in their lists of risk factors number of partners, sex of partners, IV-drug use or IV-drug-using partners (Anderson and Johnson 1990), frequency of intercourse (Aral and Cates 1989), use of condoms (Aral and Cates 1989; Stall 1988), contact with prostitutes (Reinish, Sanders, and Zeimba-Davis

1988), and sex with bisexual men (Reinish, Sanders, and Tremla-Davis 1989). This last factor has been of increasing interest, since there seems to be more bisexuality than mainstream research acknowledged previously, and because this is an obvious bridge between high- and low-HIV-rate populations, information about bisexuality has become critical. A study of lesbian women, a group usually thought of as low-risk, showed that not only had 81 percent of these women had sex with men, but at least one-third of their male partners had had sex with another man. Women with bisexual male partners were also more likely to have had anal sex (Padian et al. 1987). Bisexual men constitute a particularly great risk factor if they make regular forays into the gay-male world unbeknownst to their female partner. This proves likely to be the situation, especially among married couples or in a minority community where the behavior itself may necessitate utmost secrecy and may even be defined by the participant as "not homosexual" and therefore not risky (Carrier 1985; Blumstein, and Schwartz 1977).

Findings from a questionnaire on sexual strategies indicated that a significant number of both men and women told a lie in order to have sex.

Other, less obvious risks include the general possibility of deviousness and lies from a partner. In a poll conducted by Cochran and Mays (1990), 196 men and 226 women aged eighteen to twenty-five completed an anonymous eight-page questionnaire on sexual strategies. The findings indicated that a significant number of both men and women told a lie in order to have sex. Men lied more frequently than women, but both sexes were actively and passively willing to deceive a date.

Age itself has been studied as a high-risk factor. Teenagers have been shown to have irregular sexual contact and therefore less risk of STDs (Reinish, Sanders, and Zeimba-Davis 1988); age also correlates with significant levels of unprotected sex, including anal intercourse and multiple partners who are acquaintances or strangers (Reinish et al. 1990). College students studied by Reinish et al. (1990) were particularly casual about condom use: Less than two-thirds had used a condom in the previous year, less than one-third had used a condom the last time they had vaginal or anal intercourse, and only half had ever used contraceptive methods that protected against STD transmission. Of the respondents, those in exclusive sexual relationships reported the highest levels of intercourse. This finding prompted the researchers' concern that while it might seem that a committed sexual relationship lowered the overall risk of HIV infection by reducing the number of partners, risk might be increased because of *frequency* of relations, unless partners used condoms and knew enough *true* information about their partners' social and drug history. A recent set of qualitative research notes indicates that condom use may decrease, even among populations that most need to use them, for socioemotional reasons. Kane's population of women with HIV-probable partners in the drug culture refused, as an act of solidarity, to use condoms. These women felt that using a condom would indicate their awareness and condemnation of their partner's addiction, thereby alienating him and harming the relationship (Kane 1990).

The most voluminous risk research concerns drug users themselves. The use of alcohol and various other drugs has been shown to correlate strongly with unsafe health and sex practices (Stall et al. 1988; Stall 1988; Siegel et al. 1989). Researchers have gone on to specify when drugs are used, by whom, and so forth. For example, Leigh (1990) found that heterosexual and homosexual patterns of drug use differ: Gay men were less affected by drinking and did more risk taking when using cocaine, whereas heterosexual risk taking was predicted largely by total frequency of sex, with only a small amount of the variance explained by having partners who used drugs or alcohol. Fullilove and Fullilove (1989) found that 62 percent of the 222 black inner-city teenagers they studied used crack, and 51 percent of the users said they combined crack use with sex. Forty-one percent of the teenagers had had at least one STD; those who used crack with sex had a significantly higher rate of STD infection. The correlation between crack use, sex, and STD transmission has been found by many other investigators (Goldsmith 1988).

Researchers' concern with drug use covers not only the loss of judgment, the sale of sex for drugs, and the limited use of safe-sex practices; it has increasingly become concentrated on infection by exchange of blood by mutual use of the same needles during intravenous-drug use. In a paper by Freeman et al. (1987), a comparison of gay males and IV-drug users showed that peer support helped create safer sexual practices for gays while lack of social organization reduced IV-drug users' chances of self-protection. Of the drug users, 93 percent were well aware of their exposure, and 68 percent knew that needle sharing could transmit AIDS. Some individual attempts at decreasing the use of potentially contaminated needles had been made, but the authors felt the only way to help reduce risk in this population was to create organizations for needle dispensation, which could eventually create a culture of mutual protection.

Opinion has changed from considering IV-drug users uneducable to recognizing substantial successes in changing their drug regime to include more self-protective habits (Hopkins 1988). Still, ethnography shows that needle sharing between addicted partners is seen as an intimate and bonding behavior, and this makes change more difficult.

Perhaps the newest risk group to receive research attention is women. Since AIDS surfaced in this country among gay males, the lack of attention to women might seem reasonable—until one remembers that, as partners of bisexual men, as drug users, or as inhabitants of lands where AIDS is not a "gay disease," they would always have been at risk.

At present, the majority of women with AIDS are intravenous-drug users. The next most beset population—and one that has grown steadily—is women with a partner who is at risk for AIDS. As of November 1986, women in this latter category constituted only 7 percent of all AIDS sufferers (Guman and Hardy 1987); but by January 1989 the figure had increased to 9 percent (Campbell 1990). Most of the women in Campbell's study are in their childbearing years; 79 percent are between the ages of thirteen and thirty-nine. Slightly more than half are black; about one-fifth are Hispanic. At present, AIDS cases occur fourteen times more frequently among black women and nine times more frequently among Hispanic women than among white women.

A good deal of concern today focuses on perinatal transmission of AIDS. Children of infected mothers have about a 50 percent chance of being born with the disease (Aral and Holmes 1990), and many women, even with knowledge of this risk, choose not to abort (*Proceedings NIMH/NIDA Conference on Women and AIDS* 1989). AIDS concerns attend other reproductive issues as well, such as the safety of artificial insemination. While the American Fertility Association has guidelines that exclude high-risk men from donating sperm, methods for testing for HIV seem to be inconsistent—and private physicians may not test at all (Campbell 1990).

Tackling the problem of women and STDs on an international level presents special problems. In Asia and the Middle East, where women's sexual activity outside marriage at best damages their chance for marriage and at worst is a death sentence, getting knowledge and contraception to them is a herculean job (Leslie-Harwit and Me-heus 1989). Data indicate that these women are increasingly at risk. In Taiwan, for example, nearly 50 percent of married women aged twenty to twenty-four reported having experienced premarital intercourse, compared with 14 percent of married women aged thirty-five to thirty-nine (Cernada et al. 1986). In Thailand, women are essentially sexually ignorant, yet there are approximately 700,000 prostitutes there, most between the ages of fifteen and twenty-four and with a history of STDs. There as in other such countries, contrary to supposition, prostitutes are well utilized by indigenous men, not just by tourists and military, so STDs are regularly brought home to wives and girlfriends (Harwit-Leslie et al. 1989; Aral and Holmes 1991). In Kenya, the same study showed the incidence of general STDs for women under twenty to be 57 percent. Even more than a decade ago, similar statistics existed for Nigeria (Sogbetun et al. 1977). Miscarriages and infertility are extremely common, but unfortunately that is secondary compared with the high percentages of seropositivity for HIV now surfacing throughout Africa (Quinn et al. 1986). Besides inadequate clinical help and information, cultural norms impede self-protection.

Risk Reduction and Education

It is difficult to discuss risk without touching on risk reduction. Nonetheless, there is a literature that investigates specific risk-reduction strategies, curricula, and behavior modification, and that targets specific populations—such as gay men, minorities, teenagers, mothers, or drug users—with what is hoped to be a useful approach.

The most encouraging findings indicate that for at least one targeted group, gay men, changing risky sexual behavior is possible. This is a significant discovery, since such personal habits as drinking and overeating have been notoriously resistant to sustained modification (Research and Decisions Corporation 1984). Researchers in San Francisco, however, have found that gay men there have reduced numbers of partners and frequency of sex and increased safe-sex practices (McKeisick, Horstman, and Coates 1985; McKeisick, Wiley et al. 1985). But since much of this change is attributed to the extraordinary social power of organized homosexual groups in the city, the question arose as to whether such extraordinary change could occur among gay men operating with less daily construction and maintenance of safe-sex norms (Fisher 1988). However, change *has* happened across the United States, indicating both the strength of educational and social-control efforts among gay activists—and, perhaps, the great motivation for change when suffering and death are not only possible but probable (Feldman 1986; Martin 1987; Siegel and Glassman 1989).

If this conclusion seems self-evident, it is not, because change in gay-male circles is *not* 100 percent—or even close to it. Changes in behavior are associated with proximity to especially plagued populations; the more distance, the less change in behavior (Fox et al. 1987).

Furthermore, even in densely infected areas, a full 25 percent of HIV-negative men seem to continue risky sexual practices (Willoughby et al. 1987). There is even evidence that for some men, fear wears off and unprotected sex practices increase (Martin 1987).

Naturally, a great deal of pressure is on researchers to find out what helps all kinds of people protect themselves from AIDS. Depressingly but predictably, research finds that education alone is inadequate for behavioral change. For example, Calabrese, Harris, and Easly (1987) found that for gay men outside big cities, attendance at a safe-sex lecture, reading a safe-sex brochure, HIV-antibody testing, advice from a physician, and counseling were all inadequate. Other sex-education efforts have found limited effect and often for a limited period of time. For example, researchers assessed the impact of a ten-week university course on human sexuality and AIDS-related behavior. While students who had taken the course possessed more information about actual risk, worried about AIDS more, and asked sexual partners more questions relating to AIDS than did a control group, they did not increase their use of condoms or other contraceptives, decrease their number of sexual partners, or spend a longer time getting to know a prospective sexual partner (Baldwin, Whitely, and Baldwin 1990).

The disappointing results of sex education have caused researchers to look for other hooks. Because self-esteem and confidence give ego strength, and presumably the ability to protect oneself from others'—as well as one's own—desires, a number of researchers have pursued this avenue for AIDS prevention (Becher 1988). Role playing, assertiveness skills, and so forth are seen as having long-term payoff (Strecher et al. 1986). Some researchers reasonably argue that people have to learn the same approach to *many* risky behaviors and that consistent attitudes will help them in their sexual life as well as when they face such temptations as drugs and alcohol (Boyer 1989).

No one pretends that any one approach is appropriate for all audiences. Increasingly, this literature studies separate strategies for different groups. Students of race, ethnicity, and gender understand not only that these groups interpret language through their own matrix,

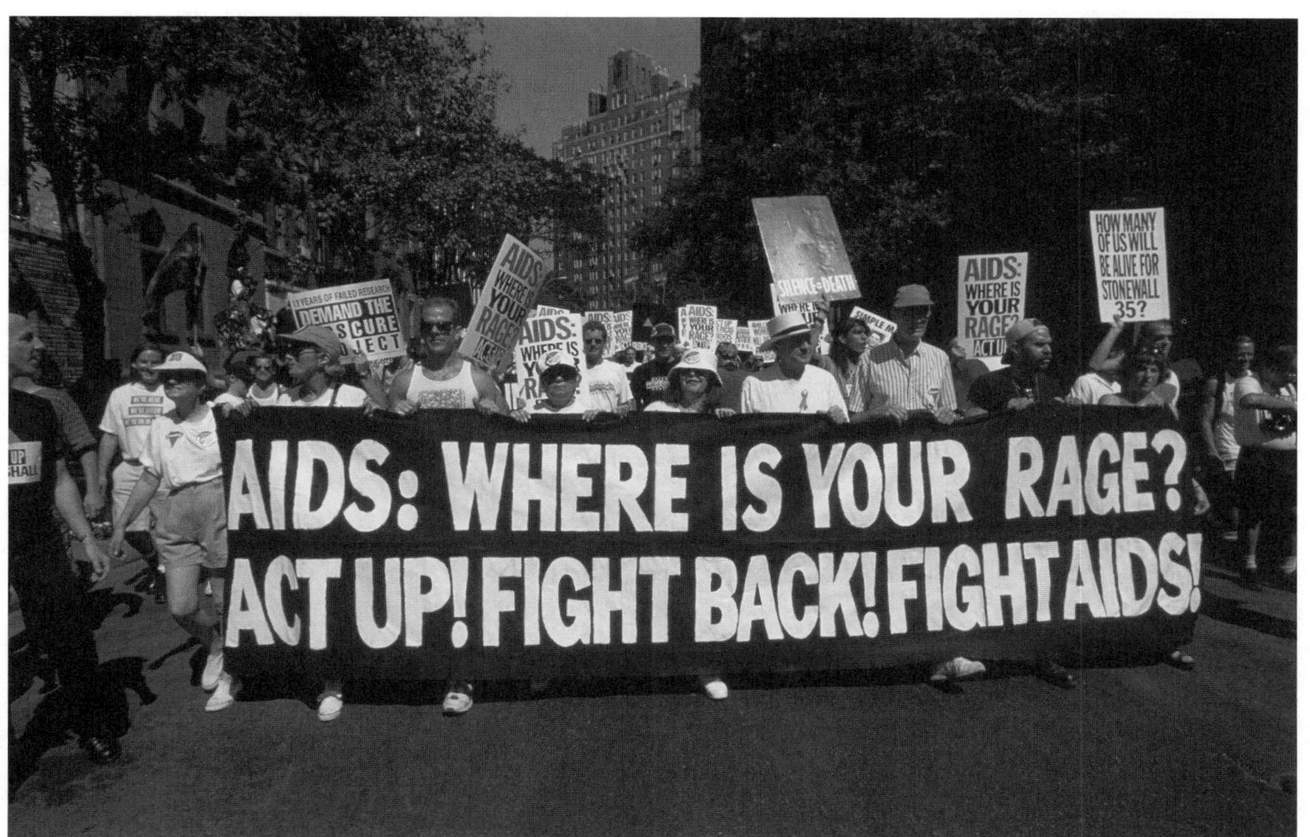

The concern of the gay and lesbian community about the AIDS epidemic helped focus attention on the social context of sexually transmitted diseases. (Michael S. Yamashita/Corbis)

but also that reality is filtered through culture. Finally, this basic sociological truism has benefited research and education among at-risk populations. An example is gender differences; Campbell (1990) noted the limitations of education programs aimed at women, especially non-IV-drug users, who resist feeling at risk. She finds partners of IV-drug users unlikely to be assertive and unable to insist on safe sex. Most of these women are already in subordinate, if not abusive, situations, and their vulnerability and passivity have to be addressed before any other kind of progress can be made. She adds that there are special issues about condom use among minority women, since minority males reject them more resolutely than do Caucasian men. Campbell also reminds the reader that educating prostitutes, both for their own safety and for that of others, needs to take in the dual issues of their gender and their profession. She also makes a good point about overreliance on women as the safety net in sexual relations.

Sex-education efforts have found limited effect and often for a limited period of time.

Among working-class and lower-income black women, gender issues often make safe-sex guidelines seem impossibly theoretical. Unemployment has set black men in more transient relations to these black women, and partners are unlikely to be engaged in the kind of cooperative communication many of the safe-sex guidelines assume (Fullilove et al. 1989). Fullilove and Fullilove also highlight black women's and teenagers' increased vulnerability to disease because of relatively high rates of nonmonogamy among potential partners. The authors feel that individual strategies are unlikely to be as powerful as a "reknitting of community connections" for the evolution of protective norms. Social disorganization further complicates things by giving less, and less accurate, information to black and Hispanic populations.

But even designing messages directly for minorities or finding community outlets for dissemination doesn't begin to handle the delicacy of reaching and influencing at-risk persons. Target audiences for the researcher are not necessarily so self-identified. For example, lesbian women who have occasional intercourse with bisexual partners may not consider themselves at risk (Reinish et al. 1990). Hispanic men irregularly visiting gay bars and having unprotected anal intercourse may not use condoms with their wives in part because, as the "activo," they do not see themselves as homosexual or having participated in a homosexual act and therefore do not perceive themselves as being at risk. Issues about identification, culture, and gender relations constantly bedevil both researcher and health worker (Magana 1990).

The emergence of AIDS as a social issue has not only revitalized interest in the social context and consequences of sexually transmitted diseases; it has finally caused medical research to understand more fully how disease can never be effectively studied outside of social conditions or without adequate information about relevant social actors. Still just in its infancy is a fuller consideration of institutional and public responses to STDs, for example, how public policy gets made and by whom (Volinn 1989), or why some communities respond with compassion, others with fear, and others not at all. The social construction of disease, and of STDs in particular, is an intriguing area of social science research.

[See also Alternative Life-Styles; Drug Abuse; Heterosexual Behavior Patterns; Sexual Behavior and Marriage; Sexual Orientation.]

BIBLIOGRAPHY

Anderson, R. M., and A. M. Johnson 1990 "Rates of Sexual Partner Change in Heterosexual and Homosexual Populations in the United Kingdom." In B. Voeller, J. M. Reinisk, and M. Gottlieb, eds., *AIDS and Sex: An Integrated Biomedical and Behavioral Approach.* New York: Oxford University Press.

Aral, S., and W. Cates 1989 "The Multiple Dimensions of Sexual Behavior as Risk Factors for Sexually Transmitted Disease: The Sexually Experienced Are Not Necessarily Active." *Sexually Transmitted Diseases* 16:173–177.

Aral, S., and K. Holmes 1990 "Epidemiology of Sexually Transmitted Diseases." In K. Holmes, P. A. Mardh, P. F. Sparling, and P. J. Wiesner, eds., *Sexually Transmitted Diseases.* New York: McGraw-Hill.

——— 1991 "Sexually Transmitted Diseases in the AIDS Era." *Scientific American* 264 (February):62–69.

Baldwin, J. I., S. Whitely, and J. D. Baldwin 1990 "Changing AIDS and Fertility Related Behavior: The Effectiveness of Sexual Education." *Journal of Sex Research* 27:245–262.

Becher, M. H. 1988 "AIDS and Behavior Change." *Public Health Review* 16:1–11.

Boyer, R. 1989 *Private Acts, Social Consequences.* New York: Free Press.

Blumstein, P., and Pepper Schwartz 1977 "Male Bisexuality." *Urban Life.*

Brandt, A. M. 1985 *No Magic Bullet.* New York: Oxford University Press.

Calabrese, L. H., B. Harris, and K. Easly 1987 "Analysis of Variables Impacting on Safe Sexual Behavior among Homosexual Men in an Area of Low Incidence for AIDS." Paper presented at the Third International Conference on AIDS, Washington, D.C.

Campbell, Carol A. 1990 "Women and AIDS." *Social Science and Medicine* 30:407–415.

Carrier, J. M. 1985 "Mexican Male Bisexuality." *Journal of Homosexuality* 1:75–85.

Cernada, G. P., M. Chang, H. Lin, T. Sun, and C. Cernada 1986 "Implications for Adolescent Sex Education in Taiwan." *Studies in Family Planning* 17:181–187.

Cochran, S. D., and V. M. Mays 1990 "Sex, Lies and HIV." *New England Journal of Medicine* 322:774–775.

Crosby, A. W. 1969 "The Early History of Syphillis: A Reappraisal." *American Anthropologist* 71:218–227.

Darrow, William 1979 "Sexually Transmitted Diseases in Gay Men: An Insider's View." *Sexually Transmitted Diseases* 6:278–280.

Feldman, D. A. 1986 "AIDS Health Promotion and Clinically Applied Anthropology." In D. A. Feldman and T. K. Jolinson, eds., *Method and Theory.* New York: Praeger.

Fisher, J. D. 1988 "Possible Effects of Reference Group Based Social Influence on AIDS-risk Behavior and AIDS Prevention." *American Psychologist* 43:914–920.

Fox, R., D. Ostrow, R. Valdiserri, B. Van Rader, and B. F. Pall 1987 "Changes in Sexual Activities among Participants in the Multi Center AIDS Cohort Study." Paper presented at the Third International Conference on AIDS, Washington, D.C.

Freeman, S. R., D. C. Des Jarlais, J. L. Sotheran, J. Garber, H. Cohen, and D. Smith 1987 "AIDS and Self-Organization among Intravenous Drug Users." *International Journal of Addictions* 23:201–219.

Fullilove, M. T., and R. E. Fullilove 1989 "Intersecting Epidemics: Black Teen Crack Use and Sexually Transmitted Disease." *Journal of American Medical Women's Association* 44:146–153.

Fullilove, M. T., R. E. Fullilove, K. Hayes, and S. Gross 1990 "Black Women and AIDS Prevention: A View Towards Understanding the Gender Rules," *Journal of Sex Research,* 27(1), p. 47–64.

Goldsmith, M. F. 1988 "Sex Tied to Drugs = STD Spread." *Journal of the American Medical Association* 260:2009.

Guman, M. E., and A. Hardy 1987 "Epidemiology of AIDS in Women in the United States 1981 through 1986." *Journal of American Medical Association* 257:2039–2042.

Hart, G. 1978 "Social and Psychological Aspects of Venereal Disease in Papua New Guinea." *British Journal of Venereal Disease* 54:215–217.

Hopkins, William 1988 "Needle Sharing and Street Behavior in Response to AIDS in New York City." In National Institute on Drug Abuse Research Monograph Series, Mono 80-40-58 (HV 5825 n.38a no.80).

Kalm, F. 1985 "The Two Faces of Antillean Prostitution." *Archives of Sexual Behavior* 203–217. Vol 14. No 3 June, 1985.

Kane, S. 1990 "AIDS, Addiction and Condom Use: Sources of Sexual Risk for Heterosexual Women." *Journal of Sex Research* 27:427–444.

Klovdahl, Alden S. 1985 "Social Networks and the Spread of Infectious Diseases: The AIDS Example." *Social Science Medicine* 21:1203–1216.

Leigh, B. C. 1990 "Sex and Drugs." *Journal of Sex Research* 27:199–213.

Leslie-Harwit, M., and A. Meheus 1989 "Sexually Transmitted Disease in Young People: The Importance of Health Education." *Sexually Transmitted Diseases.*

Magana, Raul 1990 "Bisexuality Among Hispanics." Paper Presented at *CDC Workshop on Bisexuality and AIDS, American Institutes for Research.*

Martin, J. L. 1987 "The Impact of AIDS on Gay Male Sexual Behavioral Patterns in New York City." *American Journal of Public Health* 77:578–584.

McCormack, W. M., B. Rosner, D. E. McComb et al. 1985 "Infection with Chlamydia Trachimates in Women College Students." *American Journal of Epidemiology* 121:107–115.

McKeisick, L., W. Horstman, and T. J. Coates 1985 "AIDS and Sexual Behavior Reported by Gay Men in San Francisco." *American Journal of Public Health* 75:493–496.

McKeisick, L., J. A. Wiley, T. J. Coates, R. Stall, G. Sarka, S. Morin, K. Charles, W. Horstman, and M. A. Conant 1985 "Recent Reported Changes in Sexual Behavior of Men at Risk for AIDS in San Francisco 1982–1984. The AIDS Behavioral Research Project." *Public Health Report* 100:622–629.

Mirotznik, J., R. D. Shapiro, O. E. Steinhart, and O. Gillespie 1987 "Genital Herpes: An Investigation into Its Attitudinal and Behavioral Correlates." *Journal of Sex Research* 23:266–272.

O'Reilly, K. R., and S. O. Aral 1985 "Adolescence and Sexual Behavior: Trends and Implications for STDs." *Journal of Adolescent Health Care* 6:262–270.

Padian, N., L. Marquis, D. P. Francis, R. E. Anderson, G. W. Rutherford, P. M. O'Malley, and W. Winkelstein 1987 "Male to Female Transmission of Human Immunodeficiency Virus." *Journal of the American Medical Association* 258:788–790.

Peterman, T. A., and J. W. Curran 1986 "Sexual Transmission of Human Immunovirus." *Journal of American Medical Association* 256:2222–2226.

Poherat, J. J., R. Rothenberg, and D. C. Bross 1981 "Gonorrhea in Street Prostitutes: Epidemiology and Legal Implications." *Sexually Transmitted Diseases* 8:241–244.

Porde, S. 1987 "Sexually Transmitted Disease in Ethiopia: Social Factors Contributing to Their Speed and Implications for Developing Countries." *British Journal of Venereal Disease* 557:357–362.

Quinn, T. C., J. M. Mann, J. W. Curran, and P. Piot. "AIDS in Africa." *Science* 234:955–963.

Proceedings NIMH/NIDA Conference on Women and AIDS: Promoting Health Behavior 1989 Washington, D.C.: American Psychiatric Press.

Reinish, J. M., C. A. Hill, S. A. Sanders, and M. Ziemba-Davis 1990 "Sexual Behavior among Heterosexual College Students." *Focus 5:3.*

Reinish, J. M., S. A. Sanders, and M. Ziemba-Davis 1989 "Self-labeled orientation, sexual behavior and knowledge about AIDS; Implications for biomedical research and education programs." In S. J. Blumenthal, A. Eichler, and G. Weissman, eds., *Proceedings of NIMH/NIDA Workshop on Women and AIDS: Promoting Health Behavior.* Washington, D.C.: American Psychiatric Press.

Reinish, J., S. Sanders, and Mary Zeimba-Davis 1988 "The Study of Sexual Behavior in Relation to the Transmission of Human Immunovirus." *American Psychologist* 43:11,921–927.

Research and Decisions Corporation 1984 "Designing an Effective AIDS Prevention Campaign Strategy for San Francisco: Results from the First Probability Study of an Urban Gay Male Community." San Francisco AIDS Foundation. Also see Second Probability Study, 1985.

Ross, M. W. 1984 "Sexually Transmitted Diseases in Homosexual Men: A Study of Four Societies." *British Journal of Venereal Disease* 60:52–66.

Shilts, Randy 1987 *And the Band Played On.* New York: St. Martin's.

Siegel, K., F. P. Mesagno, J. Y. Chen, and G. Christ 1989 "Factors Distinguishing Risky and Safer Sex." *Social Science and Medicine* 28:561–569.

Siegel, Karolyn, and Marc Glassman 1989 "Individual and Aggregate Level Change in Sexual Behavior among Gay Men at Risk for AIDS." *Archives of Sexual Behavior* 18:335–348.

Sion, F. S., C. A. Morais De Sa, M. C. Rachid DeLacerda, E. P. Quinhoes, M. S. Pereira, B. Galvao, and E. A. Casrilno 1988 "The Importance of Anal Intercourse in Transmission to Women." Paper presented at the Fourth Annual International Conference on AIDS, Stockholm Abstract 4007.

Sogebetun, A. O., K. O. Alausa, and A. O. Osaba. "Sexually Transmitted Diseases in Ibadan, Nigeria." *British Journal of Venereal Disease* 53:155–160.

Stall, R. 1988 "The Prevention of HIV Infection Associated with Drug and Alcohol Use During Sexual Activity." *Advances in Alcohol and Substance Abuse* 7:73–88.

———, S. McKeisick, J. A. Wiley, T. J. Coates, and S. Ostrow 1988 "Alcohol and Drug Use During Sexual Activity and Compliance with Safe Sex Guidelines for AIDS: The AIDS Behavioral Research Project." *Health Education Quarterly* 13:359–371.

Strecher, V. J., B. M. DeVellis, M. H. Becher, and I. M. Resenstock 1986 "The Role of Self Efficacy in Achieving Health Behavior Change." *Health Education Quarterly* 13:73–92.

Voeller, B. 1989 "Heterosexual Anal Intercourse." Mariposa Occasional Paper 1B. New York: Mariposa Education and Research Foundation.

Volinn, Isle 1989 "Issues of Definitions and Their Implication: AIDS and Leprosy." *Social Science and Medicine* 20:1157–1162.

Washington, A. E., R. L. Sweet, and M. A. B. Shafer 1985 "Pelvic Inflammatory Disease and Its Sequellae in Adolescents." *Journal of Adolescent Health Care* 6:298–310.

Willoughby, B., M. T. Scheiter, W. J. Boyko, K. J. P. Craib, M. S. Weaver, and B. Douglas 1987 "Sexual Practices and Condom Use in a Cohort of Homosexual Men: Evidence of Differential Modification Behavior Between Seropositive and Seronegative Men." Paper presented at the Third International Conference on AIDS, Washington, D.C.

Winkelstein, W., D. H. Lyman, N. Padian, R. Grant, M. Samuel, J. A. Wilay, R. W. Anderson, W. Lang, J. Riggs, and J. A. Levy 1987 "Sexual Practices and Risk of Infection by the Human Immunodeficiency Virus." Journal of the American Medical Association 16:321–325.

Wood, C. S. 1978 "Syphillis in Anthropological Perspective." *Social Science Medicine* 12:47–55.

Zelnik, M., and M. Kanter 1980 "Sexual Activity, Contraceptive Use and Pregnancy among Metropolitan Area Teenagers 1971–1979." *Family Planning Perspectives* 12:230–237.

——— 1977 "Contraceptive Experience of Young Unmarried Women in the United States 1976–71." *Family Planning Perspectives* 9:55–71.

SEXUAL ORIENTATION

As Nietzsche observed, "[O]nly that which has no history is definable" (1968, p. 516). By these terms the concept of *sexual orientation* may be difficult to define with any assurance of general agreement. It is mired in conflicting interpretations of the history of the behaviors presumed to be the expression of specific orientations and, perhaps more important, mired in an unresolved history of attempts to define the very meaning of the concept. The question of sexual orientation currently is something of a conceptual battleground where some of the most critical issues regarding the nature of human sexuality, if not the human condition itself, are being debated.

Sexual orientation generally can be described as the integration of the ways individuals experience the intersection of sexual desires and available sexual social roles. For some, this is experienced happily, as an unproblematic confluence; for others, it is experienced as a persistent conflict; and for still others, as an occasion for experimentation, compromise, and, sometimes, change, both in how they see themselves and in how they present themselves to others.

The question of sexual orientation is a conceptual battleground where some of the most critical issues regarding the nature of human sexuality are being debated.

Sexual orientation is also part of the conceptual apparatus of contemporary scientific and popular discourse; it becomes a way in which we recognize and "explain" sexual behavior. It is as if, to establish an individual's sexual orientation, however inaccurately, is enough to explain most of what need be known about that individual's sexuality.

Sexual Orientation and Gender

Following Freud's 1905 distinction between the "object" (the "who") and the "aim" (the "what") of sexual desire (1953), current conceptions of sexual orientation can be said to focus primarily upon the nature of the object defined in narrow terms. This almost exclusive distinction derives from the dimorphic nature of the human species, that is, two genders giving rise to three possible categories: homosexual, heterosexual, and bisexual, although within each of these categories there is a wide range of variations in both sexual and nonsexual attributes of individuals and many aspects of sexual preference that are shared across these categories. Among such aspects of desire would be the other's age, race, social class, or ethnic status; the nature of the emotional bond; and the conventions of physical beauty.

Important differences regarding sexual aims, such as sadomasochism, pedophilia, and transvestism, are most often subsumed within each of these gender-based categories. Most often, they become adjectives modifying the label *homosexual* or *heterosexual*.

The significance of gender may reflect the fact that, within modern Western societies, gender is possibly the last fully pervasive aspect of identity, serving to provide cohesion to our increasingly complex components of identity. Such distinctions establish the *sexual identity* of others and ourselves. The gender of the object of our desires has come to dominate the meaning of sexual orientation to the exclusion of almost all the other attributes of potential partners that contribute to, or preclude, sexual interest or excitement.

This emphasis upon the gender of the desired object may be a culturally specific development. Some, for example, have argued that, in other cultural or historical contexts, gender may be less significant in defining categories of legitimate sexual access than other social distinctions. Thus, the acceptability of same-gender sexual contacts among males in ancient Greece was contingent upon differences in age (adult versus youth) or social status (free citizen versus slave) and required that there be no direct reciprocity, that the "active" role (the seeking of sexual pleasure) and the "passive" role (the providing of sexual pleasure) remain respectful of social status (Halperin 1989). Men engaging in such behavior were viewed as conventional so long as these rules were maintained.

Such examples remind us that not all persons engaging in sexual acts experience their participation as erotic, experience such activities in the context of what might be termed *sexual excitement.* And, by the same token, they also remind us that not all motives for engaging in specific sexual acts derive from intrinsically sexual motives.

Through much of the twentieth century the question of sexual orientation would not have appeared problematic. In a range of theoretical positions, from Freud's 1905 assumption of an inherent bisexuality (1953) to those postulating an exclusive heterosexuality, sexual orientation was taken as being so firmly rooted in the "natural" processes of human psychosexual development that it was treated as a transcultural phenomenon (Simon 1989). This was true for heterosexuality, which often was, and for many still is, viewed as being phylogenetically programmed as a requirement of species survival (Symons 1979). Homosexuality and bisexuality were viewed either as a disturbance of "normal" development (Freud 1953), an inherited decadence (Ellis 1937), a gender-discordant development (Krafft-Ebing [1896] 1965) or, more recently, a normal, but minor, genetic variant (Kinsey, Pomeroy, and Martin 1948).

Explanations of sexual orientation currently might be described as a continuum anchored at one polar position by the assumption of an entirely biological or phylogenetic source (essentialism) and at the other pole by sources reflecting the adaptation of specific individuals within given sociocultural settings (constructionism).

ESSENTIALIST PERSPECTIVES. The commitment of the extreme essentialist position leads to a view of sexual orientation (as gender preference) potentially present in all human populations, varying only in its manifest expression as a result of differing qualities of encouragement or repression (Gladue 1987; Boswell 1983; Whitam 1983). Other biologically oriented explanations are those linking biological developments with experiential adaptations. Typically, such approaches link variations in such phenomena as prenatal hormonal chemistry with critical, but often unpredictable, postnatal experiences in the shaping of sexual orientation (Money 1988).

The essentialistic end of the conceptual continuum shares the assumption that, at some basic level of character or personality, there are objective, constitutional sources of sexual orientation (Green 1988). It is almost as if such approaches viewed different categories of sexual orientation as different species or subspecies, as if all included within a specific category of sexual interactions shared some common origin. A commitment to such permanent distinctions is often evident in the use of a concept like *latent homosexuality,* which implies that, even where such differences fail to be manifested or are manifested late in life, this orientation is viewed as the "real" one.

CONSTRUCTIONIST PERSPECTIVES. At the other end of this continuum are constructionists, who view sexual orientation as the product of specific historical contingencies, as something to be acquired or perhaps even "an accomplishment" (Stoller 1985a). Most of those holding this position reject the idea of a sexual drive or, at best, see such a drive as an unformed potential largely dependent upon experience to give it power and directionality. "Every culture has a distinctive cultural configuration with its own 'anthropological' assumptions in the sexual area. The empirical relativity of these configurations, their immense variety, and luxurious inventiveness, indicate that they are products of man's own socio-cultural formations rather than a biologically fixed human nature" (Berger and Luckman 1966, p. 49).

For most constructionists, sexual orientation is a reflection of the more general practices of a time and place, and it is expressive of social power (Foucault 1976; Weeks 1985; Padgug 1979; Greenberg 1988; Halperin 1989). Others would add concern for the specific contexts of interaction and the management of identities and social roles (Simon and Gagnon 1967; McIntosh 1976; Plummer 1975; Ponse 1968; Weinberg 1983) and still others would add concern for the experiences that constitute primary socialization (Gagnon and Simon 1973; Stoller 1985b; Simon and Gagnon 1986; Mitchell 1988).

From a constructionist perspective, the concept of sexual orientation itself is viewed as an aspect of the very cultural practices that sustain the differential evaluations of the sexual behaviors the concept purports to explain. The focusing of attention on something that can be called sexual orientation is seen as signifying an importance to be assigned to the sexual that may not be intrinsic to it but that may derive from the evolved meanings and uses that constitute the sexual.

Where essentialists tend to view the sexual as a biological constant that presses upon evolving social conventions, constructionists view the sexual as the product of the individual's contingent response to the experiencing of such social conventions. For the former, the sexual might be said to develop from the inside out, whereas, for the latter, the sexual, like most other social practices, is learned from the outside in. A middle ground is taken by many that view sexual behavior as the outcome of a dialectical relationship between biology and culture (Erikson 1950).

Current Concepts

If only in recognition of the enormous diversity of sexual practices in different cultural and historical settings, despite the relative stability of human physiology, almost all who have approached the study of human sexuality admit the need for some degree of sociological explanation of specific patterns of sexual interaction and the significance accorded them (Gregersen 1983). The question of homosexuality was the dominant issue in most discussions of sexual orientation. Heterosexuality, insofar as it was viewed as doing what came naturally, seemingly required no "explanation," unless it was expressed in unconventional ways. Rather, it was homosexuality that was viewed as problematic, if not pathological, and whose explanation was more urgent. The medicalization of same-gender sexual preference, which preceded the initial public uses of such terms as homosexuality and heterosexuality in 1880 (Herzer 1985), involved the "disease" model of seeking a specific cause, as well as a mode of prevention and possible cure. This implicitly homophobic commitment continues to persist in some parts of the scientific community's considerations of homosexuality (Irving 1990).

The increasing acceptance of homosexuality as an alternative life-style, however, did not necessarily require abandonment of concern for explaining its appearance; it merely made it more obvious that heterosexuality could not be taken for granted, that it also might require explanation (Katz 1990). One characteristic of the modern Western condition is that it has made sexual orientation and the closely related issue of sexual identity problematic. The question, What will I be when I grow up? is asked of an ever-growing number of dimensions of life, including the sexual, and asked with an increasing uncertainty regarding possible answers.

HETEROSEXUALITY. Heterosexuality, defined as *cross-gender sexual intercourse,* has been a preference in all societies, though not necessarily an exclusive preference in all societies. Nor does the universality of this preference limit definitions of with whom, when, where, or in what manner it should occur. Thus, outside of incest taboos involving immediate family members and a variable list of other close relatives, varied cultures and periods of history have defined legitimate and illegitimate sexual contacts in dramatically contrasting ways (Bullough [1978] 1980). These differences involve not only what might be called the mechanics of sexual acts, that is, matters of relationship, time, place, costume, sequence of gestures, and positions but also the determinants of their relative significance.

The question, What will I be when I grow up? is asked of an ever-growing number of dimensions of life, including the sexual.

The potential reproductive consequences of heterosexual, genital intercourse inevitably led to linking the desire for sex with some conscious or unconscious desire for reproduction. This view has been criticized as resting upon the questionable assumption of a biologically rooted commitment to species survival (Beach 1956). Valid or not, such views constitute a cultural legacy that gives credence to many current norms regarding sexual acts, norms that enhance the social regulation of reproduction in the name of some assumed natural mandate.

More specifically, expectations regarding gender and family, influenced by many aspects of social life, have generally shaped the social meaning of sexual acts. Our current language for describing cross-gender sexual contacts explicitly assumes a relationship to the family—marital sex, premarital sex, postmarital sex, and extramarital sex—and implicitly evaluates behaviors in terms of their "distance" from location within the family.

Similarly, genital intercourse is still commonly viewed as the ultimate form of sexual exchange, as the "fulfillment of nature's intent." As a result, it continues to serve as the measure of the "normality" of alternative forms of sexual contact. This was reflected in the historic, but declining, practice of criminalizing not only sexual acts occurring outside of marriage but also those involving oral or anal contact, or viewing masturbation as pathogenic when practiced by the young and symptomatic when practiced by adults.

Many of the conventions surrounding gender expectations also directly reinforced the "scripting," or construction, of heterosexuality. This involves presenting images of the sexual that both naturalize and normalize evolved Western heterosexual practices, making them appear unquestionably proper. The terms *active* and *passive,* terms that had application in many domains of social life, virtually became synonymous with *masculine* and *feminine,* respectively. Even physical position—"Who is on top?"—often has had to pay honor to prevailing patterns of social domination.

The nineteenth century witnessed the elaboration of images of the female as fragile, domestic, nurturant, receptive, and either only minimally sexual or capable of insatiable lusts. These images of femininity were complemented by images of the male as strong, given to exploratory curiosity, possessively protective, and aggressively lustful. Though applied diffusely, these implicit norms were not always applied equally. The restraint and fragility of the female found more common application in the parlors and bedrooms of the urban middle class and rural gentry and far less in the fields, factories, servants' quarters, and brothels of the day.

While the images of heterosexuality reinforced patterns of family life and gender differentiation, it is equally appropriate to speak of the ways in which patterns of family life and gender differentiation reinforced prevailing concepts of heterosexuality. This same gender-based division of labor within the family was taken for granted by mid-twentieth-century sociological theorists (Parsons and Bales 1955), as it was inscribed in the most widely held views regarding "normal" human development (Erikson 1950).

From the late nineteenth century on concepts of the family became substantially more voluntary and egalitarian. However, such modifications served to further empower the heterosexual scenario, which now serves an even more important role in the creation of marital bonding and the preservation of the nuclear family. Heterosexuality simultaneously became a near-constant threat and vital aspect of family life.

This greater emphasis placed upon the heterosexual scenario led, in turn, to greater emphasis upon the subjective aspects of one's sexual orientation. Faith in the mute logic of "nature's" intent gave way to concerns for the fashioning and maintenance of individual desire. Women were increasingly expected not only to be receptive but to desire and be desirable, as men were increasingly expected to use the sexual to affirm their masculinity not only by their ability to find sexual pleasure, but also by their ability to provide pleasure to their partners. Heterosexual preference continued to be taken for granted while heterosexual competence was being placed on the agenda in new and unanticipated ways.

In recent years, evident trends call into question many of these practices, challenging many of the previous basic expectations regarding family and gender. The conjugal family is no longer the exclusive social address for heterosexuality. Premarital sex has become statistically normal at all social levels, and it approaches becoming attitudinally normative. Moreover, the age at which sexual intercourse first occurs has declined, particularly for females (by age eighteen over half are no longer virgins, which is more than double the proportion of nonvirgins reported a generation ago), which suggests that most of what occurs can be described as premarital, as much of this early sexual behavior occurs outside of the context of family-forming courtship, where much of the premarital experiences of older generations took place.

Similarly, at both the stages of premarital and postmarital, there has been increasing acceptance of nonmarital cohabitation, in the sense that it tends to be more openly acknowledged, with little anticipation of social rejection or stigmatization. And, while the number of middle- to upper-middle-class females who have deliberately borne children without marriage or an acknowledged male partner is not great, that this practice has achieved considerable legitimacy is itself significant.

Reflecting the diffusion of feminist values, support for women, with regard to sexual interest, sexual activity, and, especially, sexual competence, the latter as measured by capacities for achieving orgasm, has visibly increased (Ehrenreich, Hess, and Jacobs 1986). As a result, gender stereotypes with regard to sexual behavior have also experienced changes; changes that, for the most part, served to blur many of the gender distinctions that previously appeared to give heterosexuality its distinctive complementarity.

Specific behaviors, such as oral sex, that once were associated with devalued sexual actors, homosexuals and prostitutes, in recent years have become a conventional part of the heterosexual script. This is particularly true at higher social class levels, where it tends to occur regularly, often substituting for genital intercourse (Gagnon and Simon 1987; Blumstein and Schwartz 1983).

Heterosexuality remains the dominant erotic imagery of Western societies. However, changing concerns for reproduction, continuing changes in the organization of family life, and the constraints describing gender presentations would indicate that present trends toward a pluralization of the ways in which heterosexuality is experienced and in the contexts within which it is expressed will continue into the imaginable future.

HOMOSEXUALITY. Same-gender sexual interactions have been reported in a sufficient number of social settings to suggest that they fall within the normal range of human behaviors (Ford and Beach 1951; Gregersen 1983). As Alfred Kinsey (Kinsey, Pomeroy, and Martin 1948) observed, "The homosexual has been a significant part of human sexual activity ever since the dawn of history, primarily because it is an expression of capacities that are basic in the human animal" (p. 666). This essentialist view implies that predispositions to same-gender sexual acts are immutable facts of nature, like gender and race and, as such, are totally independent of personal preferences and societal values (Green 1988).

At the same time, the facts that same-gender sexual involvements fail to be reported or to occur as atypical behaviors in sufficient numbers suggests that there is little about them upon which to predicate some universal or singular explanation. The specific forms of homosexual behavior, kinds of sexual acts and the relationships within which they occur, like those of most aspects of heterosexuality, vary so much that understanding must be sought in terms of the contingent features of specific social contexts. In other words, apparent uniformity of acts, such as members of the same gender engaging in sexual acts, allows us to assume very little, if any, uniformity of actors, of their development, of their motives, or of the social and personal meanings of the behavior.

When constructionists assert that the homosexual is an invention of the modern world, they are not suggesting that same-gender sexual contacts were unknown in earlier periods of Western history or in other cultural settings. What they do suggest is that the processes that constitute the behavior, that give it meaning, that transform otherwise identical forms of "behavior" into different forms of evaluated "conduct" may be of a fundamentally different character.

The variety of meanings given to same-gender "sexual" contacts is as wide as that given to cross-gender contacts. ("Sexual" is placed in quotation marks as a reminder that, while genital contact and orgasm may be present, in many instances the behavior is not necessarily experienced as sexual in the contemporary Western sense of that word.) Such same-gender, genital contacts range from those that are incidental to religious rites or rites of puberty, to those that are specific to certain statuses that may be temporary and that are not, in themselves, significant aspects of the individual's social identity, to those in which such same-gender contacts are defined as permanent features of the individual's character.

An example of the age-specific, same-gender, sexual contact can be found among the Sambians of New Guinea. Male children at about age six are removed to the men's hut, where they ingest semen, viewed as necessary for full masculine development, by engaging in fellation with older, unmarried, fellow villagers. At puberty, such males enter the role of semen donor by making their penises available to their younger fellow villagers. During early adulthood, they enter arranged marriages and are expected to exclusively practice heterosexual sex for the remainder of their lives. Observers report a near universal absence of fixation with regard to the activities of earlier stages or a reversal of age roles (Herdt 1981; Stoller 1985a).

This, of course, stands in dramatic contrast with the modern Western experience, in which the imagery of the behavior is associated with powerful meanings such that their very invocation is often capable of exciting intense emotional responses of all kinds. Thus, negative images promote strong feelings of homophobia and, at times, cause "homosexual panic." At the same time, the possibility of same-gender sexual contacts often generates responses sufficiently strong to allow many individuals to experience and accept themselves as being homosexual despite the antihomosexual character of their social settings (Bell and Weinberg 1979; Weinberg 1983).

In the examples of both the Sambians and the contemporary Western experience the biological processes associated with arousal and orgasm are undoubtedly the same. What differs are the meanings and their representation that occasion arousal. As Beach noted, "Human sexual arousal is subject to extensive modification as a result of experience. Sexual values may become attached to a wide variety of biologically inappropriate stimulus objects or partners" (1956, p. 27).

Patterns of homosexual behavior, like those of heterosexual behavior, have manifested persistent change. While same-gender sexual contact was known in premodern Europe and severely sanctioned, often treated as a capital offense, it was not viewed as being the behavior of a different kind of person but as moral failing, a sin, to which all might be vulnerable (Bray 1982). Some have argued that a conception of homosexuality as a sexual orientation involving a distinct kind of person was a correlate of many of the changing patterns and values associated with the emergence of urban, industrial capitalism (Adam 1878; Hocquenghem 1978).

Within the category of male homosexuality, different styles of homosexual activity predominated in different periods of history and in different social settings. If the concept of homosexuality is to have any meaning, such variations suggest that modern forms of homosexuality reflect an eroticization of gender and not a fixation upon a specific form of sexual activity. In other words, it is the gender of the participants that generates and sustains sexual interest and only secondarily the specific form of sexual activity (Gagnon 1990; Simon, Kraft, and Kaplan forthcoming).

The significance of gender in considerations of homosexuality has marked much of its recent history. Initial nineteenth-century views defined, and implicitly explained, homosexuality as an inversion of gender. Lesbians were often viewed as "men trapped in women's bodies" and gay men the reverse. Consistent with this, a common designation was "invert." Despite this early view, more recent research indicates that in many regards lesbians and gay men tend in their sexual development and subsequent behavior to approximate their gender. This suggests that sexual development tends to follow gender socialization: Gender roles influence sexuality more often than sexuality prompts changes in gender identity (Gagnon and Simon 1973; Blumstein and Schwartz 1983).

It is the gender of the participants that generates and sustains sexual interest and only secondarily the specific form of sexual activity.

Change in sexual patterns has been a critical aspect of recent social history. Whereas heterosexual practice might be described as being increasingly privatized and disassociated from the major institutions of society, homosexual practice has moved from the margins of society to sharing the central stage. Whereas the family becomes less and less the exclusive legitimate context for heterosexual activities, the appearance and survival of bonded relationships among homosexuals, particularly gay men, have visibly increased. Whereas the larger community appears increasingly anomic, gay communities (which once were limited to bars, discreet networks of friends, and, for gay men, locations for anonymous sexual contacts) now rival even the most solidary of ethnic groups. There is a flowering of recreational, religious, welfare, political, and other affinity groups and organizations, as well as of areas of residential dominance (Epstein 1987; Escoffier 1985; Levine 1986).

Homosexuality remains negatively valued, remains stigmatized. Discrimination in employment and housing, instances of "gay bashing," and criminalization of same-gender sexual activity in some jurisdictions speaks directly to continued homophobic practices and fears. However, on the whole, the 1960s, 1970s, and 1980s witnessed increasing acceptance of both homosexuality and the homosexual. Even the identification of gay men with the transmission of the HIV virus, which initially was associated with an incipient moral panic and occasioned expressions of antihomosexual attitudes, became an occasion for sympathetic representation in the major public media and broadened understanding of gay men, of their life-styles, and of the many roles they play in, and contributions they make to, the larger society.

Two kinds of questions have persisted, those of cause and of numbers. Many explanations for the development of either a homoerotic preference or a homoerotic capacity have been offered. None of these has found general support, from the psychoanalytic emphasis upon internal family dynamics to the emphasis on genetic predispositions (Bell, Weinberg, and Hammersmith 1981). What is clear is that there may be many more reasons for developing a homosexual orientation than there are ways of giving it expression. What once was viewed as a single phenomenon is now more generally seen as pluralized. It now encompasses different developmental histories, affording different ways of incorporating a homoerotic commitment within a specific life history. The same, it might be said, is true for the development of a heterosexual orientation (Murray 1984; Stoller 1985a).

Aspects of development such as variations in the development of a gender identity may be significant in the development of homosexual orientations for some individuals (Harry 1982; Green 1987), but these may have to be reconsidered as society modifies its more general beliefs and practices regarding gender identity. For example, the question must be asked, On what basis should "effeminacy" in male children be treated as symptomatic of some pathology, any more than comparable displays of "effeminacy" in female children? Or the reverse, regarding what is commonly referred to as *tomboyishness* among young females? Similarly we might ask, What basis exists for looking at heterosexual preferences as more desirable outcomes of the child-rearing process than homosexual preferences? This is not to suggest that gender stereotyping and a societal preference for heterosexual outcomes are about to disappear but that the very meaning of all sexual orientations may be in the process of change.

While individuals with a marked homosexual preference appear in virtually all social contexts—within different types of community settings; at different class levels; in all racial, ethnic and religious categories; and from all manner of family background (Gebhard and Johnson 1979; Bell, Weinberg, and Hammersmith 1981)—absence of unbiased and comprehensive data makes it difficult to determine with any confidence whether there are significant effects associated with possible differentials. An equal sense of uncertainty surrounds the question of numbers. Answers depend upon definitions of what constitutes homosexuality or homosexuals. All existing estimates are based upon data that are limited in their ability to provide reliable population projections. However, for what they are worth, these suggest that exclusive homosexual behavior describes about 3 percent to 5 percent of men, with about 10 percent to 12 percent having had a more than casual or experimental period of homosexual activity. Estimates for lesbian experience tend to be somewhat less than these percentages. There is reason to suspect that such statistics can provide only an approximation of current populations and a very poor guide to future developments, developments that depend more on society's conceptions and uses of sex and gender, which appear to be in continuing transition.

BISEXUALITY. Bisexuality is a complex concept; it can refer to behavior (those who have had both homosexual and heterosexual experience), to psychic response (those capable of being erotically aroused by both homosexual and heterosexual imagery), and to either social or self-labeling. Substantial numbers have had, if only incidentally, both homosexual and heterosexual experiences while retaining a firm self-identity as being one or the other. Still larger numbers have or can be assumed to have experienced sexual arousal in association with both heteroerotic and homoerotic imagery (Kinsey, Wardell, and Clyde 1948; Kinsey et al. 1952; Bell and Weinberg 1978; Bell, Weinberg, and Hammersmith 1981). Few, however, would conceive of themselves as bisexual or would be labeled as such, particularly if the concept were defined as an attraction to both genders and an attraction for the sexual behaviors commonly attributed to both genders. That is, the mere experience of having sex with members of both genders may not be sufficient to justify the application of the term *bisexual.* Thus, situational, same-gender, sexual contacts, as occur in single-sex penal institutions, may represent little more than conventionally styled heterosexual orientations expressed in restrictive circumstances (Gagnon and Simon 1973).

Many whose sexual histories involve interactions with both genders still see themselves as being either homosexual or heterosexual in orientation. This may be a reflection of the fact that outside of relatively few "bisexual support groups," neither heterosexual nor homosexual social worlds appear to accept or validate such an identity. Though a large number of the psychotherapeutic communities accept bisexuality as a distinct type of psychosexual development (Hill 1989), even among those who identify themselves as bisexual are some who tend to have patterns of sexual behavior that are "amazingly diverse and that [their] day to day life styles are greatly different from one another . . . [and] it is clear that the people come to bisexuality in an incredibly diverse number of ways" (Blumstein and Schwartz 1976, p. 180).

Until recently the very concept of bisexuality, when used to refer to a specific type of person, was viewed with skepticism (Tripp 1987). Most commonly, having bisexual interests was viewed as a mask or apology for an underlying homosexual orientation. Undoubtedly, for some the bisexual label served as a transitional phase in the often complicated task of identity transformation.

Bisexuality, as denoting a special orientation, tends to be a recent conceptualization, one that reflects increased consideration of gender as crystallizations of erotic responses that are not necessarily constrained by the logic of an excluding complementarity. Prior images of bisexuality reflected the assumed differences of masculinity and femininity such as the persistently masculinized dominant sexual actor or the individual who could switch between stereotypical presentations of gender. Increased recognition of a bisexual possibility follows the recognition of the possible absence of complementarity, that is, each participant providing what is absent in and desired by the other, within many heterosexual and homosexual relationships and a calling into question of an implicit complementarity within existing conceptions of gender.

TRANSVESTISM AND TRANSSEXUALITY. These two concepts do not represent discrete categories so much as a continuum describing the degree to which an individual biologically of one gender desires and enacts the role or aspects of the role of the other (Feinbloom 1976). For an unknown number this is limited to using the clothing of the other gender to illicit sexual excitement, with little more involved. For most, however, more is involved; for most it involves adopting and enacting, if only for an audience of oneself, aspects of the identity and selected roles of the other gender, not merely cross-dressing but cross-gendering. However, for transvestites, cross-dressing is temporary, and they do not abandon their primary gender identity; they play at being the other (Newton 1979).

At the other end of the continuum is the transsexual who ideally seeks to adopt permanently the gender, costumes, and roles of the other gender (Green 1974). And, while an absolute realization of this aspiration is impossible, combined modern surgical and pharmacological techniques and permissive bureaucracies (the former cosmetically "redesigning" the body, while the latter allows for a redesigning of one's identifying credentials) have brought us to the possibility of coming close to allowing some to more fully realize their aspiration to live their lives, as fully as possible, in the costumes and roles of the other gender (Bolin 1988; Lothstein 1983).

The desirability of supporting transsexuality remains a matter of continuing contention involving issues of mental health and gender. Several medical centers that once maintained programs of "surgical gender reassignment" have suspended such programs, reporting results that were too mixed to justify their continuation. Additionally, feminists have criticized such programs as catering to the desire to enact some of the most extreme forms of gender stereotypes (Irving 1990).

Midway between these extremes, between the erotic fetishizing of the clothing of the opposite gender and the desire to become the opposite gender, are those who prefer the costumes and behavior styles of the opposite gender without wanting to or needing to abandon their own initial gender. This ranges from those who deliberately blur costumes and the coding or semiotic of gestures to obscure distinctions—women who have masculinized or men who have feminized their presentation of self—to those who experience a continuing conflict between a "masculine self" and a "feminine self," feeling that each of these components of a divided self requires its own costumes, vocabulary of gestures, and social space.

Again, as is true for most forms of stigmatized behavior, estimates of how many individuals are involved in such practices are virtually impossible to determine with any accuracy. Across this continuum of cross-gendering, both males and females can be observed. Most researchers speculate that more males than females are involved, if only generalizing the apparent tendency for significantly more males than females to be involved in various kinds of sexual deviance.

This speculation is made additionally plausible by the manifest tendency for violations of gender expectations by men to generate more nervousness and be more heavily sanctioned against than might comparable violations by females. It is possible for many females to mask their transvestic desires by the broader range of fashion available to women. By way of example, female cross-dressing in film and literature often involves the

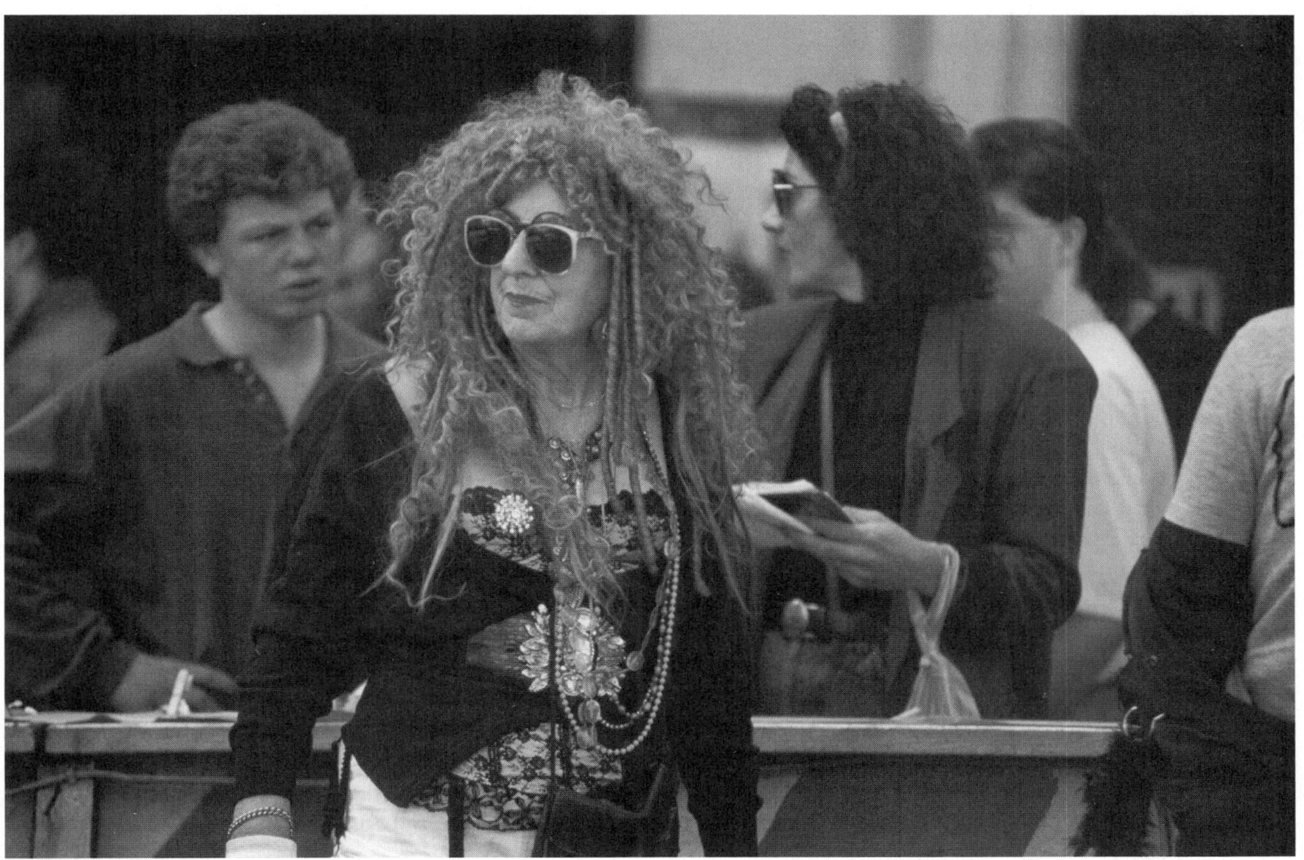

Transvestites adopt styles and roles of the opposite gender for temporary periods but return to and maintain their primary gender identity. (K.M. Westermann/Corbis)

beginnings of romantic involvement, while male cross-dressing is almost entirely restricted to the comic mode.

These two concepts, transvestism and transsexuality, perhaps more than any other, speak to the powers of gender and its multiple correlates. They speak, as well, to the complex relationship between gender and sexuality. For relatively few are gender presentations altered to facilitate some specific sexual aim; more often the sexual is organized to facilitate desired gender effects. Little that is manifestly sexual appears in the cross-gendering of some, as would be true of many male heterosexual transvestites. In the case of the transsexual, surgical procedures often diminish orgasmic capacity. However, confirmation of gender is often one of the major motives for engaging in sexual behavior and a major source of its capacity to gratify.

Conclusions

Sexual orientation is a complex construct, rather than a simple thing. While it tends to identify individuals in terms of commitment to similar sexual preferences, it also has the capacity to mask differences among those who appear to otherwise share identical orientations. This is not surprising. Sexual behaviors, like other aspects of the human that are rooted in biology, are also historical and given to change and, as such, reflect the very connections of the sexual ultimately to the total fabric of social life.

Until recently, having bisexual interests was viewed as a mask or apology for an underlying homosexual orientation.

At the same time, concepts of sexual orientation are aspects of the cultural apparatus of a time and place and are used to explain the behavior of others, as well as our own. As such they have the capacity to influence the very behaviors that they appear merely to describe. Thus, to view the sexual in isolation from the continuing dynamic of social life, which until recently has largely been its fate, is to run the risk of transforming the science of social life into an unselfconscious instrument of social life.

[See also Alternative Life-Styles; Heterosexual Behavior Patterns; Sexual Behavior and Marriage.]

BIBLIOGRAPHY

Adam, Barry 1978 "Capitalism, the Family, and Gay People." *Sociologists Gay Caucus Working Papers 1.*

Beach, Frank A. 1956 "Characteristics of Masculine 'Sex Drive.' " In Marshall R. Jones, ed., *Nebraska Symposium on Motivation.* Lincoln: University of Nebraska Press.

Bell, Allen C., and Martin S. Weinberg 1978 *Homosexualities. A Study of Diversity Among Men and Women.* New York: Simon and Schuster.

Bell, Allen C., Martin S. Weinberg, and Susan Hammersmith 1981 *Sexual Preference.* Bloomington: Indiana University Press.

Berger, Peter, and Thomas Luckman 1966 *The Social Construction of Reality.* Garden City, N.Y.: Doubleday.

Blumstein, Phillip W., and Pepper Schwartz 1976 "Bisexuality in Women." *Archives of Sexual Behavior* 5(2):171–181.

——— 1983 *The American Couple.* New York: Morrow.

Bolin, Anne 1988 *In Search of Eve: Transsexual Rites of Passage.* South Hadley, Mass.: Bergin and Garvey.

Boswell, John 1983 "Revolutions, Universals, and Sexual Categories." *Salmagundi* 58–59:89–113.

Bray, Alan 1982 *Homosexuality in Renaissance England.* London: Gay Men's Press.

Bullough, Vern L. (1978) 1980 *Sexual Variance in Society and History.* Chicago: University of Chicago Press.

DuBay, William H. 1987 *Gay Identity: The Self Under Ban.* Jefferson, N.C.: McFarland.

Ehrenreich, Barbara, Elizabeth Hess, and Gloria Jacobs 1986 *Remaking Love. The Feminization of Sex.* New York: Doubleday, Anchor.

Ellis, Havelock 1937 *Studies in the Psychology of Sex,* Vol. 2. New York: Random House.

Epstein, Steven 1987 "Gay Politics, Gay Identity: The Limits of Social Construction." *Socialist Review* 93/94:9–53.

Erikson, Erik H. 1950 *Childhood and Society.* New York: Norton.

Escoffier, Jeffery 1985 "Sexual Revolution and the Politics of Gay Identity." *Socialist Review* 82/83:119–153.

Feinbloom, Deborah 1976 *Transvestites and Transsexuals: Mixed Views.* New York: Delacorte.

Ford, Clellan, and Frank A. Beach 1951 *Patterns of Sexual Behavior.* New York: Harper.

Foucault, Michel 1978 *The History of Sexuality.* Vol. I: *An Introduction.* New York: Pantheon.

Freud, Sigmund (1905) 1953 "Three Essays on the Theory of Sexuality." *Collected Works,* Vol. 7, pp. 125–243. London: Hogarth.

Gagnon, John H. 1990 "Gender Preferences in Erotic Relations, the Kinsey Scale, and Sexual Scripts." In David McWhorter, Stefanie Sanders, and June Reinisch, eds., *Heterosexuality, Homosexuality, and the Kinsey Scale.* New York: Oxford University Press.

———, and William Simon *1973 Sexual Conduct: The Social Sources of Human Sexuality.* Chicago: Aldine.

——— 1987 "The Sexual Scripting of Oral Genital Contacts." *Archives of Sexual Behavior* 16(1):1–25.

Gebhard, Paul H., and Alan B. Johnson 1979 *The Kinsey Data: Marginal Tabulations of the 1938–1963 Interview Conducted by the Institute for Sex Research.* Philadelphia: Saunders.

Gladue, Brian A. 1987 "Psychobiological Contributions." In Louis Diamant, ed., *Male and Female Homosexuality: Psychological Approaches,* pp. 129–154. New York: Hemisphere.

Green, Richard 1974 *Sexual Identity Conflict in Children and Adults.* New York: Basic.

——— 1987 *The "Sissy Boy Syndrome" and the Development of Homosexuality.* New Haven, Conn.: Yale University Press.

——— 1988 "The Immutability of (Homo)Sexual Orientation: Behavioral Science Implications for a Constitutional (Legal) Analysis." *Journal of Psychiatry and Law* Winter: 537–557.

Greenberg, David F. 1988 *The Construction of Homosexuality.* Chicago: University of Chicago Press.
Gregersen, Edgar 1983 *Sexual Practices. The Story of Human Sexuality.* New York: Franklin Watts.
Halperin, David M. 1989 *One Hundred Years of Homosexuality: And Other Essays on Greek Love.* New York: Routledge, Chapman, and Hall.
Harry, Joseph 1982 *Gay Children Grow Up.* New York: Praeger.
Herdt, Gilbert H. 1981 *Guardians of the Flute: Idioms of Masculinity.* New York: McGraw-Hill.
Herzer, Manfred 1985 "Kertbeny and the Nameless Love." *Journal of Homosexuality* 12(1):1–23.
Hill, Ivan (ed.) 1989 *The Bisexual Spouse: Different Dimensions in Human Sexuality.* New York: Harper, Perennial.
Hocquenghem, Guy 1978 *Homosexual Desire,* trans. Danniella Dangoor. London: Allison and Busby.
Irvine, Janice M. 1990 *Disorders of Desire: Sex and Gender in Modern American Sexology.* Philadelphia: Temple University Press.
Katz, Jonathan H. 1990 "The Invention of Heterosexuality." *Socialist Review* 90/91:7–34.
Kinsey, Alfred C., Wardell B. Pomeroy, and Clyde E. Martin 1948 *Sexual Behavior in the Human Male.* Philadelphia: Saunders.
Kinsey, Alfred C., Wardell B. Pomeroy, Clyde E. Martin, and Paul H. Gebhard 1953 *Sexual Behavior in the Human Female.* Philadelphia: Saunders.
Krafft-Ebing, Richard von (1886) 1965 *Psychopathia Sexualis,* trans. Harry E. Wedeck. New York: Putnam's.
Levine, Martin P. 1986 *The Gay Clone.* Ph.D. diss., New York University.
Lothstein, Leslie 1983 *Female to Male Transsexualism: Historical, Clinical, and Theoretical Issues.* Boston: Routledge and Kegan Paul.
Mitchell, Stephan A. 1988 *Relational Concepts in Psychoanalysis.* Cambridge, Mass.: Harvard University Press.
McIntosh, Mary 1976 "The Homosexual Role." *Social Problems* 16(2):182–192.
Money, John 1988 *Gay, Straight, and In-Between: The Sexology of Erotic Orientations.* New York: Oxford University Press.
Murray, Stephen 1984 *Social Theory, Homosexual Reality.* New York: Gay Academic Union.
Nietzsche, Frederic (1887) 1968 *On the Genealogy of Morals.* In Walter Kaufmann trans., *The Basic Writings of Nietzsche.* New York: Modern Library.
Newton, Esther 1979 *Mother Camp: Female Impersonators in America.* Chicago: University of Chicago Press.
Padgug, Robert A. 1979 "Sexual Matters: On Conceptualizing Sexuality in History." *Radical History Review* 20:3–33.
Parsons, Talcott, and Robert F. Bales 1955 *Family Socialization and Interaction Process.* New York: Free Press.
Plummer, Kenneth 1975 *Sexual Stigma: An Interactionist Approach.* London: Routledge and Kegan Paul.
Ponse, Barbara 1978 *Identity in the Lesbian World.* Westport, Conn.: Greenwood.
Simon, William 1989 "The Postmodernization of Sex." *Journal of Psychology and Human Sexuality* 2(1): 9–37.
———, and John H. Gagnon 1967 "Homosexuality: The Formulation of a Sociological Perspective." *Journal of Health and Human Behavior* 8(1): 77–85.
——— 1986 "Sexual Scripts: Permanence and Change." *Archives of Sexual Behavior* 15(2):97–120.
Simon, William, Diane Kraft, and Howard Kaplan forthcoming "Oral Sex: A Critical Overview." In J. Reinisch, B. Vollmer, and R. Goldstein, eds., *AIDS and Sex: A Biomedical and Behavioral Approach.* New York: Oxford University Press.
Stoller, Robert J. 1985a *Observing the Erotic Imagination.* New Haven, Conn.: Yale University Press.
——— 1985b *Presentations of Gender.* New Haven, Conn.: Yale University Press.
Symons, Donald 1979 *The Evolution of Human Sexuality.* New York: Oxford University Press.
Tripp, Clarence A. 1987 *The Homosexual Matrix,* 2nd ed. New York: New American Library.
Weeks, Jeffrey 1985 *Sexuality and Its Discontents: Meanings, Myths, and Modern Sexualities.* London: Routledge and Kegan Paul.
Weinberg, Thomas S. 1983 *Gay Men, Gay Selves.* New York: Irvington.
Whitam Frederic L. 1983 "Culturally Invariable Properties of Male Homosexuals." *Archives of Sexual Behavior* 12:207–222.

– WILLIAM SIMON

SEXUAL VIOLENCE AND ABUSE

Sexual violence and abuse are social problems that remained relatively invisible as research topics until the late 1960s. For purposes of this presentation the focus is primarily on rape, various types of child abuse, and related issues.

The Problem of Rape

Rape was not conceptualized as a major problem in the United States until the late 1960s, an awareness that came with the resurrected women's movement and the establishment of the National Center for the Prevention and Control of Rape. After this awakening, enough information was generated to document the fact that there were more than biological and psychological explanations for rape. Society, its institutions, laws, and attitudes were seen as greatly contributing to the problem. During the 1970s rape became clearly defined as a social problem.

Rape was not conceptualized as a major problem in the United States until the late 1960s.

The definition of rape that served as the basis for most rape laws is grounded in English common law: "the unlawful carnal knowledge of a woman by force and against her will" (Green 1988, p. 6). At the national level the definition has not changed, although clinical definitions are less restrictive. During the 1970s many states redefined rape laws to more comprehensively describe those behaviors that constituted rape and age of consent. The concept of spousal immunity was challenged, and some states rewrote their laws so that women could bring marital rape charges. By the end of the decade, forty-one states had also passed some form

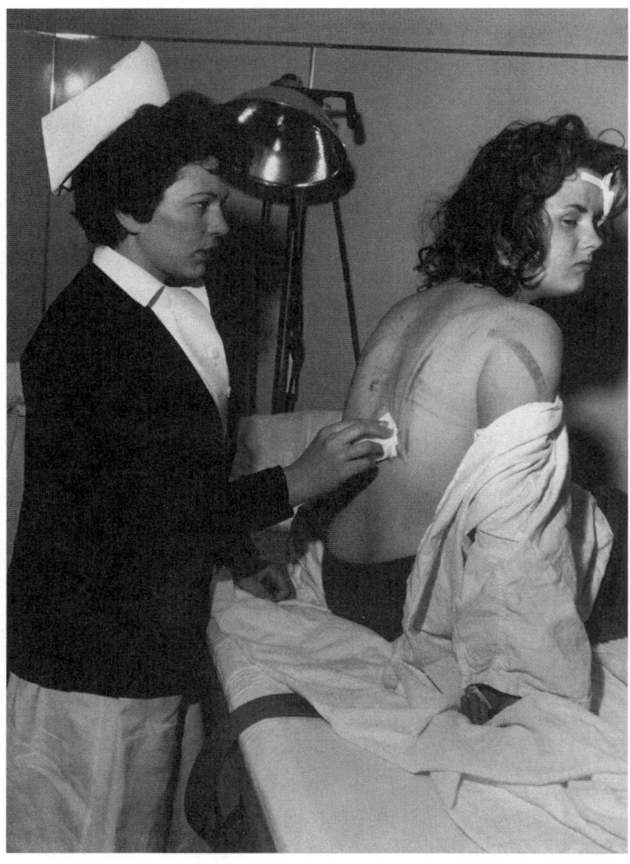

Sexual violence and abuse remained relatively unexamined social problems until the late 1960s when the women's movement focused attention on the issue. (UPI/Corbis-Bettmann)

of rape shield laws that limited admissibility of victims' prior sexual conduct with persons other than the offender (Green 1988, pp. 16–40).

Considered the second most serious crime indexed in the Uniform Crime Reports, in 1988 there were officially 92,486 reported rapes in the United States (U.S. Department of Justice 1989, p. 16), a 2-percent increase over 1987. According to a recent ABC news report by Carole Simpson (ABC American Agenda News Report, January 7, 1991), rape is currently the fastest growing crime in the United States. In some major cities, rape increased by 50 percent in 1990. Increases across the United States are attributed not only to increased reporting but also to increases in incidents. Some estimate that, for every rape reported, three to ten are not. And, while trend research has shown a general escalation, with the most dramatic increases occurring before 1981 (Russell 1984, p. 29), the 1990s appear to be ushering in a significant upward swing.

Victimization studies such as the National Crime Survey (NCS) and other research projects were initiated to get better estimates of rape. These studies show that the amount of rape is greatly underestimated, although prevalence rates vary from study to study and are hard to reconcile, due to variations in research designs, samples, and geographic locations.

Rape is described in a number of ways. Sometimes it is discussed in terms of the number of offenders per victim: the single-offender; two-offender; or multiple, group, or gang rape. Victimization statistics for these are respectively, 81 percent, 10 percent, and 8 percent (Koss and Harvey 1987, p. 10). Rape is also classified as stranger rape, when the victim and offender have no relationship to one another, or acquaintance rape, which includes date rape and rape between individuals who knew each other prior to the assault. NCS's rape statistics indicate that 60 percent to 75 percent of rapes that happen to women aged 16–24 are stranger rapes and that 27 percent of rapes involve multiple offenders. Warshaw (1988, chap. 1) citing statistics from the *MS. Magazine* Project on Campus Assault, reports fewer stranger (16 percent) and group rapes (15 percent), however, with the vast majority of incidents being individual assaults (95 percent) that involve acquaintances or dates (84 percent). A third type of rape, marital rape, occurs when the victim and offender are spouses or living in a spouselike arrangement. Although this was thought to be rare, Russell (1984, p. 59) found that 8 percent of ever-married women in her study reported being raped by their husbands.

Rape is sometimes defined in terms of motivation. While earlier researchers viewed rape as sexually motivated, more recent ones refer to it as power- or anger-motivated rape. Power rapes are motivated by a need to dominate the victim, whereas anger rapes are driven by a hatred of the victim or hatred of women in general (Groth, 1979). Further, most rapes, particularly group rapes, are planned, not impulsive, acts (Warshaw, 1988). Some rapes do appear to happen, however, simply because opportunities arise.

Researchers generally agree that the social characteristics of rapists and their victims are similar for most types of rape. While exact age ranges vary among studies, both rapists and their victims appear to be young (less than twenty-five), nonwhite (overrepresentation of Afro-Americans), and from the lower socioeconomic classes. Victims tend to be single, with more variations in marital status occurring among offenders. Rural/urban and regional rates vary and appear to be somewhat related to population density.

Explanations for Rape

Explanations for rape come from a variety of disciplines, although most explanations have been dominated by the psychiatric perspective and the medical model (Koss and Leonard 1984, pp. 213–232). The basic assumption underlying this thinking is that rapists are psychologically sick and that rape is sexually motivated. Hence, many explanations focus on developing profiles of rapists (e.g., Groth, Burgess, and Holmstrom 1977), a body of research whose validity is questioned because it is based primarily on non-representative clinical or prison populations (Schwendinger and Schwendinger 1983; Russell 1984, chap. 4).

Cross-cultural support for the biological explanation of rape is provided by Levine (1977), although his work also supports a sociocultural explanation, because the Gussi in Kenya are characterized by male dominance, low female status, and high rates of crime and violence.

Sociological explanations of rape focus on the social dynamics of society that promote, treat, or proscribe such behaviors and include sociocultural, sociohistorical, and sociopsychological analyses. While these types of explanations lagged behind those of psychology and biology, they offer an alternative to the individual-based theories.

Sociocultural explanations of rape are supported by large cross-cultural studies of tribal societies (Sanday 1981) and by large studies of nonindustrialized nations (Reiss 1986). All studies draw similar research conclusions. Rape-prone societies endorse the macho personality and fundamental belief in the inferiority of females, a belief system that incorporates an acceptance of physical aggression, a high amount of risk taking, and a casual attitude toward sex. Schwendinger and Schwendinger (1983) note that rape is also related to a culture's socioeconomic structure.

Among industrialized societies, the United States has substantially higher rape rates. In 1996, the Bureau of Justice reported a rape rate of 36.1 per 100,000 population for the United States, compared with a 5.4 average for European nations (Abramson and Hayashi 1984). Some researchers argue that the higher incidence of rape in the United States indicates that it has cultural and societal supports, one of which increasingly appears to be college campuses (Martin and Hummer 1989).

Baron and Straus's (1989, p. 180) state-level analyses show that rape rates vary by region and state within the United States and that rates are positively related to the amount of social disorganization, sex magazine circulation (pornography), and gender inequality in the state or region. This adds weight to earlier research that ties rape-specific myths and attitudes to a larger attitudinal construct supportive of sex-role stereotyping, violence against women, and adversarial sexual beliefs.

The sociocultural and sociopsychological explanations of rape support the sociohistorical analysis of feminist writer Susan Brownmiller (1975). While Brownmiller has been criticized for exaggerating the notion of male intimidation, sociological and anthropological research does indicate that rape is a socially created phenomenon that is much more likely to happen in cultures that support patriarchy and violence. Sociocultural explanations may also explain why the majority of offenders are male, irrespective of whether the victims are male or female, adult or child (Finkelhor and Russell 1984, chap. 11). Further, these explanations, combined with the legal definition of rape, might explain the lack of research on male victims.

Rape is a socially created phenomenon that is much more likely to happen in cultures that support patriarchy and violence.

Regardless of the varied theoretical perspectives, most researchers agree that multifactor (psychological and sociological factors), as compared with single-factor, explanations are better predictors of rape. Russell (1984, p. 111) notes that most rape theories could fit into Finkelhor's (1984) four-factor explanation of child sexual abuse discussed below.

The Problem of Child Sexual Abuse

Since the mid-1970s there has been increased interest in understanding child sexual abuse. This concern has led to the founding of the National Center on Child Abuse and Neglect and the passage of the 1977 Protection of Children Against Sexual Exploitation Act. A review of the child sex abuse research (Finkelhor et al. 1986) demonstrates many similarities with what we know about rape. Paralleling Brownmiller's (1975) historical analysis of rape, for example, is Florence Rush's (1980) analysis of child sexual abuse. Like Brownmiller, Rush elevates child sexual abuse to the level of a social problem by tracing its roots to patriarchal societies and their social institutions, belief systems, and myths. It should be noted, however, that there are groups that do not view child–adult sex as a problem (e.g., North American Man Boy Love Association). In fact, they advocate it.

In contrast to the concept of rape, researchers have not reached a consensus on what to call sexual relations between adults and children. Those who study victims tend to refer to the behavior as child sexual abuse, assault, maltreatment, or exploitation, whereas offender researchers call it child molestation or pedophilia. As with the definitional problems associated with rape, researchers likewise place varying limits on the ages of victims and offenders, the acts that are considered abuse, and the relationship of the victim and offender

(Araji and Finkelhor 1986, pp. 89–91; Russell 1984, p. 177; Bolten, Morris, and MacEachron 1989, pp. 31–35).

While all states consider child sexual abuse a crime, definitions vary from state to state, and some even leave the interpretation to the courts. As an ever-increasing number of child sexual abuse cases move into the court systems, particularly in cases involving divorce and custody, concern for balancing the needs of the legal system against those of children has arisen (Bolten, Morris, and MacEachron, 1989, chap. 10). Placing children in the courtroom subjects them to many of the same problems faced by rape victims: victim blaming and other courtroom-produced traumas. Although still in the early stage, reforms are being suggested and implemented (Bolten and Bolten 1987, chap. 10; Bulkley and Davidson 1981), with one of the largest areas of legislative reform having focused on increasing convictions and penalties of offenders.

As interest in understanding child sexual abuse grew, so did incidence and prevalence studies. Statistics provided by the American Humane Association (1981) and the 1981 national incidence study (National Center on Child Abuse and Neglect 1981) were used to arrive at national prevalence estimates. Today there is little agreement among social scientists as to the true extent of child sexual abuse (Peters, Wyatt, and Finkelhor 1986, p. 16), but all concede that the number of reported cases is increasing significantly and that the actual numbers are underestimated, particularly for males (Bolten, Morris, and MacEachron 1989, chap. 2). A comparison of national findings with less comprehensive research studies reveals conflicting estimates of the incidence of child sexual abuse. Still, commonly cited estimates suggest that one in four girls and one in nine boys will be sexually abused by the time they reach eighteen (Peters, Wyatt, and Finkelhor 1986, chap. 1).

At present, it is too early to make accurate cross-national comparisons of the extent of child sexual abuse. Some research has been conducted in several European countries, and recent reports from Great Britain (Glaser and Frosh 1988) and Sweden (Finkelhor et al. 1986, pp. 5–6) suggest that, as in the United States, the problem is widespread.

In contrast with rape, studies do not support a general, social-characteristics profile of victims or offenders of child sexual abuse, although females tend to be at greater victimization risk than males and males are overwhelmingly the offenders. The ages of greatest risk for victimization appear to be between eight and twelve (Finkelhor et al. 1986, pp. 61–66). Against the tide of current myths, most offenders are either known by or related to their victims and are not old. The largest groups are teenagers and young adults (Finkelhor 1979, pp. 73–74). In a review of studies, Finkelhor et al. (1986, pp. 67–71) found no consistent link between social class and sexual abuse, although the lower socioeconomic class is most likely overrepresented. He also found no consistent significant differences between racial groups.

Explanations of Child Sexual Abuse

The development of child sexual abuse explanations is similar to that of rape, as most early studies focused on offenders' psychopathological or biological motivations, or attempted to develop profiles of child molesters, victims, and families, or both. As with rape, most explanations offered only single-factor explanations, an approach criticized by Finkelhor et al. (1986, chap. 4). As an alternative, he proposed a four-factor explanation of child sexual abuse that includes the categories of emotional congruence, sexual arousal, blockage, and disinhibition. Respectively, these factors incorporate explanations of why an adult would have an emotional need to relate to a child, could be sexually aroused by a child, would not have alternative sources of gratification, and would not be deterred from such an interest by normal prohibitions (Araji and Finkelhor 1986, p. 117). The model includes both individual (e.g., arrested emotional development) and sociocultural (pornography) factors. As previously noted, Russell (1984, p. 111) believes that this model could be adapted to explain rape.

Incest

Most researchers and practitioners consider incest different from child sexual abuse, with incest viewed as *intrafamilial* and child sexual abuse as *extrafamilial* sexual relations. While some argue that the two types of abuse have much in common, one of the most significant differences between child sexual abuse and incest is that the victims of incest are always betrayed by someone who has been charged with loving and protecting them. Such experiences can have extremely destructive results.

The most common type of incest researched and written about is between father and daughter (Herman and Hirschman 1981), although the most common type may be brother-sister (Finkelhor 1979, p. 89). An emerging concern as more stepfamilies are formed is the probability of increased incestuous relationships involving stepfathers.

Incest has been viewed as a threat to societies and, as such, called the "ultimate taboo." This, combined with other reasons suggested by Rush (1980, chap. 7) and Finkelhor (1979, pp. 9, 11), may have led to a covering up of the prevalence of this act. Rates recently coming to light show estimates ranging from a high of 38 percent of females in Russell's 1983 study to about 25 percent in several other survey studies (e.g., Finkelhor 1979).

The victims of incest are always betrayed by someone who has been charged with loving and protecting them.

The same research problems surrounding rape and child sexual abuse extend to the incest literature: underestimating the extent of the crime, not accurately defining it, facing theory and sample problems.

Treatment and Prevention

A considerable body of literature on prevention and treatment of sexual violence and abuse has emerged from applied disciplines such as social work and clinical psychology, as well as from various community and feminist organizations. An extensive discussion is beyond the scope of this entry, so only a few generalizations are noted.

First, as treatment programs follow from the variety of theories of sexual abuse and violence previously discussed, it is not surprising that an array of treatment programs exist (Bolten, Morris, and MacEachron 1989, chap. 5, 6). With respect to offenders, most programs focus on punishment and/or rehabilitation (Groth 1979; Conte and Berliner 1981), and many are based on the psychiatric or medical model. In cases of child sexual abuse and incest, programs typically focus on helping the victims and their families through the crisis (Giaretto 1981). In the area of rape, programs have been primarily aimed at treating victims and families for the *rape trauma syndrome.* Treatment programs have also been developed to deal with the short- and long-term effects of victims' abuse (Brown and Finkelhor 1986) and can be either clinically or community based (Koss and Harvey 1987). Some are also beginning to focus on sex and ethnic differences. At present, however, there remain debates among professionals and practitioners as to what the appropriate treatments are, which ones work, and how well.

Stemming from myths and callous societal attitudes toward sexual aggression and the extensive involvement of feminists, prevention programs have followed a *victim advocacy* model (Araji 1989, chap. 17). Under this concept, potential victims are taught, in various ways, how to protect themselves from becoming victims. Some newer programs are aimed at males and promote the development of a nurturant, rather than macho, male image.

Pornography, Sexual Violence, and Abuse

A discussion of sexual assault would not be complete without some mention of pornography, a concept that challenges definition and remains a source of confusion and controversy. With respect to the rape-pornography connection, many feminists believe that pornography causes rape (Russell 1988); a scientific link, however, has yet to be established. With regard to social policy, some feminists advocate censorship of such materials while researchers Baron and Straus (1989, pp. 188–191) argue against this position.

Beginning in 1977 as a moral crusade, the child pornography movement led to the 1978 signing of Public Law 95–225, an amendment to the United States code concerning use of children in obscene materials. In spite of this, pornography continues to increase at alarming rates, and, as a research topic, the issue of pornography shares many of the previously noted problems associated with studying rape and child sexual abuse.

Other Areas of Sexual Abuse

Several other areas of sexual abuse that are gaining increasing attention are pre-adolescent and adolescent sexual abuse, abuse of very young children, and sexual harassment. One of the reasons that researchers and practitioners are becoming interested in the first two issues is the realization of how prominently youth figure as both victims and offenders in sexual assault statistics (Becker 1988; Herman 1989) and how very young some of the offenders and victims are. There is also an increasing interest in the belief that offenders against young children may actually begin before or at the time they enter adolescence (Knopp 1982). Sexual harassment is generating increased interest because it is viewed as one more form of violence against women and those in less powerful positions.

Summary and Conclusions

Extensive public and professional attention to sexual violence and abuse has come about only since 1960 and has been primarily a grass-roots movement. As a result, a large body of cross-discipline literature has developed, and various reforms have taken place, with more planned. While no consensus exists as to the scope of the problems, rates at which they are increasing, definitions, explanations, social policies, and solutions, sociologists, particularly feminists, conclude that sexual violence and abuse will never be reduced or eliminated until societies stop supporting and/or promoting aggression, violence, and inequality.

[See also Family Violence; Incest.]

BIBLIOGRAPHY

Abramson, P., and H. Hayashi 1984 "Pornography in Japan." In N. Malamuth and E. Donnerstein, eds., *Pornography and Sexual Aggression.* New York: Academic Press.

American Humane Association 1981 *National Study on Child Neglect and Abuse Reporting.* Denver, Colo.: AHA.

Araji, S. 1989 "The Effects of Advocates on Prevention." In N. C. Barker, ed., *Child Abuse and Neglect. An Interdisciplinary Method of Treatment.* Dubuque, Iowa: Kendall/Hunt.

———, and D. Finkelhor 1986 "Abusers: A Review of the Research." In D. Finkelhor, S. Araji, L. Baron, A. Brown, S. Doyle Peters, and G. E. Wyatt, eds., *A Sourcebook on Child Sexual Abuse.* Beverly Hills: Sage Publications.

Baron, L., and M. Straus 1989 *Four Theories of Rape in American Society.* New Haven, Conn.: Yale University Press.

Becker, J. V. 1988 "The Effects of Sexual Abuse on Adolescent Sexual Offenders." In G. W. Wyatt and G. J. Powell, eds., *Lasting Effects of Child Sexual Abuse.* Beverly Hills, Calif.: Sage.

Bolton, F. G., and S. R. Bolton 1987 *Working with Violent Families.* Beverly Hills, Calif.: Sage.

Bolton, F. G., Jr., L. A. Morris, and A. E. MacEachron 1989 *Males at Risk: The Other Side of Child Sexual Abuse.* Beverly Hills, Calif.: Sage.

Brown, A., and D. Finkelhor 1986 "Impact of Child Sexual Abuse: A Review of the Research." *Psychological Bulletin* 99:16–77.

Brownmiller, S. 1975 *Against Our Will: Men, Women, and Rape.* New York: Simon and Schuster.

Bulkley, J., and H. Davidson 1981 *Child Sexual Abuse: Legal Issues and Approaches.* Washington, D.C.: American Bar Association, National Resource Center for Child Advocacy and Protection.

Conte, J. R., and L. Berliner 1981 "Prosecution of the Offender in Cases of Sexual Assault against Children." *Victimology* 6:102–109.

Finkelhor, D. 1979 *Sexually Victimized Children.* New York: Free Press.

——— 1984 *Child Sexual Abuse: New Theory and Research.* New York: Free Press.

———, S. Araji, L. Baron, A. Brown, S. Doyle Peters, and G. E. Wyatt 1986 *A Sourcebook on Child Sexual Abuse.* Beverly Hills, Calif.: Sage.

———, and D. Russell 1984 "Women as Perpetrators: Review of the Evidence." In David Finkelhor, ed. *Child Sexual Abuse: New Theory and Research.* New York: Free Press.

Giaretto, H., 1981. "A Comprehensive Child Sexual Abuse Treatment Program." *Child Abuse and Neglect* 6:263–278.

Glaser, D., and S. Frosh 1988 *Child Sexual Abuse.* Chicago: Dorsey Press.

Green, W. M. 1988 *Rape.* Lexington, Mass.: Lexington Books.

Groth, A. N. 1979 *Men Who Rape.* New York: Plenum.

———, A. W. Burgess, and H. Holmstrom 1977 "Rape: Power, Anger and Sexuality." *American Journal of Psychiatry* 134:1239–1243.

Herman, D. F. 1989 "The Rape Culture." In J. Freeman, ed., *Women: A Feminist Perspective.* Mountain View, Calif.: Mayfield.

Herman, J. L., and L. Hirschman 1981 *Father–Daughter Incest.* Cambridge, Mass.; Harvard University Press.

Knopp, F. H. 1982 *Remedial Intervention in Adolescent Sex Offenders: Nine Program Descriptions.* New York: Safer Society Press.

Koss, M., and M. Harvey 1987 *The Rape Victim: Clinical and Community Approaches to Treatment.* Lexington, Mass.: Stephan Green Press.

Koss, M. P., and K. E. Leonard 1984 "Sexually Aggressive Men: A Review of Empirical Findings." In N. Malamuth and E. Donnerstein, eds., *Pornography and Sexual Aggression.* New York: Academic Press.

Levine, R. A. 1977 "Gussi Sex Offenses: A Study in Social Control." In D. Chappell, R. Geis, and G. Geis, eds., *Forcible Rape: The Crime, the Victim, and the Offender.* New York: Columbia University Press.

Martin, P. Y., and R. A. Hummer 1989 "Fraternities and Rape on Campuses." *Gender and Society* 3:457–473.

National Center on Child Abuse and Neglect 1981 *Study Findings: National Study of Incidence and Severity of Child Abuse and Neglect.* Washington, D.C.: Department of Health, Education and Welfare.

Peters, S. D., G. E. Wyatt, and D. Finkelhor 1986 "Prevalence." In D. Finkelhor, S. Araji, L. Baron, A. Browne, S. Doyle Peters, and G. E. Wyatt, eds., *A Sourcebook on Child Sexual Abuse.* Beverly Hills, Calif.: Sage.

Reiss, I. L. 1986 *Journey into Sexuality: An Exploratory Voyage.* Englewood Cliffs, N.J.: Prentice-Hall.

Rush, F. 1980 *The Best Kept Secret: Sexual Abuse of Children.* New York: McGraw-Hill.

Russell, D. 1983 "Incidence and Prevalence of Intrafamilial and Extrafamilial Sexual Abuse of Female Children." *Child Abuse and Neglect* 7:133–146.

——— 1984. *Sexual Exploitation, Rape, Child Sexual Abuse, and Workplace Harassment.* Beverly Hills, Calif.: Sage.

——— 1988 "Pornography and Rape: A Causal Model." *Political Psychology* 9:41–73.

Sanday, P. R. 1981 "The Socio-cultural Context of Rape: A Cross-cultural Study." *Journal of Social Issues* 37:5–27.

Schwendinger, J. R., and H. Schwendinger 1983 *Rape and Inequality.* Beverly Hills, Calif.: Sage.

U. S. Department of Justice, Federal Bureau of Investigation 1989 *Crime in the United States: Uniform Crime Reports, 1988.* Washington, D.C.: U.S. Government Printing Office.

Warshaw, R. 1988 *I Never Called It Rape.* New York: Harper & Row.

– SHARON K. ARAJI
PEPPER SCHWARTZ

SLAVERY AND INVOLUNTARY SERVITUDE

Although many observers view slavery and freedom as polar opposites, both slave and free wage labor systems rely upon compulsion. Slave systems depended ultimately upon physical coercion to force slaves to work for masters although cultural, ideological, and economic pressures typically augmented the effectiveness of force. Wage labor systems, by contrast, depend upon workers being free "in the double sense" (Marx 1967, pp. 168–169). Not only must they be free, non-slave workers, who can seek employment from others as they wish, but they must be free of all other means of subsistence that would permit voluntary withdrawal from the labor market. In the absence of subsistence alternatives, economic necessity compels "free" workers to exchange labor services for wages. Nevertheless, cultural expectations, ideological appeals, and physical coercion have often been used to reinforce market mechanisms, especially during periods of declining profits. Thus, large-scale labor systems are typically maintained by a mixture of physical and economic coercion that varies with the availability of subsistence alternatives.

How the actual constellation of physical and economic coercion and subsistence alternatives is determined by the power of contending groups as well as by historically specific cultural and ideological factors has been of great interest to social scientists. Perhaps the simplest and most durable statement of the causes of slavery is a classic conjecture known as the Nieboer-Domar hypothesis (Nieboer 1900; Domar 1970; Engerman 1986a; see Patterson 1977b for a critique), which links slavery to an abundance of arable land combined with a shortage of labor. After distinguishing slavery from other forms of involuntary servitude, this hypothesis is amended below to provide a provisional explanation for the worldwide trend from slavery toward freedom in large-scale labor systems during the past several hundred years.

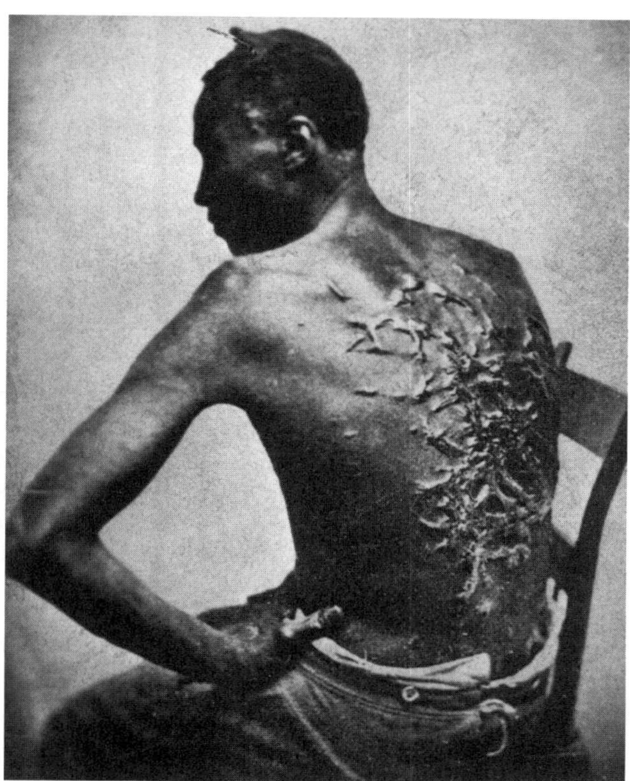

The whip marks on this plantation slave's back testify to a primary condition of slavery, which is the ability of the master to dominate the slave physically through violence or the threat of violence. (Corbis-Bettmann)

Slavery and Other Forms of Involuntary Servitude

Patterson (1982, p. 13) argues that slavery is defined by three conditions. First, slaves suffer perpetual domination that is ultimately enforced by violence. The permanent subjugation of slaves is predicated upon the capacity of masters to coerce them physically. Second, slaves suffer natal alienation, which is the severance of all family ties and the nullification of all claims of birth. They inherit no protection or privilege from ancestors, nor can they convey protection or privilege to their descendents. Finally, slaves are denied honor whereas masters are socially exalted. This last condition appears to be derivative, rather than definitive, of slavery because all hierarchical social systems develop legitimating ideologies that elevate elites and denigrate those at lower levels. The first two conditions, which distinguish slavery from other forms of involuntary servitude, constitute the working definition used here.

In chattel slave systems, slaves are movable property owned by masters and exchanged through market processes. Because some societies constructed elaborate slave systems without well-developed notions of property and property rights, property relationships cannot be an essential defining element of slavery (Patterson 1982; Patterson 1977a). Nevertheless, property relations and economic processes had important effects on slavery and other forms of unfree labor in the Americas, Europe, and Africa from the fifteenth century on, which is the major focus of this analysis.

No unfree laborer can voluntarily terminate service to a master once the servile relationship is established. Slavery maximizes the subordination of servant to master. Other servile workers, such as indentured and contract laborers, debt servants, peons, and pawns are less dominated than slaves and they do not suffer natal alienation. Pawns, for example, were offered by their families in return for loans. Pawns maintained kinship ties to their original families, which provided them some protection, and were freed once the loans were repaid. Indentured servants were bound to a master for a specific term, such as seven years, to which they agreed in exchange for passage to America, for example (Morris 1946; Smith 1947; Morgan 1975). Contract laborers were also bound for specified terms but could not be sold against their will to other masters, as was the case with indentureds. Debt servitude consists of labor service obligations that are not reduced by the amount of work performed (Morris 1946; Sawyer 1986). Peons are tied to land as debt servants and owe labor services to a landlord. Serfs are not debt servants, but they are tied to land and perform labor services on their lords' estates.

The right to labor services enjoyed by European feudal lords was vested in their political authority rather than land ownership, although serfs were reduced to slaves in all but name in some instances (e.g., Russia in the nineteenth century, Kolchin 1987).

Slaves suffer natal alienation, which is the severance of all family ties and the nullification of all claims of birth.

Indentured servants and contract laborers may agree to the initial terms of their servitude, but they cannot willingly end it during its term once it begins. Usually some form of coercion, such as poverty, debt, or impending imprisonment, was necessary to force people to agree to terms of contractual servitude or pawnship. By contrast, the status of slave, serf, peon, and debt servant was typically inherited or imposed on workers against their will.

Slavery, The Land/Labor Ratio, and The State

In its simplest form, the Nieboer-Domar hypothesis states that abundant free land makes it impossible for free workers and nonworking landowners to coexist. If free land is available and laborers can desert landowners whenever they choose, landlords will be unable to keep enough workers to maintain their status as nonworkers. If landlords can compel workers to perform labor services despite the availability of free land, then landlords become labor lords, and workers are not free. On the other hand, scarce land combined with an abundant labor supply drives wages down making wage laborers less expensive than slaves or other servile workers.

The model appears deficient in at least four ways. First, as Domar recognized, political factors determine the degree of freedom enjoyed by workers. Chief among these is the extent to which the state protects the interests of landowners when they conflict with those of laborers. Large-scale slave labor systems cannot exist in the absence of states that defend the power of slave masters to control and utilize the labor of slaves. A powerful state is essential for protecting slave masters against slave rebellions, capturing runaways, and enforcing slave discipline. State power is required for the enslavement of new supplies of slaves. If the state is responsive to the demands of workers, or if workers can voluntarily withdraw labor services as they choose, unfree labor systems cannot be maintained.

Second, the model presumes that slave masters exploit slaves in response to economic incentives. But slaves and other unfree laborers often performed military, administrative, domestic, and sexual services that were largely unrelated to economic activities (Roberts and Miers 1988; Patterson 1982). The Nieboer-Domar hypothesis therefore does not apply to societies that employ slaves and other servile workers in noncommercial or minor economic roles (Lovejoy 1983; Finley 1968). Nor does it apply to states that use race, religion, gender, or other status criteria to restrict the freedom of workers for reasons other than economic ones (James 1988).

Third, the key issue from an employer's perspective is not simply the ratio of land to labor but the relative costs and benefits of different forms of labor that can be profitably employed using existing capital (including land). A more general version of the Nieboer-Domar model compares the stock of available capital to the availability of different forms of labor at prevailing prices. Thus, labor scarcity means the scarcity of labor at prices that can be profitably employed.

Finally, the simple version of the Nieboer-Domar hypothesis ignores the organizational capacities of workers and capitalists' capacities to adopt labor-saving innovations. If workers demand concessions that threaten profits or engage in strikes and other production disruptions, capitalists experience "labor shortages" that stem not from insufficient numbers but from the organized resistance of workers who are present (Miles 1987). Faced with such disruptions, capitalists with sufficient capital may adopt labor-saving innovations if they are available. When capitalists are unable to adopt labor-saving innovations, they often resort to labor coercive strategies to curb workers' market-based demands (Paige 1975). This case contradicts the Nieboer-Domar hypothesis, which assumes that high labor to capital (or land) ratios make coercive labor control strategies unnecessary.

Unfree Labor in the Americas

From the fifteenth through the nineteenth centuries, Europe, Africa, and the Americas became closely linked by flows of people and commodities (Lovejoy 1983; Eltis 1987). The colonization of the Americas by strong European states provided vast, lightly populated lands for commercial exploitation. Expanding commodity markets in Europe for sugar, cotton, tobacco, coffee, and other products stimulated the demand for greater supplies of servile labor to work the plantations and mines of the Americas. Weak states throughout large areas of sub-Saharan Africa left large populations vulnerable to the armed predations of stronger states that supplied the expanding markets for slaves.

Estimates of the numbers of bondsmen and slaves transported to the Americas are subject to sizable errors, given the paucity and unreliability of existing records, but relative magnitudes are thought to be reasonable (see Table 1). Differences in the sources of servile labor produced different racial compositions across American regions. Slaves from Africa outnumbered arrivals from Europe nearly four to one before 1820, and most were bound for sugar cane plantations in Brazil and the West Indies. British North America was atypical because its early immigrants were predominantly white indentured servants from Britain, Ireland, and Germany; perhaps two-thirds of the white immigrants who arrived before the American Revolution were bonded servants (Smith 1947, p. 336). Before being displaced by African slaves, white bondsmen were the principal source of labor in the plantation regions of all British colonies, including those in the Caribbean (Engerman 1986a; Galenson 1981).

Indentured servitude was the principal method of defraying the costs of supplying the colonies with workers. British laws and customs regulating master-servant relationships were modified significantly to adapt them to American circumstances (Galenson 1981). Because of the high cost of transatlantic passage, longer periods of service were required, typically four to seven years rather than the one year or less in England. English servants could not be sold against their will to another master, but the practice was sanctioned in colonial laws and customs because European servants could not negotiate terms with prospective masters before passage to America. Finally, opportunities for escape were much greater in America. Consequently, elaborate state enforcement mechanisms were implemented to discourage runaways and to catch, punish, and return those who did. Most indentured servants were transported to plantation regions because plantation labor produced greater returns than any other economic activity in the Americas (Galenson 1981). Employers in areas such as New England could afford few or no servants because they spe-

TABLE 1

IMMIGRATION TO AND POPULATIONS OF REGIONS IN THE AMERICAS (IN THOUSANDS)

	Total Immigration to the Americas up to circa 1820			
	African	**European**	**Total**	**% African**
United States	550	651	1,201	46
Continental Spanish America	1,072	750	1,822	59
Brazil and the West Indies	6,777	964	7,741	88
Totals	8,399	2,365	10,764	78
	Total population circa 1650			
	Native Americans & Mestizos	**Europeans**	**Blacks & Mulattoes**	**Total**
North America	860 (86%)	120 (12%)	22 (2%)	1,002 (100%)
Continental Spanish America (excluding Peru)	8,773 (90%)	575 (6%)	437 (4%)	9,785 (100%)
Brazil, the West Indies, and the Guyanas	843 (51%)	154 (9%)	667 (40%)	1,664 (100%)
Totals	10,476 (84%)	849 (7%)	1,126 (9%)	12,451 (100%)
	Total Population circa 1825			
	Native Americans & Mestizos	**Europeans**	**Blacks & Mulattoes**	**Total**
North America	423 (4%)	9,126 (80%)	1,920 (17%)	11,469 (100%)
Continental Spanish America (excluding Peru)	12,660 (79%)	2,937 (18%)	387 (2%)	15,984 (100%)
Brazil, the West Indies, and the Guyanas	381 (5%)	1,412 (20%)	5,247 (75%)	7,040 (100%)
Totals	13,464 (39%)	13,475 (39%)	7,554 (22%)	34,493 (100%)

Sources: Immigration rates are adapted from Eltis (1983, p. 278). Population figures are adapted from Slicher Van Bath (1986, p. 21), in which the West Indies include the Spanish Islands but exclude the Bahamas.

cialized in trades with lower labor productivities and lower profit margins.

White servile labor was replaced by black slavery throughout the Americas between 1600 and 1800, and although racial prejudice encouraged the shift, it probably was not decisive (Morgan 1975). First, the limited supply of indentured servants could not satisfy the demand for servile labor, whereas the supply of African slaves was almost completely elastic. Improving economic conditions in Britain and state restrictions on the emigration of British servants reduced the numbers seeking passage to America, causing the price of servants to increase. As the price of servants exceeded the price of slaves, first for unskilled and later for skilled workers, slaves were preferred to bonded servants (Galenson 1981). Second, Africans were better acclimated to the diseases of the tropics, where the most important export crops were grown (Eltis 1983).

Slave plantations prefigured the discipline of workers in the great factories of industrial capitalism.

Third, slaves could be compelled to comply with the labor-intensive plantation work regime that developed (Fogel 1989). Slaves were more efficient and profitable than free or indentured workers in sugar, cotton, coffee, rice, and tobacco because the work required by these crops could be efficiently performed by slave work gangs. Work gangs were organized according to specialized tasks, and slaves were assigned to particular gangs according to their skills and capacities. The work was performed under close supervision to maintain work intensity and quality. Slave masters often used brutal violence to enforce slave discipline, but naked force may have been used less than was previously thought. Slave masters experimented with different mixtures of positive and negative incentives in order to encourage slaves to maximize output (Fogel 1989). Thus, slave plantations prefigured the discipline of workers in the great factories of industrial capitalism, in which assembly lines regulate the rhythms and intensity of work.

Forced migration from Africa greatly exceeded all migration from Europe as sugar production became the greatest consumer of servile labor in the Americas. High death rates and a preference for male slaves in the sugar producing regions led to net population declines among blacks and mulattoes (compare immigration numbers to population sizes in Table 1). Nevertheless, the proportion of blacks in the British West Indies increased from 25 to 91 percent between 1650 and 1770 (Fogel 1989, p. 30). By the 1820s, the proportion of blacks and mulattoes in Brazil, the Guyanas, and the West Indies together reached 75 percent.

British North America was an exception to this pattern as both black and white populations had high rates of natural increase. Almost all major slave societies were unable to maintain the size of slave populations without continuous replenishment from outside sources. By contrast, the United States slave population multiplied because of unusually high fertility rates and lower mortality rates than elsewhere (see Table 1 and Fogel 1989).

Political factors also encouraged the transition from white servitude to black slavery (Engerman 1986b; Galenson 1981). As British citizens, indentured servants retained state protected natal rights, which their masters were obliged to respect. For example, masters could beat servants and slaves to enforce work discipline, but colonial courts protected servants against unfair punishment (Smith 1947). Importantly, Europeans could choose the place of their servitude and most refused transportation to the plantation regions from the eighteenth century on. African slaves could not avoid the plantation regions and were citizens of no state in Africa or America that would defend their interests.

Because Spain conquered the continental regions with the largest Native American populations (Table 1), it had less need of African slaves to satisfy labor shortages there. Instead, Spanish colonists installed a coercive labor system patterned on Spanish feudalism that forced natives to work part-time on colonial estates although slavery was still preferred in the mines (Slicher Van Bath 1986; Kloosterboer 1960). Unfree labor markets and compulsory labor endured for 400 years, eventually evolving into debt servitude by the nineteenth century. Consequently, Native Americans and mestizos composed nearly 80 percent of the population of continental Spanish America by 1825 but were almost annihilated in the West Indies (Table 1).

Nowhere in the Americas was slavery in danger of withering away economically at the time that it was abolished (Eltis 1987). Strong states with dynamic economies based upon free wage labor where abolitionist ideologies flourished imposed abolition on weaker states. A principal exception was Haiti where slave owners were deposed by a slave revolt in 1804. Although Britain controlled one-half of the world's exports in sugar and coffee and one-half of the transatlantic commerce in slaves by the early nineteenth century (Eltis 1987), it played the dominant role in abolishing the transatlantic slave trade and, finally, in the worldwide abolition of slavery. Britain outlawed the slave trade in 1808 and freed the slaves in its West Indian colonies in 1833 over the strenuous objections of slave owners. The

United States prohibited the importation of slaves after 1808 and Civil War led to abolition in 1865. By the 1870s, all of the major European and American maritime and commercial powers had acquiesced to British pressure and outlawed the slave trade. Brazil became the last state in the Americas to abolish slavery in 1888.

The land/labor ratio strongly affected planters' responses to abolition. Where ex-slaves could find no alternative to plantation work, such as on Barbados and Antigua, the transition to free labor was rapid, and plantation production did not decline appreciably (Boogaart and Emmer 1986). Where land or alternative employment was available as in Jamaica and Trinidad, the ex-slaves abandoned the plantations, and plantation productivity declined (Engerman 1985). In response, planters implemented a variety of servile labor systems with mixed results. A second wave of indentured servants was imported chiefly from Asia, especially China and India, which more than compensated for the labor shortages induced by abolition in some cases such as Mauritius and British Guiana (Engerman 1985, 1986b). China and colonial India eventually banned servant recruitments because of objections to employers' poor treatment of servants, and Brazil was never able to negotiate access to Asian indentured laborers (Boogaart and Emmer 1986).

Where planters retained a degree of political power, as in the West Indies and Brazil, vagrancy statutes and other compulsory labor schemes were used to force workers to accept wages below free market levels (Kloosterboer 1960; Huggins 1985). Indentured labor and other forms of involuntary servitude were banned in the United States by the Thirteenth Amendment (1865) to the U.S. Constitution, but planters regained substantial influence over black workers through their control of racially discriminatory state and local governmental institutions (James 1988). Blacks were disfranchised by 1900, which made them especially vulnerable to racial segregation, physical coercion, and economic discrimination. The extent to which racial discrimination interfered with free labor markets in the South is controversial (e.g., Wright 1986). Nevertheless, the most determined resistance to the civil rights movement of the 1960s was located in the plantation regions (James 1988).

Unfree Labor in Africa and Asia

Slavery was an indigenous institution in Africa and Arabia for centuries before Europeans entered the African slave trade. While approximately 9.9 million Africans were transported to the Americas before the Atlantic slave trade was suppressed (Fogel 1989), an additional 5.2 million African slaves were transported across the Sahara, Red Sea, and Indian Ocean into the Islamic world between 1500 and 1900. Moreover, perhaps 6.4 million more were exported to Islamic societies between A.D. 650 and 1500 ("a rough approximation," Lovejoy 1983, p. 24). Millions more were enslaved in African societies.

Whereas chattel slavery in the Americas was predicated upon profit making, African slavery typically had no such narrow economic basis. African slaves were menial servants and field workers, but they might also have been concubines, surrogate kin, soldiers, commercial agents, and candidates for human sacrifice (Roberts and Miers 1988, p. 5). Female slaves were especially valued because women performed most agricultural and domestic work. African societies were based upon kinship relations in which all individuals were linked in a complex network of dependency. Because power in kinship systems depends on the size of social groups, slave masters could increase their power by obtaining more slaves. Furthermore, slaves were immune to the appeals of their master's rivals within kin groups because they had no kinship ties that mediated their subordination to their masters.

Islamic slavery also differed from chattel slavery in important ways. Islamic law prohibited the enslavement of Muslims but permitted the enslavement of persons born to slave parents or captured for the purpose of conversion to Islam (Gordon 1989). Concubines could not be sold if they bore a child to their master and the child could not be enslaved. Allowing slaves to purchase their freedom brought honor to former masters. Manumitting slaves was also meritorious and could atone for certain sins and public offenses.

Islamic slaves were typically employed as household servants, domestic workers, concubines, and, to a lesser extent, soldiers. Female slaves typically brought higher prices than males because the heads of patriarchal Muslim families prized female slaves for assignment to sexual and domestic roles in their households. Slave eunuchs performed special tasks in large households and usually brought higher prices than female slaves. Consequently, pre-twentieth-century slave traders castrated large numbers of African slave boys in crude operations, which killed perhaps 90 percent of them (Gordon 1989, pp. 91–97). But Islamic slave masters also responded to economic incentives, as did their American counterparts, when market opportunities arose. During the nineteenth century, over 750,000 slaves were transported to the clove plantations on Zanzibar and other locations on the east coast of Africa, for example (Cooper 1977; Lovejoy 1983, p. 151).

British diplomatic and military pressure finally led to the suppression of the Islamic and African slave trades as it did with the transatlantic traffic. In 1890, all of the European powers agreed to suppress slave trading and slave raiding and to assist ex-slaves, a commitment that legitimated the conquest of Africa in the eyes of European citizens. But European colonial administrators were reluctant abolitionists (Roberts and Miers 1988). Inadequate military and administrative power, fear of economic and political disruptions, and unfamiliarity with African customs delayed the process.

Female slaves brought higher prices than males because the heads of patriarchal Muslim families prized female slaves for sexual and domestic roles in their households.

Colonial governments essentially ended slavery in sub-Saharan Africa by the 1930s, but involuntary servitude persisted. Roberts and Miers (1989, pp. 42–47) identify three factors that retarded the emergence of free labor markets in Africa. The first two were responses to abundant land and scarce labor, at least in part. First, colonial states conscripted natives, imposed labor levies that local chiefs had to fill, and implemented other compulsory labor mechanisms to maintain a supply of cheap labor for European employers and administrators. Second, many Africans had access to land or livestock and were unwilling to work for wages. Colonial states tried to reduce the attractiveness of nonwage occupations by, for example, raising taxes above what peasant agriculturalists and pastoralists could pay, and prohibiting Africans from growing lucrative cash crops. In settler colonies such as South Africa, Africans were pushed off the land and confined to strictly regulated labor markets by pass laws. Third, Africans resorted widely to pawnship after abolition.

The reluctance of colonial administrators and the power of postcolonial states allowed slavery to survive in some Islamic nations of North Africa and the Arabian Peninsula well into the twentieth century. Pressure from the United Nations and world opinion finally led to formal abolition in the remaining slave states: Ethiopia in 1942; Saudi Arabia in 1962; Muscat and Oman in 1970; Mauritania for the third time in 1980. Nevertheless, reports of slavery persist. Saudi Arabia allegedly failed to free some 250,000 slaves in the late 1960s; an estimated 100,000 chattel slaves existed in Saharan regions of Mauritania in 1980, but most, if not all, were freed by 1984; nomadic tribesmen allegedly held 250,000 slaves in the Sahelian districts of Mali in 1984 (Gordon 1989, pp. 232–234; United Nations 1984, pp. 18–19; United Nations 1988, p. 197; Sawyer 1986, p. 14).

Other forms of servitude persist, although they are illegal in most nations. For example, India outlawed bondage in 1976, but a survey found more than 2.5 million bonded workers in 1978; only 163,000 had been freed by 1985 (Sawyer 1986, pp. 124–134). Debt servitude was reported since 1970 among landless peasants in India and Nepal and Native American rubber collectors in the Peruvian Amazon. As late as 1986, the Dominican Republic used the army to round up Haitian immigrants and forced them to work on sugar plantations during the harvest season (Plant 1987).

Current Patterns of Slavery and Unfree Labor

States have shaped the persistence and patterns of slavery and other forms of unfree labor since the fifteenth century. For most of this period, states defended the interests of slave masters, slave raiders, slave traders, merchants, landlords, planters, capitalists, state officials, and others who benefited from the services of unfree workers. The Nieboer-Domar hypothesis, suitably modified, provides a preliminary explanation for the persistence of slavery and unfree labor in the Americas and some parts of Africa during this period (see Patterson 1977b for an opposing view) but cannot account for the patterns of nonchattel slavery in Africa and Asia, where political and cultural factors were key.

The expansion of capitalism and increasing world population displaced large numbers from subsistence agriculture and other means of support in many regions. Great disparities between rich and poor nations drive many people across state boundaries in search of jobs and improved living conditions. State power still plays a crucial role in shaping migration and in molding the relationship between capital and labor, but states with expanding economies now prevent the entrance of many willing workers rather than compel the entrance of the unwilling. The whip of unemployment and poverty replaces the slave master's lash as free labor replaces slavery.

All nations regulate the passage of individuals across their boundaries and universally assign superior rights and privileges to citizens as compared to noncitizens. In the advanced capitalist democracies with ostensibly free labor markets, the state-enforced distinction between citizen and noncitizen is a key mechanism in maintaining dual labor markets that disproportionately relegate noncitizens to the lowest paying jobs (e.g., Thomas 1985; Miles 1987; Cohen 1987). Typically, noncitizen "guest workers" are less likely to enjoy state protection and are more vulnerable to discrimination. Any reemergence of large-scale, state-enforced slave systems in countries with expanding economies will probably be for political or cultural rather than economic reasons. Because the demand for cheap labor can be satisfied largely by choosing among citizens and noncitizens who have no other labor market alternatives, democratic states can regulate noncitizens' access to domestic labor markets rather than forcibly import unfree workers from foreign lands.

But many modern states are not liberal democracies. Thousands were confined for political reasons in forced labor camps during the Stalin era in the USSR. Nazi Germany forced Jews and other minorities into slavery where they were to be "worked to death" (Sawyer 1986). Blacks were disfranchised and rigidly segregated in the southern United States for much of the twentieth century, making them vulnerable to coercive labor practices. The Republic of South Africa's policy of apartheid denied citizenship status to native blacks, who composed 70 percent of the population and are an essential component of the work force. Claiming the right to regulate immigration as all nations do, South Africa used citizenship status to create unfree labor markets that benefited white employers and imposed severe burdens on disfavored racial and ethnic groups.

Slavery has been formally abolished everywhere, but many states do not provide equal protection of the law to all groups. Race and ethnic violence is severe in many places (e.g., Senegal, Mauritania, Sri Lanka, Somalia, India), which creates great pressure for states to enforce racial or ethnic bias. Nevertheless, state-enforced racial and ethnic distinctions are almost universally condemned by international organizations. Many nations enforced sanctions against South Africa because of its blatant racial bias, for example, but discrimination against disfavored ethnic groups has persisted in a number of other countries (U.S. Department of State 1990). For example, ethnic Albanians cannot buy real property in the Yugoslavian province of Serbia. Ethnic hiring quotas for government positions are observed in Nigeria. State-enforced race or ethnic discrimination was also reported in China, Romania, Rwanda, Burundi, Mauritania, Senegal, Sudan, and India (U.S. Department of State 1990).

State-enforced religious bias appears to be more widespread than race discrimination. Most Islamic nations impose restrictions on non-Muslims, but Saudi Arabia and Iran are especially harsh. For example, all citizens of Saudi Arabia must be Muslims and conversion to a different religion is punishable by death (U.S. Department of State 1990). Saudi Arabia also prohibits the public or private practice of non-Muslim religions and restricts economic opportunities for non-Muslims and Shi'a Muslims. Iran imposes barriers to education, jobs, and public accommodations for Christians, Jews, Zoroastrians, and Bahais. Although religious discrimination is officially prohibited in India, China, and Israel, religious minorities in these nations continue to complain of state-enforced biases.

Discrimination against women is more widespread and pernicious than other forms of state-enforced status bias, and even extreme cases seldom provoke criticism from other nations (U.S. Department of State 1990). Sex discrimination in varying degree is characteristic of Islamic nations. Saudi Arabian women have few political rights: they cannot travel abroad without permission from their nearest male relative, cannot operate automobiles or travel alone, must keep their faces covered in public, and inherit smaller amounts than their brothers. In Pakistan, press reports suggest an increase in the number of newlywed wives who are thought to have been murdered, often by burning, by husbands who were dissatisfied with the size of their wives' dowries. Violence against women is seldom investigated or punished (Muslim advice columns in Saudi Arabia and Pakistan advocate wife beating as an appropriate form of discipline).

All citizens of Saudi Arabia must be Muslims and conversion to a different religion is punishable by death.

Most Islamic states discriminate against women in the inheritance and ownership of property and in family and marriage issues, but similar biases exist in African and Asian non-Muslim nations, where traditional courts or Muslim minorities are allowed to adjudicate these issues as in Sudan, South Africa, Mauritania, Senegal, Chad, Nigeria, Rwanda, and India, for example (U.S. Department of State 1990). South African women of all races can be legally dismissed from their jobs if they become pregnant. Dowry deaths seldom result in convictions in India.

Most of the remaining countries officially condemn discrimination against women, but state-enforced bias persists (U.S. Department of State 1990). For example, women in the Philippines have restricted rights to buy and sell property. China enforces sex differences in access to jobs and education, and a number of nations in the Americas enforce some form of sex bias.

The historic decline in the land/labor ratio did not produce the abolition of slavery and involuntary servitude as the simple version of the Nieboer-Domar hypothesis suggests. Many states still enforce race, religious, sex, and other status and class distinctions among citizens that discriminate against unfavored groups or make them vulnerable to coercive labor relations and slaverylike practices. The exercise of political power, the pressure of economic necessity, and cultural practices are inextricably linked.

[See also African-American Studies; Apartheid, Prejudice, Segregation and Desegregation; Social Inequality; Social Stratification.]

BIBLIOGRAPHY

Boogaart, Ernst van den, and P.C. Emmer 1986 "Colonialism and Migration: An Overview." In P. C. Emmer, ed., *Colonialism and Migration.* Dordrecht, The Netherlands: Martinus Nijhoff.

Cohen, Robin 1987 *The New Helots.* Brookfield, Vt.: Gower Publishing.

Cooper, Frederick 1977 *Plantation Slavery on the East Coast of Africa.* New Haven, Conn.: Yale University Press.

Domar, Evesy D. 1970 "The Causes of Slavery or Serfdom: A Hypothesis." *Journal of Economic History* 30:18–31.

Eltis, David 1983 "Free and Coerced Transatlantic Migrations: Some Comparisons." *American Historical Review* 88:251–280.

——— 1987 *Economic Growth and the Ending of the Transatlantic Slave Trade.* New York: Oxford University Press.

Engerman, Stanley L. 1985 "Economic Change and Contract Labour in the British Caribbean." In D. Richardson, ed., *Abolition and Its Aftermath.* London: Frank Cass.

——— 1986a "Slavery and Emancipation in Comparative Perspective: A Look at Some Recent Debates." *Journal of Economic History* 46:317–339.

——— 1986b "Servants to Slaves to Servants: Contract Labour and European Expansion." In P. C. Emmer, ed., *Colonialism and Migration,* Dordrecht, The Netherlands: Martinus Nijhoff.

Finley, M. I. 1968 "Slavery." *International Encyclopedia of the Social Sciences,* Vol. 14, pp. 307–313. New York: Macmillan and Free Press.

Fogel, Robert W. 1989 *Without Consent or Contract.* New York: Norton.

Galenson, David W. 1981 *White Servitude in Colonial America.* New York: Cambridge University Press.

Gordon, Murray 1989 *Slavery in the Arab World.* New York: New Amsterdam Books.

Huggins, Martha K. 1985 *From Slavery to Vagrancy in Brazil.* New Brunswick, N.J.: Rutgers University Press.

James, David R. 1988 "The Transformation of the Southern Racial State: Class and Race Determinants of Local-State Structures." *American Sociological Review* 53:191–208.

Kloosterboer, W. 1960 *Involuntary Labour Since the Abolition of Slavery.* Leiden: E. J. Brill.

Kolchin, Peter 1987 *Unfree Labor: American Slavery and Russian Serfdom.* Cambridge: Harvard University Press.

Lovejoy, Paul E. 1983 *Transformations in Slavery.* Cambridge: Cambridge University Press.

Marx, Karl (1867) 1967 *Capital,* Vol. 1. New York: International Publishers.

Miles, Robert 1987 *Capitalism and Unfree Labour.* London: Tavistock.

Morgan, Edmund S. 1975 *American Slavery, American Freedom.* New York: Norton.

Morris, Richard B. 1946 *Government and Labor in Early America.* New York: Columbia University Press.

Nieboer, Herman J. 1900 *Slavery as an Industrial System.* The Hague: Martinus Nijhoff.

Paige, Jeffery 1975 *Agrarian Revolution.* New York: Free Press.

Patterson, Orlando 1977a "Slavery." *Annual Review of Sociology* 3:407–449.

——— 1977b "The Structural Origins of Slavery: A Critique of the Nieboer Domar Hypothesis." *Annuals New York Academy of Sciences* 292:12–34.

——— 1982 *Slavery and Social Death.* Cambridge, Mass.: Harvard University Press.

Plant, Roger 1987 *Sugar and Modern Slavery.* London: Zed.

Roberts, Richard, and Suzanne Miers 1988 "The End of Slavery in Africa." In S. Miers and R. Roberts, eds., *The End of Slavery in Africa.* Madison: University of Wisconsin Press.

Sawyer, Roger 1986 *Slavery in the Twentieth Century.* London: Routledge and Kegan Paul.

Slicher Van Bath, B. H. 1986 "The Absence of White Contract Labour in Spanish America During the Colonial Period." In P. C. Emmer, ed., *Colonialism and Migration.* Dordrecht, The Netherlands: Martinus Nijhoff.

Smith, Abbot Emerson 1947 *Colonists in Bondage.* Chapel Hill: University of North Carolina Press.

Thomas, Robert J. 1985 *Citizenship, Gender, and Work.* Berkeley: University of California Press.

United Nations 1984 "Slavery: Report Prepared by B. Whitaker, Special Rapporteur of the Sub-Commission on Prevention of Discrimination and Protection of Minorities." New York: United Nations.

——— 1988 "United Nations Action in the Field of Human Rights." New York: United Nations.

United States Department of State 1990 *Country Reports on Human Rights Practices for 1989.* Washington, D.C.: U.S. Government Printing Office.

Wright, Gavin 1986 *Old South, New South.* New York: Basic Books.

— DAVID R. JAMES

SOCIAL CHANGE

Social change is ubiquitous. Although earlier sociologists often treated stability as normal and significant social change as an exceptional process deserving special explanation, scholars now expect to see some continuous level of change in all social organizations. Sharp, discontinuous changes are of course rarer but still a normal part of social life. As Bourdieu (1990) and Giddens (1986) suggest, we need to see human social life as always structured but incompletely so. "Structuration" is as much a process of change as a reflection of stability. Indeed, the existence of stable social patterns over long periods of time requires at least as much explanation as does social change.

Cumulative social change must be distinguished from the universal, processual aspect of all social life. Sociologists do study the latter, for example by focusing attention on those dynamic processes through which particular characteristics of social life may change, even though overall patterns remain relatively constant. Marriages and divorces are thus major changes in particular social relationships, but a society may have a roughly constant marriage or divorce rate for long periods of time. Likewise, markets involve a continuous flow of changes in who holds money or goods, who stands in the position of creditor or debtor, who is employed or unemployed, and so forth. These specific changes, however, generally do not alter the nature of the markets themselves. Sociologists both study the form of particular transactions and develop models to describe the dynamics of large-scale statistical aggregations of such processes.

Sometimes, specific processes of social life undergo long-term transformations. These transformations in the nature, organization, or outcomes of the processes themselves are what is usually studied under the label "social change." Social life always depends, for example, on the processes of birth and death, which reproduce populations through generations. These rates (adjusted for the age of populations) may be in equilibrium for long periods of time, resulting in little change in the overall size of populations. Or birthrates may exceed death rates most of the time, resulting in gradual population growth, but periodic disasters like war, famine, and pestilence may cut the population back. In the latter case, the population may show little or no cumulative growth but rather a dynamic equilibrium in which every period of increase is offset by a rapid decline. Approximations to these two patterns characterize a great deal of world history. Population growth has generally been quite slow—though in fact periodic declines have not offset all increases. In the last 300 years, however, a new phenomenon has been noted. As societies industrialize and generally grow richer and change the daily lives of their members, they undergo a "demographic transition." First, death rates are apt to drop rapidly as a result of better nutrition, sanitation, and health care. This results in rapid population growth. Eventually, fertility rates (birthrates standardized by the number of women of childbearing age) tend also to drop, and a new equilibrium may be reached; population growth will slow or stop. This is a cumulative transition because after it the typical rates of both birth and death are much lower, though the total population may be much larger. A variety of other changes may be related to this. For example, family life may change with declining numbers of children; parents' (especially women's) lives are apt to change as fewer of their years are devoted to bearing and raising children; childhood deaths will become rarities rather than common experiences.

Human social history is given its shape by cumulative social changes. Many of these are quite basic, like the demographic transition or the creation of the modern state; others are more minor, like the invention of the handshake as a form of greeting; most, like the development of team sports, fast-food restaurants, and international academic conferences lie in the broad area in between. Thus, cumulative social changes may take place on a variety of different scales, from the patterns of small group life through institutions like the business corporation or church to overall societal arrangements. Significant changes tend to have widespread repercussions, however, and so it is rare that one part of social life changes dramatically without changes occurring in others. While some important changes are basically linear—like increasing population—others are discontinuous. There are two senses of discontinuity. The first is abruptness, like the dramatic shrinkage of the European population in the wake of the plague and other calamities of the fourteenth century, or the occurrence of the Russian Revolution after centuries of Czarist rule and failed revolts. Second, some social changes alter not just the values of variables but their relationship to each other. Thus, for much of history the power (and wealth) of a ruler was directly related to the number of subjects; growing populations meant an increasing total population from which to extract tribute, taxes, or military service. With the transformation first of agriculture and then of industrial production in the early capitalist era (or just before it), this relationship was in many cases upset. From the sixteenth through the eighteenth centuries, for example, the heads of Scottish clans increasingly found that a small population raising sheep could produce more wealth than a large one farming; their attempt to maximize this advantage helped to cause the migration of Scots to Ireland and America. This process was of course linked also to growing demand for wool and the development of industrial production of textiles. These in turn involved new divisions of social labor and increased long-distance trade. At the same time, the development of industrial production and related weapons technologies reduced the military advantages of large population size, in contrast to epochs when wars were generally won by the largest armies; indeed, population may even come to be inversely related to power if it impedes industrialization.

Sociologists have generally taken three approaches to studying cumulative social changes. The first is to look for generalizable patterns in how all sorts of changes occur. Sociologists may thus look for characteristic phases through which any social innovation must pass—for example, skepticism, experimentation, early diffusion among leaders, and later general acceptance. Ogburn (1950) was a pioneer in this sort of research, examining topics like the characteristic "lag" between cultural innovations and widespread adjustments to them or exploitation of their potentials. For example, when improved health care and nutrition make it possible for nearly all children to survive to adulthood, it takes a generation or two before parents stop having extremely large families as "insurance policies" to provide for their support in old age. Earlier researchers often hoped to find general laws explaining the duration of such lags and accounting for other features of all processes of social change. Contemporary sociologists tend to place much more emphasis on differences among various kinds of social changes and their settings. Their generalizations are accordingly more specific. Researchers may limit their studies to the patterns of innovation among business organizations, for example, recognizing that these may act quite differently from others; or they may ask questions such as why do innovations gain acceptance more rapidly in formal organizations (like businesses) than in informal, primary groups (like families), or what sorts of organizations are more likely to innovate? The changes may be very specific—like the introduction of new technologies of production—or very general, like the Industrial Revolution as a whole (e.g., Smelser 1958). The key distinguishing feature of all these sorts of studies is that they regard changes as individual units of roughly similar sorts and aim at generalizations about them.

The second major sociological approach to cumulative change has been to seek an explanation for the whole pattern of cumulation. The most important such efforts are based on evolutionary theories. The most prominent contemporary social evolutionist, Gerhard Lenski, has thus argued that increases in technological capacity (including information processing as well as material production, distribution, etc.) account for most of the major changes in human social organization. In his synthesis (Lenski, Lenski, and Nolan 1990) he arranges the major forms of human societies in a hierarchy based on their technological capacity and shows how other features such as their typical patterns of religion, law, government, class inequality, or relations between the sexes are rooted in these technological differences. In support of the notion that there is an overall evolutionary pattern, sociologists like Lenski point to the tendency of social change to move only in one direction. Thus, there are many cases of agricultural states being transformed into industrial societies but very few (if any) of the reverse. Moreover, states with more-advanced technology tend to dominate regional or even broader social processes. Of course, Lenski acknowledges that human evolution is not completely irreversible; he notes, however, not only that cases of reversal are relatively few but that they commonly result from some external cataclysm. Similarly, Lenski indicates that the direction of human social evolution is not strictly dictated from the start but channeled in certain directions only. There is room for human ingenuity to determine the shape of the future through a wide range of potential differences in invention and innovation.

There are a number of other important versions of the evolutionary approach to cumulative social change. Some stress different material factors such as human adaptation to ecological constraints (Harris 1979; White 1949); others stress culture and other patterns of thought more than material conditions (Parsons 1968; Habermas 1978). Some versions of Marxism have attempted a similar explanation of all historical social change in terms of a few key factors—notably improvement in the means of production and class struggle (e.g., Engels 1972). Other readings of Marx suggest that his mature theory is better understood as specific to capitalism (Postone forthcoming).

The development of the modern world system has fundamentally altered the conditions of future social changes.

Adherents to the third major approach to cumulative social change argue that there can be no single evolutionary explanation for all the important transitions in human history. They also stress differences among the particular instances of specific sorts of changes. These historical sociologists place their emphasis on the importance of dealing adequately with particular changes by locating them in their historical and cultural context (Abrams 1982; Calhoun 1991). Weber was an especially important pioneer of this approach (though as noted Marx can be interpreted as also offering an argument for historical specificity of explanatory categories). Historical sociologists have argued that a particular sort of transformation—like the development of a capacity for industrial production—may result from different causes and hold different implications on different occasions. The Industrial Revolution in eighteenth- and nineteenth-century Britain thus developed with no advance model and without competition from any established industrial powers. Countries industrializing today are influenced by both models and competition from existing industrial countries (not to mention influences from multinational corporations). The development of the modern world system has thus fundamentally altered the conditions of future social changes, making it misleading to lump together cases of early and late industrialization for generalization (Wallerstein 1974–88).

The development of the modern world system, however, may not have been the result of a process of evolution either. Rather, accident and disorder may have played a crucial role (Simmel 1977; Boudon 1984). Thus, Wallerstein shows the centrality of historical conjunctures and contingencies—the partially fortuitous relationships between different sorts of events. For example, the outcomes of military battles between Spain (an old-fashioned empire) and Britain (the key industrial-capitalist pioneer) were not foregone conclusions. There was room for bravery, weather, strategy, and a variety of other factors to play a role. But certain key British victories (notably in the sixteenth century) helped to make not only British history but world history different by creating the conditions for the modern world system to take the shape it did. The importance of contingency and conjunctures is not the only argument historical sociologists pose against evolutionary explanation. A crucial one is that different factors explain different transformations. Thus, no amount of study of the factors that brought about the rise of capitalism and industrial production would provide the necessary insight into the decline of the Roman Empire and the eventual development of feudalism in Europe, or into the consolidation of China's very different regions into the world's most enduring empire and most populous state. These different kinds of events have their own, different sorts of causes.

Predictably, some sociologists seek ways to combine some of the benefits of each sort of approach to explaining cumulative social change. Historical sociologists who emphasize the singularity of specific transformations can nonetheless learn from comparisons among such changes and can achieve at least partial generalizations about them. Thus, different factors are involved in every social revolution, yet certain key elements seem also to be present, like crises (often financial) in the existing government's capacity to rule. Recognizing this (following Skocpol 1979) helps to avoid placing exclusive stress on the revolutionaries and their ideologies and actions, as some previous histories had done, and focuses attention on structural factors that may help to create potentially revolutionary situations. Similarly, even though there may be a variety of specific factors determining the transition to capitalism or industrial society in every instance, some version of a demographic transition does seem to play a role in nearly all cases. Even evolutionary explanation, which is widely dismissed by historical sociologists, might be of more use. In fact, many historical sociologists who do not fully adhere to evolutionary explanations nonetheless look to them for suggestions as to what factors might be important. Thus, Lenski's emphasis on technology or Marx's on the relations of production and class struggle can provide foci for research, and that research can help to determine whether these factors are equally important in all societal transformations and whether they work the same way in each. More radically, evolutionary sociology might follow biology in focusing less on the selection of whole populations (societies) for success or failure and look instead at the selection of specific social practices (e.g., the bearing of large numbers of children) for reproduction or disappearance. Such an evolutionary theory might provide a great deal of insight into how practices become more or less common, following biology in looking for something like mechanisms of reproduction and inheritance, the initiation of new practices (mutation), the clustering of practices in interacting groups (speciation), as well as selection. It would, however, necessarily give up the capacity to offer a single explanation for all the major transitions in human social history, which is one of the attractions of evolutionary theory to its adherents.

Certain basic challenges are particularly important to the study of cumulative social change today. In addition to working out a satisfactory relationship among the three main approaches, perhaps the most important challenge is to distinguish those social changes that are basic from those that are more ephemeral or less momentous. Sociologists, like historians and other scholars, need to be able to characterize broad patterns of social arrangements. This is what we do when we speak of "modernity" or "industrial society." Such characterizations involve at least implicit theoretical claims as to what are the crucial factors distinguishing these eras or forms. In the case of complex, large-scale societal processes, these are hard to pin down. How much industrial capacity does a society need to have before we call it industrial; how small must employment in its increasingly automated industries become before we call it postindustrial? Is current social and economic "globalization" the continuation of a long-standing trend or part of a fundamental transformation? Though settling such questions is hard, debating them is crucial, for we are unable to get an adequate grasp on the historical contexts of the pheomena we study if we try to limit ourselves only to studying particulars or seeking generalizations from them without seeking to understand the differences among historical epochs (however hard to define sharply) and cultures (however much these may shade into each other with contact). Particularly because of the many current contentions that we stand on the edge of a new age—postmodern, postindustrial, or something else—sociologists need to take on the challenge of developing theories capable of giving strong answers to the question of what it means to claim that one epoch ends and another begins.

Many of the most prominent social theorists have treated all of modernity as a continuous era and stressed its distinction from previous (or anticipated future) forms of social organization. Durkheim (1893) argued that a new, more complex division of labor was central to a dichotomous distinction of modern (organically solidary) from premodern (mechanically solidary) society. Weber (1922) saw Western rationalization of action and relationships as basic and as continuing without rupture through the whole modern era. Marx (1867) saw the transition from feudalism to capitalism as basic but held that no change in modernity would be fundamental unless it overthrew the processes of private capital accumulation and the commodification of labor. Recent Marxists thus argue that the social changes of the last 300 to 500 years are phases within capitalism, not breaks with it (Mandel 1974; Wallerstein 1974–88; Harvey 1989). Many sociologists would add a claim about the centrality of increasing state power as a basic, continuous process of modernity (e.g., Tilly 1990 emphasizes the distinctive form of the nation-state). More generally, Habermas (1984–88) has stressed the split between a lifeworld in which everyday interactions are organized on the basis of mutual agreement, and an increasingly prominent systemic integration through the impersonal relationships of money and power outside the reach of linguistically mediated cooperative understanding. Common to all these positions is the notion that there is a general process (not just a static set of attributes) common to all modernity. Some would also claim to discern a causal explanation; others only point to the trends, suggesting these may have several causes but no single "prime mover" to explain an overall pattern of evolution. All would agree that no basic social change can be said to have occurred until the fundamental processes they identify have been ended or reversed. Obviously, a great deal depends on what processes are taken to be fundamental.

Rather than stressing the common processes organizing all modernity, some other scholars have pointed to the disjunctures between relatively stable periods. Foucault (1973), for example, has emphasized basic transformations in the way knowledge was constituted and an order ascribed to the world of things, people, and ideas. Renaissance culture was characterized by an emphasis on resemblances among the manifold different elements of God's single, unified creation. Knowledge of fields as diverse (to our eyes) as biology, aesthetics, theology, and astronomy was thought to be unified by the matching of similar characteristics, with those in each field serving as visible signs of counterparts in the others. The "classical" modernity of the seventeenth and early eighteenth centuries marked a radical break by treating the sign as fundamentally distinct from the thing it signified—noting, for example, that words have only arbitrary relationships to the objects they name. The study of representation thus replaced that of resemblances. In the late eighteenth and early nineteenth centuries, still another rupture came with the development of the modern ideas of classification according to hidden, underlying causes (rather than superficial resemblances) and an examination of human beings as the basic source of systems of representation. Only this last period could give rise to the "human sciences"—psychology, sociology, and so forth—as we know them. Where most theories of social change emphasize processes, Foucault's "archaeology of knowledge" emphasizes the internal coherence of relatively stable cultural configurations and the ruptures between them.

Foucault's work has recently been taken as support for the claim (which he never endorsed) that the modern era has ended. Theories of "postmodernity" (reviewed well in Harvey 1989; see also Lash 1990) argue that at some point the modern era gave way to a successor. Generally, they hold that where modernity was rigid, linear, and focused on universality, postmodernity is flexible, fluidly multidirectional, and focused on difference. Some postmodernist theories emphasize the impact of new production technologies (especially computer-assisted flexible automation), while others are more exclusively cultural. The label *postmodernity* has often been applied rather casually to point to interesting features of the present period without clearly indicating why they should be taken as revealing a basic discontinuous shift between eras.

At stake in debates over the periodization of social change is not just the labeling of eras but the analysis of what factors are most fundamentally constitutive of social organization. Should ecology and politics be seen as determinative over, equal to, or derivative of the economy? Is either demography or technological capacity prior to the other? What gives capitalism, feudalism, a kinship system, or any other social order its temporary and relative stability? Such questions must be approached not just in terms of manifest influence at any one point in time or during specific events but also in terms of the way particular factors figure in long-term processes of cumulative social change.

[See also Evolution: Biological, Social, Cultural; Technology and Society.]

BIBLIOGRAPHY

Abrams, P. 1982 *Historical Sociology.* Ithaca, N.Y.: Cornell University Press.

Boudon, R. 1986 *Theories of Social Change.* Cambridge: Polity Press.

Bourdieu, P. 1990 *The Logic of Practice.* Stanford, Calif.: Stanford University Press (orig. 1980, trans. by R. Nice. Paris: Editions de Minuit).

Calhoun, C. 1991 "Culture, History, and the Problem of Specificity in Social Theory." In S. Seidman and D. Wagner, eds., *Postmodernism and General Social Theory.* New York and Oxford: Basil Blackwell.

Durkheim, Emile 1893 *The Division of Labor in Society.* New York: Free Press.

Engels, Friedrich 1972 *The Origin of the Family, Private Property, and the State.* London: Lawrence and Wishart.

Foucault, M. 1973 *The Order of Things: An Archaeology of the Human Sciences.* New York: Random House.

Giddens, A. 1986 *The Constitution of Society.* Berkeley: University of California Press.

Habermas, J. 1978 *Communication and the Evolution of Society.* Boston: Beacon Press.

——— 1984–88 *The Theory of Communicative Action,* 2 vols. Boston: Beacon Press.

Harris, Marvin 1979 *Cultural Materialism.* New York: Vintage.

Harvey, D. 1989 *The Postmodern Condition.* Oxford: Basil Blackwell.

Lash, S. 1990 *Postmodern Sociology.* London: Routledge.

Lenski, G., J. Lenski, and P. Nolan 1990 *Human Societies.* New York: McGraw-Hill.

Mandel, E. 1974 *Late Capitalism.* London: New Left Books.

Marx, Karl 1867 *Capital (Das Kapital),* vol. 1. London: Lawrence and Wishart.

Ogburn, W. F. 1950 *Social Change with Respect to Culture and Original Nature.* New York: Viking.

Parsons, Talcott 1968 *The Evolution of Societies.* New York: Free Press.

Postone, M. Forthcoming *The Present as Necessity: The Marxian Critique of Labor and Time.* New York: Cambridge University Press.

Simmel, Georg 1977 *The Problem of the Philosophy of History.* New York: Free Press.

Skocpol, T. 1979 *States and Social Revolutions.* New York: Cambridge University Press.

Smelser, N. J. 1958 *Social Change in the Industrial Revolution.* London: Routledge and Kegan Paul.

Tilly, C. 1990 *Coercion, Capital, and European States, AD 990–1990.* Oxford: Basil Blackwell.

Wallerstein, I. 1974–88 *The Modern World System,* 3 vols. San Diego: Academic Press.

Weber, Max 1922 *Economy and Society.* Berkeley: University of California Press.

White, Leslie A. 1949 *The Science of Culture.* New York: Grove Press.

– CRAIG CALHOUN

SOCIAL GERONTOLOGY

Social gerontology, or the sociology of aging, has two primary foci: (a) social factors during later life and (b) social antecedents and consequences of the aging process. Thus, social gerontology includes examination of both the status of being old and the process of becoming old. This is a vast arena, and the substance of social gerontology is appropriately informed by the theories and methods of many sociological subspecialties ranging from macro historical comparative and demographic perspectives to the micro orientations of social psychology and ethnomethodology.

Historically, social gerontology emerged from a social-problems orientation and focused on the deprivations and losses that were expected to characterize late life (Maddox and Campbell 1985). Early research in social gerontology focused on issues such as poverty during later life; old age as a marginal status, reflecting problems of social integration; adjustment to losses of old age; negative effects of institutionalization and poor quality of long-term care; and ageism and age discrimination. A significant proportion of recent research also focuses on the deprivations of old age. Investigators remain concerned about social integration and adjustment to loss. The majority of funding for gerontological research is provided by the National Institute on Aging, which is mandated to support health-related research. Consequently, much of social gerontology focuses on illness and the health care delivery system. The dramatic aging of populations in industrialized societies (Myers 1990) leads to questions about the capacities of social institutions and public policies to meet the needs of an unprecedented number and proportion of older adults. Scholars using the perspectives of political economy focus on the ways in which societies respond to the dependency needs of older adults and the social implications of those responses (Quadagno 1988).

Rather than representing involuntary loss of a treasured role, retirement is actively sought by the majority of older workers and seldom poses adaptive problems.

Although much gerontological research remains focused on the problems of later life, sociologists now recognize the broader importance and implications of old age and aging. Two factors appear to account for this broader and more complex view. First, despite the social-problem orientation of earlier research, empirical data failed to confirm a bleak picture of old age. For example, in spite of higher rates of illness and disability, the vast majority of older adults are competent and able to live independent, autonomous lives (U.S. Public Health Service 1987). Similarly, rather than representing involuntary loss of a treasured role, retirement is actively sought by the majority of older workers and seldom poses adaptive problems (Palmore et al. 1985). In addition, some of the problems observed in early studies have been remedied by the increased resources that recent cohorts have brought to late life and by effective public policies (Crystal 1982). Thus, although health care costs remain a burden for many older adults,

Medicare and Medicaid substantially reduced barriers to health care among older people. Similarly, as a result of improvements in Social Security benefits and increased participation in private pensions, older Americans now are no more likely to live in poverty than younger adults and, indeed, are less likely to live in poverty than children. Such findings pushed social gerontology toward more complex and empirically defensible perspectives on old age and aging.

Second, sociologists now recognize that age plays a fundamental role in social structure and social organization. Age is a major factor in the organization of society, affecting the allocation of social resources and social roles. Along with sex and race, age is an ascribed status, in that it is immutable and cannot be voluntarily chosen. But age also is unique among ascribed statuses in that it changes over time, and movement across age categories results in changing expectations for behavior, changing access to social resources, and changing personal and social responsibilities. Because of the fundamental role of age in social structure and personal biography, sociologists are committed to better understanding age groups and the aging process.

Isolating the effects of age and characterizing the aging process are difficult tasks, and available research represents only beginning efforts toward those goals. Because many factors affect social structure and individual behavior, it is always difficult to isolate the effects of one particular factor. But this task is even more difficult with regard to age, because it is inherently confounded with the effects of two other factors: cohort and time of measurement (Rodgers 1982). *Age,* of course, refers to time since birth, and *age effects* refers to patterns resulting from the passage of time or sheer length of life. *Cohorts* refers to persons born at the same or approximately the same time (e.g., the 1920 cohort, the 1940–1944 cohort). There are two primary kinds of *cohort effects.* One type results from historical factors. For example, cohorts that lived through the Great Depression or World War II had different life experiences than cohorts that were not exposed to these historical events (Elder 1974). Those life experiences may have implications for late life. The second type of cohort effect reflects compositional characteristics. Thus, large cohorts (such as the Baby Boomers) may face greater competition for social resources than smaller cohorts (such as those born during the Great Depression, when fertility rates were low), and differential access to social resources may affect status and well-being in old age (Easterlin 1980). *Period effects* (also called *time of measurement effects*) result from events or situations that happen at a particular time. For example, faith in government decreased among all Americans (regardless of age or cohort) at the time of the Watergate scandal.

Age, cohort, and period effects are intertwined. If one knows when an individual was born and also knows the time of measurement, simple subtraction provides accurate information about the individual's age. Similarly, if one knows an individual's age and time of measurement, one can easily calculate date of birth or birth cohort. There are no easy methods for disentangling age, period, and cohort effects. In general, however, the most compelling research results are those that are based on examination of multiple cohorts measured at different times (Rodgers 1982). If the same age patterns are observed across different cohorts measured at different times, those patterns are likely to reflect age effects. If patterns are not similar across cohorts and times of measurement, however, they are unlikely to reflect age effects.

Age, cohort, and period effects are all important in gerontological research. Age effects provide information about human development as it unfolds in social context. Cohort effects permit us to observe the social implications of shared history and cohort composition. Period effects provide information about the effects of contemporaneous events and situations on social structure and individual behavior. Although social factors are relevant to age, cohort, and period effects, distinguishing among them has important implications for generalization of research results. Age effects are the same or highly similar across time and place; thus, they are generalizable. In contrast, cohort and period effects are, by definition, variable across time. Consequently, generalization is limited.

Older adults are satisfied with life when they perceive their life conditions to be fair and just.

Examination of age, period, and cohort effects requires large databases in which multiple cohorts are observed on multiple occasions, often over long periods of time. Because of these stringent requirements, few studies in social gerontology focus specifically upon disentangling these confounded factors. But recognition of these sources of confounding appropriately tempers investigators' generalizations. In addition, this issue has sensitized investigators to the need to examine change over time, with the result that longitudinal studies, in which individuals are observed at multiple points in time, have become the dominant research design in efforts to characterize the aging process.

Not all studies in social gerontology focus on isolating the effects of age or characterizing the aging process. Another major focus of social gerontology is examining the heterogeneity, or variability, among older persons. The older population is highly heterogeneous, and there is evidence that variability is greater among older than younger adults. It is important to understand the sources and consequences of this diversity. In addition, recognition of this variability helps to avoid narrow, sterotypic images of old age. For example, some investigators are interested in identifying the social factors associated with different levels of financial resources during later life. Similarly, some researchers study the implications of varying levels of social integration on perceptions of well-being among older adults. Cross-sectional research designs, in which study participants are observed at a single time, are sometimes appropriate for such studies, although longitudinal research is also valuable for understanding the antecedents and consequences of heterogeneity in the older population. Also, even when the research focus is variability among older adults, investigators need to recognize that their findings may not generalize to other cohorts or times of measurement.

No single theme nor easily summarized list of topics does justice to the scope and diversity of research in social gerontology. Nonetheless, brief review of several major research areas can provide a general sense of the important themes in social gerontology.

Age Stratification

Stratification refers to the ranking of categories or classes in a hierarchical system. Because of their hierarchical form, stratification systems involve inequality; that is, some classes or categories are more highly valued and receive more social resources than others. *Age stratification* refers to the division of society into meaningful age groups that differ in social value and allocation of social resources (e.g., Riley 1985). The concept of age stratification has proven to be useful in a variety of ways. At the broadest level, it reminds us that age is a fundamental parameter of social organization and social structure. Age stratification has proven particularly useful in helping to account for age-related roles and norms. Reminders to "act our age" testify to the presence of age-related norms, and society allocates substantial numbers of roles on the basis of age, ranging from the right to vote and drive a car to eligibility for Social Security and Medicare. Age stratification has a social psychological parameter also: age consciousness or awareness of and identification with members of one's age group. Evidence indicates that most older adults are reluctant to label themselves as such, probably because of ageism and negative attitudes toward aging and old age (George 1985).

Status of Old Age

Two research traditions inform us about the status of old age. The first focuses on the emergence of late life as a distinctive and socially recognized segment of the life course. Old age did not emerge as a socially meaningful concept until social, health, and environmental conditions reached a level that resulted in significant proportions of persons living to advanced age (Clausen 1986). Thus, industrialization, public health measures, and technological development played critical roles in leading to the distinction between middle and old age. Life expectancy and preservation of health and autonomy in late life continue to increase, leading some observers to hypothesize that the distinction between "young-old" and "old-old" is increasingly salient (Neugarten and Neugarten 1986). The second research tradition focuses on the social value placed upon old age and the extent to which older persons receive inferior, equal, or superior treatment, compared to other age groups. Early research suggested that old age was valued less in modern, industrialized societies than in less-developed societies. More recent research, however, indicates that this conclusion is oversimplified (Keith, Fry, and Ikels 1990). The status of old age depends on a broad mix of social factors including cultural and religious traditions, family structure, and the social organization of the means of production. Although it is not possible to make broad statements about the relationship between modernization and the status of the elderly, negative stereotypes of older people and age discrimination are common in American society.

Old Age as the Culmination of Life-Course Experiences

Congruent with sociologists' increasing attention to the life course as a whole, gerontological research reveals that the past is indeed prologue to the future. Thus, status and personal well-being in late life depend in large part on events and achievements experienced earlier in the life course. Research on socioeconomic status (SES) in later life provides an excellent illustration of this research tradition (O'Rand 1990). There is compelling evidence that the economic resources available to older people are a function of educational, occupational, and economic decisions made in early and middle adulthood. In the occupational arena, factors such as occupational sector, length and continuity of job history, and pension coverage are important predictors of SES in old age. Personal decisions about savings and home ownership also affect financial resources in later life. The increased poverty of older women and older minority groups reflects the culmination of life-course experiences. Compared to white men, women and members of minority groups have shorter, more discontinuous job histories, are employed in occupations with lower pay and less opportunity for advancement, and are less likely to have private pensions. Marriage and fertility patterns in early and middle adulthood also have important implications for later life (Hagestad 1988). Financial resources, health, and perceptions of well-being during late life are enhanced by stable marriages. The age difference between spouses is significantly associated with the timing and length of widowhood. Children and grandchildren typically enhance well-being in later life and provide important sources of assistance for frail or dependent older adults.

Perceptions of Well-Being in Later Life

Study of life satisfaction, or perceptions of well-being, has been the dominant theme in social gerontology since the late 1950s. The gerontological research community has been particularly intrigued by the degree to which and the ways in which older people sustain a sense of well-being despite age-related losses of social and personal resources and increased proximity to death. Research strongly indicates that the vast majority of older people experience high life satisfaction and a sense of well-being (George 1990). Indeed, levels of life satisfaction are at least as high among older adults as among middle-aged and younger adults, and may be somewhat higher. For older adults, as for the population generally, perceived well-being is strongly related to the availability of social resources and meaningful ties to social structure. Thus, the determinants of life satisfaction in later life (and during adulthood generally) include financial resources, meaningful relationships with family and friends, and a sense that the physical and social environments are secure and supportive. Despite similarities in the predictors of life satisfaction, there are two ways in which perceived well-being differs for older and younger adults. First, there is clear evidence that older adults express high levels of life satisfaction in the presence of less attractive objective conditions than is true for younger and middle-aged adults. For example, older people are satisfied with far fewer financial resources and lower levels of health than their younger peers. Second, the processes or mechanisms by which objective life conditions affect perceptions of life quality appear to differ for older and younger adults. It appears that these two differences are related such that younger persons evaluate their life quality on the basis of comparisons of desired and actual levels of resources, whereas older adults evaluate their life quality on the basis of perceptions of equity (Carp and Carp 1982). Thus, young and middle-aged adults are satisfied with their lives when their achievements match their aspirations; older adults are satisfied with life when they perceive their life conditions to be fair and just. It remains unclear whether these age differences reflect age changes in perceptions of well-being or whether they are cohot effects.

Environment and Aging

A major tenet of sociology is that the physical and social environments, or, as more recently termed, *social context,* are important for understanding individual attitudes and behavior. Despite the importance of this proposition in social science theory, it is difficult to measure environments and document their effects. One contribution of gerontological research is its support of the importance of environment. Many older persons live in restricted or bounded environments such as nursing homes and retirement communities. Measuring environmental dimensions and observing their effects is considerably easier in restricted environments than in broader, more complex, social settings. In addition, there is evidence that, because of increased illness and frailty, older adults are often more sensitive to environmental demands than are younger adults (Lawton 1974). Thus, even rather small differences in environments can have substantial impact on older persons' attitudes and behaviors. Research on environments and aging documents the importance of environment, or context, for behavior during later life. Among the consistent findings are (a) that physical environments can be manipulated to facilitate or impede social interaction and the development of social bonds, (b) that objective environmental parameters are strongly associated with the perceived stressfulness of specific environments, and (c) that environments that foster a sense of personal control are associated with better health and functioning, as well as with higher levels of perceived well-being (George and Maddox 1989). These findings are of practical and theoretical value; dimensions of the physical and social environment can be purposely manipulated to generate favorable outcomes.

Social gerontology is an important field. It provides us with information about what it means to be "old," about the antecedents and consequences of stability and change during later life, and about the ways that older adults negotiate the development of meaningful lifestyles. Social gerontology is especially important in that it focuses sociologists' attention on the dynamics of process and change and on the intersections of social structure, social change, and personal biography. At its best, social gerontology effectively links processes and dynamics at the macro historical and societal levels with individual attitudes and behaviors. In addition, later life provides an excellent context for testing and, indeed, challenging some commonly held assumptions and hypotheses about the dynamics of social influence. In this way, it offers valuable insights and information to the larger sociological enterprise.

[See also Death and Dying; Filial Responsibility; Intergenerational Relations; Long-Term Care; Retirement; Widowhood.]

BIBLIOGRAPHY

Carp, Frances M., and Abraham Carp 1982 "Test of a Model of Domain Satisfactions and Well-being: Equity Considerations." *Research on Aging* 4:503–522.

Clausen, John A. 1986 *The Life Course.* Englewood Cliffs, NJ.: Prentice-Hall.

Crystal, Stephen 1982 *America's Old Age Crisis: Public Policy and the Two Worlds of Aging.* New York: Basic Books.

Easterlin, Richard A. 1980 *Birth and Fortune: The Impact of Numbers on Personal Welfare.* New York: Basic Books.

Elder, Glen H., Jr. 1974 *Children of the Great Depression.* Chicago: University of Chicago Press.

George, Linda K. 1985 "Socialization to Old Age: A Path Analytic Model." In E. Palmore, J. Nowlin, E. W. Busse, I. C. Siegler, and G. L. Maddox, eds., *Normal Aging III.* Durham, N.C.: Duke University Press.

——— 1990 "Social Structure, Social Processes, and Social-Psychological States." In R. H. Binstock and L. K. George, eds., *Handbook of Aging and the Social Sciences,* 3rd ed. New York: Academic Press.

———, and George L. Maddox 1989 "Social and Behavioral Aspects of Institutional Care." In M. G. Ory and K. Bond, eds., *Aging and Health Care: Social Science and Policy Perspectives,* London: Tavistock.

Hagestad, Gunhild O. 1988 "Demographic Change and the Life Course: Some Emerging Trends in the Family Realm." *Family Relations* 37:405–410.

Keith, Jennie, Christine L. Fry, and Charlotte Ikels 1990 "Community as Context for Successful Aging." In J. Sokolovsky, ed., *The Cultural Context of Aging: Worldwide Perspectives.* New York: Greenwood Press.

Lawton, M. Powell 1974 "Social Ecology and the Health of Older People." *American Journal of Public Health* 64:257–260.

Maddox, George L., and Richard T. Campbell 1985 "Scope, Concepts, and Methods in the Study of Aging." In R. H. Binstock and E. Shanas, eds., *Handbook of Aging and the Social Sciences,* 2nd ed., New York: Van Nostrand Reinhold.

Myers, George C. 1990 "Demography of Aging." In R. H. Binstock and L. K. George, eds., *Handbook of Aging and the Social Sciences,* 3rd ed. New York: Academic Press.

Neugarten, Bernice L., and Dale A. Neugarten 1986 "Age in the Aging Society." *Daedalus* 115:31–49.

O'Rand, Angela M. 1990 "Stratification and the Life Course." In R. H. Binstock and L. K. George, eds., *Handbook of Aging and the Social Sciences,* 3rd ed. New York: Academic Press.

Palmore, Erdman, Bruce M. Burchett, Gerda G. Fillenbaum, Linda K. George, and Laurence Wallman 1985 *Retirement: Causes and Consequences.* New York: Springer.

Quadagno, Jill 1988 *The Transformation of Old Age Security.* Chicago: University of Chicago Press.

Riley, Matilda White 1985 "Age Strata in Social Systems." In R. H. Binstock and E. Shanas, eds., *Handbook of Aging and the Social Sciences,* 2nd ed. New York: Van Nostrand Reinhold.

Rodgers, Willard L. 1982 "Estimable Functions of Age, Period, and Cohort Effects." *American Sociological Review* 47:774–787.

U.S. Public Health Service 1987 *Current Estimates from the National Health Interview Survey, United States, 1986* (DHHS Pub. No. PHS 87–1592). Washington, D.C.: U.S. Government Printing Office.

— LINDA K. GEORGE

SOCIAL INEQUALITY

Social inequality refers to the graduated dimensions (Blau 1977), vertical classifications (Ossowski 1963; Schwartz 1981), or hierarchical relations (Burt 1982) by which human populations at varying levels of aggregation are differentiated. As such, this concept is among the oldest and most diversely defined in sociology, extending back at least as far as Plato's conception of the Republic and developed subsequently in the social theories of Marx (1859), Mosca (1939), Weber (1947), Simmel (1896), Sorokin (1941), Eisenstadt (1971), Merton (1968), and others. The construct is often used interchangeably with such related (though relatively more specific) concepts as social class, social stratification, socioeconomic status, power, privilege, accumulative advantage, dependence, and dominance. And it is relevant for the study of social systems that range in size from the dyad (Simmel 1896) to the modern world-system (Wallerstein 1974).

Social Inequality as a Graduated Dimension

When social inequality is conceptualized as a graduated dimension, it is treated as a distributional phenomenon. Here the approach is to define inequality in terms of the distribution of socially valued attributes, such as education, income, information, health, and influence, in a population. However, distributional phenomena can be examined from one of two very different assumptions. The first views inequality as an outcome of, or generated by, the underlying distribution(s) of valued traits among individuals. In this sense, it refers to "regular differences in power, goods, services, and privileges among defined sets" of actors (Granovetter and Tilly 1988). The second assumption views inequality strictly as a system-level property with individual-level differences defined as derivative rather than generative (Blau 1977). Distributions such as the size of the system and its total volume of resources are examined as higher levels of aggregation, with the goal of determining the overall level of inequality (oligarchy) across systems and without reference to individual differences (e.g., Lenski 1966; May-hew 1973; Mayhew and Schollaert 1980).

Both approaches parameterize populations along criteria usually measurable at the level of individual actors (persons, races, gender categories, organizations, nation-states) in a system. Early applications of the first assumption can be found in Pareto's ([1897] 1980) examinations of income distributions and of the circulation of elites. He proposed that economic and political inequality emerged from the distribution and redistribution of "congenital abilities" valued within social systems. Sorokin (1941) proposed similar arguments to explain social and cultural processes of mobility and inequality.

Among the most influential and controversial conceptualizations of inequality as a graduated dimension emerging from individual differences was Davis and Moore's (1945) functionalist statement of the principles of stratification. They argued that social inequality results from the differential distribution of societal rewards to individuals based on their relative achievement of ranked social positions. This achievement process, with its implications for social mobility, was formally specified by Blau and Duncan (1967), who established that educational attainment mediated the process of intergenerational social mobility among men. They defined social inequality as socioeconomic status based on the economic and prestige rewards accorded achieved occupational positions in American society. The strong parallel between this model of inequality and the neoclassical model of human capital and economic inequality (see Becker 1964) is well established (Wright 1978).

Social inequality in industrial society developed along economic and political dimensions to produce the multidimensional bases of inequality: class, status, and party.

The most prominent distributional theories of inequality, however, are founded on macrosocial views regarding the division of labor, the rationalization of authority, and the distribution of social and economic rewards in industrial societies. Weber's (1947) theory of economic organization proposed that capitalist systems of property, power, and prestige developed out of the conjunction of changing systems of economic exchange (money economies) and accounting (double-entry bookkeeping) with rationalized systems of social control (rational-legal authority). Thus, social inequality in industrial society developed along economic and political dimensions to produce the multidimensional bases of inequality: class, status, and party. Lenski's (1966) comparative study of the evolution of inequality attempted a direct test of Weber's rationalization thesis that inequality evolves necessarily (functionally) with increasing differentiation in the direction of systems of privilege based on rational authority and away from socially illegitimate systems of force or economic dominance.

Accordingly, distributional inequality can be concerned with more than the single dimension of individual socioeconomic outcomes. It also addresses macrosocial patterns of inequality (Eisenstadt 1971). The parameters of social structure, according to Blau (1977), include inequality and heterogeneity—or graduated and nominal dimensions, respectively—which intersect to constrain and differentiate individuals' opportunities, as well as their motivations and outcomes. The intersection of graduated and nominal parameters creates diverse systems or populations with differing distributional properties that cannot be reduced to an original individual source. Blau's distributional theory is "macrosocial in the sense that the 'cases' are populations or communities and the 'variables' measure some aspect (a rate or a distributional property) of these populations" (Skvoretz and Fararo 1986, p. 30). Following this approach, indicators of inequality can be defined in such terms as Lorenz curves (e.g., Gini indices), social welfare functions, or similar distributional properties (see Allison 1978).

Thus, economic inequality may intersect with the nominal category of race, for example, and produce more diverse outcomes than traditional functional or neoclassical economic theories would predict. Examinations of patterns of interracial/interethnic marriage, for example, indicate that the association between occupational achievement and race is mediated by the extent of interracial/interethnic marriage in a community (see Blum 1984; Blau, Blum, and Schwartz 1982). This treatment of inequality, based on notions of dispersion and association, departs from the simple reduction of unequal outcomes to individual attributes and embeds the process in extended distributional contexts.

Other distributional approaches introduce mesoscopic constructs to explain inequality at levels above individual attributes, although individuals usually remain the units of analysis. Spatial and temporal contexts, for example, define and constrain distributions of individual outcomes. The examination of occupational mobility within organizational or labor-market contexts attempts to nest the process of inequality in the workplace within organizational and occupational boundaries. The availability of occupational positions within a system is independent of the motivations and other attributes of workers. White's (1970) influential notion of "vacancy chains" exemplifies this approach with its argument that job vacancies produce opportunity structures for individual mobility and define the mobility chances, and distributional outcomes, of individuals. Vacancy-chain models have been particularly useful for examining closed opportunity systems, such as internal labor markets (Sorensen 1977).

Distributions of individuals in systems of inequality are also influenced by temporal factors. Merton's (1968) provocative discussion of the "Matthew Effect" in scientific career systems argues that, over time, initial inequalities in a system bias distributional outcomes in favor of initial advantage. Formal extensions and applications of Merton's notion of accumulative advantage have been applied across contexts (Cole and Cole 1973; Allison and Stewart 1974) to establish patterns of temporal regulation of distributional outcomes over and above the attributes of individuals over time.

Social Inequality as a Vertical Classification

When social inequality is conceptualized as a vertical classification system, it is treated as an oppositional phenomenon. Here the approach is to define inequality in terms of "the relative position in a matrix of oppositions" (Schwartz 1981, p. 94) of social categories that determine relations of dominance, such as class, race, and gender. Vertical classifications grow out of antagonistic and contradictory interests in the relations of "objective" positions in the social division of labor, not out of the dispersed motivations and interests of individuals. Dominance and subordination emerge from the objective opposition of social categories. Dichotomous, binary, and polar conceptions of inequality (e.g., ruler–ruled, rich–poor, white–black, masculine–feminine) generally subscribe to an oppositional framework. Some have argued that this approach to inequality may be the most ancient in human social consciousness (Ossowski 1963; Schwartz 1981).

Class theories following Marxian frameworks dominate this approach (Braverman 1974; Wright 1985). Marx's theory of class proposes that class relations in capitalist systems are inevitably in conflict. Since all value is ultimately produced by labor, all (capitalist) profit must be at the expense of labor. The objective positions of owning class (bourgeoisie) and laboring class (proletariat), therefore, are necessarily antagonistic. Advanced capitalist systems sustain the exploitation of labor through rationalized job-definition systems and the degradation of work (Braverman 1974). Wright (1978) has argued, furthermore, that in advanced capitalist societies the elaborate differentiation of functions originally embodied in entrepreneurial capitalism into many different categories has not overcome the fundamental oppositional inequality of its origins; contradictory class positions continue to exist as a result of the underlying structure of capitalist relations.

Oppositional frameworks lend themselves to the examination of such classlike relations as those observable in race- and gender-centered systems of inequality. Oppositional approaches to the examination of race inequality can be traced to Myrdal's (1944) pioneering analysis of racial exploitation in the U.S. context. These approaches argue that race is an invariant principle of vertical classification masked by ideologies of economic progress and attainment (Pinkney 1984). Debates regarding the inevitability of racial opposition as the basis of inequality center on the substitutability of race and class as categories in the recent history of U.S. inequality. Wilson (1980) has proposed the controversial argument that class inequality has superseded race inequality as the basis of cross-race differences in economic and social outcomes.

Theories of gender inequality extend back to Mill's 1859 libertarian essay on the subjection of women and to Engels's Marxian analysis, written two decades later, of the relationship between private property and the stratification of family (gender) roles. But contemporary feminist theories provide the strongest argument for gender inequality as an oppositional, vertical classification system. The sex/gender system, it is argued, subordinates women in patriarchal relations that exist over and above class relations (Jaggar 1984), since male dominance over women's productive and reproductive roles predates the emergence of capitalism (Harding 1983). This system of inequality leads inevitably to a conflict of interests and to the emergence of competing ideologies.

Since the notion of dominance is central to vertical-classification approaches to inequality, these are also readily applied to the analysis of large-scale systems of inequality, such as the state (Skocpol 1979) and the modern world-system (Wallerstein 1974). Mechanisms of domination extend beyond class (or classlike) interests alone and are observable in the historical relations of nation-states (Reddy 1987) and multistate sectors of the modern world-system (Wallerstein 1974). Asymmetrical relations of exchange and dependence between states and geopolitical state sectors create relations of dominance, which define global inequalities. Such inequalities can be formulated as distributional phenomena following a functional framework; however, the historical analysis of dominance systems lends itself more readily to oppositional analysis. The classification of the world-system into core and periphery sectors that resulted from historically contingent factors introduces notions of centrality and dominance that suggest more than an underlying distribution of resources (Wallerstein 1974).

Social Inequality as Hierarchical Relations

When social inequality is conceptualized as hierarchical relations, it is treated as a system of interactions or interdependencies characterized by relative symmetry (equality) and asymmetry (inequality) among relations. Here the approach is usually to define the form of social relations rather than the attributes of individuals in these relations and to account for patterns of unequal relations without necessary reference to oppositions. Inequality or dominance stems from positions in hierarchical relations, not from the a priori possession or control of resources or power by individuals, groups, or categories (Marsden 1983). This relational approach to inequality can be traced to Simmel (1896), whose studies of the structures of superordination-subordination by persons, groups, and principles continue to inform research on hierarchical relations and social networks in modern life (Coleman 1982).

Because social relationships have such formal properties as connectedness, transitivity, reciprocity, and multiplexity, they are measurable units of analysis for the study of social inequality within populations at all levels, from siblings to communities to transnational trading systems (Lin and Marsden 1982). These social units make up complex configurations of social relations within which distinctive positions of relative equivalence or centrality can be revealed (Burt 1982). Thus, in their study of coalitions and elite structures in a German community named Altneustadt, Laumann and Pappi (1976) determined the relational bases of influence between natives and newcomers using network techniques emphasizing associational patterns over personal attributes. Patterns of social distance and connectedness among corporate actors, not the preexisting distribution of resources, defined the influence process in this community.

A provocative study by Granovetter (1974) of the job-search process clearly demonstrates the relative utility of relational over distributional approaches to inequality. Granovetter demonstrates that weak ties, rather than strong ties, in a community prevail in the successful job search. The "strength of weak ties" hypothesis (related to Simmel's *tertius gaudens,* or the third who enjoys) provides the counterintuitive argument that weaker (secondary) social contacts increase individuals' access to jobs more than stronger (primary) ties. These ties operate independently of the attributes of individual job seekers.

The "strength of weak ties" phenomenon can be extended beyond the job-search process to examine structures of relational inequality in different contexts. Studies of interlocking directorates and informational brokerage systems, for example, demonstrate that loosely coupled relational systems of different forms produce different systems of social inequality (Burt 1982). The network of ties constitutes a social-constraint context within which actors are "captured." Burt's (1983) study of corporate philanthropy as a cooptive relation is a specific example of the relational bases of inequality in a market context. Using Internal Revenue Service data on firm expenditures on advertising and philanthropy, Burt demonstrates that firm philanthropy coopts the household sector by legitimizing the firm to the public as a protector and by improving the ability of specific classes to purchase the firm's products (Burt 1983, p. 424). The strength of this approach is that advertising, which is more blatantly cooptive, does not escape public suspicion where philanthropy does more easily. Firms in an economic sector perform unequally as a result of their relative cooptive relations with the public; and the public exists in a cooptive relationship as consumers in this context.

Firm philanthropy coopts the household sector by legitimizing the firm to the public as a protector.

Finally, it should be mentioned that, despite the rationale provided above for the bulk of sociological research on relational inequality, the relational approach has been used to examine the importance of individual resources for social inequality. Indeed, early experimental efforts to study small-group processes of inequality demonstrated that both individual resources and social relations can create systems of inequality, whether measured as leadership processes or communication networks (Thibaut and Kelley 1959). And, more recently, studies of what Burt (1982) has termed "ego-centered" networks examine network position itself as an individual resource with implications for social inequality.

Approaches to Social Inequality

The three major approaches to the study of social inequality outlined above have different implications for theory as well as for method. The distributional approach that examines social inequality as a graduated dimension depends primarily upon sample data and can be directed toward individual as well as structural explanations of inequality. The oppositional approach to vertical classifications may use sample data but has tended to adopt historical and qualitative approaches to study the institutionalization of dominance in various forms, that is, as class, race, or gender or as other forms of subordination. Finally, the relational approach, which provides a direct method for examining the social context of inequality, may use sample or case data to map the configurations of the relations of inequality with implications for explanation at both the individual and structural levels.

[See also Equality of Opportunity; Social Stratification.]

BIBLIOGRAPHY

Allison, Paul D. 1978 "Measures of Inequality." *American Sociological Review* 43:865–880.

———, and John A. Stewart 1974 "Productivity Differences among Scientists: Evidence for Accumulative Advantage." *American Sociological Review* 39:596–606.

Becker, Gary S. 1964 *Human Capital.* Chicago: University of Chicago Press.

Blau, Peter M. 1977 *Inequality and Heterogeneity.* New York: Free Press.

———, Terry C. Blum, and Joseph E. Schwartz 1982 "Heterogeneity and Intermarriage." *American Sociological Review* 47:45–62.

———, and Otis Dudley Duncan 1967 *The American Occupational Structure.* New York: John Wiley.

Blum, Terry C. 1984 "Racial Inequality and Salience: An Examination of Blau's Theory of Social Structure." *Social Forces* 62:607–617.

Braverman, Harry 1974 "Labor and Monopoly Capital: The Degradation of Work in the Twentieth Century." *Monthly Review* 26:1–134.

Burt, Ronald S. 1982 *Toward a Structural Theory of Action: Network Models of Social Structure, Perception, and Action.* New York: Academic Press.

——— 1983 "Corporate Philanthropy as a Cooptive Relation." *Social Forces* 62:419–449.

Cole, Jonathan R., and Stephen Cole 1973 *Social Stratification in Science.* Chicago: University of Chicago Press.

Coleman, James S. 1982 *The Asymmetric Society.* Syracuse, N.Y.: Syracuse University Press.

Davis, Kingsley, and Wilbert E. Moore 1945 "Some Principles of Stratification." *American Sociological Review* 10:242–249.

Eisenstadt, S. M. 1971 *Social Differentiation and Stratification.* Glencoe, Ill.: Scott Foresman.

Engels, Frederick (1884) 1942 *The Origin of the Family, Private Property and the State.* New York: International Publishers.

Granovetter, Mark 1974 *Getting a Job.* Cambridge: Harvard University.

———, and Charles Tilly 1988 "Inequality and Labor Processes." In Neil J. Smelser, ed., *Handbook of Sociology.* Beverly Hills, Calif.: Sage.

Harding, Sandra G. 1983 *Discovering Reality: Feminist Perspectives on Epistemology, Metaphysics Methodology, and Philosophy of Science.* Dordrecht, Holland: D. Reidel.

Jaggar, Alison M. 1984 *Feminist Frameworks: Alternative Theoretical Accounts of the Relations Between Men and Women,* 2nd ed. New York: McGraw-Hill.

Laumann, Edward O., and Franz U. Pappi 1976 *Networks of Collective Action: A Perspective on Community Influence Systems.* New York: Academic Press.

Lenski, Gerhard E. 1966 *Power and Privilege.* New York: McGraw-Hill.

Lin, Nan, and Peter V. Marsden (eds.) 1982 *Social Structure and Network Analysis.* Beverly Hills, Calif.: Sage.

Marsden, Peter V. 1983 "Restricted Access in Networks and Models of Power." *American Journal of Sociology* 88:686–717.

Marx, Karl (1859) 1976–1978 *Capital: A Critique of Political Economy.* Harmondsworth, England: Penguin Books.

Mayhew, Bruce H. 1973 "System Size and Ruling Elites." *American Sociological Review* 38:468–475.

———, and Paul T. Schollaert 1980 "The Concentration of Wealth: A Sociological Model." *Sociological Focus* 13:1–35.

Merton, Robert K. 1968 "The Matthew Effect in Science." Science 159:56–63.

Mill, John Stuart (1859) 1970 *The Subjection of Women.* New York: Source Book Press.

Mosca, G. 1939 *The Ruling Class.* New York: McGraw-Hill.

Myrdal, Gunnar 1944 *An American Dilemma: The Negro Problem and Modern Democracy.* New York: Harper and Brothers.

Ossowski, Stanislav 1963 *Class Structure in the Social Consciousness.* New York: Free Press.

Pareto, Vilfredo (1897) 1980 *Compendium of General Sociology.* Minneapolis: University of Minnesota Press.

Pinkney, Alphonso 1984 *The Myth of Black Progress.* New York: Cambridge University Press.

Reddy, William 1987 *Money and Liberty in Modern Europe.* Cambridge: Cambridge University Press.

Schwartz, Barry 1981 *Vertical Classification.* Chicago: University of Chicago Press.

Simmel, Georg 1896 "Superiority and Subordination as Subject Matters of Sociology," trans. A. Small. *American Journal of Sociology* 2:167–189, 392–415.

Skocpol, Theda 1979 *States and Social Revolutions.* New York: Cambridge University Press.

Skvoretz, John, and Thomas J. Fararo 1986 "Inequality and Association: A Biased Net Theory." *Current Perspectives in Social Theory* 7:29–50.

Sorensen, Aage 1977 "The Structure of Inequality and the Process of Attainment." *American Sociological Review* 42:965–978.

Sorokin, Pitirim A. 1941 *Social and Cultural Dynamics.* New York: Bedminster.

Thibaut, John W., and Harold H. Kelley 1959 *The Social Psychology of Groups.* New York: Wiley.

Wallerstein, Immanuel Maurice 1974 *The Modern World System.* New York: Academic Press.

Weber, Max (1947) 1978 *Economy and Society,* Vols. I and II. Berkeley: University of California Press.

White, Harrison C. 1970 *Chains of Opportunity.* Cambridge, Mass.: Harvard University Press.

Wilson, William J. 1980 *The Declining Significance of Race: Blacks and Changing American Institutions.* Chicago: University of Chicago Press.

Wright, Erik Olin 1978 *Class, Crisis, and the State.* London: NLB.

———1985 *Classes.* London: Verso.

– ANGELA M. O'RAND

SOCIALIZATION

Socialization has had a diversity of meanings in the social sciences, partly because a number of disciplines claim it as a central process. In its most common and general usage, socialization refers to the process of interaction through which an individual (a novice) acquires the norms, values, beliefs, attitudes, and language characteristics of his or her group. In the course of acquiring these cultural elements, the individual self and personality are created and shaped. Socialization, therefore, addresses two important problems in social life: the problem of societal continuity from one generation to the next, and the problem of human development.

Different disciplines, however, have emphasized different aspects of this process. Anthropologists tend to view socialization primarily as cultural transmission from one generation to the next, sometimes substituting the term "enculturation" for socialization (Herskovits 1948). Anthropological interest in socialization or "enculturation" coincides with the emergence of the "culture and personality" orientation in the late 1920s and 1930s. During this period, the works of Margaret Mead (1928), Ruth Benedict (1934), and Bronislaw Malinowski (1927) focused on cultural practices affecting child rearing, value transmission, and personality development and helped shape the anthropological approach to socialization. Much of the work in the culture and personality field was influenced by psychoanalytic theory.

Psychologists have been less likely to emphasize the transmission of culture and more likely to emphasize various aspects of the individual's development (see Goslin 1969). There is considerable diversity within psychology regarding the aspect of socialization studied. For developmental psychologists, particularly those influenced by Piaget (1926), socialization is largely a matter of cognitive development, which is typically viewed as a combination of social influence and maturation. For behavioral psychologists, socialization is synonymous with learning patterns of behavior. For clinical psychologists and personality theorists, socialization is viewed as the establishment of character traits usually within the context of early childhood experiences. The subfield of child development is most closely associated with the topic of socialization within psychology, where socialization is largely equated with child rearing (see Clausen 1968 for a historical overview of socialization in these disciplines).

Political science has also shown some interest in socialization, but in a much more limited sense. Its interests have not gone much beyond political socialization—that is, the process by which political attitudes and orientations are formed. However, a different and more esoteric usage of the term occasionally appears in this literature: socialization as "collectivization," that is, the transformation of capitalism to socialism and/or communism.

Within sociology there have been two main orientations to socialization. One views socialization primarily as the learning of social roles. From this perspective, individuals become integrated members of society by learning and internalizing the relevant roles and statuses of the groups to which they belong (Brim 1966). This view has been present in some form from the beginnings of sociology as a discipline but has been most closely associated with structural-functionalist perspectives (Clausen 1968).

The other, and more prevalent, sociological orientation views socialization mainly as self-concept formation. The development of self and identity in the context of intimate and reciprocal interaction is considered to be the core of socialization. This view of socialization is closely associated with the symbolic interactionist perspective—a synthesis of various strands of pragmatism, behaviorism, and idealism that emerged in the 1920s and 1930s in the writings of a number of scholars at the University of Chicago, especially George H. Mead (1934). In Mead's writings, the self is a reflexive, thoroughly social phenomenon that develops through language or symbolic interaction. Through role-taking the individual is able to view himself or herself from the perspective of another. This becomes the basis for selfhood and also for the interpenetration of self and society. Mead and other symbolic interactionists have argued that self and society are two sides of the same coin. The basis for this assertion is that the contents of self-conceptions (e.g., identities) reflect those aspects of the social process with which the individual is involved, through the internalization of role identities, values, and meanings. This internalization, in turn, reproduces society. From the interactionist perspective, both self and society depend on the same process of social interaction whereby "realities" are created and constantly negotiated (Gecas 1982, 1986).

For contemporary interactionists as well, socialization is distinguished from other types of learning and other forms of social influence by its relevance for self-conceptions—that is, for our thoughts and feelings about ourselves. As such, socialization is not merely the process of learning rules or norms or behavior patterns. It is learning these things only to the extent that they become part of the way in which we think of ourselves. The mark of successful socialization is the transformation of social control into self-control. This is largely accomplished through the development of identities, the various labels and characteristics attributed to the self. Commitment to identities (such as son, mother, professor, honest person) is a source of motivation for individuals to act in accordance with the values and norms implied by these identities (Foote 1951; Stryker 1980; Gecas 1986). The focus on identity also emphasizes the membership component of socialization: To be socialized is to belong, via idealification with one's group.

Socialization as identity formation occurs through a number of more specific processes associated with self-concept development: reflected appraisals, social comparisons, self-attributions, and identification (see Gecas 1982, 1986 and Rosenberg 1979 for discussions of these processes). Reflected appraisals, based on Cooley's (1902) "looking-glass self" metaphor, refers to our perceptions of how others see us and evaluate us. To some extent we come to see ourselves as we think others (particularly significant others) see us (see Shrauger and Schoeneman [1979] for a review and assessment of the research on this proposition). We also develop conceptions of ourselves with regard to specific attributes by comparing ourselves to others (social comparisons) and by making self-inferences from observing our own actions and their consequences (self-attributions). Particularly important to socialization as identity formation is the process of identification. Initially used by Sigmund Freud, it refers to the child's emotional attachment to the parent and desire to be like the parent, as a consequence of which the child internalizes and adopts the parent's values, beliefs, and other characteristics. Among other things, through identification with the parent the child becomes more receptive to parental influence.

Identification is also used to refer to the imputation or ascription of identities. Here the focus is on the establishment of identities in social interaction and is an important aspect of defining situations and constructing realities. This also has important socializing consequences, as much of the literature on labeling, stereotyping and expectancy effects attests (see Jones 1977).

Content and Contexts of Socialization

Much of the research on socialization has been concerned with identifying what aspects of the socializee's development are affected by which agents and contexts of socialization and through what processes. Most of the focus has been on the family context, where the initial or *primary* socialization of the individual takes place. Studies of childrearing in "normal" as well as "abnormal" situations (e.g., institutionalized children, "closet children," "feral children") have identified a number of conditions that must be present for primary socialization to take place—that is, for the child to become a person. These include the use of symbolic interaction (language) in the context of an intimate, nurturant relationship between an adult and a child. These conditions are necessary for the initial sense of self to emerge and for normal cognitive development and even physical development to take place. The claim that the family (in some form) is a universal feature of human societies is based in large part on this important socialization function (Weigert and Thomas 1971).

Parental support continues to be important in the socialization of offspring through childhood, adolescence, and beyond. It is one of the most robust variables in the literature on child rearing. Parental support has been found to be positively related to the child's cognitive development, moral behavior, conformity to adult standards, self-esteem, academic achievement, and social competence (see Rollins and Thomas 1979; Peterson and Rollins 1987; and Thomas et al. 1974 for reviews). Conversely, lack of parental support is associated with negative socialization outcomes for children and adolescents: low self-esteem, delinquency, deviance, drug use, and various other problem behaviors.

Parental support has been found to be positively related to the child's cognitive development, moral behavior, self-esteem, academic achievement, and social competence.

Parental control is almost as important as support in the socialization literature. "Control" refers to the degree and manner in which parents attempt to place constraints on the child's behavior. Other terms used for this dimension of parenting are punishment, discipline, restrictiveness, permissiveness, protectiveness, supervision, strictness, and monitoring. Parental control is a more complicated variable than is parental support. It is necessary to distinguish different types or styles of control because they frequently have opposite socialization consequences. An important distinction is between "authoritarian" and "authoritative" control (Baumrind 1978) or "coercion" and "induction" (Rollins and Thomas 1979). Authoritarian or coercive control (i.e., control based on force, threat, or physical punishment) is associated with negative or unfavorable socialization outcomes, whereas authoritative or inductive control (i.e., control based on reason and explanation) has positive outcomes.

The most powerful models of parental influence in the socialization of children are those that combine the dimensions of support and control. Parents are most effective as agents of socialization when they express a high level of support and exercise inductive control. Under these conditions, children are most likely to identify with their parents, internalize parental values and expectations, use parents as their models, and become receptive to parental influence attempts. Conversely, low parental support combined with reliance on coercive control are associated with unfavorable socialization outcomes (for reviews of this literature see Peterson and Rollins 1987; Maccoby and Martin 1983; Rollins and Thomas 1979).

Parental support and control cover much of the ground in the literature on child rearing, but not all of it. Other important socialization variables are extent of parental involvement with the child (e.g., time spent); extent to which political or religious beliefs and value systems are taught to the child by the parent; and various characteristics of the parent, such as patience, tolerance, honesty, integrity, competence, and age, as well as the sex of the parent and of the child. Many factors affect the process and outcomes within family socialization.

Much of the socialization that takes place in the family involves learning appropriate role behavior associated with the various family positions. For the child, the most significant of these are sex and age roles. Through processes of reinforcement from parents and others, through identification with various role models, and through parental admonitions and instructions, the child is socialized into the behavioral expectations associated with these roles. Of the two, sex roles have received most of the research attention on role-learning in the family (see Maccoby and Jacklin 1974 and Block 1983 for reviews). This research suggests that sex-role socialization is extensive (usually starting at birth with differential treatment of male and female infants), pervasive (by various agents and contexts of socialization), and consequential for a wide range of other individual and social outcomes. A prominent theme in much of the contemporary research on sex-role socialization is that the differential treatment of boys and girls that emphasizes "masculine" characteristics for boys and "feminine" characteristics for girls is detrimental to the development of both girls and boys and to the relationship between the sexes (see Bem 1974 on the virtues of androgyny). This research reflects the ethos of equality between the sexes evident in most modern societies.

Most studies of socialization within the family assume a unidirectional influence, from parent to child. Parents are typically viewed as agents of socialization (part of the job description of "parent") and children as objects of socialization, and given the disparities in power, status, and competence between parent and child, it is justifiably assumed that the direction of influence is mainly from parent to child. However, it is also increasingly evident that socialization is a reciprocal process of influence, with children influencing parents as well as the reverse. Over the past few decades, the thinking with regard to socialization processes has shifted from unidirectional to bidirectional and reciprocal models (Peterson and Rollins 1987; Gecas 1981). For example, in considering the association between parental punishment and a child's deviant behavior, it can be argued that the child's behavior is both a consequence and a cause of the parental behavior. Socialization is increasingly viewed as reciprocal, even though the degree of influence is typically not equal.

Besides parents and other adult kin, siblings serve as agents of socialization within the family context. For that matter, as family size increases, more of the socialization of the younger children is taken on by their older siblings, either by default or because parents delegate this responsibility to the older children. Some have argued that this puts younger children in large families at a disadvantage (with regard to cognitive development), since they have relatively less contact with the most competent and committed family members, the parents (Zajonc 1976). However, these findings, based mostly on cross-sectional data, have not gone unchallenged (Galbraith 1982).

An increasingly pervasive agent of socialization within contemporary families is television. Children spend more time watching television than at any other activity except school and sleep (Bronfenbrenner 1970). The purpose of most television programs that children watch is typically not to socialize or educate children, but to entertain and to sell products. However, a good deal of unintended socialization is likely to occur, from shaping conceptions of reality (e.g., sex roles) to styles of behavior and tastes. In general, television is perceived as having a negative influence on children (with the exception of a few educational programs on public television). Much of the concern has focused on the extensive violence and aggression in television programs. Bandura et al.'s (1963) work on modeling has persuasively shown that exposure to aggressive behavior tends to increase aggression in the viewer. Along with the undesirable consequences for child socialization of the content of television programs, Bronfenbrenner (1970) observes that television is detrimental to child development with regard to the behavior it prevents—that is, the human interaction forgone in the course of being a passive viewer. The role of television as an agent of socialization in families seems to be increasing by default, as the amount of contact between parents and their children decreases. Various social forces (especially proportion of working mothers, dual-career families, and professionalization of child care) have operated to decrease the amount of parent/child interaction and hence the parent's role as a socializing agent. This vacuum, Bronfenbrenner (1970) argues, has been increasingly filled by the child's involvement with television and with peers. For children in American society, television, peer group, and school are increasingly important agents of socialization.

Like the family, the school is an institution whose mandate is to socialize children. The school's mission, however, is more narrowly defined than is that of the family and is primarily concerned with the formal instruction of children and the development of their cognitive skills. In this sense, the school context is less involved in *primary* socialization (i.e., the development of basic values, beliefs, motivations, and conceptions of self) and more involved in *secondary* socialization (i.e., the development of knowledge and skills). This is not a very precise distinction, however. In the course of the socialization experienced in the school, things other than skills and knowledge are also learned, such as norms, values, and attitudes, and various aspects of the child's personality and self-concept are affected. Much more is typically learned in school than what is explicitly taught.

Many of the activities associated with the school (specifically within the classroom) have implications for the child's self-concept. For example, one of the most important activities involves evaluation of the student's performance by the teacher. Success in various evaluated activities, based on one's own efforts, is good for self-esteem and builds confidence in one's abilities. But failure is not, and *public* failure is worse. The school provides numerous opportunities to the child for public failure as well as for public success. One of the consequences of performance evaluations may be the categorization or "labeling" of students, by teachers as well as others, as "smart," "dumb," "slow learner," "underachiever," etc. Negative as well as positive labels affect the way in which others respond to the person, and through their responses reinforce and shape the person in the labeled direction. This process is called "expectancy effects" (Jones 1977) or "self-fulfilling prophecy" (Merton 1957). Rosenthal and Jacobson (1968) found that teachers' expectations of students, even when based on erroneous information, had a significant effect on how these students developed over the course of the school year: When the teacher was led to believe that a student in her class would be a "slow learner," the stu-

The role of television as an agent of socialization has increased by default among American children as parent-child contact has decreased. (Jennie Woodcock; Reflections Photolibrary/Corbis)

dent was more likely to do poorly in class. Labeling and expectancy effects occur in most socialization contexts and have important consequences for self-concept development.

Failure-avoiding strategies are attempts to disassociate one's performance from one's ability and worth.

But students, like other socializees, are not passive recipients of the pressures they experience. Covington and Beery (1976) propose that two fundamentally different motivation patterns emerge in schools as a result of these pressures: one is oriented toward striving for success; the other is oriented toward avoiding failure. Failure-avoiding strategies (such as nonparticipation, withdrawal, procrastination, and putting off work assignments until too late) are attempts to disassociate one's performance from one's ability and worth. Failure, then, can be attributed to lack of effort or to various external circumstances (less damaging attributions for self) and not to one's lack of ability (a more damaging attribution). This is a form of role-distancing, the separation of self from the behavior required of a role occupant. It is also an obstacle to school achievement. As Covington and Beery (1976) point out, failure-avoiding strategies are self-defeating: In their attempts to avoid the feelings of failure, these students increase the probability of actual failure. For some students this is one of the unintended and undesirable consequences of classroom socialization. In the process of socializing students toward achievement and mastery (desirable socialization outcomes), pressures are generated that may result in undesirable adaptations.

The third most important context for the socialization of children, especially adolescents, is the peer group. In terms of structure and function, the peer group is a very different context of socialization from family and school. Unlike the previous two contexts, it is not the "job" of peers to socialize each other, even though a great deal of childhood socialization occurs in this context—some of it in reaction against the socialization experienced in family and school.

There are several important features of the peer group as a context of socialization. Most important, it is a *voluntary* association. For most children, it is their first. This permits greater freedom of choice regarding associations in the group. A second important feature is that association is between status equals. Consequently, interaction is more likely to be based on egalitarian norms. Status distinctions do emerge, of course, but are more likely to be based on achievement and negotiation. But the basic relationship within peer groups is not hierarchical; rather it is a friendship bond based on equality, mutual tolerance, and concern. Third, the peer group is an arena for the exercise of independence from adult control. As such, it is often the context for the development of values, norms, and behavior in opposition to those of adults (such as the subcultures described by Coleman 1961 and in much of the literature on juvenile delinquency). Fourth, children's peer groups (in contemporary American society at least) are typically segregated by sex. An important socialization consequence of intensive association with same-sex peers and involvement in sex-typed activities is that it strongly reinforces identification and belongingness with members of the same sex. Not only sex-role identity but also much of the sexual socialization during childhood occurs in the context of peer rather than parent-child associations (Fine 1987). Peers provide an alternate reference group for children as well as an alternate source of self-esteem and identity. For these reasons, attachment to peers may be even stronger than attachment to family, especially for adolescents.

The socialization experienced by adults generally falls in the category of secondary socialization, building on the socialization experiences of childhood. Much of this is role-specific (Brim 1968)—that is, learning the knowledge and skills required for the performance of specific adult roles (e.g., occupation, marriage, parenthood). As individuals become committed to the roles they play, they come to identify themselves and think of themselves in terms of these role identities (Stryker 1980).

Since work is a dominant activity and setting for most adult men and women in our society, much of adult socialization involves either preparation for an occupation or career (which usually takes place within specialized schools or training programs—e.g., law school, medical school, college), or on-the-job training. The work setting itself can have a substantial socializing effect on workers, affecting more than just their knowledge and skills. Kohn and Schooler (1983) have shown how certain occupational conditions affect the development of the worker's values and personality. Specifically, they found that work that is routine, closely supervised, and relatively uncomplicated gives rise to values of conformity in workers, whereas work that is complex and encourages self-direction increases the value workers place on independence and autonomy. Kanter (1977) also found that the nature of work relations, particularly the structure of opportunity on the job, affects workers' attitudes and behaviors as a consequence of their adaptations to the work situation. Workers' adaptations to their work situations do not necessarily imply commitment to the job or self-investment in terms of the occupational role. On the contrary, a prevalent theme in much of the sociological literature on work and workers (especially from a Marxist perspective) deals with the alienating consequences of work in capitalist societies.

Many other contexts have socializing consequences for adults: family, political and religious organizations, recreational settings, and various voluntary associations. The socialization that takes place within these contexts can be considered "developmental" (Wheeler 1966) because it builds on previous socialization and is a continuation and expansion of past socialization experiences. *Resocialization,* however, refers to socialization experiences representing a more radical change in the person. Resocialization contexts (e.g., mental hospitals, some prisons, reform schools, therapy groups, political indoctrination camps, religious conversion settings) have as their explicit goal the transformation of the individual. An important feature of resocialization is the replacement of one's previous set of beliefs, values, and (especially) conceptions of self with a new set grounded in the new group's ideology or worldview. This has been described as a process of death and rebirth of the self (Lifton 1963). Typically this is accomplished through intense small-group interaction, in which the physical and symbolic environments are highly controlled by the agents of socialization. It is an experience that usually involves considerable stress for the socializee (see Gecas 1981 for an analysis and comparison of contexts of socialization).

Socialization Over the Life Course

Socialization is a lifelong process of change. Even though the socialization experienced in the family is in some ways the most consequential, there are important socializing experiences that individuals typically have throughout their lives. A central theme in the life course literature is the degree of continuity and consistency in personality as the individual moves through the life course (Mortimer and Simmons 1978). Positions on this issue range from the claim that personality is largely shaped during early childhood (most likely held by those with a psychoanalytic orientation) to the position that people are thoroughly malleable, changing across situations and throughout their lives (characteristic of situational orientations to personality and behavior). The majority appear to argue for an intermediate position, maintaining that the "core" personality or self-conception develops in early socialization experiences, while various other characteristics are added to self through the acquisition of new roles, identities, and socializing experiences (Brim 1966, 1968; Clausen 1986). The previous discussion suggests how contexts of socialization, which are typically age-graded, can contribute to the development of different aspects of individuals associated with different ages and stages of life.

Some of the important socializing experiences and changes individuals undergo are keyed to developmental or maturational considerations: The concerns and capabilities of children tend to be different from those of adolescents; young adults from those in middle age and from those in old age. Erikson's (1959) developmental scheme, building on the Freudian theory of psychosexual development in childhood, has emphasized the different developmental tasks associated with different stages of life. The challenges or developmental tasks proposed by Erikson are: (1) trust vs. mistrust; (2) autonomy vs. shame; (3) initiative vs. guilt; (4) industry vs. inferiority; (5) identity vs. identity confusion; (6) intimacy vs. isolation; (7) generativity vs. self-absorption; and (8) integrity vs. despair. Most of the socialization research guided by Erikson's formulations has focused on stage 5, adolescence, and the developmental task highlighting identity concerns. Adolescence, in our society, has long been considered a time when self-concept concerns increase in prominence. Physiological changes and changes in social circumstances (e.g., high school, dating, career considerations) contribute to an increase in self-awareness and concern about how one is viewed by others. Research by developmental psychologists has generally found that good family relations (i.e., those high in parental support, communication, involvement, and inductive control) facilitate the development of ego identity in adolescence (see Gecas and Seff 1990 for a review). By adolescence, however, the influence of parents is substantially less than it was during childhood. Increasingly other agents and contexts of socialization become important to the adolescent: peers, school, friends, coaches, etc. The adolescent's struggles with identity need to be worked out in a number of competing arenas.

Identity concerns are not limited to adolescence, of course. If we consider socialization to be a process of self-concept formation and a lifelong process, then matters of identity are important at various stages of the individual's development. Identity concerns are most likely to be accentuated during periods of transition, particularly those involving entrance into or exit from social statuses and roles. Some of these role transitions are institutionalized and highly ritualized. The rites of passage in various cultures marking the transition from childhood to adulthood can be quite elaborate and dramatic. Sometimes this involves acquiring a new name as well as a new status (as in many of the Plains Indian cultures). In contemporary Western societies, these status passages may be less dramatic but still quite consequential for the person: getting a driver's license; high-school graduation; marriage; divorce; first full-time job; retirement; widowhood. In general, each major transition initiates a new socializing experience or situation, having implications for the individual's self-concept.

Each major transition in life initiates a new socializing experience or situation, having implications for the individual's self-concept.

Some stage theorists have focused on transitions in adulthood (Levinson 1978) and examined the circumstances that can lead to a "midlife crisis," an acute reexamination of self. But the middle years of life are still relatively neglected by life-course scholars, compared to studies of childhood, adolescence, and (increasingly) old age.

In considering socialization over the life cycle, we need to take history and culture into account. Not just the content of socialization during various "stages" of life, but also the stages themselves vary by culture and historical context. For example, adolescence as an identifiable stage of life is a relatively recent historical emergent in Western societies, closely associated with the extension of formal education to high school (Gecas and Seff 1990). Even childhood, as Aries (1960) amply documents, is not universally considered as a distinct stage of life. The modern conception of childhood as an identifiably distinct stage emerged during the European Renaissance, partly as a consequence of the emergence of parochial schools. More recently, Elder (1974) has shown a historical consciousness in his life-course analyses, by examining how specific historical events (e.g., the Great Depression, World War II) differentially affected two cohorts of children and their families. Whether there are eight stages of life, or four stages, or seven stages (as Shakespeare observed) depends on the society and on one's analytical purposes.

Contemporary Issues and Themes in Socialization Research

In the past, the concept of socialization has been heavily imbued with the notion of adaptation and conformity of the individual to societal expectations (Zigler and Seitz 1978). The past few decades, however, have seen a marked shift to a more active view of the self, to an emphasis on self-socialization. Renewed interest in the self-concept as a source of motivation (Gecas 1986) and as an agent in its environment has contributed to this shift, as has the increased interest in adult socialization (Mortimer and Simmons 1978; Bush and Simmons 1981). But even in studies of parent-child interaction, the child (even the infant) is increasingly viewed as an active partner in his or her socialization (Rheingold 1969). In short, the outcomes of socialization (whether these are conceptualized as values, self-conceptions, behavior patterns, or beliefs) are increasingly viewed as the products of reciprocal interactions between agent and socializee (itself a somewhat arbitrary distinction).

A concern with social structure and its effects on the process and outcomes of socialization is still the hallmark of the sociological orientation to socialization, from social class influences (see Gecas 1979) to the effects of family structure. Changes in family structure over the past few decades have increased interest in the effects of single-parent families, reconstituted families, and day care for child socialization. Rarely are these changes viewed as favorable for child socialization (Bronfenbrenner 1979). But the evidence is inconclusive on just how negative their consequences may be for child socialization. Given the increasing rate of social and cultural change in contemporary societies, it is clear that socialization of children and adults is becoming increasingly problematic.

[See also Adulthood; Gender; Moral Development; Parental Roles; Sex Differences.]

BIBLIOGRAPHY

Aries, Phillip 1960 *Centuries of Childhood: A Social History of Family Life.* New York: Random House.

Bandura, Albert, Dorothea Ross, and Sheila A. Ross 1963 "Imitation of Film-Mediated Aggressive Models." *Journal of Abnormal and Social Psychology* 66:3–11.

Baumrind, Diana 1978 "Parental Disciplinary Patterns and Social Competence in Children." *Youth and Society* 9:239–276.

Bem, Sandra L. 1974 "The Measurement of Psychological Androgyny." *Journal of Consulting and Clinical Psychology* 42:155–162.

Benedict, Ruth 1934 *Patterns of Culture.* Boston: Houghton Mifflin.

Block, Jean H. 1983 "Differential Premises Arising from Differential Socialization of the Sexes: Some Conjectures." *Child Development* 54:1335–1354.

Brim, Orville G., Jr. 1966 "Socialization Through the Life Cycle." In O. G. Brim, Jr., and S. Wheeler, eds., *Socialization After Childhood: Two Essays.* New York: Wiley.

——— 1968 "Adult Socialization." In J. A. Clausen, ed., *Socialization and Society.* Boston: Little, Brown.

Bronfenbrenner, Urie 1970 *Two Worlds of Childhood: U.S. and U.S.S.R.* New York: Russell Sage Foundation.

——— 1979 *The Ecology of Human Development: Experiments by Nature and Design.* Cambridge, Mass.: Harvard University Press.

Bush, Diane M., and Roberta G. Simmons 1981 "Socialization Processes over the Life Course." In M. Rosenberg and R. H. Turner, eds., *Social Psychology: Sociological Perspectives.* New York: Basic Books.

Clausen, John A. 1968. "A Historical and Comparative View of Socialization Theory and Research." In J. A. Clausen, ed., *Socialization and Society.* Boston: Little, Brown.

——— 1986 *The Life Course: A Sociological Perspective.* Englewood Cliffs, N.J.: Prentice-Hall.

Coleman, James S. 1961 *The Adolescent Society.* New York: Free Press.

Cooley, Charles H. (1902) 1964 *Human Nature and the Social Order.* New York: Scribners.

Covington, Martin V., and Richard G. Beery 1976 *Self-Worth and School Learning.* New York: Holt, Rinehart, and Winston.

Elder, Glen H., Jr. 1974 *Children of the Great Depression.* Chicago: University of Chicago Press.

Erikson, Erik H. 1959 *Identity and the Life Cycle.* New York: International Universities Press.

Fine, Gary A. 1987 *With the Boys: Little League Baseball and Preadolescent Culture.* Chicago: University of Chicago Press.

Foote, Nelson N. 1951 "Identification as the Basis for a Theory of Motivation." *American Sociological Review* 16:14–21.

Galbraith, Robert C. 1982 "Sibling Spacing and Intellectual Development: A Closer Look at the Confluence Models." *Development Psychology* 18:151–173.

Gecas, Viktor 1979 "The influence of social class on socialization." In W. R. Burr, R. Hill, F. I. Nye, and I. L. Reiss, eds., *Contemporary Theories About the Family,* Vol. 1. New York: Free Press.

——— 1981 "Contexts of Socialization." In M. Rosenberg and R. H. Turner, eds., *Social Psychology: Sociological Perspectives.* New York: Basic Books.

——— 1982 "The Self-Concept." In R. H. Turner and J. F. Short, Jr., eds., *Annual Review of Sociology,* Vol. 8. Palo Alto, Calif.: Annual Reviews.

——— 1986 "The Motivational Significance of Self-Concept for Socialization Theory." In E. J. Lawler, ed., *Advances in Group Processes,* vol. 3. Greenwich, CT: JAI Press.

———, and Monica Seff 1990 "Families and adolescents: 1980s Decade Review." *Journal of Marriage and the Family* 52:941–958.

Goslin, David A. 1969 *Handbook of Socialization Theory and Research.* Chicago: Rand McNally.

Herskovits, Melville J. 1948 *Man and His Works: The Science of Cultural Anthropology.* New York: Alfred A. Knopf.

Jones, R. A. 1977 *Self-Fulfilling Prophecies: Social Psychological and Physiological Effects of Expectancies.* New York: Wiley.

Kanter, Rosabeth M. 1977 *Men and Women of the Corporation.* New York: Basic Books.

Kohn, Melvin L., and Carmi Schooler 1983 *Work and Personality: An Inquiry into the Impact of Social Stratification.* Norwood, N.J.: Ablex.

Levinson, Daniel J. 1978 *The Seasons of a Man's Life.* New York: Alfred A. Knopf.

Lifton, Robert J. 1963 *Thought Reform and the Psychology of Totalism: A Study of "Brainwashing" in China.* New York: W. W. Norton.

Maccoby, Eleanor E., and Carol N. Jacklin 1974 *The Psychology of Sex Differences.* Stanford, Calif.: Stanford University Press.

Maccoby, Eleanor E., and John A. Martin 1983 "Socialization in the Context of the family: Parent-Child Interaction." In P. H. Mussen, ed., *Handbook of Child Psychology,* vol. 4. New York: Wiley.

Malinowski, Bronislaw (1927) 1953 *Sex and Repression in Savage Society.* London: Routledge.

Mead, George H. 1934 *Mind, Self, and Society.* Chicago: University of Chicago Press.

Mead, Margaret 1928 *Coming of Age in Samoa.* New York: William Morrow.

Merton, Robert K. 1957 *Social Theory and Social Structure.* New York: Free Press.

Mortimer, Jeylan T., and Roberta G. Simmons 1978 "Adult Socialization." In R. H. Turner, J. Coleman, and R. C. Fox, eds., *Annual Review of Sociology,* vol. 4. Palo Alto, Calif.: Annual Reviews.

Peterson, Gary W., and Boyd C. Rollins 1987 "Parent-Child Socialization: A Review of Research and Applications of Symbolic Interaction Concepts." In M. B. Sussman and S. K. Steinmetz, eds., *Handbook of Marriage and the Family.* New York: Plenum Press.

Piaget, Jean 1926 *The Language and Thought of the Child.* London: Kegan Paul.

Rheingold, Harriet L. 1969 "The Social and Socializing Infant." In D. A. Goslin, ed., *Handbook of Socialization Theory and Research.* Chicago: Rand McNally.

Rollins, Boyd C., and Darwin L. Thomas 1979 "Parental Support, Power, and Control Techniques in the Socialization of Children." In W. R. Burr, R. Hill, F. I. Nye, and I. L. Reiss, eds., *Contemporary Theories About the Family,* vol. 1. New York: Free Press.

Rosenberg, Morris 1979 *Conceiving the Self.* New York: Basic Books.

Rosenthal, Robert, and L. Jacobson 1968 *Pygmalion in the Classroom.* New York: Holt, Rinehart, and Winston.

Shrauger, J. S., and T. J. Schoeneman 1979 "Symbolic Interactionist View of Self-Concept: Through the Looking-glass Darkly." *Psychological Bulletin* 86:549–573.

Stryker, Sheldon 1980 *Symbolic Interactionism: A Social Structural Version.* Menlo Park, Calif.: Benjamin/Cummings.

Thomas, Darwin L., Viktor Gecas, Andrew Weigert, and Elizabeth Rooney 1974 *Family Socialization and the Adolescent.* Lexington, Mass.: D. C. Heath.

Weigert, Andrew J., and Darwin L. Thomas 1971 "Family as a Conditional Universal." *Journal of Marriage and the Family* 33:188–196.

Wheeler, Stanton 1966 "The Structure of Formally Organized Socialization Settings." In O. G. Brim, Jr., and S. Wheeler, eds., *Socialization After Childhood: Two Essays.* New York: Wiley.

Zajonc, Robert B. 1976 "Family Configuration and Intelligence." *Science* 192:227–236.

Zigler, Edward, and Victoria Seitz 1978 "Changing Trends in Socialization Theory and Research." *American Behavioral Scientist* 21:731–756.

– VIKTOR GECAS

SOCIAL MOBILITY

Social mobility has been defined as movement through "social space" from one status category (the origin) to another status category (the destination). In general, *vertical mobility* refers to individual or group movement upward or downward in the social hierarchy, but the possibility of downward mobility is seldom considered. *Horizontal mobility* involves moving from one social status to another of about equal rank. Other nonvertical forms of mobility have been discussed, most often in terms of movement across social categories not typically defined as hierarchical, such as religion, political party affiliation, age, citizenship, and so forth (Schnore 1961; Sorokin 1927).

Social mobility, then, is reflected as changes in relative social standing or status. Social status has been defined as one's community standing (e.g., one's position of power or influence), organizational membership, kinship relations, property ownership, education, and wealth or income, among other criteria. Yet empirical studies of social mobility have focused almost entirely on occupational positions as the sole indicator of social status. And while occupations differ in terms of prestige, income, influence, access to valued resources, and relationship to the mode of production, studies have overwhelmingly relied on occupational prestige scores to measure occupational achievement. Supporters of this method argue that in an industrial-urban society, occupational prestige is the best singular indicator of social status. It is a particularly useful measure in that it is linked to economic status and educational background and is, therefore, correlated with the "pattern of living" of an individual. In addition, several studies have shown a stable relationship between occupation and prestige that is attached to the position but is occupied by the individual (Treiman 1977). Occupations have also been shown to be strongly related to a class concept (Wright et al. 1982).

Those who argue against such a unidimensional perspective of social status point out that respondents asked to rate occupations consider a variety of factors, such as the level of information, or lack thereof, concerning the occupation, the occupation's relation to their own position (Goldthorpe and Hope 1974), the income of the occupation, and the typical sex of the occupation's incumbents (Bose 1973).

Most research on mobility has focused on *intergenerational mobility,* which refers to a change of social status from one generation to the next. The change is typically measured by comparing the son's occupation to his father's. *Intragenerational mobility,* on the other hand, typically refers to the vertical mobility experienced by an individual within his or her own lifetime, as through job promotions and other career advancements.

Although most work in the field has taken place in the post-World War II era, social mobility has been seen since Plato's time as providing efficiency and stability in state formation and maintenance. In his *Republic* (c. 380 B.C.) Plato described individuals as being of gold, silver, or bronze thread. While heredity of social status was expected, Plato argued that gold children of bronze parents should be promoted to their rightful place of leadership. Likewise, gold parents of bronze children need to recognize their children's limitations, for the ruin of the state was prophesied if it came to be led by men of bronze. In addition, Plato's student Aristotle, (c. 384–322 B.C.) discussed class formation and the logic of state rule by the middle class. Citizens among the "mean" were thought to counter the political ambitions of the two extremes.

Even Marx recognized the stabilizing effects of upward mobility for the ruling class. He believed that the high rates of mobility that characterize the United States were partly responsible for the lack of organized labor. A class that is self-recruiting will more readily develop class consciousness. On the other hand, high rates of upward mobility between classes acts as a safety valve, keeping down the pressure of the discontented lower class (Marx 1958).

Landmarks

Sorokin's classic work, *Social Mobility* (1927), is often considered the first modern treatise in the field. The basic outline of Sorokin's argument is that there are certain permanent and universal bases of occupational inequality: "At least two conditions seem to have been fundamental. . . . First, the importance of an occupation for the survival and existence of a group as a whole; second, the degree of intelligence necessary for a successful performance of an occupation" (pp. 100–101).

Without the lure of the power and privilege associated with social mobility, incompetent people are found in positions of importance, resulting in inefficiency.

Social mobility is necessary to secure the allocation of talents to occupations. Without the lure of the power and privilege associated with social mobility, incompetent people are found in positions of importance, resulting in inefficiency and possible disruption. Like the sentiments voiced by Marx, Sorokin believed that social mobility provided motivation to members of the lower class and thus, "instead of becoming leaders of a revolution, they are turned into protectors of social order" (p. 533). Although Sorokin argued for the inevitability of social mobility, one of the underlying themes of his work is the lack of a linear progression. He saw no definite perpetual trend toward either an increase or a decrease of the intensity and generality of mobility.

In the early post–World War II period, a major concern of mobility studies was the determination of the rate of mobility of a society, community, or population. This concern stemmed from interest in the degree of "openness" referring to the fluidity of movement among social strata in societies, which was thought to be a measure of inequality. A society is characterized as open, fair, or equitable depending on how advantages are passed from one generation to the next. Early comparative research within this theme was supported and encouraged by the International Sociological Association, which sought comparative studies in Britain, Scandinavia, and the United States.

Since Sorokin's work, little theoretical advancement has been made to accompany the major breakthroughs in data collection and analysis. The first general population study concerning intergenerational social mobility was carried out by David Glass in 1949 (*Social Mobility in Britain*). Glass began a new trend in social mobility studies: a focus on social inequalities rather than on societal stability, as was seen in Plato, Marx, and Sorokin. The main findings from the analysis of movement from father's occupation to son's occupation was that Great Britain "exhibited a considerable amount of relatively short-range mobility coupled with a higher degree of rigidity and self-recruitment at the extremes, and in particular at the upper levels of the social structure where there was the strongest tendency for sons to follow in their father's footsteps and enter broadly comparable occupations" (Heath 1981, p. 31). The line between manual and nonmanual labor has been seen as a barrier to long-range movement on the order of rags to riches or vice versa (see Westergaard and Resler 1975).

Only a decade after Glass's study in Great Britain, Lipset and Bendix (1959) set out to better understand mobility patterns in industrial societies through a secondary analysis of data available from nine industrialized societies: Denmark, France, Germany, Great Britain, Italy, Japan, Sweden, Switzerland, and the United States. By reassigning respondents to either manual or non-manual occupational positions, they examined upward and downward mobility as a measure of the total vertical mobility between middle and working classes. Contrary to their expectations, Lipset and Bendix found no evidence that the United States was more open than the traditional societies of Europe. What they did find was that virtually all the nine countries exhibited similar, high rates of total vertical mobility.

The consequences that social mobility held for the individual and society became the theme that dominated this analysis. Additional work by Lipset (1960) was primarily concerned with the stability of American society. While he acknowledged the perspective of prior theorists who viewed social mobility as contributing to stability, Lipset placed most of his emphasis on the *destabilizing* processes of too much mobility. The source of this destabilizing effect is the problem of "status inconsistency." Lipset viewed stratification as a multidimensional system containing a number of different hierarchies based on status, class, and authority. From this perspective, one individual may be mobile on one dimension but not on another. For example, a person may acquire a high occupational position but encounter social ostracism because of his or her low social origins. On the other hand, an upper-class family may become economically impoverished but retain its high social position. Lipset saw this type of disjunction or inconsistency as a possible source of frustration; such frustration may predispose individuals to accept extremist politics.

A stimulating conclusion in terms of inspiring additional research was the "industrialization hypothesis" developed by Lipset and Zetterberg (1956). These researchers observed that during the nineteenth century, the proportion of the labor force in urban occupations increased while the proportion in agriculture decreased. This observation led to the hypothesis that the overall pattern of social mobility appears to be much the same in industrialized societies of various Western countries. Additionally, they felt that a threshold effect was operating; social mobility would become high once the level of industrialization and economic expansion reached a certain level. Lipset and Zetterberg predict that as societies industrialize, they require a set of standardized features from social institutions: smaller, nuclear, and socially mobile families, mass education, a pluralistic political structure, and social mobility based on meritocratic lines (Heath 1981). Many critics argue that the authors were providing support for the functional perspective of the American stratification system. Tests and elaborations of this hypothesis are further addressed below.

Perhaps the most influential and important work in the 1960s is Blau and Duncan's *The American Occupational Structure* (1967). In the tradition of Glass's *Social Mobility in Britain,* this work focused on the issue of status attainment and inequality. Blau and Duncan recognized the basis of the American stratification system as determined by the individual's position in the occupational structure. This structure is also seen as the connecting link between different social institutions and spheres of social life. The processes of intra- and intergenerational occupational mobility are reflected in the dynamics of the occupational structure. Blau and Duncan attempted to analyze social mobility by investigating the patterns of movement between occupations, the conditions that affect those movements, and their consequences. Focusing on allocation factors, such as education, they examined what influence different factors had on occupational achievement and how these factors modify the effects of social origins on achievement. The basic question they addressed was how the status that individuals "achieve" is affected by the statuses "ascribed" to them earlier in life.

Expanding earlier work that focused on a simple dichotomy of manual and nonmanual workers, Blau and Duncan used seventeen occupational categories in examining movement from father's occupation to son's. The results of this analysis found that upward mobility was primarily the result of an expansion of opportunity in occupational categories of higher status and a contraction of opportunity in lower-level categories. In addition, fertility rates in occupations at the top of the hierarchy were lower than those at the bottom, creating occupational openings. The combination of these factors created a chain-reaction "pull" from the top and "push" from the bottom, which has been termed *structural mobility.* Structural mobility is due to structural changes in the economic sphere that "force" sons into alternative occupational categories from those of their fathers. The most commonly cited explanation of structural mobility is the shift from farm labor to urban labor resulting from an increase in industrialization (Lipset and Zetterberg 1956), technological progress, immigration, and differential fertility (Sibley 1942).

An important contribution made by this work was in the application of new statistical techniques. Blau and Duncan have been credited with providing the first major empirical application of path analysis to sociological data. The basic model involves five variables: father's education, father's occupation, respondent's education, respondent's first job, and respondent's occupation in 1962. This model is then elaborated in various ways to take into account additional ascribed statuses. Similar to Glass's findings, Blau and Duncan found most occupational movement within short ranges. Contrary to Glass, however, they found the American stratification system to be divided into three social categories, white collar, blue collar, and farm, with semipermeable class boundaries prohibiting long-range movement.

International Comparisons

Several problems arise in attempts to compare social mobility across different societies; of these, finding an appropriate measure is foremost. Two primary problems in measuring social mobility have been discussed (Raftery 1985). First, studies of social mobility most often use mobility tables that are a cross-classification of occupational categories for sons and fathers; change in occupational category from his father's represents mobility for the son. Because of the inconsistency in data collection across countries, crude dichotomies or trichotomies are used in an effort to obtain the data in parallel form. The problem lies in what to do with the farm category. For example, the son of a large farm owner is forced into manual labor because of the loss of jobs in agriculture resulting from economic or technological shifts. This move would likely be classified as upward mobility, yet the impact for the individual is downward (from a self-employed farm owner to a manual laborer). In addition, much apparent mobility is primarily due to shifts in occupational categories or "shifts in the marginals." The problem in using two or three occupational categories to examine social mobility is that much short-range mobility is missed. It also gives equal weight to movements across the manual nonmanual boundary, be they short-range or long-range.

A second problem in measuring mobility involves the variability among countries as to the structure of their stratification systems (Tyree, Semyonov, and Hodge 1979). Some countries have obvious delineations between social strata, while others possess systems that form a continuum of occupational categories without obvious breaks. This second group of societies, and the inherent problems of investigating social mobility within them, was first discussed by Tyree et al., who referred to them as "glissandos," as opposed to the first group, which contained "gaps" between occupational categories or groupings. If social stratification is of the "glissando" type, the crude categories used to create mobility tables will hide much mobility. For example, the respondents lying on the diagonal (the immobiles) may in fact have experienced mobility that would be revealed if the categories were smaller or otherwise differently defined.

The total amount of social mobility found can be decomposed into circulation mobility and structural mobility (sometimes also called "net" and "exchange" mobility). *Circulation mobility* is defined as the residue remaining after structural mobility has been accounted for. It, therefore, is the difference between total and structural mobility. "Circulatory mobility can be viewed as a zero-sum game. Net of movement forced by changes in the occupational structure over time and differential fertility, one's move up implies another's move down" (Tyree, Semyonov, and Hodge 1979, p. 413).

Given these conceptual and methodological difficulties, comparative studies must be reviewed with caution. Several recent international comparisons find that total mobility seems to have increased in most Western countries. This increase is primarily due to increasing structural mobility and, especially, increasing nonmanual employment and diminishing agricultural employment. The trends in circulation mobility are much less clear

(Matras 1980). Overall, comparative studies have found that the United States and Great Britain appear to have consistently high levels of intergenerational mobility, Spain and the Philippines have consistently low levels, and Denmark, Sweden, and Belgium have consistently intermediate levels.

The industrialization thesis, as previously discussed, has been specified more precisely by Treiman (1970), who held that total and circulation mobility increase with increasing industrialization. This hypothesis has not received convincing support in the more extensive comparative studies (Hazelrigg and Garnier 1976; Tyree, Semyonov, and Hodge 1979), but it has received some support from studies that examined trends over time in conjunction with studies of changing occupational composition (Rogoff-Ramsoy 1977; Hauser and Featherman 1977; Goldthorpe, Payne, and Llewellyn 1978).

Additional work by Featherman, Jones, and Hauser (1975) suggests an alternative hypothesis (referred to as the FJH hypothesis) that variations in intergenerational mobility emerge from historical or cultural differences in occupational structure, but not from differences in exchanges between occupations. It is predicted, therefore, that "mobility chances are invariant once variations in origin and destination distributions have been controlled" (Grusky and Hauser 1984, p. 19).

Questioning the process by which economic development would decrease inequality (an assumed result of increased social mobility), Rubinson (1976) developed an alternative model that views cross-national differences in inequality as the result of differing relations of the states to the world-economy. This model is based on two assumptions: The first is that countries are not autonomous units of production but share in a world economic system of production, which contains multiple political units. Second, the model assumes that the social control and organization of production determines the distribution of income. Rubinson hypothesizes that the "greater the economic dominance and influence that states . . . have in the world-economy, the more equal the distribution of power within states, and consequently, the more equal the distribution of rewards" (p. 640).

Social Mobility of Blacks and Women

The majority of social mobility studies have focused on the dominant male population. In Western Europe and the United States, this means there are extensive data and analyses of the mobility patterns of white males but very little information on the mobility patterns of blacks and women. Part of this problem lies in the focus on occupations as the measure of achieved status, since nonmajority groups may focus their energies on other forms of achievement, such as family formation. In addition, special consideration needs to be given to the history of discrimination, which has traditionally disadvantaged minority members and may act as a barrier to their chances for mobility.

In order to compensate for some of these problems, many researchers have directed their research on changes over time. Farley (1984) operationalizes inequality as differences in level of education, occupational prestige, and income. He shows that income disparities between blacks and whites in the United States have narrowed between 1960 and 1980, that there has been a trend toward equity in educational attainment between blacks and whites, and that race differences in occupations have declined. Featherman and Hauser (1978) examine class inheritance and find that the profiles of black and white men are growing more similar. In fact, blacks gained more than whites in socioeconomic status between 1962 and 1973 although in 1973 they still lagged behind the occupational status of 1962 white men (a sure indication that they had a lot of catching up to do). The researchers also found that the effect of first job on occupational status in 1973 was similar for blacks and whites. These changes appear to be most evident with younger men, indicating positive trends for the future.

Examining mobility between 1962 and 1973, Hout (1984) shows that intergenerational mobility patterns were appreciably different for blacks and whites in those years, and that there was an increase in net upward mobility for black men. Regarding intragenerational mobility of blacks, he argues that class effects were more important than race effects. Hout cautions that, although his finding is positive in terms of blacks' occupational standing, they still receive lower returns for schooling than do whites. His research supports the notion that as the American population becomes more educated (particularly college educated), there appears to be more universalism and increasing social mobility (Hout 1988).

Mobility is less extensive for blacks than for whites, and more restricted to short-range mobility.

Rosenberg (1980), examining a dual labor market model, compared black and white mobility from their first job to their job in 1970. Rosenberg found that white men were more likely to move upward than blacks, though the differentials were modest. Examining upward mobility from a set of low-paying occupations to a mainstream stratum consisting of all occupations that pay at least moderately well, Pomer (1984, 1985) found marked black white differentials for the period 1965 to 1970. Using the 1973 Occupational Change in a Generation (OCG) data, he found that one's position in a segmented labor market is important in accounting for differential mobility patterns for blacks and whites (Pomer 1986). Mobility is less extensive for blacks than for whites, and more restricted to short-range mobility.

The strategy most often used by status attainment and mobility researchers to cope with issues of inequality between men and women is to absorb sex as a variable into existing models. Methods and measures previously developed to study men have been applied to women. In spite of some differences in labor market experiences between men and women the most consistent and surprising findings are that the occupational and marital mobility patterns of women are not much different from those of men (Tyree and Treas 1974; Dunton and Featherman 1983). In addition, females' occupational prestige scores are either equal to or higher than men's (Featherman and Hauser 1976; Farmer et al. 1990). Yet these findings should not be taken as evidence of gender equality. The finding of equal occupational prestige is an artifact of the truncated/clustered distribution of female prestige scores (Bose 1973). Hauser and Featherman (1977), examining social mobility for men and women, find that the destinations for women are very different from those of men.

Additional Considerations

A serious question remains concerning just what is being measured and described by the overall level of mobility. In the traditional measures of total or circulation mobility, the concept refers to an actual or adjusted percentage of respondents who report occupations different (or in a different category) from those of their fathers; in the more recent log linear measures it refers to the size (smallness) of statistical interactions between occupations of respondents and those of their father's in the various time periods, cohorts, or societies. One occupational category may be relatively open while another is relatively closed—a fact that is obscured in "overall" measures. Within countries or societies the rules for classifying occupations and for determining sameness or difference in occupational category are often the same across cohorts or time periods, but this is not often the case for cross-national comparisons. "But even when we assume that the classifications and rules are uniform across countries, generations, cohorts, time periods, etc., the meaning of the mobility rate of a country, or of the differences between the mobility rates of two or more countries, is still in question" (Matras 1980, p. 413).

It was noted above that social mobility was defined as movement through social space. While this movement has been described as both vertical and horizontal, few researchers have systematically evaluated nonvertical forms of social mobility (see Sorokin 1927 for one example). In fact, the primary has been on vertical occupational changes from one generation to the next. While a small number studies have recognized the influence on differential stratification structures and the influence of economic systems, few if any have acknowledged differential bases of stratification other than occupational or economic. There is a vast array of ways in which people organize and categorize themselves, from membership by virtue of birth (ascribed) to voluntary membership (achieved). Within these social categories, divisions and hierarchies emerge based on a variety of criteria. For example, societies have based their stratification regime on kinship structures, such as through rules of membership, including patrilineal, matrilineal, and bilineal systems. Other stratification regimes are based on religion, as is found in the Indian caste system. Here, social mobility theoretically occurs with reincarnation or, in rare cases, when an individual can "pass" as a member of a higher strata. Occupational position is ascribed by religious doctrine, and typical social mobility studies would not tap into issues of inequality as culturally defined by these societies. Other societies stratified on the bases of race, ethnicity, gender, age, and so forth demand different questions and measures.

[See also Education and Mobility; Occupational and Career Mobility; Social Inequality; Social Stratification.]

BIBLIOGRAPHY

Aristotle (384–322 B.C.) 1943 *Politics,* trans. Benjamin Jawett. New York: Modern Library.

Blau, Peter M., and Otis Dudley Duncan 1967 *The American Occupational Structure.* New York: Wiley.

Bose, Christine E. 1973 *Jobs and Gender: Sex and Occupational Prestige.* Baltimore: Johns Hopkins University, Center of Metropolitan Planning and Research.

Dunton, Nancy, and David L. Featherman 1983 "Social Mobility Through Marriage and Careers." In Janet T. Spence, ed., *Achievement and Achievement Motives.* San Francisco: Freeman.

Farley, Reynolds 1984 *Blacks and Whites: Closing the Gap?* Cambridge, Mass.: Harvard University Press.

Farmer, Yvette, Lynn M. Ries, David G. Nickinovich, Yoshinori Kamo, and Edgar F. Borgatta 1990 "The Status Attainment Model and Income." *Research on Aging* 12:113–132.

Featherman, David, and Robert Hauser 1976a "Sexual Inequalities and Socioeconomic Achievement in the U.S., 1962–1973." *American Sociological Review* 41:462–483.

——— 1976b "Changes in the Socioeconomic Stratification of the Races, 1962–1973." *American Journal of Sociology* 82:621–651.

———, F. L. Jones, and R. M. Hauser 1975 "Assumptions of Social Mobility Research in the U.S.: The Case of Occupational Status." *Social Science Review* 4:329–360.

Glass, David, ed. 1949 *Social Mobility in Britain.* London: Routledge and Kegan Paul.

Goldthorpe, J. H., and K. Hope 1974 *The Social Grading of Occupations: A New Approach and Scale.* New York: Oxford Books.

Goldthorpe, J. H., C. Payne, and C. Llewellyn 1978 "Trends in Class Mobility." *Sociology* 12:441–468.

Grusky, David, and Robert Hauser 1984 "Comparative Social Mobility Revisited: Models of Convergence and Divergence in 16 Countries." *American Sociological Review* 49:19–38.

Hauser, Robert M., and D. L. Featherman 1977 "The Measurement of Occupation in Social Surveys." In Robert M. Hauser and David L. Featherman, eds., *The Process of Stratification: Trends and Analyses.* New York: Academic Press.

Hauser, Robert M., and David B. Grusky 1988 "Cross-National Variation in Occupational Distributions, Relative Mobility Chances, and Intergenerational Shifts in Occupational Distributions." *American Sociological Review* 53:723–741.

Hazelrigg, L. E., and M. A. Garnier 1976 "Occupational Mobility in Industrial Societies: A Comparative Analysis of Differential Access to Occupational Ranks in Seventeen Countries." *American Sociological Review* 41:498–511.

Heath, Anthony 1981 *Social Mobility.* Glasgow: Fontana.

Horan, Patrick 1978 "Is Status Attainment Research Atheoretical?" *American Sociological Review* 43:534–541.

Hout, Michael 1984a "Occupational Mobility of Black Men: 1962 to 1973." *American Sociological Review* 49:308–322.

——— 1984b "Status, Autonomy, and Training in Occupational Mobility." *American Sociological Review* 2:114–137.

——— 1988 "More Universalism, Less Structural Mobility: The American Occupational Structure in the 1980s." *American Journal of Sociology* 93:1358–1400.

Lipset, Seymour M. 1960 *Political Man: The Social Bases of Politics.* New York: Doubleday.

———, and R. Bendix 1959 *Social Mobility in Industrial Society.* Berkeley: University of California Press.

———, and H. Zetterberg 1956 "A Theory of Social Mobility." *Transactions of the Third World Congress for Sociology* 66:16–22.

Marx, Karl 1958 *Selected Works.* Moscow: Foreign Language Publishing House.

Matras, Judah 1980 "Comparative Social Mobility." *Annual Review of Sociology* 6:401–431.

Plato (c. 380 B.C.) 1955 *The Republic,* trans. H. D. P. Lee. Harmondsworth, England: Penguin.

Pomer, Marshall I. 1984 "Upward Mobility of Low-Paid Workers: A Multivariate Model for Occupational Changers." *Sociological Perspectives* 27:427–442.

——— 1985 "The Immobility of Low-Paid Workers." *Journal of Sociology and Social Welfare* 12:287–310.

——— 1986 "Labor Market Structure, Intragenerational Mobility, and Discrimination: Black Male Advancement out of Low-Paying Occupations, 1962–1973." *American Sociological Review* 51:650–659.

Raftery, Adrian 1985 "Social Mobility Measures for Cross-National Comparisons." *Quality and Quantity* 19:167–182.

Rogoff-Ramsoy, Natalie 1977 "Social Mobility and Changes in the Economy." Paper presented at ISA Research Committee on Social Stratification meeting, Dublin, April 5–7.

Rosenberg, Sam 1980 "Male Occupational Standing and the Dual Labor Market." *Industrial Relations* 19:34–49.

Rubinson, Richard 1976 "The World Economy and the Distribution of Income Within States: A Cross-National Study." *American Sociological Review* 41:638–659.

Schnore, Leo 1961 "Social Mobility in Demographic Perspective." *American Sociological Review* 26:407–423.

Sibley, Elbridge 1942 "Some Demographic Clues to Stratification." *American Sociological Review* 7:322–330.

Sorokin, P. A. 1927 *Social Mobility.* New York: Harper.

Treiman, Donald J. 1970 "Industrialization and Social Stratification." In Edward O. Laumann, ed., *Social Stratification: Research and Theory for the 1970s.* Indianapolis: Bobbs-Merrill.

——— 1977 *Occupational Prestige in Comparative Perspective.* New York: Academic Press.

Tyree, A., M. Semyonov, and R. W. Hodge 1979 "Gaps and Glissandos: Inequality, Economic Development, and Social Mobility in 24 Countries." *American Sociological Review* 44:410–424.

Tyree, Andrea, and Judith Treas 1974 "The Occupational and Marital Mobility of Women." *American Sociological Review* 39:293–302.

Westergaard, J., and H. Resler 1975 *Class in a Capitalist Society: A Study of Contemporary Britain.* London: Heinemann.

Wright, Erik O., C. Costello, D. Hachen, and J. Sprague 1982 "The American Class Structure." *American Sociological Review* 42:709–726.

– LYNN M. RIES

SOCIAL MOVEMENTS

Social movements are described most simply as collective attempts to promote or resist change in a society or a group. The degree of change advocated and the level at which changes are pursued vary across all types of social movements, be they religious, political, or student. Some movements clamor for sweeping, revolutionary transformations, whereas others pursue specific, moderate reforms. The level at which changes are sought varies from global and national alterations of social structures to attitudinal, spiritual, or life-style changes.

Types of Movements

Revolutionary movements, like the Bolshevik, Palestinian, Islamic jihad, and Irish Republican movements, seek fundamental structural changes. Such movements pursue radical changes in a society's basic institutions or, in some cases, major changes in the world order.

Some reform movements blend a plethora of political and life-style objectives.

Because they challenge the legitimacy of extant authorities, powerful elites typically use every available means, including violence, to repress revolutionary movements.

Reform movements, on the other hand, seek to modify structural relations without seriously threatening existing institutions. Consequently, while some elites oppose any reforms, they are usually more tolerant of reform movements than they are of revolutionary ones. Some reform movements, such as the peace, women's, and environmental movements, are general in scope (Blumer 1946). They often blend a plethora of political and life-style objectives (Turner and Killian 1987, p. 221). Peace movements, for example, not only pursue a variety of political objectives (e.g., preventing and stopping wars, opposing specific weapons, promoting disarmament, seeking foreign policy changes, establishing conflict resolution institutions), they also strive to convince individuals to change their attitudes and live more peaceful everyday lives.

Other reform movements, such as the antiabortion, women's temperance, and the anti-drunken-driving movements, focus on quite specific issues. Although specific reform movements are considerably narrower in scope than general reform movements, they too sometimes organize around both political and life-style objectives (Staggenborg 1987).

Still other reform movements, such as various self-help, human potential, and "New Age" movements (e.g., EST, rebirthing, transcendental meditation), focus almost exclusively on life-style issues. In contrast to other movements, these tend to disregard social structural issues. Instead, they concentrate on changing individuals.

Finally, social movements frequently generate organized opposition in the form of countermovements. Countermovements seek to prevent revolutionary or reform movements from securing the changes they promote. Given their counterreformist tendencies, most countermovements (e.g., anti-busing, McCarthyist, stop-ERA, and moral majority movements) are conservative (Lo 1982). That is, they seek to preserve extant institutions and life-styles.

Regardless of the particular type of social movement and the scope and level of change it advocates or opposes, all movements share some common characteristics of interest to social scientists. First, all movements emerge under a specific, complex set of historical, cultural, and structural conditions. Second, as a movement emerges, a variety of participation issues arise, including recruiting new members, building commitment, and sustaining participation. Third, every movement is organized to some degree. The most visible manifestations of movements are their social movement organizations and their strategies and tactics. Last, by virtue of their existence, every social movement has some consequences, however minimal they might be. Though researchers are frequently concerned with the extent to which movements affect social change, definitive answers to this question have proved illusory.

Movement Emergence

Social scientists have devoted considerable attention to the factors associated with the emergence of social movements. Early theory and research asserted that movements arise when societies undergo structural strain, as during times of rapid social change (Smelser 1962). These "breakdown theories" posited that "large structural rearrangements in societies—such as urbanization and industrialization"—lead to dissolution of social controls and heighten "the impulse toward antisocial behavior" (Tilly, Tilly, and Tilly 1975, p. 4). Hence, these systemic "breakdowns" were said to cause an increase in strikes, violent collective action, and social movements.

Contemporary movement scholars criticized breakdown theories on empirical and theoretical grounds. Rather than viewing movement emergence and participation as aberrations, scholars now view them as "simply politics by other means,' often the *only* means open to relatively powerless challenging groups" (McAdam 1988, pp. 127–128). To understand the conditions that affect the likelihood that such challenging groups will mobilize, researchers turned to the structural factors conducive to movement emergence.

One macro structural factor concerns the "structure of political opportunities" (Eisinger 1973). This refers to "the receptivity or vulnerability of the political system to organized protest" by a social movement (McAdam, McCarthy, and Zald 1988, p. 699). Research on the civil rights movement, for example, indicates that the movement's emergence was facilitated by a series of interrelated changes in the structure of political opportunities. These included the decline of cotton markets, black migration to the North, the expansion of the black vote, and the electoral shift to the Democratic party (McAdam 1982).

Another macro factor researchers have identified is the absence of repression. Social movements are sometimes spared a violent or otherwise repressive response from authorities, not only during times of breakdown or regime crisis (Skocpol 1979), but also during periods of expanding political opportunities. Continuing with the example of the civil rights movement, Doug McAdam (1982) documents how black lynchings declined as blacks' political opportunities increased from 1930 to 1955.

Research suggests that the relationship between collective action and repression is bell-shaped (Tilly 1978). Authorities' initial attempts to repress movements often fan the flames of discontent and fuel further protest activities. However, if authorities respond by increasing the severity of the repression, as when Chinese authorities ordered tanks and troops into Tiananmen Square to fire on student demonstrators, the costs of collective action usually become too high for movements to continue their challenges.

Indigenous organization constitutes a third major structural factor associated with movement emergence (Morris 1984). Pre-existing organizations serve as communication networks for discontented members of a population (Freeman 1973). They also provide a base for mobilizing the resources needed to sustain a movement. Various churches, for example, were important indigenous organizations that contributed to the emergence of the contemporary peace, civil rights, and Moral Majority movements.

Finally, several European scholars contend that state intervention into private domains of life have generated "new social movements." According to this perspective, various structural changes in Western industrialized societies, especially changes in the system of production, led the state to seek control over previously private domains. Consequently, private domains such as sexual relations, biological identity, birth and death, illness and aging, and one's relationship to nature "have entered the realm of 'public' conflict" (Melluci 1980, p. 219). New social movements (e.g., women's, gay rights, euthanasia, environmental) emerged to reclaim those areas from the state.

The foregoing indicates that numerous structural factors are crucial to the emergence of social movements. Yet structural factors alone cannot account for the rise of a particular movement. Why is it that when the structural conditions appear to be ripe for the emergence of a particular movement, frequently no movement appears? To address this question, some researchers have begun to investigate the micro interactional factors associated with social-movement emergence.

The bulk of this research focuses on grievance interpretation processes. These refer to the means by which people collectively arrive at similar definitions of the situation or "interpretive frames" regarding social changes they support or oppose (Snow et al. 1986).

Repression of a social movement fuels protest activity such as this demonstration in China. But when authorities react harshly, such as ordering tanks into Tiananmen Square to crush this gathering, the cost to the protestors becomes too high for the movement to challenge authorities further. (Kevin R. Morris/Corbis)

Before an aggrieved, but previously unmobilized, category of people are likely to engage in sustained protest activity, they must revise the manner in which they look at some problematic condition or aspect of life. Social arrangements that were ordinarily considered "just and immutable" must come to be seen as "unjust and mutable" (Piven and Cloward 1977, p. 12). This "cognitive liberation" process typically involves an attributional shift from blaming oneself to blaming the system for particular problems (McAdam 1982). In sum, social movements are most likely to emerge when the structural conditions for mobilization are ripe and when the collective interpretation of grievances produces cognitive liberation.

Movement Participation

Closely related to the issue of movement emergence are questions regarding movement participation. Who joins and why? What conditions affect the likelihood of participating? How do movements build membership commitment and sustain participation? Initial attempts to address questions concerning movement participation were also influenced by breakdown theories. Movement participation was viewed as an irrational response to social-structural strains. The factors regarded as key determinants of movement participation ranged from alienation and social isolation to status strains and relative deprivation (for reviews, see Gurney and Tierney 1982; Zurcher and Snow 1981). Each of these approaches suggested that some sort of psychological malaise or personality defect predisposed some individuals to react to structural strains by participating in social movements.

The outburst of collective action and the proliferation of social movements in the 1960s led many social scientists to reconsider breakdown-theory assumptions (Jenkins 1983). Some theorists redefined movement participation as a rational choice (Oberschall 1973). According to this perspective, potential participants take part in social movement activities only when they perceive that the anticipated benefits outweight the expected costs of participation (Klandermans 1984). An avalanche of research on the conditions affecting cost-benefit participation decisions (e.g., Oliver 1984) indicates that it is a complex process involving numerous structural and social-psychological factors.

Social networks are another crucial factor that affect differential recruitment to social movements. Movements tend to recruit the majority of their new members from the networks of existing members (Snow, Zurcher, and Ekland-Olson 1980). A person typically decides to attend their first movement function because a friend, coworker, or relative invited them. Those outside such networks are less likely to be aware of the existence of specific movement groups. Moreover, they are less likely to attend a movement function if they are not sure there would be others present whom they know.

Social ties in the form of family and career attachments can constrain movement participation.

While having social ties to people who are movement participants increases the likelihood of movement participation, other social ties can diminish that probability. Social ties in the form of family and career attachments can constrain movement participation in a number of ways. For one, these competing commitments may result in role conflict. The demands of being a movement participant and the demands of being a parent or employee may at times be incompatible. Married persons who have parental responsibilities as well as full-time jobs may not have sufficient discretionary time to participate in social movements (McCarthy and Zald 1973). Furthermore, spouses and employers can be displeased by a person's movement participation.

To justify their movement participation to themselves and others, participants develop vocabularies of motives (Snow and Benford 1988). These are rationales that offer compelling reasons for their participation, particularly when their actions are called into question by employers, family members, or friends. Research suggests that movement participants socially construct these vocabularies of motive as they interact with one another (Benford 1988). Activists, in turn, employ these rationales as motivational prods to encourage sympathizers and adherents to take action on behalf of movement goals.

Vocabularies of motive not only facilitate recruitment to movements, but also serve as commitment-building mechanisms. They help participants justify to themselves making sacrifices on behalf of a cause. The more sacrifices they make, the more costly leaving the movement seems to be. As they relinquish old attachments in favor of new ones, their commitment grows deeper (Kanter 1968). Research indicates that such conversion and commitment-building processes are, contrary to popular myths regarding participation in new religious movements and cults, typically voluntary (Snow and Machalek 1984).

Taken together, research on social movements reveals that participation motives and experiences are quite diverse. No single explanation suffices to account for movement participation. Rather, a confluence of factors affect the decision to participate. Likewise, there are a variety of ways individuals may participate, ranging from those that require little commitment of time, such as signing a petition or writing a letter to a political official, to those requiring extensive commitment, such as coordinating national campaigns or committing acts of civil disobedience.

Movement Organizations

The activities of movements and their participants are coordinated by social movement organizations (SMOs) (Zald and Ash 1966). Most general reform movements spawn numerous SMOs. For example, by 1984, the U.S. nuclear-disarmament movement included some 3,000 independent SMOs as well as another 1,000 local chapters of national organizations. Specific reform movements, by contrast, tend to generate fewer SMOs. Regardless, SMOs are formal movement groups that can be thought of as "the command posts of movements" (McAdam, McCarthy, and Zald 1988). They acquire and deploy resources, mobilize adherents, and plot movement strategy.

Resource mobilization theorists were among the first to emphasize the importance of SMOs in performing these functions. In particular, they point out that in the absence of an organization it is difficult for movements to acquire the resources needed to sustain their challenges (Tilly 1978). Contemporary movements require money for advertising, printing, postage, lobbying, staff, and the like.

Other resource-mobilization theorists have suggested that studying SMOs reveals how the macro and micro levels are reciprocally linked (McAdam, McCarthy, and Zald 1988). For example, the resource level of a society affects the resources available to SMOs, which in turn affect recruitment efforts (McCarthy and Zald 1977). During times of economic prosperity, as in the 1960s, the entire social-movement sector expands. There are simply more discretionary resources available for movements during these periods. In this illustration, the macro level (a society's surplus resources), mediated by SMOs, affects the micro level (individual participation).

Yet many movements also seek to affect the macro level from below. Again, SMOs play a mediating role. Individuals with similar grievances get together in an informal, small group setting, what McAdam (1988) refers to as a "micromobilization context." Sometimes participants at these ad hoc meetings decide to establish a more formal, enduring organization to act on the participants' collective grievances (i.e., an SMO). The SMO in turn devises a strategy aimed at changing the system in some way. Occasionally, SMOs succeed in bringing about macro-level changes.

The tactics and strategies a movement employs in pursuit of its objectives are typically selected or devised by SMOs. A movement strategy refers to the "broad organizing plans" for the acquisition and use of resources toward achieving movement goals (Turner and Killian 1987, p. 286). For example, as previously suggested, movements may pursue social change by devising strategies aimed at changing structural arrangements or at changing people or both. Similarly, movements may choose between legal and illegal strategies, and between violent and nonviolent strategies.

Tactics refer to the specific techniques movements employ to carry out their strategies. Teach-ins, sit-ins, marches, rallies, strikes, and mass mailings are but a few of the tactics contemporary reform movements typically utilize. There appears to be considerable tactical borrowing across the political spectrum. Conservative movements of the 1980s and 1990s, such as the Moral Majority and the anti-abortion movements, for example, used many of the tactics of the civil rights and New Left movements of the 1960s.

Charles Tilly made a similar observation regarding the eighteenth-century American revolutionary-movement tactics he studied. He accounted for tactical simiiarities across movements and SMOs by noting that every place and time has limited "repertoires of collective action" that are well defined but limited compared to the various tactical options theoretically available. These "standard forms are learned, limited in scope, slowly changing, and peculiarly adapted to their settings" (Tilly 1979, p. 131).

While tactical diffusion across movements and SMOs occurs, a division of tactical labor also commonly arises within movements (Benford and Zurcher 1990). Each SMO tends to develop its own specific tactical preferences and expertise. These specializations arise as a consequence of cooperation and competition among the various SMOs that comprise a movement (Zald and McCarthy 1980). By refining and employing specialized tactics, an SMO is able to carve out a niche within the movement that distinguishes it from other SMOs.

Once an SMO establishes an organizational identity, it is in a position to build a stable resource base. Indeed, some SMOs have been so successful in that regard that they survive the decline of a movement. Recent research on the women's movement indicates that such "abeyance organizations" provide continuity from one cycle of movement activity to the next (Taylor 1989). They do so by sustaining activist interaction and commitment during periods when the opportunity structures are unfavorable to mass mobilization. In sum, SMOs contribute at least some temporary stability to what is otherwise a fluid, emergent phenomenon.

Movement Outcomes

What effects, if any, do social movements actually have on social change? This obviously crucial question is not as easy to answer as might be assumed. Because of the difficulties associated with studying a large sample of movements, most researchers choose to study movements one at a time. Whereas these case studies provide researchers with rich, detailed data on a specific movement, they are not very helpful in making generalizations. But even with case studies, the question of the effects of a particular movement is difficult to answer. First, the logic employed is counterfactual (Moore 1978). That is, in evaluating the effects of a particular movement, researchers are in a position of having to speculate on what the outcome would have been had the movement *not* existed. Second, the effects of movements are not always immediate and apparent. Some movements, like the civil rights and women's movements, produce rippling effects that gradually engulf society's institutions, at times generating effects several decades after the movement's most intense period of agitation has ceased.

Some movements, like the civil rights and women's movements, produce rippling effects that gradually engulf society's institutions.

In general, movements seem to be more effective in producing cultural rather than structural changes. The enduring legacy of the movements of the 1960s, for example, appears to be cultural. These cultural changes are reflected in attitudinal shifts regarding women and minorities (liberalized), fashion trends (relaxed), lifestyles (hedonistic), and the like. Nevertheless, the movements of the sixties had a rather negligible impact on structural changes. While it is true that civil rights legislation helped dismantle caste restrictions and nearly equalized voting rights in the South, blacks continued to suffer "grinding poverty" and "persistent institutional discrimination in jobs, housing, and education" (McAdam 1982, p. 234). Women realized even fewer structural gains than blacks. Despite popular myths to the contrary, they still suffer gross inequities in the workplace and at home. Finally, the sweeping changes in the economic, political, and educational institutions advocated by student activists never came to pass.

That does not mean that movements always fail to achieve their structural objectives. In the late 1980s and early 1990s, grass-roots movements radically transformed the totalitarian political structures of a number of Eastern European countries into more democratic states. The mid-nineteenth-century abolitionist movement succeeded in abolishing slavery. Similarly, today's global movement against apartheid has produced a number of reforms in the treatment of blacks in South Africa. In short, although movements do occasionally achieve such dramatic outcomes, social structures initially tend to be more resistant than cultures to the revolutionary or reform efforts of social movements.

William Gamson (1990) is one of the few researchers who has attempted to identify systematically the conditions under which social movements are likely to achieve their objectives. He traced the activities of a representative sample of fifty-three "challenging groups," SMOs that emerged in the United States between 1800 and 1945. Gamson measured the relative success or failure of the SMOs in terms of whether or not they (1) gained new advantages and/or (2) gained acceptance from their antagonists. He found that thirty-one (58 percent) of the SMOs either gained new advantages or acceptance; twenty (38 percent) gained both.

One of Gamson's strongest findings pertained to the degree of change advocated. Movement groups that sought to displace extant elites rarely succeeded. Gamson reported that the SMOs most likely to succeed exhibited the following additional characteristics: selective incentives for participants (some form of inducement, including rewards or punishment, to participate); unruly tactics (e.g., strikes, violence), especially when the target was relatively weak; bureaucratic, centralized organizational structures; and the absence of factional splits within the group. Although Gamson's research has been criticized as simplistic, it does identify several factors that affect the outcomes of social movements.

Frequently, before social movements are able to change social structures, they must change the way at least some people view or "frame" a social issue or domain of life. Movement activists devote considerable time to the task of transforming people's interpretive frames (Snow et al. 1986). If the movement's framing efforts are successful, a general shift in public opinion can occur, as has been the case for the movement against drunk driving (Gusfield 1981). Those who were once thought of as foolish or careless have been redefined as "killer drunks." Subsequently, the movement has found it relatively easy to secure legislation raising minimum drinking ages and increasing the penalties for driving under the influence of alcohol. Although favorable public opinion is not a sufficient condition for social change to occur, it can lead to advantageous changes in the opportunity structure as well as the availability of resources.

Social movements may not always succeed in achieving their goals. Movements have, however, played a significant role in most societal reforms, revolutions, and changes in the world order.

[See also Collective Behavior; Labor Movements and Unions; Protest Movements; Religious Movements; Revolutions; Social Change; Student Movement.]

BIBLIOGRAPHY

Benford, Robert D. 1988 "Motivational Framing: The Social Construction of Motives within the Nuclear Disarmament Movement." Paper presented at the Annual Meetings of the Midwest Sociological Society, Minneapolis, Minn., April.

———, and Louis A. Zurcher 1990 "Instrumental and Symbolic Competition among Peace Movement Organizations." In Sam Marullo and John Lofland, eds., *Peace Action in the Eighties.* New Brunswick, N.J.: Rutgers University Press.

Blumer, Herbert 1946 "Collective Behavior." In A. M. Lee, ed., *A New Outline of the Principles of Sociology.* New York: Barnes and Noble.

Eisinger, Peter K. 1973 "The Conditions of Protest Behavior in American Cities." *American Political Science Review* 67:11–28.

Freeman, Jo 1973 "The Origin of the Women's Liberation Movement." *American Journal of Sociology* 78:792–811.

Gamson, William A. 1990 *The Strategy of Social Protest,* 2nd ed. Belmont, Calif.: Wadsworth.

Gurney, Joan Neff, and Kathleen J. Tierney 1982 "Relative Deprivation and Social Movements: A Critical Look at Twenty Years of Theory and Research." *Sociological Quarterly* 23:33–47.

Gusfield, Joseph R. 1981 *The Culture of Public Problems: Drinking-Driving and the Symbolic Order.* Chicago: University of Chicago Press.

Jenkins, J. Craig 1983 "Resource Mobilization Theory and the Study of Social Movements." *Annual Review of Sociology* 9:527–553.

Kanter, Rosabeth M. 1968 "Commitment and Social Organization: A Study of Commitment Mechanisms in Utopian Communities." *American Sociological Review* 33:499–517.

Klandermans, Bert 1984 "Mobilization and Participation: Social-Psychological Expansions of Resource Mobilization Theory." *American Sociological Review* 49:583–600.

Lo, Clarence Y. 1982 "Countermovements and Conservative Movements in the Contemporary U.S." *Annual Review of Sociology* 8:107–134.

McAdam, Doug 1982 *Political Process and the Development of Black Insurgency, 1930–1970.* Chicago: University of Chicago Press.

——— 1988 "Micromobilization Contexts and Recruitment to Activism." *International Social Movement Research* 1:125–154.

———, John D. McCarthy, and Mayer N. Zald 1988 "Social Movements." In N. Smelser, ed., *Handbook of Sociology.* Newbury Park, Calif.: Sage Publications.

McCarthy, John D. 1977 "Resource Mobilization and Social Movements: A Partial Theory." *American Journal of Sociology* 82:1212–1241.

———, and Mayer N. Zald 1973 *The Trend of Social Movements in America: Professionalization and Resource Mobilization.* Morristown, N.J.: General Learning Press.

Melluci, Alberto 1980 "The New Social Movements: A Theoretical Approach." *Social Science Information* 19:199–226.

Moore, Barrington, Jr. 1978 *Injustice: The Social Bases of Obedience and Revolt.* White Plains, N.Y.: M. E. Sharpe.

Morris, Aldon D. 1984 *The Origins of the Civil Rights Movement: Black Communities Organizing for Change.* New York: Free Press.

Oberschall, Anthony 1973 *Social Conflict and Social Movements.* Englewood Cliffs, N.J.: Prentice-Hall.

Oliver, Pamela 1984 " 'If You Don't Do It, Nobody Else Will': Active and Token Contributors to Collective Action." *American Sociological Review* 49:601–610.

Piven, Frances Fox, and Richard A. Cloward 1977 *Poor Peoples' Movements: Why They Succeed, How They Fail.* New York: Vintage.

Skocpol, Theda 1979 *States and Social Revolutions.* New York: Cambridge University Press.

Smelser, Neil J. 1962 *Theory of Collective Behavior.* New York: Free Press.

Snow, David A., and Robert D. Benford 1988 "Ideology, Frame Resonance, and Participant Mobilization." *International Social Movement Research* 1:197–217.

Snow, David A., and Richard Machalek 1984 "The Sociology of Conversion." *Annual Review of Sociology* 10:167–180.

Snow, David A., E. Burke Rochford, Jr., Steven K. Worden, and Robert D. Benford 1986 "Frame Alignment Processes, Micromobilization, and Movement Participation." *American Sociological Review* 51:464–481.

Snow, David A., Louis A. Zurcher, Jr., and Sheldon Ekland-Olson 1980 "Social Networks and Social Movements: A Microstructural Approach to Differential Recruitment." *American Sociological Review* 45:787–801.

Staggenborg, Suzanne 1987 "Life-style Preferences and Social Movement Recruitment: Illustrations from the Abortion Conflict." *Social Science Quarterly* 68:779–797.

Taylor, Verta 1989 "Social Movement Continuity: The Women's Movement in Abeyance." *American Sociological Review* 54:761–775.

Tilly, Charles 1978 *From Mobilization to Revolution.* Reading, Mass.: Addison-Wesley.

——— 1979 "Repertoires of Contention in America and Britain, 1750–1830." In M. N. Zald and J. D. McCarthy, eds., *The Dynamics of Social Movements.* Cambridge, Mass.: Winthrop.

———, Louise Tilly, and Richard Tilly 1975 *The Rebellious Century: 1830–1930.* Cambridge: Harvard University Press.

Turner, Ralph H., and Lewis M. Killian 1987 *Collective Behavior,* 3rd ed. Englewood Cliffs, N.J.: Prentice-Hall.

Zald, Mayer N., and Roberta Ash 1966 "Social Movement Organizations: Growth, Decay and Decline." *Social Forces* 44:327–341.

Zald, Mayer N., and John D. McCarthy 1980 "Social Movement Industries: Competition and Cooperation among Movement Organizations." In L. Kriesberg, ed., *Research in Social Movements, Conflict and Change.* Greenwich, Conn.: JAI Press.

Zurcher, Louis A., and David A. Snow 1981 "Collective Behavior: Social Movements." In M. Rosenberg and R. H. Turner, eds., *Social Psychology: Sociological Perspectives.* New York: Basic Books.

– ROBERT D. BENFORD

SOCIAL SECURITY SYSTEMS

In the United States, Social Security refers to a set of programs, including old-age, survivors, and disability insurance, directed toward the elderly and their dependents. This particular usage of the term *social security* relates as much to the special and delimited character of the welfare state in the United States as it does to the generally accepted meaning of the term. For organizations such as the International Labour Office and the International Social Security Association, and for scholars concerned with comparative studies, social security refers to a wider variety of programs than those aimed at the elderly. For instance, in its volume *Social Security throughout the World,* the Social Security Administration states

> The term "social security" in the context of this report refers to programs established by government statutes which insure individuals against interruption or loss of earning power, and for certain special expenditures arising from marriage, birth, or death. (1985, p. ix)

The concept of social protection underlying this definition includes unemployment programs to cover involuntary, temporary loss of work, sickness programs to cover loss of income from sickness and the cost of medical care, disability or occupational injury programs to cover physical limitations to work, family allowances to cover loss of economic status from addition of members to the family, and social assistance to cover other circumstances such as family disruption causing income to fall below specified levels. Protection of earning power from loss of work or from health conditions associated with old age also remains crucial. Still, many of the other programs, more common among advanced welfare systems of Western European nations than in the United States, must still be considered part of social security systems.

The relative size of programs devoted to the elderly perhaps warrants the special attention to old age in social security systems. Of all expenditures for education and social security programs, those for old-age pensions represent the largest component, averaging 36 percent across high income nations in 1985 (Organization for Economic Development and Cooperation 1988, Tables 1 and 3). The next largest component, 22 percent, is devoted to health care, which also disproportionately benefits the elderly. Furthermore, the growth rate of programs for the aged has exceeded those for other programs, and in the future expenditures for such programs will consume an even greater proportion of the total. Spending for unemployment, family allowances, and social assistance represents a relatively small part of social security programs. As Myles (1984) notes, the welfare state is primarily a welfare state for the elderly.

The need for collective protection—for the aged or otherwise—stems from the existence of economic insecurity. Loss of earning power from poor health, old age, or unemployment remains a possibility for nearly all participants in a market economy but at the same time is uncertain enough to make it difficult to predict loss of income or future savings potential. Traditional protection against such risk in preindustrial societies developed informally through the family. Children and relatives, under ideal circumstances, could support parents unable to provide for themselves or desiring to step down from their economic role of provider. Social security thus took the form of an intergenerational contract, based on norms of filial piety and parental control over wealth, between children or other relatives and parents (Simmons 1960). Never a guaranteed source of protection, however, other family members became an even less reliable source of support with the decrease in family size, increase in mobility, and industrialization of labor that accompanied the demographic and industrial transitions. With the development of large-scale corporate capitalism in the late nineteenth and early twentieth centuries, the risks of forced retirement and unemployment also grew. Systems of social security collectivized and formalized the relationship between young workers and elderly, unemployed, or disabled nonworkers. Workers would contribute support to certain categories of nonworkers in return for the expectation they would be covered should they be unable to work.

The state has always played a crucial role in the collectivized contract by making participation in the system compulsory for most workers. Voluntary programs of saving for unexpected contingencies are insufficient because many people are not rational in saving for events that may not occur or may occur only in the far future. Private compulsory systems within industries, unions, or businesses likewise face problems of incomplete coverage, financial insolvency, and job movement. In contrast, collectivizing social security provides for reliable funding, and it is easier to predict events for a group than for individuals.

Most nations provide for more than social security alone. The broader welfare state in capitalist societies also supports education, retraining, full employment, business regulation, price supports, infrastructure, and legal rights. In socialist societies, social security systems exist but involve broader social protection through guaranteed employment, subsidized food, housing, and energy prices, and the reduced importance of market performance as the primary criterion for economic support. Still, market-oriented reforms in Eastern Europe may yet expand the emphasis on social security systems as typically and more narrowly defined in capitalist societies.

If motives of social protection are common to social security systems, the coverage of the population and the distribution of benefits show wide variation. Benefits may be distributed on the basis of at least four criteria, each of which may be emphasized or deemphasized in particular systems. First, citizenship entitlement provides basic benefits—usually in the form of flat-rate cash payments—to individuals or families as a right of citizenship, regardless of work history, contributions, or income. Second, employment-related criteria base eligibility on wage or payroll contributions made before the contingency causing earnings to cease. As a form of public or social insurance, these benefits reinforce market criteria of income determination. Third, need-based criteria provide benefits by comparing resources against a standard typically based on subsistence needs. Means-tested or social assistance programs target benefits at the most needy, usually those otherwise not covered by citizenship or insurance programs. Fourth, entitlement is sometimes granted on the basis of marital or family status, usually to women and homemakers, or to families with young children.

To a large extent, nations mix their degree of reliance on the different criteria. Nations that began with universal systems added earnings-based supplements (e.g., Sweden), and those originally enacting earnings-based benefits have added universal benefits (e.g., Great Britain) or some form of minimum benefit (e.g., the United States). Similar claims have been made about the mix of public and private systems. Nations that have traditionally relied on private systems (e.g., the United States) have, to limit inequality, increasingly expanded public system benefits, while nations relying traditionally on public system benefits (e.g., West Germany) have increasingly expanded private benefits for high-income workers wanting more return on their contributions.

Some argue that social citizenship remains the most important component of social protection because security is not complete until the state grants alternative means to economic welfare to the market (Esping-Andersen 1989; Korpi 1989). Because meager means-tested benefits are structured to avert work disincentive effects, they fail to emancipate individuals from market dependence. Because social insurance benefits stem from labor-based contributions—that is, qualification based on previous contributions defines the right to benefits—they maintain links to the market. And because family benefits depend on qualification of others by virtue of need or contribution, they likewise fail to detach distribution from the market mechanism. A definition of social security would thus require decommodifying labor or insulating workers from dependence on the market for economic support. According to Esping-Anderson, in decommodifying welfare states

> citizens can freely, and without potential losses of job, income or general welfare, opt out of work under conditions when they themselves consider it necessary for reasons of health, family, age or even educational self-improvement; when, in short, they deem it necessary for participating in the social community. (1989, p. 22)

Few if any nations meet the high standards defined by citizenship rights or decommodification. Nearly all nations rely at least partially on earnings-related benefits to supplement universal benefits; flat-rate benefits available to all are too expensive to provide generously for all elderly persons. Still, the trend is toward expanded social rights. Recent efforts to gain the right to protection from economic insecurity follow efforts in previous centuries to gain civil rights such as freedom of speech and equality before the courts and political rights for universal voting (Marshall 1964). This highlights the dynamic meaning of social security and the continuing evolution of its definition.

Recent efforts to gain the right to protection from economic insecurity follow efforts in previous centuries to gain civil rights such as freedom of speech.

Political debate over how far governments should go in extending definitions of social security to include citizenship rights reflects larger tensions between the relative roles in the market and the state in public policy (Myles 1984). On one hand, inequality in earnings and contributions during work life means the market remains a strong influence on social security benefits and on the financial circumstances of nonworkers. On the other hand, equality of participation in the democratic political system provides impetus for equality in benefits unrelated to the market. The underlying dynamics of market and democracy— differentiation versus equality—both show in varying degrees in the benefit structures of different systems and in debates over the appropriate definition of what social security should provide.

Historical Background

A formal social security system was slow to come to the United States. The first public social security system (albeit one limited in coverage and generosity) emerged in Bismarckian Germany in 1889 and was followed within the next several decades by systems in Denmark in 1891, New Zealand in 1898, Austria in 1906, and Australia and Great Britain in 1908 (Social Security Administration 1985). Yet legislation was not passed at the national level in the United States until 1935, and the first old-age pension was not paid until 1940. In part, the expansion of disability benefits to Civil War veterans (even if they had not been injured or seen combat) in 1890 provided a de facto pension system for northern whites but did not promote implementation of a more general national pension system for nonveterans as well (Orloff and Skocpol 1984).

The reasons Civil War pensions did not lead to a more comprehensive social security system have been examined extensively. A historical persistence of individualist, laissez-faire values obstructed public support for public programs (Rimlinger 1971). Big business preferred private negotiation with labor, and small business wanted to avoid altogether the cost of social security provisions. Relative to a powerful business community, weak, decentralized labor unions in the United States were unable to agree on a common approach or push redistributive public programs as they did in several European nations (Stephens 1979). Relatedly, the United States did not have a socialist or social democratic party closely committed to labor goals, as regional, ethnic, and racial divisions split clearly defined class interests in support of social legislation. Southern congressional representatives, who desired to maintain cheap agricultural (particularly black) labor in their region, used their power in a committee-dominated federal legislature to block legislation (Quadagno 1988). Finally, the lack of a professional civil-service bureaucracy to administer the program, and the existence of often corrupt patronage politics at the local level, may have limited public support for a large public social security system (Skocpol and Ikenberry 1983). All of these forces had some role in blocking attempts during the first several decades of the twentieth century to expand protection beyond the veteran's pension and partial state-based programs for mothers' pensions or industrial accidents.

The impetus for passage of old-age and unemployment social security came from the Great Depression. Rapidly expanding costs of private pensions and a crisis of capitalist growth lessened opposition of big business to federal pension legislation and a more general role of the government in the capitalist economy (Jenkins and Brents 1989). Southern congressmen were persuaded to support legislation by excluding agricultural and domestic workers and by insisting that means-tested levels for old-age assistance be set at the state level. Both would limit disruption of the low-wage southern economy. Popular demands during the early 1930s of several hundred thousand supporters of the Townsend movement for a federal government pension to each citizen over sixty may have hastened enactment (Williamson, Evans, and Powell 1982). Ultimately, the goal of reducing unemployment by removing older workers from the labor force and of supporting at least temporarily those who were unemployed proved crucial in passing the initial legislation in 1935 (Schulz 1988; Graebner 1980).

The original 1935 Social Security Act mandated only limited coverage and benefit levels for old-age retirement. Only 60 percent of the work force was covered: agricultural, domestic, and self-employed workers, military personnel, federal, state, and local employees, and employees of nonprofit, tax-exempt organizations were all excluded. Moreover, benefit levels were quite low: policy makers intended not to replace work income fully or assure maintenance of the workers' preretirement standard of living but to supplement private sources of retirement income with minimal public benefits (Achenbaum 1986). Social Security benefits would alone hardly meet what at the time would be considered poverty levels in many states (Quadagno 1984).

The initial structure of the social security system, along with incremental changes made in the following decades, was for the most part market-conforming. Early debates over the degree to which the program should redistribute income across classes were settled in favor of those who desired to maintain the connection between contributions and benefits (Cates 1983). Funding from general revenues was rejected in favor of contribution-based financing, which reinforced the view of the system as an insurance system. Flat-rate benefits were rejected as unsuitable for a nation of such regional and social heterogeneity; benefits were instead to reflect preretirement income levels. A cap placed on taxable wages, which ostensibly concentrated both contributions and benefits for ordinary, middle-income wage workers, introduced some regressiveness into the formula. The major exception to this strategy was that benefits for low-wage workers were higher, relative to contributions, than those for high-wage workers (Myers 1981). Also, provisions for unemployment, aid to dependent children, and relief for the blind targeted modest benefits for needy groups (Achenbaum 1989). The system thus began and remains as a mixture of social insurance based on contributions and social adequacy based on social need (Munnell 1977).

Expansion of the system began before the first benefits were ever paid out and continued on for several more decades. In 1939, dependents and survivors were made eligible for benefits. Coverage was extended in the 1950s to include most self-employed, domestic, and agricultural workers, and participation of state and local employees was made elective (federal employees kept their own system until 1984). In 1956, actuarially reduced benefits were made available at ages sixty-two to sixty-four for women, and in 1961 the same option for early retirement was made available to men—an option now exercised by a majority of new beneficiaries. Also in the 1950s, benefits equal to those for retirees were added for disabled persons ages fifty to sixty-four and still later for disabled workers of all ages. In 1965, Medicare for the elderly and Medicaid for the poor were added to provide protection from the high costs of medical care. Benefit and contribution levels also rose with extensions of coverage and disability. Ad hoc adjustments to benefit levels, which well exceeded inflation (Tomasson 1984), were common until 1972 when benefits were linked to yearly increases in the consumer price index. Payroll taxes and the maximum taxable wage also increased.

Growth of benefits and coverage nonetheless proceeded more quickly than contributions, and by the late 1970s this situation resulted in funding problems. The concept of accumulation of a reserve was replaced very quickly by a pay-as-you-go system in which current workers paid for current retirees (with surplus enough to cover year-to-year fluctuations). In the early years of the system, the ratio of one retiree to 120 workers made such funding workable. By the 1970s, the ratio of retirees to workers was one to five. Combined with increasingly high benefit levels, the growing dependency ratio resulted in payments that exceeded contributions. Amendments in 1977 "deliberalized" benefits for the first time by, among other things, freezing minimum benefits and making the earnings test more stringent (Tomasson 1984). Far from sufficient to deal with the implications of higher benefits and an older age structure, the changes only delayed more serious restructuring. A $17 billion deficit in 1983 required further deliberalization. In 1981, a Reagan administration proposal to lower benefits, change the retirement age, delay cost-of-living increases, and reduce family benefits for dependents and survivors was met with near universal opposition. To move negotiation out of the public eye, where painful and politically unpopular choices could be agreed upon, a bipartisan commission was appointed to develop proposals to deal with both short-term and long-term funding problems (Light 1985). The commission offered a compromise plan that was quickly passed by Congress and signed by President Reagan.

To summarize a complex 1983 amendment, a number of major changes were made in the direction the system was to take compared to previous decades. For the first time, Social Security benefits above specified levels were to be taxed. The age of eligibility for full retirement benefits was to be extended gradually to age sixty-seven beginning in 1999. And payroll taxes were to be increased along with the maximum taxable wage base. All these changes have had the desired effect: Contributions now exceed benefits paid. The long-run projection is that the surplus accrued during the next thirty years will likely balance the expected deficit when large, baby-boom cohorts reach retirement age (Social Security Administration 1989). The surplus, however, is by law used to purchase Treasury bonds, which fund deficits in general revenue spending. Since the bonds will need to be paid off by the taxpayers through general income taxes later on, funding problems will not disappear.

The cumulative changes in the system now result in coverage of over 90 percent of the workers, who qualify for benefits by satisfying forty quarters or ten years of covered employment. Besides the basic benefit, a minimum benefit is available for those with long-term covered employment at low wages, a dependent's benefit at 50 percent of spouses' benefits is available to spouses, and a survivor's benefit is available at 100 percent of the deceased spouse's benefits. Supplemental Security Income (SSI) provides cash assistance—unrelated to contributions and funded from general revenues—for needy aged, disabled, and blind persons who meet the means test. Among the elderly, 38 percent of all income comes from Social Security and a majority of the elderly depend on Social Security income for more than half of their income (Sherman 1987).

The position of the U.S. Social Security system relative to other nations depends on how generosity is measured. As a percent of gross domestic product (GDP), the United States ranks quite low. Considering pensions alone, however, a measure of the benefit of a new retiree as a percent of the wage of the average manufacturing worker ranks the United States higher. It falls slightly below average for single workers and slightly above average for married workers (Aldrich 1982). Part of the discrepancy stems from the concentration of public spending on pensions in the United States to the neglect of other programs. Family allowance spending and free health care for the non-aged common in other advanced industrial democracies are absent altogether in the United States (except for need-based public assistance such as Aid to Families with Dependent Children and Medicaid). The United States provides well for those whose contributions during their work lives are high—the average retiree in other words—but spends less in the aggregate for those who are not covered. Finally, the low percentage aged in the United States relative to other advanced industrial nations makes it possible to replace an above-average proportion of preretirement wages while spending a below-average fraction of GDP.

Comparative Perspectives

Many developing nations have begun to implement more formal social security systems, primarily for the benefit of urban workers and civil servants, but seldom have the economic resources to provide more than minimal coverage or protection from economic contingencies (Midgley 1984). Comparative studies have instead concentrated on the historical emergence and current policies of mature welfare states in advanced industrial nations.

Among the high-income democracies, substantial variation exists in spending levels and the structure of benefit distribution. Including pensions, health care, occupational injury, unemployment, family allowances, public assistance, and related programs for civil servants and veterans, mean spending as a percent of GDP in 1980 is 19 percent (International Labour Organization 1985). Nations spending the most include Sweden (31.2 percent), the Netherlands (27.6 percent), Denmark (26.2 percent), and France (25.5 percent), and nations spending the least are Japan (9.8 percent), Italy (11.3 percent), Australia (11.6 percent), and the United States (12.2 percent). As discussed earlier, nations also vary in the extent to which they rely on universal benefits relative to insurance or need-based benefits. According to Esping-Andersen (1989), Sweden and Norway, in particular, have the most equalizing social security programs; Finland, Denmark, Belgium, and the Netherlands also structure benefits on the basis of citizenship rights. English-speaking nations and Switzerland tend to base their systems most on market-related criteria.

Comparison of maximum and minimum benefit levels of pensions further illustrates important country differences. In the United States, the difference between the maximum and minimum benefit in dollars is $9,900; in West Germany it is $11,000 (Social Security Administration 1985). These figures contrast with those for nations with primarily flat-rate systems such as Canada ($500), Denmark ($1,300), or the Netherlands ($0). Nations differ as well on the frequency of adjustment for the cost of living, the ages of eligibility for early or normal retirement, the degree of retirement required for receipt of benefits upon reaching retirement age (i.e., the existence of a retirement test), and the wage ceiling for social security taxation. Scales summarizing national differences on all these dimensions provide an overview of the divergence in pensions (Day 1978; Myles 1984).

Scholars during the 1950s and 1960s predicted convergence in social security systems as advanced industrial technology spread. The standardizing effects of technology would reduce preexisting cultural and political differences among the economically developed nations. The need for a recently trained, highly educated, and geographically mobile labor force in industrial economies made older workers superfluous to the production process. Without means of employment, the elderly depended on government programs for economic support. In this functionalist framework, the state meets the needs of business for a differentiated labor force while simultaneously meeting the financial needs of surplus labor unable to find employment (Wilensky 1975). Hence, retirement and social security grew rapidly among all developed nations, especially during the decades after World War II.

Similar convergence in social security systems is predicted by neo-Marxist theories of monopoly capitalism. Here the focus is on the requirements of the capitalist mode of production and on the power of the capitalist elite. State-sponsored insurance subsidizes the costs of production of capital, and state-sponsored social assistance helps maintain legitimacy of the political-economic system in the face of discontent among the superfluous population (O'Connor 1973). The standardizing force is therefore the needs of increasingly monopolized capital to maintain high profit and investment, but the consequence is still the expansion of the state in similar forms among advanced industrial nations. Partisan democratic politics play little role in either the industrialist or capitalist logic.

The corporatist bargain has been for labor to hold down wage demands in return for full employment and generous, redistributive welfare spending.

The fact that, in contrast to predictions of convergence theories, expenditure levels have continued to diverge across nations over the last several decades has led more recently to a number of political explanations of variation in social security. The most common explanations focus on the differential political power of labor unions across the advanced industrial democracies. Where labor is centralized and has high membership, it gains power in negotiation with capital but can also contribute to the election of socialist, social democratic, or labor parties that best represent their interests. As a result, social legislation decreasing the scope of the market and emphasizing distribution based on political power emerges where labor is strong and where leftist parties have ruled for significant periods. Where labor is weaker and more fragmented, rightist parties are more powerful, and market-reinforcing programs with low benefits are common. Relatedly, the emergence of corporatist bargaining structures in which officially designated representatives of labor and capital negotiate economic policy with state managers has emerged in some nations—usually small nations with strong political representation of labor. The corporatist bargain has been for labor to hold down wage demands in return for full employment and generous, redistributive welfare spending (Goldthorpe 1984).

Other theories agree with the importance of political forces in generating divergence but focus on the political activity of the aged and other ascriptive groups as well as on classes (Pampel and Williamson 1989). Even among the advanced industrial nations, substantial differences in the percent aged exist and appear related to welfare spending through both demographic and political channels. Given the same benefit level in 1980 as in 1960, aging of the population can account for only some of the observed increase in pension spending. However, the size of benefit increases over time correlates closely with the size of the elderly population. Beyond just demographic effects, then, the elderly would appear in at least some countries to be an influential political interest group in support of higher pension and health care spending.

Still others have emphasized the role of the state in divergent social security policies. Beginning with the assumption that public policies cannot be reduced to the demands and preferences of any social group, state-based theories have examined how the structure of relatively autonomous state agencies and the interests of state managers can shape the way demands are expressed and translated into legislation. Qualitative studies have identified, within specific historical and national contexts, the state characteristics important for the particular policy outcomes. The quantitative literature, however, has had less success relating state characteristics such as size or centralization to measures of social security spending or citizenship rights.

Any resolution to the theoretical debates and mixed empirical results will come from synthetic efforts at theory building and statistical analysis. Class, status-demographic, political, productive, and state factors may all prove important for understanding social security system development once theories and models more clearly specify how one set of factors varies by the level of the others. Efforts to estimate nonlinear, interactive models are already under way and should prove crucial for future research (Hicks, Swank, and Ambuhl 1989; Pampel, Williamson, and Stryker 1990).

Consequences

A huge literature on the consequences of social security spending for social equality and social behavior can only be given the broadest overview. Controversy exists not so much on whether spending has any effect but on what kinds of social phenomena it most affects.

One view is that social security spending directly reduces economic inequality without substantially changing social behavior such as labor force participation, living arrangements, or savings. The major evidence in favor of the redistributive consequences comes from studies that subtract transfers from total income and compare inequality with and without the transfers included (Smeeding, Torrey, and Rein 1988). In the United States and a number of European nations, pretransfer inequality and poverty are higher than for post-transfer income distribution. Particularly egalitarian, according to the results of this methodology, are expenditures for pensions. However, advocates of this view have been less willing to accept the claim that transfers promote inequality by providing incentives to leave the labor force—in other words, by inducing behavior that indirectly contributes to higher poverty and inequality. Implicitly, unemployment and low income are seen as the result of discrimination and lack of opportunities—situations that do not change with the receipt of benefits.

Other views weigh the behavioral responses to transfers as important relative to the redistributive consequences. If transfers themselves induce labor force and living arrangement changes that make pretransfer income distribution less egalitarian than it would otherwise be if transfers were not present, the evidence of redistribution cited above would be flawed (Danziger, Haverman, and Plotnick 1981). For instance, pensions have the largest effect in reducing pretransfer inequality but also induce voluntary retirement that lowers earnings relative to what they would be without pensions or retirement. Similarly, transfers increase an individual's ability to afford independent living arrangements, which makes pretransfer income figures misleading.

Trends in poverty and inequality do not provide unambiguous evidence for either view. Certainly the absolute income of the elderly in the United States has risen with the growth of Social Security benefits. As Social Security benefits rose dramatically during the last several decades, poverty among the aged declined from a level of 35 percent (compared to 22 percent for the population) in 1960 to a level of 12 percent (compared to 13 percent for the population) by 1987 (U.S. Bureau of the Census 1989). However, the improved economic position of the elderly also stems from the fact that recent cohorts entering old age have been better off financially than previous cohorts and more likely to have accumulated private pensions and savings to support them. For overall income inequality, the trend shows little change (at least until 1980) despite the massive growth of transfers (Levy 1987). Either transfers were not redistributive or pretransfer inequality increased. Perhaps household changes, in part an indirect response to transfers, balanced the direct effects of transfers on inequality (Treas 1983). After 1980 inequality grew, but, again, separating the effects of changes in the occupation structure from changes in real Social Security benefits for the poor and unemployed is difficult.

Comparative evidence on the relationship between social security spending and inequality across advanced industrial nations is also mixed (compare Pampel and Williamson 1989 with Esping-Andersen 1985). Nations with high spending levels and benefit structures based on citizenship rights such as in Scandinavia have always had lower levels of income inequality among both the aged and the general population. Yet, establishing a causal association between those levels and social security benefits across nations that differ in so many other social and economic characteristics is difficult.

Given the mixed empirical evidence, views on the redistributive consequences of the welfare state reflect theoretical assumptions about the determinants of social security spending levels and structure. Neo-Marxist theories of monopoly capitalism, assuming high inequality is an inherent and necessary feature of advanced capitalism, argue social security systems help maintain that structure rather than change it. Interest-group or neopluralist theories see middle-class, politically powerful groups as the primary recipients of most spending, which limits the extent of redistribution to the poor. Other theories claim just the opposite. For industrialism theories, spending is directed at surplus workers most in need. For social democratic theories, spending is directed to the working class and poor represented by leftist parties and unions. Still others would claim that the state and institutional context shapes the ability of spending to reduce inequality. As in the study of the determinants of spending, interactive or contextual studies will likely be needed to make sense of the comparative experience.

Issues

A number of issues or problems face policymakers dealing with social security systems. A few of these can be reviewed briefly. Some apply especially or primarily to the United States, while others apply to all advanced industrial nations or to third-world nations.

First, concern has been expressed over the inequitable treatment of women in earnings-related social security systems. When receipt of benefits for women in old age depends on the benefits of spouses, high rates of marital breakup and widowhood make reliance on this source of financial security risky. When receipt of benefits of women in old age depend on wage contributions, the discontinuous labor force participation during years of childbearing penalizes women. Universal benefits provide some support for older women, but other policy options are emerging to deal more directly with the gender-based problems. Some nations give social security contribution credits to women out of the labor force to raise children or split earned credits of a couple equally between the spouses.

Second, the improved economic position of the elderly, declining poverty rates, and higher public benefits during the 1970s and the 1980s contrast with the declining real level of benefits and increasing poverty among children in the United States. The improved position of the elderly relative to children may stem from the increasing size (and political power) of elderly cohorts compared to the smaller-sized cohorts of children (Preston 1984). That benefits for children take the form of means-tested social assistance—a type of program that receives weak public support relative to pensions because it is not shared by large parts of the population—also contributes to the inequality. Other nations that have family allowance systems to provide cash benefits to all or nearly all parents have experienced little in the way of concern over generational equity.

Critics have argued that the rising costs of social security contribute to economic problems of inflation and unemployment by reducing savings and productivity.

Third, after decades of expansion, policymakers must face problems of balancing continued demands for more spending with limits on taxation. On one hand, given problems of support that still exist among certain vulnerable groups such as the oldest old, minorities, and widowed women, more spending is needed. Increasingly expensive health and long-term care for the elderly and disabled add particularly to the cost of social security systems. Despite the cost, support for pension and health care continues strong (Coughlin 1980). On the other hand, critics have argued that the rising costs of social security contribute to economic problems of inflation and unemployment by reducing savings and productivity. Others who are more sociologically oriented suggest that high expenditures tend to weaken community and family bonds, which ultimately are the source of protection for those in need (Glazer 1988). Certainly concern with high tax levels has led politicians to attempt to control spending and reduce taxes in nearly all advanced industrial democracies. Balancing these goals without deficit spending will remain the task of governments in the decades to come.

Fourth, concern over population aging relates to debates over controlling costs of social security. Whatever the difficulties in meeting funding demands, they are likely to worsen in the next century with the entrance of large baby-boom cohorts into old age. In part, the problem is one of declining fertility, which reduces the size of younger, working cohorts relative to older, retired cohorts. In the recent past, when the relative sizes of working and elderly cohorts were reversed, social security recipients were treated generously: They received benefits worth five to six times their contributions and interest (Wolff 1987). Future retiring cohorts are not likely to experience such high returns on their contributions (and are sometimes skeptical of receiving any at all). Still, funding problems for aging populations are not insurmountable. Many European nations, whose fertility levels fell faster than those in the United States, already have aged populations as large as 17 percent of the total—levels not to be reached for thirty years in the United States. Through appropriate political and economic policy, the United States can meet the needs of its elderly population (Aaron, Bosworth, and Burtless 1989).

Finally, these same issues are emerging as important in third-world nations. Though the percentage aged in these nations is small, and social security remains primarily a family rather than a state responsibility, the situation can change quickly. Rapid declines in fertility sharply increase the percent aged, make family care for the elderly difficult, and generate demands for public support. With scare resources, the state may risk being overwhelmed by the demands. Our understanding of the process of building social security systems for these nations remains meager.

[See also: Government Regulation; Retirement; Social Gerontology.]

BIBLIOGRAPHY

Aaron, Henry J., Barry P. Bosworth, and Gary Burtless 1989 *Can America Afford to Grow Old? Paying for Social Security.* Washington D.C.: Brookings Institution.

Achenbaum, W. Andrew 1986 *Social Security: Visions and Revisions.* Cambridge: Cambridge University Press.

——— 1989 "Public Pensions as Intergenerational Transfers in the United States." In Paul Johnson, Christoph Conrad, and David Thomson, eds., *Workers Versus Pensioners: Intergenerational Justice in an Aging World.* Manchester: Manchester University Press.

Aldrich, Jonathan 1982 "The Earnings Replacement Rate of Old-Age Benefits in Twelve Countries, 1969–80." *Social Security Bulletin* 445(12): 3–11.

Cates, Jerry R. 1983 *Insuring Inequality: Administrative Leadership in Social Security, 1935–53.* Ann Arbor: University of Michigan Press.

Coughlin, Richard M. 1980 *Ideology, Public Opinion, and Welfare Policy.* Berkeley: Institute of International Studies, University of California.

Danziger, Sheldon, Robert H. Haverman, and Robert Plotnick 1981 "How Income Transfer Programs Affect Work, Savings, and the Income Distribution: A Critical Review." *Journal of Economic Literature* 19:975–1,028.

Day, Lincoln 1978 "Government Pensions for the Aged in Nineteen Industrialized Countries." *Comparative Studies in Sociology* 1:217–234.

Esping-Andersen, Gosta 1985 "Power and Distributional Regimes." *Politics and Society* 14:222–255.

——— 1989 "The Three Political Economies of the Welfare State." *Canadian Review of Sociology and Anthropology* 26:10–35.

Glazer, Nathan 1988 *The Limits of Social Policy.* Cambridge, Mass.: Harvard University Press.

Goldthorpe, John H. 1984 "The End of Convergence: Corporatist and Dualist Tendencies in Modern Western Societies." In John H. Goldthorpe, ed., *Order and Conflict in Contemporary Capitalism.* Oxford: Clarendon.

Graebner, William 1980 *A History of Retirement.* New Haven: Yale University Press.

Hicks, Alexander, Duane Swank, and Martin Ambuhl 1989 "Welfare Expansion Revisited: Policy Routines and Their Mediation by Party, Class, and Crisis, 1959–1982." *European Journal of Political Research* 4:401–430.

International Labour Organization 1985 *The Cost of Social Security.* Geneva: International Labour Organization.

Jenkins, J. Craig, and Barbara G. Brents 1989 "Social Protest, Hegemonic Competition, and Social Reform: A Political Struggle Interpretation of the Origins of the American Welfare State." *American Sociological Review* 54:891–909.

Korpi, Walter 1989 "Power, Politics, and State Autonomy in the Development of Social Citizenship: Social Rights during Sickness in Eighteen Countries since 1930." *American Sociological Review* 54:309–328.

Levy, Frank 1987 *Dollars and Dreams: The Changing American Income Distribution.* New York: Russell Sage.

Light, Paul 1985 *Artful Work: The Politics of Social Security Reform.* New York: Random House.

Marshall, T. H. 1964 *Class, Citizenship, and Social Development.* Chicago: University of Chicago Press.

Midgley, James 1984 *Social Security, Inequality, and the Third World.* New York: Wiley.

Munnell, Alice H. 1977 *The Future of Social Security.* Washington D.C.: Brookings Institution.

Myers, Robert J. 1981 *Social Security.* Rev. ed. Homewood, Ill.: Irwin.

Myles, John 1984 *Old Age in the Welfare State: The Political Economy of Public Pensions.* Boston: Little, Brown.

O'Connor, James 1973 *The Fiscal Crisis of State.* New York: St. Martin's.

Organization for Economic Cooperation and Development 1988 *The Future of Social Protection.* OECD Social Policy Studies No. 6. Paris: Organization for Economic Cooperation and Development.

Orloff, Ann Shola, and Theda Skocpol 1984 "Why Not Equal Protection? Explaining the Politics of Public Social Spending in Britain, 1900–1911, and the United States, 1880–1920s." *American Sociological Review* 49:725–750.

Pampel, Fred C., and John B. Williamson 1989 *Age, Class, Politics, and the Welfare State.* Cambridge: Cambridge University Press.

Pampel, Fred C., John B. Williamson, and Robin Stryker 1990 "Class Context and Pension Response to Demographic Structure." *Social Problems* 37:535–550.

Preston, Samuel H. 1984 "Children and the Elderly: Divergent Paths for America's Dependents." *Demography* 21:435–457.

Quadagno, Jill S. 1984 "Welfare Capitalism and the Social Security Act of 1935." *American Sociological Review* 49:632–647.

——— 1988 *The Transformation of Old Age Security: Class and Politics in the American Welfare State.* Chicago: University of Chicago Press.

Rimlinger, Gaston 1971 *Welfare Policy and Industrialization in Europe, America, and Russia.* Toronto: John Wiley.

Schulz, James 1988 *The Economics of Aging.* Dover, Mass.: Auburn House.

Sherman, Sally R. 1987 "Fast Facts and Figures about Social Security." *Social Security Bulletin* 50(5): 5–25.

Simmons, Leo 1960 "Aging in Preindustrial Societies." In Clark Tibbits, ed., *Handbook of Social Gerontology.* Chicago: University of Chicago Press.

Skocpol, Theda, and John Ikenberry 1983 "The Political Formation of the American Welfare State in Historical and Comparative Perspective." *Comparative Social Research* 6:87–148.

Social Security Administration 1985 *Social Security throughout the World.* Washington D.C.: U.S. Government Printing Office.

——— 1989 "Actuarial Status of the OASI and DI Trust Funds." *Social Security Bulletin* 52(6): 2–7.

Smeeding, Timothy, Barbara Boyle Torrey, and Martin Rein 1988 "Patterns of Income and Poverty: The Economic Status of Children and the Elderly in Eight Countries." In John L. Palmer, Timothy Smeeding, and Barbara Boyle Torrey, eds., *The Vulnerable.* Washington D.C.: Brookings Institution.

Stephens, John D. 1979 *The Transformation from Capitalism to Socialism.* London: Macmillan.

Tomasson, Richard F. 1984 "Government Old Age Pensions under Affluence and Austerity: West Germany, Sweden, the Netherlands, and the United States." *Research in Social Problems and Public Policy* 3:217–272.

Treas, Judith 1983 "Trickle-Down or Transfers? Postwar Determinants of Family Income Inequality." *American Sociological Review* 48:546–559.

U.S. Bureau of the Census 1989 *Statistical Abstract.* Washington D.C.: U.S. Government Printing Office.

Wilensky, Harold 1975 *The Welfare State and Equality.* Berkeley: University of California Press.

Williamson, John B., Linda Evans, and Lawrence Powell 1982 *The Politics of Aging.* Springfield, Ill.: Charles C. Thomas.

Wolff, Nancy 1987 *Income Redistribution and the Social Security Program.* Ann Arbor: University of Michigan Press.

– FRED C. PAMPEL

SOCIAL STRATIFICATION

In all complex societies, the total stock of valued resources is distributed unequally, with the most privileged individuals or families enjoying a disproportionate share of property, power, or prestige. Although it might be possible to construct an exhaustive rank-ordering of individuals based on their control over these resources, most scholars attempt to identify a set of classes or strata that reflect the major cleavages in the population. The task of stratification research is to describe the structure of these social groupings and to specify the processes by which they are generated and maintained. The following types of questions are central to the field:

1. What are the major forms of stratification in human history? Is stratification an inevitable feature of human life?
2. Are there well-defined classes or status groupings in advanced industrial societies? If so, what are the principal features of these groupings?
3. What types of social processes and institutions serve to maintain or alter ascriptive forms of stratification (e.g., racial stratification, gender stratification)? Are these ascriptive processes weakening with the transition to advanced industrialism?
4. How frequently do individuals move across class, status, or occupational boundaries? Is the process of occupational attainment governed by ascriptive traits (e.g., family background) or by achieved characteristics (e.g., education)?

There is a long tradition of commentary on questions of this kind. For the greater part of history, the stratification regime was regarded as an immutable feature of society, and the implicit objective of commentators was to explain or justify the existing order in terms of religious or quasi-religious doctrines (see Bottomore 1965). It was only with the Enlightenment that a "rhetoric of equality" emerged in opposition to the legal and political advantages accorded to privileged status groupings. After the latter privileges were weakened in the nineteenth century, this egalitarian ideal was redirected against emerging forms of economic stratification; the result was the rise of socialist and Marxist interpretations of human history. It is out of this conflict between egalitarian values and the brute facts of economic inequality that modern theories of stratification emerged.

This is not to imply that the field of stratification has been dominated by a simple Marxist model. It would be no exaggeration, in fact, to say that much of modern stratification theory has been formulated in *reaction* to Marxist and neo-Marxist theories. Indeed, the term *stratification* is often seen as anti-Marxist, since it places emphasis on the purely hierarchical ranking of classes rather than the exploitative relations between them.

Moreover, modern scholars have typically attempted to adopt a value-free orientation, with their research focusing on description and analysis rather than "praxis" in its purest form.

Forms of Stratification

The starting point for any theory of stratification is the purely descriptive task of classification. It is conventional among contemporary theorists to distinguish between modern *class systems* and the *estates* or *castes* found in advanced agrarian societies (e.g., Mayer and Buckley 1970). As shown in table 1, this conventional typology can be elaborated by introducing additional categories for tribal systems (panel A), slave systems (panel B), and state socialist societies (panel C). It should be kept in mind that these various forms of stratification are best seen as ideal types rather than descriptions of existing societies. Indeed, the stratification systems of advanced societies are complex and multidimensional, if only because their past institutional forms tend to persist despite the emergence of new forms. It follows that most systems of stratification are a complex mixture of elements from several of the ideal-typical forms specified in Table 1 (for related topologies, see Wright 1985; Runciman 1974).

The first panel in this table lists some of the basic principles underlying tribal systems of stratification (see line Al). It should be emphasized that the most extreme forms of inequality were eliminated from these societies through gift exchanges and other redistributive practices (Lenski 1966, pp. 102–112). In fact, some of the early students of tribal societies spoke of a "primitive communism," since the means of production (i.e., land) were communally owned, and other forms of property were distributed evenly among tribal members. This is not to say, of course, that a *perfect* equality prevailed. After all, some of the more powerful medicine men ("shamans") lived off the surplus production of others, and the tribal chief often exerted considerable influence on the political decisions of the day. The important point, however, is that these residual forms of power and privilege could not be inherited; it was only by demonstrating superior abilities in hunting, magic, or leadership that tribal members could secure political office or acquire prestige. It might be said, then, that tribal systems rested on meritocratic principles of a most basic kind.

With the emergence of agrarian forms of production, the economic surplus became large enough to support more complex systems of stratification. The Indian caste system, for example, is based on an elaborate and intricate classification of hereditary groupings. As indicated in Table 1, these groupings can be ranked on a continuum of ethnic purity, with the highest positions in the system reserved for castes that prohibit activities or behaviors that are seen as "polluting" (e.g., eating meat, scavenging). Although a caste system of this kind is often taken to be the limiting case of stratification, it should be noted that feudal systems were also based on a rigid system of quasi-hereditary groups. The distinctive feature of feudalism was the institution of personal bondage; that is, medieval serfs were obliged to live on a manor and pay rents of various kinds (e.g., "corvée labor"), since the feudal lord held the legal rights to their labor power (see line B3). If a serf fled to the city, this was considered a form of theft; the serf was stealing

TABLE 1

THE PRINCIPAL ASSETS, MAJOR STRATA, AND JUSTIFYING IDEOLOGIES FOR SIX FORMS OF SOCIAL STRATIFICATION

System	Principal Assets	Major Strata	Justifying Ideology
A. *Hunting and Gathering Society*			
1. Tribal System	Hunting Skills and Magic	Chiefs, Shamans, and Followers	Meritocratic Selection
B. *Horticultural and Agrarian Society*			
2. Feudal System	Land and Labor Power	Kings, Lords, and Serfs	Tradition and Religious Doctrine
3. Slave System	Human Property	Owners and Slaves	Natural and Social Inferiority
4. Caste System	Ethnic Purity	Castes	Tradition and Religious Doctrine
C. *Industrial Society*			
5. Class System	Means of Production	Capitalists and Workers	Classical Liberalism
6. State Socialism	Organizational and Party Assets	Managers and Managed	Marxism and Leninism

that portion of his labor power owned by his lord (Wright 1985, p. 78). It must be stressed, however, that the serfs of feudal society typically retained some degree of control over their labor power. If this control is completely stripped away, then workers become nothing more than *human* property, and the distinction between feudalism and slavery disappears (see line B4).

The most striking development of the modern era has been the rise of egalitarian ideologies. This can be seen, for example, in the revolutions of the eighteenth and nineteenth centuries, where the ideals of the Enlightenment were directed against the privileges of rank and the political power of the aristocracy. In the end, these struggles eliminated the last residues of feudal privilege, but they also made possible the emergence of new forms of inequality and stratification. It is usually argued that a *class system* developed in the early-industrial period, with the major inequalities in this system defined in economic terms and legitimated as the natural outcome of individual competition (i.e., "classical liberalism"). There is, however, considerable controversy over the contours and boundaries of these economic classes. As indicated in line C5, a simple Marxist model might focus on the cleavage between capitalists and workers, whereas other models represent the class structure as a continuous graduation of "monetary wealth and income" (Mayer and Buckley 1970, p. 15).

Only by demonstrating superior abilities in hunting, magic, or leadership could tribal members secure political office or acquire prestige.

Whatever the relative merits of these models might be, the Marxist one became the ideology for the socialist revolutions of the nineteenth and twentieth centuries. The intellectual heritage of these revolutions can again be traced to the Enlightenment; however, a new "rhetoric of equality" was fashioned for the times, with the attack now focusing on the economic power of the capitalist class rather than the privileges of the aristocracy. The available evidence from Eastern Europe and elsewhere suggests that this egalitarian rhetoric was only partially realized (see, e.g., Lenski 1992). To be sure, private property was largely eliminated in socialist societies, yet various commentators have suggested that new lines of stratification crystallized in the "secondary stage" of socialist development (Kelley 1981; Giddens 1973). It is often claimed, for instance, that an intellectual or bureaucratic elite emerged under state socialism to take the place of the old capitalist class (see, e.g., Gouldner 1979; Djilas 1965). Of course, this elite cannot formally own the means of production, yet it does control the production of goods and the allocation of valued resources. There is an emerging consensus, moreover, that the power of intellectuals has been *further* strengthened with the antisocialist revolutions in Eastern Europe (e.g., Szelényi 1992). The obvious irony of this development is that the intellectual elite may ultimately be sowing the seeds of its own demise by reconstituting the old capitalist class.

Sources of Stratification

The foregoing sketch makes it clear that a wide range of stratification systems has emerged over the course of human history. The question that naturally arises, then, is whether some form of stratification is an inevitable feature of human societies. In addressing this question, it is useful to begin with the functionalist approach (Davis and Moore 1945), since this is the best-known attempt to understand "the universal necessity which calls forth stratification in any system" (p. 242; also, see Davis 1953; Moore 1963a; 1963b). The starting point for Davis and Moore (1945) is the premise that all societies must devise some means to motivate the best workers to fill the most important and difficult occupations. This "motivational problem" might be addressed in a variety of ways, but perhaps the simplest solution is to construct a hierarchy of rewards (e.g., prestige, property, power) that privileges the incumbents of functionally significant positions. As noted by Davis and Moore (1945, p. 243), this amounts to setting up a system of institutionalized inequality (i.e., a "stratification system"), with the occupational structure serving as a conduit through which unequal rewards and perquisites are disbursed. The stratification system may be seen, therefore, as an "unconsciously evolved device by which societies insure that the important positions are conscientiously filled by the most qualified persons" (Davis and Moore 1945, p. 243). Under the Davis-Moore formulation, the only empirical claim is that *some form* of inequality is needed to allocate labor efficiently; the authors are silent, however, when it comes to specifying *how much* inequality is sufficient for this purpose. It is well to bear in mind that the extreme forms of stratification found in existing societies may exceed the "minimum . . . necessary to maintain a complex division of labor" (Wrong 1959, p. 774).

The Davis-Moore hypothesis has come under considerable criticism from several quarters (see Huaco 1966 for an early review). The prevailing view, at least among the postwar commentators, is that the original hypothesis cannot adequately account for inequalities in "stabilized societies where statuses are ascribed" (Wesolowski 1962, p. 31; Tumin 1953). Indeed, whenever the vacancies in the occupational structure are allocated on *purely* hereditary grounds, the stratification system is no longer ensuring that the most important positions are "conscientiously filled by the most qualified persons" (Davis and Moore 1945, p. 243). What must be recognized, however, is that a purely hereditary system is rarely achieved in practice; in fact, even in the most rigid caste societies, the most talented and qualified individuals may have some opportunities for upward mobility. Under the Davis-Moore formulation (1945), this slow trickle of mobility is regarded as essential to the functioning of the social system, so much so that elaborate systems of inequality have been devised to ensure that the trickle continues (see Davis 1948, pp. 369–370, for additional and related comments). This suggests, then, that the Davis-Moore hypothesis might be used to explain inequalities in societies with relatively rigid mobility regimes. However, when opportunities for mobility are completely closed off, most commentators would concede that the original hypothesis becomes somewhat less credible.

Whereas the early debates addressed conceptual issues of this kind, the focus ultimately shifted to constructing "critical tests" of the Davis-Moore hypothesis. This research effort continued apace throughout the 1970s, with some commentators reporting evidence consistent with functionalist theory (e.g., Cullen and Novick 1979), and others being somewhat less sympathetic in their assessments (e.g., Broom and Cushing 1977). Although the following decade was a period of relative quiescence, the debate over functionalism resurfaced when Lenski (1992) suggested that "many of the internal, systemic problems of Marxist societies were the result of inadequate motivational arrangements" (p. 6). This analysis focused on the unintended consequences of the socialist "experiments in destratification" (Lenski 1978); that is, Lenski argued that the socialist commitment to wage leveling made it difficult to recruit and motivate highly skilled workers, while the "visible hand" of the socialist economy could never be calibrated to mimic the natural incentive of capitalist profit-taking. These results led Lenski to conclude that "successful incentive systems involve . . . motivating the best qualified people to seek the most important positions" (p. 11). It remains to be seen whether this interpretation will generate a new round of functionalist theorizing and debate.

The Structure of Modern Stratification

The recent history of stratification theory is in large part a history of debates about the contours of class, status, and prestige hierarchies in advanced industrial societies. These debates have been waged on a wide variety of fronts; however, for the present essay, it will suffice to focus on three distinct schools of thought (see Wright 1979, pp. 3–18, for a comprehensive review). The various debates within these schools might appear to be nothing more than academic infighting, but in fact they have been regarded by many postwar European intellectuals as a "necessary prelude to the conduct of political strategy" (Parkin 1979, p. 16). This form of political strategizing plays an especially prominent role within Marxist and neo-Marxist circles; for instance, a good deal of energy has been devoted to drawing the correct dividing line between the working class and the bourgeoisie, since the task of identifying the oppressed class is seen as a prerequisite to devising a political strategy that might appeal to it. It goes without saying that political and scholarly goals are often conflated in such mapmaking efforts; and, consequently, the assorted debates in this subfield are infused with more than the usual amount of normative excitement.

MARXISTS AND NEO-MARXISTS. The debates within the Marxist and neo-Marxist camps have been especially contentious, not only because of the foregoing political motivations, but also because the discussion of class within *Capital* (Marx [1894] 1972) is too fragmentary and unsystematic to adjudicate between various competing interpretations. At the end of the third volume of *Capital,* we find the now-famous fragment on "the classes" (Marx [1894] 1972, pp. 862–863), but this discussion breaks off at just that point where Marx appeared ready to advance a formal definition of the term. It is clear, nonetheless, that his abstract model of capitalism was resolutely dichotomous, with the conflict between capitalists and workers constituting the driving force behind further social development. This simple two-class model should be viewed as an ideal type designed to capture the "developmental tendencies" of capitalism; indeed, whenever Marx carried out concrete analyses of *existing* capitalist systems, he acknowledged that the class structure was complicated by the persistence of transitional classes (i.e., landowners), quasi-class groupings (e.g., peasants), and class fragments (e.g., the lumpen-proletariat). It was only with the progressive maturation of capitalism that Marx expected these complications to disappear as the "centrifugal forces of class struggle and crisis flung all *dritte Personen* to one camp or the other" (Parkin 1979, p. 16).

The recent history of modern capitalism suggests that the class structure has not evolved in such a precise and tidy fashion. To be sure, the available evidence makes it clear that the old middle class of artisans and shopkeepers has declined in relative size (Gagliani 1981; cf.

Steinmetz and Wright 1989), yet a "new middle class" of managers, professionals, and nonmanual workers has expanded to occupy the newly vacated space. The last fifty years of neo-Marxist theorizing might be seen as an "intellectual fallout" from this development, with some commentators seeking to minimize its implications, and others putting forward a revised mapping of the class structure that accommodates the new middle class in explicit terms. Within the former camp, the principal tendency is to claim that the lower sectors of the new middle class are in the process of being proletarianized, since "capital subjects [nonmanual labor] . . . to the forms of rationalization characteristic of the capitalist mode of production" (Braverman 1974, p. 408). This line of reasoning suggests that the working class may gradually expand in relative size and thereby regain its earlier power.

At the other end of the continuum, Poulantzas (1974) has argued that most members of the new intermediate stratum fall *outside* the working class proper, since they are engaged in "unproductive labor" of various kinds. This approach may have the merit of keeping the working class conceptually pure, but some commentators have noted that it also reduces the size of this class to trivial proportions. The latter result has motivated contemporary scholars to develop class models that fall somewhere between the extremes advocated by Braverman (1974) and Poulantzas (1974). For example, the neo-Marxist model proposed by Wright (1978) generates an American working class that is acceptably large (i.e., approximately 46 percent of the labor force), yet the class mappings in this model still pay tribute to the various cleavages and divisions among workers who sell their labor power (also, see Wright et al. 1982). In fact, the model places professionals in a *distinct* "semi-autonomous class" by virtue of their control over the work process, while upper-level supervisors are located in a "managerial class" by virtue of their authority over workers (Wright 1978; also, see Wright 1985; Westergaard and Resler 1975). It should be noted that the dividing lines proposed in these neo-Marxist class models often rest on concepts (e.g., authority relations) that were once purely the province of "bourgeois sociology," This development led Parkin (1979) to conclude that "inside every neo-Marxist there seems to be a Weberian struggling to get out" (p. 25).

WEBERIANS AND NEO-WEBERIANS: The rise of the "new middle class" is less problematic for scholars working within a Weberian framework. Indeed, the class model advanced by Weber suggests a *multiplicity* of class cleavages, because it equates the economic class of workers with their "market situation" (Weber [1922] 1968, pp. 926-940). This model implies that wealthy property-owners are in a privileged class; after all, members of this class can outbid workers for valued goods in the commodity market, and they can also convert their wealth to capital and thereby monopolize entrepreneurial opportunities. However, Weber emphasized that skilled workers are also privileged under modern capitalism, since their services are in high demand on the labor market. The end result, then, is a new middle class of skilled workers that intervenes between the "positively privileged" capitalist class and the "negatively privileged" mass of unskilled laborers (Weber [1922] 1968, pp. 927-928). At the same time, the stratification system is further complicated by the existence of *status groupings,* which Weber saw as forms of social affiliation that often competed with class-based forms of organization. Although an economic class is merely an aggregate of individuals in a similar market situation, a status grouping is defined as a community of individuals who share a "style of life" and interact as status equals (e.g., the nobility, an ethnic caste, etc.). Under some circumstances, the boundaries of a status grouping are determined by purely economic criteria, yet Weber notes that "status honor need not necessarily be linked with a class situation" (Weber [1922] 1968, p. 932). The *nouveaux riches,* for instance, are never immediately accepted into "high society," even when their wealth clearly places them in the uppermost economic class (Weber [1922] 1968, pp. 936–937).

The nouveaux riches *are never immediately accepted into "high society," even when their wealth clearly places them in the uppermost economic class.*

The Weberian approach has been elaborated and extended by sociologists seeking to understand the "American form" of stratification. During the decades following World War II, American sociologists typically dismissed the Marxist model of class as overly simplistic and one-dimensional, whereas they celebrated the Weberian model as properly distinguishing between the numerous variables that Marx had conflated in his definition of class (see, e.g., Barber 1968). In the most extreme versions of this approach, the dimensions identified by Weber were disaggregated into a multiplicity of stratification variables (e.g., income, education, ethnicity), and the correlations between these variables were then shown to be weak enough to generate various forms of "status inconsistency" (e.g., a poorly educated millionaire). The resulting picture suggested a "pluralistic model" of stratification; that is, the class system was represented as intrinsically multidimensional, with a host of crosscutting affiliations producing a complex patchwork of internal class cleavages. Although one well-known critic has remarked that the multidimensionalists provided a "sociological portrait of America as drawn by Norman Rockwell" (Parkin 1979, p. 604), it must be kept in mind that some of these theorists also emphasized the seamy side of pluralism. In fact, Lenski (1954) and others (e.g., Lipset 1959) have argued that the modern stratification system might be seen as a breeding ground for personal stress and political radicalism, since individuals with contradictory statuses may feel relatively deprived and thus support "movements designed to alter the political *status quo*" (Lenski 1966, p. 88). This interest in the consequences of status inconsistency died out in the early 1970s under the force of negative and inconclusive findings (e.g., Jackson and Curtis 1972). However, among recent researchers and commentators, there appears to be a resurgence of interest in issues of status disparity and relative deprivation. It is notable that American scholars have *not* been the driving force behind this "second wave" of multidimensional theorizing; to be sure, some Americans have participated in the revival (e.g., Baron 1992), but most of the new theorizing is European in origin (e.g., Beck 1987) and focuses on the generic properties of all "post-modern" stratification systems.

It would be a mistake, of course, to regard these multidimensionalists as the *only* intellectual descendants of Weber. In fact, some neo-Weberians contend that identifiable classes can develop under modern capitalism, despite the fragmenting effects of crosscutting affiliations and cleavages (e.g., Goldthorpe 1980). The prevailing view within this revisionist camp is that various forms of *social closure* and *exclusion* play an important role in generating social classes with a shared culture and style of life (e.g., Giddens 1973; Breiger 1981). In modern industrial societies, there are no legal sanctions that prevent labor from freely flowing across class boundaries, but there are various social, cultural, and institutional mechanisms that effectively "channel" children into occupations that are similar to those of their parents. These exclusionary mechanisms produce a class structure with a relatively stable and permanent membership; as a result, a set of distinctive class cultures may emerge, and this in turn may generate a minimal level of class awareness and identification. In most countries, one would expect to see a fundamental "class divide" between manual and nonmanual labor, since the strongest barriers to mobility are found precisely at this boundary. Although barriers of this kind are not the only source of class structuration (e.g., see Giddens 1973, pp. 107-112), they may well contribute to the formation of identifiable "collar classes" under modern industrialism.

GRADATIONAL MODELS. The distinction between categorical and gradational models of stratification has long been important in American sociology. Whereas neo-Marxists seek to describe the stratification system with a small number of discrete categories (i.e., "classes"), gradational theorists map the contours of modern stratification in terms of *ordered levels* (see Ossowski 1963). This distinction played an especially prominent role in the community studies completed after World War II; for instance, Lenski (1952) emphasized that the residents of a New England mill town were stratified into "graded prestige levels" rather than "discrete social classes," while Landecker (1960) attempted to locate the "natural breaks" and cleavages within the status hierarchy of Detroit. As the discipline matured, the focus shifted away from critical tests of this kind, and the two approaches developed into distinct research traditions with their own methods of inquiry. It is commonly argued that American sociologists have an "elective affinity" for gradational models; in fact, when Ossowski (1963) surveyed the history of stratification research, he concluded that the "American class structure is [typically] interpreted . . . in terms of a scheme of gradation" (p. 102).

The gradational approach can be operationalized by measuring the income, prestige, or status of individuals. While there is some sociological precedent for treating income as an indicator of class distinctions (e.g., Mayer and Buckley 1970, p. 15), most sociologists seem content with a disciplinary division of labor that leaves the income distribution to economists. This is perhaps unfortunate; after all, if one is indeed intent on assessing the "market situation" of workers, there is much to recommend a direct measurement of their income and wealth. Despite the merits of this method, it never enjoyed much popularity: the preferred approach is to define classes as "groups of persons who are members of effective kinship units which, as units, are approximately equally valued" (Parsons 1954, p. 77). The latter method was operationalized in the postwar community studies (e.g., Warner 1949) by constructing broadly-defined categories of reputational equals (i.e., "upper-upper class," "upper-middle class," etc.). However, when the disciplinary focus shifted to national surveys, the measure of choice soon became interval-level scales constructed from detailed occupational codes (see, e.g., Duncan 1961; Siegel 1971; Treiman 1977). These scales now serve as standard measures of "class background" in sociological research of all kinds.

Ascriptive Forms of Stratification

The long-standing tendency within both the Marxist and non-Marxist schools has been to treat ethnicity, race, and gender as purely "secondary forces" in history.

There was always considerable disagreement within these schools over the appropriate way to define social classes; nevertheless, despite these various conflicts and disputes, the shared presumption was that modern society is essentially a *class system.* In almost all formulations, the nuclear family was seen as the elemental unit of stratification, with the *occupation* or *employment status* of the family head (i.e., the husband) defining the class position of all its members. This approach had the effect of reducing various types of intraclass cleavages (e.g., ethnic cleavages, gender-based cleavages) to the status of "complicating factors" or historically contingent developments (see Parkin 1979, pp. 29-31, for an incisive review). To be sure, it was typically recognized that the competing bonds of race or ethnicity were still salient for some individuals, yet these ties were viewed as vestiges of traditional loyalties that would ultimately wither away under the rationalizing influence of capitalism or industrialism. It was often argued that this decline in purely ascriptive forces proceeded from the functional requirements of modern industrial societies (e.g., Levy 1966).

This so-called "conventional model" of stratification has come under criticism on both empirical and theoretical grounds. The first step in the gradual breakdown of this model was the fashioning of a multidimensional approach to stratification systems (see earlier section on the Structure of Modern Stratification). Whereas the conventional model gave theoretical and conceptual priority to the economic dimension of stratification, the multidimensionalists emphasized that the status of individuals reflected a wider array of ascriptive and achieved outcomes (e.g., race, gender, education, occupation). This approach had the obvious effect, then, of forcing sociologists to attend more closely to ascriptive sources of status and solidarity. The breakdown of the conventional model was further accelerated by the accumulating evidence in the 1970s that racial, ethnic, and gender-based conflicts were emerging in intensified form. Far from withering away under the force of industrialism, the bonds of ethnicity appeared to be alive and well; the consensus view was that "there had been a . . . sudden increase in tendencies by people in many countries and many circumstances to insist on the significance of their group distinctiveness" (Glazer and Moynihan 1975, p. 3). At the same time, the 1970s witnessed a concurrent growth in various types of feminist movements, which had the effect of politicizing the *gender* of individuals. These developments made it manifestly clear that ascriptive forms of solidarity continue to be salient in modern industrial societies.

The radical response to this evidence was to proclaim that the ascriptive factors of race, ethnicity, or gender are the driving forces behind further social development. In their latest formulation, Glazer and Moynihan (1975) conclude that "property relations [formerly] obscured ethnic ones" (p. 16), but now it is "property that begins to seem derivative, and ethnicity that seems to become a more fundamental source of stratification" (p. 17). There is, of course, an analogous position within the field of gender stratification; the "radical wing" within feminist circles has long argued for the "primacy of men's dominance over women as the cornerstone on which all other oppression (class, age, race) rests" (Hartmann 1981, p. 12; Firestone 1972). It should be noted, however, that the latter formulations beg the question of timing; after all, if the forces of ethnicity or gender are truly primordial, it is natural to ask why they only began expressing themselves with relative vigor in recent decades. In addressing this issue, Bell (1975) has suggested that a trade-off exists between class-based and ethnic forms of solidarity, with the latter strengthening as the former weaken. With the institutionalization of industrial conflict in modern societies (i.e., the rise of "trade unionism"), Bell argues that class-based affiliations gradually lost their *moral* or *affective* content; it was ethnic groups, then, that filled the gap by providing individuals with a new sense of identification and commitment (see Olzak 1983 for a comprehensive review of competing theories). It might be added that for some individuals it was gender politics that apparently filled the "moral vacuum" (Parkin 1979, p. 34) brought about by the weakening of class-based ties.

It may be misleading, of course, to treat the competition between ascriptive and class-based forces as a sociological horse race in which one, and only one, of these two principles can ultimately win out. In a pluralist society of the American kind, workers can *choose* an identity appropriate to the situational context; a modern-day individual might behave as "an industrial worker in the morning, a black in the afternoon, and an American in the evening" (Parkin 1979, p. 34). Although this "situational model" of status has not been widely adopted in contemporary research, there is nonetheless an emerging tendency among scholars to take into account the multiple affiliations of individuals. The preferred approach, especially among feminist theorists, is to assume that the major status groupings in contemporary societies are defined by the *intersection* of ethnic, gender, or class-based affiliations (e.g., black working-class women, white middle-class men, etc.). The theoretical framework motivating this approach is not always well-articulated, but the implicit claim seems to be that these subgroupings shape the "life chances and experiences" of individuals (Ransford and Miller 1983, p. 46) and define the social settings in which subcultures typically emerge (also, see Gordon 1978; Baltzell 1964). The obvious effect of this approach is to invert the traditional post-Weberian perspective on status groupings; indeed, whereas orthodox multidimensionalists described the stress experienced by individuals in inconsistent statuses (e.g., poorly-educated doctors), these new multidimensionalists emphasize the shared cultures generated within commonly encountered status sets (e.g., black working-class women).

The popularity of this revised form of multidimensionalism reflects, at least in part, a growing dissatisfaction with classical sociological theories that take the nuclear family to be the elementary unit of stratification (e.g., Parsons 1954). As was noted earlier, the "conventional model" of class represents the stratification system as a graded hierarchy of households, with the socioeconomic standing of all household members (e.g., wives) determined by the occupation or employment status of the family head. While most scholars agree that this model has been serviceable in describing past stratification systems, there is some concern that it no longer adequately represents the life chances and class situation of women in advanced industrial societies. Among the various positions that have emerged in this debate, the following ones have achieved some prominence:

1. According to some scholars, the conventional class system is receding in significance, and the *individual* is emerging as the new "elementary unit" of stratification. This revolution in class structure and identification is typically linked to the breakdown of the nuclear family, the growth of an autonomous female labor force, and the rise of individualist values (e.g., Szelányi 1988; also, see Davis and Robinson 1988).
2. At the other end of the continuum, Britten and Heath (1983) continue to see the nuclear family as the basic unit of stratification, yet they modify the conventional model by taking into account the work situation of *both* husbands and wives. This approach makes it possible to identify and describe various types of "cross-class families" in which the husband and wife work in different class situations.
3. The conventional model has also been defended in its original form (e.g., Goldthorpe 1983). Although this defense has been waged on a variety of fronts, the main point emphasized by Goldthorpe (1983) and others (e.g., Giddens 1973, p. 288) is that the male head still makes the *principal* commitment to paid employment, whereas the female spouse typically enters the labor force in "an intermittent and limited" fashion (Goldthrope 1983, p. 481). The implication, therefore, is that ongoing changes in female labor force participation have not undermined the conventional model to the extent that some critics have supposed.

Within American sociology, the first of these three positions has become the *de facto* standard; it is now common practice to carry out virtually all types of stratification analysis with separate male and female subsamples. The analytic assumptions underlying these analyses are not typically spelled out, but it would be difficult indeed to reconcile this form of subsampling with a conventional class model in its original or modified form.

Generating Stratification

The language of stratification research makes a sharp distinction between the structure of *socioeconomic inequality* (i.e., the "class structure") and the structure of *opportunities* by which individuals are allocated into differential outcomes (i.e., the "opportunity structure"). Whereas most Americans are willing to tolerate sizable inequalities in the distribution of resources, they typically insist that individuals from all backgrounds should have an equal opportunity to secure these resources. It might be said, then, that our primary interest rests in "running the race fairly" rather than equalizing the rewards distributed at the finish line (see, e.g., Hochschild 1981; Kluegel and Smith 1986). Whatever the wisdom of this logic might be, sociologists have long sought to explore its factual underpinnings; there is a substantial body of research that seeks to measure the objective opportunities for mobility against our shared expectations for a "fair race." This research agenda might be operationalized in various ways; the standard starting point, however, is to construct a mobility table that cross-classifies the occupational origins and destinations of individuals. Although most of the current research has focused on parent-child comparisons ("intergenerational mobility"), there is also a parallel tradition of work examining the contours of mobility within the life course of individuals ("intragenerational mobility"). These various types of mobility tables have served as the "anvil for sociological craftwork since the days when blacksmiths outnumbered social scientists" (Breiger 1981, p. 604).

The primary interests of most Americans rests in "running the race fairly" rather than equalizing the rewards distributed at the finish line.

It is no easy task to analyze tables of this kind. As is often the case, substantive issues turn on technical matters; the history of mobility research is marked by methodological signposts as much as substantive ones. The driving force behind these methodological developments has been the longstanding attempt to distinguish between *structural* and *circulation* mobility. This conceptual distinction derives, of course, from the well-known fact that social mobility is generated by structural shifts in the shape of the class structure as well as

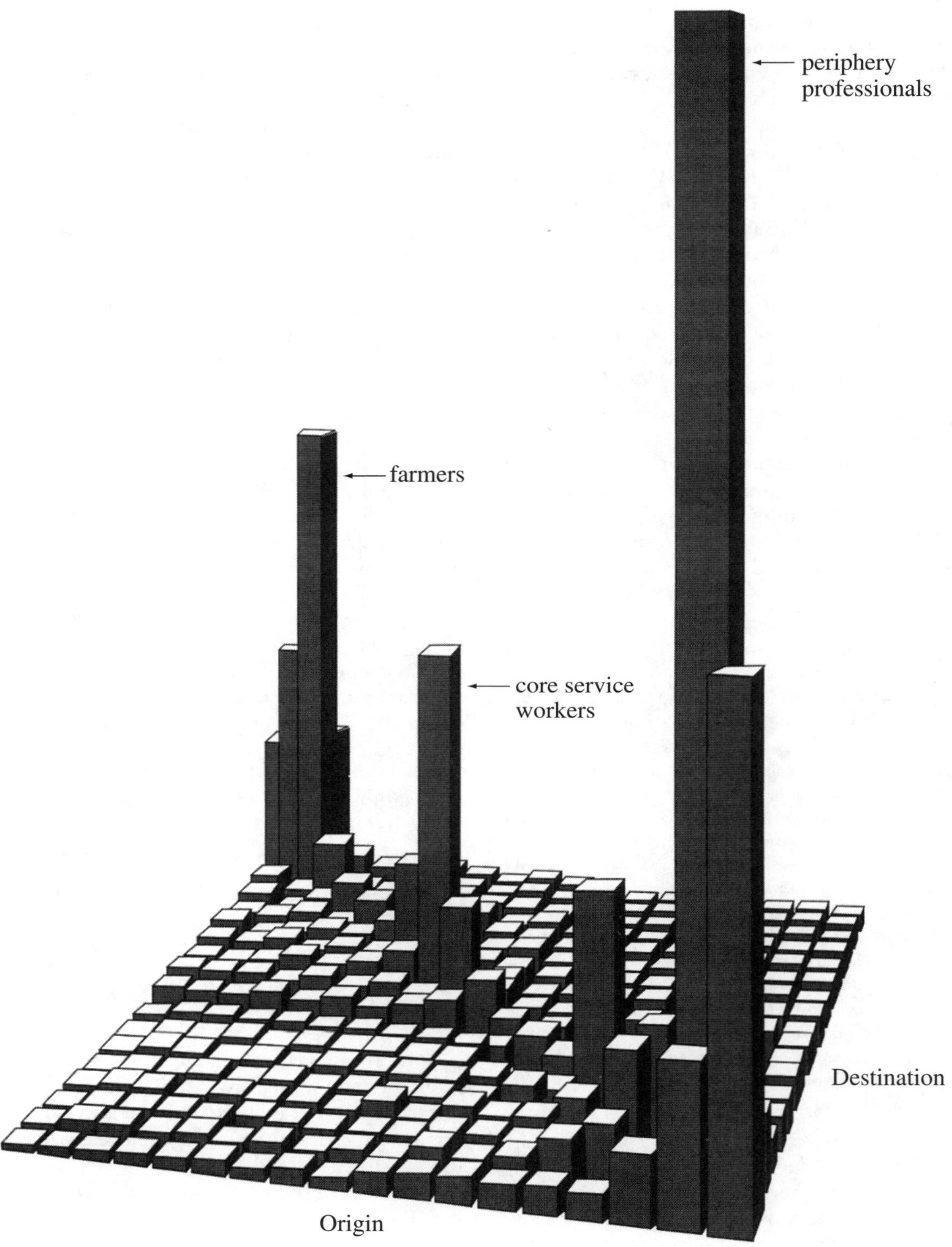

Figure 1. Densities of Mobility and Immobility for an 18 × 18 Intragenerational Table.

underlying patterns of exchange between classes (see Duncan 1966 for details and qualifications). The former component is often regarded as a nuisance factor, whereas the latter pertains to the openness of the mobility regime and the contours of class-based differences in life chances. While the verbal distinction between structural and circulation mobility is easy to maintain, it turns out to be difficult to represent this distinction in formal models of the mobility regime. It was only with the emergence of log-linear modeling in the early 1970s that the fundamental problem of "structurally induced" mobility was finally solved (see, e.g., Goodman 1972; Hauser 1978; Hout 1983; Sobel, Hout, and Duncan 1985).

The descriptive power of this approach is best demonstrated by turning directly to an illustrative analysis based on a major survey of stratification outcomes and processes (see Featherman and Hauser 1978). The densities plotted in Figure 1 refer to patterns of career mobility over the period between the point of first entry into the labor force ("first occupation") and the time when the survey was administered ("current occupation"). As indicated in the stub to this figure, the rows and columns of the matrix index the origin and destination occupations, and the vertical dimension maps the estimated densities of career persistence and mobility for our sample of American males (see Stier and Grusky 1990 for further details). The height of the bars refers to the relative likelihood of persistence or mobility after the structural forces of occupational supply and demand have been purged from the data. The topography of this simple figure suggests the following five conclusions:

1. The towering peaks on the main diagonal testify to the strength of occupational persistence within the life course. The farming peak, for example, indicates that workers originating as farmers are 69.7 times more likely to remain in that occupation than to move to the top of the class structure (Stier and Grusky 1990, p. 747).
2. The clustering on the main diagonal follows a W-shaped pattern. Although the tallest peaks are found at the two extremes of the hierarchy, a set of secondary peaks emerge in the center of the class structure. This result indicates that *some* sectors of the middle class (i.e., service sectors) are relatively successful in retaining their incumbents.
3. The strength of the manual-nonmanual divide reveals itself in a low-lying ridge marking out the northwest and southeast quadrants. At the top of each ridge, the mobility data form a broad plateau; the height of these plateaus speak to the "holding power" of the manual and nonmanual strata.
4. The distribution of destination points for long-distance movers is surprisingly uniform. The valleys in the northeast and southwest quadrants are flat and uncontoured; there is no evidence, then, of a "distance gradient" that channels long-distance movers into the closest occupations.
5. The design matrix is symmetric around the main diagonal. The implication is that patterns of occupational inflow and outflow are identical once the structural forces of supply and demand are controlled (see Hauser 1981).

Taken as a whole, the figure suggests a broad valley rising into a pair of low-lying plains, with the plains then rising into a jagged mountain ridge that cuts across the valley (see Featherman and Hauser 1978 for a similar description). While this overall picture can be generated under a wide range of log-linear specifications (Stier and Grusky 1990), it is always possible to devise competing models that yield somewhat different interpretations (see, e.g., MacDonald 1981). These differences have generated a continuing debate over the merits or shortcomings of particular types of log-linear models (e.g., Pöntinen 1982; Grusky and Hauser 1984; Kim 1987).

It should be emphasized that the preceding figure can only be used to characterize the structure of male career mobility in the early 1970s. Although the available evidence suggests a "family resemblance" in the basic topology of all mobility regimes, it is clear that systematic variations in the contours of mobility can also be found. The last decade of stratification research has been devoted, in large part, to documenting the structure of these differences across subpopulations defined by nation, region, gender, race, or time (e.g., Hout 1984; Grusky and Hauser 1984). The latter research effort has been complemented by a parallel stream of research focusing on the mediating variables (e.g., education) that account for the origin-by-destination association in a mobility table. It could well be argued that these two subfields are producing new findings "faster and more furiously . . . than any other [subfields] in sociology" (Hout 1984, p. 1379).

[See also Ethnicity; Income Distribution in the United States; Slavery and Involuntary Servitude.]

BIBLIOGRAPHY

Baltzell, Edward Digby 1964 *The Protestant Establishment.* New York: Random House.

Barber, Bernard 1968 "Social Stratification." In D. L. Sills, ed., *International Encyclopedia of the Social Sciences.* New York: Macmillan and Free Press.

Baron, James N. 1992 "Reflections on Recent Generations of Mobility Research." In David B. Grusky, ed., *Social Stratification: Class, Race, and Gender in Sociological Perspective.* Boulder, Colo.: Westview.

Beck, Ulrich 1987 "Beyond Status and Class: Will There be an Individualized Class Society?" In Volker Meja, Dieter Misgeld, and Nico Stehr, eds., *Modern German Sociology.* New York: Columbia University Press.

Bell, Daniel 1975 "Ethnicity and Social Change." In Nathan Glazer and Daniel P. Moynihan, eds., *Ethnicity: Theory and Experience.* Cambridge: Harvard University Press.

Bottomore, Thomas B. 1965 *Classes in Modern Society.* London: Allen and Unwin.

Braverman, Harry 1974 *Labor and Monopoly Capital.* New York: Monthly Review Press.

Breiger, Ronald L. 1981 "The Social Class Structure of Occupational Mobility." *American Journal of Sociology* 87:578–611.

Britten, Nicky, and Anthony Heath 1983 "Women, Men and Social Class." In Eva Gamarnikow, David H. J. Morgan, June Purvis, and Daphne E. Taylorson, eds., *Gender, Class and Work.* London: Heinemann.

Broom, Leonard, and Robert G. Cushing 1977 "A Modest Test of an Immodest Theory: The Functional Theory of Stratification." *American Sociological Review* 42 (1):157–169.

Cullen, John B., and Shelley M. Novick 1979 "The Davis-Moore Theory of Stratification: A Further Examination and Extension." *American Journal of Sociology* 84 (6):1424–1437.

Davis, Kingsley 1948 *Human Society.* New York: Macmillan.

——— 1953 "Reply." *American Sociological Review* 18:394–397.

Davis, Kingsley, and Wilbert E. Moore 1945 "Some Principles of Stratification." *American Sociological Review* 10:242–249.

Davis, Nancy J., and Robert V. Robinson 1988 "Class Identification of Men and Women in the 1970s and 1980s." *American Sociological Review* 53:103–112.

Djilas, Milovan 1965 *The New Class.* New York: Praeger.

Duncan, Otis Dudley 1961 "A Socioeconomic Index for All Occupations." In Albert J. Reiss, Jr., ed., *Occupations and Social Status.* New York: Free Press.

——— 1966 "Methodological Issues in the Analysis of Social Mobility." In Neil J. Smelser and Seymour M. Lipset, eds., *Social Structure and Mobility in Economic Development.* Chicago: Aldine.

Featherman, David L., and Robert M. Hauser 1978 *Opportunity and Change.* New York: Academic.

Firestone, Shulamith 1972 *The Dialectic of Sex.* New York: Bantam.

Gagliani, Giorgio 1981 "How Many Working Classes?" *American Journal of Sociology* 87:259–285.

Giddens, Anthony 1973 *The Class Structure of the Advanced Societies.* London: Hutchinson.

Glazer, Nathan, and Daniel P. Moynihan 1975 "Introduction." In Nathan Glazer and Daniel P. Moynihan, eds., *Ethnicity: Theory and Experience.* Cambridge: Harvard University Press.

Goldthorpe, John H. 1980 *Social Mobility and Class Structure in Modern Britain.* Oxford, England: Clarendon Press.

——— 1983 "Women and Class Analysis: In Defence of the Conventional View." *Sociology* 17: 465–488.

Goodman, Leo A. 1972 "Some Multiplicative Models for the Analysis of Cross-Classified Data." In *Proceedings of the Sixth Berkeley Symposium on Mathematical Statistics and Probability.* Berkeley: University of California Press.

Gordon, Milton M. 1978 *Human Nature, Class, and Ethnicity.* New York: Oxford University Press.

Gouldner, Alvin 1979 *The Future of Intellectuals and the Rise of the New Class.* New York: Seabury.

Grusky, David B., and Robert M. Hauser 1984 "Comparative Social Mobility Revisited: Models of Convergence and Divergence in 16 Countries." *American Sociological Review* 49:19–38.

Hartmann, Heidi 1981 "The Unhappy Marriage of Marxism and Feminism: Towards a More Progressive Union." In Lydia Sargent, ed., *Women and Revolution.* Boston: South End Press.

Hauser, Robert M. 1978 "A Structural Model of the Mobility Table." *Social Forces* 56: 919–953.

——— 1981 "Hope for the Mobility Ratio." *Social Forces* 60:572–584.

Hochschild, Jennifer L. 1981 *What's Fair? American Beliefs about Distributive Justice.* Cambridge: Harvard University Press.

Hout, Michael 1983 *Mobility Tables.* Beverly Hills: Sage.

——— 1984 "Status, Autonomy, and Training in Occupational Mobility." *American Journal of Sociology* 89:1379–1409.

Huaco, George A. 1966. "The Functionalist Theory of Stratification: Two Decades of Controversy." *Inquiry* 9:215–240.

Jackson, Elton F., and Richard F. Curtis 1972 "Effects of Vertical Mobility and Status Inconsistency: A Body of Negative Evidence." *American Sociological Review* 37:701–713.

Kelley, Jonathan 1981 *Revolution and the Rebirth of Inequality.* Berkeley: University of California Press.

Kim, Jae-On 1987 "Social Mobility, Status Inheritance, and Structural Constraints: Conceptual and Methodological Considerations." *Social Forces* 65:783–805.

Kluegel, James R., and Eliot R. Smith 1986 *Beliefs About Inequality: Americans' Views of What Is and What Ought to Be.* New York: Aldine.

Landecker, Werner S. 1960 "Class Boundaries." *American Sociological Review* 25:868–877.

Lenski, Gerhard E. 1952 "American Social Classes: Statistical Strata or Social Group?" *American Journal of Sociology* 58:139–144.

——— 1954 "Status Crystallization: A Non-vertical Dimension of Social Status." *American Sociological Review* 19:405–413.

——— 1966 *Power and Privilege.* New York: McGraw-Hill.

——— 1978 "Marxist Experiments in Destratification: An Appraisal." *Social Forces* 57:364–383.

——— 1992 "New Light on Old Issues: The Relevance of 'Really Existing Socialist Societies' for Stratification Theory." In David B. Grusky, ed., *Social Stratification: Class, Race, and Gender in Sociological Perspective,* Boulder, Colo.: Westview.

Levy, Marion, Jr. 1966 *Modernization and the Structure of Societies.* Princeton, N.J.: Princeton University Press.

Lipset, Seymour Martin 1959 *Political Man: The Social Bases of Politics.* Baltimore, Md.: Johns Hopkins University Press.

MacDonald, K. I. 1981 "On the Formulation of a Structural Model of the Mobility Table." *Social Forces* 60:557–571.

Marx, Karl (1894) 1972 *Capital,* 3 vols. London: Lawrence and Wishart.

Mayer, Kurt B., and Walter Buckley 1970 *Class and Society.* New York: Random House.

Moore, Wilbert E. 1963a "But Some Are More Equal Than Others." *American Sociological Review* 28:13–28.

——— 1963b "Rejoinder." *American Sociological Review* 28:27.

Olzak, Susan 1983 "Contemporary Ethnic Mobilization." *Annual Review of Sociology* 9:355–374.

Ossowski, Stanislaw 1963 *Class Structure in the Social Consciousness.* New York: Free Press.

Parkin, Frank 1979 *Marxism and Class Theory: A Bourgeois Critique.* New York: Columbia University Press.

Parsons, Talcott 1954 *Essays in Sociological Theory.* Glencoe, Ill.: Free Press.

Pöntinen, Seppo 1982 "Models and Social Mobility Research: A Comparison of Some Log-Linear Models of a Social Mobility Matrix." *Quality and Quantity* 16:91–107.

Poulantzas, Nicos 1974 *Classes in Contemporary Capitalism.* London: Verso.

Ransford, H. Edward, and Jon Miller 1983 "Race, Sex and Feminist Outlooks." *American Sociological Review* 48:46–59.

Runciman, Walter G. 1974 "Towards a Theory of Social Stratification." In Frank Parkin, ed., *The Social Analysis of Class Structure.* London: Tavistock.

Siegel, Paul M. 1971 *Prestige in the American Occupational Structure.* Unpublished Ph.D. dissertation, University of Chicago.

Sobel, Michael E., Michael Hout, and Otis D. Duncan 1985 "Exchange, Structure, and Symmetry in Occupational Mobility." *American Journal of Sociology* 91:359–372.

Steinmetz, George, and Erik O. Wright 1989 "The Fall and Rise of the Petty Bourgeoisie: Changing Patterns of Self-Employment in the Postwar United States." *American Journal of Sociology* 94:973–1018.

Stier, Haya, and David B. Grusky 1990 "An Overlapping Persistence Model of Career Mobility." *American Sociological Review* 55:736–756.

Szelényi, Ivan 1992 "Post-industrialism, Post-communism, and the New Class." In David B. Grusky, ed., *Social Stratification: Class, Race, and Gender in Sociological Perspective.* Boulder, Colo.: Westview.

Szelényi, Szonja 1988 "Economic Subsystems and the Occupational Structure," Unpublished paper, Dept. of Sociology, Stanford University.

Treiman, Donald J. 1977 *Occupational Prestige in Comparative Perspective.* New York: Academic.

Tumin, Melvin M. 1953 "Some Principles of Stratification: A Critical Analysis." *American Sociological Review* 18:378–394.

Warner, W. Lloyd 1949 *Social Class in America.* Chicago: Science Research Associates.

Weber, Max (1922) 1968 *Economy and Society.* Berkeley: University of California Press.

Wesolowski, Wlodzimierz 1962 "Some Notes on the Functional Theory of Stratification." *Polish Sociological Bulletin* 3–4:28–38.

Westergaard, John, and Henrietta Resler 1975 *Class in a Capitalist Society: A Study of Contemporary Britain.* London: Heinemann.

Wright, Erik O. 1978 *Class, Crisis, and the State.* London: New Left Books.

——— *Class Structure and Income Determination.* New York: Academic.

——— 1985 *Classes.* London: Verso.

Wright, Erik O., Cynthia Costello, David Hachen, and Joey Sprague 1982 "The American Class Structure." *American Sociological Review* 47:709–726.

Wrong, Dennis H. 1959 "The Functional Theory of Stratification: Some Neglected Considerations." *American Sociological Review* 24:772–782.

– DAVID B. GRUSKY
AZUMI ANN TAKATA

SPORTS

The emergence of sports as a major social institution is inextricably linked to general trends of modernization. The twentieth century especially has seen a progressive shift from informal, participant-oriented amateur sports to highly organized, spectator-oriented professional sports. The accompanying shifts from local or regional events to national and international events and from individual to team activities are part of the evolution of sports as big business.

Sporting institutions cannot be understood in isolation from the prevailing social structure. They are inseparable from historical context, technological development, and shifting ideologies. An essential ingredient for the emergence of big-time sports was the development of mass leisure. Although play and games have been a part of every known society (Huizinga 1955), the growth of leisure institutions as a segregated part of life available to the masses required several changes, including the move from rural to urban life, the separation of the workplace from the home, and shorter work schedules. A supportive value system was also essential. For example, not until the mid-nineteenth century did old Puritanical prohibitions on sports and other amusements begin to break down in North America. Expanding railroad networks and local transit systems played an indispensable role in popularizing spectator sports and in the creation of national leagues (Betts 1980).

By the beginning of the twentieth century the newspaper sports page had arrived.

A system of mass communications was also required for sporting events to become part of mass culture. In the second half of the nineteenth century, fans in Europe and the United States could get instantaneous reports on some events, particularly boxing and horse racing, through the expanding telegraph network, and they could read journalistic accounts in proliferating magazines and newspapers (Betts 1980). By the beginning of the twentieth century the newspaper sports page had arrived, some two decades later came radio, and by midcentury, television. The expansion of cable television in the latter part of the century brought its viewers 24-hour sports coverage. Satellites permit live transmission of televised sports events that reach audiences around the world. Comparative data on audiences for satellite-televised events show that major international sporting contests draw together more spectators than anything else (Lever 1983).

Sports promote connections, from the momentary bonding of two strangers at a game to the creation of a global village. Organized sports parallel the weave of government agencies in their structure: Small towns, even rural areas, are linked to each other and to the big cities for state and regional championships; major cities are knit together into national leagues; and nations that play the same sports are drawn into relationships with one another through continental and worldwide federations that stage international contests. Nationalistic feelings get fanned while, simultaneously, people are united into a global folk culture. The paradox of sport is that it bonds even as it divides. The same event can serve as an occasion for patriotic display while easing diplomatic relations (Lever 1983).

International sports have succeeded as a basis for global community by providing a common frame of reference and rules that transcend cultural, political, and language barriers. Yet the same sport can be played differently in different places. For example, in Japan baseball games can end in a tie and the emphasis is on team rather than individual achievement. Sports mirror each society as they reflect, while reinforcing, social and cultural values. For this reason sports are ideal for both comparative and historical study.

Across time and place, sports promoters—whether communist or capitalist, private or public management, or mass media executives—have told fans that they can properly assume a victory as their own. Disseminating propaganda, building solidarity, and making profits by selling tickets, media rights, and advertising space are the primary rewards for the promoters. Identification of fans with athletes—whether in terms of a common school, city, nation, race, or religion—and the concomitant sense of collective identity and pride are the primary rewards for the spectators (Roberts 1976). As objects of conversation, publicity, and mass media coverage, organized sports have served to involve people jointly and focus community social life everywhere (Luschen and Sage 1981).

Sports and Social Structure

Whether one sees the consequences of sports as beneficial or harmful to society depends on which of two competing theoretical approaches—functionalist or conflict—is adopted (Coakley 1984). The functionalist perspective leads social scientists to examine the ways in which sports contribute to the smooth operation of society as a whole. The benefits of sports are seen to include the promotion of values such as the importance of rules, hard work, organization, and a defined authority structure; the legitimation of the goals of success

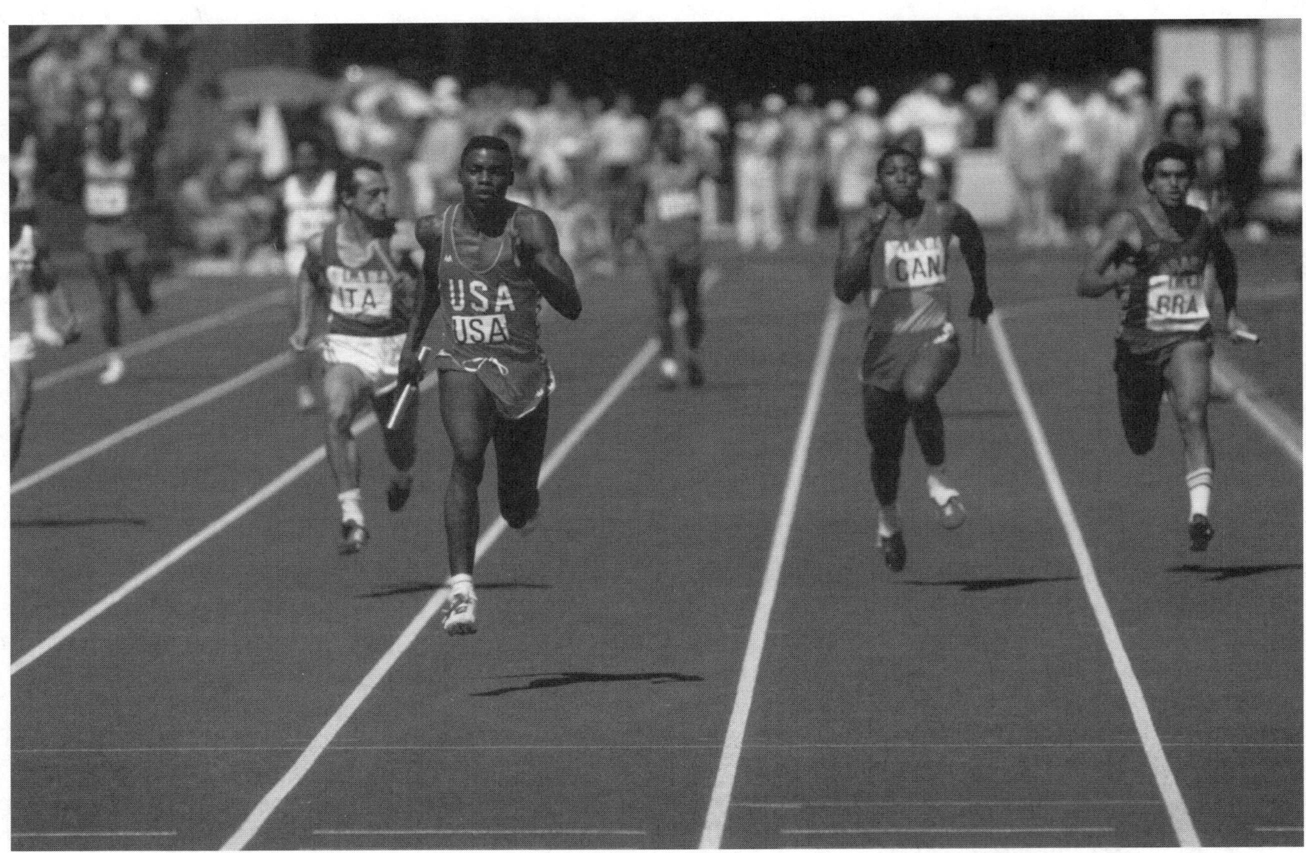

As an organized sporting event, the Olympics increase national pride while also building international unity. (Neal Preston/Corbis)

and achievement; the social integration or reaffirmation of linkages of collectivities represented; and the development of physical skills and the promotion of physical well-being among people who lead otherwise sedentary lives in industrial and postindustrial cities.

Conflict theorists do not disagree that widespread interest in commercialized sports leads to such consequences; rather, their perspective leads them to view those consequences as harmful. Critics of the status quo recognize the role of sports in socializing the young to fit into a regimented, bureaucratic mold. Organized sports as mass entertainment spectacles are viewed as a "mass narcotic" that provides escape and excitement, thus making participation in political or revolutionary organizations less likely (Hoch 1972).

Furthermore, conflict theorists argue that commercialized sports reduce players to material commodities exploited by others for the sake of profit, and the pressure to perform takes its toll on athletes' bodies through injury or the inducement to take harmful drugs (Shaw 1972). The highly visible rewards given to athletes in turn publicize an ideology of upward mobility. Conflict theorists point out that athletes' fame creates illusions about individualism by presenting a model in which success depends on hard work and perseverance, thus distracting attention from organizational bases for blocked mobility (Hoch 1972; Lipsyte 1975). Sports also separate the sexes and idealize an exaggerated notion of masculinity. Finally, fans' identification with athletes is used to sell a host of consumer goods, and the proliferation of participant sports has spawned a huge leisure industry in capitalist societies.

Functionalist theorists have been criticized for ignoring the possibility that sports may benefit some members of society more than others and for failing to note the exploitation found in organized sports. Conflict theorists have been criticized for overemphasizing the influence of capitalism when in fact contemporary sports function much the same way in socialist and communist societies. Perceptive analysts have noted that theorists tend to apply the functionalist model to social systems they support and the conflict model to those they criticize (Coakley 1984).

The contours of sports specific to a culture shed light on its other institutions, values, myths, and inequalities. In the United States, for example, racial integration in team sports awaited the breakdown of societal segregation, then hastened its demise by virtue of the attendant publicity (Koppett 1981). Yet blacks remain largely absent from elite sports and are excluded from many leadership and management positions in team sports. Media attention to female athletes remains minimal despite women's increased participation in sports.

Sports and Aggression

A different type of controversy surrounds one function of sports presumed to hold true across time and place, namely, that sports serve as a societal safety valve. Sporting rituals have long been thought to be cathartic. Roman elites believed that a diet of "bread and circuses" would keep workers from revolt. Neo-Freudians view the buildup of tension and frustration as inevitable and see violent sports as a healthy channel for expression and control of aggression for participant and spectator alike.

Contemporary empiricists (Goldstein 1983) raise two questions about these assumptions. First, they point out that games and sports are consistent with broader cultural patterns. Cooperative societies encourage noncompetitive sports; societies that stress individual achievement and success encourage competitive sports. Violent societies endorse violent sports. In U.S. football, for example, most of the violence is within the rules, or normative, and even violence outside the rules is often rewarded by coaches, communities, and the media. More than a reflection of societal values, sports as an instrument of socialization also reinforce aggression because they condone it.

Second, it is clear that not all expressions of aggression by fans are harmless; rather, collective violence at sporting events has emerged as a major social problem for many nations. Do aggressive sports attract violence-prone fans, or do they create in them an inclination toward the display of violence? A decade of empirical research suggests that combative sports, as a mirror of cultural norms, teach and stimulate violence. It is not competition per se that increases hostility but rather the aggressive nature of that competition. Those who participate in combative sports show more aggression in response to anger and frustration than those who participate in noncontact sports. Of course, it is also likely that more aggressive people show a preference for combative over noncontact sports. In any case, athletes in combative sports are more likely than others to suffer from hypertension, a finding that further undermines the notion of sports as catharsis (Goldstein 1983).

Whether releasing or promoting aggression is a consequence, what is certain is that sports provide an emotional outlet with few equals in the world of entertainment. Contests offer excitement and drama because the outcome is uncertain, and both luck and injury can intervene. The action is live, not scripted. Each contest is unique, unrehearsed, and finite with a clear-cut beginning, middle, and end. Sport is special because it stands apart from routine reality. The demonstration of the exuberance not only shows the audience's appreciation of effort and skill but is rooted in the fan's personal involvement in the team's or athlete's fate (Lever 1983).

The Sociological Study of Sport

People devote more time and affect in playing, watching, and discussing sport than in any other organized activity in public life. Millions of children are enrolled in sports leagues, high school and collegiate sports share the business orientation of the professional teams, and millions of adults organize their leisure time around playing amateur sports and watching professional athletes. Sports are a major factor in modern nations' economies insofar as billions of dollars are paid for admission tickets, telecast and advertising rights, recreational equipment, and both legal and illegal gambling. Sports so permeate culture that everyday language incorporates game images and metaphors that shape—some would say distort—the way people think about social reality (Koppett 1981).

Given the tremendous emotional and monetary investment in sports, one could rightfully expect it to be a major focus for sociological research, especially in the United States, where interest in sports ranks very high by any measure. However, the study of sport emerged only in the early 1950s in Western Europe and not until the late 1960s in the United States. To date, the subdiscipline is still underdeveloped and unfashionable in the United States, as measured by the relative handful of sociologists who declare the field as their specialty and by the few courses on the subject offered at the graduate level in major universities (Loy, Kenyon, and McPherson 1987).

Sports are largely taken for granted. Intellectuals, viewing play and games as trivial and inconsequential, feel little need for scientific scrutiny of the frivolous side of life. Journalists and philosophers have contributed interesting speculations more often than social scientists have provided empirical data (Weiss 1969). The careful examination of the role of sports in society remains minimal despite growing recognition that leisure pursuits, like occupations, are salient bases for identification in modern life.

BIBLIOGRAPHY

Betts, John R. 1980 "The Technological Revolution and the Rise of Sport, 1850–1900." In George H. Sage, ed., *Sport and American Society.* 3rd ed. Reading, Mass.: Addison-Wesley.

Coakley, Jay J. 1984 "Sport in Society: An Inspiration or an Opiate?" In D. Stanley Eitzen, ed., *Sport in Contemporary Society.* 2nd ed., New York: St. Martin's.

Goldstein, Jeffrey H. (ed.) 1983 *Sports Violence.* New York: Springer-Verlag.

Hoch, Paul 1972 *Rip Off the Big Game: The Exploitation of Sports by the Power Elite.* New York: Doubleday.

Huizinga, Johan 1955 *Homo Ludens: A Study of the Play Element in Culture.* Boston: Beacon Press.

Koppett, Leonard 1981 *Sports Illusion, Sports Reality.* Boston: Houghton Mifflin.

Lever, Janet 1983 *Soccer Madness.* Chicago: University of Chicago Press.

Lipsyte, Robert 1975 *Sportsworld: An American Dreamland.* New York: Quadrangle.

Loy, J., G. Kenyon, and B. McPherson 1987 "The Emergence and Development of the Sociology of Sport as an Academic Specialty." In A. Yiannakis, T. McIntyre, M. Melnick, and D. Hart, eds., *Sport Sociology.* 3d ed. Dubuque, Iowa: Kendall/Hunt.

Luschen, G., and G. H. Sage 1981 *Handbook of Social Science of Sport.* Champaign, Ill.: Stipes.

Roberts, Michael 1976 *Fans! How We Go Crazy over Sports.* Washington, D.C.: New Republic Books.

Shaw, Gary 1972 *Meat on the Hoof.* New York: Dell.

Weiss, Paul 1969 *Sport: A Philosophic Inquiry.* Carbondale, Ill.: Southern Illinois University Press.

– JANET LEVER

STUDENT MOVEMENTS

Student movements are generally college student movements. Such young adult movements have a long history and have been evident in widely differing societies (Altbach and Lomotey, 1990; Feuer 1969; Lipset 1971). Some have been related to direct student redress of situational grievances such as the seventeenth-century sacking of their own English Jesuit College of La Fleche to protest a rigid, strained regimen and the student protests led by African-Americans on over one hundred campuses in the 1980s to protest cutbacks in governmental aid and scholarships for lower income students. Other student protest movements have been related to larger social movements such as the nineteenth-century Russian revolutionary student movement, the American civil rights and antiwar student movements of the 1930s and 1960s, and the ill-fated Chinese Tiananmen Square democratic movement in the 1980s.

Other examples could be noted extending back a millennium or more in other societies. What is different about contemporary student movements is a combination of their frequency and their social change consequences on society. This is a reflection of the central role that an extended formal education has on economic and social stability and development globally in both advanced technological societies and developing societies (Gordon 1988, pp. 97–98; Meyer et al. 1977).

The massive growth of higher education is evident from the change in the proportion of young adults in their late teens and early twenties attending college. Prior to World War II, even in the advanced industrial nations of Japan, the United States, and Canada, as well as in Great Britain and Western Europe, less than 10 percent of the young adult age cohort attended college. The figure was less than 1 percent in what is now generally referred to as emerging, often former colonial, developing nations. In contrast, by the late twentieth-century, close to half of young adults were in college in advanced technological societies, and the fastest growing student body in developing countries was collegiate (Meyer et al. 1977). Overall, instead of a few thousand students, major state universities in the United States now generally range between 20,000 and 40,000 or more students, with long-established private universities typically having over 10,000 students. Similarly, large national universities like those in Mexico City and Beijing have student bodies larger than the largest U.S. state universities.

The growth of public education generally and, in particular, collegiate education has placed young adult students in a strategic position respecting protest movement potential for inducing social change. It is not only that college students represent a high proportion of future economic, political, and social influentials. The growth of colleges since the mid-twentieth century is also an international reflection of the general publics' and the democratic or authoritarian regimes' recognition that students represent a key element in the effective future of their various societies.

Strategic positioning aside, there has been extensive research on what motivates consequential proportions of students to periodically engage in protest movements. College students represent a relatively privileged and prospectively influential group in society. These characteristics are generally associated with support for the established social order. Yet students are often in the activist forefront of protest movements.

This dilemma has been addressed in intergenerational conflict terms since at least Socrates and Plato. In sociology, Karl Mannheim (1952) addressed specific attention to this phenomenon as part of his sociology of knowledge concerns. Building upon Mannheim's analyses, Feuer (1969) holds that the need for the emerging young to replace the older adults in societies generates inherent intergenerational conflict that crystallizes in the increasingly influential collegiate settings.

In this context, it is held that students act out their traditional intergenerational conflicts in a setting that is particularly conducive to challenging the older generation. Colleges, and to a lesser extent primary and secondary schools, remove students from familial and kinship settings. While faculty present an adult schooling influence, within the increasingly large school settings, students are placed in a peer-related situation removed from both direct familial influences and the later pressures of occupational positions.

The relatively separated, student peer-influenced, life pattern is evident in the precipitating protest actions of many student movements. Most sociological research attention has been on student participation in major protest movements involving civil rights, environmental protection, war, and other momentous public issues. Yet a review of the student movement literature demonstrates that often the early motivation for student protestors against university administrators and more general societal authorities has been related to specific student-experienced grievances over such American situational concerns as poor dormitory food in the 1950s and Italian and Chinese student concerns in the 1960s and 1980s, respectively, that growing numbers of college graduates were either unemployed or receiving less pay than undegreed manual laborers (Altbach and Peterson 1971; Borgatta 1990; Lipset 1971).

Early motivation for student protestors has been related to specific student-experienced grievances over such American situational concerns as poor dormitory food in the 1950s

Such immediate student self-interest can often be seen in respect to student participation in larger social movements also. This has been evident in respect to direct student concerns about conscription and being forced into combat situations. The 1860s Harvard University student anti-conscription protests during the Civil War helped precipitate the congressional and state legislative acts to enable those with several hundred dollars to commute their draft status to the next young person called up, which in turn was a central factor in the Irish Catholic, New York City, conscription riots of 1863 that left several hundred dead (Catton 1960, p. 485).

Similar immediate self-interest was a part of the American Student Union antiwar movement in the 1930s, as well as of the anti-Vietnam War movement led by the Students for a Democratic Society (SDS) in the 1960s. These student protests partially reflected general public divisiveness over war support, but the most common thread was that of immediate student interest. A particularly clear case of student self-interest was the high involvement of African-American students in the civil rights student movements of the 1960s, working for more openings and support for African-

Americans who had long been excluded from equal higher educational opportunity (Edwards 1970).

Yet immediate self-interest does not explain student movements in support of disadvantaged minority and low-income groups, such as extensive involvement in the Student Non-Violent Coordinating Committee and other American civil rights organizations in the 1960s or the 1989 student effort to establish democracy in China. In this respect, students tend to activate ideals and values that are perceived to be falling too short in their implementation (Davies 1969). What has become evident in the extensive empirical research on student movement participants since the 1960s is that the conflict of generations thesis advanced by Mannheim, Feuer, and others is less a conflict of generations than an active attempt among the student generation to realize the values they have been socialized to by the parental generation.

Rather than challenging the values of the parental generation, student activists generally support those values and act to see them actualized (DeMartini 1985). A polar case in point is the background characteristics of students who were active in the liberal, politically left SDS, which was strongly against the Vietnam War, and those in the conservative, politically right Young Americans for Freedom (YAF), which was strongly supportive of the Vietnam War. As Lipset (1968) reports, SDS students were largely from high-status, Protestant backgrounds and homes where secular, liberal values prevailed. In contrast, but in intergenerational concurrence, YAF student activists were generally drawn from strongly religious and conservative homes in lower middle-class and working-class settings. Another example of this intergenerational confluence is Bell's (1968) documentation that the largest proportion of white student activists in the Congress of Racial Equality (CORE) were Jewish and actively expressing their home-based familial values in support of minority rights.

Student movement concerns with actualizing ideals have been a dynamic aspect of such movements. The national student Free Speech Movement in 1964 was

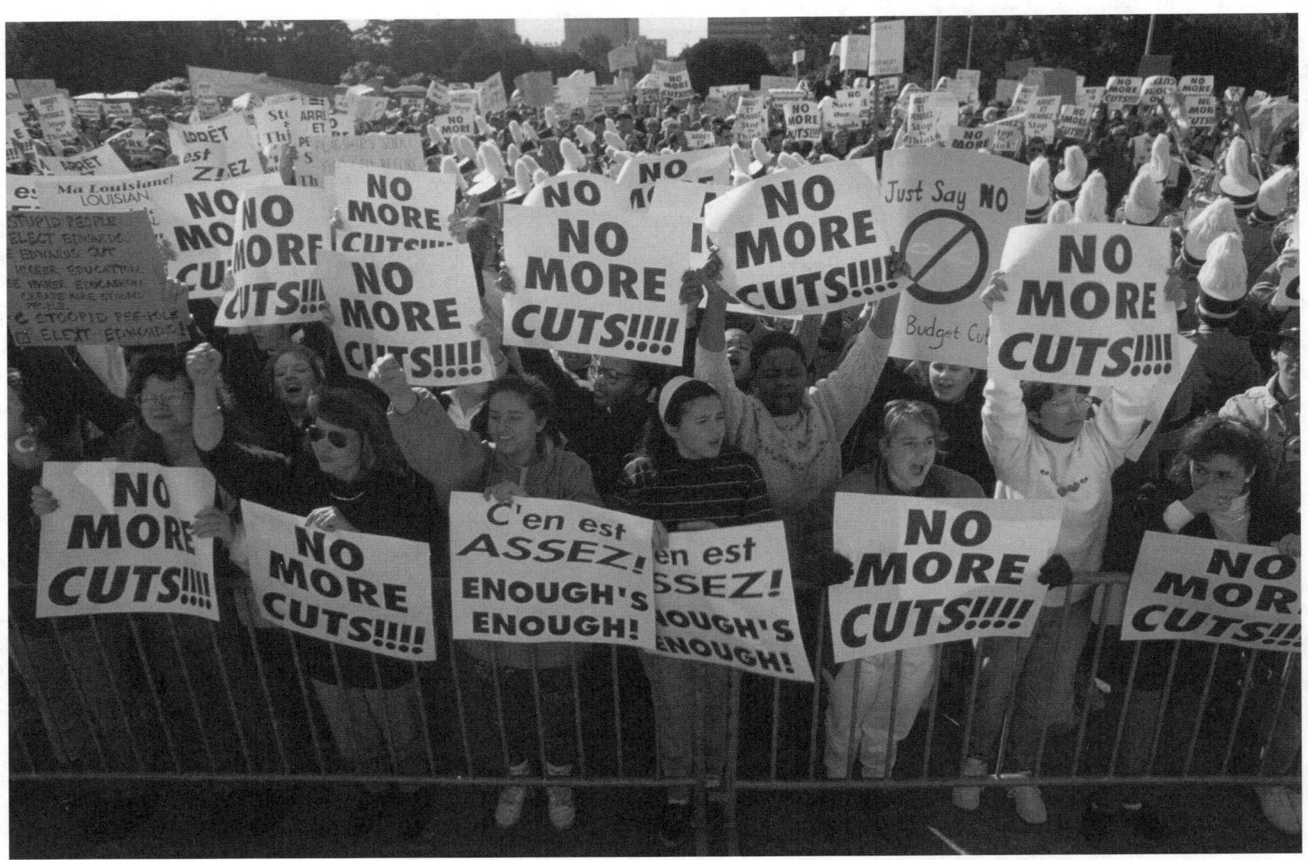

Student protests generally stem from specific issues, such as this group's concern about funding cuts at Louisiana State University. (Philip Gould/ Corbis)

precipitated by University of California at Berkeley students who protested a specific ban on allowing a CORE civil-rights-information table on the campus in an open mall area. While a relatively small number of students were actively involved with the CORE table, a large majority of students, first at Berkeley and then nationally, supported the right of open expression and led to the larger Free Speech Movement (Altbach and Peterson 1971; Lipset 1968, 1971).

Protest movements are time delimited generally. Given the relatively short age cohort dimensions of student status, student movements tend to have even shorter time constraints. Even with time and leadership delimitations, student movements are sufficiently frequent and consequential that more systematic research is needed on not only who the student protestors are but also where they go after a student activist movement ends.

It is clear that most student activists enter into business and professional, high socioeconomic status positions. What is not clear is to what extent they continue to adhere to the values and related issues that motivated them to engage in one or more student movements. Research in this area of student movement concern may demonstrate additional social change consequences on society long after specific student movements have ended.

[See also Protest Movements; Social Movements.]

BIBLIOGRAPHY

Altbach, Philip G., and Kofi Lomotey (eds.) 1990 *The Racial Crisis in Higher Education.* Buffalo: State University of New York Press.

Altbach, Philip G., and Patti Peterson 1971 "Before Berkeley: Historical Perspectives on American Student Activism." *Annals of the American Academy of Political and Social Science* 395:1–14.

Bell, Inge Powell 1968 *CORE and the Strategy of Non-Violence.* New York: Random House.

Borgatta, Edgar F. January 3, 1990 Correspondence with author on Student Movements.

Catton, Bruce 1960 *The Civil War.* New York: American Heritage.

Davies, James C. 1969 "The J-Curve of Rising Expectations and Declining Satisfactions as a Cause of Some Great Revolutions and Contained Rebellions." In H. Graham and T. Gurr, eds., *Violence in America.* New York: Bantam.

DeMartini, Joseph R. 1985 "Change Agents and Generational Relationships: A Reevaluation of Mannheim's Problem of Generations." *Social Forces* 64:1–16.

Edwards, Harry 1970 *Black Students.* New York: Macmillan.

Feuer, Lewis S. 1969 *The Conflict of Generations: The Character and Significance of Student Movements.* New York: Basic Books.

Gordon, Leonard 1988 "The Sociology of Education." In E. Borgatta and K. Cook, eds., *The Future of Sociology.* Beverly Hills, Calif.: Sage.

Lipset, Seymour M. 1968 "The Activists: A Profile." *Public Interest* 13:46–50.

——— 1971 *Rebellion in the University.* Boston: Little, Brown.

Mannheim, Karl 1952 *Essays on the Sociology of Knowledge,* pp. 276–322. New York: Oxford University Press.

Meyer, John W., Francisco O. Ramirez, Richard Rubinson, and John Boli 1977 "The World Educational Revolution: 1950–1970." *Sociology of Education* 50:242–258.

— LEONARD GORDON

SUBURBANIZATION

Suburbanization is one aspect of the more general process of the expansion and spatial reorganization of metropolitan settlements. Settled areas beyond the historical boundaries of what have been considered cities, but still clearly functionally linked to the cities, may be considered suburban, or they may not. What is suburban is a matter of social definition. For example, when small cities are enveloped by the expansion of larger cities, at what point shall they be considered suburbs, if at all? As some cities extend their boundaries outward, will newly settled areas not be considered suburban if they are within the new boundaries?

Many researchers in the United States have chosen to adopt conventions established by the Bureau of the Census. Suburban is the portion of a metropolitan area that is not central city. This definition, then, depends on what is defined as metropolitan and central city, and these definitions change over the years. Such changes are not simply technical adjustments; they respond (among other criteria) to presumptions about what cities and suburbs are. For example, as many U.S. "suburbs" have become employment centers in the last two decades, altering traditional patterns of commuting to work, Bureau scientists have adjusted the definition of "central city" to include some of these peripheral areas.

For many purposes, it may be preferable to avoid these categories altogether. "Suburban" may be intended to reflect distance from the city center, recency of development, residential density, or commuting patterns—all of which can be measured directly. The main substantive rationale for accepting definitions tied to the juridical boundaries of cities is to emphasize the differences between cities and suburbs (and among suburbs) that are due to municipal governance. An important class of issues revolves around disparities in public resources: In what parts of the metropolis are taxes higher, where are better schools available, where is police protection greater? What are the effects of these differences on opportunities available to people who live in different parts of the metropolis? Another dimension concerns local politics: How do localities establish land use and budget policies, and what are their effects on growth?

Because many suburban residents have traditionally worked in central cities while paying taxes in the suburbs, John Kasarda has described the city-suburb relationship in terms of "exploitation." Political scientists in particular have studied this issue in terms of arguments for the reform of metropolitan governance structures. The normative implications of their arguments have explicit ideological underpinnings. Some, like Dennis Judd, emphasize the values of equality of life chances and interpret differences between cities and suburbs as disparities; others (public choice theorists such as Elinor Ostrom) emphasize freedom of choice and interpret differences as opportunities for the exercise of choice.

Sociologists on the whole have been less willing to be proponents of metropolitan solutions, and they have shown more interest in the causes than in the consequences of suburbanization. Nevertheless, there are differences in theoretical perspective that closely parallel those in political science, and they hinge in part on the importance of political boundaries and the political process. The main lines of explanation reflect two broader currents in sociological theory: structural functionalism is found in the guise of human ecology and neoclassical economics, and variants of Marxian and Weberian theory have been described as the "new" urban theory.

Ecologists and many urban economists conceptualize suburbanization as a process of decentralization, as reflected in Burgess's (1967) concentric zone model of the metropolis. Burgess accepted the postulate of central place theory that the point of highest interaction and most valued land is naturally at the core of the central business district. The central point is most accessible to all other locations in the metropolis, a feature that is especially valuable for commercial firms. At the fringes of the business district, where land is being held for future commercial development, low-income and immigrant households can compete successfully for space, though only at high residential densities. Peripheral areas, by contrast, are most valued by more affluent households, particularly those with children and preferences for more spacious surroundings.

The key to this approach is its acceptance of a competitive land market as the principal mechanism through which locational decisions are reached. More specific hypotheses are drawn from theories about people's preferences and willingness (and ability) to pay for particular locations, or about structural changes (e.g., elevators, transportation technology, or space needs of manufacturers) that affect the value of central location. Many researchers have focused particularly on gradients linking distance from the center to various compositional characteristics of neighborhoods: their population density (Treadway 1969), household composition (Guest 1972), and socioeconomic status (Choldin and Hanson 1982). Comparatively little research has been conducted on the preferences of residents or the factors that lead them to select one location or another.

Other sociologists have argued that growth patterns result from conscious policies and specific institutional interventions in the land and housing markets. Representative of this view is Checkoway (1980), who emphasizes the role of federal housing programs and institutional support for large-scale residential builders in the suburbanization of the 1950s. The move to suburbs, he argues, was contingent on the alternatives offered to consumers. The redlining of inner city neighborhoods by the Federal Housing Administration, its preference for large new subdivisions, and its explicit discrimination against minority homebuyers are among the major forces structuring these alternatives.

There have been few studies of the housing market from an institutional perspective, although the restructuring of real estate financing and the emergence of new linkages between large-scale developers and finance capital have begun to attract attention. More consideration has been given to the explicitly political aspects of land development (Logan and Molotch 1987). Following Hunter (1953), who believed that growth questions were the "big issue" in local politics, recent studies find that the most powerful voices in local politics are the proponents of growth and urban redevelopment and, in this sense, that the city is a growth machine.

Applying this model to suburbs, most observers portray suburban municipalities as "exclusionary." Suburban municipalities have long used zoning to influence the location and composition of land development. Since environmentalism emerged as a formidable political movement in the early 1970s, it has become commonplace to hear of localities that exercise their powers to preserve open space and historic sites, that impose restraints or even moratoria on new development. The "no-growth movement" is a direct extension of earlier exclusionary zoning policies.

Socioeconomic Differences Between Cities and Suburbs

These two theoretical perspectives can be illustrated through their application to research on socioeconomic differences between cities and suburbs. It is well known that central cities in most metropolitan regions have a less affluent residential population than their surrounding suburbs. There is much debate, however, whether this class segregation between cities and their suburbs is a natural sorting out of social classes through the private market or whether its causes are political and institutional. Similar debate surrounds the phenomenon of differentiation *within* suburbia, where there is great variation in economic function, class and racial composition, and other characteristics of suburbs.

Research from an ecological perspective has stressed a comparison between the older, larger, denser cities of the North and the more recently growing cities of the South and West. The principal consistent findings have been that (1) the pattern of low central city relative to suburban social status is more pronounced in older metropolitan regions, but, (2) controlling for metropolitan age, there appears to be a universal generalization of this pattern over time (Guest and Nelson 1978). These sociologists propose that suburbs have natural advantages over central cities. For example, their housing stock is newer, suburban land is less expensive, and suburbs are more accessible to freeways and airports. The socioeconomic differences between cities and suburbs reflect those advantages.

Others argue that disparities are generated primarily by political structures that allocate zoning control and responsibility for public services to local governments and require these governments to finance services from such local sources as the tax on real property. They propose that the typical fragmentation of metropolitan government creates the incentive and opportunity for suburbs to pursue exclusionary growth policies (Danielson 1976).

Seeking to test these theories, Logan and Schneider (1982) found greater disparities in metropolitan areas where central cities were less able to grow through annexation (thus, where suburban municipal governments were more autonomous) and where localities were more reliant on local property taxes (hence, had greater incentive to pursue exclusionary policies). They also found a significant racial dimension: Greater disparities were evident in both 1960 and 1970 in metropolitan areas in the North with a larger proportion of black residents. (The same did not hold for the South and West, however.) This is due both to the concentration of lower income blacks in central cities and to a greater propensity of higher status whites to live in suburbs in these metropolitan areas. This finding is reinforced by William Frey (see Frey and Speare 1988), who reported

Suburban areas of the 1990s, such as these developments spreading out from Las Vegas, Nevada, often became employment centers themselves, altering trends in commuting to work. (James Marshall/Corbis)

that the central city proportion of black residents is a significant predictor of white flight, independent of other causes.

If suburbs follow exclusionary growth policies, it seems counterintuitive that suburbs have experienced much more rapid growth than did cities in the postwar decades. The findings on city-suburb disparities, of course, indicate that exclusion has selective effects. Nevertheless, it is surprising that Baldassare and Protash (1982), in a study of northern California cities, found that communities with more restrictive planning controls actually had higher rates of population growth during the 1970s. Similarly, Logan and Zhou (1989) found that suburban growth controls had little if any impact on development patterns (population growth, socioeconomic status, or racial composition). In their view, the exclusionary policies of suburbs may be more apparent than real. The more visible actions, like growth moratoria, are often intended to blunt criticisms by residents concerned with problems arising from rapid-development. Unfortunately, few studies have looked in depth at the political process within suburbs; there is as little direct evidence on the role of local politics as there is on the operation of the land market. Most research from both the ecological and political-institutional perspectives has inferred the *processes* for controlling growth from evidence about the *outcomes.*

Suburbanization of Employment

A central problem for early studies of suburban communities was to identify the patterns of functional specialization among them. It was recognized that older industrial satellites coexisted with dormitory towns in the fringe areas around central cities. Both were suburban in the sense that they were integrated into a metropolitan economy dominated by the central city. Their own economic role and the nature of the populations that they housed were quite distinct, however. The greatest population gains in the 1950s were made by residential suburbs, communities that were wealthier, younger, newer, and less densely settled than those towns on the fringes of the region that had higher concentrations of employment. Leo Schnore (see Schnore and Winsborough 1972) distinguished "suburbs" from "satellites" to acknowledge these different origins.

The metaphors of suburbs and satellites reflected the reality of early postwar suburbanization, a period when established towns and small cities were surrounded by successive waves of new subdivisions. The metaphors are no longer appropriate. Since the late 1950s, the bulk of new manufacturing and trade employment in the metropolis is located in small- and middle-sized cities in the suburban ring (Berry and Kasarda 1977, Chapter 13). Downtown department stores compete with new suburban shopping malls. The highly developed expressway network around central cities frees manufacturing plants to take advantage of the lower land prices and taxes and the superior access to the skilled workforce offered by the suburbs. For the period of 1963 to 1977, in the largest twenty-five metropolitan areas, total manufacturing employment in central cities declined by about 700,000 (19 percent), while their suburbs gained 1.1 million (36 percent). At the same time, total central city retail and wholesale employment was stagnant (dropping by 100,000). Trade employment in the suburbs increased by 1.8 million (or 110 percent) in this period. Thus, total employment growth in the suburbs outpaced the growth of population (Logan and Golden 1986).

The central city proportion of black residents is a significant predictor of white flight, independent of other causes.

How has suburbanization of employment affected suburban communities? According to microeconomic and ecological models, locational choices by employers reflect the balance of costs and benefits of competing sites. New employment maintains old patterns because the cost-benefit equation is typically stable, including such important considerations as location relative to work-force, suppliers, markets, and the local infrastructure. In the terms commonly used by urban sociologists, this means that communities find their "ecological niche." Stahura's (1982) findings of marked persistence in manufacturing and trade employment among suburbs from 1960 to 1972 supports this expectation. Once "crystallized," the functional specialization of communities changes only under conditions of major shifts in the needs of firms.

To the extent that changes occur, in this view, they follow a natural life cycle (Hoover and Vernon 1962). Residential suburbs in the inner ring, near the central city, tend over time to undergo two related transformations: first, to higher population density and a conversion to nonresidential development, and second, to a lower socioeconomic status. Thus, inner suburbs that gain employment are—like older satellites—less affluent than residential suburbs.

By contrast, those who emphasize the politics of land development suggest very different conclusions. A growing number of suburbs perceive business and industry as a significant local resource. Once shunned by the higher status suburbs, they now contribute to both property values and the local tax base. Prestigious communities such as Greenwich, Connecticut, and Palo Alto, California, house industrial parks and corporate headquarters. The "good climate for business" that they offer includes public financing of new investments, extensive infrastructure (roads, utilities, parking, police and fire protection), and moderate taxes (Logan and Molotch 1987).

Competition among suburbs introduces a new factor that has the potential to reshape suburban regions. Schneider (1989) reports that location of manufacturing firms is affected by the strength of the local tax base, suggesting that wealthy suburbs are advantaged in this competition. Logan and Golden (1986) find that newly developing suburban employment centers have higher socioeconomic status, as well as stronger fiscal resources, than other suburbs; this is a reversal of the pattern of the 1950s.

Minority Suburbanization

The suburbanization process also increasingly involves minorities and immigrants, and the incorporation of these groups into suburban areas has become an important topic for research on race and ethnic relations. As Massey and Denton (1987) document, the rate of growth of nonwhites and Hispanics in metropolitan areas is far outstripping the rate of growth of non-Hispanic whites. Much of this growth is occurring in suburbs. During the 1970s, for example, the number of blacks in the non-central-city parts of metropolitan areas increased by 70 percent, compared to just 16 percent in central cities; and the number of other nonwhites in them shot up by 150 percent, compared to approximately 70 percent in central cities. One reason for the rapidly increasing racial and ethnic diversity of suburbs may be that some new immigrant groups are bypassing central cities and settling directly in suburbs. Equally important is the increasing suburbanization of older racial and ethnic minorities, such as blacks (Frey and Speare 1988).

This phenomenon has encouraged researchers to study suburbanization as a mirror on the social mobility of minorities. Consistent with classical ecological theory, suburbanization has often been portrayed broadly as a step toward assimilation into the mainstream society and as a sign of the erosion of social boundaries. For European immigrant groups after the turn of the century, residential decentralization appears to have been part of the general process of assimilation (Guest 1980).

Past studies have found that suburbanization of Hispanics and Asians in a metropolitan area is in fact strongly associated with each group's average income level (Massey and Denton 1987, pp. 819–820; see also Frey and Speare 1988, pp. 311–315). Further, again for Hispanics and Asians, Massey and Denton demonstrate that suburban residence is typically associated with lower levels of segregation and, accordingly, higher probabilities of contact with the Anglo majority. But these and other authors report very different results for blacks. Black suburbanization is unrelated to the average income level of blacks in the metropolitan area, and suburbanization does not result in higher intergroup contact for blacks. The suburbanization process for blacks appears largely to be one of continued ghettoization (Farley 1970), as indicated by high and in some regions increasing levels of segregation and by the concentration of suburban blacks in communities with a high incidence of social problems (e.g., high crime rates), high taxes, and underfunded social services (Logan and Schneider 1984).

These findings regarding black suburbanization have been interpreted in terms of processes that impede the free mobility of racial minorities: steering by realtors, unequal access to mortgage credit, exclusionary zoning, and neighbor hostility (Foley 1973). Home ownership indeed may be one of the gatekeepers for suburban living. Stearns and Logan (1986) report that blacks were less likely to live in suburban areas where higher proportions of the housing stock were owner-occupied.

Further evidence is offered by Alba and Logan (1991), who based their article on an analysis of individual-level data from the 1980 census. They find that suburban residence is more likely among homeowners and persons of higher socioeconomic status. There are stronger effects of family status (marriage and the presence of children in the household) and measures of cultural assimilation (English language use, nativity, and period of immigration). Assimilation is evidently a major part of the suburbanization process for most groups, especially those arising out of immigration.

At the same time, however, they report important differences among ethnic groups. The first is the unusually small effect of family status among blacks, Mexicans, and Puerto Ricans (all three groups rank near the bottom in terms of overall likelihood of suburbanization). In these groups, married couples with young children are more likely than others to be found in suburbs. But the difference made by family type tends to be small, indicating that families with children are comparatively disadvantaged in achieving suburban residence. A second difference is in the magnitude of the socioeconomic gradient in suburbanization. For members of the non-Hispanic white majority, household income has only a small effect (and education has no effect at all). But socioeconomic status is strongly related to suburbanization for some minorities, for example, the Chinese and Puerto Ricans. This gradient appears to indicate that suburban residence does, in fact, "cost" some minorities more than it does members of the majority. A final difference is in the effects of metropolitan characteristics. Some groups face a substantial disadvantage in metropolitan areas where home ownership is a requirement for suburban entry or where the income differential between suburb and city is large (thus indicating that the suburban ring has generally higher status than the central city). Although these factors have little impact on the suburbanization of whites, they have a sizable negative influence on suburbanization for blacks and the Hispanic groups. This suggests that some minorities face obstacles to suburban residence in precisely those metropolitan areas where suburban locations are most desirable.

Home ownership indeed may be one of the gatekeepers for suburban living.

Parallel results are found for the racial and ethnic sorting process within a suburban region (the New York-New Jersey suburban region, as reported by Logan and Alba 1991). Two sorts of analyses were conducted. First, members of different racial and ethnic groups were compared on the average characteristics of suburbs in which they reside. Second, regression models were estimated for members of each major racial or ethnic group to predict several of these indicators of place advantages or community resources.

There are important differences between whites, blacks, Hispanics, and Asians in the kinds of suburbs that they live in. As some researchers have suspected, suburban Asians have achieved access to relatively advantaged communities, similar in most respects to those of suburban non-Hispanic whites. Hispanics in the New York region have not. Suburban Hispanics, by and large, live in communities that are about the same as black suburbs: communities with low average income levels and low rates of home ownership.

Is the disadvantage of blacks and Hispanics attributable to individual qualities of group members, or do these groups face collective disadvantages? Analysis of individual characteristics that may predict the quality of suburb that one resides in shows that the same location process does not apply equally to all minorities. The pattern for whites, who are relatively advantaged in access to community resources, lends clear support to assimilation theory. Human capital and indicators of cultural assimilation are strongly associated with access to higher status suburbs. The same can be said of Asians (who are relatively advantaged overall), with the exception that cultural assimilation variables seem not to be important for Asians.

Results for blacks strongly call attention to processes of racial stratification. Even controlling for many other individual characteristics, blacks live in suburbs with lower ownership and income levels than do non-Hispanic whites. Further, most human capital and assimilation variables have a smaller payoff for blacks than for whites. The findings for Hispanics are supportive of the assimilation model in several respects. Hispanics gain more strongly than whites from most human capital characteristics; therefore, at higher levels of socioeconomic achievement and cultural assimilation, Hispanics come progressively closer to matching the community resources of whites. It should be noted, however, that Hispanics begin from a lower starting point and that black Hispanics face a double disadvantage that is inconsistent with an assimilation perspective.

Looking to the Future

Suburbanization continues to be a key aspect of metropolitan growth. The political boundaries among cities and suburbs accentuate interest in substantive issues of metropolitan inequalities. They also create special opportunities for theories of urbanization to go beyond economic models and to incorporate an understanding of the political process. Research on suburbanization has been most successful in describing patterns of decentralization and spatial differentiation. The movements of people and employment, and the segregation among suburbs by social class, race, ethnicity, and family composition, have been well documented. But these patterns are broadly consistent with a variety of interpretations, ranging from those that assume a competitive land market (human ecology) to those that stress the institutional and political structuring of that market.

The principal gaps in knowledge concern the key processes that are central to these alternative interpretations. Few sociologists have directly studied the housing market from the perspective of either demand (how do people learn about the alternatives, and how do they select among them?) or supply (how does the real estate sector operate, how is racial and ethnic segmentation of the market achieved, how is the complex of construction industries, developers, and financial institutions tied to the rest of the economy?). Rarely have sociologists investigated government decisions (at any level) that impinge on development, from the point of view neither of their effects nor of the political process that led to them. Of course, these observations are not specific to research on suburbanization. It is important to bear in mind that neither the theoretical issues nor the research strategies in this field distinguish suburbanization from other aspects of the urban process.

[See also Cities; Community; Urbanization.]

BIBLIOGRAPHY

Alba, Richard D., and John R. Logan 1991 "Variations on Two Themes: Racial and Ethnic Patterns in the Attainment of Suburban Residence." *Demography,* forthcoming.

Baldassare, Mark, and William Protash 1982 "Growth Controls, Population Growth, and Community Satisfaction." *American Sociological Review* 47:339–346.

Berry, Brian, and John Kasarda 1977 *Contemporary Urban Ecology.* New York: Macmillan.

Burgess, Ernest W. 1967 "The Growth of the City." In R. E. Park, E. W. Burgess, and R. D. McKenzie, eds., *The City.* Chicago: University of Chicago Press.

Checkoway, Barry 1980 "Large Builders, Federal Housing Programmes, and Postwar Suburbanization." *International Journal of Urban and Regional Research* 4:21–44.

Choldin, Harvey M., and Claudine Hanson 1982 "Status Shifts Within the City." *American Sociological Review* 47:129–141.

Danielson, Michael 1976 *The Politics of Exclusion.* New York: Columbia University Press.

Farley, Reynolds 1970 "The Changing Distribution of Negroes Within Metropolitan Areas: The Emergence of Black Suburbs." *American Journal of Sociology* 75:512–529.

Foley, Donald 1973 "Institutional and Contextual Factors Affecting the Housing Choices of Minority Residents." In Amos Hawley and Vincent Rock, eds., *Segregation in Residential Areas.* Washington, D.C.: National Academy of Sciences.

Frey, William, and Alden Speare 1988 *Regional and Metropolitan Growth and Decline in the United States.* New York: Russell Sage Foundation.

Guest, Avery M. 1972 "Patterns of Family Location." *Demography* 9:159–171.

——— 1980 "The Suburbanization of Ethnic Groups." *Sociology and Social Research* 64:497–513.

———, and G. Nelson 1978 "Central City/Suburban Status Differences: Fifty Years of Change." *Sociological Quarterly* 19:7–23.

Hoover, Edgar, and Raymond Vernon 1962 *Anatomy of a Metropolis.* Garden City, N.Y.: Doubleday.

Hunter, Floyd 1953 *Community Power Structure.* Chapel Hill: University of North Carolina Press.

Logan, John R., and Richard Alba 1991 "Locational Returns to Human Capital: Minority Access to Suburban Community Resources." Paper presented at the annual meeting of the American Sociological Association, Cincinnati, August 23–27.

Logan, John R., and Reid Golden 1986 "Suburbs and Satellites: Two Decades of Change." *American Sociological Review* 51:430–437.

Logan, John R., and Harvey L. Molotch 1987 *Urban Fortunes: The Political Economy of Place.* Berkeley: University of California Press.

Logan, John R., and Mark Schneider 1982 "Governmental Organization and City-Suburb Income Inequality, 1960–1970." *Urban Affairs Quarterly* 17:303–318.

——— 1984 "Racial Segregation and Racial Change in American Suburbs: 1970–1980." *American Journal of Sociology* 89:874–888.

Logan, John R., and Min Zhou 1989 "Do Growth Controls Control Growth?" *American Sociological Review* 54:461–471.

Massey, Douglas, and Nancy Denton 1987 "Trends in the Residential Segregation of Blacks, Hispanics, and Asians: 1970–1980." *American Sociological Review* 52:802–825.

Schneider, Mark 1989 *The Competitive City: The Political Economy of Suburbia.* Pittsburgh: University of Pittsburgh Press.

Schnore, Leo, and Hal Winsborough 1972 "Functional Classification and the Residential Location of Social Classes." In Brian Berry, ed., *City Classification Handbook: Methods and Application.* New York: Wiley.

Stahura, John 1982 "Determinants of Suburban Job Change in Retailing, Wholesaling, Service, and Manufacturing Industries: 1960–1972." *Sociological Focus* 15:347–357.

Stearns, Linda, and John Logan 1986 "The Racial Structuring of the Housing Market and Segregation in Suburban Areas." *Social Forces* 65:28–42.

Treadway, Roy C. 1969 "Social Components of Metropolitan Population Densities." *Demography* 6:55–74.

– JOHN R. LOGAN

SUICIDE

To many, suicide, or intentional self-killing, seems like the ultimate asocial act of an individual. Yet sociology itself grew out of Emile Durkheim's argument that suicide rates are social facts and reflect variation in social regulation and social interaction (Durkheim [1897] 1951). The concept of suicide derives from the Latin *sui* ("of oneself") and *cide* ("a killing"). Edwin Shneidman defines suicide as "currently in the Western world a conscious act of self-induced annihilation best understood as a multidimensional malaise in a needful individual who defines an issue for which suicide is perceived as the best solution" (1985, p. 203). Several conceptual implications follow from this definition.

Although suicidal types vary, there probably are some common traits that most suicides share (Shneidman 1985). People who choose suicide tend to

- seek a solution to their life problems by dying;
- want to cease consciousness;
- try to reduce intolerable psychological pain;
- have frustrated psychological needs;
- feel helpless and hopeless;
- be ambivalent about dying;
- be perceptually constricted and rigid thinkers;
- manifest escape, egression, or fugue behaviors;
- communicate their intent to commit suicide or die;
- have lifelong self-destructive coping responses (sometimes called "suicidal careers").

Completed suicides need to be differentiated from nonfatal suicide attempts, suicide ideation, and suicide talk or gestures. Sometimes one speaks of self-injury, self-mutilation, accident proneness, failure to take needed medications, and the like—where suicide intent cannot be demonstrated—as "parasuicide." The most common of all self-destructive behaviors are indirect, for example, alcoholism, obesity, risky sports, gambling, and so forth. There are also mass suicides (Jonestown, Guyana, 1978, and Masada in Roman-ruled Palestine, 73 A.D.) and murder-suicides. Individual and social growth probably require some partial self-destruction.

Although most suicides have much in common, suicide is emphatically not one type of behavior. Suicidology will never be an exact science until it carefully specifies its dependent variable. The predictors or causes of suicide vary immensely with the specific type of suicidal outcome. Suicidologists tend to recognize three to six basic types of suicide, each with two or three of their own subtypes (Maris et al. 1991, chap. 4). For example, Durkheim ([1897] 1951) thought all suicides were basically anomic, egoistic, altruistic, or fatalistic. Freud ([1917] 1953) and Menninger (1938) argued that psychoanalytically all suicides were based on hate or revenge (a "wish to kill"); on depression, melancholia, or hopelessness (a "wish to die"); or on guilt or shame (a "wish to be killed"). Finally, Baechler (1979) added "oblative" (i.e., sacrifice or transfiguration) and "ludic" (i.e., engaging in ordeals or risks and games) suicidal types.

Epidemiology, Rates, and Predictors

Suicide is a relatively rare event, one to three in 10,000 in the general U.S. population per year. In 1994 there were 31,142 suicides (about 1.4 percent of all deaths). This number amounts to an overall suicide rate of 12.0 suicides per 100,000 population. Suicide is now the ninth leading cause of death, ranking just ahead of homicide and legal intervention and just behind HIV infection. Suicide has been moving up the ladder of the leading causes of death in this century.

Suicide rates in the United States vary considerably by sex, age, and race. The highest rates are observed consistently among white males, who constitute roughly 70 percent of all suicides. White females make up about 20 percent of all suicides. American blacks (especially

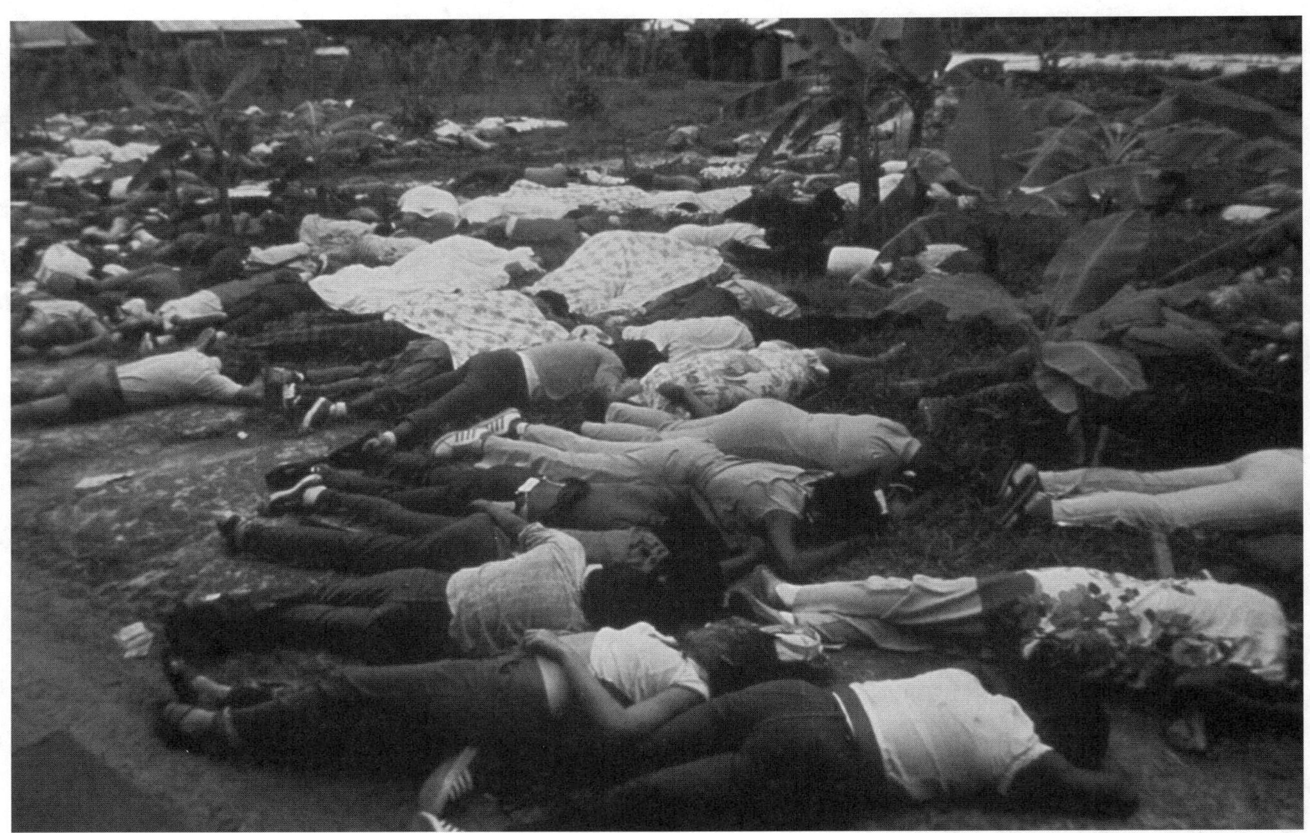

Followers of a religious leader named Jim Jones committed mass suicide under his orders in 1978 in their jungle camp in Guyana. (UPI/Corbis-Bettmann)

TABLE 1

TEN LEADING CAUSES OF DEATH IN THE UNITED STATES, 1994

Rank	Cause of death	Rate*	No. of deaths
1	Disease of the heart	281.3	732,409
2	Malignant neoplasms (cancer)	205.2	534,310
3	Cerebrovascular disease (stroke)	58.9	153,306
4	Chronic obstructive pulmonary disease	39.0	101,628
5	Accidents	35.1	91,437
6	Pneumonia	31.3	81,473
7	Diabetes	21.8	56,692
8	HIV infection	16.2	42,114
9	Suicide	12.0	31,142
10	Homicide and legal intervention	(NA)†	(NA)

* Per 100,000 population.
† Not available.
Total number of deaths (all causes) in 1994: 2,278,994.
Source: U.S. Census Bureau; Vital Statistics; Section 2; 1998.

TABLE 2

RATES OF COMPLETED U.S. SUICIDE BY RACE AND GENDER FOR 1987*

Race-gender group	Number of suicides	Percent of suicides	Rate per 100,000
White males	22,188	72.0	22.1
White females	6,029	19.6	5.7
Black males	1,635	5.3	11.6
Black females	328	1.1	2.1
Other males*	449	1.5	11.6
Other females*	167	0.5	2.5
Totals	30,796	100.0	12.7

* Includes American Indian, Chinese, Hawaiian, Japanese, Filipino, Other Asian or Pacific Islander, and Other.
Source: Data from National Center for Health Statistics, 1990.

TABLE 3

RATES OF COMPLETED U.S. SUICIDE PER 100,000 POPULATION BY YEAR AND AGE

	Year			
Age*	1957	1967	1977	1987
5–14	0.2	0.3	0.5	0.7
15–24	4.0	7.0	13.6	12.9
25–34	8.6	12.4	17.7	15.4
35–44	12.8	16.6	16.8	15.0
45–54	18.0	19.5	18.9	15.9
55–64	22.4	22.4	19.4	16.6
65–74	25.0	19.8	20.1	19.4
75–84	26.8	21.0	21.5	25.8
85 and over	26.3	22.7	17.3	22.1
Totals	9.8	10.8	13.3	12.7

* No suicide reported for individuals under five years of age.
Source: Data from National Center for Health Statistics, 1990.

TABLE 4

PERCENT OF COMPLETED U.S. SUICIDES (1987) BY METHOD AND GENDER

	Gender	
Method	Male %	Female %
Firearms (E955.0–955.4)	64.0	39.8
Drugs/Medications (E950.0–950.5)	5.2	25.0
Hanging (E953.0)	13.5	9.4
Carbon monoxide (E952.0–952.1)	9.6	12.6
Jumping from a high place (E957)	1.8	3.0
Drowning (E954)	1.1	2.8
Suffocation by plastic bag (E953.1)	0.4	1.8
Cutting/Piercing instruments (E956)	1.3	1.4
Poisons (E950.6–950.9)	0.6	1.0
Other*	2.5	3.2
Totals	100.0	100.0

* Includes gases in domestic use (E951), other specified and unspecified gases and vapors (E952.8–952.9), explosives (E955.5), unspecified firearms and explosives (E955.9), and other specified or unspecified means of hanging, strangulation, or suffocation (E953.8–953.9).
Source: Data from National Center for Health Statistics, 1990.

females) rarely commit suicide (except for some young urban males). Some scholars have argued that black suicides tend to be disguised as homicides or accidents. In general, male suicides outnumber female suicides three or four to one. Suicide rates also increase gradually with age and then drop off some at the very oldest ages. Female suicide rates tend to peak earlier than those of males. Note (in Table 3) that from about 1967 to 1977 there was a significant increase in the suicide rate of fifteen- to twenty-four-year-olds and that elderly suicide rates seem to be climbing again.

Typically, marrying and having children protect one against suicide. Usually suicide rates are highest for the widowed, followed by those of the divorced and the never-married or single. Studies of suicide rates by social class have been equivocal. Within each broad census occupational category there are job types with both high and low suicide rates. For example, psychiatrists have high suicide rates, but pediatricians and surgeons have low suicide rates. Operatives usually have low rates, but policemen typically have high suicide rates.

The predominant method of suicide for both males and females in 1987 was firearms. The second most common method among males is hanging and among females is drug and medicine overdoses. Females use a somewhat greater variety of methods than males do. Suicide rates tend to be higher on Mondays and in the springtime (Gabennesch 1988).

Prediction of suicide is a complicated process (Maris et al. 1991). As with other rare events, suicide prediction generates many false positives (i.e., identifying some deaths as suicides when they are in fact not suicides). Correctly identifying true suicides is referred to as "sensitivity," and correctly identifying true nonsuicides is called "specificity." In one celebrated study using common predictors (see Table 5) Porkorny (1983) correctly predicted fifteen of sixty-seven suicides among 4,800 psychiatric patients, but he also got 279 false positives.

Table 5 lists fifteen major predictors of suicide. Single predictor variables seldom if ever correctly identify suicides. Most suicides have "comorbidity" (i.e., several key predictors are involved), and specific predictors vary with the type of suicide and other factors. Depressive disorders and alcoholism are two of the major predictors of suicide. Robins (1981) found that about 72 percent of all completed suicides were either depressed or alcoholic. Roughly 15 percent of all those with depressive illness and 18 percent of all alcoholics will eventually commit suicide. Repeated depressive illness that leads to hopelessness is especially suicidogenic.

Nonfatal suicide attempts, talk about suicide or dying, and explicit plans or preparations for dying or suicide all increased suicide risk. However, for the paradigmatic suicide (older white males) 85 to 90 percent of them make only one fatal suicide attempt and seldom explicitly communicate their suicidal intent or show up at hospitals and clinics. Social isolation (having no close friends, living alone, being unemployed, unmarried, etc.) and lack of social support is more common among suicides than among controls. Suicide tends to run in families, which suggests both modeling and genetic influences. There are some important biological and sociobiological predictors of suicide emerging, especially low central spinal fluid serotonin in the form of 5-HIAA (Maris et al. 1991).

TABLE 5

COMMON SINGLE PREDICTORS OF SUICIDE

1. Depressive illness, mental disorder
2. Alcoholism, drug abuse
3. Suicide ideation, talk, preparation, religion
4. Prior suicide attempts
5. Lethal methods
6. Isolation, living alone, loss of support
7. Hopelessness, cognitive rigidity
8. Older white males
9. Modeling, suicide in the family, genetics
10. Work problems, economics, occupation
11. Marital problem, family pathology
12. Stress, life events
13. Anger, aggression, irritability, 5-HIAA
14. Physical illness
15. Repetition and comorbidity of factors 1–14, suicidal careers

Source: Maris et al., 1991, chap. 1.

History, Comparative Studies, and Social Suicedologists

The incidence and study of suicide has a long history and was fundamental to the foundation of sociology. The earliest known visual reference to suicide is Ajax falling on his sword (c. 540 B.C.). Of course, we know that Socrates (about 399 B.C.) drank the hemlock. In the Judeo-Christian scriptures there were eleven men (and no women) who died by suicide (most notably Samson, Judas, and Saul). Common biblical motives for suicide were revenge, shame, or defeat in battle. Other famous suicides in art history include paintings of Lucretia stabbing herself (after a rape), Dido, and work by Edvard Munch and Andy Warhol.

The earliest known visual reference to suicide is Ajax falling on his sword (c. 540 b.c.).

Suicide varies with culture and ethnicity. Most cultures have at least some suicides. However, suicide is rare or absent among the Tiv of Nigeria, Andaman islanders, and Australian aborigenes and relatively infrequent among rural American blacks and Irish Roman Catholics. The highest suicide rates in the world are found in Hungary, the Federal Republic of Germany, Austria, Scandinavia, and Japan (see Table 6). The lowest rates are found in several South American, Pacific Island, and predominantly Roman Catholic countries (including Antigua, Jamaica, New Guinea, the Philippines, Mexico, Italy, and Ireland).

The sociological study of suicide, of course, started with Durkheim ([1897] 1951) and has continued to the present day, primarily by the following sociologists: Henry and Short (1954); Gibbs and Martin (1964); Gibbs (1988); Douglas (1967); Maris (1969; 1981); Phillips (1974; 1991); Stack (1982); Wasserman (1989); and Pescosolido and Georgianna (1989). It is impossible in an encyclopedia to do justice to the full account of the sociological study of suicide. For a more complete review, see Maris (1989). What follows is only a sketch.

TABLE 6

SUICIDE RATES (PER 100,000 OF POPULATION) IN 62 COUNTRIES: 1980–1986

Country	Rate	Country	Rate
1. Hungary	45.3	32. Uruguay	9.6
2. Federal Republic of Germany	43.1	33. Northern Ireland	9.3
3. Sri Lanka	29.0	34. Portugal	9.2
4. Austria	28.3	35. England and Wales	8.9
5. Denmark	27.8	36. Trinidad and Tobago	8.6
6. Finland	26.6	37. Guadeloupe	7.9
7. Belgium	23.8	38. Ireland	7.8
8. Switzerland	22.8	39. Italy	7.6
9. France	22.7	40. Thailand	6.6
10. Suriname	21.6	41. Argentina	6.3
11. Japan	21.2	42. Chile	6.2
12. German Democratic Republic	19.0	43. Spain	4.9
13. Czechoslovakia	18.9	44. Venezuela	4.8
14. Sweden	18.5	45. Costa Rica	4.5
15. Cuba	17.7	46. Ecuador	4.3
16. Bulgaria	16.3	47. Greece	4.1
17. Yugoslavia	16.1	48. Martinique	3.7
18. Norway	14.1	49. Colombia	2.9
19. Luxembourg	13.9	50. Mauritius	2.8
20. Iceland	13.3	51. Dominican Republic	2.4
21. Poland	13.0	52. Mexico	1.6
22. Canada	12.9	53. Panama	1.4
23. Singapore	12.7	54. Peru	1.4
24. United States	12.3	55. The Philippines	0.5
25. Hong Kong	12.2	56. Guatemala	0.5
26. Australia	11.6	57. Malta	0.3
27. Scotland	11.6	58. Nicaragua	0.2
28. The Netherlands	11.0	59. Papua New Guinea	0.2
29. El Salvador	10.8	60. Jamaica	0.1
30. New Zealand	10.3	61. Egypt	0.1
31. Puerto Rico	9.8	62. Antigua and Barbuda	—

Source: Diekstra 1990.

Durkheim claimed that the suicide rate varied inversely with social integration and that suicide types were primarily ego-anomic. However, Durkheim did not operationally define "social integration." Gibbs and Martin (1964) created the concept of "status integration" to correct this deficiency in Durkheim. They hypothesized that the less frequently occupied status sets would lead to lower status integration and higher suicide rates. Putting it differently, they expected status integration and suicide rates to be negatively associated. In a large series of tests from 1964 to 1988 Gibbs found his primary hypothesis to be confirmed only for occupational statuses (which Durkheim also had said were of central importance).

Henry and Short (1954) expanded Durkheim's concept of external and constraining social factors to include interaction with social-psychological factors of "internal constraint" (such as strict superego restraint) and frustration-aggression theory. Henry and Short reasoned that suicide rates would be highest when external restraint was low and internal restraint was high (and that homicide rates would be high when internal restraint was low and external restraint was high).

A vastly different sociological perspective on suicide originated with the work of ethnomethodologist Jack Douglas. Douglas (in the tradition of Max Weber's subjective meanings) argued that Durkheim's reliance on official statistics (like death certificates) as the data base for studying suicide was fundamentally mistaken (Douglas 1967). What Douglas said we need to do is to observe the accounts or situated meanings of actual individuals who are known to be suicidal, not some third-party official like a coroner or medical examiner who is not a suicide and who may use ad hoc criteria to classify a death as a suicide. There are probably just about as many official statistics as there are officials.

Maris (1981) extended Durkheim's empirical survey of suicidal behaviors, but not just by measuring macrosocial and demographic or structural variables. Instead Maris focused on actual interviews ("psychological autopsies") of the intimate survivors of suicides (usually their spouses) and compared these cases with control or comparison groups of natural deaths and nonfatal suicide attempters. Maris claimed that individuals who committed suicide had long "suicidal careers" involving complex mixes of biological, social, and psychological factors.

Phillips (1974) differed with Durkheim's contention that suicides are not suggestable or contagious. In a pioneering and stage-setting paper in the *American Sociological Review* in 1974, Phillips demonstrated that front-page newspaper coverage of celebrity suicides was associated with a statistically significant rise in the national suicide rate seven to ten days after the publicized suicide. The rise in the suicide rate was greater the longer the front-page coverage, greater in the region where the news account ran, and higher if the stimulus suicide and the person supposedly copying the suicide were similar. In a long series of similar studies Phillips and others expanded and documented the suggestion effect for other types of behavior and for other groups. For example, the contagion effect appears to be especially powerful among teenagers. Nevertheless, contagion accounts for only a 1 to 6 percent increase over normal expected suicide rates in a population.

Newspaper coverage of celebrity suicides has been associated with a statistically significant rise in the national suicide rate seven to ten days after the publicized suicide.

Phillips's ideas about contagion have dominated the sociological study of suicide in the 1980s. Work by Stack (1982), Wasserman (1989), Kessler and Stripp (1984), and others have produced equivocal support for the role of suggestion in suicide (Diekstra et al. 1989). Wasserman feels the business cycle and unemployment rates must be controlled for. Some have claimed that imitative effects are statistical artifacts. Most problematic is that the theory of imitation in suicide is underdeveloped.

The most recent sociologist to study suicide is medical sociologist Bernice Pescosolido. She has claimed, contrary to Douglas, that the official statistics of suicide are acceptably reliable and (as Gibbs said earlier) that they are the best basis available for the foundation of a science of suicide. Her latest paper (Pescosolido and Georgianna 1989) examined Durkheim's claim that religious involvement protects against suicide. Pescosolido finds that Roman Catholicism and evangelical Protestantism do protect one against suicide (institutional Protestantism does not) and that Judaism has a small, inconsistent protective effect. Pescosolido concludes that with disintegrating network ties, individuals who were denied both integrative and regulative supports commit suicide more often.

Issues and Future Directions

Much of current sociological research on suicide appears myopic and sterile, compared to early work by Durkheim ([1897] 1951), Douglas (1967), and Garfinkel (1967). Not only is the scope of current research limited, there is very little theory and few book-length publications. Almost no research monographs on the sociology of suicide were written in the 1980s. Highly focused scientific journal articles on imitation have predominated. However, none of these papers has been able to establish if suicides ever in fact were exposed to the original media stimulus! Since suicide does not just concern social relations, the study of suicide needs more interdisciplinary syntheses. The dependent variable (suicide) needs to include comparisons with other types of death and violence, as well as more nonsocial predictor variables (Holinger 1987).

A second issue concerns methods for studying suicide (Lann, Mościcki, and Maris 1989). There has never been a truly national sample survey of suicidal behaviors in the United States. Also, most suicide research is retrospective and based on questionable vital statistics. More prospective or longitudinal research designs are needed, of course, with adequate sample sizes and comparison or control groups. Models of suicidal careers should be analyzed with specific and more appropriate statistical techniques (like logistic regression, log-linear procedures, and event or hazard analysis). It should be noted that federal funds to do any major research on suicide are in short supply and that this is probably the single major obstacle to the contemporary scientific study of suicide.

Third, most studies of suicide are cross-sectional and static. Future research will, it is hoped, include more social developmental designs (Blumenthal and Kupfer 1990). We still have very little solid knowledge about the social dynamics or "suicidal careers" of eventual suicides (Maris 1990). For example, it is well known that completed suicides tend to be socially isolated at the time of death, but how they came to be that way is less well understood. Fourth, in passing it must be noted that even after almost a hundred years of research the relationship of suicide to social class, occupation, and socioeconomic status is still not clear.

Finally, a major issue in the study of suicide is rational suicide, active euthanasia, the right to die, and appropriate death. With a rapidly aging and more secular population and the spread of the AIDS virus, the American public is demanding more information about and legal rights for voluntary assisted death (see the case of Nico Speijer in the Netherlands, Diekstra 1986). The right to die and assisted suicide have been the focus of a few recent legal cases (Humphry and Wickett 1986; Battin and Maris 1983). Rosewell Gilbert, an elderly man who was sentenced to life imprisonment in Florida for the mercy killing of his sick wife, was pardoned in 1990 by the governor of Florida. However, in 1990 the U.S. Supreme Court (*Cruzon* v. *the State of Missouri*) ruled that hospitals have the right to continue to force-feed even brain-dead patients. The Hemlock Society was founded by Derek Humphry to assist those who wish to end their own lives, make living wills, or pass living-will legislation in their states (however, see the *New York Times,* February 8, 1990, A18). Of course, the state must be cautious that the right to die does not become the obligation to die (e.g., for the aged). These issues are further complicated by strong religious and moral persuasions.

[See also Death and Dying; Deviance Theories; Mental Illness and Mental Disorders.]

BIBLIOGRAPHY

Alcohol, Drug Abuse, and Mental Health Administration 1989 *Report of the Secretary's Task Force on Youth Suicide,* Vols. 1–4. Washington, D.C.: U.S. Government Printing Office.

Baechler, Jean 1979 *Suicides.* New York: Basic Books.

Battin, Margaret P., and Ronald W. Maris (eds.) 1983 *Suicide and Ethics.* New York: Human Sciences Press.

Blumenthal, Susan J., and David J. Kupfer (eds.) 1990 *Suicide over the Life Cycle: Risk Factors, Assessment, and Treatment of Suicidal Patients.* Washington, D.C.: American Psychiatric Press.

———, and René F. W. Diekstra 1986 "The Significance of Nico Speijer's Suicide: How and When Should Suicide Be Prevented?" *Suicide and Life-Threatening Behavior* 16 (1):13–15.

——— 1990 "An International Perspective on the Epidemiology and Prevention of Suicide." In Susan J. Blumenthal and David J. Kupfer, eds., *Suicide of the Life-cycle.* Washington, D.C.: American Psychiatric Press.

———, Ronald W. Maris, Stephen Platt, Armin Schmidtke, and Gernot Sonneck (eds.) 1989 *Suicide and Its Prevention: The Role of Attitude and Imitation.* Leiden: E. J. Brill.

Douglas, Jack D. 1967 *The Social Meanings of Suicide.* Princeton, NJ.: Princeton University Press.

Dunne, Edward J., John L. McIntosh, and Karen Dunne-Maxim (eds.) 1987 *Suicide and Its Aftermath.* New York: W. W. Norton.

Durkheim, Emile (1897) 1951 *Suicide.* New York: Free Press.

Evans, Glen, and Norman L. Farberow (eds.) 1988 *The Encyclopedia of Suicide.* New York: Facts On File.

Freud, Sigmund (1917) 1953 "Mourning and Melancholia." In James Strachey, ed., *Standard Edition of the Complete Works of Sigmund Freud.* London: Hogarth Press.

Gabennesch, Howard 1988 "When Promises Fail: A Theory of Temporal Fluctuations in Suicide." *Social Forces* 67:129–145.

Garfinkel, Harold 1967 *Studies in Ethnomethodology.* Englewood Cliffs, N.J.: Prentice-Hall.

Gibbs, Jack, and Mark C. Stafford 1988 "Change in the Relation Between Marital Integration and Suicide Rates." *Social Forces* 66:1060–1079.

Gibbs, Jack P., and W. T. Martin 1964 *Status Integration and Suicide.* Eugene: University Of Oregon Press.

Gibbs, Jewelle Taylor (ed.) 1988 *Young, Black, and Male in America: An Endangered Species.* Dover, Mass.: Auburn House.

Henry, Andrew F., and James F. Short 1954 *Suicide and Homicide.* New York: Free Press.

Holinger, Paul C. 1987 *Violent Deaths in the United States: An Epidemiological Study of Suicide, Homicide, and Accidents.* New York: Guilford.

Humphry, Derek, and Ann Wickett 1986 *The Right to Die: Understanding Euthanasia.* New York: Harper and Row.

Jacobs, Douglas, and Herbert N. Brown (eds.) 1989 *Suicide, Understanding, and Responding: Harvard Medical School Perspectives.* Madison, Conn.: International Universities Press.

Kessler, Ronald C., and H. Stripp 1984 "The Impact of Fictional Television Stories on U.S. Fatalities: A Replication." *American Journal of Sociology* 90:151 –167.

Lann, Irma S., Eve K. Mościcki, and Ronald W. Maris (eds.) 1989 *Strategies for Studying Suicide and Suicidal Behavior.* New York: Guilford.

Maris, Ronald W. 1969 *Social Forces in Urban Suicide.* Chicago: Dorsey Press.

——— 1981 *Pathways to Suicide: A Survey of Self-Destructive Behaviors.* Baltimore: Johns Hopkins University Press.

——— 1986 *Biology of Suicide.* New York: Guilford.

——— 1989 "The Social Relations of Suicide." In Douglas Jacobs and Herbert N. Brown, eds., *Suicide, Understanding, and Responding: Harvard Medical School Perspectives.* Madison, Conn.: International Universities Press.

——— 1990 "The Developmental Perspective of Suicide." In Antoon Leenaars, ed., *Life Span Perspectives of Suicide.* New York: Plenum.

———, Alan L. Berman, John T. Maltsberger, and Robert I. Yufit (eds.) 1991 *Assessment and Prediction of Suicide.* New York: Guilford.

Menninger, Karl 1938 *Man Against Himself.* New York: Harcourt, Brace.

Pescosolido, Bernice A., and Sharon Georgianna 1989 "Durkheim, Suicide, and Religion: Toward a Network Theory of Suicide." *American Sociological Review* 54:33–48.

Pfeffer, Cynthia R. (ed.) 1989 *Suicide Among Youth: Perspectives on Risk and Prevention.* Washington, D.C.: American Psychiatric Press.

Phillips, David P. 1974 "The Influence of Suggestion on Suicide." *American Sociological Review* 39:340–354.

———, Katherine Lesyna, and Daniel J. Paight 1991 "Suicide and the Media." In Ronald W. Maris et al., eds., *Assessment and Prediction of Suicide.* New York: Guilford.

Porkorny, Alex D. 1983 "Prediction of Suicide in Psychiatric Patients." *Archives of General Psychiatry* 40:249–257.

Robins, Eli 1981 *The Final Months.* New York: Oxford University Press.

Shneidman, Edwin S. 1985 *Definition of Suicide.* New York: Wiley-Interscience.

Stack, Stephen 1982 "Suicide: A Decade Review of the Sociological Literature." *Deviant Behavior* 4:41–66.

Stafford, Mark C., and Jack P. Gibbs 1988 "Change in the Relation between Marital Integration and Suicide Rates." *Social Forces* 66:1060–1079.

Wasserman, Ira M. 1989 "The Effects of War and Alcohol Consumption Patterns on Suicide: United States, 1910–1933." *Social Forces* 67:129–145.

– RONALD W. MARIS

T

TECHNOLOGICAL RISKS AND SOCIETY

Sociologists have long been interested in phenomena that harm people and what they value. Until recently, most such work concentrated on harm from natural events such as earthquakes, floods, and tornadoes. While we have learned much from that research, there is another class of threats that sociologists are now according more attention—"technical or technological risks." Within this class sociologists study a large number of topics, ranging from how individuals think about risks to how nation-states develop strategies to mitigate threats from failures of advanced technology. Some are even interested in risks that might be faced by societies far into the future. Toxic threats have drawn particularly close scrutiny from scholars, and indeed there are important sociological studies of Love Canal, Three Mile Island, Chernobyl, Bhopal, nuclear waste, and nuclear weapons. (It is a somewhat depressing area of study.) One reason toxic risks are so interesting is that they invert the way natural disasters do their damage. Rather than assaulting people from the outside, as do natural calamities, toxic hazards assault bodies from within. Toxic injuries also have no definable end, so victims can never know when they are safe from further damage. The meaning of toxic risks, it seems, is fundamentally different from that of natural disasters (Couch and Kroll-Smith 1985; Erikson 1990).

Toxic injuries have no definable end, so victims can never know when they are safe from further damage.

In general, the sociology of risk is concerned with researching and explaining how interactions between technology and modes of social organization create hazards, or the potential for hazards (Short 1984). "Hazards" can mean actual threats to people's lives (toxic chemical contamination, for example) or the *perception* that there is a threat. Indeed, many researchers focus their intellectual attention on risk perception—what people think is dangerous, and why they think what they do (Freudenburg 1988). The word *technology* in my definition means the social and mechanical tools people use to accomplish something—the design of a nuclear power plant, or even vocabularies used by experts when they talk of effectively evacuating an urban area after a major radiation release from a nuclear power plant (Perrow 1984). "Modes of social organization" refers to both social structure (e.g., the hierarchy of power found in an organization) and culture (e.g., the degree of legitimacy we grant experts). As we move into the twenty-first century, society will continue its seemingly inexorable march toward social and technical complexity, a complexity driven, at least in substantial part, by a distinctly modern capacity to create machines and institutional arrangements that are at once grand and terrifying. With these developments, it seems, the public is increasingly aware of the potentially devastating consequences of modern risks, even as it enjoys the cornucopia engendered by modern social organization and modern technology.

As is true of much sociology, research on risk can be classified into micro and macro studies. Both micro and macro studies have made significant contributions to understanding the connections between risk, technology, and society. Micro-level research, generally speaking, is concerned with personal, political, and social dilemmas, posed by technology and activities, that threaten the quality of people's lives. Macro-level work on risk does not by any means deny the importance of micro-oriented research, but asks different questions, and seeks answers to those questions at an institutional level of analysis.

As some of the examples below illustrate, much macro work emphasizes the importance of the institutional context within which decisions about risk are made. Sociologists of risk are keen to distinguish between public and private decisions. Put differently, some people make choices that affect mainly themselves, while those who are in positions of authority make choices that have significant implications for others. This is only one among many ways in which the sociology of risk is crucially concerned with issues of power and the distribution of hazards and benefits.

Since the theories, methods, and findings in the sociology of risk cannot possibly be reviewed here, some examples will be used to illustrate the kinds of things sociologists of risk try to understand. It should be noted that this subfield is still very much in its formative stages, so it has no clearly delimited intellectual history to serve as an organizing device for an encyclopedia article. A couple of examples from the micro level of analysis follow.

A substantial body of work has demonstrated that the public overestimates threats that are dramatic (e.g., from airplane accidents), particularly violent (e.g., handguns), and potentially catastrophic (e.g., from nuclear power plants). Similarly, people tend to underestimate more prosaic, chronic threats, such as those from botulism or asthma. Why is this so? Several explanations have been proposed, but the one that is most convincing focuses on the mechanisms through which information about risks is channeled to people (Kahneman, Slovic, and Tversky 1982; Heimer 1988). Specifically, the media—especially newspapers and television—are more likely to feature dramatic, violent, or catastrophic calamities compared with less sensational threats. Pushing the analysis further, we see that one reason the media find such risks more interesting is that they are easier to cover, and hence more easily fit into tight deadlines. Covering prosaic risks is also more time-consuming than covering short, dramatic accidents. What all this adds up to is that there are several fairly good structural reasons why the media pay more attention to high-drama risks and neglect low-drama risks. Thus, sociologists are able to explain why the public holds biased estimates of risk by focusing on the structural connections between people and media, and more specifically on the constraints that lead the media to be biased about certain types of information.

Another example at the micro level of analysis is in the fascinating work of Carol A. Heimer (forthcoming), who has been studying how information is used and transmitted in intensive care units for infants. Heimer's study is cast at a fairly micro level of analysis in the sense that one of her concerns is with how parents think about information regarding terribly sick babies. But like all good sociological studies, Heimer's connects what parents think with the social contexts in which they find themselves. For example, one of Heimer's findings is that when hospital personnel transmit information to parents about their infants, that process is

The public overestimates the danger of death by airplane, for example, which is statistically unlikely to happen to an individual. Meanwhile, people underestimate danger from less dramatic though more common causes such as asthma or smoking. (Paul A. Souders/Corbis)

structured to protect the hospital from lawsuits, and only secondarily to apprise parents of the precise condition of their children. Hence, Heimer tells us how parents think, much as a psychologist might, but also demonstrates that how they think is contingent on the organizational needs of hospitals.

Macro-level work on risk includes research on how professionals influence the behavior of regulatory agencies, how organizations blunder and break down, how social movements arise to push certain issues into public debate, even how national cultures shape which risks are considered acceptable (Douglas 1985). Many macro theorists are deeply concerned with how the institutional structure of society makes some risks rather than others more likely to gain political and intellectual attention (Clarke 1988). Consider, for instance, motor vehicle risks. Nearly 50,000 people are killed on U.S. highways every year, which most would agree is an appalling mortality rate. Now, although it is a commonplace that half of those deaths are alcohol-related, the truth of the matter is that we don't really know how much of the carnage is, in fact, due to alcohol (Gusfield 1981). Nevertheless, we can probably reasonably assume that some serious proportion is caused by drunken drivers (even 10 percent would be 5,000 deaths). Most people would agree that 5,000 deaths per year is grounds for concern. Yet we also know that high rates of fatal traffic accidents are associated with speeding, wrong turns, and improper passing. Objectively, there is no difference between a death caused by someone making a wrong turn and one caused by a drunken driver. And yet most nations' cultures say the two deaths are in fact very different indeed. In the United States there is even a small social movement galvanized around the issue of drunken drivers, one example of which is the organization called Mothers Against Drunk Drivers. But why is there no organization called Mothers Against Improper Passers? A sociological answer is that most cultures frown on using drugs to alter one's degree of self-control, and one who does so is defined as morally decadent and lacking social responsibility. Therefore, the ardent opprobrium unleashed on drunken drivers has less to do with the objective magnitude of the problem than the apparent danger such drivers represent to the cultural value of self-control. This type of analysis tells much about the conditions under which phenomena become socially constructed as social problems.

Another example of macro work on risk, this time concerning organizations, is the massive oil spill from the *Exxon-Valdez* tanker in March 1989. At the time, the spill was the worst ever to occur in U.S. waters, leaking at least 11 million gallons of oil into Prince William Sound and the Gulf of Alaska. The accident caused massive loss of wildlife, and although no people died, it did cause massive disruptions in social relationships, created a political crisis, and reoriented debates about the safety of oil transportation systems in the United States. From a sociological point of view, one of the most interesting things about the Exxon spill has to do with how corporations and regulatory agencies plan for large oil spills. Sound research shows there really isn't much that can be done about large amounts of spilled oil (Clarke 1990). And yet, organizations continue to create elaborate plans for what they will do to contain large spills, and for how they will clean the oil from beaches and shorelines. They do this even though there has never been a case of successful containment or recovery on the open seas. Organizations create plans that will never work because such plans are master metaphors for taming the wild, subjugating uncertainty, and proclaiming expertise. We live in a world in which expert knowledge and rational organization are of paramount importance, and we now seem to have an institutionalized incapacity to admit that some things may be beyond our control.

Yet another example is the 1984 tragedy in Bhopal, India. At least 2,600 people died when a very complex accident in a Union Carbide plant released toxic chemicals into the environment. At the time, Bhopal was the worst single industrial accident in history (the nuclear meltdown at Chernobyl in 1986 will eventually be responsible for more deaths). The Bhopal tragedy was certainly an organizational failure, as a number of studies have documented (Shrivastava 1987). For our purposes here, however, what was interesting about the Bhopal accident was that the risk created by the Union Carbide chemical plant had become institutionalized to the point where very few if any of the key players were worried about potential catastrophe. The poor people who lived next to the plant seemed to have accepted official assurances that they were safe (and in any case had little choice in the matter). Government officials—the ones assuring those who lived near the plant of safety—seemed to have accepted the catastrophic potential of the plant as part of the price of having a large corporation in their country. For their part, corporate officials and experts seem to have given insufficient thought to the possibility of killing several thousand Indians. One reason the Bhopal disaster is sociologically interesting is the degree to which individuals, groups, and organizations come to accept risk as part of their everyday lives. The same observation might be made of automobile driving, nuclear power plants, and lead-contaminated water pipes (even brass pipes have about 7 percent lead in them).

We shall consider one final example of a macro analysis of risk. Every year our natural environment seems more polluted than the preceding year. Why? A common-sense explanation might claim that people just don't care enough about the environment, perhaps attributing callous attitudes or personal greed to politicians and corporations. Such an explanation would focus on the motives of individual managers and politicians, but from a sociological point of view would miss the all-important institutions in which such decision makers are embedded. Sociologists know that those who occupy top positions in government and corporate organizations are not without intelligence and good sense. Such decision makers may even be individually quite concerned about environmental degradation. But because of their structural locations, they are subject to pressures that may be at odds with environmental health and welfare. These pressures originate in specific social structures that create institutional interests that may be contrary to individual preferences (Clarke 1988; 1989). The corporate executive seeks (and *must* seek) to remain in business, if necessary at the expense of others' well-being or the environment. A similar explanation accounts for why Ford president Lee Iacocca marketed Pintos in the 1970s that had an extraordinary propensity to explode and burn. In other words, market institutions are arranged so that it is sensible for any individual, or individual organization, to force negative externalities on society. For its part, one of the key functions of government is to maintain a political and economic environment that is favorable to business. Thus, an explanation that centers on the institutional constraints and incentives that shape decisions about pollution is better able to account for the behavior of organizations, experts, and officials than an explanation that focuses on their personal characteristics (Vaughan 1990).

One reason the Bhopal disaster is sociologically interesting is the degree to which individuals and groups came to accept risk as part of their lives.

Future developments in the sociology of risk will likely revolve around issues of social conflict—its bases, its meaning, its role in spurring social change. Society, and sociology, will be confronted with some fundamental dilemmas in the next century. Modernity, as Max Weber foresaw, brings both fruits and poisons. The fruits include convenience, longer lives, and high standards of living. Yet, many of our most frightening threats—nuclear meltdowns near large cities, toxic leachate in water tables, ozone destruction, explosions of liquefied natural gas from supertankers, failure to contain nuclear waste—almost seem to be beyond our ability to control them. It may well be the case that before we can better control political and technological systems, we must admit that some aspects of the technical world are not within our control. Such an admission would be anathema to cultures dedicated to the notion of personal, social, and environmental mastery.

[See also Human Ecology and the Environment.]

BIBLIOGRAPHY

Clarke, Lee 1988 "Explaining Choices Among Technological Risks." *Social Problems* 35 (1):501–514.

——— 1989 *Acceptable Risk? Making Decisions in a Toxic Environment.* Berkeley: University of California Press.

——— 1990 "Oil Spill Fantasies." *Atlantic Monthly* (Nov.):65–77.

Couch, Stephen R., and J. Stephen Kroll-Smith 1985 "The Chronic Technical Disaster." *Social Science Quarterly* 66 (3):564–575.

Douglas, Mary 1985 *Risk Acceptability According to the Social Sciences.* New York: Russell Sage Foundation.

Erikson, Kai 1990 "Toxic Reckoning: Business Faces a New Kind of Fear." *Harvard Business Review* 90 (1):118–126.

Freudenburg, William R. 1988 "Perceived Risk, Real Risk: Social Science and the Art of Probabilistic Risk Assessment." *Science* 242. (October 7):44–49.

Gusfield, Joseph 1981 *The Culture of Public Problems: Drinking-Driving and the Symbolic Order.* Chicago: University of Chicago Press.

Heimer, Carol A. 1988 "Social Structure, Psychology, and the Estimation of Risk." *Annual Review of Sociology* 14:491–519.

——— Forthcoming "Your Baby's Fine, just Fine: Certification Procedures, Meetings, and the Supply of Information in Neonatal Intensive Care Units." In James F. Short, Jr., and Lee Clarke, eds., *Risky Decision Making: Complexity and Context.*

Kahneman, Daniel, Paul Slovic, and Amos Tversky 1982 *Judgment under Uncertainty: Heuristics and Biases.* Cambridge: Cambridge University Press.

Perrow, Charles 1984 *Normal Accidents: Living with High Risk Technologies.* New York: Basic Books.

Short, James F., Jr. 1984 "Toward the Social Transformation of Risk Analysis." *American Sociological Review* 49 (6):711–755.

Shrivastava, Paul 1987 *Bhopal: Anatomy of a Crisis.* Cambridge: Ballinger.

Vaughan, Diane 1990 "Autonomy, Interdependence, and Social Control: NASA and the Space Shuttle Challenger." *Administrative Science Quarterly* 35 (2):225–257.

– LEE CLARKE

TECHNOLOGY AND SOCIETY

Popularization of the word *technology* in the early nineteenth century indicated that an organized body of knowledge was developing about how to produce various useful material objects. The word came to be employed in a way that suggested an awareness that technological change could be directed to specific ends and that the conscious control of technology could be a means of shaping the future direction of society. Thus was inaugurated the explicit relationship between technology and society, a relationship that had previously been implicit.

The technology of a society encompasses the tools its members use and the procedures involved in inventing, producing, maintaining, and using them. Some observers define the term more broadly to include all practices employed in a rational way to achieve specific ends, even if material tools are not directly involved. Popular discussions of technology focus largely on recent and anticipated advances in, and problems related to, weaponry, medicine, computing, communication, transportation, spaceflight, and agricultural and industrial production. However, old and simple tools such as toothpicks, flyswatters, hammers, and baskets are also part of technology, and they do not necessarily disappear as newer and more complicated forms of technology arise.

A major technological item requires an infrastructure, or supporting system. Thus, the automobile as a major element in a society's transportation calls for paved roads, service and repair stations, spare parts, trained drivers, automobile mechanics, traffic laws and authorities to enforce them, and arrangements for manufacturing or importing autos. An inadequate supporting system may inhibit adoption of certain technologies. On the other hand, when the drive to adopt a particular technological item is strong enough, social pressures may be generated to develop the necessary supporting system, which, in turn, may involve major social changes.

Technological determinism, illustrated by the works of Leslie White (1949) and Jacques Ellul (1964), conceives of the technology-society relationship as primarily unidirectional, with technology developing autonomously and shaping the course of development of society, but without having its own developmental direction strongly shaped by society in turn.

In support of technological determinism one might cite numerous instances in which a seemingly minor technological development has had drastic social consequences. Adoption of the stirrup, which enabled warriors on horseback to brace themselves while charging, helped to make possible the fighting style characteristic of medieval knights and the feudal social system centering on knighthood (White 1946). A transition from dry rice cultivation (on hillside land that had to be abandoned after a few years because the soil became depleted) to wet rice cultivation (on low-lying land that could be cultivated year after year without interruption) caused the Tanala tribe of Madagascar to abandon a nomadic life-style and adopt a settled way of life, with consequent changes in diverse institutions (Linton 1957). More recently, the elevator has made possible a life-style centering on skyscrapers, and air conditioning has enormously increased the potential attractiveness of geographical locations with hot climates (making possible, for example, the explosive growth of Phoenix, Arizona).

Evidence against technological determinism includes the fact that the consequences of a technological innovation sometimes vary from one social setting to another. Thus, gunpowder, printing, and the compass had effects in Western Europe very different from their effects when introduced earlier in China. Printing, for example, facilitated standardization of official government documents in China, while in Western Europe printing facilitated an explosive diversification of published literature (Needham 1969). Similarly, computers may have either centralizing or decentralizing effects, depending on the social context. This casts doubt on the variant of technological determinism that sees modern technologies as increasingly requiring economies of scale that reinforce tendencies toward bureaucratic centralization in modern society (Etzkowitz 1991).

Also opposed to technological determinism and favoring a conception of technological dependence on society is the idea, emphasized by Mumford (1967) and others, that society can choose among alternative technologies. Once a particular technology is chosen (often because it fits in better with established social arrangements than the rejected alternatives would), these alternatives are often largely forgotten, and the commitment to the chosen technology is reinforced by further investment in it and in the social patterns associated with it. What was chosen then appears in retrospect to have been inevitable, even though it actually was not. Examples include the post' World War II American commitment to nuclear power that fit in with the bureaucratic structure of established power companies and the concomitant neglect of a solar-energy alternative that might have bypassed these companies in favor of more decentralized arrangements (Etzkowitz 1984); the selection of the internal-combustion engine for automobiles, with electric and steam-driven models disappearing from public awareness (see Flink 1975); and the American commitment to the automobile while urban public transit systems deteriorated.

Regardless of the causal relationships between technology and society, there are striking structural similarities between some machines that modern technology has given us and some organizational arrangements prevailing in technologically advanced societies. The standardization of machine components that permits their routine replacement with "spare parts" parallels the bureaucratic expectation that performances by certain organizational personnel be standardized. The process of automatic adjustment to changing circumstances as illustrated by the thermostat is also illustrated by arrangements that provide for automatic cost-of-living salary adjustments to inflation and for automatic reapportionment of legislative bodies when new census data are obtained (Richter 1982).

The technologies of the simplest human societies involve few if any *secondary tools* (tools used to make other tools), entail relatively little specialization of human activity, rely primarily on human muscles and on natural rather than artificially produced substances, and focus on adaptation to natural environments rather than on efforts to transform these environments (e.g., on adapting to forest life rather than on wiping out the forest).

The major civilizations of the ancient world, technologically advanced far beyond the level of the simplest societies, produced great engineering feats that are still admired today: impressive buildings, irrigation systems, fortifications, and highways. Ancient technology nevertheless developed very slowly by modern standards, as illustrated by the several thousand years that elapsed between the earliest domestication of horses and the widespread adoption of the stirrup. In recent times the pace of technological change has drastically accelerated, exponentially according to some observers. The Industrial Revolution, developing over several centuries, reaching a climax in late eighteenth- and early nineteenth-century England, and centering around steam power and coal, led to a second great technological transformation centering around electricity and chemistry and to still another transformation now taking place centering on information technology (Bell 1989). Technological innovation has manifestly transformed human life, yet new technology sometimes has conservative, stabilizing implications. Thus, the shift from wood to coal as a fuel in eighteenth-century England helped preserve an established way of life that was threatened by a growing wood shortage (Richter 1980, pp. 69–79).

A major technological task in ancient times was to figure out ways in which the muscles of numerous individual people (or, in some cases, domestic animals) could be effectively combined, e.g., how the muscles of hundreds of oarsmen could be coordinated to propel a large oared ship. Modern technology, in contrast, commonly tends to displace human labor, although movement in this direction is inhibited where labor costs are low relative to other costs. Thus, where farm labor is cheap and abundant while good farmland is scarce and expensive, agricultural technology seeks to maximize production per acre rather than production per farm worker. Modern businesses also sometimes transfer work from their employees to their customers, rather than transferring it from employees to labor-saving machinery. Thus, in an American supermarket customers (rather than employees or machinery) typically move down the aisles to collect items to be purchased and transport these items to the checkout counter.

Modern technology and modern science powerfully reinforce one another. For example, nuclear science has provided the foundation for nuclear technologies (weapons and power plants), while computer technology has opened up numerous new possibilities for scientific research. However, technology in relatively simple forms developed slowly over many millennia before science came into existence. To understand prescientific technologies we must realize that, even without the systematically controlled observation and experimentation of science, ordinary trial-and-error methods can produce substantial practical knowledge if continued over a long time and also that effective technologies can sometimes develop even without much comprehension of how or why they work (e.g., traditional folk medicine, which is sometimes surprisingly effective even though its practitioners have no adequate theoretical conception of the mechanisms through which their results are obtained).

Even after the rise of modern science in the seventeenth century, technological progress in many areas continued for a long time to occur primarily through craft traditions quite separate from science. Thus, eighteenth-century productive enterprises such as brickmaking and glassblowing were based on the accumulated knowledge and experiences of craftsmen, which were passed on to apprentices through observation and practice under the guidance of a master. Occasionally in the course of making a product, an anomaly would occur that was found to produce an improvement. This improvement might then be incorporated into future production, without necessarily being fully understood or put into writing.

In medieval Europe, and in some other preindustrial civilizations as well, craft traditions and scholarly traditions tended to be sharply separated (Mason 1962). The coming together of these traditions in the sixteenth and seventeenth centuries facilitated the rise of modern science. Engineering disciplines, in turn, emerged in the nineteenth century from a mixture of modern science with craft traditions. These disciplines utilized mathematical and experimental techniques derived from science to organize and expand the knowledge of craft practitioners, who passed on this knowledge to students through schools and written formulations rather than through apprenticeships. Today, much new technology comes from engineers, but some comes from scientists directly, and some still comes from craftspeople, as in the distant past.

In the twentieth century, research and development (R & D) has come to constitute a distinctive and separate activity within industrial corporations, and companies devoted exclusively or primarily to R & D have emerged. The management of technology has become a distinctive occupational specialty, and research managers directing groups of engineers and scientists have become a driving force in technological advance. In the United States these developments have taken place primarily within the private sector. In Japan and Europe governments have come to play a greater direct role in coordinating the relationship between technological change and the economy.

Innovations ranging from streetlights to anesthesia were initially opposed by some on the ground that they interfered with God's plans.

Technological developments have produced diverse, and often negative, reactions. Innovations ranging from streetlights to anesthesia were initially opposed by some on the ground that they interfered with God's plans. The Luddites were English workers in 1811–1816 who smashed machines that they blamed for unemployment and low wages. Many more recent workers have also opposed technological innovations that threaten their jobs. Some business corporations have tried to discourage new technologies that might destroy the market for their existing products. One way they have done this is by obtaining patent rights to products that they then decline to produce and also prevent other corporations from producing (see Stern 1959). Military organizations have often resisted new technologies. Reactions against big technology and a preference for locally controlled, small-scale, technological arrangements have been expressed in an "Appropriate Technology" movement (see Schumacher 1973). There is also considerable concern today about technology-induced damage to the environment and to human health and about dangerous implications of modern technologies of war.

In addition, new technological capacities impose new decision-making burdens on the political system. Technological knowledge must be taken into account in making decisions about weapons procurement, pollution control, funding of medical care, and innumerable other governmental matters. And new technology makes citizens' preferences about various matters relevant to the political process in new ways. If we ever learn to control the weather, our political system will have to cope with the fact that different people have different weather preferences, a fact that has always existed but that will become politically relevant only if and when significant weather-controlling capacities arise.

Despite problems associated with modern technology, we have become fundamentally dependent upon it. For example, without modern technologies of agriculture and transportation we could not feed our population that has grown far beyond the premodern level. Furthermore, we depend on further technological progress to help us overcome problems associated with the technology we already have. Thus, we need new energy sources to enable us to avoid the polluting effects of fuels we use today. Pressure for still further technological innovation arises from unsatisfied needs, from profit-making motives, and from challenges posed by technologically advancing competitors.

The sociological importance of technology is reflected in the fact that technological criteria are often used by sociologists to distinguish among types of societies. Thus we have *hunting and gathering, horticultural, agrarian* and *industrial* societies distinguished on the basis of their levels of technological achievement (see Lenski and Lenski 1982). The importance of technology has also led to numerous attempts to distinguish between good and bad technologies, but such a distinction is complicated not only by the absence of agreement as to what is good or bad but also by the fact that a given technological item may have highly diverse uses and implications. Thus, the same biological knowledge may be used for curing illness and for biological warfare. And the importance of technology has inspired innumerable attempts to predict its future development and implications, often with results that can provide amusement for subsequent generations, such as a wildly overpessimistic prediction in 1903 (a few months before the Wright brothers' first flight) that heavier-than-air machines would never fly, and an overoptimistic prediction by the sociologist William Fielding Ogburn (1946) that numerous Americans would soon acquire private airplanes that would be "roadable" (i.e., convertible to automobiles for ground travel).

Paradoxically, the importance of technology in society has not caused the "sociology of technology" to become an especially prominent sociological specialty. Instead, studies of different kinds of technology have become recognized as belonging to different sociological specializations. Thus, the sociological study of weaponry is part of *military sociology,* while the sociological study of medical technology is part of *medical sociology.* However, this situation now appears to be changing, as a coherent body of sociological knowledge concerning the general relationship between technology and society has been emerging (see Bijker, Hughes, and Pinch 1987; Mackenzie and Wajcman 1985; Richter 1982; Shrum 1985; Westrum 1991).

[See also Inventions; Technological Risks and Society.]

BIBLIOGRAPHY

Bell, Daniel 1989 "The Third Technological Revolution." *Dissent* (Spring); 164–176.

Bijker, Wiebe E., Thomas P. Hughes, and Trevor J. Pinch (eds.) 1987 *The Social Construction of Technological Systems.* Cambridge, Mass.: MIT Press.

Ellul, Jacques 1964 *The Technological Society,* trans. John Wilkinson. New York: Knopf.

Etzkowitz, Henry 1984 "Nuclear vs. Solar Energy: Autonomous or Dependent Technology?" *Social Problems* 31:417–434.

——— 1991 "Technology and Social Change." In Henry Etzkowitz and Ronald Glassman, eds., *The Renascence of Sociological Theory.* Itasca, Ill.: F. E. Peacock.

Flink, James J. 1975 *The Car Culture.* Cambridge, Mass.: MIT Press.

Lenski, Gerhard, and Jean Lenski 1982 *Human Societies: An Introduction to Macrosociology.* New York: McGraw-Hill.

Linton, Ralph 1957 *The Tanala: A Hill Tribe of Madagascar.* Chicago: Field Museum of Natural History.

Mackenzie, Donald A., and Judy Wajcman (eds.) 1985 *The Social Shaping of Technology: How the Refrigerator Got Its Hum.* New York: Taylor and Francis.

Mason, Stephen F. 1962 *A History of the Sciences.* New York: Collier.

Mumford, Lewis 1967 *Technics and Human Development.* New York: Harcourt, Brace, and World.

Needham, Joseph 1969 *The Grand Titration: Science and Society in East and West.* Toronto: University of Toronto Press.

Ogburn, William Fielding 1946 *The Social Effects of Aviation.* Boston: Houghton Mifflin.

Richter, Maurice N., Jr. 1980 *Society: A Macroscopic View.* Cambridge, Mass.: Schenkman.

——— 1982 *Technology and Social Complexity.* Albany, N. Y.: State University of New York Press.

Schumacher, E. F. 1973 *Small Is Beautiful: Economics As If People Mattered.* New York: Harper and Row.

Shrum, Wesley 1985 *Organized Technology: Networks and Innovation in Technical Systems.* West Lafayette, Ind.: Purdue University Press.

Stern, Bernhard J. 1959 "Restraints upon the Utilization of Inventions." In *Historical Sociology.* New York: Citadel Press.

Westrum, Ron 1991 *Technologies and Society: The Shaping of People and Things.* Belmont, Calif: Wadsworth.

White, Leslie A. 1949 *The Science of Culture.* New York: Farrar, Straus, and Cudahy.

White, Lynn 1946 *Medieval Technology and Social Change.* Oxford: Clarendon Press.

– HENRY ETZKOWITZ
MAURICE N. RICHTER, JR.

TERRORISM

Terrorism became an issue of worldwide concern during the last third of the twentieth century. Terrorist tactics themselves were not new—they had been used for centuries before being defined as terrorism. The word *terror* entered the political lexicon during the French Revolution's "reign of terror." In the late nineteenth century, the beginning of the twentieth, and again in the 1920s and 1930s—significantly, all periods between major wars on the European continent—terrorism became a technique of revolutionary struggle. Stalin's regime in the 1930s and 1940s was called a reign of terror, but from the late 1940s to the 1960s the word was associated primarily with the armed struggles for independence waged in Palestine and Algeria, from which later generations of terrorists took their inspiration and instruction. Following World War II, "terror" emerged as a component of nuclear strategy; the fear of mutual destruction that would deter nuclear war between the United States and the Soviet Union was referred to as a "balance of terror."

Here was a concept on the move. By the 1970s, *terrorism* became a fad word, promiscuously applied to a wide spectrum of conditions and actions. Bombs in public places were one form of terrorism, but some people asserted that poverty and hunger were also a form of terrorism. Some governments labeled as terrorism all violent acts committed by their opponents, while antigovernment extremists claimed to be, and often were, the victims of government terror.

In an effort to get a firm hold on a slippery subject, those wishing to study the phenomenon of terrorism were obliged to define it more precisely. Terrorism could be described simply as the use or threat of violence, calculated to create an atmosphere of fear and alarm and thereby to bring about some political result. But making this definition operative in political debate, rules of war, or criminal codes was anything but easy. Is all politically motivated violence terrorism? How does terrorism differ from ordinary crime? Should terrorism be considered a crime at all, or should it be seen as simply another form of armed conflict, no less legitimate than any other form of war? Is the term properly reserved for those trying to overthrow governments, or can governments also be terrorists?

Definition was crucial because it ultimately determined the way in which terrorism has been studied. A major problem was that terrorism almost always has a pejorative connotation and thus falls in the same category of words as *tyranny* and *genocide,* unlike such relatively neutral terms as *war* and *revolution.* One can aspire to objective and dispassionate research, but one cannot be neutral about terrorism any more than one can be neutral about torture. Thus, defining terrorism became an effort not only to delineate a subject area but also to maintain its illegitimacy. Even the most clinical inquiry was laden with values and, therefore, political issues. The very study of terrorism implied to some a political decision.

Terrorism can be defined objectively by the quality of the act, not by the identity of the perpetrators or the nature of their cause. All terrorist acts are crimes, and many would also be war crimes or "grave breaches" of the rules of war if one accepted the terrorists' assertion that they wage war. All terrorist acts involve violence or the threat of violence, sometimes coupled with explicit demands. The violence is directed against noncombatants. The purposes are political. The actions are often carried out in a way that will achieve maximum publicity, and the perpetrators are usually members of an organized group.

The hallmark of terrorism is that terrorist acts are intended to produce psychological damage.

Terrorist organizations are by necessity clandestine, but, unlike other criminals, terrorists often claim credit for their acts. And finally—the hallmark of terrorism—the acts are intended to produce psychological damage. This introduces a distinction between the actual victims of terrorist violence and the target audience. The connection between the victim and the target of terrorism can be remote. The identity of the victims may be secondary or even irrelevant to the terrorist cause. "Pure terrorism" is entirely indiscriminate violence.

Terrorism differs from ordinary crime in its political purpose and in its primary objective. But not all politically motivated violence is terrorism, nor is terrorism synonymous with guerilla war or any other kind of war.

Terrorist techniques can be used by governments or those fighting against governments; however, scholars generally use the term *terror* when discussing fear-producing tactics employed by governments and *terrorism* when referring to tactics used by those fighting against governments. The distinction is primarily semantic. Both groups may use threats, assassinations, or abductions, but government terror may also include arbitrary imprisonment, concentration camps, torture, mind-affecting techniques, and the use of drugs for political purposes. Antigovernment terrorists generally lack the infrastructure for such tactics. Government terror produces more victims than terrorism does. Terrorists tend to seek more publicity than do governments.

The term *international terrorism* refers to terrorist attacks on foreign targets or the crossing of national frontiers to carry out terrorist attacks. It was the dramatic rise in international terrorism—especially in the form of attacks on diplomats and commercial aviation in the late 1960s—that caused mounting alarm on the part of governments not directly involved in these local conflicts.

The 1980s recognized a new form of international terrorism—state-sponsored terrorism. Some governments began to use terrorist tactics themselves or to employ terrorist tactics as a mode of surrogate warfare. Unlike government-directed terror, which is primarily domestic, state-sponsored terrorism is directed against foreign governments or domestic foes abroad.

Despite great differences in political perspectives and outlook toward armed conflict, the international community gradually came to accept at least a partial definition of terrorism and prohibited certain tactics and attacks on certain targets. This approach reflected that of the academic community, focusing on the terrorist act and rejecting judgment based on the political objective or cause behind the act. Thus, by 1985, the United Nations General Assembly unanimously condemned international terrorism, including but not limited to those acts covered by previous treaties against airline hijacking and sabotage of aircraft, attacks in any form against internationally protected persons (i.e., diplomats), and the taking of hostages.

This covered roughly half of all incidents of international terrorism but omitted primarily bombings of targets other than airlines or diplomatic facilities. One difficulty in delineating this type of terrorist act is the problem of distinguishing between terrorist bombings and aerial bombardment, which is considered a legitimate form of war. The rules of war prohibit indiscriminate bombing, thus providing at least a theoretical distinction between war and terrorism, although, even with modern precision-guided munitions, collateral civilian casualties from aerial bombing in populated areas vastly exceed casualties caused by the deliberate, indiscriminate bombs of terrorists.

Research has focused narrowly on the phenomenon of terrorism. In part, this reflects the desire of researchers to avoid the murky, politically loaded area of underlying causes, where any discussion might be seen as condemnation or the rationalization of terrorist violence. Nonetheless, there have been some excellent case studies of individual groups and their tactics.

Defining terrorism in terms of the act has enabled researchers to maintain a theoretically objective approach and conduct at least some primitive quantitative analysis. Event-based analysis has enabled them to discern broad patterns and trends and to chart the growth of terrorism and its diffusion around the globe. They have been able to demonstrate statistically that as terrorism has increased in volume it has also become bloodier. Researchers have been able to illustrate a clear trend toward incidents of large-scale indiscriminate violence in the 1980s and to infer that terrorists tend to be more imitative than innovative in their tactics. Event-based analysis has also permitted researchers to distinguish the operational profiles of specific terrorist groups, and these profiles have been useful in identifying changes in a group's *modus operandi.*

At the same time, event-based analysis has led the analysts into some methodological traps. An exclusive focus on terrorist actions, for example, resulted in terrorists being viewed first as if they were all part of a single entity and second as if they were almost extraterrestrial. While there are connections and alliances among some terrorist groups, the only thing the terrorists of the world have in common is a propensity for violence and certain tactics. Moreover, each group is rooted in its own social, political, and cultural soil, and cross-national comparisons are difficult. This has led to the question of whether there are terrorist-prone societies.

Researchers' attempts to discern deeper causes or conditions that lead to high levels of terrorism in certain societies have produced meager results. Terrorism is not demonstrably a response to poverty or political oppression. The liberal democracies of Western Europe have suffered high levels of terrorist violence, while totalitarian states are virtually free of terrorism. Overall, countries with perceived terrorist problems tend to be comparatively advanced politically and economically. They are more highly urbanized, have higher per capita incomes, larger middle classes, more university students, and higher rates of literacy. One may ask whether political and economic advance simply brings a more modern form of political violence.

An obstacle to linking high levels of terrorism with environmental factors is the problem of measuring terrorism. For the most part, this has consisted of counting terrorist incidents. But international terrorism, as we have seen, was narrowly and, more important, artificially defined to include only those incidents that cause international concern, a distinction that has meant very little to the terrorists. Counting *all* terrorist incidents, both local and international, is better but still inadequate. Terrorist tactics, narrowly defined, represent most of what some groups, particularly those in Western Europe, do; but for other groups, terrorism repre-

The international community considers terrorist acts, such as the bombing of the American embassy in Beirut, Lebanon, in 1983, as crimes. (UPI/Corbis-Bettmann)

sents only one facet of a broader armed conflict. And what about the extensive uncounted political and communal violence in the rural backlands of numerous third world countries? Broad statements about terrorist-prone or violence-prone societies simply cannot be made on the basis of measuring only a thin terrorist crust of that violence.

Many terrorists have been urban middle and upper class males, in their early twenties, with university or at least secondary school educations.

If terrorism cannot be explained by environmental factors, then we must look into the mind of the individual terrorist for an explanation. Are there individuals who are prone to becoming terrorists—a preterrorist personality? Encouraged by superficial similarities in the demographic profiles of the terrorists—many of them have been urban middle and upper class (not economically deprived) males, in their early twenties, with university or at least secondary school educations—researchers searched for common psychological features.

Behavioral analysts painted an unappealing portrait: The composite terrorist appeared to be a person who was narcissistic, emotionally flat, easily disillusioned, incapable of enjoyment, rigid, and a true believer who was action-oriented and risk-seeking. Psychiatrists could label terrorists as neurotic, possibly sociopathic, but they found that most of them were not clinically insane. Some behavioral analysts looked for deeper connections between the terrorists' attitude toward parents and their attitudes toward authority. A few went further in claiming a physiological explanation for terrorism based upon inner ear disorders, but these assertions were not given wide credence in the scientific community. The growing number of terrorists apprehended and imprisoned in the 1980s permitted more thorough studies, but while these occasionally unearthed tantalizing similarities, they also showed terrorists to be a diverse if dangerous lot.

Much of the research on terrorism has been government-sponsored and therefore oriented toward the practical goal of understanding terrorism in order to defeat it. While social scientists looked for environmental or behavioral explanations for terrorism, other researchers attempted to identify terrorist vulnerabilities and successful countermeasures. They achieved a measure of success in several areas. Studies of the human dynamics of hostage situations led to the development of psychological tactics that increased the hostages' chances of survival and a better understanding (and therefore more effective treatment) of those who had been held hostage. In some cases, specific psychological vulnerabilities were identified and exploited. With somewhat less success, researchers also examined the effects of broader policies, such as not making concessions to terrorists holding hostages or military retaliation. The conclusions in this area were less clear-cut.

A final area of research concerned the effects of terrorism on society. Here, researchers viewed terrorism as comprising not only the sum of terrorist actions but also the fear and alarm produced by those actions. Public opinion polls, along with measurable decisions like not flying or avoiding certain countries, provided the measure of effect.

Over the years, research on terrorism has become more sophisticated, but in the end, terrorism confronts us with fundamental philosophical questions: Do ends justify means? How far does one go on behalf of a cause? What is the value of an individual human life? What obligations do governments have toward their own citizens, if, for example, they are held hostage? Should governments; or corporations ever bargain for human life? What limits can be imposed on individual liberties to ensure public safety? Is the use of military force, as a matter of choice, ever appropriate? Can assassination ever be justified? These are not matters of research. They are issues that have been debated through the ages.

[See also International Law; Revolutions; Violent Crime; War.]

BIBLIOGRAPHY

Kurz, Anat (ed.) 1987 *Contemporary Trends in World Terrorism.* Tel Aviv, Israel: The Jaffee Center for Strategic Studies.

Laqueur, Walter 1976 *Guerrilla—A Historical and Critical Study.* Boston: Little, Brown.

——— 1977 *Terrorism.* Boston: Little, Brown.

O'Sullivan, Noel (ed.) 1986 *Terrorism, Ideology and Revolution.* Boulder, Colo.: Westview Press.

Schmid, Alex P., and Albert J. Jongman 1988 *Political Terrorism.* Amsterdam/Oxford/New York: North Holland.

Thackrah, John Richard 1987 *Terrorism and Political Violence.* London: Routledge & Kegan Paul.

Wilkinson, Paul, and Alasdair M. Stewart (eds.) 1987 *Contemporary Research on Terrorism.* Aberdeen, Scotland: Aberdeen University Press.

– BRIAN MICHAEL JENKINS

U

URBANIZATION

Urbanization is the process of expansion in the entire system of interrelationships by which a population maintains itself in its habitat (Hawley 1981, p. 12). The most evident consequences of the process, and the most common measures of it, are an increase in the number of people at points of population concentration, an increase in the number of points at which population is concentrated, or both (Tisdale 1942). Theories of urbanization attempt to explain how human settlement patterns change as technology expands the scale of social systems.

Because technological regimes, population growth mechanisms, and environmental contingencies change over time and differ in different regions of the world, variations in the pattern of distribution of human settlements can generally be understood by attending to these related processes. In the literature on urbanization, interest in organizational forms of systems of cities is complemented by interest in how growth is accommodated within cities themselves through changes in density gradients, in the location of socially meaningful population subgroups, and in patterns of urban activity. Although the expansion of cities has been the historical focus for describing the urbanization process, revolutionary developments in transportation, communication, and information technology since 1950 have expanded the scale of urban systems and focused attention on the broader system of organization within which cities emerge and grow.

Much of the research on the urbanization process is descriptive in nature, emphasizing the identification and measurement of patterns of change in demographic and social organization within a territorial frame of reference. Territorially circumscribed environments employed as units of analysis include administrative units (villages, cities, counties, states, nations), population concentrations (places, agglomerations, urbanized areas), and networks of interdependency (neighborhoods, metropolitan areas, daily urban systems, city systems, earth).

A *city* is an administratively defined unit of territory containing "a relatively large, dense and permanent settlement of socially heterogeneous individuals" (Wirth 1938, p. 1). *Urban* refers to a set of specialized, nonagricultural activities that are characteristic of, but not exclusive to, city dwellers. A ruling class with a capacity for taxation and capital accumulation and writing and its application to predictive sciences, artistic expression, and trade for vital materials are the kinds of specialized activities necessary to the definition of the emergence of a truly urban place (Childe 1950). Specialized activities such as administration, commerce, and manufacturing have historically been centered in cities, but the scale of the system of interdependence and exchange involved in such activity can range from the immediate hinterland of the earliest known cities to the entire world of today. Urban activities and associated outlooks of people engaged in them are no longer found only in the city.

Less than 4 percent of the American labor force is engaged in agricultural occupations.

The extent to which dispersed population is involved in urban systems is quite variable. An estimated 90 percent of the American population now lives within a Daily Urban System (DUS). These units are constructed from counties that are allocated to economic centers on the basis of commuting patterns and economic interdependence. Residents of the DUS are closely tied together by efficient transportation and communication technology. Each DUS has a minimum population of 200,000 within its labor shed and constitutes "a multinode, multiconnective system (which) has replaced the core dominated metropolis as the basic urban unit" (Berry and Kasarda 1977, p. 304). Less than 4 percent of the American labor force is engaged in agricultural occupations. Residents even of remote rural areas are mostly urban in their activities and outlook.

In contrast, many residents inhabiting uncontrolled developments on the fringes of emerging mega-cities in less developed countries are practically isolated from the urban center and carry on much as they have done for generations. Over one-third of the population of the largest cities in India was born elsewhere, and maintenance of rural ways of life in the cities is common due to lack of urban employment, maintainance of village kinship ties, and seasonal circulatory migration to rural areas. And, although India has three of the ten largest cities in the world, it remains decidedly rural, with 75 percent of the population residing in agriculturally oriented villages (Nagpaul 1988).

Measurement of the rate at which urbanization takes place is confounded by the fact that concentrations of population do not correspond to administrative definitions of a city. Although data on population change for cities is widely reported and quite useful for administrative purposes, relatively fixed boundaries of political units make them less useful for examining change. The concept of an *urbanized area* (UA) is based upon a density criterion. In the United States a UA refers to a city of 50,000 or more inhabitants and all of the adjacent area built up to densities of 1,000 or more people per square mile. The UA was developed to be more consistent with the notion of population concentration, and it corresponds roughly with the pattern of lights that can be seen at night from an aircraft. Its boundaries change to reflect changes in concentration of numbers. A *metropolitan statistical area* (MSA) is based on a high degree of social and economic interdependence between a large population nucleus and adjacent communities that, together, are considered part of an integrated urban system. An MSA consists of a politically incorporated *central city* (CC) of 50,000 or more inhabitants (or twin cities meeting similar criteria), the county it is in, and a adjacent counties economically tied to the central city. The area outside the political boundaries of the central city, but within the MSA, is referred to as the *ring* and contains suburban population. When MSAs expand to the borders of adjacent MSAs such as in the New York and Los Angeles areas, these agglomerations of MSAs are referred to as *consolidated metropolitan statistical areas* (CMSA) and their component parts are called *primary metropolitan statistical areas* (PMSA) (U.S. Bureau of the Census 1989).

As of 1987, there were 282 MSAs and CMSAs containing just over three-quarters of the population of the United States. The remaining 25 percent of Americans resided in counties not economically tied to a city of 50,000 or more and were classified as nonmetropolitan. In 1950, just over half of all Americans (56 percent) lived in the 169 metropolitan areas in existence at that time. In 1980, the largest population agglomeration in the United States was the New York–Northeastern New Jersey CMSA, with 17,539,000 residents, 15,584,000 of whom resided in the densely built-up UA. The New York PMSA had 8,275,000 residents, and New York City proper numbered only 7,072,000 (U.S. Bureau of Census 1989).

Units for analysis must be carefully chosen to best represent research interests. Much of what is known about the direction and pace of change in the internal structure of American cities is derived from dicennial census reports for city blocks and census tracts within MSAs. A census tract is a small geographic subarea containing from one to ten thousand people for which detailed socioeconomic characteristics are reported.

The American urban system is suburbanizing and deconcentrating. One measure of suburbanization is the ratio of the rate of growth in the ring to the rate of growth in the central city over a decade (Schnore 1959). While some MSAs began suburbanizing in the late 1800s, the greatest rates for the majority of places occurred in the decades of the 1950s and 1960s. Widespread use of the automobile, inexpensive energy, efficient production of materials for residential infrastructure, and federal housing policy allowed metropolitan growth to be absorbed by sprawl rather than by increased congestion at the center.

As the scale of territorial organization increased, so did the physical distances between black and white, rich and poor, young and old, and other meaningful population subgroups. The Index of Dissimilarity measures the degree of segregation between two groups by computing the percentage of one group that would have to reside on a different city block in order for it to have the same proportional distribution across urban space as the group to which it is being compared (Taeuber and Taeuber 1965). While there was some decline in indices of dissimilarity between African-Americans and white Americans in the 1960s and 1970s, owing in part to increasing Africa-American suburbanization, the 1980 mean index for central cities of the large MSAs was slightly above 80, meaning that 80 percent of the African-Americans would have to live on different city blocks to have the same distribution in space as whites. A very high degree of residential segregation remains (Taeuber 1983). Although there is great diversity in social status within central cities, and increasing diversity within suburban rings, disadvantaged and minority populations are over-represented in central cities, while the better educated and more affluent are overrepresented in suburban rings.

A related process, deconcentration, involves a shedding of urban activities at the center and is indicated by greater growth in employment and office space in the ring than in the central city. This process was well under way by the mid-1970s and continued unabated through the 1980s. A surprising turn of events in the late 1970s was mounting evidence that nonmetropolitan counties were, for the first time since the depression of the 1930s, growing more rapidly than metropolitan counties (Lichter and Fuguitt 1982). This process has been referred to as *deurbanization* and as *the nonmetropolitan turnaround.* It is unclear whether this trend represents an enlargement of the scale of metropolitan organization to encompass more remote counties or whether new growth nodes are developing in nonmetropolitan areas.

The American urban system is undergoing major changes as a result of shifts from a manufacturing to a service economy, the aging of the population, and the expansion of organizational scale from regional and national to global decision-making contingencies. Older industrial cities in the Northeast and the Midwest lost population as the locus of economic activity shifted from heavy manufacturing to information and residentiary services. Cities in Florida, Arizona, California, and the Northwest have been the recipients of growing numbers of retirees seeking environmental, recreational, and medical amenities not tied to economic production. Investment decisions regarding the location of office complexes, the factories of the future, are made more on the basis of availability of an educated labor pool, favorable tax treatment, and availability of amenities than upon the access to raw materials that underpinned the urbanization process through the mid-twentieth century.

These same shifts are reflected in the internal reorganization of American cities. The scale of local communities expanded from the central-business-district-oriented city to the multinodal metropolis. Daily commuting patterns have been shifting from radial trips between bedroom suburbs and workplaces in the central city to lateral trips among highly differentiated subareas throughout urban regions. Urban villages of affluent residences, high-end retail minimalls, and office complexes are emerging in nonmetropolitan counties beyond the reach of metropolitan political constraints, creating even greater segregation between the most and least affluent Americans.

While suburbanization and deconcentration were general phenomena for most metropolitan areas throughout the 1960s and 1970s, shifts in the economy, in household composition, and in contingencies influencing

In 1980, the largest population agglomeration in the United States was the New York-Northwestern New Jersey consolidated metropolitan statistical area, with about 17.5 million residents. (Paul A. Souders/Corbis)

corporate-development decision making produced quite different growth patterns in different cities across the country in the 1980s. Many older central cities tied to the heavy manufacturing economy of the past have continued to decline while suburbanization and deconcentration continue. Other cities such as San Francisco, Seattle, and Denver, which offer amenities of climate or natural beauty, have witnessed massive investment in their downtown central business districts. Corporate and government office buildings that provide administrative and control functions for national and global organizations have mushroomed as new forms of private-public partnerships have been created to take advantage of existing infrastructure for traffic and other urban services and to protect existing investments in land and real estate in the central business district.

Deteriorating residential and warehousing districts adjacent to new downtown office complexes are being rehabilitated for residential use by childless professionals, or "gentry." The process of *gentrification,* or the invasion of lower-status, deteriorating neighborhoods of absentee-owned rental housing by middle- to upper-status home or condominium owners is driven by the desire for accessibility to nearby white-collar jobs and cultural amenities, as well as by the relatively higher costs of suburban housing pushed up by competing demand in these rapidly growing metropolitan areas. Although the number of people involved in gentrification is too small to have reversed the overall decline of central cities, the return of affluent middle-class residents has reduced segregation to some extent. Gentrification is positive in that it reclaims deteriorated neighborhoods, but a negative side is the displacement of the poor who have no place else to live at rents they can afford (Feagin and Parker 1990).

The pace and direction of the urbanization process are closely tied to technological advance. As industrialization proceeded in Western Europe and the United States over a 300-year period, an urban system emerged that reflected the interplay between the development of city-centered heavy industry and requirements for energy and raw materials from regional hinterlands. The form of city systems that emerged has been described as *rank-size.* Cities in such a system form a hierarchy of places from large to small such that the number of places of a given size decreases proportionally to the size of the place. Larger places are fewer in number, are more widely spaced, and offer more specialized goods and services than smaller places (Christaller 1933).

City systems that emerged in less industrialized nations are *primate* in character. In a primate system, the largest cities absorb far more than their share of societal population growth. Sharp breaks exist in the size hierarchy of places, with one or two very large, several medium-sized, and many very small places. Rapid declines in mortality beginning in the 1950s, coupled with traditionally high fertility, created unprecedented rates of natural increase. Primate city systems developed with an orientation more toward export of raw materials to the industrialized world than toward manufacturing and development of local markets. As economic development proceeds, it occurs primarily in the large primate cities with very low rates of economic growth in rural areas. Consequently, nearly all the excess of births over deaths in the nation is absorbed by the large cities, which are more integrated into the emerging global urban system (Dogan and Kasarda 1988).

In 1800 only two urbanized areas, London and Beijing, exceeded one million. By 1990, 298 had reached that size, with 408 expected by the year 2000. Between 1960 and 1990, the urbanized area of Mexico City grew from 4.9 to 19.4 million. Sao Paulo increased from 4.7 to 18.4 million. Tokyo-Yokohama doubled to 20.5 million, while New York grew from 14.2 to only 15.7 million over the same period. As of 1990, these were the four largest population agglomerations on the planet. In 1960 only four urbanized areas exceeded 10 million (Tokoyo, New York, Shanghai, and London). Twenty-five cities are expected to be over 10 million by the year 2000, eighteen of them in the less-developed world (U.S. Bureau of the Census 1989, pp. 818–819).

The territorial bounds of the relevant environment to which a population collectively adapts have expanded from the immediate hinterland to the entire world.

Mega-cities of over 10 million are a very recent phenomenon, and their number is increasing rapidly. Their emergence can be understood only within the context of a globally interdependent system of relationships. The territorial bounds of the relevant environment to which a population collectively adapts have expanded from the immediate hinterland to the entire world in the short span of only half a century.

Convergence theory suggests that cities throughout the world will come to exhibit organizational forms increasingly similar to one another, converging on the North American pattern, as technology becomes more accessible throughout the global system (Young and Young 1962). Divergence theory suggests that increasingly divergent forms of urban organization are likely to emerge due to differences in the timing and pace of the urbanization process, differences in the position of cities within the global system, and increasing effectiveness of deliberate planning of the urbanization process by centralized governments holding differing values and, therefore, pursuing a variety of goals for the future (Berry 1981).

The importance of understanding this process is suggested by Amos H. Hawley (1981, p. 13).

> Urbanization is a transformation of society, the effects of which penetrate every sphere of Personal and collective life. It affects the status of the individual and his opportunities for advancement, it alters the types of social units in which people group themselves, and it sorts people into new and shifting patterns of stratification. The distribution of Power is altered, normal social process are reconstituted, and the rules and norms by which behavior is guided are redesigned.

[See also Cities; Suburbanization; Urban Underclass.]

BIBLIOGRAPHY

Berry, Brian J. L. 1981 *Comparative Urbanization: Divergent Paths in the Twentieth Century.* New York: St. Martin's Press.

———, and John D. Kasarda 1977 *Contemporary Urban Ecology.* New York: Macmillan.

Childe, V. Gordon 1950 "The Urban Revolution." *Town Planning Review* 21:4–7.

Christaller, W. 1933 *Central Places in Southern Germany,* trans. C. W. Baskin. Englewood Cliffs, N.J.: Prentice-Hall.

Dogan, Mattei, and John D. Kasarda 1988 "Introduction: How Giant Cities Will Multiply and Grow." In Mattei Dogan and John D. Kasarda, eds., *The Metropolis Era: A World of Giant Cities,* vol. 1. Newbury Park, Calif.: Sage.

Feagin, Joe R., and Robert Parker 1990 *Building American Cities: The Urban Real Estate Game,* 2nd ed. Englewood Cliffs, N.J.: Prentice-Hall.

Hawley, Amos H. 1981 *Urban Society: An Ecological Approach.* New York: Wiley.

Lichter, Daniel T., and Glenn V. Fuguitt 1982 "The Transition to Nonmetropolitan Population Deconcentration." *Demography* 19:211–221.

Nagpaul, Hans 1988 "India's Giant Cities." In Mattei Dogan and John D. Kasarda, eds., *The Metropolis Era: A World of Giant Cities,* vol. 1. Newbury Park, Calif.: Sage.

Schnore, Leo F. 1959 "The Timing of Metropolitan Decentralization." *Journal of the American Institute of Planners* 25:200–206.

Taeuber, Karl E. 1983 *Racial Residential Segregation, 28 Cities, 1970–1980* (working paper 83–12). Madison: University of Wisconsin, Center for Demography and Ecology.

———, and Alma F. Taeuber 1965 *Negroes in Cities: Residential Segregation and Neighborhood Change.* Chicago: Aldine.

Tisdale, Hope 1942 "The Process of Urbanization." *Social Forces* 20:311–316.

U.S. Department of Commerce, Bureau of the Census 1989 *Statistical Abstract of the United States: 1989,* 109th ed. Washington, D.C.: U.S. Government Printing Office.

Wirth, Louis 1938 "Urbanism as a Way of Life." *American Journal of Sociology* 44:1–24.

Young, Frank, and Ruth Young 1962 "The Sequence and Direction of Community Growth: A Cross-Cultural Generalization." *Rural Sociology* 27:374–386.

– LEE J. HAGGERTY

URBAN UNDERCLASS

Perhaps no social science concept has generated more discussion and controversy in recent years than that of the urban underclass. Some argue that it is little more than new wine in old bottles—a pithy and stigmatizing term for poor or lower-class persons who have always existed in stratified societies (Gans 1990; Jencks 1989; Katz 1989; McGahey 1982). Others contend that the underclass is a distinct and recent phenomenon, which reflects extreme marginalization from mainstream economic institutions, and its aberrant behavior (drug abuse, violent crime, out-of-wedlock births), reached catastrophic proportions in the inner cities by the mid-1970s (Glasgow 1980; Auletta 1982; Reischauer 1987; Nathan 1987; Wilson 1987). Despite the multifaceted, subjective, and often ambiguous definitions of the urban underclass, common to almost all are the notions of weak labor-force attachment and persistent low income (Jencks and Peterson 1991; Sjoquist 1990). Indeed, the first scholar to introduce the term *underclass* to the literature labeled its members as an emergent substratum of permanently unemployed, unemployables, and underemployed (Myrdal 1962).

Widely differing interpretations of the causes of the underclass have been offered, ranging from Marxist to social Darwinist. The most influential contemporary analysis of the urban underclass is William Julius Wilson's (1987) *The Truly Disadvantaged.* In this treatise, Wilson links the origins and growth of the urban underclass to the structure of opportunities and constraints in American society. Its roots are hypothesized to lie in historical discrimination and the mass migration of blacks to Northern cities during the first half of this century. Its more recent growth and experiences are posited to rest with industrial and geographic changes occurring in Northern metropolitan economies since 1970, in particular the economic transition in central cities, where goods-processing industries have been replaced by information-processing industries and where blue-collar jobs have dispersed and relocated in the suburbs. These changes led to dramatic increases in joblessness among inner-city minorities who neither had the skills to participate in new urban growth industries nor the logistical or financial means to commute or relocate to the suburbs. Rapidly rising joblessness among inner-city blacks, in turn, triggered high concentrations

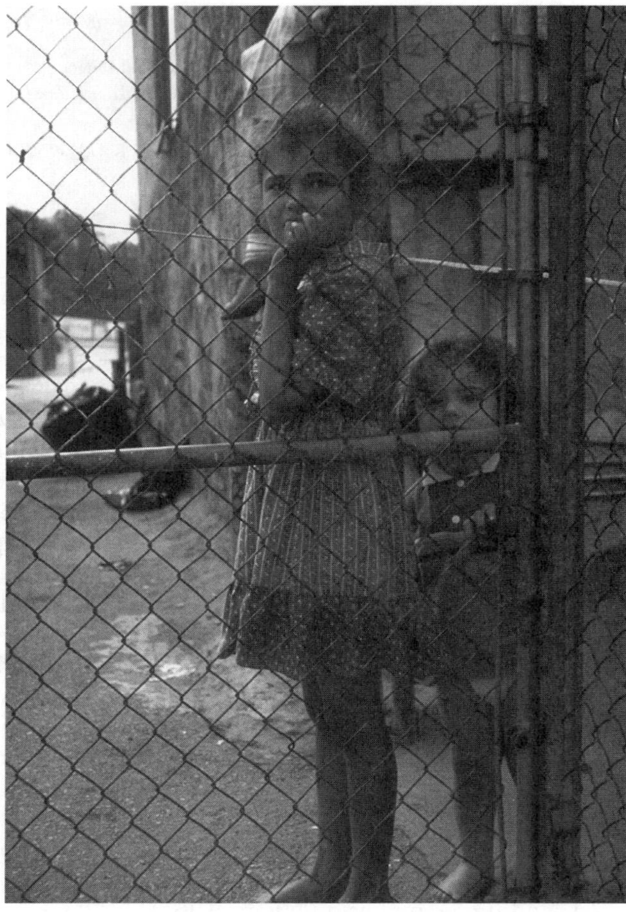

These children in a Los Angeles ghetto belong to the persistent urban underclass, the causes of which have been analyzed from numerous perspectives. (Joseph Sohm; ChromoSohm Inc./Corbis)

of poverty and related social problems that characterize its definitions (see also Kasarda 1985, 1988; Wilson 1991).

Alternative views on the causes of the underclass can be found in the works of Murray (1984) and Mead (1988). These conservative scholars look at underclass behaviors as rational adaptations to the perverse incentives found in government welfare programs plus a lack of individual responsibility for actions harmful to themselves and to others. Abetted by well-intentioned but misguided social programs, joblessness and persistent poverty are seen more as consequences of the deviant behaviors frequently noted in underclass definitions, rather than as causes of these behaviors.

Measurement of the size of the underclass varies as much as definitions of it. A number of researchers have focused on individual-level indicators of persistent poverty, defined as those who are poor for spells from n to $n + x$ years (Levy 1977; Duncan, Coe, and Hill 1984; Bane and Ellwood 1986) or long-term AFDC recipients (Gottschalk and Danziger 1987). For example, Levy (1977), using the Panel Study of Income Dynamics for years 1967 to 1973, estimated that approximately eleven million Americans were persistently poor for at least five years. When the underclass is defined as being persistently poor for eight or more years, six million people were found to be members of the underclass (Duncan, Coe, and Hill 1984). This represents approximately one-fifth of the thirty-two million Americans living in poor households in 1988 (Mincy, Sawhill, and Wolf 1990).

Another measurement strategy focuses on the geographic concentration of the poor in urban areas. Using Bureau of the Census tract-level definitions of local poverty areas, Reischauer (1987) reports that, of the nation's population living in such poverty areas, central cities housed over half in 1985, up from just one-third in 1972. Jargowsky and Bane (1990) documented that the number of poor people living in extreme poverty tracts in cities (i.e., census tracts where more than 40 percent of the residents fall below the poverty line) expanded by 66 percent between 1970 and 1980, from 975,000 to 1,615,000. Moreover, just four Northern cities (New York, Chicago, Philadelphia, and Detroit) accounted for two-thirds of this increase.

Mincy (1988) further documented that concentrated poverty is predominantly a minority problem. His analysis of extreme poverty tracts in the 100 largest central cities in 1980 showed that of the approximately 1.8 million poor people residing in these tracts, fewer than 10 percent were non-Hispanic white (175,178), while nearly 70 percent were black (1,248,151). Nearly all of the remainder were Hispanic.

As noted above, the concept of underclass is typically considered to entail more than poverty. It is also posited to incorporate certain behavioral characteristics conflicting with mainstream values: joblessness, out-of-wedlock births, welfare dependency, school dropout, and illicit activities.

While considerable debate continues to surround definitions (or even the existence) of the underclass, attempts have been made to measure its size by using multiple "behavioral" indicators derived from census data. Ricketts and Sawhill (1988) measured the underclass as people living in neighborhoods whose residents in 1980 simultaneously exhibited disproportionately high rates of school dropout, joblessness, female-headed families, and welfare dependency. Using a composite definition where tracts must fall at least one standard deviation above the national mean on *all* four characteristics, they found that approximately 2.5 million people lived in such tracts in 1980 and that these tracts were disproportionately located in major cities in the Northeast and Midwest. They reported that in underclass tracts, on average, 63 percent of the resident adults had less than a high school education, that 60 percent of the families with children were headed by women, that 56 percent of the adult men were not regularly employed, and that 34 percent of the households were receiving public assistance. Their research also revealed that, although the total poverty population grew by only 8 percent between 1970 and 1980, the number of people living in the underclass areas grew by 230 percent, from 752,000 to 2,484,000.

With the exception of tracts made up of public-housing projects, there is considerable diversity in resident income, education levels, and joblessness within urban neighborhoods.

Such location-based aggregate measures have been criticized on the grounds that, aside from race, most urban census tracts are quite heterogeneous along economic and social dimensions. Jencks (1989; Jencks and Peterson 1991), for example, observes that, with the exception of tracts made up of public-housing projects, there is considerable diversity in resident income and education levels, joblessness, and public assistance recipiency within urban neighborhoods. According to his calculations, even in extreme poverty tracts only about 50 percent of all families had incomes in 1980 below the poverty line, and some reported incomes up to four times the poverty level. He further notes Ricketts and Sawhill's findings that within the worst urban neighborhoods (those they define as underclass areas) more than 50 percent of the working age adults held steady jobs and only 33 percent of the households received public assistance. Conversely, considerable numbers of urban residents who are poor, jobless, and dependent on public assistance live in census tracts where fewer than 20 percent of the families fall below the poverty line.

Nevertheless, while most scholars concur that behaviors linked to underclass definitions and measurement are found throughout society, it is the concentration of these behaviors in economically declining inner city areas that is said to distinguish the underclass from previously impoverished urban subgroups. Geographic concentration, it is argued, magnifies social problems and accelerates their spread to nearby households through social contagion, peer pressure, and imitative behavior (Wilson 1987). Economically stable households seeking to avoid these problems selectively flee the neighborhood. Left behind in increasingly isolated concentrations are those with the least to offer in terms of marketable skills, role models, and familial stability. The result is a spiral of negative social and economic outcomes for the neighborhoods and the households that remain.

Incorporating the efforts of neighborhoods and social-transmission processes means that the future research agenda on the urban underclass will be qualitative as well as quantative in approach. Ethnographic studies of underclass neighborhoods, family systems, and individual development will complement growing numbers of surveys and sophisticated statistical analyses on the persistence and intergenerational transfer of urban poverty. In fact, some cynics have suggested that a profitable academic industry may well emerge from studying the ghetto poor.

[See also Cities; Community; Poverty; Segregation and Desegregation; Urbanization.]

BIBLIOGRAPHY

Auletta, Ken 1982 *The Underclass.* New York: Random House.

Bane, Mary Jo, and David Ellwood 1986 "Slipping Into and Out of Poverty: The Dynamics of Spells." *Journal of Human Resources* 21:1–23.

Duncan, G. J., R. D. Coe, M. S. Hill 1984 In *Years of Poverty, Years of Plenty.* Ann Arbor: Institute of Social Research, University of Michigan.

Gans, Herbert J. 1990 "Deconstructing the Underclass: The Term's Danger as a Planning Concept." *Journal of the American Planning Association,* pp. 271–277.

Glasgow, Douglas G. 1980 *The Black Underclass: Poverty, Unemployment, and Entrapment of Ghetto Youth.* San Francisco: Jossey-Bass.

Gottschalk, P. and S. Danziger 1987 Testimony on Poverty, Hunger, and the Welfare System, 5 August 1986, *Hearing Before the Select Committee on Hunger, House of Representatives,* 99th Cong., 2nd Sess., ser. no. 23. Washington, D.C.: U.S. Government Printing Office.

Jargowsky, Paul A., and Mary Jo Bane 1990 *Neighborhood Poverty: Basic Questions.* Discussion Paper Series, #H-90-3. Cambridge, Mass.: Malcolm Wiener Center for Social Policy, John F. Kennedy School of Government, Harvard University.

Jencks, Christopher 1989 "What Is the Underclass—And Is It Growing?" *Focus* 12:14–31.

———, and Paul Peterson (eds.) 1991 *The Urban Underclass.* Washington, D.C.: The Brookings Institution.

Kasarda, John D. 1985 "Urban Change and Minority Opportunities." In P. Peterson, ed., *The New Urban Reality.* Washington D.C.: Brookings Institution.

——— 1988 "Economic Restructuring and America's Urban Dilemma." In M. Dogan and J. D. Kasarda, eds., *The Metropolis Era: A World of Giant Cities.* Newbury Park, Calif.: Sage.

Katz, Michael 1989 *The Undeserving Poor: From the War on Poverty to the War on Welfare.* New York: Pantheon Books.

Levy, Frank 1977 "How Big Is the American Under-class?" Washington, D.C.: Urban Institute.
McGahey, R. 1982 "Poverty's Voguish Stigma," *The New York Times,* March 12.
Mincy, Ronald B. 1988 "Industrial Restructuring, Dynamic Events, and the Racial Composition of Concentrated Poverty." Paper prepared for Planning Meeting of Social Science Research Council on Industrial Restructuring, Local Political Economies, and Communities and Neighborhoods. New York, September 21–23, 1988.
———, Isabel V. Sawhill, Douglas A. Wolf 1990 "The Underclass: Definition and Measurement." *Science* 248:450–53.
Myrdal, Gunner 1962 *Challenge to Affluence.* New York: Pantheon.
Nathan, Richard P. 1987 "Will the Underclass Always Be with Us?" *Society* 24:57–62.
Reischauer, Robert D. 1987 *The Geographic Concentration of Poverty: What Do We Know?* Washington, D.C.: The Brookings Institution.
Ricketts, Erol, and Isabel Sawhill 1988 "Defining and Measuring the Underclass." *Journal of Policy Analysis and Management* 7:316–325.
Sjoquist, David "Concepts, Measurements, and Analysis of the Underclass: A Review of the Literature." Georgia State University. Typescript.
Wilson, William Julius 1987 *The Truly Disadvantaged: The Inner City, the Underclass, and Public Policy.* Chicago: University of Chicago Press.
——— 1991 "Studying Inner-City Social Dislocations." *American Sociological Review* 56:1–14.

– JOHN D. KASARDA

V

VIOLENT CRIME

Violent crime is commonly defined as occurring when one person illegally and intentionally physically injures, or threatens to physically injure, another. Assault, robbery, rape, and murder are the classic examples of serious violent crime. This definition is beguilingly simple, however, and one of the first lessons learned in studying violent crime is how much disagreement is possible over its definition and, thus, over its measurement, description, and explanation (Nettler 1982). There are problems in defining intent, in documenting physical injuries, and in determining how threat is perceived. Measuring and comparing both amounts and public conceptions of violent crime in different times and places are problematic for these and other reasons.

Most research on violent crime accepts the legal definitions germane to the jurisdiction under study and relies on official crime reports based on these legal definitions. (Most developed nations compile annual reports on the incidence of crime. For example, in Canada, the Canadian Centre for Justice Statistics publishes Canadian Crime Statistics; in the United States, the Federal Bureau of Investigation publishes the Uniform Crime Reports.) There are two principal difficulties with this approach to measuring crime. While legal definitions and official statistics provide a reliable guide to what is designated as crime *within* a given society, they may not in themselves accurately indicate differences *among* societies in similar types of behavior. This is because the definition of even the most serious violent crimes, including murder, can vary. Abortion, infanticide, and some deaths caused by drivers of motor vehicles have been considered criminal homicide in some societies and not in others. The acceptance of legal definitions as given neglects the issue of why certain acts are defined as crime in some places or eras and not others.

The second difficulty with using legal definitions and official statistics to define the field of study is more serious. Official statistics simply do not accurately measure levels of violent crime even within a single society. Using legal definitions typically directs researchers to official agencies such as the police, the courts, and the coroner for data, but characteristics of these agencies inevitably influence how these acts are interpreted and reported. Furthermore, some acts that appear to fit the legal definitions may only infrequently be subject to criminal enforcement, such as forms of white collar or corporate crime. Since the public is the primary means by which officials learn about violent crime, popular views on both crime and the agencies that deal with it also determine which acts are reported. Less than half of all rapes and assaults are reported to the police in most Western nations. As a result, official statistics on violent crime reflect both more and less than its true incidence (O'Brien 1985). Moreover, reliance on only official statistics neglects the issue of why laws are enforced against certain acts or persons and not others.

Some researchers have attempted to avoid these problems by using victimization surveys and self-report studies, in which people are asked about their experiences as either victims or perpetrators of certain acts. These provide higher estimates of the incidence of violent crime than do official statistics, and they describe the types of acts and actors that are less likely to appear in official statistics. Both have been criticized, however, for their reliance on the honesty and comprehension of respondents and for sometimes including trivial acts that should not be considered "real crime" (O'Brien 1985).

Differences in Violent Crime Over Time, Place, and Persons

To describe trends over time or differences among societies in violent crime, researchers presently must rely on official statistics, since self-report and victimization studies are not extensive enough. In so doing, the problems with comparing data from various official sources need to be kept in mind. The most reliable information is for the most serious crimes, especially murder and robbery. This information suggests that rates of violent crime declined over the last several centuries in Western societies, reached a low point in the first half of the twentieth century, and then increased sharply, beginning in the late 1960s. Shorter term crime waves during the early stages of urbanization and industrialization, and after wars, disrupted the general downward trend (Gurr 1989). At present, rates of violent crime are highest in several Latin American and Caribbean countries and lowest in northern and western Europe. The United States is anomalous among developed nations for its level of violent crime: Its rate of homicide is as much as ten times greater than European rates, and its robbery rate is at least thirty times that of Japan's (Archer and Gartner 1984).

Violent crime is unevenly distributed not only *among* but also *within* societies. Large regional differences are common in many countries. For example, rates of violent crime are higher in southern Italy, the southwestern and southern United States, and the western provinces of Canada. Violent crime also tends to be concentrated in urban areas, especially within developed countries. For the most serious of these crimes, offenders are predominantly young adult males, and members of disadvantaged racial and ethnic minority groups tend to be overrepresented among offenders. The majority of violent offenders have a criminal record, but few specialize in a particular type of crime (Miller, Dinitz, and Conrad 1982). Most violent crimes involve little planning, skill, or attention to their consequences.

The rate of homicide in the United States is as much as ten times greater than European rates.

Victims of violent crime, with the exception of rape victims, generally share many of the characteristics of their victimizers, most being young, economically disadvantaged males. Females make up a larger proportion of victims than they do offenders, the majority victimized by a male they are related to or acquainted with. A substantial number of violent crimes occur among family members, though this proportion is smaller in the United States than other nations and has declined in recent years. In contrast, over one-third of violent crimes in the United States are committed against strangers, a much higher proportion than in most developed nations.

Explaining Violent Crime

There are three levels of analysis that frame sociological explanations of violent crime: the individual, the situational, and the structural-cultural. Individual-level analyses typically look for characteristics of offenders that either predispose them to violence or fail to discourage them from it. Many individual-level theories focus on how violence is learned, or how restraint is not learned, from family, peers, the media, or the broader culture (Wilson and Herrnstein 1985). The intergenerational transmission of violence and the effects of the mass media on violent behavior are two issues recently addressed by learning theories (Straus and Gelles 1990; Phillips 1983). While learning theories have garnered much support, more systematic evidence of the link between exposure to "lessons" in violence and a person's violent behavior is needed to substantiate them.

Situational approaches focus on the more immediate factors and processes surrounding violent crime (Luckenbill 1984). The interaction of participants, the nature of the conflict, the presence of alcohol, drugs, or weapons, all are examined to understand how conflicts escalate to violence. Situational analyses also emphasize the subjective, symbolic aspects of violent crime. Saving face by responding to insults or resistance with violence and creating a stance of moral superiority in relation to the victim are common themes in accounts of murder, robbery, and rape (Katz 1988).

Structural-cultural approaches tend to emphasize broader social forces, processes, and value systems that affect the motivations, controls, or opportunities for violent crime. Both structural and cultural analyses attempt to explain variations in rates of violent crime among population aggregates: cities, states, regions, and nations. These two approaches differ, however, in the importance placed on individual cognitions and propensities toward violence. Cultural accounts typically see these as crucial for explaining the distribution of violent crime among different groups, whereas structural accounts do not. Instead, structural analyses examine how social conditions either promote violence or distribute opportunities for victimization in a population. Structural analyses have found that the potential for violent conflicts and, hence, rates of violent crime are greater where the distribution of economic resources is more unequal, ethnic or racial heterogeneity and inequality are greater, and divorce rates are higher (Blau and Blau 1982; Gartner 1990). The routine-activity perspective is a structural approach that focuses on the distribution of opportunities for violent crime in social space (Cohen and Felson 1979). According to this perspective, major social changes since World War II, especially the movement of women into the labor force and the dispersion of daily activities away from the home, have increased the opportunities for victimization.

The best-known example of a cultural approach to explaining violent crime begins with the observation that certain groups in a population (e.g., African-Americans in the United States, aborigines in Canada), certain geographic regions of nations (e.g., Sardinia in Italy, southern states in the United States), or certain nations (e.g., Colombia, Mexico) have especially high rates of violent crime. According to this subcultural perspective, norms and values supporting the use of force in interpersonal and group relations are transmitted by group members through social learning (Wolfgang and Ferracuti 1967). A quite different sort of cultural approach, which integrates structural themes, attributes differences in violent crime between Canada and the United States to differences in political ideologies grounded in historical contingencies (Hagan and Leon 1977).

Controlling Violent Crime

Each type of explanation has implications for crime-control policies. Incapacitation through long prison sentences or capital punishment, deterrence through increased certainty and severity of punishment, and rehabilitation through individually designed treatment programs are individual-level approaches to controlling violent crime. On the whole, such programs have not been found to be very effective (Martinson 1974). Stricter limits on access to guns, alcohol, and drugs are often proposed as a means to decrease the likelihood that conflictual situations will escalate to serious violence. Here, too, there is much debate and little evidence that such policies could reduce violent crime more than marginally (see, for example, Wright, Rossi, and Daly 1984). Policies designed to reduce economic and racial discrimination, or increase legitimate opportunities, assume that crime prevention requires major structural change. Such policies have been under attack in recent years from those who claim any gains are outweighed by their costs (Wilson 1983).

Pessimism over our ability to control violent crime has not discouraged researchers from posing new approaches and investigating neglected areas. Important advances have been made in research on family violence (Straus and Gelles 1990), violence against women (Gordon and Riger 1988), careers of violent offenders (Miller, Dinitz, and Conrad 1982), and terrorism (Gibbs 1989). Concepts from other disciplines are being integrated to create innovative new frameworks for future analyses (Cohen and Machalek 1988). Together these efforts demonstrate the continued vitality of the sociological study of criminal violence.

[See also Family Violence; Sexual Violence and Abuse; Terrorism.]

BIBLIOGRAPHY

Archer, Dane, and Rosemary Gartner 1984 *Violence and Crime in Cross-National Perspective.* New Haven, Conn.: Yale University Press.

Blau, Judith R., and Peter Blau 1982 "The Cost of Inequality: Metropolitan Structure and Urban Crime." *American Sociological Review* 48:34–45.

Cohen, Lawrence E., and Marcus Felson 1979 "Social Change and Crime Rate Trends: A Routine Activities Approach." *American Sociological Review* 44:558–607.

Cohen, Lawrence E., and Richard Machalek 1988 "A General Theory of Expropriative Crime: An Evolutionary Ecological Approach." *American Journal of Sociology* 94:465–501.

Gartner, Rosemary 1990 "The Victims of Homicide: A Temporal and Cross-National Comparison." *American Sociological Review* 55:92–106.

Gibbs, Jack P. 1989 "Conceptualization of Terrorism." *American Sociological Review* 54:329–340.

Gordon, Margaret T., and Stephanie Riger 1988 *The Female Fear.* New York: Free Press.

Gurr, Ted Robert 1989 "Historical Trends in Violent Crime: Europe and the United States." Pp. 21–54 in *Violence in America,* vol. 1. Newbury Park, Calif.: Sage.

Hagan, John, and Jeffrey Leon 1977 "Philosophy and Sociology of Crime Control." *Sociological Inquiry* 47:181–208.

Katz, Jack 1988 *Seductions of Crime: Moral and Sensual Attractions of Doing Evil.* New York: Basic Books.

Luckenbill, David F. 1984 "Murder and Assault." In Robert F. Meier, ed., *Major Forms of Crime.* Beverly Hills, Calif.: Sage.

Martinson, Robert 1974 "What Works? Questions and Answers about Prison Reform." *Public Interest* 35: 22–54.

Miller, Stuart J., Simon Dinitz, and John P. Conrad 1982 *Careers of the Violent.* Lexington Mass.: Lexington Books.

Nettler, Gwynn 1982 *Killing One Another.* Cincinnati, Ohio: Anderson.

O'Brien, Robert M. 1985 *Crime and Victimization Data.* Beverly Hills, Calif.: Sage.

Phillips, David 1983 "The Impact of Mass Media Violence on U.S. Homicides." *American Sociological Review* 48:560–568.

Straus, Murray A., and Richard J. Gelles 1990 *Physical Violence in American Families.* New Brunswick, N.J.: Transaction.

Wilson, James Q. 1983 *Thinking about Crime,* rev. ed. New York: Basic Books.

———, and Richard J. Herrnstein 1985 *Crime and Human Nature.* New York: Simon & Schuster.

Wolfgang, Marvin E., and Franco Ferracuti 1967 *The Subculture of Violence: Towards an Integrated Theory in Criminology.* London: Tavistock.

Wright, James, Peter Rossi, and Kathleen Daly 1984 *Under the Gun: Weapons, Crime, and Violence in America.* New York: Aldine.

– ROSEMARY GARTNER

VOLUNTARY ASSOCIATIONS

Within four years after Mikhail Gorbachev came to power as head of the USSR in 1985, people in the Soviet Union were forming what they called "informal groups," which have the characteristics of voluntary associations as we know them in the West. That is, these groups were independent of control from sources outside themselves, people were free to join or leave, and members established their own objectives and goals and the means to achieve them.

One of the major manifestations of the movement toward political change in Eastern Europe since 1988 has been the emergence of voluntary associations, especially political parties. These have brought with them personal and social freedoms long suppressed.

On the other hand, these voluntary associations emerged because the people valued them and were ready to organize. At the same time, President Gorbachev allowed them to emerge, even encouraged their existence.

In his commentary on American society, Alexis de Tocqueville (1956) took particular note of the degree to which Americans formed groups to serve personal interests and to solve problems, from the most mundane to the most profound. Perhaps New England small-town government acted in important ways as a type of voluntary association, with "town meetings" designed to solve its own problems, from building schools to constructing roads to caring for the poor. Indeed, American nostalgia for local control may owe much to this early form of voluntary association. Certainly the autonomous religious congregations coupled with local governments gave impetus to the growth of voluntary associations in the nineteenth and twentieth centuries. Today these associations are a ubiquitous part of American society.

Characteristics and Objectives of Voluntary Associations

In 1967, Arnold Rose estimated that there were over 100,000 such organizations in the United States (Rose 1967). While no recent census is known to have been taken, it is widely believed that the number may now be close to 200,000. These voluntary associations are diverse in character and have a variety of sizes, structures, and objectives. Some groups, such as neighborhood improvement associations and local bowling leagues, are loosely structured, have relatively few members, and may be short-lived, while organizations such as the American Sociological Association, the American Civil Liberties Union, and the Ku Klux Klan have thousands of members and persist over long periods of time. Furthermore, the structure of voluntary associations can range from highly bureaucratic to very informal. There can be high fees to join some organizations such as a yacht club, or there can be little or no fees to join an organization such as a bowling club.

Political parties are the quintessential voluntary associations of Western democracies.

Voluntary associations also exist for differing reasons and with varying objectives. While some (such as a lobbying organization or a community service group) exist to attain specific external goals, there are others (such as biking clubs or prayer groups) whose goals are more internal. The latter exist as ends in themselves, with objectives that may be religious, social, or recreational. Voluntary associations have also been identified as instrumental or expressive. Of course, some organizations have the characteristics of both types, in which case they would be labeled as expressive—instrumental or instrumental—expressive, depending on the primacy of focus (Gordon and Babchuk 1959). The Rotary and the Elks clubs are two examples of such associations. Furthermore, it is possible that an association, in addition to its expressed objectives and actual functions, may also fulfill certain latent functions for the members, for society, or both. For example, a neighborhood association whose expressed objective is to increase the quality of life of its residents (manifest function) may also provide members with opportunities to gain leadership and organizational skills (latent function) that may later lead them into politics at the local, state, or even national level.

Voluntary associations may serve a number of personal as well as societal functions. For example, researchers have found that membership in voluntary associations provides individuals with the opportunity to learn social norms, acquire information, and develop organizational and leadership skills. In addition, it has been hypothesized that membership serves to combat loneliness, increase self-esteem, and decrease members' sense of powerlessness (Sills 1968). Support groups, as varied as the American Legion and Alcoholics Anonymous, are good examples of organizations that serve the latter set of functions.

At the societal level, voluntary associations have many functions. Clearly, they serve an important governing role at the local, regional, and national level and perform tasks as varied as community decision making, emergency relief, fund-raising, public information campaigns, and professional licensing (Sills 1968). Voluntary associations also provide arenas for social change, the integration of subgroups, and power distribution (Sills 1968). For example, members of minority groups have formed voluntary associations such as the National Association for the Advancement of Colored People (NAACP) and the Mexican-American Legal Defense Education Fund (MALDEF) to increase political power and ensure equal rights. Political parties are the quintessential voluntary associations of Western democracies.

Membership in Voluntary Associations

Researchers studying voluntary associations have found varying support for Tocqueville's assessment of the United States as a nation of "joiners." Hyman and Wright (1971) reported that in 1962 57 percent of the adult population did *not* belong to a voluntary association. At about the same time, local and regional studies found higher participation rates. For example, Babchuk and Booth's Nebraska study (1969) found that 80 percent of the adult population belonged to at least one voluntary association. More recently, Knoke observed that "perhaps a third of U.S. adults belong to no formal voluntary organization, and only a third hold membership in more than one (not including churches)" (Knoke 1986, pg. 3). It is not clear from the research whether the differences are a function of different or better samples or of a growth in the number and attraction of voluntary associations.

One of the most consistent findings of voluntary association participation is that individuals with a higher socioeconomic status (SES) are more likely to participate in voluntary associations (Cutter 1976). Age, race, and gender (while influenced strongly by SES) are also identified as being important factors in membership, with middle-aged persons, whites, and males more likely to be members.

Gender differences in voluntary association membership have been studied in terms of rates of participation as well as differences in the types of organizations to which each sex belongs. Historically, women's participation rates in voluntary associations have been lower than men's. Furthermore, the groups to which women belonged tended to be smaller, single-sex, and expressive (rather than instrumental). There is some evidence that the gender gap in participation rates is lessening (Knoke 1986). That is, more and more women are participating in voluntary associations. Due in part to the increased participation of women in the labor force, it is hypothesized that women's participation in less segregated, more instrumental associations would increase (i.e., membership in professional organizations; Knoke 1986). In a study of voluntary associations in Nebraska, McPherson and Smith-Lovin (1986) found, however, that the organizations to which women belonged continued to be predominantly female (one-half of the groups were exclusively female, while one-fifth of them were all male). They also found that instrumental groups were more likely than expressive groups to be sex heterogeneous.

Studies of the effect of race on voluntary association membership provide inconsistent findings. For example, Hyman and Wright (1971) documented a sharp increase in membership among blacks between 1955 and 1962 (sharper than that among whites); however,

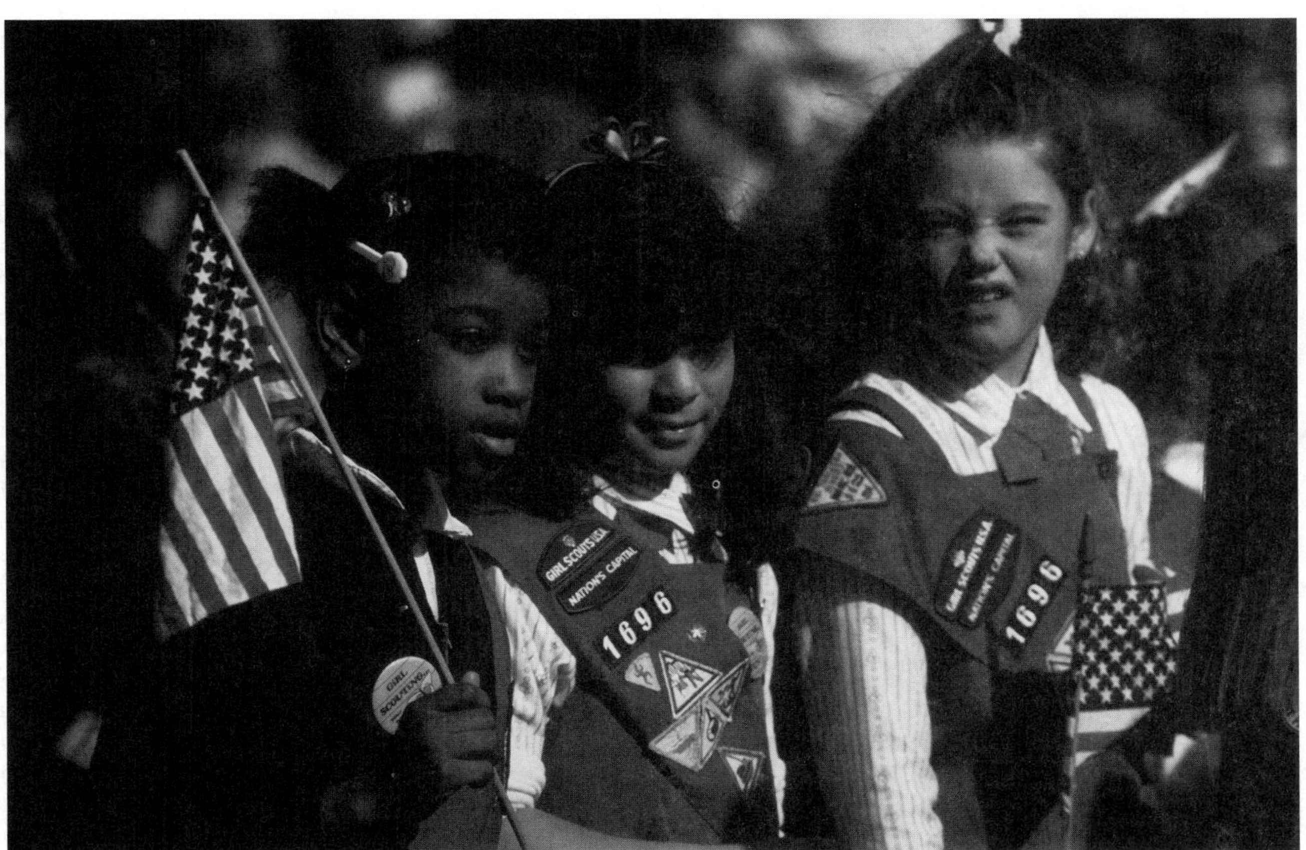

Voluntary associations such as the Girl Scouts provide members with opportunities to learn social norms and acquire organizational and leadership skills. (Richard T. Nowitz/Corbis)

blacks continued to be less likely to belong to a voluntary association. By contrast, a 1973 Texas study found that black participation rates in voluntary associations were higher than both whites and Mexican-Americans (Williams, Babchuk, and Johnson 1973). Knoke summarized more recent research with the statement that "researchers generally found that blacks' participation rates fell below whites' but disagreed on whether the gap could be traced to black SES disadvantages" (Knoke 1986, p. 4).

In addition to studying differences in voluntary association membership due to SES, race, gender, and age, many researchers have examined the relationship between political participation and voluntary association membership. Researchers studying voting behavior and political participation have found that those individuals who are members of organizations are more likely to vote and participate in politics (see, e.g., Wolfinger and Rosenstone 1980; Milbrath and Goel 1977; Sigelman et al. 1985; Rogers, Bultena, and Barb 1975).

Some organizations like the American Medical Association, labor unions, and churches that are hierarchic in structure or practice infant baptism may have some of the characteristics of voluntary associations, but they are not seen as such in the definition adopted here.

In sum, voluntary associations are generally seen as central ingredients of the pluralist, democratic society. Whatever their number in Western societies, their ability to claim legitimacy for themselves and to have the claim accepted by political authorities constitutes a social fact of the free society (D'Antonio and Form 1965).

[See also Community.]

BIBLIOGRAPHY

Babchuk, Nicholas, and Alan Booth 1969 "Voluntary Association Membership: A Longitudinal Analysis." *American Sociological Review* 34:31–45.

Cook, Terence E., and Patrick M. Morgan 1971 *Participatory Democracy.* San Francisco: Canfield Press.

Cutler, Stephen J. 1976 "Age Differences in Voluntary Association Membership." *Social Forces* 55:43–58.

D'Antonio, William V., and William H. Form 1965 *Influentials in Two Border Cities.* South Bend, Ind.: University of Notre Dame Press.

Gordon, C. Wayne, and Nicholas Babchuk 1959 "A Typology of Voluntary Associations." *American Sociological Review* 24:22–29.

Hyman, Herbert H., and Charles R. Wright 1971 "Trends in Voluntary Association Memberships of American Adults: Replication Based on Secondary Analyses of National Sample Surveys." *American Sociological Review* 36:191–206.

Knoke, David 1986 "Associations and Interest Groups." *Annual Review of Sociology* 12:1–21.

McPherson, J. Miller, and Lynn Smith-Lovin 1986 "Sex Segregation in Voluntary Associations." *American Sociological Review* 51:61–79.

Milbrath, Lester W., and M. L. Goel 1977 *Political Participation.* Chicago: Rand McNally.

Rogers, David L., Gordon L. Bultena, and Ken H. Barb 1975 "Voluntary Association Membership and Political Participation: An Exploration of the Mobilization Hypothesis." *The Sociological Quarterly* 16:305–318.

Rose, Arnold M. 1967 *The Power Structure.* New York: Oxford University Press.

Sigelman, Lee, Philip W. Roeder, Malcolm E. Jewell, and Michael A. Baer 1985 "Voting and Nonvoting: A Multi-Election Perspective." *American Journal of Political Science* 29:749–765.

Sills, David L. 1968 "Voluntary Associations: Sociological Aspects." In David L. Sills, ed., *International Encyclopedia of the Social Sciences,* Vol. 16. New York: Macmillan and Free Press.

Smith, Constance, and Ann Freedman 1972 *Voluntary Associations: Perspectives on the Literature.* Cambridge, Mass.: Harvard University Press.

Tocqueville, Alexis de 1956 *Democracy in America,* ed. and abridged Richard D. Heffner. New York: Mentor.

Williams, J. Allen, Jr., Nicholas Bahchuk, and David R. Johnson 1973 "Voluntary Associations and Minority Status: A Comparative Analysis of Anglo, Black, and Mexican Americans." *American Sociological Review* 38:637–646.

Wolfinger, Raymond E., and Steven J. Rosenstone 1980 *Who Votes?* New Haven, Conn.: Yale University Press.

– MARIA KRYSAN
WILLIAM D'ANTONIO

VOTING BEHAVIOR

In addition to sociologists, scholars from many different fields such as history, political science, psychology, and geography have studied elections and voting behavior. In current American sociology, however, these topics are largely neglected. Major advances have been made in neighboring disciplines. Yet, as one of the pioneers, sociologist Stuart Rice (1928, p. vii), succinctly stated: "The phenomena of politics are functions of group life. The study of group life per se is a task of sociology." In general terms, notwithstanding shifts in emphasis between different approaches, the sociological study of voting behavior, then, is concerned with the way individuals obtain, select, and process information related to the political arena, the various forces shaping this process, the relevance individuals attribute to the political sphere, and how individuals decide upon or refrain from specific political action. Elections provide a convenient focus, a point where the often elusive and latent processing of political information renders manifest behavioral correlates: voting or abstaining, supporting one candidate or the other. Forecasting election returns, however, is not a primary goal of the sociological study of voting behavior, while the general public, parties, and politicians are mostly interested in this aspect. Much (applied) research has served these immediate needs and interests, in the past and to this very day. In the field of voting behavior, pure (academic) and applied research peacefully coexist; cross-fertilization rather than mutual irreverence characterizes their relationship.

The study of voting behavior began as early as the late eighteenth century (Jensen 1969), though most of the very early work does not meet strict scholarly standards. In the course of its development as an academic discipline, two different strands—still discernible today—have emerged. The first strand, *aggregate data analysis,* is characterized by the use of actual election returns compiled for geopolitical units like wards, districts, counties, and so forth. These returns are compared with census data, rendering a socio-demographic profile of the same areal units. Starting with the late nineteenth century, there developed a school of quantitative historiography that made extensive use of maps representing voting and census information by different shades and colors (Frederick Jackson Turner in the United States, André Siegfried in France). The mere visual inspection and somewhat subjective interpretation of these maps by the Turner school was later supplemented and replaced by more vigorous statistical techniques, in particular correlation analysis, inspired by sociologist Franklin Giddins at Columbia. One of Giddins's students, Stuart Rice (1928), persuasively demonstrated the utility of quantitative methods in politics. At the University of Chicago, interdisciplinary cooperation in the social sciences produced some of the most outstanding work at the time (e.g., Gosnell 1930). The advent of modern survey research in the 1930s and 1940s, however, then obscured the aggregate approach for quite some time.

Polling individuals about their vote intentions or about past voting decisions started in the late nineteenth century.

The second strand in the study of voting behavior, the *analysis of survey data,* had some early forerunners as well. Polling individuals about their vote intentions ("straw polls") or about past voting decisions started in the late nineteenth century. In one of the most extensive efforts, more than one-quarter million returns from twelve mid-western states were tabulated by a Chicago newspaper for the 1896 presidential contest between McKinley and Bryant. In the 1920s, straw polls conducted by newspapers and other periodicals were quite common and enjoyed great popularity. Their reputation was ruined, though, by the giant failure of the *Literary Digest* poll to foresee the landslide victory of Franklin D. Roosevelt in the 1936 elections (predicting a victory by Alf Landon instead). At this time, however, pioneers of public opinion research like George Gallup, Archibald Crossley, and Elmo Roper had started to use more rigorous sampling methods as well as trained interviewers to ensure a proper representation of all strata of the electorate (Gallup [1944] 1948).

Interest in voting and political behavior and concern with mass communication, marketing strategies, and the public's attitude toward World War II stimulated the rapid development of modern survey research from about the mid-1930s through the 1940s and led to the establishment of survey research centers in both the academic and the commercial sector (Converse 1986). These include the Survey Research Center/Institute for Social Research (ISR) at the University of Michigan and the National Opinion Research Center (NORC) at the University of Chicago on the academic side, and Gallup's American Institute of Public Opinion on the commercial side—to name a few early organizations still prevalent today.

Modern voting research based on the survey method typically uses rather small but randomly selected samples of about 1,000 (rarely more than 2,000) eligible voters. Information is collected by use of standardized questionnaires administered by trained interviewers in person or over the phone. "Standardized" means that the question wording is predetermined by the researcher and that the interviewer is supposed to read the questions exactly as stated and in the prearranged order. For the most part, the response alternatives are also predetermined ("closed questions"); sometimes—and for select questions—verbatim answers are recorded ("open questions") and later sorted into a categorical scheme. In contrast to aggregate level analysis and the use of official election returns, survey-based research on voting behavior, then, relies on self-reports by individual citizens. Thus, it is subject to bias and distortion due to insensitive questions, dishonest answers, memory failure, and last-minute mood changes—even if the sample is properly drawn. Its major advantage, though, is the unequivocal linkage of individual traits (such as age, sex, ethnicity, and social class) and political attitudes and behavior.

Aggregate Data Analysis

The use of aggregate data in studying voting behavior poses formidable methodological problems, yet it is the only approach open for the study of voting behavior prior to the mid-1930s. For example, the Germans voted Hitler into power by genuinely democratic elections in the late 1920s and early 1930s. Explaining the voting behavior of the Germans in the Weimar Republic has been subject to much debate and controversy in political sociology. The earlier consensus, that Hitler's support came predominantly from the lower middle classes, has been challenged by more recent studies (e.g., Childers 1983; Falter 1991) contending that this support had a much wider base cutting across all social groups.

Findings based on aggregate data analysis often depend heavily on seemingly technical details of preparing the data base and the choice of specific statistical techniques. As a rule, findings are more reliable if the geopolitical units are small. Still, even if the greatest care is exercised, there is always the danger of an "ecological fallacy." To use a contemporary example, if the vote for a white candidate increases with a rising percentage of white voters across voting districts, it is plausible to assume that people voted along racial lines. Yet this need not be the case. It may be that ethnic minorities in predominantly white districts are more likely than minorities elsewhere to vote for a white candidate. So they—and not the additional white voters—may be responsible for the increased share of the white candidate.

In spite of all its shortcomings, aggregate data analysis is an indispensable tool for tracing patterns of voting behavior over time (e.g., Silbey, Bogue, and Flanigan 1978) in a sociohistorical analysis or to analyze contemporary voting behavior in the absence of sufficiently detailed and reliable survey data. Particularly for local or regional studies, there may not be sufficient funds to conduct appropriate surveys, or the research interest develops only after the elections have taken place.

Survey-Based Voting Research

THE COLUMBIA SCHOOL. Four landmark studies connected with the presidential elections of 1940, 1948, 1952, and 1956 mark the establishment of scholarly survey-based research on voting behavior (Rossi 1959). In essence, these studies still provide the core of the concepts and models used in contemporary voting research. Reviewing these studies, then, provides an introduction to present-day theories of voting behavior in presidential elections, as far as the United States are concerned. Congressional elections here typically follow a very simple pattern: Incumbents are rarely defeated.

The first two studies were conducted by Paul F. Lazarsfeld and his associates at Columbia University. Their main intention was to analyze the developing process, "to relate preceding attitudes, expectations, personal contacts, group affiliations and similar data to the final decision" (Berelson, Lazarsfeld, and McPhee 1954, p. viii) and to trace changes of opinion over the course of the campaign. Emphasizing the particular set of political and social conditions, and its importance for this process, the Columbia group restricted each of their studies to one particular community (Erie County, Ohio, in 1940 and Elmira, New York, in 1948), and they interviewed the same respondents repeatedly—up to seven times in 1940, four times in 1948. Repeated interviews—or the "panel design"—became a standard feature of more sophisticated voting studies, while the major studies to come abandoned the focus on one community in favor of nationwide representation.

Several major findings emerged from the Erie County study (Lazarsfeld, Berelson, and Gaudet [1944] 1968). First, people tend to vote as they always have, in fact as their families had. In the Michigan school of voting behavior (see below), this attitude stability was then conceptualized as "party identification," a stable inclination toward a particular party largely developed during adolescence and early adulthood.

Second, attitudes are formed and reinforced by individuals' membership in social groups such as their social class, their ethnic group, their religious group, and the associations they belong to. More concretely, the research team found that people of lower social status, people in urban areas, and Catholics tended to be Democrats, while people of higher social class, people in rural areas, and Protestants were more likely to be Republicans. Subsequently, the alliance of particular segments of the population with specific parties has been amply documented, some modifications of its particular form notwithstanding. More so than in the United States, voting behavior in the major European democracies (most notably Britain and West Germany) can be explained largely by the links between social groups and particular parties (Lipset and Rokkan 1967).

Third, change does occur and people under cross-pressures are most likely to change. A cross-pressure occurs when the set of different group memberships provides conflicting stimuli. For example, in 1940, Protestant blue-collar workers experienced a pull toward the Republicans because of their religious affiliation and at the same time a pull toward the Democrats due to their class position. In the United States today, the impact of religious affiliation is more complicated, but the general notion of cross-pressure remains important.

Fourth, Lazarsfeld and colleagues developed the concept of a "two-step flow of information." According to this concept, most people are not directly persuaded by mass media, even if they are susceptible to change. Rather, they tend to follow opinion leaders. These are informal leaders in the various social networks (family, friends, associates at the work place) in which individuals are involved. These leaders pay close attention to the media; they redisseminate and validate media messages. Given the ever-increasing impact of mass media (television) over the last fifty years, this last result of the

1940 study may not accurately reflect the situation today. However, with respect to media effects the empirical evidence is still shaky. Several studies suggest a more direct and stronger impact of media (e.g., Iyengar and Kinder 1987), but a generally accepted model of this process has not emerged.

The 1948 Elmira study was designed to test further and—if necessary—modify the findings of the earlier study and to integrate the results into the body of existing knowledge (see Berelson, Lazarsfeld, and McPhee 1954, pp. 327–347 for a comparative synopsis of several major studies). In fact, its main contribution lies in the refinement of several aspects insufficiently covered in the Erie County study. However, the Elmira study still failed to show systematically the links between the efforts of the various institutions in the community and the decisions of the voters themselves. And the focus on these links was the key rationale for limiting these studies to one particular community, at the same time inviting doubt whether the findings can be generalized to American voting behavior in general.

THE MICHIGAN SCHOOL. The sociological approach of the Columbia school was subsequently overshadowed by the social psychological model of the Michigan school, which came to dominate survey-based voting research for many years. After a smaller study in 1948 (Campbell and Kahn 1952), the Michigan team, led by Angus Campbell, conducted two major studies in 1952 and 1956 (Campbell, Gurin, and Miller 1954; Campbell et al. 1960). In contrast to Lazarsfeld and associates, the studies used national samples—expanding geographical coverage—but only two interviews, shortly before and shortly after the elections. In addition, the Michigan group introduced far-reaching changes in the conceptualization of the voting process. On the basis of their national study of 1948, they felt that social group memberships had little direct impact on the voting decision. Instead, they focused on "the psychological variables which intervene between the external events of the voter's world and his ultimate behavior" (Campbell, Gurin, and Miller 1954, pp. 85–86). In particular, they considered three concepts labeled "party identification," "issue orientation," and "candidate orientation." *Party identification* refers to a sense of personal attachment an individual feels toward a party, irrespective of formal membership or direct in-

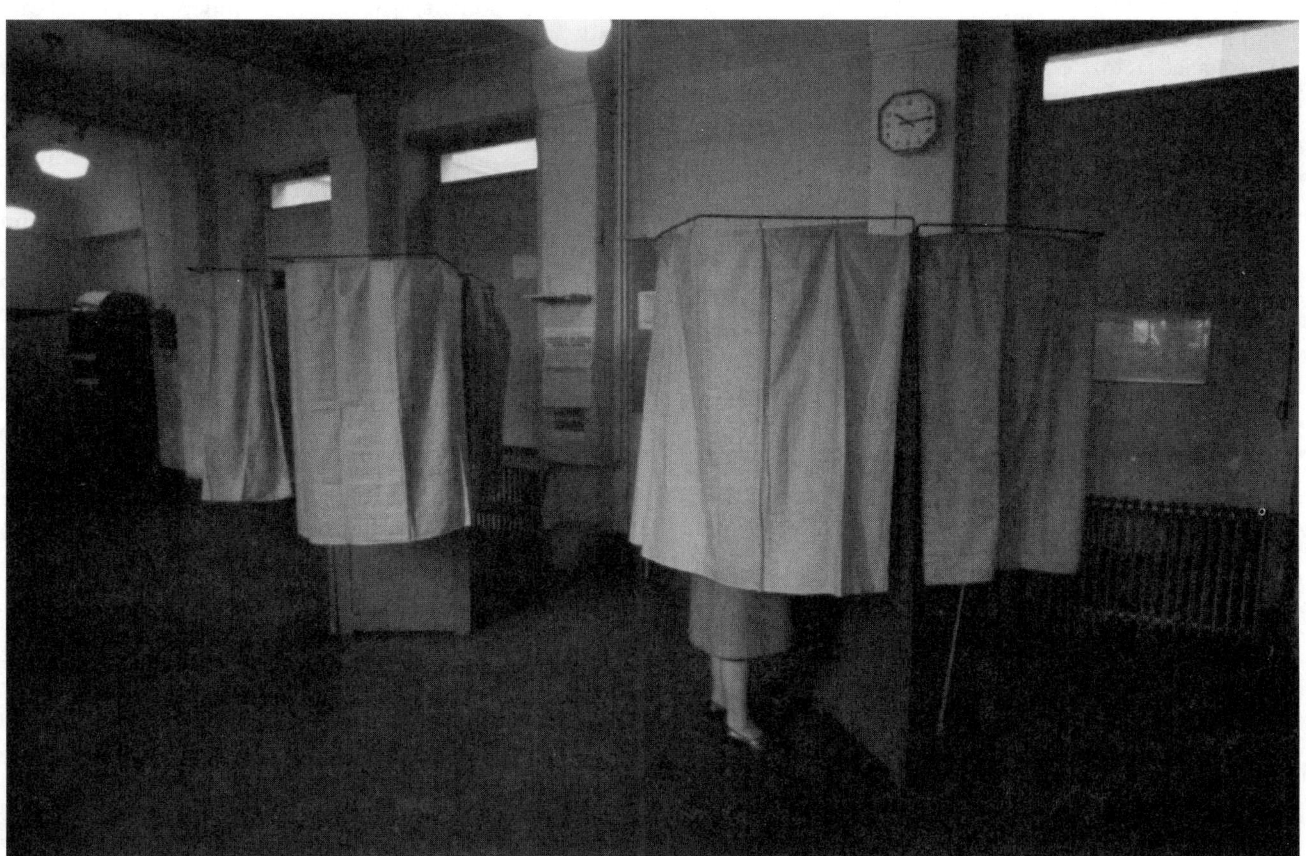

Voters tend to maintain an inclination toward a certain political party that they developed in their youth. (Marc Garanger/Corbis)

volvement in the party's activities. It is thought of as a stable attitude developed early in life. In contrast, both issue and candidate orientations depend on the context of a particular election. *Issue orientation* refers to the individuals' involvement in issues they perceive as being affected by the outcome of an election. For example, if individuals are concerned with the economy and feel that it makes a difference whether the country has a Democratic or a Republican president, then this will have an impact on their voting decision. Similarly, *candidate orientation* refers to the individuals' interest in the personality of the candidates and to a possible preference based on the personal traits of the candidates. For example, Ronald Reagan portrayed himself as a firm and determined leader but also as a caring and understanding father. In this way he was able to attract many voters otherwise attached to the Democrats.

Ronald Reagan portrayed himself as a firm leader but also as a caring father. In this way he was able to attract many Democratic voters.

The Michigan model posits a "funnel of causality." The social factors emphasized in the Columbia school are not dismissed outright, but they are viewed as at the mouth of this funnel, having an indirect effect only via the three central psychological variables, particularly party identification. Party identification, in turn, affects issue and candidate orientations besides exercising a direct effect on the voting decision. The simplicity of this model is both its strength and its weakness. It clearly marks the shift of emphasis to psychological processes of individual perception and evaluation, but it does not explicitly address the social and political context. However, in *The American Voter* (Campbell et al. 1960) the Michigan group presents a much more comprehensive analysis after the 1956 elections. There they address topics like the role of group membership, social class, and the political system—without, however, explicitly elaborating the basic model.

Additional concepts that have been used widely in further research include the concept of a *normal vote* and the typology of elections as *maintaining, deviating,* or *realigning* (Campbell et al. 1966) and an assessment of mass belief systems (Converse 1964). The normal vote concept follows directly from the basic model: If all voters follow their long-standing inclinations (i.e., vote according to their party identification), they produce a normal vote. Comparing actual election returns with the (hypothetical) normal vote allows one to assess the impact of contemporaneous, mostly short-term factors. In a maintaining election the party with the larger number of partisans wins, but its vote share may be somewhat different from its normal share because of short-term factors. If short-term factors lead to the defeat of this party, the election is considered as deviating. Realigning elections, finally, mark a major shift in basic allegiances. Such shifts are rare and are not typically accomplished in a single election. During the 1930s, the American electorate shifted toward the Democrats as a consequence of economic depression and Roosevelt's New Deal, which promised a way out. However, given their long-term nature, processes of dealignment and realignment are difficult to determine in strict empirical terms (Dalton, Flanagan, and Beck 1984).

With respect to the nature of mass belief systems, Converse's (1964) article triggered a long-lasting debate, which was never finally settled. Converse asserted that the vast majority of the American public has little interest in politics, that their opinions on issues lack consistency and stability over time, and that these opinions are mostly "non-attitudes." Consequently, a large portion of the electorate does not vote at all; and if they do, their vote is based mostly on partisanship or candidate personality but not on an independent and careful evaluation of the issues at stake.

CRITIQUE OF *THE AMERICAN VOTER*. Like other landmark empirical studies, *The American Voter* was not safe from sometimes radical critique, which can be categorized as follows: First, challenges of the allegedly derogatory image of the American electorate and its implications for the democratic process; second, assertions that the findings are valid for the specific period of the 1950s only; and third, methodological critique of operationalization, measurement, and model specification. Most of the methodological critique, however, is too technical to be discussed here (but see, e.g., Asher 1983).

One of the earliest and most vocal critics was V. O. Key (1966). Based on a reanalysis of Gallup data from 1936 to 1960, he developed a typology of "standpatters," "switchers," and "new voters" and asserted that the global outcome of the elections followed a rational pattern based on an appraisal of past government performance. Hence, as a whole, the electorate acts responsibly—notwithstanding "that many individual voters act in odd ways indeed" (Key 1966, p. 7).

The most comprehensive effort to review American voting behavior over time, a critique of the second kind, was presented by Nie, Verba, and Petrocik (1976) and was based on the series of Michigan election studies from 1952 to 1972. Still working within the framework of the Michigan model, they found significant changes in the relative importance of its three central factors: a steady decrease in the level of party identification—particularly among young age groups—and a much stronger relative weight of issue and candidate orientations. In a turbulent period of internal strife and social change (civil rights, the Vietnam war, Watergate), the electorate became more aware of issues and much more critical of parties and the established political process. Nie, Verba, and Petrocik found a decomposition of the traditional support bases for both Democrats and Republicans, all adding up to an " 'individuation' of American political life" (1976, p. 347).

MORE RECENT STUDIES AND APPROACHES. Still largely following the path led by the Michigan school, much research in the 1980s was directed toward issue voting that reflected a continued decline of stable party attachments via political socialization or group memberships. In particular, the impact of economic conditions on electoral outcome was investigated both in the United States and in other major Western democracies (Eulau and Lewis-Beck 1985; Lewis-Beck 1988; Norpoth, Lewis-Beck, and Lafay 1991). The findings were diverse, contingent upon specification of the research question and national context. Yet one general pattern clearly emerged: Perceived competence of political actors in economic matters is strongly related to the individual voting decision.

As a distinct break with the Michigan tradition, rational choice models of voting behavior were developed (e.g., Page 1978; Enelow and Hinich 1984; Himmelweit, Humphreys, and Jaeger 1985). Following economic theory, these models see the voter as carefully evaluating pros and cons of each party or candidate, assessing their utility (consumer models) or their proximity (spatial models) to the voter's own position, and then voting for the closest or most useful party or candidate. Rational choice models have become increasingly popular in the explanation of a wide range of social behavior, not just voting behavior. However, in the basic form described here, these models are hardly adequate to portray the process of the voting decision—except for a small segment of the electorate: the highly informed and highly motivated citizens. Conceptually, most of the existing theories can be integrated into a rational choice framework (Bennett and Salisbury 1987). Then, however, an empirical test becomes very difficult, if not impossible.

Fiorina (1981) has presented an attempt to combine the basics of the Michigan model with a rational choice approach. His concept of *retrospective voting* posits that both party identification and issue orientation are largely dependent on the evaluation of past government performance. Party identification thus represents a sort of running tally of past experience. It is still a long-term influence, but it is subject to gradual change, and it is much more based on cognition than on affection compared with its original conceptualization.

Two other strands that have expanded and elaborated the Michigan model have emerged in recent years. In one, the formation and change of political evaluations and orientations are subjected to further scrutiny by employing concepts developed in cognitive psychology (e.g., Lau and Sears 1986). In the other, an attempt is made to assess the impact of the local context on the decision making of the individual. Context information is gathered either by using block level census data or by tracing and interviewing members of the social network of the primary respondents (Huckfeldt 1986; Huckfeldt and Sprague 1987).

VOTING BEHAVIOR IN OTHER NATIONAL CONTEXTS. The Michigan school of voting behavior has had a major impact on survey-based voting research in other Western democracies (see, e.g., Beyme and Kaase 1978; Butler and Stokes 1976; Heath, Jowell, and Curtice 1985; Kaase and Klingemann 1990; Rose 1974). A strict replication of the basic model, however, has not been feasible because of considerable differences in political systems, party organization, and electoral rules. In Europe, fairly homogeneous political parties rather than presidential candidates dominate the political contest, and social cleavages relating to class, religion, or both are powerful determinants of voting behavior—though their impact is slowly declining. But various concepts of the Michigan school have been adopted to supplement the dominant explanation based on social group membership (Lipset and Rokkan 1967). Attempts to operationalize the key concept of party identification, though, have produced mixed results at best (e.g., Budge, Crewe, and Fairlie 1976).

Much of current European debate is focused on the evolving changes in the electorate. The once-stable alliances between parties and certain segments in the electorate along social cleavages have begun to deteriorate; the voters have become more volatile; and electoral change is imminent (Crewe and Denver 1985; Franklin, Mackie, and Valen 1991; Miller et al. 1990). Recently, Rose and McAllister (1990) have proposed a *lifetime learning model,* which seeks to integrate various factors in a time-hierarchical model starting with family loyalties in step 1 and gradually proceeding to evaluations of the current government in step 5. Though they explicitly abandon the concept of party identification, their model can be seen as a modification and expansion of the Michigan model.

Another major democracy, Japan, displays even more marked systemic differences from the United States than do the European democracies. In Japan, personal social networks and intraparty competition are important components in the process of forming a voting

The once-stable alliances in Europe between parties and certain segments in the electorate along social cleavages have begun to deteriorate.

decision. Still, the Michigan model has guided much research on Japanese voting behavior as well (Flanagan et al. 1991).

Outlook

The widespread but eclectic use of the Michigan model does not compensate for the lack of genuinely comparative cross-national research on voting behavior. Some progress may be made by recent projects, for example, a study in the twelve member states of the European Community on the occasion of the concurrent elections to the European Parliament in 1989 (Schmitt and Mannheimer 1991). However, the theory of voting behavior is still fragmented, and the predominant use of the survey method and of national samples has led to stagnation. It is time to bring sociology back in and to develop more imaginative research designs that mix qualitative and quantitative approaches and use data from various sources. The design of the early Columbia studies still awaits full realization.

[See also Democracy.]

BIBLIOGRAPHY

Asher, Herbert B. 1983 "Voting Behavior Research in the 1980s." In Ada W. Finifter, ed., *Political Science.* Washington, D.C.: American Political Science Association.

Bennett, W. Lance, and Bart R. Salisbury 1987 "Rational Choice: The Emerging Paradigm in Election Studies." In Samuel Long, ed., *Research in Micropolitics.* Greenwich, Conn.: JAI Press.

Berelson, Bernard, Paul F. Lazarsfeld, and William N. McPhee 1954 *Voting: A Study of Opinion Formation in a Presidential Campaign.* Chicago: University of Chicago Press.

Beyme, Klaus von, and Max Kaase (eds.) 1978 *Elections and Parties.* London: Sage.

Budge, Ian, Ivor Crewe, and Dennis Fairlie (eds.) 1976 *Party Identification and Beyond.* London: Wiley.

Butter, David, and Donald Stokes 1976 *Political Change in Britain.* 2nd ed. New York: St. Martin's Press.

Campbell, Angus, and Robert L. Kahn 1952 *The People Elect a President.* Ann Arbor: University of Michigan, Institute for Social Research.

Campbell, Angus, Gerald Gurin, and Warren E. Miller 1954 *The Voter Decides.* Evanston, Ill.: Row, Peterson and Co.

Campbell, Angus, Philip E. Converse, Warren E. Miller, and Donald E. Stokes 1960 *The American Voter.* New York: Wiley.

——— 1966 *Elections and the Political Order.* New York: Wiley.

Childers, Thomas 1983 *The Nazi Voter.* Chapel Hill: University of North Carolina Press.

Converse, Jean M. 1986 *Survey Research in the United States: Roots and Emergence.* Berkeley: University of California Press.

Converse, Philip 1964 "The Nature of Belief Systems in Mass Publics." In David Apter, ed., *Ideology and Discontent.* New York: Free Press.

Crewe, Ivor, and David Denver (eds.) 1985 *Electoral Change in Western Democracies: Patterns and Sources of Electoral Volatility.* New York: St. Martin's Press.

Dalton, Russell J., Scott C. Flanagan, and Paul Allen Beck (eds.) 1984 *Electoral Change in Advanced Industrial Democracies: Realignment or Dealignment?* Princeton: Princeton University Press.

Enelow, James M., and Melvin J. Hinich 1984 *The Spatial Theory of Voting.* New York: Cambridge University Press.

Eulau, Heinz, and Michael Lewis-Beck (eds.) 1985 *Economic Conditions and Electoral Outcomes: The United States and Western Europe.* New York: Agathon Press.

Falter, Järgen W. 1991 *Hitler's Wähler.* Munich: Beck.

Fiorina, Morris P. 1981 *Retrospective Voting in American National Elections.* New Haven: Yale University Press.

Flanagan, Scott C., Shinsaku Kohei, Ichiro Miyake, Bradley M. Richardson, and Joji Watanuki 1991 *The Japanese Voter.* New Haven: Yale University Press.

Franklin, Mark, Tom Mackie, and Henry Valen (eds.) 1991 *Electoral Change: Responses to Evolving Social and Attitudinal Structures in Seventeen Democracies.* Cambridge: Cambridge University Press.

Gallup, George (1944) 1948 *A Guide to Public Opinion Polls.* Princeton: Princeton University Press.

Gosnell, Harold 1930 *Why Europe Votes.* Chicago: University of Chicago Press.

Heath, Anthony, Roger Jowell, and John Curtice 1985 *How Britain Votes.* New York: Pergamon Press.

Himmelweit, Hilde, Patrick Humphreys, and Marianne Jaeger 1985 *How Voters Decide.* Milton Keynes, England: Open University Press.

Huckfeldt, Robert 1986 *Politics in Context: Assimilation and Conflict in Urban Neighborhoods.* New York: Agathon Press.

———, and John Sprague 1987 "Networks in Context: The Social Flow of Political Information." *American Political Science Review* 81:1,197–1,216.

Iyengar, Shanto, and Donald Kinder 1987 *News That Matters.* Chicago: University of Chicago Press.

Jensen, Richard 1969 "American Election Analysis: A Case History of Methodological Innovation and Diffusion." In Seymour M. Lipset, ed., *Politics and the Social Sciences.* New York: Oxford University Press.

Kaase, Max, and Hans-Dieter Klingemann (eds.) 1990 *Wahlen and Wähler.* Opladen, Germany: Westdeutscher Verlag.

Key, Valdimer Orlando, Jr. 1966 *The Responsible Electorate.* Cambridge, Mass.: Belknap Press, Harvard University Press.

Lau, Richard, and David Sears 1986 *Political Cognition.* Hillsdale, N.J.: Erlbaum.

Lazarsfeld, Paul F., Bernard Berelson, and Hazel Gaudet (1944) 1968 *The People's Choice.* 3rd ed. New York: Columbia University Press.

Lewis-Beck, Michael 1988 *Economics and Elections: The Major Western Democracies.* Ann Arbor: University of Michigan Press.

Lipset, Seymour Martin, and Stein Rokkan (eds.) 1967 *Party Systems and Voter Alignments.* New York: Free Press.

Miller, William L., Harold D. Clarke, Lawrence Leduc, and Paul Whiteley 1990 *How Voters Change.* New York: Oxford University Press.

Nie, Norman H, Sidney Verba, and John R. Petrocik 1976 *The Changing American Voter.* Cambridge, Mass.: Harvard University Press.

Norpoth, Helmut, Michael Lewis-Beck, and Jean-Dominique Lafay (eds.) 1991 *Making Governments Pay.* Ann Arbor: University of Michigan Press.

Page, Benjamin 1978 *Choices and Echoes in Presidential Elections.* Chicago: University of Chicago Press.

Rice, Stuart A. 1928 *Quantitative Methods in Politics.* New York: Alfred A. Knopf.

Rose, Richard (ed.) 1974 *Electoral Behavior: A Comparative Handbook.* New York: Free Press.

Rose, Richard, and Ian McAllister 1990 *The Loyalties of Voters: A Lifetime Learning Model.* London: Sage.

Rossi, Peter A. 1959 "Four Landmarks in Voting Research." In Eugene Burdick and Arthur Brodbeck, eds., *American Voting Behavior.* Glencoe, Ill.: Free Press.

Schmitt, Hermann, and Renato Mannheimer (eds.) 1991 *The European Elections of 1989* (special issue). *European Journal of Political Research* 19(1).

Silbey, Joel H., Allan G. Bogue, and William H. Flanigan (eds.) 1978 *The History of American Electoral Behavior.* Princeton: Princeton University Press.

– MANFRED KUECHLER

WAR

The ubiquity and importance of war have made analyses of its causes a central concern of scholars for over two millennia. Although many of the fundamental questions about the causes of war were raised first by Thucydides (fifth century B.C.), the vast amount of work on the topic since has produced ongoing debates instead of generally accepted answers. Some debates focus on characteristics of the interstate system that are thought to increase or decrease war. Are wars more likely during periods of economic prosperity or economic contraction? Which is more likely to maintain peace, a balance of power in the international system or a situation in which one state is hegemonic? Social scientists also disagree about the effects of political and economic factors within states on war. Do capitalist economics make states more or less likely to initiate wars? Do democratic states start wars less often than autocracies? There is also no consensus on which model of individual decision making is most appropriate for the study of war. Is the decision to go to war based on a rational calculation of economic costs and benefits, or is it an irrational outcome of distortions in decision making in small groups and bureaucracies?

Studies of war can be divided into three broad categories (reviews of the literature using similar frameworks are provided by Waltz 1959; Bueno de Mesquita 1980; and Levy 1989). The first type takes the system as whole as the unit of analysis and focuses on how characteristics of the interstate system affect the frequency of war. States are the unit of analysis in the second type, which explores the relationships among political, economic, and cultural features of particular states and their propensity to initiate wars. The third type analyzes war as an outcome of choices made by individual leaders, using models of individual and small-group decision making.

The Interstate System and War

Most studies of war that take the interstate system as the unit of analysis begin with assumptions from the "realist" paradigm. States are seen as unitary actors in realist theories, and their actions are explained in terms of structural characteristics of the system. The most important feature of the interstate system is that it is anarchic. Unlike politics within states, relations between states take place in a Hobbesian state of nature. Since an anarchic system is one in which all states constantly face actual or potential threats, their main goal is security. Security can only be achieved in such a system by maintaining power. In realist theories, the distribution of power in the interstate system is the main determinant of the frequency of war.

Although all realist theories agree on the importance of power distributions in determining war, they disagree about which types of power distributions make war more likely. Balance-of-power theories (Morgenthau 1967) suggest that an equal distribution of power in the system facilitates peace and that unequal power distributions lead to war. They argue that parity deters all states from aggression and that an unequal power distribution will generally result in the strong using force against the weak. When one state begins to gain a preponderance of power in the system, a coalition of weaker states will form to maintain their security by blocking the further expansion of the powerful state. The coalitions that formed against Louis XIV, Napoleon, and Hitler seem to fit this pattern.

Some maintain that major wars will be more frequent during periods of economic expansion because only then will states have the resources necessary to fight.

Hegemonic stability theory (Gilpin 1981) suggests exactly the opposite, that unequal power in the system produces peace and that parity results in war. When one state has hegemony in the world system, it has both the incentive and the means to maintain order in the system. It is not necessary for the most powerful state to fight wars, since their objectives can be achieved in less costly ways, and it is not rational for other states to challenge a state with overwhelming power. Gilpin notes that the periods of British and U.S. hegemony were relatively peaceful and that World Wars I and II occurred during intervening periods in which power was more equally distributed. Since balance-of-power and hegemonic stability theories each seem to explain some but not all of the cases, what is needed is a theory specifying the conditions under which either parity or hegemony lead to war.

Balance-of-power and hegemonic stability arguments are not applicable to all wars, only those between great powers. A third attempt to explain great-power war is power transition theory (Organski 1968). Power transition theory suggests that differential rates of economic growth create situations in which rising states rapidly catch up with the hegemonic state in the system, and that this change in relative power leads to war. Organski argues that the rising state will initiate a war to displace the hegemonic state. This final part of the argument is questionable, since it seems at least as plausible that the hegemonic state would initiate the war against the rising challenger in an attempt to keep the small and fleeting advantage it still has (Levy 1989, p. 253).

Another ongoing debate about systemic causes of war concerns the effects of long cycles of economic expansion and contraction. Some scholars argue that economic contraction will increase war, since the increased scarcity of resources will lead to more conflict. Others have suggested the opposite: Major wars will be more frequent during periods of economic expansion because only then will states have the resources necessary to fight. Goldstein's (1988) research suggests that economic expansion tends to increase the severity of great-power wars but that economic cycles have no effect on the frequency of war.

Theoretical debates about the systemic causes of war have not been resolved, in part because the results of empirical research have been inconclusive. To take just one example, equality of power in the interstate system decreased war in the nineteenth century and increased war in the twentieth century. Each theory can point to specific cases that seem to fit its predictions, but each must also admit to many cases that it cannot explain.

Economic interests are often at stake in a war. Many people believed that the United States engaged in the Persian Gulf War of 1991, above, to protect its oil interests in the Middle East. (U.S. Department of Defense/Corbis)

At least part of the problem is that systemic theories have not incorporated causal factors at lower levels of analysis, such as internal economic and political characteristics of states. Since the effects of system-level factors on war are not direct but are always mediated by the internal political economy of states and the decisions made by individual leaders, complete theories of the causes of war must include these factors as well.

Capitalism, Democracy, and War

One of the longest and most heated debates about the causes of war concerns the effects of capitalism. Beginning with Adam Smith, liberal economists have argued that capitalism promotes peace. Marxists, on the other hand, suggest that capitalism leads to frequent imperialist wars.

Liberal economic theories point to the wealth generated by laissez-faire capitalist economies, the interdependence produced by trade, and the death and destruction of assets caused by war. Since capitalism has both increased the benefits of peace (by increasing productivity and trade) and the costs of war (by producing new and better instruments of destruction), it is no longer rational for states to wage war. The long period of relative peace that followed the triumph of capitalism in the nineteenth century and the two world wars that came after the rise of protectionist barriers to free trade are often cited in support of liberal economic theories, but the same facts can be explained by hegemonic stability theory as a consequence of the rise and decline of British hegemony.

In contrast to the sanguine views of capitalism presented by liberal economic theories, Marxists argue that economic problems inherent in advanced capitalist economics create strong incentives for war. First, the high productivity of industrial capitalism coupled with a limited home market due to the poverty of the working class result in a chronic problem of "underconsumption" (Hobson [1902] 1954). Capitalists will thus seek imperial expansion to control new markets for their goods. Second, Lenin ([1919] 1939) argued that capitalists will fight imperialist wars to gain access to more raw materials and to find more profitable outlets for their capital. These pressures will lead first to wars between powerful capitalist states and weaker peripheral states, and next to wars between great powers over which of them will get to exploit the periphery.

In contrast to the stress on the political causes (power and security) of war in most theories, the Marxist theory of imperialism has the virtue of drawing attention to economic causes. However, there are several important problems with the economic causes posited in theories of imperialism. Like most Marxist arguments about politics, theories of imperialism assume that states are controlled (directly or indirectly) by dominant economic classes and thus that state policies will reflect dominant class interests. Since states are often autonomous from dominant class control, and since many groups other than capitalists often influence state policies, it is much too simplistic to view war as a reflection of the interests of capitalists. Moreover, in light of the arguments made by liberal economists, it is far from clear that capitalists will prefer war to other means of expanding markets and increasing profits.

The form of government in a country may also determine how often that country initiates wars. Kant ([1795] 1949) argued that democratic states (with constitutions and separation of powers) will initiate wars less often than autocratic states. This conclusion follows from a simple analysis of who pays the costs of war and who gets the benefits. Since citizens are required to pay for war with high taxes and their lives, they will rarely support war initiation. Rulers of states, on the other hand, have much to gain from war and can pass on most of the costs to their subjects. Therefore, when decisions about war are made only by rulers (in autocracies), war will be frequent, and when citizens have more control of the decision (in democracies), peace will generally be the result.

Empirical research indicates that democratic states are less likely than nondemocratic states to initiate wars, but the relationship is not strong (Levy 1989, p. 270). Perhaps one reason for the weakness of the relationship is that the assumption that citizens will oppose war initiation is not always correct. Many historical examples indicate that in at least some conditions citizens will support war even though it is not in their economic interests to do so. Nationalism, religion, and other cultural factors are often cited as important causes of particular wars in journalistic and historical accounts, but we still have no general theory of the conditions under which these factors will modify or even override economic interests. This raises the general issue of the factors affecting the choices individuals make about war initiation: Can these be modeled as rational maximization of interests, or is the process more complex?

Decision Making and War

Although they may be only implicit or undeveloped, all theories of war must contain some assumptions about individual decision making. However, few theories of war focus on the individual level of analysis. One notable exception is the rational-choice theory of war developed and tested by Bueno de Mesquita (1981).

Bueno de Mesquita begins by assuming the decision to initiate war is made by a single dominant ruler who is a rational expected-utility maximizer. Utilities are defined in terms of state policies. Rulers fight wars to affect the policies of other states, essentially to make other states' policies more similar to their interests. Rulers calculate the costs and benefits of initiating war, and the probability of victory. War will be initiated only when rulers expect a net gain from them.

This parsimonious set of assumptions has been used to generate several counterintuitive propositions. For example, common sense might suggest that states would fight their enemies and not their allies, but Bueno de Mesquita argues that war will be more common between allies than between enemies. Wars between allies are caused by actual or anticipated policy changes that threaten the existing relationship. The interventions of the United States in Latin America and of the USSR in Eastern Europe since World War II illustrate the process. Other counterintuitive propositions suggest that under some conditions a state may rationally choose to attack the stronger of two allied states instead of the weaker, and under some conditions it is rational for a state with no allies to initiate war against a stronger state with allies. Although these propositions and others derived from the theory have received strong empirical support, many have argued that the basic rational choice assumptions of the theory are unrealistic, and have rejected Bueno de Mesquita's work on those grounds.

Other analyses of the decision to initiate war focus on how the social features of the decision-making process lead to deviations from rational choice. Allison (1971) notes that all political decisions are made within organizations and that this setting often influences the content of the decisions. He argues that standard operating procedures and repertoires tend to limit the flexibility of decisions and make it difficult to respond adequately to novel situations. Janis (1972) focuses on the small groups within political organizations (such as executives and their cabinet advisers) that actually make decisions about war. He suggests that the cohesiveness of these small groups often leads to a striving for unanimity that prevents a full debate about options and produces a premature consensus. Other scholars have discussed common misperceptions that distort decisions about war, such as the tendencies to underestimate the capabilities of enemies and to overestimate one's own. In spite of these promising studies, work on the deviations from rational choice is just beginning, and we are still far short of a general theoretical model of the decision to initiate war.

Conclusion

The failure to develop a convincing general theory of the causes of war has convinced some scholars that no such theory is possible, that all we can do is describe the causes of particular wars. This pessimistic conclusion is premature. The existing literature on the causes of war provides several fragments of a general theory, many of which have some empirical support. The difficult goal of theory and research on war in the future will be to combine aspects of arguments at all three levels of analysis to create a general theory of the causes of war.

[See also Peace; Revolutions; Terrorism.]

BIBLIOGRAPHY

Allison, Graham 1971 *Essence of Decision.* Boston: Little, Brown.

Bueno de Mesquita, Bruce 1980 "Theories of International Conflict: An Analysis and Appraisal." In Ted Robert Gurr, ed., *Handbook of Political Conflict.* New York: Free Press.

——— 1981 *The War Trap.* New Haven, Conn: Yale University Press.

Gilpin, Robert 1981 *War and Change in World Politics.* Cambridge: Cambridge University Press.

Golstein, Joshua 1988 *Long Cycles.* New Haven, Conn: Yale University Press.

Hobson, J. A. (1902) 1954 *Imperialism.* London: Allen and Unwin.

Janis, Irving 1972 *Victims of Groupthink.* Boston: Houghton Mifflin.

Kant, Immanuel (1795) 1949 "Eternal Peace." In C. J. Friedrich, ed., *The Philosophy of Kant.* New York: Modern Library.

Lenin, V. I. (1917) 1939 *Imperialism.* New York: International.

Levy, Jack S. 1989 "The Causes of War: A Review of Theories and Evidence." In Philip E. Tetlock, Robert Jervis, Paul Stern, and Charles Tilly, eds., *Behavior, Society, and Nuclear War.* Oxford: Oxford University Press.

Morgenthau, Hans 1967 *Politics Among Nations.* New York: Alfred A. Knopf.

Organski, J. F. K. 1968 *World Politics.* New York: Alfred A. Knopf.

Waltz, Kenneth 1959 *Man, the State, and War.* New York: Columbia University Press.

— EDGAR KISER

WHITE-COLLAR CRIME

Edwin Sutherland, the originator of the concept, defined white-collar crime as "a crime committed by a person of respectability and high social status in the course of his occupation" (Sutherland 1961). Sutherland listed the following as white-collar crimes: violations of antitrust laws; misrepresentation in advertising; infringements of patents, trademarks, and copyrights; violations of labor laws; and breaches of trust of various types. A businessperson who committed a murder or rape, whether in a business office or out of it, would not have committed a white-collar crime, nor would a lawyer who committed an aggravated assault upon another person, even though the act occurred in the lawyer's office or in the courtroom.

When Sutherland introduced the concept, he was primarily interested in formulating an overall theory of

criminal behavior. He rejected the conventional explanations of criminality because he felt they were based on statistics that indicated a concentration of crime in the lower socioeconomic class of our society. The statistics, he believed, were distorted by two factors: Upperclass persons who commit crimes are frequently able to escape arrest and conviction because their money and social position make them more powerful politically; and laws that apply exclusively to business and the professions, and that therefore involve only upper-class people, are seldom dealt with by criminal courts.

Herbert Edelhertz, a former chief of the fraud section of the Criminal Division of the U.S. Department of Justice, found Sutherland's definition too restrictive, in that it limited the concept to crimes committed in the course of one's occupation. Edelhertz included as white-collar crime filing false income tax returns, making fraudulent claims for social security benefits, concealing assets in personal bankruptcy, and buying on credit with no intention or capability of ever paying for the purchases. He also included the criminal manipulations of "con" games operated in a business milieu. His definition of white-collar crime was that it was an illegal act or series of illegal acts committed by nonphysical means and by concealment of guile to obtain money or property, to avoid the payment or loss of money or property, or to obtain business or personal advantage, including all of the above-described activities. The common elements that Edelhertz saw as basic to all white-collar crimes were (1) intent to commit a wrongful act or to achieve a purpose inconsistent with law or public policy; (2) disguise of purpose or intent; (3) reliance by perpetrator on ignorance or carelessness of victim; (4) acquiescence by victim in what she or he believes to be the true nature and content of the transaction; (5) concealment of crime by preventing the victim from realizing there has been victimization, or relying on the fact that only a small percentage of victim react to what has happened, by making provisions for restitution to, or other handling of, the disgruntled victim; or paper, organizational, or transactional facade to disguise the true nature of what has occurred (Edelhertz 1970).

A study conducted in 1985 by sociologist Amitai Etzioni found that two-thirds of the nation's five hundred largest industrial corporations were convicted of such serious crimes as bribery, falsification of records, tax law violations, and gross violations of workplace safety rules. The findings might not surprise many Americans. A poll, conducted in 1988 by the Roper Organization, concluded that 62 percent of American adults thought that white-collar crime was a "serious and growing problem that shows a real decline in business ethical behavior."

Hardly a week goes by without a newspaper account of charges filed by the government against some large corporation alleging the fixing of prices, the rigging of bids, the forming of illegal combinations in restraint of trade, the making of false claims in its advertising, or the undertaking of some other business activity in violation of the law. Business executives and the corporations with which they are associated are occasionally convicted of such violations. The punishment imposed is usually in the form of a fine. When executives are sentenced to jail, the terms are short, seldom in excess of thirty days.

When executives are sentenced to jail, the terms are short, seldom in excess of thirty days.

In the over one-hundred-year history of the Sherman Antitrust Act, businesspeople have been sent to jail on very few occasions. A question raised is, How can jurors send that well-dressed, white, wealthy father of three to jail with unkempt, nonwhite, poor, uneducated criminals? For example, in one recent case of white-collar crime, the executives of seven electrical manufacturing corporations convicted of a price conspiracy involving over $1 billion were sentenced to thirty days in jail each. In the judicial process, severer sentences are meted out to poor people convicted of more petty crimes.

This condition of unequal sentencing was revealed in a 1987 United States Justice Department research report. The researcher revealed that the incarceration rate was only 40 percent of convicted white-collar criminals in 1985, compared with 54 percent of the non-white-collar criminals. The study concluded that financial losses caused by white-collar crime dwarf the amounts lost through other types of crime.

There are many forms of white-collar crime. Following are a number of prototypical cases revealing the dynamics and complexity of white-collar crimes.

Corporate Tax Fraud

According to a recent commissioner of the Internal Revenue Service, corporate tax avoidance schemes have reached shocking proportions. Known losses from corporate tax avoidance have increased enormously. He states, "It is unbelievable that large, publicly held corporations engage in such schemes. Yet, they do. This is flouting the law—deliberate, willful attempts to avoid and evade taxes."

Defense Contract Fraud

In 1988, a Pentagon procurement scandal was brought to light. Defense contractors used lobbyists and others to illegally acquire data from the Pentagon that would give these companies an edge in the competition for billions of dollars' worth of defense contracts.

Stock Market White-Collar Crime

Previous white-collar crimes involving stock manipulations have been dwarfed by recent criminal capers. American white-collar crimes appear to increase with time. The ingenious white-collar crimes of Ivan Boesky, Michael Milken, and many other tycoons who operated like them in the late 1980s, shook the foundation of Wall Street and the world financial market.

Boesky's criminal activities in the stock market were revealed in 1986. Essentially, those activities involved trading on insider information not known to the general public. His illicit profits came from taking unfair advantage of price movements in a broad range of stocks.

On November 14, 1986, the Securities and Exchange Commission announced that Boesky, forty-nine, one of America's most eminent and successful stock market speculators, had been caught in an ongoing probe of insider trading. Boesky agreed to pay $100 million in penalties, to return profits, and to cease to trade stock professionally for the rest of his life. In December 1986 Boesky was sentenced to a three-year term in prison,

Shortly after the Boesky incident, the public learned of even more astounding crimes in the Wall Street investment firm of Drexel Burnham Lambert, and the alleged illegal activity of its California branch's high-yield bond investment chief executive, Michael Milken. On April 14, 1988, after months of negotiations, Drexel Burnham Lambert and the Securities and Exchange Commission reached a settlement on civil charges involving securities law violations, with the influential Wall Street firm agreeing to sweeping changes in how it does business and how it will be regulated in the future by the government.

The settlement ended a two-and-a-half-year investigation into Drexel's trading practices at its junk bond unit in Beverly Hills, California. *Junk bonds,* risky high-

Ivan Boesky ranked among the most successful stock market speculators before he went to prison for illegal trading activities in the mid-1980s. (UPI/Corbis-Bettmann)

yield bond issues, were developed by Milken and used as part of the financial packages in flamboyant corporate takeovers in the 1980s. Drexel agreed to plead guilty to criminal charges and to pay $650 million in fines and other penalties. Also, as part of its settlement with government prosecutors, Drexel was required to dismiss Milken. Milken was later indicted and convicted on criminal charges including racketeering, securities fraud, and mail fraud.

Fraud in Banks and Savings and Loan Companies

Two hundred ten savings and loan companies failed in the United States between 1984 and 1988. Regulators have found serious abuse, fraud, and misconduct in half, according to the Federal Savings and Loan Insurance Corporation, which regulates the industry. In California, the rate is as high as 77 percent. The thirty-one savings and loans in California seized or closed by regulators between 1984 and 1988 cost the Federal Savings and Loan Insurance Company an estimated $5.6 billion. That is more than half the $10.8 billion Congress appropriated in 1988 to rescue the insolvent deposit insurance fund.

It takes much more time and experience for law enforcement officials to unravel the sophisticated plots of savings and loan insiders than, say, the plots of ordinary bank robbers. And, as indicated, sentences for white-collar criminals, when they are caught and convicted, can be light in comparison with those for robbers who make off with a fraction of the cash.

Most white-collar crime simply involves the theft of considerable money from citizen victims who are usually unaware they are being robbed. The money finds its way into corporate coffers, and the top executives in these companies personally benefit through lucrative stock splits, high salaries, and bonuses. In some cases, however, white-collar crime can result in bodily harm and death. The violence may be indirect and hard to trace, but the results are, nevertheless, assaults on people.

Criminal behavior involves either the commission of an act or the omission, in which someone neglects to do something prescribed by law. Notable in this latter context are neglect in cleaning up pollution-producing industrial wastes, oil spills, and proper health and safety measures for employees. Such white-collar crimes and others that lead to bodily harm, to violence to citizens, are committed to maximize the profits of corporations placing the value of the dollar above the value of the human.

This pattern of white-collar crime is illustrated by the marketing and/or use of substances whose toxic effects are not known, and in some cases cannot be known, until people become ill or die. For example, asbestos fibers, the synthetic hormone diethylstilbestrol (DES), and the defoliant Agent Orange are among the substances that have led to litigation related to white-collar crimes, a notable case being the Lockheed litigation.

In 1988, a number of Lockheed Aircraft employees who were working on the stealth bomber in a hangar full of chemicals instituted a lawsuit because they had a variety of illnesses. The paradox in their case was that, because of security issues, they could not reveal the type of work they performed in the hangar. Among the problems in such cases are the fact that the victim may not discover the injury or harm until years after exposure to the substance and the difficulty of showing a direct link between the substance and the injury. These tend to work to the benefit of the corporate white-collar criminal and to point out the degree to which current laws pertaining to violent, corporate, white-collar crime are outmoded.

The success of white-collar criminals tends to make them models for some people in lower social strata, many of whom decide that these deviant values are worth imitating. The behavior patterns of the con artist, the professional thief with the highest status, closely resemble those of the businessperson engaged in white-collar crime. Despite the sharp increase in the unethical practices and criminal activities that characterize white-collar crime, the great majority of people working in corporate America are ethical, law-abiding citizens.

[See also Crime Theories; Criminology; Organized Crime; Political Crime.]

BIBLIOGRAPHY

Edelhertz, Herbert 1970 *Nature, Impact, and Prosecution of White-Collar Crime.* Washington, D.C.: U.S. Government Printing Office.

Sutherland, Edwin H. 1961 *White Collar Crime.* New York: Holt, Rinehart and Winston.

Yablonsky, Lewis 1990 *Criminology.* New York: Harper and Row.

– LEWIS YABLONSKY

WIDOWHOOD

Marriages that do not end in divorce eventually dissolve through the death of a spouse. Much of the stress of bereavement derives from the disorganization caused by the loss of the deceased from the social support system of the survivor. The difficult and sometimes devastating transition to widowhood (or widowerhood) necessitates a reintegration of roles suitable to this new status. If children are present, parental death precipitates a reorganization of the family as a social system. Roles and status positions must be shifted, values reoriented, and personal and family time restructured. The potential for role strains and interpersonal conflicts becomes evident as relationships are lost, added, or redefined (Pitcher and Larson 1989). Loneliness emerges as a major problem. In many modern societies this adaptive process typically proceeds with few or no guidelines because the role of the widowed person tends to be "roleless," lacking clear norms or prescriptions for behavior (Hiltz 1979).

While the survivors face some common problems and role strains both within and outside the immediate family, it is difficult to specify a normative course of adjustment. This is because the widowed are a heterogeneous group characterized by wide differences in social and psychological characteristics. It is also due to the fact that spousal loss evokes a panorama of emotional and behavioral responses from survivors, depending on such factors as the timing and the circumstances under which death occurred. For example, a wife whose husband was killed in military battle will respond differently than if he had committed suicide or suffered a long terminal illness. Many other antecedent conditions, such as the quality of the marital relationship, affect the bereavement reactions and coping strategies employed by survivors.

The Demographics of Widowhood

Census data for the United States show that at the end of the 1980s there were more than 13.5 million widowed persons, 85 percent of whom were women. However, people in the widowed category may exit it through remarriage. Hence, the number of people having ever experienced spousal loss is much greater than is indicated by the census.

For some decades the widowed female has outnumbered her male counterpart by an ever-widening margin. Three factors largely account for this: (1) mortality among females is lower than among males and, therefore, greater numbers of women survive to advanced years; (2) wives are typically younger than their husbands and, consequently, have a greater probability of outliving them; and (3) among the widowed, remarriage rates are significantly lower for women than for men. Other factors that contribute to the buildup of widows are war, depressions, and disease pandemics.

For various reasons widowhood has become largely a problem of the aged woman. Advances in medical technology and pervasive health programs have greatly extended life expectancy. The probabilities of mortality prior to middle age have decreased, and widowhood has for the most part been postponed to the latter stages of the life cycle. The gains in longevity have been more rapid for women than for men. Thus, the growing proportion of elderly females accents their more dramatic rates of widowhood. About one-fourth of all married women will become widows by age 65, and one-half of the remaining women will be widowed by age 75. During the same age span, only one-fifth of the men will lose their wives. It is projected that the ratio of widows to widowers will increase dramatically, from five to one currently to ten to one in twenty-five years.

Research Findings on Widowhood

In making the transition from married to widowed status, the bereaved are often confronted with a variety of personal and familial problems. They are not always successful in adapting to these circumstances. This is reflected in the findings that, as compared with married persons, the widowed rather consistently show higher rates of mortality, mental disorders, and suicide (Balkwell 1981). While there is a general consensus that bereavement is stressful, research on its effects on physical health has yielded inconsistent results. The evidence does show that the widowed experience poorer health than the married, but the reasons for this difference remain unclear.

Because widowhood is most likely to occur in the elderly, research has focused on that population. However, there is some evidence that the transition to widowhood varies by developmental stages. Older widows adapt more readily because losing a spouse at advanced ages is more the norm, thus making acceptance of the loss easier than for those who are young and widowed. Grieving over the death of a husband or wife at older ages can be exacerbated if additional significant others also die, requiring multiple grieving. This can cause *bereavement overload,* which makes it difficult for the survivor to complete the grief work and bring closure to the bereavement process (D. Berardo 1988). There is general consensus that the distress associated with conjugal bereavement diminishes over time. Grief becomes less intense as years pass, but this is not a simple, linear process. The emotional and psychological traumas of grief and mourning may recur sporadically long after the spouse has died.

The issue of gender differences in adaptation to widowhood has been widely debated. The evidence suggests a somewhat greater vulnerability for widowers (Stroebe and Stroebe 1983). Men are less likely to have same-sex widowed friends, more likely to be older and less healthy, have fewer family and social ties, and experience greater difficulty in becoming proficient in domestic roles (F. Berardo 1968, 1970). Higher mortality and suicide rates also suggest somewhat greater distress among widowers.

Continuous widowhood has been associated with loss of income and increased risk of poverty. Two-fifths of widows fall into poverty at some time during the five years following the death of their husbands. There is some evidence that widowers also suffer a decline in economic well-being, albeit to a lesser degree than their female counterparts (Zick and Smith 1988). Poor adjustment to widowhood may be related to lack of adequate finances. Elderly individuals often have below-average incomes prior to the death of their spouse. They may be unwilling or unable to seek employment and are likely to face discrimination in the labor market (Morgan 1989). The younger widowed are more likely to have lost a spouse suddenly and may be, therefore, unprepared to cope with lowered financial status.

Widowhood often leads to changes in living arrangements. Reduced income may force surviving spouses to seek more affordable housing. They may also choose to relocate for other reasons such as future financial and health concerns, desire to divest of possessions, or desire to be near kin or friends (Hartwigsen 1987). Most often, the people living alone are women—usually elderly widows. Isolation and lack of social support can lead to deterioration in their physical and mental wellbeing. Compared with elderly couples, they are much more likely to live in poverty and are less likely to receive medical care when needed (Kasper 1988).

Widows tend to idealize the former partner, a process known as sanctification.

The probability for remarriage is significantly less for widows than for widowers, especially at the older ages. Widows may feel they are committing *psychological bigamy* and therefore reject remarriage as an option (DiGiulio 1989). There is also a tendency to idealize the former partner, a process known as *sanctification* (Lopata 1979). This makes it difficult for widows to find a new partner who can compare favorably with the idealized image of the deceased (D. Berardo 1982). Widows remarry less frequently than widowers also because of the lack of eligible men and because of the existence of cultural norms that degrade the sexuality of older women and discourage them from selecting younger mates. Many women manage to develop and value a new and independent identity beyond widowhood, leading them to be less interested in reentering the marriage market.

There are other barriers to remarriage for the widowed. Dependent children limit the opportunities of their widowed parents to meet potential mates or to develop relationships with them. Older children may oppose remarriage out of concern for their inheritance. Widowed persons who cared for a dependent spouse through a lengthy terminal illness may be unwilling to risk this burden again.

Widowhood and Mortality

The increased risk of mortality for widowed persons has been widely reported. Men are at a greater risk than women following bereavement. The causes of these differences are unknown. Marital selection theory posits that healthy widowers remarry quickly, leaving a less healthy subset, which experiences premature mortality. Other factors, such as common infection, shared environment, and lack of adequate daily care may also influence the higher mortality rates of the widowed.

Timing and Mode of Death

Studies of whether *anticipatory grief,* or forewarning of the pending death of a spouse, contributes to bereavement adjustment have yielded conflicting results (Roach and Kitson 1989). Some suggest that anticipation is important because it allows the survivor to begin the process of role redefinition prior to the death, whereas unanticipated death will produce more severe grief reactions. Survivors who experienced unexpected deaths of their spouses report more somatic problems and longer adjustment periods than those who anticipated the loss. Anticipatory role rehearsal does not consistently produce smoother or more positive adjustment among the bereaved. It appears that the coping strategies employed by survivors vary with the timing and mode of death, which in turn influence the bereavement outcome.

Social Support and Reintegration

It has been suggested that social support plays an important role in bereavement outcome and acts as a buffer for stressful life events, but the research is inconclusive. Nevertheless, there is evidence that the extent to which members of the social network provide various types of support to the bereaved is important to the pattern of recovery and adaptation. Available confidants and access to self-help groups to assist with emotional management can help counter loneliness and promote the survivor's reintegration into society. The social resources of finances and education have been found to be particularly influential in countering the stresses associated with the death of a husband or wife. Community programs that provide education, counseling, and financial services can facilitate the efforts of the widowed and their families to restructure their lives.

[See also Death and Dying; Filial Responsibility; Remarriage; Social Gerontology.]

BIBLIOGRAPHY

Balkwell, Carolyn 1981 "Transition to Widowhood: A Review of the Literature." *Family Relations* 30:117–127.

Berardo, Donna H. 1982 "Divorce and Remarriage at Middle-Age and Beyond." *Annals of the American Academy of Political and Social Science.* 464:132–139.

———1988 "Bereavement and Mourning." In Hannelore Wass, Felix M. Berardo, and Robert A. Neimeyer, eds., *Dying: Facing the Facts.* 2nd ed. New York: Hemisphere Pub. Co.

Berardo, Felix M. 1968 "Widowhood Status in the United States: A Neglected Aspect of the Family Life-Cycle." *Family Coordinator* 17:191–203.

———1970 "Survivorship and Social Isolation: The Case of the Aged Widower." *Family Coordinator* 19:11–25.

Clark, Philip G., Robert W. Siviski, and Ruth Weiner 1986 "Coping Strategies of Widowers in the First Year." *Family Relations* 35:425–430.

DiGiulio, R. C. 1989 *Beyond Widowhood.* New York: Free Press.

Dimond, Margaret, Dale A. Lund, and Michael S. Caserta 1987 "The Role of Social Support in the First Two Years of Bereavement in an Elderly Sample." *Gerontologist* 27:599–604.

Hartwigsen, G. 1987 "Older Widows and the Transference of Home." *International Journal of Aging and Human Development* 25:195–207.

Hiltz, Starr R. 1979 "Widowhood: A Roleless Role." In Marvin B. Sussman, ed., *Marriage and Family.* Collected Essay Series. New York: Hayworth Press.

Kasper, Judith D. 1988 *Aging Alone: Profiles and Projections.* Baltimore: Commonwealth Fund.

Lopata, Helen Z. 1973 *Widowhood in an American City.* Cambridge, Mass.: Schenkman.

———1979 *Women as Widows.* New York: Elsevier.

Morgan, Leslie 1989 "Economic Well-Being Following Marital Termination: A Comparison of Widowed and Divorced Women." *Journal of Family Issues* 10:86–101.

Pitcher, Brian L., and Don C. Larson 1989 "Elderly Widowhood." In Stephen J. Bahr and Evan T. Peterson, eds., *Aging and the Family.* Lexington, Mass.: D.C. Heath and Co.

Roach, Mary J., and Gay T. Kitson 1989 "Impact of Forewarning and Adjustment to Widowhood and Divorce." In Dale A. Lund, ed., *Older Bereaved Spouses.* New York: Hemisphere.

Stroebe, Margaret S., and Wolfgang Stroebe 1983 "Who Suffers More: Sex Differences in Health Risks of the Widowed." *Psychological Bulletin* 93:279–299.

Zick, Cathleen D., and Ken R. Smith 1988 "Recent Widowhood, Remarriage, and Changes in Economic Well-Being." *Journal of Marriage and the Family* 50:233–244.

– FELIX M. BERARDO

WOMEN'S MOVEMENT

The reemergence of the women's movement in the United States in the late 1960s is commonly referred to as the second wave of feminism, which serves to distinguish it from the period more than a century earlier when women first organized around demands for full citizenship. While this modern wave of feminism changed during its first three decades, the demand for greater equity and self-determination for women in the United States remained its core. Through its many struggles and achievements, the women's movement remained a salient force for social justice and equity in the 1990s. The roots of the second wave lay in large-scale structural changes that occurred in the United States after 1960. Demographic change, including a rapidly falling birth rate, increased longevity, a rising divorce rate, and an increase in the age at which people married, radicalized the expectations of girls and women. They flooded into the full-time labor force, stayed in school longer, secured college and postgraduate degrees in increasing numbers, and linked their newfound sexual freedom with the desire to control their own reproduction.

What women found as they emerged from the relative shelter of wife and mother roles, however, was a society reluctant to accept them as full and equal participants. This contradiction variously produced disappointment, outrage, anger, and finally a social movement determined to acquire for women full rights of citizenship. The earliest organized forms of second-wave feminism were modeled on the civil rights movement's successful challenge to racial injustice in the United States. Many early activists in the women's movement had participated in the civil rights and antiwar movements or in the New Left politics and counterculture of the 1960s. The organizing lessons learned and the contacts developed served as the basis for their own attempts at change.

The ideology of the movement was diverse from the beginning, but there were underlying themes common to all those who sought to improve women's status. One was that of sexism—the notion that there are political and social institutions as well as deep-seated cultural attitudes that discriminate against women, denying them the opportunity to reach their fullest potential. A second theme was the goal of individual self-determination—the claim that women should be free to choose their own paths in life, perhaps helped by but not constrained by men or other women. Finally, perhaps the most widely publicized theme was that the "personal is political," the conviction that the only way to change women's individual problems in the form of battering, rape, low-paying jobs, unfair divorce laws, discriminatory education, or degrading notions of femininity is through political organizing and political struggle.

Organizations and small groups appeared in the late 1960s and the 1970s as feminists grappled with the difficult question of how to act on these themes and insights. The largest and most structured of the new feminist organizations, the National Organization for

Women (NOW), founded in 1966, fought legal and legislative battles in an unsuccessful attempt to secure passage of the Equal Rights Amendment, intended to eliminate discrimination against women in education and the labor force and safeguard women's reproductive freedom. In contrast, the small, loosely organized consciousness-raising groups typical of the early women's liberation movement held intimate discussions in which women explored their struggles to become more assertive and to resist a socialization process that had taught them to be passive and self-denigrating.

What women found as they emerged from the relative shelter of wife and mother roles was a society reluctant to accept them as full and equal participants.

Some feminists believed that street protests were the most effective way to communicate feminism's message to large numbers of people. Direct-action tactics included protests at the Miss America pageant in 1968; the hexing of the New York Stock Exchange by women dressed as witches; the Women's Strike for Equality on Aug. 26, 1970, involving more than 100,000 women throughout the country; and, later, huge demonstrations to assert women's right to abortion. Other activists worked for a feminist vision of change by organizing alternative institutions. Rape hot lines and battered women's shelters were established; women's health clinics, food stores, publishers, a symphony orchestra, art galleries, bookstores, banks, and bars provided outlets for creative energies and entrepreneurial skills. Although there was much disagreement within the movement about which of these disparate tactics was most effective, their combined effect was staggering. They touched the lives of millions of Americans and began to transform the ways people thought about and acted toward women.

In the 1990s the women's movement faced new challenges and problems. Despite substantial gains in many areas over thirty years, sexist attitudes and behavior endured. The gap between women's and men's incomes narrowed but persisted, with women earning approximately 25 percent less than men regardless of education. Abortion rights, while guaranteed, came under renewed attack and in some states were eroded. Sexual harassment was a recognized crime but continued to compromise women's full equality. More women were running for and winning elective office than ever before but in 1994 women constituted only 10 percent of the Congress. Many women earning their own incomes had to work a "second shift" because they remained responsible for most or all of their families' care, even in two-earner households. These and other concerns shaped the ideological debates within feminism at the end of the twentieth century. The women's movement continued to contain within itself a plethora of differing analyses and opinions concerning women and social change.

One such debate focused on the issue of sexual violence. Feminists were divided about the role of pornography in engendering and encouraging the sexual violence rampant in the United States. Many who believed that pornography was a major cause of woman-centered violence called for strict regulation or outlawing of pornography as a violation of women's civil rights. Other feminists were concerned about the difficulty of defining pornography, claiming that the real causes of violence against women are complex and rooted deep within our culture and social institutions. They argued that pornography is a form of free speech—however abhorrent—that must be tolerated in a democratic society. Disagreements were apparent as well on the question of how to define and punish such problems as sexual harassment, date rape, and marital rape. Some questioned the legitimacy of a "battered woman defense," giving women victims of systematic violence the right to strike back against their abusers. While all feminists agreed that gender-based crimes against women, including violent acts against lesbian women, were a virulent form of sexism that must be eradicated, they differed in their analyses of and remedies for these problems.

Another debate divided "difference" feminists from "equality" feminists. Difference feminists stressed that women resemble one another and differ from men in fundamental ways. They focused on the value of presumed feminine characteristics, claiming women's greater empathy, cooperation, intuition, and care and posited these as superior to those thought to characterize men. Although they frequently pointed to socialization rather than biology as the source of sex differences, these feminists believed women's characteristics are shared by all women and difficult if not impossible to alter. Equality feminism, in contrast, rejected the view that there are basic social and psychological differences between women and men. It focused on eliminating barriers to fulfilling individual potential. Equality feminism defined social justice in a gender-neutral fashion, anticipating a future that would provide women and men with opportunities to exercise individual choice on a wide range of issues, including reproduction, education, employment, legal rights, sexual orientation, and personal relationships. It rejected the traditional idea that women's differences from men are inherent or can ever be legitimately used to justify either sex's exclusion from any aspect of society or social life. The political ramifications of difference and equality feminism were many. They divided feminists who advocated special provisions for women in the labor force and the law from those who wanted equal treatment for women and men. One practical aspect of this debate concerned the appropriate remedy for the persistent disadvantages of women in the labor force. When compared to men, women earned less, were promoted less frequently, and continued to be segregated in "female" occupations. Most harmful of all was the pattern of interrupted work histories that characterized large numbers of women as they continued to drop out of the labor force in order to almost single-handedly rear children and care for their homes.

Insisting on preserving women's special relationship to home and children, difference feminists addressed women's disadvantaged position in the workforce with such solutions as the "mommy track." This special arrangement of part-time work enables female lawyers, for example, to spend more time at home without forgoing their law practices. Women retain their relationships with firms even though the ability to qualify as partners is delayed and salaries are considerably lower than are those of full-time lawyers. Equality feminists, however, rejected such special protections. Their search for remedies focused rather on finding ways to equalize men's and women's responsibilities for home and child care. Many equality feminists believed that parental leaves of absence from work when children are young or ill, expanded availability of low-cost and high-quality day care, and greater participation of men in fairly dividing responsibilities for housework and child rearing were the only real solutions to women's dual-workload problem. By the middle of the 1990s, however, neither difference nor equality feminists had been able to exercise the political power necessary to

These women cheered the extension of the ratification period for the Equal Rights Amendment to the Constitution in 1978, but the amendment later failed to pass. (UPI/Corbis-Bettmann)

resolve women's continuing disadvantages in the labor force.

The ideologies of difference and equality separated feminists with respect to strategies for building the movement itself. Difference feminists tended to be wary of coalitions, especially those with men. They were generally pessimistic about the possibility of changing what they saw as men's essentially intractable sexist attitudes and behavior and frequently claimed that only women can understand and fight women's oppression. As a result, feminists influenced by a difference model tended to be separatist, inward looking, and focused on what they saw as women's inevitable victimization. Their activism often took the form of trying to shield women from sexism, especially by separating them from its sources. Thus, one of their primary goals was the creation of all-women environments that were considered safe spaces, such as those at women's music festivals or retreats.

The ideology of equality feminism, in contrast, concentrated on eradicating sexism by removing its causes. For many equality feminists this included working in coalition with men to change their attitudes and behavior toward women. They focused on issues that could unite women and men of different social classes and races, such as the disproportionate poverty of U.S. women and their children, federal funding for abortions, and the need for day care. Their goal was to change those aspects of the society that engender sexism. They fought for fair laws and nonsexist legislation and staged large demonstrations and protests to create a broad-based, diverse, and effective movement for ending sexism.

The difference and equality debate raged within academic institutions. The establishment of women's studies courses and programs in almost every institution of higher education in the country was unquestionably one of the women's movement's most significant achievements. These programs and the women's centers with which they were often associated on college campuses altered the way scholars and students thought about issues of gender. Reversing a situation in which women and their contributions to history, science, and society were almost entirely ignored, women's studies courses educated millions of young people about the importance of both women and men to our cultural heritage and contemporary world. Despite their success, women's studies programs faced an identity crisis in the 1990s. On one side, equality feminists argued that the subjects of women and gender should be integrated into the curriculum and not require separate courses or programs. To them the primary goal of women's studies programs was to facilitate that integration. In contrast, difference feminists claimed that only an independent women's studies curriculum could fulfill the continuing need for courses dedicated to women's unique place in and approach to the world. Thus, feminists celebrated the many accomplishments of women's studies programs even as they disagreed about the strategy that should be adopted by such programs.

The women's movement remained a forum for debate, with issues, strategies, and tactics subject to controversy. While such diversity may have confused a public looking for simple definitions or perplexed those who wanted to know, finally, "What do women want?" its multifaceted nature was the movement's strength. The women's movement had room for everyone who agreed that sexism has no place in a society dedicated to social justice. The most important contribution of the women's movement of the late twentieth century was to improve women's lives by reducing obstacles to the full expression of their desires and choices. Feminists contributed to the wider society as well, because their activism was an important element in the continuing struggle for a more equitable and just society for all.

– JOAN D. MANDLE

WORK AND OCCUPATIONS

In modern society, work is a defining force in people's lives. It shapes people's identity, places them in the stratification system by influencing their social and economic positions, and affects their physical and emotional well-being. People's jobs determine the conditions under which they spend many of their waking hours and influence the quality of their lives. Although the term *work* is popularly used to denote the exertion of effort toward some end (e.g., we speak of "working" on one's backstroke), in an economic sense, work refers to activities oriented to producing goods and services for one's own use or for pay. Unpaid work includes that done in the home (indeed, in 1990 more people were employed at homemaking than any other occupation).

Historical Evolution of Work

Although contemporary work differs dramatically from the work of our forebears, the evolution of the organization of production and people's attitudes toward work have important legacies for today's workers. For much of human history, work and home lives were integrated: Most work was done at or near the home, and people consumed the products of their labor.

The predecessors of the modern labor force were nonagricultural workers including skilled artisans who, under the control of guilds, made and sold products. The development of *industrial* work supplemented human effort with machines, introduced a division of labor that assigned specialized tasks to different workers, and ushered in a wage economy. In Europe, industrial work began as cottage industry in which middlemen brought unfinished goods to cottagers, often women and children, who manufactured products. However, the exploitation of new energy sources that could run large machines, the growing number of displaced peasants forced to sell their labor, and the expansion of markets for industrial goods made it economical to shift industrial work from cottages to factories. The resulting industrial revolution sounded the death knell for artisanal work, while laying the foundation for modern work. It also created the labor force.

The Labor Force

From a tiny fraction of the population of medieval societies, the labor force, people employed or seeking paid work, has grown steadily to absorb an increasing share of adults in developed societies. In Western industrialized nations it ranged in the late 1980s from about half of the civilian adults for Italy and the Netherlands to about two-thirds in Sweden, Canada, and the United States. In the United States by 1990 the labor force comprised about 125 million persons. Over time, labor force composition changed. Although women and children were well represented in the earliest labor force, as industrial work replaced agricultural work, the labor force became increasingly male. By the late nineteenth century, five out of six American workers were male, and the first half of the twentieth century witnessed children's exodus from the labor force. The growth of jobs that societies label "women's work" brought women back into the work force in ever-increasing numbers (Oppenheimer 1970). By 1990 women made up slightly more than 45 percent of the U.S. labor force, compared with less than 15 percent in Muslim North Africa and a high of 47 percent in Central Eastern Europe.

Employers design some jobs as part-time to avoid paying fringe benefits.

The amount of their time people spend at paid work has changed throughout the centuries. In the early decades of industrialization, adults and children often worked fourteen-hour days, six days a week. Workdays shrank in the West after labor organizations won maximum-hours laws and, through collective bargaining, secured unionized workers right to overtime pay. After 1973, the average work week declined for European and American workers, largely because more workers, especially married women with children, worked less than full-time, either to make time for unpaid family work or because they could not find full-time jobs. Indeed, employers design some jobs as part-time to avoid paying fringe benefits. However, in the 1980s American women increased their working hours, and by 1990 three-quarters of employed women worked full-time. The incidence of women's part-time employment varied sharply cross-nationally, with 43 percent of Swedish women employed less than full-time in contrast with less than 11 percent of Italian women.

People wanting paid work have usually outnumbered jobs, at least in capitalist societies, leaving some would-be workers unemployed. In advanced industrialized nations in the late 1980s, unemployment varied from 2 percent to 3 percent in Sweden and Japan to over 10 percent in France and the United Kingdom. Official estimates set the U.S. unemployment rate at 5.2 percent in 1990. Critics charge that official statistics underestimate the actual level of unemployment in the United States by disregarding "discouraged workers" who have stopped searching for jobs because they believe none exist for which they qualify. The risk of unemployment for racial/ethnic minorities (10.8 percent for African-Americans and 7.7 for Hispanics) and teenagers (14.5 percent) substantially exceeds that for white Anglo-American adults.

The Work People Do: Jobs and Occupations

To refer to the work people do, social scientists use the terms *jobs* and *occupations.* A job is a set of work activities that one or more people perform in a specific setting. The 1977 edition of the Department of Labor's *Dictionary of Occupational Titles* listed over 12,000 job titles (Miller et al. 1980). The approximately 120 million employed persons hold about one million different jobs. Occupations, in contrast, refer to related jobs that represent a single economic role and, hence, are transferable across employers and work settings. In 1990 the U.S. Census Bureau distinguished 503 such "detailed" occupations (for example, funeral director, meter reader, janitor, accountant) that it grouped into six broad categories: managerial and professional specialties; technical, sales, and administrative-support occupations; service occupations; precision production, craft, and repair occupations; operation, fabrication, and labor occupations; and farming, forestry, and fishing occupations. A steady growth in the number of occupations since the industrial revolution reflects the increasing division of labor in complex societies.

OCCUPATIONAL STRUCTURE. A tabulation of the number of workers in each occupation in a society pro-

vides a snapshot of its occupational structure. Comparing societies' occupational—and industrial—structures at different times or across nations reveals a lot about their economic and technological development and the job opportunities available to their members. For example, in 1870 agriculture employed half of all American workers; in 1990 it provided jobs for about 2 percent of workers. The decline of smokestack industries in the United States and the explosion of service jobs illustrates the result of changing occupational and industrial structures: A worker's odds of getting a well-paid craft job have fallen sharply, so groups that have historically lacked access to these jobs (minorities, women) are unlikely to appreciably increase their representation. In contrast, the growing number of management jobs in the United States led to a record number of managerial positions for women and minorities in the 1980s.

Preparing for and Getting a Job

EDUCATION AND VOCATIONAL TRAINING. Workers education affects the jobs they get for several reasons. Schools teach vocational skills, including literacy and numeracy, inculcate traits that employers value, such as punctuality, deference to authority, and competence in dealing with bureaucracies; and provide credentials that suggest that employers can train prospective workers for skills that jobs require. In Germany, for example, vocational training is a major way that workers acquire job skills. In the United States, in contrast, many workers, especially in traditionally male blue-collar jobs, acquire most skills on the job. However, clerical occupations, the professions, and the "semiprofessions" require workers to acquire relevant skills before employment.

JOB OUTCOMES. People end up in particular jobs because of their personal characteristics, the constraints the occupational structure imposes, and the operation of labor markets, mechanisms that match workers to jobs and set wages. Although people decide whether to accept job offers, a minority of workers can be said to have freely chosen their occupations from the full range of possibilities. Labor markets, along with the educational system, limit people's options by restricting their knowledge of job openings, their qualifications, and their access to particular jobs.

Although thousands of distinct labor markets serve different locales and occupations, to understand the job-allocation process it is useful to distinguish *primary* markets that fill jobs characterized by high wages, pleasant working conditions, the chance to acquire skills, job security, and opportunities to advance from *secondary* markets that serve low-paid, dead-end, low-security jobs. Firms in the primary sector fill non-entry-level jobs through *internal labor markets* that provide employees with "ladders" that connect their jobs to related jobs higher in the organization. The failure of secondary-market jobs to provide job ladders that reward seniority and these jobs general undesirability encourage high turnover (Gordon 1972). Both statistical discrimination and prejudice disproportionately relegate certain workers—the young, inexperienced, and poorly educated; racial and ethnic minorities; immigrants; and women—to jobs filled in secondary labor markets. As a result, one of the most enduring features of the occupational structure is the concentration of workers of different sexes, races, and ethnicities in different occupations. For example, before World War II, American blacks were segregated into farming, service, and unskilled-labor jobs in the secondary sector of the economy, such as domestic worker, porter, and orderly. War-induced labor shortages opened the door for African-Americans to a wider range of jobs, and antidiscrimination regulations (especially Title VII of the 1964 Civil Rights Act) spurred by the Civil Rights Movement helped to expand African-Americans' opportunities. As a result, race segregation has declined sharply in the United States since 1940, especially among women.

Sex segregation, which exists in every society, has been more resilient. In the United States in 1980, of all gainfully employed women, 28 percent were concentrated in just five occupations: secretary, bookkeeper, manager/administrator, clerk, and registered nurse. Over half of employed women worked in just 19 of the 503 occupations the Census Bureau distinguished. Men, in contrast, were spread more evenly across all occupations: The top five—manager/administrator, production supervisor, truck driver, sales supervisor, and wholesale sales representative—accounted for 19 percent of all employed men (Taeuber and Valdisera 1986). The extent of occupational sex segregation varies sharply across nations. In advanced industrial nations, it tends to be higher when more women are in the labor force (Bakker 1988) and in countries that provide paid maternity leaves (Rosenfeld and Kalleberg 1990).

Given the diversity of jobs within the same occupational titles, *job segregation* is more pervasive than *occupational segregation.* Data for 393 California firms revealed that only about 10 percent of employees worked side by side in the same job with someone of the other sex (Bielby and Baron 1986). Thus, evidence of declining occupational-level sex segregation masks continued job-level segregation (Reskin and Roos 1990). Many scholars favor enforcing existing antidiscrimination laws and affirmative-action regulations and training workers for nontraditional jobs as the most effective remedies for job segregation.

Rewards of Employment

People seek jobs to maximize *extrinsic* rewards—a high income, prestige, a good chance for promotion, and security (Rothman 1987; Jencks, Perman and Rainwater 1988)—as well as *intrinsic* rewards—satisfaction, autonomy, and variety.

EARNINGS. Earnings are the most important job reward for many workers. Although one's age, race, sex, and education influence one's earnings, their effects are largely mediated through occupation. Economic theory holds that supply and demand determine earnings, but sociologists recognize that both employers and workers influence supply and demand (for example, unions and professional associations restrict competition and construe their work as skilled and, hence, meriting high compensation) and that prejudice prompts some employers to make decisions at odds with market principles (Granovetter 1981). As a result, considerable income inequality exists across individuals and social groups. Substantial race, sex, and ethnic inequality in earnings characterizes all industrial societies. In the United States African-Americans have always earned much less than same-sex whites. In 1963 the Equal Pay Act outlawed wage discrimination by race, national origin, and sex. That law and declining occupational segregation by race have reduced the race gap in earnings among men and almost eliminated it among women. The disparity in earnings between American women and men has proven more robust because segregation continues to relegate most women to low-paying jobs and because jobs in which women predominate pay less. Hence, in 1989 female full-time year-round workers earned 65 percent of men's annual earnings. The wage gap varies across nations (and across occupations and industries within countries). In the 1980s Australia came closest to equal pay (female full-time year-round workers earned 80 percent of what men made), compared with 47 percent in Japan (Kafleberg and Rosenfeld 1990). Factors that can reduce the wage gap among

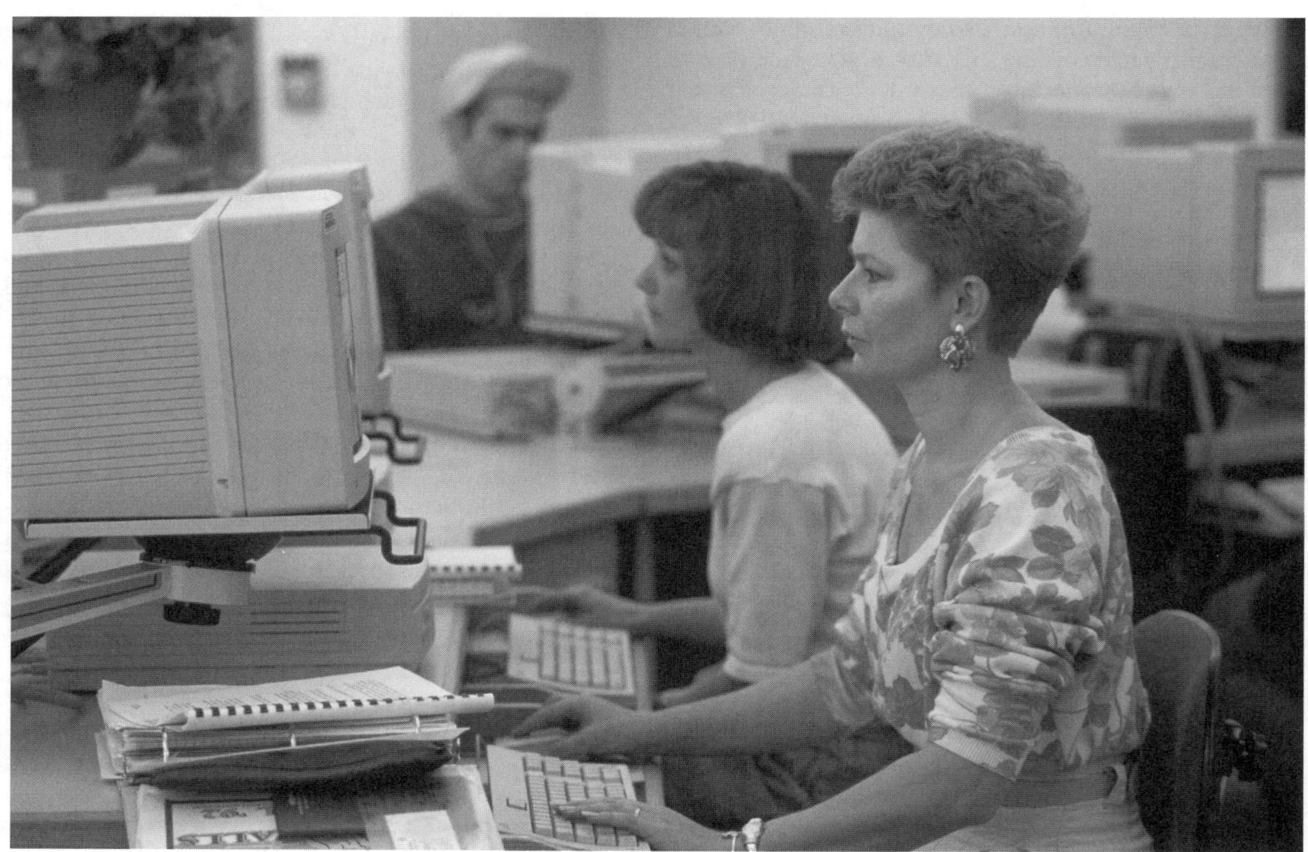

Working women in the United States remain concentrated in certain occupations. Many of them are secretaries, bookkeepers, manager/administrators, clerks, and registered nurses. (Bob Rowan; Progressive Image/Corbis)

full-time workers include equalizing the sexes' educational attainment and labor-market experience, integrating jobs, and implementing pay schemes that compensate workers for the worth of jobs regardless of their sex composition.

OCCUPATIONAL PRESTIGE. People assign prestige to workers partly on the basis of their occupations. In the past, the distinction between blue-collar and white-collar jobs served as a rough proxy for workers' social status. However, as the occupational structure became increasingly complex, social scientists developed more sophisticated ways to measure occupational prestige. The most commonly used is the Duncan Socioeconomic Index (Duncan 1961), which assigns a score to each occupation on the basis of its incumbents' average educational and income levels. The occupational prestige scores permit scholars to study the distribution, determinants, and stability of occupational prestige. Researchers have found that the occupational-status hierarchy has been remarkably stable over time and across cultures (Treiman 1977) and that the occupational standing of American workers is highly stratified. Most people work in occupations with relatively low socioeconomic scores, and only 5 percent hold occupations with scores above 80 (on a scale from 1 to 100).

Japanese and German workers, who have shown the lowest levels of job satisfaction, were among the world's most productive workers.

INTRINSIC REWARDS: JOB SATISFACTION. Contemporary workers see their jobs as places to find personal fulfillment, self-expression, and satisfaction (Katieberg 1982), and they seek jobs that will provide these and other psychic rewards such as autonomy (Jencks, Perman, and Rainwater 1988). Workers in routine jobs try to imbue them with challenge or meaning, in part by creating a workplace culture. These adaptations contribute to the high levels of satisfaction Americans report with their jobs. Nonetheless, not all jobs are satisfying, nor are all workers satisfied. Although some assume that dissatisfied workers are less productive, James Lincoln and Arne Kalleberg (1990) found that Japanese and German workers, who showed the lowest levels of satisfaction, were among the world's most productive workers. Nonetheless, some employers in the United States and elsewhere have devised strategies such as workplace democracy, job-enrichment programs, and "quality circles" to enhance workers' involvement in their jobs.

Work and Family

In moving paid work out of the home, the Industrial Revolution in the West laid the foundation for the separation of work and family and cemented a division of labor that mandated domestic work for women and market work for men. Although married women increasingly hold paid jobs, doing so has not exempted them from primary responsibility for domestic tasks. The resulting time pressures are stressful for employed women, especially mothers, although those whose husbands share child care and who have no difficulty arranging child care fare better on measures of emotional well-being than nonemployed women (Mirowsky and Ross 1989). Women have adapted by cutting down on domestic work, sacrificing leisure time, renegotiating the domestic division of labor with their families, purchasing more services, and working part-time. The tendency to purchase more services has fueled the growth of service jobs in fast-food chains, day-care centers, and cleaning services and, in turn, the demand for low-wage workers. A growing number of mostly women workers are doing paid work at home in what some see as a return to cottage industry (Boris and Daniels 1989).

As more married women work outside the home (by 1989, 58 percent of American women did so), the "role overload" under which they labor has become a societal problem. European countries have responded with paid parental leave and state-run nurseries. American women are increasingly appealing to employers and policymakers for similar solutions: flextime, parental leave, and assistance with child care. At the start of the 1990s, a limited number of U.S. firms voluntarily offered these options, but employers' increasing reliance on women and politicians' concern with women's votes should make them more heedful of women's needs.

Trends in Work and Occupations

CHANGES IN LABOR FORCE COMPOSITION. The Bureau of Labor Statistics has projected a slowdown in U.S. labor force growth through the 1990s, with a work force of about 140 million in the year 2000. That labor force will be older, and have more female and minority workers than in the past. African-Americans, Asian-Americans, Hispanics, and other races are expected to make up about 57 percent of the labor force growth between 1986 and 2000. In fact, native white males are expected to make up only 15 percent of the labor force entrants from 1985 to 2000. Thus, in 2000 the U.S. labor force is projected to be 47 percent female and 15.5 percent minority (Johnston and Packer 1987), compared with 45 percent female and 14.2 percent minority in 1990. The shrinking number of young workers in the baby bust generation that followed the baby boom will orient employers to other labor sources, such as immigrants, to fill low-wage, entry-level jobs.

CHANGES IN TECHNOLOGY, THE PRODUCTION PROCESS, AND THE OCCUPATIONAL STRUCTURE. The history of work can be seen as a battle between employers and workers over output, autonomy, and remuneration. Employers, taking advantage of their control over the tools of production, have tried to control the labor process through close supervision, embedding control into work technology, deskilling work, and implementing bureaucratic controls such as regular evaluations and career ladders (Edwards 1979). Workers have resisted through collective action and work cultures that enforced production norms (Simpson 1989).

In their search for greater profits and control, U.S. employers have increasingly subcontracted work outside the firm and exported jobs to the Pacific Rim, Mexico, and the Caribbean, where labor has been cheap and tractable. Since the late 1960s hundreds of thousands of American jobs have been lost to automation or exportation. In the 1980s, fewer than 6 percent of Americans worked on assembly lines, and by 2000 fewer than 14 percent are expected to hold manufacturing jobs. The United States and other advanced industrial nations have become *postindustrial societies* that specialize in producing services rather than goods (Bell 1973). Thus, service occupations in the United States are projected to add six million jobs by the year 2000 (Johnston and Packer 1987). The export of manufacturing jobs from advanced industrial nations, fueled by the growth of multinational corporations, is fostering an international division of labor in which workers in less developed countries manufacture products under conditions resembling those of early European industrialization.

The other strategy in employers' efforts to control labor and contain costs has been technological innovations that have transformed the production of goods and services. In the 1990s, innovations in microprocessor technology will permit advances in robotics and information processing that will further revolutionize the production process and the workplace. Robots work around the clock, can handle hazardous tasks, and are cheap to operate. Pessimists fear that technical innovations will eliminate or deskill many jobs and subject workers to close technological control. Optimists stress the job-creating and job-enhancing potential of these advances. Randy Hodson and Robert Parker's (1988) review of research on high-technology industries suggests that sophisticated technologies, while increasing productivity, are likely to eliminate more jobs, particularly relatively less-skilled jobs, than they create and to erode skills in mid- to low-skill jobs. Clerical jobs are especially vulnerable. While robots may take over some dangerous jobs, Hodson and Parker conclude that technological advances may make the high-technology workplace more stressful and less healthy.

Expected job shortages can create opportunities for historically disadvantaged groups, especially those with education adequate to exploit job opportunities. However, in postindustrial societies, knowledge and technical expertise have become increasingly important, and a growing number of jobs require at least some college education, so workers without a high school diploma will face difficulties finding jobs that pay well and provide advancement opportunities. Moreover, workers will need different skins from those that traditional work required, so job training and retraining will become increasingly important. In the years ahead, societies will have to grapple with the effects of technological innovations on workers' opportunities and experiences in the workplace.

[See also Comparable Worth; Labor Force; Occupational and Career Mobility; Professions.]

BIBLIOGRAPHY

Bakker, Isabella 1988 "Women's Employment in Comparative Perspective." In Jane Jenson, Elisabeth Hagen, and Reddy Ceallaigh, eds., *Feminization of the Labor Force.* New York: Oxford University Press.

Bell, Daniel 1973 *The Coming of Post-Industrial Society.* New York: Basic Books.

Bielby, William T., and James N. Baron 1984 "Men and Women at Work: Sex Segregation and Statistical Discrimination." *American Journal of Sociology* 91:759–799.

Boris, Eileen, and Cynthia R. Daniels (eds.) 1989 *Homework: Historical and Contemporary Perspectives on Paid Labor at Home.* Urbana: University of Illinois Press.

Duncan, Otis Dudley 1961 "A Socioeconomic Index for All Occupations." In Albert J. Reiss et al., (eds.) *Occupations and Social Status.* New York Free Press.

Edwards, Richard 1979 *Contested Terrain: The Transformation of the Workplace in the Twentieth Century.* New York: Basic Books.

Gordon, David M. 1972 *Theories of Poverty and Unemployment.* Lexington, Mass.: Lexington Books.

Granovetter, Mark 1981 "Toward a Sociological Theory of Income Differences." In Ivar Berg, ed., *Sociological Perspectives on Labor Markets.* New York: Academic Press.

Hodson, Randy, and Robert E. Parker 1988 "Work in High Tech Settings: A Literature Review." In Richard L. Simpson and Ida Harper Simpson, eds., *Research in the Sociology of Work,* vol. 4. Greenwich, Conn.: JAI Press.

Jencks, Christopher, Lauri Perman, and Lee Rainwater 1988 "What Is a Good job?" *American Journal of Sociology* 93:1322–1357.

Johnston, William B., and Arnold E. Packer 1987 *Workforce 2000: Work and Workers for the Twenty-first Century.* Washington, D.C.: U.S. Government Printing Office.

Kalleberg, Arne L. 1982 "Work: Postwar Trends and Future Prospects." *Business Horizons* July/August, pp. 78–84.

———, and Rachel A. Rosenfeld July, 1990 "Gender Inequality in the Labor Market: A Cross-National Perspective." Presented at the 12th World Congress of Sociology, Madrid.

Lincoln, James R., and Arne L. Kalleberg 1990 *Culture, Control and Commitment: A Study of Work Organization and Work Attitudes in the U.S. and Japan.* New York: Cambridge University Press.

Miller, Ann R., Donald J. Treiman, Pamela S. Cain, and Patricia A. Roos (eds.) 1980 *Work, Jobs, and Occupations: A Critical Review of the Dictionary of Occupation at Titles.* Washington, D.C.: National Academy Press.

Mirowsky, John, and Catherine E. Ross 1989 *Social Causes of Psychological Distress.* New York: Aldine.

Oppenheimer, Valerie K. 1970 *The Female Labor Force in the United States: Demographic and Economic Factors Governing Its Growth and Changing Composition.* Westport, Conn.: Greenwood Press.

Reskin, Barbara F., and Patricia A. Roos 1990 *Job Queues, Gender Queues: Explaining Women's Inroads into Male Occupations.* Philadelphia: Temple University Press.

Rosenfeld, Rachel A., and Arne L. Kalleberg 1990 "A Cross-National Comparison of the Gender Gap in Income." *American Journal of Sociology* 96:69–106.

Rothman, Robert A. 1987 *Working: Sociological Perspectives.* Englewood Cliffs, NJ.: Prentice Hall.

Simpson, Ida Harper 1989 "The Sociology of Work: Where Have the Workers Gone?" *Social Forces* 67:945–964.

Taeuber, Cynthia M., and Victor Valdisera 1986 *Women in the American Economy.* Current Population Report P-23, Series P-23, No. 146. Washington, D.C.: U.S. Government Printing Office.

Treiman, Donald J. 1977 *Occupational Prestige in Comparative Perspective.* New York: Academic Press.

– BARBARA F. RESKIN

WORLD RELIGIONS

Religious life throughout the world, regardless of the specific tradition, exhibits both personal/psychological and communal/social aspects. Of course, people within the diverse religious traditions of the world understand the spiritual dimension of their faith to transcend both individual psychological and emotional as well as the corporate and social aspects of their faiths' expressions. Nonetheless, two major academic strands of religious studies over the past century have focused primarily on either the psychological (e.g., James 1961; Freud 1928; or Jung 1938) or the social (e.g., Weber 1963; Durkheim. 1965; or Wach 1958) dimensions of religion. An example of an Oglala Lakota's ("Sioux," in Algonquian) vision reveals these two interactive aspects of religion.

The Plains Indians in America were noted for their vision quests and, quite often, periods of fasting and life-cycle rituals were associated with the quests. However, the vision of Black Elk, a Lakota shaman (healer and diviner), occurred spontaneously when he was nine years old and was ill with fever and other physical maladies (Neidardt 1972, pp. 17–39). His vision began with two men dressed in traditional garb but shaped like slanting arrows coming from the sky to get him. As a little cloud descended around him the young Black Elk rose into the sky and disappeared into a large cloudbank. He saw an expansive white plain, across which he was led by a beautiful bay horse. As he looked in the four directions, he saw twelve black horses in the west, twelve white horses in the north, twelve sorrel horses in the east, and twelve buckskin horses in the south. Upon the arrival of Black Elk, the horses formed into lines and formations to lead Black Elk to the "Grandfathers." As this heavenly parade proceeded, horses appeared everywhere, dancing and frolicking and changing into all types of animals, such as buffalo, deer, and wild birds. Ahead lay a large tepee.

As Black Elk entered the rainbow door of the tepee, he saw six old men sitting in a row. As he stood before the six, he was struck that these old men reminded him of the ancient hills and stars. The oldest spoke, saying, "Your grandfathers all over the world are having a council, and they have called you here to teach you." Black Elk later remarked of the speaker, "His voice was very kind but I shook all over with fear now, for I knew that these were not old men but the Powers of the World and the first was the Power of the West; the second, of the North; the third, of the East; the fourth, of the South; the fifth, of the Sky; the sixth, of the Earth."

Religious experiences codified in the social institutions of the world's religions are not fully captured by either psychological or sociological explanation.

The spokesman of the elders gave Black Elk six sacred objects. First, he received a wooden cup full of water, symbolizing the water of the sky that has the power to make things green and alive. Second, he was given a bow, which has within it the power to destroy. Third, he was given a sacred name, "Eagle Wing Stretches," which he was to embody in his role as shaman for his tribe. Fourth, he was given an herb of power that would henceforth allow him to cleanse and to heal those who were in sick in body or in spirit. Fifth, he was given the sacred pipe, which had as its purpose a strengthening of the collective might of the Lakota tribe and was intended to heal divisions among the Lakota that would allow them to live in peace and harmony. And finally Black Elk received a bright red stick, which was the "center of the nations circle" or hoop. This stick symbolized a sacred centering of the Lakota nation and linked the Lakota to their ancestors as well as to those who would follow after them.

Black Elk's vision ended with a flight into the foreboding future in which the Lakota would encounter the white-skinned "bluecoats" who would threaten the sacred hoop of the Lakota nation. Many years later, as Black Elk reflected on his vision, he realized that even in the devastating upheaval caused by the wars between his Lakota nation and the "bluecoats," his people had been given the sacred objects and rituals that were necessary to rise above mundane exigencies and to heal the nation and restore the hoop in times of trouble.

The vision of Black Elk makes clear that what sometimes appear to be perfunctory religious rituals, fantastic myths, or arcane ethical injunctions often have their roots in a deep sense of the contact between humans and that which they have experienced as a divine power. While the emphasis in this article will be on social aspects of world religions, it is important to keep in mind that the religious experiences codified in the social institutions of the world's religions are not fully captured by either psychological or sociological explanation. There has been a tendency in the academic study of religion to reduce religious experience and behavior to either their psychological or their social antecedents. For example, Freud (1928) reduces religion to unconscious projections of human needs, which he likens to infantile fantasies that rational humans should grow beyond. On the other hand, a contemporary of Freud, Durkheim (1965, p. 466), has a tendency to reduce religions to their social functions: "If religion has given birth to all that is essential in society, it is because the idea of society is the soul of religion."

While the pioneering work of Weber and Durkheim laid the groundwork for much of contemporary social analysis of religion, comparative sociologists of religion such as Joachim Wach (1958) have tempered earlier tendencies toward sociological reductionism. Wach sought to understand the nature of religion by examining traditions throughout the world and noting the primary elements they shared in common. He identified religious experience as the basic and formative ele-

Religious beliefs and traditions can transcend social and cultural distinctions. In this Roman Catholic ceremony, Native Americans join the pope in naming the first American Indian Catholic saint, Kateri Tekakwitha. (Vittoriano Rastelli/Corbis)

ment in the rise of religious traditions around the world, then sought to understand the expression of this experience in thought, action, and community.

Wach said that a symbiotic relationship exists between religion and society. On the one hand, religion influences the form and character of social organizations or relations in the family, clan, or nation and also develops new social institutions, such as the Christian church, the Buddhist *sanga,* or the "Takota nation." On the other hand, social factors shape religious experience, expression, and institutions. For example, in Black Elk's vision the role of the warrior in Lakota society is expressed through the two men who come to escort Black Elk into the sky and, in his later mystical venture into the future, Black Elk as Lakota shaman *(wichash* wakan is one who converses with and transmits the Lakota's ultimate spiritual powers or wakan) becomes the ultimate warrior who battles a "blue man" (perhaps representing personified evil or the dreaded "bluecoats"). Lakota social conventions that name the natural directions as four (north, south, east, and west) are modified by Black Elk's vision to include Sky and Earth, making six vision directions that influence the number of elders Black Elk encounters in the heavenly tepee and the number of sacred objects he is given. Here the vision modifies social conventions, only to create a social subconvention for other visionaries who name the directions as six. The objects themselves are conventional implements of Black Elk's culture that are empowered to serve symbolically as multivocal conveyors of sacred knowledge and wisdom. Finally, Black Elk's vision can be viewed sociologically as confirming the corporate sacredness (the sacred hoop) of the nation of the Lakota. For example, a Lakota's vision was powerful and meaningful only to the extent that the tribe accepted it. In this sense one can understand why Durkheim would say that religion, in this case the Lakota's, is society write large up on the sky.

However, for Wach, and scholars such as Ninian Smart (1969) who follow his lead, the form and expressions of religious life are best understood as emanating from religious experience. Smart identifies six dimensions that all religions throughout the world share: (1) ritual; (2) mythological; (3) doctrinal; (4) ethical; (5) social; and (6) experiential. This author has provided an interpretative framework for understanding the necessary interdependence of these six elements of religious traditions in his book *Two Sacred Worlds: Experience and Structure in the World's Religions* (1977). These six dimensions of the religious life, therefore, form the structure of this analysis of the social aspect of world religions.

Religious Experience

Building on the insights of William James (1961) and Rudolph Otto (1946), more contemporary scholars such as Wach, Smart, and Mircea. Eliade (1959) seek the origin of religion in the religious experience of a founder or religious community. These scholars assert that genuinely religious experiences include an awareness or an immediate experience of an ultimate reality or sacred power. James suggests that transcendental or mystical experiences are immediate apprehensions of the divine that are marked by their ineffability, noetic quality, transiency, and passivity. From one perspective, ineffability can be understood as the inability of language to relay the emotional and cognitive content of a peak religious experience. Ineffability may also be described as a failure of language to capture the divine subject of such an experience—that is, the ultimate reality itself. Nonetheless, religious experiences are inevitably understood as providing new states of knowledge that cannot be grasped fully by the discursive intellect. This "noetic" dimension of religious experience is often described as the revelation of new knowledge (i.e., illumination) that is provided by religious experiences. In fact, it is precisely an awareness of an encounter with a sacred reality in religious experiences that differentiates these experiences from other peak experiences. It is also the case that religious experiences are usually marked by brevity (i.e., transiency) and the passivity of the one receiving the experience. While aesthetic, political, or erotic peak experiences may be characterized by ineffability, transiency, and passivity, only religious experiences bring with them a consciousness of an encounter with a "holy other" sacred reality.

Whether a founding religious experience is immediate and direct, such as the Buddha's enlightenment experience of Nirvana, or cumulative and indirect, as was the exodus experience of the Hebrews, religious experiences are, in Wach's (1958) terms, "the most powerful, comprehensive, shattering, and profound experience" of which humans are capable (p. 35). Wach concluded that a necessary criterion of genuine religious experience "is that it issues in action. It involves imperative; it is the most powerful source of motivation and action" (p. 36). Consequently, religious experiences may be viewed as the wellspring of religion both in the formation of a new religious tradition as well as in the origin of faith of later generations.

Even accepting the primacy of religious experience, it is important to note that founding religious experiences are deeply immersed in the social and cultural realities of their time and place. For example, whether immediate and dramatic or cumulative and more intuitive, religious experiences are inevitably expressed in the language and concepts of the person and culture in which they arose. Black Elk's vision of Wakan in the form of the six grandfathers clearly reflects the Lakota's social and political structure as well as their idealized notions of nation and nature. The Thunder Beings and Grandfathers who are the personifications of Wakan Tanka ("Great Power") obviously arise from the natural, linguistic, and social environments of the Lakota. So does the conception of Wakan itself as a pervasive power permeating animal and human life as well as that of nature. A contemporary Lakota has said, "All life is *Wakan.* So also is everything which exhibits power whether in action, as in the winds and drifting clouds, or in passive endurance, as the boulder by the wayside."

Religious experiences occur to persons who have previous socialization. The most obvious social tool is the language used to express even the most profound religious experiences. The ineffable nature of religious experiences requires the use of metaphors or extensions of everyday language, as in the case of Black Elk. Nonetheless, to some extent the experience itself is shaped by the language in which it is expressed.

Divine names themselves are usually borrowed from the social and linguistic environment of the founder or the founding community. For example, the exodus experience of the Hebrew people was interpreted by them as a liberating religious experience fostered by the God of Abraham, Isaac, and Jacob. This God, whose name is given in the book of Exodus as "Yahweh" ("I am who I am"), is also called El Elyon (God most high), El Shaddai (God of the mountain), and Elohim (though a plural noun, usually translated "God"). Moses likely borrowed the name Yahweh from the Midianites. El Elyon was the high god of Salem (later called Jerusalem) and was worshiped by King Melchizedek. It is also known that the Canaanite high god of the same period was named El and appears in different cultic sites throughout the ancient Near East. While it is clear that the Hebraic religious texts understand Yahweh and El quite differently from their known local counterparts, it cannot be ignored that the Hebrew high god embraced the local deity nomenclatures while modifying their meanings.

In a similar fashion the divinity of the man Jesus is acknowledged in early Christian texts by references to earlier Jewish apocalyptic language and expectations. In the Jewish apocalyptic literature (e.g., I Enoch) the Son of man appears as a righteous judge who will come on earth to signal the beginning of the heavenly kingdom and God's rule. As an eternal savior, the Son of man will come to save righteous followers of God and destroy all those who ignore him. In such linguistic borrowings, however, significant modifications of the original conceptions are made to adjust the titles and expectations to the man Jesus as perceived by his followers. For example, Jesus comes as the Son of man not primarily as a stern and revengeful judge but rather as a savior who is himself the sacrifice. This linguistic and conceptual transformation reflects the dependence of language on experience as much as it reveals the social dimensions of religious experience.

Similar examples of borrowed—and transformed—god names abound in religious literature and history throughout the world. In Saudi Arabia in the sixth century of this era, Muhammad elevated a local polytheistic Meccan god, Allah, to an international deity. In tenth-century Indian Puranic literature, devotees of the god Vishnu promote his *avatar,* Krishna, to a supreme theistic position as the god above all gods. Although the *Bhagavata Purana* recounts the *lilas* or play of Krishna as though the author were describing a historic figure, it is clear to textual scholars that two essentially distinct and dynamic story traditions arise from the Brahminical Krishna of *Bhagavad Gita* fame and from the indigenous cowherd, Gopala, Krishna associated with the Western Indian Abhira tribes.

Although there is no doubt that devotees either of Allah or of Krishna now perceive their divinity and his name as having been "from the beginning," there is little doubt that the local social and linguistic environments provided both some of the content and context for the names of the sacred in these two traditions. Perhaps the most radical example of theistic amalgam is that of the Indian goddess Kali. Described in medieval Indian texts as being synonymous with literally dozens of local and regional goddess names and traditions, Kali is a latecomer to the Indian theistic scene as one who is given the primary attributes of many gods and goddesses. The mythological tale of the birth of Kali reveals an amalgamation process that gave birth to this great goddess now worshiped by millions in India as the "Supreme Mother."

What should be clear from the above examples is that while religious experience of the sacred may be the initiating point of the world's religious traditions or of an individual's faith, that experience is given shape and substance by the linguistic and social context out of which it arises. It is still the case, however, that such life-altering religious experiences as those described above also shape the language and traditions they borrow. We will see this symbiotic relationship repeated in the other dimensions of religious life that are shared by the world's religions.

Myth and Ritual

Formative religious experiences contain within them impulses to expression (myth) and re-creation (ritual) that later become routinized and, finally, institutionalized. Core myths and rituals, therefore, attempt to convey and re-create the experience of the founder or religious community. Both myths and rituals rely on symbols whose content must be shared in order for them to have meaning for the religious group that uses them. Symbols have not only shared cognitive meanings but also common emotional significance and value—that is, symbols do not simply convey intellectual understanding, they also engender an emotive response. Furthermore, religious symbols are integrative and transforming agents as they attempt to point to realities that have been encountered but are hidden from everyday vision and experience. Ricoeur (1972) says that symbols yield their meaning in enigma and not through literal or direct translation. Therefore, symbols suggest rather than explicate; they provide "opaque glimpses" of reality rather than definitive pictures. Understood in this fashion, the journey from symbol to myth is a short one for Ricoeur, who takes the latter to be a narrative form of the former. Put very simply, myths are narratives or stories of the sacred and human encounters with it.

Nearly every extant religious tradition tells and retells its sacred narrative of the founder's or founders' encounter with the sacred reality.

As stories of sacred powers or beings, myths fall into two basic categories: expressive and reflective. Expressive myths are those sacred narratives that attempt to relate the founding or codifying religious experience or experiences of a religious tradition, while reflective stories are composed subsequently to integrate the sacred experience into everyday life. For example, Black Elk's retelling of his vision experience becomes an expressive myth or sacred narrative for the Oglala Lakota, to which they refer again and again in other reflective stories of the Thunderbeings or the Grandfathers, where the Lakota attempt to extend the lessons of this experience to later problems they encountered. Nearly every extant religious tradition tells and retells its sacred narrative of the founder's or founders' encounter with the sacred reality. Black Elk's vision becomes such a story for the Oglala Lakota.

The story of the exodus of the Hebrews is still recounted for contemporary Jewish people as a symbolic and founding narrative of God's liberation. The stories of the life, death, and resurrection of Jesus from the core myths of Christians when one understands the term to mean sacred narrative rather than "untrue story." Likewise, the arduous meditative journey culminating in attainment of Nirvana by the Buddha serves to inspire religious thought and behavior throughout all Buddhist lands even today. Similarly, Muhammad's auditory experience of Allah on Mount Hira that resulted in his recitations of the Qur'an constitutes the sacred history of millions of Muslims on all continents. And finally, even though scholars have been quite confident in their judgment that the life of Krishna as told in the tenth century *Bhagavata Purana* is really an anthology of stories borrowed from various earlier Krishna traditions, these *lilas* or "playful" episodes in the life of Krishna have inspired religious experiences, poetry, and rituals that still enliven the lives of millions of Hindhus throughout the world. From even this selective set of examples of founding myths, it is clear how deeply they drink from the social, linguistic, and institutional contexts of their time and place.

The generative function of core myths is shared by certain rituals that attempt to re-present in a spatial and physical context the core experience of a religious tradition. From one perspective, core rituals are those that emerge from sacred narratives or myths as their active component. From a second perspective, core rituals represent repetitive, institutionalized behavior and clearly are immersed in the social sphere of religious life. For example, the Christian narrative that relates the "Last Supper" of Jesus as a sacramental event (e.g., Mark 14:12–26) is physically presented in the early Christian love feast that later becomes the Lord's Supper (Eucharistic ritual or Mass) of the Christian churches. The work of Victor Turner (1969) in a traditional African religious context provides vocabulary for the religious and social transactions that take place in core myths and rituals. He says the three phases in ritual reenactments attempt (1) to separate or detach the participant from everyday consciousness and social position; (2) to provide a moment of *liminality* and *communitas* of shared experience with ritual participants; and then (3) to reintegrate ritual participants back into everyday life with its social roles and structure. *Liminality* is that psychological and social state of transition between one's former consciousness and social roles and the new status that one assumes beyond the ritual. *Communitas* for Turner is a mode of social relationship that is marked by egalitarianism uncommon in the stratified roles and relationships of the everyday world. Consequently,

Turner would argue that religious rituals may provide an in-between or "liminal" moment of social and psychological experience that religious devotees often assert includes an encounter with their sacred power or reality.

The Passover narrative in the biblical Book of Exodus provides one good example of a core myth that is later enacted in a Passover meal. In its literal meaning, the Passover myth simply refers to the tenth plague, when the angel of death killed Egyptian firstborn children while sparing the Hebrew children just prior to the exodus journey itself. In its symbolic sense, the Passover story that is represented in the Passover sacrificial meal symbolizes Yahweh's power of liberation. To the extent that the story of the exodus reveals the beginning of Yahweh's covenant relationship to the Hebrew people, the Passover ritual attempts to re-create or revivify that relationship.

Beyond the social embodiment of the community in recounting the sacred story of Israel's encounter with Yahweh in a festive and communal sacrificial ritual of the Passover, the social aspects of both the myth and the ritual are obvious. Sacrifices were the common mode of worship for the pre-Mosaic tribal religions as well as for the contemporary cults in Moses' day. It is very likely that the Passover ritual described in Exodus 12 actually derives from a combination of a nomadic animal sacrifice and an agricultural feast of unleavened cakes, both of which predate the exodus event. While the Hebrews' experience of Yahweh in the exodus journey reshapes both the story and the ritual as a liberation event, both the Hebrew myth and ritual have antecedents in the social and religious world of which they were a part.

In a similar fashion, the baptism and Eucharist rituals in the Christian faith are core rituals that stem from the religious narratives that gave birth to them. Likewise, traditional Theravada forms of Buddhist meditation appear to stem directly from the stories of the Buddha's own spiritual struggle and release, but also draw on Jain and Hindu forms that predate it. Among the Oglala Lakota, the horse dance ritual was taught by Black Elk to his tribe in a fashion that replicated as closely as possible the vision he received. Therefore, the six old grandfathers, the horses representing the four cardinal directions, and the various sacred implements he was given all become central elements of the horse dance ritual.

In Islam, the Hajj is one of the five pillars of faith that are incumbent on all Muslims to perform. The Hajj is a pilgrimage reenacting the spiritual journey of Muhammad with periods of fasting, prayer, and meditation that culminate with ritual circumambulations of the Ka'ba, which is the seat of Allah's throne. In the Hindu devotional traditions, it is common for dramatic presentations, stylized ritual dance forms such as the Bharata Natyam, and temple dramatic readings all to convey episodes of the encounter of devotees with the divine. Consequently, dramatic productions of the *lilas* or playful pastimes of the cowherd god Krishna are enjoyed by villagers throughout India not simply as theatrical events but also as re-presentations of Krishna's delightful divine play. The daily ritual reenactment that occurs before the shrines of Krishna or Kali or other Indian divinities is called *puja* and is a ritual ceremony that likely emanates from the stylized honorific behavior one accords to a royal guest. Here the social precursors to religious ritual are obvious, even though they are transformed by the religious narrative and ritual context into which they are placed.

Scholars across a variety of disciplines and perspectives have asserted the interconnection of myth, ritual, and the religious community. Perhaps the clearest summary of this relationship is given by Bronislaw Malinowski when he says, "an intimate connection exists between the word, the mythos, the sacred tales of a tribe, on the one hand and their ritual acts, their moral deeds, their social organization, and even their practical activities on the other" (1954, p. 96). Malinowski reminds us that while core myths and rituals may have their origin in founding religious experiences, they also serve as social "warrants" for social beliefs of the society out of which they arise and that they help shape. From this perspective, myths and rituals serve primarily as vehicles that legitimate social institutions. Core myths and rituals appear to be charged with the difficult task of re-presenting and re-creating founding religious experiences. As we have seen, they, too, reflect and embrace their social and cultural contexts. Furthermore, not all myths and rituals serve this primary and essentialist function. As we will see shortly, certain myths, rituals, and religious behavior diverge considerably from the impetus that the core narrative seems to suggest.

Ethics

Malinowski and Wach make clear that ethics arise partly as a result of religious experience but also participate fully in social processes. While it may be that religious experiences give rise to immediate expression (core myths) and reenactments (core rituals), they also give impetus to new attitudes and intentions that are reflected in norms for behavior. In the Christian context such behavior is claimed to be the mark of a "reborn" person whose conduct represents the tangible effects of an experience of God. On the other hand, the ethical norms and traditions that arise within a religious institution may reflect as much the mores of the surround-

ing culture and society as they do the experience on which the institution was founded. Social factors (such as language, family roles, and social customs) play a role in the process of the externalization of the religious life in ethical laws. William James says simply that subsequent behavior is the empirical criterion for determining the quality and validity of a religious experience. The distinction he makes between the person who has a religious experience and the one who undergoes religious conversion is the distinction between having a highly charged peak experience and that of living a new life born of that experience.

It appears that all religious traditions evidence an interdependent and necessary relationship of conduct to

Spiritual pilgrimages form an essential part of Muslim worship. These pilgrims are praying in the Old Courtyard of the Shrine of Iman Riza in Mashhad, Iran. (Roger Wood/© Corbis)

experience such that what is experienced as ecstatic encounter is expressed as a whole mode of living. The committed ethical life of a devotee, then, is ideally understood as an active extension of religious experience expressed through communal or shared norms. While an immediate religious experience may provide a core religious impulse (e.g., to love in the Christian context, or to fear Allah in the Muslim context), that intentional force or impetus gains objectivity in the concrete situations of social behavior. For example, the enlightenment experience of the Buddha resulted in a sense of detachment from the world that was linked to enduring traditions of *metta* and *karuna* (love and compassion) and resulted in "detached compassion" as the complex ethical norm that the Buddha required of his disciples.

The most obvious intrusion of social norms and processes into the religious life occurs in moral decision making. It is the world and living in it that provide the situations and problems that require an ethical response. Consequently, life in the world poses many situations not anticipated in the religious texts and routinized ethical norms of religious traditions. As a result, ethical systems over time often come to reflect the surrounding secular culture and social norms as much as they do the basic religious impulse from which they are supposed to derive their direction. This problem is mediated during the life of the founder or founders whose authority and behavior provide a model for action. In subsequent generations, however, it is often social roles and institutions such as that of the pope, the Buddhist *sanga* (community of elders), or the Lakota tribal council that determine the ethical norms of a community. When ethical statements and positions stray too far from their initial impulses, they are in danger of mirroring the society they intend to make sacred. Put simply, while ethical impulses may originate from religious experiences, the ethical laws, norms, and traditions that are constituted in scriptures and institutional pronouncements often distort the imperative by rationalizations that conform to social and not religious expectations.

An example of the difference between ethical impulse and moral law can be found in the Hebrew notion of a covenant relationship with God. The experience of Moses and the exodus tribes was of a compassionate, mighty, jealous, and demanding God. The laws of the early Hebrews, therefore, were viewed not simply as commandments arising from a stern leader or group of legalistic lawmakers but rather as expressions of an appreciative and liberating relationship to God. The Sinai story of the transmission of the Ten Commandments is intended to reveal the Hebrews' ethical relationship to Yahweh. It was on that holy mountain that the covenant between Yahweh and his people was given concrete expression. However, it is also clear that this relationship was marked by infidelity on the part of Yahweh's people. Therefore, for many of them the codes of conduct contained in the Ten Commandments and the Levitical Code were experienced as oppressive laws of a judgmental God.

Jesus summarized the essence of ethical behavior in a twofold commandment of love of God and love of neighbor that was enjoined on all who would count themselves as disciples of God. However, the teachings of Jesus and the commandment of love have led over the centuries to disputes about whether Christians should engage in war, permit abortions, treat homosexuals as equals in the church, or allow divorces. Institutionalized Christian churches in their many forms have decreed what proper ethical conduct is with regard to such issues, and these norms vary and even contradict each other across traditions. This is the difference between the imperative to love God and to love neighbor, and ethical laws that must express such divine love in complex and rapidly changing social contexts and situations. A seemingly universal law such as "Do not kill" means quite different things to a Lakota warrior, who may kill (and sometimes scalp) his enemy (but not a tribesman); to a Muslim, who is encouraged to kill an infidel who defames Allah; and to a Buddhist, who is enjoined not to harm *any* animal or human life.

Institutionalized Christian churches in their many forms have decreed what proper ethical conduct is and these norms vary and even contradict each other across traditions.

Even within seemingly similar traditions, such as the Hindu devotional sects, the ethical norms can vary immensely. In the Kali goddess tradition, animal sacrifice is still commonly practiced as a way of returning to the goddess the life-giving force she has bestowed on her creation. Some devotees of Kali have interpreted her mythological destruction of demons to be a model for their own behavior and have followed suit as thieves and murderers in the Indian Thuggi tradition. On the other hand, Kali devotees such as Rahmakrishnan understand Kali to be a transcendent "ocean of bliss" who engenders peacefulness and noninjury in her disciples.

What is true of all the above-mentioned religious traditions around the world is that persons are usually taught what constitutes proper or ethical behavior, and in this context ethics are learned conceptions born of

the social process and its experiences. Consequently, ethical norms and their expression often reflect the social environment in which religious traditions arise. A clear expression of this fact is found in the Hindu religious tradition's embracing of the caste system that sacralizes a socially elitist and patriarchal social system that predates Hinduism. The mythical and theological texts of the Hindu tradition that sacralize caste distinctions simply serve as warrants for social roles and norms that under-gird not only the Hindu traditions but also those of the Buddhists and Jains in India as well.

Theology/Doctrine

Just as religious experience may result in the formation of a religious movement that tells the founding story of contact with a sacred power (core myth), tries to recreate that experience for the beginning and subsequent communities (core rituals), and impels new believers to act in accordance with this vision or revelation (ethical impulse leading to institutionalized ethics), so it is that even very early in a religious tradition's history questions and criticisms arise that must be answered. Religious reflection takes a variety of forms that touch the total corporate life of a religious community. Sacred scriptures often encompass expressive myths that relate in narrative form the founder's or founders' contact with the sacred; core rituals in outline or in full; ethical njunctions and moral codes; and reflective myths, doctrines, and explications that attempt to answer the believers' questions and the opponents' criticisms. Almost inevitably a religious community is provoked from without and within to explain how the sacred reality is related to the origin of the community and, perhaps, even to the origin of the world. Consequently, reflective myths that represent second-level or posterior reflection are incorporated to explain such beginnings.

Three distinct but interrelated purposes and functions of reflective myths are (1) an explanation of origins; (2) a rationalization of aspects of core beliefs; and (3) an apologetic defense of the faith to disbelieving insiders or outsiders. A good example of reflective theologizing is the development of the biography of the Buddha. The oldest Pali texts essentially begin the life of the Buddha with his disillusionment with the world at age twenty-nine, when he was already a husband and a father. The early texts indicate that his name was Siddhartha and that his father, Suddhodana, ruled a small district in the North Indian republic of the Sakyas. This early story indicates that Siddhartha was married at age sixteen or seventeen, had a son, and then became disillusioned with the human suffering he saw around him and renounced the world to seek spiritual liberation while leaving his family behind.

Approximately five hundred years after the death of the Buddha, two separate "biographies" were written containing accumulated legends not only of the miraculous birth of the Buddha but also of the "great renunciation" itself. The birth story is replete with the descent of the Buddha from the heavens as a white elephant who miraculously enters his mother's side, only to be born nine months later as a fully functioning adultlike child. These biographies describe the Buddha's physical features (captured in religious images and icons) as including the lengthened ears of an aristocrat, a smooth-shaped conical bump on his head indicating his intelligence, and other such marks that foretold his later enlightenment.

Likewise, these latter-day scriptures recount his renunciation from the world in a full-blown theologized story of encounters with an ill man, a decrepit old man, a dead man, and a religious ascetic. What the story of the Buddha's four visions accomplishes is a fuller explication of the reasons for his renunciation. Both the birth story (confirming the Buddha's sacred origins) and the story of the four visions of the Buddha (a rationalization of his renunciation) represent reflective myths that fill in biographical gaps in earlier stories of his life in light of his later enlightenment status.

Parallels to the biographical history of the Buddha can be found in the scriptural stories of the miraculous births of Jesus, Mahavira (founder of the Jains), Krishna, Kali, and Muhammad, among others. A similar genre of reflective myths may be found in the creation stories that often are added dozens of years or even centuries after the founding experience. Good examples of this process are the Hebrew creation stories told in Genesis 1 and Genesis 2. God's creation in seven days is the youngest creation story (the priestly story of the seventh century B.C. and told in Genesis 1:1–2:4a) and is placed at the beginning of the Book of Genesis. It is likely that the Akkadian myth of Tiamat served as a model for this story of the creation of the world out of a watery chaos.

The older Yahwist creation story found in Genesis 2:4b ff. is set in a desert environment instead of a primeval ocean and stems very likely from the tenth century B.C. A decidedly more anthropomorphic story, the Yahwist Garden of Eden represents a story that was added at least three hundred to four hundred years after the exodus experience itself. Neither the priestly nor Yahwist stories received their present form until the sixth or seventh century B.C., as they were called upon to explicate the creative power of their Hebrew God set against a seasonal set of mythologies from the Canaanites, whom the Hebrews encountered in Palestine. For the Palestine farmer, Canaanite, or Israelite, the question was, "Is it Yahweh or Baal to whom one should offer sacrifices and give allegiance if one's crops are to prosper?" The two Genesis creation stories provide not only the answer of who is responsible for the origin of life on earth but also how one can explain human illness, suffering, and death in the context of the God who led the Hebrews out of Egypt. In Africa and in India, the numerous and sometimes contradictory creation stories one finds within a single religious tradition reveal less about the illogical nature of such reflective myths than they do about the human need to have questions of birth, suffering, social relationships, the founding of a tribe, and the death event placed in the context of a tradition's ultimate reality.

When religious traditions develop full-fledged social institutions, it is quite common for sacred texts or other interpretative theological texts to explain the necessity of such a religious organization and its officials. Whether it is the early church fathers' explanations of the seat of Peter on which the pope sits in the Roman Catholic tradition, or a Lakota visionary myth that explains the role of the shaman in their community, reflective myths and theologies develop as intellectual and institutional rationalizations for the extension of the founding tradition into all aspects of life and society. Religious councils, theological traditions, sectarian disputes, and doctrinal formulas all arise as socialized institutions that attempt to explicate, defend, and provide an apology for a religious faith firmly embedded in the personal and social lives of its people. For example, Islamic theology extends the influence of the Qur'anic faith into the economic, political, and social lives of the Muslim people. Likewise, from birth and family relationships through wars and death, the Lakota's life was incorporated within the sacred hoop.

The kind of extension of religious faith into all aspects of life is justified in scriptures and doctrinal tracts by the reflective process of mythmaking and theologizing. Berger (1969) calls such activity the construction of a *nomos.* A theological *nomos* is essentially a socially constructed worldview that attempts to order all human experience in the context of the sacred. Such reflection is determined to a great extent by the social and human circumstances that give rise to the questions that must be answered as well as the language and social conventions through which the reflections are expressed. However, Wach reminds us that the prophetic function of religious traditions often shapes the social environment to a religious vision and not simply vice versa.

Institutions

Religious institutions arise as the fullest and most obvious social expression of a religious faith. They are equally the home for the core myths and rituals to be enacted as well as the loci of the religious community whose individual and collective needs must be met. Religious institutions vary from formal collectivities such as the Christian church, the Muslim mosque, the Hindu temple, or the Buddhist *sangha* to their extended representations in festivals and ceremonial events such as weddings and funerals. It is within the social institution that *communitas* understood as a spiritual leveling of religious adherents exists alongside a religious community where social differentiation and hierarchies usually persist. Religious institutions are usually the most deeply embedded social aspect of religion, since it is their primary task to control the external conduct of their members through rites, rituals, and ethical norms while providing an economic and political power base through which they may compete with other social institutions. Simply put, religious institutions are, to a great extent, socially constructed realities that provide for the habituation and rationalization of religious thought and behavior.

Religious institutions are usually the most deeply embedded social aspect of religion, since it is their primary task to control the conduct of their members.

William James viewed the church, synagogue, or religious organization as a "secondhand" extension of the religious life. Abraham Maslow (1970) goes so far as to distinguish a category of "prophets" for those who found the religion, as separate from the "legalists," who regulate, systematize, and organize religious behavior in institutional forms. Even from this brief discussion of the interrelationships of the primary aspects of the religious life, it should be apparent why Michael Novak can say, "Institutions are the normal, natural expression of the human spirit. But that spirit is self-transcending. It is never satisfied with its own finite expressions" (1971, p. 156). Novak says that the basic conflict is between the human spirit and all institutions.

No religious institution has escaped criticisms of its creeds, dogmas, ethics, or authoritative pronouncements from those within the tradition who insist that the essential faith demands revisions of the institutions' expressions of that faith. Such criticisms give rise not only to reform movements but also to schisms and new sects that emerge as a result of the clash between the received faith in its textual and social forms and the

religious experiences and impulses of a reformer or critic within that organization. Martin Luther is an example of one reformer whose critique of his received Roman Catholic heritage was both personal and theological. Similarly, the numerous Buddhist sects that arose within the first hundred years after the death of the Buddha gained their impetus from quarrels over doctrine, life-style, or interpretations of the essential nature of the faith. The Sunna and Shi'a branches of Islam have dozens of contemporary expressions that emanate from a fundamental split in the tradition that occurred shortly after the death of Muhammad and that focused on the source of authority for future proclamations in Islam. Typical of other religious traditions, Islam gave early birth to a pietistic mystical tradition, known as Sufism, which has consistently criticized both of the major theological branches of Islam for their legalistic and worldly focus to the detriment of the nourishment of the spiritual life. From one perspective, sectarian and schismatic movements are attempts to recapture the original experience and spirit of a religious tradition. In every case, however, the new movement incorporates the same social dimensions discussed previously as they articulate their message and seek to institutionalize their recommended changes.

Conclusion

Clifford Geertz argues that each world religion is essentially "(1) a system of symbols which acts (2) to establish powerful, pervasive, and long-lasting moods and motivation in men by (3) formulating conceptions of a general order of existence and (4) clothing these conceptions with such an aura of factuality that (5) the moods and motivations seem uniquely realistic" (1968, p. 1). This social-anthropological definition of religion embraces in a clear and simple fashion most of the underlying interpretation of relationships that this article has attempted to describe. Religion as a system of symbols simultaneously attempts to express and reveal dimensions of experience beyond that of the everyday, while doing so in socially conditioned language and conceptions. Likewise, the general order of existence *(nomos)* that is formulated in the myths, rituals, and ethical norms of a religious tradition emerge from the social consciousness, communal norms, and shared conceptions of the community that give rise to them. Finally, what Peter Berger calls "legitimation" and Clifford Geertz calls "factuality" are nothing other than broad-based social acceptance of certain religious beliefs. Consequently, from their inception in religious experience to their full social expression in concrete institutions, religious traditions involve an interplay between personal and social forces. No aspect—experiential, mythical, ritual, ethical, doctrinal, or institutional—of any of the world's religious traditions escapes some social conditioning. Likewise, no culture or society is left unchallenged by its religious expressions and lifestyles.

BIBLIOGRAPHY

Berger, Peter 1969 *The Sacred Canopy: Elements of a Sociological Theory of Religion.* Garden City, N.Y.: Doubleday.

———, and Thomas Luckmann 1967 *The Social Construction of Reality.* Garden City, N.Y.: Doubleday.

Durkheim, Emile 1965 *The Elementary Forms of the Religious Life,* trans. Joseph Ward Swain. New York: Free Press.

Eliade, Mircea 1959 *The Sacred and the Profane,* trans. Willard R. Trask. New York: Harper and Brothers.

Freud, Sigmund 1928 *The Future of an Illusion,* trans. W. D. Robson-Scott, Horace Liveright, and the Institute of Psychoanalysis. London: Hogarth Press.

Geertz, Clifford 1968 "Religion as a Cultural System." In Michael Banton, ed., *Anthropological Approaches to the Study of Religion.* London: Tavistock.

James, William 1961 *The Varieties of Religious Experience: A Study in Human Nature.* New York: Collier Books.

Jung, Carl 1938 *Psychology and Religion.* New Haven, Conn.: Yale University Press.

Malinowski, Bronislaw 1954 "Myth in Primitive Psychology." In Malinowski, *Magic, Science and Religion.* Garden City, N.Y.: Doubleday.

Maslow, Abraham H. 1970 *Religions, Values, and Peak Experiences.* New York: Penguin Books.

Neidardt, John G. 1972 *Black Elk Speaks.* New York: Pocket Books (from field notes contained in Raymond J. DaMillie 1984 *The Sixth Grandfather: Black's Teachings given to John Neihardt.* Lincoln: University of Nebraska Press).

Novak, Michael 1971 *Ascent of the Mountain, Flight of the Dove.* New York: Harper and Row.

Otto, Rudolph 1946 *The Idea of the Holy,* trans. J. W. Harvey. London: Oxford University Press.

Ricoeur, Paul 1972 "The Symbol Gives Rise to Thought." In Walter H. Capps, ed., *Ways of Understanding Religion.* New York: Macmillan.

Shinn, Larry D. 1977 *Two Sacred Worlds: Experience and Structure in the World's Religions.* Nashville, Tenn.: Abingdon.

Smart, Ninian 1969 *The Religious Experience of Mankind.* New York: Scribners.

Turner, Victor 1969 *The Ritual Process: Structure and Anti-Structure.* Chicago: Aldine.

Wach, Joachim 1958 *The Comparative Study of Religions.* New York: Columbia University Press.

Weber, Max 1963 *The Sociology of Religion,* trans. Ephraim Fischoff. Boston: Beacon.

– LARRY DWIGHT SHINN

Index

D

Q

R

S

T

Y

Z